Contemporary Authors

Contemporary Authors

**A Bio-Bibliographical Guide to
Current Writers in Fiction, General Nonfiction,
Poetry, Journalism, Drama, Motion Pictures,
Television, and Other Fields**

FRANCES CAROL LOCHER
Editor

volumes 73-76

GALE RESEARCH COMPANY • BOOK TOWER • DETROIT, MICHIGAN 48226

CONTEMPORARY AUTHORS

Published by
Gale Research Company, Book Tower, Detroit, Michigan 48226
Each Year's Volumes Are Revised About Five Years Later

Frederick G. Ruffner, *Publisher*   James M. Ethridge, *Editorial Director*

Christine Nasso, *General Editor, Contemporary Authors*

Frances Carol Locher, *Editor*
Martha J. Abele, Michael L. Auty, James Carlton Obrecht,
Nancy M. Rusin, Susan A. Stefani, Leslie D. Stone, and
Barbara A. Welch, *Assistant Editors*
Johanna P. Zecker, *Research Assistant*
Norma Sawaya and Shirley Seip, *Editorial Assistants*

Otto Penzler, *Contributing Editor*
Barbara Bedway, Conrad Corda, Andrea Geffner, Carole Potter,
Frank M. Soley, Joseph Sullivan, Arlene True,
and Benjamin True, *Sketchwriters*
Eunice Bergin, *Copy Editor*
Michaeline Nowinski, *Production Manager*

Special recognition is given to the staffs of
Journalists Biographical Master Index
and
Yesterday's Authors of Books for Children

Copyright © 1978
GALE RESEARCH COMPANY

ISBN 0-8103-0031-1

Questions and Answers About
Contemporary Authors

What types of authors are included in *Contemporary Authors*? More than 50,000 living authors of nontechnical works (and such authors who have died since 1960) are represented in the series. *CA* includes writers in all genres—fiction, nonfiction, poetry, drama, etc.—whose books are issued by commercial, risk publishers or university presses. Authors of books published only by known vanity or author-subsidized firms are not generally included. Since native language and nationality have no bearing on inclusion in *CA,* authors who write in languages other than English are also included in *CA* if their works have been published in the United States or translated into English.

Although *CA* focuses primarily on persons whose work appears in book form, the series now also encompasses prominent writers of interest to the public whose work appears in other media: newspaper and television reporters and correspondents, columnists, newspaper and periodical editors, syndicated cartoonists, screenwriters, television scriptwriters, and other media people.

Among the authors and media people of particular interest included in this volume are Brendan Behan, Jimmy Breslin, Claude Brown, Archibald Cox, E. E. Cummings, Erich Fromm, John Huston, Erica Jong, Norman Lear, Joseph Mankiewicz, Mao Tse-tung, Kate Millett, Harold Robbins, Margaret Chase Smith, and Paul Zindel.

How is *Contemporary Authors* **compiled?** Most of the material in *CA* is furnished by the authors themselves. Questionnaires are sent regularly to authors as their new books appear and are reviewed as well as to prominent media personalities. Information provided by the authors in their questionnaires is then written in the distinctive *CA* format, and the proposed entries are sent to the authors for review and approval prior to publication.

How are entries prepared if authors do not furnish information? If authors of special interest to *CA* users fail to reply to requests for information, material is gathered from various other reliable sources. Biographical dictionaries are checked (a task made easier through the use of Gale's *Biographical Dictionaries Master Index* and *Author Biographies Master Index*), as are bibliographical sources, such as *Cumulative Book Index, The National Union Catalog,* etc. Published interviews, feature stories, and book reviews are examined, and often material is supplied by the authors' publishers.

As with entries prepared from questionnaires, sketches prepared through extensive research are also sent to the authors for approval prior to publication. If the authors do not respond, the listings are published with an asterisk (*) following them to indicate that the material has not been personally verified by the authors.

Will you please explain the unusual numbering system used for *Contemporary Authors* **volumes?** The unusual four-volume numbering system used today reflects *CA*'s publication history. To meet the urgent need for information about authors as quickly as possible, *CA* began as a quarterly publication, with each book carrying a single volume number. The numbering system was changed to double-volume numbers when Volumes 5-6 was published with twice as many entries as a quarterly volume. With the appearance of Volumes 25-28, the numbering system was altered once more to indicate that each physical volume of *CA* represents four of the original quarterly volumes.

Now, all *CA* volumes are available as four-volume units, including the revised volumes. As early volumes of *CA* were revised, they were combined into the four-volume units presently being issued. For example, when Volumes 1, 2, 3, and 4 were revised, the material was updated, merged into a single alphabet, and is available today as Volumes 1-4, First Revision.

An unusual number of biographical publications have been appearing recently, and the question is now often asked whether a charge is made for listings in such publications. Do authors listed in *Contemporary Authors* make any payment or incur any other obligation for their listings? Some publishers charge for listings or require purchase of a book by biographees. There is, however, absolutely no charge or obligation of any kind attached to being included in *CA*. Copies of the volumes in which their sketches appear are offered at courtesy discounts to persons listed, but less than five percent of the biographees purchase copies.

Cumulative Index Should Always Be Consulted

Since *CA* is a multi-volume series which does not repeat author entries from volume to volume, the cumulative index published in alternate new volumes of *CA* should always be consulted to locate an individual author's listing. Each new volume contains authors not previously included in the series and is revised approximately five years after its original publication. The cumulative index indicates the original or revised volume in which an author appears. Authors removed from the revision cycle and placed in the *CA Permanent Series* are listed in the index as having appeared in specific original volumes of *CA* (for the benefit of those who do not hold *Permanent Series* volumes), *and* as having their finally revised sketches in a specific *Permanent Series* volume.

CONTEMPORARY AUTHORS

Indicates that a listing has been compiled from secondary sources believed to be reliable, but has not been personally verified for this edition by the author sketched.

ABBOTTS, John 1947-

PERSONAL: Born May 14, 1947, in Sapulpa, Okla.; son of Eunice Gene Smith. *Education:* Princeton University, A.B., 1969. *Office:* Public Interest Research Group, P.O. Box 19312, Washington, D.C. 20036.

CAREER: Public Interest Research Group, Washington, D.C., staff member, 1974—. *Military service:* U.S. Navy, Nuclear Submarine Service, nuclear propulsion officer, 1969-74; became lieutenant.

WRITINGS: (With Ralph Nader) *The Menace of Atomic Energy,* Norton, 1977.

SIDELIGHTS: Abbotts' present employer is a Ralph Nader organization. Abbotts writes: "I am continuing my primary functions of research and testimony on energy policy, monitoring federal agencies and filing administrative petitions."

* * *

ACKER, Helen

PERSONAL: Born in Niagara Falls, N.Y.; married Arthur B. Anderson. *Education:* Earned B.A. and M.A. from University of Minnesota. *Residence:* Minneapolis, Minn.

CAREER: Writer. Has also worked as a teacher in Puerto Rico and at University of Minnesota.

WRITINGS: Three Boys of Old Russia, Thomas Nelson, 1944; *Four Sons of Norway,* Thomas Nelson, 1948, reprinted, Books for Libraries, 1970; *Five Sons of Italy,* Thomas Nelson, 1950; *The School Train,* Abelard, 1953; *Lee Natoni: Young Navajo,* Abelard, 1958.*

* * *

ACKERMAN, Carl W(illiam) 1890-1970

PERSONAL: Born January 16, 1890, in Richmond, Ind.; son of John F. and Mary Alice (Eggemeyer) Ackerman; married Mabel Vander Hoof, 1914; children: Robert Vander Hoof. *Education:* Earlham College, B.A., 1911, M.A., 1917; Columbia University, B.Litt., 1913. *Home:* Briar Patch, Lambertville, N.J. *Office:* Pulitzer Building, Columbia University, New York, N.Y. 10027.

CAREER: Journalist, United Press International, 1915; *New York Tribune,* New York City, special writer, 1915-16; *Saturday Evening Post,* Indianapolis, Ind., correspondent in

Mexico, Spain, France, and Switzerland, 1917-18; *New York Times,* New York City, correspondent in Siberia, 1918-19; *Philadelphia Ledger,* Philadelphia, Pa., director of foreign news service, 1919-21; president and head of public relations, Carl W. Ackerman, Inc., 1921-30; General Motors Corp., Detroit, Mich., assistant to president, 1930-31; Columbia University, Graduate School of Journalism, New York City, dean, 1931-70. *Awards, honors:* LL.D. from University of Richmond, Northwestern University, and Earlham College; Doctor honoris causa from University of Havana, 1944.

WRITINGS: Germany, the Next Republic? (nonfiction), Hodder & Stoughton, 1917; *Mexico's Dilemma* (nonfiction), Doran 1918, Gordon Press, 1976; *Trailing the Bolsheviki* (nonfiction), Scribner, 1919; *Dawes, the Doer* (biography), Houghton, 1930; *Biography of George Eastman,* Houghton, 1930. Also author of articles, pamphlets, and reports on journalism and related affairs.

SIDELIGHTS: Carl W. Ackerman was noted as a champion of freedom of the press, especially in World Wars I and II, and for his distinguished tenure as dean of the Graduate School of Journalism at Columbia University. Mr. Ackerman's public life and writings dealt largely with journalism and world affairs during the years from World War I through World War II.

Reviewer Ward Swain said of *Germany, the Next Republic?:* "We knew very little of Germany before the war, and we know practically nothing of what has been going on in that country since August, 1914. Our conception of the whole war is confined to some trite phrase, such as 'democracy against autocracy.' In view of this deplorable situation, it is fortunate that Mr. Ackerman has written this book; it is a book that every American, and especially every American liberal, should find of the greatest value." The *London Times Literary Supplement* commented: "For the serious student of affairs the importance of the book lies in the large mass of information which it contains as to the struggle which was going on all the time in Germany between the two great parties, the Pan-Germans and the party of comparative moderation which centered round the Foreign Office."

Mexico's Dilemma was considered "topical," "limited in scope and subject," and of "little relevance." *Trailing the Bolsheviki* was similarly received. As a biography, *Dawes, the Doer* was panned as "poorly handled," whereas *Biogra-*

phy of George Eastman was called by the *New York Tribune* "objective in the sense that it holds strictly to the drama of events in justification of its hero. This makes it eminently readable, even exciting at times, purely as an epic of success achieved, a sort of 'Pilgrim's Progress' of business."

Mr. Ackerman was an outspoken advocate of a journalism foundation in the United States "dedicated to the study of the daily newspaper and government." He explained, "We need scientific studies of the press by the press, and for the press, which will contribute to the progress of journalism as the great educational foundations have advanced medicine."

BIOGRAPHICAL/CRITICAL SOURCES: Dial, August 16, 1917, September 6, 1919; *London Times Literary Supplement,* January 3, 1918; *New York Times,* July 20, 1919; *New York Herald Tribune,* August, 1930.

OBITUARIES: New York Times, October 10, 1970; *Washington Post,* October 10, 1970; *Newsweek,* October 19, 1970; *Time,* October 19, 1970.*

(Died October 9, 1970)

* * *

ADAMS, James E(dward) 1941-

PERSONAL: Born March 28, 1941, in Charleston, Ark.; son of Herman M. (a businessman) and Rose (Walbe) Adams; married Patty Shaughnessy, June, 1971; children: Brian, Mary Brigid, Elizabeth Ann. *Education:* St. Bernard College, B.A., 1963; University of Dayton, M.A., 1967; McGill University, graduate study. *Religion:* Roman Catholic. *Office:* St. Louis Post-Dispatch, 900 North 12th Blvd., St. Louis, Mo. 63101.

CAREER: St. Louis Review, St. Louis, Mo., reporter, 1968; *St. Louis Post-Dispatch,* St. Louis, reporter and religion editor, 1969—. *Military service:* Air National Guard, 1965-69. *Awards, honors:* Award from local chapter of Sigma Delta Chi, 1974.

WRITINGS: Preus of Missouri (biography), Harper, 1977.

WORK IN PROGRESS: Easter Mountain, a novel.

SIDELIGHTS: James Adams told *CA:* "My goal in both nonfiction and fiction writing is essentially journalistic: to create highly readable narratives that explain things and people to outsiders. Although journalists are often rightly criticized for giving simplistic accounts, I believe making complex events simple for mass audiences remains the heart of journalism, and writing generally. The publishing world is still too much under the sway of academicians who let their material dominate them and who do not feel the need to shape their subjects into disciplined narratives."

* * *

ADKINS, Nelson F(rederick) 1897-1976

PERSONAL: Born Feburary 3, 1897, in Hartford, Conn.; married Lillian Bixler, 1950. *Education:* Trinity College (Conn.), A.B., 1920, A.M., 1921; Yale University, Ph.D., 1925. *Home:* 19 Christopher St., New York, N.Y. 10014. *Office:* Department of American Literature, New York University, Washington Sq., New York, N.Y. 10003.

CAREER: New York University, New York City, instructor, 1924-31, assistant professor, 1931-47, associate professor, 1947-52, professor of American literature, 1952-70, professor emeritus, 1970-76. *Member:* Modern Language Association of America, Bibliographical Society of America, Emerson Society, Mark Twain Research Foundation.

WRITINGS: Fitz-Green Halleck: An Early Knickerbocker

Wit and Poet, Yale University Press, 1930; *Philip Freneau and the Cosmic Enigma: The Religious and Philosophical Speculations of an American Poet,* New York University Press, 1949, reprinted, Russell & Russell, 1971; (author of introduction) Mary Griffith, *Three Hundred Years Hence,* Gregg, 1950; (editor) *Thomas Paine: Common Sense & Other Political Writings,* Bobbs-Merrill, 1953. Also co-author of *Courses of Reading in American Literature with Bibliography.* Contributor to *Colophon, Bibliographical Society of America-Papers,* and *PMLA.*

OBITUARIES: New York Times, July 30, 1976.*

(Died July 27, 1976, in New York, N.Y.)

* * *

ADLER, Jack

PERSONAL: Born in New York City; son of Isidor and Anna Adler; married; children: Tor, Sture. *Education:* University of California at Berkeley, B.A. *Politics:* Independent. *Office:* 6122 Shadyglade Ave., North Hollywood, Calif. 91606.

CAREER: Paterson Morning Call, Hackensack, N. J. staff reporter, 1964-65; *Travel Weekly,* New York City, feature editor, 1965-68; Laurence Laurie & Associates (public realtions), Los Angeles, Calif., account executive, 1968-72; writer and playwright, 1972—. Columnist. Travel assignments have included Soviet Union, India, Ceylon, Nicaragua, Israel, France, Finland, Sweden, West Germany, Norway, and Zambia. *Member:* Society of American Travel Writers, Writers Guild West. *Awards, honors:* Yaddo Foundation grant for playwrighting, 1962.

WRITINGS: Exploring Historic California, Ward, Ritchie, 1974.

Plays: "The Bed," first produced in New York City at Eleanor Gould Theatre, May, 1961; "Why Wash?," first produced in New York City at Jack Manning Theatre, August, 1961; "The Window," first produced in New York City at Gallery Theatre, July, 1962; "Webs," first produced in New York City at Gramercy Arts, Theatre, August, 1965; "The Retreat," first produced in New York City at Gramercy Arts Theatre, August, 1965; "The Sophistication of America," first produced in New York City at New York Theatre Ensemble Company, August, 1968; "Looking for Rosa," first produced in New York City at New York Theatre Ensemble Company, October, 1968; "Winds of Change," first produced in Los Angeles, at Evergreen Stage, May, 1971. Author of staged readings "The Fat Jewish Policeman," and "On Pass," both first produced in Los Angeles at Evergreen Stage, 1972.

Also author with Jerry Fonarow of screenplay for feature film, "The Delegate." Author of bi-monthly newspaper humor column "With a Smile," syndicated by Trans-World News Service, 1975—. Contributor to *People's Almanac* and *World Travel Almanac.* Book review editor of *Singles Critique.*

* * *

ADRIAN, Edgar Douglas 1889-1977

November 30, 1889—August 4, 1977; British physiologist and author of books in his field. Adrian was co-winner of the Nobel Prize for medicine in 1932 for his discoveries about the functions of the neuron. In 1955, he was made a baron by Queen Elizabeth II. Adrian served as chancellor of Cambridge University from 1968 to 1975. Obituaries: *New York Times,* August 6, 1977.

AGUERO, Kathleen 1949-

PERSONAL: Born June 5, 1949, in New York; daughter of Herbert J. (an engineer) and Ruth (Rumbold) Aguero. *Education:* Attended University of Edinburgh, 1969-70; Tufts University, B.A., 1971; Boston University, M.F.A., 1973. *Politics:* Feminist. *Home:* 77 Bonnair St., Somerville, Mass. 02145.

CAREER: University of New Hampshire, Durham, visiting lecturer in English, 1973-74; poet and writer, 1974—. Participant in New Hampshire's Poetry-in-the-Schools program, 1974-77; part-time instructor at University of New Hampshire, Merrimack Valley Branch, 1976. Co-coordinator of Concord Women's Center. *Awards, honors:* Fellowship from Massachusetts Creative Artists Services, 1975.

WRITINGS: Thirsty Day (poems), Alice James Books, 1977. Contributor to literary journals, including *Conch, Massachusetts Review, Grist,* and *Ataraxia.*

WORK IN PROGRESS: Another book of poems.

* * *

AINSWORTH, G(eoffrey) C(lough) 1905-

PERSONAL: Born October 9, 1905, in Birmingham, England; son of Percy Clough (a Wesleyan clergyman) and Gertrude (Fisk) Ainsworth; married Frances Hilda Bryan, September 30, 1931; children: two daughters. *Education:* University College of Nottingham, B.Sc., 1930, Ph.D., 1934, both conferred as external degrees by University of London. *Home:* 42 Monmouth St., Topsham, Exeter EX3 OAJ, England.

CAREER: Experimental and Research Station, Cheshunt, England, plant pathologist, 1930-39; Commonwealth Mycological Institute, Kew, England, assistant mycologist, 1939-45; University of Exeter, Exeter, England, lecturer, 1948-51, reader in mycology, 1951-57; Commonwealth Mycological Institute, assistant director, 1957-64, director, 1964-68; writer and researcher, 1968—.

MEMBER: Institute of Biology (fellow), British Mycological Society (honorary member), Mycological Society of America (corresponding member), Linnean Society of London (fellow).

WRITINGS: The Plant Diseases of Great Britain: A Bibliography, Chapman & Hall, 1937; (with G. R. Bisby) *A Dictionary of Fungi,* Commonwealth Mycological Institute, 1943, 6th edition, 1971; (with Kathleen Sampson) *The British Smut Fungi,* Commonwealth Mycological Institute, 1950; *Medical Mycology,* Pitman, 1952; (with P.K.C. Austwick) *Fungal Diseases of Animals,* CAB, 1959, 2nd edition, 1973; (editor with A. Sussman and F. K. Sparrow) *The Fungi,* five volumes, Academic Press, 1965-73; *Introduction to the History of Mycology,* Cambridge University Press, 1976. Contributor of more than a hundred articles to scientific journals.

WORK IN PROGRESS: A history of plant pathology.

* * *

ALBARET, Celeste (Gineste) 1891-

PERSONAL: Born May 17, 1891, in Auxillac, France; daughter of Sylvain (a farmer) and Celestine (a miller; maiden name, Privat) Gineste; married Odilon Albaret, March 27, 1913 (deceased); children: Odile Regine Marcelle (Mrs. Jean-Jacques Gevaudan). *Education:* Attended a convent school in La Canourgues, France. *Religion:* Catholic. *Home:* 16 avenue de la Gare, 78490 Montfort

L'Amaury, France. *Agent:* Opera-Mundi, 100 avenue Raymond Poincare, 75016 Paris, France.

CAREER: Housekeeper for Marcel Proust in Paris, France, 1913-22; hotel owner in Paris, 1923-58; Musee Maurice Ravel, Montfort L'Amaury, France, museum curator, 1958-70. *Wartime service:* Member of the French Resistance, 1941-44. *Awards, honors:* Medaille de la Qualite Francaise, 1953; Prix Verite, 1973.

WRITINGS: Monsieur Proust, R. Laffont, 1973, translation by Barbara Bray published as *Monsieur Proust: A Memoir,* McGraw, 1976.

SIDELIGHTS: Celeste Albaret told *CA* that she hid more than two thousand persons hunted by the German occupation forces (including Jews, resisters, escaped prisoners, Britons, and Americans) in her Paris hotel between 1941 and 1944. Apart from this, she writes that she "has dedicated her life to the work of Marcel Proust and to his memory."

* * *

ALBERT, Marvin H.
(Anthony Rome)

PERSONAL: Born in Philadelphia, Pa.; married Vivian Coleman.

CAREER: Author and editor. Has worked in various positions, including copyperson for the *Philadelphia Record,* magazine editor, researcher for *Look* magazine, and television scriptwriter. *Military service:* Chief Radio Officer on Liberty ships during World War II.

WRITINGS: Lie Down With Lions, Gold Medal Books, 1955; *The Law and Jake Wade,* Fawcett, 1956, reprinted, Jenkins, 1969; *Broadsides and Boarders,* Appleton-Century, 1957; *The Long White Road* (for young people; illustrated by Patricia Windrow), McKay, 1957; *Apache Rising,* Gold Medal Books, 1957; *The Bounty Killer,* Gold Medal Books, 1958; *Party Girl,* Gold Medal Books, 1958; *Renegade Posse,* Gold Medal Books, 1958; (with Theodore R. Seidman) *Becoming a Mother,* Premier Books, 1958, reprinted, Fawcett, 1966; *That Jane from Maine,* Gold Medal Books, 1959; *Pillow Talk,* Gold Medal Books, 1959; *Rider from Wind River,* Gold Medal Books, 1959; *The Reformed Gun,* Gold Medal Books, 1959, reprinted, Jenkins, 1969; (under pseudonym Anthony Rome) *Miami Mayhem,* R. Hale, 1961; (under Rome pseudonym) *The Lady in Cement,* R. Hale, 1962; *The Outrage* (based on an original screenplay by Michael Kanin), Pocket Books, 1964; *Goodbye Charlie,* Dell, 1964; *The Divorce,* Simon & Schuster, 1965; *The Gargoyle Conspiracy,* Doubleday, 1975. Also author of *The Man in Black, The Don Is Dead,* and *The VIP's.*

Screenplays: "The VIP's" (based on own novel), Metro-Goldwyn-Mayer, 1963; "Bullet for a Badman" (based on own novel *Renegade Posse*), Universal, 1964; "Duel at Diablo" (based on own novel *Apache Rising*), United Artists, 1966; "Rough Night in Jericho" (based on own novel *The Man in Black*), Universal, 1967; (under Rome pseudonym) "Tony Rome" (based on own novel *Miami Mayhem*), Twentieth Century-Fox, 1967; (under Rome pseudonym) "Lady in Cement" (sequel to "Tony Rome"), Twentieth Century-Fox, 1968; "A Twist of Sand" (based on novel by G. Jenkins), United Artists, 1968; "The Ugly Ones" (based on own novel *The Bounty Killers*), United Artists, 1968; "The Don Is Dead" (based on own novel), Universal, 1974.

SIDELIGHTS: Albert's novel *The Gargoyle Conspiracy* concerns a Moroccan terrorist who plots with Libyan extremists to assassinate both the king of Jordan and the U.S. secretary of state. Burke Wilkinson praised the book for its excitement: "As the tangled web draws tight, the reader becomes totally absorbed. And the climactic shoot-out at the Valasi cook-out is stunning indeed, for the author has a gift for direct and explicit action. He does not mince words." Newgate Callendar, however, was less enthusiastic: "The hero of this book goes through a lot of slow, slogging investigation before putting everything together. 'The Gargoyle Conspiracy' is stodgy in its writing, predictable in its ending. The central situation, however, is dynamite, and most readers will enjoy following the author through his painstaking mosaic."

BIOGRAPHICAL/CRITICAL SOURCES: Christian Science Monitor, November 7, 1957, July 23, 1975; *New York Times Book Review,* August 10, 1975.

* * *

ALBERT, Mimi (Abriel) 1940-

PERSONAL: Born June 18, 1940, in New York, N.Y.; daughter of Jacob Milton and Judith (Rochester) Ginsberg; married D. S. Alberts (divorced January, 1971). *Education:* Hunter College of the City University of New York, B.A., 1963; graduate study at University of Pennsylvania, 1965-67; Columbia University, M.F.A., 1969. *Residence:* New York. *Agent:* Ellen Levine, Curtis Brown Ltd., 60 East 56th St., New York, N.Y. 10022.

CAREER: Fordham University, Lincoln Center, New York, N.Y., English and creative writing teacher, 1969-70; Brooklyn College of the City University of New York, Brooklyn, N.Y., English and creative writing teacher, 1970-76, writer-member of the Fiction Collective, 1975—. *Awards, honors:* Yaddo Foundation grant for fiction, 1975; New York State Council on the Arts grant for fiction, 1977.

WRITINGS: The Small Singer (collection of short stories and poems), Shameless Hussy Press, 1975; *The Second Story Man* (novel), Fiction Collective/Braziller, 1975. Contributor of stories to periodicals, including *Pequod, Transatlantic Review, Phoenix, Works, Shameless Hussy Review, Big Deal, Moving Out, Off Our Backs, New Fiction,* and to anthologies, including *Statements II.*

WORK IN PROGRESS: A Daughter's Book, a novel; a second collection of stories.

SIDELIGHTS: Albert told *CA:* "A New Yorker by circumstance and eventually prejudice, (a *metropolitan* New Yorker, that is), I have recently been sampling the taste of rural living, first in upstate New York (please note that I am still a New York resident), and now most recently in Sonoma County, California, a place which is famous for its communes and its redwoods, both of which are becoming familiar to me. Life is very quiet. I cannot even say, like Allen Ginsberg, that I am a fanatical Buddhist. Nothing so glamorous or explicable."

* * *

ALBRECHT, William P(rice) 1907-

PERSONAL: Born June 25, 1907, in Wilkinsburgh, Pa.; son of Frederick Carl (a sales manager) and Althea (Price) Albrecht; married Jane Lanier Moses, July 17, 1931; children: William Price, Jr., Thomas Frederick, Jane Lanier Alix. *Education:* Carnegie Institute of Technology (now Carnegie-Mellon University), B.S., 1929; University of Pittsburgh, M.A., 1934; University of Chicago, Ph.D., 1943. *Politics:* Democrat. *Religion:* Presbyterian. *Home:*

1163 University Dr., Lawrence, Kan. 66044. *Office:* Department of English, University of Kansas, Lawrence, Kan. 66045.

CAREER: Westinghouse Electric Corp., technical writer, 1929-32; Carnegie Institute of Technology (now Carnegie-Mellon University), Pittsburgh, Pa., instructor, 1934-37, assistant professor of English, 1946; University of Pittsburgh, Pittsburgh, instructor in English, 1939-42; Bucknell University Junior College, Wilkes-Barre, Pa., assistant professor of English, 1942-43; University of New Mexico, Albuquerque, 1946-57, began as assistant professor, professor of English, 1954-56; University of Kansas, Lawrence, professor of English, 1957—, chairman of department, 1957-63, dean of Graduate School, 1963-72. Consultant to Southern Illinois University, 1959, 1963, 1973, U.S. Office of Education, 1962-63, 1965-67, University of Wyoming, 1964, and Michigan State University, 1968-69; consultant–examiner, North Central Association of Colleges and Universities, 1964-72. *Military service:* U.S. Naval Reserve, active duty, 1943-46; retired as commander.

MEMBER: Modern Language Association of America, International Association of University Professors of English, American Association of University Professors (president of New Mexico conference, 1954), Midwest Modern Language Association (president, 1959-60), Alpha Tau Omega, Phi Kappa Phi. *Awards, honors:* Ford Foundation faculty fellow at Oxford University, 1952-53; Alumni Merit Award, Carnegie-Mellon University, 1973.

WRITINGS: William Hazlitt and the Malthusian Controversy, University of New Mexico Press, 1950; (contributor) Richard Walser, editor, *The Enigma of Thomas Wolfe,* Harvard University Press, 1953; *The Loathly Lady in "Thomas of Erceldoune,"* University of New Mexico Press, 1954; (with C. V. Wicker) *The American Technical Writer,* American Book, Co., 1960; (contributor) H. Orel and G. J. Worth, editors, *Six Studies in Ninteenth-Century English Literature and Thought,* University of Kansas Press, 1962; *Hazlitt and the Creative Imagination,* University of Kansas Press, 1965; (contributor) Orel and Worth, editors, *The Nineteenth-Century Writer and His Audience,* University of Kansas Press, 1969; (contributor) Paschal Reeves, compiler, *Studies in "Look Homeward, Angel,"* C. E. Merrill, 1970; (contributor) W. P. Elledge and R. L. Hoffman, editors, *Romantic and Victorian: Studies in Memory of William H. Marshall,* Fairleigh Dickinson University Press, 1971; *The Sublime Pleasures of Tragedy,* University Press of Kansas, 1975. Contributor to *Encyclopedia Americana.* Also contributor of articles and reviews to various journals. Editor, *Journal of the Proceedings and Addresses of the Association of Graduate Schools,* 1970-72.

* * *

ALD, Roy A.

PERSONAL—Education: Privately educated. *Home:* 75-51 187th St., Jamaica Estates, N.Y. 11366.

CAREER: Free-lance writer of sports, Western, and science fiction material; president and publisher of *Coupon;* president of Creative Publications; editor for Fawcett World Library. Physical fitness authority, specializing in geriatric rehabilitation. Executive director of Creative Marketing and Merchandising Development (former president); co-owner of Strength and Health Gymnasiums; initiated federal efficiency program for Mental Industry for National Development. President of Council for the Investigation of Psionic Phenomena and of International Doll Museum. Consultant to Restaurant Cuisine Associates and Standard Reference Works Publishing Corp. *Military service:* U.S. Army, information specialist. *Member:* Societe des Gourmets Internationales (member of board of directors), National Jump-rope Association (past executive director).

WRITINGS: Favorite Recipes of Famous Men, Ziff-Davis, 1949.

Low Carbohydrate Diet Cookbook, Lancer Books, 1967; *Physical Fitness After Thirty-Five,* Essandess, 1967; *The Cheerful Cat Cookbook,* Essandess, 1968; *Cycling: The Rhythmic, Respiratory Way to Physical Fitness,* Grosset, 1968; *The Happy Dog Cookbook,* Essandess, 1968; *The Side Dish Cookbook,* Essandess, 1968; *Sex Off Campus,* Grosset, 1969; *The Complete Soup Cookbook,* Prentice-Hall, 1969.

The Youth Communes, Tower, 1970; *The Skinnylook Cookbook,* New American Library, 1970; *The Man Who Took Trips: A True Experience in Another Dimension,* Delacorte, 1971; *Jump for Joy!,* Geis, 1971; *Casseroles by Candlelight,* Pyramid Publications, 1971; *Creative Wine Cookery,* Pyramid Communications, 1972.

Also author of *Jogging, Aerobics, and Diet, Cycling for Fitness, Campus Relations,* and with Richard Hoffman, *Celluloid Womb.*

WORK IN PROGRESS: The World Cancer: Experts Make Matters Worse; Robots of Consumption: The Shopping Addicts; Natural Lifetimekeeping: The Premature Aging Dilemma; research on the restabilization of disordered systems.

SIDELIGHTS: Ald comments that among his interests are investigations and lectures in the area of parapsychology as it relates to probability systems. Several communes have been established under his guidelines. Among his projects are the organization of "minimarkets," the "Pride in America" program, Housewives Sales Force, and *Sunday Junior News.*

* * *

ALDRIDGE, Josephine Haskell

PERSONAL: Married Richard Aldridge (a poet), October, 1958; children: Abigail Nancy. *Home:* Sebasco Estates, Me.

CAREER: Artist and author of books for children. *Awards, honors: Reasons and Raisins* was selected as one of the books in the American Institute of Graphic Arts Children's Book Show, 1971-72.

WRITINGS: A Penny and a Periwinkle (illustrated by Ruth Robbins), Parnassus Press, 1961; *The Best of Friends* (illustrated by Betty F. Peterson), Parnassus Press, 1963; *Fisherman's Luck* (illustrated by Robbins), Parnassus Press, 1966; (with husband, Richard Aldridge) *Reasons and Raisins* (illustrated by John Larrecq), Parnassus Press, 1972.*

* * *

ALEXANDER, Conel Hugh O'Donel 1909-1974

PERSONAL: Born April 19, 1909 in Cork, Ireland; son of C.W.L. (a professor) and H. B. (Bennett) Alexander; married Enid Constance Crichton Neate, 1934; children: Michael, Patrick. *Education:* King's College, Cambridge, earned degree with first class honors, 1931. *Home:* Old Bath Lodge, Thirlestaine Rd., Cheltenham, Gloucestershire G153 7AS, England.

CAREER: Schoolmaster at private school in Winchester, England, 1932-38; employed by John Lewis Partnership,

1938-39; British Foreign Office, 1939-45, John Lewis Partnership, 1945-46, and British Foreign and Commonwealth Office, Cheltenham, England, 1946-71; writer, 1971-74. Member of British Chess Team, 1931-58, non-playing captain, 1964-72. *Member:* Savile Club. *Awards, honors:* British Chess Champion, 1938; Order of the British Empire, 1946, commander of Order of the British Empire, 1955, companion of the Order of St. Michael and St. George, 1970.

WRITINGS: Chess, Pitman, 1937, 5th edition, 1968; (editor) Aleksandr Aleksandrovich Alekhin, *Alekhine's Best Games of Chess,* Volume I: 1938-45, G. Bell, 1949, Harcourt, 1950, McKay, 1972; (with Thomas John Beach) *Learn Chess: A New Way for All,* Volume I: *First Principles,* Volume II: *Winning Methods,* Pergamon, 1963; *Fischer versus Spassky: Reykjavic, 1972,* edited by Derek Birdsall, Vintage, 1972; *The Penguin Book of Chess Positions,* Penguin, 1973; *A Book of Chess,* edited by Birdsall, Harper, 1973; *Alexander on Chess* (based on first book, *Chess*), Pitman, 1974. General editor of "Pergamon Chess Series," Pergamon, 1963-74. Chess correspondent for *Sunday Times, Financial Times,* and *South African Durban News.*

AVOCATIONAL INTERESTS: Bridge, croquet, philately, reading.

(Died February, 1974)

* * *

ALEXANDER, George Jonathan 1931-

PERSONAL: Born March 8, 1931, in Berlin, Germany; naturalized U.S. citizen, 1944; son of Walter and Sylvia Alexander; married Katharine Sziklia, September 6, 1958; children: Susan, George Jonathan, Jr. *Education:* University of Pennsylvania, A.B. (major honors), 1953, J.D. (cum laude), 1959; Yale University, LL.M., 1965, J.S.D., 1969. *Office:* School of Law, University of Santa Clara, Santa Clara, Calif. 95053.

CAREER: University of Chicago, Chicago, Ill., instructor in law, 1959-60; Syracuse University, Syracuse, N.Y., professor of law, 1960-70, associate dean of College of Law, 1968-70; University of Santa Clara, Santa Clara, Calif., professor of law, 1970—, dean of School of Law, 1970—. Member of Bar in California, Illinois, and New York; member of Bar of the U.S. Supreme Court. Instructor at Naval Reserve Officers School, 1959-60; visiting assistant professor at University of Southern California, summer, 1963. Member of International Institute of Space Law (of International Federation of Aeronautics and Astronautics; life member; director of U.S. executive committee), 1968—; member of International Commission for Human Rights (honorary member of advisory committee), 1972—; consultant to U.S. Commission on Civil Rights, Educational Policies Research Center, and White House Conference on Aging. *Military service:* U.S. Naval Reserve, 1953-64, active duty, 1953-56.

MEMBER: American Association for the Abolition of Involuntary Mental Hospitalization (co-founder; member of board of directors), American Psychology-Law Society, American Bar Association, Society of American Law Teachers (member of board of governors, 1974—; member of executive committee, 1975—), California Bar Association (chairman of committee on the legal problems of aging, 1976—), Coif (president of Syracuse chapter, 1968-70), Justinian Honor Society (honorary member), Phi Alpha Delta (faculty adviser, 1967-70).

WRITINGS: (With others) *Cases and Materials for Legis-*

lation and Legislative Drafting, University of Chicago Law School, 1960; *Cases and Materials for Legal Method,* Syracuse University Press, 1962; *Civil Rights, U.S.A.: Public Schools–Cities in the North and West,* U.S. Government Printing Office, 1963; (contributor) H. L. Pinner, editor, *World Unfair Competition Law,* Sijthoff, 1965; *Jury Instructions on Medical Issues: A Compilation of Forms for Instructions Covering Medical Issues in Personal Injury Cases,* Allen Smith, 1966; *Cases on Antitrust,* Syracuse University Press, 1966; *Honesty and Competition: False-Advertising Law and Policy under Federal Trade Commission Administration,* Syracuse University Press, 1967; (contributor) Farrell, editor, *Aircraft Litigation,* Practicing Law Institute, 1970; (with Travis H. D. Lewin) *The Aged and the Need for Surrogate Management,* Syracuse University Press, 1972; *Commercial Torts,* Allen Smith, 1973. Also contributor to *Changing Aspects of Business Law,* edited by Zelermeyer, 1965. Author of film "Sources of Legal Research," 1966. Contributor of about thirty articles to law journals.

WORK IN PROGRESS: The Right to Be Responsible; Public Tort Liability; International Anti-trust.

* * *

ALEXANDER, James E(ckert) 1913-

PERSONAL: Born September 4, 1913, in Zanesville, Ohio; son of James Rufus and Nellie (Hunter) Alexander; married Jean Kathryn Crew, July 1, 1940; children: James C., Jean (Mrs. Joseph D. Small III), John R. *Education:* Washington and Jefferson College, A.B., 1935. *Politics:* Democrat. *Religion:* Presbyterian. *Home:* 633 Rock Springs Rd., Pittsburgh, Pa. 15228. *Office:* Pittsburgh Post-Gazette, 50 Boulevard of the Allies, Pittsburgh, Pa. 15222.

CAREER/WRITINGS: Akron Beacon Journal, Akron, Ohio, reporter, 1937; *Pittsburgh Press,* Pittsburgh, Pa., reporter, 1937-38; *Zanesville News,* Zanesville, Ohio, editor, 1939-42; *Minneapolis Star-Journal and Tribune,* Minneapolis, Minn., Sunday editor, 1942-45; Minnesota and Ontario Paper Co., Minneapolis, public relations executive, 1946; *Akron Beacon Journal,* reporter, 1947-48; *Pittsburgh Post-Gazette,* Pittsburgh, book critic, 1949—, writer and editor, 1949-65, city editor, 1965-72, assistant managing editor, 1972-73, managing editor, 1973—. Professor at University of Pittsburgh, 1963-65. Literary critic for KDKA-TV in Pittsburgh, 1963-67. *Member:* International Press Institute, Society of American Travel Writers, Beta Theta Pi, Pittsburgh Press Club, Montour Heights Country Club.

* * *

ALGER, Leclaire (Gowans) 1898-1969
(Sorche Nic Leodhas)

PERSONAL: Born May 20, 1898, in Youngstown, Ohio; daughter of Louis Peter Gowans; married Amos Risser Hoffman, 1916 (died, 1918); married second husband several years later; children: Louis. *Education:* Graduated from Carnegie Library School, 1929.

CAREER: Author and librarian. Began writing as a child; started as a page with Carnegie Library of Pittsburgh, 1915; worked for New York Public Library, 1921-25; employed as a librarian in several branches of Carnegie Library, 1929-66; full-time writer, 1966-69. *Awards, honors:* Runner-up for Lewis Carroll Shelf Award, 1962, and for Newbery Medal, 1963, both for *Thistle and Thyme.*

WRITINGS: Jan and the Wonderful Mouth Organ (illus-

trated by Charlotte Becker), Harper, 1939; *Dougal's Wish* (illustrated by Marc Simont), Harper, 1942; *The Golden Summer* (illustrated by Aldren Watson), Harper, 1942.

Under pseudonym Sorche Nic Leodhas: (Editor) *Heather and Broom: Tales of the Scottish Highland* (illustrated by Consuelo Joerns), Holt, 1961; (editor) *Thistle and Thyme: Tales and Legends from Scotland* (illustrated by Evaline Ness), Holt, 1962; *All in the Morning Early* (illustrated by Ness), Holt, 1963; *Gaelic Ghosts* (illustrated by Nonny Hogrogian), Holt, 1963; *Ghosts Go Haunting* (illustrated by Hogrogian), Holt, 1965; *Always Room for One More* (illustrated by Hogrogian), Holt, 1965; (editor) *Claymore and Kilt: Tales of Scottish Kings and Castles* (illustrated by Leo and Diane Dillon), Holt, 1967; *Sea-Spell and Moor Magic: Tales of the Western Isles* (illustrated by Vera Bock), Holt, 1968; *Kellyburn Braes* (illustrated by Ness), Holt, 1969; *The Laird of Cockpen* (illustrated by Adrienne Adams), Holt, 1969; (editor) *A Scottish Song Book* (illustrated by Ness), Holt, 1969; (editor) *By Loch and by Lin: Tales from Scottish Ballads* (illustrated by Bock), Holt, 1969; *Twelve Great Black Cats, and Other Eerie Scottish Tales* (illustrated by Bock), Dutton, 1971.

SIDELIGHTS: Many of Leclaire Alger's writings were based on old Scottish folk tales passed down through oral tradition. The author preferred to collect and retell folklore which had never been previously published. Her skill in researching and adapting the tales into modern English has been highly praised by literary critics. In reviewing Alger's first collection of folklore, *Heather and Broom,* a critic for the *Chicago Sunday Tribune* noted, "even television has not learned to spin richly imaginative adventures to match those . . . from the storyteller's heart. . . ."

In addition to Gaelic folklore, the author's works have also been influenced by folk songs from Scotland. Alger's *Always Room for One More* was derived from the Scottish folk song about Lachie MacLachlan whose kind hospitality and open heart proved more than his small house could hold. She gathered information from old Scottish ballads for her *By Loch and by Lin.* "These good yarns of brawny lads and bonnie lasses gleam with lessons, magic, chivalry, trickery, wisdom and adventure," commented a critic for the *Christian Science Monitor.*

BIOGRAPHICAL/CRITICAL SOURCES: Chicago Tribune, November 6, 1960; *Saturday Review,* October 16, 1965; *Christian Science Monitor,* November 9, 1969.*

(Died November 14, 1969)

* * *

ALLARDT, Erik 1925-

PERSONAL: Born August 9, 1925, in Helsinki, Finland; son of Arvid (a registrar) and Marita (a teacher; maiden name, Heikel) Allardt; married Sagi Nylander, September 7, 1947; children: Jorn, Monica, Barbro. *Education:* University of Helsinki, M.S.S., 1947, Ph.D., 1952; postdoctoral study at Columbia University, 1953-54. *Home:* Unionsgaten 45 B 40, Helsingfors 17, Finland. *Office:* University of Helsinki, Mariegatan 10 A 13, Helsinki 00170, Finland.

CAREER: University of Helsinki, Helsinki, Finland, instructor in sociology, 1948-53; School of Social Sciences, Helsinki, research director, 1955-57; University of Helsinki, professor of sociology, 1958-70; Academy of Finland, Helsinki, research professor of sociology at University of Helsinki, 1971—. Visiting professor at University of California, Berkeley, 1962-63, University of Illinois, 1966-67, and University of Wisconsin, Madison, 1970.

MEMBER: Amnesty International (chairman of Finnish section, 1977—), International Sociological Association, Finnish Academy of Sciences, Finnish Sociological Association (chairman, 1961-66), Finnish Political Science Association (chairman, 1972-75), American Sociological Association. *Awards, honors:* Rockefeller fellowship, 1953-54.

WRITINGS: Syntyperaeae ja sosiaalista kohoamista koskevat arvostukset (title means "Value Orientations as Regards Social Origin and Social Mobility"), Karisto, 1956; *Social struktur och politisk aktivitet: En studie av vaeljaraktiviteten vid riksdagsvalen i Finland, 1945-1954* (title means "Social Structure and Political Activity: A Study of Electoral Participation at the Parliamentary Elections In Finland, 1945-1954), Soederstroems, 1956; (with Pentti Jartti, Faina Jyrkilae, and Yrjoe Littunen) *Tyoelaeisnuorison harrastustoiminta* (title means "The Social Activities of Working Class Youth"), Tammi, 1956; (with Jartti, Jyrkilae, and Littunen) *Nuorison harrastukset ja yhteisoen rakenne* (title means "The Leisure Use of Youth and Social Structure), Soederstroem Osakeyhtoe, 1958; (with Littunen) *Sosiologia* (title means "Sociology"), Soederstroem Osakeyhtoe, 1958, fourth revised edition, 1972; abridged edition published as *Sosiologian perusteet* (title means "Introductory Sociology"), third edition, 1972; *Yhteiskunnan rakenne ja sosiaalinen paine* (title means "Social Structure and Social Pressures"), Soederstroem Osakeyhtoe, 1964; (editor with Littunen) *Cleavages, Ideologies, and Party Systems: Contributions to Comparative Political Sociology,* Academic Bookstore for Westermarck Society, 1964; *Foerankringar* (title means "Solidarities"), Soederstroems, 1970; (editor with Stein Rokkan) *Mass Politics: Studies in Political Sociology,* Free Press, 1970; (with Klaus Waris and Osmo A. Wiio) *Valinnan yhteiskunta* (title means "A Society of Options"), Weilin & Goeoes, 1970; *Att ha, att aelska, att vara: Om vaelfaerd i Norden* (title means "To Have, to Love, to Be: On Well-being in Nordic Countries"), Argos, 1975; *Hyvinvoinnin ulottuvuuksia* (title means "About Dimensions of Welfare'), Soederstroem Osakeyhtoe, 1976.

Contributor: R. L. Merritt and Stein Rokkan, editor, *Comparing Nations: The Use of Quantitative Data in Cross-National Research,* Yale University Press, 1966; (with Pertti Pesonen) Seymour M. Lipset and Rokkan, editors, *Party Systems and Voter Alignments,* Free Press, 1967; J. A. Jackson, editor, *Social Stratification,* Cambridge University Press, 1968; (with Richard F. Tomasson) Lipset and P. G. Altbach, editors, *Students in Revolt,* Houghton, 1969; M. Dogan and Rokkan, editors, *Quantitative Ecological Analysis in the Social Sciences,* M.I.T. Press, 1969; (and editor with Rokkan) *Mass Politics: Studies in Political Sociology,* Free Press, 1970; M. Rejai, editor, *Decline of Ideology?,* Aldine, 1971; A. Pizzorno, editor, *Political Sociology,* Penguin, 1971; *Industrialization, Urbanization, and Ways of Life,* Hungarian Academy of Science, 1971; P. Birnbaum and Francois Chazel, editors, *Sociologie politique, tome I* (title means "Political Sociology"), Librarie Armand Colin, 1971; A. W. Finifter, editor, *Alienation and the Social System,* Wiley, 1972; Nancy Hammond, editor, *Social Science and the New Societies: Problems in Cross-Cultural Research and Theory Building,* Michigan State University, Social Science Research Bureau, 1973; S. N. Eisenstadt and Rokkan, editors, *Building States and Nations: Models and Data Resources,* Sage, 1973; Candido Mendes, editor, *O Outro Desenvolvimento* (title means "The Other Development") Editora Artenova, 1973; R. P. Mohan and D. Martindale, editors, *Handbook of Contemporary Developments in World Sociology,* Greenwood Press, 1975; R. Dubin, editor, *Handbook of Work, Organization, and Society,* Rand McNally, 1976.

Contributor of numerous articles to sociology journals in the United States and Europe. Chief editor of *Acta Sociologica,* 1967-70, and *Scandinavian Political Studies,* 1973-76. Member of editorial board of International Sociological Association, 1976—.

WORK IN PROGRESS: Ethnic Boundaries and Ethnic Identity, with a focus on the Swedish-speaking population in Finland.

*   *   *

ALLEN, Jay Presson 1922-

PERSONAL: Born March 3, 1922, in San Angelo, Tex.; daughter of Albert Jeffrey (a department store owner) and Wilhilmina (a buyer; maiden name, Miller) Presson; married Lewis Maitland Allen (a producer), March 17, 1955; children: Anna Brooke. *Education:* Educated in Dallas, Tex. *Residence:* Roxbury, Conn. *Agent:* International Creative Management, 40 West 57th St., New York, N.Y. 10019.

CAREER: Novelist, playwright, and author of screenplays and teleplays; American Broadcasting Co. (ABC), New York, N.Y., creator of television series "Family," 1976—. *Awards, honors:* Humanities Award, 1976.

WRITINGS: Spring Riot, Rinehart, 1948; *Just Tell Me What You Want* (novel), Dutton, 1975.

Plays: *The Prime of Miss Jean Brodie* (three-act; first produced in Torquay, England, at Princess Theatre, April 5, 1966), Samuel French, 1969; *Forty Carats* (two-act; first produced on Broadway at Morosco Theatre, December 26, 1968), Random House, 1969; "I and Albert," first produced in London at Piccadilly Theatre, November 6, 1972.

Screenplays: "Marnie," Universal, 1964; "The Prime of Miss Jean Brodie," Twentieth Century-Fox, 1969; "Travels with My Aunt," Metro-Goldwyn-Mayer, 1972; "Cabaret," Allied Artists, 1972; "Funny Lady," Columbia, 1975.

Contributor of teleplays to "Philco Playhouse," "Playhouse 90," and "Hallmark Hall of Fame."

WORK IN PROGRESS: "Just Tell Me What You Want," "Mayberly's Kill," and "Grand Hotel," films; an English television series based on *The Prime of Miss Jean Brodie.*

SIDELIGHTS: Allen, whose dramatization of Muriel Spark's novel *The Prime of Miss Jean Brodie* lured such actresses as Vanessa Redgrave, Zoe Caldwell, and Maggie Smith to the title role, discussed the difficulties of adapting the book: "I love the book. I found it very difficult to do what you have to do in any adaptation, and that's rape and dismember it. The more you like a book the harder it is. It's easier to take something that's fragmented or that you like a part of or that you think you can improve on. But it's painful to take a novel you really admire and to do what has to be done with a novel—to remove a great amount of the subtlety and make it a much more direct and obvious thing."

BIOGRAPHICAL/CRITICAL SOURCES: New York Times, March 3, 1968.*

*   *   *

ALLEN, Leslie Christopher 1935-

PERSONAL: Born December 25, 1935, in Bristol, England; son of Bertie (a metalworker) and Dorothy (Harp) Allen; married Elizabeth Ruth Gulliver (a teacher), August 21, 1965; children: Jeremy Lawrence, Miriam Ishmahanna (both adopted). *Education:* Corpus Christi College, Cambridge,

M.A., 1960; University of London, Ph.D., 1968. *Politics:* "Right-wing socialist." *Religion:* Christian Brethren. *Home:* 22 Rosecroft Walk, Pinner, Middlesex HA5 1LL, England. *Office:* London Bible College, Green Lane, Northwood, Middlesex, England.

CAREER: London Bible College, Northwood, England, lecturer in Old Testament languages and literature, 1960—. *Member:* Society for Old Testament Study, Evangelical Race Relations Group.

WRITINGS: The Greek Chronicles, two volumes, E. J. Brill, 1974; *The New International Commentary on the Old Testament: The Books of Joel, Obadiah, Jonah, and Micah,* Eerdmans, 1976. Contributor to *A New Testament Commentary* and to theology journals.

WORK IN PROGRESS: "Psalms 73-150," to be included in a commentary on the Old Testament, for Pickering & Inglis.

SIDELIGHTS: Allen writes: "My field is the text and exegesis of the Old Testament; my overall aim is to communicate the message of the Old Testament in its cultural setting, as an interaction of divine revelation and human response." *Avocational interests:* Race relations, gardening (especially designing gardens).

*   *   *

ALLEY, Rewi   1897-

PERSONAL: Born December 2, 1897, in Springfield, New Zealand; son of Frederick James (a schoolmaster) and Clara (Buckingham) Alley; children: Alan, Michael (both adopted). *Education:* Educated in New Zealand. *Home and office:* 1 Tai Chi Chang, Peking, China.

CAREER: Chief factory inspector in Shanghai, China, 1927-38; organizer of Gung Ho (Chinese industrial cooperatives), 1938-43; director of Sandan Bailie Industrial School, 1944-53; New Zealand representative for the Asian and Pacific Peace Liaison Committee, 1952-66. Writer. *Military service:* New Zealand Expeditionary Force during World War I; received Military Medal. *Awards, honors:* Don Doctor of Literature, Victoria University, Wellington, New Zealand.

WRITINGS: The Chinese Industrial Cooperative, China Information Publishing Co. (Chungking), 1940; *Two Years of Indusco,* Promotion Committee (Hong Kong), 1940; *Yo Banfa!* (title means "We Have a Way!"), New World Press (Peking), 1952; *The People Have Strength,* [Peking], 1954; *Man Against Flood,* New World Press, 1956; *Spring in Vietnam,* Raven Press, 1956; *Land of the Morning Calm,* Raven Press, 1956; *Buffalo Boys of Vietnam,* Foreign Language Publishing House, 1956; *Children of the Dawn: Stories of Asian Peasant Children,* New World Press, 1956; *Journey to Outer Mongolia: A Diary with Poems,* Caxton (Christchurch), 1957; *Human China: A Diary,* New Zealand Peace Council, 1957; *Peking Opera,* New World Press, 1957; *Stories Out of China,* New World Press, 1958; *Sandan: An Adventure in Creative Education,* Caxton, 1959.

Towards a People's Japan, Caxton, 1960; *Three Conferences to Cairo, New Delhi, and Bandung,* Caxton, 1961; *China's Hinterland in the Leap Forward,* New World Press, 1961; *Land and Folk in Kiangsi,* New World Press, 1962; *Our Seven—Their Five,* New World Press, 1963; *Among the Hills and Streams of Hunan,* New World Press, 1963; (with Shou Tseng Meng) *Cooperative Management,* National Cooperative Union of India (New Delhi), 1964; *In the Spirit of Hunghu: A Story of Hupeh Today,* New World Press, 1966; *For the Children of the World,* Far East Reporter,

1966; *Fruition: The Story of George Alwin Hogg,* Caxton, 1967; *The Influence of the Thought of Mao Tse-tung,* Far East Reporter, 1969.

Oceania, Caxton, 1971; *Some Chinese Children,* Caxton, 1972; *The Prisoners: Shanghai 1936,* Caxton, 1972; *A Highway and an Old Chinese Doctor,* Caxton, 1973; *The Rebels,* [Aukland], 1973; *Taiwan,* China Society and Progressive Book Society, 1973; *Travels in China,* New World Press, 1973; *Children: 1962-1972* (photographs), [Peking], 1973; (with Hans Miller) *Vaster Landets Imperialism I Kana,* [Stockholm], 1974. Also author of *La Chine: Une Autre Qualitie du Vie* with Wilfred Burchett, translation published as *China: The Quality of Life,* Penguin, 1976.

Poems: *Gung Ho,* Caxton, 1948; *Leaves from a Sandan Notebook,* Caxton, 1950; *This Is China Today,* Caxton, 1951; *Fragments of Living Peking,* Peace Council, 1955; *Beyond the Withered Oaks Ten Thousand Saplings Grow,* Caxton, 1962; *Who Is the Enemy?,* New World Press, 1964; *Not a Dog: An Ancient Thai Ballad,* New World Press, 1966; *In Southeast Asia Today: The United States, Vietnam, China,* Far East Reporter, 1966; *What Is Sin,* Caxton, 1967; *Twenty-five Poems of Protest,* Caxton, 1970; *Upsurge, Asia and the Pacific,* Caxton, 1970; *73—Man to Be,* Caxton, 1971; *Winds of Change,* Caxton, 1972; *Poems for Aotea-roa,* China Society and Progressive Book Society, 1972; *Walkabout,* Australia-China Society, 1973; *Over China's Hills of Blue,* Caxton, 1974; *Snow Over the Pines,* Progressive Books, 1977; *The Freshening Breeze,* New World Press, 1977.

Translator from the Chinese; all poems: *Peace Through the Ages,* [Peking], 1954; *The People Speak Out,* [Peking], 1954; *The People Sing,* [Peking], 1958; *Lament of a Soldier's Wife,* Foreign Publishing House (Hanoi), 1959; *Poems of Revolt,* New World Press, 1962; *The Eighteen Laments,* New World Press, 1963.

WORK IN PROGRESS: Manuscripts on five Americans in China, on the provinces of Hupeh, Shansi, and Honan, on ancient and modern pottery kilns in China, and on travels in China, 1971-76; translations of Li Pai and Pai Chu-yi.

SIDELIGHTS: With his lengthy list of publications, Alley's fame rests to a large extent upon his role in the industrialization of China. He cites the importance of change in that nation, and the effect of one quarter of mankind upon the rest of the world, as a major motivation of his life and work. Behind his writings, he says, has been the feeling "that there is so much more to be said than has been said already."

After a childhood on the frontier of what was then a wild and rugged New Zealand, a young adulthood in active service during World War I, and a failed attempt at sheep ranching, Alley went to China in 1927. The Kuomintang revolution was in full swing, but he found work for the Shanghai Municipal Council, initially as a factory inspector of the Shanghai Fire Brigade, later as chief factory inspector of the Council's Industrial Department.

Thus exposed to the inhuman factory conditions of the time, Alley soon initiated a program of reform, writing pamphlets and articles and pressing for the establishment of new factory regulations. After the Japanese bombing of Shanghai in 1937, however, he turned his attention to the survival of Chinese industry. In the face of the demolition of ninety per cent of China's east-coast industry, he saw the need "to start thousands of small 'semi-mobile' cooperative industries, located in the hinterland close to unexploited raw materials, using salvaged tools and machinery." Thus he conceived the development of China's guerrilla industry and became an active member of Chinese Industrial Cooperatives, commonly known as Indusco.

Alley's publications have come out of his experiences among the Chinese workers, but go far beyond descriptions and analyses of industrial conditions. Fluent with a number of Chinese dialects, he has translated several books of Chinese poetry and has written, as well, many volumes of original verse.

BIOGRAPHICAL/CRITICAL SOURCES: Willis Thomas Goodwin Airey, *Learner in China: A Life of Rewi Alley,* Caxton, 1970.

* * *

ALLISON, John Murray 1889-

PERSONAL: Born September 28, 1889, in Noble County, Ohio; son of Jesse J. (a farmer) and Mary (Green) Allison; married Hazel Dye, January 1, 1912 (deceased); married Eva Randell, January 19, 1939; married Elizabeth Fralick, December 13, 1952; children: (first marriage) John Murray, Jr., Harriet Jean (Mrs. Arthur J. Wojnowski). *Education:* Attended College of Wooster, 1908-09; University of Chicago, Ph.B., 1915. *Politics:* Independent. *Home and office:* 8 Zoar Ave., Albany, N.Y. 12209.

CAREER: High school teacher in Leadville, Colo., 1915-18; Y.M.C.A., Great Lakes, Ill., war secretary, 1918-19; Congregational minister in Amery, Wis., 1919-25, Twinsburg, Ohio, 1925-29, and Berea, Ohio, 1929-36; minister of Congregational Christian Churches (now United Church of Christ) in Zanesville, Ohio, 1937-39, Euclid, Ohio, 1939-42, Marietta, Ohio, 1943-48, Elcho, Wis., 1948-52, and Medusa, N.Y., 1953-57; Registrar of Hudson River Association of Congregational Christian Churches, 1954-63; secretary of Hudson Mohawk Association, United Church of Christ, 1963—.

WRITINGS: Adams and Jefferson: The Story of a Friendship, University of Oklahoma Press, 1966; *Ambassador from the Prairie, or Allison Wonderland,* Houghton, 1973.*

* * *

ALLON, Yigal 1918-

PERSONAL: Name originally Yigal Paicovich; born October 10, 1918, in Kfar Tabor, Israel; son of Reuben and Haia (Schwartz) Paicovitch; married Ruth Appisdorf, 1938; children: Gomi, Iftach. *Education:* Attended Kadourie Agricultural College, Hebrew University, and Oxford University. *Home:* Kibbutz Ginossar, Israel. *Office:* Knesset, Jerusalem, Israel.

CAREER: Kibbutz Ginossar, Israel, founder, 1937—; joined Hagana (underground Jewish defense organization), 1937; founding member of Palmah (Hagana's striking force), 1941, commander-in-chief, 1945-48; head of Hagana operations, Palestine, 1945-47; served in War of Independence, 1948-49; Israel Defense Forces Reserves, major-general, 1948—; member of Knesset (Israeli Parliament), 1954—; minister of labor, 1961-67; deputy prime minister, 1967—; minister of immigrant absorption, 1967-69; minister of education and culture, 1969-74; minister of foreign affairs, 1974-77. Sergeant, Jewish Settlement Police, 1939; research fellow, Oxford University, 1960; acting Premier of Israel, February 26-March 17, 1969. Leader of Labor Party and the Labor-Mapam Alignment; member of Cabinet Committee for Defense; member of secretariat of Kibbutz Meuhad Movement.

WRITINGS: Ma'arkhot Palmah (Title means "Campaigns of the Palmah"), HaKibbutz HaMeuhad Publishing House (Tel Aviv), 1951; *Massakh Shel Hol* (title means "Curtain of Sand"), HaKibbutz HaMeuhad Publishing House, 1959; *The Making of Israel's Army,* Universe Books, 1970; *Shield of David: The Story of Israel's Armed Forces,* Random House, 1970; *Thalath Hurub Wa-Salem Wahad* (title means "Three Wars and One Peace"), Al-Nahda (Nazareth), 1970; *Beit Avi,* HaKibbutz HaMeuhad Publishing House, 1974; *My Father's House,* Norton, 1976. Contributor to *International Affairs* and other periodicals.

* * *

ALLVINE, Glendon 1893(?)-1977

1893(?)—November 5, 1977; American movie producer, theatrical and film publicity agent, playwright, and author of a biography. Allvine was associated with Paramount, Fox Film Company, and RKO Radio Pictures. He wrote a biography about the film mogul William Fox. He died in East Atlantic Beach, N.Y. Obituaries: *New York Times,* November 8, 1977.

* * *

ALMOND, Paul 1931-

PERSONAL: Born April 26, 1931, in Montreal, Canada. *Education:* Attended McGill University and Balliol College, Oxford.

CAREER: Author of screenplays, producer and director.

WRITINGS—Screenplays: "Isabel," 1968; "Act of the Heart," 1970; "Journey," 1972.

SIDELIGHTS: In a review of "Isabel," Vincent Canby stated that "only Eugene O'Neill could have made ultimate sense out of the exposition that is as tangled as seaweed on a Gaspe shore." Canby noted that, although the film "starts off on a low, promisingly ominous key," it soon deteriorates "into an irritating and pretentious movie, too posey and superficial to be much of a psychological study of sexual repression and too intelligent really to be effective as Gaspe-gothic romance."

BIOGRAPHICAL/CRITICAL SOURCES: New York Times, July 24, 1968.*

* * *

ALPERN, David M(ark) 1942-

PERSONAL: Born August 21, 1942, in Brooklyn, N.Y.; son of Jerome I. (a textile salesman) and Libbie (a secretary; maiden name, Roginsky) Alpern. *Education:* Columbia University, B.A., 1963. *Home:* 424 East 57th St., New York, N.Y. 10022. *Agent:* Wendy Weil, Julian Bach Agency, 3 East 48th St., New York, N.Y. 10022. *Office: Newsweek* Magazine, 444 Madison Ave., New York, N.Y. 10022.

CAREER/WRITINGS: New York Post, New York City, copy boy and campus stringer, 1960-63; *Elizabeth Daily Journal,* Elizabeth, N.J., reporter, 1961; United Press International, New York City, newsman, 1962-65; *Newsweek,* New York City, general editor for national affairs, 1966—. Notable assignments include coverage of the national political conventions of 1968, 1972, and 1976, and the Senate Watergate hearings, 1974; interviews with Harry Truman, Sophia Loren, Nelson Rockefeller, and Jimmy Carter. Principal work includes *Newsweek* cover stories on the 1976 presidential campaign, Watergate, Nixon impeachment, CIA-FBI scandals, welfare, campaign finance, television, and other political matters. Contributor of articles to *More* magazine and *New York Times* travel section. *Military service:* U.S. Army Reserve, 1964-70. *Awards, honors:* Nicholas Murray Butler journalism awards, 1960 and 1961, both for work on Columbia College *Daily Spectator;* Association of Trial Lawyers award, 1973, for story "Living With Crime"; American Bar Association Silver Gavel, 1974, for story "All About Impeachment"; Aviation/Space Writers Association award, 1977, for story "The Concorde Furor."

* * *

ALTMAN, Robert 1925-

PERSONAL: Born February 20, 1925, in Kansas City, Mo.; married third wife, Kathryn; children: (first marriage) Christine, (second marriage) Michael, Stephen, (third marriage) Bobby, Matthew (adopted). *Religion:* "Hedonist." *Residence:* Malibu Beach, Calif. *Office:* Lion Gate Productions, Los Angeles, Calif.

CAREER: Film director and writer. Began career as a writer, photographer, editor, and director of industrial films for Calvin Co., Kansas City, Mo. during late 1940's and early 1950's; wrote, produced, and directed independent feature film "The Delinquents," 1955; co-producer and director of "The James Dean Story," Warner Brothers, 1957; writer, producer, and director of television programs, 1957-65, including "The Roaring Twenties," "Bonanza," "Combat," "Suspense Theatre," "The Millionaire," "Whirlybirds," and others; director of films for various studios, 1965—, including "Nightmare in Chicago," Universal, 1967; "Countdown," Warner Bros.-Seven Arts, 1968; "That Cold Day in the Park," Commonwealth United, 1969 (see also, *WRITINGS*); president, Lion Gate Productions, Los Angeles, Calif. *Military service:* U.S. Army, 1943-47. *Awards, honors:* Recipient of numerous awards for "M*A*S*H" including grand prize at Cannes Film Festival, 1970; best film award and best director award, New York Film Critics, 1975, for "Nashville"; nominated for two Academy Awards by Academy of Motion Picture Arts and Sciences.

WRITINGS—Screenplays: (Co-author with Ring Lardner, Jr.; also producer and director) "M*A*S*H" (adapted from novel by Richard Hooker), Twentieth Century-Fox, 1970; (also director) "Brewster McCloud," Metro-Goldwyn-Mayer, 1970; (co-author; also director) "McCabe & Mrs. Miller," Warner Bros., 1971; (also director) "Images," Columbia, 1972; (also director) "The Long Goodbye" (adapted from novel by Raymond Chandler), United Artists, 1973; (co-author with Joan Tewkesbury; also director) "Thieves Like Us," United Artists, 1974; (also director) "California Split," Columbia, 1974; (co-author with Tewkesbury; also director and producer) "Nashville," Paramount, 1975; (co-author with Alan Rudolph) *Buffalo Bill & the Indians; or, Sitting Bull's History Lesson* (screenplay; produced as feature film, 1976), Bantam, 1976; (also director) "Three Women," 1977; (also director) "A Wedding," 1978.

WORK IN PROGRESS: "Quintet," a film about which Altman says: "It's a very strange kind of story, based on an idea of mine and written by Patricia Resnick and myself. I want to keep the story under wraps though, so that it won't be overanticipated or overhyped."

SIDELIGHTS: Robert Altman is an unconventional filmmaker. He ignores scripts in favor of improvisation, the weather, the way he feels that morning. He provides his actors with an unstructured, creative atmosphere, an ambience that reveals real human behaviour and not the contrived gesticulations of mere role playing. "I'm interested in the behavior pattern of the characters," Altman states, "not in

what they say." A screenplay, for him, is a "selling tool to get financing; afterwards, it's not much more than a production schedule."

Altman's first major film was "M*A*S*H," and he took the job only after fourteen "more acceptable" directors had turned it down. Already forty-five years of age, he commented: "I just had a long gestation period. I think if I'd made a big success in my 20's, if I had gotten a big film, I wouldn't have been sitting here now. I think I really would have succumbed to the rewards of all that. It would have destroyed me." Collaborating on the screenplay with Ring Lardner, Jr., who admitted "Mr. Altman does not treat a script very carefully," Altman insisted that his main contribution to "M*A*S*H" was "the basic concept, the philosophy, the style, the casting, and then making all those things work. Plus all the jokes, of course!"

Altman described his next film, "Brewster McCloud," as "adult fairytale about a man who lives in the Astrodome and learns to fly. It's about insanity. It's about cruelty." Though popular with a cult of those who see it again and again, this film did not meet with unanimous acclaim.

"Nashville" is Altman's most important picture to date, and it is in "Nashville" that his essentially documentary style is revealed. Intended loosely as a portrait of the southern town, "Nashville" subordinates plot to the welter of action, light and sound that is the undisciplined nature of life as we perceive it daily. The camera is distant, a detached observer before whom the actors improvise among themselves, reacting naturally, reciting lines they themselves most probably have written. *Newsweek* called the film "everything a work of social art ought to be but seldom is, immensely moving yet terribly funny, chastening yet ultimately exhilarating. It is also that rarest thing in comtemporary movies, a work of art that promises to be hugely popular." In an interview with *Film Quarterly,* Altman stated: "Well, you take from 'Nashville' what you can understand. For example, my grandmother saw it and she has a totally different consciousness than I do, and she liked it. A lot of people went and saw a country-western musical, and lot of people saw a soap opera, or a political film. Or a lot of people just saw a long, pointless movie. People see what they are able to see and what they want to see."

A filmmaker who doesn't think of himself as a "man with a message," Altman commented: "I don't have anything to say. I really don't have a statement. I don't have a crusade. I just discover things about myself, looking back over the films. Looking back, not looking forward, I think that the reason my work can be identified as my work is because everything passes through me like a sieve, and it's bound to have my shape."

In a recent interview with the *New York Times* Altman said; "I cannot do 'Rocky' or 'One Flew Over the Cuckoo's Nest' and all those films where there's no question about the way the audience is going to feel at the end. I think sad people laugh, happy people cry, and brave people are frightened. Cowards are brave. There's total contradiction. The minute you plot something and say this is going to be this way because of this, you're wrong."

BIOGRAPHICAL/CRITICAL SOURCES: New York Times Magazine, June 20, 1971; *Christian Science Monitor,* October 24, 1974; *Newsweek,* March 11, 1974; *New Times,* June 13, 1975, April 15, 1977; *Rolling Stone,* June 17, 1975; *Film Quarterly,* winter, 1975-76; *London Times,* August 19, 1976; *New York Times,* April 15, 1977, June 13, 1977, June 19, 1977, October 28, 1977; *Saturday Review,* April 16, 1977.*

ALZAGA, Florinda 1930-

PERSONAL: Born July 26, 1930, in Camaguey, Cuba; daughter of Apolinar L. (an administrator of a sugar mill) and Nena (Loret de Mola) de Alzaga; married Pedro J. Romanach, 1955 (divorced, 1972); children: Pierre A. Romanach. *Education:* University of Havana, Ph.D., 1956; University of Miami, M.A., 1971; graduate study at Barry College, 1970-72; further study at Miami Dade Junior College, 1972-73. *Religion:* Catholic. *Home:* 725 Northeast 87th St., Miami, Fla. 33138. *Office:* 11300 Northeast Second Ave., Miami Shores, Fla. 33161.

CAREER: Nuestra Senora del Rosario, Dominicas Francesas (high school), Havana, Cuba, professor of Spanish, philosophy, logic, sociology, and history, 1953-54; Universidad Catolica de Santo Tomas de Villanueva, Havana, professor of oral expression and grammar, 1958-59; Universidad de La Habana, Havana, instructor of history of philosophy, 1959-60; Dade County Schools Program, Miami, Fla., teacher of English as a second language, 1962; Notre Dame Academy, Miami, professor of English and American literature, 1962-63, professor of Spanish and head of languages department, 1963-66; Barry College, Miami Shores, Fla., associate professor of Spanish and philosophy, 1966—. Professor of Cuban history in cooperation with the Junta Educacianal Patriotica Cubana, Miami, 1964-65; professor of teaching methods for Spanish in Dade County Public School Systems, Miami, 1972; part-time professor of English as a second language at Miami Dade Junior College, 1972-73; Miami Dade Community College, director of English as a second language program, 1974, part-time professor of literature, philosophy, and English as a second language, 1974—. *Member:* American Catholic Association of Philosophy, American Association of University Professors, Association of Teachers of Spanish and Portuguese, Instituto de Cultura Hispanica, Alpha Mu Gamma (faculty member of Miami chapter), Cuban Women's Club (chairman of cultural section, 1974-76), Municipios de Cuba en el Exilio (Miami), Cruzada Educativa Cubana (Miami). *Awards, honors:* Florida Star Award from Florida Chamber of Commerce, 1966, in recognition of teaching achievement; Diploma of Honor Lincoln-Marti from U.S. Department of Health, Education, and Welfare, 1970, for service to the Cuban Refugee Program; various literary and community service awards from more than ten Cuban organizations, schools, colleges, and community organizations.

WRITINGS: (With Ana Rosa Nunez) *Ensayo de Diccionario del Pensamiento Vivo de la Avellaneda* (title means "Dictionary of Ideas in the Works of la Avellaneda"), Ediciones Universal (Miami), 1975; (with Nunez) *Antologia de la Poesia Religiosa de la Avellaneda* (title means "Anthology of the Religious Poetry of la Avellaneda"), Editiones Universal, 1975; *Ensayo sobre El Sitio de Nadie de Hilda Perera* (title means "Essay on 'A Place for None' by Hilda Perera"), Editiones Universal, 1975; *Raices del Alma Cubana* (title means "Roots of the Cuban Soul"), Editiones Universal, 1976. Contributor of articles to *Diario Las Americas, El Tiempo, Diario de la Marina,* and other periodicals and newspapers. Editor of the literature section, *Afan* (Cuban monthly review), 1957; *El Habanero,* editor of children's literature and historical section, "Menique," 1968-72, editor with Ana Rosa Nunez of literature section, "Horas Blancas," 1972—; editor of Cuban page, *Diario Las Americas,* 1971-72.

WORK IN PROGRESS: A manuscript, "Ortega y Gasset: Metaphysics, Ethics and Theory of Knowledge"; three

books, *Cuentos Cortos, Antologia de la Literatura Cubana desde 1604 al Modernismo; Jose de la Luz y Caballero.*

SIDELIGHTS: Alzago told *CA:* "The circumstance of having come to the U.S.A. as a Cuban refugee escaping communism is basic in my outlook in life. One of my basic aims is to concentrate on Cuban culture and Cuban literature courses and writings so as to give the Cuban youth in exile a knowledge of their culture and deeper sense of identity. Teaching implies a definite vocation and sense of mission." Basic authors in the formation of her thought include Ortega y Gasset, Miguel de Unamuno, Jose Marti, and Jose de la Luz y Caballero. Also her Catholic religion has been fundamental, she reported. Besides her native language of Spanish, she speaks English and French and has a general knowledge of Latin and Greek. She has traveled in Spain, France, Switzerland, Italy, Mexico, and the United States.

BIOGRAPHICAL/CRITICAL SOURCES: Voice, October 12, 1962; *Diario Las Americas,* April 27, 1969, February 21, 1971, October 7, 1971; *Hourglass,* October 27, 1975.

*   *   *

AMBASZ, Emilio 1943-

PERSONAL: Born June 13, 1943, in Argentina; son of Abraham and Julia (van Paats) Ambasz. *Education:* Princeton University, M.F.A., 1965. *Home and office:* 295 Central Park West, New York, N.Y. 10024.

CAREER: Princeton University, Princeton, N.J., assistant professor of architecture, 1966-68, Philip Freneau Bicentennial Preceptor of Architecture, 1968-69; Museum of Modern Art, New York City, curator of design, 1970-76; free-lance architect, 1977—. Architectural projects include a computer center near Mexico City, a community arts center in Grand Rapids, Mich., a series of educational and agrarian community centers in Peru, and the installation of the exhibition "Italy: The New Domestic Landscape," at the Museum of Modern Art. Co-director of "New Cities Project," 1969-70; director of research program "Institutions for a Post Technological Society: The Universitas Project," 1970-72. Lecturer, Hochschule fuer Gestaltung (Germany), 1967. Institute for Architecture and Urban Studies, co-founder, 1967, fellow, 1970-72. *Awards, honors:* Cover Award from the American Institute of Graphic Arts, 1973, 1976; Prix Jean de la Fontaine award, 1975, for *Working Fables: A Collection of Design Tales for Skeptic Children;* Progressive Architecture Award, 1976, for design of a community center; Institutional and Business Designer's Top Award, Gold Medal, 1977; Resources Council's Award, 1977.

WRITINGS: (Editor) *Italy: The New Domestic Landscape,* Museum of Modern Art, 1972; *The Universitas Project: Institutions for a Post-Technological Society,* Museum of Modern Art, 1972; (editor) *Designing Programmes/lla, 1975; (with Brian Richards, R. Gearpanos, and Martin Wohl)* The Taxi Project, *Museum of Modern Art, 1976;* The Architecture of Luis Barragan, *Museum of Modern Art, 1976.*

Contributor of more than twenty articles to journals in his field.

WORK IN PROGRESS: The Alternative Home Catalogue, a book proposing the use of industrial products as alternatives for use in a domestic environment.

SIDELIGHTS: Emilio Ambasz told *CA:* "I am an object maker, whether products or buildings. As for my attitude toward problem-solving in design, I can distinguish two features of my work. First, I try to go beyond the problem-at-hand. The second characteristic of my approach is that I always look around to see whether there is not something already existent which I may re-utilize.

"Since I feel slightly guilty for having betrayed our forefathers' blind trust in progress, and their belief in new products as the healers of mankind's problems, I have felt compelled to develop a little philosophical theory to justify such behaviour. It goes, more or less, as follows:

"Europe's eternal quest remains Utopia, the myth of the end. America's returning myth is Arcadia, the eternal beginning. While the traditional vision of Arcadia is that of a humanistic garden, America's Arcadia has turned into a man-made nature, a forest of artificial trees and of mental shadows.

"Like the first chair-maker who used the wood of surrounding trees, so are now some of America's designers beginning to use the objects and processes (and sometimes, the memories) surrounding them. But, since no more trees remain, just chairs, they have to be careful their creations are either capable of returning to their previous state, or of being re-utilized, lest they find themselves the gardeners of a man-made desert. The designer, that old thaumaturgus of the eternal gesture, must now learn both how to celebrate the ritual of the beginning and how to design for the ceremony of the end.

"The principle underlying such notions of order is the concept of open-ended systems, where the possibilities for changing patterns of relationships remain always open, but where each of the component elements maintains its irreducible identity.

"The methodological principle guiding my work is to search for prototypical or pilot solutions which can first be formulated into a general method, and then applied to solve specific problems.

"I believe the designer's real task begins once functional and behavioural needs have been satisfied. We create objects not only because we hope to satisfy the pragmatic needs of man, but mainly because we need to satisfy the demands of our passions and imagination. It is not hunger, but love and fear, and sometimes wonder, which make us create. The poetic principle is the fundament of our creating objects. The designer's milieu may have changed but the task, I believe, remains the same: to give poetic form to the pragmatic."

Examples of Ambasz's design work were acquired in 1967 and 1977 for the permanent design collection of the Museum of Modern Art in New York City. He contributed a special project to the section representing American architecture at the 1976 Venice Biennale, and presented a special exhibition of his architectural, industrial, and graphic design work in Tokyo, Japan, during the month of September, 1977.

Ambasz is competent in English, Spanish, Italian, French, and German.

BIOGRAPHICAL/CRITICAL SOURCES—Books: Mildred Constantine, *Word and Image*, Museum of Modern Art, 1968; Ada Louise Huxtable, *Kicked a Building Lately?*, Quadrangle, 1976; Martin Fox and Edward K. Carpenter, *The Best in Exhibition Design*, RC Publications, 1977; Marina Waisman, *Emilio Ambasz*, Editorial Summa, 1977.

Periodicals: *Progressive Architecture*, March, 1975, May, 1975, January, 1976, May, 1977; *Space/Design* (Japan), August, 1975; *Architecture and Urbanism* (Japan), January, 1977.

AMBHANWONG, Suthilak 1924-
(Suthinee)

PERSONAL: Born January 22, 1924, in Saraburi, Thailand; daughter of Luang Prasarnsindu and Pismai (Kupirom) Ambhanwong. *Education:* Chulalongkorn University (Thailand), B.A., 1943; Simmons College, M.S., 1953. *Religion:* Buddhism. *Home:* 200/1 Silom Rd., Bangkok 5, Thailand. *Office:* Department of Library Science, Chulalongkorn University, Bangkok 5, Thailand.

CAREER: Chulalongkorn University, Bangkok, Thailand, assistant lecturer, 1947-54, assistant librarian, 1947-56, lecturer in charge of department of library science, 1955-62, chief librarian, 1957-75, assistant professor in charge of department of library science, 1963-64, associate professor, 1965-66, head of department of library science, 1965—, professor of library science, 1967—. *Member:* International Association of Orientalist Librarians, American Library Association, Thai Library Association (member of executive committee, 1975-76). *Awards, honors:* National Book Week Award for Best Book for Young Adults, 1975, for *Bang-Pa-In Summer Palace.*

WRITINGS: Four Periods in the Thai Literature: An Annotated Bibliography, Tai Library Association, 1951, 2nd edition, 1972; *Introduction to Librarianship: Use of Books and Libraries,* Thai Watana Panich (Thailand), 1959, 4th edition, 1972; (compiler) *A Bibliography of Material about Thailand in Western Languages,* Chulalongkorn University Central Library, 1960; *Cataloging Rules for Thai Books and Subject Headings,* Thai Library Association, 1963; *Dr. Frances Lander Spain: Founder of Modern Library Service in Thailand* (monograph), Department of Library Science, Chulalongkorn University, 1965; *A Chronology of Libraries and Librarianship in Thailand* (monograph), Department of Library Science, Chulalongkorn University, 1967; *Complete Cataloging Rules for Thai Books with Card Samples,* Thai Watana Panich, 1967.

Sud-thi-rug (title means "The Dearest"), Banakit Trading, 1974; *Wat Pra Jetubon* (name of a Thai temple), Teachers Council Press, 1974; *Literature of Thai Librarianship,* Department of Library Science, Chulalongkorn University, 1975; *Bang-Pa-In Summer Palace* (young adult), Teachers Council Press, 1975; *Chulalongkorn University* (young adult), Teachers Council Press, 1976; *Siamese Cats* (young adult), Teachers Council Press, 1977; *Use of Libraries* (textbook), Teachers Council Press, 1977.

Also author, under name Suthinee, of column "Life Is a Journey" in *Rojana* (Thai magazine). Contributor of articles to *Journal of Education for Librarianship, Journal of Library History, International Library Review, UNESCO Bulletin for Libraries,* and *Thai Library Association Bulletin.*

Member of international advisory board, *Journal of Library History, Philosophy and Comparative Librarianship,* 1966-76; member of board of contributing consultants, *International Library Review,* 1969—.

WORK IN PROGRESS: A Bibliography of Material about Thailand in Western Languages, First Supplement, 1960-1973; Foundation of Librarianship; Prince Sitthatha.

SIDELIGHTS: Ambhanwong told *CA:* "My favorite book is *Sud-thi-rug,* a collection of articles published in Siam Samai weekly newspapers written under pseudonym Suthinee. Many articles in this book have been included in textbooks in Thai writing for school and college students in Thailand as examples for a good style of writing. My extensive travelling abroad has made it possible for me to write for *Rojana* a regular column entitled "Life Is a Journey" focusing on my reminiscences and observations made of my various trips. In fact, I enjoy writing as well as teaching library science."

* * *

AMES, Gerald 1906-

PERSONAL: Born October 17, 1906; married second wife, Rose Wyler, 1948; children: (first marriage) Eva Lee Baird, (stepchildren) Joseph, Karl. *Home:* New York City.

CAREER: Author of books for children. *Member:* Authors Guild.

WRITINGS—All with wife, Rose Wyler: *Life on Earth* (self-illustrated), H. Schuman, 1953; *Restless Earth,* Abelard-Schuman, 1954; *The Golden Book of Astronomy* (illustrated by John Polgreen), Simon & Schuster, 1955, revised edition published as *The New Golden Book of Astronomy,* Golden Press, 1965; *The Story of the Ice Age* (illustrated by Thomas W. Voter), Harper, 1956; *The Earth's Story,* Creative Educational Society, 1957, reprinted, 1967; *First Days of the World* (illustrated by Leonard Weisgard), Harper, 1958; *What Makes It Go?* (illustrated by Bernice Myers), Whittlesey, 1958; *The First People in the World* (illustrated by Weisgard), Harper, 1958.

The Giant Golden Book of Biology (illustrated by Charles Harper), Golden Press, 1961, revised edition published as *The Golden Book of Biology,* 1967; *Planet Earth* (illustrated by Cornelius De Witt), Golden Press, 1963; *Prove It!* (illustrated by Talivadis Stubis), Harper, 1963; *Food and Life,* Creative Educational Society, 1966; *Magic Secrets* (illustrated by Stubis), Harper, 1967; *Spooky Tricks* (illustrated by Stubis), Harper, 1968; *Secrets in Stone* (photographs by Ames), Four Winds Press, 1970; *Funny Magic: Easy Tricks for Young Magicians* (illustrated by Stubis), Parents' Magazine Press, 1972; *Funny Number Tricks: Easy Magic with Arithmetic* (illustrated by Stubis), Parents' Magazine Press, 1976.

Contributor of articles on scientific subjects to popular magazines.

SIDELIGHTS: Ames's books have been generally praised for presenting scientific facts to children in the clearest possible language. *New York Herald Tribune* called *The Story of the Ice Age* "one of the most precise and scholarly as well as one of the simplest and most effective informational books for children." In a review of *First Days of the World, Christian Science Monitor* stated, "It presents a scientifically complex subject in terms of its central and easily understood concepts, dropping complicated explanations in favor of clarity." Accordingly, *New York Times Book Review* applauded *The Giant Golden Book of Biology:* "Much of the excitement in modern biological science is captured.... Scientific experiments of the past are included also to point out that real progress in understanding comes less from answering questions than by learning to ask better, more sophisticated questions. This view of science is seldom presented so clearly."

BIOGRAPHICAL/CRITICAL SOURCES: New York Herald Tribune, August 12, 1956, June 15, 1958; *Christian Science Monitor,* May 8, 1958; *New York Times Book Review,* January 28, 1962.

* * *

AMMON, Harry 1917-

PERSONAL: Born September 4, 1917, in Waterbury,

Conn.; son of G. Harry and Lena (Farrell) Ammon. *Education:* Georgetown University, B.S., 1939, M.A., 1940; University of Virginia, Ph.D., 1948. *Home:* 318 West Oak St., Carbondale, Ill. 62901. *Office:* Department of History, Southern Illinois University, Carbondale, Ill. 62901.

CAREER: Tulane University, New Orleans, La., assistant professor of history, 1945-47; Sweet Briar College, Sweet Briar, Va., assistant professor of history, 1947-48; *Maryland Historical Magazine,* Annapolis, Md., editor, 1948-50; Southern Illinois University, Carbondale, assistant professor, 1950-54, associate professor, 1954-67, professor of history, 1967—. Fulbright lecturer at University of Vienna, 1954-55; visiting professor at University of Virginia, 1969-70. *Member:* American Historical Association, Southern Historical Association, Phi Beta Kappa.

WRITINGS: James Monroe: Quest for National Identity, McGraw, 1971; *The Genet Mission,* Norton, 1973. Contributor of articles and reviews to history journals.

WORK IN PROGRESS: A study of the Monroe administration, for University of Nebraska Press; research on the history of historical writing.

SIDELIGHTS: Ammon writes briefly that his "primary vocational interest is early American history and the history and philosophy of history." *Avocational interests:* Travel (to Mexico to study pre-Columbian ruins, and to Europe), music, painting, architecture.

* * *

AMRINE, Michael 1919(?)-1974

PERSONAL: Born in Council Grove, Kan.; married wife, Renee; children: Neil, Eric, Douglas. *Education:* Attended Kansas State Teachers College and Columbia University. *Office:* National Heart and Lung Institute, 9600 Rockville Pike, Bldg. 31, Bethesda, Md. 20014.

CAREER: Science writer and public relations counsel to scientific organizations. Has also worked as a journalist with the *Emporia Gazette* and as assistant to the director of the National Heart and Lung Institute. First staff member, Federation of Atomic Scientists.

WRITINGS: All Sons Must Say Goodbye (novel), Harper, 1942; *Secret* (novel), Houghton, 1950; *The Great Decision: The Secret History of the Atomic Bomb,* Putnam, 1959; *This Is Humphrey: The Story of the Senator,* Doubleday, 1960; *This Awesome Challenge: The Hundred Days of Lyndon Johnson,* Putnam, 1964; *The Safe Driving Handbook,* Grosset, 1970. Also author of scientific articles and papers.

SIDELIGHTS: As the first staff member of the Federation of Atomic Scientists, Amrine was influential in the creation of the Atomic Energy Commission. In addition, *New York Times* reported, "he was instrumental in bringing public attention to the early battles by scientists of the Manhattan atom-bomb project for civilian, rather than military, control of nuclear energy."

OBITUARIES: New York Times, February 19, 1974.*

(Died February 17, 1974)

* * *

ANAND, Valerie 1937-
(Fiona Buckley)

PERSONAL: Born July 6, 1937, in London, England; daughter of John McCormick (a proofreader) and Florence (a dressmaker; maiden name, Sayers) Stubington; married Dalip Singh Anand (a civil servant), March 26, 1970. *Educa-*

tion: Attended convents and local public school. *Politics:* "Not much, as ideologies seem to me to be 'package deals' in ideas. ..." *Residence:* Surrey, England. *Office:* Matthew Hall & Co. Ltd., 101 Tottenham Court Rd., London W1A 1BT, England.

CAREER: Secretary and typist, 1956-59; *Quarry Managers Journal,* London, England, secretary and sub-editor, 1959-60; Institute of British Launderers, London, assistant public relations officer, 1960-63; *Accountancy,* London, reporter on office equipment, 1963-66; *Index to Office Equipment,* Croyden, Surrey, England, reporter and feature writer, 1966-68; E. J. Poole Associates, London, public relations officer and feature writer on business systems, 1968-71; Heal's (furnishing company), London, assistant editor of house organ, 1971-72, editor, 1972-75; Matthew Hall & Co. Ltd. (engineering group), London, editor of house magazine, 1975—. *Member:* British Association of Industrial Editors.

WRITINGS: Gildenford (historical novel), Scribner, 1977. Author of cooking columns in Heal's house magazine. Contributor of short stories (under pseudonym Fiona Buckley) to *Evening News,* and of articles to *Surrey Life* and *Accountancy.*

WORK IN PROGRESS: Research on the Norman Conquest, with a historical novel expected to result.

SIDELIGHTS: Valerie Anand writes: "I first became interested in history at the age of fifteen when I saw MGM's film of *Ivanhoe.* I began reading history in secret, due to the fear that, if the school found out, I would be pounced on and forced to take it seriously, which would wreck the fun and sense of adventure. The deception worked. I enjoyed history on the side and my school reports complained bitterly of my lack of interest in this subject.

"I picked historical fiction as opposed to any other sort of writing, because I was in love with a bit of history. I regard a novelist's function primarily as entertainment: it doesn't matter what you write about as long as it can take someone's mind off his income tax or his influenza.

"I never planned my career (my chief philosophy of life is that it's for living) but took it as it came, though with strong bias toward traditionally masculine fields. I regard ordinary women's journalism as dull and trivial. The only exception to this is cookery.

"My husband is Punjabi-born, Sikh by religion. I have found the resultant introduction into Indian society an enthralling experience. It is very interesting to get 'inside' a culture other than one's own. This may have something to do with the attraction history has for me."

AVOCATIONAL INTERESTS: Horseback riding, flying (once had private pilot's license), trying to learn chess and Hindi, reading, cats, rumpsteak, good wine, the southwest corner of England, Shirley Bassey.

*   *   *

ANDERSON, Carolyn   1941-

PERSONAL: Born August 20, 1941, in Evansville, Ind.; daughter of Maurice O. (a social worker) and F. Helen (a teacher; maiden name, Burnau) Hunt; married Gerald L. Anderson (president of American Gas & Chemical Co.), June 5, 1965; children: Clifford Blake, Gwendolyn Cheryl. *Education:* Attended Lycoming College, 1959-61; Boston University, B.A., 1963; Columbia University, M.S., 1965; New York School of Interior Design, certificate, 1968. *Religion:* Protestant. *Home:* 138 Clapboard Ridge Rd., Greenwich, Conn. 06830. *Agent:* Brandt & Brandt, 101 Park Ave., New York, N.Y. 10017.

CAREER: New York Community Service Society, New York, N.Y., caseworker for family agency, 1966-67; Carolyn Anderson Corp. (interior design firm), Greenwich, Conn., president, 1968—. *Member:* Field Club (Greenwich, Conn.).

WRITINGS: The Complete Book of Homemade Ice Cream, Milk Sherbet, and Sherbet, Saturday Review Press, 1972.

WORK IN PROGRESS: With John Wilson, *Skiing: A Sport for Children.*

*   *   *

ANDERSON, Clarence William   1891-1971

PERSONAL: Born April 12, 1891, in Wahoo, Neb.; married Madeline Paltenghi (a poet). *Education:* Studied at the Art Institute of Chicago. *Residence:* Mason, N.H.

CAREER: Author and illustrator of books about horses. Worked his way through art school as a school teacher for two years; moved to New York, 1925, became a free-lance artist, developing an interest in horses; later qualified as a judge of hunters and jumpers by the American Horse Shows Association. His works have been displayed in galleries and museums throughout the United States. *Member:* American Society of Etchers, Society of American Graphic Artists.

WRITINGS—"Billy and Blaze" series; all self-illustrated and published by Macmillan, except as noted: *Billy and Blaze,* 1936, reprinted, 1969; *Blaze and the Gypsies,* 1937, reprinted, 1962; *Blaze and the Forest Fire,* 1938, reprinted, Collier Books, 1972; *Blaze Finds the Trail,* 1950; *Blaze and Thunderbolt,* 1955; *Blaze and the Mountain Lion,* 1959; *Blaze and the Indian Cave,* 1964; *Blaze and the Lost Quarry,* 1966; *Blaze and the Gray Spotted Pony,* 1968; *Blaze Shows the Way,* 1969; *Blaze Finds Forgotten Roads,* 1970.

Fiction; all self-illustrated and published by Macmillan, except as noted: *And So to Bed,* Loring & Mussey, 1935; *Salute,* 1940, reprinted, 1966; *High Courage,* 1941; *Bobcat,* 1949; *A Pony for Linda,* 1951; *Linda and the Indians,* 1952; *The Crooked Colt,* 1954; *The Horse of Hurricane Hill,* 1956; *Afraid to Ride,* 1957; *Pony for Three,* 1958; *A Filly for Joan,* 1960; *Lonesome Little Colt,* 1961; *Great Heart,* 1962; *Twenty Gallant Horses,* 1965; *Another Man o' War,* 1966; *C. W. Anderson's Favorite Horse Stories,* 1967; *The Outlaw,* 1967; *Phantom: Son of the Gray Ghost,* 1969; *The Blind Connemara,* 1971; *The Rumble Seat Pony,* 1971.

Nonfiction; all self-illustrated: *Black Bay and Chestnut: Profiles of Twenty Favorite Horses,* Macmillan, 1939; *Deep Through the Heart: Profiles of Twenty Valiant Horses,* Macmillan, 1940, reprinted, 1961; *Thoroughbreds,* Macmillan, 1942; *Big Red,* Macmillan, 1943; *Heads Up, Heels Down: A Handbook of Horsemanship and Riding,* Macmillan, 1944, reprinted, 1961; *A Touch of Greatness,* Macmillan, 1945; *Tomorrow's Champion,* Macmillan, 1946; *Sketchbook,* Macmillan, 1948; *All Thoroughbreds,* Harper, 1948; *Post Parade,* Harper, 1949; *Horses Are Folks,* Harper, 1950; *Horse Show,* Harper, 1951; *Turf and Bluegrass,* Harper, 1952; *The Smashers,* Harper, 1954; *Grey, Bay, and Chestnut,* Harper, 1955.

Colts and Champions, Harper, 1956; *Accent on Youth,* Harper, 1958; *Bred to Run,* Harper, 1960; *Complete Book of Horses and Horsemanship,* Macmillan, 1963; *The Look of a Thoroughbred,* Harper, 1963; *The World of Horses,* Harper, 1965; *Before the Bugle,* Macmillan, 1968; *Horse of the Century: Man o' War,* Macmillan, 1970; *The Miracle of Greek Sculpture,* Dutton, 1970.

SIDELIGHTS: Anderson began writing childrens books at age forty-five. All of his drawings are in pen and ink because he rejected the notion that children's books must be illustrated in color. If the drawings were realistic and lively enough, he felt, children would be unaware of the lack of color. Anderson found that lithography was the most perfect way to reproduce his drawings, and many of his books were done directly on stone.

OBITUARIES: New York Times, March 28, 1971; Publishers Weekly, April 26, 1971; Antiquarian Bookman, May 17, 1971.*

(Died March 26, 1971)

*   *   *

ANDERSON, Robert David 1942-

PERSONAL: Born July 11, 1942, in Cardiff, Wales. Education: Oxford University, B.A., 1963, D.Phil., 1967. Agent: A. D. Peters, 10 Buckingham St., London, England. Office: Department of History, University of Edinburgh, Edinburgh, Scotland.

CAREER: University of Glasgow, Glasgow, Scotland, assistant lecturer, 1967-69; University of Edinburgh, Edinburgh, Scotland, lecturer in history, 1969—.

WRITINGS: Education in France, 1848-70, Clarendon Press, 1975; France, 1870-1914: Politics and Society, Routledge & Kegan Paul, 1977.

WORK IN PROGRESS: A History of Education in the Nineteenth Century, emphasizing Scotland.

*   *   *

ANDERSSON, Nic
    See TOFTE, Arthur

*   *   *

ANDRES, Glenn M(erle) 1941-

PERSONAL: Born July 15, 1941, in Chicago, Ill.; son of Harold William (a businessman) and Amanda (Breuhaus) Andres; married Barbara Hamm, August 26, 1967; children: Christopher, Melissa. Education: Cornell University, B.Arch., 1964; Princeton University, M.F.A., 1967, Ph.D., 1971; American Academy in Rome, graduate study, 1967-69. Politics: Independent. Religion: Congregationalist. Residence: Salisbury, Vt. Office: Johnson Memorial Building, Middlebury College, Middlebury, Vt. 05753.

CAREER: Middlebury College, Middlebury, Vt., assistant professor, 1970-78, associate professor of art, 1978—, associate director of Johnson Gallery, 1976—. Tour guide in Italy, 1969. Member of Middlebury Townscape Improvement Committee, 1974-76, and Frog Hollow Federation, 1974-75. Trustee of Sheldon Museum, 1975—. Member: National Trust for Historic Preservation, Society for the Preservation of New England Antiquities (member of Vermont council, 1975—), Tau Beta Pi, Phi Kappa Phi. Awards, honors: Danforth fellowship, 1964-70; Woodrow Wilson fellowships, 1964-65, 1967-68; Rome Prize and fellowship from American Academy in Rome, 1967-69.

WRITINGS: A Walking History of Middlebury, Vermont, Addison Press, 1975; The Villa Medici in Rome, Garland Publishing, 1976. Contributor to exhibition catalogs and to professional and local journals.

WORK IN PROGRESS: Research for a book on Middlebury, Vt., as a microcosm of nineteenth-century American planning and building; research for a reconstruction of the life and work of sixteenth-century Italian architect Nanni di Baccio Bigio.

SIDELIGHTS: Andres writes: "I am an architectural historian seeking to communicate a sense of architecture and the built environment as a physical manifestation of history (personal, technical, economic, and cultural). By this means I hope to contribute to the appreciation and preservation of this environment and to an understanding of the ways in which it can respond to, influence, and serve society."

*   *   *

ANGEBERT, Jean
    See BERTRAND, Michel

*   *   *

ANGEBERT, Jean-Michel
    See BERTRAND, Michel

*   *   *

ANGEBERT, Michel
    See BERTRAND, Michel

*   *   *

ANGELO, Valenti 1897-

PERSONAL: Born June 23, 1897, in Massarosa, Tuscany, Italy; came to the United States, 1905; son of Augustino and Viclinda (Checchi) Angelo; married Maxine Grimm, July 23, 1923; children: Valdine, Peter. Education: Attended schools in Italy and California. Religion: Catholic. Residence: Bronxville, N.Y.

CAREER: Author and illustrator. Worked in a paper mill at the age of fifteen; later worked as a laborer in rubber, steel, and glass works; employed for three years at a photoengraving firm; began illustrating books for Grabhorn Press, 1926; became a free-lance artist, 1933; turned to writing children's books, 1937. Awards, honors: Since 1927, thirty-seven books illustrated by Angelo have been included in the American Institute of Graphic Arts' Fifty Books of the Year Exhibits.

WRITINGS—All self-illustrated; all published by Viking, except as noted: Nino, 1938; Golden Gate, 1939, reprinted, Arno, 1975; Paradise Valley, 1940; A Battle in Washington Square, Golden Cross Press, 1942; Hill of Little Miracles, 1942; Look Out Yonder, 1943; The Rooster Club, 1944; The Bells of Bleecker Street, 1949, reprinted, 1969; The Marble Fountain, 1951; Big Little Island, 1955; The Acorn Tree, 1958; The Honey Boat, 1959; The Candy Basket, 1960; Angelino and the Barefoot Saint, 1961; The Merry Marcos, 1963; The Tale of a Donkey, 1966.

Illustrator: Walt Whitman, Leaves of Grass, Random House, 1930; Alexander Dumas, Three Musketeers, Illustrated Editions Co., 1935; Nathaniel Hawthorne, House of the Seven Gables, Limited Editions Club, 1935; Ruth Sawyer, Roller Skates, Viking, 1936; Charles George Soulie, editor and translator, Chinese Love Tales, Illustrated Editions Co., 1936; Richard Francis Burton, F. Kasidah of Haji Abdu el-Yezdi: A Lay of the Higher Law, Limited Editions Club, 1937; Clement Clarke Moore, Visit from St. Nicholas, Hawthorne, 1937; Charles K. Scott Moncrieff, toanslator, Song of Roland, Limited Editions Club, 1938; Marguerite Vance, Paula, Dodd, 1939.

John Fante, Dago Red, Viking, 1940; Sawyer, Long Christmas, Viking, 1941; Bret Harte, Luck of Roaring Camp and

Other Stories, Peter Pauper Press, 1943; *Psalms of David in the King James Version,* Peter Pauper Press, 1943; Annie Thaxter Eaton, *The Animals' Christmas,* Viking, 1944, reprinted, 1966; Elizabeth Barrett Browning, *Sonnets from the Portuguese,* Heritage Press, 1945; Edwin Arnold, *Light of Asia,* Peter Pauper Press, 1946; Burton, translator, *Book of the Thousand Nights and a Night,* Heritage Press, 1946; Floy Perkinson Gates, *Hey, Mr. Grasshopper!,* privately printed, 1949.

Clyde Robert Bulla, *Song of St. Francis,* Crowell, 1952; Sterling North, *Birthday of Little Jesus,* Grosset, 1952; Delos Wheeler Lovelace, *Journey to Bethlehem,* Crowell, 1953; Francis Thompson, *Hound of Heaven,* Peter Pauper Press, 1953; Eaton, *Welcome Christmas,* Crowell, 1955; William Shakespeare, *The Tragedy of Hamlet,* Peter Pauper Press, 1956; *The Book of Proverbs,* Heritage Press, 1963; Bulla, *St. Valentine's Day,* Crowell, 1965; Hawthorne, *Twice-Told Tales,* edited by Wallace Stegner, Limited Editions Club, 1966. Also illustrator of *Benito,* by Bulla, published by Crowell.

SIDELIGHTS: As a child growing up in Italy, Angelo was encouraged by the village wood-carver to become an artist. He has since decorated and illustrated more than two hundred children's books. At the age of forty Angelo also began writing stories, based largely on his own childhood memories. Reviewing one of these stories, *The Candy Basket, Christian Science Monitor* stated, "Valenti Angelo can spin a tale as fragile and as colorful as his cooks can fashion a basket."

BIOGRAPHICAL/CRITICAL SOURCES: Christian Science Monitor, September 8, 1960.

*   *   *

ANICAR, Tom
See RACINA, Thom

*   *   *

ANSEL, Walter (Charles) 1897-1977
August 25, 1897—November 26, 1977; American career naval officer and writer of books on Hitler. Ansel, who served in both world wars, retired as rear admiral. He died in Annapolis, Md. Obituaries: *Washington Post,* November 28, 1977. (See index for *CA* sketch)

*   *   *

ANTHONY, Edward 1895-1971
PERSONAL: Born August 4, 1895, in New York, N.Y.; son of Robert and Rose (Friedman) Anthony; married Esther H. Howard (an artist and editor), December 17, 1928; children: Richard W. *Residence:* New Milford, Conn. *Agent:* Paul R. Reynolds, Inc., 12 East 41st St., New York, N.Y. 10017.

CAREER: Author, newspaperman, and publisher. Member of the staff of the *Bridgeport Herald* and the *New York Herald;* became publisher of *Woman's Home Companion,* 1943, and *Collier's,* 1949. Publicity director of Herbert Hoover's presidential campaign, 1928. *Member:* National Press Club, P.E.N., Dutch Treat Club, Players Club.

WRITINGS: Merry-Go-Roundelays, Century, 1921; (for children) *The Pussycat Princess,* Century, 1922; (with Joseph Anthony) *The Fairies Up-to-Date* (illustrated by Jean de Bosschere), Little, Brown, 1923; *"Razzberry!",* Holt, 1924; (editor) *How to Get Rid of a Woman* (illustrated by George de Zayas), Bobbs-Merrill, 1928; (with Frank Buck)

Bring 'Em Back Alive, Simon & Schuster, 1930; (with Buck) *Wild Cargo,* Simon & Schuster, 1932; (with Clyde Beatty) *The Big Cage,* Century, 1933; (with Gordon B. Enders) *Nowhere Else in the World,* Farrar, Straus, 1935; (with Abel A. Schechter) *I Live on Air,* F. A. Stokes, 1941; *The Sex Refresher* (illustrated by George Price), Howell, Soskin, 1943; *Every Dog Has His Say* (poems; illustrated by Morgan Dennis), Watson-Guptill, 1947; (for children) *Oddity Land* (illustrated by Erik Blegvad), Doubleday, 1957; *This Is Where I Came In: The Impromptu Confessions of Edward Anthony* (autobiography), Doubleday, 1960; *O Rare Don Marquis: A Biography,* Doubleday, 1962; (with C. Beatty) *Facing the Big Cats,* Doubleday, 1965; (with Henry Trefflich) *Jungle for Sale,* Hawthorn Books, 1967; (with Eric Sloane) *Mr. Daniels and The Grange,* Funk & Wagnalls, 1968; *Astrology and Sexual Compatibility,* Essandes, 1971.

SIDELIGHTS: Saturday Review's analysis of *I Live on Air* included: "Mr. Schechter and his co-author have an agreeable talent for story-telling, and a racy style marked by a fondness for homespun American idiom. They write from the inside with all the data at their disposal. The result is a readable, in parts highly entertaining volume on a subject that so far has not been adequately covered. Anyone interested in news coverage in general or radio in particular might do well to have a copy of [this book] on his desk." The *New York Times* added, "It is a scattered and hectic account, racy and enthusiastic and laid out on the carefree principle that when one good story reminds the teller of another, it should be told at once, even if it properly belongs in another chapter."

Oddity Land, a book of nonsense verse, was reviewed by a *New York Herald Tribune* critic who wrote, "This is nonsense that will be enjoyed beyond the nursery. The antic rhymes, smooth and clever or mischievously odd, the artfully crazy images that seem to be created because a rhyme is necessary, are strung together in groups with brief rhyming introductions. It is just plain fooling and good fooling."

A *New York Herald Tribune* review of *This Is Where I Came In,* Anthony's autobiography, said, "Though he packs his book with the names of the famous and illustrious people he knew and worked with, Anthony himself emerges as an unpretentious humor-loving individual who makes no personal claim to fame. He has no recognizable philosophy; he has no deep meaning message; he possesses no great literary style. But he is highly enjoyable because he writes out of the richness of a full and varied life in the world of words he loves." Quentin Reynolds, writing in *Saturday Review* added, ". . . There isn't a dull page in *This Is Where I Came In* because there hasn't been a dull page in the life of Ed Anthony."

Universal Pictures adapted Anthony's and Clyde Beatty's work, *The Big Cage,* into a motion picture of the same name in 1933.

BIOGRAPHICAL/CRITICAL SOURCES: New York Times, March 2, 1941; *Saturday Review,* April 26, 1941, April 30, 1960; *New York Herald Tribune,* November 17, 1957, May 22, 1960; *This Is Where I Came In: The Impromptu Confessions of Edward Anthony,* Doubleday, 1960.

OBITUARIES: New York Times, August 18, 1971; *Washington Post,* August 20, 1971; *Publishers Weekly,* September 13, 1971.*

(Died August 16, 1971)

ANTIN, David 1932-

PERSONAL: Born February 1, 1932, in New York, N.Y.; son of Max and Mollie (Kitzes) Antin; married Eleanor Fineman (an artist and poet) December 16, 1960; children: Blaise Cendrars. *Education:* City College of New York (now of the City University of New York), B.A., 1955; New York University, M.A., 1966. *Home address:* P.O. Box 1147, Del Mar, Calif. 92014. *Office:* Department of Visual Arts, University of California, La Jolla, Calif. 92037.

CAREER: Poet and art critic. University of California, San Diego, professor of visual arts, 1968—, curator and director of "The Gallery." *Awards, honors:* Longview award for poetry published in small magazines, 1960; Herbert Lehman fellowship from New York University, 1966-68; creative arts award from University of California, 1972.

WRITINGS: definitions (poetry), Caterpillar Press, 1967; *Autobiography,* Something Else Press, 1967; *code of flag behavior* (poetry), Black Sparrow Press, 1968; *Meditations* (poetry), Black Sparrow Press, 1971; *Talking* (poetry), Kulchur Foundation, 1972; *After the War: A Long Novel with Few Words,* Black Sparrow Press, 1973; (contributor) Ira Schneider and Beryl Korot, editors, *Video Art,* Harcourt, 1976; *Talking at the Boundaries,* New Directions, 1976.

Translator: Bernard Pullman, *Modern Theory of Molecular Structure,* third edition, Dover, 1962; Heinrich Dorrie, *One Hundred Great Problems of Elementary Mathematics: Their History & Solution,* Dover, 1965; Werner A. Gunther, *Physics of Modern Electronics,* revised edition, Dover, 1966.

Contributor of poems and articles to *Stony Brook Journal, Some/Thing, Caterpillar, Poems from the Floating World, Trobar, Kayak, Nation, Art News, Kulchur, Journal of the History of Ideas, Arts Magazine, Boundary-2,* and other periodicals. Editor with Jerome Rothenberg, *Some/Thing,* 1965-70; contributing editor, *Alcheringa: A Journal of Ethnopoetics.*

SIDELIGHTS: David Antin, poet and art critic, is associated with a group of artists, working out of New York City, who brought new definitions and ambitions to poetry in the early 1970's. When one thinks of the context of Antin's work, poets like Jerome Rothenberg and Armand Schwerner come to mind, for they are two writers who have done much to revive, or rather establish, interest in primitive poetry.

Antin told *CA:* "While I have a considerable interest in what is called primitive art and primitive poetry, I have not really been as involved in translating or adapting it as Rothenberg. My background in linguistics and my background in science reflect my interest in the human significance of language structures; this extended to the work of American, Indian, and African poets, though I did no work in it. *Definitions* reflects my interest in the language of science and its implications, *Code of Flag Behavior,* my interest in the pop vernacular and cliche. The term 'found poetry' with its suggestion of the 'trouvaille' and estheticism of junk sculpture was always far from my concerns. I am interested in the lethal implications of socially debased language, at least I was at the time of *Code of Flag Behavior,* which has something in common with the pop Art strategies of Warhol, Lichtenstein and Wesselman. Contrary to the beliefs of many poets, all language is 'found', but some language is not only found, but second and third and hundreth hand."

With regard to "talk poems" he commented: "The 'talk poems' are improvised talk pieces, pieces I go to some particular place to create—in public, as improvisations. I go to a particular place with something in mind but no clear way of saying it, and in the place I come to I try to find some way to deal with what I am interested in, in a way that is meaningful to both the audience and myself. I tape record the pieces, and if I was successful I have something I can transcribe, that may be worth publishing. If it is, I publish it; if not, I forget it. So the 'talk poems' are more or less adapted notations of performances, done somewhere. I've been doing improvised 'talk poems' since 1972. My first book to include a 'talk poem' was *Talking.*"

BIOGRAPHICAL/CRITICAL SOURCES: Poetry, April, 1968, August, 1968; *New York Times,* August 25, 1968; *Virginia Quarterly Review,* 1969; *New York Times Book Review,* November 28, 1976; *Nation,* December 11, 1976; *New Republic,* March 5, 1977.

* * *

ANTON, Hector R(oque) 1919-

PERSONAL: Born March 14, 1919, in El Paso, Tex.; son of Roque and Luisa (Guerra) Anton; married Lois Miriam Triggs, 1949; children: John R., David L., Mary F., Susan C. *Education:* Attended Los Angeles City College, 1938-39; University of California, Los Angeles, B.S., 1942, M.B.A., 1947; University of Minnesota, Ph.D., 1953. *Home:* 7 Mortar Rock Rd., Westport, Conn. 06880.

CAREER: Ivar Pally, Beverly Hills, Calif., junior accountant, 1946; University of Minnesota, Minneapolis, instructor in business administration, 1947-50; University of Washington, Seattle, assistant professor of business administration, 1950-54; University of California, Berkeley, professor of accounting and business administration, beginning 1954, chairman of department of accounting, 1964-68, associate research economist, 1959, 1960, research economist, 1968, 1972, associate dean of Graduate School of Business Administration, 1969-72, retired as professor emeritus; Haskins & Sells (certified public accountants), New York, N.Y., faculty consultant, 1972, partner, 1973—. Certified public accountant in California, Louisiana, and North Carolina. Instructor at University of California, Los Angeles, summer, 1948; visiting professor at University of Minnesota, 1958-59, University of Washington, Seattle, summer, 1965, and Victoria University of Wellington, 1966; Fulbright professor in Finland, 1961-62; Ford Foundation visiting professor at University of Chicago, 1968-69. Adviser to Accounting Principles Board, 1972-73; consultant to government agencies and business firms in the United States, Ireland, and Japan. *Military service:* U.S. Naval Reserve, active duty, 1942-46.

MEMBER: American Accounting Association (research director and member of executive committee, 1970-72), American Economic Association, American Sociological Association, American Association for the Advancement of Science, American Institute of Certified Public Accountants, National Association of Accountants, Institute of Management Sciences, Scandinavian Foundation, Finnish-American Foundation, Finnish Academy of Science (foreign member), Beta Gamma Sigma, Beta Alpha Psi, Alpha Kappa Psi. *Awards, honors:* Grants from Ford Foundation, 1957, 1959-60, 1964, Marcus Wallenberg Foundation, for Stockholm School of Economics, 1964, and National Science Foundation, 1968-69.

WRITINGS: Accounting for the Flow of Business Funds, Houghton, 1962; (with Wayne S. Boutell) *Fortran and Business Data Processing,* McGraw, 1968.

Contributor: L. Schloss and other editors, *Accounting*

Teachers' Guide, American Accounting Association, 1953; R. Dickey, editor, *Cost Accounts Handbook,* Ronald, 1960; *Management Controls: New Directions in Basic Research,* McGraw, 1964; Davidson and other editors, *An Income Approach to Accounting Theory,* Prentice-Hall, 1964; (and editor with Peter Firmin) *Contemporary Issues in Cost Accounting,* Houghton, 1966, 2nd edition, 1972; R. K. Jaedicke and other editors, *Basic Research in Accounting Measurements,* American Accounting Association, 1966; T. H. Williams and C. H. Griffin, editors, *Management Information: A Quantitative Accent,* Irwin, 1967; S. Davidson, editor, *Accounting Handbook,* McGraw, 1970, revised edition, 1977. Contributor of articles and reviews to accounting and economic journals.

*   *   *

ANTONIONI, Michelangelo 1912-

PERSONAL: Born September 29, 1912, in Ferrara, Italy; son of Ismaele (a landowner) and Elisabetta (Roncagli) Antonioni; married Flora Lampronti, 1942 (divorced). *Education:* Attended University of Bologna; Centro Sperimentale (Italian national film school), diploma, 1941. *Home:* Via Vincenzo Tiberio 18, Rome, Italy.

CAREER: Worked as film critic for *Il Corriere Padano* (newspaper) and as bankteller in Ferrara, Italy; moved to Rome, 1940; worked various jobs, including one briefly as staff writer for *Cinema,* 1940; began working in films, 1942, as assistant director and co-scenarist with Robert Rossellini, Enrico Fulchignoni, and Marcel Carne; worked on films at night and on leave from army, 1942-43; film critic for various journals, 1943-50; documentary film maker, 1945-50; credited with being one of early practitioners in neorealistic film with documentary "Gente del Po," filmed in 1943, but not released until 1947; full-length feature film director and scenarist, 1950—. *Military service:* Italian Army, 1942-45.

AWARDS, HONORS: Grand prize for direction at Festival of Punta del Este, 1951, for "Cronaca di un amore"; Golden Bear award from Berlin International Film Festival, 1960, for "La Notte"; "L'Avventura" was voted second best motion picture in film history, 1962, in poll conducted by British Film Institute; Grand prize from Venice Film Festival, 1964, for "Il Deserto rosso"; Academy Award nomination, 1966, for "Blow-Up."

WRITINGS—Documentary films: "Gente del Po" (title means "People of the Po"; first released in 1947), 1943; "N.U. [Netezza urbana]" (title means "Sanitation Department"), 1948; "L'Armorosa menzogna" (title means "Illusory Love"), 1949; "Superstizione" (title means "Superstitions"), 1949; "Sette canne un vestito" (title means "Seven Spindles Make One Suit"), 1949; "La Villa dei Mostri" (title means "The Villa Mostri"), 1950; "La Funivia del Faloria" (title means "The Funicular Railway of Faloria"), 1950; "Uomini in Piu," 1955; "Chung Kuo," 1972, broadcast as "China," by American Broadcasting Corp., 1973.

Screenplays; all as director: "Cronaca di un amore," 1953, released in United States as "Story of a Love," 1975; "I Vinti" (title means "The Beaten Ones"), 1952; "La Signora senza camelie," 1953, released in United States as "Camille Without Camelias," 1965; (with Suso Cecchi d'Amico and Alba de Cespedes) "Le Amiche" (title means "The Girl Friends"; based on short story, "Tra donne sole," by Cesare Pavese), 1955; (with Elio Bartolini and Ennio De Concini) "Il Grido" (title means "The Outcry"), 1957, released in United States, 1961; (with Bartolini and Tonino Guerra) *L'Avventura* (title means "The Adventure"; 1960, released

in United States, 1961), edited by Tommaso Chiaretti, Cappelli (Bologna, Italy), 1960, English translation, Grove, 1969; (with Ennio Flaiano and Guerra) "La Notte" (1961, released in United States as "The Night," 1962), translated from the Italian into French by Michele Causse and published as *La Nuit: La Notte,* Buchet/Chastel (Paris), 1961; (with Guerra, Bartolini, and Ottiero Ottieri) *L'Eclisse* (1962, released in United States as "The Eclipse," 1962), edited by John Francis Lane, Cappelli, 1962; (with Guerra) *Il Deserto rosso* (1964, released in United States as "The Red Desert," 1965), Cappelli, 1964; (with Guerra and Edward Bond) *Blow-Up* (1966), Einaudi (Turin, Italy), 1968, Simon & Schuster, 1971; (with Guerra, Sam Shepard, Fred Graham, and Clare Peploe) *Zabriske Point* (1969), Cappelli, 1970; (with Mark Peploe and Peter Wollen) *The Passenger* (1974), Grove, 1976.

Contributor to films: (Co-scenarist) Enrico Fulchignoni, director, "I Due Foscari," 1942; (co-scenarist) Roberto Rossellini, director, "Un Pilota ritorna," 1942; (co-scenarist) Giuseppe De Santis, director, "Caccia tragica," 1947; (screenwriter and director of "Tentato suicido" segment) "L'Amore in citta," 1952; (co-scenarist) Federico Fellini, director, "Lo Sceicco Bianco," 1952; (screenwriter and director of "Prefazione" episode) "I Tre Volti," 1965.

Collected screenplays: *Screenplays of Michelangelo Antonioni* (includes "Il Grido," "L'Avventura," "La Notte," and "L'Eclisse"), translated by Roger J. Moore and Louis Brigante, Orion Press, 1963; *Sei Film* (includes "Le Amiche," "Il Grido," "L'Avventura," "La Notte," "L'Eclisse," and "Il Deserto rosso"), Einaudi, 1964; *Antonioni: Four Screenplays* (includes "L'Avventura," "Il Grido," "L'Eclisse," and "La Notte"), Grossman, 1971; *Red Desert* [and] *Zabriskie Point,* Simon & Schuster, 1972; *Il Primo Antonioni: I Cortometraggi* (includes "Cronaca di un amore," "I Vinti," "La Signora senza camelie," and "Tentato suicido"), edited by Carlo Di Carlo, Cappelli, 1973.

Also author, with Elio Bartolini, of play, "Scandali Segreti." Contributor of articles and film criticism to film journals and magazines in Italy, 1940-50.

SIDELIGHTS: Antonioni's early films were reviewed as mature and substantial work in Europe but, before 1961 and "L'Avventura," Antonioni was practically unknown in the United States. Only one film had been shown here and it received little notice. "L'Avventura" marks the turning point in Antonioni's recognition because of an intense negative reaction at the 1960 Cannes Film Festival. The film, a drastic departure for an audience in 1960, was booed and heckled at the festival. One-third of the way into the film, Anna, supposedly the main character, disappears and her disappearance is never explained. Her friend, Claudia, becomes the new main character as she takes up with Anna's lover. By the end of the movie the lover has already been unfaithful to Claudia and she rapidly accepts the infidelity without any explanation, or so it seemed to the audience. Owing to the audience's reaction, the film was going to be withheld from commercial release until sympathetic critics and directors voiced their support.

The reviews that appeared soon after the film's release echoed the dismay of the Cannes audience. In time, a highly favorable review appeared, then another, and another, and in 1962, "L'Avventura" was voted the second best film ever made in a poll of critics conducted by the British Film Institute. Later evaluations of the film have called it a masterpiece, a milestone of cinema history, and along with Godard's "Breathless" one of the two great path-breaking films for the sixties. Antonioni's next two films, "La Notte" and "Eclipse" have shared in the favorable evaluation of "L'Avventura." They form a loose trilogy with that film and are also generally regarded to be high points in motion picture achievement.

In 1964 "The Red Desert" appeared, Antonioni's first color film. It received deliberate, lengthy, and serious debate; critics roughly taking two sides. One faction liked the use of color but found the movie thematically lacking. The other side maintained it was a truer form of cinema, a courageous attempt to make the visual expression carry the thematic concerns. For this film, Antonioni painted streets, building interiors, grass, and other objects when he preferred a color other than natural.

His next film, "Blow-up," began the fierce critical controversy that has since followed Antonioni's work. For this film he left Italy and worked in London. When the Motion Picture Association of America required deletions before it would give the finished film a production code seal, Antonioni refused. An interview with the director, which some labeled a poison ink portrait of arrogance, was printed in the *New York Times*. MGM called the refusal to make the cuts artistic integrity and released the film without a code. When the film finally did make its American appearance, some critics bitterly attacked it as a superficial moral waste and blasted the views of society, of London, and of youth they saw in it. Other critics praised the film as a complex work of art, and cheered Antonioni for radically condensing the narration and creating a personal reality, a new world on film that radically cut cinema off from theatre by doing something that was impossible on the stage. The controversy worsened when critics began attacking critics.

After "Blow-up" Antonioni began work on his next project. "When MGM asked me if I would be interested in doing a movie set in the United States the idea intrigued me, but I said I'd have to have some direct contact with America and Americans before I decided. So in May of 1967 I began my travels. I flew to Southern California and into that smoggy basin known as greater Los Angeles. Do you know what impressed me most? How photogenic everything was. The blocks and blocks of used-car lots, and the endless freeways curling like gigantic snakes around the mountains. And the steel buildings shining through clouds of pollution. The billboards—JESUS SAVES—DRINK PEPSI—all over—like the huge eyes of Dr. T. J. Eckleburg in the *Great Gatsby*."

In contrast to the excellent reviews received in Europe, most American critics could hardly contain their disgust for the film he made in America—"Zabriskie Point." It was placed among the ten worst films of 1970 by the *New York Times*. Judith Crist said, "the film is a depressingly adolescent vision of this country, depicted in elliptical and meandering and, by now, trite terms." Arthur Schlesinger, Jr. said: "As anger had eroded Antonioni's subtlety, it has also eroded his originality.... Every artist has a right to his own vision. The sadness of *Zabriskie Point* is that anger had led a notably subtle director to make an exceedingly simpleminded hymn to violence. His hatred of America has given a vision without nuance or complexity and has thereby betrayed him as an artist." This disfavor was reminiscent of some of the uncomfortable reactions toward the perceived view of London in "Blow-up."

Not all Americans were so unkind. William Pechter said: "I find something a good deal more than that unmitigated disaster it was generally taken to be.... And far from being the hysterical, anti-American travelogue-of-ugliness its hostile critics labeled it, *Zabriskie Point* seems to me marked by its open, curious, and surprised response to the rough, outsized, but not unbeautiful look of its Western American setting."

It has been suggested that the London of "Blow-up" and the America of "Zabriskie Point" should be seen as settings for films rather than political statements, and that American critics were too involved in the setting to be objective about the rest of the film. Antonioni apparently agrees. "My own cultural lugguage, my education, can be useful for what I face in a new country," he said. "But in Italy, I can't see at all. You are blind in your own country.... That's why everyone got so angry when I showed 'Zabriskie Point.' That's one of the reasons. They got so furious, they couldn't see what was good in that film, and there was much that was good."

Samplings from the response to the filmmaker's latest feature show the agitation that continues to surround Antonioni's work. John Simon said: "If vacuity had any weight, you could kill an ox by dropping on it Michelangelo Antonioni's latest film, *The Passenger*." Paul Zimmerman voted it: "Antonioni's most beautiful cinematic canvas and certainly one of the most stunning visual voyages ever filmed." Andrew Sarris called the final sequence "one of the greatest conjunctions of cinema as narrative and cinema as art object." Lee Atwell said: "This seems to me an over-reaction to what is certainly a minor, uneven work in the Antonioni *oeuvre*. After much vehement opposition and blatant misunderstanding from unsympathetic voices, Antonioni is certainly due recognition as a master film-maker, but in the case of *The Passenger*, it is misplaced and tends to ignore the weaknesses of a work that exhibits an uneasy blend of commercialism and art, ultimately satisfying the demands of neither."

Some critics propose the main point and recurring theme of Antonioni's work, especially evident in "The Red Desert," is that industrialization is dehumanizing and that Antonioni is disgusted with the aimlessness, corruption, alienation, and sterility of the modern world. "It simplifies things too much," answers Antonioni, "(as many have done) to say that I accuse this inhuman, industrialized world in which the individual is crushed and led to neurosis. My intention, on the contrary (moreover, we may know very well where we start but not at all where we'll end up), was to translate the beauty of this world, in which even the factories can be very beautiful.... The line, the curves of factories and their smoke-stacks, are perhaps more beautiful than a row of trees—which every eye has already seen to the point of monotony. It's a rich world—living, useful."

Another group contends that the most significant aspect of Antonioni's work is the visual effect. This group points out the importance of "still lives" which reverberate with a residue of momentous and ineffable action, highlighted by the famous final sequences which sum up each film in visual terms. They believe that "a richly sensuous employment of color for no other sake than its own" dominates his work.

When the *Wilson Library Bulletin* reviewed his collected screenplays, it said: "Fundamentally he gives us characters whose drama arises out of facing life minute after minute, day after day, rather than in moving through selected synoptic arrangements of events, like the usual plot, with neatly articulated obstacles to overcome or to founder on: men and women who love and die without the comfort of a divinity that understands them, that sees their secret sufferings and will reward them. All this is put in a visually exquisite texture that does not merely 'contain' the actors and story and settings but is an organic part of the drama.''

"Because, again," continued Antonioni, "my films mirror life and life is lived mainly from day to day without unusual incident, without melodrama, without moments of bombast and high emotion. More than anything, I hate melodrama, as in the films of a director like Visconti. Melodrama is the easiest thing in the world to do—the scene with the drunken whore or the brutal, shouting father—and it is the cheapest thing to do too. And so not worth doing. Far more difficult, more complicated, and thus more artistically challenging is to make a film that reflects the true rhythms of life. In fact, while I mean in no way to suggest that we are comparable artists, you must think when looking at my films of the novels of Proust, 'A la recherche du temps perdu,' rather than other films. That is, my films are, as you put it, 'slow paced' and 'without dramatic incident' in the same way Proust is.''

Several critics have seen his latest film as a crucial turning point in the director's career. It is difficult to determine whether or not Antonioni heeds this sort of observation. He has recently said: "As Brecht used to say about his English, 'I say what I can say, not what I want to say.' I have to complicate my thoughts. I have to change my nature and think in terms of Americans or English. The same force that pushes me to make the film pushes my mentality. It has to be the same for an actor who has to change many parts, he has to change many times. . . . I am never satisfied. I amuse myself from experimenting. It's an illusion to think that with movie people, our lives stop when we are finished shooting a film. Everything keeps going on. It's part of my life. . . . My experience is deeper now. Even technically, I am more mature. I don't have any technical problems, I never cared about grammar. Now everything I have to say comes out fluently. I'm still never happy while I'm shooting a film. I don't know why.''

AVOCATIONAL INTERESTS: Tennis, ping pong, painting, studying architecture, collecting blown glass.

BIOGRAPHICAL/CRITICAL SOURCES—Books: Pierre Leprohon, *Michelangelo Antonioni,* Seghers (Paris), 1961, 4th edition, 1969, translation by Scott Sullivan published as *Michelangelo Antonioni: An Introduction,* Simon & Schuster, 1963; W. R. Robinson and George Garrett, editors, *Man and the Movies,* Louisiana State University Press, 1967; Ian Cameron and Robin Wood, *Antonioni,* Studio Vista, 1968, Praeger, 1969, revised edition, 1971; Edward S. Perry, *A Contextual Study of Michelangelo Antonioni's Film, "L'Eclisse",* University of Iowa, 1968; Charles T. Samuels, *Encountering Directors,* Putnam, 1972; Robert J. Lyons, *Michelangelo Antonioni's Neo-Realism: A World View,* Arno, 1976.

Articles: *New York Times,* September 8, 1964, December 19, 1966, January 3, 1971, April 14, 1975, May 4, 1975; *Wilson Library Bulletin,* May, 1965; *Sight and Sound,* spring, 1965, summer, 1975; *Cahier du Cinema* (England), January, 1966; *Commentary,* April, 1967, August, 1975; *American Scholar,* winter, 1967; *Holiday,* March, 1969; *New York,* February 23, 1970; *Vogue,* April 1, 1970; *Film Quarterly,* fall, 1970, summer, 1975; *Horizon,* autumn, 1972; *Saturday Review World,* May 18, 1974; *New Republic,* April 19, 1975; *Esquire,* July, 1975.

*   *   *

APGAR, Virginia   1909-1974

PERSONAL: Born June 7, 1909, in Westfield, N.J.; daughter of Charles Emory (a businessman and teacher of sales-

manship) and Helen May (Clarke) Apgar. *Education:* Mount Holyoke College, B.A., 1929; Columbia University, M.D., 1933; Johns Hopkins University, M.P.H., 1959. *Religion:* Methodist. *Home:* 30 Engle St., Tenafly, N.J. 07607. *Office:* The National Foundation, 800 Second Ave., New York, N.Y. 10017.

CAREER: Presbyterian Hospital, New York City, intern in surgery, 1933-35; University of Wisconsin and Bellevue Hospital, New York City, resident in anesthesiology, 1937; Columbia University, New York City, instructor, 1936-38, assistant professor, 1938-42, associate professor, 1942-49, professor of anesthesiology, 1949-59, clinical director of department of anesthesiology at Columbia-Presbyterian Medical Center, 1938-59; National Foundation-March of Dimes, New York City, head of division on congenital malformations, 1959-68, director of basic research department, 1967-74, vice-president for medical affairs, 1968-73, senior vice-president for medical affairs, 1973-74. Diplomate, American Board of Anesthesiology, 1937. Member, Methodist Board of Hospitals and Homes, 1965; member of board of trustees, Mount Holyoke College, 1965-71; lecturer at Cornell University, 1965-71, and at Johns Hopkins University, 1973. Consultant to National Research Council and to hospitals.

MEMBER: American College of Anesthesiology (fellow; chairwoman of board of governors, 1950-52), American Society of Anesthesiology (treasurer, 1939-45), American Association for the Advancement of Science, American College of Obstetrics and Gynecology (fellow), American Pediatric Society, American Academy of Pediatrics, American Society of Human Genetics, American Eugenics Society, American Public Health Association, Teratology Society, Harvey Society, A. O. Whipple Surgical Society, Pan-American Congress of Anesthesiology, Pediatric Society of the Dominican Republic, Irish-American Pediatric Society, Congress of Anomalies Research Association (Japan), New York Academy of Medicine, New York Academy of Sciences, New York State Society of Anesthesiology, Alaska Medical Society, Washington State Obstetrical Society, American Philatelic Society, Ubitquiteers (treasurer, 1959), Amateur Chamber Music Players, Catgut Acoustical Society (treasurer, vice-president), Alpha Omega Alpha.

AWARDS, HONORS: Alumnae award, Mount Holyoke College, 1954; Elizabeth Blackwell award, 1960; distinguished service award from American Society of Anesthesiology, 1961; Med.Sc.D. from Women's Medical College, 1964, and from New Jersey College of Medicine and Dentistry, 1967; Sc. D. from Mount Holyoke College, 1965, and from Boston University, 1967.

WRITINGS: (With Joan Beck) *Is My Baby All Right?* (nonfiction), Trident, 1972. Contributor of some fifty articles to medical journals. Trustee, *Teratology Society Journal,* 1967-74.

SIDELIGHTS: In 1952 Virginia Apgar developed what has come to be known as the Apgar score, a method of determining a newborn baby's condition and chance for survival. The test is given within the first sixty seconds after birth. An anesthesiologist who attended the births of more than seventeen thousand babies, Apgar devised the test as a means of focusing delivery-room attention on the baby, who previously had been neglected to its occasional detriment.

The Apgar score itself consists of five categories: heart rate, respiration, muscle tone, reflexes, and color. The baby is scored on the basis of these categories, each of which can receive zero to two points. A perfect score of ten indicates an excellent chance for survival and normality. The average score is eight to ten points, and a score below three gives the infant a poor chance for survival and the possibility of grave abnormalities if the infant does survive the first critical weeks. Use of the Apgar score signals immediate medical intervention for the gravely ill newborn.

National Observer's Joe Western notes that Apgar "was the first woman physician ever appointed a full professor at the Columbia College of Physicians and Surgeons . . . [and that] over the years . . . Ginnie Apgar became mother-confessor to many of [her students], counseling them on matters of life and love." Apgar's energy was remarkable. According to Western, during her years at Mount Holyoke College "she was on eleven class athletic and academic teams and on seven varsity teams, reported for the college newspaper, acted in college dramas, played violin in the college orchestra. And she did all this while working her way through school by opening the college library every morning, taking care of the anatomy lab, waiting on tables, selling Puerto Rican linens, and catching stray cats for comparative anatomy classes."

Although Virginia Apgar initially trained for surgery, she later determined that the specialty of anesthesiology held more career opportunities for a female physician. Joe Western wrote that "at Columbia University, Dr. Apgar built up one of the strongest anesthesiology departments in the world. . . . Her drive and devotion enabled her to do her research under the perpetual emergency conditions of the delivery room." Apgar's research resulted in her contributing to medical journals more than fifty articles concerning prenatal care and teratology, the study of birth defects. Her book, *Is My Baby All Right?*, is a compilation, written for the pregnant woman, of her theories of prenatal care and the avoidance of abnormalities.

Additionally Apgar was a musician skilled at both the viola and the cello. *New York Times* writer Werner Bamberger noted that "she performed with the Teaneck . . . Symphony and other ensembles." She was also a member of the Catgut Acoustical Society, a group devoted to crafting their own stringed musical instruments.

AVOCATIONAL INTERESTS: Playing the violin, making stringed instruments, stamp collecting, photography, fishing, gardening, golf.

BIOGRAPHICAL/CRITICAL SOURCES: National Observer, June 6, 1966; *Woman's Day,* September, 1966; *New York Post,* January 20, 1967; *New York World-Telegram,* December 19, 1967.

OBITUARIES: New York Times, August 8, 1974; *Current Biography,* October, 1974.*

(Died August 7, 1974, in New York City)

*   *   *

ARENS, Richard 1921-

PERSONAL: Born November 24, 1921, in Lithuania; came to the United States in 1939, naturalized citizen, 1943; son of Theodore (a business executive) and rose (a dentist; maiden name, Goldberg) Arens; divorced. *Education:* University of Michigan, A.B., 1946; Yale University, J.D., 1948, LL.M., 1950. *Politics:* Democrat. *Religion:* "Unaffiliated." *Home address:* 18th St. & Parkway, Philadelphia, Pa. 19103. *Office:* School of Law, Temple University, Philadelphia, Pa. 19102.

CAREER: University of Buffalo (now State University of New York at Buffalo), Buffalo, N.Y., visiting assistant pro-

fessor of law, 1950-51; assistant staff member on California Tidelands Case before U.S. Supreme Court, 1951-52; Yale University, research associate in Law School, 1952-53; University of Buffalo, 1953-57, began as assistant professor, became associate professor of law; attorney in private practice in Washington, D.C., 1958-64; Catholic University of America, Washington, D.C., professor of law, 1964-66; McGill University, Montreal, Quebec, professor of law, 1966-69; University of Toronto, Toronto, Ontario, professor of law, 1969-72; Temple University, Philadelphia, Pa., professor of law, 1972—. Visiting professor of criminal justice at State University of New York at Albany, 1968-69; lecturer in international law in Indonesia, 1964. *Military service:* U.S. Army, 1943-46; served in Europe. *Member:* Amnesty International, International League for Human Rights (member of board of directors), Phi Beta Kappa.

WRITINGS: (With H. D. Lasswell) *In Defense of Public Order,* Columbia University Press, 1961; *Insanity Defense,* Philosophical Library, 1974; (editor and contributor) *Genocide in Paraguay,* Temple University Press, 1976. Contributor to law journals and to *Nation.*

WORK IN PROGRESS: Torture in Political and Criminal Interrogation in the World Community.

SIDELIGHTS: In 1966, Arens was the first attorney to win a juvenile court case asserting the right of the child to counsel and full disclosure before the U.S. Supreme Court. He also won the first ruling by the Inter-American Human Rights Commission in 1977, recognizing human rights violations inflicted upon the Ache Indians in Paraguay. He writes: "I was impelled to begin work on *Genocide in Paraguay* by my recollection of Nazi extermination and concentration camps I saw after their liberation by the U.S. Army, and by the disclosure of Paraguayan genocidal practices by western European media while American media remained almost wholly silent."

*   *   *

ARGO, Ellen 1933-

PERSONAL: Born July 25, 1933, in Fort Monroe, Va.; daughter of Reamer Welker (an Army officer) and Ellen (Tierney) Argo; married Mendal W. Johnson (a writer; died February 6, 1976). *Education:* Attended Dunbarton College and George Washington University. *Home:* 63 Conduit St., Annapolis, Md. 21401. *Agent:* Julian Bach Literary Agency, Inc., 3 East 48th St., New York, N.Y. 10017.

CAREER: Writer. Has worked as a secretary, office manager, comptroller, executive, board member, accountant, consultant, and director of a state legislative staff.

WRITINGS: Jewel of the Seas (novel), Putnam, 1977.

WORK IN PROGRESS: The Crystal Star and *The Yankee Girl,* Volumes II and III of the trilogy begun with *Jewel of the Seas.*

SIDELIGHTS: Ellen Argo writes: "I have always been a teller of stories, and when I discovered that I could set them down on paper, I was delighted, which is, I suppose, what motivated me to become a writer. In living and traveling all over the world with my parents and later with my husband, I saw the possibilities for stories everywhere around me. Since I was born practically at sea, and have usually lived on or very near the water, it is my first and most enduring love, and it is the theme for the trilogy upon which I am now engaged."

ARMES, Roy   1937-

PERSONAL: Born in 1937, in England. *Home:* 19 New End, Hampstead, London NW 3, England.

CAREER: Film critic for *London Magazine;* senior lecturer in film at Middlesex Polytechnic; writer in the field of cinema. *Awards, honors:* Research Fellow in Film and Television Studies, Hornsey College of Art.

WRITINGS: French Cinema Since 1946, two volumes, A. S. Barnes, 1966; *The Cinema of Alain Resnais,* A. S. Barnes, 1968; *French Film,* E. P. Dutton, 1970; *Patterns of Realism,* A. S. Barnes, 1972; *Film and Reality: An Historical Survey,* Penguin, 1974; *The Ambiguous Image,* Indiana University Press, 1976.

SIDELIGHTS: A cinema enthusiast, Armes believes that "the cinema is the most exciting medium for the expression of modernist ideas: creating its own space-time continuum, mixing the real and the fictional, objective narration and subjective viewpoint, and building up a multiple perspective in the manner of cubist painting." John Coleman finds *Patterns of Realism* a "very sensible and well-documented book, a model of its kind, [which] starts earlier and ends later in defining its territory. With admirable delicacy and self-control, he avoids the semantic pyrotechnics latent in any discussion of words like 'real' and 'neo-realism', offering a useful quote from Lukacs, putting down the ineffable Kracauer, all the time quietly moving towards an examination of the hard stuff itself: the films. . . . I am grateful for this scholarly and entertaining survey, one of the few film books to achieve the professional level of observation, insight and argument that we take for granted in other disciplines."

BIOGRAPHICAL/CRITICAL SOURCES: New Statesman, September 1, 1971; *Journal of Aesthetic and Art Criticism,* winter, 1974; *Encounter,* January, 1975.*

* * *

ARMSTRONG, (Walter) Alan   1936-

PERSONAL: Born December 25, 1936; son of Walter Henry and Elsie (Carter) Armstrong; married Heather Ruth Ann Davies (a teacher), August 11, 1962; children: Alison, Jonathan Alan. *Education:* University of Birmingham, B.A., 1960, Ph.D., 1967. *Home:* Woodside, Adisham, near Canterbury, Kent, England. *Office:* Eliot College, University of Kent, Canterbury, Kent, England.

CAREER: University of Nottingham, Nottingham, England, assistant lecturer, 1962-64, lecturer in economic and social history, 1964-68; University of Warwick, Coventry, England, lecturer in history, 1968-69; University of Kent, Canterbury, England, lecturer, 1969-72, senior lecturer in economic and social history, 1972-77, reader in social and demographic history, 1977—. British Council visitor to universities in the Netherlands, 1973. *Military service:* Royal Air Force, 1955-57. *Member:* Royal Historical Society (fellow).

WRITINGS: (Contributor) E. A. Wrigley, editor, *Introduction to English Historical Demography,* Weidenfeld & Nicolson, 1966; (contributor) H. J. Dyos, editor, *The Study of Urban History,* Edward Arnold, 1968; (editor) J. D. Chambers, *Population, Economy and Society in Pre-Industrial England,* Oxford University Press, 1972; (contributor) Wrigley, editor, *Nineteenth Century Society,* Cambridge University Press, 1972; (contributor) Peter Laslett, editor, *Household and Family in Past Time,* Cambridge University Press, 1972; *Stability and Change in an English County*

Town: A Social Study of York, 1801-51, Cambridge University Press, 1974. Contributor of articles and reviews to learned journals.

WORK IN PROGRESS: "The Enumerators," to be included in *British Censuses of the Nineteenth Century,* edited by R. A. Lawton, for Frank Cass; a chapter on labor, to be included in *The Agrarian History of England and Wales,* Volume VI: *1750-1850,* edited by G. E. Mingay and J. Y. Higgs, publication by Cambridge University Press expected in 1980; "The Flight from the Land," to be included in *The Victorian Countryside,* edited by Mingay.

SIDELIGHTS: Armstrong remarks: "I am interested in the application of quantitative techniques and social science perspectives to social history—a trend evident in Britain and Europe, as well as North America, in recent years. Such approaches do however make for problems of communication with a wider audience of which I am no doubt not alone in becoming increasingly conscious."

AVOCATIONAL INTERESTS: Vegetable gardening, collecting trade tokens.

* * *

ARMSTRONG, Richard G.   1932-

PERSONAL: Born February 21, 1932, in Bronx, N.Y.; son of Arthur J. (a businessman) and Anna (McCaffrey) Armstrong. *Education:* Maryknoll College, B.A., 1954; Maryknoll Seminary, M.A., 1959; Columbia University, M.S. (cum laude), 1960. *Politics:* Independent. *Religion:* Roman Catholic. *Home:* 104 East 31st St., New York, N.Y. 10016. *Office:* Edna McConnell Clark Foundation, 250 Park Ave., New York, N.Y. 10017.

CAREER: Ordained Roman Catholic Maryknoll priest, 1959; Christophers, New York City, assistant director, 1960-68, director, 1969-77; Edna McConnell Clark Foundation, New York City, consultant, 1977—.

WRITINGS: This Is Your Day, Christophers, 1969; *How to Make Your Life Worthwhile,* Trident, 1970; *Now Is the Time,* Christophers, 1970; *Add Meaning to Your Life,* Christophers, 1971; *Christopher Prayers for Today,* Paulist/Newman, 1972; *Make the Most of Your Day,* Christophers, 1973; *It's Your Life,* Christophers, 1974; *Powered Ships: The Beginnings,* Rowman & Littlefield, 1975; *Bits and Pieces: A Treasury of Christopher Quotes,* Christophers, 1975; *The Time of Your Life,* Christophers, 1976; *This Could Be Your Day,* Christophers, 1977.

WORK IN PROGRESS: You Can Still Change the World; magazine articles "on conditions of and prospects for migrant and seasonal farm workers."

SIDELIGHTS: Armstrong writes: "I have to write because it's a way of expressing myself to others—and of finding out what I think. Most of my works to date have been of an inspirational quality, a reflection of my association with the Christophers. It's been a satisfaction to know that what I have written has helped many people through difficult personal crises. Although I have left the Christophers and am embarking on other fields of endeavor, I expect this aspect of my writing will not be left behind. Fresh experiences, however, will lead me to think and express my thoughts in a wider variety of ways."

* * *

ARNO, Peter   1904-1968

PERSONAL: Original name, Curtis Arnoux Peters, Jr.;

name legally changed; born January 8, 1904, in New York, N.Y.; son of Curtis Arnoux (a judge) and Edith (Haymes) Peters; married Lois Long, 1927 (divorced, 1931); married Mary Livingston Lansing, 1953 (divorced); children: (first marriage) Patricia. *Education:* Attended Yale College (now University). *Residence:* Harrison, N.Y. *Office:* New Yorker Magazine, Inc., 25 West 43 St., New York, N.Y. 10036.

CAREER: Worked as professional musician; New Yorker Magazine, Inc., New York, N.Y., cartoonist, 1925-68.

WRITINGS—All published by Simon & Schuster: *Whoops Dearie!*, 1927; *Peter Arno's Circus*, 1931; *Hullabaloo*, 1931; *Peter Arno's Favorites*, 1932; *For Members Only*, 1935; *Cartoon Revue*, 1942; *Man in the Shower*, 1944; *Sizzling Platter*, 1949; *Peter Arno's Ladies and Gentlemen*, 1952; *Peter Arno's Hell of a Way to Run a Railroad*, 1956; *Peter Arno's Lady in the Shower*, 1967.

SIDELIGHTS: Arno, the son of a prominent New York family, changed his name to "protect the family's respectability." Brendan Gill in *Here at the New Yorker* recalled, "Peter was a classic harum-scarum young man-about-town in that day of the speak-easy, the flapper, and the Stutz Bearcat." A *New York Times* interviewer remembered Arno as "tall, urbane, impeccable dressed, with the kind of firm-jawed good looks popularized in old Arrow collar ads."

Music, rather than art, was to have been Peter Arno's profession. While still at Yale he organized a small band in which he played the banjo and other instruments. Brendan Gill also noted that Arno dropped out of Yale in 1923 to become the bandleader of a nightclub group called "Rendez-vous."

Two years later, the *New Yorker,* then a fairly new publication, bought Arno's first cartoon. Art replaced music, and Peter Arno began his lifelong association with the New Yorker. In his career of forty-three years, Arno became one of the magazine's most celebrated cartoonists along with James Thurber, William Steig, and Saul Steinberg. Brendan Gill credited him with having done much to "set the tone and direction" of the *New Yorker* at a time when the "raciness of his art frightened many of the older generation."

"At no time in the history of the world have there been so many damned morons gathered together in one place as here in New York right now. The town squirms with them," said Arno in a *New York Times* interview. According to James Thurber in *The Years with Ross,* Arno's double-entendres often made his editor, the late Harold W. Ross, squirm.

Arno's first targets, which Brendan Gill called the "imperious dowagers" and "choleric, Roosevelt-hating clubmen," gave way to more current satire. In his tribute to Arno in the *New Yorker,* Gill observed that "his subject range widened as his social interest narrowed." Arno, in his later years, lived a solitary life in the country. Gill remarked, however, that his "drawings remained very much in and of the world."

In the *New York Times,* Arno was quoted: "I had a really hot impulse to go and exaggerate their ['the fatuous, ridiculous people's'] ridiculous aspects. That anger gave my stuff punch and made it live." Out of this social anger came eleven anthologies of cartoons celebrated for their wit and irony.

Arno's *Whoops Dearie!*, the first such collection, was taken from his popular weekly feature, "The Whoops Sisters." A reviewer for *Books* typified its reception: "Whether parading their pet elephant, picnicking in Central Park with the lit-

tle orphan, Foster, or otherwise stopping traffic, they are to be depended upon for slapstick fun. There's a happy ending, too. If the text doesn't get you the pictures must." Yet, a reviewer, writing for the *Saturday Review of Literature,* criticized the forced plot and length of the book: "The big laugh has gone out of the material. It might have been expected."

Hullabaloo, Arno's second book, received even greater praise. W. R. Brooks in *Outlook* cited Benchley's introductory remark: "The old, feeble two-line joke practically disappeared, and in its place came a fresh and infinitely more civilized form—the illustrated single remark." One look at Arno's pictures, Brooks said, and "the incongruity, the implications, strike you and your guffaws shake the house." A *New York Times* reviewer commenting on several cartoons not considered suitable or proper for Ross's magazine said, "This is no book to be left in the guest room when Aunt Sarah comes for a visit. And then, again, you never know."

Arno's other collections, though not widely reviewed, were well received. Brendan Gill recognized Arno's almost intense dedication to his work when he said, "He worked hard to give delight, and it must have pleased him to think of thousands of perfect strangers laughing out loud over what had cost him so much serious effort." Arno told a *New York Times* interviewer; "My ideas are produced with blood, sweat, brainracking toil, the help of the New Yorker art staff, and the collaboration of keen-eyed operatives." His favorite collaborator was Richard McCallister, who frequently offered material for Arno's drawings and jokes.

Of Arno's art, Brendan Gill wrote: "With every year, Arno's work in black and white grew simpler and stronger and more playful, and the colors he employed in his superb covers grew brighter. One could spot them a long way off, blazing with a kindergarten fierceness of sky blue, apple red, sea green." Arno's acknowledged debt to the style of Honore Daumier and his appreciation of the work of Georges Rouault marked his own artistic technique.

The final tribute given to Arno's work came from a colleague who had never actually met the reclusive artist. Brendan Gill quoted from that colleague's letter in his *New Yorker* obituary for Arno. After hearing of Arno's death, the man commented on the universal appeal of Arno's work: "In 1956, I found a copy of an old Arno drawing framed in a bar in Salerno. I came on another last summer in Greece. I expect to be finding Arno drawings for years to come, wherever I go, all over the world."

BIOGRAPHICAL/CRITICAL SOURCES: Saturday Review of Literature, June 11, 1927; *Books,* July 17, 1927; *Nation,* December 10, 1930; *Outlook,* December 10, 1930; *New York Times,* December 14, 1930, February 23, 1968; *New Republic,* December 17, 1930; *New Yorker,* March 9, 1968; Brendan Gill, *Here at the New Yorker,* Random House, 1975.

OBITUARIES: New York Times, February 23, 1968; *Time,* March 1, 1968; *Newsweek,* March 4, 1968; *Publishers Weekly,* March 4, 1968; *New Yorker,* March 9, 1968; *Current Biography,* April, 1968.

(Died February 22, 1968)

* * *

ARNOTT, (Margaret) Anne 1916-

PERSONAL: Born September 8, 1916, in Bath, England; daughter of Thomas (a doctor) and Louisa (a mathematics teacher; maiden name, Story) Wilson-Smith; married Thomas Grenfell Arnott (an Anglican clergyman), February

16, 1942; children: David, Christopher, Catherine. *Education:* University of London, B.A., 1938. *Religion:* Church of England. *Home:* The Rectory, Brandesburton, Driffield, East Yorkshire, England.

CAREER: Teacher in Newcastle-upon-Tyne, 1938-41, and in Bath, England, 1964-73; served as justice of the peace in Newcastle-upon-Tyne and Weston-Super-Mare, England, 1968-71; Dame Allen's Schools, Newcastle-upon-Tyne, England, governor, 1969—. *Member:* York Diocese Mother's Union. *Awards, honors:* Received top book award in the youth category from Religious Publishers, 1975, for *The Secret Country of C. S. Lewis.*

WRITINGS: The Brethren, Mowbray, 1969; *Journey into Understanding,* Mowbray, 1971; *The Secret Country of C. S. Lewis,* Eerdmans, 1975; *Wife to the Archbishop,* Mowbrays, 1976. Regular contributor to *Sign.*

SIDELIGHTS: Arnott told *CA:* "I grew up in an unusual home. My dedicated doctor factor was a Puritan, a Plymouth Brother, right outside mainstream denominations. My brilliant academic mother, a vicar's daughter, left her church to marry him. Their fascinating characters and the influence of my home (a period piece) is the matter of my first two books, seen from a child's point of view, pictorially. The third book, which I was commissioned to write for children and young people, deals with the life of C. S. Lewis. My fourth book deals with the life of Jean Coggan, wife to our present Archbishop of Canterbury. Writing is a great relaxation, though in fact writing is always hard and demanding. But it is fun to stop and do one's own thing!"

* * *

ARONSON, Shlomo   1936-

PERSONAL: Born October 13, 1936, in Tel-Aviv, Israel; son of Jacob (an engineer) and Bella Aronson; married wife, Dalia (a teacher), June 1, 1958; children: Roa, Nili, Dan. *Education:* Hebrew University of Jerusalem, B.A., 1959; graduate study at University of Munich, 1962; Free University of Berlin, D.Phil., 1967. *Religion:* Jewish. *Home:* 12 Ramat-Denia, Jerusalem, Israel. *Office:* Department of Political Science, Hebrew University of Jerusalem, Jerusalem, Israel.

CAREER: Israel Broadcasting Authority, Jerusalem, news editor, 1958-62, correspondent from Berlin, 1962-67; Hebrew University of Jerusalem, Jerusalem, Israel, instructor, 1967-69, lecturer, 1969-72, senior lecturer, 1972-77, associate professor of political science, 1977—. Head of news and current affairs for Israel Television, 1968-69. *Military service:* Israel Defense Forces, 1954-56; became lieutenant. *Member:* International Political Science Association, International Studies Association, American Political Science Association.

WRITINGS: The Beginning of the Gestapo System: The Bavarian Model in 1933, Israel Universities Press, 1969; *Reinhard Heydrich und die Fruehgeschichte von Gestapo und S.D.,* Deutsche Verlags-anstalt, 1971; *Conflict and Bargaining in the Middle East, 1960-1977,* Johns Hopkins Press, 1977. Contributor to professional journals.

WORK IN PROGRESS: Contemporary Europe, for Brookings Institution; *Nuclear Proliferation.*

SIDELIGHTS: Aronson comments that his writing and research is stimulated by the Jewish Holocaust and the Arab-Israeli conflict.

ARTHUR, Alan
See EDMONDS, Arthur Denis

* * *

ARTOBOLEVSKY, Ivan I.   1905-1977

October 9, 1905—September 22, 1977; Russian scientist, originator of the Soviet theory on mechanisms and machines, and author of the first textbook in the field. He was also editor of several standard texts in related subjects. Artobolevsky was vice-president of the Institute of Soviet-American Relations for several years. He died in Moscow, U.S.S.R. Obituaries: *New York Times,* September 23, 1977.

* * *

ASHBAUGH, Nancy   1929-

PERSONAL: Born June 9, 1929, in Rochester, N.Y.; daughter of Thomas (a builder) and Daisy (a ballet dancer; maiden name, Artelli) Gould; married James Ashbaugh, December 23, 1945 (deceased); children: James. *Education:* Educated in New York City. *Politics:* "The Gentle Cynic." *Religion:* "Who knows whether spirit of man goes upward and the spirit of the beast goes down to earth." *Home:* 3667 Twain Circle, Las Vegas, Nev. 89121.

CAREER: Has worked as a dancer, publicist, teacher, journalist, typist, and singer; writer.

WRITINGS: Turn Left or Be Killed, Vanguard, 1971. Author of radio plays, including "The Story of Bill Abrams" series, 1957-58. Contributor of short stories to periodicals, including *Canadian Forum, Artesian,* and *Vegan.*

WORK IN PROGRESS: Stoop and Pick Up Nothing, about a theatre family; *The Blonde Barracuda at the Tangerine; The Prey,* an ecology novel; *Blood Sport; Dede; Year of the Ferret.*

SIDELIGHTS: Ashbaugh told *CA* her philosophy "is stolen from Ecclesiastes, 'chasing after wind.' Ends or goals for which people live, brings 'vanity and vexation of spirit.' The more one learns the more dissatisfied one becomes with that which he has already attained. The righteous man fares no better than the wicked, some times not as well. I find a resolution to make the best of a crooked world most comforting, unlike Job, all wrought up over situations. Be moderate in all things, the happy medium. A writer is or should be an observer, he does not get into the middle and shake his fist, he observes the others doing this."

* * *

ASHER, Don   1926-

PERSONAL: Born March 7, 1926, in Worcester, Mass.; son of Daniel (a chemist) and Marcia (Smith) Asher. *Education:* Cornell University, B.A., 1947, M.S., 1948. *Home:* 46 Ord Ct., San Francisco, Calif. 94114. *Agent:* James Brown, 22 East 60th St., New York, N.Y. 10022.

CAREER: Jazz pianist on East and West coasts, 1941—; writer, 1955—. Organic research chemist in Cranston, R.I., 1949-50. *Awards, honors:* Ascap-Deems Taylor Award, 1975, for *Raise Up Off Me.*

WRITINGS: The Piano Sport, Atheneum, 1966; *Don't the Moon Look Lonesome,* Atheneum, 1967; *The Electric Cotillion,* Doubleday, 1970; *The Eminent Yachtsman and the Whorehouse Piano Player,* Coward, 1973; (with Hampton Hawes) *Raise Up Off Me,* Coward, 1974; *Blood Summer,* Putnam, 1977.

WORK IN PROGRESS: A new novel.

SIDELIGHTS: Asher told *CA:* "I've used my musical experience as background in several novels. The rhythms of music and speech are complementary and reinforcing; perhaps this is why the writing of dialogue comes easy to me."

* * *

ASHFORD, Douglas E(lliott) 1928-

PERSONAL: Born August 8, 1928, in Lockport, N.Y.; son of Howard and Doris (Saunders) Ashford; married Marguerite Anderson, June, 1954 (divorced, 1971); married Karen Knudson (a nurse), June 8, 1974; children: (first marriage) Elizabeth, Douglas Elliott, Jr., David, Michael; (second marriage) Matthew. *Education:* Brown University, B.A., 1950; Oxford University, M.A., 1952; Princeton University, Ph.D., 1960. *Office:* Center for International Studies, 170 Uris Hall, Cornell University, Ithaca, N.Y. 14853.

CAREER: Indiana University, Bloomington, assistant professor of political science, 1959-62; Johns Hopkins University, Baltimore, Md., visiting professor of political science, 1962-63; Cornell University, Ithaca, N.Y., fellow of Center for International Studies, 1963-64, associate professor, 1964-68, professor of political science, 1968—. Lecturer for Foreign Service Institute, 1962-69, and Peace Corps, 1963; visiting fellow at University of Sussex, 1969-70, and Netherlands Institute for Advanced Study, 1977-78. *Military service:* U.S. Air Force, 1952-55; became first lieutenant.

MEMBER: American Political Science Association, American Society for Public Administration, Middle East Institute, Phi Beta Kappa. *Awards, honors:* American Council of Learned Societies-Social Science Research Council fellowships, 1958-60, 1963-64; Rhodes scholar, 1950-52.

WRITINGS: Political Change in Morocco, Princeton University Press, 1961; *Perspectives of a Moroccan Nationalist,* Bedminster, 1964; *The Elusiveness of Power: The African Single Party State,* Cornell University Center for International Studies, 1965; *National Development and Local Reform,* Princeton University Press, 1967; (with Chandler Morse) *Modernization by Design,* Cornell University Press, 1969; *Ideology and Participation,* Sage Publications, 1972; *Politics of Consensus,* Cornell Western Societies Program, 1976; *Decentralization, Democracy, and Decisions,* Sage Professional Papers, 1976; (editor) *Yearbook of Public Policy 1977,* Sage Publications, 1977; (coauthor) *Comparative Bibliography of Public Policy,* Sage Publications, 1977.

WORK IN PROGRESS: British Idealism and French Pragmatism: The Politics of Local Reorganization, tentative title.

SIDELIGHTS: Ashford told *CA* that his "basic concern has been difficulties of exercising democratic control; more recently in policy process in advanced industrial states."

* * *

ASHTON, (Margery) Violet 1908-

PERSONAL: Born February 5, 1908, in Sasketchewan, Canada; came to the United States in 1924, permanent resident of United States; daughter of Charles A. and Harriet (a writer; maiden name, Gledstanes-Richard) Brown; married second husband, Arthur Thomas Ashton (a trick-shot golfer; deceased); children: (first marriage) Jo-Ann Margaret Oaks (Mrs. Jack Seiquist), Michael Oaks, Leo Oaks. *Education:* Educated privately. *Politics:* "I am a Liberal in the tradition of my forebears." *Residence:* South Gate, Calif. *Agent:* Howard Moorepark, 444 East 82nd St., New York, N.Y. 10028.

CAREER: Writer.

WRITINGS: Love's Triumphant Heart, Fawcett, 1977; *House on Royal Street,* Fawcett, 1978.

Work anthologized in *Choicest.* Contributor of stories and poems to magazines, including *Escapade.*

WORK IN PROGRESS: A historical novel, set in Russia in 1913.

SIDELIGHTS: Violet Ashton writes that she is descended from Jonathan Swift, Dinah Mullock Craik, and Irish poet Ethna Carberry.

* * *

ASKIN, A. Bradley 1943-

PERSONAL: Born November 16, 1943, in Washington, D.C.; son of Leonard (in newspaper business) and Hilda (Thyrring) Askin. *Education:* Lafayette College, B.A. (with distinction), 1965; Massachusetts Institute of Technology, Ph.D., 1970; also attended University of California, Los Angeles, 1970. *Residence:* Washington, D.C. *Office:* Federal Energy Administration, Room 8222C, 2000 M St. N.W., Washington, D.C. 20461.

CAREER: Maryland-National Capital Park and Planning Commission, Silver Spring, Md., economist, 1966; U.S. Bureau of the Budget (now Office of Management and Budget), Washington, D.C., economist, 1967; Massachusetts Institute of Technology, Cambridge, part-time instructor in economics, 1968; University of California, Irvine, acting assistant professor, 1969-70, assistant professor of administration, 1970-75; Federal Energy Administration, Washington, D.C., economist in Office of Economic Impact Analysis, 1974-75, chief of National Impact Division, 1975—. Associate professorial lecturer at George Washington University, 1975; professorial lecturer at Georgetown University, 1976-77. Consultant to RAND Corp., Pacific Marine Acceptance Corp., and Price Commission.

MEMBER: American Economic Association, Society of Government Economists, Atlantic Economic Society, Southern Economic Association, Western Economic Association. *Awards, honors:* Fellow at University of California, Los Angeles; fellowship from American Assembly of Collegiate Schools of Business, 1974-75; certificate of special achievement from Federal Energy Administration, 1976.

WRITINGS: An Economic Analysis of Black Migration, National Technical Information Service, 1971; (with John Kraft) *Econometric Wage and Price Models: Assessing the Impact of the Economic Stabilization Program,* Heath, 1974; (contributor) Kraft and Blaine Reports, editors, *Wage and Price Controls: The U.S. Experiment,* Praeger, 1975; (editor with Kraft, and contributor) *Econometric Dimensions of Energy Demand and Supply,* Heath, 1976; (editor and contributor) *How Energy Affects the Economy,* Heath, in press. Contributor to economics journals. Referee-reviewer for *Growth and Change,* 1970, 1971, *Western Economic Journal,* 1971, and *Urban Studies,* 1973.

WORK IN PROGRESS: Continuing research on energy and the economy and on inflations.

SIDELIGHTS: Bradley told *CA* he is "interested in applying quantitative economic analysis to policy questions."

* * *

ASTON, James
See WHITE, T(erence) H(anbury)

ASTON, Margaret   1932-

PERSONAL: Born October 9, 1932, in London, England; daughter of Edward Ettingdene (a civil servant) and Katharine Dianthe (a musician; maiden name, Farrer) Bridges; married Trevor Aston, August 7, 1954 (divorced); married Paul Buxton (a civil servant), September 17, 1971; children: (second marriage) Sophia Frances, Hero Elizabeth. *Education:* Lady Margaret Hall, Oxford, B.A. and M.A., 1954, D.Phil., 1962. *Home:* Castle House, Chipping Ongar, Essex, England.

CAREER: Oxford University, St. Anne's College, Oxford, England, lecturer in history, 1956-59; Cambridge University, Newnham College, Cambridge, England, research fellow and lecturer in history, 1961-66; Catholic University of America, Washington, D.C., lecturer in history, 1967-68; writer. Research fellow at Folger Shakespeare Library and Harry E. Huntington Library, both 1967-68. *Member:* Royal Historical Society (fellow). *Awards, honors:* American Philosophical Society grant, 1967-68.

WRITINGS: Thomas Arundel: A Study of Church Life in the Reign of Richard II, Clarendon Press, 1967; *The Fifteenth Century: The Prospect of Europe,* Harcourt, 1968; (contributor) Richard L. DeMolen, editor, *The Meaning of Renaissance and Reformation,* Houghton, 1974. Contributor to history journals.

WORK IN PROGRESS: England's Iconoclasts.

*   *   *

ATKINS, Kenneth R(obert)   1920-

PERSONAL: Born November 19, 1920, in England; came to the United States in 1954, son of Percy (a lathe machinist) and Florrie (Roberts) Atkins; married Kathleen Mary James, January 3, 1943; children: Susan Mary Atkins Quigley, Brian Robert, Richard Henry. *Education:* Trinity College, Cambridge, B.A., 1942, Ph.D., 1949. *Religion:* Atheist. *Home:* 555 Colonel Dewees Rd., Wayne, Pa. 19087. *Office:* Department of Physics, University of Pennsylvania, Philadelphia, Pa. 19174.

CAREER: Admiralty Radar Establishment, Witley, England, physicist, 1942-45; Cambridge University, Cambridge, England, fellow of Trinity College, 1948-52; University of Toronto, Toronto, Ontario, associate professor of physics, 1951-54; University of Pennsylvania, Philadelphia, associate professor, 1954-56, professor of physics, 1956—. *Member:* American Physical Society, American Association of Physics Teachers, American Astronomical Society, American Association for the Advancement of Science, Institute of Physics (London), Sigma Xi.

WRITINGS: Liquid Helium, Cambridge University Press, 1959; *Physics,* Wiley, 1965, revised edition, 1976; *Physics Once Over Lightly,* Wiley, 1972; (with John R. Holum and Arthur N. Strahler) *Essentials of Physical Science,* Wiley, in press.

WORK IN PROGRESS: Research on relativity, gravitation, and cosmology.

SIDELIGHTS: Atkins writes: "My primary motivation is the belief that scientific theory provides the most reliable clues to the nature and purpose of the universe." *Avocational interests:* Bird watching, gardening, reading fiction, classical music.

ATKINS, Oliver F.   1916-1977
    (Ollie Atkins)

PERSONAL: Born February 18, 1916, in Hyde Park, Mass.; son of Oliver Fraser and Annie Sally (McLeod) Atkins; married Marjorie Neola Deakin, August 10, 1940; children: Randi Claire, Dale Ann. *Education:* University of Alabama, A.B., 1938. *Home address:* Route 1, Box 128-B, Washington, Va. 22747. *Office:* Curtis Publishing, Inc., 1100 Waterway Blvd., Indianapolis, Ind. 46206.

CAREER: Birmingham Post, Birmingham, Ala., staff and chief photographer, 1939-40; *Washington Daily News,* Washington, D.C., staff photographer, 1940-42; foreign correspondent and photographer, 1942-45; *Saturday Evening Post,* New York, N.Y., Washington photographer, 1945-69, foreign correspondent and photographer in Korea and Japan, 1951; *Washington Post,* Washington, D.C., photography columnist, 1947-50; personal photographer to the president of the United States and chief White House photographer, 1969-74; Curtis Publishing Co., Indianapolis, Ind., vice-president, 1974-77. *Wartime service:* Served with Red Cross during World War II. *Member:* National Press Photographers' Association (chairman of freedom of information committee), American Overseas Association, White House News Photographers Association (president, 1964), U.S. Senate Photographers Gallery (chairman of inaugural committee). *Awards, honors:* White House News Photographers' Association grand award, 1943; Graflex All-American Photo Contest portrait award, 1946; National Press Photographers' Association personalities award, 1952; received citation from American Red Cross for overseas service.

WRITINGS—Under name Ollie Atkins: (With Charles Baptie) *Camera on Assignment,* Fairfax Publication Society, 1957; *The White House Years: Triumph and Tragedy,* Playboy Press, 1977. Contributor of photographs to books, including *Eye on Nixon,* edited by William Safine, Hawthorn, 1972.

SIDELIGHTS: As the presidential photographer, Atkins traveled everywhere with Richard Nixon, He was summoned to take pictures of the Nixon family in private quarters on the president's last day in office.

OBITUARIES: New York Times, January 11, 1977.*

    (Died January 10, 1977, in Washington, Va.)

*   *   *

ATKINS, Ollie
    See ATKINS, Oliver F.

*   *   *

ATKINSON, Margaret Fleming

PERSONAL: Born in Washington, D.C. *Residence:* Washington, D.C.

CAREER: Author and illustrator of books for young people. Has worked as a department store art director and as an organizer of Cooperative Handicrafts, Inc., in Puerto Rico, 1936.

WRITINGS: How to Raise Your Puppy (self-illustrated), Greenberg, 1944; *Care for Your Kitten,* Greenberg, 1946; *It's Fun to Help at Home* (self-illustrated), Greenberg, 1947; (with Nancy Draper) *Ballet for Beginners,* Knopf, 1951, reprinted, 1964; (with May B. Hipshman) *Dancers of the Ballet,* Knopf, 1955, 3rd edition, 1965.

SIDELIGHTS: "The mere sight of this volume," wrote *New Yorker* of Atkinson's *Dancer of the Ballet,* "with its stunning photographs of forty outstanding dancers of the United States, England, and France, is likely to raise girls of over eight *sur les pointes*. The accompanying biographies are written in a chatty and somewhat breathless style, though less disturbingly so than most books on the subject." A reviewer for the *San Francisco Chronicle* added: "Obviously designed for the young adult market, it is apt to smack of the sugar-plum-fairy backstage atmosphere in the hands of the mature reader. However, for its very scope alone, it is not without a certain value to the adult balletomane."

BIOGRAPHICAL/CRITICAL SOURCES: San Francisco Chronicle, March 27, 1955; *New Yorker,* November 26, 1955.*

*   *   *

ATKINSON, Walter S(ydney) 1891-1978

1891—January 9, 1978; American eye doctor, surgeon, and author of books and articles on the diagnosis and treatment of diseases of the eye. Atkinson died in Watertown, N.Y. Obituaries: *New York Times,* January 10, 1978.

*   *   *

ATLAS, Samuel 1899-1977

December 5, 1899—July 27, 1977; Lithuanian-born rabbi, educator, and author and editor of books on philosophy and Jewish oral law. Atlas was professor emeritus of philosophy and Talmud at Hebrew Union College-Jewish Institute of Religion. He died in Liberty, N.Y. Obituaries: *New York Times,* July 29, 1977.

*   *   *

ATWATER, Montgomery Meigs 1904-

PERSONAL: Born October 21, 1904, in Baker City, Ore.; son of Maxwell W. (a mining engineer) and Mary (a writer and designer; maiden name, Meigs) Atwater; married Joan Hamill, May, 1956; *Education:* Harvard University, B.S., 1926.

CAREER: Author and avalanche specialist. Began writing after graduating from college; held various jobs as athletic director, fur farmer, cattle rancher, and guide; joined the U.S. Forest Service to research avalanche control at the end of the World War II; retired from the Forest Service to become a private consultant on snow and avalanche problems, 1964. *Military service:* U.S. Army, 1942; supervised a military ski and winter warfare school, Camp Hale, Colo.; commanded a reconnaissance unit in Europe.

WRITINGS: Government Hunter (illustrated by Fred C. Rodewald), Macmillan, 1940; *Flaming Forest* (illustrated by R. Farrington Elwell), Little, Brown, 1941; *Ski Patrol,* Random House, 1943; *Hank Winton, Smokechaser* (illustrated by E. Joseph Dreany), Random House, 1947; (with Sverre Engen) *Ski with Sverre: Deep Snow and Packed Slope Ski Technique,* New Directions, 1947; *Smoke Patrol,* Random House, 1949; *Avalanche Patrol,* Random House, 1951; *Rustlers on the High Range,* Random House, 1952; (with F. C. Koziol) *The Alta Avalanche Studies,* United States Forest Service, 1953; (with Koziol) *Avalanche Handbook,* United States Forest Service, 1953; *Cattle Dog,* Random House, 1954; *The Trouble Hunters,* Random House, 1956; *The Ski Lodge Mystery,* Random House, 1959; *Snow Rangers of the Andes,* Random House, 1957; *The Avalanche Hunters* (introduction by Lowell Thomas), Macrae Smith, 1968; *The Forest Rangers,* Macrae Smith, 1969.*

AUNE, Bruce (Arthur) 1933-

PERSONAL: Surname is pronounced *Aw*-nee; born November 7, 1933, in Minneapolis, Minn.; son of Arthur Berg and Doris (Bowler) Aune; married Ilene Mae Carlson (a social worker), August 20, 1955; children: Alison Judith, Patricia Marion, Kirsten Marie. *Education:* University of Minnesota, B.A. (magna cum laude), 1955, M.A., 1957, Ph.D., 1960; University of California, Los Angeles, graduate study, 1957-58. *Residence:* Amherst, Mass. *Office:* Department of Philosophy, University of Massachusetts, Amherst, Mass. 01002.

CAREER: Minnesota Center for the Philosophy of Science, Minneapolis, Minn., reserach assistant, 1960; Oberlin College, Oberlin, Ohio, instructor in philosophy, 1960-62; University of Pittsburgh, Pittsburgh, Pa., assistant professor, 1963-65, associate professor of philosophy, 1965-66; University of Massachusetts, Amherst, professor of philosophy, 1966—, head of department, 1966-70. Visiting professor at University of Michigan, summer, 1965, University of Minnesota, autumn, 1965, and Mount Holyoke College, autumn, 1976; fellow of Center for Advanced Study in the Behavioral Sciences, 1974-75; director of National Endowment for the Humanities summer seminar, 1977—.

MEMBER: American Philosophical Association, American Psychological Association, Mind Association, Phi Beta Kappa. *Awards, honors:* National Science Foundation Fellowship, 1959; Charles E. Merrill fellowship, 1963-64; Guggenheim fellowship, 1963-64.

WRITINGS: Knowledge, Mind, and Nature, Random House, 1967; *Rationalism, Empiricism, Pragmatism,* Random House, 1970; *Reason and Action,* D. Reidel, 1977.

Contributor: Grover Maxwell and Paul Feyerabend, editors, *Matter, Mind and Method,* University of Minnesota Press, 1965; Max Black, editor, *Philosophy in America,* Humanities Press, 1966.

Contributor to *Encyclopedia of Philosophy* and to scholarly journals.

WORK IN PROGRESS: Kant's Moral Philosophy; Semantics and Logic, with Martin Steinmann, Jr.

*   *   *

AUSTIN, Allan Edward 1929-

PERSONAL: Born June 17, 1929, in Niagara Falls, N.Y.; son of Albert (a merchant) and Margery Austin; married Margaret Olivia Stone, 1953; children: Jeffrey, Pree. *Education:* Michigan State University, B.A., 1959; University of Rochester, Ph.D., 1963. *Office:* Department of English, University of Guelph, Guelph, Ontario, Canada N1G 2W1.

CAREER: Worked as journalist until middle 1950's; Russell Sage College, Troy, N.Y., lecturer, 1962-63, assistant professor, 1963-65; University of Guelph, Guelph, Ontario, assistant professor, 1965-71, associate professor, 1971—.

WRITINGS: Elizabeth Bowen, Twayne, 1971; *Roy Fuller,* Twayne, in press.

WORK IN PROGRESS: Collection of short stories.

*   *   *

AUSTIN, Lewis 1936-

PERSONAL: Born June 7, 1936, in New York, N.Y.; son of Robert W. (a professor) and Mary Lewise (Carpenter) Austin; married Susan Fogg, August 24, 1961 (divorced); children: Charles, Alison. *Education:* Harvard University,

B.A., 1958; Columbia University, M.A., 1963; Massachusetts Institute of Technology, Ph.D., 1970. *Residence:* Santa Cruz, Calif. *Office:* Monterey Institute, 425 Van Buren St., Monterey, Calif. 93940.

CAREER: First National City Bank, Tokyo, Japan, promanager, 1963-66; Yale University, New Haven, Conn., assistant professor of political science, 1970-76; University of California, Santa Cruz, lecturer in political science, 1976-77; Monterey Institute, Monterey, Calif., associate professor of political science, 1977—. *Military service:* U.S. Army, 1958-61; became Spec 5. *Member:* American Political Science Association, Association for Asian Studies.

WRITINGS: Saints and Samurai: The Political Culture of the American & Japanese Elites, Yale University Press, 1975; (editor) *Japan: The Paradox of Progress,* Yale University Press, 1976.

* * *

AUSTIN, Richard B(uckner), Jr. 1930-

PERSONAL: Born December 31, 1930, in Dallas, Tex.; son of Richard Buckner Austin; married, 1953 (divorced); children: Richard Buckner III. *Education:* University of Texas, B.B.A., 1953, M.A., 1958, Ph.D., 1960. *Religion:* Christian. *Home:* 2206-B Nantucket, Houston, Tex. 77057. *Agent:* Roslyn Targ Literary Agency, Inc., 250 West 57th St., Suite 1932, New York, N.Y. 10019. *Office:* 5100 Westheimer, Suite 185, Houston, Tex. 77056.

CAREER: Del Mar Technical School, Corpus Christi, Tex., instructor in human relations, 1960-61; private practice in clinical psychology, 1961—. Instructor at Del Mar College and Texas A. & I. University—Corpus Christi. Psychologist at Parent-Child Guidance Center, 1960-61; director of psychology department at Seaview Psychiatric Hospital. Texas representative on examination board of American Association of State Psychology Boards, 1966-67; adviser to Nueces City Alcoholism Council and to Youth City. *Military service:* U.S. Navy. *Member:* American Group Psychotherapy Association (fellow), American Psychological Association, Southwestern Group Psychotherapy Society (president, 1971-73), Texas Psychological Association, Corpus Christi Psychological Association (president, 1964-65).

WRITINGS: (Contributor) *Ideas for Action,* Texas Association for Children with Learning Disabilities, 1966; *How to Make It with Another Person: Getting Close, Staying Close,* Macmillan, 1976. Also author of *Alpha Meditation: A New Approach to Growth,* 1977. Contributor to psychology journals.

WORK IN PROGRESS: What You Can Do About a Child's Learning Problems.

* * *

AVERY, Burniece 1908-

PERSONAL: Born June 12, 1908, in Alabama; daughter of John E. (a miner) and Elizabeth (an evangelist) Crews; married Robert H. Avery, 1933 (died October 16, 1977); children: Shirley. *Education:* Wayne State University, B.S. *Politics:* Democrat. *Religion:* Protestant. *Home:* 141 Longfellow, Detroit, Mich. 48202.

CAREER: Elementary school teacher in Detroit, Mich., 1954-73; writer, 1973—. Actress, performing in Detroit, Ann Arbor, Rochester, and Flint, Mich., and Louisville, Ky.; director and talent coordinator for WGPR-Television, 1975; founder of Proscenium Players, Outlet for Opportunity, and

Search, Explore, Expand Knowledge (SEEK). *Member:* Detroit Women Writers, Carver Progressive Club (charter member).

WRITINGS: Walk Quietly through the Night and Cry Softly (novel), Balamp, 1977.

Plays: "What Makes Suzy Run?" (three-act), first produced in Detroit at Central Methodist Church, 1971; "Death Rehearsal" (one-act), produced at Detroit Institute of Arts, 1971; "As Others See Us" (two-act), produced in Detroit at Considine Recreation Center, 1973.

Author of television play, "Smouldering," broadcast on WTVS-Television.

WORK IN PROGRESS: Readin' Ridin' and Ruthlessness, a novel; "Mortgage Payment," a short story; rewriting plays.

SIDELIGHTS: Burniece Avery remarks: "I feel compelled to express any situation from *my* point of view. I am hopeful that an additional viewpoint will aid people to arrive at solutions that will be representative of all of us. I am extremely interested in people as *individuals.* I deplore being referred to as the victim of the attitude 'they are all alike.' "

* * *

AYER, Frederick, Jr. 1917(?)-1974

PERSONAL: Born in Topsfield, Mass.; married Ann Moody; children: David, Ruth. *Education:* Harvard University, B.A., 1937, LL.B., 1941. *Residence:* Wenham, Mass.

CAREER: Federal Bureau of Investigation, Washington, D.C., special agent and chief of personnel of European theatre of operations, 1941-45; attorney in Boston, Mass., 1945-52; Office of the Secretary of the Air Force, Washington, D.C., special assistant for intelligence, 1953-60; attorney in Washington, D.C., 1961-74. Republican candidate for attorney general of Massachusetts, 1950.

WRITINGS: Yankee G-Man (autobiography), Regnery, 1957; *Walter, the Improbable Hound,* Regnery, 1959; *Where No Flags Fly* (novel), Regnery, 1961; *Before the Colors Fade: Portrait of a Soldier, George S. Patton, Jr.,* Houghton, 1964; *The Man in the Mirror* (novel), Regnery, 1965.

SIDELIGHTS: Ayer is credited with laying the groundwork that led to the solution of the 1948 murder of Columbia Broadcasting System correspondent George Polk.

Retired U.S. Army Brigadier General S.L.A. Marshall reviewed *Before the Colors Fade* for the *New York Times Book Review:* "In a very real sense [Ayer] grew up in his famous uncle's shadow. During the campaigns in Europe, Ayer was present doing counterintelligence duty. Anecdotal material from that period, heart-to-heart conversations between uncle and nephew during drinking bouts amid Patton's greatest campaigns, enrich the story and reveal the general's character as nothing else has done."

BIOGRAPHICAL/CRITICAL SOURCES: Frederick Ayer, Jr., *Yankee G-Man,* Regnery, 1957; *New York Times Book Review,* June 21, 1964. Obituaries: *New York Times,* January 5, 1974.*

(Died January 4, 1974, in Tucker's Town, Bermuda)

* * *

AYLING, (Harold) Keith (Oliver) 1898-1976

PERSONAL: Born in 1898, in Headley, Hampshire, England; came to United States, 1941; naturalized U.S. citizen; married Lorraine Sydor; children: Rex, Donald, David, Lowell, Susan, Leila. *Residence:* Long Island, N.Y.

CAREER: Worked as free-lance writer and journalist in England until 1941; warfare analyst for *New York Post,* 1942-43; writer of radio programs for Lowell Thomas, 1946-49; writer, 1949-76. Notable assignments include coverage of aero-warfare techniques in Germany, Italy, France, and in Spain during its civil war. *Military service:* Royal Air Force.

WRITINGS: R.A.F.: The Story of a British Fighter Pilot, Holt, 1941; *Calling All Women,* Harper, 1942; *How Every Boy Can Prepare for Aviation Service,* Garden City, 1942; *Flying Furies,* Thomas Nelson, 1942; *They Fly For Victory,* Thomas Nelson, 1943; *Semper Fidelis: The U.S. Marines In Action,* Houghton, 1943; *Combat Aviation,* Military Service, 1943; *. . . Bombers . . . ,* Crowell, 1944; *Bombardment Aviation,* Military Service, 1944; *Old Leatherface of the Flying Tigers: The Story of General Chennault,* Bobbs-Merrill, 1945; *SAAB Guide,* Sports Car Press, 1961; *The Auto Union-DKW Guide,* Sports Car Press, 1961; *Gas, Guts, and Glory: Great Moments in International Auto Racing,* Abelard, 1970. Also author of programs for British Broadcasting Corporation. Contributor to *London Times, Sketch,* and other periodicals.

OBITUARIES: New York Times, August 11, 1976.*

(Died, August 9, 1976, in Long Island, N.Y.)

* * *

BACKLUND, Ralph T. 1918-

PERSONAL: Born August 3, 1918, in Hoffman, Minn.; son of Adolph and Grace (Sheppard) Backlund; married Carolyn Beardsley Hillman Eckel (an art librarian), May 18, 1956; children: Nicholas Sheppard. *Education:* University of Minnesota, B.A., 1940. *Religion:* Episcopalian. *Home:* 3827 Massachusetts Ave. N.W., Washington, D.C. 20016. *Office: Smithsonian,* 900 Jefferson Dr., Washington, D.C. 20560.

CAREER/WRITINGS: Minnesota Stock Co., Minneapolis, Minn., publicity director, 1940-41; *Ortonville Independent,* Ortonville, Minn., associate editor, 1941-42; University of Minnesota, Minneapolis, instructor, 1946-50; WCCO-Radio, Minneapolis, news writer, 1946-50; Columbia Broadcasting System (CBS), New York City, producer, 1950-55; CBS-Radio, New York City, executive director of public affairs programs, 1955-58, moderator of "Invitation to Learning" program, 1957-58; *Horizon,* New York City, associate editor, 1958-64, managing editor, 1964-66; Department of State, Washington, D.C., special assistant for the arts, 1966-69; *Smithsonian,* Washington, D.C., member, board of editors, 1969-76, executive editor, 1976—. *Military service:* 1942-46, 1951-52; became first lieutenant. *Awards, honors:* Heywood Broun Award from American Newspaper Guild, 1948, for a radio series on racial discrimination.

* * *

BADGER, Ralph E(astman) 1890-1978

February 3, 1890—January 18, 1978; American author, economist, security analyst and investment adviser. He served as economic adviser to Iran, Puerto Rico, and Guam. Badger died in Boca Raton, Fla. Obituaries: *New York Times,* January 19, 1978. (See index for *CA* sketch)

* * *

BAECHLER, Jean 1937-

PERSONAL: Born March 28, 1937, in Thionville, France; son of Maurice (a merchant) and Marie (Hoss) Baechler; married Fabienne Scheffler, December 24, 1959; children: Anne, Beatrice, Sabine, Laurent. *Education:* University of Paris, Agregation, 1962, Docteur es Lettres, 1975. *Politics:* "Liberal, in the European sense of the word." *Religion:* "Tolerant agnostic." *Home:* 4 Avenue de Rocroy, 91380 Chilly-Mazarin, France.

CAREER: Taught history and geography in a secondary school in LeMans, France, 1962-66; Centre National de la Recherche Scientifique, Paris, France, researchist, 1966—. *Awards, honors:* Prize from Fondation de la Paix, 1974, for *Les Phenomenes Revolutionnaires;* prize from *Spectacle du Monde,* 1976, for *Les Suicides.*

WRITINGS: (Editor) *Politique de Trotsky* (title means "The Politics of Trotsky"), Armand Colin (Paris), 1968; *Les Phenomenes revolutionnaires,* Presses Universitaires de France, 1970, translation by Joan Vickers published as *Revolution,* Harper & Row, 1975; *Les Origines du capitalisme,* Gallimard, 1971, translation by Barry Cooper published as *The Origins of Capitalism,* Basil Blackwell, 1975; *Les Suicides,* Calman-Levy (Paris), 1975, translation by Barry Cooper published as *Suicides,* Basil Blackwell, 1978; *Qu'est-ce que l'ideologie?* (title means "What is Ideology?"), Gallimard, 1976. Member of editorial committees of *European Journal of Sociology* and *Commentaires.*

WORK IN PROGRESS: A study of power, which will develop a "general and comparative theory of political regimes, of their history and sociology since the Paleolithic age."

SIDELIGHTS: Baechler writes: "I detest confidences and distrust authors who succumb to their narcissism. I shall say simply that the duty of a man of science is to concentrate exclusively upon the discovery of that which is true for the moment, to flee with horror from the role of the prince's advisor, to seek to enlighten men, and to commit himself to always write in language directly accessible to those who wish to be enlightened."

* * *

BAILEY, Carolyn Sherwin 1875-1961

PERSONAL: Born October 25, 1875, in Hoosick Falls, N.Y.; daughter of Charles Henry (a scientist) and Emma Frances (a teacher and writer; maiden name, Blanchard) Bailey; married Eben Clayton Hill (a radiologist), 1936. *Education:* Columbia University, graduated, 1896; attended Montessori School (Rome), and the New York School of Social Work. *Politics:* Republican. *Religion:* Episcopalian. *Home:* "Hillcrest," Temple, N.H.

CAREER: Author and editor of books for children. Worked as a teacher in New York and as a principal in Springfield, Mass.; did social work at Warren Goddar House in New York. Editor of the children's department of *Delineator,* and of *American Childhood,* 1924-35. *Member:* Pen and Brush Club (New York); Mount Vernon Town Club (Baltimore). *Awards, honors:* Newbery Medal, 1947, for *Miss Hickory.*

WRITINGS—For children: The Peter Newell Mother Goose (illustrated by Peter Newell), Holt, 1905; (editor with Clara M. Lewis) *For the Children's Hour* (illustrated by G. William Breck), M. Bradley, 1906, reprinted, Gale, 1974; *Firelight Stories* (illustrated by Diantha W. Horne), M. Bradley, 1907; *Stories and Rhymes for a Child* (illustrated by Christine Wright), M. Bradley, 1909; *Girls' Make-at-Home Things,* F. A. Stokes, 1912; (with sister, Marian Elizabeth Bailey) *Boys' Make-at-Home Things,* F. A. Stokes,

1912; *For the Story Teller*, M. Bradley, 1913, reprinted, Gale, 1975; *The Children's Book of Games and Parties*, M. A. Donohue, 1913; *Every Child's Folk Songs and Games*, M. Bradley, 1914; *Stories for Sunday Telling*, Pilgrim Press, 1916; (editor) *Stories Children Need*, M. Bradley, 1916; *For the Children's Hour*, two volumes (illustrated by Frederick A. Nagler), M. Bradley, 1916; *Stories for Any Day*, Pilgrim Press, 1917; *Boys and Girls of Colonial Days* (illustrated by Uldene Shriver), A. Flanagan, 1917.

What to Do for Uncle Sam, A. Flanagan, 1918; *Stories for Every Holiday*, Abingdon Press, 1918, reprinted, Gale, 1974; (editor) *Tell Me Another Story*, M. Bradley, 1918; *Once upon a Time Animal Stories*, M. Bradley, 1918; *The Outdoor Story Book*, Pilgrim Press, 1918; *Stories of Great Adventures (Adapted from the Classics)* (illustrated by Clara M. Burd), M. Bradley, 1919; *Folk Stories and Fables* (illustrated by Nagler), M. Bradley, 1919; *Hero Stories* (illustrated by Frederick Knowles), M. Bradley, 1919; *Broad Stripes and Bright Stars: Stories of American History* (illustrated by Power O'Malley), M. Bradley, 1919, reprinted as *Boy Heroes in Making America* (illustrated by Lea Norris and O'Malley), A. Flanagan, 1931; *Everyday Stories* (illustrated by Knowles), M. Bradley, 1919.

The Enchanted Bugle, and Other Stories, *F. A. Owen, 1920;* Wonder Stories: The Best Myths for Boys and Girls *(illustrated by Burd), M. Bradley, 1920; (editor)* Merry Tales for Children: Best Stories of Humor for Boys and Girls, *M. Bradley, 1921;* The Torch of Courage, and Other Stories, *M. Bradley, 1921;* Flint: The Story of a Trail *(illustrated by Charles Lassell), M. Bradley, 1922;* Friendly Tales: A Community Story Book, *M. Bradley, 1923;* Bailey's In and Outdoor Play-Games: Boys' and Girls' Book of What to Play and Make *(illustrated by Cobb Shinn), A. Whitman, 1923;* When Grandfather Was a Boy, *Pilgrim Press, 1923;* Reading Time Stories, *A. Whitman, 1923;* Stories from an Indian Cave: The Cherokee Cave Builders *(illustrated by Joseph Eugene Dash), A. Whitman, 1924;* Boys and Girls of Pioneer Days, from Washington to Lincoln, *A. Flanagan, 1924;* Little Men and Women Stories, *A. Whitman, 1924;* Lincoln Time Stories, *A. Whitman, 1924; (editor)* In the Animal World, *M. Bradley, 1924;* All the Year Play Games: Boys' and Girls' Book of Merry Pastimes *(illustrated by Shinn), A. Whitman, 1924.*

The Wonderful Tree and Golden Day Stories (illustrated by Dash), A. Whitman, 1925; *The Wonderful Days* (illustrated by C. B. Falls), 1925; *Boys and Girls of Discovery Days* (illustrated by Dorothy Dulin), A. Flanagan, 1926; *The Wonderful Window, and Other Stories* (illustrated by Katherine R. Wireman), Cokesbury Press, 1926; *Untold History Stories* (illustrated by Lillian O. Titus), F. A. Owen, 1927; *Forest, Field, and Stream Stories* (illustrated by Dulin), A. Flanagan, 1928; *Sixty Games and Pastimes for all Occasions* (illustrated by Shinn), A. Whitman, 1928; *Boys and Girls of Today: A First Book of Citizenship*, A. Flanagan, 1928; *Read Aloud Stories* (illustrated by Hildegard Lupprian), M. Bradley, 1929; *Boys and Girls of Modern Days* (illustrated by Dulin), A. Flanagan, 1929; *Garden, Orchard, and Meadow Stories* (illustrated by Dulin), A. Flanagan, 1929.

Plays for the Children's Hour, M. Bradley, 1931; (editor) *Stories Children Want* (illustrated by Jack Perkins), M. Bradley, 1931; (editor) *Schoolroom Plans and Projects*, M. Bradley, 1932; (editor) *The Story-Telling Hour*, Dodd, 1934; *Tell Me a Birthday Story* (illustrated by Margaret Ayer), F. A. Stokes, 1935; *Children of the Handcrafts* (illustrated by Grace Paull; Junior Literary Guild selection), Viking, 1935, reprinted, 1962; *Tops and Whistles: True Stories of Early*

American Toys and Children (illustrated by Paull), Viking, 1937; *From Moccasins to Wings: Stories of Our Travel Ways* (illustrated by Margaret Ayer), M. Bradley, 1938; *Li'l Hannibal*, Platt, 1938.

Homespun Playdays (illustrated by Paull), Viking, 1941; *Country-Stop* (illustrated by Paull), Viking, 1942 (published in England as *Wishing-Well House*, Muller, 1950); *Pioneer Art in America* (illustrated by Paull; Junior Literary Guild selection), Viking, 1944, reprinted, 1966; *The Little Rabbit Who Wanted Red Wings* (illustrated by Dorothy Grider, Platt, 1945, reprinted, 1961; *Miss Hickory* (illustrated by Ruth Gannett; Junior Literary Guild selection), Viking, 1946, reprinted, 1968; *Merry Christmas Book* (illustrated by Eunice Young Smith), A. Whitman, 1948; *Old Man Rabbit's Dinner Party* (illustrated by Robinson), Platt, 1949, reprinted, 1961; *Enchanted Village* (illustrated by Eileen Evans), Viking, 1950; *Finnegan II, His Nine Lives* (illustrated by Kate Seredy), Viking, 1953, reprinted, 1968; *A Candle for Your Cake: Twenty-Four Birthday Stories of Famous Men and Women* (illustrated by M. Ayer), Lippincott, 1952; *The Little Red Schoolhouse* (illustrated by Dorothy Bayley Morse), Viking, 1957; *Flickertail* (illustrated by Garry MacKenzie), H. Z. Walck, 1962; *A Christmas Party* (poems; illustrated by Cyndy Szekeres), Pantheon, 1975.

Other: (With Clara M. Lewis) *Daily Program of Gift and Occupation Work*, M. Bradley, 1904; *Montessori Children*, Holt, 1915; (with E. Hershey Sneath, George Hodges, and Henry H. Tweedy) *The Way of the Gate*, Macmillan, 1917; *The Carolyn Sherwin Bailey Historical Collection of Children's Books: A Catalogue*, edited by Dorothy R. Davis, Southern Connecticut State College Press, 1966.

Also editor of editions of *The Three Musketeers* by Alexandre Dumas, *Lorna Doone* by Richard D. Blackmore, and *Evangeline* by Henry Wadsworth Longfellow. General editor, with Alice Hanthorn, of "Little Readers" series (illustrated by Ruth M. Hallock), McLoughlin Brothers, beginning 1934.

SIDELIGHTS: Carolyn Sherwin Bailey's first literary endeavor—a story dictated to her mother at age five—won second prize of $25 in a *St. Nicholas* magazine contest.

Atlantic described *Miss Hickory*, the 1947 Newbery Medal winner as, "a skillful blending of fact, fantasy, and woodsy detail—told in prose as clear and delicate as an etching. *Little Red Schoolhouse* was written, noted the *New York Times*, "with the same feeling for the beauty of the countryside that flavored her Newbery Medal Book, *Miss Hickory*."

Many of Miss Bailey's books have been translated into braille, as well as several foreign languages. However, they were banned in the Soviet Union for being "too idealistic."

She traveled extensively in Europe and in the Caribbean countries, and when at home, devoted much time to the family apple orchard and scientific apple cultivation.

A dramatization of *Miss Hickory* was adapted by Ray Fowler and Barrett Clark as a Viking recorded book in 1972.

BIOGRAPHICAL/CRITICAL SOURCES: Atlantic, December, 1946; *New York Times*, May 19, 1954; *Carolyn Sherwin Bailey, 1875-1961: Profile and Bibliography*, Eastern Press, 1967. Obituaries: *New York Times*, December 25, 1961; *Publishers Weekly*, January 8, 1962.*

(Died December, 1961)

BAKER, Donald W(hitelaw) 1923-

PERSONAL: Born January 30, 1923, in Boston, Mass.; son of Merrill Ellsworth (a cabdriver) and Ida Margaret (Dempsey) Baker; married Natalie Jane Krentz, May 2, 1945; children: Pamela Jane, Alison Jean. *Education:* Brown University, A.B., 1947, A.M., 1949, Ph.D., 1955; also attended Harvard University, summers, 1950-51. *Politics:* Left. *Religion:* None. *Home:* 16 Harry Freedman Pl., Crawfordsville, Ind. 47933. *Agent:* John A. Sterling, Paul R. Reynolds, Inc., 12 East 41st St., New York, N.Y. 10017. *Office:* Department of English, Wabash College, Crawfordsville, Ind. 47933.

CAREER: Brown University, Providence, R.I., instructor in English, 1948-53; Wabash College, Crawfordsville, Ind., assistant professor, 1953-58, associate professor, 1958-69, professor of English, 1969-76, Milligan Professor of English, 1976—, director of drama, 1954-60, poet-in-residence, 1964—. *Military service:* U.S. Army Air Forces, aerial navigator, 1942-46; became first lieutenant.

MEMBER: American Association of University Professors, National Council of Teachers of English (member of national achievement awards advisory board, 1968-71), Modern Language Association of America, Great Lakes Colleges Association (director of new writer's awards, 1976—), Phi Beta Kappa. *Awards, honors:* McClain-McTurnan award from Wabash College, 1967; National Endowment for the Arts fellowship, 1974-75.

WRITINGS: Twelve Hawks and Other Poems, Sugar Creek Series, 1974.

Work represented in many anthologies, including *Sound and Sense,* edited by Perrine, 5th edition, and *Literature,* edited by Hogins. Contributor of poems to about sixty magazines, including *Saturday Review, Nation, Atlantic, Poetry,* and *Carolina Quarterly.*

WORK IN PROGRESS: Losing the Cities, a book of short stories; a novel.

SIDELIGHTS: Baker writes: "My politics are left, without current affiliation. I have been a Democrat, but 1968, among other things, ended that. My writing is at present without much system. I'm not prolific and have a lot of trouble producing anything at all. Some of my poems persist: one of them, 'Formal Application,' is still being reprinted in anthologies. I'm happy about that. I hope to go on writing and teaching for a long time. I've done a lot of readings and workshops, and they're among my greatest pleasures, sharing what I've written and what I've learned with people who want to know."

*   *   *

BAKER, Ivon 1928-

PERSONAL: Born June 25, 1928, in London, England; son of Willim and Edith (Nuttman) Baker; married Barbara Dainty (a teacher), August 11, 1956; children: Aidan St. John, Hugh Crispin, Felicity Clare, Sarah Francesca, Giles Alban. *Education:* Attended Handsworth College, 1951-54; St. Augustine's College, diploma, 1960. *Religion:* Church of England. *Home:* Gringley on the Hill, Doncaster DN10 4QP, England.

CAREER: Ordained minister of Methodist Church, 1954, minister in Brighton, Sussex, rural Yorkshire, Nottinghamshire, and Derbyshire, 1954-59; ordained priest in Church of England Southwell Minster, 1961; chaplain to Cadet Battalion, Sherwood Foresters Regiment, 1961; vicar of Gringley on the Hill parish, 1962—. Chaplain, Borstal Institution (a penal establishment), 1962—. Lecturer. *Military service:* British Air Force, 1946-49.

WRITINGS—All novels: Death in Sanctuary, Hale, 1970; *Days Among the Dead,* Hale, 1971; *Grave Doubt,* McKay, 1972; *The Pandora Feature,* Hale, 1973; *Justice for Judas,* Hale, 1974; *Peak Performance,* St. Martin's, 1976; *Death and Variations,* St. Martin's, 1977.

Plays: "To See Ourselves" (three-act), first produced in London at The Central Hall, 1950; "Son et Lumiere," first produced in Norwell, England, at Norwell Parish Church, 1967; "This Ringing Anvil," first produced in England at Wingerworth Parish Church, 1978.

Also author of "From the Hills . . . A Stranger" filmscript, 1959. Contributor to over a dozen periodicals, including *Guardian, Country Life, Woman's Own, Norsk Ukeblad,* and *Motor Boat and Yachting.*

WORK IN PROGRESS: A novel "chronicling further adventures of David Meynell and his wife, Anne."

SIDELIGHTS: "Interest in history and archaeology," Baker told *CA,* is reflected in my writing, particularly "Son et Lumiere" and "Panodrama" productions commissioned to dramatise the story of ancient buildings or sites from earliest days. Much of my current poetic output appears in these scripts. My suspense novels, while owing much to my travels in France, Spain, Israel, and Jordan, are set mainly in the midland and northern English shires I have come to know and love.

"I often write about people whose expertise (bellringing, poetry, archaeology) puts them, often unwillingly, one jump ahead of professional crime investigators.

"I'm simply a story-teller; no axe to grind, no points to score. My job is to entertain, intrigue and inform. Golden rule: *Never insult your readers' intelligence.* If they get as much enjoyment from solving the mystery as I get from creating it, that (plus royalties!) is all I could ask."

*   *   *

BAKER, William W(allace) 1921-

PERSONAL: Born July 2, 1921, in Kansas City, Mo.; son of William Reaune (a lawyer) and Grace (Wallace) Baker; married Virginia Graham, December 21, 1941; children: William, Jr. (deceased). *Education:* University of Michigan, A.B., 1947. *Religion:* Episcopal. *Home:* 4900 West 64th St., Prairie Village, Kan. 66208. *Office: Kansas City Star,* 18th and Grand, Kansas City, Mo. 61408.

CAREER/WRITINGS: Kansas City Star, Kansas City, Mo., reporter, copy editor, and picture editor, 1947-54, editorial writer, 1954-63, associate editor, 1963-67, editor, 1967—, executive vice-president, 1972-75, president and chief executive officer, 1976—. Member, board of trustees, William Allen White Foundation; member, board of regents, Rockhurst College; trustee, University of Missouri at Kansas City. *Military service:* U.S. Army, 1941-45; received Bronze Star. *Member:* American Society of Newspaper Editors, American Newspaper Publishers Association, National Conference of Editorial Writers, Kansas City Press Club, Sphinx, Sigma Delta Chi, Phi Beta Kappa, Phi Kappa Phi, Phi Eta Sigma.

SIDELIGHTS: Baker told *CA:* "My principal extra-curricular work has been as an active lay leader of the Episcopal Church—deputy to past five national conventions from Diocese of Kansas, and I was formerly a member of the Standing Committee of the Diocese and am now a member of the board of trustees.

"I have travelled through the Middle East on assignment for *The Star,* and more recently, while on vacation, I made several trips to Africa.

"My motivation in newspaper work is simple: I am a dedicated professional journalist, convinced of the importance of a free press to our society." Baker has been an active participant in the Editor-in-Residence program of the Newspaper Fund and the American Society of Newspaper Editors.

*   *   *

BAKKER-RABDAU, Marianne K(atherine)   1935-
(Marianne Rabdau)

PERSONAL: Born February 24, 1935, in Spokane, Wash.; daughter of James Michael (employed by U.S. Department of Agriculture) and Mildred Ellen (in banking and accounting; maiden name, Owen) Rabdau; married Cornelius B. Bakker (a physician and professor of psychiatry), June 11, 1955; children: Paul Michele, James William, Gabrielle Suzanne. *Education:* Sacred Heart School of Nursing, Spokane, Wash., R.N., 1955. *Home address:* P.O. Box 3, Mukilteo, Wash. 98275. *Office:* Adult Development Program, University of Washington, Seattle, Wash. 98105.

CAREER: Kirkwood Publishing Co., Seattle, Wash., president, 1969-71; University of Washington, Seattle, psychiatric nurse practitioner and member of staff of Adult Development Program, 1971—. President of Wonder Mother Records. Associate of Individual Development Center, 1974-76; chairman of board of directors of Rosehill Community Center, 1974-77. *Member:* American Nurses Association, Broadcast Music, Inc., Washington State Nurses Association.

WRITINGS: No Trespassing: Explorations in Human Territoriality, Chandler & Sharp, 1973.

Author of script "Verboden Toegang" (title means "No Trespassing"), for Belgium National Television. Contributor to magazines and music journals.

WORK IN PROGRESS: Reflections on Narcissus: Understanding Human Behavior; The Loyal Opposition, a book on marriage; research on assertiveness, aggressiveness, hostility, marital bargaining, affiliation and shyness, and behavior change modalities.

SIDELIGHTS: Marianne Bakker-Rabdau is a semi-professional folksinger and songwriter. She lived in the Netherlands for two years and translates Dutch folksongs. She teaches folksinging and folk guitar as a volunteer service for community colleges and community school programs. For one year she managed a rock group.

She has also lectured as a patient rights advocate, and comments: "The price of freedom is responsibility, the cost of contentment, commitment. There is no free lunch!"

AVOCATIONAL INTERESTS: Gourmet cooking, travel (Europe, Mexico).

*   *   *

BALCON, Michael   1896-1977

May 19, 1896—October 16, 1977; British film executive, producer, and author of his autobiography. He was best known for the comedies made under his supervision in the late 1940's and early 1950's at Ealing Studios. Balcon was associated with several production companies in England. Among his more notable productions are Alfred Hitchcock's "The 39 Steps," Robert Flaherty's "Man of Iran," and the historical adventures, "Rhodes of Africa" and "Scott of the Antarctic." He was knighted in 1948. Balcon died in Sussex, England. Obituaries: *Washington Post,* October 19, 1977.

*   *   *

BALFORT, Neil
See FANTHORPE, R(obert) Lionel

*   *   *

BALL, George W(ildman)   1909-

PERSONAL: Born December 21, 1909, in Des Moines, Iowa; son of Amos and Edna (Wildman) Ball; married Ruth Murdoch, September 16, 1932; children: John Colin, Douglas Bleakly. *Education:* Northwestern University, B.A., 1930, J.D., 1933. *Home:* 860 United Nations Plaza, New York, N.Y. 10017. *Office:* Lehman Brothers, 1 William St., New York, N.Y. 10004.

CAREER: Admitted to Illinois Bar, 1934, and Washington, D.C. Bar, 1946. U.S. Government, Washington, D.C., lawyer in Farm Credit Administration, 1933-34, and in Treasury Department, 1934-35; private practice of law, Chicago, Ill., 1935-42; U.S. Government, Washington, D.C., associate general counsel of Lend-Lease Administration, 1942-43, and of Foreign Economic Administration, 1943-44, civilian member of Air Force Evaluation Board in Paris, France, 1944, director of U.S. Strategic Bombing Survey, London, England, 1944-45; Cleary, Gottlieb, Steen and Ball (law firm; now Cleary, Gottlieb, Steen and Hamilton), Washington, D.C., and New York City, founding partner, 1945-61, partner, 1966-68, consultant, 1969—; U.S. Department of State, Washington, D.C., Undersecretary for Economic Affairs, 1961, Undersecretary of State, 1961-68; Lehman Brothers (investment bankers), New York City, senior partner, 1969—. U.S. Permanent Representative to United Nations, 1968. Member of board of directors, Standard Oil Co. of California and Singer Co. *Awards, honors:* U.S. Medal of Freedom; Officer, French Legion of Honor; Grand Cross of the Order of the Crown (Belgium).

WRITINGS: The Discipline of Power: Essentials of a Modern World Structure, Atlantic, 1968; (editor) *Global Companies,* Prentice-Hall, 1975; *Diplomacy for a Crowded World,* Little, Brown, 1976.

SIDELIGHTS: George W. Ball's years in government service, particularly his tenure as Undersecretary of State for Presidents Kennedy and Johnson, have provided him with ample material for *The Discipline of Power.* He indicates, however, that the book "is not a personal memoir. It reveals no state secrets. It discloses no personal confidences. It is instead a book of argument—an attempt to illuminate the central problem that has absorbed my interest in and out of government for 35 years: how free men can organize their power in a rational way." He feels that the key to this organization of power is the unification of Western Europe into a super-power which would include the United Kingdom. This unification would provide a link between the United States and Soviet Russia. If there is not some intervening body between the two existing powers the danger of nuclear disaster would be so great that it could occur even though it would not really be wanted by either side. The idea of a third power would also prove helpful in settlements in the Middle East and Vietnam. Ball came out against the war in Vietnam because he felt that it was not of enough importance. He did, however, support Johnson's policies on the war. He believes also that there must be some kind of recognition of the problems and needs of the weaker, poorer, Southern Hemisphere, although he does not feel that this area is nearly as important as the northern half of the world.

Philip Gayelin believes that "the virtue of [Ball's] book is not its treatment of current events, but its message for the future." Eliot Fremont-Smith points out that the book is addressed not only to Americans but to Europeans as well. He says that "Mr. Ball is a knowledgeable and forceful writer, and his book is intellectually stimulating and full of acute assessments and persuasive ideas, particularly on what power is and what nations require to exercise it now." He feels, though, that "there is a sense here that systems operate without personalized responsibility, and Mr. Ball is quite haughty toward those who might think otherwise." Ronald Steel writes: "Vigorous, opinionated, and informative, Ball's 'book of argument' is a lucid exposition of the conventional politics of the cold war era we are now moving out of. For all its minor iconoclasms—opposition to the bombing of North Vietnam and indifference to communist regimes in small African states—it is profoundly rooted in an imperial view of American world responsibility and the immutable struggle against Soviet communism." Gayelin concluded by saying that "Ball is a compelling and engaging advocate. Even those who can't accept his Grand Concept will find in *The Discipline of Power* all the rewards of a lively and stimulating debate."

BIOGRAPHICAL/CRITICAL SOURCES: Washington Post, April 6, 1968; *New York Times,* April 8, 1968; *Best Sellers,* April 15, 1968; *Virginia Quarterly Review,* summer, 1968; *New York Review of Books,* September 12, 1968.*

* * *

BALSDON, John Percy Vyvian Dacre 1901-1977 (Dacre Balsdon)

November 4, 1901—September, 1977; British essayist and novelist specializing in Roman antiquity. Balsdon is known for scholarly works, including *The Emperor Gaius* and *Life and Leisure in Ancient Rome,* as well as satirical novels published under the name Dacre Balsdon. He died in England. Obituaries: *AB Bookman's Weekly,* January 30, 1978. (See index for *CA* sketch)

* * *

BAN, (Maria) Eva 1934-

PERSONAL: Born March 16, 1934, in Brazil; daughter of Adalberto (a physician) and Clara Ban. *Education:* Pensionat Mont'Olivet, Lausanne, Switzerland, B.A.; attended University of Curitiba; University of Rio de Janeiro, Ph.D.; attended University of Porto Alegre. *Politics and religion:* "I fight for social justice; no defined parties or religions have my allegiance." *Home:* 153 East 57th St., Apt. 9C, New York, N.Y. 10022; and Avenue Copacabana 959, Apt. 503, Rio de Janeiro, Brazil. *Agent:* Danilo Martinovich, 745 Fifth Ave., New York, N.Y. 10022.

CAREER/WRITINGS: Folha da Tarde, Porto Alegre, Brazil, reporter, 1948; Radio Gaucha, Porto Alegre, host of disc-poetry program, 1948; *Vanguarda,* Rio de Janeiro, Brazil, crime reporter, 1950; *Noite Ilustrada,* Rio de Janeiro, roving foreign correspondent, 1949-51; *Diario da Noite,* Rio de Janeiro, roving foreign correspondent, 1951-58; *Cruzeiro,* Rio de Janeiro, roving foreign correspondent, 1958-64; *Diario da Noite,* roving foreign correspondent, 1964-67; *Cruzeiro,* foreign correspondent in the United States, 1967-74; free-lance correspondent for about forty outlets worldwide, 1974—. Notable assignments include spending two months as a member of a drug-smuggling ring, posing as a beggar for story on panhandlers, climbing the walls of a women's prison for a story, and many interviews with world leaders.

Teacher in journalism, University of Rio de Janeiro. Poetry represented in anthologies, including *From Deborah and Sapho to the Present,* edited by Anca Vrbovska and Alfred Dorn, New Orlando, 1975.

MEMBER: International Association of Journalists (international vice-president and Brazilian president, 1976), Associacao Brasilerira de Imprensa (Brazil), Sindicato dos Jornalistas Liberais (Brazil), Foreign Press Association (New York), Academia de Letras (Brazil), Poetry Society of America. *Awards, honors:* Recipient of many awards for reporting and creative writing, the most recent being named outstanding international media woman of the year by New York chapter, National Association of Media Women, 1975.

WORK IN PROGRESS: A nonfiction book entitled *Criminals, Politicians and I,* to be published in Brazil.

SIDELIGHTS: Eva Ban wrote: "I know six languages, write in two; found English easy, maybe because Portuguese is so complicated. As far back as I can remember, I wanted to be a writer. I became one, when I wrote my first fairy tale at the age of seven, my first poem when I was eight, and I became a crusading reporter when, in the newspaper of my little town, I denounced in fiery words the only cinema. I was eleven years old and had found out about its exploitation and abuse. I have fought these ever since then, to the point that my first editor-in-chief still calls me a "female Don Quixote." I was born liberated, always felt completely sure of myself (it is funny, but at the same time, until I was about 25, I was timid in secret). Sex was and is very natural; I have no hangups, had many lovers and have now a companion for over (I think) 13 years. I do not want to marry and I never wanted children. Very early in my career I made the choice: I could do more for the children of the world, by writing, than having children of my own. Another choice I made was to live from writing only. Because of this and because I never did or wrote anything which would go against my code of ethics, I have had a hard life and went hungry many times, which was good for my writing. I know I can't be bought, because big multinational companies have offered me, at least two times, signed checks which I threw into their collective faces and went on rapping them on their greedy little knuckles.... So, more or less, I am happy with my life, but think I have not done enough yet. I have a very active social conscience, damn it! I owe it to my father.

"I have a quarrel with what American reporters consider 'objectivity.' Being objective, for me, is to *get proof* for everything I write. Once I had a judge, two doctors, and a detective witness how I opened the grave of a small boy who, it had come to me on my private "bas-fond" line, had been killed by a beating. The institute where he had been sent for petty stealing, officially stated that he died from a heart-attack. Well, I proved the truth, the director and guards went to jail and, at least for some months, they didn't kill other little boys.... This kind of reporting I consider to be objective. I would *not* publish the director's defense speech, after having proved that it was done with his knowledge.

"Journalism for some years now, has the Telex-machine which is cold and gives facts with no human striving for justice. The journalist does not, should not be a Telex-machine, but a fighter for justice, using words *based on facts.* When the Biafra children were dying (they still are) of hunger and I went there to do the story, would it have been objective to also defend the countries that were selling the weapons that helped to build up conditions giving rise to such atrocities?! I do not think that would have been journalistic objectivity. That would have been accomodation or even cowardice.

"I practice Rafa-Ioga and because of this, I am satisfied with three or four hours of sleep. Am now thinking of leaving journalism next year, to write books, short stories and poems. As most journalists, I have printer's ink in my veins and can't live well without the smell of newsprint. That is why, even after some years in TV, my real love is still the written press. So maybe I will have to do with one hour less sleep and whatever I want to write must be done this way. After all, I have to leave something important to the world. Journalism is today's fresh bread and tomorrow it will be fed to the pidgeons.... I want to live until I am 120 years old, but do not want to look worse then I do now. There is so much to see!"

* * *

BANISTER, Margaret   1894(?)-1977

1894(?)—November 18, 1977; American public relations specialist and novelist. Banister worked in public relations for Sweet Briar College and the Pentagon before retiring in 1956 to write novels. Obituaries: *Washington Post,* November 23, 1977.

* * *

BANNING, Evelyn I.   1903-

PERSONAL: Born December 10, 1903, in Oakdale, Mass.; daughter of Marshall Parker (a grocer) and Edith E. (Abbott) Banning. *Education:* Boston University, student, 1922-24; University of California, Los Angeles, A.B. (honors), 1926; Mills College, M.A., 1928; Harvard University, D.Ed., 1952. *Politics:* Democrat. *Religion:* Unitarian Universalist. *Home:* 1015 Whalley Ave., B-14, New Haven, Conn. 06515. *Office:* Wheaton College, Norton, Mass. 02766.

CAREER: Wheaton College, Norton, Mass., assistant professor, 1953-56, associate professor and chairman of department of psychology and education, 1956-59, professor of education, 1959-69, professor emeritus, 1969—, chairman of department of education, 1966-69, associate dean, 1966-69. *Member:* American Association of University Professors (chapter president, 1958-59), American Association of University Women (Boston branch), National Education Association, Cooperative Bureau for Teachers (member of governing board, 1961-63), Alumni Council of Harvard Graduate School of Education (secretary, 1958-59), Norton Historical Society, Pi Lambda Theta.

WRITINGS: Mary Lyon of Putnam's Hill, Vanguard, 1965; *Helen Hunt Jackson,* Vanguard, 1973. Contributor to *Encyclopedia of Educational Research* and to journals.

WORK IN PROGRESS: A biography for young people.

AVOCATIONAL INTERESTS: Collecting early textbooks; doing research on early schools in New England; drama; knitting; and gardening.*

* * *

BARACH, Alvan L(eroy)   1895-1977

February 22, 1895—December 13, 1977; American physician, pioneer in respiratory therapy, and author of books and more than three hundred articles, as well as a novel. Barach developed the first practical oxygen tent and other devices to facilitate breathing for patients with respiratory disorders. He was professor of clinical medicine at Columbia University and Presbyterian Hospital in New York City for many years. Barach died in New York City. Obituaries: *New York Times,* December 14, 1977.

BARBARE, Rholf
See VOLKOFF, Vladimir

* * *

BARBEAU, Clayton C(harles)   1930-

PERSONAL: Born April 11, 1930, in Sacramento, Calif.; son of Louis Albert and Bertha (DeGnath) Barbeau; married Myra Ellen Chorley, May 1, 1953; children: Michael Conrad, Amy Elizabeth, Rose-Marie, Margaret Ann, Mark Jerome, Daniel Joseph, Jennifer Irene, Christopher Charles. *Education:* Attended Sacramento Junior College, 1948-49, 1954-55; University of Santa Clara, B.S. (cum laude), 1959; Lone Mountain College, M.A., 1977. *Religion:* Roman Catholic. *Home:* 842 Clayton St., San Francisco, Calif. 94117. *Agent:* Marilyn Marlow, Curtis Brown Ltd., 60 East 56th St., New York, N.Y. 10022.

CAREER: Free-lance author and lecturer, 1959-64; *Way: Catholic Viewpoints,* San Francisco, Calif., managing editor, 1964-67, editor-in-chief, 1967-70, editor-at-large, 1970-73, editor, 1973; free-lance writer, 1973—. Communications counselor for Marriage Preparation Centers of San Francisco; member of board of trustees of Haight-Ashbury Ecumenical Ministry, 1967-70. Administrative director of Barbwire Theatre, 1972-73. Member of Conference on Religion and Peace, 1964—, and World Without War Council of Northern California, 1965—. Has given public lectures all over the United States; lay consultant to U.S. Catholic Conference, 1968—. *Military service:* U.S. Army, 1951-53. *Awards, honors:* James D. Phelan Award for Fiction, 1958, for *The Ikon;* author's award from *Spiritual Life,* 1961, for *The Head of the Family.*

WRITINGS: The Ikon (novel), Coward, 1961; *The Head of the Family* (nonfiction), Regnery, 1961; (contributor) Henry M. Christman, editor, *Peace and Arms: Reports from "The Nation",* Sheed, 1964; (editor) *Art, Obscenity, and Your Children,* Abbey Press, 1967; (contributor) Raban Hathorn, William Genne, and Mordecai Brill, editors, *Marriage: An Interfaith Guide for All Couples,* Association Press, 1970; (contributor) Frank Dickson and Sandra Smythe, editors, *Handbook of Short Story Writing,* Writer's Digest, 1970; (editor) *The Generation of Love,* Macmillan, 1971; (editor) *The Future of the Family,* Macmillan, 1971; *Dante and Gentucca* (historical fiction), Capra, 1973; *Creative Marriage: The Middle Years,* Seabury, 1976.

Author of television script "The Head of Thomas More," 1961, and filmstrip script "Creating a Marriage," Paulist/Newman, 1977. Also author of cassette lecture series, for St. Anthony Messenger Tapes, "Creative Marriage," 1975, and "The Art of Loving," 1977. Contributor to *New Catholic Encyclopedia,* 1965, and of several hundred articles to magazines.

WORK IN PROGRESS: The Long Journey, a historical novel about Dante; "The Male Condition," a nonfiction work.

SIDELIGHTS: Barbeau writes: "All my works deal with love—or the lack of it. My novel based on Korean combat experiences was devoted to exploration of themes of love and death. My nonfiction work deals with loving in the family, parent-child, husband-wife, as well as building up the community of love in the larger sphere. I am very much into counseling work with persons married and single, young and old; but the major thrust of my literary work is two novels now in progress. My completed novel on Dante Alighieri—the first full-scale recreation of his life—is much too long for today's publishers.'' Barbeau's book, *The Head of the Family,* has been published in Italian and continues to be in print seventeen years after publication.

AVOCATIONAL INTERESTS: Trout fishing in the Sierras (''For me, the ultimate in satori is to be knee-deep in a rushing river casting for a German Brown or a brookie''), deep sea fishing, camping, hiking.

* * *

BARBOUR, George 1890-1977

August 22, 1890—July 11, 1977; Scottish-born geologist, educator, and author. Barbour took part in geological expeditions around the world, most notably in China and South Africa, and was associated with the discovery of the Peking man. He was professor emeritus and dean of the College of Arts at the University of Cincinnati for more than twenty years. He collaborated on a book with Teilhard de Chardin entitled *In the Field With Teilhard de Chardin.* Barbour died in Cincinnati, Ohio. Obituaries: *New York Times,* July 13, 1977.

* * *

BARCLAY, William 1907-1978

1907—January 24, 1978; Scottish biblical scholar, educator, and author of books on religion. Barclay rewrote the New Testament in colloquial English and his *Daily Study Bible* sold more than five million copies. He was a professor at Glasgow University. Barclay died in Glasgow, Scotland. Obituaries: *New York Times,* January 25, 1978.

* * *

BARKER, Albert W. 1900-

PERSONAL: Born in 1900; son of Edwin L. (an editor) and Jessie (Wineman) Barker; married Gertrude Rozan. *Address:* 15 St. Andrews Pl., Yonkers, N.Y. 10705. *Agent:* Oliver Swan, Collier Associates, 280 Madison Ave., New York, N.Y. 10016.

WRITINGS: Black on White and Read All Over: The Story of Printing (juvenile), Messner, 1971; *The Straw Virgin,* Popular Library, 1975.

Adult novels; ''Reefe King'' series: *Gift From Berlin,* Award Books, 1969; *Apollo Legacy,* Award Books, 1970.

''Hawk Macrae'' series; all published by Curtis Books: *If Anything Should Happen to Me,* 1973; *The Big Fix,* 1973; *The Dragon in Spring,* 1973; *The Blood of Angels,* 1974; *The Diamond Fix,* in press.

WORK IN PROGRESS: A new novel.

* * *

BARLTROP, Robert 1922-
(Robert Coster)

PERSONAL: Born November 6, 1922, in London, England; son of Edwin John (a horsefood dealer) and Madeline (Lancaster) Barltrop; married Mary Gleeson, July 18, 1947; children: Christopher, Nicholas, Jonathan. *Education:* Educated in London, England. *Politics:* Socialist. *Religion:* None. *Home:* 34 St. Martin's Ave., East Ham, London E6 3DX, England.

CAREER: Has worked as a clerk, shop assistant, laborer, professional boxer, lorry driver, grave digger, strip-cartoonist, schoolteacher, and sign painter; writer, 1974—. *Member:* Socialist Party of Great Britain.

WRITINGS: The Monument: Story of the Socialist Party of Great Britain, Urizen Books, 1975; *Jack London: The Man, the Writer, the Rebel,* Urizen Books, 1977; (editor and author of introduction) Jack London, *Revolution: Stories and Essays,* Journeyman Press, 1978. Contributor of articles to *Socialist Standard, Western Socialist* (U.S.), *Socialist Leader, Freethinker, Freedom,* and *Essex Countryside.* Editor, *Socialist Standard,* 1972—.

WORK IN PROGRESS: A Part of Man's Life, a novel; a book based on teaching experiences; an outline for a commissioned work entitled *Radical London.*

SIDELIGHTS: Robert Barltrop wrote to *CA:* ''My motivation comes entirely from my working-class upbringing and identifications. As for subject matter—nothing which is human is alien, etc. I often stay and work (also draw and paint) in circuses, where I have many friends.'' *Avocational interests:* ''Books, books, more books,'' talking, sports of all kinds, tracing family history (village blacksmiths in Essex as far back as the 1400's).

* * *

BARNARD, John Lawrence 1912(?)-1977

1912(?)—August 5, 1977; American foreign service agent, novelist, and author of an autobiography. Barnard served as American consul in Antwerp and as consul general in Aruba and the Bahamas. He wrote two novels, *Revelry by Night* and *Land of Promise,* as well as his autobiography, *Gently Down the Stream.* Barnard died in New York, N.Y. Obituaries: *New York Times,* August 7, 1977; *AB Bookman's Weekly,* October 17, 1977.

* * *

BAROLINI, Helen 1925-

PERSONAL: Born November 18, 1925, in Syracuse, N.Y.; daughter of Anthony S. (a merchant) and Angela (Cardamone) Mollica; married Antonio Barolini (a writer), July 26, 1950 (died, 1971); children: Teodolinda, Susanna, Nicoletta. *Education:* Syracuse University, A.B., 1947; University of Florence, diploma di profitto, 1950; Columbia University, M.L.S., 1959. *Home and office:* 33 Ellis Pl., Ossining, N.Y. 10562. *Agent:* Liz Trupin, Jet Associates, 124 East 84th St., New York, N.Y. 10028.

CAREER: Translator and free-lance writer, 1948—; Trinity College, Hartford, Conn., teacher of translation and the Italian short story in a program in Rome, Italy, 1971-73; Kirkland College, Clinton, N.Y., instructor in Italian, 1974-75; teacher of oral history for adult education program in Dobbs Ferry, N.Y., 1976; town historian for Ossining, N.Y., 1977—.

MEMBER: International P.E.N. (American branch), Authors Guild, American Italian Historical Association, Ossining Historical Society (member of board of trustees, 1976—), Phi Beta Kappa. *Awards, honors:* Marina-Velca Journalism Prize from Ente Provinciale Turismo (Viterbo, Italy), 1970, for ''Etruscan Places Today''; MacDowell Colony fellow, 1974; National Endowment for the Arts grant for fiction writing, 1976.

WRITINGS: (With husband, Antonio Barolini) *Duet* (poems), Neri Pozza, 1966; ''Margaret Fuller'' (radio play), first broadcast in Rome, Italy, January 29, 1971.

Translator: Anthony Barolini, *Our Last Family Countess,* Harper, 1960; A. Barolini, *A Long Madness,* Pantheon, 1964; Terisio Pignatti, *History of Painting,* Newsweek Books, 1974; Francesco Arcangeli, *Graham Sutherland,* Abrams, 1975; Giancarlo Zizola, *John XXIII,* Orbis, 1978.

Author of scripts for Italian radio. Contributor of articles, stories, poems, and translations to American and Italian magazines, including *Cosmopolitan, Quarterly Review of Literature, Paris Review, New Yorker, Ms., New York Review of Books, Antioch Review, Yale Review,* and *Kenyon Review.* Associate editor of *Westchester Illustrated,* 1976—.

WORK IN PROGRESS: Two novels, *The Last Abstraction* and *Umbertina;* a book of short stories; an oral history of Ossining, N.Y.

SIDELIGHTS: Helen Barolini comments: "My husband was Italian, I lived in Italy for over ten years, and my children went to school there. Much of my writing reflects the Italian influence in my life, which is strong, fundamental, and abiding. It has also put into proper perspective my own Italian-American background."

* * *

BARON, Othello
    See FANTHORPE, R(obert) Lionel

* * *

BARRETT, Bob 1925-

PERSONAL: Born June 27, 1925, in Rogers City, Mich.; son of Paul Morse and Thelma (Stephens) Barrett; married Dessie Bryant (a store operator), August 16, 1973; children: Bruce, Joyce, Judy, Ruth. *Education:* Michigan State University, B.A., 1952. *Home address:* P.O. Box 742, Safford, Ariz. 85546.

CAREER: High school teacher of English and journalism in Bad Axe, Mich., 1953-58; *Huron News,* Bad Axe, Mich., editor, 1958-64; Fairchild Publications, bureau chief in Milwaukee, Wis., 1965-70, and Boston, Mass., 1970-72; Dessie's Idea Shop, Safford, Ariz., partner, 1972—. *Military service:* U.S. Navy, 1943-46.

WRITINGS: Delay at Parson's Flat (western), Doubleday, 1976; *Pembrook versus the West* (western), Doubleday, 1977.

WORK IN PROGRESS: Pen and Six-Gun, a Western novel.

SIDELIGHTS: Barrett told *CA:* "I try to write stories that a discriminating adult will enjoy reading more than once."

* * *

BARRETT, William R. 1922(?)-1977

1922(?)—November 14, 1977; American reporter and news service editor. Barrett was a newspaper, radio, and television reporter for fourteen years before joining United Press International in 1955. He was most recently assistant managing editor for the wire service. Barrett died in New York, N.Y. Obituaries: *New York Times,* November 15, 1977.

* * *

BARTON, Erle
    See FANTHORPE, R(obert) Lionel

* * *

BARTON, Lee
    See FANTHORPE, R(obert) Lionel

* * *

BARTON, Lew(is Randolph) 1918-

PERSONAL: Born June 4, 1918, near Maxton, N.C.; son of

Harker Randolph (a tenant farmer) and Catherine Anne (Dial) Barton; married Mary T. Warriax; children: Mary Ruth, Bruce, Renee, Ernie, Garry, Connee, Roger Dale, Ricky Mitchel, Gloria. *Education:* Attended King's Business College, 1950, and Bufner School for the Blind, 1954; Pembroke State University, B.A., 1957; University of North Carolina, M.A., 1964. *Home address:* P.O. Box 35, Pembroke, N.C. 28372. *Agent:* Bruce Barton, c/o *Carolina Indian Voice,* Pembroke, N.C. 28372. *Office:* 126 Austin St., Maxton, N.C.

CAREER: Held positions as editor of a newspaper in Pembroke, N.C., public relations officer at American Indian Study Center, Baltimore, Md., and public school teacher in N.C.; currently artist employed by North Carolina Arts Council, Raleigh, N.C., and writer. *Military service:* U.S. Navy; served in European and Asian-Pacific theaters. *Member:* Mystic Order of the Golden Dragon. *Awards, honors:* Marder Award, 1957; Henry Berry Lowry Memorial Award, 1972.

WRITINGS: Land of Promise (on Israel), W. Laurie, 1956; *Rhythm a Little Lumbee,* Amerind Good Will Publications, 1963; *"Way Out" in Carolina,* privately printed, 1963; *The Most Ironic Story in American History: An Authoritative, Documented History of the Lumbee Indians of North Carolina,* privately printed, 1967. Also author of *The Story of a Robeson Indian,* 1954, and *Up from Dust and Darkness,* 1977. Contributor of several hundred stories and articles to magazines and newspapers.

WORK IN PROGRESS: Interviews for an oral history program at University of Florida.

SIDELIGHTS: Barton writes: "I write because I could not do otherwise, not and be the kind of personality I am. In 1972, I originated two of the top ten newspaper stories of my area; I also became the second native of my county to appear on a North Carolina literary map (the *only* native born in this century to do so)."

* * *

BASSETT, (Mary) Grace 1927-

PERSONAL: Born August 17, 1927, in Spokane, Wash.; daughter of Joseph Elliott (an investor) and Jane Olive (a teacher; maiden name, Jones) Bassett. *Education:* Whitman College, B.A., 1947; Columbia University, M.S., 1948; further study at University of Paris and University of Frankfurt, 1950-51. *Home:* 2704 N St. N.W., Washington, D.C. 20007. *Office:* Department of Housing and Urban Development, 451 7th St. S.W., Washington, D.C. 20410.

CARREER/WRITINGS: Washington Post, Washington, D.C., staff writer on urban affairs, 1952-57; *Washington Star,* Washington, D.C., Congressional correspondent, 1957-67; King Features Syndicate, Washington, D.C. writer on politics and domestic and urban affairs, 1969-76; Department of Housing and Urban Development, Washington, D.C., assistant to secretary, 1976—. Notable assignments include coverage of the White House, Congress, and presidential campaigns. Assistant campaign manager, Eugene McCarthy presidential campaign, 1968; urban consultant, 1968-70. *Awards, honors:* Russell Sage fellow, 1966-67; American Political Science Association outstanding political writing citation; Newspaper Guild prize for series on Washington school integration; co-winner of Pulitzer Prize.

* * *

BATCHELOR, C(larence) D(aniel) 1888-1977

April 1, 1888—September 5, 1977; American cartoonist.

Batchelor's cartoons appeared in the *New York Daily News* from 1931 to 1969. He won a Pulitzer Prize for a cartoon in 1937. Batchelor died in Deep River, Conn. Obituaries: *New York Times,* September 7, 1977; *Time,* September 19, 1977.

* * *

BATHURST, Sheila
See SULLIVAN, Sheila

* * *

BATSON, George (Donald) 1918-1977

1918—July 25, 1977; American playwright and producer best known for his satires and comedies. Batson's plays include "Treat Her Gently," "Punch and Julia," "Ramshackle Inn," and "A Date With April," with starring roles performed by such notables as Gregory Peck, Jackie Cooper, Julie Harris, Zasu Pitts, Tallulah Bankhead, and Ethel Waters. He died in New York, N.Y. Obituaries: *New York Times,* July 30, 1977. (See index for *CA* sketch)

* * *

BAUER, George C. 1942-

PERSONAL: Born July 11, 1942, in Chicago, Ill.; son of George Charles and Helen (Laue) Bauer; married Linda Freeman (a teacher), December 29, 1968. *Education:* University of Illinois at Chicago Circle, B.Arch., 1967; Oberlin College, M.A., 1969; Princeton University, Ph.D., 1975. *Home:* 3403 Seashore Dr., Newport Beach, Calif. 92663. *Office:* School of Fine Arts, University of California, Irvine, Calif. 92717.

CAREER: University of California, Irvine, assistant professor of art history, 1973—. *Member:* College Art Association.

WRITINGS: Bernini in Perspective, Prentice-Hall, 1975. Contributor to *Art Bulletin.*

WORK IN PROGRESS: Bernini's Architecture and Decoration.

* * *

BAUER, Raymond A(ugustine) 1916-1977

September 7, 1916—July 10, 1977; American social psychologist and author of books in his field. Bauer won notoriety as director of a team conducting research on thousands of Russians who fled to Western Europe after World War II. This study led to Bauer's books *Man in Soviet Psychology, Nine Soviet Portraits,* and the co-authored *How the Soviet System Works.* Bauer also published studies on advertising and the politics of foreign trade. He died in Cambridge, Mass. Obituaries: *New York Times,* July 11, 1977. (See index for *CA* sketch)

* * *

BAUMANN, Charles Henry 1926-

PERSONAL: Born October 24, 1926, in Brooklyn, N.Y.; son of Charles (a florist) and Christina (Bauer) Baumann; married Nancy Nicholas (a teacher), 1951; children: Barbara, William. *Education:* Washington University, St. Louis, Mo., B.S., 1951; Pratt Institute, M.A.L.S., 1952; University of Wyoming, further study, 1956-61; University of Illinois, Ph.D., 1969. *Religion:* Unitarian-Universalist. *Home:* 481 North Third, Cheney, Wash. 99004. *Office:* Library, Eastern Washington University, Cheney, Wash. 99004.

CAREER: Champlain College, Plattsburgh, N.Y., assistant librarian, 1952-53; Niagara Falls Public Library, Niagara Falls, N.Y., branch librarian and reference librarian, 1953-54; University of Wyoming, Laramie, documents librarian, 1954-55, acquisitions librarian, 1956-61, assistant director of library, 1961-69; Eastern Washington State College (now Eastern Washington University), Cheney, college librarian, 1969—, trustee of Tamarack Festival, 1972—. Chairman of library services committee of Western Interstate Commission on Higher Education, 1968-69; chairman of steering committee of Washington State Advisory Council on Libraries for "Expo '74," 1972-73; chairman of administrative council of Spokane Regional Agency on Aging, 1975-77. *Military service:* U.S. Navy, 1944-46.

MEMBER: American Library Association, Association of College and Research Libraries, Freedom to Read Foundation (member of board of directors, 1975—), Phi Delta Kappa, Beta Phi Mu.

WRITINGS: The Influence of Angus Snead MacDonald and the Snead Book Stack on Modern Library Architecture, Scarecrow, 1972. Contributor to library journals. Member of editorial board of "Publications on Librarianship," Association of College and Research Libraries, 1976—.

WORK IN PROGRESS: Bernard Richardson Greene: Engineer and Library Planner.

* * *

BAVIN, Bill 1919-

PERSONAL: Legal name, William Stanley Bavin; born January 6, 1919, in London, England; son of Will Nicholas (an engineer) and Dorothy (a couturiere; maiden name, Towns) Bavin; married wife (died); children: Jacqueline Valerie, Stephanie Lynne (Mrs. Roger Mantle). *Education:* Educated in England. *Politics:* Conservative. *Religion:* Church of England. *Residence:* Tucson, Ariz. *Agent:* Lew Weitzman & Associates, 9171 Wilshire Blvd., Suite 406, Beverly Hills, Calif. 90210.

CAREER: Property developer; broker for Lloyds of London; writer, 1957—. Associate of the Corporation of Insurance Brokers, 1948—. Chairperson of London Chamber of Commerce. Has made numerous appearances on television shows in the United Kingdom, South Africa, Rhodesia, and the United States. *Military service:* British Army; served in artillery; mentioned in dispatches at Dunkirk. *Member:* Royal Society of Arts (fellow), Crime Writers' Association, Valuers' Institute (fellow), British Parachute Association, Rotary, Round Table, United Wards Club (London), London Sketch Club.

WRITINGS: One Man's War, Hutchinson, 1968; *Dead Regimental,* Hutchinson, 1969; *The Extortionists,* Universal/Tandem, 1970; *The Strange Death of Freddie Mills,* Howard Baker, 1975; *The Destructive Vice,* Universal/Tandem, 1977. Contributor of short stories and articles to British periodicals.

WORK IN PROGRESS: Rhodesian Rape, a book dealing with several periods in Rhodesia and South Africa; two novels, *Acapulco Gold* and *Cry from the Dungeon,* both about visits to Mexico and the undercover work of secret service narcotics agents.

SIDELIGHTS: Bavin told *CA:* "Both *The Extortionists* and *The Strange Death of Freddie Mills* were dangerous to research since they involved London and South African gangsters. I believe one cannot write unless personal experiences of the subject have been gained first hand. Most of my work is fiction based on actual fact.'' Bavin has originated a ''world-wide and very exclusive club called 'The Nobles.' There are only twenty/thirty members but they range from here to Hong Kong. There are no fees and no compulsion except to comport oneself without 'bull' and the idea is that every member will know where he can contact someone of integrity wherever he finds himself in the world.'' He has pilot licenses in England and the U.S. and a British Parachutist's License.

AVOCATIONAL INTERESTS: Travel, riding, squash, and pistol shooting.

* * *

BAXTER, James Sidlow 1903-

PERSONAL: Born February 25, 1903, in Sydney, Australia; son of John (an insurance broker) and Alice (a police court missionary; maiden name, Berry); married Ethel Smith, January 30, 1928; children: Miriam E. *Education:* Attended Spurgeon's Theological College, 1924-28. *Religion:* Evangelical Baptist. *Home:* 79 Virginia Lane, Santa Barbara, Calif. 93108.

CAREER: Writer. Entered Christian ministry, 1923; served as pastor of churches in Northampton, England, Sunderland, England, and Edinburgh, Scotland.

WRITINGS: Enter Ye In, Marshall, Morgan & Scott, 1939; *His Part and Ours,* Marshall, Morgan & Scott, 1948, Zondervan, 1960; *The Best Word Ever,* Marshall, Morgan & Scott, 1949; *God So Loved,* Marshall, Morgan & Scott, 1949, Zondervan, 1960; *Mark These Men,* Marshall, Morgan & Scott, 1949, Zondervan, 1960; *Studies in Problem Texts,* Marshall, Morgan & Scott, 1949, Zondervan, 1960; *Explore the Book,* 6 volumes, Marshall, Morgan & Scott, 1951-55, Zondervan, 1957, one volume edition, Marshall, Morgan & Scott, 1960; *Going Deeper,* Marshall, Morgan & Scott, 1957, Zondervan, 1960.

Awake My Heart, Zondervan, 1960; *A New Call to Holiness,* Marshall, Morgan & Scott, 1967, Zondervan, 1973; *His Deeper Work in Us,* Zondervan, 1967; *Our High Calling,* Zondervan, 1967; *The Strategic Grasp of the Bible,* Zondervan, 1968; *Does God Still Guide?,* Marshall, Morgan & Scott, 1968, Zondervan, 1971; *The Master Theme of the Bible,* Tyndale House, 1973; *Rethinking Our Priorities: The Church, Its Pastor and People,* Zondervan, 1974; *Christian Holiness: Restudied and Restated,* Zondervan, 1977. Also author of *Divine Healing of the Body.*

SIDELIGHTS: Baxter is well known to Evangelicals as a preacher, lecturer, and author. He has traveled in Australia, the United States, Canada, Britain, South Africa, and Rhodesia as a minister. He has also visited many missionary fields around the world.

* * *

BAYLES, Ernest E(dward) 1897-

PERSONAL: Born October 31, 1897, in Auburn, Kan.; son of Joseph William (a Baptist minister) and Lillian (Potter) Bayles; married Lucene Spencer, August 25, 1920; children: Spencer, Hugh G., Lewis A., John E. *Education:* Attended Ottawa University, Ottawa, Kan., 1915-18; University of Kansas, A.B., 1919, M.A., 1922; University of Chicago, summer graduate study, 1926, 1927; Ohio State University, Ph.D., 1932. *Home:* 1911 Oxford Rd., Lawrence, Kan. 66044. *Office:* School of Education, University of Kansas, Lawrence, Kan. 66044.

CAREER: High school natural science teacher in Iola,

Kan., Newton, Iowa, and Lawrence, Kan., 1919-22; Central Missouri State Teachers College (now Central Missouri State University), Warrensburg, associate professor of science teaching, 1922-28; University of Kansas, Lawrence, 1928—, began as assistant professor, professor of education, 1946-68, professor emeritus, 1968—. Visiting summer professor at University of Missouri, 1936-38, University of Kansas City (now University of Missouri, Kansas City), 1956, Wayne State University, 1958, Fresno State College (now California State University, Fresno), 1960, and Michigan State University, 1966; distinguished professor of comparative education and educational philosophy, Western Michigan University, summer, 1962. Conducted classes in teaching theory for inmates at the Federal Penitentiary, Leavenworth, Kan., 1956-57. Consultant to Institute for Educational Leadership, Japan, for Secretary of the U.S. Army, 1949-50. *Military service:* U.S. Naval Reserve, 1918.

MEMBER: Philosophy of Education Society (president, 1961-62), Comparative Education Society, History of Education Society, National Society of College Teachers of Education (former vice-president; president, 1967-68), American Association of University Professors (chapter president, 1959-61), John Dewey Society, Southwestern Philosophical Society, Phi Delta Kappa (past representative, Southwestern district).

WRITINGS: (With R. Will Burnett) *Biology for Better Living* (high school text), Silver Burdett, 1941; (contributor) S. Eldridge and others, editors, *Development of Collective Enterprise,* Kansas University Press, 1943; (with Arthur L. Mills) *Basic Chemistry* (high school text), Macmillan, 1947; *The Theory and Practice of Teaching,* Harper, 1950; (contributor) W. A. Fullagar and others, editors, *Readings for Educational Psychology,* Crowell, 1956; *Democratic Educational Theory,* Harper, 1960; (contributor) Alfred E. Kuenzli, editor, *Reconstruction in Religion: A Humanist Symposium,* Beacon, 1961; (with Bruce L. Hood) *Growth of American Educational Thought and Practice,* Harper, 1966; *Pragmatism in Education,* Harper, 1966; *The Insight Theory in Learning and Teaching,* Pageant-Poseidon, 1976. Author of monographs on teaching theory; contributor to *Encyclopedia of Educational Research* and of about 100 articles to educational journals.

General editor of Harper's ''Series on Teaching'' and ''Philosophy of Education Series''; editor and publisher, *Proceedings* of the Annual Meeting of the Philosophy of Education Society, 1958-65; occasional consultant, Coronet Educational Films.*

* * *

BEAL, M. F. 1937-

PERSONAL: Born September 6, 1937, in New York, N.Y.; daughter of Edwin F. and Mary (Peer) Beal. *Education:* Barnard College, B.A., 1960; University of Oregon, M.F.A., 1970. *Agent:* Betty Anne Clarke, International Creative Management, 40 West 57th St., New York, N.Y. 10019.

CAREER: California State University, Fresno, associate professor of writing and literature, 1970—. Founding member of Women's Resource Center of Lincoln County, Ore. *Member:* International P.E.N.

WRITINGS: Amazon One (novel), Little, Brown, 1975; *Safe House* (essays), Northwest Matrix, 1976; *Angel Dance* (novel), Daughters, Inc., 1977.

Work anthologized in *Best American Short Stories,* 1972.

WORK IN PROGRESS: Dead Time, a novel.

BEALE, Betty

PERSONAL: Born in Washington, D.C.; daughter of William Lewis (a banker) and Edna (Sims) Beale; married George K. Graeber (a manufacturer's representative), February 15, 1969. *Education:* Smith College, A.B. *Religion:* Christian Scientist. *Home and office:* 2926 Garfield St. N.W., Washington, D.C. 20008.

CAREER/WRITINGS: Washington Post, Washington, D.C., columnist, 1937-40; *Washington Evening Star,* Washington, D.C., author of column, 1945—; Field Newspaper Syndicate, Chicago, Ill., author of "Betty Beale's Washington" weekly column, 1953—. Notable assignments include the White House functions under six presidents, every national political convention since 1952, the Kennedy and Johnson presidential campaigns, and interviews with Harry Truman, the King of Morocco and Queen of Spain, the Empress of Iran, Richard Nixon, Gerald Ford, and every first lady since 1952. *Member:* Washington Press Club. *Awards, honors:* Freedom Foundation Award, 1969.

SIDELIGHTS: Beale told *CA* she has "a passion for accuracy and fairness; a contempt for hypocrisy and an innate preference for the constructive rather than the destructive—plus an interest in a wide variety of subjects." But her main interest, she said, "is the political pictures as viewed from the White Houe."

* * *

BEALES, Derek (Edward Dawson) 1931-

PERSONAL: Born June 12, 1931, in Felixstowe, England; son of Edward and Dorothy Kathleen (Dawson) Beales; married Sara Jean Ledbury (a teacher of classics), August 14, 1964; children: Christina Margaret, Richard Derek. *Education:* Sidney Sussex College, Cambridge, B.A., 1953, M.A. and Ph.D., both 1957. *Religion:* Anglican. *Office:* Department of History, Sidney Sussex College, Cambridge University, Cambridge, England.

CAREER: Cambridge University, Cambridge, England, fellow of Sussex College, 1958—, university assistant lecturer, 1962-65, university lecturer in history, 1965—. *Member:* Royal Historical Society (fellow). *Awards, honors:* Prince Consort Prize and Seeley Medal from Cambridge University, 1960, for *England and Italy, 1859-60.*

WRITINGS: England and Italy, 1859-60, Thomas Nelson, 1961; *From Castlereagh to Gladstone,* Thomas Nelson, 1969; *The Risorgimento and the Unification of Italy,* Allen & Unwin, 1971. *Historical Journal,* editor, 1971-75, member of editorial board, 1975—.

WORK IN PROGRESS: A book on Joseph II; research on Gladstone's career and importance, especially his first ministry, 1868-74.

AVOCATIONAL INTERESTS: Music (piano and organ), travel, and bridge.

* * *

BEAN, Mabel Greene 1898(?)-1977
(Mabel Greene)

1898(?)—July 4, 1977; American journalist. She was a feature writer and fashion editor for the *New York Sun.* Among her principal journalistic assignments were coverage of fashion shows in Paris and the trial of Bruno Hauptmann for the murder of Charles Lindbergh's son. She died in Queens, N.Y. Obituaries: *New York Times,* July 5, 1977.

BEAR, John 1938-

PERSONAL: Born March 14, 1938, in New York; son of John Klempner (a writer) and Tina (a teacher; maiden name, Minsker) Bear; married first wife, Helen, August 20, 1960 (died December 15, 1962); married Marina Dorrow (a carpenter), August 14, 1963; children: Mariah, Susannah, Tanya. *Education:* Reed College, student, 1955-58; University of California, Berkeley, B.A., 1959, M.J., 1960; Michigan State University, Ph.D., 1966. *Politics:* Democrat. *Religion:* Jewish. *Home address:* Drawer H, Little River, Calif. 95456.

CAREER: Center for the Gifted Child, Inc., San Francisco, Calif., director, 1963-65; Bell & Howell Co., Chicago, Ill., research director in human development, 1966-68; University of Iowa, Iowa City, associate professor of journalism, 1968-69; Midas-International Corp., Chicago, Ill., director of advertising, 1968-70; consultant, 1970-74; writer, 1974—. Consultant to Xerox Corp., General Motors, *Encyclopaedia Britannica,* the Grateful Dead, and Teknekron, Inc.

WRITINGS: The Something Went Wrong, What Do I Do Now Cookbook, Harcourt, 1970, also published as *Common Cooking Crises,* Reader's Digest Press, 1972, and *The Something Went Wrong, What Do I Do Now Cookery Book,* Macdonald & Co., 1973; *Signals and Messages,* Macdonald Educational, 1973; *San Francisco: An Unusual Guide to Unusual Shopping,* Price, Stern, 1972; *Communication,* Macdonald Educational, 1974; *The United States of America: The Land and Its People,* Macdonald Educational, 1974; *So You're in Your Teens,* Price, Stern, 1975; *So You're in Your Twenties,* Price, Stern, 1975; *So You're in Your Thirties,* Price, Stern, 1975; *So You're in Your Forties,* Price, Stern, 1975; *So You're in Your Fifties,* Price, Stern, 1975; *So You're in Your Sixties,* Price, Stern, 1975; *College Degrees by Mail: A Comprehensive Guide to Alternative Degree Programs,* Rafton & Bear, 1975, 4th edition, 1978; *The World's Worst Maxims,* Price, Stern, 1976.

SIDELIGHTS: Bear comments: "I have taken two to three years off to build a house on the shores of the eastern Pacific Ocean. I am co-owner of an ice cream manufacturing business, and am involved in selling a wide variety of products (books to waterbeds to candy) by mail. Perhaps because my father was a successful writer of fiction books in the 1930's and 1940's, I have been disinclined or intimidated from moving in that direction. But I have enough splendid nonfiction ideas to keep me going for the balance of years probably allotted me."

* * *

BEATY, Betty
(Karen Campbell, Catherine Ross)

PERSONAL: Born in Farsley, Yorkshire, England; daughter of Harry Brooke and Catherine Campbell (McNeill) Smith; married David Beaty (a writer); children: Susan, Carole, Karen. *Education:* University of Leeds, diploma in social science and public administration. *Residence:* Woodside, Hever, Kent, England. *Agent:* Curtis Brown Ltd., 13 King St., Covent Garden, London W.C.2, England.

CAREER: Former stewardess for British European Airways, London, England; has also held positions in the medical field including medical social worker at Pensbury Hospital in England; currently full-time writer.

WRITINGS—Novels; all published by Mills & Boon: *Maiden Flight,* 1956; *South to the Sun,* 1957; *The Atlantic Sky,* 1957; *Amber Five,* 1958; *The Butternut Tree,* 1958; *The*

Path of the Moonfish, 1964; *Miss Miranda's Walk,* 1967. Also author of *The Swallows of San Fedora, Love and the Kentish Maid,* and *Head of Chancery.*

Under pseudonym Karen Campbell: *Suddenly in the Air,* Stein & Day, 1969; *Thunder on Sunday,* Bobbs-Merrill, 1972, *Wheel Fortune,* Collins, 1974; *Death Descending,* Collins, 1976.

Under pseudonym Catherine Ross: *The Colours of the Night,* M. Joseph, 1962; *The Trysting Tower,* M. Joseph, 1964; *From This Day Forward,* J. Cape, 1968.

*   *   *

BEAUCHAMP, Tom L.   1939-

PERSONAL: Born December 2, 1939. *Education:* Southern Methodist University, B.A., M.A., 1963; Yale University, B.D. (cum laude), 1966; Johns Hopkins University, Ph.D., 1970. *Office:* Kennedy Institute, Center for Bioethics, Georgetown University, Washington, D.C. 20057.

CAREER: Georgetown University, Washington, D.C., associate professor of philosophy and senior research scholar. Staff philosopher for National Commission for the Protection of Human Subjects (of National Institutes of Health). Visitng professor at Dalhousie University. Referee of articles, projects and manuscripts for Prentice-Hall, Dickenson, McGraw, Wadsworth, National Science Foundation, and *Philosophy of Science. Member:* American Philosophical Association (chairman of sub-committee on employment services, 1976—), Washington Philosophy Club (president, 1976-77).

WRITINGS: Philosophical Problems of Causation, Dickenson, 1974; *Ethics and Public Policy,* Prentice-Hall, 1975; *Distributive Justice,* National Commission for the Protection of Human Subjects, 1976; (contributor) R. Almeder and J. Humber, editors, *Biomedical Ethics and the Law,* Plenum, 1976; (editor with Stephen F. Barker) *Thomas Reid: Critical Interpretations,* Philosophical Monographs, 1976; (editor with LeRoy Walters) *Contemporary Issues in Bioethics,* Dickenson, 1977; (contributor) William T. Blackstone and R. Heslep, editors, *Social Justice and Preferential Treatment,* University of Georgia Press, 1977; (contributor) T. Mappes and J. Zembaty, editors, *Social Ethics,* McGraw, 1977; (editor with Seymour Perlin) *Death and Dying,* Prentice-Hall, 1977; (editor with Blackstone and Joel Feinberg) *Contemporary Introduction to Philosophy,* Dickenson, in press; (contributor) A. W. Siemsen and other editors, *Emerging Medical, Moral, and Legal Concerns: Extraordinary Therapeutic Procedures,* University Press of Hawaii, in press. Contributor to *Encyclopedia of Bioethics* and to philosophy journals.

*   *   *

BECK, Helen L(ouise)   1908-

PERSONAL: Born January 3, 1908, in Vienna, Austria; came to the United States in 1940, naturalized in 1944; daughter of Oskar and Julie Beck. *Education:* Bryn Mawr College, M.S.W., 1946. *Home:* 41 Wolfpit Ave., Norwalk, Conn. 06851. *Office:* Center for Lifetime Learning, Fairfield University, Fairfield, Conn. 06430.

CAREER: Teacher in nursery and elementary schools in Vienna, Austria; Psychoanalytic Institute of Vienna, Vienna, member, 1928-38; Wartime Day Nursery School, London, England, co-founder and administrator, 1938-40; worked in the field of family welfare after arriving in the United States; instructor in residential therapy, Medical School, University of Cincinnati, Cincinnati, Ohio; worked as admission supervisor in a treatment hospital for mentally ill adults; chief psychiatric social worker in handicapped children's unit, St. Christopher's Hospital for Children; associate professor of social work in department of pediatrics, Medical School, Temple University, Philadelphia, Pa.; instructor in Center for Lifetime Learning, Fairfield University, Fairfield, Conn.

MEMBER: World Federation of Mental Health, American Orthopsychiatric Association, Association for Retarded Children, Connecticut Association of Children with Learning Disabilities (member of board of directors).

WRITINGS: Going to Camp, Stephen Day Press, 1949; *The Closed, Short Term Group* (monograph), U.S. Children's Bureau, 1965; *Social Services to the Mentally Retarded,* C. C Thomas, 1969; *Don't Push Me, I'm No Computer,* McGraw, 1973. Contributor to education and mental health journals, and to *Parents' Magazine.*

SIDELIGHTS: Helen Beck writes: "My interest has always been in young children, because of the preventive aspect of any service and program for them. My work with parents individually and in groups is stimulated by the same motivation." *Don't Push Me, I'm No Computer* has been translated into Dutch and German.

*   *   *

BECKMAN, Aldo Bruce   1934-

PERSONAL: Born December 24, 1934, in Lima, Ill.; son of Aldo H. (a farmer) and Mildred (Lummis) Beckman; married Marijo Walsh, November 4, 1961 (divorced May 7, 1973); children: Teri, Tricia, Jennifer, Mary Kay, Eugene. *Education:* Attended Bradley University, 1952-53; Western Illinois University, B.S., 1956. *Religion:* Methodist. *Home:* 1913 Key Blvd., Arlington, Va. 22201. *Office:* Chicago *Tribune,* 1707 H St., N.W., Washington, D.C. 20006.

CAREER/WRITINGS: United Press International, Chicago, Ill., writer for national radio, 1958-59; *Chicago Tribune,* Chicago, Ill., reporter, 1959—, covered Capitol Hill, 1966-70, White House correspondent, 1970-77, Washington bureau chief, 1977—. Notable assignments include coverage of President Nixon from 1970 until his resignation, and President Ford. Member, board of directors, Western Illinois Foundation. *Military service:* U.S. Army, 1956-58. *Member:* White House Corrrespondents Association (secretary and vice-president, 1976-77, president, 1978—), National Press Club. *Awards, honors:* Beck Award from the *Chicago Tribune,* 1966 and 1972, for best story of year; Western Illinois University distinguished alumni award, 1973; Merriman Smith Award from White House Correspondents Association, 1976, for coverage of Sara Jane Moore's attempted assassination of President Ford.

SIDELIGHTS: Beckman told *CA:* "I nurtured ambitions to be a reporter since high school. I believe reporters provide vital service in a democracy by providing information to citizens. I abhor participatory journalism. A reader should never be able to guess the politics of a reporter. Ideally, a reporter should have no strong political views and should be an observer, not a shaper, of events."

*   *   *

BECKWITH, B(rainerd) K(ellogg)   1902-

PERSONAL: Born December 11, 1902, in New York; son of S. Vilas and Julia (Rogers) Beckwith; married Katherine Buntin; children: Brainerd Kellogg, Jr. *Education:* Attended

Yale University, 1921-22. *Politics:* Republican. *Religion:* Episcopalian. *Home:* 333 West California Blvd., Pasadena, Calif. 91105.

CAREER: Newspaper journalist and publicity director. Owned cattle ranches in Mexico, Oregon, Wyoming, and California. *Wartime service:* American Red Cross field officer with U.S. Air Force.

WRITINGS: Spinning Dust (novel), Wallace Hebberd, 1928; *Galloping Down* (novel), Century Co., 1931; *Seabiscuit: The Saga of a Great Champion,* W. Crowell, 1940; *Step and Go Together: The World of Horses and Horsemanship,* A. S. Barnes, 1967; *The Longden Legend,* A. S. Barnes, 1973; *The Story of Santa Anita,* Los Angeles Turf Club, 1975. Also author of *The Thoroughbred in California.*

SIDELIGHTS: Beckwith comments that his writings are "largely confined to horses and the people connected with them."

*   *   *

BEEBE, (Charles) William   1877-1962

PERSONAL: Born July 29, 1877, in Brooklyn, N.Y.; son of Charles and Henrietta Marie (Younglove) Beebe; married Mary Blair (divorced); married Elswyth Thane (an author), September, 1927. *Education:* Columbia University, B.S., 1898, graduate study, 1898-99. *Residence:* New York, N.Y.

CAREER: Naturalist and author. Became curator of ornithology, New York Zoological Park (also known as the Bronx Zoo), 1899; director of the Zoological Society's department of tropical research, 1899-1962; director of the British Guiana Zoological Station. *Military service:* U.S. Army. *Member:* American Association for the Advancement of Science, American Ornithologists' Union, Societe d'-Acclimatation de France, Zoological Society (New York and London), New York Academy of Sciences (fellow), Audubon Society, Ecological Society, Linnaean Society, Society of Mammologists. *Awards, honors:* Sc.D., Tufts College and Colgate University, both 1928; also received Elliot Medal and John Burroughs Medal.

WRITINGS—Nonfiction: *Two Bird-Lovers in Mexico,* Houghton, 1905; *The Bird: Its Form and Function,* Holt, 1906; *The Log of the Sun: A Chronicle of Nature's Year* (illustrated by Walter King Stone), Holt, 1906; (with first wife, Mary Blair) *Our Search for a Wilderness: An Account of Two Ornithological Expeditions to Venezuela and to British Guiana,* Holt, 1910; (with G. Inness Hartley and Paul G. Howes) *Tropical Wild Life in British Guiana,* New York Zoological Society, 1917; *Jungle Peace,* Holt, 1918; *A Monograph of the Pheasants,* Witherby, 1918-22, published as *Pheasants: Their Lives and Homes,* Doubleday, Page, 1926; *Edge of the Jungle,* Holt, 1921, reprinted, Duell, Sloan, 1956; *Galapagos: World's End* (illustrated by Isabel Cooper and John Tee-Van), Putnam, 1924; *Jungle Days,* Putnam, 1925; *The Arcturus Adventure: An Account of the New York Zoological Society's First Oceanographic Expedition,* Putnam, 1926; *Pheasant Jungles,* Putnam, 1927; *Beneath Tropic Seas: A Record of Diving Among the Coral Reefs of Haiti,* Putnam, 1928.

Exploring with Beebe: Selections for Younger Readers, Putnam, 1932; *Nonsuch: Land of Water,* Brewer, Warren, 1932; (with John Tee-Van) *Field Book of the Shore Fishes of Bermuda,* Putnam, 1933, published as *Field Book of the Shore Fishes of Bermuda and the West Indies,* Dover, 1970; *Half Mile Down,* Harcourt, 1934, reprinted, Duell, Sloan, 1965; *Zaca Venture,* Harcourt, 1938; *Book of Bays,* Har-

court, 1942; (editor) *The Book of Naturalists: An Anthology of the Best Natural History,* Knopf, 1944; *High Jungle,* Duell, Sloan, 1949; *Unseen Life of New York* (illustrated by Donald T. Carlisle), Duell, Sloan, 1953; *Adventuring with Beebe,* Duell, Sloan, 1955. Contributor to *Atlantic Monthly.*

SIDELIGHTS: Beebe made his first of several international expeditions when he journeyed with his wife, Mary Blair (who later became well known as novelist Blair Niles) to Mexico in the early 1900's. Following his Mexican expedition, Beebe travelled to the Zoological Society's research station in British Guiana. His studies of the South American environment are published in *Tropical Wild Life, Monographs of the Pheasants,* and *Jungle Life.*

During the First World War, Beebe served as an aviator and bomber. Troubled by his war experiences, he returned to Guiana to renew his spirits. While there he wrote a collection of papers which was later published as *Jungle Peace.* Teddy Roosevelt reviewed the book as "one of the rare books which represent a positive addition to the sum total of genuine literature. . . . It will stand on the shelves of cultivated people, of people whose taste in reading is both wide and good, as long as men and women appreciate charm of form in the writings of men who also combine love of daring adventure with the power to observe and vividly to record the things of strange interest which they have seen."

Beebe made a record breaking descent of 3,028 feet into the ocean in a bathyspere designed by Otis Barton. He told of his findings in *Half Mile Down.*

High Jungle, a recounting of Beebe's expeditions ot the Venezuelan Andes, was reviewed by *Saturday Review:* "The factual discoveries and revelations of nature made by Beebe and his enthusiastic assistants in the Venezuelan jungles are so legionary as to defy review."

A selection of Beebe's writings are collected in *Adventuring with Beebe.*

BIOGRAPHICAL/CRITICAL SOURCES: Saturday Review, September 3, 1949; Frederick Wagner, *Famous Underwater Adventurers,* Dodd, 1962; (for children) Bernadine Freeman Bailey, *Famous Modern Explorers,* Dodd, 1963; *Reader's Digest,* July, 1968; Robert Henry Welker, *Natural Man: The Life of William Beebe,* Indiana University Press, 1975.

OBITUARIES: New York Times, June 6, 1962; *Illustrated London News,* June 16, 1962; *Newsweek,* June 18, 1962; *Publishers Weekly,* June 18, 1962.*

(Died June 4, 1962)

*   *   *

BEGNAL, Michael H(enry)   1939-

PERSONAL: Born October 17, 1939, in Wahsington, D.C.; son of Henry I. (a social worker) and Kate (a social worker; maiden name, Kilmartin) Begnal; married Cynthia Marion Finch, January 16, 1965; children: Michael S., Anthony A. *Education:* University of Connecticut, B.A., 1961; Pennsylvania State University, M.A., 1963; University of Washington, Seattle, Ph.D., 1968. *Home:* 100 West Hamilton Ave., State College, Pa. 16801. *Office:* Department of English, Pennsylvania State University, University Park, Pa. 16802.

CAREER: Colgate University, Hamilton, N.Y., instructor in English, 1963-65; Pennsylvania State University, University Park, assistant professor, 1968-71, associate professor of English and comparative literature, 1972—. Fulbright senior lecturer, Charles University, Prague, 1973-74 and 1976-77.

WRITINGS: Joseph Sheridan Le Fanu, Bucknell University Press, 1971; *A Conceptual Guide to Finnegans Wake,* Pennsylvania State University Press, 1975; *Narrator and Character in Finnegans Wake,* Bucknell University Press, 1976.

WORK IN PROGRESS: James Joyce; Contemporary Experimental Literature; Eastern European Literature.

SIDELIGHTS: Bengal commented: "most of my writing relates to mythology, especially in relation to *Finnegans Wake.*"

*   *   *

BEHAN, Brendan   1923-1964

PERSONAL: Born February 9, 1923, in Dublin, Ireland; son of Stephen (a house painter, labor leader, and soldier) and Kathleen (Kearney) Behan; married Beatrice ffrench-Salkeld (a painter); children: one daughter. *Education:* Attended Irish Catholic schools. *Religion:* Roman Catholic. *Residence:* London, England.

CAREER: Apprenticed as a house painter, 1937; arrested in Liverpool, England, 1939, convicted of possessing explosives and sent to Borstal (a reform school), 1939-42; arrested and convicted in Dublin, 1942, for revolutionary activities and sentenced to three years in an Irish prison, 1942-45; worked as house painter, seaman, free-lance journalist, and writer, 1945-64. Member, Fianna Eireann (youth organization), and Irish Republican Army (IRA).

WRITINGS: The Quare Fellow: A Comedy-Drama (three-act play; first produced in Dublin at Pike Theatre, 1954), Grove, 1956; *Borstal Boy,* Hutchinson, 1958, Knopf, 1959; *The Hostage* (three-act play; first produced in Dublin, 1958), Grove, 1958, third revised edition, Methuen, 1962; *Brendan Behan's Island: An Irish Sketch-Book,* Geis, 1962; *Hold Your Hour and Have Another* (collected articles), Little, Brown, 1963; *Brendan Behan's New York,* Geis, 1964; *The Scarperer,* Doubleday, 1964; *Confessions of an Irish Rebel,* Hutchinson, 1965, Geis, 1966; Al Simpson, editor, *Richard's Cork Leg,* Grove, 1974.

Omnibus volume: *The Quare Fellow and The Hostage: Two Plays,* Grove, 1964.

SIDELIGHTS: Once characterized as "a professional young Irishman," Brendan Behan, in both his life and work, took the role to heart. Even before his early death in 1964 from alcoholism, jaundice, and diabetes, he had become a legend. Stories of his drunken antics and of his youthful "terrorist" activities for the IRA prevailed in the media over mention of his literary creations. His work was often dismissed as the careless outpouring of a sensation-hungry revolutionary without a revolution.

But serious connections have been drawn between the content of Behan's writing, particularly his major plays "The Quare Fellow" and "The Hostage," his politics, and his self-destructive drinking. In his work, as in his life, laughter and the despair of dying are commingled with intoxicating effect. Behan himself once said that he possessed "a sense of humor that would cause me to laugh at a funeral, providing it wasn't my own." About his comedies critic Alfred Kazin stated: "There is the constant suggestion in Behan's work that the laughter which supports despair does not always hide despair. But Behan's is the despair of an authentic predicament, of the actualities of life at the present time." Ted Boyle, in his book *Brendan Behan,* commented: "A good deal of the comedy in Behan's plays portrays the hysteria which overcomes the human being caught in a situation over which he has no control." The criminal about to be hanged in "The Quare Fellow" and the British soldier being held for exchange with a captured IRA member in "The Hostage" are both examples of this comedic circumstance.

Behan's work is also characterized by his talent for realistic dialogue, the gift of his "tape-recorder ear." His later works in fact were taken down on tape, transcribed, and then edited by others. But even in his earlier writing there is the same fidelity to common speech patterns. Kazin commented: "What Behan has done, coming in too late to participate in the Irish literary renaissance, is to identify himself not with the abstract cause of art but with the profane and explosive speech of the streets, the saloons, the prisons."

In 1970 Frank McMahon adapted *Borstal Boy* for the theater. The dramatization, like the book, portrays Behan's early prison years, incorporating the addition of a narrator, the older Behan, who relates the story from downstage. The play conveys, as critic Alan Bunce wrote, "a florid reflection of Behan's adult personality—mellow, tartly philosophical, a mixture of Hibernian ruefulness with lambent humor." The play received both the Antoinette Perry Award and the New York Drama Critics Circle Award as best play of the 1969-70 season.

Both "The Quare Fellow" and "The Hostage" have been made into films. His writings have been translated into Italian, French, and German.

BIOGRAPHICAL/CRITICAL SOURCES: Alfred Kazin, *Contemporaries,* Little, Brown, 1959; Alan Simpson, *Beckett and Behan and a Theatre in Dublin,* Routledge & Kegan Paul, 1962; Brooks Atkinson, *Tuesdays and Fridays,* Random House, 1963; Dominic Behan, *My Brother Brendan,* Frewin, 1965, Simon & Schuster, 1966; Rae Jeffs, *Brendan Behan: Man and Showman,* Hutchinson, 1966, World Publishing, 1968; Sean McCann, *The World of Brendan Behan,* Frewin, 1966; Frederick Lumley, *New Trends in 20th Century Drama,* Oxford University Press, 1967; *Books Abroad,* spring, 1967; Ted E. Boyle, *Brendan Behan,* Twayne, 1969; *Christian Science Monitor,* April 8, 1970; *Contemporary Literary Criticism,* Volume I, Gale, 1973.*

(Died March 20, 1964)

*   *   *

BELL, Carol
See FLAVELL, Carol Willsey Bell

*   *   *

BELL, James (Adrian)   1917-

PERSONAL: Born November 12, 1917, in Altoona, Kan.; son of George Andrew (an engineer) and Fay (Commons) Bell; married Virginia Gray, July 8, 1941; children: Jane Robertson, George. *Education:* University of Kansas, B.A., 1940. *Home:* 224 Marlborough St., Boston, Mass. 02116. *Office: Time,* 2285 Prudential Center, Boston, Mass. 02199.

CAREER/WRITINGS: Topeka Daily Capital, Topeka, Kan., reporter, 1940-41; *Time,* New York, N.Y., correspondent from Chicago, 1942-48, White House correspondent, 1948-50, chief of New York bureau, 1950, war correspondent, 1950, Middle East bureau chief, 1951-54, Central European bureau chief, 1954-56, China and Southeast Asia bureau chief, 1956-59, chief of Africa bureau, 1959-61, chief of European central bureau, 1961-66, chief of New York bureau, 1966-68, chief of London bureau, 1968, chief of Rome bureau, 1968-73, chief of Atlanta bureau, 1973-76, senior correspondent, 1976—. Contributor to *Time, Life, Fortune,* and other periodicals. Notable assignments include coverage of the Korean War and the White House. *Military service:* U.S. Army, 1942-45; became second lieutenant. *Awards, honors:* University of Kansas distinguished service award, 1961.

SIDELIGHTS: Bell told *CA* that the most challenging aspect of his work as a foreign bureau chief is "bringing complex political situations not fully understood in the U.S. into proper perspective. An example would be the Arab-Israeli confrontation and the plight of Palestinian refugees in the years immediately following the war of 1948. We Americans often tend to see only one side of the question."

* * *

BELL, Thornton
See FANTHORPE, R(obert) Lionel

* * *

BELPRE, Pura

PERSONAL: Name is pronounced *Poo*-rah *Bell*-pray; born in Cidra, Puerto Rico; came to the United States in the 1920's; married Clarence Cameron White (a musician and composer). *Education:* Educated in Puerto Rico, later attended the New York Public Library School. *Residence:* New York, N.Y.

CAREER: Author and puppeteer-storyteller. Began telling stories to children as part of the New York Public Library program, later became interested in designing puppets to enhance her stories. *Awards, honors:* Brooklyn Art Books for Children citation, 1973, for *Santiago.*

WRITINGS—Fiction, except as noted: *Perez and Martina: A Portorican Folktale* (illustrated by Carlos Sanchez), Warne, 1932, new edition, 1961; *The Tiger and the Rabbit, and Other Tales* (illustrated by Kay Peterson Parker), Houghton, 1946, new edition (illustrated by Tomie de Paola), Lippincott, 1965; *Juan Bobo and the Queen's Necklace: A Puerto Rican Folk Tale* (illustrated by Christine Price), Warne, 1962; *Ote: A Puerto Rican Folk Tale* (illustrated by Paul Galdone), Pantheon, 1969: *Santiago* (illustrated by Symeon Shimin), Warne, 1969; (with Mary K. Conwell) *Libros en Espanol: An Annotated List of Children's Books in Spanish* (nonfiction), New York Public Library, 1971; *Dance of the Animals: A Puerto Rican Folk Tale* (illustrated by P. Galdone), Warne, 1972; *Once in Puerto Rico* (illustrated by C. Price), Warne, 1973.

Translator into Spanish: Munro Leaf, *El Cuento de Ferdinand* (title means "The Story of Ferdinand"), Viking, 1962; Crosby N. Bonsall, *Caso del Forastero Hambriento* (title means "Case of the Hungry Stranger"), Harper, 1969; Carla Greene, *Camioneros: Que Hacen?* (title means "Truck Drivers: What Do They Do?"), Harper, 1969; Syd Hoff, *Danielito y el Dinosauro* (title means "Danny and the Dinosaur"), Harper, 1969; Leonard Kessler, *Aqui Viene el Ponchado* (title means "Here Comes the Strikeout"), Harper, 1969; Else Holmelund Minarik, *Osito* (title means "Little Bear"), Harper, 1969; Millicent E. Selsam, *Teresita y las Orugas* (title means "Terry and the Caterpillas"), Harper, 1969; Paul Newman, *Ningun Lugar para Jugar* (title means "No Place to Play"), Grosset, 1971.

BIOGRAPHICAL/CRITICAL SOURCES: Lee Bennett Hopkins, *Books Are by People,* Citation, 1969.*

BELSER, Lee 1925-

PERSONAL: Born September 7, 1925, in Martinsburg, W.Va.; daughter of Noland Claxton and Emily (Fellows) West; children: William Gordon III. *Education:* University of South Carolina, B.S., 1948. *Politics:* Independent. *Religion:* Lutheran. *Home:* 1604 32nd St. N.W., Washington, D.C. 20007. *Office:* 1701 Pennsylvania Ave. N.W., Washington, D.C. 20007.

CAREER/WRITINGS: International News Service, Los Angeles, Calif., columnist, 1952-58; *Los Angeles Mirror,* Los Angeles, columnist, 1958-60; *Los Angeles Herald-Examiner,* Los Angeles, reporter, 1960-62; Hearst Headline Service, Washington, D.C., correspondent from Paris and Rome, 1962-63, Washington correspondent, 1972—; *Baltimore News American,* Baltimore, Md., reporter, 1966-72, author of "This Week on Capitol Hill" weekly column, 1972—. Notable assignments include coverage of Capitol Hill, the Flying Tigers plane crash, the Finch-Gregoff murder trials, the criminal libel trial of *Confidential,* and the Lana Turner-Johnny Stompanato case. Contributor to *Coronet,* 1969-72. *Member:* Washington Press Club. *Awards, honors:* Hearst Award, 1976.

SIDELIGHTS: Belser told *CA:* "As a woman, I found it challenging trying to get ahead in a man's world, but I cannot be stereotyped as a 'women's libber.' My career began long before women's lib so I never really thought in those terms and never considered myself anthing other than equal to the men I worked with. Perhaps being a news reporter was somewhat of an advantage in this respect. In the 1960's I switched from Hollywood to Capitol Hill and politics. My main concern is reporting the news fairly and honestly. My main grievances certainly include the stupidity of Congress and its preoccupation with itself rather than diligently pursuing the interests of the people it represents.

"I'm very interested in travel, and have made numerous trips to Europe."

* * *

BEMELMANS, Ludwig 1898-1962

PERSONAL: Born April 27, 1898, in Meran, Tyrol, Austria (now part of Italy); came to United States in 1914, naturalized in 1918; son of Lambert (a Belgian painter) and Frances (Fisher) Bemelmans; married Madeline Freund, November, 1935; children: Barbara. *Education:* Attended public and private schools in Austria. *Residence:* New York, N.Y.

CAREER: Writer, humorist, illustrator, painter, and author of books for children. Worked in hotels and restaurants, 1914-17 and after World War I, became waiter, and later part owner of Hapsburg House on New York's East Side. Designed settings for a Broadway play and did an unsuccessful comic strip for the *New York World. Military service:* U.S. Army during World War I, as an attendant in a mental hospital and instructor of German-speaking recruits. *Awards, honors:* Caldecott Medal, 1953, for *Madeline's Rescue;* New York Times Choice for Best Illustrated Children's Books of the Year, 1953, for *Madeline's Rescue,* and 1955, for *Parsley;* New York Herald Tribune Children's Spring Book Festival Award, 1950, for *Sunshine,* and 1957, for *Madeline and the Bad Hat.*

WRITINGS: Small Beer, Viking, 1939; *At Your Service: The Way of Life in a Hotel,* Row, Peterson, 1941; *Hotel Splendide,* Viking, 1941, *Rosebud,* Random House, 1942; *I Love You, I Love You, I Love You* (short stories), Viking, 1942; *Now I Lay Me Down to Sleep* (novel), Viking, 1943;

Hotel Bemelmans (autobiographical short stories), Viking, 1946; *Dirty Eddie* (novel), Viking, 1947; *A Tale of Two Glimps,* Columbia Broadcasting System, 1947; *The Eye of God* (novel), Viking, 1949; *Father, Dear Father* (autobiographical), Viking, 1953; *To the One I Love Best,* Viking, 1955; *The World of Bemelmans: An Omnibus,* Viking, 1955; *The Woman of My Life,* Viking, 1957; *My Life in Art,* Harper, 1958; *How to Have Europe All to Yourself,* European Travel Commission, 1960; *Are You Hungry, Are You Cold,* World Publishing, 1960; *Marina,* Harper, 1962; *On Board Noah's Ark,* Viking, 1962; *The Street Where the Heart Lies,* World Publishing, 1963.

All self-illustrated: *My War with the United States,* Viking, 1937; *Life Class,* Viking, 1938; *The Donkey Inside,* Viking, 1941; *The Blue Danube,* Viking, 1945; *The Best Times: An Account of Europe Revisited,* Simon & Schuster, 1948; *How to Travel Incognito,* Little Brown, 1952; *The Happy Place,* Little, Brown, 1952; *The High World,* Harper, 1954; *Italian Holiday,* Houghton, 1961.

For children; all self-illustrated: *Hansi,* Viking, 1934, reprinted, 1966; *The Golden Basket,* Viking, 1936; *The Castle Number Nine,* Viking, 1937; *Quito Express,* Viking, 1938, reprinted, 1965; *Madeline,* Simon & Schuster, 1939, reprinted, Viking, 1969; *Fifi,* Simon & Schuster, 1940; *Sunshine: A Story about the City of New York,* Simon & Schuster, 1950; *Madeline's Rescue,* Viking, 1950, reprinted, 1973; *Parsley* (an earlier version appeared in *Womans Day* under the title, "The Old Stag and the Tree"), Harper, 1955; *Madeline and the Bad Hat,* Viking, 1956, reprinted, 1968; *Madeline and the Gypsies,* Viking, 1959, reprinted, 1973; *Madeline in London,* Viking, 1961, reprinted, 1972.

Other: (illustrator) Munro Leaf, *Noodle,* F. A. Stokes, 1937, reprinted, Four Winds, 1969; (illustrator) Leonard J. Mitchell, *Luechow's German Cookbook,* Doubleday, 1952; (contributor) *Best of Modern Humor* (anthology), edited by Pelham G. Wodehouse and Scott Meredith, Washburn, 1952; (contributor) *Empire City: A Treasury of New York,* edited by Alexander Klein, Rinehart, 1955; (compiler and illustrator) *Holiday in France,* Houghton, 1957; (contributor) *Hallmark Christmas Festival,* edited by Carl Beier, Compass Productions, 1959; *Welcome Home!,* Harper, 1960; *La Bonne Table* (selections), edited by Donald and Eleanor Friede, Simon & Schuster, 1964.

Contributor of articles and stories to *New Yorker, Vogue, Town and Country, Stage,* and other periodicals.

SIDELIGHTS: A visit by May Masse, Viking children's book editor, to Ludwig Bemelmans's New York apartment launched his career as an author-illustrator. What she saw there were landscapes of his native Tyrol painted on the window shades to ease his homesickness, and furniture, that he could not afford to buy, painted on the walls. This convinced her that he should write for children.

Bemelmans was a spirited man who enjoyed life, but who insisted that writing was always difficult for him. He claimed that he began writing because he suffered from insomnia, and added that if it were ever cured, he would quit. He also believed that his best writing and drawing was accomplished while soaking in a hot bathtub.

All of Bemelmans's works were based on his own experiences. The "Madeline" books, which have sold over a quarter of a million copies, were named after his wife. *Madeline's Rescue,* which as the sequel to *Madeline* received the Caldecott Medal in 1953, was reviewed by a *Saturday Review* critic as "not only an amusing story, but a trip to Paris for adults as well as children! And you will want to take it

over and over again." Describing the illustrations, which are usually in water color, *Opectator* said that "the gaiety, clarity, and richly right colours of Bemelmans' pictures make them live and joyous scenes."

Bemelmans's works have been adapted as motion pictures. "Yolanda and the Thief" was produced by Metro-Goldwyn-Mayer in 1945, and "Madeline" by Columbia Pictures in 1952.

BIOGRAPHICAL/CRITICAL SOURCES: Saturday Review, May 16, 1953; *Spectator,* December 4, 1953; *Publishers Weekly,* March 20, 1954, November 14, 1960.

OBITUARIES: New York Times, October 2, 1962; *Publishers Weekly,* October 8, 1962; *Time,* October 12, 1962; *Illustrated London News,* October 13, 1962; *Newsweek,* October 15, 1962; *Wilson Library Bulletin,* November, 1962; *Current Biography,* December, 1962.*

(Died October 1, 1972)

*   *   *

BENDER, Thomas 1944-

PERSONAL: Born April 18, 1944, in San Mateo, Calif.; son of Joseph C. (a politician) and Catherine (McGuire) Bender; married Sally Hill (a librarian), June 18, 1966; children: David. *Education:* University of Santa Clara, B.A., 1966; University of California, Davis, M.A., 1967, Ph.D., 1971. *Residence:* New York, N.Y. *Office:* New York Institute for the Humanities, New York University, Washington Square, New York, N.Y. 10003.

CAREER: University of Wisconsin—Green Bay, assistant professor of history and urban studies, 1971-74; New York University, New York, N.Y., assistant professor, 1974-76, associate professor of history, 1976-77, Samuel Rudin Professor of the Humanities, 1977—. Visiting assistant professor at University of California, Davis, summer, 1972. *Member:* American Historical Association, Organization of American Historians, American Studies Association, Columbia University Seminar on the City (chairman, 1976—), New York Institute for the Humanities. *Awards, honors:* Frederick Jackson Turner Prize from Organization of American Historians, 1975, for *Toward an Urban Vision.*

WRITINGS: Toward an Urban Vision: Ideas and Institutions in Nineteenth-Century America, University Press of Kentucky, 1975; *Community: Social Change in America,* Rutgers University Press, 1978; (with Edwin Rozwenc) *The Making of American Society,* Knopf, 1978. Contributor to history and education journals, and to literary magazines, including *New England Quarterly.*

WORK IN PROGRESS: Research on the cultural history of American cities, and on the social foundations of intellectual life in cities, especially New York City.

*   *   *

BENEDICTUS, David (Henry) 1938-

PERSONAL: Born September 16, 1938, in London, England; son of Henry Jules and Kathleen Constance (Ricardo) Benedictus; married. *Education:* Balliol College, Oxford, B.A., 1959; further study at University of Iowa. *Home:* The Pelican, 20 Alexandra Rd., East Twickenham, Middlesex, England.

CAREER: British Broadcasting Corp. (BBC), London, England, assistant trainee, 1963-64, drama director, 1964-65, story editor, "Wednesday Play," 1967; Thames Television, Bristol, England, trainee director, 1969-70; novelist, playwright, and author of short stories.

WRITINGS—Novels: *The Fourth of June,* Blond, 1962, Dutton, 1963; *You're a Big Boy Now,* Blond, 1963, Dutton, 1964; *This Animal Is Mischievous,* New American Library, 1965; *Hump; or, Bone by Bone, Alive,* Blond, 1967; *The Guru and the Golf Club,* Blond, 1969; *The World of Windows,* Weidenfeld & Nicolson, 1971; *The Rabbi's Wife,* M. Evans, 1976.

Plays: "The .Fourth of June," first produced in London, 1964; "Angels (Over Your Grave) and Geese (Over Mine)," first produced in Edinburgh at the Traverse Theatre, 1967; "Dromedary," first produced in Newcastle upon Tyne, 1969; "What a Way to Run a Revolution!," first produced in London, 1971.

Contributor of short stories to *Seventeen, Pointer, Penthouse, Men Only,* and other periodicals.

SIDELIGHTS: New Yorker reviewed *The Fourth of June:* "The extremely promising and funny first novel of a young Englishman, David Benedictus, who is as clever as paint and at great pains to hide from his readers the secret that what he is offering them is a warmhearted and humane tract aimed at making Eton think twice about itself." The *New York Herald Tribune* claimed Benedictus "springs from the British tradition of undergraduate arrogance that propelled Beerbohm and Waugh into their first printings and he remains eminently cool."

BIOGRAPHICAL/CRITICAL SOURCES: New York Herald Tribune, October 21, 1962; *New Yorker,* February 16, 1963.*

* * *

BENJAMINSON, Peter   1945-

PERSONAL: Born August 19, 1945, in Washington, D.C.; son of Albert (a rancher and electronics consultant) and Florence (a legal secretary; maiden name, Galinson) Benjaminson. *Education:* University of California, Berkeley, A.B., 1967; Columbia University, M.S., 1968. *Residence:* Miami, Fla.

CAREER: Detroit Free Press, Detroit, Mich., reporter and city-county bureau chief, 1970-76; writer. *Military service:* U.S. Army, 1968-70; became lieutenant. *Member:* Investigative Reporters and Editors. *Awards, honors:* Sloan fellow, Woodrow Wilson School of Public and International Affairs, Princeton University, 1976-77.

WRITINGS: (With David Anderson) *Investigative Reporting,* Indiana University Press, 1976; *Motown,* Grove Press, 1978.

SIDELIGHTS: CA asked Benjaminson how he felt the investigative reporting demonstrated in the Watergate investigation affected reporters. He responded: "I, along with many other reporters, feel that the Watergate investigation a) showed what beneficial results could be achieved from an investigation partly based on not telling the truth (Woodward and Bernstein lying to the committee for the Re-election of the President employees they interviewed, as they themselves admit), and bending, if not breaking, the law and some ethical codes (interviewing or attempting to interview grand jurors, looking at other people's telephone bills, etc.) and b) made a lot of reporters and editors too arrogant and sure of themselves and too ready to see wrongdoing where there is none, or at least none that the public should be concerned about other than for reasons of gossip (as the post-Elizabeth Ray sex scandals, and perhaps even the Ray scandal itself, showed.)

"I think the Watergate investigation also showed, once again, that nothing should be left to experts. I may be over-reflecting my own experiences, but I believe along with many others that war shouldn't be left to the generals, nor White House reporting to White House reporters, nor music industry reporting to music biz critics or executives."

CA asked Benjaminson about *Motown:* "I see the Motown story," he said, "as a story of race in America and as a reflection of racial struggles—and of the eventually more-or-less successful integration of American society—in the music of that society. In most important ways, the Motown book will be much more interpretive than investigative, at least in the traditional sense in which those words are used."

* * *

BERG, Lasse   1943-

PERSONAL: Born July 1, 1943, in Sweden; son of Edvard and Ebba (Kaeding) Berg; married Lisa Edfelt (a writer), 1965; children: Josefin, Mia. *Education:* University of Stockholm, Fil. Kand,, 1970. *Agent:* Gidlunds Bokfoerlag, P.O. Box 12016, 112 41 Stockholm, Sweden.

CAREER: Writer, 1970—.

WRITINGS: (With wife, Lisa Berg) *Ansikte mot ansikte: Fascister och revolutionaerer i Indien,* Raben & Sjoegren, 1970, English translation by Norman Kurtin published as *Face to Face: Fascism and Revolution in India,* Ramparts, 1971, revised edition, 1972; (with L. Berg and Stig T. Karlsson) *Varfoer jobbar Chand?* (juvenile ; title means "Why Is Chand Working?"), Gidlund, 1971; (with L. Berg) *Uppvaknandet: Japan idag* (title means "Awakening: Japan Today"), Raben & Sjoegren, 1972; (with L. Berg) *Japan i Asien* (title means "Japan and Asia"), Utrikespolitiska Instituet, 1972; (with L. Berg) *Barn paa Bali* (juvenile; title means "Children in Bali"), Gidlund, 1974; (with L. Berg and Karlsson) *Japan: Framtiden har redan boerjat* (title means "Japan: The Future Has Started"), Gidlund, 1974; (with L. Berg and Karlsson) *Vi bor i vaerldens stoersta stad* (title means "Living in the Biggest City in the World"), Gidlund, 1974; (with L. Berg) *Att leva i Bangladesh* (juvenile; title means "Living in Bangladesh"), Esselte Studium, 1975. Author of documentary radio and television scripts for Swedish Broadcasting Corp. Contributor to *Vi* and *Dagens Nyheter.*

WORK IN PROGRESS: Tredje vaerlden–ett tvaersnitt (title means "The Third World"), reporting from Papua-New Guinea, South Asia, and North Africa, dealing with the struggle for a new international order on different levels.

SIDELIGHTS: Berg told *CA:* "By mixing grass-root level close-ups with analytical overviews we want to report on the historical fight of our era by the peoples of the Third World to liberate themselves from oppression.

"By writing for children we want to give them a realistic view on the day to day situation of the majority of mankind, and even more importantly, to help them through increased knowledge to identify with the poor in the Third World."

* * *

BERGAUST, Erik   1925-

PERSONAL: Born March 23, 1925, in Baerum, Oslo, Norway; came to the United States, 1949, naturalized, 1956; married Jean Cameron Somers, January 13, 1951; children: Christine, Erik, Paul, Jane. *Education:* Frogner Gymnasium, B.S., 1943; attended Oslo Handelgymnasium, 1944. *Residence:* Falls Church, Virginia.

CAREER: Author, editor, and publisher. Editor and publisher of numerous publications concerning air and sea exploration, 1946—; manager of airplane and helicopter services, 1948-52; free lance aviation writer, 1949-52; president, North Springs, Inc., 1962-64. Conducted a weekly radio program, "Washington Radio Features" and has been associated with the Voice of America. Chairman, Republican Advisory Committee on Space and Aerospace, 1962—. *Military service:* Served with the Norwegian Resistance Movement, 1943, and Norwegian Exile Army, 1944-45. *Member:* National Press Club, Aviation and Space Writers Association, Author's Guild, Environmental Writers Association of America (member of board of directors, 1972—), National Space Club (founder; president, 1957-1959), American Helicopter Society, American Military Engineers, American Rocket Society, Convertible Aircraft Pioneers, Norsk Astronautisk Forening, Mason.

WRITING: All published by Putnam, except as noted: (With Gunnar Oxaal) *Reisen til Manen Blir Alvor,* Fabritius (Oslo), 1952; (with Bernt Balchen) *The Next Fifty Years of Flight,* Harper, 1954; (with William Beller) *Satellite!,* Hanover House, 1956; *Rockets and Missiles,* 1957; *Rockets around the World,* 1958; (with Seabrook Hull) *Rocket to the Moon,* Van Nostrand, 1958; *Rockets of the Navy,* 1959; *Satellites and Space Probes,* 1959; *First Men in Space,* 1960; *Reaching for the Stars,* Doubleday, 1960; *Rockets of the Air Force,* 1960; *Rockets of the Army,* 1960; *Birth of a Rocket,* 1961; *Rocket Aircraft: U.S.A.,* 1961; *Rockets to the Moon,* 1961; *Rockets to the Planets,* 1961; (with Thorstein Thelle) *Romfartens ABC,* P. F. Steensballes boghandels (Oslo), 1961; (with William O. Foss), *Coast Guard in Action,* 1962; (with Foss) *Helicopters in Action,* 1962; *Our New Navy,* 1962; *Rocket Power,* 1962; *Saturn Story,* 1962; *Space Stations,* 1962; *Rocket City: U.S.A.,* Macmillan, 1963; *The Next Fifty Years in Space,* Macmillan, 1964.

(With W. O. Foss) *The Marine Corps in Action,* 1965; (with W. O. Foss) *Skin Divers in Action,* 1965; (editor) *Illustrated Space Encyclopedia,* 1965, revised edition published as *The New Illustrated Space Encyclopedia,* 1971; *Rockets of the Armed Forces,* 1966; *Aircraft Carriers in Action,* 1968; *Mars: Planet for Conquest,* 1968; *Murder on Pad 34,* 1968; (with Foss) *Oceanographers in Action,* 1968; *Convertiplanes in Action: The VTOL Success Story,* 1969; *The Russians in Space,* 1969; (with Thelle) *Havforsking,* B.H. Reenskaug (Oslo), 1970; (editor) *The Illustrated Nuclear Encyclopedia,* 1971; *National Outdoorsmen's Encyclopedia,* Remington & Ross, 1973; *The Next Fifty Years on the Moon,* 1974; *Rescue in Space: Lifeboats for Astronauts and Cosmonauts,* 1974; *Colonizing the Planets,* 1975; *Colonizing the Sea,* 1976.

* * *

BERN, Maria Rasputin Soloviev 1900(?)-1977
(Maria Rasputin)

1900(?)—September 28, 1977; Russian-born dancer, circus performer, and author. The daughter of the czarist "Mad Monk," Gregory Rasputin, Bern wrote the book, *Rasputin: The Man Behind the Myth.* She toured Europe with a circus as an animal trainer before settling in the United States in 1935. She died in Los Angeles, Calif. Obituaries: *New York Times,* September 29, 1977; *Newsweek,* October 10, 1977.

* * *

BERNA, Paul 1910-
PERSONAL: Born February 21, 1910, in Hyeres, France;

married Jany Saint-Marcoux (a writer); children: Bernard, Philippe. *Education:* Attended Villa Saint-Jean, Fribourg, Switzerland. *Residence:* Paris, France.

CAREER: Author. Worked as an accountant, insurance man, secretary, film distributor, and at other various jobs before starting a full-time writing career; reporter for a suburban Paris newspaper, 1930-36; accepted a position with the French Ministry of Communications at the end of the second World War. *Awards, honors:* The Mystery Writers of America award, 1967, for *The Secret of the Missing Boat.*

WRITINGS: Le Piano a bretelle (illustrated by Pierre Dehay), Editions G.P. (Paris), 1956, translation by John Buchanan-Brown published as *The Street Musician,* Bodley Head, 1960; *Le Carrefour de la Pie,* Editions G.P., 1957, translation by Helen Woodyatt published as *Magpie Corner,* Hamish Hamilton, 1966; *Le Cheval sans tete,* 1955, translation by J. Buchanan-Brown published as *A Hundred Million Francs,* Bodley Head, 1957, published in America as *The Horse without a Head,* Pantheon, 1959; *Le Kangourou volant* (illustrated by Pierre Le Guen), Editions G.P., 1957, translation by H. Woodyatt published as *The Golden Fish,* Hamish Hamilton, 1963; *Millionaires en herbe* (illustrated by G. de Sainte-Croix), Editions G.P., 1958, translation by J. Buchanan-Brown published as *The Knights of King Midas,* Pantheon, 1961; *Les Pelerins de Chiberta* (illustrated by G. de Sainte-Croix), Editions G.P., 1958, translation by J. Buchanan-Brown published as *The Mystery of the Cross-Eyed Man,* Bodley Head, 1965; *La Porte des etoiles* (illustrated by Geraldine Spence), translation by J. Buchanan-Brown published as *Threshold of the Stars,* Bodley Head, 1958, Abelard, 1961; *Le Champion* (illustrated by P. Le Guen), Editions G.P., 1959; *Le Continent du ciel,* translation by J. Buchanan-Brown published as *Continent in the Sky,* Bodley Head, 1959, Abelard, 1963.

La Grande Alerte (illustrated by Jacques Pecnard), Editions G.P., 1960, translation by J. Buchanan-Brown published as *Flood Warning,* Bodley Head, 1962, Pantheon, 1963; *La Piste du souvenir,* translation by J. Buchanan-Brown published as *The Mystery of Santi-Salgue,* Bodley Head, 1963, Pantheon, 1964; *Le Temoignage du chat noir* (illustrated by Daniel Dupuy), Editions G.P., 1963, translation by J. Buchanan-Brown published as *The Clue of the Black Cat,* Bodley Head, 1964, Pantheon, 1965; *La Volle rouge,* translation by J. Buchanan-Brown published as *The Secret of the Missing Boat,* Bodley Head, 1966, Pantheon, 1967; *Le Commissaire Sinet et le mystere de l'autoroute sud* (illustrated by D. Dupuy), Presses de la Cite (Paris), 1967, translation by J. Buchanan-Brown published as *The Mule on the Motorway,* Bodley Head, 1967, published in America as *The Mule on the Expressway,* Pantheon, 1968; *Le Commissaire Sinet et le mystere des poissons rouges* (illustrated by D. Dupuy), Presses de la Cite, 1968, translation by J. Buchanan-Brown published as *A Truckload of Rice,* Pantheon, 1968; *L'Epave de la Berenice,* Editions G.P., 1969; *Un Pays sans legende,* Editions G.P., 1969, translation by J. Buchanan-Brown published as *They Didn't Come Back,* Pantheon, 1969; *Le Grand Rallye de Mirabal,* translation by J. Buchanan-Brown published as *The Vagabonds Ashore,* Bodley Head, 1973; *Les Vagabonds du Pacifique,* translation by J. Buchanan-Brown published as *Vagabonds of the Pacific,* Bodley Head, 1973; *La Derniere Aube,* Editions G.P., 1974.

Also author of *Le Bout du monde* and *Operation oiseau-noir,* both published by Editions G.P.

SIDELIGHTS: Reviews of Paul Berna's *Threshold of the*

Stars range from that of a *Kirkus* critic who called it "good adventure, and so well translated, [with] a number of characters who have a thoroughly adult quality, and the ideas of what the future holds are made credible," to the comment by a *New York Herald Tribune* writer who described it as "both dull and inaccurate." His work, however, has been generally well received. A critic for *Young Readers' Review* termed *The Clue of the Black Cat,* a sequel to *The Mule on the Expressway,* "A bit more far fetched than [its predecessor], but just as suspenseful and just as cleverly plotted. The riddle unfolds slowly, but the action is fast and readers will be mystified until the very end. This book has a dry humor which is not every child's cup of tea, but it is a superior mystery and one which is worth reading."

BIOGRAPHICAL/CRITICAL SOURCES: Kirkus, November 1, 1960; *New York Herald Tribune,* May 14, 1961; *Christian Science Monitor,* November 14, 1963; *Times Literary Supplement,* November 26, 1964; *New York Times Book Review,* November 7, 1965; *Young Readers' Review,* December, 1968.*

* * *

BERNARD, George 1939-

PERSONAL: Born May 18, 1939. in New York, N.Y. *Education:* City College of the City University of New York, B.B.A., 1961. *Home and office:* 345 East 73rd St., New York, N.Y. 10021.

CAREER: Worked as broadcast executive at WINS-Radio and WIP-Radio, and as station manager of TeleGuide, 1961-64; *National Enquirer,* Lantana, Fla., reporter, 1964-68; Columbia Broadcasting System (CBS), New York, N.Y., manager of press services, 1968-72; World Team Tennis, New York City, vice-president and general manager, 1972, 1973; World Football League, New York City, director of press relations, 1973, 1974; free-lance writer, 1975-77; Panax Newspapers, East Lansing, Mich., New York bureau chief, 1977—. *Military service:* U.S. Army Reserve, 1961-67.

WRITINGS: Inside the National Enquirer: Confessions of an Undercover Reporter, Ashley Books, 1977.

Author of screenplays "The Madness of Herman Plotkin," "Last Cha Cha in Brooklyn," and "Al, Baby!".

Contributor of articles and photographs to magazines and newspapers, including *People, Gentleman's Quarterly,* and *Penthouse.*

SIDELIGHTS: Bernard writes: "My first, and only, book was dedicated to the memory of my father. I have dedicated my life to exposing injustices in the system. For five years, I did the same for the *Enquirer.* And, when they attempted on at least two occasions to stop my book, I fought back. A third publisher, Ashley Books, joined me in fighting for the right to publish and distribute my work. I am now exposing corruption in government. My position in New York affords me the opportunity to explore the world of politics, entertainment, science, religion, the unpredictable—and the unexplained. In this respect, I consider myself to be most fortunate."

* * *

BERRY, Wendell (Erdman) 1934-

PERSONAL: Born August 5, 1934, in Henry County, Ky.; married Tanya Amyx, May 29, 1957; children: Mary Dee, Pryor Clifford. *Education:* University of Kentucky, A.B., 1956, M.A., 1957. *Home:* River Rd., Port Royal, Ky. 40058. *Office:* Department of English, University of Kentucky, Lexington, Ky. 40506.

CAREER: University of Kentucky, Lexington, member of faculty, 1964-70, distinguished professor of English, 1971-72, professor of English, 1973—. *Awards, honors:* Bess Hokin Prize, 1967, for "Six Poems"; National Institute of Arts and Letters Literary award, 1971; recipient of Guggenheim Foundation grant, and Rockefeller grant.

WRITINGS: Nathan Coulter, Houghton, 1960; *November Twenty-six Nineteen Hundred Sixty-Three,* Braziller, 1964; *The Broken Ground,* Harcourt, 1964; *A Place on Earth,* Harcourt, 1967; *The Rise,* University of Kentucky Library Press, 1968; *Openings: Poems,* Harcourt, 1968; *The Long-legged House,* Harcourt, 1969; *Findings,* Prairie Press, 1969.

Farming: A Handbook, Harcourt, 1970; *The Hidden Wound,* Houghton, 1970; (with R. E. Meatyard and A. Gassan) *Ralph Eugene Meatyard,* Gnomon Press, 1970; (with Meatyard) *The Unforeseen Wilderness: An Essay on Kentucky's Red River Gorge,* University Press of Kentucky, 1971; *A Continuous Harmony: Essays Cultural and Agricultural,* Harcourt, 1972; (contributor) James Lane Allen, *The Blue Grass Region of Kentucky, and Other Kentucky Articles,* Books for Libraries, 1972; *The Country of Marriage,* Harcourt, 1973; *The Eastward Look,* Sand Dollar Press, 1974; *The Memory of Old Jack,* Harcourt, 1974; *Horses,* Larkspur Press, 1975; *To What Listens,* Best Cellar Press, 1975; *Sayings and Doings,* Gnomon Press, 1975; *The Kentucky River: Two Poems,* Larkspur Press, 1976; *There Is Singing Around Me,* Cold Mountain Press, 1976; *Clearing,* Harcourt, 1977; *Three Memorial Poems,* Sand Dollar Press, 1977; *The Unsettling of America: Culture and Agriculture,* Sierra Books, 1977.

Contributor to *Nation, New World Writing, New Directions Annual, Prairie Schooner, Contact, Chelsea Review, Quarterly Review of Literature,* and others.

SIDELIGHTS: Berry is a poet, novelist, and essayist whose work reflects a concern with the despoilation of his native Kentucky.

Reviewer Jonathan Yardly states that although Berry deals primarily with Kentucky and its people, "one would be hard pressed to dismiss him as a mere regionalist. Perhaps his problem is that he is quite old-fashioned: his work is rooted in the land and in the values of an older America, and though nostalgia is much in vogue these days, the same cannot be said of the morality to which Americans of half a century ago clung."

Another reviewer, Roland Sawyer, said that Berry "left his native hills and valleys for a time but returned in the conviction that in the surroundings to which a man is closest, which he loves and understands best, he makes his greatest contribution to his fellowmen."

BIOGRAPHICAL/CRITICAL SOURCES: National Review, November 14, 1967; *Shenandoah,* autumn, 1969; *Poetry,* May, 1974; *Parnassussus: Poetry in Review,* spring/summer, 1974; *Sewanee Review,* summer, 1974; *Contemporary Literary Criticism,* Gale, Volume 4, 1975, Volume 6, 1976; *New York Times Book Review,* September 25, 1977.

* * *

BERRY, William D(avid) 1926-

PERSONAL: Born May 20, 1926, in California; son of Harvey R. (an electrical engineer) and Ruth (Black) Berry; married Elizabeth M. Lambert (a potter), April 27, 1952; children: Mark Fraser, Paul Norman. *Education:* Attended Art Center School of Los Angeles, 1943, School of Allied

Arts, Glendale, Calif., 1947-50, Glendale Junior College, 1949-50, and University of Alaska, Fairbanks, 1971. *Politics:* "No hard line." *Religion:* "No organized religion." *Home and office:* Miller Hill, Star Rt. Box 20063, Fairbanks, Alaska 99701.

CAREER: California Junior Museum, Sacramento, curator of science, 1951-52; National Park Service, Western Museum Laboratory, San Francisco, Calif., preparator, 1958-60; Denver Museum of Natural History, Denver, Colo., staff artist, 1973-74; Tanana Valley Community College, Fairbanks, Alaska, instructor in art, 1975—. Free-lance artist and writer. Technical consultant to Walt Disney Enterprises, 1956-57. *Military services:* U.S. Army, 1944-47; received Bronze Star. *Member:* Alaska Conservation Society. *Awards, honors:* Has received several prizes for paintings and prints in regional shows.

WRITINGS—All self-illustrated: (With wife, Elizabeth M. Berry) *Mammals of the San Francisco Bay Region,* University of California Press, 1959; *Buffalo Land,* Macmillan, 1961; *Deneki,* Macmillan, 1965.

Illustrator: George Willett, *Birds of the Southern California Deserts,* Los Angeles County Museum, 1951; Fran Hubbard, *Animal Friends of the Sierra,* Awani, 1955; Hubbard, *Animal Friends of the Northwest,* Awani, 1957; Vinson Brown, *How to Understand Animal Talk,* Little, Brown, 1958; Charles A. McLaughlin, *Mammals of Los Angeles County,* Los Angeles County Museum, 1959; Herbert H. Wong, *Ducks, Geese, and Swans,* Lane, 1960; William O. Pruitt, *Animals of the North,* Harper, 1966.

Contributor of articles to *Audubon* Magazine and *North American Review.*

WORK IN PROGRESS: A book on drawing animals and humans; a book using his wildlife sketches.

SIDELIGHTS: Berry wrote: "From early childhood until the age of thirty-five I had one overriding interest: animals. Starting about age three, I drew them, studied books about them, kept them as pets, observed them in zoos and in the wild. Unable to make up my mind whether I wanted to be a wildlife artist or a biologist, I settled on a sort of compromise between the two. As a child I loved the magic worlds of Dr. Doolittle and the Oz Kingdom, where no hard line separated human beings from the rest of the animal world. I collected all the *National Geographic* magazines and *Nature* magazines—then illustrated largely with paintings of wildlife rather than photographs—I could lay my hands on. But my enthusiasm was not without criticism. If the living animals did not turn out to look as they had been depicted in the illustrations, I felt as if I had been misled somehow, and resolved that any paintings I did would attempt to show animals and birds as accurately as possible. (I was as keen on imaginary animals as real ones, and although I separated the world of fantasy from the world of science, the scientific attitude crept into the fantasy world to produce a kind of science-fiction result.) Above all, I was enchanted with Walt Disney's animated films, and the possibilities the movie animation offered the artist to create his own moving, speaking world. Second choice lay in the field of comic strips, much more accessible to individual effort. Another type of 'world' existed in the museum diorama, with its painted background and mounted animals. As a child I spent many hours trying to construct miniature dioramas; my room was always a combination of a museum collection and cartoon factory.

"With adolescence the world of human beings began increasingly to invade my interest, but, like Mowgli, it was as if I had been raised in the forest and had never quite learned the language of humanity. The behavior of animals seemed to make much more 'sense' to me than the behavior of my own species. When I met the girl I was to marry, it was her background in biology and her own love of animal life that enabled us to communicate, and certainly it was her training in the sciences that, coupled with my own mania for 'accuracy,' tended to steer my work, at the beginning of my professional career, into scientific and natural history illustration with an educational intent. Not until *Buffalo Land* and *Deneki* was I allowed the freedom to present the material in my own way, however.

"Just after the completion of *Buffalo Land,* events in my own life brought the 'conversion to humanity' to completion. Suddenly I could identify wholly with my fellow man, and animals—which had always seemed more individual to me, somehow, than the masses of people—were just as suddenly seen in a different light; a host of hoofed, furred, and feathered creatures whose minds could never be truly known to me, and in fact whose world had much less to offer than my 'own.' *Deneki* was produced just at this time, and is in a sense a fond look back at a world I had once pretended to inhabit, but now seen from the outside, from the viewpoint of Man trying to look objectively at another species and its environment. Most 'animal stories,' enchanting as they may be, are myths about mankind given animal form, and I suppose *Deneki* was an attempt to create a primarily visual book (with traces of museum-exhibit, animation, and comic-strip-sequence style) that would tell the 'true' story about a young moose's growing-up: that there is no 'moral lesson' to be learned by us from any other species, for their individual struggles are not ours. 'Deneki' is just a moose, no more (except, possibly, in a very general metaphorical sense), but his world and his means of coping with his environment are of interest in themselves, valuable to us because in our attempts to understand them, we develop ways of understanding ourselves."

"It may be of interest that *Deneki* was conceived and illustrated on the spot where the story takes place, so that although the books is fiction based on many facts, it is in a sense a portrait of an area done from life, for the land, the weather, the vegetation, and the animals surrounded my studio, daily shaping the nature of the book during the three years it was in progress.

"For the past ten years most of my work—although still dealing primarily with wildlife—has been devoted to individual paintings, drawings, or sculpture, or to a series of limited-edition prints, almost all dealing with Alaskan subjects."

BIOGRAPHICAL/CRITICAL SOURCES: Alaska Journal, summer, 1973.

*   *   *

BERTHOLD, Margot 1922-

PERSONAL: Born November 8, 1922, in Markersdorf, Germany; daughter of Curt and Lina (Klaus) Berthold. *Education:* Attended University of Berlin, 1946-49; University of Munich, Dr.phil., 1951. *Home:* Reitmorstrasse 26, 8 Munich 22, West Germany.

CAREER: Writer, 1952—. Instructor in film, University of Munich, 1968-73.

WRITINGS: Weltgeschichte des Theaters, Kroener-Verlag, 1968, translation by Edith Simmons published as *A History of World Theater,* Ungar, 1972.

BERTRAM, Noel
See FANTHORPE, R(obert) Lionel

* * *

BERTRAND, Michel 1944-
(Jean Angebert, Jean-Michel Angebert, Michel Angebert)

PERSONAL: Born January 16, 1944, in Carcassonne, France; son of Paul (a secondary school principal) and Suzanne (a teacher; maiden name, Isnard) Bertrand; married. *Education:* University of Aix-en-Provence, licence (law), 1969, licence (history), 1971. *Religion:* Roman Catholic. *Home:* 6 rue Alasseur, 75015 Paris, France. *Office:* Editions Albin Michel, 22 rue Huyghens, 75014 Paris, France.

CAREER: French National Radio and Television, Paris, France, assistant for language commission, 1971-73; Council of Europe, Strasbourg, France, assistant to deputy director of environment and local powers, 1973-74; Editions Albin Michel (publisher), Paris, writer and director of collection, 1975—. *Military service:* French Navy, 1966-69; became petty officer. *Member:* Societe des Gens de Lettres de France, Syndicat des Ecrivains (committee chairman), Association des Ecrivains de Langue Francaise (ADELF).

WRITINGS: Histoire secrete de la Provence (title means "Secret History of Provence"), A. Michel, 1978.

With Jean Angelini, under pseudonym Jean-Michel Angebert: *Hitler et la tradition cathare,* Laffont, 1971, translation (under pseudonyms Jean Angebert and Michel Angebert) published as *The Occult and the Third Reich,* Macmillan, 1974, translation by Lewis A. M. Sumberg published as *The Occult and the Third Reich: The Mystical Origins of Nazism and the Search for the Holy Grail,* McGraw, 1975; *Les Mystiques du soleil* (title means "The Mysteries of the Sun"), Laffont, 1971; *Le Livre de la tradition* (title means "The Book of Tradition"), Laffont, 1972; *Les Cites magiques* (title means "Magical Cities"), A. Michel, 1974.

Also author of conference proceedings with Jean Angelini, under pseudonym Jean Angebert. Contributor to *Folklore, Atlantis, Gazette des Uniformes,* and other French periodicals. Editor-in-chief of *De Bello* (military history journal), 1975-76.

WORK IN PROGRESS: Translations of his works into Spanish, Portuguese, Italian, and English.

SIDELIGHTS: Bertrand writes: "Departing from esoterism, I have progressively discovered the sense of holiness and tradition as the unique source of spirituality (which is the 'true religion' of Saint Augustine which goes back to Adam). This has permitted me to find faith once again in God and in his son, Jesus Christ, the most important event of my life (1976). Now I hope to write better books which will help men to live and not fear death.

"My return to faith made me understand something I hadn't seen before: the transcendent unity of religions in the divine plan which we can perceive intuitively but which does not permit us to put ourselves in the place of God. This conviction implies a union 'at the summit' and not at the foundation (which excludes syncretism); that is to say we must remain faithful to the faith we have received. I would say in closing that it is better to be converted inwardly (in depth) than to be converted horizontally (to change religions): it is the heart that must be changed, not the mind. Don't the Hindus themselves ask Westerners who come to find them, 'Isn't Christ sufficient for you?'

"If I write other books about esoterism, history of religions, or metaphysics perhaps, it will be to share my experience and to avoid disagreements with those who search for truth in a world where it is difficult to perceive. Personal experience should serve to clarify permanent, impersonal values which can be useful to everyone. The books I'd like to write would be placed in this perspective of 'Servant of True Spirituality.'"

Bertrand has participated in radio broadcasts in France, Switzerland, Belgium, and Canada, and in numerous conferences in France.

* * *

BETTELHEIM, Charles 1913-

PERSONAL: Born November 20, 1913, in Paris, France; son of Henri and Lucienne (Jacquemin) Bettelheim; married Lucette Beauvallet, February 18, 1937; children: Henri, Elisabeth, Daniel (deceased), Sophie. *Education:* University of Paris, Licence et Diplome d'Etudes Supérieures de Philosophie, 1937; Doctorat d'Etat, 1939. *Office:* Ecole des Hautes Etudes en Sciences Sociales, 54 Blvd. Raspail, 75006 Paris, France.

CAREER: University of Caen, Caen, France, deputy lecturer, 1939-40; Centre des Etudes Sociales et Internationales du Ministere du Travail, Paris, France, director, 1944-48; Ecole des Hautes Etudes en Science Sociales, Paris, France, director of studies, 1948—; Francois Maspero Editeur, Paris, director of edition collection, 1964—. Professor, Ecole Nationale d'Administration, 1948-52, Institut d'-Etudes du Developpement Economique et Social, 1958-64. *Awards, honors:* Laureat de l'Academie Francaise, 1963.

WRITINGS: La Planification sovietique (title means "Soviet Planning"), M. Riviere, 1939, 3rd edition, 1945; *Problemes theoriques et pratiques de la planification,* Presses Universitaires de France, 1946, 3rd edition, Maspero, 1966, translation by Brian Pearce published as *Studies in the Theory of Planning,* Asia Publishing House, 1959; *L'-Economie allemande sous le nazisme: Un Aspect de la decadence du capitalisme* (title means "The German Nazi Economy: An Aspect of Capitalism's Decay"), M. Riviere, 1946; *Bilan de l'economie francaise, 1919-1946* (title means "Balance Sheet of France's Economy 1919-1946"), Presses Universitaires de France, 1947; *Esquisse d'un tableau economique de l'Europe* (title means "Outline of an Economic Tableau of Europe"), Dornat, 1948; *Le Probleme de l'-emploi et du chomage dans les theories economiques* (title means "The Employment and Unemployment Problem in Economic Theories"), Centre de Documentation Universitaire, 1949; (with Suzanne Frere) *Auxerre en 1950: Une Ville francaise moyenne; Etude de structure social et urbaine* (title means "Auxerre in 1950, a Medium-sized Town in France: A Study in Social and Urban Structure"), A. Colin, 1950; *Les Theories contemporaines de l'emploi* (title means "Contemporary Employment Theories"), Centre de Documentation Universitaire, 1951; *Problemes monetaires contemporains* (title means "Contemporary Monetary Problems"), A. Colin, 1951.

Some Basic Planning Problems, Asia Publishing House, 1961; *L'Inde independante,* A. Colin, 1962, translation by W.A. Caswell published as *India Independent,* MacGibbon & Kee, 1968, Monthly Review Press, 1969; *Planification et croissance acceleree: Recueil d'articles et d'etudes inedites* (title means "Planning and Accelerated Growth"), Maspero, 1964, 2nd edition, 1965; (with Jacques Charriere and Helene Marchisio) *La Construction du socialisme en Chine* (title means "Social Construction in China"), Maspero, 1965; *La Transition vers l'economie socialiste,* Maspero, 1968, translation by Brian Pearce published as *The Transition to Socialist Economy,* Humanities, 1975; (with Paul Sweezy) *Lettres sur quelques problemes actuels du socialisme,* Maspero, 1970, revised edition, 1972, translation published as *On the Transition to Socialism,* 2nd enlarged edition, Monthly Review Press, 1972; *Calcul economique et formes de propriete,* translation by John Taylor published as *Economic Calculation and Forms of Property,* Monthly Review Press, 1975; *Revolution culturelle et organisation industrielle en Chine,* Maspero, 1973, translation by Alfred Ehrenfeld published as *Cultural Revolution and Industrial Organization in China: Changes in Management and the Division of Labor,* Monthly Review Press, 1974; *Les Luttes de classes en URSS* (title means "Class Struggles in the USSR"), Maspero/Seuil, Volume I: *1917-1923,* 1974, Volume II: *1924-1929,* 1977.

WORK IN PROGRESS: Volume III of *Les Luttes de classes en URSS.*

* * *

BEUTTLER, Edward Ivan Oakley
(Ivan Butler)

PERSONAL: Born in Heswell, Cheshire, England; married; children: one son. *Education:* Attended Central School of Speech Training and Dramatic Art. *Home:* Northwood, Middlesex, England.

CAREER: Writer. Worked in professional theatre as actor and producer. Member of lecture panel, British Film Institute. Director of seminars on the cinema.

WRITINGS—All under pseudonym Ivan Butler: *Crime Out of Mind,* Tooks Court, 1950; *Columbine in Camberwell,* Deane, 1953; *The Wise Children,* Stacey Publications, 1954; (with Falkland L. Cary) *The Paper Chain,* French, 1953; *Tranquil House,* Stacey Publications, 1954; (with Cary) *Danger Inside,* Samuel French, 1960; *Producing Pantomime and Revue,* W. & G. Foyle, 1962; *The Horror Film,* A. S. Barnes, 1967; *Religion in the Cinema,* A. S. Barnes, 1969; *Horror in the Cinema,* 2nd revised edition, A. S. Barnes, 1970; *The Cinema of Roman Polanski,* A. S. Barnes, 1970; *The Making of Feature Films: A Guide,* Penguin, 1971; *"To Encourage the Art of the Film": The Story of the British Film Institute,* R. Hale, 1971; *Choosing a Play for Your Amateur Group,* Taplinger, 1972; (compiler) *The 100 Best Full-length Plays for Amateurs,* Pelham, 1972; *Cinema in Britain: An Illustrated Survey,* A. S. Barnes, 1973; *Murderer's England,* R. Hale, 1973; *Murderer's London,* R. Hale, 1973; *The War Film,* A. S. Barnes, 1974; (editor) Carl Allensworth, Dorothy Allensworth, and Clayton Rawson, *The Complete Play Production Handbook,* R. Hale, 1976; *Trials of Brian Donald Hume,* David and Charles, 1976. Also author of radio and television scripts.*

* * *

BHAKTIVEDANTA, A. C.
See PRABHUPADA, Bhaktivedanta

* * *

BHAKTIVEDANTA SWAMI, A. C.
See PRABHUPADA, Bhaktivedanta

BIDDLE, Katherine Garrison Chapin   1890-1977
(Katherine G[arrison] Chapin)

September 4, 1890—December 30, 1977; American poet, playwright, and literary critic. The widow of former Attorney General Francis Biddle, she was best known for her books of poetry and a play, "Sojourner Truth," written under her maiden name. Several of her works have been set to music. Biddle died in Devon, Pa. Obituaries: *Washington Post,* December 31, 1977; *New York Times,* January 2, 1978; *AB Bookman's Weekly,* February 20, 1978. (See index for *CA* sketch)

* * *

BIENEK, Horst   1930-

PERSONAL: Born May 7, 1930, in Gleiwitz, Poland; son of Hermann and Valeska (Piontek) Bienek. *Education:* Attended Berliner Ensemble, 1951. *Religion:* Roman Catholic. *Home:* Isarweg 2, Muenchen-Ottobrunn, West Germany 8012.

CAREER: Editor at radio station in Frankfurt, West Germany, 1957-62; Deutscher Taschenbuch, Munich, West Germany, reader, 1962-72; director of documentary and feature films, 1966—, including "Ezra Pound, 80," 1966; "Jean Tinquely," 1968; "Marie Luise Kaschnitz," 1972; "The Cell," 1973. *Member:* German Academy for Language and Poetry, Bavarian Academy of Fine Arts. *Awards, honors:* Literature Prize of Bremen, 1968; Bundesfilmpreis in gold, for best young director, 1971, for "The Cell"; Hermann-Kesten-Preis, 1975.

WRITINGS: Traumbuch eines Gefangenen (title means "Dreambook of a Prisoner"), Hanser, 1957; *Nachstuecke* (title means "Nightpieces"), Hanser, 1959; *Werkstattgespraeche mit Schriftstellern* (title means "Writers at Work, Fifteen Interviews"), Hanser, 1962; *Die Zelle,* Hanser, 1968, translation by Ursula Mahlendorf published as *The Cell,* Unicorn (Santa Barbara, Calif.), 1972; *Selected Poems,* translated by Ruth Mead and Mathew Mead, Unicorn Press, 1969; *Vorgefundene Gedichte* (title means "Found Poems"), Hanser, 1969; *Bakunin, eine Invention* (title means "Bakunin, an Invention"), Hanser, 1970; (with Johannes Bobrowski) *Selected Poems,* translated by R. Mead and M. Mead, Penguin, 1971; *Solschenizyn und andere* (title means "Solzhenitsyn and Other Essays"), Hanser, 1972; *Die Zeit danach: Gedichte* (title means "The Time Thereafter"), Eremiten-Presse, 1974; *Die erste Polke* (title means "The First Polka"), Hanser, 1975; *Gleiwitzer Kindheit: Gedichte aus zwanzig Jahren* (title means "Childhood in Gleiwitz: Poems from Twenty Years"), Hanser, 1976; *Septemberlicht* (title means Septemberlight"), Hanser, 1977.

Editor: (With Friedrich Ege) *Finnische Lyrik aus hundert Jahren* (title means "Poems from Finland"), Merlin, 1973; *The Work of Ivan Bunin,* Piper, 1973.

WORK IN PROGRESS: A cycle of novels about the former province of Upper Silesia.

SIDELIGHTS: "I feel influenced by American literature," Bienek wrote, "especially Faulkner, Carson McCullers, Thomas Wolfe, and early Truman Capote. Also Borges and Ezra Pound. I made the last documentary film on Pound in 1966. My feature film 'The Cell' is dedicated to Amnesty International."

Bienek was arrested in 1951 in East-Berlin and sentenced to twenty-five years in a labor camp. He was released four years later by an amnesty issued after the death of Stalin.

BIOGRAPHICAL/CRITICAL SOURCES: Contemporary Literary Criticism, Volume 7, Gale, 1977.

* * *

BINDOFF, Stanley Thomas 1908-

PERSONAL: Born April 8, 1908; son of Thomas Henry and Mary Bindoff; married Marjorie Blatcher, 1936; children: one son, one daughter. *Education:* University of London, B.A. (honors), 1929, M.A. (with distinction), 1933. *Home:* 5 Carlton Rd., New Malden, Surrey, England.

CAREER: Secretary at Netherlands Information Bureau, 1933-34; University of London, University College, London, England, 1935-45, began as assistant lecturer, became lecturer in history; University of London, reader in modern history at University College, 1945-51, professor of history at Queen Mary College, 1951—, fellow of University College, 1958—. Visiting professor at Columbia University, 1960, Claremont Graduate School, 1966, Wellesley College and Harvard University, 1968; Cornell Lecturer at Swarthmore College, 1973. *Military service:* British Royal Navy, Intelligence Division, 1942-45; became admiral. Royal Historical Society (fellow; vice-president, 1967), Royal Dutch Society of Literature, Utrecht Historical Society, Reform Club. *Awards, honors:* Alexander Medal from Royal Historical Society, 1935.

WRITINGS: (Editor with E. F. Malcolm Smith and C. K. Webster) *British Diplomatic Representatives, 1789-1852,* Royal Historical Society, 1934; *The Scheldt Question to 1839,* Allen & Unwin, 1945; *Ket's Rebellion, 1549,* G. Philip, 1949, Historical Association, 1968; *Tudor England,* Penguin, 1959; (editor with J. Hurstfield and C. H. Williams) *Elizabethan Government and Society: Essays Presented to Sir John Neale,* Athlone Press (of University of London), 1961; (editor with James T. Boulton) *Research in Progress in English and Historical Studies in the Universities of the British Isles,* St. Martin's, 1971; *The Fame of Sir Thomas Gresham,* Humanities, 1973. Contributor of articles and reviews to proceedings of the British Academy, transactions of the Royal Historical Society, and history journals.

AVOCATIONAL INTERESTS: Walking and climbing, watching games.*

* * *

BINGER, Carl A(lfred) L(anning) 1889-1976

PERSONAL: Born August 26, 1889, in Long Branch, N.J.; son of Gustav and Frances (Newgass) Binger; married Clarinda Garrison, June 3, 1926; children: David G., Beatrice, Katherine G. *Education:* Harvard University, A.B., 1910, M.D. (cum laude), 1914. *Home:* 21 Lowell St., Cambridge, Mass. 02138.

CAREER: Harvard University, Cambridge, Mass., lecturer in history of science, 1914; after World War I, was associated with Rockefeller Institute Hospital in New York City until 1928; studied psychiatry with Carl Jung in Zurich, Switzerland, 1929; practiced psychiatry in New York City, 1929-33; New York Hospital, New York City, assistant attending physician, 1933-47, associate attending psychiatrist, 1947-54. Diplomate of American Board of Internal Medicine and American Board of Neurology and Psychiatry. Cornell University Medical College, assistant professor, 1933-47, associate professor of clinical psychiatry, 1947-54; lecturer in psychiatry at Harvard Medical School, 1954-56; visiting professor of psychiatry at Cincinnati Medical College, 1956-68. Associated with rehabilitation clinic of Payne Whitney Clin-

ic, 1943-46; visiting psychiatrist at Massachusetts General Hospital, 1954-58, physician, 1958-76; consulting psychiatrist at Radcliffe College medical department, 1954-76; consultant to Harvard University Health Services, 1968-76. Member of board of directors, National Committee for Mental Hygiene; member of International Committee on Mental Hygiene of World Health Organization; member of International Congress on Mental Health and Mental Health Film Board (president, 1952). *Military service:* Served during World War I as first lieutenant in the Medical Corps; received Purple Heart and Order of St. George (Greece).

MEMBER: American Medical Association, American Academy of Arts and Sciences, American Psychiatric Association, American Psychoanalytic Association, Association for Psychoanalytic Medicine (president, 1943-44), American Psychosomatic Society (founding member; president, 1963-69), Group Advancement for Psychiatry, New York Academy of Medicine, Massachusetts Psychoanalytic Association, Massachusetts Medical Society for Clinical Investigation, Harvey Society, American Legion, Harvard Club, Century Association, Sakonnet Yacht Club, Alpha Omega. *Awards, honors:* Norton Award, 1945, for *The Doctor's Job.*

WRITINGS: The Doctor's Job, Norton, 1945; (with N. W. Ackerman, A. E. Cohn, H. A. Schroeder, and J. M. Steele) *Personality in Arterial Hypertension,* American Society for Research in Psychosomatic Problems, 1945; *More About Psychiatry,* University of Chicago Press, 1949; *Post Meridian* (poetry), privately printed, 1959; *Revolutionary Doctor: Benjamin Rush, 1746-1813,* Norton, 1966; *The Two Faces of Medicine* (essays), Norton, 1967; *Thomas Jefferson: A Well-Tempered Mind,* Norton, 1970. *Psychosomatic Medicine,* revision editor, 1945-47, editor-in-chief, 1947-62, member of editorial board, 1962-76.*

(Died March 22, 1976, in Cambridge, Mass.)

* * *

BINNS, Archie (Fred) 1899-

PERSONAL: Born July 30, 1899, in Port Ludlow, Wash.; son of Frank and Atlanta Sarah (McQuah) Binns; married Mollie Windish, 1923; children: Jacqueline, Georgia. *Education:* Stanford University, B.A., 1922. *Residence:* Menlo Park, Calif.

CAREER: Novelist and historian. Served on a lightship crew near Cape Flattery, Wash., 1917; Washington correspondent for Scripps-Howard newspapers, 1923; employed as editor of the Leonard Scott Publication Company during 1920's; creative writing instructor, University of Washington, Seattle, 1950—. *Military service:* U.S. Army, 1918-23; became second lieutenant.

WRITINGS—All fiction, except as noted: (With Felix Riesenberg) *The Maiden Voyage,* Day, 1931; *Lightship* (also see below), Reynal & Hitchcock, 1934; *Backwater Voyage* (excerpts of *Lightship),* Reynal & Hitchcock, 1936; *The Laurels Are Cut Down,* Reynal & Hitchcock, 1937, reprinted, Literary Guild of America, 1967; *The Land Is Bright,* Scribner, 1939; *Mighty Mountain,* Scribner, 1940, reprinted, Binfords, 1975; *Northwest Gateway: The Story of the Port of Seattle* (nonfiction), Doubleday, Doran, 1941; *The Roaring Land* (nonfiction), R. M. McBride, 1942; *The Timber Beast,* Scribner, 1944; *You Rolling River,* Scribner, 1947, reprinted, Ballantine, 1971.

The Radio Imp (illustrated by Rafaello Busoni), J. C. Winston, 1950; *Secret of the Sleeping River* (illustrated by Busoni), J. C. Winston, 1952; *Sea in the Forest* (nonfiction), Doubleday, 1953; *Sea Pup* (illustrated by Robert Candy), Duell, Sloan, 1954, published as *Here, Buster*, Scholastic Book Services, 1972; (with Olive Kooken) *Mrs. Fiske and the American Theatre* (nonfiction), Crown, 1955; *The Enchanted Islands* (illustrated by Neil Meitzler), Duell, Sloan, 1956; *The Headwaters: A Novel*, Duell, Sloan, 1957; *Sea Pup Again*, Duell, Sloan, 1965; *Peter Skene Ogden: Fur Trader* (nonfiction), Binfords, 1967.*

*   *   *

BIRN, Randi (Marie) 1935-

PERSONAL: Born February 25, 1935, in Tromsoe, Norway; came to the United States in 1960, naturalized citizen, 1971; and daughter of Didrik (a sea captain) and Solveig (Brocks) Ingebrigtsen; married Raymond Birn (a professor), July 18, 1960; children: Eric, Laila. *Education:* University of Oslo, cand.philol., 1960; University of Illinois, Ph.D., 1965. *Home:* 2140 Elk Ave., Eugene, Ore. 97403. *Office:* Department of Romance Languages, University of Oregon, Eugene, Ore. 97403.

CAREER: University of Oregon, Eugene, assistant professor, 1965-70, associate professor, 1970-76, professor of French, 1976—. *Member:* Modern Language Association of America, American Association of Teachers of French, Society for the Advancement of Scandinavian Studies. *Awards, honors:* Grants from American Philosophical Society, 1966, 1977.

WRITINGS: Johan Borgen, Twayne, 1974; *Johan Borgen, en litteraer biografi* (title means "Johan Borgen, A Literary Biography"), Gyldendal, 1977. Contributor to literary journals.

WORK IN PROGRESS: Editing *Orion Blinded*, essays on Claude Simon, with Karen Gould.

SIDELIGHTS: Randi Birn writes: "I am a Norwegian by birth, and I am consequently interested in combining research in contemporary French and Norwegian literature. I lived in Norway until I was twenty-five years old, and I have spent several years in France and Belgium."

*   *   *

BIRT, David 1936-

PERSONAL: Born January 15, 1936, in London, England; married; children: one son. *Education:* Cambridge University, B.A. (honors), 1960. *Home:* Bramble Hill, Shelsley Beauchamp, Stanford Bridge, near Worcestershire, England.

CAREER: Abberley Hall School, North Worcestershire, England, head of history department, 1960-71; Repton School, Derbyshire, England, member of English and history departments, 1971-75; Abberley Hall School, head of history department, 1975—. Gives lectures on "simulations and mixed-ability teaching to various teachers' groups and conferences."

WRITINGS—All juvenile: (With Jon Nichol) *Games and Simulations in History*, Longman, 1975; (with Peter Tinniswood) *Bank Loan: A Simulation*, Longman, 1975.

"History Games" series; all with Nichol, all published by Longman, all 1973: *The Norman Conquest; The Development of the Medieval Town; Trade and Discovery; Frontier; Ironmaster; Village Enclosure.*

"Middle Ages" series (with teacher's unit); all with Nichol; all published by Longman, all 1974: *The Norman Conquest;*

The Medieval Village; Knights and Tournaments; Stephen and Matilda; The Murder of Becket; The First and Third Crusades; King John; The Castle; The Monestary; Edward I; The Black Prince; The Black Death; The Peasants' Revolt; Battle of Agincourt; Joan of Arc; Marco Polo; Ships and Voyages; The Medieval Town; The Wars of the Roses; Richard III.

"The Tudors" series (with teacher's unit); all published by Longman, all 1975: *The Great Cardinal; King and Pope; The Oxford Martyrs; Drake's World Voyage; Elizabeth and Her Court; Mary, Queen of Scots; The Tudor Navy; Rogues and Vagabonds; The Elizabethan Theatre; Tudor London; The Field of Cloth of Gold; The Pilgrimage of Grace; The Nine Days' Queen; Raiding and Trading; To Entertain a Queen; The Babington Plot; Drake and the Spanish Armada; The London Underworld; The Globe Playhouse; Plots and Plays.*

"Roman Britain" series (with teacher's unit); all published by Longman, all 1976: *Invasion; The Roman Conquest of Britain; A Roman Soldier in Britain; Hadrian's Wall; Roads; Travel and Trade; The Roman Villa; The Roman Town; Religion in Roman Britain; The Legions of Leave; Everyday Life in Roman Britain; Britain Before the Romans; Attacking the Wall; Roman Mosaics; Boudicca's Revolt; Investigating the Druids; Roman Ships; Gladiators; Investigating King Arthur; Pottery in Roman Britain; Siege Machines.*

"The Stuarts" series (with teacher's unit); all published by Longman, all 1976: *The Guy Fawkes File; The Stuart Navy; The Eleven Years' Tyranny; The Civil War; Cromwell; Restoration England; Science and Superstition; Plague and Fire; The Invasion of 1688; Marlborough's Wars; Stuart Fashion; Buckingham's Expeditions; The Pilgrim Fathers; The Battle of Naseby; Execution of Charles I; Popish Plot; The Witch Finder; The Rebuilding of St. Paul's; Monmouth's Rebellion; The March to Blenheim.*

"The Saxons and Vikings" series (with teacher's unit); all published by Longman; all 1977: *The Saxon Invasions; The Coming of Christianity; The Celtic Realms; The Cross and the Crescent; Viking Ships; The Vikings in England; King Alfred; Viking Voyages; Viking Life; Life in Anglo-Saxon England; The Saxon Home; King Offa of Mercia; Celtic Knotwork; Trade and Traders; A Longship; The Battle of Maldon; Schools and Education; Sea Routes: A Game; The Iceland Settlement; Crime and Punishment.*

"Yesterday Today" series; all published by Edward Arnold: *Castles*, 1977; *Roads*, 1978.

"Communications" series; all published by Longman, all 1978: *Something to Sell: Propaganda; Something to Sell: Advertising; Signs and Symbols; You Out There; Language Lives!; Wordless Messages; Our Daily Spread; Watch Your Language; Freedom and Censorship; Bumf.*

"Involvement in History" series; all with Robin Acland; all published by Edward Arnold: *The Middle Ages I*, 1978; *Middle Ages II*, in press.

WORK IN PROGRESS: "Network English" series with Robin Acland and Tricia Acland, for Longman, publication expected 1979.

*   *   *

BISHOP, Claire (Huchet)

PERSONAL: Born in Brittany, France; later became an American citizen; married Frank Bishop (a pianist). *Education:* Attended the Sorbonne, Paris. *Religion:* Catholic. *Residence:* New York, N.Y.

CAREER: Author and poet. Instrumental in opening "L'-Heure Joyeuse," the first children's library in France, 1924; worked on the staff of the *Nouvelle Revue Francaise;* joined the staff of the New York Public Library upon her arrival in the United States; served for a times as children's book editor for the *Commonweal;* has traveled America as a lecturer and storyteller; lecturer and writer for various social movements in France. *Awards, honors:* New York Herald Tribune Spring Book Festival prize, 1947, for *Pancakes-Paris;* Well-Met Children's Book Award, 1952, for *Twenty and Ten.*

WRITINGS—Fiction: *The Five Chinese Brothers* (illustrated by Kurt Wiese), Coward, 1938, reprinted, Scholastic Book Services, 1965; *The Kings' Day* (illustrated by Doris Spiegal), Coward, 1940; *The Ferryman* (illustrated by K. Wiese), Coward, 1941, reprinted, Viking, 1974; *The Man Who Lost His Head* (illustrated by Robert McCloskey), Viking, 1942; *Augustus* (illustrated by Grace Paull), Viking, 1945; *Pancakes-Paris* (illustrated by Georges Schreiber), Viking, 1947; *Blue Spring Farm,* Viking, 1948; *Christopher the Giant* (illustrated by Berkeley Williams, Jr.), Houghton, 1950; *Bernard and His Dogs* (illustrated by Maurice Brevannes), Houghton, 1952; (with Janet Joly) *Twenty and Ten* (illustrated by William Pene du Bois), Viking, 1952; *All Alone* (illustrated by Feodor Rojankovsky), Viking, 1953; *The Big Loop* (illustrated by Charles Fontsere), Viking, 1955; (editor) *Happy Christmas: Tales for Boys and Girls* (illustrated by Ellen Raskin), Stephen Daye Press, 1956; *Toto's Triumph* (illustrated by Claude Ponsot), Viking, 1957; *A Present from Petros* (illustrated by Dimitris Davis), Viking, 1961; *Twenty-Two Bears* (illustrated by K. Wiese), Viking, 1964; *The Truffle Pig* (illustrated by K. Wiese), Coward, 1971; *Georgette* (illustrated by Ursula Landshoff), Coward, 1973.

Biographies: *Martin de Porres: Hero* (illustrated by Jean Charlot), Houghton, 1954; *Lafayette: French American Hero* (illustrated by M. Brevannes), Garrard, 1960; *Yeshu: Called Jesus* (illustrated by Donald Bolognese), Farrar, Straus, 1966; *Mozart: Music Magician* (illustrated by Paul Frame), Garrard, 1968; *Johann Sebastian Bach: Music Giant* (illustrated by Russell Hoover), Garrard, 1972.

Nonfiction: *French Children's Books for English Speaking Children,* Sheridan Square Press, 1938; *France Alive,* McMullen, 1947; *All Things Common,* Harper, 1950; *French Roundabout,* Dodd, 1960, revised edition, 1966; *Here Is France,* Farrar, Straus, 1969; *How Catholics Look at Jews,* Paulist Press, 1974. Also contributor of poetry to French avant-garde literary magazines and other periodicals.

SIDELIGHTS: Claire Huchet Bishop became a children's author as a direct result of being an oral storyteller. She told the story, "The Five Chinese Brothers" to a New York audience, was pleased with her English translation, and decided to write it down. Its publication began her writing career.

Commonweal called *Mozart: Music Magician* "a sensitive introduction to the bitter-sweet history of one of the very greatest composers who ever lived. Young readers will pay this gifted biographer the best compliment of all by consulting the 'listening choices' she appends." Another biography, *Yeshu, Called Jesus* was described by *Young Readers' Review* as "the day to day and year to year life as Jesus, a Jewish boy in a small village, might have lived it, an objective, logical, and carefully developed book which breathes the spirit of ecumenism."

AVOCATIONAL INTERESTS: Music, cooking, gardening, reading.

BIOGRAPHICAL/CRITICAL SOURCES: Commonweal, May 22, 1964, May 24, 1968; *Young Readers' Review,* December, 1966.*

*　　*　　*

BLACK, Creed C(arter) 1925-

PERSONAL: Born July 15, 1925, in Harlan, Ky.; son of Creed C. and Mary (Cole) Black; married Mary C. David, December 28, 1947 (divorced); children: Creed C., Jr., Steven, Douglas. *Education:* Northwestern University, B.S., 1949; University of Chicago, M.A., 1952. *Politics:* Independent. *Religion:* Protestant. *Home:* Society Hills Towers-North, Apt. 29B, 200 Locust St., Philadelphia, Pa. 19106. *Office: Philadelphia Inquirer,* 400 North Broad St., Philadelphia, Pa. 19101.

CAREER/WRITINGS: Paducah Sun-Democrat, Paducah, Ky., editor, 1942-43, 1946; *Chicago Sun-Times,* Chicago, Ill., copy editor, 1949; *Chicago Herald-American,* Chicago, copy editor, 1950; *Nashville Tennessean,* Nashville, Tenn., editorial writer, 1950-57, executive editor, 1957-59; *Savannah Morning News and Evening Press,* Savannah, Ga., executive editor and vice-president, 1959-60; *Wilmington Morning News and Evening Journal,* Wilmington, Del., executive editor and vice-president, 1960-64; *Chicago Daily News,* Chicago, executive editor, 1964-68; Department of Health, Education and Welfare, Washington, D.C., assistant secretary for legislation, 1969-70; *Philadelphia Inquirer,* Philadelphia, Pa., editor and vice-president, 1970—. *Military service:* U.S. Army, 1943-45; received Bronze Star. *Member:* American Society of Newspaper Editors (former secretary and member of board), National Conference of Editorial Writers (president, 1962), Philadelphia Foreign Relations Committee, Philadelphia Racquet Club, Philadelphia Country Club, Sigma Delta Chi, Kappa Tau Alpha. *Awards, honors:* Pennsylvania Society of Newspaper Editors first prize for editorial writing, 1970; Northwestern University Alumni Medal, 1973.

SIDELIGHTS: Black was a member of the American Society of Newspaper Editors' delegation to Russia in 1963 and the People's Republic of China in 1975.

*　　*　　*

BLACK, William Joseph 1934(?)-1977

1934(?)—December 17, 1977; American architect, educator, and author. Black was an expert on the social dynamics and architecture of Harlem. He was the author of several articles on the subject and of a book, *Visions of Harlem: Past, Present, and Future.* Black died in Silver Spring, Md. Obituaries: *New York Times,* December 21, 1977; *Washington Post,* December 23, 1977.

*　　*　　*

BLACKBURN, Thomas (Eliel Fenwick) 1916-

PERSONAL: Born February 10, 1916, in Cumberland, England; married wife Margaret (a school teacher); children: Julia. *Education:* Earned B.A. and M.A. from University of Durham. *Home:* 4 Luttrell Ave., London S.W.5, England. *Agent:* David Higham Associates Ltd., 76 Dean St., London W.1, England.

CAREER: Teacher in elementary schools. Writer. *Member:* Royal Society of Literature (fellow). *Awards, honors:* Gregory Fellow of Poetry at University of Leeds.

WRITINGS: The Outer Darkness (poems), Hand and Flower Press, 1951; *The Holy Stone* (poems), Hand and Flower Press, 1954; (editor with Philip Arthur Wayne) *The Middle School Book of Verse,* Harrap, 1955; *In the Fire* (poems), Putnam, 1956; *The Next Word* (poems), Putnam, 1958.

(Editor) *Forty-Five to Sixty: An Anthology of English Poetry, 1945-60,* Putnam, 1960; *A Smell of Burning* (poems), Putnam, 1961, Morrow, 1962; *The Price of an Eye* (poems), Morrow, 1961; *The Judas Tree: A Musical Drama of Judas Iscariot* (libretto; music by Peter Dickinson), Novello, 1963; *A Breathing Space* (poems), Dufour, 1964; (editor) *Presenting Poetry: A Handbook for English Teachers,* Methuen, 1966; (editor) *Gift of Tongues: A Selection from the Work of Fourteen Twentieth-Century Poets,* Thomas Nelson, 1967; *Robert Browning: A Study of His Poetry,* Eyre & Spottiswoode, 1967, Rowman & Littlefield, 1974; *A Clip of Steel: A Picaresque Autobiography,* MacGibbon & Kee, 1969; *Thomas Blackburn and John Heath-Stubbs* (poems), Longmans, 1969.

The Feast of the Wolf (novel), MacGibbon & Kee, 1971; *The Fourth Man* (poems), MacGibbon & Kee, 1971; *Selected Poems of Thomas Blackburn,* Hutchinson, 1975; *The Devil's Kitchen,* Chatto & Windus, 1975.

WORK IN PROGRESS: A second autobiography; *Inroads on Dying.*

AVOCATIONAL INTERESTS: Mountaineering.

*   *   *

BLACKIE, John (Ernest Haldane)   1904-

PERSONAL: Born June 6, 1904, in Limpsfield, England; son of Ernest Morell (a bishop) and Caroline (Stewart) Blackie; married Kathleen Mary Creswell, September 4, 1933 (died January, 1941); married Pamela Althea Vernon Margetson (a writer), May 22, 1942; children: Carolyn Blackie De Grey, David, Sebastian, Catherine Blackie Shepherd. *Education:* Magdalene College, Cambridge, M.A., 1926. *Politics:* "No political affiliations—outlook Tory Radical." *Religion:* Anglican. *Home:* The Bell House, Alconbury, Huntingdon, Cambridgeshire PE17 SDT, England.

CAREER: Assistant master of English and French at a school in Lawrenceville, N.J., 1926-27, and in Berkshire, England, 1928-33; Department of Education, Her Majesty's inspector of schools, 1933-36, district inspector in Manchester, England, 1936-47, divisional inspector in eastern division, 1947-51, chief inspector of further education, 1951-58, chief inspector of primary education, 1958-66; Cambridge University, Homerton College, Cambridge, England, part-time lecturer, 1966-70. Secretary of State's assessor on Central Advisory Council, 1963-66; senior counsellor, Open University, New York City, 1970-74; Consultant to Ford Foundation, 1971; trustee of National Extension College, 1972—. *Military service:* British Home Guard, 1940-44. *Member:* Royal Entomological Society (fellow). *Awards, honors:* Coronation Medal, 1952; Companion of the Bath, 1959.

WRITINGS: (With Robert Newton) *The Passing of the Queen,* Heffers (Cambridge), 1924; *The A B C of Art,* Vanguard, 1927; *Thought and Feeling in English Verse,* Heinemann, 1930; (editor) A. C. Swinburne, *Atlanta in Calydon,* Macmillan, 1930, 2nd edition, 1940; *Good Enough for the Children?,* Faber & Faber, 1963; *Inside the Primary School,* H.M.S.O., 1967, 2nd edition, 1968, Schocken, 1971; *English Teaching for Non-Specialists,* Faber & Faber, 1969; *Inspecting and the Inspectorate,* Routledge & Kegan Paul, 1970; (editor with Holly Brearley and others) *English Primary Schools Today,* Citation Press, 1971; *Changing the Primary School,* Macmillan, 1974, published as *Transforming the Primary School,* Schocken, 1975; *Bradfield, 1850-1975,* Bradfield College, 1976. Editor of "What Do They Do?" series, Macmillan. Contributor of articles to *Entomologist, The Stewarts,* and various official publications.

WORK IN PROGRESS: An autobiography; *The English Gentleman Observed.*

SIDELIGHTS: Blackie writes that he enjoys a happy home and family life with his wife in their seventeenth century country house. He balances his academic interests in history, English, and French with his social concern, which he expresses through his work with the handicapped and elderly in his community. He and his wife serve as volunteer librarians in a local hospital and are non-resident members of a Christian community. Blackie has traveled throughout western and eastern Europe, and to Egypt, Ceylon, Australia, New Zealand, Fiji, Central and South America, and the United States.

*   *   *

BLADES, Brian Brewer   1906-1977

July 4, 1906—September 28, 1977; American thoracic surgeon, educator, author of textbooks in his field, and editor of professional journals. He served as chairperson of the surgery department at George Washington University from 1946 to 1970. Blades died in Washington, D.C. Obituaries: *New York Times,* September 30, 1977; *Washington Post,* September 30, 1977.

*   *   *

BLAIR, John M(alcolm)   1914-1976

PERSONAL: Born in 1914, in Aurora, Ill.; married Saidee Finney. *Education:* Tulane University, B.A., 1936; American University, Ph.D., 1941. *Residence:* St. Petersburg, Fla. *Office:* Department of Economics, University of South Florida, Tampa, Fla. 33620.

CAREER: Bureau of Labor Statistics, Washington, D.C., economist for Temporary National Economic Committee, 1938-44; Department of Commerce, Washington, D.C., chief of the Office of Regional Economics, beginning 1945; Federal Trade Commission, Washington, D.C., assistant chief economist, until 1957; chief economist of the Subcommittee on Antitrust and Monopoly of the U.S. Senate Judiciary Committee, 1957-70; University of South Florida, Tampa, professor of economics, until 1976.

WRITINGS: Seeds of Destruction: A Study in the Functional Weaknesses of Capitalism, Covici, 1938; (contributor) Helmut Arndt, editor, *Recht, Macht and Wirtschaft* (title means "Justice, Power, and the Domestic Economy"), Duncker & Humblot, 1968; (with Harrison F. Houghton and Matthew Rose) *Economic Concentration and World War II,* Johnson Reprint, 1972; *Economic Concentration: Structure, Behavior, and Public Policy,* Harcourt, 1972; *The Control of Oil,* Pantheon, 1977.

OBITUARIES: New York Times, December 23, 1976; *Washington Post,* December 23, 1976.*

(Died December 21, 1976, in St. Petersburg, Fla.)

BLATCHFORD, Christie 1951-

PERSONAL: Born May 20, 1951, in Noranda, Quebec, Canada; daughter of Ross Thomas (a manager) and Kathleen (Lytle) Blatchford. *Education:* Ryerson Polytechnical Institute, diploma, 1973. *Home:* 500 Duplex Ave., Apt. 2006, Toronto, Ontario, Canada. *Office: Globe and Mail,* 444 Front St. W., Toronto, Ontario, Canada.

CAREER/WRITINGS: Globe and Mail, Toronto, sports reporter, 1973-74, general reporter, 1974-75, sports columnist, 1975—. Notable assignments include coverage of Prince Charles' royal tour, 1975, and a trip up the Yukon River, by raft, with thirty members of the Canadian Army. Contributor to *Weekend* and Canadian Broadcasting Co. (CBC) Radio. *Member:* Football Reporters of Canada, National Hockey League Writers, Toronto Press Club. *Awards, honors:* Joe Perlove Award, 1973.

* * *

BLOCH, Ernst 1885-1977

July 8, 1885—1977; German philosopher, educator, and prolific writer of philosophy and theology books. *Das Prinzip Hoffnung* ("The Principle of Hope") is considered by many to be Bloch's master work and is said to have laid the groundwork for Juergen Moltmaan's "philosophy of hope." Bloch died in Stuttgart, West Germany. Obituaries: *Washington Post,* August 5, 1977; *Time,* August 15, 1977. (See index for *CA* sketch)

* * *

BLOOD, Charles Lewis 1929-

PERSONAL: Born December 24, 1929, in New Jersey; son of Lewis H. (a chemical engineer) and Ethel (a teacher; maiden name, Lewis) Blood. *Education:* Columbia University, B.F.A., 1954; Art Students League of New York, certificate in advanced art, 1954; graduate study at University of Pittsburgh, 1955-56. *Office:* Hera Associates, 18 Village Lane, Middletown, N.J. 07748.

CAREER: Performer on New York City network radio, 1937-43; actor in New York city productions, 1948-58; performer on television series, including "Armstrong Circle Theatre" and "My True Story," during middle 1950's; Young & Rubicam, New York City, creative supervisor, 1958-73; employed at Hera Associates, Middletown, N.J., 1972—; J. Walter Thompson, New York City, group head, 1974—. Instructor at Los Angeles Valley State College, 1970—. *Military service:* U.S. Air Force, 1950-54; served in Korea, became staff sergeant. *Awards, honors:* Received fifty-eight national and international advertising awards.

WRITINGS: The Goat in the Rug (juvenile), Parents' Magazine Press, 1976. Author of "More Letters from the Earth," a weekly column in *Middletown Courier.* Contributor to magazines.

WORK IN PROGRESS: A book on American Indian games and another on the Navajo coyote legend; a series of about fifty volumes and twenty-one films on American Indians; an educational entertainment television series for juveniles, tentatively titled "All About Everything"; a children's television special about flight.

SIDELIGHTS: Blood attributes his interest in American Indians to the fact that he is himself part Indian. He is currently focusing his work on a notorious ancestor, Colonel Thomas Blood, the only man ever to steal the British crown jewels from the Tower of London.

BLUMBERG, Harry 1903-

PERSONAL: Born August 27, 1903, in New York, N.Y.; son of Philip (a merchant) and Hannah (Sabsevitz) Blumberg; married Ann Kamber (a teacher), October 25, 1931; children: Judith Blumberg Redlich, Paul Noam. *Education:* New York University, B.S., 1924; Columbia University, M.A., 1925; Harvard University, Ph.D., 1929. *Home:* 18a Bet Hakerem St., Jerusalem, Israel.

CAREER: Principal of Hebrew school in Philadelphia, Pa., 1929-32, and Brooklyn, N.Y., 1933-36; instructor at Flatbush Yeshivah, Brooklyn, 1936-39, and James Monroe High School, Bronx, N.Y., 1939-56; Hunter College of the City University of New York, New York, N.Y., assistant professor, 1956-60, associate professor, 1960-64, professor of Hebrew, 1964-69, professor emeritus, 1969—, head of Hebrew Division, 1956-69. Visiting professor at Tel-Aviv University, 1969-74. Chairman of examining committee for Hebrew, College Entrance Examination Board, 1959-62.

MEMBER: National Association of Professors of Hebrew (president, 1967-68), American Oriental Society, Mediaeval Academy of America, Modern Language Association of America, American Council on the Teaching of Foreign Languages, Societe Internationale pour l'Etude de la Philosophic Medievale, American Association of University Professors, Histadruth Ivrith, American Friends of Hebrew University of Jerusalem, American Jewish Congress Bnai Zion. *Awards, honors:* American Council of Learned Societies traveling fellow in the humanities, 1932-33.

WRITINGS: (With Mordecai Lewittes) *Select Readings in Hebrew Literature,* Hebrew Publishing, 1942; (with Lewittes) *Modern Hebrew,* Hebrew Publishing, Volume I, 1946, revised edition, 1963, Volume II, 1952; (editor with Emily L. Shields) *Averroes Cordubensis Compendia Librorum Aristotelis qui Parva Naturalia Vocantur,* Mediaeval Academy of America, 1949; (editor) *Sefer ha-Hush ve-ha Muhash le Abu'l Walid ibn Rushd,* Mediaeval Academy of America, 1954, English translation with introduction and notes, Mediaeval Academy of America, 1961; *Modern Hebrew Grammar and Composition,* Hebrew Publishing, 1955; (editor and author of introduction and notes in Arabic) *Kitab al-Hiss w'al Mahsus le Abu'l Walid ibn Rushd,* Mediaeval Academy of America, 1973.

SIDELIGHTS: Harry Blumberg speaks Hebrew, Yiddish, French, Spanish, and German; he reads Arabic, Aramaic, Latin, and Greek. He has traveled in eastern Europe, Scandinavian countries, Greece, Turkey, Israel, and Egypt in search of manuscripts relating to his field.

* * *

BLUME, Friedrich 1893-1975

PERSONAL: Born January 5, 1893, in Schluchtern, Germany; son of Emil (a civil servant) and Clara (Sommerburg) Blume; married Gabriele Mohrig, 1922 (died November 7, 1949); married Christiane Stemmer, May 25, 1950; children: Eva Blume Herrmann, Ruth, Cornelia Blume Eichberg, Georg. *Education:* Attended University of Munich, 1911-14; University of Leipzig, Ph.D., 1921; Humboldt University of Berlin, habilitation, 1926. *Religion:* Evangelical Lutheran. *Home:* Feierabendgrund 21, D-6490 Schluchtern, Hessen, West Germany.

CAREER: Assistant to Hermann Abert, 1921-27; acting chairman of Institute of Musicology, 1927-29; University of Kiel, Kiel, Germany, assistant professor, 1933-38, professor of musicology, 1938-58, professor emeritus, 1958-75. President of German Society for Music Research, 1947-67. Chairman of "Das Erbe Deutscher Musik" (collection of German music), 1939-45, New Heinrich Schutz Society, 1942-45, Joint Commission for International Inventory of Musical Sources, 1952-73, and Commission of Music History, 1953-65; founder and chairman of Kassel archives, 1953-65, and Joseph Haydn Institute of Cologne, 1955-73. *Military service:* German Army, 1914-19. *Member:* International Society of Musicology (member of executive board, 1948-58; president, 1958-61), International Association of Music Libraries (founder, 1950), Daenischen Akademie der Wissenschaften, Schwedischen Akademie der Musik.

WRITINGS: Das monodische Prinzip in der protestantischen Kirchenmusik (title means "The Monodic Principle in Protestant Church Music"), Breitkopf & Haertel, 1925; *Studien zur Vorgeschichte der Orchestersuite im 15. und 16. Jahrhundert* (title means "Studies in the Prehistory of the Suite for Orchestra in the Fifteenth and Sixteenth Centuries"), Kistner & Siegel, 1925; *Die evangelische Kirchenmusik,* Akademische Verlagsgesellschaft Athenaion, 1931, 2nd revised and enlarged edition published as *Geschichte der evangelischen Kirchenmusik,* Barenreiter, 1965, translation by Ludwig Finscher and others published as *Protestant Church Music: A History,* Norton, 1974; *Das Rasseproblem in der Musik, entwurf zu einer Methodologie musikwissenschaftlicher rasseforschung* (title means "The Problem of Race in Music"), G. Kallmeyer, 1939; *Johann Sebastian Bach im Wandel der Geschichte,* Barenreiter, 1947, translation by Stanley Godman published as *Two Centuries of Bach: An Account of Changing Taste,* Oxford University Press, 1950; *Goethe und die Musik* (title means "Goethe and Music"), Barenreiter, 1948; *Renaissance and Baroque Music: A Comprehensive Survey* (essays), translated by M. D. Herter Norton, Norton, 1967; *Classic and Romantic Music: A Comprehensive Survey* (essays), translated by Norton, Norton, 1970.

Editor: *Gedenkschrift fuer Hermann Abert von seinen schulern* (title means "In Memoriam: Hermann Abert"), M. Niemeyer, 1928, 2nd edition, Schneider, 1974; (with Hermann Abert) *Gesammelte Schriften und Vortraege* (title means "Collected Writings and Lectures [of Hermann Abert]"), M. Niemeyer, 1929, 2nd edition, Schneider, 1968; (with Martin Ruhnke and Anna Amalie Abert) *Syntagma musicologicum: Gesammelte Reden und Schriften* (title means "Collected Lectures and Writings"), Barenreiter, Volume I, 1963, Volume II, 1973.

Editor of the collection "Das Chorwerk," Moeseler, 1929-75; editor of *Enzyklopaedie Die Musik in Geschichte un Gegenwart* (title means "Music in the Past and the Present"), Barenreiter, 1949-75.

BIOGRAPHICAL/CRITICAL SOURCES: Music Library Association Notes, March, 1968; *Choice,* Spring, 1975; *Christian Century,* September 17, 1975.

(Died November 22, 1975, in Schluchtern, Germany)

[Sketch verified by wife, Christiane Blume]

* * *

BLUMENTHAL, Monica David 1930-

PERSONAL: Born September 1, 1930, in Tuebingen, Germany; married Frank S. Blumenthal (a physician); children: Martin Benno, Holly Patricia. *Education:* University of Michigan, B.A. (honors), 1952, M.S., 1953, M.D., 1957; University of California, Berkeley, Ph.D., 1962. *Home:* 2074 Beechwood Blvd., Pittsburgh, Pa. 15217. *Office:* West-

ern Psychiatric Institute & Clinic, University of Pittsburgh, Pittsburgh, Pa. 152   1.

CAREER: University of Michigan, Ann Arbor, associate research clinical biochemist on schizophrenia and psychopharmacology project, 1962-63, instructor, 1965-66, assistant professor, 1967-72, associate professor, 1972-76, professor of psychiatry, 1976, research associate at Institute for Social Research, 1969-71, program director, 1971-76, senior staff psychiatrist at Neuropsychiatric Institute, 1972-76; University of Pittsburgh, Pittsburgh, Pa., professor of psychiatry and program director of geriatric psychiatry at Western Psychiatric Institute & Clinic, both 1976—. Visiting associate professor at Stanford University, 1974-75. Member of technical advisory committee of Adult Services/Area Agency on Aging, 1977—; reviewer for National Science Foundation, 1974—.

MEMBER: American Medical Association, American Association for the Advancement of Science, American Psychiatric Association (fellow), Society of Biological Psychiatry, American Association of University Professors, American Geriatric Society, Gerontological Society, Pennsylvania Medical Association, Pennsylvania Psychiatric Society, New York Academy of Sciences, Allegheny County Medical Association, Women's Research Club, Phi Beta Kappa, Sigma Xi, Alpha Epsilon Iota. *Awards, honors:* National Institute of Mental Health grants, 1959-62, 1962-68, 1964-66, 1971-74; National Science Foundation grants, 1969-71, 1971-74, 1972-76; prize from American Psychiatric Association, 1972, for outstanding research on aggression and violence.

WRITINGS: (Contributor) D. V. S. Sankar, editor, *Schizophrenia: Current Concepts and Research,* P.J.D. Publications, 1969; (with R. L. Kahn, F. M. Andrews, and K. B. Head) *Justifying Violence: Attitudes of American Men,* Institute for Social Research Publications, University of Michigan, 1972; (contributor) J. A. Murray, editor, *Alienation and Violence in the North American Community,* University of Windsor Press, 1972; (contributor) P. Zimbardo and C. Maslach, editors, *Psychology for Our Times: Readings,* Scott, Foresman, 1973; (contributor) J. D. Ben-Dak, editor, *The Future of Collective Violence: Societal and International Perspectives,* Studentlitteratur, 1974; (with L. B. Chadiha, G. A. Cole, and T. E. Jayaratne) *More About Justifying Violence: A Methodological Study of Attitudes and Behavior,* Institute for Social Research Publications, University of Michigan, 1975; (contributor) Leonard Solomon, editor, *An Experiential Approach to Psychology,* Spaulding Press, in press. Contributor of about twenty-five articles and reviews to scholarly publications, including economics, philosophy, social science, and medical journals. Member of editorial board of *Research Communications in Psychology, Psychiatry, and Behavior;* reviewer for *Archives of General Psychiatry.*

WORK IN PROGRESS: The Elderly Depressed Person: Should Drug Treatment Be Considered?, for School of Medicine, University of Pittsburgh; "Attitudes Toward Violence: 1969 and 1974," to be included in a book on violence, edited by D. Hamburg; research on the problems and prevalence of chronic organic brain syndromes, on geriatric psychiatry, and on survey research and epidemiology.

* * *

BODANSKY, Oscar 1901-1977

August 21, 1901—August 21, 1977; Russian-born American biochemist and author of two textbooks. Bodansky was a pioneer in the detection of diseases, especially cancer, using biochemistry. He was associated with Sloan-Kettering Institute for Cancer Research for several decades. Bodansky died in New York, N.Y. Obituaries: *New York Times,* August 23, 1977.

* * *

BODKER, Cecil 1927-

PERSONAL: Born March 27, 1927, in Fredericia, Denmark; daughter of H. P. (an author and artist) and Gertrude (Mathiesen) Jacobsen; married; children: (daughters) Dorete, Mette, Tadjure, Madena. *Education:* Completed four year apprenticeship to a silversmith in Fredericia, Denmark. *Agent:* V. Allen Jensen, International Children's Book Service, Kildeskovsvej 21, Gentofte, Denmark DK-2820.

CAREER: Silversmith Georg Jensen (silversmith workshop), Copenhagen, Denmark, silversmith, 1948-51; Silversmith Markstroems, Stockholm, Sweden, silversmith, 1951-52; writer, 1955—.

AWARDS, HONORS: Edith Rodes grant 1956, for *Luseblomster* and *Fygende Heste;* Morten Nielsens Memorial Award, 1960; Critics' Prize, 1961, for *Oejet;* Otto Benzon's author fellowship, 1963; anniversary prize from Arena, 1963; Louisiana Prize, 1964; state arts grant, 1965; first and only prize ever bestowed by Danish Academy for a children's book, 1967, and best children's book of the year award from Danish Ministry of Cultural Affairs, 1968, both for *Silas og den sorte hoppe;* nominated for International Board on Books for Young People (IBBY) Hans Christian Andersen Medal, 1970, received diploma as highly commended author, 1974, and awarded IBBY Hans Christian Andersen Medal, 1976, for her works for children; second prize from Danish Mission Society, 1970, for short story "Hyaenenatten"; received Silver Pencil from Netherlands, 1972, and the 1975 Mildred Batchelder Award from American Library Association, 1977, both for *Leoparden;* Drachmann prize, 1973, for her poetry, prose, and children's books; Ingrid Jespersen Prize from Danish Women's Organization, 1974; Tagea Brandts travel fellowship, 1975.

WRITINGS—Juveniles in English translation: *Silas og den sorte hoppe,* Branner & Korch, 1967, translation published as *Silas and the Black Mare,* Seymour Lawrence, in press; *Leoparden,* Branner & Korch, 1970, translation by Gunnar Poulsen and Solomon Deressa published as *The Leopard,* Atheneum, 1975.

Other juveniles: *Silas og Gen-Godik* (title means "Silas and Foot-Godik"), Branner & Korch, 1969; *Timmerlis* (title means "Timanna"), Branner & Korch, 1969; *Dimma Gole* (collection of short stories; title means "Dimma Gole"), illustrated by Arne Bodker, Branner & Korch, 1971; *Silas fanger et firspand* (title means "Silas Rescues Two Four-in-Hand"), Branner & Korch, 1972; *Barnet i sivkurven* (title means "The Child in the Basket of Rushes"), P. Hasse & Soens, 1975; *Jerutee fra Raeveroed* (title means "Jerutte of Fox Clearing"), Arena, 1975; *Jerutte redder Tom og Tinne* (title means "Jerutte Saves Tom and Tinne"), Arena, 1975; *Da jorden forsvandt* (title means "When the Earth Disappeared"), P. Haase & Soens, 1975; *Jerutte og bjornen paa Raeverod* (title means "Jerutte and the Bear at Fox Clearing"), Arena, 1976; *Silas stifter familie* (title means "Silas Starts a Family"), Branner & Korch, 1976; *Silas paa Sebastianbjerget* (title means "Silas on Sebastian Mountain"), Branner & Korch, 1977; *Jerutte besoger Hundejens* (title means "Jerutte Visits Dog-Jens"), Arena, 1977; *Den udvalgte* (title means "The Chosen One"), P. Haase & Soens, 1977.

Poems: *Luseblomster* (title means "Lice Flowers"), Arena, 1955; *Fygende heste* (title means "Drifting Horses"), Arena, 1956; *Anadyomene* (title means "Aphrodite"), Arena, 1959, 2nd edition, 1961; *Samlede digte* (title means "Collected Poems"), S. Hasselbalch, 1964; *I vaedderens tegn* (title means "In the Sign of the Ram"), Arena, 1968.

Short Stories: *Oejet* (title means "The Eye"), Arena, 1961; *Tilstanden Harley* (title means "The State of Harley"), Arena, 1965; *Fortaellinger Omkring Tavs* (title means "Stories about Tav"), Arena, 1971.

Novels: *Pap* (title means "Cardboard"), Arena, 1967; *Salthandlerskens Hus* (title means "The Salt Dealer's House"), Arena, 1972; *En Vrangmaske I Vorherres Strikketoej* (title means "A Wrong Stitch in Our Lord's Knitting"), Arena, 1974.

Plays: *Latter* (radio play; title means "Laughter"), Arena, 1964; "Badekarret" (radio play; title means "The Bathtub"), 1965; "Dukke Min" (radio play; title means "Doll of Mine"), 1968; "Kvinden Som Gik Bort Over Vandet" (radio play; title means "The Woman Who Walked Away over the Water"), 1971; "Skyld" (stage play; title means "Guilt"), first produced in Denmark, 1972.

WORK IN PROGRESS: More English translations of Bodker's "Silas" books are in preparation by Sheila Le Farge for Seymour Lawrence and Oxford University Press.

SIDELIGHTS: Bodker wrote: "People frequently ask me why I almost always write about boys and hardly ever about girls. Perhaps it is because my childhood was full of boys—or perhaps because I found what boys did more interesting than what girls did.

"When I was young, most children's books were written especially for boys or especially for girls—at least, that was true in Denmark where I live. I preferred to read the books for boys until I began reading adult books. Those written for girls usually seemed boring and sentimental.

"I never played with dolls for I found them boring, too. Once I was given a doll buggy. I used it as a soapbox car until it fell apart.

"I liked skating, sledding, sailing, biking, and camping. We lived out in the country, near the sea and not far from a town, with a beach to one side and open fields and the forest to the other.

'We were six children, five of them boys. I wore boy's clothing at a time when other girls wore only dresses; slacks and jeans didn't exist. Since we had a long, cold bike ride to school, my mother reasoned that I should be warmly dressed for the winter. So I was outfitted with knickers, a lumberjacket, a dark brown sheepskin cap, and leather boots that laced to the knees—just like my brothers.

"Was I teased about my clothes?

"To be honest, I don't remember, but probably.

"In Denmark people have titles according to their occupations and so people used to ask me *what* my father was. I didn't know how to answer, not because I didn't *know* what he was but because he was so many things. He was trained as a house painter and he was an author and an artist, but he earned a living as a designer in a silversmith's factory. He called himself 'draftsman.' Many people thought that was a strange thing to be. I could see it on their faces.

"After I finished high school, I became an apprentice at the factory where my father worked but this didn't change my situation. Counting all of us in the various workshops at the factory, there were fifty apprentices and I was the only girl.

We attended technical schools in the evenings, where—again—I was the only girl. At the time I must have seen the world with the eyes of a boy.

"After four years as an apprentice, I received a silversmith's certificate and moved to Copenhagen, where I worked in the Georg Jensen silversmith workshop. I stayed there for three years and later spent one year as a silversmith at Markstroem's model workshop in Uppsala, Sweden.

"All this time I was writing and my poetry was piling up. I don't think I was more than ten when I wrote the first poem, but not until I was twenty-eight were any of my poems published. By then I had assembled an impressive number from which to choose the first collection.

"The critics gave this first volume an excellent reception and as a result I received my first writer's grant: five hundred Danish crowns. I decided to buy a typewriter with the money, to drop my work as a silversmith, and to concentrate on writing. Something inside me said that this was the right thing to do.

"Apparently that 'something' advised me well.

"My husband is a farmer. We are a good match. Half of his life is books and half of mine is the soil. We have just bought a good-sized farm in a beautiful part of Jutland. Now both of us must work very hard to develop it the way we want it to be, but we enjoy doing it together.

"I am often asked why I began to write and I must answer truthfully that I do not know. I just did. On the other hand, I do know why I continue to write: partly because I cannot help it and partly because I want to produce books so tightly-knit and so exciting that the children and young people who read them will experience them as intensely as I experienced books when I was their age. Even though my stories are mostly about boys, I hope that they will be read by both boys and girls, and sometimes by grownups, too."

BIOGRAPHICAL/CRITICAL SOURCES: Bookbird, Number 2, 1976, Number 4, 1976.

*　　*　　*

BOETTINGER, Henry M(aurice) 1924-

PERSONAL: Born December 3, 1924, in Baltimore, Md.; son of Jacob Wilfred (a foreman) and May Josephine Boettinger; married Shirley Louise Greaves, May 15, 1976; children: Ellen Christine, Carol-Ann Greaves. *Education:* Johns Hopkins University, B.E., 1948; graduate study at University of Michigan, New York University, and University of Pennsylvania. *Religion:* Episcopalian. *Home:* Gentle Knight, Crackington Haven, Cornwall, England.

CAREER: Worked as draftsman, 1941, surveyor, 1942, and electronics testman, 1943; Chesapeake & Potomac Telephone Co. of Maryland, Baltimore, traffic assistant, 1948-50, staff assistant in accounting, 1950-51, plant supervisor, 1951; American Telephone & Telegraph Co., New York, N.Y., staff assistant on inflation studies, 1952; Chesapeake & Potomac Telephone Co. of Maryland, division auditor of receipts in Baltimore, 1953, western district traffic manager in Hagerstown, 1954, auditor of disbursements in Baltimore, 1955; American Telephone & Telegraph Co., assigned to temporary investments in Financial Division, 1955, general financial supervisor of treasury department, 1956-58, stock transfer manager, 1958-59, general financial supervisor, 1959; Michigan Bell Telephone Co., Detroit, vice-president and comptroller, 1959-60; American Telephone & Telegraph Co., assistant vice-president in planning, 1960-62, assistant comptroller in operations, 1962-68, assistant comptroller in

management sciences, 1968-71, director of management sciences, 1971-72, director of corporate planning, 1972-76, director of corporate planning research, 1976-77, assistant vice-president in executive department, 1977; free-lance writer, 1977—. Adjunct professor at Pace University; visiting fellow at Oxford University Centre for Management Studies. Past member of advisory council of American Foundation for Management Research; member of management training panel for Boy Scouts of America. *Military service:* U.S. Army Air Forces, navigator, 1943-46; served in Pacific theater. U.S. Army, Signal Corps, 1946; served in Japan. U.S. Army Reserve, 1946; became captain.

MEMBER: International Academy of Management (fellow), Institute of Electrical and Electronics Engineers, American Academy of Political and Social Science, American Association for the Advancement of Science, Institute for the Future (member of board of trustee), Committee for Economic Development (member of board of trustees; chairman of design committee on technology policy), Financial Executives Institute (chairperson of education committee, 1969-71), Tau Beta Pi, Beta Alpha Psi, New York Chamber of Commerce, New York University Club, Johns Hopkins Club, Fencers Club of New York, Century Association. *Awards, honors:* Award of distinction in technical communication from Society for Technical Communication, 1976, and certificate of excellence for distinguished achievement in the communicating arts from Communication Collaborative, both for *The Telephone Book.*

WRITINGS: Moving Mountains: On the Art and Craft of Letting Others See Things Your Way, Macmillan, 1969; *Some Aspects of Management and Technology* (lectures), British Institute of Management, 1970; *Essays on Public Utility Pricing and Regulation: Comment on Professor Oliver E. Williamson's Paper on "Administrative Controls and Regulatory Behavior"* (edited by H. M. Trebing), Graduate School of Business Administration, Michigan State University, 1971; *A Design for Business Vitality* (lecture), British Institute of Management, 1971; *The Telephone Book: Bell, Watson, Vail, and American Life, 1876-1976,* Riverwood, 1976.

Contributor: Peter F. Drucker, editor, *Preparing Tomorrow's Business Leaders Today,* Prentice-Hall, 1969; *Improving Management for More Effective Government,* U.S. General Accounting Office, 1971; Robert J. Mockler, editor, *Readings in Business Planning and Policy Formulation,* Appleton, 1972; David Ewing, editor, *Challenge to Leadership: Managing in a Changing World,* Free Press, 1973; Ithiel de Sola Pool, editor, *The Social Impact of the Telephone,* M.I.T. Press, 1976; R. I. Tricker, editor, *The Individual, the Enterprise, and the State,* Halsted, 1977.

Creator of numerous videotape and audiotape programs, 1969—.

Contributor of about thirty-five articles to business, management, and telephone company journals. Member of international board of *Telecommunications Policy.*

WORK IN PROGRESS: The Organization of Ignorance, essays in management and planning; *The Rewards of Incompetence,* about the social and historical impact of incompetence in all aspects of the human condition; a historical novel set in the time of the Industrial Revolution in England and America, all with wife, Shirley Boettinger.

SIDELIGHTS: Boettinger told *CA:* "*The Telephone Book* was conceived as the saga of how the telephone and the U.S. grew together and influenced each other's development over the last one hundred years. Particular stress is placed on the crucial role of individual creativity, nerve, and vision, and the dramatic clashes of great social changes in a new nation.''

Boettinger retired from business to ''devote full time and thought to writing in rural England. Themes will be affirmative excursions in fiction and non-fiction on technology's history, nature studies, and social change. My wife, Shirley, will work on all projects as editor, photographer, designer, and researcher.''

AVOCATIONAL INTERESTS: Painting, music, horseback riding, golf, and fencing.

* * *

BOGAN, Louise   1897-1970

PERSONAL: Born August 11, 1897, in Livermore Falls, Me.; daughter of Daniel Joseph and Mary Helen (Shields) Bogan; married Curt Alexander, 1916 (died, 1920); married Raymond Holden (a poet), 1925 (divorced, 1937); children: (first marriage) Mathilde. *Education:* Attended Boston University, 1915-16. *Residence:* New York City.

CAREER: Poet and critic. Poetry editor of *New Yorker,* 1931-70. Visiting professor at University of Washington, Seattle, 1948, University of Chicago, 1949, University of Arkansas, 1952, Seminar in American Studies, Salzburg, Austria, 1952, and Brandeis University, Waltham, Massachusetts, 1964-65. *Member:* American Academy of Arts and Letters. *Awards, honors:* John Reed Memorial Prize, 1930, and Helen Haire Levinson Memorial Prize, 1937, both from *Poetry;* Guggenheim fellowship, 1933 and 1937; Library of Congress Fellowship in American Letters, 1944; Harriet Monroe Poetry Award, 1948; National Institute of Arts and Letters grant, 1951; Bollingen Prize in Poetry, 1955, for *Collected Poems;* Academy of American Poets fellowship, 1958; Brandeis University Creative Arts Award in Poetry, 1961; Library of Congress Chair in Poetry, 1945-46; L.H.D., 1956, from Western College for Women; Litt.D., 1960, from Colby College.

WRITINGS—Poems: *Body of This Death,* McBride, 1923; *Dark Summer,* Scribner, 1929; *The Sleeping Fury,* Scribner, 1937; *Poems and New Poems,* Scribner, 1941; *Collected Poems, 1923-1953,* Noonday Press, 1954; *The Blue Estuaries: Poems, 1923-1968,* Farrar, Straus, 1968.

Other: *Achievement in American Poetry* (criticism), H. Regnery, 1951; *Selected Criticism: Prose, Poetry,* Noonday Press, 1955; (translator) Iwan Goll, *The Myth of the Pierced Rock,* Allen Press, 1962; (editor and translator with Elizabeth Roget) Jules Renard, *The Journal of Jules Renard,* Braziller, 1964; (editor with William J. Smith) *The Golden Journey: Poems for Young People,* Reilly & Lee, 1965; (author of afterword) Virginia Woolf, *A Writer's Diary, Being Extracts from the Diary of Virginia Woolf,* New American Library, 1968; *A Poet's Alphabet: Reflections on the Literary Art and Vocation,* McGraw-Hill, 1970; (translator) Johann Wolfgang von Goethe, *The Sorrows of Young Werther, and Novella,* Random House, 1971; *What the Woman Lived: Selected Letters of Louise Bogan,* edited by Ruth Limmer, Harcourt, 1973.

Contributor of verse to *New Republic;* contributor of literary criticism to *New Yorker, Nation, Poetry: A Magazine of Verse,* and *Atlantic Monthly.*

SIDELIGHTS: Louise Bogan has been called by some critics the most accomplished woman poet of our time. Her subtle, restrained, intellectual style was greatly influenced by the English metaphysical poets. Many have placed her in the same category with George Herbert, John Donne, and Henry Vaughan. Bogan belonged to a group of brilliant minor poets described by some as the ''reactionary generation.'' Aware of the success of Ezra Pound and T. S. Eliot, Bogan and others chose to follow the traditional English form of expression of the seventeenth century, which included the use of meters. Although she utilized traditional techniques, her poetry is modern, her language immediate and contemporary. Bogan's poetry contains a personal quality derived from personal experience, but it is not private. Her poems, most critics agree, are economical in words and masterpieces of crossed rhythms in which the meter opposes word groupings.

Sleeping Fury was one of the earlier published books of poems by Louise Bogan. The *Springfield Republican* noted that ''Miss Bogan's poetry appeals to the comparative few who appreciate delicacy and artistry in verse.'' *Books* review said Bogan ''has achieved a mastery of form rare in the realm of modern poetry. There is creative architecture in even the slightest of her lyrics. Miss Bogan works not as a landscape painter (while her visual imagery is exact, it does not depend on color alone), nor yet as a musician—although in many of her poems, the auditory imagery is superior to the visual: the ear listens, even as the eye sees. Her art is that of a sculpture.'' A *Nation* critic wrote, ''Distinguished is the word one always thinks of in connection with Louise Bogan's poetry. Whatever form she tries, her art is sure, economical, and self-definitive. There is never in her poems a wasted adjective or phrase but always perfect clarity and a consistent mood precisely set down. She can write the completely artless lyric or the very subtle poem worked out through complex imagery.''

Reviewing *Poems and New Poems* in *Saturday Review,* William Rose Benet noted, ''Her poetry is, and always has been, intensely personal. She has inherited the Celtic magic of language, but has blended it somehow with the tartness of New England.'' Marianne Moore further observed in *Nation,* ''Women are not noted for terseness, but Louise Bogan's art is compactness compacted. Emotion with her, as she has said of certain fiction is 'itself form, the kernel which builds outward form from inward intensity.' She uses a kind of forged rhetoric that nevertheless seems inevitable.''

Collected Poems, 1923-53 was reviewed in the *New York Times* by Richard Eberhart. ''Louise Bogan's poems adhere to the center of English with a dark lyrical force, ''wrote Eberhart. ''What she has to say is important. How she says it is pleasing. She is a compulsive poet first, a stylist second. When compulsion and style meet, we have a strong, inimitable Bogan poem.'' *Saturday Review* commented, ''Louise Bogan is mistress of precise images and commands an extensive range of poetic accents and prosodic effects; she is also a musician, whose notes are as crystalline as those of Chopin's Preludes. More than this, one cannot read far in her pages without realizing that at the core of her poetry is mindstuff which it is fashionable to call metaphysical.'' These poems are also important because they deal intelligently with the themes of sexual love and bodily decay.

The Blue Estuaries was the final collection of poems published before Louise Bogan's death. The *New York Times* reviewed the book: ''Now that we can see the sweep of 45 years work in this collection of over a hundred poems, we can judge what a feat of character it has been. . . . [Her diction] stems from the severest lyrical tradition in English. . . . [Her language is] as supple as it is accurate, dealing with things in their own tones.''

With the assistance of William Jay Smith, Louise Bogan compiled an anthology of poems for children. *The Golden Journey*, with poems ranging from Shakespeare to Dylan Thomas, was described by James Dickey as possibly "the best general anthology of poems for young people ever compiled. By the poems they present, by their arrangement and timing, the editors subtly hold out the possibility that a child—though a child—is capable of rising to good poems, and so of becoming, through an encounter which also requires much of him, something more than he was. . . . [This book] could have been selected only by poets as distinguished as these two, and by human beings who realize that to make the wrong concessions to children is injurious to them."

Louise Bogan also wrote a great deal of criticism. *Achievement in American Poetry, 1900-1950* was a brief account of American poetry during the first half of this century. The *Chicago Tribune* described the book as " . . . a delight. Like all Miss Bogan's criticism, this book is full of acute, spirited, and authoritative judgments of writers and works, expressed with grace and wit." The *New York Times* added, "Louise Bogan not only manages to compress a formidable amount of factual information into her small compass, but also contrives to do a great deal of satisfactory talking about her facts." The *United States Quarterly Book Review* commented, "Miss Bogan's clarity of style, her ability to compress a great deal of information into a few lucid, interesting phrases, and her severely just appraisal form the chief atrractions of this volume."

BIOGRAPHICAL/CRITICAL SOURCES: Saturday Review, April 18, 1937, April 25, 1942, July 3, 1954, February 21, 1970; *Nation*, April 24, 1937, November 15, 1941; *Books*, May 30, 1937; *Chicago Tribune*, November 4, 1951; *New York Times*, November 25, 1951, May 30, 1954; *United States Quarterly Book Review*, March, 1952; *New York Times Book Review*, November 7, 1965, October 13, 1968; Ruth Zimmer, editor, *What the Woman Lived: Selected Letters of Louise Bogan, 1920-1970*, Harcourt, 1973; *Contemporary Literary Criticism*, Volume IV, Gale, 1975.

OBITUARIES: New York Times, February 5, 1970; *Washington Post*, February 6, 1970; *New Yorker*, February 14, 1970; *Antiquarian Bookman*, February 16, 1970; *Newsweek*, February 16, 1970; *Time*, February 16, 1970, *Publishers Weekly*, February 23, 1970.*

(Died February 4, 1970)

*   *   *

BOLDING, Amy 1910-

PERSONAL: Born January 10, 1910, in Shawnee, Okla.; daughter of John H. and Monnie (Donnell) Ward; married James T. Bolding (a minister), May 21, 1928; children: Genelle (Mrs. Roy Carpenter), James, Rebecca (Mrs. Howard Greer). *Education:* Attended Burleson College, 1926-28, Hardin Simmons College (now University), 1929-30, and Southwestern Baptist Theological Seminary, 1937-40. *Politics:* Democrat. *Religion:* Baptist. *Home:* 4802 West Tenth, Lubbock, Tex. 79416.

MEMBER: South Plains Writers.

WRITINGS—All published by Baker Book, except as noted: *Please Give a Devotion*, 1963; *Please Give Another Devotion*, 1964; *Please Give a Devotion of Gladness*, 1965; *Words of Welcome*, 1965; *Please Give a Devotion for Young People*, 1966; *Kind Words for Sad Hearts*, 1967; *Please Give a Devotion for All Occasions*, 1967; *Handy Introduc-*

tions and Replies, 1968; *Day by Day with Amy*, 1968; *Installation Services for All Groups*, Broadman, 1969; *Please Give a Devotion for Juniors*, 1969, published as *Please Give a Devotion for Active Teens*, 1974; *Please Plan a Program*, 1971; *New Welcome Speeches*, 1971; *Simple Welcome Speeches and Other Helps*, 1973; *Women's Devotional Discussion Guide*, 1973; *Please Give a Devotion for Women's Groups*, 1976; *Day by Day*, 1976. Contributor to *Home Life*.

WORK IN PROGRESS: A book for young women.

*   *   *

BOLLES, Donald F. 1928-1976

PERSONAL: Born in 1928, in Milwaukee, Wisc.; married second wife, Rosalie, June 2, 1968; children: seven. *Education:* Graduated from Beloit College, 1950.

CAREER/WRITINGS: Associated Press, New York, N.Y., sports editor and rewriter, 1953-62; *Arizona Republic*, Phoenix, investigative reporter, 1962-76. Notable assignments include an expose of a land fraud scheme involving Western Growth Capital Corp., and a series of stories on Emprise Corp., owner of Arizona dog and horse racing tracks. *Member:* Investigative Reporters and Editors. *Awards, honors:* Nominated for a Pulitzer Prize, 1965, for stories on bribery and kickbacks in Arizona state tax and corporation commissions; named reporter of the year by Arizona Press Club, 1974, for a series of stories on a conflict-of-interest scandal in the Arizona legislature; John Peter Zenger Award, granted posthumously, from Arizona Newspaper Association.

SIDELIGHTS: Bolles's managing editor at the *Arizona Republic*, J. Edward Murray, commented: "In 14 years of trying Don Bolles was not able to make a sufficient dent on the Arizona criminal scene to prevent his own murder." In the months before his death, it was apparent to Bolles's colleagues that he was frustrated by the lack of attention paid to the corruption he uncovered; his reports were ignored by the public, by law enforcement agents, and by the political establishment in Arizona. He reportedly complained about the "official gutlessness in town." Shortly before his death, he asked to be reassigned to the paper's capitol bureau, and evidently had no intention of returning to investigative reporting. The *Republic's* city editor told Jon Bradshaw: "I've seen the same things happen to many reporters in many places. After about ten years of investigative work it gets to you and you need a break. Don worked *all* the time, including weekends. Investigative reporting has been glamorized recently. There's nothing glamorous about it. It's little more than patient drudgery. You get untold harassment from lawyers, a lot of nasty rumors spring up around you, and you get enormous pressure from your family. Add to that the frustration of nothing ever happening and all of a sudden you want to lead a normal life."

Nevertheless, on May 27, 1976, when he received a phone call from a man who claimed to have information which could link important political figures to a land fraud deal, Bolles agreed to meet him. On June 2 the man failed to show up for the scheduled meeting at a Phoenix hotel, but apparently called Bolles at the hotel to cancel the appointment. As Bolles drove his car out of the parking lot, a dynamite bomb, set off by a remote control device, exploded and wounded Bolles critically. He died eleven days later.

Bolles's last words were "Mafia . . . Emprise . . . They finally got me. . . . John Adamson . . . find him." Emprise, a Buffalo, N.Y., based enterprise that along with the Funk family of Arizona controlled dog and horse racing tracks in the state, had been the subject of a series of Bolles's articles. Adamson, a greyhound breeder, was arrested two hours after Bolles's death. At the time it was generally believed that he was only part of a larger conspiracy to murder Bolles, and the investigation centered on both members of the Mafia and local criminals.

When Adamson stood trial in January, 1977, he pleaded guilty to second-degree murder and agreed to talk to authorities in exchange for a maximum sentence of twenty years and two months. The story that emerged from Adamson's allegations led to wholesale liquor dealer Kemper Marley, one of Arizona's largest landowners. Adamson claimed that Max Dunlap, a wealthy contractor who had been raised by Marley, had hired him to kill Bolles; Dunlap, in turn, was acting on instructions from Marley who was angry about a series of articles Bolles had written about him the previous March. At that time there had been a legislative move under way to break up the race track monopoly of Emprise and the Funks, and Marley had let it be known that he would like to be nominated to the state racing commission, which regulates dog and horse racing. The legislature recommended Marley's appointment, although they did so reluctantly after hearing vague allegations about improper behavior against him by a former employee, and after Marley refused to say that he favored breaking up the dog racing monopoly. Eight days later, Bolles published a story bringing up some of Marley's past legal problems. Robert Lindsey commented that the article was "hardly Woodward and Bernstein investigative reporting—just a straightforward report that Bolles probably assembled after digging into his own memory and his newspaper's files—but apparently it was enough to kill the nomination." Lindsey continued: "Marley announced that if, 'as a matter of pride,' the Legislature gave him the job, he would resign from it after a few days. He was confirmed, and quit one week later."

Dunlap and plumber James Robison, the man who Adamson claimed detonated the device that triggered the explosion, were arrested and ordered to stand trial for first degree murder. Both pleaded not guilty. On November 6, 1977, both Dunlap and Robison were convicted of first degree murder and conspiracy. They were sentenced to death on January 10, 1978. Authorities were unable to attain enough evidence to corroborate Adamson's allegations about Marley, and he remains free.

The public outrage which immediately followed Bolles's death has since subsided. There has been moderate reform of some of the illegal activities Bolles uncovered, and although Emprise (which has since changed its name) and the Funks still control dog racing, they must divest themselves of two of their six tracks by the end of 1978. But members of Bolles's profession have not forgotten his death. In October, 1976, a group of top investigative reporters from a dozen newspapers across the country convened in Phoenix to continue the investigation of Bolles's death. The unique team will compile a series of articles which will be published in each of their representative papers and then will be offered to any other paper that wishes to publish them.

BIOGRAPHICAL/CRITICAL SOURCES: Newsweek, June 11, 1976, September 20, 1976; *Washington Post,* June 14, 1976; *Time,* June 28, 1976; *New York,* September 6, 1976; *New York Times Magazine,* February 20, 1977; *Bulletin of the American Society of Newspaper Editors,* March, 1977; *Detroit Free Press,* November 7, 1977.*

(Died June 13, 1976, in Phoenix, Ariz.)

BONNER, Mary Graham   1890-1974

PERSONAL: Born September 5, 1890, in Cooperstown, N.Y.; dual citizen of the United States and Canada; daughter of George William Graham (a bank manager) and Margaret Cary (Worthington) Bonner. *Education:* Attended Halifax Ladies' College and Halifax Conservatory of Music in Nova Scotia. *Home:* New York, N.Y.

CAREER: Author of books, magazine articles, stories, and reviews. *Awards, honors:* Constance Lindsay Skinner Award from the Women's National Book Association, 1943, for *Canada and Her Story.*

WRITINGS: Daddy's Bedtime Animal Stories (illustrated by Florence Choate and Elizabeth Curtis), F. A. Stokes, 1916; *Daddy's Bedtime Fairy Stories* (illustrated by Choate and Curtis), F. A. Stokes, 1916; *Daddy's Bedtime Bird Stories* (illustrated by Choate and Curtis), F. A. Stokes, 1917; *365 Bedtime Stories* (illustrated by Choate and Curtis), F. A. Stokes, 1923; *A Parent's Guide to Children's Reading,* Funk, 1926; *The Magic Map* (illustrated by Luxor Price), Macaulay, 1927; *Mrs. Cucumber Green* (illustrated by Janet L. Scott), Milton Bradley, 1927; *Magic Journeys* (illustrated by Price), Macaulay, 1928; *Miss Angeline Adorable* (illustrated by Scott), Milton Bradley, 1928; *Madam Red Apple* (illustrated by Scott), Milton Bradley, 1929; *The Magic Music Shop* (illustrated by Price; with music by Harry Meyer), Macaulay, 1929.

Etiquette for Boys and Girls: A Handbook for Use by Mothers, Governesses and Teachers, McLoughlin, 1930; *A Hundred Trips to Storyland* (illustrated by Hildegard Lupprian), Macaulay, 1930; *The Magic Universe* (illustrated by Price), Macaulay, 1930; *The Big Baseball Book for Boys* (edited by Alan Gould; introduction by Ty Cobb), McLoughlin, 1931; *The Magic Clock* (illustrated by Price), Macaulay, 1931; *The Animal Map of the World* (illustrated by Price), Macaulay, 1932; *Adventures in Puddle Muddle* (illustrated by William A. Kolliker), Dutton, 1935; *Rainbow at Night,* L. Furman, 1936; *A World of Our Own* (illustrated by William A. Kolliker), Dutton, 1936; (editor) *Every Child's Story Book,* McLoughlin, 1938; *A Story Teller's Holiday* (illustrated by Scott), McLoughlin, 1938; (editor) *A.B.C. Nursery Rhyme Book,* McLoughlin, 1939.

Sir Noble, the Police Horse, Knopf, 1940; *Danger on the Coast: A Story of Nova Scotia,* Knopf, 1941; *Canada and Her Story,* Knopf, 1942, 2nd edition, revised, 1950; *Made in Canada,* Knopf, 1943; *Couriers of the Sky: The Story of Pigeons,* Knopf, 1944, 2nd edition, revised, published as *Couriers of the Sky: Pigeons and Their Care,* 1952; *The Surprise Place* (illustrated by Lois Lenski), Knopf, 1945; *Something Always Happens* (illustrated by Avery Johnson), Knopf, 1946; *Out to Win: A Baseball Story* (illustrated by Howard Butler), Knopf, 1947, reprinted, 1965; *Hidden Village Mystery* (illustrated by Bob Meyers), Knopf, 1948; *The Mysterious Caboose,* Knopf, 1949.

The Haunted Hut: A Winter Mystery (illustrated by Meyers), Knopf, 1950, published as *Mystery of the Haunted Hut* (illustrated by Norman Baer), Scholastic Books, 1969; *Winning Dive: A Camp Story* (illustrated by Meyers), Knopf, 1950; *The Base-Stealer* (illustrated by Meyers), Knopf, 1951; *Wait and See* (illustrated by John N. Barron), Knopf, 1952; *Dugout Mystery* (illustrated by Jonathan David), Knopf, 1953; *Baseball Rookies Who Made Good,* Knopf, 1954; *How to Play Baseball* (illustrated by Bernard Krigstein), Knopf, 1955; (editor) Rebecca McCann, *Complete Cheerful Cherub,* Crown, 1956 ; *The Real Book about Crime Detection* (illustrated by Vincent Fodera), Garden

City Books, 1957; *Wonders around the Sun,* Lantern Press, 1957; *The Real Book about Sports* (illustrated by Albert Orbaan), Garden City Books, 1958; *Two-Way Pitcher* (illustrated by Victor Prezio), Lantern Press, 1958; *Spray Hitter* (illustrated by Prezio), Lantern Press, 1959.

The Real Book about Journalism (illustrated by Albert Orbaan), Garden City Books, 1960; *Wonders of Invention* (illustrated by Carol Cobbledick), Lantern Press, 1961; *Mystery at Lake Ashburn,* Lantern Press, 1962; *Wonders of Musical Instruments* (illustrated by Carol Cobbledick), Lantern Press, 1963.

Author of over 3,000 "Sundown Stories" syndicated daily by the Associated Press during a ten-year period.

AVOCATIONAL INTERESTS: Playing basketball, hockey, and rounders (British baseball), swimming, high diving, skating, ice boating, and camping.

OBITUARIES: New York Times, February 13, 1974; *Publishers Weekly,* March 4, 1974.*

(Died February 12, 1974)

*　*　*

BONNEY, (Mabel) Therese 1897-1978

American journalist and photographer. Bonney founded the first American illustrated press service in Europe. She was a columnist and war correspondent for *Le Figaro,* the French daily newspaper, and wrote several travel books. Bonney died in Paris, France. Obituaries: *New York Times,* January 26, 1978.

*　*　*

BONSALL, Crosby Barbara (Newell) 1921-
(Crosby Newell)

PERSONAL: Born January 2, 1921, in New York, N.Y.; married George Bonsall. *Education:* Attended American School of Design and New York University. *Residence:* Hillsgrove, Pa.

CAREER: Author and illustrator of books for children. Has also worked for advertising agencies.

WRITINGS—Under name Crosby Bonsall; all published by Harper: *Listen, Listen!* (illustrated by Ylla), 1961; *Tell Me Some More* (illustrated by Fritz Siebel), 1961; *Look Who's Talking* (illustrated by Ylla), 1962; *Who's a Pest?* (self-illustrated), 1962; *The Case of the Hungry Stranger* (self-illustrated), 1963; *What Spot?* (self-illustrated), 1963; *I'll Show You Cats* (illustrated by Ylla), 1964; *It's Mine!* (self-illustrated), 1964; *The Case of the Cat's Meow* (self-illustrated), 1965; *The Case of the Dumb Bells* (self-illustrated), 1966; *Here's Jellybean Reilly* (illustrated by Ylla), 1966; *Whose Eye Am I?* (illustrated by Ylla), 1968; *The Case of the Scaredy Cats,* 1971; *The Day I Had to Play with My Sister* (self-illustrated), 1972; *Mine's the Best* (self-illustrated), 1973; *Piggle* (self-illustrated), 1973; *And I Mean It,* 1974; *Twelve Bells for Santa,* 1977.

Under name Crosby Newell: (With George Bonsall) *What Are You Looking At?,* Treasure Books, 1954; (with G. Bonsall) *The Helpful Friends,* Wonder Books, 1955; *The Surprise Party* (self-illustrated), Wonder Books, 1955; *Captain Kangaroo's Book* (illustrated by Evan Jeffrey), Grosset, 1958; *Polar Bear Brothers* (illustrated by Ylla), Harper, 1960; *Kippy the Koala* (illustrated by George Leavens), Harper, 1960; *Hurry up, Slowpoke* (self-illustrated), Grosset, 1961.

Illustrator—under name Crosby Bonsall: Joan L. Noodset,

Go Away, Dog, Harper, 1963; Phil Ressner, *August Explains,* Harper, 1963; Joan Kahn, *Seesaw,* Harper, 1964; Ralph Underwood, editor, *Ask Me Another Riddle,* Grosset, 1964; Oscar Weigle, editor, *Great Big Joke and Riddle Book,* Grosset, 1970.

Under name Crosby Newell: George Bonsall, *The Really Truly Treasure Hunt,* Treasure Books, 1954; G. Bonsall, *The Big Joke,* Wonder Books, 1955.

BIOGRAPHICAL/CRITICAL SOURCES: Saturday Review, April 22, 1961; *New York Times Book Review,* May 9, 1965.*

*　*　*

BOON, Louis-Paul 1912-
(Boontje)

PERSONAL: Born March 15, 1912, in Aalst, Belgium; son of Joseph (a painter) and Estella (Verbestel) Boon; married Jeanette De Wolf; children: Joseph Clement. *Education:* Attended Municipal Academy of Aalst, Belgium. *Home:* Vogelzang, Erembodegem, Belgium.

CAREER: Writer and painter. *Member:* Honest Arts Movement. *Awards, honors:* Leo J. Krijn Prize, 1942, for *De Voorstad groeit;* Henriette Roland Holst Prize, 1957, for *De kleine Eva uit de kromine bijlstraat;* Constantijn Huygens Prize, 1966; Belgian State Prize, 1971; Multatuli Prize, 1972, for *Pieter Daens.*

WRITINGS—In English: *De Kapellekensbaan* (novel), Arbeiderspers, 1953, translation by Adrienne Dixon published as *Chapel Road,* Twayne, 1972.

Other: *De voorstad groeit* (title means "The Suburb Grows"), Manteau, 1943; *Vergeten straat* (novel; title means "Obscure Street"), Manteau, 1946; (under pseudonym, Boontje) *Boontje's reservaat* (title means "Boontje's Reserve"), Arbeiderspers, 1954, reissued as *Reservaat,* 1965; *Menuet* (short novel; title means "Minuet"), Arbeiderspers, 1955; *Wapenbroeders: Een getrouwe bewerking der aloude boeken over Reinaert en Isengrimus* (title means "Comrades in Arms: A True Adaptation of the Ancient Books about Reynard and Isengrim"), Arbeiderspers, 1955; *De kleine Eva uit de kromme bijlstraat* (title means "Little Eve from Crooked Axe Street"), Arbeiderspers, 1956; *Niets gaat en onder* (title means "Nothing Perishes"), Arbeiderspers, 1956, reprinted, 1970; *Zomer te Ter Muren* (novel; title means "Summer at Ter-Muren"), Arbeiderspers, 1956; *De bende van Jan de Lichte* (novel; title means "Jan de Lichte's Gang"), Arbeiderspers, 1957; *Grimmige sprookjes voor verdorven kinderen* (title means "Grimm Fairy Tales for Depraved Children"), Arbeiderspers, 1957; *De paradijsvogel* (novel; title means "Bird of Paradise"), Arbeiderspers, 1958; *Vaarwel krokodil, of De prijslijst van het geluk, een groteske* (titlte means "Goodbye Crocodile, or the Pricelist of Happiness, a Grotesque"), Arbeiderspers, 1959.

Mijn kleine oorlog (novel; title means "My Little War"), Querido, 1960; *De zoon van Jan de Lichte* (title means "Jan de Lichte's Son"), Arbeiderspers, 1961; *Blauwbaardje in wonderland: En andere grimmige sprookjes voor verdorven kinderen* (title means "Little Bluebeard in Wonderland and Other Fairy Tales for Depraved Children"), Arbeiderspers, 1962; *Dag aan dag* (title means "Day by Day"), Arbeiderspers, 1963; *Het nieuwe onkruid* (title means "The New Weeds"), Arbeiderspers, 1964; *Dorp in Vlaanderen* (title means "Village in Flanders"), Arbeiderspers, 1966; (under pseudonym Boontje) *Wat een leven* (title means "What a Wretched Life"), Arbeiderspers, 1967; *Kleine omnibus:*

Twee spoken; De kleine Eva uit de Kromme Bijlstraat; Vaarwel krokodil (collected work; title means "Small Omnibus: Two Spectres; Little Eve from Crooked Axe Street; Goodbye Crocodile"), ABC-Boeken, 1967; *Abel Gholaerts,* Querido, 1968; *De bom* (title means "The Bomb"), Uitgeverij De Kentaur, 1968; *Drie mensen tussen nuren* (title means "Three People Between Walls"), Querido, 1969; *Geniaal: Maar met te korte beentjes* (essays; title means "Brilliant: But Legs Too Short"), Arbeiderspers, 1969.

Negentig mensen (title means "Ninety People"), Arbeiderspers, 1970; *Pieter Daens: Of hoe in de negentiende eeuw de arbeiders van Aalst vochten tegen armoede en onrecht* (title means "Pieter Daens: Or the Struggle of the Workers of Aalst Against Poverty and Injustice in the Nineteenth Century"), Querido, 1971; (under pseudonym, Boontje) *Boon apartjes* (title means "Boon Asides"), Bruna, 1971; *Als het onkruid bloeit* (title means "When the Weeds Are in Bloom"), Arbeiderspers, 1972; *Eten op zijn Vlaams* (nonfiction; title means "Eating the Flemish Way"), Arbeiderspers, 1972; *Mieke Maaike's obscene jeugd* (title means "Mieke Maaike's Obscene Youth"), Arbeiderspers, 1972; *Zomerdagdroom* (title means "Summer Daydream"), Querido, 1973; *De meisjes van Jesses* (title means "Jesse's Girls"), Querido, 1973; *Blauwbaardje in de ruinte* (title means "Little Bluebeard in Space"), Manteau, 1973; *Davids jonge dagen* (title means "David's Young Days"), Querido, 1974; *Menuet en audere verhalen* (collected work; title means "Minuet and Other Stories"), Querido, 1974; (under pseudonym, Boontje) *Verse Boontjes* (title means "Boon's Fresh Beans"), Orion, 1974; *Verscheurd jeugdportret* (title means "Torn Youthportrait"), Querido, 1975; *Memoires van de Heer Daegeman* (title means "Memoirs of Mr. Daegeman"), Arbeiderspers, 1975; *De Zwarte Hand: Of Het anarchisme van de negentiende eeuw in het industriestadje Aalst* (title means "The Black Hand: Or the Anarchism of the 19th Century in the Small Industrial Town of Aalst"), Arbeiderspers, 1976.

WORK IN PROGRESS: A book; film scripts.

BIOGRAPHICAL/CRITICAL SOURCES: Louis Julien Weverbergh, *Boonbock,* Manteau, 1972.

*   *   *

BOONTJE
See BOON, Louis-Paul

*   *   *

BOORSTEIN, Edward   1915-

PERSONAL: Born August 23, 1915, in New York, N.Y.; son of Jacob (a laundryman) and Sophie (a laundrywoman; maiden name, Fishman) Boorstein; married Regula Simons (a journalist), September 5, 1948. *Education:* City College (now of the City University of New York), B.S.S., 1936; Columbia University, M.A., 1940; further study at University of Paris, 1950-51. *Home:* 4410 Cayuga Ave., Apt. 1F, Bronx, N.Y. 10471.

CAREER: Federal Reserve Board, Washington, D.C., junior economist, 1940-42; economist in the United States and abroad, 1946-60; adviser to the president of Cuba's National Bank and Cuban minister of foreign trade, 1960-63; writer and lecturer, 1964-68; Cornell University, Ithaca, N.Y., visiting lecturer, 1969-70; Chile Trading Corp., New York, N.Y., assistant to president, 1970-71; assistant to the Chilean president's economic adviser, 1972-73; writer and lecturer, 1973—, *Military service:* U.S. Army, 1943-46.

WRITINGS: The Economic Transformation of Cuba, Monthly Review Press, 1968; *Allendes' Chile: An Inside View,* International Publishers, 1977.

WORK IN PROGRESS: An analysis of the crisis in the U.S. economy.

SIDELIGHTS: Boorstein commented: "My interest in the first two books was to explain to the ordinary American reader the Cuban and Chilean revolutions and the steps the U.S. Government took to try to stop them. My current interest is to analyze the crisis in the U.S. economy in plain simple English."

*   *   *

BOREL, Raymond C.   1927-

PERSONAL: Born August 24, 1927, in Murol, France; married Adelheid Guthman, December 23, 1957; children: Michael, Nathalie. *Education:* Ecole des Beaux Arts de Paris, B.F.A., 1946; St. Charles Institute, B.A.; Sorbonne, University of Paris, M.A., 1959; graduate of Ecole Superieure de Journalisme and Institut des Hautes Etudes Internationales. *Politics:* Socialist. *Religion:* Roman Catholic. *Home:* 102 Ave. Charles de Gaulle, 92200 Neuilly, France. *Office: Edita,* 29 Rue du Faubourg Poissonniere, 75009 Paris, France.

CAREER: Painter; assistant to motion picture directors in Africa, Brazil, and Mexico; television screenwriter in Hollywood, Calif.; editor of *Detective* (French weekly magazine); publisher of *Tonus* (medical newspaper); correspondent for several European newspapers; *Edita,* Paris, France, currently president and director general. *Military service:* U.S. Army, cameraman in Signal Corps during Korean War. *Member:* Screen Writers Guild.

WRITINGS: L'Affaire Gregory (spy novel; title means "The Gregory Case"), Albin Michel, 1968; *La Garde meurt a French Creek* (novel), Stock Publishing, 1973, English translation published as *Death at French Creek,* McGraw, 1975.

Screenplays: "O.S.S. in Corsica," 1959; "Banco in Bangkok," 1960. Also author of "The Old Master," "Along Came Death," and "Study for a Masterpiece."

WORK IN PROGRESS: A Gentleman from Nowhere, a novel on Jean Laffite.

SIDELIGHTS: Born of American parents in France, Borel spent his childhood traveling between Pennsylvania and well-known palaces in Europe, where his father was "chef de cuisine." He writes that he always considers himself "un Francais d'Amerique" and "an American in Paris." He spent the World War II years with his father in Brittany, on the west coast of France.

He comments that his first book sets a new literary style in spy novels, and that his second book, although fiction (on Napoleonic exiles in America), is "more than sufficiently rich in references to be of the greatest value to the historian and to all interested in human epics."

*   *   *

BORGESE, Elisabeth Mann   1918-

PERSONAL: Born April 24, 1918, in Munich, Germany; daughter of Thomas (a writer) and Katia (Pringsheim) Mann; married G. A. Borgese (a writer), November 23, 1939 (deceased); children: Angelica Borgese Colocci, Dominica. *Education:* Conservatory of Music, Zurich, diploma, 1938; University of Chicago, further study, 1939-41. *Religion:* "I do not belong to organized religion." *Home address:* San Domenico, Florence, Italy. *Agent:* John Schaffner Literary Agency, 425 East 51st St., New York, N.Y. 10022. *Office:* International Ocean Institute, University of Malta, Msida, Malta.

CAREER: Writer. Senior fellow at Center for the Study of Democratic Institutions, 1964-76; chairman of planning council for International Ocean Institute at University of Malta, 1972—; adviser to Austrian delegation to the United Nations Conference on the Law of the Sea. *Member:* American Anthropological Association, American Academy of Political Science, American Society of International Law, Authors Guild of Authors League of America.

WRITINGS: To Whom It May Concern (short stories), Braziller, 1962; *Ascent of Woman,* Braziller, 1964; *The Language Barrier,* Holt, 1965; *The White Snake,* MacGibbon & Kee, 1966; *The Ocean Regime,* Center for the Study of Democratic Institutions, 1968; *The Drama of the Oceans,* Abrams, 1976; *Seafarm,* Abrams, in press.

Also author of plays. Contributor to journals. Editor of *Common Cause,* 1948-52; executive secretary of board of editors of *Encyclopaedia Britannica,* 1964-66.

WORK IN PROGRESS: Law of the Sea; The New International Economic Order; research on agriculture and sea-farming.

SIDELIGHTS: Elisabeth Borgese's books have been published in French, Italian, and German. She writes: "I have a life-long commitment to socialism, developing countries, and world order."

*   *   *

BORSKI, Lucia Merecka

PERSONAL: Born in Warsaw, Poland; came to the United States; married Stephen Borski Szczepanowicz. *Education:* Earned B.A. from New York University, and B.S. from Columbia University.

CAREER: Translator of Polish folk tales. Worked for the New York Public Library, and for the Library of Congress, 1944-46.

WRITINGS: (Translator with Kate B. Miller) *The Jolly Tailor, and Other Fairy Tales* (illustrated by Kazimir Klepacki), Longmans, Green, 1928, reprinted, D. McKay, 1966; (translator with Miller) *The Gypsy and the Bear, and Other Fairy Tales* (illustrated by James Reid), Longmans, Green, 1933; (translator and adaptor) *Polish Folk Tales* (illustrated by Erica Gorecka-Egan), Sheed & Ward, 1947; (translator and compiler) *Good Sense and Good Fortune* (illustrated by Gorecka-Egan), D. McKay, 1970; (translator) Jerzy Ficowski, *Sister of the Birds, and Other Gypsy Tales,* Abingdon, 1976.

SIDELIGHTS: Lucia Borski first heard the stories that she adapted for publication as *Polish Folk Tales* during her childhood in Poland. She has told the sixteen religious tales to children at the New York Public Library. *Saturday Review* said, "In translating the old Polish legends Mrs. Borski preserves their curious simplicity and their humor. They are not told for children, but there is a great deal in them that boys and girls will enjoy."

BIOGRAPHICAL/CRITICAL SOURCES: Saturday Review, March 13, 1948.*

*   *   *

BORSODI, Ralph   1888-1977

1888—October 27, 1977; American economist and author. The founder of the School of Living colony in Suffern, N.Y., Borsodi advocated the "city-farmer" plan, by which city families grow enough food to be self-sufficient. *Flight From the City* was his best-known book. He died in Exeter, N.H. Obituaries: *New York Times,* October 28, 1977.

*   *   *

BOSTON, Lucy Maria (Wood)   1892-

PERSONAL: Born 1892, in Southport, Lancashire, England; daughter of James (an engineer) and Mary (Garrett) Wood; married a military officer, 1917 (marriage dissolved, 1935); children: Peter. *Education:* Attended Somerville College, Oxford. *Home:* Hemingford Grey, Huntingdonshire, England.

CAREER: Author of children's books, 1954—. Served as a nurse in France during World War I. *Awards, honors:* Carnegie Medal, 1961, for *A Stranger at Green Knowe;* Lewis Carroll Shelf Award, 1969, for *The Children of Green Knowe.*

WRITINGS—Fiction, except as noted: *The Children of Green Knowe* (illustrated by son, Peter Boston), Faber, 1954, Harcourt, 1955; *Yew Hall,* Faber, 1954; *Treasure of Green Knowe* (illustrated by P. Boston), Harcourt, 1958 (published in England as *The Chimneys of Green Knowe,* Faber, 1958); *The River at Green Knowe* (illustrated by P. Boston), Harcourt, 1959; *A Stranger at Green Knowe* (illustrated by P. Boston), Harcourt, 1961; *An Enemy at Green Knowe* (illustrated by P. Boston), Harcourt, 1964; *The Castle of Yew* (illustrated by Margery Gill), Harcourt, 1965; *The Sea Egg* (illustrated by P. Boston), Harcourt, 1967; (contributor) Kathleen Lines, editor, *The House of the Nightmare and Other Eerie Tales,* Bodley Head, 1967, Farrar, Straus, 1968; *The House that Grew* (illustrated by Caroline Hemming), Faber, 1969; *Strongholds,* Harcourt, 1969 (published in England as *Persephone,* Collins, 1969).

The Horned Man; or, Whom Will You Send to Fetch Her Away? (play), Faber, 1970; (contributor) M. R. Hodgkin, editor, *Young Winter's Tales, I,* Macmillan, 1970; *Nothing Said* (illustrated by P. Boston), Harcourt, 1971; *Memory in a House* (nonfiction), Bodley Head, 1973, Macmillan, 1974; *The Guardians of the House* (illustrated by P. Boston), Bodley Head, 1974, Atheneum, 1975; *The Fossil Snake* (illustrated by P. Boston), Atheneum, 1975; *The Stones of Green Knowe* (illustrated by P. Boston), Atheneum, 1976.

SIDELIGHTS: In 1939, Lucy Boston purchased Manor House near Cambridge, England, and with the help of her son, restored it to its original beauty and dignity. It stood for a way of life to Mrs. Boston, and had a great impact on her writing. When she began writing at age sixty, Manor House became Green Knowe—an old, haunted house. This house dominates all of her principle books, except *The Sea Egg,* and is said to be their central character.

According to John Rowe Townsend in *A Sense of Story,* "Mrs. Boston is not an explicitly moral writer, but her values are clearly to be seen. She believes in the goodness of the natural living creature, in roots, in continuity; and she is able to symbolize these values in the house, itself built of natural materials, which she has said she cannot think of as 'a thing.'"

New Yorker described *Children of Green Knowe,* Lucy Boston's first book, as "an uncommon tale for literate young ones, told with a gratifying blend of the eerie, the sinister, and the familiar."

Strongholds was Boston's first adult novel to be published in

America. *Saturday Review* said, "Lucy Boston achieves the same gentle, romantic mood and the same cameo style that have made her 'Green Knowe' books so popular for children ... each setting is brilliantly conceived, the characters are perceptively etched, and the elegance of the writing compensates for the fact that the primary story line is sentimental in woman's magazine style."

Boston's stories have been used regularly on the BBC's children's storyreading hour.

BIOGRAPHICAL/CRITICAL SOURCES: New Yorker, November 26, 1955; Jasper A. Rose, *Lucy Boston,* Bodley Head, 1965; *Saturday Review,* May 10, 1969; *Times Literary Supplements,* July 20, 1970; John Rowe Townsend, *A Sense of Story,* Longman, 1971; Lucy M. Boston, *Memory in a House,* Bodley Head, 1973, Macmillan, 1974; Justin Wintle, *The Pied Pipers,* Paddington, 1974; *Children's Literature Review,* Volume 3, Gale, 1978.*

*   *   *

BOTTOMS, A(nthony) E(dward) 1939-

PERSONAL: Born August 29, 1939, in Shillong, Assam, India; son of James William (a medical missionary) and Dorothy Ethel (Barnes) Bottoms; married Janet Freda Wenger (a lecturer in English literature), August 18, 1962; children: Catharine, Stephen, Erica. *Education:* Corpus Christi College, Oxford, B.A., 1961, M.A., 1965; Corpus Christi College, Cambridge, diploma in criminology, 1962; University of Sheffield, Ph.D., 1974. *Politics:* Labour. *Religion:* Christian. *Residence:* Sheffield, England. *Office:* Centre for Criminological Studies, University of Sheffield, Crookesmoore Building, Conduit Rd., Sheffield S1O 1Fl, England.

CAREER: Essex Probation Service, Basildon, England, probation officer, 1962-64; Cambridge University, Cambridge, England, research officer at Institute of Criminology, 1964-68; University of Sheffield, Sheffield, England, lecturer, 1968-72, senior lecturer, 1972-76, professor of criminology and director of Centre for Criminological Studies, both 1976—. Visiting fellow at Cambridge University, 1977. Part-time member of Parole Board for England and Wales, 1974-76.

WRITINGS: (With F. H. McClintock) *Criminals Coming of Age: A Study of Institutional Adaptation in the Treatment of Adolescent Offenders,* Heinemann, 1973; (with J. D. McClean) *Defendants in the Criminal Process,* Routledge & Kegan Paul, 1976; (with J. Baldwin and Monica A. Walker) *The Urban Criminal,* Tavistock Publications, 1976.

Contributor: Peter Watson, editor, *Psychology and Race,* Penguin, 1973; Martin Wright, editor, *Use of Criminology Literature,* Butterworth & Co., 1974; Roger Hood, editor, *Crime, Criminology and Public Policy: Essays in Honor of Sir Leon Radzinowicz,* Heinemann, 1974, Free Press, 1975; F. J. Ebling, editor, *Racial Variation in Man,* Institute of Biology, 1975. Contributor to professional and popular journals, including *New Society, Race,* and *Times Literary Supplement.* Editor of *Howard Journal of Penology and Crime Prevention,* 1975—.

WORK IN PROGRESS: English Penal Policy, 1948-1977, for Blackwood of Oxford; research on Sheffield Study of Urban Social Structure and Crime, a sequel to *The Urban Criminal.*

AVOCATIONAL INTERESTS: Visiting historic buildings (especially English cathedrals).

BOUCE, Paul-Gabriel 1936-

PERSONAL: Surname is pronounced Boo-*say;* born January 26, 1936, in Versailles, France; son of Gabriel (a headmaster) and Andree (Roublot) Bouce; married Paulette Joyeux (a teacher), December 29, 1959; children: Hugh, Anne. *Education:* University of Lyons, licence, 1957, diplome d'etudes superieures, 1958, CAPES, 1959, agregation, 1960; Sorbonne, University of Paris, D.Litt., 1970. *Home:* 36 Ave. Rabelais, 92160 Antony, France. *Office:* Department of English, University of Paris III, 5 Rue de l'Ecole de Medecine, 75006 Paris, France.

CAREER: University of Paris III, Sorbonne Nouvelle, Paris, France, assistant professor, 1963-67, associate professor, 1967-70, professor of English, 1971—, chair of studies in eighteenth-century English literature and civilization, 1971—. Member of Wolfson College, Cambridge. *Military service:* French Naval Reserve, active duty, 1960-62. *Member:* Societe d'Etudes Anglo-Americaines des Dix-septieme et Dix-huitieme siecles, Societe des Anglicistes de l'Enseignement Superieur, British Society for Eighteenth Century Studies.

WRITINGS: (With G. S. Rousseau) *Tobias Smollett,* Oxford University Press, 1971; *Les Romans de Smollett,* Didier, 1971, translation published as *The Novels of Smollett,* Longman, 1976. Contributor of numerous articles and reviews to both British and American literature and philology journals. Associate editor of *Etudes Anglaises;* member of editorial board of "The Works of Tobias Smollett," University of Delaware Press.

WORK IN PROGRESS: A critical edition of *Roderick Random,* publication by Oxford University Press expected in 1980.

SIDELIGHTS: Bouce writes: "As a French academic, with a bilingual education, I can only regret the present lack of interest of most of our undergraduates—not all!—for eighteenth-century literature, both in France and in England, and probably in America. The fact that so much is being published *about* eighteenth-century literature does not mean that it is actually being *read* by Johnson's beloved 'common readers.' Whose fault? The constant brainwashing and messageless massaging of the media? The selfishness of ivory-tower academics more bent on their personal research than on awakening a genuine interest in their subject among their undergraduates? Or the idiotic, indiscriminate condemnation of non-contemporary literature by pseudo-leftist, but genuinely suicidal, intellectual (?) gurus? A novel by Fielding, Richardson, Sterne, or Smollett is every bit as 'modern' as the latest ephemeral fictional trash extolled to pitiful literary heaven by crazed critics: with the major difference that eighteenth-century novels will still be as 'modern' in a couple of centuries' time."

*   *   *

BOUGHTON, Willis A(rnold) 1885-1977

1885—August 7, 1977; American chemist and author of more than forty books. His works include fiction, poetry, history, biography, and children's books. Boughton died in Fort Lauderdale, Fla. Obituaries: *New York Times,* August 19, 1977; *AB Bookman's Weekly,* October 17, 1977.

*   *   *

BOWEN, Robert Sydney 1900-1977
(James Robert Richard)

PERSONAL: Born in 1900, in Boston, Mass.; married wife,

Mary Ann; children: three sons, one daughter. *Residence:* Honolulu, Hawaii.

CAREER: Author, editor, and journalist. Began working as a journalist, 1918, for *London Daily Mail, Chicago Tribune* in Paris, and for two Boston newspapers; served as editorial director for the International Civil Aeronautics Conference in Washington, D.C.; editor-in-chief, *Aviation Magazine;* also editor of *Flying News* and several motor magazines; free-lance writer of fiction, 1930-77. *Military service:* U.S. Aviation Service, 1914-18; qualified as ace fighter pilot by shooting down eight enemy aircraft. *Member:* American Society for Promotion of Aviation (publicity director). *Awards, honors:* A gold medal and certificates from Boy's Clubs of America.

WRITINGS—All published by Lothrop, except as noted: *Flying From the Ground Up,* McGraw, 1931; *The Winning Pitch,* 1948; *Player, Manager,* 1949; *Fourth Down,* 1949; *Ball Hawk,* 1950; *Blocking Back,* 1950; *Hot Corner,* 1951; *Touchdown Kid,* 1951; *Canyon Fury,* 1952; *Pitcher of the Year,* 1952; *Behind the Bat,* 1953; *Infield Spark,* 1954; *The Million-Dollar Fumble,* 1954; *The Big Inning,* 1955; *The Last White Line,* 1955; *The 4th Out,* 1956; *No Hitter,* 1957; *The Big Hit,* 1958; *Triple Play,* 1959.

Hot Rod Angels, Chilton, 1960; *Pennant Fever,* 1960; *Million-Dollar Rookie,* 1961; *Bat Boy,* 1962; *Flight Into Danger,* Chilton, 1962; *Wings for an Eagle,* Chilton, 1962; *Perfect Game,* 1963; *Dirt Track Danger,* Doubleday, 1963; *They Found the Unknown: The Stories of Nine Great Discoveries in the Field of Medical Knowledge,* Macrae, 1963; *Hot Corner Blues,* 1964; *Hot Rod Rodeo,* Criterion, 1964; *Rebel Rookie,* 1965; *They Flew to Glory: The Story of the Lafayette Flying Corps,* 1965; *Hot Rod Patrol,* Criterion, 1966; *Man on First,* 1966; *Hot Rod Showdown,* Criterion, 1967; *Lightning Southpaw,* 1967; *Hot Rod Outlaws,* Chilton, 1968; *Wipeout,* Criterion, 1969; *Infield Flash,* 1969; *Born to Fly,* Criterion, 1971; *Hot Rod Doom,* Criterion, 1973.

"Dave Dawson" series; all published by Crown: *Dave Dawson at Dunkirk,* 1941; *. . . in Libya,* 1941; *. . . on Convoy Patrol,* 1941; *. . . with the Pacific Fleet,* 1942; *. . . at Casablanca,* 1944; *. . . at Truk,* 1946.

Under pseudonym James Robert Richard; all published by Lothrop, except as noted: *The Club Team,* 1950; *Fighting Halfback,* 1952; *Quarterback, All-American,* 1953; *Phantom Mustang,* 1954; *The Purple Palomino,* 1955; *The Appaloosa Curse,* 1956; *Snow King, Lippizan Horse,* 1957; *Double M for Morgans,* 1958; *Joker, the Polo Pony,* 1959.

OBITUARIES: New York Times, April 13, 1977.*

(Died, 1977, in Honolulu, Hawaii)

* * *

BOWMAN, Bob
    See BOWMAN, Robert T.

* * *

BOWMAN, Robert T. 1910-
    (Bob Bowman)

PERSONAL: Born February 5, 1910, in Prescott, Ontario, Canada; son of Charles Arthur (a newspaper editor) and Ruth (Laing) Bowman; married Marguerite Bessie Ross, December 11, 1934; children: Elisabeth, Charles. *Education:* McGill University, B.Comm., 1932. *Home and office:* 4494 James St., Vancouver, British Columbia, Canada, V5V3J1.

CAREER: British Broadcasting Corp. (BBC), London, England, commentator, 1934-36; Canadian Broadcasting Corp. (CBC), Ottawa, Ontario, director of special events, 1936-43; Southam Newspapers of Canada, Toronto, Washington correspondent, 1943-46; manager of radio stations in Canada, including CJCH Halifax, CKMO Vancouver, CFBC St. John, and CKLG Vancouver, 1947-62; Toronto Sun Syndicate, Toronto, author of "Washback on Canada" column syndicated to about thirty newspapers, 1962—. *Member:* Canadian War Correspondents Association, Vancouver Teachers Association.

WRITINGS: Bob Bowman on the Ice, Barker, 1936; *Dateline Canada,* Holt, 1967.

SIDELIGHTS: Bowman told *CA* that he is "presently concentrating on Canadian history, bringing out events and personalities little known to Canadians."

An extensive traveler, Bowman has visited Europe, the Far East, and the Canadian Arctic.

* * *

BOYCE, (Joseph) Chris(topher) 1943-

PERSONAL: Born September 12, 1943, in Glasgow, Scotland; son of Peter (a laborer) and Anne (Flanagan) Boyce; married Angela M. Mullane (a lawyer), July 3, 1973. *Education:* Attended Scottish College of Commerce, 1964-65. *Politics:* "Fried eggs." *Religion:* "Boiled eggs." *Home:* 11 Dowanside Rd., Glasgow G12 9YB, Scotland. *Agent:* Angela M. Mullane, 11 Dowanside Rd., Glasgow G12 9YB, Scotland. *Office: Daily Record,* Anderston Quay, Glasgow, Scotland.

CAREER: Glasgow Public Libraries, Glasgow, Scotland, library assistant, 1962-68; Lewis's Department Store, Glasgow, furniture deliverer, 1969; Strathclyde University, Glasgow, traffic flow evaluator, 1969; Springfield Post Office, Glasgow, postal and telegraph officer, 1970; *Daily Record,* Anderston Quay, Glasgow, librarian, 1970—. Writer. *Member:* British Interplanetary Society, Association in Scotland to Research Astronautics (A.S.T.R.A.). *Awards, honors:* Victor Gollancz/Sunday Times Science Fiction Award, 1975, for *Catchworld.*

WRITINGS: Catchworld, Gollancz, 1975, Doubleday, 1977; (contributor) Duncan Lunan, *Interstellar Contact,* Regnery, 1975. Contributor of short stories to *Impulse Science Fiction.*

WORK IN PROGRESS: Forbidden Colour, a thriller; a science fiction novel, *Brain Fix;* a book on the psychological implications of extra-terrestrial contact provisionally titled *Encounter.*

SIDELIGHTS: Chris Boyce told *CA:* "Being amazingly arrogant I am furiously purveying my personal view, nay, vision, of man's future over the next few hundred years, by the end of which time our distant offspring may regard themselves as human but I doubt very much if we would agree."

In conjunction with his writing his interests include ethology, behavioural science, artificial intelligence, space science, and CETI/SETI (Contact with, Search for, Extra-Terrestrial Intelligence). In 1969 he traveled overland to India and back. He is a student of English and "Glaswegian."

AVOCATIONAL INTERESTS: Modern war gaming, eggs.

* * *

BOYD, Ann S.
    See SCHOONMAKER, Ann

BOYLSTON, Helen (Dore) 1895-

PERSONAL: Born April 4, 1895, in Portsmouth, N.H.; daughter of Joseph and Fannie Dore (Wright) Boylston. *Education:* Graduated from Massachusetts General Hospital School of Nursing, 1915. *Home:* Westport, Connecticut.

CAREER: Nurse and author. Enlisted in Harvard Medical Unit, served with British Expeditionary Force during World War I, 1915-19; joined Red Cross after the war, doing reconstruction work in Europe for a year and a half; returned to Massachusetts General Hospital, teaching nose and throat anesthesia for two years. Has also worked as a psychiatric nurse.

WRITINGS: Sister: The War Diary of a Nurse, I. Washburn, 1927; *Sue Barton, Student Nurse* (illustrated by Forrest W. Orr), Little, Brown, 1936; *Sue Barton, Senior Nurse* (illustrated by Orr), Little, Brown, 1937; *Sue Barton, Visiting Nurse* (illustrated by Orr), Little, Brown, 1938; *Sue Barton, Rural Nurse* (illustrated by Orr), Little, Brown, 1939; *Sue Barton, Superintendent of Nurses* (illustrated by Orr), Little, Brown, 1940; *Carol Goes Backstage* (illustrated by Frederick E. Wallace), Little, Brown, 1941; *Carol Goes on the Stage* (illustrated by Wallace), J. Lane, 1943; *Carol Plays Summer Stock* (illustrated by Major Felton), Little, Brown, 1942; *Carol on Broadway* (illustrated by Felton), Little, Brown, 1944; *Carol on Tour* (illustrated by Felton), Little, Brown, 1946; *Sue Barton, Neighborhood Nurse,* Little, Brown, 1949; *Sue Barton, Staff Nurse,* Little, Brown, 1952; *Clara Barton: Founder of the American Red Cross* (illustrated by Paula Hutchison), Random House, 1955.

Contributor to magazines including *Atlantic Monthly, Harper's, Forum, Country Gentlemen, McCall's,* and *Liberty.*

SIDELIGHTS: While serving as a nurse with the British Expeditionary Force, Mrs. Boylston kept a diary which was later serialized in the *Atlantic Monthly.* Discovering she could earn a living by writing, the author based many of her stories on her own nursing experiences and became a leading contributor of career novels for young people. *Avocational interests:* Photography.*

*   *   *

BRADSHAW, Brendan 1937-

PERSONAL: Born May 28, 1937, in Limerick, Ireland; son of Kevin (a businessman) and Annie (Harrison) Bradshaw. *Education:* National University of Ireland, B.A., 1964, M.A., 1966; Holy Cross College, Dublin, B.D., 1970; Cambridge University, Ph.D., 1975. *Office:* Department of History, Queen's College, Cambridge University, Cambridge CB3 9ET, England.

CAREER: Irish Civil Service, Department of Posts and Telegraphs, Dublin, executive officer, 1955-60; entered Society of Mary, 1960, ordained Roman Catholic priest, 1969; Cambridge University, Cambridge, England, fellow of St. John's College, 1973-75; Mary Immaculate College of Education, Limerick, Ireland, lecturer in history, 1975-77; Cambridge University, lecturer in history at Queen's College and Girton College, 1977—. *Member:* Royal Historical Society (fellow). *Awards, honors:* Alexander Prize from Royal Historical Society, 1976.

WRITINGS: (Contributor) Brian Farrell, editor, *The Irish Parliamentary Tradition,* Gill & Macmillan, 1973; *The Dissolution of the Religious Orders in Ireland under Henry VIII,* Cambridge University Press, 1974; (contributor) Nicholas Canny and other editors, *The Westward Enterprise,* University Press, 1977. Contributor to history journals.

WORK IN PROGRESS: A history of sixteenth-century Ireland.

*   *   *

BRADY, George Stuart 1887-1977

1887—August 11, 1977; American engineer, former army colonel, and author. Brady was an engineer on the construction of the Panama Canal, served in the Roosevelt administration in various capacities, and served in both world wars and in the Korean conflict. He contributed articles and short stories to periodicals and wrote several books, including an encyclopedia for executives. Brady died in Bethesda, Md. Obituaries: *Washington Post,* August 16, 1977.

*   *   *

BRAGDON, Lillian Jacot

PERSONAL: Born in New Jersey. *Education:* Attended University of Lausanne, Switzerland. *Residence:* Connecticut.

CAREER: Author and lecturer. Worked as a children's book editor and editorial consultant.

WRITINGS: Tell Me the Time, Please (illustrated by Frank and Margaret Phares), F. A. Stokes, 1936; *The Land of William Tell,* F. A. Stokes, 1938, revised edition published as *The Land and People of Switzerland,* Lippincott, 1961; *Words on Wings: The Story of Communication* (illustrated by James MacDonald), Farrar & Rinehart, 1938; *The Land of Joan of Arc,* F. A. Stokes, 1939, revised edition published as *The Land and People of France,* Lippincott, 1972; (editor with others) *Color Guide to Home Decoration,* Sterling, 1956; *Let There Be Light* (illustrated by Leonard Shortall), Lippincott, 1959; *Luther Burbank: Nature's Helper* (illustrated by Frederick T. Chapman), Abingdon, 1959; *Abraham Lincoln: Courageous Leader* (illustrated by Edward Shenton), Abingdon, 1960; *It's Fun to Speak French* (illustrated by Judith Brown), Abingdon, 1962; *Meet the Remarkable Adams Family* (illustrated by Chapman), Atheneum, 1964.*

*   *   *

BRAHTZ, John F(rederick) Peel 1918-

PERSONAL: Born January 29, 1918, in St. Paul, Minn.; son of John H. A. (an engineer) and Charlotte Beatrice (a teacher; maiden name, Peel) Brahtz. *Education:* California Institute of Technology, student, 1935-36; Stanford University, A.B., 1939, M.S., 1948, Ph.D., 1951. *Residence:* La Jolla, Calif. *Office address:* P.O. Box 825, La Jolla, Calif. 92038.

CAREER: Consolidated Aircraft Corp., San Diego, Calif., structural research engineer, 1939-41; Stanford University, Stanford, Calif., acting instructor in engineering mechanics, 1946-51; J. H. Pomeroy & Co., Inc., San Francisco, Calif., field engineer, 1950-51; Northrop Aircraft Co., Hawthorne, Calif., project engineer, 1951-53; University of California, Los Angeles, director of off-campus graduate program and associate professor of engineering, 1953-57; J. H. Pomeroy & Co., Inc., vice-president and director of engineering, 1957-59; John F. Brahtz Associates (consulting engineers), Los Angeles, Calif., director of operations, 1959-60; Stanford Research Institute, Menlo Park, Calif., manager of construction systems research, 1960-63; University of California, Los Angeles, lecturer in engineering, 1963-70; California State University, San Diego, lecturer in civil engineering, 1970-73, director of Construction Systems Institute,

1970—. Special lecturer and later postdoctoral scholar at University of California, Los Angeles, 1960-61, 1970-73; instructor and academic adviser in construction management, tutorial degree program, University of California, San Diego, 1977—. Registered civil and mechanical engineer in California; staff consultant to director, Naval Civil Engineering Laboratory and Naval Electronics Laboratory Center, 1963-70. Chairman-elect of Technical Council on Ocean Engineering; consultant to National Council on Marine Resources and Engineering Development and Aerophysics Development Corp. *Military service:* U.S. Naval Reserve, 1941-69, active duty as procurement officer, 1941-46; became commander.

MEMBER: American Society of Civil Engineers (fellow; member of construction Division Committee on Estimating and Cost Control), American Institute for Aeronautics and Astronautics (associate fellow), Marine Technology Society, Sigma Xi.

WRITINGS: (Contributor) *California and Use of the Ocean,* Institute of Marine Resources, University of California, 1956; (editor and contributor) *Ocean Engineering: System Planning and Design,* Wiley, 1968; (editor and contributor) *Coastal Zone Management: Multiple Use with Conservation,* Wiley, 1972; (editor) H. N. Ahuja, *Construction Performance Control,* Wiley, 1976; (editor) Stanley Goldhaber, Chandra K. Jha, and Manual C. Macedo, *Construction Management: Principles and Practices,* Wiley, 1977. Editor of Wiley's "Series in Construction Management and Engineering." Contributor to professional publications.

WORK IN PROGRESS: Construction management books for Wiley; research on personal and managerial productivity in the construction industry.

SIDELIGHTS: Brahtz's current research focuses on the impact of modern technology in areas of socioeconomic activity on the American scene. He writes: "When considering the pressures and constraints of the world economic environment, we recognize an increasing trend toward large-scale operations and greater complexity in the construction product. To improve productivity and maintain acceptable performance standards, today's construction practitioner must broaden his concept of innovation and seek to achieve excellence through knowledgeable utilization of the resources. Therefore our focus is on skills and disciplines that support productivity, quality, and optimization in all aspects of the total facility acquisition process and at all levels of the management hierarchy."

*   *   *

BRAIN, Robert 1933-

PERSONAL: Born in 1933, in Tasmania, Australia. *Education:* University of Tasmania, B.A. (honors), 1956; University of London, Ph.D., 1964. *Home:* 11 Convento Batignano, Provincia de Grosseto 58041, Italy. *Agent:* Curtis Brown Ltd., 60 East 56th St., New York, N.Y. 10022.

CAREER: University of London, University College, London, England, lecturer in anthropology, 1965-69; free-lance writer and translator, 1970—. Visiting lecturer in anthropology at University of Urbino, Italy, 1975.

WRITINGS: (With Adam Pollock) *Bangwa Funerary Sculpture,* Duckworth, 1971; *Bangwa Kinship and Marriage,* Cambridge University Press, 1972; *Into the Primitive Environment: Survival on the Edge of Our Civilization,* Prentice-Hall, 1972; (with Tambi Eyongetah) *A History of*

the Cameroon, Longman, 1974; *Friends and Lovers* (nonfiction), Basic Books, 1976; *The Last Primitive Peoples,* Crown, 1976; *Kolonialagent,* Harper, 1977; *Art and Society in Africa,* Longman, 1978.

Translator: Marcel Mauss, *A General Theory of Magic,* Routledge & Kegan Paul, 1972; (with Luisa Saviori) Edmund Leach, editor, *Claude Levi-Strauss: Strutturalismo del mito e del totemismo* (title means "Structuralism of Myth and Totemism"), Newton Compton Editori, 1975; Maurice Godelier, *Perspectives in Marxist Anthropology,* Cambridge University Press, 1977.

WORK IN PROGRESS: Black and White: A Comparative Study of Aboriginal and European Australians; The Clitoris, a novel; *Ritual in Western Society.*

SIDELIGHTS: Brain commented briefly: "I am specifically interested in transferring anthropological interest in primitive society to modern western urban society."

*   *   *

BRANDI, John 1943-

PERSONAL: Born November 5, 1943, in Los Angeles, Calif.; married Gioia Tama, 1968; children: two. *Education:* California State College, B.F.A., 1965. *Home address:* Box 356, Guadalupita, N.M. 87722.

CAREER: Writer and artist. Served as a Peace Corps volunteer in South America, 1965-68. *Awards, honors:* Portland *State Review* prize for prose, 1971.

WRITINGS—Poetry: Poem Afternoon in a Square of Guadalajara, Maya Press, 1970; *Emptylots: Poems of Venice and LA,* Nail Press, 1971; *Field Notes from Alaska,* Nail Press, 1971; *Firebook,* Smoky the Bear Press, 1974; *In a December Storm,* Tribal Press, 1975; *Looking for Minerals,* Cherry Valley Editions, 1975; *Poems from Four Corners,* Great Raven Press, 1977.

Short Stories: *Desde Alla,* Tree Books, 1971; *One Week of Mornings at Dry Creek,* Christopher's Press, 1971; *Y aun Hay Mas, Dreams and Explorations: New and Old Mexico,* Christopher's Press, 1972; *Narrowgauge to Riobamba,* Christopher's Press, 1973, *Memorandum from a Caribbean Isle,* Blackberry Editions, 1977.

Other: *Towards a Happy Soltice,* Christopher's Press, 1971; *San Francisco Lastday Homebound Hangover Highway Blues,* Nail Press, 1973; *A Partial Exploration of Palo Flechado Canyon,* Nail Press, 1973; *The Phoenix Gas Slam,* Nail Press, 1974.

SIDELIGHTS: Brandi is interested in working in prisons, drug rehabilitation centers, and old age homes.

*   *   *

BRANZBURG, Paul M(arshal) 1941-

PERSONAL: Born June 25, 1941, in New York, N.Y.; son of Louis (a mechanical engineer) and Mary (an insurance claims auditor; maiden name, Poholsky) Branzburg; married Marian Gayle Kuhn (a librarian), December 16, 1969. *Education:* Cornell University, A.B., 1963; Harvard University, J.D., 1966; Columbia University, M.S. (with honors), 1967. *Home:* 3816 Devon Rd., Royal Oak, Mich. 48073.

CAREER/WRITINGS: Harvard Law Record, Cambridge, Mass., president, 1965-66; *Louisville Courier-Journal,* Louisville, Ky., investigative reporter, 1967-71; *Detroit Free Press,* Detroit, Mich., investigative reporter, 1971-74. Notable assignments include a series on illegal drug use in Louisville, Ky., which led to the 1972 U.S. Supreme Court decision, *Branzburg* v. *Hayes;* and coverage of a Lousiville race riot, agricultural frauds, wasteful expenditures in refurbishing the Michigan Capitol building, and an expose of Michigan attorneys and policemen involved in an ambulance chasing racket. Lecturer at colleges and universities, including University of Southern Illinois, Dartmouth College, University of Michigan, Michigan State University, University of Illinois, and Wayne State University. Civil rights worker for Law Students Civil Rights Research Council, Tampa, Fla., and Monroe, La., 1964, and for the National Association for the Advancement of Colored People (NAACP) in Greenville and Greenwood, Miss., 1965. *Member:* Newspaper Guild of Detroit (vice-president, 1974), Sigma Delta Chi.

AWARDS, HONORS: American Political Science Association public affairs reporting award, 1968, for series on meat inspection, and 1970, for series on drug abuse; Independent Natural Gas Association of America-University of Missouri Business Journalism Awards certificate of outstanding merit, 1968, for agricultural fraud story; Indiana Associated Press Managing Editors Award, 1969, for story about an Indiana town fearing invasion by motorcycle "outlaws"; Silver Gavel Award from the American Bar Association, 1970, for examination of Louisville courts; Columbia University Journalism Alumni Award, 1973; has also been nominated for two Pulitzer Prizes.

SIDELIGHTS: In early 1969, Branzburg wrote a series on the illegal use of drugs for the *Louisville Courier-Journal.* The series, he told *CA,* "was based on almost three months spent with the whole spectrum of drug users—from the high school student who smokes marijuana to the professional criminal with a $150 a day heroin habit." In November, 1969, using the same sources he had developed in writing the drug series, Branzburg wrote a short feature story about two young men operating a makeshift laboratory to convert marijuana to hashish. "The men had agreed to let me visit their laboratory to watch them work," Branzburg said. "They had done so only after I had promised never to reveal their identities. I even showed one of them a copy of Kentucky Revised Statutes 421.100 which provided, in part, that 'No person shall be compelled to disclose . . . before any grand . . . jury . . . the source of any information procured or obtained by him, and published in a newspaper . . . by which he is engaged or employed.'"

A few days after the hash laboratory story was published, Branzburg was subpoenaed to appear before the Jefferson County grand jury. He refused to identify the hash manufacturers on the grounds of the First Amendment and the Kentucky statute. "I think the First Amendment is a newsman's privilege statute," Branzburg explained, "because freedom of the press does not mean only the freedom to publish the news, but the freedom to gather it. And investigative reporters must often gather information from people who will not talk without a promise that their names and certain other details will be kept confidential. Obviously, sources are more likely to help if they know the journalist has a legally recognized privilege to refuse to identify confidential sources." The judge refused to recognize Kentucky Revised Statute 421.100 and threatened to hold Branzburg for contempt of court if he refused to identify the hash manufacturers. The case was appealed to the Kentucky Court of Appeals.

Branzburg was subpoenaed by the Franklin County grand jury in January, 1971, to testify on a story he had written on illegal drug use in Frankfort, Ky. "In researching that story," Branzburg said, "I had spent several weeks in Frank-fort talking to about thirty illegal drug users. I had, of course, witnessed a number of drug offenses." Branzburg refused to enter the grand jury room because "merely to have entered would have chilled my relationship with my sources. Grand jury testimony is secret and none of the thirty people could know whether or not I had betrayed them. With a group that large, a few were likely to get arrested and they would naturally suspect that I had put the police on their trail."

The Kentucky Court of Appeals ruled against Branzburg in both cases, holding that Kentucky Revised Statute 421.100 did not apply since the people Branzburg interviewed were not the "source of information," but that Branzburg's own observations were the source of information. "This interpretation," Branzburg said, "has been widely ridiculed, from the U.S. Senate to the *Kentucky Law Journal.*"

Both cases went to the U.S. Supreme Court, and on June 29, 1972, the court issued its opinion in *Branzburg* v. *Hayes.* The Court ruled five-to-four that the First Amendment does not afford newsmen the privilege of either refusing to respond to grand jury subpoenas or of withholding confidential information from grand juries. Branzburg said: "It was the first time in American legal history that the high court had dealt with the competing claims of grand juries for information and of journalists for immunity from grand jury demands for confidential information. The decision has been generally denounced in legal periodicals throughout the nation."

"The loser, of course, is the public. To the extent that reporters now cannot ferret out certain stories, it is the public that remains ignorant. For example, had Woodward and Bernstein been subpoenaed to identify their confidential sources early in their Watergate coverage, those sources would probably have dried up, leaving the two reporters—and the nation—possibly unable to learn the full scope of the scandal.

"Policemen and prosecutors are also losers when sources dry up. Earl Caldwell of the *New York Times* was giving the nation the finest reporting available about the Black Panthers, but after a federal grand jury subpoenaed him, his coverage ceased. In my case, the stories about the drug culture came to an end. Before the Supreme Court decision, the police could read everything we knew—except for a few confidential details. After the Supreme Court decision, they could read nothing."

Branzburg left Kentucky in 1971. On September 1, 1972, two months after the Supreme Court ruling, he was sentenced to six months imprisonment for contempt of the Jefferson County court. No longer a resident of Kentucky, he refused to return voluntarily. Michigan Governor William G. Milliken refused Kentucky's request for extradition.

CA asked Branzburg his opinion of contemporary American journalism. He responded, "I have a strong love-hate relationship with journalism.

"I love the power of the press to bring about reform, when that power is used forcefully and responsibly. I also love the variety and excitement of reporting.

"But, I agree with H. L. Mencken that 'most of the evils that continue to beset American journalism . . . are not due to the rascality of owners nor even to the Kiwanian bombast of business managers, but simply and solely to the stupidity, cowardice and Philistinism of working newspapermen. The majority of them, in almost every American city, are still ignoramuses, and proud of it. . . . I know of no subject, in truth, save perhaps baseball, on which the average American newspaper, even in the larger cities, discourses with unfailing sense and understanding.'

"Reporters and editors today are undoubtedly better educated and trained than in Mencken's day. But American newspapers are still justly considered disreputable and ignorant, with a few dozen exceptions.

"Nevertheless, I love journalism."

AVOCATIONAL INTERESTS: Jogging, comparative religion, book collecting, hiking, art history.

BIOGRAPHICAL/CRITICAL SOURCES: New York Times, February 24, 1972, June 30, 1972, July 1, 1972, September 2, 1972, October 27, 1972; *Nation,* September 18, 1972; *Newsweek,* October 16, 1972; *Time,* October 16, 1972; *New York Times Magazine,* December 17, 1972; *Harvard Civil Rights–Civil Liberties Law Review,* January, 1973; *New Republic,* May 5, 1973; *Congressional Digest,* Volume 52, May, 1973; *Yale Law Journal,* May, 1973; *Journal of Criminal Law and Criminology,* June, 1973; *Harper's,* August, 1973; *Catholic University Law Review,* Winter, 1973; *Newsmen's Privilege: Hearings Before the Subcommittee on Constitutional Rights of the Committee on the Judiciary, United States Senate,* U.S. Government Printing Office, 1973; *Syracuse Law Review,* 1973; *Harvard Journal on Legislation,* February, 1974; *University of San Francisco Law Review,* spring, 1974; *Texas Law Review,* May, 1974; *American Bar Association Journal,* June, 1974; *Loyola Law Review,* 1974; *Hastings Law Journal,* January, 1975; *University of Pennsylvania Law Review,* November, 1975; *UCLA Law Review,* October, 1976.

*   *   *

BRAWLEY, Paul L(eroy)   1942-

PERSONAL: Born September 27, 1942, in Granite City, Ill.; son of Paul Virgil and Lucille Melba (Holm) Brawley. *Education:* Southern Illinois University, B.A., 1965; Simmons College, M.S., 1968; further graduate study at University of Oklahoma, 1969. *Home:* 55 West Chestnut St., Chicago, Ill. 60610. *Office:* American Library Association, 50 East Huron St., Chicago, Ill. 60611.

CAREER/WRITINGS: Boston Public Library, Boston, Mass., records librarian, 1965-66, audio-visual librarian, 1966-68; *The Booklist* (of Library Association), Chicago, Ill., editor of nonprint reviews, 1969-73, editor-in-chief, 1973—. Co-director of summer workshops in library science at Kent State University, Long Island University, Dalhousie University, Syracuse University, and University of Washington, Seattle. *Member:* American Library Association, Sigma Pi, Phi Eta Sigma.

*   *   *

BRAWNE, Michael   1925-

PERSONAL: Born May 5, 1925; married; children: three. *Education:* Attended University of Edinburgh, 1942-43, and Architectural Association School of Architecture, 1948-53; Massachusetts Institute of Technology, A.A., 1953, M.Arch., 1954; Cambridge University, M.A., 1977. *Office:* Michael Brawne & Associates, 42 Earlham St., London WC2H 9LA, England.

CAREER: Soullee Steel Co., San Francisco, Calif., architectural designer, 1954-56; Architects' Co-Partnership, London, England, architect, 1956-59; architect, British Transport Commission, 1959-61, and Denys Lasdun & Partners, 1961-64; currently partner, Michael Brawne & Associates, London, England. Member of teaching staff, Depart-

ment of Architecture, Cambridge University, 1963—; British Council lecturer in India, 1968; lecturer at universities in Germany, England, Scotland, and the United States, including University of Illinois and Boston Architectural Center. Has designed several dozen exhibitions, including work for Tate Gallery and Royal Academy; member of International Colloquium on the Technical Equipment of Central Libraries, 1974; consultant to Arts Council of Great Britain, British Council, and UNESCO. *Member:* Royal Institute of British Architects (fellow). *Awards, honors:* Smith-Mundt fellow at Massachusetts Institute of Technology, 1953.

WRITINGS: The New Museum: Architecture and Display, Architectural Press, 1965, Praeger, 1966; (editor) *University Planning and Design: A Symposium,* Lund Humphries, 1967; *Libraries: Architecture and Equipment,* Praeger, 1970. Contributor to *A Dictionary of Modern Thought.* Contributor of more than twenty-five articles and reviews to architecture journals.

WORK IN PROGRESS: Exhibition Design, for Verlag Gerd Hatje; *Architectural Issues: A Study of the Relation of the Philosophy of Karl Popper to Architecture,* for Lund Humphries.

SIDELIGHTS: Brawne's books have been published in German, Italian, and Spanish.

*   *   *

BRAYMAN, Harold   1900-

PERSONAL: Born March 10, 1900, in Middleburgh, N.Y.; son of Channing and Minnie (Feeck) Brayman; married Martha Witherspoon Wood, January 25, 1930; children: Harold Halliday, Walter Witherspoon. *Education:* Cornell University, A.B., 1920. *Residence:* Greenville, Wilmington, Del. 19807. *Mailing address:* Rooms 3 and 4, Suite 1250, Wilmington Trust Bldg., Wilmington, Del. 19801.

CAREER: High school teacher in Fort Lee, N.J., 1920-22; began newspaper career as reporter for the *Evening Journal,* Albany, N.Y., 1922-24, and then became Albany correspondent for *New York Evening Post,* New York, N.Y., 1924-28; Washington correspondent for *New York Evening Post,* 1928-33, *Philadelphia Evening Ledger,* 1933-40, and *Houston Chronicle,* 1940-42; also syndicated columnist, "The Daily Mirror of Washington," 1937-40, and "Washington Preview," 1940-42, and correspondent on the presidential campaign trains of Alfred E. Smith, 1928, Franklin D. Roosevelt, 1932, Alfred M. Landon, 1936, and Wendell L. Willkie, 1940; joined E. I. duPont de Nemours & Co., Wilmington, Del., as assistant director of public relations, 1942-44, director of public relations, 1944-65. First corporate executive in residence at American University, Washington, D.C., 1967-68. Director of Continental American Life Corp. Member of board of visitors, School of Public Communication, Boston University, 1951-72; chairman of advisory council, Graduate School of Business, Cornell University, 1960-65, and of Cornell Council, 1961-63, and longtime member of both councils. Trustee of Foundation for Public Relations Research and Education, 1956-62; trustee of Gettysburg College and Wilmington Medical Center.

MEMBER: National Press Club (president, 1938), Gridiron Club (president, 1941), and Overseas Writers (all Washington, D.C.); Wilmington Club (board member, 1952-64), Du Pont Country Club, and Rotary Club (all Wilmington); University Club (New York). *Awards, honors:* Named Public Relations Professional of 1963 by *Public Relations News;* citation of Public Relations Society of America, 1963, for distinguished service in the advancement of public relations;

LL.D. from Gettysburg College, 1965; Golden Plate Award of American Academy of Achievement, 1965.

WRITINGS: Corporate Management in a World of Politics, McGraw, 1967; (with A.O.H. Grier) *A History of the Lincoln Club of Delaware,* Lincoln Club of Delaware, 1970; *The President Speaks . . . off the Record,* edited by Steve Hegaard, Dow Jones, 1976. Also author of *Developing a Philosophy for Business Action,* 1969. Contributor to magazines and newspapers. Editor, *Public Relations Journal* (publication of Public Relations Society of America), 1956.

BIOGRAPHICAL/CRITICAL SOURCES: L.L.L. Golden, *Only by Public Consent,* Hawthorn, 1968.

* * *

BRECHT, Arnold 1884-1977

1884—September 11, 1977; German-born American educator, government official in pre-Hitler Germany, and author. As representative from Prussia, Brecht defied Hitler, the newly designated chancellor, in the last free speech given in Germany's parliament. A short time later he was dismissed from his post and came to the United States. Brecht joined the faculty of the University in Exile, which became the core of the graduate school of the New School for Social Research. He wrote five books and an autobiography. Brecht died while vacationing in Eutin, West Germany. Obituaries: *New York Times,* September 15, 1977; *Time,* September 26, 1977; *AB Bookman's Weekly,* January 30, 1978.

* * *

BRENNER, Marie 1949-

PERSONAL: Born December 15, 1949, in San Antonio, Tex.; daughter of Milton Conrad (a business executive) and Thelma (a psychiatrist; maiden name, Long) Brenner. *Education:* Attended University of Pennsylvania, 1967-69; University of Texas, B.F.A., 1970; New York University, M.A., 1971. *Religion:* Jewish. *Residence:* New York, N.Y. *Agent:* Owen Laster, William Morris Agency, 1350 Avenue of the Americas, New York, N.Y. 10019.

CAREER: Paramount Pictures, New York City, story editor, 1973-75; *New York* Magazine, New York City, contributing editor, 1975-76; writer.

WRITINGS: Tell Me Everything, Dutton, 1976; *Going Hollywood,* Delacorte, 1977. Contributor of articles to *New York Times* Magazine, *Film Critic, New York* Magazine, *New West, Redbook, Cosmopolitan, Village Voice,* and *Los Angeles* Magazine. Contributing editor, *Texas Monthly,* 1976—.

WORK IN PROGRESS: A new novel; "Acting Like Children," a two-act play, with Carla Heffner.

* * *

BRENT, Stuart

PERSONAL: Surname was originally Brodsky; born in Chicago, Ill.

CAREER: Former professor of philosophy; lecturer; critic; TV and radio reviewer, and host of "Books and Brent," 1959-60, a series of book reviews presented on WBKB television and WLS radio of the American Broadcasting Co. (ABC), Chicago, Ill.; author of children's books; bookseller beginning 1946.

WRITINGS: The Seven Stairs (autobiographical), Houghton, 1962; *The Strange Disappearance of Mr. Toast* (illustrated by Leslie Goldstein), Viking, 1964; *Mr. Toast and the*

Woolly Mammoth (illustrated by Lilian Obligado), Viking, 1966; *Mr. Toast and the Secret of Gold Hill* (illustrated by George Porter), Lippincott, 1970.

SIDELIGHTS: Stuart Brent's love for good books is what made him want to be a bookseller. In 1946, with a G.I. loan, Brent bought three hundred dollars worth of books, borrowed some more, and opened a small store fifteen feet long and nine feet wide. The original store, called "The Seven Stairs," also sold records, with the idea being, according to Brent, that anyone with literary taste would have the equivalent taste in music. With the help of newspaper columnists, the word was spread about Brent's bookstore. In 1968, the store, located at 670 Michigan Ave. in Chicago, Ill., was remodeled into what Brent described as an American version of Blackwell's in Oxford, England.

BIOGRAPHICAL/CRITICAL SOURCES: Stuart Brent, *The Seven Stairs,* Houghton, 1962; *Publishers Weekly,* September 30, 1968, March 12, 1973, March 11, 1974.*

* * *

BRESLIN, James 1930-
(Jimmy Breslin)

PERSONAL: Born October 17, 1930, in Jamaica, N.Y.; son of James Earl and Frances (a high school teacher and social worker; maiden name, Curtin) Breslin; married Rosemary Dattolico, December 26, 1954; children: James and Kevin (twins), Rosemary, Patrick, Kelly. *Education:* Attended Long Island University, 1948-50. *Residence:* Queens, New York. *Agent:* Sterling Lord, 660 Madison Ave., New York, N.Y. 10021.

CAREER: Began as copyboy with the *Long Island Press,* 1948; sportswriter for several newspapers, including the *New York Journal-American,* all in New York City, 1950-63; *New York Herald Tribune* (later *New York World Journal Tribune*), New York City, began as sportswriter, became columnist, 1963-67; *New York Post,* New York City, columnist, 1968-69; author and free-lance journalist in New York City, 1969—; *New York Daily News,* New York City, columnist, 1976—. Contributing editor and initiating writer, *New York* magazine, 1968-71, *New Times* magazine, 1973; commentator, WABC-TV, 1968-69, WNBC-TV, 1973; Democratic primary candidate for president of New York City council, 1969; delegate to Democratic National Convention, 1972; actor in television programs and commercials. *Member:* American Federation of Television and Radio Artist, Screen Actors Guild, New York Boxing Writers Association. *Awards, honors:* Award for general reporting from Sigma Delta Chi and Meyer Barger Award from Columbia University, both 1964, both for article on death of President Kennedy; New York Reporters Association Award, 1964.

*WRITINGS—*All under name Jimmy Breslin: *Sunny Jim: The Life of America's Most Beloved Horseman, James Fitzsimmons* (nonfiction), Doubleday, 1962; *Can't Anybody Here Play This Game?: The Improbable Saga of the New York Mets, First Year* (nonfiction), Viking, 1963; *The World of Jimmy Breslin* (collected articles), annotated by James G. G. Bellows and Richard C. Wald, Viking, 1967; (with Norman Mailer, Peter Maas, Gloria Steinem, and others) *Running Against the Machine: The Mailer-Breslin Campaign* (collected speeches, policy statements, interviews, etc.), edited by Peter Manso, Doubleday, 1969; *The Gang That Couldn't Shoot Straight* (novel), Viking, 1969; *World Without End, Amen* (novel; Book-of-the-Month Club alternate selection), Viking, 1973; *How the Good Guys Finally Won: Notes from an Impeachment Summer* (nonfiction), Viking, 1975.

Contributor to numerous newspapers and to magazines, including *Penthouse, Sports Illustrated, Saturday Evening Post, Time,* and *New York.*

SIDELIGHTS: When Jimmy Breslin made the jump from sportswriter on the *New York Tribune* to featured columnist, the New York literary circle was startled. He had been accused of being a drunk, a bully, a clown. It was said he invented quotes; his politics were extreme right-wing. Yet anyone who worked with him disagreed, and Tom Wolfe was later to credit him with being one of the first of the new journalists.

No one can deny that Breslin is colorful. He sued the *New York Times* and a reporter for one million dollars in a libel suit in 1970 and he was a co-defendant in a plagiarism and literary piracy suit in 1975. He placed a huge sign on the front lawn of his Long Island home which listed all the neighbors he hated and wasn't speaking to. "When the list included the whole block" remembers Breslin, "I moved away amidst cheers and lawsuits." Breslin quit his column at the *New York Post* in 1969 by placing an advertisement to the *Post*'s publisher on the front page of the *New York Times*. It read: "ROBERT J. ALLEN: You are on your own. I am giving up my newspaper column. Jimmy Breslin." Rumor has it that he was followed by a saloon keeper when he went to pick up the five-hundred-dollar Meyer Barger award from Columbia University, because the saloon keeper wanted to collect a two hundred and forty-five dollar bar bill.

In 1969, Breslin ran for president of the New York City council on the ticket with Norman Mailer, who was running for mayor. They urged that New York City become the 51st state; that Coney Island become the Las Vegas of the East. They campaigned for Sweet Sundays—Sundays on which cars would be outlawed in the city. They wanted to build a monorail around Manhattan, create autonomous neighborhoods, and hold street olympics. They lost.

While Breslin was still a newspaper columnist, Josh Greenfeld wrote: "Among the recent practitioners of daily journalism in New York, Breslin is a stickout. For he is that rarity—'real' or unreal, intelligent or stupid—someone in the word business who actually knows how to put one word after another so it all comes out sounding right. In fact, all Breslin can do is write, which sort of makes him the Eddie Stanky of letters."

Jack Newfield admitted he had heard all the stereotypes about Breslin. "But each day, week after week, it was Breslin whose copy most truthfully communicated the human essence of the day's events. Time after time I would watch Breslin, with his ferocious energy, put in the longest day, throw away first drafts anyone else would be proud to publish, labor in his motel room past midnight, and finally create the next day's most realistic and perceptive piece of work."

In his book *The New Journalism,* Tom Wolfe claims the novel has been overtaken as the leading literary genre in the United States by a new style of journalism, and high among the early experimenters in this new trade, he places Jimmy Breslin. But Breslin looks back on his years as a journalist without any such fond or proud memories. "Life must pass me by. You can't dwell on the past. I can't remember the joint [the *Tribune*] now. I got too many mouths to feed. If it was that exciting for Wolfe, then God bless him. . . . I never had an easy day in the newspaper business. It's murder. You get short-sighted editors who want everybody to write the same way, and you wind up having to scream and abuse people and search for someone who can think and read. Most years the Pulitzer should go to readers. . . . You work

four, five hours a day, say, and the paper goes onto the floor of the subway anyway. You wind up being the best known person in the saloon and so what?"

Breslin quite the *Post* in 1969 to become a novelist and a contributing editor at *New York* magazine. Clay Felker, his editor on the *Tribune* and again at *New York,* watched Breslin's development from his early years. He said: "Jimmy works harder than anyone else. For day in day out performance, I think he is the best journalist in the country. Jimmy's judgments about things are sound, they stand up. He's got more original story ideas than most editors. He's got an instinct for reality. He's tuned into what's actually going on. He still lives in Queens. He knows what ordinary people are feeling. He knows this city. . . . He may have begun as a conservative Queens Catholic. But he has been changed, by going to Vietnam, seeing the ghettos, going to the campuses, becoming a friend of Bobby Kennedy's. If you're in the middle of that many big stories, you grow."

Upon hearing the news that Breslin was working on his first novel, a newsman was said to have commented: "So what? He's been writing fiction for years." More encouraging were others. At that time, Josh Greenfeld said: "Lack of refinement, calculated boorishness, tough stances are, of course, the traditional posturing of a young and thin-skinned artistic sensitivity. The work of a maturer Breslin—he is now only 37—is something to look forward to, I think, in a literary as well as journalistic sense. He may yet develop an artistic courage commensurate to his uncommonly huge talent. He may yet decide to write completely for the expression of a probing and articulate self rather than for the entertainment of some vague tired reader, clutching a subway strap."

When his first novel, *The Gang that Couldn't Shoot Straight,* did appear, it received some bad reviews, with the *New York Times* and *Newsweek* among those panning the book. Breslin admitted: "It's a terrible feeling when they say something bad about my product. I get very, very jumpy. When they knock your product it's very upsetting. It's always done by people I don't know. I don't know what they can do." However, most criticism was favorable. The book became a best-seller and was made into a movie.

At the appearance of Breslin's next novel, Peter Straub said: "Jimmy Breslin, who used to write an aggressive, vivid column for a New York newspaper, recently made a very public decision to give up security for the sake of writing novels. His second effort, *World Without End, Amen,* demonstrates that he was not conning himself: when he is dealing with the tough New York world of cops, bartenders and thieves his writing is totally convincing, sharply focused on the sort of details and gestures which reveal in implication entire histories of uncomprehended fear and repression."

Breslin's latest book, *How the Good Guys Finally Won,* was hailed as one of the best books about the fall of the Nixon administration. Martin F. Nolan noted: "Breslin's prose style has changed. It isn't slam-bang sixties anymore. It is more subtle, but equally concise, slightly subdued and even alas, more literary. But we're all 10 years older and we can't buy the *New York Herald Tribune* anymore. What hasn't changed about Breslin is his instinct to be at the right place at the right time, his internal radar that guides him to the conclusion that good guys are better copy than bad guys. More sweeping, more ponderous and stuffier books will be written about the summer of 1974, but none will be zestier or funnier. None will convey a more vivid sense of the authenticity of the author's presence than *How the Good Guys Finally Won.*" This internal radar that guides him may be what continues to keep Breslin close to, if not actually in, the newspaper business. He'll still drop a manuscript at a moment's notice to cover a good story.

When Eugene Kennedy asked Breslin if he could be labeled an Irish Catholic writer, Breslin responded: "Yes, I would definitely lean to that background. But as far as Irish Catholics writing in this country goes, forget about it. We have a great heritage of using words and I'm puzzled why more Irish don't write. We've got that wonderful natural use of words and the Irish have been storytellers all through history but nobody writes anything much." In his writing Breslin counts more on this ethnic background than on any literary one. "I'm the first of the electronic generation. I don't read too much. The greatest article I ever read was 'The Brownsville Bum' by W. C. Heinz (about the late Brooklyn welterweight, Al 'Bunny' Davis). The next best writer I ever read was Tony Betts (former racing writer for the *Daily Mirror*).... I don't read the good guys because of my inherent larceny. If I liked them, I'd steal whole sentences."

As a novelist, Breslin hasn't slowed his newsman's pace. "I like to get started early in the morning, around seven if possible, and work through until about three. I want to improve on what I've written. In that book [*World Without End, Amen*] I stayed with what I believe to be interesting. I'm going to stay with these characters; I should never have gotten away from them. Writing is like building. You've gotta work, polish, scrub, hammer, and pound. That to me is very hard manual labor. The main game is writing. Writers who get away from it make a big mistake."

BIOGRAPHICAL/CRITICAL SOURCES: Book Week, June 18, 1967; *New York,* March 17, 1969; *Village Voice,* July 31, 1969; *Newsweek,* November 24, 1969; *New York Times,* November 28, 1969; *Vogue,* February 1, 1970; *Publisher's Weekly,* August 27, 1973; *Baltimore News-American,* September 2, 1973; *New Statesman,* April 26, 1974; *The Critic,* December, 1974.*

* * *

BRESLIN, Jimmy
See BRESLIN, James

* * *

BRETT, Dorothy 1883-1977

1883—August 27, 1977; Children's book illustrator and author. The last living member of novelist D. H. Lawrence's circle, Brett wrote about him in *Lawrence and Brett: A Friendship.* She died in Taos, N.M. Obituaries: *New York Times,* September, 29, 1977.

* * *

BRETT, Leo
See FANTHORPE, R(obert) Lionel

* * *

BRIDGMAN, Elizabeth 1921-

PERSONAL: Born April 9, 1921, in Charlottesville, Va.; daughter of Walter L. and Lucille (Collie) Pierce; married Luther H. Bridgman (an insurance executive), March 14, 1945; children: Torrey, Sara, Benjamin. *Education:* Graduated from Stephens College, 1941; further study at Art Students League of New York, 1942-43. *Residence:* Wings Point, Charlotte, Vt. 05445. *Agent:* William Reiss, Paul Reynolds, Inc., 12 East 41st St., New York, N.Y. 10017.

CAREER: Life, New York, N.Y., employed in "picture morgue," 1943-45; free-lance artist and illustrator, 1960—. Writer. Member of board of trustees of Stowe School, 1973-75.

WRITINGS: If I Were a Horse (self-illustrated children's book), Dodd, 1977.

Illustrator: Joan Kahn, *You Can't Catch Me,* Harper, 1976; Margaret K. McElderry, *All the Little Bunnies,* Atheneum, 1977.

WORK IN PROGRESS: Picture books, *Life and Times of Granny Bear, The Dog Next Door.*

AVOCATIONAL INTERESTS: Sailing, tennis.

* * *

BRIGGS, Ellis O(rmsbee) 1899-1976

PERSONAL: Born December 1, 1899, in Watertown, Mass.; son of James (an insurance broker) and Lucy (Hill) Briggs; married Lucy Barnard, May 26, 1928; children: Lucy, Everett. *Education:* Dartmouth College, A.B., 1921. *Home:* 3 Pleasant St., Hanover, N.H. 03755.

CAREER: Robert College, Constantinople, Turkey, instructor, 1921-23; free-lance writer, 1923-25; U.S. Department of State, Washington, D.C., foreign service officer on duty in Peru, Liberia, Cuba, Chile, and Washington, D.C., 1925-44, appointed ambassador to Dominican Republic, 1944, minister-counselor to the American Embassy in Chungking, China, 1945; Office of American Republic Affairs, Washington, D.C., director, 1945-47; U.S. Department of State, ambassador to Uraguay, 1947-49, Czechoslovakia, 1949-52, Korea, 1952-55, Peru, 1955-56, Brazil, 1956-59, Greece, 1959-61, and Spain, 1961-62, became Career Ambassador, 1960; writer. Visiting professor, University of Southern California, 1965. Trustee, American Farm School; chairman, Dartmouth Alumni College.

MEMBER: Metropolitan Club, Chevy Chase Club, University Club, Brook Club, Century Club, Dartmouth Club of Rio de Janeiro (president, 1956-59). *Awards, honors:* Presidential Medal of Freedom, 1955, for meritorious service as ambassador to Korea; LL.D. from Dartmouth College, 1955, and from Bowdoin College, 1959; Dartmouth Alumni Award, 1957.

WRITINGS: Shots Heard Round the World: An Ambassador's Hunting Adventures on Four Continents, Viking, 1957; *Farewell to Foggy Bottom: The Reflections of a Career Diplomat,* McKay, 1964; *Anatomy of Diplomacy: The Origin and Execution of American Foreign Policy,* McKay, 1968. Contributor of articles on diplomacy and foreign affairs to *Reader's Digest, Saturday Evening Post, Show, Esquire,* and other periodicals.

SIDELIGHTS: In his book, *Farewell to Foggy Bottom,* Ellis Briggs criticizes both the habitual overstaffing of foreign embassy offices and the custom of frequent transfer. However interesting a regular change of country makes a personal career, he argued that to be effective one must at least be given time to adjust to the new situation.

Brigg's work in Korea with General Mark W. Clark and secret negotiations with the opposing Syngman Rhee government prepared the way to armistice. A truce was signed July 27, 1953, by the United Nations and the Communists.

OBITUARIES: New York Times, February 23, 1976; *Washington Post,* February 23, 1976; *AB Bookman's Weekly,* April 12, 1976; *Current Biography,* April, 1976.*

(Died February 21, 1976, in Gainesville, Fla.)

BRIGGS, Fred 1932-

PERSONAL: Born May 31, 1932, in Chicago, Ill.; son of Finney and Leona (Fay) Briggs; married Dorothy Wagner, May 20, 1961; children: Lowell. *Education:* Attended University of Louisville, 1954-58. *Religion:* Methodist. *Home:* Eppinger Strasse 11, Berlin 33, West Germany. *Office:* NBC News, Kurfuerstendamm 26-A, Berlin 15, West Germany.

CAREER/WRITINGS: WSB-TV, Atlanta, Ga., correspondent, 1960-66; National Broadcasting Co. (NBC) News, New York City, correspondent from Cleveland, Ohio, 1966-70, Chicago, Ill., 1970-74, San Francisco, Calif., 1974-75, Berlin, West Germany, 1975—. Notable assignments include coverage of black lung disease, 1969, the United Mine Workers Union, 1969-70, the Yablonski murders, 1970, the energy crisis, 1972, Wounded Knee occupation, 1973, a profile of Federico Fellini, 1975, and the crisis in Uganda, 1977. *Military service:* U.S. Army, 1950-52. *Awards, honors:* Radio-TV News Directors Association Award and Ohio State Award, both 1965, for "Foot in a New Door" documentary; Emmy Award, 1969, for series on black lung disease.

*   *   *

BRIGGS, Raymond Redvers 1934-

PERSONAL: Born January 18, 1934, in London, England; married Jean Taprell Clark (a painter), 1963. *Education:* Attended Wimbledon School of Art and Slade School of Fine Art. *Residence:* Sussex, England.

CAREER: Illustrator and author of books for children, 1957—. Part-time faculty member at Brighton College of Art, 1961—. *Military service:* British Army. *Member:* Society of Industrial Artists, Dairy Farmer's Association. *Awards, honors:* Kate Greenaway Medal, runner-up, 1964, for *Fee Fi Fo Fum,* and winner, 1966, for *Mother Goose Treasury.*

WRITINGS—All self-illustrated: *Midnight Adventure,* Hamish Hamilton, 1961; *The Strange House,* Hamish Hamilton, 1961; *Ring-a-Ring o' Roses,* Coward, 1962; *Sledges to the Rescue,* Hamish Hamilton, 1963; (editor) *The White Land,* Coward, 1963; (editor) *Fee Fi Fo Fum,* Coward, 1964; (editor) *The Mother Goose Treasury,* Coward, 1966; *Jim and the Beanstalk,* Coward, 1970; *Father Christmas,* Coward, 1973; *Father Christmas Goes on Holiday,* Coward, 1975.

Illustrator: (With others) Julian Sorell Huxley, *Wonderful World of Life,* Doubleday, 1958; Ruth Manning-Sanders, *Peter and the Piskies,* Oxford University Press, 1958, Roy, 1966; Alfred Leo Duggan, *Look at Castles,* Hamish Hamilton, 1960, published as *The Castle Book,* Pantheon, 1961; A. L. Duggan, *Arches and Spires,* Hamish Hamilton, 1961, Pantheon, 1962; Jacynth Hope-Simpson, editor, *Hamish Hamilton Book of Myths and Legends,* Hamish Hamilton, 1964; William Mayne, *Whistling Rufus,* Hamish Hamilton, 1964, Dutton, 1965; Manning-Sanders, editor, *Hamish Hamilton Book of Magical Beasts,* Hamish Hamilton, 1965, published as *A Book of Magical Beasts,* Thomas Nelson, 1970.

James Aldridge, *The Flying 19,* Hamish Hamilton, 1966; Bruce Carter, *Jimmy Murphy and the White Duesenberg,* Coward, 1968; *Carter Nuvolari and the Alpha Romeo,* Coward, 1968; Nicholas Fisk, *Lindbergh: The Lone Flier,* Coward, 1968; Fisk, *Richtofen: The Red Baron,* Coward, 1968; Mayne, editor, *The Hamish Hamilton Book of*

Giants, Hamish Hamilton, 1968, published as *William Mayne's Book of Giants,* Dutton, 1969; Michael Brown, *Shackelton's Epic Voyage,* Coward, 1969; Elfrida Vipont Foulds, *The Elephant and the Bad Baby,* Coward, 1969; Showell Styles, *First up Everest,* Coward, 1969; James Reeves, *Christmas Book,* Dutton, 1970; Ian Serraillier, *The Tale of Three Landlubbers,* Hamish Hamilton, 1970, Coward, 1971; Virginia Haviland, editor, *The Fairy Tale Treasury,* Coward, 1972; Manning-Sanders, editor, *Festivals,* Heinemann, 1972, Dutton, 1973. Also illustrator of a book of Cornish fairy stories, Oxford University Press, 1957.

SIDELIGHTS: Briggs originally wanted to be a cartoonist, studied instead to be a painter, and became an illustrator. The eight hundred ninety-seven illustrations that he did for *The Mother Goose Treasury* won the Kate Greenaway Medal in 1966. These drawings established Briggs' reputation as one of the finest modern illustrators.

Briggs created a sequel to *Jack and the Beanstalk. Jim and the Beanstalk* portrays a giant too old to digest children, and in need of glasses, new teeth, and a toupee. *Commonweal* called it "a hilarious, modern sequel to the famous tale . . . [with] wonderful pictures," while the *New York Times Book Review* described it as a "gigantic delight."

AVOCATIONAL INTERESTS: Reading, gardening, growing fruit, and modern jazz.

BIOGRAPHICAL/CRITICAL SOURCES: Lee Bennett Hopkins, *Books Are by People,* Citation, 1969; *Times Literary Supplement,* October 16, 1969; *New York Times Book Review,* November 8, 1970; *Commonweal,* November 20, 1970.*

*   *   *

BRIGGS, Vernon M(ason), Jr. 1937-

PERSONAL: Born June 29, 1937, in Washington, D.C.; son of Vernon Mason (a builder) and Ann Marie (Cox) Briggs; married Martijna Aarts, December 29, 1971; children: Vernon Mason III, Kees Kanen. *Education:* University of Maryland, B.S., 1959; Michigan State University, M.A., 1960, Ph.D., 1965. *Politics:* Democrat. *Religion:* Roman Catholic. *Home:* 8602 Green Valley Dr., Austin, Tex. 78759. *Office:* Department of Economics, University of Texas, Austin, Tex. 78712.

CAREER: University of Texas, Austin, assistant professor, 1964-68, associate professor, 1968-73, professor of economics, 1973—. Research director of U.S. Department of Health, Education & Welfare committee on administration of training programs, 1967-68; member of National Council on Employment Policy, 1977—. *Member:* American Economic Association, Industrial Relations Research Association, Phi Sigma Kappa, Omicron Delta Kappa.

WRITINGS: (With F. Ray Marshall) *The Negro and Apprenticeship,* Johns Hopkins Press, 1967; *Chicanos and Rural Poverty,* Johns Hopkins Press, 1973; (with Walt Fogel and Fred Schmidt) *The Chicano Worker,* University of Texas Press, 1977; (with John Adams, Brian Rungeling, and Lewis Smith) *Employment, Income, and Welfare in the Rural South,* Praeger, 1977. Contributor to economic, labor and industrial relations, and social science journals.

WORK IN PROGRESS: Research on youth employment issues and the input of illegal aliens on domestic labor markets.

*   *   *

BRIGHT, Robert 1902-

PERSONAL: Born August 5, 1902, in Sandwich, Mass.;

son of Edward and Blanche (Denio) Bright; married Katherine Eastman Bailey; children: two. *Education:* Princeton University, B.A., 1923. *Residence:* La Jolla, Calif.

CAREER: Author and illustrator. Has also worked as a reporter and editor for newspapers, including *Baltimore Sun* and *Paris Time,* and in advertising.

WRITINGS—All published by Doubleday, except as indicated: *The Travels of Ching* (self-illustrated), W. R. Scott, 1943; *The Life and Death of Little Jo,* 1944; *The Intruders,* 1946; *The Olivers: The Story of an Artist and His Family,* 1947; *Me and the Bears* (self-illustrated), 1951; *Richard Brown and the Dragon* (self-illustrated), 1952; (with Dorothy Brett) *Hurrah for Freddie!,* 1953; *Miss Pattie* (self-illustrated), 1954; *I Like Red* (self-illustrated), 1955; *The Spirit of the Chase* (illustrated by Mircea Vasiliu), Scribner, 1956; *The Friendly Bear* (self-illustrated), 1957, reprinted, 1971; *My Red Umbrella* (self-illustrated), Morrow, 1959; *My Hopping Bunny* (self-illustrated), 1960; *Which Is Willy?* (self-illustrated), 1962; *Gregory: The Noisiest and Strongest Boy in Grangers Grove* (self-illustrated), 1969.

"Georgie" series; all self-illustrated; all published by Doubleday: *Georgie,* 1944; *Georgie to the Rescue,* 1956; *Georgie's Halloween,* 1958; *Georgie and the Robbers,* 1963; *Georgie and the Magician,* 1966; *Georgie and the Noisy Ghost,* 1971; *Georgie Goes West,* 1973; *Georgie's Christmas Carol,* 1975.

SIDELIGHTS: Bright, who spent his childhood in Goettingen, Germany, lived in New Mexico for fifteen years. His affection for the surrounding Spanish community in New Mexico is said to have inspired him to write his first novel, *The Life and Death of Little Jo.*

Two of Bright's books, *Georgie* and *Georgie to the Rescue,* were made into motion pictures. Composer J. Donald Robb made *The Life and Death of Little Joe* into an opera which premiered in Albuquerque, N.M.*

* * *

BRINDZE, Ruth 1903-

PERSONAL: Born in 1903, in New York, N.Y.; married Albert W. Fribourg (a lawyer). *Education:* Graduated from Columbia University. *Home:* Mt. Vernon, N.Y.

CAREER: Author. Worked on various newspaper staffs. *Awards, honors: New York Herald Tribune* Children's Book Festival Prize, 1945, for *The Gulf Stream;* Honorable mention in Children's Science Book category, from New York Academy of Sciences, 1975, for *Look How Many People Wear Glasses: The Romance of Lenses.*

WRITINGS: How to Spend Money: Everybody's Practical Guide to Buying, Vanguard, 1935, published as *How to Spend Money: How to Get Your Money's Worth,* Garden City Publishing, 1938; *Not to Be Broadcast: The Truth about the Radio,* Vanguard, 1937, reprinted, Da Capo Press, 1974; *Johnny Get Your Money's Worth* (illustrated by Emery I. Gondor), Vanguard, 1938; *Seamanship below Deck,* Harcourt, 1939; *Daily Bread and Other Foods* (illustrated by Harry Daugherty), Row, Peterson, 1941; *Stretching Your Dollar in Wartime,* Vanguard, 1942; *You Can Help Your Country Win* (illustrated by Gondor), Vanguard, 1943; *The Gulf Stream* (illustrated by Helene Carter; Junior Literary Guild selection), Vanguard, 1945; *Boating Is Fun* (illustrated by Kurt Wiese), Dodd, 1949; *The Story of Our Calendar* (illustrated by Carter), Vanguard, 1949.

The Story of the Totem Pole (illustrated by Yeffe Kimball), Vanguard, 1951; *The Story of Gold* (illustrated by Robert Bruce), Vanguard, 1955; *The Experts' Book of Boating* (illustrated by Fred Wellbrock), Prentice-Hall, 1959; *All about Undersea Exploration,* Random House, 1960; *The Story of the Trade Winds* (illustrated by Hilda Simon), Vanguard, 1960; *All about Sailing the Seven Seas,* Random House, 1962; *All about Courts and the Law* (illustrated by Leonard Slonevsky), Random House, 1964; *The Rise and Fall of the Seas: The Story of the Tides* (illustrated by Felix Cooper), Harcourt, 1964; *Investing Money: The Facts about Stocks and Bonds,* Harcourt, 1968; *The Sea: The Story of the Rich Underwater World,* Harcourt, 1971; *Charting the Oceans,* Vanguard, 1973; *Hurricanes: Monster Storms from Sea,* Atheneum, 1973; *Look How Many People Wear Glasses: The Romance of Lenses,* Atheneum, 1975.

AVOCATIONAL INTERESTS: Reading, writing, cooking, gardening, and sailing.

* * *

BRINKMAN, Grover 1903-

PERSONAL: Born February 27, 1903, in Illinois; son of John (a farmer) and Sarah Jane (Friend) Brinkman; married Leona May Stricker, July 21, 1925; children: Gene H., Shirley Jane Brinkman McDannold. *Education:* Attended Belleville College of Business. *Religion:* Methodist. *Home and office:* 101 East High St., Okawville, Ill. 62271.

CAREER: Okawville Times, Okawville, Ill., editor and publisher, 1925-47; free-lance writer and photographer, 1947—. *Member:* Lions Club.

WRITINGS: Night of the Blood Moon, Independence Press (Independence, Mo.), 1976. Also editor of *This Is Washington County,* 1968, and *Grover Brinkman's Southern Illinois,* 1976. Also author of a four-part detective novel series published in Scandinavia.

Contributor to more than two hundred magazines and newspapers, including *Life.* Editor of *Back Home in Illionis,* a regional magazine.

WORK IN PROGRESS: Research for a historical novel centered around the Kaskaskia Bell.

SIDELIGHTS: Brinkman comments: "I work with my wife as a writing-photographic team; I sold my first piece of fiction to *Grit* at the age of sixteen; since then have been selling on the regional, national, and international level. I have more than a hundred thousand photographic negatives on file, the work of forty years behind the camera. In other words, I'm a working freelance and we make a living at it. I write fiction 'just for fun.'"

* * *

BRITTAIN, John A(shleigh) 1923-

PERSONAL: Born September 10, 1923, in Chicago, Ill.; son of Ashleigh Woodruff and Louise (Hulbert) Brittain; married Geraldine Marcus (a social worker), April 23, 1949; children: Mark, Erica. *Education:* Knox College, A.B., 1944; attended London School of Economics and Political Science, 1954; University of California, Berkeley, Ph.D., 1958. *Home:* 7704 Marbury Rd., Bethesda, Md. 20034. *Office:* Economic Studies Program, Brookings Institution, 1775 Massachusetts Ave. N.W., Washington, D.C. 20036.

CAREER: National Defense Research Committee, Washington, D.C. and Cumberland, Md., research associate in mathematics, 1943-46; U.S. Naval Ordnance Research, Pasadena, Calif., mathematician, 1946; Mexico City College, Mexico City, Mexico, professor of economics, 1950-

51; University of Leeds, Leeds, England, lecturer in economics, 1955-56; Cornell University, Ithaca, N.Y., assistant professor of statistics, 1956-59; Vanderbilt University, Nashville, Tenn., assistant professor, 1959-61, associate professor of economics, 1961-64; Brookings Institution, Washington, D.C., senior fellow in economics, 1964—. Has testified before U.S. Senate and House of Representatives committees.

WRITINGS: Corporate Dividend Policy, Brookings Institution, 1966; *The Payroll Tax for Social Security,* Brookings Institution, 1972; *The Inheritance of Economic Status,* Brookings Institution, 1977; *Inheritance and the Inequality of Material Wealth,* Brookings Institution, 1978. Contributor of articles and reviews to economic, law, and statistics journals.

WORK IN PROGRESS: The Role of Private Pensions in Maintaining the Economic Status of the Aged.

SIDELIGHTS: Brittain told *CA:* "Irresponsible journalists and others have exaggerated the problems of the Social Security system. Its financial backing is sound, and no one need fear for his or her pension. However, I would prefer to see some of the increased financing drawn from several revenues rather than from taxes or wages and salaries alone."

* * *

BRITTER, Eric V(alentine) B(lakeney)   1906-1977

February 14, 1906—September 2, 1977; Indian-born journalist. Britter was a foreign correspondent for the *London Times* in several Asian countries, and for fourteen years, was its New York correspondent concentrating on the United Nations. He died in St. Georges, Grenada. Obituaries: *New York Times,* September 4, 1977.

* * *

BROADUS, Robert N(ewton)   1922-

PERSONAL: Born December 3, 1922, in Stanford, Ky.; son of Earl N. (a postal clerk) and Elizabeth Lambert (Carter) Broadus; married Mary Eleanor Hammond (a librarian), December 15, 1948; children: John Robert, Earl William. *Education:* David Lipscomb College, student, 1941-43; Pepperdine College (now University), B.A., 1945; University of Chicago, B.L.S., 1947; University of Southern California, Ph.D., 1952. *Politics:* Republican. *Religion:* Church of Christ. *Home address:* Sycamore Dr., Mount Bolus, Chapel Hill, N.C. 27514. *Office:* School of Library Science, University of North Carolina, Chapel Hill, N.C. 27514.

CAREER: Pepperdine College (now University), Los Angeles, Calif., librarian, 1947-53; David Lipscomb College, Nashville, Tenn., librarian, 1953-55; Northern Illinois State College (now University), De Kalb, associate professor of library science, 1955-56; Sperry Rand Corp., Chicago, Ill., library specialist, 1956-61; Northern Illinois University, associate professor, 1961-65, professor of library science, 1965-76; University of North Carolina, Chapel Hill, professor of library science, 1976—.

MEMBER: American Library Association, American Association of University Professors, Association of American Library Schools, Southeastern Library Association, North Carolina Library Association, Phi Kappa Phi.

WRITINGS: (Editor with Louis Glorfeld and Tom Kakonis) *The Short Story: Ideas and Backgrounds,* C. E. Merrill, 1967; *Selecting Materials for Libraries,* H. W. Wilson, 1973. Contributor to academic journals in sociology, education, speech, and library science.

WORK IN PROGRESS: Revising *Selecting Materials for Libraries,* completion expected in 1980; a book on library buildings and equipment.

AVOCATIONAL INTERESTS: Letterpress printing, woodworking, reading.

* * *

BROADWELL, Martin M.   1927-

PERSONAL: Born February 15, 1927, in Nashville, Tenn.; son of William Ernest (an engineer) and Jessie (Bell) Broadwell; married Patricia Breeding (an elementary school science teacher), December 29, 1951; children: Martin M., Jr., Timothy W., Patricia Carol. *Education:* George Peabody College for Teachers, B.S., 1948; graduate study at Wittenburg College and University of Tennessee; National Christian University, M.A., 1975. *Politics:* Conservative. *Religion:* Conservative. *Home:* 2882 Hollywood Dr., Decatur, Ga. 30033. *Office:* Resources for Education and Management, Inc., 544 Medlock Rd., Decatur, Ga. 30033.

CAREER: High school teacher of science and mathematics in Xenia, Ohio, 1948-51; Bell System in Tennessee, Georgia, and Kentucky, engineer, 1951-56; technical writer, 1956-57, in public relations, 1957-59, personnel director, 1959-63, director of technical training, 1964-70; Resources for Education and Management, Inc., Decatur, Ga., co-founder and partner, 1968—. Co-founder and director of Publishing Systems, Inc., 1972—; consultant to major business firms. *Military service:* U.S. Navy, radarman, 1944-45.

MEMBER: American Society for Training and Development, American Society for Engineering Education, Institute of Electrical and Electronic Engineers, National Society for Performance and Instruction. *Awards, honors:* Blue ribbon from American Film Festival, 1969, for writing and producing "The Managerial Skills."

WRITINGS: The Supervisor as an Instructor: A Guide to Classroom Training, Addison-Wesley, 1968, 3rd edition, in press; *The New Supervisor,* Addison-Wesley, 1972; *Success at Bible Teaching,* Publishing Systems, Inc., 1974; *The Supervisor and On-the-Job Training,* Addison-Wesley, 1974, 2nd edition, 1975; (with Brij Kapur) *The New Manager,* Shri Ram Centre for Industrial Relations, 1977; *The Practice of Supervising: Making Experience Pay,* Addison-Wesley, 1977; (with Nancy Diekelmann) *The New Hospital Supervisor,* Addison-Wesley, 1977; *Moving Up to Supervision: How to Become a Supervisor,* Addison-Wesley, in press. Author of monthly column "Questions and Answers About Training" in *Training.* Contributor to trade journals in the United States and abroad.

WORK IN PROGRESS: Two trade books; three novels.

SIDELIGHTS: Broadwell writes: "As a consultant, I've traveled around the world twice, with three trips to Australia. I spent weeks in my favorite outside-the-United States country: India. I have worked and/or traveled in twenty-six different countries. All this travel is intended to support my fiction writing hobby when I grow up. I have skiied in the Canadian Rockies, ridden elephants to the Amber Palace in India, hiked in the Himalayas, boated past the wats of Thailand and explored Singapore, Amsterdam, Stonehenge, and the wilds of Alaska. From the steps of the Parthenon to the ruins of Delphi and old Corinth, I've tried to feel at home, know the people and the places. Being a country boy keeps me awed by all that's outside my day-to-day world."

BROCKMAN, Norbert 1934-

PERSONAL: Born March 2, 1934, in Cincinnati, Ohio; son of Norbert C. and Mary E. (Hasdorff) Brockman. *Education:* University of Dayton, A.B., 1955; Catholic University of America, M.A., 1958, Ph.D., 1963; United Theological Seminary, S.T.M., 1972. *Politics:* Democrat. *Religion:* Roman Catholic. *Home address:* P.O. Box 1283, Dayton, Ohio 45401. *Office:* Bergamo Center, 4435 East Patterson Rd., Dayton, Ohio 45430.

CAREER: Ordained Roman Catholic priest of Society of Mary, 1973; University of Dayton, Dayton, Ohio, assistant professor of politics, 1962-68, associate professor of politics, 1968-71, member of board of trustees, 1970-71; St. Louis University, St. Louis, Mo., visiting scholar, 1971-73; Bergamo Center, Dayton, director of programming, 1973-76; member of corporate board of University of Dayton, 1973-77; director of Marianist Training Network, 1973—; freelance consultant, 1977—. Member of Ohio Constitution Revision Commission, 1970-71.

MEMBER: Association for Creative Change (member of board of directors, 1971-73, 1976-77), National Organization for Continuing Education of Catholic Clergy, Dignity.

WRITINGS: (With Richard Sullivan) Community Action, *Fides, 1968; (editor with Nicholas Piediscalzi)* Contemporary Religion and Social Responsibility, *Alba, 1971;* Ordained to Service, *Exposition, 1976. Contributor to theology and law journals.*

WORK IN PROGRESS: Charism and Community, to develop the theme of group identity and religious self-identity.

SIDELIGHTS: Brockman told *CA:* "Bergamo Center is an adult religious conference center, one of the largest in the U.S. I direct programs in various areas of religious/spiritual growth and adult development. As director of the Marianist Training Center (MTN), I offer similar workshops throughout the country."

* * *

BRONDFIELD, Jerome 1913-
(Jerry Brondfield)

PERSONAL: Born December 9, 1913, in Cleveland, Ohio; son of Nathan (a businessman) and Pauline (Solomon) Brondfield; married Ruth Weisenfeld, December 8, 1940; children: Eric S., Ellen Brondfield King. *Education:* Ohio State University, B.S., 1936. *Home:* 30 Holly Lane, Roslyn Heights, N.Y. 11577. *Agent:* Harold Ober Associates, Inc., 40 East 49th St., New York, N.Y. 10017. *Office:* Scholastic Magazines, Inc., 50 West 44th St., New York, N.Y. 10036.

CAREER: Columbus Dispatch, Columbus, Ohio, sports writer, 1935-37; Newspaper Enterprise Association, Cleveland, Ohio, sports writer, 1937-40; International News Service, Cleveland, Ohio, reporter, 1940-41; Associated Press, New York, N.Y., reporter, 1942-44; RKO-PATHE, New York City, writer of film documentaries, 1944-57; Scholastic Magazines, Inc., New York City, staff editor, 1958—. President of local Little League, 1955, and local Booster Club, 1956.

WRITINGS: Bittersweet (juvenile), Scholastic Book Services, 1962; (under name Jerry Brondfield; with Kenneth L. Wilson) *The Big Ten,* Prentice-Hall, 1967; (under name Jerry Brondfield) *One Hundred Years of Football* (juvenile), Scholastic Book Services, 1969; (under name Jerry Brondfield) *Woody Hayes and the Hundred-Yard War,* Random House, 1974; (under name Jerry Brondfield) *Rockne: A Legend Revisited,* Random House, 1976.

Documentary films include: "This Is America," "Below the Sahara," and "Louisiana Territory."

Author of television scripts for Columbia Broadcasting System. Contributor of stories and articles to popular magazines, including *American, Collier's, Liberty, Esquire, Family Circle, Reader's Digest* and *Redbook.*

* * *

BRONDFIELD, Jerry
See BRONDFIELD, Jerome

* * *

BRONSON, Wilfrid Swancourt 1894-

PERSONAL: Born October 24, 1894, in Chicago, Ill. *Education:* Attended Chicago Art Institute School. *Residence:* Warwick, N.Y.

CAREER: Author and illustrator. Worked as a mural painter's assistant in several studios in New York after the first World War; accompanied four scientific marine expeditions as a staff artist, resulting in the creation of numerous nature books for children; expedition paintings were presented to the Peabody Museum at Yale. *Military service:* U.S. Army, served during first World War.

WRITINGS—All self-illustrated; all published by Harcourt, except as noted: *Fingerfins: The Tale of a Sargasso Fish,* Macmillan, 1930; *Paddlewings: The Penguin of Galapagos,* Macmillan, 1931; *Pollwiggle's Progress,* Macmillan, 1932; *Water People,* Wise-Parslow, 1935; (with William Maxwell Reed) *Sea for Sam,* 1935, revised edition, 1960; *The Wonder World of Ants,* 1937; *The Chisen-Tooth Tribe,* 1939; *Children of the Sea,* 1940; *Horns and Antlers,* 1942; *Stooping Hawk and Stranded Whale: Sons of Liberty,* 1942; *The Grasshopper Book,* 1943; *Hooker's Holiday,* 1944; *Turtles,* 1945; *Coyotes,* 1946; *Pinto's Journey,* Messner, 1948; *Starlings,* 1948; *Cats,* 1950; *Freedom and Plenty: Ours to Save,* 1953; *Goats,* 1959; *Beetles,* 1963; *Dogs: Best Breeds for Young People,* 1969.

Illustrator: Alice C. Desmond, *Lucky Llama,* Macmillan, 1939; A. C. Desmond, *Feathers: The Story of a Rhea,* Macmillan, 1940; Will Henry, *Wolf-Eye: The Bad One,* Messner, 1951. Contributor of articles and illustrations to various periodicals.

SIDELIGHTS: Wilfrid Swancourt Bronson's favorite subjects have always been wild animals. Bronson has also written books about conservation. Of *Freedom and Plenty: Ours to Save,* a *Saturday Review* critic wrote, "in a series of unusually attractive drawings, lovely in design and touched with humor, Mr. Bronson presents the story of America's failures and successes in conserving its natural resources."

BIOGRAPHICAL/CRITICAL SOURCES: Kirkus, September 1, 1950; *Chicago Sunday Tribune,* November 12, 1950; *Saturday Review,* October 31, 1953; *New York Times,* July 5, 1959; *Christian Science Monitor,* November 14, 1963.*

* * *

BROOKS, Douglas
See BROOKS-DAVIES, Douglas

* * *

BROOKS, James L. 1940-

PERSONAL: Born May 9, 1940, in Brooklyn, N.Y.; son of Edward M. and Dorothy Helen (Sheinheit) Brooks; married

Marianne Catherine Morrissey, July 7, 1964 (divorced, 1971); children: Amy Lorraine. *Education:* Attended New York University, 1958-60. *Residence:* Malibu, Calif. *Office:* C.B.S., 4024 Radford Ave., Studio City, Calif. 91604.

CAREER/WRITINGS: Columbia Broadcasting System (CBS) News, New York, N.Y., reporter and writer, 1964-66; Wolper Productions, Los Angeles, Calif., writer and producer of documentaries, 1966-67; American Broadcasting Co. (ABC), Los Angeles, executive story editor and creator of television series "Room 222," 1968-69; CBS, Studio City, Calif., executive producer and creator of television series "Mary Tyler Moore Show," 1970, producer and writer of "Thursday Game," 1971—, producer of "The End," 1973, co-executive producer and co-creator of "Rhoda," 1974—. Lecturer, Stanford University. *Member:* Writers Guild, Television Academy of Arts and Sciences. *Awards, honors:* Emmy Award from National Academy of Television Arts and Sciences, 1969, for creation of "Room 222," and 1970, 1975, and 1976, for "Mary Tyler Moore Show"; Golden Globe Award from Hollywood Foreign Press Corp, 1974, for "Rhoda."

WORK IN PROGRESS: A film adaption of Dan Wakefield's *Starting Over;* "The Lou Grant Show" for CBS; co-writing and co-producing "Cindy," a musical for television to be aired on ABC in 1978; a column for *Los Angeles Times.*

SIDELIGHTS: Brooks, who has achieved considerable success with his television shows, recalled his early career as a newswriter: "I still, today, have warm thoughts about getting back into news. It was like being a kid in a toy store. There was no caste system, no bureaucracy, in the newsroom. Everybody shared their feelings with everybody else. Edward R. Murrow—Eric Sevareid—Fred Friendly—Hughes Rudd—emotional people with great, great integrity. Every day was a thrilling new experience."

Writing for television comedy shows, Brooks told Rowland Barber, is not devoid of excitement: "That great feeling when you're getting a run! You're stuck, then suddenly it all breaks loose, and you start dictating like crazy, laughing all the way."

"I find that the best motivation for a writer who hopes to produce good work is terror," Brooks added.

BIOGRAPHICAL/CRITICAL SOURCES: TV Guide, February 8, 1975.

*   *   *

BROOKS, Richard 1912-

PERSONAL: Born May 18, 1912, in Philadelphia, Pa.; married second wife, Jean Simmons (an actress), 1961 (divorced, 1976); children: Kate. *Education:* Attended Temple University. *Residence:* Bel Aire, Calif. *Agent:* Irving Paul Lazar Agency, 211 South Beverly Dr., Beverly Hills, Calif. 90212. *Office:* c/o Metro-Goldwyn-Mayer, 10202 Washington Blvd., Culver City, Calif. 90230.

CAREER: Writer of novels and screenplays, 1942—; director of films, 1950—, producer, 1966—. Reporter, *New York World Telegram;* radio writer, narrator, and commentator, National Broadcasting Co. (NBC). *Military service:* U.S. Marine Corps. *Member:* Writers Guild of America, Academy of Motion Picture Arts and Sciences, Screen Directors Guild. *Awards, honors:* Oscar from the Academy of Motion Picture Arts and Sciences (Academy Award), 1961, for "Elmer Gantry"; Writers Guild of America Laurel Award, 1967, for "In Cold Blood."

WRITINGS: Brick Foxhole, Harper, 1945; *Boiling Point,* Harper, 1948; *The Producer,* Simon & Schuster, 1951.

Screenplays: (Contributor of additional dialogue) "Don Winslow of the Coast Guard," released by Universal, 1942; "White Savage" (adapted from story by Peter Milne), Universal, 1943; "Cobra Woman" (adapted from story by W. Scott Darling), Universal, 1944; "My Best Gal," Republic, 1944; "Swell Guy" (adapted from play "The Hero" by Gilbert Emery), Universal, 1947; "Brute Force" (adapted from story by Robert Patterson), Universal, 1947; "To the Victor," Warner Bros., 1948; (with John Huston) "Key Largo" (adapted from play by Maxwell Anderson), Warner Bros., 1948; "Any Number Can Play" (adapted from novel by Edward Heth), Metro-Goldwyn-Mayer, 1949.

(With Sydney Boehm) "Mystery Street" (adapted from story by Leonard Spigelgass), Metro-Goldwyn-Mayer, 1950; (and director) "Crisis" (adapted from "The Doubters" by George Tabori), Metro-Goldwyn-Mayer, 1950; (with Daniel Fuchs) "Storm Warning," Warner Bros., 1951; (and director) "The Light Touch" (adapted from story by J. Harris and T. Reed), Metro-Goldwyn-Mayer, 1952; (and director) "Deadline, U.S.A.," Twentieth Century-Fox, 1952; "Battle Circus" (adapted from story by Allen Rinkin and Laura Kerr), Metro-Goldwyn-Mayer, 1953; (with Julius J. and Philip G. Epstein, and director) "The Last Time I Saw Paris" (adapted from "Babylon Revisited" by F. Scott Fitzgerald), Metro-Goldwyn-Mayer, 1954; (and director) "The Blackboard Jungle" (adapted from novel by Evan Hunter), Metro-Goldwyn-Mayer, 1955; (and director) "The Last Hunt" (adapted from novel by Milton Lott), Metro-Goldwyn-Mayer, 1956; (and director) "Something of Value" (adapted from novel by Robert C. Ruark), Metro-Goldwyn-Mayer, 1957; (and director) "The Brothers Karamazov" (adapted from novel by Fyodor Dostoyevsky), Metro-Goldwyn-Mayer, 1958; (with James Poe, and director) "Cat on a Hot Tin Roof" (adapted from play by Tennessee Williams), Metro-Goldwyn-Mayer, 1958.

(And director) "Elmer Gantry" (adapted from novel by Sinclair Lewis), United Artists, 1960; (and director) "Sweet Bird of Youth" (adapted from play by Tennessee Williams), Metro-Goldwyn-Mayer, 1962; (and director) "Lord Jim" (adapted from novel by Joseph Conrad), Columbia, 1965; (producer and director) "The Professionals" (adapted from *A Mule for the Marquesa* by Frank O'Rourke), Columbia, 1966; (producer and director) "In Cold Blood" (adapted from novel by Truman Capote), Columbia, 1967; (and director) "The Happy Ending," United Artists, 1969; "$" [i.e., "Dollars"], Columbia, 1971; (and director) "Bite the Bullet," Paramount, 1975; (and director) "Looking for Mr. Goodbar" (adapted from novel by Judith Rossner), Paramount, 1977.

SIDELIGHTS: Richard Brooks is known around Hollywood as a tough guy. He is almost always the second or third choice for a film, and he continues to terrify Hollywood producers and to bully them into doing things his way. He refuses, for example, to show a finished script to the producers, or even to the actors in his films. They get their lines the night before, and then only for the up-coming scene. He insists and gets total control in the editing room, in the script writing, and in the directing. Therefore, it is fair to say that when a film is a bomb, it is a Richard Brooks bomb, and almost entirely his fault.

From his earliest days Brooks has been a rebel. He left college when he found out that his parents were taking a loan to send him through, and rode the rails during the Depression trying to find a job. He said it was during that period that he met the person who had the most influence in his life. Brooks recalled: "He was about forty, but seemed like an old man then. This guy knew everything about freight trains. This guy asks me, 'So you want to be a writer, eh?' He says, 'What kind?' I say, 'I don't know. Newspaper, I guess.' He says, 'Do much reading? Dostoyevski, Flaubert, Tolstoy? Willa Cather?' I said, 'No.' He said, 'Listen, kid, for every word you write you oughta read at least a thousand. And even that's a little low. You're not a writer till then.' That was the beginning of my education."

Maybe it dates back to those days, but Brooks is considered one of Hollywood's more literate director-writers, having tackled, with varying degrees of success, "The Brothers Karamazov," "Lord Jim," "Elmer Gantry," and two Tennessee Williams plays. One of his most powerful and successful films was "Blackboard Jungle." It established the realistic style, the tough, uncompromising quality that characterizes his most successful films, a strength at its best in the movie "In Cold Blood."

When writer John Mariani asked Brooks whether he thought the ideal of the "man's man" had lost its impact with the public, Brooks answered: "I think the real man is ashamed to show himself. Men have been told it's a shame to cry, or for him to put it on the line. It's now every man for himself. Why worry about the other guy. What was Watergate all about? The big man doesn't have to bare his chest and kick the shit out of somebody. He's not afraid to be laughed at, to feel emotion. It's the man who knows what he believes that's a real man, not a guy who believes what others tell him to. I'm no flagwaver, but people are ashamed to be Americans. Americanism is about doing what you can to help the underdog.

"There is no commitment today," continued Brooks. "It's all operating on the pleasure principle. People are disillusioned. When I was in college, if a public official was corrupt, we went after him. We protested against the Sacco-Vanzetti case. The kids today have been burned, left without heroes by Vietnam."

Brooks has been known for his share of "he-man" movies, although they have not always been successful. "The Professionals" and "Bite the Bullet" were good examples of this particular "Brooksian ideal of courage."

Brooks himself is an ardent student of the cinema and has a vast collection (well over five hundred) of films which he gladly shows to film buffs and serious students alike. He studies past films and learns the old techniques. He is one of Hollywood's historians.

BIOGRAPHICAL/CRITICAL SOURCES: New York Herald Tribune, November 4, 1951; *Saturday Review,* March 6, 1965; *New York Post,* December 15, 1967; *Life,* January 12, 1968; *New York Times,* January 18, 1970; *Time,* February 2, 1970; *After Dark,* January, 1975; *Millimeter,* July/August, 1977; *New York,* September 19, 1977.*

* * *

BROOKS, Thomas R(eed) 1925-

PERSONAL: Born April 25, 1925, in Shrewsbury, Mass.; son of Norman E. (a handyman) and Mildred A. (Reed) Brooks; married Harriet L. Schumacher (an executive secretary), October 8, 1949; children: Christopher N., William F., Karin L. *Education:* Harvard University, A.B. (cum laude), 1950. *Politics:* Social Democrat. *Religion:* None. *Home:* 236 Clinton St., Brooklyn, N.Y. 11201. *Agent:* Knox

Burger Associates Ltd., 39½ Washington Sq. S., New York, N.Y. 10012.

CAREER: Socialist Party of New York City, New York City, city secretary, 1950; International Ladies Garment Workers Union, New York City, assistant to the director of education, 1951; Transport Workers Union, New York City, assistant editor, 1952-55; free-lance writer, 1956; *Business Week,* New York City, assistant labor editor, 1956-61; *Current,* New York City, associate editor, 1962; free-lance writer, 1962—. Member of board of directors of Joint Apprenticeship Training Program. *Military service:* U.S. Army, 10th Mountain Division, 1943-45; received Bronze Star.

MEMBER: League for Industrial Democracy (president, 1976—), Authors Guild, Social-Democrats of the United States.

WRITINGS: Toil and Trouble: A History of American Labor, Delacorte, 1964, 2nd edition, 1971; *Picket Lines and Bargaining Tables,* Grosset, 1968; *Walls Come Tumbling Down: A History of the Civil Rights Movement, 1940-1970,* Prentice-Hall, 1977; *Communications Workers of America,* Mason/Charter, 1977. Author of monthly column in *New America.* Contributor to magazines.

WORK IN PROGRESS: Biographies of labor intellectual Clinton S. Golden and of Carl Schurz.

* * *

BROOKS-DAVIES, Douglas 1942-

PERSONAL: Original name, Douglas Brooks; name legally changed in 1976; born March 10, 1942, in London, England; son of Douglas (an industrial chemist) and Margaret (Dean) Brooks; married Stevie Davies (a university lecturer and writer), February 12, 1976; children: Emily Jane. *Education:* Brasenose College, Oxford, B.A., 1965; University of Liverpool, Ph.D., 1967. *Politics:* "Democratic socialist." *Religion:* "Superstitious atheist." *Home:* 5 Brixham Ave., Cheadle Hulme, Cheshire, England. *Office:* Department of English, University of Manchester, Manchester, Lancashire, England.

CAREER: University of Leeds, Leeds, England, lecturer in English literature, 1967-70; University of Manchester, Manchester, England, lecturer in English literature, 1970—.

WRITINGS: (Editor, under name Douglas Brooks) Henry Fielding, *Joseph Andrews and Shamela,* Oxford University Press, 1971; (editor with A. R. Humphreys; under name Douglas Brooks) Fielding, *Jonathan Wild and a Voyage to Lisbon,* Dent, 1973; (under name Douglas Brooks) *Number and Pattern in the Enghteenth-Century Novel,* Routledge & Kegan Paul, 1973; (editor) *Spenser: The Faerie Queene, a Selection,* Dent, 1976; *Spenser's Faerie Queene: A Critical Commentary on Books I and II,* Manchester University Press, 1977. Contributor to literature and language journals, including *Ariel.*

SIDELIGHTS: Brooks-Davies comments: "I find many academic books (and academics) rather distrubingly impersonal. All my early writing was, similarly, impersonal. I hope I have now discovered the beauty and power of personal feeling and that this is now reflected in my writing and teaching." *Avocational interests:* Music (plays recorder, oboe, and viola), gardening.

* * *

BROUGHTON, Jack(sel Markham) 1925-

PERSONAL: Born January 4, 1925, in Utica, N.Y.; son of

Jacksel M. N. (a salesman) and Elizabeth (McGinley) Broughton; married Alice Joy Owen, December 26, 1951; children: Mark, Sheila, Maureen, Kathleen. *Education:* U.S. Military Academy, B.S., 1945; George Washington University, M.S., 1965; also attended Air Command & Staff College and National War College. *Politics:* Conservative. *Religion:* Episcopal. *Home:* 4096 Bonita View Dr., Bonita, Calif. 92002. *Office:* Air Cushion Systems, 290 Trousdale Dr., Chula Vista, Calif. 92010.

CAREER: U.S. Air Force, career officer, 1945-68, combat qualified pilot on fighters and interceptors (flew more than two hundred single engine fighter combat missions), vice-commander of fighter wings, commander of demonstration team "The Thunderbirds," served in Germany, Korea, Turkey, Japan, Southeast Asia, Greece, France, England, Mexico, Guatemala, the Philippines, Australia, Singapore, and Okinawa, also member of Defense Department's Weapons System Evaluation Group, 1968, retiring as colonel; Antilles Airboats, Fajardo, P.R., director of operations, 1965; Mobil Oil Corp., Anchorage, Alaska, director of air cargo support in Alaska, 1966; Air Cushion Systems, Chula Vista, Calif., president, 1966—.

AWARDS, HONORS—Military: Forty-two decorations, including Air Force Cross, two Silver Stars, and Legion of Merit.

WRITINGS: Thud Ridge, Lippincott, 1969.

WORK IN PROGRESS: A book on Southeast Asia.

SIDELIGHTS: Broughton writes: "I have built and tested six prototype ACVs and a production demonstration ACV which made a successful public debut at the National Petroleum Show. I have been through all the joys and frustrations of building a better mousetrap. I have developed some degree of expertise in marketing, corporate structuring, financing, budget, legal and accounting matters, patent procedures, personnel management, procurement, relations with larger corporations, tax structures, and many other overall facets of management.

"Technically, I have lived with the machinery, including propellers, engines, controls, lift fans, skirting materials, internal and external environmental control and all the things that bind these components into a machine—primarily fiberglass and associated plastics. I can, and have, gotten my fingernails dirty.

"My primary goal has been to bring the air cushion vehicle to a point where the technology and components could generate a safe, reliable and practical machine capable of doing a job in obvious markets."

Regarding his writing, he comments: "I wanted to document the air war over Korea, but when I got home I found I had not properly recorded my thoughts. I found the Southeast Asia war to be even a worse mess, so I documented my thoughts to tell the story as clearly as possible. I wanted people to know what it was like without any baloney."

*   *   *

BROWN, Arthur A(llen)   1900-

PERSONAL: Born February 5, 1900, in Norcatur, Kan.; son of Ora L. (a clergyman, teacher, and farmer) and Catharine (Farlee) Brown; married Claire Sicher (a high school teacher and executive director of Girl Scouts of America), May 30, 1925; children: Alline Marie Brown Sontag, Yvonne Elise Brown Browning. *Education:* University of Michigan, B.S.F., 1922; University of California, Berkeley, graduate study, 1935-37. *Religion:* Presbyterian. *Home:* 15006 Candover Court, Silver Spring, Md. 20906.

CAREER: U.S. Forest Service, Washington, D.C., junior forester at Coeur d'Alene, Idaho, 1922-26, assistant forest supervisor at Helena National Forest, 1926-27, and Jefferson National Forest, 1927-30; Forest Experiment Station, Berkeley, Calif., leader of projects in planning fire control systems, 1930-37; U.S. Forest Service, chief of forest fire control in the Rocky Mountain region, 1937-44, national assistant chief of forest fire control, 1944-47, chief of forest fire control, 1947-48, director of Division of Forest Fire Research, 1948-64. Writer. Past member of Committee on Fire Research of National Academy of Sciences-National Research Council; Fulbright lecturer in Australia, 1967; staff member of International Senior Girl Scout Roundup; operator of Girl Scout Ranger Aid Camp, 1965-66.

MEMBER: Society of American Foresters, American Association for the Advancement of Science (fellow), American Horticulture Society, Phi Sigma, Kiwanis, Cosmos Club. *Awards, honors:* Citations from American Meteorological Society, 1960, and National Academy of Sciences-National Research Council, 1965.

WRITINGS: (With A. D. Folweiler) *Fire in the Forests of the United States,* John S. Swift, 1953; (with Kenneth P. Davis) *Forest Fire: Control and Use,* McGraw, 1973. Contributor to professional journals.

SIDELIGHTS: Brown began his career as timber cruiser, log scaler, timber sale administrator, and fire fighter. Early assignments included administering range lands and creating areas for recreational use by the public. But his expertise in dealing with forest fires led to a specialization that continued until his retirement in 1964. He worked on fire lookout systems, communication systems, road networks, and scientific research assignments to increase efficiency.

AVOCATIONAL INTERESTS: European travel.

*   *   *

BROWN, Cecil M.   1943-

PERSONAL: Born July 3, 1943, in Bolton, N.C. *Education:* Columbia University, B.A., 1966; University of Chicago, M.A., 1967. *Residence:* Berkeley, Calif.

CAREER: Writer. Lecturer in English, University of Illinois, University of California, Berkeley, and Merrit College.

WRITINGS: The Life and Loves of Mr. Jiveass Nigger (novel), Farrar, Straus, 1970. Author of plays, including "The African Shades: A Comedy in One Act," "The Gila Monster," and "Our Sisters Are Pregnant." Contributor of articles to *Partisan Review, Black World, Kenyon Review, Yardbird Reader, Evergreen Review, Negro Digest,* and other periodicals.

BIOGRAPHICAL/CRITICAL SOURCES: Time, February 2, 1970; *New Statesman,* June 19, 1970.*

*   *   *

BROWN, Claude   1937-

PERSONAL: Born February 23, 1937, in New York, N.Y.; son of Henry Lee (a railroad worker) and Ossie (a domestic; maiden name, Brock) Brown; married Helen Jones (a telephone operator), September 9, 1961. *Education:* Howard University, B.A., 1965; further study at Stanford University and Rutgers University. *Home:* 2736 8th Ave., New York, N.Y. 10039.

CAREER: Member of Harlem Buccaneers Gang's "Forty Thieves" division and served three terms at Warwick

School, New York City, during 1940's; worked confidence games and dealt in drugs, New York City, 1953-54; worked as a busboy, watch crystal fitter, shipping clerk and jazz pianist in Greenich Village, 1954-57; writer and lecturer. *Member:* Harlem Improvement Group. *Awards, honors:* Metropolitan Community Methodist Church grant, 1959; *Saturday Review* Ansfield-Wolf Award, for furthering intergroup relations.

WRITINGS: Manchild in the Promised Land, Macmillan, 1965; *The Children of Ham,* Stein & Day, 1976. Contributor of articles to *Dissent, Esquire,* and other periodicals.

SIDELIGHTS: "There is no doubt that Negroes have much to be angry about," William Mathes wrote in 1965, "and I'm all for anger, righteous or otherwise. Not hate, but anger. There is room for dialogue in that emotion. It get things moving; someone answers with shock; someone applauds; something happens." Tired of the "high-pitched" anger of James Baldwin and the "too fraught-with-love" anger of Roy Wilkins and James Farmer, Mathes called for "words that convey hurt and deprivation themselves, words that can permit many people—especially white people—to identify with the Negro. So far we have lacked words that impart the feelings of what it is to be a Negro in this country at this time." The words, Mathes and other social commentators agreed, came with *Manchild in the Promised Land.* Its publication caused Tom Wolfe to write: "Claude Brown makes James Baldwin and all that old Rock of Ages rhetoric sound like some kind of Moral Rearmament tourist from Toronto come to visit the poor."

Brown, a survivor of Harlem's "Bebopping gang," the Bucaneers, received his primary education from two reformatories and years of "roaming the streets with junkies, whores, pimps, hustlers, the 'mean cats' and the numbers runners." By the time he was thirteen he had been struck by a bus, chain-whipped, tossed into a river, and shot in the stomach. Four years later he decided to resume his formal education and moved from his home, a move, he wrote, "away from fear, toward challenges, towards the positive anger that I think every young man should have."

Encouraged by Ernest Papanek, his former mentor at Wiltwyck School, Brown wrote an article on Harlem for *Dissent.* After its publication, Macmillan offered Brown an expense account to write a book about his life in Harlem. By 1963 he completed a 1,537 page manuscript of *Manchild in the Promised Land.*

Praised by critics for its deft realism and remarkable clarity, Brown's book became a harbinger of hope to the civil rights movement as it drew increasing interest and concern to the plight of urban blacks. "I want to talk about the experiences of a misplaced generation," Brown began, "of a misplaced people in an extremely complex, confused society. This is a story of their searching, their dreams, their sorrows, their small and futile rebellions, and their endless battle to establish their own place in America's greatest metropolis—and in America itself." Romulus Linney wrote that *Manchild in the Promised Land* "is written with brutal and unvarnished honesty in the plain talk of the people, in language that is fierce, uproarious, obscene and tender, but always sensible and direct. And to its enormous credit, this youthful autobiography gives us its devastating portrait of life without one cry of self-pity, outrage or malice, with no caustic sermons or searing rhetoric. Claude Brown speaks for himself—and the Harlem people to whom his life is bound—with open dignity, and the effect is both shattering and deeply satisfying." More than a decade later, George Davis in *New York*

Times Book Review claimed that *Manchild in the Promised Land* "remains one of the great personal, nonideological view, of life in the rawest parts of Harlem."

Brown's second book, *The Children of Ham,* is an account of a group of Harlem teenagers who banded together and transformed abandoned apartments into "spots" where they could "interact free of the 'monster' heroin that dominated their homes and the narrow Harlem side street out front." The group maintained little connection to anything except themselves, their religion was survival and they "encouraged each other to stay clean and stay in school, or to develop whatever latent talents each might have."

"As a child," Brown wrote in *Manchild in the Promised Land,* "I remember being morbidly afraid. It was a fear that was like a fever that never lets up. Sometimes it became so intense that it would just swallow you. At other times, it just kept you shaking. But it was always there. I suppose, in Harlem, even now, the fear is still there." *The Children of Ham* reportrays Harlem, and finds it to be a neighborhood "that ten years of neglect has rubbed even more raw."

BIOGRAPHICAL/CRITICAL SOURCES: Claude Brown, *Manchild in the Promised Land,* Macmillan, 1965; *Antioch Review,* fall, 1965; *New Statesman,* August 5, 1966; *Detroit Free Press,* March 12, 1967; *New York Times Book Review,* August 15, 1976.*

* * *

BROWN, Daniel Russell
　　See CURZON, Daniel

* * *

BROWN, (Ernest) Francis 1903-

PERSONAL: Born December 31, 1903, in Amherst, Mass.; son of Ernest G. and Jessie A. (Scott) Brown; married Mary Elizabeth Adden, June 8, 1940; children: Victoria Allen, Francis Scott. *Education:* Dartmouth College, B.S., 1952; Columbia University, M.A., 1927, Ph.D., 1931. *Home:* 165 West St., Amherst, Mass. 01002.

CAREER: Current History (magazine), New York City, associate editor, 1930-36; *New York Times,* New York City, member of staff, 1936-45; *Time,* New York City, senior editor, 1945-49; *New York Times Book Review,* New York City, editor, 1949-70. Trustee of Barlow School, 1964-73. *Member:* Massachusetts Historical Society, Century Association (New York City), Phi Beta Kappa. *Awards, honors:* Decorated Order of Bernardo O'Higgins (Chile), 1948; Litt.D. from Dartmouth College, 1952.

WRITINGS: Joseph Hawley: Colonial Radical, Columbia University Press, 1931; *Edmond Nyles Huyck: The Story of a Liberal,* Dodd, 1936; *The War in Maps,* Oxford University Press, 1942; *Raymond of the Times,* Norton, 1951, revised, 1970; (editor) *Highlights of Modern Literature,* New American Library, 1954; *Opinions and Perspectives,* Houghton, 1964; (editor) *Page Two: The Best of "Speaking of Books" From the New York Times Book Review,* Holt, 1969; *A Dartmouth Reader,* Dartmouth Publications, 1969.

* * *

BROWN, George Isaac 1923-

PERSONAL: Born March 14, 1923, in Hanover, N.H.; son of Daniel H. (an engineer) and Yetta (Caplan) Brown; married wife, Judith (a therapist), August 29, 1948; children: Joshua, Elissa, Ethan, Adam. *Education:* University of New Hampshire, B.A., 1949, Ed.M., 1952; University of

London, certificate, 1949; Harvard University, Ed.D., 1958. *Home:* 2141 Ridge Lane, Santa Barbara, Calif. 93103. *Agent:* Sterling Lord Agency, Inc., 660 Madison Ave., New York, N.Y. 10021. *Office:* Graduate School of Education, University of California, Santa Barbara, Calif. 93106.

CAREER: University of New Hampshire, Durham, lecturer in educational psychology, 1958; University of Delaware, Newark, associate professor of curriculum and psychology, 1958-61; University of California, Santa Barbara, associate professor, 1961-68, professor of confluent education, 1969—. Visiting clinical professor at Harvard University, summer, 1963; guest professor at University of Rotterdam, spring, 1974. Gestalt therapist, 1964—, trainer of therapists, 1970—. Member of advisory board of Psychosynthesis Research Foundation; has particpated in workshops and seminars in the United States, Norway, England, Germany, and the Netherlands. *Military service:* U.S. Army, Combat Infantry, 1942-45; served in European theater.

MEMBER: Association for Humanistic Psychology, American Educational Research Association. *Awards, honors:* Grant from Fund for the Advancement of Education, 1967-68; Ford Foundation grants, 1970-74, 1973-74, 1974-76.

WRITINGS: Now: The Human Dimension (monograph), Esalen Institute, 1968; (contributor) H. Otto and J. Mann, editors, *Ways of Growth,* Grossman, 1968; *Affectivity, Classroom Climate and Teaching* (monograph), American Federation of Teachers, 1971; (with John M. Shiflett) *Confluent Education: Attitudinal and Behavioral Consequences of Confluent Teacher Training* (monograph), University Center, University of Michigan, 1972; *Human Teaching for Human Learning,* Viking, 1971; (contributor) B. Joyce and M. Weil, editors, *Perspectives for Reform in Teacher Education,* Prentice-Hall, 1972; *The Live Classroom: Innovations Through Confluent Education and Gestalt,* Viking, 1974. Contributor of more than forty articles and reviews to education journals. Member of board of advisors of *Humanizing Education.*

SIDELIGHTS: Brown writes: "I seem to like to avoid boredom by staying on the frontiers of whatever I am involved in. This is compounded by a combination of anger at injustice and a political sense of what it is possible to change and how. I enjoy contact that is real in the sense of being present. I avoid phoniness when I can, including my own."

* * *

BROWN, Letitia Woods 1915-1976

PERSONAL: Born October 24, 1915, in Tuskegee Institute, Ala.; daughter of Matthew (an instructor at Tuskegee Institute) and Evadne (an instructor at Tuskegee Institute; maiden name, Adams) Woods; married Theodore E. Brown (an economist with the State Department), 1947; children: Lucy Brown Franklin, Theodore, Jr. *Education:* Tuskegee Institute, B.S., 1935; Ohio State University, M.A., 1937; Harvard University, Ph.D., 1966. *Home:* 4311 18th St., Washington, D.C. 20011.

CAREER: Teacher in Macon County, Ala., 1935-36; Tuskegee Institute, Tuskegee Institute, Ala., instructor in history, 1937-40; LeMoyne-Owen College, Memphis, Tenn., tutor, 1940-45; Howard University, Washington, D.C., 1961-70, began as instructor, became associate professor of history; professor at Federal Executive Institute, 1970-71; George Washington University, Washington, D.C., associate professor of history and American civilization, 1971-76. Senior Fulbright lecturer at Monash University and Australian National University, 1968. Consultant to Federal Executive Institute, 1971-73; member of committee on objectives for National Assessment of Educational Progress, 1972-73. *Member:* American Historical Association, Organization of American Historians, Association for the Study of Afro-American Life and History, Southern Historical Association, African Heritage Studies Association of Afro-Americans in Washington D.C.

WRITINGS: Free Negroes in the District of Columbia, 1790-1846, Oxford University Press, 1972. Contributor to *Journal of Negro Education.*

OBITUARIES: New York Times, August 5, 1976; *Washington Post,* August 5, 1976.*

(Died August 3, 1976, in Washington, D.C.)

* * *

BROWN, Marian A. 1911-

PERSONAL: Born December 10, 1911, in Clarkson, N.Y.; daughter of George Henry (a farmer and politician) and Laura (a teacher; maiden name, Mathewson) Rayburn; married Ralph Adams Brown (a professor of history and writer), February 8, 1947; children: Richard Adams, Linda Viola Brown Kerr. *Education:* State University of New York College at Buffalo, B.S., 1935; University of Rochester, M.S., 1939; Columbia University, Ed.D., 1950; postdoctoral study at New School for Social Research, and Cornell University. *Politics:* Republican. *Religion:* Presbyterian. *Home:* 44 West Court St., Cortland, N.Y. 13045.

CAREER: Teacher of English and social studies in Huntington, N.Y., 1937-39, guidance director, 1939-45; Columbia University, New York, N.Y., research assistant in Bureau of Administrative Research, 1946-47; Cornell University, Ithaca, N.Y., vocational counselor, 1948-50; State University of New York College at Cortland, dean of women, 1956-58; private testing and consulting psychologist, 1952-76; writer, 1976—. Psychologist for Cortland County Board of Cooperative Educational Services, 1965-68; counselor at State University of New York College at Cortland, 1969; psychologist for schools in Homer, N.Y., 1971-73. Visiting professor at Stetson University, 1970. Owner and manager of a girls' day camp in Huntington, 1940; counselor for Christian refugees, 1942; member of Cortland County Mental Health Board, and Council of Social Agencies. *Member:* American Psychological Association, National Association of School Psychologists, School Psychologists of Upper New York State, Young Women's Christian Association.

WRITINGS: Impressions of America, two volumes, Harcourt, 1965; *American History Reading List for High Schools,* National Council for the Social Sciences, 1967; *Cluster Biographies,* four volumes, McGraw, 1969; (editor with Ralph Adams Brown) *Europeans Observe the American Revolution,* Messner, 1976. Also contributor to *Exploring with American Heroes,* Follett, 1964. Book review editor of *Social Education,* 1960-63.

WORK IN PROGRESS: Research on the results of placement in small classes, and the use of special techniques and testing with children of average or low-average intelligence who normally fail in school; research on parent-child relationships, and on methods of increasing the individual's intelligence.

SIDELIGHTS: Marian Brown wrote: "Ever since I can remember, I have scribbled stories and poems. I was obsessed by a curiosity about people; how they thought and reacted, what they valued, what motivated them and what fostered or hindered their development—the personality, backgrounds, intelligence, situations and people that formed them. Thus history with its fascinating individuals, guidance and psychology, as well as writing and reviewing, interested me.

"Vocationally I am interested in clinical assessment, counseling, and education as well as in writing and have returned to the former intermittently while, and after, raising a family. I believe practicing one's profession is essential to keeping alert in one's field, but I also believe it may have to be abandoned, at times, for the immediate needs and overall good of the family."

AVOCATIONAL INTERESTS: Bridge, golf, antiques, art, gardening, European travel.

* * *

BROWN, Raymond Lamont 1939-

PERSONAL: Born September 20, 1939, in Leeds, England; son of James (a civil engineer) and Margaret Isabella (Johnston) Brown; married Jean Elizabeth Adamson, April 14, 1973. *Education:* Institute of Engineering Technology, M.A., 1963; also attended London School of Oriental and African Studies, 1965. *Home:* 34 Spottiswoode Gardens, St. Andrews, Scotland.

CAREER: Yorkshire Electricity Board, Bradford, England, staff member in commercial and accounting departments, 1959-65; free-lance writer, 1965—. Extra-mural lecturer at University of St. Andrews. Founder of Japan Research Projects, 1965. Editor of M. B. Publications, Ltd., 1967-69. *Member:* International P.E.N., Royal Geographical Society, Royal Asiatic Society, Japan Society, Society of Authors, Society of Scottish Antiquaries.

WRITINGS: History of St. Mark's Church, Dewsbury, 1865-1965, Birkdale Books, 1965; *A Book of Epitaphs,* Taplinger, 1967; *Doncaster Rural District Official Guide,* Directory Publications, 1967; *Clarinda: The Intimate Story of Robert Burns and Agnes Maclehose,* M. B. Publications, 1968; *Sir Walter Scott's Letters on Demonology and Witchcraft,* Citadel, 1968; *Robert Burns's Commonplace Book,* S. R. Publishers, 1969.

A Book of Superstitions, Taplinger, 1970; *A Book of Proverbs,* Taplinger, 1970; *A Book of Witchcraft,* Taplinger, 1971; *General Trade in Berwick-on-Tweed, 1894,* Bell, 1972; *Charles Kirkpatrick Sharpe's Historical Account of the Belief of Witchcraft in Scotland,* S. R. Publishers, 1972; *Phantoms of the Sea,* Taplinger, 1972; *Robert Burns's Tour of the Borders,* Boydell Press, 1972; *Phantoms, Legends, Customs, and Superstitions of the Sea,* Taplinger, 1972; *The Magic Oracles of Japan,* Fowler, 1972; *Robert Burns's Tour of the Highlands and Stirlingshire,* Boydell Press, 1973; *A New Book of Epitaphs,* Frank Graham, 1973; *A Casebook of Military Mystery,* Drake, 1974; *Phantoms of the Theatre,* Thomas Nelson, 1977; *Epitaphs Hunting,* Thornhill Press, 1977; *Scottish Epitaphs,* Thornhill Press, 1977.

Contributor of about two hundred fifty articles to magazines all over the world.

WORK IN PROGRESS: Dictionaries and reference books on literature and history; anthropological studies of Oriental peoples.

SIDELIGHTS: Brown writes briefly: "I strive, through the written word, to bring a greater understanding of the motivation of the 'Oriental mind' to the West. I have travelled widely in the Far East, and promoted English literature in the Orient."

BROWN, Richard E(ugene) 1937-

PERSONAL: Born June 30, 1937, in Little Falls, N.Y.; son of Edward S. Brown and Mary E. (Metz) Lynch; married Beverly Ann Shaffer (a teacher); children: Kelly (daughter), Christopher, Kirsten. *Education:* Hope College, B.A., 1959; University of Michigan, M.P.A., 1962; Harvard University, D.P.A., 1968. *Office:* Mills Building, Suite 301, Topeka, Kan. 66612.

CAREER: Tennessee Valley Authority, Knoxville, management intern, member of research, planning, and budget staffs, and assistant to general manager, 1960-69; State of New York, Legislative Commission on Expenditure Review, Albany, director of research operations and project manager, 1970-75; State of Kansas, Topeka, legislative post auditor, 1975—. Faculty member at University of Tennessee, 1965, College of William and Mary, 1969-70, Russell Sage College, 1971-74, State University of New York at Albany, 1972-74, and University of Kansas, 1976—. Member of National Conference of State Legislatures (member of executive committee) and National Auditors Training Committee.

MEMBER: American Society for Public Administration (local vice-president), American Academy of Political and Social Science, Institute of Internal Auditors, Association of Government Accountants.

WRITINGS: A Review of Employee Evaluation Systems, Public Personnal Association, 1963; *The GAO: Untapped Source of Congressional Power,* University of Tennessee Press, 1970; (editor with Ray D. Pethtel, and contributor) *Legislative Review of State Program Performance* (monograph), Eagleton Institute of Politics, Rutgers University, 1972; (editor with Don E. Fehrenbacher) *Tradition, Conflict and Modernization: Perspectives on the American Revolution,* Academic Press, 1977. Contributor to auditing, public administration, and economic journals.

WORK IN PROGRESS: Editing *Legislative Performance Auditing and Evaluation,* for Fagleton Institute, Rutgers University, with Meredith Williams; a text about performance auditing.

SIDELIGHTS: Richard Brown writes: "Like public budgeting and budget systems, which became the focus of so much attention a generation ago, auditing is growing in awareness and importance in the minds of scholars and praticioners alike. In an age of increasing accountability, this is inevitable." *Avocational interests:* Chess, music, swimming, sailing, tennis, handball, racquet ball, cycling, hiking.

* * *

BROWNE, Howard 1908-
(John Evans)

PERSONAL: Born April 15, 1908, in Omaha, Neb.; son of George (a bakery owner) and Rose (Carlton) Browne; married Esther Levy, June 28, 1931 (divorced, June 10, 1959); married Doris Ellen Kaye, June 12, 1959; children: Allen Myles, Sue Ann (Mrs. Richard Bailey), Melissa (adopted). *Education:* Educated in Lincoln, Neb. *Politics:* Non-partisan. *Religion:* None. *Home:* 3303 La Costa Ave., Carlsbad, Calif. 92008. *Agent:* Eisenbach-Green-Duchow, 760 N. La Cienega Blvd., Los Angeles, Calif. 90069.

CAREER: Worked as a department store credit manager in Chicago, Ill., 1929-41; Ziff-Davis Publishing Co., New York, N.Y., and Chicago, Ill., editor, 1941-56; novelist, motion picture and television writer. Instructor, University of California, San Diego, 1973—. *Member:* Writers Guild of America, Mystery Writers of America.

WRITINGS: Warrior of the Dawn, Reilly & Lee, 1943; (under pseudonym John Evans) *Halo in Blood,* Bobbs-Merrill, 1946; (under pseudonym) *If You Have Tears,* Mystery House, 1947; (under pseudonym) *Halo for Satan,* Bobbs-Merrill, 1948; (under pseudonym) *Halo in Brass,* Bobbs-Merrill, 1949; *Thin Air,* Simon & Schuster, 1954; *The Taste of Ashes,* Simon & Schuster, 1957.

Author of screenplays, including "Portrait of a Mobster," "St. Valentine's Day Massacre," and "Capone." Author of over one hundred twenty-five television scripts for programs including "Columbo," "Destry," "77 Sunset Strip," "Maverick," "Bus Stop," "Mannix," "Alias Smith & Jones," "Cheyenne," "Playhouse 90," "The Fugitive," "The Virginian," "Kraft Mystery Theatre," "The Bold Ones," and "Mission Impossible."

Contributor of over three hundred short stories, articles, and novelettes to pulp magazines, 1939-55, and also to *Cosmopolitan, Redbook, American Magazine, Esquire,* and other periodicals.

WORK IN PROGRESS: A mystery novel, tentatively titled *The Paper Gun.*

SIDELIGHTS: "In an effort to escape from a nine-to-five desk job," Browne told *CA,* "I turned to writing pulp fiction as a hobby in 1939. In 1941 I became a magazine editor and my spare time was devoted to novel writing. Early on I came under the influence of Raymond Chandler's writing and his style, as well as the style of James M. Cain. They were doing the kinds of books I had wanted to do before I had read—or even heard of—either man. In 1956, a Hollywood producer, having read my work, brought me to Los Angeles to try my hand at screenwriting. For the past twenty years I've written nothing except for the screen. Now, semi-retired, I'm going back to writing books."

*   *   *

BROWNE, Raymond 1897-

PERSONAL: Born October 26, 1897, in New York, N.Y.; son of Raymond A. (a composer) and Julia (Manley) Browne; married Margaret Lewerth (a dramatist and novelist), April 10, 1959. *Education:* Columbia University, student, 1915-16. *Politics:* "No party. Social Patriot." *Religion:* "No church, white Gentile." *Home and office address:* Post Office Rd., Waccabuc, N.Y. 10597. *Agent:* Paul R. Reynolds, Inc., 12 East 41st St., New York, N.Y. 10017.

CAREER: J. Walter Thompson Co., New York City, account executive and copy group head, 1925-33; Texaco, New York City, advertising manager, 1937-41; Foote, Cone & Belding, New York City, account executive and advertising copywriter, 1945-49; Young & Rubicam, Inc., New York City, account executive, 1949-53; Rogers, Slade & Hill, Inc., New York City, vice-president; writer. Certified emergency medical technician in Lewisboro, N.Y. *Military service:* Canadian Army, Infantry, 1917-19.

WRITINGS: (With Lee H. Hill) *Upward in the Black,* Prentice-Hall, 1966; *Making a Success of Your Food Garden,* Doubleday, 1976. Contributor to newspapers, including *New York Times, Westchester Weekly,* and *Christian Science Monitor.*

WORK IN PROGRESS: Grow Your Own Soil (tentative title); experiments with innovative gardening practices; continuous color photographs of plant-growth stages.

SIDELIGHTS: Browne has prepared an expose of organic gardening, dealing with fallacies and a possibility of mail

order fraud. He is also concerned with "the actual rather than the romanticized nature of today's criminal types, with candid consideration of racial differences." *Avocational interests:* Fox hunting, beagling, sailing.

*   *   *

BROYLES, William Dodson, Jr. 1944-

PERSONAL: Born October 8, 1944, in Houston, Tex.; son of William Dodson and Elizabeth (Bills) Broyles; married Sybil Newman (an art director), August 15, 1973. *Education:* Rice University, B.A., 1966; Oxford University, M.A., 1968. *Office address: Texas Monthly,* P.O. Box 1569, Austin, Tex. 78767.

CAREER/WRITINGS: U.S. Naval Academy, Annapolis, Md., instructor in philosophy, 1970-71; Houston Public Schools, Houston, Tex., assistant superintendent, 1971-72; *Texas Monthly,* Austin, Tex., editor, 1972—; Texas Monthly Press, Austin, editor, 1975—. *Military service:* U.S. Marine Corps, 1969-71; became captain; received Bronze Star. *Member:* Texas Institute of Letters. *Awards, honors:* National Magazine Award, 1974.

SIDELIGHTS: Broyles told *CA:* "Being an editor is its own reward."

*   *   *

BRUGGER, Bill
See BRUGGER, William

*   *   *

BRUGGER, William 1941-
(Bill Brugger)

PERSONAL: Born January 9, 1941, in Brighton, England; son of William Brugger; married Suzanne Mary Pollard; children: Katherine Mary Elizabeth, Antony William Fabian, Max William Eugene. *Education:* School of Oriental and African Studies, London, B.A., 1964, M.Sc., 1968, Ph.D., 1972. *Home:* 58 Kildonian Rd., Warradale, South Australia, Australia 5046. *Office:* School of Social Sciences, The Flinders University of South Australia, Bedford Park, South Australia, Australia 5042.

CAREER: Peking Second Foreign Languages Institute, Peking, China, teacher, 1964-66; University of London, London, England, member of staff of Contemporary China Institute, 1968-71; Flinders University of South Australia, Bedford Park, lecturer, 1972-75, senior lecturer in politics, 1976—.

WRITINGS: Democracy and Organisation in the Chinese Industrial Enterprise, 1948-53, Cambridge University Press, 1976; *Contemporary China,* Croom Helm, 1977; (editor) *China: The Impact of the Cultural Revolution,* Croom Helm, 1978.

*   *   *

BRUNHOFF, Laurent de 1925-

PERSONAL: Born August 30, 1925, in Paris, France; son of Jean (an author and illustrator) and Cecile (Sabouraud) de Brunhoff; children: Ann, Antoine. *Education:* Attended Academie de la Grande Chaumiere. *Residence:* Paris, France.

CAREER: French author and illustrator. Began to work seriously at painting during World War II; at the same time he became involved in continuing the "Babar" picture book series his father had originated; his works have been exhibited in the Galeire Maeght and the Salon de Mai. *Awards, honors: New York Times* Choice of Best Illustrated Books of the Year, 1956, for *Babar's Fair.*

WRITINGS—All self-illustrated: *Serafina le Girafe,* Editions du Pont Royal, 1961, translation published as *Serafina the Giraffe,* World Publishing, 1961; *Serafina's Lucky Find,* World Publishing, 1962; *Captain Serafina,* World Publishing, 1963; *Anatole and His Donkey,* translation from the French by Richard Howard, Macmillan, 1963; *Bonhomme,* translation from the French by Howard, Pantheon, 1965; *Gregory et Dame Tortue,* Ecole Loisirs, 1971, translation by Howard published as *Gregory and Lady Turtle in the Valley of the Music Trees,* Pantheon, 1971; *Bonhomme et la grosse bete qui avait des escailles sur le dos,* Grasset, 1974, translation by Howard published as *Bonhomme and the Huge Monster,* Pantheon, 1974.

"Babar" series: *Babar et ce coquin d'Arthur,* Hachette, 1947, translation by Merle Haas published as *Babar's Cousin: That Rascal Arthur,* Random House, 1948; *Pique-Nique Chez Babar,* Hachette, 1949, translation by Haas published as *Babar's Picnic,* Random House, 1949; *Babar dans l'Ile aux oiseaux,* Hachette, translation by Haas published as *Babar's Visit to Bird Island,* Random House, 1952; *La Fete de Celesteville sera ouverte dimanche prochain,* Hachette, 1954, translation by Haas published as *Babar's Fair Will Be Opened Next Sunday,* Random House, 1954.

Babar et le Professeur Grifaton, Hachette, 1956, translation by Haas published as *Babar and the Professor,* Random House, 1957; *Le Chateau de Babar,* Hachette, 1961, translation by Haas published as *Babar's Castle,* Random House, 1962; *Babar's French Lessons,* Random House, 1963; *Babar's Spanish Lessons* (Spanish words by Roberto Eyzaguirre), Random House, 1965; *Babar en Amerique,* Hachette, translation by M. Jean Craig published as *Babar Comes to America,* Random House, 1965; *Babar à New York,* Hachette, 1966; *Babar Loses His Crown,* Beginner Books, 1967.

Babar fait du ski, Hachette, 1967, translation by Haas published as *Babar Goes Skiing,* Random House, 1969; *Babar jardinier,* Hachette, c.1967, translation by Haas published as *Babar the Gardener,* Random House, 1969; *Babar en promenade,* Hachette, c.1967, translation by Haas published as *Babar Goes on a Picnic,* Random House, 1969; *Babar's Games,* Random House, 1968; *Babar à la mer,* Hachette, translation by Haas published as *Babar at the Seashore,* Random House, 1969.

Babar et le docteur, 6th edition, Hachette, 1969, translation published as *Babar and the Doctor,* Random House, 1971; *Babar's Trunk* (contains *Babar at the Seashore, Babar Goes on a Picnic, Babar Goes Skiing,* and *Babar the Gardener*), Random House, 1969; *Babar Learns to Drive,* translation from the French by O. Jones, Methuen, 1969; *Babar aux sports d'hiver,* 7th edition, Hachette, 1969; *Babar Goes Visiting,* translation from the French by O. Jones, Methuen, 1969; *Babar's Moon Trip,* Random House, 1969; *Tele-Babar,* Hachette, 1969.

L'Anniversaire de Babar, Hachette, 1970, translation published as *Babar's Birthday Surprise,* Random House, 1970; *Babar Keeps Fit,* translation from the French by O. Jones, Methuen, 1970; *Babar the Artist,* Random House, 1971; *Babar the Camper,* Random House, 1971; *Babar sur la planete molle,* Hachette, 1972, translation by Haas published as *Babar Visits Another Planet,* Random House, 1972; *Meet Babar and His Family,* Random House, 1973.

Babar aviateur, Hachette, 1974; *Babar's Bookmobile,* Random House, 1974; *Babar patissier,* Hachette, 1974; *Babar and the Wully-Wully,* Random House, 1975; *Babar Saves the Day,* Random House, 1976.

Foreign language textbook series, published by Hachette: *Je parle allemand avec Babar; Je parle anglais avec Babar; Je parle espagnol avec Babar; Je parle italien avec Babar.*

Also author of *Babar chez le docteur, Babar et l'arbre de Noel,* and *Babar musicien,* all published by Hachette. Joint author of Jean de Brunhoff's *Albums roses "Babar,"* Volume VI, Hachette, 1951-53; editor of Jean de Brunhoff's *Les aventures de Babar,* Hachette, 1959; illustrator of Auro Roselli's *The Cats of the Eiffel Tower,* Dial, 1967.

SIDELIGHTS: Laurent de Brunhoff was five years old when his father, Jean de Brunhoff, first created Babar the elephant. As he grew older, the younger Brunhoff waivered between becoming a painter and carrying on his father's work. By the time he was twenty-one, however, Laurent decided to commit himself to writing more of Babar's adventures in much the same style in which they were originally produced. In addition to the regular cast of animals in the Babar books, Laurent de Brunhoff created new characters based on his own children for the book, *Babar and the Professor.* First published in French, these famous elephant picture-books have been published in German, Spanish, Danish, Dutch, Hungarian, and Japanese, as well as English.

In reviewing *Babar's Birthday Surprise,* a *Time* magazine critic said that the "charm of the Babar stories is that they can be read with equal pleasure by kids who have barely heard of Paris and francophile parents."

In 1971, *Babar Comes to America* was made into a film by Random House with narration by Peter Ustinov.

AVOCATIONAL INTERESTS: Gardening, bird watching, and his Siamese cat.

BIOGRAPHICAL/CRITICAL SOURCES: Publisher's Weekly, November 20, 1961; *Life,* November 26, 1965; *Time,* December 21, 1970.*

* * *

BRUS, Wlodzimierz 1921-

PERSONAL: Born in 1921, in Poland; married; three children. *Education:* Attended Free University of Warsaw, 1938-39, and Lvov Institute of Commerce, 1940-41; Institute of Planning, Saratov, Soviet Union, M.A., 1942; University of Leningrad, graduate study, 1942-44; Central School of Planning and Statistics, Warsaw, Poland, Ph.D., 1951. *Office:* Wolfson College, Oxford University, Oxford, England.

CAREER: Wage-clerk and planner for industrial enterprises in Saratov, Soviet Union, 1942-44; Central School of Planning and Statistics, Warsaw, Poland, assistant professor of political economy, 1949-52; University of Warsaw, Warsaw, Poland, professor of planning and statistics, 1952-65, professor of political economy, 1965-68, dean of Faculty of Economics, 1958-60; Institute of Housing, Warsaw, Poland, research worker, 1968-72; University of Glasgow, Glasgow, Scotland, visiting research fellow in international economic studies, 1972-73; Oxford University, Oxford, England, senior research fellow at St. Antony's College, 1973-76, lecturer in modern Russian and East European studies, and fellow of Wolfson College, both 1976—. Professor at Central School of Planning and Statistics (Warsaw), 1952-65; visiting professor at University of Rome, 1971, and Catholic University of Louvain, 1973. Chairman of department of political economy at the Institute of Social Sciences (of central committee of Polish United Workers Party), 1950-56; director of bureau of research at Planning Commission of Poland, 1956-58; vice-chairman of Polish Economic Council, 1957-63; member of Polish group of Economic Commission (of Council of Mutual Economic Assistance), 1957-64. *Awards, honors:* Ford Foundation fellowship for the United States, 1961.

WRITINGS—All published by Routledge & Kegan Paul: (Co-author) *Main Trends in Economics,* 1970; *The Market in Socialist Economy,* 1972; *Economics and Politics of Socialism,* 1973; *Socialist Ownership and Political Systems,* 1975. Also author of six books not, as yet, translated into English.

Contributor: R. C. Tucker, editor, *Stalinism: Essays in Historical Interpretation,* Norton, 1977; E. Eshag, editor, *Michel Kalecki Memorial Lectures,* Institute of Economics and Statistics, Oxford University, 1977. Also contributor to *Problems in Economic Development,* 1965; *The Socialist Idea: A Reappraisal,* 1974; *An Economic History of Eastern Europe, 1919-1949,* in press.

Contributor to political and economic journals in the United States, Poland, England, Italy, France, Czechoslovakia, Germany, and the Soviet Union.

*   *   *

BRUSH, Stephen G(eorge)

PERSONAL: Born in Bangor, Maine; son of Edward N. (a professor of psychology) and Lillian (a psychologist; maiden name, Hatfield) Brush; married Phyllis Egbert, October 8, 1960; children: Denise, Nicholas. *Education:* Harvard University, A.B., 1955; Oxford University, D.Phil., 1958. *Office:* Institute for Physical Science and Technology, University of Maryland, College Park, Md. 20742.

CAREER: Lawrence Radiation Laboratory, Livermore, Calif., physicist, 1959-65; Harvard University, Cambridge, Mass., research associate, 1965-68, lecturer in physics and the history of science, 1966-68; University of Maryland, College Park, associate professor, 1968-71, professor of history of science, 1971—. U.S. national representative to Commission on the Education of Historians of Science, sponsored by International Union for the History and Philosophy of Science, 1971—. *Member:* American Physical Society, History of Science Society. *Awards, honors:* Rhodes scholarship, 1955-58; research grants from National Science Foundation, 1958-59.

WRITINGS: Kinetic Theory, three volumes, Pergamon, 1965-72; (editor) *Resources for the History of Physics,* University Press of New England, 1972; (editor with A. L. King) *History in the Teaching of Physics,* University Press of New England, 1972; *Introduction to Concepts and Theories in Physical Science,* Addison-Wesley, 1973; *The Kind of Motion We Call Heat: History of Kinetic Theory,* North-Holland Publishing, 1976; *The Temperature of History: Phases of Science and Culture in the Nineteenth Century,* B. Franklin, 1977. Contributor to physics and history of science journals.

WORK IN PROGRESS: A history of geophysics and astrophysics.

SIDELIGHTS: Brush writes: "I started as a theoretical physicist, changed to history of science. My best-known technical article explains how stars may become solid at high pressure. My best-known article on science education is 'Should the History of Science Be Rated X?'"

BRYAN, C(ourtlandt) D(ixon) B(arnes) 1936-

PERSONAL: Born April 22, 1936, in New York, N.Y.; son of Joseph III and Katharine (Barnes) Bryan; married Phoebe Miller, December 28, 1961 (divorced, 1966); married Judith Snyder, December 21, 1967; children: (first marriage) J. St. George III, Lansing Becket; (second marriage) Amanda Barnes. *Education:* Yale University, B.A., 1958. *Home:* 56 Union St., Guilford, Conn. 06437. *Agent:* Brandt & Brandt, 101 Park Ave., New York, N.Y. 10022.

CAREER: Editor, *Monocle* (magazine), 1961—; writer. Writer-in-residence, Colorado State University, winter, 1967; visiting lecturer in writers workshop, University of Iowa, 1967-69; special editorial consultant, Yale University, 1970; visiting professor, University of Wyoming, 1975. *Military service:* U.S. Army, 1958-60, 1961-62. *Member:* Yale Club. *Awards, honors:* Harper Prize Novel Contest award, 1965, for *P. S. Wilkinson; Friendly Fire* named among top five nonfiction books of the year by *Time,* and rated best nonfiction book of the year by *New York Daily News,* both 1976.

WRITINGS: P. S. Wilkinson (novel; Literary Guild selection), Harper, 1965; *The Great Dethriffe* (novel), Dutton, 1970; *Friendly Fire* (nonfiction; Book-of-the Month Club selected alternate), Putnam, 1976. Also author of narration for Swedish film, "The Face of War," 1963. Contributor to *New York Times Magazine, Holiday, New Yorker* and other periodicals.

SIDELIGHTS: Bryan's book, *The Great Dethriffe,* has been likened to *The Great Gatsby* by at least two reviewers. In *New York Times Book Review,* Jonathan Yardley points to Bryan's "effort to translate the Gatsby story into contemporary terms." A *New Republic* reviewer, after remarking upon the "laborious parallel between Scott Fitzgerald's characters and Bryan's," calls *The Great Dethriffe* "remarkable for its grace and depth of perception." Geoffrey Wolff of *Newsweek* notes the improvement of Bryan's second book over his first, calling *The Great Dethriffe* "droll" and "articulate."

Friendly Fire, Bryan's most acclaimed work to date, is an attempt to supply a satisfactory explanation for the death of Michael Mullen, an American soldier in Vietnam. The title itself is the Pentagon's euphemism for accidental death by American artillery. In contrast to the somewhat mixed reactions of critics to his previous books, Bryan's *Friendly Fire* has received approbation from nearly every reviewer. Peter Gardner of *Saturday Review* stated that Bryan's book "is objective despite the tug of compassion, and is powerfully affecting in its evocation of trapped grief." Gardner notes, in addition, that "Bryan's account focuses less on Michael's death than on what it did to his parents, who now had lost faith in their country. Explicitly and implicitly, it's dramatic comment on what the war did to America." Walter Clemons, in an article for *Newsweek,* applauded Bryan's treatment of the Mullens' "conspiracy theory," which they formulated in their grief, frustrated by their inability "to decode government communications about the circumstances of their son's death." *Friendly Fire* is the nonfictional account of grief transformed to rage. R. Z. Sheppard of *Time* says *Friendly Fire* "is as close to elemental tragedy as any nonfiction account to come out of the war. Bryan conveys grief and rage with purity and tact."

Friendly Fire has been adapted for television by American Broadcasting Co.

BIOGRAPHICAL/CRITICAL SOURCES: Time, February 5, 1965, April 19, 1976; *Saturday Review,* February 6,

1965, January 22, 1972, May 15, 1976; *New York Times Book Review,* November 1, 1970, May 9, 1976; *New Republic,* November 7, 1970; *Newsweek,* November 23, 1970, May 17, 1976; *Christian Science Monitor,* June 11, 1976; *Atlantic,* July, 1976; *New York Review of Books,* August 5, 1976; *Best Sellers,* September, 1976.

* * *

BRYAN, J(ack) Y(eaman) 1907-

PERSONAL: Born September 24, 1907, in Peoria, Ill.; son of James Yeaman (an insurance executive) and Regina (Gibson) Bryan; married Margaret Gardner, June 21, 1934; children: Joel Yeaman, Guy Kelsey, Donna Gardner, Kirsten Stuart (Mrs. Sidney Bruce Kelley, Jr.). *Education:* Attended University of Chicago, 1925-27; University of Arizona, B.A. (with high distinction), 1932, M.A., 1933; Duke University, postgraduate study, 1933-35; University of Iowa, Ph.D., 1939. *Home:* 3594 Ramona Dr., Riverside, Calif. 92506. *Office:* University of California, Riverside, Calif. 92502.

CAREER: Federal Emergency Relief Association, Washington, D.C., research analyst, 1935-36; University of Maryland, College Park, 1936-48, began as instructor in English, became professor of journalism and head of department; U.S. Office of Civilian Defense, Washington, D.C., public relations adviser, 1942-43; Cleveland Welfare Federation, Cleveland, Ohio, director of public relations, 1943-45; United Nations Relief and Rehabilitation Administration, public information officer in England and France, 1945-46; U.S. Department of State, cultural affairs officer at American Embassy, Manila, Philippines, 1948-51, chief of program planning at International Exchange Service, Washington, D.C., 1951-53; U.S. Information Agency, public affairs officer in Bombay, India, 1953-54, and Bangalore, India, 1954-55; U.S. Department of State, cultural affairs officer at embassies in Cairo, Egypt, 1956, and Teheran, Iran, 1956-58, chief of cultural affairs in Karachi, Pakistan, 1958-63, officer in charge of special recruitment program for Bureau of Educational and Cultural Affairs, Washington, D.C., 1963-68; University of California, Riverside, lecturer in creative photography, 1968—. Chairman of publications board at University of Maryland, 1946-48; chairman of board of directors of U.S. Educational Foundation in Philippines, 1949-51, and in Pakistan, 1958-63. Has exhibited photographs in one-man shows in India, Pakistan, and Washington, D.C.; a collection of his Asian photographs was exhibited at colleges and universities throughout the United States.

MEMBER: American Museum of Natural History, National Audubon Society, Texas Institute of Letters, Texas State Historical Association, Phi Delta Theta, Phi Gamma Mu, Delta Sigma Rho. *Awards, honors:* Jesse H. Jones Award in fiction of Texas Institute of Letters and Summerfield G. Roberts Award of Sons of the Republic of Texas, both 1964, for *Come to the Bower;* short story award of Texas Institute of Letters, 1974.

WRITINGS: Come to the Bower (novel), Viking, 1963. Stories anthologized in *Best Short Stories,* 1942. Contributor to periodicals, including *Story, Atlantic Monthly, Collier's, Southwest Review, Toronto Star-Weekly, Arizona Quarterly, National Parks Magazine,* and *South Atlantic Quarterly.*

WORK IN PROGRESS: Beyond Bounds, a sequel to *Come to the Bower* and second novel in a trilogy about the American thrust across the Southwest; *Eye on Asia,* a book of photographs and commentary with historical perspective, completion expected in 1976.

AVOCATIONAL INTERESTS: Photography, horsemanship, ecology, travel (has been in fifty-four countries in all parts of the world).

* * *

BRYANT, Gay 1945-

PERSONAL: Born October 5, 1945, in Newcastle, England; came to the United States in 1969; daughter of Richard King and Catherine (Shiel) Bryant. *Education:* Attended elementary and secondary schools in Ireland and England. *Home:* 34 Horatio St., New York, N.Y. 10014. *Agent:* John Cushman Associates, 25 West 43rd St., New York, N.Y. 10036. *Office: New Dawn,* 99 Park Ave., New York, N.Y. 10016.

CAREER: Telefis Eireann (Irish Television), Dublin, assistant producer, 1965-66; *Queen,* London, England, assistant reviews editor, 1966-67, merchandising editor, 1967-68; Penthouse/Viva International, New York, N.Y., fiction editor of *Penthouse,* 1968-74, and senior editor of *Viva,* 1973-74; Playboy Publications, New York City, New York editor of *Oui,* 1974-75; *New Dawn,* New York City, founder and editorial director, 1975—.

WRITINGS: Underground Travel Guide, Award Books, 1973; (with Bockris Wylie) *How I Learned to Like Myself,* Warner Paperback, 1975. Contributor to magazines in the United States and abroad, including *Nova, Gallery, Cosmopolitan,* and *Moneysworth.*

WORK IN PROGRESS: A book for Bobbs-Merrill.

SIDELIGHTS: Bryant told *CA:* "I am editing *New Dawn* for the contemporary young women who have such a wide variety of exciting options open to them that they can do almost anything they want! Producing a women's magazine to meet such a challenge is stimulating work!"

* * *

BRYERS, Paul 1945-

PERSONAL: Born August 1, 1945, in Liverpool, England; son of Richard (a businessman) and Helen (Hunter) Bryers. *Education:* Graduated from University of Southampton (honors), 1966. *Politics:* Socialist. *Religion:* Roman Catholic. *Home:* 44 Washington St., Brighton, England. *Agent:* A. D. Peters, 10 Buckingham St., Adelphi, London WC2N 6BU, England; and Peter H. Matson, Harold Matson Co., Inc., 22 East 40th St., New York, N.Y. 10016. *Office:* Southern Television, Duke St., Brighton, England.

CAREER: London Daily Mirror, London, England, reporter in London, Manchester, and Belfast, 1970-73; Southern Television, Brighton, England, reporter and interviewer on current affairs program "Day by Day," and documentary series "Southern Report," 1973-77. Labour candidate for Parliament from Torbay, England, 1968-70. *Awards, honors:* Award from Southeast Arts Association, 1976, for the best first novel, *Hollow Target.*

WRITINGS: Target Plutex (novel), Doubleday, 1976, published in England as *Hollow Target,* Deutsch, 1976.

WORK IN PROGRESS: The Cat Trapper, a thriller about big business deals with the Soviet Union, to be published by Andre Deutsch; a behind-the-scenes film of the October 1977 European tour of the Peter Gabriel band.

SIDELIGHTS: Bryers writes: "My main professional interest at present is making television documentaries. Most of those I've been involved with have been of a social or political nature. They include 'For the Love of Helen,' about a firm of private eyes who specialise in snatching children involved in 'tug-of-love' custody cases, 'The Cartland Affair,' about the murder of a former British intelligence officer in the south of France, 'The Forgotten Children,' about conditions in unlicensed foster homes for children from London's deprived areas, 'The Falklands: Islands on the Edge of Nowhere,' about the problems facing Britain's colony in the South Atlantic facing the threat of an Argentine take-over, 'What Do You Think of It So Far?,' about a party of Massachusetts state policemen and their wives on a week's tour of the United Kingdom, and 'Every Wednesday There's a War,' about the Royal Navy's response to the threat posed by Warsaw Pact fast patrol boats armed with surface-to-surface missiles.''

BIOGRAPHICAL/CRITICAL SOURCES: Liverpool Daily Post, September 13, 1976.

*   *   *

BUCCHIERI, Theresa F.   1908-

PERSONAL: Surname (pronounced Bu-cary) was originally Bicchieri; born October 4, 1908, in Philadelphia, Pa.; daughter of Anthony (a grocery store owner) and Josephine (Passalacqua) Bicchieri. *Education:* Attended Temple University, 1921-31. *Politics:* Democrat *Religion:* Roman Catholic. *Home:* 931 Pierce St., Philadelphia, Pa. 19148.

CAREER: Began free-lance writing for a South Philadelphia weekly and Italian-language newspapers in Philadelphia and New York during college days; later regular free lancer for *Philadelphia Public Ledger,* doing feature stories on opera stars and visiting Italian dignitaries; after *Ledger* ceased publication, worked briefly for Pennsylvania Department of Public Assistance; federal employee with U.S. Department of Labor, 1940-68, as Wage Hour Law enforcement specialist.

WRITINGS: Feasting with Nonna Serafina, A. S. Barnes, 1966; *Keep You Old Folks at Home,* Alba Books, 1975. Contributor of culinary and travel features to newspapers, including *Philadelphia Evening Bulletin, New York Times,* and *Chambersburg Public Opinion.*

WORK IN PROGRESS: Two novels.

SIDELIGHTS: Theresa Bucchieri's gourmet tastes began in South Philadelphia where she watched her grandmother preparing Italian dishes (such as filet of flounder simmered in wine, and spiked with plump oysters and shrimp). She wrote her first book, technically classed as a cookbook, around these culinary adventures, and the customs and ways of life in an Italian-American community of that day.

AVOCATIONAL INTERESTS: Music (opera-goer and symphony regular since youth), travel, photography.

BIOGRAPHICAL/CRITICAL SOURCES: Chambersburg Public Opinion, September 17, 1966.*

*   *   *

BUCHAN, Alastair (Francis)   1918-1976

PERSONAL: Born September 9, 1918, in London, England; son of John (former governor general of Canada, novelist) and Susan Charlotte (Grosvenor) Buchan; married Hope Gordon Gilmour, April 11, 1942; children: David John, Benjamin William, Anna Virginia. *Education:* Christ Church, Oxford, M.A., 1939. *Home:* Waterloo House, Brill, Buckinghamshire, England. *Office:* Balliol College, Oxford, England.

CAREER: Economist (weekly), London, England, assistant editor, 1948-51; *Observer,* London, Washington correspondent, 1951-55, diplomatic and defense correspondent, 1955-58; Institute for Strategic Studies, London, founder and director, 1958-69; Royal College of Defense Studies, London, commandent, 1970-72; University of Oxford, Oxford, England, Montagu Burton Professor of International Relations, 1972-76. Reith Lecturer, 1973; fellow, Woodrow Wilson International Center for Scholars of the Smithsonian Institution, 1973-74. *Military service:* Canadian Army, 1939-45; became lieutenant colonel. *Awards, honors:* Named Member of the Order of the British Empire, 1944, named Commander, 1968.

WRITINGS: (With Oliver Villiers) *Twenty-five Years: Major Alastair Guy Spens Campbell, M.C., F.R.G.S.,* Alcuin Press, 1952; *The Spare Chancellor: The Life of Walter Bagehot,* Chatto & Windus, 1959, Michigan State University Press, 1960; *NATO in the 1960's: The Implications of Interdependence,* Praeger, 1960, revised edition, 1963; (with Philip Windsor) *Arms and Stability in Europe,* Praeger, 1963; *The U.S.A.,* Oxford University Press, 1963, 3rd edition, 1971; (editor) *China and the Peace of Asia,* Praeger, 1965; *Crisis Management: The New Diplomacy,* Atlantic Institute, 1966; *War in Modern Society: An Introduction,* Watts (London), 1966, Harper, 1968; (editor) *A World of Nuclear Powers?,* Prentice-Hall, 1966; *The Future of NATO,* Carnegie Endowment for International Peace, 1967; (editor) *Europe's Futures, Europe's Choices: Models of Western Europe in the 1970's,* Columbia University Press, 1969.

(Editor) *Problems of Modern Strategy,* Praeger, 1970; (with others) *The Atlantic Papers: Political and Strategic Studies,* Dunellen, 1971; *Power and Equilibrium in the 1970's,* Praeger, 1973; *The End of the Postwar Era: A New Balance of World Power,* Saturday Review Press, 1974; *Change Without War: The Shifting Structures of World Power,* Chatto & Windus, 1974, St. Martin's Press, 1975. Contributor of articles on foreign policy to periodicals.

WORK IN PROGRESS: A history of American postwar foreign policy.

SIDELIGHTS: Renowned as an expert in international relations and military affairs, Alastair Buchan was responsible for eliciting the participation of many prominent and powerful men in the work carried on by the International Institute of Strategic Studies which he founded. The Institute's value in the assessment of defense strategy and world security in our nuclear age is officially recognized.

OBITUARIES: Washington Post, February 5, 1976; *New York Times,* February 7, 1976; *AB Bookman's Weekly,* March 1, 1976.

(Died February 3, 1976, in Buckinghamshire, England)

*   *   *

BUCHANAN, William J(esse)   1926-

PERSONAL: Born January 30, 1926, in Morganfield, Ky.; son of William Jesse (a penologist) and Margaret Evelyn (Kagey) Buchanan; married Milli Sites, December 15, 1950; children: William Jesse III, Steven, James, Rebecca. *Education:* University of Louisville, B.S., 1950. *Politics:* ''Mossback Democrat.'' *Religion:* Protestant. *Home:* 11421 Key West Dr., Albuquerque, N.M. 87111. *Agent:* Ann Elmo Agency, Inc., 52 Vanderbilt Ave., New York, N.Y. 10017.

CAREER: U.S. Air Force, 1944-46, 1950-70; served as a radar operator during World War II, as technical intelligence officer in Japan, Korea, Taiwan, and Hong Kong, 1950-60, as communications officer in Iceland, 1963, Alaska, 1968-70, retiring as lieutenant colonel; writer, 1966—. Guest lecturer at University of New Mexico; has lectured in Japanese elementary schools. *Member:* Authors Guild, Authors League of America, Rio Grande Writers Association. *Awards, honors:* Freedoms Foundation award for writing, 1965, for "I Am All American"; First Person Award from *Reader's Digest,* 1967, for "One Last Time, Amigo".

WRITINGS: A Shining Season (biography of mile-runner, John Baker), Coward, 1978.

Work represented in anthologies, including *The Rhetoric of Our Times,* edited by J. Jeffery Aver, Appleton-Century-Crofts, 1969; *Black Military Experience in the American West,* edited by John M. Carrol, Liveright, 1971. Contributor to popular magazines, including *True, Saturday Evening Post, Americas,* and *Mankind.*

WORK IN PROGRESS: One Last Time, Amigo, based on *Reader's Digest* article of the same title; a novel on command intrigue and influence on a highly publicized military court-martial in 1972.

SIDELIGHTS: Buchanan, who began writing long before his retirement from the Air Force, spends a great deal of time on research. He has traveled in Europe and spent a lot of time in the Orient, especially Japan, where he researched the samurai era. Some of his articles have been made available in Portuguese and Spanish, by the Organization of American States. His works are often found in high schools and colleges in the United States and overseas.

Buchanan's *A Shining Season* was the basis for a television film of the same title by Columbia Broadcasting System.

AVOCATIONAL INTERESTS: Camping, trout fishing.

* * *

BUCK, Lewis 1925-

PERSONAL: Born February 16, 1925, in Norfolk, Va.; son of Ernest Robert (a mechanic) and Florence (Thompson) Buck; married Georgia Allen Weaver, June 26, 1953; children: Eric Banning, Peter Carson. *Education:* Duke University, A.B., 1947; College of William and Mary, M.F.A., 1952. *Home address:* Clark Island Rd., Spruce Head, Maine 04859.

CAREER: High school teacher of English and art in Poquoson, Va., 1952-53; tour guide in Europe and North Africa, 1953-54; Barney Neighborhood House, Washington, D.C., art teacher and social worker, 1954-57; American University, Washington, D.C., draftsman and illustrator for Human Relations Area Files, 1957-59; National Rehabilitation Association, Washington, D.C., administrative assistant, 1960-67; *Journal of Rehabilitation,* Washington, D.C., editor, 1967-70; Craignair at Clark Island, Spruce Head, Maine, innkeeper and artist, 1970—. *Military service:* U.S. Naval Reserve, 1943-59. *Member:* Mid Coast Audubon Society (member of board of directors, 1976-77).

WRITINGS: Wetlands: Bogs, Marshes, and Swamps (juvenile), Parents' Magazine Press, 1974.

WORK IN PROGRESS: The Craignair Papers: The First Thing They Do Is Cut Their Toenails, letters to and from two innkeepers and their friends.

SIDELIGHTS: Buck writes: "The book, *Wetlands,* was done at the suggestion of friends, Rose Wyler and Gerald Ames, who have written many science books for children. From our many field trips together, they felt that I was quali-

fied to write this one that they knew Parents' Magazine Press hoped to produce. To my surprise, the editor accepted my initial chapter and outline, and I wrote the book in a month.

"While our sons were small we took often to the woods and mountains and became interested in natural history and ecology. When we moved to Maine, we continued to lead guests at our inn on natural history field trips. All of this was volunteer work. We made our living in other ways.

"Both of our sons are now away at college. With our jobs as parents over, we expect to pursue art careers fulltime. As soon as we can sell the inn, we will open an intaglio workshop in Camden, Maine."

* * *

BUCKINGHAM, Burdette H. 1907(?)-1977

1907(?)—November 4, 1977; American physicist and author. Buckingham most recently was assistant to the director of the applied physics laboratory at Johns Hopkins University. He was co-author of a high school science textbook. Obituaries: *Washington Post,* November 6, 1977.

* * *

BUCKLAND, Raymond 1934-
(Tony Earll, Jessica Wells)

PERSONAL: Born August 31, 1934, in London, England; son of Stanley Thomas and Eileen E. (Wells) Buckland; married Rosemary June Moss, November 19, 1955 (divorced December 19, 1973); married Joan Helen Taylor (a teacher), February 15, 1974; children: Robert Charles H., Regnauld Hugh C. *Education:* Attended high school in London, England. *Home address:* P.O. Box 9729, Wright Station, Norfolk, Va. 23505. *Agent:* Donald MacCampbell, Inc., 12 East 41st St., New York, N.Y. 10017.

CAREER: James Brodie (publishers), London, England, retail manager, 1959-62; British Airways, New York, N.Y., publications editor, 1962-71; writer and illustrator, 1971—. Director of Weirs Beach Chamber of Commerce, 1973-75. Consultant to Witches Cauldron, Inc. *Military service:* Royal Air Force, 1957-59.

WRITINGS: A Pocket Guide to the Supernatural, Ace Books, 1969, revised edition, 1975; *Practical Candleburning Rituals,* Llewellyn, 1970, revised edition, 1976; *Witchcraft Ancient and Modern* (self-illustrated), House of Collectibles, 1970; (under pseudonym Tony Earll) *Mu Revealed* (self-illustrated; novel), Paperback Library, 1970; *Witchcraft from the Inside* (self-illustrated), Llewellyn, 1971, revised edition, 1975; *Here Is the Occult,* House of Collectibles, 1974; *The Tree: Book of Saxon Witchcraft* (self-illustrated), Samuel Weiser, 1974; *Amazing Secrets of the Psychic World,* Parker, 1975; *Anatomy of the Occult,* Samuel Weiser, 1977; *The Magick of Chant-O-Matics,* Parker, 1978; *Practical Color Magic: Chromopathy and Chromology* (self-illustrated), Llewellyn, in press.

Illustrator: *A Science Encyclopedia for Junior Schools,* Brodie, 1962.

WORK IN PROGRESS: Fletcher's Folly, a gothic novel, under pseudonym Jessica Wells; *The Wiitiko Inheritance,* a novel.

SIDELIGHTS: Buckland told *CA:* "My interest in Witchcraft and the Occult has developed over twenty-five years. My approach is an anthropological one, showing Witchcraft in its pre-Christian origins through to its contemporary practice. In 1966 I founded this country's first museum devoted exclusively to the subject, and ran it successfully until 1976. I have recently shifted my writing emphasis from non-fiction to fiction, using my background to write the occult-accented gothic horror novel.''

* * *

BUCKLEY, Fiona
See ANAND, Valerie

* * *

BUCKLEY, Michael J(oseph) 1931-

PERSONAL: Born October 12, 1931, in San Francisco, Calif.; son of Michael T. (a U.S. Army career man and professor of mathematics) and Eleanor (a high school teacher; maiden name, Fletcher) Buckley. *Education:* Gonzaga University, B.A., 1955, M.A., 1956; Mount St. Michael's, Ph.L., 1956; Alma College, Los Gatos, Calif., S.T.L., 1963; University of Santa Clara, S.T.M., 1963; University of Chicago, Ph.D., 1967. *Office:* Department of Historical and Systematic Theology, Jesuit School of Theology at Berkeley, 1735 LeRoy Ave., Berkeley, Calif. 94709.

CAREER: Entered Society of Jesus (Jesuits), 1949, ordained Roman Catholic priest, 1962; University of Chicago, Chicago, Ill., lecturer, 1967-68; Gonzaga University, Spokane, Wash., assistant professor of philosophy, 1968-71; Jesuit School of Theology at Berkeley, Berkeley, Calif., associate professor of philosophic theology, 1971-73; Pontifical Gregorian University, Rome, Italy, visiting professor of systematic theology, 1973-74; Jesuit School of Theology at Berkeley, associate professor of spirituality and systematic theology, 1975—. Associate professor at Graduate Theological Union, 1971—. Rector of Jesuit community at Jesuit School of Theology at Berkeley, 1969-73. Member of board of trustees of Loyola University, Los Angeles, Calif., 1969-70, University of San Francisco, 1969-72, and Jesuit School of Theology at Berkeley, 1969-73. Representative to general congregation of Society of Jesus, 1974-75. *Member:* Metaphysical Society of America, American Catholic Philosophical Association, American Philosophical Association, Alpha Sigma Nu.

WRITINGS: Motion and Motion's God, Princeton University Press, 1971. Contributor to philosophy and history of philosophy journals.

WORK IN PROGRESS: Research for a book on atheism.

* * *

BUDBILL, David 1940-

PERSONAL: Born June 13, 1940, in Cleveland, Ohio; married wife, Lois; children: Gene. *Education:* Attended Muskingum College and Columbia University; earned M.Div. from Union Theological Seminary, New York, N.Y. *Residence:* Wolcott, Vt.

CAREER: Writer. Has worked variously as short order cook, gardener, grounds keeper, street gang worker, manager of a coffee house, research assistant, carpenter's apprentice, forester, day laborer, and English teacher.

WRITINGS: Mannequins' Demise (play), Baker's Plays, 1964; *Barking Dog* (poems), Barking Dog Press, 1968; *Christmas Tree Farm* (juvenile), Macmillan, 1974; *Snowshoe Trek to Otter River* (stories), Dial, 1976; *The Chainsaw Dance* (poems), Crow's Mark Press, in press; *The Bones on Black Spruce Mountain* (novel), Dial, in press.

Also author of "Knucklehead Rides Again" (play), first produced in 1966.

* * *

BUEL, Richard (Van Wyck), Jr. 1933-

PERSONAL: Born July 22, 1933, in Morristown, N.J.; son of Richard V. W. (an accountant) and Frances (Thompson) Buel; married Joy Evelyn Margaret Day, June 5, 1964; children: Margaret Alexandra. *Education:* Amherst College, B.A., 1955; Harvard University, M.A., 1957, Ph.D., 1962. *Home:* Walkley Barn, Walkley Hill Rd., Haddam, Conn. 06438. *Office:* Department of History, Wesleyan University, Middletown, Conn. 06457.

CAREER: Wesleyan University, Middletown, Conn., 1962—, began as assistant professor, become professor of history. Member of Haddam Board of Finance, 1972-74. *Member:* American Historical Association, Institute for Early American History and Culture, Phi Beta Kappa. *Awards, honors:* American Council of Learned Societies fellowship, 1966-67; fellowship from Charles Warren Center, Harvard University, 1966-67; National Endowment for the Humanities junior fellowship, 1971-72.

WRITINGS: Securing the Revolution: Ideology in American Politics, 1789-1815, Cornell University Press, 1972. Contributor to *William and Mary Quarterly.* Associate editor of *History and Theory,* 1970—.

WORK IN PROGRESS: Continuing research on Revolutionary America.

SIDELIGHTS: Buell told *CA* that his book, *Securing the Revolution,* "treats the effort to consolidate revolutionary achievements in an unfriendly world from the multiple perspectives of ideology, politics, and diplomacy." He is currently working on a "preliminary exploration of the political economy of the Revolutionary War." And, he added, "I hope to follow it shortly with a book-length study of the revolutionary mobilization done from the perspective of Connecticut. My long term ambition is to develop as synthetic an understanding of the Revolution as possible."

* * *

BUGG, Ralph 1922-

PERSONAL: Born October 12, 1922, in Notasulga, Ala.; son of Thomas Samuel and Esperance (Flurry) Bugg; married Mary Jo Smith, November 18, 1943; children: Barbara Bugg Tootle, Randy, Larry, Jennifer. *Education:* University of Alabama, B.A., 1947; graduate study at Emory University. *Politics:* Democrat. *Religion:* Methodist. *Home and office:* 1310 Stillwood Dr. N.E., Atlanta, Ga. 30306.

CAREER: Birmingham-Southern College, Birmingham, Ala., assistant professor of journalism and head of department, 1947-49; *Post Herald,* Birmingham, copy editor, 1949; *Atlanta Constitution,* Atlanta, Ga., night city editor, 1949-64; writer, 1964—. *Member:* American Society of Journalists and Authors.

WRITINGS: When Your Family Goes Camping, United Methodist Church, 1967; *The Times of Our Lives,* United Methodist Church, 1970; *Job Power,* Pyramid Publications, 1977. Contributor of several hundred articles to magazines.

WORK IN PROGRESS: Several volumes of fiction and nonfiction.

SIDELIGHTS: Bugg comments that the areas he covers in his writings are work, leisure, the family, and the outdoors.

BUGLIOSI, Vincent T. 1934-

PERSONAL: Born August 18, 1934, in Hibbing, Minn.; son of Vincent and Ida (Valerie) Bugliosi; married Gail Margaret Talluto, July 21, 1956; children: Wendy Suzanna, Vincent John. *Education:* University of Miami, Florida, B.B.A., 1956; University of California, Los Angeles, LL.B., 1964. *Politics:* Democrat. *Office:* 9171 Wilshire Blvd., Beverly Hills, Calif. 90210.

CAREER: Admitted to California bar, 1964; Los Angeles County Office of District Attorney, Los Angeles, Calif., deputy district attorney, 1964-72; Steinberg & Bugliosi, Beverly Hills, Calif., partner, 1972—. Professor of criminal law, Beverly Hills School of Law, 1968-74. Democratic candidate for district attorney, Los Angeles County, 1972, and California Attorney General, 1974. *Military service:* U.S. Army, 1957; became captain.

WRITINGS: (With Curt Gentry) *Helter Skelter: The True Story of the Manson Murders,* Norton, 1974.

SIDELIGHTS: Bugliosi successfully prosecuted five members of the Manson Family in connection with the 1969 Tate-LaBianca murders. In attempting to reconstruct the motive of the seemingly senseless killings, Bugliosi commented, "The prosecution does not have the legal burden of providing motive. But motive is extremely important evidence. A jury wants to know why."

The motive, Bugliosi discovered, was encapsulated in Charles Manson's phrase "helter-skelter"—a vague prediction of a forthcoming apocalyptic war between races that only the Family, safely inside Death Valley, would survive. Manson was convinced that the Beatles, who recorded the song "Helter Skelter" on their "White" album in 1968, were sending him messages. "As family members testified at the trial," *New Republic* reported, Manson "had worked out with scholarly precision correlations between his murderous doctrine and virtually every line of every lyric; more than that he had searched beyond his origins in the Beatles to *their* origins in *Book of Revelations,* where in the ninth chapter he found the 'four angels' with 'faces as the faces of men' but 'hair as the hair of women'; even mention of their electric guitars ('breastplates of fire') and much else besides. There was work of a fifth angel, and the family knew who that had to be. One translation of *Revelations* calls him Exterminans."

Bugliosi's *Helter Skelter,* which traces the murders, the bungled police investigation, and the trial itself, was generally received by critics as "a valuable book on a lurid subject ... a record of savagery and official bungling." W. C. Woods called it "an indifferently written social document of rare importance." "It is quickly clear," *New York Times* writer Michael Rogers said, "that Bugliosi's concern is at least as much with the intellectual process of investigation and prosecution as with the crime and the criminals themselves." Manson's words after his conviction, *New Republic* contends, "give reason enough why we all should know all of his story." Manson stated, "Mr. and Mrs. America—you are wrong. I am not the King of the Jews nor am I a hippy cult leader. I am what you have made me and the mad dog devil killer fiend leper is a reflection of your society.... Whatever the outcome of this madness that you call a fair trial or Christian justice, you can know this: In my mind's eye my thoughts light fires in your cities."

BIOGRAPHICAL/CRITICAL SOURCES: Time, November 4, 1974; *New York Times Book Review,* November 17, 1974; *New Republic,* January 4, 1975; *New Statesman,* April 25, 1975.

BULLEN, Dana R(ipley) 1931-

PERSONAL: Born August 6, 1931, in Boston, Mass. *Education:* University of Florida, B.S.J., 1953, LL.B., 1956. *Home:* 2716 P St. N.W., Washington, D.C. 20016. *Office: Washington Star,* 225 Virginia Ave. S.E., Washington, D.C. 20061.

CARRER/WRITINGS: Washington Star, Washington, D.C., U.S. Supreme Court reporter, 1962-69, syndicated columnist, 1966-69, U.S. Senate reporter, 1969-71, assistant national editor, 1972-76, foreign editor, 1976—. Research fellow, East Asian Research Center, Harvard University, 1971. *Military service:* U.S. Marine Corps Reserve, 1956-58; became lieutenant. *Awards, honors:* American Bar Association Gavel Award, 1964 and 1970; Nieman fellow, 1966-67; American Political Science Association award, 1970.

* * *

BURDA, R(obert) W(arren) 1932-

PERSONAL: Born January 16, 1932, in Chicago, Ill.; son of Joseph J. (a surveyor) and Lillian (Johnson) Burda; married, 1962 (divorced, May, 1974); children: James Russell. *Education:* Northwestern University, B.S., 1952; Union Theological Seminary, New York, N.Y., M.Div., 1955; San Francisco State University, M.A., 1965; also attended University of Minnesota, Wheaton College, University of Chicago, Georgetown University, Harvard University, and University of Iowa. *Residence:* Bloomington, Ill. *Agent:* Fox Chase Agency, Inc., 419 East 57th St., New York, N.Y. 10022. *Office:* Department of English, Illinois Wesleyan University, Bloomington, Ill. 61701.

CAREER: Illinois Wesleyan University, Bloomington, assistant professor, 1965-71, associate professor of English, 1971—, chairman of department, 1970-73, coordinator of international studies, 1971-73. *Awards, honors:* National Endowment for the Humanities grant, summer, 1974.

WRITINGS: The Pilgrim Thief (novel), Doubleday, 1977. Also author of a play, "The Quarantined Woman," 1978.

WORK IN PROGRESS: Clinemark's Tale, a novel set in Africa; *Yeats: The Myth of a Child; Outside In,* a novel; "Quixote at Elsinore," a play.

SIDELIGHTS: Although only one novel has been published so far, Burda has written ten novels in the last twenty years. He has traveled widely, especially in the non-Western world, and none of his novels is set in the United States.

* * *

BURGESS, Linda Cannon 1911-

PERSONAL: Born March 18, 1911, in Cambridge, Mass.; daughter of Walter Bradford (a physiologist) and Cornelia (a writer; maiden name, James) Cannon; married Charles Harry Burgess (a geologist), May 24, 1934 (divorced, 1954); children: W. Pierce, Heather Burgess Pentland, James, Pamela Burgess Southworth, Martha Burgess Talamas. *Education:* Attended Constantinople Women's College, 1928-29, and Boston University, 1931-32; Simmons College, M.A., 1934. *Politics:* Democrat. *Religion:* Unitarian-Universalist. *Home:* 2820 Hurst Ter., Washington, D.C. 20016.

CAREER: Children's Hospital, Boston, Mass., medical social worker, 1934-35; Highland Park Mental Health Clinic, Highland Park, Ill., psychiatric social worker, 1952-53; Evanston Hospital, Evanston, Ill., medical social worker, 1953-54; Barker Foundation, Washington, D.C., adoption agency director, 1954-60; Peirce-Warwick Adoption Service, Washington, D.C., director, 1961-72; member of planning boards, counselor, and writer, 1972—. *Member:* National Association of Social Workers.

WRITINGS: The Art of Adoption, Acropolis Books, 1977. Contributor to *Washington Post.*

WORK IN PROGRESS: Articles on adoptees, teenage pregnancies, and male domestication.

SIDELIGHTS: Linda Burgess writes: "The lives of the parties to adoption—adopting parents, birth parents, adoptees, and social workers—are inexorably bound to one another, but they live in different worlds of perception. I hope my book helps them to understand each other in a freer way."

Avocational interests: Painting, playing the accordion, travel to orphanages in the Near East, India, Nepal, and Africa.

*   *   *

BURGESS, Thornton Waldo   1874-1965
(W. B. Thornton)

PERSONAL: Born January 14, 1874, in Sandwich, Mass.; son of Thornton Waldo and Caroline F. (Hayward) Burgess; married Nina E. Osborne, June 30, 1905 (died, 1906); married Fannie P. Johnson, April 30, 1911; children: Thornton Waldo. *Education:* Attended business college in Boston for one year. *Residence:* Hampden, Mass.

CAREER: Editor and author of books for children. Held early jobs as a cashier and assistant bookkeeper in a shoe store. Began working for the Phelps Publishing Company as an office boy, 1895, became a reporter for one of the firm's weekly magazines, 1895-1911, and literary and household editor for Orange Judd weeklies, 1901-11; associate editor of *Good Housekeeping,* 1904-11; founded and directed the Burgess Radio Nature League, where for six years he gave weekly talks. *Awards, honors:* Litt.D., from Northwestern University, 1938.

WRITINGS—"Old Mother West Wind" series, published by Little, Brown: *Old Mother West Wind* (illustrated by George Kerr), 1910, reissued, 1960; *Mother West Wind's Children* (illustrated by Kerr), 1911 [reprinted edition illustrated by Harrison Cady, 1962]; *Mother West Wind's Animal Friends* (illustrated by Kerr), 1912; *Mother West Wind's Neighbors* (illustrated by Kerr), 1913 [reprinted edition illustrated by Cady, 1968]; *Mother West Wind "Why" Stories* (illustrated by Cady), 1915; *Mother West Wind "How" Stories* (illustrated by Cady), 1916; *Mother West Wind "Where" Stories* (illustrated by Cady), 1918.

"Boy Scouts" series, published by Penn Publishing: *The Boy Scouts of Woodcraft Camp* (illustrated by C. S. Corson), 1912; *The Boy Scouts on Swift River* (illustrated by Corson), 1913; *The Boy Scouts on Lost Trail* (illustrated by Corson), 1914; *The Boy Scouts in a Trapper's Camp* (illustrated by F. A. Anderson), 1915.

"Bedtime Story-Books" series, all original editions published by Little, Brown and illustrated by Harrison Cady, except as noted: *The Adventures of Johnny Chuck,* 1913; . . . *of Reddy Fox,* 1913; . . . *of Unc' Billy Possum,* 1914; . . . *of Mr. Mocker,* 1914; . . . *of Jerry Muskrat,* 1914, reprinted, Grosset & Dunlap, 1962; . . . *of Peter Cottontail,* 1914, reprinted, Grosset & Dunlap, 1970 [an abridged edition illustrated by Phoebe Erickson, Grosset & Dunlap, 1967]; . . . *of Grandfather Frog,* 1915; . . . *of Chatterer, the Red Squirrel,* 1915; . . . *of Danny Meadow Mouse,* 1915; . . . *of Sammy Jay,* 1915, reprinted, Grosset & Dunlap, 1962; . . . *of Old Mr. Toad,* 1916; . . . *of Old Man Coyote,* 1916, reprinted, Grosset & Dunlap, 1962; . . . *of Buster Bear,* 1916; . . . *of Prickly Porky,* 1916; . . . *of Poor Mrs. Quack,* 1917, reprinted, Grosset & Dunlap, 1962; . . . *of Paddy the Beaver,* 1917; . . . *of Jimmy Skunk,* 1918; . . . *of Bobby Coon,* 1918; . . . *of Ol' Mistah Buzzard,* 1919; . . . *of Bob White,* 1919.

"Wishing Stone" series: *Tommy and the Wishing Stone* (illustrated by Cady), Century, 1915, reprinted, Grosset & Dunlap, 1959; *Tommy's Change of Heart* (illustrated by Cady), Little, Brown, 1921, reprinted, Grosset & Dunlap, 1959; *Tommy's Wishes Come True* (illustrated by Cady), Little, Brown, 1921, reprinted, Grosset & Dunlap, 1959.

"Green Meadow" series, published by Little, Brown—*Happy Jack* (illustrated by Cady), 1918; *Mrs. Peter Rabbit* (illustrated by Cady), 1919; *Old Granny Fox* (illustrated by Cady), 1920; *Bowser the Hound,* 1920.

"Green Forest" series, published by Little, Brown, except as noted—*Lightfoot the Deer* (illustrated by Cady), 1921; *Whitefoot, the Wood Mouse* (illustrated by Cady), 1922, reprinted, Grosset & Dunlap, 1962; *Blacky the Crow* (illustrated by Cady), 1922; *Buster Bear's Twins* (illustrated by Cady), 1923, reprinted, Grosset & Dunlap, 1970.

"Smiling Pool" series, published by Little, Brown, except as noted: *Billy Mink* (illustrated by Cady), 1924; *Little Joe Otter* (illustrated by Cady), 1925; *Jerry Muskrat at Home* (illustrated by Cady), 1926, reissued, Grosset & Dunlap, 1962; *Longlegs the Heron* (illustrated by Cady), 1927.

"Little Color Classics" series, published by McLoughlin—*Little Pete's Adventure* (illustrated by Cady), 1941; *Little Red's Adventure* (illustrated by Cady), 1942; *Little Chuck's Adventure* (illustrated by Cady), 1942.

Animal stories: *The Burgess Animal Book for Children* (illustrated by Louis Agassiz Fuertes), Little, Brown, 1920, reprinted, Grosset & Dunlap, 1965; *The Christmas Reindeer* (illustrated by Rhoda Chase), Macmillan, 1926; *Happy Jack Squirrel Helps Unc' Billy* (illustrated by Cady), Stoll & Edwards, 1928; *Grandfather Frog Gets a Ride* (illustrated by Cady), Stoll & Edwards, 1928; *A Great Joke in Jimmy Skunk* (illustrated by Cady), Stoll & Edwards, 1928; *The Neatness of Bobby Coon* (illustrated by Cady), Stoll & Edwards, 1928; *Baby Possum's Queer Voyage* (illustrated by Cady), Stoll & Edwards, 1928; *Digger the Badger Decides to Stay* (illustrated by Cady), Stoll & Edwards, 1928.

Tales from the Storyteller's House (illustrated by Lemuel Palmer), Little, Brown, 1937; *While the Story-Log Burns* (illustrated by Palmer), Little, Brown, 1938; *The Three Little Bears,* Platt & Munk, 1940; *Reddy Fox's Sudden Engagement,* Platt & Munk, 1940; *Peter Rabbit Proves a Friend,* Platt & Munk, 1940; *Paddy's Surprise Visitor,* Platt & Munk, 1940; *Bobby Coon's Mistake,* Platt & Munk, 1940; *Young Flash, the Deer,* Platt & Munk, 1940; *Animal Stories* (illustrated by Cady), Platt & Munk, 1942, reprinted as *The Animal World of Thornton Burgess,* 1961; *Baby Animal Stories* (illustrated by P. Erickson), Grosset & Dunlap, 1949; *Peter Rabbit and Reddy Fox* (illustrated by Mary and Carl Hauge), Wonder Books, 1954.

Nature stories: *The Burgess Bird Book for Children* (illustrated by L. A. Fuertes), Little, Brown, 1919, reprinted, Grosset & Dunlap, 1965; *The Burgess Flower Book for Children,* Little, Brown, 1923; *The Burgess Seashore Book for Children* (illustrated by W. H. Southwick and George Sutton), Little, Brown, 1929; *Wild Flowers We Know,* Whitman, 1929; *On the Green Meadows: A Book of Nature Sto-*

ries (illustrated by Cady), Little, Brown, 1944; *At the Smiling Pool: A Book of Nature Stories* (illustrated by Cady), Little, Brown, 1945; *The Crooked Little Path: A Book of Nature Stories* (illustrated by Cady), Little, Brown, 1946; *The Dear Old Briar Patch: A Book of Nature Stories* (illustrated by Cady), Little, Brown, 1947; *Along Laughing Brook: A Book of Nature Stories* (illustrated by Cady), Little, Brown, 1949; *Nature Almanac* (illustrated by Erickson), Grosset & Dunlap, 1949; *At Paddy Beaver's Pond: A Book of Nature Stories* (illustrated by Cady), Little, Brown, 1950; *The Littlest Christmas Tree* (illustrated by M. and C. Hauge), Wonder Books, 1954; *The Burgess Book of Nature Lore: Adventures of Tommy, Sue, and Sammy with Their Friends of Meadow, Pool, and Forest* (illustrated by Robert Candy), Little, Brown, 1965.

Other: (Author of text with others) *The Bride's Primer: Being a Series of Quaint Parodies on the Ways of Brides and Their Misadventures Interlarded with Useful Hints for Their Advantage* (illustrated by F. Strothmann), Phelps Publishing, 1905; *The Burgess Big Book of Green Meadow Stories* (illustrated by Cady), Little, Brown, 1932; *The Wishing-Stone Stories* (illustrated by Cady), Little, Brown, 1935; *A Robber Meets His Match*, Platt & Munk, 1940; *A Thornton Burgess Picture Book* (illustrated by Nino Carbe), Garden City Publishing, 1950; *Aunt Sally's Friends in Fur; or, The Woodhouse Night Club* (with photographs by the author), Little, Brown, 1955; *Stories Around the Year* (illustrated by Erickson), Grosset & Dunlap, 1955; *50 Favorite Burgess Stories: On the Green Meadows* [and] *The Crooked Little Path* (illustrated by Cady), Grosset & Dunlap, 1956; *Thornton W. Burgess Bedtime Stories* (illustrated by C. and M. Hauge), Grosset & Dunlap, 1959, reprinted, 1977; *Now I Remember: Autobiography of an Amateur Naturalist*, Little, Brown, 1960; *The Million Little Sunbeams* (illustration by Cady), Six Oaks Press, 1963.

Contributor to magazines, including *Country Life in America* (under pseudonym W. B. Thornton), and *Good Housekeeping*.

SIDELIGHTS: One of Burgess's last books was his autobiography, *Now I Remember: Autobiography of an Amateur Naturalist. Kirkus Reviews* said, "His loosely autobiographical style is seldom stimulating, but the trials and 'thrills' of the selfmade man are always readable, and one is comforted by the fact that Mr. Burgess' life work was educational, informative, and entertaining to children of all ages." *New York Times Book Review* commented, "Mr. Burgess actually belongs to a long line, one that reaches at least as far back as Aesop. But he won't discuss this in his autobiography. One wishes he had. Then one remembers that he really is Peter Rabbit and has been Peter Rabbit for a long time."

In 1973, *The Adventures of Jimmy Skunk* was recorded as a ninety-minute-long phonotape by Taped Book Projects.

BIOGRAPHICAL/CRITICAL SOURCES: J. Bryan, *Saturday Review Gallery*, Simon & Schuster, 1959; Thornton Waldo Burgess, *Now I Remember: Autobiography of an Amateur Naturalist*, Little, Brown, 1960; *Nature*, January, 1956; *Kirkus Reviews*, July 15, 1960; *New York Times Book Review*, September 25, 1960; *Life*, November 14, 1960; *Audubon*, September, 1964; *Readers Digest*, October, 1967.

OBITUARIES: New York Times, June 6, 1965, June 7, 1965; *Publishers Weekly*, June 14, 1965; *Time*, June 18, 1965; *Newsweek*, June 21, 1965.*

(Died June 5, 1965)

BURGESS-KOHN, Jane 1928-

PERSONAL: Born January 1, 1928, in Stevens Point, Wis.; daughter of Karl W. and Alice (Bruce) Menzel; married Samuel G. Burgess (died, 1964); married Willard K. Kohn (a plant manager), November 29, 1974; children: (first marriage) David Bruce, Elizabeth Burgess Erven. *Education:* University of Wisconsin, Stevens Point, B.S., 1964; University of Wisconsin, Milwaukee, M.S., 1965; University of Illinois, Ph.D., 1972. *Residence:* Menomonee Falls, Wis. *Office:* Department of Sociology, University of Wisconsin, Waukesha, Wis. 53186.

CAREER: University of Wisconsin, Waukesha, assistant professor, 1967-71, associate professor of sociology, 1972—. Member of Groves Family Conference. Lecturer to single adults and single parent groups and to high school students and businesses. *Member:* National Council of Family Relations, Altrusa, Midwest Sociological Association, Wisconsin Sociological Association (president, 1975-76), Wisconsin Family Life Association (vice-president, 1974—). *Awards, honors:* Grant from University of Oslo, 1970; travel grant from University of Wisconsin, for Oslo, 1970.

WRITINGS: (Contributor) Charles Zastrow and Zae H. Chang, editors, *What Do I Do Now?*, Spectrum, 1976; (with husband, Willard K. Kohn) *The Widower*, Beacon Press, 1978. Contributor of more than twenty articles and reviews to sociology journals, *Parents' Magazine*, and newspapers.

WORK IN PROGRESS: Sex and the High School Senior; analyzing data on sex communication between parents and children: research on children's attitudes toward death; research on people who have reached retirement age.

SIDELIGHTS: Jane Burgess-Kohn writes: "My own experience as a widow for ten years, and the fact that I was unable to locate books for formerly married men to help them with their own unique problems, prompted me to begin research for the book, *The Widower*. My husband and I met while I was collecting data for this book and, after we married, we decided to join forces in writing *The Widower*."

* * *

BURGIN, C(harles) David 1939-

PERSONAL: Born February 12, 1939, in Somerset, Ky.; son of Lester E. and Lillian (Mounce) Burgin; married Diane Josephy, December 14, 1968 (divorced, 1974). *Education:* Miami University, B.A., 1962. *Politics:* Democrat. *Religion:* Protestant. *Home:* 2413 Tunlaw Rd. N.W., Washington, D.C. 20007. *Office: Patterson News,* 1 News Plaza, Patterson, N.J. 07509.

CAREER/WRITINGS: New York Herald Tribune, New York City, reporter, 1963-66; Newspaper Enterprise Association, New York City, news editor and Washington correspondent, 1966-68; *Washington Daily News,* Washington, D.C., Washington correspondent and sports editor, 1968-69; *San Francisco Examiner,* San Francisco, Calif., sports editor, 1969-71; *Washington Star,* Washington, D.C., sports editor, 1971-73, metropolitan editor, 1973-75, assistant managing editor, 1975-77; *Patterson Morning and Evening News,* Patterson, N.J., executive editor, 1977—. *Military service:* U.S. Army, 1962-63; became sergeant.

* * *

BURKE, (Omar) Michael 1927-

PERSONAL: Born April 18, 1927, in Lahore, India; son of Claude William (a landowner) and Mary Violet Burke. *Education:* Educated privately. *Adress:* c/o Octagon Press, 14 Baker St., London W1M 2HA, England.

CAREER: Import-export executive and writer.

WRITINGS: Among the Dervishes, Octagon, 1973, Dutton, 1975.

WORK IN PROGRESS: A biography of the Sayed Idries Shah, "authority on Sufi thought and eminent Middle Eastern personality descended from the Prophet Mohammed."

SIDELIGHTS: Burke has traveled in Sudan and Egypt, Afghanistan, Pakistan, India, and Iran, gathering material on little-known Sufi and other spiritual communities. He speaks and writes Persian and Urdu. He comments that he is "especially interested in the dramatic dissonance between what people in the West imagine about Eastern spiritual systems and their reality on the ground."

* * *

BURKE, Tom

PERSONAL: Education: Attended Columbia University. *Home:* 48 Gramercy Park, New York, N.Y. 10010.

CAREER: Ghost-writer, 1963; former columnist and editor of *Gentlemen's Quarterly;* writer, 1968—. *Member:* Writer's Bloc.

WRITINGS: Burke's Steerage (collection of profiles and essays), Putnam, 1976. A contributing editor of *Rolling Stone.* Contributor to *New York Times, Los Angeles Times, Village Voice, Esquire, TV Guide, Cosmopolitan,* and other publications.

WORK IN PROGRESS: A novel.

SIDELIGHTS: As a child, Burke was pressured by his father into becoming an opera singer. "But there was a problem," stated Burke: "I didn't have a voice. As a boy soprano I'd sounded like Beverly Sills, but after puberty, forget it." After some professional acting as a teenager, Burke decided to write about performers rather than be one: "It struck me that never, in any other culture, had there ever been such a thing as a movie or TV star. That no entertainer had ever before been loved by so many as these people are. I wanted to find out what being so mythical did to their psyches."

Burke claims to have no hobbies.

* * *

BURNET, (Frank) Macfarlane 1899-

PERSONAL: Born September 3, 1899, in Traralgon, Victoria, Australia; son of Frank (a bank manager) and Hadassah (Mackay) Burnet; married Edith Linda Marston Druce, July 10, 1929 (died November 10, 1973); married Hazel Foletta Jenkin, January 16, 1976; children: Elizabeth (Mrs. Paul Dexter), Ian, Deborah (Mrs. John Giddy). *Education:* University of Melbourne, M.B. and B.S., both 1923, M.D., 1924; University of London, Ph.D., 1928. *Home:* 48 Monomeath Ave., Canterbury, Victoria, Australia 3126. *Office:* Department of Microbiology, University of Melbourne, Parkville, Victoria, Australia 3052.

CAREER: Melbourne Hospital, Melbourne, Australia, resident pathologist, 1923-24; Lister Institute, London, England, Beit fellow in medical research, 1926-27; Walter & Eliza Hall Institute for Medical Research, Melbourne, Australia, assistant director, 1928-31; National Institute for Medical Research, Hampstead, England, visiting worker, 1932-33; Walter & Eliza Hall Institute for Medical Research, assistant director, 1934-44, director, 1944-65, Rowden White research fellow in microbiology, 1966-67; writer, 1967—. University of Melbourne research professor, 1944-66, pro-

fessor emeritus and guest professor, 1966—. Dunham lecturer at Harvard University, 1944; Croonian lecturer for Royal Society; Herter lecturer at Johns Hopkins University, 1950; Abraham Flexner lecturer at Vanderbilt University, 1958. Member of World Health Organization medical research advisory committee in Geneva, 1957-60; chairman of medical research advisory committee in Papua New Guinea, 1962-69; chairman of board of trustees of Commonwealth Foundation (London), 1966-69.

MEMBER: Australian Academy of Science (president, 1965-69), Royal Australian College of Physicians (fellow), Australian Medical Association, Royal Society (fellow), Royal College of Physicians (fellow), Royal College of Surgeons (honorary fellow), Pathological Society of the United Kingdom, National Academy of Sciences (United States; foreign associate), American College of Physicians (fellow), American Academy of Arts and Sciences (foreign member), Swedish Royal Academy of Science. *Awards, honors:* Royal Medal from Royal Society, 1947, Copley Medal, 1959; knighted, 1951, named knight commander of the British Empire, 1969; Order of Merit, 1958; Von Behring Prize from University of Marburg, 1952; Lasker Award from Lasker Foundation, 1952; Galen Medal in Therapeutics from Society of Apothecaries, 1958; co-winner of Nobel Prize for Medicine, 1960; Sc.D. from Cambridge University, 1946; D.Sc. from Oxford University, 1968.

WRITINGS: Changing Patterns (autobiography), Heinemann, 1968, American Elsevier, 1969; *Dominant Mammal,* Heinemann, 1970, St. Martin's, 1972; *Walter and Eliza Hall Institute, 1915-1965,* Melbourne University Press, 1971; *Endurance of Life,* Melbourne University Press, in press.

Scientific works: *Biological Aspects of Infectious Disease,* Cambridge University Press, 1940, 2nd edition published as *Natural History of Infectious Disease,* 1953, 4th edition (with D. O. White), 1972; *Virus as Organism,* Harvard University Press, 1945; *Viruses and Man,* Penguin, 1953, 2nd edition, 1955; *The Clonal Selection Theory of Acquired Immunity,* Vanderbilt University Press, 1959; *The Integrity of the Body,* Harvard University Press, 1962; *Cellular Immunology,* Cambridge University Press, 1969; *Immunological Surveillance,* Pergamon, 1970; *Genes, Dreams, and Realities,* Medical & Technical Publishing, 1971; *Intrinsic Mutagenesis,* Medical & Technical Publishing, 1974. Also author of other books on technical subjects.

WORK IN PROGRESS: Research on various aspects of aging and the genetic components of human behavior.

SIDELIGHTS: Burnet writes: "Two autobiographical books, *Changing Patterns* and *Walter and Eliza Hall Institute* present personal pictures of my own scientific development and the growth of an Australian laboratory. Since my retirement, I have written extensively on aspects of human biology in the broad sense, mostly as lectures to professional groups of various sorts. *Dominant Mammal* summarized my 1970 attitudes without attracting much attention. *Endurance of Life* is more ambitious and more controversial, with a strong bias toward stressing the importance of genetics in all behavioural as well as structural aspects of the human being. The social implications of such a viewpoint are already becoming evident."

BIOGRAPHICAL/CRITICAL SOURCES: Lancet, Volume I, 1965; Macfarlane Burnet, *Changing Patterns,* Heinemann, 1968, American Elsevier, 1969; Burnet, *Walter and Eliza Hall Institute, 1915-1965,* Melbourne University Press, 1971.

BURNINGHAM, John Mackintosh 1936-

PERSONAL: Born April 27, 1936, in Farnham, England; son of Charles and Jessie (Mackintosh) Burningham; married Helen Gillian Oxenbury (a designer), 1964; children: one son, one daughter. Education: Attended Central School of Art, London, 1956-59. Residence: Hampstead, London, England.

CAREER: Author, illustrator, and free-lance designer. Worked as a farmer, builder, in forestry, and with Friend's Ambulance Unit during 1950's. Awards, honors: Kate Greenway Medal, 1963, for Borka: The Adventure of a Goose with No Feathers, and 1970, for Mr. Grumpy's Outing; New York Times best illustrated book of the year award, 1971; Boston Globe-Horn Book award for illustration, 1972.

WRITINGS—All self-illustrated: Borka: The Adventures of a Goose with No Feathers, Random House, 1963; ABC, J. Cape, 1964, Bobbs-Merrill, 1967; Trubloff: The Mouse Who Wanted to Play the Balalaika, J. Cape, 1964, Random House, 1965; Humbert, Mister Firkin, and the Lord Mayor of London, J. Cape, 1965, Bobbs-Merrill, 1967; Cannonball Simp, J. Cape, 1966, Bobbs-Merrill, 1967; Harquin: The Fox Who Went Down to the Valley, J. Cape, 1967, Bobbs-Merrill, 1968; Seasons, J. Cape, 1969, Bobbs-Merrill, 1971; Mr. Grumpy's Outing, Holt, 1970; (adaptor) Around the World in Eighty Days, J. Cape, 1972; Mr. Gumpy's Motor Car, Macmillan, 1975.

"Little Book" series: The Rabbit, J. Cape, 1974, Crowell, 1975; The School, J. Cape, 1974, Crowell, 1975; The Snow, J. Cape, 1974, Crowell, 1975; The Baby, Crowell, 1975; The Blanket, J. Cape, 1975, Crowell, 1976; The Cupboard, J. Cape, 1975, Crowell, 1976; The Dog, J. Cape, 1975, Crowell, 1976; The Friend, J. Cape, 1975, Crowell, 1976.

Illustrator: Ian Fleming, Chitty Chitty Bang Bang: The Magical Car, Random House, 1964; Letta Schatz, editor, The Extraordinary Tug-of-War, Follett, 1968.

SIDELIGHTS: Burningham uses a wide assortment of materials and techniques in his illustrations, including crayons, charcoal, and india ink. He has designed murals, exhibitions, three-dimensional models, magazine illustrations, and advertisements. Some of his works have been exhibited by the American Institute of Graphic Arts.*

* * *

BURRINGTON, David E. 1931-

PERSONAL: Born March 11, 1931, in Rapid City, S.D.; son of Therlo (a dentist) and Mary (Nissen) Burrington. Education: Attended South Dakota School of Mines and Technology, 1949-50; University of Minnesota, B.A., 1953, M.A., 1959; further study at Sorbonne, University of Paris, 1956-57, and University of California at Los Angeles, 1963-64. Politics: Independent. Home: 1104 West Blvd., Rapid City, S.D. 57701. Office: NBC News, 30 Rockefeller Plaza, New York, N.Y. 10020.

CAREER/WRITINGS: National Broadcasting Co. (NBC) News, New York City, correspondent from Saigon, Viet Nam, 1966-67, Los Angeles, Calif., 1967-69, Paris, 1969-71, Tel Aviv, Israel, 1971-74, Rome, 1974—. Notable assignments include coverage of the Viet Nam War, assassinations of Martin Luther King and Robert Kennedy, the 1968 presidential campaign, the 1971 Indian-Pakistan War, the 1973 Arab-Israel War. Military service: U.S. Army, 1954-56. Member: Overseas Press Club, Foreign Press Club in Rome and Madrid. Awards, honors: David Sarnoff fellowship, 1963-64.

SIDELIGHTS: "In TV news," Burrington told CA, "I feel the film should tell the story insofar as is possible. Commentary is frequently used as a crutch, and often gets in the way of most effective film use. TV news has so far not learned how to make science, medicine, and economics interesting—this I see as a major challenge."

AVOCATIONAL INTERESTS: Ancient history, archaeology.

* * *

BURROUGHS, William, Jr. 1947-

PERSONAL: Born July 21, 1947, in Conroe, Tex.; son of William Seward (a writer) and Joan (Vollmer) Burroughs; married Karen Perry (separated). Education: Attended a private school. Politics: "Gandhi." Religion: Christian. Agent: Peter Matson, Harold Matson Co., Inc., 22 East 40th St., New York, N.Y. 10016.

CAREER: Has worked as a crewman on a commercial fishing boat in Homer, Alaska, as a ski beveller in Boulder, Colo., as an exterminator in Savannah, Ga., and variously as a short-order cook, a gas station attendant, a kitchen steward, and a confidence therapist for children with behavioral disorders; now a writer.

WRITINGS: Speed (novel), Olympia, 1970; Kentucky Ham (autobiography), Dutton, 1973. Contributor to Esquire and Crawdaddy.

WORK IN PROGRESS: "Research on proofs of Absolute Reality as opposed to the Eastern concept of Totally Illusory Cosmology."

SIDELIGHTS: New York Times book reviewer, Anatole Broyard, quoted from Kentucky Ham that Burroughs was "making a plea for the integrity of insanity" and "loonies are our greatest planetary resource." Broyard called this "junkyards of bombast," but Burroughs told CA that he views "senseless benevolence as opposed to senseless violence" as "really an increasing phenomenon" given to "aiding and abetting kind lunatics." Broyard admitted that the younger Burroughs had the "handicap of being the son of the drug scene's grand guru," while a reviewer for New Yorker said that Burroughs's "I've-seen-it-all-toughness" writing style "bears a striking resemblance to the enthusiastic, naive, sloppy, populist, and, at its best, fascinating writing of the Beats." Richard Brickner comments on Burroughs's "Perelmanic yet personal style that takes advantage of his over-developed sense of passivity to describe himself and others as if they were constantly being jerked about, forced to perform with exquisite clumsiness. The effect is frequently as funny as one's most beloved slapstick routines."

Of his work in progress, Burroughs says he hopes to "hash it together within a year if the creek don't rise or the whole civilization doesn't back up five hundred years suddenly."

BIOGRAPHICAL/CRITICAL SOURCES: New York Times, June 24, 1973; Best Sellers, July 1, 1973; New York Times Book Review, July 29, 1973; New Yorker, August 20, 1973; William Burroughs, Jr., Kentucky Ham, Dutton, 1973.

* * *

BUTLER, Ivan
See BEUTTLER, Edward Ivan Oakley

* * *

BUTLER, Octavia E(stelle) 1947-

PERSONAL: Born June 22, 1947, in Pasadena, Calif.;

daughter of Laurice and Octavia M. (Guy) Butler. *Education:* Pasadena City College, A.A., 1968; California State University, Los Angeles, student, 1969—. *Home address:* P.O. Box 6604, Los Angeles, Calif. 90055.

CAREER: Free-lance writer, 1970—. *Member:* Science Fiction Writers of America.

WRITINGS—Science fiction novels: *Patternmaster,* Doubleday, 1976; *Mind of My Mind,* Doubleday, 1977; *Survivor,* Doubleday, 1978.

Work represented in anthologies, including *Clarion,* edited by Robin Scott Wilson, New American Library, 1970, and *The Last Dangerous Visions,* edited by Harlan Ellison, Harper, 1978.

WORK IN PROGRESS: To Keep Thee in All Thy Ways (tentative title), "a quiet little horror story of the antebellum South."

SIDELIGHTS: Octavia Butler writes: "I began writing when I was about ten years old for the same reason many people begin reading—to escape loneliness and boredom. I didn't realize then that writing was supposed to be work. It was too much fun. It still is. I began writing fantasy and science fiction because both inspire a high level of creativity and offer a great deal of freedom. However, I remember that when I began reading science fiction, I was disappointed at how little this creativity and freedom was used to portray the many racial, ethnic, and class variations. Also, I could not help noticing how few significant women characters there were in science fiction. Fortunately, all of this has been changing over the past few years. I intend my writing to contribute to the change."

* * *

BYRNE, Donald E(dward), Jr. 1942-

PERSONAL: Born January 7, 1942, in St. Paul, Minn.; son of Donald Edward (a postal employee) and Edna Marie (Reinhart) Byrne; married Mary Anne Tietjen, August 4, 1967; children: Julie, Donald Edward III, Clare, Mary. *Education:* St. Paul Seminary, St. Paul, Minn., B.A., 1963; Marquette University, M.A., 1966; Duke University, Ph.D., 1972. *Politics:* Democrat. *Religion:* Roman Catholic. *Home:* 515 East Main St., Annville, Pa. 17003. *Office:* Department of Religion, Lebanon Valley College, Annville, Pa. 17003.

CAREER: College of St. Catherine, St. Paul, Minn., instructor in theology, 1967-68; Lebanon Valley College, Annville, Pa., assistant professor, 1971-77, associate professor of religion, 1977—. *Member:* American Association of University Professors, American Folklore Society, American Academy of Religion, American Society of Church History.

WRITINGS: No Foot of Land: Folklore of American Methodist Itinerants, Scarecrow, 1975; (with Arthur Ford and Philip Billings) *Three Voices* (poetry chapbook), privately printed, 1976.

WORK IN PROGRESS: Studying ethnic festivals in central Pennsylvania.

SIDELIGHTS: Byrne told *CA:* "There is a gulf between religious behavior as perceived by historians and religious behavior as practiced by ordinary people. The study of religious folklore may help to bridge that gap."

* * *

BYRNE, Robert 1930-

PERSONAL: Born May 22, 1930, in Dubuque, Iowa; son of Thomas Edward (a contractor) and Clara (Loes) Byrne; married Josefa Heifetz (a pianist), May 3, 1959 (divorced); children: Russell. *Education:* University of Colorado, B.S., 1954. *Politics:* Democrat. *Religion:* None. *Home:* 201 Roundtree Way, San Rafael, Calif. 94903. *Agent:* Knox Burger Associates Ltd., 39½ Washington Sq., New York, N.Y. 10012.

CAREER: Editor in San Francisco, Calif., 1961-73; writer, 1973—.

WRITINGS: Writing Rackets, Lyle Stuart, 1968; *Memories of a Non-Jewish Childhood,* Lyle Stuart, 1969; *McGoorty,* Lyle Stuart, 1972; (editor) *Mrs. Byrne's Dictionary,* University Books, 1974; *The Tunnel,* Harcourt, 1977; *The Ultimate Book of Pool and Billiards,* Harcourt, in press.

SIDELIGHTS: Byrne remarks: "A person should write only if he or she feels more miserable not writing. I would rather play three-cushion billiards than anything else in life. Too bad there's no money in it."

* * *

CAIN, James M(allahan) 1892-1977

July 1, 1892—October 27, 1977; American novelist best known for mystery crime novels, including *The Postman Always Rings Twice, Double Indemnity,* and *Mildred Pierce.* Cain's writing style is said to have influenced the writing of Albert Camus. He died in University Park, Md. Obituaries: *New York Times,* October 29, 1977; *Washington Post,* October 29, 1977; *Time,* November 7, 1977; *Newsweek,* November 7, 1977. (See index for *CA* sketch)

* * *

CAIN, Maureen 1938-

PERSONAL: Born March 10, 1938, in England; daughter of Lewis Arthur (an electrical engineer) and Norah Elizabeth (a teacher; maiden name, Heard) Cain; children: Daniel John. *Education:* London School of Economics and Political Science, B.A., 1959, Ph.D., 1963. *Politics:* Socialist. *Religion:* Roman Catholic. *Office:* Department of Sociology, Brunel University, Uxbridge, Middlesex, England.

CAREER: University of Manchester, Manchester, England, fellow, 1964-65; Brunel University, Uxbridge, England, research fellow, 1968-69, lecturer, 1969-75, senior lecturer in sociology, 1975—. *Member:* British Sociological Association, British Society of Criminology, International Sociological Association (member of sociology of law committee), Institute of Sociology of Law for Europe (board member), University Women's Club.

WRITINGS: (Contributor) Ben Whitaker, editor, *The Police,* Penguin, 1964; (contributor) Stanley Cohen, editor, *Images of Deviance,* Penguin, 1971; *Society and the Policeman's Role,* Routledge & Kegan Paul, 1973. Contributor to law and sociology journals.

WORK IN PROGRESS: Research on solicitor-client relationships, and on Marx and Engels on the law.

* * *

CALDWELL, John 1928-

PERSONAL: Born November 28, 1928, in Detroit, Mich.; son of John Homer and Dorothy (Briggs) Caldwell; married Hester Goodenough (a teacher), July 5, 1952; children: Timothy John, Sverre, Peter James, Jennifer. *Education:* Dartmouth College, B.A., 1950; Wesleyan University, M.A.L.S., 1965. *Home address:* Putney, Vt. 05346. *Office:* Putney School, Putney, Vt. 05346.

CAREER: Putney School, Putney, Vt., teacher, 1953—. Also works as athletic coach and ski instructor. *Military service:* U.S. Navy, 1950-52; became lieutenant junior grade.

WRITINGS: *The Cross-Country Ski Book,* Stephen Greene Press, 1964; *The New Cross-Country Ski Book,* Stephen Greene Press, 1970; *Caldwell on Cross-Country,* Stephen Greene Press, 1975; *Cross-Country Skiing Today,* Stephen Greene Press, 1977. Contributing editor of *Skiing.* Editorial adviser for *Nordic Skiing.*

WORK IN PROGRESS: Research on training, technique, and waxing for cross-country skiing.

SIDELIGHTS: Caldwell remarks: "I enjoy teaching. I think there is an important connection between the mental processes used in the teaching (and doing) of mathematics and the coaching of skiing. One must develop highly analytical thinking processes and then be able to express them." *Avocational interests:* Gardening.

* * *

CALLEN, Larry
See CALLEN, Lawrence Willard, Jr.

* * *

CALLEN, Lawrence Willard, Jr. 1927-
(Larry Callen)

PERSONAL: Born April 3, 1927, in New Orleans, La.; son of Lawrence Willard and Emily (Barrouquere) Callen; married Willa Carmouche (a learning disabilities diagnostician), December 6, 1958; children: Erin Andree, Alex David, Dashiel Noel, Holly Willa. *Education:* Attended Tulane University, 1944-45, 1953-54, and Loyola University, New Orleans, La., 1950-52; Florida State University, B.S., 1957; Louisiana State University, graduate study, 1960-63. *Home:* 1117 Tiffany Rd., Silver Spring, Md. 20904. *Office:* U.S. Department of Labor, 601 D St. N.W., Washington, D.C. 20213.

CAREER: *Jefferson Herald,* New Orleans, La., associate editor, 1952-55; H. L. Peace Publications, New Orleans, associate editor of a fishing industry magazine, 1958-59; Louisiana Department of Employment Security, Baton Rouge, in unemployment insurance and employment services, 1959-63; U.S. Department of Labor, Washington, D.C., in unemployment insurance, 1963—. *Military service:* U.S. Navy, 1945-46. U.S. Air Force, 1955-58.

WRITINGS—Under name Larry Callen: *Pinch* (juvenile novel), Little, Brown, 1976; *Deadly Mandrake* (juvenile novel), Little, Brown, 1978.

WORK IN PROGRESS—Under name Larry Callen: "a third book about people in Four Corners"; "the great American mystery novel."

SIDELIGHTS: Callen wrote to *CA:* "There is a rather delicate middle ground between stories for children and stories for grownups. It's an elusive target. Story tellers who find it entertain both groups. I'm trying to find it.

"I am also totally sold on the value of the family in the mental, moral and emotional growth of the individual. I've indicated that in the two books published so far.

"Maybe you would also like to know that most of *Pinch* was written on a commuter bus between my home in Silver Spring, Md., and my job in Washington, D.C. And a goodly portion of *Deadly Mandrake* was written in a carpool over the same distance, and benefited from a great deal of kibitzing from fellow drivers.

"My hobbies are unrelated to writing. First is kid raising. We have four, ranging from six to eleven years of age. Second and third are a tie. I have several tanks of tropical and salt water fish and have plans to do some breeding of tropicals. Also have a cowrie collection that is a beautiful thing to see. Cowries are salt water snails. I collect the shells. Also have a half dozen or so live cowries in my salt water tanks. Hobby number four is geneology. I occasionally dabble at this, trying to trace my family's journey prior to settling in Louisiana. We are Scotch-Irish. Progress is slow. I've only made it back to North Carolina."

* * *

CALVERT, John
See LEAF, (Wilbur) Munro

* * *

CAMERON, A(rchibald) J(ames) 1920-

PERSONAL: Born October 3, 1920, in Fife, Scotland; son of Archibald James (a policeman) and Florence Mary (a nurse; maiden name, Blair) Cameron; married Patricia Mary Coward (a bank official), September 5, 1953; children: Fiona Mary, Catriona, Duncan, Roderick. *Education:* Attended University of London, 1955-66; University of Durham, diploma, 1969, M.Ed., 1973, M.Sc., 1976. *Politics:* "Floating voter, tending toward the right." *Religion:* Church of England. *Home:* The Folly, Hillcrest, Durham DH1 1RB, England. *Office:* Department of Education, New College Durham, Durham DH1 4SY, England.

CAREER: Electrical engineer, 1937-41; teacher of mathematics and head of department at schools in Essex, England, 1948-66; Neville's Cross College, Durham, England, lecturer, 1966-70, senior lecturer in mathematics, 1970-77; New College Durham, Durham, England, senior lecturer in statistics and quantitative methods, 1977—. *Military service:* Royal Navy, 1941-46; served in Mediterranean and Pacific theaters. *Member:* Institute of Mathematics and Its Applications (associate fellow).

WRITINGS: *Mathematical Enterprises for Schools,* Pergamon, 1966, revised edition, 1968; *A Guide to Graphs,* Pergamon, 1970.

WORK IN PROGRESS: *Mathematical Enterprises for the Middle School;* a television play.

SIDELIGHTS: Cameron comments: "As the archetypal 'Late Developer' I feel that my career is of interest only in as far as it illustrates the great improvement in educational opportunity in England and Wales since the war. (Scotland has always had a completely different educational and legal, etc., system)." He feels that his first book played a part in the changes in British mathematical education that have occurred in the last ten years.

AVOCATIONAL INTERESTS: Foreign travel.

* * *

CAMERON, David R(obertson) 1941-

PERSONAL: Born January 19, 1941, in Vancouver, British Columbia, Canada; married wife, Stephanie; children: Tassie, Amy. *Education:* University of British Columbia, B.A., 1963, graduate study, 1963-64; London School of Economics and Political Science, London, M.Sc,, 1966, Ph.D., 1969. *Home address:* R.R. 3, Keene, Ontario, Canada K0L 2G0. *Office:* Department of Politics, Peter Robinson College, Trent University, Peterborough, Ontario, Canada K9J 7B8.

CAREER: Member of research staff of Royal Commission on Bilingualism and Biculturalism, 1964-65, summer, 1967; University of London, London, England, part-time tutor at Imperial College, 1966-67; Trent University, Peter Robinson College, Peterborough, Ontario, member of faculty in department of politics, 1968—, chairman of department, 1970-75, dean of Arts and Science, 1975—.

MEMBER: Institute of Public Administration of Canada, Canadian Political Science Association, Canadian Society for Eighteenth Century Studies, Canadian Association of Deans of Arts and Science, American Society for Political and Legal Philosophy, Political Studies Association (England). *Awards, honors:* Canada Council fellowship, 1965, 1966, 1967, 1969, 1974-75; I.O.D.E. fellowship, 1966, 1967.

WRITINGS: (Contributor) *The Federal Capital: Government Institution,* Volume I, Royal Commission on Bilingualism and Biculturalism, 1969; *The Social Thought of Rousseau and Burke: A Comparative Study,* Weidenfeld & Nicolson, 1973; *Nationalism, Self-Determination and the Quebec Question,* Macmillan (Canada), 1974; (contributor) John Redekop, editor, *Approaches to Canadian Politics,* Prentice-Hall, 1977. Contributor to political studies and Canadian studies journals. Associate editor of *Journal of Canadian Studies,* 1975—; member of editorial board of *Canadian Forum,* 1976—.

* * *

CAMPA, Arthur L(eon)   1905-

PERSONAL: Born February 20, 1905, in Guaymas, Mexico; naturalized U.S. citizen; son of Daniel and Delfina (Lopez) Campa; married Lucille Cushing, April 23, 1943; children: Mary Del (Mrs. Larry Price), Danielle, Arthur, Jr., Nita, David. *Education:* University of New Mexico, B.A., 1928, M.A., 1930; Columbia University, Ph.D., 1940. *Politics:* Republican. *Religion:* Protestant. *Home:* 2031 South Madison, Denver, Colo. 80210. *Office:* Department of Modern Languages, University of Denver, Denver, Colo.

CAREER: Columbia University, New York, N.Y., instructor in Spanish, 1930-31; University of New Mexico, Albuquerque, instructor, 1932-33, assistant professor, 1935-37, associate professor, 1937-41, professor of modern languages, 1942-46; University of Denver, Denver, Colo., professor of modern languages, chairman of department, and director of Center for Latin American Studies, 1946—, chairman of Division of Languages and Literature, 1946-50. U.S. Department of State, lecturer in Spain, 1953-54; U.S. Embassy, Lima, Peru, cultural attache, 1955-57; Peace Corps, training project director and Denver University liaison officer. President, National Folk Festival Association, Inc., Washington, D.C. *Military service:* U.S. Army Air Forces, 1942-45; served in European theater; became major; received Bronze Star Medal and ten campaign stars.

MEMBER: American Association of Teachers of Spanish and Portuguese, Modern Language Association of America, American Anthropological Association, National Folklore Festival Association, American Folklore Society, Westerners (Denver Posse), Colorado Folklore Society (president, 1948-55), Colorado Authors League (president, 1953), Pan American Club of Denver (president, 1948, 1952). *Awards, honors:* Spanish Arts Foundation fellow, 1932; Rockefeller research grant, 1933-34; Guggenheim fellowship, 1952; Top Hand Award of Colorado Authors League for nonfiction article, 1955, 1964, for non-fiction book, 1963.

WRITINGS: Acquiring Spanish, Macmillan, 1944; *Mastering Spanish,* Macmillan, 1945; *Spanish Folk-Poetry in New Mexico,* University of New Mexico Press, 1946; *Treasure of the Sangre de Cristos,* University of Oklahoma Press, 1963; *Hispanic Folklore Studies of Arthur Campa: An Original Anthology,* edited by Carlos Coates, Arno, 1976. Also author of more than seventy monographs, bulletins, and articles for folklore and other professional journals. Editor, *Westerners Roundup* (monthly magazine).

WORK IN PROGRESS: A book of proverbs and sayings of the Southwest; *Hispanic Culture in the Southwest.*

* * *

CAMPBELL, Dennis M(arion)   1945-

PERSONAL: Born August 23, 1945, in Dalhart, Tex.; son of Frances Marion (a businessman) and Margaret (Osterberg) Campbell; married Leesa Heydenreich (a college administrator), June 13, 1970; children: Margaret Heyden. *Education:* Duke University, A.B., 1967, Ph.D., 1973; Yale University, B.D., 1970. *Politics:* Rupublican. *Religion:* Mehtodist. *Home:* 416 Harrell Dr., Spartanburg, S.C. 29302. *Office:* Department of Religion, Converse College, Spartanburg, S.C. 29301.

CAREER: Ordained minister of United Methodist Church; minister of Trinity United Methodist Church, Durham, N.C., 1970-73; Converse College, Spartanburg, S.C., assistant professor of religion and chairperson of department, 1974—. *Member:* American Academy of Religion, American Society of Christian Ethics, Phi Beta Kappa, Omicron Delta Kappa.

WRITINGS: Authority and the Renewal of American Theology, Pilgrim Press, 1976.

WORK IN PROGRESS: Theology and Social Location.

* * *

CAMPBELL, Ewing   1940-

PERSONAL: Born December 26, 1940, in Alice, Tex.; son of James Vernon and Marie (Crofford) Campbell; married Lois R. Glenn (an editor), April, 1972. *Education:* North Texas State University, B.B.A., 1968; University of Southern Mississippi, M.A., 1972. *Politics:* "Apolitical." *Religion:* "Irreligious." *Home and office:* 3955 Shoal Creek Blvd., #104, Austin, Tex. 78756.

CAREER: Writer, 1967—. *Military service:* U.S. Army, 1959-62. *Member:* Phi Kappa Phi.

WRITINGS: Weave It Like Nightfall (novel), Nefertiti Head Press, 1977.

Work represented in anthologies, including *Intro Five.* Contributor to literary journals, including *Prairie Schooner, Dalhousie Review,* and *Cimarron Review.*

WORK IN PROGRESS: The Way of Sequestered Places, the second half of *The Rincon Diptych,* of which *Weave It Like Nightfall* is the first half.

SIDELIGHTS: Campbell writes: "I wrote *Weave It Like Nightfall* in order to make permanent something that had long since passed out of existence except in my mind; I am writing *The Way* in order to complete the circle begun when I started the first book."

* * *

CAMPBELL, James Marshall   1895-1977

PERSONAL: Born September 30, 1895, in Warsaw, N.Y. *Education:* Hamilton College, A.B., 1917; graduate study at Princeton University, 1917-18; Catholic University of

America, M.A., 1920, Ph.D., 1923. *Home:* 222 H St. N.W., Washington, D.C. 20002.

CAREER: Ordained Roman Catholic priest, 1926; Catholic University of America, Washington, D.C., instructor in classics, 1921-27, associate professor, 1927-32, professor of Greek, 1932-66, professor emeritus, 1967-77, director of Pacific Coast branch, summers, 1932-66, dean of college of arts and sciences, 1934-66. *Member:* American Philological Association, Mediaeval Academy of America. *Awards, honors:* LL.D. from Dunbarton College, 1960; Litt.D. from Hamilton College, 1962; L.H.D. from Catholic University of America, 1966.

WRITINGS: The Influence of the Second Sophistic on the Style of the Sermons of St. Basil the Great, Catholic University of America, 1922; *The Greek Fathers,* Longman, Green, 1929, reprinted, Cooper Square, 1963; (editor with Martin R. P. McGuire) *The Confessions of St. Augustine,* Prentice-Hall, 1966. Also co-author of *Concordance of Prudentius.*

OBITUARIES: Washington Post, March 26, 1977.*

(Died March 25, 1977, in Washington, D.C.)

* * *

CAMPBELL, Karen
See BEATY, Betty

* * *

CAMPBELL, Robert 1922-1977

January 20, 1922—October 2, 1977; American author and documentary filmmaker. Campbell died in Boonton, N.J. Obituaries: *New York Times,* October 4, 1977; *AB Bookman's Weekly,* January 30, 1978. (See index for *CA* sketch)

* * *

CANNING, Jeff(rey Michael) 1947-

PERSONAL: Born July 3, 1947, in Tarrytown, N.Y.; son of John R. (a newspaper pressman) and Dolores A. (a secretary; maiden name, Schaefer) Canning. *Education:* Manhattan College, Bronx, N.Y., B.A., 1969. *Religion:* Roman Catholic. *Residence:* Tarrytown, N.Y. *Office: Port Chester Daily Item,* 33 New Broad St., Port Chester, N.Y. 10573.

CAREER: Tarrytown Daily News, Tarrytown, N.Y., reporter, 1965-69; Westchester Rockland Newspapers, County News Bureau, White Plains, N.Y., night copy editor, 1972-73; *Mamaroneck Daily Times,* Mamaroneck, N.Y., news editor, 1973-74; *Port Chester Daily Item,* Port Chester, N.Y., news editor, 1974—. Member of transportation council of the Village of Tarrytown; executive secretary of Old Mill Singers (community chorus), 1974—. *Military service:* U.S. Army, 1969-72. *Member:* Westchester County Pilots Association.

WRITINGS: (With Wally Buxton) *History of the Tarrytowns,* Harbor Hill, 1975; (author of preface) William Abbott, *The Crisis of the Revolution,* Harbor Hill, 1976.

Co-author of "Something Extra" (three-act musical comedy).

WORK IN PROGRESS: A two-volume history of Hudson River communities from Hastings to Peekskill, with Wally Buxton; a political novel; a military novel; a three-act comedy about life in the Hudson Valley.

SIDELIGHTS: Canning writes: "*History of the Tarrytowns* was the outgrowth of a special edition Wally Buxton

and I put together for *Tarrytown Daily News,* on the one hundredth anniversary of the village's incorporation in 1970. As natives of a community whose population is slowly shifting from lifetime residents to transients and commuters, we felt it was important to record local history before those who lived it, or at least knew it, passed away. The fact that both of us were born and raised in the Tarrytowns made it possible for us to bring to our work an extra dimension that no outsider possibly could, no matter how diligent his or her research.

"In other words, you don't capture the special flavor of the community by reading a couple books and walking around town for a few days; you have to stay around awhile and soak up the spirit through osmosis.

"Also, I don't believe that you can approach the future with confidence if you don't know where you are or where you've been, whether as a person, a community, or a nation.

"My lone overnight trip outside the United States took me to South Viet Nam during my vacation in October, 1973, at my own expense. I wanted to visit some pen pals and a girl I was sponsoring in an orphanage, and in general observe the country first hand and form my own impressions of that embattled land. My ability to speak Vietnamese (albeit haltingly) melted barriers and I spent a most delightful two weeks in Saigon and vicinity. Although my company did not underwrite any expenses of this trip, upon my return I wrote a three-part series on my impressions of Viet Nam.

"In addition to English and Vietnamese, I also speak Russian and Spanish fairly fluently plus a little Chinese Mandarin.

In general, I find the Orient and its people fascinating; while not shortchanging the importance of our own Western Civilization, I wish our education syllabus could be rearranged to include a little more emphasis on the history and people of the Orient and other areas beyond North America and Europe."

AVOCATIONAL INTERESTS: Singing, flying (private pilot's license), railroads.

* * *

CAPUTO, Philip 1941-

PERSONAL: Born June 10, 1941, in Chicago, Ill.; son of Joseph (a plant manager) and Marie Ylonda (Napolitan) Caputo; married Jill Esther Ongemach (a librarian), June 21, 1969; children: Geoffrey Jacob, Marc Antony. *Education:* Attended Purdue University; Loyola University (Chicago), B.A., 1964. *Politics:* Democrat. *Religion:* Roman Catholic. *Residence:* Key West. Fla.

CAREER: 3-M Corp., Chicago, Ill., promotional writer and member of staff of a house paper, 1968-69; *Chicago Tribune,* Chicago, local correspondent, 1969-72, correspondent in Rome, Beirut, Saigon, and Moscow, 1972-77; writer and lecturer. Notable assignments include coverage of violence in Beirut, Yom Kippur War, Ethiopian Civil War, Turkish invasion of Cyprus, fall of Saigon, 1975. *Military service:* U.S. Marine Corps, 1964-67. *Member:* Italian Foreign Press Association, Sigma Delta Chi. *Awards, honors:* Pulitzer Prize, with William Hugh Jones, 1972, for coverage of primary election fraud; George Polk Award, 1973, for coverage of captivity by Palestinian guerrillas; also received Illinois Associated Press Award, Illinois United Press Award, and Green Gavel Award from American Bar Association.

WRITINGS: A Rumor of War, Holt, 1977.

WORK IN PROGRESS: A novel set in war-torn Ethiopia.

SIDELIGHTS: "On March 8th, 1965," wrote Caputo, "as a young infantry officer, I landed at Danang with a battalion of the 9th Marine Expeditionary Brigade, the first U.S. combat unit sent to Indochina." Young enough to exult in seeing his platoon perform well in its first battle, Caputo was soon overwhelmed by the heat, "malevolent and alive," the jungle, "where men thrashed aimlessly about and nothing ever happened according to plan," the casualties, and fatigue. Perhaps the most difficult war experience to bear was the range of extreme, conflicting emotions felt by each man: "This inner, emotional war produces a tension almost sexual in its intensity," wrote Caputo in *A Rumor of War.* "It is too painful to endure for long. All a soldier can think about is the moment when he can escape his impotent confinement and release this tension. All other considerations, the rights and wrong of what he is doing, the chances for victory or defeat in the battle, the battle's purpose or lack of it, become so absurd as to be less than irrelevant. Nothing matters except the final, critical instant when he leaps out into the violent catharsis he both seeks and dreads." Before his stint in Vietnam was up, *Time* reported, Caputo admittedly learned to hate and to enjoy killing: "We were past feeling anything for ourselves, let alone for others."

After sixteen months of duty in Vietnam, "much of it pointless," Caputo thought about writing a novel of his experiences, but soon realized he couldn't: "Hemingway once said it's difficult to write imaginatively when you know too much about something. It wasn't working primarily because I was emotionally too close to it." On his way back to the United States, Caputo spent six weeks in England and there encountered the poetry of Wilfred Owen and Siegfried Sassoon: "The emotions they felt," Caputo said, "were the same I had in Vietnam."

Even as a successful reporter for the *Chicago Tribune* Caputo was unable to escape the war. "I'd be walking in the woods," he wrote, "and without even trying, I'd say to myself that'd make a good ambush site. When the rain fell, it reminded me of monsoons . . . the war had a grip and you couldn't get free." The *Tribune* sent Caputo to Rome, and in March of 1974, while sitting a few blocks from where Caesar's legions once marched out, Caputo made his decision to write *A Rumor of War.* "Suddenly," he said, "I saw the whole thing, each segment and shape of it, and the moral tale as well."

A Rumor of War was hailed by critics as an accurate memoir of the Vietnam War. "This book," wrote Caputo in the prologue, "does not pretend to be history. It has nothing to do with politics, power, strategy, influence, national interests, or foreign policy; nor is it an indictment of the great men who led us into Indochina and whose mistakes were paid for with the blood of quite ordinary men. In a general sense, it is simply a story about war, about the things men do in war and the things war does to them. More strictly, it is a soldier's account of our longest conflict, the only one we have ever lost, as well as the record of a long and sometimes painful experience." What Caputo achieves, reviewers agree, is a portrait of the war never seen by television cameras, a view "deep into the jungle, where the heat was so oppressive, packs so heavy, nerves so frayed, muscles so tired, men so weary, numbed, frustrated, that an outsider can understand the inevitable savagery of a My Lai."

AVOCATIONAL INTERESTS: Deep sea and fly fishing.

BIOGRAPHICAL/CRITICAL SOURCES: New York Times, May 26, 1977, May 29, 1977; *Newsweek,* June 6, 1977; *Saturday Review,* June 11, 1977; *Washington Post,* June 12, 1977; *Time,* July 4, 1977.

CAREY, Jane Perry (Clark) 1898-

PERSONAL: Born in 1898, in Washington; daughter of John C. and Addie (Burr) Clark; married Andrew Galbraith Carey (a political scientist), Januray 10, 1942. *Education:* Vassar College, A.B.; Columbia University, A.M., Ph.D., 1931. *Politics:* Democrat. *Religion:* Methodist. *Home:* 78 Godfrey Rd., Weston, Conn. 06880; and 30 Sutton Pl., New York, N.Y. 10022.

CAREER: Research secretary for International Migration Service, 1922-28; Mount Holyoke College, South Hadley, Mass., instructor in economics, 1928-29; Barnard College, New York City, assistant professor of government, 1938-53; Columbia University, New York City, assistant professor of government until 1953. Staff member of President's Committee on Economic Security, 1934-35; member of federal and state wage boards, 1934-40; principal training specialist for U.S. Civil Service Commission, 1943; assistant adviser on displaced persons to U.S. Department of State, 1944-46. Research guest of the Governments of Greece, 1965, Sweden, 1968, 1970, Turkey, 1969, and Iran, 1970; member of U.S. Fulbright Commission for Italy, 1953-54. President of New York's Consumers League, 1941-42. Trustee of Vassar College, 1943-51, and Mount Vernon Junior College and Seminary for Girls; member of board of directors of Robert College (Istanbul) and Anatolia College (Thessaloniki). Past member of board of directors of American Women's Volunteer Service.

MEMBER: International Political Science Association, American Political Science Association, American Society for Public Administration, American Academy of Political Science, American Society for International Law, American Society of Public Administrators, Society of Women Geographers, Cosmopolitan Club (New York City). *Awards, honors:* Research awards from Council for Research in the Social Sciences, 1935, 1938, 1948; Star of Solidarity (Italy).

WRITINGS: Deportation of Aliens from the United States to Europe, Columbia University Press, 1931, reprinted, AMS Press, 1968; *The Rise of a New Federalism: Federal-State Cooperation in the United States,* Columbia University Press, 1938, reprinted, Russell & Russell, 1965; *The Role of Uprooted People in European Recovery,* National Planning Association, 1948; (with husband, Andrew Galbraith Carey) *Italy, Change and Progress,* Foreign Policy Association, 1963; (with A. G. Carey) *The Web of Modern Greek Politics,* Columbia University Press, 1968. Contributor to professional journals.*

*   *   *

CARIGIET, Alois 1902-

PERSONAL: Given name is pronounced al-*wah;* surname is pronounced cah-ree-*jyay;* born August 30, 1902, in Truns (Grisons), Switzerland; son of Alois (a peasant farmer) and Barbara Carigiet. *Education:* Attended schools in Chur, Switzerland for ten years. *Residence:* Zurich, Switzerland.

CAREER: Artist, and author and illustrator of children's books. Apprenticed to a decorator at age seventeen; later worked as a commercial artist, designing magazine covers, tourist posters, and theatrical scenery. *Awards, honors: Florina and the Wild Bird* (written by Selina Choenz; illustrated by Carigiet) was among the New York Times Choice of Best Illustrated Children's Books of the Year in 1953; Hans Christian Andersen International Children's Book Medal, 1966; Swiss Juvenile Book Prize, 1966, for *Anton the Goatherd; The Pear Tree, the Birch Tree, and the Barberry*

Bush appeared on the honor list of the German Juvenile Book Prize in 1968.

WRITINGS—All self-illustrated: *Platengia: Eine Kunstmappe,* Desertina Verlag, 1960; *Zottel, Zick, und Zwerg,* Schweizer, Spiegel, 1965; *Anton the Goatherd* (English translation), H. Z. Walck, 1966; *Birnbaum, Birke, Berberitze,* Schweizer, Spiegel, 1967, translation published as *The Pear Tree, the Birch Tree, and the Barberry Bush,* H. Z. Walck, 1967; *Maurus und Madleina,* Schweizer, Spiegel, 1969, translation by Refna Wilkin published as *Anton and Anne,* H. Z. Walck, 1969.

Illustrator: Selina Choenz, *Bell for Ursli* (English translation), Oxford University Press, 1950; Choenz, *Flurina und das Wildvoeglein,* Schweizer, Spiegel, 1952, translation published as *Florina and the Wild Bird,* Oxford University Press, 1953, reprinted, H. Z. Walck, 1966; Choenz, *The Snowstorm* (English translation), H. Z. Walck, 1958.

SIDELIGHTS: The friendship between Carigiet and poet, Selina Choenz, began in 1940. A visit to Zurich at that time resulted in their collaboration on several children's books. The books, set in the Alps of Carigiet's youth, were written in the Swiss dialect, Romansh, and later translated into several languages. The two developed the layout of the books, which often had full-page color illustrations by Carigiet preceding the written text. The illustrations for one such book, *Florina and the Wild Bird,* were described by *Christian Science Monitor* as "utterly delightful."

Following the collaborations with Choenz came requests from many other authors who wanted Carigiet to illustrate their books. Many of the offers were refused because Carigiet felt that he could only illustrate what he himself had experienced.

Carigiet later authored as well as illustrated books for children, but these were less enthusiastically received. *Anton the Goatherd,* for example, drew these comments from *Horn Book:* "Slightness of text is a weakness of all the Carigiet picture books, but those written by Selina Choenz are more interesting than this one." The review also stated that the book's illustrations "have lovely colors and interesting detail, but are lacking in depth." A *Christian Science Monitor* critic, was more impressed with the art work: "So good are the illustrations, that the mediocre [story] (perhaps the fault of the translator) [is] easily forgiven and forgotten."

BIOGRAPHICAL/CRITICAL SOURCES: Horn Book, February, 1967; *Christian Science Monitor,* May 4, 1967.*

* * *

CARLISLE, Fred 1915-
(K. F. Murray)

PERSONAL: Born June 29, 1915, in Liverpool, England; son of Walter and Kathleen M. (Hudson) Carlisle; married Kathryn Walker, June 2, 1945; children: Mary B., Nora K. *Education:* Attended secondary school in Liverpool, England. *Politics:* "Right of Centre: Free Enterprise." *Residence:* Scarborough, Ontario, Canada.

CAREER: Has worked as an insurance agent in Scarborough, Ontario; writer, 1942—. *Military service:* Royal Air Force, 1941-46; became sergeant.

WRITINGS: Journey with Caravel, De Graff, 1971. Contributor of stories and articles to Canadian and British magazines, under pseudonym K. F. Murray.

WORK IN PROGRESS: Suspense fiction set on ocean-going sailing craft.

SIDELIGHTS: Carlisle writes that his wartime contact with the ocean "led to an interest in adventure and sailing, so I aimed at early retirement, and in 1965, at age fifty, I bought a forty-foot trimaran and took my wife and two daughters (then aged six and eight) on a five-year cruise on the North Atlantic, Mediterranean, and Caribbean. I have now bought a thirty-six-foot motor sailor ("Caravel III") as more suitable for a man in his sixties, but I am continuing a similar life-style. I have also traveled extensively by truck camper in North America, Mexico, and Europe."

* * *

CARLSON, Avis D(ungan) 1896-

PERSONAL: Born June 25, 1896, in Moline, Kan.; daughter of C. O. (a stockman) and Mamie (Howard) Dungan; married Harry G. Carlson (an attorney), August 5, 1917 (died March 31, 1970); children: Eric D., Jill C. (Mrs. James K. Marsh). *Education:* Southwestern College, Winfield, Kan., A.B., 1917; University of Illinois, A.M., 1922, further graduate study, 1922-25. *Religion:* Methodist. *Home:* 6163 McPherson, St. Louis, Mo. 63112. *Agent:* Roy E. Porter, 215 West Ohio, Chicago, Ill. 60610.

CAREER: Free-lance journalist, 1927-43; active in civic affairs, 1943-70; writer, 1970—. Past member of St. Louis Council on Human Rights (now Civil Rights Enforcement Agency), Commission on Community Services, and Citizens' Bond Issue Supervising Committee. *Member:* Urban League, Missouri Association for Social Welfare, Adult Education Association of Greater St. Louis, St. Louis League of Women Voters (past president).

WRITINGS: Small World, Long Gone (memoirs of childhood), Chicago Review Press, 1975; *In the Fullness of Time,* Regnery, 1977. Also author of *The First Forty Years* (on St. Louis League of Women Voters), 1959.

Contributor of articles to *Harper's, Atlantic Monthly, New Republic, Nation,* and other magazines, and of short stories to *American, Chatelaine,* and *Maclean's.*

WORK IN PROGRESS: "Going through old papers and letters as material for a description of a young professional family's experience in Wichita, Kansas, during the 1930's."

SIDELIGHTS: Avis Carlson writes: "*Small World, Long Gone* was written mostly as a result of my son's prodding and nagging, to write down what it was like to grow up a rural child in the Kansas of the early twentieth century, that is, in a world long gone. The book, *In the Fullness of Time,* is an account of the experience of growing old, written from the *inside,* instead of the outside, as the middle-aged gerontologists and crusading young journalists who have been flooding the markets with books about 'aging' must necessarily do."

* * *

CARLSON, Richard 1912(?)-1977

1912(?)—November 25, 1977; American television, stage, and screen actor, director, screenwriter, and author of fiction. Carlson was best known for his role in the television series "I Led Three Lives," broadcast in the early 1950's. He died in Los Angeles, Calif. Obituaries: *Washington Post,* November 27, 1977.

* * *

CARR, William 1921-

PERSONAL: Born April 1, 1921, in Workington, England;

son of William (a cashier) and Eleanor (Stewart) Carr; married Kathleen Mary Williams (a teacher), December 28, 1950; children: Mary Louise. *Education:* University of Birmingham, B.A. (honors), 1948; University of Sheffield, D.Phil., 1955. *Politics:* Labour. *Religion:* Roman Catholic. *Home:* 22 Southbourne Rd., Sheffield S10 2QN, England. *Office:* Department of History, University of Sheffield, Sheffield S10 2TN, England.

CAREER: University of Sheffield, Sheffield, England, assistant lecturer, 1949-52, lecturer, 1952-63, senior lecturer, 1963-70, reader in European history, 1970—. Lecturer at University of Nebraska, summer, 1970, and University of Pennsylvania, summer, 1972. Magistrate of Sheffield, 1970—; member of board of visitors at Wakefield Prison, 1967—. Member of National Health Service Executive for Sheffield, 1966-71. *Military service:* British Army, Royal Artillery, interrogation officer, 1941-47; served in Germany. *Member:* Historical Association, Royal Historical Society (fellow), Society for the Study of Labour History, Gesellschaft fuer Schleswig-holsteinische Geschichte.

WRITINGS: Schleswig-Holstein, 1815-1848: A Study in National Conflict, Manchester University Press, 1963; *A History of Germany, 1815-1945,* Edward Arnold, 1969; *Arms Autarky and Aggression: German Foreign Policy, 1933-1939,* Edward Arnold, 1972; *Adolf Hitler: A Study in Personality and Politics,* Edward Arnold, in press.

Contributor: M. Bruce, editor, *The Shaping of the Modern World 1870-1939,* Hutchinson, 1958; C. B. Cox and A. E. Dyson, *The Twentieth Century Mind,* Oxford University Press, 1972; W. Laqueur, editor, *Fascism,* University of California Press, 1976.

Reviewer for *English Historical Review* and *History.*

WORK IN PROGRESS: A collection of documentary material illustrating national socialism, 1919-1945, for Edward Arnold.

SIDELIGHTS: Carr writes: "The Second World War was, I suppose, a turning point in my academic life for it brought me into close contact with Germany at a crucial point in that country's history. Though I studied German at University, I had still not visited the country until 1945.

"I chose for my B.A. dissertation subject the theme of the development of German nationalism in Schleswig-Holstein, 1848-1948. I was fortunate in having been in that part of Germany and had observed the growth of the pro-Danish movement in the border land with Denmark in 1946-47 so that my hundred-year survey had topicality. I pursued my interest in Schleswig-Holstein further in my doctoral thesis, examining the early nineteenth-century origins of German national feeling in that area. Subsequently, I decided to look at the Danish national movement in the area and try to compare the two movements.

"After trying my hand at a modestly successful general history of Germany, I turned to Nazi Germany and have been engaged in work in that field ever since. I suppose I am attracted to this period by the amount of work being done on it, and probably by my own involvement in the period. I have no plans in the immediate future to abandon this area.

"I have been a frequent visitor to Germany in recent years working in the archives and lecturing at German universities. My knowledge of German is now very good."

* * *

CARTER, Don E(arl) 1917-

PERSONAL: Born June 22, 1917, in Plains, Ga.; son of William Alton and Annie Laurie (Gay) Carter; married Carolyn McKensie, October 3, 1942. *Education:* Attended Georgia Southwestern College, 1934-46; University of Georgia, A.B.J., 1938. *Religion:* Protestant. *Home address:* P.O. Box 684, 244 DeSoto St., Sea Island, Ga. 31561. *Office:* One Herald Plaza, Miami, Fla. 33101.

CAREER/WRITINGS: Atlanta Journal, Atlanta, Ga., city editor, 1951-59; *Wall Street Journal* newspaper fund, New York, N.Y., executive director, 1959-61; *National Observer,* Silver Spring, Md., founding managing editor, 1961-67; *Paterson Morning Call,* Paterson, N.J., executive editor, 1967-69; *Hackensack Record,* Hackensack, N.J., executive editor, 1967-71; *Macon Telegraph & News,* Macon, Ga., executive editor, 1971-75; *Lexington Herald and Leader,* Lexington, Ky., publisher, 1975-77; Knight-Ridder Newspapers, Detroit, Mich., vice-president of news, 1976—. Notable assignments include visiting People's Republic of China with first group from American Society of Newspaper Editors, 1972. Journalism teacher at Georgia State College, 1950-59; lecturer for American Press Institute, 1953—. Member of board of directors of Newspaper Fund, 1959—; Pulitzer Award juror, 1968-70. Trustee of Ramapo College, N.J., 1969-70; advisory board member at University of Georgia School of Journalism, 1972—. *Military service:* U.S. Army, 1941-45; became captain; received Bronze Star.

MEMBER: American Society of Newspaper Editors, American Council on Education for Journalism (president, 1973—), National Press Club, American Newspaper Publishers Association News Research Committee, Associated Press Managing Editors (president, 1971), Sigma Delta Chi (president of Atlanta chapter, 1957-59; national director, 1958-59, 1966-67, 1969-71), Phi Beta Kappa, Omicron Delta Kappa, Phi Kappa Phi, Phi Delta Epsilon, Kappa Tau Alpha, Macon Rotary Club, Atlanta Athletic Club, Idle Hour Golf and Country Club (Macon). *Awards, honors:* Citation for service to journalism from Theta Sigma Phi, 1961, and from University of Nebraska School of Journalism, 1962; Special Sigma Delta Chi Award, 1973, for China series.

* * *

CARTEY, Wilfred 1931-

PERSONAL: Born July 19, 1931, in Trinidad, British West Indies. *Education:* University of the West Indies, B.A., 1955; Columbia University, M.A., 1956, Ph.D., 1964. *Residence:* New York, N.Y. *Office:* City College of the City University of New York, 139th St. & Amsterdam, New York, N.Y. 10031.

CAREER: Columbia University, New York City, instructor in Spanish, 1957-62, associate professor of comparative literature, 1963-69; City College of the City University of New York, New York City, professor of comparative literature, 1969-72; Brooklyn College of the City University of New York, Brooklyn, N.Y., Martin Luther King Distinguished Professor of Comparative Literature, 1972-73; City College of the City University of New York, distinguished professor, 1973—. Visiting scholar and lecturer at University of Puerto Rico, summer, 1959; visiting professor at University of Vermont, summer, 1964; visiting professor at University of the West Indies, summer, 1965, resident professor, summer, 1972; visiting professor at University of Ghana, 1967-68; adjunct professor at Columbia University, 1969—.

MEMBER: African Studies Association of America; Black Academy of Arts and Letters. *Awards, honors:* French Consul Prize, 1949, for French; Spanish Consul Prize, 1950, for Spanish; Fulbright travel grant, 1955-59.

WRITINGS: *Some Aspects of African Literature,* University of Vermont, 1964; *The West Indies: Islands in the Sun,* Thomas Nelson, 1967; (contributor) *The African Experience,* Northwestern University Press, 1968; *Whispers from a Continent: Literature of Contemporary Black Africa,* Random House, 1969.

(With J. G. Colmen and others) *The Human Uses of the University: Planning a Curriculum in Urban and Ethnic Affairs at Columbia University,* Praeger, 1970; (author of introduction) Norman Shapiro, editor and translator, *Negritude: French African and Caribbean Poets,* October House, 1970; (author of introduction) Cheikh Hamidou Kane, *Ambiguous Adventure,* Collier Books, 1970; (author of introduction) *Black African Voices,* Scott, Foresman, 1970; (author of introduction) Peter Abrahams, *Tell Freedom,* Collier Books, 1970; (with Marlin Kilson) *The African Reader,* Volume I: *Colonial Africa,* Volume II: *Independent Africa,* Random House, 1970; *Palaver: Critical Anthology of African Literature,* Thomas Nelson, 1970; *Black Images: The Evolution of the Image of the Black Man in the Poetry of Spanish-English-French-Speaking Caribbean, the United States, Latin America, and West Africa,* Teachers College Press, 1970; *House of Blue Lightning* (poems), Emerson Hall, 1973; *Waters of My Soul,* Printed Word, 1975; *Red Rain,* Emerson Hall, 1977. Co-editor of "Documents in Afro-American History" series, Random House, 1970—. Work represented in *Forum Anthology,* Columbia University Press, 1968. Contributor to *Grolier Encyclopedia, Encyclopedia Americana,* and *Standard Reference Encyclopedia.* Contributor of articles and reviews to professional journals and national magazines, including *Commonwealth, New Republic,* and *Negro Digest.* Literary editor of *African Forum,* 1967-68; member of executive board of *Pan African Journal,* 1970—; contributing editor of *Confrontation: A Journal of Third World Literature,* 1970—, and *SAVACOU,* 1970—.

WORK IN PROGRESS: *Suns and Shadows,* poems; *Whispers from the Caribbean,* a critique of the literature of the Caribbean world; a study of Black autobiography.

* * *

CARTNER, William Carruthers 1910-

PERSONAL: Born January 22, 1910, in South Shields, England; son of Edward (a police officer) and Margaret (Graham) Cartner; married Lillian Armstrong, August 4, 1941; children: Elizabeth Anne. *Education:* School of Art, art teaching diploma, 1930. *Home:* 2 Ryelands Park, Easington, Saltburn, Cleveland, England.

CAREER: Writer and illustrator. Middlesbrough College of Art, Middlesbrough, Yorkshire, England, lecturer in graphics and typography, 1949-70. *Military service:* Royal Air Force, 1941-46; became flying officer. *Member:* Printing Historical Society, Society for Italic Handwriting.

WRITINGS—For children: *Fun With Architecture,* Kaye & Ward, 1969; *The Young Calligrapher,* Warne, 1969; *Fun With Palaeontology,* Kaye & Ward, 1971, published as *What Happened on Earth Before Man Arrived,* Sterling, 1972; *Fun With Geology,* Kaye & Ward, 1972; *Fun With Botany,* Kaye & Ward, 1973.

Illustrator: G. Watson, *Fun With Ecology,* Kaye & Ward, 1968.

WORK IN PROGRESS: *Fossils of the Yorkshire Lias: Jurassic.*

SIDELIGHTS: Cartner wrote: "To counter the social problems of city life, children should be encouraged by all possible means to follow an interest in crafts and hobbies and outdoor activities and nature study." *Avocational interests:* Outdoor pursuits in natural sciences, wildlife preservation.

* * *

CARTWRIGHT, Joseph H. 1939-

PERSONAL: Born May 16, 1939, in Nashville, Tenn.; son of Howard W. (a salesman) and Frances (Mosier) Cartwright; married Pamela Callaway (a teacher), July 11, 1959; children: Keith, Jeffrey. *Education:* Vanderbilt University, M.A., 1968, Ph.D., 1973. *Home:* 1623 Keenland Dr., Murray, Ky. 42071. *Office:* Department of History, Murray State University, Murray, Ky. 42071.

CAREER: Murray State University, Murray, Ky., assistant professor, 1970-75, associate professor of history, 1975—. *Member:* Organization of American Historians, Southern Historical Association, Phi Alpha Theta.

WRITINGS: *The Triumph of Jim Crow,* University of Tennessee Press, 1976. Contributor of articles and reviews to history journals.

WORK IN PROGRESS: *Tennessee Republicans and Reconstruction, 1862-1870* (tentative title), completion expected in 1979.

SIDELIGHTS: Cartwright writes: "My major areas of interest include southern history, race relations, and the period in United States history from the Civil War to World War I.

"My interest in southern history, especially southern race relations, stems, in part, from curiosity aroused by growing up in the South during the 1950's. When legalized segregation came under increasing attack during my undergraduate and graduate school years in the 1960's, my interests, like those of others, were drawn to questions about the origins of that system. Furthermore, there were gaps in research in southern race relations that seemed to offer exciting possibilities of satisfying personal curiosity while addressing a socially significant issue.

"The history of the South continues to fascinate me because its study offers an opportunity to examine some of the most significant issues in American history while at the same time observing the lives of a people, black and white, whose experiences frequently have varied significantly from the national norm."

AVOCATIONAL INTERESTS: Jogging, backpacking, listening to classical guitar music.

* * *

CASEMORE, Robert 1915-

PERSONAL: Born June 30, 1915, in Detroit, Mich.; son of Richard (a builder) and Mildred (a teacher; maiden name, Wolcott) Casemore; married Rosemarie Lammers, April 18, 1945; children: Richard II, David John. *Education:* Wayne State University, B.A., 1957. *Residence:* Birmingham, Mich. *Agent:* Blanche Gregory, No. 2 Tudor City Place, New York, N.Y. 10017.

CAREER: Simons-Michelson Advertising, Detroit, Mich., radio, television, and advertising copywriter, 1946-50; Jim Handy Organization, Inc., Detroit, commercial and public relations film writer, 1951-68; Teletape Productions, Detroit, television and film writer, 1968-72; free-lance writer, 1972—. Assistant district commissioner, North Trails District, Boy Scouts of America, 1964-67. *Military service:* U.S. Army, 1941-45. U.S. Army Reserves, 1946-65; became lieutenant colonel. *Member:* Adcraft Club, Alpha Kappa Delta. *Awards, honors:* Freedom Foundation of Valley Forge medal, 1955, for essay "My Stake in the American Way."

WRITINGS: Splendid Morning, Angus & Robertson, 1944; *There Were Twelve,* National Council of Churches, 1965.

Plays: "End of the Day" (one-act), first produced in Detroit, Mich., at Players Barn Theatre, June, 1961; "Just a Minute" (one-act), first produced in Toronto, at Royal York, April, 1976. Also author of over fifty public relations motion picture and television scripts. Contributor of short stories and articles to *Argosy* and other periodicals.

WORK IN PROGRESS: The Fencers, an Eastern European novel on Baltic intrigue; *Back to the Blanket;* a three-act comedy.

SIDELIGHTS: Casemore told *CA:* "I am a free-lance writer primarily in the field of industrial and public relations films, but work in the fiction field as well." An extensive traveller, Casemore maintains a residence in France.

* * *

CASEY, Lawrence B. 1905-1977

PERSONAL: Born September 6, 1905, in Rochester, N.Y.; son of Joseph L. and Agnes M. (Switzer) Casey. *Education:* Attended St. Bernard's Theological Seminary, 1924-30. *Home:* 178 Derrom Ave., Paterson, N.J. 07504. *Office:* 24 De Grasse St., Paterson, N.J. 07505.

CAREER: Ordained Roman Catholic priest, 1930; Diocese of Rochester, Rochester, N.Y., vice-chancellor, 1932-46; pastor in Rochester, 1946-52; Sacred Heart Cathedral, Rochester, rector, 1952; titular bishop of Cea and auxiliary to bishop of Rochester, 1953-66; Diocese of Paterson, Paterson, N.J., bishop, 1966-77. *Awards, honors:* Best column award from Catholic Press Association, 1977, for "By the Way."

WRITINGS: The Heart Remembers, Too, Paulist/Newman, 1977. Weekly columnist, "By the Way," in the *Beacon.* Founder of the *Beacon* (diocesan newspaper).

SIDELIGHTS: In 1975 Bishop Casey received national attention for supporting the Quinlan family's request to remove their daughter Karen Anne from the respirator that was keeping her alive. Because there was no reasonable hope for her recovery, he maintained that Roman Catholic ethics did not require extraordinary means to sustain life.

OBITUARIES: New York Times, June 16, 1977.*

(Died June 15, 1977, in Paterson, N.J.)

* * *

CASTELLANO, Giuseppe 1893-1977

1893—July 31, 1977; Italian general and author of two books of memoirs. Castellano signed the Italian armistice with General Dwight Eisenhower in 1943. He died in Porretta Terme, Italy. Obituaries: *Washington Post,* August 5, 1977.

* * *

CATALA, Rafael 1942-

PERSONAL: Born September 26, 1942, in Cuba; son of Rafael Enrique (a businessman) and Caridad (a housewife; maiden name, Gallardo) Catala. *Education:* New York University, B.A., 1970, M.A., 1972, Ph.D., 1976. *Home*

address: R.D. 1, Box 356, Hampton, N.J. 08827. *Office:* Department of Languages, Lafayette College, Easton, Pa. 18042.

CAREER: Lafayette College, Easton, Pa., instructor of languages, 1977—. *Member:* International Institute of Ibero-American Literature, American Association of Teachers of Spanish and Portuguese, Modern Language Association of America, Carl Jung Foundation, Hispanic Graduate Association of New York University.

WRITINGS: Caminos/Roads (bilingual edition with English translation by Nancy Sebastiani), Hispanic Press, 1972; (editor) *Romanica,* New York University, 1973-75; *Circulo cuadrado,* Anaya-Las Americas, 1974; *Ojo sencillo/Triqui-traque,* Editorial Cartago, 1975; (with Luis Jimenez, Gladys Zaldivar, Concepcion Alzola, Arthur Natella) *Cinco approximaciones a la narrativa hispanoamericana,* Playor, 1977; (with Raysa Amador, Maria Paz, Charles V. Aubrun, Giovanni Bertini, Pedro Bovi-Guerra, Narciso Bruzzi Castas, and others) *Estudios de Historia, Literatura y Arte Hispanicos,* Ediciones Insula, 1977.

Contributor to *Romanica, Irish Review, Norte, El Diario, Victoria de las Tunas, ARE Newsletter, Septagon, Boreal, Ventana, Dialogos, Point of Contact, Puerto Norte y Sur, Caribe, La Noticia Aqui, La Gaceta Literaria de Auditorium, El Tiempo,* and *Impacto.*

WORK IN PROGRESS: Ojo de gato, poetry; *Cause,* a play; *The Lesser Known Poets of the Caribbean,* literary criticism.

SIDELIGHTS: Catala told *CA:* "For me writing is an act of listening, as if I were an instrument of an universal text that is unfolding. I am a tool through which this text comes forth into expression.

"Writing is my work. It requires some studying. I think I'll always be a student. Learning is fun and it's beautiful, what thrills me about learning is that everything is connected whether it's math, science, literature, art of physics. Writing is learning to listen to what is inside me. To me inside and outside are one and the same.

"Writing is work, and real work is play. I believe that I am at play most of the time not only when writing or studying but when gardening, cycling, teaching or hiking."

BIOGRAPHICAL/CRITICAL SOURCES: El Tiempo, March 2, 1975; *Romanica,* 1975; *The Lafayette,* October 28, 1977.

* * *

CATE, Benjamin W(ilson) 1931-

PERSONAL: Born September 28, 1931, in Paris, France; son of Karl Springer (a businessman) and Josephine (Wilson) Cate; married Monique Soulon, 1963 (divorced, 1976); children: Christopher, Stephanie. *Education:* Yale University, B.A., 1955. *Home:* 200 E. Delaware Pl. 14-E, Chicago, Ill. 60611. *Office:* Time-Life Building, 303 E. Ohio St., Chicago, Ill. 60611.

CAREER/WRITINGS: St. Petersburg Times, St. Petersburg, Fla., reporter, 1955-60; *Time,* New York City, correspondent in Boston, Mass., 1960-61, Los Angeles, 1961-62, Detroit, Mich., 1962-65, bureau chief in Houston, Tex., 1965-68, deputy bureau chief in Paris, France, 1968-69, bureau chief in Bonn, Germany, 1969-72, deputy chief of correspondents in New York City, 1972-75, Midwest bureau chief, 1975—. Notable assignments include the Gemini space program, revolution in France, May, 1968, the Berlin

Big Four agreement, beginning of detente, Willy Brandt's Ostpolitik. *Military service:* U.S. Army, 1956-58; became sergeant.

AVOCATIONAL INTERESTS: Photography, skiing, and recreational athletics.

* * *

CATE, Dick
   See CATE, Richard Edward Nelson

* * *

CATE, Richard Edward Nelson   1932-
   (Dick Cate)

PERSONAL: Born March 31, 1932, in Durham, England; son of Richard (a shopkeeper) and Ivy (Nelson) Cate; married Elizabeth Alexander (a teacher), February 11, 1956; children: Nicholas, Catherine, Jonathan, Rosemary. *Education:* Leeds College of Education, diploma, 1954; Goldsmiths' College, London, diploma, 1955; Bretton Hall College, diploma, 1971. *Politics:* Labour. *Religion:* None. *Home:* Ashfield, 2 Bank Lane, Denby Dale, Huddersfield HD8 8QP, England. *Office:* The Grammar School, Penistone, Barnsley, England.

CAREER: Resident teacher in services school in Hamm, Westphalia, Germany, 1961-70; The Grammar School, Barnsley, England, remedial teacher, 1970-73, deputy head of English department, 1973—. *Military service:* British Army, Durham Light Infantry, 1950-52. *Member:* Denby Dale Workingmen's Club.

WRITINGS—Childrens books: *On the Run* (short stories), Macmillan, 1973; *Flying Free,* Hamish Hamilton, 1975, Thomas Nelson, 1976; *Funny Sort of Christmas,* Hamish Hamilton, 1976, published as *Never Is a Long Long Time,* Thomas Nelson, in press; *One of the Gang* (short stories), Macmillan, in press; *Old Dog, New Tricks,* Hamish Hamilton, in press; *Where's Grandma,* Hamish Hamilton, in press.

Author of scripts for plays and stories broadcast on British Broadcasting Corp.-Radio and poems broadcast on British Broadcasting Corp.-Television. Contributor to education journals.

WORK IN PROGRESS: A science fiction novel for older children; a psychological crime story for adults.

SIDELIGHTS: "Writing, for me, is very much a matter of exploration and discovery, "Cate told *CA.* "I'm not a prolific writer, but I often have the feeling that the process of waiting is a door that opens into an infinity of wonders. I mean, there's always something else there, waiting to be written. But it does take an effort. A writer has to get up from the chair by the fire and go into a room and write.

"When I'm not writing, I feel half alive. To be a writer and not have anything to write about is to understand that the concept of the zombie is not altogether without foundation in actuality. About reading, just as in writing, there's always something waiting to be discovered. Writing and reading are ways of seeing infinity."

* * *

CAVALIERO, Glen   1927-

PERSONAL: Born June 7, 1927, in Eastbourne, England; son of Clarence John (a stockbroker) and Mildred (Tilburn) Cavaliero. *Education:* Oxford University, M.A., 1948; Cambridge University, M.A., 1967, Ph.D., 1972. *Home:* 29 Portugal Pl., Cambridge, England.

CAREER: Curate of Church of England parishes in Margate, 1952-55, and Canterbury, England, 1955-56; chaplain at Lincoln Theological College, 1956-60, and Edinburgh University, 1960-64; Cambridge University, Cambridge, England, fellow of St. Catharine's College, 1967-71, member of faculty of English, 1971—. *Military service:* Royal Air Force, 1948-50.

WRITINGS: John Cowper Powys: Novelist, Oxford University Press, 1973; *The Ancient People* (poems), Carcanet, 1973; *The Rural Tradition in the English Novel, 1900-1939,* Macmillan, 1977; *Paradise Stairway* (poems), Carcanet, 1977.

WORK IN PROGRESS: A Study of E. M. Forster.

* * *

CAZEMAJOU, Jean   1924-

PERSONAL: Born June 2, 1924, in Auros, France; son of Pierre (in farming and timber trade) and Ernestine (Nestier) Cazemajou; married Denise Caraby, August 9, 1951; children: Agnes. *Education:* University of Toulouse, License es lettres, 1945, Maitrise d'anglais, 1947; University of Bordeaux, Agregation d'anglais, 1952, doctorat d'Etat, 1970. *Religion:* Catholic. *Home:* 24 rue Rosny, Bordeaux 33200, France. *Office:* University of Bordeaux III, Talence 33405, France.

CAREER: University of West Virginia, Morgantown, instructor in English, 1957-58; University of Bordeaux, Bordeaux, France, part-time instructor in English, 1959-62; University of Toulouse, Toulouse, France, instructor, 1962-65, assistant professor, 1965-67, associate professor of English, 1967-68; University of Bordeaux, associate professor, 1968-72, professor of English, 1972—. Visiting professor at University of California, Davis, 1973-74. *Member:* Societe des Anglicistes de l'Enseignement Superieur, Association francaise d'etudes americaines. *Awards, honors:* Fulbright and Smith-Mundt awards for research, summers, 1961 and 1966; Palmes Academiques (Chevalier) award from the French Ministry of Education Nationale, 1963.

WRITINGS: Stephen Crane, ecrivain journaliste, Didier, 1969; *Stephen Crane: The Red Badge of Courage et Maggie, a Girl of the Streets,* Armand Colin, 1969; *Stephen Crane,* Minnesota University Press, 1969; *Presse, Radio, et Television aux Etats-Unis,* Armand Colin, 1972. Editor of *Annales du C.R.A.A.* (publication of University of Bordeaux III).

WORK IN PROGRESS: Research in the field of American Literary Naturalism.

SIDELIGHTS: Cazemajou told *CA:* I have always been a voracious reader of English and American books, but the beginning of my interest in American literature probably goes back to the year 1952 when I became a fully qualified teacher of English. Soon after that I saw John Huston's screen adaptation of *The Red Badge of Courage* in Paris, and I discovered the fascination of Stephen Crane's masterwork (although the film does not always give a faithful rendering of Crane's intentions).

"This interest in Crane was to take root and develop" Cazemajou continued, "and I was to devote about ten years of my life to exploring the strange and haunting quality of this writer's achievements in many fields: fiction, poetry, reportage, essay-writing. Although war is one of Crane's favorite themes, I think that I was more attracted by the skill and modernity of his poetics than by the fact that he made a name for himself thanks to a war novel.

"The difficulty to circumscribe a mode of writing with such terms as 'realism' or 'naturalism' was part of the challenge I tried to meet when I decided to study a writer who was hailed by many critics as the pioneer of American naturalism. However, such terms soon appeared to me as almost irrelevant apart from their association with a literary zeitgeist which, in some way or other, colored all contemporary literary production. To me Crane's message lay somewhere else, in his personal way of dealing with words and in his constant urge to explore a mysterious no man's land between life and death."

Cazemajou added that he has "a great interest in country things, and a great affinity with anything that is linked with the traditions and folklore of my French province, Gascony. I am very proud to have in my literary heritage such prestigious names as Montaigne, Montesquieu, and Francois Mauriac."

*   *   *

CHACKO, George K(uttickal) 1930-

PERSONAL: Born July 1, 1930, in Trivandrum, India; son of Geevarghese (a technical school principal) and Thankamma (Matthew) Chacko; married Yo Yee (a social worker), August 10, 1957; children: Rajah Yee, Ashia Yo. *Education:* Madras University, M.A., 1950; Indian Statistical Institute, certificate, 1951; Calcutta University, B.Commerce, 1952; New School of Social Research, Ph.D., 1959. *Politics:* Democrat (registered). *Religion:* "Mar Thoma Syrian Church of India, believed to have been founded by Doubting Disciple Thomas in 52 A.D.; member of National Presbyterian Church, Washington, D.C." *Home:* 6809 Barr Rd., Washington, D.C. 20016. *Office:* University of Southern California Eastern Region, 5510 Columbia Pike, Arlington, Va. 22204.

CAREER: Indian Finance, Calcutta, India, assistant editor, 1951-53; *Times of India,* Calcutta, commercial correspondent, 1953; Princeton University, Princeton, N.J., assistant in research, 1953-54; Educational Testing Service, Princeton, associate in mathematics test development, 1955-57; Royal Metal Manufacturing Co., New York City, director of marketing and management research, 1958-60; Hughes Semiconductor Division, Newport Beach, Calif., manager of operations research department, 1960-61; University of California, Los Angeles, assistant professor of business administration, 1961-62; Union Carbide Corp., New York City, operations research consultant, 1962-63; Research Analysis Corp., McLean, Va., staff member, 1963-65; MITRE Corp., Arlington, Va., staff member, 1965-67; TRW Systems Group, Washington, D.C., senior staff scientist, 1967-70; University of Southern California, Los Angeles, visiting professor, 1970-71, professor of systems management, 1971—. Research fellow at Western Management Sciences Center, University of California, Los Angeles, 1961; lecturer at U.S. Department of Agriculture Graduate School, 1965-67; George Washington University, assistant professorial lecturer, 1965-68, Ph.D. thesis director, 1968-70; American University, professorial lecturer, 1967-70, Ph.D. examiner, 1969-70, adjunct professor, 1970. Youth consultant, World Council of Churches, 1954. Systems management consultant to numerous corporations and governmental organizations, including Rand Corp., Macro Systems, Inc., U.N. Public Administration Division, U.S. Air Force Logistics Systems Command, and Fujitsu Ltd.

MEMBER: World Future Society, American Association for the Advancement of Science (fellow; national council

member, 1968-73; symposium chairman, 1971, 1972, 1974, 1976), American Astronautical Society (national vice-president for publications, 1969-71; director, 1972-74), Operations Research Society of America (national vice-chairman of health applications section, 1966-68; national meeting arrangements chairman, 1970), Institute of Management Sciences, Washington Operation Research Council (Technical Colloquia chairman, 1967-68; trustee, 1968-70), Policy Sciences Association, American Association of University Professors, Societe des Consultants Independants et neutres de la Communaute European (corresponding member), Kiwanis (support churches committee chairman, 1955-56; first vice-president, 1961; international relations committee chairman, 1966-67; director, 1967-69, 1972-74; division chairman, 1968-70, 1971-72; charter president of Friendship Heights club, 1972-73).

WRITINGS: India: Toward an Understanding, College and University Press, 1959; *International Trade Aspects of Indian Burlap: An Econometric Study,* Bookman Associates, 1961; *Today's Information for Tomorrow's Products: An Operations Research Approach,* Thompson Book Co., 1966; *Studies for Public Men,* International Christian Leadership, 1969; (editor and contributor) *The Recognition of Systems in Health Services,* Health Applications Section, Operations Research Society of America, 1969; (editor) *Reducing the Cost of Space Transportation,* American Astronautical Society, 1969.

(Editor with William J. Burnsmall and George W. Morgenthaler) *Planning Challenges of the 70's in the Public Domain,* American Astronautical Society, 1971; *Applied Statistics in Decision Making,* American Elsevier, 1971; *Computer-Aided Decision-Making,* American Elsevier, 1972; (editor) *Alternative Approaches to the National Delivery of Health Care,* Health Applications Section, Operations Research Society of America, 1972; *Systems Approach to Environmental Pollution,* Health Applications Section, Operations Research Society of America, 1972; *Technological Forecontrol: Prospects, Problems, and Policy,* North-Holland Publishing, 1975; *Applied Operations Research/Systems Analysis in Hierarchical Decision-Making,* Volume I: *Systems Approach,* Volume II: *Operations Research Approach: Systems Approach to Public and Private Sector Problems,* North-Holland Publishing, 1976; *Operations Research Approach to Problem Formulation and Solution,* North-Holland Publishing, 1976; (editor with Harry E. Emlet, Jr.) *Systems Approach to Strokes and Heart Diseases,* Health Applications Section, Operations Research Society of America, 1977; (editor and contributor) *Health Handbook, 1978: An International Reference on Care and Cures,* North-Holland Publishing, 1978.

Contributor: C. West Churchman and M. Verhulst, editors, *Management Sciences: Models and Techniques,* Pergamon, 1960; Joseph P. Martino, editor, *Long Range Forecasting Methodology,* Office of Aerospace Research, 1968; *Systems Technology Applied to Social and Community Problems,* U.S. Government Printing Office, 1969; *Congressional Recognition of Goddard Rocket and Space Museum,* U.S. Government Printing Office, 1970; Robert L. Chartrand, editor, *Hope for the Cities,* Spartan Book (New York City), 1971; *TWR's PROBE of the Future,* TWR, Inc., 1971; *The Use of Modern Management Techniques in the Public Administration of Developing Countries,* United Nations, 1972; G. Majone and S. Eduade, editors, *Pitfalls in Analysis and Analysis of Pitfalls,* International Institute for Applied Systems Analysis, 1978; Harold E. Bamford, editor, *Beyond*

Gutenburg: Communication Without Paper?, Society for Technical Communications, 1978.

Has edited technical newsletters for organizations, including Operations Research Society of America (Health Applications Section), 1966-72, Washington Operations Research Council, 1967-68, American Astronautical Society, 1968-70, and Kiwanis, 1968-70. Contributor of numerous articles to professional journals in his field. *Journal of Astronautical Sciences,* acting managing editor, 1969-70, managing editor, 1971-74.

WORK IN PROGRESS: Trauma and Triumph of Travel: An Average Asian-American Family's Unaverage Experiences in Asia and Europe; Incomplete Information Systems for Effective Management; Organismic Organizational Systems for Effective Management; and *Expectative Economic Systems.*

SIDELIGHTS: Chacko writes: "Insight and incisiveness are what I strive for in my writing, which must always teach *me* something new and/or novel in the process of explaining to practitioners, preceptors, and policymakers what I have learned from life. Whatever the disciplinary specialty, my focus is upon the relevance to problems, not merely the elegance of solutions. As one who was born into a Christian family which has been Christian as far as tradition can trace, all the way to the founding in the year 52 of the Mar Thoma Church in Southwest India by Thomas, the Doubting Disciple of Christ, and as one who has personally accepted Jesus Christ as Lord when 13, I look upon the exciting encounters I have had with new ideas (such as Theory of Games when I was 19), and new professions (such as Operations Research and Systems Analysis) as precious talents over which I exercise stewardship by enjoying excellence of effort and exposition.

"Not only intellectual and professional encounters, but also personal encounters have been most fulfilling, as seen from the dedication of my book, *Technological Forecontrol:* 'Dedicated affectionately to YO YEE, my vivacious partner in dreams and deeds for seventeen years, with whom it is exciting to pursue a better tomorrow at home and abroad.' The two-year trip abroad of the family is captured in one of the current manuscripts, *Trauma and Triumph of Travel.*"

* * *

CHAFETZ, Henry 1916-1978

May 2, 1916—January 5, 1978; American editor, writer, publisher, and antiquarian book dealer. Chafetz is known for his critically acclaimed children's books, including *The Lost Dream* and *Thunderbird and Other Stories.* He died in New York, N.Y. Obituaries: *New York Times,* January 8, 1978; *AB Bookman's Weekly,* January 30, 1978. (See index for *CA* sketch)

* * *

CHAIS, Pamela (Herbert) 1930-

PERSONAL: Born April 4, 1930, in Los Angeles, Calif.; daughter of F. Hugh (a writer) and Arline LaVerne (Appleby) Herbert; married Stanley Chais (a private investor), October 15, 1960; children: Mark Hugh, William Frederick, Emily. *Education:* Attended University of California, Los Angeles, 1947-49. *Politics:* Liberal. *Religion:* None. *Home and office:* 611 North Oakhurst Dr., Beverly Hills, Calif. 90210. *Agent:* William Morris Agency, 151 El Camino Dr., Beverly Hills, Calif. 90210.

CAREER: Has worked in various public relations positions.

Writer of comedy pilots, episodes, and motion pictures for television.

WRITINGS: Split Ends (novel), Lippincott, 1977. Also author of a produced play and television scripts.

WORK IN PROGRESS: A play; two novels; writing for television.

* * *

CHALKER, Jack L(aurence) 1944-

PERSONAL: Born December 17, 1944, in Norfolk, Va.; son of Lloyd Allen, Sr. and Nancy Alice (an artist; maiden name Hopkins) Chalker. *Education:* Towson State College, B.S., 1966; Johns Hopkins University, M.L.A., 1969. *Home:* 5111 Liberty Heights Ave., Baltimore, Md. 21207. *Agent:* Eleanor Wood, Spectrum Literary Agency, Suite 303-East, 200 Park Ave., New York, N.Y. 10021. *Office:* Mirage Press Ltd., P.O. Box 7687, Baltimore, Md. 21207.

CAREER: Mirage Press Ltd., Baltimore, Md., editor, 1960-72, editorial and marketing director, 1961—. Social science teacher in public schools in Baltimore, Md., 1966—. Lecturer at University of Maryland and Smithsonian Institution. Consultant to World Science Fiction Conventions. *Military service:* U.S. Air Force, air commando with Special Forces, 1968-71. Maryland Air National Guard, 1968-73; became staff sergeant. *Member:* World Science Fiction Society, Science Fiction Writers of America, American Federation of Labor-Congress of Industrial Organizations, Washington Science Fiction Association, New York Science Fiction Society, United Teachers of Baltimore, Pacific Northwest National Parks Association. *Awards, honors:* Nominated for John W. Campbell Award by reader vote of World Science Fiction Convention, 1977, for best new science fiction writer.

WRITINGS: (Editor) *H. P. Lovecraft Bibliography,* Mirage Press, 1961, revised edition, 1973; (editor) *In Memoriam: Clark Ashton Smith,* Mirage Press, 1963; (editor) *Mirage on Lovecraft,* Mirage Press, 1964; (editor with Mark Owings) *Index to Science Fiction Publishers,* Mirage Press, 1966, revised edition, 1978; (editor with Owings) *The Necronomicon: A Study,* Mirage Press, 1968; *An Informal Biography of Scrooge McDuck,* Mirage Press, 1974; *A Jungle of Stars* (science fiction novel), Ballantine, 1976; *Midnight at the Well of Souls* (science fiction novel), Del Rey, 1977; *Afterglow* (science fiction novel), Del Rey, 1978; *The Web of the Chosen* (science fiction novel), Del Rey, in press; *The Identity Matrix* (science fiction novel), Berkeley, in press.

Contributor of stories to *Analog* and *Stellar Three.*

WORK IN PROGRESS: The Wars of the Well, a two volume novel for Del Rey; *The Devil Will Drag You Under,* for Fantasy Publishing.

SIDELIGHTS: Chalker told *CA:* "As a trained historian, I am almost unique in writing science fiction. My concerns are not basically new technology or applications, but their effects on mankind. I see a certain historical universality in human nature which is essentially pessimistic, however, in my futures man is still going and still expanding—although the more things change the more they stay the same. My works strongly attack authoritarianism, elitism, and dogmatic ideas whether they be political or otherwise. My general humanistic themes are contemporary; the translation to an exotic (and, of course, technically accurate) science fictional background makes it easier to illustrate and explore the human condition, for the contrast of human beings with exotic backgrounds tends to isolate the universals I wish to address. Individual themes concern alienation, loneliness, and the increasing dehumanization of people by the technology and fast changes that grow around them. The strong individual's attempt to maintain sanity and balance in such a dehumanized society (which is, after all, a reflection of trends I see today) and the social and psychological price that must be paid are common to my works.

"Science fiction, long the stepchild of literature, has, I believe, come of age. In no other form of literature may serious questions be addressed as freely and serious issues isolated more clearly. I am, however, a strong believer in verisimilitude in creating societies and backgrounds, and a believer in the strong surface plot, often intricate, through which the themes are woven rather than dominating the work. One need not be a bore to address serious themes."

AVOCATIONAL INTERESTS: Travel (including Europe and Australia), "riding every ferryboat in the world," esoteric audio-high fidelity, tape recording, art auctioneering, conservation, national parks.

* * *

CHALLINOR, John 1894-

PERSONAL: Born November 30, 1894, in Leek, Staffordshire, England; son of William Edward and Catherine (Allen) Challinor; married Mary Winifred Atkins, July 17, 1928. *Education:* Trinity College, Cambridge, B.A., 1916, M.A., 1922. *Home:* Broncastell, Capel Bangor, Aberystwyth, Wales.

CAREER: University College of Wales, Aberystwyth, assistant lecturer, 1919-22, lecturer, 1922-42, senior lecturer in geology, 1942-60; writer, 1960—. *Military service:* British Army, Royal Artillery, 1917-19; became lieutenant. *Member:* Geological Society, Geologists' Association, North Staffordshire Field Club, East Midlands Geological Society (honorary member). *Awards, honors:* Garner Medal from North Staffordshire Field Club, 1948; Spanton Medal from North Staffordshire Field Club, 1961.

WRITINGS: (With J. I. Platt) *Simple Geological Structures,* Murby & Co., 1930, 5th edition, 1974; *Dictionary of Geology,* University of Wales Press, 1961, 5th edition, in press; *History of British Geology,* David & Charles, 1971; (with D.E.B. Bates) *Geology Explained in North Wales,* David & Charles, 1973. Contributor to scientific journals.

WORK IN PROGRESS: Research on history and philosophy of geology.

SIDELIGHTS: "In my current geological writing," Challinor told *CA,* "I am chiefly concerned in discussing certain important aspects of the science that are apt to be neglected on the mistaken supposition that they are already well understood; e.g., the definition and content of geology, 'economy of hypothesis' applied to geological reasoning, controversial questions in geomorphology, confusion between certain concepts in structural geology, the definition, meaning, and application of certain leading terms."

* * *

CHAMBERS, William E. 1943-

PERSONAL: Born October 9, 1943, in Brooklyn, N.Y.; son of William R. (a truck driver) and Julia (Lynch) Chambers; married Marie Antoinette Kaczanowski (a bookkeeper), August 29, 1964. *Education:* Educated in Brooklyn, N.Y. *Office:* New York Telephone Co., 125 Barclay St., New York, N.Y. 10003.

CAREER: New York Telephone Co., New York City, deskman; writer. *Member:* Mystery Writers of America (member of board of directors, 1976—), Authors Guild.

WRITINGS: Death Toll (mystery novel), Popular Library, 1976; (contributor) Joe Gores and Bill Prozini, editors, *Tricks and Treats,* Doubleday, 1976. Contributor of short stories to *Mike Shayne's Mystery Magazine* and *Alfred Hitchcock's Mystery Magazine.*

WORK IN PROGRESS: Satan's Circle; short stories.*

* * *

CHAPIN, Katherine G(arrison)
See BIDDLE, Katherine Garrison Chapin

* * *

CHAPLIN, Charles Spencer 1889-1977
(Charlie Chaplin)

April 16, 1889—December 25, 1977; British motion picture actor, producer, director, and screenwriter. Chaplin's career spanned more than fifty years and began almost with the film industry itself. He was best known for his role of the Tramp, a character he created in 1914 and which he played in more than eighty films in thirty years. Altogether, Chaplin wrote and directed more than eighty of his eighty-nine films. Considered a pioneer in the cinema, he was among the first filmmakers to address such subjects as the Depression, World War I, the factories, class distinction, and the Nazis. His most popular films include "Shoulder Arms," 1918, "The Kid," 1921, "The Gold Rush," 1925, "City Lights," 1931, "Modern Times," 1936, "The Great Dictator," 1940, and "Limelight," 1952, in which he appeared with fellow film comedian, Buster Keaton. Chaplin's last film was "A Countess From Hong Kong," 1967, which he wrote, directed, produced, and appeared in briefly. He wrote his autobiography, *My Autobiography.* Chaplin died in Vevey, Switzerland. Obituaries: *New York Times,* December 26, 1977; *Washington Post,* December 26, 1977; *Newsweek,* January 9, 1978.

* * *

CHAPLIN, Charlie
See CHAPLIN, Charles Spencer

* * *

CHAPMAN, Christine 1933-

PERSONAL: Born June 10, 1933, in Detroit, Mich.; daughter of Duncan Stewart (a businessman) and Esther (a teacher; maiden name, Goodrich) Patton; married William Thomas Chapman (a foreign correspondent), September, 1956; children: Peter T., Daniel S. *Education:* Wells College, B.A., 1954; George Washington University, M.A., 1965. *Politics:* Democrat. *Residence:* Tokyo, Japan. *Agent:* Helen Brann Agency, 14 Sutton Pl. S., New York, N.Y. 10022.

CAREER: Scholastic, New York, N.Y., staff writer, 1954-56; *Charleston News & Courier,* Charleston, S.C., part-time staff writer, 1956-58; teacher of English at private schools in Charleston, S.C., 1958-60, and Washington, D.C., 1962-66; Sidwell Friends School, Washington, D.C., English teacher, 1966-77; writer, 1976—.

WRITINGS: America's Runaways, Morrow, 1976.

WORK IN PROGRESS: A novel dealing with the contemporary family; research on the history of upstate New York in the late nineteenth and early twentieth centuries, with a novel expected to result.

SIDELIGHTS: Christine Chapman writes: "Federal and state governments, the police, psychiatry, and the schools contribute, erroneously, to the idea of runaways as delinquents or as mentally ill children. In *America's Runaways* I tried to show what was happening to more than a million children who leave home suddenly each year for many reasons, most centering on the family. At home, then out in the streets, they are like the child victims of a Dickens' novel. In my novel I concentrate on two teen-agers, not runaways, and the fantasy world they live in, Washington, D.C. Having taught prep school students in Washington for fifteen years, I'm familiar with the territory."

* * *

CHARQUES, Dorothy (Taylor) 1899-1976
(R. D. Dorothy)

PERSONAL: Born June 4, 1899, in Arrow, Warwickshire, England; daughter of Benjamin (a schoolmaster) and Florence Margaret (Price) Taylor; married Richard Denis Charques (a journalist, author and critic), November 9, 1929 (marriage terminated); married S.A.G. Emms (an inventor and consultant engineer), 1964. *Education:* University of Sheffield, B.A. (history; with honors), 1922, B.A. (economics; with honors), M.A., 1923. *Home:* 143 Loxley Rd., Stratford upon Avon, Warwickshire, England.

CAREER: Fabian Society, London, England, researcher, 1925-31. Writer, 1937-76. Lecturer.

WRITINGS: (Under pseudonym R. D. Dorothy, with husband Richard Charques) *Above and Below,* Secker & Warburg, 1929; (under pseudonym R. D. Dorothy, with R. Charques) *After the Party,* Secker & Warburg, 1933; *The Tramp and His Woman,* Macmillan, 1937; *Between Sleeping and Waking,* Macmillan, 1938; *Time's Harvest* (first novel in trilogy; also see below), Hamish Hamilton, 1940; *The Running Heart* (second novel in trilogy; also see below), Hamish Hamilton, 1943; *Between the Twilights* (third novel in trilogy; includes *Time's Harvest, The Running Heart, Between the Twilights*), J. Murray, 1949; *Men Like Shadows,* J. Murray, 1952, Coward, 1953; *The Valley,* J. Murray, 1954; *The Dark Stranger,* J. Murray, 1956, Coward, 1957; *The Nunnery,* J. Murray, 1959, Coward, 1960; *A Wind from the Sea,* J. Murray, 1971.

WORK IN PROGRESS: A historical novel set in the reign of Henry VIII.

SIDELIGHTS: Dorothy Charques has been acclaimed by critics as a historical novelist of remarkable sensibility and talent. Growing up in a land so rich with history, she became immersed in those legends and tales that survive the great figures of Warwickshire's past, the battles fought, the triumphs and beginnings of a noble heritage. Her ancestors were farmers from the rugged north and west of England. *Time's Harvest,* the first volume in a trilogy of that title, recounts the tragedy experienced by her mother's family in the 1870's when murrain killed their cattle and the loss ruined them.

Her other novels, *The Tramp and His Woman* and *Between Sleeping and Waking,* are tales of rural English life. *Men Like Shadows* tells of the Third Crusade, and *The Dark Stranger* of the Royalist-Roundhead struggles in the seventeenth century.

AVOCATIONAL INTERESTS: Walking, and sitting.

OBITUARIES: AB Bookman's Weekly, May 17, 1976.*

(Died March 20, 1976, in England)

* * *

CHEN, Janey 1922-

PERSONAL: Born February 5, 1922, in Fatshan, Kwangtung, China; came to United States in 1976; daughter of Ching Choy (a merchant) and Sik Yu (Li) Chou; married Ti Kang Chen (a government worker), July 25, 1943; children: David, Julia, Helen. *Education:* National Southwest Associated Universities (China), B. Sc., 1944; Heavenly People Theological Seminary, M.R.E., 1968. *Religion:* Christian. *Home:* 4 Derby Rd., 1st Floor, Kowloon Tong, Kowloon, Hong Kong. *Office:* c/o Leona Froggatt, 95 Marietta Dr., San Francisco, Calif. 94127.

CAREER: First Middle School, Kuangchouwan, China, instructor in English, 1945-56; Taiwan Theological Seminary, Taiwan, interpreter and translator, 1954-64; Taipei Language Institute, Taiwan, senior instructor, 1957-64; Alliance Press and Salvation Army, Hong Kong, book translator, 1964-72; Hong Kong Language Institute, Hong Kong, supervisor and principal, 1971-75; World Home Bible League, Hong Kong, director, 1972—. Senior instructor in languages, Chinese University, New Asia College, Yale-in-China, Chinese Language Center, 1964-71. Proprietor, J. C. Publications, 1968—. *Member:* Hong Kong Evangelical Fellowship, Christian and Missionary Alliance.

WRITINGS: Christmas in the Market Place, Presbyterian Church of Formosa, 1962; *A Language Bridge for the Gospel of John,* Christian and Missionary Alliance, 1967; *Conversation Drills in Everyday Cantonese,* J. C. Publications, 1969; *A Practical English-Chinese Pronouncing Dictionary,* Tuttle, 1969; *Cantonese Pattern Drills,* J. C. Publications, 1971; *300 Common Chinese Characters, Book I,* Hong Kong Language Institute, 1973; *Cantonese Dialogues,* Hong Kong Language Institute, 1973; *Clinical Material,* Hong Kong Language Institute, 1973; *Conversational Stories,* Hong Kong Language Institute, 1973; *Educational Material,* Hong Kong Language Institute, 1973; *Guided Conversational Material,* Hong Kong Language Institute, 1973; *300 Common Chinese Characters, Book II,* Hong Kong Language Institute, 1974; *Common Hospital, Medical and Herbal Terms in Mandarin and Chinese,* J. C. Publications, 1974.

WORK IN PROGRESS: Revising teaching materials; language books.

SIDELIGHTS: "Since I am a U.S. immigrant as of 1976" Chen told *CA,* "I desire an opportunity to teach the Chinese language, both Mandarin and Cantonese. I am very much interested in helping prospective missionaries who have a need to learn the Chinese language. I have had the experience of setting up a language school in Hong Kong, perhaps such an institution could be set up in the States if the funds were available."

* * *

CHENEY, Roberta Carkeek 1912-

PERSONAL: Born April 18, 1912, in Montana; daughter of George A. (a rancher) and Pearl (Storey) Carkeek; married Truman M. Cheney (a psychologist), June 7, 1934; children: Karen Cheney Shores, Maureen Cheney Curnow, Larry. *Education:* University of Montana, B.A., 1932; graduate study at Columbia University, Oregon State University, and University of Nevada. *Religion:* Episcopalian. *Residence:* Cameron, Mont. 59720.

CAREER: High school English teacher in Montana, 1933-35, and Idaho, 1944-46; Family Counseling Service, Portland, Ore., secretary, 1952-59; free-lance writer, 1970—. Director of writers' workshops. *Member:* Western Writers of America (president, 1978; past vice-president), National League of American Pen Women, American Association of University Women. *Awards, honors:* Western Heritage Award from Cowboy Hall of Fame (Oklahoma City), 1975-76, for *Hans Kleiber;* Emmie Award from Wyoming Writers Association, 1976, for outstanding service to Wyoming writers; state and national journalism awards.

WRITINGS: Names on the Face of Montana, University of Montana Press, 1971; (with Emmie Mygatt) *Your Personal Writer's Workshop,* Sol III Publications, 1975; (with Mygatt) *Hans Kleiber: Artist of the Big Horn Mountains,* Caxton, 1976; (editor with Mygatt) *This Is Wyoming: Listen,* Bighorn Books, 1977; *Big Missouri Winter Count,* Naturegraph, 1978. Contributor to a wide variety of magazines, including *True West, Rotarian, Jack and Jill, Farm Wife,* and *Collector's World,* and to newspapers.

WORK IN PROGRESS: Revising *Names on the Face of Montana;* a book on Montana's first dude ranch.

SIDELIGHTS: Roberta Cheney told *CA* that she lectures in Montana and Wyoming about place names. *Avocational interests:* European travel (especially France).

* * *

CHERNOFSKY, Jacob L. 1928-

PERSONAL: Born April 11, 1928, in New York, N.Y.; son of Max (an attorney) and Bertha (Cohen) Chernofsky; married Ellen Jung, March 6, 1955; children: Meir Dan, Michael A., Brynna, Eva Miriam. *Education:* Attended Polytechnic Institute of Boston, 1945-49; New York University, B.A., 1953. *Home:* 7 Dunhill Lane, Monsey, N.Y. 10952. *Office address: AB Bookman's Weekly,* Box 1100, Newark, N.J. 07101.

CAREER/WRITINGS: AB Bookman's Weekly, Clifton, N.J., managing editor, 1972-74, editor and publisher, 1975—.

* * *

CHERNOWITZ, Maurice E. 1909-1977

1909—July 4, 1977; Educator and author. He was professor of fine arts at Yeshiva University, wrote *Proust and Painting,* and was editor of *Bitzaron,* the monthly Hebrew magazine. He died in New York, N.Y. Obituaries: *New York Times,* July 6, 1977; *AB Bookman's Weekly,* August 5, 1977.

* * *

CHESSMAN, Caryl (Whittier) 1921-1960

PERSONAL: Born May 27, 1921, in Michigan; married in 1940 (divorced, 1945). *Education:* Self-educated. *Home:* California State Prison, San Quentin, Calif. 94964.

CAREER: Writer. Arrested, January 23, 1948, and charged with being California's "Red Light Bandit"; convicted by Los Angeles County Superior Court of seventeen charges, including kidnapping for robbery with bodily harm, and sentenced to death, May 18, 1948; entered death row, California State Prison at San Quentin, July 3, 1948, and won eight stays of execution over the following twelve years; executed, May 2, 1960.

WRITINGS: Cell 2455, Death Row (autobiography), Prentice-Hall, 1954; *Trial by Ordeal* (autobiography), Prentice-Hall, 1955; *The Face of Justice,* Prentice-Hall, 1957; *The Kid Was a Killer* (novel), F. Muller, 1960. Also author of radio scripts for "San Quentin on the Air."

SIDELIGHTS: Caryl Chessman's father, a drifter who worked variously as a carpenter, poultry butcher, and yardman, and his mother, an invalid paralyzed from the waist down, raised young Caryl in the Glendale section of Los Angeles. An undersized, sickly child, Chessman excelled in school. His first encounters with the law, by his own accounts, began during his early teens when he started pilfering and joyriding in stolen cars. Arrested for auto theft at sixteen, Chessman was taken to a juvenile hall for medical examination. He climbed through a window, jumped into a truck and drove it to the wall, climbed on top of the truck and escaped. He was arrested the next morning while looting a drugstore. Chessman spent the next eight months at the Preston State Industrial School at Ione, Calif.

Chessman was arrested for auto theft again a few months after his release from Preston. With his previous records, the eighteen-year old faced a term in San Quentin. Summoning his talent for words, Chessman wrote a long essay which declared "a sense of repulsion against all things criminal, including myself for having become ensnared in its brutal grip during my formative years." The impressed Superior Court judge put Chessman on probation.

Chessman was convicted of five counts of robbery and assault a year later and was sent to San Quentin. At San Quentin he learned to type, completed his high school equivalency qualifications, and began taking college correspondence courses. He also edited the prison newspaper and taught illiterate prisoners to read. After two years, as a reward for good behavior, he was sent to the open prison at Chino. He escaped and returned to stealing. Apprehended and sent to Folsom Prison, Chessman was released on parole four years later in December, 1947.

During the month after Chessman's release from Folsom, Los Angeles' lovers lanes were terrorized by what local newspapers termed the "Red Light Bandit." The bandit, who drove a grey Ford coupe and flashed a red spotlight as if he were a policeman, robbed parked couples at gunpoint. On at least two occasions in three days he forced women victims into his car and, as indictments charged, had them perform an "unnatural sex act." One victim, a seventeen-year old who had been mentally ill since age twelve, was later confined to a state hospital after becoming schizophrenic. The day after the final Red Light Bandit crime, Los Angeles police were summoned to apprehend two men who had robbed a clothing store and escaped in a grey Ford. After a high-speed chase through the city, officers apprehended the suspects. The driver was Caryl Chessman.

Charged with being the Red Light Bandit as well as the clothing store robber, Chessman elected to act as his own defense counsel. The jury was comprised of eleven women and one man, and the presiding judge, Charles W. Fricke, was famous for having sentenced more people to death than any other judge in the history of the state of California. At the trial victims of the Red Light crimes identified a pistol Chessman threw from the Ford during the chase. A nut was found in Chessman's pocket which the prosecution said was used to attach red cellophane to the car's spotlight. Most damaging of all, three victims identified Chessman as the Red Light Bandit. Throughout the trial Chessman maintained his innocence in the Red Light crimes. Chessman was convicted by the Los Angeles County Superior Court on a total of seventeen counts, including kidnapping for robbery with bodily harm, a capital offense which the prosecution argued Chessman committed by robbing the two women victims, forcing them into his car, and sexually assaulting them. Judge Fricke sentenced Chessman to death.

Chessman entered the death house at San Quentin on July 3, 1948. For the next twelve years he lived in a small cell where, according to his own accounts, he "read or skimmed 10,000 legal books" and wrote "between two and three million words." Celebrated attorney Melvin Belli called Chessman "one of the sharpest and best-trained lawyers I have met." In defense of his claims of innocence, Chessman appealed his case to the U.S. Supreme Court seventeen times and engaged in a long series of legal maneuvers which "brought him from the obscurity of death row to world-wide notoriety." Chessman's major appeal revolved around the two thousand page transcript of the trial taken by court reporter Ernest Perry. Perry died after only one-third of his shorthand notes had been transcribed. Judge Fricke also committed a serious error in mid-1949, according to the U.S. Supreme Court, when he certified the transcript prepared by another reporter without allowing Chessman to be present at the hearing. Chessman appealed Fricke's denial through the courts and won six stays of execution. In 1957 the U.S. Supreme Court ruled that Fricke's denial violated Chessman's due process rights. A new hearing was held, and a Superior Court judge ordered more than two thousand changes in the transcript. Chessman, unsatisfied with the changes, again took his case to the Supreme Court. In December, 1959, after ordering a seventh stay of execution, the Supreme Court rejected Chessman's appeal for a review of the state court decision and upheld the transcript. The Superior Court set February 19, 1960, as Chessman's new execution date.

Chessman had become by this time the "world's most famous prisoner" and the "center of impassioned arguments on both sides of the Atlantic." His bestselling *Cell 2455, Death Row,* published in 1954, was translated into twelve languages. In the introduction, Chessman wrote: "I feel impelled to add that the book has been written for one purpose only—because its author is both haunted and angered by the knowledge that his society needlessly persists in confounding itself in dealing with the monstrous twin problems of what to do about crime and what to do with criminals. Pled, consequently, is the cause of the criminally damned and doomed. It's time their voice was heard. And understood." Through his writing Chessman had become a vividly living personality to people worldwide and, inevitably, the symbolic cause for those opposed to capital punishment, particularly because he was never convicted of killing anyone. Brazilian Supreme Court Justice Nelson Hungria, who also was principal author of Brazil's penal code, summed up the feelings of Chessman supporters: "Caryl Chessman is the most eloquent assurance of the need to wipe out once and for all the death penalty, that ugly stain on civilization." The save-Chessman agitation, according to *Time,* arose "partly out of compassion, sometimes tinged with admiration, for his twelve year battle to stave off execution—his self-publicized role as underdog, fighting alone against the impersonal power of the state, his sheer persistence in teaching himself law, drafting appeals, writs and briefs in a double-locked Death Row cell, smuggling out one writ on sheets of toilet paper, concealing the manuscript of a book by typing it lightly on carbon paper after prison authorities ordered him not to write any more for publication. But the Number 1 argument of the spare-Chessman camp is that he has already suffered enough." "Death row," wrote Chessman, "is always a place of horrors even for those able to

hold the horror at arm's length. For death itself always is your mocking, obscene companion."

As the February 19th execution date approached, thousands of save-Chessman messages poured into the office of California Governor Edmund G. Brown. Messages from abroad included letters from members of European parliaments; a telegram arrived from Belgium's Queen Mother, and a Dutch invalid offered to die in Chessman's place. A petition to spare Chessman gathered more than 2.5 million signatures in Brazil. The Vatican's *L'Osservatore Romano* described Chessman's long wait as "a punishment more tremendous than death" and claimed "no one can deny that he has expiated his guilt, however grave, because a more severe penalty than this does not reasonably exist." Ten hours before Chessman was scheduled to die, Governor Brown received a State Department telegram that warned that the government of Uruguay feared hostile demonstrations against President Eisenhower's scheduled visit because of the strong Chessman sentiment in South America. Brown granted a sixty-day reprieve.

Brown, a long time opponent of capital punishment, called a special session of the California legislature to consider his proposal to abolish capital punishment. The legislature's sentiment was four-to-one against saving Chessman, and Brown channeled his proposal through the senate judiciary committee, where it was voted down eight-to-seven. Brown, "deeply sorry" about the committee's decision, declared, "The regular schedule of executions will continue under the constitutions and laws of the State of California." The new date set for the execution was May 2, 1960.

George Davis, one of Chessman's three attorneys, appealed the sentence based on the claim that Chessman's twelve years on death row constituted "cruel and unusual punishments" and thus violated the Eighth Amendment to the U.S. Constitution. Chessman himself had little hope: "I have had nine execution dates, and have been spared eight times. I do not want to be credited with more lives than a cat." On the morning of May 2, 1960, the California State Supreme Court denied Chessman's petition for a writ of habeus corpus and a stay of execution. Davis immediately asked for a stay of execution pending a U.S. Supreme Court appeal, which was also denied. Less than an hour later, U.S. Supreme Court Justice William O. Douglas received a petition for a stay of execution, which he denied. Federal District Judge Louis E. Goodman, wishing an hour to consider defense attorneys' pleas, ordered the stay. Goodman's secretary misdialed the number, and by the time the call was completed, Chessman's execution had begun. In front of sixty witnesses, Chessman was executed in the gas chamber in San Quentin. His last words, according to witnesses, were "Tell Rosalie goodby" (directed to Rosalie Asher, one of his attorneys). In a statement he had prepared to be issued after his death, Chessman said, "In my lifetime I was guilty of many crimes, but not those for which my life was taken." Shortly before his execution he wrote, "Now that the state has gained its vengeance, I should like the world to consider what has been gained."

According to Free Press Wire Services, Chessman's execution sparked a "worldwide wave of denunciation that erupted into open anti-American outbursts in Europe and South America." Protesting demonstrators shattered windows of the U.S. Embassy in Lisbon; students gathered in front of U.S. Embassies in Quinto, Ecuador, and Montevideo, Uruguay, shouting "murderers" and "assassins." In Scandinavia feeling ran particularly high and police were called to surround the U.S. Embassy in Stockholm. The

London Daily Herald wrote, "there must be in the hearts of most honest-to-goodness Americans great shame over the execution of Caryl Chessman." In Italy and Belgium, papers reported, "the general reaction was one of shock." In California, young people picketed the capitol and governor's mansion, and students walked from San Francisco to San Quentin to demonstrate their support of Chessman.

The night before he died, Chessman wrote a number of letters, including one to Will Stevens of the *San Francisco Examiner*. "What impels me to write this letter," Chessman told Stevens, "is because I earnestly believe more is involved than the death of one man. I am writing it because I have heard humanity's voice raised in my behalf—and because I have seen too much of man-inflicted death.

"I must believe and I do believe that before too many more years have passed we will realize the senseless tragedy and the witless futility of that 'relic of human barbarism,' capital punishment, and that we will have the courage and vision to eliminate it."

BIOGRAPHICAL/CRITICAL SOURCES: Caryl Chessman, *Cell 2455, Death Row,* Prentice-Hall, 1954; Chessman, *Trial by Ordeal,* Prentice-Hall, 1955; *Newsweek,* November 2, 1959, February 29, 1960, March 21, 1960, May 2, 1960, May 9, 1960; *Life,* February 29, 1960, May 9, 1960; *Time,* March 21, 1960; *Saturday Review,* April 23, 1960; *San Francisco Examiner,* May 2, 1960, May 3, 1960; *Detroit Free Press,* May 3, 1960; *Nation,* May 21, 1960; *Reporter,* May 26, 1960; Elinor L. Horwitz, *Capital Punishment, U.S.A.,* Lippincott, 1973.*

(Died May 2, 1960, in San Quentin, Calif.)

* * *

CHIANG Yee 1903-1977

May 19, 1903—October 17, 1977; Chinese-born American educator, artist, poet, and author. Chiang was professor emeritus at Columbia University where he had taught painting, sculpture, calligraphy, and East Asian languages and cultures. He was governor of four Chinese provinces before a dispute with a warlord caused him to leave China in 1933. Chiang was the author and illustrator of more than twenty-five books, including his well-known art-travel series. He died in Peking, China. Obituaries: *New York Times,* October 21, 1977. (See index for *CA* sketch)

* * *

CHICKERING, Roger (Philip) 1942-

PERSONAL: Born August 15, 1942, in San Francisco, Calif.; son of Roger W. (in insurance) and Margaret (a writer; maiden name, Yoerck) Chickering; married Wendy Phillips, December 18, 1965; children: Roger Allen, David Maxwell. *Education:* Cornell University, B.A., 1964; Stanford University, M.A., 1965, Ph.D., 1968. *Residence:* Eugene, Ore. *Office:* Department of History, University of Oregon, Eugene, Ore. 97403.

CAREER: Stanford University, Standord, Calif., instructor in western civilization, 1967-68; University of Oregon, Eugene, assistant professor, 1968-74, associate professor of history, 1974—. *Member:* American Historical Association, American Civil Liberties Union, Conference Group on Central European History, Conference on Peace Research in History, Conference Group on the Uses of Psychology in History, Phi Beta Kappa. *Awards, honors:* National Endowment for the Humanities fellowship, 1970-71; North Atlantic Treaty Organization fellowship, 1971-72; Fulbright fellowship, 1976-77.

WRITINGS: Imperial Germany and a World without War: The Peace Movement and German Society, 1892-1914, Princeton University Press, 1975. Contributor to history journals.

WORK IN PROGRESS: Patriotic Societies in Imperial Germany, 1890-1914.

* * *

CHILDS, James Bennett 1896-1977

June 2, 1896—May 14, 1977; American bibliographer and author. Childs was a specialist in government document bibliography with the Library of Congress and wrote several pioneering bibliographies in the field. Obituaries: *AB Bookman's Weekly,* October 10, 1977.

* * *

CHOMSKY, William 1896-1977

January 15, 1896—July 19, 1977; Russian-born grammarian, educator, and author. One of the world's foremost Hebrew grammarians, Chomsky taught at Gratz College and at Dropsie University. *Hebrew, the Eternal Language* is among his best-known books. He died in Philadelphia, Pa. Obituaries: *New York Times,* July 22, 1977.

* * *

CHRISTIAN, Marcus Bruce 1900-

PERSONAL: Born March 8, 1900, in Houma, La. *Education:* Attended Dillard University, 1936-39. *Home address:* Box 50094, New Orleans, La. 70150.

CAREER: Louisiana Weekly, New Orleans, La., poetry editor and special feature writer, 1932—; Dillard University, New Orleans, assistant librarian, 1944-50; Bruce Printing and Publishing Co., New Orleans, founder, 1950; Louisiana State University, New Orleans, instructor in history and director of poetry workshop, 1969—. *Awards, honors:* Rosenwald fellow, 1943-44; Arthur Springarn Crisis outstanding book award, 1948, for *The Common Peoples Manifesto;* also received Sesquicentennial Commission of the Battle of New Orleans bronze medal.

WRITINGS: The Common Peoples Manifesto of World War II, Les Cenelles Society of Arts, 1948; *High Ground,* Southern Publishing, 1958; *Negro Ironworkers of Louisiana,* Pelican, 1972. Also author of *From the Deep,* 1937; *In Memoriam: Franklin Delano Roosevelt,* 1945; *Negro Soldiers in the Battle of New Orleans,* 1965.

Work represented in anthologies, including *Ebony Rhythm,* edited by Beatrice M. Murphy, Exposition Press, 1948; *American Negro Poetry,* edited by Arna Bontemps, Hill & Wang, 1963; *The Poetry of the Negro: 1746-1970,* edited by Langston Hughes and Bontemps, Doubleday, 1970.

Contributor of articles and poetry to *Crisis, Opportunity,* and other periodicals.*

* * *

CHRISTOPHER, John
See YOUD, Samuel

* * *

CHRISTY, Teresa E(lizabeth) 1927-

PERSONAL: Born March 31, 1927, in Brooklyn, N.Y.; daughter of James P. (a fireman) and Charlotte (Pardy) Christy. *Education:* Manhattanville College of the Sacred

Heart, B.S., 1949; De Paul University, M.S., 1957; Columbia University, Ed.D., 1968. *Home:* 1615 Ridge Rd., Iowa City, Iowa 52240. *Office:* College of Nursing, University of Iowa, Iowa City, Iowa 52240.

CAREER: Halloran Veterans Administration Hospital, Staten Island, N.Y., operating room staff nurse, 1947-48; French Hospital, New York, N.Y., labor and delivery room staff nurse, 1949-50; St. Joseph's Hospital, Joliet, Ill., instructor in nursing arts, 1950-60; Molloy College, Rockville Centre, N.Y., assistant professor of medical-surgical nursing, 1960-64, chairman of department of nursing, 1963-64; Columbia University, Teachers College, New York, N.Y., instructor, 1966-67, lecturer, 1967-68, assistant professor of nursing education, 1968-70; Adelphi University, Garden City, N.Y., associate professor of nursing, 1970-74; University of Iowa, Iowa City, associate professor, 1974-75, professor of nursing, 1975—. Registered in New York, Illinois, and Iowa. Visiting professor at University of Illinois at Chicago Circle, 1977—. Member of Nassau County Civil Defense Committee, 1963-64; member of board of directors of Iowa Citizens' League for Nursing, 1977. Has given dozens of lectures all over the United States.

MEMBER: American Nurses Association (chairman of Hall of Fame committee, 1977), National League for Nursing, American Association of University Professors, American Public Health Association, American Historical Association, National Organization for Women, Pi Lambda Theta, Kappa Delta Pi, Sigma Theta Tau. *Awards, honors:* Centennial scholar award for Johns Hopkins University, 1976; Columbia University Teachers College distinguished alumni achievement award, 1976, for research and scholarship; Sigma Theta Tau Founders Award for research, 1977.

WRITINGS: Cornerstone for Nursing Education: A History of the Division of Nursing Education of Teachers College, Columbia University, 1899-1947, Teachers College Press, 1969. Contributor to nursing journals.

WORK IN PROGRESS: Research for a biography of Lavinia Lloyd Dock and for a history of the School of Nursing at the University of Minnesota.

SIDELIGHTS: Teresa Christy writes: "In current feminist writings, the work of the great leaders in nursing has been overlooked. It is as though nurses were non-existent as scholars or academicians. I am researching and writing about the lives of great American nurses who were intelligent, industrious, dedicated visionaries—people whom nurses of the present could emulate."

* * *

CIRIA, Alberto 1934-

PERSONAL: Born January 27, 1934, in Buenos Aires, Argentina; son of Nicolas (a clerk) and Maria (de Miguel) Ciria; married Raquel Esperanza Gonzalez (a translator), August 18, 1966. *Education:* Colegio Nacional de Buenos Aires, B.A., 1952; University of Buenos Aires, J.D., 1959; graduate study at London School of Economics and Political Science, London, 1963-64. *Home:* No. 403, 5450 Empire Dr., Burnaby, British Columbia, Canada V5B 1N4. *Office:* Department of Political Science, Simon Fraser University, Burnaby, British Columbia, Canada V5A 1S6.

CAREER: University of Buenos Aires, Faculty of Law, Buenos Aires, Argentina, assistant professor of political law, 1965-66; University of California, Riverside, visiting research assistant professor of political science, 1966; University of North Carolina, Chapel Hill, visiting assistant

professor of political science, 1966-67; Rutgers University, Douglass College, New Brunswick, N.J., lecturer in political science, 1967-68; Simon Fraser University, Burnaby, British Columbia, assistant professor, 1969-70, associate professor, 1970-77, professor of political science, 1977—. *Military service:* Argentine Army, 1954-55. *Member:* Canadian Association of Latin American Studies, Canadian Political Science Association, Latin American Studies Association, Southern Political Science Association, Simon Fraser University Faculty Association.

WRITINGS: (With Horacio Sanguinetti) *Universidad y estudiantes* (title means "University and Students"), Ediciones Depalma, 1962; *Partidos y poder en la Argentina moderna, 1930-46,* Jorge Alvarez, 1964, translation by Carlos A. Astiz and Mary F. McCarthy published as *Parties and Power in Modern Argentina, 1930-46,* State University of New York Press, 1974, 3rd Spanish edition, Ediciones de la Flor, 1975; (translator and editor) *Montesquieu,* Centro Editor de America Latina, 1967; *Cambio y estancamiento en America Latina* (title means "Change and Stagnation in Latin America"), Jorge Alvarez, 1967; (editor and contributor) *Brecht,* Jorge Alvarez, 1967; (with Sanguinetti) *Los Reformistas* (title means "The [University] Reformers"), Jorge Alvarez, 1968; (translator and editor) *Sorel,* Centro Editor de America Latina, 1968; *America Latina: Contribuciones al estudio de su crisis* (title means "Latin America: Contributions to the Study of Its Crisis"), Monte Avila, 1969; (with Arturo Jauretche, Norberto Galasso, and others) *La decada infame* (title means "The Infamous Decade"), C. Perez, 1969.

Peron y el justicialismo (title means "Peron and His Doctrine of 'Justicialismo'"), Siglo Veintiuno, 1971; (with Dario Canton and Jose Luis Moreno) *La democracia constitucional y su crisis* (title means "The Crisis of Constitutional Democracy"), Paidos, 1972; *Estados Unidos nos mira* (title means "The United States Is Watching Us"), La Bastilla, 1973.

Translator: (From the French) Edgar Morin, *Las estrellas del cine* (title means "The Movie Stars"), Eudeba, 1964; Gustave Flaubert, *Diccionario de los Lugares comunes* (title means "Dictionary of Common Places"), Jorge Alvarez, 1966; (from the English) Matysa Navatto Gerassi, *Los Nacionalistas* (title means "The Nationalists"), Jorge Alvarez, 1968; Federico G. Gil, *El sistema politica de Chile* (title means "The Political System of Chile"), Editorial Juridica "Andres Bello", 1969; Robert Michels, *Introduccion a la sociologia politica* (title means "Introduction to Political Sociology"), Paidos, 1969; Karl W. Deutsch, *Los nervios del gobierno* (title means "The Nerves of Government"), Paidos, 1969; Richard R. Fagen, *Politica y comunicacion* (title means "Politics and Communication"), 1969.

Columnist, *Marcha* (a Uraguayan political weekly), 1960-69. Contributor of articles to *Sais Review, Latin American Research Review, Latin American Perspectives, Journal of International Studies, Revista del Instituto de Ciencias Sociales,* and other journals in his field. Participating editor, *Latin American Perspectives,* 1974—.

WORK IN PROGRESS: A History of Peronism in Argentina, 1943-76; Ideology, Classes, and Dependence in Mexico, Peru, and Argentina; editing *A Life History of a Spanish Immigrant to Argentina.*

SIDELIGHTS: Ciria told *CA:* "My main interests are teaching and research on Latin American politics, both at the academic level and the general one. I try to present a realistic assessment of those problems to counterbalance the

North American Mass-media's simplistic view of that continent." Ciria has traveled frequently to Latin America (Mexico, Argentina, and Peru) and also to Europe. He characterizes himself as a movie buff.

* * *

CLARE, Josephine 1933-

PERSONAL: Born June 5, 1933, in Sigmaringen, Germany; daughter of Franz Valentin (a railroad mechanic and engine driver) and Maria (Ott) Wirkus; married Anselm Hollo (a poet, translator, and teacher), December 23, 1957; children: Hannes, Kaarina, Tamsin. *Education:* Attended Academy of Music (Stuttgart), 1952-54. *Politics:* "Against authoritarianism in all its manifestations—in international and national affairs, in public and private life." *Home:* 112 Washington St., Geneva, N.Y. 14456.

CAREER: Worked as an actress at Thespiskarren Theatre in Tuebingen, Germany, and Unity Theatre, London, England, 1956-61; British Broadcasting Corp. (BBC), London, actress in radio plays, 1964-66, translator, 1964-68; Hobart and William Smith College, Geneva, N.Y., instructor in creative writing, 1973-76; poet. *Awards, honors:* New York State Creative Artists Public Service Program fellowship in poetry, 1977.

WRITINGS: Deutschland, Morgan Press, 1970; *Deutschland & Other Places,* North Atlantic, 1974; *Mammatocumulus,* Ocotillo Press, 1977.

Translator into German: (With husband, Anselm Hollo) William Carlos William, *Paterson,* Henry Goverts, 1970; (with A. Hollo, Rolf John, and Ralf-Rainer Rygulla) Ron Padgett, *Grosse Feuerbaelle* (from English edition, *Great Balls of Fire*), Rowohlt Verlag, 1974.

Contributor to literary magazines, including *Ambit, Chicago, Hills, New Letters,* and *Sumac.*

WORK IN PROGRESS: Poetry.

SIDELIGHTS: Clare told *CA:* "So much I do in my poetry I do without knowing why. As far as I can recognize, there seems to be a force at work to constantly reconstruct the constantly disintegrating world; my own personal world I share with a few, and the world at large I share with everyone. Ever since, as a child in Germany in World War II, I watched the world I thought I knew utterly change and take on monstrous features, I felt a stubbornness grow in me to refuse to aid the forces of destruction. The enemy has picked up the gauntlet I flung down then. The fight is real, exciting too because so real; the lines blur; at times I recognize the enemy as part of myself; at times I am weary. I am interested in the borderline on which the two forces meet—can they merge? Can they cease to be opposites? The outcome, for me, is utterly uncertain."

* * *

CLARK, Jerry E(ugene) 1942-

PERSONAL: Born March 1, 1942, in Eldora, Iowa; son of Harold A. (a laborer) and Avis (Hoversten) Clark; married Lora Lee, June 19, 1965 (divorced, July, 1974); children: Anthony, Sarah. *Education:* Westmar College, B.A., 1964; University of Wisconsin, Madison, M.A., 1966; University of Kentucky, Ph.D., 1974. *Home:* 5807 Grant St., Omaha, Neb. 68104. *Office:* Department of Sociology and Anthropology, Creighton University, Omaha, Neb. 68178.

CAREER: Marshalltown Community College, Marshalltown, Iowa, instructor in sociology, 1966-67; Luther Col-

lege, Decorah, Iowa, instructor in sociology and anthropology, 1967-70; Blackburn College, Carlinville, Ill., teacher of sociology and anthropology, 1974-76; Creighton University, Omaha, Neb., assistant professor of anthropology, 1976—. *Member:* American Society for Ethnohistory, Nebraska Academy of Science.

WRITINGS: The Shawnee, University Press of Kentucky, 1977. Contributor to scientific and archaeology journals.

WORK IN PROGRESS: Christian Missions and the Shawnee Indians.

SIDELIGHTS: Clark writes: "My basic research interest is the study of history, especially ethnohistory. It is my intent to make history interesting, not by dwelling on the spectacular, but by humanizing the people that I write about. My specific interest is in American Indians and their cultural heritage. My goal is to develop an understanding of Indian-White relations from the cultural perspective of the Indians themselves."

* * *

CLARK, Marion L. 1942(?)-1977

1942(?)—September 4, 1977; American journalist and author. Clark was editor of the *Washington Post*'s *Potomac* Magazine and was a member of the team that first reported the Wayne Hays sex scandal. She was co-author of the book, *Public Trust, Private Lust: Sex, Power and Corruption on Capitol Hill.* Clark died in East Tawas, Mich. Obituaries: *New York Times,* September 6, 1977; *Washington Post,* September 6, 1977.

* * *

CLARKE, P(eter) F(rederick) 1942-

PERSONAL: Born July 21, 1942, in England; son of John William (a government official) and Winifred (Hadfield) Clarke; married Dillon Cheetham (a studio glass artist), March 29, 1969; children: Liberty Lucy, Emily Jane. *Education:* St. John's College, Cambridge, B.A., 1963, M.A., 1967, Ph.D., 1967. *Politics:* Labour. *Home:* 69 Grasmere Rd., London N. 10, England. *Office:* Department of History, University College, University of London, London W.C.1, England.

CAREER: University of London, London, England, lecturer in history, 1966—. *Member:* Royal Historical Society (fellow).

WRITINGS: Lancashire and the New Liberalism, Cambridge University Press, 1971; (editor and author of introduction) L. T. Hobhouse, *Democracy and Reaction,* Harvester, 1972; (editor and author of introduction) J. A. Hobson, *The Crisis of Liberalism,* Harvester, 1974; *Liberals and Social Democrats,* Cambridge University Press, 1978. Contributor of articles and reviews to history journals and *Times Literary Supplement.*

SIDELIGHTS: Clarke told *CA:* "*Lancashire and the New Liberalism* was a major reassessment of the role of the Liberal party in Britain before World War I. It challenged the commonly accepted view that the party's electoral position had already been fatally undermined by the rise of Labour and instead made an influential case for the continuing vitality of Liberalism. *Liberals and Social Democrats* takes up some of these themes in terms of intellectual developments. It mounts strong arguments for seeing new Liberals like Hobhouse and Hobson as major figures within a reform tradition running from the work of the early Fabians in the 1880's to that of J. M. Keynes in the 1930's."

CLARKSON, L(eslie) A(lbert)   1933-

PERSONAL: Born January 27, 1933, in London, England; son of Leonard (a carpenter) and Rosina (Downes) Clarkson; married Rosalind M.C. Addison (a teacher), August 7, 1955; children: Christine, Stephen, Jane, Helen, Michael. *Education:* University of Nottingham, B.A., 1954, Ph.D., 1960. *Home:* 49 Marlborough Park S., Belfast, Northern Ireland. *Office:* Department of Economic History, Queen's University, Belfast, Northern Ireland.

CAREER: University of Melbourne, Parkville, Australia, lecturer in economic history, 1958-61; University of Western Australia, Nedlands, lecturer in economics, 1962-65; Queen's University, Belfast, Northern Ireland, lecturer, 1965-70, senior lecturer, 1970-76, reader in economic and social history, 1976—. *Member:* Economic History Society of Great Britain (member of council, 1977—), Economic History Society of Ireland.

WRITINGS: The Pre-Industrial Economy in England, 1500-1750, Batsford, 1971; *Death, Disease, and Famine in Pre-Industrial England,* Gill & Macmillan, 1975. Contributor to journals.

WORK IN PROGRESS: Labour in England and Ireland, 1500-1800; English Industrial History, 1500-1800.

SIDELIGHTS: Clarkson told *CA:* "I am interested, generally, in pre-industrial economics and in England and Ireland, particularly, by accident of birth and residence. I believe that comparative studies are useful and that Irish history has frequently suffered by being too insular."

* * *

CLAYTON, Charles C(urtis)   1902-

PERSONAL: Born June 3, 1902, in Cambridge, Neb.; son of Curtis Stanton (an accountant) and Clara (Richardson) Clayton; married Mary Elizabeth Elliott, June 3, 1925; children: Carol Roma (Mrs. William G. Hill), Charles Stephen. *Education:* Attended University of Nebraska, 1919-23; University of Missouri, B.J., 1925. *Politics:* Independent. *Religion:* Presbyterian. *Home:* 805 Taylor Dr., Carbondale, Ill. 62901.

CAREER: St. Louis Globe-Democrat, St. Louis, Mo., reporter, 1925-29, assistant city editor, 1929-39, literary editor, 1937-39, city editor, 1940-42, editorial writer, 1942-52, executive assistant to the publisher, 1954-55; Southern Illinois University, Carbondale, professor of journalism, 1956-72, professor emeritus, 1972—. Lecturer in journalism at Washington University, St. Louis, 1927-28, Webster College, 1940-53, Lindenwood College, 1940-52, and University of Missouri, 1947-50, fall, 1972; visiting professor of journalism at National Chengchi University, Taipei, Formosa, 1961-62, and 1971-72. Established School of Journalism and the Mass Communications Center at Chinese University of Hong Kong, and served as director of mass communications and journalism, 1965-66. Member of Carbondale City Plan Commission, 1957-61. *Member:* Association for Education in Journalism, Sigma Delta Chi (national president, 1951-52; chairman of executive council, 1952-53), Kappa Tau Alpha, Circumnavigators Club, Carbondale Rotary Club. *Awards, honors:* University of Missouri Medal for distinguished service to journalism, 1952; honorary professor (for life), National Chengchi University, 1962; guest editor of *The China Post,* Taipei, 1971-72.

WRITINGS: Newspaper Reporting Today, Odyssey, 1947; *Fifty Years for Freedom,* Southern Illinois University Press, 1959; *Little Mack: Joseph B. McCullagh of the St. Louis Globe-Democrat,* Southern Illinois University Press, 1969; (contributor) John A. Lent, editor, *The Asian Newspapers' Reluctant Revolution,* Iowa State University Press, 1971. Contributor to magazines. Editor, *Quill,* 1956-61, advisory editor, 1961—.

SIDELIGHTS: Clayton has been around the world twice, visiting thirty-five countries. *Avocational interests:* gardening.

* * *

CLEAVER, Bill

PERSONAL: Born in Seattle, Wash.; married wife, Vera (a writer).

CAREER: Author of books for children. *Military service:* U.S. Air Force. *Awards, honors:* Finalist for the National Book Award, Children's Book Category, 1971, for *Grover.*

WRITINGS—All with wife, Vera Cleaver: *Ellen Grae* (illustrated by Ellen Raskin), Lippincott, 1967; *Lady Ellen Grae* (illustrated by E. Raskin), Lippincott, 1968; *Where the Lilies Bloom* (illustrated by Jim Spanfeller), Lippincott, 1969; *Grover* (illustrated by Frederic Marvin), Lippincott, 1970; *The Mimosa Tree,* Lippincott, 1970; *I Would Rather Be a Turnip,* Lippincott, 1971; *The Mock Revolt,* Lippincott, 1971; *Delpha Green and Company,* Lippincott, 1972; *The Whys and Wherefores of Littabelle Lee,* Atheneum, 1973; *Me Too,* Lippincott, 1973; *Dust of the Earth,* Lippincott, 1975; *Trial Valley,* Lippincott, 1977.

Contributor of stories to *McCall's* and *Woman's Day* magazines.*

* * *

CLEAVER, Hylton Reginald   1891-1961
(Reginald Crunden)

PERSONAL: Born in 1891, in London, England. *Education:* Educated in London, England.

CAREER: Evening Standard, London, England, sports writer, 1937-1960; author of children's books and playwright. *Military service:* British Army.

WRITINGS: The Tempting Thought, Mills & Boon, 1917; *Brother o' Mine: A School Story,* Oxford University Press, 1920; *The Sporting Spirit, and Other Stories,* G. Newnes, 1920; *The Harley First XI,* Oxford University Press, 1920; *Roscoe Makes Good: A Story of Harley,* Oxford University Press, 1921; *Captains of Harley: A School Story,* Oxford University Press, 1921; *On with the Motley,* Mills & Boon, 1922; *The Old Order: A Public School Story,* Oxford University Press, 1922; *The Harley First XV,* Oxford University Press, 1922; *Second Innings: A School Story,* Oxford University Press, 1924; *One Man's Job,* Collins, 1926; *Rugger! The Greatest Game,* Christophers, 1927; *The Greyminster Mystery,* Collins, 1927; *The Short Term at Greyminster,* Collins, 1928; *Fox-Bound: A Novel,* Hutchinson, 1928; *Captains of Greyminster,* Collins, 1929.

A House Divided, Collins, 1930; *The Term of Thrills,* F. Warne, 1931; *The Secret Service of Greyminster,* Collins, 1932; *The New Boy at Greyminster,* Collins, 1932; *Captains of Duke's,* F. Warne, 1933; *Buttle Butts In: A Story of Duke's,* F. Warne, 1933; *The Ghost of Greyminster,* Collins, 1933; *The Forbidden Study,* Collins, 1934, reprinted, Childrens Press, 1955; *Boxing for Schools: How to Learn It and How to Teach It,* Methuen, 1934; *The Phantom Pen: A Story of Duke's School,* F. Warne, 1934; *They Were Not Amused,* Methuen, 1934; *The Haunted Holiday,* F. Warne,

1934; *The Happy Company,* [Dublin], 1934; *The Test Case,* Collins, 1934; *Gay Charade,* Methuen, 1934.

The Hidden Captain, F. Warne, 1935; *The Further Adventures of the Happy Company,* [Dublin], 1935; *The School That Couldn't Sleep,* F. Warne, 1936; *Double Room,* Methuen, 1936; *The Pilot Perfect,* F. Warne, 1937; *Leave It to Craddock,* F. Warne, 1937; *Sport Problems: One Hundred and Fifty Intricate Sports Questions and Authoritative Rulings,* F. Warne, 1937; *The Blaze at Baron's Royal,* F. Warne, 1938; *The Forgotten Term,* F. Warne, 1939; *The Knight of the Knuckles,* F. Warne, 1940; *Dawnay Leaves School,* F. Warne, 1947; *The Deputy Detective,* Bruce Publishing, 1947; *St. Benedict's Goes Back,* F. Warne, 1948; *Dead Man's Tale: A Detective Story,* F. Warne, 1949; *No Rest for Rusty,* F. Warne, 1949.

Lawson for Lord's, F. Warne, 1950; *Lucky Break,* F. Warne, 1950; *Captain of Two Schools,* F. Warne, 1950; *Sporting Rhapsody* (autobiography), Hutchinson, 1951; *Danger at the Ringside,* Hutchinson, 1952; *Dusty Ribbon,* F. Warne, 1952; *The Vengeance of Jeremy,* F. Warne, 1953; *Nizefela Makes a Name* (the autobiography of Wilf White as told to Hylton Cleaver), Museum Press, 1955; *They've Won Their Spurs,* R. Hale, 1956; *A History of Rowing,* H. Jenkins, 1959, reprinted, 1967; *Their Greatest Ride,* R. Hale, 1959; *Before I Forget,* R. Hale, 1961.

Contributor of serials, sometimes under pseudonym Reginald Crunden, to boys periodicals, including *Boy's Own Paper, Chums,* and *The Captain.**

(Died September 9, 1961, in London, England)

*   *   *

CLEAVER, Vera

PERSONAL: Born in Virgil, S.D., married Bill Cleaver (an author).

CAREER: Author of books for children with husband, Bill Cleaver. *Awards, honors:* Finalist for the National Book Award, Children's Book Category, 1971, for *Grover.*

WRITINGS—All with husband, Bill Cleaver, except as noted: (Sole author) *The Nurse's Dilemma,* Avalon Books, 1966; *Ellen Grae* (illustrated by Ellen Raskin), Lippincott, 1967; *Lady Ellen Grae* (illustrated by Raskin), Lippincott, 1968; *Where the Lilies Bloom* (illustrated by Jim Spanfeller), Lippincott, 1969; *Grover* (illustrated by Frederic Marvin), Lippincott, 1970; *The Mimosa Tree,* Lippincott, 1970; *I Would Rather Be a Turnip,* Lippincott, 1971; *The Mock Revolt,* Lippincott, 1971; *Delpha Green and Company,* Lippincott, 1972; *The Whys and Wherefores of Littabelle Lee,* Atheneum, 1973; *Me Too,* Lippincott, 1973; *Dust of the Earth,* Lippincott, 1975; *Trial Valley,* Lippincott, 1977.

Contributor of stories to *McCall's* and *Woman's Day* magazines.*

*   *   *

CLEMENS, Alphonse H.   1905-1977

1905—September 19, 1977; American sociologist, educator, and author. Clemens taught sociology at Catholic University for twenty-five years and wrote and edited several books on marriage and family life. He died in Bethesda, Md. Obituaries: *Washington Post,* September 21, 1977.

*   *   *

CLEMHOUT, Simone   1934-

PERSONAL: Born June 16, 1934, in Tubize, Belgium; came to the United States in 1958, permanent resident of United States. *Education:* University of Liege, lic. es sciences economiques, 1957; International Institute for Social Studies, dipl. planning, 1958; Massachusetts Institute of Technology, Ph.D., 1963. *Home address:* P.O. Box 631, Ithaca, N.Y. 14850.

CAREER: United Nations, New York City, intern at Bureau of Economic Affairs, 1957, research assistant to chief of department of industrial statistics, 1961-62; International Institute for Social Studies, The Hague, Netherlands, researcher, 1962-63; United Nations, research associate of Bureau of Economic Affairs, 1963; City University of New York, New York City, lecturer in economics, 1963-64; United Nations Research Institute for Social Development, Geneva, Switzerland, consultant, 1965; University of California, Berkeley, lecturer in economics, 1966-68, research economist at Institute of International Studies, 1966-69, and School of Engineering, 1969-70; Cornell University, Ithaca, N.Y., associate professor of economics, 1970—, research economist at Center for Urban Development Research, 1970-72, member of its publication committee, 1972-74, member of executive committee of Center for Quantitative and Mathematical Research in Economics and Management, 1970—. Lecturer at Harvard University and fellow of Radcliffe Institute, both 1976-77. Participant in international conferences and symposia.

MEMBER: American Council on Consumer Interests, Econometric Society, Consumer Research Association. *Awards, honors:* Travel grant from University of Liege, summer, 1956, for Zaire; fellowship for European University Center, Nancy, France, 1957; fellowship from Belgian Government, 1958-60, for International Institute for Social Studies, 1958, and for study in England and the Netherlands, 1963; Fulbright fellowship and fellowship from American Association of University Women, 1958-60, for study in the United States; research grant from Belgian National Science Foundation, 1965; Ford Foundation grant, 1966-70; National Science Foundation grants, 1969, 1970, 1971 (for Japan), 1972; research grant from New York Urban Development Corp., 1971-72; U.S. Manpower Administration grant, 1974.

WRITINGS: Patterns of Public Expenditures and Revenues of the Budget in the Congo Under the Ten-Year Plan, 1950-1959, Bureau of Economic Affairs, United Nations, 1957; *Models for Projections of Economic Aggregates for Latin America with a View of Determining the Trade Gaps* (monograph), Bureau of Economic Affairs, United Nations, 1963; *The Social Thresholds: Patterns Associated with Economic Growth* (monograph), United Nations Research Institute for Social Development, 1967.

(Contributor) K. C. Parsons and others, editors, *Public Land Acquisition for New Communities and the Control of Urban Growth: Alternative Strategies,* Center for Urban Development, Cornell University, 1972; (contributor) H. Hess, editor, *General Production Functions and Production Structures,* Hiepenheuer & Witsch, 1973; (contributor) G. Leitmann, editor, *Multicriteria Decision Making and Differential Games,* Plenum, 1976; (contributor) Y. C. Ho and S. K. Mitter, editors, *Directions in Large-Scale Systems: Many-Person Optimization and Decentralized Control,* Plenum, 1976; *Perspectives for Public Policy: An Environmental View on Human Ecology,* University Press of America, 1977.

Contributor of more than thirty articles and reviews to scholarly journals in the United States and abroad, and to newspapers. Referee for *Mathematical Reviews, American Economic Review, Journal of International Studies, International Economic Review, Review of Economic Studies,* and *Western Economic Journal.*

WORK IN PROGRESS: Welfare Economics: Groundings for a Strategy for Consumer Interests.

SIDELIGHTS: Simone Clemhout writes: "I am a strong advocate of the role to be played by consumers/citizens in the process of-social and economic change as indicated in my book.

"I have taught undergraduate and graduate courses in economic theory, monetary theory and banking, economic development, models for planning, welfare economics with applications to public policy in education, urban problems, consumer economics, health, environmental issues, etc. My interests in public policy cover organization and decision making of the household, community and government institutions. I am interested in decision making from a dynamic point of view, and as part of complex systems of interrelated and interactive processes."

* * *

CLEMONS, Lulamae 1917-

PERSONAL: Born December 27, 1917, in Widener, Ark.; daughter of William and Mamie (Moore) Clemons; married Frank Clay McClanahan, Jr.; children: Frank Clay III. *Education:* Earned R.N. from a Missouri general hospital, 1942; Lincoln University (Jefferson City, Mo.), B.S. (cum laude), 1945; Columbia University, M.A., 1951; University of Southern California, Ed.D., 1964; Harvard University, certificate, 1967. *Religion:* Protestant. *Home:* 5837 Walter St., Riverside, Calif. 92504. *Office:* Kaiser Foundation Hospitals, 9961 Sierra Ave., Fontana, Calif. 92335.

CAREER: Lincoln University, Jefferson City, Mo., director of student health services, 1945-46; Riverside County Schools, Riverside, Calif., director of health education, 1956-70; California State College at Fullerton, instructor in multi-cultural education, 1969-70; University of California at Riverside, director of General Assistance Center, 1971-74; Kaiser Foundation Hospitals, Fontana, Calif., director of education and training, 1975—. Member of executive committees and/or board of directors of service organizations, including United Fund/Way, Economic Opportunity Board, Girl Scouts of America, Community Relations Commission, Riverside Urban Coalition, Riverside County Heart Association, Health & Tuberculosis Association of Riverside County; member of executive committee of California Legislature; member of local advisory committees. *Member:* National Association for the Advancement of Colored People (N.A.A.C.P.; president, Riverside chapter), National Education Association (N.E.A.), American Association of University Women, Alpha Kappa Alpha.

WRITINGS: (With Gordan Gardner and Erwin Hollitz) *The American Negro,* McGraw, 1965. Contributor to professional journals.

* * *

CLIFFORD, Martin
See HAMILTON, Charles Harold St. John

* * *

CLIFTON, Harry
See HAMILTON, Charles Harold St. John

CLIFTON, Lewis
See LINEDECKER, Clifford L.

* * *

CLIVE, Clifford
See HAMILTON, Charles Harold St. John

* * *

COBHAM, Sir Alan
See HAMILTON, Charles Harold St. John

* * *

COCHRAN, Hamilton 1898-1977

September 9, 1898—July 27, 1977; American historian and author of thirteen books. He died in Upland, Pa. Obituaries: *New York Times,* August 2, 1977. (See index for *CA* sketch)

* * *

CODEL, Michael R(ichard) 1939-

PERSONAL: Born April 20, 1939, in Baltimore, Md.; son of Edward and Roslyn (Segal) Codel; married Birte Elise Nielsen, May 27, 1967; children: Edward Kai, Kirsten Roslyn. *Education:* Oberlin College, A.B., 1960. *Home and office:* 6534 North 28th St., Arlington, Va. 22213.

CAREER: Associated Press, foreign correspondent in Kinshasa, Congo, 1965-67, and London, England, 1967-69; *Business International SA,* Geneva, Switzerland, associate editor, 1969-72; free-lance writer (specializing in African affairs and international economics), 1972—. Spent two years in the Congo (now Zaire), providing daily coverage of political and economic events. Lecturer on Africa. Member of board of experts for WRC Radio, Washington; consultant to U.S. Congress. *Military service:* U.S. Air Force Reserve, 1960-66. *Member:* National Press Club, Public Relations Society of America, Washington Independent Writers, Sigma Delta Chi.

WRITINGS: Prospects for Business in Developing Africa, Business International SA, 1970; *Sweden: Toward a Post-Industrial Economy,* Business International SA, 1971; (editor) *Africa '73,* Africa Journal Ltd., 1973. Contributor of several hundred articles to magazines and newspapers, including *Nation, Africa Report, Development Forum,* and *Denmark Review.* Former associate editor of *Business Europe.*

WORK IN PROGRESS: Articles on Africa and international economics.

SIDELIGHTS: Codel, one of America's most experienced analysts of African affairs, writes: "I have had sixteen years' involvement with Africa, including residence in Nigeria, the Congo (Zaire), and Ghana, and travel in about thirty other countries. My writings reflect my firm belief that African events stem from local politics and economics, not Big Power rivalries. I have worked as consultant to multinational corporations on responsible investment in, and social obligations toward, developing countries. I am also a specialist on international trade and economics in general, and on Scandinavia."

* * *

COHN, Elchanan 1941-

PERSONAL: Born January 16, 1941, in Tel-Aviv, Israel; came to the United States in 1961, naturalized citizen, 1972; son of Alexander (an engineer) and Klara (Joshua) Cohn;

married Sharon May (a teacher), December 22, 1963; children: David, Klara. *Education:* University of Minnesota, B.A., 1963, M.A., 1965; Iowa State University, Ph.D., 1968. *Politics:* Independent. *Religion:* Jewish. *Office:* Department of Economics, University of South Carolina, Columbia, S.C. 29208.

CAREER: University of Minnesota, Minneapolis, instructor in economics, 1964-65; Iowa State University, Ames, instructor in economics, 1965-68; Pennsylvania State University, University Park, assistant professor, 1968-71, associate professor of economics, 1971-74; University of South Carolina, Columbia, professor of economics, 1974—. *Military service:* Israeli Army, 1958-61. *Member:* American Economic Association, American Statistical Association, American Education Finance Association, Western Economic Association, Omicron Delta Epsilon. *Awards, honors:* National Science Foundation institutional grant for Pennsylvania State University, 1968-71; research grants from U.S. Department of Labor, 1968-71, Governor's Office of the Commonwealth of Pennsylvania, 1969-72, Michigan Advisory Council for Vocational Education, 1971-72, U.S. Bureau of Mines, 1972-73, National Institute of Education, 1972-73 and 1973-74, South Carolina Commission of Higher Education, 1975, and General Services Administration, 1975.

WRITINGS: The Economics of Education, Heath, 1972; *Public Expenditure Analysis: With Special Reference to Human Resources,* Heath, 1972; *Economics of State Aid to Education,* Heath, 1974; *Input/Output Analysis in Public Education,* Ballinger, 1975; (contributor) *The Bituminous Coal Industry: A Forecast,* Institute for Research on Human Resources, Pennsylvania State University, 1975; (contributor) S. J. Bernstein and W. G. Mellon, editors, *Selected Readings in Quantitative Urban Analysis,* Pergamon, 1977.

Contributor of nearly fifty articles and reviews to economic journals. Member of editorial board of *Educational Economics* and *Wall Street Review of Books.*

WORK IN PROGRESS: Revising *The Economics of Education,* for Ballinger; a book on goal programming in educational planning; continuing research on the economics and financing of education.

SIDELIGHTS: Cohn writes: "A major impetus to my writing has been the apparent need for a dialogue between educators and economists. My work is an attempt to provide readable material on the role of economics in education. In the process, I have also endeavored to make modest contributions to the economics of human resources, especially in the areas of benefit/cost analysis, educational input/output analysis, and the finance of education."

*   *   *

COLE, Annette
See STEINER, Barbara A(nnette)

*   *   *

COLE, Burt 1930-

PERSONAL: Born May 30, 1930, in Lambertville, N.J.,; married Maria Argentina Florentina Varella, 1953; children: Maria Regina, Julia Remedios. *Education:* Attended Bethany College, 1949-50. *Politics:* "Left Alone." *Religion:* "Survival." *Residence:* Franklin, N.J. *Agent:* A. L. Hart, Fox Chase Agency, Inc., 419 East 57th St., New York, N.Y. 10022.

CAREER: Writer. Employed by various newspapers, ad-

vertising agencies, and magazines, 1960—. *Military service:* U.S. Army, 1950-51; served in Korea.

WRITINGS: Subi: The Volcano, Macmillan, 1957; *The Longest Way Round,* Macmillan, 1958; *Olimpia,* Macmillan, 1959; *The Funco File,* Doubleday, 1969; *The Book of Rook,* Doubleday, 1971; *Sahara Survival,* Harper Magazine Press, 1973; *The Blue Climate,* Harper, 1977.

WORK IN PROGRESS: Kindred and *Shaman,* two novels dealing with the overthrow of the United States by violence and subversion.

SIDELIGHTS: Cole told *CA:* "I traveled extensively in Asia, Europe, and Africa for ten years (see adventure books), until I was partially disabled by injuries (see office jobs)." He added, "Tis better to have tried and failed than never to have tried—but not much."

Cole's novel *Olimpia* was adapted as a screenplay and released by Warner Brothers in 1968 under the title "The Bobo."

*   *   *

COLEMAN, A(llan) D(ouglass) 1943-

PERSONAL: Born December 19, 1943, in New York, N.Y.; son of Earl M. (a publisher) and Frances (a publisher and photographer; maiden name, Allan) Coleman; married Alexandra L. Blomberg, October 21, 1968 (divorced, November, 1976); children: Edward Allan. *Education:* Hunter College of the City University of New York, B.A., 1964; San Francisco State College (now University), M.A., 1967. *Politics:* Radical. *Religion:* None. *Home and office:* 465 Van Duzer St., Staten Island, N.Y. 10304.

CAREER: Da Capo Press, Inc., New York, N.Y., assistant editor, 1967-68; New School for Social Research, New York City, instructor in photography, 1970-71; Pratt Institute, Brooklyn, N.Y., instructor in photography, 1971-72; free-lance photography critic and lecturer, 1972—. Visiting lecturer at Maryland Institute College of Art, 1971-73; visiting critic at San Francisco Art Institute, summer, 1974; instructor in photography at University of California, San Francisco Extension, spring, 1974. Critic-in-residence at Center for Photographic Studies (Louisville, Ky.), 1977. Co-director of Center for Visual Communication (Staten Island, N.Y.); founder and organizer of Conference on Photographic Criticism; curator of exhibits at University of Bridgeport Art Gallery, 1976, 1977. Has delivered dozens of lectures at schools, museums, photography center, and workshops; guest on radio and television programs in Toronto, Atlanta, New York, and Columbus, Ohio, and on national programs. *Awards, honors:* Art critic's fellowship from National Endowment for the Arts, 1976-77.

WRITINGS: (Editor and author of introduction) Robert Delford Brown, *First-Class Portraits,* First National Church of the Exquisite Panic, 1973; *Carbon Copy* (with own photographs), ADCO Enterprises, 1973; *Confirmation* (with own photographs), ADCO Enterprises, 1975; (contributor) Richard Kostelanetz, editor, *Younger Critics of North America,* Margins Press, 1977; *The Grotesque in Photography,* Ridge Press, 1977; *Re:vision: Essays on the Transformation of Photography into Culture,* Da Capo Press, in press.

Author of foreword and/or introduction: Leslie Krims, *Eight Photographs,* Doubleday, 1970; Krims, *The Little People of America,* Humpy Press, 1972; Edward S. Curtis, *Portraits from North American Indian Life,* Outerbridge & Dienstfrey, 1972; *Brassai Portfolio,* Witkin-Berley, 1973; Man

Ray, *Man Ray: Photographs, 1920-1934,* East River Press, 1975; Curtis, *The Sioux and the Apsaroke,* Harper, 1975; *Arthur Tress: Theater of the Mind,* Morgan & Morgan, 1976; Archibald MacLeish, *Land of the Free,* Da Capo Press, 1977.

Author of columns "Latent Image," in *Village Voice,* 1968-73, "Shows We've Seen," in *Popular Photography,* 1969-74, and "Photography," in *New York Times,* 1970-74. Contributor to *Collier's Encyclopedia* and *Columbia Encyclopedia.* Contributor to art and photography magazines and to newspapers, including *Artforum, Eye, Art in America,* and *Infinity.* Contributing editor of *Camera 35.*

WORK IN PROGRESS: Research on "the autobiographical mode in photography and contemporary erotic photography," with books expected to result.

SIDELIGHTS: Coleman remarks that some of his current interests are "various forms of image-making and the possibilities of combining words and photographs in different ways." *Avocational interests:* Music (former rock and roll musician), sociology.

BIOGRAPHICAL/CRITICAL SOURCES: Camera 35, March, 1972.

* * *

COLEMAN, Lucile

PERSONAL: Born in New York, N.Y.; daughter of Myron H. (a writer and attorney) and Della (a pianist; maiden name, Konski) Lewis; married Denzil R. Coleman (a physician); children: Joseph. *Residence:* North Miami, Fla. *Office:* P.O. Box 610813, North Miami, Fla.

CAREER: A-to-Z Book Service (mail order search service), North Miami, Fla., owner, 1961—. Founder and chairperson of Staten Island Poetry Day, 1949, and New York State Poetry Day, 1950; poetry counselor at University of Tampa, 1952. *Member:* International League of American Booksellers, Antiquarian Booksellers of America, Poetry Society of America. *Awards, honors:* Received several awards for poetry, including prize from Michigan Conference for Writers, 1947, prize from American Poetry League, 1949, first prize from Texas Poetry Society, 1949, award from *Gemini,* 1950, first prize from Southwest Writers Conference, 1952, William A. Woods Memorial Prize from Poetry Society of Georgia, 1952; award from India Journalists Association, 1962, for *This Laughing Dust.*

WRITINGS: Strange Altar (poems), privately printed, 1947; (editor) *First Music* (poems), Staten Island Poetry Society, 1947; (editor) *Second Chorus* (poems), Staten Island Poetry Society, 1949; *This Laughing Dust* (poems), privately printed, 1951; (editor and contributor) *Singing Warriors* (collected by Ellwood C. Nance), Marshall Jones, 1952; *Once Upon a Rhyme* (poems for children), privately printed, 1957; *The Lyric Return* (poems), Valkyrie Press, 1977. Also editor, with others, of *New Orlando Poetry Anthology,* 1958.

Author of "From Where I Sit" (one-act play), first produced in Staten Island, N.Y., March 21, 1969.

Author of "My Days Are Just an Interlude," a song, Clarence Williams Publishing, 1938.

Work represented in anthologies, including *Omnigatherum,* 1977, *Modern Fantasies,* and *Golden Year.* Contributor of several thousand stories and poems to literary journals, science fiction magazines, and popular magazines in the United States and abroad, including *Tiger's Eye, True Confessions,*

and *Today's Health,* and to newspapers. Co-editor of *Manhattan Memo,* 1949; founding member of editorial board of *Pegasus,* 1952.

WORK IN PROGRESS: A portfolio of song lyrics; five or more books of poems, including love lyrics, seasonal verse, religious verse, humorous poems, poems for the family, and for children.

SIDELIGHTS: Coleman writes briefly: "I believe that rhythm and rhyme in poetry adds to its life—and is a cause for remembrance."

Recordings have been made of poems originally published in *This Laughing Dust* and *Singing Warriors.* Readings of Coleman's poetry have been performed on radio programs in Texas, Pennsylvania, California, Arkansas, and Florida.

* * *

COLLINGS, Ellsworth 1887-

PERSONAL: Born October 23, 1887, in McDonald County, Mo.; son of Thomas Jefferson and Sallie Betheny (McBee) Collings; married Lessie Lee Garren, December 25, 1907; children: Jewell Opal. *Education:* University of Missouri, B.S., 1917; Columbia University, M.A., 1922, Ph.D., 1924. *Politics:* Democrat. *Religion:* Baptist. *Residence:* Norman, Okla.

CAREER: University of Oklahoma, Norman, dean of School of Education, 1926—; author and educator. *Member:* National Education Association, American Association for the Advancement of Science, Progressive Education Association, Oklahoma Education Association, Oklahoma Academy of Science, Kappa Delta Pi, Phi Beta Sigma, Phi Delta Kappa.

WRITINGS: An Experiment with a Project Curriculum, Macmillan, 1923; *School Supervision in Theory and Practice,* Crowell, 1927; *A Syllabus in Project Teaching (Secondary Schools),* Edwards Brothers, 1928; *Project Teaching in Elementary Schools,* Century, 1928; *Psychology for Teachers: Purposive Behavior, the Fundamentals of Learning,* Scribner, 1930; *Progressive Teaching in Secondary Schools,* Bobbs-Merrill, 1931; *The Community in the Making: An Experiment in Community Organization,* Economy, 1932; *Supervisory Guidance of Teachers in Secondary Schools,* Macmillan, 1934.

(With Alma Miller) *The 101 Ranch,* University of Oklahoma Press, 1937, reprinted, 1974; *Adventures on a Dude Ranch,* Bobbs-Merrill, 1940; *The Old Home Ranch: The Will Rogers Range in the Indian Territory,* Redlands Press, 1964.

SIDELIGHTS: The 101 Ranch traces the life and activities of the Millers in founding the 101 Ranch, its rise to become an empire, and its eventual fall. *New York Times* wrote, "It is an amazing and a vitally interesting story, not merely of work and adventure against the background of the old West but of the development of 'the greatest diversified farm in the world' and its transformations from the simplicities of a cattle range."

BIOGRAPHICAL/CRITICAL SOURCES: New York Times, July 11, 1937.*

* * *

COLLINS, Arnold Quint 1935-

PERSONAL: Born March 19, 1935, in New York, N.Y.; son of Julius Maurice (a lawyer) and Ethel (Quint) Collins. *Education:* Harvard University, A.B., 1957; University of Pennsylvania, M.A., 1961. *Office:* ABC News, 22 Avenue d'Eylau, Paris 16, France.

CAREER/WRITINGS: WTOP-TV, Washington, D.C., production manager, 1962-64; United Press International Newsfilm, New York City, assignment editor, 1964-65; American Broadcasting Co. (ABC) News, New York City, operations supervisor, 1965-67; free-lance journalist in Middle East, 1967; National Broadcasting Co. (NBC) News, New York City, West Coast assignment manager, 1968-69; ABC News, correspondent in Cairo, Egypt, 1969-74, correspondent in Rome, 1974-75, Asia producer in Hong Kong, 1976, bureau manager in Paris, 1977—. *Military service:* U.S. Naval Reserve, active duty, 1957-60; became lieutenant.

* * *

COLLINS, Desmond 1940-

PERSONAL: Born May 28, 1940, near Reading, England; son of Harold Kennedy (a company director) and Ivy Kathleen A. Collins; married Ann Alen (a teacher), December 20, 1965; children: Simon Alen. *Education:* Cambridge University, B.A. (honors), 1962. *Politics:* "Liberal Social Democrat, eugenicist and idealist." *Home:* 27 Belsize Sq., London N.W.3, England.

CAREER: University of London, London, England; lecturer, 1963-1972, senior lecturer in extramural studies, 1972—. Member of board of directors of Abington Finance Trust Ltd. and John Kennedy Investments Ltd., 1956—. *Member:* Society of Antiquaries of London (fellow), Current Anthropology (associate). *Awards, honors:* M.A. from Cambridge University.

WRITINGS: (With Ruth Whitehouse, Martin Henig, and David Whitehouse) *Background to Archaeology,* Cambridge University Press, 1972; (editor and contributor) *The Origins of Europe,* Allen & Unwin, 1975, Apollo, 1976; *The Human Revolution,* Dutton, 1976; *Early Man in West Middlesex: The Yiewsley Palaeolithic Sites,* H.M.S.O., 1978.

WORK IN PROGRESS: Palaeolithic Europe, publication expected in 1980.

SIDELIGHTS: Collins, who has done field work in Spain, Germany, Israel, and Britain, is currently excavating in West Heath, Hamstead, England. He told *CA:* "My main interest is solving general problems related to human emergence; especially the Neanderthal problem. I am the originator of the theory of evolution of Neanderthal man into Cro-Magnon man by neoteny—the chief selective mechanism being the difficulty of childbirth of big-brained Neanderthal infants."

* * *

COLUM, Padraic 1881-1972

PERSONAL: Born December 8, 1881, in Longford, Ireland; came to the United States in 1914; son of Padraic (a warehouse master) and Susanna (MacCormack) Colum; married Mary Gunning Maguire (a writer), 1912 (died, 1957). *Education:* Educated at local schools. *Religion:* Catholic.

CAREER: Playwright, essayist, novelist, poet, and author of books for children; worked briefly for a railroad; became full-time writer in Dublin, Ireland, 1901; was a founder of the Irish National Theatre (later known as the Abbey), and co-founder and editor for a time of the *Irish Review.* Visited Hawaii, 1923, at the request of its legislature to reshape the island's traditional stories. *Member:* Irish Academy of Literature, American Academy of Arts and Letters, Poetry Society of America (president, 1938-39). *Awards, honors:* Runner-up for the Newbery Medal, 1922, for *The Golden*

Fleece and the Heroes Who Lived Before Achilles, 1926, for *Voyagers,* and 1934, for *Big Tree of Bunlahy;* American Academy of Poets Award, 1952; Gregory Medal of the Irish Academy of Letters, 1953; Regina Medal, 1961; Boston Arts Festival Poet, citation, 1961; Georgetown University 175th Anniversary Medal of Honor, 1964; Litt.D., Columbia University, 1958, and Trinity College, Dublin, 1958.

WRITINGS—Children's stories: *A Boy in Eirinn,* Dutton, 1913, revised edition illustrated by Jack B. Yeats, Dutton, 1929; *The King of Ireland's Son* (illustrated by Willy Pogany), Holt, 1916, reprinted, Macmillan, 1967; (editor) Jonathan Swift, *Gulliver's Travels* (an abridged edition for children; illustrated by W. Pogany), Macmillan, 1917, reprinted, 1964; *The Adventures of Odysseus [and] The Tale of Troy* (illustrated by W. Pogany), Macmillan, 1918, as *The Children's Homer: The Adventures of Odysseus [and] The Tale of Troy,* 1962; *The Boy Who Knew What the Birds Said* (illustrated by Dugald S. Walker), Macmillan, 1918; *The Girl Who Sat by the Ashes* (illustrated by D. S. Walker), Macmillan, 1919, revised edition illustrated by Imero Gobbato, Macmillan, 1968; *The Children of Odin* (illustrated by W. Pogany), Macmillan, 1920, reprinted, 1962; *The Boy Apprenticed to an Enchanter* (illustrated by D. S. Walker), Macmillan, 1920, reprinted, 1966.

The Golden Fleece and the Heroes Who Lived Before Achilles (illustrated by W. Pogany), Macmillan, 1921, reprinted, 1962; *The Children Who Followed the Piper* (illustrated by D. S. Walker), Macmillan, 1922; (editor) *A Thousand and One Nights: Tales of Wonder and Magnificence,* Macmillan, 1923; *The Six Who Were Left on a Shoe,* Macmillan, 1923, reprinted, McGraw-Hill, 1968; *The Peep-Show Man* (illustrated by Lois Lenski), Macmillan, 1924; *The Forge in the Forest* (illustrated by Boris Artzybasheff), Macmillan, 1925; *The Voyagers* (illustrated by Wilfred Jones), Macmillan, 1925; *The Fountain of Youth* (illustrated by Jay Van Everen), Macmillan, 1927, excerpt from *The Fountain of Youth* published separately as *Story Telling New and Old* (illustrations from J. Van Everen), Macmillan, 1968; *Three Men: A Tale,* Matthews & Marrot, 1930; *The Big Tree of Bunlahy* (illustrated by J. Yeats), Macmillan, 1933; *The White Sparrow* (illustrated by Lynd Ward), Macmillan, 1933, reprinted, McGraw-Hill, 1972; *Where the Winds Never Blew and the Cocks Never Crew* (illustrated by Richard Bennett), Macmillan, 1940; *The Stone of Victory, and Other Tales* (illustrated by Judith Gwyn Brown), McGraw-Hill, 1966.

Poems: *Heather Ale: A Book of Verse,* [Dublin], 1907; *Wild Earth: A Book of Verse,* Maunsel (Dublin), 1907; *Wild Earth, and Other Poems,* Holt, 1916; (editor) *Poems of the Irish Revolutionary Brotherhood,* Small, Maynard, 1916; *Dramatic Legends, and Other Poems,* Macmillan, 1922; (editor) *An Anthology of Irish Verse,* Boni & Liveright, 1922, reissued, Liveright, 1972; *Creatures* (illustrated by B. Artzybasheff), Macmillan, 1927; *Old Pastures,* Macmillan, 1930; *Poems,* Macmillan, 1932, revised edition published as *Collected Poems,* Devin-Adair, 1953; *Flower Pieces,* Orwell Press, 1938; *The Vegetable Kingdom,* Indiana University Press, 1954; *Irish Elegies,* Dolmen Press (Dublin), 1958, reprinted, Dufour, 1965; *The Poet's Circuits,* Oxford University Press, 1960; (editor) Samuel Ferguson, *Poems,* Dufour, 1963; (editor) *Roofs of Gold: Poems to Read Aloud,* Macmillan, 1964; *Images of Departure,* Dolmen Press, 1969.

Plays: *The Land* (three-act), Maunsel, 1905; *The Fiddler's House* (three-act), Maunsel, 1907; *Thomas Muskerry* (three-act) Maunsel, 1910; *Three Plays: The Fiddler's House, The*

Land, Thomas Muskerry, Little, Brown, 1916, reprinted, Dufour, 1963; *Mogu, the Wanderer; or, The Desert* (three-act), Little, Brown, 1917; *The Miracle of the Corn,* Theatre Arts, 1925; *Balloon,* Macmillan, 1929; (with wife, Mary Colum) *Moytura: A Play for Dancers,* Oxford University Press, 1963.

Other: *My Irish Year* (autobiography), J. Pott, 1912; (editor) *Broad-Sheet Ballads,* Maunsel, 1913; *Castle Conquer* (novel), Macmillan, 1923; *At the Gateways of the Day* (Hawaiian legends; illustrated by Juliette M. Fraser), Yale University Press, 1924; *The Island of the Mighty* (retold from the Mabinogion), Macmillan, 1924; *The Bright Islands* (Hawaiian legends; illustrated by J. M. Fraser) Yale University Press, 1925; *The Road Round Ireland,* Macmillan, 1926; (contributor) *Book of Modern Catholic Prose,* edited by Theodore Maynard, Holt, 1928; *Orpheus: Myths of the World* (illustrated by B. Artzybasheff), Macmillan, 1930; *Cross Roads to Ireland,* Macmillan, 1930; *A Half-Day's Ride; or, Estates in Corsica* (essays), Macmillan, 1932, reprinted, Books for Libraries, 1969; *The Legend of Saint Columba* (illustrated by Elizabeth MacKinstry), Macmillan, 1935; *The Frenzied Prince* (Irish legends; illustrated by W. Pogany), McKay, 1943; (editor) *A Treasury of Irish Folklore,* Crown Publishers, 1954, reprinted, 1967; *The Flying Swans* (novel), Crown Publishers, 1957, reprinted, A. Figgis (Dublin), 1969; (with M. Colum) *Our Friend James Joyce,* Doubleday, 1958; *Ourselves Alone! The Story of Arthur Griffith and the Origin of the Irish Free State,* Crown Publishers, 1959 (published in Ireland as *Arthur Griffith,* Browne & Nolan, 1959).

SIDELIGHTS: As a young boy, Colum lived with his grandmother, where he would find himself being entertained by a storyteller narrating legends and reciting songs and poetry. These early childhood experiences would later influence the author's own writings. By the time he was twenty years old, Colum had received recognition as both a poet and playwright. His name was soon associated with William Butler Yeats, Lady Gregory, John Millington Synge, A. E. (George W. Russell), and others who made literary contributions to the period known as the Irish Renaissance. Although he was co-founder of the Irish National Theatre (later known as the Abbey), and author of its first successful play, *The Land,* Colum eventually cut his connections with the theatre over disagreement with the drama company's policy.

The Irish-American author began writing children's books after he came to the United States in 1914. According to a *New York Times* article, Colum credited his popularity with children to his belief that one should not talk down to them. The author philosophized, "If children are to will out of the imagination, and create out of the will, we must see to it that their imaginations are not clipped or made trivial."

Colum was very devoted to his wife, Mary. Together they wrote the book, *Our Friend James Joyce.* A critic for the *Chicago Sunday Tribune* reviewed the book as being "the outcome of their [the Colums] warm affection for Joyce, an affection that is all the warmer for being far from blind." Colum's respect for Joyce as a friend and peer made him a dedicated member of the James Joyce Society.

Although never quite reaching the prominence of some of his contemporaries, many of the author's poems have been set to music and have become familiar Irish folksongs. In a *New York Times* article, Colum was quoted as saying, "Poems are made to be said. They are for our voices, not just for our eyes."

BIOGRAPHICAL/CRITICAL SOURCES: Contemporary

Drama of Ireland, Little, Brown, 1917; *Tendencies of Modern English Drama,* Scribner, 1923; John C. Farrar, editor, *Literary Spotlight,* Doran, 1924; *Catholic Literary Revival,* Bruce Publishers, 1935; Lennox Robinson, editor, *Irish Theatre,* Macmillan, 1939; *Chicago Sunday Tribune,* August 24, 1958; *Catholic Library World,* December, 1960; Laura Benet, *Famous Storytellers for Young People,* Dodd, 1968; Zack R. Bowen, *Padraic Colum: A Biographical-Critical Introduction,* Southern Illinois University Press, 1970.

OBITUARIES: Detroit News, January 12, 1972; *New York Times,* January 12, 1972; *Washington Post,* January 13, 1972; *Newsweek,* January 24, 1972; *Time,* January 24, 1972; *Commonwealth,* February 11, 1972; *Publishers Weekly,* February 21, 1972.*

(Died January 12, 1972)

* * *

COMSTOCK, W(illiam) Richard 1928-

PERSONAL: Born May 16, 1928, in Bakersfield, Calif. *Education:* University of California, Berkeley, B.A., 1948; Princeton Theological Seminary, B.D., 1954, Th.M., 1959; Union Theological Seminary, New York, N.Y., Ph.D., 1963. *Office:* Department of Religious Studies, University of California, Santa Barbara, Calif. 93106.

CAREER: University of California, Santa Barbara, professor of religious studies, 1977—.

WRITINGS: (Editor) Robert D. Baird and others, *Religion and Man: An Introduction,* Harper, 1971; *The Study of Religion and Primitive Religions,* Harper, 1972.

* * *

CONDIT, Martha Olson 1913-

PERSONAL: Born September 8, 1913, in East Orange, N.J.; daughter of Olof (a machinist) and Ida Christina Olson; married Milton Armstrong Condit, June 17, 1944. *Education:* Pratt Institute, certificate, 1934; Rutgers University, B.A., 1953, M.L.S., 1958; Montclair State College, supervisor's certificate, 1971. *Religion:* Presbyterian. *Home:* 17 Lincoln Ave., Florham Park, N.J. 07932.

CAREER: Page Free Library, East Orange, N.J., part-time page, 1927-31, junior assistant, 1931-34; Hunterdon County Library, Flemington, N.J., library assistant, 1934-36; Nutley Public Library, Nutley, N.J., children's librarian, 1936-43; Forstmann Library, Passaic, N.J., children's librarian, 1943-45; East Orange Public Library, East Orange, children's librarian, 1945-56; Montclair Public Schools, Montclair, N.J., school librarian, 1956-65, coordinator of libraries and audio visual services, 1965-72; writer, 1972—. Co-adjutant staff member at Rutgers University. Vice-president of Cable Car Playhouse, West Orange, N.J.

MEMBER: American Library Association, American Association of School Librarians, National Council of Teachers of English, New Jersey Education Association, New Jersey School Library Association, Essex County School Library Association (president), Montclair Education Association, Montclair Operetta Club (life member).

WRITINGS: Something to Make, Something to Think About (juvenile), Four Winds, 1975; *Easy to Make, Good to Eat* (juvenile), Scholastic Book Services, 1976.

WORK IN PROGRESS: A juvenile biography of Thomas Alva Edison.

SIDELIGHTS: Martha Condit writes: "My original research on trade books for beginning readers, at Rutgers Graduate Library School in 1959, led to an interest in preschool-to-third grade children's literature. In spite of the rapid changes taking place in society, I find that contemporary children greet books with the same sense of excitement, anticipation, and joy as in the past." *Avocational interests:* Scandinavian travel, religious education, cooking.

* * *

CONE, Fairfax Mastick   1903-1977

PERSONAL: Born February 21, 1903, in San Francisco, Calif.; son of William H. and Isabelle F. (Williams) Cone; married Gertrude Kennedy, June 29, 1929; children: Mary Mastick (Mrs. Richard H. O'Riley). *Education:* Attended University of California, 1925. *Office:* Foote, Cone & Belding, Inc., 200 Park Ave., New York, N.Y. 10017.

CAREER: With *San Francisco Examiner,* San Francisco, Calif., 1926-29; Lord & Thomas (advertising agency), San Francisco, copywriter and account executive, 1929-38, vice-president and manager, 1938-40, vice-president in charge of creative work, New York, N.Y., 1941, executive vice-president and manager of Chicago office, 1942; Foote, Cone & Belding, Inc. (advertising agency), Chicago, Ill., chairman of executive committee, 1942-48, chairman of the board, 1942-51, president, 1951-57, chairman of executive committee, 1957-66. Member of Chicago Board of Education, 1961-63. Trustee of Chicago Educational Television, 1961-70; chairman of board of trustees of University of Chicago, 1963-70. Director of Community Fund of Chicago, 1940-63; chairman of Crusade of Mercy, 1960. *Awards, honors:* LL.D. from Mundelein College, 1961; Berkeley fellow of University of California; Distinguished Service in Advertising medal from Syracuse University.

WRITINGS: With All Its Faults: A Candid Account of Forty Years in Advertising, Little, Brown, 1969.

OBITUARIES: Time, July 4, 1977; *Newsweek,* July 4, 1977.*

(Died June 20, 1977, in Carmel, Calif.)

* * *

CONLY, Robert Leslie   1918(?)-1973
(Robert C. O'Brien)

PERSONAL: Born c. 1918.

CAREER: Author and editor. Began writing career, 1943; worked as editor, *National Geographic Magazine;* staff writer, *Newsweek;* rewrite man, *Washington Times Herald;* news editor, *Pathfinder. Awards, honors:* Lewis Carroll Shelf Award, 1972, Newbery Medal, 1972, runner-up National Book Award, 1972, Mark Twain Award, 1973, Pacific Northwest Library Association Young Readers' Choice Award, 1974, William Allan White Children's Book Award, 1974, all for *Mrs. Frisby and the Rats of NIMH.*

*WRITINGS—*Under pseudonym Robert C. O'Brien; all published by Atheneum: *The Silver Crown* (illustrated by Dale Payson), 1968; *Mrs. Frisby and the Rats of NIMH* (illustrated by Zena Bernstein), 1971; *A Report from Group 17,* 1972; *Z for Zachariah,* 1975.

SIDELIGHTS: Conly began creating imaginary worlds at a very young age, but it wasn't until he was in his late forties that he decided to share his storytelling talents with the public. In his Newbery Award acceptance speech, the author revealed his reasons for writing books for children. "I write them because a story idea pops in my mind. And since I am

in the writing business, when I get a story idea I write it down before I forget it. It isn't always for children, but those are the stories I most like to write, because children like a straightforward, honest plot with a beginning, a middle, and an end: a problem, an attempt to solve it, and at the end a success or a failure."

The author's multi-award winning book, *Mrs. Frisby and the Rats of NIMH,* spun a fantasy about a group of rodents who developed human communication and engineering skills. A reviewer for *The Junior Bookshelf* noted, "This most unusual story well deserved its Newbery Medal. It combines successfully two usually incompatible styles of narration, animals with human names and in human situations, and an accurate study of wild life. It is a beautifully written and thought-provoking book."

In his *A Report from Group 17,* Conly wove a tale involving political intrigue and scientific research. "Make no mistake about it, Robert O'Brien [Conly] is out to make our flesh creep, our spines turn icy, and our hair stand upright. It is a compulsive book, impossible to leave unfinished," commented a critic for *Christian Science Monitor.*

The posthumously published science-fiction thriller, *Z for Zachariah,* told the story of two survivors after a nuclear war. A reviewer for *Bulletin of the Center for Children's Books* observed, "The journal form is used by O'Brien very effectively, with no lack of drama and contrast, and the pace and suspense of the story are adroitly maintained until the dramatic and surprising ending."

AVOCATIONAL INTERESTS: Music, gardening, and furniture making.

BIOGRAPHICAL/CRITICAL SOURCES: Christian Science Monitor, March 23, 1972; *Junior Bookshelf,* February, 1973; *Bulletin of the Center for Children's Books,* November, 1975.

OBITUARIES: New York Times, March 8, 1973; *Publishers Weekly,* March 12, 1973; *Time,* March 19, 1973.*

(Died March 5, 1973)

* * *

CONQUEST, Owen
See HAMILTON, Charles Harold St. John

* * *

CONWAY, Gordon
See HAMILTON, Charles Harold St. John

* * *

COOK, (Harold) James   1926-

PERSONAL: Born November 9, 1926, in Schenectady, N.Y.; son of Harold James (an engineer) and Ruth May (Turner) Cook; married Claire Kehrwald, September 12, 1953; children: Karen Louise, Cassandra Claire. *Education:* Bowdoin College, A.B., 1947; Columbia University, A.M., 1948. *Home:* Twin Arch Rd., Rock Tavern, N.Y. 12575. *Office: Forbes,* 60 Fifth Ave., New York, N.Y. 10011.

CAREER/WRITINGS: Yankton College, Yankton, S.D., instructor in English and drama, 1948-49; Ohio University, Athens, Ohio, instructor in English, 1949-52; Popular Publications, New York City, western pulps editor, 1952-53; *Railroad* magazine, New York City, managing editor, 1953-55; *Forbes* magazine, New York City, associate editor, 1955-58; free-lance writer, 1958-61; *Forbes,* associate editor, 1961-64, senior editor, 1964-76, editor of *Forbes* in Arabic,

1975-76, executive editor, 1976—. Notable assignments include coverage of the state department's role in OPEC's control winning of the petroleum market, relations between 1973 oil prices and third world countries, and exposing Charles Engelhard as prototype of *Goldfinger*.

SIDELIGHTS: Cook told *CA:* "I think the U.S. and world economies are undergoing radical changes whose consequences cannot be foreseen. The occasion was the coming to power of OPEC, but this is probably simply accidental. The dynamic forces that brought affluence and prosperity to the industrial west had already begun to reverse themselves."

Asked why he preferred capitalism to other economic systems, Cook replied: "Simply because I think the discipline it provides has to come from somewhere. The limited resources of the planet are more likely to be allocated efficiently and productively by capitalism than by the direct intervention of human agencies."

* * *

COOK, Terry 1942-

PERSONAL: Born May 22, 1942, in Chicago, Ill.; son of Lewis Ray and Marie (Roberts) Cook; married Virginia Destro, August 12, 1968; children: Anastasia, Christopher. *Education:* Attended Lehigh University, 1960-64. *Home address:* P.O. Box 123, Chester, N.J. 07930.

CAREER: Writer of column, "New Jersey News" for *Drag News,* 1963; *Drag World,* Los Angeles, Calif., associate editor, 1965-66; *Car Craft,* Los Angeles, feature editor, 1966-68, editor, 1968-71; *Hot Rod,* Los Angeles, editor, 1972-74; *Vans and Trucks,* East Northport, N.Y., editor, 1975-76; *Car and Driver,* New York, N.Y., editorial staff writer, 1976—. Member of Chester Planning Board. *Military service:* U.S. Army Reserve, 1968-74.

WRITINGS: Vans and the Truckin' Life, Abrams, 1977.

WORK IN PROGRESS: Research on three-dimensional films and printed matter (including posters, books, and comics).

SIDELIGHTS: Cook remarks: "I am extremely self-motivated. During my tenure as magazine editor, newsstand sales rose substantially. When I left each magazine, its newsstand sales dropped. I believe in 'telling it like it is,' assuming you do thorough research."

BIOGRAPHICAL/CRITICAL SOURCES: Hot Rod, February, 1972; *Car Craft,* April, 1972.

* * *

COOKE, Charles Harris 1904(?)-1977

1904(?)—October 18, 1977; American federal agency employee, magazine editor and staff writer, and author. Cooke worked for several federal agencies including the Department of Health, Education and Welfare. He was a staff writer on the *New Yorker,* associate editor of *Holiday* and *Esquire* magazines, author of a novel, *Big Show,* and of a book for amateur pianists. He died in Cooperstown, N.Y. Obituaries: *New York Times,* October 20, 1977.

* * *

COOMBS, Orde M.

PERSONAL: Born in St. Vincent, West Indies. *Education:* Yale University, B.A., 1965; graduate study at Clare College, Cambridge, 1965-66; New York University, M.A., 1971. *Residence:* New York, N.Y.

CAREER: Producer of documentaries dealing with West

Indian culture, 1958-61; Doubleday & Co., New York City, associate editor, 1966-68; Western Electric Co., New York City, senior public relations specialist, 1968-69; McCall Publishing Co., New York City, senior editor, 1969—.

WRITINGS—Nonfiction: (With John H. Garabedian) *Eastern Religions in the Electric Age,* Grosset, 1968; *Do You See My Love for You Growing?,* Dodd, 1972; (with Chester Higgins, Jr.) *Drums of Life,* Doubleday, 1974; *Sleep Late with Your Dreams,* Dodd, 1977.

Editor: *We Speak as Liberators: Young Black Poets,* Dodd, 1970; *What We Must See: Young Black Storytellers,* Dodd, 1971; *Is Massa Day Dead? Black Moods in the Caribbean,* Doubleday, 1974.

Work represented in anthologies, including *Black Review No. 2,* edited by Mel Watkins, Morrow, 1971. Contributor to periodicals, including *New York Times, Harper's,* and *Black World.*

SIDELIGHTS: Liz Gant noted that Coombs dealt with "some of the toughest and longest standing problems we [Blacks] have" in the series of eleven essays which comprise *Do You See My Love for You Growing?* Gant praised Coombs for having "stirred up some things that never should have been allowed to lie still," such as the "inability to protect ourselves [and] . . . the inability to come together on common ground."

BIOGRAPHICAL/CRITICAL SOURCES: New York Times Book Review, June 20, 1971; *Black World,* February, 1973.*

* * *

COOPER, Wyatt 1927-

PERSONAL: Born September 1, 1927, in Quitman, Miss.; son of Emmett (a farmer) and Jennie (Anderson) Cooper; married Gloria Vanderbilt (an artist), December 24, 1963; children: Carter, Anderson. *Education:* Attended University of California, Los Angeles, and University of California, Berkeley,. *Politics:* Democrat. *Religion:* Unitarian-Universalist. *Home and office:* 30 Beekman Pl., New York, N.Y. 10022.

CAREER: Stage and film actor in Hollywood, Calif., appearing in "Joan of Lorraine," 1948-50; television and stage actor in New York City, appearing in "Kraft Television Theatre," "Robert Montgomery Presents," "Philco Playhouse," and in summer stock productions, 1950-56; actor in Rome, Italy, appearing in the play "Picnic" and in the film "Seven Hills of Rome," 1957; actor and technical advisor in Hollywood, 1958; free-lance writer and screenwriter, 1959—. Lecturer; television talk show guest.

WRITINGS: (Screenplay; with Don M. Mankiewicz) "The Chapman Report" (based on the novel by Irving Wallace), produced by Warner Bros., 1962; (author of introduction) Gloria Vanderbilt, *Book of Collages,* Van Nostrand, 1970; *Families: A Memoir and a Celebration,* Harper, 1975; (author of introduction) Stella Jolles Reichman, *Great Big Beautiful Doll,* Dutton, 1977. Also author of a television film "Glass House" with Truman Capote, produced by Columbia Broadcasting System (CBS), 1973. Contributor of articles to magazines, including *Town and Country, Esquire,* and *Harper's Bazaar.* Editor of *Status,* 1969-70.

* * *

COOPERSMITH, Jerome 1925-

PERSONAL: Born August 11, 1925, in New York, N.Y.;

son of Meyer (an attorney) and Henrietta (a secretary; maiden name, Miller) Kupfersmith; married Judy Loehnberg (a ballet teacher), February 14, 1956; children: Amy, Jill. *Education:* Attended City College (now of the City University of New York), 1941-43; New York University, B.A., 1947. *Agent:* William Morris Agency, 1350 Avenue of the Americas, New York, N.Y. 10019.

CAREER: Shubert Theatrical Company, New York City, office assistant, 1942; Martin Stone Associates (television production), New York City, production assistant, 1948-49, writer and producer, 1949-54; free-lance writer, 1954—. Adjunct associate professor of film writing at Hunter College of the City University of New York, 1971—. *Military service:* U.S. Army, 1943-45; received Bronze Star. *Member:* Dramatists Guild, Writers Guild of America, East (council member, 1970-74; vice-president, 1974-77). *Awards, honors:* Robert E. Sherwood Award from Fund for the Republic, 1956, for teleplay "I Was Accused"; Christopher Award from The Christophers, 1959, for teleplay "SSN 571—The Nautilus"; Tony award nomination from Antoinette Perry Awards Committee, 1965, for libretto of "Baker Street"; Isaiah Award from Jewish Chautauqua Society, 1971, for documentary film "Beyond the Mirage"; Edgar Allen Poe Special Award from Mystery Writers of America, 1974, for teleplay "Here Today, Gone Tonight"; S. Elizabeth Pope Playwriting Award from Bridgewater State College, 1976, for play "Eleanor."

WRITINGS: A Chanukah Fable for Christmas, Putnam, 1969; *Professional Writer's Teleplay/Screenplay Format,* Writers Guild of America, East, 1975.

Librettos: *Baker Street* (two-act; first produced in Boston, Mass., at Shubert Theatre, 1964; produced on Broadway, 1965), Doubleday, 1966; (with Jerry Bock and Sheldon Harnick) "The Apple Tree" (two-act), first produced in Boston at Shubert Theatre, 1966; "Mata Hari" (two-act), first produced in Washington, D.C., at National Theatre, 1967; "Ballad for a Firing Squad" (two-act), first produced in New York City at Theatre de Lys, 1968; "Swiss Family Robinson" (juvenile; one-act), first produced in Livingston, N.J., 1972; "Pinocchio" (juvenile; one-act), first produced in New York City at Bil Baird Marionette Theatre, 1973.

Play: "Eleanor" (two-act), first produced in Bridgewater, Mass., at Bridgewater State College, 1976.

Creator, writer, and producer of "Johnny Jupiter" juvenile television series, produced by Dumont Network, 1953; author of television movie "Mr. Inside/Mr. Outside," produced by National Broadcasting Company (NBC), 1974; author of "Twas the Night Before Christmas," a television special based on the poem by Clement Moore, produced by Columbia Broadcasting System (CBS), 1974; creator and writer of "The Andros Targets," a television series produced by CBS, 1977. Also contributor of scripts to television series, including "Hawaii Five-O," "Armstrong Circle Theatre," "Harry S. Truman," and "Alcoa-Goodyear Playhouse."

WORK IN PROGRESS: A Christmas special for NBC's Hallmark Hall of Fame; "The Assassins," a television movie for CBS; "The Violation," a television movie for NBC.

SIDELIGHTS: Coopersmith told *CA:* "I write because I enjoy it, and because I relish the variety and independence of a free-lance writer's life. I am primarily a dramatist; at least half the fun and excitement is seeing the material come to life on stage or screen. My main motivation is to entertain and rivet an audience; beyond that, I seek opportunities to comment on human and social conditions. I am frequently inspired by material that is historical or based on fact, though I have also written mysteries, fantasies, and adaptations of classics."

* * *

CORBIN, Sabra Lee
See MALVERN, Gladys

* * *

CORDTZ, Dan 1927-

PERSONAL: Born May 1, 1927, in Gary, Ind.; son of Edmund Richard (an army officer) and Edna (Cox) Cordtz; married Mildred Peck, September 6, 1947 (divorced, December 10, 1970); married Ann Latimer (a teacher), November 7, 1975; children: Wendy (Mrs. Sam K. Eaton, Jr.), Kay, Richard, Jeffrey. *Education:* Stanford University, B.A., 1949. *Home:* 8123 Thoreau Dr., Bethesda, Md. 20034. *Office:* ABC News, 1124 Connecticut Ave. N.W., Washington D.C. 20036.

CAREER/WRITINGS: San Francisco News, San Francisco, Calif., general assignment reporter, 1948-49; *Wall Street Journal,* New York City, copy editor of Pacific Coast edition, 1949-50; *Hanford Sentinel,* Hanford, Calif., city editor, 1950-52; *Cleveland Plain Dealer,* Cleveland, Ohio, general assignment reporter and sports writer, 1952-55; *Wall Street Journal,* feature story writer in New York City, 1955-56, manager of Detroit bureau, 1956-59, Page One editor, 1959-60, correspondent in Paris, 1960-64, senior congressional correspondent, 1964-66; *Fortune,* New York City, Washington editor, 1966-68; Urban Institute, Washington, D.C., senior research fellow and director of communication studies, 1968-69; *Fortune,* associate editor, 1969-74; American Broadcasting Co. (ABC) News, New York City, economics editor, 1974—. Notable assignments include coverage of the 1954 World Series, the automotive industry, construction of the Berlin Wall, the Algerian war, the formation of the Common Market, the U.S. presidential election, 1964, the aftermath of the Six-Day War, and an expose of racial problems in Chicago.

* * *

CORNFELD, Gaalyahu 1902-

PERSONAL: Born May 26, 1902, in Rosh Pina, Palestine (now Israel); son of Leon Arieh (a philologist) and Sarah (Korsonsky) Cornfeld; married Lilian Kert (a nutritionist and writer of cookbooks), 1924; children: Gibeon. *Education:* Lycee Francais, Cairo, Egypt. *Religion:* Jewish. *Home:* 145 Hayarkon St., Tel Aviv, Israel.

CAREER: Editor and journalist, 1942-47; Twersky Publishing House, Tel Aviv, Israel, acting director, 1945-48; in private business, 1950-52; Hebrew Book Publishers Association, Tel Aviv, general secretary, 1952-59; Hamikra Baolam Publishing Ltd., Tel Aviv, director and chief editor, 1957—. Director and chief editor, G. and L. Cornfeld, Publishers; president, Orion Records.

WRITINGS: (Editor) *Adam to Daniel: An Illustrated Guide to the Old Testament and Its Background,* Macmillan, 1960; (editor) *Daniel to Paul: Jews in Conflict with Graeco-Roman Civilization,* Macmillan, 1962; (with Valerie Mindlin) *Epic of the Maccabees,* Macmillan, 1962; (editor) *Pictorial Biblical Encyclopedia: A Visual Guide to the Old and New Testaments,* Macmillan, 1964; (with Bernard Rosenblatt) *Two Generations of Zionism,* Shengold Publishers, 1967; (compiler) *War for Redemption and Peace* (trilingual edition, Hebrew, English, and French), [Israel], 1967; (with Pirsume Yerushalayim) *Jerusalem at Large*, Jerusalem Publications, 1968; (editor with D. N. Freedman) Benjamin Mazar, *The Mountain of the Lord*, Doubleday, 1975. Also author of *This is Mesada, I Love Jerusalem*, and *Albums of Israel*, 1970 and 1972. Contributor of articles and essays to American publications since 1936.

WORK IN PROGRESS: Editing B. Mazar's, *Excavations on the Temple Mount and the City of David;* an archeological Biblical atlas, *Archeology and the Books of the Bible;* an illustrated Bible; and a Bible archaeology for young readers.

SIDELIGHTS: Cornfeld speaks French, English, Hebrew, and Arabic; he has a large photographic archive on Biblical background and Near Eastern archaeology. *Avocational interests:* Archaeology, photography, country hiking, studying nature.

*   *   *

CORTEZ, Jayne   1936-

PERSONAL: Born May 10, 1936, in Arizona; children: Denardo Coleman. *Home address:* Box 96, Village Station, New York, N.Y. 10014.

CAREER: Poet. Lecturer at Queens College, Howard University, Dartmouth College, Wesleyan College, and University of Ibadan. Co-founder, Watts Repertory Theatre, Los Angeles, Calif. *Awards, honors:* New York State Council on the Arts creative artist award for poetry, 1973.

WRITINGS: Pissstained Stairs and the Monkey Man's Wares, Phrase Text, 1969; *Festivals and Funerals*, Bola Press, 1971; *Scarifications*, Bola Press, 1973; *Mouth on Paper*, Bola Press, 1977.

Work represented in anthologies, including *We Speak as Liberators*, edited by Orde Coombs, Dodd, 1970; *The Poetry of Black America*, edited by Arnold Adoff, Harper, 1972; *A Rock Against the Wind: Black Love Poems*, edited by Lindsay Patterson, Dodd, 1973; *New Black Voices*, edited by Abraham Chapman, New American Library, 1972; *Giant Talk*, edited by Quincy Troupe and Rainer Schulte, Random House, 1975.

Contributor to *Black World, Negro American Forum, Yardbird Reader, American Dialog, Confrontation, Mundus Artium,* and other periodicals.

SIDELIGHTS: Nikki Giovanni reviewed *Pissstained Stairs and the Monkey Man's Wares:* "We haven't had many jazz poets who got inside the music and the people who created it. We poet about them, but not of them. And this is Cortez's strength. She can wail from Theodore Navarro and Leadbelly to Ornette and never lose a beat and never make a mistake. She's a genius and all lovers of jazz will need this book—lovers of poetry will want it."

Cortez read her poetry accompanied by the Clifford Thornton New Art Ensemble at Carnegie Hall in 1970. She has traveled to several Third World countries.

BIOGRAPHICAL/CRITICAL SOURCES: Negro Digest, December, 1969.

*   *   *

COSTER, Robert
See BARLTROP, Robert

*   *   *

COSTIGAN, James   1928-

PERSONAL: Born March 31, 1928, in Belvedere Gardens,

Calif.; son of Thomas Patrick (an electrical manufacturer) and Joan (Sullivan) Costigan. *Education:* Educated in Los Angeles, Calif.

CAREER: Actor, playwright, and author of teleplays. Began stage career at Wilshire-Ebell Theater, Los Angeles, 1940; actor in New York and California, 1943-45; Gretna Playhouse, Mt. Gretna, Pa., stock actor, 1948-49; ELT "Scrapbook" Productions, New York City, actor on tour, 1950-53; author of teleplays, 1952—; playwright, 1959—. *Military service:* U.S. Army, 1944-45. *Member:* Actors Equity Association, American Federation of Television and Radio Artists, Writers Guild of America, Screen Actors Guild. *Awards, honors:* Emmy Award and George Foster Peabody Award, 1958, both for "Little Moon of Alban," and 1975, for "Love Among the Ruins"; Emmy Award, 1975, for "Eleanor and Franklin."

WRITINGS—Plays: *Little Moon of Alban* [and] *A Wind from the South*, Simon & Schuster, 1959; "The Beast in Me," first produced in Westport, Conn., at Nash's Barn Theatre, 1962; *Baby, Want a Kiss?* (two-act; first produced on Broadway at Little Theatre, April 19, 1962), Samuel French, 1965.

Teleplays: "Rain No More," National Broadcasting Co. (NBC), 1953; "The Bells of Damon," Columbia Broadcasting System (CBS), 1953; "The World, My Cage," CBS, 1953; "Cradle Song," NBC, 1956 and 1960; "The Lark," NBC, 1957; "On Borrowed Time," NBC, 1957; "Wuthering Heights," CBS, 1958; "The Turn of the Screw," NBC, 1959; "A Doll's House," NBC, 1959; "A War of Children," 1972; "Love Among the Ruins," 1975; "Eleanor and Franklin," 1975. Also author of "In This House of Brede," and "F. Scott Fitzgerald and the Last of the Belles."

SIDELIGHTS: "I bewail the meaningless violence many television producers insist that writers shovel into their scripts," Costigan said in 1958. "It shows how meager are the dreams of these men." In the foreword to *Little Moon of Alban*, written the same year, Costigan foresaw "the day when a whole library of wonderful plays and wonderful musicals will be done for television."

Seventeen years later, with the highly acclaimed production of "Love Among the Ruins," Costigan noted a change in television: "There was a time when no matter what you wrote, or how good it was, you were considered a second-class writer if it was for television. That day is gone. When you can get a George Cukor to direct a film for television and a Katherine Hepburn and Laurence Olivier to act in it, it's fantastic!"

BIOGRAPHICAL/CRITICAL SOURCES: Time, April 7, 1958; *New York Times,* May 4, 1958; *New York Daily News,* March 2, 1975.*

*   *   *

COUGHLIN, Violet L(ouise)

PERSONAL: Born in Montreal, Quebec, Canada; daughter of Sydney and May Elizabeth (Gregory) Hulin; married Bernard Errol Coughlin, June 27, 1936 (deceased); children: Robert. *Education:* McGill University, B.S. (magna cum laude), 1928, B.L.S., 1938; Columbia University, M.A., 1958, D.L.S., 1966. *Home:* 666 Spadura Ave., Apt. 1810, Toronto, Ontario, Canada M5S 2H8. *Office:* Faculty of Library Science, University of Toronto, Toronto, Ontario, Canada M5S 1A1.

CAREER: Royal Victoria Hospital, Montreal, Quebec, medical technician, 1928-29; high school chemistry teacher in Montreal, 1929-34; McGill University, Montreal, cataloger at Redpath Library, 1941, librarian at Royal Victoria College, 1941-51, lecturer, 1951-57, assistant professor, 1957-65, associate professor, 1965-69, professor of library science, 1969-75, professor emeritus, 1975—, acting director of Library School, 1970-71, director, 1971-73; University of Toronto, Toronto, Ontario, visiting emeritus professor of library science, 1975—. Visiting professor at University of Pittsburgh, 1966-67, and University of Hawaii, summers, 1968, 1970.

MEMBER: Canadian Library Association, American Library Association, American Association of Library Schools, Quebec Library Association (president, 1954-55), Corporation of Professional Librarians of Quebec (member of board of directors, 1972-75), Beta Phi Mu (member of board of directors, 1965-68).

WRITINGS: (Contributor) *Library Education: An International Survey,* Graduate School of Library Science, University of Illinois, 1968; *Larger Units of Public Library Service in Canada,* Scarecrow, 1968. Contributor to *Encyclopedia of Library and Information Science* and to library journals.

SIDELIGHTS: Coughlin told *CA:* "I feel my main contribution has been in helping young people to take their place in life, first as a chemistry teacher and later as a professor in the library education field. I have felt the human side to be as important as the academic side (if not more so).

"The book published by Scarecrow has been an important contribution to the field which is greatly lacking in serious historical studies. It is *the* textbook on the subject in universities throughout Canada and also elsewhere in the United States and Great Britain."

*   *   *

COUSTILLAS, Pierre   1930-

PERSONAL: Born July 11, 1930, in Neuville-aux-Bois, France; son of Rene (a railwayman) and Marie-Therese (Lebrun) Coustillas; married Helene Albert, July 19, 1958; children: Francoise. *Education:* Sorbonne, University of Paris, licence, 1952, diplome d'etudes superieures d'anglais, 1953, agregation, 1955, Ph.D., 1967, Doctorat-es-lettres, 1970. *Religion:* None. *Home:* 10 Rue Gay-Lussac, 59110 La Madeleine, France. *Office:* Universite de Lille III, 59650 Villeneuve d'Ascq, Lille, France.

CAREER: English teacher in high schools in Charleville and Paris, France, 1957-63; University of Paris, Sorbonne, Paris, assistant professor of English, 1963-66; University of Madagascar, Tarnanarive, professor of English and head of department of modern languages, 1966-68; University of Lille III, Lille, France, senior lecturer, 1968-70, lecturer, 1970-72, professor of English, 1972—, director of Victorian Studies Centre. *Military service:* French Army, 1955-57; served in Germany and Morocco.

WRITINGS: (Editor) *The Letters of George Gissing to Gabrielle Fleury,* New York Public Library, 1965; (editor and translator) George Robert Gissing, *Les Carnets d'Henry Ryecroft* (title means "The Private Papers of Henry Ryecroft"), Aubier, 1966; (editor) *Collected Articles on George Gissing,* Barnes & Noble, 1968; *Gissing's Writings on Dickens: A Bibliographical Survey, Together with Two Uncollected Reviews by George Gissing from the Times Literary Supplement,* Enitharmon Press, 1969, 2nd edition, 1971; *George Gissing at Alderley Edge,* Enitharmon Press, 1969, 2nd edition, 1971; (editor) Gissing, *Isabel Clarendon* (novel; critical edition), Harvester Press, 1969.

(Editor and contributor with Shigero Koike, Giichi Kamo, and C. C. Kohler) *Gissing East and West: Four Aspects,* Enitharmon Press, 1970; (editor) Gissing, *Essays and Fiction* (critical edition), Johns Hopkins Press, 1970; (editor) Gissing, *My First Rehearsal and My Clerical Rival* (stories; critical edition), Enitharmon Press, 1970; (with John Spiers) *The Rediscovery of George Gissing,* National Book League, 1971; (editor with Colin Partridge) *Gissing: The Critical Heritage,* Routledge & Kegan Paul, 1972; (editor) Gissing, *Demos* (novel; critical edition), Harvester Press, 1972; (editor and author of introduction) *Henry Hick's Recollections of George Gissing, Together with Gissing's Letters to Henry Hick,* Enitharmon Press, 1973; (editor) *The Letters of George Gissing to Edward Clodd,* Enitharmon Press, 1973; (editor) *Politics in Literature in the Nineteenth Century,* Presses Universitaires de Lille, 1974; (editor) Gissing, *Our Friend the Charlatan* (novel; critical edition), Associated University Presses, 1976; (editor) George Moore, *Literature at Nurse: or, Circulating Morals* (pamphlet; critical edition), Humanities Press, 1976; (editor) *Victorian Writers and the City,* University of Lille, 1977.

Contributor: Charles Sanders, editor, *W. Somerset Maugham: An Annotated Bibliography of Writings About Him,* Northern Illinois University Press, 1970; (author of introduction) *George Gissing: A Study in Literary Leanings,* Kohler & Coombs, 1974; (author of introduction) Gissing, *Sleeping Fires,* Harvester Press, 1974; Joseph J. Wolff, editor, *George Gissing: An Annotated Bibliography of Writings About Him,* Northern Illinois University Press, 1974. Contributor to *Encyclopaedia Universalis.* Contributor of articles and reviews in English and French to literature and library journals. Editor of *Gissing Newsletter.*

WORK IN PROGRESS: Editing the novel, *The Emancipated,* by George Gissing, for Harvester Press; a two-volume biography of Gissing, Harvester Press; translating Gissing's novels, *New Grub Street, The Nether World,* and *The Odd Women;* translating Conrad's *Tales of Unrest* into French, for Bibliotheque de la Pleiade; a bibliography of Gissing; editing a five-volume collection of Gissing's short stories.

SIDELIGHTS: Coustillas told *CA:* "My interest in George Gissing dates back to my student days when I read the assessment of his work made by Louis Cazamian in his *History of English Literature.* I immediately realized that he was the author for me. Though my personal experience of life has little enough in common with his, I share many of his opinions and attitudes in many domains (political, social, spiritual, intellectual). From the first I was convinced that he had been a victim of his own youthful idealism, of social segregation, and of literary prejudice. For the last twenty years or so, I have done my best through different means (articles, books, talks, an exhibition in London, interviews on the radio) to rehabilitate him. Only two or three scholars were actively interested in him about 1960; there are now dozens. His books were scarce; they are now nearly all available. I should have been far less successful but for the disinterested assistance (and equal enthusiasm) of a number of friends in the worlds of publishing, scholarly journalism, bookselling, etc., in such countries as England, America, Japan, Italy, and France.

"Among my favourite English authors, on whom I have written are George Orwell, Thomas Hardy, Mrs. Gaskell, and Anthony Trollope. Among the French are Zola and Camus.

"More generally my interests lie in the novel, the short story, the Victorian press, the history of publishing, and bibliography."

BIOGRAPHICAL/CRITICAL SOURCES: Gissing Newsletter, July, 1970.

* * *

COVERDALE, John F(oy) 1940-

PERSONAL: Born June 20, 1940, in Chicago, Ill.; son of Philip J. (a businessman) and Kathleen M. (Biggins) Coverdale. *Education:* Attended University of Maryland, 1958-60; Lateran University, B.A., 1962; University of Navarre, M.A., 1966; University of Wisconsin, Madison, Ph.D., 1971. *Home:* 7225 North Greenview, Chicago, Ill. 60626. *Office:* Department of History, Northwestern University, Evanston, Ill. 60201.

CAREER: Princeton University, Princeton, N.J., assistant professor of history, 1971-76; Northwestern University, Evanston, Ill., associate professor of history, 1976—. Member, Columbia University Seminar on Modern Italy. *Member:* American Historical Association, Society for Spanish and Portuguese Historical Studies, Society for Italian History, Portuguese Studies Association, Conference Group on Italian Politics. *Awards, honors:* Howard R. Marraro Prize from Society for Italian History, 1976, for *Italian Intervention in the Spanish Civil War.*

WRITINGS: Italian Intervention in the Spanish Civil War, Princeton University Press, 1975; *Spanish Politics After Franco,* Praeger, 1978.

WORK IN PROGRESS: A Social and Political History of the First Carlist War in Spain, 1833-39.

* * *

COX, Archibald 1912-

PERSONAL: Born May 17, 1912, in Plainfield, N.J.; son of Archibald and Frances Bruen (Perkins) Cox; married Phyllis Ames, June 12, 1937; children: Sally, Archibald, Jr., Phyllis. *Education:* Harvard University, A.B., 1934, LL.B., 1937. *Home:* Glezen Lane, Wayland, Mass. 01775. *Office:* Harvard Law School, Cambridge, Mass. 02138.

CAREER: Circuit Court of Appeals, New York City, law clerk for Judge Learned Hand, 1937; Ropes, Gray, Best, Coolidge & Ruggs, Boston, Mass., associate, 1938-41; National Defense Mediation Board, Washington, D.C., staff member, 1941; Office of Solicitor General, U.S. Department of Justice, Washington, D.C., attorney, 1941-43; Department of Labor, Washington, D.C., associate solicitor, 1943-45; Harvard University, Cambridge, Mass., lecturer, 1945-46, professor, 1946-61, Williston Professor of Law, 1965—, Carl M. Loeb University Professor, 1976—; Wage Stabilization Board, Washington, D.C., chairman, 1952; U.S. Department of Justice, solicitor general, 1960-65; Watergate Special Prosecution Force, Washington, D.C., director, 1973. Co-chairman, Construction Industry Stabilization Commission, 1951-52; special investigator, Massachusetts Legislature, 1972; Pitt Professor of American History and Institutions. Cambridge University, 1974-75. Member, Overseers Harvard, 1962-65. *Member:* American Bar Association, American Academy of Arts and Sciences, American Bar Foundation, American Law Institute. *Awards, honors:* Received eight honorary LL.D. degrees from U.S. universities, including Loyola University (Chicago), University of Cincinnati, Rutgers University, Amherst University, and University of Michigan.

WRITINGS: (Editor, with Derek Bok) *Cases on Labor Law,* Foundation Press, 1948, 8th edition, 1976; *Law and the National Labor Policy,* University of California Institute of Industrial Relations, 1960; (with Mark deWolfe Howe and J. R. Wiggins) *Civil Rights, the Constitution and the Courts,* Harvard University Press, 1967; *The Warren Court: Constitutional Decision as an Instrument of Reform,* Harvard University Press, 1968; *The Role of the Supreme Court in American Government,* Oxford University Press, 1976.

Contributor of articles to periodicals, including *Atlantic Monthly* and *Fortune,* and to law reviews.

WORK IN PROGRESS: Revising and editing the 1976 Carpentier Lectures at Columbia University and Rosenthal Lectures at Northwestern University.

SIDELIGHTS: When Archibald Cox was selected by Attorney General-designate Elliot Richardson to become the long-sought special prosecutor for Watergate in May, 1973, he brought with him a formidable list of political and constitutional experience. During the 1940's he worked with the National Defense Mediation Board and Office of Solicitor General, and headed the Wage Stabilization Board during the Korean War (a position he resigned in protest over President Truman's granting John L. Lewis' United Mine Workers a $1.90 a day increase). Cox arbitrated nationwide labor cases in the 1950's, including the Brotherhood of Locomotive Engineers and Class 1 railroad disputes and was appointed Solicitor General in the 1960's. Most recently, he served as special mediator in the 1967 New York City school strike and as chairman of the investigation of the Columbia University riots of 1968. Cox's appointment as special prosecutor for Watergate caused Senator Edward Kennedy to remark: "Time and again he has been called to serve the public interest, and each time he has proven himself to be a man of brilliance, judgment, and sensitivity." His job, put simply, was to investigate "all allegations involving the President, members of the White House staff or Presidential appointees." "Somehow," said Cox, "we must restore confidence in the honor, integrity and decency of the government."

Cox's first action in his new position was to secure the complete independence of the special prosecutor. Richardson and Cox drew up a charter which provided, Richardson wrote, "that I, as attorney general, would delegate to the special prosecutor 'full authority' over the Watergate investigation, leaving to the attorney general only his 'statutory accountability for all matters falling within the jurisdiction of the Department of Justice.'" "The charter also reserved to the attorney general," Richardson continued, "the power to remove the special prosecutor, but only in the case of 'extraordinary improprieties on his part.'" These three provisions—the full authority of Cox, the ultimate accountability of the attorney general, and the removal clause—played a crucial part in the events of the "Saturday Night Massacre" of October 20, 1973. On May 22, 1973, President Nixon said he pledged "my full support" for the efforts of Richardson and Cox "to see the truth brought out."

By July Cox and his team of eighteen lawyers and seventeen staff members were working on what Cox termed the "five segments" of the investigation which included Watergate itself, from bugging to break-in to cover-up, operations of "the plumbers" and their raid on the office of Daniel Ellsburg's psychiatrist and the tapping of phones, the question of International Telephone and Telegraph Corp.'s campaign contributions during its antitrust settlement, the "dirty tricks" revolving around "political saboteur" Donald Segretti, and the questionable contributions to the Committee to Re-elect the President. "I am caught up on the great bulk of it," Cox said, "but I ask myself: Will one man ever be caught up on all the details." Remarking that the Teapot Dome investigation took six years, Cox told a *Time* reporter the same month, "the job might end tomorrow; on the other hand it could last the rest of my working life."

When the testimony of Alexander Butterfield to the U.S. Senate in late July revealed the existence of "wall-to-wall White House wiring," Cox issued a formal subpoena for certain presidential tapes and records which figured in his investigation. "A very grave constitutional issue is certainly precipitated," he told *Newsweek* just before asking Judge John J. Sirica to rule on Nixon's refusal to release the tapes. "When the President announced that he alone had personal control of the tapes, it made it impossible not to include his name in the subpoena. If we are to live under a rule of law, surely the regular processes of justice must be used to determine when evidence is available or when it is privileged. The mere declaration of 'Presidential papers' or 'documents' can't be enough to withhold that evidence." Judge Sirica ordered the White House tapes and papers be given to him so that he could decide what portions should be relayed to the grand jury as directed by Cox. Appealed by Nixon, the Sirica ruling was sustained by a 5-2 by the U.S. Court of Appeals on October 12. Given five days by the appellate court to file his appeal with the Supreme Court, Nixon cited a crisis in the Middle East and appealed to "an overriding national interest," and said that he would prepare a "summary" rather than submit the tapes. This summary, offered in direct defiance of a court order and now known as "the Stennis proposal," was described by Richardson: "The White House would prepare summaries of the tapes, have the summaries checked against the original tapes by Senator John C. Stennis of Mississippi, and then submit the summaries to the special prosecutor." Cox, realizing that the failure of the prosecution to produce the tapes would allow defense attornies to seek dismissals on grounds that evidence was being withheld, said "No court would accept summaries of tapes as evidence. Any judge would insist on the tapes."

On October 19, 1973, the White House issued a major statement on the tapes, containing one order aimed directly at Cox: "Though I have not wished to intrude upon the independence of the special prosecutor," Nixon said, "I have felt it necessary to direct him, as an employee of the Executive Branch, to make no further attempts by judicial process to obtain tapes, notes, or memoranda of presidential conversations." The next day Cox called a press conference and objected to the compromise, declaring that he would ask the courts to cite Nixon for contempt or clarify why the President's offer was unacceptable. Cox also stated that he could not accept such an order as it was at variance with the conditions under which he had been hired. He noted that because Richardson had been empowered to select and hire him, only Richardson could fire him, and he had no intention of resigning. Shortly after the press conference, Richardson received a message from the White House stating "Fire Cox." Rather than fire Cox, Richardson sent the President a letter of resignation in which he said that he would "not countermand or interfere with the special prosecutor's decisions or actions." Deputy Attorney General William Ruckelshaus also resigned, writing to Nixon: "I am sorry my conscience will not permit me to carry out your instructions to fire Archibald Cox." Solicitor General Robert Bork fired Cox and abolished his entire operation on October 10, 1973.

The Federal Bureau of Investigation, acting on White House orders, quickly took possession of the offices and files of the special prosecutor. On the news of his firing, Cox said: "Whether ours shall continue to be a government of laws and not of men is now for Congress and ultimately the American people to decide."

The firing of Cox and the resignations of the heads of the Department of Justice was named the "Saturday Night Massacre" by the press and created immediate public protest, called by some historians "the most tumultuous week of modern U.S. political history." *Time* was quick to note that "by firing Archibald Cox, Nixon had removed one of his best hopes of eventual vindication: a final judgment by an independent investigator that the President was in no way criminally implicated in the Watergate deceits and transgressions." Richardson remembered: "Although I could have foreseen that the firing and the two resignations would in combination produce a considerable public uproar, I could not have guessed that, all across the country, many others felt as strongly about the day's events. Three million messages descended on the Congress, the greatest outpouring of its kind that has ever taken place." The following week, two dozen resolutions to begin impeachment were introduced in the House of Representatives.

When asked shortly afterwards if his firing left him with any bitterness, Cox responded: "No, it's left me with a regenerated faith in the people's ability to make a very determined President conform to the rule of law."

BIOGRAPHICAL/CRITICAL SOURCES: Newsweek, May 28, 1973, June 11, 1973, August 6, 1973, October 29, 1973, November 5, 1973, July 29, 1974; *Time,* July 16, 1973, October 29, 1973, November 5, 1973; *Atlantic,* March, 1976.

*   *   *

COYSH, A(rthur) W(ilfred) 1905-

PERSONAL: Born July 13, 1905, in Bristol, England. *Education:* University of Bristol, M.Sc. and diploma in education, 1927. *Politics:* Liberal. *Home:* White House, Ibthorpe, Hurstbourne Tarrant, near Andover SP11 OBY, England.

CAREER: Schoolmaster in Bristol, England, 1931-42; British Broadcasting Corp. (BBC), Bristol, assistant head of programs, 1942-62; writer, 1962—.

WRITINGS: (With M. E. Tomlinson) *North America,* University Tutorial Press, 1946, 16th edition, 1975; (with Tomlinson) *The Southern Continents,* University Tutorial Press, 1951, 11th edition, 1975; (with John King) *Buying Antiques,* David & Charles, 1968; (with Tomlinson) *Africa,* University Tutorial Press, 1970, 2nd edition, 1974; *The Buying Antiques Dictionary of Names,* Praeger, 1970; *Blue and White Transfer Ware, 1780-1840,* Tuttle, 1970, revised edition, 1974; (with King) *Buying Antiques Reference Book,* David & Charles, 1971, revised edition, 1973; *Blue-Printed Earthenware, 1800-1850,* Tuttle, 1972; *Historic English Inns,* Drake, 1972, 2nd edition, 1973; *Collecting Bookmarkers,* Drake, 1974; *British Art Pottery, 1870-1940,* Tuttle, 1976.

WORK IN PROGRESS: Further research on ceramics, especially British pottery, and on printed ephemera, especially dust jackets.

SIDELIGHTS: Coysh comments: "I like to find a field which has been little explored, especially a 'collecting' field, and to write a book embodying my researches in the hope that others may take it up and take it further."

*   *   *

CRAIG, Charlotte M(arie) 1929-

PERSONAL: Born January 14, 1929, in Czechoslovakia;

came to the United States in 1949, naturalized citizen, 1954; daughter of Paul (an engineer) and Johanna Suess (Opelka) Dub; married Robert Bruce Craig (a colonel in the U.S. Army), August 14, 1954. *Education:* Los Angeles City College, A.A., 1954; University of Puget Sound, B.A., 1957; University of Arizona, M.A., 1960; Rutgers University, Ph.D., 1964; also attended University of California, Berkeley. *Religion:* Roman Catholic. *Home:* 2 Field Stone Court, Eatontown, N.J. 07724. *Office:* Department of Foreign Languages, Kutztown State College, 10 DeFrancesco Bldg., Kutztown, Pa. 19530.

CAREER: U.S. Military Government, Salzburg, Austria, interpreter and translator, 1945-49; teacher in adult foreign language program at public schools in Tacoma, Wash., 1949-50; Occidental Life Insurance Co. of California, Los Angeles, claims adjustor, 1950-55; teacher of English and history at public schools in Anchorage, Alaska, 1957-59; University of Kansas, Lawrence, assistant professor of German, 1964-68; George Washington University, Washington, D.C., lecturer in German, 1968-69; Schiller College, Heidelberg, Germany, professor of German and comparative literature, 1969-73, chairman of department, 1970-73; Kutztown State College, Kutztown, Pa., associate professor, 1974-77, professor of German, 1977—. Instructor at U.S. Armed Forces Institute, 1957-59; lecturer at University of Virginia, Arlington, 1967-69.

MEMBER: American Association of Teachers of German, Modern Language Association of America, American Society for Eighteenth Century Studies, Northeast Society for Eighteenth Century Studies.

WRITINGS: Christoph Martin Wieland as the Originator of the Modern Travesty in German Literature, University of North Carolina Press, 1970. Contributor of articles and reviews to language and literature journals and newspapers.

WORK IN PROGRESS: Research on Sophie La Roche's "enlightened Anglophilia."

SIDELIGHTS: Charlotte Craig writes: "As an immigrant, I found it necessary to establish myself, first in this country and gradually in my profession as a teacher-scholar. After marriage, my husband's career has both advanced and hampered my professional progress—travel and enrichment on the positive side of the ledger, frequent moves and resulting change of academic affiliation on the other. Teaching experience on various levels between consummation of graduate degrees is both rewarding and time-consuming. Flexibility becomes necessarily a by-product of one's development. Realization that one must excel in one's chosen field serves as impetus."

AVOCATIONAL INTERESTS: Reading, travel (Mexico, the Caribbean, Europe, North Africa, the Middle East, and Far East), walking, swimming, tennis, winter sports.

* * *

CRAIG, Don(ald) Laurence 1946-

PERSONAL: Born September 3, 1946, in Cleveland, Ohio; son of Robert Stafford (a civil servant) and Dorothy (a nurse; maiden name, Monsees) Laurence. *Education:* Attended University of Texas, 1964-66. *Office:* NBC News, 30 Rockefeller Plaza, New York, N.Y. 10020.

CAREER/WRITINGS: Ft. Worth Star-Telegram, Ft. Worth, Tex., staff writer, 1966-67; WCBS-TV, New York City, editorial producer, 1969-70; KLRN-TV, Austin, Tex., public affairs producer, 1971-73; WRGB-TV, Schenectady, N.Y., reporter, anchorman, and producer, 1973-76; National Broadcasting Co. (NBC) News, New York City, Mideast correspondent, 1976—. Notable assignments include coverage of the Lebanese Civil War, 1976. *Military service:* U.S. Naval Reserve, 1967-68.

SIDELIGHTS: Craig told *CA* he "lived in Spain and France a total of two years, working as an audio-visual producer in Paris, photographer in Madrid, and manual laborer in Chateauneuf-du-Pape."

* * *

CRAIG, James 1930-

PERSONAL: Born January 1, 1930, in Montreal, Quebec, Canada; came to the United States in 1957; son of James (a painter) and Sarah Jane (Clarke) Craig. *Education:* Earned B.F.A. from Cooper Union, and M.F.A. from Yale University. *Residence:* Holmes, N.Y. *Office:* Craig Graphics Ltd., 1515 Broadway, New York, N.Y. 10036.

CAREER: Northern Electric, Montreal, Quebec, salesman, 1947-55; General Electric, New York City, salesman, 1957-59; School of Visual Arts, New York City, part-time instructor in typography, 1966-70; Craig Graphics Ltd., New York City, owner, 1966—.

WRITINGS: Designing with Type, Watson-Guptill, 1971; *Production for the Graphic Designer,* Watson-Guptill, 1974.

WORK IN PROGRESS: A book on phototypesetting for designers.

SIDELIGHTS: Craig remarks: "I was offered a job teaching basic typography at the School of Visual Arts. During the first couple of years I was looking for a good book on the basics of typography, a book that would not only answer the questions, but graphically illustrate each point. After a while I gave up and decided to write my own book."

* * *

CRAIG, M. Jean

PERSONAL: Married Martin Craig (a sculptor); children: two daughters.

CAREER: Author of books for children. *Awards, honors: Where Do I Belong?* was a selection of the American Institute of Graphic Arts Children's Book Show, 1971-72.

WRITINGS—For children: The Dragon in the Clock Box (illustrated by Kelly Oechsli), Norton, 1962; *Boxes* (illustrated by Joe Lasker), Norton, 1964; *What Did You Dream?* (illustrated by Margery Gill; Junior Literary Guild selection), Abelard-Schuman, 1964; *Spring Is Like the Morning* (illustrated by Don Almquist), Putnam, 1965; *Dinosaurs and More Dinosaurs* (illustrated by George Solonevich), Four Winds Press, 1965; *The Long and Dangerous Journey* (illustrated by Ib Ohlsson), Norton, 1965; *The New Boy on the Sidewalk* (illustrated by Sheila Greenwald), Norton, 1967; *Summer Is a Very Busy Day* (illustrated by Almquist), Norton, 1967; *Not Very Much of a House* (illustrated by Almquist), Norton, 1967; *Questions and Answers about Weather* (illustrated by Judith Craig), Four Winds Press, 1969; *Pomando* (illustrated by Enrico Arno), Norton, 1969.

Puss in Boots (a revised edition of the fairy tale), Scholastic Book Service, 1970; *Where Do I Belong?* (illustrated by Ray Cruz), Four Winds Press, 1971; *The Three Wishes,* Scholastic Book Services, 1971; (compiler) *The Sand, the Sea, and Me* (poems; illustrated by Audrey Newell), Walker, 1972; *The Adventures of Tom Thumb* (illustrated by Haig and Regina Shekerjian), Scholastic Book Services, 1972; (with William C. Grimm) *The Wondrous World of Seedless Plants,* Bobbs-Merrill, 1973; *The Creation,* Fortress, 1976.

WORKS IN PROGRESS: Little Monsters, for Scholastic Book Services.

SIDELIGHTS: A New York Times critic wrote that in *Spring is Like the Morning* "all the wonderment of unfolding buds and of animals emerging from hibernation with their young is described in terms a child will understand, and pictures in illustrations sure to please."

Dinosaurs and More Dinosaurs was described by the *Christian Science Monitor* as written in "pellucid, kindly prose. Solonevich's dramatic pictures in greenish monochrome are probably as realistic as most. Some of the illustrations may seem terrifying to very sensitive children; some have a certain reptilian charm."

M. Jean Craig spent seven years in France with her husband. Her book *The Dragon in the Clock Box* has been printed in twelve foreign countries.

BIOGRAPHICAL/CRITICAL SOURCES: New York Times Book Review, April 26, 1964, May 9, 1965; *Christian Science Monitor,* May 7, 1964, November 7, 1968.*

* * *

CRANE, Joan St. C(lair) 1927-

PERSONAL: Born November 16, 1927, in Newport, R.I.; daughter of John Jarvis (a commander in the U.S. Navy) and Imogen (St. Clair) Crane. *Education:* Attended University of California, Berkeley, 1945-1949, Stanford University, summer, 1945, and San Francisco State Teachers College, 1953. *Home:* 1704 Mason Lane, Charlottesville, Va. 22901. *Office:* Rare Book Department, University of Virginia Library, Charlottesville, Va. 22901.

CAREER: Scribner Book Store, New York City, assistant cataloguer in rare book department, 1957-61; John Howell Rare Book Shop, San Francisco, Calif., cataloguer, 1961-63; Parke-Bernet Galleries, New York City, rare books cataloguer, 1963-65; rare book cataloguer for a private collection in Middleburg, Va., 1965-67; University of Virginia, Charlottesville, curator of American Literature Collections in library's rare book department, 1968—, sesquicentennial associate of the Center for Advanced Studies, 1978-79. *Member:* Bibliographical Society of America (member of publications committee), Manuscript Society, Bibliographical Society of the University of Virginia, Associates of the University of Virginia Library.

WRITINGS: Fifty-Five Books Printed before 1525: Representing the Works of England's First Printers, Anthoensen Press, 1968; *Robert Frost: A Descriptive Catalogue of Books and Manuscripts in the Clifton Waller Library,* University Press of Virginia, 1974; *The Fiction of James Fenimore Cooper,* University Printing Office, University of Virginia, 1974; *Carl Sandburg, Philip Green Wright, and the Asgard Press, 1900-1910,* University Press of Virginia, 1975; *Man Collecting: Manuscripts and Printed Works of William Faulkner in the University of Virginia Library,* University Printing Office, University of Virginia, 1975.

WORK IN PROGRESS: Compiling the official bibliography of the works of Willa Cather, publication by University of Nebraska expected in 1981.

* * *

CRANIN, A(braham) Norman 1927-

PERSONAL: Born June 17, 1927, in Brooklyn, N.Y.; son of Samuel L. (a physician) and Henrietta (Minkoff) Cranin; married Marilyn Sunners, 1953; children: Jonathan Blake,

Andrew Ross, Elizabeth S. *Education:* Swarthmore College, B.A., 1947; New York University, D.D.S., 1951; Institute for Graduate Dentists, postdoctoral study, 1953-54. *Home:* 209 Cedar Ave., Hewlett Bay Park, N.Y. 11557. *Office:* 2120 Ocean Ave., Brooklyn, N.Y. 11229.

CAREER: Mount Sinai Hospital, New York, N.Y., intern, 1951-52, resident in anesthesiology, 1952-53, clinical assistant in oral surgery, 1954-55, adjunct dental and oral surgeon, 1955-62, associate attending oral surgeon, 1963—, director of postgraduate courses in dentistry, 1960—, chairperson of house staff education in department of dental and oral surgery, 1960-67. Research assistant at Brooklyn Hebrew Home and Hospital for the Aged, 1959-60; associate clinical professor at Mount Sinai School of Medicine of City University of New York; clinical professor at New York University. Associate attending dental surgeon at Unity Hospital (Brooklyn), 1959-64; associate attending oral surgeon at Greenpoint Hospital Service (Mount Sinai Hospital), 1963-64; chief of Oral Surgery Division of Community Hospital of Brooklyn; director of dental and oral surgery at Brookdale Hospital Medical Center, 1966—(also member of executive medical board and chairman of committee on continuing and postdoctoral education); consulting oral surgeon for Corpus Christi Monastery and Kings County State School. Member of national advisory council for biomaterials research at Clemson University. Has given more than five hundred lectures at schools and to other professionals in the United States and abroad; has patented oral surgery instruments. Former attending oral surgeon at Hospital of Jacques Loewe Foundation. *Military service:* U.S. Naval Reserve, active duty as aviation cadet, 1945-46, and in Hospital Corps, 1947-51.

MEMBER: International Association of Dental Research, International Society of Anesthetists, American Academy of Implant Dentistry (fellow; diplomate; president, 1968-69; chairman of publications committee, 1959-68), American Academy of Oral Medicine; American Association of Dental Research, American Association of Hospital Dentists, American Society for the Advancement of General Anesthesia in Dentistry, American Dental Association, American Dental Society of Anesthesiology (fellow), American Association of Dental Schools (vice-president; chairperson of council of hospitals, 1968-72), Society for Biomaterials (charter member), American Association of Science, American Association of University Professors, American Society of Automotive Medicine, Royal Society of Health (fellow), Brazilian Society of Oral and Maxillo-Facial Surgery (honorary fellow), Society of Diplomates of New York Board of Oral Surgery (president), New York Institute of Clinical Oral Pathology, Metropolitan Conference of Hospital Dental Chiefs (president), New York University Dental Alumni Association, Swarthmore College Alumni Association, Mount Sinai Hospital Alumni Association, Second District Dental Society, Flatbush Dental Society, Woodmere Bay Yacht Club. *Awards, honors:* Gold medal from American Dental Association centennial meeting, 1959, for scientific exhibit on implants; national science writer's award from American Dental Association, 1966, for a magazine article, second prize, 1969, for scientific exhibits; legion of honor of Soberana Orden Militar de S.S.yS. Brigida de Suecia; annual biomaterials award from Clemson University, 1974.

WRITINGS: (Editor) *Oral Implantology,* C. C Thomas, 1970; *Oral Implantology: A Teaching System,* Volume I: *Subperiosteal,* Volume II: *Endosteal,* Medcom, 1970; *The Modern Family Guide to Better Dental Health,* Stein & Day, 1971; *Reconstructive and Plastic Oral Surgery: A*

Teaching System, Volume I: *Acquired Abnormalities,* Volume II: *Congenital Abnormalities,* Medcom, 1973; (contributor) Carl O. Boucher, editor, *Current Clinical Dental Terminology,* Mosby, 1974. Contributor of about sixty articles to dental and medical journals. Editor-in-chief of *Journal of Oral Implant and Transplant Surgery,* 1965-69; editor of *Oral Implantology Quarterly,* 1969-72, and New York University College of Dentistry's *Alumni Forum,* 1974; associate editor of *Journal of Prosthetic Dentistry,* 1969-72.

WORK IN PROGRESS: A novel about a resident in dentistry, entitled "Sermon on the Mount"; a short story.

SIDELIGHTS: Cranin commented that his book for laypersons, *The Modern Family Guide to Better Dental Health,* took him five years to complete and "gives me more satisfaction than anything else I have done. I can re-read it with pleasure (a problem with other things I've written). The organizations of dentistry tried to prevent its publication—an extremely counter-productive effort. As a result I lost my first publisher and it took five years more before I found another."

* * *

CRANSTON, Edward
See FAIRCHILD, William

* * *

CRIST, Raymond E. 1904-

PERSONAL: Born October 11, 1904, in Seven Mile, Ohio; son of Ollie (a farmer) and Beulah (Earley) Crist; married Hilda Buttenwieser, December 23, 1942. *Education:* University of Cincinnati, B.A., 1925; graduate study at Cornell University, 1927-28, and Universities of Zurich and Bonn, 1931-33; University of Grenoble, Dr. es lettres, 1937. *Office:* Department of Geography, University of Florida, Gainesville, Fla. 32601.

CAREER: El Aguila Refining Co., Mexico, field geologist, 1926-27; Atlantic Refining Co., Venezuela, field geologist, 1928-31; University of Illinois, Urbana, instructor in geology and geography, 1936-41; University of Puerto Rico, Mayaguez, associate professor of geography and chief of department of economic geography, 1941-46; University of Maryland, College Park, professor of geography, 1946-51; University of Florida, Gainesville, research professor of geography, 1951—, faculty lecturer, 1967-68. Teacher at Northwestern University, summers, 1936, 1938; Fulbright Professor at Universite de Toulouse, 1959. Past member of educational advisory board of Guggenheim Foundation, and of its selection committee for Latin America.

MEMBER: Association of American Geographers, American Geographical Society, Sigma Xi. *Awards, honors:* American Field Service fellowship from Institute of International Education, 1932-33; Guggenheim fellowships, 1940-41, 1954—; Rockefeller Foundation fellowship, 1951-52; Creole Petroleum Corp. grant, 1957-58; Agricultural Development Corp. grant, 1960; Fermat Medal from Academie des Sciences, Inscriptions et Belles-Lettres of Toulouse, 1967; Sc.D. from University of Cincinnati, 1969; Social Science Research Council grant.

WRITINGS: (With Raoul Blanchard) *A Geography of Europe,* Holt, 1935; *Etude Geographique des Llanos Occidentales* (monograph) Allier Pere et Fils, 1937; *The Cauca Valley, Colombia: Land Tenure and Land Use* (monograph), Waverly, 1952; *Venezuela: Around the World Program* (monograph), Nelson Doubleday Co., 1959; *Learning About*

Latin America, Silver Burdett, 1961; *Land for the Fellahin,* Schalkenback Foundation, 1961; (with E. P. Leahy) *Search for a Middle Ground,* Van Nostrand, 1969; (with C. M. Nissly) *East from the Andes,* University of Florida Press, 1973.

Contributor: *The Caribbean at Mid-Century,* University of Florida Press, 1950; *The Caribbean: The Central American Area,* University of Florida Press, 1961; *Intergroup Relations and Leadership,* Wiley, 1962; *Dictatorship in Spanish America,* Knopf, 1964; *Rural Development in Tropical America,* Cornell University Press, 1967; *Human Geography and Neighboring Disciplines,* Aldine, 1969. Has also contributed to *The Arab Far East,* 1957; *The Latin American Way of Life,* Volume II, 1968; and *Geography of Population: A Teacher's Guide,* 1969. Contributor to *Encyclopaedia Britannica.* Contributor of nearly one hundred articles to scientific journals. Member of editorial board of *American Journal of Economics and Sociology.*

SIDELIGHTS: Since 1932, Crist has carried out intensive field investigations of diverse aspects of cultural geography in the West Indies, Andean South America, and the Mediterranean Basin. He has studied land tenure systems and human migration, the peasant problem in the Arab states of the Near East, and the Indians of the Guajiro Peninsula.

* * *

CROOK, Bette (Jean) 1921-
(San Leslie)

PERSONAL: Born August 13, 1921, in Highland Park, Mich.; daughter of George William (an accountant) and Pansy Evelyn (Williams) Stevenson; married Charles L. Crook (a physician), February 15, 1941 (died, 1971); children: Bette Suzanne Crook Whyte, Charles Stevenson, Leslie Patricia. *Education:* Attended Michigan State University, 1939-40, University of Michigan, 1940-41, and Wayne State University. *Religion:* Episcopalian. *Home:* 976 Lakeview, Route 3, Gaylord, Mich. 49735. *Office:* Northeast Michigan Council of Governments, 131 Shipp St., Gaylord, Mich. 49735.

CAREER: Free-lance writer, 1946—. Information officer for Great Lakes region staff of Civil Air Patrol, 1957-60; author-in-residence, Gaylord Community Schools, 1975-76. Communications specialist for Northeast Michigan Council of Governments, 1976—. Former member of board of directors of Otsego Lake Chamber of Commerce. *Member:* Zonta International (local charter president), Ninety-Nines (international organization of women pilots), Authors Guild of Authors League of America, Aviation Space Writers' Association, Detroit Women Writers (life member; past president).

WRITINGS: (Under pseudonym San Leslie) *Shifting Shadows* (poems), Dierkes Press, 1947; *Famous Firsts in Medicine,* Putnam, 1974. Author of column "It Can't Happen to Me" in *Michigan Public Aviation News;* author of "Gaylord Gourmet," "Fashion Talk," and "Gavel Talk," columns for *Ostego County Herald Times.* Contributor of poems (under pseudonym San Leslie) and articles to aviation and travel magazines, organization newsletters, and newspapers. Associate editor of *Echoes of West Virginia.*

WORK IN PROGRESS: Juvenile and regional articles.

* * *

CROSBIE, John S(haver) 1920-
PERSONAL: Born May 1, 1920, in Montreal, Quebec,

Canada; son of Thomas Champion and Margaret Ruth (Shaver) Crosbie; married Catherine Patricia James, November 19, 1971; children: Peter, Stephen, Andrew, Kathryn, Charles. *Education:* Attended University of New Brunswick and University of Toronto. *Home:* 106 Ridge Dr., Toronto, Ontario, Canada M4T 1B8. *Agent:* William Morris Agency, 1350 Avenue of the Americas, New York, N.Y. 10019. *Office:* Magazine Association of Canada, 1240 Bay St., Toronto, Ontario, Canada M5R 2A7.

CAREER: Canadian Broadcasting Corp., Halifax, Nova Scotia and Toronto, Ontario, Canada, announcer and producer, 1942-44; Purdy Productions, Toronto, managing director, 1944-46; Dancer-Fitzgerald-Sample Ltd., Toronto, assistant general manager, 1946-49; Canadian Advertising Agency Ltd., Montreal, Quebec, Canada, general manager, 1949-50; J. Walter Thompson Co. (advertising agency), New York, N.Y., employed in Toronto office, 1950-58, became vice-president in Chicago, Ill., 1958-64, and San Francisco, Calif., 1965-66; Magazine Association of Canada, Toronto, president, 1967—. Director and former chairman of Canadian Advertising Advisory Board; former vice-chairman of United Appeal, Toronto. *Military service:* Canadian Army, 1940-42; became lieutenant.

MEMBER: International Advertising Association, Travel Industry Association of Canada, National Parks Association, Canadian Club (New York City; director), Granite Club.

WRITINGS: Canada and Its Leaders, Baxter, 1968; *Crosbie's Dictionary of Puns,* Simon & Schuster (Canada), 1972; *The Mayor of Upper Upsalquitch,* McGraw, 1973; *The Incredible Mrs. Chadwick,* McGraw, 1975; *Crosby's Dictionary of Puns,* Crown, 1977. Also author of radio and television scripts. Contributor to magazines.

SIDELIGHTS: The film version of *The Incredible Mrs. Chadwick* is scheduled for release in 1978.

* * *

CROSBIE, Sylvia Kowitt 1938-
(Sylvia Kowitt)

PERSONAL: Born June 17, 1938, in New York, N.Y.; daughter of David (an interior decorator) and May (a teacher; maiden name, Wiesenberger) Kowitt; married Angus Duncan Crosbie IV (a model builder), February 27, 1971; children: Angus Duncan V, Samuel Morgan. *Education:* Bryn Mawr College, B.A., 1959; Columbia University, M.A., 1961, Ph.D., 1970; also attended Institut d'Etudes Politiques. *Politics:* Democrat. *Religion:* Jewish. *Residence:* Van Nuys, Calif. *Office:* Department of History and Government, Immaculate Heart College, 2021 North Western Ave., Los Angeles, Calif. 90027.

CAREER: Israel Ministry for Foreign Affairs, Department of International Cooperation, Jerusalem, assistant director of publications, 1961-63; high school teacher of English, French, civics, and geography in Eilat, Israel, 1963-65; Carnegie Endowment for International Peace, New York, N.Y., editor, 1965-66; Iona College, New Rochelle, N.Y., assistant professor of government, 1969-71; Plymouth State College, Plymouth, N.H., adjunct professor of government, 1974-75; Immaculate Heart College, Los Angeles, Calif., associate professor of government, 1975—.

WRITINGS: A Tacit Alliance: France and Israel from Suez to the Six-Day War, Princeton University Press, 1974.

Contributor: E. K. Ettinger, editor, *International Handbook of Management,* McGraw, 1965; J. C. Hurewitz, editor,

Soviet-American Rivalry in the Middle East, Praeger, 1969; Richard P. Stebbins and Alba Amoia, editors, *Political Handbook and Atlas of the World,* Simon & Schuster, 1970.

Contributor of articles and reviews (sometimes under name Sylvia Kowitt) to periodicals and political science journals, including *Journal of International Affairs, International Concilation, Political Science Quarterly,* and *New Africa.*

WORK IN PROGRESS: America in the 60's: A Nation's Foreign Policy.

SIDELIGHTS: "In addition to research and teaching," Crosbie told *CA,* "I am totally involved in raising our two young sons, struggling to find the time to continue painting (watercolors and oils). I am also on the local educational council for gifted children."

* * *

CROSBY, Bing
See CROSBY, Harry Lillis

* * *

CROSBY, Harry Lillis 1904-1977
(Bing Crosby)

May 2, 1904—October 14, 1977; American singer, actor, and author of his autobiography. Crosby began his entertainment career in 1927 singing with Paul Whitman's Band. In the next fifty years, he made 850 records which sold 300 million copies. Crosby's acting career was marked by films such as "The Bells of St. Mary's," "The Country Girl," and "Going My Way" for which he was awarded an Academy Award for best actor. He also appeared in several films with Bob Hope and Dorothy Lamour, including "The Road to Singapore," "The Road to Hong Kong," and "The Road to Bali." Referred to as "The Groaner" and "Der Bingle," Crosby was an avid golfer and sponsored his own tournament. He died near Madrid, Spain. Obituaries: *Washington Post,* October 15, 1977; *New York Times,* October 16, 1977; *Newsweek,* October 24, 1977; *Time,* October 24, 1977.

* * *

CROSBY, Philip B(ayard) 1926-

PERSONAL: Born June 18, 1926, in Wheeling, W.Va.; son of Edward Karg (a podiatrist) and Mary (Campbell) Crosby; married Shirley Jones (a book store co-owner), May 1, 1947; children: Philip Bayard, Jr., Phylis B. *Education:* Attended West Liberty State College, 1946, and Western Reserve University (now Case Western Reserve University), 1946-49; Ohio College of Podiatry, Dr.Surg.Chiropody, 1950; Industrial College of the Armed Forces, graduate study, 1964. *Politics:* Republican. *Religion:* Presbyterian/Congregationalist. *Home:* 614 Lyon Farm, Greenwich, Conn. 06830. *Agent:* Richard Curtis, 156 East 52nd St., New York, N.Y. 10022. *Office:* International Telephone & Telegraph Corp., 320 Park Ave., New York, N.Y. 10022.

CAREER: Crosley Corp., Richmond, Ind., junior technician, 1953-55; Bendix Corp., Mishawa, Ind., reliability engineer, 1955-57; Martin-Marietta Corp., Orlando, Fla., manager of quality, 1957-65; International Telephone & Telegraph Corp. (ITT), New York, N.Y., vice-president and director of quality, 1965—. Chairman of Little i Foundation, 1966—. *Military service:* U.S. Naval Reserve, active duty as hospital corpsman, 1944-46, 1951-52.

MEMBER: American Society for Quality Control, New York Athletic Club, International Golf Club, Stanwich Country Club, John's Island Club. *Awards, honors:* Distinguished civilian service medal from U.S. Army, 1972, for creating the concept of zero defects.

WRITINGS: Cutting the Cost of Quality, Cahners, 1966; *The Strategy of Situation Management,* Cahners, 1971; *The Art of Getting Your Own Sweet Way,* McGraw, 1972; *Quality Is Free,* McGraw, 1977. Contributor of several hundred articles to professional journals.

WORK IN PROGRESS: You Are What You Hate.

SIDELIGHTS: Crosby writes: "Working as an international business executive, I have learned to carry a typewriter along on the frequent (fifty per cent of the time) business trips and write in the evenings. The material is nontechnical and understandable to all business people. In this fashion, I have created improvement programs such as Buck a Day, Zero Defects, Make Certain, and others which thousands of corporations use for cost reduction and quality improvement."

* * *

CROSLAND, (Charles) Anthony (Raven) 1918-1977

PERSONAL: Born August 29, 1918, in London, England; son of Joseph Beardsel (a civil servant) and Jessie (a lecturer in medieval languages; maiden name, Raven) Crosland; married Hilary Anne Sarson, 1952 (divorced, 1957); married Susan Catling, 1964. *Education:* Trinity College, Oxford (first class honors), 1946. *Politics:* Grimsby Labour. *Home:* 37 Lansdowne Rd., London W.11, England.

CAREER: Oxford University, Trinity College, Oxford, England, lecturer in economics, 1947-50; elected member of British Parliament, 1950-55, 1959-63; British government official, serving as secretary of independent commission of inquiry into the cooperative movement, 1956-58, minister of state for economic affairs, 1964-65, secretary of state for education and science, 1965-67, president of board of trade, 1967-69, secretary of state for local government and regional planning, 1969-70, minister of environment, 1974-76, foreign Secretary, 1976-77, member of European Community's Council of Ministers, 1976-77. Member of executive committee for Town and Country Planning Association, 1971-77. *Military service:* British Army, 1940-45; became captain.

WRITINGS: Britian's Economic Problem, J. Cape, 1953; *The Future of Socialism,* J. Cape, 1956, Macmillan, 1957, revised and abridged edition, Schoken, 1964; *The Conservative Enemy; A Programme of Radical Reform for the 1960's,* J. Cape, 1962, Schoken, 1963; *Socialism Now and Other Essays,* J. Cape, 1974. Also author of pamphlets.

OBITUARIES: Newsweek, February 28, 1977; *Time,* February 28, 1977; *Current Biography,* April 11, 1977.*

(Died February 19, 1977, in Oxford, England)

* * *

CROSS, John Keir 1914-1967
(Stephen MacFarlane, Susan Morley)

PERSONAL: Born August 19, 1914, in Carluke, Scotland.

CAREER: Author of books for children. Was an insurance clerk, hobo, and traveling busker/ventriloquist before joining the staff of the BBC in 1937; worked in the drama, variety, features, and Children's Hour departments writing and producing radio plays and features, as well as adapting stories and books for broadcasting, 1937-46. Left the BBC in 1946 to freelance, but from 1962-67, he was co-writer of its daily radio series, "The Archers."

WRITINGS—For children: *Aspect of Life: An Autobiogra-*

phy of Youth, Selwyn & Blount, 1937; *Studio J Investigates: Spy Story for Children* (illustrated by Joseph Avrach), P. Lunn, 1944 [reprinted edition illustrated by John Worsley, P. Lunn, 1946]; *Jack Robinson* (illustrated by John R. Parsons), P. Lunn, 1945; *The Angry Planet: An Authentic First-Hand Account of a Journey to Mars in the Spaceship Albatross* (illustrated by Robin Jacques), P. Lunn, 1945, Coward-McCann, 1946; *The Owl and the Pussycat* (illustrated by Jacques), P. Lunn, 1946, published in America as *The Other Side of Green Hills,* Coward-McCann, 1947; *The Man in the Moonlight* (illustrated by Jacques), J. Westhouse, 1947; *The White Magic,* J. Westhouse, 1947; (editor) *The Children's Omnibus* (illustrated by H. M. Brock), P. Lunn, 1948.

Blackadder: A Tale of the Days of Nelson (illustrated by Jacques), F. Muller, 1950, Dutton, 1951; *The Red Journey Back: A First-Hand Account of the Second and Third Martian Expeditions by the Spaceships Albatross and Comet* (illustrated by Jacques), Coward-McCann, 1954; *The Flying Fortunes in an Encounter with Rubberface!,* F. Muller, 1952, published in America as *The Stolen Sphere: An Adventure and a Mystery,* Dutton, 1953; *SOS from Mars,* Hutchinson, 1954; *The Dancing Tree,* Hutchinson, 1955, reprinted, World Distributors, 1963; (editor) *Best Horror Stories,* Faber, 1957, reprinted, 1962; *The Sixpenny Year: A Country Adventure,* Hutchinson, 1957; *Elizabeth in Broadcasting,* Hutchinson, 1957; (editor) *Black Magic Stories,* Faber, 1960; (editor) *Best Horror Stories 2,* Faber, 1965.

Under pseudonym Stephen MacFarlane: *Detectives in Greasepaint* (illustrated by Avrach), P. Lunn, 1944; *Lucy Maroon: The Car that Loved a Policeman* (illustrated by Bruce Angrave), P. Lunn, 1944; *Mr. Bosanko, and Other Stories* (illustrated by Angrave), P. Lunn, 1944; *The Strange Tale of Sally and Arnold,* P. Lunn, 1944; *Blue Egg,* P. Lunn, 1944; *The Story of a Tree* (illustrated by R. A. Brandt) P. Lunn, 1946.

For adults: *The Other Passenger: Eighteen Strange Stories* (illustrated by B. Angrave), J. Westhouse, 1944, Lippincott, 1946, reissued, Ballantine Books, 1961; (under pseudonym Susan Morley) *Mistress Glory,* Dial Press, 1948 (published in England under the author's real name as *Glory,* W. Laurie, 1951); (under pseudonym Susan Morley) *Juniper Green,* Dial Press, 1953 (published in England under the author's real name, W. Laurie, 1952, reprinted, Hamilton & Co., 1962).*

(Died January 22, 1967)

* * *

CROUCH, Thomas W(illiam) 1932-

PERSONAL: Born July 29, 1932, in Pecos, Tex.; son of Frank Malcolm (a teacher) and Lois (Richardson) Crouch; married Nancy D. Johnson (a social worker), August 6, 1965. *Education:* University of Texas, Arlington, student, 1949-50; Texas Tech University, B.A., 1953; University of Texas, Austin, M.A., 1959, Ph.D., 1969. *Home:* 705 Battle Bend Blvd., Austin, Tex. 78745.

CAREER: Texas A. & I. University, Kingsville, instructor in history, 1960-61; Southwest Texas State University, San Marcos, instructor in history and government, 1963; Memphis State University, Memphis, Tenn., assistant professor of history, 1968-75; free-lance writer, 1975—. *Military service:* U.S. Army, Corps of Engineers, 1953-55; served in West Germany.

MEMBER: Organization of American Historians, American Historical Association, Southern Historical Association, Western Historical Association, Texas State Historical Society, Phi Alpha Theta, Pi Sigma Alpha.

WRITINGS: A Yankee Geurrillero: Frederick Funston and the Cuban Insurrection, 1896-1897, Memphis State University Press, 1975; *A Leader of Volunteers: Frederick Funston and the Twentieth Kansas Volunteers in the Philippines, 1898-1899,* Coronado Press, in press. Contributor of articles and reviews to history journals.

WORK IN PROGRESS: Border Command: Frederick Funston and the Southern Department, 1915-1917.

SIDELIGHTS: Crouch told *CA:* "Frederick Funston was a most interesting figure on the American scene at the turn of the century. Personally, he was colorful, dashing, and courageous. As an historical figure, he was the epitome of the confident, aggressive, and expansion-minded element in the United States in the early 20th century." *Avocational interests:* Playing guitar, gardening, travel (especially visiting historical areas in the southwestern United States), reading history and biography, swimming, jogging, Mexican music and cooking, Spanish.

* * *

CROWLEY, Mart 1935-

PERSONAL: Born August 21, 1935, in Vicksburg, Miss. *Education:* Attended Catholic University, Washington, D.C., and University of California, Los Angeles. *Agent:* Audrey Wood, International Creative Management, 40 West 57th St., New York, N.Y. 10019. *Office:* c/o Dramatists Guild, 234 West 44th St., New York, N.Y. 10036.

CAREER: Playwright and screenwriter. Worked for Martin Manulis Productions, 1963, Four Star Television, 1964; secretary to actress Natalie Wood, 1964-66.

WRITINGS—Plays: Boys in the Band (first produced Off-Broadway at Theatre Four, April 14, 1968; produced in London at Wyndham's, February 11, 1969), Farrar, Straus, 1968; "Remote Asylum," first produced in Los Angeles at Ahmanson Theatre, 1970; *A Breeze from the Gulf* (first produced in Pennsylvania at Bucks County Playhouse, February, 1973; produced Off-Broadway at Eastside Playhouse, October, 1973), Farrar, Straus, 1974. Also author of "Cassandra at the Wedding" (screenplay), and co-author of "Fade-In" (screenplay).

SIDELIGHTS: Perhaps it will remain that Mart Crowley's contribution to the American stage will be the first honest portrayal of homosexuals on the stage. His "Boys in the Band" was a landmark play, and under the direction of William Friedkin its popularity was extended into film.

Clive Barnes of the *New York Times* called it "the frankest treatment of homosexuality I have ever seen on stage. We are a long way from 'Tea & Sympathy' here. The point is that this is not a play about a homosexual, but a play that takes the homosexual milieu, and the homosexual way of life, totally for granted and uses that as a valid basis of human experience. The power in the play is in the way in which it remorselessly peels away the pretensions of its characters and reveals a pessimism so uncompromising in its honesty that it becomes in itself an affirmation of life."

Crowley himself stated: "There was a little of me in all the characters in that play. I was determined to write a new kind of drama about homosexuality. All the plays I had ever seen on the subject were stereotyped, sensational, embarrassed or evasive. I tried to be thoughtful and honest and adult. It was, I think, a major breakthrough."

Rex Reed, writing for the *New York Times,* said that it had the best "bitchy dialogue" since "All About Eve." Reed went on to say that "most such plays have basically avoided the real nature of the subject. And homosexuals have always paid for their sins onstage. 'Boys in the Band' has changed all that. The 'boys' in Mart Crowley's band are human beings and, like human beings, they have fun, too. They don't kill themselves or want to get married or spend the rest of their lives tortured by conscience. The only way they 'pay' is to know who they are. They go to bed with a hangover and start all over again the next day. Like life."

After "Boys in the Band," Crowley wrote "A Breeze from the Gulf," a play which had a short, unhappy run. "I suppose almost all playwrights do semi-biographical plays," said Crowley. "My new play has the feeling of thoughts going around in the head of a person drowning, or maybe waiting for a street light to change. It all swirls quickly in the mind. I'm able to do this play only after six years of analysis and two other plays. This is my personal play. It is set in a small town in Mississippi, similar to the one where I grew up. My father was a drunkard and my mother was a hypochondriac, dependent upon drugs.

"I started to write the play down in Puerto Rico about a year ago, although my notes on the theme go all the way back to 1959. When I sat down to write it, I said to myself: 'Can I face it.' Well, the first week I stayed dead drunk. Finally I went on a strict discipline. I didn't drink and I didn't smoke. It was so very rough the first weeks. I'd go on crying jags as I remembered all those things about my past life. My father's death. So many painful memories."

BIOGRAPHICAL/CRITICAL SOURCES: New York Times, April 15, 1968, February 18, 1969, July 13, 1969, March 18, 1970; *Time,* April 26, 1968; *Nation,* April 29, 1968; *Life,* May 24, 1968, April 10, 1970; *Partisan Review,* summer, 1968; *New Statesman,* January 10, 1969, February 21, 1969; *Punch,* February 19, 1969; *Newsweek,* April 29, 1969, March 30, 1970; *Cue,* June 21, 1969; *National Observer,* March 30, 1970; *National Review,* June 29, 1971.*

* * *

CROWTHER, James Gerald 1899-

PERSONAL: Born in 1899, in Lightcliffe, Yorkshire, England. *Education:* Educated in England. *Address:* 2 Mytre Ct., Johns Mews, London WC1N 2PA, England.

CAREER: Manchester Guardian, Manchester, England, scientific correspondent, 1928-48; British Council, London, director of the science department, 1941-46; free-lance writer. *Member:* Association of Scientific, Technical, and Managerial Staffs.

WRITINGS: Science for You, Brentano's, 1928; *Short Stories in Science,* Routledge, 1929; *Science in Soviet Russia,* Williams & Norgate, 1930; *An Outline of the Universe,* Dodd, 1931; *The ABC of Chemistry,* Kegan Paul, 1932; *Osiris and the Atom,* Routledge, 1932; *Industry and Education in Soviet Russia,* Heinemann, 1932; *The Progress of Science: An Account of Recent Fundamental Researches in Physics, Chemistry, and Biology,* Kegan Paul, 1934; *British Scientists of the Nineteenth Century,* Kegan Paul, 1935, reprinted, 1962, published as *Men of Science: Humphry Davy, Michael Faraday, James Prescott Joule, William Thomson, James Clerk Maxwell,* Norton, 1936; *Famous American Men of Science,* Norton, 1937, reprinted, Books for Libraries, 1969; *Science and Life,* V. Gollancz, 1938; *About Petroleum,* Oxford University Press, 1938.

The Social Relations of Science, Macmillan, 1941, revised edition, Dufour, 1967; (with Richard Whiddington) *Science at War,* McLeod, 1948; *Science in Liberated Europe,* Pilot, 1949; *Six Great Inventors: Watt, Stephenson, Edison, Marconi, Wright Brothers, [and] Whittle,* Hamish Hamilton, 1954; *Sciences of Energy,* Muller, 1954; *Discoveries and Inventions of the Twentieth Century,* 4th edition (Crowther was not associated with earlier editions), Dutton, 1955, 5th edition, 1966; *Nuclear Energy in Industry,* Pitman, 1956; *Science Unfolds the Future,* Muller, 1956; *Six Great Doctors: Harvey, Pasteur, Lister, Pavlov, Ross, [and] Fleming,* Hamish Hamilton, 1957; *The Story of Agriculture,* Hamish Hamilton, 1958; *Six Great Engineers: De Lesseps, Brunel, Westinghouse, Parsons, Diesel, [and] Hinton,* Hamish Hamilton, 1959.

Francis Bacon, the First Statesman of Science, Cresset, 1960; *Founders of British Science: John Wilkins, Robert Boyle, John Ray, Christopher Wren, Robert Hooke, Isaac Newton,* Cresset, 1960; *Six Great Scientists: Copernicus, Galileo, Newton, Darwin, Marie Curie, Einstein,* Hamish Hamilton, 1961; *Radioastronomy and Radar* (illustrated by David A. Hardy), Criterion, 1961; *Six Great Astronomers: Tycho Brahe, Kepler, Halley, Herschel, Russell, Eddington,* Hamish Hamilton, 1961; *Electricity* (illustrated by D. A. Hardy), Methuen, 1961; *Scientists of the Industrial Revolution: Joseph Black, James Watt, Joseph Priestley, Henry Cavendish,* Cresset, 1962, Dufour, 1963; *The Young Man's Guide to Civil Engineering,* Hamish Hamilton, 1963; *Statesmen of Science: Henry Brougham, William Robert Grove, Lyon Playfair, the Prince Consort, the Seventh Duke of Devonshire, Alexander Strange, Richard Burdon Haldane, Thomas Tizard, [and] Frederick Alexander Lindemann,* Cresset, 1965, Dufour, 1966.

Science in Modern Society, Cresset, 1967, Schocken Books, 1968; *Scientific Types,* Cresset, 1968, Dufour, 1970; *A Short History of Science,* Methuen, 1969; *Fifty Years with Science,* Barrie & Jenkins, 1970; *Alexander Fleming,* Heron Books, 1971; *Ernest Rutherford,* Methuen, 1972; *Charles Darwin,* Methuen, 1972; *Josiah Wedgwood,* Methuen, 1972; *The Cavendish Laboratory, 1874-1974,* Science History Publications, 1974.

Editor, *Science and Mankind,* 1949.

SIDELIGHTS: Crowther has lectured in Canada and in the United States, and has made several trips to the Soviet Union.*

* * *

CRUMP, (James) Irving 1887-

PERSONAL: Born December 7, 1887, in Saugerties, N.Y.; son of William Russell and Emma F. (Peters) Crump; married Marguerite Duryea Whitney, April 4, 1910; children: Marguerite Whitney, James Irving. *Education:* Attended Columbia University. *Politics:* Republican. *Religion:* Baptist.

CAREER: Associate editor, *Edison Monthly,* 1912-14; editor, *Boy's Life,* 1918-23; managing editor, *Pictorial Review,* 1923-24; author and writer for radio. *Member:* Ulster Company Society of New York, Omega Gamma Delta.

WRITINGS: Jack Straw in Mexico: How the Engineers Defended the Great Hydro-Electric Plant (illustrated by Leslie Crump), McBride, Nast, 1914; *Jack Straw, Lighthouse Builder* (illustrated by L. Crump), R. M. McBride, 1915; *The Boys' Book of Firemen,* Dodd, 1916; *The Boys' Book of Policemen,* Dodd, 1917; *The Boy Scout Fire Fight-*

ers (illustrated by Charles L. Wrenn), Barse & Hopkins, 1917; *The Boys' Book of Mounted Police,* Dodd, 1917; *Conscript 2989: Experiences of a Drafted Man* (illustrated by H. B. Martin), Dodd, 1918; *Og: Son of Fire* (illustrated by Charles Livingston Bull), Dodd, 1922; *The Boys' Book of Forest Rangers,* Dodd, 1924; *Og: Boy of Battle* (illustrated by Bull), Dodd, 1925; *The Boys' Book of Arctic Exploration,* Dodd, 1925; *The Boys' Book of the U. S. Mails,* Dodd, 1926; *The Boys' Book of Airmen* (with an introduction by Richard E. Byrd), Dodd, 1927; *The Boys' Book of Coast Guards,* Dodd, 1928; *The Pilot of the Cloud Patrol* (illustrated by William Heaslip), Grosset, 1929; *The Cloud Patrol* (illustrated by Heaslip), Grosset, 1929.

Mog, the Mound Builder (illustrated by Remington Schuyler), Dodd, 1931; *Craig of the Cloud Patrol* (illustrated by Heaslip), Grosset, 1931; *The Boys' Book of Fisheries,* Dodd, 1933; *The Boys' Book of Newsreel Hunters,* Dodd, 1933; *"Making" the School Newspaper,* Dodd, 1933; *The Boys' Book of Cowboys,* Dodd, 1934; (with John W. Newton) *Our Police,* Dodd, 1935; *Og of the Cave People* (illustrated by Jack Murray), Dodd, 1935; (with J. W. Newton) *Our Airmen,* Dodd, 1936; (with Newton) *Our G-Men,* Dodd, 1937; *Our Firemen,* Dodd, 1938; *Scouts to the Rescue,* Rand McNally, 1939; (with Norman Maul) *Our Airliners,* Dodd, 1940; *Our Movie Makers,* Dodd, 1940; *Out of the Woods* (illustrated by Enos B. Comstock), Dodd, 1941; *Our United States Secret Service,* Dodd, 1942; *Our Marines,* Dodd, 1944; *Teen-Age Boy Scout Stories;* illustrated by Ronald Gaschke), Lantern Press, 1948; *Our Oil Hunters,* Dodd, 1948; (editor) *Dog Stories,* Thomas Nelson, 1949.

(Editor) *Adventure Stories,* Thomas Nelson, 1950; *Our Tanker Fleet,* Dodd, 1952; (editor) *Book of Scout Stories,* Doubleday, 1952; *Our Army Engineers,* Dodd, 1954; *Our State Police,* Dodd, 1955; *The Birdsong Boys* (illustrated by Cyrus Le Roy Baldridge), Friendship Press, 1955; *Our Merchant Marine Academy, Kings Point,* Dodd, 1958; *Our United States Coast Guard Academy,* Dodd, 1961; (with son, James Irving Crump) *Dragon Bones in the Yellow Earth,* Dodd, 1963; *Og: Son of Og,* Dodd, 1965; *Biography of a Borough—Oradell,* [Oradell, N.J.], 1969.

SIDELIGHTS: Irving Crump wrote *Our G-Men* with John W. Newton. *Books* said, "The book is concerned only with the problem of apprehension of criminals. This grim business is written up almost as a sporting affair, with the G-man as the hero. All in all, however, the brief presentations will meet with the approval of readers young or old, if only for the abundance of exciting elements provided by the authors. The *New York Herald Tribune* wrote of our *Tanker Fleet:* "In war and peace, many of us have had reason to say, 'Thank the tankers.' Especially dramatic was their contribution to our victory in the Pacific in World War II. Mr. Crump has written a book about them that is both informative and exciting."

In 1938-39, Universal Pictures produced a movie series entitled, "Scouts to the Rescue," based on Crump's book of the same name, and starring Jackie Cooper.

BIOGRAPHICAL/CRITICAL SOURCES: Books, January 2, 1938; *New York Times,* August 10, 1941; *New York Herald Tribune,* March 2, 1952; *Kirkus,* July 15, 1955.*

* * *

CRUNDEN, Reginald
See CLEAVER, Hylton Reginald

CRUZ, Joan Carroll 1931-

PERSONAL: Born September 10, 1931, in New Orleans, La.; daughter of Daniel Joseph (a radio operator) and Josephine (an organist; maiden name, Eiffert) Carroll; married Louis Edgar Cruz, June 12, 1954; children: Louis Edgar, Jr., Tommy, Michael, Jeannine, Carolyn. *Education:* Attended Tulane University, 1950, and Notre Dame Junior College (now St. Louis University), 1951-52. *Religion:* Roman Catholic. *Home:* 5705 Pasteur Blvd., New Orleans, La. 70122.

CAREER: Has worked as a secretary for a local utility company and as a legal secretary for an attorney; writer, 1970—.

WRITINGS: Desires of Thy Heart (novel), Tandem Press, 1977; *The Incorruptibles* (nonfiction), Tan Books, 1978.

WORK IN PROGRESS: Love Endures Forever, a novel; *Relics,* a compilation of major Roman Catholic relics throughout the world.

SIDELIGHTS: Joan Cruz writes: "The School Sisters of Notre Dame, who educated me throughout my academic life, profoundly influenced my life, thinking, and ambitions. Because of their influence, I could not do otherwise than bring a high moral element to my writings. This is brought out in *Desires of Thy Heart* and in the two novels I am presently working on. I believe novels can be both moral and highly romantic. It is regrettable that so many writers do not hold to this viewpoint."

AVOCATIONAL INTERESTS: "My interests are quite varied, ranging from football to grand opera."

*   *   *

CSIKOS-NAGY, Bela 1915-

PERSONAL: Born September 9, 1915, in Szeged, Hungary; son of Jozsef (a lawyer) and Jolan (Jedlicska) Csikos-Nagy; married Livia Kneppo (a guide), September 19, 1944; children: Katalin, Zsuzsanna. *Education:* University of Szeged, J.D., 1937; University of Pecs, Doctor of Social Sciences, 1942; Hungarian Academy of Sciences, Doctor of Economic Sciences, 1967. *Politics:* Hungarian Socialist Workers Party. *Religion:* Roman Catholic. *Home:* 26/c Varosmajor utca, Budapest, Hungary. *Office:* Board of Prices and Materials, 23.Guscev utca, Budapest, Hungary.

CAREER: Hungarian Government, Budapest, general secretary of Ministry of Finance, 1941-45, secretary of Government of Economic Committee, 1945-47, chief of Department of Economic Planning Committee, 1947-51, deputy of Ministry of Light Industry, 1951-55, president of Board of Prices and Materials, 1959—. Karl Marx University of Economic Sciences, Budapest, Lecturer, 1959-64, university professor, 1964—. *Member:* International Economic Association (member of executive committee), Hungarian Economic Association (president), Energy Policy Club. *Awards, honors:* Hungarian State Prize.

WRITINGS—In English: Bevezetes a Gazdasagpolitikaba, Kossuth, 1969, translation by Elek Helvei published as *Socialist Economic Policy,* St. Martin's, 1973; *Socialist Price Theory and Price Policy,* translated by Helvey and Istvan Veges, International Publications Service, 1976.

Other: *Helyi Iparunk a Fejlodes Utjan,* Koennyueipari, 1954; *Arpolitika az Atmenti Gazdasagban,* Koezgazdasagi & Jogi, 1958, revised edition published as *A Szocialista Arkepzes,* 1961; *Arpolitika a mai Kapitalizmusban,* Kossuth, 1964; *Hongaarse Recepten,* Becht, 1964; *Ezkoezgazdalkodas es Arrendeszer,* Kossuth, 1964; *Szocialista Arelmelet*

es Arpolitika, Kossuth, 1966; *Altalanos es Szocialista Arelmemet,* Kossuth, 1968; *Problemi Monetari del Comecon,* ISDEE, 1974.

WORK IN PROGRESS: In For a New Price Revolution?

*   *   *

CUISENIER, Jean 1927-

PERSONAL: Born February 9, 1927, in Paris, France; son of Andre (a teacher) and Therese (Tostain) Cuisenier; married Solange Moreau (a teacher), July 20, 1950; children: Francois, Isabelle, Laurent, Emmanuelle. *Education:* Sorbonne, University of Paris, agrege de philosophie, 1954, Docteur es lettres et sciences humaines, 1971. *Home:* 24 Les Passereaux, DFSA, 78170 La Celle St. Cloud, France. *Office:* Musee Arts Traditions Populaires, 75116 Paris, France.

CAREER: Philosophy teacher in secondary schools in Caen, France, 1950-54, and Carthage, Tunisia, 1954-55; Institut des Hautes Etudes de Tunis, Tunisia, professor of sociology, 1956-59; Centre National de la Recherche Scientifique, Paris, France, staff member, 1959-71, research director, 1971—, also member of various councils. Chief curator at Musee National des Arts et Traditions Populaires, Paris, 1968—; director of the Centre d'ethnologie francaise, Paris, 1968—; lecturer at l'Ecole Normale Superieure, Paris, 1968; director of graduate studies in social and historical anthropology at the Ecole des Hautes Etudes en Sciences Sociales, Paris, 1975—. Member of various councils of the Institut National d'Etudes Demographiques and the Direction des Musees de France. *Military service:* French Air Force, 1951-52; became lieutenant. *Member:* Societe Internationale d'Ethnologie et de folklore, Societe francaise de Sociologie, Societe d'Ethnologie Francaise. *Awards, honors:* Chevalier de la Legion d'Honneur.

WRITINGS: L'Ansarine: Contribution a la sociologie du developpement (title means "The Ansarine: Contribution to the Sociology of Development"), Presses Universitaires Francaises, 1962; *Economie et parente* (title means "Economy and Kinship"), Mouton, 1975; *L'Art populaire en France,* Office du Livre, 1975, translation by Thomas Lyman published as *French Folk Art,* Kodansha International Ltd. (New York), 1977.

Editor: *Problemes du developpement economique dans les pays mediterraneens* (title means "Problems of Economic Development in the Mediterranean Countries"), Mouton, 1963; (with Hubert Mace and Philippe Pigelet) *Le Tourisme balneaire en Languedoc et en Roussillon* (title means "Seaside Resort Tourism in Languedoc and Rousillon"), Documentation Francaises, 1967; (with Martine Segalen) *The Family Life Cycle in European Societies,* Mouton, 1977; *Europe as a Cultural Area,* Mouton, 1979.

Contributor: *L'Etat et le citoyen* (title means "The State and the Citizen"), Le Seuil, 1961; *Espana en el desarollo mediterraneo* (title means "Spain in Mediterranean Development"), Ediciones Insula, 1964; Pierre-Henri Simon and others, editors, *L'Avenir* (title means "The Future"), C.C.I.F. and Fayard (Paris), 1964; Jacques Berque, Jean-Pierre Charnay, and others, editors, *De l'imperialisme a la decolonisation* (title means "From Imperialism to Decolonization"), Les Editions de Minuit, 1966; Darras, editor, *Le Partage des benefices* (title means "The Division of Profits"), Les Editions de Minuit, 1966; Jean-Daniel Reynaud, editor, *Tendances et volomtes de la societe francaise* (title means "Tendencies and Whims of French Society"), S.E.D.E.I.S. (Paris), 1966; Guy Palmade, editor, *L'Econ-*

omique et les sciences sociales (title means "The Economy and the Social Sciences"), Dunod, 1967.

Ester Boserup and Ignacy Sachs, editors, *Foreign Aid to Newly Independent Countries,* Mouton, 1971; Jean Pouillon and Pierre Maranda, editors, *Echanges et Communications* (title means "Exchanges and Communication"), Mouton, 1970; Jean-Claude Casanova, editor, *Science et conscience de la societe* (title means "Knowledge and Conscience of Society"), Calmann-Levy, 1971; John Peristiany and others, editors, *Modernization and Family Life in Mediterranean Societies,* American Universities Field Staff (Rome), 1976; Peristiany, editor, *The Family in the Mediterranean Countries,* Cambridge University Press, 1976. Also contributor to *Kinship and Social Organization in the Tuzko-Mongolian Cultural Area,* edited by Robert Forster and Orest Ranum, Johns Hopkins Press.

Director and editor of the series "Memoires d'Anthropologie Francaise," "Archives d'Anthropologie Francaise," "L'Architecture rurale francaise," 1977—, "Contes et recits populaires," 1977—, and "Sources regionales," 1978. Contributor to *Encyclopaedia Universalis, Esprit, Cahiers de Tunisie, Etudes Rurales, L'Homme, Revue Francaise de Sociologie,* and other journals in his field. Director and editor of *Ethnologie Francaise,* 1971—.

SIDELIGHTS: Cuisenier writes: "As a young professor of philosophy, I first taught psychology, metaphysics, logic, and history of philosophy, as is the tradition in the French university. Appointed to the University of Tunis, I discovered a society and a culture well known from the geographical and historical points of view, but scarcely studied from the anthropological point of view. On the advice of my masters at that time, Raymond Aron and Claude Levi-Strauss, I engaged in intensive field work in the mountains of northern Tunisia, especially in a group of villages, the cheikhat of the Ansarine. I was able to unravel how the French colonial system hinged upon a traditional society, and how the Arab society reacted to the instruments, the ideas, and the values introduced by the French colonization. Not only did I collect the material for my further publications during these five years, but more importantly I discovered the quality and intensity of the social relations in a highly structured society, as was the Arab Tunisian society between 1955 and 1960. This is undoubtedly the reason I gave so much attention to biographies as sources for the understanding of kinship and economic relations in my publications (as in my book *Economie et Parente*).

"Next I was appointed assistant director of the laboratory of Raymond Aron at the Sorbonne. I worked on the Mediterranean societies, and especially on Yugoslavia and Turkey, which led me to compare the social organization of villages with closely related economic levels, but with different culture, language and religion. Thus I stayed twice in Anatoly, in the Taurus mountains, at the home of the Yuruks (shepherds and nomads) and the peasants of the Eregli region, and two times in fourteen villages of Croatia, Serbia, etc. I was thoroughly involved in these comparative ethnographical studies of Mediterranean societies when, at the proposal of Claude Levi-Strauss and, Andre Malraux, the Minister of Culture at that time, I was called to direct the new Musee National des Arts et Traditions populaires and the Centre d'ethnologie francaise in 1968. It was necessary to finish the construction, set up the collections, recruit and organize the staff, and to develop the specialized educational program which would make this establishment a veritable Institut d'Ethnologie Francaise.

"I have devoted myself to this establishment since then, opening the research laboratories in 1969, the student galleries in 1972, and the public galleries in 1975. At the same time I found it necessary to give researchists, amateurs, and interested laymen the appropriate means to become better acquainted with ethnography and the popular arts and traditions of France; the magazine, *Ethnologie Francaise,* and the different series, "Architecture Rurale," "Contes et recits," and "Sources Regionales" all have this goal. The book, *French Folk Art,* is the first synthesis written on this subject. It proposes principles of analysis which it applies to precise written and figurative documentation, and it works as a real guide for the amateur."

AVOCATIONAL INTERESTS: Sailing in the Mediterranean.

*　　*　　*

CULLEN, Maurice R(aymond), Jr. 1927-

PERSONAL: Born May 18, 1927, in Cambridge, Mass.; son of Maurice Raymond (a businessman) and Kathryn (Burgess) Cullen; married Mary Kathryn Maloney (a dean's assistant), September 7, 1957; children: Mary Pat, Kathleen, John, Maureen. *Education:* Boston University, B.S., 1954, M.S., 1955; Michigan State University, Ph.D., 1966. *Politics:* Democrat. *Religion:* Roman Catholic. *Home:* 1040 West Grand River Ave., East Lansing, Mich. 48823. *Agent:* Curtis Brown Ltd., 575 Madison Ave., New York, N.Y. 10022. *Office:* School of Journalism, Michigan State University, East Lansing, Mich. 48824.

CAREER: Boston Post, Boston, Mass., reporter, 1951-53; *Cambridge Chronicle-Sun,* Cambridge, Mass., staff writer and reporter, 1953-55; *Olean News,* Olean, N.Y., editor, 1956-58; University of South Carolina, Columbia, assistant professor of journalism, 1958-64; Rutgers University, New Brunswick, N.J., assistant professor of journalism, 1966-68; Boston University, Boston, Mass., associate professor of journalism, 1968-73; Michigan State University, East Lansing, associate professor, 1973-76, professor of journalism, 1976—. Instructor at St. Bonaventure University, 1955-58. Director of Dental Editor's Seminar for American Dental Association. *Military service:* U.S. Navy, 1944-46.

MEMBER: Association for Education in Journalism, American Association of University Professors, Early American Society, Sigma Delta Chi, Phi Kappa Phi.

WRITINGS: Battle Road: Birthplace of the American Revolution, Chatham Press, 1970. Contributor of articles and reviews to journalism and education journals and other magazines, including *Extension, Family Digest,* and *Male Adventure.*

WORK IN PROGRESS: Bulwark of Liberty: The Struggle for Freedom of the Press in Early America; The Mass Media and the First Amendment, for W. C. Brown.

*　　*　　*

CUMES, J(ames) W(illiam) C(rawford) 1922-
(C. W. James)

PERSONAL: Born August 23, 1922, in Rosewood, Queensland, Australia; son of Roy Augustus (a public servant) and Ruby Constance (Crawford) Cumes; married Anita Mary Sargent, October 4, 1947 (divorced January 10, 1968). *Education:* University of Queensland, B.A., 1945; Canberra University College, diploma in diplomatic studies, 1945; London School of Economics and Political Science, London, Ph.D., 1951. *Politics:* "No formal party—about centre-leftish.'' *Religion:* Church of England. *Home:* Peter Jordan Strasse 35, Vienna, Austria 1190. *Office:* Australian Embassy, Mattiellistrasse 2-4, Vienna, Austria 1040.

CAREER: Australian Department of Foreign Affairs, diplomat in Paris, 1949, and London, 1949-51, charge d'-affaires in Bonn, 1955-56, diplomat in Berlin, 1956-58, head of economic relations in Canberra, 1958-61, assistant secretary of foreign affairs and charge d'affaires in Belgium and for Australian missions to European Economic Community and Euratom, 1961-65, Australian high commissioner to Nigeria, 1965-67, first assistant secretary in Canberra, 1968-74, ambassador to Belgium, Luxembourg, and European Communities, 1975-77, ambassador to Austria and Hungary and resident representative to International Atomic Energy Agency and United Nations Industrial Development Organization, 1977—. Member of Australian delegations to United Nations and international conferences, including United Nations General Assembly, 1963, 1967, 1970, 1971, Third Antarctic Conference in Brussels, 1964, Commonwealth Prime Ministers' Conference in Lagos, 1966, second United Nations Conference on Trade and Development in New Delhi, 1968, ministerial meeting of Organization for Economic Co-operation and Development in Paris, 1970, 1972, 1973, 1974, and Anzus Council Meeting, 1974. Leader of Officials' Delegation to Colombo Plan Conference in Wellington, 1973. *Military service:* Australian Army, 1942-44.

WRITINGS: The Indigent Rich, Pergamon Press, 1971; *Inflation: A Study in Stability,* Pergamon Press, 1974; *Their Chastity Was Not Too Rigid,* Longman, 1978. Author of short stories under pseudonym C. W. James and contributor of articles to periodicals.

WORK IN PROGRESS: Haverleigh, a novel of life in southern Queensland, publication expected in 1979.

SIDELIGHTS: Cumes told *CA: "The Indigent Rich* was written to identify the economic problems which I saw to be emerging for the developed countries in the 1970's, and the impact these problems would have on the developing countries. Up until July, 1969, the United States tried to do too much in terms of social welfare, defense, space research, the Vietnam war, and so on, and its economy had been afflicted with what was, by later standards, modest inflation. It tried conventional methods of reducing economic acitivty, with the result that unemployment and unused productive capacity emerged but inflation got worse. In January, 1971, the American government reflated by the conventional method of expanding consumption. It was better than the worst but much worse than the best. Unemployment got temporarily better, the balance of payments got worse, and the United States exported its inflation, inter alia, by allowing imports to flood in and the dollar to devalue.

"The Indigent Rich put forth the view that developed economies had undergone such growth and stability of their private and government consumption expenditure that conventional Keynesian methods of managing the boom at the top of the cycle would no longer work, but would rather make things worse. The attempt to reduce economic activity at the top of the boom would reduce production and investment, but both personal and governmental consumption would remain high and some government expenditures would even increase because of such compensating payments as unemployment benefits. Unemployment would increase and inflation would get worse too, resulting in the stag-flation that we have since become so accustomed to. The solution, I suggested, was not to reduce economic activity at the top of the boom but rather to increase it (and give further stimuli to

investment) while seeking not to give any further stimulus to personal or governmental consumption. This would enable governments to maintain activity in the fields of social welfare, education, transport infrastructure, the environment, aid to developing countries, and so on—while maintaining a reasonable level of prices.

"The Indigent Rich was reasonably well received but had virtually no impact on national or international policies. Conventional Keynesian policies continued to be applied by all the developed countries, with varying but universally deleterious effects on employment and inflation.'' Deeply concerned about the deterioration of economic stability throughout the Western world, Cumes wrote a second book on inflation that presented a more sophisticated version of his theories and proposed specific solutions. But this book had no impact on policy-makers, either. ''After that,'' Cumes commented, ''I concentrated on a book on Australian social history. *Their Chastity Was Not Too Rigid* describes the way in which the earliest Australian settlers of European origin used their leisure time during the years from the first European settlement in 1788 to the eve of the gold rushes in 1850.''

BIOGRAPHICAL/CRITICAL SOURCES: Canberra Times, October 1, 1971.

*   *   *

CUMMINGS, Betty Sue   1918-

PERSONAL: Born July 12, 1918, in Big Stone Gap, Va.; daughter of Howard Lee and Hattie (Bruce) Cummings. *Education:* Longwood College, B.S., 1939; University of Washington, Seattle, M.A., 1949. *Agent:* Virginia Kidd, P.O. Box 278, Milford, Pa. 18337.

CAREER: Teacher of English at public schools in Norton, Va., 1939-41, Richmond, Va., 1941-42, Buckingham, Va., 1945-46, Thermopolis, Wyo., 1950-57; Brevard County Schools, Titusville, Fla., teacher of English, 1957-73. Writer. *Military service:* U.S. Coast Guard, SPARS, 1942-45. *Member:* National League of American Pen Women, Writers-in-Company. *Awards, honors:* Award from Rollins College Writers' Conference, 1973, for short story ''Three Days''; plaque from Writers-in-Company, 1977.

WRITINGS: Hew Against the Grain (novel), Atheneum, 1977; *Let a River Be* (novel), Atheneum, in press.

WORK IN PROGRESS: Now, Ameriky, about a young woman coming from Ireland during the potato famine.

SIDELIGHTS: Betty Cummings writes: ''In my lifetime I have known many brave women, young and old, and I have a strong need to *record* their courage, both historically and contemporarily speaking. My first book concerned a brave young woman in Civil War days, my second a brave old woman fighting river pollution today.''

*   *   *

CUMMINGS, E(dward) E(stlin)   1894-1962

PERSONAL: Born October 14, 1894, in Cambridge, Mass.; son of Edward (a professor and Congregational minister) and Rebecca Haswell (Clarke) Cummings; married first wife, Elaine (divorced); married Anne Barton, May 1, 1929 (divorced); married Marion Morehouse; children: Nancy. *Education:* Harvard University, A.B., 1915, M.A., 1916. *Home:* 4 Patchin Place, New York, N.Y. 10011; and Joy Farm, Silver Lake, N.H. 03875.

CAREER: Served as an ambulance driver with the Norton

Harjes Ambulance Service in France, 1917; imprisoned in a French detention camp, 1917; studied art and painting in Paris, 1920-24; poet, painter, novelist, playwright, and lecturer. Charles Eliot Norton lecturer at Harvard University, 1952-53. *Military service:* U.S. Army, 1918-19. *Member:* National Academy of Arts and Letters. *Awards, honors:* Dial Award, 1925, for distinguished service to American literature; Academy of American Poets fellowship, 1950; National Book Award special citation, 1955, for *Poems, 1923-1954;* Bollingen Prize in Poetry, 1957.

WRITINGS: (Contributor) *Eight Harvard Poets,* L. J. Gomme, 1917; *The Enormous Room* (novel), Boni & Liveright, 1922, reissued with a new introduction, Modern Library, 1934; *Tulips and Chimneys* (poems), T. Seltzer, 1923; *Puella Mia* (poem), Golden Eagle Press, 1923; *XLI Poems,* Dial, 1925; *&* (poems), privately printed, 1925; *is 5* (poems), Boni & Liveright, 1926; *Him* (three-act play; first produced in New York at Provincetown Playhouse, April 18, 1928), Boni & Liveright, 1927; *Christmas Tree,* American Book Bindery, 1928.

By E. E. Cummings (poems), Covici Friede, 1930; *CIOPW* (paintings and drawings), Covici Friede, 1931; *W [ViVa]* (poems), Liveright, 1931; *Eimi* (a travel diary), Covici Friede, 1933, 4th edition, Grove, 1958; (translator) Louis Aragon, *The Red Front,* Contempo, 1933; *Tom* (a ballet), Arrow, 1935; *No Thanks* (poems), Golden Eagle Press, 1935; *1/20* (poems), R. Roughton, 1936; *Collected Poems,* Harcourt, 1938.

50 Poems, Duell, Sloan & Pearce, 1940; *1 x 1* (poems), Holt, 1944; *Anthropos: The Future of Art,* Golden Eagle Press, 1944; *Santa Claus: A Morality* (play), Holt, 1946; *Xaipe* (poems), Oxford University Press, 1950; *i:six nonlectures,* Harvard University Press, 1953; *Poems, 1923-1954,* Harcourt, 1954; *95 Poems,* Harcourt, 1958; *E. E. Cummings: A Miscellany,* edited by George J. Firmage, Argophile Press, 1958, revised edition, October Press, 1965; *100 Selected Poems,* Grove, 1959.

Selected Poems, 1923-1958, Faber, 1960; (with wife, Marion Morehouse) *Adventures in Value,* Harcourt, 1962; *73 Poems,* Harcourt, 1963; *A Selection of Poems,* Harcourt, 1965; *Fairy Tales,* Harcourt, 1965; *Three Plays & A Ballet,* edited by Firmage, October House, 1967; *Complete Poems,* MacGibbon & Kee, 1968; *Selected Letters of E. E. Cummings,* edited by F. W. Dupee and George Stade, Harcourt, 1969; *Complete Poems, 1913-1962,* Harcourt, 1972.

Contributor of poems to *Atlantic, Encounter, Evergreen Review, New Yorker, Poet, Poetry, Poetry London, Quarterly Review of Literature, Shenandoah, Spearhead, Wake,* and other periodicals.

SIDELIGHTS: In the final moments of his last Charles Eliot Norton lecture at Harvard University in 1953, E. E. Cummings attempted to answer the question "who, as a writer, am I?": "I am someone who proudly and humbly affirms that love is the mystery-of-mysteries, and that nothing measurable matters 'a very good God damn': that 'an artist, a man, a failure' is no mere whenfully accreting mechanism, but a givingly eternal complexity—neither some soulless and heartless ultrapredatory infra-animal nor any un-understandingly knowing and believing and thinking automation, but a naturally and miraculously whole human being—a feelingly illimitable individual; whose only happiness is to transcend himself, whose every agony is to grow."

Celebration of the individual in a world of "mostpeople" pervades Cummings's work, from his first published book, *The Enormous Room,* a novel of his experiences in a French

internment camp in World War I, to *73 Poems,* written more than a half century later. In the introduction to the 1934 edition of *The Enormous Room* Cummings wrote: "When this book wrote itself, I was observing a negligible portion of something incredibly more distant than any sun; something more unimaginably huge than the most prodigious of all universes—Namely?

"The Individual."

To engender each man to be alive and "feeling" became Cummings's major thematic occupation, and in *Collected Poems* he carefully described the unfeeling masses, "mostpeople": "What does it mean to be mostpeople? Catastrophe unmitigated. Socialrevolution. The cultured aristocrat yanked out of his hyperexclusively ultravoluptuous superpalazzo, and dumped into an incredibly vulgar detentioncamp swarming with every conceivable species of undesirable organism. Mostpeople fancy a guaranteed birthproof safetysuit of nondestructible selflessness. If mostpeople were to be born twice they'd probably call it dying—

"you and I are not snobs. We can never be born enough. We are human beings; for whom birth is a supremely welcome mystery, the mystery of growing: the mystery which happens only and whenever we are faithful to ourselves."

Full engagement of life, Cummings insisted, comes with recognition of miracles in the commonplace and God. He wrote in *50 Poems:*

> "(now the ears of my ears awake and
> now the eyes of my eyes are opened)."

Throughout his writing, Cummings experimented with the English language, using compressed language, dislocated syntax, experiments in typography, line division, and capitalization to bring a freshness of perception to his work and to the language itself. Fellow poet William Carlos Williams called Cummings's language a "private" language, a "christian language—addressing to the private conscience of each of us in turn." Williams saw Cummings as "Robinson Crusoe at the moment when he first saw the print of a naked human foot in the sand. That, too, implied a new language—and a readjustment of conscience." Cummings himself, in the introduction Boni & Liveright requested he write for *is 5,* described his theory of technique: "I can express it in fifteen words, by quoting The Eternal Question And Immortal Answer of burlesk, viz. 'Would you hit a woman with a child?—No, I'd hit her with a brick.' Like the burlesk comedian, I am abnormally fond of that precision which creates movement."

Despite his typographical extravaganzas, Cummings, in his sense of individualism, his continual theme of love ("love is whole and more than all"), and his satires against politicians, salesmen, and businessmen, is in the Emersonian tradition of romantic transcendentalism. Though his themes remain consistent, in his later poems there is a deepening awareness of his special lyrical gift as a poet of celebration and some abandonment of earlier sallies into ideology and criticism.

In a letter to the Ottawa Hills High School newspaper, the *Spectator,* Cummings gave his advice to young poets: "As for expressing nobody-but-yourself in words, that means working just a little harder than anybody who isn't a poet can possibly imagine. Why? Because nothing is quite so easy as using words like somebody else. We all of us do exactly this nearly all of the time—and whenever we do it, we're not poets.

"If, at the end of your first ten or fifteen years of fighting and working and feeling, you find you've written one line of one poem, you'll be very lucky indeed.

"And so my advice to all young people who wish to become poets is:do something easy,like learning how to blow up the world—unless you are not only willing,but glad,to feel and work and fight till you die.

"Does this sound dismal? It isn't.

"It's the most wonderful life on earth.

"Or so I feel."

BIOGRAPHICAL/CRITICAL SOURCES: *is 5,* Boni & Liveright, 1926; *The Enormous Room,* Modern Library, 1934; *50 Poems,* Duell, Sloan & Pearce, 1940; *Harvard Wake,* 5, Spring, 1946; *i:six nonlectures,* Harvard University Press, 1953; *Spectator* (Grand Rapids, Mich.), October 26, 1955; Charles Norman, *The Magic Maker: E. E. Cummings,* Macmillan, 1958; Norman Friedman, *E. E. Cummings: The Growth of a Writer,* Southern Illinois University Press, 1964; *Complete Poems, 1913-1962,* Harcourt, 1972; *Contemporary Literary Criticism,* Gale, Volume 1, 1973, Volume 3, 1975, Volume 8, 1978.*

(Died September 3, 1962, in North Conway, N.H.)

* * *

CUNNINGHAM, Barry 1940-

PERSONAL: Born December 29, 1940, in Pittsburgh, Pa.; son of John Milton and Sara (a kindergarten teacher; maiden name, Yellig) Cunningham; married Laura Weiss (a novelist), January 4, 1967. *Education:* Attended University of Pittsburgh, 1960-62; New York University, B.S., 1967. *Agent:* Don Congdon, Harold Matson Co., Inc., 22 East 40th St., New York, N.Y. 10016. *Office: New York Post,* 210 South St., New York, N.Y. 10002.

CAREER: *New York Journal-American,* New York City, reporter and correspondent, 1965-66; *New York Post,* New York City, reporter and correspondent, 1966—. *Military service:* U.S. Army, Cavalry, 1962-63, Medical Corps, 1963-64; served in Japan. *Member:* Sigma Delta Chi. *Awards, honors:* James Fenimore Cooper Award from New York University, 1966, for the article "Conscience of a Southern Town"; Citizens Budget Award from Citizens Budget Committee, 1967, for his expose of the surrogate court patronage scandal in New York; Page One Award from New York Newspaper Guild, 1973, for the series "Growing Old in New York"; co-winner of Meyer Berger Award from Columbia University, 1973, for distinguished journalism in New York City.

WRITINGS: (With Mike Pearl) *Mr. District Attorney: The Story of Frank S. Hogan and the Manhattan District Attorney's Office,* Mason/Charter, 1977.

Contributor of several hundred articles to magazines and newspapers, some of which have been published in foreign languages.

WORK IN PROGRESS: A novel.

SIDELIGHTS: Cunningham writes: "Since joining the staff of the *New York Post,* I have been on assignment throughout Southeast Asia, Europe, and North America. At age twenty-five, I became one of the youngest American correspondents covering the battlefield war in Vietnam. Returning home in 1967, I was an eyewitness to the major domestic convulsions of that period: the 'moratorium' marches on Washington, D.C., the 1968 SDS rebellions at Columbia, Cornell, and Harvard, and the black riots of Newark, Plainfield, and Cleveland.

"In 1969, I traveled to more than a dozen military installations around the country, gathering material for a series of articles on dissent in the Army. I covered the South Carolina court-martial of Captain Howard Levy. I traced Army deserters to Canada in order to get their stories.

"During the later Nixon years, I began examining the inner workings of the criminal justice system. I wrote hundreds of articles based on my observations inside prisons, police stations, and courtrooms, and chronicled the lives of criminals and their victims. On one occasion, I dove under the polluted East River with New York scuba police, searching for the body of a drowned murder victim. In 1972, I traced the pipeline of French heroin smuggling from a secret opium refinery in Marseilles to a junkie's needle in Harlem.

"As a journalist for all seasons, I have covered virtually every topic from acupuncture to yogurt. In addition to reports on crime and disaster, there have been show business articles, personality profiles, industry pieces, book and author reviews, and first-person, Walter Mittyesque adventure sagas."

AVOCATIONAL INTERESTS: Tennis, squash, skiing, magic.

BIOGRAPHICAL/CRITICAL SOURCES: M. L. Stein, *Under Fire: The Story of American War Correspondents,* Messner, 1968.

* * *

CUNNINGHAM, Paul James, Jr. 1917-

PERSONAL: Born August 13, 1917, in New Rochelle, N.Y.; son of Paul James (an engineer) and Mary-Ada (Morris) Cunningham; married Constance Morton, February 13, 1954 (died, 1968); married Maaike Agnes van Haren, September 21, 1970; children: Paul, III, McAllister, Meredith, Marieka, Ian-Thomas. *Education:* Attended New York University, 1936; University of Minnesota, B.A., 1946. *Religion:* Catholic. *Home:* Oak End Way, Gerrards Cross, Buckinghamshire SL9 8BZ, England. *Office:* National Broadcasting Co., 25 St. Jameses St., London SW1, England.

CAREER/WRITINGS: Meinhard Greff & Co., New York City, clerk, 1935-37; Insurance Company of North America, New York City, clerk, 1937-39; *Minneapolis Star,* Minneapolis, Minn., staff member, 1946-48; National Broadcasting Co. (NBC), New York City, newswriter and correspondent, 1949—. Notable assignments include coverage of Fidel Castro and the Cuban Revolution, the war in Vietnam, interviews with John F. Kennedy, Hubert Humphrey, and Emperor Haile Selassie. Reporter-at-large for "Today" show, 1961-76. *Military service:* U.S. Army, 1941-45; became staff sergeant. *Awards, honors:* Albert Lasker Award for medical journalism, 1966.

SIDELIGHTS: Cunningham told *CA* he is "satisfied to be a news reporting journalist for television and radio network news."

* * *

CURRAN, Phil(ip) R(ead) 1911-

PERSONAL: Born April 27, 1911, in Mullan, Idaho; son of Michael Patrick (a baker) and Grace Ernestine (a home economist; maiden name, Read) Curran; married Shirley Joy Scott (a television fashion coordinator); children: Craig, Terry, Kent. *Education:* Attended Reed College, 1929-31. *Politics:* Independent. *Religion:* Protestant. *Home:* 2149 Vista Entrada, Newport Beach, Calif. 92660. *Office:* United Feature Syndicate, 200 Park Ave., New York, N.Y. 10017.

CAREER/WRITINGS: United Press International, New York City, United States war correspondent, 1941-45; Southwest Pacific manager in Sydney, Australia, 1945-47; British United Press, Montreal, Canada, managing director, 1948-58; United Press International, New York City, director of client relations, 1958-62; United Feature Syndicate, New York City, western manager in Los Angeles, Calif., 1962-75. *Member:* Overseas Press Club, Society of Professional Journalists, Players Club.

SIDELIGHTS: "I've traveled and worked in eighty countries," Curran told *CA.* "I can get by in French and Spanish sufficiently to eat, drink, and sleep."

*   *   *

CURRER-BRIGGS, Noel   1919-

PERSONAL: Born November 21, 1919, in Leeds, England; son of Reginald Martin (a colliery owner) and Doris May (Greener) Currer-Briggs; married Barbara Hey, 1948 (separated, 1971). *Education:* St. Catharine's College, Cambridge, M.A. (honors), 1948. *Home and office:* Flint Cottage, Wendens Ambo, Saffron Walden, Essen CB11 4UL, England. *Agent:* Jon Thurley, 78 New Bond St., London W.1, England.

CAREER: British Foreign Office, London, England, member of staff, 1947-48; farmer in Gloucestershire, England, 1948-61; genealogical and historical research consultant, 1956—. Consultant to *Burke's Peerage, Debrett's Peerage,* and *Kluwer-Harrap Handbook of Security. Military service:* British Army, cryptanalyst in Intelligence, 1940-47; became major; mentioned in dispatches. *Member:* Society of Genealogists (fellow; member of executive committee), Association of Genealogists and Record Agents, Legion of Frontiersmen of the Commonwealth. *Awards, honors:* Fellowship from Society of Genealogists, 1969.

WRITINGS: (Editor) *Security Attitudes and Techniques for Management,* Hutchinson, 1968; (editor) *Contemporary Observations on Security,* Chubb, 1968; *Virginia Settlers and English Adventurers,* Phillimore, 1969; *Dr. Ferranti,* Hutchinson Benham, 1970; (with Jane Paterson and Brian Kennett) *Handwriting Analysis in Business,* ABP, 1971; *English Adventurers and Colonial Settlers,* Phillimore, 1971; *English Wills of Colonial Families,* Polyanthos, 1972; (translator) *Letters of Carl Maria von Weber,* Oswald Wolff, 1976; *The Complete Family Historian,* Routledge & Kegan Paul, in press. Contributor to genealogy journals in the United States and England.

SIDELIGHTS: Currer-Briggs writes of *The Complete Family Historian:* "This book will be a study of the family as an institution and the place of genealogy in all branches of modern life, including medicine, psychology, demography, designed especially for those living in the New World wishing to trace their roots in the Old."

He adds: "We live in an age threatened by materialism in the shape of Marxist dogma, in which the values and institutions of the past are at risk. My writing is designed to point out those risks and to strengthen belief in the value of traditional institutions, though not to adhere to them slavishly and without criticism. New approaches are needed to bring them up to date. My forthcoming book, which has taken four years to write, attempts to channel the current interest in genealogy and family history along positive and thought-provoking lines, as well as to be a practical encyclopaedic guide to those wishing to establish their family origins."

CURRIE, Lauchlin   1902-

PERSONAL: Born October 8, 1902, in West Dublin, Nova Scotia, Canada; came to United States in 1925, naturalized in 1934; son of Lauchlin and Alice (Eisenhauer) Currie; married Dorothy York Bacon, 1927; married second wife, Elvira Wiesner, May 16, 1954; children: (first marriage) Morgan, Roderick; (second marriage) Ronald, Elizabeth. *Education:* Attended St. Francis Xavier University, Antigonish, Nova Scotia, 1920-22; London School of Economics and Political Science, B.Sc., 1925; Harvard University, Ph.D., 1931. *Religion:* Roman Catholic. *Home:* Carrera 5, 25-A-28, Bogota, Colombia.

CAREER: Harvard University, Cambridge, Mass., instructor and tutor, 1927-34; Fletcher School of Law and Diplomacy, Medford, Mass., professor of international economics, 1933-34; U.S. Federal Reserve System, Board of Governors, Washington, D.C., assistant director of research and statistics, 1934-39; Office of the President (Franklin D. Roosevelt), White House, Washington, D.C., administrative assistant, 1939-45; Fundacion para el Progreso de Colombia, Colombia, director, 1961-67; National University of Colombia, Bogota, director of studies, Center of Development Research, and director of department of economics, 1966-67. Head of U.S. Economic Mission to China, 1941, International Bank Mission to Colombia, 1949-50, and Colombian Joint Commission to Venezuela, 1966; consultant to Colombian Government agencies, 1951-67. Lecturer at University of California, Berkeley, and other U.S. and Canadian universities, 1965-67. *Awards, honors:* Decorations from governments of Nationalist China and Venezuela.

WRITINGS: The Supply and Control of Money in the United States, Harvard University Press, 1934, reprinted with "A Proposed Revision of the Monetary System of the United States," Russell, 1968; *Basis of a Program for Colombia,* Johns Hopkins Press, 1950; (with Hugo Belalcazar) *Proyecciones de la demanda de construcciones y de materiales para construccion en Colombia, para el periodo 1962-1970,* [Bogota], 1963; (with Alfredo G. Samper) *El Manejo de cuencas en Colombia,* Ediciones Tercer Mundo, 1965; *Una politica urbana para los paises en desarrollo,* Ediciones Tercer Mundo, 1965; *Accelerating Development: The Necessity and the Means,* McGraw, 1966; *Ensenanza universitaria en los estudios sociales,* Ediciones Tercer Mundo, 1967; *Obstacles to Development,* Michigan State University Press, 1967; *Taming the Megalopolis: A Design for Urban Growth,* Pergamon, 1976. Writer of reports and articles in English and in Spanish.*

*   *   *

CURTIS, Tony   1925-

PERSONAL: Born June 3, 1925, in New York, N.Y.; son of Manuel (a tailor) and Helen (Klein) Schwartz; married Janet Leigh, June 4, 1951 (divorced); married Christine Kaufman, February 8, 1963 (divorced); married Leslie Allen (a model), April 20, 1968; children: Kelly, Jamie, Alexandra, Allegra. *Education:* Educated in New York City. *Politics:* None. *Religion:* "Born a Jew." *Home:* 737 Sarborne Road, West Los Angeles, Calif. 90025. *Agent:* Irving Paul Lazar, 211 South Beverly Dr., Beverly Hills, Calif. 90212. *Office:* 49 Chester Sq., London SW1, England.

CAREER: Actor. Began acting career with small supporting role in "Criss Cross," 1948; signed with Universal Pictures, 1948, and has appeared in over fifty motion pictures, including "City Across the River," 1949, "Wincester 73," 1950, "The Prince Who Was a Thief," 1951, "Houdini," 1953,

"The Black Shield of Falworth," 1954, "Beach Head," 1954, "Six Bridges to Cross," 1955, "Trapeze," 1956, "Mister Cory," 1957, "The Sweet Smell of Success," 1957, "The Vikings," 1958, "The Defiant Ones," 1959, "Some Like It Hot," 1959, "Operation Petticoat," 1959, "Sparticus," 1960, "The Great Imposter," 1960, "Forty Pounds of Trouble," 1962, "Taras Bulba," 1962, "Captain Newman MD," 1963, "The Great Race," 1965, "Boeing Boeing," 1965, "The Boston Strangler," 1968, "You Can't Win Them All," 1970, "Third Girl from the Left," 1973. *Military service:* U.S. Navy, 1944-46; served in submarine service.

WRITINGS: Kid Andrew Cody and Julie Sparrow, Doubleday, 1977.

*   *   *

CURZON, Daniel
(Daniel Russell Brown)

PERSONAL: Original name, Daniel Russell Brown; born in Illinois. *Education:* University of Detroit, Ph.B., 1960; Kent State University, M.A., 1961; Wayne State University, Ph.D., 1969. *Home:* 328 San Carlos, San Francisco, Calif. 94110. *Agent:* Arnold Goodman, 500 West End Ave., New York, N.Y. 10024.

CAREER: University of Detroit, Detroit, Mich., instructor in English, 1962-65; Wayne State University, Detroit, instructor in English, 1965-69; University of Maryland, London Division, London, England, lecturer in English, 1970-72; University of Maryland, Far East Division, Japan, Vietnam, and Thailand, lecturer in English, 1972-74; California State University, Fresno, lecturer in English, 1974-76; writer and director, 1976—.

WRITINGS: Something You Do in the Dark (novel), Putnam, 1971; *The Misadventures of Tim McPick* (novel), John Parke Custis Press, 1975; *The Revolt of the Perverts* (short stories), Leland Mellott Books, 1978; *Among the Carnivores* (novel), Ashley Books, 1978.

Play: "Sex Show: Comedy Madness," first performed in San Francisco at Leavenworth St. Theatre, 1977.

Contributor of poetry to *College English, St. Andrew's Review, Manroot,* and journals, of short stories to *Kansas Quarterly, GPU News, Vector, Quorum,* and other literary journals, and of articles to *Modern Fiction Studies, Journal of Aesthetics and Art Criticism,* and other journals and newspapers.

WORK IN PROGRESS: Boys Don't Jump Rope, a novel.

SIDELIGHTS: Curzon told *CA:* "I write because I want to capture the various realities of human experience and make them bearable and beautiful. Where life disappoints and confuses and hurts, literature satisfies—maybe.

"In particular I like to write about gay people because their worlds have been unreported except in the most censorious and demeaning ways for centuries and centuries. Gay people, however, are human beings, no more, no less. I hope, in time, that those reluctant to grant full literary and emotional value to gay writing will overcome their bias. As it stands now, there is still great fear and hatred of homosexuality, making it difficult for anyone who chooses to write on this topic to reach the larger audience beyond the ghetto. But the day of greater openness may be dawning."

*   *   *

DAKIN, D(avid) Martin   1908-

PERSONAL: Born March 13, 1908, in Halifax, Yorkshire, England; son of David Samuel (a Congregational minister) and Annie Elizabeth (a teacher and missionary; maiden name, Ffrench) Dakin; married Jennie Eileen Wright (a schoolmistress), August 4, 1936; children: Alison Eileen. *Education:* Queen's College, Oxford, B.A., 1931, M.A., 1949; University of Hull, teaching diploma, 1932. *Politics:* "Unorthodox Socialist." *Religion:* United Reformed Church. *Home:* 61 Suttons Lane, Hornchurch, Essex RM12 6RL, England.

CAREER: Assistant master at primary schools in Hull, England, 1932-44, and Wigton, England, 1945-48; high school teacher of religious knowledge in Aveley, England, 1948-49; County High School, Dagenham, England, master for religious knowledge, 1950-70; writer, 1956—. *Member:* Fellowship of Reconciliation (past member of General Committee), Peace Pledge Union, Lewis Carroll Society, Sherlock Holmes Society (London; past member of council), Hornchurch Historical Society (president, 1975—).

WRITINGS: Peace and Brotherhood in the Old Testament, Bannisdale Press, 1956; *A Sherlock Holmes Commentary,* Drake, 1972; *Holmesian Clerihews,* Luther Norris, 1975.

WORK IN PROGRESS: London Curiosities; Dictionary of Nicknames; Bible Commentary for Schools, a multi-volume work.

SIDELIGHTS: Dakin told *CA:* "I am a Christian Pacifist. I believe in renunciation of war and unilateral disarmament: hence my first book. I'm a Modernist, believing in the progressive revelation of the Bible and in religious education in schools (naturally, having taught it full and part time for thirty-eight years). I am a Christian Socialist but NOT a Communist. But we all need light relief at times—hence my interest in detective fiction and nonsense writing, Conan Doyle and Lewis Carroll being my two favourite authors."

AVOCATIONAL INTERESTS: Book collecting ("to read, not first editions!"), reading (especially detective fiction and its history), color photography, ancient buildings.

*   *   *

DALGLIESH, Alice   1893-

PERSONAL: Born October 7, 1893, in Trinidad, British West Indies; naturalized U.S. citizen; daughter of John and Alice (Haynes) Dagliesh. *Education:* Attended Pratt Institute; earned B.A. and M.A. from Columbia University. *Residence:* Brookfield, Conn.

CAREER: Editor and author of children's books. Has also worked as an elementary school teacher and as a lecturer.

WRITINGS—For children: A Happy School Year (illustrated by Mary Spoor Brand), Rand, McNally, 1924; *West Indian Play Days* (illustrated by Margaret Evans Price), Rand, McNally, 1926; *The Little Wooden Farmer [and] The Story of the Jungle Pool* (illustrated by Theodora Baumeister), Macmillan, 1930, published as *The Little Wooden Farmer,* Collier Books, 1971; *The Blue Teapot: Sandy Cove Stories* (illustrated by Hildegard Woodward), Macmillan, 1931; *First Experiences with Literature,* Scribner, 1932; *The Choosing Book* (illustrated by Eloise Burns Wilkin), Macmillan, 1932; *Relief's Rocker: A Story of Sandy Cove and the Sea* (illustrated by Woodward), Macmillan, 1932; *America Travels: The Story of a Hundred Years of Travel in America* (illustrated by Woodward), Macmillan, 1933, reprinted, 1961; (compiler) *Christmas: A Book of Stories Old and New* (illustrated by Woodward), Scribner, 1934; *Roundabout: Another Sandy Cove Story* (illustrated by Woodward), Macmillan, 1934.

Sailor Sam (self-illustrated), Scribner, 1935; *The Smiths and Rusty* (illustrated by Berta and Elmer Hader), Scribner, 1936; *Long Live the King!* (illustrated by Lois Maloy), Scribner, 1937; *Wings for the Smiths* (illustrated by B. and E. Hader), Scribner, 1937; *America Builds Homes: The Story of the First Colonies* (illustrated by Maloy), Scribner, 1938; *America Begins: The Story of the Finding of the New World* (illustrated by Maloy), Scribner, 1938; (compiler) *Once on a Time* (illustrated by Katherine Milhous), Scribner, 1938; *The Young Aunts* (illustrated by Charlotte Becker), Scribner, 1939; (compiler) *Happily Ever After* (selected fairy tales; illustrated by Milhous), Scribner, 1939; *The Hollyberrys* (illustrated by Pru Herric), Scribner, 1939.

A Book for Jennifer (illustrated by Milhous), Scribner, 1940; *Wings Around South America* (illustrated by Milhous), Scribner, 1941; *Three from Greenaways* (illustrated by Gertrude Howe), Scribner, 1941; *They Live in South America* (illustrated by Milhous), Scribner, 1942; *Gulliver Joins the Army* (illustrated by Ellen Segner), Scribner, 1942; *The Little Angel: A Story of Old Rio* (illustrated by Milhous), Scribner, 1943; *The Silver Pencil* (illustrated by Milhous), Scribner, 1944; *Along Janet's Road* (illustrated by Milhous), Scribner, 1946; *Reuben and His Red Wheelbarrow* (illustrated by Ilse Bischoff), Grosset & Dunlap, 1946; (compiler) *The Enchanted Book* (illustrated by Concetta Cacciola), Scribner, 1947; *The Davenports Are at Dinner* (illustrated by Flavia Gag), Scribner, 1948; *The Davenports and Cherry Pie* (illustrated by Gag), Scribner, 1949.

The Bears on Hemlock Mountain (illustrated by Helen Sewell), Scribner, 1952; *The Thanksgiving Story* (illustrated by Sewell), Scribner, 1954; *The Courage of Sarah Noble* (illustrated by Leonard Weisgard), Scribner, 1954; *The Columbus Story* (illustrated by Leo Politi), Scribner, 1955; *Ride on the Wind* (illustrated by Georges Schreiber), Scribner, 1956; *The Fourth of July Story* (illustrated by Marie Nonnast), Scribner, 1956; *Adam and the Golden Cock* (illustrated by Weisgard), Scribner, 1959.

Book review editor, *Parents Magazine.*

SIDELIGHTS: Dagliesh has spent many summers in Sandy Cove, Nova Scotia, which became the setting for three of her books—*Roundabout, The Blue Teapot,* and *Relief's Rocker.* Two other books, *The Silver Pencil* and its sequel, *Along Janet's Road,* are semi-autobiographical.*

* * *

D'ALLENGER, Hugh
See KERSHAW, John (Hugh D'Allenger)

* * *

DALRYMPLE, Douglas J(esse) 1934-
PERSONAL: Born October 1, 1934, in Lockport, N.Y.; son of M. Daniel and S. Esther Dalrymple; married Nancy Justin (a teacher), December 20, 1958; children: Jill, Craig, Lynn. *Education:* Cornell University, B.S., 1956, M.S., 1959; Michigan State University, D.B.A., 1964. *Home:* 2312 Montclair Ave., Bloomington, Ind. 47401. *Office:* Department of Marketing, Indiana University, 570D Business, Bloomington, Ind. 47401.

CAREER: Cornell University, Ithaca, N.Y., research specialist, 1958-60; Michigan State University, East Lansing, assistant instructor in business administration, 1960-62; University of California, Los Angeles, assistant professor of business administration, 1963-68; Indiana University, Bloomington, associate professor of business administra-

tion, 1968—. *Military service:* U.S. Army Reserve, 1956-64, active duty, 1957; became second lieutenant. *Member:* American Marketing Association, Institute of Management Science, American Institute for Decision Sciences.

WRITINGS: Measuring Merchandising Performance in Department Stores, National Retail Merchants Association, 1964; *Retail Management Cases,* Free Press, 1969; *Retailing: An Economic View,* Free Press, 1969; *Marketing Management: Text and Cases,* Wiley, 1976. Contributor to business, economic, advertising, and management journals. Member of editorial board of *Journal of Retailing.*

WORK IN PROGRESS: Research on use of Box-Jenkins techniques in sales forecasting.

SIDELIGHTS: Dalrymple told *CA:* "My philosophy of business education is that maximum learning takes place when students apply basic principles to solve realistic business cases." *Avocational interests:* Growing roses, sailing, reading, and swimming.

* * *

DAMAS, Leon 1912-1978
March 28, 1912—January 23, 1978; French Guianan politician and author. Damas was best known as a pioneer, with Leopold Sedar Senghor and Aime Cesaire, in creating the cultural and literary Negritude movement in the 1930's. Although he served in the French Assembly for six years, he was primarily known as a writer and was the author of ten books of prose and verse, as well as journalism. *Pigments* and *Retour de Guyana* are among his most important works. Damas died in Washington, D.C. Obituaries: *Washington Post,* January 24, 1978.

* * *

DAMOR, Hakji
See LESSER, R(oger) H(arold)

* * *

D'ANDREA, Kate
See STEINER, Barbara A(nnette)

* * *

DANIEL, Anne
See STEINER, Barbara A(nnette)

* * *

DANIELOU, Alain 1907-
PERSONAL: Born October 4, 1907, in Neuilly-sur-Seine, France; son of Charles (a writer and politician) and Madeleine (an educator and founder of religious order; maiden name, Clamorgan) Danielou. *Education:* Educated in France, India, and the United States. *Religion:* Hindu. *Home:* Colle Labirinto, Zagarolo, 00039 Rome, Italy. *Office:* Institute for Comparative Music Studies, Fondazione Cini, San Giorgio, Venice, Italy.

CAREER: Hindu University, Benares, India, research professor of Sanskrit literature on music, 1949-54; International Institute for Comparative Music Studies, Venice, Italy, and Berlin, Germany, director, 1962—. *Member:* French Institute of Indology, Ecole Francaise d'Extreme-Oreint. *Awards, honors:* Chevalier Legion d'honneur, 1967; Chevalier Arts et Lettres, 1970; Officier Merite National, 1975.

WRITINGS: Le Betail des dieux (title means "The Cattle of the Gods"), Buchet-Chastel, 1962; *Hindu Polytheism,*

Princeton University Press, 1964; (translator) Ilango Adrigal, *Shilappadikaram: The Ankle Bracelet,* New Directions, 1965; *Inde du norde: Collection "Les Traditions Musicales"* (title means "Musical Traditions of Northern India"), Buchet-Chastel, 1966; *Semantique musicale* (title means "Musical Semantics"), Hermann, 1967; *The Raga-s of Northern Indian Music,* Barrie & Rockliff, 1968.

Histoire de l'Inde (title means "History of India"), Fayard, 1971; *Situation de la musique et des musiciens dans les pays d'orient,* Olschki, 1971, translation by author published as *Music and Musicians in the Countries of the Orient,* Olschi, 1971; *Yoga: Methode de reintegration,* L'Arche, 1973, translation by author published as *Yoga: The Method of Reintegration,* University Books, 1973; *La Sculpture erotique hindoue* (title means "Erotic Hindu Sculpture"), Buchet-Chastel, 1975; *Les Fous de dieu: Contes gangetiques* (title means "God's Madmen"), Buchet-Chastel, 1976; *Les Quatre Sens de la vie: La Structure sociale de l'Inde traditionnelle* (title means "The Four Aims of Life: Social Structures of Traditional India"), Buchet-Chastel, 1976; (translator) *Theatre de Harsha* (title means "The Plays of Harsha"), Buchet-Chastel, 1977; *Le Temple hindou* (title means "The Hindu Temple"), Buchet-Chastel, 1977. Also author of *La Musique dans la societe et la vie de l'Inde,* and translator of *Le Shiva Svarodaya-Ancien traite de presages et premonitions d'apres le Souffle Vital.*

Editor of UNESCO collection of Oriental and traditional music recordings.

WORK IN PROGRESS: Shiva et Dionysos: Mythes et rites d'une religion pre-aryenne; Le Sangita-Shirmani et le Dattilam.

SIDELIGHTS: Alain Danielou told *CA* that his "main interest is explaining Hindu traditional civilization, religion and culture to the outside world." He continued: "Hinduism especially in its oldest, Shivaite form, never destroyed its past. It is the sum of human experience from the earliest times. Non-dogmatic, it allows every one to find his own way. Ultimate reality being beyond man's understanding, the most contradictory theories or beliefs may be equally inadequate approaches to reality. Ecological (as we would say today), it sees man as part of a whole where trees, animals, men and spirits should live in harmony and mutual respect, and it asks everyone to cooperate and not endanger the artwork of the creator. It therefore opposes the destruction of nature, of species, the bastardisation of races, the tendency of each one to do what he was not born for. It leaves every one free to find his own way of realization human and spiritual be it ascetic or erotic or both. It does not separate intellect and body, mind and matter, but sees the Universe as a living continuum. It refuses the absurdity of seeing in man a unique being entitled to enjoy and destroy the world for his own benefit as do most of the modern creeds that lead mankind towards its doom.

"I believe any sensible man is unknowingly a Hindu and that the only hope for man lies in the abolition of the erratic, dogmatic, unphilosophical creeds people today call religions."

Danielou speaks English, Hindi, and Italian.

AVOCATIONAL INTERESTS: Painting, playing Western and Indian music.

*   *   *

DARBY, Patricia (Paulsen)
PERSONAL: Married Raymond Darby, October 26, 1954;

children: Glen, Jessica, Grant, Raymond, Jr., Edward, Rebecca. *Home:* 2527 Hereford Rd., Thousand Oaks, Calif. 91360. *Agent:* August Lenniger, Lenniger Literary Agency, 11 West 42nd St., New York, N.Y. 10036.

CAREER: Author. Has also worked as a physical therapist.

WRITINGS: (With husband, Ray Darby) *Your Career in Physical Therapy,* Messner, 1969; (with R. Darby) *Conquering the Deep Sea,* McKay, 1971.

SIDELIGHTS: Science Books reviewed *Conquering the Deep Sea* as "one of the best descriptive analyses of man's exploration of the ocean."

BIOGRAPHICAL/CRITICAL SOURCES: Science Books, September, 1972.

*   *   *

DASSONVILLE, Michel A(uguste) 1927-
PERSONAL: Born December 27, 1927, in Lille, France; came to the United States in 1960, naturalized citizen, 1971; son of Rene R. (an executive in the textile industry) and Leonie (Rouze) Dassonville; married Therese Ennaert, July 18, 1949; children: Marie-France Dassonville Mignon, Jean-Louis, Pierre-Olivier. *Education:* University of Lille, B.A., 1946, lic. es lettres, 1948; University of Sacre-Coeur, M.A., 1951; Laval University, Dr. es lettres, 1953. *Politics:* Democrat. *Home:* 3607 Cherry Lane, Austin, Tex. 78703. *Office:* Department of French and Italian, Sutton Hall 215, University of Texas, Austin, Tex. 78712.

CAREER: Laval University, Quebec, Quebec, assistant professor, 1953-55, associate professor of French literature, 1955-58; University of Paris, Catholic Institute, Paris, France, professeur de licence, 1958-60; University of Texas, Austin, assistant professor, 1960-61, associate professor, 1961-62, professor of Romance languages, 1963—. *Member:* Alliance Francaise (local president, 1963-67), South Central Modern Language Association. *Awards, honors:* Casgrain Award from Laval University, 1958, for *L'Analyse de Texte;* Piper Professorship from Minnie Stevens Piper Foundation, 1965; Palmes Academiques from French Government, 1976; also received research grants from French Government, 1953, 1958, and Canada Arts Council, 1957, and Texas University Research Institute, 1967, 1975.

WRITINGS: Comment ecrire une dissertation litteraire (title means "How to Write an Essay"), Presses Universitaires, 1955, 2nd edition, 1961; (with Philippe Deschamps) *De l'Explication Francaise a la redaction* (title means "From Reading to Writing"), Presses Universitaires, 1955, 2nd edition, 1958; *Cremazie: Collection des Classiques Canadiens* (title means "Texts of Octave Cremazie"), Fides, 1956, 2nd edition, 1962; *L'Analyse de Texte* (title means "Literary Analysis"), Presses Universitaires, 1957; *Frechette: Collection des Classiques Canadiens* (title means "Texts of Louis Frechette"), Fides, 1958; *Initiation a la Recherche Litteraire* (title means "Introduction to Literary Research"), Presses Universitaires, 1959.

Pierre de la Ramee: Dialectique (title means "Petrus Ramus' Dialectic in French"), Droz, 1964; *Ronsard: Etude historique et litteraire* (title means "Ronsard: A Historical and Literary Study"), Droz, Volume I: *Les Enfances Ronsard: 1536-1545* (title means "The Formation Years"), 1968, Volume II: *A la Conquete de la toison d'or, 1545-1550* (title means "The Quest of the Golden Fleece"), 1970, Volume III: *Prince des Poetes ou Poete des Princes, 1550-1556* (title means "Prince of the Poets or Poet of the Princes"), 1976. Contributor of about twenty articles to language and literature journals.

WORK IN PROGRESS: *Ronsard: Etude historique et litteraire,* Volume IV: *Grandeurs et Servitudes, 1560-1574* (title means "Grandeur and Servitude"), Volume V: *La Jeunesse des Dieux, 1574-1585* (title means "An Eternal Youth").

* * *

DAUGHERTY, Charles Michael 1914-

PERSONAL: Born November 17, 1914, in New York, N.Y.; son of James (an artist and author) and Sonia (a children's author; maiden name, Medwedeff) Daugherty. *Education:* Attended Yale University and the Art Students League. *Residence:* Westport, Conn.

CAREER: Author and illustrator of books for children. *Military service:* U.S. Army, 1941-45.

WRITINGS: *So Sailors Say* (self-illustrated), Holt, 1941; *Street of Ships* (self-illustrated), Holt, 1942; *Let 'Em Roll* (self-illustrated), Viking, 1950; *Where the Condor Nests* (self-illustrated), Viking, 1955; *Good News* (self-illustrated), Viking, 1956; *The Army: From Civilian to Soldier* (self-illustrated), Viking, 1957; *Wider than the Sky: Aviation as a Career,* Harcourt, 1958; *Mirror with a Memory: The Art of Photography,* Harcourt, 1959; *Wisher* (illustrated by James Daugherty), Viking, 1960; *Searchers of the Sea: Pioneers in Oceanography* (illustrated by Don Miller), Viking, 1961; *The Great Archaeologists* (illustrated by Leonard E. Fisher), Crowell, 1962; *City under the Ice: The Story of Camp Century,* Macmillan, 1963; *Robert Goddard: Trail Blazer to the Stars* (illustrated by J. Daugherty), Macmillan, 1964; *Benjamin Franklin: Scientist-Diplomat* (illustrated by John Falter), Macmillan, 1965; *Samuel Clemens* (illustrated by Kurt Werth), Crowell, 1970; (editor) *Six Artists Paint a Portrait: Alfred Chadbourn, George Passantino, Charles Reid, Ariane Beigneux, Robert Baxter, Ann Toulmin-Rothe,* North Light, 1974.

Illustrator: Katherine B. Shippen, *Bright Design,* Viking, 1949; Eric P. Swenson, *South Sea Shilling,* Viking, 1952.

SIDELIGHTS: Charles Michael Daugherty's first book was *So Sailors Say,* of which the *New York Times* commented: "This is a first book that promises well. The author's style is pleasant and easy and he combines an interesting, swiftly moving tale with enough practical information about boat building and sailing to encourage any boy who lives near a pond to follow Davey's example and build a boat of his own." *Street of Ships,* his second effort, was reviewed by a *Books* critic, who wrote: "The straightforwardness of the story is convincing; the events are so striking that a lurid style would have spoiled them. As for South Street itself, the special charm of that waterfront pervades the story, and inspires most of its line drawings of the period." The *New York Times* added, "Mr. Daugherty has the knack of telling a lively tale that sustains the interest; he knows ships and writes of them with contagious enthusiasm."

Speaking of *Let 'Em Roll,* the *New York Herald Tribune* wrote: "The style is brisk, and the sketches are excellent and helpfully factual at the right places. Any boy of about twelve who is interested in movies from any angle will be absorbed. This is no very special piece of good writing, and the adventure is, of course, a fantastic bit of luck. But it is good to suggest that boys take an attitude toward the movies which is both critical and creative." The *New York Times* added; "In a pleasing style, mature but never heavy, the author succeeds, though his central character sometimes seems secondary to the information."

The *Chicago Tribune* review of *Where the Condor Nests* included: "Charles Daugherty, the author, and Peter Winkler, the young man in his book, both joined archaeological expeditions as photographers. As a result the reader gets the benefit of imagination and reality blended very neatly, with adventure coming out on top." *Kirkus* commented; "A fanciful story set in Peru combines photography, archaeology, and illegal treasure hunting for the stuff of its adventure, but the result is over dressed melodrama rather than real excitement."

Mirror with a Memory was reviewed by a *New York Times* critic who called it "a broad and stimulating introduction for the young to the whole of photography. The emphasis throughout is on developing individual ability to see and to feel more than the obvious and to produce photographs that have significance and beauty."

The *Christian Science Monitor* called *The Great Archaeologists* "a lively history of the development of modern archaeology told in terms of the men who contributed to its early days. Each chapter has its suspense and climax, each its appeal to spirited young adventurers." It then described *Robert Goddard: Trail Blazer to the Stars:* "The life story of America's greatest rocket pioneer, Robert Goddard, written by Charles Daugherty and illustrated by his father, James, reads like a joint labor of love. Youngsters nine and up will find it warm, humorous, and often moving, yet compact and succinct."

AVOCATIONAL INTERESTS: Traveling.

BIOGRAPHICAL/CRITICAL SOURCES: *New York Times,* June 29, 1941, August 2, 1942, May 14, 1950; *Books,* May 10, 1942; *New York Herald Tribune Book Review,* May 7, 1950; *Kirkus,* July 1, 1955; *Chicago Sunday Tribune,* November 13, 1955; *New York Times Book Review,* October 18, 1959; *Christian Science Monitor,* November 14, 1963, December 31, 1964.*

* * *

DAUGHERTY, James (Henry) 1889-1974

PERSONAL: Born June 1, 1889, in Asheville, N.C.; son of Charles M. and Susan Peyton (Telfair) Daugherty; married Sonia Medwedeff (a children's author), 1913; children: Charles M. (Chris). *Education:* Attended Cocoran School of Art and studied art with Frank Brangwyn in London. *Residence:* Westport, Conn.

CAREER: Author and illustrator of books for children. Early jobs included camouflaging ships and designing war posters for the Navy during World War I, and mural painting on public buildings. *Member:* Author's Guild, P.E.N., Silvermine Guild. *Awards, honors:* Runner-up for the Caldecott Medal, 1939, for *Andy and the Lion,* and 1957, for *Gillespie and the Guards* (the latter written by Benjamin Elkin); Newberry Medal, 1940, for *Daniel Boone.*

WRITINGS—All self-illustrated: *Andy and the Lion,* Viking, 1938, reprinted, 1970; *Daniel Boone,* Viking, 1939, reprinted, 1966; *Poor Richard,* Viking, 1941, reprinted, 1966; *Abraham Lincoln,* Viking, 1943, reprinted, 1966; *An Outline of Government in Connecticut,* Case, Lockwood, 1944, 7th edition, revised, 1968; *The Wild, Wild West,* D. McKay, 1948; *The Landing of the Pilgrims,* Random House, 1950; *Of Courage Undaunted: Across the Continent with Lewis and Clark,* Viking, 1951, reprinted, 1967; *Trappers and Traders of the Far West,* Random House, 1952; *Marcus and Narcissa Whitman: Pioneers of Oregon,* Viking, 1953; *The Magna Charta,* Random House, 1956; *West of Boston,* Viking, 1956; *The Picnic,* Viking, 1958; *William Blake,* Viking, 1960.

Illustrator: Richard H. Horne, *King Penguin,* Macmillan, 1925; Stewart E. White, *Daniel Boone, Wilderness Scout,* Doubleday, 1926; Arthur T. Quiller-Couch, *Splendid Spur,* Doran, 1927; Washington Irving, *Knickerbocker's History of New York,* Doubleday, 1928; Arthur Conan Doyle, *White Company,* Harper, 1928; Carl Sandburg, *Abe Lincoln Grows Up,* Harcourt, 1928; William Shakespeare, *Three Comedies,* Harcourt, 1929; Harriet B. Stowe, *Uncle Tom's Cabin,* Coward-McCann, 1929; The Bible, *Kingdom, and the Power, and the Glory,* Knopf, 1929; Stephen Vincent Benet, *John Brown's Body,* Doubleday, 1930; C. Sandburg, *Early Moon,* Junior Literary Guild, 1930, reprinted, Harcourt, 1958; W. Irving, *Bold Dragoon,* Knopf, 1930, reprinted, 1958.

Francis Parkman, *Oregon Trail,* Farrar, Straus, 1931; Benvenuto Cellini, *Memoirs* (translated from the Italian by Robert H. Cust), Duffield, 1932; Sonia M. Daugherty, *Mashinka's Secret,* F. A. Stokes, 1932; Mark Twain, *Adventures of Tom Sawyer,* Harper, 1932; S. M. Daugherty, *Vanka's Donkey,* F. A. Stokes, 1940; Cornelia Lynde Meigs, *Call of the Mountain,* Little, Brown, 1940; Margaret I. Ross, *Morgan's Fourth Son,* Harper, 1940; S. M. Daugherty, *Wings of Glory,* Oxford University Press, 1940; Charles Dickens, *Barnaby Rudge,* Heritage, 1941; S. M. Daugherty, *Way of an Eagle,* Oxford University Press, 1941; The Bible, *In the Beginning,* Oxford University Press, 1941; Willis Thornton, *Almanac for Americans,* Greenburg, 1941; Daniel A. Poling, compiler, *Treasury of the Best-Loved Hymns,* Greenburg, 1942.

Irwin Shapiro, *Yankee Thunder,* Messner, 1944, reprinted, 1966; Abraham Lincoln, *Lincoln's Gettysburg Address,* A. Whitman, 1947; I. Shapiro, *Joe Magarac and His U.S.A. Citizen Papers,* Messner, 1948; Alfred Powers, *Long Way to Frisco,* Little, Brown, 1951; David Appel, *Comanche,* World Publishing, 1951; S. M. Daugherty, *Ten Brave Men,* Lippincott, 1951; S. M. Daugherty, *Ten Brave Women,* Lippincott, 1953; Benjamin Elkin, *Loudest Noise in the World,* Viking, 1954; Earl S. Miers, *Rainbow Book of American History,* World Publishing, 1955, revised edition, 1968; B. Elkin, *Gillespie and the Guards,* Viking, 1956; (and editor) *Walt Whitman's America,* World Publishing, 1964; (and editor) *Henry David Thoreau: A Man for Our Time,* Viking, 1967; Ralph Waldo Emerson, *The Sound of Trumpets,* Viking, 1971.

SIDELIGHTS: Daugherty spent his early childhood on a farm in southern Indiana and a small town in southern Ohio. Surrounded by the quiet wildlife of the South, one of the author-illustrator's fondest memories was of his grandfather telling him tales of Daniel Boone. Many years later, quite by coincidence, Daugherty's first assignment as a book illustrator was to draw pictures for Stewart Edward White's *Daniel Boone.*

As a young man studying art in London, Daugherty had his first taste of Walt Whitman's writings. It filled him with the desire to return to America, and by 1964, the author-illustrator, undertook the task of editing and illustrating *Walt Whitman's America.* A *New York Times* book reviewer wrote that Daugherty "gives well-selected excerpts from [Whitman's] poems . . . and prose. . . . He then illustrates these passages with magnificent drawings which convey the spirit of the poet's themes. . . . These drawings, bold, heroic, and colorful, interpret the poetry and prose better than words. . . ."

Daugherty's well-known children's story *Andy and the Lion* has been produced as an educational movie, 1955, and filmstrip, 1959, by Weston Woods Studios.

BIOGRAPHICAL/CRITICAL SOURCES: (For children) Elizabeth Rider Montgomery, *Story Behind Modern Books,* Dodd, 1949; *Newbery Medal Books, 1922-1955,* edited by Bertha E. (Mahony) Miller and E. W. Field, Horn Book, 1955; *New York Times Book Review,* October 11, 1964; *Newsweek,* November 1, 1965.

OBITUARIES—New York Times, February 22, 1974; *Publishers Weekly,* March 18, 1974; *Current Biography,* April, 1974.*

(Died February 21, 1974)

* * *

DAVES, Delmer Lawrence   1904(?)-1977

1904(?)—August 17, 1977; American film director, producer, and screenwriter. During his forty-year career, Daves worked on eighty films for Warner Bros. and Twentieth Century-Fox. Among his best-known films are "Destination Tokyo," "Dark Passage," "The Hanging Tree," and "An Affair to Remember." He died in La Jolla, Calif. Obituaries: *New York Times,* August 19, 1977; *Washington Post,* August 19, 1977.

* * *

DAVIDSON, Marion
See GARIS, Howard Roger

* * *

DAVIDSON, Max D.   1899(?)-1977

1899(?)—September 9, 1977; American rabbi and author. Davidson was active in several Jewish organizations including the Rabbinical Assembly, the Synagogue Council of America, and the Jewish Welfare Board. He wrote *The Golden Chain* and was a frequent contributor to *Commentary.* Davidson died in Perth Amboy, N.J. Obituaries: *New York Times,* September 11, 1977.

* * *

DAVIDSON, Philip (Grant)   1902-

PERSONAL: Born May 28, 1902, in Omaha, Neb.; son of Philip Grant, Sr. and Jessie (Hartwell) Davidson; married Jane Campbell Foot, August 10, 1922; children: Ada Page Davidson Clayton, Philip Grant III. *Education:* University of Mississippi, B.S. (honors), 1922; University of Chicago, M.A., 1925, Ph.D., 1929. *Politics:* Democrat. *Religion:* Episcopalian. *Home:* 3830 Cross Creek Rd., Nashville, Tenn. 37215.

CAREER: Agnes Scott College, Decatur, Ga., professor of history, 1928-42; Vanderbilt University, Nashville, Tenn., professor of history and dean of graduate school, 1942-51; provost of undergraduate colleges, 1948-51; University of Louisville, Louisville, Ky., professor of history and president of the university, 1951-68, emeritus professor and emeritus president, 1968—. President of Conference of Deans of Southern Graduate Schools, 1949, and Southern Universities Conference, 1957-58; program adviser to Ford Foundation in Bangkok, 1968-73; consultant to board of trustees of Shakertown at Pleasant Hill.

MEMBER: Organization of American Historians, American Historical Association, English-Speaking Union, Association of Urban Universities (president, 1957-58), Southern

Historical Association, Association of Consultants in Education (Florida). *Awards, honors:* Litt.D. from University of the South, 1954, and Bellarmine College, 1967; LL.D. from University of Akron, 1960, and University of Kentucky, 1965; officer of Order of the British Empire, 1960; D.H. from University of Louisville, 1974.

WRITINGS: (Editor and contributor) *The History of Georgia,* Science Research Associates, 1940; *Propaganda and the American Revolution,* University of North Carolina Press, 1941, reprinted, Norton, 1975. Contributor to professional journals.

SIDELIGHTS: Davidson comments: "After forty-two I became involved more and more in university administration and my study and writing has been in that field. I am currently educational consultant to the trustees of Shakertown at Pleasant Hill, Ky., a restored Shaker Village, and am doing my studying in that field."

* * *

DAWSON, Richard E(vans) 1939-

PERSONAL: Born March 2, 1939, in Columbus, Ohio; son of Harold H. (an engineer) and Katharine Anne (a preschool teacher; maiden name, Evans) Dawson; married Karen S. Smith (a political scientist), August 8, 1965; children: Andrew E., Kathryn M., Eric D. *Education:* Ohio Wesleyan University, B.A., 1960; Northwestern University, Ph.D., 1963. *Home:* 6624 Waterman, St. Louis, Mo. 63130. *Office:* Department of Political Science, Washington University, St. Louis, Mo. 63130.

CAREER: Washington University, St. Louis, Mo., assistant professor, 1963-66, associate professor, 1966-73, professor of political science, 1973—. Political science program director for National Science Foundation, 1976-78; election consultant for American Broadcasting Co.—Television, 1968-74. *Member:* American Political Science Association, American Association for Public Opinion Research, American Association for the Advancement of Science, Midwest Political Science Association. *Awards, honors:* Ford Foundation fellowship, 1968-69; National Science Association grant, 1970-71.

WRITINGS: (Contributor) *The American Party Systems,* Oxford University Press, 1967; (contributor) *Political Science Annual,* Bobbs-Merrill, 1967; (with Kenneth Prewitt) *Political Socialization,* Little, Brown, 1969, 2nd edition (with Prewitt and wife, Karen S. Dawson), 1977; (contributor) *Politics in the American States,* Little, Brown, 1972; *Public Opinion and Contemporary Disarray,* Harper, 1973. Contributor to political science journals.

* * *

DEACON, Richard
See McCORMICK, (George) Donald King

* * *

DEAN, Stanley (Rochelle) 1908-

PERSONAL: Born February 13, 1908, in Stamford, Conn.; son of Jacob and Gerda (Rochelle) Dean; married Belle Katzman, March 4, 1934 (died, 1966); married Marion Jamison, November 7, 1967; children: (first marriage) Michael Lewis, Lori Dean Schonfeld. *Education:* University of Michigan, B.S. (cum laude), 1930, M.D. (cum laude), 1934. *Home and office:* 1800 Northeast 114th St., Miami, Fla. 33181. *Agent:* Ruth Hagy Brod Literary Agency, 15 Park Ave., New York, N.Y. 10016.

CAREER: Taunton State Hospital, Taunton, Mass., resident in psychiatry, 1935-37; Fairfield State Hospital, Fairfield, Conn., senior physician, 1937-40; private practice of psychiatry in Stamford, Conn., 1940-65; private practice of psychiatry, specializing in family and marriage counseling, Miami, Fla., 1964—; clinical professor of psychiatry at University of Florida, Gainesville, University of Miami, Miami, 1965—. Founder of Research in Schizophrenia Endowment (RISE). *Member:* American Psychiatric Association (fellow), American College of Psychiatry (fellow), Royal College of Medicine, Royal College of Psychiatry.

WRITINGS: Schizophrenia: The First Ten Dean Awards, MSS Corp., 1972; *Psychiatry and Mysticism,* Nelson-Hall, 1975. Contributor of over seventy-five articles and book chapters on psychiatry and related subjects.

WORK IN PROGRESS: Psychiatry in the Bible; Food and Religion; Sex from Eight to Eighty.

* * *

DEASON, Hilary J(ohn) 1903-

PERSONAL: Born May 21, 1903, Park City, Utah; son of John A. (a machinist) and Meta Marie (Sorensen) Deason; married Hetty Bourne, April 15, 1944 (deceased). *Education:* University of Michigan, A.B., 1927, A.M., 1928, Ph.D. (zoology), 1936. *Religion:* Episcopalian. *Office:* American Association for the Advancement of Science, 1515 Massachusetts Ave. N.W., Washington, D.C. 20005.

CAREER: U.S. Bureau of Fisheries, Ann Arbor, Mich., aquatic biologist, 1928-41; U.S. Fish and Wildlife Service, Washington, D.C., associate aquatic biologist, 1941-43, senior aquatic biologist, 1943-46, assistant to deputy coordinator of fisheries, 1943-45, chief officer for foreign activities, 1945-52; Episcopal Diocese of Washington, Washington, D.C., research consultant, 1953-55, secretary, 1956—; American Association for the Advancement of Science, Washington, D.C., bibliographer and director of libraries, 1955-71. Technical advisor to U.S. delegation, International Whaling Conference, 1945, 1946, and International Fishery Conference, 1948, 1949, 1951. *Member:* American Association for the Advancement of Science (fellow), National Science Teachers Association, National Education Association, American Library Association, American Society of Zoologists, Sigma Xi.

WRITINGS—All published by American Association for the Advancement of Science, except as indicated: (Compiler) *The Travelling High School Science Library,* 1955-57; (compiler) *An Inexpensive Science Library,* 1957, 5th edition, 1961; (compiler) *The AAAS Science Book List,* 1959, revised edition published as *The AAAS Science Book List for Young Adults,* 1964, 3rd edition published as *The AAAS Science Book List: A Selected and Annotated List of Science and Mathematics Books for Secondary School Students, College Undergraduates and Nonspecialists,* 1970; (compiler with Ruth N. Foy) *The Science Book List for Children,* 1960, 2nd edition (with Nora Beust) published as *The AAAS Science Book List for Children,* 1963, 3rd edition (sole compiler) published as *The AAAS Science Book List for Children: A Selected and Annotated List of Science and Mathematics Books for Children in Elementary Schools, and for Children's Collections in Public Libraries,* 1972; (compiler with William B. Blacklow) *Careers in Science,* 1961, 2nd edition, 1962; (editor with Blacklow) *A Guide to Science Reading,* New American Library, 1963, 2nd revised edition (sole editor), 1966.

Editor, *Science Books: A Quarterly Review,* for American Association for the Advancement of Science, 1965.*

d'EASUM, Cedric (Godfrey) 1907-
(Dick d'Easum)

PERSONAL: Born April 29, 1907, in Canada; came to the United States in 1910, naturalized citizen; son of Basil C. (a priest) and Ethel A. (Stacey) d'Easum; married Mary E. Williamson, June 18, 1935. *Education:* University of Idaho, B.A., 1930; also attended Colorado State University and University of Wyoming. *Politics:* Republican. *Religion:* Episcopalian. *Home and office:* 1086 Krall St., Boise, Idaho 83702.

CAREER: Idaho Statesman, Boise, reporter and author of column "Two Cents Worth," 1932-43; State Fish and Game Department, Boise, Idaho, news director, 1943-49; University of Idaho, Extension Service, Boise, editor, 1949-72; writer, 1972—. Member of Boise Green Belt Committee, 1974—. *Military service:* U.S. National Guard, 1926-29. U.S. Army Reserve, Infantry, 1930-40. *Member:* Kiwanis (president, 1972), Masons (state grand historian, 1969), Elks.

WRITINGS—Under name Dick d'Easum: *Fragments of Villainy* (essays), Caxton, 1959; *Sawtooth Tales,* Caxton, 1977. Author of weekly column in *Idaho Statesman,* 1943-76.

WORK IN PROGRESS: Biography of Permeal French, former dean of women at University of Idaho.

* * *

d'EASUM, Dick
See d'EASUM, Cedric (Godfrey)

* * *

DeBAKEY, Michael E(llis) 1908-

PERSONAL: Born September 7, 1908, in Lake Charles, La.; son of Shaker Morris (a businessman) and Raheega (Zorba) DeBakey; married Diana Cooper (a nurse), October 15, 1936 (died, 1972); married Katrin Fehlhaber, August, 1975; children: (first marriage) Michael Maurice, Ernest Ochsner, Barry Edward, Denis Alton; (second marriage) Olga Katerina. *Education:* Tulane University, B.S., 1930, M.D., 1932, M.S., 1935. *Politics:* Democrat. *Religion:* Episcopalian. *Home:* 5323 Cherokee, Houston, Tex. 77005. *Office:* College of Medicine, Baylor University, 1200 Moursund, Houston, Tex. 77030.

CAREER: Charity Hospital, New Orleans, La., intern, 1932-33, resident with Tulane Surgical Service, 1933-35; University of Strasbourg, Strasbourg, France, resident, 1935-36; University of Heidelberg, Heidelberg, Germany, resident, 1936; Tulane University, New Orleans, instructor, 1937-40, assistant professor, 1940-46, associate professor of surgery, 1946-48; Baylor University, Houston, Tex., professor of surgery and chairman of department, 1948—, distinguished service professor, 1968—, director of National Heart and Blood Vessel Research and Demonstration Center, 1976—, vice-president for medical affairs and chief executive officer of College of Medicine, 1968-69, president of college, 1969—. Certified by National Board of Medical Examiners, 1933; diplomate of American Board of Surgery, 1939, and American Board of Thoracic Surgery, 1948. Clinical professor at University of Texas, Houston, 1952—; distinguished professor at Texas A & M University, 1972—; director of Cardiovascular Research and Training Center at Houston's Methodist Hospital, 1964-75. Surgeon at several hospitals. Member of numerous advisory boards and executive committees of hospitals, medical organizations, governmental bodies, and universities in the United States and abroad. *Military service:* U.S. Army Reserve, began as assistant director, became director of Surgical Consultants Division, Office of the Surgeon General, active duty, 1942-46; became colonel; received Legion of Merit.

MEMBER: Member, honorary member, or executive member of about one hundred medical organizations throughout the world, including International Cardiovascular Society (president, 1959; North American president, 1964), World Medical Association (associate member), and American Heart Association (fellow; founding member of several councils); member of numerous social clubs and fraternal organizations. *Awards, honors:* Honorary degrees from more than twenty colleges and universities, including University of Lyon, University of Michigan, Tulane University, and University of Cincinnati; recipient of over fifty awards from scientific and medical organizations throughout the world, including Albert Lasker Award for Clinical Research, 1963; Alexander Vasilievich Vishnevsky Medal from Academy of Sciences (Soviet Union), 1965; award from American Medical Writers Association, 1966, for textbooks; International Dag Hammarskjold Prize (Milan), 1967; Eleanor Roosevelt Humanities Award, 1969.

WRITINGS: (With Robert A. Kilduffe) *The Blood Bank and the Technique and Therapeutics of Transfusions,* Mosby, 1942; (with Gilbert W. Beebe) *Battle Casualties: Incidence, Mortality, and Logistic Considerations,* C. C Thomas, 1952; (editor with Alton Ochsner) *Christopher's Minor Surgery,* 7th edition (DeBakey was not associated with earlier editions), Saunders, 1955, 8th edition, 1959; (editor with Daniel C. Elkin, and contributor) *Vascular Surgery in World War II,* Office of the Surgeon General, Department of the Army, 1955; (with Bernard M. Cohen) *Buerger's Disease: A Follow-Up Study of World War II Army Cases,* C. C Thomas, 1963; *A Surgeon's Diary of a Visit to China,* Phoenix Newspapers, 1974; (with Antonio Gotto) *The Living Heart,* McKay, 1977.

Contributor of chapters to over one hundred fifty medical textbooks. Contributor of nearly a thousand articles to medical journals in the United States and abroad. Editor or member of editorial staff of more than twenty professional journals.

SIDELIGHTS: DeBakey is one of the most prominent physicians in the United States. He was the surgeon who, in 1966, implanted the first artificial heart in a man. As early as 1936, he was among the first physicians to educate the public regarding the relationship of cigarette smoking to lung cancer. Since then, he has been responsible for many surgical procedures and techniques within his specialty. Out of necessity he has devised his own surgical instruments.

Unlike many surgeons, however, DeBakey does not confine himself to the operating room and the classroom, but is concerned about the role of the physician in society. His name is known all over the world; he has visited the Soviet Union and China, and has broadcast over Voice of America.

AVOCATIONAL INTERESTS: Music, hunting, fishing.

BIOGRAPHICAL/CRITICAL SOURCES: Time, June 22, 1959; *New York Post,* November 1, 1963.

* * *

DeBERARD, Ella 1900-

PERSONAL: Born October 22, 1900, in Laurens, S.C.; daughter of Edwin Fuller and Loulee (Hudgens) Teague; married Philip Edwin DeBerard (a banker), April 13, 1922; children: Philip Edwin, Jr., Jeanne DeBerard Bakken, Anne

DeBerard Brown. *Education:* Attended Northwestern University, 1920-22. *Politics:* Democrat. *Religion:* Episcopal. *Home:* 620 Tuxedo Ave., DeLand, Fla. 32720.

CAREER: Writer. Member of DeLand Players at Shoestring Theatre (first president); teacher of creative writing to children and senior citizens; active in community affairs; public lecturer. *Member:* National League of American Pen Women, Inc. (Florida president, 1968-70), Authors League of America (member of Dramatists Guild), Florida Watercolor Society, Florida Theatre Conference (life member), West Volusia Artists.

WRITINGS: Steamboats in the Hyacinths, College Publishing Co., 1954; *Retirement for Two,* Everett/Edwards, 1964.

Plays: "Love and Politics" (three-act comedy), first produced in DeLand, Fla., at Shoestring Theatre, 1951; "Thelma" (three-act comedy), first produced in DeLand, Fla., at Shoestring Theatre, 1952; (co-author) "Dessie Bar the Door" (three-act comedy), first produced in DeLand, Fla., at Shoestring Theatre, 1955; "The Magic Mushroom" (three-act fantasy), first produced in Daytona Beach, Fla., at Daytona Plaza Hotel, 1961; "Vacancy" (three-act tragi-comedy), first produced in DeLand, Fla., at Shoestring Theatre, May 9, 1963; "The Sexagenarians" (three-act comedy), first produced in DeLand, Fla., at Shoestring Theatre, May 17, 1972.

Also author with Frank Yakots of "The Last Estate," a three-act musical, as yet neither published nor produced. Contributor of articles and a story to *Woman's Day, Motor Boating,* and newspapers.

WORK IN PROGRESS: A novel (social commentary); research toward alleviating boredom in senior citizens' activities; "The Matriarch," a three-act play; a collection of poems.

SIDELIGHTS: DeBerard told *CA:* "I became interested in playwriting when I was a student at Northwestern University. A professor asked for a show of hands of those who would write a play for the freshman class. I held up my hand—looked around—and was the only one who volunteered! I bought a book on how to write a play, and the result was 'The Fool,' a one-act play." In addition to her writing, she also enjoys painting, and has lectured widely on adjusting to retirement.

* * *

DE BORCHGRAVE, Arnaud 1926-

PERSONAL: Born October 26, 1926, in Brussels, Belguim; son of Baudouin (a diplomat) and Audrey (a writer; maiden name, Townshend) de Borchegrave; married Eileen Ritschel, March 30, 1959 (divorced, 1969); married Alexandra Villard (a photographer), May 10, 1969; children: Arnaud, Jr., Trisha. *Education:* Education in England and Belguim. *Residence:* Geneva, Switzerland. *Agent:* Harry Walker, 350 Fifth Ave., New York, N.Y. 10001. *Office: Newsweek,* 444 Madison Ave., New York, N.Y. 10022.

CAREER: United Press International, New York City, chief of Brussels bureau, 1948-50; *Newsweek,* New York City, bureau chief in Paris, 1951-54, foreign editor, 1955-59, chief European correspondent, 1959-62, foreign editor, 1962-63, chief foreign correspondent, 1963—. Notable assignments include coverage of the Marshall Plan, the creation of NATO, twelve wars, including seven tours of duty in Vietnam, confrontations in South Africa, and interviews with foreign leaders, including Golda Meir, Anwar Sadat, Gamal

Nasser, and Levi Eshkol. *Military service:* British Navy, 1942-46. *Member:* United Nations Correspondents Association, Anglo-American Press Club, Travellers Club, Racquet and Tennis Club (New York). *Awards, honors:* Overseas Press Club Prize for best magazine reporting from abroad, 1969, 1971, and 1975; Page One Award for foreign corresponding from New York Newspaper Guild, 1973, 1974, and 1975.

WRITINGS: Toward a Wiser Colossus, Purdue University Press, 1972.

* * *

DE BRUNHOFF, Laurent
See BRUNHOFF, Laurent de

* * *

DEEMER, Charles (Robert, Jr.) 1939-

PERSONAL: Born October 26, 1939, in Norfolk, Va.; son of Charles Robert and Florence (Lear) Deemer; married Judi Dell, November, 1960 (marriage ended, 1968); married Polly Stewart (a folklorist), August 19, 1968; children: Christine. *Education:* Attended California Institute of Technology, 1957-59; Pasadena City College, A.A., 1964; University of California, Los Angeles, B.A., 1966; University of Oregon, M.F.A., 1973. *Religion:* "Brunist." *Home and office address:* Route 5, Box 478, Salisbury, Md. 21801.

CAREER: Northwest Mobile-Home News, Portland, Ore., editor, 1967-69; University of Oregon, Eugene, part-time instructor in English, 1969-71; free-lance writer, 1971—. Part-time disc jockey on WSSC-Radio, 1974—. Actor in local theater productions; performs folk songs at benefit performances. *Military service:* U.S. Army, Russian linguist for Security Agency, 1959-62. *Member:* Phi Beta Kappa. *Awards, honors:* Fellowship from University of Colorado's writers' conference, 1971, for the play "The Profession"; Ward Foundation fellowship, 1976-77.

WRITINGS: Reports and Confessions (stories), privately printed, 1973.

Plays: "Above the Fire" (one-act), first produced in Eugene, Ore., at University of Oregon, February, 1970; "The Profession" (two-act), first produced in Eugene at University of Oregon, March, 1971; "Sir Lancelot and the Dragon" (one-act; adapted from Russian), first produced in Eugene at University of Oregon, August, 1971; "The Library of Our Lives" (television serial), first produced in Eugene, Ore., on PL-3 TV, January-March, 1972; "The Flooding of West Rapids" (one-act), first produced in Eugene at Barn Theatre, July, 1972; "The Battle of the Ages" (two-act), first produced in Salisbury, Md., at Salisbury State College, February, 1976.

Unproduced plays: (With Mark Falcoff) "A Brown Man's Burden," 1973; "Mercy to the Patriot," 1976; "The Death Cycle" (one-act plays; contains "The Stiff," "The Obscene Interruptions of War," and "The Death of Ten Yin-Feng"), 1975.

Work represented in *Best American Short Stories,* 1971, 1972, 1974. Contributor to professional journals, to *New Republic,* and to newspapers. Feature writer for *Portland Oregonian* and *Northwest,* 1966-73.

WORK IN PROGRESS: The Pardon (tentative title), a novel set in Maryland, dealing with the return of a draft dodger to the United States after President Carter's pardon; short stories with a local setting; a play with a local setting.

SIDELIGHTS: Deemer writes: "I came to writing slowly, via mathematics. Having arrived at writing, I had a long interest in avant-garde writing; that is, work which takes major narrative risks: as a result, I have six unpublished novels, three of which I still 'own up to'—*Farther You Go, Faster I Come,* 1967, *Necrophiles,* 1969, and *The Death of the Rainbow,* 1973. My interest in fiction has slowly moved, perhaps from the discouragement of the earlier work, to more traditional story-telling modes. But in fact, my whole career is in flux at the moment; sometimes I think my interest (flirtation) with Zen will lead to Silence and the abandonment of writing entirely.

"My motivations bewilder me, my circumstances being invisibility. These are questions best ignored, I think. I tend to write what matters to me in fall and winter; in spring and summer, I generally drink too much, and otherwise pass the time until the next season.

"I find American contemporary literature rather unimpressive, although I am convinced the best work remains invisible. I prefer the fiction of South America, the drama of Eastern Europe.

"My thematic interests have long centered on race-war: that is, on the conditions of it, the parameters of a racist society: note that I am white. Whatever my ill-defined politics, I am anti-capitalist. But I am perhaps only anti-*corporate*-capitalist, since there is a good deal of the rugged individualist in me. Hence, my fifties 'Oldies' radio show and the emergence of white rock-n-roll from black rhythm-n-blues, is one of my central focuses in fiction."

*   *   *

de FOX, Lucia Ugaro
    See LOCKART, Lucia A(licia) Fox

*   *   *

DeGRAFT, Joseph Coleman   1932-

PERSONAL: Born in 1932, in Ghana. *Office:* UNESCO, POB 30592, Nairobi, Kenya.

CAREER: Novelist, poet, and playwright. Founder of the Drama and Theatre Studies Division, University of Ghana, Legon, and director of the Ghana Drama Studio, Accra, in the 1950's; teacher of English for UNESCO in Nairobi, Kenya, in the 1970's.

WRITINGS: Sons and Daughters (play), Oxford University Press, 1964; *The Secret of Opokuwa: The Success Story of the Girl with a Big State Secret* (novel), Anowuo Educational Publications, 1967; *Visitors from the Past* (novel), Anowuo Educational Publications, 1968; *Through a Film Darkly* (play; first produced as "Visitors from the Past" in Accra, Ghana, at Ghana Dance Studio, September, 1962), Oxford University Press, 1970.

Unpublished plays: "Ananse and the Glue Man," first produced in 1961; "Old Kweku," first produced in 1965.

Also author of "Hamile," an adaptation of Shakespeare's *Hamlet,* first produced by National Educational Television, 1970. Work represented in *Messages: Poems from Ghana,* edited by Awoonor and Adali-Mortty, Heinemann, 1971. Contributor to *Okyeame.**

*   *   *

DE HAAN, Margaret
    See FREED, Margaret De Haan

DELANY, Kevin F(rancis) X(avier)   1927-

PERSONAL: Born August 26, 1927, in Brooklyn, N.Y.; son of John J. (a physician) and Anna C. (Gallagher) Delany. *Education:* Williams College, A.B., 1950; Columbia University, M.S., 1952, M.A., 1962. *Home:* 3025 Orchard Lane N.W., Washington, D.C. 20007. *Office:* American Broadcasting Co. News, 1124 Connecticut Ave. N.W., Washington, D.C. 20036.

CAREER/WRITINGS: New York World Telegram & Sun, New York City, reporter and television columnist, 1955-57; Columbia Broadcasting System, Inc. (CBS) News, New York City, reporter and assignment editor, 1957-63, Hong Kong correspondent, 1958-59; Peace Corps, Washington, D.C., evaluator of overseas programs, 1963-65, deputy and acting director of East Asia and Pacific region, 1965-68, director in Thailand, 1968-70; American Broadcasting Co. (ABC) News, Washington, D.C., bureau chief in Vietnam, 1971-73, director of television news in Washington bureau, 1973—. Notable assignments include coverage of Cuban missile crisis and early space shots for CBS, the North Vietnamese Easter offense and fall of Saigon for ABC. *Military service:* U.S. Navy, 1945-46, 1952-55.

*   *   *

DELCROIX, Carlo   1896-1977

1896—October 25, 1977; Italian author best known for *Fiori di Sacrificio.* Delcroix became a champion of handicapped war veterans after losing his sight and hands in World War I. He died in Rome, Italy. Obituaries: *New York Times,* October 27, 1977.

*   *   *

DELDERFIELD, Ronald Frederick   1912-1972

PERSONAL: Born February 12, 1912, in Greenwich, London, England; married May Evans, 1936; children: one son, one daughter. *Education:* Educated in England. *Residence:* Sidmouth, Devon, England.

CAREER: Author, playwright, and newspaperman. Worked in various capacities on the country newspaper that his father owned, 1929-40. *Military service:* Royal Air Force, 1940-45, as a public relations officer in Europe.

WRITINGS—Plays: (With Basil Thomas) *This Is My Life* (three-act), C. H. Fox, 1944; *Peace Comes to Peckham* (three-act), Samuel French, 1948; *All Over Town* (three-act), Samuel French, 1948; *Worm's Eye View* (three-act), Samuel French, 1948; *The Queen Came By* (three-act), Baker, 1949; *Sailors Beware* (one-act), H. F. W. Deane, 1950; *Waggonload o' Monkeys* (three-act), H. F. W. Deane, 1952; *The Old Lady of Cheadle* (one-act), H. F. W. Deane, 1952; *Misow! Misow!* (one-act), Samuel French, 1952; *Made to Measure* (one-act), Samuel French, 1952; *The Bride Wore an Opal Ring* (one-act), Samuel French, 1952; *Absent Lover* (one-act), Samuel French, 1953; *Smoke in the Valley* (one-act), Samuel French, 1953; *Spark in the Juince* (three-act), F. de Wolfe & R. Stone, 1953; *The Testimonial* (one-act), Samuel French, 1953; *The Orchard Walls* (three-act), Samuel French, 1954; *And Then There Were None* (one-act), Samuel French, 1954; *The Guinea-Pigs* (one-act), H. F. W. Deane, 1954; *Home Is the Hunted* (one-act), Samuel French, 1954; *Where There's a Will* (three-act), Samuel French, 1954; *The Rounderlay Tradition,* H.F.W. Deane, 1954; *Ten till Five* (one-act), F. de Wolfe & R. Stone, 1954; *Musical Switch* (one-act), F. de Wolfe & R. Stone, 1954; *The Offending Hand* (three-act), H. F. W. Deane, 1955;

Uncle's Little Lapse (three-act), F. de Wolfe & R. Stone, 1955; *Flashpoint* (three-act), Samuel French, 1958; *The Mayerling Affair* (three-act), Samuel French, 1958; *Wild Mink* (one-act), Samuel French, 1962; *Once Aboard the Lugger* (three-act), Samuel French, 1962.

Histories: *Napoleon in Love,* Hodder & Stoughton, 1959, Little, Brown, 1960; *The March of the Twenty-Six: The Story of Napoleon's Marshals,* Hodder & Stoughton, 1962; *The Golden Millstones: Napoleon's Brothers and Sisters,* Weidenfeld & Nicolson, 1964, Harper, 1965; *Napoleon's Marshals,* Chilton Books, 1966; *The Retreat from Moscow,* Atheneum, 1967; *Imperial Sunset: The Fall of Napoleon, 1813-14,* Chilton, 1968.

Other writings: *These Clicks Made History,* Raleigh Press, 1946; *Seven Men of Gascony* (novel), Bobbs-Merrill, 1949, reprinted, Simon & Schuster, 1973; *Farewell the Tranquil,* Dutton, 1950 (published in England as *Farewell the Tranquil Mind,* Hodder & Stoughton, 1950, reprinted, 1974); *Nobody Shouted Author* (autobiographical), W. Laurie, 1951; *Bird's Eye View* (autobiographical), Constable, 1954; *The Adventures of Ben Gunn* (based on Robert Louis Stevenson's *Treasure Island;* illustrated by William Stobbs), Hodder & Stoughton, 1956, published in America as *The Adventures of Ben Gunn: A Story of the Pirates of Treasure Island,* Bobbs-Merrill, 1957; *The Avenue Goes to War,* Hodder & Stoughton, 1958, Ballantine, 1964; *The Dreaming Suburb,* Ballantine, 1958; *Diana,* Putnam, 1960 (published in England as *There Was a Fair Maid Dwelling,* Hodder & Stoughton, 1960); *Stop at a Winner,* Hodder & Stoughton, 1961; *The Unjust Skies,* Hodder & Stoughton, 1962; *Mr. Sermon* (novel), Simon & Schuster, 1963 (published in England as *The Spring Madness of Mr. Sermon,* Hodder & Stoughton, 1963); (editor) *Tales Out of School: An Anthology of West Buckland Reminiscences, 1895-1963,* H. E. Warne, 1963; *Under an English Sky,* Hodder & Stoughton, 1964; *Too Few for Drums,* Simon & Schuster, 1964, reprinted, Pocket Books, 1975; *The Avenue* (originally published separately as *The Avenue Goes to War* and *The Dreaming Suburb*), Simon & Schuster, 1964, reprinted, Hodder & Stoughton, 1972.

The Horseman Riding, Hodder & Stoughton, 1966, Simon & Schuster, 1967; *Post of Honor,* Ballantine, 1966, reprinted, 1974; *Return Journey,* Simon & Schuster, 1967, reprinted, Pocket Books, 1975 (published in England as *Cheap Day Return,* Hodder & Stoughton, 1967, reprinted, Corgi Books, 1972); *For My Own Amusement* (autobiographical), Hodder & Stoughton, 1968, Simon & Schuster, 1972; *The Green Gauntlet,* Simon & Schuster, 1968; *Come Home Charlie and Face Them,* Hodder & Stoughton, 1969, published in America as *Charlie Come Home,* Simon & Schuster, 1976; *God Is an Englishman,* Simon & Schuster, 1970; *Overture for Beginners* (autobiographical), Hodder & Stoughton, 1970; *Theirs Was the Kingdom,* Simon & Schuster, 1971; *To Serve Them All My Days,* Simon & Schuster, 1972; *Give Us This Day,* Simon & Schuster, 1973.

SIDELIGHTS: Delderfield began his career as a writer after World War II. Since that time he estimated that he had written 4,000 words a day, every day of the year. One of his earliest novels was *Seven Men of Gascony,* a historical novel set during the Napoleonic wars. *A Christian Science Monitor* reviewer wrote: "Well conceived and well-executed, Mr. Delderfield's story of Napoleon's last six years pulses with the devotion of unnamed hundreds of thousands and the horrors of a Continent at war—all expressed in realistic terms of ordinary, naturally decent men. The *New York Herald Tribune* added: "The author has achieved a war chronicle of breadth and vigor admirably more devoted to the sources of human behavior than to the mechanics of warfare."

The *New York Times* found that Delderfield's book *Diana,* about a romance between a Cockney orphan and a wealthy heroine, "recaptures with refreshing simplicity the awkwardness, excitement, and delights of youth.... This is a charming novel both in its understanding of the ironic predicaments of the lovers and in their identification with an enchanted setting." A reviewer for the *New Yorker* commented: "A very long and romantic English novel with a run-of-the-mill air that does not really detract from its pale but solid virtues; it is a carefully written work, and has not only a plot that unravels smoothly but enough logic to leave the reader without anything to wonder about."

God Is an Englishman was one of Delderfield's last novels. The *New York Times Book Review* observed: "A cheerful anachronism in the world of letters, Mr. Delderfield writes with vigor, unceasing narrative drive and a high degree of craftsmanship. At his best he may remind one of Trollope, at his worst of Hugh Walpole.... He is a storyteller, which is no small thing to be. But he is not a novelist who can create characters so individual or so universal that they linger in the memory.... Although difficult to take seriously, [this book] provides a good bird's-eye view of Victorian England and contains numerous snippets of social history.... There is a place for the conventional, traditional, lively and amusing sort of fiction."

Delderfield's books have sold at least a million copies in the United States alone. According to Simon & Schuster, *God Is an Englishman* and *Theirs Was the Kingdom* have each sold over 65,000 copies in hardcover.

BIOGRAPHICAL/CRITICAL SOURCES: New York Herald Tribune, February 13, 1949; *Christian Science Monitor,* March 3, 1949; Ronald Frederick Delderfield, *Nobody Shouted Author,* Laurie, 1951; Delderfield, *Bird's Eye View: Autobiography,* Constable, 1954; *Kirkus Reviews,* June 15, 1960; *New Yorker,* September 17, 1960; *New York Times Book Review,* September 18, 1960, September 13, 1970; Delderfield, *Overture for Beginners,* Hodder & Stoughton, 1970; Delderfield, *For My Own Amusement,* Simon & Schuster, 1972.

OBITUARIES: New York Times, June 27, 1972; *Washington Post,* June 28, 1972; *National Observer,* July 8, 1972; *Newsweek,* July 10, 1972; *Publishers Weekly,* July 17, 1972.*

(Died June 24, 1972)

* * *

de LEEUW, Hendrik 1891-1977

1891—July 23, 1977; Dutch-born American traveler, lecturer, broadcaster, and author. He died in New York, N.Y. Obituaries: *New York Times,* July 25, 1977.

* * *

de LEIRIS, Alain 1922-

PERSONAL: Born August 7, 1922, in Paris, France; married wife, Mary (a slide curator), August 16, 1949; children: Daniel, Lucia. *Education:* Rhode Island School of Design, B.F.A., 1948; Harvard University, Ph.D., 1957. *Home:* 4009 Cleveland St., Kensington, Md. 20795. *Office:* Department of Art, University of Maryland, College Park, Md. 20742.

CAREER: University of the South, Sewanee, Tenn., assistant professor of art and chairman of department, 1955-58; Brandeis University, Waltham, Mass., assistant professor of art history, 1958-64; University of Maryland, College Park, professor of art history, 1965—. *Military service:* U.S. Army Air Forces, 1943-45; became second lieutenant. *Member:* College Art Association.

WRITINGS: The Drawings of Edouard Manet, University of California Press, 1969. Contributor to art history journals and exhibition catalogs.

WORK IN PROGRESS: Research on the nineteenth-century French painter Philippe Auguste Jeanron and on the French salon exhibitions of the same period.

SIDELIGHTS: De Leiris comments briefly: "I began my career as a painter, then developed an interest in art historical teaching and research. My painting activity is now avocational."

* * *

DELLA-PIANA, Gabriel M. 1926-

PERSONAL: Born April 4, 1926, in East Boston, Mass.; son of Leandro (a cabinet maker) and Elisa (Savini) Della-Piana; married Ilene Brown, and later Linda Thament (both marriages terminated); married third wife, Sarah Hatch; children: Joseph, Marla, Vernal Lee, Ralph, Risa, Gina, Ben, Dylan. *Education:* Brigham Young University, A.B., 1950; University of Illinois, M.S., 1953, Ph.D., 1956. *Politics:* Independent. *Residence:* Salt Lake City, Utah. *Office:* Department of Educational Psychology, University of Utah, Salt Lake City, Utah 84112.

CAREER: Elementary school teacher, and director of curriculum and guidance for public schools in Highwood, Ill., 1955-58; University of Utah, Salt Lake City, director and professor of educational psychology, 1958—. U.S. Agency for International Development lecturer in India, 1970; director of intercultural reading and language program for Northwest Regional Laboratory, 1974-75. Member of Salt Lake Community Mental Health Advisory Council, 1976—. Consultant on educational research and development and educational evaluation. *Military service:* U.S. Marine Corps, 1942-45.

MEMBER: International Reading Association, American Educational Research Association, American Psychological Association, National Society for Performance and Instruction (vice-president, 1966; president, 1967), Phi Delta Kappa.

WRITINGS: Student Guide for Cronbach's Educational Psychology, Harcourt, 1965, revised edition published as *U.S. Armed Forces Institute Study Guide,* 1969; *Handbook for Instructors of Educational Psychology,* University of Illinois, 1965; *Reading Diagnosis and Prescription,* Holt, 1968, 2nd edition, in press; *How to Talk with Children (And Other People),* Wiley, 1973; *How to Establish a Behavior Observation System,* Educational Technology Publications, 1975; *Be What You Want to See,* Designers Provision, 1977.

WORK IN PROGRESS: A book of poems; research for *The Revision Process in Writing.*

SIDELIGHTS: Della-Piana writes: "I was most influenced by my parents to *do something,* by the U.S. Marine Corps to learn something, by my children to write *How to Talk with Children,* by M. W. Poulson to be a psychologist, by Sam Kirk to write *Reading Diagnosis,* by students to revise *Reading Diagnosis,* by Northwest Indians to give what is needed and be open to receiving what is needed, by the Sufi and my wife 'to be what I want to see,' by Joe Kirk to study

revision process of writers, by Norm Wallen to play handball and tennis. I believe the three essential catalysts for any work (including rearing children, business, yourself) are: immersion (get completely into it), integrity (say what you see), and ignorance (provide a continuous polarity to what you know). Without these three there is no art. With them, all work is art-work. It's no accident that all the catalysts begin with 'I'."

* * *

DELMAR, Roy
See WEXLER, Jerome (LeRoy)

* * *

De LUCA, Charles J. 1927-

PERSONAL: Born April 3, 1927, in U.S. Canal Zone, Panama; son of Philip J. (in U.S. Navy) and Theresa (a government employee; maiden name, Marcucci) DeLuca; married Diana Macintyre (a college teacher), March 21, 1962; children: David Edward. *Education:* University of Hawaii, B.A., 1956. *Home:* 2333 Kapiolani Blvd., #402, Honolulu, Hawaii 96826. *Office:* Waikiki Aquarium, University of Hawaii, 2777 Kalakaua Ave., Honolulu, Hawaii 96815.

CAREER: News and program director in broadcasting, Honolulu, Hawaii, 1956-69; University of Hawaii, Honolulu, curator of Waikiki Aquarium, 1969—. Member of University Marine Council. *Military service:* U.S. Navy, 1943-46; served in Asia, the Pacific, and the Philippines. *Member:* Hawaiian Malacological Society.

WRITINGS: (With Spencer W. Tinker) *Sharks and Rays,* Tuttle, 1973; (with wife, Diana Macintyre DeLuca) *Pacific Marine Life,* Tuttle, 1976. Editor of *Directory of the Public Aquaria of the World* and *Directory of Aquarium Specialists, 1974-75.*

WORK IN PROGRESS: Literature and the Sea, with wife, Diana Macintyre DeLuca, "a collection of about three thousand passages from works dealing in whole or in part with the sea, juxtaposed with scientific facts or theories about the ocean and its many facets."

* * *

DENHOLTZ, Elaine 1932-

PERSONAL: Born September 17, 1932, in Paterson, N.J.; daughter of Maurice (a musician) and Lillian (Sachs) Grudin; married Melvin Denholtz (a dentist), December 18, 1949; children: Jeffrey, Steven, Lisa. *Education:* Bucknell University, B.A., 1950; Seton Hall University, M.A.T., 1966. *Residence:* Livingston, N.J. *Agent:* Marian Searchinger Associates, c/o C.T.W., 1 Lincoln Plaza, New York, N.Y. 10023. *Office:* Melaine Productions, 114 West Mt. Pleasant Ave., Livingston, N.J. 07039.

CAREER: Fairleigh Dickinson University, Wayne, N.J., lecturer in English, 1966—. Vice-president of Melaine Productions, 1970—. Lecturer at Bergen Community College and University of Texas. Playwright, 1970—; filmmaker, scriptwriter, and performer, 1977.

MEMBER: American Association of University Professors, Authors League of America, Women in Communications, Phi Beta Kappa. *Awards, honors:* Fiction prize from Philadelphia Writer's Conference, 1963, for story, "A Time for Everything"; short story award from *Writer's Digest,* 1965, for "Obviously It Was a Wooden Leg"; Kahn Fiction Award from Purdue University Research Foundation, 1965, for story, "Nothing Comes Easy"; first prize from Philadelphia Writers Conference, 1968, for article, "Gino Holland-er, American Expatriate"; Doris Bell Paiss Drama Award from Philadelphia Writer's Conference, 1968, for one-act play, "Judge Not"; Fenimore Players Annual Playwrighting Award, 1971, MacArthur Playwrighting Prize from University of Florida, 1973, annual drama award from New York City's Courtyard Playhouse, 1973, and Russell A Sharp Drama Prize from Willow Grove, Mo., 1973, all for "Some Men Are Good at That"; distinguished achievement award from Educational Press Association of America, 1974, for excellence in educational journalism; finalist in American Film Festival career category, 1974, for "The Dental Auxiliary"; University of Texas Drama Prize from E. P. Conkle Workshop, 1974, for "The Highchairs"; Eugene O'Neill National Playwriting Award from O'Neill Theatre Conference, 1977, for television drama, "Another Mother."

WRITINGS: (Contributor) Frank R. Krajewsky and Gary L. Peltier, editors, *Education: Where It's Been, Where It's At, Where It's Going,* C. E. Merrill, 1973; *The Highchairs* (two-act play; first produced in Austin at University of Texas E. P. Conkle Workshop for Playwrights, 1974), Dramatic Publishing Co., 1975; (with husband, Melvin Denholtz) *How to Save Your Teeth and Your Money,* Van Nostrand, 1977.

Unpublished plays: "Frozen" (one-act), first produced in New York City at Clark Center for Performing Arts, 1969; "Some Men Are Good at That" (one-act), first produced in New York City at the Assembly, 1970; "The Dungmen Are Coming" (one-act), first produced in Lewisburg, Pa., at Bucknell University Cocktail Theatre, 1972; "Hey Out There, Is There Anyone Out There?" (one-act), first produced in New York City at New York Theatre Ensemble, 1972.

Filmscripts: "Summerhill" (documentary), Melaine Productions, 1972; "The Dental Auxiliary," Melaine Productions, 1974; "Waiting: The Life Styles of the Elderly," Melaine Productions, 1975; "What's Inside" (documentary), Puerto Rico Television, 1976.

Also writer of "Judge Not," "An Even Exchange," and "Fresh Bread and Strawberry Ice Cream," plays as yet unproduced, and "Henry Funke," "Another Mother," and "Not Coming Home," filmscripts as yet unproduced. Scriptwriter and performer for "Your Money and Your Health," a television series on health consumerism, 1977. Contributor of stories and articles to magazines.

WORK IN PROGRESS: Having It Both Ways: Married Women with Lovers; The Dental Face Lift; "The Assertive Training of Henry Funkel," a radio play.

SIDELIGHTS: Denholtz told *CA* that she appears as a speaker at writer's conferences and that she writes and performs commercials for television.

*　　*　　*

DENNES, William Ray 1898-

PERSONAL: Born April 10, 1898, in Healdsburg, Calif.; son of Edward Frederick (a merchant) and Harriet (Ray) Dennes; married Margaret Munroe Stevenson, June 22, 1923; children: Richard, Margaret (Mrs. Edwin Honig). *Education:* University of California, Berkeley, A.B., 1919, M.A., 1920; Corpus Christi College, Oxford, D.Phil., 1923. *Politics:* Democrat. *Home:* 2265 Virginia St., Berkeley, Calif. 94709.

CAREER: University of California, Berkeley, instructor, 1923-24, assistant professor, 1924-27, associate professor,

1927-32, 1933-36, professor of philosophy, 1936-65, Mills Professor of Intellectual and Moral Philosophy and Civil Polity, 1958-65, professor emeritus, 1965—, chairperson of department, 1941-43, 1944-48, dean of Graduate Division, 1948-55. Visiting associate professor at Yale University, 1932-33; visiting professor at Harvard University, 1935, Stanford University, 1941, 1943, Southern Illinois University, 1966, University of Virginia, 1967, and University of California, Santa Cruz, 1970-71; Woodbridge Memorial Lecturer in Philosophy at Columbia University, 1958. Assistant director of Manhattan District of Los Alamos Project, 1943. *Military service:* U.S. Naval Reserve, 1918-21, active duty, 1918.

MEMBER: American Philosophical Association (president of Pacific Division, 1945), American Association for the Advancement of Science (fellow), Conference on Science, Philosophy, and Religion, Association of American Universities (president of graduate school association, 1952), Association of Land-Grant Colleges and Universities (chairman of graduate council, 1952), Royal Society of Arts (fellow), Mind Society of Great Britain, Phi Beta Kappa (president of Alpha chapter, 1941-42), Alpha Kappa Lambda, Faculty Club (Berkeley). *Awards, honors:* Rhodes scholar, 1920-23; Guggenheim fellow in Germany and England, 1929-30; LL.D. from New York University, 1951, and University of California, 1965.

WRITINGS: The Method and Presuppositions of Group Psychology, University of California Press, 1924, reprinted, Johnson Reprint, 1969; (with John Dewey and others) *Naturalism and the Human Spirit,* Columbia University Press, 1944; *Civilization and Values,* University of California Press, 1945; *Conflict,* University of California Press, 1946; *Meaning and Interpretation,* University of California Press, 1950; (with others) *East-West Philosophy,* University Press of Hawaii, 1951; (with others) *Symbols and Values,* University of California Press, 1954; *Some Dilemmas of Naturalism,* Columbia University Press, 1960. Also author of *C. I. Lewis on the Morally Imperative,* 1969. Co-editor of "Publications in Philosophy," University of California Press, 1941-65.

WORK IN PROGRESS: Research on the metaphysics of Aristotle and on epistemology of David Hume.

*　　*　　*

DENNIS, Arthur
See EDMONDS, Arthur Denis

*　　*　　*

DENNIS, Lawrence 1893-1977

December 25, 1893—August 20, 1977; American diplomat, economist, and author. Dennis, who advocated fascism for the United States, was one of twenty-nine people tried by the federal government in 1944 on charges of sedition. A mistrial was subsequently declared. Dennis was formerly in foreign service in five posts. He wrote books on political systems and published the *Weekly Foreign Letter* and *Appeal to Reason.* Dennis died in Spring Valley, N.Y. Obituaries: *New York Times,* August 21, 1977.

*　　*　　*

DENNIS, Patrick
See TANNER, Edward Everett III

DENNISON, Shane 1933-

PERSONAL: Born December 29, 1933, in Tsawwassen, British Columbia, Canada; son of Bill (a cobbler) and May F. Zoe (a gardener; maiden name, Owen) Dennison; married Maryan Embree (a laboratory technician), September 5, 1959; children: Zoe, Lake. *Education:* Attended schools in British Columbia. *Politics:* "Whee! I'm a capitalist." *Religion:* "Ah ho ha hee hoo hoo boy." *Home address:* P.O. Box 1581, 11729 Reynolds Ave., Summerland, British Columbia, Canada V0H 1Z0.

CAREER: Farmer, logger, fisherman, miner, salesman, importer in Hong Kong, and truck driver, 1951-76; writer. Past president of Summerland Singers and Players; past producer of Penticton Dramatic Society; actor in Stratford Little Theatre. *Military service:* Served in Royal Canadian Air Force.

WRITINGS: Sidehill Gouger; or, What's So Deadly About Caterpillars?, Doubleday, 1977; *"Run Like Hell! The Bureaucrat is Coming!",* Doubleday, 1978.

SIDELIGHTS: "The only subject I consider vital is me," Dennison wrote. "However I'm interested in such non-vital subjects as education, bureaucrazy, unionism, and conglomeration. I see these four mystiques as the religions of our day and they are the subjects I write at. Just the same, my main interest is in living happily ever after. Therefore I do not take the four sects mentioned very seriously, especially since *they* take themselves seriously."

* * *

DENOON, Donald (John Noble) 1940-

PERSONAL: Born July 29, 1940, in Scotland; son of Alexander (an engineer) and Elspeth (a secretary; maiden name, Noble) Denoon; married Pamela Bavin Tod (a sociologist), January 8, 1966; children: Louise, Alexander, Gordon. *Education:* University of Natal, B.A. (honors), 1961; Cambridge University, Ph.D., 1965. *Office:* Department of History, University of Papua New Guinea, Port Moresby, Papua New Guinea.

CAREER: Makerere University, Kampala, Uganda, lecturer in history, 1966-72; University of Papua New Guinea, Port Moresby, professor of history, 1972—.

WRITINGS: A Grand Illusion, Longman, 1972; *Southern Africa in 1800,* Longman, 1972; (editor) *Uganda Before 1900,* Volume II, East African Publishing House, in press; (editor with Kieth Rennie) *Uganda and Rwanda,* East African Publishing House, in press.

WORK IN PROGRESS: A biography of Ulli Beier; *A History of Agriculture in Papua New Guinea,* completion expected in 1979; *Colonies of White Settlement in the Southern Hemisphere, 1899-1915,* 1979.

SIDELIGHTS: Denoon comments: "My main concern is to explore the impact of white colonists and individuals in non-European communities during the past hundred years."

* * *

DEPEL, Jim 1936-

PERSONAL: Born July 4, 1936, in Oklahoma City, Okla.; son of William Emil (a mechanic) and Ruby (Osterlow) Depel; married Diane Pope, 1969 (divorced). *Education:* Attended Central State College, Edmond, Okla. and Coffeyville Junior College. *Home:* 9021 South Shartel, #204, Oklahoma City, Okla. 73139.

CAREER: Junior high and high school teacher and coach in New Orleans, La., 1962-63, Bowie, Ariz., 1963-64, Magnum, Okla., 1964-65; Putnam City School System, Oklahoma City, Okla., teacher of social studies and coach, 1965-73; teacher of social studies and football and golf coach at Western Oaks Junior High, 1973—. *Military service:* U.S. Marine Corps Reserve, 1955-63.

WRITINGS: The Baseball Handbook for Coaches and Players, Scribner, 1976.

* * *

DE POLNAY, Peter 1906-

PERSONAL: Born March 8, 1906; married Margaret Mitchell-Banks, 1942 (died, 1950); married Daphne Taylor, 1952; married Maria del Carmen Rubio y Caparo, 1955; children: one son. *Education:* Privately educated in England, Switzerland, Italy, and Hungary. *Home:* 33 Percy St., London W.1, England.

CAREER: Author, 1932—; farmed in Kenya, beginning 1932; moved to Paris before the beginning of World War II; joined the French Resistance, and was discovered and imprisoned for several months until his escape to England.

WRITINGS: Angry Man's Tale (novel), Secker & Warburg, 1938, Knopf, 1939, revised edition, Hutchinson, 1947; *Children, My Children!,* Secker & Warburg, 1939; *Boo,* Secker & Warburg, 1941, published as *The Magnificent Idiot,* Doubleday, 1942; *Death and To-morrow* (personal narratives), Secker & Warburg, 1942, published as *The Germans Came to Paris,* Duell, Sloan & Pearce, 1943; *Water on the Steps: A Novel,* Secker & Warburg, 1943; *Two Mirrors,* Constable, 1944, Creative Age Press, 1946; *A Letter to an Undertaker,* Home & Van Thal, 1946; *The Umbrella Thorn* (novel), Hutchinson, 1946, Creative Age Press, 1947; *A Pin's Fee,* Hutchinson, 1947; *The Fat of the Land,* Hutchinson, 1948; *The Moot Point,* Creative Age Press, 1948; *Into an Old Room: A Memoir of Edward FitzGerald,* Creative Age Press, 1949 (published in England as *Into an Old Room: The Paradox of E. FitzGerald,* Secker & Warburg, 1950); *Out of the Square,* Creative Age Press, 1949; *Somebody Must,* Hutchinson, 1949.

The Next Two Years, Hamish Hamilton, 1951; *Death of a Legend: The True Story of Bonny Prince Charlie,* Hamish Hamilton, 1952; *An Unfinished Journey to South-Western France and Auvergne,* Wingate, 1952; *A Beast in View: A Novel,* W. H. Allen, 1953; (translator with Elspeth Grant) Odette Joyeux, *Open Arms,* Wingate, 1954; *When Time Is Dead,* W. H. Allen, 1954; *Before I Sleep,* W. H. Allen, 1955; *Fools of Choice* (autobiography), R. Hale, 1955; *Descent from Burgos* (travel), R. Hale, 1956; *The Shorn Shadow,* W. H. Allen, 1956; *The Clap of Silent Thunder,* W. H. Allen, 1957, Random House, 1958; *The Night of the Hyrax,* W. H. Allen, 1958; *Peninsular Paradox* (nonfiction), McGibbon & Kee, 1958; *The Scales of Love,* W. H. Allen, 1958; *A Door Ajar* (autobiography), R. Hale, 1959; *The Shriek of the Gull,* W. H. Allen, 1959; *Travelling Light: A Guide to Foreign Parts,* Hollis & Carter, 1959; *The Uninvolved* (novel), W. H. Allen, 1959.

The Crack of Dawn: A Childhood Fantasy, Hollis & Carter, 1960; *The Gamesters,* W. H. Allen, 1960, Frank R. Walker, 1962; *Garibaldi: The Legend and the Man,* Hollis & Carter, 1960, published as *Garibaldi: The Man and the Legend,* Thomas Nelson, 1961; *Mario,* W. H. Allen, 1961; *No Empty Hands,* Bobbs-Merrill, 1961; *A Queen of Spain: Isabel II,* Hollis & Carter, 1962; *A Man of Fortune,* W. H. Allen, 1963; *The Run of Night* (novel), W. H. Allen, 1963; *Three Phases of High Summer,* W. H. Allen, 1963; *A Home of*

One's Own, W. H. Allen, 1964; *The Plaster Bed,* W. H. Allen, 1964; *As the Crow Flies,* W. H. Allen, 1965; *In Raymond's Wake,* W. H. Allen, 1965; *The Centre-Piece,* W. H. Allen, 1966; *Not the Defeated,* W. H. Allen, 1966; *A Winter's Promise,* W. H. Allen, 1967; *The World of Maurice Utrillo,* Heinemann, 1967, revised edition published as *Enfant Terrible: The Life and World of Maurice Utrillo,* Morrow, 1969; *Aspects of Paris,* W. H. Allen, 1968, published as *Paris: An Urbane Guide to the City and Its People,* Regnery, 1970; *The Second Death of a Hero* (novel), W. H. Allen, 1968; *Madame de Maintenon,* Heron Books, 1969; *The Patriots,* W. H. Allen, 1969; *A Tower of Strength,* W. H. Allen, 1969; (translator) Maurice David-Darnac, *The True Story of the Maid of Orleans,* W. H. Allen, 1969.

Napoleon's Police, W. H. Allen, 1970; *The Permanent Farewell,* W. H. Allen, 1970; *Sarah Bernhardt,* Heron Books, 1970; *Spring Snow and Algy,* W. H. Allen, 1970, St. Martin's, 1975; *A Tale of Two Husbands,* W. H. Allen, 1970; *A Life of Ease,* W. H. Allen, 1971; *The Grey Sheep,* W. H. Allen, 1972; *The Loser,* W. H. Allen, 1973; *The Moon and the Marabou Stork,* Elek, 1973; *The Price You Pay,* W. H. Allen, 1973; *The Crow and the Cat,* W. H. Allen, 1974; *Indifference,* W. H. Allen, 1974.

AVOCATIONAL INTERESTS: Shooting, collecting French furniture, French history.*

* * *

DERY, Tibor 1894-1977

1894—August 18, 1977; Hungarian anti-establishment intellectual and author of novels and short stories. A leading figure in the intellectual movement in Hungary before the anti-Soviet Hungarian uprising of October, 1956, Dery was sentenced to nine years imprisonment for "hostile activities." Dery was also imprisoned just before World War II for translating a book by Andre Gide. Though still considered highly controversial, Dery holds a firm place in Hungarian literature. He died in Budapest, Hungary. Obituaries: *New York Times,* August 19, 1977; *AB Bookman's Weekly,* October 17, 1977.

* * *

de STE. CROIX, G(eoffrey) E(rnest) M(aurice) 1910-

PERSONAL: Born February 8, 1910, in Macao, China; son of Ernest Henry (in Chinese customs) and Florence Annie (Macgowan) de Ste. Croix; married Lucile Hyneman, September 7, 1932 (divorced, 1959); married Margaret Knight, September 3, 1959; children: (first marriage) Carolyn (deceased); (second marriage) Richard, Julian. *Education:* University of London, B.A. (first class honors), 1949. *Politics:* Socialist. *Religion:* Atheist. *Home:* Evenlode, Stonesfield Lane, Charlbury, Oxford OX7 3ER, England.

CAREER: Solicitor in London, England, 1932-40; University of London, London, England, assistant lecturer in ancient economic history, 1950-53; Oxford University, Oxford, England, lecturer in ancient history and fellow of New College, 1953-77, emeritus fellow of New College, 1977—; writer, 1977—. J. H. Gray Lecturer at Cambridge University, 1973. *Military service:* Royal Air Force, 1940-46; became acting flight lieutenant. *Member:* British Academy (fellow). *Awards, honors:* M.A. from Oxford University, 1953.

WRITINGS: The Origins of the Peloponnesian War, Cornell University Press, 1976; *The Class Struggle in the Ancient Greek World,* Duckworth, in press.

Contributor: A. C. Littleton and B. S. Yamey, editors, *Studies in the History of Accounting,* Sweet & Masewell, 1956; *Ancient Society and Institutions: Studies Presented to V. Ehrenberg,* Basil Blackwell, 1966; Arnold Toynbee, editor, *The Crucible of Christianity,* Thames & Hudson, 1969; M. I. Finley, editor, *Studies in Ancient Society,* Routledge & Kegan Paul, 1974; B. S. Yamey and Harold Edey, editors, *Debits, Credits, Finance, and Profits,* Sweet & Masewell, 1974; Barbara Levick, editor, *The Ancient Historian and His Materials,* Gregg International, 1975. Contributor of articles and reviews to professional journals.

WORK IN PROGRESS: Thucydides: Ancient and Modern Historian, publication by Duckworth expected in 1981.

SIDELIGHTS: De Ste. Croix remarks briefly: "I am a Marxist, increasingly interested in historiographical method." *Avocational interests:* Walking, listening to music.

* * *

de SELINCOURT, Aubrey 1894-1962

PERSONAL: Born June 7, 1894, in London, England; son of Martin de Selincourt; married Irene Rutherford McLeod, 1919; children: two daughters. *Education:* University College, Oxford, M.A.

CAREER: Author and translator. Has also worked as a headmaster for schools in England. *Military service:* Royal Air Force. *Member:* P.E.N., Oxford University Authentics, Royal Cruising Club.

WRITINGS: Streams of Ocean, Heinemann, 1923; *Family Afloat* (illustrated by Eileen Verrinder and Guy de Selincourt), Routledge & Kegan Paul, 1940; *Three Green Bottles* (illustrated by G. de Selincourt), Routledge & Kegan Paul, 1941; *One Good Tern* (illustrated by G. de Selincourt), Routledge & Kegan Paul, 1943; *One More Summer* (illustrated by G. de Selincourt), Routledge & Kegan Paul, 1944; (with wife, Irene de Selincourt) *Six o'Clock and After, and Other Rhymes for Children* (illustrated by John Morton Sale), Muller, 1945; *Calicut Lends a Hand* (illustrated by G. de Selincourt), Routledge & Kegan Paul, 1946; *Dorset* (illustrated by Barbara Jones), Elck, 1947; *Micky* (illustrated by G. de Selincourt), Routledge & Kegan Paul, 1947; *A Capful of Wind* (illustrated by G. de Selincourt), Methuen, 1948; *Isle of Wight* (illustrated by Kenneth Rowntree), Elck, 1948; *The Young Schoolmaster* (illustrated by F. M. Middlehurst), Oxford University Press, 1948; *Kestrel* (illustrated by G. de Selincourt), Routledge & Kegan Paul, 1949; *Mr. Oram's Story: The Adventures of Captain James Cook* (illustrated by John Baynes), Methuen, 1949; *The Ravens Nest* (illustrated by G. de Selincourt), Routledge & Kegan Paul, 1949; *Sailing: A Guide for Everyman* (illustrated by G. de Selincourt), Lehmann, 1949.

Odysseus the Wanderer (illustrated by Norman Meredith), G. Bell, 1950; *The Schoolmaster,* Lehmann, 1951; *On Reading Poetry,* Swallow, 1952, reprinted, Folcroft, 1970; *The Channel Shore,* R. Hale, 1953; *Six Great Englishmen,* Hamish Hamilton, 1953; (translator and author of introduction) Herodotus, *Herodotus: The Histories,* Penguin, 1954, revised edition, 1972; *Horatio Nelson,* Hamish Hamilton, 1954; *Cat's Cradle,* M. Joseph, 1955; *Six Great Poets,* Hamish Hamilton, 1956, reprinted, Folcroft, 1973; *Nensen* (illustrated by Ian Ribbons), Oxford University Press, 1957; (translator) Flavius Arrianus, *The Life of Alexander the Great,* Penguin, 1958, published as *The Campaigns of Alexander,* 1976; *Six Great Thinkers,* Hamish Hamilton, 1958, reprinted, Folcroft, 1977; *Six Great Playwrights,* Hamish

Hamilton, 1960, reprinted, Folcroft, 1974; (translator and author of introduction) Titus Livius, *The Early History of Rome: Books I-V of The History of Rome from Its Foundation,* Penguin, 1960, reprinted, Heritage Press, 1972; (editor) *The Book of the Sea,* Eyre & Spottiswoode, 1961, Norton, 1963; *The World of Herodotus,* Secker & Warburg, 1962, Little, Brown, 1963; (translator) T. Livius, *The War with Hannibal: Books XXI-XXX of The History of Rome from Its Foundation,* edited by Betty Radice, Penguin, 1965.

Editor, *Oxford Magazine,* 1927-29.

SIDELIGHTS: New York Times reviewed *Odysseus the Wanderer* as a "smooth-paced retelling of the epic marked by unerring taste in the selection and treatment of incidents and the haunting echoes of Homeric phraseology." *Avocational interests:* Yacht cruising.

BIOGRAPHICAL/CRITICAL SOURCES: New York Times, April 22, 1956.*

(Died in 1962)

*   *   *

DESMOND, John   1909(?)-1977

1909(?)—August 20, 1977; American journalist. Desmond was assistant Sunday editor of the *New York Times* and was known principally for his work in the "Week in Review" section. He died in Riverhead, N.Y. Obituaries: *New York Times,* August 21, 1977.

*   *   *

DESMOND, Robert W(illiam)   1900-

PERSONAL: Born July 31, 1900, in Milwaukee, Wis.; son of William John (in real estate) and Lillian Amy (Wilce) Desmond; married Dorothy Christian, 1927 (deceased); married Emily Virginia Wall, March 17, 1949; children: (first marriage) Richard S.; (second marriage) Christopher R., Carolyn V. *Education:* University of Wisconsin, Madison, A.B., 1922; School of International Studies, Geneva, Switzerland, certificate, 1929; University of Minnesota, M.A., 1930; London School of Economics and Political Science, University of London, Ph.D., 1936. *Home:* 314 Ricardo Pl., La Jolla, Calif. 92037.

CAREER: Milwaukee Journal, Milwaukee, Wis., reporter, rewriter, and on copydesk, 1922-25; *Miami Herald,* Miami, Fla., on copydesk and city desk, 1925-26; *New York Herald,* Paris edition, Paris, France, on copydesk, 1926-27; University of Michigan, Ann Arbor, instructor in journalism, 1927-28; University of Minnesota, Minneapolis, instructor, 1928-29, assistant professor of journalism, 1929-32; *Christian Science Monitor,* Boston, Mass., editorial writer, editor, and roving reporter in London bureau, 1931, 1933-38; Northwestern University, Evanston, Ill., professor of journalism, 1938-39; University of California, Berkeley, professor of journalism, 1939-68, professor emeritus, 1968—, chairperson of department, 1939-54, 1962-63, 1967; *San Diego Union,* San Diego, Calif., on copydesk and other departments, 1969-74; free-lance writer, 1974—. Visiting professor at Stanford University, 1938; Fulbright lecturer at University of Amsterdam, 1955-56, University of Baghdad, 1965-66, and University of Teheran, 1968-69; lecturer at University of Strasbourg, 1956, 1958, 1960. Member of press staff at Williamstown Institute of Politics, 1932; on foreign desk at *New York Times,* 1941; worked for *San Francisco Examiner,* 1942, *Louisville Courier-Journal,* summer, 1955, North American Newspaper Alliance (NANA), 1955-56, *Hartford Times,* summer, 1964, and *San Francisco Chronicle,* 1968;

academic director of foreign assignment tour in Europe, 1952; author of "Conceived in Liberty," a column syndicated by Copley News Service, 1971-75. News commentator on KSFO-Radio, 1941-42; member of UNESCO Commission on Technical Needs of the Mass Media, 1947, 1949; consultant to *Encyclopedia Americana* and International Press Institute. *Military service:* U.S. Army, Infantry, 1918, 1943-44; served in European theater; became major.

MEMBER: American Association of Schools and Departments of Journalism (president, 1947-48), Association for Education in Journalism, Torch Club (local president, 1976-77), Sigma Delta Chi (and its Key Club). *Awards, honors:* Citation from California State Senate, 1968.

WRITINGS: Newspaper Reference Methods, University of Minnesota Press, 1933; *Press and World Affairs,* Appleton, 1937; (with Francis James Brown, Charles Hodges, Joseph Slabey Roucek) *Contemporary World Politics,* Wiley, 1940, revised edition, 1941; *The Professional Training of Journalists* (brochure), UNESCO, 1949; *Les tendances de l'enseigement du journalisme aux Etats-Unis* (title means "Trends in the Teaching of Journalism in the United States"), Etudes de Press, 1959; *Professional Secrecy and the Journalist,* International Press Institute, 1962; *The Information Process: World News Reporting to the Twentieth Century,* University of Iowa Press, 1977. Contributor to magazines. Member of editorial staff of *Journalism Quarterly,* 1955-65.

WORK IN PROGRESS: Two books on the history of international news coverage.

SIDELIGHTS: Desmond writes: "My professional activities, as noted, have been divided between active journalism and teaching journalism, with the two often combined, or with return to active journalism in summer months (while teaching). All graduate work was in the area of political science and international relations, with a special research and professional interest in the area of world news reporting. Travel beyond the United States and Canada has been concentrated in Europe and the Middle East, but has also included the Far East, parts of Africa, Cuba, Mexico, and the West Indies."

*   *   *

DES PRES, Terrence   1939-

PERSONAL: Born December 26, 1939; divorced; children: Jean-Paul. *Education:* Southeast Missouri State College, B.A., 1962; Washington University, M.A., 1965, Ph.D., 1968. *Home:* 1 Preston Hill Rd., Hamilton, N.Y. 13346. *Agent:* Georges Borchardt, Inc., 145 East 52nd St., New York, N.Y. 10022. *Office:* Department of English, Colgate University, Hamilton, N.Y. 13346.

CAREER: Colgate University, Hamilton, N.Y., Crawshaw Chair in English Literature, 1973—. Judge, National Book Award, 1978. *Member:* National Humanities Institute (Yale University; fellow), American Association of University Professors, Writers Guild, Amnesty International.

WRITINGS: The Survivor: An Anatomy of Life in the Death Camps, Oxford University Press, 1976. Contributor to *Encounter, Harper's, Partisan Review, Sports Illustrated,* and other periodicals.

*   *   *

DE TOLNAY, Charles Erich   1899-
(Karoly Tolnai, Vagujhelyi Karoly Tolnai)

PERSONAL: Born May 27, 1899, in Budapest, Hungary;

came to United States in 1939, naturalized citizen, 1945; son of Arnold and Anna (Pilk) de Tolnay; married Rina Ada Clara Bartolucci, 1930 (died, 1965). *Education:* Studied at University of Berlin, 1920-21, and University of Frankfurt, 1922; University of Vienna, Ph.D., 1925; postdoctoral study in Rome, Italy. *Home:* Casa Buonarroti, Via Ghibellina 70, Florence, Italy.

CAREER: University of Hamburg, Hamburg, Germany, privat-docent and lecturer in history of art, 1929-33; University of Paris, Sorbonne, Paris, France, visiting lecturer in art and archaeology, 1934-39; Institute for Advanced Study, Princeton, N.J., member of staff, 1939-48; Columbia University, New York, N.Y., visiting lecturer in art, 1954-64; Casa Buonarroti, Florence, Italy, director, 1965—. Professor at University of Hamburg, 1957; visiting lecturer at University of London, 1935, University of Gand, 1936, University of Utrecht, 1937, Harvard University, 1939, Princeton University, 1939, 1958, College de France, 1948, University of Basel, 1951, and Columbia University, 1954-64.

MEMBER: College Art Association, Accademia dell' Arte Disegno (honorary member), Accademia di San Luca (honorary member), Accademia Nazionale dei Lincei, Athenaeum Club. *Awards, honors:* U.S. laureate of Academie des Inscriptions et Belles Letteraria, 1937, Fould Prize, 1937, Bordin Award, 1939; Guggenheim fellowships, 1948-49, 1953-54; honorary doctorate from University of Rome, 1964, and University of Budapest, 1969; premio Internazionale Galileo Galilei, 1965.

WRITINGS—Some originally published under names Karoly Tolnai or Vagujhelyi Karoly Tolnai: *Pierre Bruegel l'ancien* (title means "Peter Bruegel the Elder"), Volume I: *Texte,* Volume II: *Planches,* Nouvelle societe d'editions, 1935, translation published as *Drawings of Peter Bruegel the Elder,* Zwemmer, 1952; *Hieronymus Bosch* (in German), two volumes, Holbein, 1937, translation published under same title, Reynal, 1966; *Le retable de l'Agneau mystique des freres van Eyck,* Editions de la Connaissance, 1938; *Le Maitre de Flemalle et les freres Van Eyck,* Editions de la Connaissance, 1939.

Michelangelo, six volumes, Princeton University Press, Volume I: *The Youth of Michelangelo,* 1943, 2nd edition, 1969, Volume II: *The Sistine Chapel,* 1945, 2nd edition, 1969, Volume III: *The Medici Chapel,* 1948, 2nd edition, 1970, Volume IV: *The Tomb of Julius Two,* 1954, 2nd edition, 1970, Volume V: *The Final Period: Last Judgment, Frescoes of the Pauline Chapel, Last Pietas,* 1960, 2nd edition, 1970, Volume VI: *Michelangelo: Architect,* 1967, condensed edition in one volume published as *Michelangelo: Sculptor, Painter, Architect,* 1975; *The History and Technique of Old Master Drawings: A Handbook,* H. Bittner, 1943, Hacker, 1972; *Werk und Weltbild des Michelangelo,* Rhein-Verlag, 1949, English translation by Nan Buranelli published as *The Art and Thought of Michelangelo,* Pantheon, 1964.

Die Zeichnungen Pieter Bruegels, mit einem kritischen Katalog und 188 Abbildungen, Rascher, 1952.

Apercus sur l'art francais: Formes et esprit, Vallecchi, 1960; *"Michel-Ange dans son atelier"* par Delacroix, Gazette des beaux-arts, 1962; *Conceptions religieuses dans la peinture de Piero della Francesca,* Tipocolor, 1963; *Disegni di Michelangelo,* Silvana editoriale d'arte, 1964; *Michelangelo: Artista, pensatore, scrittore,* Istituto geografico de Agostini, 1965; *Nuove ricerche riguardanti la casa de Michelangelo in via Ghibellina,* Accademia nazionale dei Lincei, 1966; *Le madonne di Michelangelo: Nuove ricerche sui disegni,* Ac-

cademia nazionale dei Lincei, 1968; *Nuove osservazioni sulla Cappella Medicea,* Accademia nazionale dei Lincei, 1969.

Michel-Ange (in French), Arts et metiers grapiques, 1970; *Il riordinamento delle collezioni della casa Buonarroti a Firenze, i principi deguiti: Nuove scoperte e acquisizioni,* Accademia nazionale dei Lincei, 1970; *La Casa Buonarroti,* Arnaud, 1970; *Alcune recenti scoperte e risultati negli studi michelangioleschi,* Accademia nazionale dei Lincei, 1971; *L'omaggio a Michelangelo di Albrecht Duerer,* Accademia nazionale dei Lincei, 1971; *I disegni di Michelangelo nelle collezioni italiane,* Centro Di, 1972. Contributor to professional journals in the United States and Europe.

* * *

DEVIEW, Lucille 1920-

PERSONAL: Born December 9, 1920, in Detroit, Mich.; daughter of John Arthur and Viola (Jonske) Starkey; divorced; children: Robin Pappas, Harden, Jr. *Education:* Attended Wayne State University. *Religion:* Christian Scientist. *Home:* 2165 Burns, Detroit, Mich. 48214. *Office:* *Detroit News,* 615 Lafayette Blvd., Detroit, Mich. 48231.

CAREER: DeView Advertising (public relations), Traverse City, Mich., co-owner and manager, 1955-65; *Southfield News,* Southfield, Mich., women's editor, 1968-69; Detroit Area Weekly Newspapers, East Detroit, Mich., associate editor, 1969-71; *Detroit News,* Detroit, staff writer and columnist, 1971—. Founded Grand Traverse League of Women Voters, 1964. *Member:* Women in Communications, National Federation of Press Women, Michigan Women's Press Club, American Civil Liberties Union. *Awards, honors:* Has received several awards for advertising; several awards from Michigan Women's Press Club; award from United Press International, 1975 and 1977, for investigative reporting; award from Associated Press, 1977, for reporting; award from Detroit Press Club Foundation, 1977, for reporting.

WRITINGS: Up North: A Contemporary Woman's Walden (essays and poems), Indian Village Press, 1977. Author of column "Kids" in *Detroit News,* 1976—.

Contributor of articles to periodicals, including *Christian Science Monitor, McCalls,* and *Motor News.*

WORK IN PROGRESS: A novel.

SIDELIGHTS: DeView's notable assignments include an investigative report of abortion referral agencies, juvenile crime, marriage and family relationships, the women's movement, science, and homicide. She told *CA:* "In these rapidly changing and complex times, I believe in 'problem-solving journalism.' It is not sufficient to probe problems and recite facts. We must also point to possible solutions. For example, in a series of articles on juvenile crime, it became evident there was a lack of counseling for the family when children become involved with the law. I was able to recommend in a final article that an anonymous self-help group be formed for this purpose and several community agencies rallied to this need. In this way, the journalist becomes 'part of the solution'—and for the sake of the individual and the human family in need, I feel journalists should become 'involved.'"

* * *

DEVINE, (Joseph) Lawrence 1935-

PERSONAL: Born September 21, 1935, in New York, N.Y.; son of John Justin (an advertising executive) and

Hazel (Tippit) DeVine; married Jane Christian, August 29, 1959 (divorced April, 1968); married Lucy Memory Williamson (an educator), July 26, 1968; children: John Justin II, Ellen Morse. *Education:* Attended Georgetown University, 1953-54; Northwestern University, B.S., 1957. *Religion:* Roman Catholic. *Home:* 1050 Van Dyke, Detroit, Mich. 48214. *Office: Detroit Free Press,* 321 West Lafayette Blvd., Detroit, Mich. 48214.

CAREER/WRITINGS: Miami Herald, Miami, Fla., reporter, columnist, and drama critic, 1962-67; *Los Angeles Herald-Examiner,* Los Angeles, Calif., entertainment editor, 1967-68; *Detroit Free Press,* Detroit, Mich., drama critic, 1968—. Instructor in drama criticism at University of Detroit, 1974; fellow, National Endowment for the Humanities Seminar for Critics of the Arts, 1977. Associate director of National Critics Institute, Eugene O'Neill Theater Center, Waterford, Conn., 1973—. Contributor to *Grolier's Encyclopedia Yearbook,* 1970-74, to *Yale Drama Review,* Knight-Ridder news syndicate, and other magazines and newspapers. *Military service:* U.S. Army Counter Intelligence Corps, 1958-62; served as Russian and German language specialist. *Member:* American Theatre Critics Association (director, 1977—), Sigma Delta Chi, Beta Theta Pi. *Awards, honors:* National Endowment for the Humanities fellowship at University of Michigan, 1975-76.

SIDELIGHTS: DeVine shared these thoughts with *CA:* "Is television the enemy? Is a man who gives you free candy an enemy? Well, television itself does not bother me; I do not have to deal with it. I have never seen a Lucille Ball or a Mary Tyler Moore show, for instance. Television's effects *do* bother me. So many children spend, mutely, more hours in front of their sets than they do in school. In the art form of the millions, TV's few meaningful shows sink beneath the sins of the many. When it comes to personal involvement, the theater is the lone survivor. The face-to-face confrontation is being more and more intelligently exploited by creative men. 'Equus' put the audience on stage. Richard Schechner put the actors in our laps. Try that with a Met tenor, let alone a TV set. Easy psychology suggests that the growing impersonality of our art forms makes the intelligent soul long for honest-to-God live people. You gain entrance to parking lots by putting a coded card into a slot. Television's surveys and computers do the same thing with our intellects. Theater speaks, breathes, pauses; it is neither cinema's celluloid nor video's microdots. If you like humanity, it's all you have left."

*   *   *

DeWEERD, Harvey A. 1902-

PERSONAL: Born September 21, 1902, in Holland, Mich.; son of Walter (a machinist) and Gertrude (Arendsen) DeWeerd; married Nellie Kole, August 5, 1926; children: Mary Jane, Evelyn DeWeerd Ewing. *Education:* Hope College, A.B., 1924; University of Michigan, M.A., 1925, Ph.D., 1937. *Home:* 503 Muskingum Ave., Pacific Palisades, Calif., 90272. *Office:* RAND Corp., 1700 Main St., Santa Monica, Calif. 90406.

CAREER: Michigan State College of Agriculture and Applied Science (now Michigan State University), East Lansing, instructor in history, 1926-28; Wittenberg University, Springfield, Ohio, assistant professor of history, 1928-39; Denison University, Granville, Ohio, associate professor of history and government, 1939-46; University of Missouri, Columbia, professor of history, 1946-53, chairman of department, 1950-53; RAND Corp., Santa Monica, Calif., senior

staff member, 1953-67, resident consultant, 1967—. Member, Institute for Advanced Study, Princeton, N.J., 1941-42; lecturer in political science, University of California, Los Angeles, 1962-68. Lecturer and consultant, Air War College, 1955-59; consultant, Systems Development Corp., 1967-69, and Computer-Based Center for Behavioral Studies, University of California, Los Angeles, 1971-73. *Military service:* U.S. Army, 1942-46; Historian Operations Division, War Department General Staff, 1945-46; became lieutenant colonel. *Member:* American Historical Association, American Military Institute.

WRITINGS: Great Soldiers of the Two World Wars, Norton, 1941; *Great Soldiers of World War II,* Norton, 1944; (with Roger Shugg) *World War II: A Concise History,* Infantry Journal Press, 1946; *President Wilson Fights His War,* Macmillan, 1968; (editor) *Selected Speeches and Statements of General of the Army George C. Marshall,* Do Capo, 1973. Editor, *Military Affairs* (journal of American Military Institute), 1937-42; associate editor, *Infantry Journal,* 1942-45.

*   *   *

DEWEY, Godfrey 1887-1977

September 3, 1887—October 18, 1977; American educator and exponent of a simplified method of spelling based on phonetics, and writer of many books and articles in his field. Dewey died in Lake Placid, N.Y. Obituaries: *New York Times,* October 20, 1977. (See index for *CA* sketch)

*   *   *

DIAMOND, Martin 1919-1977

December 19, 1919—July 22, 1977; American political scientist, professor, and author of books on American politics. He held the Thomas and Dorothy Leavey chair on the Foundation of American Freedom at Georgetown University, and was recognized for his studies of the American founders. He died in Washington, D.C. Obituaries: *New York Times,* July 23, 1977.

*   *   *

DICKINSON, A(lan) E(dgar) F(rederic) 1899-

PERSONAL: Born in 1899, in London, England; son of F. W. (an editor) and M. B. (Kuhr) Dickinson; married Ethel Mary McWilliam, 1937; children: Belinda, Brian. *Education:* Balliol College, Oxford, B.A., 1921, M.A., 1926, B.Mus., 1926; Royal College of Music, A.R.C.M., 1925. *Politics:* "Left centre." *Religion:* Ecumenical. *Home:* Toutley Hall, Wokingham, Berkshire, England.

CAREER: Music teacher and director of music at secondary schools in Belfast, Northern Ireland, 1929-36, and Reading, England, 1941-46; University of Durham, Durham, England, lecturer in music, 1946-54. Writer. *Military service:* British Army, Royal Garrison Artillery, 1918. *Member:* Penn Club.

WRITINGS: The Art of J. S. Bach, Hinrichsen, 1936, revised edition, 1950; *Beethoven,* Thomas Nelson, 1941; *Bach's Fugal Works,* Pitman, 1956; *Vaughan Williams,* Faber, 1963; *The Music of Berlioz,* Faber, 1972; *Holst's Music,* Dobson, 1977. Contributor to music journals.

WORK IN PROGRESS: Wagner's Musical Dramas: Structure.

SIDELIGHTS: Dickinson comments that he regards: "Music first: 1) structure, 2) texture; background second: 1) literary text, 2) conjecture; life third."

DLUZNOWSKY, Moshe 1906-1977

February 22, 1906—July 30, 1977; Polish-born Jewish novelist, playwright, and essayist. Dluznowsky's stories deal with Jewish life in France, Morocco, New York City, and other parts of the world where he had lived. He received the Jacob L. Gladstein Award of the Jewish Culture Congress in 1975. He died in Manhattan, N.Y. Obituaries: *New York Times,* August 1, 1977.

* * *

DOBSON, Julia M(argaret) 1937-

PERSONAL: Born August 1, 1937, in Lincoln, Neb.; daughter of Donald Duane (a U.S. State Department employee) and Carolyn (Van Anda) Dobson. *Education:* University of New Mexico, B.A., 1959; American University, M.A., 1963. *Home:* 2400 Virginia Ave. N.W., Washington, D.C. 20037. *Office:* U.S. Information Agency, 1750 Pennsylvania Ave. N.W., Washington, D.C. 20547.

CAREER: Georgetown University, Washington, D.C., instructor in English as a foreign language at English Language Institute in Ankara, Turkey, 1957, instructor in English as a foreign language, 1960; Turkish Air Force Language School, Izmir, instructor in English as a foreign language, 1960-62, supervisor, 1963-65; free-lance writer, 1965-67; U.S. Information Agency, Washington, D.C., foreign service officer, English teaching consultant, 1968-73, English teaching program adviser, 1973-74, writer-editor for Office of Policy and Plans, 1974—. Has lectured on linguistics and English teaching methodology in Afghanistan, Bolivia, Brazil, Cameroon, Canada, Colombia, Costa Rica, Czechoslovakia, Jordan, Laos, Malagasy Republic, Mexico, Morocco, Paraguay, Peru, Poland, Portugal, Spain, Thailand, Turkey, Uruguay, and Venezuela. *Member:* Teachers of English to Speakers of Other Languages, Middle East Institute, Phi Kappa Phi, International Club.

WRITINGS: The American Language Course Dictionary, Turkish Air Force Press, 1964; *Effective Techniques for English Conversation Groups,* Newbury House Publishers, 1974; (with Frank Sedwick) *Conversation in English: Points of Departure,* American Book Co., 1975. Contributor to *English Teaching Forum.*

WORK IN PROGRESS: Conversation in English: Professional Careers, with Gerald S. Hawkins, for American Book Co.; *A Dictionary of Dialogues,* illustrating English communication in hundreds of scenarios.

SIDELIGHTS: Dobson, whose career experiences have ranged from teaching in a Turkish aircraft hanger to dodging bullets in Amman, writes that her interests are in "cross-cultural communication, English phonology, and psycholinguistics. I particularly focus on the communicative phase of language teaching—the 'voice connection' which sustains a community and welds civilizations. Accurate verbalizing is the key to successful inter-personal relations, and I believe in launching a student into creative conversation at the earliest possible phase of language teaching."

* * *

DODD, Ed(ward) Benton 1902-

PERSONAL: Born November 7, 1902; in LaFayette, Ga.; son of Jesse Mercer (a Baptist minister) and Effie (Cooke) Dodd; married Rebecca Bowles, 1930 (divorced, 1932); married Miriam Croft, February 26, 1938 (died, 1943); married Elsa Norris (an artist), July 25, 1958 (divorced, 1968). *Education:* Studied at Georgia Institute of Technology, 1921-22, and Art Students' League of New York, 1923-24; studied animal drawing and illustration under Dan Beard. *Politics:* Republican. *Religion:* Presbyterian. *Home:* 6955 Brandon Mill Rd. N.E., Atlanta, Ga. 30328. *Agent:* Toni Mendez, Inc., 140 East 56th St., New York, N.Y. 10022.

CAREER: Dan Beard Camp for Boys, instructor, later director, 1920-38; New York Military Academy, Cornwall, N.Y., instructor in outdoor activities, 1926-27; commercial artist, New York, N.Y., 1929-30; cartoonist doing "Back Home Again," for United Feature Syndicate, 1930-45, and "Mark Trail" for Hall Syndicate, 1946—. National chairman, National Wildlife Week, 1952, 1953. *Member:* National Press Club (Washington, D.C.), Outdoor Writers of America, Delta Tau Delta, Homassassa Atlanta Club (Homassassa, Fla.), Piedmont Driving Club (Atlanta), Campfire Club (New York). *Awards, honors:* Award from Delta Sigma Chi for best cartoon strip, 1948; special award for outdoor writing, Georgia Sportsman Federation, 1960; awards for service to conservation from National Forest Association, 1951, Men's Garden Clubs of America, 1964, National Wildlife Federation (for greatest contribution to conservation in the United States), 1967, and other organizations; National Achievement award, Delta Tau Delta, 1972.

WRITINGS—Self-illustrated: Mark Trail's Book of North American Mammals, Hawthorn, 1955; *Chipper the Beaver* (juvenile), Putnam, 1968; *Flapfoot* (juvenile), Random House, 1968; *Mark Trail's Camping Tips,* Essandess, 1969; *Mark Trail's Fishing Tips,* Essandess, 1969; *Mark Trail's Hunting Tips,* Essandess, 1969; *Careers for the Seventies: Conservation,* Crowell, 1971; *Mark Trail's Boating Tips,* Essandess, 1971; *Mark Trail's Cooking Tips,* Essandess, 1971; *Mark Trail's Family Camping Tips,* Essandess, 1971. Author of NBC-TV documentary "Our Endangered Wildlife," and "Mark Trail's Man in Atlanta," for WAII-TV, Atlanta. Contributor to national magazines.

SIDELIGHTS: Ed Dodd has traveled extensively throughout the United States, Canada, Alaska, and visited in Europe, Central America, and Cuba. *Avocational interests:* Fishing, outdoor cooking, horse training, reading, and wing shooting.

* * *

DOLAN, Anthony R(ossi) 1948-

PERSONAL: Born July 7, 1948, in Norwalk, Conn.; son of Joseph W. (a businessman) and Margaret (Kelley) Dolan. *Education:* Yale University, B.A., 1970. *Religion:* Roman Catholic. *Home:* 256 Shippan Ave., Stamford, Conn. 06902. *Office: Stamford Advocate,* 258 Atlantic St., Stamford, Conn. 06904.

CAREER/WRITINGS: Has worked as a press consultant for U.S. Senate and gubernatorial campaigns, 1970-73; *Stamford Advocate,* Stamford, Conn., investigative reporter, 1973—. Notable assignments include exposure of municipal corruption in Stamford, Conn. *Military service:* U.S. Army Reserves, 1970-76. *Member:* Association of Composers, Authors, and Publishers. *Awards, honors:* New England Press Association citation, 1975, for exposure of civil service scandal; National Headliners Award, 1976, for "exposing crooked cops, the mob, and a corrupt political machine."

SIDELIGHTS: Roland Blais, editor of the *Stamford Advocate,* told *CA:* "Dolan's wide ranging investigations into Stamford city government has led to five major investigations by the U.S. Attorney's Office, the F.B.I. and grand juries, as well as dismissals or resignations of seven major city officials and numerous policemen. His studies have led to reform of the city civil service system and the appointment of a new 'reform' police chief. Dolan has also exposed abuses in a chain of nursing homes in Connecticut that led to a federal investigation into financial irregularities as well as a special investigation ordered by Governor Ella Grasso. Dolan's stories ended in the closing of one nursing home, the disclosure of conflicts of interests on the part of state health officials, and reforms in the state health inspection system.''

BIOGRAPHICAL/CRITICAL SOURCES: New York Times, June 11, 1977.

* * *

DONABEDIAN, Avedis 1919-

PERSONAL: Born January 7, 1919, in Beirut, Lebanon; came to the United States in 1955, naturalized citizen, 1960; son of Samuel (a physician) and Maritza (Der-Hagopian) Donabedian; married Dorothy Salibian (a professor of nursing), September 15, 1945; children: Haig, Bairj, Armen. *Education:* American University of Beirut, B.A., 1940, M.D., 1944; Harvard University, M.P.H., 1955. *Politics:* "Equal opportunity elitist!" *Religion:* Protestant. *Home:* 1739 Ivywood, Ann Arbor, Mich. 48103. *Office:* School of Public Health, University of Michigan, 109 Observatory St., Ann Arbor, Mich. 48109.

CAREER: English Mission Hospital, Jerusalem, Israel, physician and acting superintendent, 1945-47; American University of Beirut, Beirut, Lebanon, instructor in physiology, 1948-50, clinical assistant in dermatology, 1948-54, university physician, 1949-54, director of University Health Service, 1951-54; United Community Services of Metropolitan Boston, Boston, Mass., medical associate, 1955-57; New York Medical College, New York, N.Y., assistant professor, 1957-60, associate professor of preventive medicine, 1960-61; University of Michigan, Ann Arbor, associate professor, 1961-64, professor of medical care organization, 1964—. Emeritus member of National Academy of Sciences Institute of Medicine.

MEMBER: American Public Health Association (fellow), Association of Teachers of Preventive Medicine. *Awards, honors:* Dean Conley Award from American College of Hospital Administrators, 1969; Norman A. Welch Award from National Association of Blue Shield Plans, 1976, for *Benefits in Medical Care Programs.*

WRITINGS: Aspects of Medical Care Administration: Specifying Requirements for Health Care, American Public Health Association, 1969; *A Guide to Medical Care Administration,* Volume II: *Medical Care Appraisal: Quality and Utilization,* Harvard University Press, 1973; *Benefits in Medical Care Programs,* Harvard University Press, 1976. Contributor to medical and public health journals.

WORK IN PROGRESS: Research on the assessment and monitoring of the quality and appropriateness of medical care.

SIDELIGHTS: Donabedian writes briefly: "For some years now my major interest has been in collecting and systematizing available information in the field of health services administration. This work will continue probably until my retirement and will represent my contribution to my field.''

* * *

DONALDSON, Kenneth 1908-

PERSONAL: Born May 22, 1908, in Erie, Pa.; son of Wil-

liam T. (a machinist) and Marjorie K. (Whitbeck) Donaldson; children: David K., Beverly Ann Donaldson Reaves, Peter A. *Education:* Attended Syracuse University. *Politics:* Democrat. *Home and office address:* P.O. Box 1145, York, Pa. 17405. *Agent:* Maxwell Aley Associates, 145 East 35th St., New York, N.Y. 10016.

CAREER: Worked as a salesperson, factory machine operator, carpenter, and builder in Syracuse, N.Y., Tucson, Ariz., St. Louis, Mo., Los Angeles, Calif., and Philadelphia, Pa., 1938-56; writer and lecturer in Syracuse, N.Y., 1971-73; writer and lecturer in York, Pa., 1973—. *Member:* Mental Health Association of York County. *Awards, honors:* Has received awards from Mental Health Association; Ralph E. Kharas Award, 1977, from the central New York chapter of the American Civil Liberties Union.

WRITINGS: Insanity Inside Out, Crown, 1976.

WORK IN PROGRESS: A fictional account of his legal case; a nonfiction elaboration of testimony given before a Senate subcommittee on the aging.

SIDELIGHTS: In 1957, Donaldson was committed to a Florida state mental hospital by his father. Although he was diagnosed as a paranoid schizophrenic, Donaldson says that his illness was mainly that he "refused to admit I was ill when I first went there. From what I've seen and heard, that is the worst disease you can have—refusing to admit that you have a disease.''

He refused, as well, to accept his involuntary confinement. After three years as a "patient" (he received virtually no psychiatric treatment), he began petitioning state and federal courts for his release. During the nineteenth round of appeals, under the direction of his lawyer Morton Birnbaum, with an *amicus curiae* brief by the New York Civil Liberties Union, plus briefs from three other organizations, the hospital set him free with no strings attached, July 31, 1971, about ten days before he was to appear in federal court on a writ of habeas corpus.

Then, under the direction of Attorney Bruce Ennis, of the Mental Health Law Project, Donaldson won a judgment against two of the hospital doctors, including punitive damages. This was the first judgment ever against a state hospital doctor. On appeal, the damages award was vacated by the U.S. Supreme Court because of a technicality. More importantly, the court ruled in *O'Connor v. Donaldson* on June 26, 1976, that "a state cannot constitutionally confine without *more* a nondangerous individual who is capable of surviving safely in freedom.''

Donaldson's book *Insanity Inside Out,* which the *New York Times* called a "powerful story of the injustices that are done in the name of caring for the mentally ill,'' is an account of his experiences. He told *CA:* "My writings represent my crusade to inform the American public that we have a misconception of our state mental hospitals. I feel that very few people need to be confined because of so-called mental illness.''

BIOGRAPHICAL/CRITICAL SOURCES: Bruce Ennis, *Prisoners of Psychiatry,* Harcourt, 1972; *Time,* July 7, 1975; *Newsweek,* July 7, 1975; *New York Times Book Review,* July 18, 1976; *New Republic,* September 18, 1976; *Village Voice,* November 22, 1976.

* * *

DONOHUE, James F(itzgerald) 1934-

PERSONAL: Born June 11, 1934, in New York, N.Y.; son of Harold J. (a hotel manager) and Josephine (Hamel) Donohue; married Muriel Lyford, July 26, 1965; children: Catherine, Deborah. *Education:* St. Mary's University, B.A., 1957. *Politics:* Independent. *Religion:* Roman Catholic. *Residence:* Scituate, Mass. *Agent:* Otte Co., 9 Park St., Boston, Mass. 02108. *Office:* Cahners Publishing Co., Inc., 221 Columbus Ave., Boston, Mass. 02116.

CAREER: Gainesville Daily Times, Gainesville, Ga., reporter, 1959-60; *Charlotte Observer,* Charlotte, N.C., reporter, 1960-62; *Greensboro News,* Greensboro, N.C., reporter, 1962-64; Associated Press, Boston, Mass., reporter, 1964-67; Carl Byoir & Associates (public relations firm), New York, N.Y., in press relations, 1967-70; Weber Donohue Cooper, Inc. (public relations and advertising firm), Weymouth, Mass., co-owner, 1970-74; Cahners Publishing Co., Inc., Boston, managing editor of *Purchasing,* 1974—. *Military service:* U.S. Air Force Reserve, 1958-64. *Awards, honors:* Silver Anvil from Public Relations Society of America, 1968.

WRITINGS: Spitballs and Holy Water (novel), Avon, 1977.

WORK IN PROGRESS: Starr Carr, a novel.

SIDELIGHTS: Donohue writes: "If you can write, I think you have an obligation to do it. That's using a rare talent. You should determine what you want to accomplish with what you write. I write mainly for enjoyment for my readers and myself. I think it is helpful to write from experience, but not necessary. I think it is helpful to learn something (from research, possibly) and pass that on to your reader. Then you both learn something. I am not black, but I gave a great deal of information about the Negro Leagues in *Spitballs and Holy Water* because I found that period historically fascinating."

* * *

DONOVAN, Bonita R. 1947-
(Bonnie Donovan)

PERSONAL: Born January 1, 1947, in Waycross, Ga.; daughter of Frederick J. and Evon (Strickland) Rose; married second husband, William S. Donovan (in international planning and development); children: (first marriage) Jon Bradley Pease; (second marriage) Sarah Meade. *Education:* Attended Long Island University (C. W. Post College). *Politics:* Liberal. *Religion:* Unitarian-Universalist. *Home address:* Camp Parker, Pembroke, Mass. 02359.

CAREER: Massachusetts League of Cities and Towns, Boston, secretary, 1966-67; *Newburyport Daily News,* Newburyport, Mass., advertising saleswoman, 1968; licensed real estate broker in Newburyport, 1969-74; South Shore Hospital, South Weymouth, Mass., associate cesarean childbirth educator, 1974-77; Jordan Hospital, Plymouth, Mass., cesarean childbirth educator, 1977—. Writer, 1973—. Adviser to Cesarean Support Group of Vermont.

MEMBER: International Childbirth Education Association (state coordinator), 1977-78), Nurses Association of the American College of Obstetricians and Gynecologists (NAACOG; associate member), National Association of Parents and Professionals for Safe Alternatives in Childbirth.

WRITINGS: The Cesarean Birth Experience, Beacon Press, 1977. Contributor to nursing journals.

WORK IN PROGRESS: (Under name Bonnie Donovan) *How Are Cesarean Babies Born?,* for children; *Supernatural Childbirth or Technological Joyland?,* a childbirth book dealing with iatrogenesis; *Plastic Straws and Silver Spoons* (tentative title), a satirical semi-erotic feminist novel; a trilogy of nonsexist contemporary fantasies for children; *Black Mesa, Blue Tacos,* a short novel set in New Mexico; poetry and song lyrics.

SIDELIGHTS: Bonnie Donovan writes: "Wordsmith, childbirth educator, public speaker, consumer advocate, familywoman: my careers are not always interrelated nor are they mutually exclusive. Like other women with families, mine is a classic problem of trying to find time to do all the jobs well without neglecting one or another. No longer do I consider myself a strident feminist. My sense of outrage, of injustice, of bitterness has been replaced by a more holistic, humanistic equilibrium—and a sense of humor. Having just hit the Catch-30 crossroads of my life, instead of being in a crisis, I find that I'm only now hitting my stride, just beginning to give birth to myself. I find the renascence exhilarating. Being able to accept change, to grow with it means that my life has been enriched, expanded, and diversified. So has my writing.

"An interesting sidelight to my writing has been invitations to do public appearances, give lectures, and be a guest on television shows including, most recently, 'The Today Show.' Not only does this offer me the opportunity to travel, it has also helped me overcome the phobia of addressing large groups of people—a situation that was formerly so intimidating that as a member of the audience I could barely summon the courage to ask a question of the speaker. No more!"

* * *

DONOVAN, Bonnie
See DONOVAN, Bonita R.

* * *

DORAN, Charles F(rancis) 1943-

PERSONAL: Born January 31, 1943, in Mankato, Minn.; son of Francis George (in agriculture) and Harriet (a teacher; maiden name, Wallace) Doran; married Barbara Giusti (a writer and educational consultant), December 29, 1967; children: Charles Francis, Jr., Brent. *Education:* Harvard University, A.B., 1964; Johns Hopkins School of Advanced International Studies, M.A., 1966; Johns Hopkins University, Ph.D., 1969. *Home:* 5006 Wigton, Houston, Tex. 77096. *Office:* Department of Political Science, Rice University, Houston, Tex. 77001.

CAREER: Texas A & M University, College Station, assistant professor of political science, 1968-69; Rice University, Houston, Tex., assistant professor, 1969-74, associate professor of political science, 1974—. Member of Houston Committee on the Humanities. *Member:* International Studies Association, American Political Science Association, Peace Science Society (southern vice-president, 1974-75).

WRITINGS: The Politics of Assimilation: Hegemony and Its Aftermath, Johns Hopkins Press, 1973; (with Manfred Hinz and P. C. Mayer-Tasch) *Umweltschutz: Politik des peripheren Eingriffs—Einführung in die politische okologie,* Sammlung Luchterland, 1974; *Domestic Conflict in State Relations: The American Sphere of Influence,* Sage Publications, 1976; *Myth, Oil and Politics: An Introduction to the Political Economy of Petroleum,* Free Press, 1977. Contributor to professional journals. Member of editorial board of *Comparative Sociology.*

WORK IN PROGRESS: Continuing research on international energy politics, conflict analysis, political risk analysis, international relations, and U.S. foreign policy.

DORFMAN, Nat N. 1895-1977

1895—July 3, 1977; American theatre press agent, journalist, and playwright. Dorfman began his career as a reporter for the *American,* and contributed humorous articles to such magazines as *Collier's, Saturday Evening Post, Vanity Fair,* and *Life.* Choosing the theatre over newspaper work, he became a press agent and represented more than three hundred Broadway plays. He also served as public information director of the New York City Opera, handling such personalities as Beverly Sills, Maralin Niska, Norman Treigle, and Spiro Malas. He was the author of such plays as "Errant Lady," "Take My Tip," and "Rhapsody in Black." He died in New York, N.Y. Obituaries: *New York Times,* July 7, 1977; *Time,* July 18, 1977.

* * *

DORIA, Charles 1938-

PERSONAL: Born April 18, 1938, in Cleveland, Ohio; son of Louis (a lawyer) and Alice (a teacher; maiden name, Farinacci) Doria; children: Diana. *Education:* Western Reserve University (now Case Western Reserve University), B.A., 1960; Harvard University, M.A., 1964; State University of New York at Buffalo, Ph.D., 1966. *Politics:* Anarchist. *Religion:* Polytheist. *Home:* 106 Spring St., New York, N.Y. 10012.

CAREER: State University of New York at Buffalo, instructor in English, 1964-66; University of Texas, Austin, assistant professor of classics, 1967-74; free-lance writer, 1974—. Visiting professor at State University of New York at Buffalo, summer, 1973; visiting lecturer at University of Utah, spring, 1976. *Awards, honors:* Fulbright grant for travel in Italy, 1960-61; grant from Italian Government, 1960-61; Woodrow Wilson fellowship, 1961-63; Fulbright student in Vienna, 1966-67.

WRITINGS: (Contributor) Gareth Morgan, editor, *The Fourth Skill* (college Latin textbook), Austin Printing, 1970, revised edition, 1972; (contributor) Joan McIntyre, editor, *Mind in the Waters,* Scribner, 1974; (editor and translator, with Harris Lenowitz) *Origins: Creation Texts from the Ancient Mediterranean,* Doubleday, 1976; (editor and translator) *The Tenth Muse: Classical Drama in Translation,* Swallow Press, 1977; *The Game of Europe* (poems), Membrane Press, 1977; (with Jerome Rothenberg, editors) *The Big Jewish Book: Poems and Other Visions of the Jews,* Doubleday, 1978; *Austin Flaco* (poems), Swallow Press, in press; (contributor) Diane DiPrima, editor, *Realms of the Goddess,* Doubleday, in press.

Represented in anthologies, including *Experiments in Prose,* edited by Eugene Wildman, Swallow Press, 1969; *New Poetry Anthology,* edited by Michael Anania, Swallow Press, 1969; *An Anthology of Greek Tragedy,* edited by A. S. Cook and Edwin Dolin, Bobbs-Merrill, 1972. Contributor of articles and translations to scholarly journals. Co-editor of *Audit/Poetry,* 1963-66; contributing editor of *Alcheringa: Ethnopoetics,* 1973—; guest editor of *Margins,* 1976.

WORK IN PROGRESS: Translating *Carmina Burana* and Giordano Bruno; poems and translations for *New Wilderness.*

SIDELIGHTS: Doria writes: "My aims include reviving interest in the classics; translation as literature; poetry as a synthesis of time and personal experience; and breaking new ground when- and wherever possible. My present home is New York City—a place where all human dreams have a way of coming true." *Avocational interests:* Visual arts, rock and roll.

DORIAN, Harry
See HAMILTON, Charles Harold St. John

* * *

DORMAN, Sonya 1924-

PERSONAL: Born June 4, 1924, in United States; daughter of Louis (a merchant) and Grace (a dancer and model; maiden name, Brown) Hess; first marriage ended in divorce, 1946; married Jack Dorman (an engineer), 1950; children: Sherri. *Politics:* "Fluctuating." *Religion:* "Taoist inclinations." *Residence:* Connecticut. *Agent:* John Schaffner, 425 East 51st St., New York, N.Y. 10022.

CAREER: Has been employed variously as cook, receptionist, flamenco dancer, kennel maid, and stable maid. Writer. *Member:* Poetry Society of America, P.E.N., Science Fiction Writers of America.

WRITINGS: Poems, Ohio State University Press, 1970; *Stretching Fence,* Ohio University Press, 1975; *Planet Patrol* (juvenile novel), Coward, 1978. Also author of *A Paper Raincoat,* Puckerbrush Press. Contributor of poems to periodicals, including *Nation, Saturday Review, Harper's,* and *Southern Poetry Review;* contributor of short stories to periodicals, including *Redbook, Cosmopolitan,* and *Fantasy & Science Fiction,* and to numerous science-fiction anthologies.

WORK IN PROGRESS: Every Link Is Just the Same, a completed, as yet unpublished, novel; *The Lost Traveller,* a book of poetry.

SIDELIGHTS: Dorman told *CA* that "periods of residence at the MacDowell Colony have been of great importance to me; many of my best poems were written there, and collections of poetry put together at the Colony." She wrote that she is "interested in and influenced by organic gardening, land and water resources, and rock hunting as a hobby, all of which I share with my husband." They have visited Finland, Norway, New Zealand, Australia, Iles de la Madaleine, and plan to hunt rocks in Washington, Oregon, and British Columbia.

* * *

DOROTHY, R. D.
See CHARQUES, Dorothy (Taylor)

* * *

DOUGLAS, David C(harles) 1898-

PERSONAL: Born January 5, 1898, in London, England; son of John Josiah (a physician) and Margaret (Peake) Douglas; married Evelyn Helen Wilson, June 7, 1932; children: Ann Margaret. *Education:* Keble College, Oxford, B.A. (first class honors), 1921. *Home:* 4 Henleaze Gardens, Bristol BS9 4HJ, England.

CAREER: University of Glasgow, Glasgow, Scotland, lecturer in history, 1924-34; University of Exeter, Exeter, England, professor of history, 1934-39; University of Leeds, Leeds, England, professor of medieval history, 1939-45; University of Bristol, Bristol, England, professor of history, 1945-63; writer, 1963—. Ford's Lecturer at Oxford University, 1962-63. Member of board of trustees of London Museum, 1945-70. *Member:* British Academy (fellow). *Awards, honors:* James Tait Black Prize, 1939, for *English Scholars;* honorary fellow of Keble College, Oxford, 1960; D.Litt. from University of Caen, 1957, University of Wales, 1966, and University of Exeter, 1974.

WRITINGS: *English Scholars,* Jonathon Cape, 1939; *Domesday Monarchorum,* Historical Society of Great Britain, 1944; (editor with G. W. Greenaway) *English Historical Documents,* Oxford University Press, Volume I, 1953, Volume II, 1953; *William the Conqueror: The Norman Impact upon England,* University of California Press, 1964; *The Norman Achievement, 1050-1100,* University of California Press, 1969; *The Norman Fate, 1100-1154,* University of California Press, 1976; *Time and the Hour,* Metheun, 1977. Also editor of *English Monarchs.* Contributor of articles and reviews to scholarly journals.

WORK IN PROGRESS: Further research in Anglo-Norman history.

* * *

DOUGLAS, Roy (Ian) 1924-

PERSONAL: Born December 28, 1924, in London, England; son of Percy Oswald (a company secretary) and Lilian (Bowley) Douglas; married Jean Rosemary Roberts, January, 1955; children: Alison, Michael, Bruce, Nigel. *Education:* University of London, B.Sc., 1946; University of Edinburgh, Ph.D., 1952. *Politics:* "Liberal (nineteenth-century type!)." *Home:* 26 Downs Rd., Coulsdon, Surrey CR3 1AA, England. *Agent:* Curtis Brown Ltd., 1 Craven Hill, London W2 3EP, England. *Office:* University of Surrey, Guildford, Surrey GU2 5XH, England.

CAREER: Barrister-at-law; called to the Bar in 1956; University of Surrey, Guildford, Surrey, England, lecturer, 1955-76, senior lecturer, 1976—. Liberal Parliamentary candidate, 1950, 1951, 1955, 1959, 1964.

WRITINGS: *Law for Technologists,* Gee, 1964; *The History of the Liberal Party, 1895-1970,* Sidgwick & Jackson, 1971; (contributor) K. D. Brown, editor, *Essys in Anti-Labour History,* Macmillan, 1974; (contributor) A.J.A. Morris, editor, *Edwardian Radicalism,* Routledge & Kegan Paul, 1974; *Land, People, and Politics,* St. Martin's, 1976; *In the Year of Munich,* Macmillan, 1977. Contributor to learned journals.

WORK IN PROGRESS: *The Advent of War,* a sequel to *In the Year of Munich.*

* * *

DOUGLASS, Herbert Edgar 1927-

PERSONAL: Born May 16, 1927, in Springfield, Mass.; son of Herbert Edgar, Sr. (a plant manager) and Mildred (a nurse; maiden name, Munson) Douglass; married Vivienne Trask, June 15, 1947 (divorced); married Norma Campbell (a medical secretary), November 16, 1974; children: Janelle Douglass Voorhees, Herbert Edgar III, Reatha Douglass Van Dolson, Vivienne Sue Douglass Rampton. *Education:* Atlantic Union College, A.B. (summa cum laude), 1947; Andrews University, M.A., 1956, B.D. (magna cum laude), 1957; Pacific School of Religion, Th.D., 1964. *Home:* 419 Browning Ave., Bismarck, N.D. 58501.

CAREER: Ordained clergyman of Seventh-day Adventist Church, 1951; pastor of Seventh-day Adventist churches in Illinois, 1947-53; Pacific Union College, Angwin, Calif., assistant professor of religion, 1953-60; Atlantic Union College, South Lancaster, Mass., professor of religion and head of department, 1960-64, dean, 1964-67, president of college, 1967-70; *Review & Herald,* Washington, D.C., associate editor, 1970-76; Carlson Mortgage & Development, Bismarck, N.D., president, 1976—. Chairman of board of directors of Trans World Foundation, 1971—; vice-president

of Wilderness Survival Seminar, 1975—; general partner of Sligo-Colonial Partnership, 1976—. *Member:* Rotary International.

WRITINGS: *If I Had One Sermon to Preach,* Review & Herald, 1971; *Why I Joined,* Review & Herald, 1972; *What Ellen White Means to Me,* Review & Herald, 1973; *We Found This Faith,* Review & Herald, 1974; *Perfection: The Impossible Possibility,* Southern Publishing, 1975; *Why Jesus Waits,* Review & Herald, 1976; *Jesus: The Benchmark of Humanity,* Southern Publishing, 1977. Contributor to *These Times, Ministry,* and *Review & Herald.*

WORK IN PROGRESS: *Faith That Works; Hastening God's Harvest.*

SIDELIGHTS: Douglass mentions that he has led two tours through Europe and the Near East, and has made five visits to Scotland. *Avocational interests:* Gardening, remodeling homes, horse riding.

* * *

DOUGLASS, Malcolm P(aul) 1923-

PERSONAL: Born August 18, 1923, in Pullman, Wash.; son of Aubrey A. (an educator) and Mary Evelyn (Fitzsimmons) Douglass; married Enid Marie Hart (an oral historian), August 28, 1948; children: Malcolm Paul, Jr., John Aubrey, Susan Enid. *Education:* Pomona College, B.A., 1947; Columbia University, M.A., 1948; Stanford University, Ed.D., 1954. *Home:* 1195 Berkeley Ave., Claremont, Calif. 91711; and Mt. Desert, Me. 04660. *Office:* Center for Developmental Studies in Education, Claremont Graduate School, Claremont, Calif. 91711.

CAREER: Teacher in public schools in Sacramento, Calif., 1948-50, and San Lorenzo, Calif., 1952-54, administrator in San Lorenzo, 1950-54; Claremont Graduate School, Claremont, Calif., assistant professor, 1954-58, associate professor, 1958-63, professor of education, 1963—, chairman of department, 1961-68, 1975—, member of advisory board of George G. Stone Center for Children's Books, 1966—, director of Center for Developmental Studies in Education, 1971—. *Military service:* U.S. Army, 1943-45; served in European theater. *Member:* International Reading Association, International Society for the Study of Behavioral Development, American Association of University Professors, National Council of Teachers of English, National Council for the Social Studies, Society for Research in Child Development, California Curriculum Forum.

WRITINGS: *Reading Meaning into Maps Through the Camera Lens,* Curriculum Materials Center, 1961; (contributor) Maury Hillson, editor, *Change and Innovation in Elementary School Organization: Selected Readings,* Holt, 1965; *Social Studies: From Theory to Practice in Elementary Education,* Lippincott, 1967; (contributor) Willard W. Hartrup and Jan de Wit, editors, *Determinants of Behavioral Development,* Academic Press, 1972; (contributor) Madelon Stent and others, editors, *Cultural Pluralism in Education,* Appleton, 1973; (editor) *Reading in Education: A Broader View,* C. E. Merrill, 1973.

Editor; "Claremont Reading Conference" series; all published by Claremont Graduate School: *Marks of Superiority in Reading Instruction,* 1960; *Facing the Issues in Reading,* 1961; *Reading in a Responsible Society,* 1962; *Readers for the Twenty-first Century,* 1963; *Reading and Emerging Cultural Values,* 1964; *On Becoming a Reader,* 1965; *Beyond Literacy,* 1966; *Imprints of Culture,* 1967; *Self and Society,* 1968; *Sign and Significance,* 1969; *Reading and School Life,*

1970; *The Many Facets of Reading,* 1971; *The Person in a Mass Society,* 1972; *Reading Between and Beyond the Lines,* 1973; *Reading, Thought, and Language,* 1974; *Reading the Teaching Learning Process,* 1975; *A Little Revolution Now and Then,* 1976; *All Things Considered . . .,* 1977.

Author of filmstrip series, "Maps and Map Reading." Contributor to *New World Dictionary* and to educational journals.

WORK IN PROGRESS: Reading in America (tentative title).

SIDELIGHTS: Malcolm Douglass told *CA:* "My primary interests in research and teaching have focused on the teaching-learning process, especially upon the education of the young child, the processes by which curriculum is developed and put into practice in our schools, and the role of the school in social education. I have had a long-standing interest in the reading process broadly viewed. As a result, I have been engaged for many years in studying the growth of map-reading abilities in addition to being concerned with reading (and writing) the verbal mode in communication. I believe we have treated reading as an end rather than as a means to an end, that we have failed to see it as a very natural process, one in which all persons may easily engage, if the educative conditions are conducive to the evocation of the process rather than being based upon invoking this much sought after behavior. Currently, I am engaged in studying how reading emerges in a natural setting, prior to the child's entry into the formal school system."

*   *   *

DOYLE, James (Stephen) 1935-

PERSONAL: Born June 18, 1935, in Boston, Mass.; son of Donald Joseph (a cabinet maker) and Catherine (MacDonald) Doyle; married Ann Grady (a tutor), December 28, 1960; children: Katherine, Rebecca. *Education:* Boston College, B.S., 1956; Columbia University, M.A., 1961. *Politics:* Constitutionalist. *Religion:* Roman Catholic. *Home:* 6401 Tone Dr., Bethesda, Md. 20034. *Office: Newsweek,* 1750 Pennsylvania Ave. N.W., Washington, D.C. 20006.

CAREER: Boston Globe, Boston, Mass., political reporter, 1961-65, Washington bureau chief, 1965-70; *Washington Star,* Washington, D.C., national correspondent, 1970-73; Watergate Special Prosecution Force, Washington, D.C., special assistant and spokesman, 1973-75; *Newsweek,* Washington, D.C., correspondent, 1976-77, deputy bureau chief, 1977—. *Military service:* U.S. Navy, 1957-60; became lieutenant, junior grade. *Member:* Reporter's Committee for Freedom of the Press (founding member), Authors Guild, Society of Nieman Fellows, Merrimack Park Citizens Association (past president), National Symphony Association, Federal City Club, International Club, Potomac Appalachian Trail Club. *Awards, honors:* Pulitzer Prize, 1965, for meritorious public service; Nieman fellow, 1965.

WRITINGS: Not Above the Law: The Battles of Watergate Prosecutors Cox and Jaworski, Morrow, 1977. Contributor of articles to *Newsweek, New Republic, Reporter, Progressive, Boston, Forum,* and *New York Times.*

WORK IN PROGRESS: Research on "Institutional folkways of U.S. Senate"; research on the future of American political parties.

SIDELIGHTS: In June, 1973, Doyle became special assistant to the Watergate Special Prosecution Force and served as spokesman and adviser to Archibald Cox, Leon Jaworski, and Henry S. Ruth, Jr. "With the announced intention of

writing of my experience," Doyle told *CA,* "I kept a diary recording the internal debates and conflicts within the Watergate Special Prosecution Force. After the 'Saturday Night Massacre' when Cox was fired, the subsequent revelation of the White House tapes' contents, the resignation of Richard Nixon and his pardon by Gerald Ford, I began interviewing all the participants for *Not Above the Law,* which in manuscript form ran to more than 300,000 words. A revision, running to 150,000 words, was published in June 1977.

"I believe the book will be a recognized source for historians. While I will go on to write others, this will be my most important and enduring book. It records the inequities of the American criminal justice system in the late 20th century, but its real contribution is as an antidote to the nihilistic view of the Washington of Vietnam and Watergate.

"One who reads Jonathon Schell's *A Time of Illusion* will read *Not Above the Law* to discover that in the end democracy was vindicated. My story shows that Gladstone was right: the United States Constitution is the most remarkable political document produced by the human intellect in modern times."

When asked by *CA* if he felt that Watergate helped purge American politics, Doyle responded: "Despite the revisionist history being set down, often at great financial profit, by Richard Nixon and other leading participants in the Watergate obstruction of justice, what will endure into the coming generations is the evidence that Watergate tested the strength of the government structures set down 200 years earlier by the Founders, and the edifice held.

"This was our most profound Constitutional crisis, in which an elected chief executive was subjected to criminal investigation under traditional procedures administered by the Executive branch; with the aggressive oversight of the Legislative branch; with the diligent supervision of the Judicial branch, from a District Court to the full bench of the Supreme Court of the United States.

"The performances of the three branches, and of the American press, has not purged American politics of its traditions of plunder and corruption. But it will be a long time before another President tries to steal from us our Constitution. Hopefully it will never happen again."

*   *   *

DRAKE, Frank
See HAMILTON, Charles Harold St. John

*   *   *

DREGER, Ralph Mason 1913-

PERSONAL: Born April 18, 1913, in Chicago, Ill.; son of E. Herbert (an accountant) and Clara (a bookkeeper; maiden name, Mason) Dreger; married G. Ellen Mills, July 24, 1936 (deceased); married Alice May Hill (a production worker), April 14, 1973; children: Philip Alan, Patricia Jean, David Herbert. *Education:* Wheaton College, Wheaton, Ill., A.B. (cum laude), 1935; Garrett-Evangelical Theological Seminary, M.Div. (with distinction), 1938; Northwestern University, M.A., 1939; University of Southern California, Ph.D., 1950. *Politics:* Democrat. *Home:* 2106 Lee Dr., Baton Rouge, La. 70808. *Office:* Department of Psychology, Louisiana State University, Baton Route, La. 70803.

CAREER: Ordained Methodist minister, 1939; pastor of Methodist churches in Illinois and California, 1935-47; teacher of psychology and literature to adults in public schools in Los Angeles, Calif., 1948; George Pepperdine

College (now Pepperdine University), Los Angeles, Calif., instructor in psychology, 1948-49; Florida State University, Tallahassee, assistant professor of psychology, 1949-56; Child Guidance and Speech Correction Clinic, Jacksonville, Fla., director, 1956-60; Jacksonville University, Jacksonville, Fla., professor of psychology, 1960-64; Louisiana State University, Baton Rouge, professor of psychology, 1964—. Member of Florida State Board of Examiners in Psychology, 1958-61, Florida Cooperating Council on Children and Youth, 1961-63, Florida Council on Human Relations (member of board of directors, 1956-64; member of executive committee, 1962-63; president, 1963), Louisiana Advisory Committee to U.S. Civil Rights Commission, 1964—, Louisiana Council on Human Relations (member of board of directors, 1965—; member of executive committee, 1967—; president, 1972—), Southern Regional Council, 1964—, and Uniting Campus Ministry (member of board of directors, 1965-76; president, 1970-72).

MEMBER: American Association for the Advancement of Science (fellow), American Association of University Professors, American Psychological Association (fellow), Society for Research in Child Development, Southeastern Psychological Association (president, 1965-66), Southeastern Society for Multivariate Experimental Psychology (chief executive officer, 1969-70), Florida Psychological Association (president, 1959-60), Louisiana Psychological Association (member of executive committee, 1965—), Phi Beta Kappa, Sigma Xi (local vice-president, 1960-62), Sigma Pi Sigma. *Awards, honors:* Visiting scientist for National Academy of Sciences and American Psychological Association, 1974.

WRITINGS: Fundamentals of Personality, Lippincott, 1962; *Multivariate Personality Research,* Claitors, 1972; (co-editor) *Comparative Studies of Blacks and Whites in the United States,* Seminar Press, 1973; *Handbook of Modern Personality Theory,* Wiley, 1977.

Contributor: I. A. Berg and L. A. Pennington, editors, *An Introduction to Clinical Psychology,* Ronald, 1966; G. P. Bowers and W. Baskin, editors, *New Outlooks in Psychology,* Philosophical Library, 1969.

Contributor of more than sixty articles and reviews to scientific journals. Consulting editor of *Journal for the Scientific Study of Religion* and *Journal of Abnormal Child Psychology;* reviewer for *Journal of Clinical and Consulting Psychology* and *Psychological Bulletin.*

WORK IN PROGRESS: A manual and handbook for a children's behavioral classification project, on children's emotional disorders.

SIDELIGHTS: Dreger comments that his most current concerns are his work in the area of human rights and his work on microcomputer applications. He adds that some books that have influenced his work are the Hebrew Bible, Deissman's *Light from the Ancient East,* and Fenichel's *Psychoanalytic Theory of Neurosis.*

* * *

DREHER, Carl 1896-1976

PERSONAL: Born February 17, 1896, in Vienna, Austria; came to United States in 1898; son of Julius (a businessman) and Cecelia Dreher; married wife, Rose, April 13, 1925. *Education:* College of the City of New York (now City College of the City University of New York), B.S., 1917. *Residence:* New York.

CAREER: Sound engineer for Radio-Keith-Orpheum

(RKO) studios, Hollywood, Calif., 1929-37, and for RCA Corporation and the National Broadcasting Company (NBC); science editor for *Nation,* New York, N.Y., 1961-75. *Military service:* U.S. Air Force, 1942-45; became major. *Member:* Radio Club of America (fellow), American Institute of Electrical and Electronic Engineers (fellow).

WRITINGS: The Coming Showdown, Little, Brown, 1940 (published in England as *The Coming Future,* John Lane, 1943); *Automation,* Norton, 1957; *Sarnoff, An American Success,* Quadrangle, 1977. Contributor of stories and articles to popular magazines and engineering journals.

OBITUARIES: Nation, July 31, 1976.

(Died July 13, 1976, in New York)

[Sketch verified by wife, Rose Dreher]

* * *

DRUMMOND, Maldwin Andrew Cyril 1932-

PERSONAL: Born April 30, 1932, in London, England; son of Cyril Augustus (a soldier) and Mildred (Humphreys) Drummond; married Susan Cayley, August 21, 1955; children: Frederica, Annabella. *Education:* Attended Royal Agricultural College; University of Southampton, certificate in environmental science (with distinction), 1972. *Religion:* Church of England. *Home and office:* Manor of Cadland, Fawley, Southampton, England. *Agent:* Lady Avebury, Strathmore Literary Agency, 145 Park Rd., St. John's Wood, London N.W.8, England.

CAREER: Manor of Cadland, Cadland Farms, Fawley, England, owner, 1956—. Director of Newtown Oyster Co. and Rothesay Seafoods; senior partner of Inland and Waterside Planners. Member of New Forest District Council, 1958-67, Hampshire County Council, 1967-75, and Southampton Harbour Board, 1967-73; chairman of Hamble River Management Committee, 1973-75; verderer of New Forest, 1961—. Member of council of Maritime Trust (vice-chairman, 1971—); member of management committee of Royal National Life-Boat Institution, 1971—. *Military service:* British Army, Rifle Brigade, 1950-52, Queen's Royal Rifles, 1952-64; became captain.

MEMBER: Geologist Association, Palaeontographical Association, Marine Biological Association, Brackish Water Association, Solent Protection Society (chairman, 1969-71), Society for Environmental Improvement (member of council, 1974—), Royal Yacht Squadron, Royal Cruising Club, Royal Ocean Racing Club.

WRITINGS: (Editor) *The Secrets of George Smith, Fisherman* (self-illustrated), Ilex Press, 1973; *Conflicts in an Estuary,* Ilex Press, 1973; (editor) *Esturine Pollution,* University of Southampton Press, 1974; *Tall Ships,* Angus & Robertson, 1976. Yachting correspondent for *Field,* 1964-69.

WORK IN PROGRESS: A book devoted to explaining the natural environment to the amateur sailor; a novel concerning sailing, curses, and the West Coast of Scotland; research on ships in trust.

SIDELIGHTS: Drummond writes briefly: "The sea provides my main motivation, though I am interested and worried about the effects of man on other environments. My books have been devoted to salt water."

* * *

DUCKHAM, A(lec) N(arraway) 1903-

PERSONAL: Born August 23, 1903, in London, England;

son of Alexander (a chemist) and Violet Ethel (Narraway) Duckham; married Audrey Mary Polgreen, November 23, 1932 (died, 1969); children: Shelagh Frances Duckham Cox, Bruce, Katherine Duckham Westbrook. *Education:* Clare College, Cambridge, M.A. (honors), diploma in agricultural science (with distinction), 1926. *Politics:* "Centre." *Home:* 5 Woolacombe Dr., Elm Rd., Reading RG6 2WA, England. *Office:* Department of Agriculture, University of Reading, Earley Gate, Reading RG6 2AT, England.

CAREER: Conducted research and advisory work on animal husbandry in Cambridge, England, Aberdeen, Scotland, and Belfast, Northern Ireland, 1927-39; Ministry of Food, London, England, chairman of home and overseas agricultural supplies committees and director of Supply Plans Division, 1941-45; British Embassy, Washington, D.C., agricultural attache, 1945-50; Ministry of Agriculture and Fisheries, London, England, assistant secretary, 1950-54; University of Reading, Reading, England, professor of agriculture, 1955—. Vice-chairman of Alexander Duckham & Co. Ltd., 1945-70. Agricultural adviser to United Kingdom high commissioner in Ottawa, Ontario, 1945-50; liaison officer to Minister of Agriculture, Fisheries, and food, 1965-70. *Member:* Institute of Biology (fellow). *Awards, honors:* Silver Research Medal from Royal Agricultural Society, 1926; Officer of the Order of the British Empire, 1945, Commander, 1950.

WRITINGS: Animal Industry in the British Empire, Oxford University Press, 1932; *American Agriculture,* H.M.S.O., 1952; *The Fabric of Farming,* Chatto & Windus, 1958; *Agricultural Synthesis: The Farming Year,* Chatto & Windus, 1963; (with G. B. Masefield) *Farming Systems of the World,* Chatto & Windus, 1970; (editor with J. G. W. Jones and E. H. Roberts) *Food Production and Consumption,* American Elsevier, 1976. Co-editor of *Journal of Agricultural Administration.*

WORK IN PROGRESS: A book on agricultural administration, publication expected in 1979; research on food resource management.

SIDELIGHTS: Duckham comments that his main professional interest has been "feeding the world." *Avocational interests:* Oil painting, music (especially opera), reading nonfiction and poetry.

* * *

DUDLEY, Louise 1884-

PERSONAL: Born November 15, 1884, in Georgetown, Ky.; daughter of Richard Moberley (a teacher) and Mary (Henton) Dudley. *Education:* Georgetown College, Georgetown, Ky., A.B., 1905; Bryn Mawr College, Ph.D., 1910. *Politics:* Democrat. *Religion:* Baptist. *Residence:* Columbia, Mo. *Office:* Department of English, Stephens College, Columbia, Mo. 65201.

CAREER: Member of English faculty at Mount Holyoke College, South Hadley, Mass., 1910-11, Stephens College, Columbia, Mo., 1913-14, Sarah Lawrence College, Bronxville, N.Y., 1914-18, and Stephens College, 1919—. Young Women's Christian Association worker in munitions factory in France, 1918-19.

WRITINGS: The Egyptian Elements in the Legend of the Body and Soul, Furst, 1911; *The Study of Literature,* Houghton, 1928, reprinted, Richard West, 1973; (with Austin Faricy) *The Humanities: Applied Aesthetics,* McGraw, 1940, 5th edition (with Bernard S. Myers), 1974.

WORK IN PROGRESS: Sixth edition of *The Humanities: Applied Aesthetics.*

DUERR, Edwin 1904-

PERSONAL: Born February 21, 1904, in Las Vegas, N.M.; son of Frank H. (a railroad employee) and Celia (Connell) Duerr. *Education:* University of California, Berkeley, B.A., 1926; Cornell University, M.A., 1931. *Politics:* Democrat. *Religion:* Roman Catholic. *Home:* 10906 Cord Ave., Downey, Calif. 90241.

CAREER: University of Nevada, Reno, instructor in public speaking and English and theater director, 1926-30; University of California, Berkeley, theater director, 1931-40; Western Reserve University (now Case Western Reserve University), Cleveland, Ohio, assistant professor of theater, theater director, 1940-42; Carnegie Institute of Technology (now Carnegie-Mellon University), Pittsburgh, Pa., visiting lecturer, 1943; Young & Rubicum (advertising), New York, N.Y.; radio and television director, 1943-62; free-lance writer, 1963-64; California State University, Fullerton, professor of theater and theater director, 1964-74. Director of the radio show "The Aldrich Family."

WRITINGS: Radio and Television Acting, Rinehart, 1950; *The Length and Depth of Acting,* Holt, 1962. Also author of two produced plays, "Doctor for a Dumb Wife," 1934, and "Return to Laughter," 1935; adapted for the stage *The Tower Beyond Tragedy* by Robinson Jeffers; co-translated Moliere's *Tartuffe,* 1932, and *Intermezzo* by Jean Giraudoux, 1935; compiled several original musical revues, 1934-39. Contributor of numerous articles and reviews to speech and theater journals.

WORK IN PROGRESS: The Design of Acting; Men of the Theater; A Twentieth Century Solo; revising *The Length and Width of Acting.*

SIDELIGHTS: Duerr writes that he has directed 116 full-length stage productions. Among his former students are screen actor Gregory Peck, stage actor Barry Nelson, theater producer Robert Fryer, and television producers Ralph Edwards and Mark Goodson.

* * *

DUFFEY, Margery 1926-

PERSONAL: Born March 30, 1926, in Fairmont, Minn.; daughter of Edwin W. (a farmer) and Mary Catherine (Murphy) Duffey. *Education:* College of St. Teresa, B.S., 1949; Western Reserve University (now Case Western Reserve University), M.S., 1954; University of Minnesota, Ph.D., 1967. *Home:* 8807 Riggs Circle, Overland Park, Kan. 66212. *Office:* School of Nursing, University of Kansas, 39th & Rainbow Blvd., Kansas City, Kan. 66103.

CAREER: College of St. Teresa, Winona, Minn., assistant professor of nursing, 1954-59; University of Minnesota, Minneapolis, instructor in nursing, 1959-64; University of Kansas, Kansas City, assistant professor, 1965-68, associate professor, 1968-72, professor of nursing, 1972—, associate dean of School of Nursing, 1974—. Consultant to Council of Graduate Schools. *Member:* American Council of Nursing Researchers, American Educational Research Association, National League for Nursing (Council of Baccalaureate and Higher Degree Programs), Sigma Theta Tau. *Awards, honors:* Mayo scholarship.

WRITINGS: (Contributor) Betty Bergersen editor, *Pharmacology in Nursing,* Mosby, 10th edition (Duffey was not included in earlier editions), 1966; (editor with Bergersen, Edith H. Anderson, Mary Lohr, and Marion H. Rose) *Current Concepts in Clinical Nursing,* four volumes, Mosby, 1967-73; (editor) *Case Studies of Nursing Intervention,* McGraw, 1974. Contributor to nursing journals.

WORK IN PROGRESS: A comparative study of two different curricula in nursing.

* * *

DUGGAN, Alfred Leo   1903-1964

PERSONAL: Born in 1903, in Buenos Aires, Argentina; emigrated with his family to England in 1905; son of Alfred Hubert and Grace (Hinds) Duggan; married Laura Hill, 1953; children: one son. *Education:* Attended Eton College and Balliol College, Oxford. *Residence:* Herefordshire, England.

CAREER: Author of historical fiction and books for young people. Collected specimens for the British National Museum, which took him all over the world. *Military service:* Served in the London Irish Rifles (T.A.) in Norway, 1938-41; employed in airplane factory, 1941-45.

WRITINGS—Historical fiction: *Knight with Armour,* Coward, 1950, reprinted, New English Library, 1973; *Conscience of the King,* Coward, 1951; *Thomas Becket of Canterbury,* Faber, 1952, published in America as *The Falcon and the Dove: A Life of Thomas Becket of Canterbury,* Pantheon, 1966; *The Little Emperors,* Coward, 1953; *The Lady for Ransom,* Coward, 1953; *Leopards and Lilies,* Coward, 1954; *My Life for My Sheep,* Coward, 1955 (published in England as *God and My Right,* Faber, 1955); *Julius Caesar: A Great Life in Brief,* Knopf, 1955; *Winter Quarters,* Coward, 1956.

Devil's Brood (illustrated by G. Hartmann), Coward, 1957; *He Died Old: Mithradates Eupator, King of Pontus,* Faber, 1958, published in America as *King of Pontus: The Life of Mithradates Eupator,* Coward, 1959; *Three's Company,* Coward, 1958; *Children of the Wolf,* Coward, 1959 (published in England as *Founding Fathers,* Faber, 1959); *Family Favourites,* Faber, 1960, Pantheon, 1961; *The Cunning of the Dove,* Pantheon, 1960; *The Right Line of Cerdic,* Pantheon, 1961 (published in England as *The King of Athelney,* Faber, 1961); *Lord Geoffrey's Fancy,* Pantheon, 1962; *Besieger of Cities,* Pantheon, 1963 (published in England as *Elephants and Castles,* Faber, 1963); *The Story of the Crusades, 1097-1291* (illustrated by C. Walter Hodges), Faber, 1963, Pantheon, 1964; *Count Bohemond,* Faber, 1964, Pantheon, 1965.

For children: *The Castle Book* (illustrated by Raymond Briggs), Pantheon, 1960 (published in England as *Look at Castles,* Hamish Hamilton, 1960); *Look at Churches* (illustrated by R. Briggs), Hamish Hamilton, 1961, published in America as *Arches and Spires: A Short History of English Churches from Anglo-Saxon Times,* Pantheon, 1962; *Growing Up in Thirteenth Century England* (illustrated by C. W. Hodges), Pantheon, 1962 (published in England as *Growing Up in the Thirteenth Century,* Faber, 1962); *The Romans* (illustrated by Richard M. Powers), World Publishing, 1964; *Growing Up with the Norman Conquest* (illustrated by C. W. Hodges), Faber, 1965, Pantheon, 1966.

Other: (Author of introduction) William A. Taylor, *Historical Fiction,* Cambridge University Press, 1957.

SIDELIGHTS: In 1924, Alfred Duggan sailed a 600-ton barquentine from England to the Galapagos Islands, becoming one of the few people to cross the Atlantic Ocean under sail.

Duggan began his writing career in 1950. The *New York Times* review of *Besieger of Cities* said: "[The author] has combined wit and scholarship to provide his readers with an insight into a complex age through the re-creation of a char-acter whom previous biographers had reduced to caricature. His Demetrius has the complexity of a credible cosmopolite. His third-century B.C. settings have the authenticity of controlled scholarship. His style has the urbanity of the age he is dramatizing, and his characters become intelligible as they lead the reader to understanding."

Of *The Romans,* the *Christian Science Monitor* wrote: "The author succeeds by giving 12's-on-up the bare bones of Roman history largely devoid of color and spectacle usually associated with that city. In its way this is all to the good for the reader gains a beginning understanding of the political movements and clashes of factions."

The Falcon and the Dove: A Life of Thomas Becket of Canterbury, published posthumously in America, was reviewed by a *Saturday Review* critic, who wrote: "Always impressive by the extent to which he could simultaneously entertain and instruct, the late Mr. Duggan is again superb. His candid, percipient biography of Becket gives a marvelous picture of the intricacies of twelfth-century feudal society and of the complexity of the relations between Church and State."

BIOGRAPHICAL/CRITICAL SOURCES: New York Herald Tribune Book Review, January 17, 1954, October 24, 1954; *New York Times Book Review,* September 22, 1963; *Christian Science Monitor,* May 7, 1964; *America,* October 24, 1964; *Saturday Review,* December 10, 1966; *The Times Literary Supplement, 1969-1973,* Oxford University Press, 1970-74.

OBITUARIES: New York Times, April 5, 1964; *History Today,* June, 1964; *London Spectator,* July 10, 1964.*

(Died April 4, 1964)

* * *

DUGGAN, Maurice   1922-1975

PERSONAL: Born November 25, 1922, in Auckland, New Zealand; married Barbara Platts, 1945; children: one. *Education:* Attended University of Auckland. *Home:* 58 Forrest Hill Rd., Takapuna, Auckland 10, New Zealand.

CAREER: Worked in advertising, beginning 1961; J. English Wright Advertising Ltd., Auckland, New Zealand, staff member, beginning 1965; writer. *Awards, honors:* Hubert Church Memorial Award, 1957; Esther Glenn Award, 1959; Katherine Mansfield Award, 1959; Robert Burns Fellow at Otago University, 1960; New Zealand Literary Fund scholarship, 1966; Freda Buckland Award, 1970.

WRITINGS: Immanuel's Land (short stories), Pilgrim Press, 1956; *Falter Tom and the Water Boy* (juvenile), Blackwood & Janet Paul, 1957, Criterion, 1958; (with others) *New Authors: Short Stories 1,* Hutchinson, 1961; *Summer in the Gravel Pit* (short stories), Blackwood & Janet Paul, 1965; *O'Leary's Orchard and Other Stories,* Caxton Press, 1970.

SIDELIGHTS: According to R. A. Copland, Duggan's stories "represent as it were a carving down from the block of experience rather than the modelling up from the imagination that they display within themselves very little growth, little energy of an expanding sort, little plot and no great exploration of character." Copland found Duggan's stories to be reductions of experience to moments of crisis, written both skillfully and economically, trimmed away so much "that occasionally it seems that only the human circumstance remains, almost independently of the humans who create it."

Such a narrow range of tone and theme, though, "may become a virtue," wrote Lawrence Jacobs, "if it encourages intensity, as Joyce's *Dubliners* illustrates. Such a world as Mr Duggan's needs to be presented in the Joycean static mode, in stories that depend more on the revelation than the resolution of conflict, more on image and mood than on plot." Jacobs felt that "to achieve intensity such stories require an economical choice of telling details that will cumulatively form a revelation of a character and his situation to the reader (and sometimes to himself). The style must be precise, close to poetry in the range and control of connotation. Judged by these criteria," Jacobs commented, "Mr Duggan's technique is not always adequate. . . . Often the setting is beautifully evoked in vivid detail and is made quite relevant to the characters. . . . However, there is often a loss in clarity and economy through full development."

Terry Sturm agreed that "in almost all [Duggan's] stories there is a careful stress on meticulously observed physical detail, to establish a solidly realistic environment for his characters, but this detail is also used to create a mood and atmosphere—an emotional tone which envelops the stories as a whole." Mindful of criticism leveled against Duggan's use of detail in his short stories, Sturm observed that "one often detects, in comments about Duggan's style, an impatience that he hasn't said 'what he has to say' more directly, or more simply." Sturm called Duggan, especially in his later stories, a difficult writer: "The general development of his style has been from a relatively bare selective realism in the manner of the early Joyce, to a much denser, evocative prose working through overtones, allusion, suggestion." Sturm pointed out, however, that "the exploitation of perspective, of the angle of vision, is crucial to the effect of a Duggan story; there is always some kind of ironic distance between Duggan's total perspective on the world he creates in his stories and the partial or limited perspective of individual characters."

While Jacobs noted that "Duggan's characters . . . are primarily members of the submerged society of the lonely, the repressed, and the futile that has populated much of British short fiction since Joyce's *Dubliners* . . . the general tone . . . reminds one of Joyce's dead Dubliners and the 'young man carbuncular' of Eliot's London." But Sturm remarked about Duggan's gloomy characters: "Occasionally [they] reach a moment of self-awareness, a dim recognition which breaks through defense mechanisms and rationalizations, habitual ways of thinking and feeling and reacting. More often, though, they remain tragically or pathetically imprisoned, victims (at some crisis of commitment on which the stories characteristically focus) of a radical failure of will in themselves or in others." Sturm concluded: "Duggan's interest in this aspect of human experience has produced writing of increasing complexity and depth. It could perhaps be described as his individual variation of the theme of 'man alone.'"

BIOGRAPHICAL/CRITICAL COURCES: Landfall, March, 1957, September, 1965, March, 1971; *London Magazine,* September, 1970.

OBITUARIES: AB Bookman's Weekly, February 3, 1975.*

(Died January, 1975)

*   *   *

DULOUP, Victor
See VOLKOFF, Vladimir

DUMAS, Andre 1918-

PERSONAL: Born December 7, 1918, in Montauban, France; son of Andre (a doctor) and Therese (a professor; maiden name, Maury) Dumas; married Francine Buss (a social worker), July 11, 1944; children: Michel, Annick (Mrs. Christian Guillemot). *Education:* University of Montpellier, licence (philosophy), 1939, licence (Protestant theology), 1941. *Religion:* Protestant. *Home:* 45 rue de Sevres, 75006 Paris, France. *Office:* Faculte de Theologie, 83 Blvd. Arago, 75014 Paris, France.

CAREER: Social worker in internment camps in southern France, 1942-43; general secretary of the French student movement in Paris, France, 1943-49; pastor of the French Reformed Church in Pau, France, 1949-56; student chaplain in Strasbourg, France, 1959-61; University of Paris, professor on faculty of Protestant theology, 1961—. *Member:* World Council of Churches.

WRITINGS—In English: *Une Theologie de la realite: Dietrich Bonhoeffer,* Labor (Geneva), 1968, translation by Robert McAfee Brown published as *Dietrich Bonhoeffer: Theologian of Reality,* Macmillan, 1971.

Other works: *La Guerre d'Algerie* (title means "The Algerian War"), Zollikon (Zurich), 1959; *Le Controle de naissances* (title means "Birth Control"), Bergers & Mages (Paris), 1965; *Foi et ideologie* (title means "Faith and Ideology"), Tempoe Presenca (Rio de Janeiro), 1968; *Croire et douter* (title means "Believing and Doubting"), Saint-Paul (Paris), 1971; *Prospective et prophetie* (title means "Futurology and Prophecy"), Cerf (Paris), 1971; *Theologies politiques et vie de l'eglise* (title means "Political Theologies and Church Life"), Chalet (Paris), 1977; *Dieu et ses lieux* (title means "God and His Places"), Cerf, 1978; *Comment Nommer Dieu?* (title means "Names for God"), Centurion, 1978; *L'Amour humain, recompense de Dieu* (title means "Human Love as Reward for God"), Centurion, 1978.

WORK IN PROGRESS: An English translation of *Theologies politiques et vie de l'Eglise* for S.C.M. Press.

SIDELIGHTS: Dumas told *CA:* "My interest has been to look at the consistency of biblical analogy in confrontation with actual questioning situations, like sexuality, industrial society, the common good and the battle of classes, epistomological shifts. . . ."

BIOGRAPHICAL/CRITICAL SOURCES: Christian Century, December 1, 1971; *Commonweal,* September 29, 1972.

*   *   *

DUMONT, Jean-Paul 1940-

PERSONAL: Born May 23, 1940, in Vendome, France; son of Paul-Ursin (a physician) and Genevieve Dumont. *Education:* Sorbonne, University of Paris, A.B., 1964; University of Pittsburgh, Ph.D., 1972. *Office:* Department of Anthropology, University of Washington, Seattle, Wash. 98195.

CAREER: Anthropological fieldwork among Panare Indians of Venezuelan Guiana, 1967-69; Fordham University, Bronx, N.Y., instructor, 1970-71, assistant professor of anthropology, 1972; University of Washington, Seattle, Wash., assistant professor, 1975—. Visiting assistant professor at universities of Paris, Nantes, and Tours, 1972, and at Queens College of City University of New York, 1973-74; visiting lecturer, Princeton University, 1974-75. *Member:* American Anthropological Association, Societe des Americanistes.

WRITINGS: (With J. Monod) *Le Foetus Astral,* Bourgois, 1970; *Hasard Coagule* (poetry), Bourgois, 1970; *Flocs* (poetry), Bourgois, 1972; *Under the Rainbow: Nature and Supernature Among the Panare Indians,* University of Texas Press, 1976; (contributor) E. B. Basso, editor, *Essays on the Carib Culture, Society and Language,* Arizona University Press, 1977; (contributor) W. C. McCormack and S. A. Wurm, editors, *Language and Thought: Anthropological Issues,* Mouton, 1977; (contributor) S. A. Freed, editor, *Anthropology and the Climate of Opinion,* Annals of the New York Academy of Sciences, 1977.

WORK IN PROGRESS: Another book on the Panare.

* * *

DUNCAN, Irma 1897-1977

February 26, 1897—September 20, 1977; German-born American dancer, teacher, and writer. She was one of Isadora Duncan's six foster children who toured as the "Isadorables." She became director of the Duncan School of modern dance after Isadora Duncan left the Soviet Union in 1924. In 1931 she opened the first American Isadora Duncan School of Dance in New York City. Irma Duncan died in Santa Barbara, Calif. Obituaries: *New York Times,* September 22, 1977; *Time,* October 3, 1977. (See index for *CA* sketch)

* * *

DUNKEL, Richard H(adley) 1933-

PERSONAL: Born March 21, 1933, in Dayton, Ohio; son of Richard C. (a journalist) and Ruth (Hadley) Dunkel; married Lee (a photographer), April 8, 1958; children: Robert, Richard, Jr. *Education:* Attended Wittenberg University, 1952-53. *Home and office:* 94 Ormond Parkway, Ormond Beach, Fla. 32074.

CAREER/WRITINGS: Los Angeles Times, Los Angeles, Calif., news editor, 1958-68; *Philadelphia Bulletin,* Philadelphia, Pa., Sunday and magazine editor, 1968-72; *Daytona Beach News-Journal,* Daytona Beach, Fla., Sunday editor, 1973—. Author and owner, Dick Dunkel's College Football and Basketball Index, 1972—.

SIDELIGHTS: CA asked Dunkel how college football has changed in recent years. He wrote: "It's gotten more and more expensive—therefore the same great power at the top—but with many small colleges continuing to entertain fans and alumni albeit with restricted funds. Somehow the game will survive inflation and the continuing energy crisis!"

* * *

DUNLOP, Eileen (Rhona) 1938-

PERSONAL: Born October 13, 1938, in Scotland; daughter of James and Grace (Love) Dunlop. *Education:* Moray House College of Edinburgh, teacher's diploma, 1959. *Religion:* Presbyterian. *Home:* 23 Paton St., Alloa FK10 2DY, Scotland.

CAREER: Eastfield Primary School, Penicuik, Scotland, assistant mistress, 1959-62; Abercromby Primary School, Tullibody, Scotland, assistant mistress, 1962-64; Sunnyside School, Alloa, Scotland, assistant mistress, 1964-70, assistant headmistress, 1970—. *Member:* International P.E.N. (Scottish Centre), Educational Institute of Scotland.

WRITINGS—For children: *Robinsheugh,* Oxford University Press, 1975, published as *Elizabeth Elizabeth,* Holt, 1976; *A Flute in Mayferry Street,* Oxford University Press, 1976, published as *The House on Mayferry Street,* Holt, 1977.

WORK IN PROGRESS: Fox Farm, a children's novel with a Scottish setting.

SIDELIGHTS: Eileen Dunlop writes: "In my writing I have tried to place my characters in settings which are meaningful to me, where I have myself been aware of the 'spirit of place.' I like to imagine the working of that spirit on the minds and hearts of my characters—the effect of the past on the present. Although I have travelled in Europe, moving from place to place does not mean much to me; I am concerned with 'rootedness,' with the continuity of human experience, and the power of the historical imagination. This is summed up for me in the first lines of "Burnt Notions" in T. S. Eliot's *Four Quartets*:

> 'Time present and time past
> Are both perhaps present in time future.
> And time future contained in time past.
> If all time is eternally present
> All time is unredeemable.
> What might have been is an abstraction
> Remaining a perpetual possibility
> Only in a world of speculation.' "

AVOCATIONAL INTERESTS: Reading, going to the theater.

* * *

DUNN, Esther Cloudman 1891-1977

May 5, 1891—August 1, 1977; American professor and author of books on English literature. She was a noted authority on Shakespeare and Elizabethan writers, and taught at Smith College. Her books included *Shakespeare in America* and *Literature of Shakespeare's England.* She died in Northampton, Mass. Obituaries: *New York Times,* August 5, 1977.

* * *

DUNN, James D(ouglas Grant) 1939-

PERSONAL: Born October 21, 1939, in Birmingham, England; son of David and Agnes (Orr) Dunn; married Meta Russell (a teacher), July 25, 1963; children: Catriona, David, Fiona. *Education:* University of Glasgow, M.A. (honors), 1961, B.D. (with distinction), 1964; Cambridge University, Ph.D., 1968. *Religion:* "Christian—or more precisely, Methodist-Presbyterian with Baptist leanings and Pentecostal interests." *Home:* 167 Sutton Passeys Cres., Wollaton Park, Nottingham NG8 1EA, England. *Office:* Department of Theology, University of Nottingham, Nottingham NG7 2RD, England.

CAREER: Senior assistant pastor of Church of Scotland in Glasgow, 1967-68; chaplain to overseas students in Edinburgh, Scotland, 1968-70; University of Nottingham, Nottingham, England, lecturer in New Testament, 1970—. Chairman of Nottingham Area Council for Overseas Student Affairs, 1976—. *Member:* Society for New Testament Studies, Society for the Study of Theology, Association of University Teachers. *Awards, honors:* B.D. from Cambridge University, 1976, for *Jesus and the Spirit.*

WRITINGS: Baptism in the Holy Spirit: A Reexamination of the New Testament Teaching on the Gift of the Holy Spirit in Relation to Pentecostalism Today, S.C.M. Press, 1970, Westminster, 1977; *Jesus and the Spirit: A Study of the Religious and Charismatic Experience of Jesus and the First Christians as Reflected in the New Testament,* Westminster, 1975; *Unity and Diversity in the New Testament: An Inquiry into the Character of Earliest Christianity*, Westminster, 1977.

WORK IN PROGRESS: A study in New Testament Christology; *A History of First-Century Christianity*.

SIDELIGHTS: Dunn writes: "Recognizing the considerable importance of Christianity both past and present, the overall concern of my larger writing is to gain as clear a perception as possible of what Christianity's beginnings were. I hope thus to help provide some insights into Christianity's original character which will serve as reference points for critiques of modern Christianity and which hopefully may offer guidelines for the development of Christianity into the future in respect both to its message and its structures. For the same reasons I am also a sympathetic supporter and critic of the current charismatic movement, and take an active part in the worship and life of the local Methodist circuit. Bound up with all this is a concern for the character of human relationships in the various societies of which I am a member; hence my involvement with staff-student affairs in my present university, with particular reference to the welfare and position of overseas students."

*   *   *

DUNNAM, Maxie D(enton)   1934-

PERSONAL: Born August 12, 1934, in Demer, Miss.; son of Murdoc M. (a welder) and Cora (Malone) Dunnam; married Jerry Morris (an artist), March 15, 1957; children: Kim, Kerry, Kevin. *Education:* University of Southern Mississippi, B.S., 1955; Emory University, M.Th., 1958. *Politics:* Democrat. *Home address:* Route 1, Kin Cove, Mount Juliet, Tenn. 37122. *Office:* 1908 Grand Ave., Nashville, Tenn. 37203.

CAREER: Ordained Methodist minister, 1958; pastor of Methodist churches in Gulfport, Miss. 1959-64, San Clemente, Calif., 1964-69, and Anaheim Calif., 1969-75; *Upper Room*, Nashville, Tenn., editor, 1975—. *Awards, honors:* D.D. from Asbury Theological Seminary, 1977.

WRITINGS: Direction and Destiny, Abingdon, 1963; *Channels of Challenge*, Abingdon, 1966; *The Manipulator and the Church*, Abingdon, 1970; *Be Your Whole Self*, Revell, 1972; *The Workbook of Living Prayer*, Upper Room, 1975; *Barefoot Days of the Soul*, Word, Inc., 1976; *Dancing at My Funeral*, St. Mary's College Press, 1977. Also author of *Direction and Destiny*, 1963.

WORK IN PROGRESS: A sequel to *The Workbook of Living Prayer*, for Upper Room.

*   *   *

DUSCHA, Julius (Carl)   1924-

PERSONAL: Born November 4, 1924, in St. Paul, Minn.; son of Julius William and Anna (Perlowski) Duscha; married Priscilla Ann McBride, August 17, 1946; children: Fred C., Steve D., Suzanne, Sally Jean. *Education:* Attended University of Minnesota, 1943-47; American University, A.B., 1951; graduate study at Harvard University, 1955-56. *Home:* 3421 Raymond St., Chevy Chase, Md. 20015. *Office:* Washington Journalism Center, 2401 Virginia Ave. N.W., Washington, D.C. 20037.

CAREER: St. Paul Pioneer Press & Dispatch, St. Paul, Minn., reporter, 1943-47; American Federation of Labor, Washington, D.C., writer for Labor's League for Political Education, 1949-52; International Association of Machinists, Washington, D.C., writer for *Machinist*, 1952-53;

Lindsay-Schaub Newspapers, Decatur, Ill., editorial writer, 1954-58; *Washington Post*, Washington, D.C., national affairs reporter, 1958-66; Stanford University, Stanford, Calif., associate director of professional journalism fellowships program, 1966-68; Washington Journalism Center, Washington, D.C., director, 1968—. Publicist for Democratic National Committee, 1948, 1952.

MEMBER: National Press Club, Kappa Sigma. *Awards, honors:* Nieman fellow at Harvard University, 1955-56; award from Sigma Delta Chi, 1961, for work as Washington correspondent.

WRITINGS: Taxpayers' Hayride: The Farm Problem from the New Deal to the Billie Sol Estes Case, Little, Brown, 1964; *Arms, Money, and Politics: The Economics and Politics of the Defense Program*, Washburn, 1965. Contributor to popular magazines, including *Washingtonian, Harper's, Atlantic,* and *New Republic*.

WORK IN PROGRESS: A book on the New Deal period in Washington.

*   *   *

DYE, Anne G.
See PHILLIPS, Anne G(arvey)

*   *   *

EAGAN, Andrea Boroff   1943-

PERSONAL: Born July 26, 1943, in New York, N.Y.; daughter of Daniel A. (an immunologist) and Dorothy (a lawyer; maiden name, Protter) Boroff; married Richard M. Eagan (a cabinetmaker), April 28, 1958; children: Molly Maeve. *Education:* Bennington College, student, 1960-61; Columbia University, B.S., 1969. *Politics:* "Socialist/ feminist." *Home:* 23 South Elliott Pl., Brooklyn, N.Y. 11217. *Agent:* Susan Ann Protter, 156 East 52nd St., New York, N.Y. 10022.

CAREER: Writer. *Member:* Health Right, Inc.

WRITINGS: Why Am I So Miserable, If These Are the Best Years of My Life?, Lippincott, 1976. Author of street play "She's Beautiful When She's Angry." Author of pamphlets on women's health. Contributor to magazines, including *Leviathan*. Member of editorial board of *Health Right*.

WORK IN PROGRESS: "A book on the post-partum period" for Lippincott; a pamphlet on breast cancer for Health Right, Inc.

*   *   *

EAGER, Edward McMaken   1911-1964

PERSONAL: Born in 1911, in Toledo, Ohio; children: Fritz. *Education:* Attended Harvard University.

CAREER: Playwright and lyricist. Author of children's books, 1951-64. *Awards, honors:* Ohioana Book Award, 1957, for *Knight's Castle*, and 1963, for *Seven-Day Magic*.

WRITINGS—All illustrated by Nils Mogens Bodecker and published by Harcourt, except as noted: *Red Head* (illustrated by Louis Slobodkin), Houghton, 1951, reprinted, E. M. Hale, 1961; *Mouse Manor* (illustrated by Beryl Bailey-Jones), Ariel Books, 1952; *Half Magic*, 1954, reprinted, 1970; *Playing Possum: Story* (illustrated by Paul Galdone), Putnam, 1955; *Knight's Castle*, 1956, reprinted, 1965; *Magic by the Lake*, 1957; *The Time Garden*, 1958; *Magic or Not?*, 1959; *The Well-Wishers*, 1960; *Seven-Day Magic*, 1962.

Plays: "Two Misers," 1943; (lyricist) "Dream with Music," 1944; (lyricist) "Sing out Sweet Land," 1944; (with Alfred Drake) "The Liar" (based on work by Carlo Goldoni), 1950; (with Drake) "The Gambler" (based on work by Ugo Betti), 1952; (lyricist) *Adventures of Marco Polo: A Musical Fantasy* (book by William Friedberg and Neil Simon; music by Clay Warnick and Mel Paul; first produced as a television special, 1956), Samuel French, 1959; (with Drake) "Dr. Willy Nilly," 1959; "Call It Virtue" (based on the play "The Pleasure of Respectability" by Luigi Pirandello), 1963; (with Drake) "Rugantino," 1964; "The Happy Hypocrite," 1968.

Also adapter of numerous operas and operettas for television, including Jacques Offenbach's "Orpheus in the Underworld" and Mozart's "Marriage of Figaro," both produced by NBC-TV, 1954.

SIDELIGHTS: In his childhood, Eager was fascinated by L. Frank Baum's "Oz" books. As an adult reading to his own young son, Eager became a devoted admirer of E. Nesbit, whose children's books influenced his own magic stories. One of Eager's early fantasy books, *Half-Magic,* received mixed reviews. A *Horn Book* reviewer found it "an unusually good book; the humor never falls flat; the author never rides any situation to death; the story holds up to the very end." However, a critic for the *New York Times* noted that "The children are credible and fun to read about, though too often the comments are coy and the jokes and situations more fit for animated cartoons and comic strips than for a story." Reflecting on the diversity of opinion about the book, a reviewer for the *New York Herald Tribune* wrote: "The value and charm of this unusual modern fantasy have been debated by critics and will be by children too. They will either appreciate heartily or dislike the honest child talk of these three girls and one brother."

Despite criticism of his books' format, Eager wrote six other magic books in the same style. In reviewing the author's latest work, *Seven-Day Magic,* a writer for *Horn Book* commented: "Mr. Eager makes the reading of books an exciting part of life and the sharing of magic a believable adventure for the reader.... Although he, like E. Nesbit, always writes the same kind of magic book, the magic itself is always different and never forseeable."

BIOGRAPHICAL/CRITICAL SOURCES: New York Times, April 18, 1954; *New York Herald Tribune,* May 16, 1954; *Horn Book,* June 1954, December 1962.

OBITUARIES: New York Times, October 24, 1964; *Publishers Weekly,* November 9, 1964.*

(Died October 23, 1964, in Connecticut)

* * *

EARLE, William
See JOHNS, William Earle

* * *

EARLL, Tony
See BUCKLAND, Raymond

* * *

EATON, Jeanette 1886-1968

PERSONAL: Born November 30, 1886, in Columbus, Ohio. *Education:* Vassar College, B.A., 1908; Ohio State University, M.A., 1910.

CAREER: Author of books for children. Early jobs included editorial work for the New York Board of Education and editor of *Story Parade* magazine. *Awards, honors:* Ohioana Book Award, 1959, for *America's Own Mark Twain.*

WRITINGS: (With Bertha M. Stevens) *Commercial Work and Training for Girls,* Macmillan, 1915; *The Story of Transportation* (illustrated by Maurice Day), Harper, 1927; *The Story of Light* (illustrated by Max Schwartz), Harper, 1928; *A Daughter of the Seine: The Life of Madame Roland,* Harper, 1929; *Jeanne d'Arc: The Warrior Saint* (illustrated by Harve Stein), Harper, 1931; *The Flame: Saint Catherine of Siena,* Harper, 1931; *Young Lafayette* (illustrated by David Hendrickson), Houghton, 1932; *Behind the Show Window,* Harcourt, 1935; *Betsy's Napoleon* (illustrated by Pierre Brissaud), Morrow, 1936; *Leader of Destiny: George Washington, Man and Patriot* (illustrated by Jack Manley Rose), Harcourt, 1938, reprinted, 1965.

Narcissa Whitman: Pioneer of Oregon (illustrated by Woodi Ishmael), Harcourt, 1941; (with Jean Adams and Margaret Kimball) *Heroines of the Sky,* Doubleday, 1942, reprinted, Books for Libraries, 1970; *Lone Journey: The Life of Roger Williams* (illustrated by W. Ishmael), Harcourt, 1944, reissued, 1966; *David Livingstone: Foe of Darkness* (illustrated by Ralph Ray), W. Morrow, 1947; *That Lively Man, Ben Franklin* (illustrated by Henry C. Pitz), Morrow, 1948; *Buckey O'Neill of Arizona* (illustrated by Edward Shenton), Morrow, 1949; *Leaders in Other Lands,* Heath, 1950; *Ghandi: Fighter without a Sword* (illustrated by R. Ray), Morrow, 1950, reprinted, 1963; *Washington: The Nation's First Hero* (illustrated by Ray), Morrow, 1951; *Lee: The Gallant General* (illustrated by Harry Daugherty), Morrow, 1953; *Trumpeter's Tale: The Story of Louis Armstrong* (illustrated by Elton C. Fax), Morrow, 1955; *The Story of Eleanor Roosevelt,* Morrow, 1956; *America's Own Mark Twain* (illustrated by Leonard E. Fisher), Morrow, 1958.

SIDELIGHTS: In reviewing Jeanette Eaton's *Trumpeter's Tale: The Story of Young Louis Armstrong,* Langston Hughes, writing in the *New York Times* said: "*Trumpeter's Tale* is an accurate tribute to the great part the Negroes played in the creation of America's favorite music. Elton Fax has given the book excellent illustrations. An ideal way to read this book is with a pile of Armstrong's records at hand, so one can hear the pieces Louis has played as one reads."

The Story of Eleanor Roosevelt was reviewed by *Saturday Review* as a "warm, intimate biography of Eleanor Roosevelt. Jeanette Eaton with her usual skill, adds another name to her list of great people. She tells the absorbing story of this unselfish woman, who, with extraordinary self-discipline, moved from periods of loneliness, timidity, and self-doubt to eminent places as wife of a governor, wife of a President, and in her own right an international leader for peace."

Of Jeanette Eaton's last book, *America's Own Mark Twain, Kirkus* said: "Though many fictional devices are used by the author, the facts presented are clearly documented and will give the Twain enthusiast a stimulating insight into the world and personages which he so lovingly incorporates into his classic novels and essays."

BIOGRAPHICAL/CRITICAL SOURCES: New York Times, February 27, 1955; *Kirkus,* March 1, 1956, July 15, 1958; *Saturday Review,* May 12, 1956.*

(Died February 19, 1968)

EBERHART, Mignon G(ood) 1899-

PERSONAL: Born July 6, 1899, in Lincoln, Neb.; daughter of William Thomas and Margaret Hill (Bruffey) Good; married Alanson C. Eberhart (a civil engineer), December 29, 1923 (divorced); married John P. Hazen Perry, 1946 (divorced); remarried Alanson C. Eberhart, 1948. *Education:* Attended Nebraska Wesleyan University, 1917-20. *Address:* c/o Popular Library, 355 Lexington Ave., New York, N.Y. 10017. *Agent:* Brandt & Brandt, 101 Park Ave., New York, N.Y. 10017.

CAREER: Author, 1930—. *Member:* Society of Midland Authors, P.E.N., Art Club, Fortnightly Club (both Chicago). *Awards, honors:* Scotland Yard Prize, 1930, for *While the Patient Slept;* D.Litt., Nebraska Wesleyan University, 1935.

WRITINGS—All mystery novels; all published by Random House, except as noted: *The Patient in Room 18,* Doubleday, 1929, revised edition, Popular Library, 1972; *While the Patient Slept,* Doubleday, 1930; *The Mystery of Hunting's End,* Doubleday, 1930; *From this Dark Stairway,* Doubleday, 1931; *Murder by an Aristocrat,* Doubleday, 1932 (published in England as *Murder of My Patient,* John Lane, 1934); *The White Cockatoo,* Doubleday, 1933; *The Dark Garden,* Doubleday, 1933 (published in England as *Death in the Fog,* John Lane, 1934); *The House on the Roof,* Doubleday, 1935; *Fair Warning,* Doubleday, 1936; *Danger in the Dark,* Doubleday, 1936; *The Pattern,* Doubleday, 1937; *Hasty Wedding,* Doubleday, 1938; *The Glass Slipper,* Doubleday, 1938; *The Chiffon Scarf,* Doubleday, 1939.

The Hangman's Whip, Doubleday, 1940; *Stranger in Flight,* Bantam, 1940, enlarged edition published as *Speak No Evil,* Random House, 1941; *With This Ring,* 1941; *Wolf in Man's Clothing,* 1942; *The Man Next Door,* 1943; *Unidentified Woman,* 1943; *Escape the Night,* 1944; *Wings of Fear,* 1945; *The White Dress,* 1946; *Five Passengers from Lisbon,* 1946; *Another Woman's House,* 1947; *House of Storm,* 1949.

Hunt with the Hounds, 1950; *Never Look Back,* 1951; *Dead Men's Plans,* 1952; *The Unknown Quantity,* 1953; *Man Missing,* 1954; *Postmark Murder,* 1956; *Another Man's Murder,* 1957; *Melora,* 1959.

Jury of One, 1960; *The Cup, the Blade, or the Gun,* 1961 (published in England as *The Crime at Honotassa,* Collins, 1962); *Enemy in the House,* 1962; *Run Scared,* 1963; *Call After Midnight,* 1964; *R.S.V.P. Murder,* 1965; *Witness At Large,* 1966; *Woman on the Roof,* 1968; *Message from Hong Kong,* 1969.

El Rancho Rio, 1970; *Two Little Rich Girls,* 1971; *Murder in Waiting,* 1973; *Danger Money,* 1975.

Collected works: *The Cases of Susan Dare* (short stories), Doubleday, 1934; *Mignon G. Eberhart Omnibus* (includes *The Patient in Room 18, While the Patient Slept,* and *Murder by an Aristocrat*), Grosset, 1936; *Mignon G. Eberhart's Mystery Book* (includes *Speak No Evil* and *With This Ring*), World Publishing, 1945; *Deadly Is the Diamond and Three Other Novelettes of Murder* (includes "Deadly Is the Diamond," "Bermuda Grapevine," "The Crimson Paw," and "Murder in Waltz Time"), Random House, 1958.

Detective Book Club combined novels; all published by W. J. Black: *With This Ring, The Mighty Blockhead,* [*and*] *The D. A. Cooks a Goose* (the first by Eberhart, the second by Frank Gruber, the third by Erle Stanley Gardner), 1942; *Five Passengers from Lisbon, Wake for a Lady,* [*and*] *The Murder in the Stork Club* (the first by Eberhart, the second

by H. W. Roden, the third by Vera Caspary), 1946; *Postmark Murder, Inspector Maigret and the Burglar's Wife,* [*and*] *Wanted for Murder* (the first by Eberhart, the second by Simenon, the third by Nancy Rutledge), 1956; *Another Man's Murder, Back to the Wall,* [*and*] *The Death of Humpty Dumpty* (the first by Eberhart, the second by Robert P. Hansen, the third by David Alexander), 1957; *Deadly Is the Diamond* [*and*] *Dishonor Among Thieves* (the first by Eberhart, the latter by Prentice Winchell), 1958; *Melora, The Black Gold Murders,* [*and*] *Prelude to Murder* (the first by Eberhart, the second by John B. Ethan, the third by Anthony Gilbert), 1959; *Jury of One, A Borderline Case,* [*and*] *The Aluminum Turtle* (the first by Eberhart, the second by Brad Williams, the third by Baynard Kendrick), 1960; *The Cup, the Blade, or the Gun, Search for a Sultan,* [*and*] *Night of the Kill* (the first by Eberhart, the second by Manning Coles, the third by Breni James), 1961; *Enemy in the House, A Dead Ending,* [*and*] *Repent at Leisure* (the first by Eberhart, the second by Judson Philips, the third by Rae Foley), 1962; *Run Scared, The 12th of Never,* [*and*] *Run to Evil* (the first by Eberhart, the second by Douglas Heyes, the third by Lesley Egan), 1963; *Call After Midnight, Hang the Little Man,* [*and*] *One-Man Jury* (the first by Eberhart, the second by John Creasey, the third by Stephen Ransome), 1964.

SIDELIGHTS: Mignon Eberhart's name has appeared in many film credits. She wrote the story for the film "The Murder of Dr. Harrigan" released by Warner Bros. in 1939; six of her novels were adapted for films, "The White Cockatoo," Warner Bros., 1935, "While the Patient Slept," First National, 1935, "Murder by an Aristocrat," Warner Bros., 1936, "Patient in Room 18," Warner Bros., 1936, *Mystery of Huntings End,* filmed as "Mystery House," Warner Bros., 1937, and *Hasty Wedding,* filmed as "Three's a Crowd," Republic, 1945; and finally, a short story was filmed, "The Great Hospital Mystery," Twentieth Century-Fox, 1937.*

*   *   *

ECHEWA, T(homas) Obinkaram 1940-

PERSONAL: Born December 16, 1940, in Nigeria; came to the United States in 1961; son of Nwaigwe (a farmer) and Ojiugo (Nwaohamuo) Echewa; married Mae Whittler (a teacher), June 5, 1965; children: Martin, Chinyere, Olenga. *Education:* University of Notre Dame, B.S., 1965; Columbia University, M.S., 1966; University of Pennsylvania, M.A., 1972. *Residence:* Philadelphia, Pa. *Agent:* Max Gartenberg, 331 Madison Ave., New York, N.Y. 10017. *Office:* Department of English, Cheyney State College, Cheyney, Pa. 19319.

CAREER: Grambling College, Grambling, La., instructor in English, 1967-70; School District of Philadelphia, Pa., research assistant, 1973; State University of New York College at Oswego, instructor in English, 1973-74; Cheyney State College, Cheyney, Pa., associate professor of English, 1974—. *Member:* International Communication Association. *Awards, honors:* Award from English-Speaking Union, 1976, for *The Land's Lord.*

WRITINGS: The Land's Lord (novel), Lawrence Hill, 1976. Also author of "Abstract Nouns" (three-act play).

WORK IN PROGRESS: Caricaturing I (With Footnotes), a novel.

SIDELIGHTS: Echewa writes: "I have been side-stepping along in my career looking for an outlet. Perhaps I will find it in writing serious fiction. Meanwhile I am completing a doctoral degree in organizational communication. I wish I could begin college again and study philosophy or political science.''

* * *

EDDY, Edward D(anforth, Jr.)   1921-

PERSONAL: Born May 10, 1921, Saratoga Springs, N.Y.; son of Edward Danforth (a lawyer) and Martha (a university professor; maiden name, Henning) Eddy; married Mary Allerton Schurman, June 23, 1949; children: Edward Danforth III, Mary Isabel Eddy Cunningham, Catherine Schurman, David Henning. *Education:* Cornell University, B.A., 1944, Ph.D., 1956; Yale University, M.Div., 1946. *Religion:* Presbyterian. *Home:* 2604 Tall Cedar Circle, State College, Pa. 16801. *Office:* Office of the Provost, Pennsylvania State University, University Park, Pa. 16802.

CAREER: Cornell University, Ithaca, N.Y., associate director of interfaith office, 1946-49; University of New Hampshire, Durham, instructor in English and assistant to the president, 1949-54, acting president, 1954-55, vice-president and provost, 1955-60; Chatham College, Pittsburgh, Pa., president, 1960-77; Pennsylvania State University, University Park, provost and deputy president, 1977—. Commissioner of Pennsylvania Public Television Network; member of executive board of HERS-Mid-Atlantic; member of board of directors of Pittsburgh Symphony Orchestra; member of advisory board of Pittsburgh Public Theatre; trustee of Wheaton College (Norton, Mass.) and Presbyterian-University Hospital (Pittsburgh). Vice-chairman of board of directors of WQED-Television, 1960-77, and Henry C. Frick Educational Commission, 1964-77; founding president of Pittsburgh Council on Public Education, 1963-65, and Pittsburgh Council on Higher Education, 1964-67; member of board of directors of Pittsburgh Chamber Music Society, 1967-77; member of Illinois Commission to Study Non-Public Higher Education, 1967-69; chairman of Pennsylvania Commission for Independent Colleges and Universities, 1973-75. Former member of Pennsylvania Commission on Post-Secondary Education; former member of executive committee of Women's College Coalition; former chairman of board of trustees of Ruud Foundation.

MEMBER: Sigma Phi, Omicron Delta Kappa, Phi Delta Kappa, Duquesne Club, Pennsylvania Society, Newcomen Society, Yale Club of Pittsburgh (past governor). *Awards, honors:* Honorary degrees include LL.D. from Thiel College, 1962, D.Litt. from Duquesne University, 1966, Let.D. from Saint Vincent College, 1967, LL.D. from University of New Hampshire, 1967, L.H.D. from Keuka College, 1968, and L.H.D. from Chatham College, 1977; national brotherhood award from National Conference of Christians and Jews, 1977.

WRITINGS: Colleges for Our Land and Time, Harper, 1957; *The College Influence on Student Character,* American Council on Education, 1959; *Los Centros de Ensenanza Norteamericanso en la Actualidad* (title means "Contemporary Teaching Centers in North America"), Editorial Reverte, 1962; *Une Solution Democratique de l'Enseignement* (title means "A Democratic Solution for Education"), Intercontinental Editions, 1965; (co-author) *The Public Schools and the Public: A Study of the Pittsburgh School Board,* Chatham College, 1969; *The Twelve College Cost-Quality Study,* McKinsey & Co., 1972; *The Twelve College Faculty Appointment and Development Study,* Institute for Educational Development, 1973. Contributor to education, history, and rhetoric journals.

WORK IN PROGRESS: Research on student values and on structure and financing of higher education.

SIDELIGHTS: Eddy wrote *CA* that Chatham College has named its Edward Danforth Eddy Theatre in his honor for "his lifelong interest in the arts and especially in theatre."

* * *

EDDY, John J(ude)   1933-

PERSONAL: Born March 6, 1933, in Perth, Australia; son of William (a civil servant) and Mary (Crosse) Eddy. *Education:* University of Melbourne, B.A. (honors), 1958; Canisius College, Sydney, Australia, graduate study; Oxford University, D.Phil., 1968. *Home:* 122 Empire Circuit, Yarralumga, Australian Capital Territory 2600, Australia. *Office:* Department of History, Research School of Social Sciences, Australian National University, Canberra, Australian Capital Territory 2600, Australia.

CAREER: Entered Society of Jesus (jesuits), 1950, ordained Roman Catholic priest, 1963; University of Melbourne, Parkville, Victoria, tutor, 1959, senior tutor in history, 1964; Australian National University, Canberra, research fellow, 1968, fellow, 1968-73, senior fellow, 1973—.

WRITINGS: Britain and the Australian Colonies, 1818-31, Clarendon Press, 1969.

WORK IN PROGRESS: Research on Australian, British, and Commonwealth history.

* * *

EDDY, Paul   1944-

PERSONAL: Born December 14, 1944, in England; son of Ernest (an accountant) and Doris (a buyer; maiden name, Zeirsen) Eddy; married Elaine Davenport (a writer), August, 1977; children: (from previous marriage) Nicolas, Simon. *Education:* Attended King Edward VIth school in Stratford-upon-Avon, England. *Home:* 30 Baker St., London W.1, England. *Agent:* Robert Ducas, 201 East 42nd St., Room 2900, New York, N.Y. 10017. *Office: Sunday Times,* 200 Grays Inn Rd., London, W.C.1, England.

CAREER: Morning News, Leamington Spa, England, reporter, 1961-64; East London News Agency, London, England, reporter, 1964-65; freelance writer in Europe, 1965-71; *Sunday Times,* London, investigative reporter, 1971—. Has traveled on assignment to Northern Ireland, Hong Kong, the Middle East, Spain, Rhodesia, and Isreal. Notable assignments include coverage of the last years of Howard Hughes.

WRITINGS: (With Bruce Page and Elaine Potter) *Destination Disaster,* Quadrangle, 1976; (with Elaine Davenport and Mark Hurwitz) *The Hughes Papers,* Ballantine, 1976.

SIDELIGHTS: Eddy writes that his aim is: "To investigate complex affairs and write about them in a way that the largest possible number of people will find them understandable and interesting. It seems to me that in a world that is increasingly bureautcratic and polarised we need to understand what is really going on around us. One way of assisting in that process is to take events, exhaustively investigate them and place them in a context and a perspective that people can readily understand. Obviously, this can become a fairly depressing vocation because we tend to concentrate on the less attractive sides of life—war, corruption, accidental slaughter and so on—and so in my spare time I like to 'escape' by travelling widely and, particularly, by sailing. My ability to speak foreign languages is pathetic but I have a passion to learn."

EDGE, David O(wen) 1932-

PERSONAL: Born September 4, 1932, in High Wycombe, Buckinhamshire, England; son of Stephen Rathbone Holden (an industrial chemist) and Kathleen Edith (a music teacher; maiden name, Haines) Edge; married Barbara Corsie (a social worker), February 21, 1959; children: Aran Kathleen, Alastair Clouston, Gordon. *Education:* Caius College, Cambridge, B.A., 1955, M.A., 1959, Ph.D., 1959. *Politics:* "Community Action (Liberal/Labour)." *Religion:* Methodist. *Home:* 25 Gilmour Rd., Edinburgh EH16 5NS, Scotland. *Office:* Science Studies Unit, University of Edinburgh, 34 Buccleuch Pl., Edinburgh EH8 9JT, Scotland.

CAREER: Teacher of physics at a grammar school in Cambridge, England, 1959; British Broadcasting Corp., London, England, producer of science talks, 1959-66; University of Edinburgh, Edinburgh, Scotland, senior lecturer in science and director of science studies unit, 1966—. *Military service:* Royal Air Force, 1950-52. *Member:* Royal Society of the Arts (fellow), Royal Astronomical Society (fellow), Scout and Guide Graduate Association (president, 1976—), Society for Social Studies of Science, British Society for Social Responsibility in Science, British Society for the Philosophy of Science, British Association for the Advancement of Science, American Asssociation for the Advancement of Science.

WRITINGS: (Editor) *Experiment* (script), British Broadcasting Corp., 1963; (editor with J. N. Wolfe) *Meaning and Control,* Tavistock Publications, 1973; (with Michael J. Mulkay) *Astronomy Transformed: The Emergence of Radio Astronomy in Britain,* Wiley, 1976.

Editor of scripts for British Broadcasting Corp.: "Quanta and Reality," 1962, "Relativity Today," 1963, "Cells and Embryos," 1963, "A New Kind of Physics?", 1964, "A Few Ideas," 1964, "The Formative Years," 1968.

Author of hymn "Lord, We Are Blind." Contributor of articles to learned journals. Joint editor of *Science Studies,* 1971-74, and *Social Studies of Science,* 1975—.

WORK IN PROGRESS: A popular monograph on philosophical theology, based on lecture notes; studies in the sociology of contemporary physics.

SIDELIGHTS: Edge comments: "My 'radical' approach in both politics and religion was much influenced by my training as a 'social group worker/youth leader.' I am incurably anti-authoritarian. My experience at British Broadcasting Corp. led to a belief in the ineffectiveness of mass media as an agent of social change, slowly leading to despair as to the effectiveness of *any* agent of social change. I am fascinated by social, political, and ethical problems of scientific practice."

AVOCATIONAL INTERESTS: Watching sport (European and/or American), listening to music, going to the opera, "introducing my children to the delights of hill-walking."

* * *

EDINBOROUGH, Arnold 1922-

PERSONAL: Born August 2, 1922, in Donington, England; son of Frank and Sarah Ann (Clark) Edinborough; married Letitia Mary Wolley, January 16, 1946; children: Christine Ann, Alastair Michael, Sarah Jane. *Education:* St. Catharine's College, Cambridge, B.A. (honors), 1947, M.A. (honors), 1949. *Religion:* Anglican. *Home:* 190 Douglas Dr., Toronto, Ontario, Canada. *Office:* Saturday Night Publications, Toronto, Ontario, Canada.

CAREER: Queen's University, Kingston, Ontario, assistant professor of English, 1947-54; *Kingston Whig-Standard,* Kingston, Ontario, editor, 1954-58; *Saturday Night,* Toronto, Ontario, editor, 1958-62; Saturday Night Publications, Toronto, Ontario, president, 1963-68, chairman of board of directors, 1968—. President of Edina Publications, Ltd. Visiting lecturer at University of Lausanne, 1947; special lecturer at Royal Military College (Canada), 1948-52, 1957-58. Chairman of board of directors of New Symphony Association, 1954-58; chairman of East Ontario Drama League, 1955-56; member of board of directors of National Ballet School of Canada, Elliot Lake Centre for Continuing Education, and Bishop Strachan School; member of board of governors of Dominion Drama Festival, 1956-58. Member of Toronto Planning Board, 1965-68; director of Canadian Institute of Public Affairs. Panelist on Canadian Broadcasting Corp. and Canadian Television network programs. *Military service:* British Army, Royal Artillery, 1942-45; served in North Africa and Italy; became captain; received Military Cross.

MEMBER: Magazine Publishers Association (president, 1961-62), John Howard Society (national director; director of Ontario section), Humanities Association of Canada, Shakespeare Society of America, Albany Club, Arts and Letters Club (Toronto). *Awards, honors:* LL.D. from University of Guelph, 1968.

WRITINGS: Canada, Doubleday, 1962; (editor with Philip LeBlanc) *One Church, Two Nations?,* Longmans Canada, 1968; *A Personal History of the Toronto Symphony* (souvenir edition), Rothmans of Pall Mall (Canada), 1972. Also author of *The Restless Church,* 1966, and *Why the Sea Is Boiling Hot,* 1966.

Author of columns in *Financial Post* and *Canadian Churchman.* Contributor to magazines. Canadian correspondent for *Shakespeare Quarterly* and *Shakespeare Survey,* 1952.

AVOCATIONAL INTERESTS: Amateur theatricals.*

* * *

EDINGTON, Andrew 1914-

PERSONAL: Born January 15, 1914, in Mobile, Ala.; son of David Henry (a judge) and Blanche (Planck) Edington; married Marguerite Haas, June 4, 1940; children: Rita Edington Odom, David Henry. *Education:* Southwestern College at Memphis, A.B., 1934; University of Alabama, M.A., 1938. *Religion:* Presbyterian. *Home:* 503 Fairway Dr., Kerrville, Tex. 78028. *Office:* Schreiner College, Kerrville, Tex. 78028.

CAREER: Athletic coach at military school in Mobile, Ala., 1934-36; Springhill College, Mobile, Ala., coach, 1936-38; Southwestern College at Memphis, Memphis, Tenn., assistant to the president, 1938-40; Schreiner College, Kerrville, Tex., president, 1950-71, president emeritus, 1971—; writer, 1971—. President of Peterson Foundation. Member of board of directors of local First National Bank. *Military service:* U.S. Navy, captain of "PC 1206" and "PGM 17," 1942-45; received Admiral's Award, President's Citation, and General Foch Medal of France. *Awards, honors:* LL.D. from Austin College, 1951.

WRITINGS: The Big Search, (popular theology) Pageant, 1955; *Some Folks Wonder,* Herring Printing, 1972; *The Word Made Fresh,* John Knox, Volume I, 1972, Volume II, 1974, Volume III, 1976; *First Aid for the Soul,* Herring Printing, 1973. Also author of *Monkeying With the Flood,* and *The Camels Are Coming,* both for children.

WORK IN PROGRESS: Bible stories for children, including *The Camels Are Coming; The Donkey and His Grandson; The Number One Snake;* and *The Eagle Book.*

SIDELIGHTS: Edington has traveled in England, Germany, France, Italy, Egypt, the Holy Land, South America, and Okinawa. *Avocational interests:* Fishing, golf.

* * *

EDMONDS, Alan
    See EDMONDS, Arthur Denis

* * *

EDMONDS, Arthur Denis   1932-
    (Alan Arthur, Arthur Dennis, Alan Edmonds,
    Elizabeth Graham)

PERSONAL: Born September 23, 1932, in London, England; son of Arthur, Sr. (a mailman) and Sarah Ann (Goodwin) Edmonds; married Elizabeth Hancock, October, 1965 (divorced, April, 1971); children: John Graham, David Mark, Sarah Elizabeth. *Education:* Attended secondary school in London, England. *Home and office:* 26 Castleview Ave., Toronto, Ontario, Canada.

CAREER: Brighton Evening Argus, Brighton, England, reporter, 1953-54, sub-editor, 1954, author of bi-weekly humor feature, 1955; *Daily Express,* London, England, reporter and correspondent, 1955-60; *Toronto Star Weekly,* Toronto, Ontario, editor and contributor, 1960-62; *Toronto Daily Star,* Toronto, reporter and correspondent, 1962-65; *Maclean's Magazine,* Toronto, writer and editor, 1965-71; free-lance writer and editor, 1971-73; senior writer for *Canadian* (magazine), 1973-74; *Toronto Sun,* Toronto, associate editor, 1974-75; free-lance writer, 1975—. *Member:* Periodical Writers Association of Canada.

WRITINGS: (With Susan Cartwright; under pseudonym Alan Edmonds) *Capital Cookery,* Pagurian Press, 1970; (under pseudonym Alan Edmonds) *Voyage to the Edge of the World,* McClelland & Stewart, 1972; (under pseudonym Alan Edmonds) *The Prime Minister's Cook Book,* McGraw, 1976; (with Fred Soyka; under pseudonym Alan Edmonds) *The Ion Effect,* Dutton, 1976. Author of scripts and commentaries for television documentary films, including Public Broadcasting System's series "Best Kept Secrets." Contributor, usually under pseudonym Alan Edmonds, to Canadian consumer magazines, *Canadian,* and newspapers.

WORK IN PROGRESS: A book on the social history of the 1960's.

SIDELIGHTS: Edmonds writes: "I am a rare bird—a professional writer not employed by any specific publication; if you like, a pen for hire. That does not, however, imply that the views I express are in any way coloured by the fact that, usually, I am being paid at the time I'm writing (as opposed to after the fact, as is the case with fiction writers). I am perhaps best known as a popularizer of complex scientific, political, and sociological material. As such I am an interpreter; a necessary animal in an incredibly complex society where knowledge is power and it grows increasingly necessary to reduce that knowledge to lay language so that the power does not become concentrated into few hands."

* * *

EDMUNDS, Malcolm   1938-
PERSONAL: Born July 24, 1938, in Harlow, England; son

of Frank (a heating engineer) and Mary (a poultry farmer; maiden name, Warner) Edmunds; married Janet Holmes, January 2, 1963; children: Julia, Helen. *Education:* Queen's College, Oxford, B.A., 1960, D.Phil., 1963. *Religion:* Society of Friends (Quakers). *Home:* Mill House, Mill Lane, Goosenargh, near Preston PR3 2JX, England. *Office:* Division of Biology, Preston Polytechnic, Corporation St., Preston PR1 2TQ, England.

CAREER: University of Ghana, Legon, lecturer, 1963-69, senior lecturer in zoology, 1969-73; University of Exeter, Exeter, England, senior research fellow, 1973-74; Preston Polytechnic, Preston, England, senior lecturer, 1974-75, principal lecturer in zoology, 1975—, head of Division of Biology, 1976—. *Member:* Institute of Biology, British Ecological Society, Marine Biological Association, Botanical Society of the British Isles, Linnean Society (fellow), Malacological Society (London).

WRITINGS: Defence in Animals: A Survey of Anti-Predator Defences, Longman, 1974; (contributor) D. W. Ewer and J. B. Hall, editors, *Ecological Biology,* Volume II, Longman, 1977. Contributor of more than thirty articles to scientific journals.

WORK IN PROGRESS: Research on anti-predator defenses of animals (behavioral and ecological) and on taxonomy of sea slugs.

SIDELIGHTS: Edmunds comments: "I am interested in problems of the third world, following ten years of work in Africa. I am concerned about the problems posed by economic development and high-level technology, and prefer solutions at the local, low-level technology level. The world is drifting toward 'big is better' and it can be obtained only by force or threat of force. This must be reversed—and the population pressure plus selfishness exacerbates the problem. We must aim for a stable population and minimal reliance on non-renewable resources."

* * *

EDSON, Peter   1896-1977
February 8, 1896—July 14, 1977; American journalist. Edson's article about an expense fund maintained by friends of Richard Nixon led to Nixon's famous "Checkers" speech which saved his place on the Republican ticket with Dwight D. Eisenhower in 1952. Edson's Washington column appeared in more than seven hundred fifty newspapers, making him one of the most widely syndicated columnists in the nation. He died in Washington, D.C. Obituaries: *Washington Post,* July 16, 1977; *New York Times,* July 17, 1977.

* * *

EDWARDS, A. W. F.   1935-
PERSONAL: Born April 10, 1935, in London, England; son of Harold Clifford (a surgeon) and Ida (Phillips) Edwards; married Catharina Edlund, August 9, 1958; children: Ann, Thomas, Charlotte. *Education:* Earned B.A., M.A., Ph.D. and Sc.D. from Cambridge University. *Office:* Gonville & Caius College, Cambridge University, Cambridge, England.

CAREER: Cambridge University, Cambridge, England, fellow of Gonville & Caius College and assistant director of research at the university, 1970—.

WRITINGS: Likelihood, Cambridge University Press, 1972, corrected edition, 1975; *Foundations of Mathematical Genetics,* Cambridge University Press, 1977.

WORK IN PROGRESS: Mathematical Methods of Human Genetics.

EDWARDS, Lynne   1943-

PERSONAL: Born June 25, 1943, in Essex, England; daughter of John Richard (an engineer) and Kathrine (a hairdresser; maiden name, Johnson) Saunders; married Brian Henry Edwards (an illustrator), August 14, 1965; children: Dickon, Thomas. *Education:* Weymouth Training College, teaching certificate (with merit), 1964. *Home:* 88 High St., Bildeston, Ipswich, Suffolk, England.

CAREER: Elementary school teacher in London, England, 1964-67, and Suffolk, England, 1967—.

WRITINGS: Dead as the Dodo, Words Work, 1973; *The Dodo Is a Solitary Bird,* Words Work, 1977.

WORK IN PROGRESS: Mad Dan Dodo in Outer Space.

SIDELIGHTS: Lynne Edwards told *CA:* "My husband, who illustrates our books, and I work as a close team in the production of each book. While each has as its hero a Dodo, the individual stories stand as entities on their own, and are primarily picture-books, with full-page illustrations throughout. The appeal is to children of pre-school age up to seven or eight, but we hope the humour is witty enough to entertain adults and children alike.

"My husband is a full-time illustrator, working on our books and on a complex comic-strip fantasy of his own devising. In between writing our Dodo books, about every eighteen months or so, I teach eight hours a week a handicapped boy in his home as a government-appointed home teacher."

AVOCATIONAL INTERESTS: Making corn dollies, patchwork quilts, and cushions.

*   *   *

EGGELING, Hans Friedrich   1878-1977

October 22, 1878—October, 1977; Scottish writer and teacher of German at Edinburgh University for more than forty years. Eggeling died in London, England. Obituaries: *AB Bookman's Weekly,* January 30, 1978. (See index for *CA* sketch)

*   *   *

EHRENREICH, Barbara   1941-

PERSONAL: Born August 26, 1941, in Butte, Mont.; daughter of Ben Howes and Isabelle Oxley (Isely) Alexander; married John Ehrenreich (a teacher), August 6, 1966; children: Rosa, Benjamin. *Education:* Reed College, B.A., 1963; Rockefeller University, Ph.D., 1968. *Politics:* "Socialist and feminist." *Religion:* None. *Home:* 16 Walters Ave., Syosset, N.Y. 11791.

CAREER: Health Policy Advisory Center, New York City, staff member, 1969-71; State University of New York College at Old Westbury, assistant professor of health sciences, 1971-74; writer, 1974—.

WRITINGS: (With husband, John Ehrenreich) *Long March, Short Spring,* Monthly Review Press, 1969; (with J. Ehrenreich) *American Health Empire,* Random House, 1970; (with Deirdre English) *Witches, Midwives, and Nurses,* Feminist Press, 1972; (with English) *Complaints and Disorders: The Sexual Politics of Sickness,* Feminist Press, 1973; (with English) *The Last Romance: Women and the Experts,* Doubleday, 1978. Author of column in *In These Times.* Contributor to magazines, including *Socialist Revolution, Radical America, Nation,* and *Liberation.* Member of editorial board of *Health Right* and *Social Policy.*

SIDELIGHTS: Barbara Ehrenreich writes: "My writing is

motivated by my commitment to social justice. I have been involved in the anti-war movement and the women's movement and have recently been involved in the women's health movement."

*   *   *

EICHELBAUM, Stanley   1926-

PERSONAL: Born October 5, 1926, in Brooklyn, N.Y.; son of Sam (a baker) and Rebecca (Rosen) Eichelbaum. *Education:* City College (now of the City University of New York), B.A. (summa cum laude), 1947; Columbia University, M.A., 1948; Sorbonne, University of Paris, Diplome d'Etudes, 1949. *Politics:* Democrat. *Religion:* Jewish. *Home:* 333 Green St., San Francisco, Calif. 94133. *Office: San Francisco Examiner,* 110 Fifth St., San Francisco, Calif. 94119.

CAREER/WRITINGS: New Yorker, New York, N.Y., editorial reporter and researcher, 1949-58; *San Francisco Examiner,* San Francisco, Calif., feature editor, 1958-61, film and theater critic, 1961—. Notable assignments include annual coverage of European filmmaking and film festivals, and theater in London, New York, and Los Angeles. Lecturer at various colleges and universities, 1961—; instructor in critical writing workshop, University of California, San Francisco, 1968—. Member of selections committee, San Francisco International Film Festival, 1962-65; member of program, San Francisco Art Institute, 1968-70. Contributor of free-lance articles on film and theater to *Christian Science Monitor, Hollywood Reporter, Theater Arts, San Francisco, Ramparts,* and *Playbill. Member:* American Theater Critics Association, California Historical Society, Phi Beta Kappa.

SIDELIGHTS: Eichelbaum has exhibited his paintings in a group show at the Forum Gallery in New York City. He was appointed to the American committee for the Shakespeare Quadricentennial in 1964.

*   *   *

EISELEY, Loren Corey   1907-1977

September 3, 1907—July 9, 1977; American educator, anthropologist, poet, and author. Eiseley was best known for his ability to combine poetic style with scholarly subjects. His philosophy and writings often insisted on the need for man to envision and imagine. He believed that reason, embraced by itself, would destroy man. Among his most notable works are *The Immense Journey,* the autobiographical *All the Strange Hours,* and *Darwin's Century.* Eiseley died in Philadelphia, Pa. Obituaries: *New York Times,* July 11, 1977; *Washington Post,* July 11, 1977; *Newsweek,* July 25, 1977; *Time,* July 25, 1977. (See index for *CA* sketch)

*   *   *

EISEN, Jack   1925-

PERSONAL: Born April 22, 1925, in California; son of Charles E. and Davina Prendergast (Kosh) Eisen; married Lucy Utterback, December 18, 1950; children: Peter, Mark. *Education:* Attended San Francisco State College, 1946-47; Antioch College, A.B., 1951. *Home:* 7234 Jillspring Ct., Springfield, Va. 22152. *Office: Washington Post,* 1150 15th St. N.W., Washington, D.C. 20071.

CAREER/WRITINGS: San Rafael Independent-Journal, San Rafael, Calif., reporter and editor, 1942-52; *San Francisco Chronicle,* San Francisco, Calif., reporter, 1943; *Louisville Times,* Louisville, Ky., reporter, editor, and columnist, 1952-56; currently employed by *Washington Post,* Washington, D.C. Notable assignments include coverage of the U.S. urban riots of the 1960's and transportation. Staff assistant to a U.S. Congressman, 1950; lecturer in journalism, George Washington University, 1956-68; consultant to United Nations Economic Commission for Europe, 1976. *Military service:* U.S. Army, 1943-46; became sergeant. *Awards, honors:* American Society of Planning Officials special award, 1963.

* * *

EISENBERG, Ronald L(ee) 1945-

PERSONAL: Born July 11, 1945, in Philadelphia, Pa.; son of Milton (a physician) and Betty (Klein) Eisenberg; married Zina Leah Schiff (a concert violinist), September 19, 1970; children: Avlana Kinneret. *Education:* University of Pennsylvania, A.B., 1965, M.D., 1969. *Home:* 2A Greenwood Cove Dr., Tiburon, Calif. 94920. *Office:* Department of Radiology, Veterans Administration Hospital, San Francisco, Calif. 94121.

CAREER: Mount Zion Hospital, San Francisco, Calif., intern, 1969-70; Massachusetts General Hospital, Boston, Mass., resident in radiology, 1970-71; University of California, San Francisco, resident in radiology, 1973-75, assistant professor of radiology, 1975—. Chief, gastrointestinal radiology, at Veterans Administration Hospital (San Francisco), 1975—. *Military service:* U.S. Army, 1971-73; became major. *Member:* American Roentgen Ray Society, San Francisco Radiology Society, Phi Beta Kappa, Alpha Omega Alpha.

WRITINGS: The Iguana Corps of the Haganah, Bloch Publishing, 1977. Contributor to professional journals.

WORK IN PROGRESS: "A juvenile book describing the experimental 'kibbutz' in Nazi Germany (prior to future settlement in Palestine) by Jews, unknown to the German authorities."

SIDELIGHTS: Eisenberg writes: "The idea of writing seriously (other than medical articles) arose during my years in the Army. When I was on call every fourth night I had to remain on the base. Rarely was I called on to see a patient. With a great deal of time on my hands, I began to write.

"The subject of my writing was iguanas—primarily because we had one named Waverly. This, coupled with a visit to Israel and the reading of a work about a dog-parachutist by the present head of the Israeli Army, led me to write about the Iguana Corps of the Haganah. (It is a story, probably fictitious, about the use of the large lizards to carry messages, guns, and explosives to the Israeli agents behind Arab lines.)"

AVOCATIONAL INTERESTS: Playing the piano, collecting Israel stamps (almost a complete set).

* * *

EISENHOWER, Milton S(tover) 1899-

PERSONAL: Born September 15, 1899, in Abilene, Kan.; son of David Jacob (an engineer) and Ida E. (Stover) Eisenhower; married Helen Elsie Eakin, October 12, 1927; children: Milton, Ruth. *Education:* Kansas State University, B.S., 1924. *Home:* 5 Roland Mews, Baltimore, Md. 21210. *Office:* 4545 North Charles St., Baltimore, Md. 21210.

CAREER: U.S. Department of State, Washington, D.C., vice-consul in Edinburgh, Scotland, 1926-28; U.S. Department of Agriculture, Washington, D.C., director of informa-

tion, 1928-42, land use coordinator, 1937-42; War Relocation Authority, Washington, D.C., director, 1942; Office of War Information, Washington, D.C., associate director, 1942-43; Kansas State University, Manhattan, president, 1943-50; Pennsylvania State University, University Park, president, 1950-56; Office of Latin American Affairs, Washington, D.C., special ambassador and personal representative of the president, 1953-60; Johns Hopkins University, Baltimore, Md., president, 1956-67, 1971-72; writer, 1972—. Served on several government organizations including Famine Emergency Relief Committee, National Committee for Economic Development, President's Advisory Committee on Government Organization, Problems and Policy Committee of the American Council on Education, President's Commission on the Causes and Prevention of Violence (chairman); also participated in UNESCO. Directorships and trusteeships include Maryland Academy of Sciences, 1961—, Commercial Credit Company, 1963-75, Greater Baltimore Medical Center, 1967—, and Chicago Board of Trade, 1968-71. *Military service:* U.S. Army, 1918.

MEMBER: Sigma Alpha Epsilon, Phi Beta Kappa, Phi Beta Phi, Alpha Zeta, Delta Sigma Phi, Alpha Phi Omega, Omicron Delta Kappa, Sigma Delta Chi, Mason at Sight. *Awards, honors:* Awarded thirty-seven honorary doctorates from thirty-two American and five foreign universities; received highest civilian decoration from presidents of Bolivia, Brazil, Ecuador, Chile, Korea, and Panama.

WRITINGS: The Wine Is Bitter, Doubleday, 1963; *The President Is Calling,* Doubleday, 1974. Contributor to many magazines.

WORK IN PROGRESS: Books on political reform and higher education.

SIDELIGHTS: Eisenhower's forty-nine years of political service (including advisory positions with presidents Eisenhower and Johnson) form the basis of his writings. "All of my writings," he told *CA,* "deal with federal affairs and higher education as I have worked directly with eight presidents and served as president of three universities. Thus, *The Wine Is Bitter* is an analysis of our historic relations with Latin America. *The President Is Calling* is partly a memoir and partly a set of suggestions for changes in federal procedures and structure." Included among Eisenhower's suggested reforms are a single six year term for U.S. presidents and a separation of the presidency from party leadership.

Two of Eisenhower's reports were adopted as official policy while he was U.S. ambassador to Latin America.

* * *

EISERER, Leonard Arnold 1948-

PERSONAL: Born December 9, 1948, in Washington, D.C.; son of Leonard Albert and Lorraine (Hickey) Eiserer; married Patricia Anne Lemay (a journalist and actress), May 29, 1972. *Education:* University of Maine, B.A., 1970; Bryn Mawr College, M.A., 1972, Ph.D., 1974. *Home:* 1106 Aquilla Dr., Lancaster, Pa. 17601. *Office:* Department of Psychology, Whitely Psychology Laboratories, Franklin & Marshall College, Lancaster, Pa. 17604.

CAREER: Business Publishers, Inc., Silver Spring, Md., associate editor, 1972—; Keuka College, Keuka Park, N.Y., assistant professor, 1974-76; Franklin & Marshall College, Lancaster, Pa., assistant professor, 1977—. Owner and editor of *Ecology, U.S.A.,* 1976—. *Member:* American Psychological Association, Ecological Society of America,

Animal Behavior Society, National Audubon Society, National Wildlife Federation.

WRITINGS: The American Robin: A Backyard Institution, Nelson-Hall, 1976. Contributor of more than a dozen articles to journals in the behavioral sciences. Editor of *Federal Research Report.*

WORK IN PROGRESS: Animal Predators, completion expected in 1979; research on behavior of the American robin, and on early socialization in ducklings.

* * *

EISLER, Riane Tennenhaus 1931-

PERSONAL: Born July 22, 1931, in Vienna, Austria; daughter of David (a businessman) and Elisa (Greif) Tennenhaus; married George Eisler, 1953 (divorced); children: Andrea Suzanne, Loren Claire. *Education:* University of California, Los Angeles, B.A. (magna cum laude), 1952, J.D., 1965. *Agent:* Elliot Sanders, 1531 Corinth Ave., Los Angeles, Calif. 90025. *Office:* 1028 Selby Ave., Los Angeles, Calif. 90024.

CAREER: Rand-SDC, Santa Monica, Calif., social scientist, 1955-57; Zagon, Schiff, Hirsch & Levine, Beverly Hills, Calif., staff attorney, 1966-68; private law practice in Los Angeles, Calif., 1968—. Admitted to California Bar. Staff attorney for Los Angeles Women's Center, 1968-71, associate director of legal program, 1969-71. Lecturer at University of California, Los Angeles, and Immaculate Heart College. Member of Actors' Studio West, 1970-71; member of board of directors of Los Angeles Women's Clinic and Los Angeles Young Women's Christian Association. *Member:* Los Angeles County Bar Association, Women Lawyers' Association, Phi Beta Kappa, Pi Gamma Mu.

WRITINGS: Dissolution: No-Fault Divorce, Marriage and the Future of Women, McGraw, 1977. Also author of several documentary and theatrical works, including "Infinity," first produced in Pasadena, Calif., at Pasadena Art Museum, 1970, "Help Is on the Way," first produced in Los Angeles, Calif., at Immaculate Heart College, 1971, "Women Alone" (radio play), first aired on KPFK-Pacifica Radio, 1971, and "Joy," first produced in Pasadena at California Institute of Technology, 1972.

Contributor to *California Continuing Education for the Bar.* Contributor to *New Life Options, Women's Rights Law Reporter, Everywoman,* and *Social Action.*

WORK IN PROGRESS: The Gate, a book on the Equal Rights Amendment.

SIDELIGHTS: Riane Eisler comments: "I write out of deep commitment—compelling me to 'bear witness' to the human situation, and also to try somehow to contribute to its betterment, at the same time trying to juggle all my roles: mother, friend and partner, household administrator, business manager, chief cook and bottle washer, so that the end product is I think very much a reflection, not only of my aspirations, but my life."

* * *

ELDER, Gary 1939-

PERSONAL: Born April 16, 1939, in Pendleton, Ore.; son of Hiram Keith (a carpenter and businessman) and Wanita (Binder) Elder; married Audrey Albrecht (marriage ended); married Jeane Noble (a teacher and historian), April 6, 1963. *Education:* Attended Whitman College, 1957-60, and University of California, Berkeley, 1962. *Residence:* White-

thorn, Calif. *Office:* Holmgangers Press, 22 Ardith Lane, Alamo, Calif. 94507.

CAREER: Farmhand in Oregon, 1955-58; State of Oregon Highway Department, Pendleton, surveyor, 1957-59; surveyor for Umatilla County, Ore., in Pendleton, 1960-61; Neighborhood House Youth Theatre, Richmond, Calif., director, 1966-67; Holmgangers Press, Alamo, Calif., editor and publisher, 1974—. Member of East Bay Regional Park Council, and Eugene O'Neill Foundation, Tao House. *Member:* Western American Literature Association, Wilderness Society, Defenders of Wildlife.

WRITINGS: Arnulfsaga (poem), Dustbooks, 1970; *Making Touch* (poems), San Marcos Press, 1971; *Grosser Fagot Fugit,* Poetry Newsletter, 1973; *A Vulgar Elegance* (poem), Thorp Springs Press, 1974; (editor) *The Far Side of the Storm: New Ranges of Western Fiction,* San Marcos Press, 1975. Contributor to literary journals, including *Assembling, Margins,* and *West Coast Poetry Review,* and to *Journal of Popular Culture.*

WORK IN PROGRESS: Three books of poems, *Hold Fire, Texas Temper,* and *The Last Days of the Nation;* Volume II of a trilogy (*Arnulfsaga* was Volume I).

SIDELIGHTS: Elder writes: "As a poet, I've been concerned with moving beyond linear modes of perception/expression and have endeavored to make work that moves the audient-reader with at least the complex simultaneity of musical experience, particularly that of jazz—its modern structures, voicings, phrasings, rhythms, etc. *Arnulfsaga* was written from a need to get down *out* of the vacuum of violence I feel in this country; and all of my writings—fictions, plays, essays—have remained concerned therewith. And, due in some part to my Northwestern birthplace, I've been organically involved as an artist with the Western experience—with the land, its history, ecology, and with the problems of native Americans."

* * *

ELLIS, Frank Hale 1916-

PERSONAL: Born January 18, 1916, in Chicago, Ill.; son of Frank Hale and Gay (Shepherd) Ellis; married Constance Dimock, December 20, 1940; children: Gay. *Education:* Northwestern University, B.S., 1939; Yale University, Ph.D., 1948. *Home:* 146 Elm St., Northampton, Mass. 01060. *Office:* Department of English, Smith College, Northampton, Mass. 01060.

CAREER: University of Buffalo, Buffalo, N.Y., member of faculty, 1941-42; Yale University, New Haven, Conn., instructor, 1945-51, assistant professor of English literature, 1950-51; U.S. Department of State, Washington, D.C., member of staff, 1951-54; Smith College, Northampton, Mass., 1958—, professor of English literature, 1966—, Mary Augusta Jordan Professor, 1974—. *Military service:* U.S. Army, 1942-45; received Bronze Star medal. *Member:* Modern Language Association of America, Connecticut Academy of Arts and Sciences, Cum Laude Society, Phi Beta Kappa, Elizabethan Club and Lawn Club (both New Haven). *Awards, honors:* Morse fellow, 1950-51.

WRITINGS: (Editor) *Jonathon Swift: A Discourse of the Contests and Dissentions between the Nobles and Commons in Athens and Rome with the Consequences They Had upon Both Those States,* Clarendon Press, 1967; (editor) *Twentieth Century Interpretations of Robinson Crusoe: A Collection of Critical Essays,* Prentice-Hall, 1969; (editor) *Poems on Affairs of State: Augustan Satirical Verse, 1660-*

1714, Yale University Press, Volume VI: *1699-1704,* 1970. Contributor of articles to professional journals.*

* * *

ELLISTON, Thomas R(alph)   1919-1977

1919—October 20, 1977; American foreign service officer and journalist. Elliston worked for the U.S. Information Agency as a newswriter for Voice of America, covering the White House, Capitol Hill, and other government news. In 1976 he earned the Superior Honor Award from the agency for "the creation and implementation of unusually imaginative and effective election year programs." He died in Lima, Peru. Obituaries: *Washington Post,* October 23, 1977.

* * *

ELVIN, Mark   1938-

PERSONAL: Born August 18, 1938, in Cambridge, England; married Anne K. Stevenson (a poet and critic); children: two sons. *Education:* Cambridge University, B.A. (first class honors), 1959, M.A., 1964, Ph.D., 1968; attended Harvard University, 1962-64. *Politics:* "Liberal/Ecological." *Office:* St. Antony's College, Oxford University, Oxford OX2 6JF, England.

CAREER: Cambridge University, Cambridge, England, assistant lecturer in Chinese history, 1964-67, fellow of Clare Hall, 1966-67; University of Glasgow, Glasgow, Scotland, lecturer in economic history, 1968-73; Oxford University, Oxford, England, lecturer in Chinese history and fellow of St. Antony's College, 1973—. *Member:* Oxford City Liberal Association (past chairman). *Awards, honors:* Harkness-Commonwealth fellowship for Harvard University, 1962-64.

WRITINGS: (Translator) Ayao Hoshi, *The Ming Tribute Grain System,* Center for Chinese Studies, University of Michigan, 1969; (translator) Yoshinobu Shiba, *Commerce and Society in Sung China,* Center for Chinese Studies, University of Michigan, 1970; *The Pattern of the Chinese Past: A Social and Economic Interpretation,* Stanford University Press, 1973; (editor with G. W. Skinner) *The Chinese City between Two Worlds,* Stanford University Press, 1974. Contributor to Asian studies journals. Founder and editor of *Michigan Abstracts on Chinese History.*

WORK IN PROGRESS: Research on Chinese economic and social history, 1500-1900, with special emphasis on demography.

AVOCATIONAL INTERESTS: Cross-country running, canal and river boating, chess, piobaireachd (pipe music), writing children's stories.

* * *

ELY, James W(allace), Jr.   1938-

PERSONAL: Born January 20, 1938, in Rochester, N.Y.; son of James Wallace (a banker) and Edythe (Farnham) Ely; married Ruth MacCameron (a teacher), August 27, 1960; children: Elizabeth, Kimberly F., Suzanne B., James Wallace III. *Education:* Princeton University, B.A. (honors), 1959; Harvard University, LL.B., 1962; University of Virginia, M.A., 1968, Ph.D., 1971. *Religion:* Presbyterian. *Home:* 112 Lynnwood Ter., Nashville, Tenn. 37205. *Office:* School of Law, Vanderbilt University, Nashville, Tenn. 37240.

CAREER: Harris, Beach & Wilcox, Rochester, N.Y., associate, 1962-67; University of Virginia, Charlottesville, instructor in history, 1970; Virginia Commonwealth Universi-

ty, Richmond, instructor, 1970-72, assistant professor of history, 1972-73; Vanderbilt University, Nashville, Tenn., visiting assistant professor, spring, 1973, assistant professor, 1973-75, associate professor of law, 1975—. *Member:* American Society for Legal History (member of board of directors, 1977-80).

WRITINGS: The Crisis of Conservative Virginia: The Byrd Organization and the Politics of Massive Resistance, University of Tennessee Press, 1976. Contributor of about twenty articles and reviews to history and law journals.

WORK IN PROGRESS: Editing *The Legal Papers of Andrew Jackson,* for University of Tennessee Press; studying South Carolina legislation in the colonial era.

* * *

EMERY, Michael   1940-

PERSONAL: Born April 16, 1940, in Berkeley, Calif.; son of William Edwin, Jr. (a journalism historian) and Mary (McNevin) Emery; married Suzanne Steiner (a sociologist), April 27, 1963; children: Maria, Andrea, Shannon. *Education:* University of Minnesota, B.A., 1962, M.A., 1964, Ph.D., 1968. *Office:* Department of Journalism, California State University, Northridge, Calif. 96405.

CAREER: Reporter for United Press International, 1961-64; Wisconsin State University, Whitewater (now University of Wisconsin—Whitewater), faculty member in journalism department, 1964-68; California State University, Northridge, faculty member in journalism department, 1968—. Editor of opinion section, *Los Angeles Times. Military service:* U.S. Army Reserve, active duty; became first lieutenant. *Member:* Society of Professional Journalists, Association for Education in Journalism, Sigma Delta Chi.

WRITINGS: (Editor with Edwin Emery and R. Smith Schuneman) *America's Front Page News, 1690-1970,* Vis-Com, Inc., 1970; (editor with Tel C. Smythe) *Readings in Mass Communication,* W. C. Brown, 1972; (with E. Emery) *The Press and America,* Prentice-Hall, in press. Contributor to *Quill* and other journalism publications.

WORK IN PROGRESS: A new edition of *Readings in Mass Communication,* with Tel C. Smythe, publication by W. C. Brown expected in 1979.

* * *

EMIG, Janet Ann

PERSONAL: Born in Cincinnati, Ohio. *Education:* Mount Holyoke College, B.A. (magna cum laude), 1950; University of Michigan, M.A., 1951; Harvard University, Ed.D., 1969. *Office:* Graduate School of Education, Rutgers University, 10 Seminary Pl., New Brunswick, N.J. 08903.

CAREER: Has taught in public and private schools, colleges, and universities, 1951—; presently professor of English education at Rutgers University, New Brunswick, N.J. Visiting instructor at University of Alaska; member of faculty at University of Lethbridge. *Member:* National Conference on Research in English, Phi Kappa Delta, Pi Lambda Theta. *Awards, honors:* Danforth fellowship, 1962-63.

WRITINGS: (Editor with others) *Language and Learning,* Harcourt, 1966; *Writing as Process,* McKay, 1977.

Poetry anthologized in *Anthology of Sports Poems,* edited by R. R. Knudson, Dell, 1971. Contributor of about twenty-five articles to language journals. Member of editorial board of *Harvard Educational Review,* 1962-64; member of *Alumnae Quarterly* committee at Mount Holyoke College, 1968-72.

WORK IN PROGRESS: Contributing to *New Directions in Composition Research* and *The Basics and Rhetoric,* both for National Council of Teachers of English.

AVOCATIONAL INTERESTS: Playing the piano, swimming, cooking.

* * *

EPHRON, Henry   1911-

PERSONAL: Born May 26, 1911, in New York, N.Y.; son of Isaac (a carpet merchant) and Gussie (Weinstein) Ephron; married Phoebe Wolkind (a screenwriter and playwright), July 31, 1934 (died October 13, 1971); children: Nora, Delia, Hallie Ephron Touger, Amy. *Education:* Graduated from Cornell University, 1932. *Politics:* Democrat. *Religion:* Jewish. *Home:* 176 East 71st St., New York, N.Y. 10021. *Agent:* Harriet Pilpel, Wolff, Greenbaum & Ernst, 437 Madison Ave., New York, N.Y. 10017.

CAREER: Screenwriter and playwright, 1943—. Produced, with wife Phoebe Ephron, the films "Carousel," 1956, and "The Desk Set," 1957. *Member:* Writers Guild, Screenwriters Guild, Mystery Writers Guild. *Awards, honors:* Academy Award nomination for screenplay of "Captain Newman, M.D.," 1963.

WRITINGS: We Thought We Could Do Anything (memoirs), Norton, 1977.

Plays—All with wife Phoebe Ephron: "Three's A Family," first produced on Broadway at Longacre Theatre, 1944; "Take Her, She's Mine," first produced on Broadway at Biltmore Theatre, 1961; "My Daughter, Your Son," first produced on Broadway at Biltmore Theatre, 1967.

Screenplays—All with Phoebe Ephron: "Bride by Mistake," produced by RKO, 1945; "April Showers," produced by Warner Bros., 1948; "Wallflower" (based on a play by Reginald Denham and Mary Orr), produced by Warner Bros., 1948; (and with I. A. L. Diamond) "Always Together," produced by Warner Bros., 1948; (and with Marian Spitzer) "Look for the Silver Lining," produced by Warner Bros., 1949; "John Loves Mary" (based on a play by Norman Krasna), produced by Warner Bros., 1949.

"The Jackpot" (based on an article by John McNulty), produced by Twentieth Century-Fox, 1950; (and with Valentine Davies) "On the Riviera" (based on a play by Rudolph Lothar and Hans Adler), produced by Twentieth Century-Fox, 1951; "Belles on Their Toes" (based on a book by Frank B. Gilbreth and Ernestine Gilbreth Carey), produced by Twentieth Century-Fox, 1952; "What Price Glory" (based on a play by Maxwell Anderson and Laurence Stallings), produced by Twentieth Century-Fox, 1952; "There's No Business Like Show Business," produced by Twentieth Century-Fox, 1954; "Daddy Long Legs" (based on a novel by Jean Webster), produced by Twentieth Century-Fox, 1955; "Carousel" (based on the Benjamin F. Glazer adaption of the play by Ferenc Molnar), produced by Twentieth Century-Fox, 1956; "The Desk Set" (based on a play by William Marchant), produced by Twentieth Century-Fox, 1957; (and with Richard L. Breen) "Captain Newman, M.D." (based on novel by Leo Rosten), produced by Universal, 1963.

WORK IN PROGRESS: Another screenplay and a novel.

SIDELIGHTS: Ephron's book *We Thought We Could Do Anything,* a memoir of his life as a comedy screenwriter in Hollywood, reads at times "like a script for a nice commercial upbeat comedy with lots of funny lines," according to Richard R. Lingeman.

Julie Cameron wrote that the book is outstanding in the company of frequently dull movie memoirs: indeed, she found that it "justifies the genre." Mel Gussow commented that the book is an "all-American success story," told with "irrepressible ebullience," and added: "Ephron is open-eyed about his profession—and proud of his professionalism. Unlike some screenwriters, who felt that they demeaned themselves and debased their talents in Hollywood, he and his wife loved their work and reveled in transforming dross into entertainment."

While Ephron discusses movie stars "with an unfamiliar candor," Cameron found that "these character studies are simple sketches compared to Ephron's portrait of his wife. Clearly, movie stars were simply stars to him while Phoebe was the moon. *We Thought We Could Do Anything* is really a last—and lasting—love letter."

BIOGRAPHICAL/CRITICAL SOURCES: New York Times Book Review, May 15, 1977; *New York Times,* May 21, 1977; *Washington Post,* June 5, 1977.

* * *

EPSTEIN, June

PERSONAL: Born in Perth, West Australia; daughter of Simon (a businessman) and Annie (Walters) Epstein; married Julius Guest (a lecturer in mathematics), March 7, 1949; children: Katharine-Anne (Mrs. William Garland), John Casey, Philip Ross (deceased). *Education:* Trinity College of Music, Cambridge, licentiate; Royal Academy of Music, licentiate; Royal Schools of Music, licentiate. *Office:* Institute of Early Childhood Development, State College of Victoria, 4 Madden Grove, Kew, Victoria, Australia.

CAREER: Australian Broadcasting Commission, Melbourne, Australia, broadcaster and scriptwriter, 1933—. Senior lecturer at State College of Victoria, 1972—. Director of music at Melbourne Church of England Girls' Grammar School, 1946-49; foundation president of Kew Colleges Parents' Association, 1957. *Member:* Professional Musicians Union of Australia, Australian Society of Authors, Society of Women Writers. *Awards, honors:* Overseas scholar of Trinity College of Music, 1936-39; silver medal from Worshipful Company of Musicians, 1938.

WRITINGS: The Nine Muses, Robertson & Mullens, 1951; *Mermaid on Wheels: The Story of Margaret Lester,* Ure Smith, 1967, Taplinger, 1968; *Image of the King: A Parent's Story of Mentally Handicapped Children,* Ure Smith, 1970, Drake, 1971; *Enjoying Music with Young Children,* Allans, 1972; *Mr. Nightingale,* Allans, in press. Music critic for *Australian Journal of Music Education.*

Plays: "A Paltry Affair," first produced in Victoria, Australia, November, 1976. Creator of educational recordings for children and composer of music.

WORK IN PROGRESS: No Music by Request: The Biography of a Voice.

SIDELIGHTS: Epstein told *CA:* "I've always combined the two professional careers of music and writing. In music I began in childhood as a concert pianist, studied on an overseas scholarship, returned to tour Australia as a concert pianist for the Australian Broadcasting Commission, and later became involved in music education.

"In writing I have been influenced by my great interest and involvement with handicapped people and have written three full length biographies of people with different handicaps."

EPSTEIN, Leslie 1938-

PERSONAL: Born May 4, 1938, in Los Angeles, Calif.; son of Philip (a screenwriter) and Lillian (Targen) Epstein; married Ilene Gradman, November 1, 1969; children: Anya, Paul and Theo (twins). *Education:* Yale University, B.A., 1960, graduate study, 1963-65, D.F.A., 1967; Oxford University, diploma, 1962; University of California, Los Angeles, M.A., 1963. *Home:* 221 West 82nd St., New York, N.Y. 10024. *Agent:* Lois Wallace, Wallace, Aitken & Shiel, Inc., 118 East 61st St., New York, N.Y. 10024.

CAREER: Queens College of the City University of New York, Flushing, N.Y., lecturer, 1965-67, assistant professor, 1968-70, associate professor, 1970-75, professor of English, 1976—. *Member:* International P.E.N. *Awards, honors:* Rhodes scholarship, 1960-62; National Endowment for the Arts grant, 1972; Fulbright fellowship, 1972-73; CAPS grant, 1976-77; Guggenheim fellowship, 1977-78.

WRITINGS: P. D. Kimerakov (novel), Little, Brown, 1975; *The Steinway Quintet Plus Four* (stories), Little, Brown, 1976. Contributor of stories, articles, and reviews to literary journals and popular magazines, including *Atlantic Monthly, Esquire, Nation, Antaeus, Playboy,* and *Antioch Review.*

WORK IN PROGRESS: A novel, "about a Polish city, and the Jews in it, during World War II."

* * *

ERICKSON, Marilyn T. 1936-

PERSONAL: Born April 30, 1936, in Brockton, Mass. *Education:* Brown University, A.B., 1957, M.A., 1959; University of Washington, Seattle, Ph.D., 1961. *Home:* 104 W. Franklin St., Apt. 1008, Richmond, Va. 23220. *Office:* Virginia Commonwealth University, 800 West Franklin St., Richmond, Va. 23284.

CAREER: University of North Carolina, Chapel Hill, assistant professor, 1961-67, associate professor of psychology, 1967-71; University of North Carolina, Greensboro, associate professor of psychology, 1971-76; Virginia Commonwealth University, Richmond, professor of psychology, 1976—.

WRITINGS: Child Psychopathology, Prentice-Hall, 1978.

WORK IN PROGRESS: Parenting; Child Development for Preparents.

* * *

ERNY, Pierre Jean Paul 1933-

PERSONAL: Born July 7, 1933, in Colmar, France; son of Charles (a certified accountant) and Madeleine (Bronner) Erny; married Antoinette Weibel, August 22, 1963; children: Benoit, Mathieu, Marie-Claire. *Education:* University of Strasbourg, M.A. and pedagogy diploma, 1963, Ph.D. (ethnology), 1965; Ph.D. (religious sciences), 1970. *Religion:* Catholic. *Home:* 6 rue Victor Huen, 68000 Colmar, France. *Office:* Universite des Sciences humaines, 22 rue Descartes, 67084 Strasbourg, France.

CAREER: Primary school teacher in Upper Volta, West Africa, 1958-60; Center for Higher Education (now University of Brazzaville), Brazzaville, Congo, deputy lecturer, 1963-64; Centre National de la Recherche Scientifique, Paris, France, research psychologist in Brazzaville, 1964-65; University of Strasbourg, Strasbourg, France, assistant professor of ethnology, 1965-70; Official University of the Congo, Lubumbashi, professor of educational sciences, 1970-71; National University of Zaire, Kisangani, professor of educa-

tional sciences, 1971-73; National University of Rwanda, Butare, professor of philosophy and educational sciences, 1973-76; Strasbourg University of Human Sciences, assistant professor of sociology and ethnology of education, 1976—. *Member:* Societe des Africanistes, Societe de thanatologie de langue francaise, Centre d'etudes et de documentation africaines (Brussels).

WRITINGS: Histoire de l'Afrique occidentale (title means "History of West Africa"), Editions Saint-Paul, 1964; *L'-Enfant dans la pensee traditionnelle de l'Afrique Noire,* Le Livre Africain, 1968, translation published as *Childhood and Cosmos: The Social Psychology of the Black African Child,* Black Orpheus Press, 1973; *Les Premiers Pas dans la vie de l'enfant d'Afrique noire* (title means "First Steps in the Life of the Child of Black Africa"), Editions de l'Ecole, 1972; *L'Enfant et son milieu en Afrique Noire: Essais sur l'-education traditionnelle* (title means "The Child and His Environment in Black Africa: Essays on Traditional Education"), Payot, 1972; *Sur les sentiers de l'universite: Autobiographies d'etudiants zairois* (title means "On the Paths of the University: Autobiographies of Zairian Students"), La Pensee Universelle, 1977; *L'Enseignement dans les pays pauvres: Modeles et propositions* (title means "Education in the Poor Countries: Models and Proposals"), Editions de l'Harmattan, 1977.

WORK IN PROGRESS: Books on African education and the ethnology of education, including *Etude du systeme d'-enseignement de la Republique du Rwanda* (title means "Study of the Educational System in the Republic of Rwanda"), publication expected in 1979, *Ethnologie de l'-education* (title means "Ethnology of Education"), *Psychologie de l'enfant africain* (title means "Psychology of the African Child"), *Pensee pedagogique de Rudolf Steiner* (title means "The Pedagogical Thought of Rudolf Steiner"), and *L'Experience pedagogique des maisons familiales rurales* (title means "The Pedagogical Experiment of Rural Family Hotels").

SIDELIGHTS: Erny writes: "For the past several years my project has been to shed some light on the problems posed by education in Black Africa by using data from the different human sciences, particularly psychology, ethnology, and sociology. I've spent a dozen years in five African countries. In the years to come I plan to draw a certain number of more general lessons from the experience I gained there."

* * *

ESPINOSA, Rudy
See ESPINOZA, Rudolph Louis

* * *

ESPINOZA, Rudolph Louis 1933-
(Rudy Espinosa)

PERSONAL: Born September 28, 1933, in San Francisco, Calif.; son of Mercedes Max (a laborer-artist) and Rosita (Kilgore-Enriquez) Espinoza. *Education:* University of California, Berkeley, B.A., 1971; San Francisco State University, M.A., 1977. *Home address:* P.O. Box 492, Scotia, Calif. 95565. *Agent:* Roberto (TSB) Moreno, Tlamantini Associates, P.O. Box 158, Arcata, Calif. 95521.

CAREER: EMPLEO, San Quentin, Calif., public relations director, 1969-71; DQ University, Davis, Calif., counselor, 1972-73; San Francisco State University, San Francisco, Calif., lecturer in experience and literature, 1974; Contra

Costa Junior College, San Pueblo, Calif., lecturer in Chicano literature, 1974-75; Ohlone College, Fremont, Calif., instructor in English, 1975; Editorial Justa Publications, Berkeley, Calif., public relations director, 1975-76; Humboldt State College, Arcata, Calif., lecturer in ethnic studies, 1976—. *Military service:* U.S. Army, 1953-55. *Member:* Modern Language Association of America, Point Zero Literary Workshop (trustee). *Awards, honors:* Breadloaf Writers' Conference scholarship, 1962.

WRITINGS: El Grito (title means "The Cry"), Quinto Sol, 1969; *El Espejo* (title means "The Mirror"), Quinto Sol, 1969; *El Pocho Che,* El Pocho Che, 1970; "Jailed" (one-act play), published in *El Tecolote,* October 27, 1971.

WORK IN PROGRESS: A collection of short stories on "American city experience from an urban Mexican-American perspective."

SIDELIGHTS: Espinosa told *CA* that he is "interested in the development of basic reading and writing skills within the Mexican-American working community." *Avocational interests:* Ethnic literature.

* * *

ETKIN, Anne (Dunwody Little) 1923-

PERSONAL: Born June 4, 1923, in Thomasville, Ga.; daughter of Arthur Dillard Harmon (a surgeon) and Carolyn (Atkinson) Little; married Seymour Etkin (an accountant), May 25, 1944; children: Nancy, Elizabeth Bremer. *Education:* Attended University of Georgia, 1940-41, University of Maryland, 1943, and L'Ecole Francaise de Middlebury, 1943; Vanderbilt University, A.B., 1944. *Politics:* "Encourage what's suited to Hobbits, discourage what's suited to Orcs." *Religion:* Unitarian-Universalist. *Home:* 6819 Second St., Riverdale, Md. 20840.

CAREER: Mission Militaire Francaise, Washington, D.C., receptionist, 1944-45; nursery school teacher in Tacoma, Wash. and San Antonio, Tex., 1945-47, in Silver Springs, Md., 1947-48; free-lance writer and author of children's books, 1951—. French teacher in Prince George's County, Md., 1960-68. Member of board of advisors, Quest Communications, Inc.; volunteer librarian. *Member:* American Tolkien Society, Tolkien Federation, Mythopoeic Society, Tolkien Society (Britain), Markland Confederation, Phi Beta Kappa, Midgard Medieval Mercenary Militia.

WRITINGS: All at Sea, Seymour Etkin, 1961; (contributor and illustrator) Henry Mondeloff, editor, *Mon Cahier de Francais* (title means "My French Workbook"), Board of Education, Prince George's County, Md., 1965; (contributor) Ruth Berman, editor, *Rime Royal,* Society for Creative Anachronism, 1975; *Waterspout Up,* T-K Graphics, 1975; *The Magination,* T-K Graphics, 1976; (with Wendell Hill) *Handbook for the Live Ring Game,* Quest Communications, 1978; *Eglerio! In Praise of Tolkien* (includes essays by C. S. Lewis), Quest Communications, 1978. Also contributing editor of *Paint Branch Anthology,* Pat Cain Press. Contributor to *Midgard Runestone,* other medievalist and Tolkien journals, and songbooks.

WORK IN PROGRESS: Research and translation of works by Marguerite d'Angouleme; new translation of the romance of Fouke Fitzwarin; a novel, *In the Time of the Silver Stars;* two short books of interest to Tolkien fans.

SIDELIGHTS: Etkin told *CA:* "There has never been a sharp division between my vocations and avocations. For example, as a teacher I helped to write the textbook and prepared visual aids. Teaching comes into my writing and art into everything. Most of my adult life has been taken up with children and pets, but I have never stopped writing."

Etkin is fluent in several forms of French, and reads German, Middle English, and Anglo-Saxon.

* * *

EURICH, Nell 1919-

PERSONAL: Born July 28, 1919, in Norwood, Ohio; daughter of Clayton W. and Edah (Palmer) Plopper; married Alvin C. Eurich (an educator), March 15, 1953; children: Juliet Ann, Donald Alan. *Education:* Stephens College, A.A., 1939; Stanford University, B.A., 1941, M.A., 1943; Columbia University, Ph.D., 1959. *Home:* 24 West 55th St., New York, N.Y. 10019; and Hubbell Mountain Rd., Sherman, Conn. 06784. *Office:* Department of English, Manhattanville College, Purchase, N.Y. 10577.

CAREER: University of Texas, Austin, Tex., director of student union, 1942-43; Barnard College, New York City, resident counselor, 1944-46; Woman's Foundation, New York City, assistant to president, 1947-49; State University of New York, Albany, N.Y., officer in charge of public relations, 1949-52; Stephens College, Columbia, Mo., acting president, 1953-54; New York University, New York City, assistant professor of English, 1959-64; New College, Sarasota, Fla., academic dean, 1965; City of Aspen, Colo., director of project to reorganize the public high school curriculum, 1966; Vassar College, Poughkeepsie, N.Y., professor of English and dean of faculty, 1967-70; Manhattanville College, Purchase, N.Y., professor of English, 1971—, provost and dean of faculty, 1971—. National Endowment of the Humanities, member of national selection committee and chairman of Rocky Mountain regional committee, 1966-67, consultant, 1970-71; member, Middle States commission, Marshall Scholarships, 1967-68, and chairman of Northeastern region, 1969-71; member, U.S. Commission on Educational Technology, U.S. Department of Health, Education, and Welfare, 1968-69; member of judges panel for Federal Woman's award, 1969—; consultant, Academy for Educational Development, 1970-71; member of career minister review board, U.S. Department of State, 1972; member of regional panel, White House Commission on Fellows, 1973—. Trustee of New College and Salisbury School; former trustee, Bank Street College of Education, Hudson Guild Neighborhood House, Rocky Mountain School.

MEMBER: Modern Language Association of America, American Association of Colleges, World Society for Ekistics, National Council of Women of the United States (honorary member).

WRITINGS: Science in Utopia: A Mighty Design, Harvard University Press, 1967. Also author, with B. Schwenkmeyer, *Great Britain's Open University,* 1971. Contributor of articles to educational journals.*

* * *

EVANS, Eva (Knox) 1905-

PERSONAL: Born August 17, 1905, in Roanoke, Virginia; daughter of a Southern Methodist minister; married Boris Witte.

CAREER: Author. Teacher in rural and city schools, migrant labor camps, and in the demonstration school for Negro children at the University of Atlanta.

WRITINGS: Araminta (illustrated by Erick Berry), Minton, Balch, 1935; *Jerome Anthony* (illustrated by Berry), Putnam, 1936; *Key Corner* (illustrated by Berry), Putnam,

1938; *Araminta's Goat* (illustrated by Berry), Putnam, 1938; *Emma Belle and Her Kinfolks* (illustrated by Flavia Gag), Putnam, 1940; *The Lost Handkerchiefs* (illustrated by Gag), Putnam, 1941; (with Erick Berry) *Mr. Jones and Mr. Finnigan,* Oxford University Press, 1941; *A Surprise for Araminta* (illustrated by Ann Eshner), Grosset & Dunlap, 1942; *So You're Going to Teach,* Julius Rosenwald Fund, 1943; *Children and You: A Primer of Child Care* (illustrated by Mary A. Giles), Putnam, 1943; *Out under the Sky* (illustrated by Giles), West Georgia College Press, 1944; *Let's Cook Lunch* (illustrated by Giles), West Georgia College Press, 1944; *Skookum* (illustrated by Rafaello Busoni), Putnam, 1946, reprinted, Houghton, 1966; *All about Us* (illustrated by Vana Earle), Capitol Publishing, 1947; *Life around Us* (illustrated by Earle), Hinds, Hayden, 1948.

Tim's Place (illustrated by Bruno Frost), Putnam, 1950; *People Are Important* (illustrated by Earle), Capitol Publishing, 1951; *Why We Live Where We Live* (illustrated by Ursula Koering), Little, Brown, 1953; *The Story of Su-Su* (illustrated by Earle), D. McKay, 1953; *Nothing Is Dripping on Us,* Little, Brown, 1954; *The Adventure Book of Shells* (illustrated by Earle), Capitol Publishing, 1955; *The Adventure Book of Money* (illustrated by Raymond Burns), Capitol Publishing, 1956; *Where Do You Live?* (illustrated by Beatrice Darwin), Golden Press, 1960; *The Adventure Book of Forest Wonders* (illustrated by Aubrey Combs), Golden Press, 1960; *That Lucky Mrs. Plucky* (illustrated by Jo Ann Stover), D. McKay, 1961; *Home Is a Very Special Place* (illustrated by Millard McGee), Golden Press, 1961; *The Adventure Book of Archaeology,* Golden Press, 1962; *Sleepy Time* (illustrated by Reed Champion), Houghton, 1962; *The Snow Book* (illustrated by Aldren A. Watson), Little, Brown, 1965; *Rocks* (illustrated by Earle), Golden Press, 1965; *American Biographies,* Holt, 1968; *The Beginning of Life: How Babies Are Born* (illustrated by Rob Howard), Crowell-Collier, 1969; *The Dirt Book: An Introduction to Earth Science* (illustrated by Robert Quackenbush), Little, Brown, 1969; *Archaeology: Secrets of the Past,* Golden Press, 1969; *Rocks and Rock Collecting,* Golden Press, 1970.*

* * *

EVANS, Joan 1893-1977

June 22, 1893—July 14, 1977; British historian, author, and authority on medieval art. She died in England. Obituaries: *AB Bookman's Weekly,* September 5, 1977. (Sec index for *CA* sketch)

* * *

EVANS, John
See BROWNE, Howard

* * *

EVERWINE, Peter Paul 1930-

PERSONAL: Born February 14, 1930, in Detroit, Mich.; divorced; children: two. *Education:* Northwestern University, B.S., 1952; Stanford University, graduate study, 1958-59; University of Iowa, Ph.D., 1959. *Home:* 2645 Moroa, Fresno, Calif. 93704. *Office:* Department of English, California State University, Fresno, Calif. 93710.

CAREER: University of Iowa, Iowa City, instructor in English, 1959-62; California State University, Fresno, professor of English, 1962—. *Military service:* U.S. Army, 1952-54. *Member:* Philological Association of the Pacific Coast. *Awards, honors:* Lamont Award from the Academy of American Poets, 1972.

WRITINGS: In the House of Light: Thirty Aztec Poems, Stone Wall Press, 1970; *Collecting the Animals* (poems), Atheneum, 1973. Work has been anthologized in *Down at the Santa Fe Depot,* Giligia, 1969.*

* * *

EWBANK, Henry L(ee), Jr. 1924-

PERSONAL: Born March 26, 1924, in Michigan; son of Henry Lee (a professor) and Rachel (a teacher and artist; maiden name, Belt) Ewbank; married Barbara Harris (a shop owner), December 24, 1972; children: Kimberley Ewbank Reynolds, Heller Ewbank Lipsett, Mark Michael. *Education:* University of Wisconsin, Madison, A.B., 1947, M.A., 1948, Ph.D., 1952. *Home:* 627 Central Ave., Lafayette, Ind. 47905. *Office:* Department of Communication, Purdue University, West Lafayette, Ind. 47907.

CAREER: University of Hawaii, Honolulu, instructor in speech, 1949-51; Eastern Illinois University, Charleston, assistant professor of speech and director of forensics, 1951-53; Purdue University, West Lafayette, Ind., assistant professor, 1953-56, associate professor, 1956-70, professor of speech communication, 1970—, director of forensics, 1956-61, 1970—. Visiting professor at University of Hawaii, 1963. Member of Lafayette Civic Theatre. *Military service:* U.S. Army Reserve, 1941. U.S. Marine Corps, 1942-43. U.S. Naval Reserve, 1943-50.

MEMBER: Speech Communication Association of America, American Association of University Professors (local president, 1961-63; member of national council, 1967-70), Central States Speech Association (executive secretary, 1957-60; president, 1961-62), Phi Kappa Phi (founder and president of local chapter, 1971-72), Delta Sigma Rho, Tau Kappa Alpha (national secretary, 1963-65).

WRITINGS: Meeting Management, W. C. Brown, 1968. Contributor to speech journals. Editor of newsletter of Commission on American Parliamentary Practice.

WORK IN PROGRESS: Public Speaking in the Parliamentary Situation, for Science Research Associates; a chapter to be included in a book on the 1976 Presidential campaign, edited by Bruce H. Gronbeck, for Speech Communication Association of America; exploring the rhetorical uses of analogy, the analogical relationships between rhetoric and architecture, the rhetorical aspects of politics, and issues in freedom of speech.

SIDELIGHTS: Ewbank told *CA:* "People need to develop the ability to apply critical standards to political rhetoric in order to function more adequately as voters. They will also benefit from an understanding of the philosophy and principles underlying the rules of parliamentary practice, rather than the almost pathological concern for and fear of the procedural rules for meetings.

"Relationships between rhetoric and architecture range from the concept of 'building an argument' to John Ruskin's *Seven Lamps of Architecture,* and Richard McKeon's view that 'rhetoric is architectonic.' Still, there is more to be explored and ruminated upon concerning the relationships among the 'useful arts.' "

* * *

EWEN, Frederic 1899-

PERSONAL: Born October 11, 1899, in Lemberg, Austria; brought to United States in 1912, naturalized in 1912; son of Issac (a writer) and Helen (Kramer) Ewen; married Miriam Gideon (a composer), December 16, 1949; children: Joel.

Education: City College (now City College of the City University of New York), B.A., 1921; Columbia University, M.A., 1925, Ph.D., 1932. *Home:* 410 Central Park W., New York, N.Y. 10025.

CAREER: City College (now City College of the City University of New York), New York, N.Y., instructor in English, 1923-30; Brooklyn College (now Brooklyn College of the City University of New York), Brooklyn, N.Y., assistant professor of English, 1930-52. Visiting lecturer at Yeshiva University, Juilliard School of Music, Brooklyn Academy, and Master Institute of New York.

WRITINGS: The Prestige of Schiller in England, Columbia University Press, 1932; *Bibliography of Eighteenth-Century English Literature,* Columbia University Press, 1935; (with David Ewen) *Musical Vienna,* Whittlesey House, 1939; *The Poetry and Prose of Heinrich Heine,* Citadel, 1948; *Bertolt Brecht: His Life, His Art, and His Times,* Citadel, 1967; (translator) Heinrich Heine, *Self-Portrait and Other Prose Writings,* Citadel, 1974.

Dramatic adaptations: (With Phoebe Brand and John Randolph) "A Portrait of the Artist as a Young Man" (adapted from the novel by James Joyce), produced Off-Broadway at Martinique Theatre, 1962-63; (with P. Brand and J. Randolph) "Magic Mountain" (adapted from Thomas Mann's novel by the same name, originally published as *Der Zauberberg),* produced at Brandeis University, 1967. Television adaptations include "Two Jewish Stories," 1966, and "The Unknown Chekhov," 1967, both produced on Columbia Broadcasting System's "Camera Three," and Chekhov's "Ward Number 6," 1968.

WORK IN PROGRESS: A dramatic adaptation of Fedor Dostoyevski's *The Possessed;* writing *A Half-Century of Greatness: The Literary Imagination of Europe, 1830-1880.*

BIOGRAPHICAL/CRITICAL SOURCES: New York Times Book Review, December 10, 1967; *Nation,* March 4, 1968; *Books Abroad,* winter, 1969; *Observer Review,* August 9, 1970.

* * *

FABER-KAISER, Andreas 1944-

PERSONAL: Born April 5, 1944, in Barcelona, Spain; son of Will (a painter) and Emma (Kaiser) Faber; married Mercedes Castellanos, December 23, 1967; children: Sergi, Monika. *Education:* Attended University of Barcelona, 1963-67. *Religion:* "Anyone." *Home:* Lepanto 422, Barcelona, Spain. *Office: Mundo Desconocido,* Balmes 393, Barcelona 6, Spain.

CAREER: Mundo Desconocido, Barcelona, Spain, director and editor, 1976—. *Awards, honors:* National award from Agrupacion Astronautica Espanola, 1972, for "Repercusion de la Astronautica en la vida del hombre."

WRITINGS: Sacerdotes o Cosmonautas? (title means "Priests or Astronauts?"), Ate, 1971; *Cosmos: Cronologia general de la astronautica* (title means "Cosmos: General Chronology of Space Investigation"), Ate, 1973; *Em Busca dos extraterrestres* (title means "In Search of Extraterrestrials"), Editora Tres., 1973; *Jesus vivio y murio en Cachemika,* Ate, 1976, translation by Gordon R. Cremonesi published as *Jesus Died in Kashmir,* Gordon & Cremonesi, 1977.

WORK IN PROGRESS: Research on parapsychology, unidentified flying objects, astronautics, religions, and philosophy.

SIDELIGHTS: Faber comments that he is motivated by "the great mystery of human origin and the human future." He has traveled in Europe, Asia, and Latin America.

* * *

FABREGA, Horacio, Jr. 1934-

PERSONAL: Born January 6, 1934, in Philadelphia, Pa.; son of Horacio and Maria (Stewart) Fabrega; married Joan Sporkin, June 7, 1957; children: Andrea Melanie, Michele Marie. *Education:* University of Pennsylvania, B.S., 1956; Columbia University, M.D., 1960; Yale University, postdoctoral study, 1961-64. *Residence:* Pittsburgh, Pa. *Office:* Department of Psychiatry, University of Pittsburgh, Pittsburgh, Pa. 15216.

CAREER: Yale University, New Haven, Conn., resident at Medical Center, 1961-64; Baylor University, Houston, Tex., assistant professor of psychiatry, 1966-69; Michigan State University, East Lansing, professor of psychiatry and anthropology, 1969-77; University of Pittsburgh, Pittsburgh, Pa., professor of psychiatry, 1977—. Visiting professor at University of Chicago, 1972-73, and Institute of Psychiatry and Institute of Neurology (London, England). Member, research panel, President's Commission on Mental Health. *Military service:* U.S. Army, Medical Corps, 1964-66.

MEMBER: American Psychiatric Association, American Anthropological Association, American Association for the Advancement of Science, Society for Medical Anthropology (president), American Sociological Association, American Association for Physical Anthropology, American Public Health Association. *Awards, honors:* John L. Kosa Award, 1975.

WRITINGS: Illness and Shamanistic Medicine, Stanford University Press, 1973; *Disease and Social Behavior,* M.I.T. Press, 1974. Contributor of over sixty articles to medical and social science journals.

WORK IN PROGRESS: Analysis of data of longitudinal study of illness experiences and medical care practices of a panel of families in Southeastern Mexico.

SIDELIGHTS: Fabrega writes that he was raised in Panama, and is interested in the social and cultural aspects of disease, medical perspectives, and medical care practices.

* * *

FAIRCHILD, William
(Edward Cranston)

PERSONAL: Born in Cornwall, England. *Education:* Attended Royal Naval College. *Office:* c/o Robin Dalton Associates, 4 Goodwins Ct., St. Martin's Lane, London WC2, England.

CAREER: Motion picture director, screenwriter, and playwright. Trustee, Writers Guild of Great Britain. *Military service:* Royal Navy. *Member:* Society of Authors, League of Dramatists, Dramatists Club. *Awards, honors:* Venice Festival director's award, 1955, for "John and Julie."

WRITINGS: (Under pseudonym Edward Cranston) *A Matter of Duty,* Longmans, Green, 1943; *The Swiss Arrangement* (novel), St. Martin's, 1973.

Plays: *The Sound of Murder* (three-act), Samuel French, 1960; *Breaking Point* (three-act), Samuel French, 1963. Also author of "Poor Horace," "Kill-In," "No Man's Land," "The Signal," "Four Just Men," "Some Other Love," "Cunningham 5101," "The Break," and "The Two Hundred Gang."

Screenplays: "Operation Disaster," released by Universal, 1951; "The Long Dark Hall," Eagle Lion, 1951; "The Clouded Yellow," Columbia, 1952; "Outcasts of the Islands," United Artists, 1952; "Project M-7," Universal, 1954; "Malta Story," United Artists, 1954; "Value for Money," Rank, 1954; "Land of Fury," Universal, 1955; "The Silent Enemy," Universal, 1959; "Do Not Disturb," Fox, 1965; "Star!", Fox, 1968. Also author of screenplays including "Badgers Green," "Glory at Sea," "Black 13," "Front Page Story," "John and Julie," "The Extra Day," "The Horsemasters," and "The Last Shot You Hear."

Author of more than fifty short stories.*

* * *

FAIRFAX, Beatrice
    See McCARROLL, Marion C(lyde)

* * *

FAIRLEY, Irene R.   1940-

PERSONAL: Born January 2, 1940, in Brooklyn, N.Y.; daughter of Morris (an account executive) and Regina (Kalvary) Rosensweig; married; children: Gerard Tynes, Peter Raphael. *Education:* Queens College (now of the City University of New York), B.A. (cum laude), 1960; Harvard University, M.A., 1961, Ph.D., 1971. *Home:* 34 Winn St., Belmont, Mass. 02178. *Office:* Department of English, Northeastern University, Boston, Mass. 02115.

CAREER: Massachusetts Institute of Technology, Cambridge, instructor in English, summer, 1966; Long Island University, C. W. Post College, Greenvale, N.Y., instructor, 1968-72, assistant professor of English, 1972-73; Northeastern University, Boston, Mass., assistant professor of English, 1973—. Member of Millay Colony for the Arts. Has had exhibits of pencil and charcoal drawings and watercolor paintings.

MEMBER: Modern Language Association of America, Linguistic Society of America, Northeast Modern Language Association, Boston Area Stylistics Circle (founding member). *Awards, honors:* National Science Foundation travel grant, 1977; American Council of Learned Societies grant, 1977-78.

WRITINGS: (Editor with William I. Bennett and John T. Onuska) *Facing the Issues,* Sloan School of Industrial Management, Massachusetts Institute of Technology, 1966; (contributor) Charles A. Gribble, editor, *Studies Presented to Professor Roman Jakobson by His Students,* Slavica Publishers, 1968; (contributor) Don L. F. Nilsen, editor, *Meaning: A Common Ground of Linguistics and Literature,* University of Northern Iowa Press, 1973; *E. E. Cummings and Ungrammar: A Study of Syntactic Device in His Poems,* Watermill Publishers, 1975. Contributor of articles, poems, and reviews to literature journals. Member of editorial board of *Language and Style, Semiotic Scene,* and *Studies in American Fiction.*

WORK IN PROGRESS: Visual Aspects of Poems; Reader Responses to Poems: Empirical Data and Stylistic Analysis; a stylistic analysis of the poetry of William Carlos Williams.

SIDELIGHTS: Irene Fairley writes: "I have long been interested in the structure of literary creations and believe that insights come through many different approaches. My own perspective on the poetic results from a combined background in literary criticism and linguistics. I believe that the most interesting breakthrough lies ahead, in the discovery of that semiotic function of art that literature partakes of."

AVOCATIONAL INTERESTS: Ski touring, tennis, hiking, drawing and painting, travel (Mexico and Europe).

* * *

FANE, Bron
    See FANTHORPE, R(obert) Lionel

* * *

FANTHORPE, R(obert) Lionel   1935-
    (Neil Balfort, Othello Baron, Erle Barton, Lee Barton, Thornton Bell, Noel Bertram, Leo Brett, Bron Fane, Phil Hobel, Mel Jay, Marston Johns, Victor La Salle, Oban Lerteth, Robert Lionel, John E. Muller, Elton T. Neef, Peter O'Flinn, Peter O'Flynn, Lionel Roberts, Rene Rolant, Deutero Spartacus, Robin Tate, Neil Thanet, Trebor Thorpe, Trevor Thorpe, Pel Torro, Olaf Trent, Karl Zeigfreid)

PERSONAL: Born February 9, 1935, in Dereham, England; son of Robert (a shop owner) and Greta Christine (a teacher; maiden name, Garbutt) Fanthorpe; married Patricia Alice Tooke, September 7, 1957; children: Stephanie Dawn, Fiona Mary. *Education:* Norwich Teachers Training College, certificate, 1963; Open University, B.A., 1974. *Politics:* "Middle-of-the-road man, moderate Conservative." *Religion:* "Theistic humanist." *Home:* Lothlorien, 48 Fairways, Hellesdon, Norwich, Norfolk NR6 5PN, England. *Office:* Hellesdon High School, Middleton's Ln., Hellesdon, Norwich, Norfolk NR6 5SB, England.

CAREER: Worked as a machine operator, farm worker, warehouseman, journalist, salesman, storekeeper, and yard foreman during the 1950's; secondary school teacher in Dereham, England, 1963-67; Gamlingay Village College, Gamlingay, England, tutor, 1967-69; Phoenix Timber Co., Rainham, England, industrial training officer, 1969-72; Hellesdon High School, Hellesdon, England, head of English department, 1972, second master, 1973—. *Military service:* British Army, 1967-69; became first lieutenant. *Member:* Society for Psychical Research, British Institute of Management, Mensa, Genealogical Society, College of Preceptors, Norwich Science Fiction Club, Judo Club. *Awards, honors:* East of England Judo Championship silver medal, 1977.

WRITINGS—All published by Badger Books, except as indicated: *The Waiting World,* 1958; *Alien from the Stars,* 1959, Arcadia House, 1967; *Hyperspace,* 1959, Arcadia House, 1966; *Space-Borne,* 1959; *Fiends,* 1959; *Doomed World,* 1960; *Satellite,* 1960; *Asteroid Man,* 1960, Arcadia House, 1966; *Out of the Darkness,* 1960; *Hand of Doom,* 1960, Arcadia House, 1968; *Flame Mass,* 1961; *The Golden Chalice,* 1961; *Space Fury,* 1962, Vega Books, 1963; *Negative Minus,* 1963; *Neuron World,* 1965; *The Triple Man,* 1965; *The Unconfined,* 1966; *The Watching World,* 1966.

Nonfiction; all published by John Spencer: (With W. H. Farrer) *Spencer's Metric Decimal Guide,* 1970; (with wife, Patricia Fanthorpe) *Spencer's Office Guide,* 1971; (with P. Fanthorpe) *Spencer's Metric Decimal Companion,* 1971; (with P. Fanthorpe) *Decimal Payroll Tables,* 1971.

Under pseudonym Erle Barton: *The Planet Seekers,* Vega Books, 1964.

Under pseudonym Lee Barton: *The Unseen,* Badger Books, 1963; *The Shadow Man,* Badger Books, 1966.

Under pseudonym Thornton Bell: *Space Trap,* Badger Books, 1964, Arcadia House, 1966; *Chaos,* Badger Books, 1964.

Under pseudonym Leo Brett; all published by Badger Books, except as indicated: *Exit Humanity*, 1960, Arcadia House, 1965; *The Microscopic Ones*, 1960; *Faceless Planet*, 1960; *March of the Robots*, 1961; *Mind Force*, 1961, Lenox Hill, 1971; *Black Infinity*, 1961; *Nightmare*, 1962; *Face in the Night*, 1962; *The Immortals*, 1962; *They Never Came Back*, 1962; *The Forbidden*, 1963; *From Realms Beyond*, 1963; *The Alien Ones*, 1963, Arcadia House, 1969; *Power Sphere*, 1963, Arcadia House, 1968.

Under pseudonym Bron Fane; all published by Badger Books, except as indicated: *Juggernaut*, 1960, published as *Blue Juggernaut*, Arcadia House, 1965; *Last Man on Earth*, 1960; *Rodent Mutation*, 1961; *The Intruders*, 1963; *Somewhere Out There*, 1963, Arcadia House, 1965; *Softly by Moonlight*, 1963; *Unknown Destiny*, 1964; *Nemesis*, 1964; *Suspension*, 1964, Vega Books, 1965; *The Macabre Ones*, 1964; *U.F.O. 517*, 1966.

Under pseudonym Victor La Salle: *Menace from Mercury*, John Spencer, 1954.

Under pseudonym John E. Muller; all published by Badger Books, except as indicated: *The Ultimate Man*, 1961; *The Uninvited*, 1961; *Crimson Planet*, 1961, Arcadia House, 1966; *The Venus Venture*, 1961, published under pseudonym Marston Johns, Arcadia House, 1965; *Forbidden Planet*, 1961, Arcadia House, 1965; *Return of Zeus*, 1962; *Perilous Galaxy*, 1962; *Uranium 235*, 1962, Arcadia House, 1967; *The Man Who Conquered Time*, 1962; *Orbit One*, 1962, published under pseudonym Mel Jay, Arcadia House, 1966; *The Eye of Karnak*, 1962; *Micro Infinity*, 1962, *Beyond Time*, 1962, published under pseudonym Marston Johns, Arcadia House, 1966; *Infinity Machine*, 1962; *The Day the World Died*, 1962; *Vengeance of Siva*, 1962; *The X-Machine*, 1962; *Reactor XK9*, 1963; *Special Mission*, 1963; *Dark Continuum*, 1964; *Mark of the Beast*, 1964; *The Negative Ones*, 1965; *The Exorcists*, 1965; *The Man from Beyond*, 1965, Arcadia House, 1969; *Beyond the Void*, 1965; *Spectre of Darkness*, 1965; *Out of the Night*, 1965; *Phenomena X*, 1966; *Survival Project*, 1966, Arcadia House, 1968.

Under pseudonym Lionel Roberts; all published by Badger Books, except as indicated: *Dawn of the Mutants*, 1959; *Time Echo*, 1959, published under pseudonym Robert Lionel, Arcadia House, 1964; *Cyclops in the Sky*, 1960; *The In-World*, 1960, Arcadia House, 1968; *The Face of X*, 1960, published under pseudonym Robert Lionel, Arcadia House, 1965; *The Last Valkyrie*, 1961; *The Synthetic Ones*, 1961; *Flame Goddess*, 1961.

Under pseudonym Neil Thanet: *Beyond the Veil*, Badger Books, 1964; *The Man Who Came Back*, Badger Books, 1964.

Under pseudonym Trebor Thorpe: *Five Faces of Fear*, Badger Books, 1960; *Lightning World*, 1960, Arcadia House, 1964.

Under pseudonym Pel Torro; all published by Badger Books, except as indicated: *Frozen Planet*, 1960, Arcadia House, 1967; *World of the Gods*, 1960; *The Phantom Ones*, 1961; *Legion of the Lost*, 1962; *The Strange Ones*, 1963; *Galaxy 666*, 1963, Arcadia House, 1968; *Formula 29X*, 1963, published as *Beyond the Barrier of Space*, Tower Books, 1969; *Through the Barrier*, 1963; *The Timeless Ones*, 1963; *The Last Astronaut*, 1963, Tower Books, 1969; *The Face of Fear*, 1963; *The Return*, 1964, published as *Exiled in Space*, Arcadia House, 1968; *Space No Barrier*, 1964, published as *Man of Metal*, Lenox Hill, 1970; *Force 97X*, 1965.

Under pseudonym Karl Zeigfreid; all published by Badger Books, except as indicated: *Walk Through To-Morrow*, 1962, Vega Books, 1963; *Android*, 1962; *Gods of Darkness*, 1962; *Atomic Nemesis*, 1962; *Zero Minus X*, 1962, Arcadia House, 1965; *Escape to Infinity*, 1963; *Radar Alert*, 1963, Arcadia House, 1964; *World of Tomorrow*, 1963, published as *World of the Future*, Arcadia House, 1968; *The World That Never Was*, 1963; *Projection Infinity*, 1964; *No Way Back*, 1964, Arcadia House, 1968; *Barrier 346*, 1965, Arcadia House, 1966; *The Girl from Tomorrow*, 1965.

Also author of "Supernatural Stories" monographs.

Contributor to periodicals under pseudonyms Neil Balfort, Othello Baron, Erle Barton, Lee Barton, Thornton Bell, Noel Bertram, Leo Brett, Bron Fane, Phil Hobel, Oban Lerteth, Elton T. Neef, Peter O'Flinn, Peter O'Flynn, Lionel Roberts, Rene Rolant, Deutero Spartacus, Robin Tate, Neil Thanet, Trebor Thorpe, Trevor Thorpe, Pel Torro, and Olaf Trent.

WORK IN PROGRESS: The Mysterious Treasure of Rennes-le-Chateau, with wife, Patricia Fanthorpe.

SIDELIGHTS: "I started writing when I was sixteen, having read and enjoyed most of the fantasy and science fiction I could get hold of at school," Fanthorpe told *CA*. "This was a mixture of Wells, Verne, Poe, etc., plus the odd paper back by authors whose names didn't register at the time. I have always had a poor memory for authors and titles, but I can recall the plot and characters of a story I've enjoyed for years afterwards. I wrote a parody of John Masefield's 'Sea Fever' beginning—

I must go back into space again,
To the lonely space and the stars;
And all I ask is a rocket ship
And a job to do on Mars. . . ."

Fanthorpe, who wrote nearly one hundred sixty books from 1957 until 1966, recalled the beginnings of his writing career: "In those days my mother ran a small shorthand and typing school from the front room of our house, and she did all the typing for me. Demand grew over the years. I married Patricia in 1957 and she shared the typing. Demand went on growing. At its peak we were being asked to produce a book a week, or even a book in a weekend. Communications would arrive from Spencers to the effect that the printer was waiting, could I hurry up. Patricia's sister got called into the typing team. I bought tape recorders and dictated material as fast as I could, despatching reels to the various typists, proofreading the typescripts and sending the manuscripts to Spencers by express mail. They never sent proofs and on some occasions what came out of the printer's end bore only coincidental resemblance to what I'd sent in.

"Spencers almost invariably sent the cover rough to me with a request to write a selection of titles and blurbs that would fit in. When I'd send this, they'd write back saying which ones they'd selected. I wrote the back cover introductions at the same time. Most of these were in-jokes of one sort or another. For example, they produced collections of shorts and insisted that each story appeared under a different pen-name. All my pen-names with the exception of Deutero Spartacus, which is an exercise in exploring the limits of the preposterous, were extractive anagrams based on ROBERT LIONEL FANTHORPE.

"I tried to give my pen-names an international flavour, but it was in the Milligan and Sellers vein. My international authors were music hall caricatures; my Scotsmen said, 'Och aye, the noo,' as a condition of their very existence; my Welshman came out of the infinite, terminated every utterance with, 'Look you, Dai Bach,' and usually worked in coal mines near nonconformist chapels. My French author, Rene Rolant, invariably pronounced *th* as *z* and darkly hinted of his past as a *souteneur* and resistance hero. My all-American boy was Elton T. Neff, known for some obscure reason as the Manhattan Magus, who was a faint shadow of John Wayne mixed with Damon Runyon and Mark Twain. The more blatantly unbelievable it all became, the more stories they bought. Like an impoverished latter-day Sheridan I tried giving characters names that went with their temperaments. He had Mrs. Malaprop and Sir Lucius O'Trigger. I had a gigantic security man with a sloping forehead and a love of fighting. I called him Slam Croberg and featured him in *Android*. It was Kingsley Amis's misfortune to review this for the *Observer* and his delicate artistic soul never fully recovered from the trauma.

"There *are* real characters hidden in some of the stories. It was another form of in-joke. Some I liked and described accordingly. Others I didn't. The reader must guess at those—at least until my mortal remains have gone where no laws of libel can reach. I'm in some of the stories too. The man-I'd-like-to-be is only thinly disguised in "The Attic" by Deutero Spartacus. (I'm the narrator, not the senile villain who gets the chop!) The Bron Fane character *Valentine Gregory Stearman* is also made in this mould. The nearest real description as opposed to an idealised one is the character of *Trader Krells* in *The Watching World*."

Addressing himself to the question why an author writes as he does at a particular period in his life, Fanthorpe added: "I am conscious that some experiences have coloured my thinking and led me to emphasize certain characters, lifestyles and philosophies at different stages of my writing. At sixteen and seventeen I was an enthusiastic Christian, a left-wing socialist and an ardent pacifist. In my twenties I was less committed to religion and my political enthusiasm waned. In my thirties I left the church and stopped renewing my subscriptions to the Labour Party. Currently, in my forties, I'm a vaguely theistic humanist, and sufficient of a Conservative to use my car to convey Conservative voters to the polling station to oblige a friend. I believe that writing should *say* something as well as telling a story: when I was a Christian socialist I plugged Christian socialism and meant it. I no longer mean it so I no longer write about Christian socialist heroes fighting totalitarian dictators. I cannot accept that any belief which reduces human happiness can be a moral belief, and to that extent I'm an old fashioned hedonist. I'm for anything which makes people happy, and gives them the chance to develop as autonomous beings. I'm against the miserable creeds of any religious or political group which subordinate the individual to some supposed higher end or purpose. In the last analysis we're probably neither more nor less than hapless fellow passengers to the grave, and if we can make the journey pleasant for someone else that's about the most we can do.

"My major dislikes are prudery, puritanism, and the increasing fads and whims of modern bureaucratic management. Given the chance to run my own show I'd be an old-fashioned, autocratic paternalist—the one on whose desk the buck not merely stops but is brought to a crashing, juddering halt. If Moses had worked with a committee the Israelites would still be in Egypt."

*   *   *

FARAH, Madelain 1934-

PERSONAL: Born December 20, 1934, in Portland, Ore.; daughter of Sam (a merchant) and Laurice (Nasrallah) Farah; married (divorced, 1966); children: Leila Habib. *Education:* Portland State University, B.A., 1959, M.A.T., 1967; University of Utah, Ph.D., 1976; also attended University of Oregon, American University of Cairo, and University of Tehran. *Religion:* Antochian Orthodox. *Address:* P.O. Box 66395, Portland, Ore. 97266.

CAREER: Farah's Department Store, Portland, Ore., clerk, buyer, and manager, 1946-59; high school teacher of Spanish, French, English, and social studies in Portland, Ore., 1960—. Translator and secretary for U.S. Government in Washington, D.C., 1955-59; drill instructor in Arabic at Portland State University, 1966; instructor in cooking at Portland Community College, 1976-77; writer, 1977—. Has tutored high school students in Arabic and Saudi Arabian students in English; has also worked as professional model, cosmetic consultant, and in hospital personnel departments. Vice-president of Western region of Antiochian Orthodox Women of North America, 1975; Parish Council president of St. George Orthodox Church, 1976 (first woman in the history of the church). Delegate to National Conference on Citizenship, 1956; member of board of directors of local United Nations chapter, 1958-62.

MEMBER: American Association of Teachers of French, National Education Association, Oregon Education Association, Portland Association of Teachers, Smithsonian Institute. *Awards, honors:* Medals from Concours national de francais, 1951; Fulbright grant, 1961-62, for Cairo; National Defense Foreign Language fellow, 1969-71, for University of Utah; grant from American Center for Iranian Studies, summer, 1970, for University of Tehran; first place in team competition of international table tennis tournament, 1971.

WRITINGS: Lebanese Cuisine, Ryder Printing, 1972, 3rd edition, 1975. Correspondent for *Word* magazine, 1973-75. Author of "Arabesque Recipes," a column in *News Circle*, 1973-74. Contributor to Arabic studies journals.

WORK IN PROGRESS: Islamic Marital Code: Prolegomenon to and Introduction of al-Ghazali's Book on the Etiquette of Marriage in Ihya' 'Ulum al-Din; The Doctrine of the Nagshabandi Order: A Study of Mysticism in Islam.

SIDELIGHTS: Farah possesses various degrees of fluency in Arabic, Persian, French, Spanish, and Russian. She has traveled to Lebanon, Egypt, Syria, Iran, Italy, Turkey, Greece, Jordan, Kuwait, Qatar, Saudi Arabia, Germany, Austria, France, England, and Mexico.

AVOCATIONAL INTERESTS: International travel, yoga, karate, fencing, hiking, dancing, shell and rock collecting, sewing, collecting foreign coins, antiques.

*   *   *

FARLEY-HILLS, David 1931-

PERSONAL: Born July 15, 1931, in Margate, England; son of Charles and Louise (Harriman) Farley-Hills; married Marlene Muscat Manduca, September 15, 1961; children: Sandra, Elizabeth Farley-Hills Bunting, Edward, Tom. *Education:* Queen's College, Oxford, M.A., 1961, B.Litt., 1961, D.Phil., 1969. *Politics:* "I oscillate between socialist and liberal." *Religion:* Atheist. *Home:* 4 Upper Malone Rd., Belfast 9, Northern Ireland. *Office:* Department of English, Queen's University, Belfast, Northern Ireland.

CAREER: Royal University of Malta, Msida, lecturer in English, 1960-68; Queen's University, Belfast, Northern Ireland, lecturer, 1968-73, senior lecturer in English literature, 1973-78.

WRITINGS: (Contributor) D. R. Howard and C. K. Zacker, editors, *Critical Studies of Sir Gawain and the Green Knight,* University of Notre Dame Press, 1968; (editor) *Rochester, the Critical Heritage,* Barnes & Noble, 1972; *The Benevolence of Laughter: Comic Poetry, 1650-1700,* Macmillan, 1974; *Upon Nothing: The Poetry of Rochester,* G. Bell, 1978. Contributor to literature and criticism journals.

WORK IN PROGRESS: *The Comic in Comedy from Shakespeare to Etherege* (tentative title).

SIDELIGHTS: Farley-Hills writes: "I have an intense fear of human beings and most other wild animals, an intense dislike of sexual prudery (I believe prudery one of the causes of wildness). My books are a small contribution to the more open discussion of sexual matters in literature. I have a special liking for the Maltese (I married one)."

* * *

FARNIE, D(ouglas) A(ntony) 1926-

PERSONAL: Born March 31, 1926, in Salford, Lancashire, England; son of Arthur and Ethel (Farrington) Farnie; married Edna Verina Eato. *Education:* University of Manchester, B.A., 1951, M.A., 1953; University of Natal, Ph.D., 1969. *Home:* 31 Parksway, Swinton, Manchester M27 1JN, England. *Office:* Department of History, University of Manchester, Manchester M13 9PL, England.

CAREER: University of Natal, Durban, lecturer in history, 1954-60; University of Manchester, Manchester, England, lecturer, 1961-71, senior lecturer in economic history, 1972—. *Military service:* British Army, 1944-48; became sergeant. *Member:* Historical Association, Economic History Society.

WRITINGS: *East and West of Suez: The Suez Canal in History, 1854-1956,* Clarendon Press, 1969. Contributor to economic and literary journals, including *Manchester Review.*

SIDELIGHTS: Farnie told *CA:* "The theme of the Suez book, the changing pattern of relationships between Europe and Asia, was partly a delayed product of my military service in India and Egypt. During my service in the Suez Canal zone, at Ismailia and Kentara, I developed no particular interest in the history of Egypt but I read Gibbon's *Decline and Fall* as an introduction to the study of history, which to me then meant the history of Europe. When I undertook research into the history of the cotton industry in 1951-53, I became aware of the importance of the Indian market for Lancashire during the era of its greatest expansion and I also explored the influence of the opening of the Canal on the export trade to the East."

WORK IN PROGRESS: A history of the trade in cotton textiles during the nineteenth century, linking together the United States, Lancashire, and Asia.

* * *

FARR, Kenneth R(aymond) 1942-

PERSONAL: Born January 4, 1942, in Jackson, Mich.; son of Clarence K. (an inspector in a manufacturing plant) and Evelyn (a designer of women's clothing; maiden name, Gaertner) Farr; married Maria Teresa Garcia (a photographer), August 2, 1969; children: Stephanie. *Education:* Valparaiso University, B.A., 1964; University of Florida, M.A., 1965; Tulane University, Ph.D., 1971; University of Michigan, M.P.H., 1974. *Politics:* Democrat. *Religion:* Lutheran. *Home:* 19002 Coltfield Court, Gaithersburg, Md. 20760.

CAREER: University of Puerto Rico, Mayaguez, instructor, 1965-69, assistant professor of political science, 1970-73, coordinator of department, 1971-73; Areawide Comprehensive Health Planning Association, Jackson, Mich., health planner, 1973-74; Chapman College, Orange, Calif., visiting assistant professor of government for World Campus Afloat, 1974; Governors State University, Park Forest South, Ill., professor of health science, 1975; U.S. Department of Health, Education & Welfare, Washington, D.C., public health advisor for Office of International Health, 1975-76, director of health planning, 1977—. Visiting professor at University of Puerto Rico, 1972. Administrative assistant to the urban renewal director of Jackson, Mich., 1966, junior planner, 1968; consultant to World Health Organization and Pan American Health Organization.

MEMBER: American Public Health Association, Latin American Studies Association, Caribbean Studies Association, American Association of Comprehensive Health Planning. *Awards, honors:* Grant from Research Center at University of Puerto Rico, 1972.

WRITINGS: *Puerto Rico Election Factbook,* Institute of Comparative Study of Political Systems, 1968; *Historical Dictionary of Puerto Rico and the U.S. Virgin Islands,* Scarecrow, 1973; *Personalism and Party Politics in Puerto Rico,* Inter-American University Press, 1973; (contributor) Eneida Rivero and Baldomero Cores, editors, *Antologia de Ciencias Sociales* (title means "Social Science Anthology"), University of Puerto Rico, 1973; (with Richard Douglas) *Cost-Effectiveness of Alcohol-Related Crash Counter-Measures,* Highway Safety Research Institute, University of Michigan, 1974; (editor with Robert Emery and James Sarn) *Health Sector Assessment for Nicaragua,* U.S. Agency for International Development—Nicaragua, 1976.

WORK IN PROGRESS: Research on health planning and policy in Guatemala.

SIDELIGHTS: Farr writes: "I am completely fluent in Spanish and well-immersed in Latin America. I am married to an Ecuadorian-American, and have done volunteer work among Spanish-speaking groups in the United States. I have extensive travel experience in Latin America and other parts of the world."

AVOCATIONAL INTERESTS: Foreign travel, weather forecasting, raquetball, and ice skating.

* * *

FARRELL, J(ames) G(ordon) 1935-

PERSONAL: Born January 23, 1935, in Liverpool, England. *Education:* Brasenose College, Oxford, B.A., 1960. *Home:* 16 Egerton Gardens, London SW3 2DG, England.

CAREER: Writer. *Awards, honors:* Harkness Fellowship for residence in United States, 1966-68; Arts Council Award, 1970; Faber Memorial Prize, 1970, for *Troubles;* Booker Literary Prize, 1973, for *The Seige of Krishnapur.*

WRITINGS—Novels: *A Man from Elsewhere,* Hutchinson, 1963; *The Lung,* Hutchinson, 1965; *A Girl in the Head,* J. Cape, 1967, Harper, 1969; *Troubles,* J. Cape, 1970, Knopf, 1971; *The Seige of Krishnapur,* Weidenfeld & Nicolson, 1973, Harcourt, 1974.

SIDELIGHTS: Farrell's most recent novel, *The Seige of Krishnapur,* was set in India during the 1857 Sepoy Rebellion. Critic Walter Clemons noted that the novel "begins as a comedy of Victorian conventions and imperial pride. It accelerates into a terrific narration of action as the prolonged seige tests the inmates of Krishnapur with cholera, stench, despair and religious mania. Before it ends, steep clefts have opened in the assumptions of progress and civilized order." Clemons concluded his enthusiastic review by stating that the book "is a work of wit, lively historical reconstruction and imaginative intensity. Farrell is an original, and I only mean to chart rough points of reference by suggesting that his book combines the pleasures of *The Reason Why*, Cecil Woodham-Smith's astringent study of the Charge of the Light Brigade, and Richard Hughes's classic *A High Wind in Jamaica*."

Melvin Maddocks wrote: "Novelist Farrell takes his Englishmen out of a quaint hunting print and frames them in a painting by Hieronymus Bosch. The once happy few, beseiged in the compound at Krishnapur for three months, come to resemble the natives they had so exquisitely ignored. . . . Farrell can write with a fury to match his theme," Maddocks continued. "As spectacle, *The Seige of Krishnapur* has the blaze and the agony of a scenario for hell. But as moral commentary, it is overcalculated—and its ironies unsuitably neat."

L. E. Sissman commented that "Mr. Farrell's interesting and entertaining novel is merely the rather early effort of a writer who has not yet hit his stride." He criticized Farrell for attempting to cover too much ground ("its audacious idea . . . promises more than it is able to deliver.") with a plot "which is sort of pat, [and] is strung out on a series of carefully staged set pieces." But, Sissman added: "When Mr. Farrell is not caught up in an understandable desire to poke fun at his characters and their orotund respectabilities, he can be both direct and affecting; then even his ordinary diction comes to life."

BIOGRAPHICAL/CRITICAL SOURCES: Time, September 30, 1974; *Newsweek,* October 21, 1974; *New Yorker,* November 25, 1974; *Contemporary Literary Criticism,* Volume 6, Gale, 1976.

* * *

FARRINGTON, Selwyn Kip, Jr. 1904-

PERSONAL: Born May 7, 1904, in Orange, N.J.; son of Selwyn Kip and Josephine (Taylor) Farrington; married Sara Houston Chisholm, August 9, 1934. *Education:* Educated in New Jersey. *Politics:* Republican. *Religion:* Episcopalian. *Residence:* East Hampton, Long Island, N.Y.

CAREER: Author, lecturer, and sportsman. Worked in advertising with Kelly Nason, Inc., New York, N.Y., during 1940's; has appeared in seven motion pictures on salt water fishing. *Member:* American Society of Ichthyologists. *Awards, honors:* Order of Al Merito from Republic of Chile, 1943.

WRITINGS: Atlantic Game Fishing (illustrated by Lynn Bogue Hunt; introduction by Ernest Hemingway), Kennedy Bros., 1937; *Bill, the Broadbill Swordfish* (illustrated by Hunt), Coward-McCann, 1942; *Pacific Game Fishing* (illustrated by Hunt), Coward-McCann, 1942; *Railroading from the Head End,* Doubleday, Doran, 1943; *Giants of the Rails* (illustrated by Glen Thomas), Garden City Publishing, 1944; *Railroads at War,* Coward-McCann, 1944; *The Ducks Came Back* (illustrated by Hunt), Coward-McCann, 1945; *Interesting Birds of Our Country* (illustrated by Hunt), Garden City Publishing, 1945; *A Book of Fishes* (illustrated by Hunt), Blakiston, 1946; *Railroading from the Rear End,* Coward-McCann, 1946; *Ships of the U.S. Merchant Marine* (illustrated by Jack Coggins), Dutton, 1947; *Fishing the Atlantic, Offshore and On* (illustrated by Hunt), Coward-McCann, 1949; *Railroads of Today,* Coward-McCann, 1949; *Sports Fishing Boats,* W. W. Norton, 1949.

Railroading the Modern Way, Coward-McCann, 1951; *Fishing the Pacific, Offshore and On* (illustrated by Hunt), Coward-McCann, 1953; *Railroading around the World,* Coward-McCann, 1955; *Fishing with Hemingway and Glassell,* McKay, 1971; *Skates, Sticks, and Men: The Story of Amateur Hockey in the United States,* McKay, 1971; *The Santa Fe's Big Three: The Life Story of a Trio of the World's Greatest Locomotives,* McKay, 1972; *The Trail of the Sharp Cup: The Story of the Fifth Oldest Trophy in International Sports,* Dodd, 1974; *Labrador Retriever: Friend and Worker,* Hastings House, 1976; *Railroading Coast to Coast,* Hastings House, 1977.

Contributor: Eugene Virginius Connet, editor, *American Big Game Fishing,* Derrydale Press, 1935; *Fishing and Vacation Yearbook,* Garden City Publishing, 1942; *British Book of Sporting Fish,* 1947; *The Great Outdoors,* 1947.

Contributor to periodicals, including *Collier's, Cosmopolitan, Sportsman,* and *Reader's Digest.*

SIDELIGHTS: An expert fisherman, Farrington helped design the emergency fishing kits used by the U.S. Army, Navy, and Coast Guard. Farrington has held several world fishing records, and in 1937 served as captain of the U.S. team in international fishing matches in England and Cuba. During the same year, Farrington wrote his first book, *Atlantic Game Fishing.* A critic for *Saturday Review* commented that the book "is of interest to the novice as well as to the expert. . . . We feel certain that anyone who reads this book will not only enjoy its contents, but will wish to have it with him at all times, as a ready reference on the subject of big and small game fishing."

Farrington's great enthusiasm for railroads inspired him to write numerous books on the subject. In his *Railroading around the World,* Farrington examined the railroading systems outside the United States. A reviewer for the *Chicago Sunday Tribune* noted, "The author, who has written six other rail books, has a good grasp of engineering and mechanical principles. With knowledge of foreign railroading scanty in our country, his book goes a long way towards filling the gap."

BIOGRAPHICAL/CRITICAL SOURCES: Saturday Review, January 1, 1938; *Chicago Tribune,* July 24, 1955.*

* * *

FAURE, Lucie 1908-1977

1908—September 25, 1977; French editor and author. She was the wife of Edgar Faure, president of the French National Assembly and former premier. In 1943 she founded the literary and political review *La Nef* with Raymond Aron, and had edited it since then. Among her books are *Journal of a Voyage to China,* and a series of psychological novels, including the prize-winning *Filles du Calvaire.* She died near Paris, France. Obituaries: *New York Times,* September 27, 1977; *Washington Post,* September 28, 1977.

* * *

FEATHER, Norman T(homas) 1930-

PERSONAL: Born July 27, 1930, in Sydney, Australia; son of Thomas William (an insurance executive) and Lilian (England) Feather; married Daryl Raynes (a college principal), December 28, 1968; children: Mark William Norman. *Education:* University of Sydney, B.A., 1952; University of New England, M.A., 1953; University of Michigan, Ph.D., 1960. *Home:* 187 Brougham Pl., North Adelaide, South Australia. *Office:* School of Social Sciences, Flinders University of South Australia, Bedford Park, South Australia 5042.

CAREER: University of New England, Armidale, New South Wales, Australia, lecturer, 1953—, senior lecturer, 1961—, associate professor of social sciences, 1965-67; Flinders University of South Australia, Bedford Park, foundation professor of psychology, 1968—. Visiting professor at University of Michigan, 1967, and Harvard University, 1974. *Member:* Academy of Social Sciences in Australia (fellow), Australian Psychological Society (fellow), British Psychological Society (fellow), Phi Beta Kappa, Sigma Xi. *Awards, honors:* Fulbright fellowships, 1958-60, 1967-68; Marquis Award from University of Michigan, 1961.

WRITINGS: (With John W. Atkinson) *A Theory of Achievement Motivation,* Wiley, 1966; *Values in Education and Society,* Free Press, 1975.

Contributor: E. E. Sampson, editor, *Approaches, Contexts, and Problems of Social Psychology,* Prentice-Hall, 1964; D. Byrne and M. L. Hamilton, editors, *Personality Research,* Prentice-Hall, 1966; R. N. Haber, editor, *Current Research in Motivation,* Holt, 1966; L. Berkowitz, editor, *Advances in Experimental Social Psychology,* Volume III, Academic Press, 1967. Also contributor to *A Source Book for Elementary Psychology,* edited by R. C. Birney. Contributor to scholarly journals. Associate editor of *Australian Journal of Psychology.*

WORK IN PROGRESS: Research on values, sex-roles, achievement motivation, and cognitive psychology.

SIDELIGHTS: Feather writes: "I am an Australian psychologist with research interests in social psychology and the psychology of motivation and personality. I spent a year at Harvard University in 1974 where I completed the first draft of my recent book on values. I continue to be active in areas of psychology that relate to human thought and action."

* * *

FEDIN, Konstantin A(lexandrovich) 1892-1977

February 27, 1892—July 15, 1977; Soviet writer. Described as "one of the founders and creators" of Soviet literature, Fedin turned from his early experimental techniques to the officially approved school of Soviet realism. His major novels include *Rape of Europe, Brothers, An Unusual Summer,* and *First Joys.* Fedin served as head of the Soviet Writers Union. Obituaries: *New York Times,* July 18, 1977; *Washington Post,* July 18, 1977.

* * *

FEENBERG, Eugene 1906-1977

October 19, 1906—November 7, 1977; American educator, physicist, and author of books on physics. Feenberg was professor emeritus of theoretical physics at Washington University. His research contributed to the understanding of the nucleus of the atom and to the development of the theory behind atomic energy. He died in St. Louis, Mo. Obituaries: *New York Times,* November 13, 1977.

* * *

FEINBERG, Lawrence B(ernard) 1940-

PERSONAL: Born June 2, 1940, in Brooklyn, N.Y.; son of Robert E. (a buyer) and Geraldine (Goldfarb) Feinberg; married Roberta Leibman (a nursing educator), August 17, 1961; children: Ronald, Nancy. *Education:* State University

of New York at Buffalo, B.A., 1961, M.S., 1963, Ph.D., 1966. *Home:* 8405 Sugarman Dr., La Jolla, Calif. 92037. *Office:* Administration Building, San Diego State University, San Diego, Calif. 92115.

CAREER: Syracuse University, Syracuse, N.Y., assistant professor, 1966-70, associate professor of special education, 1970-74, professor of rehabilitation education, 1974-77, chairman of department, 1967-77; San Diego State University, San Diego, Calif., associate dean of graduate division and research, 1977—. Visiting professor at Utica College. Member of board of directors of Commission on Rehabilitation Counselor Certification. *Member:* American Rehabilitation Counseling Association (president), American Personnel and Guidance Association (member of board of directors), New York State Rehabilitation Counseling Association (president).

WRITINGS: (With J. S. Cohen) *Rehabilitation and Poverty: Bridging the Gap,* Syracuse University Press, 1969; (with R. W. English) *Rehabilitation in the Inner City,* Syracuse University Press, 1970; (contributor) H. A. Moses and C. H. Patterson, editors, *Research Readings in Rehabilitation Counseling,* Stipes, 1973; (with L. M. Sundblad and L. J. Glick) *Education for the Rehabilitation Services: Planning Undergraduate Curricula,* Syracuse University Press, 1974. Contributor to professional journals.

WORK IN PROGRESS: Research on biofeedback applications in counselor education.

SIDELIGHTS: Feinberg writes that his professional interest centers "around the social-psychological aspects of disability, somatopsychology, and behavior modification."

* * *

FEINSTEIN, George W(illiamson) 1913-

PERSONAL: Born December 6, 1913, in Grand Forks, N.D.; son of Jacob (a grocer) and Sarah (Odorov) Feinstein; married Edith Schmidt, October 14, 1942; children: Lisa, Susan Gurman, Margo. *Education:* University of North Dakota, B.A., 1934, M.A., 1936; further graduate study at University of Minnesota, summer, 1937, and Northwestern University, summer, 1938; State University of Iowa, Ph.D., 1945. *Home:* 1840 Sonoma Dr., Altadena, Calif. 91001. *Office:* Pasadena City College, 1570 East Colorado Blvd., Pasadena, Calif. 91106.

CAREER: High school principal in Oberon, N.D., 1934-36; University of North Dakota, Grand Forks, instructor in English, 1936-42, assistant professor of physics, 1942-44, assistant professor of English, 1945-48; John Muir College, Pasadena, Calif., instructor in humanities, 1948-54; Pasadena City College, Pasadena, Calif., instructor, 1954-63, assistant professor, 1963-70, professor of English, 1970—. Chairman of Lively Arts Forum, 1962-64, and Fireside Fellowship (lecture series), 1964-67. Member of Pasadena Community Orchestra, 1955-66.

MEMBER: National Education Association, National Council of Teachers of English, American Association of University Professors, Mark Twain Association, U.S. Chess Federation, Pasadena Chess Club, California Teachers Association, Phi Beta Kappa (president of local chapter, 1943), Sigma Xi, Phi Delta Kappa.

WRITINGS: Programed College Vocabulary 3600, with instructor's manual, Prentice-Hall, 1969; *Programed Spelling Demons,* with instructor's manual, Prentice-Hall, 1973; *Programed Writing Skills,* with instructor's manual, Prentice-Hall, 1976. Member of staff of *American People's*

Encyclopedia, 1945. Contributor of articles and reviews to magazines and newspapers, including *Twainian, Your Life,* and *Your Personality.* Editor for Western Critic Syndicate, 1964-68.

WORK IN PROGRESS: "Two books—one academic and the other sexy."

SIDELIGHTS: Feinstein writes: "Why do my textbooks deal with vocabulary and spelling? Students write that Greek epics were sung by a liar; that two straight lines form an angel; that the three wise men brought gifts of myrrh and frankfurters; that American Indians were put in reservoirs; that in the Mexican War our soldiers hollered, 'Remember the alimony!'; that Hester Prynne broke the seventh amendment; that to cure a cold you should take a catholic and go to bed. And that is why my textbooks deal with vocabulary and spelling."

*   *   *

FELDENKRAIS, Moshe (Pinchas) 1904-

PERSONAL: Born May 6, 1904, in Baranowicze, Poland; son of Aryeh (a forester) and Scheindl (a painter; maiden name, Pshater) Feldenkrais; divorced. *Education:* Ecole E.T.D., Paris, diploma in engineering, 1933; Sorbonne, University of Paris, ingenieur-docteur (first class honors), 1935. *Home:* 49 Nachmani St., Tel-Aviv 67136, Israel. *Agent:* Ron Bernstein, 12 East 53rd St., New York, N.Y. 10022. *Office:* Feldenkrais Institute, Tel-Aviv, Israel.

CAREER: Van-Steenbrugghe & Breton (surgical instrument company), Paris, France, consultant, 1935-40; National Committee for Scientific Research, Paris, staff member, 1939-40; scientific officer for British Admiralty anti-submarine experimental establishments in Portland and Scotland, 1940-46; Pioneer Films Ltd., London, England, head of research and development department, 1946-49; Ministry of Defense, Kordany, Israel, director of electronics department, 1949-52; Feldenkrais Institute, Tel-Aviv, Israel, founder and director, 1952—. Lecturer in psychology at Tel-Aviv University, 1963-67. Holder of six patents. *Member:* Jiu-Jitsu Club de France (founder and technical director, 1934).

WRITINGS—In English: *Judo: The Art of Defence and Attack* (self-illustrated), Warne, 1942, reprinted, 1972; *Practical Unarmed Combat,* Warne, 1942; *Body and Mature Behaviour: A Study of Anxiety, Sex, Gravitation, and Learning,* Routledge & Kegan Paul, 1949, International Universities Press, 1950, reprinted, 1973; *Higher Judo,* three volumes, Warne, Volume I: *Ground Work (Katame-Waza),* 1952, reprinted, 1972; *Shichlul ha-yecholet* (title means "Improving Ability: Theory and Practice"), Alef Publishers, 1967, translation published as *Awareness Through Movement: Health Exercises for Personal Growth,* Harper, 1972; *Twenty-Five Lessons,* Movement Notation Society, 1971; *Adventures in the Jungle of the Brain: The Case of Nora,* Harper, 1977; *Basic Feldenkrais,* Simon & Schuster, 1978; *Fifty Lessons in Awareness Through Movement,* Simon & Schuster, 1979.

Other works: *Jiu-Jitsu vehagana acemit* (title means "Jiu-Jitsu and Self-Defense"), Binah Publishers, 1929; *Autosugestia* (title means "Autosuggestion"), Binah Publishers, 1930; *Manuel pratique du jiu-jitsu: La defense du faible contre l'agresseur* (title means "Practical Manual of Jiu-Jitsu: Defense of the Weak Against an Agressor"), Chiron, 1932, reprinted, 1973; *ABC de Judo,* Chiron, 1937, reprinted, 1973; *Judo pour ceintures noires* (title means "Judo for Black Belts"), three volumes, Chiron, 1950, reprinted, 1972; *Prokim beshitati* (title means "From My Method"), Alef

Publishers, 1964; *L'Expression corporelle* (lectures; title means "Bodily Expression"), E. Chiron, 1965; *12 lecons de sante* (title means "Twelve Lessons for Health"), Gerard, 1973.

Contributor to French scientific journals and to *Nature.* Also author of lessons broadcast by Swiss Radio in Germany, and lessons on cassette for Ex-Libris (Zurich) and Westinghouse.

SIDELIGHTS: Feldenkrais, who holds a black belt in judo, has met Jigoro Kano, the creator of Judo, on many occasions and has letters from him in English and in Japanese. The Judo Club of France, founded and directed by Feldenkrais, has one million members today. *Avocational interests:* Soccer, ping-pong, and swimming.

*   *   *

FELDMAN, Abraham J(ehiel) 1893-1977

June 28, 1893—July 21, 1977; Ukrainian-born Jewish leader and author. Feldman was a former president of the Central Conference of American Rabbis and of the Synagogue Council of America, and was known for his ecumenical work and defense of human rights. He founded and edited the *Jewish Ledger,* and wrote many books on Judaism and the Bible. He died in West Hartford, Conn. Obituaries: *New York Times,* July 23, 1977.

*   *   *

FELDMAN, Alan 1945-

PERSONAL: Born March 16, 1945, in New York, N.Y.; son of Barney (a teacher) and Goldye (a teacher; maiden name, Abrams) Feldman; married Nanette Hass (an artist and teacher), October 22, 1972; children: Rebecca, Daniel. *Education:* Columbia University, A.B., 1966, M.A., 1969; State University of New York at Buffalo, Ph.D., 1973. *Home:* 399 Belknap Rd., Framingham, Mass. 01701. *Office:* Department of English, Framingham State College, Framingham, Mass. 01701.

CAREER: Elementary school teacher in New York City, 1966-68; Shaker Village, New Lebanon, N.Y., member of poetry staff, 1969; high school English teacher in New York City, 1970; Framingham State College, Framingham, Mass., assistant professor of English, 1972—. Instructor at Bronx Community College and Kingsborough Community College, 1970. *Awards, honors:* Short story award from *Saturday Review* and National Student Association, 1965, for "Living in the Sea"; National Endowment for the Humanities fellowship, 1977-78.

WRITINGS: The Household (poems), Columbia Review Press, 1966; *The Happy Genius* (poems), Sun Press, 1978; *Frank O'Hara,* Twayne, in press.

Stories represented in anthologies, including *My Name Aloud,* edited by Harold Ribalow, Yoseloff, 1969, and *A Cinch: Amazing Works from the Columbia Review,* Columbia University Press, 1969. Contributor of poems to literary magazines, including *Audit/Poetry, Panache, Atlantic,* and *Sun.*

WORK IN PROGRESS: Studying poetry in the schools.

SIDELIGHTS: Feldman writes briefly: "The subject of my poetry and fiction has mostly been family relations. I am concerned with taking the flow of life around me—family life so far—and composing it into some sort of intimate history."

FELDMAN, Anne (Rodgers) 1939-

PERSONAL: Born July 19, 1939, in Pittsburgh, Pa.; daughter of Bennett (a juvenile court judge) and Eleanor (Longenecker) Rodgers; married Richard Lewis Feldman (a security analyst), August 27, 1965; children: David, Mark. *Education:* Mount Holyoke College, B.A., 1961. *Politics:* Democrat. *Religion:* None. *Home:* 205 East 69th St., New York, N.Y. 10021.

CAREER: Worth Publishers, Inc., New York, N.Y., picture editor of college science textbooks, 1968—.

WRITINGS: (With Jean Ely) *The Inflated Dormouse and Other Ways of Life in the Animal World* (juvenile), Doubleday, 1970; *The Railroad Book: Trains in America* (juvenile), McKay, 1978; *Firefighters* (juvenile), McKay, 1978. *Awards, honors: The Inflated Dormouse and Other Ways of Life in the Animal World* was chosen by *Scientific American* as one of the best children's science books for 1970.

WORK IN PROGRESS: A juvenile, *To the Rescue,* "about five disasters and the rescue personnel who cope with each."

SIDELIGHTS: Anne Feldman writes: "I am interested in writing good, accurate, well-illustrated nonfiction for children. All of my books are heavily illustrated with good photographs. In fact, the photographs are a very important part of the text. They are not just an 'extra.' My feeling is that a child (especially one who doesn't really enjoy reading) will examine a good, dramatic photograph carefully and, with the addition of clear text explaining the photograph, will find himself learning from both photographs and text.

"My working method for the books on trains and fires has been to research the topic thoroughly, to decide what I want to cover, to get the photographs, and then to write the text."

AVOCATIONAL INTERESTS: Travel (Mexico, Israel, Greece, Italy, France, England), animals, hiking, photography.

*   *   *

FELDMEIR, Daryle M(atthew) 1923-

PERSONAL: Born January 28, 1923, in Froid, Mont.; son of Frank X. and Clara (Rhoda) Feldmeir; married Jeanne Elizabeth Meyer, September 24, 1949 (died, April, 1973); children: Ann, Matthew, Todd, Susan. *Education:* St. Olaf College, B.A., 1948; Harvard University, M.A., 1949; further study at University of Minnesota, 1951-52. *Home:* Aldana 45, San Miguel de Allende, Guanajuato, Mexico.

CAREER/WRITINGS: Minneapolis Tribune, Minneapolis, Minn., reporter, 1949-55, news editor, 1955, managing editor, 1956-68; *Chicago Daily News,* Chicago, Ill., managing editor, 1968-70, executive editor, 1970, editor, 1971-77, consultant to the publisher, 1977—. *Military service:* U.S. Army Air Force, 1943-45; became master sergeant. *Member:* American Society of Newspaper Editors, Sigma Delta Xi, Phi Beta Kappa.

*   *   *

FELDSTEIN, Martin S(tuart) 1939-

PERSONAL: Born November 25, 1939, in New York, N.Y.; son of Meyer and Esther (Gevarter) Feldstein; married Kathleen Foley, June 19, 1965; children: Margaret, Janet. *Education:* Harvard University, A.B. (summa cum laude), 1961; Oxford University, B.Litt., 1963, M.A., 1964, D.Phil., 1967. *Home:* 147 Clifton St., Belmont, Mass. 02178. *Office:* Department of Economics, Harvard University, 1737 Cambridge St., Cambridge, Mass. 02138.

CAREER: Oxford University, Oxford, England, lecturer in public finance and fellow of Nuffield College, 1965-67; Harvard University, Cambridge, Mass., assistant professor, 1967-68, associate professor, 1968-69, professor of economics, 1969—. Ford Research Professor at University of California, Berkeley, 1975. President of National Bureau of Economic Research, 1977—. Member of National Academy of Sciences Institute of Medicine, 1971—; senior adviser and member of Brookings Panel on Economic Activity, 1975—. Managing editor of *Studies in Public Economics.*

MEMBER: American Economic Association, American Academy of Arts and Sciences (fellow), National Academy of Sciences, Econometric Society (fellow; member of council, 1977—), Phi Beta Kappa. *Awards, honors:* Fulbright scholarship; John Bates Clark Medal from American Economic Association, 1977.

WRITINGS: Economic Analysis for Health Service Efficiency, North-Holland Publishing, 1967; *The Rising Cost of Hospital Care,* Information Resources, 1971; (contributor) Cotton M. Lindsay, editor, *New Directions in Public Health Care: An Evaluation of Proposals for National Health Insurance,* Institute for Contemporary Studies, 1976; (with Amy Taylor) *The Rapid Rise of Hospital Costs,* Council on Wage and Price Stability, 1977; (with Daniel Frisch) *Corporate Tax Integration: A Quantitative Comparison of Alternatives,* Tax Foundation, 1978. Contributor to scholarly journals. Co-editor of *Journal of Public Economics.* Member of editorial board of *Review of Economic Studies,* 1965-67, *Quarterly Journal of Economics, Review of Economics and Statistics,* and *American Economic Review.*

*   *   *

FELKER, Clay S(chuette) 1925-

PERSONAL: Born October 25, 1925, in St. Louis, Mo.; son of Carl T. (a newspaper editor) and Cora Felker; married Leslie Aldridge (divorced); married Pamela Tiffin (divorced). *Education:* Duke University, B.A., 1951. *Home:* 322 East 57th St., New York, N.Y. 10022.

CAREER: Life magazine, New York City, reporter, 1951-57; *Esquire* magazine, New York City, features editor, 1957-62; *New York Herald Tribune* (*New York World Journal Tribune* after 1966), New York City, editor of Sunday magazine, 1963-67; New York Magazine Corp., New York City, president, 1968-77, member of the board of directors, 1969-77, founder, editor, and publisher of *New York,* 1968-77, publisher of *Village Voice,* 1975-77, and of *New West,* 1976-77. Consulting editor, Viking Press, 1963-66; editor, *Infinity* (American Society of Magazine Photographers magazine), 1965-66, and *Bookweek,* 1966-67; member of board of directors of Aeneid Equities, 1969—. *Member:* Society of Professional Journalists, Sigma Delta Chi, Phi Delta Theta.

WRITINGS: Casey Stengel's Secret, Walker, 1961; (editor and compiler) *The Power Game,* Simon & Schuster, 1969.

SIDELIGHTS: Two sentences in recent write-ups in *Newsweek* and *Time* magazines describe Clay Felker in no less than sixteen adjectives, among them: brilliant, ingenuous, rapacious, mysterious, and despotic. This means Felker has picked up a little over an adjective and a half for each of the ten years he has spent building the most successful city magazine in the country.

In 1967 Felker purchased, with his severance pay, the Sunday supplement from the dying *New York Herald Tribune,* which he turned into a sophisticated and highly successful independent weekly magazine. This success largely came from Felker's uncanny ability to recognize talent in new writers and his journalistic sense to assign them to strong, sure stories. Nora Ephron said: "I've never seen anything like him. If you tell him you're having a lobotomy tomorrow, he would say: 'Hmmm, lobotomy, lobotomy, what can I do with it?' He sees stories everywhere." And besides those of Nora Ephron, he has been able to draw upon the resources of such notable journalists as Jimmy Breslin, Tom Wolfe, Gloria Steinem, Norman Mailer, Dick Schaap, Pete Hamill, and Richard Reeves for his magazine. Felker is also credited with being the first editor to seize upon this country's vast talent of women writers. In addition to Ephron and Steinem, Julie Baumgold, Jane O'Reilly, Sally Beauman, Gail Sheehy, Judy Daniels, Ellen Willis, and Judith Crist appeared in *New York* with articles whose subjects were previously reserved for men writers.

The successful formula for *New York* has been copied by other city magazines throughout the country, but in 1976 Felker got into trouble with his board of directors at New York Magazine Corp. when he tried to copy his own technique for *New West*. The board felt he was spending too much trying to get this new magazine off the ground and Felker began to look around for new backers in the western venture. One source of funds he made the mistake of turning to was Australian newspaper tycoon, Rupert Murdoch. Within four weeks Murdoch was trying to buy New York Magazine Corp. out from under Felker. The outcome of the resulting power struggle made the cover story of both *Time* and *Newsweek* when Murdoch seized over fifty per cent of the stock and won.

BIOGRAPHICAL/CRITICAL SOURCES: Newsweek, January 17, 1977; *Time,* January 17, 1977.*

* * *

FENBERG, Matilda 1888(?)-1977

1888(?)—October 23, 1977; Polish-born lawyer and author. One of the first women admitted to Yale Law School, she became an associate of Clarence Darrow and assisted him in the Leopold-Loeb murder trial. She wrote a book on women and jury service, and a uniform divorce law for the state of Illinois. An early defender of equal rights for women, she headed the Equal Rights Amendment committee in Illinois in later years. She died in Findlay, Ohio. Obituaries: *New York Times,* October 25, 1977; *Washington Post,* October 28, 1977.

* * *

FENELON, Kevin G(erard) 1898-

PERSONAL: Born December 6, 1898, in London, England; son of Martin Joseph (a civil servant) and May (Macdonell) Fenelon; married Mary Irvine (died, 1934); married Eunice Rawcliffe (an artist; died, 1970); children: Raymond, Lawrence. *Education:* University of Edinburgh, M.A., 1921, Ph.D., 1926. *Religion:* Roman Catholic. *Home:* 134 Blvd. de la Petrusse, Luxembourg.

CAREER: University of Edinburgh, Edinburgh, Scotland, lecturer in economics, 1921-31; Victoria University of Manchester, Manchester, England, director of department of industrial administration, 1931-42; Institution of Production Engineers, London, England, general secretary, 1942-43; British Engineering Association, London, chief research officer, 1943-45; British Ministry of Food, London, assistant secretary and director of statistics and economic intelligence, 1945-51; Government of Iraq, Baghdad, statistical adviser, 1951-58; American University of Beirut, Beirut,

Lebanon, professor of statistics and economics, 1958-61; Government of Kuwait, Al-Kuwait, statistical adviser, 1962-66; Government of Jordan, Amman, statistical adviser, 1966-67; Government of Bahrain, Manama, statistical adviser, 1967-70; Government of Abu Dhabi, Abu Dhabi, statistical adviser, 1970-76; writer, 1976—. *Military service:* British Army, Royal Engineers, 1917-19; became captain.

MEMBER: British Institute of Management (fellow; founding member), Chartered Institute of Transport (fellow), Royal Statistical Society (fellow). *Awards, honors:* Commander, Order of the British Empire, 1959.

WRITINGS: The Economics of Road Transport, Allen & Unwin, 1925; *Transport Coordination,* P. S. King, 1929; *Transport and Communication,* Pitman, 1931; *Railway Economics,* Methuen, 1932; *British Railways Today,* Thomas Nelson, 1939; *Management and Labour,* Methuen, 1939; *Blind Workers in Industry,* privately printed, 1944; *Planning Local Prosperity,* New Era, 1946; *The Motor Age,* Common Ground, 1949; *Britain's Food Supplies,* Methuen, 1952; *Iraq's National Income and Expenditure,* Al Rabita Press, 1958; *The Trucial States,* Khayat, 1967, revised edition, 1969; *The United Arab Emirates,* Longman, 1973, 2nd edition, 1976.

WORK IN PROGRESS: Industrial Archeology of the Middle East.

SIDELIGHTS: Fenelon writes that he has twice traveled around the world, and that he has lived in or visited practically all the countries of the Middle East.

He told *CA:* "Apart from my studies as a statistician and economist of the activities and development of Middle East and other countries, I am also interested in their way of life, folklore, and especially their traditional crafts, appliances, and machines. In the Middle East the still existing relics of the past are now rapidly disappearing. Such are the wind towers of the Gulf, the underground irrigation canals of Iran and the Gulf, the water wheels of the upper Euphrates, the silk mills of Lebanon, or the machines, tools, and equipment of weavers, shipbuilders, and potters. I hope they may be recorded, described, and photographed before it is too late, and, above all, that some examples may be preserved."

AVOCATIONAL INTERESTS: Model railways, railway travel, windmills, canals.

* * *

FENGER, Henning Johannes Hauch 1921-

PERSONAL: Born August 9, 1921, in Denmark; son of Poul Hauch and Asta Hauch (maiden name, Carlsen) Fenger; married Kirsten Wiedemann, 1945 (died, 1956); married Lise Lander (a journalist), 1974. *Education:* University of Copenhagen, M.A., 1948; University of Aarhus, Dr.Phil., 1955; Cambridge University, M.A., 1961; also attended Sorbonne, University of Paris, 1948-51, and Columbia University, 1952-53. *Home:* 5 Cite Pigalle, 75009 Paris, France.

CAREER: University of Strasbourg, Strasbourg, France, lecturer in Danish, 1954-55; University of Paris, Sorbonne, Paris, France, lecturer in Danish, 1955-61; Cambridge University, Cambridge, England, lecturer in Danish, 1961-66; University of Aarhus, Aarhus, Denmark, professor of comparative literature, 1966-72; University of Odense, Odense, Denmark, professor of comparative literature, 1972-74; writer, 1974—. Member of advisory committee on Voltaire correspondence. *Member:* Vetenskapssocieteten (Lund, Sweden), Det Laerde Selskab, Georg Brandes Society (president, 1973-74).

WRITINGS: Voltaire et le theatre anglais (title means ''Voltaire and the English Theater''), Gyldendal, 1949; *Georg Brandes' Laereaar* (title means ''The Formative Years of Georg Brandes''; includes English summary), Gyldendal, 1955; *Den unge Brandes* (title means ''The Young Brandes''), Gyldendal, 1957; *Brandes et la France* (title means ''Brandes and France''), Sorbonne, University of Paris, 1963; *The Heibergs,* Twayne, 1971; *Kierkegaard kilder og Kierkegaard-myter* (title means ''Kierkegaard Sources and Kierkegaard Myths''; includes English summary), Odense University Press, 1976. Contributor to Scandinavian and European magazines and newspapers.

WORK IN PROGRESS: An English translation of the book on Kierkegaard sources and myths for Yale University Press.

SIDELIGHTS: Fenger comments: ''Except for the book on Voltaire and the English theater, my production has been concentrated on introducing some of the greatest names in Danish literature to an international public: Kierkegaard, the four members of the Heiberg family, Hans Christian Andersen, and Georg Brandes.''

*   *   *

FERGUSON, David L.   1930-

PERSONAL: Born September 24, 1930, in Los Angeles, Calif.; son of Alvah and Margaret (Smith) Ferguson; married Katharine Crowninshield in 1958. *Education:* Received B.A. from Harvard University, and LL.B. from Georgetown University. *Religion:* Protestant. *Home:* 541 Gay St., Westwood, Mass. 02090.

CAREER: Attorney in private practice in metropolitan Boston, Mass., 1961—.

WRITINGS: Cleopatra's Barge: The Crowninshield Story, Little, Brown, 1976.

*   *   *

FETRIDGE, William Harrison   1906-

PERSONAL: Born August 2, 1906, in Chicago, Ill.; son of Matthew and Clara (Hall) Fetridge; married Bonnie Jean Clark, June 27, 1941; children: Blakely Fetridge Bundy (daughter), Clark Worthington. *Education:* Northwestern University, B.S., 1929. *Politics:* Republican. *Religion:* Episcopal. *Home:* 2430 North Lake View Ave., Chicago, Ill. 60614. *Office:* Dartnell Corp., 4660 Ravenswood Ave., Chicago, Ill. 60640.

CAREER: Northwestern University, Evanston, Ill., assistant to the dean, 1929-30; Trade Periodical Co., Chicago, Ill., editor, 1930-31; *Chicago Tribune,* Chicago, editor, 1931-34; H. W. Kastor & Son, Chicago, editor, 1934-35; Roche, Williams & Cleary, Inc., Chicago, editor, 1935-42; *Popular Mechanics,* Chicago, assistant to the president, 1945-46, vice-president, 1946-53, executive vice-president, 1953-59; Diamond T. Motor Truck Co., Chicago, vice-president, 1959-61, executive vice-president, 1961-65; Dartnell Corp., Chicago, president and chief executive officer, 1965—. Managing editor of *Republican,* 1939-42; chairman of Republican Forum, 1958-60; chairman of Midwest Volunteers for Nixon, 1960; chairman of Nixon Recount Committee; honorary president of United Republican Fund of Illinois, 1968-73; finance chairman of Illinois Republican Party, 1968-73; member of Republican National Finance Committee; vice-chairman of Citizens Honest Elections Foundation. Member of U.S. Foundation for International Scouting (president, 1971—), national vice-president of Boy Scouts of America, 1958-76, presently member of national executive board; chairman of board of directors of Johnston Scout Museum; delegate to scouting conferences all over the world. Director of Bank of Ravenswood; trustee of Jacques Holinger Memorial Association and American Humanics Foundation; past president of board of trustees of Latin School of Chicago. *Military service:* U.S. Naval Reserve, active duty on ''U.S.S. DeHaven,'' 1942-45; became lieutenant commander.

MEMBER: Navy League of the United States (past regional president), Society of Midland Authors, Illinois St. Andrew Society, Beta Theta Pi, Newcomen Society, Rotary, Chicago Club, Union League Club, Casino Club, Saddle and Cycle Club, Chikaming Country Club, Illinois Chamber of Commerce. *Awards, honors:* LL.D. from Central Michigan University, 1954; awards from Boy Scouts of America include Silver Beaver, Silver Antelope, Bronze Wolf Award, 1973, and Distinguished Eagle Award, 1976; chevalier of Grand Priory of Malta, Sovereign Order of St. John of Jerusalem.

WRITINGS: (Editor) *The Navy Reader,* Bobbs-Merrill, 1943; (editor) *The Second Navy Reader,* Bobbs-Merrill, 1944; (editor) *The American Political Almanac,* Capitol House, 1951; *The Republican Precinct Workers Manual,* URF Press, 1968; *With Warm Regards,* Dartnell Corp., 1976. Also author of *So You Want to Be a Politician,* Capitol House.

*   *   *

FETTIG, Art(hur John)   1929-

PERSONAL: Born July 5, 1929, in Detroit, Mich.; son of Arthur J., Sr. (an inventor) and Jenny (Sands) Fettig; married Ruth R. Zepke (a registered nurse), September 11, 1955; children: Nancy Lou, Daniel, Amy, David. *Education:* Attended high school in Detroit, Mich. *Religion:* Roman Catholic. *Home:* 31 East Ave. S., Battle Creek, Mich. 49017. *Office:* Grand Trunk Western Railroad Co., 25 East Dickman Rd., Battle Creek, Mich. 49016.

CAREER: Grand Trunk Western Railroad Co., Battle Creek, Mich., railroad claim agent in Detroit, 1948-60, and Battle Creek, 1960-73, company relations officer, 1973—. President of True-Fettig & Associates, 1975—. International lecturer and free-lance audio-visual producer, 1973—. Teacher of writing courses. *Military service:* U.S. Army, combat rifleman, 1951-53; served in Korea; received Purple Heart and five battle stars.

MEMBER: Toastmasters International, National Speakers Association, American Society of Training and Development, Battle Creek Chamber of Commerce. *Awards, honors:* Two awards from American Association of Railroads *Bulletin,* 1959, 1960; award from National Public Relations Association, 1977.

WRITINGS: It Only Hurts When I Frown (humor), Liguori Publications, 1973; *Selling Lucky* (true stories), Ovations Unlimited, 1977; (co-editor) Herb True, *Funny Bone,* Humor Guild of America, 1977; (contributor) Sylvia Costa, editor, *A Manager's Guide to Audio Visuals,* Peterson, 1978; *7-11* (on public speaking), Ovations Unlimited, 1978.

Work anthologized in *Forty Salutes to Michigan,* Poetry Society of Michigan. Contributor of more than a thousand articles, stories, and poems to a wide variety of magazines in the United States and abroad.

WORK IN PROGRESS: A videotape program on public speaking for executives, for Canadian National Railway; a novel, *The Girls of Eta Jima.*

SIDELIGHTS: Fettig's audio-visual presentations include: two filmstrips, "They Can't Stop," for Grand Trunk Western Railroad Co., and "Stages" (on alcoholism), both 1976; two audio cassettes, "Humor-ize Your Speaking" and "110% Effort"; and "Selling Your Writing," a cassette course for beginning writers.

Fettig writes: "My current areas of interest include creativity, selling, motivation, and humor. I lecture throughout the world on these subjects, and my research and writing in these areas continues. Currently, I am driven to learn and help others with the elusive goal of total communication. Getting through on a one-to-one basis is my goal, even when I am talking to an audience of twenty-five hundred. I want every one of my listeners or readers to feel I am talking to him."

* * *

FIELD, David D(udley)   1918-

PERSONAL: Born March 9, 1918, in New Jersey; son of Joseph (a florist) and Catherine (a nurse; maiden name, Lansdowne) Field; married Rosaland Helms, July 16, 1943; children: David D., Jr. *Education:* Colgate University, A.B. (magna cum laude), 1939; Ohio University, M.A. (honors), 1955. *Religion:* Baptist. *Home:* 2 Commander Dr., Hampton, Va. 23666. *Office:* Thomas Nelson Community College, Hampton, Va. 23670.

CAREER: U.S. Army, career officer, 1942-62; served in European theater, 1944-45, served in Korean conflict, 1950-51, on military advisory staff to South Vietnam, 1956-57, retiring as lieutenant colonel; teacher of social studies at a high school in Newport News, Va., 1962-65, administrator, 1965-68; Thomas Nelson Community College, Hampton, Va., coordinator of admissions and records, 1968-71, associate professor of psychology, 1971—.

MEMBER: American Psychological Association, Golf Writers Association of America, Phi Beta Kappa. *Awards, honors*—Military: Bronze Star Medal.

WRITINGS: (With Donald K. Wright) *A Human Relations Guide,* M.S.S. Educational Publishing, 1972. Contributor to magazines. Contributing editor of *Carolina Golfer.*

WORK IN PROGRESS: A book on religion and psychology.

SIDELIGHTS: Field writes: "Most of my writing at present is for various periodicals combining my knowledge of golf and psychology. My motivation for writing goes back to being the son of parents who were fluent with both the written and spoken word and to certain English teachers who stressed the satisfaction of expressing oneself in writing."

* * *

FIELDS, Julia   1938-

PERSONAL: Born January 18, 1938, in Bessemer, Ala. *Education:* Knoxville College, B.S., 1961; Bread Loaf School of English, M.A., 1972; further study at University of Edinburgh. *Home address:* Box 209, Scotland Neck, N.C. 27874.

CAREER: Poet. Has worked as a high school teacher in Birmingham, Ala., and as poet-in-residence at several universities and colleges, including Miles College, Hampton Institute, St. Augustine College, and East Carolina University. *Awards, honors:* National Endowment for the Arts grant, 1968; Seventh Conrad Kent Rivers Memorial Fund Award, 1972.

WRITINGS: Poems, Poets Press, 1968; *East of Moonlight,* Red Clay Books, 1973. Also author of *I Heard a Young Man Saying.*

Work represented in anthologies, including *New Negro Poets: U.S.A.,* edited by Langston Hughes, Indiana University Press, 1964; *Kaleidoscope,* edited by Robert Hayden, Harcourt, 1967; *Black Fire,* edited by LeRoi Jones and Larry Neal, Morrow, 1968; *The Poetry of the Negro, 1746-1970,* edited by Langston Hughes and Arna Bontemps, Doubleday, 1970; *The Poetry of Black America,* edited by Arnold Adoff, Harper, 1972.

Contributor of poetry and short stories to *Black World, Essence, Negro Digest,* and other periodicals.*

* * *

FIESER, Louis F(rederick)   1899-1977

April 7, 1899—July 25, 1977; American educator, chemist, and author. Fieser was credited with developing vitamin K and combat napalm, and received numerous awards for his research on cancer-producing chemicals. He was emeritus professor of organic chemistry at Harvard University, and the author of research papers and books in his field. He died in Cambridge, Mass. Obituaries: *New York Times,* July 27, 1977; *Newsweek,* August 8, 1977; *Time,* August 8, 1977.

* * *

FINKLEHOFFE, Fred F.   1910-1977

February 16, 1910—October 5, 1977; American film and stage producer, playwright, and screenwriter. Among the screenplays he co-authored were "For Me and My Gal" and "Meet Me in St. Louis," for which he received an Academy Award nomination in 1944. Finklehoffe produced numerous Broadway shows, including "The Heiress," "The Traitor," and "Ankles Aweigh." He died in Springtown, Pa. Obituaries: *New York Times,* October 7, 1977; *Time,* October 17, 1977.

* * *

FINN, David   1921-

PERSONAL: Born August 30, 1921, in New York, N.Y.; son of Jonathan (a writer) and Sadie (Borgenicht) Finn; married Laura Zeisler (a travel agent), October 20, 1945; children: Kathy Finn Bloomgarden, Dena Finn Merriam, Peter, Amy Finn Binder. *Education:* City College (now of the City University of New York), B.S., 1943. *Residence:* New Rochelle, N.Y. *Office:* Ruder & Finn, Inc., 110 East 59th St., New York, N.Y. 10022.

CAREER: Ruder & Finn, Inc. (public relations firm), New York, N.Y., co-founder, 1948, partner, 1948-56, president, 1956-68, chairman of board of directors, 1968—. Adjunct associate professor at New York University. Vice-chairman of board of directors of Jewish Museum; member of board of directors of MacDowell Colony, Jewish Theological Seminary of America, New Hope Foundation, American Crafts Council, American Friends of Hebrew University, Institute for the Future, Victor Gruen Center for Environmental Planning, Institute for Advanced Studies in the Humanities, Franklin Book Programs, Inc., Artists for the Environment Foundation, American College in Switzerland, and International Center of Photography. Member of advisory council of International Business Institute and member of advisory board of Council for the Study of Mankind, Bernard M. Baruch College of the City University of New York, New York City Office of Cultural Affairs, and Manpower Opportunities in Israel; member of board of overseers of Parsons School of Design and board of visitors of City College of the City University of New York. *Military service:* U.S. Army Air Forces, 1944; became first lieutenant.

MEMBER: International Public Relations Association, Public Relations Society of America, American Graphic Society, American Federation of Arts, American Institute of Graphic Arts (member of board of directors), Kappa Tau Alpha.

WRITINGS: Public Relations and Management, Reinhold, 1956; *The Corporate Oligarch,* Simon & Schuster, 1969.

Contributor of photographs: Gustav Vigeland, *Embrace of Life,* Abrams, 1969; Henry Moore, *As the Eye Moves,* Abrams, 1971; *Henry Moore: Sculpture and Environment,* Abrams, 1977. Also contributor of photographs to *Donatello: Prophet of Modern Vision,* and *Michelangelo's Three Pietas.* Contributor to *Handbook of Public Relations.* Contributor to professional journals and popular magazines, including *Harper's* and *Saturday Review.*

SIDELIGHTS: Finn's firm has developed new techniques and concepts in public relations and publicity in the United States, as well as Japan, Israel, Mexico, New Zealand, and Malaysia. His offices are spread out all over the world, and his books have been translated into Spanish, Japanese, Chinese, and Arabic.

Finn is also an artist (painter and sculptor), with a one-man show at New School for Social Research; paintings have been exhibited at schools and museums, including National Academy and Boston Museum of Art.

AVOCATIONAL INTERESTS: Collecting contemporary sculpture.

* * *

FINNEY, Paul B(urnham) 1929-

PERSONAL: Born October 28, 1929, in New York, N.Y.; son of Frank Burnham (an editor) and Eleanor (Axline) Finney; married Joanne Brown, December 27, 1952 (divorced October 16, 1975); children: Christopher L. B., Suzanne P. W. *Education:* Harvard University, B.A. (cum laude), 1950. *Home:* 139 East 94th St., New York, N.Y. 10028. *Office:* McGraw-Hill Publishing Co., 1221 Avenue of the Americas, New York, N.Y. 10020.

CAREER: McGraw-Hill Publishing Co., *Business Week,* New York City, served variously as London correspondent, assistant foreign editor, and New England bureau chief, 1950-60, associate managing editor, 1960-61, assistant managing editor, 1961-65, managing editor, 1966—. Member of local Citizens Advisory Committee for Transportation Quality, 1968-72. Member of Trilateral Commission. Vice-president of board of trustees of Collegiate School, 1963-71. *Military service:* U.S. Army, public information officer in Ordnance Corps, 1951-53; became lieutenant. *Member:* Overseas Press Club (past member of board of governors), Council on Foreign Relations, Harvard Club of New York.

WRITINGS: The Businessman's Guide to Europe, McGraw, 1965. Contributor to magazines and newspapers, including *Esquire* and *Travel and Leisure.*

* * *

FIORE, Robert Louis 1935-

PERSONAL: Born August 2, 1935, in New York, N.Y.; son of Anthony Francis and Rose E. (Morales) Fiore; married Jannette Carringer (a librarian), March 29, 1964; chil-

dren: David, Gabriella. *Education:* Iona College, B.A., 1961; Middlebury College, M.A., 1962; University of North Carolina, Ph.D., 1967. *Home:* 702 Snyder Rd., East Lansing, Mich. 48823. *Office:* Department of Romance Languages, Michigan State University, East Lansing, Mich. 48824.

CAREER: University of North Carolina, Greensboro, instructor in Spanish and Italian, 1962-67; Michigan State University, East Lansing, assistant professor, 1967-68, associate professor of Spanish and Italian, 1968—. Secretary-general of 26th Congress of International Institute Iberoamerica, summer, 1973. *Military Service:* U.S. Air Force, 1955-58. *Member:* Modern Language Association of America, American Association of Teachers of Spanish and Portuguese, American Association of Teachers of Italian, American Association of University Professors, Midwest Modern Language Association. *Awards, honors:* Scholarship from Instituto de la cultura hispanica of the Spanish Government.

WRITINGS: (Contributor) L. Dunham and I. Ivask, editors, *The Cardinal Points of Borges,* University of Oklahoma Press, 1971; (contributor) Jack H. Parker and Arthur M. Fox, editors, *Calderon de la Barca Studies, 1951-69,* University of Toronto Press, 1971; *Drama and Ethos: Natural-Law Ethics in Spanish Golden Age Theater,* University Press of Kentucky, 1975. Contributor to *Hispanic Review.*

WORK IN PROGRESS: Lazarillo de Tormes, for Twayne.

* * *

FIRTH, Grace (Ushler) 1922-

PERSONAL: Born August 16, 1922, in Fairfield, Conn.; daughter of Anton Edward (an accountant) and Veronica (Kabureck) Ushler; married Lewis R. Firth (a business administrator), October 10, 1953; children: Martin James, Marie Jean (Mrs. James Harrigan), Penny Louise. *Education:* Maryville Missouri State College, teaching certificate, 1942; University of Southern California, A.B., 1945; George Washington University, M.A., 1968. *Home address:* Port Republic, Md. 20676.

CAREER: Elementary school teacher in Stewartsville, Mo., 1941; State Hospital, St. Joseph, Mo., psychiatric stenographer, 1941-42; Bureau of Indian Affairs, Seward and Sitka, Ala., teacher, 1945-51; vocational rehabilitation counselor in Seward, 1951-53; Metromedia, Washington D.C., television cook and co-host, 1972—. Volunteer librarian and secretary for various civic organizations.

WRITINGS: A Natural Year, Simon & Schuster, 1972; *Living the Natural Life,* Simon & Schuster, 1974; *Stillroom Cookery,* EPM Publications, 1977.

WORK IN PROGRESS: A book on Alaskan history; researching biographical material.

SIDELIGHTS: Firth told *CA:* "At an early age I learned to enjoy the ritual of gardening and putting down produce, as well as fishing, foraging, frogging, and loafing in the sun. Was taught that waste was the killer of continents and that man thrives when he breathes joy.

"Education included interests in drama, speech and debate, dance, sports, chorus, and numerous years on the bass fiddle. Assisted with college costs by working in book binding, housework, and comedy dance in floor shows. Volunteered with USO camp show. After stenographic training, supplemented income by working as a medical office assistant.

"Upon graduation, taught in the Alaskan Native Service for

six years. Loved teaching Eskimos. As vocational rehabilitation counselor assisted in establishing a sheltered workshop for the handicapped in Alaska.

"Activities and hobbies included little theatre and community chorus, hunting, fishing, mountain climbing (first lady to hoof it above ten thousand feet on Mt. McKinley), skiing (first girl to ski across the Kenai peninsula), and panning gold (proved up on a placer claim, bought a .375 magnum rifle with nuggets).

"Earned private pilot's license, night and float ratings, 1946. Radio-telephone operator's permit. Pilot, small boat, Alaskan coastal waters. Operated crab traps and gill nets. Preserved all manner of northern abundance on my eighty acre homestead.

"Rescued four times by Air Rescue and Coast Guard (a record). 1. Plane upended on a slough, broken prop. 2. Boat sank. 3. Downed on remote sand bar, sediment bulb broke in flight. 4. Eleven days overdue because of high seas.

"After meeting Lewis (under a tractor) and marrying him, we sought our fortune in Florida phosphate fields where I shuddered at the earth's laceration. Moved to northern Virginia where our three children were reared and where we purchased a small wrinkle in the earth's surface and enjoyed wilderness weekends. It was here that I began to write. After ten years, seven Alaskan novels and hundreds of shorts that did not sell, I returned to the university (we old-timers were called retreads) and learned of Young America's interest in things natural. I subsequently wrote three books dealing with foods prepared in the early-day manner.

"My television career accidently began in 1972 when ginger ale that I was demonstrating blew its cap and suds engulfed cameras and crew. My programs are presented in a light-hearted manner because I believe that with a bright spirit everything merges in harmonious joy and hope."

*   *   *

FISCHER, Alfred (George) 1920-

PERSONAL: Born December 10, 1920, in Rothenburg, Germany; came to the United States in 1935; parents American citizens; son of George Erwin (a businessman) and Thea (Freise) Fischer; married Winnifred Varney, August 26, 1939; children: Joseph Fred, George William, Lenore Ruth. *Education:* Northwestern College, Watertown, Wis., student, 1935-37; University of Wisconsin, Madison, B.A., 1939, M.A., 1940; Columbia University, Ph.D., 1950. *Home:* 544 Alexander Rd., Princeton, N.J. 08540. *Office:* Department of Geology, Princeton University, Princeton, N.J. 08540.

CAREER: Virginia Polytechnic Institute, Blacksburg, Va., instructor in geology, 1941-43; Stanolind Oil & Gas Co., geologist in Kansas and Florida, 1943-46; University of Rochester, Rochester, N.Y., instructor in geology, 1946-47; University of Kansas, Lawrence, 1948-51, began as instructor, became assistant professor of geology; International Petroleum Co. Ltd., Lima, Peru, senior geologist, 1951-56; Princeton University, Princeton, N.J., 1956—, began as assistant professor, became associate professor, and Blair Professor of Geology.

MEMBER: American Association for the Advancement of Science, Geological Society of America, American Association of Petroleum Geologists, Paleontological Society of America, Society of Economic Paleontologists and Mineralogists, Audubon Society, Sierra Club, Palaeontologische Gesellschaft, Geologische Vereinigung, Sigma Xi. *Awards,*

honors: National Science Foundation fellowship, 1962-63; Guggenheim fellowship, 1969-70; Leopold V. Buch Medal from Deutsche Geologische Gesellschaft, 1972.

WRITINGS: (With Moore and Lalicker) *Invertebrate Fossils,* McGraw, 1952; (with Newell, Rigby, Whiteman, and Hickox) *The Permian Reef Complex,* W. H. Freeman, 1952, reprinted, Hafner, 1972; (with Honjo and Garrison) *Electron Micrographs of Limestones and Their Nanofossils,* Princeton University Press, 1967; (editor with Judson) *Petroleum and Global Tectonics,* Princeton University Press, 1975. Contributor to scientific journals.

WORK IN PROGRESS: Revising *Invertebrate Fossils,* for McGraw.

SIDELIGHTS: Fischer comments that his fundamental motivation is a "desire to understand the history of the earth and the life on it." His career has permitted extensive travel and as a child he lived in South America.

*   *   *

FISHEL, Wesley R(obert) 1919-1977

PERSONAL: Born September 8, 1919, in Cleveland, Ohio; married Jane Brudno, 1944; children: Barbara, Mary Fishel Sargent, Michael, Laurence. *Education:* Northwestern University, B.S., 1942; graduate study at University of Michigan, 1943; University of Chicago, Ph.D., 1948. *Office:* Department of Political Science, James Madison College, Michigan State University, East Lansing, Mich. 48824.

CAREER: University of California, Los Angeles, instructor in political science, 1948-51; Michigan State University, East Lansing, assistant professor, 1951-54, associate professor, 1954-57, professor, 1957-67, professor of political science in James Madison College, 1967-77. Visiting professor of government at Southern Illinois University, 1969. Chief administrator for Michigan State University Vietnam aid program in Saigon, 1956-58; board chairman of American Friends of Vietnam, 1964-66. Consultant or adviser to operations research office at Johns Hopkins University, 1952-56, Foreign Operations Administration, 1954-55, prime minister of Vietnam, 1955, International Cooperation Administration, 1955, special operations research office at American University, 1958-61, and U.S. State Department, 1963. *Military service:* U.S. Naval Reserve, 1941-42. U.S. Army, 1942-45; became lieutenant; served as military language specialist in the Pacific. *Member:* American Political Science Association, American Society of International Law, Association of Asian Studies.

WRITINGS: The End of Extraterritoriality in China, University of California Press, 1952, reprinted, Octagon, 1974; *Vietnam: Is Victory Possible?,* Foreign Policy Association, 1964; *Vietnam: Anatomy of a Conflict,* Peacock, 1968. Also author of *Problems of Freedom: South Vietnam Since Independence.* Contributor to proceedings of Conference on Social Development and Welfare in Vietnam. Editor of *Southeast Asia International Quarterly.*

OBITUARIES: New York Times, April 15, 1977.*

(Died April 14, 1977, in Lansing, Michigan)

*   *   *

FISHER, Margery (Turner) 1913-

PERSONAL: Born in 1913, in Camberwell, London, England; married James Fisher (an author, naturalist, and publisher); children: three sons, three daughters. *Education:* Earned B.Litt. and M.A. from Somerville College, Oxford. *Residence:* Ashton, Northampton, England.

CAREER: Author and critic. Teacher of English at Oundle School, 1939-45; organizer of courses on reading and writing for pleasure for the National Federation of Women's Institutes. *Awards, honors:* Eleanor Farjeon Award, 1967.

WRITINGS: Field Day, Collins, 1951; (with husband, James Fisher) *Shackleton* (illustrated by W. E. How), Barrie, 1967, published in America as *Shackleton and the Antarctic,* Houghton, 1958; (editor) *A World of Animals* (illustrated by Maurice Wilson), Brockhampton Press, 1962; *John Masefield,* H. Z. Walck, 1963; *Intent upon Reading: A Critical Appraisal of Modern Fiction for Children,* Brockhampton Press, 1961, F. Watts, 1962, revised and enlarged edition, Brockhampton Press, 1964; (editor) *Open the Doors,* World Publishing, 1965; (editor) Richard H. Horne, *Memoirs of a London Doll,* Macmillan, 1968; *Henry Treece,* Bodley Head, 1969; *Matters of Fact: Aspects of Non-Fiction for Children,* Crowell, 1972; *Who's Who in Children's Books,* Holt, 1975. Editor and publisher of *Growing Point,* 1962—.*

*   *   *

FITZGERALD, E(dmund) V(alpy) K(nox)   1947-

PERSONAL: Born January 30, 1947, in London, England; son of Desmond Lyons (a lawyer) and Penelope (a writer; maiden name, Knox) Fitzgerald; married Angelines Fernandez (a metallurgist), July 31, 1968; children: Gregory, Laurence. *Education:* Oxford University, B.A., 1968, M.A., 1972; Cambridge University, Ph.D., 1973. *Politics:* Socialist. *Religion:* Roman Catholic. *Home:* 10 Hertford St., Cambridge, England. *Agent:* Curtis Brown Academic, 13 King St., London W.C.2, England. *Office:* Faculty of Economics and Politics, Cambridge University, Cambridge, England.

CAREER: Cambridge University, Cambridge, England, assistant director of development studies, 1973—, fellow and tutor at St. Edmund's House, 1974—. Adviser to United Nations, World Bank, and British Government. *Member:* Royal Statistical Society (fellow), Royal Economic Society, Society for Latin American Studies.

WRITINGS: The State and Economic Development: Peru Since 1968, Cambridge University Press, 1976; *Public Investment Planning for Developing Countries,* Macmillan, 1977. Contributor of articles and reviews to economic, development studies, and Latin American studies journals.

SIDELIGHTS: Fitzgerald writes: "The experience of working as an adviser in development planning to a number of poor countries, particularly in Latin America, has forced me to come to terms with the reality of poverty on the one hand and of international exploitation on the other. This has understandably influenced my work, as has the respect for truth and scholarly care instilled by my parents and teachers."

*   *   *

FITZGERALD, Edward Earl   1919-

PERSONAL: Born September 10, 1919, in New York, N.Y.; son of Francis J. and Mary Leona (Morgan) Fitzgerald; married Libuse P. Ostruk, June 6, 1942; children: Eileen Frances, Kevin Paul. *Home:* 26 Claudet Way, Eastchester, N.Y. 10709. *Office:* 280 Park Ave., New York, N.Y. 10017.

CAREER: Author and editor. Reporter, Westchester County Publications, Inc., 1937-42; editor, Macfadden Publications, Inc., 1946-60; *Sport* magazine, editor-in-chief, 1951-60, editorial director men's group, 1952-60, assistant to the president, 1958-60; editor-in-chief, Literary Guild of

America, 1960-64; Doubleday & Co., vice-president, general manager of book club division, 1964-68; president, chief executive officer, McCall Publishing Co., 1968-71; vice-president, Book-of-the-Month Club, Inc., 1971—. *Military service:* U.S. Army, 1942-46. *Member:* Overseas Press Club.

WRITINGS: (With Lou Boudreau) *Player-Manager,* Little, Brown, 1949, revised edition, 1952; *College Slugger,* A. S. Barnes, 1950; *Yankee Rookie,* A. S. Barnes, 1952, reprinted, Grosset & Dunlap, 1961; *Champions in Sports and Spirit* (illustrated by De Wolfe Hotchkiss), Farrar, Straus, 1956; *The Ballplayer,* A. S. Barnes, 1957; *More Champions in Sports and Spirit* (illustrated by H. Lawrence Hoffman), Vision Books, 1959; *Johnny Unitas: The Amazing Success Story of Mr. Quarterback,* Nelson, 1961; (with Yogi Berra) *Yogi: The Autobiography of a Professional Baseball Player,* Doubleday, 1961; (with Mel Allen) *You Can't Beat the Hours: A Long, Loving Look at Big-League Baseball, Including Some Yankees I Have Known,* Harper, 1964; (with John Unitas) *Pro Quarterback: My Own Story,* Simon & Schuster, 1965.

Editor: *Tales for Males,* Cadillac, 1945; *Kick-Off!,* Bantam Books, 1948; *The Turning Point,* A. S. Barnes, 1948; *The Story of the Brooklyn Dodgers* (with an introduction by Red Barber), Bantam Books, 1949; *The Book of Major League Baseball Clubs,* A. S. Barnes, 1952; *A Treasury of Sport Stories,* Bartholomew House, 1955; *The National League,* Grosset & Dunlap, 1959, revised edition, 1966; *The American League,* Grosset & Dunlap, 1959, revised edition, 1966.

SIDELIGHTS: The *New York Times* review of Edward Fitzgerald's *Yankee Rookie* included, "This young rookie, with his love for his parents, his over-eagerness at bat, his desire not to be thought high-hat, acts and talks like a real person. Swift action, tense situations and personal crises combine to make this an exciting story." The *San Francisco Chronicle* noted, "Filled with baseball lore, the book also paints a vivid picture of a young man's struggles to reach the top in the sport he loves."

The reviews of *The Ballplayer* were mixed. The *San Francisco Chronicle* said, "This is what is called a serious novel about baseball. It would be better not so serious. . . . The author . . . knows the throw-and-catch business well. He also writes a clear declarative sentence. *New Yorker* added, "Mr. Fitzgerald knows everything about baseball, including just what Vinnie Burns, his able young player-manager of the Sox, is likely to be doing at every moment, not only on the field but in the dugout, the clubhouse, and the hotel, and on the winter-banquet circuit. Unfortunately, Mr. Fitzgerald knows very little about writing a novel, and his characters, plot, dialogue, and descriptions are all constructed of the same ready-cut fibreboard."

BIOGRAPHICAL/CRITICAL SOURCES: New York Times, November 16, 1952; *San Francisco Chronicle,* November 16, 1952, March 31, 1957; *New Yorker,* March 30, 1957; *New York Times Book Review,* June 7, 1964.*

*   *   *

FIXX, James Fuller   1932-

PERSONAL: Born April 23, 1932, in New York, N.Y.; son of Calvin Henry and Marlys (Fuller) Fixx; married Mary J. Durling, June 11, 1957 (divorced, 1973); married Alice Joy Kasman, July 21, 1974; children: Paul, John, Elizabeth, Stephen. *Education:* Attended Indiana University, 1950-52; Oberlin College, B.A., 1957. *Home:* 37 Crescent Rd., Riverside, Conn. 06878. *Office:* 730 Third Ave., New York, N.Y. 10017.

CAREER: *Sarasota Journal,* Sarasota, Fla., reporter, 1957-58; *Saturday Review,* New York City, feature editor, 1958-66; *McCall's,* New York City, executive editor, 1966-67, editor, 1967-69; *Life,* New York City, senior editor, 1969-72; *Christian Herald,* Chappaqua, N.Y., contributing editor, 1970—; contributing editor, *MBA Communications,* 1973—; *Horizon,* New York City, managing editor, 1974-76.

WRITINGS: *Games for the Superintelligent,* Doubleday, 1972; *More Games for the Superintelligent,* Doubleday, 1976; *The Complete Book of Running,* Random House, 1977. General editor, "Contemporary Issues" book series, *New York Times,* 1970-71. Editorial consultant, *New York Times,* 1969—; articles editor, *Audience,* 1971-72.

SIDELIGHTS: The author of a new book on running, Fixx explained: "I began running ten years ago because I'd pulled a muscle in my leg while playing tennis. I was really in terrible shape." He found running opened up a new life to him, one in which he felt better, dropped his excess weight, and found himself better able to cope with pressure and tension, among other benefits of the sport. He even claims that "runners who run no more than two miles a day can lose twenty-four pounds a year until the blubber is gone. Without dieting."

Fixx told *CA:* "People sometimes ask me how it happens that I've written books on such diverse subjects as human intelligence and physical fitness—i.e., running. They seem to think these an unlikely combination. But they aren't, not really. What I'm most deeply interested in is human limits and potentials. Most people, even quite ordinary people (if there is such a thing), are capable of far more than they dream of. An ordinary middle-aged man like myself can run a grueling 26.2-mile marathon with the requisite training, just as an ordinary person, if he or she works hard enough at it, may occasionally write a line or even a whole quatrain that [John] Donne would have been proud of."

BIOGRAPHICAL/CRITICAL SOURCES: *New York Post,* October 21, 1977.

* * *

FLAHERTY, Robert Joseph 1933-

PERSONAL: Born June 29, 1933, in Boston, Mass.; son of Joseph Patrick (a printer) and Mary Agnes (Healy) Flaherty; married Jean Imelda Hoffman, July 25, 1959; children: Joseph, Anne, Brian, Doreen, Edward. *Education:* Harvard University, A.B. (magna cum laude), 1955, M.B.A., 1961. *Politics:* Democrat. *Religion:* Roman Catholic. *Home:* 28 Tunstall Rd., Scarsdale, N.Y. 10583. *Office: Forbes* Magazine, 60 Fifth Ave., New York, N.Y. 10011.

CAREER/WRITINGS: *Forbes* Magazine, New York, N.Y., senior editor, 1961—. Notable assignments include coverage of the rise and fall of America's 100 largest corporations, 1917-77; twenty-seven cover stories, and profiles of fifty money managers. Contributor of articles to *Forbes* magazine. *Member:* New York Financial Writers Association (president, 1978—).

WORK IN PROGRESS: Articles for *Forbes.*

SIDELIGHTS: Flaherty told *CA:* "Ever since Polster Elmo Roper told me when I was a student at Harvard Business School, 'Find a way to get paid for doing what you like,' I have been writing about American business and I'm still having fun."

* * *

FLAHERTY, Vincent X. 1908(?)-1977

1908(?)—September 6, 1977; American journalist and screenwriter. Flaherty's syndicated sports columns helped to arouse interest in bringing major league baseball to the Pacific coast. He also wrote screenplays for "Jim Thorpe—All American" and contributed to the writing of "PT-109." He died in Los Angeles, Calif. Obituaries: *Washington Post,* September 8, 1977; *New York Times,* September 9, 1977.

* * *

FLAVELL, Carol Willsey Bell 1939-
(Carol Bell)

PERSONAL: Surname is accented on first syllable; born May 31, 1939, in Jamestown, N.Y.; daughter of Alfred Edward (a pharmacist) and Corinne (Braun) Willsey; married Ralph Ross Bell, May 17, 1958 (divorced, 1973); married Norman Lea Flavell (in numerical control for industry), July 4, 1975; children: (first marriage) Leslie Ann, Christopher K. *Education:* Attended Youngstown State University, 1974. *Religion:* Protestant. *Home:* 4649 Yarmouth Lane, Youngstown, Ohio 44512.

CAREER: Genealogist and writer, 1969—; Youngstown State University, Youngstown, Ohio, instructor in genealogy, 1971, worker in acquisitions department at library, 1974-75; Ohio Historical Society, Columbus, genealogical reference librarian, 1975. Certified by Board for Certification of Genealogists, also member of board of trustees. *Member:* Daughters of the American Revolution (Ohio Society), Daughters of American Colonists, Ohio Genealogical Society (member of board of trustees), Huguenot Society of Ohio (vice-president, 1974-76), First Families of Ohio, Western Pennsylvania Genealogical Society.

WRITINGS: (Under name Carol Bell) *1860 Columbiana County Ohio Census Index,* privately printed, 1972; (under name Carol Bell) *1850 Census: Columbiana County, Ohio,* Ohio Genealogical Society, 1973; *Greene County Ohio Area Key,* Area Keys, Inc., 1977; *Ohio Genealogical Periodical Index,* privately printed, 1977; (with Florence Clint) *Ohio Area Key,* Area Keys, Inc., 1977.

WORK IN PROGRESS: *Ohio Area Keys,* a multi-volume work, with one volume for each of Ohio's eighty-eight counties.

SIDELIGHTS: Carol Flavell writes: "My main interest is in making genealogical materials more readily available, and in guiding people in finding records within Ohio. Lecturing on the subject of genealogy is also part of my career, and I have traveled extensively doing so."

* * *

FLETCHER, Alan Mark 1928-

PERSONAL: Born May 19, 1928, in Conklin, N.Y.; son of Harley Seaver (a Presbyterian clergyman) and Anna Margaret (Pedersen) Fletcher; married Julia M. Emigh (a film librarian), June 24, 1950; children: four daughters. *Education:* Juniata College, B.S., 1950. *Religion:* Protestant. *Home:* 300 Forest Home Dr., Ithaca, N.Y. 14850. *Office:* College of Agriculture and Life Sciences, Cornell University, Ithaca, N.Y. 14850.

CAREER: Teacher of science, nature study, and world history at a private school in Stony Brook, N.Y., 1950-52; member of research staff, Pennsylvania Fish Commission, 1952; *Aquarium,* 1952-59, began as associate editor, became managing editor, then editor; managing editor of *Sunday School Times,* 1959-62; high school science teacher in Ambler, Pa., 1962; Doubleday & Co., Inc., Garden City, N.Y., senior science editor, 1962-64; J.B. Lippincott Co., Philadelphia, Pa., senior science editor, 1964-69; Cornell University Press, Ithaca, N.Y., sales manager, 1969-72, editor, 1972-73; Cornell University, Ithaca, editor of research publications and research associate in communication arts, 1973-75, head of publications for College of Agriculture and Life Sciences and College of Human Ecology, 1975—. Publications editor for Innes Publishing Co., 1956-59; consultant to Doubleday.

MEMBER: American Association for the Advancement of Science, National Science Teachers Association, American Association of Ichthyologists and Herpetologists, American Institute of Biological Sciences, American Killifish Association, Pennsylvania Academy of Science.

WRITINGS: (Editor of revision) Otto and Towle, *Modern Biology,* Holt, 1964; *The Land and People of the Guianas,* Lippincott, 1966, revised edition, 1972; *Unusual Aquarium Fishes,* Lippincott, 1968; *Fishes Dangerous to Man,* Addison-Wesley, 1969; *Fishes That Travel,* Addison-Wesley, 1970; *Fishes That Hide,* Addison-Wesley, 1973; *Fishes and Their Young,* Addison-Wesley, 1974. Contributor of several hundred articles to aquarium magazines and other journals, including *Collier's* and *Christianity Today,* and to newspapers.

SIDELIGHTS: Fletcher has made about a dozen trips to South America to study natural history. His photographs have won national aquarium fish photography contests.

* * *

FLETCHER, Anthony John 1941-

PERSONAL: Born April 24, 1941, in Llandygwyd, Wales; son of John (a dendrochronologist) and Delle Chenevix (Trench) Fletcher; married Tresna Dawn Russell (a teacher and justice of the peace), July 29, 1967; children: Crispin Hilary Trench, Dickon Anthony Railton. *Education:* Merton College, Oxford, B.A. (honors), 1962. *Home:* 59 Ranmoor Cres., Sheffield S10 3GW, England. *Office:* Department of History, University of Sheffield, Sheffield S10 2TW, England.

CAREER: Tutor at a private school in Windsor, England, 1962-63; history master at private school in London, England, 1964-67; University of Sheffield, Sheffield, England, lecturer, 1967-76, senior lecturer in history, 1976—. *Member:* Royal Historical Society (fellow), Ecclesiastical History Society, Historical Association, Association of University Teachers, Sussex Archaeological Society. *Awards, honors:* Award from *Choice,* 1976, for *A County Community in Peace and War.*

WRITINGS: Elizabethan Village, Longman, 1967; *Tudor Rebellions,* Longman, 1968; *A County Community in Peace and War,* Longman, 1975. Contributor to history, education, archaeology, and church history journals.

WORK IN PROGRESS: The Outbreak of the English Civil War, a study of the origins of the war at Westminster and in the localities, 1640-1642, publication by Edward Arnold expected in 1981.

AVOCATIONAL INTERESTS: Opera, theater, travel, hill walking.

* * *

FLORIAN, Tibor 1908-

PERSONAL: Born April 12, 1908, in Selmecbanya, Hungary; came to United States, 1949; naturalized U.S. citizen, 1956; son of Gero (a judge) and Aranka (Jaan) Florian; married Eva Felfoldy, October 28, 1945 (divorced, 1954); married Sophie Weress, March 18, 1955; children: Aniko, Zsombor, Lili, Ildiko, Claudia. *Education:* University of Kolozsvar (Romania), law degree, 1934. *Politics:* "Humanist." *Religion:* Roman Catholic. *Home:* 3 Mountain View Dr., New Milford, Conn. 06776.

CAREER: Hungaria (cultural and political weekly), Munich, Germany, literary editor, 1947-49; Radio Free Europe, New York City, announcer, 1950-60, editor, 1961-74; lecturer and free-lance writer, 1974—. Member of Pazmani Literary Association, Rumania, 1938, and of Kemeny Zsigmond Literary Association, Hungary, 1944. President of Kossuth Publishing Co., New York City and Cleveland, Ohio, 1954-60; president, Literary Branch of Arpad Academy in Cleveland, 1973—. *Member:* International P.E.N. (American Branch; honorary treasurer, 1955-71; acting honorary secretary, 1971-75; secretary-treasurer, 1976—), American Transylvanian Federation (secretary, 1966-72; vice-president, 1973—). *Awards, honors:* Letter of Merit from Zrinyi Miklos Literary Circle (Los Angeles), 1961; Silver Medal from Arpad Academy, 1964; Letter of Merit from Associatio Alumnorum Scholarum Piarum Hungariae Gratitudinem (New York), 1972; Gold Medal from Arpad Academy, 1973; 25th Anniversary Medal from Helikon Society (Toronto), 1976; Diploma from Ady Society (Netherlands), 1977.

WRITINGS—Poetry: *Above Clouds, Below Clouds,* Minerva, 1935; *Sketches,* Minerva, 1936; (translator from the Rumanian) Octavian Sireagu, *In Christ's Shadow,* Minerva, 1938; *The Stone Slabs Are Broken,* Exile Community, 1946; *New Poems,* Protestant Student Association, 1948; (editor) *Before Sunrise,* Farago (Munich), 1948; *Above the Depth,* Nyugat West, 1948; *Bitter Roots,* Pilvax, 1975; *The Man and the World,* Hungarian Life (Melbourne, Australia), 1978.

Work represented in many anthologies, including *Hungarian Anthology,* Pannonia Books, 1966; *Do You Know Us?,* Harsona (London), 1971; and *Poets of Transylvanian Helikon,* Kriterion (Bucharest, Rumania), 1973. Contributor of articles to newspapers, magazines, journals, and other periodicals.

WORK IN PROGRESS: "Essays and articles on man in nature, man in society, how we can keep second generation Hungarians bilingual, tradition and progress, the mission of the poet, respect of quality, respect of humanity, equality of man, and the Mother Earth."

SIDELIGHTS: Florian told *CA:* "Both my birthplace, and the city to which my father was transferred when I was four years old, belonged to Hungary. After World War I however, they were annexed to other countries. Therefore, my life became a typical, Central European life. Without leaving the basin of the Carpathians, and without resettling or emigrating to other countries, I had to live in three different countries and use three different languages in order to defend my rights. I was able to live in my native country for only a few years, while I spent the other years under foreign rule. I witnessed the chauvinism of overzealous nationalism and got accustomed to being treated as a citizen of secondary importance. This is how I became a poet, a fighter for human rights and freedom who fiercely opposes prejudice, privileges, and segregation. I learned to love human beings, no matter what their race, religion, or social class. My ideological background and my attitude showed me the path I had to follow after World War II. I chose the West.

"In America, for the first time in my life, I experienced real freedom and equality with everyone. In Central Europe I was considered a second-class citizen, and in Western Europe, only a homeless person. For the first time I was able to witness here the realization of a miraculous experiment in which, due to the democratic ideal, all races and religions of the world can peacefully live side by side in one single country.

"In one sentence, the philosophy which I follow in all my writings is the respect of freedom without hurting others, and love driving out hate.

"Through my articles and lectures as an exiled writer, I have always encouraged my fellow Hungarians to build upon the spiritual foundations of their Hungarian heritage, to be better, more faithful citizens in a new land, and to be defenders of a new nation and protectors of its human freedoms. Yet, at the same time, I believe we should drink deeply from the wellspring of our souls, our heritage, and our roots."

* * *

FLUSSER, Martin 1947-

PERSONAL: Born May 24, 1947, in Newark, N.J.; son of Martin W. (a real estate broker) and Janet (Romanow) Flusser; married Jorie Pepper, September 20, 1968 (marriage ended, 1973). *Education:* Harvard University, B.A. (cum laude), 1969; graduate study at New York University, 1972. *Home and office:* 230 West 79th St., New York, N.Y. 10024. *Agent:* Julian Bach Literary Agency, Inc., 3 East 48th St., New York, N.Y. 10017.

CAREER: Newsday, Garden City, N.Y., feature writer and reporter, 1969-72; School of Visual Arts, New York, N.Y., instructor in English, 1971-73; writer, 1973—.

WRITINGS: The Squeal Man (social documentary), Morrow, 1977. Contributor to magazines and newspapers, including *New York* and *Esquire.*

WORK IN PROGRESS: "A book of short stories that take place in New York City and my imagination."

AVOCATIONAL INTERESTS: Reading, playing tennis.

* * *

FODASKI-BLACK, Martha 1929-

PERSONAL: Born May 3, 1929, in Milford, Mich.; daughter of Ralph M. and Allie (Cockrell) Haller; married Sergius A. Wilde (marriage terminated); married Robert Fodaski (marriage terminated); married Kevin Sullivan (marriage terminated); married Leslie Black (an architect; marriage terminated); children: (first marriage) Steven; (second marriate) Corinna, David. *Education:* Alma College, student, 1947-49; Wayne State University, B.A. (highest honors), 1951; University of Wisconsin, Madison, M.A., 1952, Ph.D., 1960. *Home:* 69 Aspinwall Rd., Briarcliff Manor, N.Y. 10510. *Office:* Department of English, Brooklyn College of the City University of New York, Brooklyn, N.Y. 11210.

CAREER: Madison College, Harrisonburg, Va., assistant professor, 1956-60, associate professor of English, 1960-61; Brooklyn College of the City University of New York, Brooklyn, N.Y., instructor, 1962-66, assistant professor, 1966-70, associate professor, 1970-75, professor of English, 1976—. Lecturer at Scarsdale Adult School, 1968-76, Westchester Community College, summer, 1972, and Edgemont School, 1973; associate director of Institute for Irish Studies (Dublin), 1974-76, and Humanities Centre (Dublin), 1976—.

Member: Modern Language Association of America, National Council of Teachers of English.

WRITINGS: (Contributor) Oscar Williams, editor, *Masterpoems of the English Language,* Trident, 1966; *George Barker,* Twayne, 1969; *Two Notorious Women* (on Emma Goldman and Margaret Sanger), Prentice-Hall, in press. Contributor to *Encyclopedia of World Literature in the Twentieth Century,* to professional journals, and to *Explicator.*

WORK IN PROGRESS: The Last Word in Stolen-Telling, an annotated James Joyce bibliography; article on Kate Chopin's *The Awakening* "in the light of G. B. Shaw's 'Quintessence of Ibsenism'"; research on *Medea,* on irony in Joseph Conrad's "An Outpost of Progress," and on Wilde's swallow in *The Wasteland.*

SIDELIGHTS: Martha Fodaski-Black writes: "Being born a woman and becoming a mother and a professor inevitably led me to my current interest in women's studies and my work on *Medea,* Chopin, and the book on Emma Goldman and Margaret Sanger. My work in Ireland was stimulated by my interest in Anglo-Irish literature, a long friendship with Kevin Sullivan, and my teaching a graduate course in Anglo-Irish literature. During intersession I take students to Ireland where they can earn credit for a course in Irish literature, history, and culture."

* * *

FOLEY, Martha 1897(?)-1977

1897(?)—September 5, 1977; American editor, educator, and writer. For thirty-five years she edited the yearly anthology, *The Best American Short Stories.* With her former husband, Whit Burnett, she founded *Story* magazine and worked as an editor for Story Press. As a teacher at Columbia University until 1966, she sought to encourage young writers with constructive rather than destructive criticism. She died in Northampton, Mass. Obituaries: *New York Times,* September 7, 1977.

* * *

FOOTE, A(von) Edward 1937-

PERSONAL: Born September 24, 1937, in Burnsville, Miss.; son of Avon R. (a postal employee) and Lila (a teacher; maiden name, Broughton) Foote; married Dorothy Gargis (in real estate sales), March 15, 1960; children: Anthony, Kevin, Chele. *Education:* Florence State University (now University of North Alabama), B.S., 1963; University of Southern Mississippi, M.S., 1968; Ohio State University, Ph.D., 1970; also attended University of Mississippi and New York University. *Politics:* Republican. *Religion:* Methodist. *Home:* 217 Cavalier Rd., Athens, Ga. 30606. *Office:* School of Journalism, University of Georgia, Athens, Ga. 30602.

CAREER: WJOI-Radio, Florence, Ala., announcer and writer, 1958-60; WOWL-Television, Florence, production manager, director, and reporter, 1960-64; Plough, Inc. (drug and cosmetic company), Memphis, Tenn., advertising writer and coordinator, 1964-66; University of Southern Mississippi, Hattiesburg, instructor in radio and television, 1966-67; Ohio State University, Columbus, producer and director of educational television at Telecommunications Center, 1967-69; *Educational Broadcasting Review,* Washington, D.C., editor, 1969-73; University of Georgia, Athens, assistant professor of journalism and mass communications, and coordinator of graduate studies, 1974—, member of screening committee for George Foster Peabody Radio-Television Awards, 1975-76, chairperson of screening committee, 1976-77. Associate professor at University of Mississippi, 1971-72; visiting assistant professor at Ohio State University, 1973-74. Screening judge for Ohio State Awards, 1968-70, 1972-73. Project director of Ohio Valley Medical Microwave Television System for Ohio Educational Television Network Commission, 1972-74; correspondent with Aspen Institute, 1975-76; consultant to Columbus Foundation.

MEMBER: National Association of Educational Broadcasters, National Academy of Television Arts and Sciences (member of board of governors, 1970-71; regional Emmy Award judge, 1971), Broadcast Education Association, Proofreaders (charter member).

WRITINGS: (Contributor) Allen Koenig, editor, *Broadcasting and Bargaining: Labor Relations in Radio and Television,* University of Wisconsin Press, 1970; (editor) *The Challenges to Educational Communications: National Association of Educational Broadcasters Convention Report,* National Association of Educational Broadcasters, 1970; (contributor) Ronald D. McLaurin, editor, *PSYOP Casebook: An Anthology of Psychological Operations,* American Institutes for Research, 1972; (editor) *CBS and Congress: "The Selling of the Pentagon" Papers,* National Association of Educational Broadcasters, 1972.

Writer of numerous television programs for "Standard Oil News," WOWL-TV, 1960-62, "Outlook," WOWL-TV, 1961-63, "To Learn More, to Learn Better," WOSU-TV, 1969; writer of numerous radio and television commercials for stations in Alabama and Tennessee, 1958-66.

National Association of Educational Broadcasters correspondent for *EBU Review,* 1970-72. Contributor to professional journals.

WORK IN PROGRESS: From Chotank to the Corner, a popularized family history drawing from seven years of research, to be published in 1979.

SIDELIGHTS: Foote wrote of his work in progress: "The success of *Roots* spurred my intent to write a popular version of a fascinating story that touches Mount Vernon, Jefferson Davis, and the gallows. The adaptation to film or television is planned. Finally, my vocation and avocation are being merged and are providing me great delight and enjoyment." *Avocational interests:* Geneology research.

* * *

FOOTE, Horton 1916-

PERSONAL: Born March 14, 1916, in Wharton, Tex.; son of Albert (a shopkeeper) and Hallie (Brooks) Foote; married Lillian Vallish, June 4, 1945; children: Barbarie Hallie, Albert Horton, Walter Vallish, Daisy Brooks. *Education:* Studied at Pasadena Playhouse Theatre, 1933-35, and Tamara Darkarhovna Theatre School, 1937-39. *Home:* Ferris Lane, Grand View, N.Y. 10960. *Agent:* Lucy Kroll, 390 West End Ave., New York, N.Y. 10024.

CAREER: Writer for stage, screen, and television. Acted in Broadway plays, including "The Eternal Road," "The Fifth Column," "The Coggerers," "Mr. Banks of Birmingham," and "Texas Town," through 1942; operated Productions, Inc. in Washington, D.C., where he taught playwriting and acting and managed a semi-professional theatre. Writer of dramatic teleplays for Columbia Broadcasting Company (CBS), National Broadcasting Company, (NBC), and British Broadcasting Corp. (BBC); contributor of scripts to dramatic television series, including "Playhouse Ninety,"

and "Dupont Show of the Week." *Member:* Writers Guild of America, Authors Guild, Dramatists Guild, Texas Institute of Letters. *Awards, honors:* Academy Award (Oscar) for best screenplay based on another medium from Academy of Motion Picture Arts and Sciences, and Writers Guild of America Screen Award, both 1962, both for "To Kill a Mockingbird."

WRITINGS—Plays: *Only the Heart* (three-act; produced in New York City at Bijou Theatre, April 4, 1944), Dramatists Play Service, 1944; *The Chase* (three-act; first produced on Broadway at The Playhouse, April 15, 1952), Dramatists Play Service, 1952, published in novel form, under same title, Rhinehart, 1956; *Harrison, Texas: Eight Television Plays,* Harcourt, 1959; *Roots in a Parched Ground* (broadcast by CBS under title "Nights of the Storm," March, 1960), Dramatists Play Service, 1962; *Three Plays* (includes "Roots in a Parched Ground," "Old Man" [broadcast by CBS, November, 1959], and "Tomorrow"), Harcourt, 1962; *Tomorrow* (adapted from story by William Faulkner; broadcast by CBS, March, 1960), Dramatists Play Service, 1963.

Unpublished plays: "Texas Town," first produced in New York City at Provincetown Playhouse, December, 1942; "Out of My House," produced in New York City, 1942; "Celebration" (one-act), produced in New York City at Maxine Elliott Theatre, April 11, 1948; "The Trip to Bountiful" broadcast by NBC, March, 1953, produced on Broadway at Henry Miller's Theatre, November 3, 1953; "Midnight Caller" (one-act), broadcast by NBC, December, 1953, produced in New York City, 1958; "John Turner Davis" (one-act), broadcast by NBC, November, 1953, produced in New York City, 1958; "The Dancers," broadcast by NBC, March, 1954, produced in Los Angeles at Fiesta Hall, October 28, 1963; "The Traveling Lady," produced at The Playhouse, October 27, 1954. Also author of the book for "Gone With the Wind," (a musical version of Margaret Mitchell's novel), first produced on the West End at Drury Lane Theatre, May 3, 1972, produced in Los Angeles at Dorothy Chandler Pavillion, August 28, 1973.

Screenplays: "Storm Fear," United Artists, 1956; "To Kill a Mockingbird," Universal, 1962; "The Chase," Columbia, 1965; "Baby, the Rain Must Fall" (based on own play, "The Traveling Lady"), Columbia, 1965; "Hurry Sundown" (based on novel by K. B. Gilden), produced by Otto Preminger, Paramount, 1966; "The Stalking Moon," Warner Bros., 1968; "Tomorrow," Filmgroup, 1971.

Writer of more than twenty teleplays, including "The Travelers," NBC, 1952; "Young Lady of Property," NBC, 1953; "Death of the Old Man," NBC, 1953; "Shadow of Willie Greer," NBC, 1954; "Member of the Family," CBS, 1957, "The Shape of the River," CBS, 1960; "The Gambling Heart," NBC, 1964.

SIDELIGHTS: "From the beginning," Foote wrote, "most of my plays have taken place in the imaginary town of Harrison, Texas, and it seems to me a more unlikely subject could not be found in these days of Broadway and world theatre, than this attempt of mine to recreate a small Southern town and its people. But I did not choose this task, this place, or these people to write about so much as they chose me, and I try to write of them with honesty."

Foote's novel, *The Chase,* received critical acclaim for its dramatic power and strong characterizations. Anthony Boucher made these comments: "Sharply effective as a melodrama of violence, it is also powerful as a novel of character, probing deeply into many lives . . . and studying the inherent moral and psychological problems of violence." While *Commonweal*'s W. J. Smith found the book's lengthy epilogue to be ineffective, he was enthusiastic about the story itself: "The characterizations are excellent, the action is fast and suspenseful and the ramifications of the plot neatly interlocked. The novel attains a level beyond that of the mere thriller—psychological melodrama, perhaps, describes it better." A *Saturday Review* critic agreed that *The Chase* "is far more than a thriller (although it deserves a blue ribbon in that class); it is also a story of depth, fundamentally a tale of redemption and judgement." The *San Francisco Chronicle* described it as "tragic, almost entirely depressing, but powerful in its feeling of truth," and warned that "It is not meant for the type of reader who likes 'a book about nice people.'" Reviewer Anne Brooks, however, was less strongly impressed: "The dramatist who writes a novel is apt to limit himself to the stage confines of dialogue," she said. "Mr. Foote does not fall into this trap. *The Chase* is pure narrative. But still he has failed to capture the pictorial quality which gives a novel its greater breadth of fabric, and his story, while moving, is skeletal."

Another of Foote's books, *Harrison, Texas,* is a collection of television plays written and produced between January, 1953 and March, 1954. Of this collection a *Saturday Review* Critic wrote: "Television is in redemptive hands as long as it can work with art like this."

BIOGRAPHICAL/CRITICAL SOURCES: New York Herald Tribune Book Review, February 6, *Saturday Review,* February 18, 1956; *New York Times,* February 19, 1956; *San Francisco Chronicle,* February 26, 1956; *Commonweal,* March 16, 1956.

* * *

FORD, Harvey Seabury 1905(?)-1978

1905(?)—January 1, 1978; American journalist and author. Ford was associate editor of the *Toledo Blade,* and was recognized as an authority on education and an expert in history and foreign affairs. He died in Toledo, Ohio. Obituaries: *New York Times,* January 4, 1978.

* * *

FORD, Hilary
See YOUD, Samuel

* * *

FORESTER, C(ecil) S(cott) 1899-1966

PERSONAL: Born August 27, 1899, in Cairo, Egypt; son of George (a government official) and Sarah (Troughton) Forester; married Katherine Belcher, 1926 (divorced, 1944); married Dorothy Foster, 1947; children: (first marriage) John, George. *Education:* Studied medicine at Guy's Hospital. *Residence:* Berkeley, Calif.

CAREER: Novelist. Wrote film scripts in Hollywood for part of each year, 1932-39; worked as a correspondent in Spain, 1936-37, and covered the Nazi occupation of Czechoslovakia in Prague; was a member of the British Information Service, 1939-40. *Member:* Athenaeum Club, Savage Club (London), Century Club (New York). *Awards, honors:* James Tait Black Memorial Prize, 1939, for *A Ship of the Line.*

WRITINGS—"Horatio Hornblower" series: *Beat to Quarters,* Little, Brown, 1937, reprinted, Pinnacle Books, 1974 (published in England as *The Happy Return,* M. Joseph, 1937, reprinted, Nelson, 1964); *A Ship of the Line,* Little, Brown, 1938, reprinted, Pinnacle Books, 1975; *Flying Colours,* Little, Brown, 1939, reprinted, Pinnacle Books, 1975; *Captain Horatio Hornblower* (contains three novels, *Beat to Quarters, Ship of the Line,* and *Flying Colours;* illustrated by N. C. Wyeth), Little, Brown, 1939, reprinted, 1967; *Commodore Hornblower,* Little, Brown, 1945, reprinted, Pinnacle Books, 1975; *Lord Hornblower,* Little, Brown, 1946, reprinted, Pinnacle Books, 1975; *Mr. Midshipman Hornblower,* Little, Brown, 1950, reprinted, Pinnacle Books, 1974; *Lieutenant Hornblower,* Little, Brown, 1952, reprinted, Pinnacle Books, 1974; *Hornblower and the Atropos,* Little, Brown, 1953, reprinted, Pinnacle Books, 1974; *Hornblower Takes Command* (selections from *Beat to Quarters* and *Hornblower and the Atropos;* edited by G. P. Griggs; illustrated by Geoffrey Whittam), Little, Brown, 1953, reprinted, 1965; *Admiral Hornblower in the West Indies,* Little, Brown, 1958, reprinted, Pinnacle Books, 1975.

Young Hornblower, Three Complete Novels: Mr. Midshipman Hornblower, Lieutenant Hornblower, Hornblower and the Atropos, Little, Brown, 1960; *Hornblower and the Hotspur,* Little, Brown, 1962, reprinted, Pinnacle Books, 1974; *The Indomitable Hornblower: Commodore Hornblower, Lord Hornblower,* [and] *Admiral Hornblower in the West Indies,* Little, Brown, 1963; *The Hornblower Companion* (illustrated by Samuel H. Bryant), Little, Brown, 1964, reprinted, Pinnacle Books, 1974; *Hornblower's Triumph* (selections from *Commodore Hornblower* and *Lord Hornblower;* edited by G. P. Griggs; illustrated by G. Whittam), Little, Brown, 1965; *Hornblower in Captivity* (selections from *A Ship of the Line* and *Flying Colours;* edited by Griggs; illustrated by Whittam), Little, Brown, 1965; *Hornblower Goes to Sea* (selections from *Lieutenant Hornblower* and *Mr. Midshipman Hornblower*), Little, Brown, 1965; *Hornblower during the Crisis, and Two Stories: Hornblower's Temptation* and *The Last Encounter* (unfinished novel), Little, Brown, 1967.

Other writings: *A Pawn among Kings,* Methuen, 1924; *Napoleon and His Court* (biography), Methuen, 1924; *Josephine, Napoleon's Empress* (biography), Dodd, 1925; *Payment Deferred,* J. Lane, 1926, reprinted, Bodley Head, 1968; *Victor Emmanuel II and the Union of Italy,* Dodd, 1927; *One Wonderful Week,* Bobbs-Merrill, 1927 (published in England as *The Wonderful Week,* J. Lane, 1927); *Love Lies Dreaming,* Bobbs-Merrill, 1927; *The Daughter of the Hawk,* Bobbs-Merrill, 1928 (published in England as *The Shadow of the Hawk,* J. Lane, 1928); *Louis XIV, King of France and Navarre* (biography), Methuen, 1928; *Single-Handed,* Putnam, 1929 (published in England as *Brown on Resolution,* J. Lane, 1929); *Lord Nelson* (biography), Bobbs-Merrill, 1929; *The Voyage of the Annie Marble,* J. Lane, 1929; *Plain Murder,* J. Lane, 1930, reprinted, Bodley Head, 1967; *The Annie Marble in Germany,* J. Lane, 1930; *Two-and-Twenty,* D. Appleton, 1931; *Death to the French,* J. Lane, 1932, reprinted, Bodley Head, 1967; *The Gun* (novel), Little, Brown, 1933, reprinted, M. Joseph, 1968; *The Peacemaker,* Little, Brown, 1934; *The African Queen,* Little, Brown, 1935, reissued, Bantam Books, 1964.

Marionettes at Home, M. Joseph, 1936; *The General,* Little, Brown, 1936, reprinted, Bantam Books, 1967; *The Earthly Paradise,* M. Joseph, 1940, reprinted, 1960; *To the Indies,* Little, Brown, 1940; *The Captain from Connecticut,* Little, Brown, 1941; *Poo-Poo and the Dragons* (children's story; illustrated by Robert Lawson), Little, Brown, 1942, reprinted, 1968; *Rifleman Dodd* [and] *The Gun: Two Novels of the Peninsular Wars,* Readers Club, 1942; *The Ship,* Little, Brown, 1943; *The Sky and the Forest,* Little, Brown,

1948, reprinted, M. Joseph, 1960; *Randall and the River of Time,* Little, Brown, 1950, reprinted, New English Library, 1968; (editor) John Porrit Wetherell, *The Adventures of John Wetherell,* Doubleday, 1953; *The Barbary Pirates* (children's story; illustrated by Charles J. Mazoujian), Random House, 1953; *The Nightmare,* Little, Brown, 1954, reprinted, New English Library, 1970.

The Good Shepherd (Book-of-the-Month Club selection), Little, Brown, 1955, reprinted, New English Library, 1965; *The Age of Fighting Sail: The Story of the Naval War of 1812* (history), Doubleday, 1956 (published in England as *The Naval War of 1812,* M. Joseph, 1957); *The Last Nine Days of the Bismarck,* Little, Brown, 1959, also published as *Sink the Bismarck!,* Bantam Books, 1959 (published in England as *Hunting the Bismarck,* M. Joseph, 1959); *Long before Forty* (autobiography), Little, Brown, 1967; *The Man in the Yellow Raft* (short stories), Little, Brown, 1969, reprinted, Pinnacle Books, 1976; *Gold from Crete* (short stories), Little, Brown, 1970; *The Hostage* (selections from *The Nightmare*), New English Library, 1970.

SIDELIGHTS: Around 1926, Forester travelled through the rivers of England, France, and Germany in a dinghy with his first wife, Katherine Belcher. The author kept a log of his journey, which was later published as *The Voyage of the Annie Marble.* Although an attack of arteriosclerosis left him a semi-invalid later in life, Forester continued to write historical novels. Perhaps the author's most popular literary character is Horatio Hornblower.

Many motion pictures have been based on Forester's works, including "Payment Deferred," starring Charles Laughton, Maureen O'Sullivan, and Ray Milland, Metro-Goldwyn-Mayer, 1932; "Eagle Squadron," starring Robert Stack, Universal Pictures, 1942; "The Commandos Strike at Dawn," adaptation of *The Commandos,* starring Paul Muni and Lillian Gish, Columbia Pictures, 1943; "The African Queen," starring Humphrey Bogart and Katherine Hepburn, United Artists, 1951; "Captain Horatio Hornblower," starring Gregory Peck and Virginia Mayo, Warner Brother, 1951; "Sailor of the King," adaptation of *Brown on Resolution* starring Jeffrey Hunter and Michael Rennie, Twentieth Century-Fox, 1953; "The Pride and the Passion," adaptation of *The Gun,* starring Cary Grant, Frank Sinatra, and Sophia Loren, United Artists, 1957; and "Sink the Bismarck!" starring Dana Wynter, Twentieth Century-Fox, 1960.

"The African Queen" was also produced as a television special starring Warren Oates and Mariette Hartley, presented on CBS, March 18, 1977.

BIOGRAPHICAL/CRITICAL SOURCES: Saturday Evening Post, July 6, 1946, March 6, 1948; *New York Times Book Review,* April 6, 1952, April 3, 1955; *Newsweek,* July 9, 1956, September 1, 1958; *Christian Science Monitor,* August 2, 1962; C. S. Forester, *Long before Forty,* Little, Brown, 1967.

OBITUARIES—New York Times, April 3, 1966; *Time,* April 8, 1966; *Illustrated London News,* April 9, 1966; *Newsweek,* April 11, 1966; *Britannica Book of the Year,* 1967.*

(Died April 2, 1966, in Fullerton, Calif.)

*   *   *

FORSYTH, James (Law)   1913-

PERSONAL: Born March 5, 1913, in Glasgow, Scotland; son of Richard (a construction engineer) and Jessie (a teacher; maiden name, Law) Forsyth; married Helen Steward, 1938 (divorced, 1953); married Dorothy Louise Tibble (an executive secretary), August 4, 1955; children: John Antony, Richard Sandes. *Education:* Glasgow Art School, diploma in drawing and painting, 1934. *Politics:* "Non-party radical liberal." *Religion:* "Non-denominational Christian." *Home and office:* Grainloft, Ansty, Haywards Heath, Sussex RH17 5AG, England.

CAREER: Painter and sculptor in Glasgow and Edinburgh, Scotland, 1934-37; worked with General Post Office Film Unit, London, England, 1937-40; Old Vic Company, London, dramatist-in-residence, 1946-48; free-lance playwright in London and New York, 1949-61; Howard University, Washington, D.C., dramatist-in-residence, 1962; Tufts University, Medford, Mass., guest director and lecturer, 1963; Florida State University, Tallahassee, distinguished professor-in-residence, 1965; director of Tufts University Program in London, 1967-71; Forsyths' Barn Theatre, Ansty, Sussex, England, artistic director and producer, 1971—. Executive member of League of Dramatists and Society of Authors, Great Britain, 1946-75; founder member of Theatre Advisory Council of Great Britain, 1962-67. *Military service:* Scots Guards, 1940. South Wales Borderers, 1940-46; became captain; received Bronze Cross of the Netherlands. *Member:* Society of Authors, London Library. *Awards, honors:* Brooks Atkinson Critics Award nomination for most promising dramatist, 1960, for "Heloise"; IVS choice for Italia Prize, 1972, for "The Last Journey."

WRITINGS—All plays, except as noted: Three Plays (contains "The Other Heart" [also published separately; see below]; "Heloise" [also published separately; see below]; and "Adelaise" [four-act; broadcast, 1951; first produced in Ashburton, England, at Ashburton Theatre, 1953]), Heinemann, 1956; *Heloise* (three-act; broadcast, 1951; first produced in Southsea, England, at The King's Theatre, 1951; produced on the West End at Duke of York's Theatre, November 14, 1951; produced Off-Broadway at Gate Theatre, September 24, 1958), Theatre Arts, 1958; *Joshua* (libretto of oratorio; music by Franz Waxman; first produced in Dallas at Temple Emmanuel, 1960), Ricordi, 1959.

Brand (new version of Ibsen play), Heinemann, 1960; *Dear Wormwood* (three-act; first produced in Brighton, England, at Theatre Royal, 1965), Dramatic Publishing, 1961, published as *Screwtape,* 1973; *Emmanuel: A Nativity Play* (four-act; broadcast, 1950 and 1960; first produced Off-Broadway at Gale Theatre, 1960), Theatre Arts, 1963; *The Other Heart* (three-act; broadcast, 1951; first produced in the West End at Old Vic Theatre, April 15, 1952), Theatre Arts, 1964; *Cyrano de Bergerac* (five-act; first produced in Sarasota, Fla., at Asolo Theatre, 1963; produced on Broadway at Vivian Beaumont Theatre, April 25, 1968), Dramatic Publishing, 1968; *If My Wings Heal* (three-act; first produced in Stroud, England, at the parish church, 1966), Dramatic Publishing, 1968.

The Road to Emmaus: A Play for Eastertide, Theatre Arts, 1972; *Defiant Island* (three-act; first produced in Washington, D.C., at Howard University Theatre, 1962), Dramatic Publishing, 1975; *No Crown for Herod* (one-act; first produced in Ansty, Sussex, England at Forsyth's Barn Theatre, December, 1976), Dramatic Publishing, 1977.

Unpublished plays: "Trog" (three-act), broadcast, 1949, first produced in Coventry, England, at Belgrade Theatre, October 12, 1959; "The Medicine Man" (three-act), first produced in London at Embassy Theatre, February 14, 1950; "The Pier" (three-act), first produced in Bristol, England, at Bristol Old Vic Theatre, May 27, 1958; "Fifteen Strings of Money" (three-act), first produced in Pitlochry, Scotland, at Festival Theatre, April 22, 1961; "Everyman" (one-act), first produced in Coventry, England, at Coventry Cathedral, December 5, 1962; "Seven Scenes for Yeni" (three-act), first produced in Boston at Boston College Theatre, May, 1963; "Four Triumphant" (four-act), televised, 1966 and 1967, first produced as "Festival of Four" in Ansty, England, at Forsyths' Barn Theatre, 1976; "Lobsterback" (three-act), first produced in Medford, Mass., at Tufts Arena Theatre, 1975; "The Play of Alban" (two-act), first produced in St. Alban's, England, at St. Alban's Cathedral, October, 1977.

Screenplays: "The End of the Road," 1937-40; "Francis of Assisi," released by Twentieth Century Fox, 1961.

Radio and television plays: "The Bronze Horse," 1948; "The Nameless One of Europe," 1951; "For He's a Jolly Good Fellow," 1952; "Pig," 1953; "Seelkie," 1954; "The Festive Spirit," 1955; "Lisel," 1955; "Christophe," 1958; "Underground," 1958; "Old Mickmack," 1961; "Every Pebble on the Beach," 1963; "The English Boy," 1969; "The Last Journey," 1972; "The Old Man's Mountain," 1972; "Rise Above It" (documentary), 1972; "When the Snow Lay Round About," 1978.

Other writings: *Tyrone Guthrie: The Authorized Biography,* Hamish Hamilton, 1976. Also author of libretto of "Villon," an opera with music by Gardner Read, as yet unpublished.

WORK IN PROGRESS: "Bonaparte . . . Gunner," a play about Napoleon, contracted for production in Edinburgh.

SIDELIGHTS: Forsyth writes: "Having started in the visual and plastic arts and gone via poetry into drama, I am very much an all-arts playwright. I believe theatre, as a composite art form capable of being served to one end by all arts, to be the most potentially potent art form man has at his disposal, and that it belongs—as an institution—at the heart of any civilized community—starting from the earliest civilizations and deserving continuity to the end of this world. Originality is its essence, not novelty."

*   *   *

FOSTER, Marian Curtis   1909-
(Mariana)

PERSONAL: Born in 1909, in Cleveland, Ohio. *Education:* Attended Sophie Newcomb College, Art Students League, New York City; and Grande Chaumiere, Paris, France. *Residence:* New York City; and Long Island, N.Y.

CAREER: Author and illustrator of books for children.

WRITINGS—Under pseudonym Mariana; all self-illustrated: *The Journey of Bangwell Putt,* F. A. R. Gallery, 1945, reprinted, Lothrop, 1965; *Miss Flora McFlimsey's Christmas Eve,* Lothrop, 1949; *Miss Flora McFlimsey's Easter Bonnet,* Lothrop, 1951; *Miss Flora McFlimsey and the Baby New Year,* Lothrop, 1951; *Miss Flora McFlimsey's Birthday,* Lothrop, 1952; *Hotspur,* Lothrop, 1953; *Miss Flora McFlimsey and Little Laughing Water,* Lothrop, 1954; *Doki, the Lonely Papoose* (a Junior Literary Guild selection), Lothrop, 1955; *Miss Flora McFlimsey and the Little Red School House,* Lothrop, 1957; *Miss Flora McFlimsey's Valentine,* Lothrop, 1962; *Miss Flora McFlimsey's May Day,* Lothrop, 1969; *Miss Flora McFlimsey's Halloween,* Lothrop, 1972.

Illustrator: Rhoda Berman, *When You Were a Little Baby,* Lothrop, 1954; Betty Peckinpah, *Coco Is Coming,* Lothrop, 1956; Jean Y. Jaszi, *Everybody Has Two Eyes,* Lothrop,

1956; Janice, *Little Bear's Christmas,* Lothrop, 1964; Janice M. Udry, *Danny's Pig,* Lothrop, 1965; Janice, *Little Bear's Thanksgiving,* Lothrop, 1967; Janice, *Little Bear Marches in the St. Patrick's Day Parade,* Lothrop, 1967; Janice, *Little Bear Learns to Read the Cookbook,* Lothrop, 1969; Janice, *Little Bear's New Year's Party,* Lothrop, 1973.

SIDELIGHTS: As a child, Marian Curtis Foster opted for drawing lessons over piano lessons, considering the former the lesser of the two evils. Her interest in dolls began in childhood. She had a doll house in the yard big enough for a child to walk in, and numerous dolls. During the Depression, she worked on the American Index Project of the W.P.A., making drawings of early Americana at museums. The old toys and dolls in the museums fascinated her the most. In a book, *Child Life in Colonial Days,* she found a picture of a rag doll named Bangwell Putt who became the basis for *The Journey of Bangwell Putt.* At the New York Historical Society, she came upon an old doll named for the heroine of the nineteenth-century poem, *Miss Flora McFlimsey of Madison Square.* This doll became the heroine in the series of books by Marian Curtis Foster, all written under the pseudonym of Mariana.

The drawings she does for her books are usually watercolor and gouache, with black-and-white put in with a Chinese ink stick. Many of her original drawings are housed in the special Mariana Room of the Hockessin Elementary School Library in Wilmington, Delaware.

BIOGRAPHICAL/CRITICAL SOURCES: Chicago Tribune, March 18, 1951; *Life,* September 22, 1952; *New York Times,* January 24, 1954; *New York Times Book Review,* November 14, 1965.*

*   *   *

FOWLER, Robert H(oward)   1926-

PERSONAL: Born July 2, 1926, in Monroe, N.C.; son of James Wiley and Stella (Mundy) Fowler; married Beverly Jeanne Utley (a research assistant), June 30, 1950; children: Wade Utley, Alyce Mundy, Robert Howard, Jr., Susanna Jeanne. *Education:* Attended Guilford College, 1946-48; University of North Carolina, A.B., 1950; Columbia University, M.S., 1954. *Politics:* Democrat. *Religion:* Methodist. *Home:* 703 Hilltop Dr., New Cumberland, Pa. 17070. *Agent:* John Schaffner Literary Agency, 425 East 51st St., New York, N.Y. 10022. *Office:* Historical Times, Inc., P.O. Box 1831, Harrisburg, Pa. 17105.

CAREER: Reidsville Review, Reidsville, N.C., reporter, 1950; *Greensboro Daily News,* Greensboro, N.C., reporter and assistant city editor, 1950-55; *St. Petersburg Times,* St. Petersburg, Fla., city editor, 1955-56; *Harrisburg Patriot-News,* Harrisburg, Pa., editorial writer, 1956-60; Historical Times, Inc., Harrisburg, Pa., member of board of directors, 1960—, vice-president and general manager, 1960-69, president, 1968—. Member of board of directors of Commonwealth Communication Services, Inc.; director of People-to-People Book Drive, 1959. *Military service:* U.S. Naval Reserve, active duty, 1944-46.

MEMBER: American Society of Magazine Editors, National Historical Society (founder; president), Overseas Press Club, Company of Military Historians, Harrisburg Civil War Round Table, Sigma Delta Chi, Princeton Club, Savage Club. *Awards, honors:* Prizes from Pennsylvania Newspaper Publishers Association, 1957-60, for editorial and public service.

WRITINGS: Album of the Lincoln Murder, Stackpole,

1965; (with Frederick Ray) *O, Say Can You See,* Stackpole, 1970; *Jim Mundy* (novel set during the Civil War), Harper, 1977. Founding editor of *Civil War Times Illustrated,* 1959-73, and *American History Illustrated,* 1966—; founder of *British History Illustrated.*

WORK IN PROGRESS: A novel set on the Pennsylvania frontier just before the French and Indian War, dealing with tensions between the Quakers, Ulster Presbyterians, and Palatinate Germans on the one hand and various contending Indian tribes on the other.

SIDELIGHTS: Fowler told *CA:* "*Jim Mundy* is my first published novel. I have written four detective novels based on the exploits of an ex-CIA man now a professor of American history and a Civil War buff, but have not offered them to a publisher. I pay a great deal of attention to accuracy in my historical novels. The writing of fiction is a hobby with me along with sculpting, tennis, and canoeing."

* * *

FOX, Freeman
See HAMILTON, Charles Harold St. John

* * *

FOX, Lucia Ugara de
See LOCKART, Lucia A(licia) Fox

* * *

FOX, Michael W(ilson) 1937-

PERSONAL: Born August 13, 1937, in Bolton, England; came to the United States in 1962; son of Geoffrey (a banker) and Elizabeth Fox; married second wife, Deborah Johnson (a social worker), 1973; children: Michael Wilson, Jr., Camilla (first marriage). *Education:* Royal Veterinary College, London, B.Vet.Med., 1962; University of London, Ph.D., 1967, D.Sc., 1976; Alpha School of Massage, Ms.T., 1974. *Office:* Institute for the Study of Animal Problems, 2100 L St. N.W., Washington, D.C. 20037.

CAREER: Jackson Laboratory, Bar Harbor, Me., fellow, 1962-64; State Research Hospital, Galesburg, Ill., medical research associate, 1964-67; Washington University, St. Louis, Mo., assistant professor, 1967-69, associate professor of psychology, 1969-76; Institute for the Study of Animal Problems, Washington, D.C., director, 1976—. Associate professor at George Washington University. Guest on national television and radio programs.

MEMBER: Royal College of Veterinary Surgeons, Animal Behaviour Society, American Veterinary Medical Association, American Association for the Advancement of Science, American Federation of Television and Radio Artists, Authors Guild of Authors League of America. *Awards, honors:* Christopher Award for Children's Literature, 1973, for *The Wolf; Sundance Coyote* was nominated for Mark Twain Award, 1976; best science book award from National Teacher's Association, 1976, for *Ramu and Chennai.*

WRITINGS: Canine Behavior, C. C Thomas, 1965; *Canine Pediatrics,* C. C Thomas, 1966; *Integrative Development of Brain and Behavior in the Dog,* University of Chicago Press, 1971; *Behavior of Wolves, Dogs, and Related Canids,* Harper, 1971; *Understanding Your Dog,* Coward, 1972; *Understanding Your Cat,* Coward, 1974; *Concepts in Ethology: Animal and Human Behavior,* University of Minnesota Press, 1974; *Between Animal and Man: The Key to the Kingdom,* Coward, 1976; *The Dog: Domestication and Behavior,* Garland Publishing, 1978; *Pet Sense,* Coward, 1978; *One Earth, One Mind,* Coward, 1978.

Juveniles: *The Wolf,* Coward, 1973; *Vixie: The Story of a Little Fox,* Coward, 1973; *Sundance Coyote,* Coward, 1974; *Ramu and Chennai,* Coward, 1975; (with Wende Devlin Gates) *What Is Your Dog Saying?,* Coward, 1977; *Wild Dogs Three,* Coward, 1977.

Editor: *Abnormal Behavior in Animals,* Saunders, 1968; *Readings in Ethology and Comparative Psychology,* Brooks/Cole, 1973; *The Wild Canids,* Van Nostrand, 1975; (with R. K. Morris) *On the Fifth Day: Animal Rights and Human Obligations,* Acropolis Press, 1977. Contributor of about one hundred fifty articles to scientific journals.

Author of syndicated newspaper column "Ask Your Vet"; contributing editor, *McCall's* Magazine.

WORK IN PROGRESS: Animal Rights and Human Liberation; The Animal/Nature Connection: Understanding and Communion; What Is Your Cat Saying? and *Whitepaws the "Coydog,"* both for children, to be published by Coward.

SIDELIGHTS: Fox told *CA:* "My major motivation behind the adult and children's books I write is to improve the relationship between people and animals and nature; to foster compassion and responsible care through respect and understanding; in essence to encourage *humane stewardship* of all life, upon which the survival and fulfillment of our own species is wholly dependent."

* * *

FOX, Paula 1923-

PERSONAL: Born April 22, 1923, in New York, N.Y.; daughter of Paul Hervey (a writer) and Elsie (de Sola) Fox; married Richard Sigerson (divorced, 1954); married Martin Greenberg, June 9, 1962; children: (first marriage) Adam, Gabriel. *Education:* Attended Columbia University. *Residence:* Brooklyn, N.Y.

CAREER: Author. Worked in Europe for a year as a reporter for a news agency. C. W. Post College, professor of English literature, beginning 1963. *Member:* P.E.N., Author's League. *Awards, honors:* Finalist in the National Book Award Children's Book Category, 1971, for *Blowfish Live in the Sea;* National Institute of Arts and Letters Award, 1972; Guggenheim fellow, 1972; Newbery Medal, 1974, for *The Slave Dancer.*

WRITINGS: Maurice's Room (illustrated by Ingrid Fetz), Macmillan, 1966; *A Likely Place* (illustrated by Edward Ardizzone), Macmillan, 1967; *How Many Miles to Babylon?* (illustrated by Paul Giovanopoulos), David White, 1967; *Poor George,* Harcourt, 1967; *The Stone-Faced Boy* (illustrated by Donald A. Mackay), Bradbury Press, 1968; *Dear Prosper* (illustrated by Steve McLachlin), David White, 1968; *Portrait of Ivan* (illustrated by Saul Lambert), Bradbury Press, 1969; *The King's Falcon* (illustrated by Eros Keith), Bradbury Press, 1969; *Hungry Fred* (illustrated by Rosemary Wells), Bradbury Press, 1969; *Blowfish Live in the Sea,* Bradbury Press, 1970; *Desperate Characters,* Harcourt, 1970; *The Western Coast,* Harcourt, 1972; *Good Ethan* (illustrated by Arnold Lobel), Bradbury Press, 1973; *The Slave Dancer* (illustrated by Keith), Bradbury Press, 1973; *The Widow's Children,* Dutton, 1976.

SIDELIGHTS: John Rowe Townsend noticed that a recurrent theme of Fox's books for children "is that of noncommunication and lack of understanding between young and old. It is not the generation gap, exactly, but Miss Fox lives in the world we know at our nerve-ends, in which the old comfortable certainties can no longer be relied on."

The *New York Times* said of *How Many Miles to Babylon?:*

"There is a dual sense of isolation here; both the isolation of a lonely childhood and the further isolation of an impoverished urban existence. What is rare and valuable is its unblunted vision of the way things are, and its capacity to evoke the sense of what it is to live as so many people do live in this city, in this time." The *Times* also reviewed *The Stone-Faced Boy,* and commented: "The surrealistic quality of Paula Fox's writing, so ably demonstrated in *How Many Miles to Babylon?* is also present in this work. [Her] books are for discerning readers who are able to take joy in getting below the surface, readers who can take a simply-stated thought and recognize the complexities it conveys."

Fox's first adult novel, *Poor George* was described by the *Times Literary Supplement* as "a searching, gloomy look at loneliness, rootlessness, and resourcelessness, and the cool wit of the observer makes it no less depressing to contemplate." The *New Leader* described *Desperate Characters* as "A small masterpiece, a revelation of contemporary New York middle-class life that grasps the mind of the reader with the subtle clarity of metaphor and the alarmed tenacity of nightmare."

A motion picture entitled "Desperate Characters" and based on Paula Fox's novel was released by Paramount Pictures in 1970, and starred Shirley MacLaine.

BIOGRAPHICAL/CRITICAL SOURCES: Times Literary Supplement (London), August 24, 1967; *New York Times Book Review,* September 24, 1967, November 3, 1968; *New Leader,* February 2, 1970; John Rowe Townsend, *A Sense of Story,* Longman, 1971; *Contemporary Literary Criticism,* Gale, Volume 2, 1974, Volume 8, 1978; *Children's Literature Review,* Volume 1, Gale, 1976; *New York Times,* September 16, 1976.*

* * *

FOX, Ruth 1895-

PERSONAL: Born June 21, 1895, in New York, N.Y.; daughter of James Braden and Adelaide (Gomer) Fox; married McAlister Coleman, 1931 (deceased); children: McAlister Coleman, Ann Huntington (Mrs. Douglass Allen). *Education:* University of Chicago, Ph.B., 1919; University of Paris, Certificate of Chemistry and Natural Science, 1920; Rush Medical College, M.D., 1926; Flower and Fifth Avenue Hospitals, course in psychoanalysis, 1947-50. *Home and office:* 150 East 52nd St., New York, N.Y. 10022.

CAREER: Diplomate, National Board of Medical Examiners. Peking Union Medical College, Peking, China, Rockefeller Foundation intern, 1925-26; Fifth Avenue Hospital, New York, N.Y., resident fellow in pediatrics, 1927-32; physician in general practice, New York, N.Y., 1932-34; Columbia-Presbyterian Medical Center, New York, N.Y., director of laboratories at Neurological Institute, 1934-38; physician in private practice, New York, N.Y., 1938—, specializing in psychoanalysis, 1948—; National Council on Alcoholism, New York, N.Y., medical director, 1959—. Lecturer on alcoholism in United States, Europe, and the Orient. Member of Cooperative Commission for the Study of Alcoholism, and medical consultant to committee on alcoholism of Community Council of Greater New York. Member of board of directors, E. M. Jellinek Memorial Fund; trustee, American Academy of Psychoanalysis.

MEMBER: American Psychiatric Association (fellow), Association for the Advancement of Psychotherapy (fellow), American Academy of Psychoanalysis (fellow), American Public Health Association (fellow), American Medical Society on Alcoholism (co-founder; president, 1959-60; member of executive board), American Medical Association, Pan American Medical Association, American Medical Women's Association, Royal Society of Health (England), Society for the Study of Addiction to Alcohol and Other Drugs (England), American Society of Group Psychotherapy and Psychodrama, American Group Psychotherapy Association, American Orthopsychiatric Association, American Society of Clinical Hypnosis (fellow), Society of Clinical and Experimental Hypnosis, Association for Advancement of the Behavioral Therapies, New York Academy of Medicine (fellow), and county and city medical organizations. *Awards, honors:* Citation of Merit from Malvern Institute for Psychiatric and Alcoholic Studies, 1963.

WRITINGS: (With Peter Lyon) *Alcoholism: Its Scope, Cause and Treatment,* Random House, 1955; (editor) *Alcoholism: Behavioral Research, Therapeutic Approaches,* Springer, 1967; (editor with Peter G. Bourne) *Alcoholism: Progress in Research and Treatment,* Academic Press, 1973; *The Tangled Chain: The Structure of Disorder in the Anatomy of Melancholy,* University of California Press, 1976.

Contributor: Gustav Bychowski and L. Despert, editors, *Specialized Techniques of Psychotherapy,* Basic Books, 1952; Victor Eisenstein, editor, *Neurotic Interaction in Marriage,* Basic Books, 1956; Harold E. Himwich, editor, *Alcoholism: Its Basic Aspects and Treatment,* American Association for the Advancement of Science, 1957; *The Medical Clinics of North America,* Saunders, 1958; Louis Linn, editor, *Frontiers in General Hospital Psychiatry,* International Universities, 1961; *Progressive Child Psychiatry,* S. Karger, 1963; Jules M. Masserman, editor, *Current Psychiatric Therapies,* Volume V, Grune, 1965; Lawrence E. Abt and Stuart L. Weissman, editors, *Acting Out—Theoretical and Clinical Aspects,* Grune, 1965; *Alcoholism: Group Psychotherapy and Rehabilitation,* C. C Thomas, 1966. Contributor to medical journals.

WORK IN PROGRESS: Continuing clinical research in field of alcoholism.*

* * *

FRANCHERE, Ruth

PERSONAL: Born in Mason City, Iowa; daughter of H. Verne and Celta (Huffman) Myers; married Hoyt Catlin Franchere (an author), 1928; children: Julie (Mrs. E. Hugh Hinds, Jr.). *Education:* Graduated from the University of Iowa, 1930. *Residence:* Lake Oswego, Ore.

CAREER: Author of books for young people. Lecturer in English at University of Oregon, University of Washington, and Portland State University. *Member:* Author's Guild, Author's League of America.

WRITINGS: Willa (illustrated by Leonard Weisgard), Crowell, 1958; *Stephen Crane: The Story of an American Writer,* Crowell, 1961; *Jack London: The Pursuit of a Dream,* Crowell, 1962; *Hannah Herself,* Crowell, 1964; *The Travels of Colin O'Dae* (illustrated by Lorence Bjorklund), Crowell, 1966; *Stampede North,* Macmillan, 1969; *Tito of Yugoslavia,* Macmillan, 1970; *Cesar Chavez* (illustrated by Earl Thollander), Crowell, 1970; *Carl Sandburg: Voice of the People* (illustrated by Victor Mays), Garrard, 1970; *Westward by Canal,* Macmillan, 1972; *The Wright Brothers* (illustrated by Louis Glanzman), Crowell, 1972.

AVOCATIONAL INTERESTS: Travel, swimming, and gardening.*

FRANCOISE
    See SEIGNOBOSC, Francoise

*   *   *

FRANCOIS-PONCET, Andre   1887-1978
June 13, 1887—January 8, 1978; French diplomat, journalist, and author. Francois-Poncet served as French ambassador to Germany during Hitler's rise to power. Though he repeatedly warned his government of Germany's rearmament, his warning went unheeded. After the war, he held the post of French High Commissioner in West Germany until 1955 when the republic became independent and he was named French ambassador in Bonn. After his retirement from the diplomatic service, he wrote a regular column for the conservative Paris daily, *Le Figaro.* He was the author of books on German literature and politics and several volumes of memoirs. He died in Paris, France. Obituaries: *New York Times,* January 10, 1978; *Washington Post,* January 11, 1978; *AB Bookman's Weekly,* February 20, 1978.

*   *   *

FRANK, Murray   1908-1977
May 10, 1908—October 19, 1977; American journalist, educator, and author. Active in the Jewish community, Frank was director and announcer for "Voice of Israel," a weekly radio program. He was Washington correspondent for various newspapers published in Israel, Argentina, England, and New York City. Frank died in Silver Spring, Md. Obituaries: *Washington Post,* October 21, 1977. (See index for *CA* sketch)

*   *   *

FREED, Margaret De Haan   1917-
    (Margaret De Haan)
PERSONAL: Born December 16, 1917, in Santa Monica, Calif.; daughter of George (an engineer) and Marianne (a teacher; maiden name, Kater) De Haan; married Alvyn M. Freed (a psychologist, writer, and publisher), May 22, 1947; children: Lawrence Douglas, Jesse Mark. *Education:* Pasadena Junior College, A.A., 1936; University of California, Los Angeles, B.E., 1938; Columbia University, M.A., 1940; further graduate study at Bennington College and New York University. *Home:* 1129 Commons Dr., Sacramento, Calif. 95825.

CAREER: Horace Mann School, New York City, recreation director, 1938-40; Santa Barbara State College, Santa Barbara, Calif., instructor in modern dance, 1940-42; Barnard College, New York City, instructor in modern dance, 1943-46; Temple University, Philadelphia, Pa., assistant professor of modern dance, 1946-49; University of Texas, Austin, assistant professor of dramatic arts, 1952-55; high school teacher in San Juan, Calif., 1964-74; Jalmar Press, Sacramento, Calif., editor, 1974-77. Instructor, Columbia University, summers, 1943-48. *Member:* International Transactional Analysis Association, California Association of Health, Physical Education and Recreation (life member), Sacramento Mental Health Association, Crocker Art Gallery Association.

WRITINGS: (Under name Margaret De Haan; with Ruth Whitney Jones) *Modern Dance in Education,* Teachers College Press, 1948; *A Time to Teach, a Time to Dance,* Jalmar Press, 1976; (with husband, Alvyn Freed) *The New T.A. for Kids,* Jalmar Press, 1977.

SIDELIGHTS: Margaret Freed writes: "I have become very interested in the applications of Transactional Analysis to teaching youngsters to understand and express their own feelings and those of others—in order to achieve better relationships in school, home and community. In conducting workshops based on T.A. I find I use all of my teaching skills, acquired over many years of teaching at all grade levels."

*   *   *

FREEMAN, Barbara C(onstance)   1906-
PERSONAL: Born November 29, 1906, in Ealing, Middlesex, England; daughter of William (a writer) and Lucy C. (a teacher; maiden name, Rimmington) Freeman. *Education:* Attended School of Art, Kingston-upon-Thames, England. *Home:* Shirley, 62 Hook Rd., Surbiton, Surrey, England.

CAREER: Green & Abbott (wallpaperers), London, England, painter, 1926-27; free-lance illustrator of children's books, 1928-56; writer, 1956—.

WRITINGS—Self-illustrated children's books: *Two Thumb Thomas,* Faber, 1961; *Timi,* Faber, 1961; *A Book by Georgina,* Faber, 1962; *Broom Adelaide,* Faber, 1963, Atlantic Monthly Press, 1965; *The Name on the Glass,* Norton, 1964; *Lucinda,* Norton, 1965; *The Forgotten Theatre,* Faber, 1967; *Tobias,* Faber, 1967; *The Other Face,* Macmillan (London), 1975, Dutton, 1976; *A Haunting Air,* Macmillan (London), 1976, Dutton, 1977; *A Pocket of Silence,* Macmillan, 1977.

Illustrator: *The Summer Travellers,* Macmillan, 1978.

WORK IN PROGRESS: Illustrations for *Snow in the Maze,* for Macmillan.

SIDELIGHTS: Barbara Freeman writes: "I have lived for most of my life in a mid-Victorian house, with a large, rather wild garden, twelve miles from London. The house is part of several of my stories. The name, Jenny, beautifully written on one of the windows, led to *The Name on the Glass.* I've no idea who Jenny was. My grandfather and an aunt were painters. The past of ordinary people, leading day to day lives, fascinates me."

*   *   *

FREEMAN, Ira Maximilian   1905-
PERSONAL: Born August 15, 1905, in Chicago, Ill.; married Mae Blacker, 1935; children: one son, one daughter. *Education:* University of Chicago, B.S., 1925, M.S., 1926, Ph.D., 1928.

CAREER: Princeton University, Princeton, N.J., resident associate professor, 1943-45; Swarthmore College, Swarthmore, Pa., associate professor, 1945-47; Rutgers University, New Brunswick, N.J., associate professor, 1947-59, professor, 1959—; author of books on science. Fellow, Institute of International Education, Frankfort, Germany, 1928-29; fellow, von Humboldt Foundation, 1929-30; associate physicist, National Advisory Committee for Aeronautics, Langley Field, Va., 1930-31; visiting professor, Purdue University, 1942-43; member, National Defense Research Committee, 1944; science consultant, UNESCO, Paris, 1950-51; consultant on physics films to Coronet Instructional Films. *Member:* American Association for the Advancement of Science (fellow), American Association of Physics Teachers.

WRITINGS: Invitation to Experiment (photographs and drawings by the author and wife, Mae Freeman), Dutton, 1940; *Modern Introductory Physics,* McGraw-Hill, 1949;

Physics Made Simple, Cadillac Publishing, 1954, revised edition, Doubleday, 1965; *All about the Wonders of Chemistry* (illustrated by George Wilde), Random House, 1954; *All about the Atom* (illustrated by G. Wilde), Random House, 1955; *All about Electricity* (illustrated by Evelyn Urbanowich), Random House, 1957; *All about Sound and Ultrasonics* (illustrated by Irving Geis), Random House, 1961, reprinted as *Sound and Ultrasonics* (illustrated by George T. Resch), 1968; (with Arthur March) *The New World of Physics,* Random House, 1962; *All about Light and Radiation,* Random House, 1965, reprinted as *Light and Radiation* (illustrated by G. T. Resch), 1968; (with Alva Rae Patton) *The Science of Chemistry* (illustrated by Zenowij Onyshkewych), Random House, 1968; *Physics: Principles and Insights,* McGraw-Hill, 1968; *The Look-It-Up Book of Space* (illustrated by John Polgreen), Random House, 1969; (with Sean Morrison) *Your Body: Bones and Muscles,* Random House, 1970.

With wife, Mae Freeman: *Fun with Science,* Random House, 1943, revised edition, 1956; *Fun with Chemistry,* Random House, 1944, reprinted, 1967; *Fun with Figures,* Random House, 1946, reprinted, 1963; *Fun with Geometry,* Random House, 1946, reprinted, Kaye & Ward, 1969; *Fun with Astronomy,* Random House, 1953; *Fun with Your Camera,* Random House, 1955; *Your Wonderful World of Science* (illustrated by Rene Martin), Random House, 1957; *You Will Go to the Moon* (illustrated by Robert Patterson), Random House, 1959, revised edition, 1971; *The Sun, the Moon, and the Stars* (illustrated by R. Martin), Random House, 1959; *Fun with Scientific Experiments,* Random House, 1960; *The Story of the Atom* (illustrated by R. Martin), Random House, 1960; *The Story of Electricity* (illustrated by R. Martin), Random House, 1961; *The Story of Chemistry* (illustrated by Charles Goslin), Random House, 1962; *Fun with Photography* (edited by Gordon Catling), E. Ward, 1962; *Fun and Experiments with Light,* Random House, 1963, reprinted as *Fun with Light,* Kaye & Ward, 1968.

SIDELIGHTS: The *New York Times* said of Freeman's *All about the Atom:* "His explanations are, on the whole, lucid, easy to understand and his approach should help make young people feel at home in this strange new world."

A *Christian Science Monitor* reviewer said of *All about Sound and Ultrasonics:* "With the help of striking illustrations, this absorbing discussion of acoustics carries the 10-14 [years old] through all aspects of its subject. Here is an author who is not afraid to talk to his readers as intelligent young people. He has explained his subject simply and interestingly."

BIOGRAPHICAL/CRITICAL SOURCES: New York Times, November 20, 1955; *Christian Science Monitor,* November 16, 1961.*

*   *   *

FREEMAN, Mae (Blacker) 1907-

PERSONAL: Born in 1907; married Ira Maximilian Freeman, 1935; children: one son, one daughter.

CAREER: Author and photographer.

WRITINGS: Fun with Cooking, Random House, 1947; *Fun with Ballet,* Random House, 1952; *The Story of Albert Einstein, The Scientist Who Searched Out the Secrets of the Universe,* Random House, 1958; *Stars and Stripes: The Story of the American Flag* (illustrated by Lorence Bjorklund), Random House, 1964; *A Book of Real Science* (illus-

trated by John Moodie), Four Winds, 1966; *The Book of Magnets* (illustrated by Norman Bridwell), Four Winds, 1967; *Finding Out about the Past,* Random House, 1967; *When Air Moves,* McGraw, 1968; *Finding Out about Shapes* (illustrated by Bill Morrison), McGraw, 1969; *Do You Know about Water?* (illustrated by Ernest K. Barth), Random House, 1970; *Do You Know about Stars?* (illustrated by George Solonovich), Random House, 1970; *Gravity and the Astronauts* (illustrated by Beatrice Darwin), Crown, 1970; *Space Base* (illustrated by Raul Mina Mora), F. Watts, 1972; *The Wonderful Looking-Through Glass,* Scholastic Book Services, 1972; *Undersea Base* (illustrated by John Mardon), F. Watts, 1974.

With husband, Ira Maximilian Freeman: *Fun with Science,* Random House, 1943, revised edition, 1956; *Fun with Chemistry,* Random House, 1944, reprinted, 1967; *Fun with Figures,* Random House, 1946; *Fun with Geometry,* Random House, 1946, reprinted, Kaye & Ward, 1969; *Fun with Astronomy,* Random House, 1953; *Fun with Your Camera,* Random House, 1955; *Your Wonderful World of Science* (illustrated by Rene Martin), Random House, 1957; *You Will Go to the Moon* (illustrated by Robert Patterson), Random House, 1959, revised edition, 1971; *The Sun, the Moon, and the Stars* (illustrated by Martin), Random House, 1959; *Fun with Scientific Experiments,* Random House, 1960; *The Story of the Atom* (illustrated by Martin), Random House, 1960; *The Story of Electricity* (illustrated by Martin), Random House, 1961; *The Story of Chemistry* (illustrated by Charles Goslin), Random House, 1962; *Fun with Photography* (edited by Gordon Catling), E. Ward, 1962; *Fun and Experiments with Light,* Random House, 1963, reprinted as *Fun with Light,* Kaye & Ward, 1968.

SIDELIGHTS: Freeman lived for a while in Princeton, New Jersey, where she became acquainted with Albert Einstein. A result of that friendship was her biography for young readers, *The Story of Albert Einstein.* It was met with mixed reviews from critics. *Kirkus* called it "a well-realized portrait of a man who was a legend in his own lifetime. The story of Einstein is brought within the grasp of children through selected facets of his life. With today's emphasis on science, it is likely to interest youngsters and the tone is nontechnical." The *New York Times,* on the other hand, said: "Mrs. Freeman's biography of Einstein is an interesting and important book, but it is a study of the individual rather than what he created. No attempt is made to explain his theories, and although this is probably understandable when one considers their complexities, still there may be many young people who will feel dissatisfied at not being given any explanations."

Freeman is also a photographer, and took her own photographs for *Fun with Ballet,* using her 10-year old daughter for a model. *Saturday Review* said; "This is the very first book for girls who want to study the art of ballet dancing."

BIOGRAPHICAL/CRITICAL SOURCES: Saturday Review, November 15, 1952; *Kirkus,* March 1, 1958; *New York Times,* September 14, 1958.*

*   *   *

FRIED, Emanuel 1913-
(Edward Mann)

PERSONAL: Born March 1, 1913, in Brooklyn, N.Y.; son of Solomon (a small businessman) and Pauline (a small businesswoman; maiden name, Newman) Fried; married Rhoda Lurie (an artist), March 21, 1941; children: Lorrie E. Fried Rabin, Melinda. *Education:* Attended University of Iowa,

1932, and Canisius College, 1937; State University of New York at Buffalo, B.A., 1971, M.A., 1972, Ph.D., 1974. *Politics:* "Left." *Religion:* Jewish. *Home:* 1064 Amherst St., Buffalo, N.Y. 14216. *Agent:* Bertha Klausner International Literary Agency, Inc., 71 Park Ave., New York, N.Y. 10016. *Office:* Department of English, State University of New York College at Buffalo, 1300 Elmwood Ave., Buffalo, N.Y. 14222.

CAREER: Playwright. Professional actor (under stage name Edward Mann) in New York, N.Y., 1933-39; Buffalo Contemporary Theatre, Buffalo, N.Y., director, 1939-40; Curtiss-Wright Airplane Corp., Buffalo, template maker, 1940-41; United Electrical, Radio, and Machine Workers, Buffalo, organizer, 1941-56; International Association of Machinists, Buffalo, organizer, 1956; Canada Life Assurance Co., Buffalo, life insurance broker, 1957-72; State University of New York College at Buffalo, assistant professor of English, 1973—. Served as delegate to Buffalo American Federation of Labor-Congress of Industrial Organizations (AFL-CIO) central labor council. *Military service:* U.S. Army, Infantry, 1944-46; became first lieutenant.

MEMBER: Dramatists Guild, Authors League of America, United University Professions, American Federation of Labor-Congress of Industrial Organizations (member of Buffalo council). *Awards, honors:* New American playwrights award from Catawba College, 1961, for "The Dodo Bird," "Peddler," "Rose," and "Brother Gorski."

WRITINGS: The Dodo Bird (one-act play; first produced in New York City at Martinique Theatre, December 8, 1967), Labor Arts Books, 1974; *Drop Hammer* (play), West End Press, 1977.

Unpublished plays: "Mark of Success" (three-act), first produced in Salisbury, N.C., at Catawba College, March, 1963; "Peddler" (one-act), first produced in New York City at Martinique Theatre, December 8, 1967; "Rose" (three-act), first produced in New York City at Provincetown Theatre, October 28, 1969; "Brother Gorski" (two-act), first produced in New York City at Astor Palace Theatre, March 15, 1973; "The Second Beginning" (three-act), first produced in Kansas City, Mo., at Foolkiller Theatre, January 19, 1978.

Author of film script for "The Dodo Bird." Contributor of stories and articles to magazines, including *Cultural Reporter* and *Eccentric,* and newspapers.

WORK IN PROGRESS: Lasting Out, a novel; "Cocoon," a three-act play.

SIDELIGHTS: Fried remarks: "Since there are plenty of middle-class writers expressing that point of view, I am trying my best to bring union and working class life into the arts, to be a voice for working people."

* * *

FRIED, Richard M(ayer) 1941-

PERSONAL: Born April 14, 1941, in Milwaukee, Wis.; son of Richard G. and Betty (Mayer) Fried; married Barbara Brachman (a guidance counselor), August 1, 1964; children: Richard B., Gail Lynne. *Education:* Amherst College, B.A. (magna cum laude), 1963; Columbia University, M.A., 1965, Ph.D., 1972. *Residence:* Glen Ellyn, Ill. *Office:* Department of History, University of Illinois at Chicago Circle, Chicago, Ill. 60680.

CAREER: Bowling Green State University, Bowling Green, Ohio, instructor in history, 1967-70; Indiana University of Pennsylvania, Indiana, assistant professor of history,

1970-71; Fairmont State College, Fairmont, W. Va., assistant professor of history, 1971-72; University of Illinois at Chicago Circle, Chicago, assistant professor, 1972-77, associate professor of history, 1977—. Member of Glendale Heights Plan Commission, 1975-77, and Zoning Board of Appeals, 1976-77. *Member:* American Historical Association, Organization of American Historians, State Historical Society of Wisconsin, Phi Beta Kappa.

WRITINGS: (Contributor) Robert Griffith and Athan Theoharis, editors, *The Specter: Original Essays on the Cold War and the Origins of McCarthyism,* New York Viewpoints, 1974; *Men Against McCarthy,* Columbia University Press, 1976. Contributor to *Encyclopaedia of Southern History* and to history journals.

WORK IN PROGRESS: A monograph on the 1960 Presidential election; research on anti-communism in the 1940's.

SIDELIGHTS: Fried comments: "The core of my research has been in archives at the state and national level. I find it an intriguing challenge to search for the occasional crucial document which rewards the long hours of sifting through the routine correspondence of national and regional political figures. Such research took me to some forty libraries in twenty-seven states. One sees a lot of the country that way—sometimes, admittedly, from a library alcove.

"I teach recent political history, including courses on such topics as the Great Depression, the Origins of the Cold War, and American since 1945."

* * *

FRIEDMAN, Sanford 1928-

PERSONAL: Born June 11, 1928, in New York, N.Y.; son of Leonard and Madeline (Uris) Friedman. *Education:* Carnegie Institute of Technology (now Carnegie-Mellon University), B.F.A., 1949. *Residence:* New York, N.Y. *Agent:* Georges Borchardt, Inc., 145 East 52nd St., New York, N.Y. 10022.

CAREER: University Playhouse, Cape Cod, Mass., playwright-in-residence, 1947-48; clerk in London, England, 1949-50; Carnegie Hall Playhouse, New York City, producer, 1954-58; writer, 1958-75; Juilliard School, New York City, part-time instructor in drama, 1975—. *Military service:* U.S. Army, Military Police, 1951-53; served in Korea; received Bronze Star. *Member:* International P.E.N. (American Center). *Awards, honors:* O. Henry Award from Society of Arts & Sciences, 1965, for "Ocean."

WRITINGS: Totempole (novel), Dutton, 1965; *A Haunted Woman* (novel), Dutton, 1968; *Still Life* (novel), Dutton, 1975.

Plays: "Dawn From an Unknown Ocean," first produced in Mashpee, Mass., at University Theatre, August, 1947. Also author of plays, as yet neither published nor produced, including "Roderick Sorman" (two-act), 1948, "Invasion" (three scenes), 1949, "Bobby Bullard" (three-act), 1952, "Assassination" (three-act), 1953, "Horoscope" (three-act), 1957, and "The Abolitionist" (five scenes), 1959.

Contributor to magazines, including *Partisan Review* and *New World Writing.*

WORK IN PROGRESS: Rip Van Winkle, a novel.

* * *

FRISCH, Paul Z. 1926(?)-1977

1926(?)—September 18, 1977; American educator, psychotherapist, and author. Frisch was a founder and director of the Institute for Re-Creative Development, Park East Psychological Associates, and Growth Skills, Inc. He was a professor and chairman of the psychology department at Adelphi University. With his wife, Ann, he wrote *Discovering Your Hidden Self* and *Freedom in Marriage*. He died in Long Island, N.Y. Obituaries: *New York Times*, September 22, 1977.

* * *

FROHOCK, W(ilbur) M(errill) 1908-

PERSONAL: Born June 20, 1908, in South Thomaston, Me.; son of Horatio Wilbur (a physician) and Sarah (Merrill) Frohock; married Natalie Barrington (an editor), August 16, 1938; children: Natalie (Mrs. David W. Tarbet), Sarah (Mrs. W. R. C. Phelps). *Education:* Brown University, Ph.B., 1930, A.M., 1931, Ph.D., 1935. *Religion:* Roman Catholic. *Home:* 10 Shady Hill Sq., Cambridge, Mass. 02138.

CAREER: Brown University, Providence, R.I., instructor in French, 1935-37; Columbia University, New York, N.Y., instructor, 1937-42, assistant professor, 1945-48, associate professor of French, 1948-53; Wesleyan University, Middletown, Conn., professor of French, 1953-56; Harvard University, Cambridge, Mass., professor of French, 1956-76. Bacon Exchange Professor, University of Lille, 1959; visiting professor, University of Munich, 1963; visiting lecturer, University of Heidelberg, 1970. *Military service:* U.S. Naval Reserve, active duty, 1943-45; became lieutenant.

WRITINGS: The Novel of Violence in America, Southern Methodist University Press, 1950, 5th edition, 1971; *Andre Malraux and the Tragic Imagination*, Stanford University Press, 1952; *Strangers to This Ground*, Southern Methodist University Press, 1961; *Rimbaud's Poetic Practice*, Harvard University Press, 1963; *Style and Temper: Studies in French Fiction, 1925-1960*, Harvard University Press, 1967; (editor, and author of introduction) *Image and Theme: Studies in Modern French Fiction*, Harvard University Press, 1969; *Andre Malraux*, Columbia University Press, 1974.

WORK IN PROGRESS: Survivals and revivals of European literary forms and modes in American writing.

SIDELIGHTS: "In general Professor Frohock stands out as a critical nominalist, and one who refuses any simple equation between form and style," the *Times Literary Supplement* critic writes, in discussing *Style and Temper: Studies in French Fiction*. Germaine Bree says: "Meditative, engagingly modest and unpedantic, Mr. Frohock's is the work of a man immensely sensitive to literary values, conversant with the subtle but real distinctions that are involved in the craft of writing and able to show the bearing they have on the complex statements that the writer is making."

BIOGRAPHICAL/CRITICAL SOURCES: Times Literary Supplement, March 2, 1967; *Wisconsin Studies in Contemporary Literature*, autumn, 1967; *Comparative Literature*, summer, 1969.

* * *

FROMM, Erich 1900-

PERSONAL: Born March 23, 1900, in Frankfurt, Germany; came to United States in 1934; naturalized citizen, 1940; son of Naphtali (a wine merchant) and Rosa (Krause) Fromm; married Frieda Reichmann, June 16, 1926 (divorced); married Henny Gurland, July 24, 1944 (died, 1952); married Annis Freeman, December 18, 1953. *Education:* University of Heidelberg, Ph.D., 1922; attended University of Munich, 1923-24, Institute of the German Psychoanalytic Society,

1928-31, Psychoanalytic Institute (Berlin), and University of Frankfurt. *Home:* 180 Riverside Dr., New York, N.Y. 10024; and, Locarno, Switzerland.

CAREER: Psychoanalyst, philosopher, and writer, 1925—; Psychoanalytic Institute and University of Frankfurt, Frankfurt, Germany, lecturer in social psychology at Institute for Social Research, 1929-32; Columbia University, International Institute for Social Research, New York City, lecturer, 1934-39, guest lecturer, 1940-41; Bennington College, Bennington, Vt., member of faculty, 1941-50; National Autonomous University of Mexico, Medical School, professor of psychoanalysis, 1951—, head of department, 1955—; New York University, New York City, adjutant professor of psychology, 1962—; Mexican Institute for Psychoanalysis, Mexico City, Mexico, director, 1962—. Lecturer, American Institute for Psychoanalysis, 1941-42, New School for Social Research, 1946-56; member of faculty, William Alanson White Institute for Psychiatry, Psychoanalysis and Psychology, 1945—, chairman of faculty, 1947—; Terry Lecturer, Yale University, 1949-50; professor, Michigan State University, 1957-61. Diplomate in clinical psychology, American Psychological Association.

MEMBER: Mexican National Academy of Medicine, New York Academy of Science (fellow), Washington Psychoanalytic Society. *Awards, honors:* Fellow at Washington School of Psychiatry, 1940, and William Alanson White Institute for Psychiatry, Psychoanalysis and Psychology, 1945.

WRITINGS: Die Entwicklung des Christusdogmas (title means "The Development of the Dogma of Christ"), Internationaler Psychoanalytischer Verlag (Vienna), 1931; *Escape from Freedom*, Farrar & Rinehart, 1941, Avon, 1963 (published in England as *The Fear of Freedom*, Kegan Paul, Trench, Trubner & Co., 1942); *Man for Himself: An Inquiry into the Psychology of Ethics*, Rinehart, 1947.

Psychoanalysis and Religion, Yale University Press, 1950; *The Forgotten Language: An Introduction to the Understanding of Dreams, Fairy Tales, and Myths*, Rinehart, 1951; *The Sane Society*, Rinehart, 1955; *The Art of Loving*, Harper, 1956; *Sigmund Freud's Mission: An Analysis of His Personality and Influence*, Harper, 1959.

(Editor with Daisetz T. Suzuki and Richard De Martino) *Zen Buddhism and Psychoanalysis*, Harper, 1960; *Let Man Prevail: A Socialist Manifesto and Program* (booklet), Lambert Schneider (Heidelberg), 1961; (editor with Hans Herzfeld) *Der Friede: Idee und Verwirklichung* (title means "The Search for Peace"), Lambert Schneider, 1961; *May Man Prevail? An Enquiry into the Facts and Fictions of Foreign Policy*, Doubleday, 1961; (editor) *Marx's Concept of Man*, Ungar, 1961; *Is World Peace Still Possible?: An Enquiry into the Facts and Fictions of Foreign Policy*, [New York], c. 1962; *Beyond the Chains of Illusion: My Encounter with Marx and Freud*, Simon & Schuster, 1962; *War Within Man: A Psychological Enquiry into the Roots of Destructiveness*, American Friends Service Committee, 1963; *The Dogma of Christ and Other Essays on Religion, Psychology, and Culture*, Holt, 1963; *The Heart of Man: Its Genius for Good and Evil*, Harper, 1964; (editor) *Socialist Humanism: An International Symposium*, Doubleday, 1965; *You Shall Be as Gods: A Radical Interpretation of the Old Testament and Its Tradition*, Holt, 1966; (editor with Ramon Xirau) *The Nature of Man*, Macmillan, 1968; *The Revolution of Hope: Toward a Humanized Technology*, Harper, 1968.

(With Michael Maccoby) *Social Character in a Mexican Village: A Socio-Psychoanalytic Study*, Prentice-Hall, 1970;

The Crisis of Psychoanalysis (essays), J. Cape, 1970, Fawcett, 1971; *The Anatomy of Human Destructiveness,* Holt, 1973; (with Hans Juergen Schultz) *Im Namen des Lebens* (booklet; title means "In Name of Life"), Deutsche Verlagsanstalt, 1974; *To Have or To Be?,* Harper, 1976.

Contributor; Ruth N. Anshen, *Moral Principles of Action: Man's Ethical Imperative,* Harper, 1952; James R. Newman, editor, *What Is Science?,* Simon & Schuster, 1955; Clark E. Moustakas, editor, *The Self: Explorations in Personal Growth,* Harper, 1956; Ruth N. Ashen, editor, *Language: An Enquiry into Its Meaning and Function,* Harper, 1957; William Phillips, editor, *Art and Psychoanalysis,* Criterion, 1957; Abraham H. Maslow, editor, *New Knowledge in Human Values,* Harper, 1959; Ruth N. Anshen, editor, *Family: Its Function and Destiny,* revised edition, Harper, 1959; Michael Harrington and Paul Jacobs, editors, *Labor in a Free Society,* University of California Press, 1959; Huston Smith, editor, *Search for America,* Prentice-Hall, 1959; Richard A. Condon and Burton O. Kurth, editors, *Writing from Experience,* Harper, 1960; Hiram Collins Haydn and Betsy Saunders, editors, *The American Scholar Reader,* Atheneum, 1960; Donald G. Brennan, editor, *Arms Control, Disarmament, and National Security,* Braziller, 1961; Irving Louis Horowitz, editor, *The New Sociology: Essays in Social Science and Social Theory in Honor of C. Wright Mills,* Oxford University Press, 1964; Steven E. Deutsch and John Howard, editors, *Where It's At: Radical Perspective in Sociology,* Harper, 1969; *Summerhill: For and Against,* Hart Publishing, 1970.

WORK IN PROGRESS: A sequel to *To Have or To Be?;* a book on "godless religion," a study of religious experience in which the concept of god is "unnecessary and undesirable"; a book on self-analysis.

SIDELIGHTS: Critics, disciples, and objective analysts alike have been hard pressed to define Erich Fromm's role in the world of letters. As John Dollard pointed out in the *New York Herald Tribune,* Fromm is "at once sociologist, philosopher, historian, psychoanalyst, economist, and anthropologist—and, one is tempted to add, lover of human life, poet, and prophet." Fromm himself indicated the vast scope of his concerns in the foreword to his most famous book, *Escape from Freedom,* when he wrote simply that "this book is part of a broad study concerning the character structure of modern man and the problems of the interaction between psychological and sociological factors which I have been working on for several years."

Perhaps the best description of Erich Fromm would be the term "social humanist," suggested by the title of a collection of essays he edited in 1965 entitled *Socialist Humanism.* He has strived throughout his career toward an understanding of human existence based upon the breaking down of barriers—between individuals as well as between schools of thought. As his theories have developed over decades, he has incorporated knowledge and information culled from such diverse fields as Marxist socialism and Freudian psychology.

Of course, Fromm narrows his vision in individual books, and his long list of publications includes studies in a great variety of specific fields. For instance, *May Man Prevail? An Enquiry into the Facts and Fictions of Foreign Policy* is an analysis of the cold war between the United States and the Soviet Union, while *The Forgotten Language: An Introduction to the Understanding of Dreams, Fairy Tales, and Myths* was an early examination of the role fantasy and myth in the interplay between social control and individual imagi-

native freedom. In 1956 he published *The Art of Loving,* in which he maintained that "love is the only sane and satisfactory answer to the problem of human existence" and examined the many varieties and forms of the emotion.

Most of Erich Fromm's work, however, has been an application of psychoanalysis, sociology, philosophy as well as religion to the peculiar problems of man in modern industrialized society. In *Escape from Freedom* he postulated that "modern man, freed from the bonds of pre-individualistic society, which simultaneously gave him security and limited him, has not gained freedom in the positive sense of the realization of his individual self; that is, the expression of his intellectual, emotional and sensuous potentialities. Freedom, though it has brought him independence and rationality, has made him isolated and, thereby, anxious and powerless." This problem, the individual's tenuous relationship to institutions and society, became, in fact, the core of such later Fromm works as *Man for Himself: An Enquiry into the Psychology of Ethics and The Sane Society.*

Erich Fromm's most recent book is *To Have or To Be?,* which presents, as Paul Roazen pointed out in *Nation,* "the viewpoint and challenge of 'radical humanistic psychoanalysis.'" The volume has been seen as the culmination of Fromm's work to date and maintains, according to a publisher's note, "that two modes of existence are struggling for the spirit of humankind; the *having* mode, which concentrates on material possession, acquisitiveness, power, and aggression and is the basis of such universal evils as greed, envy, and violence; and the *being* mode, which is based in love, in the pleasure of sharing, and in meaningful and productive rather than wasteful activity. Dr. Fromm sees the *having* mode bringing the world to the brink of psychological and ecological disaster, and he outlines a program for socio-economic change [to] turn the world away from its catastrophic course."

BIOGRAPHICAL/CRITICAL SOURCES: New York Herald Tribune, September 4, 1955; *Saturday Review,* April 11, 1959, December 14, 1968; J. H. Schaar, *Escape from Authority: The Perspectives of Erich Fromm,* Basic Books, 1961; Ashley Montague, editor, *Culture and the Evolution of Man,* Oxford University Press, 1962; G. B. Hammond, *Man in Estrangement,* Vanderbilt University Press, 1965; J. S. Glen, *Erich Fromm: A Protestant Critique,* Westminster, 1966; Richard I. Evans, *Dialogue with Erich Fromm,* Harper, 1966; *Commonweal,* March 14, 1969, March 15, 1974, May 19, 1976; Rubin Gotesky, *Personality: The Need for Liberty and Rights,* Libra, 1967; Otto Butz, editor, *To Make a Difference,* Harper, 1967; *Book World,* November 10, 1968; *New Republic,* December 7, 1968; *Nation,* September 1, 1969; *Times Literary Supplement,* December 7, 1969, April 28, 1972, December 27, 1974; Bernard Landis and Edward S. Tauber, editors, *In the Name of Life: Essays in Honor of Erich Fromm,* Holt, 1971; Don Hausdorff, *Erich Fromm,* Twayne, 1972; *Publishers Weekly,* September 13, 1976.*

* * *

FRUGONI, Cesare 1881-1978

1881—January 6, 1978; Italian physician and author. Frugoni's patients included Marconi, the inventor of wireless telegraphy, Mussolini, the Fascist dictator, and Togliatti, a Communist Party leader. He taught in Florence, Padua, and Rome, and wrote books on diagnostics and pathology. He died in Rome, Italy. Obituaries: *New York Times,* January 10, 1978.

FRYE, William R(uggles) 1918-

PERSONAL: Born December 15, 1918, in Detroit, Mich.; son of William Caleb and Anna Mildred (Ruggles) Frye; married Joan Bogert Ripperger, June 6, 1953; children: John Randall, Nancy Bogert. *Education:* Harvard University, B.A. (cum laude), 1940. *Religion:* Christian Scientist. *Home:* 2 Tudor City Pl., New York, N.Y. 10017. *Office:* Frye Syndicate and News Service, Room 360, United Nations, New York, N.Y. 10017.

CAREER: Christian Science Monitor, Boston, Mass., local reporter, 1941-42, copy reader and assistant to foreign editor, 1946-50, United Nations correspondent and chief of United Nations News Bureau, 1950-63; Frye Syndicate, New York City, director, editor, and self-employed correspondent, covering the United Nations and diplomatic events overseas, 1963—. Lecturer on world affairs, 1948—. Radio and television news analyst for Canadian Broadcasting Corp. *Military service:* U.S. Army, on staff of *Stars and Stripes,* 1941-46; served in European theater.

MEMBER: Council on Foreign Relations, United Nations Correspondents Association. *Awards, honors:* Awards from Overseas Press Club, 1955, for world affairs reporting, and from Deadline Club of New York, 1963, for United Nations coverage.

WRITINGS: A United Nations Peace Force, Oceana, 1957; (contributor) D. G. Brennan, editor, *Arms Control, Disarmament, and National Security,* Braziller, 1961; *In Whitest Africa,* Prentice-Hall, 1968. Contributor to magazines and newspapers. Author of weekly column, "World in Focus," 1957—, "Diplomatic Pouch," an interpretive news service, 1965—, and series of travel articles, "Footloose with Frye," all self-syndicated.

SIDELIGHTS: Frye writes: "I take at least two major overseas trips a year, and some shorter ones, seeking out newsworthy events. Travel is also a source of fresh ideas and perspective. Too much journalism is superficial; I believe there is a wide audience for in-depth, three-dimensional copy if it is well written." *Avocational interests:* Sailing a twenty-three-foot sloop, contract bridge, Bible study, classical music, educational television, golf, good food.

* * *

FUCHS, Lucy 1935-

PERSONAL: Born April 13, 1935, in Ohio; daughter of Frank X. (a machinist) and Mary (Honigford) Weber; married Frank J. Fuchs (a teacher), August 14, 1971. *Education:* University of Dayton, B.S., 1961; Ohio State University, M.A., 1967; Florida State University, M.S., 1973. *Politics:* Democrat. *Religion:* Roman Catholic. *Home and office:* 505 South Oakwood Ave., Brandon, Fla. 33511.

CAREER: High school French teacher in Cincinnati, Ohio, 1966-69; Florida State University, Tallahassee, counselor, 1969-71; social worker in Tampa, Fla., 1971-73; Hillsborough County Elementary School, Hillsborough, Fla., teacher, 1974—. Instructor in sociology and French at Hillsborough Community College, 1972—. *Member:* International Reading Association.

WRITINGS: Wild Winds of Mayaland (novel), Bouregy, 1978. Contributor to education and religious periodicals and children's magazines, including *Highlights for Children, Primary Treasure,* and *Our Little Friend.*

WORK IN PROGRESS: A novel; a nonfiction book.

SIDELIGHTS: Lucy Fuchs comments: "I write because I am not happy when I am not writing. I have learned very much from other writers, both through personal conversations and from publications of writers, such as the magazines for writers. I am interested in just about everything, especially people as they relate to each other."

AVOCATIONAL INTERESTS: Travel, religion.

* * *

FUENTES, Martha Ayers 1923-
(Scat Lorimer)

PERSONAL: Born December 21, 1923, in Ashland, Ala.; daughter of William Henry (a construction foreman) and Elizabeth (a dressmaker and designer; maiden name, Dye) Ayers; married Manuel Solomon Fuentes (a jewelry manufacturer), April 11, 1943. *Education:* University of South Florida, B.A., 1969. *Religion:* Roman Catholic. *Home:* 11505 North Ola Ave., Tampa, Fla. 33612.

CAREER: Jewelry sales clerk in a department store in Tampa, Fla., 1940-43; Western Union, Tampa, Fla., bookkeeper, 1943-48; writer, 1953—. Teacher at writers' workshops. Member of Tampa Community Theatre. *Member:* Authors Guild, Authors League of America, Dramatists Guild, Society of Children's Book Writers, Southeastern Writers Association, University of South Florida Alumni Club, Blue Army, Society of the Little Flower, Infant Jesus of Prague Society. *Awards, honors:* George Sergel drama award from University of Chicago, 1969-70, for "Go Stare at the Moon."

WRITINGS: Two Characters in Search of an Agreement (one-act play), Contemporary Drama, 1970.

Unpublished plays: "Mama Don't Make Me Go to College" (one-act), first produced in Tampa, Fla. at University of South Florida, 1963; (under pseudonym Scat Lorimer) "Go Stare at the Moon" (three-act), first produced in Chicago, Ill. at University of Chicago, 1969.

Author of "The Rebel," a script for the television series "Faith for Today." Contributor of articles and stories (some for young people) to national magazines.

WORK IN PROGRESS: "Mr. Peek's Mines," a three-act play.

SIDELIGHTS: Martha Fuentes comments: "I would like to write one good play in my lifetime. My admiration for Tennessee Williams has motivated me to write about the South. I write because it is the only thing I enjoy doing: fulfillment is found in writing most of all.

"I have traveled throughout Europe, Asia, and Mexico, visiting major shrines, and religious and historical places of interest, writing and taking photographs."

AVOCATIONAL INTERESTS: Reading, France.

* * *

FUHRMAN, Lee 1903(?)-1977

1903(?)—December 8, 1977; American journalist and playwright. Fuhrman was city editor of the *Atlanta Constitution.* His comedy about the newspaper business, "The Local Angle," was produced by the Atlanta Civic Theater in 1952. Obituaries: *New York Times,* December 10, 1977.

* * *

FUHRMANN, Joseph T(heodore) 1940-

PERSONAL: Born November 29, 1940, in Gadsden, Ala.; son of Paul Traugott (a professor and writer) and Esther (a musician) Fuhrmann; married Mary C. Cook (a weaver and painter), March 1, 1969; children: Maria Kristin, Christopher Joseph. *Education:* Emory University, B.A., 1962; Indiana University, M.A., 1964, Ph.D., 1968. *Politics:* "Burkean conservative, no party attachment." *Religion:* Roman Catholic. *Home address:* Route 8, Box 178, Greeneville, Tenn. 37743. *Office:* Box 40, Tusculum College, Greeneville, Tenn. 37743.

CAREER: University of the South, Sewanee, Tenn., instructor in history, 1967-69; University of Texas, Arlington, assistant professor of history, 1969-70; Tusculum College, Greeneville, Tenn., associate professor of history, 1970—, scholar in residence, 1977—, director of Division of Historical, Philosophical, and Religious Studies, 1971-74. *Member:* American Historical Association, American Association for the Advancement of Slavic Studies, Southern Conference on Slavic Studies, Southeastern Medievalist Association (member of executive council, 1974—), *Awards, honors:* Grant from Inter-University Committee on Travel Grants, 1965-66, for University of Moscow.

WRITINGS: (Contributor) Sidney Monas, editor, *Essays on Russian Intellectual History,* University of Texas Press, 1971; *The Origins of Capitalism in Russia: Industry and Progress during the Sixteenth and Seventeenth Centuries,* Quadrangle, 1972; (author of introduction) Paul Milyukov, *The Rise of Ideology in Russia,* Academic International, 1974; *Tsar Alexis: His Reign and His Russia,* Academic International, 1978; *A History of Tusculum College,* Academic International, in press. Contributor to *The Modern Encyclopedia of Russian and Soviet History.* Contributor of articles and reviews to scholarly journals in the United States and abroad.

WORK IN PROGRESS: History of Tusculum College, 1794-1978.

AVOCATIONAL INTERESTS: Music (classical, folk, rock), old houses and antiques, vegetable gardening, dogs, hikes, travel, gourmet cooking.

*   *   *

FULLER, Paul E(ugene)   1932-

PERSONAL: Born February 11, 1932, in Chattanooga, Tenn.; son of Floyd L. (a laborer) and Mae (McKissick) Fuller; married Peggy Kistler, April 19, 1953; children: Paul Eugene, Leasa Ann. *Education:* University of Chattanooga, A.B., 1960; University of Kentucky, Ph.D., 1971. *Politics:* Democrat. *Religion:* Presbyterian. *Home:* 664 Elsmere Park, Lexington, Ky. 40508. *Office:* Department of History, Transylvania University, Lexington, Ky. 40508.

CAREER: Transylvania University, Lexington, Ky., assistant professor of history, 1964-73; Wesleyan College, Macon, Ga., professor of history and chairman of department, 1973-77; Transylvania University, professor of history, 1977—. *Military service:* U.S. Army, 1952-54; became sergeant. *Member:* Organization of American Historians, Southern Historical Association, Pi Gamma Mu, Phi Alpha Theta. *Awards, honors:* Woodrow Wilson fellowship, 1960-61.

WRITINGS: Laura Clay and the Woman's Rights Movement, University Press of Kentucky, 1975. Contributor to *Adena.*

WORK IN PROGRESS: The W.C.T.U. in the South (tentative title), focusing on the organization's educational and civic activities.

SIDELIGHTS: Fuller writes: "A subject I consider most vital is the teaching of the traditional liberal arts curriculum in our high schools and colleges. Our abandonment of the humanities and basic sciences for vocationalism and fads has left our educational system—from the public schools through the colleges—in a muddle."

*   *   *

FURGURSON, Ernest B(aker, Jr.)   1929-
(Pat Furgurson)

PERSONAL: Born August 29, 1929, in Danville, Va.; son of Ernest Baker and Passie Durham (Ferguson) Furgurson; married Mary Louise Stallings, April 6, 1954 (divorced); married Cassie Woodward Thompson, April 21, 1973; children: Ernest Baker III, Elisabeth Glynn. *Education:* Averett College, student, 1948-50; Columbia University, A.B., 1952, M.S., 1953; Georgetown University, further graduate study, 1961. *Office: Baltimore Sun,* 1214 National Press Building, Washington, D.C. 20045.

CAREER: Danville Commercial Appeal, Danville, Va., reporter, 1948-50; Associated Press, New York City, copy boy, 1950-51; *Roanoke World-News,* Roanoke, Va., reporter, 1952; *Richmond News Leader,* Richmond, Va., reporter, 1955-56; *Baltimore Sun,* Baltimore, Md., reporter and Washington correspondent, 1956-61, chief of Moscow Bureau, 1961-64, White House correspondent, 1964-68, Vietnam correspondent and chief of Saigon Bureau, 1965-66, national political correspondent, 1966-68, author of national affairs column, 1969—, chief of Washington Bureau, 1975—. Sports editor for WDVA-Radio, 1949-50. Has covered U.S. Presidential campaigns since 1960. *Military service:* U.S. Marine Corps, 1953-55; became first lieutenant. *Member:* National Press Club, Overseas Writers Club.

WRITINGS: Westmoreland: The Inevitable General, Little, Brown, 1968. Author of "By No Means Neutral," a column for Los Angeles Times Syndicate, 1970—. Contributor to popular magazines, sometimes under name Pat Furgurson. Contributing editor of *Washingtonian,* 1973—.

AVOCATIONAL INTERESTS: Birds, hiking, state and local history, photography.

*   *   *

FURGURSON, Pat
See FURGURSON, Ernest B(aker, Jr.)

*   *   *

FURTH, George   1932-

PERSONAL: Born December 14, 1932, in Chicago, Ill.; son of George R. and Evelyn (Tuerk) Schweinfurth. *Education:* Northwestern University, B.S., 1954; Columbia University, M.F.A., 1956. *Home:* 3030 Durand Dr., Hollywood, Calif. 90068. *Agent:* Arnold Steifel, 9255 Sunset, Los Angeles, Calif. 90028.

CAREER: Actor in more than thirty feature films, including "Butch Cassidy and the Sundance Kid," "Myra Breckenridge," "How to Save Your Marriage," "Airport 77," and "Shampoo," and in stage shows and television series, including "The Dumplings," "Tammy," "Broadside," and "Mary Hartman, Mary Hartman." Playwright. *Awards, honors:* Has received awards, including the Tony, Drama Critics, Outer Circle, and Evening Standard awards.

WRITINGS—Plays: "Company" (two-act), first produced on Broadway at Alvin Theatre, April 26, 1970; *Twigs* (four-act; first produced on Broadway at Broadhurst Theatre, November, 1971), French, 1977; "The Act" (two-act), first produced on Broadway at Majestic Theatre, October, 1977.

WORK IN PROGRESS: "Off the Record," a record album for Motown.

* * *

GABO, Naum 1890-1977

August 5, 1890—1977; Russian-born sculptor and writer of *The Realist Manifesto*. He founded constructivism, a twentieth-century art movement which rejected sculpture as mass and espoused the idea of space as structure. Gabo's work, fragile and fluid, laid the groundwork for kinetic sculpture. He died in Waterbury, Conn. Obituaries: *Time,* August 5, 1977. (See index for *CA* sketch)

* * *

GABRIELSON, Ira N(oel) 1889-1977

September 27, 1889—September 7, 1977; American writer and internationally recognized authority on conservation. Gabrielson served as the first director of the U.S. Fish and Wildlife Service and helped organize several national conservation associations. His study of birds and wildlife took him on expeditions to the South Pole, the Andes, the Amazon, the Mediterranean, Europe, and Alaska. He died in Washington, D.C. Obituaries: *Washington Post,* September 9, 1977. (See index for *CA* sketch)

* * *

GAEDDERT, Lou Ann (Bigge) 1931-

PERSONAL: Born June 20, 1931, in Garden City, Kan.; married Orlan M. Gaeddert; children: Andrew, Martha. *Education:* Attended Phillips University; University of Washington, B.A., 1952; attended Radcliffe College. *Politics:* Republican. *Religion:* Protestant. *Residence:* Jackson Heights, N.Y. *Agent:* Curtis Brown, Ltd., 575 Madison Ave., New York, N.Y. 10022.

CAREER: Author. *West Seattle Herald,* Seattle, Wash., writer and editor, 1952-54; worked in publicity departments of T. Y. Crowell, 1954-55, and Doubleday, 1956-61.

WRITINGS: *Noisy Nancy Norris* (illustrated by Gioia Fiammenghi), Doubleday, 1965; *The Split-Level Cookbook: Family Meals to Cook Once and Serve Twice,* Crowell, 1967; *Too Many Girls* (illustrated by Marylin Hafner), Coward, McCann, 1972; *Noisy Nancy and Nick* (illustrated by Fiammenghi), Doubleday, 1970; *All-in-All: A Biography of George Eliot,* Dutton, 1976; *Gustav the Gourmet Giant* (illustrated by Steven Kellogg), Dial, 1976; *Your Night to Make Dinner* (illustrated by Ellen Weiss), Watts, 1977.

SIDELIGHTS: Gaeddert's first book, *Noisy Nancy Norris,* grew out of her concern and experience with raising children in an apartment building. In 1967, the Communications Laboratory of Bank Street College of Education produced a motion picture which was based on *Noisy Nancy Norris* and was narrated by Shirley MacLaine.

BIOGRAPHICAL/CRITICAL SOURCES: Lee Bennett Hopkins, *Books Are by People,* Citation, 1969.

* * *

GAINZA PAZ, Alberto 1899-1977

March 16, 1899—December 26, 1977; Argentine journalist. Gainza Paz was the editor and publisher of the internationally known Argentine newspaper, *La Prensa.* During the 1940's and 1950's he was forced into exile in Uruguay and the United States because of his criticism of the Peron regime. Peron seized *La Prensa* and turned it over to the labor unions which supported him, but Gainza Paz regained control over the paper after the 1956 military coup which ousted Peron. He died in Buenos Aires, Argentina. Obituaries: *New York Times,* December 27, 1977; *Washington Post,* December 27, 1977.

* * *

GALBRAITH, Vivian Hunter 1889-1976

PERSONAL: Born December 15, 1889, in England; son of David and Eliza Davidson (McIntosh) Galbraith; married Georgina Rosalie Cole Baker, 1921; children: one son, two daughters. *Education:* Educated at Manchester University and Balliol College, Oxford. *Home:* 20A Bradmore Rd., Oxford OX2 6QP, England.

CAREER: Manchester University, Manchester, England, assistant lecturer, 1920-21; assistant keeper of the public records in London, 1921-28; Oxford University, Balliol College, Oxford, England, fellow and tutor in modern history and university reader in diplomatic, 1928-37; Edinburgh University, Edinburgh, Scotland, professor of history, 1937-44; University of London, London, director of Institute of Historical Research, 1944-48; Oxford University, Regius Professor of Modern History, 1947-57. Ford's Lecturer in English History at Oxford University, 1940-41; David Murray Lecturer at Glasgow University, 1943-44; James Bryce Memorial Lecturer at Somerville College, 1944; Creighton Lecturer at University of London, 1949; Purington Lecturer at Mount Holyoke College, 1965; Penrose Lecturer for American Philosophical Society, 1966. *Member:* Royal Commission on Ancient and Historical Monuments of England and Scotland, American Philosophical Society. *Awards, honors:* Honorary doctorates from University of Manchester, University of Edinburgh, University of Belfast, and Emory University; honorary fellow of Balliol College, Oxford, 1957; honorary fellow of Oriel College, Oxford, 1958.

WRITINGS: *The Abbey of St. Albans From 1300 to the Dissolution of the Monasteries,* B. H. Blackwell, 1911; *An Introduction to the Use of the Public Records,* Clarendon Press, 1934, reprinted with corrections by Oxford University Press, 1963; *Studies in the Public Records,* Thomas Nelson, 1948; (editor with James Tait) *Domesday Book,* J. W. Ruddock, 1950; *The Making of Domesday Book,* Clarendon Press, 1961; *The Historian at Work,* BBC Publications, 1962; *An Introduction to the Study of History,* C. A. Watts, 1964; *A Draft of Magna Carta,* Oxford University Press, 1967; (editor) *The Anonimalle Chronicle, 1333 to 1381,* Manchester University Press, 1970; *Domesday Book: Its Place in Administrative History,* Clarendon Press, 1974. Contributor to *English Historical Review.*

OBITUARIES: *London Times,* November 26, 1976; *AB Bookman's Weekly,* January 3, 1977.*

(Died November, 1976, in England)

* * *

GALDONE, Paul 1914-

PERSONAL: Born in Budapest, Hungary; came to the United States in 1914; married wife, Jannelise; children: Joanna, Paul Ferencz. *Education:* Studied art at the Art Student's League and New York School for Industrial Design. *Residence:* New York, N.Y.

CAREER: Author and illustrator of books for children. Early jobs included bus boy, electrician's helper, and fur dryer; worked for four years in the art department at Doubleday (publisher). *Military service:* U.S. Army Engineers, World War II. *Awards, honors:* Runner-up for the Caldecott Medal, 1957, for *Anatole,* and 1958, for *Anatole and the Cat* (both written by Eve Titus).

WRITINGS—All self-illustrated: (With Eve Titus) *Basil of Baker Street,* McGraw, 1958; *Paddy the Penguin,* Crowell, 1959; (with Titus) *Anatole over Paris,* McGraw, 1961; *Hare and the Tortoise,* McGraw, 1962; (with Feenie Ziner) *Counting Carnival,* Coward, 1962; *Little Tuppen,* Seabury, 1967; *The Horse, the Fox, and the Lion,* Seabury, 1968; *Life of Jack Sprat, His Wife, and Cat,* McGraw, 1969; *The Monkey and the Crocodile,* Seabury, 1969; (with Richard W. Armour) *All Sizes and Shapes of Monkeys and Apes,* McGraw, 1970; (with daughter, Joanna Galdone) *Honeybee's Party,* F. Watts, 1972; *The Moving Adventures of Old Dame Trot and Her Comical Cat,* McGraw, 1973; (with J. Galdone) *Gertrude, the Goose Who Forgot,* F. Watts, 1975; *The Magic Porridge Pot,* Seabury, 1976.

Illustrator and adapter: *Old Woman and Her Pig,* Whittlesey House, 1960; *The House That Jack Built,* Whittlesey House, 1961; *The Three Wishes,* Whittlesey House, 1961; Mother Goose, *Tom, Tom, the Piper's Son,* McGraw, 1964; Francois Rabelais, *The Wise Fool,* Random, 1968; *Henny Penny,* Seabury, 1968; *Androcles and the Lion,* McGraw, 1970; *Three Little Pigs,* Seabury, 1970; *History of Little Tom Tucker,* McGraw, 1970; *Obedient Jack,* F. Watts, 1971; *The Town Mouse and the Country Mouse,* McGraw, 1971; Aesop, *Three Aesop Fox Fables,* Seabury, 1971; *The Three Bears,* Seabury, 1972; Peter C. Asbjornsen, *The Three Billy Goats Gruff,* Seabury, 1973; Joseph Jacobs, *Hereafterthis,* McGraw, 1973; *The Little Red Hen,* Seabury, 1973; Grimm Brothers, *Little Red Riding Hood,* McGraw, 1974; Grimm Brothers, *The Frog Prince,* McGraw, 1974; *The Gingerbread Boy,* Seabury, 1975; Charles Perrault, *Puss in Boots,* Seabury, 1976.

Illustrator: Ellen MacGregor, *Miss Pickerell Goes to Mars,* Whittlesey House, 1951; Edward Fenton, *Nine Lives,* Pantheon, 1951; Ruthven Todd, *Space Cat,* Scribner, 1952; reprinted, 1971; MacGregor, *Miss Pickerell and the Geiger Counter,* McGraw, 1953; Doris T. Plenn, *Green Song,* McKay, 1954; MacGregor, *Miss Pickerell Goes to the Arctic,* McGraw, 1954, reprinted, 1967; Mary Mapes Dodge, *Hans Brinker,* Doubleday, 1954; Miriam Schlein, *How Do You Travel,* Abingdon, 1954; William O. Steele, *Winter Danger,* Harcourt, 1954; MacGregor, *Theodore Turtle,* Whittlesey House, 1955; W. O. Steele, *Tomahawks and Trouble,* Harcourt, 1955; Edward M. Eager, *Playing Possum,* Putnam, 1955; MacGregor, *Mr. Ferguson and the Fire Department,* Whittlesey House, 1956; W. O. Steele, *Lone Hunt,* Harcourt, 1956; Titus, *Anatole,* Whittlesey House, 1956; Margaret T. Burroughs, *Did You Feed My Cow?,* Crowell, 1956; Amy Hogeboom, *Audubon and His Sons,* Lothrop, 1956; Clyde T. Bulla, *Sword in the Tree,* Crowell, 1956; Todd, *Space Cat Meets Mars,* Scribner, 1957; Titus, *Anatole and the Cat,* McGraw, 1957; M. Franklin and Eleanor K. Vaughan, *Rusty Rings a Bell,* Crowell, 1957; W. O. Steele, *Flaming Arrows,* Harcourt, 1957; Bulla, *Old Charlie,* F. Watts, 1957; W. O. Steele, *Perilous Road,* Harcourt, 1958; Franklin and Vaughan, *Timmy and the Tin-Can Telephone,* Crowell, 1959; Nathaniel Hawthorne, *The Golden Touch,* McGraw, 1959; W. O. Steele, *Far Frontier,* Harcourt, 1959.

Mother Goose, *Old Mother Hubbard and Her Dog,* McGraw, 1960; Scott Corbett, *The Lemonade Trick,* Little, Brown, 1960; Eve Merriam, *A Gaggle of Geese,* Knopf, 1960; Alfred Steinburg, *Woodrow Wilson,* Putnam, 1961;

Corbett, *The Mailbox Trick,* Little, Brown, 1961; Cora Cheney and Ben Partridge, *Rendezvous in Singapore,* Knopf, 1961; Karin Anckarsvard, *Robber Ghost,* translated from the Swedish by Annabelle Macmillan, Harcourt, 1961; Esther M. Meeks, *Jeff and Mr. James' Pond,* Lothrop, 1962; Edward Lear, *The Two Old Bachelors,* McGraw, 1962; Anckarsvard, *Madcap Mystery,* translated from the Swedish by A. MacMillan, Harcourt, 1962; *The First Seven Days* (adapted from the Bible), Crowell, 1962; Alice E. Goudey, *Sunnyvale Fair,* Scribner, 1962; John G. Saxe, *The Blind Men and the Elephant,* McGraw, 1963; Henry Wadsworth Longfellow, *Paul Revere's Ride,* Crowell, 1963; Corbett, *The Disappearing Dog Trick,* Little, Brown, 1963; Wilson Gage, *Miss Osborne-the-Mop,* World Publishing, 1963; Robert Barry, *Mister Willowby's Christmas Tree,* McGraw, 1963.

Rhoda Bacmeister, *People Downstairs, and Other City Stories,* Coward-McCann, 1964; Vitali Bianki, *Peek the Piper,* Braziller, 1964; Johnston, *Edie Changes Her Mind,* Putnam, 1964; Corbett, *The Limerick Trick,* Little, Brown, 1964; Francis Hopkinson, *The Battle of the Kegs,* Crowell, 1964; Mary O'Neill, *People I'd Like to Keep,* Doubleday, 1964; Titus, *Anatole and the Poodle,* Whittlesey House, 1965; John Greenleaf Whittier, *Barbara Frietchie,* Crowell, 1965; Richard W. Armour, *The Adventures of Egbert the Easter Egg,* McGraw, 1965; Oliver Wendell Holmes, *The Deacon's Masterpiece,* McGraw, 1965; *Shadrach, Meshach, and Abednego* (adapted from the Bible), Whittlesey House, 1965; Helen E. Buckley, *The Little Boy and the Birthdays,* Lothrop, 1965; Corbett, *The Baseball Trick,* Little, Brown, 1965; Anckarsvard, *Mysterious Schoolmaster,* translated from the Swedish by A. MacMillan, Harcourt, 1965; Hans Peterson, *Brownie,* Lothrop, 1965; Dale Fife, *Who's in Charge of Lincoln,* Coward-McCann, 1965.

Titus, *Anatole and the Piano,* McGraw, 1966; Johnston, *That's Right, Edie,* Putnam, 1966; *The History of Simple Simon,* McGraw, 1966; Francis Scott Key, *The Star-Spangled Banner,* Crowell, 1966; Ivan Kusan, *Koko and the Ghosts,* Harcourt, 1966; Lear, *Two Laughable Lyrics,* Putnam, 1966; Armour, *Animals on the Ceiling,* McGraw, 1966; Wilson Gage, *The Ghost of Five Owl Farm,* World Publishing, 1966; Lee G. Goetz, *A Camel in the Sea,* McGraw, 1966; Sidney Offit, *The Adventures of Homer Fink,* St. Martin, 1966; Edgar Allan Poe, *Three Poems of Edgar Allan Poe,* McGraw, 1966; Wylly Folk St. John, *The Secrets of Hidden Creek,* Viking, 1966; Armour, *A Dozen Dinosaurs,* McGraw, 1967; Guy Daniels, *The Tsar's Riddles,* McGraw, 1967; Corbett, *The Turnabout Trick,* Little, Brown, 1967; Barbara Rinkoff, *Elbert, the Mind Reader,* Lothrop, 1967; Hawthorne, *Pandora's Box: The Paradise of Children,* McGraw, 1967; Patricia M. Martin, *Woody's Big Trouble,* Putnam, 1967; Letta Schatz, *Whiskers, My Cat,* McGraw, 1967; Judy Van der Veer, *Wallace the Wandering Pig,* Harcourt, 1967; Armour, *Who's in Holes,* McGraw, 1967; Paul Showers, *Your Skin and Mine,* Black, 1967; Franklyn M. Branley, *High Sounds, Low Sounds,* Crowell, 1967.

Armour, *Odd Old Mammals,* McGraw-Hill, 1968; W. O. Steele, *The Buffalo Knife,* Harcourt, 1968; Richard Shaw, *Budd's Noisy Wagon,* F. Warne, 1968; Augusta R. Goldin, *Sunlit Sea,* Crowell, 1968; Grimm Brothers, *The Bremen Town Musicians,* McGraw, 1968; Clement C. Moore, *A Visit from St. Nicholas,* McGraw, 1968; Peggy Mann, *The Boy with a Billion Pets,* Coward-McCann, 1968; Corbett, *The Hairy Horror Trick,* Little, Brown, 1969; H. E. Buckley, *Grandmother and I,* Lothrop, 1969; Jean Fritz, *George*

Washington's Breakfast, Coward-McCann, 1969; Carol Iden, *Sidney's Ghost,* World Publishing, 1969; Van der Veer, *To the Rescue,* Harcourt, 1969; Pura Belpre, *Ote,* Pantheon, 1969; Showers, *Look at Your Eyes,* Black, 1969, Crowell, 1976; Titus, *Anatole and the Thirty Thieves,* McGraw, 1969.

Fife, *What's New, Lincoln?,* Coward-McCann, 1970; Roberta Greene, *Two and Me Makes Three,* Coward-McCann, 1970; Titus, *Anatole and the Toyshop,* McGraw, 1970; Judith Viorst, *Try It Again, Sam: Safety When You Walk,* Lothrop, 1970; Fife, *What's the Prize, Lincoln?,* Coward-McCann, 1971; John Knoepfle, *Dogs and Cats and Things Like That* (poems), McGraw, 1971; Corbett, *The Hateful Plateful Trick,* Little, Brown, 1971; Titus, *Basil and the Pygmy Cats,* McGraw, 1971; Beatrice S. DeRegniers, *It Does Not Say Meow,* Seabury, 1972; Mary L. Solot, *100 Hamburgers: The Getting Thin Book,* Lothrop, 1972; Belpre, *Dance of the Animals: A Puetro Rican Folk Tale,* F. Warne, 1972; Zibby Oneal, *The Improbable Adventures of Marvelous O'Hara Soapstone,* Viking, 1972; Corbett, *The Home Run Trick,* Little, Brown, 1973; F. N. Monjo, *Clarence and the Burglar,* Coward-McCann, 1973; Diane Wolkstein, *The Cool Ride in the Sky,* Knopf, 1973; Titus, *Anatole in Italy,* McGraw, 1973; Edna Barth, *Jack-o'-Lantern,* Seabury, 1974; Armour, *Sea Full of Whales,* McGraw, 1974; *The History of Mother Twaddle and the Marvelous Achievements of Her Son Jack,* Seabury, 1974; Johnston, *Speak Up, Edie!,* Putnam, 1974; Corbett, *The Hockey Trick,* Little, Brown, 1974.

Dorothy Van Woerkom, *The Queen Who Couldn't Bake Gingerbread,* Random House, 1975; Mary Q. Steele, *Because of the Sand Witches There,* Greenwillow Books, 1975; Fife, *Who Goes There, Lincoln?,* Coward-McCann, 1975; Showers, *Follow Your Nose,* Crowell, 1975; Titus, *Basil in Mexico,* McGraw, 1975; Pat D. Tapio, *The Lady Who Saw the Good Side of Everything,* Seabury, 1975; Patricia Lauber, *Clarence and the Burglar,* Worlds Work, 1975; Showers, *How Many Teeth?,* Crowell, 1976; Corbett, *The Black Mask Trick,* Little, Brown, 1976; Grimm Brothers, *The Table, the Donkey, and the Stick,* McGraw, 1976; Joanna Galdone, *Amber Day,* McGraw, 1978; Hans Christian Andersen, *The Princess and the Pea,* Seabury, 1978.

SIDELIGHTS: In addition to being an illustrator of children's books (using primarily pen and ink washes), Galdone is a painter and sculptor. He and his wife, Jannelise, have also designed their own home.

A *Book World* reviewer commented: "For bright joyous drawings, one only has to turn to Paul Galdone's work. His retellings of simple animal folk tales are always clear and concise. In *The Monkey and the Crocodile* Galdone astounds the reader with the variety of colorful pictures in which just the two animals appear."

AVOCATIONAL INTERESTS: Hiking, forestry, and gardening.

BIOGRAPHICAL/CRITICAL SOURCES: Lee Bennett Hopkins, *Books Are by People: Interviews with 104 Authors and Illustrators of Books for Young Children,* Citation Press, 1969; *Book World,* November 9, 1969.*

* * *

GALICH, Alexander 1918(?)-1977

1918(?)—December 15, 1977; Soviet screenwriter, balladeer, and poet. Though once an officially approved writer of Soviet screenplays, Galich was expelled from both the Film Worker's Union and the Writer's Union in 1971. He emigrated in 1974, going to Norway, then Munich, finally settling in Paris where he joined the group of exiled Soviet dissidents there and worked for Radio Liberty. He was best known for his dissident poetry and protest songs. He died in Paris, France. Obituaries: *New York Times,* December 16, 1977; *Washington Post,* December 17, 1977.

* * *

GALLOWAY, Joseph L(ee) 1941-

PERSONAL: Born November 13, 1941, in Bryan, Tex.; son of Joseph L. and Marian (Dewvall) Galloway; married Theresa Null, September 9, 1966; children: Lee Tyler. *Education:* Attended Victoria College, 1959. *Home address:* P.O. Box 116, Refugio, Tex. 78377. *Office:* United Press International, Kutuzovsky Pr. 7/4 Apt. 67, Moscow, U.S.S.R.

CAREER/WRITINGS: Victoria Advocate, Victoria, Tex., reporter, 1959-61; United Press International, New York, N.Y., reporter in Kansas City, Mo., 1961, capital correspondent in Topeka, Kan., 1962-64, war correspondent in Saigon, 1965-66, editor in Tokyo, Japan, 1967, manager in Jakarta, Indonesia, 1968-73, manager for South Asia, New Delhi, 1973-74, manager for Southeast Asia, Singapore, 1974-75, bureau manager in Moscow, 1976—. Notable assignments include coverage of war in Indochina, India-Pakistan War of 1971, student uprisings in Sri Lanka, 1971. *Member:* Foreign Correspondents Association (president in Indonesia, 1973), Foreign Correspondents of Southeast Asia, Press Club of India.

* * *

GARARD, Ira D(ufresne) 1888-

PERSONAL: Surname is pronounced with a soft "g"; born March 19, 1888, in Dunkard, Pa.; son of Charles Alexander (a farmer) and Margaret (Herrington) Garard; married Mabel Baldwin, September 20, 1919 (died, 1971). *Education:* Graduate of Southwestern State Normal School, Calif., 1908, and Grove City College, 1911; Columbia University, M.A., 1916, Ph.D., 1918. *Home:* 410 West Belvedere St., Lakeland, Fla. 33803.

CAREER: Teacher in country schools in Pennsylvania, 1904-07; high school teacher of science and mathematics in Coraopolis, Pa., 1908-09, and Grove City, Pa., 1911-16; Rutgers University, Douglass College, New Brunswick, N.J., associate professor and chairman of department, 1919-22, professor of chemistry, 1922-55; writer, 1955—. Consulting chemist, 1931-56. *Military service:* U.S. Army, 1918-19. *Member:* American Chemical Society, American Institute of Chemists, Institute of Food Technologists, Phi Beta Kappa.

WRITINGS: Applied Chemistry, Macmillan, 1924; *Introduction to Organic Chemistry,* Wiley, 1933; *Invitation to Chemistry,* Doubleday, 1969; *The Story of Food,* Avi, 1974; *Introductory Food Chemistry,* Avi, 1976.

WORK IN PROGRESS: The Rise and Fall of Our Civilization: Exhausting Our Energy and Resources; Not So Long Ago: The History of Greene County, Pennsylvania, 1890-1918; The House Across the Creek, a mystery.

* * *

GARD, Joyce 1911-
(Joyce Reeves)

PERSONAL: Born in 1911, in London, England. *Education:* Lady Margaret Hall, Oxford, B.A. *Residence:* London, England.

CAREER: Author. Served as an adminstrative officer with the Ministry of Economic Warfare, London, England, and with the Supreme Headquarters of the Allied Expeditionary Force, Frankfurt, Germany, 1940-45; studio potter, 1947-56; has also taught school and worked for a literary agent. *Member:* Society of Authors, Nash House.

WRITINGS: (Adaptor) Jules Verne, *Journey to the Centre of the Earth,* Hutchinson Educational, 1961; *Wooroo* (illustrated by Ronald Benham), Gollancz, 1961; *The Dragons of the Hill,* Gollancz, 1963; *Talargain the Seal's Whelp,* Gollancz, 1964, published as *Talargain,* Holt, 1965; *Smudge of the Fells,* Gollancz, 1965, Holt, 1966; *The Snow Firing,* Gollancz, 1967, Holt, 1968; *The Mermaid's Daughter,* Holt, 1969. Under pseudonym Joyce Reeves, translator from the French on the subject of contemporary art.

SIDELIGHTS: Joyce Gard uses a combination of fact and fiction in her novels, which have been highly praised by numerous book reviewers. "Vivid, excellent writing, the skillful blending of fantasy and history and a plot filled with suspense make this an outstanding work," commented a *New York Times* critic about the author's novel, *Talargain.*

Of the author's latest novel, *The Mermaid's Daughter,* a review in the *Times Literary Supplement* said: "The rich and rapturous telling will undoubtedly thrill the impressionable adolescent girls of sensibility and spirituality."

AVOCATIONAL INTERESTS: Contemporary art, archaeology, walking, and gardening.

BIOGRAPHICAL/CRITICAL SOURCES: New York Times Book Review, May 23, 1964; *Times Literary Supplement,* June 26, 1969.*

* * *

GARDNER, Martin 1914-

PERSONAL: Born October 21, 1914, in Tulsa, Okla.; son of James Henry and Willie (Spiers) Gardner; married Charlotte Creenwald, October 17, 1952; children: James Emmett, Thomas Owen. *Education:* University of Chicago, B.A., 1936.

CAREER: Journalist and writer. Reporter for Tulsa Tribune; public relations staffer for University of Chicago; *Humpty Dumpty's* magazine, New York City, contributing editor, 1952-62; *Scientific American,* New York City, writer of mathematical games department, 1957—. *Military service:* U.S. Naval Reserve, 1942-46.

WRITINGS: In the Name of Science, Putnam, 1952, revised edition published as *Fads and Fallacies in the Name of Science,* Dover, 1957; *Mathematics, Magic and Mystery,* Dover, 1956; *Logic Machines and Diagrams,* McGraw, 1958, revised edition published as *Logic Machines, Diagrams, and Boulean Algebra,* Dover, 1968; *The Scientific American Book of Mathematical Puzzles and Diversions,* Simon & Schuster, 1959; *The Arrow Book of Brain Teasers,* Scholastic Book Services, 1959.

Science Puzzlers (illustrated by Anthony Ravielli), Viking, 1960; *The Second Scientific American Book of Mathematical Puzzles and Diversions,* Simon & Schuster, 1961; *Mathematical Puzzles* (illustrated by A. Ravielli), Crowell, 1961; *Relativity for the Million* (illustrated by A. Ravielli), Macmillan, 1962, revised edition published as *The Relativity Explosion,* Random House, 1976; *The Ambidextrous Universe* (illustrated by John Mackey), Basic Books, 1964, revised edition, New American Library, 1969; *Archimedes, Mathematician and Inventor* (illustrated by Leonard E. Fisher), Macmillan, 1965; *The Numerology of Dr. Matrix,*

Simon & Schuster, 1967; *The Unexpected Hanging, and Other Mathematical Diversions,* Simon & Schuster, 1969; *Perplexing Puzzles and Tantalizing Teasers* (illustrated by Laszlo Kubinyi) Simon & Schuster, 1969; *Never Make Fun of a Turtle, My Son* (illustrated by John Alcorn), Simon & Schuster, 1969.

Space Puzzles (illustrated by Ted Schroeder), Simon & Schuster, 1971; *The Sixth Book of Mathematical Games from Scientific American,* W. H. Freeman, 1971; *Codes, Ciphers, and Secret Writing,* Simon & Schuster, 1972; *The Flight of Peter Fromm,* William Kaufmann, 1973; *The Snark Puzzle Book* (illustrated by Henry Holiday), Simon & Schuster, 1973; *Mathematical Carnival,* Knopf, 1975; *The Incredible Dr. Matrix,* Scribner, 1976; *Mathematical Magic Show,* Knopf, 1977; *More Perplexing Puzzles and Tantalizing Teasers* (illustrated by L. Kubinyi), Pocket Books, 1977.

Editor: *The Wizard of Oz and Who He Was,* Michigan State University Press, 1957; *Great Essays in Science,* Pocket Books, 1957; Sam Loyd, *Best Mathematical Puzzles of Sam Loyd,* Dover, Volume I, 1957, Volume II, 1960; Lewis Carroll, *The Annotated Alice,* C. N. Potter, 1960; Charles C. Bombaugh, *Oddities and Curiosities of Words and Literature,* Dover, 1961; Lewis Carroll, *The Annotated Snark,* Simon & Schuster, 1962; Samuel Taylor Coleridge, *The Annotated Ancient Mariner,* Bramhall House, 1965; Rudolf Carnap, *Philosophical Foundations of Physics,* Basic Books, 1966, revised edition published as *An Introduction to the Philosophy of Science,* 1974; E. L. Thayer, *The Annotated Casey at the Bat,* C. N. Potter, 1967; Henry E. Dudeney, *Five Hundred Thirty-Six Puzzles and Curious Problems,* Scribner, 1967; Boris Kordemski, *Moscow Puzzles,* Scribner, 1971; Koban Fujimura, *Tokyo Puzzles,* Scribner, 1978; Lewis Carroll, *The Wasp in a Wig,* C. N. Potter, 1978.

SIDELIGHTS: Gardner's skill in combining math, science, philosophy, and literature has produced unusual books of diverse natures. The author's first book, *In the Name of Science,* was reviewed by the *San Francisco Chronicle* which noted: "Mr. Gardner has written a highly critical and at times hilariously entertaining account of cults and fad sciences in various fields." Nearly twenty years later Gardner produced a "novel of ideas" that explored conflicting points of view in Protestant theology. A *New York Times Book Review* critic reviewing *The Flight of Peter Fromm* commented: "This is a brilliantly illuminating metaphysical novel that employs ideas as adversaries and translates them into human dilemmas."

AVOCATIONAL INTERESTS: Magic, chess, musical saw.

BIOGRAPHICAL/CRITICAL SOURCES: San Francisco Chronicle, March 1, 1953; *New York Times Book Review,* December 23, 1973; *Time,* April 21, 1975; *Chicago Daily News,* August 22, 1975; *Washington Post,* March 11, 1976.

* * *

GARDNER, Wanda Kirby 1914-

PERSONAL: Born July 25, 1914, in DeWitt County, Ill.; daughter of Irvin N. (a teacher and farmer) and Pearl (Byerly) Kirby; married John P. Gardner (in security), February 22, 1935; children: Martha Rose, William, Thomas, Mary Jo. *Education:* Attended Deaconess School of Nursing. *Politics:* "Registered Republican, but vote both." *Religion:* Methodist. *Home:* 33 Keokuk St., Lincoln, Ill. 62656.

CAREER: John Warner Hospital, Clinton, Ill., nurse's aide in obstetrics, 1957-61. Writer. *Member:* National League of

American Pen Women, Illinois State Poetry Society. *Awards, honors:* Publication grants from American Poets Fellowship Society for books of poems.

WRITINGS: The Stranger on the Stage (poems), Prairie Poet Books, 1976; *These Vintage Years* (poems), Prairie Poet Books, 1977.

WORK IN PROGRESS—Novels: *The Woods Colt; My Trip to Nostalgia; Mil; Look Up.*

SIDELIGHTS: Wanda Gardner comments: "I think I decided long ago that if I was to leave a legacy of any kind it would have to be in writing. Others make quilts, needlework, paint in oil or carve; I do these things but not well. I have an uncontrollable urge to write; I get very discouraged at times and think I will stop but something pushes me on. I have not had too much training for writing, but have to do it."

* * *

GARDNER, Wayland Downing 1928-

PERSONAL: Born May 16, 1928, in Elgin, Neb.; son of Arthur C. (a newspaperman) and Bernice (Downing) Gardner; married Suzanne Roop, December 26, 1953; children: Janet, Elaine, Edward, James. *Education:* Doane College, A.B., 1950; University of Wisconsin—Madison, M.S., 1951, Ph.D., 1958. *Home:* 1011 Boswell Lane, Kalamazoo, Mich. 49007. *Office:* Department of Economics, Western Michigan University, Kalamazoo, Mich. 49008.

CAREER: North Dakota State University, Fargo, assistant professor, 1958-61, associate professor of economics, 1961-63; University of Maryland, College Park, associate professor of agricultural economics, 1963-64; Western Michigan University, Kalamazoo, associate professor of economics, 1964—. *Military service:* U.S. Army, 1953-54; became first lieutenant. *Member:* American Economic Association, Midwest Economic Association, Economic Society of Michigan.

WRITINGS: Government Finance: National, State, and Local, Prentice-Hall, 1978. Contributor to economics and tax journals. Editor of *Economic Society of Michigan Newsletter.*

WORK IN PROGRESS: An undergraduate textbook on general economics; research on government finance.

SIDELIGHTS: Gardner comments: "My chief interest is in teaching university students. My particular interest is in government finance, especially as related to democratic processes and local governments."

* * *

GARELICK, May 1910-
(Garel Clark, a joint pseudonym)

PERSONAL: Born in 1910, in Vobruisk, Russia; brought to the United States at age nine months; married Marshall McClintock (an author). *Education:* Educated in New York, N.Y.

CAREER: Author and editor. Has worked in the publishing business with jobs ranging from clerical worker to production manager. Editor of children's books for William R. Scott Company; children's European editor for publisher E. P. Dutton.

WRITINGS: (With Ethel McCullough Scott, under joint pseudonym Garel Clark) *Let's Start Cooking* (illustrated by Kathleen Elgin), W. R. Scott, 1951; (with Scott, under joint pseudonym) *The Cook-a-Meal Cook Book* (illustrated by

Leonard Kessler), W. R. Scott, 1953; *What's Inside?,* W. R. Scott, 1955, reprinted as *What's Inside: The Story of an Egg That Hatched,* Scholastic Book Services, 1970; *Manhattan Island* (illustrated by John and Clare Ross), Crowell, 1957; *Double Trouble* (illustrated by Arthur Getz), Crowell, 1958.

Where Does the Butterfly Go When It Rains (illustrated by Leonard Weisgard), W. R. Scott, 1961; *Sounds of a Summer Night* (illustrated by Beni Montresor), Young Scott Books, 1963; *Here Comes the Bride* (illustrated by Joe Lasker), Young Scott Books, 1964; *Wild Ducks and Daffodils* (illustrated by Clare Ross), Young Scott Books, 1965; *Winter's Birds* (illustrated by Clement Hurd), Young Scott Books, 1965; *What Makes a Bird a Bird?* (illustrated by Weisgard), Follett, 1969; *Look at the Moon* (illustrated by Weisgard), Young Scott Books, 1969; *Just Suppose,* Scholastic Book Services, 1971; *Who Likes It Hot?* (illustrated by Brinton Turkle), Four Winds, 1972; *Runaway Plane* (illustrated by Joezef Sumichrast), J. P. O'Hara, 1973; *Down to the Beach* (illustrated by Barbara Cooney), Four Winds, 1973; *About Owls* (illustrated by Tony Chen), Four Winds, 1975.

SIDELIGHTS: May Garelick's books have all been a response to a question in her own mind, or of one posed to her by a child. She usually reads them to a classroom of children, accepting their criticism and enjoying their comments.

BIOGRAPHICAL/CRITICAL SOURCES: Lee Benett Hopkins, *Books Are by People: Interviews with 104 Authors and Illustrators of Books for Young Children,* Citation Press, 1969.*

* * *

GARIS, Howard Roger 1873-1962
(Marion Davidson)

PERSONAL: Born April 25, 1873, in Binghamton, N.Y.; son of Simeon H. and Ellen A (Kimball) Garis; married Lillian C. McNamara (a writer), April 26, 1900 (died, 1954); children: Roger C., Cleo F. Garis Clancy. *Education:* Attended Stevens Institute of Technology. *Religion:* Roman Catholic. *Residence:* Amherst, Mass.

CAREER: Author of children's books and journalist. Worked for Stratemeyer Syndicate as one of several writers of the "Tom Swift" and "Motor Boys" series; reporter and special writer for *Newark Evening News,* 1896-1947. *Member:* National Press Club, Authors League of America, Reptile Study Society.

WRITINGS—Children's books: *With Force and Arms: A Tale of Love and Salem Witchcraft,* J. S. Ogilvie, 1902; *The King of Unadilla: Stories of Court Secrets Concerning His Majesty,* J. S. Ogilvie, 1903; *Isle of Black Fire: A Tale of Adventure for Boys,* Lippincott, 1904; *The White Crystals: Being an Account of the Adventures of Two Boys* (illustrated by Bertha Corson Day), Little, Brown, 1904; *Dick Hamilton's Fortune; or, The Stirring Doings of a Millionaire's Son,* Grosset, 1909; *Dick Hamilton's Cadet Days; or, The Handicap of a Millionaire's Son,* Grosset, 1910; *Sammie and Susie Littletail,* R. F. Fenno, 1910; *Johnnie and Billie Bushytail* (illustrated by Louis Wisa), R. F. Fenno, 1910; *Those Smith Boys; or, The Mystery of the Thumbless Man,* R. F. Fenno, 1910.

Johnnie and Jackie and Peetie Bow Wow (illustrated by Wisa), R. F. Fenno, 1912; *Lulu, Alice, and Jimmie Wibblewobble* (illustrated by Wisa), R. F. Fenno, 1912; *The Island Boys; or, Fun and Adventures on Lake Modok,* R. F. Fenno, 1912; *Those Smith Boys on the Diamond; or, Nip and Tuck for Victory,* R. F. Fenno, 1912; *Three Little Tripper-*

trots on Their Travels, the Wonderful Things They Saw, and the Wonderful Things They Did, Graham & Matlack, 1912; *Three Little Trippertrots, How They Ran Away, and How They Got Back Again,* Graham & Matlack, 1912; (under pseudonym, Marion Davidson) *Camp Fire Girls on the Ice; or, The Mystery of a Winter Cabin,* R. F. Fenno, 1913; (under pseudonym, Marion Davidson) *The Camp Fire Girls; or, The Secret of an Old Mill,* R. F. Fenno, 1913; *Bully and Bawly No-Tail, the Jumping Frogs* (illustrated by Wisa), R. F. Fenno, 1915; *Snarlie the Tiger,* R. F. Fenno, 1916; *The Venture Boys Afloat; or, The Wreck of the Fausta* (illustrated by Perc E. Cowan), Harper, 1917; *Umboo the Elephant,* R. F. Fenno, 1918; *Woo-Uff the Lion,* R. F. Fenno, 1918; *The Venture Boys in Camp; or, The Mystery of Kettle Hill,* Harper, 1918; *Toodle and Noodle Flat-Tail, the Jolly Beaver Boys* (illustrated by Wisa), A. L. Burt, 1919; *Mystery Boys in Ghost Canyon* (illustrated by H. G. Nichols), M. Bradley, 1930; *Mystery Boys at Round Lake* (illustrated by Nichols), M. Bradley, 1931.

"Great Newspaper" series; all published by Chatterton-Peek: *From Office Boy to Reporter; or, The First Step in Journalism,* 1907; *Larry Dexter, Reporter; or, Strange Adventures in a Great City,* 1907.

"Great Newspaper" series; all published by Grosset: *Larry Dexter's Great Search; or, The Hunt for the Missing Millionaire,* 1909; *Larry Dexter and the Bank Mystery; or, A Young Reporter in Wall Street,* 1912; *Larry Dexter and the Stolen Boy; or, A Young Reporter on the Lakes,* 1912.

"Uncle Wiggily" series; published by R. F. Fenno: *Uncle Wiggily's Adventures* (illustrated by Wisa), 1912; *Uncle Wiggily Longears,* 1916; *Uncle Wiggily and Alice in Wonderland,* 1916; *Uncle Wiggily's Arabian Nights,* 1916; *Uncle Wiggily and Mother Goose* (illustrated by Edward Bloomfield), 1916.

"Uncle Wiggily" series; published by A. L. Burt, except as noted: *Uncle Wiggily's Rheumatism* (illustrated by Bloomfield), 1920; *Uncle Wiggily and Baby Bounty* (illustrated by Wisa), 1920; *Uncle Wiggily's Bungalow,* 1930; *Uncle Wiggily's Travels* (illustrated by Wisa), 1931; *Uncle Wiggily's Airship* (illustrated by Wisa), 1931; *Uncle Wiggily's Picnic Party,* 1933; *Uncle Wiggily's Surprises,* Blue Ribbon Books, 1937.

"Uncle Wiggily" series; illustrated by Lang Campbell and published by C. E. Graham: *Uncle Wiggily's Ice Cream Party,* 1922; *... Woodland Games,* 1922; *... Silk Hat,* 1922; *... June Bug Friends,* 1922; *Uncle Wiggily on the Farm,* 1922; *Uncle Wiggily: Indian Hunter,* 1922; *Uncle Wiggily's Funny Auto,* 1924; *... Painting Fun,* 1924; *... Painting Play,* 1924; *Uncle Wiggily at the Beach,* 1924; *... and the Pirates,* 1924; *... on the Flying Rug,* 1924; *... Goes Swimming,* 1924; *... on Roller Skates,* 1924; *The Adventures of Uncle Wiggily: The Bunny Rabbit Gentleman with the Twinkling Pink Nose,* 1924; *The Second Adventures of Uncle Wiggily: The Bunny Rabbit Gentleman and His Muskrat Lady Housekeeper,* 1925; *Uncle Wiggily's Make Believe Tarts,* 1929; *... Ice Boat,* 1929; *... Wash Tub Ship,* 1929; *... Squirt Gun,* 1929; *... Rolling Hoop,* 1929; *Uncle Wiggily and the Alligator,* 1929; *Uncle Wiggily Plays Storekeeper,* 1929; *Uncle Wiggily's Jumping Boots,* 1931; *Uncle Wiggily Builds a Snow House,* 1931; *Uncle Wiggily Catches the Alligator,* 1931; *Uncle Wiggily's Icicle Spear,* 1931; *Uncle Wiggily Captures the Skee,* 1931; *Uncle Wiggily's Trick Skating,* 1931.

"Daddy" series; all published by R. F. Fenno, all 1916: *Daddy Takes Us Camping; ... Fishing; ... to the Circus;*

... Skating; ... Coasting; ... Hunting Flowers; ... Hunting Birds; ... to the Woods; ... to the Farm; ... to the Garden.

"Rick and Ruddy" series; published by M. Bradley: *Rick and Ruddy: The Story of a Boy and His Dog* (illustrated by John Goss), 1920; *Rick and Ruddy in Camp: The Adventures of a Boy and His Dog* (illustrated by Milo Winter), 1921; *Rick and Ruddy: The Cruise of a Boy and His Dog* (illustrated by W. B. King), 1922; *Rick and Ruddy Out West* (illustrated by King), 1923; *Rick and Ruddy on the Trail* (illustrated by King), 1924.

"Rick and Ruddy" series; published by McLoughlin: *The Face in the Dismal Cavern,* 1930; *The Mystery of the Brass Bound Box,* 1930; *On the Showman's Trail,* 1930; *Swept from the Storm,* 1930; *The Secret of Lost River,* 1930.

"Curlytops" series; published by Cupples & Leon, c. 1923: *Curlytops and Their Pets; ... and Their Playmates; ... at the Cherry Farm; ... at Silver Lake; ... at Sunset Beach* (illustrated by Julia Greene); *... at Uncle Frank's Ranch; ... in Summer Camp; ... in the Woods* (illustrated by J. Greene); *... on Star Island; ... Snowed in* (illustrated by Greene); *... Touring Around; ... Growing Up; or, Winter Sports and Summer Pleasures* (illustrated by Greene), 1928; *... at Happy House; or, The Mystery of the Chinese Vase,* 1931; *... at the Circus; or, The Runaway Elephant,* 1932.

"Two Wild Cherries" series; illustrated by John M. Foster and published by M. Bradley: *Two Wild Cherries in the Woods; or, How Dick and Janet Caught the Bear,* 1924; *Two Wild Cherries in the Country; or, How Dick and Janet Saved the Mill,* 1924; *Two Wild Cherries; or, How Dick and Janet Lost Something,* 1924; *Two Wild Cherries at the Seashore,* 1925.

"Happy Home" series; published by Grosset: *Adventures of the Galloping Gas Stove,* 1926; *... Runaway Rocker,* 1926; *... Sailing Sofa,* 1926; *... Sliding Foot Stool,* 1926; *... Traveling Table,* 1926; *... Prancing Piano,* 1927.

"Buddy" series; published by Cupples & Leon: *Buddy in School; or, A Boy and His Dog,* 1929; *... and His Winter Fun; or, A Boy in a Snow Camp,* 1929; *... on the Farm; or, A Boy and His Prize Pumpkin,* 1929; *... at Rainbow Lake; or, A Boy and His Boat,* 1930; *... and His Chum; or, A Boy's Queer Search,* 1930; *... at Pine Beach; or, A Boy on the Ocean,* 1931; *... and His Flying Balloon; or, A Boy's Mysterious Airship,* 1931; *... on Mystery Mountain; or, A Boy's Strange Discovery,* 1932; *... on Floating Island; or, A Boy's Wonderful Secret,* 1933; *... and the Secret Cave; or, A Boy and the Crystal Hermit,* 1934; *... and His Cowboy Pal; or, A Boy on a Ranch,* 1935; *... and the Indian Chief; or, A Boy Among the Navajos,* 1936; *... and the Arrow Club; or, A Boy and the Long Bow,* 1937; *... at Lost River; or, A Boy and a Gold Mine,* 1938; *... on the Trail; or, A Boy Among the Gypsies,* 1939; *... in Deep Valley; or, A Boy on a Bee Farm,* 1940; *... at Red Gate; or, A Boy on a Chicken Farm,* 1941; *... in Dragon Swamp; or, A Boy on a Strange Hunt,* 1942; *Buddy's Victory Club; or, A Boy and a Salvage Campaign,* 1943; *Buddy and the G-Man Mystery; or, A Boy and a Strange Cipher,* 1944; *... and His Fresh-Air Camp; or, A Boy and the Unlucky Ones,* 1947.

"Dick and Janet Cherry" series; published by McLoughlin: *Saving the Old Mill,* 1930; *Shipwrecked on Christmas Island,* 1930; *The Bear Hunt,* 1930; *The Gypsy Camp,* 1930.

"Rocket Riders" series; published by A. L. Burt: *Rocket Riders over the Desert; or, Seeking the Lost City,* 1933; *Rocket Riders in Stormy Seas; or, Trailing the Treasure*

Divers, 1933; *Rocket Riders across the Ice; or, Racing against Time*, 1933; *Rocket Riders in the Air; or, A Chase in the Clouds*, 1934.

"Outboard Motor Boat" series; published by A. L. Burt: *Outboard Boys at Mystery Island; or, Solving the Secret of Hidden Cove*, 1933; *Outboard Boys at Pirate Beach; or, Solving the Secret of the Houseboat*, 1933; *Outboard Boys at Shadow Lake; or, Solving the Secret of the Strange Monster*, 1933; *Outboard Boys at Shark River; or, Solving the Secret of the Mystery Tower*, 1934.

"Teddy" series; published by Cupples & Leon: *Teddy and the Mystery Monkey*, 1936; ... *Mystery Dog*, 1936; ... *Mystery Cat*, 1937; ... *Mystery Parrot*, 1938; ... *Mystery Pony*, 1939; ... *Mystery Deer*, 1940; ... *Mystery Goat*, 1941.

Contributor of stories to periodicals including *St. Nicholas* and *Collier's*.

SIDELIGHTS: In his youth Garis was not encouraged to become a writer. His father, a pioneer railroad telegrapher, felt that writing was a nonlucrative field and he sent Garis to Stevens Institute to study engineering. There Garis failed every subject except elocution and English and he was soon dismissed. He was later sent to printers trade school but when his father died he returned to his first love, writing.

Garis wrote his first novel, "A World of Women," when he was sixteen years old. He took the 400 page manuscript to Harper's with instructions that it should be thrown into the wastepaper basket if it was not good. The editors did just that. At age nineteen Garis received 9 dollars for his first published work, a short story which appeared in *Happenchance* magazine.

Garis was hired by Edward M. Stratemeyer as one of several authors of serial books written under pseudonym. Garis wrote books for the "Motor Boys" series under the pseudonym, Clarence Young, and for the "Tom Swift" series under the pseudonym, Victor Appelton. Stratemeyer would suggest an outline and Garis would write the book, not always following the outline. Due to the great success of the "Tom Swift" books, Garis's pay was raised 25 dollars above the 100 dollars per book he had been getting. It was at about this time that he met his wife, Lilly, who was writing the "Bobbsey Twins" and other series for Stratemeyer.

The first Uncle Wiggily story was written as a special assignment in addition to his regular police beat on the *Newark Evening News*. The idea of serializing children's stories came from the paper's owner and publisher, Edward M. Scudder. Beginning January 30, 1910, Garis wrote Uncle Wiggily stories averaging seven hundred words in length, six days a week for more than fifty years. The stories were syndicated in many other newspapers and the popularity of Uncle Wiggily increased when Garis began to read the stories over radio. In his lifetime, Garis wrote over 15,000 Uncle Wiggily adventures and sold over eighteen million copies of his numerous Uncle Wiggily books. In 1917 he invented the Uncle Wiggily game which soon became the largest selling children's game in the world. Other Uncle Wiggily commercial products also appeared—dolls, dishes, dress patterns, toys, wallpaper, and phonograph records—making Uncle Wiggily one of the most famous and best loved rabbits of all time.

In a *Saturday Evening Post* article written by his son, Roger, Garis was described as a happy person. His philosophy—which was also Uncle Wiggily's—was simply not to admit that any hardship or disaster was serious enough to cause one to become discouraged. According to the article, Garis would say, "Oh hum suz-duz and a basket of carrots—let's not worry. It will come out all right in the end." Garis continued to write stories until the day he died. After his eighty-ninth birthday, he worked at his typewriter until noon each day and then walked around the streets of Amherst, making up new Uncle Wiggily adventures for the children who invariably followed him. In 1962, Garis told *Look* magazine: "There's no secret to an active life, just good behavior and plenty of it."

BIOGRAPHICAL/CRITICAL SOURCES: Newsweek, October 14, 1946, November 7, 1966; *Look*, July 3, 1962; *Saturday Evening Post*, December 19, 1964; Roger Garis, *My Father Was Uncle Wiggily*, McGraw, 1966.

OBITUARIES: New York Times, November 6, 1962; *Time*, November 16, 1962; *Newsweek*, November 19, 1962; *Publishers Weekly*, November 19, 1962.*

(Died November 5, 1962)

*   *   *

GARNER, Alan   1935-

PERSONAL: Born in 1935, in Cheshire, England; children: three. *Education:* Attended Magdalen College, Cambridge. *Home:* "Toad Hall," Blackden-cum-Goostrey, Cheshire, England.

CAREER: Writer. *Military service:* British Army; became second lieutenant. *Awards, honors:* Carnegie Medal, 1967, for *The Owl Service;* Guardian Award, 1968, for *The Owl Service;* Lewis Carroll Shelf award, 1970, for *The Weirdstone of Brisingamen.*

WRITINGS: The Weirdstone of Brisingamen: A Tale of Alderley, Collins, 1960, published as *The Weirdstone: A Tale of Alderley*, F. Watts, 1961, revised edition, Walck, 1969; *The Moon of Gomrath*, Walck, 1963; *Elidor*, Walck, 1965; *The Owl Service*, Walck, 1967; *The Old Man of Mow* (illustrated by Roger Hill), Doubleday, 1967; (editor) *A Cavalcade of Goblins* (illustrated by Krystyna Turska), Walck, 1969 (published in England as *The Hamish Hamilton Book of Goblins*, Hamish Hamilton, 1969); *Red Shift*, Macmillan, 1973; *The Guizer*, Greenwillow Books, 1976.

SIDELIGHTS: Garner's writings have been strongly influenced by ancient legends, particularly the *Mabinogion*, a collection of old Welsh tales. The author's educational background plus his motivation to do extensive research for his books have resulted in stories that successfully weave folklore with modern-day settings. Garner was once quoted as saying; "The more I learn, the more convinced I am that there are no original stories: originality now means the personal colouring of existing themes."

Garner's widely acclaimed novel, *The Owl Service*, is an example that fairly well illustrates his theory. "Mr. Garner's story is remarkable not only for its sustained and evocative atmosphere, but for its implications. It is a drama of young people confronted with the challenge of moral choice; at the same time it reveals, like diminishing reflections in a mirror, the eternal recurrence of the dilemma with each generation," wrote a reviewer for *Children's Book World*. A critic for *Christian Science Monitor* commented, "In a daring juxtaposition of legend from the *Mabinogion*, and the complex relationship of two lads and a girl, old loves and hates, are, as it were, re-enacted. Mr. Garner sets his tale in a Welsh valley and touches with pity and terror the minds of the reader who will let himself feel its atmosphere. This is not a book 'for children'; its subtle truth is for anyone who will reach for it."

BIOGRAPHICAL/CRITICAL SOURCES: Christian Science Monitor, November 2, 1967; *Children's Book World,* November 3, 1968; John Rowe Townsend, *A Sense of Story: Essays on Contemporary Writers for Children,* Longman, 1971; Julie Wintle and Emma Fisher, *The Pied Pipers: Interviews with the Influential Creators of Children's Literature,* Paddington.*

*   *   *

GARNER, H(essle) F(ilmore) 1926

PERSONAL: Born February 24, 1926, in Creston, Iowa; son of Ray F. (a hotel manager) and Leda (a hotel manager; maiden name, Dickens) Garner; married Mary Craig (an art therapist), August 29, 1954; children: Ana Christina, Craig Curtis, Mark McLean, Bruce Gordon, Raquel Marie, Noel Katrine, Simone Michelle. *Education:* Iowa State University, B.S., 1950; University of Iowa, M.S., 1951, Ph.D., 1953. *Home:* 302 Park, Upper Montclair, N.J. 07043. *Office:* Department of Geology, Rutgers University, Newark, N.J. 07102.

CAREER: Standard Oil of California, Los Angeles, Calif., geologist in San Francisco, Calif., 1953-54, and in Peru and Ecuador, 1954-56; University of Arkansas, Fayetteville, assistant professor, 1956-61, associate professor of geology, 1962-67; Rutgers University, Newark, N.J., professor of geology, 1967—. *Military service:* U.S. Navy, 1944-46. *Member:* Geological Society of America (fellow), Paleontological Society, American Association of Petroleum Geologists, American Association for the Advancement of Science, National Geographic Society, New York Academy of Sciences.

WRITINGS: Permian Ammonoid Zones of the West Texas Region (guidebook), West Texas Geological Society, 1953; (contributor) H. G. Richards and other editors, *The Cretaceous Fossils of New Jersey,* Part II, New Jersey Geological Survey, 1962; (contributor) Benjamin Moulton, editor, *Readings in Earth Science,* Van Nostrand, 1972; *The Origin of Landscapes: A Synthesis of Geomorphology,* Oxford University Press, 1974; *Planet Earth: An Introduction to Physical Geology,* Wadsworth, in press. Contributor to *Encyclopedia of Geomorphology* and *Encyclopedia of Earth Sciences.* Contributor of about thirty-five articles to scientific journals, including *Scientific American.*

SIDELIGHTS: Garner writes: "*The Origin of Landscapes* was a major career objective and required about fifteen years in the compiling and writing. It was motivated by a desire to help geologists interpret the earth and by my own drive to teach and create. *Planet Earth* is an effort to bring ideas to beginning students in geology and to give ideas outlined in *The Origin of Landscapes* to a wider audience."

*   *   *

GARNETT, Tay 1894(?)-1977

1894(?)—October 4, 1977; American director and screenwriter. Among Garnett's most well-known films were "The Postman Always Rings Twice," "A Connecticut Yankee in King Arthur's Court," "Valley of Decision," and "Mrs. Parkington." Prior to becoming a director, Garnett was a writer for Mack Sennett comedies. He died in Los Angeles, Calif. Obituaries: *New York Times,* October 19, 1977.

*   *   *

GARRETT, Charles 1925-1977

November 10, 1925—September 10, 1977; American historian, educator, and author. Garrett was a professor of American history at C. W. Post College of Long Island University. He specialized in the history of twentieth-century America and New York City. He died in New York City. Obituaries: *New York Times,* September 12, 1977; *AB Bookman's Weekly,* November 21, 1977.

*   *   *

GARRETT, Clarke 1935-

PERSONAL: Born February 26, 1935, in Evanston, Ill.; son of William B. (an attorney) and Margaret (Clarke) Garrett; married Margaret Davenport (a college administrator), June 29, 1957; children: Amy, Susan, Margaret. *Education:* Carleton College, B.A., 1957; University of Wisconsin, Madison, Ph.D., 1961. *Home:* 133 East High St., Carlisle, Pa. 17013. *Office:* Department of History, Dickinson College, Carlisle, Pa. 17013.

CAREER: Wake Forest University, Winston-Salem, N.C., assistant professor of history, 1961-65; Dickinson College, Carlisle, Pa., assistant professor, 1965-67, associate professor, 1967-72, professor of history, 1972—, director of Center for European Studies in Bologna, Italy, 1969-70. Member of board of directors of Central Pennsylvania Youth Ballet Guild. *Member:* Society for French Historical Studies, American Society for Eighteenth Century Studies. *Awards, honors:* National Endowment for the Humanities fellow, 1970; Newberry Library fellow, 1970-71.

WRITINGS: Respectable Folly: Millenarians and the French Revolution in France and England, Johns Hopkins Press, 1975.

WORK IN PROGRESS: Research on witchcraft and popular culture in western Europe and on spirit possession in eighteenth-century popular religion.

SIDELIGHTS: Garrett comments: "I'm interested in using the theoretical and comparative insights of anthropology to understand the culture and religion of the popular classes of 'Old Regime' Europe."

*   *   *

GARRETT, Gerald R. 1940-

PERSONAL: Born September 21, 1940, in Mount Vernon, Wash.; son of Kenneth J. and Odessa P. (Wells) Garrett; married Marcia Pope (a professor of sociology and a lawyer), June 10, 1967. *Education:* Whitman College, A.B., 1962; Washington State University, M.A., 1966, Ph.D., 1970. *Office:* Department of Sociology, University of Massachusetts, Boston, Mass. 02125.

CAREER: University of Wisconsin, Whitewater, instructor in sociology, 1966-67; Carroll College, Waukesha, Wis., assistant professor of sociology, 1967-68; Washington State University, Pullman, research fellow in sociology, 1968-70; University of Massachusetts, Boston, associate professor of sociology, 1970—. Research associate at Columbia University, 1969, 1970; lecturer at University of Maryland, European Division (Heidelberg, Germany), 1976-77; visiting associate professor at Washington State University, 1977. Member of National Task Force on Higher Education and Criminal Justice, 1975-76. *Member:* American Sociological Association, American Society of Criminology, Massachusetts Sociological Association.

WRITINGS: (With H. M. Bahr) *Women Alone,* Heath, 1976; (with Richard Rettig and Manuel J. Torres) *Manny: A Criminal-Addict's Story,* Houghton, 1977.

Contributor: H. M. Bahr, editor, *Skid Row: An Introduction to Disaffiliation,* Oxford University Press, 1973; Jack Kinton, editor, *Police Roles in the 1970's,* Social Science & Sociological Resources, 1975; Jack and Joann Delora, editors, *Intimate Life Styles,* Goodyear Publishing, 1976. Contributor to social studies, sociology, and psychology journals.

WORK IN PROGRESS: Research on alcoholism in women, alcohol problems in the military, correctional education, and evaluations research.

* * *

GARRETT, Gerard 1928-

PERSONAL: Born May 5, 1928, in London, England; son of Thomas Hornby (a businessman) and Violet (Bush) Garrett. *Education:* Attended Salesian College. *Home:* 21 Romney Rd., New Malden, Surrey, England.

CAREER: Kensington Post, London, England, staff reporter, 1950-56; *TV Mirror,* London, England, sub-editor and feature writer, 1956-57; Rank Organisation, Pinewood Studios, Buckinghamshire, England, unit publicity director, 1957-58; *Evening Standard,* London, England, author of "Show Page," a show column, 1958-69; *Daily Sketch,* London, England, television critic, 1970-73; free-lance writer, 1973—.

WRITINGS: The Films of David Niven, LSP Books, 1975, Citadel, 1976; *The Winemaker's Log,* Collins, 1976; *Prince of Darkness* (about horror films), LSP Books, 1978. Contributor to magazines and newspapers.

WORK IN PROGRESS: A book of his collected magazine articles on winemaking; a book on cinema in the 1960's; *The Devil May Care,* a novel; a collection of stories.

SIDELIGHTS: Garrett comments: "I have no high-flown attitudes toward my vocation. I aim to please, but insinuate Reformist ideas painlessly where compatible. After years of international travel as a journalist, penning millions of words, I now prefer to produce major series or books, mainly on entertainment subjects."

AVOCATIONAL INTERESTS: Listening to music.

* * *

GARRY, Charles R. 1909-

PERSONAL: Birth-given name, Garabed Hagop Robutlay Garabedian; born March 17, 1909, in Bridgewater, Mass.; son of Hagop Robutlay (a laborer) and Varthouie (Bananian) Garabedian; married Louise Evelyn Edgar, November 9, 1932. *Education:* San Francisco Law School, J.D., 1938. *Home:* 482 Wellington, Daly City, Calif. *Agent:* Joan Daves, 515 Madison Ave., New York, N.Y. 10022. *Office:* Garry, Dreyfus, McTernan, Brotsky, Pesonen, Harndon, Inc., 1256 Market St., San Francisco, Calif. 94102.

CAREER: Admitted to California Bar, 1938; attorney in private practice, 1938-57; Garry, Dreyfus, McTernan, Brotsky, Pesonen, Herndon, Inc., San Francisco, Calif., senior partner, 1957—. *Military service:* U.S. Army, 1943-45.

WRITINGS: (Contributor) Ann Fagan Ginger, editor, *Minimizing Racism in Jury Trials: The Voir Dire Conducted by Charles R. Garry in the People of California versus Huey P. Newton,* National Lawyers Guild, 1969; (with Art Goldberg) *Streetfighter in the Courtroom,* Dutton, 1977.

SIDELIGHTS: Garry's legal clients have included the demonstrators at the 1960 San Francisco appearance of the House Un-American Activities Committee, Black Panthers Huey Newton, Bobby Seale, and Eldridge Cleaver, the Oakland Seven draft resisters, the San Quentin Six (accused of murder and conspiracy in a prison escape attempt), Inez Garcia (who murdered a man who helped rape her), and anti-war leader Rennie Davis.

According to Art Silverman, Garry's role as a radical defense lawyer has been, "to use the law against itself, to help bring about fundamental social change by keeping activists out of prison." Garry's own explanation of his purpose is "to give legal first aid. Nothing more than that. No lawyer can change the basics; the people have to do that. The best I can say is that my clients, who are part of movements for social change, get the opportunity to continue their work with some sort of freedom. It would be callous to think that we (lawyers) do anything more than that."

Hanging on the wall of Garry's San Francisco office is a framed quotation which says: "When tyranny is law, revolution is order."

BIOGRAPHICAL/CRITICAL SOURCES: San Francisco Examiner, August 12, 1977; *Berkeley Barb,* August 26, 1977; *Washington Post,* September 29, 1977.

* * *

GARVIE, A(lexander) F(emister) 1934-

PERSONAL: Born January 29, 1934, in Edinburgh, Scotland; son of Alexander (an office manager) and Edith (Tyson) Garvie; married Jane Wallace Johnstone (a teacher), August 4, 1966; children: Margaret, David. *Education:* University of Edinburgh, M.A., 1955; Cambridge University, B.A., 1959, M.A., 1964. *Religion:* Church of Scotland. *Residence:* Glasgow, Scotland. *Office:* Department of Greek, University of Glasgow, Glasgow, Scotland.

CAREER: University of Glasgow, Glasgow, Scotland, assistant lecturer, 1960-61, lecturer, 1961-73, senior lecturer in Greek, 1973—. Visiting Gillespie Professor at College of Wooster, 1967-68; visiting assistant professor at Ohio State University, 1968. *Military service:* British Army, 1955-57. *Member:* Hellenic Society (member of council, 1971-74), Classical Association, Classical Association of Scotland, Scottish-Hellenic Society.

WRITINGS: Aeschylus' Suppliants: Play and Trilogy, Cambridge University Press, 1969. Contributor of articles and reviews to classical studies journals.

WORK IN PROGRESS: Commentary on Aeschylus' *Choephori.*

SIDELIGHTS: "I am interested in Greek literature in general," Garvie told *CA,* "but more particularly in Greek poetry, with a special interest in tragedy. My book was concerned with the dating of a play, which used to be considered the earliest surviving play of Aeschylus, but which a papyrus fragment shows to be comparatively late. I agreed that this new evidence must be taken seriously, and that the internal evidence of the play itself supports (or does not conflict with) the late dating."

AVOCATIONAL INTERESTS: Music, hill walking.

* * *

GARVIN, Philip 1947-

PERSONAL: Born November 16, 1947, in New York, N.Y.; son of Gene (a businessman) and Nora (Shapiro) Garvin. *Education:* Yale University, B.A., 1969, M.F.A., 1970. *Home address:* P.O. Box 147, Ridgway, Colo. 81432. *Office:* Media Design Studio, 305 Crown St., New Haven, Conn. 06520.

CAREER: Lecturer in art, research associate, and film producer at Yale University, New Haven, Conn.; producer and director for WGBH-Television, Boston, Mass.; president of Norac, Inc., New York City. *Awards, honors:* National Book Award nominations, 1970, for *A People Apart,* and 1974, for *Religious America;* four Golden Eagle awards from Council on International Nontheatrical Events for documentary films.

WRITINGS: A People Apart: Hasidism in America, Dutton, 1970; (with Julia Welch) *Religious America,* McGraw, 1974.

WORK IN PROGRESS: "Westering," a series of dramatic films presenting the history of the American West, with a book expected to result.

*   *   *

GASSAN, Arnold 1930-

PERSONAL: Born May 2, 1930, in Alliance, Neb.; son of Edward and Ruth E. (Muzzey) Gassan; married wife Laird (a teacher), August 23, 1970; children: A. Lawrence, Richard. *Education:* University of Colorado, B.F.A., 1966; University of New Mexico, M.A., 1967. *Office:* School of Art, Ohio University, Athens, Ohio 45701.

CAREER: Engineer in Denver, Colo., 1955-60; photographer in Denver, Colo., 1960-64; Ohio University, Athens, associate professor of art, 1967—. *Military service:* U.S. Air Force, 1948-52.

WRITINGS: A Chronology of Photography, Handbook Co., 1972; *Handbook for Contemporary Photography,* Light Impressions Corp., 1977.

WORK IN PROGRESS: Fences, a book of words and photographs.

*   *   *

GASTER, T(heodor) Herzl 1906-

PERSONAL: Born July 21, 1906, in London, England; son of Moses and Lucy (Friedlander) Gaster; came to United States in 1939, naturalized citizen, 1944; married Lotta Schmitz (a college instructor); children: Corinna Michal. *Education:* University of London, B.A. (honors in classics), 1928, M.A., 1936; Columbia University, Ph.D., 1943. *Religion:* Jewish. *Home:* 390 Riverside Dr,, New York, N.Y. 10025. *Office:* 219 A Milbank Hall, Barnard College, Columbia University, New York, N.Y. 10027.

CAREER: Dropsie College, Philadelphia, Pa., professor of religion, 1944-59, visiting professor of religion, 1959-66; Fairleigh Dickinson University, Teaneck, N.J., professor of ancient civilizations, 1959-66; Columbia University, New York, N.Y., adjunct professor of religion, 1954-66, Barnard College, professor of religion, 1966-72, professor emeritus, 1972—. Chief of Hebraic section, U.S. Library of Congress, 1944-48. Fulbright professor of history of religion, University of Rome, 1951-52, and of biblical studies and history of religions, Melbourne, 1961-62; special lecturer, Yale University, 1972, and Barnard College, 1972—. *Member:* American Oriental Society, Society of Biblical Literature (honorary president, 1973-74), American Archaeological Institute, Society for Old Testament Studies (Great Britain), Society for the Study of Religion, American Academy of Religion, American Classical Society. *Awards, honors:* Guggenheim fellowships, 1954, 1959; D.D., University of Vermont, 1965; D.Litt., University of London, 1971; D.H.L., Kenyon College, 1971.

WRITINGS: Passover: Its History and Traditions, Schu-

man, 1949; *Purim and Hanukkah in Custom and Tradition: Feast of Lots and Feast of Lights,* Schuman, 1950; *Thespis: Ritual, Myth and Drama in the Ancient Near East,* Schuman, 1950, 2nd revised edition, Gordian, 1975; (editor and translator) *The Oldest Stories in the World,* Viking, 1952; *Festivals of the Jewish Year: A Modern Interpretation and Guide,* Sloane, 1953; *New Year: Its History, Customs, and Superstitions,* Abelard, 1955; *The Holy and the Profane: Evolution of Jewish Folkways,* Sloane, 1955, published as *Customs and Folkways of Jewish Life,* Apollo, 1966; (editor and translator) *The Dead Sea Scriptures in English Translation,* Anchor Books, 1956, 3rd edition, Doubleday, 1976 (published in England as *The Scriptures of the Dead Sea Sect,* Secker & Warburg, 1957); (editor) *The New Golden Bough,* Criterion, 1959; *Myth, Legend and Custom in the Old Testament,* Harper, 1969, new edition in two volumes, 1975. Contributor of numerous articles to periodicals, encyclopedias, and dictionaries.

SIDELIGHTS: Gaster works in twenty-nine languages and dialects, and has assembled a card file of seventeen thousand items concerning world folklore.*

*   *   *

GAUDET, Frederick J(oseph) 1902-1977

March 5, 1902—December 12, 1977; Canadian author and professor of psychology at Stevens Institute of Technology for more than thirty years. Gaudet specialized in the psychological aspects of labor and was consultant to various firms throughout the United States and Canada. He died in Yarmouth, Nova Scotia. Obituaries: *New York Times,* December 31, 1977. (See index for *CA* sketch)

*   *   *

GAY, Zhenya 1906-

PERSONAL: Born September 16, 1906, in Norwood, Mass. *Education:* Attended Columbia University, 1919-22; later studied in New York City under Solon Borglum and Winold Reiss, and in Paris under Gaston Dorfinant. *Residence:* Saugerties, N.Y.

CAREER: Author and illustrator. Began as a free-lance artist for motion picture posters and newspaper advertisements; worked as a costume designer for Brooks Theatrical Costumes; traveled in Central America, Europe, and Mexico, laying groundwork for future book illustrations. Works have been exhibited in many galleries and museums, including Davis Galleries, Mexico City, 1927, Montross Gallery, New York City, 1930, and American Museum of Natural History, New York City, 1935.

WRITINGS—All self-illustrated: (With Jan Gay) *Pancho and His Burro,* Morrow, 1930; (with J. Gay) *The Goat Who Wouldn't Be Good: A Story of Norway,* Morrow, 1931; (with J. Gay) *The Shire Colt,* Doubleday, Doran, 1931; *Sakimura,* Viking, 1937; (with Pachita Crespi) *A Fish Story,* Garden City Publishing, 1939; (with Crespi) *Happy Birthday,* Viking, 1939; (with Crespi) *170 Cats,* Random House, 1939; (with Crespi) *Manuelito of Costa Rica,* Messner, 1940; *Look!,* Viking, 1952; *Jingle Jangle,* Viking, 1953; *Wonderful Things!,* Viking, 1954; *What's Your Name?,* Viking, 1955; *Who Is It?,* Viking, 1957; *Bits and Pieces,* Viking, 1958; *Small One,* Viking, 1958; *The Dear Friends,* Harper, 1959; *The Nicest Time of Year,* Viking, 1960; *I'm Tired of Lions* (Junior Literary Guild selection), Viking, 1961; *Who's Afraid?,* Viking, 1965.

Illustrator: Nikolai Vasilievich Gogol, *Taras Bulba* (translation from the Russian by Isabel F. Hapgood), Knopf, 1915; Thomas De Quincey, *Confessions of an English Opium-Eater,* Limited Editions Club, 1930; J. Gay, *Town Cats,* Knopf, 1932; Gaius Valerius Catullus, *Poems* (English translation by Horace Gregory), Covici-Friede, 1933; Frances Clarke Sayers, *Mr. Tidy Paws,* Viking, 1935; Idwal Jones, *Whistler's Van,* Viking, 1936; Oscar Wilde, *Ballad of Reading Gaol,* Limited Editions Club, 1937; Eleanor Hoffmann, *Travels of a Snail,* Stokes Publishing, 1939; Gretchen McKown and Florence S. Gleeson, *All the Days Were Antonia's,* Viking, 1939.

Hoffmann, *Cat of Paris,* Stokes Publishing, 1940; Rutherford George Montgomery, *Troopers Three,* Caxton, 1940; Crespi, *Cabita's Rancho: A Story of Costa Rica,* Messner, 1942; Antoni Gronowicz, *Bolek,* Thomas Nelson, 1942; Melicent H. Lee, *Village of Singing Birds,* Harper, 1942; Agnes Fisher, *Once Upon a Time: Folk Tales, Myths, and Legends of the United Nations,* Thomas Nelson, 1943; Arkadii Petrovich Gaidar, *Timur and His Gang* (translation by Zina Voynow), Scribner, 1943; Walt Whitman, *There Was a Child Went Forth,* Harper, 1943; Helen Acker, *Three Boys of Old Russia,* Thomas Nelson, 1944; (with Edmund Monroe) Raymond Will Burnett, *To Live in Health,* Duell, 1944; Janette S. Lowrey, *In the Morning of the World,* Harper, 1944; Irving Robert Melbo and others, *Young Neighbors in South America,* Silver Burdett, 1944; Hilda T. Harpster, *Insect World,* Viking, 1947; Irma Black, *Toby: A Curious Cat,* Holiday House, 1948.

Ruth Tooze, *Tim and the Brass Buttons,* Messner, 1951; Elizabeth Helfman, *Milkman Freddy,* Messner, 1952; Joseph Eugene Chipperfield, *Beyond the Timberland Trail,* Longmans, Green, 1953; Frances Louise Lockridge, *Lucky Cat,* Lippincott, 1953; Miriam Evangeline Mason, *Major and His Camels,* Macmillan, 1953; Mason, *Sugarbush Family,* Macmillan, 1954; Jane Quigg, *Jiggy Likes Nantucket,* Oxford University Press, 1954; Elizabeth Jane Coatsworth, *Peddler's Cart,* Macmillan, 1956; Christine Von Hagen, *Pablo of Flower Mountain,* R. Hale, 1956.*

*   *   *

GEARE, Mildred Mahler   1888(?)-1977

1888(?)—November 26, 1977; American journalist. Geare was an early defender and proponent of women's rights. Her notable journalistic assignments included coverage of the Russian revolution in 1917 and national presidential conventions from 1932 to 1960. Obituaries: *New York Times,* November 28, 1977; *Washington Post,* November 29, 1977.

*   *   *

GEBHARD, Bruno (Frederic)   1901-

PERSONAL: Born February 1, 1901, in Rostock, Germany; came to United States in 1937, naturalized in 1944; son of Fritz William (a custodian) and Meta (Ross) Gebhard; married Gerta Adolph, April 8, 1927 (died, 1975); children: Susanna (Mrs. Alvin Goodman), Christine (Mrs. Bernard McCabe), Ursula (Mrs. Raymond Fink). *Education:* Attended University of Munich, 1921-22, and University of Berlin, 1922-23; University of Rostock, M.D., 1925. *Politics:* Democrat. *Religion:* Congregational. *Home:* 3276 Braemar, Shaker Heights, Ohio 44120. *Office:* Cleveland Health Museum, 8911 Euclid Ave., Cleveland, Ohio 44100.

CAREER: Children's Hospital, Dortmund, Germany, resident physician, 1926; German Hygiene Museum, Dresden, Germany, curator, 1927-32; Exhibition Office, Berlin, Germany, director of research and planning, 1932-37; New York

World's Fair, New York, N.Y., consultant in medicine and public health, 1937-40; Cleveland Health Museum, Cleveland, Ohio, director, 1940-65, director emeritus, 1965—. Associate in health education at Western Reserve University (now Case Western Reserve University), 1940-65; delegate to International Council of Museums, Paris, 1948; consultant to Army Medical Museum, 1951. *Member:* Swedish Academy of Association (honorary member of history section), American Medical Association (fellow), American Public Health Association, American Association of the History of Medicine, American Association of Museums, Hertzler Research Foundation (honorary life member), Cleveland Academy of Medicine (distinguished member), Rotary International, Rowfant Club (Cleveland). *Awards, honors:* Austrian Red Cross Award, 1930; Olympic Games award, 1936; Elizabeth S. Prentiss award, 1965; Golden Door award from Nationality Services Center, 1968.

WRITINGS: (Editor with Herbert Michael, Gerhard Brecher, and Hatto Weiss) *Wunder des Lebens* (title means "Wonder of Life"), Union Deutsche Verlag, 1936; *Das Leben der Frau* (title means "The Life of Women in Health and Disease"), Union Deutsche Verlag, 4th edition, 1937; *Im Strom und Gegenstrom* (title means "With and Against the Stream: Autobiography, 1919-1937"), Steiner, 1976; *Two Lives,* Cleveland Health Museum, in press. Contributor of more than one hundred eighty articles to professional journals of medicine and museum work.

SIDELIGHTS: Gebhard commented about his work: "The Cleveland Health Museum is the first of its kind in the United States. It features thirteen teaching laboratories used by thirty thousand pupils during the school year. The exhibit space deals with human biology, personal health care, and public health."

*   *   *

GECK, Francis J(oseph)   1900-

PERSONAL: Born December 20, 1900, in Detroit, Mich.; son of Jacob C. (a grocer) and Anna (Angermeier) Geck; married Evelyn M. Sturdyvin, July 22, 1937. *Education:* Studied painting privately in Detroit, Mich., and interior design at Paris Atelier of New York School of Fine and Applied Art (now Parsons School of Design); Syracuse University, M.F.A., 1946. *Home:* 407 Sixteenth St., Boulder, Colo. 80302. *Office:* Department of Fine Arts, University of Colorado, Boulder, Colo. 80302.

CAREER: New York School of Fine and Applied Art (now Parsons School of Design), New York, N.Y., instructor in interior architecture and decoration at Paris Atelier, Paris, France, 1925-27; William Wright Co., Detroit, Mich., interior architect and designer, 1927-30; University of Colorado, Boulder, instructor, 1930-35, assistant professor, 1935-44, associate professor, 1944-65, professor of fine arts, 1965-69, professor emeritus, 1969—, curator of exhibits, 1947-57. Director of Sherwood Art Gallery, Boulder, 1937-40; director of exhibits for Boulder Historical Society, 1944-58, and Pioneer Museum, 1958—; design consultant to Mullins Plastics, 1969—. Work as an artist and designer has been exhibited at museums, art institutes, and universities and colleges throughout the country. Associate for research of Historic Boulder, Inc., 1972—; member of Boulder advisory council of Colorado Centennial-Bicentennial Commission, beginning 1972.

MEMBER: Mediaeval Academy of America, Bibliographical Society of America, American Artists Professional League, Renaissance Society of America, American Institute of Interior Designers (education associate; honorary fellow), American Society of Interior Design (honorary fellow), Interior Design Educators Council (member of executive committee, 1963-65; emeritus member, 1969—), American Association of University Professors, Michigan Watercolor Society, Boulder Artists Guild (president, 1944-46, 1971), Boulder Historical Society (president, 1948-50, 1952-53, 1970), Parson School of Design Alumni Council (vice-president, 1952-55), Delta Phi Delta (national treasurer, 1940-48; national president, 1954-58), Theta Xi, Knights of Columbus. *Awards, honors:* Honorable mention, Florida International Art Exhibition, 1952; Grumbacker Award of Merit for outstanding contribution to the arts, 1952; Gold Award, American Artists Professional League National Show, 1953; American Institute of Interior Designers citation of merit, 1963; Tommaso Campanella silver metal, Accademia Internazionale di Lettere-Arti-Scienze, 1970; Benedictine Art Award honorable mention, 1971.

WRITINGS: French Interiors and Furniture: The Historical Development, University of Colorado, 1932; *Bibliographies of Italian Art,* University of Colorado, Volume V: *Bibliography of Italian Gothic Art,* 1935, Volume VI: *Bibliography of Italian Early Renaissance Art,* 1932, Volume VII: *Bibliography of Italian High Renaissance Art,* 1933, Volume VIII: *Bibliography of Italian Late Renaissance Art,* 1934, Volume IX: *Bibliography of Italian Baroque Art,* 1937, Volume X: *Bibliography of Italian Rococo Art,* 1941; *Art: The Period Styles,* University of Colorado, 1945; *Exercises in Perspective,* University of Colorado, 1948; *Introduction to Interior Decoration,* W. C. Brown, 1951; *Interior Design and Decoration: An Outline,* W. C. Brown, 1962, 4th edition, 1971; *Dial-a-Style: English Period Furniture,* Pruett, 1966. Contributor to *Palette, School Executive, Journal of Educational Research,* and other journals of art and education.

* * *

GEGA, Peter C(hristopher) 1924-

PERSONAL: Surname is pronounced *Gay*-ga; born April 9, 1924, in Newark, N.J.; son of Benjamin (a stationary engineer) and Anna (Mazich) Gega. *Education:* University of Southern California, A.B., 1949, M.S., 1952, Ed.D., 1955. *Office:* Department of Elementary Education, San Diego State University, San Diego, Calif. 92182.

CAREER: San Diego State University, San Diego, Calif., assistant professor, 1955-59, associate professor, 1960-64, professor of elementary education, 1964—. *Member:* Council for Elementary Science International (past president), National Science Teachers Association.

WRITINGS: Science in Elementary Education, Wiley, 1966, 3rd edition, 1977; (with Milo K. Blecha and Muriel Green) *Exploring Science,* six volumes, Laidlaw Brothers, 1976.

AVOCATIONAL INTERESTS: Flying, golf, bicycling.

* * *

GEIPEL, John 1937-

PERSONAL: Born January 25, 1937, in Richmond, England; son of Eric (a bank chief accountant) and Gwen Geipel; divorced. *Education:* Attended high school in Berkshire, England. *Home and office:* 1 Cranes Park Cres., Surbiton, Surrey, England.

CAREER: Free-lance writer and illustrator, 1959—. Has worked on animated television series for British Broadcast-

ing Corp., Associated Television Ltd., and Thames Television, and on "Dodo the Space Kid," for National Broadcasting Co. (NBC)—Television; scriptwriter and designer of commercial and educational films, filmstrips, and other audio-visual presentations; film producer and writer for Central Office of Information, 1966-68; has appeared on television and radio programs. Medical writer for Sterling Drug, 1968-73; sports and topical cartoonist for London *Evening News,* 1973-76; translator from Danish to English; lecturer at universities in England, Denmark, and the United States. *Military service:* British Army, 1957-59.

WRITINGS: The Europeans, Longmans, Green, 1969; *Anthropologie de l'Europe* (title means "Anthropology of Europe"), Laffont, 1970; *The Viking Legacy,* A. S. Barnes, 1970; *The Cartoon,* A. S. Barnes, 1970; *Soul—An Afro-American Music,* Dobson, 1974; *Great Adventures of the Vikings,* Rand McNally, 1977.

Illustrator: *Kari and the Stallo,* MacDonald Educational, 1975; *Toytown Annual,* World Distributors, 1975; *Basil Brush,* Purnell, 1975; *Funky Phantom Annual,* Brown Watson, 1975; *Scooby-Doo Annual,* Brown Watson, 1976. Also illustrator of *Barnaby Annual,* Stafford Pembeam; *Magic Roundabout Scrapbook,* Purnell; *Pink Panther Scrapbook,* Purnell.

Contributor of cartoons to comic books and local newspapers. Editor of "Philips Merchandiser," for Philips Industries, 1976-77.

WORK IN PROGRESS: A children's version of *The Europeans;* a book on the general historical linguistics of Europe; illustrations for a book on safety at work; a book on Parkinson's Disease for Lederle Laboratories.

SIDELIGHTS: Geipel writes: "I have scripted and designed several hundredweight of commercial films, filmstrips, and other audio-visual presentations for such international companies as Coca Cola, Shell, and Holiday Inns. I worked for two years at the Halas and Batchelor Cartoon Studio in London, writing and designing language-teaching film series (English, German, and Russian) in collaboration with advisers from the University of Surrey. I also do regular translation work for commercial organisations, such as furniture and chipboard importers, and have made occasional, self-financed trips to such parts of the world as the American Deep South and Soviet Central Asia in search of first-hand material for my books and lectures.

"As, like most authors, I am unable to make even a modest living from my books and lectures, I am forced to work mostly in such fields as commercial copywriting, film-scripting, writing, and editing, cartooning, and book illustration—not particularly stimulating work, but they pay the mortgage, and for the occasional trip overseas."

* * *

GELBART, Larry (Simon) 1923-

PERSONAL: Born February 25, 1923, in Chicago, Ill.; son of Harry (a barber) and Frieda Gelbart; married Patricia Marshall (a singer and actress), November 25, 1956; children: three sons, two daughters. *Education:* Educated in public schools in Chicago, Ill. *Residence:* Los Angeles, Calif.

CAREER: Comedy writer for radio, television, films, and theatre, 1939—. *Military service:* U.S. Army, 1946-47. *Member:* Writers Guild of America, Dramatists Guild, American Society of Composers, Authors, and Publishers (ASCAP). *Awards, honors:* Emmy Award from the National Academy of Television Arts and Sciences and Sylvania Award, both 1958, for "Art Carney Special"; Antoinette Perry Award (Tony), 1963, for "A Funny Thing Happened on the Way to the Forum"; Emmy Award, 1973, and George Foster Peabody Award, 1975, for "M*A*S*H."

WRITINGS—Plays: "The Conquering Hero," first produced in New York City, January, 1961; (with Burt Shevelove) "A Funny Thing Happened on the Way to the Forum" (adaptation of work by Plautus), first produced on Broadway at Alvin Theatre, May 8, 1962; "Sly Fox" (based on "Volpone" by Ben Jonson), first produced on Broadway at Broadhurst Theatre, October 14, 1976. Also author of "Jump," first produced in London, England.

Screenplays: "The Notorious Landlady," 1962; (author of story) "The Thrill of It All," 1963; (with Burt Shevelove) "The Wrong Box," 1966; (with Norman Panama and Peter Barnes) "Not with My Wife, You Don't," 1966; (with Shevelove) "A Funny Thing Happened on the Way to the Forum," 1966; "Oh, God," 1977.

Television scripts: "The Red Buttons Show," 1952; "The Patrice Munsel Show," 1954-62; "The Sid Caesar Show," 1955-57; (with Gene Reynolds, and producer) "M*A*S*H," 1972—; (with Reynolds, and producer) "Karen," 1975. Also writer for several Art Carney specials, Sid Caesar specials, Barbra Streisand specials, and "The Marty Feldman Show."

Radio scripts: "Command Performance" for the Armed Forces Radio, 1947; "The Bob Hope Show," 1949-52. Also writer for "The Fanny Brice Show," "Duffy's Tavern," "The Joan Davis Show," and "The Jack Paar Show."

WORK IN PROGRESS: Two screenplays, "Hadrian VII" and "Double Feature" (which contains two forty-five-minute scripts); a musical, "Baxter Beauties of 1935"; "Dynamite Hands."

SIDELIGHTS: Gelbart considers his recreation "raising and enjoying my five children." He spends most of his time, however, writing very funny scripts which have been known to make people laugh and cry at once. "I make jokes all the time," Gelbart told Mel Gussow. "It's a tic—a way of making myself comfortable. I can't imagine not having humor to lean on. I tend to write things with a circus-like atmosphere. In my mind, there's a circus—three rings—all the time."

Gelbart started as a gag writer, which lead him into script writing. "For a long time," he said, "I didn't think of it as writing. I thought of it as a specialty. To think of myself as a writer was—cheeky." Asked to explain his basic themes, Gelbart responded "Death, sex, and money, in order of height. I guess I'm in awe of all three. They show how scary death is, and maybe how scary sex is, and how greedy I am."

The play "A Funny Thing Happened on the Way to the Forum," which he wrote with Burt Shevelove, was praised by critic Howard Taubman, who also pointed out that no one on the stage ever sets out to go to the "Forum," but that seemed to be beside the point. Abe Laufe wrote: "Just how much of the plot Shevelove and Gelbart borrowed from Plautus was not so important as the fact that they maintained the spirit of the old comedies. 'A Funny Thing' would never win any prizes for literary merit or for subtlety, but it proved that lowbrow humor could still be very entertaining if done properly." Most of the theatrical critics agreed that the show lived up to its title, because it was funny in the same way that burlesque was funny. Gelbart admittedly hated the film version of his play, which Richard Lester directed: "It was gratuitously written and grotesquely directed. Watching that movie is like being run over by a truck and then having it back over you for one and a half hours."

When "Sly Fox" came to Broadway, Gelbart said: "I'm the only one who expected it to be as funny as it is. 'Volpone' preaches. I'd rather write in a lighter way, without underlining a message. I'm clearly trying to entertain the audience." Gelbart even envisioned "Sly Fox" as becoming "a Saturday morning kid's show, about a cute, sly fox cheating the other animals out of chestnuts!"

BIOGRAPHICAL/CRITICAL SOURCES: Abe Laube, *Broadway's Greatest Musicals,* Funk, 1970; *New York Times,* January 5, 1977.*

* * *

GEORGOPOULOS, Basil S(pyros) 1926-

PERSONAL: Born October 15, 1926, in Greece; came to the United States in 1948, naturalized citizen, 1960; son of Spyros Elias and Eurydice A. (Anagnostopoulos) Georgopoulos; married Julia Jeanette Fedeli (a registered nurse), June 25, 1955; children: Liana E., Lona M., Melissa H. *Education:* Bowling Green State University, B.A. (magna cum laude), 1952; University of California, Los Angeles, M.A., 1953; University of Michigan, Ph.D., 1957. *Home:* 3140 Charing Cross, Ann Arbor, Mich. 48104. *Office:* Institute for Social Research, University of Michigan, Ann Arbor, Mich. 48104.

CAREER: University of Michigan, Ann Arbor, assistant study director of Survey Research Center at Institute for Social Research, 1954-56, study director, 1956-64, senior study director, 1964-66, program director, 1966—, research coordinator, 1971-74, research scientist, 1974—, lecturer at university, 1959-61, assistant professor, 1961-64, associate professor, 1964-69, professor of psychology, 1969—, associate director of Health Services Research Center and chairman of doctoral program in organizational psychology, 1976—. Visiting professor at Northwestern University, spring, 1975, and University of Iowa, 1976; member of visiting committee at Vanderbilt University, 1968-74. Member of board of trustees of American Nurses' Foundation, 1967-71; member of health services research study section, U.S. Department of Health, Education & Welfare, and U.S. Public Health Service, 1972-75; consultant to National Science Foundation and National Academy of Sciences. *Military service:* Greek Navy, 1946-48.

MEMBER: International Sociological Association, American Psychological Association (fellow), American Association for the Advancement of Science (fellow), American Sociological Association (fellow), American Academy of Political and Social Science, American Association of University Professors, New York Academy of Science (fellow), Sigma Xi. *Awards, honors:* Book award from American College of Hospital Administrators, 1964, for *The Community General Hospital,* and 1974, for *Organization Research on Health Institutions;* grants from U.S. Department of Health, Education & Welfare and U.S. Public Health Service, 1952-70.

WRITINGS: (With F. C. Mann) *The Community General Hospital,* Macmillan, 1962; (editor) *Organization Research on Health Institutions,* University of Michigan Press, 1972; *Hospital Organization Research: Review and Source Book,* Saunders, 1975. Contributor to scientific journals and journals in the social sciences. Consulting editor of *Journal of Personality and Social Psychology.*

WORK IN PROGRESS: A comparative study of hospital emergency services, to assess organization and effectiveness; a manuscript based on data from a major organizational (controlled) experiment in the area of role specialization in relation to organizational effectiveness; a major text on organization theory.

SIDELIGHTS: Georgopoulos writes that his main interests are "organizations as complex work-performing and problem-solving systems, the social psychology of organizations, open-system theory, management and administration of complex organizations, health services research, and complexity and specialization in organizations."

AVOCATIONAL INTERESTS: Foreign travel.

*   *   *

GERHARDIE, William Alexander   1895-1977
(William Alexander Gerhardi)

November 21, 1895—July 15, 1977; British novelist. During his most prolific period, the 1920's and 1930's, Gerhardie published one novel per year. Among the works for which he received critical acclaim are *Ressurection, The Polyglots, Futility,* and *Of Mortal Love.* Gerhardie died in London, England. Obituaries: *New York Times,* July 16, 1977; *AB Bookman's Weekly,* September 5, 1977. (See index for *CA* sketch)

*   *   *

GEROSA, Guido   1933-
(Sergio Guado)

PERSONAL: Born June 22, 1933, in Fiume, Italy; son of Giuseppe (a military officer) and Egle (Smozuina) Gerosa; married Adelaide Zoffili, June 11, 1960; children: Mario, Alberto. *Education:* University of Milan, law degree, 1957. *Religion:* Roman Catholic. *Home:* 311 East 54 St., New York, N.Y. 10022. *Office:* Rizzoli Editore, 712 Fifth Ave., New York, N.Y. 10019.

CAREER: La Notte (daily newspaper), Milano, Italy, special correspondent, 1953-61; *Epoca* (weekly magazine), Milano, U.S. and special correspondent, 1962-1967; *Europeo* (weekly magazine), Milano, U.S. and special correspondent, 1967—. Editor-in-chief of *Playboy*'s Italian edition, 1972. Notable assignments include coverage of the wars in the Middle East, 1956, 1967, and 1973, and interviews with Marc Chagall, Georges Braque, Alvar Aalto, and other art personalities. Lecturer in Italian universities. *Awards, honors:* Foreign press award from University of California, Los Angeles, 1965, for reporting on the 1964 elections; Premiolino Bagutta (Italy), 1968, for story on Bikini Island population fleeing after explosion of H-Bomb.

WRITINGS—Nonfiction: *Da Giarabub a salo* (title means "From Giarabub to Salo"), Cinema Nuovo, 1963; *L'Arno non gonfia d'acqua chiara* (title means "Arno Doesn't Swell of Clear Water"), Mondadori, 1967; *Cronache dell'eta atomica* (title means "History of the Floods in Florence"), Sei, 1972; *Cronache dell'eta atomica* (title means "Chronicles of the Atomic Age"), Societa editrice internazionale, 1972; *Chi na ucciso Ben Barka?* (title means "Who Killed Ben Barka?"), Fabbri, 1973; *Il Delitto Matteotti* (title means "The Maneotti Crime"), Mondadori, 1973; *La Tragedia di Dallas* (title means "The Tragedy of Dallas"), Mondadori, 1974; *I Missili di Cuba* (title means "The Cuban Missiles"), Mondadori, 1974; *I Cannoni del Sinai* (title means "The Guns of Sinai"), Sei, 1975; *L'Bano: Un popolo muore,* Sei, 1976.

Biographies: *Pietro Nenni,* Longanesi, 1972; *Martin Luther King,* Mondadori, 1973; *Winston Churchill,* Mondadori, 1973; *Napoleone,* De Agostini, 1975; *Nelson,* De Agostini, 1976.

Also author of *Libano* (history of Lebanon), 1977, and *Scheda Bianca* (novel; title means "White Ballot"), 1977.

Also author of Italian filmscripts, sometimes under pseudonym Sergio Guado. Writer of foreign policy columns in *Europeo* and *Epoca.* Contributor to *Paris Match, Stern, Manchete* (Brazil), and *Politika* (Jugoslavia).

WORK IN PROGRESS: A book about the first year of Carter's presidency.

SIDELIGHTS: "My major interests are in foreign policy and history," wrote Gerosa. "My aim is to write biographies of major characters in history and famous events with scientific accuracy and journalistic style."

*   *   *

GHEDDO, Piero   1929-

PERSONAL: Born March 10, 1929, in Tronzano, Vatican City; son of Giovanni (a land surveyor) and Rosa (Franzi) Gheddo. *Education:* Attended Pontifical Institute for Mission Extension (P.I.M.E.) Theological Seminary, 1949; Urbaniana University (Rome), degree in missiology, 1956; Bonn University, diploma in German language, 1956; University of Social Studies (Rome), diploma in journalism, 1957. *Home:* 94 Via Mose Bianchi, Milano, Italy 20149.

CAREER: Ordained Roman Catholic priest, 1953; director of *Mondo e Missione* (magazine), 1959—; director of *Italia Missionaria* (magazine for young adults), 1975—. Correspondent for *Avvenire* (Catholic daily newspaper) and other Italian newspapers and magazines, 1956—; member of the staff of EMI (Italian missionary publisher), 1956—. *Member:* Italian Institute for Africa, Societe des Etudes Indochinois, Italian Institute for Middle and Far East, Pro Mundi Vita, P.I.M.E. Missionary Society. *Awards, honors:* Italian journalism prize, Campione d'Italia, 1972, for *Terzo Mondo: Perche povero?*

WRITINGS: Il risveglio dei popoli di colore (title means "Rousing Colored People"), Editrice missionaria italiana, 1956, 2nd edition, 1957; *Giornalismo missionario in Italia* (title means "Missionary Journalism in Italy"), Editrice missionaria italiana, 1958.

Il Concilio ecumenico e le missioni (title means "The Ecumenical Council and Mission"), Pontificio Istituo missioni estere, 1962; (with Domenico Colombo) *L'opera missionaria ed ecumenica* (title means "Missionary and Ecumenical Work"), Pontificio Istituto missioni estere, 1963; (compiler) *Sono fuggito dalla Cina rossa!* (title means "I Run Away from Red China"), Pontificio Istituto missioni estere, 1963; *Concilio e terzo mondo* (title means "Council and the Third World"), Editrice missionaria italiana, 1964; *L'Occidente cristiano ed i paesi in via di sviluppo* (title means "The Western Christian and Countries Under Development"), Pontificio Istituto missioni estere, 1964; (compiler) *Il problema della fame: Documenti pontifici* (title means "The Problem of Hunger: Pontifical Documents"), Editrice missionaria italiana, 1965; (editor) *L'Eglise du tiers-monde* (title means "The Church in the Third World"), Centurion, 1965; *Il difficile cammino dell'India* (title means "The Difficult Rousing of India"), Massimo, 1967; (with Grazioso Ceriani and C. Melzi) *Commento all'enciclica Populorum progressio sullo sviluppo dei popoli* (title means "Comment to the Encyclical Letter: 'Populorum Progressio'"), Massimo, 1967; *Cattolici e buddisti nel Vietnam: Il ruolo delle comunita religiose nella costruzione della pace,* Vallecchi, 1968, translation by Charles Underhill Quinn published as *The Cross and the Bo-tree: Catholics and Buddhists in Vietnam,* Sheed, 1970.

L'annima della politica (title means "The Interior of Politics"), Mani tese, 1971; *Processo alle missioni* (title means "Trial to the Missions"), Editrice missionaria italiana, 1971; *Terzo mondo: Perche povero?,* P.I.M.E., 1971, translation by Kathryn Sullivan published as *Why Is the Third World Poor?,* Orbis, 1973; *I libri dell'impegno* (title means "The Books Which Commence"), Tipo-lito M.E., 1971; *Razzismo: Cancro del nostro tempo* (title means "Racism: Cancer of Our Time"), Editrice missionaria italiana, 1972; *Dove va la Cina?* (title means "Where Is China Going?"), Editrice missionaria italiana, 1972; *Cile: Una Chiesa nella rivoluzione* (title means "Chile: A Church in Revolution"), Gribaudi, 1973; *Vietnam, cristiani e comunisti* (title means "Vietnam, Christians, and Communists"), Societa editrice internazionale, 1976. Also author of *Cambodia: Rivoluzione senza amore* (title means "Cambodia: Revolution Without Love"), 1977.

WORK IN PROGRESS: Research on Cambodia, Vietnam, and India.

SIDELIGHTS: Gheddo writes: "As a priest and a missionary I am interested in the problems of the missionary church as well as in the problems of the Third World and Latin America which I know quite well because I have travelled a lot, both in Asia and Africa, as well as in Latin America. I have been interested, above all, in the Southeast Asian continent (Vietnam, Cambodia, Laos) which I have visited several times. I've written books and many articles on the subject of these countries. I speak very often about these problems and those of the Third World on both Italian and Swiss television." Besides making a significant journalistic contribution, Gheddo gives the world an ideal of universal brotherhood and service to the poor through his writings.

BIOGRAPHICAL/CRITICAL SOURCES: Christian Century, March 18, 1970; *Commonweal,* September 18, 1970.

* * *

GIFFIN, Sidney F. 1907-1977

1907—December 17, 1977; American military officer, strategic adviser, and author. Giffin served in the Army Air Corps and then the Air Force, retiring as brigadier general. Among his posts were vice commandant of the Air War College, and director of the Office of Armed Forces Information and Education. After his retirement from the Air Force, Giffin was program director for the Institute for Defense Analyses. He died in Annapolis, Md. Obituaries: *Washington Post,* December 31, 1977.

* * *

GILDRIE, Richard P(eter) 1945-

PERSONAL: Born April 18, 1945, in Norfolk, Va.; son of C. J. (a teacher) and Virginia (Smith) Gildrie; married Meredith Miller, June 18, 1966; children: Elizabeth, Evelyn. *Education:* Eckerd College, B.A., 1966; University of Virginia, M.A., 1968, Ph.D., 1971. *Politics:* "America's favorite blood sport—serious Democrat." *Religion:* "Calvinist (circa 1680)." *Residence:* Clarksville, Tenn. *Office:* Department of History, Austin Peay State University, Clarksville, Tenn. 37040.

CAREER: Austin Peay State University, Clarksville,

Tenn., assistant professor, 1970-73, associate professor of history, 1973—. *Member:* American Historical Association, American Association of University Professors, Essex Institute, Institute of Early American History and Culture, American Civil Liberties Union, Common Cause, New England Historical and Genealogical Society.

WRITINGS: Salem, Massachusetts, 1626-1683: A Covenant Community, University Press of Virginia, 1975. Contributor to *Essex Institute Historical Collections.*

WORK IN PROGRESS: "I'm trying to discover and describe popular culture or 'subcultures' in seventeenth-century Massachusetts and understand 'leadership style' in that society. To that end I'm pursuing, fitfully, a number of projects, including a collection of articles, written by others and myself, on social order and tension in early New England (co-edited by Charles Sorenson) and a couple of other articles on Puritans. I'd like to write a social history of Puritan Essex County, concentrating on social and political development and conflicting values. Puritanism was not monolithic."

SIDELIGHTS: Gildrie writes: "I am part academic drudge and part humanist social reformer. During the 1960's I was a 'sunshine soldier' in the civil rights and peace movements, but I learned that my talents are limited to spectator and commentator. I love to kibitz. America's early history holds me enthralled. The western world from 1500-1800 holds the keys to grasping much of who we are and what we ought to do."

* * *

GILES, James R(ichard) 1937-

PERSONAL: Born October 26, 1937, in Bowie, Tex.; son of Roger (a butcher) and Eva (a school tax assessor; maiden name, Walker) Giles; married Wanda Hancock (a mental health worker), September 1, 1968; children: Morgan. *Education:* Texas Christian University, B.A., 1960, M.A., 1961; University of Texas, Ph.D., 1967. *Home:* Suburban Apts., #901, DeKalb, Ill. 60115. *Office:* Department of English, Northern Illinois University, DeKalb, Ill. 60115.

CAREER: North Texas State University, Denton, instructor, 1966-67, assistant professor of English, 1967-70; Northern Illinois University, DeKalb, assistant professor, 1970-73, associate professor of English, 1973—.

WRITINGS: Claude McKay, G. K. Hall, 1976.

Anthologized in *Innovative Fiction,* Dell; *No Signs from Heaven,* Dell. Contributor of articles and stories to magazines, including *Quartet, Descant, Phylon,* and *Studies in Black Literature,* and newspapers.

WORK IN PROGRESS: A book on James Jones, for Twayne.

SIDELIGHTS: Giles comments: "My writing is of two kinds: critical, focusing primarily on Black American and post-World War II American literature, and supplementing my vocation as a college English teacher; and 'creative,' essentially short fiction about various aspects of 'the Texas experience,' because that is what I write about most convincingly."

* * *

GILL, Brendan 1914-

PERSONAL: Born October 4, 1914, in Hartford, Conn.; son of Michael Henry Richard and Elizabeth (Duffy) Gill; married Anne Barnard, June 20, 1936; children: Brenda,

Michael, Holly, Madelaine, Rosemary, Kate, Charles. *Education:* Yale University, B.A., 1936. *Office: New Yorker,* 25 West 43rd St., New York, N.Y. 10036.

CAREER: New Yorker, New York, N.Y., regular contributor, 1936—, film critic, 1960-67, drama critic, 1968—. *Member:* Irish Georgian Society (board member), Institute for Art and Urban Resources (president), Victorian Society (vice-president), New York Landmark Conservancy (board chairman), Municipal Art Society (board chairman), Film Society of Lincoln Center (vice-president). *Awards, honors:* National Institute of Arts and Letters grant, 1951; National Book Award, 1951, for *The Trouble of One House.*

WRITINGS: Death in April and Other Poems, Hawthorne House, 1935; *The Trouble of One House* (novel), Doubleday, 1950; *The Day the Money Stopped* (novel), Doubleday, 1957; (with Robert Kimball) *Cole: A Book of Cole Porter Lyrics and Memorabilia,* Holt, 1972; *Tallulah,* Holt, 1972; (author of introduction) *The Portable Dorothy Parker,* Viking, 1973; (editor) *Happy Times,* photography by Jerome Zerbe, Harcourt, 1973; *Ways of Loving: Two Novellas and Eighteen Short Stories,* Harcourt, 1974; (editor) Philip Barry, *States of Grace: Eight Plays,* Harcourt, 1975; *Here at the New Yorker,* Random House, 1975; *Lindbergh Alone,* Harcourt, 1977; *Summer Places,* photography by Dudley Witney, Stewart & McClelland, 1977.

Also author of "La Belle," (play), first produced in Philadelphia, 1962.

Contributor of short stories to *Saturday Review, New Yorker, Collier's,* and *Virginia Quarterly Review.*

WORK IN PROGRESS: A biography of Stanford White, for Viking; a collection of essays, *Thirties People,* for Harcourt.

SIDELIGHTS: Disdaining the tortured artist myth, Gill writes fondly of his career at *New Yorker:* "I started out at the place where I wanted most to be and with much pleasure and very little labor have remained here since." Unlike his colleagues, whom he describes as "lonely, molelike creatures, who work in their own portable if not peasant darkness and who seldom utter a sound above a groan," Gill is amused by his talent. "I am always so ready to take a favorable view of my powers," writes Gill, "that even when I am caught out and made a fool of, I manage to twist this circumstance about until it becomes a proof of how exceptional I am."

Gill, a diversified writer who has produced novels, short stories, essays, film and drama reviews, told *CA:* "Fiction is my chief interest, followed by architectural history, followed by literary and dramatic criticism. If these fields were to be closed to me, I would write copy for a bird-seed catalogue. In any event, I would write."

Author of the popular bestseller, *Here at the New Yorker,* which *New York Times Book Review* called "delightful" and *Time* termed an "account laced with some acid," Gill is sentimental of the past spent there: "Looking back, I shake my head, not without wonder, at that arrogant, confident beginner." But he is not cynical of the future. "Today I feel emerging on the threshold of old age the latest of the many persons I have been, and even this person may prove, with luck and discipline, only the latest me and not the last."

Gill's *The Day the Money Stopped* was produced as a play by Maxwell Anderson.

BIOGRAPHICAL/CRITICAL SOURCES: New York Times Book Review, February 16, 1975; *Time,* February 24, 1975; Brendan Gill, *Here at the New Yorker,* Random House, 1975.

GILLESPIE, John T(homas) 1928-

PERSONAL: Born September 25, 1928, in Fort William, Ontario, Canada; came to the United States in 1955, naturalized citizen, 1963; son of William and Jean (Barr) Gillespie. *Education:* University of British Columbia, B.A., 1948; Columbia University, M.S., 1957; New York University, Ph.D., 1970. *Home:* 360 East 72nd St., New York, N.Y. 10021. *Office:* Palmer Graduate Library School, C. W. Post Center, Long Island University, Greenvale, N.Y. 11548.

CAREER: Elementary school teacher in British Columbia, 1950-55; school librarian in Hicksville, N.Y., 1956-57, and Roslyn, N.Y., 1957-63; Long Island University, C. W. Post Center, Greenvale, N.Y., associate professor, 1963-71, professor of library science, 1971—, dean of Palmer Graduate Library School, 1971-76. Adjunct assistant professor at Long Island University, 1960-63. Circulation librarian at Hunter College of the City University of New York, 1959-61.

MEMBER: American Library Association, Association of American Library Schools, Association for Educational Communication and Technology, National Education Association, American Association of University Professors, New York Library Association (member of board of directors; president, 1962), New York Library Club, Nassau-Suffolk School Library Association (president, 1960), Phi Delta Kappa, Kappa Delta Pi.

WRITINGS: (With Diana L. Lembo) *Juniorplots,* Bowker, 1966; *The Secondary School Library as an Instructional Materials Center,* New York State Department of Education, 1969; (with Lembo and Ralph J. Folcarelli) *Library Learning Laboratory,* Fordham Publishing, 1969; (with Lembo) *Introducing Books,* Bowker, 1970; (with Diana L. Spirt) *The Young Phenomenon: Paperbacks in Our Schools,* American Library Association, 1971; *Paperback Books for Young People,* American Library Association, 1971, 2nd edition, 1977; (with Spirt) *Creating a School Media Program,* Bowker, 1973; *More Junior Plots,* Bowker, 1977; *A Model School District Media Program,* American Library Association, 1977.

WORK IN PROGRESS: Building School Media Center Collections, publication by Libraries Unlimited expected in 1979; *Encyclopedia of Children's Literature,* publication by Crowell expected in 1979.

SIDELIGHTS: Gillespie told *CA:* "The basic principles of learning have remained the same throughout the years: children learn as individuals, children learn at various rates, children learn according to different styles and patterns, and education is a continuous process. In an attempt to translate these principles into practice, educators have realized that a unified media program involving all forms and types of educational materials and equipment is a necessity. There has been increased support of the library media center concept from many agencies, organizations, and professional personnel because those who are involved in education now realize that a sound media program is a prerequisite for high quality education."

* * *

GILLIES, John 1925-

PERSONAL: Born December 15, 1925, in Chicago, Ill.; son of Anton J. (a clergyman) and Anna (a social worker; maiden name, Batutis) Gillies; married Carolyn Young (a librarian), March 18, 1950; children: Laurie Gillies Fraites, Stephen, Andrew. *Education:* Attended Wheaton College, Wheaton,

Ill., 1945, 1947, Northwestern University, 1947-49, and University of Texas, 1956-57. *Politics:* Independent. *Religion:* Presbyterian. *Home:* 9303 Hunters Trace E., Austin, Tex. 78758. *Office:* 2704 Rio Grande, #9, Austin, Tex. 78705.

CAREER: Presbyterian Church of the United States, Atlanta, Ga., audiovisual director, 1961-65; Christian Rural Overseas Program/Church World Service, Elkhart, Ind., communication director, 1965-72; communications consultant, 1972-74; State Department of Public Welfare, Austin, Tex., director of educational media production, 1974-77; Christian Rural Overseas Program, Austin, Tex., regional director for Texas, 1977—. Has also worked as mass communications missionary in Brazil, advertising executive, announcer, television director, and newscaster. *Military service:* U.S. Army, 1945-46.

MEMBER: American Federation of Television and Radio Artists, Screen Actors Guild, Authors Guild of Authors League of America, Religious Public Relations Council (past member of board of governors). *Awards, honors:* Blue ribbon from Educational Film Library Association, 1964, for filmstrip script "Gold D. Lox and the Five Bears"; bronze medal from Religious Arts Festival, 1973, for "The Retreat."

WRITINGS: A Primer for Christian Broadcasters, Moody, 1955; *The Martyrs of Guanabara,* Moody, 1976.

Plays: "The Retreat" (one-act), first produced in Sacramento, Calif., at Religious Arts Festival, 1973; and "The Firemakers" (musical play), first produced in Bristol, Ind., at Frontier Theatre, July 1, 1974. Author of several dozen radio, film, filmstrip, and television scripts.

WORK IN PROGRESS: Research on nineteenth-century Evangelical Anglican social reformers in England, for a novel; compiling a collection of one-act plays for chancel dramatic use; exploring family roots in Lithuania and elsewhere.

SIDELIGHTS: Gillies writes: "I am vitally interested in history, believing that there are authentic heroes and heroines yet to be described and popularized. I have found many of these in church history, particularly in script assignments; I am infatuated with the sometimes not-so-saintly saints who have made life and our world more livable. I am a first-generation American and I still have hope and excitement about this country."

AVOCATIONAL INTERESTS: Travel (Europe and the Middle East; has lived in Argentina), amateur photography, semi-professional singer and actor.

* * *

GILMORE, Thomas B(arry, Jr.) 1932-

PERSONAL: Born November 29, 1932, in Chicago, Ill.; son of Thomas Barry (a lawyer) and Sarah (Parmele) Gilmore; married Virginia Arbuckle (a teacher), June 15, 1957; children: Owen, Miles, Frank. *Education:* University of Michigan, A.B., 1954, A.M., 1955; University of Illinois, Ph.D., 1964. *Home:* 1601 Tamarack Trail, Decatur, Ga. 30033. *Office:* Department of English, Georgia State University, Atlanta, Ga. 30303.

CAREER: Queens College of the City University of New York, Flushing, N.Y., lecturer, 1962-64, instructor in English, 1964-65; Cornell College, Mount Vernon, Iowa, assistant professor of English, 1965-69; Georgia State University, Atlanta, associate professor of English, 1969—. *Military service:* U.S. Army, Quartermaster Corps, 1955-57. *Mem-*

ber: Modern Language Association of America, American Society for Eighteenth-Century Studies. *Awards, honors:* Fellow of Newberry Library, 1967-68.

WRITINGS: (Editor and author of introduction) Walter Harte, *An Essay on Satire,* Augustan Reprint Society, 1968; *The Eighteenth-Century Controversy over Ridicule as a Test of Truth: A Reconsideration,* Arts & Science Research Papers, University of Georgia, 1970; (editor and author of introduction) *Early Eighteenth-Century Essays on Taste,* Scholars' Facsimiles & Reprints, 1972. Contributor to *PMLA.*

WORK IN PROGRESS: Samuel Johnson's Dictionary.

AVOCATIONAL INTERESTS: Traditional jazz.

* * *

GINSBURG, Herbert (Paul) 1939-

PERSONAL: Born September 26, 1939, in New York, N.Y.; son of Isaiah (an occupational therapist) and Lillian (Ringler) Ginsburg; married Jane Knitzer (a psychologist), November 24, 1974; children: Deborah, Rebecca, Jonathan. *Education:* Harvard University, B.A., 1961; University of North Carolina, Ph.D., 1965. *Office:* Department of Psychology, University of Maryland, 5401 Wilkens Ave., Baltimore, Md. 21045.

CAREER: Cornell University, Ithaca, N.Y., assistant professor, 1965-69, associate professor of psychology, 1969-76; University of Maryland, Baltimore, professor of psychology, 1976—.

WRITINGS: (With Sylvia Opper) *Piaget's Theory of Intellectual Development,* Prentice-Hall, 1969; *The Myth of the Deprived Child,* Prentice-Hall, 1972; *Children's Arithmetic: The Learning Process,* Van Nostrand, 1977.

WORK IN PROGRESS: Cross-cultural research on intellectual development in Africa.

* * *

GIRVAN, Helen (Masterman) 1891-

PERSONAL: Born in 1891, in Minneapolis, Minn.; married Colin Girvan. *Education:* Graduated from junior college; attended art school and secretarial school.

CAREER: Author of books for young people. Employed for two years as secretary to the vice-president and general manager of the Conde Nast publications.

WRITINGS: Blue Treasure: The Mystery of Tamarind Court (illustrated by Harriet O'Brien), Farrar & Rinehart, 1937; *Phantom on Skis* (illustrated by Alan Haemer), Farrar & Rinehart, 1939; *The House at 231* (illustrated by A. Haemer), Farrar & Rinehart, 1940; *Felicity Way* (illustrated by Gertrude Howe), Farrar & Rinehart, 1942; *The White Tulip* (illustrated by Howe), Farrar & Rinehart, 1944; *The Light in the Mill* (illustrated by Joseph Hopkins, Jr.), Rinehart, 1946; *The Seventh Step: Mystery at Cedarhead* (illustrated by Howe), Rinehart, 1949.

Hidden Pond (illustrated by Albert Orbaan), Dutton, 1951; *End of a Golden String* (illustrated by Vaika Low), Dutton, 1952; *Patty and the Spoonbill* (illustrated by V. Low), Funk & Wagnalls, 1953; *Down Bayberry Lane,* Westminster Press, 1955; *The Clue in the Antique Clock,* Westminster Press, 1957; *Disappearance at Lake House,* Westminster Press, 1959; *Mystery of the Unwelcome Visitor,* Westminster Press, 1961; *The Frightened Whisper,* Westminster Press, 1963; *The Missing Masterpiece,* Westminster Press, 1965; *The Hidden Treasure,* Westminster Press, 1968; *Shadow in the Greenhouse,* Westminster Press, 1970.

AVOCATIONAL INTERESTS: Art, theatre, cooking, boating.*

*   *   *

GIUDICI, Ann Couper 1929-
(Ann Tucker, Ann Tucker-Fettner)

PERSONAL: Born February 25, 1929, in New York, N.Y.; daughter of Samuel Edward (an importer) and Ann Couper; children: Carey, John, Wright, Farley, Peter, David. *Education:* Studied at High Museum of Art, Atlanta, 1946-48. *Home:* 3426 Selwyn Ave., Charlotte, N.C. 28209. *Agent:* Julian Bach, 3 East 48th St., New York, N.Y.

CAREER: East Side Settlement House, New York City, public relations director, 1959-60; WBAI-Public Radio, New York City, arts programming director, 1960; director of four Off-Broadway plays, New York City, 1960-63; freelance writer and director of educational and industrial documentaries, including films for Ford Motor Co., Ayerst Pharmaceuticals, Texaco, Monsanto, and McGraw-Hill, 1965-70; Robert Rogers Films, Charlotte, N.C., partner in writing and directing short promotional films for businesses, 1976—. *Awards, honors:* Received award from American Medical Association, 1971, for film, "Alcoholism: Disease in Disguise."

WRITINGS: (Under name Ann Tucker) *Potpourri, Incense, and Other Fragrant Concoctions,* Workman Publishing, 1972, revised edition (under name Ann Tucker-Fettner), 1977.

Writer of four-part film series on black history for high school students, released by *New York Times,* 1971; writer and director of three short filmscripts for "Sesame Street," 1971. Contributor of poems and articles to periodicals, including *Family Circle, Charlotte Magazine, Outsider,* and *Sandlapper.*

WORK IN PROGRESS: A semi-autobiographical novel; a book of short stories.

SIDELIGHTS: Giudici told *CA:* "Raised to be a southern lady, I broke out in 1959 to find a way to live. I wrote as a means of survival, until recently when I finally learned to write.

"My children range in age from four to thirty, so I've had a good deal of distraction as well as having learned a great deal from them as they've grown. Aside from the novel on which I am working, my prime interest and research concern trying to find a way to mass-communicate for pre-literate people." She concluded: "I believe a writer's mission is to question all that is taken for granted."

BIOGRAPHICAL/CRITICAL SOURCES: Tucson Citizen, August 14, 1972; *Los Angeles Times,* October 1, 1972; *Chicago Tribune,* October 5, 1972; *New York Post,* October 18, 1972; *Seventeen,* summer, 1973; *Miami Herald,* June, 1973; *South Carolina Gardener,* May, 1974.

*   *   *

GLAD, Paul W(ilbur) 1926-

PERSONAL: Born August 15, 1926, in Salt Lake City, Utah; son of Carl Arthur (a clergyman) and Ethel Marie (Julin) Glad; married Carolyn Louise Biede (in retail jewelry and gift business), February 4, 1948; children: Thomas, Susan Glad Peterson, Richard, Steven. *Education:* Purdue University, B.S., 1947; Indiana University, M.A., 1949, Ph.D., 1957. *Office:* Department of History, University of Oklahoma, Norman, Okla. 73019.

CAREER: Hastings College, Hastings, Neb., 1950-55, began as instructor, became assistant professor of history; Coe College, Cedar Rapids, Iowa, 1955-64, began as assistant professor, became associate professor of history; University of Maryland, College Park, associate professor of history, 1964-66; University of Wisconsin, Madison, professor of history, 1966-77; University of Oklahoma, Norman, Merrick Professor of History, 1977—. Fulbright lecturer at University of Marburg, 1961-62; visiting professor at University of Oklahoma, 1971-72. *Military service:* U.S. Naval Reserve, active duty, 1944-46.

MEMBER: American Historical Association, Organization of American Historians, State Historical Society of Wisconsin. *Awards, honors:* Guggenheim fellowship, 1962-63; American Philosophical Society fellowship, 1967; fellow of National Humanities Institute at University of Chicago, 1977-78.

WRITINGS: The Trumpet Soundeth: William Jennings Bryan and His Democracy, 1896-1912, University of Nebraska Press, 1960; *McKinley, Bryan, and the People,* Lippincott, 1964; (editor) *William Jennings Bryan: A Profile,* Hill & Wang, 1968; (editor) *The Dissonance of Change,* Random House, 1969; *Progressive Century: The American Nation in Its Second Hundred Years,* Heath, 1975. Contributor to history journals.

WORK IN PROGRESS: Wisconsin Between the Wars, 1915-1940, Volume V of a six-volume series, for State Historical Society of Wisconsin.

SIDELIGHTS: Glad comments: "Beginning with an investigation of the transition from the nineteenth to the twentieth century, I have moved toward an effort to understand the changes that have accompanied modernity. I am concerned with technological, demographic, environmental, economic, and other influences that have shaped the modes of thought and politics in American life. In this endeavor I have come to recognize the importance of using non-print and quantitative materials along with verbal, written materials in historical analysis."

BIOGRAPHICAL/CRITICAL SOURCES: Abraham S. Eisenstadt, *American History: Recent Interpretations,* Book II: *Since 1865,* Crowell, 1962, 2nd edition, 1969.

*   *   *

GLASS, Bill 1935-

PERSONAL: Born August 16, 1935, in Texarkana, Tex.; son of Vernon and Mary Glass; married Mavis Irene Knapp, March 2, 1957; children: Billy, Bobby, Mindy. *Education:* Baylor University, B.A., 1957; Southwestern Baptist Theological Seminary, B.D., 1963. *Home:* 1023 Green Valley Lane, Duncanville, Tex. 75137. *Office:* Bill Glass Evangelistic Association, 616 Carriage Way, Duncanville, Tex. 75137.

CAREER: Professional football player on Canadian team, 1957-58; Detroit Lions professional football team, Detroit, Mich., player, 1958-62; Cleveland Browns professional football team, Cleveland, Ohio, all-pro defensive end, 1962-69; Bill Glass Evangelistic Association, Duncanville, Tex., evangelist, 1969—. *Awards, honors:* Named to Texas Football Hall of Fame for Professionals, as All-Pro.

WRITINGS: Get in the Game, Word, Inc., 1965; *Stand Tall and Straight,* Word, Inc., 1967; *My Greatest Challenge,* Word, Inc., 1968; (with Bill Pinson) *Don't Blame the Game,* Word, Inc., 1972; (with Bill Pinson) *Positive Power for Successful Salesmen,* Crescendo, 1972; *Free at Last,* Words, Inc., 1976.

SIDELIGHTS: Glass writes: "Even though I have finished seminary training, I have remained a layman in order to have entry into prisons and schools and other areas where the normal ordained minister cannot go. In addition to a city-wide, interdenominational, interracial ministry (much like Billy Graham's, except in smaller cities), our organization conducts a very extensive prison ministry which is discussed in detail in the book *Free at Last.*"

* * *

GLASSER, William 1925-

PERSONAL: Born May 11, 1925, in Cleveland, Ohio; son of Ben and Betty (Silverberg) Glasser; married Naomi Judith Silver, September 20, 1946; children: Joseph, Alice, Martin. *Education:* Case Institute of Technology (now Case Western Reserve University), B.S., 1945; Case Western Reserve University, M.A., 1948, M.D., 1953; attended University of California, Los Angeles, and Veterans Administration Center, Los Angeles. *Residence:* Los Angeles, Calif. *Office:* 1163 San Vicente Blvd., Suite 107, Los Angeles, Calif. 90049.

CAREER: California Youth Authority, Ventura, Calif., psychiatric consultant, 1956-57; Orthopaedic Hospital, Los Angeles, Calif., psychiatrist, 1957-66; psychiatrist for California public schools in Sacramento, Palo Alto, and Los Angeles, 1960-67; psychiatrist for adult narcotic program in California, 1963-66; Institute for Reality Therapy, Los Angeles, founder and president, 1967—. Lecturer. *Military service:* U.S. Army, 1946-47. *Member:* American Psychiatric Association.

WRITINGS: Mental Health or Mental Illness?: Psychiatry for Practical Action, Harper, 1961; *Reality Therapy: A New Approach to Psychiatry,* Harper, 1965; *Schools Without Failure,* Harper, 1969; *Identity Society,* Harper, 1972, revised edition, 1976; *Positive Addiction,* Harper, 1976; (contributor) Alexander Bassin, Thomas Edward Bratter, and Richard L. Rachin, editors, *The Reality Therapy Reader: A Survey of the Work of William Glasser, M.D.,* Harper, 1976. Contributor of articles to periodicals.

WORK IN PROGRESS: A book about "how reality therapy, positive addiction and brain function all fit and support each other."

SIDELIGHTS: Glasser told *CA:* "It doesn't get easier, it really gets harder as you continue to write. Maybe standards go up, maybe more ideas are around and interfere, but it does. But the urge to write grows stronger and that compensates, at least it does for me."

Glasser's books have been translated into Danish, French, German, Italian, Japanese, Portuguese, and Spanish.

* * *

GLEASON, Robert J(ames) 1906-

PERSONAL: Born January 19, 1906, in Seattle, Wash.; son of Homer E. (an owner of a lighting manufacturing company) and Grace (Stevens) Gleason; married Elisabeth Spencer, June 21, 1934 (divorced, 1947); married Rea Delamater Rhode, December 18, 1948 (died, April 7, 1969); married Eloise Poorman Clingerman, February 14, 1970; children: Robert, Daniel; stepchildren: Michael Rhode, David Rhode, Sally Clingerman Pierce, Susan Clingerman Wick. *Education:* University of Washington, B.S., 1931. *Home:* 3734 Ramsgate Dr., Annapolis, Md. 21403.

CAREER: Pan American World Airways, New York, N.Y., communications superintendent of Alaska Division,

1932-42, of Pacific-Alaska Division, 1945-47, and of Latin America Division, 1947-49; Aeronautical Radio, Inc. (ARINC), Annapolis, Md., operations director, 1949-51, executive vice-president, 1951-72, director of ARINC and of ARINC Research Corp., 1957-73, executive vice-president of ARINC Research Corp., 1958-72; writer, 1973—. *Military service:* U.S. Army Air Forces, 1942-45; became lieutenant colonel; received Bronze Star. *Member:* American Radio Relay League, Institute of Electrical and Electronic Engineers, Quarter Century Wireless Association, Society of Wireless Pioneers, Veteran Wireless Operators Association.

WRITINGS: Icebound in the Siberian Arctic, Alaska Northwest, 1977. Contributor to *Alaskan Journal.*

WORK IN PROGRESS: Researching Pacific Alaska Airways and Washington-Alaska Military Cable and Telegraph System.

SIDELIGHTS: Gleason told *CA:* "The depression and my Arctic experiences combined to put me in Alaska and airline work. When the airforce 'drafted' me, it took me more into management and eventually out of Alaska and into the whole world." *Avocational interests:* Golf, model building, amateur radio.

* * *

GODFREY, William
See YOUD, Samuel

* * *

GODIN, Gabriel 1929-

PERSONAL: Born October 11, 1929, in Montreal, Quebec, Canada; son of Raymond (a lawyer) and Cecile (Coulombe) Godin. *Education:* University of Montreal, B.A., 1948; McGill University, B.Sc. (honors), 1952, M.Sc., 1953; University of Toronto, M.A., 1959; University of Liverpool, Ph.D., 1964. *Religion:* Roman Catholic. *Home:* 253 McLeod, Ottawa, Ontario, Canada K2P 1A1. *Office:* Department of the Environment, 580 Booth, Ottawa, Ontario, Canada.

CAREER: Teacher of mathematics at military school in St. Jean, Quebec, 1955; Laval University, Quebec, Quebec, instructor in physics, 1956; Department of the Environment, Ottawa, Ontario, oceanographer, 1960—. *Awards, honors:* Medal from the governor general in Ottawa, Ontario, 1947; centennial medal from Canadian secretary of state, 1967.

WRITINGS: (Translator from French) Rene Rohr, *Sundials,* University of Toronto Press, 1971; *The Analysis of Tides,* University of Toronto Press, 1972.

* * *

GOETZ, Delia 1898-

PERSONAL: Born in June, 1898, near Wesley, Iowa; daughter of Joseph (a farmer) and Elizabeth (Matern) Goetz. *Education:* Graduated from Iowa State Teachers' College, 1922.

CAREER: Author, translator, and teacher. Has taught in many places, including Panama, Cuba, and Guatemala, as well as Minot Teacher's College in North Dakota. Translator at the Guatemalan Embassy in Washington, D.C.; later worked for the Foreign Policy Association and, during World War II, for the Pan American Union and the U.S. Office of Education; staff member of the U.S. Office of Education, Division of International Educational Relations, beginning 1946.

WRITINGS: *The Good Neighbors: The Story of the Two Americas* (illustrated by Juan Oliver), Foreign Policy Association, 1939; *Neighbors to the South,* Harcourt, 1941, revised edition, 1956; *Letters from Guatemala* (illustrated by Katharine Knight), D. C. Heath, 1941; *Panchita, a Little Girl of Guatemala* (illustrated by Charlotte A. Chase), Harcourt, 1941; *The Incas,* [Washington, D.C.], 1942; *Teamwork in the Americas* (illustrated by Aline Appel), Foreign Policy Association, 1943; *Half a Hemisphere: The Story of Latin America* (illustrated by Chase), Harcourt, 1943; *The Dragon and the Eagle: America Looks at China* (illustrated by Thomas Handforth), Foreign Policy Association, 1944; *Russia and America: Old Friends-New Neighbors* (illustrated by Louis Slobodkin), Foreign Policy Association, 1945; *The Burro of Barnegat Road* (illustrated by Hilda Van Stockum), Harcourt, 1945.

Education in Panama, Office of Education, Federal Security Agency, 1948; *Other Young Americans: Latin America's Young People,* Morrow, 1948; *Education in Venezuela,* Office of Education, Federal Security Agency, 1948; *World Understanding Begins With Children,* Office of Education, Federal Security Agency, 1949; *The Hidden Burro* (illustrated by Dorothy B. Morse), Morrow, 1949; *Let's Read about South America,* Fideler, 1950; *Deserts* (illustrated by Louis Darling), Morrow, 1956; *Tropical Rain Forests* (illustrated by Darling), Morrow, 1957; *South America,* Fideler, 1958; *The Arctic Tundra* (illustrated by Darling), Morrow, 1958; *At Home Around the World,* Ginn, 1958, reissued, 1965; *Grasslands* (illustrated by Darling), Morrow, 1959.

At Home in Our Land, Ginn, 1961; *Swamps* (illustrated by L. Darling), Morrow, 1961; *Mountains* (illustrated by Darling), Morrow, 1962; *Islands of the Ocean* (illustrated by Darling), Morrow, 1964; (translator with Adrian Recinos) *The Annals of Cakchiquels,* University of Oklahoma Press, 1967; *Rivers* (illustrated by John Kaufman), Morrow, 1969; *State Capital Cities,* Morrow, 1971; *Lakes* (illustrated by Lydia Rosier), Morrow, 1973. Also author of pamphlets for the Pan American Union and the Foreign Policy Association.*

* * *

GOLDBERG, M(elvyn) Hirsh 1942-

PERSONAL: Born September 21, 1942, in Baltimore, Md.; son of Herman (an attorney) and Ida (Noonberg) Goldberg; married Barbara Lea Weiser, June 30, 1963; children: Aviva, Stuart, Jonathan (deceased), Seth. *Education:* Johns Hopkins University, B.A., 1963, M.A.T., 1964; University of Maryland, further graduate study, 1964-65. *Religion:* Jewish. *Residence:* Randallstown, Md. *Agent:* Rhoda Weyr, William Morris Agency, 1350 Avenue of the Americas, New York, N.Y. 10019.

CAREER: High school English teacher in Baltimore, Md., 1963-64; University of Maryland, College Park, instructor, 1964-65; Baltimore Public Relations Agency, Baltimore, editor and writer, 1964-66; press secretary for Maryland gubernatorial candidate, 1966; press secretary to the mayor of Baltimore, 1966-67; director of public information and education for the attorney general of Maryland, 1967-69; Rouse Co., Columbia, Md., director of advertising, 1971-72; Baltimore City Public Schools, Baltimore, director of public information, 1972-74; Community College of Baltimore, Baltimore, chief of Office of Communications, 1974—. Public relations consultant. Active in local charitable work. *Member:* National Foundation of Ileitis and Colitis (founding member and president of local chapter; member of national board of trustees, 1976—). *Awards, honors:* Public service award from American Cancer Society; Smolar Award for excellence in Jewish journalism, 1974.

WRITINGS: *The Jewish Connection,* Stein & Day, 1976. Author of column "Reflections" in *Baltimore Jewish Times,* 1968—. Contributor of about fifty articles to magazines and newspapers. Editor of *Times of Israel* and *Mosaic.*

WORK IN PROGRESS: Nonfiction books.

SIDELIGHTS: Goldberg told *CA:* "I began writing at the age of eight, and throughout grammar school I wrote short stories, edited my own newspaper, tried a novel (when my brother typed it up and it ran only twenty-eight pages I almost ended my writing career in despair), and even tried one afternoon to begin an encyclopedia.

"But I also had another interest during this time. I was fascinated with the ironies, coincidences and unusual facts that fill our lives. I was an early collector of Ripley's Believe It Or Not!, as well as the unusual facts that came with Double-Bubble Gum and the fillers of information on the bottom of newspaper pages. While other kids saved stamps and coins, I was saving bags of facts.

"As I grew older, though, I drifted away from being such an avid collector because so many of these offerings of facts were basically trivia. But about four years ago I came across some startling ironies about significant events in Jewish history. It was then that I thought that there may be a whole new way of looking at the Jewish people by searching out and studying the incredible, ironic and bizarre in the Jewish experience. But I was also interested in seeing how, by researching what I called the "nook and cranny concept of history," I might shed some new light on world history in general because the world at large does share much in common with the Jews—through the Judeo-Christian heritage, through a common reverence for the Bible, through the widespread belief in monotheism.

"Out of this effort came my first book, 'The Jewish Connection,' which is subtitled 'the incredible, ironic, bizarre, funny, and provocative in the story of the Jews.' I am presently at work on a follow-up book which will explore how misunderstandings and errors basic to the human condition have had unusual—and ironic—results."

BIOGRAPHICAL/CRITICAL SOURCES: *Baltimore Magazine,* May, 1967; *Baltimore News American,* December 2, 1973; *Baltimore Jewish Times,* November 5, 1976; *Baltimore Morning Sun,* November 11, 1976.

* * *

GOLDMARK, Peter 1906-1977

December 2, 1906—December 7, 1977; Hungarian-born American scientist, inventor, and author. Goldmark invented the long-playing record and contributed significantly to the development of color television and electronic video recording technology during his years as an engineer and executive for Columbia Broadcasting System. In his autobiography he emphasized that his contributions were not so much his inventions as their spurring effects upon the industry. He died in Port Chester, N.Y. Obituaries: *New York Times,* December 8, 1977; *Washington Post,* December 9, 1977.

* * *

GOLDSTEIN, Arthur D(avid) 1937-

PERSONAL: Born May 21, 1937, in Brooklyn, N.Y.; son of

Alexander E. (an attorney) and Eve (Weinstein) Goldstein; married Lynne Milstein, December, 1967 (marriage ended, 1975). *Education:* Ohio University, B.A., 1958. *Religion:* Jewish. *Agent:* Henry Morrison, Inc., 68 West 10th St., New York, N.Y. 10011.

CAREER: Marine Engineers Beneficial Association, Brooklyn, N.Y., editor, 1963-65; Hal Leyshon & Associates (public relations firm), New York City, account executive, 1965-67; Gilbert A. Robinson, Inc. (public relations firm), New York City, account executive, 1967-68; *Securities,* New York City, editor, 1968-70; American Stock Exchange, New York City, editor, 1970-75; writer, 1975—. *Military service:* U.S. Army, 1961-63. *Member:* Authors Guild of Authors League of America, Mystery Writers of America. *Awards, honors:* Special award from Mystery Writers of America, 1973, for *A Person Shouldn't Die Like That.*

WRITINGS—Mystery novels: *A Person Shouldn't Die Like That,* Random House, 1972; *You're Never Too Old to Die,* Random House, 1974; *Nobody Was Sorry He Got Killed,* Random House, 1976. Author of a book under a pseudonym.

WORK IN PROGRESS: Another book.

AVOCATIONAL INTERESTS: Sculpting, reading, tennis, jogging.

* * *

GOLDSTEIN, Jack 1930-

PERSONAL: Born February 27, 1930, in Detroit, Mich.; son of Ruben (a salesman) and Dorothy (Zalkowitz) Goldstein; married Corinne Dorb (an art teacher), August 26, 1956; children: Irwin Brian, Darryl Louis. *Education:* Attended Wayne State University, 1947-48; Illinois College of Podiatric Medicine, D.P.M. (honors), 1952. *Politics:* "I vote for whoever I feel is best." *Religion:* Jewish. *Home:* 23171 Radclift, Oak Park, Mich. 48237. *Office:* 28200 West Seven Mile Rd., Livonia, Mich. 48152.

CAREER: Podiatrist and surgeon, 1954—. Member of Foundation for Alternative Cancer Therapies; gives public lectures; guest on local and national television and radio programs. *Military service:* U.S. Army, 1952-54; served in Korea; became staff sergeant; received two battle stars. *Member:* International Association of Cancer Victims and Friends, American Podiatry Association, American Association of Hospital Podiatrists, National Health Federation, American Natural Hygiene Society (member of board of directors; past president), Americans United to Combat Fluoridation (member of board of directors), Consumers for Pure Food, Michigan State Podiatry Association.

WRITINGS: Triumph Over Disease: By Fasting and Natural Diet, Arco, 1977.

WORK IN PROGRESS: A book on proper nutrition, for pregnant women, infants, and children, based on a vegetarian diet; a semi-humorous book on his podiatry practice.

SIDELIGHTS: When Goldstein developed a pre-cancerous disease, specialists told him that only radical surgery would prolong his life. He then decided to reject all conventional medical care, and began fasting, under the supervision of a natural hygiene practitioner. He is now a vegetarian who has no symptoms of the disease that changed his life.

He writes: "I wrote the book because people have a right to know there is another approach to health besides the 'establishment' way. The book shows the fallacy of general medical philosophy and that disease will persist and be worsened by medicines (poisons). The ingestion of chemical additives is also responsible for diseases."

AVOCATIONAL INTERESTS: Organic gardening, baseball, chess, clarinet, tennis, jogging.

* * *

GOOD, Robert Crocker 1924-

PERSONAL: Born April 7, 1924, in Mount Vernon, N.Y.; son of Alfred and Josephine (Crocker) Good; married Nancy Louise Cunningham, August 21, 1946; children: Stephen L., Karen L., Kathleen J. *Education:* Haverford College, B.A., 1945; Yale University, B.D., 1951, Ph.D., 1956. *Politics:* Democrat. *Religion:* Unitarian-Universalist. *Home:* 111 Chapin Pl., Granville, Ohio 43023. *Office:* Denison University, P.O. Box B, Granville, Ohio 43023.

CAREER: American Friends Service Committee, relief worker in Italy, 1946, director of operation in Frankfurt am Main, Germany, 1947, administrator of international student seminar program in Philadelphia, Pa., 1948; University of Denver, Social Science Foundation, Denver, Colo., instructor, 1953-56, assistant professor of international relations, 1956-58, also in charge of radio and television programming; Johns Hopkins University, School of Advanced International Studies, Baltimore, Md., research associate at Washington Center of Foreign Policy Research, 1958-61; Carnegie Endowment Seminars in Diplomacy, Washington, D.C., director, 1960-61; Neighbors, Inc., Washington, D.C., president, 1962-65; U.S. ambassador to Zambia, 1965-69; University of Denver, professor of international relations, dean of Graduate School of International Studies, and director of Social Science Foundation, 1970-76; Denison University, Granville, Ohio, president of the university, 1976—. Member of United Nations Relief & Rehabilitation Administration Italian mission, 1946; director of John F. Kennedy's Task Force on Africa, 1960; director of U.S. Department of State Office of Research and Analysis for Africa (Bureau of Intelligence and Research), 1961. Research associate at Johns Hopkins University School of Advanced International Studies, 1969-70. Member of board of directors of Center for Global Perspectives, 1974—, Global Perspectives in Education, Inc., 1975—, Council on Religion in International Affairs, 1975—, University of Kentucky School of International Diplomacy and Commerce, 1975—, and member of board of governors, National University of Lesothe.

MEMBER: International Studies Association, American Political Science Association, African Studies Association, Society for Values in Higher Education, Phi Beta Kappa. *Awards, honors:* Award from National Association of Educational Broadcasters, 1957, for television series, "Twentieth Century Revolutions in World Affairs"; superior honor award from U.S. Department of State, 1964; Haverford Award from Haverford College, 1976.

WRITINGS: (Contributor) Arnold Wolfers, editor, *Alliance Policy in the Cold War,* Johns Hopkins Press, 1959; (editor with Harry R. Davis) *Reinhold Niebuhr on Politics,* Scribner, 1960; *Congo Crisis: The Role of the New States* (monograph), Washington Center of Foreign Policy Research, Johns Hopkins University, 1961; (contributor) Laurence W. Martin, editor, *Neutralism and Non-Alignment: The New States in World Affairs,* Praeger, 1962; (with others) *The Mission of the Christian College in the Modern World,* Council of Protestant Colleges and Universities, 1962; (editor with Roger Hilsman, and contributor) *Foreign Policy in the Sixties: Issues and Instrumentalities,* Johns

Hopkins Press, 1965; *U.D.I.: The International Politics of the Rhodesian Rebellion,* Princeton University Press, 1973.

Author of "Twentieth Century Revolutions in World Affairs," a television series for University of Denver, 1957. Contributor to learned journals. Contributing editor of *Worldview.*

* * *

GOODELL, John S. 1939-

PERSONAL: Born September 2, 1939, in Brooklyn, N.Y.; son of Reuben S. and Mildred (a secretary and bookkeeper; maiden name, Martin) Goodell; married Paulette Margaret Genest (a catalog librarian), May 28, 1966. *Education:* Lafayette College, B.A., 1961; Florida State University, M.S., 1965, A.M.L.S., 1969, Ph.D., 1971. *Home:* Unit 5, 7 Robinson St., Coorparoo, Queensland, Australia 4151. *Office:* Department of Librarianship, Queensland Institute of Technology, P.O. Box 2434, North Quay, Queensland, Australia 4001.

CAREER: Frostburg State College, Frostburg, Md., cataloger at Jerome Framptom Library, 1965-67; Lee County Public Library System, Fort Myers, Fla., director, 1967-68; Emporia State University, Emporia, Kan., assistant professor of library science, 1971-76; Queensland Institute of Technology, Brisbane, Australia, lecturer in librarianship, 1977—. *Military service:* U.S. Army, 1961-64. *Member:* American Library Association, Association of College and Research Libraries, Association of American Library Schools, New Zealand Library Association, Library Association of Australia.

WRITING: Libraries and Work Sampling, Libraries Unlimited, 1975; (with Marjorie Sullivan) *Media Use in the Study of Minorities,* Emporia Kansas State College, 1975.

SIDELIGHTS: Goodell writes: "In a world of rapidly expanding knowledge, the librarian's role has become more significant than ever before. In order to perform his function in the most effective manner possible, the librarian must use modern managerial techniques such as work sampling. Hence, my interest in presenting this technique in an easily understood form in the hope that librarians and, of course, anyone else who is interested, may be able to understand and apply it."

AVOCATIONAL INTERESTS: Jogging, travel, gardening, current events.

* * *

GOODING, Judson 1926-

PERSONAL: Born October 12, 1926, in Rochester, Minn.; son of Arthur Faituoute (a broker) and Frances (Judson) Gooding; married Francoise Ridoux, June 21, 1952; children: Anthony, Amelie, Timothy. *Education:* Yale University, B.A. (cum laude), 1948; University of Paris, diploma, 1950. *Politics:* Independent. *Religion:* Episcopal. *Home address:* Box 183, RFD #2, East Middle Patent Rd., Bedford, N.Y. 10506. *Office:* Trend Analysis Associates, P.O. Box 542, Bedford, N.Y. 10506.

CAREER: Department of the Army, European Command Headquarters, Heidelberg, Germany, staff writer, 1949-52; Affiliated Film Producers, Inc., New York City, staff writer, 1952-53; WCCO-CBS Radio, Minneapolis, Minn., staff writer, 1953; *Minneapolis Tribune,* Minneapolis, reporter, 1954-56, business editor, 1956-57; *Life,* New York City, reporter and correspondent in Paris, 1957-62; *Time,* New York City, correspondent in Paris, 1962-66; Time-Life

News Service, San Francisco, Calif., chief of San Francisco Bureau, 1966-68; *Time,* education editor, 1968-69; *Fortune,* New York City, staff writer and associate editor, 1969-72; *Trend Report,* Chicago, Ill., co-founder and editor-in-chief, 1972-74; Trend Analysis Associates, Bedford, N.Y., president, 1974—. Member of board of directors of Martin Hotel Co.; consultant to Urban Research Corp. and Ford Foundation. *Military service:* U.S. Naval Reserve, active duty on a destroyer, 1944-46; served in Pacific theater.

MEMBER: World Future Society, Common Cause, Historic Preservation Society, Middle Patent Association (director), Elizabethan Club (New Haven, Conn.), Century Association, Yale Club (New York City), Bedford Bicycle Polo Association, Harvard Business School Club of New York.

WRITINGS: (Contributor) Joe David Brown, editor, *The Hippies,* Time-Life, 1967; (contributor) edited by the editors of *Fortune* magazine, *The Environment,* Harper, 1969; (contributor) Roger Revelle, A. Khosla, and M. Vinorskis, editors, *The Survival Equation,* Houghton, 1971; *The Job Revolution,* foreword by Senator Charles Percy, Walker & Co., 1972; (contributor) Alfred J. Marrow, editor, *The Failure of Success,* Amacom, 1973; (contributor) M. C. Sonfield, editor, *Analysis of Organizations,* Simon & Schuster, 1973; (contributor) Kenneth S. Knodt, editor, *Pursuing the American Dream,* Prentice Hall, 1975; (contributor) D. M. Boje, D. J. Brass, and L. R. Pondy, editors, *Managing,* Xerox Education Group, 1976. Contributor to popular magazines, including *Reader's Digest, Travel and Leisure, New York Times Magazine,* and *Money,* and to business journals.

WORK IN PROGRESS: Books on the influence of the press on the news, and on the white Protestant minority group in America; research on prisoner-treatment reform, Holiday Inns, and California wines.

SIDELIGHTS: Gooding writes: "My continuing interest is in observing, analyzing, and writing about social change. This I find far more stimulating than watching rising or falling interest rates and the like, if less rewarding financially." He has reported, during his career, from forty-two countries, and his book has been published in Japanese.

* * *

GOODMAN, Ronald A. 1938-

PERSONAL: Born September 20, 1938, in Boston, Mass.; son of Arnold G. (a businessman) and Caryl (Weissman) Goodman; married Judith Skeist (an editor); children: Sarah, David. *Education:* Harvard University, A.B., 1960; Tufts University, M.A., 1962, also doctoral study. *Home:* 68 Sea Ave., Quincy, Mass. 02169. *Office:* Department of English, Quincy Junior College, Quincy, Mass. 02169.

CAREER: Worked as loan officer, writer, photographer, realtor,and teacher; currently professor of English and photography at Quincy Junior College. *Military service:* U.S. Army Reserves, 1961-68. *Member:* American Association of University Professors, Modern Language Association of America.

WRITINGS: (With L. S. B. Leakey) *Adam or Eve,* Schenkmen, 1972. Also author of *Fenwick Tweedy.* Contributor to *Bosarts, American Baby, New Hampshire Times, Quincy Times Sun,* and other periodicals.

WORK IN PROGRESS: A Thematic Approach to American Literature, a study guide for Houghton.

SIDELIGHTS: Goodman told *CA:* "L. S. B. Leakey has helped me to realize the possibilities of man; possible not as

245

'progress,' but possible as to the inherent mystery of existence.'' *Avocational interests:* Tennis, squash, fresh air and water.

* * *

GORDON, Dorothy 1893-1970

PERSONAL: Born April 4, 1893, in Odessa, Russia; daughter of Leo (an international lawyer) and Rose (Schwarz) Lerner; married Bernard Gordon (a lawyer), June 28, 1910; children: Frank, Lincoln. *Education:* Hunter College (now of the City University of New York), B.A.; graduate study at the Sorbonne, University of Paris. *Politics:* Independent. *Home:* Chetwood, George's Mills, N.H.

CAREER: Writer; radio and television moderator. Concert folksinger, 1923-29; producer of programs for children for the British Broadcasting Corp. (BBC) in London, 1929; director of music programs for the "American School of the Air" on Columbia Broadcasting Co. (CBS), 1931-38; producer of "The Children's Corner," 1936-38; member of the Mutual Broadcasting System staff, 1938-39; consultant for children's programs on NBC, and director and actress for "Yesterday's Children," 1939-40; producer of a news program for children on station WQXR, 1940-42; director of children's radio programs for the Office of War Information, 1942-44; moderator for the "New York Times Youth Forum," 1944-61. Consultant for youth activities for the *New York Times. Member:* Overseas Press Club.

AWARDS, HONORS: National Conference of Christians and Jews award, 1948-55; School Broadcast Conference award, 1949; Institute of Education by Radio award, 1949-51; New York State Mother of the Year award, 1951; McCall's Gold Mike award, 1951; George Foster Peabody award, 1951, 1964, 1966; Federation of Jewish Women's Organizations award, 1952; Town Hall award, 1953; Columbia University Scholarship Press gold key, 1954; Ohio State University award for education on radio and TV, 1955; General Federation of Women's Clubs award, 1955; LL.D., 1959, from Fairleigh Dickinson University; Thomas Alva Edison award for scientific information to youth through the mass media; Williamsburg Settlement award for developing youth interest in world affairs; Governor's Award, Academy of Television Arts and Sciences, 1965.

WRITINGS: (Editor) *Sing It Yourself* (illustrated by Alida Conover), Dutton, 1928; *Around the World in Song* (illustrated by Conover), Dutton, 1930; *Dorothy Gordon's Treasure Bag of Game Songs* (illustrated by Veronica Reed), Dutton, 1939; *Come to France* (illustrated by Reed), American Book Co., 1940; *Knowing the Netherlands* (illustrated by Reed), American Book Co., 1940; *All Children Listen,* G. W. Stewart, 1942; *You and Democracy* (illustrated by Lois Fisher and Karl Murr), Dutton, 1951; *Who Has the Answer: An Inquiry into the Behavior of Today's Teenagers,* Dutton, 1965.

OBITUARIES: New York Times, May 12, 1970.*

(Died May 11, 1970)

* * *

GORENSTEIN, Shirley 1928-

PERSONAL: Born April 3, 1928, in New York; daughter of Harry (a restaurateur) and Mary (a restaurateur; maiden name, Pfeffer) Slotkin; married Samuel Gorenstein (a systems analyst), 1948; children: Ethan Ezra, Gabriel William. *Education:* Queens College (now of the City University of New York), B.A., 1949; Columbia University, M.A., 1953,

Ph.D., 1963. *Religion:* Jewish. *Home:* 2433 21st St., Troy, N.Y. 12180. *Office:* Department of Anthropology, Rensselaer Polytechnic Institute, Troy, N.Y. 12181.

CAREER: Columbia University, New York, N.Y., lecturer, 1963-71, assistant professor, 1971-74, associate professor of anthropology, 1974-75; Rensselaer Polytechnic Institute, Troy, N.Y., associate professor of anthropology, 1975—. Member of New York State Board for Historic Preservation. *Member:* American Anthropological Association (member of executive board), Society for American Archaeology, Association for Field Archaeology (member of executive board).

WRITINGS: Introduction to Archaeology, Basic Books, 1965; *Tepexi el Viejo* (title means "Ancient Tepexi"), American Philosophical Society, 1973; (editor) *Prehispanic America,* St. Martin's, 1975; (editor) *North America,* St. Martin's, 1976; *Not Forever on Earth,* Scribner, 1976. Contributor to *Natural History* and *American Antiquity.*

WORK IN PROGRESS: A History of American Archaeology.

* * *

GORNEY, Roderic 1924-

PERSONAL: Born August 13, 1924, in Grand Rapids, Mich.; son of Abraham and Edelaine (Roden) Gorney. *Education:* Attended Antioch College, 1942-43, Yale University, 1944, and University of Louisville, 1944-46; Stanford University, B.A., 1948, M.D., 1949; Southern California Psychoanalytic Institute, Ph.D., 1977. *Home:* 635 Walther Way, Los Angeles, Calif. 90049. *Office:* Department of Psychology, School of Medicine, University of California, Los Angeles, Calif. 90024.

CAREER: San Francisco City and County Hospital, San Francisco, Calif., intern, 1948-49; Bellevue Hospital, New York, N.Y., resident in psychiatry, 1949-50; Hillside Hospital, New York City, resident in psychiatry, 1950-52; Stanford Hospital, San Francisco, Calif., resident in psychiatry, 1952-53; private practice of psychiatry in San Francisco, Calif., 1953-62; University of California, Los Angeles, assistant professor, 1962-71, associate clinical professor, 1971-73, adjunct associate professor of psychiatry, 1973—, lecturer at School of Social Welfare, 1972-73, staff psychiatrist at Neuropsychiatric Institute, 1962-71. Licensed to practice in New York, 1949, and California, 1951; certified by American Board of Psychiatry and Neurology, 1955. Assistant clinical professor at Stanford University, 1953-62, and University of California, San Francisco, 1958-62; faculty member at Southern California Psychoanalytic Institute, 1970—, University of California, San Francisco Extension, 1974, Occidental College, 1975, and San Francisco State College, 1975; lecturer in the United States and Europe to professionals and laymen; guest on radio program "The Search for Health," in Illinois. Volunteer physician for Los Angeles Free Clinic, 1966-71; organized Willowbrook Volunteer Health Center, 1967-68; organized Human Agenda Associates, 1971—. Consultant to Committee for the Future and President's Committee on Mental Retardation. *Military service:* U.S. Army Air Forces, Medical Corps, 1943-46.

MEMBER: World Future Society, American Psychiatric Association (fellow), American Medical Association, American Group Psychotherapy Association, American Association for the Advancement of Science (fellow), Group for the Advancement of Psychotherapy, Committee for the Future, California Medical Association, Southern California Psychiatric Society, Southern California Psychoanalytic Institute and Society, Los Angeles County Medical Association (associate member), Los Angeles Group Psychotherapy Society. *Awards, honors:* Grants from G.D. Searle & Co., 1966-67, and Lilly Endowment, 1974—; award from American Psychiatric Association, 1971, for article "Interpersonal Intensity, Competition, and Synergy: Determinants of Achievement, Aggression, and Mental Illness"; Pulitzer Prize nomination, 1972, for *The Human Agenda;* National Book Award nomination, 1972; gold medal from Societe Academique of L'Academie Francaise, 1976.

WRITINGS: The Human Agenda, Simon & Schuster, 1972; (contributor) S. A. Pasternak, editor, *Violence and Victims,* Spectrum, 1975; (contributor) Jules Masserman, editor, *The Range of Normal in Human Behavior,* Grune & Stratton, 1976. Contributor to *International Encyclopedia of Neurology, Psychiatry, Psychoanalysis, and Psychology.* Contributor to medical, law, and communications journals.

WORK IN PROGRESS: Research on the effects of television drama on adults and on the cultural factors that lead to high or low levels of achievement, aggression, and mental illness.

* * *

GOUDEY, Alice E. 1898-

PERSONAL: Born January 3, 1898, in Junction City, Kan.; daughter of John West and Elizabeth (Poland) Edwards; married Wayne G. Martin, Jr., August 29, 1918 (divorced, 1945); married Earl S. Goudey, June 2, 1947; children: (first marriage) Dorothy (Mrs. William Sheeham, Jr.); (stepchildren) Pelton Goudey, Joyce Goudey (Mrs. William Smykal). *Education:* Attended Columbia University, 1946, New School of Social Research, and New York University, 1947-48. *Residence:* Morrill, Me.

CAREER: Author of books for children. Teacher in Kansas elementary schools, 1915-18; editorial work for *Western Grain Journal,* Kansas City, Mo., 1919. *Member:* Authors Guild.

WRITINGS: The Good Rain (illustrated by Nora S. Unwin), Aladdin Books, 1950; *The Merry Fiddlers* (illustrated by Bernard Garbutt), Aladdin Books, 1951; *Danny Boy, the Picture Pony* (illustrated by Paul Brown), Scribner, 1952; *Smokey, the Well-Loved Kitten* (illustrated by Meg Wohlberg), Lothrop, 1952; *Jupiter and the Cats* (illustrated by P. Brown), Scribner, 1953; *Here Come the Bears!* (illustrated by Garry MacKenzie), Scribner, 1954; *Here Come the Deer!* (illustrated by G. MacKenzie), Scribner, 1955; *Here Come the Elephants!* (illustrated by G. MacKenzie), Scribner, 1955; *Here Come the Whales!* (illustrated by G. MacKenzie), Scribner, 1956; *Here Come the Lions!* (illustrated by G. MacKenzie), Scribner, 1956; *Here Come the Seals!* (illustrated by G. MacKenzie), Scribner, 1957; *Here Come the Beavers!* (illustrated by G. MacKenzie), Scribner, 1957; *Here Come the Wild Dogs!* (illustrated by G. MacKenzie), Scribner, 1958; *Houses from the Sea* (illustrated by Adrienne Adams), Scribner, 1959; *Here Come the Raccoons* (illustrated by G. MacKenzie), Scribner, 1959.

Here Come the Bees! (illustrated by G. MacKenzie), Scribner, 1960; *The Day We Saw the Sun Come Up* (illustrated by A. Adams), Scribner, 1961; *Here Come the Dolphins!* (illustrated by G. MacKenzie), Scribner, 1961; *Here Come the Squirrels!* (illustrated by G. MacKenzie), Scribner, 1962; *Sunnyvale Fair* (illustrated by Paul Galdone), Scribner, 1962; *Butterfly Time* (illustrated by A. Adams), Scribner, 1964; *Graywings* (illustrated by Marie Nonnast), Scribner, 1964; *Here Come the Cottontails* (illustrated by G. Mac-

Kenzie), Scribner, 1965; *Red Legs* (illustrated by M. Nonnast), Scribner, 1966.

SIDELIGHTS: Alice E. Goudey began writing children's stories as supplementary reading material for her students while teaching in Kansas. Throughout her writing career this has been her main goal.

Her first published book, *Good Rain,* was reviewed by a *New York Herald Tribune* critic who commented: "This is a charming idea for a small child's picture book, and Miss Unwin has interpreted it happily, with pictures full of feeling."

Of *Butterfly Time,* a critic for the *New York Times Book Review* said: "Poetic words and delicate full-color illustrations evoke the wonder and beauty of butterflies without any sacrifice of accuracy." *New Yorker* commented: "The drawings are so good that one can't help wishing that the text, a dialogue between brother and sister, were a little less wooden. But, this is not, perhaps, important, since the intention—to make butterflies irresistible—has been accomplished."

BIOGRAPHICAL/CRITICAL SOURCES: New York Herald Tribune Book Review, November 12, 1950; *New York Times Book Review,* May 10, 1964, May 8, 1966; *New Yorker,* December 5, 1964.*

* * *

GOULD, Leslie 1902-1977

February 8, 1902—September 23, 1977; American journalist. Gould was the financial editor of the old *New York Journal-American* and a former syndicated columnist for King Features. He died in Naples, Fla. Obituaries: *New York Times,* September 24, 1977.

* * *

GOURLEY, Jay 1947-

PERSONAL: Born November 20, 1947, in Henryetta, Okla.; son of Leland (a publisher) and Billijo (an interior designer; maiden name, Simpson) Gourley. *Education:* University of Oklahoma, B.A., 1970; Georgetown University, graduate study, 1976—. *Politics:* Democrat. *Religion:* None. *Home and office:* 147 11th St. N.E., Washington, D.C. 20002. *Agent:* Aaron M. Priest Literary Agency, 15 East 40th St., New York, N.Y. 10016.

CAREER: Daily Oklahoman, Oklahoma City, Okla., reporter, 1965-67; *Hawaii Tribune-Herald,* Hilo, reporter, 1967; *Los Angeles Herald-Examiner,* Los Angeles, Calif., reporter, 1968; *Oklahoma Journal,* Oklahoma City, reporter, 1968-70; Tulakes Aviation, Oklahoma City, pilot, 1970-71; *Kentucky Post,* Covington, Ky., city editor, 1971-72, bureau chief, 1972-73; Scripps-Howard Newspapers, Washington, D.C., reporter, 1973-74; *National Enquirer,* Lantana, Fla., reporter, 1974-78. *Member:* National Press Club, Sigma Delta Chi.

WRITINGS: Great Lakes Triangle, Fawcett, 1977; (with Vance Trimble) *Cloakroom* (on the U.S. Senate), Dial, 1978. Contributor to magazines.

WORK IN PROGRESS: Research in formal logic.

SIDELIGHTS: Gourley comments briefly: "My interest in writing is purely professional. Accuracy, clarity, and significance to the reader are the most important qualities of nonfiction." *Avocational interests:* Soaring (sailplanes), rock climbing, mountaineering, skiing, snorkeling, scuba diving.

GRAAF, Peter
See YOUD, Samuel

* * *

GRABNER-HAIDER, Anton 1940-

PERSONAL: Born May 19, 1940, in Pollau, Austria; son of Anton (a farmer) and Helen (Toglhofer) Grabner-Haider; married Elke Hillmar (an economist), August 28, 1969. *Education:* Attended University of Graz, University of Tubingen, and University of Bonn, 1959-65; University of Graz, D.Th., 1965, Habilitation, 1976. *Politics:* "Not conservative." *Religion:* "Roman Catholic, but liberal." *Home:* Ragnitzstrasse 173, A-8010 Graz, Austria. *Office:* University of Graz, Philosophisches Institut, Heinrichstrasse 26/VI, A-8010 Graz, Austria.

CAREER: Padagogische Akademie, Graz, Austria, assistant professor of religious education, 1967-70; University of Graz, Graz, researchist, 1970-75, lecturer in philosophy of religion, 1976—. Publisher's reader and free-lance writer. *Member:* Semiotische Gesellschaft (Austrian Semiotics Society).

WRITINGS—In English: *An einen jungen Priester: Briefe eines Laisierten,* Veritas, 1973, translation published as *Letters to a Young Priest from a Laicized Priest,* Abbey Press, 1975.

Other works: *Paraklese und Eschatologie bei Paulus: Mensch und Welt im Anspruch der Zukunft Gottes* (title means "Exhortation and Eschatology in the Writings of the Apostle Paul"), Aschendorff, 1968; *Verkuendigung als Einladung* (title means "Preaching as Invitation"), Matthias Gruenewald, 1969; *Semiotik und Theologie: Religioese Rede zwischen analytischer und hermeneutischer Philosophie* (title means "Semiotics and Theology: Religious Speech between Analytic and Hermeneutic Philosophy"), Kosel, 1973; *Sprachanalyse und Religionspadagogik* (title means "Language Analysis and Religious Education"), Benziger, 1973; *Thema Mensch* (title means "Theme: Man"), Herder, 1974; *Theorie der Theologie als Wissenschaft* (title means "Theory of Theology as a Science"), Kosel, 1974; *Glaubenssprache: Ihre Struktur und Anwendbarkeit in Verkundigung und Theologie* (title means "Language of Faith: Its Structure and Applicability in Preaching and Theology"), Herder, 1975; *Sprechen und Glauben* (title means "To Speak and to Believe"), Aucr, 1975; *Eros und Glaube: Erotische Lebenskultur* (title means "Sex and Faith: Erotic Culture of Life"), Pfeiffer, 1976; *Vernunft und Religion: Ansaetze analytisches Religiousphilosophie* (title means "Reason and Religion: Onsets of Analytic Philosophy of Religion"), Styria, 1978.

Editor: *Praktisches Bibellexikon* (title means "Practical Lexicon of the Bible"), Herder, 1969; *Die Bibel und unsere Sprache* (title means "The Bible and Our Language"), Herder, 1970; *Recht auf Lust?* (title means "Right of Sexual Pleasure?"), Herder, 1970; *Gott* (title means "God"), Matthias Gruenewald, 1970; (with Kurt Luethi) *Der befreite Eros: Ein Dialog zwischen Kuenstlern, Kritikern und Theologen* (title means "The Liberated Eros: A Dialogue between Artist, Critic, and Theologians"), Matthias Gruenewald, 1972; *Jesus N.,* Benziger, 1972; (with wife, Elke) *Kleines Laienbrevier* (title means "A Little Breviary for Laymen"), Styria, 1972.

WORK IN PROGRESS: Research on the philosophy of religion, the transformation of religion in modern society, ethics, and humanistic psychology; *Neue Werte: Humanistische Psychologie und moderne Ethik* (title means "Transformed Values: Humanistic Psychology and Modern Ethics"); *Ideologiekritik und Religionskritik* (title means "Critics of Ideology and Religion"), publication expected in 1980.

AVOCATIONAL INTERESTS: Modern literature (including the writings of Peter Handke, Franz Kafka, and Victor Frankl), transactional analysis, encounter groups, psychodrama, gestalt therapy, youth culture (beat culture, body language, modern dance, erotic culture), bioenergetics, humanistic psychology.

* * *

GRAHAM, Desmond 1940-

PERSONAL: Born January 12, 1940, in Cobham, Surrey, England; son of Harry (a commercial traveler) and Evelyn (Dolan) Graham; married Alison Wood (a lecturer), July, 1961; children: Dominic, Katherine. *Education:* University of Leeds, B.A., 1961, Ph.D., 1969. *Home:* 8 The Grove, Gosforth, Newcastle-upon-Tyne 3, England. *Office:* Department of English Literature, University of Newcastle-upon-Tyne, Newcastle-upon-Tyne NE1 7RU, England.

CAREER: University of Tuebingen, Tuebingen, Germany, lecturer in English literature, 1961-62; University of Rhodesia, Salisbury, assistant lecturer in English literature, 1962-63; University of Sierra Leone, Freetown, lecturer in English literature, 1963-66; University of Munich, Munich, Germany, lecturer in English literature, 1968-70; University of Mannheim, Mannheim, Germany, lecturer in English literature, 1970-71; University of Newcastle-upon-Tyne, Newcastle-upon-Tyne, England, lecturer in English literature, 1971—. Broadcaster for Sierra Leone Schools Broadcasting, 1965-67.

WRITINGS: Introduction to Poetry, Oxford University Press, 1968; *Keith Douglas, 1920-1944: A Biography,* Oxford University Press, 1974; (editor) Keith Douglas, *Complete Poems,* Oxford University Press, 1978. Reporter for Southern Germany for *Opera News,* 1969-71. Poetry reviewer for *Stand,* 1975—.

WORK IN PROGRESS: Research on the place of war in twentieth century poetry.

* * *

GRAHAM, Eleanor 1896-

PERSONAL: Born in 1896, in London, England; daughter of P. Anderson Graham (editor of *Country Life* magazine). *Education:* Educated in London, England.

CAREER: Author, editor, and reviewer of books for children. Worked in a bookstore, a publishing house, and a children's library, 1927-34; selector and secretary of the Junior Book Club, 1934-38; editor of Penguin Books' "Puffin Story Books," 1941-62; editor of Methuen's children's books, 1943-57. *Awards, honors:* Eleanor Farjeon Award, 1973.

WRITINGS: The Night Adventures of Alexis (illustrated by Winifred Langlands), Faber & Gwyer, 1925; *High Days and Holidays: Stories, Legends, and Customs of Red-Letter Days and Holidays* (illustrated by Priscilla M. Ellingford), E. Benn, 1932, published as *Happy Holidays: Stories, Legends, and Customs of Red-Letter Days and Holidays,* Dutton, 1933; *Six in a Family* (illustrated by Alfred Sindall), [London], 1935; *Change for a Sixpence,* University of London Press, 1937; *When the Fun Begins,* University of London Press, 1937; *Christmas in Old England,* Silver Burdett, 1938; *The Children Who Lived in a Barn* (illustrated by J. T.

Evans), Routledge & Kegan Paul, 1938, Penguin Books, 1975.

The Making of a Queen: Victoria at Kensington Palace, J. Cape, 1940; *Favorite Nursery Tales* (illustrated by Rachel Taft Dixon), Wonder Books, 1946; (adapter) *Famous Fairy Tales: Jack and the Beanstalk, The Fisherman and His Wife, The Real Princess, and Hansel and Gretel* (illustrated by Mervin Jules), Wonder Books, 1946; (adapter) *Bedtime Stories: Cinderella, Snow White, The Emperor's New Clothes, and Why the Sea Is Salt* (illustrated by Masha, pseudonym of Marie Stern), Wonder Books, 1946; *Head o'Mey* (illustrated by Arnold Bond), E. Benn, 1947; *The Story of Charles Dickens* (illustrated by Norman Meredith), Methuen, 1952, Abelard-Schuman, 1954; *The Story of Jesus* (illustrated by Brian Wildsmith), Hodder & Stoughton, 1960, Penguin Books, 1961, revised edition, Penguin Books, 1971; *J. M. Barrie's Peter Pan: The Story of the Play* (illustrated by Edward Ardizzone), Scribner, 1962; *Kenneth Grahame,* H. Walck, 1963.

Editor: *Welcome Christmas!* (illustrated by Ellingford), E. Benn, 1931, Dutton, 1932; *A Puffin Book of Verse* (illustrated by Claudia Freeman), Penguin Books, 1953; *A Puffin Quartet of Poets: Eleanor Farjeon, James Reeves, E. V. Rieu, and Ian Serraillier* (illustrated by Diana Bloomfield), Penguin Books, 1958; *A Thread of Gold: An Anthology of Poetry* (illustrated by Margery Gill), Bodley Head, 1964, Books for Libraries, 1969; Robert Herrick, *The Music of a Feast,* Bodley Head, 1968. Also general editor, "Puffin Story Books" series, Penguin Books, 1941-62.

Contributor of children's book reviews to *Bookman, London Sunday Times, Junior Bookshelf,* and *Times Literary Supplement.*

SIDELIGHTS: Graham's book, *The Story of Charles Dickens,* was received with general enthusiasm. The *Chicago Tribune* stated: "It is difficult to see how anybody could produce a better life of Charles Dickens for young readers than Eleanor Graham has written. . . . Her book is saner and better balanced than many studies of Dickens intended for adult readers, and she is free of condenscension toward subject and audience alike."

BIOGRAPHICAL/CRITICAL SOURCES: Chicago Tribune, November 14, 1954.*

*   *   *

GRAHAM, Elizabeth
    See EDMONDS, Arthur Denis

*   *   *

GRAHAM, Lee E.   1913(?)-1977

1913(?)—September 6, 1977; American radio and television commentator and author. Her best known programs were "Lee Graham Interviews" and a radio program for the Asia Society. Graham wrote two self-help books for women. She died in New York, N.Y. Obituaries: *New York Times,* September 7, 1977; *AB Bookman's Weekly,* November 21, 1977.

*   *   *

GRAHAM, W(illiam) S(ydney)   1918-

PERSONAL: Born November 19, 1918, in Greenock, Scotland; son of Alexander (an engineer) and Margaret (Macdiarmid) Graham; married Nessie Dunsmuir, 1954; children: Rosalind. *Education:* Educated in Scotland. *Politics:* Left. *Religion:* Presbyterian. *Home:* 4 Mountview Cottages, Madron, Penzance, Cornwall, England.

CAREER: Poet. Lecturer, New York University, 1947-48. *Awards, honors:* Atlantic Award, 1947.

WRITINGS: Cage Without Grievance, Parton Press, 1942; *The Seven Journeys,* Maclellan, 1944; *2nd Poems,* Nicholson & Watson, 1945; *The Voyages of Alfred Wallis,* Anthony Froshang, 1948; *The White Threshold,* Faber, 1949; *The Nightfishing,* Faber, 1955; *Malcolm Mooney's Land,* Faber, 1970; *Implements in Their Places,* Faber, 1977. Contributor to periodicals, including *Times Literary Supplement, Encounter, Poetry, Listener, Nation, New Statesman, London Magazine,* and *Observer.*

WORK IN PROGRESS: "New poems towards a book still unamed."

SIDELIGHTS: Graham told *CA:* "It is like this. I think we are all essentially alone. Some of us bear the aloneness less painfully than others. Writing poetry makes a life for me to live in and at the same time, I hope, communicates with other people.

    "'Somewhere our belonging particles
    Believe in us. If we could only find them.'"

*   *   *

GRANT, Madeleine Parker   1895-

PERSONAL: Born in 1895. *Education:* Graduated from Simmons College; Radcliffe College, M.A., Ph.D.

CAREER: Author and educator. Sarah Lawrence College, Bronxville, N.Y., professor emeritus of biology. *Awards, honors:* Whitney Fellowship; Margaret Snell Fellowship of the American Association of University Women.

WRITINGS: Biology and World Health (illustrated by Bunji Tagawa), Abelard, 1955, revised edition, 1970; *Wonder World of Microbes* (illustrated by Clifford N. Gleary), Whittlesey House, 1956, new second edition, McGraw-Hill, 1964; *Louis Pasteur: Fighting Hero of Science* (illustrated by C. N. Gleary), Whittlesey House, 1959; *Alice Hamilton: Pioneer Doctor in Industrial Medicine,* Abelard, 1967.

SIDELIGHTS: Kirkus reviewed *Louis Pasteur: Fighting Hero of Science:* "Despite the available material on this popular chemist and bacteriologist, Dr. Grant's biography makes a further contribution. [It] combines a precise scientific analysis with a well-paced story of his personal life." *Booklist* said that it, "not only portrays Pasteur's personal life and traces his scientific career and achievements, but [also] describes in specific detail and in understandable terms his work in crystals, microbes, fermentation, and vaccines."

BIOGRAPHICAL/CRITICAL SOURCES: Kirkus, March 1, 1959; *Booklist,* July 15, 1959; *New York Times,* November 1, 1959.*

*   *   *

GRANT, Zalin (Belton)   1941-

PERSONAL: Born April 17, 1941, in Cheraw, S.C.; son of Thurmon B. and Barbara (Smith) Grant. *Education:* Clemson University, B.A., 1963. *Politics:* Independent. *Religion:* Protestant. *Home:* 815 South Church St., Cheraw, S.C. 19520; and Apartado 30, Alhaurin el Grande, Malaga, Spain.

CAREER: Time, New York, N.Y., reporter in Saigon, Vietnam and Washington, D.C., 1965-68; *New Republic,* Washington, D.C., Southeast Asia correspondent, 1968-70, contributing editor, 1970-72; free-lance writer, 1972—. *Military service:* U.S. Army, Intelligence, 1963-65; served in Vietnam.

WRITINGS: Survivors (non-fiction), Norton, 1975.

WORK IN PROGRESS: *Juliana Cash,* a historical novel set in South Carolina; a series of sketches on rural life in southern Spain; an account of the newsmen missing in Indochina.

AVOCATIONAL INTERESTS: "Off-the-beaten-track traveling (once drove a V.W. camper from Singapore to Paris)."

* * *

GRASSO, Domenico 1917-

PERSONAL: Born June 26, 1917, in Rocca, Italy; son of Carmine and Carmen (Santoro) Grasso. *Education:* University of Naples, D. Litt., 1944; Gregorian University, S.T.P., 1950. *Home:* Piazza della Pilotta 4, Rome 00187, Italy.

CAREER: Entered Society of Jesus (Jesuits), 1936, ordained Roman Catholic priest, 1947; Gregorian University, Rome, professor of pastoral theology, 1950—; theologian and writer.

WRITINGS: *Il cristianesimo di Ernesto Buonaiuti,* Morcelliana, 1953; *Gesu Cristo e la sua opera,* A.V.E. (Rome), 1956; *La conversione e l'apostasia di Giorgio Tyrrell,* P.U.G. (Rome), 1957; *E possibile l'unione delle chiese?,* Nuova Accademia Editrice, 1960; *L'annuncio della salvezza,* d'Auria, 1965, translation published as *Proclaiming God's Message,* University of Notre Dame Press, 1965; *Dialogo con i teologi,* Edizioni Paoline, 1967; *La Chiesa nel mondo,* A.V.E., 1967; *La Figura di Cristo,* E.R.I., 1968; *La predicazione alla comunita cristiana,* Edizioni Paoline, 1969; *The Problem of Christ,* Alba House, 1969; *Why does God ...?,* St. Paul, 1970; *Dobbiamo ancora battezzare i bambini?,* Cittadella editrice, 1972; *Il massaggio di Cristo,* Cittadella editrice, 1976.

WORK IN PROGRESS: A book on pastoral theology.

* * *

GRATTAN-GUINNESS, I. 1941-

PERSONAL: Born June 23, 1941, in Bakewell, England; son of Gerald Henry (an educator) and Mary Helena (Brown) Grattan-Guinness; married Enid Neville, January 9, 1965. *Education:* Wadham College, Oxford, B.A., 1962, M.A., 1967; London School of Economics and Political Science, London, M.Sc., Ph.D. *Residence:* Barnet, England. *Office:* Middlesex Polytechnic, Enfield, Middlesex EN3 4SF, England.

CAREER: EMI Electronics, Feltham, England, research mathematician, 1962-63; Middlesex Polytechnic, Enfield, England, 1964—, began as lecturer, became principal lecturer. Consultant to *Flying Saucer Review. Member:* History of Science Society, British Society for the History of Science, Society for the History of Technology, Institute of Mathematics and Its Applications.

WRITINGS: *The Development of the Foundations of Mathematical Analysis from Euler to Riemann,* M.I.T. Press, 1970; (with J. R. Ravetz) *Joseph Fourier, 1768-1830,* M.I.T. Press, 1972; *Dear Russell—Dear Jourdain: A Commentary on Russell's Logic,* Duckworth, 1977; (editor and contributor) *From the Calculus to Set Theory, 1630-1910: An Introductory History,* Duckworth, 1977. Contributor of articles on history of mathematics and science, philosophy, mathematics education, and psychic phenomena, and of reviews to academic journals. Editor of *Annals of Science.* Associate editor of *Historia Mattematica.*

WORK IN PROGRESS: *The Golden Section: Its History and Place in Man and Nature;* a history of the philosophy of mathematics, 1880-1930.

SIDELIGHTS: Grattan-Guinness writes: "I am very interested in the educational implications of the history of science, especially mathematics. No wonder that students turn away from mathematics, given the ahistorical and acultural, excessively unmotivated way in which it is taught. I am also against the 'two cultures' stuff. There is only one culture: culture."

AVOCATIONAL INTERESTS: Singing in small choirs, travel, reading, photography.

* * *

GRAVES, Nora Calhoun 1914-

PERSONAL: Born August 11, 1914, in Lake, Miss.; daughter of Willis W. (a clergyman) and Nora Emmie (Calhoun) Graves. *Education:* Whitworth College, A.A., 1934; Millsaps College, B.A., 1936; University of Mississippi, M.A., 1938; University of Southern Mississippi, Ph.D., 1967. *Religion:* Methodist. *Home address:* Rolling Green, Sylva, N.C. 28779. *Office:* Department of English, Western Carolina University, Cullowhee, N.C. 28723.

CAREER: Whitworth College, Brookhaven, Miss., instructor in English, 1938-44; high school English teacher in Boone, N.C., 1944-45; Southwest Junior College, Summit, Miss., instructor in English and head of department of English, 1945-46; Erskine College, Due West, S.C., assistant professor of English, 1946-51; Perkinston College, Perkinston, Miss., instructor in English and head of department, 1951-65; Western Carolina University, Cullowhee, N.C., associate professor, 1968-72, professor of English, 1972—. Past member of Mississippi English Commission. Part-time interviewer for Research Council, Inc.

MEMBER: Modern Language Association of America, National Council of Teachers of English, Conference on College Composition and Communication, American Association of University Women, Society for the Study of Southern Literature, South Atlantic Modern Language Association.

WRITINGS: *The Two Culture Theory in C. P. Snow's Novels,* University Press of Mississippi, 1971. Contributor to literature journals.

WORK IN PROGRESS: A study of Eudora Welty's novels; research on John Updike, Patrick White, C. P. Snow, Pamela Hansford Johnson, and John Cheever.

SIDELIGHTS: Nora Graves told *CA:* "In his lectures and writings, C. P. Snow has discussed at some length the intellectual rift in Western society between the literary (non-scientific) and the scientific cultures. *The Two Culture Theory in C. P. Snow's Novels,* by providing an understanding of the conflicting cultures, affords a greater appreciation of, and a keener sensitivity to the characters, structures and themes in all fourteen of Lord Snow's novels."

* * *

GRAY, J(esse) Glenn 1913-1977

May 27, 1913—October 30, 1977; American author and educator. Gray served as general editor, in charge of translating the works of Martin Heidegger, at Harper & Row. He died in Colorado Springs, Colo. Obituaries: *New York Times,* October 31, 1977; *AB Bookman's Weekly,* January 30, 1978. (See index for *CA* sketch)

GRAY, John S(tephens) 1910-

PERSONAL: Born August 11, 1910, in Chicago, Ill.; son of Joseph William (an investment banker) and Carrie (Weston) Gray; married Elma Nash, June 15, 1935; children: Ann R. Gray Riggs, Ginger B. Gray Minelli. *Education:* Knox College, B.S., 1932; Northwestern University, M.S., 1934, Ph.D., 1936, M.D., 1946. *Home and office:* 1408 West Lake St., Fort Collins, Colo. 80521.

CAREER: Northwestern University, School of Medicine, Chicago, Ill., instructor, 1934-36, assistant professor, 1936-45, associate professor, 1946, Nathan Smith David Professor of Physiology, 1946-70, professor of physiology, 1970-74, professor emeritus, 1974—, chairman of department, 1946-70. Aviation physiology researcher at U.S. Army Air Forces School of Aviation, 1942-45. *Member:* Western History Association, Chicago Westerners, Fort Collins Westerners, Sigma Xi, Phi Gamma Delta. *Awards, honors:* Guggenheim fellowship, 1962; Westerners International Jedediah Smith Award, 1970, for the discovery of Captain Walter Clifford's 1876 campaign diary, and award for best non-fiction book of 1976, for *Centennial Campaign: The Sioux War of 1876.*

WRITINGS: Pulmonary Ventilation and Its Physiological Regulation, C. C Thomas, 1950; (senior historical editor) *The Poudre River,* Bruce E. Berends, 1976; *Centennial Campaign: The Sioux War of 1876,* Old Army Press, 1976. Contributor of more than a hundred-thirty articles to biomedical journals and history magazines.

WORK IN PROGRESS: Fort Collins: Army Post on the Cache la Poudre; historical research.

SIDELIGHTS: Gray writes: "My passion is research and the communication of its results. When administrative duties as department chairman began to choke off my research in biomedical science, I developed a hobby of historical research that fit into spare moments. By retirement from the university, I was ready for full-time research and writing in history. My goal in both areas has always been to dig and dig for facts, analyzing them repeatedly in every way I can, discarding in the process whole series of unsatisfactory interpretations until I find one that holds up even as more facts come in. Should I ever end up with a picture remotely resembling my initial ignorant idea, I will know that I have neither researched nor learned."

* * *

GRAY, Lee Learner 1924-

PERSONAL: Born September 27, 1924, in New York, N.Y.; daughter of Benjamin (a sales manager) and Carolyn (Bimberg) Learner; married Lawrence E. Gray (an attorney), September 10, 1950; children: Nathaniel, Harold Adam, Joshua. *Education:* Pennsylvania State University, B.A., 1944. *Home:* 4018 Wexford Dr., Kensington, Md. 20795. *Office:* U.S. Department of Transportation, Washington, D.C. 20590.

CAREER: Scholastic, New York, N.Y., assistant editor, 1946-52; free-lance writer and editor, 1953-63; U.S. Department of Health, Education & Welfare, Washington, D.C., editor and writer, 1964-68; *Changing Times,* Washington, D.C., associate editor, 1968-70; U.S. Department of Health, Education & Welfare, editor and writer, 1970-77; U.S. Department of Transportation, Washington, D.C., coordinator of consumer communications, 1977—. Vice-president of Montgomery County Consumer Advisory Committee. Has given readings from her poetry at local gatherings. *Member:* National Association of Government Communicators, League of Women Voters, Interagency Council on Citizen Participation, Montgomery County Writers' Center.

WRITINGS: How We Choose a President (juvenile), St. Martin's, 1964, 3rd edition, 1976. Author of government pamphlets. Contributor to professional journals and popular magazines, including *Ladies Home Journal, American Home, Pageant,* and *Coronet.* Editor of *American Education.* Editor of consumer newsletters.

WORK IN PROGRESS: Writing poetry.

SIDELIGHTS: Lee Gray writes: "My own intense interest in political action prompted me to write *How We Choose a President,* and it is indeed gratifying that St. Martin's Press has considered it successful enough to keep it in print, through successive revisions, for twelve years. I am constantly amazed at how much updating each new edition, every four years, requires—and my only regret is that now, as a Federal employee, the Hatch Act prevents me from being involved in political activity."

* * *

GRAY, Stephen E. 1925-

PERSONAL: Born May 31, 1925, in Seattle, Wash.; son of Leo E. (a naval officer) and Marion (Paul) Gray; married Barbara Wilkins, May 31, 1950; children: William E., Kenneth E. *Education:* U.S. Military Academy, B.S., 1946; Baylor University, M.H.A., 1966; George Peabody College for Teachers, Ph.D., 1971. *Home:* 8220 Brentmoor, Wichita, Kan. 67206. *Office:* Department of Health Care Administration, Wichita State University, Wichita, Kan. 67208.

CAREER: U.S. Army, career officer, 1946-69, retiring as colonel; Xavier University, Cincinnati, Ohio, assistant professor, 1970-73; Wichita State University, Wichita, Kan., associate professor of health care administration, 1973—. *Member:* Mensa, American College of Hospital Administrators, American Hospital Association, Phi Delta Kappa, Phi Kappa Phi. *Awards, honors—*Military: Distinguished Service Cross, Silver Star, Bronze Star.

WRITINGS: Health Now, Macmillan, 1976.

WORK IN PROGRESS: Community Health Today.

* * *

GRAYSON, Ruth (King) 1926-

PERSONAL: Born January 12, 1926, in Merton, England; daughter of Charles (an accountant) and Elsie (Munford) King; married David Grayson, March 21, 1953 (died, 1977); children: Jeremy, Timothy. *Education:* Educated in England. *Politics:* Conservative. *Home:* Kings Barton, Green St., Kempsey, Worcester WR 5 3QB, England. *Agent:* Daniel P. King, 5125 North Cumberland Blvd., Whitefish Bay, Wis. 53217.

CAREER: Writer. Has also worked as a secretary. *Member:* Crime Writers Association.

WRITINGS: Thieves' Highway, R. Hale, 1973; *Yesterday's Poison,* R. Hale, 1975.

WORK IN PROGRESS: Living Tiger and *Second Chance,* mystery thrillers.

SIDELIGHTS: Grayson told *CA:* "Recovering from major surgery for cancer in 1966, I spent the months of enforced idleness writing the book I had always wanted to write. I tried to put into fictional form my reaction to my situation and my urge to go on fighting for life. The exercise was valuable and taught me a lot about writing in book form.

"Eventually I turned to thriller or suspense fiction writing, of which I had long been an avid reader myself. As a family we have had many caravanning holidays in Europe and I felt that I had a lot of useful material in my notebooks (which I always carry). As well as this, I could turn for technical information to a son who is a helicopter pilot and a husband who at the time was selling light aircraft and whom I sometimes accompanied on his travels. The result was *Thieves' Highway,* which found a publisher.

"Travel always fascinates me and sparks off the germ of an idea for another thriller—the characters follow naturally. I enjoy the discipline and the form of this type of writing, and I am always interested in what makes humans tick and their behavior under stress. If I can, I always like to try to put over the idea of how the human spirit can triumph over impossible odds, since I have experienced this in my own life.

"Joining the Crime Writers Association has widened my horizons still further, as talking to other writers has taught me a great deal that is valuable to me in my own work, and it is always interesting to meet those whose books have given me so much pleasure over the years."

*   *   *

GREEN, Andrew (Malcolm) 1927-

PERSONAL: Born July 28, 1927, in London, England; son of Arthur Alfred (a secretary) and May Edith (Simpson) Green; married Hazel Hunter, September 8, 1951 (divorced, 1971). *Education:* Educated in England. *Politics:* "Democratic." *Home:* Rothersby, Wittersham Rd., Iden, Near Rye, East Sussex, England.

CAREER: G. B. Kalee, London, England, assistant general manager, 1952-54; S. N. Bridges, London, advertising and publicity manager, 1954-64; Trade and Technical Press, Morden, England, editor, 1964-67; Thomas Organisation, London, managing editor, 1967-71; Malcolm Publications, London, managing director, 1972-75; writer, 1972—. *Member:* National Federation of Psychical Research Societies (co-founder, 1951), Institute of Service Management (founder, 1961), National Servicing Council (secretary general, 1972-74), Royal Society of Arts (fellow), Society for Psychical Research, Borderline Science Investigation Group (president, 1977). *Awards, honors:* M.Ph., 1975.

WRITINGS: Mysteries of Surrey, Napier, 1972; *Mysteries of Sussex,* Napier, 1973; *Mysteries of London,* Napier, 1973; *Ghost Hunting: A Practical Guide,* Garnstone, 1973, John M., Fontana, 1977; (editor) *Our Haunted Kingdom,* Wolfe, 1973, F. Watts, 1975; *Ghosts of the South East,* David & Charles, 1976; *Haunted Houses,* Shire, 1976; *Phantom Ladies,* Bailey Bros. & Swinfen, 1977. Contributor to *Times Educational Supplement, Prediction, Nursing Times, Wireless World,* and other periodicals. Editor, *Freight Forwarder,* 1971-75, *Mobil News for Industry,* 1972-75.

WORK IN PROGRESS: An autobiography; a science fiction novel; a political murder novel.

SIDELIGHTS: Green told *CA:* "My constant aim is to promote parapsychology and the serious study of this neo-science." His purpose for writing "is to provide constant evidence of genuine phenomena, to strengthen the need for a rational approach and to offset distortions and sensationalism by the popular media." *Avocational interests:* Archaeology and gardening.

*   *   *

GREEN, Gil(bert) 1906-

PERSONAL: Born September 24, 1906, in Chicago, Ill.; son of Isaac and Elizabeth (Chusid) Green; married; three children. *Education:* Educated in Chicago, Ill. *Politics:* Communist. *Home:* 321 West 24th St., New York, N.Y. 10011.

CAREER: Has worked as a blue collar worker in oil refineries, machine shops, fur dressing, and construction. National president, Young Communist League, 1932-39. Member, Central Committee of the Communist Party.

WRITINGS—All published by International Publishers: *The Enemy Forgotten,* 1956; *Revolution—Cuban Style,* 1969; *The New Radicalism—Anarchist or Marxist?,* 1971; *Portugal's Revolution,* 1976; *What's Happening to Labor,* 1976. Author of articles, pamphlets and brochures.

WORK IN PROGRESS: A personal account of the McCarthy era.

SIDELIGHTS: Green told *CA:* "In 1949, during McCarthy hysteria, I was convicted under the Smith Act for being a leader of the Communist Party. I spent four and one-half years in underground activity and subsequently served an eight year prison term in Leavenworth Penitentiary."

CA asked Green how he was treated after his conviction for his political beliefs. He answered: "A number of times my life was in danger and only the good relations I established with the great majority of inmates saved me from physical harm. With the exception of one person in the prison administration who inspired the threats of physical assault, the others were personally neutral in their attitudes although they felt compelled to treat me more severely for fear that word would get out, especially to members of Congress, that a Communist was being favored. For this reason I was not granted parole and was compelled to serve the maximum time permitted by law. As for the majority of inmates, they first looked upon me as some kind of queer duck, refusing to accept the fact that I was in prison because of my political beliefs and affiliations. As they learned to know me as a human being and finally realized that it was not mercenary gain that had caused my incarceration, their respect grew.

"On my own part, the years of rotting in prison were not exactly enjoyable, yet I did learn something about human nature and how social conditions cripple human beings who could under other circumstances make valuable contributions to society. My closest friends in prison were the Puerto Rican Nationalists fighting for the independence of their country, with whom I also practiced Spanish as we walked in the prison yard. But I also made friends with inmates found guilty of criminal offenses, some of whom were influenced in another direction by their contact with me.

"One general observation: justice would be greatly served if every judge were compelled to serve an indefinite term in prison. He would then realize that our prison system makes a mockery of the word rehabilitation, and that the punishment meeted out only accomplishes the opposite of that intended."

Green's books have been translated into Spanish, Hungarian, Japanese, and Russian.

*   *   *

GREEN, Hannah

PERSONAL: Born in Cincinnati, Ohio; daughter of Matthew Addy (a foreign patent and trademark agent) and Mary McAlpin (Allen) Green; married John Wesley (a painter), December, 1971. *Education:* Wellesley College, B.A., 1948; Stanford University, M.A., 1956. *Home:* 52 Barrow St., New York, N.Y. 10014. *Agent:* Timothy Seldes, Russell & Volkening, Inc., 551 Fifth Ave., New York, N.Y. 10017.

CAREER: Church World Service Language Institute, teacher of English in Camp for Displaced Persons, Ulm, Germany, 1949-50; Stanford University, Stanford, Calif., instructor in English composition and creative writing, 1954-57; research assistant to author Matthew Josephson, 1961-65; Columbia University, New York, N.Y., professor of fiction in School of the Arts, 1970—. Assistant to editor of *Pacific Spectator,* 1953-54. *Member:* P.E.N., Authors Guild, MacDowell Colony Fellows (president of executive committee, 1976—). *Awards, honors:* MacDowell Colony fellow, 1960, 1964, 1967, 1969, 1970, 1975, 1978; Ohioana Library Award for the best novel by an Ohioan in 1972, 1973, for *The Dead of the House;* Creative Artists Public Service award from New York State Council on the Arts, 1973-74; Mary Elvira Stevens Traveling Fellowship from Wellesley College, 1974-75; National Endowment for the Arts grant, 1978.

WRITINGS: (Contributor) Wallace Stegner and Richard Scowcroft, editors, *Stanford Short Stories,* Stanford University Press, Volume II: *1954,* 1954, Volume III: *1955,* 1955; *The Dead of the House,* (novel), Doubleday, 1972. Contributor to periodicals, including *Mademoiselle, Unmuzzled Ox,* and, primarily, *New Yorker* (in which most of Green's works are published).

WORK IN PROGRESS: Two autobiographical novels, *College Days* and *Dreams and Early Memories;* a novel which is a historical reverie about Saint Foy at Conques.

SIDELIGHTS: The Dead of the House, a novel more than ten years in the making, is rooted in Green's family and their lives and past in Cincinnati, Ohio. "Framed by the twenty years between the 1930's and the 1950's," wrote critic L. J. Davis, "it ranges as far back as the War of Austrian Succession and sketches whole lifetimes with what seems an effortless stroke of the pen. *The Dead of the House* is less a novel than a kind of dream, a protracted prose poem of singular delicacy, filled with generosity, love, and wisdom, and steeped in lore. [It] is a deeply felt, uniquely American fiction. . . . It is hard to remember a book as superbly balanced in all its parts."

New York Times reviewer Thomas Lask noted that Green's book was "not the usual family chronicle." He observed, "She writes under the eye of eternity. . . . Time flows in and around the events of her book like some tune that ties all meanings together. . . . Throughout the novel the wisdom of the blood takes over, almost, from the wisdom of the head. . . . It is a work of recovery, a love note to the past—something to shore the spirit against the ruins."

"In writing this book I began for the first time to write in my own way," Green recalled in an essay in the Hungarian magazine *Nagyvilag.* "At the time (in the early fifties) it seemed to me that most of the women writers who were discussed in the writing courses of the period wrote as if they were bodiless; often they chose male narrators or heroes representing themselves as men, and I felt there was something basically false in this. I was very conscious from the start of wanting to write as a woman, to have my particular womanly sensuality and sensibility to be a part of the texture and life of the book."

Green's novels in progress will draw further from the history and lives of her Ohio family, and as such will again show "what love and memory can rescue from the great enemy time," as *Atlantic Monthly* observed about her first novel. "In life," Green told *CA,* "time *is* my foe—I do not use it well—but in art I fall on my knees before its mysteries and transmute its secrets to the best of my abilities."

BIOGRAPHICAL/CRITICAL SOURCES: New York Times, February 12, 1972; *New York Times Book Review,* February 13, 1972; *Washington Post Book World,* February 27, 1972; *Boston Globe,* March 6, 1972; *Wall Street Journal,* March 7, 1972; *New Republic,* March 11, 1972; *New York Post,* March 25, 1972; *Atlantic Monthly,* May, 1972; *Saturday Review,* May 27, 1972; *Hudson Review,* October, 1972; *Southern Review,* summer, 1973; *Contemporary Literary Criticism,* Volume 3, Gale, 1974.

* * *

GREENE, Mabel
See BEAN, Mabel Greene

* * *

GREENE, Ruth Altman 1896-

PERSONAL: Born March 21, 1896, in Madisonville, Ohio; daughter of Daniel Lee (a Methodist minister) and Flavella (an organist; maiden name, Light) Altman; married Phillips Foster Greene (a missionary and physician), June 17, 1920 (died, 1967); children: Anne Greene Judy, Frederick Davis II, Margaret Greene Dickson. *Education:* Wellesley College, B.A., 1918. *Politics:* "Registered Republican—always vote Independent." *Religion:* Protestant. *Home address:* P. O. Box 67, New Richmond, Ohio 45157. *Agent:* Yale-China Association, 905A Yale Station, New Haven, Conn. 06520.

CAREER: Teacher of English to Chinese medical students in Changeha, China, 1933-36; General Hospital, Rangoon, Burma, English teacher, 1957; writer. Founding member of the China Institute, Upper Montclair, N.J., 1943; founding member of Historic New Richmond, 1972—. *Member:* League of Women Voters, Phi Beta Kappa.

WRITINGS: Hsiang-Ya Journal, Shoe String, 1977. Contributor to church and civic magazines and to *Yale Quarterly Review.*

WORK IN PROGRESS: Studying development in mainland China and on Taiwan, with a view toward helping to improve future relations between the United States and China.

SIDELIGHTS: Ruth Greene comments that, as a minister's daughter married to a missionary from a long line of missionaries, her life in missionary work was a natural development. She adds: "What was unusual about it was that it coincided with periods in the rise and development of nationalism in the Middle East, Far East, and Southeast Asia (Turkey, China, and Burma). This has given me a good half-century-perspective on present-day history for which I am very grateful. At eighty-one, I am not likely to write another book, but I shall go on writing and speaking on these themes—and what I have learned—as long as I am physically able to do so."

AVOCATIONAL INTERESTS: Local history (her great-great-grandfather built the first cabin in New Richmond in 1797, and planned the town in 1814).

* * *

GREENFIELD, James Lloyd 1924-

PERSONAL: Born July 16, 1924, in Cleveland, Ohio; son of Emil and Belle (Speiser) Greenfield; married Margaret Ann Schwertly, July 16, 1954. *Education:* Harvard University, B.A., 1949. *Home:* 850 Park Ave., New York, N.Y. 10021. *Office: New York Times,* 229 West 43rd St., New York, N.Y. 10036.

CAREER/WRITINGS: Worked for *Cleveland Press,* 1939-41, and Voice of America, 1949-50; *Time* magazine, correspondent in Korea and Japan, 1951-55, bureau chief in New Delhi, India, 1956-57, deputy bureau chief in London, England, 1958-61; Time-Life, Washington, D.C., chief diplomatic correspondent, 1961-62; U.S. State Department, Washington, D.C., deputy assistant secretary of state for public affairs, 1962-64, assistant secretary of state for public affairs, 1964-66; Continental Airlines, Los Angeles, Calif., assistant vice president for international affairs, 1966-68; Westinghouse Broadcasting Co., New York City, vice president, 1968-69; *New York Times,* New York City, foreign editor, 1969—. *Member:* Reform Club (London, England), Harvard Club (New York).

* * *

GREENING, Hamilton
See HAMILTON, Charles Harold St. John

* * *

GREENWAY, Hugh D(avids) S(cott) 1935-

PERSONAL: Born May 8, 1935, in Boston, Mass.; son of James C. (a naturalist) and Helen (Scott) Greenway; married Joy Brooks, June 11, 1960; children: Julia, Alice, Sarah. *Education:* Yale University, B.A., 1954; further study at Oxford University, 1960-62. *Office: Washington Post,* 11 Disraeli St., Jerusalem, Israel.

CAREER/WRITINGS: Time, New York, N.Y., correspondent in London, 1962-63, Washington, D.C., 1963-64, Boston, Mass., 1964-66, Saigon, 1967-68, Bangkok, Thailand, 1968-70, United Nations correspondent, 1970-72; *Washington Post,* Washington, D.C., State Department reporter, 1972, correspondent in Hong Kong, 1973-76, Israel, 1976—. Notable assignments include coverage of the Tet offensive in Viet Nam, 1968, overthrow of Sinanouk and the Cambodian civil war, Bangla Desh, 1971, the fall of Saigon, 1975, and the visit of Anwar Sadat to Jerusalem. *Military service:* U.S. Navy, 1958-60; became lieutenant, junior grade. *Member:* Yale Club, Hong Kong Club. *Awards, honors:* Nieman fellow, 1971-72.

SIDELIGHTS: Greenway told *CA:* "The Sadat visit to Jerusalem ended Israel's conviction that no Arab country was ready to accept Israel as a legitimate neighbor in the Middle East but few Israelis believe that a true peace is just around the corner."

* * *

GREENWOOD, Val D(avid) 1937-

PERSONAL: Born July 14, 1937, in Murray, Utah; son of David Hartley (a farmer) and Mary Thelma (Cox) Greenwood; married Margaret Ann Turner, July 3, 1964; children: Yvonne, Cherie, Karen. *Education:* Brigham Young University, B.S., 1962; University of Idaho, J.D., 1974. *Politics:* Republican. *Religion:* Church of Jesus Christ of Latter-day Saints (Mormons). *Home:* 2422 Surrey Rd., Salt Lake City, Utah 84118. *Office:* Genealogical Department, Latter-day Saints Church, 50 East North Temple, Salt Lake City, Utah 84150.

CAREER: Latter-day Saints Church, Salt Lake City, Utah, researcher for genealogical department, 1962-65; Ricks College, Rexburg, Idaho, professor of genealogy, 1965-71; Latter-day Saints Church, writer for genealogical department, 1974-75, temple ordinance specialist, 1976-77, group manager of special services, 1977—. *Military service:* Utah Army National Guard, 1959-65.

MEMBER: Utah Geanealogical Association (member of board of directors, 1975-77; president, 1977), Utah State Bar Association. *Awards, honors:* Fourth place national winner of Nathan Burkan Memorial Copyright Competition, sponsored by American Society of Composers, Authors and Publishers, 1974, for "Fair Use and Photocopy."

WRITINGS: The Researcher's Guide to American Genealogy, Genealogical Publishing, 1973. Contributor to genealogy journals and church publications.

WORK IN PROGRESS: Encyclopedic Dictionary of American Genealogy, tentative title, for Genealogical Publishing.

SIDELIGHTS: Greenwood writes: "*The Researcher's Guide* . . . was written to meet the need for a comprehensive general textbook on the sources (major sources) available for use by those interested in tracing their American ancestors. Prior to the publication of this book there was no such book available and it was very frustrating to try to teach the subject. I felt that I had the ability and knowledge to meet that need. It is not a difficult book to understand even though it deals with a complicated subject."

* * *

GREGG, Walter H(arold) 1919-

PERSONAL: Born April 7, 1919, in Columbus, Ohio; son of Herbert L. (a building contractor) and Lula B. (Pettibone) Gregg; married Betty Louise Harrold, March 28, 1938; children: Sue Ellen Gregg Roupas, Jay Harrold. *Education:* Ohio State University, B.Sc., 1941, M.A., 1947; Columbia University, Ed.D., 1954. *Office:* Department of Health and Physical Education, Northwestern University, Evanston, Ill. 60201.

CAREER: Teacher of mathematics, health, and physical education, and athletic coach, 1941-42; Slippery Rock State College, Slippery Rock, Pa., instructor in education and coach of football, swimming, and baseball, 1947-51; Miami University, Oxford, Ohio, 1951-57, began as assistant professor, became associate professor of health, physical education, and recreation, also health coordinator and director of graduate studies; Northwestern University, Evanston, Ill., professor of health and physical education, 1957—, chairman of department. Member of Illinois governor's advisory committee for Division of Alcoholism, Department of Mental Health. Spokesperson for California Raisin Advisory Board. *Military service:* U.S. Naval Reserve, Air Force, active duty, 1942-46.

WRITINGS: A Boy and His Physique (booklet), National Dairy Council, 1961, revised edition, 1970; *Physical Fitness Through Sports and Nutrition* (juvenile), Scribner, 1975. Contributor to health and education journals.

WORK IN PROGRESS: Preparing books on eating patterns of high school athletes, financing of high school athletic programs, and a children's book on basic skills for sports.

* * *

GREGORY, Kenneth (Malcolm) 1921-

PERSONAL: Born January 25, 1921, in Bath, England; son of Wilfred Malcolm (a teacher) and Ethel (a teacher; maiden name, Holley) Gregory; married Hilary Anne Berry (a physician), May 29, 1954 (died January 5, 1968); children: Julian Mark. *Education:* Attended Exeter College, Oxford. *Politics:* "If I may paraphrase Oscar Wilde, I have no politics—I am a member of the Conservative Party." *Home:* Cedarwood, Camilla Dr., Westhumble, Dorking, Surrey

RH5 6BU, England. *Agent:* A. P. Watt, Bedford Row, London W.C.2, England.

CAREER: Polish Air Force Resettlement Camp, Castle Combe, England, teacher of English, 1946-51; reporter for *Sheffield Telegraph,* 1951-52; *London Times,* London, England, member of editorial staff, 1953; full-time free-lance writer, 1954—. *Military service:* Royal Air Force, Intelligence, 1941-46; became first lieutenant.

WRITINGS: (Contributor) Kenneth Young, editor, *The Bed Post,* Macdonald & Co., 1962; (contributor) Jack Singleton, editor, *Home This Afternoon,* Lutterworth, 1967; (editor and author of introduction) *The First Cuckoo: Letters to the Times, 1900-1975,* Allen & Unwin, 1976, published in the United States as *Your Obedient Servant: A Selection of the Most Witty, Amusing, and Memorable Letters to the London Times, 1900-1975,* Two Continents Publishing, 1976; (editor) *In Celebration of Cricket,* Hart-Davis, 1978. Contributor to magazines, including *Queen,* and newspapers, including *London Times.*

WORK IN PROGRESS: Editing a theater anthology.

SIDELIGHTS: Gregory told *CA:* "In late 1973 a satirical article by myself appeared in the *London Times;* it dealt with the Personal column of the paper in former years when lovesick males, having glimpsed a ravishing maiden riding in Rotten Row, would pour out their hearts in the hope that the aforesaid maiden would agree to a meeting in some nook near the National Gallery or in St. James' Park. Also touched on, in contrast, was the current Personal column in a famous left-wing weekly which is doubtless at this moment including something on the lines of 'Lesbian in Hampstead seeks meeting with ditto in Highgate with view to adopting child.'

"Now for some years prior to 1973, the editorial director of the publishers Allen & Unwin had been unsuccessfully approaching the *Times* in the hope of printing a selection of letters to that paper. After many refusals, the *Times* finally relented. As they did so, the editorial director of Allen & Unwin read my satirical article, and wrote asking me if I would be interested in being the editor of a book of *Letters to the Times* as he thought I possessed the right irreverent touch. Intrigued by the thought of being paid to read the best *unpaid for* prose in the world, I agreed with alacrity.

"There was a catch," Gregory continued. "I had to consult only one feature in each edition of the *Times* over a seventy-five year period. But everyone seems to have converted their newspaper files into microfilm, and it is infinitely easier to flick over the pages of bound newspapers than it is to turn the knobs on a machine, changing the film frequently, and squinting at small type. The nearest library to keep bound files of the *Times* was the one at London's famous Guildhall. Six hours a day and five days a week, for more than four months, I invaded the vaults of Guildhall where much dust had accumulated. (I remembered to carry my own soap and washed up at a nearby public lavatory.) Ironically, a few months after I had finished selecting my choicest letters, the Guildhall's new library was opened—except that food is not provided, the interior bears a close resemblance to London's Hilton Hotel."

Gregory recalled that there were other problems: "The reader response to the project was mixed when permission to reprint the letters was sought. (The copyright of all letters to the *Times* remains with the writers or their executors.) Some wished to polish their phrases (not permitted); some insisted they had not written the letters appearing over their names, or, if they did, they were drunk at the time. Some,

like Swift, read what they had written years or decades before, and muttered 'What genius I had then!'"

Gregory also mentioned that "Response to *Your Obedient Servant* has been overwhelming. Retired generals have written to me emphasizing that the book shows why England has gone to the dogs. An Irishman expressed thanks at being shown why he has always disliked the English. A Canadian lady wished to know why letter-writing of the calibre of Bernard Shaw and Logan Pearsall Smith cannot be taught in school. An aged Australian pointed out that he takes the book to bed nightly and falls asleep laughing, insanely, within ten minutes. Several British correspondents point out that Bishops of the Church of England no longer write witty letters to the *Times* and want to know why—is it God's fault or that of a declining Britain? I have carefully acknowledged all letters," he concluded, "exonerating God from any blame."

AVOCATIONAL INTERESTS: Theatre (especially George Bernard Shaw), music (especially Mozart), reading (especially P. G. Wodehouse).

*   *   *

GRELE, Ronald J(ohn) 1934-

PERSONAL: Surname is pronounced *Gray-*lee; born June 8, 1934, in Naugatuck, Conn.; son of John R. (an accountant) and Martha (an accountant; maiden name, Painter) Grele; married Gaile Anderson (a librarian), June 10, 1959; children: John R., Michael A., Eric E., Christine T. *Education:* University of Connecticut, B.A., 1958, M.A., 1959; Rutgers University, Ph.D., 1971. *Home:* 615 South First Ave., Highland Park, N.J. 08904. *Agent:* Balkin Agency, 403 West 115th St., New York, N.Y. 10025.

CAREER: Ford Foundation, New York, N.Y., assistant director of oral history project, 1971-75; Rutgers University, New Brunswick, N.J., assistant professor of history, 1975-76; University of Indonesia, Jakarta, professor of history, 1976-77; director of oral history program, New Jersey Historical Commission, 1977—. Member of advisory council of National Archives' Regional Records Center, 1975-76. Chairman of Highland Park Rent Leveling Board, 1975-77. *Member:* American Historical Association, American Studies Association, Oral History Association.

WRITINGS: Where Cities Meet: The Urbanization of New Jersey, Van Nostrand, 1964; *Envelopes of Sound* (non-fiction), Precedent Publishing, 1975. Contributor to *American Quarterly, Journal of Library History, Oral History Newsletter.*

WORK IN PROGRESS: A handbook for oral history; interviews of American workers.

SIDELIGHTS: Grele told *CA:* "My major interest for the past ten years has been oral history, in particular the theoretical problems involved in the practice. Lately I have also been advising Asian scholars on the techniques of oral history."

*   *   *

GRIFFIN, Walter 1937-

PERSONAL: Born August 1, 1937, in Wilmington, Del.; son of William Samuel and Nina Opal (Blalock) Griffin; children: Paul Anthony. *Education:* Ohio State University, B.A., 1960; also attended Sorbonne, University of Paris. *Home address:* P.O. Box 674, East Point, Ga. 30344.

CAREER: Poet, 1955—. Has worked in poets-in-the-schools programs involving elementary and secondary schools, colleges, and prisons; has given readings throughout the South, in San Francisco, and in Ohio. Founder and director of Atlanta Poets Workshop; founder of "Atlanta Poetry Reading Series." Taught poetry course at Emory University, summers, 1970-71. *Military service:* U.S. Army, 1955-57. *Awards, honors:* International Small Press Book Award from Nirvana Publications, 1974, for *Nightmusic;* named author of the year by Southeastern Regional Council of Authors and Journalists, 1976, for *Nightmusic;* Pulitzer Prize nomination for poetry, 1977, for *Port Authority.*

WRITINGS—All volumes of poetry: *Leaving for New York,* Nirvana Publications, 1968; *Other Cities,* Hartford Press, 1971; *Bloodlines,* Purdue University English Department, 1972; *Ice Garden,* Wisconsin Review Press, 1973; *Machineworks,* Sweetwater Press, 1976; *Port Authority,* Vanderbilt University Press, 1976; *Skull Dreamer,* Border Mountain Press, 1977.

Contributor to more than three hundred magazines, including *Atlantic Monthly, Evergreen Review, Paris Review,* and *Prairie Schooner.*

WORK IN PROGRESS: Two novels; another book of poems.

SIDELIGHTS: Griffin told *CA:* "As a poor white kid in the South, I wore faded 'Captain Marvel' sweatshirts to school and had my shoes resoled at least four times per year. I have returned to the South and still look for the poetry in those days. Poetry has always been the 'glue that holds me together.' But of course it is much more than that to me. Poetry is the most personal of all art forms. The poet's poems reconcile the paradox of experience and thought, and in so doing, provide a base for sanity or what passes for sanity. Poems become still photographs of the poet's life, mind's eye, and imagination. They *are* his life.

"In my poems, I attempt to deal with middle America and the isolation, the inherent loneliness of the human spirit. They are about white frame houses passed long ago in the night. And the vagrant stranger who walks by lighted windows at dusk, feeling the traveler in us all. And that particular part of us that always, persistently tries to 'go home again.'"

* * *

GRIFFITH, Kathryn 1923-

PERSONAL: Born June 19, 1923, in Mankato, Kan.; daughter of Fred A. (a builder) and Grace (Wall) Pearcy; married Alfred Eugene Griffith (an appliance distributor), December 10, 1944. *Education:* Attended University of Kansas, 1941-42; Wichita University (now Wichita State University), A.B., 1947; Syracuse University, M.P.A., 1954; University of Chicago, Ph.D., 1967. *Home:* 525 Tara Lane, Wichita, Kan. 67206. *Office:* Department of Political Science, Wichita State University, Wichita, Kan. 67208.

CAREER: Wichita State University, Wichita, Kan., assistant to the president, 1949-63, assistant professor, 1957-63, associate professor, 1963-69, professor of political science, 1969—. *Member:* American Political Science Association, Conference of Political Thought, League of Women Voters (member of local board of directors, 1951-54; local president, 1952-54; member of state board of directors, 1956-57), Midwest Political Science Association, Southwestern Social Science Association.

WRITINGS: Judge Learned Hand and the Role of the Federal Judiciary, Oklahoma University Press, 1973.

WORK IN PROGRESS: Understanding Democracy (tentative title), which "seeks to provide an understanding of three types or models of democracy through an examination of the varying philosophical principles upon which each is based."

* * *

GRIGGS, Earl Leslie 1899-

PERSONAL: Born April 15, 1899, in New York, N.Y.; son of Edward Howard and Mary P. (Little) Griggs; married Grace Evelyn Riley, July 30, 1923. *Education:* Princeton University, student, 1917-19; University of Colorado, A.B., 1922; Columbia University, A.M., 1923; University of London, Ph.D., 1927. *Religion:* Episcopalian. *Home:* 3323 Cliff Dr., Santa Barbara, Calif 93109.

CAREER: University of Minnesota, Minneapolis, instructor in English, 1923-25; University of Oregon, Eugene, assistant professor of English, 1927-28; University of Michigan, Ann Arbor, assistant professor, 1928-34, associate professor of English, 1934-39; University of Pennsylvania, Philadelphia, professor of English, 1939-47; University of California, Los Angeles, professor of English, 1947-62, faculty research lecturer, 1961; University of California, Santa Barbara, dean of Graduate Division, 1962-67, director of education abroad program in England and Ireland, 1967-69. Visiting professor at University of Colorado, summers, 1934, 1936, and 1938, Duke University, 1937-41, Ohio State University, 1942, University of California, 1945-46, and New York University, 1950; honorary research associate at University College, University of London, 1968-69. *Military service:* U.S. Army, 1918.

MEMBER: Modern Language Association of America, Charles Lamb Society (vice-president), Royal Society of Literature (fellow), Phi Beta Kappa, Phi Kappa Phi, Phi Delta Kappa, Kappa Delta Pi, Cosmos Club. *Awards, honors:* Lloyd traveling fellowship, 1930-31; Henry Russell Award, 1931; Huntington Library fellowship, 1945-46; D.Litt. from University of London, 1956.

WRITINGS: Harley Coleridge: His Life and Work, University of London Press, 1929, reprinted, Folcroft, 1971; (editor) *Unpublished Letters of Samuel Taylor Coleridge,* two volumes, Constable, 1932; (editor) *The Best of Coleridge,* [London], 1934; (editor with Edmund Blunden) *Coleridge: Studies by Several Hands on the Hundredth Anniversary of His Death,* Constable, 1934, reprinted, Folcroft, 1973; (editor with wife, Grace E. Griggs) *Letters of Hartley Coleridge,* Oxford University Press, 1936; *Thomas Clarkson: The Friend of Slaves,* Allen & Unwin, 1936, Negro Universities Press, 1970; (editor) *Wordsworth and Coleridge: Studies in Honor of George McLean Harper,* Princeton University Press, 1939, Russel & Russell, 1962; *Coleridge Fille: A Biography of Sara Coleridge,* Oxford University Press, 1940, reprinted, Folcroft, 1972; (editor) *New Poems of Hartley Coleridge,* Oxford University Press, 1942; (editor) *Henry Christophe and Thomas Clarkson: A Correspondence,* University of California Press, 1952; (editor) *Collected Letters of Samuel Taylor Coleridge, 1772-1834,* Volumes I-VI, Clarendon Press, 1956-71. Contributor to professional journals in England and the United States.

* * *

GROF, Stanislav 1931-

PERSONAL: Born July 1, 1931, in Prague, Czechoslovakia; son of Stanislav (a chemical engineer) and Maria (Petnik) Grof; married Joan Halifax (an anthropologist), June 12,

1972 (divorced, 1977). *Education:* Charles University (Prague), M.D., 1956; Czechoslovak Academy of Sciences (Prague), Ph.D., 1964. *Home:* Buck Creek, Big Sur, Calif. 93920. *Agent:* John Brockman, 241 Central Park West, New York, N.Y. 10024. *Office:* Esalen Institute, Big Sur, Calif. 93920.

CAREER: State Mental Hospital, Kosmonosy, Czechoslovakia, member of staff, 1956-60; Psychiatric Research Institute, Prague, Czechoslovakia, research scientist, 1960-67; Johns Hopkins University, Baltimore, Md., clinical and research fellow, 1967-69; Maryland Psychiatric Research Center, Cantonsville, Md., chief of psychiatric research, 1967-73; Johns Hopkins University, assistant professor of psychiatry, 1969-73; Esalen Institute, Big Sur, Calif., scholar-in-residence, 1973—. *Member:* American Academy of Psychoanalysis. *Awards, honors:* Kuffner Award for best research of the year from the Czechoslovak Psychiatric Association, 1958, for study of anticholinergic hallucinogens.

WRITINGS: Realms of the Human Unconscious: Observations from LSD Research, Viking, 1975; (with Joan Halifax) *The Human Encounter with Death,* Dutton, 1977. Contributor of over sixty articles to books and professional journals.

Consulting editor, *Journal of Transpersonal Psychology, Synthesis,* and *Journal for the Study of Consciousness.*

WORK IN PROGRESS: Principles of LSD Psychotherapy.

SIDELIGHTS: Stanislav Grof told *CA* that his primary interest is in "unusual states of consciousness and their relevance for health, religion, and society."

His work at the Esalen Institute in Calif., a forum for the multitude of disciplines, theories, and techniques used in the "new consciousness" movement today, involves the "synthesis of ancient wisdom and modern science, Eastern and Western thought."

BIOGRAPHICAL/CRITICAL SOURCES: Joseph Campbell, *Myths to Live By,* Bantam, 1972; Huston Smith, *Forgotten Truth: The Primordial Tradition,* Harper, 1976.

* * *

GROSMAN, Brian A(llen) 1935-

PERSONAL: First syllable of surname rhymes with "loss"; born May 20, 1935, in Toronto, Ontario, Canada; son of Morris (a pharmacist) and Bessie (a law office manager; maiden name, Benson) Grosman; married Penny-Lynn Cookson (an art historian), September 1, 1967; children: John Shain. *Education:* University of Toronto, B.A., 1956, LL.B., 1960; attended Osgoode Hall Law School, 1961; McGill University, LL.M., 1967. *Home:* 1101 Temperance St., Saskatoon, Saskatchewan, Canada S7N 0N7. *Office:* Law Reform Commission of Saskatchewan, 201 21st St. E., Suite 1003, Saskatoon, Saskatchewan, Canada.

CAREER: Barrister and solicitor in Toronto, Ontario, 1962-65; McGill University, Montreal, Quebec, assistant professor of law, 1965-71; University of Saskatchewan, Saskatoon, professor of law, 1971-73; Law Reform Commission of Saskatchewan, Saskatoon, chairman, 1973—. Member of Ontario Bar, Saskatchewan Bar, Canadian Bar Council, and American Law Institute. Executive member of Canadian Human Rights Foundation; Saskatchewan commissioner of Uniform Law Conference of Canada, 1974-77.

MEMBER: International Association of Criminal Law, International Society for the Study of Comparative Law (life

member), International Association of Sociologists of Law, Society of Public Teachers of Law, American Society of Criminology (executive member), American Judicature Society. *Awards, honors:* Award from Canadian Bar Foundation, 1966; Beccaria Award from the solicitor general of Quebec, 1971; presidential citation from American Society of Criminology, 1975.

WRITINGS: The Prosecutor: An Inquiry into the Exercise of Discretion, University of Toronto Press, 1969; *Justice in Crisis* (booklet), University of Saskatchewan, 1971; (contributor) Craig Boydell and Paul Whitehead, editors, *The Administration of Criminal Justice in Canada,* Holt, 1974; *Police Command: Decisions and Discretion,* Macmillan (Canada), 1975. Also contributor to *Politics, Crime, and the International Scene,* edited by Freda Adler and G. O. Mueller, 1972. Contributor to *Criminal Law Quarterly* and other legal journals, and to Canadian newspapers. Editor of *Criminology: An Interdisciplinary Journal,* 1976-77.

WORK IN PROGRESS: Research on criminal law, criminology, medical-legal questions, and the role of the legal profession.

* * *

GROVE, Pearce S(eymour) 1930-

PERSONAL: Born September 21, 1930, in Augusta, Ga.; son of Howard Moseley and Mary Jane (Wells) Grove; married Elaine Adams, January 16, 1953; children: Brenda, Darrel, Marlene, Wayne, Kent, Alan. *Education:* University of Florida, B.A., 1956, M.Ed., 1957; University of Illinois, M.S.L.S., 1958; Eastern New Mexico University, further graduate study. *Religion:* Methodist. *Office:* Library, Western Illinois University, Macomb, Ill. 61455.

CAREER: University of Illinois, Urbana, assistant librarian, 1958-60; University of Illinois at Chicago Circle, Chicago, acquisitions and serials librarian, 1960-61; Colorado Women's College, Denver, head librarian, 1961-64; Kansas State University, Manhattan, assistant director of libraries, 1964-66; Eastern New Mexico University, Portales, library director, 1966-75; Western Illinois University, Macomb, director of libraries, 1975—. Director of U.S. Office of Education Media Administration Institute, 1969-70. Member of American National Standards Institute and Llano Estacado Southwest Heritage.

MEMBER: American Library Association, American Association of University Professors, Association for College and Research Libraries, U.S. Naval Reserve Association, Southwestern Library Association (life member; president, 1973-74), Illinois Library Association, Phi Delta Kappa, Phi Kappa Phi, Kiwanis.

WRITINGS: (Editor) *Strategic Intelligence: A Naval Reserve Training Manual,* Ninth District, U.S. Naval Reserve, 1958; *Faculty Publications and Research at Eastern New Mexico University,* Eastern New Mexico University, 1970; (editor) *A Selected List of Materials Relating to Mexican-Americans,* Eastern New Mexico University, 1970; (editor) *An Introductory Bibliography of Black Study Resources in the Eastern New Mexico University Library,* Eastern New Mexico University, 1970; *A Directory of New Mexico Libraries,* New Mexico Library Association, 1970; (with Evelyn G. Clement) *Systems and Standards for the Bibliographic Control of Nonprint Media,* American Library Association, 1972; *Forty Years of Navy Reserve Intelligence Activity in the Lubbock Area,* U.S. Naval Reserve, 1974; *Nonprint Media in Academic Libraries,* American Library Association, 1975; *New Mexico Newspapers: A*

Comprehensive Guide to Bibliographical Entries and Locations, University of New Mexico Press, 1975; (editor) *Native American Studies,* Eastern New Mexico University, 1975. Contributor of more than twenty articles to professional journals. Editor of *Library Trends,* October, 1975.

WORK IN PRIGRESS: Editing *The Genealogy of Roosevelt County Pioneers,* with Dona Stone, for local Daughters of the American Revolution.

*　*　*

GROW, Lawrence 1939-

PERSONAL: Born July 2, 1939, in Geneva, Ill.; son of Milton Dwight (a clinical psychologist) and Mary (Stuart) Grow. *Education:* Wesleyan University, B.A., 1961; also attended University of Chicago, 1961-63, and University of Paris, 1963-65. *Politics:* Democrat. *Religion:* Episcopalian. *Home address:* Pinegrove, R.D.1, Pittstown, N.J. 08867. *Office:* Main Street Press, 42 Main St., Clinton, N.J. 08809.

CAREER: Bobbs-Merrill, Inc., New York, N.Y., editor, 1965-67; McGraw-Hill Book Co., New York City, editor, 1967-69; G.P. Putnam's Sons, New York City, editor and publicity director, 1969-70; Pyne Press, Princeton, N.J., editorial director, 1970-75; Main Street Press, Clinton, N.J., president, 1975—.

WRITINGS: (Editor) *The Old House Catalogue,* Universe Books, 1976; (editor) *Waiting for the 5:05,* Universe Books, 1977; (editor) *The Old House Catalogue II,* Universe Books, in press; *Old House Plans,* Universe Books, 1977. Contributor to *Americana.*

WORK IN PROGRESS: A book on suburban railroads and stations, publication expected in 1979.

*　*　*

GRULIOW, Leo 1913-

PERSONAL: Born May 27, 1913, in Bayonne, N.J.; son of George (a watchmaker) and Rebecca (Kagan) Gruliow; married Agnes J. Forrest (an artist), September 22, 1945; children: Frank Forrest, Rebecca. *Education:* Educated in Elizabeth, N.J. *Residence:* Columbus, Ohio. *Office: Current Digest of the Soviet Press,* 2043 Millikin Rd., Columbus, Ohio 43201.

CAREER: Elizabeth Evening Times, Elizabeth, N.J., copy boy and reporter, 1930; *New York Democrat,* New York City, reporter and makeup man, 1930-33; *Moscow Daily News,* Moscow, U.S.S.R., makeup man, 1933-38; Washington bureau feature writer, Transradio Press Service, 1939-40; worked at copy desks of *Washington Daily News* and *Washington Times-Herald,* 1941; Russian War Relief, Inc., New York City, research director, 1941-42, field representative in the Soviet Union, 1943-45; lecturer in United States, 1946; lecturer, Grinnell College, Antioch College, and New School for Social Research, 1946-47; American Council of Learned Societies, Washington, D.C., translator, 1948; *Current Digest of the Soviet Press,* Columbus, Ohio (formerly in New York City), founder and editor, 1949—. Correspondent in Moscow, *Christian Science Monitor,* 1972-74, Curtis Publications, 1975. Adjunct professor, Ohio State University, 1969-72, 1975—; guest professor, Graduate Institute of International Studies, Switzerland, 1959-60, and Antioch College, 1963-64; lecturer at various U.S. colleges and universities, 1952-77; broadcast commentator for various radio and television stations, 1953-69.

MEMBER: American Association for the Advancement of Slavic Studies. *Awards, honors:* Labor Distinction Medal of the U.S.S.R., 1945, for work as U.S. field representative of Russian War Relief; senior fellowship, National Endowment for the Humanities, 1974-75, Woodrow Wilson National Fellowship Foundation, 1974—.

WRITINGS: (Translator) *Soviet Views on the Postwar World Economy: An Official Critique of Eugene Varga's Changes in the Economy of Capitalism Resulting from the Second World War,* Public Affairs Press, 1948; (editor and author of forewords) *Current Soviet Policies,* Praeger, Volume I, 1953, Volume II, 1957, Columbia University Press, Volume III, 1960, Volume IV (with Charlotte Saikowski), 1962, American Association for the Advancement of Slavic Studies, Volume VII, 1976; (editor and author of foreword) Anatoly Kuznetsov, *Babi Yar,* Dial, 1966; (co-author with the editors of Time-Life Books) *The Great Cities: Moscow,* Time-Life, 1977. ,

WORK IN PROGRESS: A study of the Soviet press and Soviet internal propaganda; a book on the Soviet Union east of the Urals-Siberia and Central Asia.

SIDELIGHTS: Gruliow told *CA:* "Travels in Russia began with the accident of obtaining a job assignment in Moscow for a time during the depression of the 1930's. I learned Russian, and returned to the Soviet Union on assignments in the wartime 1940's, at the end of the 1950's, and in the 1970's. In repeated visits, I crisscrossed that country from the Ukraine to the shore of the Bering Strait and from the Siberian Arctic to Central Asia in the south. Interest in Russia and in newspaper work became my education; I'm still learning. The two interests combined to inspire the idea of a weekly digest of the Soviet press. With the support of the U.S. academic community and funds from the Rockefeller and later the Ford foundations, I began to publish this magazine in the early postwar period, when Stalinist censorship extended even to deleting some quotations of the official Soviet press itself from American correspondents' dispatches out of Moscow—although that same Soviet press was available on U.S. newsstands. I have edited this *Current Digest of the Soviet Press* for almost thirty years, while continuing to engage in newspaper work, writing, translation, broadcasting and lecturing."

*　*　*

GRUND, Josef Carl 1920-

PERSONAL: Born February 18, 1920, in Duernberg, Germany; son of Johann (a miner) and Anna (Siegl) Grund; married Margarete Pelz, July 9, 1944 (died, 1967); married Ingrid Bauer (a teacher), December 27, 1968; children: (first marriage) Manfred, Gertraud, Eva. *Education:* Graduated from Teacher's College in Mies, Germany, 1939. *Politics:* Liberal. *Religion:* Roman Catholic. *Home and office:* Trierer Strasse 176, D-8500 Nuremberg, West Germany. *Agent:* Auteursbureau Greta Baas-Jelgersma, Den Heuvel 73, Velp, Netherlands.

CAREER: Teacher and assistant headmaster in secondary schools in Nuremberg, West Germany, 1946-73; university lecturer in history, Nuremberg, 1973-75; full-time writer, 1975—. City official in Nuremberg, 1945-75. *Military service:* German Luftwaffe (air force), 1939-45; became first lieutenant; received Iron Cross and Knight's Cross. *Member:* Boedeckerkreis (a German writers' association).

WRITINGS—In English translation: *Du hast einen Freund, Pietro,* Boje, 1961, translation by Margaret Mutch published as *You Have a Friend, Pietro* (Junior Literary Guild selection), Little, Brown, 1966; *Jenseits der Brucke,* Bahn, 1961, translation by Lucile Harrington published as

Beyond the Bridge, Little, Brown, 1968; *Flakhelfer Briel,* Sebaldus, 1965, translation by Harrington published as *Never to Be Free,* Little, Brown, 1970.

Other works; juvenile fiction: *Lucia, der Fratz* (title means "Lucia, the Little Devil"), Boje, 1956; *Rosita, das Zigeunermaedchen* (title means "Rosita, the Gypsy Girl"), Ensslin & Laiblin, 1957; *Jenny und ihr Pony* (title means "Jenny and Her Pony"), Bayerische Verlagsanstalt, 1959.

Bravo, Peng! (title means "Bravo, Bang"), Bayerische Verlagsanstalt, 1960; *Eva: Geschichte eines musikbegabten Maedchens* (title means "Eva: Story of a Girl Skilled in Music"), Bayerische Verlagsanstalt, 1961; *Das Maedchen im blauen Kleid* (title means "The Girl in the Blue Dress"), Bayerische Verlagsanstalt, 1962; *Die Bueffelranch* (title means "Buffalo Ranch"), Spectrum, 1964; *In der Praerie* (title means "In the Prairie"), Spectrum, 1965; *Cowboy Harry,* Spectrum, 1965; *Du hast Freunde, Angelina* (title means "You Have Friends, Angelina"), Spectrum, 1965; *Ruf aus dem Dunkel* (title means "A Voice out of the Dark"), Schwabenverlag, 1965.

Harry kehrt zurueck (title means "Harry Returns"), Spectrum, 1966; *Karin und die 12 Gestreiften* (title means "Karen and the Twelve Striped Creatures"), Spectrum, 1966; *Der Sohn des Verbannten* (title means "The Son of the Exiled"), Spectrum, 1967; *Hi, der Poltergeist* (title means "Hi, Goblin!"), Loewes, 1967; *Tschip, der Klabautermann* (title means "Tschip, the Bogey Man"), Loewes, 1968; *Der Mann aus Prag: Eine Erzahlung aus unserer juengsten Vergangenheit* (title means "The Man from Prague: A Story of the Post War Period"), Arena, 1968; *Wo steckt Zacharias?* (title means "Where Is Zacharias?"), Arena, 1968.

Purzel (title means "Purzel, the Teddy Bear"), Spectrum, 1970; *Knacks ist immer dabei* (title means "Snap Is Always Present"), Spectrum, 1970; *Tick, der Wieselwicht* (title means "Tick, the Goblin"), Spectrum, 1971; *Brigitte und die silberne Spinne* (title means "Brigitte and the Silver Spider"), Bahn, 1971; *Der Mann mit der Narbe: Eine Erzaehlung aus Korsika* (title means "The Man with the Scar: A Story from Corsica"), L. Auer, 1971; *Krach auf der Rollmopsinsel* (title means "Quarrel on Pickled Herring Island"), Spectrum, 1971; *Das Gespenst mit der roten Nase* (title means "The Ghost with the Ruby Nose"), Loewes, 1971; *Der Talisman des Haeuptlings* (title means "The Chief's Talisman"), 1972; *Fabian Flunkerstein und der 32 Maerz* (title means "Fabian the Storyteller and the 32nd of March"), Loewes, 1973; *Abenteuer auf der Rollmopsinsel* (title means "Adventure on Pickled Herring Island"), Spectrum, 1973; *Fabian Flunkerstein und der kleine Clown* (title means "Fabian the Storyteller and the Little Clown"), Loewes, 1973.

Fabian Flunkerstein und das Schluckauf-Gespenst (title means "Fabian the Storyteller and the Hiccup Ghost"), Loewes, 1974; *Weiter Weg durch wildes Land* (title means "A Long Way through Wild Country"), Spectrum, 1974; *Hilfe fuer Castor* (title means "Help for Castor"), Spectrum, 1974; *Nachruf auf Harald N.* (JUBU-Crew selection; title means "In Memory of Harald N."), Bahn, 1974; *Die Rache des Herrn Egerli* (title means "Mr. Egerli's Revenge"), Herold, 1975; *Verschwoerung des Schweigens* (title means "Conspiracy of Silence"), Otto Maier, 1975; *Das Maedchen vom Trevi-Brunnen* (title means "The Girl of the 'Fontana di Trevi' in Rome"), Spectrum, 1976; *Max Mogelmeier und die Hellseher* (title means "Tricky Max and the Clairvoyants"), Herold, 1977; *Inspektor Naseweis* (title means "Detective Jackanapes"), Schneider, 1977; *Venedig*

soll nicht sterben (title means "Venice Must Not Die"), Goldmann-Jugendtaschenbuch, 1977.

Travel: *Suedtirol ist eine Reise wert* (title means "South Tyrol: Worth Seeing"), Staehle & Friedel, 1971; *Vom Gardasee zur Adria* (title means "From Lake Garda to Venice"), Staehle & Friedel, 1973; *Liebenswertes Oesterreich* (title means "Amiable Austria"), Staehle & Friedel, 1975.

Plays: "Kalif Storch" (one act; title means "California Stork"), first produced in Venice, Italy, at Teatro Ridotto, 1966; "Frau Holle" (three-act), first produced in Nuremberg, West Germany, 1967; "Der zweite Stern" (three-act; title means "The Second Star"), first produced in Nuremberg, 1969; "Spezialpraeparat" (four-act; title means "Special Preparation"), first produced in Mellrichstadt, West Germany, 1971; "Der Froschkoenig" (three-act; title means "The Frog King"), first produced in Heidenheim, West Germany, 1972.

WORK IN PROGRESS: A travel book, *Deutsches Alpen-und Voralpenland* (title means "German Alps and the Alpine Foothills"); two children's books to be published by Schneider, *Der Poltergeist mit dem Holzbein* (title means "The Pollinger Kids and the Ghost with the Wooden Leg"), and *Unsere Klasse schwaermt fuer Freddy* (title means "Everybody Is in Raptures about Freddy").

SIDELIGHTS: Grund told *CA:* "Above all, I write against war and violence. I know the war from my own experience and was seriously wounded. To me, violence (except self defense) is no means of settling conflicts and is not worthy of human beings. This is the way the characters of my books act." When asked about his views on the recent upsurge of terrorism and violence in West Germany, Grund commented: "In my opinion, the terrorism of our day is not only a German phenomenon but concerns the whole world. One of the reasons might be that many ideals and hopes have crumbled to pieces."

AVOCATIONAL INTERESTS: Mountain climbing, gardening, cooking.

BIOGRAPHICAL/CRITICAL SOURCES: New York Times Book Review, April 3, 1966; *Christian Science Monitor,* May 5, 1966; *America,* July 2, 1966.

*   *   *

GRUNDY, Kenneth W(illiam) 1936-

PERSONAL: Born August 6, 1936, in Philadelphia, Pa.; son of William and Alma (Hahn) Grundy; married Martha J. Paxson, June 25, 1960; children: William MacIntyre, Thomas Paxson, Anne Edmunds. *Education:* Ursinus College, B.A. (honors), 1958; Pennsylvania State University, M.A., 1961, Ph.D., 1963. *Home:* 2602 Exeter Rd., Cleveland Heights, Ohio 44118. *Office:* Department of Political Science, Case Western Reserve University, Cleveland, Ohio 44106.

CAREER: San Fernando Valley State College (now California State University), Northridge, Calif., assistant professor of political science, 1963-66; Case Western Reserve University, Cleveland, Ohio, associate professor, 1966-74, professor of political science, 1974—. Visiting assistant professor at Pennsylvania State University, summer, 1965; visiting senior lecturer at Makerere University, 1967-68; Fulbright professor at University of Zambia, 1977. Visiting scholar at Institute of Social Studies (the Hague), 1972-73.

MEMBER: International Studies Association, African Studies Association (fellow), Inter-University Seminar on the Armed Forces and Society (member of executive council, 1976—). *Awards, honors:* Rockefeller Foundation grant for Uganda, 1967-68; grant from Center on International Race Relations for southern Africa, 1969-71; Social Science Research Council grant for England and the Netherlands, 1972-73; Hoover Institution grant, 1978.

WRITINGS: (Contributor) William H. Friedland and Carl G. Rosberg, Jr., editors, *African Socialism,* Stanford University Press, 1964; *Conflicting Images of the Military in Africa,* East African Publishing House, 1968; *Guerrilla Struggle in Africa: Analysis and Preview,* Grossman, 1971; *Confrontation and Accomodation in Southern Africa: The Limits of Independence,* University of California Press, 1973; (with Michael Weinstein) *The Ideologies of Violence,* C. E. Merrill, 1974; *We're Against Apartheid, But . . .* (monograph), University of Denver, 1974; *Defense Legislation and Communal Politics* (monograph), Ohio University, 1978. Contributor of more than seventy-five articles and reviews to academic and literary journals and popular magazines, including *Saturday Review, Yale Review,* and *Virginia Quarterly.* Special editor of *Armed Forces and Society,* January, 1976.

WORK IN PROGRESS: An extended study of South African defense and foreign policy, especially relating to the use of non-whites in the armed forces.

SIDELIGHTS: Grundy writes: "Writing for me is a joy, not a chore. I regret how difficult it is to find the time to do as much as I would like to do. This is so, not because all other tasks are unpleasant, but because so many other tasks are also fun. Teaching is pleasant. So is doing things with my family. So, choices have to be made from among a variety of enjoyments, and herein lies the dilemma—how to squeeze forty hours out of a day without becoming thoroughly frustrated."

* * *

GRUNFELD, Frederic V. 1929-

PERSONAL: Born June 2, 1929, in Berlin, Germany; came to the United States in 1939, naturalized citizen, 1944; son of Franz V. (an industrialist) and Elli E. (a fashion designer; maiden name, Neumann) Grunfeld; married Dorothy Miles Gregory, March 21, 1947 (divorced, 1960); married Ann Mary O'Sullivan (an artist), December 16, 1976; children: Foster V., Laura E. *Education:* University of Chicago, Ph.B., 1949; Columbia University, M.F.A., 1974. *Home and office address:* Son Rullan, Deya, Mallorca, Spain. *Agent:* Wallace & Sheil, Inc., 118 East 61st St., New York, N.Y. 10021.

CAREER: WQXR-Radio, New York, N.Y., commentator, 1950-55; Bourree Productions, New York City, vice-president, 1955-58; *Reporter,* New York City, European cultural correspondent, 1958-65; *Horizon,* New York City, roving editor, 1966-77; writer, 1977—. *Member:* Society of the Classic Guitar (fellow), Overseas Press Club, Reform Club (London), Real Club Nautico (Spain).

WRITINGS: Music and Recordings, Oxford University Press, 1955; *The Art and Times of the Guitar,* Macmillan, 1970, published as *The Art and Times of the Guitar: An Illustrated History of Guitars and Guitarists,* 1974; *Music,* Newsweek Books, 1973; *The Hitler File: A Social History of Germany and the Nazis, 1918-1945,* Random House, 1974; (editor) *Games of the World,* Holt, 1975; *Berlin,* Time-Life, 1977. Contributor to magazines, including *Horizon, Saturday Review,* and *Reporter.* Consulting editor of *Queen,* 1965-70.

WORK IN PROGRESS: A biography of Auguste Rodin; a cultural history of the Weimar intellectuals.

SIDELIGHTS: Grunfeld comments: "I have heard much music and seen much art, principally in America, Europe, and Asia. I am fascinated by the geosyncline of cultures circling the globe, and enjoy writing about aspects of it, notably primitive art, music, and theatre. For many years I covered such things for *Horizon* and have also taken many photographs. One day I hope to put together an encyclopedia of tribal crafts as a companion piece to the book on ethnic games I edited some years ago."

* * *

GUADO, Sergio
See GEROSA, GUIDO

* * *

GUARE, John 1938-

PERSONAL: Born February 5, 1938, in New York, N.Y.; son of Edward and Helen Claire (Grady) Guare. *Education:* Georgetown University, A.B., 1961; Yale University, M.F.A., 1963. *Residence:* New York, N.Y. *Agent:* R. Andrew Boose, Greenbaum, Wolf & Ernst, 437 Madison Ave., New York, N.Y. 10032.

CAREER: Playwright. Playwright-in-residence at New York Shakespeare festival, 1977. *Military service:* U.S. Air Force Reserve, 1963. *Member:* Authors League, Dramatists Guild (member of board of directors), Eugene O'Neill Playwrights' Conference (founding member). *Awards, honors:* Obie Award, 1968, for "Muzeeka"; Obie Award as New York Drama Critics Most Promising Playwright, 1968-69, for "Cop-Out"; New York Drama Critics Circle Award for Best American Play, 1971, for "The House of Blue Leaves"; Outer Critics Circle Prize for playwrighting, 1971; New York Drama Critics Circle Award for Best Musical of 1971-72, for "Two Gentlemen of Verona"; Antoinette Perry (Tony) Awards for Best Musical and for Best Libretto, 1972, for "Two Gentlemen of Verona"; Rockefeller grant in playwrighting; Joseph Jefferson award for playwriting, 1977, for "Landscape of the Body."

WRITINGS—Plays: "Universe," first produced in New York, 1949; "Did You Write My Name in the Snow?", first produced in New Haven, Conn., 1962; "To Wally Pantoni, We Leave a Credenza," first produced in New York, 1964; *The Loveliest Afternoon of the Year,* [and] *Something I'll Tell You Tuesday* (both first produced Off-Off Broadway at Cafe Cino, 1966), Dramatists Play Service, 1968; *Muzeeka and Other Plays: Cop-Out, Home Fires* (includes "Muzeeka," first produced in Waterford, Conn., 1967, produced in New York, 1968; "Cop-Out" and "Home Fires," both first produced in Waterford, 1968, produced in New York, 1969), Grove, 1969; (contributor) John Lahr, editor, *Showcase 1: Plays from the Eugene O'Neill Foundation,* Grove, 1969; "A Play by Brecht" (a musical based on "The Exception the Rule" by Bertolt Brecht; music by Leonard Bernstein; lyrics by Stephen Sondheim), first produced on Broadway at Broadhurst Theatre, February 18, 1969.

(Contributor) *Off-Broadway Plays,* Volume I, Penguin (London), 1970; *Kissing Sweet, and A Day for Surprises: Two Short Plays* ("Kissing Sweet," first produced on television, 1969; "A Day for Surprises," first produced in London, 1971), Dramatists Play Service, 1970; (with Milos Forman) *Taking Off* (screenplay), New American Library, 1971; "Un Pape a New York," first produced in Paris at Gaiete-Montparnesse, 1972; *The House of Blue Leaves: A*

Play (first produced Off-Broadway, 1971), Viking, 1972; (with Mel Shapiro and Galt MacDermot) *Two Gentlemen of Verona* (adaptation of the play by Shakespeare; first produced in New York, 1971), Holt, 1973; "Rich and Famous," first produced Off-Broadway at Public Theatre, 1976; "Marco Polo Sings a Solo," produced Off-Broadway at New York Shakespeare Festival, 1977; "Landscape of the Body," first produced in Lake Forest, Ill., at Academy Festival Theatre, 1977, produced Off-Broadway at Public Theatre, 1977.

*SIDELIGHTS:*Clive Barnes, in his review of "Marco Polo Sings a Solo," refers to Guare as "one of our most inventive playwrights. He has a great wit and, perhaps more importantly for the theater, an immaculate sense of the ridiculous." Richard Eder agrees, "he is one of the most personal and valuable figures among our stage writers."

In the preface to a published version of "The House of Blue Leaves," Guare briefly summarized his ideas as a playwright: "I think the only playwrighting rule is that you have to learn your craft so that you can put on stage plays *you* would like to see."

"I started writing plays at 11," Guare told an interviewer. "And I've written a play every year since 1956, when I was 18. How many of my plays have been produced? 'Marco Polo' will be my thirteenth. When a play of mine closes, I want a new play to go to. That's how I wrote 'Marco Polo.' I had the music from 'Two Gentlemen of Verona' ringing in my ears. I had to get the music out. So, I was coming back from the London production of 'Verona' and I said 'I'm not going to land in New York without having a new play finished.' I wrote the second act of 'Marco Polo' on the plane. That was almost four years ago. You know what one of the real pains is of being a playwright?" he continued. "It's going around and not being connected to a theatre. It's bad when you have a production, and then it's over, and there's no place to go."

While reworking "Marco Polo Sings a Solo," Guare explained Polo's journey from childishness to maturity. He defined maturity as "a creating of your own structure that allows you to flourish." In many ways this paralleled Guare's own career. While studying at Yale, with the late John Gassner, Guare found himself rejecting the emphasis on logic and good construction. Later, he studied with Arnold Weinstein and found he loved the idea of disregarding both logic and the conventional modes of construction in order to find his own way. He began writing one-act plays.

"I'm very obsessive about work," Guare commented. "Work for me is all voyaging, a kind of emotional serendipity. I write to get objectivity on things that have happened. Life is the unconscious, writing the conscious."

BIOGRAPHICAL/CRITICAL SOURCES: New Yorker, April 19, 1969; *New York Post,* February 26, 1971; Bruce Mailman and Albert Poland, *Off-Off Broadway Book,* Bobbs-Merrill, 1972; *Saturday Review,* November 20, 1973; *New York Times,* December 10, 1976, February 7, 1977, October 14, 1977.

*   *   *

GUENTHER, Herbert V. 1917-

PERSONAL: Born March 17, 1917, in Bremen, Germany; son of Reinhold Friedrich Karl (an engineer) and Dorothea (Meyer) Guenther; married Ilse Rossrucker (a music teacher), June 15, 1944; children: Edith, Kimbell, Nora. *Education:* University of Munich, Ph.D., 1939; University of Vi-

enna, Ph.D., 1943. *Home:* 1320 13th St. E., Saskatoon, Saskatchewan, Canada S7H 0C6. *Agent:* Sam Berelholz, P.O. Box 271, Boulder, Colo. 80302. *Office:* Department of Far Eastern Studies, University of Saskatchewan, Saskatoon, Saskatchewan, Canada S7N 0W0.

CAREER: University of Vienna, Vienna, Austria, docent, 1943-50; University of Lucknow, Lucknow, India, assistant professor of Indian and Tibetan studies, 1950-58; Varanasi Sanskrit University, Varanasi, India, assistant professor of Indian and Tibetan studies, 1958-64; University of Saskatchewan, Saskatoon, professor of Indian and Tibetan studies, 1964—. *Member:* Association for Asian Studies.

WRITINGS: Das Seelenproblem in Altern Buddhismus Curt Weller, 1949; *Yuganaddha: The Tantric Way of Life,* Chowkhamba, 1952; *Der Buddha und Seine Lehre,* Rascher & Co., 1956; *Buddhism and Psychology in the Abhidharma,* Buddha Vihara, 1957, revised edition, Shambhala, 1974; *Sgam-po-pa: The Jewel Ornament of Liberation,* Rider & Co., 1959; *The Life and Teaching of Naropa,* Clarendon Press, 1963; *Tibetan Buddhism Without Mystification,* E. J. Brill, 1966; *The Royal Song of Sahara,* University of Washington Press, 1969.

Treasures on the Tibetan Middle Way, Shambhala, 1971; *Buddhist Philosophy in Theory and Practice,* Penguin, 1972; *The Tantric View of Life,* Shambhala, 1972; *Tantra als Leben-Anschauung,* Barth Verlag, 1974; (with Choegyam Trungpa) *The Dawn of Tantra,* Shambhala, 1975; (with Leslie S. Kawamura) *Mind in Buddhist Psychology,* Dharma Publishing, 1975; *Kindly Bent to Ease Us,* Dharma Publishing, Volume I: *Mind,* 1975, Volume II: *Meditation,* 1976, Volume III: *Wonderment,* 1976; *Tibetan Buddhism in Western Perspective,* Dharma Publishing, 1977.

Contributor: *Twenty-Five Hundred Years of Buddhism,* Government of India, 1956; (author of foreword) Lama Mipham, *Calm and Clear,* Dharma Publishing, 1973; Genjun W, Sasaki, editor, *A Study of Klesa: A Study of Impurity and Its Purification in Oriental Religions,* Shimizukobundo Ltd., 1975. Also contributor to *A New Tibeto-Mongol Pantheon,* 1961; *History of Religions,* Volume II, 1963, Volume VI, 1966; and *An Introduction to Tantric Buddhism.*

Contributor to *Encyclopaedia Britannica.* Contributor of about eighty-five articles and reviews to journals.

WORK IN PROGRESS: Buddhist Philosophy in Tibetan Development.

BIOGRAPHICAL/CRITICAL SOURCES: Leslie S. Kawamura and Keith Scott, editors, *Buddhist Thought and Asian Civilization,* Dharma Publishing, 1977.

*   *   *

GUESS, Edward Preston 1925-
(Edward Preston)

PERSONAL: Born January 11, 1925, in Rome, Miss.; son of Thomas Lonzo (a plantation manager) and Ralda (Bailey) Guess; married Barbara Remington, August 12, 1967 (divorced). *Education:* Attended McNeese College, 1942-43, University of Washington, Seattle, 1944-45, and University of Miami, Coral Gables, Fla., 1947-48. *Residence:* New York, N.Y.

CAREER: Free-lance writer and editor, 1950—. Has worked as foreign correspondent in England and Germany for newspapers, including *San Francisco Chronicle,* 1963-71, and *Paris Herald Tribune,* 1963-66. *Military service:* U.S. Army, 1946.

WRITINGS—All under Edward Preston: *Fighter for Freedom* (biography of Martin Luther King, Jr.), Doubleday, 1968; *How to Buy Land Cheap,* Boggle Publications, 1977. Contributor of stories to *Bizarre* and *Fiba International.*

* * *

GUIMARY, Donald L(ee) 1932-

PERSONAL: Born June 10, 1932, in Portland, Ore.; son of Adrian A. and Ellen J. (Lund) Guimary; married Florence Lee (a cartographer), December 21, 1956; children: Stuart, Michael. *Education:* University of Oregon, B.A., 1959, M.A., 1966, PH.D., 1973. *Home:* 4022 Elmran Dr., West Linn, Ore. 97068. *Office:* Department of Journalism, Portland State University, P.O. Box 751, Portland, Ore. 97207.

CAREER: Portland State University, Portland, Ore., assistant professor, 1969-75, associate professor of journalism, 1975—. Lecturer at Universiti Sains Malaysia, 1973-74. *Member:* American Association of University Professors, Oregon United Nations Association (past member of board of directors), Sigma Delta Chi.

WRITINGS: Citizens Groups and Broadcasting, Praeger, 1975. Contributor to journalism periodicals and local newspapers.

WORK IN PROGRESS: Third World Journalism; A History of Salmon Cannery Workers; The Decline and Death of the Portland Daily Reporter Newspaper.

SIDELIGHTS: Guimary comments that his main interests are "international communications systems and citizen feedback, and the mass media." He has studied Chinese, Japanese, and Spanish.

* * *

GWINUP, Thomas 1932-

PERSONAL: Born April 8, 1932, in Denver, Colo.; son of William DuMont Gwinup (a businessman) and Zelma (Nash) Failor. *Education:* University of Denver, B.A., 1954, M.A. in L.S., 1968; Indiana University, M.A., 1959. *Politics:* Liberal. *Religion:* None. *Home:* 7138 Saranac, #34, La Mesa, Calif. 92041. *Office:* Library, San Diego State University, San Diego, Calif. 92182.

CAREER: Southern Illinois University, Carbondale, assistant professor of sociology, 1960-61; San Diego County Probation Department, San Diego, Calif., senior probation officer, 1962-67; San Diego State University, San Diego, librarian, 1968-74, associate librarian, 1974—. *Military service:* U.S. Air Force, 1955-57; became first lieutenant. *Member:* Phi Beta Kappa.

WRITINGS: (With Fidelia Dickinson) *Greek and Roman Authors: A Checklist of Criticism,* Scarecrow, 1973. Contributor to library journals.

WORK IN PROGRESS: Residential Condominiums—Caveat Emptor: An Annotated Bibliography Relating to Problems and Pitfalls; a supplement to *Greek and Roman Authors,* completion expected in 1980; *A Bibliography of Irreligious Thought.*

SIDELIGHTS: Gwinup writes: "My bibliographical interests are varied. Perceiving a gap in the literature is my usual motivation. I am concerned with and write on librarianship as a profession, the failure of librarians to attain true professional status, the problem of bureaucracy in librarianship, the inadequacy of library administration, and the failures of library education."

GYLLENHAMMAR, Pehr G(ustaf) 1935-

PERSONAL: Born April 28, 1935, in Gothenburg, Sweden; son of Pehr (a managing director of insurance companies) and Aina (Kaplan) Gyllenhammar; married Christina Engellau; children: Cecilia, Charlotte, Oscar, Sophie. *Education:* University of Lund, LL.B., 1959; also attended Centre d'-Etudes Industrielles, 1968. *Office:* Volvo, 405 08 Gothenburg, Sweden.

CAREER: Mannheimer & Zetterloef Advokatbyra, Gothenburg, Sweden, member of staff, 1959; Amphion (insurance company), Stockholm, Sweden, member of staff, 1960-65; Skandia (insurance company), Stockholm, assistant administrative manager, 1965, in corporate long-term planning, 1966-70, president and chief executive officer, 1970-71; Volvo, Gothenburg, Sweden, president and chief executive officer, 1971—. Chairman of Swedish Ships Mortgage Bank and Center d'Etudes Industrielles Foundation board of directors; member of board of directors of Custos, Gustaf Horwitz, Investment Asken, and Teijin-Volvo Corp. Member of advisory committees of Chase Manhattan Bank and Organization for Economic Co-Operation and Development; member of United Nations group of experts on international auditing. Member of board of trustees of Aspen Institute.

WRITINGS: Mot sekelskiftet paa maafaa, Bonnier, 1970, published as *Toward the Turn of the Century at Random,* Askild & Kaernekull, 1971; *Jag tror paa Sverige,* Askild & Kaernekull, 1973, published as *I Believe in Sweden,* 1973; *People at Work* (juvenile), Addison-Wesley, 1977.

* * *

HAAS, Ben(jamin) L(eopold) 1926-1977
(John Benteen, Thorne Douglas, Richard Meade)

July 21, 1926—October 27, 1977; American novelist best known for his works concerning the South in transition. Haas wrote more than one hundred books, including *The Foragers, Look Away, Look Away, Daisy Canfield, The House of Christina,* and many mysteries and westerns published under pseudonyms. He died in New York, N.Y. Obituaries: *New York Times,* October 29, 1977. (See index for *CA* sketch)

* * *

HAAS, Charlie 1952-

PERSONAL: Born October 22, 1952, in Brooklyn, N.Y.; son of Philip (an attorney) and Eunice (Dillon) Haas; married Janet Dodson (a radio producer), September 9, 1976. *Education:* University of California, Santa Cruz, B.A., 1974. *Politics:* Democratic socialist. *Residence:* Los Angeles, Calif. *Agent:* Writers & Artists, 9720 Wilshire Blvd., Beverly Hills, Calif. 90212.

CAREER: Warner Brothers Records, Burbank, Calif., copywriter and editorial director, 1974-76; *Chic,* Los Angeles, Calif., associate editor, 1976; *New West;* Beverly Hills, Calif., contributing editor, 1977—.

WRITINGS: (With Tim Hunter) *The Soul Hit,* Harper, 1976. Co-author of the screenplay "Mousepacks." Work anthologized in *Universe Sex,* Doubleday, 1976.

WORK IN PROGRESS: A screenplay, with Tim Hunter; a novel, with Hunter.

SIDELIGHTS: Haas writes: "Fiction continues to be the most hospitable medium for dealing with the signal issue of our age: how the individual mind can apprehend and reconcile an information-glutted environment. This question is something of an obsession with me. Eventually I hope to be capable of coming to grips with it on the page."

*   *   *

HABE, Hans   1911-1977

February 12, 1911—September 29, 1977; Hungarian-born journalist and author of more than twenty-four critically acclaimed novels. Habe is best known for *A Thousand Shall Fall,* his story of the defeated French Army in 1940. Enlisting in first the French and then the American armies, he became editor-in-chief of eighteen U.S. newspapers published in occupied Germany after World War II. He was once described by Thomas Mann as "a born novelist." Habe died in Locarno, Switzerland. Obituaries: *New York Times,* October 1, 1977; *Washington Post,* October 2, 1977; *Time,* October 10, 1977; *Newsweek,* October 10, 1977; *AB Bookman's Weekly,* January 30, 1978. (See index for *CA* sketch)

*   *   *

HABER, Heinz   1913-

PERSONAL: Born May 15, 1913, in Mannheim, Germany; came to the United States in 1946; son of Karl (a business executive) and Maria (Saar) Haber; married Anneliese Huendle (a technical research assistant), February 15, 1940; children: Kai (son), Cathleen. *Education:* University of Berlin, Ph.D. (physics), 1939, Ph.D. (astronomy and astrophysics), 1944. *Religion:* Lutheran.

CAREER: Physicist and author. Kaiser Wilhelm Institute for Physical Chemistry, Germany, head of department of spectroscopy, 1942-45; United States Air Force School of Aviation Medicine, Randolph Field, Texas, assistant professor of astrophysics, 1946-52; became associate physicist with the Institute of Transportation and Traffic Engineering, University of California, Los Angeles, 1952; later produced television science programs in Germany. *Member:* American Aero-Medical Association, American Space-Medical Association (co-founder), Optical Society of America, Sigma Xi.

WRITINGS: (Contributor) J. P. Marbarger, editor, *Space Medicine,* University of Illinois Press, 1951; (contributor and co-editor) *Physics and Medicine of the Upper Atmosphere,* University of Mexico Press, 1952; *Man in Space* (illustrated by Jerry Milord), Bobbs-Merrill, 1953; *The Physical Environment of the Flyer,* USAF School of Aviation Medicine, 1954; *The Walt Disney Story of Our Friend the Atom* (illustrated by the Walt Disney Studio), Dell, 1956, a later edition published as *Our Friend the Atom,* L. W. Singer, 1959; *Lebendiges Weltall: Menschen, Sterne und Atome,* Bluechert Verlag (Hamburg), 1959, translation published as *Stars, Men, and Atoms,* Golden Press, 1962, revised edition, Washington Square Press, 1966; *Unser Blauer Planet: Die Entwicklungsgeschichte der Erde,* Deutsche Verlags-Anstalt (Stuttgart), 1965, translation by Ernst Stuhlinger published as *Our Blue Planet: The Story of the Earth's Evolution,* Scribner, 1969; *Der Stoff der Schoepfung,* Deutsche Verlags-Anstalt, 1966; *Das Mathematische Kabinett,* Deutsche Verlags-Anstalt, 1967; *Space Science: A New Look at the Universe,* Golden Press, 1967; *Der Offene Himmel: Eine Moderne Astronomie,* Deutsche Verlags-Anstalt, 1968; *Unser Mond,* Deutsche Verlags-Anstalt, 1969.

Brueder im All, Deutsche Verlags-Anstalt, 1970; (editor) *Mit der Erde durchs All,* Deutsche Verlags-Anstalt, 1970; (editor) *Neue Funde aus Alter Zeit,* Deutsche Verlags-An-

stalt, 1970; *Bausteine Unserer Welt,* Deutsche Buch-Gemeinschaft (Berlin), 1971, another edition published as *Drei Welten,* Deutsche Verlags-Anstalt, 1971; (editor) *Naturvoelker in Unserer Zeit,* Deutsche Verlags-Anstalt, 1971; (with Irmgard Haber) *Sterne Erzaehlen Ihre Geschichten,* Deutsche Verlags-Anstalt, 1971; *Unser Wetter,* Deutsche Verlags-Anstalt, 1971; *Stirbt Unser Blauer Planet?,* Deutsche Verlags-Anstalt, c. 1973; (with Wolfgang Wesely and others) *Der Auftrag Der Naturwissenschafter in der Erwachsenenbildung,* Neckar-Verlag, 1974; *Gefangen in Raum und Zeit,* Deutsche Verlags-Anstalt, 1975.

Also contributor to *Colliers* and *Scientific American.* Editor of a German science magazine.

SIDELIGHTS: While an instructor at the United States Air Force School of Aviation, Haber, in collaboration with Hubertus Strughold, introduced the study of space medicine. The author-scientist's research on the physical problems the human body would encounter in a high altitude environment played an important role in the first manned space launching.

Haber has lectured before scientific and civic groups throughout the United States and has written books for children as well as adults. The author's book, *Space Science: A New Look at the Universe,* was written for young people. A reviewer for the *Christian Science Monitor* wrote that Haber "takes teenage readers on a fascinating tour of the techniques and discoveries of space exploration. . . . His mastery both as science expert and as writer makes this book a delight. The field he covers is vast. But generally he presents it in good perspective, hitting the important high points."

One of Haber's later books, *Our Blue Planet,* examines the origins and the future of the earth and its properties. A critic for *Choice* commented: "Haber has the remarkable gift of describing a deep philosophical aspect of science with such simplicity and clarity that the nonscientific reader, as well as any scientist, will obtain a taste . . . of the adventure, the romance, and the mystery of science."

AVOCATIONAL INTERESTS: Chess, reading, and writing.

BIOGRAPHICAL/CRITICAL SOURCES: Christian Science Monitor, November 2, 1967; *Choice,* March, 1970.*

*   *   *

HACKETT, Blanche Ann   1924-

PERSONAL: Born June 14, 1924, in New York; daughter of John (a farmer) and Emity (Roman) Barrios; married Robert Hackett (a manager), August 7, 1949; children: Lynn, Carol. *Education:* Attended Hunter College (now of the City University of New York) and University of Wisconsin, Madison. *Office:* 303 Concord St., Cresskill, N.J. 07626.

CAREER: Free-lance writer, 1945-60; *Valley Star,* Englewood, N.J., reporter and feature writer, 1960-62; *Suburbanite,* Englewood, reporter, 1963-65; free-lance writer, 1965-70; Cresskill Library, Cresskill, N.J., librarian, 1970—. Teacher of creative writing in local adult education programs. *Member:* American Society of Journalists and Authors, Authors Guild of Authors League of America.

WRITINGS: Man in Action, two volumes, Prentice-Hall, 1960; "Inside Cresskill" (three-act play), first produced in Cresskill, N.J., 1964; "Pocahantas" (three-act play), first produced in 1978. Also ghost writer of five books, 1976-77.

WORK IN PROGRESS: All About Trains, for children; *Pocahantas: The Mother of Our Country; Quilting for Be-*

ginners; a history column, "Did You Know?"; a travel column, "Your Travel Questions."

* * *

HACKETT, Charles J(oseph) 1915-

PERSONAL: Born September 18, 1915, in New York, N.Y.; son of James Winfield and Catherine Pauline (Eilert) Hackett; married Mary Ellen Ryan, January 25, 1955 (died January 11, 1956); children: Charles Peter. *Education:* Attended Brooklyn College (now of the City University of New York), 1933-34, and Columbia University, 1939-40; Columbia University, Biarritz, France, B.A., 1946. *Politics:* Independent. *Religion:* Roman Catholic. *Home:* 107 Baldwin Ave., Point Lookout, N.Y. 11569. *Office:* 800 Front St., Hempstead, N.Y. 11550.

CAREER: Commandant of military academy in Oakland, N.J., 1949-50; Hackensack Hospital, Hackensack, N.J., associate administrator, 1951-60; Hempstead General Hospital, Hempstead, N.Y., assistant administrator, 1961-65, administrator, 1965—. Adjunct professor at C. W. Post College of Long Island University. Member of Nassau County emergency medical services committee. Member of board of directors of National Conference of Christians and Jews, 1967—. *Military service:* U.S. Army, 1942-48; became major.

MEMBER: International Association of Chiefs of Police, American College of Hospital Administrators, American Academy of Medical Administrators, American Society of Hospital Public Relations Directors (charter member), Reserve Officers Association, New York State Public Health Association, Long Island Association of Chiefs of Police, Hempstead Chamber of Commerce (member of board of directors, 1967—; president, 1974), Newman Alumni Association, Hofstra University Club (member of board of directors, 1966—), University Club, Garden City Golf Club, Lions.

WRITINGS: The Last Happy Hour (novel), Doubleday, 1976. Author of poetry column in *Journal of the Hospital Financial Management Association.* Contributor to hospital administration journals.

WORK IN PROGRESS: The Wind in the Sky, a novel.

SIDELIGHTS: Hackett writes: "When my son became eighteen years of age and subject to the draft board, I became a pacifist and so wrote a novel, *The Last Happy Hour,* to prove by satire that war, although necessary at times, when the dignity of man is being threatened, is nonetheless ridiculous and juvenile."

* * *

HADER, Berta (Hoerner) 1890(?)-1976

PERSONAL: Born c.1890, in San Pedro, Coahuila, Mexico; daughter of Albert and Adelaide (Jennings) Hoerner; married Elmer Stanley Hader (a writer and illustrator), July 14, 1919 (died, 1973). *Education:* Attended University of Washington, Seattle, 1909-12, California School of Design, San Francisco, 1915-18. *Residence:* Grand View-on-Hudson, N.Y.

CAREER: Author and illustrator. Began as a fashion designer, 1914; worked as a newspaper artist, *San Francisco Bulletin,* 1916-18; became a miniature portrait painter, 1916-37; illustrator for children's books, national magazines, and newspapers, beginning, 1919. *Awards, honors:* Caldecott Medal, runner-up, 1940, for *Cock-a-Doodle Doo,* and 1944, for the *Mighty Hunter,* winner, 1949 for *The Big Snow.*

WRITINGS—All written and illustrated with husband, Elmer Hader: *The Picture Book of Travel: The Story of Transportation,* Macmillan, 1928; *Two Funny Clowns,* Coward, 1929; *What'll You Do When You Grow Up?,* Longmans, Green, 1929; *Lions and Tigers and Elephants Too,* Longmans, Green, 1930; *Under the Pig-Nut Tree,* Knopf, 1930; *The Farmer in the Dell,* Macmillan, 1931; *Tooky: The Story of a Seal Who Joined the Circus,* Longmans, Green, 1931; *Berta and Elmer Hader's Picture Book of the States,* Harper, 1932; *Chuck-a-Luck and His Reindeer,* Houghton, 1933; *Spunky,* Macmillan, 1933; *Whiffy McMann,* Oxford University Press, 1933; *Midget and Bridget,* Macmillan, 1934; *Jamaica Johnny,* Macmillan, 1935; *Billy Butter,* Macmillan, 1936; *Green and Gold: The Story of the Banana,* Macmillan, 1936; *Stop, Look, Listen,* Longmans, Green, 1936; *The Inside Story of the Hader Books,* Macmillan, 1937; *Tommy Thatcher Goes to Sea,* Macmillan, 1937; *Cricket: The Story of a Little Circus Pony,* Macmillan, 1938; *Cock-a-Doodle Doo: The Story of a Little Red Rooster,* Macmillan, 1939, reprinted, 1966.

The Cat and the Kitten, Macmillan, 1940; *Little Town,* Macmillan, 1941; *The Story of Pancho and the Bull with the Crooked Tail,* Macmillan, 1942; *The Mighty Hunter,* Macmillan, 1943, reprinted, 1961; *The Little Stone House: A Story of Building a House in the Country,* Macmillan, 1944, reprinted, 1970; *Rainbow's End,* Macmillan, 1945; *The Skyrocket,* Macmillan, 1946; *Big City,* Macmillan, 1947, reprinted, 1967; *The Big Snow,* Macmillan, 1948, reprinted, 1972; *Little Appaloosa,* Macmillan, 1949.

Squirrely of Willow Hill, Macmillan, 1950; *Lost in the Zoo,* Macmillan, 1951; *Little White Foot: His Adventures on Willow Hill,* Macmillan, 1952; *The Friendly Phoebe,* Macmillan, 1953; *Wish on the Moon,* Macmillan, 1954; *Home on the Range: Jeremiah Jones and His Friend Little Bear,* Macmillan, 1955; *The Runaways: A Tale of the Woodlands,* Macmillan, 1956; *Ding, Dong, Bell: Pussy's in the Well,* Macmillan, 1957; *Little Chip of Willow Hill,* Macmillan, 1958; *Reindeer Trail: A Long Journey from Lapland to Alaska,* Macmillan, 1959; *Mister Billy's Gun,* Macmillan, 1960; *Quack Quack: The Story of a Little Wild Duck,* Macmillan, 1961; *Little Antelope: An Indian for a Day,* Macmillan, 1962; *Snow in the City: A Winter's Tale,* Macmillan, 1963; *Two Is Company, Three's a Crowd,* Macmillan, 1965.

Illustrator; all with Elmer Hader: Cornelia Lynde Meigs, *Wonderful Locomotive,* Macmillan, 1928; Octave Feuillet, *Story of Mr. Punch* (translation from the French by J. Harris Gable), Dutton, 1929; Hamilton Williamson, *Monkey Tale,* Doubleday, Doran, 1929; Dorothy Walter Baruch, *Big Fellow at Work,* Harper, 1930; Madge A. Bigham, *Sonny Elephant,* Little, Brown, 1930; Elinor Whitney, *Timothy and the Blue Cart,* Stokes Publishing, 1930; Williamson, *Baby Bear,* Doubleday, Doran, 1930; Williamson, *Little Elephant,* Doubleday, Doran, 1930; *Berta and Elmer Hader's Picture Book of Mother Goose,* Coward, 1930; Anne Stoddard, *Bingo Is My Name,* Century, 1931; Stoddard, *Good Little Dog,* Century, 1931; Williamson, *Lion Cub: A Jungle Tale,* Doubleday, Doran, 1931; Stoddard, *Here Bingo,* Century, 1932; Prescott Lecky, *Play-Book of Words,* Stokes Publishing, 1933; Jane Miller, *Jimmy the Groceryman,* Houghton, 1934; Alice Dalgliesh, *Smiths and Rusty,* Scribner, 1936; Dalgliesh, *Wings for the Smiths,* Scribner, 1937; Julia Letheld Hahn, *Who Knows: A Little Primer,* Houghton, 1937; Melicent Humason Lee, *Marcos: A Mountain Boy of Mexico,* Albert Whitman, 1937; Henry Bolles Lent, *Farmer,* Macmillan, 1937; Williamson, *Humpy: Son of the Sands,* Doubleday, Doran, 1937; Phillis Garrard, *Banana*

Tree House, Coward, 1938; Williamson, *Stripey: A Little Zebra,* Doubleday, Doran, 1939; Miriam Evangeline Mason, *Timothy Has Ideas,* Macmillan, 1943; Louise Hunting Seaman, *Mr. Peck's Pets,* Macmillan, 1947.

Also illustrator, with Elmer Hader, of the "Happy Hour" series, Macmillan, c. 1927.

BIOGRAPHICAL/CRITICAL SOURCES: New York Herald Tribune, November 7, 1954; *Saturday Review,* November 13, 1954, November 16, 1957; *New York Times Book Review,* February 21, 1960. *Obituaries: AB Bookman's Weekly,* May 17, 1976.*

(Died February 6, 1976)

* * *

HADER, Elmer Stanley 1889-1973

PERSONAL: Born September 7, 1889, in Pajaro, Calif.; son of Henry and Lena (Nyberg) Hader; married Berta Hoerner (a writer and illustrator), July 14, 1919 (died, 1976). *Education:* Attended California School of Design, San Francisco, 1907-10; Julian Academy, Paris, France, 1912-14. *Residence:* Grand View-on-Hudson, N.Y.

CAREER: Author and illustrator. Worked as a silversmith's assistant, surveyor's assistant, and locomotive fireman before turning his interest to painting; spent three years as a vaudevillian in Paris; became a landscape artist and portrait painter, 1914; illustrator for children's books, national magazines, and newspapers, beginning 1919. Served as zoning administrator for the Village of Grand View-on-Hudson, N.Y., beginning 1925; member of the advisory board of directors, Hudson River Conservation Society. *Military service:* U.S. Army, 1918-19; served in the Camouflage Corps, American Expeditionary Forces. *Awards, honors:* Caldecott Medal runner-up, 1940, for *Cock-a-Doodle Doo,* and 1944, for *Mighty Hunter,* winner, 1949, for *The Big Snow.*

WRITINGS—All written and illustrated with wife, Berta Hader: *The Picture Book of Travel: The Story of Transportation,* Macmillan, 1928; *Two Funny Clowns,* Coward, 1929; *What'll You Do When You Grow Up?,* Longmans, Green, 1929; *Lions and Tigers and Elephants Too,* Longmans, Green, 1930; *Under the Pig-Nut Tree,* Knopf, 1930; *The Farmer in the Dell,* Macmillan, 1931; *Tooky: The Story of a Seal Who Joined the Circus,* Longmans, Green, 1931; *Berta and Elmer Hader's Picture Book of the States,* Harper, 1932; *Chuck-a-Luck and His Reindeer,* Houghton, 1933; *Spunky,* Macmillan, 1933; *Whiffy McMann,* Oxford University Press, 1933; *Midget and Bridget,* Macmillan, 1934; *Jamaica Johnny,* Macmillan, 1935; *Billy Butter,* Macmillan, 1936; *Green and Gold: The Story of the Banana,* Macmillan, 1936; *Stop, Look, Listen,* Longmans, Green, 1936; *The Inside Story of the Hader Books,* Macmillan, 1937; *Tommy Thatcher Goes to Sea,* Macmillan, 1937; *Cricket: The Story of a Little Circus Pony,* Macmillan, 1938; *Cock-a-Doodle Doo: The Story of a Little Red Rooster,* Macmillan, 1939, reprinted, 1966.

The Cat and the Kitten, Macmillan, 1940; *Little Town,* Macmillan, 1941; *The Story of Pancho and the Bull with the Crooked Tail,* Macmillan, 1942; *The Mighty Hunter,* Macmillan, 1943, reprinted, 1961; *The Little Stone House: A Story of Building a House in the Country,* Macmillan, 1944, reprinted, 1970; *Rainbow's End,* Macmillan, 1945; *The Skyrocket,* Macmillan, 1946; *Big City,* Macmillan, 1947, reprinted, 1967; *The Big Snow,* Macmillan, 1948, reprinted, 1972; *Little Appaloosa,* Macmillan, 1949.

Squirrely of Willow Hill, Macmillan, 1950; *Lost in the Zoo,* Macmillan, 1951; *Little White Foot: His Adventures on Willow Hill,* Macmillan, 1952; *The Friendly Phoebe,* Macmillan, 1953; *Wish on the Moon,* Macmillan, 1954; *Home on the Range: Jeremiah Jones and His Friend Little Bear,* Macmillan, 1955; *The Runaways: A Tale of the Woodlands,* Macmillan, 1956; *Ding, Dong, Bell: Pussy's in the Well,* Macmillan, 1957; *Little Chip of Willow Hill,* Macmillan, 1958; *Reindeer Trail: A Long Journey from Lapland to Alaska,* Macmillan, 1959; *Mister Billy's Gun,* Macmillan, 1960; *Quack Quack: The Story of a Little Wild Duck,* Macmillan, 1961; *Little Antelope: An Indian for a Day,* Macmillan, 1962; *Snow in the City: A Winter's Tale,* Macmillan, 1963; *Two Is Company, Three's a Crowd,* Macmillan, 1965.

Illustrator; all with Berta Hader, except as noted: Cornelia Lynde Meigs, *Wonderful Locomotive,* Macmillan, 1928; Octave Feuillet, *Story of Mr. Punch* (translation from the French by J. Harris Gable), Dutton, 1929; Hamilton Williamson, *Monkey Tale,* Doubleday, Doran, 1929; Dorothy Walker Baruch, *Big Fellow at Work,* Harper, 1930; Madge A. Bigham, *Sonny Elephant,* Little, Brown, 1930; Elinor Whitney, *Timothy and the Blue Cart,* Stokes Publishing, 1930; Williamson, *Baby Bear,* Doubleday, Doran, 1930; Williamson, *Little Elephant,* Doubleday, Doran, 1930; *Berta and Elmer Hader's Picture Book of Mother Goose,* Coward, 1930; Anne Stoddard, *Bingo Is My Name,* Century, 1931; Stoddard, *Good Little Dog,* Century, 1931; Williamson, *Lion Cub: A Jungle Tale,* Doubleday, Doran, 1931; Stoddard, *Here Bingo,* Century, 1932; Prescott Lecky, *Play-Book of Words,* Stokes Publishing, 1933; Jane Miller, *Jimmy the Groceryman,* Houghton, 1934; Alice Dalgliesh, *Smiths and Rusty,* Scribner, 1936; Dalgliesh, *Wings for the Smiths,* Scribner, 1937; Julia Letheld Hahn, *Who Knows: A Little Primer,* Houghton, 1937; Melicent Humason Lee, *Marcos: A Mountain Boy of Mexico,* Albert Whitman, 1937; Henry Bolles Lent, *Farmer,* Macmillan, 1937; Williamson, *Humpy: Son of the Sands,* Doubleday, Doran, 1937; Phillis Garrard, *Banana Tree House,* 1938; Williamson, *Stripey: A Little Zebra,* Doubleday, Doran, 1939; Mary Margaret McBride, *How Dear to My Heart* (E. S. Hader, sole illustrator), Macmillan, 1940; Miriam Evangeline Mason, *Timothy Has Ideas,* Macmillan, 1943; Louise Hunting Seaman, *Mr. Peck's Pets,* Macmillan, 1947.

Also illustrator, with Berta Hader, of the "Happy Hour" series, Macmillan, c.1927.

SIDELIGHTS: Hader and his wife Berta built their own stone house near Nyack, New York. It was located in a deep hillside at the site of an old quarry. One of the many unique features was the waterfall which ran from the roadway to the house to a pool at the foot of large willow trees. The Haders had no blue prints, so the house just grew from one stage to the next. It accommodated fourteen guests, and they were constantly surrounded by friends. Their studio, with a 25-foot cathedral ceiling and floor-to-ceiling windows, was a copy of a studio that Elmer lived in as a student in Paris. Their story, *The Little Stone House,* describes the building of this house.

BIOGRAPHICAL/CRITICAL SOURCES: Saturday Review, November 10, 1951; *New York Herald Tribune,* November 11, 1951, November 13, 1955; *Kirkus Reviews,* September 1, 1955, September 1, 1960; *New York Times,* November 13, 1955.*

(Died, 1973)

HAGGETT, Peter 1933-

PERSONAL: Born January 24, 1933, in England; son of Charles and Elizabeth Haggett; married Brenda Woodley, 1956; children: two sons, two daughters. *Education:* St. Catharine's College, Cambridge, M.A., Ph.D. *Home:* 5 Tun Bridge Close, Chew Magna, Somerset, England.

CAREER: University of London, London, England, assistant lecturer in geography, 1956; Cambridge University, Cambridge, England, lecturer in geography, 1958, fellow of Fitzwilliam College, 1964; University of Bristol, Bristol, England, professor of urban and regional geography, 1966—. Visiting professor at University of California, Berkeley, Pennsylvania State University, and University of Western Ontario. Member of Southwest Planning Council, 1967—; governor of Centre for Environmental Studies, 1975—.

AWARDS, HONORS: Leverhulme fellow in Brazil, 1959; Cullam Medal from American Geographical Society, 1969; meritorious award from Association of American Geographers, 1973.

WRITINGS: Locational Analysis in Human Geography, St. Martin's, 1965, revised edition, two volumes, (with others) Halstead Press, 1977; (editor with R. J. Chorley) *Frontiers in Geographical Teaching,* Methuen, 1965; *Models in Geography,* Barnes & Noble, 1967; (with Chorley) *Network Analysis in Geography,* Edward Arnold, 1969; *Progress in Geography,* seven volumes, Edward Arnold, 1969; *Geography: A Modern Synthesis,* Harper, 1972, revised edition, 1975; (with A. D. Cliff and others) *Elements of Spatial Structure,* Cambridge Book Co., 1975. Also author of *Regional Forecasting,* 1971, and *Processes in Physical and Human Geography: Bristol Essays,* 1975. Contributor to professional journals.

AVOCATIONAL INTERESTS: Natural history.

* * *

HAGIWARA, Michio Peter 1932-

PERSONAL: Born November 23, 1932, in Tokyo Japan; came to the United States in 1952, naturalized citizen, 1974; son of Shinichi (a writer) and Michiko (Enomoto) Hagiwara; married Anne Lindell Shlionsky (an instructor in English as a second language), May 12, 1967; children: Jennifer. *Education:* University of Missouri, Kansas City, B.A., 1956; Washington University, St. Louis, Mo., M.A., 1958; University of Michigan, Ph.D., 1966. *Home:* 1571 Covington Dr., Ann Arbor, Mich. 48103. *Office:* Department of Romance Languages, University of Michigan, Ann Arbor, Mich. 48109.

CAREER: University of Michigan, Ann Arbor, instructor, 1962-64, lecturer, 1964-66, assistant professor, 1966-71, associate professor of French, 1971—. Visiting assistant professor at University of Missouri, Kansas City, summers, 1961 and 1962, Utah State University, summer, 1964, and Harvard University, 1969-1970 and summers, 1967 and 1970. *Member:* Modern Language Association of America, Linguistic Society of America, American Association of Teachers of French, American Council on the Teaching of Foreign Languages, American Association of University Professors.

WRITINGS: (With R. L. Politzer) *Active Review of French: Selected Patterns, Vocabulary, and Pronunciation Problems for Speakers of English,* Ginn, 1963; (with J. R. Carduner) *L'Echelle: Structures essentielles du francais* (title means "The Ladder: Basic Structures of French"), with laboratory workbook and teachers' manual, Blaisdell, 1966; (with Politzer) *Continuons a Parler* (title means "Let's Con-

tinue Speaking"), Blaisdell, 1967; *Trends in the Training and Supervision of Graduate Assistants,* American Council on the Teaching of Foreign Languages, 1970; *French Epic Poetry in the Sixteenth Century,* Mouton, 1972; (with Jaqueline Morton) *Mosaique,* Van Nostrand, 1977; *Studies in Romance Linguistics,* Newbury House Publishers, 1977; (with Francoise DeRocher) *Theme et Variations* (title means "Theme and Variations"), Wiley, 1977. Contributor of articles and reviews to professional journals.

WORK IN PROGRESS: A Manual of French Phonetics, with Sylvie Carduner; *Intensive English for Communication,* for people learning English as a foreign language, with wife, Anne Hagiwara; a book on applied linguistics; a review grammar in French.

AVOCATIONAL INTERESTS: Travel, music, photography, model making, astronomy.

* * *

HAIGHT, Anne Lyon 1895-1977

May 11, 1895—August 8, 1977; American author, rare book collector, and Indian cultures enthusiast. While doing research on Indians for the American Museum of Natural History, she participated in several expeditions to the Isthmus of Panama. Haight is also credited with starting the Children's Book of the Month Club. She died in Litchfield, Conn. Obituaries: *New York Times,* August 9, 1977; *AB Bookman's Weekly,* September 12, 1977. (See index for *CA* sketch)

* * *

HAINAUX, Rene 1918-

PERSONAL: Born April 29, 1918, in Thouars, France; son of Etienne and Lucie (Lepere) Hainaux; married Simone De Loneux (a teacher of French literature), January 9, 1943 (died August 12, 1977); children: Anne, Bernard. *Education:* University of Liege, licence, 1941. *Home:* 12 Avenue du Marechal, 1180 Brussels, Belgium. *Office:* Conservatoire de Liege, 14 rue Forgeur, 4000 Liege, Belgium.

CAREER: Free-lance actor, beginning 1943; Conservatoire Royal de Liege, Liege, Belgium, professor of dramatic art, beginning 1963; National Institute of Performing Arts (I.N.S.A.S.), Brussels, Belgium, lecturer in the history of theatre and scenography, beginning 1964; University of Liege, Liege, lecturer, beginning 1972. *Member:* International Theatre Institute.

WRITINGS: Spectacles 70-75 dans le monde, Meddens, 1975, translation by Michael Nash published as *Stage Design Throughout the World, 1970-75,* Theatre Arts, 1976; (with Paul Doyen) *The Physical Theatre,* University of Liege, 1976.

Editor with Yves Bonnat: *Stage Design Throughout the World Since 1935,* Theatre Arts, 1956, 3rd edition, Meddens (Brussels), 1964; *Stage Design Throughout the World Since 1950,* Theatre Arts, 1964; *Stage Design Throughout the World Since 1960,* Theatre Arts, 1973.

WORK IN PROGRESS: Bibliographie francaise selective des arts du spectacle (title means "A Selective French Bibliography of the Performing Arts"), first volume of a projected international bibliography of the performing arts.

SIDELIGHTS: Hainaux told *CA:* "For several years, I've been most particularly interested in focusing upon a semiotic method of analysis of the theatre as entertainment, and its application to the education of producers."

HALE, Kathleen 1898-

PERSONAL: Born May 24, 1898, in Scotland; daughter of Charles Edward and Ethel Alice Aylmer (Hughes) Hale; married Douglas McClean (a doctor), 1926 (died, 1967); children: two sons. *Education:* Attended Manchester School of Art, Reading University College of Art, Central School of Arts and Crafts, London, and East Anglican School of Painting and Drawing. *Home:* Tod House, Forest Hill, Oxford, England.

CAREER: Author and illustrator. Worked for the Ministry of Foods, England, 1917; after the war, held various jobs such as caring for children, mending, and collecting bad debts for a window cleaner; later began designing book jackets and posters. Her works have been exhibited at numerous galleries, including Grosvenor Galleries, Vermont Gallery, and Leicester Galleries. *Member:* Society of Industrial Arts (fellow).

WRITINGS—All self-illustrated: *Henrietta: The Faithful Hen,* Transatlantic, 1943, reprinted, Allen & Unwin, 1967; *Manda,* J. Murray, 1952, Coward, 1953; *Henrietta's Magic Egg,* Allen & Unwin, 1973.

"Orlando" series; self-illustrated: *Orlando (the Marmalade Cat): A Camping Holiday,* Scribner, 1938; *Orlando's Evening Out,* Penguin, 1941; *Orlando's Home Life,* Penguin, 1942; *Orlando (the Marmalade Cat) Buys a Farm,* Transatlantic, 1942; *Orlando (the Marmalade Cat) Becomes a Doctor,* Transatlantic, 1944; *Orlando (the Marmalade Cat): His Silver Wedding,* Transatlantic, 1944; *Orlando's Invisible Pyjamas,* Transatlantic, 1947, new edition, J. Murray, 1964; *Orlando (the Marmalade Cat) Keeps a Dog,* Transatlantic, 1949; *Orlando (the Marmalade Cat): A Trip Abroad,* Country Life, 1949; *Orlando the Judge,* J. Murray, 1950; *Orlando (the Marmalade Cat): A Seaside Holiday,* Country Life, 1952; *Orlando's Zoo,* J. Murray, 1954; *Orlando (the Marmalade Cat): The Frisky Housewife,* Country Life, 1956; *Orlando's Magic Carpet,* J. Murray, 1958; *Orlando (the Marmalade Cat) Buys a Cottage,* Country Life, 1963; *Orlando and the Three Graces,* J. Murray, 1965; *Orlando (the Marmalade Cat) Goes to the Moon,* J. Murray, 1968; *Orlando (the Marmalade Cat) and the Water Cats,* J. Cape, 1972.

Illustrator: Mary Rachel Harrower, *I Don't Mix Much with Fairies,* Eyre & Spottiswode, 1928; M. R. Harrower, *Plain Jane,* Coward, 1929; *Puss in Boots,* Houghton, 1951.

AVOCATIONAL INTERESTS: Painting.

BIOGRAPHICAL/CRITICAL SOURCES: New York Times, November 30, 1947; *Christian Science Monitor,* December 12, 1947; *New York Herald Tribune,* July 15, 1951.*

* * *

HALL, Alice Clay 1900-

PERSONAL: Born December 25, 1900, in Campbell County, Va.; daughter of John W. (a county treasurer) and Gertrude Lee (an educator; maiden name, Butler) Clay; married Vernon Addison Hall, October 22, 1924; children: Cynthia. *Education:* Attended Randolph-Macon Woman's College, College of William & Mary, and University of Florida. *Religion:* Protestant. *Home:* 109 Saddletree Rd., San Antonio, Tex. 78231.

CAREER: Poet and writer. Co-owner of Alice Clay Hall Museum. Has given dramatic readings. *MEMBER:* International Platform Association (fellow),

Intercontinental Biographical Association (fellow), World Poetry Society Intercontinental, International Academy of Poets (founder; life fellow), Avalon World Arts Academy (honorary life member), National Travel Club, National Society of Arts and Letters, American Academy of Poets (affiliate), Association for Research and Enlightenment, Poetry Society of Texas (member of area council; organizer and first president of local chapter), Poetry Society of Virginia (member of founding group, 1923), Texas Fine Arts Association, Shavano Park Woman's Club, San Antonio Art League, Ruth Taylor Fine Arts Center, William and Mary Alumni Association, Salem Alumnae Association, Randolph-Macon Alumnae Association, Sorosis Club.

WRITINGS: April Hunger (poems), Different Press, 1958; *Chaliced Atoms* (poems), Villiers Publications, 1972.

Work represented in anthologies, including *The New Angelus,* 1972, and *The Golden Anniversary Anthology of Poems by Member Poets of the Poetry Society of Virginia,* 1974. Contributor of poems to magazines and newspapers.

WORK IN PROGRESS: "Compiling a book of poems by the late poet and founder-director of Avalon. Lilith gave me a notebook of her poems from which to compile a book, requesting that it be titled: *Beyond the Last Frontier.*"

SIDELIGHTS: Alice Hall writes: "I am interested in all life and my relationship to its totality in all planes of cosmic existence. My profession is poetry. I have received prizes for my oil paintings and charcoal drawings as well as for my poetry. Due to lack of time and energy I have passed up many opportunities for wider publication.

"For over fifty years I have been collecting boxes of my handwritten notebooks and miscellaneous unrevised poems and work samples of prize-winning poems. In fact, I have collected a rather objective history of my life in the arts. This includes family heirlooms, a library, a wooded estate where my husband and I have lived for nearly thirty years, making history all the time. We have a complete museum on a small scale."

* * *

HALL, C(onstance) Margaret 1937-

PERSONAL: Born August 11, 1937, in Lancashire, England; came to the United States in 1962; daughter of John (a quarry owner) and Madeline (a teacher; maiden name, Brooks) Hall; married Robert T. Cole (a lawyer, in international law), October 25, 1959; children: Elizabeth Anne, Tanya Helen, Judith Amy. *Education:* London School of Economics and Political Science, London, B.Sc. (honors), 1960; American University, M.A., 1969, Ph.D., 1970. *Home:* 4846 Langdrum Lane, Chevy Chase, Md. 20015. *Office:* Department of Sociology, Georgetown University, Washington, D.C. 20015.

CAREER: Instructor at English state schools, 1957-59, and private schools in Belgium, 1960-62; American University, Washington, D.C., professorial lecturer in sociology, 1970; Georgetown University, Washington, D.C., assistant professor, 1970-75, associate professor of sociology, 1975—, chairman of department, 1976—, research associate of Family Center, 1976—. Research associate of Kennedy Institute Center for Population Research, 1975—; clinical consultant to Frederick Community Mental Health, 1971-76.

MEMBER: International Sociological Association, American Sociological Association (chairman of committee on public issues and the family), Sociologists for Women in Society, Society for the Study of Social Problems, Society for the Scientific Study of Religion, Groves Conference, British Sociological Society, Eastern Sociological Association, District of Columbia Sociological Society, Phi Kappa Phi.

WRITINGS: The Sociology of Pierre Joseph Proudhon, 1809-1865, Philosophical Library, 1971; *Vital Life: Questions in Social Thought,* Christopher, 1973. Contributor to *Journal of Family Counseling.*

WORK IN PROGRESS: Books on development of family theory, on application of family theory to the position of women in society, and on application of family theory to social problems; research includes cross-cultural substantiation of family theory and social behavior.

SIDELIGHTS: Margaret Hall comments: "I am interested in the publication of books as a means of communication with others. I am motivated to write in part due to benefits in practice for clarifying thinking and congruence of ideas. My major project is exploratory research in general theory development—with reference to society beyond the U.S. context. I have a substantial interest in fertility and population growth in the world at large, in possibilities for planning and decision-making for the future, based on past experience, and in the importance of biography and history combined with each other."

*   *   *

HALL, Gladys 1891(?)-1977

1891(?)—September 18, 1977; American writer. Hall wrote for such Hollywood fan magazines as *Photoplay, Modern Scren,* and *Screenland,* and was best known for her interviews with Hollywood stars. She also co-authored a book about dog care. She died in Huntington, N.Y. Obituaries: *New York Times,* September 22, 1977.

*   *   *

HALL, Robert Lee 1941-

PERSONAL: Born January 15, 1941, in San Francisco, Calif.; son of Leroy Oran (a typographer) and Ruth (owner and operator of a private school; maiden name, Goodale) Hall; married Joan Helen Hall, January 20, 1963 (divorced); children: Brian William. *Education:* Attended University of California, Berkeley, 1958-60; California College of Arts and Crafts, B.A.Ed., 1964, B.F.A., 1965, M.F.A., 1968. *Residence:* Oakland, Calif. *Agent:* Mitchell J. Hamilburg Agency, 292 South La Cienega Blvd., Suite 212, Beverly Hills, Calif. 90211.

CAREER: Has worked in art departments of advertising agencies; California High School, San Ramon, Calif., teacher of art and English, 1964—. *Member:* Mystery Writers of America, Baker Street Irregulars (Scowrers Branch), California Writer's Club. *Awards, honors:* Local awards for paintings exhibited in the San Francisco Bay area.

WRITINGS: Exit Sherlock Holmes (mystery novel), Scribner, 1977.

WORK IN PROGRESS: The Assassination Papers, an Edwardian novel; *Vanishing Act,* a contemporary suspense novel.

SIDELIGHTS: Hall writes: "For many years, while I was a public school teacher, I stole evenings, weekends, and vacations to paint and exhibit in the San Francisco Bay area. I wanted to be a good painter, to do something original, mine. Yet I had always loved words and books. On a sabbatical to study etching I began to write short stories. My first novel is a short story that got out of hand. Now I seem to be

launched on a writing career. In it, too, I hope to do something all my own. However, the reader, like a superego, is always in the back of my mind. I think a writer must ask himself if the reader will understand."

*   *   *

HALLIER, Amedee 1913-

PERSONAL: Born March 25, 1913, in Peillac, France; son of Joseph (a farmer) and Marie-Francoise (maiden name, Hurtel) Hallier. *Education:* Attended Highlands College, 1927-30, and Pontifical Gregorian University, 1949-52, 1954-55; Pontifical College S. Anselmo, Th.D., 1957. *Home:* Notre-Dame de Grace, 50260 Bricquebec, France.

CAREER: Highlands College, Isle of Jersey, professor of French literature, 1936-39; Abbaye Notre-Dame de Grace, Bricquebec, France, professor of theology, 1957—.

WRITINGS: Un educateur monastique, Aereld de Rievaulx, Gabalda, 1959, translation by Columban Heaney published as *The Monastic Theology of Aelred de Rievaulx,* Cistercian Publications, 1969. Contributor to *Citeaux.*

SIDELIGHTS: When asked about the controversy surrounding Bishop Lefebvre, Hallier commented: "In the light of history, which illuminates two thousand years in the life of the church, the 'Lefebvre affair' takes on a *very relative* importance. It appears to be only a 'rear-guard action.'" *CA* also asked Hallier about his views on the refusal of Pope Paul VI to retire at age eighty. He replied: "Since Pope Paul VI is Bishop of Rome, he could resign at age seventy-five like his brothers. But because of his role as 'successor to Peter,' he is invested with a spiritual authority, a sort of universal paternity, which sets him apart, with a very special responsibility towards all Catholics in the entire world."

*   *   *

HALPERIN, Maurice 1906-

PERSONAL: Born March 3, 1906, in Boston, Mass.; son of Philip (a merchant) and Ethel (Summer) Halperin; married Edith Frisch (a teacher), September 5, 1926; children: Judith Halperin Gamoran, David. *Education:* Harvard University, A.B., 1927; University of Oklahoma, M.A., 1929; Sorbonne, University of Paris, Ph.D., 1931. *Home:* 600 Smith Ave., Apt. 131-H, Coquitlam, British Columbia, Canada V3J 2W4. *Office:* Department of Political Science, Simon Fraser University, Burnaby, British Columbia, Canada V5A 1S6.

CAREER: University of Paris, Sorbonne, Paris, France, lecturer in North American civilization, 1930-31; University of Oklahoma, Norman, 1931-41, began as assistant professor, became associate professor of romance languages and civilization; Boston University, Boston, Mass., chairperson of department of Latin American regional studies, 1949-53; National University of Mexico, Mexico City, visiting professor of political science, 1954-58; Union of Soviet Socialist Republics Academy of Sciences, Institute of World Economics and International Affairs, visiting professor, 1959-62; University of Havana, Havana, Cuba, visiting professor of economic geography, 1963-67; Simon Fraser University, Burnaby, British Columbia, professor of political science, 1968—. *Military service:* U.S. Army, chief of Latin America Division of Office of Strategic Services, 1942-46. *Awards, honors:* Order of the Southern Cross, from the Government of Brazil, 1952.

WRITINGS: Le Roman de Tristan et Iseult dans la Litterature Anglo-Americaine (title means "The Romance of Tristan and Iseult in Anglo-American Literature''), Jouve et Cie, 1931; *La America Latina en Transicion* (title means "Latin America in Transition"), National University of Mexico, 1956; *The Rise and Decline of Fidel Castro: An Essay in Contemporary History*, University of California Press, 1973. Contributor to academic journals and periodicals, including *New Republic, New York Times Magazine*, and *Foreign Affairs*.

WORK IN PROGRESS: Another book on Cuba.

SIDELIGHTS: Halperin commented: "In my writing on Cuba and other subjects in later years, I have tried to illustrate Shakespeare's dictum that 'all that glitters is not gold.'"

*   *   *

HALTON, David 1940-

PERSONAL: Born May 28, 1940, in Beaconsfield, England; son of Matthew Henry (a journalist) and Jean (Campbell) Halton; married Zoai Titova, September 12, 1968; children: Julian Alexander, Daniel. *Education:* University of Paris, Sorbonne, diploma, 1958; University of Toronto, B.A. 1962; Institute of Political Studies (Paris), certificate, 1963. *Home:* 14 Oakhill Ave., London NW3, England. *Office:* 43-51 Great Titchfield St., London, England.

CAREER/WRITINGS: Time, New York, N.Y., contributing editor in Montreal, 1964-65; Canadian Broadcasting Corp. (CBC), Toronto, correspondent in Paris, 1966-67, Moscow, 1967-68, Paris, 1969-71, Montreal, 1971-73, London, England, 1973—. Notable assignments include coverage of the Six Day War, Vietnam War, Nasser's funeral, war in Rhodesia, and Canadian federal elections. *Member:* Foreign Press Association, Association of Canadian Broadcasting Corp. Correspondents. *Awards, honors:* Association of Canadian Television and Radio Artists best newscaster award, 1975; Anik Award for best news broadcast, 1976.

*   *   *

HAMIL, Thomas Arthur 1928-

PERSONAL: Born in 1928. *Education:* University of Washington, Ph.D.

CAREER: Painter and author. *Awards, honors: Brother Alonzo*, was chosen for the American Institute of Graphic Arts exhibit of outstanding children's books, 1957.

WRITINGS: Brother Alonzo (self-illustrated), Macmillan, 1957; *Hans and the Golden Flute* (self-illustrated), Macmillan, 1958.

Illustrator: James Kendrick Noble, *Ploob: A Midshipman's First Year at Annapolis*, Noble & Noble, 1949, revised edition published as *Ploob: The Fortunes and Misfortunes of a Midshipman's First Year at the United States Naval Academy*, Noble & Noble, 1957; Ashraf Siddiqui, *Bhombal Dass: The Uncle of Lion*, Macmillan, 1959; Patricia Miles Martin, *Calvin and the Cub Scouts*, Putnam, 1964; P. M. Martin, *Kumi and the Pearl*, Putnam, 1968; P. M. Martin, *There Goes the Tiger!*, Putnam, 1970.

SIDELIGHTS: Hamil lived for a time in California. His book, *Hans and the Golden Flute* told the story of a shepherd boy, his magical flute, and the lesson he learned about humility. A reviewer for *Kirkus* noted, "Tom Hamil both in his text and in his illustrations happily combines whimsy with morality."

BIOGRAPHICAL/CRITICAL SOURCES: Kirkus, September 1, 1958.*

HAMILTON, Charles Harold St. John 1875-1961
(Martin Clifford, Harry Clifton, Clifford Clive, Sir Alan Cobham, Owen Conquest, Gordon Conway, Harry Dorian, Frank Drake, Freeman Fox, Hamilton Greening, Cecil Herbert, Prosper Howard, Robert Jennings, Gillingham Jones, T. Harcourt Llewelyn, Clifford Owen, Ralph Redway, Ridley Redway, Frank Richards, Hilda Richards, Raleigh Robbins, Robert Rogers, Eric Stanhope, Robert Stanley, Nigel Wallace, Talbot Wynyard)

PERSONAL: Born August 8, 1875 (or 1876, according to some sources), in Ealing, Middlesex (now London), England; son of John Hamilton (a master carpenter). *Education:* Attended a local private school. *Home:* "Rose Lawn," Kingsgate, Broadstairs, Kent, England.

CAREER: Author of stories for children. Creator of a series of school and adventure stories for numerous boys' magazines, 1906-1940; a renewed interest in his fictional characters after World War II encouraged him to write a new series of stories at the age of seventy.

WRITINGS—All fiction, except as noted; under pseudonym Owen Conquest: *The Rivals of Rookwood School*, Mandeville, 1951.

Under pseudonym Martin Clifford: *Tom Merry and Co. of St. Jim's*, Mandeville, 1949; *The Secret of the Study*, Mandeville, 1949; *Rallying around Gussy*, Mandeville, 1950; *The Scapegrace of St. Jim's*, Mandeville, 1951; *Talbot's Secret*, Mandeville, 1951; *Gold Hawk Books* (a series of tales), Hamilton & Co., 1952.

Under pseudonym Frank Richards: "Schoolboy Series," W. C. Merrett, beginning 1946; "Mascot Schoolboy Series," J. Matthew, beginning 1947; *Jack of All Trades*, Mandeville, 1950; *The Autobiography of Frank Richards* (nonfiction), C. Skilton, 1952, memorial edition, 1962.

"Billy Bunter" series; under pseudonym Frank Richards: *Billy Bunter of Greyfriars School* (illustrated by R. J. Macdonald), C. Skilton, 1947; *Billy Bunter's Banknote*, C. Skilton, 1948; *Billy Bunter's Barring-Out* (illustrated by Macdonald), C. Skilton, 1948; *Billy Bunter in Brazil*, C. Skilton, 1949; *Billy Bunter's Christmas Party* (illustrated by Macdonald), C. Skilton, 1949.

Billy Bunter Among the Cannibals (illustrated by Macdonald), C. Skilton, 1950; *Billy Bunter's Benefit* (illustrated by Macdonald), C. Skilton, 1950; *Billy Bunter Butts In* (illustrated by Macdonald), C. Skilton, 1951; *Billy Bunter's Postal Order* (illustrated by Macdonald), C. Skilton, 1951; *Billy Bunter's Beanfeast* (illustrated by Macdonald), Cassell, 1952; *Billy Bunter and the Blue Mauritius* (illustrated by Macdonald), C. Skilton, 1952; *Billy Bunter's Brain-Wave* (illustrated by Macdonald), Cassell, 1953; *Billy Bunter's First Case* (illustrated by Macdonald), Cassell, 1953; *Billy Bunter the Bold* (illustrated by Macdonald), Cassell, 1954; *Bunter Does His Best!* (illustrated by Macdonald), Cassell, 1954; *Backing Up Billy Bunter* (illustrated by Charles H. Chapman), Cassell, 1955; *Billy Bunter's Double* (illustrated by Macdonald), Cassell, 1955; *The Banishing of Billy Bunter* (illustrated by Chapman), Cassell, 1956; *Lord Billy Bunter*, Cassell, 1956; *Billy Bunter Afloat* (illustrated by Chapman), Cassell, 1957; *Billy Bunter's Bolt* (illustrated by Chapman), Cassell, 1957; *Billy Bunter's Bargain* (illustrated by Chapman), Cassell, 1958; *Billy Bunter the Hiker* (illustrated by Chapman), Cassell, 1958; *Bunter Comes for Christmas* (illustrated by Chapman), Cassell, 1959; *Bunter Out of Bounds* (illustrated by Chapman), Cassell, 1959.

Bunter the Bad Lad, Cassell, 1960; *Bunter Keeps It Dark* (illustrated by Chapman), Cassell, 1960; *Billy Bunter at Butlin's* (illustrated by Chapman), Cassell, 1961; *Billy Bunter's Treasure-Hunt* (illustrated by Chapman), Cassell, 1961; *Bunter the Ventriloquist* (illustrated by Chapman), Cassell, 1961; *Just like Bunter* (illustrated by Chapman), Cassell, 1961; *Billy Bunter's Bodyguard* (illustrated by Chapman), Cassell, 1962; *Bunter the Caravanner* (illustrated by Chapman), Cassell, 1962; *Big Chief Bunter* (illustrated by Chapman), Cassell, 1963; *Bunter the Stowaway* (illustrated by Chapman), Cassell, 1964; *Thanks to Bunter* (illustrated by Chapman), Cassell, 1964; *Bunter's Holiday Cruise,* May Fair Books, 1965; *Bunter's Last Fling* (illustrated by Chapman), Cassell, 1965; *Bunter and the Phantom of the Towers,* May Fair Books, 1965; *Bunter the Racketeer,* May Fair Books, 1965; *Bunter the Sportsman* (illustrated by Chapman), Cassell, 1965; *Bunter the Tough Guy of Greyfriars,* May Fair Books, 1965; *Billy Bunter and the Bank Robber,* Paul Hamlyn, 1968; *Billy Bunter Sportsman!,* Paul Hamlyn, 1968; *Billy Bunter of Bunter Court,* Howard Baker, 1969.

Under pseudonym Hilda Richards: "Headland House Series," W. C. Merrett, beginning 1946; "Mascot Schoolgirl Series," J. Matthews, beginning 1947; *Bessie Bunter of Cliff House School* (illustrated by Macdonald), C. Skilton, 1949.

Contributor under various pseudonyms to periodicals including *Modern Boy, Funny Cuts, Boys Friend Weekly, Vanguard Library, Ranger, Popular,* and *Picture Fun.*

SIDELIGHTS: Charles Hamilton used over twenty different pseudonyms during his writing career, and more may still be undiscovered. It was estimated that the author created over one hundred fictional schools as a backdrop for his more than five thousand stories. A popular writer for several boy's magazines, Hamilton turned to writing books when the outbreak of World War II brought a close to many juvenile magazines in England. Though Hamilton suffered from ill-health and failing eyesight toward the end of his life, he continued to write stories and correspond with his many readers, both young and old.

AVOCATIONAL INTERESTS: Chess, music.

BIOGRAPHICAL/CRITICAL SOURCES: Frank Richards, *The Autobiography of Frank Richards,* C. Skilton, 1952; W.O.G. Lofts and D.J. Adley, *The Men Behind Boys' Fiction,* Howard Baker, 1970.*

(Died December 24, 1961)

*   *   *

HAMILTON, Peter (Edward) 1947-

PERSONAL: Born August 27, 1947, in Bromley, England; son of Juan Edward (a clerical worker) and Nora (a florist; maiden name, Buckland) Hamilton; married Susan Mary Richardson, November 30, 1972; children: Toby, Oliver, Max. *Education:* Brunel University, B.Sc. (honors), 1972; London School of Economics and Political Science, London, graduate study, 1972-77. *Politics:* "Left of centre." *Religion:* None. *Home:* 4 Estover Way, Chinnor, Oxford 0X9 4TE, England. *Office:* Faculty of Social Sciences, Open University, Milton Keynes, England.

CAREER: Photographer in London, England, 1963-68; Open University, Milton Keynes, England, lecturer in sociology, 1973—. *Member:* European Rural Sociology Society, British Sociological Association.

WRITINGS: Knowledge and Social Structure, Routledge & Kegan Paul, 1974; *Pre-Industrial Society,* Open University Press, 1975; *Social Interaction,* Open University Press, 1975; *Science and Social Change,* Open University Press, 1975; *Power and Social Structure,* Open University Press, 1975; *Work and Social Theory,* Open University Press, 1976. Author of radio and television scripts for British Broadcasting Corp.-Open University Productions, 1973-77. Contributor to sociology and education journals.

WORK IN PROGRESS: A major comparative study of rural social structures in Great Britain and France, concentrating on modernization and change processes; research on the work of Talcott Parsons.

SIDELIGHTS: Hamilton writes: "As a professional sociologist I have two main objectives: to produce a form of sociology which approaches important areas of life in a clear and revealing way, and to carry out research projects which have some practical relevance." *Avocational interests:* Ornithology, photography, racing cars, wine.

*   *   *

HAMNER, Earl (Henry), Jr. 1923-

PERSONAL: Born July 10, 1923, in Schuyler, Va.; son of Earl Henry and Doris Marion (Gianinni) Hamner; married Jane Martin, October 16, 1954; children: Scott Martin, Caroline Spencer. *Education:* Attended University of Richmond, 1940-43, and Northwestern University, 1946; College of Music of Cincinnati, B.F.A., 1958. *Residence:* Studio City, Calif. *Office:* Lorimer Productions, Inc., 4000 Warner Blvd., Burbank, Calif. 91522.

CAREER: WLW-Radio, Cincinnati, Ohio, writer, 1946-48; National Broadcasting Co. (NBC), New York City, radio and television writer, 1949-60; free-lance television and film writer in Hollywood, Calif., 1961—; Columbia Broadcasting System (CBS), New York City, creator and executive producer of "The Waltons" television series, 1971—. President, Amanda Productions. *Military service:* U.S. Army, 1943-46. *Awards, honors:* TV-Radio Writers award, 1967; Writers Guild prize, 1969, for "Heidi"; George Foster Peabody Award, 1972; Christopher Award, 1973; Virginian of the Year award from Virginia Press Association, 1973; Emmy Award, 1974; National Association of Television Executive Man of the Year award, 1974; Virginian Association of Broadcasters award, 1975; L.H.D. from Berea College and Loyola University, and D.F.A., from Morris Harvey College, all 1975.

WRITINGS—All novels: *Fifty Roads to Town,* Random House, 1953; *Spencer's Mountain,* Dial, 1961; *You Can't Get There from Here,* Random House, 1965; *The Homecoming,* Random House, 1970.

Screenplays: "Spencer's Mountain," Warner Bros., 1963; "Palm Springs Weekend," Warner Bros., 1963.

Teleplays: "Highway," 1954; "Heidi," 1969; "Appalachian Autumn," 1970; "Aesop's Fables," 1971; "The Homecoming," for CBS, 1971; "Where the Lilies Bloom," 1972.

WORK IN PROGRESS: Fenwick's Landing, a novel.

SIDELIGHTS: The success of the 1971 Columbia Broadcasting System Christmas teleplay, "The Homecoming," gave rise to the successful television series, "The Waltons." Margaret Tanguay asked Hamner how his own family, after whom the Walton characters are largely patterned, had reacted to the series. "Not [with] shock, but delight at reliving old times," Hamner said. "You know, Thomas Wolfe 'couldn't go home again' because of the things he'd written, but I can go home, and do, because I've written with affection about our life together."

BIOGRAPHICAL/CRITICAL SOURCES: Variety, December 22, 1971.*

* * *

HAMSCHER, Albert N(elson) 1946-

PERSONAL: Born August 19, 1946, in Philadelphia, Pa.; son of Albert Nelson (a plant manager) and Florence (a bank teller; maiden name, Wagner) Hamscher. *Education:* Pennsylvania State University, B.A., 1968; Emory University, M.A., 1970, Ph.D., 1973. *Home:* 1901 Rockhill Rd., Manhattan, Kan. 66502. *Office:* Department of History, Kansas State University, Manhattan, Kan. 66506.

CAREER: Kansas State University, Manhattan, assistant professor, 1972-76, associate professor of history, 1977—. *Member:* American Historical Association, American Catholic Historical Association, Society for French Historical Studies, Phi Beta Kappa, Phi Alpha Theta. *Awards, honors:* Ford Foundation fellow at Emory University, 1968-72; National Endowment for the Humanities summer fellowship, 1976.

WRITINGS: The Parlement of Paris After the Fronde, 1653-1673, University of Pittsburgh Press, 1976. Contributor to history journals.

WORK IN PROGRESS: A book on judicial reform in seventeenth- and eighteenth-century France.

* * *

HANKINS, Clabe
See McDONALD, Erwin L(awrence)

* * *

HANLEY, James 1901-
(Patric Shone)

PERSONAL: Born 1901, in Dublin, Ireland. *Home:* The Cottage, Llanfechain, Monmouthshire, Wales. *Agent:* David Higham Associates, 5/8 Lower John St., Golden Sq., London W1R 4HA, England.

CAREER: Novelist, short story writer, and playwright. Wrote first story at age of eight; went to sea in 1915, jumped ship in Canada, 1917; after World War I worked a variety of jobs, including free-lance journalist, railway porter, and racecourse cashier; full-time author in Wales, 1930—. *Military service:* Canadian Expeditionary Force, during World War I.

WRITINGS—Novels: Drift, Eric Partridge, 1930, complete and limited edition, Boriswood, 1931; *Boy,* Boriswood, 1931, Knopf, 1932; *Ebb and Flood,* John Lane, 1932; *Captain Bottell,* limited edition, Boriswood, 1933, Panther Books, 1965; *Resurrexit Dominus,* limited edition, privately printed, 1934; *The Furys* (first book of "The Furys" chronicle), Macmillan, 1935; *Stoker Bush,* Chatto & Windus, 1935, Macmillan, 1936; *The Secret Journey* (second book of "The Furys" chronicle), Macmillan, 1936; *Hollow Sea,* John Lane, 1938, reprinted, Panther Books, 1965.

Our Time Is Gone (third book in "The Furys" chronicle), John Lane, 1940, revised edition, Phoenix House, 1949, published as a trilogy with first two books of "The Furys" chronicle, Dent, 1949; *The Ocean,* Morrow, 1941, reprinted, Mayflower Books, 1965; *No Directions,* Faber, 1943; *Sailor's Song,* Nicholson & Watson, 1943; *What Farrar Saw,* Nicholson & Watson, 1946; *Emily,* Nicholson & Watson, 1948; *Winter Song* (fourth book of "The Furys" chronicle), Dent, 1950; (under pseudonym Patric Shone) *The*

House in the Valley, J. Cape, 1951; *The Closed Harbour,* Macdonald & Co., 1952, published as *The Closed Harbor,* Horizon Press, 1953; *The Welsh Sonata: Variations on a Theme,* Derek Verschoyle, 1954; *Levine,* Horizon Press, 1956; *And End and a Beginning,* Horizon Press, 1958.

Say Nothing (adapted from his own play), Horizon Press, 1962; *Another World,* Horizon Press, 1972; *A Woman in the Sky,* Horizon Press, 1973; *A Dream Journey,* Horizon Press, 1976.

Short stories: *A Passion Before Death,* privately printed, 1930; *The Last Voyage: A Tale,* limited edition, William Jackson, 1931; *Men in Darkness: Five Stories,* preface by John Cowper Powys, John Lane, 1931, Knopf, 1932, reprinted, Books for Libraries Press, 1970; *Stoker Haslett: A Tale,* Joiner & Steele, 1932; *Aria and Finale and Other Stories,* Boriswood, 1932; *Quartermaster Clausen,* Arlan, 1934; *The German Prisoner,* introduction by Richard Aldington, privately printed, c. 1935; *At Bay,* Grayson, 1935; *Half an Eye: Sea Stories,* John Lane, 1937; *People Are Curious: Short Stories,* John Lane, 1938.

At Bay: Tales (includes "Beyond the Horizon," "Jacob," "The Butterfly," "The Brothers," "People Are Curious," "At Bay" "The Tale," "Fog," "The Sea," and "Brother Geoffrey"), Faber, 1944; *Crilly and Other Stories,* Nicholson & Watson, 1945; *Selected Stories,* Fridberg (Dublin), 1947; *A Walk in the Wilderness* (includes "A Walk in the Wilderness," "Afterwards," "The Road," "Another World," and "It Has Never Ended"), Dent, 1950; *Collected Stories,* Macdonald & Co., 1953; *Don Quixote Drowned* (includes "Don Quixote Drowned," "Smiler," "Oddfish," "A Writer's Day," "Ship in the Snow," and "Anatomy of Llangyllwch"), Macdonald & Co., 1953; *The Darkness,* Covent Garden Press, 1973.

Plays: "Say Nothing," first broadcast, 1961, first produced in Stratford at Theatre Royal, August 14, 1962, produced in New York, 1965; *The Inner Journey: A Play in Three Acts* (first produced in Hamburg, 1967, produced in New York at Forum Theatre, March 20, 1969), Horizon Press, 1965; "Forever and Forever," first produced in Hamburg, 1966; *Plays One* (includes "The Inner Journey" and "A Stone Flower"), Kaye & Ward, 1968; "It Wasn't Me," first produced in London, 1968; "Leave Us Alone," first produced in London, 1972.

Television plays: "The Inner World of Miss Vaughan," 1964; "Another Port, Another Town," 1964; "Mr. Ponge," 1965; "Day Out for Lucy," 1965; "A Walk in the Sea," 1966; "That Woman," 1967; "Nothing Will Be the Same Again," 1968.

Radio plays: "S.S. Elizabethan," 1941; "Freedom's Ferry," 1941; "Open Boat," 1941; "Return to Danger," 1942; "A Winter Journey," 1958; "I Talk to Myself," 1958; "A Letter in the Desert," 1958; "Gobbet," 1959; "The Queens of Ireland," 1960; "Miss Williams," 1960; "Say Nothing," 1961; "A Pillar of Fire," 1962; "A Walk in the World," 1962; "A Dream," 1963; "One Way Out," 1967; "The Silence," 1968; "Sailor's Song," 1970; "One Way Only," 1970.

Other: *Broken Water: An Autobiographical Excursion,* Chatto & Windus, 1937; *Grey Children: A Study in Humbug and Misery* (sociological study of unemployment among coal miners in South Wales), Methuen, 1937; *Between the Tides,* Methuen, 1939; *Towards Horizons* (on life at sea), Mellifont Press, 1949; (editor and compiler with Nina Froud) Fedor Ivanovich Shaliapin, *Chaliapin: An Autobiography as Told to Maxim Gorky,* Stein & Day, 1967; *J. C. Powys: A Man in the Corner,* limited edition, K. A. Ward, 1969; *The Face of Winter* (poem), limited edition illustrated by wife Liam Hanley, K. A. Ward, 1969; *Herman Melville: A Man in the Customs House,* limited edition, Dud Norman Press, 1971.

Plays anthologized in *Plays of the Year,* Volume 27, edited by J. C. Trewin, Elek, 1963; *Plays and Players,* volumes 10 and 11, edited by Peter Roberts, Hansom Books, 1963. Also author with others of special issue, on John Cowper Powys, of *Dock Leaves* (literary journal), spring, 1956.

AVOCATIONAL INTERESTS: Fishing, music.

BIOGRAPHICAL/CRITICAL SOURCES: Time, February 18, 1974; *Contemporary Literary Criticism,* Gale, Volume 3, 1975, Volume 5, 1976; *Publisher's Weekly,* December 27, 1976.*

* * *

HANN, Jacquie 1951-

PERSONAL: Born May 18, 1951, in New York; daughter of Walter and Irmgard (Pach) Hann. *Education:* University of Wisconsin, Madison, B.S., 1972; also attended Parsons School of Design, 1973-74, and School of Visual Arts, 1974. *Home and office:* 20 Jane St., New York, N.Y. 10014.

CAREER: Writer, 1975—. *Member:* Illustrators Guild.

WRITINGS—Self-illustrated children's books: *That Man Is Talking to His Toes,* Four Winds, 1976; *Where's Mark?,* Four Winds, 1977; *Up Day, Down Day,* Four Winds, 1978; *Big Trouble,* Four Winds, 1978.

WORK IN PROGRESS: Writing and illustrating children's books.

SIDELIGHTS: Jacquie Hann Writes: "As a child, I never was interested in reading books, but I always wrote stories and drew pictures. I never wanted to be told anything, I wanted to experience everything for myself. Doing children's books intrigued me for a long time—it was an even blend of words and pictures, and it was art for a purpose.

"I wrote my first children's book in college with a friend. I illustrated it, set the type, printed it, and bound it. We had fantasies of being sent on a world tour for our 'Caldecott winner'—but of course it never even got published.

"I think the most important component in children's books is humor. It can be in any form—whimsy, satire, nonsense—but I have yet to see a strong children's book without this ingredient.

"I try to write books about kids as they really are, and I usually do that by delving into my own childhood to remember what I thought and felt. I don't believe in preaching morals to kids. I think kids have a great deal of common sense and just need the encouragement to think for themselves and use their imaginations."

* * *

HANSEN, Donald A(ndrew) 1933-

PERSONAL: Born July 17, 1933, in Red Wing, Minn.; son of Andrew (a mechanic) and Alice (Sorensen) Hansen; married Vicky Almona Johnson (a psychologist), April 1, 1972. *Education:* University of Minnesota, B.A., 1955, M.A., 1958, Ph.D., 1962; Northwestern University, Ph.D., 1962; also attended University of Chicago, 1951-52. *Home:* 866 El Pintado, Danville, Calif. 94526. *Office:* University of California, 3647 Tolman, Berkeley, Calif. 94720.

CAREER: Minneapolis Tribune, Minneapolis, Minn., feature writer, 1957-59; University of Otago, Dunedin, New Zealand, lecturer in education, 1962-63; Purdue University, West Lafayette, Ind., assistant professor of sociology, 1964-65; University of California, Santa Barbara, assistant professor of sociology, 1965-68; University of California, Berkeley, associate professor of education and affiliate professor of sociology, 1968—. Member of board of directors of Boyd & Fraser Publishing Co. *Member:* American Sociological Association.

WRITINGS: (Editor with Joel Gerstl) *On Education: Sociological Perspectives,* Wiley, 1967; (with J. H. Parsons) *Mass Communication: A Research Bibliography,* Glendessary, 1968; (editor) *Explorations in Sociology and Counseling,* Houghton, 1969; *An Invitation to Critical Sociology,* Free Press, 1976.

WORK IN PROGRESS: Education and Social Theory.

* * *

HANSEN, Harry 1884-1977

PERSONAL: Born December 26, 1884, in Davenport, Iowa; son of Hans and Christine (Jochims) Hansen; married Ruth McLernon, April 29, 1914; children: Ruth Eleanor, Marian Hope Stankard. *Education:* University of Chicago, Ph.B., 1909. *Office:* 10 East 40th St., New York, N.Y. 10016.

CAREER: University of Chicago, Chicago, Ill., alumni secretary and editor of magazine, 1909-11; *Chicago Daily News,* Chicago, war correspondent in Baltic zone, 1914-16, correspondent at Paris Peace conference, 1919, literary editor, 1920-26; *New York World,* New York City, literary editor, 1926-31; *New York World-Telegram,* New York City, literary editor, 1931-48; editor of *World Almanac,* 1948-65; Hastings House Publishers, Inc., New York City, vice-president, 1965-77. Member of editorial boards of East and West Association and Armed Services Editions. *Member:* Overseas Press Club, Illinois Historical Society, Historical Society of Iowa, Sigma Alpha Epsilon, Dutch Treat Club (New York City), Coffee House Club (New York City), Tavern Club (Chicago).

WRITINGS: The Adventures of the Fourteen Points, Century Co., 1919; (translator from the German) Friedrich Freksa, *A Peace Congress of Intrigue,* Century Co., 1919; *Midwest Portraits,* Harcourt, 1923; *Carl Sandburg: The Man and His Poetry,* Haldeman-Julius, 1925; (translator from the German) Jacob Wasserman, *Faber,* Harcourt, 1925; *Your Life Lies Before You* (novel), Harcourt, 1935; *The Chicago,* Farrar & Rinehart, 1942.

North of Manhattan, Hastings House, 1950; *Scarsdale: Colonial Manor to Modern Community,* Harper, 1954; *Old Ironsides,* Random House, 1955; *The Story of Illinois,* Garden City Books, 1956, revised edition, Hastings House, 1974; *The Civil War,* New American Library, 1961; *The Boston Massacre,* Hastings House, 1970; *Longfellow's New England,* Hastings House, 1972. Also co-author of *Writing Up the News,* 1940; *Journalism in Wartime,* 1943; *The Aspirin Age,* 1949.

Editor: *The Stories of O. Henry,* Heritage Press, 1965; *New England Legends and Folklore,* Hastings House, 1967; *Texas: A Guide to the Lone Star State,* revised edition, Hastings House, 1969; *Colorado: A Guide to the Highest State,* revised edition, Hastings House, 1970; *Louisiana: A Guide to the State,* revised edition, Hastings House, 1971. Also editor of *Colorado,* 1969, and an edition of *All Quiet on the Western Front,* 1969.

Editor of the "American Guide" series, 1966. Editor of

Prize Short Stories: The O. Henry Awards, 1933-40. Contributor to *Encyclopaedia Britannica* and *Universal Jewish Encyclopedia.*

OBITUARIES: New York Times, January 3, 1977; *AB Bookman's Weekly,* March 20, 1977.*

(Died January 2, 1977, in New York, N.Y.)

*   *   *

HANSON, Earl D(orchester) 1927-

PERSONAL: Born February 15, 1927, in Shahjahanpur, India; son of Harry Albert (a missionary) and Jean (Dorchester) Hanson; married Carlota Ferne Kinzie, June 10, 1948 (divorced August 30, 1973); married Evelyn Fairheller (a university administrator), January 4, 1975; children: (first marriage) Mardi Jean Hanson d'Alessandro, Stanley Royce, Kenric Mark. *Education:* Bowdoin College, A.B. (cum laude), 1945; Indiana University, Ph.D., 1954. *Office:* College of Science in Society, Wesleyan University, Middletown, Conn. 06457.

CAREER: Yale University, New Haven, Conn., instructor, 1954-57, assistant professor of zoology, 1957-60; Wesleyan University, Middletown, Conn., associate professor, 1960-63, professor of biology, 1963-72, Fisk Professor of Natural Science, 1972—, chairman of department of biology, 1968-71, chairman of College of Science in Society, 1975—. Research associate at Osaka University, 1960-61; guest professor at University of Tuebingen, 1967-68. Commission on Undergraduate Education in the Biological Sciences, member, 1963-67, member of executive committee, 1963-65; chairman, 1965-67; member of regional selection board for Woodrow Wilson fellowships, 1964-65; member of Haddam Conservation Commission, 1969-73. Member of corporation of Bermuda Biological Station, 1959—, and Middlesex Memorial Hospital, 1967-75. *Military service:* U.S. Marine Corps Reserve, active duty, 1945-46.

MEMBER: American Association for the Advancement of Science, American Association of University Professors, American Institute of Biological Sciences (member of governing board, 1971-74), Genetics Society of America, Society of Protozoologists, Federation of American Scientists, New York Academy of Sciences, Connecticut Academy of Arts and Sciences, Connecticut Academy of Science and Engineering, Phi Beta Kappa, Sigma Xi. *Awards, honors:* Lalor faculty summer research awards, 1956, 1957; Fulbright fellowship, 1960-61; Guggenheim fellowship, 1960-61; Harbison Distinguished Teaching Award from Danforth Foundation, 1970; National Science Foundation grants.

WRITINGS: Animal Diversity, Prentice-Hall, 1961, 3rd edition, 1972; (editor with E. C. Dougherty, Z. N. Brown, and W. D. Hartman, and contributor) *The Lower Metazoa: Comparative Biology and Phylogeny,* University of California Press, 1963; (contributor) G. W. Kidder, editor, *Chemical Zoology,* Volume I, Academic Press, 1967; (contributor) Robert G. Page, editor, *Preparation for the Study of Medicine,* University of Chicago Press, 1969.

(Contributor) W. J. van Wagtendonk, editor, *Paramecium: A Current Survey,* Elsevier, 1973; (contributor) D. H. Prescott, editor, *Methods in Cell Physiology,* Volume III, Academic Press, 1974; *The Origin and Early Evolution of Animals,* Wesleyan University Press, 1977. Contributor to *Encyclopaedia Britannica.* Contributor of about fifty articles to scientific journals.

WORK IN PROGRESS: Biology: The Science of Life a high school textbook, with David Lockard and Peter Jensch.

SIDELIGHTS: Hanson comments: "The motivation behind my books is to transform the treatment of organismic diversity from a compendium of facts to a conceptual analysis based on testable theories. In particular, Darwinian natural selection is extended from the origin of species to the origin of the major evolutionary innovations."

*   *   *

HANZLICEK, C(harles) G(eorge) 1942-

PERSONAL: Born August 23, 1942, in Owatonna, Minn.; son of George John (a machinist) and Freda (Schuenke) Hanzlicek; married Dianne Staley, May 11, 1968. *Education:* University of Minnesota, B.A., 1964; University of Iowa, M.F.A., 1966. *Politics:* "Irrational." *Religion:* "Without." *Home:* 738 East Lansing Way, Fresno, Calif. 93704. *Office:* Department of English, California State University, Fresno, Calif. 93740.

CAREER: California State University, Fresno, 1966—, began as assistant professor, professor of English, 1975—. *Awards, honors:* Fellowship from National Endowment for the Arts, 1976; Devins Award from the Devins Foundation, 1977-78, for *Stars.*

WRITINGS: The Voices (translations of Rainer Maria Rilke), Is It As Press, 1970; *Living in It* (poems), Stone Wall Press, 1971; *A Bird's Companion* (versions of American Indian songs), Licklog Press, 1974; *Stars* (poems), University of Missouri Press, 1977.

WORK IN PROGRESS: A book of poems dealing primarily with the death of his father.

SIDELIGHTS: Hanzlicek writes: "My main teaching interests are in the fields of creative writing and literature of the American Indian. My chief aim as a poet is to write with clarity, total clarity. If I am misunderstood, I have written badly. In terms of subject matter, I am more interested in emotions than in ideas, more drawn to the life of the body than the life of the mind. The great Irish poet, W. B. Yeats, said somewhere that the only two things worth writing about are sex and death. He meant that in the broadest sense, of course, and I tend to agree. I take poetry seriously, and therefore try to write serious poems."

AVOCATIONAL INTERESTS: Photography.

*   *   *

HARAWAY, Donna Jeanne 1944-

PERSONAL: Born September 6, 1944, in Denver, Colo.; daughter of Frank O. (a sports writer) and Dorothy (Maguire) Haraway; married B. Jaye Miller, July 11, 1970 (divorced, 1974). *Education:* Colorado College, B.A., 1966; Yale University, M.Phil., 1969, Ph.D., 1972. *Office:* Department of the History of Science, Johns Hopkins University, Baltimore, Md. 21218.

CAREER: University of Hawaii, Honolulu, assistant professor of general science, 1970-74; Johns Hopkins University, Baltimore, Md., assistant professor of the history of science, 1974—. *Member:* History of Science Society, Institute of Society, Ethics, and the Life Sciences, Science for the People.

WRITINGS: Crystals, Fabrics, and Fields: Metaphors of Organicism in Twentieth-Century Developmental Biology, Yale University Press, 1976. Contributor to history of science journals, to *Soundings,* and to feminist publications.

WORK IN PROGRESS: A History of Primate Behavior Studies.

SIDELIGHTS: "I am interested in the political and social dimensions of science," Haraway told CA. "My recent work has centered around the use of animals as models for human nature and history. I think it is important to use one's specialized training to contribute to the development of a socialist and feminist society. Biological and biosocial disciplines have been important parts of belief and value systems which may function as expressive social control or may be reclaimed for other ends. So I see the history of science as a disciplined craft which should lead to a critical understanding of important relations of science and other human activities and purposes."

* * *

HARDY, Alan 1932-

PERSONAL: Born March 24, 1932, in Newcastle-upon-Tyne, England; son of John Robert and Emily Hardy; married Betty Howe, July 17, 1972. Education: University of Manchester, B.A., 1953; Institute of Historical Research, London, M.A., 1956. Politics: Conservative. Religion: Church of England. Home: 18 Meadowside, Cambridge Park, Twickenham, England.

CAREER: Research assistant to Sir Lewis Namier, 1955-56; London Municipal Society, London, England, research officer and deputy director, 1956-63; affiliated with British Secretariat, Council of European Municipalities, 1963-67; Greater London Council, member, 1967—, chairman of its finance and establishment committee, 1977—. Past vice-chairman of London's Historic Buildings Board; member of board of directors of Harlow New Town Development Corp., 1968—.

WRITINGS: Queen Victoria Was Amused, J. Murray, 1976, Taplinger, 1977.

WORK IN PROGRESS: Research on the influence of mistresses of British monarchs since Charles II.

SIDELIGHTS: Hardy told CA that he is "primarily concerned with royal themes in British history. The writing of Queen Victoria Was Amused was motivated by a desire to correct the common misconception of Queen Victoria as humourless. The book was reviewed by the Prince of Wales who confirmed that my interpretation was the one passed on to him by elderly relations who knew her."

* * *

HARDY, Jason
See OXLEY, William

* * *

HARGRODER, Charles M(erlin) 1926-

PERSONAL: Born September 5, 1926, in Franklin, La. Education: Attended Louisiana State University, 1943-47. Home: 10157 Runnymede Ave., Baton Rouge, La. 70815. Office address: Box 44122 Capitol Station, Baton Rouge, La. 70804.

CAREER/WRITINGS: Baton Rouge Morning Advocate, Baton Rouge, La., member of staff, 1947-50; Monroe Morning World, Monroe, La., member of staff, 1952-53; executive assistant to the governor of Louisiana, 1953-56; public relations assistant to Congressman Hale Boggs, 1956-57; Inter-Industry Highway Safety Committee, Washington, D.C., field representative, 1957-58; New Orleans Times-Picayune, New Orleans, La., editorial writer, 1959-61, political writer and author of "Louisiana Capitol Report" column, 1961—. Notable assignments include coverage of Re-

publican National Conventions since 1964. Military service: U.S. Army Signal Corps, 1950-52; became sergeant. Member: Louisiana Capitol Correspondents Association (president, 1972-73, treasurer, 1974-78).

* * *

HARKABI, Yehoshafat 1921-

PERSONAL: Born September 21, 1921, in Haifa, Israel; son of Zidkiahv (a judge) and Haya (Stamper) Harkabi; married Miryam Manzon (a medical secretary), March 23, 1953; children: Irit, Dan. Education: Hebrew University of Jerusalem, M.A., 1949, Ph.D., 1968; Harvard University, M.P.A., 1960. Religion: Jewish. Home: 6 Bar Kokhva St., French Hill, Jerusalem, Israel. Office: Department of International Relations, Hebrew University of Jerusalem, Jerusalem, Israel.

CAREER: Israel Defence Forces, director of military intelligence, 1950-59, leaving service as major general; Ministry of Defence, Tel-Aviv, Israel, in strategic research, 1963-68; Hebrew University of Jerusalem, Jerusalem, Israel, professor of international relations, 1968—.

WRITINGS: Nuclear War and Nuclear Peace, Israel Program for Scientific Translations, 1964; Arab Attitudes to Israel, Israel University Press, 1971; Palestinians and Israel, Keter Publishing House, 1974; Arab Strategies and Israel's Response, Free Press, 1977.

WORK IN PROGRESS: A work on the philosophy of international relations.

* * *

HARMAN, Gilbert H(elms) 1938-

PERSONAL: Born May 26, 1938, in East Orange, N.J.; son of William Henry (a businessman) and Marguerite Veriel (Page) Harman; married Lucy Newman, August 14, 1970; children: Elizabeth. Education: Swarthmore College, B.A., 1960; Harvard University, Ph.D., 1964. Home: 106 Broadmead, Princeton, N.J. 08540. Office: Department of Philosophy, Princeton University, Princeton, N.J. 08540.

CAREER: Princeton University, Princeton, N.J., instructor, 1963-64, assistant professor, 1964-68, associate professor, 1968-71, professor of philosophy, 1971—. Member: American Philosophical Association, Linguistic Society of America.

WRITINGS: (Editor with Donald Davidson) Semantics of Natural Language, D. Reidel, 1972; Thought, Princeton University Press, 1973; (editor) On Noam Chomsky, Anchor Books, 1974; (editor with Davidson) The Logic of Grammar, Dickenson, 1975; The Nature of Morality, Oxford University Press, 1977.

WORK IN PROGRESS: Research on the nature of reasoning.

* * *

HARNDEN, Ruth Peabody

PERSONAL: Born in Boston, Mass.; daughter of Edward Warren (a lawyer) and Alice (Goldthwait) Harnden. Education: Radcliffe College, B.A.; also attended Trinity College, University of Dublin. Politics: Independent. Religion: Unitarian-Universalist. Home address: Box 301, Plymouth, Mass. 02360. Agent: Russell & Volkening, Inc., 551 Fifth Ave., New York, N.Y. 10017.

CAREER: Writer. Awards, honors: Annual award from Child Study Association of America, for The High Pasture.

WRITINGS: Bright Star or Dark (fiction), McGraw, 1945; *I, a Stranger* (fiction), Whittlesey House, 1950; *Golly and the Gulls* (juvenile), Houghton, 1962; *The High Pasture* (juvenile), Houghton, 1964; *Summer's Turning* (juvenile), Houghton, 1966; *Runaway Raft* (juvenile), Houghton, 1968; *Next Door* (novel), Houghton, 1970; *Wonder Why* (juvenile verse), Houghton, 1971.

Contributor of stories to magazines.

*　　*　　*

HARRINGTON, Alan 1919-

PERSONAL: Born January 16, 1919, in Newton, Mass.; son of Eugene and Gwyneth (Browne) Harrington; married Margaret Young (a medical researcher), January 18, 1968; children: Stephen, John, Susan. *Education:* Harvard University, B.A., 1939. *Home:* 2831 N. Orlando Ave., Tucson, Ariz. 85712. *Agent:* International Creative Management, 40 West 57th St., New York, N.Y. 10019.

CAREER: Transradio Press, New York City, reporter, 1946-47; Information Office, Republic of Indonesia, New York City, editor, 1950-54; Standard-Vacuum Oil Co., White Plains, N.Y., employed in public relations department, 1954-58; International Telephone and Telegraph (ITT), New York City, employed in public relations department, 1950-60; writer. *Military service:* U.S. Army Air Forces, Weather Service, 1942-46, became staff sergeant. *Member:* P.E.N.

WRITINGS: The Revelations of Dr. Modesto (novel), Knopf, 1955; *Life in the Crystal Palace* (nonfiction), Knopf, 1959; *The Secret Swinger* (novel), Knopf, 1966; *The Immortalist* (nonfiction), Random House, 1969, revised edition, Celestial Arts, 1977; *Psychopaths . . .* (case histories), Simon & Schuster, 1972; (with Dan Sakall) *Love and Evil: From a Probation Officer's Casebook* (nonfiction), Little, Brown, 1974; *Paradise I,* Little, Brown, 1978. Contributor to *Harper's, Atlantic, Esquire, Playboy, Penthouse, Nation, New Republic,* and *Chicago Review.*

WORK IN PROGRESS: A novel, *Paradise II,* completion expected, 1978.

SIDELIGHTS: Harrington told *CA:* "*The Immortalist* theorized that humanity's main drive and motivation is its disguised drive to achieve physical immortality, replacing all the old gods, becoming divine ourselves. First sentence: 'Death is an imposition on the human race, and no longer acceptable.' *Paradise I* and *Paradise II* are novels working out fictional possibilities inherent in achieving immortality. Most of my work in the future will have to do with slowing down, stabilizing, and ultimately reversing the aging process, and dealing with all consequences arising from this enroute and once there."

Harrington's first novel, *The Revelations of Dr. Modesto,* was generally criticized for a lack of discipline and structure. Some reviewers, however, recognized the author's potential for humor and inventiveness. Carolyn Stull noted: "There are times when Mr. Harrington succeeds in creating a fictional atmosphere that is vaguely, even if very vaguely, reminiscent of the work of Sinclair Lewis in his *Main Street—Elmer Gantry* period. If he acquires some of Lewis' discipline and workmanship, he will be able to give better voice to his talent." In a review for *New York Times,* Ben Crisler commented that Harrington's "ingenious workmanship excites interest and admiration, whereas the essentially inutile nature of his enterprise can inspire little save sympathetic head-shakings and tongue-clickings." *Commonweal*'s

Frank Getlein referred to *The Revelations of Dr. Modesto* as a "fantasy-satire . . . [that] isn't funny." Getlein added that "there is a kind of comic *hubris* necessary in such work, and here it is completely lacking." *Kirkus Reviews* focused on the novel's "abysmal confusion and boredom," while Sylvia Stallings observed that Harrington "has not given his plot enough stamina to support the weight of his text." However, *Saturday Review*'s Jerome Stone praised Harrington's comedic talents in drawing scenes that "are rooted in reality . . . on a base of intellectual criticism."

Life in the Crystal Palace relates Harrington's experiences in the public relations department of a large corporation. According to *New York Herald Tribune Book Review,* Harrington "feels that the Crystal Palace, with its exclusive suburban headquarters, splendid working conditions, blandly generous employee relations, may one day fall of its dead weight, of its slow accumulation of mediocrities and incompetents and its multiplying inefficient practices." *Atlantic* reviewer Charles Rolo wrote that the "appeal of Harrington's essay is that his personal findings constitute in effect a condensation and summation of what has been said in a variety of places, and they are presented in a telling and most readable manner." A reviewer for *Christian Century* called Harrington's book "an excellent, first-hand account of what work may be for most Americans in another generation," and *San Francisco Chronicle* declared it the "strangest, most disturbing and without doubt the most controversial of all recent 'Organization Man' type of books." Dissenting views came from *Management Review*'s T. B. Dolmatch, who called the book "petty" and a "cartoon version" of "corporate life in America," and from a reviewer for *London Times Literary Supplement* who termed it a "blown-up article . . . too perfunctory for the seriousness of [its] subject."

The Secret Swinger concerns a middle-aged man's realization of the purposelessness of his life and the steps he takes to amend his situation. *America*'s Catharine Hughes reported that although Mr. Harrington is an "extraordinarily fine writer, with pages approaching sheer brilliance, he is ultimately the victim of his desire to 'tell all' about the decline and fall of [the hero]. Or, more accurately, to tell 'all' several times." John Knowles, in an article for *New York Times Book Review,* stated that a "study of male menopause does not seem the ideal theme for contemporary fiction. Futility, inertia, immobility threaten not only the protagonist of such a novel but also the novel itself." Knowles further claimed that Harrington "has cut away all the fat from this study, leaving only undiluted gristle. Instead of a wallowing futile tale, he has produced a headlong, even arrogant book about a failure."

The Immortalist: An Approach to the Engineering of Man's Divinity is Harrington's projection of a future utopia in which death will be vanquished by technological advances to come, and immortality will thereby be attained. R. G. Hazo called Harrington's treatise a "remarkably bold, ingenious, profoundly and intentionally shocking, undoubtedly sincere and utterly diabolical book." Hazo noted, however, that this "otherwise thoughtful book is tarnished by the absence of a single argument for the atheist position." Geoffrey Wolff admitted that Harrington's "thesis is persuasive" but found that *The Immortalist . . .* "occasionally chops logic and frequently refuses to imagine the condition of the planet groaning under successive generations whose numbers will be reduced only as the result of accident." Wolff continued that Harrington "writes . . . from anger barely under control. His clipped sentences suggest a man writing in haste, and under great pressure, and the effect is to excite sensations of urgency in the reader. He mounts an unrelenting assault against everything that would dilute the blunt fact of death.''

In *Psychopaths ...*, a compilation of selective case histories, Harrington postulated his theory of the difference between "traditional" psychopathy and the *carpe diem* psychopathy deliberately assumed in the last few years in reaction to the encroaching technology. Walter Clemons of *Newsweek* stated that "Harrington's case histories ... are melodramatically but diffusely recorded. Plausibility isn't exactly the problem, but lack of resonance." Clemons added that although Harrington's "argument ... is often brilliantly suggestive ... it is when Harrington turns from description to prescription that most readers will shy off.''

Love and Evil: From a Probation Officer's Casebook cites case histories from co-author Dan Sakall's experiences as a probation officer, and delves into the problems of the American court system. *Atlantic* reviewer Phoebe Adams noted that the "purpose of [the] book is to urge reconsideration of the system of justice," and she deemed the authors successful in presenting their "strong doubts about the court system designed to control" the "gaggle of criminal unfortunates roaming through these memoirs.''

BIOGRAPHICAL/CRITICAL SOURCES: Kirkus Reviews, June 15, 1955; *New York Herald Tribune Book Review,* August 21, 1955, November 8, 1959; *New York Times,* August 21, 1955, June 20, 1969; *Commonweal,* September 2, 1955; *San Francisco Chronicle,* October 25, 1959; *Atlantic,* November, 1959, July, 1974; *Christian Century,* December 16, 1959; *Times Literary Supplement,* April 1, 1960; *New York Times Book Review,* April 17, 1966; *America,* May 7, 1966; *Newsweek,* June 30, 1969, June 5, 1972; *Life,* July 4, 1969; *Time,* July 11, 1969; *Book World,* July 13, 1969.

*   *   *

HARRIS, R(ansom) Baine   1927-

PERSONAL: Born June 5, 1927, in Hudson, N.C.; son of Ransom Z. and Hettie (Crouch) Harris; married Ettie Jeanne Johnson, June 8, 1958; children: Nancie Elizabeth, Lori Ann. *Education:* Mars Hill Junior College, A.A., 1946; University of Richmond, B.A., 1948, M.A., 1954; Southern Baptist Theological Seminary, B.D., 1951; Emory University, M.A., 1960; Temple University, Ph.D., 1971; also attended Duke University and University of Virginia. *Politics:* Democrat. *Religion:* Baptist. *Home:* 4037 Windymille Dr., Portsmouth, Va. 23703. *Office:* Department of Philosophy, Old Dominion University, Norfolk, Va. 23508.

CAREER: University of Richmond, Richmond, Va., instructor in philosophy and religion, 1953-54; Georgia Institute of Technology, Atlanta, instructor in philosophy and social sciences, 1956-60; Frederick College, Portsmouth, Va., professor of philosophy and chairman of department, 1960-65; Clemson University, Clemson, S.C., assistant professor of philosophy and director of studies in philosophy and religion, 1965-70; Eastern Kentucky University, Richmond, associate professor, 1970-71, professor of philosophy and chairman of department, 1971-73; Old Dominion University, Norfolk, Va., professor of philosophy and chairman of department, 1973—, also named Eminent Scholar. Adjunct professor at George Washington University, 1963-65; visiting professor at University of Richmond, summer, 1964.

MEMBER: International Society for Neoplatonic Studies (founding member; executive director), American Philosophical Association, Metaphysical Society of America, American Academy of Religion, Society for Philosophy of Religion, Eastern Virginia Theological Society (organizer), Southern Society for Philosophy and Religion, Southern Society for Philosophy and Psychology, Virginia Philosophical Society, Washington, D.C. Philosophical Society. *Awards, honors:* Fellowship from Emory University, 1969; grant from Lilly Foundation, summer, 1971.

WRITINGS: (Editor) *The Significance of Neoplatonism,* State University of New York Press, 1976; (editor) *Neoplatonism: Ancient and Modern,* State University of New York Press, 1976; (editor) *Authority: A Philosophical Analysis,* University of Alabama Press, 1976. Contributor to *Quote,* and to journals in his field. Guest editor of *Southern Journal of Philosophy,* 1970.

WORK IN PROGRESS: The Collected Essays of Dean Inge, five volumes; *Neoplatonism Reconsidered: Recent Essays on Neoplatonism; Chance, Choice, and God.*

SIDELIGHTS: Harris told *CA* his "current academic interests include the comparison and contrast of Christianity and Neoplatonism and leading in the work of the International Society for Neoplatonic Studies.''

*   *   *

HARRIS, Thomas O(rville)   1935-

PERSONAL: Born March 4, 1935, in Miami, Okla.; son of Orville F. (an auditor) and Muriel (Barnes) Harris; married Maxine Young, June 25, 1954; children: Lee Ann Harris Perez, Timothy, Christopher, Jennifer. *Education:* Attended Northeastern Oklahoma Agricultural and Mechanical Junior College, 1953-54, and Joplin Junior College, 1958-59; Kansas State College (now Pittsburg State University), B.S., 1962, M.S., 1963; Kansas State University, Ph.D., 1975. *Religion:* Protestant. *Home:* 401 Utah, Pittsburg, Kan. 66762. *Office:* Department of Vocational-Technical Education, Pittsburg State University, Pittsburg, Kan. 66762.

CAREER: High school teacher of industrial training and vocational education in Baxter Springs, Kan., 1962-64, Girard, Kan., 1964-67, and Pratt, Kan., 1967-68; Schafer Plow, Inc., Pratt, Kan., executive vice-president, 1968-69; Pittsburg State University, Pittsburg, Kan., assistant professor, 1969-75, associate professor of vocational-technical education, 1975—. Instructor at Pratt Junior College, 1967-68; visiting professor at Oregon State University, summer, 1976. Consultant to industry and health facilities.

MEMBER: American Vocational Association (life member), Vocational Industrial Clubs of America (charter professional member; local executive secretary, 1966-75; member of state board of directors), National Association of Industrial and Technical Educators, National Association of Trade and Industrial Instructors, National Association of Trade and Industrial Education, Kansas Vocational Association (life member; past executive secretary), Kansas Industrial Education Association, Kansas Coordinator-Instructor Association (president), Epsilon Pi Tau, Phi Delta Kappa, Kappa Delta Pi.

WRITINGS: (With Robert E. Scott) *Trade and Industrial Education Notebook,* Interstate, 1968; *Organization and Administration of Vocational Club Activities,* Professor Publications, 1973; (with Scott) *Model Personnel Policy Manual and Job Descriptions,* American Health Care Association, 1974. Contributor to professional journals.

WORK IN PROGRESS: Journalism.

SIDELIGHTS: Harris comments: "My major purpose in writing is to help others do a better job in their positions. The majority of my publications are 'no-fee' type, so I'm certainly not in it for the money. The major thrust in my writing is that of synthesizing much information into simple, readable, useable information. I am basically lazy and thus have become highly efficient and organized.''

AVOCATIONAL INTERESTS: Tinkering.

*   *   *

HARRISON, Keith Edward   1932-

PERSONAL: Born in 1932, in Melbourne, Australia; came to the United States in 1966; son of Harvey Herbert and Jessie Gladys Harrison; children: Katrina, Rebecca. *Education:* Attended Melbourne Teachers College, 1951; University of Melbourne, B.A., 1954; University of Iowa, M.A., 1967. *Home address:* Route 1, Northfield, Minn. 55057. *Office:* Department of English, Carleton College, Northfield, Minn. 55057.

CAREER: High school teacher of French, English, and music in Victoria, Australia, 1954-57; City Literary Institute, London, England, lecturer in English, 1959-65; University of Iowa, Iowa City, visiting poet, 1966; York University, Toronto, Ontario, lecturer in English, 1966-68; Carleton College, Northfield, Minn., assistant professor, 1968-73, associate professor of English, 1974—, director of arts program, 1969-75. Free-lance poet, journalist, and broadcaster, 1958-66; chief administrator and producer of "Poets in Public" readings at Edinburgh International Festival, 1965; has given readings on radio and at centers of learning in the United States, Canada, and Australia. Tutor at University of London, 1963-65. *Awards, honors:* Award from British Arts Council, 1972, for *Songs from the Drifting House.*

WRITINGS—Books of poems: (Editor with Peter Brent) *Young Commonwealth Poets '65,* Heinemann, 1965; *Points in a Journey,* Macmillan (London), 1966, Dufour, 1967; *Two Variations on a Ground,* Turret Books, 1967; *Songs from the Drifting House,* Macmillan, 1972; *The Basho Poems,* Cyathus Press, 1975.

Poems anthologized in *Australian Voices,* 1975, *Twenty-Five Minnesota Poets,* 1976, and *Winter Tales for Children.* Contributor of articles, poems, and reviews to magazines in the United States and abroad, including *Atlantic Monthly, New Statesman, Western Humanities Review,* and *Observer. Carleton Miscellany,* guest editor, winter, 1971-72, editor, 1976—.

WORK IN PROGRESS: Time of the Goat, a short novel.

SIDELIGHTS: Harrison told *CA:* "I think American society—modern society in general—is in the throes of a very complex sickness. One possible way out of the sickness is to emphasize the interdependence of the human community. The writing, reading, and discussion of literature is one way—but only one way—of doing that."

*   *   *

HARRISS, R(obert) P(reston)   1902-

PERSONAL: Born August 19, 1902, in Fayetteville, N.C.; son of Frank MacCullough and Harriet W. (Anderson) Harriss; married Margery Orem Willis, June 21, 1934; children: Clarinda Harriss Lott. *Education:* Duke University, A.B., 1926; graduate study at Ecole d'Art Animalier, 1929-30, and Sorbonne, University of Paris, 1930-31. *Politics:* Democrat. *Religion:* Episcopalian. *Home:* 306 Suffolk Rd., Baltimore, Md. 21218. *Office: Baltimore News American,* Baltimore, Md. 21203.

CAREER: Employed by *Baltimore Sun,* Baltimore, Md., 1927-29; *New York Herald Tribune,* New York City, reporter from Paris, 1929-33; *Baltimore Sun,* member of editorial staff, 1934-43, senior associate editor and acting editor, 1943-46; employed by *Gardens, Houses and People,* 1947-57; *Baltimore News American,* Baltimore, art, music, and drama editor, 1957—. American press representative, under auspices of U.S. State Department, to Anglo-American Caribbean Commission in Barbados during World War II.

MEMBER: American Theater Critics Association, Poe Society (past member of board of directors), Association of American Mammalogists, Sons of the American Revolution, Maryland Historical Society, Baltimore Friends of Peale Museum, Friends of H. L. Mencken, Baltimore Art Museum, Walters Art Gallery, Maryland Club, Fourteen West Hamilton Street Club, Baltimore Country Club, Johns Hopkins Faculty Club, Phi Beta Kappa, Sigma Phi Epsilon. *Awards, honors:* Steadman Essay Medal from British Book Society, 1937, for *The Foxes.*

WRITINGS: The Foxes (novel), Houghton, 1936. Also editor of *The Archive Anthology of Poetry,* Duke University Press. Contributor of articles, poems, and stories to magazines.

SIDELIGHTS: Harriss writes: "In my early years, I did general reporting, racing, features, etc., but most of my career has been devoted to criticism and essays and articles on music, art, drama, ballet, architecture."

He comments that an original idea of his is "that symphonic music is and has always been strongly influenced by transportation in the composer's own time. Examples: J. S. Bach by trotting, carriage horses (contrapuntal); Haydn, father of the symphony, likewise. Beethoven by boat and canal travel as well as horse drawn. Later nineteenth century composers by steam. Contemporary composers by jet, etc."

AVOCATIONAL INTERESTS: Gardening.

*   *   *

HARTING, Emilie Clothier   1942-

PERSONAL: Born February 12, 1942, in Staten Island, N.Y.; daughter of James A. and Dorothy (Meyer) Clothier; married Robert M. Harting (an executive), August, 1965; children: Morgan C., Thea E. *Education:* Keuka College, B.A., 1963; Seton Hall University, M.A., 1968; further graduate study at University of Pennsylvania. *Home:* 7143 Ardleigh St., Philadelphia, Pa. 19119. *Office:* Community College of Philadelphia, 34 South 11th St., Philadelphia, Pa. 19119.

CAREER: High school teacher of English in Haverford, Pa., 1964-65, and Lambertville, N.J., 1965-66; Community College of Philadelphia, Philadelphia, Pa., assistant professor of English, 1971—. Instructor at Rider College, 1968-70. Organized education program for ex-drug addicts at New Jersey Neuropsychiatric Institute, 1965-66. *Member:* National Council of Teachers of English, Philadelphia Writers Conference.

WRITINGS: Literary Tour Guide to England and Scotland, Morrow, 1976; *Literary Tour Guide to the Northeast,* Morrow, in press. Editor of *Schuylkill Post,* 1970.

WORK IN PROGRESS: Research on literary people and places.

SIDELIGHTS: Emilie Harting explains that her books cover "spots associated with major authors and give background on each place and show how it was part of the author's world.'' The books contain directions and maps that are ''limited to places which are visible and accessible (though not all necessarily open), as opposed to the *Oxford Literary Guide to the British Isles,* which is a digest and gives a few facts on hundreds of places.''

* * *

HARTLEY, Shirley Foster 1928-

PERSONAL: Born September 25, 1928, in Chicago, Ill.; daughter of Paul Bauman and Frances (Smith) Pederson; married David E. Hartley (an investment banker), June 18, 1950; children: Laurelle Hartley Kinney, Wallace. *Education:* University of California, Berkeley, B.S., 1950, Ph.D., 1969; San Jose State University, M.S., 1963. *Home:* 15 Van Tassel Lane, Orinda, Calif. 94563. *Office:* Department of Sociology, California State University, Hayward, Calif. 94542.

CAREER: California State University, Hayward, 1968—, began as assistant professor, became associate professor, then professor of sociology. Community service worker for Palo Alto's Retarded Children's Guild, 1957-62, Santa Clara Valley Migrant Farm Workers Service, 1958-62, and member of Contra Costa County Social Services Advisory Board, 1966-70.

MEMBER: International Sociological Association, International Union for the Scientific Study of Population, Population Association of America (member of board of directors, 1973-76), American Sociological Association, National Council on Family Relations, Society for the Study of Social Problems, Sociologists for Women in Society.

WRITINGS: Population: Quantity versus Quality, Prentice-Hall, 1972; (contributor) Donald R. MacQueen, editor, *Understanding Sociology Through Research,* Addison-Wesley, 1973; *Illegitimacy* (monograph), University of California Press, 1975. Also contributor to *The History of Illegitimacy,* edited by Peter Laslett. Contributor to journals in the social sciences. Associate editor of *Contemporary Sociology.*

WORK IN PROGRESS: The Status of Women: A World Profile, with Nadia Youssef; ''Biomedical Research and Human Values,'' a questionnaire on attitudes toward genetic research and cloning; research on the stratification of nations.

SIDELIGHTS: Hartley wrote to *CA:* ''The study of human social behavior is endlessly fascinating and increasingly important in a world of fast-paced travel and communication and deadly technology. Rapidly increasing technology and population numbers make it more difficult for individuals to feel a sense of control over their lives, while the maintenance of our fragile ecological balance requires responsible individual action. Thus, communication in writing and by lecture on the importance of considering long-range consequences of current behaviors is a personal goal.''

AVOCATIONAL INTERESTS: Travel (more than forty countries in Europe, the Far East, the Middle East, Africa, India, and the Caribbean).

* * *

HARVEY, Nigel 1916-
(Hugh Willoughby)

PERSONAL: Born August 8, 1916, in Oxford, England; son of Godfrey Eric (a civil servant in India) and Stella Hope (Garratt) Harvey; married Barbara Anne Skemp; children: Charles Frazer, Geoffrey Rowland. *Education:* Exeter Col-

lege, Oxford, M.A. (honors), 1938. *Home:* 41 Corringham Rd., Golders Green, London N.W.11, England.

CAREER: Ministry of Agriculture, Fisheries, and Food, London, England, staff member, 1944-58; Agricultural Research Council, London, staff member, 1958-76; full-time writer, 1976—. Agricultural history adviser to Old Fort William project in Ontario for National Heritage Ltd. (Toronto). *Member:* Royal Institution of Chartered Surveyors (associate).

WRITINGS: The Story of Farm Buildings, National Federation of Young Farmers Clubs, 1953; *The Farming Kingdom,* Turnstile, 1955; *Ditches, Dykes, and Deep Drainage,* National Federation of Young Farmers Clubs, 1956; (under pseudonym Hugh Willoughby) *Amid the Alien Corn,* Bobbs-Merrill, 1958; *Farm Work Study,* Farmer & Stockbreeder, 1958; *A History of Farm Buildings in England and Wales,* David & Charles, 1970; *Old Farm Buildings,* Shire Publications, 1975; *Fields, Hedges, and Ditches,* Shire Publications, 1976; *Farms and Farming,* Shire Publications, 1977. Contributor to agriculture journals and to *New Statesman* and *Country Life.*

WORK IN PROGRESS: The Industrial Archeology of Farming, for Batsford.

SIDELIGHTS: Harvey is a professional agriculturist writing on the history of his work. Some of his books are technical publications, but most are farming histories of interest to the general reader. *Amid the Alien Corn* is a collection of Harvey's letters from Purdue University to his home. He told *CA:* ''My letters were never intended for publication, of course. When I got home, I had copies run-off, omitting personal matters, to give to friends and one of them took it to Bobbs-Merrill who offered to publish it.'' The *Christian Science Monitor* wrote, ''Since he combines intellect with wit, his views make fast and easy reading, having for Americans all the fascination inherent in a chance to look over someone's shoulder and read private correspondence about ourselves.''

BIOGRAPHICAL/CRITICAL SOURCES: Christian Science Monitor, December 6, 1958.

* * *

HASAN, Saiyid Zafar 1930-

PERSONAL: Born July 5, 1930, in Gopalipur, India; son of Saiyid Akhtar (a civil servant) and Alia (Khatoon) Hasan; married Nuzhat Ara, November 3, 1961; children: Shirin, Simin, Akbar, Jafar. *Education:* University of Lucknow, B.A. (honors), 1948, M.A., LL.B., 1949, diploma in social services, 1950; Columbia University, M.S.S.W., 1955, D.S.W., 1958. *Religion:* Islam. *Home:* 1315 Beulah Park, Lexington, Ky. 40502. *Office:* Department of Social Work, University of Kentucky, Lexington, Ky. 40506.

CAREER: University of Lucknow, Lucknow, India, research assistant, 1950-51, lecturer, 1951-54, reader, 1958-65, professor of social work and head of department of sociology and social work, 1965-71; University of Kentucky, Lexington, 1971—, began as visiting professor, became professor of social work. *Member:* National Association of Social Workers, American Society for Public Administration, Council on Social Work Education, Indian Association of Trained Social Workers (life member). *Awards, honors:* United Nations social welfare scholarship to the United States, 1954.

WRITINGS: Federal Grants and Public Assistance: A Study of Policies and Programmes in the U.S.A. and India, Kitab Mahal, 1963; (contributor) Shirley Jenkins, editor,

Social Security in International Perspective, Columbia University Press, 1969; (contributor) V. B. Singh, editor, *Labour Research in India,* Prakashan, 1970; (contributor) G. C. Hallen and R. P. Saksena, editors, *Half a Century of Sociology in India,* Satish Book Enterprise, 1970; (editor and contributor) *Research in Sociology and Social Work,* Department of Sociology and Social Work, University of Lucknow, 1971; (author of foreword) G. R. Madan, *Social Change and Problems of Development in India,* Allied Publishers Private Ltd., 1971; (author of foreword) Brij Mohan, *India's Social Problems: Analyzing Basic Issues,* Indian International Publications, 1972; (author of foreword) Surendra Singh, *Indian Industrial Labour* (in Hindi), Upper India Publishing House, 1972; (author of foreword) Kirpal Singh Soodan, *Aging in India,* Minnerva Associates Publishers, 1975. Contributor to *Encyclopedia of Social Work in India.* Contributor of about twenty-five articles and reviews to sociology and social work journals.

WORK IN PROGRESS: Research on social policy, in the areas of income maintenance, corrections, and minorities.

SIDELIGHTS: Hasan writes that his inspiration comes from Indian and American scholars, including R. K. Mukerjee, B. Singh, Gardner Murphy, E. M. Burns, Nathan Cohen, and A. J. Kahn.

BIOGRAPHICAL/CRITICAL SOURCES: Indian Journal of Social Research, Volume XI, number 1, 1970.

*   *   *

HASSALL, Mark (William Cory)   1940-

PERSONAL: Born June 13, 1940, in Oxford, England; son of William Owen (a university librarian) and Averil (a teacher of art history; maiden name, Beaves) Hassall; married Catherine Ward-Perkins (a picture restorer), September 16, 1972. *Education:* Magdalen College, Oxford, B.A., 1963; Institute of Archaeology, London, diploma, 1965. *Politics:* "Utilitarian." *Religion:* "Humanism (informal)." *Home:* 25 Bewdley St., London N1 1HB, England. *Office:* Institute of Archaeology, University of London, 31-34 Gordon Sq., London WC1 HOPY, England.

CAREER: University of London, Institute of Archaeology, London, England, assistant lecturer, 1966-68, lecturer in archaeology of the Roman Empire, 1968—. *Member:* Society of Antiquaries, Royal Archaeological Institute (member of council, 1972-75), Society for the Promotion of Roman Studies (member of council, 1972-75), British Interplanetary Society. *Awards, honors:* Inherited the title of freeman of the City of Chester, 1973.

WRITINGS: The Romans, Putnam, 1971. Contributor to professional journals.

WORK IN PROGRESS: The Roman Frontier in Britain (tentative title), for Collins; research on Roman inscriptions (especially from England) and the Roman army.

SIDELIGHTS: Hassall writes: "Since my mother taught me to look for fossils and flint arrowheads I have been interested in the past. I think it's a worthwhile study now, because we'd be less than human if we didn't know where we came from and weren't interested in where we're going. Besides, when the technological utopia comes along we'll need something to amuse ourselves and archaeology is fun! I've excavated in Britain and Europe, Turkey and Libya, and visited sites in the Near East, and Central and South America."

AVOCATIONAL INTERESTS: Horseback riding, tracing his family tree, "putting on magic shows for my nephews and nieces."

HASSLER, Jon (Francis)   1933-

PERSONAL: Born March 30, 1933, in Minneapolis, Minn.; son of Leo Blaise (a grocer) and Ellen (a teacher; maiden name, Callinan) Hassler; married Marie Schmitt, August 18, 1956; children: Michael, Elizabeth, David. *Education:* St. John's University, Collegeville, Minn., B.A., 1955; University of North Dakota, M.A., 1960. *Religion:* Roman Catholic. *Residence:* Brainerd, Minn.

CAREER: High school English teacher in Melrose, Minn., 1955-56, Fosston, Minn., 1956-69, Park Rapids, Minn., 1959-65; Bemidji State University, Bemidji, Minn., instructor in English, 1965-68; Brainerd Community College, Brainerd, Minn., instructor in English, 1968—.

WRITINGS: Four Miles to Pinecone (novel for young adults), Warne, 1977; *Staggerford* (novel), Atheneum, 1977. Contributor of short stories to literary journals.

WORK IN PROGRESS: The Maiden, a novel for young adults.

SIDELIGHTS: Hassler comments: "At the age of six I began to think of myself as a writer. At the age of thirty-seven I began to write. Now after seven years of constant writing (and after eighty-five rejection slips) I have the good fortune to see two of my novels published almost simultaneously. Since I was a year old, I have lived in Minnesota small towns, so it's no wonder that most of my fiction focuses on small-town culture, particularly the various gaps and bridges between the young and the old."

AVOCATIONAL INTERESTS: "Landscapes (gazing at them, walking through them, and painting pictures of them)."

*   *   *

HASTINGS, Robert Paul   1933-

PERSONAL: Born October 27, 1933, in Birmingham, England; son of Robert (a railway employee) and Ethel Mary (a teacher; maiden name, Pretty) Hastings; married Olive Mary Richardson (a teacher), October 24, 1964; children: Robert. *Education:* University of Birmingham, B.A. (honors), 1954, certificate, 1956, M.A., 1959. *Home:* 11 North Side, Green, Hutton Rudby, Yarm, North Yorkshire, England. *Office:* Department of History, Middletown St. George College of Education, near Darlington, County Durham, England.

CAREER: History master at comprehensive schools in Birmingham, England, 1956-66; Hereford College of Education, Hereford, England, lecturer in history, 1966-68; Middleton St. George College of Education, near Darlington, England, principal lecturer in history and head of department, 1968—, Part-time lecturer at University of Birmingham, 1960-63, 1967-68, University of Durham, 1971-72, University of Leeds, 1972—. Governor of Hurworth Comprehensive School and Egglescliffe Comprehensive School, 1970—. Parish councillor, 1976—. *Member:* Society of Authors, Durham County Local History Society, Cleveland and Teesside Local History Society, Hutton Rudby Local History Society.

WRITINGS: (With V. H. T. Skipp) *Discovering Bickenhill: The History of a North Warwickshire Parish* (booklet), Extra-Mural Department, University of Birmingham, 1963; *Between the Wars,* Benn, 1968; *The Cold War,* Benn, 1969; *Railroads: An International History,* Praeger, 1972; *Medicine: An International History,* Praeger, 1974; (contributor) Jeffrey Skelley, editor, *The General Strike,* Lawrence & Wishart, 1976. General editor of "Industries and Inventions

Series," for Benn. Contributor to regional history journals. Editor of bulletin of Durham County Local History Society, 1972—.

WORK IN PROGRESS: Books on poverty and its treatment in the north riding of Yorkshire, 1780-1850, on the Birmingham Labour movement, 1900-1945, on Chartism in north Yorkshire and south Durham, 1938-39, and on the north Yorkshire linen industry.

SIDELIGHTS: Hastings comments that his principal interests are British local and regional history, particularly of the eighteenth and nineteenth centuries, British Labour history, Victorian studies, and contemporary world history. *Avocational interests:* Archaeology.

* * *

HATHAWAY, William 1944-

PERSONAL: Born December 18, 1944, in Madison, Wis.; son of Baxter L. (a professor) and Sherry (an art gallery owner; maiden name, Kitchen) Hathaway; married Dixie Blaszek (a store manager), February 28, 1966; children: Jesse, Nathaniel, Susanne. *Education:* Attended American College in Paris and Cornell University; University of Montana, B.A., 1967; University of Iowa, M.F.A., 1969. *Home:* 2101 Hollydale, Baton Rouge, La. 70808. *Office:* Allen Hall, Louisiana State University, Baton Rouge, La. 70803.

CAREER: Cornell University, Ithaca, N.Y., instructor in English, 1969-70; Louisiana State University, Baton Rouge, assistant professor of English, 1970—. *Member:* Associated Writing Programs.

WRITINGS: True Confessions and False Romances (poetry), Ithaca House, 1971; *A Wilderness of Monkeys* (poetry), Ithaca House, 1975. Contributor of poems to literary journals.

WORK IN PROGRESS: The Gymnast of Inertia, a book of poems.

SIDELIGHTS: Hathaway writes: "My poems are generally 'accessible' poems about interpersonal relations and travel. I work in both closed and open forms and I like to read poetry aloud. I am less interested in the confessional mode than I used to be, but that element will always be there."

* * *

HATTWICK, Richard E(arl) 1938-

PERSONAL: Born January 23, 1938, in Chicago, Ill.; son of Melvin S. (a business executive) and La Berta (a psychologist; maiden name, Weiss) Hattwick; married Maria de Nazareth Toledo Lobato, August 10, 1963; children: Philip, Patricia. *Education:* Ohio Wesleyan University, B.A., 1960; Vanderbilt University, Ph.D., 1963. *Politics:* Republican. *Religion:* Methodist. *Home:* 20 Indian Trail Rd., Macomb, Ill. 61455. *Office:* Center for Business and Economic Research, Western Illinois University, Macomb, Ill. 61455.

CAREER: University of Houston, Houston, Tex., assistant professor, 1963-69; Western Illinois University, Macomb, associate professor, 1969-74, professor of economics, 1974—, director of Center for Business and Economic Research, 1969—. President of Illinois Business Hall of Fame. *Member:* American Economic Association, American Association for the Advancement of Science, Macomb Area Chamber of Commerce (member of board of directors), Phi Beta Kappa.

WRITINGS: (With Bernard Brown and Joe Sailors) *De-*

mand, *Supply and the Market Mechanism,* Prentice-Hall, 1972; (with David Beveridge, James Niss, Mike Pledge, and others) *The New Illinois Method of Forecasting Job Opportunities for Graduates of Local Vocational Education Programs,* Center for Business and Economic Research, Western Illinois University, 1976. Author of scripts for slide presentations.

WORK IN PROGRESS: The Economics of Corporate Strategic Planning; Profiles of Business Courage: Biographical Sketches of the Members of the Illinois Business Hall of Fame; research on the economic aspects of perinatal health care.

* * *

HAVENS, George R(emington) 1890-1977

August 25, 1890—September 28, 1977; American author, editor, and authority on eighteenth-century thought and literature, Havens's books include *The Age of Ideas.* He died in Columbus, Ohio. Obituaries: *New York Times,* October 4, 1977. (See index for *CA* sketch)

* * *

HAWKINS, Jim 1944-

PERSONAL: Born June 1, 1944, in Superior, Wis.; son of Lawrence A. (a laborer) and Edna (Grinnell) Hawkins; married Penelope Johnson (an artist), September 4, 1965; children: Leslie, Mark. *Education:* University of Wisconsin, Madison, B.A., 1966. *Residence:* West Bloomfield, Mich. *Agent:* Zander Hollander, 370 Lexington, New York, N.Y. 10017. *Office: Detroit Free Press,* 321 West Lafayette, Detroit, Mich. 48231.

CAREER: Wilmington News-Journal, Wilmington, Del., sportswriter, 1966-67; *Baltimore Evening Sun,* Baltimore, Md., sportswriter, 1968-69; *Detroit Free Press,* Detroit, Mich., baseball writer, 1970—, also author of column "Jim Hawkins." *Member:* Baseball Writers Association of America. *Awards, honors:* Named sportswriter of the year by National Sportscaster and Sportswriters Association, 1969.

WRITINGS: (With Jim Benagh) *Go Bird Go,* Dell, 1976; *Breakout,* Harper, 1978.

Anthologized in *Best Sports Stories,* 1970, 1972-75. Correspondent for *Sporting News.* Contributor to popular magazines, including *True, Popular Sports,* and *Young Athlete.*

SIDELIGHTS: Hawkins writes that he began covering the Detroit Tigers at age twenty-five, and was the youngest regular baseball writer in the United States.

* * *

HAWKS, Howard (Winchester) 1896-1977

May 30, 1896—December 26, 1977; American film director and screenwriter. Among his best known films were "Sergeant York," "Only Angels Have Wings," "To Have and Have Not," "I Was a Male War Bride," and "Rio Lobo." In 1924 he wrote the script for the film "Tiger Love." Hawks was awarded an honorary Oscar in 1975. He died in Palm Springs, Calif. Obituaries: *New York Times,* December 28, 1977.

* * *

HAWKSWORTH, Henry D. 1933-

PERSONAL: Born March 12, 1933, in Oakland, Calif.; son of Arthur Henry and Kathleen (Williams) Hawksworth; married Ann M. McPhee, September 11, 1954; children:

Linda, Dave, Scott. *Education:* Attended high school in California. *Politics:* "Libertarian." *Religion:* "Mystical." *Home and office address:* P.O. Box 219, Brookdale, Calif. 95007.

CAREER: General manager of an appliance store in Calif., 1954-60; district manager for a life insurance company in Calif., 1960-65; general manager of a department store in Calif., 1973-75; writer, 1975—. *Military service:* U.S. Marine Corps, 1951-54; became sergeant; received Bronze Star Medal. *Member:* American Society of Writers.

WRITINGS: (With Ted Schwartz) *The Five of Me: The Autobiography of a Multiple Personality,* Regnery, 1977. Contributor of poems to literary magazines.

WORK IN PROGRESS: The Second Coming of H.H.; The Crisis Ward; Reverend Helen.

SIDELIGHTS: Hawksworth comments: "Because of my years of mental illness and unusual psychic experiences, I feel well-equipped to write on both subjects. It is also my desire to inform the readers, in lay words, of what's happening in the world of the 'mind doctors.'"

*   *   *

HAYDEN, Naura   1942-

PERSONAL: Born September 29, 1942, in Los Angeles, Calif.; daughter of John E. (a newspaperman) and N. Elizabeth (Bussins) Hayden; married Theodore Geiser (an attorney), June 4, 1975. *Education:* Attended University of California at Los Angeles and Berkeley. *Religion:* "Believer in Love." *Agent:* Julian Bach, 3 East 48th St., New York, N.Y. 10017.

CAREER: Actress, singer, and writer on health. *Member:* International Academy of Preventive Medicine (honorary fellow).

WRITINGS: The Hip, High-Prote, Low-Cal, Easy-Does-It Cookbook, Dodd, 1973; *Everything You've Always Wanted to Know About Energy But Were Too Weak to Ask,* Hawthorn, 1976.

SIDELIGHTS: "My profession is acting and singing, both of which I love to do," Hayden told *CA,* "but I also love to write books, write music, make television appearances as a personality, come up with business ideas, and turn people on to health! I have enormous energy and love to use it constructively. I have a new record album out titled 'And Then She Wrote,' and I will be starring in an Off-Broadway musical, 'Be Kind to People Week,' in 1978. I have also completed a movie in which I star, 'The Perils of P. K.'"

BIOGRAPHICAL/CRITICAL SOURCES: People, May 30, 1977.

*   *   *

HEIM, Ralph Daniel   1895-

PERSONAL: Born September 26, 1895, in Pickaway County, Ohio; son of Emanuel and Hattie (Dumond) Heim; married Leona Kuhlman, August 20, 1927; children: Paul, Martha (Mrs. Arrigo Raho). *Education:* Wittenberg College, A.B., 1919, M.A., 1923; studied at Chicago Lutheran Theological Seminary, 1919-20, and Chicago Lutheran Divinity School, 1920-21; Hamma Divinity School, B.D., 1923; University of Chicago, additional study, 1926; Northwestern University, Ph.D., 1929. *Politics:* Democrat. *Home:* 130 South Hay St., Gettysburg, Pa. 17325.

CAREER: Ordained minister of Lutheran Church, Ohio Synod, 1923; associate pastor in Chicago, Ill., 1923-26; Thiel

College, Greenville, Pa., professor of Bible and religion, 1927-32, dean of men, 1929-31; Hartwick College, Oneonta, N.Y., professor of religion and religious education, 1932-39, dean of the college, 1934-39; Lutheran Theological Seminary, Gettysburg, Pa., professor of Christian education and English Bible, 1939-68, registrar, 1940-52. Visiting professor, Garrett Theological Seminary, 1956. Lecturer in India and Japan, 1958, in Europe, Africa, Australia, and South America, 1962. Member of board of publication, United Lutheran Church, 1946-58; member of North American Committee, World Council of Christian Education, 1949—, and Commission on General Christian Education, National Council of Churches of Christ. Participant in World Institutes on Christian Education in Canada, 1950, Japan, 1958, and Ireland, 1962. *Military service:* U.S. Navy, 1917-18. *Member:* Religious Education Association (member of board of directors, 1958—), Royal Philatelic Society (London; fellow), Phi Delta Kappa, Torch Club. *Awards, honors:* D.D., Wittenberg College, 1948.

WRITINGS: A Harmony of the Gospels, for Students (revised standard version), Muhlenberg Press, 1947; *Leading a Sunday Church School,* Muhlenberg Press, 1950, published as *Leading a Church School,* Fortress, 1968; *Youth's Companion to the Bible,* Muhlenberg Press, 1959; (contributor) Marvin J. Taylor, editor, *Religious Education: A Comprehensive Survey,* Abingdon, 1960; (editor with Howard N. Bream, Elizabeth Achtemeier and others), *A Light Unto My Path: Old Testament Studies in Honor of Jacob M. Myers,* Temple University Press, 1974; *Reader's Companion to the Bible,* Fortress, 1975.

Workbooks: *Workbook for Old Testament Study,* Nelson, 1938; *Workbook for New Testament Study,* Ronald, 1948. Author of other curriculum materials, booklets, and leader guides. Contributor to *Westminster Dictionary of Christian Education,* 1963, *The Encyclopedia of the Lutheran Church,* 1965. Also contributor to *Lutheran* and other church periodicals. Chairman of editorial council, *Lutheran Quarterly,* 1960-64.

AVOCATIONAL INTERESTS: Gardening, philately, photography, and music.

*   *   *

HEIMBERG, Marilyn Markham   1939-

PERSONAL: Born November 3, 1939, in San Diego, Calif.; daughter of Glenn J. (a businessman) and Dorothy (a real estate broker; maiden name, Scudder) Markham; married T. M. Ross; children: Scott, Steve, Kevin, Laurie. *Education:* Attended San Diego State University. *Home:* 1340 Tourmaline St., San Diego, Calif. 92109.

CAREER: San Diego-South Bay Trade Schools, San Diego, Calif., director of marketing, 1969-74; marketing consultant, advertising copywriter, and writer, 1974—. Instructor, San Diego Community College District, 1975-77. Member of board of directors of Research Electronics Co. *Member:* National Federation of Press Women, National Genealogical Society. *Awards, honors:* First place in nonfiction from Southern Division of California Press Women, 1977, for "Business Bites Back at Internal Crime."

WRITINGS: Discover Your Roots: A New, Easy Guide for Tracing Your Family Tree, Communication Creativity, 1977. Ghost writer and editor. Contributor to over fifteen magazines, including *Essence, National Enquirer, Coronet, Catholic Digest,* and *Westways.* Editor of "People in Motion" (company newsletter), 1971-74.

WORK IN PROGRESS: Creative Loafing: A Shoestring Guide to New Leisure Fun.

SIDELIGHTS: Heimberg writes: "To me, communication is a vital facet of life. It is the catalyst that helps us understand ourselves and others better. I hope to use the written word to enlighten and entertain on a broad scope. It is important to me that others be encouraged to enjoy the abundance in life that I have discovered. My major interests are continuing personal growth and actualization and perpetuating a beautiful marriage relationship. I enjoy ideas, people, nature, any creative pursuit."

* * *

HEINZERLING, Larry E(dward) 1945-

PERSONAL: Born August 28, 1945, in Elyria, Ohio; son of Lynn Louis (a journalist) and Agnes (Dengate) Heinzerling; married Sharyn Jorgensen, January 11, 1969; children: Jesse, Kristen. *Education:* Ohio Wesleyan University, B.A., 1967; Ohio State University, M.A., 1968. *Religion:* Catholic. *Home:* 11 Primrose Dr., Victory Park, Johannesburg, South Africa. *Office:* Associated Press, 52 Simmonds St., Johannesburg, South Africa.

CAREER/WRITINGS: Plain Dealer, Cleveland, Ohio, newsman, 1966-67; Associated Press, New York, N.Y., intern newsman in Lagos, Nigeria, 1968, newsman in Columbus, Ohio, 1969-71, correspondent in Lagos, 1971-74, chief of Johannesburg, South Africa bureau, 1974—. Notable assignments include the West African draught, 1972-74, Angolan Civil War, 1975, the Soweto riots, 1976, and guerilla war in Rhodesia. Instructor in journalism, Ohio Wesleyan University, 1968-69. *Member:* Sigma Delta Chi. *Awards, honors:* Headliners Award, 1976, for coverage of Africa.

SIDELIGHTS: Heinzerling told *CA:* "Africa is a writer's dream. It is still an emerging continent, politically, economically, and technologically. What is left of the colonial era in southern Africa will be a source of news for years to come, a problem of fascinating complexity for those reporting it and tragic for those it involves of all races.

"Covering Africa means interviewing a variety of people from urban government leaders with an education at Harvard, Oxford or the Sorbonne or illiterate villagers. I prefer the villagers who are unfailingly kind and helpful and usually somewhat amazed that a foreign correspondent takes more interest in their problems than their own government. Government officials in Africa rarely tolerate a free press in their own country and prefer in general to avoid the scrutiny of foreign newsmen.

"I have visited over thirty of Africa's forty-nine independent states on behalf of Associated Press and read widely about the continent."

* * *

HELD, Jacqueline 1936-

PERSONAL: Born May 27, 1936, in Poitiers, France; daughter of Raymond (a teacher) and Simone (a teacher; maiden name, Gazeau) Bonneau; married Claude Held (a poet and teacher), March 25, 1961; children: Luc, Pascale, Veronique. *Education:* Sorbonne, University of Paris, licence and secondary teaching certificate (C.A.P.E.S.), 1958. *Home:* Les Tertres, 45800 Boigny-sur-Bionne, France.

CAREER: Taught philosophy and child psychology in Laon, France, 1960-67; teacher of psychology and juvenile literature in Orleans, France, 1967—. Member of Board of Administration of Centre de recherche et d'information sur la litterature pour la jeunesse (research and information center for children's literature), 1973—. *Awards, honors:* Television prize of juvenile literature, 1970; Best Book Award from "Loisirs Jeunes" for *Poiravechiche,* 1973, and *Le Navire d'Ika,* 1975.

WRITINGS—Juvenile: *Patatou, l'hippopotame* (title means "Patatou the Hippopotamus"), Dupuis, 1970; *Le Chat de Simulombula* (title means "The Cat of Simulombula"), Harlin Quist, 1970; *Les Piquants d'Arsinoe* (title means "Arsinoe's Prickles"), Magnard, 1970; *La Tortue pattue, trapue, ventrue, barbue* (title means "The Fat Squat Bearded Tortoise"), Dessain & Tolra, 1971; *Jil et Jacinthe a la mer* (title means "Jil and Jacinthe at the Sea"), Dessain & Tolra, 1972; *Jil et Jacinthe au cirque* (title means "Jil and Jacinthe at the Circus"), Dessain & Tolra, 1972; *Jil et Jacinthe au zoo* (title means "Jil and Jacinthe at the Zoo"), Dessain & Tolra, 1972; *Le Pommier des Perloupette* (title means "The Perloupettes' Apple-Tree"), L'Ecole des Loisirs, 1972; *Le Lion de Bouddha* (title means "The Lion of Buddha"), L'Ecole des Loisirs, 1973; *Arsinoe et Mr. Printemps* (title means "Arsinoe and Mr. Spring"), Magnard, 1973; *La Part du vent* (title means "This Side of the Wind"), Duculot, 1974; *Le Navire d'Ika* (title means "Ika's Ship"), La Farandole, 1974.

Petipaton le garcon-poisson, Flammarion, 1975, published as *Fabian, the Fish-Boy,* Addison-Wesley, 1976; *Objet volant non identifie* (title means "Unidentified Flying Object"), La Farandole, 1975; *La Tortue, le hamster, le chat, la lune, et la television* (title means "The Turtle, the Hamster, the Cat, the Moon, and the Television"), La Farandole, 1975; *Mais ou est donc Arsinoe?* (title means "But Where Then is Arsinoe?"), Magnard, 1976; *Teddy-douce-oreille* (title means "Sweety-Ear Teddy"), Magnard, 1976; *Les Enfants d'Aldebaran* (title means "The Children of Aldebaran"), La Farandole, 1976; *Dikidi et la sagesse, antifables* (title means "Dikidi and Wisdom, Antifables"), Delarge-Ruy Vidal, 1976; (with husband, Claude Held) *Le Chat qui n'etait pas botte* (title means "The Cat That Had No Boots"), Oeuvre Suisse, 1976; *La Voiture-baobab* (title means "The Baobab-Automobile"), Duculot, 1977; *Le journal de Manou* (title means "Manou's Diary"), Hatier-Bibliotheque de l'Amitie, 1977; *L'Imaginaire au pouvoir: Les Enfants et la litterature fantastique* (title means "For a Rising Power of Imagination: Children and Fantasy Literature"), Editions Ouvrieres, 1977.

Books of poems with husband, Claude Held: *Poiravechiche (Les Legumes)* (title means "About Vegetables"), Grasset, 1973; *Hamster rame* (title means "Mr. Hamster Rows"), L'Ecole des Loisirs, 1974; *Lune vole* (title means "The Moon Flies"), L'Ecole des Loisirs, 1976.

Contributor to *Cricket* magazine.

WORK IN PROGRESS: Several manuscripts in collaboration with her husband, Claude Held, including poems, fantastic tales, three short science fiction novels, and a play entitled "The Other Man of Starros."

SIDELIGHTS: Held writes: "Inside the literary field for the young, I feel spontaneously attracted by the poetic and fantastic trends. Writing in the twentieth century for children of the twentieth century, I try to point out the possibilities of strangeness and dream that lie constantly under the most obvious elements of everyday life: the telephone, the car, the fridge, the plane. . . . Such dream is no evasion but, on the contrary, a way of rediscovering the world, a way of taking possession of it."

HELLER, Jean 1942-

PERSONAL: Born October 14, 1942, in Warren, Ohio; daughter of Robert N. (an attorney) and Dorothy (a teacher; maiden name, Schetzer) Heller; married Preston R. Stevens (a journalist), May 2, 1971. Education: Attended University of Michigan, 1960-62; Ohio State University, B.A., 1964. Home: 10208 Carol St., Great Falls, Va. 22066. Office: Newsday, Suite 304, 1750 Pennsylvania Ave. N.W., Washington, D.C. 20006.

CAREER/WRITING: Associated Press, New York, N.Y., general assignment reporter, 1964-67, investigative reporter in Washington, D.C., 1967-74; Cox Newspapers, Washington, D.C., investigative reporter, 1974-76; Newsday, Washington, D.C., investigative and political reporter, 1976—. Notable assignments include coverage of the Tuskegee syphilis study, every national political convention since 1968, and the 1976 U.S. presidential campaign. Awards, honors: Worth Bingham Prize, 1968, for general investigative reporting; Polk Award, Clapper Award, and Robert F. Kennedy Memorial Award, all 1972, all for Tuskegee study disclosures.

*   *   *

HELLMAN, Geoffrey T(heodore) 1907-1977

February 13, 1907—September 26, 1977; American writer. Hellman contributed humorous profiles to New Yorker for nearly fifty years. He died in New York, N.Y. Obituaries: Time, October 10, 1977; Newsweek, October 10, 1977; AB Bookman's Weekly, January 30, 1978. (See index for CA sketch)

*   *   *

HELMER, William J(oseph) 1936-
(Horace Naismith)

PERSONAL: Born March 6, 1936, in Iowa City, Iowa; son of Albert Joseph and Myrtle (Curl) Helmer; married Pat Thompson, September, 1958 (divorced, 1966); married Jean Brockman (a free-lance illustrator), August 6, 1971; children: Marc, Jan. Education: University of Texas, B.J., 1959, M.A., 1968. Politics: "Fanatically moderate libertarian." Religion: None. Home: 726 South Blvd., Evanston, Ill. 60202. Office: Playboy, 919 North Michigan, Chicago, Ill. 60611.

CAREER: Worked as editor of several men's, trade, and special interest magazines, including Escapade, Aramco World, and True West, 1959-63; University of Texas, Austin, supervisor of student magazines, 1965-66; National Commission on the Causes and Prevention of Violence, Washington, D.C., staff member, 1968-69; Playboy, Chicago, Ill., senior editor, 1969—. Military service: U.S. Naval Reserve, 1953-61; became radioman first class. Member: John Dillinger Died for You Society, Discordian Society, Bavarian Illuminati. Awards, honors: Named honorary deputy sheriff of Travis County, Tex., 1964.

WRITINGS: The Gun That Made the Twenties Roar: A Social History of the Thompson Submachine Gun, Macmillan, 1969. Contributor of articles (including humor, under pseudonym Horace Naismith) to popular magazines, including Harper's, Texas Observer, Texas Monthly, and Playboy.

SIDELIGHTS: Helmer comments: "I got into and have remained in writing, editing and journalism mainly because I never figured out another way to make a living. I'd much rather be a fireman, but I'm past the age limit. I confess to an impulse to do good things for mankind, to dispel ignorance and combat stupidity, but I recognize this as a neurotic personal need and a waste of time."

*   *   *

HELOISE
See REESE, Heloise (Bowles)

*   *   *

HELPERN, Milton 1902-1977

PERSONAL: Born April 17, 1902, in New York City; son of Moses (a businessman) and Bertha (Toplon) Helpern; married Ruth Vyner, 1927 (marriage terminated, 1953); married Beatrice Leibowitz Nightingale (an executive), January 1, 1955; children: Nancy (Mrs. Edward Moldover), Susan (Mrs. Paul Nettler), Alice, William (stepson), Stuart (stepson). Education: College of the City of New York (now City College of the City University of New York), B.S., 1922; Cornell University, M.D., 1926. Politics: "No specialty in politics." Religion: Jewish. Home: 303 East 57th St., New York, N.Y. 10022.

CAREER: Bellevue Hospital, New York, N.Y., intern, 1927-29, resident and assistant pathologist, 1929-31; Cornell University, Ithaca, N.Y., lecturer in legal medicine, 1932-35; New York University, New York City, assistant professor, 1935-49, associate professor, 1949-54, professor of forensic medicine and chairman of department, 1954-74, professor emeritus, 1974-77, adjunct professor, 1963-77, founder of Institute of Forensic Medicine, 1968, director, 1968-77. Licensed in New York, 1926; diplomate of National Board of Medical Examiners, 1929; certified by American Board of Pathology in pathologic anatomy, 1938, and forensic pathology, 1959. Lecturer at Cornell University, 1935-77, assistant clinical professor, 1940-67, visiting professor, 1966-74, professor emeritus, 1975-77; honorary lecturer at University of Southern California, 1953-68, emeritus lecturer, 1968-77; visiting professor at South Carolina Medical College, 1969-77, and Korea University, 1974-77; distinguished visiting professor at City College of the City University of New York, 1974-77. City of New York, assistant medical examiner, 1931-43, deputy chief, 1943-54, chief medical examiner, 1954-74, consultant, 1974. Hospital for Special Surgery, acting director of laboratories, 1941-45, director, 1945-58, consultant, 1958-68, chief of pathology emeritus, 1968-74, honorary chief of pathology, 1974-77. Vice-president of International Congress of Legal Medicine and Social Medicine of the French Language, 1966-74; member of board of trustees of Milton Helpern Library of Legal Medicine, 1962-77, and Forensic Sciences Foundation, Inc., 1972-73; member of board of directors of Hebrew University's Hadassah Medical School, 1958-70, State of New York Athletic Commission, 1965-76, Godfrey Nurse Fund, 1965-77 (chairman, 1975-77), National Foundation for Sudden Infant Death, 1967-71, Guild for Infant Survival, Inc., 1967-77, Foundation for the Advancement of Medical Knowledge, 1969-77, Andrew Menchell Infant Survival Foundation, 1969-77, Collectors' Editions-Medecina Rara, 1970-73, National Foundation for the March of Dimes, 1970-77, Alcoholism Recovery Institute, 1972-74, City College's Center for Biomedical Education, 1973-77, National Council on Alcoholism, 1974-77 (member of executive committee, 1975), and Medical Liability Mutual Insurance Co., 1976-77. Consultant to Armed Forces Institute of Pathology, Federal Aviation Agency, and U.S. Department of Justice. Military service: U.S. Army Air Forces, Aero-Medical Laboratory, 1943-45; served in England.

MEMBER: International Association for Accident and Traffic Medicine (member of New York City founding committee, 1960; president, 1966-69), International Academy of Legal Medicine and Social Medicine (vice-president, 1961-70), International College of Surgeons (fellow), American Academy of Compensation Medicine (fellow; president, 1961-65, 1976—), American Academy of Forensic Sciences (fellow; member of founding committee, 1949; president, 1962-63), National Association of Medical Examiners (founder; president, 1968-70; member of board of directors, 1970), Society of Medical Jurisprudence (member of board of trustees, 1955—; president, 1965-67), American College of Legal Medicine (fellow), American Heart Association (fellow), American Medical Association (fellow), American Society of Clinical Pathologists (fellow), College of American Pathologists (fellow), National Association for Prevention of Addiction to Narcotics (member of board of trustees, 1961-74), World Medical Association. Honorary member of more than fifteen national and international organizations, including Mystery Writers of America and American Society of Forensic Odontology. Member of more than fifteen state and local medical organizations. Phi Beta Kappa (vice-president, 1975-76; president of Gamma chapter, 1977), Alpha Omega Alpha. *Awards, honors:* Gold medals from University of Texas Law Sciences Institute and Foundation, 1958, Phi Lambda Kappa, 1964, and Virchow Medical Society, 1972; Raven Award from Mystery Writers of America, 1965; Redway Medal from *New York State Journal of Medicine,* 1966; special award from American Physicians Art Association, 1966; officer of Order of Leopold II of Belgium, 1968; silver medal from Oscar Freire Institute, 1968; award from American Medical Writers Association, 1969; Ward Burdick Award from American Society of Clinical Pathologists, 1972; LL.D. from University of Ghent, 1970, City College of the City University of New York, 1972, and New York Law School, 1976; D.Hum. from Pan American Medical Association, 1976; Milton Helpern Library of Legal Medicine, 1962, Milton Helpern International Center for Forensic Sciences in Wichita, Kan., 1974, and Milton Helpern Lectureship on International Forensic Sciences at Wichita State University, 1975, were all named in his honor.

WRITINGS: (With Thomas A. Gonzales and Morgan Vance) *Legal Medicine and Toxicology,* Appleton, 1937; (with Gonzalez, Vance, and Charles J. Umberger) *Legal Medicine, Pathology, and Toxicology,* Appleton, 2nd edition, 1954; (author of foreword) R. T. Long, *Physician and the Law,* Appleton, 1955; (contributor) Larry Alan Bear, editor, *Law, Medicine, Science, and Justice,* C. C Thomas, 1964; (author of introduction) Lawrence G. Blochman, *Clues for Dr. Coffee,* Lippincott, 1964; (contributor) C. W. M. Wilson, editor, *Adolescent Drug Dependence,* Pergamon, 1968; (author of foreword) Cyril H. Wecht, editor, *Legal Medicine Annual 1969,* Appleton, 1969; (author of foreword) Jaroslav Nemec, *International Bibliography of Medico-Legal Serials, 1736-1967,* National Library of Medicine, 1969; (contributor) C. George Tedeschi, editor, *Neuropathology: Methods and Diagnosis,* Little, Brown, 1970; (contributor) *Chemical and Biological Aspects of Drug Dependence,* C.R.C. Press, 1972; (contributor) Wolfram Keup, editor, *Drug Abuse: Current Concepts and Research,* C. C Thomas, 1972; (author of introduction) Vincent J. Fontana, *Somewhere a Child Is Crying,* Macmillan, 1973; (author of introduction) Paulette Cooper, *The Medical Detectives,* McKay, 1973; (author of foreword) Angela Roddey Holer, *Medical Malpractice Law,* Wiley, 1975; (author of foreword) C. G. Tedeschi, William Eckert, and Luke G.

Tedeschi, editors, *Forensic Medicine,* volumes I-III, Saunders, 1977; (with Bernard Knight) *Autopsy: Memoirs of Dr. Milton Helpern, the World's Greatest Medical Detective,* St. Martin's, 1977.

Contributor to *Atlas of Legal Medicine* and *Encyclopedia Americana.* Contributor of more than one hundred articles to medical journals. Editor of *International Microfilm Journal of Legal Medicine,* 1965-77, and *Zeitschrift fuer Rechtsmedizin: Journal of Legal Medicine,* 1969-77; associate editor of *Journal of Forensic Medicine,* 1964-71; member of editorial board of *General Practice* and *American Family Physician,* 1969-77, *Bulletin de Medecine Legale et de Toxicologic Medicale,* 1971-77, and *Journal of the Medical Society of the State of New York,* 1968-77; member of editorial advisory board of *Postgraduate Medicine,* 1954-68.

SIDELIGHTS: During Helpern's forty-year career as medical examiner for New York City he and his staff investigated approximately 34,000 deaths a year and performed over 80,000 autopsies. He was well-known as an expert prosecution witness, especially in the sensational murder trials of Carl Coppolino and Alice Crimmins in the 1960's. Other important investigative work by Helpern resulted in the disclosure of the cause of a malaria outbreak in New York City, and the discovery that faulty gas refrigerators leaking carbon monoxide were frequently the cause of death of people who were believed to have died of cerebral hemorrhages.

The textbook *Legal Medicine, Pathology, and Toxicology,* which he wrote with three others, is regarded as the definitive work in its field and is frequently consulted by mystery writers, although Helpern reportedly never read mystery fiction himself.

AVOCATIONAL INTERESTS: Photography, map collecting, and coin collecting.

BIOGRAPHICAL/CRITICAL SOURCES: Marshall Houts, *Where Death Delights,* Coward, 1967; Milton Helpern and Bernard Knight, *Autopsy: Memoirs of Milton Helpern, the World's Greatest Medical Detective,* St. Martin's, 1977.

OBITUARIES: *New York Times,* April 23, 1977; *Newsweek,* May 2, 1977; *Current Biography,* June, 1977.

(Died April 22, 1977, in San Diego, Calif.)

[Sketch verified by wife, Beatrice Helpern]

* * *

HEMINGWAY, Mary Welsh 1908-

PERSONAL: Born April 5, 1908, in Walker, Minn.; daughter of Thomas James (a lumberman) and Adeline (Beeler) Welsh; married Ernest Hemingway (a writer), March 21, 1946 (died July 2, 1961). *Education:* Attended Northwestern University, 1930. *Politics:* Liberal. *Religion:* Christian. *Residence:* New York City.

CAREER: *American Florist,* Chicago, Ill., editor, 1930-32; *Chicago Daily News,* Chicago, reporter, 1932-37; *London Daily Express,* London, England, reporter, 1937-40; Time, Inc., New York City, correspondnet in London bureau, 1940-45; writer, 1945—. *Member:* P.E.N., Overseas Press Club of America.

WRITINGS: *How It Was* (autobiography), Knopf, 1976. Also contributor to *I Can Tell It Now,* Dutton. Contributor of articles to magazines, including *Life, Look, Vogue, Saturday Review, Sports Illustrated,* and *Cosmopolitan.*

SIDELIGHTS: *How It Was* is Mary Welsh Hemingway's

autobiography and chronicle of her life with Ernest Hemingway. Mary Hemingway worked as a reporter before her marriage to Hemingway and "it is as a reporter that she has written this account of her life with Ernest; that is, she avoids speculation and editorializing," according to *Atlantic*. But V. S. Pritchett argued that in places her reporting is "rather too photographic in the how-it-was manner. . . . It is all very well for her to say that good reporting always implies or suggests the feelings involved. If it is self-effacing, yes; but that Mary Hemingway is not. Stoical, perhaps." *Newsweek* found the book marred by "fancy writing" and "whimsy." Vance Boujaily, however, spoke admirably about Mary Hemingway's writing, and cited one particularly well-written passage. He wrote that her account of the Hemingways' series of plane crashes in Africa and their effects on Ernest is "everything it should be: precise, vivid, stoic, harrowing, beautifully underwritten and immensely moving." In fact, he found it a better piece of writing than Hemingway's own published account.

The book is rich in the domestic detail of their marriage (Pritchett said the book "sounds like a brochure on a marriage on wheels"), and includes portions of Hemingway's previously unpublished letters to Mary. Some reviewers found themselves overwhelmed by this accretion of detail. Michael Malone commented on this problem, which he finds common to biographies of Hemingway. He said: "It is as if the sheer multiplicity of things in Hemingway's energetic and extroverted life (trips, sports, wars, wives, injuries, illnesses, heroines, quarrels, and conquests) so inundate his biographers that they lose perspective, and give us works as confusedly packed as his life was—with anecdotes, lists of camping equipment, snatches of dialogue, disconnected data. They seem to find the content of lived experience too large or too chaotic to find the form to fit it."

Bourjaily wrote that by the end of the chapter on the war and her courtship with Ernest, Mary Hemingway "stands as close beside the subject of her monument in its pages as she stood to him in life for 17 years of marriage, and it is as true now as it must have been during those 17 years that she adds to the celebrated figure the defining image of chosen partner in love-making, work, adversity, carousing, adventuring and sparring."

Mary Hemingway told *CA:* "It never occurred to me to write a book about my life until I had finished a piece about the blitz on London (1940-41) for a book published in the middle sixties by the Overseas Press Club of America, entitled *I Can Tell It Now*. It consisted of stories which various foreign correspondents could not send during World War II because of censorship. When the blitz story was finished, I realized there was much more to it than I'd written for the Overseas Press Club book. Also I remembered that *Vogue* had published a sketch I had written about my father in Minnesota. Both of these pieces had been fun to do. So, with no ultimate book specifically in mind, no deadline, no consultation with any publisher, I began filling in the gaps between my Minnesota childhood, a job on the *Chicago Daily News*, a switch to the *London Daily Express*, covering the Munich Agreement (1938) and the blitz on London, and simply went on from there.

"The diaries I'd been in the habit of keeping for years (so many days so exciting I couldn't bear not to record them) proved useful in confirming the accuracy of names, dates, and places. I still have fifteen to twenty of them beginning with my first crossing of the Atlantic by boat in 1936. The actual quotations I've used from them may amount to one one-hundredth of all their verbiage.

"The most difficult part of the book was that about Ernest's developing mental illness. I wanted it to be truthful but not clogged and befuddled with emotions, on the theory that the recording of the facts would signify the accompanying feelings to any perceptive reader."

BIOGRAPHICAL/CRITICAL SOURCES: Newsweek, September 27, 1976; *Saturday Review,* October 2, 1976; *Time,* October 18, 1976; *Esquire,* October, 1976; *New Yorker,* November 1, 1976; *Atlantic,* December, 1976; *Harper's,* December, 1976.

*   *   *

HEMINGWAY, Patricia Drake   1926-1978

November 29, 1926—January 11, 1978; American author and restaurateur. Hemingway died in New York, N.Y. Obituaries: *New York Times,* January 13, 1978. (See index for *CA* sketch)

*   *   *

HENDERSON, Laurance G.   1924(?)-1977

1924(?)—August 11, 1977; American housing and urban planning administrator and author. Henderson contributed to the reorganization plan establishing the Housing and Home Finance Agency and to the drafting of the 1949 Housing Act. His other professional positions included staff director of the Senate Small Business Committee and adviser to the Interior Department. He died in Washington, D.C. Obituaries: *Washington Post,* August 17, 1977.

*   *   *

HENDERSON, Thomas W(alter)   1949-

PERSONAL: Born June 5, 1949, in Jackson, Miss.; son of Thomas Walter (a clergyman) and Mildred Beatrice (Roberson) Henderson; married Tommye Corley (a teacher), March 25, 1972. *Education:* University of Southern Mississippi, B.A., 1971; Florida State University, M.S.L.S., 1975. *Politics:* Independent. *Religion:* United Methodist. *Home:* 515 Sycamore St., Starkville, Miss. 39759. *Office:* University Library, Mississippi State University, Box 5408, Mississippi State, Miss. 39762.

CAREER: Mississippi Department of Archives and History, Jackson, archivist, 1971-74; Mississippi State University, Mississippi State, librarian, 1975—. *Member:* American Library Association, Mississippi Library Association (member of Junior Members Roundtable), Mississippi Historical Society, Mississippi Genealogical Society, Phi Alpha Theta, Beta Phi Mu.

WRITINGS: (With Ronald E. Tomlin) *Guide to Official Records in the Mississippi Department of Archives and History,* Mississippi Department of Archives and History, 1975. Contributing editor, *Mississippi Genealogical Exchange.*

WORK IN PROGRESS: Index and introduction for Robert Lowry's *History of Mississippi.*

*   *   *

HENDRICKS, Gay   1945-

PERSONAL: Born January 20, 1945, in Leesburg, Fla.; son of Leonard G. (a farmer) and Norma (a writer; maiden name, Canaday) Hendricks; married Linda Fry, May 5, 1966 (divorced, 1972); children: Amanda Delle. *Education:* Rollins College, B.A., 1968; University of New Hampshire, M.Ed., 1970; Stanford University, Ph.D., 1974. *Office:*

School of Education, University of Colorado, Colorado Springs, Colo. 80907.

CAREER: Stanford University, Stanford, Calif., psychologist, 1973-74; University of Colorado, Colorado Springs, assistant professor of education, 1974—. *Member:* Association for Transpersonal Psychology.

WRITINGS: (With Russel Wills) *The Centering Book,* Prentice-Hall, 1975; (with James Fadiman) *Transpersonal Education,* Prentice-Hall, 1976; (with Thomas B. Roberts) *The Second Centering Book,* Prentice-Hall, 1977; (with Caral Leavenworth) *Living: A How-To Manual,* Prentice-Hall, in press.

WORK IN PROGRESS: On Being a Therapist.

SIDELIGHTS: Hendricks told *CA:* "In education and in psychotherapy, my writings attempt to develop a whole-person approach which unifies fact and feeling, cognitive and affective. The centering books contain activities to help people relax, meditate, get in touch with feeling, intuition and the mystical side of ourselves.

"Most of the information comes from my work as a therapist and teacher, as well as my own processes of personal unification."

* * *

HENISCH, Heinz K.   1922-
(Benjamin Spear)

PERSONAL: Born April 21, 1922, in Neudek, Germany; son of Leo (an attorney) and Fanny (Soycher) Henisch; married Bridget Ann Wilsher (a writer), February 6, 1960. *Education:* University of Bristol, B.Sc., 1940; University of Reading, B.Sc., 1942, Ph.D., 1949. *Home:* 346 West Hillcrest Ave., State College, Pa. 16801. *Office:* 249 Materials Research Laboratory, Pennsylvania State University, University Park, Pa. 16802.

CAREER: Royal Aircraft Establishment, Farnborough, England, junior scientific officer, 1942-46; University of Reading, Reading, England, lecturer in physics, 1948-62; Pennsylvania State University, University Park, professor of physics, 1963—, professor of the history of photography, 1974—, associate director of Materials Research Laboratory, 1968-75. Visiting scientist at Sylvania Electric Products, 1955-56; Samuel Newton Taylor Lecturer at Goucher College, 1973; lecturer at colleges and universities in Israel, Switzerland, Czechoslovakia, Romania, Peru, Venezuela, Mexico, Austria, and all over the United States, as well as on television. Co-director of exhibition "Beauty in Science: Science in Art" at Central Pennsylvania Festival of the Arts, 1973, 1974; has attended international conferences all over the world; has eight patents, all on various aspects of semiconductor technology. Member of Volunteers in Technical Assistance; member of scientific advisory board of Tem-Pres Research, Inc., 1966-70. Chairman of Pennsylvania State University Press committee, 1973-75. Consultant to Philco Corp., Polaroid Corp., Energy Conversion Devices, Inc., and Carborundum Co.

MEMBER: American Physical Society (fellow), Institute of Physics (fellow), Royal Photographic Society (fellow), Deutsche Gesellschaft fuer Photographie (corresponding member). *Awards, honors:* Honorary fellow of A74 Group of Photographers, Warsaw, 1975.

WRITINGS: Metal Rectifiers, Oxford University Press, 1949; (editor) *Semiconductor Materials,* Butterworth & Co., 1951; *Rectifying Semiconductor Contacts,* Oxford University Press, 1957; *Electroluminescence,* Pergamon, 1962; (editor with others) *Silicon Carbide,* Pergamon, 1969; *Crystal Growth in Gels,* Pennsylvania State University Press, 1970; (with wife, B. A. Henisch) *Chipmunk Portrait,* Carnation Press, 1970. Contributor to journals, sometimes under pseudonym Benjamin Spear. Editor of "International Series of Monographs on Semiconductors," Pergamon, 1959-67, and *History of Photography;* joint editor-in-chief of *Materials Research Bulletin;* member of editorial board of *Journal of the Physics of Chemical Solids,* 1957—, *Journal of Solid State Electronics,* 1958—, *Physica Status Solidi,* 1961-63, *Penn State Studies,* 1963-66, and *Progress in Crystal Growth and Assessment.*

WORK IN PROGRESS: Early Photography in Eastern Europe: First Exposure; Early Photography and Its Public; Semiconductor Contacts.

SIDELIGHTS: Henisch writes that he studies "science as an exercise in aesthetics, and science as literature." *Avocational interests:* Photography.

* * *

HENLE, Fritz   1909-

PERSONAL: Born June 9, 1909, in Dortmund, Germany; came to the United States in 1936, naturalized citizen, 1942; son of Adolf (a surgeon) and Tina (Lang) Henle; married Marguerite Williams, April 10, 1954; children: Jan, Maria, Christina, Martin. *Education:* Attended University of Heidelberg, 1929, University of Munich, 1930, and Staats-Lehranstalt fuer Lichtbildwesen, 1930-31. *Home address:* P.O. Box 723, Christiansted, St. Croix 00820, U.S. Virgin Islands. *Agent:* Photo-Editors, 60 East 56th St., New York, N.Y. 10022.

CAREER: Photographer and writer, 1931—. Photographer for *Life,* 1938-42. Work represented in private collections and at Museum of Modern Art; also exhibited in museums and galleries in the United States and Europe, and with Smithsonian Traveling Exhibition Service. *Wartime service:* U.S. Office of War Information, photographer, 1942-44. *Member:* International Center of Photography, Professional Photographers of America, Overseas Press Club of America, Society of Photographers in Communications (co-founder; past member of board of trustees), Academy of Arts and Letters (Virgin Islands). *Awards, honors:* Photography prizes include awards from *Popular Photography* and Art Directors Club of Philadelphia.

WRITINGS—With own photographs: *This Is Japan,* Heering Verlag, 1937; (author of introduction and captions) *Mexico,* Ziff-Davis, 1945; *Fritz Henle's Figure Studies,* Studio Publications, 1954; *Fritz Henle's Guide to Rollei Photography,* Studio Publications, 1956; (with P. E. Knapp) *The Caribbean: A Journey with Pictures,* Studio Publications, 1957; *With the Eyes of a Rollei Photographer,* Heering Verlag, 1964; *A New Guide to Rollei Photography,* Viking, 1965; *Fritz Henle* (memoirs, with introduction by Allen Porter and dedication by Pablo Casals), privately printed, 1973; (author of introduction and photographic essay) *Casals,* American Photographic Book Publishing, 1975.

Photographer: Kwok Ying Fung, *China,* Holt, 1943; Elliot Paul, *Paris,* Ziff-Davis, 1947; Norman Wright, *Hawaii,* Hastings House, 1948; Vivienne Winterry, *The Virgin Islands,* Hastings House, 1949; Winterry, *Fritz Henle's Rollei,* Hastings House, 1950; Mike Kinzer, *Photography for Everyone,* Viking, 1959; Anne Freemantle, *Holiday in Europe,* Viking, 1963.

Films: "Virgin Islands, U.S.A."; "The Trinidad Carnival''; (with Joffrey Holder) ''Shango'' (dance film); (with Holder) ''Yanvallou'' (dance film). Author of ''Twin Lens,'' a column in *Popular Photography*. Contributor of articles and photographs to photography journals and national magazines, including *Fortune, Harper's Bazaar,* and *Holiday*.

WORK IN PROGRESS: Life, showing the development of human relationships from early age to the faces of very old people, and showing the beauty of the human body.

SIDELIGHTS: Henle writes: ''Photography has fascinated me ever since I was a little boy and my father took the pictures of the family in the living room of our home in Dortmund. I built my first crude darkroom in the basement. It was the size of a telephone booth and it was put together with sheets of cardboard which I nailed against the wooden frame. A little red glass gave me the necessary light to watch the development of my films. The enlargements had to be done at night so that I was not disturbed by any daylight. This setup served me for many years. When I look at some of the photographs which were the result of my early efforts, I am amazed at how they have withstood time.

''I was never a slow student and I even managed to get a trip into my studies which took me to the Near East with the result of some of my pictures which since then have become well known, like 'The Pyramid.' These were still taken on a glass plate.

''After my studies in Munich, I found myself on my first job in Florence, Italy. I became acquainted with the treasures of the Renaissance in a most intimate way since many of my photographs demanded hour-long exposures. It was a beautiful experience and invaluable training.

''After finishing this assignment, I found myself on my way to India, where I met my Hindu friend, Narendra, and travelled all over this strangely beautiful country. The Far East, China, and Japan were my next steps. Both assignments resulted in extensive collections.

''After a brief stay in Germany in 1936, I accepted the assignment to photograph the United States with great pleasure. It was a fascinating time for a young European, and photography was greatly appreciated.

''In 1947 an assignment for *Holiday* brought me to the American Virgin Islands. In a way the islands reminded me of my trips to Hawaii and I liked them so much that I returned every winter, doing a lot of assignments in the sun of the Caribbean. I became intimately acquainted with practically all the islands in the Caribbean, especially Trinidad and its famous and incredibly colorful 'carnival.' The film I made in 1953, 'Trinidad Carnival,' helped to focus attention on this beautiful event. In 1958 I became a permanent resident of St. Croix.''

BIOGRAPHICAL/CRITICAL SOURCES: Popular Photography, November, 1964; *Modern Photography,* March, 1970.

* * *

HENRI, Florette 1908-
(Marjorie Winters)

PERSONAL: Born July 8, 1908, in New York, N.Y.; daughter of Louis Peine (a businessman) and Rachel (Goldstein) Holzgasser; married Raymond Henri (a Marine Corps colonel), May 14, 1935; children: Franklin D. *Education:* Barnard College, B.A., 1929; Columbia University, M.A., 1931. *Residence:* Centerport, N.Y.

CAREER: Staff editor of *Merit Students Encyclopedia,*

1961-65, and *Collier's Encyclopedia,* 1965-66; U.S. Information Agency, Washington, D.C., publications editor, 1968-71; writer, 1971—. *Member:* American Academy of Political and Social Science, Library of Congress (associate). *Awards, honors:* Maxwell Anderson Prize, 1935, for ''Surrey.''

WRITINGS: Kings Mountain (historical novel), Doubleday, 1950; (under pseudonym Marjorie Winters) *For Love of Martha,* Messner, 1956; (adapter) Marie Killilea, *Karen,* Noble & Noble, 1967; (adapter) Gordon Parks, *A Choice of Weapons,* Noble & Noble, 1967; *Bitter Victory: Black Soldiers in World War I* (juvenile), Doubleday, 1970; *George Mason of Virginia* (juvenile), Macmillan, 1971; (with Arthur Barbeau) *The Unknown Soldiers: Black American Troops in World War I,* Temple University Press, 1974; (contributor) *People and Culture,* Noble & Noble, 1974; *Black Migration: Movement North, 1900-1920,* Doubleday, 1975; *Tenants at Will: The Southwest Indians and Benjamin Hawkins,* Temple University Press, in press.

Plays: ''Surrey'' (tragedy in blank verse), first produced in Pasadena, Calif., at Pasadena Playhouse; ''The Sword of Gideon'' (historical drama), first produced in Kings Mountain National Park, summer, 1955. Contributor to *New Century Handbook of English Literature* and *Encyclopedia Americana*.

SIDELIGHTS: Henri told *CA:* ''While doing graduate work in English literature of the sixteenth century, I found my interest shifting from the purely literary to the historical interest of the period. Thenceforward, English and American history have been my major fields, and a growing sense of social commitment had led me to write historical studies of minority groups. I have lived in New York and Washington, D.C.; traveled in England, France, Switzerland, Italy, and Greece.

AVOCATIONAL INTERESTS: Cooking.

* * *

HEPWORTH, James Michael 1938-

PERSONAL: Born December 21, 1938, in Wakefield, England; son of James (a tax inspector) and Mary (Stockdale) Hepworth; married Marian Byewell (a television researcher), April 20, 1974; children: Rachel, Virginia. *Education:* University of Hull, B.A., 1961. *Home:* Rose Cottage, Whiterashes, Aberdeen AB5 0QP, Scotland. *Agent:* Curtis Brown Academic Ltd., 1 Craven Hill, London W2 3EP, England. *Office:* Department of Sociology, King's Cottage, University of Aberdeen, Old Aberdeen, Scotland.

CAREER: County Council of Warwickshire, Sutton Coldfield, England, assistant careers advisory officer, 1961-65; Sunderland Education Committee, Sunderland, England, assistant lecturer in social studies, 1965-66; Teeside Polytechnic, Middlesborough, England, lecturer in sociology, 1967-71; Lancaster Polytechnic, Coventry, England, senior lecturer in sociology, 1971; University of Aberdeen, Aberdeen, Scotland, lecturer in sociology, 1972—. *Member:* British Sociological Association, Socio-Legal Group, Crime Writers Association, Scottish Association for the Study of Delinquency.

WRITINGS: (Contributor) Stanley Cohen, editor, *Images of Deviance,* Penguin, 1971; (with others) *The Sociology of Deviance: A Bibliography,* National Deviancy Conference, 1973; (contributor) R. V. Bailey and J. Young, editors, *Contemporary Social Problems in Britain,* Saxon House, 1973; (contributor) Paul Rock and Mary McIntosh, editors, *Devi-*

ance and Social Control, Tavistock Publications, 1974; *Blackmail: Publicity and Secrecy in Everyday Life,* Routledge & Kegan Paul, 1975; (contributor) Herman Bianchi, editor, *Deviance and Control in Europe,* Wiley, 1975. Contributor of articles to *British Journal of Law and Society, International Journal of Criminology and Penology,* and other periodicals.

WORK IN PROGRESS: Murder Confessions, with Bryan Turner; *Confessing to Murder,* for Routledge & Kegan Paul; a revision of *Blackmail: Publicity and Secrecy in Everyday Life;* fiction.

SIDELIGHTS: Hepworth told *CA:* "My interest in crime began with an academic commitment to teaching a sociological approach to criminology. I am now returning to my earlier interest in crime fiction as a historical phenomenon and its relation to varying stages of social development. This is not to say that I see fiction as in some way totally buried beneath the weight of social determinism but rather as a creative and imaginative activity which can illuminate the darker aspects of criminal motivation (in particular I am thinking of murder and the more disturbing crimes of violence) sometimes as effectively as academic or forensic analysis. One of my major interests therefore is the comparative status of popular fiction as 'public knowledge' of criminal activity.

"My other current research interest is an investigation of the missing persons problem in the north east of England and its relationship to the so-called 'mid life crisis.'"

* * *

HERALD, George William 1911-

PERSONAL: Born January 3, 1911, in Berlin, Germany; came to the United States in 1941, naturalized citizen, 1943; son of Bruno H. and Paula (Levy) Herald; married Martha Alexandra Dubois, March 24, 1948; children: Steve Andrew, Patricia Claudia. *Education:* University of Basle, LL.D., 1934; also attended Columbia University, 1950-52. *Home:* 40 Rue de la Bienfaisance, Paris 8e, France. *Office: Vision,* 641 Lexington Ave., New York, N.Y. 10022.

CAREER: Paris correspondent for American and British newspapers, 1935-39; political writer for magazines, 1941-43; U.S. Embassy, London, England, intelligence officer, 1944-45; International News Service, New York City, staff European correspondent, 1945-46, bureau chief in Berlin, 1946-48, head of Vienna bureau, 1948-50; United Features, Inc., New York City, special writer and editor, 1950-52; *United Nations World,* New York City, European editor, 1952-54; *Vision,* New York City, chief of Paris bureau, 1953—. *Military service:* U.S. Army Air Forces, 1942-43. U.S. Army, Psychological Warfare Branch, 1944-45; became captain. *Member:* International Press Institute, Overseas Press Club of America, American Society of Journalists and Authors, Anglo-American Press Club (Paris).

WRITINGS: My Favorite Assassin, Vanguard, 1943; (with others) *Off the Record,* Doubleday, 1952; (with others) *The Double Dealers,* Lippincott, 1958; (with Soraya Esfandiary) *My Life as an Empress,* Doubleday, 1962; (with Edward Radin) *The Big Wheel,* Morrow, 1962; *Airlift: The Tale of the Berlin Blockade,* Springer, 1978. Author of "Tatiana," a film for CBS-TV, 1957. Contributor to *American People's Encyclopedia.* Contributor to popular magazines, including *Harper's, Reader's Digest, Coronet,* and *Reporter.*

WORK IN PROGRESS: My Wife Anastasia, with John Emanahan; *The Passion of Art Collecting,* with G. Jaeckel.

SIDELIGHTS: Herald comments: "Rightly or wrongly, I see myself as one of the world's genuine cosmopolitans in the same vein (though on a somewhat lower orbit) as Henry Kissinger, Willy Brandt, or Marlene Dietrich. I have written in English, French, and German, and am an inveterate traveler in the United States and Europe. My favorite countries, outside the United States, are Canada and Brazil, which I know well. But, in principle, I consider nation states totally outdated."

* * *

HERAUD, Brian J(eremy) 1934-

PERSONAL: Born October 21, 1934, in London, England. *Education:* London School of Economics and Political Science, B.Sc., 1958; University of London, Ph.D., 1972. *Home:* 42 Willoughby Rd., London N.W.3, England. *Agent:* Curtis Brown Ltd., 1 Craven Hill, London W.2, England.

CAREER: Purser in British Merchant Navy, 1951-53; civil servant, 1961-63; Polytechnic of North London, London, England, principal lecturer in sociology, 1964—. Visiting lecturer in sociology at Bucknell University, 1969-70; assistant professor of sociology at City University of New York, 1971. *Member:* British Sociological Association. *Awards, honors:* John Madge memorial scholarship from Regional Studies Association, 1971.

WRITINGS: Sociology and Social Work, Pergamon, 1970. Contributor to social work, sociology, and planning journals, and to *New Society.*

WORK IN PROGRESS: Community development project analysis.

* * *

HERBERG, Will 1909-1977

PERSONAL: Born August 4, 1909, in New York, N.Y.; son of Hyman Lewis and Sarah (Wolkov) Herberg; married (wife deceased). *Education:* Columbia University, B.A., 1928, M.A., 1930, Ph.D., 1932. *Home:* 17 Madison Ave., Madison, N.J. 07940. *Office:* Graduate School, Drew University, Madison, N.J. 07940.

CAREER: Research analyst and educational director for International Ladies Garment Workers Union, 1935-48; lecturer and writer, 1948-55; Drew University, Madison, N.J., graduate professor of Judaic studies and social philosophy, 1955-63, graduate professor of philosophy and culture, 1963-76. Consultant to Doubleday & Co., 1957-61, and Macmillan Co., 1961-62. *Member:* American Philosophical Association, American Sociological Association, American Historical Association, Metaphysical Society of America, American Studies Association, Mediaeval Academy of America, American Theological Society, American Judicature Society, Philosophy of Education Society, Society of Biblical Literature. *Awards, honors:* L.H.D. from Park College, 1956; Litt.D. from Franklin and Marshall College, 1960; LL.D. from Ohio Wesleyan University, 1963.

WRITINGS: Judaism and Modern Man: An Interpretation of Jewish Religion, Farrar, Straus, 1951; *Protestant, Catholic, Jew,* Doubleday, 1955, revised edition, 1960; *The Writings of Martin Buber,* Meridian, 1956; (editor) *Four Existentialist Theologians: A Reader from the Works of Jacques Maritain, Nicolas Berdyaev, Martin Buber, and Paul Tillich,* Doubleday, 1958, reprinted, Greenwood Press, 1975; (editor) *Community, State, and Church,* Doubleday, 1960; (with others) *Religious Perspectives in American Culture,* Princeton University Press, 1961; (contributor) Charles

Wellborn, editor, *Challenge to Morality,* Florida State University, 1966; (with others) *On Academic Freedom,* American Enterprise Institute for Public Policy Research, 1971. Contributor to *National Review* and *New Republic.*

BIOGRAPHICAL/CRITICAL SOURCES: John P. Diggins, *Up From Communism,* Harper, 1975.

OBITUARIES: New York Times, March 28, 1977; *Washington Post,* March 29, 1977; *Time,* April 11, 1977.*

(Died March 27, 1977, in Chatham, New Jersey)

*   *   *

HERBERT, Cecil
See HAMILTON, Charles Harold St. John

*   *   *

HERRINGTON, James L(awrence)   1928-

PERSONAL: Born July 15, 1928, in Greenville, Pa.; son of James L. (a doctor) and June (a nurse; maiden name, Thompson) Herrington; married Maxine Calvert (a secretary), June 14, 1952; children: James L. IV, Douglas, Lauren. *Education:* Northwestern University, B.A., 1955. *Office:* WXYZ-TV (ABC), 20777 West 10 Mile, Southfield, Mich. 48075.

CAREER/WRITINGS: WEAW-Radio, Evanston, Ill., sportscaster and host of talk show, 1951-56; *Evanston Review,* Evanston, sports writer, 1951-56; WJIM-TV, Lansing, Mich., newsman and sports broadcaster, 1956-58; WNEM-TV, Saginaw, Mich., production director, 1958-63; WKNX-TV, Saginaw, reporter, 1964-65; WXYZ-TV, Southfield, Mich., reporter, 1966—. Notable assignments include all national political conventions since 1952, the 1967 Detroit riots, and U.S. presidents. *Military service:* U.S. Navy, 1946-51. *Member:* Detroit Press Club (vice-president, 1977—), Sigma Delta Xi. *Awards, honors:* National Headliners Award and Detroit Press Club Foundation Award, both 1967, both for coverage of Detroit riot; Detroit Press Club Foundation award for documentary, 1969 and 1970.

SIDELIGHTS: Herrington told *CA* that the most engaging aspect of his work is "awareness of the value of communication and an informed people and my role in that." *Avocational interests:* History, English literature, music, travel, reading, gardening, sports, conversation.

*   *   *

HERSH, Burton   1933-

PERSONAL: Born September 18, 1933, in Chicago, Ill.; son of Maurice H. (a manufacturer) and Florence (Shapiro) Hersh; married Ellen Eiseman (a language teacher), August 3, 1957; children: Leo J., Margery C. *Education:* Harvard University, B.A. (magna cum laude), 1955; further study at University of Freiburg, 1955-56, University of Innsbruck, 1959-60, and Cale School, 1974. *Home and office address:* P.O. Box 204, Bradford, N.H. 03221. *Agent:* Curtis Brown Ltd., 575 Madison Ave., New York, N.Y. 10022.

CAREER: Free-lance writer, 1955—. Albert Cobb Memorial Lecturer at Blake School, 1973. Chairman of Bradford Conservation Commission, 1972-75. *Military service:* U.S. Army, 1957-59. *Member:* Authors Guild, Phi Beta Kappa. *Awards, honors:* Fulbright fellowship, 1955-56; fellow at Bread Loaf Writers Conference, 1964.

WRITINGS: The Ski People (novel), McGraw, 1968; *The Education of Edward Kennedy,* Morrow, 1972. Contributor of articles and a story to magazines, including *Holiday, Esquire, Venture, Show,* and *Transatlantic Review.*

WORK IN PROGRESS: A book about the Mellon family; continuing research on Mexico.

SIDELIGHTS: Hersh writes: "I began free-lancing while a Fulbright scholar in West Germany, and never did go straight after that. I lived six years in Europe, and traveled widely there. I have had several winters of residence in Mexico." *Avocational interests:* Sports (skiing, tennis), graphics (prints).

*   *   *

HERSH, Seymour M.   1937-

PERSONAL: Born April 8, 1937, in Chicago, Ill.; son of Isadore and Dorothy (Margolis) Hersh; married Elizabeth Sarah Klein (a medical student), May 31, 1964; children: Matthew, Melissa. *Education:* University of Chicago, B.A., 1958, graduate study, 1959. *Home:* 284 West 11th St., New York, N.Y. 10014. *Office:* 229 West 43rd St., New York, N.Y. 10036.

CAREER: City News Bureau, Chicago, Ill., police reporter, 1959-60; United Press International, correspondent in Pierre, S.D., 1962-63; Associated Press, correspondent in Chicago and Washington, D.C., 1963-67; *New York Times,* reporter in Washington bureau, 1972-75, in New York City, 1975—. Press secretary to Senator Eugene J. McCarthy during presidential campaign, 1968. *Awards, honors:* George Polk award, Worth Bingham prize, Sigma Delta Chi distinguished service award, and Pulitzer Prize for international reporting, all 1970, all for stories on the My Lai massacre; *My Lai Four* was named one of the best nonfiction books of the year by *Time,* 1970; Front Page award, Scripps-Howard service award, and George Polk award, all 1973, all for stories on bombing in Cambodia; Sidney Hillman award and George Polk award, both 1974, both for stories on CIA domestic spying.

WRITINGS: Chemical and Biological Warfare: America's Arsenal, Bobbs-Merrill, 1968; *My Lai Four: A Report on the Massacre and Its Aftermath,* Random House, 1970; *Cover-Up: The Army's Secret Investigation of the Massacre of My Lai Four,* Random House, 1972. Contributor to magazines.

SIDELIGHTS: Hersh's many front page disclosures have led him to the fore of investigative reporting in the United States. They've caused *Time* magazine to call him the "unrivaled master of the government expose." He has scored an impressive list of firsts over the past eight years: the massacre at My Lai, the secret bombing of Cambodia, the military's unauthorized bombing of North Vietnam, the wiretapping of aides by Secretary of State Henry Kissinger, the theft of papers from Kissinger's office by the Pentagon, the CIA's involvement in the Chilean coup against President Allende, and the CIA's operation of domestic spying.

"I hate secrets," Hersh explained to a lecture audience at the University of Michigan. "I don't think there should be secrets. I'm awfully tired of people in Washington telling me something is secret in the name of national security. I happen to believe that making sure that every car gets twenty-five miles to the gallon is the most important kind of national security."

His first book, *Chemical and Biological Warfare,* drew the same criticism of indiscretion concerning national security. Reviewers, though, were all impressed by the amount of fresh information, the accuracy of the information, and the digging it represented, and most of them couldn't help but fall prey to the intentions of the author. With so much information available, reviews became thinly disguised arguments for and against chemical and biological warfare research and stockpiling. Only a few reviewers suggested that Hersh's real story might be about the all too frequent incompetence in handling these weapons and that the terrifying nature of the work by necessity leads the military to ever higher realms of double-talk and obfuscation. The reaction to his newspaper work and the books on the massacre at My Lai Four and the subsequent cover-up was well publicized in both its attitude and volume. The reviews were serious, well thought out, and sober. The mail was sometimes not. Hersh's favorite reaction was from one man who called him a "sleazy goon" and a "heinous hack."

Hersh claims no advocacy for reform in his motives—"I just want the people to know the truth," he often says—but he does admit the tedious and unending effort needed to squeeze the story out and to get it right. Enormous piles of background material are read and countless interviews are conducted with anyone who might know something. After competing with Hersh on a story, Jack Anderson said, "Every place we went, Hersh had been there."

"Being an investigative reporter is like being a freak," comments Hersh. "You're trying to get information other people don't want you to have. I don't make deals, I don't party and drink with sources, and I don't play a game of leaks. I read, I listen, I squirrel information. It's fun."

BIOGRAPHICAL/CRITICAL INFORMATION: Time, January 6, 1975, June 23, 1975; *Commonweal,* February 1, 1975; *Detroit Free Press,* February 23, 1975; *Newsweek,* March 31, 1975; *New Republic,* July 4, 1975.*

* * *

HERTZ, Karl H(erbert) 1917-

PERSONAL: Born April 9, 1917, in Medicine Hat, Alberta, Canada; came to the United States in 1935; son of Ernst Gottlieb (a clergyman) and Adele (Fischer) Hertz; married Barbara M. Shephard, November 27, 1947; children: Paul Richard, Judith Ann. *Education:* Capital University, B.A., 1937; Brown University, M.A., 1938; Lutheran Theological Seminary, further graduate study, 1946-48; University of Chicago, Ph.D., 1948. *Home:* 619 Faculty Court, Springfield, Ohio 45504. *Office:* Hamma School of Theology, Wittenberg University, Springfield, Ohio 45501.

CAREER: Capital University, Columbus, Ohio, instructor, 1938-42, assistant professor of sociology, 1948-53; Wittenberg University, Springfield, Ohio, associate professor, 1953-60, professor of sociology, 1953-67, chairman of department, 1959-63, professor of church and society, 1967—. Springfield city commissioner, 1964-67; Clark County Democratic Committee, member, 1962—, chairman, 1971-76; Commission on Studies of the Lutheran World Federation, member, 1970-77, chairman, 1975-77. *Military service:* U.S. Army, 1942-45; served in European theater; received two battle stars.

MEMBER: American Association of University Professors, American Sociological Association, American Society of Christian Ethics, Institute on Religion in the Age of Science, Society for the Scientific Study of Religion, North Central Sociological Association.

WRITINGS: (Translator, with wife, Barbara Hertz) Karl Holl, *The Cultural Significance of the Reformation,* Meridian, 1959; *Every Man a Priest,* Fortress, 1960; (translator with B. Hertz) George Vicedom, *The Challenge of the World Religions,* Fortress, 1963; (translator) Heinrich Bornkamm, *Luther's Doctrine of the Two Kingdoms in the Con-*

text of His Theology, Fortress, 1966; *Ecological Planning for Metropolitan Areas,* Zygon, 1970; *Politics Is a Way of Helping People,* Augsburg, 1974; (editor) *Two Kingdoms and One World: A Sourcebook in Christian Social Ethics,* Augsburg, 1976; (editor) *The Identity of the Church and Its Service to the Whole Human Being,* Volume II: *Summary, Analysis, Interpretation,* Department of Studies, Lutheran World Federation, 1977.

Contributor: H. C. Letts, editor, *Christian Social Responsibility,* three volumes, Muhlenberg, 1957; Walter Kloetzli, editor, *Challenge and Response in the City,* Augsburg, 1962; Robert W. Bertram, editor, *Theology in the Life of the Church,* Fortress, 1963; Philip J. Hefner, editor, *The Scope of Grace,* Fortress, 1964; D. B. Robertson, editor, *Voluntary Associations,* John Knox, 1966; Kyle Haselden and Hefner, editors, *Changing Man,* Doubleday, 1968; Herbert T. Neve and Benjamin A. Johnson, editors, *The Maturing of American Lutheranism,* Fortress, 1968; Franklin Sherman, editor, *Christian Hope and the Future of Humanity,* Augsburg, 1969; Gerd Decke, editor, *The Encounter of the Church with Movements of Social Change in Various Cultural Contexts,* Department of Studies, Lutheran World Federation, 1977; Ulrich Duchrow, editor, *Zwei Reiche und Regimente,* Gerd Mohn, 1977. Contributor of articles and translations to *Lutheran Quarterly, City Church, Lutherische Monatshefte,* and *Religion in Life.*

SIDELIGHTS: Hertz writes: "I find myself increasingly concerned for questions of political ethics and ecumenical Christianity."

* * *

HERTZBERG, Hazel W(hitman) 1918-

PERSONAL: Born September 16, 1918, in Brooklyn, N.Y.; daughter of Charles Theodore (an accountant) and Grace (Wood) Whitman; married Sidney Hertzberg (a writer), August 25, 1941; children: Hendrik, Katrina Hertzberg McClintock. *Education:* University of Chicago, A.B., 1958; Columbia University, M.A., 1961, Ph.D., 1968. *Politics:* Democrat. *Religion:* Society of Friends (Quakers). *Home:* 35 Iroquois Ave., Palisades, N.Y. 10964. *Office:* Department of Social Studies, Teachers College, Columbia University, 525 West 120th St., New York, N.Y. 10027.

CAREER: High school teacher of social studies and English in Suffern, N.Y., 1957-62; Columbia University, Teachers College, New York, N.Y., instructor, 1963-68, assistant professor, 1968-69, associate professor of history and education, 1970—. Member of board of directors of Social Science Education Consortium, 1974—; member of history and social studies committee of Educational Testing Service, 1975—; consultant to Microfilming Corp. of America.

MEMBER: National Council for the Social Studies, American Historical Association, Organization of American Historians, American Association of University Professors, American Association of University Women, Annual Conference of Iroquois Research. *Awards, honors:* National Endowment for the Humanities fellowship, 1974-75; Woodrow Wilson fellowship, 1975.

WRITINGS: Anthropological Contribution to the Teaching of State History, American Anthropological Association, 1965; *Teaching the Age of Homespun,* State University of New York Press, 1965; *Teaching Population Dynamics,* Teachers College Press, 1965; (contributor) Martin Feldman and Eli Seifman, editors, *The Social Studies: Structure, Models and Strategies,* Holt, 1966; *Teaching a Pre-Columbian Culture: The Iroquois,* State University of New York

Press, 1966; *The Great Tree and the Long House: The Culture of the Iroquois,* with teacher's manual, Macmillan, 1966; (with husband, Sidney Hertzberg) *The United Nations and the Age of Change,* United Nations Association, 1966, 4th edition, 1969; *Historical Parallels for the Sixties and Seventies: Primary Sources and Core Curriculum Revisited,* Social Science Education Consortium, 1971; *The Search for an American Indian Identity: Modern Pan-Indian Movements,* Syracuse University Press, 1971; (contributor) Mary Alice White, editor, *Education: A Conceptual and Empirical Approach,* Holt, 1973. Contributor to *Handbook of North American Indians.* Contributor of articles and reviews to history, social studies, and education journals.

WORK IN PROGRESS: How to Study and Serve the Local Community: A Guide to Analysis, Projects, and Resources (tentative title); *American Indian Rights Movements Since 1928;* research on student perceptions of time in history and on oral history.

SIDELIGHTS: Hazel Hertzberg writes briefly: "My work is an attempt to bridge the gap between scholar and teacher, partly by being both."

*   *   *

HESSLER, Gene   1928-

PERSONAL: Born July 13, 1928, in Cincinnati, Ohio; son of Joseph (a tailor) and Clara M. (Schmidt) Hessler. *Education:* University of Cincinnati, B.S., 1955; Manhattan School of Music, M.M., 1957; also attended Columbia University, 1962-63, and Cincinnati Conservatory of Music. *Office:* Money Museum, c/o Chase Manhattan Bank, 30 Rockefeller Plaza, New York, N.Y. 10020.

CAREER: Professional trombonist with Stan Kenton, Woody Herman, Buddy Rich, Broadway musicals, and orchestras, 1948— ; Chase Manhattan Bank, New York, N.Y., curator of Money Museum, 1967-77; numismatist, 1967— . Made concert tours abroad for U.S. State Department. Has lectured in California, Connecticut, New York, Pennsylvania, Virginia, and at the United Nations; guest on television and radio programs, including "Today Show," "What's My Line," and "Money Facts." *Military service:* U.S. Army, 1951-53.

MEMBER: International Bank Note Society, American Numismatic Association, American Numismatic Society, Society of Paper Money Collectors, Numismatic Literary Guild, Royal Numismatic Society. *Awards, honors:* Award from Society of Paper Money Collectors, 1974, and from Professional Numismatists Guild, 1975, both for *The Comprehensive Catalog of U.S. Paper Money.*

WRITINGS: Buy and Sell Price Guide to U.S. Coins, Dafran, 1971, fifth edition, 1975; *Buy and Sell Price Guide to U.S. Currency,* Dafran, 1971, fifth edition, 1975; *The Comprehensive Catalog of U.S. Paper Money,* Regnery, 1974, second edition, 1977; (editor) *Standard U.S. Coin Catalogue,* Scott Publishing, 1976, second edition, 1977; (editor) *Standard U.S. Paper Money Catalogue,* Scott Publishing, 1976, second edition, 1977. Contributor to numismatic journals.

WORK IN PROGRESS: U.S. Paper Money Essais, Specimens, Experimental and Trial Pieces, completion expected in 1979.

SIDELIGHTS: Hessler told *CA:* "I do most of the photographic work for my articles and other publications. *Avocational interests:* Travel (western Europe, Africa, Asia, the Near East), photography, oenology.

HEUYER, Georges   1884-1977

January 30, 1884—October 23, 1977; French physician, educator, and author. One of the world's leading neuropsychiatrists for children, Heuyer held an honorary chair at the University of Paris medical school. His books included studies on juvenile delinquency and suicide. He died in Paris, France. Obituaries: *New York Times,* October 25, 1977.

*   *   *

HEWLETT, Roger S.   1911(?)-1977

1911(?)—November 14, 1977; American journalist. After a brief acting career, Hewlett turned to writing, and served as an editor for *Time* and later *Sports Illustrated.* Because of his interest in yachting, he often covered the America's Cup competition. He died in Middleton, Conn. Obituaries: *New York Times,* November 15, 1977.

*   *   *

HEYWOOD, Lorimer D.   1899(?)-1977

1899(?)—July 18, 1977; American journalist. Heywood worked for Associated Press and several newspapers, including the *Bronx Home News, Philadelphia Public Ledger, Rochester Democrat and Chronicle,* and *New York Herald Tribune.* He died in Doylestown, Pa. Obituaries: *New York Times,* July 20, 1977.

*   *   *

HICKMAN, Peggy   1906-

PERSONAL: Born July 22, 1906, in Stoke d'Abernon, Surrey, England; married Dennis Hickman (a company director; died, 1967); children: Susan Hickman Horner, Stephen. *Education:* Educated in private schools in England and Switzerland. *Politics:* Conservative. *Religion:* Church of England. *Residence:* Sussex, England.

CAREER: Writer. Organized exhibition at National Portrait Gallery, 1973.

WRITINGS: The History of Shipley: A Village in the Sussex Weald, Greenfields, 1948; *Silhouettes,* Walker & Co., 1968; *Silhouettes: Celebrities in Profile,* A. & C. Black, 1971; *Silhouettes: A Living Art,* St. Martin's, 1975; (contributor) Honoria D. Marsh, editor, *Shades from Jane Austen,* Parry Jackman, 1975, Schram, 1976; *A Jane Austen Household Book,* David & Charles, 1977. Also author of an exhibition catalog of National Portrait Gallery (London), H.M.S.O., 1973. Contributor to magazines, including *Antique Collector, Connoisseur, Country Life,* and *Womans Home Journal.*

SIDELIGHTS: Peggy Hickman now lives in a quiet Sussex village, but she spent many years traveling with her late husband through Europe. Her main research interests are history, especially local history, and antiques. *Avocational interests:* Reading (collects eighteenth-century biographies and diaries), gardening, collecting antiques.

*   *   *

HICKOK, Dorothy Jane   1912-

PERSONAL: Born May 24, 1912, in Cascade, Iowa; daughter of Samuel R. (in real estate) and Jennie L. Hickok. *Education:* Attended Drake University, 1930-34, University of Rochester, 1937-39, and University of North Carolina. *Home:* 5153 Franklin, Oswego, N.Y. 13126.

CAREER: Instrumental music teacher in Des Moines, Iowa, and Buffalo, N.Y.; assistant professor of instrumental music at State University of New York College at Oswego. Created "Miss Dottie's Music Box," a television program for children, on WUNC-Television, and "Watch and Listen," for a children's series on WHEN-Television. *Member:* Zonta Club (past local president).

WRITINGS: (With James A. Smith) *Creative Teaching of Music in the Elementary School,* Allyn & Bacon, 1974.

WORK IN PROGRESS: Short stories for children.

* * *

HICKOK, Lorena A. 1892(?)-1968

PERSONAL: Born in East Troy, Wisc. *Education:* Attended University of Minnesota. *Politics:* Democrat. *Residence:* Hyde Park, N.Y.

CAREER: Writer. Reporter for *Minneapolis Tribune* in the early 1920's; became reporter for Associated Press in New York, N.Y., in mid-1920's; served as aide to head of Works Projects Administration; member of staff of president of New York World's Fair, 1939-40; served in women's division of Democratic National Committee until her retirement in 1945.

WRITINGS: (With Eleanor Roosevelt) *Ladies of Courage,* Putnam, 1954; *The Story of Franklin D. Roosevelt* (illustrated by Leonard Vosburgh), Grosset, 1956; *The Story of Helen Keller* (illustrated by Jo Polsano), Grosset, 1958, reissued, 1974; *The Story of Eleanor Roosevelt* (illustrated by William Barss), Grosset, 1959; *The Touch of Magic: The Story of Helen Keller's Great Teacher, Anne Sullivan Macy,* Dodd, 1961; *The Road to the White House,* Chilton, 1962; (with Jean Gould) *Walter Reuther: Labor's Rugged Individualist,* Dodd, 1972.

BIOGRAPHICAL/CRITICAL SOURCES: Christian Science Monitor, May 27, 1954; *New Republic,* June 14, 1954; *New York Times,* January 27, 1957; *Saturday Review,* February 21, 1960; *New York Times Book Review,* July 30, 1972. *Obituaries: Washington Post,* May 4, 1968.*

(Died May 3, 1968, in Rhinebeck, N.Y.)

* * *

HICKS, Ronald G(raydon) 1934-

PERSONAL: Born November 29, 1934, in Shongaloo, La.; son of Graydon and Estelle Hicks; married Helen Lucille Mitchell (a secretary), November 20, 1955; children: Ronald Gregory, Karen Elaine, Rexford Graydon. *Education:* Louisiana State University, B.A.J., 1960, M.A.J., 1961, Ph.D., 1970. *Politics:* Independent. *Home:* 16460 Fulwar Skipwith Rd., Baton Rouge, La. 70808. *Office:* School of Journalism, Louisiana State University, Baton Rouge, La. 70803.

CAREER: WXOK-Radio, Baton Rouge, La., copywriter, 1958-59; Community Newspaper Representatives, Baton Rouge, La., advertising salesman, 1959-61; Louisiana State University, Baton Rouge, professor of journalism, 1962—, director of Journalism Extension Service, 1962—. Editor and publisher of *Baker Observer,* 1963. Manager for Louisiana Press Association, 1962-74. *Military service:* U.S. Navy, 1954-57; became petty officer first class.

MEMBER: International Newspaper Advertising Executives, International Weekly Newspaper Publishers, Association for Education in Journalism, Society of Professional Journalists, American Sociological Association, Newspaper Association Managers, Louisiana Press Association.

WRITINGS: A Survey of Mass Communication, Pelican, 1977. Contributor to journalism and sociology journals.

SIDELIGHTS: Hicks writes: "My interest in journalism is based on the view that the mass media are important forces shaping modern society; my concern is with the long term effects, both positive and negative, which the media have." His travels have taken him to England, France, Spain, Germany, Italy, Monaco, Japan, and Belgium.

AVOCATIONAL INTERESTS: Painting, music, literature, metaphysics, Oriental religion, philosophy.

* * *

HIERONYMUS, Clara (Booth) 1913-

PERSONAL: Born July 25, 1913, in Drew, Miss.; daughter of Bruce Charles (a painter) and Maude (a teacher; maiden name, Watson) Wiggins; married Senator Cleo Hieronymus (a banker), April 24, 1937; children: Bruce Lee, Jane (Mrs. David Henri Piller). *Education:* University of Tulsa, B.A. (cum laude), 1932; University of Oklahoma, M.S.W., 1936. *Politics:* Democrat. *Religion:* Methodist. *Home:* 2200 Hemingway Dr., Nashville, Tenn. 37215. *Office: Tennessean,* 1100 Broad St., Nashville, Tenn. 37202.

CAREER: Young Women's Christian Association, Tulsa, Okla., employment counselor, 1936-38; U.S. Employment Service, Tulsa, labor market analyst, 1938-50; free-lance writer, 1951-56; *Tennessean,* Nashville, Tenn., home furnishing editor and author of column, 1956—. Instructor in sociology at University of Tulsa, 1938-50. Labor market analyst for War Manpower Commission and Oklahoma State Employment Service. Presented book review program on KFMJ-Radio, and children's story-telling program on WSM-Television, 1950—; has performed in theater programs in Tennessee, Kentucky, and North Carolina; member of Nashville Children's Theater (past member of board of directors); professional critic at International Children's Theater's world congresses and American College Theater Festivals; member of advisory board of Tennessee Performing Arts Foundation, 1974—. Guest lecturer at National Critics Institute. Charter member of board of directors of Historic Sites Federation, 1968, and Chet Atkins Guitar Festival, 1970—; member of national editorial advisory committee of public relations program "Debut '73" for the home furnishing industry. Member of board of directors of regional chapter of National Arthritis Foundation, 1968—, and National Hemophilia Society, 1969—; member of Tennessee Fine Arts Center and Botanical Gardens and Cheekwood Fine Arts Center. President of Samaritans, Inc., 1968-70, presently member of board of directors.

MEMBER: Association International du Theatre pour les Enfants et Jeunesse, International Association for Children's Theatre, American Society of Interior Designers (press affiliate), National Society of Interior Designers (press member), American Theater Critics Association (member of first governing board and executive committee, 1974—), Women in Communications, Tennessee Artist-Craftsman Association (honorary member), Centennial Club (Nashville), Ladies Hermitage Association, Le Petit Salon (charter member; president, 1976-77). *Awards, honors:* Dorothy Dawe Award from American Furniture Mart, 1960, 1963, 1965, and 1969, for journalism in the home furnishings field; award from Dallas Market Center, 1965, for home furnishings writing; named woman of the year by Nashville Business and Professional Women, 1966; Ford Foundation fellowship, 1967; Burlington Award, 1969, 1970, 1971, and 1974, for stories on Nashville area homes; honored by Printing Industry of Nashville, 1972.

WRITINGS: (With Barbara Izard) *Requiem for a Nun: On*

Stage and Off, Aurora, 1970. Contributor to *BMI* and to theater magazines in the United States and England. Book reviewer for Sunday Page of *Tulsa Daily World.*

WORK IN PROGRESS: A book on Tennessee crafts and craftsmen.

SIDELIGHTS: Clara Hieronymus has conducted interviews with performers Helen Hayes and Carol Channing, among others. But her career has not been limited to writing. In 1972, she was a member of a national panel to select five children's theaters to perform at a world congress of Association International pour les Enfants et Jeunesse. She has conducted theater tours to New York City and London, and has organized and directed home tours, shows of table settings, and theater benefits. As an actress she appeared in "Spoon River Anthology" at Vanderbilt University. She comments that her book is the only one written about William Faulkner's sole play.

*   *   *

HIGGINS, Chester (Archer, Jr.) 1946-

PERSONAL: Born November 6, 1946, in Lexington, Ky.; son of Chester Archer (a journalist) and Varidee (a teacher; maiden name, Young) Higgins; married Renelda Meeks (a painter), April 22, 1971; children: Nataki Olamina, Chester Damani III. *Education:* Tuskegee Institute, B.S., 1970. *Politics:* "The correct way." *Home:* 575 Main St., Roosevelt Island, N.Y. 10044. *Agent:* Renaca Photography Ltd., 350 Fifth Ave., Suite 7920, New York, N.Y. 10001. *Office: New York Times,* 229 West 43rd St., New York, N.Y. 10036.

CAREER: New York University, New York City, instructor in fine arts, 1975-77; *New York Times,* New York City, staff photographer, 1975—. *Awards, honors:* Ford Foundation fellowships, 1972-74; Gational Endowment for the Arts, fellow, 1973; Rockefeller Foundation fellowship, 1974; *Graphis* and *Print* magazines awards, 1974 and 1975.

WRITINGS: Student Unrest at Tuskegee Institute, Behavioral Science Research Institute, Tuskegee Institute, 1968; (with Harold McDougall) *Black Woman* (photo-essay), McCall's, 1970; (with Orde Coombs) *Drums of Life* (photo-essay), Doubleday, 1974; (with Amanda Ambrose) *My Name Is Black* (photo-essay), Scholastic Book Services, 1974; (with Kathryn Parker) *The Day We Won* (photo-essay), Doubleday, 1977; (with Coombs) *Some Time Ago* (photo-essay), Doubleday, 1978.

WORK IN PROGRESS: Studies Made in Africa; and *The Cultural Aspects of Lines.*

SIDELIGHTS: Higgins writes: "I believe in the possibility, potential and desirability of balanced and total evolution of our species. I work for clarity; I work to learn worthy things that I can share with those I love and care about in the desperate hope that the encounter improves us all."

*   *   *

HIGGINS, James E(dward) 1926-

PERSONAL: Born April 1, 1926, in New York, N.Y.; son of Peter J. (an electrician) and Loretta (Ford) Higgins; married Emily M. Annette, July 10, 1949; children: Ellen (Mrs. Jeffrey Kaye), John, Nancy, Peter. *Education:* St. Bonaventure University, B.A., 1949; Columbia University, M.A., 1950, Ed.D., 1965; St. John's University, Brooklyn, N.Y., B.L.S., 1952. *Politics:* Independent. *Religion:* Roman Catholic. *Home:* 8 Shetland Lane, Stony Brook, N.Y. 11790. *Office:* Department of Elementary Education, Queens College of the City University of New York, Flushing, N.Y. 11367.

CAREER: Librarian and teacher at private school in Brooklyn, N.Y., 1950-53, and public school in Levittown, N.Y., 1953-65; State University of New York at Stony Brook, assistant professor, 1965-68, associate professor of education, 1968-70; Queens College of the City University of New York, Flushing, N.Y., professor of education, 1970—. Visiting professor at State University of New York at Stony Brook, summer, 1971, and in Bermuda, summer, 1976; adjunct professor at Columbia University, summer, 1976. Librarian at Columbia University, Teachers College, Agnes Russell Center, 1961-62. Member of national editorial board of Lucky Book Club, 1975—; consultant of Macmillan and Guidance Associates, Inc. *Military service:* U.S. Army Air Forces, 1943-44.

MEMBER: Association for Childhood Education International, National Council of Teachers of English, American Library Association, National Education Association, Association for Supervision and Curriculum Development, New York Library Association.

WRITINGS: (Contributor) Leland B. Jacobs, editor, *Using Literature With Children,* Teachers College Press, 1965; (contributor) Elinor Whitney Field, editor, *Horn Book Reflections,* Horn Book, 1969; *Beyond Words: Mystical Fancy in Children's Literature,* Teachers College Press, 1970; (contributor) Monroe D. Cohen, editor, *Literature With Children,* Association for Childhood Education, 1972; (contributor) Carl B. Smith and Ronald Wardhaugh, editors, *Teacher's Resource Book: Series R Reading Program,* Macmillan, 1975. Author of teachers' manuals. Contributor of articles and reviews to professional journals.

SIDELIGHTS: Higgins writes: "My professional efforts have always been directed toward attempting to remove those obstacles which seem to be inherent in our culture and educational institutions that prevent young readers from truly making their own responses to stories and poetry—allowing young readers to experience the raw impact of literature without having to sift it through adult critical criteria."

AVOCATIONAL INTERESTS: Baseball.

*   *   *

HIGHET, Gilbert 1906-1978

June 22, 1906—January 20, 1978; Scottish-born American classicist, critic, poet, author, and professor emeritus of Latin language and literature at Columbia University. At one time Highet served as chief literary critic for *Harper's.* His fourteen books include *The Classical Tradition, The Anatomy of Satire,* and *The Immortal Profession.* Highet died in New York, N.Y. Obituaries: *New York Times,* January 21, 1978; *Washington Post,* January 23, 1978; *Newsweek,* January 30, 1978; *Time,* January 30, 1978; *AB Bookman's Weekly,* April 3, 1978. (See index for *CA* sketch)

*   *   *

HILFER, Anthony Channell 1936-

PERSONAL: Born October 19, 1936, in Los Angeles, Calif.; son of Harry (a chemist) and Ruth (a librarian; maiden name, Channell) Hilfer; married Marybeth Wilson (a teacher), June 18, 1961; children: Thomas Hailey. *Education:* Middlebury College, B.A., 1958; Columbia University, M.A., 1960; University of North Carolina at Chapel Hill, Ph.D., 1963. *Politics:* Democrat. *Religion:* Polytheistic. *Home:* 1908 Robin Hood Trail, Austin, Tex. 78703. *Office:* Department of English, University of Texas, Austin, Tex. 78712.

CAREER: University of Texas, Austin, assistant professor, 1963-69, associate professor of English, 1969—. *Member:* Modern Language Association of America.

WRITINGS: The Revolt from the Village, 1915-1930, University of North Carolina Press, 1969.

WORK IN PROGRESS: The Ethics of Intensity (tentative title), on desire and ethos in works by Whitman, Howells, Henry James, William James, Dreiser, and Gertrude Stein.

SIDELIGHTS: Hilfer writes: "In *The Ethics of Intensity* I am trying to demonstrate a major shift in how a protagonist's consciousness is judged—no longer, as in the Victorian ethos, in terms of selfishness versus self-abnegation, but in terms of the intensity and daring of his or her desires. Yet I show a continuity between the selfish egoist of Victorian fiction and the solipsistic retreater from passion of turn-of-the-century fiction. I also show the parallels in the new processual rendering of consciousness to radical empiricist philosophy. The book is not polemic but the problems it discusses are live issues, involving real choices of identity. My attempt is to define, rather than solve, these problems."

*   *   *

HILGER, Sister Mary Inez   1891-1977

PERSONAL: Born October 16, 1891, in Roscoe, Minn.; daughter of William Frederick and Elizabeth (Terres) Hilger. *Education:* University of Minnesota, B.A., 1923; Catholic University of America, M.A., 1925, Ph.D., 1939. *Home:* St. Benedict's Convent, St. Joseph, Minn. 56374.

CAREER: Roman Catholic nun, member of Order of St. Benedict, 1910-77; teacher in elementary and high schools in Minnesota and Wisconsin, 1911-24; College of St. Benedict, St. Joseph, Minn., head of department of sociology, 1925-32, dean of college, 1925-29; instructor in sociology, psychology, and psychiatry in schools of nursing, 1939-57, primarily those connected with Catholic hospitals in St. Cloud, Minn., Bismarck, N.D., and Charlotte, N.C.; College of St. Benedict, St. Joseph, special lecturer in anthropology, 1957-62. Visiting professor of anthropology at St. Joseph College, West Hartford, Conn., 1960, and at University of Tokyo, Keio University, and Japan Women's University, 1962-63. Lecturer in cultural anthropology at Instituto Social Leon XIII (affiliate of University of Madrid), 1955, for American Anthropological Association at colleges and universities in United States, 1960-62, 1964-65, and at Japanese universities, University of Taiwan, Hebrew University of Jerusalem, University of Heidelberg, and other institutions abroad, 1962-63.

MEMBER: American Anthropological Association (fellow), American Association for the Advancement of Science (fellow), Instituto Indigenista Interamericano, Catholic Anthropological Association, American Benedictine Academy, Minnesota Academy of Science, Delta Epsilon Sigma. *Awards, honors:* Research grants from Social Science Research Council, 1939-40, 1940, 1942-43, American Council of Learned Societies, 1941, 1942, American Philosophical Society for field work in Chile, 1945-47, for field work in Argentina, 1951-52, Wenner-Gren Foundation for field work in Argentina, 1951-52, and National Geographic Society for field work in Japan, 1965-66; American Catholic Sociological Society Award in recognition of outstanding research, as reported in *Araucanian Child Life and Its Cultural Background,* 1958; Catholic University of America Alumni Association Award in science and research, 1961; D.Litt., College of St. Benedict, 1971.

WRITINGS: Social Survey of One Hundred Fifty Chippewa Indian Families on the White Earth Reservation of Minnesota, Catholic University of America Press, 1939; *Chippewa Child Life and Its Cultural Background,* Smithsonian Institution Press, 1951; *Arapaho Child Life and Its Cultural Background,* Smithsonian Institution Press, 1952; (contributor) Robert E. Spencer, editor, *Method and Perspective in Anthropology,* University of Minnesota Press, 1954; *Araucanian Child Life and Its Cultural Background,* Smithsonian Institution Press, 1957; *Field Guide to the Ethnological Study of Child Life,* Human Relations Area File Press, 1960, 2nd edition, 1966; (with Margaret Mondloch) *Huehun Namku: An Araucanian Indian of the Andes Remembers the Past,* University of Oklahoma Press, 1966; *Together with the Ainu, A Vanishing People,* University of Oklahoma Press, 1971.

Contributor of more than forty other articles to yearbooks, professional journals, and magazines, including *Scientific Monthly, National Geographic, Catholic Digest, Mid-America, American Anthropologist, Primitive Man,* and *Journal de la Societe des Americanistes.*

WORK IN PROGRESS: A book, tentatively entitled, *The Ainu Then and Now: A Photographic Essay,* based on ethnological field notes collected among the Ainu in Japan; *Grandmothers' Stories from Many Parts of the World,* a collection of favorite stories collected in various countries.

SIDELIGHTS: Hilger's collections resulting from her field studies are exhibited at Chicago Natural History Museum, in Explorers' Hall of the National Geographic Society, and in the anthropology museum of the University of Minnesota.

(Died May 18, 1977 in St. Joseph, Minn.)

*   *   *

HILL, Adrian   1895-1977

March 24, 1895—June 22, 1977; English artist and author. Hill was best known for his self-help art books and art instruction television program. His book *Art Versus Illness* contributed significantly to the art therapy movement. He died in England. Obituaries: *AB Bookman's Weekly,* September 5, 1977.

*   *   *

HILL, Frank Ernest   1888-1969

PERSONAL: Born August 29, 1888, in San Jose, Calif.; son of Andrew P. and Florence (Watkins) Hill; married Elsa Hempl, 1915 (divorced, 1936); married Ruth Arnold Nickel, May 27, 1938; children: (first marriage) Russell, Anabel (Mrs. Allan Barahal). *Education:* Stanford University, B.A., 1911, M.A., 1914. *Politics:* Democrat. *Religion:* Unitarian. *Residence:* New York, N.Y.

CAREER: Stanford University, Stanford, Calif., instructor in English, 1913-16; Columbia University, New York City, faculty member in extension department, 1916-17; *New York Globe and Commercial Advertiser,* New York City, editorial writer, 1920-23; *New York Sun,* New York City, editorial writer, 1923-25, literary editor, 1925; Longmans, Green, & Co., New York City, editor-in-chief, 1925-31; writer and researcher on radio, 1931—. *Military service:* U.S. Army; served in Signal Corps during World War I.

WRITINGS: The American Legion Auxiliary: A History, [Indianapolis, Ind.], 1926; (with Joseph Auslander) *The Winged Horse* (illustrated by Paul Honore), Doubleday, 1927, reprinted, Haskell House, 1969; *Stone Dust,* Longmans, Green, 1928; (editor, with J. Auslander) *The Winged*

Horse Anthology, Doubleday, 1929; *What is American?,* Day, 1933; *The Westward Star,* Day, 1934; *The American Legion Auxiliary: A History, 1924-1934,* American Legion Auxiliary, 1935; *The School in the Camps: The Educational Program of the Civilian Conservation Corps,* American Association for Adult Education, 1935; *Listen and Learn: Fifteen Years of Adult Education on the Air,* American Association for Adult Education, 1937; *Man-Made Culture: The Educational Activities of Men's Clubs,* American Association for Adult Education, 1938; *Educating for Health: A Study of Programs for Adults,* American Association for Adult Education, 1939.

Training for the Job: Vocational Education for Adults, American Association for Adult Education, 1940; (with William E. Williams) *Radio's Listening Groups: The United States and Great Britain,* Columbia University Press, 1941; (with Kenneth Holland) *Youth in the CCC,* American Council on Education, 1942, reprinted, Arno, 1974; *India,* Columbia University Press, 1942; (translator) Geoffrey Chaucer, *The Canterbury Tales: Done into Modern English Verse,* Heritage Press, 1946, reprinted, McKay, 1962; *To Meet Will Shakespeare* (illustrated by Addison Burbank), Dodd, 1949, reprinted, Books for Libraries, 1970; *The King's Company* (illustrated by A. Burbank), Dodd, 1950; (with Bob Allison) *The Kid Who Batted 1,000* (illustrated by Paul Galdone), Doubleday, 1951, reprinted, Scholastic Book Services, 1972; (with Allan Nevins) *Ford,* Scribner, Volume I: *The Times, the Man, the Company,* 1954, Volume II: *Expansion and Challenge, 1915-1933,* 1957, Volume III: *Decline and Rebirth, 1933-1962,* 1963, all volumes, reprinted, Arno, 1976; (with Mira Wilkins) *American Business Abroad: Ford on Six Continents,* Wayne State University Press, 1964; *The New World of Wood,* Dodd, 1965; *Famous Historians,* Dodd, 1966; *The Automobile: How It Came, Grew, and Has Changed Our Lives,* Dodd, 1967.

SIDELIGHTS: Ford: The Times, the Man, the Company was reviewed by an *American Historical Review* critic, who wrote, "There is much human interest in this story, but the book as a whole is a cool and accurate account of Ford and his place in the automobile industry. It is no glorification of Ford or big business; Ford was the antithesis of the typical business magnate. . . . The Ford Motor Company was one of the few that survived among the scores of automobile concerns that started in the early chaotic years. Its history is fascinating, and the book does it justice." *Catholic World* commented that the authors "have written in entertaining style an excellent history of the beginning of an era and the man and his company that finally dominated it. They have examined a wealth of material and honestly reported their findings." *Ford: Expansion and Challenge, 1915-1933* was described by the *New York Times* as "a great book about a leading American figure and the manner in which he modified the American way of life." *New Yorker* said, "The present volume is a sound piece of scholarship combined with careful, popular writing, and it contains a telling likeness of one of the most uncommon men ever to walk the earth."

BIOGRAPHICAL/CRITICAL SOURCES: New York Times, October 16, 1949, January 7, 1951, September 15, 1957; *New York Herald Tribune,* December 4, 1949, December 17, 1950; *Christian Science Monitor,* February 3, 1951; *Catholic World,* June, 1954; *American Historical Review,* July, 1954; *New Yorker,* November 30, 1957. *Obituaries: New York Times,* November 4, 1969.*

(Died November, 1969)

HILL, Larry D(ean) 1935-

PERSONAL: Born April 25, 1935, in McAllen, Tex.; son of A. B. (a produce shipper) and Harriet (Lohr) Hill; married Doris Schaefer, June 2, 1956; children: Lea Ann, Jeffrey Dean. *Education:* Pan American College, B.A., 1962; Louisiana State University, M.A., 1965, Ph.D., 1971. *Home:* 1806 Sabine Court, College Station, Tex. 77843. *Office:* Department of History, Texas A & M University, College Station, Tex. 77840.

CAREER: Farmer in Edinburg, Tex., 1955-56, 1958-60; secondary school teacher in Pharr, Tex., 1960-63; Texas A & M University, College Station, instructor, 1967-71, assistant professor, 1971-74, associate professor of history, 1974—. *Military service:* U.S. Army, Signal Corps, 1956-58. *Member:* Organization of American Historians, Phi Alpha Theta.

WRITINGS: Emissaries to a Revolution: Woodrow Wilson's Executive Agents in Mexico, Louisiana State University Press, 1974. Contributor to *Americas.*

WORK IN PROGRESS: Woodrow Wilson and Mexican Neutrality in World War I.

SIDELIGHTS: Hill told *CA:* "My interest in Wilson's involvement in Mexico developed out of curiosity over the counterrevolutionary nature of United States foreign policy in the twentieth century. Yet the United States has at the same time been anti-colonial and pro-national self-determination. This paradox is nowhere more obvious than in Wilson's relations with Mexico."

*   *   *

HILL, Reginald (Charles) 1936-
(Dick Morland, Patrick Ruell, Charles Underhill)

PERSONAL: Born April 3, 1936, in West Hartlepool, England; son of Reginald and Isabel (Dickson) Hill; married Patricia Ruell, August 30, 1960. *Education:* St. Catherine's College, Oxford, B.A. (with honors), 1960. *Politics:* "Agnostic." *Religion:* "Cynic." *Home:* 89 Armthorpe Rd., Doncaster, South Yorkshire, England. *Agent:* A. P. Watt, 26/28 Bedford Row, London WC1R 4ML, England.

CAREER: Worked as a secondary school teacher in England, 1961-66; Doncaster College of Education, Doncaster, England, lecturer in English literature, 1966—; writer. *Military service:* National Service, 1955-57. *Member:* Crime Writers Association.

WRITINGS–All published by Collins, except as noted: *A Clubbable Woman,* 1970; *Fell of Dark,* 1971; *An Advancement of Learning,* 1971; *A Fairly Dangerous Thing,* 1972; *Ruling Passion,* 1973, Harper, 1977; *A Very Good Hater,* 1974; *An April Shroud,* 1975; *Another Death in Venice,* 1976.

Under pseudonym Dick Morland: *Heart Clock,* Faber, 1973; *Albion! Albion!,* Faber, 1976.

Under pseudonym Patrick Ruell; all first published by Hutchinson: *The Castle of the Demon,* 1971, Hawthorne, 1972; *Red Christmas,* 1972, Hawthorne, 1973; *Death Takes the High Road,* 1974; *Urn Burial,* 1975.

Under pseudonym Charles Underhill: *Captain Fantom,* Hutchinson, 1978.

WORK IN PROGRESS: A Pinch of Snuff, a detective thriller.

SIDELIGHTS: Hill told *CA:* "Literature is my primary interest both vocationally and avocationally. I lead a quiet life punctuated by loud bursts of laughter at its absurdity. I play tennis, squash and golf to as low a standard as possible without running out of partners. My wife and I devote ouselves to looking after two Siamese cats who are the only living creatures whose lot I envy."

* * *

HILLARD, James M(ilton) 1920-

PERSONAL: Born September 27, 1920, in Nortonville, Ky.; son of Cornelius (a farmer) and Leona L. (Hicks) Hillard; married Ella Louise Winzenried (a school librarian), December 23, 1944; children: James Randolph, Jerrold Manley. *Education:* Ohio University, B.A. (honors), 1947; University of Illinois, M.L.S. (high honors), 1948. *Politics:* "Independent but conservative." *Religion:* Protestant. *Home:* 203 Carolina Blvd., Isle of Palms, S.C. 29451. *Office:* Daniel Library, Citadel, Charleston, S.C. 29409.

CAREER: Free Public Library, Summit, N.J., assistant librarian, 1948-50; Carnegie City Library, Fort Smith, Ark., city librarian, 1950-52; Curtis Memorial Library, Meriden, Conn., director of library services, 1952-55; U.S. Military Academy, West Point, N.Y., associate director of library, 1955-57; Citadel, Charleston, S.C., director of Daniel Library, 1957—. *Military service:* U.S. Army, 1942-46; became sergeant. *Member:* American Library Association, American Association of University Professors, Southeastern Library Association, South Carolina Library Association, Optimists.

WRITINGS: Where to Find What, Scarecrow, 1975; *Where to Find More,* Scarecrow, 1977. Contributor of articles and reviews to history and library journals.

WORK IN PROGRESS: A library manual for students of education.

SIDELIGHTS: Hillard told *CA* his books "were intended to provide help to the reference personnel in libraries or others seeking a subject approach to reference materials." *Avocational interests:* Travel (Europe, Asia, Africa, Oceania), tennis, golf, and bridge.

* * *

HILLENBRAND, Barry R. 1941-

PERSONAL: Born September 30, 1941, in Chicago, Ill.; son of George C. and Mary (Trout) Hillenbrand; married Nguyen Thi Phuong Nga (a photographer), September 21, 1974. *Education:* Loyola University (Chicago), B.S., 1963; New York University, M.A., 1967. *Home:* Rua Joaquim Nabuco, 171, Apto 204, Rio de Janeiro, Brazil. *Office: Time,* Time-Life Building, New York, N.Y. 10020.

CAREER/WRITINGS: Peace Corps, Washington, D.C., teacher in Debre Markos, Ethiopia, 1963-65; Time-Life News Service, New York, N.Y., correspondent in Boston, Mass., 1968-70, San Francisco, Calif., 1970-71, Los Angeles, 1971-72, Saigon, Vietnam, 1972-74, bureau chief in Rio de Janeiro, Brazil, 1974—. Notable assignments include student unrest on campus, 1968-72, Bobby Fischer's chess championship, 1972, Vietnam War and war in Cambodia, 1972-74, coup in Thailand, 1973, war in Angola, 1976.

* * *

HILLERS, H(erman) W(illiam) 1925-
(Wilhelm Hillus)

PERSONAL: Born September 29, 1925, in Chana, Ill.; son of Berrnd Heinrick (a farmer) and Antje (a farmer; maiden name, Ennenga) Hillers; married Vernice A. Gustafson (a

ward secretary), February 20, 1949; children: Michelle, Michael, Marcia. *Education:* Attended University of Dubuque, 1956-57, and Coe College, 1957-59. *Politics:* Independent. *Religion:* Calvinist. *Office:* Hillers Sales & Service, 1720 Martin Rd., Bloomer, Wis. 54724.

CAREER: Worked as a farmer, machine operator, sales clerk, electrician, salesman, teller, and industrial engineer, 1946-63; Hillers Sales & Service, Bloomer, Wis., owner, 1964—. *Military service:* U.S. Navy, 1944-46.

WRITINGS—Under pseudonym Wilhelm Hillus: *The Mocking of America,* Gateway Press, 1976.

WORK IN PROGRESS: The Big Ripoff; The Unethical Society.

SIDELIGHTS: Hillers told *CA:* "*The Mocking of America* should not be classified as biographical, however, only real life experiences are used throughout the book to make the point as absolute as possible."

* * *

HILLINGER, Brad 1952-

PERSONAL: Born February 8, 1952, in Hollywood, Calif.; son of Charles Edward (a writer) and Arliene (Otis) Hillinger. *Education:* Attended University of Idaho and University of California, Los Angeles (extension). *Home:* 3131 Dianora Dr., Rancho Palos Verdes, Calif. 90274. *Agent:* Paul R. Reynolds, Inc., 12 East 41st St., New York, N.Y. 10017.

CAREER: Lifeguard with Los Angeles County Department of Beaches; actor in films and on television; writer. *Member:* National Surf Life Saving Association, Phi Delta Theta.

WRITINGS: (With Henery S. Bloomgarden) *The Wings Are Gone,* Morrow, 1976.

WORK IN PROGRESS: Five novels.

SIDELIGHTS: Hillinger writes: "I am very new in the writing world yet I come from a heritage of writers. My father is a feature writer for the *Los Angeles Times.* I seem to develop my stories from events that are close to me. My first book is a biography. I find that there are so many great stories being lived each day that there is not enough time to live them all. I believe that every story is worth relating and try in my writing to express true human adventures."

* * *

HILLUS, Wilhelm
See HILLERS, H(erman) W(illiam)

* * *

HINER, Louis C(hase) 1919-

PERSONAL: Born April 19, 1919, in Astoria, Ore.; son of Louis C. (a newspaperman) and Rubye (Isaacs) Hiner; married Marian Kendall, June 5, 1940 (divorced November, 1947); married Phyllis Clark, March, 1950; children: Carolyn (Mrs. J. William Wright III), Gregory C., Brad C. *Education:* Attended Indiana University, 1939-41. *Politics:* Independent-Republican. *Religion:* Protestant. *Home:* 3426 Farm Hill Dr., Falls Church, Va. 22044. *Office: Indianapolis News, Phoenix Gazette,* and *Muncie Evening Press,* 641 National Press Bldg., Washington, D.C. 20045.

CAREER/WRITINGS: Editor of local newspapers in Rushville, Ind., 1941, and Martinsville, Ind., 1946-47; *Indianapolis News,* Indianapolis, Ind., statehouse reporter, 1947-52, Washington correspondent, 1953—; Washington correspondent for *Muncie Evening Press,* 1953—, and *Phoenix Gazette,* 1955—. Notable assignments include coverage of all national political campaigns since 1948 and the space program. Editorial columnist, travel and aviation writer. *Military service:* U.S. Army Air Corps, 1942-46. *Member:* National Press Club, White House Washington Correspondents, American Legion, Elks Lodge, Sigma Delta Chi.

SIDELIGHTS: Hiner told *CA* that his ancestors published one of the first papers in Indiana in the town of Rising Sun around 1820, and that "newspapering" has been a family tradition ever since. For twenty years Hiner has written a regular series on waste in federal government spending, and he wrote a special series on "off beat things" for bicentennial visitors to see in the Washington area.

* * *

HINMAN, George W., Jr. 1891-1977

December 7, 1891—September 22, 1977; American military officer and journalist. Hinman's Army career positions included service with the Adjutant General's office, the General Staff Corps, and the Office of the Quartermaster General, where he served as a liason officer until retiring with the rank of colonel. During his career as a journalist, he was a foreign correspondent and news executive for the Hearst newspaper chain. He died in Washington, D.C. Obituaries: *New York Times,* September 29, 1977.

* * *

HINTON, Sam 1917-

PERSONAL: Born March 21, 1917, in Tulsa, Okla.; married Leslie Forster (a musician and singer). *Education:* Attended Texas A. & M. University, 1934-36; graduated from the University of California at Los Angeles, 1940.

CAREER: Early jobs included singing, sign painting, and selling snake venom; Desert Museum, Palm Springs, Calif., director, 1940-43; curator of aquarium and museum at University of California's Scripp's Institution of Oceanography, beginning 1943; assistant director of the Office of School Relations, University of California, beginning 1964. Teacher of college extension courses in biology and folklore, beginning 1948; taught folk music courses on educational television, 1962, 1967; featured singer on several LP's in the 1950's and 1960's; singer at campus folk song concerts; performer and discussion leader at Berkeley Folk Festival, beginning 1957.

WRITINGS: Exploring Under the Sea (illustrated by Rudolph Freund), Garden City Books, 1957; *Seashore Life of Southern California,* University of California Press, 1969. Author of newspaper feature, "The Ocean World," for the *San Diego Union,* beginning 1958.

SIDELIGHTS: Although Sam Hinton once remarked that he has always sung, his "career" as a folksinger began in 1936 when he won a Major Bowes Amateur contest. At that time, he left school to travel with one of the Bowes troupes, and for the next two years sang throughout the United States and Canada. When he tired of traveling, he returned to college, but his singing helped to pay tuition. Hinton's first recording was an album of Anglo-Irish ballads and songs, "Buffalo Boy American Folk Songs," released in 1947. His first commercial recording was "Old Man Atom" in 1950 for Columbia Records. In the early 1950's, Hinton recorded several songs for Decca Records' Children's Series which included "The Barnyard Song," "Country Critters," "The Frog Song," and "The Greatest Sound Around."

"Folk Songs of California and the Old West," was Sam Hinton's first LP, recorded for Bowmar Records in 1952. With Alan Lomax and Si Rady, he worked on the selection and arrangement of material for an RCA album, "How the West Was Won," on which he sang nine songs. He recorded several albums for Decca in the mid-1950's, including "Singing Across the Land," "A Family Tree of Folk Songs," and "The Real McCoy." In the 1960's, he was featured on such albums as "American Folk Songs and Balladeers" for the Classics Record Library, "Newport Folk Festival, 1963," for Vanguard, and "The Songs of Men," "Whoever Shall Have Some Peanuts," and "The Wandering Folksong," for Folkway Records.

Hinton also appeared in the musical comedy, "Meet the People," in Los Angeles, which featured Nanette Fabray and Jack Gilford.

BIOGRAPHICAL/CRITICAL SOURCES: San Francisco Chronicle, November 10, 1957; *New York Times,* December 8, 1957.*

* * *

HINTON, Ted C. 1904(?)-1977

American law enforcement officer and writer. Hinton participated in the six-man force that ambushed Bonnie and Clyde in 1934. In an unpublished book about the Parker-Barrow gang, Hinton contended that Bonnie died in Clyde's arms. Hinton later served as a deputy United States marshal. He died in Dallas, Tex. Obituaries: *New York Times,* October 29, 1977.

* * *

HIRSCH, Barbara B. 1938-

PERSONAL: Born July 5, 1938, in Chicago, Ill., daughter of Maurice L. and Ruth (Hartman) Hirsch. *Education:* Attended University of Illinois, 1956-58, and Northwestern University, 1959; DePaul University, LL.B., 1966. *Office:* 208 South LaSalle, Chicago, Ill. 60604.

CAREER: Admitted to Illinois bar, 1966; Chadwell, Keck, Kayser & Ruggles, Chicago, Ill., attorney, 1966-70; attorney in private practice in Chicago, 1970—. Lecturer at DePaul University and Chicago College of Law, 1971. Member of executive board of American Jewish Committee, 1971—. *Member:* American Bar Association, Federal Bar Association, Illinois Bar Association, Chicago Bar Association.

WRITINGS: Divorce: What a Woman Needs to Know, Regnery, 1973; *Living Together: A Guide to the Law for Unmarried Couples,* Houghton, 1976. Contributor to magazines and newspapers.

* * *

HIXON, Don L(ee) 1942-

PERSONAL: Born August 9, 1942, in Columbus, Ohio; son of Elbert and Nellie (Hayden) Hixon. *Education:* California State University, Long Beach, A.B., 1965, M.A., 1967; University of California, Los Angeles, M.S.L.S., 1967. *Politics:* Democrat. *Home:* 9392 Mayrene Dr., Garden Grove, Calif. 92641. *Office:* Acquisitions Department, Library, University of California, Irvine, Calif. 92716.

CAREER: University of California, Irvine, reference librarian, 1967-74, fine arts librarian, 1974—. *Member:* International Association of Music Libraries, International Musicological Society, American Musicological Society, Music Library Association (president of southern California chapter, 1977-78), University of California Music Librarians (chairman, 1977—).

WRITINGS: Music in Early America, Scarecrow, 1970; (with Don A. Hennessee) *Women in Music: A Biobibliography,* Scarecrow, 1975; (with Hennessee) *Nineteenth-Century American Drama: A Finding Guide,* Scarecrow, 1977.

WORK IN PROGRESS: A computer-assisted biobibliography of musicians.

SIDELIGHTS: Hixon told *CA:* "My chief interest lies in classical music. I have studied piano with Lura Soderstrom since 1956, and the composers who are most meaningful to me include Bach, Schumann, Schubert, and Poulenc. As an adjunct to this interest, I have assembled a record collection including more than five thousand LP's, in addition to over five hundred albums of 78 rpm recordings."

AVOCATIONAL INTERESTS: Travel (particularly desert backroads and wilderness areas of the American Southwest), nature photography, HO model railroading.

* * *

HOBEL, Phil
See FANTHORPE, R(obert) Lionel

* * *

HOCKENBERRY, Hope
See NEWELL, Hope Hockenberry

* * *

HODGES, Herbert Arthur 1905-1976

PERSONAL: Born January 4, 1905; son of Willis and Lily Malaingre (Dyson) Hodges; married Vera Joan Willis, 1939; children: two sons, one daughter. *Education:* Balliol College, Oxford, B.A., 1926; University of Reading, M.A., D.Phil., 1932. *Home:* 3 Grahame Ave., Pangbourne, Berkshire RG8 7LF, England.

CAREER: University of Reading, Reading, Berkshire, England, professor of philosophy, 1934-69, professor emeritus, 1969-76. Member of Royal Commission on Betting, Lotteries, and Gaming, 1949-51. *Member:* Guild of St. George (master).

WRITINGS: Wilhelm Dilthey: An Introduction, K. Paul, Trench, Trubner & Co., 1944, Fertig, 1969; *Christianity and the Modern World View,* SCM Press, 1949; *The Philosophy of Wilhelm Dilthey,* Routledge & Kegan Paul, 1952, reprinted, Greenwood Press, 1974; *Languages, Standpoints, and Attitudes,* Oxford University Press, 1953; *Anglicanism and Orthodoxy: A Study in Dialectical Churchmanship,* SCM Press, 1955; *The Pattern of Atonement,* SCM Press, 1955; *Death and Life Have Contended,* SCM Press, 1964. Also author of pamphlets.

OBITUARIES: AB Bookman's Weekly, October 4, 1976.*

(Died October 4, 1976, in England)

* * *

HOFSINDE, Robert 1902-1973

PERSONAL: Born December 10, 1902, in Odense, Denmark; emigrated to the United States in 1922; married wife, Geraldine, 1937. *Education:* Attended Royal Art Academy, Copenhagen, Denmark, 1916-22, Minneapolis School of Art. *Residence:* Monroe, N.Y.

CAREER: Author and illustrator of books for children. With his wife, had daily radio program, "Gray-Wolf's Ti-pi"

in Chicago, beginning 1937; through Junior Programs of New York, organized school assemblies on Indian lore throughout the country, beginning 1940. Has designed scenery for the Circus Saints and Sinners Club, illustrations for the New York Railroad Club, and numerous murals.

WRITINGS—All self-illustrated; all published by Morrow: *The Indian's Secret World,* 1955; *Indian Sign Language,* 1956; *Indian Games and Crafts,* 1957; *Indian Beadwork,* 1958; *Indian Picture Writing,* 1959; *The Indian and His Horse,* 1960; *The Indian and the Buffalo,* 1961; *Indian Hunting,* 1962; *Indian Fishing and Camping,* 1963; *Indians at Home,* 1964; *Indian Warriors and Their Weapons,* 1965; *The Indian Medicine Man,* 1966; *Indian Music Makers,* 1967; *Indian Costumes,* 1968; *Indians on the Move,* 1970; *Indian Arts,* 1971.

Illustrator: Allan A. Macfarlan, *Indian Adventure Trails,* Dodd, 1953.

Contributor of articles on Indian lore to *Popular Mechanics* and *Popular Science.*

SIDELIGHTS: Hofsinde was born next door to Hans Christian Andersen's house. His interest in the American Indian culture began with a painting trip to the north woods of Minnesota. One day, he came upon a young Indian boy who had fallen into a pit trap and suffered a compound fracture of the leg. Hofsinde rescued the boy, set the break, and carried him back to his village on a sled. In gratitude, Hofsinde was made a blood brother of the Ojibwa tribe and was given the name Gray-Wolf. He enjoyed sketching the Ojibwas and became so interested in their culture that he stayed with them for three years. He returned to Minneapolis, but still wanted to know more about the Indians. He set off on a research and sketching trip which lasted sixteen years. He visited the Ojibwa and Blackfeet tribes, traveling on horseback from Montana to Arizona. He was accepted among all the Indians as a friend, and allowed to participate in their ceremonies, sit in their councils, and smoke with the men. His wife often traveled with him, and the Indians gave her the name Morning Star.

BIOGRAPHICAL/CRITICAL SOURCES: Kirkus Reviews, July 1, 1955; *Chicago Tribune,* November 13, 1955; *Young Readers' Review,* May, 1967; *Christian Science Monitor,* June 22, 1967.*

(Died November 26, 1973)

* * *

HOGBEN, Lancelot T. 1895-1975

PERSONAL: Born December 9, 1895, in Southsea, England; son of Thomas (a seaman's parson) and Margaret Alice (Prescott) Hogben; married Dr. Enid Charles (a scientist), 1918 (divorced, 1957); married Sarah Jane Evans, 1957; children: (first marriage) two daughters, two sons. *Education:* Trinity College, Cambridge, M.A. *Residence:* Glynceiriog, North Wales.

CAREER: University of London, Imperial College of Science, London, England, lecturer in zoology, 1919-22, assistant director of animal breeding research department, 1923; University of Edinburgh, Edinburgh, Scotland, lecturer in experimental physiology, 1923-25; McGill University, Montreal, Quebec, assistant professor of zoology, 1925-27; University of Cape Town, Cape Town, South Africa, professor of zoology, 1927-30; University of London, professor of social biology, 1930-37; University of Aberdeen, Aberdeen, Scotland, Regius Professor of Natural History, 1937-41; University of Birmingham, Birmingham, England, Mason

Professor of Zoology, 1941-47, professor of medical statistics, 1947-61, emeritus honorable senior fellow in linguistics, 1961-64; University of Guyana, Georgetown, Guyana, vice-chancellor, 1963-65. *Awards, honors:* Awarded gold medal and elected a fellow of the Royal Society of Edinburgh, 1936; Croonian Lecturer, 1942; LL.D., University of Birmingham, 1964; D.Sc., University of Wales, 1964.

WRITINGS—Nonfiction: *The Pigmentary Effector System: A Review of the Physiology of Colour Response,* Oliver & Boyd, 1924; *An Introduction to Recent Advances in Comparative Physiology,* Collins, 1924; *Comparative Physiology,* Macmillan, 1926 (published in England as *The Comparative Physiology of Internal Secretion,* Cambridge University Press, 1927); *Principles of Evolutionary Biology,* Juta, 1927; *The Nature of Living Matter,* Keegan Paul, 1930; *Principles of Animal Biology,* Christophers, 1930; *Genetic Principles in Medicine and Social Science,* Williams & Norgate, 1931; *Nature and Nurture,* Norton, 1933; *Mathematics for the Million* (illustrated by J. F. Horrabin), Allen & Unwin, 1936, Norton, 1937, 4th edition, revised, Norton, 1968; *The Retreat from Reason,* Watts, 1936, Random House, 1937; *Science for the Citizen* (illustrated by J. F. Horrabin), Knopf, 1938, 4th edition, revised, Allen & Unwin, 1966; (editor) *Political Arithmetic: A Symposium of Population Studies,* Allen & Unwin, 1938; *Lancelot Hogben's Dangerous Thoughts,* Allen & Unwin, 1939, published as *Dangerous Thoughts,* Norton, 1940.

Principles of Animal Biology (illustrated by J. F. Horrabin), Norton, 1940; *Interglossa: A Draft of an Auxiliary for a Democratic World Order* (illustrated by Otto Neurath), Penguin, 1943; *An Introduction to Mathematical Genetics,* Norton, 1946; (editor) Henry Hamilton, *England: A History of the Homeland,* Norton, 1948; *From Cave Painting to Comic Strip: A Kaleidoscope of Human Communication,* Chanticleer Press, 1949; *Chance and Choice by Card Pack and Chessboard: An Introduction to Probability in Practice by Visual Aids,* Chanticleer Press, 1950; *Statistical Theory: The Relationship of Probability, Credibility, and Error,* Allen & Unwin, 1957, Norton, 1968; (with K. W. Cross) *Design of Documents: A Study of Mechanical Aids to Field Enquiries,* Macdonald & Evans, 1960; *Mathematics in the Making,* Crescent Books, 1960; (editor) Frederick Bodmer, *The Loom of Language,* Allen & Unwin, 1961; *Essential World English, Being a Preliminary Mnemotechnic Programme for Proficiency in English Self-Expression for International Use, Based on Semantic Principles,* Norton, 1963; *Science in Authority: Essays,* Norton, 1963; *The Mother Tongue,* Secker & Warburg, 1964, Norton, 1965; (with Maureen Cartwright) *The Vocabulary of Science,* Heinemann, 1969, Stein & Day, 1970; *The Beginnings of Science,* Heinemann, 1970, St. Martin's, 1974.

For children: (Editor) *The First Great Inventions,* Chanticleer Press, 1950, 6th edition, Parrish, 1964; (editor) *How the First Men Lived,* Chanticleer Press, 1950; *The Wonderful World of Mathematics* (illustrated by Charles Keeping and Kenneth Symonds), Garden City Books, 1955, revised and enlarged edition, Doubleday, 1968; *The Wonderful World of Energy* (illustrated by Eileen Aplin), Garden City Books, 1957, revised and enlarged edition, Doubleday, 1968 (published in England as *Men, Missiles, and Machines: The Wonderful World of Power,* Rathbone Books, 1957); *The Wonderful World of Communication,* Garden City Books, 1959, revised and enlarged edition, Doubleday, 1969 (published in England as *The Signs of Civilisation,* Rathbone Books, 1959); *Beginnings and Blunders; or, Before Science Began,* Grosset, 1970; *Astronomer Priest and Ancient Mari-*ner, Heinemann, 1972, St. Martin's, 1974; *Maps, Mirrors, and Mechanics,* St. Martin's, 1973.

Other: *Alfred Russel Wallace: The Story of a Great Discoverer,* Society for Promoting Christian Knowledge, 1918; *Author in Transit,* Norton, 1940; *Whales for the Welsh: A Tale of War and Peace,* Rapp & Carroll, 1967.

SIDELIGHTS: Many of Hogben's books were sincere attempts to bring scientific and mathematical subjects within the understanding of all literate persons. "*Mathematics for the Million,*" a *Chicago Daily Tribune* reviewer wrote, "is really a popular textbook on all the phases of mathematics, including the calculus, but so brilliantly has its author written it that he has succeeded in getting his readers really excited." *Times Literary Supplement* described the book as "anything but dull. The nonmathematician who is willing to give it the thought it deserves will be repaid with a stimulating experience, with an adventure which opens out to him a new horizon; and the mathematician will find a refreshingly different outlook brought to bear on what is perhaps too familiar to him in a book that bears no trace of the professional mathematician." *New Statesman and Nation* added: "At times the author sacrifices accuracy and precision for the sake of a gibe or a bon mot. That matters little.... What matters indeed is that there should be someone alive who can produce a work like this." The book has sold well over 70,000 copies in the United States alone.

Science for the Citizen was Hogben's second effort in popularizing difficult subjects for the layman. *Books* wrote, "Professor Hogben has a style of his own. It is insidious. There is no obvious effort to be entertaining, shocking, elegant, or ... jazzy. Like his heroes, Faraday, Tyndall, and T. H. Huxley, he is not afraid of simplicity. He writes directly of worthwhile things with the intention of instructing his readers. He believes that the citizen will read science just as he reads the directions for hooking up his new radio or any other explanation of something he finds worthwhile. Clearness, exactitude, relation to genuine interests characterize such writing; and these are the virtues that make Mr. Hogben's style fascinating." *Nation* commented that, "Lancelot Hogben has written of science from out of the depths of his knowledge, yet he has not divorced it from everyday life or made it seem the playground of the wizard and the aesthete. His concept of science is so fundamental that many a scientist may read this book with profit." *Saturday Review* remarked, "One may disagree with the author's views regarding certain philosophers and scientists and his prescriptions for the disorders of the human race, but one can have nothing but praise for the delightful and thought-provoking qualities of the book."

Author in Transit was based on Hogben's personal experience. He and his daughter were caught in Oslo, Norway when the Germans invaded in April, 1940. The only way to return to England seemed to be along a 20,000 mile detour through Sweden, Russia, Siberia, Japan, and the United States. A *Current History and Forum* review said, "This is not a joke book. It is a super-readable job of comment and observation, flexible as an old shoe, and frequently as informal. Hogben has written a short book which does for politics and nations what his *Mathematics for the Million* did for calculation and computation. So doing he reveals himself as never before as the heir presumptive to Bernard Shaw." The *Christian Science Monitor* added, "The story is delightfully entertaining.... All Professor Hogben's observations are interesting. Some of them are undoubtedly accurate. As to which are, and which are not, that is up to the reader to decide for himself."

Beginnings and Blunders; or, Before Science Began was one of Hogben's more recent efforts for children. According to a *Books* critic, "Hogben describes science as 'the written record of reliable knowledge about nature, including human nature,' and his book is the exhilarating account of how men and women made it possible for science in this sense to begin." *Saturday Review* commented, "There is nothing here that hasn't been covered before, but this is a competent synthesis of knowledge, stolidly written though not ponderous."

AVOCATIONAL INTERESTS: Building furniture and designing gardens.

BIOGRAPHICAL/CRITICAL SOURCES: New Statesman and Nation, November 14, 1936; *Times Literary Supplement,* November 21, 1936; *Chicago Daily Tribune,* March 27, 1937; *Books,* September 25, 1938, November, 1970; *Nation,* October 8, 1938; *Saturday Review,* October 8, 1938, May 15, 1971; *Current History and Forum,* November 7, 1940; *Christian Science Monitor,* December 21, 1940.

OBITUARIES: New York Times, August 23, 1975; *Washington Post,* August 24, 1975; *Newsweek,* September 1, 1975; *Publishers Weekly,* September 29, 1975.*

(Died August 22, 1975)

* * *

HOHENBERG, Dorothy Lannuier 1905(?)-1977

1905(?)—September 2, 1977; American journalist. Hohenberg was a feature writer and columnist for the *New York Post.* She died in Southampton, N.Y. Obituaries: *New York Times,* September 3, 1977.

* * *

HOIJER, Harry 1904-1976

PERSONAL: Born September 6, 1904, in Chicago, Ill.; son of John Oscar and Agnes Sophia (Peterson) Hoijer; married Dorothy Jared, June 7, 1927; children: Peter, Charlotte Teeples, Susan Loraine. *Education:* University of Chicago, A.B., 1927, A.M., 1929, Ph.D., 1931. *Home:* 191 Beloit Ave., Los Angeles, Calif. 90049.

CAREER: University of Chicago, Chicago, Ill., instructor in anthropology, 1931-40; University of California, Los Angeles, assistant professor, 1940-46, associate professor, 1946-48, professor of anthropology, 1948-72, professor emeritus, 1972-76, chairman of department of anthropology, 1948-51. Fellow, Center for Advanced Study in the Behavioral Sciences, 1959-60. *Member:* American Anthropology Association (fellow; vice-president, 1949; president, 1958), Linguistic Society of America (vice-president, 1951; president, 1959), Southwest Anthropology Association (vice-president, 1945; president, 1946), Sigma Xi.

WRITINGS: Tonkawa, an Indian Language of Texas, J. J. Agustine, 1933; *Chiricahua and Mescalero Apache Texts,* University of Chicago Press, 1938; *Navaho Phonology,* University of New Mexico Press, 1945; *An Analytical Dictionary of the Tonkawa Language,* University of California Press, 1949; (with Ralph Beals) *An Introduction to Anthropology,* Macmillan, 1953, 4th edition, 1971; (editor) *Language in Culture: Proceedings of a Conference on the Interrelations of Language and Other Aspects of Culture,* University of Chicago Press, 1954; *Linguistic Structures of Native America,* edited by Cornelius Osgood, Johnson Reprint, 1963; *Studies in the Athapaskan Languages,* University of California Press, 1963; (editor) Leonard Bloomfield, *Language History,* Holt, 1965; (with Edward Sapir) *The*

Phonology and Morphology of the Navaho Language, University of California Press, 1967; (editor) *The Social Anthropology of Latin America,* University of California Press, 1970; *Tonkawa Texts,* University of California Press, 1972; *A Navajo Lexicon,* University of California Press, 1974. Contributor of articles and reviews to professional journals.

Associate editor, *Memoirs* of American Anthropology Association, 1948-52, *International Journal of American Linguistics,* 1964-76.

OBITUARIES: New York Times, March 6, 1976; *AB Bookman's Weekly,* May 17, 1976.*

(Died March 11, 1976, in Santa Monica, Calif.)

* * *

HOKE, Helen L. 1903-
(Helen Sterling)

PERSONAL: Born in 1903; married John Hoke (an editor); married second husband, Franklin Watts (a publisher), May 25, 1945; children: (first marriage) John Lindsay. *Home:* 11 Belgravia House, 2 Halkin Place, London S.W. 1, England. *Office:* F. Watts Ltd., 1 Vere St., London W1N 9HQ, England.

CAREER: Franklin Watts, Inc., vice-president and editor-in-chief, beginning 1948, became director of international projects; president of Helen Hoke Associates (consulting and publishing firm), 1956—; author and editor of books for children.

WRITINGS: Mr. Sweeney (illustrated by William Wills), Holt, 1940; (with Richard C. Gill) *Paco Goes to the Fair: A Story of Far-Away Ecuador* (illustrated by Ruth Gannett), Holt, 1940; (with Gill) *Story of the Other America* (illustrated by Manuel R. Regalado), Houghton, 1941; (with Miriam Teichner) *The Fuzzy Kitten* (illustrated by Meg Wohlberg), Messner, 1941; *Major and the Kitten* (illustrated by Diana Thorne), Holt, 1941; (with Natalie Fox) *The Woolly Lamb* (illustrated by Sally Tate), Messner, 1942; *The Furry Bear* (illustrated by Tate), Messner, 1943; *Doctor, the Puppy Who Learned* (illustrated by Thorne), Messner, 1944; *Shep and the Baby* (illustrated by Thorne), Messner, 1944; *The Shaggy Pony* (illustrated by Dick Hart), Messner, 1944; *Mrs. Silk* (illustrated by Thorne), Veritas Press, 1945; *The Fuzzy Puppy* (illustrated by Hart), Messner, 1945; *Rags' Day* (illustrated by Thorne), Veritas Press, 1945; *Grocery Kitty* (illustrated by Harry Lees), Reynal & Hitchcock, 1946; *Too Many Kittens* (illustrated by Lees), McKay, 1947; *Factory Kitty* (illustrated by Lees), F. Watts, 1949.

The First Book of Dolls (illustrated by Jean Michener), F. Watts, 1954; (with Walter Pels) *The First Book of Toys* (illustrated by Michener), F. Watts, 1957; (with son, John Hoke) *Music Boxes: Their Lore and Lure* (illustrated by Nancy Martin), Hawthorn Books, 1957; *The First Book of Tropical Mammals* (illustrated by Helene Carter), F. Watts, 1958; *One Thousand Ways to Make $1,000 in Your Spare Time,* Bantam, 1959; *Arctic Mammals* (illustrated by Jean Zallinger), F. Watts, 1969; *The Big Dog and the Very Little Cat* (illustrated by Thorne), F. Watts, 1969; *Etiquette: Your Ticket to Good Times* (illustrated by Carol Wilde), F. Watts, 1970; *Ants* (illustrated by Arabelle Wheatley), F. Watts, 1970; *Jokes and Fun* (illustrated by Tony Parkhouse), F. Watts, 1972; (with Valerie Pitt) *Whales* (illustrated by Thomas R. Funderburk), F. Watts, 1973; *Hoke's Jokes, Cartoons, and Funny Things* (illustrated by Eric Hill), F. Watts, 1973; (with Pitt) *Fleas,* F. Watts, 1974; (with Pitt) *Owls* (illustrated by Robert Jefferson), F. Watts, 1974;

Riddle Giggles (illustrated by Parkhouse), F. Watts, 1975; (with Oliver Neshamkin) *Jokes, Fun, and Folly,* F. Watts, 1975.

Under pseudonym Helen Sterling: *Little Choo Choo* (illustrated by Denison Budd), F. Watts, 1944; *The Horse That Takes the Milk Around* (illustrated by Marjorie Hartwell), F. Watts, 1946; *Little Moo and the Circus* (illustrated by Lees), F. Watts, 1945; *The Biggest Family in the Town* (illustrated by Vance Locke), McKay, 1947.

Editor: *Jokes, Jokes, Jokes* (illustrated by Richard Erdoes), F. Watts, 1954; *The Family Book of Humor,* Hanover House, 1957; (with Boris Randolph) *Puns, Puns, Puns* (illustrated by Seymour Nydorf), F. Watts, 1958; *Witches, Witches, Witches* (illustrated by W. R. Lohse), F. Watts, 1958; *Alaska, Alaska, Alaska* (illustrated by R. M. Six), F. Watts, 1960; *Nurses, Nurses, Nurses,* F. Watts, 1961; *Patriotism, Patriotism, Patriotism* (illustrated by Leonard E. Fisher), F. Watts, 1963; *More Jokes, Jokes, Jokes* (illustrated by Erdoes), F. Watts, 1965; *Spooks, Spooks, Spooks* (illustrated by Lohse), F. Watts, 1966; *The Big Book of Jokes* (illustrated by Erdoes), F. Watts, 1971; *Dragons, Dragons, Dragons* (illustrated by C. Barker), F. Watts, 1972; *Weirdies, Weirdies, Weirdies* (illustrated by Charles Keeping), F. Watts, 1973; *Jokes, Jests, and Jollies* (illustrated by True Kelley), Ginn, 1973; *Jokes, Jokes, Jokes, 2* (illustrated by Haro), F. Watts, 1973, reprinted as *Jokes, Giggles, and Guffaws,* 1975; *Monsters, Monsters, Monsters* (illustrated by Keeping), F. Watts, 1974; *Devils, Devils, Devils* (illustrated by C. Baker), F. Watts, 1976; *More Riddles, Riddles, Riddles* (illustrated by Haro), F. Watts, 1976; *Ghosts and Ghastlies* (illustrated by Bill Prosser), F. Watts, 1976.

BIOGRAPHICAL/CRITICAL SOURCES: Kirkus, May 15, 1949; *New York Times,* July 17, 1949; *Publishers Weekly,* September 1, 1975.*

*   *   *

HOLCOMBE, Arthur N(orman) 1884-1977

November 3, 1884—December 9, 1977; American educator and writer, credited with having expanded Harvard University's government curriculum with the inclusions of political philosophy and theory. Among his former students are Henry Kissinger and Henry Cabot Lodge. In 1949, Holcombe assisted Chiang Kai Shek in drafting a constitution for the Republic of China. He died in Gwynned, Pa. Obituaries: *New York Times,* December 14, 1977. (See index for *CA* sketch)

*   *   *

HOLDEN, David (Shipley) 1924-1977

November 20, 1924—December, 1977; British journalist and author. Holden was chief foreign correspondent for *London Times.* He died in Cairo, Egypt. Obituaries: *Detroit Free Press,* December 12, 1977. (See index for *CA* sketch)

*   *   *

HOLLAND, Janice 1913-1962

PERSONAL: Born May 23, 1913, in Washington, D.C. *Education:* Attended Corcoran School of Art and Pratt Institute. *Residence:* Washington, D.C.

CAREER: Author and illustrator of books for children.

WRITINGS—All self-illustrated: *They Built a City: The Story of Washington, D.C.,* Scribner, 1953; *Pirates, Plant-*

ers, and Patriots: The Story of Charleston, South Carolina, Scribner, 1955; *Christopher Goes to the Castle,* Scribner, 1957; *The Apprentice and the Prize,* Vanguard Press, 1958; *Hello, George Washington!,* Abingdon, 1958; (adapter) *You Never Can Tell* (adapted from *The Book of Huai-nan-tzu*), Scribner, 1963.

Illustrator: Janette S. Lowrey, *Rings on Her Fingers,* Harper, 1941; Frances Cavanagh, *Our Country's Story,* Rand McNally, 1945; Mary Alice Jones, *Bible Story of the Creation,* Rand McNally, 1946; Maria C. Chambers, *Three Kings,* Oxford University Press, 1946; Andrew Lang, *Yellow Fairy Book,* Longmans, Green, 1948, reprinted, McKay, 1966; Catherine C. Coblentz, *Blue Cat of Castle Town,* Longmans, Green, 1949, reprinted, Countryman Press, 1974; Alberta P. Graham, *Christopher Columbus, Discoverer,* Abingdon, 1950; Siddie Joe Johnson, *Cat Hotel,* Longmans, Green, 1955; Lillian Quigley, *The Blind Men and the Elephant,* Scribner, 1959.

BIOGRAPHICAL/CRITICAL SOURCES: New York Times, February 15, 1953, October 20, 1957; *Chicago Tribune,* November 17, 1957, March 29, 1959; *New York Herald Tribune,* June 16, 1963.*

(Died, 1962)

*   *   *

HOLLIDAY, Barbara Gregg 1917-

PERSONAL: Born August 28, 1917, in Little River, Kan.; daughter of Ray Brooks (a teacher) and Nina (Cook) Brooks Gregg; married Robert B. Holliday (a minister), March 6, 1937 (died December, 1957); children: Nina (Mrs. Charles Sanford, Jr.), Gregg, Mindy (Mrs. Thomas J. Vranich), Susan (Mrs. Donald Lee Turney). *Education:* Christian College (now Columbia College), A.A., 1937; University of Missouri, B.J., 1939, M.A., 1967. *Religion:* Protestant. *Home:* 15802 Birwood, Birmingham, Mich. 48009. *Office: Detroit Free Press,* 321 W. Lafayette, Detroit, Mich. 48231.

CAREER/WRITINGS: Columbia Daily Tribune, Columbia, Mo., feature writer, 1958-60; *Detroit Free Press,* Detroit, Mich., copy editor, 1960-61, reporter, 1961-65, member of magazine staff, 1965-67, assistant Sunday editor, 1967-70, features editor, 1970—, book editor, 1973—. Notable assignments include a series on the John Birch Society. Contributor of articles to *Ford Times, House Beautiful,* and *Esquire.* Speaker and moderator, Oakland Writers Conference, 1970-75. *Member:* Society of Professional Journalists (member of board, 1971-76, vice-president, 1974, treasurer, 1976—).

SIDELIGHTS: Holliday told *CA:* "I was sure I wanted to be in the field of journalism at an early age and found much inspiration in a teacher and friend, Mary Paxton Keeley, first woman graduate of the University of Missouri School of Journalism. Earl English, dean emeritus, was another prodder whom I'm deeply indebted to." *Avocational interests:* Reading, archaeology, anthropology, the American Southwest.

*   *   *

HOLLIS, (Maurice) Christopher 1902-1977

PERSONAL: Born March 29, 1902, in England; son of George Arthur (an Anglican bishop) and Mary Cordelia (Burn) Hollis; married Margaret Madeline King, 1929; children: three sons, one daughter. *Education:* Attended Balliol College, Oxford. *Politics:* Conservative. *Religion:* Roman Catholic. *Home:* Little Claveys, Mells, Somerset, England.

CAREER: Author and journalist. Toured United States, New Zealand, and Australia as member of Oxford Union Debating Society, 1924-25; Stonyhurst College, Lancashire, England, assistant master, 1925-35; Notre Dame University, Notre Dame, Ind., economics researcher, 1935-39; Conservative member of Parliament, 1945-55; chairman of the board, Hollis and Carter (publishing firm). *Military service:* Royal Air Force, 1939-45.

WRITINGS: The American Heresy, Sheed (London), 1927, Minton, Balch & Co., 1930; *Dr. Johnson,* Gollancz, 1928, Holt, 1929; *The Monstrous Regiment,* Sheed, 1929, Minton, Balch & Co., 1930; *European History, 1713 to 1914,* Macmillan (London), 1929; *Saint Ignatius,* Harper, 1931; *Erasmus,* Bruce Publishing, 1933; *Dryden,* Duckworth, 1933, Folcroft, 1969; *Thomas More,* Bruce Publishing, 1934 (published in England as *Sir Thomas More,* Sheed, 1934, revised edition, Burns & Oates, 1961); *The Breakdown of Money: An Historical Explanation,* Sheed, 1934; *The Two Nations: A Financial Study of English History,* G. Routledge and Sons, 1935, Gordon Press, 1975; *Foreigners Aren't Fools,* Longmans, Green, 1936, Frederick A. Stokes Co., 1937; *We Aren't So Dumb,* Longmans, Green, 1937; *Lenin,* Bruce Publishing, 1938; *Foreigners Aren't Knaves,* Longmans, Green, 1939; *Our Case,* Longmans, Green, 1939.

Italy in Africa, Hamish Hamilton, 1941; *Noble Castle,* Longmans, Green, 1941; *Death of a Gentleman: The Letters of Robert Fossett,* Burns & Oates, 1943; *Fossett's Memory,* Hollis & Carter, 1944; *Quality or Equality?,* Signpost Press, 1944; (editor with E. H. Carter) *History of Britain in Modern Times, 1688-1939,* Hollis & Carter, 1946; *Letters to a Sister,* Hollis & Carter, 1947, published as *With Love, Peter,* McMullen, 1948; *The Rise and Fall of the Ex-Socialist Government,* Hollis & Carter, 1947; *Can Parliament Survive?,* Hollis & Carter, 1949, Kennikat Press, 1971.

A Study of George Orwell: The Man and His Works, Regnery, 1956; *The Ayes and the Noes,* MacDonald, 1957; *Along the Road to Frome,* Harrap, 1958; *Eton: A History,* Hollis & Carter, 1960; *Christianity and Economics,* Hawthorn, 1961; *The Homicide Act,* Gollancz, 1964; *The Papacy: An Illustrated History from St. Peter to Paul VI,* Macmillan, 1964; *The Oxford Union,* Evans Brothers, 1965; *The Achievements of Vatican II,* Hawthorn, 1967; *Newman and the Modern World,* Hollis & Carter, 1967, Doubleday, 1968; *The Jesuits: A History,* Macmillan, 1968 (published in England as *A History of the Jesuits,* Weidenfeld & Nicolson, 1968); (with Ronald Brownrigg) *Holy Places: Jewish, Christian, and Muslim Monuments in the Holy Land,* Praeger, 1969.

The Mind of Chesterton, University of Miami Press, 1970; *Parliament and Its Sovereignty,* Hollis & Carter, 1973; *The Seven Ages: Their Exits and Their Entrances,* Heinemann, 1974; *Oxford in the Twenties: Recollections of Five Friends,* Heinemann, 1976. Contributor of articles to periodicals and newspapers. Member of editorial board, *Tablet;* member of board, *Punch.*

SIDELIGHTS: The son of an Anglican Bishop, Hollis converted to Catholicism when he was twenty-two years old. *Avocational interests:* Tennis, watching cricket, squash rackets.

OBITUARIES: AB Bookman's Weekly, May 9, 1977; *Washington Post,* May 9, 1977; *New York Times,* May 9, 1977.*

(Died May 5, 1977 in Somerset, England)

HOLLOWAY, (Rufus) Emory 1885-1977

March 16, 1885—July 30, 1977; American educator and biographer of Walt Whitman. Holloway won a Pullitzer Prize for his 1927 work, *Whitman: An Interpretation in Narrative.* Serving as both chairperson of the department of English and of the curriculum committee at Queens College, Holloway established a collection of Whitmaniana in the college's Walt Whitman Hall. He died in Bethlehem, Pa. Obituaries: *New York Times,* August 1, 1977. (See index for *CA* sketch)

* * *

HOLSOPPLE, Barbara 1943-

PERSONAL: Born April 30, 1943, in Youngwood, Pa.; daughter of Ernest Weaver and Alice (Brush) Holsopple. *Education:* Attended Seton Hill College, 1961-62; University of Pittsburgh, B.A., 1965. *Home:* 133 Lee St., Carnegie, Pa. 15106. *Office: Pittsburgh Press,* 34 Blvd. of Allies, Pittsburgh, Pa. 15230.

CAREER: Greensburg Tribune-Review, Greensburg, Pa., proofreader and assistant women's editor, 1962-63, women's editor, 1963-64; *Pittsburgh Press,* Pittsburgh, Pa., women's page feature writer, 1964-68, general assignment feature writer, 1968-70, magazine feature writer, 1970-72, TV-Radio editor and author of "Holsopple on TV" daily column, 1972—. *Member:* Television Critics Association, Press Club of Pittsburgh, Sigma Delta Chi. *Awards, honors:* Girl Scouts of Western Pennsylvania service award, 1964 and 1965; Pennsylvania Association of Retarded Children service award, 1965; Pittsburgh Zoological Society service award, 1966; United Fund of Allegheny County award, 1967; Golden Quill of Western Pennsylvania award, 1967 and 1968; Western Pennsylvania Hearing and Speech Society award, 1970; American Dental Association Science Writing award, 1972; Press Club of Pittsburgh award, 1975.

* * *

HONIG, Louis 1911-1977

1911—July 15, 1977; American advertising executive and author. Besides his position as board chairman of Roote, Cone & Belding/Honig Inc., Honig was also an investor and backer of *Ramparts* magazine. After a trip to North Vietnam in 1972, he wrote a novel about Central Intelligence Agency involvement there. He died in San Francisco, Calif. Obituaries: *New York Times,* July 19, 1977.

* * *

HONNALGERE, Gopal 1944-

PERSONAL: Born December 20, 1944, in Bijapur, India; son of H. Ramaswamy (an engineer) and Rajalakshmi (a musician; maiden name, Rajalakshmi) Honnalgere. *Education:* Attended Calcutta University, 1964; Mysore University, B.S., 1967. *Politics:* "No interest." *Home:* Oasis School, Hyderabad, 500 008, India.

CAREER: Teacher of English and creative writing at Oasis School, Hyderabad, India, 1969-70, Blue Mountains School, Ooty, India, 1971-76, and Greenfingers School, Akluj, India, 1977—. Lecturer and poet. *Member:* Indian P.E.N. *Awards, honors:* World Poet Award from World Poetry Society, 1973; Madras and Illinois Creative Writing Award, 1976.

WRITINGS—All poetry: *A Wad of Poems,* Writers Workshop (Calcutta), 1968; *A Gesture of Fleshless Sound,* Writers Workshop, 1970; *Zen Tree and the Wild Innocents,* Gray Books (Cuttack), 1972; *The Nudist Camp,* Release, 1976.

Contributor of articles to periodicals, including *Journal of Indian Writing in English, Graybook, Poet,* and *Thought.*

WORK IN PROGRESS: A monograph on Thomas Merton; a study of American confessional poetry; a book on the influence of Eastern religions on modern American poetry; poetry.

SIDELIGHTS: "The Indian poetry writing in English today," Honnalgere told *CA,* "is mostly dominated by academicians who are mostly English teachers in universities. My writing is not in the main stream. I believe that I write poetry altogether with a different sensibility, which is non-academic and naturally calls for a non-academic critic to make a study of it."

CA asked Honnalgere what he considered to be the major thematic differences between American and Indian poetry today. "The Indian poetry in English is still written with a lot of overtones," he wrote. "When it adorns the Indian cultural ethos it seems to have a lot of sentimental overtones and when it rejects, it seems to have once again the overtones of protest poetry. It is most derivative and often indulges in academic exercises. It does not show the vitality of the poet and the flexibility of language to communicate a feeling that someone is feeling somewhere something which is real. (My own poetry too is sometimes not free from these limitations.)

"The Modern American poetry on the other hand, in spite of its leg pulling experiments for experiment's sake, seems to have a primitivism, a primal innocence which is trying to create new forms, new themes, while working towards a universalism and a breakthrough in the conventional language structures. This makes American poetry most cherishable. My guiding influences have been, to name a few: Whitman, Roethke, Dickey, Carlos Williams, James Wright, Frost, Robert Lowell, William Stafford, and Thomas Merton."

* * *

HOOKE, Nina Warner 1907-

PERSONAL: Born 1907, in England; married Gilbert Thomas (a writer), December 14, 1940. *Education:* Attended Oxford University. *Politics:* Radical. *Religion:* Atheist. *Home:* Little Durnford, Langton, Matravers, Swanage, Dorsetshire, England. *Agent:* Curtis Brown Ltd., 575 Madison Ave., New York, N.Y. 10022.

CAREER: Professional writer since the age of nineteen.

WRITINGS: The Striplings (trilogy), Dutton, 1934-38; *Home Is Where You Make It,* Dutton, 1953; *Darkness I Leave You,* R. Hale, 1937; *The Deadly Record,* R. Hale, 1961; *The Seal Summer,* Harcourt, 1964; (with husband, Gilbert Thomas) *Marshall Hall: A Biography,* Barker, 1966; *White Christmas,* Barker, 1967, published as *The Starveling,* John Day, 1968; *Moon on the Water,* BBC Publications, 1975.

Plays: *No Man's Land,* Evans, 1958; *The Godsend* (one-act), Samuel French, 1959; *Festival Nightmare* (one-act), Samuel French, 1959; *Dear Madam* (two-act), Samuel French, 1960; *Dead Ernest* (three-act), Deane, 1961; *Not in the Contract* (one-act), Samuel French, 1961; *The Picnic on the Hill* (one-act), Samuel French, 1961; *The Sugar Bowl* (three-act), Deane, 1962; *Deadly Record: A Suspense in Three Acts,* Samuel French, 1965. Also author of sketches and monologues published by French, and "The Striplings," produced in London, 1964. Contributor of short stories and articles to *Cosmopolitan, Good Housekeeping,*

Saturday Evening Post, Woman's Day and to British magazines.

WORK IN PROGRESS: A play, "Kingdom Come"; a book about an abandoned cat.

SIDELIGHTS: Nina Hooke speaks French, Spanish, and Italian. Her novels, *Darkness I Leave You* and *The Deadly Record* were made into films in England. *Avocational interests:* Animal welfare, wildlife conservation, swimming, and travel.

* * *

HOOPES, Clement R. 1906-

PERSONAL: Born October 28, 1906, in Philadelphia, Pa.; son of Macmillan (with E. I. Du Pont & Co.) and Helen (Massey) Hoopes; married Marcia Meigs, June 5, 1936; children: David, Matthew, Thomas. *Education:* Princeton University, B.A., 1929; University of Pennsylvania, law student for one year. *Religion:* Episcopalian. *Home:* Windfall Farm, R.F.D. 2, West Grove, Pa. 19390. *Agent:* Jacqueline Harvey Associates, 124 East 40th St., New York, N.Y. 10016.

CAREER: Harper & Brothers (now Harper & Row), New York City, editorial and advertising work, 1934-42; Time, Inc., New York City, advertising staff, 1947-49; Economic Cooperation Administration (Marshall Plan), assignment in Dublin, Ireland, 1950-53; U.S. Information Agency, writer in Washington, D.C., and abroad, 1954-57; engaged in farming and real estate ("with writing thrown in"), 1957—. Commissioner, Brandywine Battlefield Park; member of board of directors, National Wax Museum, Washington, D.C. President, Chester County (Pa.) Mental Health Clinic, 1957. *Military service:* U.S. Navy, 1942-46; became lieutenant commander. *Member:* National Trust for Historic Preservation, Chester County Historical Society (member of board of directors).

WRITINGS: Angry Dust (novel), Devin, 1967; *A Frolic of His Own,* Devin, 1969; *The Courier,* Dorrance, 1973. In the 1940's had a short story published in *Harper's* and a golf story in *Liberty.*

BIOGRAPHICAL/CRITICAL SOURCES: New York Times Book Review, May 28, 1967; *Best Sellers,* November 15, 1967, March 15, 1970.

* * *

HOPPE, Eleanor Sellers 1933-

PERSONAL: Born August 23, 1933, in Abilene, Tex.; daughter of Erle Dees (a physician) and Nellie (Parramore) Sellers; married Robert H. Hoppe (a businessman), September 4, 1954; children: Erle, Mark, Ann. *Education:* College of William and Mary, student, 1951-52; University of Texas, B.A., 1954; Hardin-Simmons University, M.A., 1974. *Religion:* Episcopalian. *Home:* 1902 Campbell Dr., Abilene, Tex. 79602.

CAREER: Writer, 1967—. Member of board of directors of West Texas Rehabilitation Center. *Member:* American Association of University Women, Abilene Writers Guild, Junior League of Abilene (president).

WRITINGS: (With Dilworth Parramore Sellers) *The Parramore Sketches: Scenes and Stories of West Texas,* Texas Western Press, 1975. Contributor to *Sunday Digest.* Editor of community newsletter *Commentator.*

WORK IN PROGRESS: A biography for children; historical research on West Texas.

SIDELIGHTS: Hoppe told *CA:* "I plan to have more time to devote to writing now that my children are in college. I write articles but also enjoy writing fiction."

* * *

HORNBLOW, Leonora (Schinasi) 1920-

PERSONAL: Born in 1920, in New York, N.Y.; married Arthur Hornblow (a film producer and writer); children: one son. *Residence:* New York, N.Y.

CAREER: Author. Has also written for magazines and newspapers. *Member:* Authors Guild.

WRITINGS: Memory and Desire, Random House, 1950; *The Love-Seekers,* Random House, 1957; *Cleopatra of Egypt* (illustrated by W. T. Mars), Random House, 1961; (editor with Bennett Cerf) *Bennett Cerf's Take Along Treasury,* Doubleday, 1963; (with husband, Arthur Hornblow) *Birds Do the Strangest Things* (juvenile, illustrated by Michael W. Frith), Random House, 1965; (with A. Hornblow) *Fish Do the Strangest Things* (juvenile; illustrated by M. K. Frith), Random House, 1966; (with A. Hornblow) *Insects Do the Strangest Things* (juvenile; illustrated by M. K. Frith), Random House, 1968; (with A. Hornblow) *Reptiles Do the Strangest Things* (juvenile; illustrated by M. K. Frith), Random House, 1970; *Prehistoric Monsters Did the Strangest Things* (juvenile; illustrated by M. K. Frith), Random House, 1974.

SIDELIGHTS: Leonora Hornblow's first book was *Memory and Desire,* the story of a Hollywood love affair. *Saturday Review* wrote: "Mrs. Hornblow is a strong and skillful writer, witty, perceptive, not banal. The style and texture of the book are reminiscent of Evelyn Waugh or Dawn Powell. Her characters do convince us that they live and that there are legion like them, more's the pity." The *New York Herald Tribune* commented: "Mrs. Hornblow has a polished talent for describing sensitively landscape, light, the sky, flowers, or hotel furniture. Her taut, springy dialogue has charm. Like all first novels, this one has defects. Perhaps it is glib in spots and strains too much for effect. Mrs. Hornblow's next will be much better. Even so, *Memory and Desire* is a remarkably spirited and competent performance."

Speaking of *The Love-Seekers,* the *New York Herald Tribune* said it "explores the special world it has staked out with an unabashed candor which is often startling. But the author never seems to be proffering sensuality for its own sake. She is simply writing, with great frankness and understanding, her version of certain experiences and their significance in the lives of her modern 'love-seekers.'" The *San Francisco Chronicle* found the book to be "a much more polished affair than most in this general classification—the dialogue much truer and there is some attempt at characterization and a certain amount of suspense and compelling interest. All in all, this is several cuts above the average and if Mrs. Hornblow turns her attention to something slightly less familiar and standardized than the plot she used here, the results can be very welcome."

BIOGRAPHICAL/CRITICAL SOURCES: Saturday Review, April 11, 1950; *New York Herald Tribune Book Review,* March 26, 1950, July 14, 1957; *San Francisco Chronicle,* July 28, 1957.*

* * *

HOUGH, Hugh 1924-

PERSONAL: Born April 15, 1924, in Sandwich, Ill.; son of Forrest E. and Lila (Legner) Hough; married Ellen Marie Wesemann, September 8, 1948; children: Hollis A. Hough Bahnsen, Heidi A., Peter C., Christopher H. *Education:* University of Illinois, B.S., 1951. *Home:* 747 North Catherine, LaGrange Park, Ill. 50525. *Office: Chicago Sun-Times,* 401 North Wabash, Chicago, Ill. 60611.

CARREER/WRITINGS: Dixon Evening Telegraph, Dixon, Ill., sports editor, 1951-52; *Chicago Sun-Times,* Chicago, Ill., reporter and rewriter, 1952—, author, with Art Petacque, of Sunday column, "Out Front." *Military service:* U.S. Air Force, served in World War II. *Awards, honors:* Pulitzer Prize, 1974, for local reporting.

* * *

HOWARD, Ben(jamin Willis) 1944-

PERSONAL: Born June 22, 1944, in Iowa City, Iowa; son of Marion C. (a school principal) and J. Elizabeth (Nehrkorn) Howard; married Susan Carson Hepner (a teacher), July 26, 1969; children: Alexander Benjamin. *Education:* Attended University of Leeds, 1964-65; Drake University, B.A. (highest honors), 1966; Syracuse University, M.A., 1969, Ph.D., 1971; also attended Johns Hopkins University, summer, 1975. *Home address:* R.D. 1, Andover, N.Y. 14806. *Office:* Division of Humanities, Alfred University, Alfred, N.Y. 14802.

CAREER: Alfred University, Alfred, N.Y., assistant professor, 1969-75, associate professor of English, 1976—, lecturer in music, 1970—. *Member:* Modern Language Association of America, American Association of University Professors, Associated Writing Programs, Phi Beta Kappa. *Awards, honors:* Woodrow Wilson fellowship, 1966; National Endowment for the Humanities fellowship, 1975.

WRITINGS: Father of Waters (poems), Cummington Press, 1978. Work represented in anthology, *From Out of the Salt Mound: An Anthology of Poetry,* Salt Mound Press, 1968. Contributor of poems, articles, and reviews to literary journals, including *Ontario Review, Epoch, Poetry, Midwest Quarterly,* and *Carolina Quarterly.*

WORK IN PROGRESS: New poems; research on the epistolary tradition in English verse, and on post-war British poetry.

SIDELIGHTS: Howard told *CA:* "Up to now, most of my poems could be described as acts of seeing and interior dialogues. I have worked within the English meditative-descriptive tradition, with some excursions into myth and fable. Of late I've been turning to poems about people rather than the natural world and to forms such as the verse letter and the dramatic monologue. The poems are becoming more personal and more expansive.

"I have lived in the country since 1971. Much of my spare time is spent in coping with the problems of rural living—frozen pipes and whatnot. I enjoy the woods, except during deer season, when it's dangerous to be anywhere near the woods."

AVOCATIONAL INTERESTS: Playing classical guitar.

* * *

HOWARD, Prosper
See HAMILTON, Charles Harold St. John

* * *

HOWELL, Thomas 1944-

PERSONAL: Born January 20, 1944, in Houston, Tex.; son of John T. and Hazel (Hall) Howell; married Donna Walker (a teacher), August 14, 1971. *Education:* Louisiana College, B.A., 1964; Louisiana State University, M.A., 1966, Ph.D., 1971. *Office:* Department of History, Louisiana College, Pineville, La. 71360.

CAREER: Louisiana College, Pineville, instructor, 1966-69, assistant professor, 1969-71, professor of history, 1971—, chairperson of department, 1975—. *Member:* Organization of American Historians, Southern Historical Association, Phi Theta Kappa, Omicron Delta Kappa.

WRITINGS: Writers War Board (history), Eagle Press, 1974. Author of performing arts column "Back Seat Critic" in *Ready.* Contributor of articles and reviews to historical journals.

WORK IN PROGRESS: Research on American propaganda.

SIDELIGHTS: Howell commented: "I have always sought to maintain the broadest possible scope of interests—from history to organized athletics to foreign travel to the performing arts to literature—in the belief that a narrow specialization, however productive, produces a narrow mind and an undeveloped personality."

* * *

HUBERT, James Lee   1947-
(Jim Hubert)

PERSONAL: Born March 6, 1947, in Kankakee, Ill.; son of Paul Clifford (a businessman) and Dorothy (Dionne) Hubert. *Education:* Attended San Bernardino Valley College, 1965-67, and University of California, Riverside, 1967-69; San Francisco State University, B.A., 1974, M.A., 1975. *Home:* 170 Welt Olive St., San Bernardino, Calif. 92410.

CAREER: Teacher's aide at a day care center in San Bernardino, Calif., summer, 1968; tutor for public schools in Riverside, Calif., 1969, and San Francisco, Calif., 1972-73; free-lance writer, 1973—. Has given readings from his poetry in the San Francisco area and in Texas.

WRITINGS—Under name Jim Hubert: *My Lost Family* (poetry chapbook), Aisling, 1975. Contributor of poems and reviews to literary journals and popular magazines, including *Esquire, Sou'westerner, Loon,* and *Poetry Texas.* Contributing editor of *Aisling,* 1973—, editor, 1977.

WORK IN PROGRESS—Under name Jim Hubert: *Without Ceremony,* a poetry chapbook; *The Bone Trophies,* urban poems, poems written in Europe, and love poems; a series of poems based on paintings of Georges Rouault; "In Any Country's Darkness," a short story.

SIDELIGHTS: Hubert writes: "For over ten years I've been interested in painting. I have done over two hundred water colors, some thirty oils, and over a hundred ink drawings. I have also dabbled in linoleum carvings—all to my own edification, as I do not fool myself that I am anything but a poet. I am especially interested in the Impressionists and the Expressionists, though the latter seem to talk more to my life and its expression. In the literature of the Expressionists, I found an invaluable book by Walter H. Sokle called *The Writer in Extremis.* The book deals almost exclusively with German Expressionism where the movement had its inception with Kafka, Benn, Wedekind, Trakl, and others. I believe their revolt was much more significant, at least to me, than Existentialism or Surrealism, both movements grounded in intellectualism. And here, I'll go with Crane and William Carlos Williams about the intellect. Eliot's poetry is great but it lives too much in the mind. Robert Bly once said that English poetry was essentially of the

mind, that Latin American poetry was basically of the senses and emotions, and that American poetry was somewhere in between. I believe, as does Bly, that we have more to learn from the Latins than we do from the Anglo-Saxons. I have responded to that idea by translating some poems from the Spanish of Miguel Hernandez.

"Several writers have influenced my poetry. The Latin American Writers, especially Neruda and Vallejo, have been great forces in my work, though they haven't particularly influenced my line or style. If I should choose four American poets who have made deep impressions on my imagination and style they would be Stephen Crane, Robert Lowell, James Wright, and Jim Harrison."

* * *

HUBERT, Jim
See HUBERT, James Lee

* * *

HUMPHREY, Hubert Horatio   1911-1978

May 27, 1911—January 13, 1978; U.S. vice-president, senator, educator and author. Known as a "public man" to both constituents and the American public in general, Humphrey's distinguished political career spanned twenty-three years in the U.S. Senate and a term as vice-president during the Johnson administration. Humphrey was the prime mover behind medicare, the Peace Corps, the U.S. Arms Control and Disarmament Agency, the Civil Rights Act of 1964, and other landmark legislation. He was Senate Whip from 1961 to 1964, and in January, 1977, he was unanimously elected Deputy President pro tem of the Senate. Humphrey made an unsuccessful bid for the U.S. presidency in 1968. His memoirs, *The Education of a Public Man,* were published shortly before his death. Humphrey died in Waverly, Minn. Obituaries: *New York Times,* January 14, 1978, January 16, 1978; *Washington Post,* January 16, 1978; *Newsweek,* January 23, 1978; *Time,* January 23, 1978. (See index for *CA* sketch)

* * *

HUNT, Richard (Paul)   1921-

PERSONAL: Born October 25, 1921, in Streator, Ill.; son of Percy John (an auto dealer) and Lillian (Wanenmacher) Hunt; married Toni Adams, June, 1954 (divorced); married Carla Fitch (a travel executive), June 14, 1962; children: Christopher Charles, Abigail Louise. *Education:* Yale University, B.A., 1942. *Home:* 180 Riverside Dr., New York, N.Y. 10024. *Office:* NBC News, 30 Rockefeller Plaza, New York, N.Y. 10020.

CAREER/WRITINGS: Geneva Daily Times, Geneva, N.Y., reporter, 1950-53; Associated Press, New York City, reporter in Albany, N.Y., 1953-55; *New York Times,* New York City, correspondent in Africa and the Middle East, 1955-64; National Broadcasting Co. (NBC) News, New York City, correspondent in Japan, 1969, Southeast Asia, 1970-71, and Middle East, 1971-73, United Nations correspondent, 1973—. Notable assignments include coverage of the Iraq Revolution of 1958, Lebanese Civil War, 1958, war in Vietnam and Cambodia, war in Pakistan, 1972, and the Paris Peace Conference. *Military service:* U.S. Navy, 1943-45; became lieutenant, senior grade. *Member:* United Nations Correspondents Association, Association of Radio and Television News Analysts, Yale Club.

SIDELIGHTS: CA asked Hunt his opinion of the visit of Anwar Sadat to Israel in late 1977. Hunt responded: "Sadat's visit has made me optimistic about the Middle East for the first time in the twenty years I've been covering some aspect of the story. Not very optimistic, but optimistic, that a fifth war can be postponed.

"The Middle East question cannot be resolved finally without: 1) Settlement of the Palestinian refugee problem; 2) Settlement of territorial questions arising out of the wars of '48, '56, '67, and '73; 3) Settlement of religious problems centred around Jerusalem and Jewish shrines in the Arab world; 4) Settlement of the Jewish refugee problem; 5) Settlement of competing requirements for water.

"These problems cannot finally be solved without war as long as Israel and Arab irredentist movements co-exist."

Hunt has travelled to more than fifty-four countries in the course of his work, and has lived five years in the Middle East.

* * *

HUNT, Virginia Lloyd 1888(?)-1977

1888(?)—November 17, 1977; American artist and author. Hunt was an accomplished goldsmith and painter. Her book, *How to Live in the Tropics,* grew out of her experience of living with her husband in South America. She died in Springfield, Ohio. Obituaries: *New York Times,* November 21, 1977.

* * *

HUSTON, John (Marcellus) 1906-

PERSONAL: Born August 5, 1906, in Nevada, Mo.; son of Walter (an actor) and Rhea (a writer and reporter; maiden name, Gore) Huston; married Dorothy Harvey (marriage ended); married Leslie Black, 1937 (marriage ended); married Evelyn Keyes, July 23, 1946 (marriage ended); married Enrica Soma, 1949 (deceased, 1969); married Celeste Shane, 1972 (divorced, 1976); children: Walter Anthony, Anjelica, Pablo Alberran (adopted). *Education:* Attended parochial and public schools in Los Angeles, Calif. *Home:* St. Clerans, Craughwell, County Galway, Ireland; and Puerto Vallarta, Mexico. *Agent:* Paul Kohner, Los Angeles, Calif.

CAREER: Director, writer, producer, and actor. Left high school to become professional boxer, 1922; actor in Greenwich Village, appearing in Sherwood Anderson's "Triumph of the Egg," and "Ruint," 1924-25; became reporter for *Graphic,* New York, N.Y.; worked briefly as writer for Metro-Goldwyn-Mayer Studios in California and for Gaumont-British in England; studied art in Paris in the early 1930's; returned to New York and became editor of *Mid-Week Pictorial;* Warner Brothers Studios, Hollywood, Calif., writer, beginning 1938, and director, 1941-42, 1945-48, assignments included "Across the Pacific," 1942, and "No Exit," 1945 (see also, *WRITINGS*); founded Horizon Films with S. P. Eagle; Metro-Goldwyn-Mayer, Hollywood, writer and director, 1949— (see also, *WRITINGS*). Director of Broadway plays, 1939-41, including "A Passenger to Bali," 1939, and "In Time to Come," 1940; director of screenplays, including "The Barbarian and the Geisha," Twentieth Century-Fox, 1958; "The Roots of Heaven," Twentieth Century-Fox, 1958; "The Unforgiven," United Artists, 1960; "The Misfits," United Artists, 1961; "The List of Adrian Messenger," Universal, 1963; "The Bible," Twentieth Century-Fox, 1966; "The Mines of Sulphur" (opera), 1966; "La Scala" (opera), 1966; "Reflections in a Golden Eye," Warner Bros.-Seven Arts, 1967; "Sinful Davey," United Artists, 1969; "A Walk with Love and

Death," Twentieth Century-Fox, 1969; "Fat City," Columbia, 1972; "The Life and Times of Judge Roy Bean," National General, 1973; "The Mackintosh Man," Warner Bros., 1973. Actor in numerous films, including "The Cardinal," 1963; "The Bible," 1966; "DeSade," 1969; "Candy," 1969; "Myra Breckenridge," 1970; "Man in the Wilderness," 1971; "The Life and Times of Judge Roy Bean," 1973; "Chinatown," 1974; "The Wind and the Lion," 1975 (see also, *WRITINGS*). *Military service:* Mexican Cavalry, 1925-27; became lieutenant. U.S. Army, 1942-45; became major.

AWARDS, HONORS: New York Drama Critics Circle Award, 1939, for "In Time to Come"; Academy Awards for best director and best screenplay from Academy of Motion Picture Arts and Sciences, 1949, both for "Treasure of Sierra Madre"; New York Film Critics award for best director, 1949, for "Treasure of Sierra Madre"; Writers Guild Award, 1949, for "Treasure of Sierra Madre"; One World Award, 1949, for "Treasure of Sierra Madre"; Screen Directors Guild Award, 1950, for "The Asphalt Jungle"; nominated for Academy Award, 1950, for "The Asphalt Jungle," 1951, for screenplay "The African Queen," and 1962, for screenplay "Freud"; New York Film Critics award for best director of the year, 1956, for "Moby Dick"; recipient of award from National Board of Review of Motion Pictures, 1956; Silver Laurel award from Screen Writers Guild, 1963, for "Night of the Iguana"; Silver Directors Guild award, 1964, for "Night of the Iguana"; Martin Buber award, 1966, for "The Bible"; David di Donatello award, 1966, for "The Bible"; Motion Pictures Exhibitors' International Laurel award, 1968, for "Reflections in a Golden Eye"; D.Litt., Trinity College, 1970.

WRITINGS—Screenplays: "A House Divided," 1932; "Law and Order," 1932; "Murders in Rue Morgue," 1932; (with John Wexley) "The Amazing Dr. Clitterhouse" (adapted from play by Barre Lyndon), Warner Bros., 1938; (with Aeneas MacKenzie and Wolfgang Reinhardt) "Juarez" (adapted from play by Franz Werfel and *The Phantom Crown* by Bertita Harding), Warner Bros., 1939.

(With Heinz Herald and Norman Burnside) "Doctor Ehrlich's Magic Bullet," Warner Bros., 1940; (with Abem Finkel, Harry Chandlee, and Howard Koch) "Sergeant York," Warner Bros., 1941; (with W. R. Burnett) "High Sierra" (adapted from novel by Burnett), Warner Bros., 1941; (and director) "Maltese Falcon" (adapted from novel by Dashiell Hammett; also see below), Warner Bros., 1941; (and director) "Report from the Aleutians," produced for the U.S. Army, 1943; (and director) "The Battle of San Pietro," produced for the U.S. Army, 1944; (and director) "Let There Be Light," produced for the U.S. Army, 1945; (with Koch) "Three Strangers," Warner Bros., 1946; (and director) "Treasure of Sierra Madre" (adapted from novel by B. Traven), Warner Bros., 1948; (with Richard Brooks, and director) "Key Largo" (adapted from play by Maxwell Anderson), Warner Bros., 1948; (with Peter Wiertel, and director) "We Were Strangers" (adapted from story by Robert Sylvester), Columbia, 1949.

(With Ben Maddow, and director) "The Asphalt Jungle" (adapted from novel by Burnett), Metro-Goldwyn-Mayer, 1950; (and director) "The Red Badge of Courage" (adapted from novel by Stephen Crane), Metro-Goldwyn-Mayer, 1951; (with James Agee, and director) "The African Queen" (adapted from novel by C. S. Forester), United Artists, 1951; (with A. Veiller, producer and director) "Moulin Rouge" (adapted from novel by Pierre La Mure), United Artists, 1952; (with Truman Capote, producer and director)

"Beat the Devil" (adapted from novel by James Helvick), United Artists, 1954; (with Ray Bradbury, producer and director) "Moby Dick" (adapted from novel by Herman Melville), Warner Bros., 1956; (with John Lee Mahin, and director) "Heaven Knows, Mr. Allison" (adapted from novel by Charles Shaw), Twentieth Century-Fox, 1957.

(With Charles Kaufman and Reinhardt, and director) "Freud," Universal, 1962; (with Veiller, producer and director) "The Night of the Iguana" (adapted from play by Tennessee Williams), Metro-Goldwyn-Mayer, 1964; (with Wolf Mankowitz, John Law, and Michael Sayers, actor and director) "Casino Royale" (adapted from novel by Ian Fleming), Columbia, 1967; (co-author and director) "The Kremlin Letter," Twentieth Century-Fox, 1970; (with Gladys Hill, and director) "The Man Who Would Be King" (adapted from story by Rudyard Kipling) Persky-Bright/Devon, 1975; "Independence," 1976.

Other: *Frankie and Johnny* (play), Boni, 1930; (with Howard Koch, and director) "In Time to Come," first produced in New York, 1940; *The Maltese Falcon* (published version of Huston's screenplay adapted from the novel by Dashiell Hammett), edited by Richard J. Anobile, Macmillan, 1974.

Work represented in anthologies, including *The Best Plays of 1941-42*, edited by Burns Mantle, Dodd, 1942; *Twenty Best Film Plays*, edited by John Gassner and Dudley Nichols, Crown, 1943; *New Stories for Men*, edited by Charles Grayson, Garden City Books, 1943. Contributor of short stories to *American Mercury*.

WORK IN PROGRESS: A screenplay based on Ernest Hemingway's "Across the River and into the Trees."

SIDELIGHTS: John Huston made his debut in the film world with the direction of "The Maltese Falcon." This film established Huston as an innovative and challenging stylist. Working in close cooperation with the cameraman, he began with this film the characteristically cold scrutiny, the heavily shadowed study of existentially helpless men, that marks the majority and best of his later work. Now, more than thirty-five years later, he is still a talent to be reckoned with. His last film, "The Man Who Would Be King," which opened in late 1975, was viewed by many critics as a stunning comeback for Huston after a decade of generally bad films. "I think," he admitted, "I've made only three good films in the last decade: 'Reflections in a Golden Eye,' 'Fat City' and now 'The Man Who Would Be King.' I found myself going over Kipling's ground, looking for that world he's written about. 'The Man Who Would Be King' appeals to the child in me, to the child in all of us, that adventure of going into strange latitudes where reckoning ceases to count, the embarking on a voyage where you can't see the end."

Huston, the artist, is thought by critics to be uneven and unpredictable. Sometimes he has shown genius and sometimes his films have been worse than mediocre. He has, in fact, been accused outright of bad taste. By his own admission he is not a wholly intellectual director-writer. "I don't set out to tell *one* story. Still, it is not by accident that I choose my material. It is just so deep that I don't think about it. Some of the great directors, like Bergman, are totally involved in their own thing. Well, I'm more frivolous. Oh, I guess I could be pompous and say *catholic* or something like that, but I simply like to jump around in life and films."

The tendency to "jump around" has caused Huston to reflect more than once on the world he has built for himself. "I wonder with a bit of envy about those people who only do one thing all their lives. Maybe there are advantages I've missed. Well, I knew from the beginning that a picture-mak-er's life is fragmented. And I used to feel very sad when a film was over, when I realized this particular experience would never happen again, these people would never come together again. It is an end of a world."

Huston is a director who almost always writes his own material, and frequently directs himself in a character role. Some critics say, for instance, that the best part of "The Bible" was actor Huston as Noah preparing for the flood. About his work he commented: "When I cast a picture, I do most of my directing right there in finding the right person. I use actors with strong personalities, ones who are like the characters they play. I do as little directing as possible. Occasionally, there's an actor who likes to talk about his role, so I'll talk with him. But that doesn't happen very often."

Huston, the man, is a constant contradiction. Producer Jules Buck said: "As an actor he is very competent; as a writer he is brilliant; as a director he is magnificent. But John gets bored easily. He needs new people to feed on all the time. The desert is littered with their bones." And James Agee called Huston: "A natural-born authoritarian individualistic libertarian anarchist, without portfolio. He is wonderful company, almost anytime, for those who can stand the pace. One of the ranking grasshoppers of the Western Hemisphere, John was well into his twenties before anyone could imagine he would ever amount to more than an awful nice guy to get drunk with. He operates largely by instinct, unencumbered by any serious self-doubt. Incapable of boot-licking, he instantly catches fire in resistance to authority. His vocabulary ranges with the careless ease of a mountain goat between words of eight syllables and four letters. A rangy, leaping, thrusting kind of nervous vitality binds his pictures together."

BIOGRAPHICAL/CRITICAL SOURCES: William F. Nolan, *John Huston: King Rebel*, Sherbourne, 1965; Tozzi, *John Huston: A Pictorial Treasury of His Films*, Crown, 1971; *People*, April 21, 1975; *New York Post*, August 30, 1975; *Variety*, October 15, 1975: *New York Times*, February 15, 1976.*

* * *

IACUZZI, Alfred 1896-1977

1896—December 6, 1977; Italian-born educator and author. Iacuzzi was chairman of the Romance languages department at the Baruch School of the City College of New York. He died in Brooklyn, N.Y. Obituaries: *New York Times*, December 9, 1977.

* * *

INDELMAN-YINNON, Moshe 1895(?)-1977

1895(?)—September 24, 1977; Jewish scholar, journalist, and translator. Indelman-Yinnon edited Hebrew and Yiddish publications in Berlin, Warsaw, Jerusalem, and New York City. He was widely known for his translations of works by Martin Buber and A. I. Heschel into Hebrew. He died in Miami, Fla. Obituaries: *New York Times*, September 29, 1977.

* * *

INGATE, Mary 1912-

PERSONAL: Born April 12, 1912, in Halesworth, England; daughter of Alfred and Lucy (Meadows) Calver; married John Lewis Ingate (a farmer), February 4, 1939; children: John, Diana (Mrs. Lou Brissie), Nicola (Mrs. Graham Palmer). *Religion:* Church of England. *Residence:* Suffolk,

England. *Agent:* Macmillan Publishers, Ltd., Little Essex St., London, England.

CAREER: Writer. *Member:* Society of Authors, Crime Writers Association, Society of Women Writers and Journalists, East Anglian Writers, Norwich Writers (vice-president). *Awards, honors:* Cooper Memorial Prize for Best Short Story, 1972; Best Crime Novel by a Woman award from Macmillan and Pan (England), and Dell and Dodd, Mead & Co., 1973, for *The Sound of the Weir.*

WRITINGS: The Sound of the Weir, Dodd, 1974, published as *Remembrance of Miranda,* Dell, 1977; *This Water Laps Gently,* Macmillan (London), 1977. Also author of short stories for British Broadcasting Corp. radio and New Zealand radio. Contributor to *Glasgow Herald, Homes and Gardens, Woman's Realm, Women's Own, East Anglia Magazine, Good Housekeeping* (Ireland), and several Scandanavian magazines.

WORK IN PROGRESS: A suspense novel; revision of *Jessie Tallent,* a historical novel; a novel set in Suffolk at the time of World War II.

SIDELIGHTS: Mary Ingate told *CA:* "I do not find it necessary to travel to get color for my work. I have such a wealth of memory that I do not think I will exhaust it in a lifetime. In a future book I hope to bring in the pathos of the clouds of planes going out nightly from the American base three miles away—the sky was black with them—and then listening in the night as they (perhaps just a few) staggered home."

Ingate continued: "I have seen such changes in country living, agricultural revolutions, and its effect on the characters of the people. I wrote my books late in life because, being a farmer's wife, I had had little time." She explained that she lost the use of her legs in a car accident, and commented; "The accident and nearness of death had a profound effect on me—giving me a detached feeling, that of an onlooker (a recorder), rather than a participant of life."

BIOGRAPHICAL/CRITICAL SOURCES: Londoner's Diary, November 2, 1973; *Daily Express* (London), November 2, 1973; *London Letter-Eastern Daily Press,* November 2, 1973; *Smith's Trade News,* November 3, 1973; *The Bookseller,* November 3, 1973; *East Anglian Daily Times,* August 5, 1974; *Farmer's Weekly,* October 4, 1974.

*　　*　　*

INGERSOLL, John H. 1925-

PERSONAL: Born October 14, 1925, in Philadelphia, Pa.; son of Howard H. (in sales) and Margaret (Wall) Ingersoll; married Claris McGalliard, June 15, 1951 (divorced, 1960); married Georgia-Jean Cookson (an editor and writer), July 2, 1960; children: John H., Jr., Suzanne, Benton Howard, Evan Wall. *Education:* Lehigh University, A.B. and B.S., both 1950. *Politics:* Democrat. *Religion:* Episcopalian. *Home:* 520 East 20th St., New York, N.Y. 10009. *Office: House Beautiful,* 717 Fifth Ave., New York, N.Y. 10022.

CAREER: Worked as managing editor, Cantor Publishing Co., New York City; Simmons-Boardman, New York City, associate editor, 1957-58; *American Home,* New York City, building editor, 1958-62; free-lance writer, 1962-67; *House Beautiful,* New York City, senior building editor, 1967—. *Military service:* U.S. Army, 1943-46. *Member:* American Society of Journalists and Authors (vice-president, 1967).

WRITINGS: Guide to New England, Consolidated Book Publishers, 1954; *How to Buy a House,* Universal Publishing & Distributing, 1968. Contributor to magazines, including *Better Homes and Gardens, Popular Science, True, Modern Bride,* and *Holiday.*

SIDELIGHTS: Ingersoll comments: "When there's time, and that's seldom, I turn to the camera and woodworking, in that order, to siphon off work tensions. Most of the time, I'm writing for my employer or on assignment. Even my avocations are pragmatic, since much of my photography is for *House Beautiful* and much of my woodworking is, out of necessity, for our home."

*　　*　　*

INGHAM, Daniel
   See LAMBOT, Isobel

*　　*　　*

IORIZZO, Luciano J(ohn) 1930-

PERSONAL: Born March 31, 1930, in Brooklyn, N.Y.; son of John (a musician) and Adolorata (Veneziale) Iorizzo; married Marilee Bridges, December 13, 1952; children: Luciano J., Jr., Dolores, J. Thaddeus, F. Thomas, Joseph C. *Education:* Syracuse University, B.A., 1957, M.A., 1958, Ph.D., 1966. *Politics:* Democrat. *Religion:* Roman Catholic. *Home:* 134 West Seneca, Oswego, N.Y. 13126. *Office:* Department of History, State University of New York College at Oswego, Oswego, N.Y. 13126.

CAREER: History teacher at junior high schools in Vernon, Verona, and Sherrill, N.Y., 1958, and at public schools in Syracuse, N.Y., 1958-62; State University of New York College at Oswego, instructor, 1962-63, assistant professor, 1963-66, associate professor, 1966-71, professor of history, 1971—. Oswego city clerk, 1976-77. Consultant to Urban Institute. *Military service:* U.S. Air Force, 1951-55. *Member:* American Historical Association, Organization of American Historians, American Italian Historical Association (president, 1975-78), New York State Justice Educators Association (historian), Oswego County Historical Society (president, 1976-78). *Awards, honors:* Fulbright award, 1962 (declined); award from American Association for State and Local History, 1967; awards from New York State Research Foundation, 1967, 1968, 1971.

WRITINGS: (With Salvatore Monoello) *The Italian Americans,* Twayne, 1971. Contributor of articles and reviews to history and sociology journals.

WORK IN PROGRESS: Research on aspects of Italian immigration and ethnicity, especially at the local level and dealing with intermarriage and crime.

SIDELIGHTS: Iorizzo writes: "My research indicates that the history of organized crime today is little understood by many experts and lay people alike. They correctly see the dangers it poses for the United States, chiefly its threat to American institutions brought on by fostering attitudes which feed corruption and contribute to a general societal decay from within. They seek to stamp out the problem but fail to realize what it is that they must fight. These people view organized crime as an import, a problem carried to America, that can be solved, somehow, by attacking these 'alien' forces. But they ignore its origins in the American milieu and its dependency on cooperative politicians, on law enforcement personnel, and on the public. They miss its multi-ethnic and multi-racial character.

"I would like to be counted in a small but growing group of scholars who are working to illuminate this neglected field. If successful, the danger of organized crime to our society may be minimized."

IRELAND, Joe C. 1936-

PERSONAL: Born August 24, 1936, in New Orleans, La.; son of Charles B. (a career army sergeant) and Margaret (a microbiologist; maiden name, Johnson) Ireland; married wife Della, 1952 (divorced, 1960); married Carroll Jean, 1961 (divorced, 1963); married Trudence Reed, 1965 (divorced, 1966); married Virginia Dee, 1966 (divorced, 1967). *Education:* University of New Orleans, B.S., 1963; Louisiana State University, M.S., 1969. *Politics:* Anarchist. *Religion:* "Irish Catholic." *Home:* 3020 Rue Parc Fontaine, Apt. 803, New Orleans, La. 70114. *Office:* Algiers Regional Library, 3014 Holiday Dr., New Orleans, La. 70114.

CAREER: Worked as grainworker, parking meter collector, and exterminator in New Orleans, La., 1957-66; Algiers Regional Library, New Orleans, head librarian, 1967—. Instructor in creative writing, Delgado College, New Orleans, La. *Military service:* U.S. Naval Reserve, 1953-61. *Member:* International Poetry Society, Southwestern Library Association, New Orleans Poetry Forum, West Bank Poets. *Awards, honors:* City of New Orleans Poetry prize, 1976; Reynard Odenheimer Memorial Poetry Award, 1977, for "Tijuana Saturday Night".

WRITINGS: (Editor) *New Orleans Poets: Anthology,* Library Press, 1972; *Short Order: A Book of Poems,* Forum Press, 1974; (with James Morris) *Anthology of 2,* Printery, 1977. Contributor of poems to *Poet Lore, The Smith, Cafe Solo, Exiles, Sparrow, Bitterroot, Prism,* and other periodicals.

WORK IN PROGRESS: A book of poetry; a book of poems for children entitled *Finger in the Dike.*

SIDELIGHTS: Ireland told *CA:* "I write in spurts of perhaps twenty-thirty poems at a time. Maybe one or two of these make it. This happens several times a year. Greatest influence on my work has been Robert Bly; not his poetry but his person. My whole philosophy is summed up in this poem:

> *Short Order*
> What moon is this
> on my plate?
> Take it back waiter.
> I ordered
> the sun.

"[I] am very different when writing, but mostly I'm indifferent to what's going on around me. My life's hope would be to see Ireland as a unified country, Joan Baez receive the Nobel Peace Prize, and the U.S. not have any more mediocre press.

"I prefer my life to go on a day by day throw, just going to the edge, taking risks, and trying to catch the morning intact. Sometimes it works, sometimes it doesn't. I hope God has a sense of humor, after all He created the toucan and the giraffe."

AVOCATIONAL INTERESTS: Working with younger poets, gambling, photography, Irish whiskey, beautiful women, country music.

*   *   *

IRELAND, Kevin (Mark) 1933-

PERSONAL: Born July 18, 1933, in Auckland, New Zealand. *Home:* The Studio, 223A Randolph Ave., London W.9, England.

CAREER: Poet.

WRITINGS: Face to Face, Pegasus Press, 1963; *Educat-*

ing the Body, Caxton Press, 1967; *A Letter from Amsterdam,* Amphedesma Press, 1973; *Orchids Hummingbirds & Other Poems,* Oxford University Press, 1974; *A Grammar of Dreams,* Wai-Te-Ata Press, 1975; *Literary Cartoons,* Hurricane Press, 1977.

Founding editor of *Mate.*

*   *   *

IRWIN, James W. 1891(?)-1977

1891(?)—October 14, 1977; American attorney, government official, and author. Irwin was chief hearing examiner of the Civil Service Commission and an authority on the Hatch Act. He died in Pulaski, Tenn. Obituaries: *New York Times,* October 27, 1977.

*   *   *

ISHAM, Charlotte H(ickock) 1912-

PERSONAL: Surname is pronounced *Eye*-shum; born May 17, 1912, in Waterbury, Conn.; daughter of Austin (a farmer) and Sarah (Mattoon) Isham. *Education:* Danbury State Teachers College, B.E., 1940; Yale University, M.A., 1948; Harvard University, Ed.D., 1967. *Politics:* Republican. *Religion:* Congregationalist. *Home:* 153B Washington Rd., Woodbury, Conn. 06798. *Office:* Department of Education, Western Connecticut State College, White St., Danbury, Conn. 06810.

CAREER: Elementary school teacher in Plymouth, Conn., 1935-36, Harwinton, Conn., 1936-39, and Litchfield, Conn., 1939-43; teacher and principal of elementary school in Newtown, Conn., 1943-47; elementary supervisor of region including Newtown, Southbury, Woodbury, and Bethlehem, Conn., 1947-50, region including Woodbury, Southbury, and Bethlehem, 1950-53, and region including Woodbury and Bethlehem, 1953-54; supervisor of instruction in Woodbury, Conn., 1954-64; Western Connecticut State College, Danbury, assistant professor, 1964-67, associate professor, 1967-71, professor of children's literature, 1971-76. Member of Waterbury Greater Chamber of Commerce Resource Center, 1972.

MEMBER: National Education Association (life member), Association for Supervision and Curriculum Development, American Association of University Women, New England Reading Association, New England Association for Supervision and Curriculum Development, Connecticut Teachers Association, Connecticut Department of Higher Education, Connecticut Association for Supervision and Curriculum Development, Old Woodbury Historical Society (librarian), Delta Kappa Gamma, Eastern Star (past matron).

WRITINGS: The Face of Connecticut, Sugar Ball Press, 1952; *The History of North Congregational Church,* privately printed, 1966; *Freddie* (juvenile), Franklin Publishing (Philadelphia, Pa.), 1972; *Freddie's Discoveries* (juvenile), Franklin Publishing, 1974. Author of pamphlets for Old Woodbury Historical Society. Contributor to education journals.

WORK IN PROGRESS: Continuing research on the history of Woodbury, Conn.

SIDELIGHTS: Charlotte Isham's children's books are set nearly in her own back yard. She draws heavily on natural surroundings, especially the Weekeepeemee River near her home. Her books are intended to assist the beginning reader without boring him, and she insists that they be inexpensive and widely available to children.

ISH-KISHOR, Sulamith 1896-1977

PERSONAL: Born in 1896, in London, England; daughter of Ephraim and Fanny Ish-Kishor. *Education:* Attended Hunter College (now of the City University of New York). *Residence:* New York, N.Y.

CAREER: Author. *Awards, honors:* Schwartz Juvenile Award from the National Jewish Welfare Book Board Council, 1964, for *A Boy of Old Prague.*

WRITINGS: *The Bible Story,* United Synagogue of America, 1921; *The Heaven on the Sea, and Other Stories* (illustrated by Penina Ish-Kishor), Bloch Publishing, 1924; *Children's Story of the Bible,* Hebrew Publishing, 1930; *Children's History of Israel from the Creation to the Present Time,* Hebrew Publishing, 1933; *Magnificent Hadrian: A Biography of Hadrian, Emperor of Rome* (introduction by Theodore Dreiser), Minton, Balch, 1935; *Jews to Remember* (illustrated by Kyra Markham), Hebrew Publishing, 1941; *American Promise: A History of the Jews in the New World* (illustrated by Grace Hick), Behraman, 1947; *Everyman's History of the Jews,* Fell, 1948; *The Palace of Eagles, and Other Stories* (illustrated by Alice Horodisch), Shoulson Press, 1948; *Friday Night Stories,* Women's League of the United Synagogue of America, 1949.

A Boy of Old Prague (illustrated by Ben Shahn), Pantheon, 1963; *The Carpet of Solomon: A Hebrew Legend* (illustrated by Uri Shulevitz), Pantheon, 1966; *Pathways through the Jewish Holidays,* edited by Benjamin Efron, Ktav, 1967; *Our Eddie,* Pantheon, 1969; *Drusilla: A Novel of the Emperor Hadrian* (illustrated by Thomas Morley), Pantheon, 1970; *The Master of Miracle: A New Novel of the Golem* (illustrated by Arnold Lobel), Harper, 1971.

Contributor of articles and stories to *New York Times, New Yorker, New York Herald-Tribune, Menorah Journal,* and other periodicals.

OBITUARIES: *New York Times,* June 25, 1977; *A. B. Bookman's Weekly,* September 5, 1977.*

(Died June 23, 1977, in New York City)

* * *

IVERSEN, Nick 1951-

PERSONAL: Born December 25, 1951, in Des Moines, Iowa; son of Robert W. (a teacher) and Mary (a program coordinator; maiden name, Drake) Iversen. *Education:* Columbia University, B.A., 1973, M.F.A., 1978. *Agent:* Anthony Gardner, 1290 Sixth Ave., New York, N.Y. 10019.

CAREER: Yanomamo Enterprises, New York City, partner, 1970-72; writer, 1972—; Naked Turkey Renovations, New York City, partner, 1975-76; Naked Turkey Painting, New York City, partner, 1977. *Member:* American Museum of Natural History.

WRITINGS: *Record Makers and Record Breakers,* Jonathan David, 1977. Contributor to *Connection.*

WORK IN PROGRESS: A fictional biography of Peter Lorre; fiction concerning communication.

SIDELIGHTS: Iversen comments: "I work so I can earn money so I don't have to work so I can write," and adds: "I have played in several popular music combos, worked as carpenter, painter, sewer cleaner, bellboy, mailman, paper pusher, switchboard operator, gift shop manager, gardener, furniture mover, lifeguard, and physical education instructor."

AVOCATIONAL INTERESTS: Archaeology, astronomy, crime, baseball, auto racing, the jungle.

* * *

IWAMATSU, Jun Atsushi 1908-
(Taro Yashima)

PERSONAL: Born September 21, 1908, in Kagoshima, Japan; emigrated to the U.S. in 1939; son of a country doctor; married wife, Mitsu (an artist); children: Mako (son), Momo (daughter). *Education:* Studied art at the Imperial Art Academy, Tokyo, 1927-30, and at the Art Students League, New York City, 1939-41. *Residence:* Los Angeles, Calif.

CAREER: Author and illustrator of books for children. *Military service:* Served in the U.S. Army in the Office of War Information and in the Office of Strategic Services during World War II. *Awards, honors:* Child Study Association of America/Wel-Met Children's Book Award, 1955, for *Crow Boy;* New York Times Choice of Best Illustrated Children's Books of the Year, 1967, for *Seashore Story;* Southern California Council on Literature of Children and Young People Award for significant contribution in the field of illustration, 1968.

WRITINGS—Under pseudonym Taro Yashima; self-illustrated: *The New Sun,* Holt, 1943; *Horizon Is Calling,* Holt, 1947; *The Village Tree,* Viking, 1953; (with Mitsu Yashima, pseudonym of wife, Tomoe Iwamatsu) *Plenty to Watch,* Viking, 1954; *Crow Boy* (Junior Literary Guild selection), Viking, 1955; *Umbrella* (Junior Literary Guild selection), Viking, 1958; (with M. Yashima) *Momo's Kitten,* Viking, 1961; *Youngest One,* Viking, 1962; *Seashore Story,* Viking, 1967.

Illustrator: Eleanore M. Jewett, *Which Was Witch?,* Viking, 1953; (and translator) Hatoju Muku, *The Golden Footprints,* World Publishing, 1960; June Behrens, *Soo Ling Finds a Way,* Golden Gate Junior Books, 1965.

SIDELIGHTS: Jun Iwamatsu began using the name Taro Yashima during World War II. Because of his involvement with the Office of Strategic Services, he could not use his real name.

His first book, *The New Sun,* is an autobiography. The *New York Times* called it, "A simple and moving document. It is particularly in his account of [his] jail experience, of its anguish and degradation and the indomitable courage and comradship of the underground fellowship, that the artist's talent achieves its best dimensions. The black and whites tell the story with an economy and eloquence that might readily have turned into melodrama in an idiom less personal and stenographic that Mr. Yashima's own."

His first book for children was written in answer to his daughter's question about what he did as a boy in Japan. A *New York Times* critic wrote: "The work of Taro Yashima leaves this reviewer with a strong feeling that here is an artist-writer who knows children, respects and loves them deeply. With both words and pastel-and-ink strokes he has captured their simplicity, gaiety, and sense of wonder."

Taro Yashima has had several one-man shows of his works in such cities as New York, Los Angeles, and Pasadena. His paintings have been bought for permanent collections in several museums, including the Phillips Memorial Museum in Washington, D.C. Yashima also directs the Yashima Art Institute where he teaches fundamental techniques and methods of art instruction. His son, Mako, is an actor and was nominated for an Academy Award in 1967 as best supporting actor for his performance in "The Sand Pebbles."

Crow Boy, The Village Tree, and *Umbrella* have all been adapted into educational movies and filmstrips for children.

BIOGRAPHICAL/CRITICAL SOURCES: Taro Yashima, *The New Sun,* Holt, 1943; *New York Times,* November 21, 1943, November 15, 1953; T. Yashima, *Horizon Is Calling,* Holt, 1947.*

* * *

JACKSON, Robert L(owell) 1935-

PERSONAL: Born May 11, 1935, in St. Louis, Mo.; son of Lowell H. (a businessman) and Jacqueline (Walker) Jackson; married Mary Jane Flickinger (an educator), June 27, 1959; children: Julia, Patricia, Margaret. *Education:* St. Louis University, B.A., 1956, M.A., 1960. *Religion:* Roman Catholic. *Home:* 4844 Van Ness N.W., Washington, D.C. 20016. *Office: Los Angeles Times,* 1700 Pennsylvania Ave. N.W., Washington, D.C. 20006.

CAREER: St. Louis Globe-Democrat, St. Louis, Mo., reporter, 1959-60; *Los Angeles Times,* Los Angeles, Calif., investigative reporter, 1965-67, Washington correspondent and investigative reporter, 1967—. Notable assignments include coverage of the Watergate scandal, including the break in, burglary trials, Senate Watergate hearings, tape hearings, the cover up trial, and resignation of Richard Nixon. *Awards, honors:* Fulbright fellowship for study in Denmark, 1961-62; Con Lee Kelliher Award from Sigma Delta Chi, 1963, for excellence of local reporting; co-winner of Pulitzer Prize Gold Medal, 1965, for coverage of Watts riots; Los Angeles Times Editorial Award for outstanding local reporting, 1967, for investigation of California tax assessment scandal; co-winner of Pulitzer Prize, 1969, for investigation of Los Angeles Harbor Department; Sigma Delta Chi Award, 1970, for excellence of Washington correspondence in the Justice Abe Fortas case.

WORK IN PROGRESS: Investigating the Park-Korean involvement with Congressmen.

* * *

JACKSON, Wilma 1931-

PERSONAL: Born December 17, 1931, in Chicago, Ill.; daughter of R. L. (a minister) and Sophia (a beautician and teacher; maiden name, Shaw) Littlejohn; married Gordon Chester Jackson (an auto company employee); children: Carole Lynn Harris, Linda Kathryn, Jill, Shelley Susanne. *Education:* Attended Wilson Junior College and Flint Community College; Michigan State University, certificate in Counseling-Substance Abuse, 1976; University of Michigan, B.G.S., 1977. *Politics:* Democrat. *Religion:* Protestant. *Home:* 2018 Whittlesey St., Flint, Mich. 48503. *Agent:* Scott Meredith, 845 Third Ave., New York, N.Y. 10021. *Office:* Medi-Rary Literary Agency, 615 Lippincott Blvd., Flint, Mich. 48503.

CAREER/WRITINGS: Chicago Defender, Chicago, Ill., feature writer, 1955-57; *Flint Herald,* Flint, Mich., social news columnist, 1956-58; Associated Negro Press, women's editor, 1957-62; *Chicago Defender,* columnist, 1959-60; Negro Press International, theatrical editor, 1962-63; *Sepia* magazine, writer of column "Just Ask Me," 1963-78; Medi-Rary Literary Agency, Flint, director, 1972—. Columns contributed to teen magazines include "Confidentially Speaking," "Guess Who?," "Data 'N Chatter," "Dear Soul Sister," "Star Treks," "Where the Soul Is," and "Star O Scope," 1957-78. Contributor of articles to *Negro Digest, Tan,* and *Ebony* magazine. Member of board of directors,

Flint Gazette. Owner and operator, Wilma's Beauty Box; market research interviewer for Barlow Survey Service, 1958-60; teacher of creative writing; lecturer in creative writing, University of Michigan, 1977. *Member:* National Association of Media Women (founder of Flint, Mich. chapter; president, 1977), National Negro Business and Professional Women's Clubs, Inc., Urban League Guild, Flint Writer's Club. *Awards, honors:* Journalism awards from Flint Writer's Club, 1969-73, 1975, 1977.

WORK IN PROGRESS: Just Ask Me Again, a collection of advice columns.

SIDELIGHTS: Wilma Jackson told *CA:* "I like people. I have always found meeting and sharing and exchanging ideas an enriching experience. One is naturally limited to one-to-one sort of conversations because of lack of time, proximity and other variables. So I wander, explore, ponder and put it all down on paper so I can 'talk' to the masses. Places visited can be seen again and the adventure comes alive for me (and I hope others) when recollections are put down in print. I write also, I must confess, for the sheer joy of writing. Letting thoughts leap to life on paper. Life is a venture. Writing is THE adventure."

* * *

JACOBS, Diane 1948-

PERSONAL: Born October 26, 1948, in New York; daughter of Richard Alan (an advertising executive) and Patricia (an actress; maiden name, Breschel) Jacobs. *Education:* University of Pennsylvania, B.A., 1970; Columbia University, M.F.A., 1973. *Home and office:* 220 East 63rd St., Apt. 5B, New York, N.Y. 10021.

CAREER: Writer, 1966—. Assistant at Ogilvy & Mather, summers, 1969-70; manuscript reader and reviewer for United Artists Corp., 1974; researcher at Film Study Center, Museum of Modern Art, 1972.

WRITINGS: Hollywood Renaissance (critical study of new American film directors), A. S. Barnes, 1977. Author of columns "Film " in *Changes,* 1972-75, "Film" in *Gallery,* 1975—, and "On Film" in *Soho Weekly News.* Publicity writer for *Paperback News.* Contributor to popular magazines and newspapers, including *Viva, Film Comment,* and *McCall's.*

WORK IN PROGRESS: "Sea-Changes" (tentative title), a screenplay; research for a book on French filmmaker Claude Chabrol.

SIDELIGHTS: Diane Jacobs remarks: "All my life I have been interested in writing and books. A fascination with the current artists working in Hollywood spurred me to write *Hollywood Renaissance.* I have traveled twice to the Cannes Film Festival, and have visited most of Europe."

* * *

JACOBS, Leland Blair 1907-

PERSONAL: Born February 12, 1907, in Tawas City, Mich.; married; children: Allan D. *Education:* Earned A.B. from Michigan State Normal College (now University), M.A. from University of Michigan, and Ph.D. from Ohio State University.

CAREER: Writer. Has worked as teacher of all grades and as elementary school principal; taught education courses at various colleges and universities; became professor of elementary education, and later professor emeritus of education at Columbia University. Lecturer at various universities, including University of Hawaii, Northwestern University, Kent State University, and University of Florida. Consultant and lecturer for state educational associations, national organizations, and school systems. *Member:* International Association for Childhood Education, International Reading Association, National Conference on Research in English, National Council of Teachers of English, Association for Supervision and Curriculum, Authors Guild, Weekly Reader Club (member of selection committee). *Awards, honors:* New Jersey Reading Teachers Association distinguished service award, 1977; received distinguished teaching award from Mills College; chosen to represent Columbia University Teachers College on television series, "Meet the Professor"; received distinguished alumni award from Ohio State University Teachers College.

WRITINGS—All juvenile: *Good Night, Mr. Beetle* (illustrated by Gilbert Riswold), Holt, 1963; *Just around the Corner* (illustrated by John E. Johnson), Holt, 1964; *Old Lucy Lindy* (illustrated by Ed Renfro), Holt, 1964; (with Allan D. Jacobs) *Behind the Circus Tent,* Lerner, 1967; *Is Somewhere Always Far Away?* (illustrated by Johnson), Holt, 1967; *Alphabet of Girls* (illustrated by Johnson), Holt, 1969; *The Monkey and the Bee,* Western Publishing, 1969; *The Stupid Lion, and Other Stories* (illustrated by Karl Stuecklen), L. W. Singer, 1969; *I Don't, I Do* (illustrated by Frank Carlings), Garrard, 1971; *What Would You Do?* (illustrated by Carlings), Garrard, 1972; *April Fool!* (illustrated by Lou Cunette), Garrard, 1973; *Teeny-Tiny* (illustrated by Marilyn Lucey), Garrard, 1976.

Editor: (And reteller) *Belling the Cat, and Other Stories* (illustrated by Harold Berson), Golden Press, 1960; (with Eleanor Murdoch Johnson) *Treat Shop,* enlarged editon, C. E. Merrill, 1960; *Delight in Numbers* (illustrated by Kiyoaki Komoda), Holt, 1964; (with Sally Nohelty) *Poems for Young Scientists* (illustrated by Ed Young), Holt, 1964; *Using Literature with Young Children,* Teachers College Press, 1965; (with Johnson and Jo Jasper Turner) *Adventure Lands,* C. E. Merrill, 1966; (with Johnson) *Enchanted Isles,* C. E. Merrill, 1966; (with Turner) *Happiness Hill,* C. E. Merrill, 1966; (with Shelton L. Root) *Ideas in Literature,* C. E. Merrill, 1966; *Poetry for Autumn* (illustrated by Stina Nagel), Garrard, 1968; *Poetry for Chuckles and Grins* (illustrated by Tomie de Paola), Garrard, 1968.

Poetry for Bird Watchers (illustrated by Ted Schroeder), Garrard, 1970; *Poetry for Summer* (illustrated by Joann Stover), Garrard, 1970; *Poetry for Winter* (illustrated by Kelly Oechsli), Garrard, 1970; *Poetry of Witches, Elves, and Goblins* (illustrated by Frank Aloise), Garrard, 1970; *All about Me: Verses I Can Read* (illustrated by Hertha R. Depper), Garrard, 1971; *Animal Antics in Limerick Land* (illustrated by Edward Malsberg), Garrard, 1971; (with A. D. Jacobs) *Arithmetic in Verse and Rhyme* (illustrated by Oechsli), Garrard, 1971; *Funny Folks in Limerick Land* (illustrated by Raymond Burns), Garrard, 1971; *Playtime in the City* (illustrated by Oechsli), Garrard, 1971; *Poems about Fur and Feather Friends* (illustrated by Aloise), Garrard, 1971; *Poetry for Space Enthusiasts* (illustrated by Aloise), Garrard, 1971; *The Read-It-Yourself Storybook,* Golden Press, 1971; *Hello, People!* (illustrated by Malsberg), Garrard, 1972; *Hello, Pleasant Places* (illustrated by Oechsli), Garrard, 1972; *Hello, Year!* (illustrated by Aloise), Garrard, 1972; *Holiday Happenings in Limerick Land* (illustrated by Malsberg), Garrard, 1972; *Funny Bone Ticklers in Verse and Rhyme* (illustrated by Malsberg), Garrard, 1973; (with A. D. Jacobs) *Sports and Games in Verse and Rhyme,* Garrard, 1975.

Author or co-author of various English textbooks. Creator of educational materials and teaching aids, including record albums and tape cassettes.

Contributor of articles to education journals, including *Elementary English, Childhood Education, Education, Reading Teacher,* and *Today's Child.*

BIOGRAPHICAL/CRITICAL SOURCES: New York Herald Tribune, May 8, 1960; *Young Reader's Review,* December, 1967.

*   *   *

JACOBS, Paul 1918-1978

August 24, 1918—January 3, 1978; American journalist and self-proclaimed radical activist. Jacobs dedicated himself to causes of the underprivileged and supported the rights of the individual. He also worked for many years in the labor movement. Jacob's eight books include the autobiographical *Is Curly Jewish?.* He died in San Francisco, Calif. Obituaries: *New York Times,* January 5, 1978; *Washington Post,* January 5, 1978; *Time,* January 16, 1978.

*   *   *

JACOBSEN, Phebe R(obinson) 1922-

PERSONAL: Born March 24, 1922, in Baltimore, Md.; daughter of Orris Gravenor (a clergyman) and Dorothy (an organization president; maiden name, Medders) Robinson; married Bryce DuVal Jacobsen (a professor), October 16, 1943; children: Eric Gravenor, Kristin Bryce. *Education:* Western Maryland College, A.B., 1943. *Politics:* Democrat. *Religion:* Quaker. *Home:* 735 Glenwood St., Annapolis, Md. 21401. *Office address:* Maryland Hall of Records, Box 828, Annapolis, Md. 21404.

CAREER: Pennsylvania Historical and Museum Commission, Division of Public Records, Harrisburg, Pa., archivist, 1953-58; Historic Annapolis, Inc., Annapolis, Md., researcher, 1958-59; Maryland Hall of Records Commission, Annapolis, archivist, 1960—. Advisory board member of Historic Annapolis, Inc., Interpretations Center, and Swarthmore College Peace Collection. *Member:* Society of American Archivists, Mid-Atlantic Regional Archives Conference, Maryland Historical Society (advisory board member). *Awards, honors:* Waldo Gifford Leland award from Society of American Archivists, 1964, for *The Records.*

WRITINGS: (With Morris L. Radoff and Gust Skordas) *County Court Houses and Records of Maryland,* Volume II (Jacobsen was not associated with Volume I): *The Records,* Maryland Hall of Records Commission, 1964; *Quaker Records in Maryland,* Maryland Hall of Records Commission, 1967; (with Gregory A. Stiverson) *William Paca: A Biography,* Maryland Historical Society, 1976. Contributor of articles to *Maryland* magazine.

WORK IN PROGRESS: Documentation of historical buildings and areas; research in church records, local history, military history, ethnic history, and geneology.

SIDELIGHTS: Phebe Jacobsen told *CA:* "My interest in Maryland history began with stories of the Civil War. Besides, both of my parents were history majors and we all read a great deal."

BIOGRAPHICAL/CRITICAL SOURCES: American Archivist, Volume 27, 1964; *Finding Aids,* Volume 30, 1967; *Maryland Historical Magazine,* winter, 1976; *Journal of Southern History,* May, 1977.

JAFFE, Rona 1932-

PERSONAL: Born June 12, 1932, in New York, N.Y.; daughter of Samuel (an elementary school teacher and principal) and Diana (a former teacher; maiden name, Ginsberg) Jaffe. *Education:* Radcliffe College, B.A., 1951. *Residence:* New York, N.Y. *Agent:* Ephraim London, London, Buttenwieser, Bonem, and Valente, 575 Madison Ave., New York, N.Y.

CAREER: File clerk and secretary, New York City, 1952; Fawcett Publications, New York City, associate editor, 1952-56; writer, 1956—.

WRITINGS—All published by Simon & Schuster, except as indicated: *The Best of Everything* (novel), 1958; *Away from Home* (novel), 1960; *The Last of the Wizards* (juvenile), 1961; *Mr. Right Is Dead* (novella and five stories), 1965; *The Cherry in the Martini* (novel), 1966; *The Fame Game* (novel), Random House, 1969; *The Other Woman* (novel), Morrow, 1972; *Family Secrets* (novel), 1974; *The Last Chance* (novel), 1976. *Away from Home* was published as *Carvinal in Rio* in Europe, South America and Scandinavia.

WORK IN PROGRESS: Rona Jaffe told *CA:* "I am hard at work on a new novel."

SIDELIGHTS: Rona Jaffe's first novel, *The Best of Everything,* was published when the author was twenty-six years old. About "young career women who went to New York to find 'terrific jobs and terrific husbands,'" observed Joan O'Sullivan, it was born "when editor Jack Goodman of Simon and Schuster read a seventy-five-page novella she'd submitted, and asked her to write a full-length book." Jaffe explained: "That book was about me and my friends, the experiences we had as working girls. I got the idea and then I began talking to career girls in New York and California, getting their life stories. I made up a composite of five girls and wrote the book." It took her, she noted more precisely, "five months, five days and 26 years" to write the novel, which subsequently became a best-seller.

Following *The Best of Everything,* Jaffe has published a book almost every two years. She writes, explained Elizabeth Bennett, "five days a week from about 10 a.m. to 5 p.m., sets herself a goal of 10 typewritten pages a day and does very little rewriting." Jaffe plans the books carefully; she told O'Sullivan: "I can't stand the thought of looking at a blank page in the typewriter. It's too defeating. Before I start to write, I've thought the book out, I know all the characters, even the minor ones and what's going to happen to them." ["If I waited for 'inspiration,'" Jaffe remarked to Kay Holmquist, "I'd get too scared to write at all."]

Family Secrets, for example, gestated for fifteen years. Jane Ulrich noted that Jaffe "planned the whole book in her head, made an extensive list of each generation of the Saffron family . . . and minor characters, chose names from 'What Shall We Name the Baby' and from a box of soap, researched, plotted her material and worked until she finished." The result, said Ulrich, was an "absorbing and warm and human" book.

Jaffe herself described her reasons for writing *Family Secrets:* "I wanted to show the falling apart of the American family, and why—but I didn't know why when I started the book. The reason I found is that the times and needs are different for each generation."

C. M. Siggins found *Family Secrets* "excessively detailed rather than selective, overdone, overdrawn, overscrupulous in showing a Jewish family from the inside with all its weaknesses and strengths. Some of the characters are interesting as human beings, others are flat and not in any way stimulating enough to spend time with." Elaine Dundy, however, described the character delineation in *Family Secrets* as "precise" and Jaffe as "a good storyteller who is a good storywriter as well." She continued: "Jaffe has written a very good novel indeed: the sort you carry with you on trains and buses and taxis and that very nearly makes you overrun your destination, so compelling is the narration. I defy anyone to open it at random and not find himself immediately immersed."

Jaffe's most recent novel, *The Last Chance,* has also received mixed reviews. Although the *New Yorker* labeled it "a soap-operaish novel that carries stern, if muddled, warnings to the New Woman about the pitfalls of the liberated life," *New York Times Book Review* noted, "You have to keep reading Jaffe, she's competent and dependable, and she piles on the delicious details."

The Best of Everything was made into a movie of the same title, Twentieth Century-Fox, 1959, and produced on television under the same title, ABC-TV, 1970.

BIOGRAPHICAL/CRITICAL SOURCES: *Saturday Review,* September 6, 1958; Roy Newquist, *Conversations,* Rand McNally, 1967; *Listener,* January 25, 1968; *New York Times Book Review,* September 28, 1969, October 27, 1974, September 5, 1976; *New York Times,* October 2, 1969; *Book World,* November 9, 1969; *Best Sellers,* November 15, 1974, December, 1976; *Houston Post,* November 21, 1974; *Dallas News,* November 21, 1974; *Fort Worth Star-Telegram,* November 25, 1974; *Long Island Press,* January 4, 1975; *Publishers Weekly,* February 17, 1975; *New Statesman,* May 9, 1975; *Times Literary Supplement,* August 8, 1975; *New Yorker,* August 30, 1976; *Virginia Quarterly Review,* winter, 1977.

* * *

JAGODA, Robert 1923-

PERSONAL: Born November 18, 1923, in Kansas City, Mo.; son of Gilbert and Ruth Jagoda; married Kitty Kuhne, April 7, 1948; children: Eric Allen. *Education:* Northwestern University, B.S., 1949. *Politics:* "Liberal Democrat to Independent." *Religion:* Agnostic. *Home:* 136 Roaring Brook Rd., Chappaqua, N.Y. 10514. *Agent:* George Wieser, Wieser & Wieser, 52 Vanderbilt Ave., Room 1402, New York, N.Y. 10017. *Office:* International Business Machines, Old Orchard Rd., Armonk, N.Y. 10504.

CAREER: Union Carbide Corp., New York, N.Y., publicity manager and editor of house publication, 1953-60; Business Communications, Inc., New York, N.Y., vice-president, 1959-60; International Business Machines, Armonk, N.Y., manager of advertising services, 1960—. *Military service:* U.S. Army, Infantry, 1942-45, prisoner of war, 1944-45 (escaped); served in Europe; became sergeant; received Purple Heart and Bronze Star. *Member:* Mystery Writers of America.

WRITINGS: *A Friend in Deed* (mystery novel), Norton, 1977. Contributor to magazines.

WORK IN PROGRESS: *Multiple Choice,* a humorous novel.

SIDELIGHTS: Jagoda commented: "Fiction writing, at the moment (and as it always has been), is an avocation. It is my intent, however, to make it my principal vocation when one of my novels sells well enough to make that possible, or when I retire from my work at I.B.M.—whichever comes first. I intend to continue writing and publishing one novel a year in which there is no common denominator beyond the use of humor. Like Thorne Smith did, in his time, my primary wish is to entertain.''

BIOGRAPHICAL/CRITICAL SOURCES: Patent Trader, September 17, 1977.

* * *

JAMES, C. W.
See CUMES, J(ames) W(illiam) C(rawford)

* * *

JAUSSI, Laureen Richardson 1934-

PERSONAL: Surname is pronounced *Yow*-si; born August 4, 1934, in Longview, Wash.; daughter of Bertram Haldon (a farmer) and Laurice (Burch) Richardson; married August Wilhelm Jaussi (a college professor), December 23, 1955; children: Haldon Richard, Susan Marie, Kurt Christian, Clayton Lenox, Paul Gottfried, Laura Berdell. *Education:* Brigham Young University, B.S., 1956, A.S., 1966. *Religion:* Church of Jesus Christ of Latter-day Saints (Mormons). *Home:* 284 East 400th S., Orem, Utah 84057. *Office:* Genealogy Tree, 31 East 2050 North, Provo, Utah 84601.

CAREER: Oklahoma State University, College of Veterinary Medicine, Stillwater, medical technologist, 1956; Professional Medical Center, Stillwater, Okla., medical technologist, 1960-61; Genealogy Tree, Provo, Utah, partner and genealogical consultant, 1976—. Professional genealogist; research director of Orem's bicentennial history. *Member:* Genealogical Society, Utah Genealogical Association (vice-president, 1974-76; local president, 1976), Utah Daughters of the American Revolution (chairman of genealogical research and records).

WRITINGS—All with Gloria Chaston: *Fundamentals of Genealogical Research,* Deseret, 1966; *Register of LDS Church Records,* Deseret, 1968; *Genealogical Records of Utah,* Deseret, 1974. Contributor to *Genealogical Journal.*

WORK IN PROGRESS: Genealogical Research in England; Genealogical Research in the United States; How to Teach Genealogy with Continuing Workshops.

SIDELIGHTS: Laureen Jaussi writes: "Twenty years ago I took up genealogical research as a hobby to overcome the doldrums caused by the three 'D's' of dirt, diapers, and dishes. I quickly realized there were no basic textbooks and no organized approaches to genealogical research. Teachers used the 'shotgun' method and students were continually dependent upon the teacher for their next idea. I decided to approach genealogy from the scientific viewpoint. I teamed with Gloria Chaston, an experienced genealogist and an outstanding executive secretary, and we developed a textbook with lesson assignments for genealogy home study. We next developed a continuing workshop teaching method for group study and now have a genealogy course where students can become independent researchers.''

* * *

JAY, Mel
See FANTHORPE, R(obert) Lionel

* * *

JEFFERSON, Omar Xavier
See JEFFERSON, Xavier T(homas)

JEFFERSON, Xavier T(homas) 1952-
(Omar Xavier Jefferson)

PERSONAL: Born January 4, 1952, in Philadelphia, Pa.; son of Roosevelt (a painter) and Ada Bell (Hurley) Jefferson; married Lynne Elaine Smith (a manager for a book distributor), October 2, 1972; children: Toby Bryant, Omar Xavier. *Education:* Attended College of St. Thomas, 1969-71, and University of Minnesota. *Home:* 2110 First Ave. S., Minneapolis, Minn. 55404. *Office:* Manchild World Corp., P.O. Box 104, Minneapolis, Minn. 55440.

CAREER: New Art Workshop, Philadelphia, Pa., director, 1969-70; Inner City Youth League, St. Paul, Minn., director of communications department, 1976—. Alderman of Methuslah Bradley, Minn. Consultant to Manchild World Corp. *Member:* National Society of Literature and the Arts, National Historical Society, National Symposium for Contemporary Arts, American Film Institute, American Museum of Natural History, Smithsonian Associates.

WRITINGS: Blessed Are the Sleepy Ones (novel), Ashley Books, 1977; *The Killing Force* (novel), Ashley Books, 1978; *No Great Heroes, No Great Villains* (novel), Ashley Books, 1978.

Plays; under name Omar Xavier Jefferson: "Gravity" (two-act), first produced in St. Paul, Minn., at I.C.Y.L. Theater, August 10, 1976; "Feelings" (two-act musical), first produced in St. Paul, at I.A. O'Shaugnessy Auditorium, September 11, 1977.

WORK IN PROGRESS: Deathwatch, nonfiction on modern society's way of dealing with and viewing death; *The Triple Cross,* a mystery novel; *The Oscar John Method,* a novel about two con artists; *Jade* (tentative title), a novel.

SIDELIGHTS: Jefferson writes: "The primary motivation for all my work is the desire to communicate a message, idea, or thought to a wider audience. In writing, fiction has provided the best medium of expression, although I am now writing nonfiction. *Blessed Are the Sleepy Ones* is important to me because I was able to bring together all the facets I felt good modern fiction should have: an interesting topic—justice in this instance, an entertaining book with sidebars of humor and a camera-like view of our times as well as some basic philosophical ideas in terms of literature and style.

"Besides writing—and I write poetry as well as books and plays—I'm into directing, acting, and producing theatre.

"My latest undertaking is painting (I'm having several exhibitions this year). I feel confident and excited by this particular form of artistic expression.

"My personal belief is that art is in the mind—art is a mental process—the modus operandi is merely the tool by which we take what is in our minds and make it applicable and available to a larger audience.

"When composing, for the musicals, etc., the art process works at its zenith in terms of speed.''

AVOCATIONAL INTERESTS: The classics (literature), jazz, playing the piano.

BIOGRAPHICAL/CRITICAL SOURCES: Twin Cities Courier, August 4, 1977; *Minneapolis Tribune,* September 10, 1977.

* * *

JEFFREY, Christopher
See LEACH, Michael

JENKINS, (Margaret) Elizabeth (Heald) 1905-

PERSONAL: Born October 31, 1905, in Hitchin, England; daughter of James Heald (a headmaster) and Theodora (Caldicott Ingram) Jenkins. *Education:* Attended Newnham College, Cambridge, 1924-27. *Home:* 8 Downshire Hill, Hampstead N.W.3., England.

CAREER: Senior English mistress at King Alfred School, 1929-39; British civil servant during World War II; researcher and writer, 1945—. *Awards, honors:* Femina Vic Heureuse prize, 1934, for *Harriet.*

WRITINGS: Virginia Water (novel), Gollancz, 1930; *The Winters* (novel), Gollancz, 1931, 2nd edition, 1947; *Lady Caroline Brown: A Biography,* Little, Brown, 1932; *Portrait of an Actor* (novel), Gollancz, 1933; *Harriet* (novel), Doubleday, 1934; *Doubtful Joy* (novel), Doubleday, 1935; *The Phoenix Nest* (novel), Gollancz, 1936; *Jane Austen: A Biography,* Gollancz, 1938, 2nd edition, 1947; *Henry Fielding* (biography), Gollancz, 1947, 2nd edition, Baker, 1966; *Six Criminal Women* (nonfiction), Gollancz, 1949, Books for Libraries, 1971; *The Tortoise and the Hare* (novel), Gollancz, 1954; *Ten Fascinating Women* (nonfiction), Gollancz, 1955, Coward, 1968, revised edition, MacDonald, 1968; *Elizabeth the Great* (biography), Coward, 1958; *Joseph Lister* (juvenile), Gollancz, 1960; *Elizabeth and Leicester* (biography), Coward, 1961, *Brightness* (novel), Gollancz, 1963, Coward, 1964; *Honey* (novel), Coward, 1968; *Dr. Gully* (novel), M. Joseph, 1972, published as *Dr. Gully's Story,* Coward, 1972; *The Mystery of King Arthur* (nonfiction), Coward, 1975.*

*   *   *

JENNINGS, Robert
    See HAMILTON, Charles Harold St. John

*   *   *

JENNISON, Keith Warren 1911-

PERSONAL: Born December 12, 1911, in Winnipeg, Manitoba, Canada. *Education:* Attended Williams College and University of Toronto.

CAREER: Writer. Was apprenticed to a Vermont printer, and worked in shipping room of A. S. Barnes & Co. prior to 1935; Harcourt, Brace & Co., Inc., New York City, salesman, 1935-41; Henry Holt & Co., Inc., New York City, sales manager, 1941-46; William Sloane Associates, Inc., New York City, vice-president, 1946-49; Viking Press, Inc., New York City, editor, 1949-58; David McKay Co., Inc., New York City, vice-president and editor-in-chief, 1959-62. Assistant director, New York University Graduate Institute of Book Publishing, beginning 1958. *Military service:* Served in Office of War Information during World War II.

WRITINGS: Vermont Is Where You Find It, Harcourt, 1941; *The Maine Idea,* Harcourt, 1943; (editor) *Dedication: Text and Pictures of the United Nations,* Holt, 1943; *New Hampshire,* Holt, 1944; *New York and the State It's In,* Sloane Associates, 1949; *The Half-Open Road: A Handy Guide to Chaos on the Highway* (illustrated by George Price), Doubleday, 1953; *The Green Place* (novel), Funk, 1954; *Green Mountains and Rock Ribs,* Harcourt, 1954; *The Boys and Their Mother,* Viking, 1956; (with John Tebbel) *The American Indian Wars,* Harper, 1960; *From This to That* (illustrated by Kathleen Elgin), McKay, 1961; *Remember Maine,* Durrell, 1963; (with Kathryn Sisson Phillips) *My Room in the World,* Abingdon, 1964; *The Humorous Mr. Lincoln,* Crowell, 1965; *To Massachusetts with Love,* Durrell, 1970; (editor) *The Concise Encyclopedia of Sports,* F. Watts, 1970; *Yup . . . Nope, and Other Vermont Dialogues,* Countryman Press, 1976.

BIOGRAPHICAL/CRITICAL SOURCES: Christian Century, November 12, 1941; *New Republic,* November 24, 1941; *Chicago Tribune,* July 26, 1953; *Saturday Review,* March 17, 1956.*

*   *   *

JENYNS, R(oger) Soame 1904-1976
    (Soame Jenyns)

PERSONAL: Married Margaret Jourdain.

CAREER: Writer. Deputy keeper of Oriental Antiquities of the British Museum; specialist in Far Eastern decorative arts, especially Chinese and Japanese porcelain, lacquer, and cloisonne.

WRITINGS—All under name Soame Jenyns, except as noted: *A Background to Chinese Painting,* Sidgwick & Jackson, 1935, Schocken, 1966; (translator from the Chinese, under name R. Soame Jenyns) Chu Sun, compiler, *Selections from the Three Hundred Poems of the T'ang Dynasty,* Murray, 1940; (translator from the Chinese, under name R. Soame Jenyns) Sun, compiler, *A Further Selection from the Three Hundred Poems of the T'ang Dynasty,* Murray, 1940; (with wife, Margaret Jourdain) *Chinese Export Art in the Eighteenth Century,* Scribner, 1950; *Chinese Archaic Jades in the British Museum,* The Trustees of the British Museum, 1951; *Later Chinese Procelain: The Ch'ing Dynasty, 1644-1912,* Faber & Faber, 1951, 4th edition, 1971, Yoseloff, [New York], 1965; *Ming Pottery and Porcelain,* Faber & Faber, 1953, Pittman, 1954; (with William Watson; under name R. Soames Jenyns) *Chinese Arts, the Minor Arts: Gold, Silver, Bronze, Cloisonne, Cantonese Enamel, Lacquer, Furniture, Wood,* Universe Books, 1960; (with William Watson; under name R. Soame Jenyns) *Chinese Arts, the Minor Arts II: Textiles, Glass and Painting on Glass, Carvings in Ivory and Rhinoceros Horn, Carvings in Hardstones, Snuff-Bottles, Inkcakes and Inkstones,* Universe Books, 1965; *Japanese Porcelain,* Praeger, 1965; *Japanese Poettery,* Praeger, 1971.

OBITUARIES: AB Bookman's Weekly, December 20, 1976.*

(Died October 14, 1976, in England)

*   *   *

JENYNS, Soame
    See JENYNS, R(oger) Soame

*   *   *

JOBSON, Hamilton 1914-

PERSONAL: Born April 3, 1914, in London, England; son of William Hamilton (an engineer) and Anne (Lines) Jobson; married Mabel Eileen Boniface, February 8, 1941; children: Beryl Ann (Mrs. Alan Pride). *Education:* Educated in England. *Home:* 77 Westbury Rd., Southend-on-Sea, Essex, England. *Agent:* A. M. Heath, Ltd., 40 William IV St., London WC2N 4DD, England. *Office:* 43 Crosby Rd., Westcliff-on-Sea, Essex, England.

CAREER: Writer. Worked as a commercial artist in London, England, 1931-34; owner of a commercial library in Langdon Hills, England, 1934-37; insurance agent for Prudential Insurance, 1937-38; police officer in Southend-on-Sea, England, 1938-68. *Military service:* Royal Air Force,

1943-45. *Member:* British Crime Writers Association, National Book League, P.E.N., Royal Overseas League.

WRITINGS: Therefore I Killed Him, John Long, 1968; *Smile and Be a Villain,* John Long, 1968, Abelard-Shuman, 1971; *Naked to My Enemy,* John Long, 1969; *The Silent Cry,* John Long, 1970; *The House with Blind Eyes,* John Long, 1971; *The Shadow that Caught Fire,* John Long, 1972, Scribner, 1976; *The Sand Pit,* John Long, 1973; *Contract with a Killer,* John Long, 1974; *The Evidence You Will Hear,* Scribner, 1975; *Waiting for Thursday,* Collins, 1971, St. Martin's, 1978.

WORK IN PROGRESS: Judge Me Tomorrow, a novel.

SIDELIGHTS: Jobson told *CA* of his motivation to write: "I suppose it is an egocentric desire to create, with the abilities at my disposal, especially as the end product may give pleasure to others and provide money for me. However, I do become absorbed in the characters of a story I am writing, sharing their vicissitudes and triumphs, if any, so in a sense it becomes compulsive. With the main theme in mind, I allow my stories to evolve through the nature of my characters (with an occasional nudge from me). I do not like contrived situations. I feel that human nature has so many facets that relationships (which is what nearly all novels are about) have never-ending permutations."

"Having been for nearly thirty years a policeman," Jobson added, "I have naturally acquired a fairly wide experience of human beings and the situations in which they become involved. This has helped me as a writer."

"I do need encouragement. I am inclined at times to be overcritical of my work. Each book is written and typed four times."

*　　*　　*

JOHNS, Marston
See FANTHORPE, R(obert) Lionel

*　　*　　*

JOHNS, William Earle   1893-1968
(William Earle)

PERSONAL: Born February 5, 1893, in Hertford, England; son of William Richard Eastman Johns. *Education:* Educated at local grammar schools. *Home:* Hampton Court Palace, Middlesex, England.

CAREER: Journalist and author of books for children. Was apprenticed to a local surveyor at age 16, but entered the Army in 1913, serving in the Middle East, 1914-18, transferred to the R.F.C. (Royal Flying Corps), 1916-30, serving on flying duties at home and abroad; shot down over Germany, September, 1918, and was a prisoner of war for the remainder of the war; retired to the Reserves, 1930, retaining rank of captain; took up journalism as an air correspondent to several British and overseas newspapers and magazines. Lectured to air cadets, 1939, and worked for the Ministry of Information, 1939-45.

WRITINGS: (Editor) *Wings: A Book of Flying Adventures,* J. Hamilton, 1931; (under pseudonym William Earle) *Mossyface,* Mellifont Press, 1932; *Fighting Planes and Aces,* J. Hamilton, 1932; *The Camels Are Coming,* J. Hamilton, 1932; *The Spy Flyers* (illustrated by Howard Leigh), J. Hamilton, 1933; (editor) *Thrilling Flights,* J. Hamilton, 1935; *The Raid,* J. Hamilton, 1935; *Some Milestones in Aviation,* J. Hamilton, 1935; *The Air V.C.'s,* J. Hamilton, 1935; *Steeley Flies Again,* Newnes, 1936; *Sky High,* Newnes, 1936; *Blue Blood Runs Red,* Newnes, 1936; *The*

Passing Show: A Garden Diary by an Amateur Gardener, My Garden, 1937; *Murder by Air,* Newnes, 1937, revised edition, Latimer House, 1951; *Desert Night,* J. Hamilton, 1938; *Champion of the Main* (illustrated by H. Gooderham), Oxford University Press, 1938; *The Murder at Castle Deeping,* J. Hamilton, 1938; *Wings of Romance,* Newnes, 1939; *Modern Boy's Book of Pirates,* Amalgamated Press, 1939.

The Unknown Quantity, J. Hamilton, 1940; *Sinister Service,* Oxford University Press, 1942; *King of the Commandos* (illustrated by Leslie Stead), University of London Press, 1943, reprinted, May Fair Books, 1963; *Comrades in Arms,* Hodder & Stoughton, 1947; *The Rustlers of Rattlesnake Valley,* Thomas Nelson, 1948; *Short Stories,* Latimer House, 1950; *Sky Fever, and Other Stories,* Latimer House, 1953; *Kings of Space: A Story of Interplanetary Exploration* (illustrated by Stead), Hodder & Stoughton, 1954; *Adventure Bound* (illustrated by Douglas Relf), Thomas Nelson, 1955; *Return to Mars* (illustrated by Stead), Hodder & Stoughton, 1955; *Now to the Stars,* Hodder & Stoughton, 1956; *To Outer Space* (illustrated by Stead), Hodder & Stoughton, 1957; *Adventure Unlimited* (illustrated by Relf), Thomas Nelson, 1957; *No Motive for Murder,* Hodder & Stoughton, 1958; *The Edge of Beyond* (illustrated by Stead), Hodder & Stoughton, 1958; *The Man Who Lost His Way,* Macdonald, 1959; *The Death Rays of Ardilla* (illustrated by Stead), Hodder & Stoughton, 1959.

Adventures of the Junior Detection Club, M. Parrish, 1960; *Where the Golden Eagle Soars* (illustrated by Colin Gibson), Hodder & Stoughton, 1960; *To Worlds Unknown: A Story of Interplanetary Exploration,* Hodder & Stoughton, 1960; *The Quest for the Perfect Planet,* Hodder & Stoughton, 1961; *Worlds of Wonder: More Adventures in Space,* Hodder & Stoughton, 1962; *The Man Who Vanished into Space,* Hodder & Stoughton, 1963.

"Biggles" series: *The Cruise of the Condor,* J. Hamilton, 1933, reprinted as *Biggles in the Cruise of the Condor,* Thames, 1961; *Biggles of the Camel Squadron,* J. Hamilton, 1934, reprinted, Thames, 1961; *. . . Flies Again,* J. Hamilton, 1934, reprinted, Thames, 1961; *The Black Peril,* J. Hamilton, 1935, reprinted as *Biggles and the Black Peril,* Thames, 1961; *Biggles in Africa,* Oxford University Press, 1936, reprinted, May Fair Books, 1965; *. . . and Company,* Oxford University Press, 1936; *. . . Flies West* (illustrated by Leigh and Alfred Sindall), Oxford University Press, 1937; *. . . Air Commodore* (illustrated by Leigh and Sindall), Oxford University Press, 1937, reprinted, Collins, 1966; *. . . Flies South,* Oxford University Press, 1938; *. . . Goes to War,* Oxford University Press, 1938; *The Rescue Flight,* Oxford University Press, 1938, reprinted as *Biggles, The Rescue Flight,* May Fair Books, 1965; *Biggles Flies North,* Oxford University Press, 1939; *. . . in Spain,* Oxford University Press, 1939, reprinted, May Fair Books, 1963.

Biggles—Secret Agent, Oxford University Press, 1940; *. . . in the South Seas,* Oxford University Press, 1940; *. . . in the Baltic,* Oxford University Press, 1940, reprinted, May Fair Books, 1963; *The Third Biggles Omnibus* (contains *Biggles in Spain, Biggles Goes to War,* and *Biggles in the Baltic*), Oxford University Press, 1941; *Biggles Defies the Swastika,* Oxford University Press, 1941, reprinted, May Fair Books, 1965; *. . . Sees it Through,* Oxford University Press, 1941; *Spitfire Parade: Stories of Biggles in War-Time,* Oxford University Press, 1941; *Biggles Flies East,* Hodder & Stoughton, 1942, reprinted, May Fair Books, 1963; *. . . Sweeps the Desert,* Hodder & Stoughton, 1942; *. . . Fails to Return* (illustrated by Stead), Hodder & Stoughton, 1943; *. . . Charter Pilot,* Oxford University Press, 1943, reprinted,

May Fair Books, 1965; ... *in Borneo,* Oxford University Press, 1943; ... *in the Orient* (illustrated by Stead), Hodder & Stoughton, 1944, reprinted, May Fair Books, 1963.

Sergeant Bigglesworth C.I.D., Hodder & Stoughton, 1946, reprinted, May Fair Books, 1963; *Biggles Delivers the Goods* (illustrated by Stead), Hodder & Stoughton, 1946; ... *Second Case* (illustrated by Stead), Hodder & Stoughton, 1948; ... *Hunts Big Game,* Hodder & Stoughton, 1948, reprinted, Brockhampton Press, 1965; ... *Breaks the Silence* (illustrated by Stead), Hodder & Stoughton, 1949; ... *Takes a Holiday* (illustrated by Stead), Hodder & Stoughton, 1949; ... *Gets His Men* (illustrated by Stead), Hodder & Stoughton, 1950, reprinted, May Fair Books, 1965; ... *Goes to School,* Hodder & Stoughton, 1951; *Another Job for Biggles* (illustrated by Stead), Hodder & Stoughton, 1951; *Biggles Works It Out* (illustrated by Stead), Hodder & Stoughton, 1951; ... *Air Detective,* Latimer House, 1952, reprinted, Dean & Son, 1967; ... *Follows On* (illustrated by Stead), Hodder & Stoughton, 1952; ... *Takes the Case* (illustrated by Stead), Hodder & Stoughton, 1952.

The First Biggles Omnibus (contains *Biggles Sweeps the Desert, Biggles in the Orient, Biggles Delivers the Goods,* and *Biggles Fails to Return),* Hodder & Stoughton, 1953; *Biggles in the Blue* (illustrated by Stead), Brockhampton Press, 1953; ... *and the Black-Raider* (illustrated by Stead), Hodder & Stoughton, 1953; ... *in the Gobi* (illustrated by Stead), Hodder & Stoughton, 1953; ... *of the Special Air Police,* Thames, 1953, reprinted, Dean & Son, 1962; ... *Pioneer Air Fighter,* Thames, 1954, reprinted, 1961; ... *and the Pirate Treasure, and Other Biggles Adventures* (illustrated by Stead), Brockhampton Press, 1954; ... *Cuts It Fine* (illustrated by Stead), Hodder & Stoughton, 1954; ... *Foreign Legionnaire* (illustrated by Stead), Hodder & Stoughton, 1954; ... *Follows On,* Transworld Publishers, 1955; ... *Chinese Puzzle, and Other Biggles Adventures* (illustrated by Stead), Brockhampton Press, 1955; ... *in Australia* (illustrated by Stead), Hodder & Stoughton, 1955; ... *Learns to Fly* (illustrated by Stead), Hodder & Stoughton, 1955, reprinted, May Fair Books, 1963.

The Biggles Air Detective Omnibus (contains *Sergeant Bigglesworth, C.I.D., Biggles' Second Case, Another Job for Biggles,* and *Biggles Works It Out),* Hodder & Stoughton, 1956; *No Rest for Biggles,* Hodder & Stoughton, 1956, reprinted, May Fair Books, 1963; *Biggles of 266,* Thames, 1956, reprinted, Dean & Son, 1962; ... *Takes Charge* (illustrated by Stead), Brockhampton Press, 1956; ... *Makes Ends Meet* (illustrated by Stead), Hodder & Stoughton, 1957; ... *of the Interpol* (illustrated by Stead), Brockhampton Press, 1957, reprinted, 1965; ... *on the Home Front* (illustrated by Stead), Hodder & Stoughton, 1957; ... *Presses On,* Brockhampton Press, 1958; ... *Buries the Hatchet* (illustrated by Stead), Brockhampton Press, 1958; ... *on Mystery Island* (illustrated by Stead), Hodder & Stoughton, 1958; ... *in Mexico* (illustrated by Stead), Brockhampton Press, 1959; ... *Combined Operation* (illustrated by Stead), Hodder & Stoughton, 1959; ... *at World's End,* Brockhampton Press, 1959; *The Biggles Book of Heroes,* M. Parrish, 1959.

Biggles and the Leopards of Zinn (illustrated by Stead), Brockhampton Press, 1960; ... *Goes Home* (illustrated by Stead), Hodder & Stoughton, 1960; ... *and the Missing Millionaire* (illustrated by Stead), Hodder & Stoughton, 1961; ... *Forms a Syndicate* (illustrated by Stead), Hodder & Stoughton, 1961; ... *and the Poor Rich Boy,* Brockhampton Press, 1961; ... *Goes Alone* (illustrated by Stead), Hodder & Stoughton, 1962; *Orchids for Biggles* (illustrated by

Stead), Brockhampton Press, 1962; *The Biggles Book of Treasure Hunting* (illustrated by William Randall), M. Parrish, 1962; *Biggles Sets a Trap* (illustrated by Stead), Hodder & Stoughton, 1962; ... *and the Plane That Disappeared* (illustrated by Stead), Hodder & Stoughton, 1963; ... *Takes It Rough,* Brockhampton Press, 1963; ... *Special Case* (illustrated by Stead), Brockhampton Press, 1963; ... *Flies to Work,* Dean & Son, 1963; ... *Takes a Hand* (illustrated by Stead), Hodder & Stoughton, 1963; ... *and the Black Mask* (illustrated by Stead), Hodder & Stoughton, 1964; ... *Investigates, and Other Stories of the Air Police,* Brockhampton Press, 1964; ... *and the Lost Sovereigns* (illustrated by Stead), Brockhampton Press, 1964.

Biggles and the Plot That Failed, Brockhampton Press, 1965; ... *and the Blue Moon,* Brockhampton Press, 1965; ... *Looks Back* (illustrated by Stead), Hodder & Stoughton, 1965; ... *Scores a Bull,* Hodder & Stoughton, 1965; *The Biggles Adventure Omnibus* (contains *Biggles Gets His Men, No Rest for Biggles, Another Job for Biggles,* and *Biggles Takes a Holiday),* Hodder & Stoughton, 1965; *Biggles in the Terai,* Brockhampton Press, 1967.

"Gimlet" series: *Gimlet Goes Again* (illustrated by Stead), University of London Press, 1944, reprinted, May Fair Books, 1963; ... *Comes Home,* University of London Press, 1946; ... *Mops Up,* Brockhampton Press, 1947, reprinted, May Fair Books, 1963; *Gimlet's Oriental Quest,* Brockhampton Press, 1948, reprinted, May Fair Books, 1963; *Gimlet Lends a Hand* (illustrated by Stead), Brockhampton Press, 1949, reprinted, May Fair Books, 1964; ... *Bores In* (illustrated by Stead, Brockhampton Press, 1950; ... *Off the Map* (illustrated by Stead), Brockhampton Press, 1951; ... *Gets the Answer* (illustrated by Stead), Brockhampton Press, 1952; ... *Takes a Job* (illustrated by Stead), Brockhampton Press, 1954, reprinted, May Fair Books, 1963.

"Worrals" series: *Worrals of the W.A.A.F.,* Lutterworth Press, 1941; ... *Flies Again,* Hodder & Stoughton, 1942; ... *Carries On,* Lutterworth Press, 1942; ... *on the War-Path* (illustrated by Stead), Hodder & Stoughton, 1943; ... *Goes East* (illustrated by Stead), Hodder & Stoughton, 1944; ... *of the Islands,* Hodder & Stoughton, 1945; ... *in the Wilds* (illustrated by Stead), Hodder & Stoughton, 1947; ... *Down Under,* Lutterworth Press, 1948; ... *Goes Afoot,* Lutterworth Press, 1949; ... *in the Wastelands,* Lutterworth Press, 1949; ... *Investigates,* Lutterworth Press, 1950.

Founder and editor of *Popular Flying,* 1932, 2nd *Flying,* 1935.

OBITUARIES: Time, June 28, 1968.*

(Died June 21, 1968)

*   *   *

JOHNSON, Barbara F(erry)   1923-

PERSONAL: Born July 7, 1923, in Grosse Pointe, Mich.; daughter of Newell (a physician) and Anna (Heyron) Ferry; married William David Johnson (an educator), September 27, 1947; children: William Green, Starr (Mrs. Ward Kellett), Charlotte Lee. *Education:* Northwestern University, B.S., 1945; Clemson University, M.A., 1964; graduate study at Oxford University. *Religion:* Episcopalian. *Home address:* Route 1, Box 214, Shallotte, N.C. 28459. *Agent:* Writers House, 30 East 31st St., New York, N.Y. 10001. *Office:* Department of English, Columbia College, Columbia, S.C. 29203.

CAREER: *American Lumberman* (magazine), Chicago, Ill., associate editor, 1945-48; high school English teacher in Myrtle Beach, S.C., 1960-62; Columbia College, Columbia, S.C., associate professor of English, 1964—. *Member:* International Arthurian Society, Modern Language Association of America, Unicorn Hunting Society. *Awards, honors:* Palmetto fiction award, 1976-77, for *Delta Blood.*

WRITINGS: Lionors (novel), Avon, 1975; *Delta Blood* (novel), Avon, 1977.

WORK IN PROGRESS: A tenth century adventure romance novel, publication by Viking expected in 1978; *Delta Fire,* sequel to *Delta Blood,* and *Sea Vixen,* both novels, both with publication expected in 1979.

SIDELIGHTS: Johnson's *Lionors* was reviewed by the *Washington Post* as one of a "new breed of romantic paperback fiction," and Jerold Savory said that "despite the plot-potential for a medieval soap opera, *Lionors* is a well-planned and well-written novel." About Johnson's second novel, Margaret N. O'Shea observed that "to Barbara Ferry Johnson's credit, she has not allowed what is generally considered to be the taste level of her target audience to drag down the overall quality of her writing, nor did she apparently yield to the crank-it-out-quick syndrome into which some paperback novelists fall. Historical research alone must have consumed a wealth of time for she writes of New Orleans before and during the Civil War as if the time and place were her own."

Johnson does not claim to have penned the great American novel, though. She told *CA,* "I write something I would enjoy reading—something light, romantic—a good story." A licensed unicorn hunter, she "seeks out peaceful, quiet places" to needlepoint and write. Currently, the Johnsons are moving to an ante-bellum house overlooking the ocean in Shallotte, N.C.

BIOGRAPHICAL/CRITICAL SOURCES: Washington Post, September 14, 1975; *Florence Morning News,* October 7, 1975; *Columbia State* (Columbia, S.C.), November 7, 1976, May 15, 1977; *South Carolina Review,* November, 1976.

* * *

JOHNSON, Carroll B(ernard) 1938-

PERSONAL: Born January 9, 1938, in Los Angeles, Calif.; married Linda Leslie Deutsch (a teacher), July 14, 1971; children: Amy. *Education:* University of California, Los Angeles, B.A., 1960, M.A., 1961; Harvard University, Ph.D., 1966. *Office:* Department of Spanish and Portuguese, University of California, Los Angeles, Calif. 90024.

CAREER: University of California, Los Angeles, acting assistant professor, 1964-66, assistant professor, 1966-72, associate professor, 1972-76, professor of Spanish and Portuguese, 1976—. *Member:* Modern Language Association of America, Renaissance Society of America. *Awards, honors:* Fulbright grant for study in Madrid, 1963-64; National Endowment for the Humanities summer grant, 1967.

WRITINGS: Matias de los Reyes and the Craft of Fiction, University of California Press, 1973; *Inside Guzman de Alfarache,* University of California Press, 1977. Contributor to Spanish studies journals.

WORK IN PROGRESS: A short book on Don Quixote, from a psychological perspective; a novel by Mateo Alenan, for University of California Press.

SIDELIGHTS: Johnson told *CA* that he is principally interested in authors and works of sixteenth and seventeenth-century Spanish literature, "both as products of a unique historical situation and as universal human documents. My critical methodology is more or less eclectic, but I am heavily indebted to Americo Castro and to Freudian psychology."

* * *

JOHNSON, E. Ned
See JOHNSON, Enid

* * *

JOHNSON, Enid 1892-
(E. Ned Johnson)

PERSONAL: Born in 1892, in Indiana. *Education:* Studied music in New York City.

CAREER: Author of books for young people. Has also worked as an executive secretary and in real estate.

WRITINGS: (With Anne Merriman Peck) *Wings over Holland* (illustrated by Peck), Macmillan, 1932; (with Peck) *Roundabout America* (illustrated by Peck), Harper, 1933; (with Peck) *Young Americans from Many Lands* (illustrated by Peck), Whitman, 1935; *Natalie* (illustrated by Lucille Wallower), Whitman, 1938; *Runaway Balboa* (illustrated by Peck), Harper, 1938; (with Peck) *Ho for Californy!* (illustrated by Peck), Harper, 1939; (with Margaret Johnson) *Mystery of the Seven Murals,* Random House, 1940; (with Peck) *Big Bright Land* (a Junior Literary Guild selection), Messner, 1947, reprinted, Grosset, 1961.

Cowgirl Kate (illustrated by Frank McCarthy), Messner, 1950; *The Right Job for Judith,* Messner, 1951; *Jerry's Treasure Hunt* (illustrated by Ursula Koering), Messner, 1951, revised edition published as *Garbage Dump Treasure,* Melmont, 1964; *Bill Williams: Mountain Man* (illustrated by Richard Bennett), Messner, 1952; *The Three J's* (illustrated by Sari), Messner, 1952; *Cochise: Great Apache Chief* (illustrated by Lorence F. Bjorklund), Messner, 1953; *Cross-Country Bus Ride* (illustrated by Louis Zansky), Messner, 1953; *Tommy and the Orange-Lemon Tree* (illustrated by Peck), Messner, 1953; (with M. Johnson) *Sally's Real Estate Venture,* Messner, 1954; *Great White Eagle: The Story of Dr. John McLoughlin,* Messner, 1954; *Nancy Runs the Bookmobile,* Messner, 1956; (under pseudonym E. Ned Johnson) *Wyatt Earp: Gunfighting Marshal* (illustrated by Bjorklund), Messner, 1956; *Second Chance,* Messner, 1958; *Rails across the Continent: The Story of the First Transcontinental Railroad,* Messner, 1965.

BIOGRAPHICAL/CRITICAL SOURCES: Books, April 24, 1938; *New York Times,* July 3, 1938; *New Republic,* December 3, 1939; *Kirkus Reviews,* August 15, 1952; *San Francisco Chronicle,* December 14, 1952; *Commonweal,* November 19, 1954.*

* * *

JOHNSON, Eyvind (Olof Verner) 1900-1976

PERSONAL: Born July 29, 1900 in Saltsjobaden, Sweden; son of Olaf and Cevia (Gustafsdatter) Johnson; married Aase Christoffersen (died, 1938); married Cilla Frankenhaeuser, 1940; children: three. *Education:* Largely self-educated. *Home:* Vittippsvagen 8, Saltsjobaden 2 Sweden.

CAREER: Writer of novels and short stories. Worked in quarries, lumber trade, and brickyards, 1914-19; newspaper correspondent in Germany, 1921-23; member of Swedish UNESCO delegation in Switzerland, England, Germany and other countries during late 1940's. *Member:* Royal Swedish Academy (member of Nobel council). *Awards, honors:* Nordic Council Prize for Literature (Helsinki, Finland), 1962; co-winner of Nobel Prize for Literature, 1974; Ph.D. from University of Gothenburg, 1953.

WRITINGS—In English: *Nu var det, 1914,* (first novel in tetralogy; see below), 1934, reprinted, A. Bonnier, 1963, translation by Mary Sandbach published as *1914,* Adams Books, 1970; *Straandernas svall,* A. Bonnier, 1948, translation by M.A. Michael published as *Return to Ithaca: The "Odyssey" Retold as a Modern Novel,* Thames & Hudson, 1952; *Hans naades tid* (novel), A Bonnier, 1960, translation by Elspeth Harley Schubert published as *The Days of His Grace,* Vanguard, 1968.

Other: *Natten aer haer* (novel), 1932, reprinted, Aldus/Bonnier, 1969; *Bobinack* (satire), 1932, Bonnier, 1960; *Romander om Olof* (autobiographical tetralogy), Volume I: *Nu var det, 1914,* 1934, reprinted, A. Bonniers, 1968, Volume II: *Haer har du ditt liv!,* 1935, reprinted, A. Bonnier, 1963, Volume III: *Se dig inte om!,* 1939, reprinted Aldus/Bonnier, 1971, Volume IV: *Slutspel i ungdomen,* A. Bonnier, 1937, reprinted, 1966, one volume edition, A. Bonnier, 1945; *Nattoeving* (novel), A. Bonnier, 1938.

Soldatens aaterkomst (short stories, contains "Soldatens aaterkomst," "Svaar stund," "Hos Hegels," "Burell tappar krafterna," "Vallberg," "En tid av oro foer Eugenia," "Aen en gaang, Kapten!," "Uppehaal i myrlandet," "... gick foerbl," "Advent paa 30-talet," "Aennu en sommar, aennu en hoest"), 1940, reprinted, A. Bonnier, 1974; *Krilon: En Romen om det sannolika,* (trilogy) A. Bonnier, Volume I: *Grupp Krilon,* 1941, reprinted, 1966, Volume II: *Krilon sjaelv,* 1943, reprinted, 1966, Volume III: *Krilons resa,* 1945, reprinted, 1966, one volume edition, 1948; (translator from the Norwegian with wife, Cilla F. Johnson) Torloff Elster, *Historien om Gottlob,* A Bonnier, 1943; (with Gunnar Almstedt) *Warszawa!,* A. Bonnier, 1944; *Dagbok fraan schweiz,* 1947-49, A. Bonnier, 1949; *Drommer om roser och eld,* 1949, reprinted, Aldus/Bonnier, 1962.

Laegg undan solen, A. Bonnier, 1951; *Stunder Vaagor,* 1951, reprinted, A. Bonnier, 1965; *Romantisk beraettelse,* A. Bonnier, 1953; *Tidens gaang: En romantisk beraettelse,* 1955; *Vinterresa i Norrbotten,* A. Bonnier, 1955; *Molnen oever Metapontion* (novel), A. Bonnier, 1957; *Nils Ahnlund,* Norstedt, 1957; *... Vaegar oever Metaponto: En resedagbok,* A. Bonnier, 1959. *Noveller* (short stories, contains "Pan mot Sparta," "En man i Etollen," "En tid av oro foer Eugenia," "Uppehaal i Myriandet," "Maan med laanga skaagg," "Eidbaarare," "Barn i kamp," "Advent paa 30-talet"), Svenska bokfoerlaget, 1962; *Livsdagen laang* (novel), A. Bonnier, 1964; *Favel ensam* (novel). A. Bonnier, 1968; *Naagra steg mot tystnaden* (novel), A. Bonnier, 1973.

Also author of *Lettre recommandee,* 1927; *Stad i moerker,* 1927; *Minnas,* 1928; *Kommentar til ett stjaernfall* (satire), 1919; *Avsked til Hamlet* (satire), 1930; *Regn i gryningen* (novel), 1933; *Den trygga vaerlden,* 1940; *Sju liv,* 1944; *Pan mot Sparta,* 1946; *Ett vaartal,* 1951; *Spaar foerbi Kolonos,* 1961.

SIDELIGHTS: Johnson's early themes range from socialist reform to Swedish culture. One work discussed the hardships of being an unknown Swedish writer living in Paris and others satirized small-town life and Stockholm's bourgeoisie. Many critics have recognized the influence of Sigmund Freud, Marcel Proust, and James Joyce in these early works (Johnson is in fact credited with having introduced Joyce's interior monologue in Sweden). But it is generally agreed that Johnson's writing talents had not reached their potential until 1934 when the first volume of *Romanen om Olof* was published. This tetrology reflects Johnson's own life, beginning at age fourteen when he worked as a lumberjack near the Arctic Circle.

Lars G. Warme comments that the "Olof" series, like other works by Johnson, is characterized by "irony, skepticism, and reflective intellectualism." Warme also explained that with the tetrology Johnson "achieved full mastery of his means. The various impulses and technical experimentations are now transmuted into a mature synthesis. The result is an integrated work of art of epic breadth, carried by a personal vision, a social and psychological documentary, and an unsentimental and deeply moving account of the years of World War I and the author's adolescence, filled with hard labor and longings of mind and body." The work was later adapted for the screen by Swedish director Jan Troell.

Beginning in the late 1930's Johnson's writing became increasingly humanistic and anti-Nazi; pleading for individual freedom and solidarity among Scandinavian countries. The allegorical "Krilon" trilogy is recognized as Johnson's masterpiece of this era. It was followed by *Return to Ithaca,* Johnson's 1946 interpretations of the *Odessey,* which marked the beginning of his long series of historical novels.

Warme succinctly described Johnson as a "rationalist and a humanist" who, in "novel after novel pleads for a liberal democracy and for common sense and common decency. With passionate anger, disguised as irony, he opposes violence, oppression, and power-hungry tyranny."

When Johnson and fellow countryman Harry Martinson were named co-winners of the Nobel Prize for Literature in 1974, the Royal Swedish Academy received much criticism for awarding the prize to two of its own members (in addition to the fact that these names were relatively unknown to world literature experts prior to the award presentation). At the time of the presentation Johnson was cited for "a narrative art, far-seeing in lands and ages." According to the *Washington Post,* however, one critic said: "Martinson and Johnson are important writers, but there is no strong international opinion speaking for them and the choice shows a lack of judgment. Mutual admiration may be one thing, but this almost smacks of embezzlement."

BIOGRAPHICAL/CRITICAL SOURCES: Dallas News, November 10, 1974. *Obituaries: New York Times,* August 16, 1976; *Washington Post,* August 27, 1976.*

(Died in Stockholm, Sweden, August 15, 1976)

*   *   *

JOHNSON, Frederick 1932-

PERSONAL: Born August 23, 1932, in New York, N.Y.; son of Charles (a subway foreman) and Ruth G. (a secretary; maiden name, Anderson) Johnson; married Gretchen Lidicker (a teacher and doctoral student), October 3, 1952; children: Conrad, Gretchen, Guy and Erika (twins). *Education:* New York University, B.S., 1958; Columbia University, M.S.W., 1962, graduate study, 1969. *Politics:* "I'm for a system that puts people before profits and I'm against that part of our system which causes us to murder people in Vietnam and Chile." *Religion:* None. *Home:* 468 Riverside Dr., New York, N.Y. 10027. *Office:* Goddard Riverside Community Center, 161 W. 87th St., New York, N.Y. 10024.

CAREER: Youth worker and community center director for various social welfare agencies in New York City, 1952-60; administrator and developer of multi-service programs in low income areas in New York City, 1962-66; Strycker's Bay Community Action Project, New York City, project director, 1966-68; Columbia University School of Social Work, New York City, field instructor, 1970-74; Goddard Riverside Youth Project (a delinquency prevention program), New York City, project director, 1976—. Member of volunteer administration staff of Medical Committee for Human Rights office in Jackson, Miss., summer, 1964; consultant to Peace Corps in Brazil, 1969; member of Task Force to Review Office of Economic Opportunity (OEO) in Washington, D.C., 1969. *Awards, honors:* MacDowell Colony fellow, 1975 and 1977.

WRITINGS: (Contributor) Bernard A. Drabeck and others, editors, *Structures for Composition,* Houghton, 1974; *The Tumbleweeds, Somersaulting Up and Out of the City Streets,* Harper, 1977. Contributor of articles about life in New York City to *New York* magazine.

WORK IN PROGRESS: Other stories about his experiences as a youth worker and social worker in New York City ghettos.

SIDELIGHTS: Johnson writes: "Since *The Tumbleweeds* is autobiographical, it constitutes a substantial statement about many of my views. In all of my articles (non-fiction only) I try to tell an interesting story. Each reader, I hope, will take from the story what he or she will. I'm not interested in fiction (the writing of) because I have had many fascinating experiences in my twenty years work in New York City neighborhoods. If I ever get those stories out of my system, I might turn to fiction.

"I still get 'high' on the exhilaration of physical movement. I was an acrobat (that was how the Tumbleweeds story began) and a good all-around athlete. Today I still keep in shape with acrobatics and tennis. Most of my avocational reading is in history, especially about China, the International Brigades during the Spanish Civil War, and autobiographies of all kinds, especially of political activists and journalists."

* * *

JONAS, Paul 1922-

PERSONAL: Born August 27, 1922, in Budapest, Hungary; came to the United States in 1957, naturalized citizen, 1963; son of Gyoergy (a gypsy musician) and Iren (Antal) Jonas; married Edith Mason Ham (an editor), June 5, 1958; children: Benjamin. *Education:* University of Technical and Economic Sciences, Budapest, Hungary, diploma, 1947, Ph.D., 1948; attended Yale University, 1957-58; Columbia University, Ph.D., 1966. *Home:* 1013 Quincy N.E., Albuquerque, N.M. 87110. *Office:* Department of Economics, University of New Mexico, 1915 Roma N.E., Albuquerque, N.M. 87137.

CAREER: Political prisoner, 1948-53; National Iron & Steel Enterprises, Budapest, Hungary, head of planning and statistical office, 1953-56; New York University, New York, N.Y., instructor in economics, 1960-63; Brooklyn College of the City University of New York, Brooklyn, N.Y., assistant professor, 1963-65, associate professor of economics, 1965-67; University of New Mexico, Albuquerque, associate professor, 1967-72, professor of economics, 1972—. Fulbright professor at University of Islamabad, 1975-76. U.S. Agency for International Development economic-statistical adviser for India, 1969-71; lecturer at Indian universities, 1976. Conducted field research in Bulgaria, Romania, Yugoslavia, and Czechoslovakia, for U.S. Treasury Department, 1974-75.

MEMBER: American Economic Association, American Statistical Association, Econometric Society, Regional Science Association, Association for the Study of Grants Economy, Foreign Policy Association, Association for Comparative Studies, Association for Asian Studies, American Association for the Advancement of Slavic Studies, Omicron Delta Epsilon. *Awards, honors:* Rockefeller Foundation fellowships, 1957-58; Ford Foundation fellowship, 1958-60; named New York State Distinguished Scholar by New York State Department of Education, 1966; Fulbright-Hays senior scholarship, 1975-76.

WRITINGS: Az anarchizmus tarsadalmies gazdasagi elmelete (title means "The Economic and Social Theory of Anarchism"), University Press (Budapest, Hungary), 1948; *A penz forgasi sebessege a magyar 1946-i szuperinflacioban* (title means "The Role of Velocity of Money in Hungary during the Super-Inflation of 1946"), East-Central European Research Institute, 1948; *Projections and Forecasts for the Indian Economy,* three volumes, U.S. Agency for International Development, 1969; *An Analysis of Bovine Milk Consumption in Major Indian Metropolitan Areas* (monograph), U.S. Agency for International Development, 1971; *Taxation of Western Enterprise in Selected Socialist Countries* (monograph), U.S. Treasury Department, 1976; (contributor) Zbigniew Fallenbuchl, editor, *Economic Development in the Soviet Union and Eastern Europe,* Praeger, 1976; *Taxation of Multinationals in Communist Countries,* Praeger, 1977; (coeditor) *The Hungarian Revolution of 1956 in Retrospect,* Columbia University Press, 1978.

Contributor to *Collier's Encyclopedia.* Contributor of more than twenty-five articles and reviews to scholarly journals and popular magazines, including *Harper's* and *American Historical Review.* Contributing editor of *Eastern European Economics,* 1965—; member of editorial advisory committee of *Soviet and Eastern European Foreign Trade,* 1963—; member of editorial committee of *Annals of Regional Science,* 1969-71; member of faculty advisory committee of *New Mexico Business,* 1974—.

SIDELIGHTS: Imprisoned by the Nazis in 1944, Jonas was liberated by the Soviet troops only to be sentenced to a forced labor camp by the Hungarian Secret Police in 1948. He spent five years at Recsk until Stalin's death in 1953 opened the way for him to receive political amnesty. Before he left Hungary in 1956, he served as the last chairman of the Petofi Circle, which was the intellectual center of the Hungarian revolution.

As an economist, Jonas's specialization is development and comparative systems. He considers himself a "pragmatist Hicksian."

Jonas has traveled widely all over the world, and lived in the Indian subcontinent for three years during two different periods. He has frequently returned to Europe for professional meetings and pleasure.

* * *

JONES, Christina Hendry 1896-

PERSONAL: Born November 8, 1896, in Greenock, Scotland; daughter of James (a craftsman) and Mary (Boss Hunter) Hendry; married A. Willard Jones, May 27, 1922 (deceased); children: Richard Hampton. *Education:* William Penn College, B.A., 1921; attended University of Chicago, 1922. *Religion:* Society of Friends. *Home:* 304 Robin Rd., Waverly, Ohio 45690.

CAREER: English teacher in Albia, Iowa, 1921-22; English

and history teacher at boys' school in Ramallah, Palestine, 1922-30, 1944-54; private school teacher in Pennsylvania, 1933-40; served variously as secretary, vice-chairman and chairman of Near East Christian Council Committee for Refugee Work, 1948-62. *Awards, honors:* Citation from Church World Service for service to Arab refugees, 1962; L.H.D. from Heidelburg College, 1969; distinguished alumna award from William Penn College, 1971; citation from Association of Arab-American University Graduates, 1976.

WRITINGS: American Friends in World Missions, Brethren Publishing, 1946; *The Untempered Wind,* Longman, 1975. Also author of English version of *The Dome of the Rock* by Aref el Aref, 1951.

Author of booklets about the Middle East. Contributor of stories, articles, and study materials to the religious press.

WORK IN PROGRESS: Sketches of life (customs, traditions, and some history) in Palestine before Partition.

SIDELIGHTS: Christina Jones writes: "*The Untempered Wind* was written to present a picture of very troubled years in Palestine as experienced by both the Mandate Government and the Palestinians. I have a continuing interest in the current history of the Middle East." She and her husband donated many of the artifacts they collected during their years in Palestine to their alma mater, William Penn College, which now houses a special Mid-East Collection in their honor.

*   *   *

JONES, David Arthur   1946-

PERSONAL: Born August 22, 1946, in Concord, N.H.; son of Arthur Leonard (a printing executive) and Pearl (Tabor) Jones; married Catherine Mita (a professor and social worker), September 17, 1971; children: Christopher. *Education:* Clark University, A.B., 1968; Union University, Albany, N.Y., J.D., 1971; State University of New York at Albany, Ph.D., 1975. *Politics:* Democrat. *Agent:* Dominick Abel Literary Services, 529 South Wabash Ave., Chicago, Ill. 60605. *Office:* 8 Bacon St., Oxford, Mass. 01540.

CAREER: University of Tennessee, Martin, assistant professor of sociology and law enforcement, 1972-73; State University of New York at Buffalo, assistant professor of criminal justice, 1973-75; private practice of law in Massachusetts, New York, and Washington, D.C., 1975—. Adjunct professor at American University, 1975-76, and University of Pittsburgh, 1977—; deputy director, Institute of Criminal Law and Procedure and member of research faculty at Georgetown University Law Center, 1975-76. Member of bars of Massachusetts, New York, District of Columbia, and U.S. Supreme Court; general counsel to National Justice Committee, Inc.; consultant to Urban Institute. *Member:* National District Attorneys Association, Association of Trial Lawyers of America, American Bar Association, American Association for Professional Law Enforcement, American Society of Criminology, Academy of Criminal Justice Sciences, Boston Bar Association, Erie County (N.Y.) Bar Association, Phi Kappa Phi.

WRITINGS: (Editor with wife, Catherine Jones) *The Sociology of Correctional Management,* MSS Educational Publishing, 1976; *The Health Risks of Imprisonment,* Heath, 1976; *Crime and Criminal Responsibility,* Nelson-Hall, in press.

WORK IN PROGRESS: The Impact of Abortion in America Since "Roe versus Wade," 1973; *The History and Phi-*

losophy of Criminology, completion expected in 1979; with Catherine Jones, *Sex with Children: How Parents Can Cope.*

SIDELIGHTS: Jones writes: "*The Health Risks of Imprisonment* was a milestone in investigative reporting within the criminal justice system. It was the first recorded effort by an impartial observer to penetrate every-day prison life and to scrutinize both health of inmates and health care delivery systems. An in-depth analysis was made, also, of prison violence and use of contraband items behind prison walls. These and other factors were measured as they contribute to psychological distress as well as physical morbidity and mortality among prisoners."

*   *   *

JONES, Gillingham
See HAMILTON, Charles Harold St. John

*   *   *

JONES, Harriet
See MARBLE, Harriet Clement

*   *   *

JONES, Iris Sanderson   1932-

PERSONAL: Born February 8, 1932, in Winnipeg, Manitoba, Canada; came to the United States in 1961; daughter of John Emile and Flora Elizabeth (Patterson) Sanderson; married Michael Owen Jones (an engineer), July 19, 1952; children: David Ralph, Eric Michael. *Education:* Attended University of British Columbia. *Residence:* Farmington Hills, Mich. *Agent:* Toni Mendez, 140 East 56th St., New York, N.Y. 10022. *Office:* 22170 West Nine Mile Rd., Southfield, Mich. 48034.

CAREER: Powell River News, Powell River, British Columbia, reporter, 1949; *Vancouver Province,* Vancouver, British Columbia, reporter, 1949-51; free-lance writer and consultant, 1967—. Media consultant at Oakland University, 1969-76; instructor at Wayne State University, 1974-76, and Farmington Community Center. Lecturer, writer, and chairman of literature advisory panel for Michigan Council for the Arts. *Member:* American Society of Journalists and Authors, Women in Communications, Midwest Travel Writers, Detroit Women Writers (past president).

WRITINGS: Early North American Dollmaking, Scribner, 1976. Contributor of several hundred articles to national magazines, including *Ebony, Redbook, Scholastic,* and *Writer's Digest,* and to newspapers. Contributing editor of *Detroit News* Sunday magazine.

SIDELIGHTS: Iris Jones writes: "I guess the geography of my life is important to me. I lived in Australia, Singapore, and New Zealand before moving to the United States. I am still a Canadian citizen. This has given me a heightened awareness of the rest of the world and of my own isolation within it. It has also made me very aware of how people grow out of their backgrounds and cultures. I am very involved with the cultural relationship between the community and the arts (and the individual artist), and the whole field of personal growth and preventive mental health."

*   *   *

JONES, James Henry   1907(?)-1977

1907(?)—August 12, 1977; American journalist and author. Jones was a sports writer and editor for several newspapers, including the *Macon Telegraph and News, Atlanta Consti-*

tution, *Richmond Times-Dispatch,* and *Louisville Courier-Journal.* He wrote a biography of heavyweight boxer Young Stribling, entitled *King of Canebreaks.* He died in Macon, Ga. Obituaries: *New York Times,* August 14, 1977; *AB Bookman's Weekly,* October 17, 1977.

* * *

JONES, Peter Gaylord 1929-

PERSONAL: Born May 11, 1929, in Tillamook, Ore.; son of Paul (a skilled laborer) and Mary Lurline (Roe) Jones; married Teresa DeRosa, June 8, 1954; children: Peter, Paul, Cathy, David. *Education:* U.S. Military Academy, B.S., 1954; Columbia University, M.A., 1965; New York University, Ph.D., 1970. *Politics:* Independent. *Religion:* Roman Catholic. *Home:* 6404 Hythe Rd., Indianapolis, Ind. 46220. *Office:* Department of English, Indiana Central University, 1400 Hanna Ave. E., Indianapolis, Ind. 46227.

CAREER: U.S. Army, career officer, 1949-77; enlisted, 1949, entered West Point by Congressional appointment, 1950, commissioned 2nd lieutenant, 1954, assigned to various positions involving missile systems, 1954-61, served as infantry battalion adviser in Vietnam, 1962-63, instructor at U.S. Military Academy, West Point, N.Y., 1965-66, assistant professor, 1966-68, associate professor of English, 1968-69, served with United Nations Command in Korea, 1970-71, chief of missile site radar division and later battalion commander at Fort Bliss, Tex., 1971-74, chief of evaluation and research division at Fort Ben Harrison, Indianapolis, Ind., 1974-77, retiring as lieutenant colonel; Indiana Central University, Indianapolis, part-time instructor in English, 1977—.

MEMBER: Modern Language Association of America, Retired Officers Association, Association of Graduates of West Point, Indiana Historical Society. *Awards, honors*—Military: Legion of Merit, Bronze Star, Combat Infantry Badge.

WRITINGS: War and the Novelist, University of Missouri Press, 1976. Contributor to *Military History Journal.*

WORK IN PROGRESS: A detailed analysis of *Gravity's Rainbow,* by Thomas Pynchon.

SIDELIGHTS: Jones writes: "My primary interest is modern literature. I am increasingly interested in the parallels between the climate of modern techno-civilization and the ambiance of war/military organization. I believe devoutly in educational balance: one must know something of the other academic half of the world. Cultural history seems to be an increasing focus of my interests."

AVOCATIONAL INTERESTS: Running, weight training, photography, classical music.

* * *

JONES, Preston 1936-

PERSONAL: Born April 7, 1936, in Albuquerque, N.M.; son of James Brooks (a former lieutenant governor of New Mexico) and Maud (St. Vrain) Jones; married Mary Sue Birkhead (an actress-designer), September 7, 1964. *Education:* University of New Mexico, B.S., 1958; Trinity University, M.A., 1966. *Politics:* Democrat. *Religion:* Roman Catholic. *Home:* 3102 Beverly Dr., Dallas, Tex., 75205. *Agent:* Audrey Wood, 40 West 57th St., New York, N.Y. 10019. *Office:* Dallas Theatre Center, 3636 Turtle Creek, Dallas, Tex. 75205.

CAREER: Dallas Theatre Centre, Dallas, Tex., actor and director, 1960—. Member of board of governors of American Playwrights Theatre, 1975—. *Member:* Texas Institute of Letters, Texas Arts and Humanities Commission. *Awards, honors: Cue* magazine Golden Apple Award, Drama Desk award, and Outer Critics award, all 1976, all for *A Texas Trilogy.*

WRITINGS—All plays: *A Texas Trilogy* (includes "LuAnn Hampton Lavery Oberlander" [three-act], "The Last Meeting of the Knights of the White Magnolias" [two-act], and "The Oldest Living Graduate" [two-act]; trilogy first produced in Dallas, Tex., at Dallas Theatre Center, November 19, 1974; produced on Broadway at Broadhurst Theatre, September 21, 1976), Hill & Wang, 1976; "A Place on the Magdalena Flats" (three-act), first produced in Dallas, Tex., at Dallas Theatre Center, January 13, 1976; "Santa Fe Sunshine" (two-act), first produced in Dallas, Tex., at Dallas Theatre Center, April 19, 1977.

SIDELIGHTS: Jones has been hailed by critics as a regional playwright who has brought the "boondocks" of west Texas to the stage and given Americans a clearer sense of their own identities. Though not a native Texan, he has lived there much of his life, and his love for the region inspired him to write the three plays which comprise *A Texas Trilogy.* "We were doing plays at the center and I couldn't find any with regional settings," Jones said. "They were all in a New York pad or a London flat. I had these memories stored up and I decided to try to write a play about west Texas." Jones laments the loss of regionalism, saying, "At one time our strength was in our regional feeling. Now we're losing it, through the TV tube, and Colonel Sanders franchises in London, New York, and Bradleyville." By writing plays about Texas and his native state of New Mexico, Jones hopes to stimulate the growth of regional writing for the American theatre.

More than fifteen years of stage acting has given Jones a sense of the importance of emotional rhythm in playwriting. "I think my acting experience has taught me to use the actor as a story teller," he commented. "I think a lot of the time the actor can tell the offstage story better than the action can be shown onstage. And just in general, it's taught me to trust actors—the bits of business, the ad libs they contribute, they're almost always right. And you'll find these scattered all through my plays. I take whatever I can get."

Calling himself a storyteller playwright, Jones related, "I think about people I've observed, and thinking about their lives started me writing the three plays that make up 'A Texas Trilogy'.... I suppose that all the plays have grown out of an accumulation of simple observations. It is the small things that trigger me." In describing the trilogy as "a long day's journey into west Texas," Jones alluded to the plays' common theme of time and its effect on people and places. "Whatever the story is," he said, "for me it would always involve 'time' because time is not the sun going up and down every day. It is not a clock. It is not a calendar. Time is an eroding, infinite mystery. Time is, in fact, a son-of-a-bitch."

BIOGRAPHICAL/CRITICAL SOURCES: Saturday Review, May 15, 1976; *Newsweek,* May 17, 1976; *Newsweek,* October 4, 1976; *New Yorker,* October 4, 1976; *New York Times,* October 17, 1976; *Smithsonian,* October, 1976.

* * *

JONES, Tristan 1924-

PERSONAL: Born May 8, 1924, in a British vessel off Tristan da Cunha, South Atlantic; son of Tristan (a captain) and Megan (Roberts) Jones. *Education:* Educated in England,

Irish Sea, Bristol Channel, North Sea, and Wales. *Politics:* "A good boat and a fair breeze for everyone." *Religion:* "Waiting to see." *Home:* 246 West 10th St., New York, N.Y. 10014.

CAREER: Sailing skipper, 1953-75; leader of Antarctic expedition, 1977-78. Lecturer on history of ocean voyaging and polar explorations. *Military service:* Royal Navy, 1940-52. *Member:* Royal Naval Sailing Association, Slocum Society, Society of Authors, Explorers Club.

WRITINGS: The Incredible Voyage: A Personal Odyssey, Sheed, 1977. Contributor of over one hundred fifty short stories and articles to periodicals, including *Explorer's Journal, Motor Boat and Yachting, Yachting Monthly, Neptune Nautisme, Seacraft, Sail, Motor Boating and Sailing,* and *Rudder.*

WORK IN PROGRESS: Ice!, an account of solo voyages to the Arctic from 1959 to 1962; *Sea Dart Across America,* a "perambulation around forty cities in the U.S.A."; *The Saga of a Wayward Sailor; Cape Stiff.*

SIDELIGHTS: In May, 1969, Jones left Westport, Conn., in his thirty-eight foot yawl, *Barbara,* and embarked on a voyage to set "the vertical sailing record of the world." Jones' initial plan was to sail the lowest body of water, the Dead Sea, and the highest, Lake Titicaca in the Peruvian-Bolivian Andes. Setting world sailing records was not new to Jones—in 1959 he performed the first solo circumnavigation of Iceland and the following year succeeded in reaching the farthest point north ever sailed. He had crossed the Atlantic in small boats under sail eighteen times, nine alone, and sailed around the world three times, twice alone. With *Barbara,* Jones predicted, "I would set a record that will not be broken until man finds water amongst the stars."

Jones encountered his first major human problem in Israel. After hauling his vessel to the Dead Sea, he was refused permission by the Israeli government to launch her. He sailed briefly in a local craft, and carted *Barbara* to the Red Sea. Sailing the Indian Ocean, the east coast of Africa to Madagascar and the Seychelles, and around the Cape of Good Hope, Jones battled tropical storms and shortages of fresh water. "I have very often been in a situation in which I did not think I would survive," Jones wrote, "but by God, I would go on trying—I was going to play the bloody game right down to the bottom line, because it's *fun.* Also it's very interesting. Also, for the time being, it's all we have."

Barbara crossed the South Atlantic to Recife, Brazil, and from Recife Jones attempted to reach Lake Titicaca via the upper reaches of the Amazon. After sailing *Barbara* further up the Amazon than any other seagoing sailing vessel had ever gone, Jones found it impossible to get far beyond Manaus, Western Brazil. In the Lesser Antilles he acquired the British-built *Sea Dart* and sailed her through the Panama Canal (another first), down the west coast of South America to Peru. *Sea Dart* reached Lake Titicaca by truck. Jones sailed the lake to Bolivia and made another portage to the "Green Hell" of the Mato Grosso plateau. In the first successful attempt to truck and sail a seagoing vessel across the South American continent, Jones fought corrupt, greedy officials, tropical jungles, high mountain peaks, and sailed his vessel down the Paraguay and Panama rivers to Buenos Aires. Throughout the six-year voyage, Jones told *CA,* he kept faith in his beliefs: "The individual is important, and can often achieve what vast organisations cannot. Mindless bureaucracy is a grave danger to the individual spirit of Man and is to be questioned and if need be attacked at every turn."

"I had started the voyage as a kind of humorous gesture to point out the ridiculous direction in which ocean cruising was heading," Jones wrote. "By offering huge sums of money, big business and the communications media had made a mockery of the sport. In the ocean there are only two competitors—the vessel and nature itself. Anything else deprives mankind of one of the last truly personal encounters between man and God, or whatever it is that makes our universe tick."

When Jones arrived in London in August, 1975, he had portaged and sailed his vessels a distance slightly longer than twice the circumference of the earth.

Jones offered this advice to anyone wishing to embark on a similar voyage: "Learn all you can about your craft, your voyage area, your destination, and your-self (and any companions), then go to it! Take a library of good books."

BIOGRAPHICAL/CRITICAL SOURCES: Washington Star, April 18, 1977; *Wall Street Journal,* August 15, 1977; *West Coast Review of Books,* September, 1977.

*   *   *

JONG, Erica 1942-

PERSONAL: Born March 26, 1942, in New York, N.Y.; daughter of Seymour (an importer) and Edith (designer of ceramic objects; maiden name, Mirsky) Mann; married Michael Werthman (divorced); married Allan Jong (a child psychiatrist; divorced September 16, 1975). *Education:* Barnard College, B.A., 1963; Columbia University, M.A., 1965. *Politics:* "Left-leaning feminist." *Religion:* "Non-practising Jew." *Residence:* Connecticut. *Agent:* c/o Sterling Lord Agency, Inc., 660 Madison Ave., New York, N.Y. 10021.

CAREER: City College of the City University of New York, member of English faculty, 1964-65, 1969-70; University of Maryland, Overseas Division, Heidelberg, Germany, member of faculty, 1966-69. Writer and lecturer. Member, New York State Council on the Arts, 1972-74. *Member:* P.E.N., Authors Guild, Writers Guild of America, Phi Beta Kappa. *Awards, honors:* American Academy of Poets Award, 1963; Borestone Mountain Award in poetry, 1971; Bess Hokin prize from *Poetry Magazine,* 1971; Alice Faye di Castagnolia Award of the Poetry Society of America, 1972; Creative Artists Public Service (CAPS) award, 1973, for *Half-Lives;* National Endowment for the Arts fellowship, 1973-74.

WRITINGS: Fruits & Vegetables (poetry), Holt, 1971; *Half-Lives* (poetry), Holt, 1973; *Fear of Flying* (fiction), Holt, 1973; *Loveroot* (poetry), Holt, 1975; *Here Comes, and Other Poems* (collection of poetry and selected prose), New American Library, 1975; *The Poetry of Erica Jong,* Holt, 1976; *How to Save Your Own Life* (fiction), Holt, 1977.

Contributor of poems and articles to *Esquire, Ladies Home Journal, Ms., Nation, Poetry, Redbook,* and other periodicals.

SIDELIGHTS: The publication of *Fear of Flying* catapulted Erica Jong into sudden, popular success. The novel became a best seller, a Book-of-the-Month Club alternate, and an erotic sensation, while the author was both celebrated and condemned as a "pioneer" of pornography from a woman's pen and point of view.

Whether read for its sex appeal or serious intent, *Fear of Flying* was nevertheless read, and widely. By early 1975 more than 2 million paperback copies had been sold. Not surprisingly, the phenomenon of success became the new focus of Jong's concerns and essentially semi-autobiographical fiction. In a lecture at the University of Houston in May 1975, she articulated her fear of success: "We all feel when something good happens the evil eye is out to get us. It makes us not enjoy anything. The evil eye is a parental voice saying life is dangerous and you should never be happy."

Then there is another problem. Many women writers, having succeeded at their craft, have taken "the suicidal path," so that, according to Jong, for "a woman artist who wants to go on, there are few role models." And even if she adjusts to success emotionally, there are still difficulties. Jong said, "I know now that what I write will be published, and if I'm not careful someone will steal my laundry list and publish it."

Articles and interviews about coping with success finally culminated in the 1977 publication of Jong's second novel, *How To Save Your Own Life*, a novel about a woman in the very throes of success.

BIOGRAPHICAL/CRITICAL SOURCES: Poetry, March, 1974; *Biography News*, May/June, 1975; *Contemporary Literary Criticism*, Gale, Volume 4, 1975, Volume 6, 1976; *Mademoiselle*, June 1976; *Publishers Weekly*, February 14, 1977; *Harpers Bazaar*, May, 1977.

* * *

JULLIAN, Philippe 1919-1977

PERSONAL: Born July 11, 1919, in Bordeaux, France. *Education:* Educated in France. *Politics:* "Right." *Religion:* Calvinist. *Home:* 54 rue Miromesnil, Paris, France.

CAREER: Writer and painter. *Member:* Travellers Club (London).

WRITINGS—Novels and stories in English: *Gilberte retrouvee*, Plon, 1956, translation published as *Gilberte Regained*, Hamish Hamilton, 1957; *Scraps*, Plon, 1959, translation by Angus Heriot published as *Scraps*, Muller, 1961; *Chateau-Bonheur*, Plon, 1960, translation by Edward Hyams published under same title, Macdonald, 1962; *La Fuite en Egypte, recit*, La Table Ronde, 1968, translation by John Haylock published as *Flight into Egypt: A Fantasy*, Viking, 1970.

Nonfiction in English: (With Michael Swan) *Memoirs* (of Chrystianne de Chatou), Prentice-Anderson, 1950; (with Angus Wilson) *For Whom the Cloche Tolls*, Methuen, 1953, Viking, 1973; (editor) *Dictionnaire du snobisme*, Plon, 1958, translation by Heriot, Julian Jebb, Anne-Marie Callimachi, and others published as *The Snob Spotter's Guide*, Weidenfeld & Nicolson, 1958; *Memoires d'une bergere*, Plon, 1959, adaptation by Violet Trefusis published as *Memoirs of an Armchair*, Hutchinson, 1960.

Edouard VII, Hachette, 1962, translation by Peter Dawnay published as *Edward and the Edwardians*, Viking Press, 1967; *Robert de Montesquiou, un prince 1900*, Perrin, 1965, translation by Haylock and Francis King published as *Prince of Aesthetes: Count Robert de Montesquiou, 1855-1921*, Viking, 1967, 2nd edition, 1968; *Les Collectionneurs*, Flammarion, 1966, translation by Michael Callum published as *The Collectors*, Tuttle, 1967, 2nd edition, 1970; *Oscar Wilde*, Perrin, 1967, translation by Violet Wyndham published under same title, Viking, 1969; *Esthetes et magiciens: L'Art fin de siecle*, Perrin, 1969, translation by Robert Baldick published as *Dreamers of Decadence: Symbolist Painters of the 1890's*, Praeger, 1971.

D'Annunzio, Fayard, 1971, translation by Stephen Hardman published under same title, Viking, 1972, 2nd edition, 1973; *Idealistes et symbolistes*, Galerie J. C. Gaubert, 1973, translation by Mary Anne Stevens published as *The Symbolists*, Phaidon, 1973; *The Triumph of Art Nouveau*, translated by Hardman, Larousse, 1974; (with John Phillips) *The Other Woman: A Life of Violet Trefusis*, Houghton, 1976; (contributor) Robert Brandau, editor, *DeMeyer*, Knopf, 1976; *Montmartre*, Elsevier, 1977, translation by Anne Carter published under same title, Dutton, 1977.

Other works; novels: *La veuve du baronet* (title means "The Baron's Widow"), Editions de Paris, 1957; *My Lord*, A. Michel, 1961; *Cafe-Society*, A. Michel, 1962; *Apollon et compagnie* (title means "Apollon and Company"), Fayard, 1974.

Nonfiction: (With Bernard Minoret) *Les Morot-Chandonneur* (title means "The Morot-Chandonneur Family"), Plon, 1955, revised and enlarged edition, 1965; *Le Cirque du Pere Lachaise* (title means "Father Lachaise's Circus"), Fasquelle, 1957; *Les Styles* (title means "Styles"), Plon, 1961; *Delacroix*, A. Michel, 1963; *Les Reines mortes du Portugal* (title means "The Dead Queens of Portugal"), Laffont, 1964; *Jean Lorrain; ou, Le Satiricon 1900*, Fayard, 1974; *L'Evangile symboliste: Carlos Schwabe, 1892* (title means "The Symbolist Gospel: Carlos Schwabe, 1892"), Galerie J. C. Gaubert, 1974; *Le Style Second Empire* (title means "Style of the Second Empire"), Baschet, 1975; *La Brocante*, Julliard, 1975; (with Philippe Neagu) *Le Nu 1900* (title means "The Nude of 1900"), A. Barret, 1976; *Sarah Bernhardt*, A. Balland, 1978.

Illustrator, Marcel Proust, *A la recherche du temps perdu* (title means "In Search of Times Past"), Gallimard, 1969. Contributor to *Vogue, Architectural Digest*, and other periodicals.

BIOGRAPHICAL/CRITICAL SOURCES: Book World, March 24, 1967; *Life*, August 4, 1967; *New York Times*, August 6, 1967, March 10, 1968, November 25, 1969, July 3, 1970, July 12, 1970, February 25, 1973; *Harper's*, September, 1967, April, 1968; *Observer*, October 15, 1967; *Listener*, December 21, 1967; *New Statesman*, December 22, 1967, February 9, 1973; *New Yorker*, April 13, 1968, August 8, 1970; *Spectator*, May 19, 1969; *Saturday Night*, September, 1969; *Atlantic*, October, 1969; *Christian Science Monitor*, December 27, 1969; *Life*, February 6, 1970; *Economist*, February 3, 1973, November 10, 1973.

(Died September 28, 1977, in Paris, France)

[Sketch verified by executor, G. de Diesbach]

* * *

JUR, Jerzy
See LERSKI, George Jan

* * *

JUTSON, Mary Carolyn Hollers 1930-

PERSONAL: Born June 5, 1930, in San Antonio, Tex.; daughter of James P. (a dentist) and Helen Marley (Knuti) Hollers; children: Robert M. T., Jr., Scott Hollers. *Education:* Mary Baldwin College, B.A., 1951; University of Texas, M.A., 1970. *Religion:* Episcopal. *Home:* 112 Anastacia, San Antonio, Tex. 78212. *Office:* Department of Art, San Antonio College, 1300 San Pedro, San Antonio, Tex. 78284.

CAREER: San Antonio College, San Antonio, Tex., assistant professor of art history, 1970—. Member of board of trustees of San Antonio Art Institute. *Member:* Society of Architectural Historians (Texas chapter president, 1978), San Antonio Museum Association, San Antonio Conservation Society, Junior League of San Antonio. *Awards, honors:* Community excellence award from San Antonio chapter of American Institute of Architects, 1973; Emily Smith Medallion for Distinguished Service from Mary Baldwin College, 1975.

WRITINGS: Alfred Giles: An English Architect in Texas and Mexico, Trinity University Press, 1972.

WORK IN PROGRESS: O'Neil Ford, Architect: His Life and Work.

* * *

KAESTNER, Erich 1899-1974

PERSONAL: Born February 23, 1899, in Dresden, Saxony (now part of East Germany); son of Emil (a harnessmaker) and Ida Amalia (Augustin) Kaestner. *Education:* Attended the Universities of Leipzig, Rostock, and Berlin, receiving a Ph.D., 1925. *Politics:* Liberal Democrat. *Religion:* Protestant. *Residence:* Munich, Germany.

CAREER: Novelist, poet, playwright, essayist, editor, social critic, and author of children's books. Worked variously as bookkeeper, publicist, researcher, and journalist. Drama critic and associate feuilleton editor of *Neue Leipziger Zeitung,* in Leipzig, 1925-27; feuilleton editor of *Neue Zeitung,* 1945-47; founder and editor of *Pinguin,* a children's magazine, 1946; founded two literary cabarets, "Schaubude," 1945, and "Die Kleine Freiheit," 1951. *Military service:* Drafted into the Imperial Army, 1917; discharged, 1918, became artillery corporal. *Member:* International P.E.N. (past vice-president; past president of German P.E.N. center), Deutsche Akademie fuer Sprache und Dichtung, Akademie der Wissenschaft und Literatur of Mainz, Akademie der Schoenen Kuenste of Bavaria. *Awards, honors:* Literature Prize of Munich, 1956; Buechner Prize, 1957; Hans Christian Andersen Award, 1960; Mildred L. Batchelder Award, 1968, for *The Little Man* (translated by James Kirkup).

WRITINGS—For children: *Emil und die Detektive,* 1928, translation by May Massee published as *Emil and the Detectives* (illustrated by Walter Trier), Doubleday, Doran, 1930; *Puenktchen und Anton,* 1931, translation by Eric Sutton published as *Annaluise and Anton* (illustrated by W. Trier), J. Cape, 1932, Dodd, 1933; *Der 35 Mai; oder, Konrad Reitet in die Suedsee,* 1931, translation by Cyrus Brooks published as *The 35th of May; or, Conrad's Ride to the South Seas* (illustrated by Trier), J. Cape, 1933, Dodd, 1934; *Das Fliegende Klassenzimmer,* F. A. Perthes, 1933, translation by C. Brooks published as *The Flying Classroom* (illustrated by Trier), J. Cape, 1966; *Emil und die Drei Zwillinge: Die Zweite Geschichte von Emil und den Detektiven,* Atrium-Verlag, 1935, translation by Brooks published as *Emil and the Three Twins: Another Book about Emil and the Detectives,* J. Cape, 1935, reprinted, F. Watts, 1961; *Das Doppelte Lottchen,* Atrium-Verlag, 1949, translation by Brooks published as *Lottie and Lisa* (illustrated by Trier), J. Cape, 1950, Little, Brown, 1951; *Die Konferenz der Tiere,* Europa Verlag, 1949, translation by Zita de Schauensee published as *The Animals' Conference* (illustrated by Trier), McKay, 1949.

Der Gestiefelte Kater, C. Ueberreuter, 1950, translation by Richard and Clara Winston published as *Puss in Boots* (Charles Perrault's fairy tale, retold by Kaestner; illustrated by Trier), J. Messner, 1957; (translator) Jonathan Swift, *Gullivers Reisen* (title means "Gulliver's Travels"), C. Ueberreuter, 1961; *Der Kleine Mann,* C. Dressler, 1963, translation by James Kirkup published as *The Little Man* (illustrated by Rick Schreiter), Knopf, 1966; *Der Kleine Mann und die Kleine Miss,* C. Dressler, 1967, translation by J. Kirkup published as *The Little Man and the Little Miss* (illustrated by Horst Lemke), J. Cape, 1969; *The Little Man and the Big Thief* (translated from the German by J. Kirkup; illustrated by Stanley Mack), Knopf, 1969; (editor) *Die Lustige Geschichtenkiste,* A. Betz, 1972.

Poems: *Herz auf Taille,* C. Weller, 1928; *Laerm im Spiegel,* C. Weller, 1929; *Ein Mann Gibt Auskunft,* Deutsche Verlags-Anstalt, 1930; *Gesang Zwischen den Stuehlen,* Deutsche Verlags-Anstalt, 1932; *Kurz und Buendig: Epigramme,* Atrium-Verlag, 1950; *Let's Face It* (a selection of Kaestner's poems translated from the German by Patrick Bridgwater and others), J. Cape, 1963; *Von Damen und Anderen Weibern,* Fackeltraeger-Verlag, 1963; (editor) *Heiterkeit in Vielen Versen,* Fackeltraeger-Verlag, 1965; *Grosse Zeiten, Kleine Auswahl,* Fackeltraeger-Verlag, 1969.

Other writings: *Fabian: Die Geschichte eines Moralisten* (semi-autobiographical novel), Deutsche Verlags-Anstalt, 1931, translation by C. Brooks published as *Fabian: The Story of a Moralist,* Dodd, 1932, reprinted, Ace Books, 1961; *Drei Maenner im Schnee* (novel), Rascher, 1934, translation by Brooks published as *Three Men in the Snow,* J. Cape, 1935; *Die Verschwundene Miniatur; oder auch, Die Abenteuer eines Empfindsamen Fleischermeisters,* [Vienna], 1936, translation by Brooks published as *The Missing Miniature; or, The Adventures of a Sensitive Butcher,* J. Cape, 1936, Knopf, 1937; *Georg und die Zwischenfaelle* (novel), Atrium-Verlag, 1938, translation by Brooks published as *A Salzburg Comedy* (illustrated by W. Trier), F. Unger, 1957; *Bei Durchsicht Meiner Buecher,* Atrium-Verlag, 1946; *Zeltbuch von Tumilad,* Insel-Verlag, 1949.

Die Kleine Freiheit: Chansons und Prosa, 1949-1952, Atrium-Verlag, 1952; *Die Dreizehn Monate,* C. Dressler, 1955; *Die Schule der Diktatoren: Eine Komoedie in Neun Bildern* (play), C. Dressler, 1956; *Eine Auswahl,* C. Dressler, 1956; *Leben und Taten des Scharfsinnigen Ritters Don Quichotte,* Ueberreuter, 1956, translation by R. and C. Winston published as *Don Quixote* (Miguel de Cervantes' novel, retold by Kaestner; illustrated by H. Lemke), J. Messner, 1957; *Als Ich ein Kleiner Junge War,* C. Dressler, 1956, translation by Isabel and Florence McHugh published as *When I Was a Little Boy* (illustrated by H. Lemke), J. Cape, 1959, F. Watts, 1961; *Rede zue Verleihung des Georg Buechner-Preises 1957,* C. Dressler, 1958; *Der Gegenwart ins Gaestebuch,* Buechergilde Gutenberg, 1958; *Gesammelte Schriften,* seven volumes, Buechergilde, 1958; (editor) *Heiterkeit in Dur und Moll,* Fackeltraeger-Verlag, 1958; *Ueber das Verbrennen von Buechern,* C. Dressler, 1959; *Heiteres von Walter Trier,* Fackeltraeger-Verlag, 1959.

(Editor) *Heiterkeit Kennt Keine Grenzen,* Fackeltraeger-Verlag, 1960; *Notabene 45: Ein Tagebuch,* C. Dressler, 1961; (editor) *Heiterkeit Braucht Keine Worte,* Fackeltraeger-Verlag, 1962; *Das Schwein beim Friseur und Anderes,* C. Dressler, 1962; *Das Erich-Kaestner-Seemaennchen,* E. Seeman, 1963; *Kurz und Buendig,* Kiepenheuer & Witsch, 1965; *Der Taegliche Kram: Chansons und Prosa,* C. Dressler, 1965; *Zwei Schueler sind Verschwunden,* Longmans, Green, 1966; *Kaestner fuer Erwachsene,* S. Fischer, 1966; *Unter der Zeitlupe,* Hyperion-Verlag, 1967; "*. . . was Nicht in Euren Lesebuechern Steht*" (selections from Kaestner's works), Fischer-Buecherei, 1968; *Kaestner fuer Studenten,* Harper, 1968; *Kennst Du das Land, wo die Kanonen Bluehn?,* Atrium-Verlag, 1968; (editor) *Heiterkeit aus Aller Welt,* Fackeltraeger-Verlag, 1968; *Wer Nicht Hoeren Will, Muss Lesen,* Fischer Taschenbuch, 1971;

Friedrich der Grosse und die Deutsche Literatur, W. Kohl-hammer, 1972.

Also author of works for children including, *Das Verhexte Telefon,* 1931, *Arthur Mit dem Langen Arm,* 1932, *Till Eulenspeigel,* 1938, *Der Gestiefelte Kater,* 1950, *Muenchhausen,* 1951, and *Die Schildbuerger,* 1954. Author of *Leben in Dieser Zeit* (radio and stage play), 1930, *Lyrische Hausapotheke* (poems), 1936, and *Der Taegliche Kram* (songs and prose), 1948.

SIDELIGHTS: Erich Kaestner's international fame rests on his children's classic, *Emil and the Detectives,* but he was also an accomplished satirist and social critic. His poems, plays, novels, and essays were an appeal for human decency and reason against the harsh reality of post-World War I Germany. With Hitler's rise to power in 1933, Kaestner was viewed as undesirable and politically unreliable because of his declared pacifism and negative views of Nazism. He considered exile, but decided, rather, to stay in Germany to be a witness and one day give evidence. Kaestner was forbidden to publish, and on May 10, 1933, his books, along with those of several other writers, were publicly burned. He continued to publish abroad until 1942, when Hitler discovered a pseudonymous film script had been written by Kaestner; he then forbade him to publish abroad.

Without trying to be overly didactic, Kaestner's children's books stress such qualities as honesty, sincerity, and altruism, through sentimental charm and verbal humor. The most successful book, *Emil and the Detectives,* has been translated into more than two dozen languages. It has also been used in at least six countries as a textbook for the study of German.

His poems all have a social purpose, and have been categorized as neorealistic, which is related to expressionism. His books of poetry have sold over a quarter of a million copies in Germany. They were first translated into English in 1963 under the title, *Let's Face It.*

Several motion pictures have been adapted from Kaestner's works. "Paradise for Three," an adaptation of *Drei Maenner im Schnee,* starring Robert Young and Mary Astor, was produced by Metro-Goldwyn-Mayer in 1938. "The Parent Trap," an adaptation of *Das Doppelte Lottchen,* starring Hayley Mills, Maureen O'Hara, and Brian Keith, was filmed by Walt Disney Productions in 1961. "Emil and the Detectives," starring Walter Slezak, was filmed by Walt Disney Productions in 1964. There was also a German version, "Emil und die Detektive," released with English subtitles in the U.S. by the International Film Bureau.

BIOGRAPHICAL/CRITICAL SOURCES: John Winkleman, *Social Criticism in the Early Work of Erich Kaestner,* University of Missouri Press, 1953; Erich Kaestner, *When I Was a Little Boy* (translated from the German by Isabel and Florence McHugh), F. Watts, 1961; Rex W. Last, *Erich Kaestner,* Humanities, 1975.

OBITUARIES: New York Times, July 30, 1974; *Washington Post,* July 30, 1974.*

(Died July 29, 1974)

*   *   *

KALASHNIKOFF, Nicholas   1888-1961

PERSONAL: Born May 17, 1888, in Minusinsk, Siberia, Russia; emigrated to the United States in 1924, naturalized in 1930; son of a farmer; married Elizabeth Lawrence (an editor). *Education:* Attended Moscow University for two years.

CAREER: Author of books for children. At age 16, participated in the 1905 rebellion of the Russian masses and was exiled by the government to northern Siberia for four years. Joined the Russian Army during World War I with the rank of captain; commanded the People's Army of Siberia as a general during the Russian Civil War, defeating Ataman Semenoff at Irkutsk, 1919. Forced to flee to China upon Bolshevik victory. *Awards, honors:* Recipient of Mac-Dowell Fellowship, for *They That Take the Sword.*

WRITINGS: They That Take the Sword, Harper, 1939; *Jumper: The Life of a Siberian Horse* (illustrated by Edward Shenton), Scribner, 1944; *Toyon: A Dog of the North and His People* (illustrated by Arthur Marokvia), Harper, 1950; *The Defender* (illustrated by Claire and George Louden, Jr.), Scribner, 1951; *My Friend Yakub* (illustrated by Feodor Rojankovsky), Scribner, 1953.

SIDELIGHTS: Nicholas Kalashnikoff's long autobiographical novel, *They That Take the Sword,* was reviewed by a *Commonweal* critic who wrote: "It is a refreshingly dispassionate account of the protagonist's life as student, idealist, revolutionary, and terrorist, told very humbly and sorrowfully in the hope, as the preface says, that other potential revolutionaries, like the author, idealistic and uninstructed, may not be moved to 'take the sword.'" The *New York Times* added: "Coming at this moment [1939] of political temper and distemper this writing will soothe no nerves. It is inflammable material more likely to confirm prejudices, both conservative and socialistic. The author writes with obvious sincerity, strength, and conviction, and political idealists of all shades of opinion may find a story of more than common excitement, and a human document of rich and incisive historical comment."

The *New York Herald Tribune*'s comments on *Toyon: A Dog of the North and His People* included: "There is a rare combination of strength and quiet gentleness, and an unforgettable portrait of the man Guran and the brave, almost human dog. The distant Yakuts here become more real to us than many a book has made our own Eskimos. The title sounds like that of another dog story for the young, but this is a deeply felt adult novel." The *Christian Science Monitor* noted: "The wild beauty of the northland, the excitement of the hunt, the warmth and companionship of the family as well as their domestic routine, and above all the quiet wisdom that is such a part of those who live close to nature is all within the story of Toyon."

Of Kalashnikoff's last book, *My Friend Yakub,* a *New York Times* critic noted: "The nostalgic details of old-time peasant life are fascinating and clearly drawn. The characters are all credible, and the narrator emerges as a convincing and appealing boy. Although the author avoids false sentimentality, there is a ring of simple, unselfconscious goodness about this book which is as rare as it is refreshing."

BIOGRAPHICAL/CRITICAL SOURCES: New York Times, September 10, 1939, November 29, 1953; *Commonweal,* December 29, 1939; *New York Herald Tribune Book Review,* September 17, 1950; *Christian Science Monitor,* November 4, 1950.*

(Died August 17, 1961)

*   *   *

KALENIK, Sandra   1945-

PERSONAL: Born October 6, 1945, in Connecticut; daughter of Leo Peter (a consultant) and Julia (a manager; maiden name, Magdon) Kalenik. *Education:* Attended Roanoke

College, 1963-65; Ohio State University, B.A., 1968. *Home:* 2829 28th St. N.W., Washington, D.C. 20008.

CAREER: Copywriter for O. M. Scott & Sons, *U.S. News and World Report,* and Adams Group, 1968-72; free-lance writer, 1972-76; Schultz & Conover, Washington, D.C., partner, 1976—. Lecturer at University of the District of Columbia. *Member:* Dramatist's Guild, Authors League of America, Washington Independent Writers. *Awards, honors:* Playwriting fellowship at American University from Sam S. Shubert Foundation, 1970, for "Prunes for Breakfast."

WRITINGS: (With Jay S. Bernstein) *How to Get a Divorce,* Washingtonian Books, 1976.

Plays: "Growth of a Person," first produced in Columbus, Ohio, at Derby Theatre; "Life in a Mayonnaise Jar," first produced in Columbus, Ohio, at Derby Theatre; (with Susan Dias) "On Behalf of the Laugh," first produced in New York City by the Merri-Mini Players, televised in New York City.

Contributor to government publications and popular magazines, including *Washington Post Sunday Magazine, Ingenue, Reader's Digest,* and *Washingtonian,* and various newspapers.

WORK IN PROGRESS: A novella, *Hill Garden Drive; How to Renovate a House (Even Though You Don't Have a Lot of Money and You're the Wrong Gender).*

SIDELIGHTS: Kalenik told *CA:* "For someone seriously considering a writing career, I have one recommendation: Be flexible. Learn advertising/public relations copywriting, news writing, feature writing, and work your way into fiction. Take any and all editing assignments. Learn as much about production as possible, including type spacing and layout. Be complete by delving into every writing field. It may be the only way you can keep from going broke. Also, one of the best pieces of advice I've ever gotten was from Jerry Lawrence ('Mame,' 'Inherit the Wind') who said, 'Telling someone about your idea before you've written it is like peeing before you go to the doctor's.' So true. One of the best ways to kill an idea is to talk about it."

*   *   *

KAMARCK, Lawrence   1927-

PERSONAL: Born June 6, 1927, in Pyrities, N.Y.; son of Martin and Frances (Earle) Kamarck; married Caroline Langmaid, June 18, 1949 (divorced, 1970); married Mary Catherine Rich, November 5, 1970; children: Jonathon, Matthew, Mitchell, Valerie. *Education:* Harvard University, A.B., 1950. *Home address:* RFD 2, Box 51, Peterborough, N.H. 03458. *Agent:* William Morris Agency, 1350 Ave. of the Americas, New York, N.Y. 10019.

CAREER: Worked as a reporter for *Newsweek* and *Forbes* and as swingman for *New Yorker* during the 1950's; Crotched Mountain Foundation, Greensfield, N.H., director of public information, 1960-66; New Hampshire Governor's Committee on Education for the Handicapped, Concord, chairman, 1967-68; writer. Member, Governor's Committee on Vocational Rehabilitation, 1969; director, New Hampshire Easter Seals, 1969-71. *Military service:* U.S. Army, 1945-47. *Member:* Authors Guild. *Awards, honors:* Edgar Allan Poe Special Award from Mystery Writers of America, 1968, for *The Dinosaur.*

WRITINGS: The Dinosaur, Random House, 1968; *The Bell Ringer,* Random House, 1969; *The Strange Butterflies of Dr. Zitzer,* Dial, 1978.

WORK IN PROGRESS: Three books; several plays; a film script.

SIDELIGHTS: Kamarck told *CA:* "I am primarily interested in story telling. Having produced what the *New York Times* chose as one of the ten best chillers in 1968 and in 1969, I'm probably well conditioned to do what it seems I do well. However, I feel that *chilling* books are central to the chilling experience of life today.

"I suspect that books that thrill and chill differ from those that don't only in their ability to lure readers to believe intensely in the threats of the *special* reality presented by the writer. The key words are probably *intensity, threat,* and *reality.* If these three can be achieved, the chiller has a chance of being good."

*   *   *

KAMINSKY, Stuart M(elvin)   1934-

PERSONAL: Born September 29, 1934, in Chicago, Ill.; son of Leo and Dorothy (Zelac) Kaminsky; married Merle Gordon, August 30, 1959; children: Peter Michael, Toby Arthur. *Education:* University of Illinois, B.S., 1957, M.A., 1959; Northwestern University, Ph.D., 1973. *Residence:* Evanston, Ill. *Agent:* Dominick Abel, 498 West End Ave., #126, New York, N.Y. 10024. *Office:* School of Speech, Northwestern University, Evanston, Ill. 60201.

CAREER: University of Chicago, Chicago, Ill., director of Office of Public Information, 1968-71; Northwestern University, Evanston, Ill., assistant professor, 1973-75, associate professor of speech, 1975—. Member of Illinois Arts Council film committee. *Military service:* U.S. Army, 1957-59. *Member:* Society for Cinema Studies, Mystery Writers of America, Popular Culture Association.

WRITINGS: "Here Comes the Interesting Part" (one-act play), first produced in New York City at New York Academy of Arts and Sciences, 1968; *Don Siegel, Director,* Curtis Books, 1974; *American Film Genres,* Pflaum/Standard, 1974, new edition, Dell, 1977; *Clint Eastwood,* New American Library, 1975; (editor) *Ingmar Bergman: Essays in Criticism,* Oxford University Press, 1976; *Bullet for a Star* (mystery novel), St. Martin's, 1977; *John Huston: Maker of Magic,* Houghton, 1978; *Murder on the Yellow Brick Road* (mystery novel), St. Martin's, 1978.

Contributor: Ralph Amelio, editor, *Hal in the Classroom,* Pflaum/Standard, 1976; Thomas Atkins, editor, *Graphic Violence on the Screen,* Simon & Schuster, 1976; Atkins, editor, *Science Fiction Film,* Simon & Schuster, 1976.

Contributor to cinema journals and other magazines, including *U.N.C.L.E.* and *New Mexico Quarterly.*

WORK IN PROGRESS: Caxton's Hill, a western novel, with Gar Simmons, under pseudonym L. C. Hartman; a novel dealing with political sabotage; a detective novel; "a multi-generational saga."

SIDELIGHTS: Kaminsky comments: "In addition to writing, I teach courses on film and television. I have made several short sound films, and plan to make more. In my fiction writing, I am particularly interested in avoiding pretension. In my nonfiction writing, I am particularly concerned with being provocative and readable."

AVOCATIONAL INTERESTS: Athletics (especially basketball and football), reading detective fiction and media history/criticism.

KANE, Henry Bugbee 1902-1971

PERSONAL: Born January 8, 1902, in Cambridge, Mass.; children: one son, one daughter. *Education:* Attended Massachusetts Institute of Technology. *Residence:* Lincoln, Mass.

CAREER: Worked in a variety of fields, including lighting engineering, kitchen design, advertising, and public relations; Massachusetts Institute of Technology, Cambridge, director of alumni fund, 1940-66; author, photographer, and illustrator for adult and juvenile magazines and books. *Military service:* Served in the U.S. Navy as a flier. *Awards, honors: The Tale of a Wood* was chosen by the *New York Times* as one of the best illustrated children's books of the year, 1962.

WRITINGS: The Alphabet of Birds, Bugs, and Beasts (self-illustrated), Houghton, 1938; *Wings, Legs, or Fins* (self-illustrated), Knopf, 1965; *Four Seasons in the Woods* (self-illustrated), Knopf, 1968; *A Care for Nature,* Norton, 1971.

"Wild World Tales" series; all self-illustrated; all published by Knopf: *The Tale of the Whitefoot Mouse,* 1940; . . . *the Bullfrog,* 1941; . . . *the Promethea Moth,* 1942; . . . *the Crow,* 1943; . . . *the White-Faced Hornet,* 1943; . . . *the Wild Goose,* 1946; *Wild World Tales: The Tale of the Mouse, the Moth, and the Crow,* 1949; *The Tale of a Meadow,* 1959; . . . *a Pond,* 1960; . . . *a Wood,* 1962.

Illustrator: Sally Carrighar, *One Day on Beetle Rock,* Knopf, 1944; Henry David Thoreau, *Thoreau's Walden: A Photographic Register,* Knopf, 1946; John James Rowlands, *Cache Lake Country,* Norton, 1947; Thoreau, *Maine Woods,* Norton, 1950; Thoreau, *Cape Cod,* Norton, 1951; Thoreau, *Walden,* Norton, 1951; David Thompson Watson McCord, *Far and Few,* Little, Brown, 1952, reprinted, Dell, 1971; Carrighar, *Icebound Summer,* Knopf, 1953; Edwin Way Teale, *Wilderness World of John Muir,* Houghton, 1954; Thoreau, *Concord and the Merrimac,* Little, Brown, 1954; Bud Helmericks, *Arctic Hunter,* Little, Brown, 1955; McCord, *Take Sky,* Little, Brown, 1962; Dudley Cammett Lunt, *The Woods and the Sea: Wilderness and Seacoast Adventures in the State of Maine,* Knopf, 1965; McCord, *All Day Long: Fifty Rhymes of the Never Was and Always Is,* Little, Brown, 1966; Louise and Norman Dyer Harris, *Flash: The Life Story of a Firefly,* Little, Brown, 1966; McCord, *For Me to Say: Rhymes of the Never Was and Always Is,* Little, Brown, 1970.

SIDELIGHTS: Though Kane became attracted to drawing and photography as a child, he only pursued his interest in the arts as an avocation until he retired in 1966. The author's earlier books in the "Wild World Tales" series, examined the life-cycle of various insects, birds, and animals. The later books in the series looked at plant and animal life from a small boy's viewpoint.

BIOGRAPHICAL/CRITICAL SOURCES: Books, April 20, 1941; *New York Times,* May 11, 1941; *Christian Science Monitor,* November 3, 1960; *Saturday Review,* February 22, 1969. Obituaries: *New York Times,* February 16, 1971.*

(Died February, 1971)

* * *

KANTOR, MacKinlay 1904-1977

February 4, 1904—October 11, 1977; American historian and author of forty-three books. Kantor was awarded the Pulitzer Prize for his portrayal of the brutalities of a Confederate prisoner of war camp in *Andersonville.* He is also known for *Long Remember, Irene, I Love You,* and *Glory for Me* which was adapted by Robert E. Sherwood to become the Oscar-winning film, "The Best Years of Our Life." Kantor died in Sarasota, Fla. Obituaries: *New York Times,* October 12, 1977; *Washington Post,* October 12, 1977; *Time,* October 24, 1977; *Newsweek,* October 24, 1977; *AB Bookman's Weekly,* January 30, 1978. (See index for *CA* sketch)

* * *

KAPLAN, Richard 1929-

PERSONAL: Born January 21, 1929, in New York, N.Y.; son of Irving A. (a salesman) and Rose (Bernstein) Kaplan; married Julia Schwartz, November 28, 1957; children: Susan, Nancy. *Education:* City College (now of the City University of New York), B.S.S., 1950; Columbia University, M.S., 1951. *Residence:* Dobbs Ferry, N.Y. *Office: Ladies' Home Journal,* 641 Lexington Ave., New York, N.Y. 10022.

CAREER: Staff member of Magazine Management Co., 1951-55; *Real* Magazine, New York City, staff member, 1955-58; *Coronet,* New York City, senior editor, 1958-61; *Saga,* New York City, executive editor, 1963-64; *Pageant,* New York City, executive editor, 1964-66; *Ladies' Home Journal,* New York City, currently executive editor. *Military service:* U.S. Marine Corps, 1951.

WRITINGS: Great Linebackers of the National Football League, Random House, 1970; *Great Upsets of the National Football League,* Random House, 1972.

WORK IN PROGRESS: A novel, with Marcia Cohen, for Putnam.

* * *

KAPPELMAN, Murray M(artin) 1931-

PERSONAL: Born July 17, 1931, in Baltimore, Md.; son of Leon (a lawyer) and Irene (an accountant; maiden name, Bassin); married Joan Goldberg (a communications specialist), June 21, 1953; children: Lee Ilene, Karen Ruth, Ross Alan, Lynn Ann. *Education:* University of Maryland, B.S., 1951, M.D., 1955. *Home:* 2124 Western Run Dr., Baltimore, Md. 21209. *Agent:* Jane Rotrosen Agency, 212 East 48th St., New York, N.Y. 10017. *Office:* 660 West Redwood St., Baltimore, Md. 21201.

CAREER: Private practice of medicine, 1960-68; University of Maryland, School of Medicine, Baltimore, associate professor, 1970-73, professor of pediatrics, 1973—, associate dean of education and special programs. Past president of board of directors of Center State (Baltimore). *Military service:* U.S. Army, 1957-59. *Member:* Dramatists Guild.

WRITINGS: The Child Healers (novel), McKay, 1971; *What Your Child Is All About,* Reader's Digest Press, 1973; *Raising the Only Child,* Dutton, 1974; *Between Parent and School,* Dial, 1977; *Sex and the American Teenager,* Reader's Digest Press, 1977; (with Paul Ackerman) *Signals: What Your Child Is Really Telling You,* Dial, 1978.

Author of "The Clinic" (three-act play), first produced in Baltimore, Md. at Center Stage. Author of "Child Concern," a column in *Family Health,* 1972. Contributor of articles and reviews to magazines, including *Glamour* and *Performance.*

* * *

KAREN, Robert L(e Roy) 1925-

PERSONAL: Born January 6, 1925, in Los Angeles, Calif.;

son of Phillip (a businessman) and Emilie Karen; married Dorothy R. Merrill (a junior high school mathematics teacher), March 31, 1951; children: Leslie R., Timothy C., Gregory M. *Education:* Attended St. Lawrence University, 1944-45; University of California, Los Angeles, B.A., 1948, M.A., 1952; Arizona State University, Ph.D., 1964. *Home:* 3575 Elsinore Pl., San Diego, Calif. 92117. *Office:* Department of Psychology, San Diego State University, San Diego, Calif. 92182.

CAREER: Long Beach State College, Long Beach, Calif., instructor in psychology, 1951-52; U.S. Navy Electronics Laboratory, San Diego, Calif., research psychologist, 1952-55; San Diego City College, San Diego, instructor in psychology, 1955-62; San Diego State University, San Diego, assistant professor, 1964-67, associate professor, 1967-71, professor of psychology, 1971—. *Military service:* U.S. Navy, 1943-45. *Member:* American Psychological Association, American Association for the Advancement of Science, Western Psychological Association, United Professors of California.

WRITINGS: An Introduction to Behavior Theory and Its Applications, Harper, 1974. Contributor of articles and reviews to psychology journals.

WORK IN PROGRESS: Dibs: Reinforcement by Another Name; reinterpreting and synthesizing earlier studies of successful community placement of the mentally retarded; studies in the behavior modification of the reatarded.

SIDELIGHTS: Karen writes: "I feel that it is vital that man's knowledge about behavior be used in 'social practice' to his benefit and that the most powerful knowledge arises from the body of knowledge known as 'behavior theory.' My interest has been to use this knowledge and to convince my colleagues, especially those of a different theoretical persuasion, of the scope and validity of behavior theory."

*   *   *

KARPAU, Uladzimir
   See KARPOV, Vladimir

*   *   *

KARPOV, Vladimir   1912(?)-1977
   (Uladzimir Karpau)

1912(?)—August, 1977; Byelorussian author. Karpov's novels included *Year After Year* and *The Bloody Banks of the Nemila.* Obituaries: *New York Times,* August 13, 1977; *AB Bookman's Weekly,* October 17, 1977.

*   *   *

KAUFMAN, Edmund George   1891-

PERSONAL: Born December 26, 1891, near Moundridge, Kan.; son of John P. (a farmer) and Carolina (Schrag) Kaufman; married Hazel Dester, 1917 (died, 1948); married Anna Miller Baumgartner, 1950 (died, 1961); married Edna Ramseyer (a home economics instructor), June 10, 1965; children: (first marriage) Kenneth (deceased), Gordon, Karolyn Kaufman Zerger. *Education:* University of Kansas, student, 1914-15; Bethel College, North Newton, Kan., A.B., 1916; Bluffton College, A.M., 1917; Garrett Theological Seminary, B.D., 1927; University of Chicago, Ph.D., 1928. *Home:* 211 East 25th St., North Newton, Kan. 67117. *Office:* Bethel College, North Newton, Kan. 67117.

CAREER: Teacher in McPherson County, Kan., 1909-12; principal of Hua Mei Academy, Hopei Province, China, and superintendent of Mennonite mission schools in Hopei,

1918-25; Bluffton College, Bluffton, Ohio, professor of education, 1929-31, acting dean, 1930-31; Bethel College, North Newton, Kan., vice-president, 1931-32, president, 1932-52, president emeritus, 1952—, professor of sociology and religion, 1931-48, professor of religion and philosophy, 1948-63, professor emeritus, 1963—. Staff member under Agency for International Development at Punjab Agricultural University, Ludhiana, India, 1965-67. Visiting professor at Mennonite Biblical Seminary, 1931, 1946, 1957, American University in Cairo, 1950-51, Bluffton College, 1959-60, and Spelman College, 1964-65. Chairman of board of education, General Conference of the Mennonite Church, 1935-52; member of board, Mennonite Biblical Seminary, 1935-65; Mennonite relief commissioner to Europe, 1946.

MEMBER: National Education Association, American Association for the Advancement of Science, American Sociological Society, American Academy of Political and Social Science, American Association for the United Nations, International Platform Association, Delta Sigma Rho, Pi Gamma Mu, National Travel Club, Rotary International. *Awards, honors:* Chinese government decoration, 1925, for educational work done in China; LL.D., Bluffton College, 1939; D.D., Bethel College, 1968.

WRITINGS: The Chinese Student Movement, Women's Missionary Society, 1925; *The Mennonite Missionary Interest,* Mennonite Book Concern, 1931; *The Mission of the Mennonite Church,* Mennonite Central Committee, 1944; (with Peter J. Wedel) *The Story of Bethel College,* Bethel College, 1954; *The Peter and Freni (Strausz) Kaufman Family Record,* Mennonite Press, 1963; *Living Creatively,* Faith & Life, 1966; *Basic Christian Convictions,* Bethel College, 1972; (compiler) *General Conference on Mennonite Pioneers,* Bethel College, 1972; (editor) *Jacob Schrag Family Record, 1836-1974,* Bethel College, 1974. Contributor to Mennonite journals.

AVOCATIONAL INTERESTS: Farming.

*   *   *

KEATS, John (C.)   1920-

PERSONAL: Born June 12, 1920, in Moultrie, Ga.; son of Harold (a lawyer) and Helen Keats; married wife Margaret, April, 1942; children: Christopher, Margaret. *Education:* Attended University of Michigan, 1938, and University of Pennsylvania, 1939. *Residence:* Philadelphia, Pa.

CAREER: Worked as copyperson and reporter for the *Washington Daily News* during the 1950's; free-lance writer, 1953—. *Military service:* U.S. Army, 1940-45.

WRITINGS: The Crack in the Picture Window, Houghton, 1956; *The Insolent Chariots,* Lippincott, 1958; *Schools Without Scholars,* Houghton, 1958; *They Fought Alone,* Lippincott, 1963; *The Sheepskin Psychosis,* Lippincott, 1965; *Howard Hughes,* Random House, 1966; *The New Romans,* Lippincott, 1967; *See Europe Next Time You Go There,* Little, Brown, 1968; *You Might as Well Live: The Life and Times of Dorothy Parker,* Simon & Schuster, 1970; *Of Time and an Island,* Charterhouse, 1974; *What Ever Happened to Mom's Apple Pie,* Houghton, 1976.

Contributor of stories and articles to periodicals, including *Atlantic, Esquire, McCalls, Horizon,* and *New York Times.*

SIDELIGHTS: "My fathers' generation," wrote Keats, "produced the hero we worshiped as boys, while we have produced the anti-hero that our children regard as cool.

"I do not mention these changes in order to plead for a return to cottage industry and a simpler life, but rather to suggest that any one of the phenomena I have mentioned would ordinarily be sufficient to give an entire generation a great many discomforts to learn to live with and put into some rational perspective. The point is that ideas in America become accomplished facts before anyone has time to debate them; that so many different, changing things clamor for our attention that it is difficult for any one of us to sit down for himself to decide what he should do about any of them or in what order they are important to him; that the nation is so much of a vast, populous, bubbling confusion of Protean transformations that it is virtually impossible for any of us to be able to say, 'I love America' or 'America is my home' because the America we might have had in mind at the moment we say this may no longer exist by the time we get to the end of the sentence, or because the tiny bit of America that each of us knows has little relevance to the rest of the nation.''

Keats and his family have an island in the Thousand Islands region of the St. Lawrence River where they spend summers.

BIOGRAPHICAL/CRITICAL SOURCES: John Keats, *The New Romans,* Lippincott, 1967; Keats, *Of Time and an Island,* Charterhouse Books, 1974.*

*   *   *

KEENAN, Joseph H(enry)   1900-1977

August 24, 1900—July 10, 1977; American engineer, educator, and author. Keenan was an internationally recognized authority on thermodynamics and professor emeritus of mechanical engineering at Massachusetts Institute of Technology. Obituaries: *New York Times,* July 20, 1977.

*   *   *

KEITHLEY, Erwin M.   1905-

PERSONAL: Born September 19, 1905, in Palmyra, Wis.; married Ethel Bergstrom; children: Cynthia (Mrs. Robert M. Kelly). *Education:* Whitewater State Teachers College (now University of Wisconsin-Whitewater), B.Ed., 1932; Northwestern University, M.S., 1935; University of California, Los Angeles, D.Ed., 1952. *Home:* 15396 Bestor Blvd., Pacific Palisades, Calif. 90272. *Office:* Graduate School of Management, University of California, Los Angeles, Calif. 90024.

CAREER: Business teacher at schools in Algoma, Wis., 1926-27, and Racine, Wis., 1927-30; Western Electric Co., Chicago, Ill., cost accountant, 1930-31; high school teacher of business subjects in Milwaukee, Wis., 1932-46; University of California, Los Angeles, 1946—, began as faculty member of School of Business Administration, currently professor of management. Trustee, Graduate Business Admissions Council. *Member:* Academy of Management, American Business Writing Association (fellow), National Business Education Association (life member), Beta Gamma Sigma, Delta Pi Epsilon, Alpha Kappa Psi. *Awards, honors:* Distinguished Alumnus Award, Wisconsin State University-Whitewater (now University of Wisconsin-Whitewater), 1967.

WRITINGS: A Manual of Style for the Preparation of Papers and Reports, South-Western Publishing, 1959; (with M. H. Thompson) *English for Modern Business,* Irwin, 1966, revised edition, 1972. Contributor to management and business journals.

KELLAM, Sheppard (Gordon)   1931-

PERSONAL: Born January 10, 1931, in Baltimore, Md.; son of Louis and Sylvia Kellam; married Margaret E. Ensminger (a sociologist), July 10, 1976; children: Jonathan, Anthony, Stephen. *Education:* Loyola College, Baltimore, Md., B.S., 1954; University of Maryland, M.D., 1956. *Home:* 1337 East 50th St., Chicago, Ill. 60615. *Office:* Social Psychiatry Study Center, University of Chicago, 5811 South Kenwood Ave., Chicago, Ill. 60637.

CAREER: Bellevue Hospital, New York, N.Y., intern, 1956-57; Yale University, New Haven, Conn., resident in psychiatry, 1957-59; National Institute of Mental Health, Bethesda, Md., research psychiatrist, 1959-63, chief of a treatment unit at the Clinical Center, 1961-63; University of Illinois, Champaign-Urbana, assistant professor of psychiatry, 1963-66; University of Chicago, Chicago, Ill., associate professor, 1966-75, director of Social Psychiatry Study Center, 1970—, professor of psychiatry, 1975—. Diplomate of American Board of Psychiatry and Neurology; licensed in Illinois, Maryland, California, and the District of Columbia. Psychiatric ward chief at St. Elizabeth's Hospital, 1959-61; co-founder and co-director of Woodlawn Mental Health Center, 1963-70, chief psychiatric consultant, 1970-74; chairman of National Institute of Mental Health mental health committee. Member of board of directors of South East Chicago Commission, 1970—. *Military service:* U.S. Army National Guard, 1949-52. U.S. Public Health Service, 1959-63.

MEMBER: American Association for the Advancement of Science, American Association of University Professors, American Orthopsychiatric Association (fellow), American Psychiatric Association (fellow), American Psychological Association, American Public Health Association, American Psychopathological Association, Group for the Advancement of Psychiatry, Psychiatric Research Society, Illinois Psychiatric Society (president, 1972-73).

WRITINGS: (With Jeanette D. Branch, Khazan C. Agrawal, and Margaret E. Ensminger) *Mental Health and Going to School: The Woodlawn Program of Assessment, Early Intervention, and Evaluation,* University of Chicago Press, 1975.

Contributor: *Endocrines and the Central Nervous System,* Williams & Wilkins, 1966; Leonard F. Dahl and Robert L. Leopold, editors, *Mental Health and Urban Social Policy,* Jossey-Bass, 1968; Stuart E. Golann and Carl Eisdorfer, editors, *Handbook of Community Mental Health,* Appleton, 1972; Bruce S. Dohrenwend and Barbara P. Dohrenwend, editors, *Stressful Life Events: Their Nature and Effects,* Wiley, 1974; Alfred M. Freedman, Harold I. Kaplan, and Benjamin J. Sadock, editors, *Comprehensive Textbook in Psychiatry,* 2nd edition (Kellam was not included in 1st edition), Williams & Wilkins, 1975; *Ward Atmosphere, Continuity of Therapy and the Mental Health System,* in press. Contributor of more than twenty-five articles and reviews to scientific journals. Research editor of *American Journal of Orthopsychiatry,* 1969-72.

SIDELIGHTS: Kellam writes that, for the past twelve years, he has been ''responsible for the development of a field laboratory for studies in social and community psychiatry and for the first seven years the design and implementation of the clinical program of a first level neighborhood mental health center. A variety of basic and applied researches have been carried out including: studies of the adaptation of young children to the social environment of the school, the relationships among the social adaptation and psychiatric symptomatology, the relationships among family life, adaptational processes and psychiatric symptoms, the development of periodic assessment systems, the evaluation of community-wide programs of prevention and early treatment, and the development of models of basing such efforts on the sanction of the local citizens and institutions of Woodlawn. These studies are concurrent and longitudinal epidemiological over ten years from 1964 to 1976.''

*   *   *

KELLER, Edward A(nthony)   1942-

PERSONAL: Born June 6, 1942, in Los Angeles, Calif.; son of Herbert J. (a cost accountant) and Mary Louise (Kennedy) Keller; married Jacqueline Jenni, June 25, 1966; children: James Edward, Sarah Kathleen. *Education:* California State University, Fresno, B.S., 1965, B.A., 1968; University of California, Davis, M.S., 1969; Purdue University, Ph.D., 1973. *Home:* 261 San Julian, Santa Barbara, Calif. 93109. *Office:* Department of Geological Sciences and Environmental Studies, University of California, Santa Barbara, Calif. 93106.

CAREER: California State University, Fresno, assistant professor of geology, 1969-70; Purdue University, West Lafayette, Ind., instructor in geology, 1970-72; University of North Carolina, Charlotte, assistant professor of geology, 1973-76; University of California, Santa Barbara, assistant professor of geology and environmental studies, 1976—. Soil conservation district supervisor in Mecklenburg County, N.C., 1975-76; consultant for Environmental Consultants, Inc.

MEMBER: Geological Society of America, Sigma Xi, Phi Kappa Phi, Blue Key. *Awards, honors:* Grants from North Carolina Department of Administration, Office of State Planning, 1974, and North Carolina Water Resources Research Institute and U.S. Office of Water Resources Research, both 1975-78.

WRITINGS: (Contributor) Marie Morisawa, editor, *Fluvial Geomorphology,* Publications in Geomorphology, State University of New York At Binghamton, 1973; *Environmental Geology,* C. E. Merrill, 1976; (contributor) D. R. Coates, editor, *Geomorphology and Engineering,* Dowden, 1976. Contributor of articles to scientific journals.

WORK IN PROGRESS: Second edition of *Environmental Geology;* four chapters for *Multi-Media Physical Geology Program,* for C. E. Merrill.

SIDELIGHTS: Keller writes: ''Environmental geology is essentially applied geology. It involves the entire spectrum of interactions between people and our physical environment. We must understand that at this time our earth is the only suitable habitat we have and that our resources are limited. Furthermore, it is impossible to maintain a population which increases exponentially on a finite resource base. I am interested in teaching these fundamental truths so that future generations will inherit a quality environment. What must be accomplished is a melding of the physical, biological, economic, social, political, and aesthetic environments in such a way that society realizes a maximum utility of all our resources while suffering a minimum of environmental degration. My textbook *Environmental Geology* is an attempt to meld some factions of our total environment and examine in depth approaches to geologic aspects of environmental problems. It is worthwhile to note that most environmental degradation transcends political, economic, and religious institutions. The historical roots of our environmental problems are inherent to the evolution of the human race, and therefore solutions to environmental problems must be attacked

at global levels that transcend institutions and governments.''

*   *   *

KELLY, John   1921-

PERSONAL: Born July 21, 1921, in Philadelphia, Pa.; son of John Thomas and Frances (Crowley) Kelly; married Elizabeth Stoughton, June 16, 1944 (divorced, February, 1965); married Joan Rotter (a microbiologist), August 17, 1965; children: Susan (Mrs. J. L. Robinson), John, Peter, Patrick. *Education:* Attended New York University, 1940-41; University of Pennsylvania, A.B. (honors), 1947, Ph.D., 1951. *Politics:* ''Variable.'' *Religion:* None. *Home and office:* 100 East Hartsdale Ave., Hartsdale, N.Y. 10530. *Agent:* L. David Otte, Otte Co., 9 Park St., Boston, Mass. 02108.

CAREER: Trader's assistant, Merrill Lynch, Pierce, Fenner & Smith, 1938-41; instructor, later professor in science departments of University of Oklahoma, Tufts University, University of Pennsylvania, Medical College of Virginia, and Mount Sinai School of Medicine of the City University of New York, 1951-72; full-time writer, 1972—. Consultant on cosmic radiation, National Aeronautics and Space Administration-Westinghouse; science advisor, Tonight Show; science advisor to various school systems in Virginia, Oklahoma, and New York. *Military service:* U.S. Navy, night fighter pilot, 1942-45; became lieutenant; received Air Medal. *Member:* Naval Aviation Commandery. *Awards, honors:* Guggenheim fellowships, Nobel Institute for Cell Research and Genetics, Stockholm, Sweden, 1957-58, 1960-61.

WRITINGS: The Metachromatic Reaction (monograph), Springer-Verlag, 1956; *The Wooden Wolf* (war novel), Dutton, 1976; *Man and the Night* (nonfiction), Dutton, 1978. Contributor of about seventy articles to scientific journals.

SIDELIGHTS: Kelly writes: ''I gave up a career that I loved (basically) in medical teaching and research to write full-time, which now seems to be what I should have been doing all along. In medicine, there were suddenly too many in charge who knew nothing about what they were doing. In writing, too, there are publishers and agents, but the writer is ultimately the 'product' and nothing can stop him if he can write well.'' *Avocational interests:* Reading fiction (especially Thomas Mann and Herman Melville) and history.

*   *   *

KELLY, Walt(er Crawford)   1913-1973

PERSONAL: Born August 25, 1913, in Philadelphia, Pa.; son of Walter Crawford (a theatrical scene painter) and Genevieve (MacAnnulla) Kelly; children: Kathleen, Carolyn, Peter, Stephen. *Education:* Attended public schools in Bridgeport, Conn.

CAREER: Post, Bridgeport, Conn., newspaper reporter, writer, and artist, 1928-35; Walt Disney Studios, Hollywood, Calif., animator, 1935-41; commercial artist in New York City, 1941-48; *New York Star* (newspaper), art director, political cartoonist, editorial adviser, and originator of daily comic strip, ''Pogo,'' 1948-49; employed by Post Syndicate (later Post-Hall) to produce syndicated ''Pogo'' comic strip, beginning 1949. *Wartime service:* Civilian employee of the U.S. Army's foreign language unit during the Second World War. *Member:* National Cartoonist Society (president, 1954). *Awards, honors:* Reuben award (''Cartoonist of the Year''), National Cartoonists Society, 1952.

WRITINGS—Cartoon books with captions, published by

Simon & Schuster, except as noted: *Pogo*, 1951; *I Go Pogo*, 1952; *The Pogo Papers*, 1953; *Uncle Pogo So-So Stories*, 1953; *The Incompleat Pogo*, 1954; *The Pogo Stepmother Goose*, 1954; *The Pogo Peek-a-Book*, 1955; *Potluck Pogo*, 1955; *The Pogo Party*, 1956; *The Pogo Sunday Book*, 1956; *Songs of the Pogo*, 1956, reprinted, 1968; *Pogo's Sunday Punch*, 1957; *Positively Pogo*, 1957; *G. O. Fizzickle Pogo*, 1958; *The Pogo Sunday Parade*, 1958; *The Pogo Sunday Brunch*, 1959; *Ten Ever-Lovin' Blue-Eyed Years with Pogo*, 1959.

Beau Pogo, 1960; *Pogo Extra*, 1960; *Gone Pogo*, 1961; *Pogo a la Sundae*, 1961; *Instant Pogo*, 1962; *The Jack Acid Society Black Book*, 1962; *Deck Us All with Boston Charlie*, 1963; *Pogo Puce Stamp Catalog*, 1963; *The Return of Pogo*, 1965; *The Pogo Poop Book*, 1966; *Prehysterical Pogo*, 1967; *Equal Time for Pogo*, 1968; *Pogo: Prisoner of Love*, 1969; *Impollutable Pogo*, 1970; *Pogo: We Have Met the Enemy and He Is Us*, 1972; (with Selby Kelly) *Pogo's Bats and the Belles Free*, 1976; (with S. Kelly) *The Pogo Candidature: A Cartoon Story for New Children*, Sheed, 1976.

Collections and selections; all published by Simon & Schuster: *Pogo Re-Runs: Some Reflections on Elections*, 1974; *Pogo Revisited*, 1974 (contains *Instant Pogo, The Pogo Poop Book,* and *The Jack Acid Society Black Book*); *Pogo Romances Recaptured*, 1976 (contains *Pogo: Prisoner of Love* and *The Incompleat Pogo*); *Pogo's Body Politic*, edited by S. Kelly, 1976.

Illustrator: Inez Bertail, editor, *Complete Nursery Song Book*, Lothrop, 1947; John O'Reilly, *The Glob*, Viking, 1952; Charles Ellis and Frank Weir, *I'd Rather Be President*, Simon & Schuster, 1956.

SIDELIGHTS: Kelly's *Pogo* comic strip came out during the post World War II years when Americans were eager to satisfy their appetite for humor. Since then his cartoons have been syndicated to more than four hundred newspapers with an estimated readership of over twenty million in the United States and abroad. In 1954, Kelly was given the distinction of becoming the first comic-strip artist to be invited to contribute his works to the Library of Congress files.

The cartoonist based the storyline of his comic strips on topical subjects and even ran a Pogo for President campaign in both 1952 and 1956. The National Broadcasting Company took an interest in Kelly's satirical approach to social issues and hired the comic-strip artist to write some skits to brighten up the long procedures during the Democratic and Republican conventions of 1956.

By 1960, Kelly had put out *Ten Ever-Lovin' Blue-Eyed Years with Pogo*, a cartoon book commemorating the tenth anniversary of his opossum character. "An uninhibitedly inventive with language as he is gifted a draftsman, Kelly furnishes in this collection . . . the continuing story of Pogo in Pogo's world. . . . [The book] belongs on the Americana book-shelf, somewhere between Krazy Kat and Charlie Brown," noted a critic for *Commonweal*.

Metro-Goldwyn-Mayer produced "The Pogo Special Birthday Special," a thirty-minute animated television program which premiered on the National Broadcasting Network, May 18, 1969. Kelly not only wrote the story and songs for the special, but provided the voice of the character P. T. Bridgeport as well.

BIOGRAPHICAL/CRITICAL SOURCES: Commonweal, December 11, 1959; Martin Levin, editor, *Five Boyhoods*, Doubleday, 1962; *Reader's Digest*, July, 1974. Obituaries: *New York Times*, October 19, 1973; *Newsweek*, October 29, 1973; *Time*, October 29, 1973; *Current Biography 1973*.*

(Died October 18, 1973)

* * *

KENNEDY, George 1899(?)-1977

1899(?)—October 28, 1977; American journalist. A feature writer and columnist for the *Washington Star*, Kennedy was best known for his column "The Rambler," which dealt with such subjects as sports, politics, medicine, law, and religion. He died in Montserrat, West Indies Federation. Obituaries: *Washington Post*, November 2, 1977.

* * *

KENNEDY, Leonard M(ilton) 1925-

PERSONAL: Born June 22, 1925, in Beaverton, Ore.; son of Lance A. and Mona (Cain) Kennedy; married Mary Wilcox, August 17, 1947; children: Beverley Kennedy Van Santen, Patricia. *Education:* Eastern Oregon College, B.S.Ed., 1950; University of Oregon, M.S.Ed., 1952; Washington State University, Ed.D., 1960. *Office:* School of Education, California State University, Sacramento, Calif. 95819.

CAREER: Elementary school teacher in Eugene, Ore., 1950-55; Eastern Washington College (now Eastern Washington State College), Cheney, assistant professor of education, 1955-58; Washington State University, Pullman, assistant professor of education, 1959-60; California State University, Sacramento, assistant professor, 1960-66, associate professor, 1966-70, professor of education, 1960—. Mathematics consultant to Ponape, Micronesia. *Military service:* U.S. Naval Reserve, active duty, 1943-46. *Member:* National Education Association, National Council of Teachers of Mathematics, California Teachers Association, California Mathematics Council.

WRITINGS: Models for Mathematics in the Elementary School, Wadsworth, 1967; (with Henry Bamman and Robert Whitehead) *Longcliff Mystery Series*. Benefic, 1969; *Guiding Children to Mathematical Discovery*, Wadsworth, 1970, revised edition, 1975; *Experiences for Teaching Children Mathematics*, Wadsworth, 1973; (with Ruth Michon) *Games for Individualizing Mathematics Learning*, C. E. Merrill, 1973.

SIDELIGHTS: Kennedy writes: "I have observed mathematics educational programs in British schools, and conducted a teachers' tour of such schools in 1973. Of particular interest were schools using a non-textbook vocabulary approach for helping children learn mathematics."

* * *

KERNOCHAN, Sarah 1947-

PERSONAL: Born December 30, 1947, in New York, N.Y.; daughter of John M. (a professor of law) and Adelaide (an international organization consultant; maiden name, Chatfield-Turner) Kernochan. *Education:* Attended Sarah Lawrence College, 1966-69. *Agent:* Ron Bernstein, 200 West 58th St., New York, N.Y. 10019.

CAREER: Writer, film director, songwriter, and singer. Writer for *Village Voice*, 1969-71; co-producer and director of "Marjoe," 1973; songwriter and singer on albums for RCA, 1973-74. *Awards, honors:* Co-winner of Academy Award for "Marjoe," 1973.

WRITINGS: Dry Hustle, Morrow, 1977. Also author of a screenplay adapted from her own novel, for United Artists.

WORK IN PROGRESS: An as yet untitled novel, publication by Putnam expected in 1979.

SIDELIGHTS: Dry Hustle had its beginnings in a magazine article Kernochan was writing on dime-a-dance girls. While researching the story, she became acquainted with the women with whom she would travel cross-country and, as she told *Ms.,* "learn dry-hustling first hand."

"What results from Kernochan's almost unique research in a gem of a novel—the hippest, raunchiest read I've had in a long time," wrote Sheila Weller. "Kernochan has captured her characters' language and psyches with a fierce fidelity," Weller continued. Instead of playing "liberal defense lawyer," a pose often taken by writers who deal with amoral characters, Weller found that Kernochan refused to patronize the main character Kristal, and so gave her "unhackneyed integrity."

Richard Lingeman commented that even though her experiences have enabled Kernochan to write with "slice-of-life authenticity," ultimately he found that "the talk and the scam become repetitious and the characters are suspended in bitter aspic. Like its namesake, *Dry Hustle* is too much talk and too little action."

Kernochan has adapted her novel into a screenplay and will direct the film for United Artists.

BIOGRAPHICAL/CRITICAL SOURCES: New York Times, March 31, 1977; *Ms.,* June, 1977.

* * *

KERSHAW, John (Hugh D'Allenger)
(Hugh D'Allenger)

PERSONAL: Born August 2, 1931, in London, England; married Olwen Earle; children: one daughter. *Education:* Attended University of London. *Residence:* Middlesex, England.

CAREER: American Broadcasting Co. (ABC), London, England, script editor of "Tempo," 1964-67; Thames Television, London, script editor of drama series "Calan," 1968-69, producer and editor of "Armchair Theatre," 1969-71; novelist, literary critic, poet, and essayist. Tutor in literature, University of London, 1961-64; lecturer, Worker's Educational Association. *Member:* Society of Authors, Writer's Guild of Great Britain.

WRITINGS: The Present Stage: New Directions in the Theatre Today, Collins, 1966. Also author of *G. M. Hopkins,* 1962, *Anglo-Jewish Poetry,* 1963, and *Edward Thomas: A Study,* 1964.

Television plays: (Under pseudonym Hugh D'Allenger) "The Lesser of Two," first produced on Thames Television, February 16, 1971. Also author of librettos for two cantatas, two song cycles, and a children's entertainment, "George and the Dragonfly."*

* * *

KERSHNER, Howard E(ldred) 1891-

PERSONAL: Born November 17, 1891, in Tescott, Kan.; son of Isaiah B. and Cora M. (Lett) Kershner; married Gertrude Elizabeth Townsend, July 6, 1915; children: Wendell Townsend, Margaret Lynette (Mrs. Stephen C. Weber), Mary Linaford (Mrs. Glenn C. Bassatt, Jr.). *Education:* Friends University, Wichita, Kan., A.B., 1914; Harvard University, graduate student, 1923-24. *Politics:* Republican. *Religion:* Society of Friends (Quaker). *Home:* 1617 Fannin St., Houston, Tex. 77002. *Office:* Two Shell Plaza, Suite 2197, Houston, Tex. 77002.

CAREER: Employed in real estate office, Boston, Mass.,

1914-16; *Dodge City Daily Journal,* Dodge City, Kan., editor and publisher, 1917-18; War Industries Board, Washington, D.C., assistant to chief of Newspaper Section, 1918; engaged in real estate operations in Massachusetts, Kansas, and Florida, 1919-27; National Americana Society, New York, N.Y., publisher, 1927-38; American Friends Committee, director of relief in Europe, 1939-42; International Committee for Child Refugees, executive vice-president and director, 1939-52, directing feeding of children in Spain during Spanish Civil War, 1939-40, and in Unoccupied France, 1940-42; Temporary Council on Food for European Children, founder and chairman, 1943-45; Christian Freedom Foundation, Inc., Los Angeles, Calif., co-founder and president, 1950-69, chairman of the board, 1969—. Minister of philosophy of freedom, First Congregational Church, Los Angeles, beginning 1967. National Committee on Food for Small Democracies, member of executive committee, 1942-44; Save the Children Federation, vice-chairman, 1945-50, secretary, 1959-69; Cooperative for American Relief Everywhere (CARE), member of board of directors, 1945-46; United Nations Children's Fund (UNICEF), special representative of Secretary General Trygve Lie on mission to Latin American countries seeking grants from governments, 1947-48. Gave more than 300 radio addresses about the plight of children in Europe, the United States, and Latin America during the war and postwar years; has broadcast "Howard Kershner's Commentary on the News," a weekly program carried by as many as 400 stations, 1958-69. Lecturer on the philosophy of freedom for three summer terms at Fuller Theological Seminary, and at more than 150 universities, colleges, and other educational institutions in America; lecturer at Pro Deo University, Rome, Italy, 1967.

MEMBER: International Platform Association, American Conservative Union, Mont Pelerin Society, American-African Affairs Association, Supreme Court Amendment League, Youth for Decency, American Society of the French Legion of Honor. *Awards, honors:* L.H.D., Washington and Jefferson College, 1941; LL.D., Friends University, Wichita, Kan., 1948; Litt.D., Grove City College, 1957; D.D., George Fox College, 1969; H.H.D., Northwood Institute, 1970; Freedoms Foundation top award medal, annually, 1952-57, 1959-61, 1965, 1967, 1971-72; foreign decorations include Order of Leopold (Belgium), Legion of Honor and Palm d'Academie (both France), Ordre de Merit, Union Internationale de Protection de l'Enfants (Switzerland).

WRITINGS: (Editor and arranger) *Air Pioneering in the Arctic,* National Americana Society, 1928; *James W. Ellsworth* (biography), National Americana Society, 1928; *Lincoln Ellsworth* (biography), National Americana Society, 1929; *William Squire Kenyon* (biography), National Americana Society, 1930; *The Menance of Roosevelt and His Policies,* Greenburg Publishers, 1936; *One Humanity,* Putnam, 1943.

Quaker Service in Modern Warfare, Prentice-Hall, 1956; *God, Gold and Government,* Prentice-Hall, 1956; *Diamonds, Persimmons and Stars,* Bookmailer, 1964; *Dividing the Wealth: Are You Getting Your Share,* Devin-Adair, 1971.

Author of a dozen pamphlets on socialism, freedom, totalitarianism, and other subjects. His "Howard Kershner's Commentary on the News" (originating as a radio program) issued in printed form; columnist, "It's Up To You," syndicated to three hundred newspapers; contributor to *New York Times Magazine, Collier's, Quaker Life,* and other journals. Editor-in-chief, *Applied Christianity* (formerly *Christian Economics*), beginning 1953.

SIDELIGHTS: Kershner has traveled in sixty countries. *Avocational interests:* Music, swimming, hiking.*

* * *

KESSLER, Henry H(oward)   1896-1978

April 10, 1896—January 18, 1978; American physician and author. Highly regarded as an orthopedic specialist, Kessler also contributed significantly to the development of rehabilitation services for the disabled throughout the world. One of his chief accomplishments was the development of a surgical technique known as cineplasty for the muscular control of artificial limbs. His books and articles dealt with the problems and treatment of the disabled. He died in Newark, N.J. Obituaries: *New York Times,* January 19, 1978.

* * *

KESTELOOT, Lilyan   1931-
(Lilyan Lagneau-Kesteloot)

PERSONAL: Born February 15, 1931, in Brussels, Belgium; daughter of Medard (a captain in the marine corps) and Marguerite (a teacher; maiden name, De Ladriere) Kesteloot; married Simeon Fongang (a physicist), 1972; children: Georges, Tenguela. *Education:* University of Brussels, Ph.D., 1961; Sorbonne, University of Paris, Ph.D., 1975. *Politics:* "Who cares?" *Religion:* "Who cares?" *Home:* Ifan, B.P. 206, Dakar, Senegal. *Office:* University of Dakar, Dakar, Senegal.

CAREER: Professor of literature at various African universities (in Camaroon, Mali, and Ivory Coast), 1961-70; professor of literature at various French universities, including Vincennes, St. Denis, and the Sorbonne, 1971-72; University of Dakar, Dakar, Senegal, professor of oral literature, 1972—. *Member:* Society of Africanists (Paris).

WRITINGS: Les Ecrivains noirs de langue francaise, Universite libre de Bruxelles, 1961, 4th edition, 1971, translation by Ellen C. Kennedy published as *Black Writers in French: A Literary History of Negritude,* Temple University Press, 1974; *Neuf Poetes camerounais, anthologie* (title means "An Anthology of Nine Cameroonian Poets"), Editions Cle, 1965, 2nd edition, 1971; *Anthologie negro-africaine* (title means "Anthology of Black African Writers") Verviers, Gerard & Co., 1967; *Negritude et situation coloniale,* Editions Cle, 1968, translation published as *Intellectual Origins of the African Revolution,* Black Orpheus Press, 1971; (with Amadou-Hampate Ba) *Kaidaba,* Armand Colin, 1969; (with Barthelemy Kotchy) *Aime Cesaire, l'homme et l'ouevre* (title means "Aime Cesaire: The Man and His Works"), Presence Africaine (Paris), 1973; (with Ba, Alpha Sow, and Christiane Seydou) *L'Eclat de l'etoile* (title means "Starburst"), Armand Colin, 1974; (with Gerard Dumestre and Jean Baptiste Traore) *La Prise de Djoukoloni, recit epique bambara,* Armand Colin, 1976; *Biton Koulibaly, fondateur de l'empire de Segou,* Collection des grandes figures de l'histoire africaine, 1978.

Editor: *Aime Cesaire,* Seghers (Paris), 1963; (with A. H. Ba) *Kaidara, recit initiatique peul,* Julliard, 1968; (and translator) *La Poesie traditionnelle* (title means "Traditional Poetry"), Nathan, 1971; (and translator) L'Epopee traditionnelle (title means "The Traditional Epic"), Nathan, 1971; (and translator with J. B. Traore, Amadou Traore, and Ba) *Da Monzon de Segou, epopee bambara,* Nathan, 1972; (and author of preface) *Anthologie, 1962,* reprint of 1961 edition

(Kesteloot was not associated with earlier edition), Nendeln, 1973; *Contes et mythes wolof,* Nouvelles Editions Africaines (Dakar), 1978.

Contributor of articles to *L'Homme, Presence Africaine, Etudes Francaises,* and other journals in her field.

WORK IN PROGRESS: Literary texts on African oral traditions, especially Bambara and Mulinke.

SIDELIGHTS: Kesteloot sums up her philosophy of life as: "Only truth is revolutionary."

* * *

KIERNAN, Walter   1902-1978

January 24, 1902—January 8, 1978; American journalist. Kiernan was known as a news broadcaster and author of the syndicated column "One Man's Opinion." Among his notable journalistic assignments were coverage of the North American visit of King George VI and Queen Elizabeth in 1939, and the election campaign of Wendell Willkie. He died in Daytona Beach, Fla. Obituaries: *New York Times,* January 10, 1978.

* * *

KIMBROUGH, Ralph B(radley)   1922-

PERSONAL: Born March 12, 1922, in Rhea Springs, Tenn.; son of Robert Bradley and Elizabeth (Crosby) Kimbrough; married Gladys King, December 21, 1946; children: Ralph Bradley, Jr. *Education:* University of Tennessee, B.S., 1948, M.S., 1949, Ed.D., 1953. *Home:* 1212 Northwest 41st Ter., Gainesville, Fla. 32605. *Office:* College of Education, University of Florida, Gainesville, Fla. 32611.

CAREER: High school teacher of bookkeeping and typing in Knoxville, Tenn., 1948-49; principal of public school in Lenoir City, Tenn., 1949-51; Southern States Cooperative Program in Educational Administration, Princeton, W.Va., coordinator of programs in local school systems, 1953-54; University of Tennessee, Knoxville, associate professor of education, 1954-58; University of Florida, Gainesville, associate professor, 1958-64, professor of education, 1966—, chairman of department of educational administration, 1966-73. *Military service:* U.S. Army Air Forces, 1943-46; served in European theater; received five Bronze Stars.

MEMBER: American Educational Research Association, American Association of University Professors, National Education Association, American Association of School Administrators, Phi Delta Kappa.

WRITINGS: (With Truman Pierce, E. C. Merrill, L. Craig Wilson) *Community Leadership for Public Education,* Prentice-Hall, 1955; *Political Power and Educational Decision-Making,* Rand McNally, 1964; (with O. B. Graff, C. M. Street, and A. R. Dykes) *Philosophic Theory and Practice in Educational Administration,* Wadsworth, 1966; *Administering Elementary Schools: Concepts and Practices,* Macmillan, 1968; (with M. Y. Nunnery) *Politics, Power, Polls, and School Elections,* McCutchan, 1971; (with Nunnery) *Educational Administration: An Introduction,* Macmillan, 1976. Contributor to education journals.

WORK IN PROGRESS: A paper on the influence of ideologies of the structure of education.

SIDELIGHTS: Kimbrough told *CA: "Political Power and Educational Decision Making* was a pioneer work on the politics of education. This book and later publications presented the view that educators should be effective political leaders for educational improvement."

KINDLEBERGER, Charles P(oor), II 1910-

PERSONAL: Born October 12, 1910, in New York, N.Y.; son of E. Crosby and Elizabeth Randall (McIlvaine) Kindleberger; married Sarah Bache Miles, May 1, 1937; children: Charles P., Richard S., Sarah, E. Randall. *Education:* University of Pennsylvania, A.B., 1932; Columbia University, M.A., 1934, Ph.D., 1937. *Home address:* Bedford Rd., Lincoln, Mass. 01773.

CAREER: Federal Reserve Bank of New York, New York City, researcher in international trade and finance, 1936-39; Federal Reserve System, Washington, D.C., member of board of governors, 1940-42; Joint Economic Committee of the United States and Canada, Washington, D.C., American secretary, 1941-42; Office of Strategic Services, Washington, D.C., American secretary, 1941-42; Office of Strategic Services, Washington, D.C., member of staff, 1942-44, 1945; U.S. Department of State, Washington, D.C., chief of German and Austrian Economic Affairs division, 1945-48; Massachusetts Institute of Technology, Cambridge, Mass., associate professor, 1948-51, professor of economics, 1951-76, professor emeritus, 1976—, chairman of faculty, 1965-67. Member of staff, Bank for International Settlements, 1939-40. *Military service:* U.S. Army, 1944-45; became major; received Bronze Star and Legion of Merit. *Member:* American Academy of Arts and Sciences, American Economic Association, St. Anthony Club, Phi Beta Kappa, Delta Psi.

WRITINGS: International Short-term Capital Movements, Columbia University Press, 1937; *The Dollar Shortage,* M.I.T. Press, 1950; *International Economics,* Irwin, 1953, revised edition, 1973; *The Terms of Trade,* M.I.T. Press, 1956; *Economic Development,* McGraw, 1958, revised edition, 1965; *Foreign Trade and the National Economy,* Yale University Press, 1962; *Economic Growth in France and Britain, 1851-1950,* Harvard University Press, 1964; *Europe and the Dollar,* M.I.T. Press, 1966; *Europe's Postwar Growth,* Harvard University Press, 1967; *American Business Abroad,* Yale University Press, 1969; *Power and Money,* Basic Books, 1970; (editor) *The International Corporation,* M.I.T. Press, 1970; (editor) *North American and Western European Economic Policies,* St. Martin's, 1971; *The Great Depression,* University of California Press, 1973.*

* * *

KINNEY, Peter 1943-

PERSONAL: Born October 16, 1943, in Lynn, Mass.; son of Cleland and Helen (Nordin) Kinney; married Dale Brabant; children: Aaron. *Education:* Syracuse University, B.A., 1965; New York University, M.A., 1968, Ph.D., 1974. *Office:* Moore College of Art, Philadelphia, Pa. 19103.

CAREER: Moore College of Art, Philadelphia, Pa., instructor in art history, 1975—.

WRITINGS: The Early Sculpture of Bartolomeo Ammanati, Garland Publishing, 1975. Contributor of poems to *Caesura* and *Lazy Fair.*

WORK IN PROGRESS: The Sculpture of Sansorino's Library in Venice; poems; paintings; sculpture.

* * *

KINOR, Jehuda
See ROTHMULLER, Aron Marko

* * *

KIRCHNER, Audrey Burie 1937-

PERSONAL: Born August 23, 1937, in Lancaster, Pa.; daughter of John Sawyer (a contractor) and Florence (Snyder) Burie; married Leo J. Kirchner (in industrial sales), April 23, 1977. *Education:* Millersville State College, B.S.Ed., 1959, M.Ed., 1961; University of Maryland, doctoral study, 1977—. *Politics:* Republican. *Religion:* Roman Catholic. *Home:* 668 West Vine St., Lancaster, Pa. 17603. *Office:* Jenkins School, Millersville State College, Millersville, Pa. 17551.

CAREER: Millersville State College, Millersville, Pa., associate professor of education, 1962—, teacher at Jenkins School for Children, 1962—. *Member:* Association for Childhood Education International, International Reading Association, Council for Exceptional Children, National Association for the Education of Young Children, Millersville State College Faculty Association.

WRITINGS: (With Mary Ann Heltshe) *Reading With a Smile,* Acropolis Books, 1975. Contributor to education journals.

WORK IN PROGRESS: The Basic Beginning: Loving to Learn, tentative title, publication expected in 1978.

SIDELIGHTS: Audrey Kirchner writes: "I have loved working with young children. Each day in the classroom has been exciting and I am deeply satisfied as I watch these children grow to adulthood. My writings are an attempt to share workable, successful learning activities with other teachers and the college students I teach."

* * *

KISOR, Henry (Du Bois) 1940-

PERSONAL: Born August 17, 1940, in Ridgewood, N.J.; son of Manown and Judith (Du Bois) Kisor; married Deborah Abbott (a librarian and children's book columnist), June 24, 1967; children: Colin, Conan. *Education:* Trinity College, B.A. (cum laude), 1962; Northwestern University, M.S.J. (with distinction), 1964. *Home:* 2800 Harrison St., Evanston, Ill. 60201. *Office: Chicago Daily News,* 401 North Wabash, Chicago, Ill. 60611.

CAREER/WRITINGS: Chicago Daily News, Chicago, Ill., book editor, 1973—, assistant arts editor, 1977—. Contributor to *World Book Encyclopedia Yearbook.* Teacher at Northwestern University, Medill School of Journalism. Director of Chicago Hearing Society. *Member:* National Book Critics Circle.

* * *

KLAITS, Barrie 1944-

PERSONAL: Born July 2, 1944, in Biloxi, Miss.; daughter of Harold A. and Ruth (Ross) Gelbhaus; married Joseph Klaits (a university teacher of history), September 5, 1965; children: Frederick, Alexander. *Education:* University of Minnesota, student, 1965-66; Barnard College, A.B., 1966. *Home:* 4317 Lanette Dr., Pontiac, Mich. 48054.

CAREER: Minnesota Mathematics and Science Teaching Project, Minneapolis, Minn., writer, 1966-67; high school Spanish teacher in New Shrewsbury, N.J., 1969; writer, 1969—. Guest researcher at Institut de Paleontologie of Museum National d'Histoire Naturelle (Paris, France), 1967-68, 1971. Volunteer teacher of science to gifted children in Waterford Township, Mich. Founder of Troy Citizens for Recycling; co-founder of Elizabeth Lake Association. *Member:* American Association for the Advancement of Science.

WRITINGS: (With Zachariah Subarsky, Elizabeth Reed,

and Edward Landin) *Living Things in Field and Classroom,* University of Minnesota Press, 1969, revised edition, 1972; (editor with husband, Joseph Klaits) *Animals and Man in Historical Perspective,* Harper, 1974; *When You Find a Rock* (juvenile), Macmillan, 1976. Contributor to paleontology journals.

WORK IN PROGRESS: Warm-Blooded Dinosaurs, for children; "Rock Hunting in the City," to be included in *New York Kids' Catalogue,* edited by Children's Writers and Artists Collaborative, for Doubleday; research for *The City that Turned to Stone: Pompeii,* for children.

SIDELIGHTS: Barrie Klaits writes: "I love my family and I love the earth. Accompanying my husband to Paris for his historical research projects, I found myself wondering about the movements of fourteen-million-year-old rhinoceroses. Museum directors there graciously helped me to pursue my questions. Home with children now, I contemplate the pebbles which the glaciers delivered to our doorstep. It's fun helping children to discover the marvelous stories in everyday stones. It's exciting to interpret for them recent scientific findings. Trying to express all of these things on paper is my favorite challenge."

* * *

KLEIN, Randolph Shipley 1942-

PERSONAL: Born June 2, 1942, in Philadelphia, Pa.; son of Randolph S. (a lawyer) and Laura Ruth (a teacher and school principal; maiden name, Murray) Klein; married Maryann Graham (a teacher), August 14, 1965; children: Pamela Jeanne, Laura Suzanne. *Education:* University of Pennsylvania, B.A., 1963; Brown University, A.M., 1966; Rutgers University, Ph.D., 1971. *Politics:* Independent. *Religion:* Christian. *Home:* 7 River Ridge Rd., New London, Conn. 06320. *Office:* Department of History, Connecticut College, New London, Conn. 06320.

CAREER: Rutgers University, Camden, N.J., lecturer in history, 1965-66; University of Wisconsin, Stevens Point, assistant professor of history, 1969-75; Connecticut College, New London, associate professor of history, 1975—. Research associate at the library of American Philosophical Society, summers, 1964-67; lecturer at Beaver College, 1965-66. *Member:* Organization of American Historians, Historical Society of Pennsylvania.

WRITINGS: Portrait of an Early American Family, University of Pennsylvania Press, 1975. Contributor of about twenty articles and reviews to history journals.

WORK IN PROGRESS: An oral history of the New London-Waterford area of Connecticut; research on Pennsylvania and Connecticut during the American Revolution.

SIDELIGHTS: Klein writes: "I find that interacting with people—friends, teachers, and others—deepens my sensitivity and appreciation of the complexity of the past. Writings in psychology, sociology, and anthropology also provide insights and suggestions about how to approach historical evidence." *Avocational interests:* Playing the banjo and singing, cross-country skiing, jogging, sailing, racket sports, gardening, building models.

* * *

KLEINE, Glen 1936-

PERSONAL: Born September 12, 1936, in St. Louis, Mo.; son of Erwin G. and Veneta (Gebhardt) Kleine; married Joan Kay Johnson (a teacher), August 31, 1960; children: Kevin, Keith, Kris. *Education:* University of Missouri,

B.S., 1957, M.A., 1959; Eastern Kentucky University, Ed.S., 1973. *Home:* 64 Frankie Dr., Route 10, Richmond, Ky. 40475. *Office:* Department of Mass Communications, Eastern Kentucky University, P.O. Box 500, Richmond, Ky. 40475.

CAREER: High school teacher of journalism in St. Louis, Mo., 1959-65; *St. Louis Post-Dispatch,* St. Louis, Mo., education writer, 1965-66; Eastern Kentucky University, Richmond, assistant professor of communications, 1967—. Lecturer at Washington University, St. Louis, Mo., summers, 1965, 1966. *Military service:* U.S. Army Reserve, 1955-63, active duty, 1958. *Member:* Society of Collegiate Journalists, National Council of College Publications Advisers. *Awards, honors:* Award of merit from National Council of College Publications Advisers, 1973.

WRITINGS: Learning About Mass Communications, Kentucky Department of Education, 1972. Contributor of articles and photographs to journals and newspapers. Contributing editor of *Photolith.* Editor of *College Press Review,* 1970-72.

SIDELIGHTS: Kleine writes: "My particular interest is in the area of the student press. I am interested in college press performance (during such momentous events as the Apollo 11 landing on the moon and the Kent State University crisis), and in the legal rights and responsibilities of the collegiate press."

BIOGRAPHICAL/CRITICAL SOURCES: Collegiate Journalist, autumn, 1971.

* * *

KLIMENKO, Michael 1924-

PERSONAL: Born August 20, 1924, in Vladimir, Ukraine; naturalized U.S. citizen, 1976; son of Jacob (a farmer) and Thekla (Podosinov) Klimenko; married Marianne L. Lanz (a registered nurse), August, 1959; children: Andreas, Markus, Anna, Martha. *Education:* Attended University of Zurich, 1953-55, and University of Basel, 1955; Zurich Theological Seminary, B.D., 1955; University of Erlangen, Ph.D., 1957. *Religion:* Eastern Orthodox. *Home:* 578C Hahaione St., Honolulu, Hawaii 96825. *Office:* Department of European Languages, University of Hawaii, honolulu, Hawaii 96822.

CAREER: University of Erlangen, Erlangen, Germany, researcher in Russian intellectual history, 1957-60; Wittenberg University, Springfield, Ohio, instructor in Russian and German, 1960-61; University of Kansas, Lawrence, professor of Slavic languages, 1961-68; University of Hawaii, Honolulu, professor of Russian and religion, 1968—. *Member:* American Association of University Professors, American Association for the Advancement of Slavic Studies, American Association of Teachers of Slavic and East European Languages, Modern Language Association of America, National Education Association, University of Hawaii Professional Assembly. *Awards, honors:* Ford Foundation grant, 1964; American Philosophical Society grant, 1970.

WRITINGS: Ansbreitung des christentums in Russland (title means "Expansion of Christianity in Russia"), Lutherisches Verlangshaus, 1969; *The Young Sholokhov,* Christopher, 1972; *St. Sergii of Radoneth,* Nordland, 1976. Contributor to *Religion in Life, Kyrios,* and *Books Abroad.*

WORK IN PROGRESS: A book on Russia's controversial novelist, Il'ya Ehrenburg.

SIDELIGHTS: Klimenko has travelled and lived in Europe for many years. He is competent in German, Russian, Ukranian, Polish and English.

KLOBUCHAR, James John 1928-
(Jim Klobuchar)

PERSONAL: Born April 9, 1928, in Ely, Minn.; son of Michael (a mining foreman) and Mary (Pucel) Klobuchar; married Rose Heuberger, August 7, 1954 (divorced, 1976); children: Amy, Beth. *Education:* Ely Junior College, A.A., 1948; University of Minnesota, B.A. (cum laude), 1950. *Office: Minneapolis Star,* Fifth & Portland, Minneapolis, Minn. 55488.

CAREER: Bismarck Tribune, Bismarck, N.D., wire editor, 1950, legislative reporter, 1952-53; Associated Press, Minneapolis, Minn., staff reporter and rewrite man, 1953-61; *Minneapolis Tribune,* Minneapolis, sports writer, 1961-65; *St. Paul Pioneer-Press Dispatch,* St. Paul, Minn., sports writer, 1965; *Minneapolis Star,* Minneapolis, author of column, 1965—. Host of television and radio programs. *Military service:* U.S. Army, in psychological warfare, 1950-52. *Member:* American Legion. *Awards, honors:* Five first prizes in newswriting from Minnesota Associated Press, 1968, 1971, 1974, 1975, 1976; award from *Inland Daily Press* for political writing, 1977.

WRITINGS—Under name Jim Klobuchar: *The Zest (and Best) of Klobuchar,* Mark Zelenovich, 1967; *The Playbacks of Jim Klobuchar,* Dillon, 1969; *True Hearts and Purple Heads,* Ross & Haines, 1970; *Will America Accept Love at Halftime?,* Ross & Haines, 1972; *Where the Wind Blows Bittersweet,* Ralph Turtinen, 1975; *Tarkenton,* Harper, 1976; *Will the Vikings EVER Win the Super Bowl?,* Harper, 1977. Contributor to sport magazines and popular journals, including *Time, Argosy, Sport,* and *Pro.*

SIDELIGHTS: Klobuchar writes: "I've been a mountain climber for twenty years. I have climbed extensively in the Grand Tetons and the Alps, including three ascents of the Matterhorn, six of the Grand Teton, and one of Devil's Tower in Wyoming and Obergabelhorn in the Alps. I bicycled around Lake Superior in a week's time in 1975, and have made other bike rides of a thousand miles or so, partly because of professional duties and partly out of personal curiosity and appetite."

AVOCATIONAL INTERESTS: The outdoors, cross-country skiing, hiking.

*   *   *

KLOBUCHAR, Jim
See KLOBUCHAR, James John

*   *   *

KLUGE, P(aul) F(rederick) 1942-

PERSONAL: Born January 24, 1942, in Berkeley Heights, N.J.; son of Walter (a machinist) and Maria (Ensslen) Kluge; married Pamela Hollie (a journalist), February 14, 1977. *Education:* Kenyon College, B.A., 1964; University of Chicago, M.A., 1965, Ph.D., 1967. *Home address:* c/o James Kluge, 93 Longhill Rd., Chatham Township, N.J. 07928. *Agent:* Betty Anne Clarke, International Creative Management, 40 West 57th St., New York, N.Y. 10019.

CAREER: Writer, 1969—. Staff reporter for *Wall Street Journal,* 1969, 1970; assistant editor of *Life,* 1970, 1971.

WRITINGS: The Day That I Die (novel), Bobbs-Merrill, 1976. Contributor to magazines and newspapers.

WORK IN PROGRESS: Two novels, set in the Pacific.

SIDELIGHTS: Kluge writes: "As a writer, I am interested in the impact, the mutations, the purposes and ironies of the American presence abroad. This interest has been concentrated on, but is not limited to, the Pacific islands captured by the United States in World War II and controlled by us since then."

*   *   *

KNAUTH, Victor W. 1895(?)-1977

1895(?)—September 2, 1977; American radio executive, publisher, and journalist. Knauth became a correspondent for United Press after working for several newspapers as a reporter. Founder of a public relations concern and a publishing company, Knauth was also the editor of the *Bridgeport Times-Star* and owner of two radio stations. He died in Wilton, Conn. Obituaries: *New York Times,* September 3, 1977.

*   *   *

KNELMAN, Martin 1943-

PERSONAL: Born June 17, 1943, in Winnipeg, Manitoba, Canada; son of John M. (an insurance executive) and Marion (Medovy) Knelman; married Bernadette Sulgit (managing editor of *Saturday Night*), June 12, 1975; children: Joshua Medovy. *Education:* University of Manitoba, B.A., 1964, B.A. (honors), 1967; University of Toronto, M.A., 1972. *Home and office:* 224 Robert St., Toronto, Ontario, Canada M5S 2K7.

CAREER: Manitoban, Winnipeg, Manitoba, editor, 1963-64; *Globe & Mail,* Toronto, Ontario, copy editor and reporter, 1964-66; *Toronto Star,* Toronto, Ontario, film critic, 1967-69; *Globe & Mail,* film critic, 1969-76; free-lance writer, 1973—. Lecturer at York University, 1970-73. *Member:* Periodical Writers Association of Canada. *Awards, honors:* Senior arts fellowship from Canada Council, 1972-73.

WRITINGS: This Is Where We Came In: The Career and Character of Canadian Film, McClelland & Stewart, 1977. Author of columns, including a theatre column in *Saturday Night,* 1975—, a film column in *Toronto Life,* 1976—, and "O Canada" in *Weekend,* 1976-77. Contributor to magazines, including *Weekend, Atlantic Monthly,* and *Maclean's.*

*   *   *

KNIGHT, David C(arpenter) 1925-

PERSONAL: Born August 6, 1925, in Glens Falls, N.Y.; son of H. Ralph (a magazine editor) and Dorothy (a painter; maiden name, Weed) Knight; married Gisela Schmidt (an indexer), May 26, 1955; children: Karin, Karla. *Education:* Attended University of Pennsylvania, summers, 1946-48; Union College, Schenectady, N.Y., B.A., 1950; Sorbonne, University of Paris, Certificat, 1951; attended Engineering Institute, Philadelphia, Pa., 1952. *Home:* 56 Briary Road, Dobbs Ferry, N.Y. 10522. *Office:* Troll Associates, 320 Rte. 17, Mahwah, N.J.

CAREER: Pacific Coast Review, San Francisco, Calif., assistant editor, 1954-55; Prentice-Hall, Inc., Englewood Cliffs, N.J., production editor, 1955-57, associate editor, trade department, 1957-59; Franklin Watts, Inc., New York City, senior editor and science editor, 1959-73; C. R. Gibson Co., Norwalk, Conn., co-director of publications, 1974-76; Troll Associates, Mahwah, N.J., executive editor, 1977—. *Military service:* U.S. Army Infantry, 1943-46; U.S. Naval Reserve, Chief Journalist, 1964-68. *Member:* American Association for the Advancement of Science, American Society for Psychical Research (lay fellow).

WRITINGS: (Editor) *American Astronauts and Spacecraft: A Pictorial History from Project Mercury through the Skylab Manned Missions* (young adult), Watts, 1971, revised edition, 1975; *Poltergeists: Hauntings and the Haunted* (young adult), Lippincott, 1972; *The Tiny Planets: Asteroids of Our Solar System* (children), Morrow, 1973; *How to Identify 101 Popular Sailboats under Thirty Feet* (adult), Ark Books, 1973; *Thirty-two Moons: Natural Satellites of the Solar System* (young adult), Morrow, 1974; *Eavesdropping on Space: The Quest of Radio Astronomy* (young adult), Morrow, 1975; *Your Body's Defenses* (young adult), McGraw, 1975; *Harnessing the Sun: The Story of Solar Energy* (young adult), Morrow, 1976; *Bees Can't Fly but They Do: Things that Are Still a Mystery to Science* (children), Macmillan, 1976; *Dinosaur Days* (children), McGraw, 1977; *The Haunted Souvenir Warehouse, and Other Haunted Places,* Doubleday, 1977; *Colonies in Orbit: The Coming Age of Human Settlement in Space,* Morrow, 1977; *True Spy Stories,* Signal Books, Doubleday, 1978.

Series: "First Book" series (children), published by Watts: *First Book of Sound,* 1960; . . . *Air,* 1961; . . . *Deserts,* 1964; . . . *Berlin,* 1967; . . . *Mars,* 1968, revised edition, 1973; . . . *Sun,* 1968; . . . *Comets,* 1968; . . . *Meteors and Meteorites,* 1969.

"Biography Series" (young adult), published by Watts: *Robert Koch: Father of Bacteriology,* 1961; *Isaac Newton: Mastermind of Modern Science,* 1961; *Johannes Kepler and Planetary Motion,* 1962; *Copernicus: Titan of Astronomy,* 1964.

"Let's Find Out" series (children), published by Watts: *Let's Find Out about Mars,* 1966; . . . *Telephones,* 1967; . . . *Magnets,* 1967; . . . *Weather,* 1967; . . . *Insects,* 1967; . . . *the Ocean,* 1970; . . . *Earth,* 1975; . . . *Sound,* 1975. Also author of *Let's Find Out About Cats* and *Let's Find Out About Stars.*

"Focus Book" series (young adult), published by Watts: *The Whiskey Rebellion: Colonists in Revolt,* 1968; *The Naval War with France, 1798-1800: "Millions for Defense, but Not One Cent for Tribute,"* 1970.

"Finding-Out Books for Science and Social Studies" series (children), published by Parents Magazine Press: *From Log Roller to Lunar Rover: The Story of Wheels,* 1974; *Those Mysterious UFO's: The Story of Unidentified Flying Objects,* 1975.

"Sources of History" series (adult), published by Cornell University Press: *Sources for the History of Science: 1660-1914,* 1975.

Work represented in anthology, *The E.S.P. Reader,* edited by David C. Knight, Grosset, 1967.

WORK IN PROGRESS: Juvenile books for Troll Associates, including two books in the "Troll Beginning Histories" series, Unit I: *Colonial Life and the Revolution,* Unit II: *Pioneer Life and Westward Expansion, Troll Prehistoric Animal Modules, Troll Childhoods of Famous People,* and juveniles for other publishers.

* * *

KNIGHT, Francis Edgar 1905-
(Frank Knight; Cedric Salter)

PERSONAL: Born in 1905, in London, England. *Education:* Attended schools in Croydon, Surrey, England.

CAREER: Writer. Served in the Merchant Navy, 1920-30, began as an apprentice, later obtained his Extra Master Mariner's Certificate, 1929; during World War II served as a navigation instructor in the Royal Air Force in Britain and South Africa; sold yachts for a time after the war.

WRITINGS—Under name Frank Knight; fiction: *The Albatross Comes Home* (illustrated by A. E. Morley), Hollis & Carter, 1949; *Four in the Half-Deck* (illustrated by S. Drigin), Thomas Nelson, 1950; *The Island of the Radiant Pearls,* Hollis & Carter, 1950; *The Golden Monkey* (illustrated by John Strickland Goodall), Macmillan, 1953; *Strangers in the Half-Deck* (illustrated by Robert Johnston), Thomas Nelson, 1953; *Acting Third Mate* (illustrated by Johnston), Thomas Nelson, 1954; *Voyage to Bengal* (illustrated by Patrick Jobson), St. Martin's, 1954; *Clippers to China* (illustrated by Jobson), St. Martin's, 1955; *Mudlarks and Mysteries* (illustrated by Jobson), Macmillan, 1955; *Family on the Tide* (illustrated by Geoffrey Whittam), St. Martin's, 1956; *The Bluenose Pirate* (illustrated by Jobson), St. Martin's, 1956; *Please Keep off the Mud* (illustrated by Jobson), St. Martin's, 1957; *He Sailed With Blackbeard* (illustrated by Jobson), St. Martin's, 1958; *The Partick Steamboat* (illustrated by Jobson), Macmillan (London), 1958, St. Martin's, 1959.

The Sea Chest: Stories of Adventure at Sea (illustrated by William Riley), Collins, 1960, Platt & Munk, 1964; *The Sea's Fool,* Ward Lock, 1960; *Shadows on the Mud* (illustrated by Jobson), Macmillan (London), 1960, St. Martin's, 1961; *Captains of the Calabar,* Ward Lock, 1961; *The Last of the Lallow's* (illustrated by William Stobbs), St. Martin's, 1961; *The Slaver's Apprentice* (illustrated by Jobson), St. Martin's, 1961; *Pekoe Reef,* Ward Lock, 1962; *Clemency Draper* (illustrated by Stobbs), St. Martin's, 1963; *The Ship That Came Home* (illustrated by Derrick Smouthy), Benn, 1963; *Up, Sea Beggars!,* Macdonald & Co., 1964; *Remember Vera Cruz!* (illustrated by H. J. Gorin), Macdonald & Co., 1965, Dial, 1966; *Olaf's Sword* (illustrated by Andrew Sier), Heinemann, 1969, F. Watts, 1970.

Nonfiction: *A Beginner's Guide to the Sea,* St. Martin's, 1955; *The Sea Story, Being a Guide to Nautical Reading from Ancient Times to the Close of the Sailing Ship Era,* St. Martin's, 1958; *Captain Anson and the Treasure of Spain,* St. Martin's, 1959; *A Guide to Ocean Navigation,* St. Martin's, 1959; *John Harrison: The Man Who Made Navigation Safe,* Macmillan, 1962; *The Young Drake* (illustrated by Azpelicueta), Parrish, 1962; *Stories of Famous Sea Fights* (illustrated by Will Nickless), Oliver & Boyd, 1963, Westminster Press, 1967; *Stories of Famous Ships* (illustrated by Nickless), Oliver & Boyd, 1963, Westminster Press, 1966; *The Young Columbus* (illustrated by Azpelicueta), Roy, 1963; *Stories of Famous Explorers by Sea* (illustrated by Nickless), Oliver & Boyd, 1964, Westminster Press, 1966; *The Young Captain Cook* (illustrated by Joan Howell), Parrish, 1964, Roy, 1966; *Stories of Famous Explorers by Land* (illustrated by Nickless), Oliver & Boyd, 1965, Westminster Press, 1966.

Stories of Famous Sea Adventures (illustrated by Nickless), Oliver & Boyd, 1966, Westminster Press, 1967; *Prince of Cavalier: The Story of the Life and Campaigns of Rupert of the Rhine* (illustrated by John Lawrence), Macdonald & Co., 1967; *Captain Cook and the Voyage of the Endeavour,* Thomas Nelson, 1968; *Rebel Admiral: The Life and Exploits of Admiral Lord Cochrane* (illustrated by Lawrence), Macdonald & Co., 1968; *The Hero: Vice-Admiral Horatio Viscount Nelson,* Macdonald & Co., 1969; *Russia Fights Japan* (illustrated by Roger Phillips), Macdonald & Co., 1969; *Ships,* Benn, 1969; *The Dardanelles Campaign* (illustrated by F. D. Phillips), Macdonald & Co., 1970; *General at Sea: The Life of Admiral Robert Blake* (illustrated by Douglas Phillips), Macdonald & Co., 1971; *The Clipper Ship,* Collins, 1973; *True Stories of Spying* (illustrated by Victor Ambrus), Benn, 1975; *The Golden Age of the Galleon,* Collins, 1976.

Under pseudonym Cedric Salter: *Flight from Poland,* Faber, 1940; *Try-Out in Spain,* Harper, 1943; *Introducing Spain,* Methuen, 1953, revised edition, 1967; *Introducing Portugal,* Methuen, 1956; *Two Girls and a Boat* (illustrated by Victor Bertoglio), Blackie & Son, 1956; *A Fortnight in Portugal,* Percival Marshall, 1957; *Introducing Turkey,* Methuen, 1961; *Portugal,* Hastings House, 1970; *Algarve and Southern Portugal,* Hastings House, 1974; *Northern Spain,* Batsford, 1975.

SIDELIGHTS: Knight's books covered various periods of navigation history. In his *Captain Anson and the Treasure of Spain,* Knight gave an account of George Anson's journey around the world during the eighteenth century. To keep the book factual, the author relied on information from the diaries, logs, and letters of the men who participated in this segment of British naval history. A reviewer for *Christian Science Monitor* wrote, "The long voyage with its incredible endurance and splendor as well as its violence . . . is told with a clipped directness and economy that is exactly right."

Captain Cook and the Voyage of the Endeavor was concerned with James Cook's trip around Cape Horn to New Zealand. Knight based his work on Captain Cook's journal of the voyage with additional notes from other sources. A critic for the London *Times Literary Supplement* observed, "Helped by his knowledge and love of the sea, he presents careful research, quietly correcting more romantic interpretations of fact in an admirable narrative style, direct and absorbing. . . ."

BIOGRAPHICAL/CRITICAL SOURCES: San Francisco Chronicle, November 15, 1953; *New York Herald Tribune Book Review,* February 13, 1955; *Christian Science Monitor,* February 5, 1960; *Times Literary Supplement,* June 26, 1969.*

*   *   *

KNIGHT, Frank
    See KNIGHT, Francis Edgar

*   *   *

KNIGHT, Hilary 1926-

PERSONAL: Born November 1, 1926, in Hempstead, Long Island, N.Y.; son of Clayton (an artist and writer) and Katharine (an artist and writer; maiden name, Sturges) Knight. *Education:* Attended Art Students League, New York, N.Y. *Home:* 300 East 51st St., New York, N.Y. 10022.

CAREER: Author, illustrator, and designer.

WRITINGS—All self-illustrated: *ABC,* Golden Press, 1961; *Angels and Berries and Candy Canes* (also see below), Harper, 1963; *A Christmas Stocking Story* (also see below), Harper, 1963; *A Firefly in a Fir Tree* (also see below), Harper, 1963; (with Clement Clarke Moore) *Christmas Nutshell Library* (contains Knight's *Angels and Berries and Candy Canes, A Christmas Stocking Story, A Firefly in a Fir Tree,* and Moore's *The Night Before Christmas*), Harper, 1963; *Where's Wallace?,* Harper, 1964; *Sylvia, the Sloth: A Round-About Story,* Harper, 1969.

Illustrator: Kay Thompson, *Eloise,* Simon & Schuster, 1955; Patrick Gordon Campbell, *Short Trot With a Cultured Mind Through Some Experiences of a Humorous Nature,*

Simon & Schuster, 1956; Jan Henry, *Tiger's Chance,* Harcourt, 1957; Betty Bard MacDonald, *Hello, Mrs. Piggle-Wiggle,* Lippincott, 1957, reprinted, 1976; MacDonald, *Mrs. Piggle-Wiggle,* Lippincott, 1957, reprinted, 1976; MacDonald, *Mrs. Piggle-Wiggle's Magic,* Lippincott, 1957, reprinted, 1976; Thompson, *Eloise in Paris,* Simon & Schuster, 1957; *Wonderful World of Aunt Tuddy,* Random House, 1958; Dorothea W. Blair, *Roger: A Most Unusual Rabbit,* Lippincott, 1958; Thompson, *Eloise at Christmas Time,* Random House, 1958; Thompson, *Eloise in Moscow,* Simon & Schuster, 1959.

Evelyn Gendel, *Tortoise and Turtle,* Simon & Schuster, 1960; Cecil Maiden, *Beginning With Mrs. McBee,* Vanguard, 1960; *Hilary Knight's Mother Goose,* Golden Press, 1962; Maiden, *Speaking of Mrs. McCluskie,* Vanguard, 1962; Margaret Stone Zilboorg, *Jeremiah Octopus,* Golden Press, 1962; Gendel, *Tortoise and Turtle Abroad,* Simon & Schuster, 1963; Marie Le Prince De Beaumont, *Beauty and the Beast,* Macmillan, 1963; Clement Clarke Moore, *The Night Before Christmas,* Harper, 1963; Charles Dickens, *Captain Boldheart [and] The Magic Fishbone,* Macmillan, 1964; Ogden Nash, *The Animal Garden: A Story,* M. Evans, 1965; Charlotte Zolotow, *When I Have a Little Girl,* Harper, 1965; Zolotow, *When I Have a Son,* Harper, 1967; Judith Viorst, *Sunday Morning: A Story,* Harper, 1968; Margaret Fishback, *A Child's Book of Natural History,* Platt & Munk, 1969; Patricia M. Scarry, *The Jeremy Mouse Book,* American Heritage Press, 1969.

Nathaniel Benchley, *Feldman Fieldmouse: A Fable,* Harper, 1971; Duncan Emrich, editor, *The Book of Wishes and Wishmaking,* American Heritage Press, 1971; Janice Udry, *Angie,* Harper, 1971; Adelaide Holl, *Most-of-the-Time Maxie: A Story,* Xerox Family Education Services, 1974; Robert Kraus, *I'm a Monkey,* Windmill Books, 1975; Marilyn Sachs, *Matt's Mitt,* Doubleday, 1975; Steven Kroll, *That Makes Me Mad!,* Pantheon, 1976; Lucille Ogle and Tina Thoburn, *The Golden Picture Dictionary: A Beginning Dictionary of More Than 2500 Words,* Western Publishing, 1976.

SIDELIGHTS: In 1966, Knight traveled extensively throughout Europe. He visited Rome, Moscow, Paris, and Panama City among other places.

BIOGRAPHICAL/CRITICAL SOURCES: New York Herald Tribune, November 12, 1961; *New York Times Book Review,* November 12, 1961; *American Artist,* March, 1963; *Saturday Review,* October 17, 1964.*

*   *   *

KNIGHT, Robin 1943-

PERSONAL: Born June 10, 1943, in Chalfont St. Giles, England; son of Cyril Ensor (an army officer) and Hazel (Heard) Knight; married Jean Sykes. *Education:* Dublin University, B.A. (with honors), 1966; Stanford University, M.A., 1968. *Office: U.S. News and World Report,* Leninsky Pr. 36, Kv. 53, Moscow, U.S.S.R.

CAREER/WRITINGS: U.S. News and World Report, Washington, D.C., foreign correspondent in London, 1968-74, bureau chief in London, 1974-76, bureau chief in Moscow, 1976—. Notable assignments include coverage of the Ulster crisis, 1969-76, turmoil in South Africa, 1971-74, and Portugal, 1974-75, and human rights in the Soviet bloc.

*   *   *

KNOWLES, Clayton 1908-1978

April 27, 1908—January 4, 1978; American journalist.

Knowles covered political and governmental news in Albany, Washington, and New York City for the *New York Times*. His most notable stories included an on-the-spot report of the 1954 attack on the U.S. House of Representatives by four Puerto Rican nationalists, and exclusive coverage of Adam Clayton Powell's surrender to authorities in 1968. Knowles was a charter member of the Newspaper Guild. He died in Largo, Fla. Obituaries: *New York Times*, January 5, 1978.

* * *

KNOX, Collie T. 1897(?)-1977

1897(?)—May, 1977; British journalist and author. Knox was a columnist for the *London Daily Express* and *Daily Mail* as well as a feature writer for other magazines and newspapers. His books included *It Had to Be Me* and *We Live and Learn*. He died in England. Obituaries: *AB Bookman's Weekly*, October 17, 1977.

* * *

KOCH, Howard 1902-

PERSONAL: Born December 12, 1902, in New York, N.Y.; son of Frederick and Helena Mabel Koch; married second wife, Anne Green (a writer); children: Hardy, Karyl, Peter. *Education:* St. Stephens College, B.A., 1922; Columbia University, LL.B., 1925. *Politics:* Liberal Independant. *Religion:* "Cosmic." *Residence:* Woodstock, N.Y. *Agent:* International Creative Management, 40 West 57th St., New York, N.Y. 10019.

CAREER: Writer for stage, screen, and radio. *Member:* Dramatists Guild, Writers Guild. *Awards, honors:* Academy Award (Oscar) for best screenplay, 1943, for "Casablanca"; H.H.D., Bard College.

WRITINGS—Books: *The Panic Broadcast*, Little, Brown, 1970; *Casablanca: Script & Legend*, Overlook Press, 1973; *As Time Goes By* (memoirs), Harcourt, 1978.

Plays: "Great Scott!," first produced in New York, 1929; "Give Us This Day," first produced in New York, 1933; "The Lonely Man," first produced in Chicago at Blackstone Theatre, 1937; "War of the Worlds" (radio play), first produced in New York at Orson Welles Mercury Theatre, 1940; (with John Huston) "In Time to Come," first produced in New York, 1940; "Dead Letters," first produced in New York, 1971. Also author of "The Albatross" first produced in San Miguel, Mexico at Instituto Allende Theatre, "The Trial of Richard Nixon," and "Skywarn."

Screenplays: "The Letter" (adapted from play by Somerset Maugham), Warner Bros., 1940; (with Seton I. Miller) "The Sea Hawk," Warner Bros., 1940; (with Anne Froelick) "Shining Victory" (adapted from play "Jupiter Laughs" by A. J. Cronin), Warner Bros., 1941; (with Abem Finkel, Harry Chandler, and John Huston) "Sergeant York," Warner Bros., 1941; "In This Our Life" (adapted from novel by Ellen Glasgow), Warner Bros., 1942; "Mission to Moscow" (adapted from nonfiction work of Joseph E. Davies), Warner Bros., 1943; (with Julius J. and Philip G. Epstein) "Casablanca" (adapted from play "Everybody Comes to Rick's" by Murray Burnett and Joan Alison), Warner Bros., 1943; (with Ellis St. Joseph) "In Our Time," Warner Bros., 1944; (with Elliot Paul) "Rhapsody in Blue" (adapted from story by Sonya Levien), Warner Bros., 1945; (with John Huston) "Three Strangers," Warner Bros., 1946; "Letter from an Unknown Woman" (adapted from story by Stefan Zweig), Universal, 1948.

"No Sad Songs for Me" (adapted from novel by Ruth Southard), Columbia, 1950; "The 13th Letter" (adapted from screenplay "The Raven" by Louis Chavance), Twentieth Century Fox, 1951; "Loss of Innocence" (adapted from novel *The Greenage Summer* by Rumer Godden), Columbia, 1961; "The War Lover" (adapted from novel by John Hersey), Columbia, 1962; (with James Clavell) "633 Squadron" (adapted from novel by Frederick E. Smith), United Artists, 1964; (with Lewis John Carlino) "The Fox" (adapted from novella by D. H. Lawrence), Columbia, 1968. Also author of screenplays "The Rules of the Game," 1950, and "The Woman of Otowi Crossing," 1974.

WORK IN PROGRESS: "Working on extending my 'Invasion from Mars' radio play into a full-length play for stage presentation."

SIDELIGHTS: "Perhaps the circumstances which most affected my life and my career," wrote Mr. Koch, "was my connection with the hardy perennials 'War of the Worlds,' 'Casablanca' and the controversial 'Mission to Moscow.' During the writing of 'Mission to Moscow'' I met my wife, Anne Green, who was assisting me in a research-secretarial capacity—and her assistance and influence has been a mainstay in my life and work ever since.

"My chief motivation is to dramatize as honestly as I can, any aspect of the human condition in its social framework, with an emphasis on life-supporting values."

What Mr. Koch doesn't say is that during the 1950's witchhunts, he was blacklisted and unable to work. A quick look at his list of credits shows a gap of ten years during which a first rate Hollywood career was stopped. During the 1940's Koch was the premiere screenwriter of Hollywood, and it was his dedication to causes and ideals which made his films more substantial than most.

"Casablanca" is Koch's best-known, best-loved film, and much of the credit for the film's lasting popularity can be attributed to what Richard Corliss called "the happy fact that it boasts some of the best dialogue to be found in an American film. The real success of 'Casablanca,'" Corliss continued, "derives from the writer's character development and from the dialogue which Bogart and Bergman complained about to the press, and which James Agree so flippantly dismissed in his *Nation* column. Ultimately, perhaps, both the 'Casablanca' script and Howard Koch's development of it comes close to defining that rarest of attitudes: grace under pressure, Hollywood-style."

In 1970, *Film Comment* magazine sent questionnaires to a handful of Hollywood screenwriters, Koch among them. Asked which scripts had given him the most satisfaction, he replied: "While I enjoy the creative process of writing a screenplay, the real satisfaction comes when the film is made with its values intact or, in some cases, enhanced. The pictures on which I worked that gave me the most satisfaction are 'The Letter,' 'Casablanca,' 'Letter from an Unknown Woman,' 'No Sad Songs for Me,' and 'Loss of Innocence.' In all of these I was fortunate in having a close association with outstanding directors."

Asked if a screenwriter has to be particularly cynical about his own work's vulnerability to stay sane in Hollywood, Koch said: "I feel if a writer becomes cynical about his work in films, he should be doing something else. I've never looked down on the film medium (or even Hollywood) in spite of its well-advertised inanities and its haphazard mass production system. Writing a screenplay in Hollywood, or anywhere else, is only part of a writer's function; struggling to preserve its values is the other part. If he cares enough, he'll do it."

Finally, Koch was asked which screenwriters he admired, and what influences can be found in his own work. "I admire many screenwriters," he said, "among them Zavatini, Trumbo, Antony Polansky, Ring Lardner, Jr., Waldo Salt, David Rintels, Joseph Moscowitz, Gore Vidal, Ellis St. Joseph, etc. I believe that a film's style should be dictated by its content—therefore I'm not aware of any stylistic influences."

In a recent talk, Koch commented on the "auteur theory." "Granting that some fictions may be necessary or even useful, this particular one, that there is a single author of a film and that the author is the director, has, to my mind, had an unfortunate effect on many of the films that are made today. I say this not as a writer but as a movie-goer and movie-lover. It has played up stylistic effect often at the expense of content. And it has put the emphasis on the package more than on what the package contains. The director has become the wrapping on that package and the star the ribbon tied on it to make the product attractive and marketable in the eyes of those who finance and distribute the film."

BIOGRAPHICAL/CRITICAL SOURCES: The Hollywood Screenwriters, Avon, 1972; *Talking Pictures,* Penguin, 1975.

*   *   *

KORBEL, Josef 1909-1977

September 20, 1909—July 18, 1977; Czechoslovakian-born American author, diplomat, and dean of Graduate School of International Studies at University of Denver. Korbel served as Czech ambassador to Yugoslavia and chairperson of the United Nations Commission for India and Pakistan. He died in Denver, Colo. Obituaries: *New York Times,* July 19, 1977. (See index for *CA* sketch)

*   *   *

KORN, Noel 1923-

PERSONAL: Born June 25, 1923, in New York, N.Y.; son of Joseph Gregory (a glass blower) and Clara (an employment counselor; maiden name, Herland) Korn; married June C. Kroutil (a union organizer), May 1, 1952; children: Michael, Kenneth, Walter. *Education:* New York University, B.A., 1944; University of California, Los Angeles, M.A., 1948. *Politics:* Independent Democrat. *Religion:* "Reconstructionist." *Home:* 6570 Zumirez Dr., Malibu, Calif. 90265. *Office:* Los Angeles Community College District, 2140 West Olympic Blvd., Los Angeles, Calif. 90006.

CAREER: Los Angeles Valley College, Van Nuys, Calif., instructor, 1950-53, assistant professor, 1953-57, associate professor, 1957-61, professor of anthropology, 1961—, coordinator of instructional media, 1968-72. Director of Learning Resource Center at California State University, Northridge, 1972-75. Vice-president of Sigma Educational Films, 1962-71. *Member:* American Anthropological Association (fellow), American Association of Physical Anthropologists.

WRITINGS: Human Evolution, Holt, 1959, 4th edition, in press; *An Atlas of Evolution,* Holt, 1971; (contributor) William Haviland, editor, *Anthropology,* Holt, 1975.

WORK IN PROGRESS: Culture: The Biological Base.

SIDELIGHTS: Korn comments briefly that he concentrates on "humanistic perspectives on human evolution and human biological diversity."

KORN, Walter 1908-

PERSONAL: Born May 22, 1908, in Prague, Czechoslovakia; came to United States, 1950; naturalized U.S. citizen, 1955; son of Bernhard (a merchant) and Clara (a concert pianist; maiden name Deutsch) Korn; married Herta Klemperer (a legal secretary), December 24, 1933 (died, 1977). *Education:* Prague Institute of Technology, Dr. rer. pol., 1938; Wayne State University, certificate, 1957-58. *Politics:* "Cynical." *Religion:* "The Golden Rule, as stated in Tobit, and by Confucius." *Home:* 816 North Delaware St., Apt. 207, San Mateo, Calif. 94401.

CAREER: Has worked as a manager in international trade, and in executive positions in volunteer, social service, and non-profit organizations and agencies for technical assistance abroad; United Nations Relief and Rehabilitation Administration (UNRRA), U.S. zone of occupation, Germany, deputy area director, 1945-47; director of administration of United Nations Joint Distribution Committee, 1960-64; State of New York Executive Department, Division of Housing and Community Renewal, New York, N.Y., civil servant, 1970-76. Writer of books and essays on chess, 1941—. Lecturer, Allied Council (England), 1941-45; consultant, Volunteers for International Technical Assistance (VITA), 1965-70. *Member:* American Judicature Society, Academy of Political Science, Press Club of San Francisco, Princeton Club of New York. *Awards, honors:* International Judge for Chess Compositions award from Federation International des Echecs, 1964.

WRITINGS: (Editor and author) *Modern Chess Openings,* 7th edition (Korn was not associated with earlier editions), Pitman, 1946, Mckay, 1948, 12th edition, McKay, 1979; *The Brilliant Touch: 240 Chess Brilliancies Collated and Commented On,* Pitman, 1950, Dover, 1966; *American Chess Art,* Pitman, 1974. General editor of "Pitman Chess Series" and "Mason/Charter Chess Series," 1973—. Contributor to *Encyclopaedia Britannica, British Chess Magazine, Chess, Chess Life, Chess Correspondent, Chess Review, Atlantic Chess News,* and other periodicals.

WORK IN PROGRESS: America's Chess Pioneers; other books on chess and on author's own experience.

SIDELIGHTS: Walter Korn told *CA:* "I consider my activity in chess rather as a vehicle for writing, striving to remain a (recreational) generalist rather than a professionalized super-specialist. Now in retirement for family reasons, I will attempt to verbalize my past (global) experience in a wider framework than chess only—publishers willing. I will try to utilize any knowledge for the benefit of constructive programs within a better, communitarian script; instead of treading the conventional waters of the status quo, by continued 'academic(al)' learning—except for the uninterrupted expansion of mind created by the changes around us. I will be interested in acquiring a magazine column on chess 'annodomini' 1999 (not 1900!). I will perhaps resume travel in consulting, volunteer capacity."

The total of copies sold of *Modern Chess Openings,* 7th through 11th editions, is a six-digit figure.

Korn has a working knowledge of several Slavonic and Romance languages.

*   *   *

KOSHETZ, Herbert 1907(?)-1977

1907(?)—October 14, 1977; American journalist. A staff member of the *New York Times* for more than fifty years, Koshetz specialized in writing about the textile industry. He reported on foreign trade and overseas business conditions, and wrote the widely read financial column, "A Merchant's View." He died in New York, N.Y. Obituaries: *New York Times,* October 15, 1977.

*   *   *

KOVACS, Alexander   1930(?)-1977

1930(?)—October 21, 1977; Rumanian-born journalist. Kovacs worked as a journalist in Hungary until 1968, when increased political repression of free speech forced him to flee to the West. He joined the U.S. Information Agency as a writer and announcer for the Hungarian service of Voice of America. He died in Alexandria, Va. Obituaries: *Washington Post,* October 24, 1977.

*   *   *

KOWITT, Sylvia
See CROSBIE, Sylvie Kowitt

*   *   *

KRAENZEL, Carl F(rederick)   1906-

PERSONAL: Born November 1, 1906, in Hebron, N.D.; son of Reinhold (a farmer) and Hulda (Weber) Kraenzel; married Margaret Powell (a writer), June 6, 1930; children: Sarah Janet Kraenzel Nagode, Frederick John, Theodore Carl, James Albert. *Education:* Elmhurst College, A.A., 1929; University of North Dakota, B.A., 1930; University of Minnesota, M.A., 1932; Harvard University, further graduate study, 1932-33; University of Wisconsin, Madison, Ph.D., 1935. *Politics:* Democrat. *Religion:* Methodist. *Home:* 2250 East Missouri, Apt. 8C, Las Cruces, N.M. 88001. *Office:* Department of Sociology, University of Texas, El Paso, Tex. 79998.

CAREER: Federal Emergency Relief Administration, Washington, D.C., research assistant, 1934; Works Progress Administration, Washington, D.C., research assistant, 1935; Montana State University, Bozeman, assistant professor, 1935-38, associate professor, 1938-49, professor of rural sociology, 1949-54; Near East Foundation, Tehran, Iran, cooperative specialist, 1954-56; Montana State University, professor of rural and general sociology, 1956-58; Near East Foundation, area program director, 1959-61; Montana State University, professor of sociology, 1961-68; University of Texas, El Paso, H. Y. Benedict Professor of Sociology, 1968-73; writer, 1973—. Lecturer at Denver Library School, 1947, University of Minnesota, 1948, University of Wisconsin, Madison, 1957, University of Denver and Iliff School of Theology, 1958, and University of Tehran, 1960-61. Member of Great Plains Health Committee, 1937-68; chairman of advisory committee and member of Great Plains Institute, 1962—; member of board of directors and chairman of advisory committee of Wright-Ingraham Institute. President of Montana Agricultural Planning Committee, 1938-43; president of Montana Conference of Social Work; member of board of directors of Western States Water & Power Consumers Conference, 1963—.

MEMBER: American Rural Sociology Society, American Sociological Association, Institute for the History of Sociology, Western States Agricultural Economics and Rural Sociology Society, Western Social Science Association, Montana Public Health Association (past president), Phi Kappa Phi. *Awards, honors:* Rockefeller Foundation fellowship, 1942; award of merit from American Association for State and Local Government, 1956, for *The Great Plains in Transition;* National Institute of Mental Health fellowship, 1963-68; Ph.D. from Montana State University, 1975.

WRITINGS: (With Watson Thomson and Glenn H. Craig) *The Northern Plains in a World of Change,* Gregory-Cartwright Ltd., 1942; *The Great Plains in Transition,* University of Oklahoma Press, 1955; (contributor) Michael P. Malone and R. B. Roeder, editors, *The Montana Past,* University of Montana Press, 1969; (contributor) C. C. Zimmerman and R. E. Duwors, editors, *Sociology of Underdevelopment,* Copp, Clark, 1970; *The Cost of Space in the Sparsely-Populated American Yonland,* Big Sky Press, 1978. Contributor of articles on population growth, migration, mental health, hospital care, old folks' homes, community, and regionalism to professional journals. Book editor for American Rural Sociology Society, 1961-69.

WORK IN PROGRESS: Minority Groups and Bilingualism as a Social Cost of Space in the Yonland.

SIDELIGHTS: Kraenzel writes: "I am interested in social living, community, and economic adaptations to aridity and semi-aridity, as in the Great Plains and the Rocky Mountain West (Yonland), where the cost of living is extraordinarily high, due to sparsity of population and destruction arising from central place facts and theory: i.e., the exploitation of the Yonland, first by mining materials, then oil, and now by coal stripping and slurrying of coal via pipelines using scarce water; also the extraordinary cost induced by bilingualism, which in fact means multi-lingualism in many parts of the Yonland (Spanish, Navajo, Hopi, Cheyenne, Crow, Sioux, and English) where services such as education and health care are already a burden if standards are to be met."

*   *   *

KRECH, David   1909-1977

March 27, 1909—July 14, 1977; Polish-born American psychologist, educator, and author. One of Krech's most important contributions dealt with specific chemical and anatomical changes in rats raised in highly stimulated environments. His research on the chemical nature of learning and memory led him to explore the social and ethical implications of such research. He was highly regarded for his warnings to Congressional committees about the possibilities and dangers of psychological manipulation of the population. He died in Berkeley, Calif. Obituaries: *New York Times,* July 16, 1977.

*   *   *

KRENSKY, Stephen (Alan)   1953-

PERSONAL: Born November 25, 1953, in Boston, Mass.; son of Paul David (a business executive) and Roselyn (Gurewitz) Krensky. *Education:* Hamilton College, B.A., 1975. *Politics:* Independent. *Home and office:* 45 Peacock Farm Rd., Lexington, Mass. 02173.

CAREER: Free-lance writer and critic, 1975—.

WRITINGS—For children: A Big Day for Scepters, Atheneum, 1977; *The Dragon Circle,* Atheneum, 1977; *Woodland Crossings,* Atheneum, 1978; *The Perils of Putney,* Atheneum, 1978. Contributor of articles and reviews to magazines and newspapers, including *Cricket.*

WORK IN PROGRESS: A collection of fairy tales entitled *Castles in the Air and Other Tales.*

SIDELIGHTS: Krensky writes: "In writing for children, I am guided by something C. S. Lewis wrote in *Of Other Worlds* . . .; i.e., 'A book worth reading only in childhood is not worth reading even then.'"

KRIKORIAN, Yervant H(ovhannes)   1892-1977

January 7, 1892—1977; Turkish educator, editor, and author. Krikorian was professor of philosophy at the City College of the City University of New York for forty years and chairman of the department for fourteen years. He was the author and editor of numerous books on philosophy as well as articles for journals. He died in Washington, D.C. Obituaries: *New York Times,* December 7, 1977; *Washington Post,* December 7, 1977. (See index for *CA* sketch)

* * *

KRONSTADT, Henry L(ippin)   1915-

PERSONAL: Born February 22, 1915, in Pruszany, Poland; came to the United States in 1922, naturalized citizen, 1929; son of Nathan and Esther (Lippin) Kronstadt; married Claire Pauls, August 12, 1939 (deceased); children: Esther, Robin. *Education:* Attended National University, 1936; American University, B.A., 1973, M.A., 1974, M.A. (creative writing), 1976; attended Worcester College, Oxford, 1976. *Politics:* Democrat. *Religion:* Jewish. *Home and office:* 4607 Connecticut Ave. N.W., Washington, D.C. 20008. *Agent:* James Seligmann Agency, 280 Madison Ave., New York, N.Y. 10016.

CAREER: Frederic Loeser's (department store), Brooklyn, N.Y., assistant art director, 1932-34; Lansburgh's (department store), Washington, D.C., assistant advertising director, 1935-37; Henry J. Kaufman (advertising and public relations firm), Washington, D.C., account executive and copywriter, 1937-39; Henry L. Kronstadt (advertising and public relations firm), Washington, D.C., owner-operator and senior partner, 1939-62; Small Business Administration, Washington, D.C., information specialist, writer, and editor, 1962-64; U.S. Public Health Service, Washington, D.C., writer-editor and assistant information officer, 1964-66; U.S. Office of Economic Opportunity, Washington, D.C., special writer, 1966-68; U.S. Peace Corps, Washington, D.C., volunteer in Colombia, 1969-70; free-lance writer and publicist, 1970—. Guest lecturer at American University, 1958. Volunteer consultant in Bangkok, Thailand, for International Executive Service Corps, 1966. Member of executive board of Brandeis Zionist district, 1936-54, vice-president, 1947-48; member of executive board of Jewish Community Council, 1950-52; member of board of directors of Jewish Social Service Agency, 1952-55; member of steering commission of Israel Bonds Development Corp., 1960-62. Member of board of directors of Colorado and G Streets Corp. *Military service:* U.S. Army, Quartermaster Corps, technical writer, 1943-45.

MEMBER: Authors Guild, Authors League of America, National Press Club, Woodmont Club. *Awards, honors:* National award from Hollander Fur Dyers copy contest, 1936.

WRITINGS: It Comes in Bunches and other Short Stories, Lippin Press, 1977. Also author of *Latitude North,* 1944, and *Fighting Fuel,* 1945. Author of column "Washington Vignettes" in Anglo-Jewish weekly newspapers, 1959-62. Contributor to popular and ethnic magazines and newspapers, including *Phoebe, American Zionist,* and *Washington Post.*

WORK IN PROGRESS: The Cantor's Son, a novel; *Going Places,* personal travel experiences.

SIDELIGHTS: Kronstadt comments: "My interest is to write on ethnic subjects. I was born in Poland, and wish to transmit, if possible, the trials and tribulations as well as the ecstasy of *Shtetel* life. I have traveled to England, France, Belgium, Holland, Italy, Greece, Poland, Russia, Rumania, Hungary, Czechoslovakia, Spain, Venezuela, Colombia, Thailand, Hong Kong, Japan, and Israel."

* * *

KRUSE, Harry D(ayton)   1900-1977

July 9, 1900—July 13, 1977; American medical researcher and author. Kruse held positions with such organizations as the Milbank Memorial Fund, the New York Academy of Medicine, the Medical Society of the State of New York, and *Medical World News.* His books dealt with nutrition, alcoholism, and mental disease. He died in Bronxville, N.Y. Obituaries: *New York Times,* July 14, 1977.

* * *

KUESEL, Harry N.   1892(?)-1977

1892(?)—October 26, 1977; American insurance executive and author. After retiring as manager of an insurance company, Kuesel wrote books on selling techniques and training. He died in Roslyn, N.Y. Obituaries: *New York Times,* October 30, 1977.

* * *

KUSTERMEIR, Rudolf   1893(?)-1977

1893(?)—December 4, 1977; German journalist who, since 1957, worked as a correspondent in Israel for D.P.A., the West German news agency. Arrested by the Nazis in 1933 and held prisoner for twelve years, Kustermeir was later influential in starting a campaign for West German retributions for Nazi victims. After World War II he became editor of *Die Welt,* a Hamburg daily. Kustermeir died in Tel Aviv, Israel. Obituaries: *New York Times,* December 7, 1977.

* * *

LABAREE, Leonard W(oods)   1897-

PERSONAL: Born August 26, 1897, in Urumia, Persia (now Iran); U.S. citizen; son of Benjamin W. (an American missionary) and Mary A. (Schauffler) Labaree; married Elizabeth Mary Calkins, June 26, 1920; children: Arthur C., Benjamin W. *Education:* Williams College, B.A., 1920; Yale University, M.A., 1923, Ph.D., 1926. *Politics:* Independent. *Religion:* Congregational. *Home:* 165 Mill Rd., Northford, Conn. 06472.

CAREER: Milford School, Milford, Conn., instructor in history, 1920-22; Yale University, New Haven, Conn., instructor, 1924-27, assistant professor, 1927-38, associate professor, 1938-42, professor of history, 1942-66, Farnam Professor of History, 1944-66, professor emeritus, 1966—. Carnegie visiting professor, Armstrong College, University of Durham, 1929-30; Anson G. Phelps lecturer, New York University, 1947. State historian of Connecticut, 1941-51. Member of North Branford (Conn.) Town Planning Commission, 1955-64. *Military service:* U.S. Army, Air Service, 1917-19; became second lieutenant.

MEMBER: American Historical Association, American Antiquarian Society, American Philosophical Society, Connecticut Historical Society, Massachusetts Historical Society (corresponding member), Colonial Society of Massachusetts (corresponding member), New Haven Colony Historical Society (vice-president, 1966—), Phi Beta Kappa, Psi Upsilon. *Awards, honors:* Justin Winsor Prize of American Historical Association, 1930, for *Royal Government in America;* Litt.D., from Williams College, 1955, Bucknell

University, 1955, Franklin College, 1956, Franklin and Marshall College, 1956, Dickinson College, 1963, and Lehigh University, 1970.

WRITINGS: Royal Government in America, Yale University Press, 1930; (editor) *Royal Instructions to British Colonial Governors,* two volumes, Appleton, 1935; (editor) *Records of the State of Connecticut,* Volumes IV-VIII (1782-96), Connecticut State Library, 1942-51; *Conservatism in Early American History,* New York University Press, 1948; (editor with Whitfield J. Bell, Jr.) *Mr. Franklin,* Yale University Press, 1956; (editor) *The Papers of Benjamin Franklin,* eighteen volumes, Yale University Press, 1959-74; (editor) *The Autobiography of Benjamin Franklin,* Yale University Press, 1964. General editor, "Yale Historical Publications," forty volumes, 1933-36.

* * *

LABYS, Walter C(arl) 1937-

PERSONAL: Born July 25, 1937, in Latrobe, Pa.; son of Walter H. and Mary H. (Markiewicz) Labys; married Jane Elizabeth Reardon (a language teacher), August 28, 1967; children: Walter P., Charlotte J. *Education:* Carnegie-Mellon University, B.S., 1959; Duquesne University, M.B.A., 1962; Harvard University, M.A., 1965; University of Nottingham, Ph.D., 1968. *Home:* 221 Grand St., Morgantown, W.Va., 26505. *Office:* College of Mineral and Energy Resources, West Virginia University, Morgantown, W.Va. 26506.

CAREER: Abt Associates, Cambridge, Mass., senior economist in modeling and econometrics, 1968-69; United Nations Conference on Trade and Development, Geneva, Switzerland, senior economist in Commodities Division, 1969-71; Graduate Institute of International Studies, Geneva, visiting professor, 1970-71; University of Rhode Island, Kingston, assistant professor of economics, 1971-72; Graduate Institute of International Studies, visiting professor, 1972-75; West Virginia University, Morgantown, associate professor of economics, 1975—. Has made field trips to the Philippines, India, Singapore, Indonesia, and Sri Lanka. Consultant to business and government organizations, including Commodities and Research Division of the United Nations Conference on Trade and Development, International Food Policy Research Institute, International Bank of Reconstruction and Development, Food and Agricultural Organization of the United Nations, and Economics and Statistics Department of Unilever Ltd. *Member:* American Agricultural Economics Association, American Institute of Mining, Metallurgical, and Petroleum Engineers (mineral economics section), American Economic Association, Econometric Society, Harvard Alumni Association of Western Pennsylvania.

WRITINGS: (With C. W. J. Granger) *Speculation, Hedging, and Commodity Price Forecasts,* Lexington Books, 1970; *Dynamic Commodity Models: Specification, Estimation, and Simulation,* Lexington Books, 1973; (editor) *Quantitative Models of Commodity Markets,* Ballinger, 1975; (editor) *Commodity Markets and Economic Development in Latin America: A Modeling Approach,* National Bureau of Economic Research, 1978.

Contributor: *Investment in South Chicago,* Abt Associates, 1969; *Study of Energy Fuel Mineral Resources,* Volume IV: *Natural Gas,* Abt Associates, 1969; *Development Planning for East Asian Countries,* Development Academy of the Philippines, 1974; Eugene Wunderlick, editor, *A Study of Alien Investment in United States Lands,* U.S. Department of Agriculture, 1976; M. Chatterji and P. Van Rumpuy, editors, *Energy, Regional Science, and Public Policy,* Springer-Verlag, 1976; G. Amihud, editor, *Bidding and Auctioning in Theory and Practice,* New York University Press, 1976; W. Driehuis, editor, *Primary Commodity Prices: Analysis and Forecasting,* University of Rotterdam Press, 1977; Radha Sinha, editor, *The World Food Problem: Consensus and Conflict,* Pergamon, 1977; F. G. Adams and S. Klein, editors, *Stabilizing World Commodity Markets: Theory and Practice,* Lexington Books, 1978; F. G. Adams and J. R. Behrman, editors, *Econometric Modeling of World Commodity Policy,* Lexington Books, 1978.

Contributor of about twenty articles to professional journals.

WORK IN PROGRESS: Price Formation on International Mineral Markets.

SIDELIGHTS: Labys writes: "I divide my time between teaching at the College of Mineral and Energy Resources at West Virginia University and occasional lecturing at the Graduate Institute of International Studies in Geneva. My main professional interests lie with the economic analysis of international commodity markets and the impacts which these markets have on developing countries. Regarding the latter, I have made six extended trips to Southeast Asia that have involved teaching and consulting as well as research. I've managed to change my pace at times, writing my books in interesting settings ranging from a chalet in Switzerland to an island off the New England coast." Labys adds, "Among the different commodities I have analyzed, I find wines to be the most interesting."

AVOCATIONAL INTERESTS: Painting, cooking, visiting vineyards, skiing.

* * *

LA FARGE, Phyllis

PERSONAL: Married Chester Johnson. *Education:* Graduated from Radcliffe College.

CAREER: Author. *Awards, honors: The Pancake King* was selected for the American Institute of Graphic Arts Children's Book Show, 1971-72, and for the American Institute of Graphic Arts Fifty Books of the Year, 1971.

WRITINGS: (Translator, with Peter H. Judd) Jean Giraudoux, *Giraudoux: Three Plays, Volume 2,* Hill & Wang, 1964; *Kate and the Wild Kittens* (illustrated by Ingrid Fetz), Knopf, 1965; *The Gumdrop Necklace* (illustrated by Alan E. Cober), Knopf, 1967; *Jane's Silver Chair* (illustrated by Robin Jacques), Knopf, 1969; (editor) Stendhal, *The Red and the Black,* Washington Square Press, 1970; *Keeping Going,* Harcourt, 1971; *The Pancake King* (illustrated by Seymour Chwast), Delacorte, 1971; *Joanna Runs Away* (illustrated by Trina Schart Hyman), Holt, 1973; *Abby Takes Over,* Lippincott, 1974; *A Christmas Adventure* (illustrated by Ray Cruz), Holt, 1974; *Granny's Fish Story* (illustrated by Gahan Wilson), Parents Magazine Press, 1975.

Contributor to magazines, including *Harper's* and *Vogue.**

* * *

LAGNEAU-KESTELOOT, Lilyan
See KESTELOOT, Lilyan

* * *

LAIRD, Dugan 1920-

PERSONAL: Born July 6, 1920, in Rockwell City, Iowa; son of Joseph D. (a farmer) and Viola Dugan (Day) Laird.

Education: University of Northern Iowa, B.A., 1941; Northwestern University, M.A., 1948, Ph.D., 1952; also attended University of Wyoming and University of Minnesota. *Home:* 9 Willowick Dr., Decatur, Ga. 30038.

CAREER: Emporia State Teachers College, Emporia, Kan., instructor in speech and theatre, 1946-47; University of Minnesota, Minneapolis, instructor in public speaking, 1947-48; Northwestern University, Evanston, Ill., instructor in speech, 1948-51; United Air Lines, Chicago, Ill., instructor and training manager, 1952-70; writer, speaker, and consultant, 1970—. *Member:* American Society for Training and Development, National Society for Performance and Instruction. *Awards, honors:* Awards from American Society of Training and Development, 1971, 1976, for contributions to the training profession.

WRITINGS: (With J. R. Hayes) *Level-Headed Letters,* Hayden, 1964; *Business Writing Skills: A Workbook,* Addison-Wesley, 1970; *Training Methods for Skills Acquisition,* American Society for Training and Development and Agency for International Development, 1972; *A User's Look at the Audio-Visual World,* National Audio-Visual Association, 1973, revised edition, 1977; *Approaches to Training and Development,* Addison-Wesley, in press; *Writing for Results: Principles and Practice,* Addison-Wesley, in press.

SIDELIGHTS: Laird writes that he is "now concerned primarily with adult learning and the science of instruction." He has led conferences and workshops for training and development in Canada, England, Europe, Morocco, and India.

*   *   *

LAIRD, Eleanor Childs 1908-

PERSONAL: Born April 15, 1908, in Lebanon, Conn.; daughter of Harry Childs (a farmer) and Jane (Carver) Leonard; married Donald Anderson Laird (a psychologist and writer), April 18, 1940. *Education:* Brown University, A.B., 1928; University of North Carolina, A.B. in Library Science, 1932. *Politics:* Republican. *Religion:* Protestant. *Home:* 921 North Grant St., West Lafayette, Ind. 47906.

CAREER: Brown University Library, Providence, R.I., assistant to reference librarian, 1928-35; Rhode Island State Library Extension Service, Providence, organizer, 1935-36; Arlington (Va.) County Libraries, organizer and head librarian, 1937-39; writer in collaboration with husband, 1940-69; University of Dubuque, Dubuque, Iowa, adjunct research librarian, 1965-73. *Member:* American Library Association, League of Women Voters of Greater Lafayette (chairman of foreign policy committee, 1958-64). *Awards, honors:* L.H.D., University of Dubuque, 1971.

WRITINGS—All with husband, Donald A. Laird; published by McGraw, except as noted: *Psychology of Supervising the Working Woman,* 1942; *The Technique of Handling People,* 1943, revised edition, 1954; *The Technique of Building Personal Leadership,* 1944; *Techniques of Personal Analysis,* 1945; *The Technique of Getting Things Done,* 1947; *The Strategy of Handling Children: Questions-and-Answers on Parents' Problems,* Funk, 1949.

Sizing Up People, 1951; *Practical Business Psychology,* Gregg, 1951, 5th edition, published as *Psychology: Human Relations and Motivation,* 1975; *Increasing Personal Efficiency,* 4th edition, Harper, 1952 (husband was sole author of first edition); *Practical Sales Psychology,* 1952, 2nd edition, 1956; *The New Psychology for Leadership,* 1956; *The*

Techniques of Delegating, 1957; *Sound Ways to Sound Sleep,* 1959; *Tired Feelings and How to Master Them: A Practical Summary of Techniques for Home and Business,* 1960; *Techniques for Efficient Remembering,* 1960; *The Dynamics of Personal Efficiency,* Harper, 1961; *Be Active and Feel Better,* 1962; *How to Get Along with Automation,* 1964.

WORK IN PROGRESS: A reference series, tentatively entitled "500 Years of the March of Progress of Science and Technology."

AVOCATIONAL INTERESTS: World affairs, U.S. foreign policy, history, archaeology, and gardening.

*   *   *

LAKIN, Martin 1925-

PERSONAL: Born June 5, 1925, in Chicago, Ill.; son of Simon (a merchant) and Hannah (Raginsky) Lakin; married Musia Gingold (a psychologist), May 3, 1944; children: Neema Lakin Dainow, Michael. *Education:* Hebrew University, Jerusalem, A.B., 1950; University of Chicago, Ph.D., 1955. *Politics:* Democrat. *Religion:* Jewish. *Home:* 2709 McDowell Rd., Durham, N.C. 27705. *Office:* Department of Psychology, Duke University, Durham, N.C. 27706.

CAREER: Indiana University, South Bend, instructor, 1953-55; University of Illinois, Urbana, clinical instructor in psychiatry, 1956-58; Duke University, Durham, N.C., assistant professor, 1958-64, associate professor, 1964-69, professor of clinical psychology, 1969—. Research associate at Northwestern University, 1956-58; assistant chief of Veterans Administration Research Hospital (Chicago), 1956-58; fellow of Tavistock Institute, 1965-66; visiting professor at Haifa University, 1972-75. *Military service:* U.S. Army Air Forces, 1943-45.

MEMBER: International Society for the Study of Behavioral Development, American Psychological Association, Institute for European and Trans-National Training, North Carolina Psychological Association. *Awards, honors:* U.S. Public Health Service research fellowship, 1955-56; National Institutes of Health grant, 1964-69; grant from Administration on Aging, 1976-78.

WRITINGS: Interpersonal Encounter: Theory and Practice in Sensitivity Training, McGraw, 1972; *Experiential Groups: The Uses of Interpersonal Encounter, Therapeutic, and Sensitivity,* General Learning Press, 1972.

Contributor: W. G. Dyer, editor, *Modern Theory and Method in Group Training,* Von Nostrand, 1972; C. Cooper, editor, *Theories of Group Process,* Wiley, 1975; *The Intensive Group Experience,* Macmillan, 1976; M. A. Litterer, editor, *Management: Concept and Controversies,* Wiley, 1977. Contributor to journals in the social sciences.

WORK IN PROGRESS: Research on group processes among the aged and on therapeutic group interventions among the aged.

SIDELIGHTS: Lakin writes: "I am motivated to help people overcome feelings of alienation and helplessness in a world where they are in fact largely unable to do much about their determining circumstances."

*   *   *

LAMBERT, Mark 1942-

PERSONAL: Born January 9, 1942, in New York, N.Y.; son of Joseph (a gas station owner) and Blanche (Posner)

Lambert; married Ellen Zetzel (a writer and teacher), July 2, 1967. *Education:* Bard College, B.A., 1962; Yale University, M.A., 1963, Ph.D., 1971. *Home:* 65 Bay State Rd., Apt. 5, Boston, Mass. 02215.

CAREER: St. Augustine's College, Raleigh, N.C., teaching intern, 1964-65; Bard College, Annandale-on-Hudson, N.Y., instructor, 1967-68, assistant professor, 1968-72, associate professor of English, 1972—. *Member:* Modern Language Association of America.

WRITINGS: Malory: Style and Vision in "Le Morte d'Arthur," Yale University Press, 1975.

WORK IN PROGRESS: A book on Dickens and Victorian prose style; research on Chaucer's *Troilus e Criseyde* and on medieval literature in general.

SIDELIGHTS: Lambert told *CA:* "I am especially interested in the study of period style and the relation between period style and the individual artist's vision."

*   *   *

LAMBOT, Isobel 1926-
(Daniel Ingham, Meriel Rees, Mary Turner)

PERSONAL: Born July 21, 1926, in Birmingham, England; daughter of John and Phyllis Mary (Turner) Birch; married Maurice Edouard Lambot, December 19, 1959. *Education:* University of Liverpool, B.A., 1947; University of Birmingham, certificate, 1958. *Politics:* Conservative. *Religion:* Roman Catholic. *Home:* 14 Stafford Rd., Lichfield, Staffordshire WS13 7BZ, England. *Agent:* J. F. Gibson, P.O. Box 173, London SW3, England.

CAREER: Lewis's Ltd., Birmingham, England, training manager, 1955-58; Birmingham Education Committee, Birmingham, teacher, 1958-59; Lichfield School of Art, Lichfield, England, tutor in creative writing, 1973—. *Military service:* Women's Royal Air Force, 1950-55. *Member:* Crime Writers Association, International P.E.N., Writers Guild of Great Britain, Society of Authors.

WRITINGS—Novels; all published by R. Hale: *Taste of Murder,* 1966; *Deadly Return,* 1966; (under pseudonym Mary Turner) *Perilous Love,* 1966; *Dangerous Refuge,* 1966; *Shroud of Canvas,* 1967; *Danger Merchant,* 1968; *The Queen Dies First,* 1968; *Killer's Laughter,* 1968; *Let the Witness Die,* 1969; *Point of Death,* 1969; *Watcher on the Shore,* 1972; (under pseudonym Daniel Ingham) *Contract for Death,* 1972; *Come Back and Die,* 1972; *Grip of Fear,* 1974; (under pseudonym Mary Turner) *The Justice Hunt,* 1975; (under pseudonym Mary Turner) *So Bright a Lady,* 1977; *The Identity Trap,* 1978. Contributor to periodicals under own name and pseudonym Meriel Rees.

SIDELIGHTS: "I began writing in my early teens," Lambot told *CA,* "but never presented anything for publication until my middle thirties. I write crime fiction because I like reading it. I have recently made an excursion—two books—into historical fiction, which is interesting but not really my line, I think. I have written one humorous book but could not get it published, so that can't be my line either.

"My aim is to entertain, not to preach, but certain moral values underlie my work all the same. I prefer old-fashioned virtues, such as Crime Does Not Pay, while obviously in real life it does! I don't like the permissive society, and make sure my heroines get decently married at the end. If any of my characters leap into bed with each other, it is essential to the plot, and they usually regret it."

An avid traveller, Lambot has visited the Far East, Jamaica, Africa, and Europe.

LANDECK, Beatrice 1904-

PERSONAL: Born April 27, 1904, in New York, N.Y.; married in 1928; children: two. *Education:* Columbia University, B.Arch., 1926; Dalcroze School of Music, certificate, 1934. *Home:* 18 Stevens Lane, Westhampton Beach, N.Y. 11978.

CAREER: Little Red School House, New York, N.Y., music director, 1937-47; Mills College of Education, head of music department, 1948-59; author and lecturer, 1960—. Member of the National Music and Education Committee of Young Audiences, Inc., 1960—; consultant, *Book of Knowledge,* and Grolier Council Educational Research, 1968. *Member:* Music Educational National Conference, National Education Association, National Association of Jazz Education.

WRITINGS: (Editor) *Git On Board: Collection of Folk Songs,* Edward B. Marks Music Corp., 1944; (editor) *Songs to Grow On: A Collection of American Folk Songs for Children* (illustrated by David S. Martin), Edward B. Marks Music Corp., 1950; *Children and Music: An Informal Guide for Parents and Teachers,* Sloane, 1952; (editor) *More Songs to Grow On: A Collection of Folk Songs for Children* (illustrated by D. S. Martin), Morrow, 1954; *Music for Living,* Silver Burdett, 1956; *Time for Music: A Guide for Parents,* Public Affairs Committee (New York), 1958; *Echoes of Africa in Folk Songs of the Americas,* McKay, 1961; *Making Music Your Own,* Silver Burdett, 1964, revised edition, 1971; (editor with Elizabeth Crook) *Wake Up and Sing!: Folk Songs from America's Grass Roots* (illustrated by Bob Blansky), Morrow, 1969; *Learn to Read, Read to Learn: Poetry and Prose from Afro-Rooted Sources* (illustrated by Michael Heming), McKay, 1975.

SIDELIGHTS: The *San Francisco Chronicle*'s review of Beatrice Landeck's *Children and Music: An Informal Guide for Parents and Teachers* included, "Parents who hope to encourage a taste and liking for music in their children will find much sound advice in this book by Mrs. Landeck. And there is pertinent information on how parents and teachers may co-operate so the home and the school can provide the best that is musically possible for the children." *Saturday Review* added: "Her faith in the children's natural feeling for music in all its forms gives her book warmth and authority."

In the early 1950's, Landeck edited a collection of American folk songs for children entitled *Songs to Grow On.* The *Christian Science Monitor* commented: "This is an outstanding collection of genuine folk songs straight from the heart of yesteryear. Most of them cannot be found except in comprehensive collections like Carl Sandburg's *American Songbag* or John and Alan Lomax's *American Ballads and Folk Songs.* The arrangements are easy enough for a child to play."

In her most recent book, *Learn to Read/Read to Learn,* Landeck sought to enrich education by providing teachers with ethnic materials to use in reading instruction, and by suggesting new attitudes for them to internalize. Richard Davidson noted, "The ethnic materials she presents, derived as they are from folk cultures with a participatory rather than competitive ethos, answer the child's impulses to find a creative process which includes every member of the group. Thus, these materials are not only going to be 'relevant' and interesting, but they are going to encourage the students to generate (as opposed to learning by rote) responses to what they read, and encourage students to help one another find a form for those responses."

Landeck told *CA:* "Throughout the years, I have become

ever more convinced of the major importance of folklore in children's lives. Experiencing the past of one's own forebears through the lore they have unconsciously created as they worked and played not only gives children security and innate pride in their roots but somehow frees the mind from distracting thoughts and opens it to learning. If only teachers who work with underprivileged groups could become aware of the richness of the heritage of these materially poor youngsters, they would draw on the children's ethnic culture as a source for teaching materials, making it a lot easier for themselves as well as for their students.''

BIOGRAPHICAL/CRITICAL SOURCES: Christian Science Monitor, October 7, 1950; *San Francisco Chronicle,* July 20, 1952; *Saturday Review,* November 15, 1952; *The Reading Teacher,* January, 1977.

*   *   *

LANGER, William L(eonard)   1896-1977

March 16, 1896—December 26, 1977; American historian specializing in the fields of European diplomacy and Middle Eastern history. Langer was also professor emeritus in history at Harvard University where he held the chair of Coolidge Professor of History from 1936 until 1964. He held several government positions, including a post with the Central Intelligence Agency, and membership in the President's Foreign Intelligence Advisory Board. Langer was best known for his policy of "psycho-history." He advised historians to combine their efforts with those of psychologists and psychoanalysts to understand and explain events of history and historical characters. Langer published more than twelve books on the subjects of European diplomacy and Middle Eastern history. He died in Boston, Mass. Obituaries: *New York Times,* December 27, 1977; *Washington Post,* December 28, 1977. (See index for *CA* sketch)

*   *   *

LANGLEY, Roger   1930-
(Rex Power)

PERSONAL: Born August 22, 1930, in Amsterdam, N.Y.; son of Walter Bernard (a farmer) and Anna Mae (a social worker and teacher; maiden name, McCaffrey) Langley; married Norma Sekinger (a teacher); children: David, Jennifer, Michael. *Education:* Syracuse University, A.B., 1958, M.A., 1965. *Politics:* Democrat. *Religion:* Catholic. *Home:* 625 Smallwood Rd., Rockville, Md. 20850. *Office:* 758 National Press Bldg., Washington, D.C. 20045.

CAREER: Newspaper reporter for New York newspapers, *Syracuse Post-Standard, Syracuse Herald-Journal,* and *Ithaca Journal,* 1959-68; *National Enquirer,* Lantana, Fla. assistant editor, 1968-74; World News Corporation, New York, N.Y., Washington Bureau Chief, 1974—. *Military service:* U.S. Navy, 1950-54. *Member:* National Press Club, Society of Professional Journalists, Toastmasters Hall of Fame. *Awards, honors:* AP Enterprise Award and Newspaper Fund Fellowship.

WRITINGS: (With Richard C. Levy) *Wife Beating: The Silent Crisis,* Dutton, 1977; (under pseudonym Rex Power) *How to Beat Police Radar,* Arco, 1977. Contributor to *New York, Time, Reader's Digest, Writer, Woman Today,* and *Cosmopolitan.*

WORK IN PROGRESS: Working on a novel about Washington, D.C.

SIDELIGHTS: "My friends say I'm funny but that may say more about them than me," Langley told *CA,* adding: ''I

hate writing because it's hard work and I'm constantly exposed to rejection but I keep at it because it's what I do best.''

*   *   *

LANGSTAFF, Nancy   1925-

PERSONAL: Born May 3, 1925, in Brooklyn, N.Y.; daughter of John (a businessman) and Elinor (a pianist; maiden name, Graydon) Woodbridge; married John Langstaff (a writer and teacher), April 3, 1948; children: John Elliot, Peter Gary, Deborah Graydon. *Education:* Vassar College, B.A., 1945; attended Art Students League of New York and Cranbrook Academy of Art, 1946-47; Lesley College, M.A., 1974. *Home:* 9 Burlington St., Lexington, Mass. 02173. *Office:* Cambridge Friends School, Cadbury St., Cambridge, Mass. 02138.

CAREER: Music teacher at an elementary independent school in McLean, Va., 1955-66; studied and traveled abroad, 1966-69; Cambridge Friends School, Cambridge, Mass., elementary school teacher, 1969—. Music teacher to President John F. Kennedy's children at the White House, 1963, at Wheelock College and Lesley College, 1974-78.

WRITINGS: A Tiny Baby for You (juvenile), Harcourt, 1956; (with husband, John Langstaff) *Jim Along Josie* (adult), Harcourt, 1970; *Teaching in an Open Classroom,* National Association of Independent Schools, 1975. Contributor to *Independent Schools Bulletin.*

WORK IN PROGRESS: "A study together with Adelaide Sproul of the many learning possibilities inherent in the in-depth exploration of a media such as clay.''

SIDELIGHTS: Langstaff told *CA:* "An absorption that is evidenced in all my work concerns the exciting potentials for learning that children evidence when encouraged to use their own initiative, responsibility and creativity.''

*   *   *

LANGWORTH, Richard M(ichael)   1941-

PERSONAL: Born July 7, 1941, in Rye, N.Y.; son of Michael P. (a florist) and Harriet H. (a florist) Langworth; married Barbara Francis (a microbiologist), February 5, 1966. *Education:* Wagner College, B.A., 1963. *Home:* 20 Hart Ave., Hopewell, N.J. 08525. *Office:* Dragonwyck Publishing Ltd., Hopewell, N.J. 08525.

CAREER: Department of Health, Harrisburg, Pa., project director, 1967-70; *Automobile Quarterly,* senior and associate editor in New York, N.Y., 1970-75; Dragonwyck Publishing Ltd., Hopewell, N.J., president, 1975—. Founder of Vintage Triumph Register, 1974. Host of Packard Club's Macauley tour to England, 1977. *Military service:* U.S. Coast Guard, 1964-67; became lieutenant.

MEMBER: International Motor Press Association, American Society of Journalists and Authors, Guild of Motoring Writers, Society of Automotive Historians, Corvair Society of America (founder, 1969), Milestone Car Society (founder, 1971). *Awards, honors:* McKean trophy from Antique Automobile Club of America and Cugnot Award from Society of Automotive Historians, both 1975, for *Kaiser-Frazer: Last Onslaught on Detroit.*

WRITINGS: (Editor) *The World of Cars,* Dutton, 1971; (co-author with Beverly Rae Kimes) *Oldsmobile: The First Seventy-Five Years,* Automobile Quarterly, 1972; *Fifty Years of Triumph,* British Leyland, 1973; *Fiat and Lancia History,* Fiat of America, 1975; *Kaiser-Frazer: Last Ons-*

laught on Detroit, Dutton, 1975; *The Postwar Chrysler,* Motorbook, 1976; *The Postwar Hudson,* Motorbook, 1977; *The Postwar Studebaker,* Motorbook, 1978; (co-author with Graham Robson) *Triumph Cars, a History,* Motor Racing Publishers, 1978; (editor) Pat Chappell, *The Hot One: Chevrolet 1955-57,* Dragonwyck Publishing, 1978.

Author of "On Tour," a column in *Car and Parts,* 1971—. Contributor to automobile and auto history magazines in the United States, England, and Germany. Publisher of *Packard Cormorant, Vintage Triumph,* and *Triumph Sports Owners Association Newsletter.* Editor and feature editor of *Car Classics,* 1975—.

WORK IN PROGRESS: Three automotive books under Dragonwyck Publishing label; encyclopedia of postwar American cars.

SIDELIGHTS: Langworth told *CA:* "Now that old cars are fashionable, there's a growing need for accurate, carefully researched information on their history or worth as investments, to replace the hastily contrived, superficial articles for general audiences of the past. I am interested in providing some, having spent ten years researching, interviewing and writing in this specialized field. Future activities include my own magazine and additional books under the Dragonwyck label."

* * *

LANNUIER, Dorothy
See HOHENBERG, Dorothy Lannuier

* * *

LA NOUE, George R(ichard) 1937-

PERSONAL: Born September 21, 1937, in Hammond, Ind.; son of George (in industrial relations) and Lois (an artist; maiden name, Lish) La Noue; married Patricia Rudy (a teacher), October 3, 1969; children: George Jefferson, Robert James Revere. *Education:* Hanover College, B.A. (magna cum laude), 1959; Yale University, M.A., 1961, Ph.D., 1966; also attended American University. *Home:* 2433 Pickwick Rd., Baltimore, Md. 21207. *Office:* Department of Political Science, University of Maryland—Baltimore County, 5401 Wilkens Ave., Baltimore, Md. 21228.

CAREER: Columbia University, Teachers College, New York, N.Y., instructor, 1964-66, assistant professor, 1966-68, associate professor of politics and education, 1968-72; University of Maryland—Baltimore County, professor of political science, 1972—, chairman of department, 1975—. Intern with Indiana State Department of Public Welfare, summer, 1960; visiting associate professor at University of Chicago, summer, 1969. Member of board of governors of Center for Research and Education in American Liberties, 1969-70. Member of Public Association Commission on New York City School Governance, 1971; assistant to the executive director of U.S. Equal Employment Opportunity Commission, 1972-73, educational policy planner, 1973-76, chairman of Task Force on Higher Education, 1974-75; member of Maryland State Advisory Commission on Public School Athletics, 1975; trial expert for U.S. Department of Labor, 1976-77. Has lectured at schools all over the United States and testified before the U.S. Senate and House of Representatives.

MEMBER: American Political Science Association, American Educational Research Association (chairman of politics of education group, 1973-75), Society for Values in Higher Education, National Municipal League, American Civil Liberties Union (member of local boards of directors, 1966-67, 1968—). *Awards, honors:* Woodrow Wilson fellowship, 1959; grants from Brookings Institution, 1964-65, National Conference of Christians and Jews, 1965-66, World Population Council, 1966-67, Center for Urban Education, 1967-69, American Civil Liberties Union, 1968-70, and Horace Mann-Lincoln Institute, 1969-71; public administration fellowship from National Association of School Public Affairs and Administration, 1972-73.

WRITINGS: (Editor and contributor) *Educational Vouchers: Concepts and Controversies,* Teachers College Press, 1972; (with Bruce Smith) *The Politics of School Decentralization,* Heath, 1973.

Contributor: Donald Giannella, editor, *Religion and the Public Order,* University of Chicago Press, Volume II, 1965, Volume III, 1966; Theodore Sizer, editor, *Religion and Public Education,* Houghton, 1967; Robert Maidment and Emanuel Hurwitz, editors, *Criticism, Conflict, and Change: Readings in American Education,* Dodd, 1970; James Mecklenberger and Richard W. Hastrop, editors, *Educational Vouchers: From Theory to Alum Rock,* E.T.C. Publications, 1972; Hans Spiegel, editor, *Citizen Participation in Urban Development: Decentralization,* Volume III, N.T.C. Learning Resources Corp., 1973; John Martin Rich, editor, *Radical and Innovative Ideas in Education,* Allyn & Bacon, 1974. Contributor to *Encyclopedia of Education.* Contributor of about forty articles and reviews to academic journals. Co-editor of *American Behavioral Scientist,* November, 1971; member of editorial board of *Education and Urban Society,* 1971-73.

WORK IN PROGRESS: Work on government regulation of education and the future of civil liberties.

SIDELIGHTS: La Noue told *CA:* "I believe my contribution to the subject of federal regulations of education has been to devise mechanisms, particularly in the area of employment discrimination, that will remedy the problem without undermining the necessary autonomy of the University. Toward that end, I have developed new grievance procedures and litigation strategies when voluntary compliance fails.

"My next research will explore the future of civil liberties if the future is an era of scarcity. My hypothesis is that American Civil liberties are dependent on 18th Century concepts of affluence, individualism and spaciousness. As these characteristics of American life disappear, our civil liberties will have to be redefined or they will not survive."

* * *

LANSING, Gerrit (Yates) 1928-

PERSONAL: Born February 25, 1928, in Albany, N.Y. *Education:* Earned B.A. from Harvard University, and M.A. from Columbia University. *Residence:* Gloucester, Mass. *Office:* c/o Matter Books, 475 Washington St., Gloucester, Mass. 01930.

CAREER: Columbia University Press, New York City, editorial assistant, 1955-60. Writer.

WRITINGS: The Heavenly Tree Grows Downward (poetry), Matter Books, 1966. Work represented in many anthologies, including *A Controversy of Poets,* Doubleday, 1965, and *Poems Now,* Kulchur Press, 1966. Contributor of poems to *Tomorrow, Caterpillar,* and *Io.* Editor, *SET* (poetry magazine).

SIDELIGHTS: On the themes and subjects of his poetry,

Gerrit Lansing commented: "I favor love, the wedding of the natural and supernatural, and visible things."

Lansing has traveled extensively in the United States and Europe.*

* * *

LAPEZA, David (Henry) 1950-

PERSONAL: Born March 28, 1950, in Birdgeport, Conn.; son of Henry Matthew (a financial executive and certified public accountant) and Ursula Elizabeth (Kroger) Lapeza. *Education:* University of Michigan, A.B., 1972, A.M., 1974, Ph.D. candidate, 1976—. *Home:* 3629 Deerfield Pl., Ann Arbor, Mich. 48104.

CAREER: Ardis Press, Ann Arbor, Mich., copy editor, 1973-75; free-lance translator of Russian and French literature, 1973—; free-lance editor of translations of critical and historical works, 1975—. *Member:* Phi Beta Kappa. *Awards, honors:* National Defense Foreign Language (NDFL) fellowships, 1972-73, 1973-74, 1974-75, and 1975-76; Fulbright-Hays fellowship for overseas research, Academy of Sciences of the U.S.S.R., Leningrad, and Helsinki University Library, Helsinki, Finland, 1976-77; International Research and Exchanges Board (IREX) graduate student/young faculty exchange between U.S. and U.S.S.R., 1976-77; Horace H. Rackham fellowship, University of Michigan, 1977-78.

WRITINGS: (Translator with Arline Boyer) Carl R. Proffer, editor, *The Unpublished Dostoevsky,* Volume III: *Diaries and Notebooks, 1876-81* (Lapeza was not associated with earlier volumes), Ardis Press, 1976; (editor and translator) Nikolai Gumilev, *On Russian Poetry,* Ardis Press, 1977; (translator) Vladimir Voinovich, *The Ivankiad,* Farrar, Straus, 1977.

Translations represented in anthologies, *Ardis Anthology of Recent Russian Literature,* edited by C. R. Proffer and Ellendea Proffer, Ardis Press, 1975; and *Modern Russian Poets on Poetry,* edited by C. R. Proffer, Ardis Press, 1976. Contributor of translations to *Russian Literary Triquarterly* and *New York Times Magazine.* Editor, *Chrysallis* (art and literary magazine), 1970-72.

WORK IN PROGRESS: A doctoral dissertation, tentatively entitled, "Literary Parody in the Russian Romantic Period."

SIDELIGHTS: David Lapeza wrote *CA:* "In Russia, literary translation is considered a high art. The greatest Russian poets have tried their hands at verse translations of Shakespeare, Goethe, or Villon, and translators of Faulkner or Joyce win praise and prestige as contributors to the Russian literary culture.

"Americans, though just as isolated as the Russians in the vastness of their own unilingualism, tend to view translation of literary works, when they bother to consider it at all, as a task only slightly less dull than proof-reading, and requiring considerably less specific training. The assumption seems to be that translation is a mechanical process (haven't they got machines to do that yet?) and any skill involved is somehow connected with the mysterious process of language acquisition itself (can't anyone who knows Russian translate it?). This vague disdain for translation as an art is aggravated by the haphazard treatment translations receive at the hands of journalists, who choose reviewers unable to read the original texts, much less judge the translations and even omit the translator's name from the bibliographycal entries at the head of the review.

"A translator must be a writer with a flair for pastiche or even parody, a linguist with a sense of style and an editor with a specialist's knowledge of a foreign literary tradition. Besides these minimum qualifications, a translator should love detective work (finding that rare word or rarer English equivalent) and should delight in puzzles, for a long translation resembles a vast crossword with Questions ranging from easy to impossible."

Lapeza is proficient in Russian, Serbo-Croatian, and French; he has a reading knowledge of Latin, Greek, Old Church Slavic, Polish, and Finnish.

AVOCATIONAL INTERESTS: "I collect American and British antiques, play clarinet and recorder in chamber ensembles, swim, lift weights."

* * *

LARDNER, George, Jr. 1934-

PERSONAL: Born August 10, 1934, in New York, N.Y.; son of George E. (a journalist) and Rosetta (a teacher; maiden name, Russo) Lardner; married Rosemary Schalk, July 6, 1957; children: Helen, Edmund, Richard, Charles, Kristin. *Education:* Marquette University, A.B. (summa cum laude), 1956, M.A., 1962. *Religion:* Roman Catholic. *Home:* 5604 32nd St. N.W., Washington, D.C. 20015. *Office:* 1150 15th St. N.W., Washington, D.C. 20071.

CAREER/WRITINGS: Bell Syndicate, New York, N.Y., part-time copy editor, summers, 1951-54; Williston Engraving, Milwaukee, Wis., photoengraving apprentice, 1956; *Milwaukee Sentinel,* Milwaukee, part-time copyboy, 1956-57; *Worcester Telegram,* Worcester, Mass., reporter, 1957-59; *Miami Herald,* Miami, Fla., reporter, 1959-63; *Washington Post,* Washington, D.C., reporter, 1963—. Notable assignments include coverage of the 1964 Alaska earthquake, the Lemuel Penn murder by the Ku Klux Klan, the "Garrison investigation" of the John F. Kennedy assassination, the Robert F. Kennedy assassination and Sirhan trial, the Wallace campaigns, Chappaquiddick, the Jock Yablonski murder, the Yuba City murders, Apollo 12, the Watergate coverup trial, and Congress. Originator and writer of the "Potomac Watch" column in *Washington Post,* 1965-66; free-lance contributor to *Esquire, Reader's Digest, New Republic, True, Nation, Progressive,* and *Washingtonian. Member:* American Newspaper Guild, Sigma Delta Chi, Alpha Sigma Nu. *Awards, honors:* Marquette University byline award, 1967; American Bar Association certificate of merit, 1977.

SIDELIGHTS: Lardner told *CA:* "In this business, the most important thing to fight against is a ready acceptance, even an expectation, of untruthfulness on the part of those we deal with. Honesty is vital in what we write and is what we should demand of the public figures we report about. I would rather suffer a bumbling politician than a dishonest one. Too many of us let our sources get away with fibs, anonymous distortions and worse. That is the very antithesis of communication and that is the business we are in." Lardner described himself as "Financially incompetent. Habitually indignant. Incapable of tooting own horn."

* * *

LARGO, Michael 1950-

PERSONAL: Born May 5, 1950, in Staten Island, N.Y.; married Rosemarie Fahey (a music teacher), October 19, 1973; children: Jared. *Education:* Brooklyn College of the City University of New York, B.A., 1975. *Home and office:* 58 St. Marks Pl., New York, N.Y. 10003.

CAREER: Writer, 1976—. *Awards, honors:* Whiteside Poetry Award from Brooklyn College, 1975, for best poems.

WRITINGS: Nails in Soft Wood (poetry), Pickadilly Press, 1976; *Southern Comfort* (novel), New Earth Books, 1977. Contributor to *New York Poetry* and *New Earth Review.*

WORK IN PROGRESS: Straw Bridge, a novel.

SIDELIGHTS: Largo writes: "I worked as a sailor for three years, watched the ocean break on the bunker, heard the gulls enough times to make my novel alive. I also worked as a guide for High Rock Conservation Center. I tattooed a pine tree to my forearm when I was seventeen to make sure I'd never forget my interest in the outdoors. I knew things would change.

"My work deals with the struggle. America sees itself turning, half tumbling. I crawl inside the voices and listen not only to the words but to the rust on the tractors and the wood gathered slightly around an old board. I try to capture, sometimes with a clear photo, and yet also attempt to achieve the abstract through total realism. Two methods. I believe fiction can include both the story and the idea. The idea comes through the senses and not the mind."

* * *

LARSEN, David C(harles) 1944-

PERSONAL: Born October 5, 1944, in St. Paul, Minn.; son of Christian A. (an insurance agent) and Vera Lou (Bowen) Larsen; married Martha Ann Turbett (a secretary), December 2, 1976. *Education:* Wisconsin State University, B.S.Ed., 1970; Illinois State University, M.A., 1971; University of Nebraska, Ph.D., 1974. *Home:* 112221 Hutchins Court, Chaska, Minn. 55318. *Office:* Wilson Learning Corp., 6950 Washington Ave. S., Eden Prairie, Minn. 55343.

CAREER: Illinois State University, Normal, director of research, 1974-76; Wilson Learning Corp., Eden Prairie, Minn., product researcher, 1976—. Consultant, County Companies Insurance Company, 1974-76.

WRITINGS: (With C. Konsky) *Interpersonal Communication,* Kendall/Hunt, 1975.

* * *

LA SALLE, Victor
See FANTHORPE, R(obert) Lionel

* * *

LASCH, Christopher 1932-

PERSONAL: Born June 1, 1932, in Omaha, Neb.; son of Robert (a journalist) and Zora (a professor; maiden name, Schaupp) Lasch; married Nell Commager (a potter), June 30, 1956; children: Robert, Elisabeth, Catherine, Christopher. *Education:* Harvard University, B.A., 1954; Columbia University, M.A., 1955, Ph.D., 1961. *Home:* 305 Genesee St., Avon, N.Y. 14414. *Office:* Department of History, University of Rochester, Rochester, N.Y. 14414.

CAREER: Williams College, Williamstown, Mass., instructor in history, 1957-59; Roosevelt University, Chicago, Ill., assistant professor of history, 1960-61; University of Iowa, Iowa City, assistant professor, 1961-63, associate professor, 1965-66, professor of history, 1965-66; Northwestern University, Evanston, Ill., professor of history, 1966-70; University of Rochester, Rochester, N.Y., professor of history, 1970—. *Awards, honors:* D.H.L. from Bard College, 1977.

WRITINGS: The American Liberals and the Russian Rev-

olution, Columbia University Press, 1962; *The New Radicalism in America, 1889-1963: The Intellectual as a Social Type,* Knopf, 1965; *The Agony of the American Left* (essays), Knopf, 1969; *The World of Nations,* Knopf, 1973, published as *World of Nations: Reflections on American History, Politics, and Culture,* Random House, 1974; *Haven in a Heartless World: The Family Besieged,* Basic Books, 1977; *The New Narcissus,* Norton, in press.

WORK IN PROGRESS: Historical Origins of the New Paternalism.

BIOGRAPHICAL/CRITICAL SOURCES: New York Times, November 28, 1977.

* * *

LASLETT, Peter 1915-
(Thomas Russell)

PERSONAL: Born in 1915, in Bedford, England; son of Russell and Eveline (Alden) Laslett; married Janet Clark; children: George Robert. *Education:* Cambridge University, M.A., 1940. *Politics:* Labour. *Agent:* Curtis Brown Ltd., 13 King St., Covent Garden, London W.C.2, England. *Office:* Trinity College, Cambridge University, Cambridge, England.

CAREER: British Broadcasting Corp., London, England, producer, 1947-55; Cambridge University, Trinity College, Cambridge, England, reader in politics and history of social structures, 1960—. *Military service:* Royal Navy, 1940-46.

WRITINGS: (Editor) *The Physical Basis of Mind: A Series of Broadcast Talks,* Blackwell, 1950; (editor) *Philosophy, Politics, and Society: A Collection,* Macmillan, 1956, revised and enlarged edition, Barnes & Noble, Volume I, 1963, Volume II (with W. G. Runciman), 1962, Volume III (with Runciman), 1967, Volume IV (with Runciman and Quentin Skinner), 1972, Volume V (with James Fishkin), 1978; (editor and author of introduction) John Locke, *Two Treatises of Government: A Critical Edition with an Introduction and Apparatus Criticus,* Cambridge University Press, 1960, 2nd edition, New American Library, 1965; *The World We Have Lost,* Methuen, 1965, 2nd edition, 1971, Scribner, 1966, 2nd edition, 1973; (editor) Locke, *The Library of John Locke,* Oxford University Press, 1965, 2nd edition, Clarendon Press, 1971; (editor) *Anglo-American Conference on the Mechanization of Library Services, Brasenose College, Oxford University, 1966,* Mansell, 1967; (editor with Richard Wall, and author of introduction) *Household and Family in Past Time: Comparative Studies in the Size and Structure of Domestic Group over the Last Three Centuries in England, France, Serbia, Japan, and Colonial North America, with Further Materials from Western Europe,* Cambridge University Press, 1972; *Family Life and Illicit Love in Earlier Generations,* Cambridge University Press, 1977.

WORK IN PROGRESS: Bastardy and Its Comparative History, publication by Arnold expected in 1979; *The Statistical Imagination and the Historical Sociologist,* tentative title, for Academic Press.

SIDELIGHTS: Laslett also has a phonotape, "Historical Demography, 1450-1800," B.F.A. Educational Media, 1972.

BIOGRAPHICAL/CRITICAL SOURCES: L'Express, October 6, 1969.

* * *

LATHAM, Joyce 1943-

PERSONAL: Born April 19, 1943, in Lexington, Ky.;

daughter of Henry Cooper (a restaurant manager) and Lucy (a restaurant manager; maiden name, Duncan) Latham. *Education:* University of Kentucky, B.A., 1967. *Politics:* Liberal. *Religion:* None. *Home and office:* 3900 16th St. N.W., #330, Washington, D.C. 20011.

CAREER: U.S. Department of Housing & Urban Development, Washington, D.C., program assistant in publications section of Equal Opportunity Division, 1968-72; free-lance journalist, 1972—. Editor for U.S. Department of Justice, National Trust For Historic Preservation, two Ralph Nader groups, and others. *Member:* Washington Independent Writers, Writers Center of Washington. *Awards, honors:* Award from U.S. Department of Housing & Urban Development, 1972, for community volunteer work.

WRITINGS: Runaway Youth in the Washington Area, Metropolitan Washington Council of Governments, 1974; (editor) David F. Bergwall, Philip N. Reeves, and Nina B. Woodside, *Introduction to Health Planning,* Information Resources Press, revised edition (Latham was not associated with 1st edition), in press. Contributor to magazines, including *Encore, Historic Preservation, Freedomways,* and *Journal of Popular Culture.* Contributing editor of *Wilson Quarterly.*

WORK IN PROGRESS: A novel; research on America's runaway youths.

SIDELIGHTS: Joyce Latham writes that her "major vocational interests are criminal justice (especially youth problems), civil/minority/women's rights, urban problems, psychology, health, aging, American history and historic preservation, environment-ecology, and media." Her favorite aspect of the work is interviewing and travel. In 1970, she spent a short time on an Indian reservation in South Dakota, working on a filmstrip.

AVOCATIONAL INTERESTS: Photography, films, theater, twentieth-century novels, sports (horseback riding, hiking, racquet games), automobile mechanics.

* * *

LATHROP, Dorothy P(ulis) 1891-

PERSONAL: Born April 16, 1891, in Albany, N.Y.; daughter of Cyrus Clark (a businessman) and I. (a painter; maiden name, Pulis) Lathrop. *Education:* Graduated from Columbia University; further study at Pennsylvania Academy of Fine Arts and Art Students League. *Residence:* Falls Village, Conn.

CAREER: Author and illustrator of children's books. Has also worked as a high school teacher. *Member:* National Association of Women Painters and Sculptors. *Awards, honors:* Co-winner of Newbery Medal, 1930, for *Hitty;* Caldecott Medal, 1938, for *Animals of the Bible;* Eyre Medal from the Pennsylvania Academy of Fine Arts, 1941; Library of Congress prize, 1946.

WRITINGS—All self-illustrated; all published by Macmillan: *The Fairy Circus,* 1931; *Who Goes There?,* 1935, reprinted, 1963; *Bouncing Betsy,* 1936, reprinted 1964; *Hide and Go Seek,* 1938; *Presents for Lupe,* 1940; *The Colt from Moon Mountain,* 1941; *Puppies for Keeps,* 1943; *The Skittle-Skattle Monkey,* 1945; *Let Them Live,* 1951, reprinted 1966; *Puffy and the Seven-Leaf Clover,* 1954; *The Littlest Mouse,* 1955; *Follow the Brook,* 1960; *The Dog in the Tapestry Garden,* 1962.

Other writings: *The Little White Goat,* Macmillan, 1933; *The Lost Merry-Go-Round,* Macmillan, 1934; *The Snail Who Ran,* F. A. Stokes, 1934; *An Angel in the Woods,* Macmillan, 1947.

Illustrator: Walter de la Mare, *Three Mulla-Mulgars,* Knopf, 1919; William Henry Hudson, *A Little Boy Lost,* Knopf, 1920; de la Mare, *Down-Adown-Derry,* Constable, 1922; de la Mare, *Crossings,* Knopf, 1923; Hilda Conkling, *Silverhorn,* F. A. Stokes, 1924; George MacDonald, *Light Princess,* Macmillan, 1926; Jean Ingelow, *Mopsa the Fairy,* Harper, 1927; MacDonald, *Princess and Curdie,* Macmillan, 1927; Rachel Field, *Hitty,* Macmillan, 1929, reprinted 1968; Sara Teasdale, *Stars Tonight,* Macmillan, 1930; Nathaniel Hawthorne, *Snow Image,* Macmillan, 1930; W. de la Mare, *Dutch Cheese,* Knopf, 1931; Caroline Dale Snedeker, *Forgotten Daughter,* Doubleday, 1933; Helen D. Fish, *Animals of the Bible,* F. A. Stokes, 1937, reprinted, Lippincot, 1969; Sant Ram Mandal, *Happy Flute,* F. A. Stokes, 1937; Hans Christian Andersen, *Little Mermaid,* Macmillan, 1939; W. de la Mare, *Bells and Grass,* Viking, 1942; de la Mare, *Mr. Bumps and His Monkey,* Winston, 1942.*

* * *

LATUKEFU, Sione 1927-

PERSONAL: Born April 16, 1927, in Kolovai, Tonga; married Ruth Annette; children: Lotte M. V., Alopi S. *Education:* Queensland University, B.A., 1957, diploma in education, 1958, B.Ed., 1961; Australian National University, M.A.Q., 1962, Ph.D., 1967. *Religion:* United Church. *Office:* Department of History, University of Papua New Guinea, Port Moresby, Papua New Guinea.

CAREER: University of Papua New Guinea, Port Moresby, associate professor of history, and acting head of department, 1968, 1972. Executive officer of Te Rangi Hiroa Fund, 1969—. International visitor to U.S. State Department Bureau of Educational and Cultural Affairs, 1975. Member of United Church board of ministerial studies, 1974-76.

MEMBER: Papua New Guinea Society (president, 1970-71), Pacific Islands Association (president, 1975-76), Rugby Union Club (at University of Papua New Guinea; patron, 1974, 1976). *Awards, honors:* Scholarships from Methodist Overseas Missions of Australasia, 1956-58, and Commonwealth of Australia, 1962-63; research grant from Myer Foundation, 1974-75.

WRITINGS: (Contributor) J. W. Davidson and D. Scarr, editors, *Pacific Island Portraits,* Australian National University Press, 1970; (contributor) *Source Materials Related to Research in the Pacific Area,* Australian Government Publishing Service, 1973; *Church and State in Tonga,* University Press of Hawaii, 1974; *The Tongan Constitution: A Brief History to Celebrate Its Centenary,* Tonga Traditions Committee, 1975; (contributor) Noel Rutherford, editor, *History of the Friendly Islands,* Oxford University Press, 1976; (contributor) J. Boutilier, D. Hughes, and S. W. Tiffany, editors, *Mission, Church, and Sect in Oceania,* University Press of Hawaii, 1976. Contributor to history and Pacific studies journals.

WORK IN PROGRESS: Missionary Triumph and Defeat: The Case of the Roreinang Methodist Mission Station Near Kieta, Bougainville; "Life Histories and Oral Testimonies: The Case of Pacific Islands Missionaries in Papua New Guinea," to be included in *Theory and Practice of Oral History in Melanesia.*

* * *

LAWLESS, Gary 1951-

PERSONAL: Born April 30, 1951, in Belfast, Me.; son of Richard Alexander (a policeman) and Ruth (a sales clerk;

maiden name, Dow) Lawless. *Education:* Colby College, B.A., 1973. *Politics:* "Bioregional." *Religion:* "Animistic shamanism." *Residence:* South Harpswell, Me. *Office address:* Blackberry, P.O. Box 186, Brunswick, Me. 04011.

CAREER: Bookland, Brunswick, Me., assistant manager, 1973—. Has worked as lobsterman and lifeguard. Editor and publisher for Blackberry.

WRITINGS: Full Flower Moon (poetry), Blackberry, 1976; *Wintering* (poetry), Salt Works Press, 1976; *Two Owls* (poetry), White Pine Press, 1976; *Dark Moon/White Pine,* Great Raven Press, 1977; (editor) *Gulf of Maine Reader, Number One,* Blackberry, 1977.

WORK IN PROGRESS: Editing *Gulf of Maine Reader, Number Two;* research for a book about the islands of the Gulf of Maine.

SIDELIGHTS: Lawless writes: "I am interested in myth, stories, folktales, songs, and poems native to a particular place, especially Gulf of Maine coastal areas. I first became interested while lobstering during summers while in college. Then I spent six months living with poet Gary Snyder in California, and returned to work in my home area, with new ways of seeing gained from my time in California. The work goes on—slowly learning cycles, rhythms, local wisdom, and traditions."

* * *

LAWRENCE, Berta

PERSONAL: Born in North Marston, England; daughter of Henry James (a farmer) and Mary Anne (Price) Buckingham; married John F. Lawrence; children: John Christopher, Suzette Catherine Lawrence West. *Education:* University of London, B.A. (first class honors), 1927; University of Reading, diploma in education, 1928. *Home:* 17 Wembdon Hill, Bridgwater, Somerset, England.

CAREER: University of Clermont, Ferrand, France, lecturer in English, 1928-30; writer, 1943—. Has also worked as a teacher in grammar schools in England and France. *Member:* International P.E.N., Society of Authors, West Country Writers Association (committee member).

WRITINGS: A Somerset Journal, Westaway Books, 1951; *Quantock Country,* Westaway Books, 1952; *The Bond of Green Withy* (Country Book Club selection), T. Werner Laurie, 1954; *The Nightingale in the Branches,* T. Warner Laurie, 1955; *Coleridge and Wordsworth in Somerset,* David & Charles, 1970; *Somerset Legends,* David & Charles, 1973; *Discovering the Quantreks,* Shire Books, 1975. Author of children's stories for British Broadcasting Corp. (BBC) Television, and for radio. Contributor of articles, stories, and poems to magazines, including *Child Education, Good Housekeeping, Lady, Countryman,* and *Exmoor Review,* and to newspapers.

WORK IN PROGRESS: Editing *A Somerset Anthology;* research on Coleridge, Wordsworth, and Southey in the West Country of England.

SIDELIGHTS: Lawrence told *CA:* "My writing is not devoted entirely to the West Country: short stories are set in other places. It is, however, the region I know best and am most attached to. I aim at portraying its landscape and people with fidelity and without sentimentality, and at revealing to readers its special character and beauty that are inevitably changing and in many instances threatened with extinction.

"The work and literary fame of the following writers extend far beyond the boundaries of the English West Country.

They are, however, West Country writers as much of their work interprets West Country history and landscape from divergent view-points. I read the following with pleasure and admiration. The histories, autobiography, biography, and poetry of A. L. Rouse, the poetry and history of Robin Hoohill, the poetic dramatic work of Christopher Fry, and the work of the late Henry Williamson that so beautifully illumines the West Country scene."

* * *

LAWRENCE, David, Jr. 1942-

PERSONAL: Born March 5, 1942, in New York, N.Y.; son of David (a newspaperman) and Nancy (Bissell) Lawrence; married Roberta Fleischman, December 21, 1963; children: David III, Jennifer Beth. *Education:* University of Florida, B.S., 1963. *Home:* 800 Edgehill Rd., Charlotte, N.C. 28207. *Office:* 600 S. Tryon St., Charlotte, N.C. 28201.

CAREER/WRITINGS: St. Petersburg Times, St. Petersburg, Fla., news editor, 1963-67; *Washington Post,* Washington, D.C., news editor, 1967-69; *Palm Beach Post,* West Palm Beach, Fla., managing editor, 1971-75; *Charlotte Observer,* Charlotte, N.C., executive editor, 1975-76, editor 1976—.

* * *

LAWS, Priscilla W(atson) 1940-

PERSONAL: Born January 18, 1940, in New York, N.Y.; daughter of Morris Clemens (a newspaperman) and Frances (in public relations; maiden name, Fetterman) Watson; married Kenneth L. Laws (a physicist), June 3, 1965; children: Kevin, Virginia. *Education:* Reed College, B.A., 1961; Bryn Mawr College, M.A., 1963, Ph.D., 1966. *Politics:* Democrat. *Home:* 136 North College St., Carlisle, Pa. 17013. *Office:* Department of Physics, Dickinson College, Carlisle, Pa. 17013.

CAREER: Bell Telephone Laboratories, Murray Hill, N.J., senior technical aide, 1962; Dickinson College, Carlisle, Pa., assistant professor, 1965-70, associate professor of physics, 1970—. Member of Carlisle Hospital Authority, 1973; president of board of directors of Carlisle Day Care Center, 1973-74; member of medical radiation advisory committee of Bureau of Radiation Health, Food and Drug Administration, U.S. Department of Health, Education & Welfare, 1974-78.

MEMBER: American Association of Physics Teachers, Federation of American Scientists, Health Physics Society, Pennsylvania Alliance for Returnables, Cumberland Conservancy (president, 1974), Sigma Xi, Sigma Pi Sigma.

WRITINGS: Medical and Dental X-rays, Health Research Group, 1974; *X-Rays: More Harm Than Good?,* Rodale Press, 1977. Contributor to professional journals and to organic gardening and environmental action magazines.

SIDELIGHTS: Priscilla Laws writes: "My major concerns center around the uses and misuses of technology to further human welfare. My writings have focused on environmental issues, nutrition, and health care technologies. I am interested in interpreting those scientific and technological developments which affect people in terms that are readily understandable."

AVOCATIONAL INTERESTS: Camping, jogging, canoeing.

LAWSON, John Howard 1894-1977

September 25, 1894—August 11, 1977; American playwright, screenwriter, and member of the "Hollywood Ten." Lawson was blacklisted for his refusal to report to a Congressional committee about his political allegiance. He was, on two separate occasions, arrested for his support of Sacco and Vanzetti and for his denouncement of Ku Klux Klan activities in the state of Alabama. Lawson was one of the first screen writers to become involved in writing for the talkies. He was best known for such films as "Action in the North Atlantic," "Algiers," "Blockade," and "Sahara." Lawson was co-founder of the Screen Writers Guild and was its first president. He died in San Francisco, Calif. Obituaries: *New York Times*, August 14, 1977; *Washington Post*, August 14, 1977. (See index for *CA* sketch)

* * *

LAZARSFELD, Paul F(elix) 1901-1976

PERSONAL: Born February 13, 1901, in Vienna, Austria; came to United States, 1933, naturalized citizen, 1943; son of Robert and Sofie (a lay analyst; maiden name, Munk) Lazarsfeld; married second wife, Herta Herzog, February 29, 1936; married third wife, Patricia Kendall (a professor), November 21, 1949; children: (first marriage) Lotte Lazarsfeld Bailyn, (third marriage) Robert Kendall. *Education:* University of Vienna, Ph.D., 1924. *Home:* 50 West 96th St., New York, N.Y. 10025.

CAREER: Teacher of mathematics at a junior college in Vienna, Austria, 1929; University of Vienna, Vienna, 1929-33, began as instructor in psychology at Psychological Institute, became director of division of applied psychology; received grant from Rockefeller Foundation for psychological research in the United States, 1933-37; Princeton University, Princeton, N.J., director of Office of Radio Research established by Rockefeller Foundation, 1937-40; Columbia University, New York, N.Y., associate professor, 1940-62, Quetelet Professor of Social Science, 1963-76, director of bureau of applied social research, 1940-50, chairman of graduate sociology department, 1949-59; University of Pittsburgh, Pittsburgh, Pa., distinguished professor, 1970-76. Visiting professor at University of Oslo, 1948-49, and the Sorbonne, University of Paris, 1962-63, 1967-68. Consultant to government organizations and business. *Member:* American Statistical Association (fellow), American Sociological Association (past president), American Marketing Association, American Psychological Association, American Association for Public Opinion Research (past president), National Academy of Science, National Academy of Education, Academy of Arts and Sciences. *Awards, honors:* Award from Sigma Delta Chi, 1941, and from Kappa Tau Alpha, 1948, for research in journalism; award from American Association for Public Opinion Research, 1955; award from Conference on Enlightened Public Opinion, 1958; L.H.D. from Yeshiva University, 1966; LL.D. from University of Chicago, 1966, and Columbia University, 1970; Eastern Sociological Society award, 1975; awarded only honorary degree ever conferred upon an American sociologist by the Sorbonne; received Golden Cross of the Republic of Austria, for his contributions to Austrian culture.

WRITINGS: Statistisches praktikum fuer Psychologen und Lehrer, G. Fischer, 1929; (with others) *Jugend und Beruf: Kritik und Material,* G. Fischer, 1931, reprinted, Arno, 1975; *Radio and the Printed Page,* Duell, Sloan & Pearce, 1940, reprinted, Arno, 1971; (with Bernard Berelson and Hazel Gaudet) *The People's Choice,* Duell, Sloan &

Pearce, 1944, 3rd edition, Columbia University Press, 1968; (with Harry H. Field) *The People Look at Radio,* University of North Carolina Press, 1946; (with Elihu Katz) *Personal Influence,* Free Press of Glencoe, 1955; (with Wagner Thielens, Jr.) *The Academic Mind: Social Scientists in a Time of Crisis,* Free Press of Glencoe, 1958; *Non-Intellectual Factors in the Prediction of College Success,* [Princeton, N.J.], 1959.

(With Sam D. Sieber) *Organizing Educational Research,* Prentice-Hall, 1964; (with Jane Z. Hauser) *The Admissions Officer in the American College,* Columbia University Press, 1964; (with Sieber) *The Organization of Educational Research in the United States,* Columbia University Press, 1966; *Metodologie e ricerca sociologica* (title means "Methodology and Social Research"), Il Mulino, 1967; (with Neil W. Henry) *Latent Structure Analysis,* Houghton, 1968; *Am Puls der Gesellschaft,* Europa Verlag, 1968; *L'Analyse des processus sociaux* (title means "The Analysis of Social Processes"), Mouton, 1970; (with Marie Jahoda) *Marienthal: The Sociography of an Unemployed Community,* Aldine, 1971; (with Sieber) *Reforming the University,* Columbia University Bureau of Applied Social Research, 1971; *Qualitative Analysis: Historical and Critical Essays,* Allyn & Bacon, 1972; (with Samuel A. Stouffer) *Research Memorandum on the Family in the Depression,* Arno, 1972; *Main Trends in Sociology,* Harper, 1973; (contributor) *Views from the Socially Sensitive Seventies,* American Telephone and Telegraph Co., 1973; (with Douglas C. McDonald) *Some Problems of Research Organization,* Columbia University Bureau of Applied Social Research, 1973; (with Jeffrey G. Reitz) *An Introduction to Applied Sociology,* Elsevier, 1975.

Editor: Communications Research, Harper, 1941; (with Frank N. Stanton) *Radio Research,* Duell, Sloan & Pearce, 1941; (with Robert K. Merton) *Studies in the Scope and Method of "The American Soldier,"* Free Press, 1950, reprinted, Arno, 1974; *Mathematical Thinking in the Social Sciences,* Free Press, 1954; (with Morris Rosenberg) *The Language of Social Research: A Reader in the Methodology of Social Research,* Free Press, 1955; (with Raymond Boudon) *Methodes de la sociologie* (title means "Sociological Methods"), Mouton, 1965; (with Boudon) *Le Vocabulaire des sciences sociales* (title means "The Vocabulary of the Social Sciences"), Mouton, 1965, 3rd edition, 1971; (with Boudon) *L'Analyse empirique de la causalite* (title means "The Empirical Analysis of Causality"), Mouton, 1966, 2nd edition, 1969; (with Neil W. Henry) *Readings in Mathematical Social Science,* Science Research Associates, 1966; (with William H. Sewell and Harold L. Wilensky) *The Uses of Sociology,* Basic Books, 1967; (with Ann K. Pasanella and Morris Rosenberg) *Continuities in the Language of Social Research,* Free Press, 1972.

OBITUARIES: New York Times, September 1, 1976.

(Died August 30, 1976, in New York, N.Y.)

[Sketch verified by wife, Patricia Lazarsfeld]

* * *

LEA, Alec 1907-

PERSONAL: Born in 1907, in Nova Scotia, Canada; married May Kelly (a lecturer in health education), 1958; children: Judith Verna, Kenneth Richard. *Education:* Attended Oxford University. *Politics:* Socialist. *Religion:* Society of Friends (Quakers). *Home:* Malvern, Bridge of Don, Aberdeen, Scotland. *Agent:* Laura Cecil, 10 Exeter Mansions, Shaftesbury Ave., London, England.

CAREER: Dairy farmer in Sussex and Devon, England, 1937-70; writer, 1970—.

WRITINGS: To Sunset and Beyond, Hamish Hamilton, 1970, Walck, 1971; *Temba Dawn,* Bodley Head, 1972, Scribner, 1973; *A Whiff of Boarhound,* Dobson, 1974; *Kingcup Calling,* Dobson, 1976; *Deep Down and High Up,* Dobson, 1976; *Beth Varden at Sunset* (sequel to *To Sunset and Beyond*), Dobson, 1977.

WORK IN PROGRESS: A novel for children about the future.

SIDELIGHTS: Lea told *CA:* "I am worried by the fact that the bulk of children's fiction, including my own books, are nostalgic and glorify the past, whereas it is essentially the future which belongs to today's children. Those writers who do try to imagine the future in books for children seem to lack hope and produce work which may be very exciting and realistic, but is basically depressing."

* * *

LEACH, Michael 1940-
(Christopher Jeffrey)

PERSONAL: Born August 19, 1940, in Chicago, Ill.; son of Glen E. and Sara (Giarrizzo) Leach; married Vickie Jacobi (a translator), October 3, 1969; children: Christopher, Jeffrey. *Education:* St. Mary of the Lake, Mundelein, Ill., M.A., 1966. *Politics:* Independent. *Religion:* Roman Catholic. *Home:* 84 Havemeyer Lane, Old Greenwich, Conn. 06870. *Office:* Seabury Press, 815 Second Ave., New York, N.Y. 10017.

CAREER: Maryville Academy, Des Plaines, Ill., administrator, 1966-69; Seabury Press, New York City, vice-president, director of professional services, and editor, 1969—. Roman Catholic priest, 1966-69. *Member:* Religion Publishers Association.

WRITINGS: I Know It When I See It: Pornography, Violence and Public Sensitivity, Westminster, 1975; *The Boy Who Had Everything* (juvenile), Seabury, 1977. Contributor of articles and stories, and of book reviews, under pseudonym Christopher Jeffrey, to religious and educational magazines. *New Review of Books and Religion,* managing editor, 1976—. Author of hundreds of brochures, booklets, and pamphlets for non-profit organizations.

WORK IN PROGRESS: Commuter, a book of reflections on life and values; a novel.

SIDELIGHTS: I Know It When I See It, Leach's book about pornographic and violent movies, has been praised for its conversational style and readability. L. W. Putnam wrote that Leach "has marshaled a wealth of historical, psychological and legal data with which to tackle the recurring issues posed by pornography, obscenity, and censorship. His style makes the book at once concise, lively, amusing, personal, sensible, non-moralistic, and even inspiring." Tom Wallace commented that his approach is "sane and fully concerned with the moral implications that attend both the showing of X-rated films and the attempts to ban them," and noted that Leach "seems to be at odds with the prevailing morality that is considerably softer on guns than on frontal nudity."

Leach told *CA:* "I consider myself simply a dependable wordsmith who can turn a good phrase and illumine the ordinary. I'm not an artist. I try to be an excellent craftsman. Anything human interests me. And I write about what interests me just to interest others as well. Also—let's be totally honest—because I like to see my name in print and enjoy earning a living by playing with words. Writing gives me

pleasure. And I hope that what I write gives pleasure to readers too."

BIOGRAPHICAL/CRITICAL SOURCES: Christian Century, June 2, 1976; *Advocate,* August 28, 1976; *Choice,* October, 1976.

* * *

LEACH, Paul Roscoe 1890-1977

1890—July 9, 1977; American journalist, biographer, and author of short stories. Leach began working for the *Chicago Daily News* in 1910, and became its Washington bureau chief in 1933. In 1943 he became Washington bureau chief for the Knight Newspaper chain. Leach covered every national political campaign from 1920 until his retirement in 1956, and was the author of a biography of Charles G. Dawes, the first federal budget director and vice-president of the United States under Calvin Coolidge. Leach died in Ormond Beach, Fla. Obituaries: *New York Times,* July 10, 1977; *Washington Post,* July 12, 1977.

* * *

LEAF, (Wilbur) Munro 1905-1976
(John Calvert)

PERSONAL: Born December 4, 1905, in Hamilton, Md.; son of Charles Wilbur (a painter) and Emma India (Gillespie) Leaf; married Margaret Butler Pope, December 29, 1926; children: Andrew Munro, James Gillespie. *Education:* University of Maryland, A.B., 1927; Harvard University, M.A., 1931; graduate of Army Staff and Command School, 1943. *Home:* 1330 New Hampshire Ave. N.W., Washington, D.C. 20013.

CAREER: Teacher and coach at Belmont Hill School, Belmont, Mass., 1929-30, Montgomery School, Wynnewood, Pa., 1931; Bobbs-Merrill Co., Inc., New York City, manuscript reader, 1932-33; Frederick A. Stokes Co., New York City, editor, 1932-39; writer and illustrator, 1934—. *Military service:* U.S. Army, 1942-46; became major. *Member:* Kappa Alpha, Cosmos Club (Washington), Franklin Inn Philadelphia, Players Club, Dutch Treat Club, Century Association.

WRITINGS—All self-illustrated juveniles published by Stokes Publishing, except as indicated: *Grammar Can Be Fun,* 1934, revised edition, Lippincott, 1958; *Lo, the Poor Indian,* 1934; *Robert Francis Weatherbee,* 1935; *Manners Can Be Fun,* 1936, revised edition, Lippincott, 1958; *The Story of Ferdinand* (illustrated by Robert Lawson), Viking, 1936, reprinted, 1966; *Noodle* (illustrated by Ludwig Bemelmans), 1937; *Wee Gillis* (illustrated by R. Lawson), Viking, 1938, reprinted, 1967; *Safety Can Be Fun,* 1938, revised edition, Lippincott, 1961; *Listen Little Girl, Before You Come to New York,* 1938; *A Wartime Handbook for Young Americans,* Viking, 1938; *The Watchbirds,* 1939; *Fair Play,* 1939, reprinted, Lippincott, 1967.

More Watchbirds, 1940; *John Henry Davis,* 1940; *Story of Simpson and Sampson,* Viking, 1941; *Fly Away, Watchbirds!,* 1941; *Fun Book: The Munro Leaf Big Three, Manners Can Be Fun, Grammar Can Be Fun, Safety Can Be Fun,* 1941; (editor) *Aesop's Fables,* Heritage Press, 1941; *Health Can Be Fun,* 1943; *Three and Thirty Watchbirds, a Picture Book of Behavior,* Lippincott, 1944; *Gordon the Goat,* Lippincott, 1944; *Let's Do Better,* Lippincott, 1945; *Flock of Watchbirds* (includes *Watchbirds, More Watchbirds, Fly Away, Watchbirds!*), Lippincott, 1946; *How to Behave and Why,* Lippincott, 1946; (under pseudonym John

Calvert) *Gwendolyn the Goose* (illustrated by Garrett Price), Random House, 1946; *Boo, Who Used to Be Scared of the Dark* (illustrated by Francis Tipton Hunter), Random House, 1948; *Sam and the Superdroop,* Viking, 1948; (with W. C. Menninger) *You and Psychiatry,* Scribner, 1948; *Arithmetic Can Be Fun,* Lippincott, 1949.

History Can Be Fun, Lippincott, 1950; *Geography Can Be Fun,* Lippincott, 1951, revised edition, 1962; *Reading Can Be Fun,* Lippincott, 1953; *Lucky You,* Lippincott, 1955; *Three Promises to You,* Lippincott, 1957; *The Wishing Poll,* Lippincott, 1960; *Being an American Can Be Fun,* Lippincott, 1964; *Turnabout,* Lippincott, 1967; *Who Cares? I Do,* Lippincott, 1971; *Metric Can Be Fun,* Lippincott, 1976. Also author of pamphlets "The Story of Ann," illustrated by Dr. Seuss, an unorthodox military manual on malaria, and "Who Is the Man?", an explanation of the Marshall Plan. Author of monthly column entitled "Watchwords" for *Ladies Home Journal,* 1931-67.

SIDELIGHTS: The story of a bull named Ferdinand who would rather sniff at flowers than fight in a bull ring secured renown in the world of children's literature for its author Munro Leaf. Written in forty minutes on a rainy Sunday afternoon, the book has been translated into sixteen languages and has sold over 2 million copies in the United States alone. Rights to the story were purchased by Walt Disney studio and an animated film version followed.

Leaf traveled extensively for the U.S. State Department, lecturing abroad, meeting with publishers, addressing the children of other lands. A *Washington Post* writer noted: "Last September in an interview, Mr. Leaf said he was going to do a book on how Ferdinand and his other characters as well as his extensive travels had given him a good life. 'I'm going to call it *A Little Bull Goes a Long Way,*' he said."

OBITUARIES: New York Times, December 21, 1976; *Washington Post,* December 23, 1976; *Time,* January 3, 1977; *AB Bookman's Weekly,* March 7, 1977.*

(Died December 21, 1976 in Garrett Park, Md.)

*   *   *

LEAKE, Chauncey D(epew)   1896-1978

September 5, 1896—January 11, 1978; American pharmacologist, educator, administrator, medical historian, research director, and writer of numerous books on medical ethics, disease, and pharmacology. A critic of the Food and Drug Administration on many occasions, Leake believed that a scientist should always test a new drug on himself before engaging in a test program with volunteers. He was considered a pioneer in the development of pharmacology departments in several medical schools. Leake's credits include contributions to the discovery of amphetamines, tranquilizers, and new practices in anesthesiology. He died in San Francisco, Calif. Obituaries: *New York Times,* January 13, 1978. (See index for *CA* sketch)

*   *   *

LEAN, Arthur E(dward)   1909-

PERSONAL: Surname is pronounced Lane; born December 17, 1909, in Laurium, Mich.; son of Horatio Seymour (an engineer) and Louisa Jane (James) Lean; married Bernice Ann Sievert, April 11, 1944 (died, 1953); children: Cynthia (Mrs. Wayne L. Kuntze). *Education:* Lawrence University, student, 1926-28; University of Michigan, A.B. (with distinction), 1930, Ph.D., 1948; Columbia University, M.A.,

1934. *Politics:* Democrat. *Religion:* Unitarian Universalist. *Home:* 1112 Chautauqua Ave., Carbondale, Ill. 62901. *Office:* 322 Education Building, Southern Illinois University, Carbondale, Ill. 62901.

CAREER: High school teacher of Latin and English in Michigan, New York, Arizona, and Minnesota, 1930-42; Indiana State Teachers College (now Indiana State University), Terre Haute, assistant professor of education, 1948-49; University of Michigan, Ann Arbor, assistant director of Extension Division, 1949-57; Southern Illinois University, Carbondale, professor of social and philosophical foundations of education, 1957—, chairman of department of administration and supervision, 1957-60, dean of College of Education, 1960-63. Visiting summer professor, University of Arizona, 1957. Consultant, South Vietnamese Ministry of Education, 1967. *Military service:* U.S. Army, 1942-46; became captain; received Bronze Star.

MEMBER: American Academy of Political and Social Science, Philosophy of Education Society, Comparative Education Society, John Dewey Society, History of Education Society, National Society of Professors of English (formerly National Society of College Teachers of Education; member of executive committee, 1961-64), National Education Association (life member), American Civil Liberties Union, American Humanist Association, Illinois Education Association, Phi Delta Kappa, Kappa Delta Pi, Phi Kappa Phi, Honorable Order of Kentucky Colonels. *Awards, honors:* Order of the Smaller Dragon (Vietnam); Guild of King Christian IV (Denmark).

WRITINGS: (Editor with Douglas E. Lawson, and contributor) *John Dewey and the World View,* Southern Illinois University Press, 1964; *And Merely Teach: Irreverent Essays on the Mythology of Education,* Southern Illinois University Press, 1968, 2nd edition, 1976. Contributor of articles and reviews to professional journals.

SIDELIGHTS: Arthur E. Lean studied comparative and international education in the Soviet Union, 1958, Scandinavia, 1963, and Vietnam and India, 1967.

AVOCATIONAL INTERESTS: Music (had his own orchestra at one time, and gave several piano concerts).

*   *   *

LEAR, Norman (Milton)   1922-

PERSONAL: Born July 27, 1922, in New Haven, Conn.; son of Herman (a salesperson) and Jeanette (Scicol) Lear; married second wife, Frances A. Loeb, December 7, 1956; children: Ellen Lear Reiss, Kate B., Maggie B. *Education:* Attended Emerson College, 1941-42. *Home:* 255 Chadbourne Ave., Los Angeles, Calif. 90049. *Office:* Tandem Productions, Inc., 1901 Avenue of the Stars, Los Angeles, Calif. 90067.

CAREER: Worked in public relations with George and Dorothy Ross in New York City, 1946; salesperson, photographer, and free-lance writer in Los Angeles, Calif., 1946-50; comedy writer for television shows, "Ford Star Review," "Colgate Comedy Hour," and "Martha Raye Show," 1950-54; writer and director of "George Gobel Show," 1954-59; founder and partner with Alan Yorkin of Tandem Productions, Inc. (an independent production company), Los Angeles, 1959, producer, writer, and director of television shows, 1959—; creator and producer of "All in the Family," CBS-TV, 1971—, (with Aaron Ruben and Alan Yorkin) "Sanford and Son," NBC-TV, 1972—, "Maude," CBS-TV, 1972—, "Good Times," CBS-TV, 1974—, "The Jeffersons," CBS-TV, 1974—, "Hot L Baltimore," ABC-TV, 1975, "One Day at a Time," CBS-TV, 1975—, "The Dumplings," NBC-TV, 1976, "Nancy Walker Show," ABC-TV, 1976-77, "All's Fair," CBS-TV, 1976-77, "Mary Hartman, Mary Hartman" independently distributed, 1976-77, "All That Glitters," independently distributed, 1977, "The Year at the Top," CBS-TV, 1977, "Fernwood 2 Night," independently distributed, 1977, "Forever Fernwood," independently distributed, 1977—. President of Southern California branch, American Civil Liberties Union Foundation, 1973—. *Military service:* U.S. Army Air Forces, 1941-45; served as radioman in European theatre of operations; received Air medal with four oak leaf clusters.

MEMBER: Screen Writers Guild, Screen Producers Guild (member of executive board, 1968), Directors Guild of America, Producers Guild of America, American Federation of Television and Radio Artists. *Awards, honors:* Named one of the Top Ten Producers of the Year by Motion Picture Exhibitors, 1963, 1967, and 1968; Academy Award and Writers Guild award nominations, both 1967, for "Divorce American Style"; Showman of the Year, Publicists Guild, 1971; Emmy Awards, 1971, 1972, and 1973, all for "All in the Family"; Showman of the Year, Association of Business Managers, 1972; Broadcaster of the Year, International Radio and Television Society, 1973; Man of the Year, Hollywood chapter of National Academy of Television Arts and Sciences, 1973. H.H.D., Emerson College, 1968.

WRITINGS—Screenplays: (With Herbert Baker, Walter DeLeon, and Ed Simmons) "Scared Stiff," Paramount, 1953; "Come Blow Your Horn" (from play by Neil Simon), Paramount, 1963; "Divorce American Style," Columbia, 1967; (with Arnold Schulman and Sidney Michaels) "The Night They Raided Minsky's" (from novel by Rowland Barber), United Artists, 1968; "Cold Turkey," United Artists, 1971.

Author of scripts, additional dialogue, and script revisions for numerous television shows and specials, including all those he produces and directs.

WORK IN PROGRESS: Another television series, as yet untitled, to be about a former sailor and his wife's reconstruction of their 29-year-old marriage, after being together only two months a year.

SIDELIGHTS: How does the most enterprising producer in television history see himself? "I consider myself a writer who loves to show real people in real conflict with all their fears, doubts, hopes, and ambitions rubbing against their love for one another. I want my shows to be funny, outrageous, and alive. So far, so good."

With the independent sale of "Fernwood Forever," Lear has seven shows running on television and an estimated weekly audience of more than 100 million viewers. Karl E. Meyer said: "More than anyone else, Mr. Lear has made it commercially profitable for Americans to laugh at themselves. The nature of that laughter deserves analysis. The comic center is invariably the nuclear family, notwithstanding forecasts by counter-culture prophets that the family is an obsolescent fossil. The essential core of every Lear comedy is the biting backchat of husband, wife, children, and in-laws. . . . A second common motif is the open ventilation of ethnic humor. Mr. Lear has made it possible for comic series to show that the American consensus is not so fragile that the melting pot will crack if its existence is acknowledged."

While Lear's shows are often concerned with controversial social issues, he admits that the issues themselves are not of supreme importance to him. He told Gerry Nadel: "If you're asking, 'How much do you care about what a show may or may not be saying?' My answer is that isn't what motivates me. My business is theater. It isn't that I don't care about what the shows are saying. I obviously do. But the only reason I do is that's what makes good theater—issues, ideas, topicality, content. Drama that provokes. The more you care, the harder you laugh."

In 1975 two scientific studies appeared, one conducted by the University of Georgia's department of journalism and the other published by the Annenberg School of Communications. The object of both studies was to discover the influence of Archie Bunker and his bigotry on the American public. Leonard Gross defined the cause of worry for many critics: "The operating premise of 'All in the Family' is that Archie always loses. No matter what the issue, his reasoning is cockeyed and he is made to look the fool. The program is meant to be a satire on bigots and their biases. But what if a husky segment of the television audience doesn't get the joke?" Lear personally is not overly concerned with the show's effect. "How much could I expect to happen from my silly little half-hour TV show, when the entire Judeo-Christian ethic for some 2,000 years hasn't budged race relations?"

In addition to sociologists, Lear now has the networks worried. When all three networks refused "Mary Hartman," he distributed it himself. Harry F. Water and Martin Kasindorf suggested this may be Lear's greatest, lasting influence on the television medium. "'Mary Hartman's' success could have a revolutionary impact on the way the TV industry works," they explained. "Some West Coast producers, irked at the networks' play-it-safe approach, are talking about copying Lear's method and selling their more offbeat shows directly to independent broadcasters. At the same time, the independents themselves have already begun banding together into coalitions with the financial muscle to purchase series that the networks reject. That combination could produce a spate of 'instant networks' and deal a sneak blow to the Big Three's lock on what America sees—and doesn't see."

BIOGRAPHICAL/CRITICAL SOURCES: Newsweek, November 29, 1971, May 3, 1976; *Time,* September 25, 1972, April 5, 1976; *New York Times Magazine,* May 21, 1973; *TV Guide,* November 8, 1975, June 19, 1976; *Saturday Review,* May 29, 1976; *New Times,* July 8, 1977.*

*   *   *

LEARD, John E.   1916-

PERSONAL: Born August 15, 1916, in Boston, Mass.; son of John S. H. (a physician) and Isabelle (a teacher; maiden name, Earnshaw) Leard; married: Hazel Elsie Turner, September 28, 1940; children: Linda (Mrs. Raymond B. Parkin, Jr.), Judith (Mrs. Richard Nicholas). *Education:* Bates College, A.B., 1938; Columbia University, M.S., 1939. *Religion:* Episcopalian. *Home:* 6207 Monument Ave., Richmond, Va. 23226. *Office:* Richmond Newspapers, Inc., 333 East Grace St., Richmond, Va. 23219.

CAREER/WRITINGS: Lewiston Sun-Journal, Lewiston, Me., reporter, 1937; *Richmond News Leader,* Richmond, Va., reporter and editorial assistant, 1939; *Atlantic Monthly,* Boston, Mass., assistant editor, 1940-41; *Richmond News Leader,* assistant city editor, 1941-43, 1947-51, city editor, 1951-63; *Richmond Times-Dispatch,* Richmond, managing editor, 1963-69, executive editor, 1969—; *Richmond News Leader,* executive editor, 1969—. Telegraph editor of *New Haven Register,* 1946-47; co-chairman of Virginia Press-Bar

Committee, 1968—. Has written and lectured widely on new technology for news operations. *Military service:* U.S. Army, 1943-46. *Member:* American Society of Newspaper Editors, American Newspaper Publishers Association (member of research institute, production management, and news research committees, 1973—), Associated Press Managing Editors Association (president, 1976-77), Associated Press Newspapers of Virginia (president, 1969-70), Virginia News Photographers Association, Virginia Press Association (president-elect, 1977-78), Sigma Delta Chi (Richmond chapter president, 1960-61).

SIDELIGHTS: Leard wrote: "My main vocational interests are putting out the best newspapers we can to serve our readers' interests and needs. We have professional and capable staffs who take pride in their work and generally do it well. But we constantly strive to do better. In managing, I admire outstanding work, dislike time-wasting or redoing things needlessly. Accuracy and fairness are constant objectives."

AVOCATIONAL INTERESTS: Photography, golf, tennis, travel.

* * *

LeBEAUX, Richard 1946-

PERSONAL: Born March 2, 1946, in New York, N.Y.; son of Lincoln (a physician) and Thelma (a psychologist; maiden name, Westerman) Lebeaux; married Ellen Abraham (a social worker), October 7, 1973. *Education:* Middlebury College, A.B. (summa cum laude), 1968; Harvard University, M.A.T., 1970; further graduate study at Brandeis University, 1970-71; Boston University, Ph.D., 1975. *Religion:* Jewish. *Home:* 1133C Palmer Lane, East Lansing, Mich. 48823. *Office:* Department of American Thought and Language, Michigan State University, East Lansing, Mich. 48824.

CAREER: High school English teacher in Needham, Mass., 1969-70; St. Louis Community College at Forest Park, St. Louis, Mo., instructor in American civilization and English, 1975-76; Michigan State University, East Lansing, assistant professor of American thought and language, 1976—. *Member:* American Studies Association, Modern Language Association of America, Thoreau Lyceum, Thoreau Society, Phi Beta Kappa.

WRITINGS: Young Man Thoreau, University of Massachusetts Press, 1977. Contributor to *American Examiner.*

WORK IN PROGRESS: Research on Thoreau in the post-Walden years, the "moratorium" in the lives of American writers and in American culture, life cycle studies of American writers, failure in American culture, and men and masculinity in America.

SIDELIGHTS: Lebeaux writes: "I am committed to teaching and writing which explores what it means to be human and which considers—directly and indirectly—how a life is to be lived. I am concerned with fostering human liberation and a respect for diversity, coupled with a recognition of how much we have in common, how interdependent we are, and how much we need each other."

AVOCATIONAL INTERESTS: Song writing, singing, playing the guitar, camping, hiking, sports, New England.

* * *

LEBOWITZ, Albert 1922-

PERSONAL: Born June 18, 1922, in St. Louis, Mo.; son of Jacob and Lena (Zemmel) Lebowitz; married Naomi Gordon, November 26, 1953; children: Joel Aaron, Judith Leah. *Education:* Washington University, A.B., 1945; Harvard University, LL.B., 1948. *Home:* 743 Yale Ave., St. Louis, Mo. 63130. *Office:* 1015 Locust St., St. Louis, Mo. 63101.

CAREER: Admitted to Missouri Bar, 1948; Morris, Schneider & Lebowitz, St. Louis, Mo., Partner, 1955-58; Crowe, Schneider, Shanahan & Lebowitz, St. Louis, partner, 1958-66; Murphy & Roche, St. Louis, counsel, 1966-67; Murphy & Schlapprizzi, St. Louis, counsel, 1967—. Novelist. *Military service:* U.S. Army Air Force, 1943-45; received Air Medal with three oak leaf clusters. *Member:* American Bar Association, Missouri Bar Association, St. Louis Bar Association, Phi Beta Kappa.

WRITINGS: Laban's Will, Random House, 1966; *The Man Who Couldn't Say No,* Random House, 1969. Also author of short stories. Editor, *Perspective,* 1961—.

SIDELIGHTS: Daniel Stern reviewed Lebowitz's first novel, *Laban's Will:* "One way of reading this book is as a parable with William Laban as God (the Jewish one in particular: the law-giver) teasing, mocking, forcing us all, his children, into living on the side of life. Or you can read it as a kind of mad family morality tale . . . Lebowitz, like Laban, not only preaches religious joy—he manages to contribute some."

BIOGRAPHICAL/CRITICAL SOURCES: New York Times Book Review, March 27, 1966.*

* * *

LE COCQ, Rhoda P(riscilla) 1921-

PERSONAL: Born January 31, 1921, in Lynden, Wash.; daughter of Ralph and Nellie (Straks) Le Cocq; divorced. *Education:* Stanford University, M.A., 1950; Sorbonne, University of Paris, graduate study, 1951; University of California, Santa Barbara, M.A., 1967; California Institute of Asian Studies, Ph.D., 1969. *Home:* 550 Douglas St., Apt. 75, Broderick, Calif. 95605.

CAREER: Writer and actress in radio, 1937-42; magazine writer, 1946-50; Farrar, Straus & Giroux, Inc., New York, N.Y., literary scout, 1949-55; Safeway Advertising, San Francisco, Calif., in promotion, 1955-57; Honolulu Academy of Arts School, Honolulu, Hawaii, public relations director, 1957-59; University of Hawaii, Honolulu, lecturer in business writing, 1960; City and County of Honolulu, Hawaii, civil defense education and information officer, 1961-63; California State Department of Education, editor, 1968-69; Sacramento County Department of Welfare, Sacramento, Calif., public information officer, 1969—; University of California, Davis, assistant professor of philosophy, 1970-71; California Institute of Asian Studies, San Francisco, associate professor of comparative philosophy, 1971—. *Military service:* U.S. Navy, office of chief of information for magazine and book section, 1942-46; became lieutenant senior grade. *Member:* American Society of Writers, Public Relations Society of America (member of Sacramento Chapter board of directors), Smithsonian Associate, Armed Forces Writers, Theta Sigma Phi, Mensa, Association for Transpersonal Psychology (regional speaker, 1977), Cultural Integration Fellowship, Sacramento Press Club.

WRITINGS: The Radical Thinkers: Heidegger and Aurobindo, California Institute of Asian Studies, 1972.

Author of "The Shadow Outside," for General Electric Television Theatre, 1957; "The Vision of Suprahumanity," included in collection *Toward Eternity,* 1972; "The Mother/Father Pair," to be produced at Osmania University, 1978.

Stories are anthologized in *Best Short Stories in Twenty Years,* Stanford University Press, 1966.

WORK IN PROGRESS: A novel, *The Way Beyond Janus;* a book on India's Mira Alfasso, *Woman at the Golden Door.*

SIDELIGHTS: Le Cocq told *CA:* "My interests center about writing, both fiction and non-fiction, and upon further study in world philosophy. I have made study tours to India and Nepal, am now doing research in Tibetan Buddhism and studying Vajrayana Meditation techniques under a high lama in Nepal. I am, therefore, interested in self-development and transcendence, with future writing based upon this experience. Writing itself, I find a kind of yoga."

* * *

LECOMBER, Brian 1945-

PERSONAL: Born July 12, 1945, in London, England. *Education:* Educated in Amersham, England. *Politics:* "Negligible." *Religion:* "Negligible." *Home:* 2 Station View, Trafford Rd., Gt. Missenden, Buckinghamshire, England. *Agent:* David Higham Associates, Lower John St., London W1R 4MA, England.

CAREER: Motorcycle mechanic, 1961-62; free-lance journalist, 1962-64; reporter for various newspapers in England, 1964-68; *Car Mechanics,* London, England, technical editor, 1968-70; Roaring 20's Flying Circus, Denham, England, flying instructor and stunt man, 1970-72; Antigua Aero Club, Antigua, West Indies, chief flying instructor, 1972-73; free-lance writer and pilot, 1973—. *Member:* Guild of Motoring Writers, British Aerobatic Association (committee member), Tiger Club. *Awards, honors:* McAully Aerobatic Trophy, Don Henry Aerobatic Trophy, and Esso Tigers Aerobatic Trophy, all from British Aerobatic Association, all 1977.

WRITINGS: Turn Killer (novel), Simon & Schuster, 1974; *Dead Weight* (novel), Delacorte, 1977. Contributor to motoring and flying magazines.

WORK IN PROGRESS: Talk Down; another novel on flying.

SIDELIGHTS: Lecomber writes: "My main motivation these days is to become a member of the British Aerobatic Team and to be a better display pilot than I am. I own a Stampe SV4C aerobatic biplane, and also fly the last Sopwith Camel in England at air shows.

"I write because I have to eat. I am primarily a flier who writes, not a writer who happens to fly. I can't spell to save my life. However, I do have both U.S. and British professional pilots' licences, and all the aircraft I write about I have flown extensively; my machinery and locations are real, and if I talk about any maneuver, I have carried out that maneuver in that type of aeroplane."

* * *

LEDBETTER, J(ack) T(racy) 1934-

PERSONAL: Born December 7, 1934, in Greenville, Ill.; son of Leslie Rollin and Mildred (Smith) Ledbetter; married Dolores Jean Moore (a teacher), March 27, 1955; children: Tim, James, Rebecca. *Education:* California State University, Long Beach, B.A., 1961; University of Nebraska, M.A., 1968, Ph.D., 1973. *Religion:* Lutheran. *Home:* 1335 Norman, Thousand Oaks, Calif. 91360. *Office:* Department of English, California Lutheran College, Thousand Oaks, Calif. 91360.

CAREER: Teacher and principal at Lutheran school in Harbor City, Calif., 1957-61; teacher at Lutheran elementary school in Culver City, Calif., 1961-62; high school English teacher at Lutheran school in Los Angeles, Calif., 1962-64; Concordia Teachers College, Seward, Neb., instructor in English, 1964-66; English teacher at Lutheran high school in Los Angeles, Calif., 1966-70; California Lutheran College, Thousand Oaks, assistant professor of English, 1970-72; University of Nebraska, Lincoln, instructor in English, 1972-73; California Lutheran College, associate professor of English, 1973—. Poet-in-residence at Holden Village, summers, 1974, 1975, 1977; has given poetry readings at colleges and universities all over the United States and in Hong Kong. Has had one-man shows of his art works.

WRITINGS: Song of the Omahas (poetry chapbook), Horsehead Nebula Press, 1971; *Baci Piak* (poetry chapbook; title means "Uncle Drunkard"), Dalmatia Press, 1971; *Plum Creek Odyssey* (poems), Valparaiso University Press, 1975; *Voyages* (poems), California Lutheran College Press, 1977; *Mark Van Doren* (criticism), Twayne, in press; (contributor of art work) G. F. Brommer, *Collages,* Davis Publications (Worcester, Mass.), in press.

Work anthologized in *The Clover Collection of Verse,* 1972; *New American Poetry,* McGraw, 1973; *The American Poetry Press,* [Atlanta, Ga.] 1974. Contributor of poems and articles to religious, education, and literary journals, including *Prairie Schooner, Walt Whitman Review, Explicator, Poet Lore,* and *New Voices.* Member of board of editors of *New Writers;* member of script committee for "This Is the Life," a television series.

WORK IN PROGRESS: A collection of poems based on a 1977 tour of Europe and the Middle East.

SIDELIGHTS: Ledbetter told *CA:* "My poetry about Nebraska is pastoral and continues to haunt me. The lone barn or weed-choked stream seems more important than the epic view of 'man and his world.' The poems change as I grow older; symbolic poems from early life in southern Illinois are surfacing. I'm not sure which comes first: the philosophy of life or the poems that tell you what you believe. Mark Van Doren continues to be my favorite American poet."

* * *

LEDERER, Joseph 1927-

PERSONAL: Born September 3, 1927, in Chicago, Ill.; son of Joseph M. and Beatrice (Hillman) Lederer; married Pauline Levenson (a concert pianist), September 2, 1952; children: Nancy. *Education:* Attended University of Illinois at Chicago, Roosevelt University, and South Dakota State College; University of Wisconsin, Madison, B.A., 1950. *Home:* 33 East Broad St., Mt. Vernon, N.Y. 10552.

CAREER: Il Nuovo Osservatore, Rome, Italy, U.S. correspondent, 1960-63; R. O. Lehman Foundation, Paris, France, deputy director, 1963-64; Queens College of the City University of New York, Flushing, N.Y., instructor in English, 1966-67; *Urban Review,* New York, N.Y., editor, 1968-72; free-lance writer, 1972—. Publications director for Center for Urban Education (New York City), 1970-72; has given public readings and appeared as guest on radio programs. *Military service:* U.S. Army, 1944-46. *Member:* Overseas Press Club, Alpha Kappa Delta. *Awards, honors:* Young Playwrights Competition first prize, 1948, for "The Mad Donor."

WRITINGS: Education of the Deaf (monograph), Center for Urban Education, 1968; *All Around Town,* Scribner, 1975.

Plays: "The Mad Donor" (one-act), first produced in Baton Rouge, La., at Louisiana State University, 1948; "Four People and As Many Pianos" (one-act), first produced in New York, N.Y., at American Theater Wing, 1951; "World Blood" (two-act), first produced in 1954.

Contributor of stories, articles, and translations to magazines and newspapers, including *Antioch Review, Gentleman's Quarterly, Music Review, American Film,* and *After Dark.*

WORK IN PROGRESS: What Are You Going to Be When You Grow Old? (tentative title), with Harris Dienstfrey, on alternative ways of living available to the elderly, for Bantam.

SIDELIGHTS: Lederer writes: "My writing career, to say nothing of my life, is predicated on the premise that I shall live to a hundred twenty-five at the very least. The term of apprenticeship ended, at age fifty, with my most fully realized fiction to date: "The Man Who Feared Cholesterol" in *Antioch Review.* Now come the masterworks! In magnitude, though not necessarily in amplitude. William Blake wrote of seeing infinity in a grain of sand, William De Kooning of wanting to get all the colors in the world into a single painting. Similarly, one should be able to pack, without surfeit, everything worth saying into a play or story, a 17-syllable haiku or, in light of our own tradition, a supremely crafted dirty joke. To the attentive reader, it should all be there: a sense of life's precariousness; the values of complexity (hope and skepticism, exaltation and remorse); a striving for moral courage; a puncturing of ignorance, arrogance, exploitation and greed; the mystery at the heart of human existence."

* * *

LEE, Asher 1909-

PERSONAL: Born August 27, 1909, in Plymouth, England; son of Abraham (a writer) and Esther Treibitch (Lincoln) Lee; married Mollie Hales (deceased); children: Nicolette. *Education:* University of Paris, diploma, 1929; University College, London, B.A. (first class honors), 1931; Institute of Education, London, M.A., 1937. *Politics:* "None (I don't trust any politicians)." *Religion:* "Ex-Jewish." *Home:* 12 Malcolm Rd., Wimbledon, London SW19 4AS, England. *Office:* French Service, British Broadcasting Corp., Bush House, Strand, London W.C.2, England.

CAREER: British Broadcasting Corp., London, radio producer, 1945-47, head of overseas research branch, 1947-71; London Broadcasting Co. (the first British commercial radio station), London, England, research consultant, 1971-75; artist's model and broadcaster, 1976-77. Author. Lecturer at Air War College (United States), Belgium Staff and French College, Portland State University, and British universities. *Military service:* Royal Air Force, intelligence, 1939-45, chief intelligence air officer, 1944; became wing commander. Royal Air Force Reserve, 1945-55. *Member:* Royal Air Force Club. *Awards, honors:* Commander of Order of the British Empire, 1943; Legion of Merit, 1945; Rockefeller Foundation fellowship, 1950-51.

WRITINGS: The German Air Force, Harper, 1946; *The Soviet Air Force,* Harper, 1951; *Air Power,* Praeger, 1955; (editor) *Soviet Air and Rocket Forces,* Praeger, 1956; *Hermann Goering, Air Leader,* Hippocrene, 1972; (with Louis Lundquist) *Chinese Air Power,* Duckworth, in press.

Also author of children's book, *L'Appel de l'Espace* (science fiction stories; title means "The Space Age"). Author

of several hundred radio broadcasts in English and French. Contributor to newspapers, including *London Times, Guardian, Daily Telegraph,* and *Economist.*

WORK IN PROGRESS: Modelling; Chinese.

SIDELIGHTS: Lee told *CA* he is interested in "graphology, soccer, and understanding Americans."

* * *

LEE, Christopher Frank Carandini 1922-

PERSONAL: Born May 27, 1922, in London, England; son of Geoffrey Trollope (a lieutenant-colonel in British Army) and Estelle (Carandini) Lee; married Birgit Kroencke, March 17, 1961; children: Christina Erika Carandini. *Education:* Educated in England. *Agent:* Stephanie Bennett, 148 East 53rd St., New York, N.Y. 10022. *Office:* c/o Robert Littman Co., 409 N. Camden Dr., Beverly Hills, Calif. 90210.

CAREER: Actor, author, and singer. Began acting in motion pictures in 1947, and has appeared in over one hundred thirty films, including "Moulin Rouge," 1953, "A Tale of Two Cities," 1957, "The Curse of Frankenstein," 1957, "Dracula," 1958, "The Hound of the Baskervilles," 1959, "Rasputin," 1965, "The Private Life of Sherlock Holmes," 1970, "The Wicker Man," 1972, "The Three Musketeers," 1973, "The Four Musketeers," 1974, "The Man With the Golden Gun," 1974, "How the West Was Won," 1977, "Airport 77," 1977, "Return From Witch Mountain," 1977, "Caravans," 1977. Owner and founder, Charlemagne Productions, Ltd., 1972—. *Military service:* Royal Air Force, 1941-46; became flight lieutenant; mentioned in dispatches. *Member:* Travellers Club (Paris), Buck's Club, Honourable Company of Edinburgh Golfers, Bay Hill Club, Bel-Air Country Club, Special Forces Club. *Awards, honors:* Officer Arts et Lettres (France).

WRITINGS: Christopher Lee's Treasury of Terror, Pyramid Publications, 1966; *Christopher Lee's New Chamber of Horrors,* Souvenir Press, 1974; *Christopher Lee's Archives of Terror,* Warner Books, Volume I, 1975, Volume 2, 1976; *Tall, Dark and Gruesome* (autobiography), W. H. Allen, 1977.

SIDELIGHTS: "Three films were responsible for bringing me to the fore," Lee once said. "I had my first really good part in 'A Tale of Two Cities,' playing the Marquis of St. Evremonde. This led to my playing the Creature in 'The Curse of Frankenstein' and then to my getting the title role in 'Dracula.'" With the release of "The Curse of Frankenstein" and "Dracula," Lee became the undisputed master of macabre in the British cinema. In 1957 *Variety* reviewed "The Curse of Frankenstein," saying it "deserves praise for its more subdued handling of the macabre story" and that "Christopher Lee arouses more pity than horror in his interpretation of the creature." Lee's brilliant portrayal of Dracula caused one critic to write: "Lee is an actor's actor. Watching him, one can see that he realizes the full potential of the awesome Dracula character, and has created a role which cannot be copied. Lee hasn't seen another Dracula film. He simply read and reread Stoker's novel, and remains honest to it, in no matter what situation he's put."

Lest he be typecast as the charmingly gaunt aristocrat capable of transforming himself into a vampire or ghoul, it is important to note that included in Lee's one hundred thirty motion pictures and forty television films are memorable portrayals of Henry Baskerville in "The Hound of the Baskervilles," Mycroft Holmes in "The Private Life of Sherlock Holmes," Rasputin in the movie of the same name, Lord Summerisle in "The Wicker Man," the schizophrenic in "Alias John Preston," Resurrection Joe in "Corridors of Blood," the Confederate in "Hannie Caulder," Fu Manchu in several movies, and the Comte de Rochefort in "The Three Musketeers." "It does not bother me to be labeled as a horror actor although it is rather a misnomer," Lee has said. "The important thing is to make your mark and be remembered as an actor who is different from others."

CA asked Lee what movie role he found most challenging. "All movie roles are challenging," he said, "and I have probably had to play a larger number than most people, simply because I have so frequently had to contend with poor scripts, uninspired direction and indifferent production. I cannot single out any one, although, basically, making the unbelievable believable is the hardest thing a performer can be asked to do, and I have also had my share of that!

"I do not think I have yet found the 'ideal' part. But I think that the best written character and the best performance I have given was that of Lord Summerisle in Anthony Shaffer's 'Wicker Man.'"

Lee is fluent in French, Italian, Spanish, German, Russian, Swedish, Danish, and Greek.

AVOCATIONAL INTERESTS: Music, travel, golf.

BIOGRAPHICAL/CRITICAL SOURCES: Variety, May 15, 1957; *Movie Monsters,* December, 1974; *Christopher Lee International Club Journal.*

* * *

LEE, Don L. 1942-
(Haki R. Madhubuti)

PERSONAL: Born February 23, 1942, in Little Rock, Ark.; son of Jimmy L. and Maxine (Graves) Lee. *Education:* Attended Wilson Junior College, Roosevelt University, and University of Illinois, Chicago Circle. *Office:* Institute of Positive Education, 7848 South Ellis Ave., Chicago, Ill. 60619.

CAREER: DuSable Museum of African History, Chicago, Ill., apprentice curator, 1963-67; Montgomery Ward, Chicago, stock department clerk, 1963-64; post office clerk in Chicago, 1964-65; Spiegels, Chicago, junior executive, 1965-66; Cornell University, Ithaca, N.Y., writer-in-residence, 1968-69; Northeastern Illinois State College, Chicago, poet-in-residence, 1969-70; University of Illinois, Chicago, lecturer, 1969-71; Howard University, Washington, D.C., writer-in-residence, 1970-75. Publisher and editor, Third World Press. Writer-in-residence at Morgan State College, Baltimore, Md., 1972-73. Director of Institute of Positive Education, Chicago. *Military service:* U.S. Army, 1960-63. *Member:* African Liberation Day Support Committee (vice-chairperson), Congress of African People (past member of executive council).

WRITINGS: Think Black, Broadside Press, 1967; *Black Pride,* Broadside Press, 1967; *For Black People (And Negroes Too),* Third World Press, 1968; *Don't Cry Scream,* Broadside Press, 1969; *We Walk the Way of the New World,* Broadside Press, 1970; (author of introduction) *To Blackness: A Definition in Thought,* Kansas City Black Writers Workshop, 1970; *Dynamite Voices: Black Poets of the 1960's,* Broadside Press, 1971; (editor with P. L. Brown and F. Wood) *To Gwen with Love,* Johnson Publishing Co., 1971; *Directionscore: Selected and New Poems,* Broadside Press, 1971; (under pseudonym Haki R. Madhubuti) *Book of Life,* Broadside Press, 1973; *From Plan to Planet—Life Stud-*

ies: *The Need for Afrikan Minds and Institutions,* Broadside Press, 1973. Also author of *Back, Again, Home,* 1968, *One-Sided Shootout,* 1968, and *Enemies: The Clash of Races,* 1974. Editor of *Black Books Bulletin.*

SIDELIGHTS: Helen Vendler reviewed Lee's poetry for the *New York Times Book Review:* "Lee's poems, written in a rapid, jerky, intense speech-rhythm in almost Morse shorthand, have sold over 100,000 copies without any large-scale advertising or mass distribution, a phenomenon which (like the success of Ginsberg's 'Howl') means that something is happening. Lee is not Rod McKuen or Lois Wyse; he does not sell comfortable sentimentality. He sells on nerve, stamina and satire. In him the sardonic and savage turn-of-phrase long present in black speech as a survival tactic finds its best poet."

Lee's final poem in *Think Black,* "A Message All Blackpeople Can Dig (& a few negroes too)," resonates with hope and confidence for black people:

> "we are going to do it.
> US: blackpeople, beautiful people; the sons and
>   daughters of beautiful people.
> bring it back to
> US: the impossibility.
> now is
> the time, the test . . .
> blackpeople
> are moving, moving to return
>   this earth into the hands of
> human beings."

BIOGRAPHICAL/CRITICAL SOURCES: National Observer, July 14, 1969; *Negro Digest,* December, 1969; *Poetry,* February, 1973; *Contemporary Literary Criticism,* Gale, Volume 2, 1974, (under pseudonym Haki R. Madhubuti) Volume 6, 1976.*

* * *

LEE, Hermione 1948-

PERSONAL: Born February 29, 1948, in England; daughter of Benjamin (a physician and writer of children's books) and Josephine (a writer of children's books) Lee. *Education:* Oxford University, B.A. (first class honors), 1968, B.Phil., 1970. *Office:* Department of English and Related Literature, University of York, Heslington, York YO1 5DP, England.

CAREER: College of William and Mary, Williamsburg, Va., instructor in English, 1970-71; University of Liverpool, Liverpool, England, lecturer in English, 1971-76; University of York, Heslington, England, lecturer in English, 1976—.

WRITINGS: (Contributor) R. T. Davies and B. G. Beatty, editors, *Literature of the Romantic Period,* Liverpool University Press, 1976; *The Novels of Virginia Woolf,* Methuen, 1977. Contributor to literature journals and other magazines, including *New Review, Essays in Criticism,* and *New Statesman.*

WORK IN PROGRESS: A book on Elizabeth Bowen.

* * *

LEE, L(awrence) L(ynn) 1924-

PERSONAL: Born March 4, 1924, in Vernal, Utah; son of William Leroy (an electrician) and Vinnie (Miller) Lee; married Sylvia Bobolis (a teacher), September 1, 1955. *Education:* University of Utah, B.A., 1950, M.A., 1952, Ph.D., 1959. *Home:* 863 East Douglas, Bellingham, Wash. 98225. *Office:* Department of English, Western Washington University, Bellingham, Wash. 98225.

CAREER: Deseret News, Salt Lake City, Utah, copy editor, 1952-53; New Mexico Highlands University, Las Vegas, instructor in English, 1955-56; Defiance College, Defiance, Ohio, assistant professor of English, 1958-62; Western Washington University, Bellingham, assistant professor, 1962-66, associate professor, 1966-69, professor of English, 1969—. *Military service:* U.S. Army, 1943-46. *Member:* Modern Language Association of America, Virginia Woolf Society, Western Literature Association (president, 1976).

WRITINGS: Walter Van Tilburg Clark, Boise State University, 1973; *Vladimir Nabokov,* Twayne, 1976; (editor with Merrill Lewis) *The Westering Experience in American Literature: Bicentennial Essays,* Western Washington University, 1977; (editor with Merrill Lewis) *Women, Women Writers, and the West,* Whitston, 1978; (with wife, Sylvia Lee) *Virginia Sorensen,* Boise State University, 1978. Contributor to literary journals. Editor of *Concerning Poetry,* 1968-77.

SIDELIGHTS: Lee told *CA:* "I am a bird watcher, a Sunday painter, and a reader of almost anything, including cereal boxes, all of which qualifies me as a critic."

* * *

LEE, S(amuel) E(dgar) 1894-

PERSONAL: Born December 18, 1894, in Franklin Parish, La.; son of Clarence Dawson (a farmer) and Mary E. (Richardson) Lee; married Lula Belle Wiltshire, September 3, 1916; children: Samuel E. II, Lucye Lee Brocato, Pauline Lee Stitt, Kirby E. *Education:* Attended Tyler Commercial School. *Politics:* "Registered Democrat; vote Republican nationally." *Religion:* Methodist. *Home address:* Route 3, Box 34½, Winnsboro, La. 71295.

CAREER: Worked as farmer, cross tie and stove inspector, plantation overseer and bookkeeper, 1915-23; Winnsboro Motor Co., Winnsboro, La., car salesman and bookkeeper, 1923-34; Winnsboro Farm Supply, Winnsboro, manager, salesman, and bookkeeper, 1934-37; Planters Implement Co., Winnsboro, partner and manager, 1937-47, owner, 1947—, president, 1961-67; writer, 1967—. *Member:* Lions (past president; past district deputy governor), Methodist Mens Club, Masons.

WRITINGS: Recollections of Country Joe, Pelican, 1976.

WORK IN PROGRESS: A book, fiction.

SIDELIGHTS: Lee remarks: "The book was written mostly to leave a record of country life in a southern state, as lived by me fifty to eighty years ago." He adds: "I believe in law and order, the Burger Court, and church attendance." *Avocational interests:* Travel (Europe, Mexico).

* * *

LEEMING, Jo Ann
See LEEMING, Joseph

* * *

LEEMING, Joseph 1897-1968
(Jo Ann Leeming, Merlin Swift, Professor Zingara)

PERSONAL: Born 1897, in Brooklyn, N.Y.; children: Avery Leeming Nagle (daughter). *Education:* Attended Williams College.

CAREER: Author of "Fun with" series and other craft and game books. Worked for a time in the shipping industry; traveled extensively throughout the world, including a visit to India; later did editorial and publicity work.

WRITINGS—"Fun with" series: *Fun with Boxes: How to Make Things for Pleasure and Profit,* F. A. Stokes, 1937; *... Paper: How to Fold and Cut Paper to Make Useful Articles, Toys, and Amusing Tricks,* F. A. Stokes, 1939; *... String: A Collection of String Games, Useful Braiding and Weaving, Knot Work, and Magic,* F. A. Stokes, 1940; *... Leather: How to Do Decorative Leatherwork of All Kinds,* F. A. Stokes, 1941; *... Wood: How to Whittle and Carve Wood,* F. A. Stokes, 1942; *... Magic: How to Make Magic Equipment; How To Perform Many Tricks,* F. A. Stokes, 1943; *... Clay: A Book for All Beginners,* Lippincott, 1944.

Fun with Plastics: A Beginner's Book, Lippincott, 1946; *... Puzzles: Puzzles of Every Kind for Everybody,* Lippincott, 1946; *More Fun with Puzzles: Puzzles of Every Kind for Everybody,* Lippincott, 1947; *More Fun with Magic: A Book of Magic Tricks for Everyone,* Lippincott, 1948; *Fun with Fabrics: Amusing, Interesting, and Useful Things to Make of Cloth and Felt,* Lippincott, 1950; *... Beads,* Lippincott, 1954; *... Pencil and Paper: Games, Stunts, Puzzles,* Lippincott, 1955; *... Wire,* Lippincott, 1956; *... Shells,* Lippincott, 1958; *... Artificial Flowers,* Lippincott, 1959; *... Greeting Cards,* Lippincott, 1960; (with daughter, Avery Nagle) *Fun with Naturecraft,* Lippincott, 1964.

Other craft books: *Things Any Boy Can Make: The Boy's Own Book of Home-Made Toys,* Century, 1929; *More Things Any Boy Can Make: The Book of Home-Made Toys and Games,* Appleton-Century, 1936; *The Costume Book,* F. A. Stokes, 1938, reprinted, Lippincott, 1966; *Models Any Boy Can Build,* Appleton-Century, 1938; *Toy Boats to Make at Home,* Appleton-Century, 1946; *Papercraft: How to Make Toys, Favors, and Useful Articles,* Lippincott, 1949; *Holiday Craft and Fun: Party-Craft for Holidays,* Lippincott, 1950.

Magic: *The New Book of Magic,* Doubleday, Page, 1927; *Magic for Everybody: The 250 Best and Newest Feats of Magic* (illustrated by Jay Van Everen), Doubleday, Doran, 1928; (under pseudonym Professor Zingara) *The Complete Magician's Manual,* 1935, revised edition, under Leeming, published as *How to Be the Life of the Party,* Foster & Stewart, 1946; *Tricks Any Boy Can Do,* Appleton-Century, 1938, reprinted, Hawthorn, 1975; *Card Tricks Anyone Can Do,* Appleton-Century, 1941; (under pseudonym Merlin Swift) *Secrets of Magic,* F. Watts, 1946; *The Real Book About Magic,* Garden City Books, 1951.

Games: *Games to Make and Play at Home,* Appleton-Century, 1943; *Games with Playing Cards, Plus Tricks and Stunts,* F. Watts, 1949; *The First Book of Chess,* F. Watts, 1953; *The Real Book of Games,* Garden City Books, 1953.

Other nonfiction: *Ships and Cargos: The Romance of Ocean Commerce,* Doubleday, Page, 1926; *Peaks of Invention,* Century, 1928; *The Book of American Fighting Ships,* Harper, 1939; *From Barter to Banking: The Story of the World's Coinage and Money,* Appleton-Century, 1940; *Modern Export Packing,* U.S. Government Printing Office, 1940; *Brave Ships of England and America,* Thomas Nelson, 1941, reprinted, Books for Libraries Press, 1969; *Modern Ship Stowage: Including Methods of Handling Cargo at Ocean Terminals,* U.S. Government Printing Office, 1942; *The Washington Story: Pictorial Guide to Washington D.C.,* Foster & Stewart, 1948; *Jobs That Take You Places,* McKay, 1948, revised edition, 1953.

(With Avery Leeming) *It's Easy to Make Music: How to Play All the Popular Instruments,* F. Watts, 1948, new edition published as *The Real Book about Easy Music-Making,* Garden City Books, 1952; *Money Making Hobbies: 100*

Easy Ways to Earn Extra Money (illustrated by Jessie Robinson), Lippincott, 1948; (under pseudonym JoAnn Leeming, with Margaret Gleeson) *The Complete Book of Showers and Engagement Parties,* Garden City Books, 1948, revised and enlarged edition published as *The Complete Shower Party Book,* Doubleday, 1971.

Rayon: The First Man-Made Fiber, Chemical Publishing, 1950; *The White House in Picture and Story,* G. W. Stewart, 1953; *Fun for Young Collectors: An Introduction to Thirty-Two Collection Projects* (illustrated by Jessie Robinson), Lippincott, 1953; *The Real Book of Science Experiments* (illustrated by Bette J. Davis), Garden City Books, 1954; (with Avery Nagle) *Kitchen Table Fun,* Lippincott, 1961; *Yoga and the Bible: The Yoga of the Divine Word,* Allen & Unwin, 1963.

Editor: *Riddles, Riddles, Riddles* (illustrated by Shane Miller), F. Watts, 1953; (with Helen Hoke) *Jokes, Riddles, Puns: The Best Brief Humor,* F. Watts, 1959; (with K. L. Khana) Sawan Singh, *Tales of the Mystic East,* Radha Soami Satsang (Beas, India), c. 1961, 2nd edition, 1964.

BIOGRAPHICAL/CRITICAL SOURCES: Chicago Tribune, February 28, 1954.*

(Died, 1968)

* * *

LEHMANN, Lotte   1888-1976

PERSONAL: Born February 27, 1888, in Perleberg, Prussia (now West Germany); came to the United States in 1938, naturalized citizen, 1945; daughter of Carl and Marie (Schuster) Lehmann; married Otto Krause (a cavalry officer and insurance company executive), April 28, 1926 (died, January, 1939); children: Manon, Hans, Ludwig, Peter (stepchildren). *Education:* Studied voice in Germany with Helene Jordan, Eva Reinhold, and Matilde Mallinger. *Home:* 4565 Via Huerto, Hope Ranch Park, Santa Barbara, Calif. 93105.

CAREER: Operatic soprano and lieder singer. Sang with Hamburg Municipal Theatre, 1910-13; sand with Vienna Opera, 1916-38, and at Salzburg Festival, summers, 1927-37; moved to the United States and was associated with Metropolitan Opera, San Francisco Opera, and Chicago Civic Opera, 1940-1946; gave lieder recitals until 1951; after retiring from singing, became director of Music Academy of the West in Santa Barbara, Calif.; taught voice privately and in master classes at institutions such as Manhattan School of Music, Northwestern University, and University of California at Santa Barbara; co-directed a new production of "Der Rosenkavalier" for Metropolitan Opera, 1962. Made numerous concert tours, including one in South America, 1922, and in Australia, 1939, and appeared as a guest performer in opera houses throughout the world, including Covent Garden Opera, La Scala, and Paris Opera. Held an exhibit of her watercolors at Schaeffer Galleries, New York City, 1950.

AWARDS, HONORS: Made honorary member of Vienna State Opera; Cross of Honor, first class, for science and art, from Austria; Ring of Honor from Vienna Philharmonic; Swedish Gold Medal for Art & Science, 1929; officer in the French Legion of Honor; Bon Ami Award, 1960; Grand Cross of Merit, 1963, from German Federal Republic; Great Silver Medal, 1969, from city of Salzburg; received honorary doctorates from University of Portland, 1949, Mills College, 1951, Northwestern University, 1956, and University of California at Santa Barbara, 1961.

WRITINGS: Orplid mein Land (novel), H. Reichner, 1937, translation by Elsa Krauch published as *Eternal Flight,* Putnam, 1937; *Anfang und Aufstieg: Lebenserinnerungen,* H. Reichner, translation by Margaret Ludwig published as *Midway in My Song: The Autobiography of Lotte Lehmann,* Bobbs-Merrill, 1938, reprinted, Arno, 1973; *More Than Singing: The Interpretation of Songs,* translated from the German by Frances Holden, Boosey & Hawkes, 1945, reprinted, Greenwood, 1975; *My Many Lives,* translated from the German by Holden, Boosey & Hawkes, 1948, reprinted, Greenwood, 1974; *Five Operas and Richard Strauss,* translated from the German by Ernst Pawel, Macmillan, 1964; *Eighteen Songcycles: Studies in Their Interpretation,* Cassell, 1971, Praeger, 1972. Also author of a book of poetry, *Verse in Prosa.*

SIDELIGHTS: Lotte Lehmann, the dramatic and lyric soprano who thrilled audiences with her inspired acting and warm, beautiful voice, had a repertory of about one hundred operatic roles. She appeared in all the major operas of Strauss and Wagner, as well as in operas by Puccini, Mozart, and others. Among her best-known roles were Leonore in "Fidelio," Sieglinde in "Die Walkuere," and Elsa of Brabant in "Lohengrin." But it was the role of the Marschallin in Strauss's "Der Rosenkavalier" that became "synonymous with her name," according to Alden Whitman. Harold C. Schonberg described Lehmann's Marschallin: "Talking about it, strong men snuffle and break into tears. . . . In short, she was The One: unique, irreplaceable, the standard to which all must aspire."

Lehmann made her American debut at the Chicago Civic Opera as Sieglinde in "Die Walkuere" in 1930, and sang the same role for her debut at the Metropolitan Opera in 1934. She was conducted, in the United States and abroad, by such luminaries as Bruno Walter, Arturo Toscanini, Franz Schalk, Sir Thomas Beecham, and Otto Klempere.

The soprano was also a celebrated singer of lieder—songs which she described as the "ideal union of poetry and melody." During the intermission of a lieder recital in 1951, she announced her retirement. Responding to cries of protestation from the audience, she told them: "I had hoped you would protest, but please don't argue with me. After forty one years of anxiety, nerves, strain and hard work I think I deserve to take it easy."

Lehmann made numerous recordings released by Angel, Odeon, Electrola, RCA Victor, Columbia, Victrola, and other companies. To commemorate her eightieth birthday, several albums were reissued. She also made recordings of readings from Heine and Goethe. In 1948, she appeared in the film "Big City," produced by Metro-Goldwyn-Mayer.

AVOCATIONAL INTERESTS: Horseback riding, swimming, painting, sculpting, and ceramics.

BIOGRAPHICAL/CRITICAL SOURCES: Lotte Lehmann, *Midway in My Song: The Autobiography of Lotte Lehmann,* Bobbs-Merrill, 1938, reprinted, Arno, 1973. Obituaries: *New York Times,* August 27, 1976; *Washington Post,* August 27, 1976.*

(Died August 26, 1976, in Santa Barbara, Calif.)

* * *

LELE, Uma   1941-

PERSONAL: Born August 28, 1941, in India; came to the United States in 1960; daughter of D. B. (a lawyer) and K. D. Godbole; married Jayant Lele, May 20, 1960 (divorced); married John Mellor (director of a research institute), February 17, 1973; children: one. *Education:* Ferguson College, B.A. (honors), 1960; Cornell University, M.S., 1963, Ph.D., 1965. *Home:* 511 Cameron St., Alexandria, Va. 22314. *Office:* World Bank, 1818 H St. N.W., Washington, D.C.

CAREER: Queen's University, Kingston, Ontario, assistant professor of economics, 1966; Cornell University, Ithaca, N.Y., researcher in agricultural economics, 1966-69; U.S. Agency for International Development, India, researcher, 1969-70; Twentieth Century Fund, New York, N.Y., researcher, 1971; World Bank, Washington, D.C., economist, 1971—. Visiting assistant professor at Cornell University, 1970-71, visiting associate professor and senior research fellow at Center for International Studies, 1974-75. Member of board of directors of International Voluntary Services and Private Agencies Cooperating Together. *Member:* American Economic Association, American Agricultural Economic Association, Indian Society of Agricultural Economics (life member).

WRITINGS: (With John W. Mellor, Sheldon R. Simon, and Thomas F. Weaver) *Developing Rural India: Plan and Practice,* Cornell University Press, 1968; *Food Grain Marketing in India: Private Performance and Public Policy,* Cornell University Press, 1971; *The Design of Rural Development: Lessons from Africa,* Johns Hopkins Press, 1975.

Contributor: Norman T. Uphoff and Warren F. Ilchman, editors, *The Political Economy of Development,* University of California Press, 1972; G. S. Tolley, editor, *Trade, Agriculture, and Development,* Ballinger, 1973; V. A. Pai Panandikar and N. C. Mehta, editors, *Rural Banking,* National Institute of Bank Management (Bombay, India), 1974; *Food Enough or Starvation for Millions?,* Tata McGraw, in press. Contributor of about twenty articles and reviews to professional journals.

WORK IN PROGRESS: Contributor to *Agricultural Development in India: Policy and Problems.*

*   *   *

LEMERT, James B(olton)   1935-
  (Jim Lemert)

PERSONAL: Born November 5, 1935, in Sangerfield, N.Y.; son of Jesse Raymond (a clergyman) and Caroline Elizabeth (Brown) Lemert; married Carol Rudner, May, 1962 (divorced, 1963); married Rosalie Martha Bassett, March 25, 1972. *Education:* University of California, Berkeley, A.B., 1957, M.J., 1959; Michigan State University, Ph.D., 1964. *Politics:* Democrat. *Religion:* Episcopal. *Residence:* Eugene, Ore. *Office:* School of Journalism, University of Oregon, Eugene, Ore. 97403.

CAREER: Oakland Tribune, Oakland, Calif., sports stringer, 1955-56; *Chico Enterprise-Record,* Chico, Calif., reporter, 1957; Institute of Transportation & Traffic Engineering, Richmond, Calif., publications writer and technical editor, 1957-58; *Chico Enterprise-Record,* reporter, 1958-60; Southern Illinois University, Carbondale, assistant professor of journalism, 1964-67; University of Oregon, Eugene, assistant professor, 1967-69, associate professor, 1969-76, professor of journalism, 1976—, director of Division of Communication Research, 1967—. Member of Oregon Alcohol & Drug Education Advisory Committee, 1968-69.

MEMBER: International Communication Association, American Association for Public Opinion Research, Association for Education in Journalism, American Association of University Professors, South Hills Neighborhood Association (president, 1976-77), Phi Beta Kappa, Sigma Delta

Chi (president, 1956-57), Kappa Tau Alpha. *Awards, honors:* National Science Foundation fellowship, summer, 1964.

WRITINGS: Do the Media Change Public Opinion After All?: A New Approach to Effects Analysis, Nelson-Hall, 1978. Author of *Daily Californian* columns, under name Jim Lemert: "The Muscle Shop," 1955-56, and "Poet's Corner," 1957-58. Contributor of about twenty-five articles to journalism magazines, including *Journalism Quarterly,* and to newspapers. Editor of *Daily Californian,* 1957.

SIDELIGHTS: Lemert writes: "Journalists tend to be in one of the more tradition-bound crafts, and are relatively defensive when questions are raised about habitual ways of doing things. We may be asking more of them than they can deliver, but to paraphrase an old saying 'It may be crooked, but (journalism) is the only wheel in town.' A constant underlying theme in the mass media research I do is that the research can help journalists to assess the adequacy of old habits. While most of the research I've done has been published, I'd call attention to an unpublished paper on 'Craft Attitudes' which reflects my philosophy about research."

AVOCATIONAL INTERESTS: Collecting traditional jazz recordings.

*   *   *

LEMERT, Jim
  See LEMERT, James B(olton)

*   *   *

LENHOFF, Alan (Stuart)   1951-

PERSONAL: Born July 14, 1951, in Detroit, Mich.; son of Sidney M. (employed by U.S. Department of Defense) and Sarah (an elementary school teacher) Lenhoff. *Education:* University of Michigan, A.B. (with distinction), 1973. *Office:* House Press Rm., The Capitol, Lansing, Mich. 48902.

CAREER/WRITINGS: Oakland Community Newspapers, Union Lake, Mich., reporter, 1974; *Oakland Press,* Pontiac, Mich., reporter, 1974-76, state capitol bureau chief, 1976—. *Awards, honors:* Detroit Press Club Award, 1973, for editorial writing; Associated Press Award, 1976, for investigative reporting; Morgan O'Leary Award for political reporting in Michigan, American Bar Association Silver Gavel Award, Advancement of Justice Medallion from Michigan Bar Association, honorable mention from United Press International for investigative reporting, runner-up for Detroit Press club Medallion Award, Pulitzer Prize nominee, all 1977.

*   *   *

LENSON, David (Rollar)   1945-

PERSONAL: Born June 28, 1945, in Kearny, N.J.; son of Michael (a painter) and June (an executive; maiden name, Rollar) Lenson. *Education:* Princeton University, A.B., 1967, M.A., 1970, Ph.D., 1971. *Home address:* P.O. Box 77, Sunderland, Mass. 01375. *Office:* Department of Comparative Literature, University of Massachusetts, 305 South College Hall, Amherst, Mass. 01003.

CAREER: University of Massachusetts, Amherst, assistant professor, 1971-76, associate professor of comparative literature, 1976—. Publisher, president, chairman, and editor of *Panache,* 1971—. *Member:* Modern Language Association of America, Committee of Small Magazine Editors and Publishers, Coordinating Council of Literary Magazines. *Awards, honors:* National Endowment for the Humanities younger humanist fellow, 1973-74.

WRITINGS: *Achilles' Choice* (criticism), Princeton University Press, 1975; *The Gambler* (poems), Lynx House Press, 1977. Contributor to literary journals, including *Texas Quarterly* and *Quarterly Review,* and education journals.

WORK IN PROGRESS: *Ride Through the Shadow Armed,* poems; *The Imagination,* criticism.

SIDELIGHTS: Lenson writes: "With equal background in academic criticism and non-academic poetry, I have dedicated myself to integrating the two in some personal way, but find myself more deeply into poetry at the present time. I am also active as a blues musician, and find that this form of improvisatory art has influenced my poetry. As editor of *Panache,* I am also indebted to my contemporaries all over the world, whose submissions to the magazine have kept me abreast. Prime influences are Pound, Eliot, Robert Fagles, Edmund Keeley, Theodore and Renee Weiss, Joseph Frank, and Ralph Freedman."

* * *

LENT, Henry Bolles 1901-1973

PERSONAL: Born November 1, 1901, in New Bedford, Mass.; children: Henry, David. *Education:* Attended Yale University; graduated from Hamilton College. *Residence:* Woodstock, Vt.

CAREER: Author and advertising executive.

WRITINGS: *Diggers and Builders* (self-illustrated), Macmillan, 1931; *Clear Track Ahead!* (illustrated by Earle Winslow), Macmillan, 1932; *Full Steam Ahead!* (illustrated by Winslow), Macmillan, 1933; *The Waldorf-Astoria,* privately printed, 1934; *Grindstone Farm* (illustrated by Wilfrid S. Bronson), Macmillan, 1935; *Tugboat* (illustrated by Winslow), Macmillan, 1936; *The Air Pilot* (illustrated by George and Doris Hauman), Macmillan, 1937; *The Bus Driver* (illustrated by Winslow), Macmillan, 1937; *The Captain* (illustrated by Winslow), Macmillan, 1937; *The Farmer* (illustrated by Berta and Elmer Hader), Macmillan, 1937; *The Storekeeper* (illustrated by G. and D. Hauman), 1937; *The Fire Fighter* (illustrated by Winslow), Macmillan, 1939.

Flight 17 (illustrated by G. and D. Hauman), Macmillan, 1940; *Aviation Cadet: Dick Hilton Wins His Wings at Pensacola,* Macmillan, 1941; *Sixty Acres More or Less: The Diary of a Week-End Vermonter,* Macmillan, 1941; *Air Patrol: Jim Brewster Flies for the U.S. Coast Guard,* Macmillan, 1942; *Bombardier Tom Dixon Wins His Wings with the Bomber Command,* Macmillan, 1943; *PT Boat: Bob Reed Wins His Command at Melville,* Macmillan, 1943; *Seabee: Bill Scott Builds and Fights for the Navy,* Macmillan, 1944; *Straight Down* (illustrated by Adolph Treidler), Macmillan, 1944; *Straight Up* (illustrated by Raymond Lufkin), Macmillan, 1944; *Ahoy, Shipmate! Steve Ellis Joins the Merchant Marine,* Macmillan, 1945; *"This Is You Announcer": Ted Lane Breaks into Radio,* Macmillan, 1945; *Fly It Away!,* Macmillan, 1946; *Eight Hours to Solo,* Macmillan, 1947; *I Work on a Newspaper* (photographs by James B. Walsh), Macmillan, 1948.

O.K. for Drive-Away: How Automobiles Are Built, Macmillan, 1951; *From Trees to Paper: The Story of Newsprint,* Macmillan, 1952; *Here Come the Trucks* (illustrated by Renee George), Macmillan, 1954; *The Helicopter Book,* Macmillan, 1956; *Men at Work in New England,* Putnam, 1956; *Flight Overseas,* Macmillan, 1957; *Men at Work in the South,* Putnam, 1957, reprinted, 1970; *Jet Pilot,* Macmillan,

1958; *Jet Pilot Overseas,* Macmillan, 1959; *Men at Work in the Great Lakes States,* Putnam, 1958, reissued, 1971; *Men at Work on the West Coast,* Putnam, 1959.

Men at Work in the Mid-Atlantic States, Putnam, 1961, reprinted as *Men at Work in the Middle Atlantic States,* 1970; *Man Alive in Outer Space: Our Space Surgeons' Greatest Challenge,* Macmillan, 1961; *Submarine: The Story of Basic Training at the Navy's Famed Submarine School,* Macmillan, 1962; *Your Place in America's Space Program,* Macmillan, 1964; *The Book of Cars: Yesterday, Today, Tomorrow,* Dutton, 1966; *The Peace Corps: Ambassadors of Goodwill,* Westminster Press, 1966; *Agriculture U.S.A.: America's Most Basic Industry,* Dutton, 1968; *The Automobile, U.S.A.: Its Impact on People's Lives and the National Economy,* Dutton, 1968; *What Car Is That?* (illustrated by John Raynes), Dutton, 1969; *Car of the Year, 1895-1970,* Dutton, 1970; *The X Cars: Detroit's One-of-a-Kind Autos,* Putnam, 1971.

(Died, October, 1973)

* * *

LEODHAS, Sorche Nic
See NIC LEODHAS, Sorche

* * *

LEOPOLD, Carolyn Clugston 1923-
(Carolyn Leopold Michaels)

PERSONAL: Born February 21, 1923, in Chicago, Ill.; daughter of Charles D. (a sales manager) and Alice Madelyn Clugston; married Luna B. Leopold, September 6, 1940 (divorced, 1973); married William M. Michaels (a dentist), December 29, 1973; children: (first marriage) Bruce Carl, Madelyn Dennette. *Education:* Attended William and Mary College, 1935-36; University of Maryland, B.A., 1939; Catholic University of America, M.S.L.S., 1959; attended University of California, Berkeley, 1972-73. *Politics:* Republican. *Religion:* Episcopalian. *Home:* 3506 Dunlop St., Chevy Chase, Md. 20115. *Office:* National Geographic Society, 17th & M Sts. N.W., Washington, D.C. 20036.

CAREER: Librarian at private schools in Washington, D.C., 1959-60, Bethesda, Md., 1960-64, and Washington, D.C., 1964-66, at board of education Rockville, Md., 1966-69, and at American Council on Education, 1969-72, National Geographic Society, Washington, D.C., researcher, 1974-76, researcher and writer, 1976—. Consultant to Nature Conservancy and Woman's History Research Center. *Member:* American Library Association, District of Columbia Library Association, Continuing Library Education Network and Exchange (CLENE), Phi Beta Mu, Kappa Kappa Gamma.

WRITINGS: (Editor) Aldo Leopold, Sand County Almanac, Oxford University Press, 1966; *School Libraries Worth Their Keep,* Scarecrow, 1972. Contributor of articles and reviews to library and education journals.

WORK IN PROGRESS: *For the Love of the Land* (juvenile).

SIDELIGHTS: Carolyn Leopold writes: "Published writing seems the ultimate in communication. An individually authored book displays and preserves a human personality. The message is held fast where present and future minds meet and challenge your tinkering with the wheel. Person to person—or person to multitudes of persons—but each is one to one. Drawn to writing, living with someone who did practically nothing else, becoming a writer seemed inescapable.

A substitute for grandchildren—an insidious form of immortality."

* * *

LERNER, Linda

PERSONAL: Born in New York; daughter of Philip and Frieda Lerner. *Education:* Brooklyn College of the City University of New York, B.A., 1964, M.A., 1969. *Home:* 110 Montague St., Brooklyn, N.Y. 11201.

CAREER: Brooklyn College of the City University of New York, Brooklyn, N.Y., adjunct lecturer, 1970—. Adjunct lecturer at Polytechnic Institute, 1976—.

WRITINGS: Target Practice (poems), Marco Fraticille, 1977. Contributor of more than a hundred poems to magazines, including *Epoch, Centennial Review,* and *California Quarterly.*

WORK IN PROGRESS: The Wrong Children, poems.

SIDELIGHTS: Linda Lerner writes: "Writing has always been essential to my existence. I kept a journal for ten years which I have never shown to anyone. That was before I began writing. My writing is not autobiographcal in the sense that it is faithful to the facts of my life, but it is in the psychological sense, and in the way I imaginatively view the world."

* * *

LERNER, Richard E(dward) 1941-

PERSONAL: Born December 27, 1941, in New York, N.Y.; son of Nat (a salesman) and Estelle (Cohen) Lerner; married Jan Fritz (a sociologist), August 7, 1969; children: Karin Fritz, Hyunjin Fritz. *Education:* Miami University (Ohio), B.A., 1963; Johns Hopkins University, M.A., 1965; Columbia University, M.S., 1966. *Politics:* Independent. *Religion:* None. *Home:* 505 Second St. S.E., Washington, D.C. 20003. *Office:* U.P.I., 315 National Press Building, Washington, D.C. 20045.

CAREER/WRITINGS: Ohio State University, Columbus, instructor in political science, 1966-67; United Press International, Washington, D.C., writer, editor, Congressional reporter and White House correspondent, 1968—.

* * *

LERSKI, George Jan 1917-
(Jerzy Jur)

PERSONAL: Born January 20, 1917, in Lwow, Poland; came to the United States in 1949, naturalized citizen, 1962; son of Mieczyslaw (a civil engineer) and Zofia (Gordziewicz) Lerski; married Hanna Hryniewiecka, December 13, 1945 (divorced, June, 1967); married Belva Jean Pearson (a teacher), September 27, 1967; children: Thomas M., Maile K., Dana L., Martha B., Scott E. *Education:* Attended Jan Kazimierz University, 1936-39; Oxford University, LL.M., 1946; Georgetown University, Ph.D., 1953. *Politics:* Social Democrat. *Religion:* Roman Catholic. *Home:* 560 Dewey Blvd., San Francisco, Calif. 94116. *Office:* Department of History, University of San Francisco, San Francisco, Calif. 94117.

CAREER: Private secretary to Prime Minister of Poland in London, England, 1944-45; *Polish Daily,* Detroit, Mich., political editor, 1955; Nihon University, Tokyo, Japan, professor of Western history, 1955-58; University of Karachi, Karachi, Pakistan, professor of American history and international relations, 1958-60; Asia Foundation, San Francis-

co, Calif., program specialist in review and development department, 1960-62; University of Ceylon, Peradeniya, visiting professor of political science, 1962-64; Hoover Institution on War, Revolution, and Peace, Stanford, Calif., research associate, 1964-65; Asia Foundation, senior research associate, 1965-66; University of San Francisco, San Francisco, Calif., associate professor, 1966-68, professor of history and government, 1969-70, professor of modern European history, 1970—, acting chairman of department of political science, 1968-69. Visiting lecturer for Council on Asian Affairs and Japan Institute of Foreign Affairs, 1954; lecturer at Chuo University, University of the Sacred Heart, and International Christian University, all 1955-58. Member of American-Asian Educational Exchange, Inc.; chairman of board of directors of North American Study Center of Polish Affairs, 1976—; consultant to U.S. Department of Defense and National Security Council. *Military service:* Polish Armed Forces, 1935-45, anti-aircraft artillery officer, 1939-40, officer of Polish Army in Exile, 1940-42, secret courier, under name "Jur," 1942-44; served in France and Scotland; became lieutenant; received Cross of Valor, Home Army Cross, King's Medal for Courage in the Cause of Freedom (England), and British War Medal.

MEMBER: American Historical Association, American Catholic Historical Association, American Association for the Advancement of Slavic Studies, Polish American Historical Association (president, 1974; member of advisory council), Polish Institute of Arts and Sciences in America, Polish American Congress (national director, 1975-77; regional vice-president for political affairs; board chairman of the North American Study Center for Polish Affairs), Polish Society of Arts and Sciences Abroad, Societe Historique et Litteraire Polonaise, Association of Polish University Professors Abroad, Polish Home Army Veterans Association (member of supreme council), Polish Veterans of World War II, World Affairs Council of Northern California, Pilsudski Institute of America for Research in the Modern History of Poland, University of San Francisco Faculty Association. *Awards, honors:* Best book of the year award from Polish Army Veterans Association, 1958, for *A Polish Chapter in Jacksonian America.*

WRITINGS: (Editor and contributor) *Drogi Cichociemnych,* Veritas, 1954, English translation published as *The Unseen and Silent: Adventures from the Underground Movement Narrated by Paratroops of the Polish Home Army,* Sheed, 1954; *The Economy of Poland,* Washington Council for Economic and Industry Research, 1954; *History of Western Political Thought* (translation of work by Satoshi Saito), Risosha Co., 1958; *A Polish Chapter in Jacksonian America: The United States and the Polish Exiles of 1831,* University of Wisconsin Press, 1958; *Origins of Trotskyism in Ceylon: A Documentary History of the Lanka Sama Samaja Party, 1935-1962,* Hoover Institution, 1968; (contributor) Witold S. Sworakowski, editor, *World Communism: A Handbook, 1918-1965,* Hoover Institution, 1972; *Herbert Hoover and Poland: A Documentary History of a Friendship,* Hoover Institution, 1977. Contributor of articles and reviews to history and Asian studies journals in the United States and abroad.

WORK IN PROGRESS: Anthology of the Jewish Question in Polish Democratic Thought; For Your Freedom and Mine: An Autobiography of General Sikorski's Tourist; The First American Envoy in Poland: Hugh Gibson; The Polish Prince of the Church of South Asia: Apostolic Delegate Archbishop L. M. Zaleski; war memoirs, 1935-39, 1939-45.

SIDELIGHTS: Before the beginning of World War II, Lerski was chairman of the Polish Social-Democratic Youth in Lwow, and a member of the supreme council of the Democratic Party. During the war, in addition to his military activities, which included parachuting into enemy-occupied Poland, he also served with the central authorities of the Polish Underground Government. After the war, he worked as secretary general of the Polish freedom movement known as Independence and Democracy.

His current interests are more academic, including documentary history of modern Poland, with special emphasis on its relations with the United States and the Jews. His works express his "rich experience in the struggle for social-democracy and freedom."

* * *

LERTETH, Oban
See FANTHORPE, R(obert) Lionel

* * *

LESINS, Knuts 1909-

PERSONAL: Born March 28, 1909, in St. Petersburg, Russia; came to United States, 1950; naturalized U.S. citizen, 1956; son of Woldemars (a writer) and Edvina (a teacher; maiden name, Berling) Lesins; married Valda Smits (a singer and music teacher), June 8, 1935. *Education:* Latvian State Conservatory, M.A., 1932; also studied at University of Latvia. *Religion:* Evangelical Lutheran. *Home:* 4824 14th Ave., Minneapolis, Minn. 55417.

CAREER: Worked in Riga, Latvia, as journalist, writer, and music critic, 1930-36; dramatist for Latvian National Opera, 1936-42; worked in Germany, 1944-50; writer, journalist, teacher, pianist, composer, 1950—. *Member:* National Writer's Club, Latvian Press Society. *Awards, honors:* Award for short stories, Latvian Cultural Fund, 1946, for *Reflections;* honorary mention from Minnesota Centennial distinguished book competition, 1957, for *The Wine of Eternity.*

*WRITINGS—*In English: *The Wine of Eternity,* University of Minnesota Press, 1957.

Other—In Latvian: *Zimestumsa* (short stories; title means "Omens in the Dark"), J. Valters, 1938; *Problemas un sejas latviesu muzika* (title means "Faces and Problems in Latvian Music"), A. Gulbis, 1939; *Milestibas eimogs* (novel; title means "The Seal of Love"), J. Kreismanis, 1943; *Atstari* (short stories; title means "Reflections"), A. Stals, 1946; *Lietas, kas kartojas pasas* (short stories; title means "Things That Arrange Themselves"), Latvija, 1948; *Muzibas vins* (short stories), J. Kadilis, 1949; *Janka muzikants* (novel; title means "John the Musician"), Ziemelblazma, J. Abucs, 1950; *Lepnas sirdis* (short stories; title means "The Proud Hearts"), Ziemelblazma, J. Abucs, 1952; *Akla iela* (short stories; title means "Dead End Streets"), Daugava, 1955; *Zem svesam zvaigznem* (sketches and reminiscences; title means "Under Foreign Stars"), O. Dikis, 1956; *Pedejas majas* (novel; title means "The Last Home"), Ziemelblazma, J. Abucs, 1957; *Smilgas saulrieta* (poetry; title means "Sunset in the Grass"), Alfred Kalnajs, 1962.

Contributor of short stories to *Arena, PEN Club magazine, Short Stories International,* and to Latvian periodicals.

WORK IN PROGRESS: Short stories, reminiscences.

SIDELIGHTS: Lesins told *CA:* "I was influenced by the Latvian poet and writer of modern fairy-tales Karlis Skalbe (1879-1945). I liked his lyrical style with philosophical and humanitarian implications. While studying music I was attracted to the writings of the German romanticist writer and musician E.T.A. Hoffman but I also read many German, Russian, French and English short story writers who emphasize a psychological approach to people. The short story to me presents a chance to reveal sometimes the whole essence of a character in momentary episodes and glimpses. I have also always been fascinated by the deep natural wisdom and beauty of the language of the Latvian folk-songs and fairytales. The title of one of my tales and of the book ''The Wine of Eternity'' was suggested by an ancient Latvian fairytale."

* * *

LESLIE, San
See CROOK, Bette (Jean)

* * *

LESSER, Charles H(uber) 1944-

PERSONAL: Born March 15, 1944, in DuBois, Pa.; son of Ray C. (a chemist) and Mary Ann (Huber) Lesser. *Education:* Pennsylvania State University, B.A., 1966, M.A., 1968; University of Michigan, Ph.D., 1974. *Home:* 1624 Heyward, Columbia, S.C. 29205. *Office:* South Carolina Department of Archives and History, P.O. Box 11669, Capitol Station, Columbia, S.C. 29211.

CAREER: University of Michigan, Ann Arbor, research editor at William L. Clements Library, 1972-75; South Carolina Department of Archives and History, Columbia, assistant director for archives and publications, 1975—. *Member:* Society of American Archivists, Organization of American Historians, American Historical Association, Southern Historical Association, South Carolina Historical Society, South Carolina Historical Association, South Caroliniana Society.

WRITINGS: The Sinews of Independence: Monthly Strength Reports of the Continental Army, University of Chicago Press, 1976; (with J. Todd White) *The Fighters for Independence: A Guide to Sources of Biographical Information on Soldiers and Sailors of the American Revolution,* University of Chicago Press, 1977.

WORK IN PROGRESS: Continuing research on Joseph Priestley, for a biography.

* * *

LESSER, R(oger) H(arold) 1928-
(Hakji Damor)

PERSONAL: Born May 31, 1928, in London, England; son of Harold (an accountant) and Esther (a teacher; maiden name, Rogers). *Education:* Attended St. Xavier's College (Calcutta, India), 1945-49, and St. Edmund's College (England), 1949-55. *Home and office:* The Cathedral, Ajmer, Rajasthan, India 305001.

CAREER: Ordained Roman Catholic priest, 1955; taught English, history, general science, and social studies in mission school in Udaipur, India, 1955-57; did missionary work among the Bhil tribals in South Rajasthan, India; Cathedral, Ajmer, Rajasthan, India, assistant parish priest, 1968—. Diocesan director of catechetics, liturgy, and evangelization, 1969—; liason man for mass communications media, 1969—; vigilance member for diocese, 1969—; diocesan chaplain for youth, 1970—; diocesan promoter of the biblical apostolate, 1971—; correspondent for the diocese, 1971—; regional director of natural family planning, 1977—. Preacher and lecturer. *Member:* Writer's Workshop (Calcutta).

WRITINGS: What a Wonderful World!, St. Paul Publications (India). 1958; *The Growing Youth,* St. Paul Publications, 1959.

Tales That Tell, St. Paul Publications, 1960; *More Tales That Tell,* St. Paul Publications, 1961; *I Wonder,* St. Paul Publications, 1961; *Into the World,* St. Paul Publications, 1962; *A Short Cut to Happiness,* St. Paul Publications, 1962; *My G-O-O-D Book,* St. Paul Publications, 1963; *An A-B-C of Goodness,* St. Paul Publications, 1963; *Indian Adventures,* privately printed, 1963; *Kindly Light,* three volumes, St. Paul Publications, 1964; (under pseudonym Hakji Damor) *Hak ni vat* (title means "Way of Happiness"), privately printed, 1966, 2nd revised edition (with Andrew Buria, John Sunni, George D'Souza, and Joseph Pathalil), 1968; *The Bible: My Book,* privately printed, 1969, 2nd revised edition published as *The Bible: Our Book,* Theological Publications (India), 1975.

My Place in the Family of the Trinity, privately printed, 1970; *The Church Indeed Is His Body,* St. Paul Publications, 1970; *Great Love Stories,* privately printed, 1971; *Things Worth Having,* privately printed, 1971, 2nd edition, St. Paul Publications, 1975; *Indian Mosaic,* Writers Workshop (Calcutta), 1972; *Preach the Gospel,* Pontifical Mission Aid Societies (Bangalore, India), 1972; *Peace Is Possible,* Commission for Justice and Peace (Delhi, India), 1973; *Words With God: The Psalms,* privately printed, 1973, revised edition, St. Paul printed, 1974; *The Family Prayer-Book,* St. Anselm's Press, 1975, revised edition, 1977; (editor) *Development of Personality: A Course of Morals for Non-Christian College Students,* two volumes, All India Association of Christian Higher Education, 1976-77; *The Holy Spirit and Charismatic Renewal,* Theological Publications (India), 1978.

In Hindi: *Missa Pravesh* (title means "Introduction to the Mass"), privately printed, 1967; (with Baburav Joshi) *Manzil sab ki ek: Rah alag alag* (title means "All Aim at the Same Goal: Only the Ways Then Differ"), privately printed, 1971; *Muktidan* (play, title means "Gift of Salvation"), privately printed, 1976.

Author of eight pamphlets for Amruthavani Enquiry Centre Secunderabad. Contributor of over six hundred articles, book reviews, and stories to *Catholic World, Catholic Herald, Times of India, Thought,* and other periodicals.

WORK IN PROGRESS: Third volume of *Development of Personality; Helping People to Know God Better; So You Want to Get Married; How to Marry Well; History of the Mission Sisters of Ajmer.*

SIDELIGHTS: Lesser writes: "I was the first English diocesan priest to be ordained in England by an Indian bishop for the Indian mission. My first job was teaching in a school in Udaipur. Then I was posted to work among the Bhil tribals in South Rajasthan where I was asked to start a new mission and train catechists. After fourteen enjoyable years among the tribals, I was posted to my present position. I enjoy and appreciate almost everything, especially Eastern and Western classical music and dancing. I have travelled over most of India and Sri Lanka giving retreats and seminars, and am about to give a course on the philosophy of St. Thomas Aquinas in the local government college."

* * *

LESTER, MARK
  See RUSSELL, Martin

LESTER, Robert C(arlton) 1933-

PERSONAL: Born February 1, 1933, in Lead, S.D.; son of Odell (a small businessman) and Mary (a small businesswoman; maiden name, Martin) Lester; married Donna H. Larson, April 15, 1954; children: Paul E., Charles F., Robert T. *Education:* University of Montana, B.A., 1955; Yale University, B.D., 1958, M.A., 1959, Ph.D., 1963. *Home:* 2440 Panorama Ave., Boulder, Colo. 80302. *Office:* Department of Religious Studies, University of Colorado, Boulder, Colo. 80302.

CAREER: American University, Washington, D.C., assistant professor, 1962-65, associate professor of religious studies, 1965-70; University of Colorado, Boulder, associate professor, 1970-72, professor of religious studies, 1972—. *Member:* American Academy of Religion, Society for Values in Higher Education (fellow), Association for Asian Studies. *Awards, honors:* Ford Foundation foreign area fellowship for study in India, 1960-62; Fulbright-Hays fellowships for India and Southeast Asia, 1967, 1974-75.

WRITINGS: Theravada Buddhism in Southeast Asia, University of Michigan Press, 1973; *Ramanuja on the Yoga,* Adyar Library, 1976; *The Srivacana Bhushana of Pillai Lokacharya,* Kuppuswami Sastri Research Institute, 1977.

WORK IN PROGRESS: A History of Sri-Vaishnava Thought, on South Indian Hinduism.

* * *

LETTVIN, Maggie 1927-

PERSONAL: Born March 15, 1927, in Philadelphia, Pa.; married Jerome Lettvin (a professor), 1947; children: David, Ruth Lettvin McCambridge, Jonathan. *Residence:* Cambridge, Mass. *Agent:* Helen Barrett, William Morris Agency, 1350 Ave. of the Americas, New York, N.Y. 10019.

CAREER: Massachusetts Institute of Technology, Cambridge, lecturer in physical education, 1966—. Assistant professor at Leslie College, 1976—; leader of exercises on "The Beautiful Machine," WGBH-Television, 1969—.

WRITINGS: The Beautiful Machine, Knopf, 1974; (contributor) Raymond Harris and Lawrence J. Frankle, editors, *Guide to Fitness After Fifty,* Plenum Press, 1977; *Maggie's Back Book: Healing the Hurt in Your Low Back,* Houghton, in press.

* * *

LEUBSDORF, Carl P(hilipp) 1938-

PERSONAL: Born March 17, 1938, in New York, N.Y.; son of Karl (a stockbroker) and Bertha (Boschwitz) Leubsdorf; children: Lorna Stockmeyer, Edwin Stockmeyer, Charles Stockmeyer, Claire Stockmeyer, Carl, Jr. *Education:* Cornell University, B.A. (with honors), 1959; Columbia University, M.S. (with honors), 1960. *Home:* 3102 N St. N.W., Washington, D.C. 20007. *Office: Baltimore Sun,* 1214 National Press Bldg., Washington, D.C. 20045.

CAREER/WRITINGS: Associated Press, Washington, D.C., political writer, 1963-75; *Baltimore Sun,* Baltimore, Md., White House correspondent, 1976—. Notable assignments include coverage of U.S. presidential campaigns since 1968, Spiro Agnew's foreign trips, the White House.

* * *

LEUTSCHER, Alfred (George) 1913-

PERSONAL: Surname is pronounced *Loo*-cher; born October 30, 1913, in London, England; son of Izaak and Lammegien (Huizinga) Leutscher; married Phyllis Muriel Carter, July 13, 1940 (deceased); married Barbara Joan Farr, December 13, 1971; children: (stepchildren) Kevin Maurice Farr, Victoria Jayne Farr, Anthony John Farr. *Education:* Birkbeck College, London, B.Sc. (honors), 1940. *Office:* Pixies Halt, Kedington, Haverhill, Suffolk, England.

CAREER: British Museum (Natural History), South Kensington, England, guide lecturer, 1946-50, senior guide lecturer, 1950-73; writer, 1973—. Guest on radio and television programs. *Military service:* British Army, Royal Service Corps and Education Corps, 1941-46. *Member:* British Naturalists Association (president), Wildlife Fund (committee member of Wildlife Youth Service), London Natural History Society, Zoological Society of London (fellow).

WRITINGS: Vivarium Life, Cleaver-Hume, 1952, 2nd edition, 1961; *Quiz Book on Animals,* Daily Mail Publications, 1956; *Quiz Book on Birds,* Daily Mail Publications, 1957.

The Wonderful World of Reptiles, Bruce & Gawthorn, 1960; *Pictorial Animal Book,* Daily Mail Publications, 1961; *Tracks and Signs of British Animals,* Cleaver-Hume, 1961; *A Study of Reptiles and Amphibians,* Blandford, 1963; *The Curious World of Snakes,* Bodley Head, 1963; *Life in Freshwaters,* Bodley Head, 1964; (translator) A. vanden Nieuwenhuizen, *Tropical Aquarium Fishes,* Constable, 1965; (translator) P. Brohmer and G. Stehli, *The Young Specialist Looks at Animals,* Burke Publishing, 1965; (translator) R. Mertens, *The Young Specialist Looks at Reptiles,* Burke Publishing, 1966; (translator) Hans Haas, *The Young Specialist Looks at Fungi,* Burke Publishing, 1969; *Field Natural History: An Introduction to Ecology,* G. Bell & Son, 1969.

(With Francis Rose, M. Chinory, C. M. Yange, T. Baqenal, K. Williamson, and R. Futer) *Shell Natural History of Britain,* Rainbird, 1970; *Ecology of Waterlife,* F. Watts, 1971; *Dinosaurs and Other Prehistoric Animals,* Paul Hanlyn, 1971; *Woodland Life: Badgers,* F. Watts, 1973; *Woodland Life: Deer,* F. Watts, 1973; *Woodland Life: Squirrels,* F. Watts, 1973; *Woodland Life: Woodpeckers,* F. Watts, 1973; (with others) *Book of the British Countryside,* Reader's Digest Press, 1973; *Epping Forest: Its History and Wildlife,* David & Charles, 1974; *Ecology of Towns,* F. Watts, 1975; *Keeping Reptiles and Amphibians,* David & Charles, 1976. Also author of *Animals and Their Young,* 1962. Contributor to magazines.

WORK IN PROGRESS: A children's book on prehistoric animals, for Collins; *Ecology of Mountains,* for F. Watts; consultant editor for *Joy of Nature.*

SIDELIGHTS: Leutscher's books have been published in Japanese, Esperanto, and Afrikaans. He writes: "My most rewarding experience has been in talking to and writing for the young generation (my sternest critics!). As an outlet for the enquiring young mind natural history knows no bounds, and it has been my humble privilege to encourage youngsters to follow in my footsteps.

"My love of nature stems from early childhood. Mother used to tell me that I often escaped from the playpen in the garden, to explore the exciting world of nature in the herbaceous border, collecting caterpillars, worms, spiders and other treasures which were lovingly gathered as my first 'pets.' I then went through the usual juvenile phase of keeping tadpoles, fancy mice, goldfish and similar conventional pets, but was always keen to meet the real wildlife of the countryside.

"I have always stressed the importance of taking an active part in nature pursuits, pointing out that books, lectures, radio, museum visits and other media are only guidelines to personal and practical studies, especially in the field. Even a town garden in a city environment has something to offer. My garden in London is akin to a small nature reserve, designed to attract wildlife. Indoors it is nothing unusual to find an animal or two sharing our home—a python in the bedroom, a crocodile in the bath, or a bush-baby in the morning room."

*   *   *

LEVIN, Kim
(Kim Pateman)

PERSONAL: Born in New York; daughter of Aaron A. (a physicist) and Jean (a textile designer; maiden name, Lien) Levin; married John A. Pateman (a pilot). *Education:* Vassar College, A.B.; attended Yale-Norfolk Summer School of Art; Columbia University, M.A. *Home:* 52 West 71st St., New York, N.Y. 10023.

CAREER: Artist and writer. Lecturer at Philadelphia College of Art, 1968-72, and Parsons School of Design, 1969-72. Has had solo shows at colleges and universities, museums, and Poindexter Gallery. *Awards, honors:* Award from Art Libraries Association, 1975, for *Lucas Samaras.*

WRITINGS: (Contributor) Thomas B. Hess, and John Ashbury, editors, *Light in Art,* Collier, 1969; (contributor) *Super Realism: A Critical Anthology,* edited by Gregory Battock, Dutton, 1975; *Lucas Samaras* (a monograph), Abrams, 1975. New York correspondent for *Opus International.* Contributor to art and archaeology journals. Editorial associate of *Art News,* 1964-73; contributing editor of *Arts.*

*   *   *

LEVINE, Arthur E(lliott) 1948-

PERSONAL: Born June 16, 1948, in N.Y.; son of Meyer (a postal clerk) and Katherine (an insurance technician; maiden name, Kalman) Levine; married Linda C. Fentiman (a lawyer), August 18, 1974. *Education:* Brandeis University, B.A., 1970; State University of New York at Buffalo, Ph.D., 1976. *Religion:* Jewish. *Residence:* Berkeley, Calif. *Office:* Carnegie Council on Policy Studies in Higher Education, 2150 Shattuck Ave., Berkeley, Calif. 94704.

CAREER: Brandeis University, Waltham, Mass., director of Center for Undergraduate Curriculum Evaluation, 1970-72; substitute teacher in public schools in Boston, Mass., 1971-72; State University of New York at Buffalo, adjunct lecturer in Experimental Humanities College, 1973-75; Carnegie Council on Policy Studies in Higher Education, Berkeley, Calif., senior fellow, 1975—. *Member:* American Sociological Association, American Association for Higher Education. *Awards, honors:* Book of the year award from American Council of Education, 1974, for *Reform of Undergraduate Education.*

WRITINGS: (With John R. Weingart) *Undergraduate Curriculum Evaluation: A Study of Eight Undergraduate Curriculum Structures at Twenty-Six Colleges,* U.S. Office of Education, 1972; (with Weingart) *Reform of Undergraduate Education,* Jossey-Bass, 1973; *Handbook on Undergraduate Curriculum,* Jossey-Bass, 1978; *Reflections of an Itinerant Interviewer,* Carnegie Council, 1978. Contributor to education journals.

WORK IN PROGRESS: Why Innovation Fails: The Institutionalization and Termination of Innovation in Higher Education; Brookwood Labor College and Its Times; The American College Student, for Jossey-Bass.

SIDELIGHTS: Levine writes: "I find writing painful, but can't kick the habit and have no intention of doing so." *Avocational interests:* Reading, movies, running, tennis.

* * *

LEVINE, Daniel H(arris) 1942-

PERSONAL: Born July 3, 1942, in New York, N.Y.; son of David (an architect) and Sylvia (Pargment) Levine; married Phyllis May (a social worker), February 1, 1964; children: Peter Morgan, Paul Anthony, Sarah. *Education:* Dartmouth College, A.B., 1964; London School of Economics and Political Science, London, M.Sc., 1965; Yale University, M.Phil., 1967, Ph.D., 1970. *Home:* 2034 Day St., Ann Arbor, Mich. 48104. *Office:* Department of Political Science, University of Michigan, Ann Arbor, Mich. 48109.

CAREER: University of Michigan, Ann Arbor, assistant professor, 1970-75, associate professor of political science, 1976—. Fulbright-Hays senior lecturer in Guatemala, 1978. *Member:* Latin American Studies Association.

WRITINGS: Conflict and Political Change in Venezuela, Princeton University Press, 1973. Contributor to political science and international studies journals.

WORK IN PROGRESS: Research for a book on the Roman Catholic church and politics in Venezuela and Colombia.

* * *

LEVINE, Norman 1924-

PERSONAL: Born October 22, 1924, in Ottawa, Ontario, Canada; son of Moses Mordecai and Annie (Gurevich) Levine; married Margaret Payne, January 2, 1952; children: Cass, Kate, Rachel. *Education:* McGill University, B.A. (with honors), 1948, M.A., 1949. *Home:* 45 Bedford Rd., St. Ives, Cornwall, England. *Agent:* Dr. Ruth Liepman, Maienburgweg 23, Zurich, Switzerland.

CAREER: Writer. Head of English department, Barnstaple Boys Grammar School, 1953-54; first resident writer, University of New Brunswick, 1965-66. *Military service:* Royal Canadian Air Force, 1942-45; became flying officer. *Awards, honors:* Canada Council fellowship, 1959; Canada Council arts award, 1969 and 1971.

WRITINGS: Myssium (poetry), Ryerson Press, 1948; *The Tightrope Walker* (poetry), Totem Press, 1950; *The Angled Road* (novel), Werner Laurie, 1952; *Canada Made Me* (travel), Putnam, 1958; *One Way Ticket* (stories), McClelland & Stewart, 1961; (editor) *Canadian Winter's Tales,* Macmillan, 1968; *From a Seaside Town* (novel), Macmillan, 1970; *I Don't Want to Know Anyone Too Well* (stories), Macmillan, 1971; *Selected Stories,* Oberon Press, 1975; *I Walk by the Harbour* (poetry), Fiddlehead Poetry Books, 1976; *In Lower Town,* Commoners, 1977.

Contributor of teleplays to the Canadian Broadcasting Co., and the British Broadcasting Co. Contributor of short stories to *Encounter, Queen's Quarterly,* and other periodicals.

WORK IN PROGRESS: Short stories; a novel.

SIDELIGHTS: Levine was the subject of two television films, "Norman Levine Lived Here," made by the Canadian Broadcasting Co. in 1970, and "Norman Levine's St. Ives," made by the British Broadcasting Co., 1972.

BIOGRAPHICAL/CRITICAL SOURCES: Canadian Literature 41, 1969; *Canadian Literature 45,* 1970; *London Times,* July 19, 1970; *Montreal Star,* September 26, 1970; *Queen's Quarterly,* 1976.

LEVINE, Rhoda

PERSONAL: Born in New York, N.Y. *Education:* Graduated from Bard College. *Religion:* Jewish.

CAREER: Began dancing in musicals and the New York City Opera's ballet company after college graduation; teacher at Yale Drama School, New Haven, Conn., Bard College, Annandale-on-Hudson, N.Y., and Curtis Institute, Philadelphia, Pa.; choreographer for television programs, Broadway productions, and several opera companies, including City Center Opera and the Metropolitan Opera's National Company; directed operas in Belgium and the Netherlands; author of books for children.

WRITINGS: Arthur (illustrated by Everett Aison), Atheneum, 1962; *Quiet Story* (illustrated by Rosalie Richards), Atheneum, 1963; *Three Ladies beside the Sea* (illustrated by Edward Gorey), Atheneum, 1963; *Harrison Loved His Umbrella* (illustrated by Karla Kuskia; Junior Literary Guild selection), Atheneum, 1964; *He Was There from the Day We Moved In* (illustrated by E. Gorey), Harlin Quist, 1969; *The Herbert Situation* (illustrated by Larry Ross), Harlin Quist, 1970.

SIDELIGHTS: Ms. Levine first became involved in live opera during a trip to Spoleto, Italy, in 1963. The choreographer found her background in theatrical productions an asset when she eventually began directing opera for the stage. "That transition was very easy, because really the problems in all theater are the same, in terms of character," revealed Ms. Levine in an interview for *Opera.* "Of course the emotional timing of things is often determined by the music. But when you have a librettist and a composer like Da Ponte and Mozart, they're so accurate that it's never a problem, only a help."

In December of 1975, Ms. Levine directed the world premiere of the opera "Der Kaiser von Atlantis, oder der Tot Dankt Ab" (title means "The Emperor of Atlantis, or Death Abdicates") for the Netherlands Opera. The opera was written in 1940 by two prisoners in a German concentration camp, but was never before performed publicly because of its antitotalitarian message.

In addition to her work in the theater, Ms. Levine has also written books for children. Her first book, *Arthur,* was about a bird who decided to brave the cold New York winter rather than fly south with his friends. "This story, with an Andersen quality, is for reading aloud in small bits as there is much more to it than most," commented a reviewer for the *San Francisco Chronicle.*

The Herbert Situation, Ms. Levine's latest book, concerns a small boy who cries constantly, but most of all on happy occasions—because he knows that good things must come to an end. A *New York Times* critic wrote: "It saddens me that the book doesn't work, because its charm, humor and illustrations are delightful. The trouble is that the story illustrates a very adult idea: that the postponement of pleasure can work to the detriment of pleasure itself. Children are untroubled by such problems."

BIOGRAPHICAL/CRITICAL SOURCES: San Francisco Chronicle, May 13, 1962; *New York Times Book Review,* February 15, 1970; *Opera,* February 14, 1976.*

* * *

LEVINSON, Deirdre 1931-

PERSONAL: Born October 24, 1931, in Llanelly, Wales; came to the United States in 1965; daughter of Judah (a cantor) and Miriam (Miller) Levinson; married Allen Bergson (a psychotherapist), June 4, 1968; children: Miranda, Tobias (deceased), Malachi (adopted). *Education:* St. Anne's College, Oxford, B.A., 1954, M.A., 1957, B.Litt., 1957. *Religion:* Jewish. *Home:* 220 West 93rd St., New York, N.Y. 10025. *Agent:* Peggy Caulfield, A. Watkins, Inc., 77 Park Ave., New York, N.Y. 10016. *Office:* Department of English, Queens College of the City University of New York, Flushing, N.Y. 11367.

CAREER: Oxford University, St. Anne's College, Oxford, England, part-time tutor in Old English, 1955-56; University of Cape Town, Cape Town, South Africa, lecturer in English, 1957-62; street trader in London, England, 1962-63; University of Maryland, Overseas Program in England, instructor in English, 1963-64; Tougaloo College, Tougaloo, Miss., instructor in English, 1965; New York University, New York, N.Y., instructor in English, 1965-68; Queens College of the City University of New York, Flushing, N.Y., lecturer in English, 1969—. *Awards, honors:* National Endowment for the Arts award, 1973.

WRITINGS: Five Years (novel), Deutsch, 1966. Contributor of stories to *Commentary.*

WORK IN PROGRESS: Modus Vivendi, a novel.

SIDELIGHTS: Deirdre Levinson writes: "My novel is based on my experience, emphatically political, of South Africa. In 1962 I travelled—on foot, and on passing vehicles—from South Africa up to East Africa and Sudan, then across the Sahara, to West Africa (Nigeria and Ghana)." *Avocational interests:* Works of art, "the past and future or futurelessness of the human race."

* * *

LEVINSON, Richard L. 1934-

PERSONAL: Born August 7, 1934, in Philadelphia, Pa.; son of William (a businessman) and Georgia (Harbert) Levinson; married Rosanna Huffman (an actress), April 12, 1969; children: Christine. *Education:* Earned B.S. from University of Pennsylvania. *Home:* 215 South Cliffwood, Los Angeles, Calif. *Agent:* Creative Artists Agency, Century City, Calif.

CAREER: Writer of short stories and teleplays. Columbia Broadcasting System (CBS), New York City, creator with William Link of "Mannix" television series, 1967-75; National Broadcasting Company (NBC), New York City, creator with Link of "The Bold Ones" television series (lawyers segments), 1969-73, and "The Psychiatrist" television series, 1971, creator and producer, with Link, of "Tenafly" television series, 1971, and "Columbo" television series, 1971—, developer and producer of "Ellery Queen" television series, 1975-76. *Member:* Actors Studio West (chairperson of playwrights committee), Caucus for Writers, Producers, and Directors (member of steering committee). *Awards, honors:* Emmy Award from National Academy of Television Arts and Sciences, 1970, for "My Sweet Charlie"; Golden Globe Awards from Hollywood Foreign Press Association, 1972, for "Columbo" series, and 1973, for "That Certain Summer"; Writers Guild of America award, 1973, for "That Certain Summer"; Silver Nymph Award from Monte Carlo Film Festival, 1973, for "That Certain Summer"; George Foster Peabody Award from University of Georgia, 1974, for "The Execution of Private Slovik."

WRITINGS—All with William Link: *Prescription: Murder* (three-act play), Samuel French, 1963; *Fineman* (novel), Laddin Press, 1972.

Teleplays; all with Link: "My Sweet Charlie," "That Certain Summer," "The Gun," "The Execution of Private Slovik," and "The Storyteller." Also co-author with Link of "McCloud" television pilot script. Contributor of more than one hundred scripts to television series, including "General Motors Presents," "Westinghouse Desilu Playhouse," "Dr. Kildare," "The Fugitive," "The Rogues," and "The Alfred Hitchcock Hour."

Contributor of more than thirty short stories to periodicals, including *Playboy.*

SIDELIGHTS: With William Link, a friend since high school days, Levinson created "Columbo," one of television's most popular mystery series. Detective Columbo's character evolved from the character of a policeman whom the Levinson/Link team had invented for an earlier television script, "The Storyteller." When made-for-television films became popular, the two men were asked to write another script and came up with "Prescription: Murder," introducing Detective Columbo. Two years later NBC decided that "Columbo" should become a series. At one count thirty-seven million Americans were tuning in each week to see the bumbling detective with the crumpled raincoat.

Time magazine reported: "'Columbo' is at once the most classic and the most original (of the cops-and-robbers variations). The title character's method of operation (M.O.) dates back at least to Sherlock Holmes—detection through pure deduction. There is no gunplay, no chase sequence, and the audience usually knows the identity of the culprit. The only puzzle is how and when Columbo's seemingly bumbling pursuit will lead to *the* clue—the one misstep in an otherwise perfect crime."

Because Columbo lives in an unidentified town and is never seen at home or at the police station, Levinson remarked: "Columbo exists only in the cases he investigates. He comes from limbo and goes back into limbo." Link recalled that when he and Levinson wrote the pilot for the series they aimed to "define a character who's very bright but doesn't seem to be. Somebody who's not got much of an education and no social graces but takes advantage of his shortcomings." Link further explained that Columbo was modeled after Pyotr Petrovich, the detective in Dostoevsky's *Crime and Punishment,* who pretended to defer to the murderer Raskolnikov's superior education but was actually luring Raskolnikov into revealing too much.

Several of the Levinson/Link teleplays have had controversial themes, questioning society's right to dictate morals. "My Sweet Charlie" presented an interracial relationship, "That Certain Summer" depicted male homosexual love, "The Gun" concerned the problem of handguns, and "The Execution of Private Slovick" dealt with a man's conscience. Critics have praised Levinson and Link for approaching these subjects with straightforwardness and sympathy.

Of "That Certain Summer" Merle Miller wrote: "Mr. Link and Mr. Levinson have created two people who act and talk the way I think they would act and talk, and they leave it there, which is where I think it should be left. . . . It is simply a marvelous film—beautifully written, superbly acted, and directed and produced with tender care."

Another of their films, "The Gun," was a plea for gun control laws. Levinson stated: "What we're trying to do is to tell the story of the weapon. A middle-class businessman buys it for protection. His wife won't have it around the house. He gives it away. We must remember that the gun that killed Senator Kennedy went through about five hands in three years. In doing this project we found that 20,000 people die every year from handguns. And that forty percent of all firearms fatalities involve kids under nineteen. Every four minutes, if you can believe it, someone is killed by a gun across the country. Every three minutes somebody is robbed at gunpoint. Do you want more? A handgun is sold or traded every three seconds. And five million come off the production lines every year. This is what Bill Link and I found out doing research for the program.''

BIOGRAPHICAL/CRITICAL SOURCES: New York Daily News, October 24, 1972; *Variety,* November 1, 1972; *New York Times,* November 3, 1972; *World,* August, 1973; *Time,* November 26, 1973; *New York Post,* October 25, 1974.

* * *

LEVIT, Rose 1922-

PERSONAL: Born January 30, 1922, in Chicago, Ill. *Education:* University of Chicago, A.B., 1943, A.M., 1945. *Residence:* Novato, Calif. *Agent:* E. Pomada, 1029 Jones, San Francisco, Calif. 94947.

CAREER: High school teacher of art in Evanston, Ill., 1947-48; junior high school teacher of social studies and English in Novato, Calif., 1962-66; elementary school teacher in Novato, 1966—. Faculty member at Evanston Township Junior College, 1947-48. *Member:* Phi Beta Kappa. *Awards, honors:* American Library Association named *Ellen* one of the best books for young adults in 1974.

WRITINGS: Ellen: A Short Life Long Remembered, Chronicle Books, 1974.

WORK IN PROGRESS: Evaluating Your School Board: A Consumer Approach; a novel about two young boys, their families, and their teachers.

SIDELIGHTS: Rose Levit writes: "After moving to the San Francisco Bay area, I remained at home for several years while my children were young. Later, I returned to the professional world of education. I wrote *Ellen: A Short Life Long Remembered* in 1973 after the death of my youngest daughter. At present, my interests continue to focus on children and the world of education."

* * *

LEVITT, Saul 1911(?)-1977

1911(?)—September 30, 1977; American novelist and playwright best known for his Emmy Award winning play, "The Anderson Trial." Levitt's first novel, *The Sun Is Silent,* was published in 1951; he was also co-author of "The Trial of the Catonsville Nine," a play based on the trial of the Berrigan brothers, which was produced in 1971. He died in New York, N.Y. Obituaries: *New York Times,* October 1, 1977.

* * *

LEVY, Babette May 1907-1977

1907—December 21, 1977; American professor and author of books on early New England history. Levy was a professor of English at Hunter College for thirty-seven years, and later was appointed to the Charles A. Dana Professorship at Sweet Briar College. She died in Huntington, N.Y. Obituaries: *New York Times,* December 23, 1977.

* * *

LEVY, David M(ordecai) 1892-1977

PERSONAL: Born April 27, 1892, in Scranton, Pa.; son of Benno and Sarah (Breakstone) Levy; married Adele Rosenwald, June 2, 1927 (died, 1960); children: (stepsons) Armand

Deutsch, Richard Deutsch. *Education:* Harvard University, A.B., 1914; University of Chicago, M.D., 1918. *Home:* 993 Fifth Ave., New York, N.Y. *Office:* 47 East 77th St., New York, N.Y.

CAREER: Resident physician at Chicago Psychopathic Hospital and Cook County Hospital, 1918-20; University of Illinois, Urbana, instructor in criminology, 1920-22; Illinois Institute for Juvenile Research, Chicago, acting director, 1923; Michael Reese Hospital, Chicago, director of mental-hygiene clinic for children, 1923-26; New York Institute for Child Guidance, New York City, chief of staff, 1927-33; engaged in private psychiatric practice, beginning 1933; Columbia University, New York City, clinical professor and psychiatrist, 1944-57, founder and attending psychoanalyst at Psychoanalytic Clinic for Training and Research, beginning 1944. Lecturer at University of Chicago, 1923-27, at Smith College, 1924-30, and at New School for Social Research, 1928-39; instructor at New York Psychoanalytical Institute, 1936-41. Consulting psychiatrist in personnel for Office of Strategic Services, 1944-45; director of Infantry Control Division Screening Center, 1945-46; attending psychiatrist at New York State Psychiatric Institute, 1949; consultant to Henry Ittleson Center for Child Research, beginning 1956.

MEMBER: American Psychoanalytic Association (past president), American Psychological Association, American Orthopsychiatric Association (fellow), American Neurological Association, National Committee for Mental Hygiene, Association for Research in Nervous and Mental Diseases, Association for Psychoanalytic Medicine, Association for Psychoanalytic and Psychosomatic Medicine (fellow), New York Academy of Medicine (fellow), New York Academy of Science (fellow), New York Neurological Society, New York Society for Research in Child Development, New York Society for Clinical Psychiatry.

WRITINGS: Studies in Sibling Rivalry, American Orthopsychiatric Association, 1937; *Maternal Overprotection,* Columbia University Press, 1943, reprinted, Norton, 1966; *New Fields of Psychiatry,* Norton, 1947; *Behavioral Analysis: Analysis of Clinical Observations of Behavior as Applied to Mother-Newborn Relationships,* C. C Thomas, 1958; *The Demonstration Clinic for the Psychological Study and Treatment of Mother and Child in Medical Practice,* C. C Thomas, 1959. Contributor to professional journals.

OBITUARIES: New York Times, March 4, 1977.*

(Died March 1, 1977, in New York, N.Y.)

* * *

LEVY, Harold B(ernard) 1918-

PERSONAL: Born April 27, 1918, in Shreveport, La.; son of Philip and Ida (Sperling) Levy; married Betty Friedenthal, November 29, 1942; children: James, Charles, Roger, Judy Levy Ganucheau. *Education:* Louisiana State University, B.S., 1937, M.D., 1940. *Politics:* "Registered Southern Democrat; philosophy, Anti-Socialist Republican." *Religion:* Reformed Jewish. *Home:* 6026 Dillingham, Shreveport, La. 71106. *Office:* 6300 Line Ave., Shreveport, La. 71106.

CAREER: Physician with private practice of pediatrics in Shreveport, La., 1948—. Louisiana State University, Medical Center, School of Medicine, New Orleans, clinical instructor, 1953-60, clinical assistant professor of pediatrics, 1960-67, School of Medicine, Shreveport, clinical assistant professor, 1967-70, clinical associate professor of pediatrics,

1970—. Co-medical director of Caddo Foundation for Exceptional Children; local director of Louisiana State Department of Health's Pediatric Neurology Clinic. Member of Louisiana Advisory Council on Learning Disabilities. *Military service:* U.S. Army Air Forces, Medical Corps, flight surgeon, 1941-46; served in the Aleutians. U.S. Air Force Reserve, 1946-51; became major.

MEMBER: Association for Childhood Education International, American Academy of Pediatrics (fellow), American Academy for Cerebral Palsy (fellow), American Academy of Neurology (clinical associate), Council for Exceptional Children, Orton Society, Sigma Xi.

WRITINGS: Square Pegs, Round Holds: The Learning Disabled Child in the Classroom and at Home, Little, Brown, 1973; (contributor) Betty Lou Kranville, editor, *Youth in Trouble,* Academic Therapy Publications, 1975. Contributor to *Southern Medical Journal.*

WORK IN PROGRESS: Studying learning disabilities, including dyslexia, and hyperactivity.

SIDELIGHTS: Levy writes: "As a pediatrician I am concerned about the significant number of children who fail to achieve in the classroom due to deficient language skills. Many of these children show other evidence of immaturity which can be helped by combined medical-educational intervention. Early recognition can do much to lower the appalling correlation between learning disability and juvenile delinquency."

* * *

LEVY, Marion Joseph, Jr. 1918-

PERSONAL: Born December 12, 1918, in Galveston, Tex.; son of Marion Joseph and Alma Frances (Liebman) Levy; married Joy Agnes Cohen, October 10, 1944; children: Dore Jesse, Noah Robert, Amos Marion. *Education:* Harvard University, A.B. (honors), 1939, A.M., 1943, Ph.D., 1947; University of Texas, A.M., 1940. *Home:* 102 Russell Rd., Princeton, N.J. 08540. *Office:* Department of East Asian Studies, Princeton University, Princeton, N.J. 08540.

CAREER: Princeton University, Princeton, N.J., assistant professor, 1947-51, associate professor, 1951-59, professor of sociology, 1959-71, professor of international affairs, 1965-71, Musgrave Professor of Sociology and International Affairs at Woodrow Wilson School, 1971—, director of East Asian studies program, 1971—, chairman of department of East Asian studies, 1973—. Chairman of board of directors of Destructive Critics, Inc., 1961—. Participant in conferences. *Military service:* U.S. Naval Reserve, active duty, 1942-45; became lieutenant, senior grade.

MEMBER: American Sociological Association, Sigma Xi. *Awards, honors:* Ford Foundation grant, 1958-60; National Science Foundation grant, 1960.

WRITINGS: The Family Revolution in Modern China, Harvard University Press, 1949, reprinted, Octagon, 1971; *The Rise of the Modern Chinese Business Class: Two Introductory Essays,* Institute of Pacific Relations, 1949; *Some Problems of Modernization in China,* Institute of Pacific Relations, 1949; *The Structure of Society,* Princeton University Press, 1952; (contributor) Ansley J. Coale and other editors, *Aspects of the Analysis of Family Structure,* Princeton University Press, 1965; *Modernization and the Structure of Societies: A Setting for International Affairs,* Princeton University Press, 1966; *Levy's Six Laws of the Disillusionment of the True Liberal,* Princeton University, 1966, privately reprinted as *Levy's Ten Laws,* 1972; *Modernization:*

Latecomers and Survivors, Basic Books, 1972. Contributor to professional journals. Member of editorial board of *Behavioral Science,* 1956—, and *Journal of Asian Studies,* 1956-58; advisory editor of *Sociological Abstracts,* 1958—.

SIDELIGHTS: Levy told *CA:* "I believe that the fundamental problem posed by modernization is whether human animals can adjust as readily to longevity, affluence, and peace as they have in the past to shortgevity, poverty, and war. I do not think life as likely to become solitary, poor, nasty, brutish, and short, but I think it is likely to become crowded, affluent, nasty, brutish and long. I think that anthropologists, sociologists and other special pleaders who see the family going out of existence and societies organized without them—I think those thinkers fools, some amiable, some not."

* * *

LEVY, Richard C. 1947-

PERSONAL: Born January 7, 1947, in Wilkes-Barre, Pa.; son of Sidney Z. (an attorney) and Bettie (a fashion consultant; maiden name, Abrahamson) Levy; married Sheryl Slate (a company vice-president), October 19, 1968. *Education:* Attended University of Madrid, 1966; University of Paris, Diplome de Humanite, 1967; Emerson College, B.A., 1968. *Residence:* Silver Spring, Md. *Office address:* P.O. Box 1836, Rockville, Md. 18050.

CAREER: Paramount International Pictures, New York, N.Y., assistant to the president, 1968-69; Paramount Films of Panama, Panama, director of Central American advertising and publicity, 1969; Avco Embassy Pictures Corp., New York City, director of foreign advertising and publicity, 1970-71; television and film consultant, 1972—. Director of Panama International Film Festival, 1969-70; media consultant to Panamanian General Omar Torrijos. *Member:* International Film Relations Board, Motion Picture Export Association of America, National Academy of Television Arts and Sciences.

WRITINGS: (With Roger Langley) *Wife Beating: The Silent Crisis,* Dutton, 1977. Contributor to magazines, including *Travel, Clipper, Small World, Parade,* and *Cosmopolitan,* and newspapers.

WORK IN PROGRESS: With Roger Langley, *How to Buy Real Estate with Other People's Money.*

SIDELIGHTS: Levy writes that he spends more than half of each year travelling overseas and throughout the United States. He has resided in Spain, France, Italy, and Panama. Among his successful Avco overseas publicity campaigns are twenty-five motion pictures, including "The Graduate," "Lion in Winter," and "The Producers." He has also directed Paramount campaigns in Central America for about twenty films, including "Odd Couple," "Rosemary's Baby," "Romeo and Juliet," and "Barbarella."

Levy has also produced films, including "An Mar Tule," a documentary on Cuna Indians in the San Blas Archipelago, and "Beyond the Windy Place," on the Quicke Indians of Guatemala.

Levi is the co-inventor of two electronic toys now being manufactured by Milton Bradley Co. for the 1978 season.

He speaks Spanish, French, Italian, German, and Portuguese.

* * *

LEWIN, Michael Zinn 1942-

PERSONAL: Born July 21, 1942, in Springfield, Mass.; son

of Leonard C. (a writer) and Iris (a social worker; maiden name, Zinn) Lewin; married Marianne Grewe (a social worker), August 11, 1965; children: Elizabeth, Roger. *Education:* Harvard University, A.B., 1964; further study at Cambridge University, 1964-65. *Home:* 32 Lansdown Place, Frome, Somerset, England. *Agent:* Wallace, Aitken & Sheil, Inc., 118 East 68th St., New York, N.Y. 10021.

CAREER: Worked as a high school physics teacher in Bridgeport, Conn., 1966-68, and science teacher in New York, N.Y., 1968-69; writer, 1969—. *Member:* Mystery Writers of America, Crime Writers Association, West County Writers Association, Frome Revue Group.

WRITINGS: How to Beat College Tests, Dial, 1969; *Ask the Right Question,* Putnam, 1971; *The Way We Die Now,* Putnam, 1972; *The Enemies Within,* Knopf, 1974; *Night Cover,* Knopf, 1976; *The Silent Salesman,* Knopf, 1978.

Also author of radio plays for the British Broadcasting Corp. (BBC), including "The Loss Factor," "The Way We Die Now," and "The Enemies Within." Columnist, *Somerset Standard;* contributor of articles and stories to *Sport, Penthouse,* and other periodicals.

WORK IN PROGRESS: A novel; research on basketball in the United Kingdom; research on sports, gardening, and drama.

SIDELIGHTS: Lewin wrote: "I am gradually broadening the kinds of writing I do so that it keeps being hard and so I keep learning."

*   *   *

LEWIS, Alfred Allan 1929-

PERSONAL: Born June 17, 1929, in New York, N.Y.; son of Sidney (a salesman) and Lillian (a secretary; maiden name, Gelenter) Lewis; married Nita Pessin, March, 1969 (divorced, 1971). *Education:* New York University, B.A., 1950. *Home:* 923 Fifth Ave., New York, N.Y. 10021. *Agent:* Roz Cole, Waldorf Towers, New York, N.Y. 10022.

CAREER: Professional actor (in "Lady from the Sea," "Diamond Lil," and "Julius Caesar") in New York, N.Y., 1950-51; theatrical press agent (for more than twenty Broadway plays), 1952-57; manager of the European tour of the "Porgy and Bess" company, 1959-60; writer, 1960—. *Member:* Dramatists Guild. *Awards, honors:* George Foster Peabody Award from School of Journalism at University of Georgia, 1954, for radio script, "A Tribute to Eugene O'-Neill"; Yaddo writing fellowship, 1957.

WRITINGS: (With Sylvia Sidney) *Sylvia Sidney Needlepoint,* Van Nostrand, 1968; (with Pola Negri) *Memoirs of a Star,* Doubleday, 1970; (with Gloria Vanderbilt) *Gloria Vanderbilt Collage,* Van Nostrand, 1970; (with Maggie Hayes) *Maggie Hayes Jewelry Book,* Van Nostrand, 1972; (with Constance Woodworth) *Miss Elizabeth Arden,* Coward, 1972; *Mountain Artisans Quilting Book,* Macmillan, 1973; *Decorating with Fabric,* Grosset, 1974; (with Barrie Berns) *Three Out of Four Wives,* Macmillan, 1975; (with Julienne Krasnoff) *Everybody's Weaving Book,* Macmillan, 1976; *Man of the World* (biography of Herbert B. Swope), Bobbs-Merrill, 1977; *A Wonderful Sex* (nonfiction), Doubleday, 1978.

Plays: "Gene" (on Eugene O'Neill; two-act) first produced on the West End at Duke of York's Theatre, June, 1964; "Diplomatic Relations" (three-act), first produced in Palm Beach at Royal Poinciana Playhouse, February, 1967.

Author of scripts for television and radio broadcasts, includ-

ing "A Tribute to Eugene O'Neill" (radio), 1954, and scripts for television series "Edge of Night," "The Doctors," "Dark Shadows," and "CBS Playhouse."

WORK IN PROGRESS: Two novels, *A Consuming Fire* and *Pilgrimage.*

SIDELIGHTS: Lewis writes: "It simply seemed that professional writing was the next logical step after my work in the theater. The initial encouragement of people like the late Carlotta O'Neill, James Jones, and Burroughs Mitchell, of Scribner's, were incentives. Living in London and Paris for several years certainly helped to shape my perceptions."

*   *   *

LEWIS, Felice (Elizabeth) Flanery 1920-

PERSONAL: Born October 5, 1920, in Plaquemine, La.; daughter of Lowell Baird and Emma Elizabeth (Lee) Flanery; married Francis Russell Lewis (a U.S. Army chaplain), December 22, 1944; children: John Lowell. *Education:* University of Washington, Seattle, B.A., 1947; Columbia University, M.A., 1965; New York University, Ph.D., 1974. *Residence:* Glen Cove, N.Y. *Office:* Brooklyn Center, Long Island University, Brooklyn, N.Y. 11201.

CAREER: Long Island University, Brooklyn Center, Brooklyn, N.Y., part-time lecturer in English literature, 1965-68, counselor, 1966-67, assistant to the dean of adult, evening, and continuing education, 1967-68, assistant dean, 1968-74, assistant professor of sociology, 1974—, dean of liberal arts and sciences, 1974—. *Member:* Walt Whitman Birthplace Association (vice-president and member of board of trustees).

WRITINGS: Literature, Obscenity, and Law, Southern Illinois University Press, 1976; (editor with Elmer Gertz) *Henry Miller: Years of Trial and Triumph, the Correspondence of Henry Miller and Elmer Gertz, 1962-1964,* Southern Illinois University Press, 1978. Also author of by-line society column in *Star and Herald* (Panama City), 1956-57. Contributor of articles to professional journals. Associate editor of *Adult Student Personnel Association Journal,* 1968-71.

WORK IN PROGRESS: Literature and Values: William Faulkner.

SIDELIGHTS: Felice Lewis writes that she has worked as a professional singer (church and concert soloist, choir director, and voice teacher). She has directed plays for community theater groups, and has also performed in local plays. She has lived in Puerto Rico, Panama, and Germany.

*   *   *

LEWIS, Henry T(rickey) 1928-

PERSONAL: Born October 2, 1928, in Riverside, Calif.; son of Henry Trickey and Caroline (Gregg) Lewis; married Nancy Margaret Bell, January 19, 1952; children: Robert Munro, Kevin Trickey. *Education:* Fresno State College (now California State University, Fresno), A.B., 1958; University of California, Berkeley, Ph.D., 1967. *Home:* 9134 116th St., Edmonton, Alberta, Canada T6G 1P9. *Office:* Department of Anthropology, University of Alberta, Edmonton, Alberta, Canada T6G 2H4.

CAREER: San Diego State College (now University), San Diego, Calif., assistant professor of anthropology, 1964-68; University of Hawaii, Honolulu, assistant professor of anthropology, 1968-71; University of Alberta, Edmonton, associate professor, 1971-77, professor of anthropology,

1977—. *Military service:* U.S. Army, 1947-50; became sergeant. U.S. Air Force, 1950-54; became staff sergeant.

WRITINGS: Ilocano Rice Farmers, University Press of Hawaii, 1971; *Patterns of Indian Burning in California: Ecology and Ethnohistory,* Ballena, 1973. Contributor to anthropology journals.

WORK IN PROGRESS: A Time for Burning; producing "Fire, Plants and Animals: An Indian Heritage," a film; research on communal irrigation in the northern Philippines.

SIDELIGHTS: Lewis writes: "My research and publications involve topics and approaches that are essentially scientific and technical. However, the subject matter of how Indians used fire to alter forest and grasslands and how Philippine peasants have adjusted to the so-called Green Revolution are of a wider, more general interest. Eschewing vague notions of 'primitive mystique' and 'peasant intuitiveness,' my work attempts to show, without resorting to anthropological jargon, the local logic and reasoning by which northern Canadian Indians and Philippine peasants have helped shape and, in turn, have been shaped by their respective environments."

* * *

LEWIS, Paul H. 1937-

PERSONAL: Born June 3, 1937, in Springfield, Mass.; son of Paul Lucien (a businessman) and Kathryn (in insurance; maiden name, Derenthal) Lewis; married Anne Lulka (a professor), September 6, 1965. *Education:* Attended Boston University, 1956-58; University of Florida, B.A., 1961; University of North Carolina, Ph.D., 1965. *Home:* 628 State St., New Orleans, La. 70118. *Office:* Newcomb College, Tulane University, New Orleans, La. 70118.

CAREER: North Carolina State University, Raleigh, instructor in political science, 1965; Louisiana State University, Baton Rouge, assistant professor of political science, 1965-67; Tulane University, New Orleans, La., associate professor of political science, 1967—. *Member:* Southern Political Science Association.

WRITINGS: The Politics of Exile, University of North Carolina Press, 1968; *The Governments of Argentina, Brazil, and Mexico,* Crowell, 1975.

SIDELIGHTS: Lewis comments that his main interest is politics of Latin American and Mediterranean countries.

* * *

LI, Chiang-Kwang 1915-

PERSONAL: Born March 25, 1915, in Taishan, Kwangtung, China; son of Yun Peng (a businessman) and Pak Nui (Eng) Li; married Chia Ming Lo, February 28, 1943 (died, 1970); children: Anne Mapes, Allen, Arthur. *Education:* National Peking University, B.A., 1939; further study at New York University, 1944-46. *Office:* Central News Agency, Inc., 549 National Press Bldg., Washington, D.C. 20045.

CAREER/WRITINGS: Central News Agency of China, Taiwan, Republic of China, correspondent in New York, N.Y., 1944-55, and Paris, 1955-63, bureau chief in Washington, D.C., 1963—. Notable assignments include coverage of the United Nations from its inception until 1955, the Middle East, and West Africa. *Member:* National Press Club, White House Correspondents Association, State Department Correspondents Association, International Press Institute.

LIBERMAN, Judith 1929-

PERSONAL: Born March 4, 1929, in Haifa, Israel; came to the United States in 1947, naturalized citizen, 1965; daughter of Abraham (an attorney) and Hannah (a poet and drama teacher) Weinshall; married Robert Liberman (a professor of law), September, 1953; children: David, Laura. *Education:* University of California, Berkeley, B.A., 1950; University of Chicago, M.A. 1953, J.D., 1954; University of Michigan, LL.M., 1956; Boston University, further studies, 1977—. *Religion:* Jewish. *Home and office:* 18 Van Roosen Rd., Newton, Mass. 02159.

CAREER: Tel Aviv University, Tel Aviv, Israel, visiting lecturer in law, 1954-55; free-lance artist, 1956—. Visiting artist for Newton Creative Arts Council, 1976-77; guest lecturer at schools, colleges, and libraries in the Boston area. *Member:* National League of American Pen Women, Society of Children's Book Writers, New England Authors and Illustrators of Children's Books, Phi Beta Kappa, Order of the Coif.

WRITINGS: Introduction to International Law, Tel Aviv University Student Association, 1956; *The Bird's Last Song* (self-illustrated; juvenile), Addison-Wesley, 1976. Contributor to law journals.

SIDELIGHTS: Judith Liberman comments briefly: "*The Bird's Last Song* represents the climax of twenty years of creative activity. Although it took but a few months to write and illustrate, it expresses the essence of what I have tried to say in my art about life—and death."

* * *

LICHTENBERG, Jacqueline 1942-

PERSONAL: Born in 1942; daughter of M. Kern and Mary Brice; married Salomon Lichtenberg; children: Naomi Gail, Deborah Ruth. *Education:* University of California, Berkeley, B.S., 1964. *Home:* 9 Maple Terrace, Monsey, N.Y. 10952.

CAREER: Worked as industrial chemist for two years, one of them in Israel; full-time writer, 1968—.

WRITINGS: (With Sondra Marshak and Joan Winston) *Star Trek Lives!,* Bantam, 1975; (contributor) Alice Laurence, editor, *Casandra Rising,* Doubleday, 1978.

"Sime" Novel Series: *House of Zeor,* Doubleday, 1974; *Unto Zeor, Forever,* Doubleday, 1978.

WORK IN PROGRESS: Two "Sime" novels, *First Channel* (with Jean Lorrah) and *Mahogany Trinrose,* and a book about "Star Trek" fans.

SIDELIGHTS: Fans of Lichtenberg's "Sime" series publish an amateur magazine, *Ambrov Zeor,* carrying fiction, poetry, and commentary.

* * *

LIEBER, Joel 1937-1971

PERSONAL: Born September 24, 1937, in New York, N.Y.; son of Jules (a salesman) and Minerva (a bookkeeper; maiden name, Fink) Lieber; married Sylvia Soloman (a teacher), September, 1960 (divorced); children: Alexander Isaac, Amy Tamar. *Education:* Hobart College, B.A., 1958. *Agent:* Mary Yost, 141 East 55th St., New York, N.Y. 10022.

CAREER: Worked in public relations; writer. *Military service:* U.S. Navy.

WRITINGS: Israel on $5 a Day, Arthur Frommer, 1964,

revised edition published as *Israel on $5 and $10 a Day,* 1968; *How the Fishes Live* (novel), McKay, 1967; *Move!* (novel), McKay, 1968; *America the Beautiful* (articles), David White, 1968; *The Chair* (historical novel), McKay, 1969; *The Circle Game* (novel), Simon & Schuster, 1970; *Two-Way Traffic* (novel), Doubleday, 1972. Also author of screenplay "Move!", Twentieth Century-Fox, 1970. Contributor of articles to *New York Times.*

BIOGRAPHICAL/CRITICAL SOURCES: Saturday Review, December 12, 1970, January 22, 1975; *Contemporary Literary Criticism;* Volume 6, Gale, 1976. Obituaries: *New York Times,* May 6, 1971; *Washington Post,* May 7, 1971; *Publishers' Weekly,* May 17, 1971.*

(Died May 3, 1971, in New York, N.Y.)

*   *   *

LIGHT, Ivan 1941-

PERSONAL: Born November 3, 1941, in Chicago, Ill.; married Leah Lazarovitz; children: Matthew, Nathaniel. *Education:* Harvard University, B.A. (magna cum laude), 1963; University of California, Berkeley, Ph.D., 1969. *Office:* Department of Sociology, University of California, Los Angeles, Calif. 90024.

CAREER: University of California, Los Angeles, member of staff in department of sociology. *Member:* American Association of University Professors, Sierra Club.

WRITINGS: Ethnic Enterprise in America, University of California Press, 1972. Contributor to *American Sociological Review, American Journal of Sociology.*

WORK IN PROGRESS: Research on illegal enterprise in America, Koreans in Los Angeles, and urban studies in general.

*   *   *

LILLARD, Paula Polk 1931-

PERSONAL: Born November 6, 1931, in Dayton, Ohio; daughter of Louis F. and Pauline (Chaney) Polk; married John S. Lillard (an investment counselor), September 12, 1953; children: Lisa, Lynn, Pamela, Angeline, Poppy. *Education:* Smith College, B.A., 1953; Xavier University, Cincinnati, Ohio, M.Ed., 1969. *Religion:* Episcopalian. *Office:* c/o Schocken Books, 200 Madison Ave., New York, N.Y. 10016.

CAREER: Elementary school teacher in Terrace Park, Ohio, 1956-57; Montessori assistant at a school in Cincinnati, Ohio, 1962-63; Lake Forest Country Day School, Lake Forest, Ill., kindergarten teacher, 1975—.

WRITINGS: Montessori: A Modern Approach, Schocken, 1970; (editor) Mario Montessori, Jr., *Education for Human Development,* Schocken, 1977.

WORK IN PROGRESS: A book on kindergarten teaching, using a combination of teaching philosophies, including traditional, Montessori, and "progressive" or modern.

SIDELIGHTS: Paul Lillard writes: "I am interested in the communication between advocates of differing educational approaches: specifically in the supportive aspects of traditional and modern approaches with Montessori education."

*   *   *

LIMA, Frank 1939-

PERSONAL: Born December 27, 1939, in New York, N.Y.; son of Phillip and Anita (a registered nurse; maiden name, Flores) Lima; married second wife, Roberta Antoinette Branciforti (a certified social worker), March 14, 1974; children: (first marriage) Natasha, Nanushka; (second marriage) Matthew. *Education:* Attended Brooklyn College (now of the City University of New York), 1958, Wagner College, 1960, Fordham University, 1972, and New School for Social Research, 1973; Columbia University, M.F.A., 1975. *Religion:* Catholic. *Home:* 21-34 45th Ave., Long Island City, N.Y. 11101.

CAREER: Group IV Studios (photographers), New York City, studio manager, 1965-67; Harold D. Krieger Studios (photographers), New York City, studio manager, 1967-68; Phoenix House Foundation (for drug abusers), New York City, induction director, 1968-69, director of informational services, 1969-70; Hispanic Association for a Drug Free Society, Inc., Bronx, N.Y., assistant administrator, 1970-72, deputy director for administration, 1972-75; Compass House (for youthful drug abusers), New York City, executive director, 1975-76; Logos, New York City, regional director and drug and alcohol rehabilitation administrator, 1976—. Adviser to Manhattan Veteran's Administration Hospital methadone maintenance program, 1974—; consultant to Geraldo Rivera for documentary film, "The Littlest Junky," 1974. Panelist for National Endowment for the Arts and New York State Council of the Arts, 1974. Poet-in-residence at schools in Dover, N.J., 1971, New York State University College and Yardville Prison, 1973; teacher of poetry and creative writing at schools and prisons in New York and New Jersey, 1971-73. Co-founder and member of Lower East Side Tenements' Council, 1963-64. Volunteer worker with South Bronx street gang members, 1970-74.

MEMBER: National Association of Puerto Rican Drug Abuse Programs (chairman, 1975-77). *Awards, honors:* New York Hotel Exposition French Classical Cookery Award, 1959; grants received from Gotham Book Poetry Award Fund, 1961, Academy of Poets, 1962, 1970, John Hey Whitney Foundation, 1965, 1970, and New York State Council of the Arts and National Institute of the Arts. 1972.

WRITINGS—Poetry: Inventory, Tibor de Nagy (New York), 1964; *Underground With the Oriole,* Dutton, 1972; *Angel,* Norton, 1976.

WORK IN PROGRESS: A collection of poems, *Recipes for a Small Planet.*

*   *   *

LIN, Julia C(hang) 1928-

PERSONAL: Born May 4, 1928, in Shanghai, China; came to the United States in 1949, naturalized citizen, 1963; daughter of Fu Shing (a physician) and Tsung-ts'ui (a nurse; maiden name, Sun) Tsang; married Henry Huan Lin (a college administrator), December 28, 1951; children: Tan, Maya. *Education:* Smith College, B.A., 1951; University of Washington, Seattle, M.A., 1952, Ph.D., 1965. *Home:* 30 Cable Lane, Athens, Ohio 45701. *Office:* Department of English, Ohio University, Athens, Ohio 45701.

CAREER: Ohio University, Athens, lecturer, 1965-66, assistant professor, 1966-73, associate professor of English, 1973—. *Member:* Association of Asian Studies. *Awards, honors:* Fellowship from American Council of Learned Societies and Social Science Research Council, 1968-69; younger humanist fellowship from National Endowment for the Humanities, 1975-76.

WRITINGS: Modern Chinese Poetry: An Introduction, University of Washington Press, 1972.

WORK IN PROGRESS: *Contemporary Taiwan Poetry,* completion expected in 1979.

SIDELIGHTS: Julia Lin comments: "My major area of vocational as well as avocational interest is modern literature, both Western and Eastern. I have a passion for lyric poetry, both classical and modern. Writing does not come easily for me. It is sheer agony most of the time. Still, I do find deep satisfaction in doing it."

* * *

LIN, Nan   1938-

PERSONAL: Born August 21, 1938, in Chungking, China; came to the United States in 1961. *Education:* Tunghai University, B.A., 1960; Syracuse University, M.A., 1963; Michigan State University, Ph.D., 1966. *Office:* Department of Sociology, State University of New York at Albany, 1400 Washington Ave., Albany, N.Y. 12222.

CAREER: Michigan State University, East Lansing, instructor in communication, 1965-66; Johns Hopkins University, Baltimore, Md., assistant professor of sociology, 1966-71, assistant director of research, 1968-71, research associate in population dynamics, 1971; State University of New York at Albany, associate professor, 1971-76, professor of sociology, 1976—. Member of board of trustees of Brother's Brother Foundation, 1972. *Member:* American Sociological Association, American Association for the Advancement of Science. *Awards, honors:* Grants from National Science Foundation, 1971-72, National Institutes of Health, 1971-72, and Ford Foundation, 1972-73.

WRITINGS: *The Study of Human Communication,* Bobbs-Merrill, 1973; *Foundations of Social Research,* McGraw, 1976; *Conducting Social Research,* McGraw, 1976. Contributor to academic journals.

WORK IN PROGRESS: *Social Support, Stress, and Illness; Uses of Social Relations.*

* * *

LINCOLN, Edith Maas   1891-1977

1891—August 28, 1977; American physician and author of *Tuberculosis in Children.* Lincoln was appointed in 1922 to start the chest clinic of the children's medical service at New York's Bellevue Hospital. A pioneer in the use of drugs as therapy for tuberculosis, Lincoln was awarded the Trudeau Medal of the National Tuberculosis Association in 1959. She died in North Salem, N.Y. Obituaries: *New York Times,* August 30, 1977.

* * *

LINDQUIST, Jennie Dorothea   1899-1977

PERSONAL: Born in 1899, in Manchester, N.H. *Residence:* Albany, N.Y.

CAREER: Librarian, editor, and author of books for children. Served as a children's librarian in Manchester and Albany, N.Y.; taught courses in appreciation of children's books at the University of New Hampshire and worked as a consultant in work with children and young people at the University Library; *Horn Book* magazine, Boston, Mass., managing editor, 1948-50, editor, 1951-58.

WRITINGS: (With Caroline M. Hewins) *Mid-Century Child and Her Books [and] Caroline M. Hewins and Books for Children* (the former by Hewins, the later by Lindquist), Horn Book, 1954; *The Golden Name Day* (illustrated by Garth Williams), Harper, 1955; *The Little Silver House* (il-lustrated by Williams), Harper, 1959; *The Crystal Tree* (illustrated by Mary Chalmers), Harper, 1966. Contributor of articles to periodicals.

SIDELIGHTS: Jennie D. Lindquist's grandparents were born in Sweden. They brought many Swedish customs with them when they came to America, and consequently, the family always celebrated two sets of holidays. Jennie Lindquist's writings were influenced not only by her family background, but also by her many years of close association with children.*

(Died February 8, 1977)

* * *

LINDQUIST, Willis   1908-

PERSONAL: Born June 5, 1908, in Winthrop, Minn. *Education:* Attended the University of Minnesota and George Washington University.

CAREER: Following admission to the bar, became a tax lawyer with the U.S. Internal Revenue Service; author of books for children.

WRITINGS: *Burma Boy* (illustrated by Nicholas Mordvinoff), Whittlesey House, 1953; *The Golden Stamp Book of Boats and Ships* (illustrated by Robert Doremus), Simon & Schuster, 1956; *Animals from All Over the World* (illustrated by James G. Irving and Sy Barlowe), Simon & Schuster, 1956; *Call of the White Fox* (illustrated by P. A. Hutchison), Whittlesey House, 1957; *The Red Drum's Warning* (illustrated by Harper Johnson), Whittlesey House, 1958; *Alaska, the Forty-Ninth State* (illustrated by Hutchison), McGraw-Hill, 1959; *Folktales from Many Lands* (illustrated by Gordon Laite), L. W. Singer, 1969; *Stone Soup* (illustrated by Bob Shein), Western Publishing, 1970; *Haji of the Elephants* (illustrated by Don Miller), McGraw-Hill, 1976.

Contributor of articles and photographs to various periodicals, including *National Geographic.*

SIDELIGHTS: Willis Lindquist has traveled extensively in foreign countries. His first book, *Burma Boy,* was written after a visit to Burma. The *New York Times* commented, "Willis Lindquist knows Burma at first-hand and gives us a vivid impression of the teak forests, the jungle, the native villages, all of which is repeated in Nicholas Mordvinoff's illustrations."

BIOGRAPHICAL/CRITICAL SOURCES: *New York Times,* August 16, 1953; *Chicago Tribune,* September 6, 1953; *New York Herald Tribune Book Review,* May 12, 1957.*

* * *

LINDSAY, Merrill K(irk)   1915-

PERSONAL: Born September 10, 1915, in Topeka, Kan.; son of Merrill K. (a physician) and Mary Louise (Ryan) Lindsay; married Ellen Christiana Smedley (deceased); married Patricia Coffin (a writer and editor), December 12, 1949; children: (first marriage) Merrill Kirk David, Christiana Sutor; (second marriage) Patricia Dionis Bissot. *Education:* Attended Yale University, 1937. *Home address:* Route 139, North Branford, Conn. 06471.

CAREER: Winchester Press, New York, N.Y., publisher, 1969-70; October House, New York City, editor, 1971-73; Arma Press, North Branford, Conn., publisher, 1974—. President of Eli Whitney Museum. Organized exhibit for New Haven Colony Historical Society, 1975. Consultant to Metropolitan Museum of Art.

MEMBER: American Society of Arms Collectors, Company of Military Historians, Military Order of the Loyal Legion, Academia di San Marciano (Italy), Gesellschaft fuer Historisches Waffen und Kostumkunde, Vrienden Van Het Legermuseum, Danish Arms and Armor Society, Historical Arms Collectors of New York, Armor and Arms Club (New York City), Amis de Musee d'Armes (Belgium), Amis de Musee de l'Armee (France), Antique Arms Collectors Association of Connecticut (president). *Awards, honors:* Townsend Whelan Award from *Gun Digest,* 1970, for contributions to arms and arms literature.

WRITINGS: Gunpowder; or, How It All Didn't Start, Accademia di San Marciano, 1966; *One Hundred Great Guns,* Walker & Co., 1967; *Miniature Arms,* McGraw, 1970; *Master French Gunsmiths' Designs from the Seventeenth to the Nineteenth Centuries,* Winchester Press, 1970; (editor and contributor) *Illustrated British Firearms Patents,* Winchester Press, 1970; *Twenty Great American Guns,* Accademia di San Marciano, 1971; *The Kentucky Rifle,* Arma, 1971; *The Lure of Antique Arms,* McKay, 1975; *The New England Gun: The First Two Hundred Years,* McKay, 1976.

WORK IN PROGRESS: Guns and Their Makers.

* * *

LINDSEY, (Helen) Johanna 1952-

PERSONAL: Born March 10, 1952, in Germany; daughter of Edwin Dennis (a professional soldier) and Wanda Donaldson (a personnel management specialist; maiden name, Boston) Howard; married Ralph Lindsey (an estimator), November 28, 1970; children: Alfred, Joseph, Garret. *Education:* Attended high school in Kailua, Hawaii. *Home:* 95-029 Kuahelani Ave., #132, Wahiawa, Hawaii 96789.

CAREER: Writer, 1975—.

WRITINGS: Captive Bride (historical romance), Avon, 1977; *Spirited Lady* (historical romance), Avon, 1978.

WORK IN PROGRESS: This Woman's Mine, a historical romance for Avon to be published in 1979.

SIDELIGHTS: Johanna Lindsey writes: "With my father in the Army and stationed in Europe, I lived in Germany and France for a short time, but unfortunately, I was too young to remember my travels there. My home has been Hawaii since 1964 and shall remain there." *Avocational interests:* Painting, knitting.

* * *

LINDSEY, Karen 1944-

PERSONAL: Born December 3, 1944, in California; daughter of Watson (a model) and Verna (Thomas) Lindsey. *Education:* Queens College of the City University of New York, B.A., 1967. *Politics:* "Radical Feminist." *Religion:* Agnostic. *Home and office:* 115 Museum St., Somerville, Mass. 02143. *Agent:* Sarah-Jane Freyman, 111 East 85th St., New York, N.Y. 10028.

CAREER: Newsweek, New York, N.Y., proofreader, 1962-71; free-lance writer and editor, 1972—. Member of Massachusetts governor's Commission on the Status of Women, 1975; member of board of advisers of Prostitutes Union of Massachusetts (PUMA). *Member:* Word Guild, Feminist Writers Union (New England).

WRITINGS: Falling off the Roof (poetry), Alice James Books, 1975; *A Company of Queens* (poetry), Bloody Mary Press, 1977.

Work anthologized in *Where Is Vietnam,* and *Sisterhood is Powerful.* Author of columns "Feminist Viewpoint" in *Boston Phoenix,* 1974-76, and "Feminist Perspective" in *Boston Herald American,* 1976-77. Contributor to literary and popular journals and newspapers, including *Ms., Sojourner,* and *Second Wave.*

WORK IN PROGRESS: Journey to Gomorrah, a book of poems; research on battered wives who kill their husbands, and on anti-Semitism and the women's movement.

SIDELIGHTS: Karen Lindsey writes: "Though I sometimes write on other subjects, my major personal/political/professional concern is women's lives, the women's movement and the need for social change. Most of my journalism and much of my poetry focuses on this. I have a strong interest in Tudor England, and my second book of poems is about this era. I am also interested in the Tarot, and, to a lesser extent, other areas of 'arcane' knowledge. Mostly I care about feminism."

* * *

LINE, Les 1935-

PERSONAL: Born June 24, 1935, in Sparta, Mich.; son of John Jacob (a manager) and Hazel (Light) Line; married Lois Anne Anderson, June 3, 1961; children: Michael John, Heather Lynette. *Education:* Attended Grand Rapids Junior College, and Aquinas College, 1953-56. *Office:* Audubon, 950 Third Ave., New York, N.Y. 10022.

CAREER: Midland Daily News, Midland, Mich., chief photographer and conservation editor, 1957-66; *Audubon,* New York, N.Y., editor, 1966—, vice president for publication, 1975—. *Awards, honors:* Received awards for news photography and conservation writing, 1957-66; National Magazine Award from C.U.S.J. for editing *Audubon;* Children's Science Book Award from New York Academy of Science, 1977, for *The Milkweed and Its World of Animals.*

WRITINGS: (With Axel Amuchastegui) *Some Birds and Mammals of North America,* Tryon Gallery (London), 1971; (editor) *What We Save Now: An Audubon Primer of Defense,* Houghton, 1973; (editor) *This Good Earth: The View from Audubon Magazine,* Crown, 1974; (editor) *The Pleasure of Birds: An Audubon Treasury,* Lippincott, 1975; (editor) *The Audubon Wildlife Treasury,* Lippincott, 1976; (with Franklin Russell) *The Audubon Society Book of Wild Birds,* Abrams, 1976; (with Richard Ricciuti) *The Audubon Society Book of Wild Animals,* Abrams, 1977.

Photographic illustration: Ada Graham and Frank Graham, Jr., *Puffin Island* (juvenile), Cowles, 1971; Graham and Graham, *The Mystery of the Everglades* (juvenile), Random House, 1972; Franklin Russell, *The Sea Has Wings,* Dutton, 1973; Hal Borland, *Seasons,* Lippincott, 1973; Phyllis S. Busch, *Dining on a Sunbeam: Food Chains and Food Webs* (juvenile), Four Winds Press, 1973; Graham and Graham, *Let's Discover the Floor of the Forest* (juvenile), Golden Press, 1974; Millicent Selsam, *Land of the Giant Tortoise: The Story of the Galapagos,* Four Winds Press, 1977.

SIDELIGHTS: Line has been active in citizen conservation efforts in Michigan, and was responsible for the passage of a state law granting total protection to the endangered timber wolf.

* * *

LINEAWEAVER, Thomas H(astings) III 1926-

PERSONAL: Born October 21, 1926, in Bryn Mawr, Pa.;

son of Thomas H., Jr. (a manufacturer) and Eleanor (Robb) Lineaweaver; married Anne Tilghman, June 28, 1954 (divorced, November, 1973); children: Toby T., Timothy H. *Education:* Princeton University, B.A., 1948. *Politics:* Democrat. *Religion:* Protestant. *Home address:* P.O. Box 677, Woods Hole, Mass. 02543. *Agent:* Russell & Volkening, Inc., 551 Fifth Ave., New York, N.Y. 10017. *Office:* Marine Biological Laboratory, Woods Hole, Mass. 02543.

CAREER: Worked as ranch hand, dishwasher, brick stacker, fishing guide, painter, and teacher; free-lance writer, 1948-59; *Sports Illustrated,* New York, N.Y., staff writer, 1959-61; employed at Marine Biological Laboratory, Woods Hole, Mass., 1961—; free-lance writer, 1961—. *Military service:* U.S. Navy, 1942-44. *Member:* Society of Cincinnati.

WRITINGS: (With R. H. Backus) *The Natural History of Sharks,* Lippincott, 1970. Contributor to magazines.

WORK IN PROGRESS: The History of the Gulf Stream, for Norton.

SIDELIGHTS: Lineaweaver told *CA:* "The fact that F. Scott Fitzgerald was a close friend of my father's may have had something to do with my career, but when I wanted to do my honors thesis on him at Princeton, I was told he was not a 'major' author. I switched to a history major." *Avocational interests:* Watching hockey, playing squash.

* * *

LINEBERRY, Robert L(eon) 1942-

PERSONAL: Born May 4, 1942, in Oklahoma City, Okla.; son of John and Julia (Flemming) Lineberry; married Nita Ann Ray, September 5, 1964; children: Mary Nicole, Robert Keith. *Education:* University of Oklahoma, B.A., 1964; University of North Carolina, Ph.D., 1968. *Politics:* Democrat. *Home:* 2333 Grey Ave., Evanston, Ill. 60201. *Office:* Department of Political Science, Northwestern University, Evanston, Ill. 60201.

CAREER: University of Texas, Austin, assistant professor, 1967-72, associate professor of government, 1972-74; Northwestern University, Evanston, Ill., professor of political science and urban affairs, 1974—. *Member:* American Political Science Association, Southwestern Political Science Association, Midwest Political Science Association.

WRITINGS: (Editor with Charles Bonjean and Terry Clark) *Community Politics,* Free Press, 1971; (with Ira Sharkansky) *Urban Politics and Public Policy,* Harper, 1971, 3rd edition, 1978; (editor with Louis Masotti) *The New Urban Politics,* Ballinger, 1976; *Equality and Urban Policy,* Sage Publications, 1977.

WORK IN PROGRESS: Policing the City; Politics in Chicago.

* * *

LINEDECKER, Clifford L. 1931-
(Lewis Clifton)

PERSONAL: Born June 23, 1931, in Plymouth, Ind.; son of Clifford Irvin (a factory worker) and Julia Mae (Anders) Linedecker; married Yang Soon Ri (co-owner of a liquor store), November 28, 1957. *Education:* Attended public schools in Plymouth, Ind. *Politics:* Independent. *Religion:* "Neo-pagan." *Home and office:* 553 West Belmont Ave., Chicago, Ill. 60657. *Agent:* Ruth Hagy Brod Literary Agency, 15 Park Ave., New York, N.Y. 10016.

CAREER: LaPorte Herald-Argus, LaPorte, Ind., police and government reporter, 1958-64; *Terre Haute Tribune,*

Terre Haute, Ind., police and government reporter, 1964; *Fort Wayne News Sentinel,* Fort Wayne, Ind., police reporter, 1964-65; *Rochester Times-Union,* Rochester, N.Y., reporter and rewrite man, 1966-67; *Philadelphia Inquirer,* Philadelphia, Pa., reporter and rewrite man, 1967-73; *Hammond Times,* Hammond, Ind., police and county government reporter, 1973-74; *National Tattler,* Chicago, Ill., articles editor, 1974-76; *Country Rambler,* Chicago, articles editor, 1976-77; free-lance writer, 1977—. *Military service:* U.S. Navy, journalist, 1952-58; served in Japan.

WRITINGS: Psychic Spy: The Story of an Astounding Man, Doubleday, 1976; (with Becky Yancey) *My Life with Elvis,* St. Martin's, 1977. Contributor to magazines, sometimes under pseudonym Lewis Clifton, and newspapers, including *Country Style, Modern People, Today,* and *Chicago.*

WORK IN PROGRESS: The New Burnings, on modern persecution of neo-paganism; *Country Music and the Supernatural,* for Dell; with Patricia Young, *The Man Who Became a Woman: The Story of a Transsexual,* for Confucian Press.

SIDELIGHTS: Linedecker writes that his primary areas of interest are parapsychology and the occult. He is especially concerned with parapsychological research to promote alternative methods of healing either in conjunction with or independent of conventional medicine, and also with the uses of ESP, telekinesis, clairvoyance and other unconventional "occult" tools in espionage and by the military. *Avocational interests:* Pen and ink drawings, cartooning, listening to and collecting instrumental jazz and country music.

* * *

LINK, William 1933-

PERSONAL: Born December 15, 1933, in Philadelphia, Pa.; son of William (a textile broker) and Elsie (Roerecke) Link. *Education:* Earned B.S. from University of Pennsylvania. *Office:* Universal Studios, Universal City, Calif. 91608.

CAREER: Writer of short stories, plays, and teleplays; Columbia Broadcasting System (CBS), New York City, creator, with Richard L. Levinson, of "Mannix" television series, 1967-75; National Broadcasting Co. (NBC), New York City, creator, with Levinson, of television series, "The Bold Ones" 1969-73, "Tenafly," 1971, "The Psychiatrist," 1971, "Columbo," 1971—, and "Ellery Queen," 1975-76. *Military service:* U.S. Army, 1956-58. *Member:* National Academy of Television Arts and Sciences (member of board of governors), Writers Guild of America, Caucus for Writers, Producers, and Directors. *Awards, honors:* Emmy Award, 1970, for "My Sweet Charlie," and 1972, for "Columbo" script; Image Award from National Association for the Advancement of Colored People (NAACP), 1970, for "My Sweet Charlie"; Golden Globe Award, 1972, for "Columbo" series, and 1972, for "That Certain Summer"; Silver Nymph award from Monte Carlo Film Festival, 1973, for "That Certain Summer"; George Foster Peabody Award, 1974, for "The Execution of Private Slovik."

WRITINGS—All with Richard Levinson: *Prescription: Murder* (three-act play), Samuel French, 1963; *Fineman* (novel), Laddin Press, 1972.

Teleplays—All with Levinson: "My Sweet Charlie," "That Certain Summer," "The Gun," "The Execution of Private Slovik," and "Prescription: Murder." Contributor of more than one hundred scripts to television series, including

"General Motors Presents," "Westinghouse Desilu Playhouse," "Dr. Kildare," "The Fugitive," "The Rogues," and "The Alfred Hitchcock Hour."

Contributor of more than thirty short stories to periodicals, including *Playboy*.

* * *

LINZEE, David (Augustine Anthony) 1952-

PERSONAL: Born July 26, 1952, in St. Louis, Mo.; son of Homer Edward (an economist) and Clementine (Hoffmann) Linzee. *Education:* Attended New York University, 1970-71; Vassar College, A.B., 1974. *Politics:* Democrat. *Religion:* Roman Catholic. *Home:* 7316 Pershing Ave., St. Louis, Mo. 63130. *Agent:* Ray Corsini, 12 Beekman Pl., New York, N.Y. 10022.

CAREER: Salesman and clerk, 1974-76; writer, 1976—. *Member:* Authors Guild of Authors League of America, Mystery Writers of America.

WRITINGS: Death in Connecticut (mystery novel), McKay, 1977; *Discretion* (suspense novel), Seaview Books, 1978.

WORK IN PROGRESS: Research for a novel set in the United States during the early years of World War I.

SIDELIGHTS: Linzee told *CA:* "In the classic mystery, the detective enters—and the novel begins—after the action has taken place. Left behind are a few clues (usually corpses), and the detective proceeds to unearth the action for us.

"In my novels the action is still going on. The characters don't 'solve' the mystery, they get lost in it, and have to find their way out."

* * *

LIONBERGER, Herbert F(rederick) 1912-

PERSONAL: Born March 5, 1912, in Middletown, Mo.; son of Henry Hugo (a farmer) and Caroline Wilhelmina (a farmer; maiden name, Kimmich) Lionberger; married Vivian Mae Schack (a nurse), May 9, 1942; children: Carolyn E. Lionberger Coyle, David R. *Education:* Attended Central Wesleyan College, 1931-32; Northeast Missouri State College, B.S., 1936; University of Missouri, M.E., 1941, Ph.D., 1950; also attended University of Kansas City, 1944. *Politics:* Independent. *Religion:* Baptist. *Home:* 909 South Greenwood, Columbia, Mo. 65201. *Office:* Department of Rural Sociology, University of Missouri, 101 Sociology, Columbia, Mo. 65201.

CAREER: Rural school teacher in Montgomery County, Mo., 1931-36; high school teacher of social sciences and principal in Curryville, Mo., 1936-39; U.S. Immigration & Naturalization Service, Kansas City, Mo., immigrant inspector, 1942-44, district administration and personnel officer, 1944-46; University of Missouri, Columbia, assistant professor, 1946-54, associate professor, 1954-58, professor of rural sociology, 1958—, chairman of study team in India, 1965. Lecturer at Johns Hopkins University, 1965-67; consultant to Tennessee Valley Authority, Ford Foundation, and the Government of India.

MEMBER: American Sociological Association, Rural Sociological Society, Midwest Sociological Society, Gamma Sigma Delta. *Awards, honors:* Grant from Agricultural Development Council, 1966-67, for Taiwan; award of merit from Gamma Sigma Delta, 1974.

WRITINGS: Adoption of New Ideas and Practices, Iowa State University Press, 1960; *Research in Family Planning,*

Princeton University Press, 1962; (with H. C. Chang) *Farm Information for Modernizing Agriculture: The Taiwan System,* Praeger, 1970; (contributor) Marcella R. Lawler, editor, *Strategies for Planned Curricular Innovation,* Columbia University Press, 1970; (with Gary D. Copus and Chii-Jeng Yeh) *Social Change in Communication Structure: A Comparative Study of Farmers in Two Communities,* West Virginia University, 1975. Contributor to professional journals.

WORK IN PROGRESS: Studying the development and dissemination of information in one U.S. and two Taiwan universities.

SIDELIGHTS: Lionberger writes: "My current concerns are international agriculture, with particular reference to the systems that develop and disseminate agricultural information within and between countries. My research career has been in the communication and diffusion of ideas and practices among farmers in the United States and in other countries."

* * *

LIONEL, Robert
See FANTHORPE, R(obert) Lionel

* * *

LIPPINCOTT, Joseph W(harton) 1887-1976

PERSONAL: Born February 28, 1887, in Philadelphia, Pa.; son of Joshua Bertram (a publisher) and Joanna (Wharton) Lippincott; married Elizabeth Schuyler Mills, October, 1913 (died November 20, 1943); married Virginia Jones Mathieson, September 20, 1945; children: (first marriage) Joseph Wharton, Jr., Elizabeth Schuyler (Mrs. E. Harry Wilkes), M. Roosevelt Schuyler; stepchildren: Mary O'Neill, Joan Matheison. *Education:* University of Pennsylvania, B.S., 1908. *Politics:* Republican. *Religion:* Society of Friends. *Home:* Oak Hill, Bethayres, Pa. *Office:* c/o J. B. Lippincott Co., East Washington Sq., Philadelphia, Pa. 19105.

CAREER: J. B. Lippincott Co., Philadelphia, Pa., began as office boy, 1908, became vice-president, 1915-27, president, 1927-48, chairman of the board, 1948-58. Director, Free Library of Philadelphia, Council on Books in Wartime, Inc.; chairman of the board of libraries, University of Pennsylvania; secretary and member of board of trsutees, Moore Institute of Arts, Sciences, and Industry. Member of board, Franklin Institute, Mercantile Library, Abingdon Hospital, Philadelphia City Institute. Lecturer. *Military service:* U.S. Naval Reserve; during World War I.

MEMBER: National Association of Book Publishers (president, 1929), American Booksellers Association, National Geographical Society, American Game Protective Association, Pennsylvania Audobon Society, Philadelphia Zoological Society, Sons of the Revolution, Mayflower Descendants, Explorers Club, Philadelphia Club, Racket Club, Brook Club, Publisher's Lunch Club, Downtown Club.

WRITINGS—All juveniles: Bun, A Wild Rabbit, Penn, 1918, revised edition, Lippincott, 1953; *Red Ben, the Fox of Oak Ridge,* Penn, 1919, revised edition published as *Little Red, the Fox,* Lippincott, 1953; *Gray Squirrel,* Penn, 1921, revised edition, Lippincott, 1954; *Striped Coat, the Skunk,* Penn, 1922, revised edition, Lippincott, 1954; *Persimmon Jim, the 'Possum,* Penn, 1924, revised edition, Lippincott, 1955; *Long Horn, Leader of the Deer,* Penn, 1928, revised edition, Lippincott, 1955; *The Wolf King,* Penn, 1933, reprinted, Lippincott, 1949; (with G. J. Roberts) *Animal Neighbors of the Countryside,* Lippincott, 1933; *The Red*

Roan Pony, Penn, 1934, revised edition, Lippincott, 1951; *Chisel-Tooth, the Beaver,* Penn, 1936; *Wilderness Champion: The Story of a Great Hound* (Junior Literary Guild selection), Lippincott, 1944, reprinted, Grosset & Dunlap, 1970; *Black Wings, the Unbeatable Crow,* Lippincott, 1947; *The Wahoo Bobcat,* Lippincott, 1950; *The Phantom Deer,* Lippincott, 1954; *Old Bill, the Whooping Crane,* Lippincott, 1958; *Coyote, the Wonder Wolf,* Lippincott, 1964.

SIDELIGHTS: Joseph Wharton Lippincott was the third member of his family to head the publishing firm J. B. Lippincott Company. He was involved in every aspect of book production from writing to publishing and collecting in libraries. His enthusiasm for libraries was inspired by Andrew Carnegie, a traveling companion in Europe in 1908. This interest led eventually to the creation of the Joseph Wharton Lippincott Award for outstanding achievements in librarianship in 1950.

Lippincott's love for the outdoors was reflected not only in the collection of record big game trophies to his credit, but also in his contribution to the Lippincott American Wildlife Series. His books for young readers combined fact and fantasy to achieve correct as well as memorable accounts of animal life. He was deeply concerned with conservation. His *The Phantom Deer,* the story of a nearly extinct species of deer in Florida, brought this comment from the *Chicago Tribune,* "Out of these elements the author has fashioned a fine tense story of pursuit and escape, and a powerful plea for wild-life conservation."

BIOGRAPHICAL/CRITICAL SOURCES: Chicago Tribune, November 14, 1954.

OBITUARIES: New York Times, October 23, 1976; *AB Bookman's Weekly,* November 1, 1976.*

(Died October 22, 1976 in Huntington Valley, Pa.)

*   *   *

LIPSEN, Charles B.   1925-

PERSONAL: Born February 8, 1925, in Minneapolis, Minn.; son of Morris and Pauline (Connor) Lipsen; married Janice C. Greenberg, October 12, 1946; children: Sandra Lee, Linda April, Sydney Gail. *Education:* Earned B.A., LL.B., and J.D. from University of Wisconsin, Madison. *Home:* 1826 Calvert St. N.W., Washington, D.C. 20009. *Agent:* Gerard McCauley Agency, Inc., 551 Fifth Ave., New York, N.Y. 10017. *Office:* Cramer, Haber & Becker, 475 L'Enfant Plaza S.W., Washington, D.C. 20024.

CAREER: U.S. Senate, Committee on the Post Office and Civil Service, Washington, D.C., counsel-investigator for manpower policy subcommittee, 1951-52; National Milk Producers Federation, Washington, D.C., counsel, 1952-54; Direct Mail Advertising Association, Washington, D.C., Washington counsel and Congressional representative, 1955-56; special counsel to Senator Estes Kefauver, 1956; Retail Clerks International Association, Washington, D.C., director of legislative and government relations and political action, 1956-71; National Cable Television Association, Washington, D.C., vice-president in government relations, 1971-75; Cramer, Haber & Becker, Washington, D.C., attorney, representing individual, corporate, and association clients before Congress and the administrative and executive agencies for the federal government, 1975—. *Military service:* U.S. Marine Corps, 1943-45; served in the South Pacific.

MEMBER: National Democratic Club, Capitol Hill Club, Broadcasters Club. *Awards, honors:* M.Com. from International University, 1972.

WRITINGS: (With Stephan Lesher) *Vested Interest,* Doubleday, 1977.

BIOGRAPHICAL/CRITICAL SOURCES: Liz Carpenter, *Ruffles and Flourishes,* Pocket Books, 1971.

*   *   *

LIPSKY, Mortimer   1915-

PERSONAL: Born May 6, 1915, in Brooklyn, N.Y.; son of Louis (a union delegate) and Sarah (Pappe) Lipsky; married Anne Davis (a teacher), December 15, 1941; children: Mark, Joel. *Education:* Brooklyn College (now of the City University of New York), B.A., 1936; Brooklyn Law School, LL.B., 1938, J.D., 1938; also attended New School for Social Research, 1948-51. *Home:* 11 Washington Ave., Lawrence, N.Y. 11559. *Office:* 515 Fifth Ave., New York, N.Y. 10036.

CAREER: U.S. Army, Hartford, Conn., civilian accountant in Ordnance, 1941-45; Schimmel, Rochlin, Lipsky (certified public accountants), New York, N.Y., managing partner, 1948—. Lawyer in New York City, 1973—. Has also worked as social worker, personnel director, and controller. *Member:* World Constitution and Parliament Association (member of executive cabinet), American Association of Certified Public Accountants, Authors Guild of Authors League of America, Fellowship of Reconciliation, New York Society of Certified Public Accountants, New York Council of Peace Organizations, B'nai B'rith.

WRITINGS: Quest for Peace: Story of the Nobel Award, A. S. Barnes, 1966; *A Time for Hysteria: The Citizen's Guide to Disarmament,* A. S. Barnes, 1969; *Never Again War: The Case for World Government,* A. S. Barnes, 1971; *A Tax on Wealth: An Alternative to Revolution in America,* A. S. Barnes, 1977.

WORK IN PROGRESS: Wealth: Its Story, completion expected in 1979.

SIDELIGHTS: Lipsky writes: "I consider the subjects of world peace and world government in a just world as most vital. I recently returned from the world constitutional assembly and world citizens assembly held in Innsbruck, Austria, where a proposed constitution for the Federation of Earth was adopted. I was a delegate and hope to be active in pushing adoption."

AVOCATIONAL INTERESTS: International travel.

*   *   *

LISTER, Hal
See LISTER, Harold

*   *   *

LISTER, Harold   1922-
(Hal Lister)

PERSONAL: Born October 4, 1922, in England; came to the United States in 1923, naturalized citizen, 1943; son of John W. and Hilda (Cohen) Lister; married: Marilyn Marx (a music teacher), June 9, 1945; children: Peter, Steven, Wendy (Mrs. John Beaumonte), Todd, Andrew. *Education:* Attended University of Chicago, 1945-46; University of Wisconsin-Milwaukee, B.S., 1969; University of Missouri, M.A., 1970. *Politics:* "Republican-leaning independent." *Religion:* Jewish. *Home:* 209 Maplewood, Columbia, Mo. 65201. *Office:* School of Journalism, University of Missouri, Columbia, Mo. 65201.

CAREER: Aetna Life Insurance Co., Milwaukee, Wis.,

agent and agent supervisor, 1947-54; Grede Publishing Corp., Milwaukee, news editor, 1954-60; Grolier Society, Mobile, Ala., regional sales manager, 1960-62; Southeast Wisconsin Community Newspapers, Milwaukee, managing editor, 1962-65; *Milwaukee Engineering,* Milwaukee, editor, 1965-67; University of Missouri, Columbia, instructor, 1969-72, assistant professor, 1972-76, associate professor, 1972-76, professor of journalism, 1976—. Consultant to American Telephone & Telegraph Co. and U.S. Soil Conservation Service. *Military service:* U.S. Army, Infantry, 1942-45; served in European theater; received Bronze Star with two oak leaf clusters, Purple Heart with two oak leaf clusters, Croix de Guerre, Fuerregerre, and six battle stars. *Member:* Suburban Newspapers of America, Association for Education in Journalism, Sigma Delta Chi, Kappa Tau Alpha, Kiwanis (past president).

WRITINGS: The Suburban Press: A Separate Journalism, Lucas Brothers, 1975; *Media Communications Handbook for Public Officials,* Extension Division, University of Missouri, St. Louis, 1975.

WORK IN PROGRESS: A novel, *Krantland Calling; A Primer for Publicists.*

SIDELIGHTS: Lister writes: "An area of journalism I have made my specialty is the largest and fastest-growing area of print media—the suburban press. My background and research have given me strong insights into this area of the profession. I have been in contact repeatedly over the past seven or more years with publishers and editors of more than two thousand suburban newspapers by mail, in public meetings, at conventions and seminars, etc., constantly seeking to update my information on this unique phenomenon. I plan to visit England to study that country's suburban newspapers and their development since the industrial revolution, primarily with an eye to relating their experience to that of their American counterparts."

*　　　*　　　*

LITCHFIELD, Robert O(rbin)　?-1977

?—August 15, 1977; American public relations consultant for financial and industrial firms and newspaperman. Litchfield served in France and Germany with the 42nd (Rainbow) Division of the American Expeditionary Forces. He worked as a reporter for the *New York World* during the 1920's, and was the author of a long-range weather forecasting study. He died in Washington, D.C. Obituaries: *Washington Post,* August 20, 1977.

*　　　*　　　*

LIVINGSTONE, J(ohn) Leslie　1932-

PERSONAL: Born August 29, 1932, in South Africa; came to the United States in 1961; son of Philip (an executive) and Jenny (Smulian) Livingstone; married Trudy Dorothy Zweig, August 7, 1977. *Education:* University of the Witwatersrand, B.Com., 1956; Stanford University, M.B.A., 1963, Ph.D., 1965. *Home:* 106 Adrian Place, Atlanta, Ga., 30327. *Office:* College of Industrial Management, Georgia Institute of Technology, Atlanta, Ga. 30332.

CAREER: Edgars Stores Ltd., Johannesburg, South Africa, budget director, 1958-61; Haskins & Sells, San Francisco, Calif., senior accountant, 1962; Stanford University, Stanford, Calif., instructor in business, 1963-64; Ohio State University, Columbus, associate professor, 1966-69, Arthur Young Distinguished Professor of Administrative Science, 1970-73; Georgia Institute of Technology, Atlanta, Fuller E.

Callaway Professor of Industrial Management, 1973—, member of institute's executive board, 1976—. Visiting Ford Foundation professor at Catholic University of Valparaiso, 1968-69, and University of Toronto, 1972-73; distinguished visiting lecturer at University of Florida and University of the Witwatersrand, both 1972. Member of advisory council of Catholic University of Valparaiso, 1969—; member of advisory panel for Academy for Contemporary Problems, 1971-73; member of U.S. Securities and Exchange Commission's advisory committee on replacement cost implementation, 1976—. Expert witness before local, state, and federal agencies, courts, and legislatures; consultant to government and business. Principal for Management Analysis Center, Inc.

MEMBER: American Accounting Association, American Institute for Decision Sciences, National Association of Accountants, Academy of Management, Beta Gamma Sigma. *Awards, honors:* Award from Haskins & Sells Foundation, 1963, for excellence in accounting.

WRITINGS: Management Planning and Control: Mathematical Models, McGraw, 1970; (with T. J. Burns) *Income Models and Return on Investment,* Ohio State University Press, 1971; (with Sanford Gunn) *Accounting for Social Goals: Budgeting and Analysis of Nonmarket Projects,* Harper, 1974; *Managerial Accounting: The Behavioral Foundations,* Grid Publishing, 1975; (with H. D. Kerrigan) *Modern Accounting Systems: Design and Installation,* Ronald, 4th edition (Livingstone was not associated with earlier editions), 1975; (with James A. Largay III) *Accounting for Changing Prices: Replacement Cost and General Price Level Adjustments,* Wiley/Hamilton, 1976; (with Kerrigan) *Financial Accounting: An Introductory Study,* Grid Publishing, 1977.

Contributor: W. J. Bruns, Jr. and D. T. Decoster, editors, *Accounting and Its Behavioral Implications,* McGraw, 1969; John R. Grabner and William S. Sargent, editors, *Distribution Costing: Concepts and Procedures,* Transportation & Logistic Research Foundation, Ohio State University, 1972; Robert P. Sterling, editor, *Research Methodology in Accounting,* Scholars Book Co., 1972; Joseph W. McGuire, editor, *Contemporary Management: Issues and Viewpoints,* Prentice-Hall, 1974; Michael O. Alexander, editor, *Accounting for Inflation: A Challenge for Business,* Maclean-Hunter Ltd., 1975; Hector R. Anton and Peter A. Firmin, editors, *Contemporary Issues in Cost Accounting: A Discipline in Transition,* 3rd edition (Livingstone was not included in earlier editions), Houghton, 1977. Contributor to *Handbook of Cost Accounting* and *Handbook of Modern Accounting.* Contributor to professional journals in the United States and abroad. Associate editor of *Decision Sciences,* 1973—; member of editorial boards of *Accounting Review,* 1969-72, 1976—, and *Accounting, Organizations and Society,* 1975—.

WORK IN PROGRESS: Research on replacement cost accounting, and other inflation accounting techniques, on financial aspects of public utility regulation; financial analysis of antitrust and other actions for damages; cost-effectiveness analysis of projects and programs in such areas as health care, energy, and the environment.

*　　　*　　　*

LLEWELYN, T. Harcourt
See HAMILTON, Charles Harold St. John

LLOYD, Robin 1925-

PERSONAL: Born December 24, 1925, in South Wales; came to United States in 1949, naturalized citizen, 1952; son of Albert E. (an industrialist) and Alice (Mansell) Lloyd; married Natalie Daryle, 1960 (died, 1965); children: Carlos Mansell. *Education:* Royal Naval Academy, B.Sc., 1947; University of Caracas, M.A., 1949. *Home:* 3712 Barham Blvd., C-108, Los Angeles, Calif. 90068. *Agent:* James Brown Associates, 22 East 60th St., New York, N.Y. 10022. *Office:* NBC News, 3000 West Alameda, Burbank, Calif. 91523.

CAREER: Japanese Imperial Dancers, Tokyo, Japan, music director, 1957-61; Graystone Associates (advertising), Midland, Tex., vice-president, 1961-62; *West Texan,* Midland, editor, 1962-63; KIII, Corpus Christi, Tex., news director, 1962-64; KHFI, Austin, Tex., new director, 1964-65; *Newsweek,* New York City, writer and photographer, 1965-67; *Life,* New York City, writer and photographer, 1967-70; National Broadcasting Company (NBC), New York City, member of staff in Los Angeles, 1973—. Freelance writer and photographer. *Military service:* Royal Navy, 1941-45; became lieutenant commander. Bronze Star with cluster. *Member:* Author's Guild, American Society of Magazine Photographers, Smithsonian Institution. *Awards, honors:* Has received fourteen awards in journalism, including awards for investigative reporting and documentary production from United Press International.

WRITINGS: For Money or Love (nonfiction), Vanguard, 1976; *Playland,* Blond & Briggs, 1977; *The Child Exploiters,* Coward, 1978. Contributor of articles and photographs to periodicals, including *Life, Newsweek, Time,* and *Washington Post.*

WORK IN PROGRESS: The C. Z. Project, for Vanguard; *Yesterday Was Prettier.*

SIDELIGHTS: Lloyd wrote: "I was more affected by what Hemingway did rather than by what he wrote. He was once quoted as saying 'A man has not lead a complete life until he has done four things; written a book, climbed a mountain, sired a son, and fought a bull.' Once I'd accomplished all that, I lost interest.

"Hemingway, to the best of my knowledge, did not fight a bull although he was a great aficianado and one of the leading experts on the art. I fought professionally for two very brief seasons in Mexico. It's not that big a deal. I also worked behind the counter at Walgreen's drugstore in New York, installed venetian blinds, worked at a plumbing supply house, and spent several happy years as a professional musician playing drums. I gave that up because I couldn't see any future in striking the skin of a dead animal with two wooden sticks.

"But the most important part of my life has been spent in news—ranging from editing a ribald and completely irresponsible weekly newspaper in Texas to staffing at NBC news in Los Angeles after a stint as news editor at KFWB, Westinghouse's all-news station in Hollywood. At an early age, I had to decide between honest arrogance and hypocritical humility. I chose honest arrogance and, over the years, I have seen no reason to change."

* * *

LOCKART, Lucia A(licia) Fox 1930-
(Lucia Ugaro de Fox)

PERSONAL: Born March 28, 1930, in Lima, Peru; married. *Education:* Universidad Nacional de San Marcos, M.A., 1951; University of Illinois, Ph.D., 1960. *Home:* 1049 Cressenwood Rd., East Lansing, Mich. 48823. *Office:* Department of Romance Languages, Michigan State University, East Lansing, Mich. 48824.

CAREER: University of Sonora, Sonora, Mexico, lecturer, 1961-62; instructor in high schools in Inglewood, Calif., 1962-64; Centro Venezolano-Americano, Caracas, Venezuela, lecturer, 1964-66; San Fernando Valley State College, Los Angeles, Calif., assistant professor, 1966-68; Michigan State University, East Lansing, Mich., assistant professor of romance languages, 1968—. *Member:* American Association of Teachers of Spanish and Portuguese, Institute of International Studies, Latin American Studies Association, Modern Language Association.

*WRITINGS—*Under name Lucia Ugaro de Fox: *Imagenes de Caracas* (poetry), Caracas, 1965; *Ensayos hispanoamericanos,* M. A. Garcia, 1966; *Aceleracion multiple,* Dead Weight, 1969; *Monstruos aeros y submarinos* (poetry), Superspace, 1974. Also author of *Redes,* 1967. Contributor to periodicals, including *El rosto de la patria,* and *La Tapada.*

WORK IN PROGRESS: Family, Social Class and Sexuality on Spanish and Spanish American Women Novelists; a fictional work "concerning the utopian change in Latin American society based on a new political structure with the power when an androgynous breed takes over"; studies of the role of higher education, women as motif in Peruvian poetry, and Mexican history and social institutions.

AVOCATIONAL INTERESTS: Working with Chicano and bilingual groups.

* * *

LOCKE, Michael (Stephen) 1943-

PERSONAL: Born June 12, 1943, in London, England; son of Leonard Alfred and Effie (Sheppard) Locke; married Mary Elizabeth Carter, August 23, 1968. *Education:* University of Reading, B.A., 1964. *Politics:* Socialist "radical/reforming/democratic." *Religion:* None. *Home:* 12 Bartok House, 30 Lansdowne Walk, London W.11, England. *Agent:* A. D. Peters & Co., 10 Buckingham St., London W.C.2, England.

CAREER: Envoy Journals, London, England, news editor, 1964-66; *Student News,* London, England, editor, 1966-67; *Education,* London, England, assistant editor, 1967-70; *Faculty,* London, England, deputy editor, 1970; North East London Polytechnic, London, England, research associate, 1970-72, research fellow, 1974—. *Member:* British Educational Administration Society, National Union of Journalists, Westway Nursery Association.

WRITINGS: Research Studies on College Government (booklets), five volumes, Further Education Staff College, 1972-76; (with John Pratt and others) *Your Local Education,* Penguin, 1973; *Power and Politics in the School System,* Routledge & Kegan Paul, 1974; *A Guide to Education after School,* Penguin, in press; *Tradition and Controls in the Making of a Polytechnic: Woolwich Polytechnic, 1890-1970,* Thames Polytechnic, in press.

WORK IN PROGRESS: Research on the location and organization of colleges; policy studies in British higher education.

SIDELIGHTS: Locke states that his main interests are, "The control of public institutions; processes and mechanisms of democratic decisions and of administration; methods for analysis and testing of public policies." *Avocational interests:* Travel (made London-to-Nairobi overland drive), travel books, architecture and arts in Islamic cultures, cricket.

*   *   *

LOCKERBIE, Ernajean 1938-

PERSONAL: Born December 14, 1938, in Hamilton, Ontario, Canada; daughter of Ernest A. (a clergyman) and Jeannette (a writer; maiden name, Honeyman) Lockerbie. *Education:* Methodist Hospital School of Nursing, R.N., 1958; Cedarville College, B.A., 1961. *Religion:* Baptist. *Home:* 12 Chub Hill Rd., Stony Brook, N.Y. 11790. *Office:* Association of Baptists for World Evangelism, 1720 Springdale Rd., Cherry Hill, N.J. 08034.

CAREER: Worked as registered nurse on hospital staffs, 1958-62; Association of Baptists for World Evangelism, Cherry Hill, N.J., missionary nurse in Chittagong, Bangladesh, 1963—, director of literature ministries, 1969—.

WRITINGS: On Duty in Bangladesh, Zondervan, 1973; *Gita, Girl of Bangladesh,* Regular Baptist Press, 1975. Author of teacher's manuals.

WORK IN PROGRESS: Religious material, translated into Bengali.

SIDELIGHTS: Ernajean Lockerbie, who writes in English, then translates her material into Bengali, writes: "My primary aim is to provide understandable, culturally appropriate material explaining the Christian faith. This is not an attempt to force anyone to change his beliefs but to give an opportunity to make a choice."

AVOCATIONAL INTERESTS: Travel, music.

*   *   *

LOGAN, Gerald E(lton) 1924-

PERSONAL: Born April 15, 1924, in Auburn, Calif.; son of George Elton (in agriculture) and Hildegarde (Cate) Logan; married Gisela Wittek (a teacher), August 23, 1947; children: Lucille Logan Filice, Daniel, Michael, Lynette, Andrew. *Education:* University of California, Berkeley, B.A., 1949, M.A., 1950; further study at Stanford University, 1958-59, 1961, 1963, and at Loyola University, Los Angeles, Calif., and University of Arizona. *Home:* 17875 Peak Ave., Morgan Hill, Calif. 95037. *Office:* Live Oak High School, 1505 East Main, Morgan Hill, Calif. 95037.

CAREER: Live Oak High School, Morgan Hill, Calif., teacher of German, mathematics, science, and philosophy, 1957—. Member of summer faculty at Stanford University (in Germany), 1966, 1968, San Francisco State University, 1970-71, University of Nevada, 1972, University of Washington, Seattle, 1973, and University of Louisville, 1974-76. U.S. delegate to International Seminar on Culture at Goethe Institute, 1970; has conducted workshops in the United States, Canada, Poland, Yugoslavia, and Germany. *Military service:* U.S. Army, 1943-46; served in European theater.

MEMBER: National Education Association, American Council on the Teaching of Foreign Languages, American Association of Teachers of German (president of northern California chapter; national chairman of chapter presidents, 1969), National Carl Schurz Association, California Teachers Association, California Council of Foreign Language Teachers Associations, Foreign Language Association of Northern California, Foreign Language Association of Santa Clara County, Morgan Hill Teachers Association. *Awards, honors:* Fulbright award for Duisburg, Germany, 1961-62; American Specialist Grant from U.S. State Department for Poland and Yugoslavia, 1976.

WRITINGS—All published by Newbury House: *Individualized Foreign Language Learning: An Organic Process,* 1973; *German Conversational Practice,* 1974; *French Conversational Practice,* 1975; *Spanish Conversational Practice,* 1976; *Deutsch: Kernstufe* (title means "German: Embryo Stage"), 1976; *Italian Conversational Practice,* 1977; *Deutsche: Zweite Stufe* (title means "German: Second Stage"), 1977; *Hallo Deutschland!* (title means "Hello Germany!"), 1978. Contributor to language journals. Associate editor of *Unterrichtspraxis,* 1967-78.

WORK IN PROGRESS: A book on teaching methods; elementary readers for students of German.

SIDELIGHTS: Logan told *CA:* "In 1973 I began an alternative school-within-a-school with three other teachers. We offer over one hundred subjects for one hundred-fifty students, requiring 'renaissance' type people as teachers. Credit is given only for mastery learning, but there is no traditional structure of periods and classes. Students must be self-motivating, and they plan their own learning time as need dictates. Instruction is totally individualized, consisting of independent work, small group work, seminars, etc. In addition, there is much peer-teaching. Teachers evaluate students often, but individually. I, for instance, am responsible for evaluating, instructing and assisting students in all science courses (through physics), all math courses (through advanced calculus), college preparatory expository writing, philosophy, and, of course, all German courses. The learning format makes it possible for me to take small groups of German students aside for extensive conversational work. The success of this program, especially the insistence on mastery learning of the basics without employing old-fashioned 'discipline,' has again begun to attract national attention. A book on this approach will be forthcoming when other planned writings are complete."

AVOCATIONAL INTERESTS: Gardening, camping.

*   *   *

LONGLEY, Richmond W(ilberforce) 1907-

PERSONAL: Born October 16, 1907, in Paradise, Nova Scotia, Canada; son of Joseph Spurgeon (a farmer) and Tryphena (Kinley) Longley; married Margaret Edith Gallaher, July 31, 1935; children: Douglas E., Bruce C. *Education:* Acadia University, B.Sc., 1928; Harvard University, A.M., 1929, Ed.M., 1932; University of Toronto, M.A., 1940. *Religion:* Society of Friends (Quakers). *Home:* 11333 73rd Ave., Edmonton, Alberta, Canada T6G 0C9.

CAREER: Meteorological Service of Canada, Toronto, Ontario, meteorologist, 1940-59; University of Alberta, Edmonton, assistant professor, 1959-63, associate professor, 1963-67, professor of meteorology, 1967-73; Weather Bureau of South Africa, Pretoria, meteorologist, 1974-76; writer and researcher, 1976—.

WRITINGS: (With E. Wendell Hewson) *Meteorology: Theoretical and Applied,* Wiley, 1944; *Elements of Meteorology,* Wiley, 1970; *The Climate of the Prairie Provinces,* Canadian Atmospheric Environment Service, 1972. Contributor to scientific journals.

WORK IN PROGRESS: Continuing research on the climate and weather in the Canadian prairies.

SIDELIGHTS: Longley told *CA.* "During my nineteen years with the Canadian Meteorological Service, I was forecaster for ten years, including two years at Resolute in the Canadian Arctic, teacher of meteorology, with some research, at Toronto four years, research worker at Ralston, Alberta, four years and climatologist one year.

"Much of my interest after joining the staff of the University of Alberta dealt with Alberta, and prairie weather. Two studies, completed in 1977, continued that interest. One dealt with climatic change as it affects Alberta and the other prairie provinces. The other was a climatology of the Oil Sands area.

"In South Africa, my major work was on weather maps, map typing, and weather of the Republic. I also did some teaching, and wrote a number of popular articles on South African weather, such as the variation in sailing weather along the coasts."

*   *   *

LOOK, Dennis 1949-

PERSONAL: Born August 9, 1949, in Berkeley, Calif.; son of Claude A. (a conservationist) and Mildred E. (a nursing educator) Look. *Education:* Attended high school in Los Altos, Calif. *Home:* 2727 Honeysuckle Way, Sacramento, Calif. 95826. *Agent:* Irwin Zucker, 6565 Sunset Blvd., Hollywood, Calif. 90028. *Office:* 391 Monroe St., Sacramento, Calif. 95825.

CAREER: Antelope Camping Equipment, Cupertino, Calif., machine worker, 1965-67, salesman, 1967-70, manager, 1970-75; writer, 1969—. Lecturer at American River College, Consumnes River College, University of Santa Clara, and University of California, Davis; has also taught at recreation centers and for adult education programs. *Military service:* California National Guard, 1970-76.

WRITINGS: A Basic Back Packing Manual, two volumes, Look's Books, 1971-75; *The Joy of Backpacking: People's Guide to the Wilderness,* Jalmar Press, 1977.

WORK IN PROGRESS: Dummy: Growing Up Dyslexic.

SIDELIGHTS: Look writes: "My writing career has come about from my interest in backpacking. Since I did not attend college, I decided to enter the working world at age fifteen. I started teaching backpacking at age twenty-one, and now I'm able to devote most of my time to writing. For the future, my next book will be in the area of humanities.

"I feel that educationally handicapped children need more understanding and attention. Since I was considered educationally handicapped through high school, I will do my best as a writer to portray what it is like to grow up dyslexic. As a writer I find that a challenge."

*   *   *

LORCH, Robert Stuart 1925-

PERSONAL: Born February 2, 1925, in Ames, Iowa; son of Fred W. (a professor of English) and Ruth M. (Raper) Lorch; married Barbara R. Day (a professor of sociology), December 19, 1964; children: John Day. *Education:* University of Iowa, B.A., 1949; University of Nebraska, M.A., 1950; University of Wisconsin, Madison, Ph.D., 1957. *Politics:* Republican. *Religion:* Episcopal. *Home:* 2820 Shadowglen Dr., Colorado Springs, Colo. 80907. *Office:* Department of Political Science, University of Colorado, Cragmor Rd., Colorado Springs, Colo. 80907.

CAREER: Georgia Institute of Technology, Atlanta, assistant professor of government, 1956-59; California State University, Long Beach, assistant professor, 1959-64, associate professor of government, 1964-69; University of Colorado, Colorado Springs, professor of political science, 1969—, chairman of department, 1974-77. *Military service:* U.S. Army, 1943-46; served in European theater. U.S. Air Force,

1951-53; became first lieutenant. *Member:* American Political Science Association, Western Political Science Association, Conference Group on German Politics. *Awards, honors:* Pulitzer Prize nomination, 1969, for *Democratic Process and Administrative Law.*

WRITINGS: Democratic Process and Administrative Law, Wayne State University Press, 1969; *Colorado's Government,* Colorado Associated University Press, 1976; *Public Administration,* West Publishing, 1978. Contributor of more than twenty articles and reviews to law and political science journals and to newspapers.

WORK IN PROGRESS: State and Local Government, publication expected in 1980.

*   *   *

LORIMER, Scat
See FUENTES, Martha Ayers

*   *   *

LOTH, Calder 1943-

PERSONAL: Born July 30, 1943, in Charlottesville, Va.; son of John Ellison and Jane Thayer (Turner) Loth. *Education:* University of Virginia, B.Arch.History, 1965, M.Arch.History, 1967. *Home:* 202 North Granby St., Richmond, Va. 23220. *Office:* Virginia Historic Landmarks Commission, 221 Governor St., Richmond, Va. 23219.

CAREER: Virginia Historic Landmarks Commission, Richmond, senior architectural historian, 1968—. Member of board of trustees of Historic Richmond Foundation, 1977—. *Member:* Association for Preservation Technology (member of board of directors, 1974).

WRITINGS: (With J. T. Sadler, Jr.) *The Only Proper Style: Gothic Architecture in America,* New York Graphic Society, 1975. Contributor to professional journals and popular magazines.

*   *   *

LOUISELL, David William 1913-1977

December 2, 1913—August 21, 1977; American educator and attorney. Louisell was the Elizabeth Boalt Professor of Law at the University of California in Berkeley, and the author of several books on law. He also served on the National Committee for the Protection of Human Subjects of Biomedical and Behavioral Research. He died in Berkeley, Calif. Obituaries: *Washington Post,* August 25, 1977. (See index for *CA* sketch)

*   *   *

LOVE, Philip H(ampton) 1905-1977

December 19, 1905—August 17, 1977; American editor, columnist and reporter. Love began his newspaper career as a cartoonist for the *Baltimore Times.* He began working for the *Washington Star* in 1931 as a reporter, and retired forty years later as feature editor. He was author of the nationally syndicated column, "Love on Life," which he wrote from 1963 until the day before his death. He was also an editor for Love Syndicate, and author of a biography of Andrew Mellon. Love died in Washington, D.C. Obituaries: *Washington Post,* August 18, 1977.

*   *   *

LOVELL, Ronald P. 1937-

PERSONAL: Born August 11, 1937, in Colorado Springs,

Colo.; son of Paul I. and Verna (Bickerton) Lovell. *Education:* University of California, Los Angeles, B.A., 1959, M.S., 1961. *Home:* 3843 Northwest Arrowood Cir., Corvallis, Ore. 97330. *Office:* Department of Journalism, Oregon State University, Corvallis, Ore. 97331.

CAREER/WRITINGS: McGraw Hill World News, worked as correspondent in Los Angeles, Calif., 1963-65, bureau chief in Houston, Tex., 1965-66; *Business Week,* Denver, Colo., bureau chief, 1966-68; *Creswell Chronicle,* Creswell, Ore., owner and editor, 1968-69; *Medical World News,* New York, N.Y., senior writer, 1969-71; Oregon State University, Corvallis, professor, 1971—. Notable assignments include coverage of prison medicine and the space program. Contributor to *Denver Post, Oregon Times, Finance, Electronics,* and other publications. Teacher at University of Oregon, 1968-69. Member of Corvallis Chamber of Commerce, Oregon State University Publications Committee, and Oregon State University Convocations and Lectures Committee. *Military:* U.S. Army, 1961-62. *Member:* Sigma Delta Chi, Kappa Tau Alpha. *Awards, honors:* Blue Ribbon from American Association of Agricultural College Editors, 1971-72, for "Sea Grant Annual Report"; Creative Programming award from Western Association of Summer Session Administrators, 1975, for "Pioneers."

WORK IN PROGRESS: A newswriting textbook for Wadsworth; a trade book on presidential press secretaries.

SIDELIGHTS: Lovell told *CA:* "Writing and the teaching of writing are very important to me. I have never made my living at doing anything else. I began wanting to be a political reporter but a strange twist of fate got me into technical journalism which I enjoyed but was never devoted to. I still want to be a political journalist and hope to move back into that in a year or so. Teaching has been a good pause for me before I plunge into the second half of my writing career. I've enjoyed working with students and helping them get started. But the pace is slow and the atmosphere a bit stagnating if you want to report, write, and travel."

*   *   *

LOW, D(onald) A(nthony) 1927-

PERSONAL: Born June 22, 1927, in Naini Tal, India; son of Donald Philip and Winifred (Edmunds) Low; married Isobel Smails, September 6, 1952; children: Angela Margaret, Adam Crayden, Penelope Ann. *Education:* Oxford University, B.A. (honors), 1948, M.A., 1952, D.Phil., 1957. *Religion:* Church of England. *Home:* 21 Balmain Cres., Acton, Canberra, Australian Capital Territory 2600, Australia. *Office:* Vice-chancellor, Australian National University, Box 4, Canberra, Australian Capital Territory 2600, Australia.

CAREER: University College of East Africa, Makerere, Uganda, assistant lecturer, 1951-53, lecturer, 1953-57, senior lecturer in history, 1957-58; Australian National University, Canberra, fellow, 1959-62, senior fellow in history, 1962-64; University of Sussex, Brighton, England, professor of history, 1964-72, founder and dean of School of African and Asian Studies, 1964-69, director of graduates in arts and social sciences, 1970-72; Australian National University, professor of history, 1973—, director of Research School of Pacific Studies, 1973-75, vice-chancellor, 1975—. Visiting fellow at Cambridge University, 1971-72; member of council at University of Papua New Guinea, 1974—. Kampala correspondent for *London Times,* 1952-58; East African correspondent for *Round Table,* 1953-58. *Military service:* British Army, 1949-50. *Member:* Institute of Development Studies (fellow), Academy of the Humanities (Australia; fellow), Academy of the Social Sciences (Australia; fellow).

WRITINGS: (With R. C. Pratt) *Buganda and British Overrule, 1900-1955,* Oxford University Press, 1960; (contributor) Roland Oliver and Gervaise Mathew, editors, *History of East Africa,* Volume I, Clarendon Press, 1963; (contributor) V. T. Harlow and E. M. Chilver, editors, *History of East Africa,* Volume II, Clarendon Press, 1965; (editor and contributor) *Soundings in Modern South Asian History,* University of California Press, 1968; (with J. C. Iltis and M. D. Wainwright) *Government Archives in South Asia: A Guide to National and State Archives in Ceylon, India, and Pakistan,* Cambridge University Press, 1969.

Buganda in Modern History, University of California Press, 1970; *The Mind of Buganda,* University of California Press, 1970; *Lion Rampant: Essays in the Study of British Imperialism,* Cass & Co., 1973; (editor with Alison Smith, and contributor) *History of East Africa,* Volume III, Clarendon Press, 1976; (editor and author of introduction) *Congress and the Raj: Facets of the Indian Struggle, 1917-1947,* Heinemann, 1977.

Contributor to *Encyclopaedia Britannica,* and to Asian studies and political science journals.

WORK IN PROGRESS: Writing introduction for *The Transfer of Power in Africa,* edited by Prosser Gifford and Roger Louis.

*   *   *

LOWE, William T(ebbs) 1929-

PERSONAL: Born July 21, 1929, in Louisville, Ky.; son of William H. (a manager) and Belle T. Lowe; married Shirley H. Heckman, May 21, 1953; children: Edward W., Jean Anne, Daniel D. *Education:* Attended Hanover College, 1947-49; University of Cincinnati, B.S., 1951, M.S., 1956; University of Illinois, Ed.D., 1960; postdoctoral study at Columbia University, 1966-67. *Home:* 34 Railroad Mills Rd., Pittsford, N.Y. 14534. *Office:* College of Education, University of Rochester, Rochester, N.Y. 14627.

CAREER: Junior high school and high school teacher of social studies in Cincinnati, Ohio, 1953-56, 1958-60; Cornell University, Ithaca, N.Y., assistant professor, 1960-64, associate professor of education, 1964-68, director of Office of Teacher Preparation, 1967-68; University of Rochester, Rochester, N.Y., associate professor, 1968-70, professor of education, 1970—, chairman of Center for the Study of Curriculum and Teaching. Guest member of faculty at Rochester Institute of Technology, Columbia University, and State University of New York College at Geneseo; exchange professor at University of Hull, 1975-76. Member of Social Science Education Consortium, 1973—. *Military service:* U.S. Army, 1951-53; served in Korea; became sergeant; received Bronze Star.

MEMBER: National Council for the Social Studies, American Educational Research Association, Association for Supervision and Curriculum Development, New York State Association for Supervision and Curriculum Development, New York State Council for the Social Studies (vice-president), College and University Faculty Association. *Awards, honors:* Grants from U.S. Office of Education, New York State Department of Education, New York State Council for the Social Studies, and Urban League.

WRITINGS: Structure and the Social Studies, Cornell University Press, 1969; (co-author) *Regional Educational Development in New York State,* two volumes, New York State Department of Education, 1970; *Strategies for Metropolitan Cooperation in Education,* U.S. Office of Education, 1971; *City Life,* Hayden, 1974. Contributor of articles and reviews to education and social studies journals. Editor of *Social Science Record,* 1969-71; review editor of *Social Education,* 1972-75.

WORK IN PROGRESS: Political Behavior of American Teachers; An Analysis of Three Voluntary Metropolitan Desegregation Models.

* * *

LOWELL, Robert (Traill Spence, Jr.) 1917-1977

March 1, 1917—September 12, 1977; American educator and poet. In addition to numerous other awards, Lowell won two Pulitzer Prizes for his work, one in 1947 for *Lord Weary's Castle,* and the second in 1974 for *The Dolphin.* Lowell produced seventeen volumes of poetry, some dealing with New England life and traditions. Many critics have regarded Lowell as "the best English language poet of his generation." He died in New York, N.Y. Obituaries: *New York Times,* September 13, 1977; *Washington Post,* September 14, 1977; *AB Bookman's Weekly,* November 7, 1977. (See index for *CA* sketch)

* * *

LOWITZ, Anson 1901(?)-1978

1901(?)—January 22, 1978; American advertising executive, and author and illustrator of historical books for children. Lowitz was vice-president of several advertising agencies, including the J. Walter Thompson Co. from 1937 to 1951. He died in Pebble Beach, Calif. Obituaries: *New York Times,* January 25, 1978.

* * *

LUBAR, Robert 1920-

PERSONAL: Born October 10, 1920, in New York, N.Y.; son of George H. (an engineer) and Helen (a musician; maiden name, Gang) Lubar; married Patricia Raney (a writer), August 2, 1947; children: John, Nicholas, Stephen, Andrew. *Education:* Columbia University, B.A., 1940, M.S., 1941. *Home:* 16 Davis Rd., Port Washington, N.Y. 11050. *Office: Fortune,* Time-Life Building, New York, N.Y. 10020.

CAREER/WRITINGS: New York Times, New York City, writer, 1942-43; *Time,* New York City, foreign correspondent, 1946-58; *Fortune,* New York City, associate editor, 1958-60, member of board of editors, 1960-64, assistant managing editor, 1964-70, managing editor, 1970—. Notable assignments include coverage of India after independence, the 1954 coup in Guatemala. Trustee, New York State Higher Education Services Corp., 1976—. *Military service:* U.S. Navy, 1942-46; became lieutenant. *Member:* Council on Foreign Relations.

* * *

LUDVIGSEN, Karl (Eric) 1934-
(Elliot Miles; Eric Nielssen)

PERSONAL: Born April 24, 1934, in Kalamazoo, Mich.; son of E. L. (an executive) and Virginia (Smith) Ludvigsen; married Barbara Manger (an interior decorator), December 30, 1956; children: Aari B., Miles E. *Education:* Attended Massachusetts Institute of Technology, 1952-54, and Pratt Institute, 1954-56. *Home and office:* Motortext, Inc., 1070 Esplanade, Pelham Manor, N.Y. 10803.

CAREER: General Motors, Warren, Mich., junior designer on styling staff, 1956; *Sports Cars Illustrated,* New York, N.Y., technical editor, 1956-57; *Car and Driver,* New York City, editor, 1959-61; General Motors, Detroit, Mich., press contact on public relations staff, 1961-63; General Motors, Overseas Operations Division, New York City, press officer, 1963-67; Formula 1 Enterprises, Inc., New York City, president, 1967-71; Motortext, Inc., Pelham Manor, N.Y., president, 1974—. Author of "Rotary Report" in *Road Test* and "Out of Round," a monthly column in *Motor Trend.* Member of International jury for Car-of-the-Year Competition sponsored by Autovisie. Provides editorial, design, marketing, and automotive research consulting services to clients in and associated with the automotive field. Covered the introduction of the Wankel engine in 1959 and analytic reporting on its subsequent career; has held interviews with Bill Lear, John DeLorean, Jim Bede, Eugene Bordinat, and Mark Donohue. *Military service:* U.S. Army, Signal Corps, 1957-59.

MEMBER: International Motor Press Association, Society of Automotive Engineers, Society of Automotive Historians, Sports Car Club of America (life member), Guild of Motoring Writers, American Society of Journalists and Authors, American Auto Racing Writers and Broadcasters Association, Motor Racing Safety Society (founder and first president), Milestone Car Society, Corvair Society of America, New York Athletic Club. *Awards, honors:* First- and second-place awards in journalism contests administered by American Auto Racing Writers and Broadcasters Association, 1971-76; Montagu Trophy from Guild of Motoring Writers, 1972, and Nicholas-Joseph Cugnot Award from Society of Automotive Historians, 1973, both for *The Mercedes-Benz Racing Cars;* Ken W. Purdy Award from International Motor Press Association, 1972, for writing the introduction to *At Speed.*

WRITINGS: (With John Christy) *MG Guide,* Sports Car Press, 1958, revised edition published as *The New MG Guide,* 1968; *Your Sports Car Engine,* Sports Car Press, 1958; *Mercedes-Benz Guide,* Sports Car Press, 1959; *Guide to Corvette Speed,* Sports Car Press, 1969; *The Inside Story of the Fastest Fords,* Style Auto Editrice, 1970; *Road Racing in America,* Dodd, 1971; *Group Seven,* World Publishing, 1971; *The Mercedes-Benz Racing Cars,* Bond, Parkhurst, 1971; *Corvette: America's Star-Spangled Sports Car,* Automobile Quarterly Publications, 1972; *Wankel Engines A to Z,* Ludvigsen Publications, 1973; *Opel: Wheels to the World,* Automobile Quarterly Publications, 1975; *Gurney's Eagles,* Motorbooks International, 1976; (editor) *The Best of Corvette News,* Automobile Quarterly Publications, 1976; *Porsche: Excellence Was Expected,* Automobile Quarterly Publications, 1977. Contributor to magazines, including *Signature, Playboy, Automobile Quarterly,* and *Car Graphic;* contributor, under pseudonyms Elliot Miles and Eric Nielssen, to *Auto Age* and *Car and Driver.*

WORK IN PROGRESS: Articles.

SIDELIGHTS: Ludvigsen writes: "I've been a free-lance writer in the automotive field since 1967. I continue to enjoy this work because I'm intensely curious about cars, about the way they behave and why, and about the companies and people who design, make and race them. This takes me abroad several times a year; I'm pleased about the contacts I've made and the publications for which I write in most of the countries where cars are part of the way of life. Though I've reported on all the great controversies that have swept the automotive scene in the last decade, I've concentrated on describing those events and trends as they are, not as I would like them to be. As support for my activity I've compiled an archive filling fifty-five file drawers and comprising more than one thousand books and reference works. My photo files of the automotive field since 1948 exceed forty thousand negatives and transparencies."

BIOGRAPHICAL/CRITICAL SOURCES: New Rochelle Standard-Star, May 10, 1974; *Ward's Wankel Report,* March 7, 1975.

* * *

LUISI, Billie M(eisner) 1940-

PERSONAL: Born March 5, 1940, in New York, N.Y.; daughter of Harold (a yardmaster) and Mollie (a bookkeeper; maiden name, Ulano) Meisner; married Carmen J. Luisi, May 12, 1962 (divorced, November, 1971); children: Thecla. *Education:* Attended Barnard College, 1957-59; Hunter College of the City University of New York, A.B., 1962; Fordham University, graduate study, 1962-63. *Residence:* Woodstock, N.Y. *Agent:* Betty Marks, 51 East 42nd St., New York, N.Y. 10017.

CAREER: Ceramist in New York, N.Y., 1965—. Teacher of clay arts and "life support skills," including gardening, small-scale dairying, herbalism, and alternate healing, 1970—; nutritional counselor and community organizer of women's health issues, 1972—. *Member:* Phi Beta Kappa. *Awards, honors:* Woodrow Wilson fellowship, 1962-63.

WRITINGS: Potworks: A First Book of Clay, Morrow, 1973; *Goat Yoga: A Householder's Dairying Manual,* Rodale Press, in press. Author of columns "The Organic Gardener," in *Woodstock Review,* 1972, and "Digging Clay," in *Country Women,* 1975.

WORK IN PROGRESS: The Lore Book, an alternate healing workbook, with Susun Weed; *Strong Tea: Women's Stories,* short stories.

SIDELIGHTS: Billie Luisi writes: "I have been a potter and sculptor in clay for fifteen years. My work and perspectives as a writer reflect my experiences as a woman, as an artisan-teacher, as a feminist, and as a person responsible for my own life support systems. Over the last seven years, I have become involved in the primary production of food, shelter, and warmth for my household. My energies are now focused upon integrating and communicating my rural survival skills and ecological awarenesses with my urban-derived cultural-political heritage.

"One communication vehicle is the writing of nonfiction 'reports of process,' firsthand accounts of my experiences in disciplines leading to personal independence (such as potting or small scale dairying), another channel is community organizing around women's healing issues, for I am strongly committed to the concept and practice of accessible, non-disruptive health care. The third focus of my writing energies is on the writing of fiction concerned with the lives of women. Each of these has given rise to work in progress."

BIOGRAPHICAL/CRITICAL SOURCES: Woodstock Times, November 21, 1973; *Ulster County Townsman,* October 4, 1976.

* * *

LUNDSGAARDE, Henry P(eder) 1938-

PERSONAL: Born December 22, 1938, in Copenhagen, Denmark; came to the United States in 1955, naturalized citizen, 1961; married Anette, 1967; children: Peter, Thorsten. *Education:* University of California, Santa Barbara, B.A. (honors), 1961; University of Wisconsin, Madison, M.S.,

1963, Ph.D., 1966; postdoctoral study at Harvard University, 1969-70. *Home:* 1815 Meadowlark Lane, Lawrence, Kan. 66044. *Office:* College of Medicine, University of Vermont, Burlington, Vt. 05401.

CAREER: University of Oregon, Eugene, adjunct research assistant in anthropology, 1964-65; University of California, Santa Barbara, assistant professor of anthropology, 1965-69; University of Houston, Houston, Tex., associate professor of anthropology and chairman of department, 1970-72, University of Kansas, Lawrence, professor of anthropology, 1972—, chairman of department, 1972-76. Research associate at University of Vermont, 1976-78. Conducted field research in California, Alaska, Idaho, the Gilbert Islands, Texas, Denmark, and Vermont. Guest lecturer.

MEMBER: American Anthropological Association (fellow), American Society for Criminology, Association for Social Anthropology in Oceania (fellow), Current Anthropology (associate), Society for Medical Anthropology, Association for Political and Legal Anthropology, South Pacific Social Science Association, Tungavalu Society (Gilbert Islands; honorary member). *Awards, honors:* Woodrow Wilson fellowship, 1964-65; National Institute of Mental Health grant, summer, 1966; American Council of Learned Societies fellowship, 1969-70; National Endowment for the Humanities fellowship, summer, 1972; grant from National Center for Health Services Research, 1976-78.

WRITINGS: Cultural Adaptation in the Southern Gilbert Islands, Department of Anthropology, University of Oregon, 1966; *Social Changes in the Southern Gilbert Islands, 1938-1964,* Department of Anthropology, University of Oregon, 1967; (contributor) Vern Carroll, editor, *Adoption in Eastern Oceania,* University Press of Hawaii, 1970; (contributor) T. G. Harding and B. J. Wallace, editors, *Cultures of the Pacific: Selected Readings,* Free Press, 1970; *Legal and Behavioral Perspectives on Privacy,* Sigma Information, Inc., 1972; (editor) *Land Tenure in Oceania* (monograph), University Press of Hawaii, 1974; (contributor) Niel Gunson, editor, *The Changing Pacific: Essays in Honour of H. E. Maude,* Oxford University Press, 1977; *Murder in Space City: A Cultural Analysis of Houston Homicide Patterns,* Oxford University Press, 1977; (contributor) A. Mamak and G. McCall, editors, *Paradise Postponed: Essays on Social Research and Development in the South Pacific,* Pergamon, in press. Contributor of articles and reviews to professional journals.

WORK IN PROGRESS: A research report of an anthropological study of the computerized problem-oriented medical information system, for National Center for Health Services Research; research on homicide as a public health issue and on cultural sanctions of urban homicide.

* * *

LURIA, Alexander R(omanovich) 1902-1977

July 16, 1902—August, 1977; Soviet psychologist and brain specialist, lecturer, and writer of more than three hundred books on brain disorders and the mentally retarded. Luria became involved in brain surgery because of his experiences during World War II in treating soldiers with head wounds. Much of Luria's research involved localizing such brain functions as speech and memory. Obituaries: *New York Times,* August 17, 1977. (See index for *CA* sketch)

* * *

LYNCH, James J(oseph) 1938-

PERSONAL: Born October 7, 1938, in Everett, Mass.; son

of Joseph (a railroad worker) and Elizabeth (Kelly) Lynch; married Eileen R. Devaney, September 4, 1964; children: Joseph Michael, James Joseph, Kathleen Ellen. *Education:* Boston College, B.S., 1962; Catholic University of America, M.A., 1964, Ph.D., 1965; postdoctoral study at Johns Hopkins University, 1966. *Residence:* Towson, Md. *Office:* Institute of Psychiatry and Human Behavior, School of Medicine, University of Maryland, 645 West Redwood St., Baltimore, Md. 21201.

CAREER: Pavlovian Laboratories, Veterans Administration, Perry Point, Md., research trainee, 1962-66; Johns Hopkins University, Baltimore, Md., fellow in cardiovascular physiology, 1965-66, instructor in psychiatry, 1966-68; University of Pennsylvania, Philadelphia, associate in psychology, 1968-69; University of Maryland, School of Medicine, Baltimore, associate professor, 1969-75, professor of psychiatry, 1976—, director of behavioral laboratories at Institute of Psychiatry and Human Behavior, 1969-75, scientific director of Psychosomatic Clinics, 1976—. Member of advisory council of National Institutes of Health Cancer Institute, 1973-76.

MEMBER: Pavlovian Society of North America, American Association for the Advancement of Science, American Psychosomatic Society, American Psychopathological Association, Society for Psychophysiological Research, Eastern Psychological Association, Eastern Electroencephalographic Association, Sigma Xi. *Awards, honors:* Postdoctoral fellowship from National Institutes of Health, 1966; award from Pavlovian Society of North America for contributions to the study of normal and abnormal behavior.

WRITINGS: (Contributor) Theodore Barber, Leo DiCara, and other editors, *Biofeedback and Self Control,* Aldine-Atheneum, 1972; (contributor) Lee Birk, editor, *Biofeedback: Behavioral Medicine,* Grune, 1973; (with Birk, Stephanie Stolz, and others) *Behavior Therapy: An Evaluation* (monograph), American Psychiatric Association, 1973; (with Birk, Stolz, and others) *Behavior Therapy in Psychiatry,* Jason Aronson, 1974; *The Broken Heart: The Medical Consequences of Loneliness,* Basic Books, 1977. Contributor of nearly fifty articles and reviews to professional journals. Assistant editor of *Pavlovian Journal of Biological Science,* 1968—, and *Journal of Nervous and Mental Disease,* 1975—.

WORK IN PROGRESS: Research on psychosomatic medicine, the influence of social and developmental factors on psychophysiological processes, and the electrophysiological and emotional correlates of conditioning.

* * *

LYNCH, Kathleen M(artha) 1898-

PERSONAL: Born February 5, 1898, in Littleton, N.H.; daughter of Edward B. (a merchant) and Mary (French) Lynch; children: Elizabeth (adopted; Mrs. Walter E. Rabke). *Education:* Mount Holyoke College, A.B., 1919; Columbia University, M.A., 1920; University of Michigan, Ph.D., 1924. *Home:* Plymouth Harbor, 700 John Ringling Blvd., Apt. 502, Sarasota, Fla. 33577.

CAREER: Mount Holyoke College, South Hadley, Mass., assistant professor, 1926-28, associate professor, 1928-43, professor, 1943-60, Mary Lyon Professor of English, 1960-63, professor emeritus, 1963—, chairman of department, 1957-60; writer. *Member:* Modern Language Association of America (life member), Phi Beta Kappa. *Awards, honors:* Guggenheim fellow, 1956-57.

WRITINGS: The Social Mode of Restoration Comedy, Macmillan, 1926, 2nd edition, 1965; *Travellers Must Be Content,* Putnam, 1941; *A Congreve Gallery,* Harvard University Press, 1951, 2nd edition, 1956; (contributor) John Butt, editor, *Of Books and Human Kind,* Routledge & Kegan Paul, 1964; (editor) *Congreve's The Way of the World,* University of Nebraska Press, 1965; *Roger Boyle, First Earl of Orrery,* University of Tennessee Press, 1965; *Jacob Tonson, Kit-Cat Publisher,* University of Tennessee Press, 1971. Contributor to scholarly journals.

SIDELIGHTS: Kathleen Lynch writes: "All my life I have been an enthusiastic traveler. *Travellers Must Be Content* is a small volume of reminiscences of war-time travels, when I could not get on with sedentary research in the British Museum, the Bodleian Library, and manuscript collections preserved in English country houses.

"Among my other books, *A Congreve Gallery* is its author's 'favorite child.' I have been gratified by the general acceptance of my evidence, derived from rare or long obscured documents, that Henrietta, Duchess of Marlborough, was Congreve's mistress and that Mary, Duchess of Leeds, was their child."

* * *

LYNDEN, Patricia 1937-

PERSONAL: Born September 8, 1937, in San Francisco, Calif.; daughter of Richard (a trade union officer) and Marie (a rehabilitation counselor; maiden name, Matlin) Lynden; married Allen E. Gore (a museum security manager), August 2, 1970; children: Richard Lynden. *Education:* Attended California School of Fine Arts (now San Francisco Art Institute), 1955-56; University of California, Berkeley, B.A., 1960. *Politics:* "Left." *Religion:* None. *Home:* 164 West 79th St., New York, N.Y. 10024. *Agent:* Phyllis Westberg, 40 East 49th St., New York, N.Y. 10017. *Office: Politicks & Other Human Interests,* 271 Madison Ave., New York, N.Y. 10016.

CAREER/WRITINGS: Newsweek, New York City, reporter-researcher, 1963-68, correspondent in New York Bureau, 1969-71, "Periscope Panelist" for radio broadcasting service, 1970-71, stringer, 1971-74; free-lance journalist, 1967—; *Politicks & Other Human Interests,* New York City, senior associate editor, 1977—. Contributor to *Atlantic, Cue, Ms., New Leader,* and *New York Times* magazine, 1967—. Reporter-researcher for Eliot Janeway, syndicated columnist and economist, 1969.

WORK IN PROGRESS: Research on national politics and the feminist movement.

* * *

LYNTON, Harriet Ronken 1920-
(Harriet Ronken)

PERSONAL: Born May 22, 1920, in Rochester, Minn.; daughter of Oscar Christian (a lawyer) and Lela (Larson) Ronken; married Rolf P. Lynton (a professor), April 16, 1955; children: Maya, Nandani, Devadas. *Education:* Radcliffe College, B.A., 1941. *Home:* 6170 East Shore Dr., Columbia, S.C. 29206.

CAREER: Harvard University, Cambridge, Mass., research associate, became clinical associate in human relations, 1945-54; Aloka International Training Center, Bandaragama, Ceylon, faculty member and associate director, 1955-58, faculty member and associate director in Mysore, India, 1958-60; University of North Carolina, Chapel Hill, free-lance teacher, writer, and supervisor, 1960-72, health manpower development specialist, 1972-74; full-time writer, 1974—. Past vice-president of Chapel Hill Interchurch Council for Social Service. *Member:* International Association of Applied Social Scientists (secretary and treasurer), Phi Beta Kappa.

WRITINGS: (With Paul R. Lawrence; under name Harriet Ronken) *Administering Changes,* School of Business, Harvard University, 1952; (contributor; under name H. Ronken) K. A. Andrews, editor, *Case Method of Teaching Human Relations and Administration,* Harvard University Press, 1953; (with Fritz J. Roethlisberger and George F. F. Lombard; under name H. Ronken) *Training in Human Relations,* School of Business, Harvard University, 1954; (with husband, Rolf P. Lynton) *Asian Cases: Cases from the Aloka Experience,* Wesley Press, 1960; *Self-Instructional Course for Neighborhood Health Workers,* University of North Carolina Press, 1974; (with Mohini Rajan Rojan) *The Days of the Beloved,* University of California Press, 1974. Contributor to business journals.

WORK IN PROGRESS: A biography of Sir Salar Jung I of Hyderabad, India; *Missy-Ma: Growing Up in an Alien Culture,* completion expected in 1979; "I Believe in Spring," a contemporary three-act play; "Sun and Shadow," a musical play based on *The Days of the Beloved;* "Not at Ashkelon," a three-act play.

SIDELIGHTS: Harriet Lynton writes: "*The Days of the Beloved* was written as a trade book to interest people in India by making a recent romantic period come alive. In doing [the book] I got the help of a friend who belonged to Hyderabad and so spoke the language and could interview the people."

*   *   *

LYONS, Timothy J(ames)   1944-

PERSONAL: Born July 6, 1944, in Framingham, Mass.; son of James Edward (a salesman) and Phyllis Martha (Wiggin) Lyons; married: Judith Forman (an actress), August 12, 1967; children: Halligan and Jessica (twin daughters). *Education:* University of California, Santa Barbara, B.A., 1966, M.A., 1968; University of Iowa, Ph.D., 1972. *Home:* 2541 Gypsy Lane, Glenside, Pa. 19038. *Office:* Department of Radio, Television, and Film, Temple University, Philadelphia, Pa. 19122.

CAREER: Temple University, Philadelphia, Pa., instructor, 1972-73, assistant professor, 1973-76, associate professor of communications, 1976—, chairman of department of radio, television, and film, 1976—. Visiting assistant professor at University of California, San Diego, summer, 1974. Member of steering committee for Council on International Educational Exchange, of Centre Universitaire Americain du Cinema a Paris, 1976—. Member of planning committee of Film and the Humanities National Conference. Assistant director of New England Music Camp. Consultant to Blackhawk Films, National Project Center for Film and the Humanities, and to publishing companies. *Member:* American Film Institute, American Association of University Professors, University Film Association, Society for Cinema Studies (secretary, 1975-77; president, 1977-79).

WRITINGS: (Contributor) Donald W. McCaffrey, editor, *Focus on Chaplin,* Prentice-Hall, 1971; (contributor) Christian Koch and John Powers, editors, *1972 Oberlin Film Conference: Selected Essays and Discussion Transcriptions,* Volume II, National Endowment for the Humanities, 1973; *The Silent Partner: The History of the American Film Man-*

ufacturing Company, 1910-1921, Arno, 1974; (contributor) Don Whitemore and Philip Alan Cecchettini, editors, *Passport to Hollywood,* McGraw, 1976; *Chaplin: A Research Guide,* G. K. Hall, 1978.

Contributor of articles and reviews to film and education journals. Editor of *Journal of the University Film Association,* 1975—.

WORK IN PROGRESS: A book on the historiography of film; an introductory book on film and video criticism; articles on film history and film/video education.

SIDELIGHTS: Calling himself a "student of Chaplin," Lyons explains his interest in "the most popular film star that ever lived" as "purely academic." But he quickly adds, "You can't have a genuine academic interest in a subject that you don't love!" As a teacher he "finds in Chaplin things that benefit students . . . film history, the cultural influence of his films, and the relationships of the creator and his art product." He defends the study of film, declaring, "There are some people who still think that movies are just something to go to on a Saturday night. These people don't understand that in universities today, film study has become what the sociological study of literature once was. You can find out so much about the culture—about what life was once like—through the films of those times."

AVOCATIONAL INTERESTS: Puppetry, percussion (drums).

BIOGRAPHICAL/CRITICAL SOURCES: Evening Bulletin, November 15, 1977.

*   *   *

MACCIOCCHI, Maria Antoinetta   1922-

PERSONAL: Born July 22, 1922, in Isola Liri, Italy; daughter of Antonio (an engineer) and Giuseppina (Marazzi) Macciocchi; married Alberto Jacoviello (a journalist; divorced May 29, 1952); children: Giorgina Amendola. *Education:* University of Rome, Doctor of Letters, 1958; Sorbonne, University of Paris, Docteur es science politiques, 1977. *Politics:* Marxist. *Religion:* None. *Home:* 1 Rue Bonaparte, Paris, France 75006. *Office:* University of Paris VIII, route de la Tournelle, Paris, France 75012.

CAREER: Noi Donne (magazine for women), Rome, Italy, director, 1950-55; *Vie Nuove* (weekly magazine), Rome, director, 1956-61; *L'Unita* (daily newspaper), Rome, permanent correspondent in Paris, 1962-68; deputy of the Chamber and member of Commission of the Foreign Office, Rome, 1968-73; University of Paris VIII, Paris, professor of political science, 1973—.

WRITINGS: Lettere dall'interno del P.C.I. a Louis Althusser, Feltrinelli (Milan), 1969, translation by Stephen M. Hellman published as *Letters from Inside the Communist Party to Louis Althusser,* Humanities, 1975; *Dalla Cina: Dopo la revoluzioni culturale,* Feltrinelli, 1971, translation published as *Daily Life in Revolutionary China,* Monthly Review Press, 1973; (compiler) *Polemica sulla Cina,* Feltrinelli, 1972; *Pour Gramsci,* Editions du Seuil, 1974; *Elements pour une analyse du fascisme* (title means "Elements for an Analysis of Fascism"), Christian Bourgois, 1976; *De la France* (title means "From France"), Editions du Seuil, 1977. Writer of scripts for Italian and French radio and television programs. Contributor to *Le Monde,* and contributor of literary criticism to magazines of various countries, including United States.

WORK IN PROGRESS: A country by country study of fascism and women around the world; a study of women and marxism.

SIDELIGHTS: Macciocchi's career as a political journalist has taken her around the world many times, including three trips to People's Republic of China.

* * *

MACDONALD, Kenneth 1905-

PERSONAL: Born September 3, 1905, in Jefferson, Iowa; son of William A. (a banker) and Mabel (Swearingen) MacDonald; married Helen Inman, June 17, 1929; children: Stephen. Education: University of Iowa, B.A., 1926. Religion: Episcopalian. Home: 3412 Southern Hills Dr., Des Moines, Iowa 50321. Office: Des Moines Register and Tribune Co., 715 Locust St., Des Moines, Iowa 50304.

CAREER/WRITINGS: Des Moines Register and Tribune, Des Moines, Iowa, began as reporter, 1926, and worked as copyreader, telegraph editor, city editor, managing editor, and executive editor, 1926-46, vice-president, 1946-77, editor, 1953-76, chief operating officer, 1960-70. Member of board of directors, Associated Press, 1956-65, vice-president, 1963-65. Trustee, Simpson College (chairman, 1957-59); director, Iowa Lutheran Hospital and University of Iowa Foundation. Military service: U.S. Naval Reserve, 1943-46; became air combat intelligence officer. Member: American Society of Newspaper Editors (director, 1950-56; president, 1955). Awards, honors: D.Litt. from Buena Vista College, 1957; LL.D. from Simpson College, 1959, and Central College, Pella, Iowa, 1963.

* * *

MAC FARLANE, Stephen
See CROSS, John Keir

* * *

MacGAFFEY, Wyatt 1932-

PERSONAL: Born January 8, 1932, in England; came to the United States in 1954; son of Crichton (a physician) and Jean MacGaffey; married wife, Janet; children: Neil, Andrew, Margret. Education: Cambridge University, B.A., 1954, M.A., 1957; University of California, Los Angeles, Ph.D., 1967. Residence: Haverford, Pa. Office: Department of Sociology, Haverford College, Haverford, Pa. 19041.

CAREER: American University, Washington, D.C., senior research associate in foreign area studies, 1959-62; field anthropologist in Zaire, 1964-66, 1970; Haverford College, Haverford, Pa., assistant professor, 1967-70, associate professor, 1970-75, professor of anthropology, 1975—. Military service: U.S. Army, 1954-57; became first lieutenant. Member: International African Institute, Royal Anthropological Institute (fellow).

WRITINGS: (With C. R. Barnett) Cuba, Human Relations Area File Press, 1962, published as Twentieth Century Cuba, Doubleday, 1965; Custom and Government in the Lower Congo, University of California Press, 1970; (with J. M. Janzen) Anthology of Kongo Religion, University Press of Kansas, 1974.

WORK IN PROGRESS: Kongo Religion and Social Change (tentative title).

SIDELIGHTS: MacGaffey has lived in Africa a number of years, and has visited Ethiopia and Nigeria.

* * *

MACKAL, Roy P(aul) 1925-

PERSONAL: Born August 1, 1925, in Milwaukee, Wis.; son of Roy Frank and Lilly (Fischer) Mackal; married Dolores Peters, May 1, 1962 (divorced, 1968); married Lillian Olson (a teacher), March 13, 1969; children: Paul Karl. Education: Attended University of Wisconsin, Madison, and Marquette University; University of Chicago, B.Sc., 1949, Ph.D., 1953. Politics: Independent. Religion: Atheist. Home: 9027 South Oakley Ave., Chicago, Ill. 60620. Agent: Dominick Abel Literary Services, 498 West End Ave., New York, N.Y. 10024. Office: Department of Biology, University of Chicago, 5555 South Ellis, Chicago, Ill. 60620.

CAREER: Naval Research Laboratory, Washington, D.C., researcher, 1944-45; University of Chicago, Chicago, Ill., instructor, 1953-57, assistant professor, 1957-64, associate professor of biochemistry, 1964-74, research associate, 1964—, safety director and operations analyst, 1973—. Scientific research director and director for the United States of Loch Ness Investigation Bureau Ltd., 1965—. Consultant to World Book Encyclopedia. Military service: U.S. Navy, 1943-44. U.S. Marines, 1944-46.

MEMBER: American Society of Biological Chemists, American Society of Physical Anthropology, American Association for the Advancement of Science, Society for the Protection of Old Fishes, Adventurers Club, Savages Club (London, England), Sigma Xi, Phi Eta Sigma.

WRITINGS: (With Franz Meyer and E. A. Evans, Jr.) Some Aspects of the Biochemistry of Lysogeny, Pergamon, 1961; The Monsters of Loch Ness, Swallow Press, 1976. Contributor of about twenty-five articles to scientific journals.

WORK IN PROGRESS: Expeditions, on the study and investigation of unidentified animals, completion expected in 1979.

SIDELIGHTS: Mackal writes: "Our purpose is to establish cryptozoology as a legitimate science. The search for and study of unknown animals is of great interest from both theoretical and practical viewpoints. I have been and still am involved in a variety of expeditions to investigate reports of unidentified animals."

Among his projects are design and construction of a hydrogen generating device for weather balloons, a method of attracting male mosquitoes by simulating the sound produced by the wing beat frequency of the female, design and construction of an automatic parachute and recovery system for rockets, design, construction, and testing of simple, inexpensive underwater camera devices, design and construction of a book and newspaper copying device used by photoduplication installations in such buildings as libraries, and design and construction of portions of a mechanical dialysing kidney.

* * *

MacKINTOSH, Ian 1940-

PERSONAL: Born July 26, 1940, in Inverness, Scotland; son of James (a naval officer) and Annie (a governess; maiden name, Lawrie) MacKintosh; married Sharron Lorelei Carter; children: Zoe Lorelei, Zemma Gail. Education: Attended Britannia Royal Naval College. Religion: Church of Scotland. Home: 3 Kings Rd., Richmond, Surrey TW10 6NN, England. Agent: Christopher Busby Ltd., 44 Great Russell St., London WC1B 3PA, England. Office: Yorkshire Television, 30 Old Burlington St., London W1, England.

CAREER: Royal Navy, 1958-76, served as lieutenant-commander; British Broadcasting Corp. (BBC) Television,

London, England, drama editor, 1976-77; Yorkshire Television, London, drama producer, 1977—. *Member:* Crime Writers Association, Writers Guild, Association of Directors and Producers. *Awards, honors:* Logie Award from the Australian Television Society for best television series, 1976, for "Warship"; member of Order of British Empire.

WRITINGS: A Slaying in September, R. Hale, 1967; *Count Not the Cost,* R. Hale, 1967; *A Drug Called Power,* R. Hale, 1968; *The Man from Destiny,* R. Hale, 1969; *The Brave Cannot Yield,* R. Hale, 1970; *Warship,* Hutchinson, 1973; *HMS Hero,* Arthur Barker, 1976; *Holt, RN,* Arthur Barker, 1977; *Wilde Alliance,* Severn House, 1978.

Also author of teleplays and scripts for televisions series, including "Warship." Editor, *World Airline Colour Schemes.*

WORK IN PROGRESS: Writing and producing an adventure series for Yorkshire Television.

SIDELIGHTS: MacKintosh told *CA:* "I believe travel is essential to a writer, and therefore travel extensively all over the world both professionally and privately. I am deeply interested in drama and religion of other countries—the two are usually inseparable—and most recently in the study of Balinese culture. I am also fascinated by all aspects of commercial flying, airlines, and airliners."

BIOGRAPHICAL/CRITICAL SOURCES: London Daily Mail, March 22, 1976.

* * *

MACLEISH, Kenneth 1917-1977

February 24, 1917—August 6, 1977; American pilot, diver, editor, and journalist. MacLeish worked as science editor of *Life* before he became an editor and writer for *National Geographic* in 1963. A skilled diver, he once shared the world's record for the deepest underwater dive. He was the son of American poet Archibald MacLeish. MacLeish died in Annapolis, Md. Obituaries: *New York Times,* August 7, 1977.

* * *

MACLEOD, Norman (Wicklund) 1906-

PERSONAL: Born October 1, 1906, in Salem, Ore.; son of Norman William (a stockbroker) and Alice (Wicklund) Macleod; married Catherine Herbert Stuart, 1926 (divorced, 1937); married Vivienne Koch, 1938 (divorced, 1949); married Ann Clarke, 1950 (divorced, 1956); married Fran Bowen Sterling, 1960 (divorced, 1969); children: Jocelyn Norman (Mrs. James M. Harris), Norman Griffith, Skye Wicklund. *Education:* University of New Mexico, B.A., 1930; attended University of Southern California, 1931-32, and University of Oklahoma, 1934; Columbia University, M.A., 1936; additional study at Mount Holyoke College, 1937, University of Colorado, Boulder, 1941, and California State College, Fullerton, 1960. *Home:* 609 McMillan Ave., Bay Minette, Ala. 36507. *Agent:* Robert P. Mills, 156 East 52nd St., New York, N.Y. 10022.

CAREER: Harper & Brothers (publishers), New York City, reader and circulation assistant, 1932-34; *New York City Guide,* New York City, borough editor for the Bronx, 1935-36; *New Mexico Guide Book,* Sante Fe, editor, 1936-37; Connecticut Federal Theatre, Hartford, promotion director, 1937-39; Young Men's Hebrew Association (YMHA), New York City, founder, director, and instructor in poetry at New York Poetry Center, 1939-42; Western State College of Colorado, Gunnison, lecturer in poetry and fiction writing,

1942; University of Maryland, College Park, assistant professor of English, 1942-44; Briarcliff Junior College, Briarcliff Manor, N.Y., chairperson of English department, 1944-47; Rhodes Preparatory School, New York City, instructor in English, 1948-49; New Mexico Department of Public Welfare, Santa Fe, administrative assistant in charge of public relations, 1951-53; San Francisco State College, San Francisco, Calif., assistant director of poetry center and instructor of English, 1954-55; New Mexico Boys School, Springer, public relations director, 1956-57; high school English teacher in Gardnerville, Nev., 1958-59, in Hughson, Calif., 1959-60, in Placentia, Calif., 1960-61, and in Saco, Mont., 1962; English department chairperson at high school in Chowchilla, Calif., 1962-63; University of Baghdad, Baghdad, Iraq, chairperson of English department, 1963-64; Chadron State College, Chadron, Neb., assistant professor of English, 1964-65; high school English teacher in Lac La Biche, Alberta, 1965-66; Savannah State College, Savannah, Ga., assistant professor of English, 1966-67; Pembroke State University, Pembroke, N.C., associate professor of English, poet-in-residence, and director of creative writing program, 1967-78. Lecturer in English, Ohio State University, 1947; faculty member in English (adult education), City College of New York, 1948-49. Foreign correspondent and freelance writer in Europe, summers, 1932-33; editorial assistant, University of Oklahoma Press, 1934. Field representative for New Mexico division of American Cancer Society, 1954. *Member:* P.E.N., American Association of University Professors, College English Association, North Carolina Writers Conference, Sigma Chi. *Awards, honors:* Horace Gregory Award, 1972; National Endowment for the Arts creative writing fellowship, 1974; Roanoke-Chowan Award, 1977.

WRITINGS—Novels: *You Get What You Ask For,* Harrison-Hilton, 1939; *The Bitter Roots,* Smith and Durrell, 1941.

Poems: *Horizons of Death,* Parnassus, 1934; *Thanksgiving Before November,* Parnassus, 1936; *We Thank You All the Time,* Decker, 1941; *A Man in Midpassage,* Cronos Editions, 1947; *Pure as Nowhere,* Golden Goose Press, 1962; *Selected Poems,* Ahsahta Press, 1975; *The Distance: New and Selected Poems, 1928-1977,* Pembroke, 1977.

Contributor to periodicals throughout the world, including *Esquire, New Republic, Mercure de France,* and *Mexican Life.* American editor of *Front* (the Netherlands) and *Morada* (Italy), both 1930-32; editorial director of *Maryland Quarterly,* 1942-44, and *Briarcliff Quarterly,* 1944-47; guest editor of *Cronos,* 1947; editor of *Pembroke Magazine,* 1969-78.

WORK IN PROGRESS: The Whaling Christ and Other Poems; I Never Lost Anything in Istanbul (memoirs being serialized in *Pembroke Magazine*).

SIDELIGHTS: Macleod's poetry was associated from the beginning with the Imagists, those poets of the early twentieth century who strove to free poetry from trite convention and emotion, to avoid the intellectual and abstract while stressing the concrete. Alfred Kreymborg noted that Macleod was particularly influenced by Ezra Pound and William Carlos Williams.

In a letter to the poet, dated July 15, 1954, Williams described Macleod's work in the terms of the Imagist movement. He wrote that the book of poems *Pure as Nowhere* "made a lasting impression on me. I'll never forget how excited I was over it; it had an unequalled cleanliness; a vividness and vigor in its effects, a freshness which, I think, stamp the poems as major work."

A writer for *Saturday Review* suggested that Macleod's poetry is for "tough-minded beings who seek some measure of truth in what they read. His work is in line with poets of the middle and younger generations who were torn from the roots of innocence and forced into personal and worldly dilemmas conditioned not by themselves but by men in high places whose leadership has degenerated and cast an uncertain shadow over mankind. In the midst of social, economic, and political conflicts, Macleod tries to maintain an individual view, only to find himself driven by internal conflicts reflecting the desperation of the children of Adam generally."

When asked to comment on circumstances important to his career, Macleod pointed out that he has lived in all of the United States except Alaska and Hawaii, and in Canada, England, France, Iraq, Mexico, Scotland, and the U.S.S.R. His poetry has been translated into French, German, Spanish, Italian, Russian, and Japanese, and has been published in France, Belgium, Germany, Japan, Holland, Brazil, Mexico, the U.S.S.R., Wales, Scotland, Italy, Canada, and Australia. Macleod's reading of his poetry has been recorded for the archives of the Division of Music of the Library of Congress. His papers are housed in the Yale Collection of American Literature at Yale University.

BIOGRAPHICAL.CRITICAL SOURCES: Marable and Boylan, *A Handbook of Oklahoma Writers,* University of Oklahoma Press, 1939; Frederick Hoffman and others, *The Little Magazine: A History and Bibliography,* Princeton University Press, 1947; Spiller and others, editors, *Literary History of the United States,* Macmillan, 1948; *Saturday Review of Literature,* November 11, 1936, March 24, 1948.

* * *

MacNUTT, Francis S. 1925-

PERSONAL: Born April 22, 1925, in St. Louis, Mo.; son of Joseph Scott (a portrait painter) and Agnes (a ballet dancer; maiden name, Cady) MacNutt. *Education:* Harvard University, B.A., 1948; Catholic University of America, M.F.A., 1950; Aquinas Institute of Theology, Ph.D., 1958. *Politics:* Independent. *Home:* 4453 McPherson, St. Louis, Mo. 63108.

CAREER: Entered Ordo Praedicatorum (Order of Preachers—Dominicans), 1950, ordained Roman Catholic priest, 1956; Aquinas Institute of Theology, Dubuque, Iowa, professor of homiletics, 1958-66; Catholic Homiletic Society, St. Louis, Mo., executive director, 1966-69; Thomas Merton Foundation, St. Louis, Mo., director, 1970—. National adviser to Service Committee of Catholic Charismatic Renewal Services. *Military service:* U.S. Army, Medical Corps, 1944-46.

MEMBER: National Audubon Society, Association of Christian Therapists (adviser). *Awards, honors:* Franciscan Interna Award, 1977, for contribution to the knowledge of healing through prayer; honorary warden of International Order of St. Luke.

WRITINGS: Gauging Sermon Effectiveness, Priory Press, 1960; *Teach Us to Love: Sisters' Conference Needs,* B. Herder, 1964; *How to Prepare a Sermon,* Novalis, 1970; *Healing,* Ave Maria Press, 1974; *Power to Heal,* Ave Maria Press, 1977. Founding editor of *Preaching: A Journal of Homiletics,* 1965-70.

SIDELIGHTS: Fr. MacNutt writes: "*Healing* has had an effect upon the thinking and practice of many Christians (especially Catholics) in encouraging a renewal of the practice of praying for healing. In conjunction with the writings of Ruth Stapleton, Agnes Sanford, Barbara Shlemon and many others, this book seems to have effect a real change in many churches in the past few years."

* * *

MADHUBUTI, Haki R.
See LEE, Don L.

* * *

MADUELL, Charles Rene, Jr. 1918-

PERSONAL: Born February 2, 1918, in New Orleans, La.; son of Charles Rene (an architect) and Thelma Louise (Viosca) Maduell; married Lola Rita Legier (a secretary), March 3, 1941; children: Charles Rene III, Andree Marie Maduell Wagner, Dolores Rita. *Education:* Loyola University, New Orleans, La., student, 1935-38; Louisiana State University, B.S., 1940; Tulane University, graduate study, 1940-41. *Politics:* "Registered democrat with republican tendencies." *Religion:* Roman Catholic. *Home:* 6368 Orleans Ave., New Orleans, La. 70124. *Office:* Charity Hospital of Louisiana, 1532 Tulane Ave., New Orleans, La. 70151.

CAREER: Delta Electronics, New Orleans, La., president and electronic engineer, 1945-55; Tulane University, Radiation Laboratory, New Orleans, radiation physicist, 1960-75; Touro Infirmary, New Orleans, radiation physicist, 1975—. Genealogist. Staff physicist at Charity Hospital of Louisiana, 1955—. *Member:* American Physical Society, Louisiana Historical Society, Louisiana Genealogical and Historical Society, Genealogical Research Society of New Orleans.

WRITINGS: The Romance of Spanish Surnames, privately printed, 1967; *Marriages and Family Relationships of New Orleans,* privately printed, Volume I: *1820-1830,* 1968, Volume II: *1830-1840,* 1969; *Marriage Contracts, Wills and Testaments of the Spanish Colonial Period, 1770-1804,* privately printed, 1969; *Census Tables for the French Colony,* Genealogical Publishing, 1972; *Federal Land Grants in the Territory of Orleans,* Polyanthos, 1975; *New Orleans Marriage Contracts, 1804-1820,* Polyanthos, 1977. Contributor to local genealogy journals. Contributing editor of *New Orleans Genesis;* editor for Genealogical Research Society of New Orleans.

WORK IN PROGRESS: Annotated Census of New Orleans in 1810; Biography and Genealogy of Francisco Luis Hector, Baron de Carondelet; research on the colonial Louisiana French and Spanish governors and their genealogies.

SIDELIGHTS: Maduell writes: "My major business interest is radiation physics and hospital-oriented electronics. I have also taught X-ray and nuclear physics to residents in radiology and nuclear medicine, and to technician students in both fields.

"Realizing that many Louisiana colonial documents are not available to the general public because they are written in French and Spanish, I thought that indices to these various documents as they concern marriage contracts, wills, testaments, and the like would be vital. My principal avocation is colonial Louisiana genealogy and microhistory, and the origins and spellings of surnames as found in Louisiana, especially those of French and Spanish origin."

* * *

MAERTZ, Richard Charles 1935-

PERSONAL: Born January 29, 1935, in New Prague, Minn.; son of George W. and Gustie (Zizka) Maertz; married Judith Curtis, December 19, 1964; children: Grant, Briana, Tyler. *Education:* St. Cloud State Teachers College, B.S., 1958; California State University, Long Beach, M.A., 1970. *Home:* 2428 South Redwood Dr., Anaheim, Calif. 92806.

CAREER: High school physical education teacher and wrestling coach in Buffalo Lake, Minn., 1958-61, Cambridge, Minn., 1961-65, and Calexico, Calif., 1965-67; William N. Neff High School, La Mirada, Calif., teacher of social science and wrestling coach, 1967—, chairman of department of social science, 1974—. *Military service:* U.S. Army, 1955-57. *Member:* National Education Association.

WRITINGS: Wrestling Techniques: Takedowns, A. S. Barnes, 1970; *Wrestling Teaching Guide,* A. S. Barnes, 1973; (contributor) Ray Carson, editor, *Championship Wrestling: An Anthology,* privately printed, 1974; *Techniques for Championship Wrestling,* A. S. Barnes, 1977. Contributor to *Athletic Journal.*

WORK IN PROGRESS: A novel.

SIDELIGHTS: Maertz writes: "Being fortunate enough to achieve success early in my coaching career, I felt obligated to share my wrestling ideas, philosophy, and techniques of coaching wrestling with others. At the present time, writing is really an avocational interest, but because the written word is easier for me than the spoken word, I have turned more and more to this means to say what I want."

*   *   *

MAGEE, David (Bickersteth)   1905-1977

1905—July 17, 1977; British-born American rare book dealer, novelist, and bibliographer. Magee came to the United States in 1925 and spent the next half-century as a rare book dealer in San Francisco. He is the author of an autobiography, *Infinite Riches,* and two bibliographies of the Grabhorn Press. Obituaries: *AB Bookman's Weekly,* August 1, 1977.

*   *   *

MAGUIRE, Robert A(lan)   1930-

PERSONAL: Born June 21, 1930, in Canton, Mass.; son of Frederick W. and Ruth P. Maguire. *Education:* Dartmouth College, A.B., 1951; Columbia University, M.A., 1953, Ph.D., 1961. *Religion:* Roman Catholic. *Home:* 560 Riverside Dr., Apt. 20-H, New York, N.Y. 10027. *Office:* Department of Slavic Languages, Columbia University, New York, N.Y. 10027.

CAREER: Duke University, Durham, N.C., instructor in Russian language and literature, 1958-60; Dartmouth College, Hanover, N.H., assistant professor of Russian, 1960-62; Columbia University, New York City, assistant professor, 1962-66, associate professor, 1966-70, professor of Russian literature, 1970—, chairperson of department of Slavic languages, 1977—. Visiting assistant professor at Indiana University, summer, 1961, autumn, 1966, 1969; visiting fellow at St. Anthony's College, Oxford, 1971-72. Member of selection board of International Research and Exchanges Board, 1971-74; member of advisory committee for National Endowment for the Humanities and senior Fulbright-Hays program, both 1971-74. *Military service:* U.S. Army, 1953-55. U.S. Army Reserve, 1955-61.

MEMBER: P.E.N., Modern Language Association of America, American Association for the Advancement of Slavic Studies (member of board of directors, 1977—), American Association of Teachers of Slavic and East European Languages, American Association of University Pro-

fessors, Polish Institute of Arts and Sciences, Phi Beta Kappa. *Awards, honors:* Ford Foundation foreign area fellowship, 1957-58; American Council of Learned Societies grant, 1967; Guggenheim fellowship, 1969-70.

WRITINGS: (Editor with Maurice Friedberg, and translator) *Russian Short Stories: A Bilingual Collection,* Random House, 1965; *Red Virgin Soil: Soviet Literature in the 1920's,* Princeton University Press, 1968; (contributor) Edward J. Brown, editor, *Major Soviet Writers,* Oxford University Press, 1973; *Gogol from the Twentieth Century: Eleven Essays,* Princeton University Press, 1974, revised edition, 1976; (translator with Magnus Jan Krynski) Tadeusz Rozewicz, *"The Survivor" and Other Poems,* Princeton University Press, 1976; (translator with John Earl Malmstad) Andrei Bely, *Petersburg,* Indiana University Press, 1977; (translator with Krynski), Anna Swirszczynska, *I Was Building the Barricade,* Wydawnictwo Literackie, 1978.

Contributor to *Encyclopedia of World Literature in the Twentieth Century, Encyclopedia Americana,* and *Columbia Dictionary of Modern European Literatures.* Contributor to academic journals. Member of editorial board of *Teaching Language through Literature,* 1965—, and *Slavic Review,* 1966-69; member of editorial advisory board of "Princeton Essays in Literature," Princeton University Press, 1972-77.

WORK IN PROGRESS: Gogol: A Critical Study; Bely's "Petersburg": A Critical Study, with John Earl Malmstad, completion expected in 1979; *The Problem of the General and the Particular in Russian Literature,* 1979; *Russian Literature from 1880 to 1920.*

SIDELIGHTS: Maguire comments: "Teaching literature stimulates ideas for books, and makes me aware of the problems of communicating through language. I can read Russian, Polish, German, French, Spanish with ease—but the real problem is the mind behind the screens of language. Travel helps here. So, strangely enough, does music, precisely because it is non-verbal (I have considerable professional training here)—as does religion, whose observances resemble the acts of writing and of criticism."

*   *   *

MAHAPATRA, Jayanta   1928-

PERSONAL: Born October 22, 1928, in Cuttack, India; son of Lemuel and Sudhansu (Rout) Mahapatra; married Jyotsna Rani Das, January 16, 1951; children: Mohan (son). *Education:* Ravenshaw College, B.Sc. (honors), 1946; Science College, Patna, India, M.Sc. (first class honors), 1949. *Home:* Tinkonia Bagicha, Cuttack, Orissa, India 753001. *Office:* Department of Physics, Ravenshaw College, Cuttack, Orissa, India 753003.

CAREER: Eastern Times, Cuttack, India, sub-editor, 1949; lecturer in physics at Ravenshaw College, Cuttack, 1949-58, G.M. College, Sambalpur, India, 1958-61, Regional Engineering College, Rourkela, India, 1961-62, G.M. College, 1962-65, B.J.B. College, Bhubaneswar, India, 1965-69, F.M. College, Balasore, India, 1969-70, and at Ravenshaw College, 1970—. Visiting writer, University of Iowa, 1976. Has given poetry readings at St. Andrews Presbyterian College, University of the South, University of Tennessee at Chattanooga, University of Maryland, and at East-West Center, Honolulu, Hawaii. *MEMBER:* International P.E.N., World Poetry Society International. *Awards, honors:* Second prize in *International Who's Who in Poetry* contest, 1970, for poem "The Report Card;" Jacob Glatstein Memorial Prize from *Poetry,* 1975, for a group of poems published in *Poetry;* Bisuva Milana Award for Poetry from *Prajatantra,* 1977, for translations of Oriya poetry into English.

WRITINGS—Poetry: *Close the Sky, Ten by Ten,* Dialogue Publications, 1971; *Svayamvara and Other Poems,* Writers Workshop (Calcutta), 1971; (translator) *Countermeasures,* Dialogue Publications, 1973; *A Rain of Rites,* University of Georgia Press, 1976; *A Father's Hours,* United Writers (Calcutta), 1976; (translator) *Wings of the Past,* [Calcutta], 1976.

Juveniles: *Tales from Fakir Mohan,* Cuttack Students Store, 1969; *True Tales of Travel and Adventure,* Cuttack Students Store, 1969; *Folk Lores of Ancient India,* Kalyani, in press.

Poetry represented in anthologies, including *Indian Poetry in English, 1947-72,* edited by Pritish Nandy, Oxford University Press, 1972; *Ten Twentieth-Century Indian Poets,* edited by R. Parthasarathy, Oxford University Press, 1976; *Contemporary Indian Short Stories,* edited by Ka Naa Subramanyam, Vikas Publishing, 1976; *Best Poems of 1975: The Borestone Mountain Poetry Awards* (special India Issue), Pacific Books, 1976. Contributor of poetry to publications in the United States, England, Canada, Australia, New Zealand, and India, including *Poetry, New York Quarterly, Sewanee Review, Critical Quarterly, Meanjin Quarterly, Event, Edge,* and *Quest.* Poetry editor, *Gray Book,* 1972-73; editor, *South and West, U.S.A.;* 1973.

WORK IN PROGRESS: Stone Occasions, a book of poems; translating *Selected Poems of Sitakant Mahapatra;* editing an issue of *Poetry* devoted to Indian poetry.

SIDELIGHTS: Jayanta Mahapatra told *CA:* "At times I write a piece of short fiction, but poetry is what I have done, in the main. . . . I was raised among simple people who believed (and still do) that things happen as they do because . . . of things that have happened before, and that nothing can change the sequence of things. There are my childhood memories: the lone dark house at the village's end surrounded by aging deodars, coconut palms, like dark sentinels of my own reality. And the dark door of that house, the evenings when a pretty young cousin would bang away on it to spare herself a merciless beating from her drunken husband. We had no electric lighting, and I can recollect the oil lamps stirring, twisting, looking so human, obsequious. And I found myself following a burdensome loneliness. Perhaps such things have entered my poems, perhaps it is only a world which exists in my head. What appears to disturb me is the triumph of silence in the mind; and this silence comes from the world outside of me, a world of hunger, grief, and injustice, that has to be borne somehow. And if my poems are inventions, they are also longings amid the flow of voices toward a need that I feel is defensive. A poem makes me see out of it in all directions, like a sieve, and yet it keeps me in myself.

"Recurrent themes of women appear in my poetry; I have done some short, vivid poems on women—particularly the Indian woman, who seems to have suffered so much, and who still fascinates me by her seeming contentment. I would not like myself to squeeze the last juices from life and living; I feel life has to be taken in gently, as the earth takes in the rain—and so of woman, and of the juices in her flesh. Who has heard of a bee crushing a flower when he sucks the sweet nectar? But then it is a fast changing world; it is a world of violence and terror, and the whole thing unnerves my being. And I shut myself up in my room and write—the most foolish thing to do perhaps."

AVOCATIONAL INTERESTS: Reading fiction, photography (portraiture).

* * *

MAI, Ludwig H(ubert) 1898-

PERSONAL: Born March 27, 1898, in Mannheim, Germany; came to the United States in 1950; son of Hubert C. and Anna Maria (Specht) Mai; married Ilse Behrend, February 12, 1927; children: Veronica (Mrs. J. R. Reynolds), Klaus L., Ursula (Mrs. Gordon White). *Education:* University of Mannheim, B.B.A., 1920; University of Frankfurt, M.A., 1921, Dr.Pol., 1924. *Home:* 343 Shadwell Dr., San Antonio, Tex. 78228. *Office:* Graduate School, St. Mary's University, San Antonio, Tex. 78284.

CAREER: Fressl College, Augsburg, Germany, instructor in business administration, 1922; Deutsche Farben Handelsgesellschaft, Shanghai, China, manager, 1923-45; Tientsin College, Tientsin, China, lecturer in economics, 1945-49; St. Mary's University, San Antonio, Tex., assistant professor, 1950-53, associate professor, 1953-58, professor of economics, 1958—, university professor of economics and international relations, 1967—, dean of Graduate School, 1959-68, director of Institute for International and Public Affairs, 1968—. Director of education for Texas International Trade Association, 1955-60; consultant to Southwest Research Institute, 1956-66.

MEMBER: American Economic Association, Association of Social Economics (vice-president, 1970), Association for Evolutionary Economics, Royal Economic Society, Southwest Social Science Association, Omicron Delta Epsilon, Pi Gamma Mu.

WRITINGS: Approach to Economics, Littlefield, Adams, 1966; *The Formation of Political Economy,* Astra Center, 1969; (editor) *The Economic Order,* St. Mary's University, 1972; *A Primer on the Development of Economic Thought,* St. Mary's University, 1973; *Men and Ideas in Economics,* Littlefield, Adams, 1975. Contributor to economic journals. Editor of *Forum.*

WORK IN PROGRESS: The Nature of Social Economics; The Mature Economy.

SIDELIGHTS: Mai comments that his main interest is "the change of human thought in the economic world and the formation of political economy."

BIOGRAPHICAL/CRITICAL SOURCES: Review of Social Economy, October, 1973.

* * *

MAIDEN, Cecil (Edward) 1902-

PERSONAL: Born May 3, 1902, in Southport, England; naturalized Canadian citizen; son of James Edward and Emily (Memory) Maiden; married wife Elizabeth, December 5, 1953; children: Elizabeth Lynne, Marcus, Miles. *Education:* Educated at University of Reading. *Religion:* Christian Scientist. *Home and office:* 463 Main St., Centerville, Mass. 02632. *Agent:* Shirley Burke, 370 East 76th St., Suite B-704, New York, N.Y. 10021.

CAREER: Advertising copywriter in London, England; film writer for Twentieth Century Fox; staff writer for Disney Studio; writer.

WRITINGS: One Class Only, J. Murray, 1932; *Five to the Horizon,* P. Davies, 1933; *Song of Nefertiti,* Knox Publishing, 1943; *Here I Stay,* J. Murray, 1955; *Jonathan Found,* Crowell, 1957 (published in England as *Image and Likeness,*

J. Murray, 1957); *Harp into Battle* (fiction), Crowell, 1959; *Beginning with Mrs. McBee* (juvenile), Vanguard, 1960; *The Beloved Son* (historical novel about Jesus Christ), Dodd, 1961; *Speaking of Mrs. McCluskie* (juvenile), Vanguard, 1962; *The Molliwumps*, Viking, 1967; *The Borrowed Crown* (juvenile fiction), Viking, 1968; *Malachi Mudge*, McGraw, 1968; *A Song for Young King Wenceslas* (juvenile fiction), Addison-Wesley, 1969; *The Man Before Morning*, Christian Herald Books, 1977.

WORK IN PROGRESS: The House on Straight Street for Christian Herald Books.

* * *

MAIER, Norman R(aymond) F(rederic)   1900-1977

November 27, 1900—September, 1977; American psychologist, educator, and author of numerous textbooks. Maier was professor emeritus at the University of Michigan. His research extended into such areas as animal behavior, brain physiology, frustration, industrial psychology, and executive development programs. He died in Ann Arbor, Mich. Obituaries: *New York Times*, September 27, 1977. (See index for *CA* sketch)

* * *

MALBIN, Michael J(acob)   1943-

PERSONAL: Born June 9, 1943, in Brooklyn, N.Y.; son of Irving (a salesman) and Mae (a secretary; maiden name, Levin) Malbin; married Susan Rothberg (a historian), June 14, 1969; children: Joshua Henry. *Education:* Cornell University, B.A., 1964, Ph.D., 1973; attended University of Chicago, 1964-66. *Home:* 914 Dennis Ave., Silver Spring, Md. 20901. *Office: National Journal*, 1730 M St. N.W., Washington, D.C. 20036; and American Enterprise Institute for Public Policy Research, 1150 Seventeenth St. N.W., Washington, D.C. 20036.

CAREER: New York University, New York, N.Y., visiting instructor in political science, 1971-72; Brooklyn College of the City University of New York, Brooklyn, N.Y., instructor in political science, 1972-73; *National Journal*, Washington, D.C., staff correspondent, 1973-77, reprint series editor, 1975—, contributing editor, 1977—. Associate professorial lecturer at George Washington University, spring, 1976; Catholic University of America, lecturer, 1976-77, adjunct associate professor, 1977—. Journalist in residence at American Enterprise Institute for Public Policy Research, 1977-78. *Member:* American Political Science Association, Washington Independent Writers.

WRITINGS: (With Dom Bonafede, Richard Corrigan, and John K. Iglehart) *Congress*, National Journal, 1976; *Politics, Parties, and 1976*, National Journal, 1976, 2nd edition (with Bonafede and Robert Walters), 1976; (with Bonafede, Walters, Neil Pierce, and Jerry Hagstrom) *Politics and Parties Between Elections*, National Journal, 1977; *Congressional Staffs: The New Lawmakers*, Basic Books, in press. Contributor of about eighty articles and reviews to magazines and newspapers, including *National Journal*, *New York Times*, *Public Interest*, and *Commentary*.

WORK IN PROGRESS: A book on congressional staffs, for Basic Books.

* * *

MALONEY, Frank E(dward)   1918-

PERSONAL: Born March 27, 1918, in Niagara Falls, N.Y.; son of Frank E. and Florence (Bielman) Maloney; married

Lucille Tinker, February 20, 1943; children: Frank Edward, Joann, Elizabeth. *Education:* University of Toronto, B.A., 1938, graduate study, 1938-39; University of Florida, J.D., 1942. *Home:* 1823 Northwest Tenth Ave., Gainesville, Fla. 32601. *Office:* Holland Law Center, Room 357, University of Florida, Gainesville, Fla. 32611.

CAREER: Admitted to the Bar of Florida and the Bar of U.S. Supreme Court, 1942; Jordan, Lazonby & Dell (law firm), Gainesville, Fla., attorney, 1942; University of Florida, Gainesville, associate professor, 1946-50; professor of law, 1950—, acting dean of law school, 1958-59, dean of law school, 1959-70, dean emeritus, 1970—. Graduate fellow at Columbia University School of Law, 1950-51; visiting professor of law at New York University Law School, 1957-58, George Washington University Law Center, summers, 1968-68, Vanderbilt Law School, 1970-71, and Texas Technological University School of Law, 1971. Counsel to Florida Water Resources Study Commission, 1957; principal draftsman of 1971 Tennessee Water Quality Act, and 1974 Florida Coastal Mapping Act. *Military service:* U.S. Army Air Forces, Judge Advocate General's Department Reserve, 1942-46; served in India and Burma; became colonel. *Member:* International Water Law Association, American Bar Association, American Law Institute, Association of American Law Schools (chairman of equity round table, 1955; chairman of federal legislation committee, 1964-70), Florida Bar, University of Florida Law Center Association (vice-chairman, 1961-70), Phi Beta Kappa.

WRITINGS: (With Sheldon J. Plager and Fletcher N. Balwin, Jr.) *Water Law and Administration: The Florida Experience*, University of Florida Press, 1968; (with Richard C. Ausness and J. Scott Morris) *A Model Water Code*, University of Florida Press, 1972; (editor) *Interstate Water Compacts: A Bibliography*, U.S. Department of the Interior, 1975. Contributor of more than fifty articles to professional journals.

* * *

MALVERN, Gladys   ?-1962
(Sabra Lee Corbin, Vahrah von Klopp)

CAREER: Author of books for children. Actress; also worked as an advertising manager in Los Angeles. *Awards, honors:* Julia Ellsworth Ford Prize awarded for *Valiant Minstrel*, 1943.

WRITINGS: (Under pseudonym Vahrah von Klopp) *Kin*, Dodd, 1931; *If Love Comes* (illustrated by John A. Maxwell), C. Kendall, 1932; *Love Comes Late*, Greenberg, 1934; (under pseudonym Sabra Lee Corbin) *Let's Call It Love*, Hillman-Curl, 1938; (with sister, Corinne Malvern) *Brownie: The Little Bear Who Liked People*, McLoughlin, 1939; (with C. Malvern) *The Story Book of Brownie and Rusty*, McLoughlin, 1940; *Dancing Star: The Story of Anna Pavlova* (illustrated by Susanne Suba), Messner, 1942, reprinted, 1967; *Curtain Going Up! The Story of Katherine Cornell*, Messner, 1943, reprinted, 1962; *Valiant Minstrel* (illustrated by Corinne Malvern), Messner, 1943; *Jonica's Island* (illustrated by C. Malvern), Messner, 1945; *Good Troupers All: The Story of Joseph Jefferson*, M. Smith, 1945.

Gloria: Ballet Dancer, Messner, 1946; *Ann Lawrence of Old New York* (illustrated by C. Malvern), Messner, 1947; *According to Thomas*, R. M. McBride, 1947; *Your Kind Indulgence: A Romance of the Theatre in Old New York* (illustrated by C. Malvern), J. Messner, 1948; *Eric's Girls*

(illustrated by C. Malvern), Messner, 1949; *Meg's Fortune* (illustrated by C. Malvern), Messner, 1950; *Prima Ballerina,* Messner, 1951; *Behold Your Queen!* (illustrated by C. Malvern), Longmans, Green, 1951, reprinted McKay, 1964; *Tamar* (illustrated by C. Malvern), Longmans, Green, 1952; *Dear Wife* (illustrated by C. Malvern), Longmans, Green, 1953; *Hollywood Star,* Messner, 1954; *The Foreigner: The Story of a Girl Named Ruth* (illustrated by C. Malvern), Longmans, Green, 1954, reprinted, McKay, 1967; *Mamzelle: A Romance for Teen-Age Girls Set in the Days of Dolly Madison,* Smith, 1955.

Saul's Daughter (illustrated by Vera Bock), Longmans, Green, 1956; *Stephanie,* M. Smith, 1956; *My Lady, My Love: An Historical Junior Novel about Isabella of Valois,* M. Smith, 1957; *Curtain's at Eight: A Gladys Malvern Presentation,* M. Smith, 1957; *There's Always Forever* (illustrated by Allan Thomas), Longmans, Green, 1957; *Rhoda of Cyprus,* M. Smith, 1958; *The Great Garcias* (illustrated by Alan Moyler), Longmans, Green, 1958; *Rogues and Vagabonds: A Novel about the First Acting Troupe to Play in America,* M. Smith, 1959; *Blithe Genius: The Story of Rossini* (illustrated by Donald Bolognese), Longmans, Green, 1959; *Dancing Girl,* M. Smith, 1959; *On Golden Wings: The Story of Giuseppe Verdi,* M. Smith, 1960; *Patriot's Daughter: The Story of Anastasia Lafayette for Teen-Age Girls,* M. Smith, 1960; *The Secret Sign,* Abelard-Schuman, 1961; *Wilderness Island,* M. Smith, 1961; *So Great a Love,* M. Smith, 1962; *Heart's Conquest,* M. Smith, 1962; *The Queen's Lady,* M. Smith, 1963; *The World of Lady Jane Grey,* Vanguard Press, 1964; *The Six Wives of Henry VIII,* Vanguard Press, 1969, reprinted, 1972.

BIOGRAPHICAL/CRITICAL SOURCES: Scholastic, November 5, 1952; *New York Herald Tribune,* April 26, 1959, May 8, 1960; *Chicago Tribune,* May 10, 1959, November 6, 1960; *Kirkus Reviews,* June 1, 1959; *New York Times Book Review,* November 1, 1959. Obituaries: *Publishers Weekly,* January 7, 1963.

(Died November 16, 1962)

* * *

MAMAN, Andre 1927-

PERSONAL: Born June 9, 1927, in Oran, Algeria; came to the United States in 1958; son of Elie and Mathilde Maman; married Marie Dalane (a librarian), 1957; children: Jean-Paul, Anne-Marie, Pierre, Suzanne. *Education:* University of Toulouse, LL.B., 1948, M.A. (economics), 1949, M.A. (political science), 1950, Ph.D., 1956; Sorbonne, University of Paris, M.A. (literature), 1960. *Home:* 40 Hawthorne Ave., Princeton, N.J. 08540. *Office:* Department of Romance Languages and Literature, Princeton University, Princeton, N.J. 08540.

CAREER: Mount Allison University, Sackville, New Brunswick, lecturer, 1954-55, assistant professor of French, 1955-58; Princeton University, Princeton, N.J., instructor, 1958-61, assistant professor, 1961-66, associate professor, 1966-75, professor of French language and civilization, 1975—, assistant dean, 1968-71. Director, Princeton Alumni College, Roven, France, 1977. *Military service:* French Army, 1951-52; became captain.

MEMBER: American Association of Teachers of French, Societe des professeurs Francais en Amerique (president, 1968-74), Federation des professeurs Francais resident a l'etranger (vice-president, 1972—), Central Committee of French Societies in New York (president, 1975—), Higher Council of Frenchmen Living Abroad. *Awards, honors:* Chevalier des Palmes academiques from French Government, 1973, Chevalier de la Legion d'honneur, 1976.

WRITINGS: (With R. L. Politzer, Alexander Hull, and others) *La France: Une Tapisserie* (title means "France: A Tapestry"), McGraw, 1965, revised edition, 1970; (with Politzer, Hull, and others) *Le Francais: Langue ecrite et langue parlee* (title means "French: Written and Spoken Language"), McGraw, 1967; (with D. W. Alden) *Grammaire et style* (title means "Grammar and Style"), Prentice-Hall, 1967; (with Politzer, Hull, and others) *La France: Ses grandes heures litteraires* (title means "France: Its Great Literary Hours"), McGraw, 1968. Contributor to French journals. Member of editorial board of *Bulletin de la Societe des professeurs francais en Amerique.*

WORK IN PROGRESS: Research on the French political system, trials of French political leaders and writers, educational systems of Western countries, and stylistics.

SIDELIGHTS: Maman has been elected by French associations in the United States to represent French citizens living in the United States in the Higher Council of Frenchmen Living Abroad. He flies to Paris once a month to attend meetings held in the Ministry of Foreign Affairs. As president of the Cultural Committee, grouping some forty French associations, he has to coordinate French activities in New York. He lectures to Princeton alumni groups all over the country, on French affairs and Franco-American relations.

* * *

MANCHESTER, Harland 1898-1977

March 3, 1898—November 6, 1977; American author and editor. Manchester was a roving editor for the *Reader's Digest* for thirty years, in addition to numerous other writing assignments for such magazines as *Harper's, Popular Science,* and *Saturday Review.* He was the author of books and articles on science, technology, and archaeology. Obituaries: *New York Times,* November 9, 1977. (See index for *CA* sketch)

* * *

MANCINI, Anthony 1939-

PERSONAL: Born January 17, 1939, in New York; son of Ugo (a construction foreman) and Emma (Staniscia) Mancini; married Patricia McNees (a writer and editor), April 22, 1967 (divorced); children: Romana. *Education:* Fordham University, B.A., 1961. *Politics:* None. *Religion:* Roman Catholic. *Home:* 55 Leonard St., New York, N.Y. 10013. *Agent:* Owen Laster, William Morris Agency, 1350 Avenue of the Americas, New York, N.Y. 10019. *Office: New York Post,* 210 South St., New York, N.Y. 10002.

CAREER: New York Post, New York, N.Y., reporter, 1959—. Reporter and correspondent for *Overseas Weekly* (Frankfurt, Germany), 1965-66. Adjunct professor at New York University, 1977—. *Military service:* U.S. Army, 1962-64. *Awards, honors:* First prize from Uniformed Firefighters Association, 1977, for newspaper feature "Inside a Hospital Burn Center."

WRITINGS: Minnie Santangelo's Mortal Sin (suspense novel), Coward, 1975; *Minnie Santangelo and the Evil Eye* (suspense novel), Coward, 1977. Contributor to popular magazines, including *Cosmopolitan, Penthouse,* and *Gentleman's Quarterly,* and to newspapers.

WORK IN PROGRESS: Romulus and Remus (tentative title), a novel about twins.

SIDELIGHTS: Mancini writes: "I am an identical twin. My brother Joseph is also a writer for the *New York Post*. I have lived in Germany and Italy." *Avocational interests:* Writing poetry, shooting pool, playing basketball.

* * *

MANDEL, Eli(as Wolf) 1922-

PERSONAL: Born in 1922, in Estevan, Saskatchewan, Canada. *Education:* Attended University of Saskatchewan, Saskatoon, and University of Toronto. *Office:* Division of Humanities, York University, Toronto, Ontario, Canada.

CAREER: Former teacher of English at College Militaire Royal de Saint-Jean, St. Jean, Quebec; professor of English at University of Alberta, Edmonton, beginning 1965; currently with division of humanities, York University, Toronto, Ontario. *Military service:* Canadian Army; served in medical corps. *Awards, honors:* President's medal from University of Western Ontario, 1963; Governor-General's Award, 1968; Canada Council award, 1971.

WRITING—Poetry: (With Gael Turnbull and Phyllis Webb) *Trio,* Contact Press, 1954; *Fuseli Poems,* Contact Press, 1960; *Black and Secret Man,* Ryerson Press, 1964; *An Idiot Joy,* Hurtig, 1967; *Crusoe: Poems Selected and New,* Anansi, 1973; *Stony Plain,* Porcepic, 1973.

Other: (Editor with Jean-Guy Pilon) *Poetry 62,* Ryerson Press, 1961; *Criticism: The Silent Speaking Words,* C.B.C. Publications, 1966; *Irving Layton,* Forum House, 1969; (editor) *Five Modern Canadian Poets,* Holt, 1970; (editor with Desmond Maxwell) *English Poems of the Twentieth Century,* Macmillan, 1971; (editor) *Contexts of Canadian Criticism,* University of Chicago Press, 1971; (editor) *Poets of Contemporary Canada 1960-1970,* McClelland & Stewart, 1972; (editor) *Eight More Canadian Poets,* Holt, 1972; *Another Time,* Porcepic, 1977.

Work represented in many anthologies, including *Blasted Pine,* Macmillan, 1957; *Penguin Book of Canadian Verse,* Penguin, 1958; *Oxford Book of Canadian Verse,* Oxford University Press, 1960; *Canadian Poetry: The Modern Era,* McLelland & Stewart, 1977.

Contributor to periodicals, including *Tamarack Review, Canadian Forum, Alphabet, Queen's Quarterly,* and *Fiddlehead.*

* * *

MANDEL, Loring 1928-

PERSONAL: Born May 5, 1928, in Chicago, Ill.; son of Julius I. (a physician and surgeon) and Frieda (Okun) Mandel; married Dorothy Bernstein, July 9, 1950; children: two sons. *Education:* University of Wisconsin, B.S., 1949. *Residence:* Huntington, N.Y. *Agent:* Wender & Associates, 30 East 60th St., New York, N.Y. 10022; and Major Talent Agency, Suite 515, 12301 Wilshire Blvd., Los Angeles, Calif. 90025.

CAREER: Advertising copywriter, 1950-52; playwright and screen and television writer, 1955—. Contributor of scripts to television dramatic series, including "Studio One," "Seven Lively Arts," "Armstrong Circle Theatre," "Playhouse Ninety," "CBS Playhouse," and "American Parade" for Columbia Broadcasting System (CBS), and "Kaiser Aluminum Hour," "Dupont Show of the Month," and "Prudential's On State" for National Broadcasting Company (NBC); writer of dramatic television specials for American Broadcasting Company (ABC) and Public Broadcasting System (PBS). *Military service:* U.S. Army, 1952-54, served in Korea.

MEMBER: Writers Guild of America (president of Eastern division, 1975-77; national chairman, 1977-79), National Collegiate Players (honorary member), Dramatists Guild. *Awards, honors:* "Project Immortality" received a nomination for an Emmy Award from National Association of Television Arts and Sciences, and received Sylvania Award for best original television play, both 1959; Emmy Award, 1968, for outstanding achievement in dramatic writing in "Do Not Go Gentle Into That Good Night," and nomination for an Emmy for outstanding writing in a drama series, 1974, for "The Whirlwind"; American Bar Association Gavel Award, 1976, for script "The Case Against Milligan."

WRITINGS: Advise and Consent (three-act play; based on novel by Allen Drury; first produced on Broadway at Court Theatre, November 17, 1960), Doubleday, 1961; "Project Immortality" (play), first produced in Washington, D.C., at Arena Stage, January, 1966; *Do Not Go Gentle Into that Good Night* (teleplay; broadcast by CBS, October 17, 1967), CBS Television Network, 1967; "Countdown" (screenplay; based on novel by Hank Searls), Warner Brothers/Seven Arts, 1968; (author of preface) Paul Michael and James Robert Parish, *The Emmy Awards: A Pictorial History,* Crown, 1970.

Writer of more than thirty teleplays, including "Shakedown Cruise," 1955; "Great Robbery," Parts I and II, 1962; "Shadow Game," 1969; "To Confuse the Angel," 1970; "Particular Men," 1972; "The Trial of Chaplain Jensen," 1975; and "Crossing Fox River," 1976. Work represented in many anthologies, including *Sight, Sound, and Society,* R. Everson and D. M. White, editors, Beacon Press, 1968; *Electronic Drama,* R. Everson and D. M. White, editors, Beacon Press, 1971; *Mass Media & Society,* Alan Wells, editor, National Press Books, 1972.

SIDELIGHTS: "My first produced work was in television," Mandel recalled. "It was a very deliberate selection that I made. Sitting in a Chicago advertising agency office watching the Kefauver hearings, aware of the way the entire city stopped work for three days to watch them with me, I was convinced utterly that the potential power of communication by television was many orders beyond that of motion pictures and the distant Broadway stage. For a writer who wishes to communicate, I reasoned, this must be the place."

In a 1970 article for the *New York Times,* Mandel expressed his feelings about the lack of realism in television: "Television feeds us poison by lying to us about what life is really like. Communication between people is increasingly out of sync. Television has lied to us about ourselves, and because it shovels information at us in such quantities so relentlessly, and with such impact, we believe it instead of believing our own guts. There is no neutral information," Loring continued. "Everything bears comment, and has its impact. Even the absence of meaning conveys meaning. I have been able to write toward the truth, or its essence, because I deal in an obsolete form, the television drama, where it is not quite so necessary to succumb to the dicta of mass audience programming."

If critical acclaim is a reliable indicator Mandel appears to have been successful in his attempts to inject realism into television. In his review of Mandel's teleplay, "Shadow Game," Lawrence Laurent wrote: "The drama will also be remembered as the most savage attack on corporate ethics since Rod Sterling's 'Patterns' in the 1950's. Even with its few faults, 'Shadow Game' is far superior to ninety-five percent of what is passing for entertainment these days on TV."

Of his more recent teleplay, "Particular Men," Kay Gardella said: "Playwright Loring Mandel has brilliantly met the challenge of a subject so intellectually, morally, and physically terrifying—the agonizing birth of the atomic bomb."

BIOGRAPHICAL/CRITICAL SOURCES: New York Times, July 16, 1967, March 15, 1970; *Washington Post,* May 1, 1969; *New York Daily News,* May 8, 1972.

* * *

MANGAT, J(agjit) S(ingh) 1937-

PERSONAL: Born August 3, 1937, in Kenya; son of K. S. and Gurdev (Kaur) Mangat; married Pushpinder Sundar Singh (a teacher), October 4, 1975. *Education:* University of Delhi, B.A. (honors), 1957; University of Oregon, M.A., 1960; University of London, Ph.D., 1967. *Politics:* "Belief in Democracy." *Office:* Department of History, University of Calabar, Calabar, Nigeria.

CAREER: University of Nairobi, Nairobi, Kenya, lecturer in history, 1961-69; California State College (now University), Long Beach, assistant professor of history, 1969-71; in shipping and export services, London, England, 1973-77; University of Calabar, Calabar, Nigeria, senior lecturer in history, 1977—. Visiting assistant professor at University of Oregon, summer, 1970. *Member:* Farnham Castle Association. *Awards, honors:* Fulbright scholar at University of Oregon, 1958-60.

WRITINGS: A History of the Asians in East Africa, circa 1886-1945, Clarendon Press, 1969, revised edition, 1970; (contributor) D. A. Low and Alison Smith, editors, *The History of East Africa,* Volume III, Clarendon Press, 1976. Contributor to *East Africa Journal, Journal of African and Asian Studies,* and *Proceedings of Kenya Historical Society.*

WORK IN PROGRESS: Research on African history, with publications expected to result; an article, "The Shona, Malawi and Luba-Lunda State Systems."

SIDELIGHTS: Mangat comments that his travels include England, Europe, United States, East Africa, Nigeria, and India, and that he is knowledgeable in the languages spoken in these countries. *Avocational interests:* Popular music.

* * *

MANHEIM, Sylvan D. 1897-1977

1897—September 15, 1977; American proctologist, professor, and author of a book on pathology. Manheim was chief of the proctology service at Mount Sinai Hospital in New York City. He died in New York City. Obituaries: *New York Times,* September 16, 1977.

* * *

MANKIEWICZ, Joseph L(eo) 1909-

PERSONAL: Born February 11, 1909, in Wilkes-Barre, Pa.; son of Frank (a teacher) and Johanna (Blumenau) Mankiewicz; married second wife, Rosa Strader, July 28, 1939 (died, 1958); married Rosemary Matthews, 1962; children: Eric, Christopher, Thomas, Alexandra. *Education:* Graduated from Columbia University, 1928. *Home address:* R.F.D. 2, Box 110, Bedford, N.Y. 10506. *Agent:* Robert Lantz, 114 East 55th St., N.Y. 10022.

CAREER: Began career as a journalist in the 1920's; assigned to the Berlin bureau of *Chicago Tribune* in 1928; while in Berlin, wrote silent film titles; arrived in Hollywood in 1929 and wrote titles for Paramount; writer, director, and producer of motion pictures for Metro-Goldwyn-Mayer, United Artists, and Twentieth Century-Fox, 1930-72. *Member:* Academy of Motion Picture Arts and Sciences, Screen Directors Guild (past president). *Awards, honors:* Screen Directors Guild award for "A Letter to Three Wives," 1949, and for "All About Eve," 1950; Screen Writers Guild award for "A Letter to Three Wives," 1949, and for "All About Eve," 1950; Academy Awards from the Motion Picture Academy of Arts and Sciences for direction and screenplay of "A Letter to Three Wives," 1949, and for direction and screenplay of "All About Eve," 1950; Order of Merit from the Italian government for contributions to the arts, 1965.

WRITINGS: All About Eve: A Screenplay, Random House, 1951 (see below); (with Gary Carey) *More All About Eve: A Colloquy,* Random House, 1972.

Screenplays: (With others) "Only Saps Work," 1930; (with others) "June Moon," 1931; (with others) "Skippy," 1931; (with others) "Forbidden Adventure," 1931; (with others) "Sooky," 1931; "This Reckless Age," 1932; (with others) "Sky Bride," 1932; (with others) "Million Dollar Legs," 1932; (with others) "If I Had a Million," 1932; (with others) "Diplomaniacs," 1933; (with others) "Emergency Call," 1933; "Too Much Harmony," 1933; "Alice in Wonderland," 1933; (with others) "Manhattan Melodrama," 1934; "Forsaking All Others," 1934; "I Live My Life," 1935.

(With Nunnally Johnson, and producer) "The Keys of the Kingdom," produced by Twentieth Century-Fox, 1945; (and director) "Dragonwyck," produced by Twentieth Century-Fox, 1946; (with Howard Dimsdale and director) "Somewhere in the Night," produced by Twentieth Century-Fox, 1946; (and director) "A Letter to Three Wives," produced by Twentieth Century-Fox, 1949; (with Lesser Samuels and director) "No Way Out," produced by Twentieth Century-Fox, 1950; (and director) "All About Eve," produced by Twentieth Century-Fox, 1950; (and director) "People Will Talk," produced by Twentieth Century-Fox, 1951; (and director) "Julius Caesar," produced by Metro-Goldwyn-Mayer, 1953; (and director and producer) "The Barefoot Contessa," produced by United Artists, 1954; (and director) "Guys and Dolls," produced by Metro-Goldwyn-Mayer, 1955; (and director) "The Quiet American," produced by United Artists, 1958; (with Ronald MacDougall and Sidney Buchman and director) "Cleopatra," produced by Twentieth Century-Fox, 1962; (and director) "The Honey Pot," produced by United Artists, 1967.

Contributor—All screenplays: "The Saturday Night Kid," 1929; "Fast Company," 1929; "Slightly Scarlet," 1930; "Paramount on Parade," 1930; "The Social Lion," 1930; "Sap from Syracuse," 1930; "The Gang Buster," 1930; "Finn and Hattie," 1931; "Dude Ranch," 1931; "Touchdown," 1931; "Our Daily Bread," 1934; (and producer) "Three Godfathers," 1936; (and producer) "Fury," 1936; (and producer) "The Gorgeous Hussy," 1936; (and producer) "Love on the Run," 1936; (and producer) "The Bride Wore Red," 1937; (and producer) "Double Wedding," 1937; (and producer) "Mannequin," 1937; (and producer) "Three Comrades," 1938; (and producer) "The Shining Hour," 1938; (and producer) "A Christmas Carol," 1938; (and producer) "The Adventures of Huckleberry Finn," 1939; (and producer) "Strange Cargo," 1940; (and producer) "The Philadelphia Story," 1940; (and producer) "The Wild Man of Borneo," 1941; (and producer) "The Feminine Touch," 1941; (and producer) "Woman of the Year," 1942; (and producer) "Reunion," 1942; (and director) "The Late George Apley," 1946; (and director) "The

Ghost and Mrs. Muir," 1947; (and director) "Five Fingers," 1952; (and director) "Suddenly, Last Summer," 1959; (and director) "There Was a Crooked Man," 1970; (and director) "Sleuth," 1972.

Silent film titles: "The Dummy," 1929; "Close Harmony," 1929; "The Studio Murder Mystery," 1929; "The Man I Love," 1929; "Thunderbolt," 1929; "The Mysterious Dr. Fu Manchu," 1929.

SIDELIGHTS: Mankiewicz's experience in films has been all-encompassing. He began his career as a caption writer, then wrote screenplays, and after an apprenticeship as a producer (which he called his "blackest years"), he was given the opportunity to direct. "I felt the urge to direct," he said, "Because I couldn't stomach what was being done with what I wrote." But when he first approached Louis B. Mayer and asked to direct his screenplays, the studio head told him that he must produce for a time, and said "You have to learn to crawl before you can walk." "That's the best definition of producing I've ever heard," responded Mankiewicz.

In the early days, Mankiewicz was Ernst Lubitsch's protege. He said about his mentor: "Mr. Lubitsch could do more with one shot of a woman going up to a door and opening it than any present-day director can do with all his discotheque effects. He couldn't put it on paper. Nor could a lot of other directors. It's like this: the writing of a screenplay can be the first part of a director's work, and the actual directing of a film is the second part of the screenplay-writer's job. When you write a screenplay, you have virtually directed it by the time you have finished writing."

Mankiewicz has described his brand of cinema as being dialogue-centered. Critics agree with this assessment and say that he covers his losses as a director with his intelligent, sophisticated dialogue and Shavian wit. However, some of his films have been criticized as "too talky." Richard Corliss, for example, described the Mankiewicz style as "articulate artifice; the yups and grunts of Hollywood naturalism are the enemies he has fought throughout a four-decade career. . . . Too often, Mankiewicz's admirable intention to write 'screenplays' that can practically direct themselves leads him to dip into a patchwork bag of theatrical tricks. . . . [His] style is much more appropriate to stage than to screen. The best film dialogue is tough and terse, suggesting the give-and-take of a good prize; its closest dramatic correlative is the stichomythia of Greek tragedy. . . . The sad fact is that his reluctance to edit his own scripts resulted in films whose monologues are less often elegant than elongated."

Dialogue is vital to Mankiewicz's films because, as he said: "My particular type of writing is concerned with the manner and mores of our time, and it demands an audience which is patient with *the word*. I guess that's out of favour at the moment. Audiences are conditioned to having their eyeballs jabbed.

"I don't disapprove," he continued, "but we're on a voyeuristic kick. This is a spectator society. I guess television has contributed a lot to it. The audience in the cinema, by and large, comes to be titillated by colour and effects. But the so-called innovations of recent years—indeed since the end of World War II—haven't emanated from directors, but from the laboratories and the lens makers."

In fact, Mankiewicz has admitted: "I don't know how to write films today. I couldn't cope with all the visual violence that's expected. I believe in the word, that literacy may well be worth dramatizing. I don't think that grunts will ever replace talk. Good talk. One of the reasons I'm having a hell-

uva time finding something new to do is that I want an audience that can listen as well as look."

BIOGRAPHICAL/CRITICAL SOURCES: Films and Filming, November, 1970; *Newsweek,* December 4, 1972; Joseph L. Mankiewicz, *More All About Eve: A Colloquy,* Random House, 1972; Fred Lawrence Guiles, *Hanging on in Paradise,* McGraw, 1975; Richard Corliss, *Talking Pictures,* Penguin, 1975; *Variety,* October 29, 1975; David Thomson, *A Biographical Dictionary of Film,* Morrow, 1976.

*   *   *

MANN, Edward
    See FRIED, Emanuel

*   *   *

MANN, Philip A(lan)   1934-

PERSONAL: Born May 30, 1934, in Des Moines, Iowa; son of Herrold V. (in educational administration) and Clara (a teacher; maiden name, Rasmussen) Mann; children: Marci, Jon. *Education:* Drake University, B.A., 1956, M.A., 1963; University of Michigan, Ph.D., 1968. *Office:* 2435 Kimberly Rd., Bettendorf, Iowa 52722.

CAREER: School psychologist in Woodstock, Ill., 1961-64; University of Texas, Austin, assistant professor of psychology and consultant at Psychological Service Center, 1968-71; Indiana University, Bloomington, associate professor of psychology, 1971-74; private practice in clinical psychology in Bettendorf, Iowa, 1974—. Coordinator of program evaluation and research at Davenport Community Mental Health Center, 1974—. *Military service:* U.S. Air Force, 1957-59; became captain. *Member:* American Psychological Association, Society for the Psychological Study of Social Issues, American Association for the Advancement of Science, Iowa Psychological Association.

WRITINGS: Psychological Consultation with a Police Department: A Demonstration of Cooperative Training in Mental Health, C. C Thomas, 1973; (contributor) T. R. Armstrong and K. M. Cinnamon, editors, *Power and Authority in Law Enforcement,* C. C Thomas, 1976; *Models of Community Psychology,* Free Press, 1977. Contributor of articles and reviews to psychology journals. Consulting editor of *American Journal of Community Psychology* and *Journal of Community Psychology.*

WORK IN PROGRESS: Research on community development and human adaptation.

*   *   *

MANNING-SANDERS, Ruth   1895-

PERSONAL: Born in 1895, in Swansea, Wales; daughter of a minister; married George Manning-Sanders (an artist and writer); children: Joan, David. *Education:* Attended Manchester University. *Residence:* Penzance, Cornwall, England.

CAREER: Poet and novelist prior to World War II, and author of books for children, beginning 1948. Worked for two years with a circus. *Awards, honors:* Blindman International Poetry Prize, 1926, for *The City;* Kate Greenaway Medal, 1959, for *A Bundle of Ballads.*

*WRITINGS—*Fiction, except as noted: *The Twelve Saints,* E. J. Clode, 1926; *The City* (poem), Dial Press, 1927; *Waste Corner,* Christophers, 1927, E. J. Clode, 1928; *Hucca's Moor,* Faber & Gwyer, 1929; *The Crochet Woman,* Coward, 1930; *The Growing Trees*, Morrow, 1931; *She Was Sophia*, Cobden-Sanderson, 1932; *Run Away*, Cassell, 1934; *Mermaid's Mirror*, Cassell, 1935; *The Girl Who Made an Angel*, Cassell, 1936; *Elephant: The Romance of Laura* (short stories), F. A. Stokes, 1938; *Children by the Sea* (illustrated by Mary Shepard), Collins, 1938, published as *Adventure May be Anywhere*, F. A. Stokes, 1939; *Luke's Circus*, Collins, 1939, Little, Brown, 1940; *Mystery at Penmarth* (illustrated by Susanne Suba), McBride, 1941; *The West of England* (nonfiction), B. T. Batsford, 1949; *The River Dart* (nonfiction), Westaway Books, 1951; *Seaside England* (nonfiction), B. T. Batsford, 1951.

Juvenile: *The Circus*, Chanticleer Press, 1948; *Swan of Denmark: The Story of Hans Christian Andersen* (illustrated by Astrid Walford), Heinemann, 1949, McBride, 1950, published as *The Story of Hans Andersen, Swan of Denmark*, Dutton, 1966; *The English Circus*, Laurie, 1952; *The Golden Ball: A Novel of the Circus*, R. Hale, 1954; *Melissa*, R. Hale, 1957; *Peter and the Piskies: Cornish Folk and Fairy Tales* (illustrated by Raymond Briggs), Oxford University Press, 1958, Roy, 1966.

Circus Boy (illustrated by Annette Macarthur-Onslow), Oxford University Press, 1960; *Red Indian Folk and Fairy Tales* (illustrated by C. Walter Hodges), Oxford University Press, 1960, Roy, 1962; *Animal Stories* (illustrated by Macarthur-Onslow), Oxford University Press, 1961, Roy, 1962; *A Book of Giants* (illustrated by Robin Jacques), Methuen, 1962, Dutton, 1963; *The Smugglers* (illustrated by William Stobbs), Oxford University Press, 1962; *A Book of Dwarfs* (illustrated by Jacques), Methuen, 1963, Dutton, 1964; *A Book of Dragons* (illustrated by Jacques), Methuen, 1964, Dutton, 1965.

Damian and the Dragon: Modern Greek Folk-Tales (illustrated by William Papas), Roy, 1965; *A Book of Wizards* (illustrated by Jacques), Methuen, 1966, Dutton, 1967; *A Book of Mermaids* (illustrated by Jacques), Methuen, 1967, Dutton, 1968; *Stories from the English and Scottish Ballads* (illustrated by Trevor Ridley), Dutton, 1968; *A Book of Ghosts and Goblins* (illustrated by Jacques), Methuen, 1968, Dutton, 1969; *The Glass Man and the Golden Bird: Hungarian Folk and Fairy Tales* (illustrated by Victor G. Ambrus), Roy, 1968; *The Spaniards Are Coming!* (illustrated by Jacqueline Rizvi), Heinemann, 1969, Watts, 1970; *Jonnikin and the Flying Basket: French Folk and Fairy Tales* (illustrated by Ambrus), Dutton, 1969; *A Book of Princes and Princesses* (illustrated by Jacques), Methuen, 1969, Dutton, 1970.

Gianni and the Ogre (illustrated by Stobbs), Methuen, 1970, Dutton, 1971; *A Book of Devils and Demons* (illustrated by Jacques), Dutton, 1970; *A Book of Charms and Changelings* (illustrated by Jacques), Methuen, 1971, Dutton, 1972; *A Choice of Magic*, Dutton, 1971; *A Book of Ogres and Trolls* (illustrated by Jacques), Methuen, 1972, Dutton, 1973; *A Book of Sorcerers and Spells* (illustrated by Jacques), Methuen, 1973, Dutton, 1974; *A Book of Magic Animals* (illustrated by Jacques), Methuen, 1974, Dutton, 1975; *Stumpy: A Russian Tale* (illustrated by Leon Shtainmets), Methuen, 1974; *Old Dog Sirko: A Ukrainian Tale* (illustrated by Shtainmets), Methuen, 1974; *Sir Green Hat and the Wizard* (illustrated by Stobbs), Methuen, 1974; *Tortoise Tales* (illustrated by Donald Chaffin), Nelson, 1974; *A Book of Monsters* (illustrated by Jacques), Methuen, 1975, Dutton, 1976; *Young Gabby Goose* (illustrated by J. Hodgson), Methuen, 1975; *Scottish Folk Tales* (illustrated by Stobbs), Methuen, 1976; *Fox Tales* (illustrated by Hodgson), Methuen, 1976.

Editor: *A Bundle of Ballads* (illustrated by Stobbs), Oxford University Press, 1959, Lippincott, 1961; *Birds, Beasts, and Fishes* (illustrated by Rita Parsons), Oxford University Press, 1962; *The Red King and the Witch* (illustrated by Ambrus), Oxford University Press, 1964, Roy, 1965; *The Hamish Hamilton Book of Magical Beasts* (illustrated by Briggs), Hamish Hamilton, 1965, published as *A Book of Magical Beasts*, Thomas Nelson, 1970; *A Book of Witches* (illustrated by Jacques), Methuen, 1965, Dutton, 1966; *Festivals* (illustrated by Briggs), Heinemann, 1972, Dutton, 1973.

SIDELIGHTS: Because of her close association with the circus, many of Ruth Manning-Sanders' books center around that form of entertainment. About *English Circus*, a discussion of the historical origins of the circus, a *Saturday Review* critic wrote: "No one even faintly interested in the circus—its history, traditions, and bizarre personalities—can fail to be interested in this detailed tribute.... Mrs. Manning-Sanders ... more often than not manages to bring to life the glories of 'the art that eternally contemplates the proud enchantment of its own perfection,'" and a *Times Literary Supplement* critic commented: "The book is agreeably and quietly written and contains a large amount of interesting information. Much of it has been gathered from the work of other writers and the book's main fault is that it lacks the freshness and drive of genuine originality."

Later in her career, Manning-Sanders concentrated mainly on books for children. About one of the most recent, *A Book of Sorcerers and Spells*, the *Times Literary Supplement* commented: "The frequent use of rhetorical questions and of present-tense narrative makes the style vivid and easy to read aloud, in spite of its dependence on repeated tricks. The selection of stories is pleasantly varied, most of them being the sort of European fairy stories which Lang used so extensively."

BIOGRAPHICAL/CRITICAL SOURCES: Saturday Review, April 3, 1954; *Times Literary Supplement*, November 14, 1952, September 28, 1973.*

* * *

MANNION, John J(oseph) 1941-

PERSONAL: Born September 6, 1941, in Huddersfield, Yorkshire, England; son of Patrick (a farmer) and Winnifred (McHugh) Mannion; married Maura Campion, September 21, 1966; children: Michael. *Education:* University College, National University of Ireland, B.A. (honors), 1963, M.A., 1965; University of Toronto, Ph.D., 1971. *Home:* 149 Oxen Pond Rd., St. John's, Newfoundland, Canada. *Office:* Department of Geography, Memorial University of Newfoundland, St. John's, Newfoundland, Canada.

CAREER: Memorial University of Newfoundland, St. John's, assistant professor, 1969-73, associate professor of geography, 1974—. Member of American Commission for Irish Studies; consultant to Imperial Oil and Canadian Broadcasting Corp.'s television series, "The Newcomers." *Member:* Canadian Association of Geographers.

WRITINGS: Irish Settlements in Eastern Canada, University of Toronto Press, 1974; *Point Lance in Transition: The Transformation of a Newfoundland Outport*, McClelland & Stewart, 1976; (editor) *The Peopling of Newfoundland*, Institute of Social and Economic Research, Memorial University of Newfoundland, 1977. Contributor to geography journals.

WORK IN PROGRESS: The Irish Migrations to Newfoundland, 1700-1850, completion expected in 1979.

SIDELIGHTS: Mannion told CA: "The focus of my research is on the social and economic background of the immigrants settling in Newfoundland and elsewhere in Eastern Canada." Other research Mannion is involved with concerns "the Atlantic migrations and the transfer of culture, and the adaptation of European immigrants to the new physical and cultural environment on the Canadian frontier."

* * *

MAO Tse-tung 1893-1976

PERSONAL: Born December 26, 1893, in Shao Shan, Hunan, China; son of Mao Jen-sheng (a grain merchant) and Mao Wen; married Yang K'ai-hui, 1920 (died, 1927); married Ho Tze-cheng, 1928 (divorced); married Chiang Ch'ing (an actress), 1939; children: An-ying (died, 1950), Anch'ing, Li Na. Education: Teachers' Training College at Changsha, diploma, 1918. Office: Office of Chairman, Communist Party of China, Peking, People's Republic of China.

CAREER: Founding member and chairman of Chinese Communist Party; political writer and philosopher; poet. Attended First Congress of Chinese Communist Party as one of twelve original delegates, 1921; organized labor unions in Hunan, China, 1921-27, and served as head of Chinese Communist Party Peasants' Department, 1926; led Hunan peasants in abortive Autumn Harvest Uprising and fled to Chingkangshan, China, during Chiang Kai-shek's purge of Communists, 1927; established Fourth Workers' and Peasants' Red Army, 1928, and remained in mountain base in Chingkangshan until Chiang's "final extermination campaign," 1934; on Long March to Shensi Province, China, October 1934 to October 1935; headquartered in caves of Yenan, China, 1935-45, organizing peasant masses and building the Communist Army to nine hundred thousand troops; fought Civil War with Chiang's Nationalists, 1946-49, defeating Chiang's forces and forcing them in political retreat to Taiwan; elected Chairman of People's Government, October 1, 1949, served through 1954; instituted series of rectification campaigns during early 1950's; installed as Chairman of People's Republic of China and National Defense Council, September, 1954, through 1959; launched "anti-rightist campaign" and Great Leap Forward program, 1957; directed Cultural Revolution, 1966-69; chairman of Chinese Communist Party central committee, 1967-76.

Founder, Hunan Reconstruction Alliance, 1919; teacher at First Normal School at Changsha, 1920-22; member of Koumintang, 1923-27, and director of propaganda department, 1925; president, All-China Peasants' Association, 1927; chairman, China Workers and Revolutionary Committee, 1930; chairman, Central Peasants and Workers Government, 1933; political commissar, Red 1st Front Army, 1935; chairman of politburo, Chinese Communist Party 7th Central Committee, 1945; chairman, People's Revolutionary Military Council, 1945-56; chairman, Chinese Communist Party 8th Central Committee and Standing Committee Politburo, 1956-59; chairman presidium, Chinese Communist Party 9th Congress, 1969; supreme commander, Whole Nation and Whole Army, 1970-76.

WRITINGS—In English: The New Stage, New China Information Committee, 1938; China's "New Democracy", People's Publishing House (Bombay), 1944; The Fight for a New China, New Century, 1945; China's Strategy for Victory, People's Publishing House, 1945; The Way Out of China's Civil War, People's Publishing House, 1946; Aspects of China's Anti-Japanese Struggle, People's Publishing House, 1948; Unbreakable China, translated by Hsia

Zoh-tsung, Low Phay Hock (Singapore), 1949; (with Liu Shao-chi) Lessons of the Chinese Revolution, People's Publishing House, 1950; Strategic Problems of China's Revolutionary War, People's Publishing House, 1951; On Contradiction, Foreign Languages Press (Peking), 1952; Report of an Investigation into the Peasant Movement in Hunan, Foreign Languages Press, 1953; Mind the Living Conditions of the Masses and Attend to the Methods of Work, Foreign Languages Press, 1953; The Chinese Revolution and the Chinese Communist Party, Foreign Languages Press, 1954; Strategic Problems in the Anti-Japanese Guerrilla War, Foreign Languages Press, 1954; On the Protracted War, Foreign Languages Press, 1954; On Coalition Government, Foreign Languages Press, 1955; Our Study and the Current Situation, Foreign Languages Press, 1955; Talks at the Yenan Forum on Art and Literature, Foreign Languages Press, 1956; On the Correct Handling of Contradictions Among the People, Foreign Languages Press, 1957; Nineteen Poems, Foreign Languages Press, 1958.

On Art and Literature, Foreign Languages Press, 1960; Guerrilla Warfare in China, translated by Samuel B. Griffith, Marine Corps Institute, 1960; On New Democracy, Foreign Languages Press, 1960; On Guerrilla Warfare, translated by Samuel B. Griffith, Praeger, 1961; Statement Calling on the People of the World to Unite, Foreign Languages Press, 1964; Poems, translated by Wong Man, Eastern Horizon Press (Hong Kong), 1966; Four Essays on Philosophy, Foreign Languages Press, 1966; Quotations from Chairman Mao Tse-tung, Foreign Languages Press, 1966; Mao Tse-tung on War, English Book Depot (Dehra Dun, India), 1966; Basic Tactics, translated by Samuel B. Griffith, Praeger, 1966; Ten More Poems of Mao Tse-tung, Eastern Horizon Press, 1967; The Thoughts of Chairman Mao, Gibbs, 1967; On Practice, National Book Agency (Calcutta), 1967; Why Is It that Red Power Can Exist in China?, Foreign Languages Press, 1968; Five Articles: Serve the People, China Books, 1968; On Revolution and War, edited by M. Rejai, Doubleday, 1969; Supplement to Quotations from Chairman Mao, Chih Luen Press (Hong Kong), 1969; Six Essays on Military Affairs, Foreign Languages Press, 1971; Poems of Mao Tse-tung, translated by Hua-ling Nieh Engle and Paul Engle, Simon & Schuster, 1972; Ten Poems and Lyrics by Mao Tse-tung, translated by Wang Hui-Ming, University of Massachusetts Press, 1975.

Anthologies: Maoism: A Sourcebook, edited by H. Arthur Steiner, University of California at Los Angeles, 1952; Selected Works, Lawrence & Wishart, 1954; Mao Tse-tung: An Anthology of His Writings, edited by Anne Fremantle, New American Library, 1962; The Political Thought of Mao Tse-tung, edited by Stuart Schram, Praeger, 1963; Selected Military Writings, Foreign Languages Press, 1963; Selected Works, China Books, Volume I: 1924-37, 1965, Volume II: 1937-41, 1965, Volume III: 1941-45, 1965, Volume IV: 1945-49, 1961; Selected Readings from the Works of Mao Tse-tung, Foreign Languages Press, 1967; The Wisdom of Mao Tse-tung, Philosophical Library, 1968; Mao Papers: Anthology and Bibliography, edited by Jerome Ch'en, Oxford University Press, 1970.

Also author of numerous pamphlets and speeches.

SIDELIGHTS: "The Chinese people has stood up!" With these words, spoken on October 1, 1949, from a giant rostrum overlooking Tien An Men Square in Peking, Mao Tsetung announced the beginning of the People's Republic of China. The radical transformation which followed would sweep from China virtually all traces of staid Confucian attributes of docility and resignation, and metamorphose the new republic from "a devastated, underdeveloped satellite of the Soviet Union" into a growing, fiercely independent, almost self-sufficient world power governed, at least in spirit, by Mao's Promethian notion that "the human will can solve all problems." Mao himself, a lean and hunted bandit with a bounty of nearly two hundred fifty thousand silver dollars on his head in the 1930's, rose to become "a red and gold godhead of perfection seen on banners, posters, pins and family altars—the universal metonym of China, father image to more people than any national leader, and author of 'works' officially pushed into literally billions of copies in major and minor languages." Edgar Snow, who understood China and Mao better than any other Western journalist, wrote: "My first and lasting impression of Mao Tse-tung was of a man serenely convinced that he was destined to liberate and unify China; to restore its ancient greatness; to humble tyrants and bring into the lowliest peasant a new sense of self-reliance and self-respect; and to educate young people to become nobler beings. Mao was deeply touched by the age-old reformer's *hybris*—to remodel the inner man to perfection—and the vision never entirely left him."

A revolutionary even in his youth, Mao admittedly hated his father and later recalled the aftermath of an argument they had in his fourteenth year: "I reached the edge of a pond and threatened to jump in if my father came any nearer. My father insisted that I apologize and kowtow as a sign of submission. I agreed to give a one-knee kowtow if he would agree not to beat me. Thus the war ended, and from it I learned that when I demanded my rights by open rebellion, my father relented." Three years later, as Sun Yat-sen's republican forces plotted the overthrow of the Manchu dynasty, Mao led his first revolt: he and another student cut off their pigtails (symbols of submission to Manchu rulers) and forced eight others to cut theirs.

Mao made his way to Peking in autumn, 1918. The Great War in Europe had just ended and the architects of the Versailles Treaty, ignoring Chinese demands for the abolition of unequal treaties, granted Japan the former German concessions in China. Incensed by what he considered perfidious "Western bourgoise democracy," Mao, along with hundreds of other young nationalists, turned to Marxism. In 1921 Mao was one of the twelve founding delegates at the First Congress of the Chinese Communist Party.

Returning to Hunan to organize labor unions, Mao at first followed Marx's doctrine that the industrial proletariat would lead the Communist revolution, and he ignored the long-oppressed peasants, considering them "dirty" and "uncultivated." He soon discerned, however, that the peasants had reached their limits of endurance and were near revolt. In an essay considered highly unorthodox at the time, Mao argued that the key to the revolution was in organizing China's rural masses rather than mobilizing urban workers, and he urged the Communist Party to harness the peasantry and place them in the vanguard of the revolution. "Several hundred million peasants," he predicted, would "rise like a tornado or tempest—a force so extraordinarily swift and violent that no power, however great, will be able to suppress it."

In 1927 the Chinese Communist Party underwent a series of serious reversals. Nationalist Generalissimo Chiang Kai-shek launched a bloody purge of Communists. Communist structures in the cities were shattered. After failing to capture the capitol during the Autumn Harvest Uprising, Mao and his peasant army were forced to flee Hunan to a rural mountain base in the Chingkangshan region of South Central China. Mao's sister and wife were executed by Chiang's Kuomintang troops.

For the next seven years Mao and his growing forces headquartered in Chingkangshan. At first harassed by mountain bandits, Mao shrewdly sent bandit leaders gifts and sought advice on guerrilla tactics. He developed his own highly successful formula of guerrilla warfare, summed up in one of his most quoted slogans: "The enemy advances, we retreat; the enemy camps, we harass; the enemy tires, we attack; the enemy retreats, we pursue." From Chingkangshan Mao announced his plan for a program of land reform combined with the creation of mass organizations, which succeeded in winning a large popular following for the Communist Party. By the early 1930's Mao's army—now combined with the forces of Marshal Chu Teh—numbered more than sixty thousand men.

Chiang launched a "final extermination campaign" against the Communists in 1934, and in October the Chinese Red Army was forced to abandon their Chingkangshan base and begin the six thousand mile Long March to the rocky hillsides far to the north in Yenin. Harassed and pursued by Kuomintang troops, their first three hundred miles were a disaster. Fighting nearly every step of the way, the Communists crossed eighteen major mountain ranges, twenty five rivers, and ten provinces governed by hostile warlords. When they reached the Shensi province a year later, only a tenth of the one hundred thousand troops had survived. From these hardened survivors would emerge most of the men who would govern the People's Republic of China during its first decades.

Mao headquartered in Yenan for the next decade, and it was here, historians agree, that the myth began to overshadow the man. Living in conditions austere even to rural peasants—a cave furnished with an earthen bed, a broken wooden desk, a stool, and an urn—Mao raised his own tobacco and spent his nights studying and writing political essays. Dressed in a goat's hair jacket, he received visitors and continually chain-smoked cigarettes. By 1938 he was the recognized leader and theoritician of the Communist movement. From Yenan Mao organized peasant masses, set up mutual aid teams, and organized village elections. Within a few years the party's control extended over 100 million people, and Mao's program expanded to include expropriating land from wealthy landlords and urging peasants to "speak bitterness" to local tyrants. "Revolution is a drama of passion," Mao wrote later. "We did not win the people over by appealing to reason but by developing hope, trust, fraternity."

The Communist and Kuomintang armies formed a coalition with the outbreak of war with Japan in 1937. Cooperation soon ended after skirmishes between the two armies were as frequent as skirmishes with the Japanese. The Soviet Union viewed the success of the Chinese Communists with alarm; Joseph Stalin feared that if Mao remained in control he would not follow the lead of the U.S.S.R. Mao survived plots to subvert his leadership during the war, and by 1945 the Communist Army numbered nearly a million troops and party control extended over 90 million miles. Fearing a Communist and Kuomintang civil war, President Truman dispatched General George C. Marshall to China in December, 1945. Marshall's efforts failed, and by 1946 civil war erupted. For the next three years Mao demonstrated that he had learned his guerrilla warfare lessons well. When the Communist Army crossed the Yangtse River on April 21, 1949, the end was in sight. In the final months of the war

Kuomintang cities "fell like ripe fruit," and Chiang's army retreated to Taiwan.

The centuries old dream of a unified China was realized on October 1, 1949, as Mao declared "our nation will never again be an insulted nation." The formation of the People's Republic of China signalled the end of nearly a half century of chaos and bitter civil war.

The new Chairman's first actions included organizing China's manpower to improve agricultural production, and the collectivizing of land. Kangaroo courts convicted wealthy landlords and former Kuomintang supporters of "crimes against the people," and at least one million people, Sinologists agree, were executed for these "crimes." Intellectuals and "capitalist elements" were subjected to the long and usually painful process of *ssu-hsiang kaitsao* (thought reform) in which they purged themselves of "bourgeoise, individualist" ideas. Millions were sent to re-education camps.

In December, 1949, Mao made his first trip to Moscow for nine weeks of hard bargaining with Stalin. He emerged with an alliance promising Russia the strategic bases at Dairen and Port Arthur in exchange for $60 million in yearly aid. The death of Stalin in 1953 led Mao to a renegotiation of the Sino-Soviet Treaty of Alliance which succeeded in removing all traces of foreign domination in China.

The domestic front in China during the 1950's was marked by increased grain production and dramatic expansion of steel production due, in large part, to an infusion of loans and technology from the Soviets. Fearing an insurrection at home following the Hungarian uprising of 1956, Mao declared: "let a hundred flowers blossom and a hundred schools of thought contend." The Hundred Flowers campaign caused such a huge wave of criticism from the country's intellectuals that in 1957 Mao launched an "anti-rightest campaign" and thousands of his critics were sent to *ssu-hsiang kaitsao* camps. The same year Mao journeyed to Moscow to declare "the east wind" was now stronger than "the west wind," and to ask for atomic bombs and military help in Taiwan. Khrushchev flatly refused. Mao, convinced that a heroic collective action of the Chinese people was needed to transform the nation into a great power, declared the Great Leap Forward economic experiment. "Backyard steel furnaces," eighteen hour work days, and rural communes combined with three years of bad weather to plunge China into national chaos. Economic experts, now calling it "the Great Slide Backwards," predicted that China's economic progress was set back ten years. Faced with harsh party criticism, Mao asked that he not be re-elected as Chairman of the People's Republic and was replaced by Liu Shoa-chi on April 27, 1959. Though he later complained of being treated "like a father at his own funeral," Mao retained the real power in China as Chairman of the Chinese Communist Party.

For years Mao had warned of "blind obedience" to the Russian version of socialism, and in 1960 the first anti-Soviet attacks appeared in Chinese papers. Fearing that a technocratic elite class, already visible in Russia, could destroy China, Mao sharply criticized Soviet "revisionist" leaders, and, critics proclaimed, permanently divided the world Communist movement. In November, 1965, Mao launched the Great Proletarian Cultural Revolution, the first of "an unending series of revolutions" he envisioned. When he urged China's youth to "learn revolution by making revolution," millions of Red Guards went on rampages, smashing temples and statues, arresting the "power holders taking the capitalist road," and following Mao's order to "bombard the party headquarters" by seizing ministries. The face of China—even the Great Wall itself—was plastered with slogans and posters calling for the removal of party officials. As the movement grew increasingly irrational, thousands were killed. The army was called in to quell the masses; Defense Minister Lin Piao, chosen by Mao in 1969 to be his successor, was accused of a plot to assassinate Mao and then allegedly died in a plane crash. It was at this time that Mao became nearly deified: his picture appeared on millions of posters and badges, and his *Little Red Book* became the focus of national veneration.

China entered a period of moderation following the Cultural Revolution. Chou En-lai was called to launch a policy of reconciliation with Japan and the United States, and to try to reconstruct the internal government of China. In one of his boldest political moves, Mao opened the gates of China to Richard Nixon for the Peking summit of 1972.

Politicians and leaders the world over joined in the sentiment of Japanese Prime Minister Takeo Miki when he announced on the occasion of Mao's death: "he left his great footprints on history."

BIOGRAPHICAL/CRITICAL SOURCES—Books: Edgar Snow, *Red Star Over China,* Gollancz, 1937, Random House, 1938; Benjamin Schwartz, *Chinese Communism and the Rise of Mao,* Harvard University Press, 1951; Hsiao-Yu, *Mao Tse-tung and I Were Beggars,* Syracuse University Press, 1959; Snow, *The Other Side of the River,* Random House, 1962; Jerome Ch'en, *Mao and the Chinese Revolution,* Oxford University Press, 1965; Stuart Schram, *Mao Tse-tung,* Simon & Schuster, 1966; Ch'en, *Mao,* Prentice-Hall, 1969.

Articles: *Time,* October 7, 1974, December 22, 1975, September 20, 1976, September 27, 1976; *Newsweek,* February 3, 1975, May 31, 1976, June 28, 1976, September 20, 1976, September 27, 1976, October 18, 1976; *New York Times,* September 10, 1976.*

(Died September 9, 1976, in Peking,
People's Republic of China)

*   *   *

MARBLE, Harriet Clement   1903-1975
(Harriet Jones)

PERSONAL: Born May 13, 1903, in Worcester, Mass.; daughter of William Clement (a business executive) and Mary (Happoldt) Marble; married Vernon Jones (a professor), November 2, 1929; children: Patricia Lovell, Nancy Pearson. *Education:* Smith College, B.A. (cum laude), 1924. *Politics:* Republican. *Religion:* Baptist. *Home:* 267 Salisbury St., Worcester, Mass. 01609.

CAREER: Writer. Assistant director of Clark University Press, 1925-30; member of board of directors, Curtis & Marble Corp., Worcester, Mass., 1952-75. *Member:* Daughters of the American Revolution, American Antiquarian Society of Worcester, Clark University Women's Club, Hall Club, Smith College Club, Worcester Historical Society, College Club of Worcester, Phi Beta Kappa.

WRITINGS: James Monroe: Patriot and President, Putnam, 1970. Contributor of poems and articles to children's periodicals, including *Highlights* and *Wee Wisdom.*

WORK IN PROGRESS: Pilgrims on Cape Cod; James Otis: Orator and Statesman.

SIDELIGHTS: Vernon Jones told *CA* that his wife "was

especially interested in documenting biographical material about the less well-known but important people in American history. She travelled widely in areas connected with each historical character being studied.''

(Died in Worcester, Mass., March 22, 1975)

[Sketch verified by husband, Vernon Jones]

* * *

MARBROOK, Del
See MARBROOK, Djelloul

* * *

MARBROOK, Djelloul 1934-
(Del Marbrook)

PERSONAL: Original name, Mabrouk; name legally changed in 1934; born August 12, 1934, in Algiers, Algeria; brought to the United States in 1934; son of Ben Aissa and Juanita Rice (Guccione) Mabrouk; married Wanda Ratliff, February 12, 1955 (divorced, 1963); married Marilyn Hackett (an editor), December 20, 1971; children: (first marriage) Dorothy, Darya. *Education:* Attended Columbia University, 1951-54, and University of Rhode Island, 1962. *Home:* 3850 Tunlaw Rd. N.W., Washington, D.C. 20007.

CAREER: Providence Journal-Bulletin, Providence, R.I., reporter and bureau manager, 1958-63; *Elmira Star-Gazette,* Elmira, N.Y., night editor, city editor, and executive city editor, 1963-65; *Baltimore Sun,* Baltimore, Md., copy, makeup, and foreign desks, 1965-66; *Winston-Salem Journal-Sentinel,* Winston-Salem, N.C., Sunday editor, books, features, makeup editor, and director of intern training, 1966-69; *Washington Evening Star,* Washington, D.C., makeup and news desks, 1970-71; Education Funding Research Council, Washington, D.C., co-founder, 1971-73, also founding editor of *Education Funding News;* free-lance editor, writer, researcher, and graphics consultant, 1973-74; I. Rice Pereira Foundation, Washington, D.C., manager, 1974—. *Military service:* U.S. Navy, 1954-58; became petty officer first class. *Member:* Washington Independent Writers.

WRITINGS: The Story of Federal Aid, Prentice-Hall, 1975; *Schools, Energy, and Money,* Prentice-Hall, 1976; *Empty Desks,* Prentice-Hall, 1976. Ghostwriter for other authors.

WORK IN PROGRESS: The Arab Prince at the Checkout Counter: A Westward Journey; Square Sun Meditations.

SIDELIGHTS: Marbrook told *CA:* "I have written two books in a contemplated trilogy that is the spiritual journey of an outsider burning to get in the bone, in the wood, in the steel of each moment, each place, each person. I have the conviction based on nothing at all but my life that these works may touch and lighten some few lives, addressing as they do such usual miseries and delights as life in the suburbs, alcoholism, prejudice, marriage and divorce, fear and our great loneliness for what some, like me, call God. When I have time I should like to see these works published, but there is time and it would be death to me to wish profit of them. I think of them as my life's work, and everything here is a blurt of data.''

AVOCATIONAL INTERESTS: Arab affairs, plastic arts, poetry, government, and esoteric religion.

MARCUS, Anne M(ulkeen) 1927-
(Anne Mulkeen)

PERSONAL: Born September 18, 1927, in New York, N.Y.; daughter of Patrick J. (a business executive) and Katherine (Mannix) Mulkeen; married Morton B. Marcus (an advertising executive), February 15, 1976. *Education:* College of New Rochelle, A.B., 1949; University of Wisconsin, Madison, M.A., 1965, Ph.D., 1969. *Home:* 6672 Estero Blvd., Fort Myers Beach, Fla. 33931. *Office:* Division of Humanities, Edison Community College, Fort Myers, Fla. 33901.

CAREER: Rutgers University, Camden, N.J., instructor, 1968-69, assistant professor, 1969-74, associate professor of English, 1974-77, chairman of department, 1975-77; Edison Community College, Fort Myers, Fla., chairman of Division of Humanities, 1977—. *Member:* Modern Language Association of America, National Conference of Teachers of English, American Association of University Professors.

WRITINGS—Under name Anne Mulkeen: *Wild Thyme, Winter Lightning: The Symbolic Novels of L. P. Hartley,* Hamish Hamilton, 1973, Wayne State University Press, 1974. Contributor to *Studies in the Novel.*

WORK IN PROGRESS: Research on Doris Lessing, Jean Rhys, and John Fowles.

* * *

MAREI, Sayed (Ahmed) 1913-

PERSONAL: Born August 26, 1913, in Minia el Kamh, Egypt; son of Ahmed and Zeinab (Nousair) Marei; married wife Souad; children: Nasr, Amina, Hassan. *Education:* Attended University of Cairo. *Religion:* Moslem. *Home:* 9 Shagaret El Dorr, Cairo, Egypt. *Office:* People's Assembly, Maglis El Shaab St., Cairo, Egypt.

CAREER: Farmer in Egypt, 1937-53; managing director of Agrarian Reform Agency, 1953-55; president of board of directors of Agriculture & Credit Cooperative Bank, 1955-56; served as minister of state for agrarian reform in Cairo, Egypt, 1956-57, minister of agriculture and agrarian reform, 1958-61, deputy speaker of the National Assembly, 1963-67, minister of agriculture, agrarian reform, and land reclamations, and deputy prime minister for agriculture and irrigation, both 1969-72, first secretary of central committee of Arab Socialist Union, 1972-73, and special assistant to the president of the Republic, 1973-74; currently serving with People's Assembly, Cairo. President of World Food Council; leader of delegations to Food and Agriculture Organization of the United Nations. *Awards, honors:* Honorary degree from University of Washington, Seattle.

WRITINGS: Al-Islah al-zira i fi Misr, [Cairo], 1957, translation published as *Agrarian Reform in Egypt,* Imprimerie de l'institut francais d'archeologie orientale, 1957; *Agrarian Reform Cooperatives,* Public Relations Department, Agrarian Reform Organization, 1958; *U.A.R. Agriculture Enters a New Age: An Interpretive Survey,* [Cairo], 1960; *The Agricultural Development Programmes for the Egyptian Region, U.A.R., 1960-1965,* Middle East Publications, 1960; *The Agricultural Development Programme for the Syrian Region, U.A.R., 1960-1965,* Middle East Research Centre, 1961; (contributor) *The Second Session of the A.S.U. General National Congress,* State Information Service (Cairo), 1972; *The World Food Crisis,* Longman, 1976.

Also author of *Wazir al-Dawlah lil-Islah al-Zira i,* 1957; *Al-Islah al-zira'i wamushkilat al-sukkan fi al-Qutr al-Misri,* 1963; *Al-Zira ah al-Misriyah,* 1970; *Al-Thawrah al-khadra,*

1971; *Idha arada al-Arab,* 1975; *Al-Mashru al-Arabi lil-tan-miyah,* 1975; *The Green Revolution.*

*   *   *

MARGOLIS, Gary 1945-

PERSONAL: Born May 24, 1945, in Great Falls, Mont.; son of Edward H. (a businessperson) and Pearl (Binen) Margolis; married Wendy Dorothea Lynch (a teacher), May 24, 1976. *Education:* Middlebury College, B.A., 1967; State University of New York at Buffalo, Ph.D., 1971. *Home address:* R.D. 2, Middlebury, Vt. 05753. *Office:* Middlebury College, Middlebury, Vt. 05753.

CAREER: Middlebury College, Middlebury, Vt., director of counseling, 1972—. Member of board of directors of Addison County Association for Retarded Citizens. *Military service:* U.S. Army Medical Services; became captain. *Member:* Vermont Psychological Association, American Academy of Poets. *Awards, honors:* Finalist for Emily Balch Prize, 1975, for *Virginia Quarterly Review;* finalist for Juniper Prize, 1976, from University of Massachusetts.

WRITINGS: Contributor of numerous poems to journals, including *American Scholar, Prairie Schooner, Antioch Review,* and *Virginia Quarterly Review.* Poems represented in anthologies, including *The Random House Anthology of Contemporary American Poetry,* edited by Miller Williams, Random House, 1973.

WORK IN PROGRESS: Counseling Our College Students, a textbook and guide for college workers and parents.

SIDELIGHTS: Margolis told *CA:* "I have written an unpublished book, "The Use of Poetry in Counseling Theory and Practise" which explores metaphor, art, poetry and therapy and teaches counselors how to choose poems that may be therapeutic for their clients. The book includes an anthology of poems that may be used with specific problems. In some indirect way my attention to feelings and stories—the human landscape—as a therapist has sharpened my attention as a poet."

His advice to young poets is "read Rilke's *Letters to a Young Poet,* observe the world, listen to yourself and conversation, write about anything, surround yourself with poetry, take the advice of critics who are specific with your poems and encouraging to your humanity."

Margolis was a resident at Millay Colony for the Arts, September, 1976. He spends part of his summer in his cabin in New Elm, Nova Scotia, and has worked over the past ten years for the Bread Loaf Writer's Conference.

AVOCATIONAL INTERESTS: Beekeeping, long-distance running.

*   *   *

MARIANA
See FOSTER, Marian Curtis

*   *   *

MARILL, Alvin H(erbert) 1934-

PERSONAL: Born January 10, 1934, in Brockton, Mass.; son of Morris (a jeweler) and Rose (a ballet teacher; maiden name, Sampson) Marill; married Sandra R. Lelyveld, August 30, 1959; children: James, Steven. *Education:* Boston University, B.S., 1955. *Residence:* Glen Rock, N.J. 07452.

CAREER: WBOS Radio, Boston, Mass., music director, 1958-62; WNAC Radio and Television, Boston, producer, writer, and music director, 1962-67; WRFM-WNYW Radio,

New York City, director of music programming, 1967-69; RCA Records, New York City, publicist and public information writer, 1969-73; Tatham, Laird & Kudner Direct Marketing, New York City, senior copywriter, 1973—. Free-lance publicist, 1972-73. *Military service:* U.S. Army, 1956-58. *Member:* Alpha Epsilon Rho.

WRITINGS: (With Alan G. Barbour and James R. Parish) *Boris Karloff: An Illustrated Career Study,* Cinefax, 1968; (with Barbour and Parish) *Errol Flynn: An Illustrated Career Study,* Cinefax, 1968; (with Parish) *The Cinema of Edward G. Robinson,* A. S. Barnes, 1972; *Katharine Hepburn: An Illustrated Study,* Pyramid Publications, 1973; *The Films of Anthony Quinn,* Citadel, 1975; (editor) *Moe Howard and the Three Stooges,* Citadel, 1977; *Samuel Goldwyn Presents,* A. S. Barnes, 1977; *The Films of Sidney Poitier,* Citadel, 1978; (with Dennis Belafonte) *The Films of Tyrone Power,* Citadel, 1978; *Robert Mitchum on the Screen,* A. S. Barnes, 1978. Author of "Films on Television," a monthly column in *Films in Review.* Contributor to journals, including *Screen Facts* and *Record World.*

*   *   *

MARINO, Dorothy Bronson 1912-

PERSONAL: Born November 12, 1912, in Oakland, Ore.; daughter of a teacher and bookstore owner; married John Marino; children: Nina. *Education:* Attended University of Kansas and Art Students League, New York City. *Residence:* Brooklyn, N.Y.

CAREER: Author and illustrator of books for children. *Awards, honors:* Helen Dean Fish Award for *Little Angela and Her Puppy.*

WRITINGS—All self-illustrated: *Little Angela and Her Puppy,* Lippincott, 1954; *The Song of the Pine Tree Forest,* Lippincott, 1955; *That's My Favorite,* Lippincott, 1956; *Edward and the Boxes,* Lippincott, 1957; *Good-Bye Thunderstorm,* Lippincott, 1958; *Where Are the Mothers?,* Lippincott, 1959; *Fuzzy and Alfred,* F. Watts, 1961; *Good Night Georgie,* Dial, 1961; *Now That You Are Six,* Association Press, 1963; *Moving Day,* Dial, 1963.

"Buzzy Bear" series, published by F. Watts; all self-illustrated: *Buzzy Bear Goes South,* 1961; *. . . and the Rainbow,* 1962; *. . . in the Garden,* 1963; *. . . Goes Camping,* 1964; *Buzzy Bear's Busy Day,* 1965; *. . . Winter Party,* 1967; *. . . First Day at School,* 1970.

Illustrator: Nancy W. Smith, *Ghostly Trio,* Coward, 1954; Marie H. Bloch, *Tony of the Ghost Towns,* Coward, 1956; Helen D. Olds, *Miss Hattie and the Monkey,* Follett, 1958; Myra B. Brown, *Company's Coming,* F. Watts, 1959 (published in England as *We're Having a Party Tonight,* Heinemann, 1961); Brown, *First Night Away From Home,* F. Watts, 1960; Brown, *Benjy's Blanket,* F. Watts, 1962.

BIOGRAPHICAL/CRITICAL SOURCES: New York Times, April 11, 1954; *Saturday Review,* September 17, 1955; *Bookmark,* November, 1955.*

*   *   *

MARK, Julius 1898-1977

1898—September 7, 1977; American rabbi, professor, and author of books on the Jewish faith. Mark was a longtime national leader of Reform Judaism and senior rabbi at Temple Emanu-El, the world's largest Jewish congregation. He was twice president of the Synagogue Council of America, and for fourteen years was a professor of homiletics and practical theology at the New York School of the Hebrew

Union College-Jewish Institute of Religion. Mark died in New York City. Obituaries: *New York Times,* September 8, 1977.

* * *

MARK, Max   1910-

PERSONAL: Born February 16, 1910, in Vienna, Austria; came to the United States in 1947, naturalized citizen, 1953; son of Hersh (a businessman) and Esther (Sommerstein) Mark; married Hansi Rosenbaum (a physician), December 30, 1940. *Education:* University of Vienna, J.U.D., 1933. *Religion:* Jewish. *Home:* 24270 Manistee, Oak Park, Mich. 48237. *Office:* Department of Political Science, Wayne State University, Detroit, Mich. 48202.

CAREER: Western Reserve University (now Case Western Reserve University), Cleveland, Ohio, instructor in political science, 1949-52; Wayne State University, Detroit, Mich., assistant professor, 1952-58, associate professor, 1958-63, professor of political science, 1963—. Visiting professor at Hebrew University of Jerusalem, 1971-72. *Member:* International Political Science Association, International Studies Association, American Political Science Association, American Society for Political and Legal Philosophy, Midwest Political Science Association.

WRITINGS: Beyond Sovereignty, Public Affairs Press, 1965; *Modern Ideologies,* St. Martin's, 1973.

WORK IN PROGRESS: Comparative Revolutions.

SIDELIGHTS: Mark told *CA:* "My wife and I lived in Tientsin, China as refugees from Hitler between 1941 and 1947. I consider this stay an invaluable experience because it exposed me to an impressive non-Western civilization and cured me of whatever narrow Western-based perspective I may have had before. At the same time I was able to witness the decay of a social order, in itself a significant experience. When my wife and I paid a visit in 1974 to the People's Republic of China, we were impressed by the transformation China had undergone.

Commenting on his books, Mark said, "*Beyond Sovereignty* traces the rise and then obsolescence of the nation state. Arguments about the obsolescence of the nation state include its inability under conditions of modern arms technology to be a 'unit of protection' for its inhabitants, and the emergence of international economic interdependence. *Modern Ideologies* centers on the idea of equality. It analyzes the changes in the meaning of equality, and shows the role of equality in the relationship among nations, specifically the quest for economic equality pursued by Third World countries."

* * *

MARKEL, Lester   1894-1977

January 9, 1894—October 23, 1977; American newspaper editor, journalist, and author. Markel was the editor of the Sunday sections of the *New York Times* for more than forty years. It was under his guidance that this section of the newspaper became a model for Sunday papers all across the country. In addition to expanding the Sunday section to include "Arts and Leisure," and "Business and Finance," Markel added the section that he considered most important, "The Week in Review." Markel headed a project to organize national and international news which later grew into the International Press Institute. He was also producer and host of the program "News in Perspective" for several years. He died in New York, N.Y. Obituaries: *New York Times,* October 24, 1977; *Washington Post,* October 25, 1977; *Time,* November 7, 1977; *Newsweek,* November 7, 1977. (See index for *CA* sketch)

* * *

MARKS, Henry S(eymour)   1933-

PERSONAL: Born May 26, 1933, in Greensboro, N.C.; son of Benjamin E. (a real estate broker) and Florence (a milliner; maiden name, Hirsh) Marks; married Marsha Kass (a professor of history), June 8, 1965; children: Barbara Carol. *Education:* University of Miami, B.B.A., 1955, M.A., 1956; also attended University of Alabama, 1960-61, 1962-64. *Home:* 405 Homewood Dr. S.W., Huntsville, Ala. 35801. *Office:* 301 Terry-Hutchens Building, Huntsville, Ala. 35801.

CAREER: Jacksonville State University, Jacksonville, Ala., assistant professor of history, 1958-60; Florence State University, Florence, Ala., instructor in history, 1961-62; University of Alabama, Huntsville, instructor in history, 1964-68; Alabama Agricultural & Mechanical University, Normal, assistant professor of history, 1968-69; Northeast Alabama State Junior College, Rainsville, instructor in history and economics, 1969—. Self-employed educational consultant in Huntsville, 1969—. Member of Alabama governor's staff, 1974—.

MEMBER: American Society for Public Administration (member of local council; vice-president, 1973-74; president-elect, 1974-76; president, 1976-77), American Historical Association, Organization of American Historians, Popular Culture Association (president of Southern region, 1971-73; member of advisory council, 1971-76), Community College Social Science Association, Southern Historical Association, Alabama Academy of Science, Alabama Historical Association, Florida Historical Association, Historical Association of South Florida, Huntsville Historical Society, Huntsville Literary Association (member of board of directors, 1976—), Hakluyt Society, Phi Delta Kappa, Phi Alpha Theta (president of Delta Alpha chapter, 1955), Rotary International.

WRITINGS: The Failure of the United States to Maintain the Independence of Korea and the Effect of the Failure Upon Americans in Korea, privately printed, 1962, 2nd edition, 1970; *Who Was Who in Alabama,* Strode, 1972; (contributor) Dwight L. Smith and Lloyd W. Garrison, editors, *The American Political Process: Selected Abstracts of Periodical Literature, 1954-1971,* Clio Press, 1972; *Who Was Who in Florida,* Strode, 1973; (with T. L. Turpin) *Faces and Things of First Monday* (pamphlet), privately printed, 1973; (with Gene Britt Rigs) *Rivers of Florida,* Southern Press, 1974; (contributor) Douglas State, editor, *A Source Book for Racial and Sexual Attitudes and Attitudinal Change Through Conscious-Raising and Awareness,* University of Missouri, 1974; (contributor) Smith, editor, *Afro-American History: A Bibliography,* Clio Press, 1974; *Sketches of the Tennessee Valley in Antebellum Days: People, Places, Things,* Southern Press, 1976.

Contributor to *Collier's Encyclopedia Yearbook* and *World Book Encyclopedia of the Nations.* Contributor of more than fifty articles and reviews to history, sociology, and education journals, and newspapers. Editor of *Historic Huntsville Quarterly,* 1975—, and *Huntsville Historical Review,* 1976—.

WORK IN PROGRESS: Who Was Who in Georgia, publication by Strode expected in 1980; *Women in the Making of Alabama,* for Southern Press.

SIDELIGHTS: Marks told *CA:* "I have always endeavored to write in the popular vein, probably as a result of my training under Charlton Tebeau (emeritus) of the University of Miami. My greatest pleasure in writing is to be of service and I have attempted to aid librarians in Alabama and Florida by trying to fill a void in reference works in these states. For example, there has been no compendium of deceased in Alabama since 1947 and no single-volume work which includes sports and other popular personalities other than mine.

"I am interested in local history for a number of reasons, not the least of which is the low priority placed on such history by professional historians. Local history should be an obligation and a responsibility for the trained historian. An understanding of local history is a must for the development of regional, even national concepts by the trained historian. In addition, collaboration between the amateur and the professional historian should help to greatly improve the production of both.

"My 'professional' historical interest lies in the area of Spanish exploration and early settlement of the upper Gulf of Mexico."

*   *   *

MARSDEN, George (Mish) 1939-

PERSONAL: Born February 25, 1939, in Harrisburg, Pa.; son of Robert Samuel (a clergyman) and Bertha (a teacher; maiden name, Mish) Marsden; married Lucie Commeret, June 30, 1969; children: Gregory, Brynn. *Education:* Haverford College, B.A., 1959; Yale University, M.A., 1961, Ph.D., 1965; Westminster Theological Seminary, B.D., 1963. *Politics:* Independent. *Religion:* Christian Reformed. *Home:* 844 Dallas S.E., Grand Rapids, Mich. 49507. *Office:* Department of History, Calvin College, Grand Rapids, Mich. 49506.

CAREER: Calvin College, Grand Rapids, Mich., instructor, 1965-66, assistant professor, 1966-70, associate professor, 1970-73, professor of history, 1973—. Visiting professor at Trinity Evangelical Divinity School, 1976-77. *Member:* American Historical Association, American Society of Church History, Presbyterian Historical Society, Conference on Faith and History. *Awards, honors:* Younger humanist fellowship from National Endowment for the Humanities, 1971-72.

WRITINGS: The Evangelical Mind and the New School Presbyterian Experience, Yale University Press, 1970; *The American Revolution* (pamphlet), National Union of Christian Schools, 1973; (editor with Frank Roberts) *A Christian View of History?,* Eerdmans, 1975. Contributor to church magazines. Associate editor of social sciences for *Christian Scholar's Review,* 1970-78.

WORK IN PROGRESS: Fundamentalism and American Culture.

SIDELIGHTS: Marsden comments: "My main interests are in developing a Christian perspective on the discipline of history and in uncovering the roots of current American Protestant Evangelicalism."

*   *   *

MARSH, Leonard (George) 1930-

PERSONAL: Born October 23, 1930, in Kent, England; son of Ernest Arthur and Ann (Bean) Marsh; married Ann Margaret Gilbert (a lecturer), August 21, 1953. *Education:* Attended University of London, and University of Leicester.

Religion: Church of England. *Home:* Principal's House, Bishop Grosseteste College, Lincoln LN1 3DY, England.

CAREER: Teacher of education and mathematics at a private school in Cheltenham, England, 1959-61; University of London, Goldsmiths College, London, England, lecturer, 1961-63, senior lecturer, 1963-65, principal lecturer in education and head of department, 1965-74; Bishop Grosseteste College, Lincoln, England, principal, 1974—. Visiting lecturer at Bank Street College and Virginia Commonwealth University. Member of Independent Broadcasting Authority's general advisory council; specialist for British Council in India; consultant to Organization for Economic Co-operation and Development in Portugal.

WRITINGS: Let's Explore Mathematics, Books I-IV, A. & C. Black, 1964-67; *Children Explore Mathematics,* A. & C. Black, 1967, 3rd edition, 1969; *Exploring Shapes and Numbers,* A. & C. Black, 1968, 2nd edition, 1970; *Exploring the Metric System,* A. & C. Black, 1969, 2nd edition, 1969; *Exploring the Metric World,* A. & C. Black, 1970; *Approach to Mathematics,* A. & C. Black, 1970; *Alongside the Child in the Primary School,* Harper, 1970; *Let's Discover Mathematics,* Books I-V, A. & C. Black, 1971-72; *Being a Teacher,* Praeger, 1973. Script writer for educational programs.

WORK IN PROGRESS: Books on the development of ideas about children's learning and development and on the development of British primary education since the publication of the Plowden Report; research on rural and community development.

SIDELIGHTS: Marsh writes: "I have been involved in the development of English primary education for many years both as a trainer of teachers and with local authorities, experienced teachers, and others. This work has been closely related to the professional competence of the teacher in classroom circumstances. Increasingly this takes one into wider issues of community involvement in the educational process and the present focus for writing is the nature of community support and contribution to the development of the young person."

AVOCATIONAL INTERESTS: The theater, film, television, photography, railway travel and railways.

*   *   *

MARSHALL, J(ohn) D(uncan) 1919-

PERSONAL: Born April 2, 1919, in Ilkeston, Derbyshire, England; son of George (a civil servant) and Nellie (a nurse; maiden name, Osborn) Marshall; married Audrey F. Pullinger, 1948 (divorced, 1975); married Frances Sabina Harland, April 2, 1976; children: (first marriage) Celia Jane, Alison Rosalind, Edward. *Education:* University of Nottingham, B.Sc., 1950; University of London, Ph.D., 1956. *Home:* 4 Dalton Rd., Freehold, Lancaster, England.

CAREER: Teacher, Mansfield School of Art, 1950-54; assistant lecturer, Hucknall F.E. Centre, 1954-58; head of department of general subjects, Bolton College of Education, 1958-66; University of Lancaster, Bailrigg, Lancaster, England, senior lecturer, 1966-69, reader in regional history, 1969—, founder of Centre for North-West Regional Studies, 1971. Co-founder of Bolton's Community Relations Council, 1965. *Military service:* British Army, Royal Signals, 1944-45; served in European theater. *Member:* Royal Historical Society (fellow), Oral History Society (vice-chairman, 1977), Cumberland and Westmorland Antiquarian Society (past member of council).

WRITINGS: Furness and the Industrial Revolution, Barrow Corp., 1958; (editor) *The Autobiography of William Stout,* Manchester University Press, 1966; *The Industrial Archaeology of the Lake Counties,* David & Charles, 1969, revised edition, Michael Moon, 1977; *The Lake District at Work,* David & Charles, 1971; *Old Lakeland,* David & Charles, 1972; (editor) *History of the Lancashire County Council,* Martin Robertson, 1977. Contributor to history journals.

WORK IN PROGRESS: A history of modern Cumbria, 1830-1974; a study of the social structure of peasant society in seventeenth-century England.

SIDELIGHTS: J. D. Marshall describes himself as "one of the founders of the study of oral history in England," and "a pioneer in regional historical study." He was an "early worker in industrial archaeology (in the mid-1950's, before the term became accepted), and in regional population studies." He held the first Readership in *regional* history to be conferred in British universities.

*   *   *

MARSHALL, S(amuel) L(yman) A(twood)   1900-1977

July 18, 1900—December 17, 1977; U.S. Army brigadier general, journalist, columnist, and military historian best known for *Pork Chop Hill, The River and the Gauntlet,* and *Sinai Victory.* Marshall began as a sports and city editor for the *Detroit News* in 1927 and continued working for the paper as a foreign correspondent and military analyst until 1962. He was chief historian for the European Theater of Operations in 1945, and served as an operations analyst during the Korean War. Marshall developed a technique of assembling battlefield history by interviewing survivors soon after an encounter, and he was noted for his plain-spoken sympathy for the men of the front lines. Marshall died in El Paso, Tex. Obituaries: *New York Times,* December 18, 1977; *Washington Post,* December 18, 1977; *Time,* December 26, 1977; *Newsweek,* January 2, 1978.

*   *   *

MARTIN, Barclay (Cluck)   1923-

PERSONAL: Born October 24, 1923, in Houston, Tex.; son of Louis Vance and Thelma (Cluck) Martin; married Elizabeth MacFarlane, September 2, 1950 (separated, 1977); children: Susan, Elizabeth, Laurie. *Education:* Stanford University, B.S., 1947, Ph.D., 1953. *Home:* 1439 Poinsett Dr., Chapel Hill, N.C. 27514. *Office:* Department of Psychology, University of North Carolina, Chapel Hill, N.C. 27514.

CAREER: University of Wisconsin, Madison, instructor, 1953-54, assistant professor, 1954-59, associate professor, 1959-63, professor of psychology, 1963-71; University of North Carolina, Chapel Hill, professor of psychology, 1971—. *Member:* American Psychological Association. *Awards, honors:* National Institutes of Health fellowship, 1969.

WRITINGS: Anxiety and Neurotic Disorders, Wiley, 1971; *Abnormal Psychology,* Scott, Foresman, 1973, hardcover edition, Holt, 1977. Contributor to psychology journals.

WORK IN PROGRESS: An evaluation of the effectiveness of brief family therapy.

*   *   *

MARTIN, Herbert Woodward   1933-

PERSONAL: Born October 4, 1933, in Birmingham, Ala.; son of David Nathaniel and Willie Mae (Woodward) Martin.

Education: University of Toledo, B.A., 1964; State University of New York at Buffalo, M.A., 1967; Middlebury College, M. Litt., 1972. *Religion:* Lutheran. *Home:* 715 Turner St., Toledo, Ohio 43607. *Office:* Department of English, University of Dayton, Dayton, Ohio 45469.

CAREER: State University of New York at Buffalo, instructor, summer, 1966; Aquinas College, Grand Rapids, Mich., 1967-70, began as instructor, became assistant professor and poet-in-residence; University of Dayton, Dayton, Ohio, 1970—, began as assistant professor, became associate professor of English and poet-in-residence. Visiting distinguished professor of poetry at Central Michigan University, fall, 1973. Consultant for contemporary black writers collection at University of Toledo, 1974—.

WRITINGS: "Dialogue" (one-act play), produced in New York City at Hardware Poets Playhouse, 1963; *New York: The Nine Million and Other Poems,* Abracadabra Press, 1969; *The Shit-Storm Poems,* Pilot Press, 1972; *The Persistence of the Flesh,* Lotus Press, 1976. Editor, *The Great Lakes Review,* 1978—.

Work represented in anthologies, including *The Poetry of Black America, Introduction to Black Literature, Urban Reader, 10 Michigan Poets,* and *Face the Whirlwind.* Contributor of poetry to journals, including *Obsidian, Poetry Australia,* and *Nimrod.*

WORK IN PROGRESS: Revision of *The Shit-Storm Poems; War to Escape the Body; Arias and Silences: Poems Edited for Ezra Pound; The Log of the Vigilante,* a long poem.

SIDELIGHTS: When asked to comment on his work and other interests, Martin told *CA:* "I have said so many foolish things in the past, that I think I will sit this one out."

Martin has studied with John Ciardi, Karl Shapiro, W. D. Snodgrass, John Frederick Nims, Miller Williams, Judson Jerome, Donald Hall, John Logan, Robert Creely, and Edward Albee.

In addition to having given poetry readings at several universities, Martin has performed as narrator for orchestral presentations including Aaron Copland's "A Lincoln Portrait," Sir William Walton's "Facade," Vincent Persichetti's "Second Lincoln Inaugural," and Robert Borneman's "Reformation 69/70."

*   *   *

MARTIN, James Alfred, Jr.   1917-

PERSONAL: Born March 18, 1917, in Lumberton, N.C.; son of James Alfred (a physician) and Mary (Jones) Martin; married Ann Bradsher, June 1, 1936. *Education:* Wake Forest College (now University), B.A. (magna cum laude), 1937; Duke University, M.A., 1938; Columbia University, Ph.D., 1944; also attended Union Theological Seminary, New York, N.Y., 1940-43. *Politics:* Democrat. *Religion:* Episcopalian. *Home:* 99 Claremont Ave., New York, N.Y. 10027. *Office:* Department of Religion, Columbia University, 617 Kent Hall, New York, N.Y. 10027.

CAREER: Ordained Baptist minister, 1944; assistant pastor of Baptist church in Roxboro, N.C., 1937-38; Wake Forest College (now University), Winston-Salem, N.C., instructor in philosophy and psychology, 1938-40; Amherst College, Amherst, Mass., assistant professor, 1946-47, associate professor, 1947-50, professor of religion, 1950-54, Marquand & Stone Professor, 1954-57, Crosby Professor of Religion, 1957-60; Union Theological Seminary, New York, N.Y., Danforth Professor of Religion in Higher Education, 1960-

67; Columbia University, New York, N.Y., professor of religion, 1967—, chairman of department, 1968-77. Deacon of the Episcopal Church, 1953—. Adjunct professor at Union Theological Seminary, 1967—; visiting professor at Cornell University, summer, 1948, Mount Holyoke College, 1949-50, 1952-53, 1959-60, State University of Iowa, summer, 1959, University of North Carolina, 1963, and General Theological Seminary, 1964. Associate member of East-West Philosophers' Conference at University of Hawaii, 1949. *Military service:* U.S. Naval Reserve, chaplain, active duty, 1944-46; served in Pacific theater; became lieutenant senior grade.

MEMBER: American Theological Society, American Academy of Religion, Society for Values in Higher Education (president, 1963-69), Society for Theological Discussion, Phi Beta Kappa, Omicron Delta Kappa, Pi Kappa Alpha. *Awards, honors:* Kent fellowship from Society for Religion in Higher Education; M.A. from Amherst College, 1950; research fellowship from Rockefeller foundation, 1961; Litt.D. from Wake Forest University, 1964.

WRITINGS: Empirical Philosophies of Religion, King's Crown Press, 1944, reprinted, Arno, 1970; (with J. A. Hutchison) *Ways of Faith,* Ronald, 1954, revised edition, Wiley, 1977; *Faith: Fact and Fiction,* Oxford University Press, 1960; *The New Dialogue Between Philosophy and Theology,* Seabury, 1966.

Contributor: John B. Coburn and W. Norman Pittenger, editors, *Viewpoints: Some Aspects of Anglican Thinking,* Seabury, 1959; John A. Clark, editor, *The Student Seeks an Answer,* Colby College Press, 1960; *Theology and Church in Times of Change,* Westminster, 1970; William E. Ray, editor, *Approaches to the Understanding of God,* Wake Forest University Press, 1977.

Contributor to *Encyclopedia Americana Annual.* Contributor to religious journals.

WORK IN PROGRESS: Research on the significance and role of the esthetic in theory of religion.

SIDELIGHTS: Martin told *CA:* "My last book explored the relation of analytical philosophy to Christian theology. My work in progress explores similarities and differences between aesthetic and religious apprehensions and articulations, through examination of Kant's *Critique of Judgment,* the notion of the sublime in eighteenth and nineteenth century literature, views of Jonathan Edwards, F. E. Schleiermacher, Coleridge, Ruskin, John Denver, George Santayana, Andre Malraux, and others."

AVOCATIONAL INTERESTS: Travel (Europe, Asia, South America, the Middle East).

*   *   *

MARTOS, Borys   1879-1977

1879—September 19, 1977; Ukrainian political leader and author of books on economics and political life who emigrated to the United States in the late 1940's. Martos headed the independent Ukrainian government in Kiev from 1919 until the 1920 Bolshevik takeover. He held the positions of minister of agriculture and the treasury before becoming the prime minister of the Ukrainian National Republic. Martos died in Irvington, N.J. Obituaries: *New York Times,* September 23, 1977.

*   *   *

MARVIN, Harold Myers   1893-1977

August 11, 1893—August 6, 1977; American physician,

heart specialist, and educator. Marvin was a former president of the American Heart Association and professor emeritus from Yale University. He died in Greenwich, Conn. Obituaries: *New York Times,* August 12, 1977. (See index for *CA* sketch)

*   *   *

MARX, Groucho
See MARX, Julius Henry

*   *   *

MARX, Julius Henry   1890-1977
(Groucho Marx)

October 2, 1890—August 19, 1977; American comedian and author whose career spanned vaudeville, motion pictures, radio and television. Marx began performing at age ten and later teamed with his brothers Harpo, Chico, Gummo, and Zeppo to perform in vaudeville and on Broadway. The Marx brothers appeared in several films, including "Animal Crackers," 1930, "Horse Feathers," 1932, "Duck Soup," 1933, "A Night at the Opera," 1935, and "A Day at the Races," 1937. George Bernard Shaw once claimed "Groucho Marx is the world's greatest living actor." In 1947 Groucho began hosting the radio show "You Bet Your Life," which was turned into a television series which ran from 1951 until 1962. In 1969 a *New York Times* poll found that college freshmen most admired Jesus Christ, Albert Schweitzer, and Groucho Marx, in that order. At the award ceremonies Marx quipped: "I'm sorry Jesus Christ couldn't be here. He had to be in Philadelphia." Marx was the author of three books, *The Groucho Letters, Groucho and Me,* and *Memoirs of a Mangy Lover.* He died in Los Angeles, Calif. Obituaries: *New York Times,* August 20, 1977; *Washington Post,* August 21, 1977; *Newsweek,* August 29, 1977; *Time,* August 29, 1977.

*   *   *

MASON, Edward S(agendorph)   1899-

PERSONAL: Born February 22, 1899, in Clinton, Iowa; son of Edward Luther and Kate (Sagendorph) Mason; married Marguerite Sisson La Monte, April 4, 1930; children: Jane Carroll (Mrs. Roger Manasse), Edward H. L., Robert La Monte (stepson). *Education:* University of Kansas, A.B., 1919; Harvard University, A.M., 1920, Ph.D., 1925; Oxford University, B.Litt., 1923. *Religion:* Unitarian Universalist. *Home:* 9 Channing St., Cambridge, Mass. 02138. *Office:* Department of Economics, Harvard University, Cambridge, Mass. 02138.

CAREER: Harvard University, Cambridge, Mass., instructor, 1923-27, assistant professor, 1927-32, associate professor, 1932-37, professor, 1937-58, George F. Baker Professor of Economics, 1958-61, Thomas W. Lamont Professor of Economics, 1961-70, Lamont Professor emeritus, 1970—, dean of Graduate School of Public Administration, 1947-58. Economic consultant to Department of Labor, 1938-39, and Department of State, 1946-47; member of staff of Defense Commission, 1940-41, and Office of Strategic Services, 1941-45; deputy to assistant secretary of state in charge of economic affairs, 1946; chief economic adviser at Moscow Conference, 1947; chairman of advisory committee on economic development, Agency for International Development; consultant to Development Advisory service, Center for International Affairs, 1970—. Director, Asian Development Corp., 1974—.

MEMBER: American Economic Association (president, 1962), American Philosophical Society, Royal Economic Society (London), American Academy of Arts and Sciences, Council on Foreign Relations, Phi Beta Kappa, Delta Sigma Rho. *Awards, honors:* D.Litt., Williams College, 1948; LL.D., Harvard University, 1956, Yale University, 1964, Concord College, 1971; Medal of Freedom, 1946; Star of Pakistan, 1967; honorary fellow, Lincoln College, Oxford.

WRITINGS: Controlling World Trade: Cartels and Commodity Agreements, McGraw, 1946, reprinted, Arno, 1972; *Economic Concentration and the Monopoly Problem,* Harvard University Press, 1957; *Economic Planning in Underdeveloped Areas,* Fordham University Press, 1958; (editor) *The Corporation in Modern Society,* Harvard University Press, 1959; *Foreign Aid and Foreign Policy,* Harper, 1964; *On the Appropriate Size of a Development Program,* Center for International Affairs, Harvard University, 1964; *Economic Development in India and Pakistan,* Center for International Affairs, Harvard University, 1966; *The Paris Commune,* Fertig, 1968; (with Robert E. Asher) *The World Bank Since Bretton Woods,* Brookings, 1973. Contributor to *American Economic Review* and other journals.

* * *

MASON, George Frederick 1904-

PERSONAL: Born October 18, 1904, in Princeton, Mass.; married Dorothy M. Brooks (marriage dissolved); married second wife, Caroline; children: (first marriage) Cynthia Fay, George. *Education:* Attended Worcester Art Museum School and Clark University. *Residence:* Princeton, Mass.

CAREER: Worked as a political cartoonist for a newspaper; American Museum of Natural History, New York, N.Y., employed as a staff member, later became assistant curator of its Department of Education; author and illustrator.

WRITINGS—All self-illustrated: *The Bear Family,* Morrow, 1960; *The Deer Family,* Morrow, 1962; *Ranch in the Rockies,* Morrow, 1964; *The Wildlife of North America,* Hastings House, 1966; *The Moose Group,* Hastings House, 1968.

"Animal" series; all self-illustrated; all published by Morrow: *Animal Tracks,* 1943; *... Homes,* 1947; *... Sounds,* 1948; *... Weapons,* 1949; *... Tools,* 1951; *... Clothing,* 1955; *... Tails,* 1958; *... Habits,* 1959; *... Baggage,* 1961; *... Teeth,* 1965; *... Appetites,* 1966; *... Vision,* 1968; *... Feet,* 1970.

Illustrator: Dorothy Stall, *Chukchi Hunter,* Morrow, 1946; Ivan E. Green and Alice Bromwell, *Woody, the Little Wood Duck,* Abelard, 1953; Joseph Wharton Lippincott, *Bun, a Wild Rabbit,* revised edition, Lippincott, 1953; J. W. Lippincott, *Little Red, the Fox,* revised edition, Lippincott, 1953; J. W. Lippincott, *Long Horn, Leader of the Deer,* revised edition, Lippincott, 1953; J. W. Lippincott, *Gray Squirrel,* revised edition, Lippincott, 1954; J. W. Lippincott, *Striped Coat, the Skunk,* revised edition, Lippincott, 1954; Marie H. Bloch, *Dinosaurs,* Coward, 1955; J. W. Lippincott, *Persimmon Jim, the Possum,* revised edition, Lippincott, 1955; Miriam Schlein, *Oomi, the New Hunter,* Abelard, 1955; Genevieve Gullahorn, *Zigger, the Pet Chameleon,* Abelard, 1956; Elizabeth Greenleaf, *Pricky, a Pet Porcupine,* Oddo, 1965; Dorothy Edwards Shuttlesworth, *The Wildlife of South America,* Hastings House, 1966, revised edition, 1974; D. E. Shuttlesworth, *The Wildlife of Australia and New Zealand,* Hastings House, 1967.

SIDELIGHTS: Mason's career was influenced by the farm environment he grew up in as a child and the contrasting city life he experienced as an adult. The author-illustrator's first book, *Animal Tracks,* identified the prints of forty-four common North American animals.

Animal Homes was Mason's second book about the unique characteristics of wildlife creatures. In *Animal Weapons* he discussed the various devices used by animals to protect themselves in combat. A reviewer for the *New York Times* noted: "It does not matter at all whether the nature-lover is 10 years old or 60. The youngest will have no difficulty with this author's clear, terse prose and practical line drawings, while the mature reader will be humbled to realize how little he has understood the mechanism of animal weapons."

The success of Mason's nature books was partly due to his illustrations. The author-illustrator's drawings were generally done in pen-and-ink. His book, *Animal Clothing,* studied the different structures and functions of the outer coverings of animals. A critic for *Saturday Review* commented: "Almost as valuable as the text are the line drawings which range from a comparison of a chrysalis with an Egyptian mummy to the reason why a frog's color turns from green to yellow."

In *Animal Habits* the museum curator studied the psychological reasoning behind animal behavior. A reviewer for the *Chicago Sunday Tribune* commented: "George Mason refuses to yield to misguided sentimentalism. His book, is, therefore scientifically accurate, as befits his record of many years with the American Museum of Natural History."

BIOGRAPHICAL/CRITICAL SOURCES: New York Times, October 10, 1943, October 23, 1949; *Saturday Review of Literature,* November 15, 1947, November 12, 1955; *Christian Science Monitor,* November 10, 1955; *Chicago Sunday Tribune,* November 1, 1959; *Scientific American,* December, 1971.*

* * *

MASTERSON, Patrick 1936-

PERSONAL: Born October 19, 1936, in Dublin, Ireland; son of Laurence (a physician) and Violet (Hayes) Masterson; married Frances Lenehan (a teacher), April 6, 1964; children: Rosemary, Laurence, Lucy, Naomi. *Education:* National University of Ireland, B.A., 1958, M.A., 1960; University of Louvain, Ph.D., 1962. *Religion:* Roman Catholic. *Home:* 16 Nutley Lane, Dublin 4, Ireland. *Office:* Department of Metaphysics, University College, National University of Ireland, Belfield, Dublin 4, Ireland.

CAREER: National University of Ireland, University College, Dublin, lecturer, 1963-72, professor of metaphysics, 1972—. Member of Dublin Higher Education Authority, 1972; member of high council of European University Institute. *Member:* Irish Philosophical Society (chairman, 1972), Irish Philosophical Club. *Awards, honors:* Travel scholarship from National University of Ireland, 1970-72, for University of Louvain.

WRITINGS: Atheism and Alienation: A Study of the Philosophical Sources of Contemporary Atheism, University of Notre Dame Press, 1971, revised edition, Penguin, 1973. Contributor to learned journals.

WORK IN PROGRESS: A book on philosophy of religion, examining the possibility of a contemporary philosophy of God in the light of the impact of philosophical atheism on traditional philosophical theism.

SIDELIGHTS: Masterson writes: "As both a believer and

a philosopher, an important motivation in my research and writing is to elucidate my conviction concerning the congruity of these vocations. I have a particular interest in aspects of higher education." *Avocational interests:* European affairs, modern Irish art, travel (Europe and the United States).

*   *   *

MATEJKA, Ladislav 1919-

PERSONAL: Born May 30, 1919, in Suche Vrbne, Czechoslovakia; came to the United States in 1954, naturalized citizen, 1959; son of Joseph and Anna (Kocka) Matejka; married Gudrun Ebenfelt (a librarian), 1957; children: Jan, Anne Elisabeth. *Education:* Charles University, Ph.D., 1948; Harvard University, Ph.D., 1961. *Religion:* Episcopal. *Home:* 2003 Day St., Ann Arbor, Mich. 48104. *Office:* Slavic Department, University of Michigan, Ann Arbor, Mich. 48109.

CAREER: University of Lund, Lund, Sweden, lecturer in Slavic languages and literatures, 1948-54; Harvard University, Cambridge, Mass., research assistant, 1955-59; University of Michigan, Ann Arbor, professor of Slavic languages and literatures, 1959—. *Member:* Modern Language Association of America, American Linguistic Society. *Awards, honors:* Fulbright fellowship for Yugloslavia, 1965-66; Ford Foundation fellowship, 1972-73.

WRITINGS: (with Thomas F. Magner) *Word Accent in Standard Serbocroation,* Pennsylvania State University, 1971; (editor) *Readings in Russian Poetics: Formalist and Structuralist Views,* M.I.T. Press, 1971; (editor) *American Contributions to the Seventh International Congress of Slavists,* Mouton, 1973; *Crossroads of Sound and Meaning,* Peter de Ridder Press, 1975; *Semiotics of Art: Prague School Contributions,* M.I.T. Press, 1976; *Sound, Sign, and Meaning: Quinquagenary of the Prague Linguistic Circle,* Michigan Slavic Publications, 1976. General editor of "Michigan Slavic Publications." Contributor to professional journals.

WORK IN PROGRESS: Soviet Semiotics.

*   *   *

MATHER, Richard B(urroughs) 1913-

PERSONAL: Born November 11, 1913, in Paoting, China; son of William Arnot (a missionary) and Grace (a missionary; maiden name, Burroughs) Mather; married Virginia Temple, June 3, 1939; children: Elizabeth. *Education:* Princeton University, B.A., 1935, B.Th., 1939; University of California, Berkeley, Ph.D., 1949. *Home:* 2091 Dudley Ave., St. Paul, Minn. 55108. *Office:* Department of East Asian Languages, University of Minnesota, Minneapolis, Minn. 55455.

CAREER: Ordained Presbyterian minister, 1939; pastor of Presbyterian church in Belle Haven, Va., 1939-41; University of Minnesota, Minneapolis, assistant professor, 1949-57, associate professor, 1957-64, professor of Chinese, 1964—. *Member:* American Oriental Society, Association for Asian Studies, Chinese Language Teachers Association.

WRITINGS: The Biography of Lu Kuang, University of California Press, 1959; (translator) *Shih-shuo Hsin-yu: A New Account of Tales of the World,* University of Minnesota Press, 1976. Contributor to Oriental studies and religion journals.

WORK IN PROGRESS: The Poetry and Career of Shen Yueh, 441-512, a monograph.

SIDELIGHTS: Mather writes: "I am primarily concerned with the culture of China's early middle ages (about A.D. 200-600)—the history, literature, philosophy, religion, and art. *Shih-shuo Hsin-yu* was an annotated translation of a fifth-century collection of anecdotes describing this world. The book on Shen Yueh will be focused on a single individual who played a key role in it, as poet, literary theorist, historian, and courtier."

*   *   *

MATHESON, Sylvia A.
See SCHOFIELD, Sylvia Anne

*   *   *

MATHIEU, Bertrand 1936-

PERSONAL: Born January 16, 1936, in Lewiston, Me.; son of Armand B. (a mill worker) and Loretta (Caron) Mathieu; married Eleni Fourtouni (a translator), May 23, 1959; children: Russell, Rachel. *Education:* Nasson College, B.A. (cum laude), 1962; University of Arizona, M.A. (magna cum laude), 1964, Ph.D. (magna cum laude), 1975. *Politics:* Jeffersonian Democrat. *Religion:* "Orphic/Gnostic." *Home:* 405 Main St., West Haven, Conn. 06516. *Office:* Department of English, University of New Haven, 300 Orange Ave., West Haven, Conn. 06516.

CAREER: U.S. Army, Heidelberg, Germany, lecturer in education and troop information, 1959-61, instructor in English and mathematics, 1960-61; University of New Haven, West Haven, Conn., instructor, 1965-67, assistant professor, 1967-73, associate professor, 1973-76, professor of English, 1976—, acting chairperson, 1975. Has given readings from his works and lectures. *Military service:* U.S. Army, 1956-58. *Member:* Modern Language Association of America, Alpha Sigma Lambda. *Awards, honors:* Hart Crane Prize for Poetry from *American Weave,* 1961-62, for "Odysseus Unrepentant."

WRITINGS: Landscape with Voices (poems), Delta-Tucson, 1965; *Orpheus in Brooklyn: Orphism, Rimbaud, and Henry Miller,* Mouton & Co., 1976; (translator) Arthur Rimbaud, *A Season in Hell* (preface by Anais Nin), Pomegranate Press, 1977.

Work represented in *City Lights Anthology,* edited by Lawrence Ferlinghetti, City Lights, 1974. Contributor of more than thirty articles, poems, translations, and reviews to literary journals and newspapers, including *Burning Deck, American Poetry Review,* and *Partisan Review.*

WORK IN PROGRESS: Freeing Eurydice: Anais Nin, Rimbaud, and the Gnostic Outlook; Hermes' Laughter: Humor, Hermetic Doctrine, and Lawrence Durrell; editing *New Poets of Contemporary Greece;* translating *Illuminations,* by Arthur Rimbaud (preface and illustrations by Henry Miller); translating *Christmas on the Face of This Planet,* stories by Blaise Cendrars (preface by Anais Nin); translating *The Early Poems of Arthur Rimbaud,* a bilingual edition; translating *Bumming Around,* a travel book by Cendrars, originally titled *Bourlinguer;* translating *Selected Prose of Blaise Cendrars,* for Pale Horse Press.

SIDELIGHTS: Mathieu comments: "What interests me, first and always, is poetry. I even think of the critical trilogy I'm engaged in (on the writing of Henry Miller, Anais Nin, and Lawrence Durrell) as an extended critical poem—or 'poesie critique,' in Jean Cocteau's phrase. I happen to believe that too much writing is being published at the moment. But all the writing that *counts* is poetry. If it's not poetry, it's nothing.

"The principal influences in my life (persons) have been French or Greek, and I have a passionate interest in French and Greek literature, as well as in the countries themselves. I have devoted much of my energies as a writer/translator to exploring the impact of French and Greek thought and 'myth' on American writers. I consider myself a Franco-Greek poet disguised as a New England college professor of American lit."

* * *

MATTHEWS, (Robert) Curt(is, Jr.) 1934-

PERSONAL: Born August 25, 1934, in St. Louis, Mo.; son of Robert (an artist) and Ruth (McManemin) Matthews; married Nancy Nahm, April 12, 1958 (separated); children: Robert III, Mark, Scott, Todd. *Education:* University of Notre Dame, A.B., 1956; St. Louis University, M.B.A., 1971; graduate study at Harvard University, 1974-75. *Politics:* Independent. *Religion:* Christian. *Home:* 4710 Bethesda Ave., #1117, Bethesda, Md. 20014. *Office: St. Louis Post-Dispatch,* 1701 Pennsylvania Ave. N.W., Washington, D.C. 20006.

CAREER/WRITINGS: St. Louis Post-Dispatch, St. Louis, Mo., Washington correspondent. Notable assignments include coverage of the United States Supreme Court. Lecturer. *Military service:* U.S. Army, 1958-61; became first lieutenant. *Member:* Washington Press Club, Sigma Delta Chi. *Awards, honors:* Nieman fellow, 1974.

* * *

MATTHEWS, Harry G(len) 1939-

PERSONAL: Born February 12, 1939, in Springhill, La.; son of A. J. and Opal (Wallace) Matthews; married Harriet Monroe (a political consultant), July 22, 1960; children: Elizabeth, Glen, William, Steven. *Education:* Centenary College of Louisiana, B.A., 1962; Claremont Graduate School, M.A., 1965, Ph.D., 1968. *Politics:* Democrat. *Religion:* "Unitarian Fellowship of Flagstaff." *Home:* 1710 North San Francisco, Flagstaff, Ariz. 86001. *Office:* Box 6023, Northern Arizona University, Flagstaff, Ariz. 86011.

CAREER: Northern Arizona University, Flagstaff, assistant professor, 1966-70, associate professor of political science, 1970—. Visiting fellow at University of Sussex Centre for Multi-Racial Studies (Barbados), summers, 1972-73. Member of Southwest Political Consultants. Member of Coconino Democratic Central Committee.

MEMBER: International Studies Association, Caribbean Studies Association, American Federation of Teachers, Pi Sigma Alpha, Eta Sigma Phi. *Awards, honors:* Research grants from University of the West Indies, summer, 1969, National Science Foundation, summer, 1970, University of Denver (for research in the eastern Caribbean), 1971, 1972, and Transition Foundation of Los Angeles, 1974-76.

WRITINGS: (Co-author) *Local Government in Microstates: A Probable Model* (monograph), Institute for Government Research, 1971; *Racial Dimensions of United Nations Behavior: The Commonwealth Caribbean* (monograph), Center on International Race Relations, University of Denver, 1972; (co-author) *Recall and Reform in Arizona, 1973* (monograph), Institute for Government Research, 1973; (co-author) *Responsive and Responsible Government in Arizona,* Arizona Academy, 1975; *Multinational Corporations and Black Power,* Schenkman, 1976; *International Tourism: A Social and Political Analysis,* Schenkman, 1977. Contributor to *Annals of Tourism Research* and *National Civic Review.*

WORK IN PROGRESS: A book on American corporate involvement in the eastern Caribbean and its effects on development policy.

SIDELIGHTS: Matthews has traveled extensively in the eastern Caribbean, especially Barbados and Trinidad-Tobago. He comments briefly: "I have a keen belief that American foreign policy toward and our knowledge of the Caribbean region are grossly lacking the priority they deserve."

* * *

MATTHEWS, Herbert Lionel 1900-1977

January 10, 1900—July 30, 1977; American newspaperman and writer. Matthews began his forty-five year affiliation with the *New York Times* as a correspondent with his first foreign assignment to the Paris bureau. As foreign correspondent he covered the Italian campaign in Ethiopia, the Spanish Civil War, and World War II. Matthews returned to New York in 1949 as a member of the editorial board. In 1957 Matthews, posing as a wealthy American sugar planter, gained access to Fidel Castro's jungle hideaway and conducted an interview with him while Batista's government troops were searching the region for the revolutionary leader. The three-part newspaper series based on the risky interview caused much furor in the States, but also won him the George Polk Memorial Award from the Overseas Press Club. Matthews was the author of several books based on his experiences as foreign correspondent for the *Times.* He died in Adelaide, Australia. Obituaries: *New York Times,* July 31, 1977; *Washington Post,* August 1, 1977. (See index for *CA* sketch)

* * *

MAXEY, David R(oy) 1936-

PERSONAL: Born October 22, 1936, in Boise, Idaho; son of Roy Gess (an accountant) and Betty (an artist; maiden name, Brown) Maxey; married Juliana Guenther (a writer), April 15, 1966; children: Brian. *Education:* University of Idaho, B.S., 1958; Harvard University, M.B.A., 1961. *Home and office:* 225 West 86th St., New York, N.Y. 10024.

CAREER/WRITINGS: Look, New York City, assistant editor and researcher, 1961-63, senior editor, 1964-66, administrative editor and assistant managing editor, 1967-69; *Careers Today,* Del Mar, Calif., managing editor, 1969; *Look,* Washington, D.C., bureau chief, 1969-70, managing editor in New York City, 1970-71; *Life,* New York City, staff writer, 1971-72; *Psychology Today,* New York City, editor, 1972-76; *Sports Afield,* New York City, editor, 1976-77; free-lance writer, 1978—. Notable assignments include coverage of Apollo 8 and Apollo 11 moonshots, the assassination of Robert Kennedy, the 1972 U.S. presidential election, *Life* stories on Bella Abzug and George Wallace, and *Psychology Today* interview with Walter Mondale. Contributor, *1972 Encyclopaedia Britannica Book of the Year.* Lecturer, University of Minnesota Design Conference, San Diego Art Directors' Club, and San Diego chapter of Sigma Delta Chi. *Military service:* U.S. Army, artillery, 1959-60; became second lieutenant.

WORK IN PROGRESS: Various magazine articles and speeches.

* * *

MAXWELL, Kenneth E(ugene) 1908-

PERSONAL: Born September 27, 1908, in Huntington

Beach, Calif.; son of James Baker (a rancher) and Myrtle (Wardrobe) Maxwell; married Rosemarie Greenwood, November 15, 1941; children: David James, Margaret Carolyn Maxwell Austin, Mary Jane. *Education:* University of California, Berkeley, B.Sc., 1933; Cornell University, Ph.D., 1937. *Home:* 16751 Greenview Lane, Huntington Beach, Calif. 92649. *Office:* Department of Biology, California State University, Long Beach, Calif. 90840.

CAREER: University of California, Riverside, entomologist, 1937-39; Shell Oil Co., Martinez, Calif., technologist, 1939-42; Chemurgic Corp., Richmond, Calif., manager of Agriculture Division and member of board of directors, 1945-47; Maxwell Laboratories, Riverside, consultant, 1947-50; E. I. DuPont de Nemours & Co., Yakima, Wash., entomologist, 1949-50; Agriform Co., Santa Ana, Calif., manager of insecticide department and member of board of directors, 1951-53; Monsanto Co., Santa Clara, Calif., entomologist in development department, 1953-59; Moyer Chemical Co., San Jose, Calif., technical director, 1959-63; California State University, Long Beach, assistant professor, 1963-65, associate professor, 1965-68, professor of entomology, toxicology, and environmental biology, 1968-74, professor emeritus, 1974—. *Military service:* U.S. Navy, entomologist, 1942-45; became lieutenant commander.

MEMBER: International Oceanographic Foundation, Entomological Society of America, American Chemical Society, American Association for the Advancement of Science, American Institute of Biological Sciences, Weed Science Society of America, American Mosquito Control Association, Sierra Club, Sigma Xi, Alpha Zeta.

WRITINGS: Chemicals and Life, Dickenson, 1970; *Environment of Life,* Dickenson, 1973, 2nd edition, 1976. Contributor of about fifty articles to technical journals.

WORK IN PROGRESS: Books related to environmental science and the biological sciences.

SIDELIGHTS: Maxwell writes: "My background in toxicology has led to an interest in the environmental health aspects of natural and man-made contributions to the environment. There is a great deal of misunderstanding about these environmental influences, apparently due to faulty communication between scientists and lay reporters and deep ignorance of scientific principles on the part of many of the latter. One of my major objectives is to clarify many of these issues by communicating with the public in non-technical terms."

*   *   *

MAY, Kenneth Ownsworth   1915-1977

1915—December 1, 1977; American professor and author of books on mathematics. May was founder and editor of *Historia Mathematica.* He died in Toronto, Ontario. Obituaries: *New York Times,* December 15, 1977.

*   *   *

MAY, Timothy C(laude)   1940-

PERSONAL: Born September 18, 1940, in Stratford-upon-Avon, England; son of Claude Asten Newton (a company director) and Joan Mary (Edmonds) May; married Gillian Ruth Cowton (a teacher), April 16, 1966; children: Nicholas, William, Richard. *Education:* University of Leeds, B.A., 1962, graduate study, 1962-64. *Office:* Department of Social Science, Manchester Polytechnic, Aytoun St., Manchester, England.

CAREER: Workers Educational Association, South Humberside, England, organizing tutor, 1964-67; Manchester

Polytechnic, Manchester, England, lecturer, 1967-69, senior lecturer in politics, 1969—. Part-time counselor and tutor at Open University, 1971—. *Member:* Political Studies Association.

WRITINGS: Trade Unions and Pressure Group Politics, Heath, 1975. Contributor to politics and education journals, and to *New Society.*

WORK IN PROGRESS: A textbook on political executives in the modern state; editing a reader on the state and the economy; a survey of middle class trade unionism.

*   *   *

MAYER, Albert   1897-

PERSONAL: Born December 29, 1897, in New York, N.Y.; son of Bernhard and Sophia (Buttenwieser) Mayer; married Phyllis Carter, August 20, 1925 (divorced, 1961); married Marion Mill Preminger, March 21, 1961 (died, 1972); married Magda Pastor, January, 1975; children: (first marriage) Stella, Kerry A. *Education:* Columbia University, A.B., 1916; Massachusetts Institute of Technology, B.S. in C.E., 1919. *Religion:* Jewish. *Home:* 240 Central Park S., New York, N.Y. 10019. *Office:* 235 Park Ave. S., New York, N.Y. 10003.

CAREER: Practice as structural engineer, New York City, 1918-22; J. H. Taylor Construction Co., 1922-34, started as superintendent, became president; private practice as architect and planner, New York City, 1934-39; Mayer & Whittlesey, Architects, and successor firm, Mayer, Whittlesey & Glass, New York City, partner, 1939-60; independent practice of architecture and planning, New York City, 1960—. Designer of new communities and cities, including Kitimat, British Columbia, Chandigarh, the capital of Punjab, India, and Ashdod, a new seaport in Israel; projects also include large-scale housing and community planning in American cities and abroad, and urban renewal work. Consultant to Government of India, United Nations, UNESCO, various branches of the U.S. Government, New York State, Cleveland, Dallas, and other metropolitan cities, and Puerto Rico Urban Renewal and Housing Corp. Lecturer on architecture and planning at Massachusetts Institute of Technology, Ohio State University, Columbia University, and University of Wisconsin. *Military service:* U.S. Army, second lieutenant, 1918; World War II service in Corps of Engineers, 1943-46; became lieutenant colonel.

MEMBER: American Institute of Architects (fellow; chairman of urban design committee, 1950-52), American Society of Applied Anthropology (fellow), American Institute of Planners, American Society of Civil Engineers, Housing Study Guild (co-founder), National Housing Conference (director), Phi Beta Kappa. *Awards, honors:* American Institute of Architects, New York chapter, Medal of Honor, 1952, Pioneer in Housing award, 1973; honor awards from American Society of Landscape Architects, 1962, and Federal Housing Administration, 1963; special citation from National Association of Housing and Redevelopment Officials, 1964, Metropolitan chapter Man of the Year award, 1969; and a number of other awards for designs of plazas in New York City.

WRITINGS: (With McKim Marriott and Richard L. Park) *Pilot Project India,* University of California Press, 1958; (contributor) William B. Hamilton, editor, *The Transfer of Institutions,* Duke University Press, 1964; *The Urgent Future: People, Housing, City, and Region,* McGraw, 1967; *Greenbelt Towns Re-visited* (monograph), Department of Housing and Urban Development, 1968; *Follow the River,*

Doubleday, 1969; (contributor) Arnold Whittick, editor, *Encyclopedia of Urban Planning,* McGraw, 1973; *Guide to the Albert Mayer Papers on India,* Committee on Southern Asian Studies, 1977.

BIOGRAPHICAL/CRITICAL SOURCES: Village Voice, January 11, 1968; *Best Sellers,* May 1, 1969.

* * *

MAYER, Leo V. 1936-

PERSONAL: Born August 12, 1936, in Kansas; son of Peter P. (a farmer) and Georgianna (a teacher; maiden name, Martin) Mayer; married Jo Ann Scritchfield, May 23, 1959 (divorced, July, 1976); children: Gregory Leo, David Mark. *Education:* Kansas State University, B.S., 1959, M.S., 1961; Iowa State University, Ph.D., 1967. *Home:* 5170 Maris Ave., Alexandria, Va. 22304. *Office:* Congressional Research Service, Library of Congress, Washington, D.C. 20540.

CAREER: Iowa State University, Ames, assistant professor, 1967-70, associate professor of agricultural economics, 1970-72; Council of Economic Advisers, Washington, D.C., senior staff economist, 1972-74; Library of Congress, Congressional Research Service, Washington, D.C., senior specialist for agriculture, 1974—. U.S. Information Agency lecturer in Mexico, Chile, Brazil, Barbados, Surinam, Guyana, Trinidad and Tobago, and India, 1974—. *Member:* American Agricultural Economics Association.

WRITINGS: (With Earl O. Heady, Edwin O. Haroldsen, and Luther G. Tweeten) *Roots of the Farm Problem,* Iowa State University Press, 1965; (with Heady and Howard C. Madsen) *Future Farm Programs,* Iowa State University Press, 1972; (with Heady, Uma K. Srivastava, and Keith D. Rogers) *Food Aid and International Development,* Iowa State University Press, 1977.

WORK IN PROGRESS: Research on federal dairy programs, federal sugar programs, growth and efficiency in American agriculture, size and structure of American agriculture, income distribution in American agriculture, and agricultural trade policy.

SIDELIGHTS: Mayer told *CA* that he writes with a farm background and a continuing interest in rural America. He spends summers visiting rural areas to more fully understand the current problems and prospects of American agriculture. His visits to Mexico, Chile, Brazil, India, and Russia have given him a broad understanding of world agricultural problems, including exploding population numbers in a number of developing countries.

AVOCATIONAL INTERESTS: Golf, tennis, travel (including the Soviet Union).

* * *

MAYER, Lynne Rhodes 1926-

PERSONAL: Born October 31, 1926, in New York, N.Y.; daughter of George and Frances (Goshen) Rhodes; married Harold Mayer (a film producer-director), July 3, 1958. *Education:* University of Wisconsin, Madison, B.A., 1947; also attended Queens College (now of the City University of New York). *Residence:* New York, N.Y.; and New Milford, Conn. *Office:* Harold Mayer Productions, 155 West 72nd St., New York, N.Y. 10023.

CAREER: Writer, 1947—. Scriptwriter for WHA-Radio, Madison, Wisc., 1947; writer and radio and television consultant for American Jewish Committee, 1949-53, and for

Amalgamated Clothing Workers of America, 1953-58; documentary film writer-producer for Harold Mayer Productions, 1961—. *Awards, honors:* Three nominations for Emmy Awards from Academy of Television Arts and Sciences, 1962-63, for "Exploring the Universe," 1965-66, for "Trouble in the Family," and 1967-68, for "The Way It Is"; George Foster Peabody Award from University of Georgia, 1965, for "Trouble in the Family"; Golden Eagle awards from Council on International Nontheatrical Events (C.I.N.E.), 1967, for "Schizophrenia: The Shattered Mirror," 1968, for "To Sleep, Perchance to Dream," 1968, for "The Way It Is," 1973, for "L'Chaim: To Life!" and 1975, for "Movin' On"; Sidney Hillman Foundation Award, 1967, and A. Philip Randolph Award, 1969, both for "The Way It Is"; blue ribbon from American Film Festival, 1974, for "L'Chaim: To Life!"

WRITINGS: (With Kenneth E. Vose) *Makin' Tracks* (alternate selection of Book of the Month Club; based on the film "Movin' On"), Praeger, 1975.

Films—All for Harold Mayer Productions: "Trouble in the Family," 1965; "Schizophrenia: The Shattered Mirror," 1967; "The Way It Is," 1967; "To Sleep, Perchance to Dream," 1968; "Movin' On," 1969; "The Making of a Man," 1969; "Khrushchev Remembers," 1971; "Tellin' the World," 1972; "L'Chaim: To Life!" 1973; "The People versus Willie Farah," 1973; "All in the Same Boat," 1974; "If I Forget Thee," 1975; "Testimony: Justice vs. J. P. Stevens," 1977.

WORK IN PROGRESS: A film for Women's American Organization for Rehabilitation Through Training about their unusual vocational high school in Natanya, Israel; a film for the National Science Foundation.

SIDELIGHTS: Mayer writes that the book *Makin' Tracks* grew out of the film "Movin' On." The book, based on additional research, tells "the story of the building of the Transcontinental Railroad in the words and pictures of those who were there. 'L'Chaim: To Life' tells the story of the Eastern European Jews from the 1880's through the holocaust and the formation of Israel, and has been shown theatrically as well as to 40 million people on television. 'The Way It Is' was the first film expose of the tragedy of ghetto education. 'Testimony: Justice vs. J. P. Stevens' reveals the need to boycott J. P. Stevens, as described by the workers themselves.

"I have always been interested in writing on subjects or for a point of view that I deem to be important. If I'm going through the stress and strain of writing, it might as well be on a subject I really care about."

* * *

MAYS, Buddy (Gene) 1943-

PERSONAL: Born September 11, 1943, in Albuquerque, N.M.; son of Carl (an electrician) and Ethel (Boggus) Mays; married Mary Helen Now, October 20, 1973 (divorced June 1, 1977). *Education:* Attended New Mexico State University, 1967-70. *Politics:* "Fortunately none." *Home and office address:* P.O. Box 44, Truth or Consequences, N.M. 87901. *Agent:* Pat Killings, 3181 Waverly St., Palo Alto, Calif.

CAREER: Albuquerque Tribune, Albuquerque, N.M., photographer, 1970-72; Philmont Scout Ranch, Cimarron, N.M., instructor in mountaineering, 1972; KOAT-TV, Santa Fe, N.M., reporter, 1974-75; free-lance writer, 1975—. *Military service:* U.S. Coast Guard, 1961-65; received Gold Lifesaving Medal and expert rifleman medal.

Member: Western Writers Association. *Awards, honors:* Pulitzer Prize nomination, 1977, for feature photography on the American cowboy in the Southwest.

WRITINGS: Wildwaters, Chronicle Books, 1977; *A Pilgrim's Notebook Guide to Western Wildlife,* Chronicle Books, 1977. Contributor of articles and photographs to more than one hundred popular magazines, including *Time, Newsweek, Field and Stream,* and *Boys' Life.*

WORK IN PROGRESS: The Enchanted Giant, on New Mexico; *The Cowboy: Where Is He Now?; Flyways,* on water fowl.

SIDELIGHTS: Mays writes: "My entire world revolves around nature and most of my books, articles, and photographs are aimed toward doing my part to save what is left for future generations. Hopefully both books make their readers aware that our wild land is in trouble and only they can help.

"As for myself, I'm half-Scot, half-Irish, and full of disgust at the wishy-washy way in which our contemporary life proceeds. I've traveled extensively, both in the United States and Europe, just for the sheer fun of traveling. (Nobody loves an itinerant author any more.) I'm not very tolerant of stupidity. I hate the 'great American dream' of a plastic home, three cars, two televisions, two and a half children and a job which the breadwinner dislikes. I drive a four-wheel drive automobile, do a lot of trout fishing and soul searching. I tend to get flowery when I write. I like to sit in the woods. I cannot live in cities. My goals are to live in a handbuilt house in southern Colorado and write a perfect book."

*   *   *

McCANN, Thomas   1934-

PERSONAL: Born March 8, 1934, in Brooklyn, N.Y.; son of Thomas F. and Miriam (Lynch) McCann; married Joan Frese, May, 1955; children: Alison, Lynn, Nancy, Peter. *Education:* Attended New York University. *Politics:* Independent. *Religion:* None. *Home:* 106 Shornecliffe Rd., Newton, Mass. 02158. *Agent:* David Otte, Otte Co., 9 Park St., Boston, Mass. 02108. *Office:* 309 Commonwealth Ave., Boston, Mass. 02215.

CAREER: United Fruit Co., Boston, Mass., director of public relations and advertising, 1960-66, vice-president, 1966-68; United Brands Co., Boston, Mass., vice-president, 1968-70; communications consultant in Boston, Mass., 1970-72; television producer, 1972—. Consultant on public relations and communications to publicly held companies. *Military service:* U.S. Army, Artillery, 1958-60. *Member:* Algonquin Club. *Awards, honors:* Silver Anvil from Public Relations Society of America, 1968-77, for community programs and for international programs; gold medal award for television special of the year from Virgin Islands Film Festival, 1975, for "The White House Transcripts."

WRITINGS: An American Company: The Tragedy of United Fruit, Crown, 1976. Author of television and motion picture scripts, including "Yanqui Go Home," 1969, and "Hutzler," 1970. Contributor of articles and reviews to magazines.

WORK IN PROGRESS: A book on television; a film script, with accompanying book; producing "Eyewitness," a series of television documentary-drama programs, for Public Broadcasting Service; "Ella," a television drama series.

McCANTS, Dorothea Olga   1901-

PERSONAL: Original name, Olga McCants; born November 1, 1901, in Magnolia, Miss.; daughter of Robert Sidney (a contractor) and Daisy (Coney) McCants. *Education:* St. Vincent College, Shreveport, La., certificate, 1923; Our Lady of the Lake College (now University), A.B., 1929; Loyola University, New Orleans, La., M.A., 1934; Catholic University of America, M.A., 1941; also attended George Peabody College for Teachers, Louisiana State University, Laval University, and University of Wisconsin, Madison. *Home:* 1000 Fairview, Shreveport, La. 71104.

CAREER: Roman Catholic nun of Daughters of the Cross, 1920—; St. Vincent Academy and College, Shreveport, La., faculty member in education, 1921-41, principal, 1941-43; principal of school in Marksville, La., 1943-47; teacher in Roman Catholic high school in Monroe, La., 1947-63; Marillac College for Young Sisters, St. Louis, Mo., faculty member in education and Latin, 1964-66; Daughters of the Cross Convent, Shreveport, La., archivist, 1970—.

MEMBER: National League of American Pen Women, Louisiana Historical Society, Louisiana Outdoor Drama Association, North Louisiana Historical Association, Historic Preservation (Shreveport). *Awards, honors:* Medallion Award from Louisiana Library Association, 1970, for *They Came to Louisiana.*

WRITINGS: They Came to Louisiana (translations of French historical letters), Louisiana University Press, 1970; (translator) Rodolphe Desdunes, *Our People and Our History,* Louisiana State University Press, 1973; *With Valor They Serve,* Claitors, 1975; (translator from French) G. F. de Beauvais, *The Establishment and Growth of the Daughters of the Cross,* Daughters of the Cross Publications, 1975. Author of religious pamphlets. Contributor to *Catholic Youth Encyclopedia* and *Dictionary of Religious Institutes.* Contributor of articles and reviews to religious periodicals. Contributing editor of *Vexilla Regis,* 1949-54.

WORK IN PROGRESS: Hi, Teacher (tentative title), a book on classroom teaching, based on personal reminiscences.

*   *   *

McCARROLL, Marion C(lyde)   1893(?)-1977
(Beatrice Fairfax)

1893(?)—August 1, 1977; American author and columnist best known for her "Advice to the Lovelorn" column syndicated by King Features beginning 1941. McCarroll was the first woman to be issued a press card by the New York Stock Exchange. She died in Allendale, N.J. Obituaries: *New York Times,* August 5, 1977.

*   *   *

McCARTNEY, James H(arold)   1925-

PERSONAL: Born July 25, 1925, in St. Paul, Minn.; son of Floyd (an insurance executive) and Cora (Heilig) McCartney; married Jule Graham, January 19, 1952; children: Robert J., Sharon J. *Education:* Michigan State University, B.A., 1949; Northwestern University, M.S.J., 1952; attended Harvard University, 1963-64. *Religion:* Protestant. *Home:* 5214 Albemarle St., Bethesda, Md. 20016. *Office:* Knight-Ridder Newspapers, Inc., 1195 National Press Bldg., Washington, D.C. 20045.

CAREER/WRITINGS: South Bend Tribune, South Bend, Ind., reporter, 1949-50; Michigan State University, East Lansing, Mich., public relations man, 1951-52; *Chicago*

Daily News, Chicago, Ill., reporter, city editor, and Washington correspondent, 1952-68; Knight-Ridder Newspapers, Inc., Washington correspondent, 1968—. Notable assignments include coverage of U.S. military-industrial complex, arms sales abroad, U.S.-Soviet relations, U.S. intervention in the Dominican Republic, Middle East diplomacy, and U.S. presidential election campaigns since 1960. Director of White House press relation studies, 1973, 1974. Teacher, Northwestern University, 1957-60; lecturer, American University, 1975-76. Contributor of articles to *Nation, Progressive, Columbia Journalism Review, Cosmopolitan,* and other periodicals. *Military service:* U.S. Army, 1943-46. *Member:* National Press Club, Gridiron Club and Federal City Club (both Washington, D.C.). *Awards, honors:* Sigma Delta Chi award, 1952; co-winner of Pulitzer Prize, 1955; Nieman fellow, 1963; Raymond Clapper award, 1965, for national reporting.

SIDELIGHTS: McCartney told *CA:* "As a reporter I have traveled in more than thirty countries in Europe, the Middle East, and the Soviet Union. I have been primarily interested in U.S. military influence and in peacemaking efforts."

* * *

McCLENDON, Sarah 1910-

PERSONAL: Born July 8, 1910, in Tyler, Tex.; married husband (deceased); children Sally O'Brien (Mrs. David M. MacDonald). *Education:* University of Missouri, B.J., 1931; attended Tyler Junior College, 1948. *Home and office:* 2933 28th St. N.W., Washington, D.C. 20008.

CAREER: Philadelphia Daily News, Philadelphia, Pa., Washington correspondent, 1944; writer in Washington, D.C., 1945-46; independent reporter for own news service based in Washington, D.C., 1946—. Regular guest appearances on Chicago television program for ABC-TV. Former member of Defense Advisory Committee on Women in the Services. *Military service:* Women's Army Corps, 1942-44; became lieutenant, first class. *Member:* National Press Club (past vice-president), American Newspaper Women's Club (past president), Women in Communications.

WRITINGS: My Eight Presidents, Wyden, 1977. Contributor to periodicals including *Penthouse* and *Esquire.*

WORK IN PROGRESS: Another book, publication expected in 1978.

SIDELIGHTS: McClendon has covered eight presidents since Franklin D. Roosevelt. Mainly she covers the White House, Congress, Department of Defense, Justice Department, Department of Agriculture, and Department of the Interior.

* * *

McCLINTOCK, Theodore 1902-1971

PERSONAL: Born in 1902; married Lillian Lustig (an editor). *Education:* Graduated from Harvard University, 1924. *Home:* Croton-on-Hudson, N.Y.

CAREER: Author, editor, and translator. Editor for publishers Allyn & Bacon, F. S. Crofts, and W. S. Freeman.

WRITINGS: The Underwater Zoo, Vanguard Press, 1938; *Tank Menagerie: Adventures of the Little-Game Hunters of the Fenway,* Abelard, 1954; *Animal Close-Ups* (a Junior Literary Guild selection), Abelard, 1958; (translator from the German and adapter) Hedwig Wimmer, *Maha and Her Donkey,* Rand McNally, 1965; (translator from the German and adapter) Rudolf Neumann, *The Very Special Animal,*

Rand McNally, 1965; (editor) Elizabeth C. Gaskell, *Cranford,* University of London Press, 1966.

SIDELIGHTS: Tank Menagerie: Adventures of the Little-Game Hunters of the Fenway is a retelling, in fictional form, of McClintock's first book *The Underwater Zoo.* The *New York Herald Tribune* commented, "It would have been better if not fictionalized, but the idea it carried out should interest many children under twelve who are fascinated by snails and tadpoles, and other tiny pond creatures." The *New York Times* added that "such treatment is more of a hindrance than a help in snaring the interest of older children. Solid pages of conversation between a boy and a girl about damsel-fly nymphs, scuds, snails, and tadpoles are soon boring. Youngsters who have their own tanks and an avid interest in the subject may find the story fascinating, but most young readers above the nursery age prefer their science straight."

AVOCATIONAL INTERESTS: Hiking, animals, and bird watching.

BIOGRAPHICAL/CRITICAL SOURCES: New York Herald Tribune Book Review, May 16, 1954; *New York Times,* July 4, 1954.

OBITUARIES: New York Times, November 22, 1971; *Publishers Weekly,* December 20, 1971.

(Died November 21, 1971)

* * *

McCOMBS, Maxwell E(lbert) 1938-

PERSONAL: Born December 3, 1938, in Birmingham, Ala.; son of Max E. and Gertrude (Smith) McCombs; married Zoe Helen Collins; children: Mary Elizabeth, Leslie Ann. *Education:* Tulane University, B.A., 1960; Stanford University, M.A., 1961, Ph.D., 1966. *Office:* Communications Research Center, Syracuse University, Syracuse, N.Y. 13210.

CAREER: New Orleans Times-Picayune, New Orleans, La., general assignment reporter, 1961-62, state supreme court reporter, 1962-63; University of California, Los Angeles, lecturer, 1965-66, assistant professor of journalism, 1966-67; University of North Carolina, Chapel Hill, assistant professor, 1967-69, associate professor of journalism, 1969-73; Syracuse University, Syracuse, N.Y., John Ben Snow Professor of Newspaper Research, 1973—, director of Communications Research Center, 1973—. Visiting lecturer at University of Wisconsin, Madison, summer, 1970, and Northwestern University, summers, 1974-75. *Military service:* U.S. Army Reserve, information officer, 1963-67. *Member:* Association for Education in Journalism, American Newspaper Publishers Association (director of News Research Center, 1975—), A. G. Bell Association, American Association for Public Opinion Research.

WRITINGS: Mass Communication on the Campus, Communication Board, University of California, Los Angeles, 1967; *Mass Media in the Marketplace,* Journalism Monographs, 1972; (editor with Donald Shaw and David Gray, and contributor) *Handbook of Reporting Methods,* Houghton, 1976; (editor with Shaw, and contributor) *The Emergence of American Political Issues: The Agenda-Setting Function of the Press,* West, 1977.

Contributor: *New Educational Media in Action: Case Studies for Planners,* Volume III, UNESCO, 1967; Phillip Tichenor and F. G. Kline, editors, *Current Perspectives in Mass Communication Research,* Volume I, Sage Publications, 1972; D. M. Kovenock, J. W. Prothro, and other editors,

Explaining the Vote: Presidential Choices in the Nation and the States, 1968, Institute for Research in Social Science, University of North Carolina, Chapel Hill, 1973; Roy Moore and other editors, *Gathering and Writing News: Selected Readings,* College and University Press, 1975; Steven Chaffee, editor, *Political Communication,* Sage Publications, 1975; Ronald Ostman and Hamid Mowlana, editors, *International Yearbook of Drug Addiction and Society,* Volume III: *Communication Research and Drug Education,* Sage Publications, 1976; James Grunig, editor, *Decline of the Global Village,* General Hall, 1976; Jim Richstad, editor, *New Perspectives in International Communication,* East-West Center Communications Institute, 1977; George Comstock, editor, *The Fifth Season: How TV Influences the Way People Behave—An Evaluation of the Scientific Evidence on the Effects of Television Viewing on Human Conduct,* Rand Corp., in press. Contributor of about forty articles and reviews to professional journals and to newspapers.

WORK IN PROGRESS: Overcoming the Barriers to Communication (tentative title), with Lee Becker, for Prentice-Hall.

* * *

McCONNELL, Roland C(alhoun) 1910-

PERSONAL: Born March 27, 1910, in Amherst, Nova Scotia, Canada; came to the United States in 1912, United States citizen; son of Thomas B. (a clergyman) and Helen (a clerk; maiden name, Halfkenny) McConnell; married Isabel Rossiter (employed by War Department), February 13, 1937. *Education:* Howard University, A.B., 1931, A.M., 1933; New York University, Ph.D., 1945. *Religion:* Presbyterian. *Home:* 2406 College Ave., Baltimore, Md. 21214. *Office:* Department of History, Political Science, and Geography, Morgan State University, Baltimore, Md. 21239.

CAREER: Elizabeth City State Teachers College, Elizabeth City, N.C., instructor in history, 1938-39, 1941-42; National Archives, Washington, D.C., archivist, 1943-47; Morgan State University, Baltimore, Md., associate professor, 1947-48, professor of history, 1948—, chairman of department, 1967—, chairman of Division of Social Science, 1953-55, director of Negro history workshops, 1968-69. Co-chairman of College Level Examination (CLEP) Committee for Afro-American history, 1972-73; chairman of Maryland Commission of Afro-American History and Culture, 1977—. Consultant to Afro-American Bicentennial Corp., 1972-76, National Endowment for the Humanities. *Military service:* U.S. Army, 1942.

MEMBER: American Historical Association, Association for the Study of Afro-American Life and History (member of executive council), Society of American Archivists, National Association for the Advancement of Colored People (life member), Phi Alpha Theta. *Awards, honors:* Certificate of appreciation from War Department, for patriotic civilian service.

WRITINGS: The Negro in North Carolina Since Reconstruction, Edwards Brothers, 1949; *Through the Years with Sargent, 1908-1958: Highlights in the History of Sargent Memorial Presbyterian Church,* privately printed, 1958; *Negro Troops of Antebellum Louisiana: A History of the Battalion of Free Men of Color,* Louisiana State University Press, 1968; (contributor) Morris Radoff, editor *The Old State Line: A History of Maryland,* Hall of Records (Annapolis, Md.), 1971; (contributor) Samuel Proctor, editor, *Eighteenth-Century Florida: Life on the Frontier,* Univer-

sity Presses of Florida, 1976. Contributor to *Encyclopedia of World Biography,* 1973, and to history and black studies journals.

AVOCATIONAL INTERESTS: Travel (Europe, the Caribbean).

* * *

McCORD, David (Thompson Watson) 1897-

PERSONAL: Born November 15, 1897, in New York, N.Y.; raised in Oregon; son of Joseph Alexander and Eleanore Baynton (Reed) McCord. *Education:* Harvard University, A.B., 1921, A.M., 1922. *Politics:* Republican. *Religion:* Episcopalian. *Home:* 310 Commonwealth Ave., Boston, Mass. 02115.

CAREER: Harvard Alumni Bulletin, Cambridge, Mass., associate editor, 1923-25, editor, 1940-46; *Boston Evening Transcript,* Boston, Mass., member of the drama staff, 1923-28; Harvard Fund Council, executive director, 1925-63; poet, editor, and humorist. Phi Beta Kappa poet at Harvard University, 1938, Tufts College, 1938, College of William and Mary, 1950, and Massachusetts Institute of Technology, 1973; lecturer, Lowell Institute, 1950; staff member of the Bread Loaf Writers Conference, 1958, 1960, 1962, 1964; instructor of advanced writing courses at Harvard University during the summers of 1963, 1965, 1966; visiting professor at Framingham State College, 1974; honorary curator of the Poetry and Farnsworth Rooms of the Harvard College Library; honorary associate of Dudley House, Harvard University; honorary trustee for the Boston Center for Adult Education; trustee of Historic Boston, Inc., Peter Bent Brigham Hospital, Boston, Charity of Edward Hopkins, New England College, and Boston Athenaeum; overseer, Old Sturbridge Village, Mass., and Perkins Institute for the Blind; member of the board of directors, Association of Harvard Alumni, 1965-68; member of the usage panel, *American Heritage Dictionary;* councilor to the Harvard Society of Advanced Study and Research, 1967-72.

MILITARY SERVICE: U.S. Army, 1918, served as second lieutenant. *Member:* International P.E.N., American Alumni Council, American Council of Learned Societies, American Academy of Arts and Sciences (fellow), Phi Beta Kappa, Colonial Society of Massachusetts, Massachusetts Historical Society, Harvard Club, St. Botolph Club, Tavern Club, Club of Odd Volumes (Boston), Faculty Club, Signet Club (Cambridge, Mass.), Century Club (New York City). *Awards, honors:* Golden Rose, New England Poetry Club, 1941; William Rose Benet award, 1952; Guggenheim fellow, 1954; National Institute of Arts and Letters grant, 1961; Sarah Josepha Hale medal, 1962; Litt.D., Northwestern University, 1954, University of New Brunswick, 1963, Williams College, 1971; LL.D., Washington and Jefferson College, 1955; L.H.D., Harvard University, 1956, Colby College, 1968, Framingham State College, 1975; Art.D., New England College, 1956; first recipient of the National Council of Teachers of English Award for Excellence in Poetry for Children, 1977.

WRITINGS: Oddly Enough, Washburn & Thomas, 1926; *Floodgate* (poems), Washburn & Thomas, 1927; *Stirabout* (essays), Washburn & Thomas, 1928; *The Crows* (poems), Scribner, 1934; *Bay Window Ballads* (illustrated by John Lavalle), Scribner, 1935; *Notes on the Harvard Tercentenary,* Harvard University Press, 1936; *And What's More* (poems), Coward, 1941; *On Occasion* (poems), Harvard University Press, 1943; *About Boston: Sight, Sound, Flavor, and Inflection* (illustrated by the author), Doubleday,

1948, reprinted, Little, Brown, 1973; *A Star by Day* (poems), Doubleday, 1950; *The Camp at Lockjaw* (illustrated by Gluyas Williams), Doubleday, 1952; *The Old Bateau, and Other Poems,* Little, Brown, 1953; *Odds without Ends* (poems), Little, Brown, 1954; *Sonnets to Baedeker* (illustrated by Lavalle), Scribner, 1963; *In Sight of Severn: Essays from Harvard,* Harvard University Press, 1963; *Notes from Four Cities, 1927-1953,* A. J. St. Onge, 1969.

Juvenile: *Far and Few: Rhymes of the Never Was and Always Is* (illustrated by Henry B. Kane), Little, Brown, 1952; *Take Sky: More Rhymes of the Never Was and Always Is* (illustrated by H. B. Kane), Little, Brown, 1962; *All Day Long: Fifty Rhymes of the Never Was and Always Is* (illustrated by Kane), Little, Brown, 1966; *Every Time I Climb a Tree* (illustrated by Marc Simont), Little, Brown, 1967; *For Me to Say: Rhymes of the Never Was and Always Is* (illustrated by Kane), Little, Brown, 1970; *Mr. Bidery's Spidery Garden* (illustrated by Kane), Harrap, 1972; *Away and Ago: Rhymes of the Never Was and Always Is* (illustrated by Leslie Morrill), Little, Brown, 1975; *The Star in the Pail* (illustrated by Simont), Little, Brown, 1975.

Editor: *Once and For All* (essays), Coward, 1929; *What Cheer: An Anthology of American and British Humorous and Witty Verse,* Coward, 1945, a later edition published as *The Modern Treasury of Humorous Verse,* Garden City Books, 1951; Arthur Griffin, *New England Revisited,* Houghton, 1966; *Bibliotheca Medica: Physician for Tomorrow,* Harvard Medical School, 1966; Stow Wengenroth, *Stow Wengenroth's New England,* Barre Publishers, 1969.

Contributor to *Atlantic Monthly, Harper's, Ladies' Home Journal, New Yorker, Saturday Evening Post, Saturday Review of Literature, Theatre Arts Monthly, Virginia Quarterly,* and *Yale Review.*

SIDELIGHTS: David McCord has thought of his writing as more of a hobby than a vocation, and the charm of his work lies in this quality. *About Boston* is a description of the city and its inhabitants, based on a series of radio broadcasts. *Atlantic* wrote: "His essays fall pleasantly on the ear as they did when they came to us on the air. They are full of telling and unsuspected little details of which the author is a famous collector. They have the glint of laughter and the gay and poking lilt of a writer who turns to verse when prose would be too slow. Delightful vignettes by a skilled and sensitive hand." The *New York Herald Tribune Weekly Book Review* said: "Endowed with a painter's perceptiveness and a poet's sensitivity he gives us a new appreciation of the old, overwritten town. Perhaps the freshest and most memorable things in the book have to do with 'rus in urbe', Boston as just a part of the country, or at least everywhere interpenetrated by it—not only in the parks, the gardens of Beacon Hill and dooryard of the Back Bay, the Arboretum, but somehow in the very air."

David McCord has also written several books of poetry for children. "One of the things I learned as a country boy," he wrote in the *Boston Herald-Traveler,* "was to see, hear, feel, and breathe the rhythm of the earth. This is another way of saying that I learned very early something of the poetry of life. For poetry, remember, is not rhyme or tricks with words; or wit, laughter, grief, tears, and nonsense, though all these things are a part of written poetry. Poetry is rhythm, just as the planet Earth is rhythm, the best writing, poetry or prose—no matter what the message it conveys—depends on a very sure and subtle rhythm."

McCord was influenced in his writing for children by Edward Lear and Robert Louis Stevenson. The title for *Far*

and *Few,* McCord's first book of children's poetry, is a quotation taken from Lear. The *New York Herald Tribune Book Review* noted: "Mr. McCord is a good poet. He has the requisite wonder, sympathy, tenderness of impression, gayety, fancy, and imagination. If sometimes he strives too subtly to implant a between-the-lines suggestion, if sometimes his whimsicality seems very determined, he reports well his notes on life and the world."

McCord is also a talented water-colorist, and has had several one-man exhibitions of his landscapes.

AVOCATIONAL INTERESTS: Traveling, fishing, baseball.

BIOGRAPHICAL/CRITICAL SOURCES: Atlantic, October, 1948; *New York Herald Tribune Book Review,* October 24, 1948; August 27, 1950, September 7, 1952; *Saturday Review of Literature,* October 30, 1948, November 18, 1950; *Time,* June 29, 1962; Lee Bennett Hopkins, *Books Are by People,* Citation Press, 1969; *Bulletin of the Center for Children's Books,* June, 1975.*

*   *   *

MCCORMICK, (George) Donald King   1911-
(Richard Deacon)

PERSONAL: Born December 9, 1911, in Rhyl, Wales; son of Thomas Burnside (a journalist) and Lillie Louise (King) McCormick; married Rosalind Deirdre Buchanan Scott, 1934 (divorced); married Sylvia Doreen Cade, 1947 (deceased); married Eileen Dee Challinor James, 1963; children: Anthony Stuart McCormick. *Education:* Attended Oswestry School. *Politics:* Non-party. *Home:* 8 Barry Court, 36 Southend Rd., Beckenham, Kent, BR3 2AD England. *Agent:* Hope, Leresche & Sayle, 11 Jubilee Place, London, SW3 3TE, England.

CAREER: Has worked at a variety of jobs on numerous provincial and British national newspapers, 1931-39; *Gibraltar Chronicle,* Gibraltar, Spain, editor, 1946; Kemsley Newspapers, London, England, foreign correspondent in Northwest Africa, 1946-49, Commonwealth correspondent, 1949-55; *Sunday Times,* London, foreign manager, 1963-73; writer. *Military service:* Royal Navy, 1941-46.

WRITINGS: The Talkative Muse, Lincoln Williams (London), 1934; *Islands for Sale,* Peter Garnett (London), 1950; *Mr. France: A Biography of Pierre Mendes-France,* Jarrolds (London), 1955; *The Wicked City,* Jarrolds, 1956; *The Hell-Fire Club,* Jarrolds, 1958; *The Mystery of Lord Kitchener's Death,* Putnam (London), 1959; *The Identity of Jack the Ripper,* Jarrolds, 1959, revised edition, John Long, 1970; *The Incredible Mr. Kavanagh,* Putnam (London), 1960, Devin-Adair, 1962; *The Wicked Village,* Jarrolds, 1960; *Blood on the Sea,* Muller, 1962; *Temple of Love,* Jarrolds, 1962, Citadel, 1963; *The Mask of Merlin: Biography of David Lloyd George,* Macdonald, 1963, Holt, 1965; *The Silent Killer,* Muller, 1964; *Pedlar of Death,* Holt, 1966; *The Red Barn Mystery,* John Long, 1967, A. S. Barnes, 1968; *Murder by Witchcraft,* John Long, 1968; *One Man's Wars,* Arthur Barker, 1972; *How to Buy an Island,* St. Martin's, 1973; *The Master Book of Spies,* Hodder Causton (London), 1973, F. Watts, 1974; *Islands of England and Wales,* Osprey (London), 1974; *Islands of Scotland,* Osprey, 1974; *Islands of Ireland,* Osprey, 1974; *The Master Book of Escapes,* F. Watts, 1975; *Taken for a Ride: The History of Cons and Conmen,* Harwood Smart (London), 1976; *Who's Who in Spy Fiction,* Taplinger, 1977.

Books under the pseudonym Richard Deacon, all published

by Muller (London), unless otherwise noted: *The Private Life of Mr. Gladstone*, 1965; *Madoc and the Discovery of America*, 1966, Braziller, 1967; *John Dee*, 1968; *A History of the British Secret Service*, 1969, Taplinger, 1970; *A History of the Russian Secret Service*, Taplinger, 1972; *A History of the Chinese Secret Service*, Taplinger, 1974; *William Caxton: The First English Editor*, 1976; *Matthew Hopkins: Witchfinder-General*, 1976; *The Book of Fate: Its Origins and Uses*, 1976, Citadel Press, 1977; *The Israeli Secret Service*, Hamish Hamilton, 1977.

SIDELIGHTS: McCormick told *CA:* "I have—on the principle that it helps to save one from getting stale—switched from one type of non-fiction to another in my books. My first book, *The Talkative Muse*, was a youthfully pretentious dialogue between two friends in the form of essays on a wide range of subjects. A passion for islands has led me to write *Islands for Sale, How to Buy an Island,* and three books on the islands surrounding England, Wales, Scotland and Ireland, large and small. I have also become fascinated in studying the histories of the secret services of the world. I was prompted to tackle the British Secret Service first as a result of doing a biography of John Dee, astrologer to Queen Elizabeth I, who was also a secret agent. Then I found that down the ages there were frequent links between the British and Russian secret services. Not just the notorious Philby link, but that of the quadruple agent, Sidney Reilly, and the fact that Catharine the Great stayed up late at night to decipher messages for the British Ambassador. I then switched to the Chinese secret service largely as a challenge because everybody said it was an impossible subject. I found they had a text book on espionage way back in the fourth century BC. Finally, I got down to the subject of the Israeli secret service because it seemed to me to be the youngest, smallest and yet most efficient in the whole world and very much part and parcel of the gallant little nation's fight for survival—perhaps a lesson for all of us. In the end espionage becomes something of an inescapable obsession. One escapes from it for a time to do another type of book and then, out of one's network of contacts all over the world, a new slant on it presents itself. Lo and behold, there is another book! What fascinated me most about working on *Who's Who in Spy Fiction* was the constantly recurring links between fact and fiction and fiction and fact. This is so much more marked in modern times when almost every intelligence service studies the spy fiction of its rivals just in case somebody let leak a little truth. So often the spy fiction books reveal more fact than the spymasters get from their agents! This has been markedly the case with some fiction concerning the CIA."

*   *   *

McCULLY, Helen   1902(?)-1977

1902(?)—August 24, 1977; Canadian editor, food writer, and co-author of cookbooks. McCully was food editor of *House Beautiful* and co-author of the widely read *Nobody Ever Tells You These Things.* She died in New York, N.Y. Obituaries: *New York Times,* August 25, 1977; *AB Bookman's Weekly,* October 17, 1977.

*   *   *

McDERMOTT, Geoffrey (Lyster)   1912-

PERSONAL: Born October 7, 1912, in India; son of John William (a captain in Indian Army and member of Indian Civil Service) and Grace E. (Spurgeon) McDermott; married Ruth Mary Fleming, September 10, 1937 (divorced November 15, 1947); married Elizabeth Marion Robertson,

December 3, 1947; children: (first marriage) Anthony, Jocelyn McDermott Pink; (second marriage) Evelyn, Richard. *Education:* King's College, Cambridge, B.A. (first class honors), 1933. *Politics:* Liberal. *Religion:* Church of England. *Home:* Old Rectory, Ripple, near Tewkesbury, Gloucestershire, England; and 22 Queen St., Mayfair, London W.1, England. *Agent:* David Higham Associates Ltd., Golden Sq., London W.1, England.

CAREER: British Diplomatic Service, third secretary in Foreign Office, 1935-38, and in Sofia, 1938-41, second secretary in Ankara, 1941-43, and in Foreign Office, 1943-44, first secretary in Foreign Office, 1944-46, in Cairo, 1946-48, and in Santiago, 1948-49, charge d'affaires in Santiago, 1949-51, and in Foreign Office, 1951-53, counselor and head of permanent undersecretary's department in Foreign Office, 1953-56, minister in Foreign Office, 1956-58, political representative (with ambassadorial rank) to Middle East Forces in Cyprus, 1958-61, minister in Berlin, 1961-62; writer, 1962—. Chairman of Committee for the Recognition of the German Democratic Republic, 1971-73. *Member:* Royal Society of Arts (fellow), Boodle's Club, Garrick Club. *Awards, honors:* Companion of the Order of St. Michael and St. George, 1957.

WRITINGS: Berlin: Success of a Mission?, Harper, 1963; *The Eden Legacy and the Decline of British Diplomacy,* Frewin, 1969; *Leader Lost: A Biography of Hugh Gaitskell,* Auerbach, 1972; *The New Diplomacy and Its Apparatus,* Ward, Lock, 1973. Contributor of articles and reviews to British and American periodicals and newspapers.

WORK IN PROGRESS: Writing and lecturing on defense, intelligence, international relations, and politics.

SIDELIGHTS: McDermott writes: "Having retired from the Diplomatic Service at the age of forty-nine, as a result of a disagreement with the Foreign Office, I decided to devote myself to writing on these subjects in a critical and, I hope, forward-looking style." *Avocational interests:* Walking, motoring, the arts.

*   *   *

McDERMOTT, John J(oseph)   1932-

PERSONAL: Born January 5, 1932, in New York, N.Y.; son of John J. and Helen (Kelly) McDermott; married Virginia Picarelli (a teacher), June 14, 1952; children: Marise, Michele, David, Brian, Tara. *Education:* St. Francis College, B.A., 1953; Fordham University, M.A., 1954, Ph.D., 1959. *Home:* 705 South Dexter, College Station, Tex. 77840. *Office:* Department of Philosophy and the Humanities, Texas A & M University, College Station, Tex. 77843.

CAREER: High school Latin teacher in Brooklyn, N.Y., 1953-54; St. Francis College, Brooklyn, instructor in philosophy, 1954-57; Queens College of the City University of New York, Flushing, N.Y., instructor, 1957-59, assistant professor, 1959-65, associate professor, 1965-68, professor of philosophy, 1968-77; Texas A & M University, College Station, professor of philosophy and head of department of philosophy and humanities, 1977—. Visiting professor at State University of New York at Stony Brook, 1970-77.

MEMBER: American Philosophical Association, American Studies Association, History of Science Society, Peirce Society, Conference on the Science of Philosophy and Religion, Society for the Advancement of American Philosophy (president, 1977—). *Awards, honors:* Postdoctoral fellowship from Society for Values in Higher Education, 1964-65; E. Harris Harbison Award from the Danforth Foundation, 1969-70; LL.D. from University of Hartford, 1970.

WRITINGS: (Editor) *The Writings of William James,* Random House, 1967, revised edition, University of Chicago Press, 1977; (editor) *Basic Writings of Josiah Royce,* two volumes, University of Chicago Press, 1969; (editor) *The Philosophy of John Dewey,* two volumes, Putnam, 1973; *The Culture of Experience: Philosophical Essays in the American Grain,* New York University Press, 1976. Contributor to scholarly journals. Advisory editor of "Collected Works of William James," Harvard University Press. Editor of *Cross Currents;* member of editorial board of *Transactions* of the Peirce Society.

WORK IN PROGRESS: Co-editing *An Anthology of American Writing,* two volumes, publication expected in 1980.

SIDELIGHTS: McDermott wrote: "Although a line of continuity runs through the history of philosophy, the variant styles of philosophical articulation are almost as numerable as the philosophers involved. We can say, however, that philosophical approaches and even philosophical language tends to cluster around a historical tradition. In this way, philosophers of the twentieth century announce their roots as being in, among others, Idealism, Empiricism, Phenomenology, Existentialism or Marxism. They may even proceed from a single great philosopher, such as Plato, Aristotle, Aquinas, Descartes, Kant or Hegel. Speaking in general terms, the tradition which feeds the essays in *The Culture of Experience* is that of American philosophy, especially the work of William James, John Dewey, George H. Mead and Josiah Royce. This tradition has as its major focus, the significance of philosophy for an elucidation of the fabric and import of experience. Indeed, it is the only tradition for which experience is the primary philosophical touchstone. Corollary to this emphasis on experience is the concern for relations and in Dewey and Royce, for the nature of the community.

"The essays within *The Culture of Experience* constitute an effort to analyze contemporary culture, especially in the American grain, from a philosophical vantage point traceable to James, Royce and Dewey. The problems under consideration have an immediacy in their formulation but they reflect long-standing areas of human concern too often bypassed by contemporary philosophy.

"Of particular significance is the attempt to wed a diagnosis of actual situations to a philosophical language which approximates the way in which we have our experiences. In other words, I have tried to avoid jargon or in-house philosophical terms. Nonetheless, these essays point to the implicit philosophical significance of much of the non-philosophical literature pertaining to the themes in question.

"Holding that a philosophy of relations as found in James and Dewey can cast tremendous light on many of our most obvious problems and situations, I believe that aesthetic sensibility should be at the center of all of our evaluations and of all of our strategies for social change. This belief constitutes a new cultural pedagogy, and therefore, a new politics. The essays in this book are probes in that direction, with cities, schools, the arts, and communities acting as the fulcrum for that inquiry."

* * *

McDONALD, Erwin L(awrence) 1907-
(Clabe Hankins)

PERSONAL: Born October 31, 1907, in London, Ark.; son of Frank Floyd (a clergyman) and Rebecca Geneva (Powell) McDonald; married Mary Elsie (Maria) Price, March 1, 1930; children: Avis Jeannine (Mrs. Sam H. Jones, Jr.), Judy Carole (Mrs. Jay Lucas). *Education:* Arkansas Polytechnic College, graduate, 1932; Ouachita Baptist College (now University), A.B. (magna cum laude), 1943; Southern Baptist Theological Seminary, B.D., 1947. *Politics:* Democrat. *Home:* 1419 Garland Ave., North Little Rock, Ark. 72116.

CAREER: Ordained to Baptist ministry, 1938. *Daily Courier-Democrat,* Russellville, Ark., city editor, 1937-41; *Southern Standard* (weekly newspaper), Arkadelphia, Ark., editor, 1941-43; pastor in Washington, Ark., 1942-44; Ouachita Baptist College (now University), Arkadelphia, instructor in journalism, 1943-44; pastor in Pendleton, Ky., 1944-47; Southern Baptist Theological Seminary, Louisville, Ky., director of public relations and editor of *Tie,* 1947-51; Furman University, Greenville, S.C., director of public relations and founding editor of university magazine, 1951-54; General Association of Baptists in Kentucky, Louisville, coordinator of schools and colleges, 1954-57; Arkansas Baptist Convention, Little Rock, Ark., editor and publisher of *Arkansas Baptist,* 1957-72; *Arkansas Democrat,* Little Rock, religion editor and columnist, 1972—. Visiting professor of religious journalism, Southeastern Baptist Theological Seminary, summer, 1975. Professional photographer. Member of Arkansas Advisory Committee, U.S. Commission on Civil Rights, 1965-74; chairman, Greater Little Rock Conference on Religion and Race, 1966-67; chairman of board, Economic Opportunity Agency of Pulaski County, 1967; founding member, Southern Committee on Political Ethics, beginning 1968. Trustee, Southern Baptist Theological Seminary, beginning 1959.

MEMBER: American Association for the United Nations (president of Arkansas chapter, 1963-64), Southern Baptist Press Association (president, 1965), Greater Little Rock Ministerial Association (president, 1964-65), Little Rock Chamber of Commerce, Little Rock Rotary Club. *Awards, honors:* Litt.D., Georgetown College, Georgetown, Ky., 1958; Distinguished Alumnus award, Ouachita Baptist College, 1960; Distinguished Baptist Minister award, Southern Baptist College, 1963; Alumnus of the Year award, Southern Baptist Theological Seminary, 1972.

WRITINGS: *The Church Using the Newspaper,* Convention Press, 1958; *Seventy-Five Stories and Illustrations from Everyday Life,* Baker Book, 1964; (with Ralph Creger) *A Look Down the Lonesome Road,* Doubleday, 1964; *Across the Editor's Desk,* Broadman, 1966; (editor) *The Church Proclaiming and Witnessing,* Baker Book, 1966; *Stories for Speakers and Writers,* Baker Book, 1970; *Sixty Years of Service: History of the Rotary Club of Little Rock,* Parkin Printing & Stationery Co., 1974. Creator of Clabe Hankins, a backwood's feature, in *Training Union Magazine,* 1967—; other features include Sunday School lesson quarterlies from time to time for the Southern Baptist Convention Sunday School Board, Nashville, Tenn.

AVOCATIONAL INTERESTS: Travel, books (has large private library), fishing, photography.

* * *

McDONALD, Walter (Robert) 1934-

PERSONAL: Born July 18, 1934, in Lubbock, Tex.; son of Charles Arthur (a painter) and Vera Belle (Graves) McDonald; married Carol Ham, August 28, 1959; children: Cynthia, David, Charles. *Education:* Texas Technological College (now Texas Tech University), B.A., 1956, M.A., 1957; Univery of Iowa, Ph.D., 1965. *Religion:* Christian.

Office: Department of English, Texas Tech University, Lubbock, Tex. 79409.

CAREER: U.S. Air Force, career officer, 1957-71, instructor at U.S. Air Force Academy, 1960-62, 1965-66, assistant professor, 1966, associate professor of English, 1967-71, retiring as major; Texas Tech University, Lubbock, associate professor, 1971-75; professor of English, 1975—, director of creative writing, 1972—.

MEMBER: Modern Language Association of America, National Council of Teachers of English, College English Association, Conference of College Teachers of English (member of council, 1977—), South Central Modern Language Association, Rocky Mountain Modern Language Association, Texas Association of Creative Writing Teachers (president, 1974-76). *Awards, honors:* Voertman's Poetry Award from Texas Institute of Letters, 1976, for *Caliban in Blue;* best story award from Texas Institute of Letters, 1976, for "The Track."

WRITINGS: (Editor with Frederick Kiley) A *"Catch-22" Casebook,* Crowell, 1973; *Caliban in Blue and Other Poems,* Texas Tech University Press, 1976; (editor, with James White) *Texas Prize Stories and Poems,* Texas Center for Writers Press, 1978. Contributor of stories, poems, and articles to literary journals, including *Prairie Schooner, Mississippi Review,* and *Quartet.*

WORK IN PROGRESS: Anything, Anything, poetry.

* * *

McDONOUGH, James Lee 1934-

PERSONAL: Born June 17, 1934, in Nashville, Tenn.; son of James W. (a postal supervisor) and Ora Lee (Tatum) McDonough; married Nancy Sharon Pinkston (a teacher), May 28, 1957; children: David, Sharon, Carla. *Education:* David Lipscomb College, B.A., 1956; graduate study at Vanderbilt University, 1958-60; Abilene Christian University, M.A., 1961; Florida State University, Ph.D., 1966. *Home:* 1206 Graybar Lane, Nashville, Tenn. 37215. *Office:* Department of History and Political Science, David Lipscomb College, Nashville, Tenn. 37203.

CAREER: David Lipscomb College, Nashville, Tenn., instructor, 1965-66, assistant professor, 1966-69, associate professor, 1969-75, Justin Potter Distinguished Professor of History, 1975—. Part-time instructor at University of Tennessee, Nashville. Member of U.S. Commission on Military History. *Member:* Southern Historical Association, Tennessee Historical Society.

WRITINGS: Schofield: Union General in the Civil War and Reconstruction, University Presses of Florida, 1972; *Shiloh—In Hell Before Night,* University of Tennessee Press, 1977; (with Richard Gardner) *Skyriders: A History of the 327th-401st Glider Infantry Regiment,* Battery Press, 1978.

WORK IN PROGRESS: A book on the Civil War Battle of Stones River.

SIDELIGHTS: McDonough writes: "I hope to do more work in both the World War II and the Civil War periods. I am also interested in writing a novel that would be set during World War II."

* * *

McDOUGAL, Stuart Y(eatman) 1942-

PERSONAL: Born April 10, 1942, in Los Angeles, Calif.; son of Murray (a businessman) and Marian (Yeatman) McDougal; married Menakka Weerasinghe, 1967 (divorced); children: Dyanthe Rose, Gavin Rohan. *Education:* Haverford College, B.A., 1964; University of Pennsylvania, M.A., 1965, Ph.D., 1970. *Office:* Department of English, University of Michigan, Ann Arbor, Mich. 48109.

CAREER: University of Lausanne, Lausanne, Switzerland, exchange lecturer in English, 1965-66; Gymnase de la Cite, Lausanne, professor of English, 1966; Michigan State University, East Lansing, assistant professor of English, 1970-72; University of Michigan, Ann Arbor, assistant professor, 1972-75, associate professor of English, 1975—. Fulbright professor at University of Rome, 1978. *Member:* Modern Language Association of America, Dante Society of America, English Institute. *Awards, honors:* Bredvold Award from University of Michigan, 1973, for *Ezra Pound and the Troubador Tradition;* Rackham fellowship from University of Michigan, 1974; fellowship from American Council of Learned Societies, 1974-75.

WRITINGS: Ezra Pound and the Troubador Tradition, Princeton University Press, 1973, 2nd edition, 1974. Contributor to literature and film journals.

WORK IN PROGRESS: Editing *Dante Among the Moderns,* and writing the chapter, "Eliot's Metaphysical Dante"; *Dante, Pound, and Eliot: A Study in Poetic Influence; Literature and Film,* for Houghton.

* * *

McELROY, Thomas P(arker), Jr. 1914-

PERSONAL: Born September 19, 1914, in Pennsylvania; son of Thomas P. (a baker) and Mabel I. (Potts) McElroy; married Hannah Himmelsbach (a teacher), November 23, 1939; children: Thomas P. III, Gayle McElroy Pallesen. *Education:* Attended West Chester State Teachers College, 1932-34. *Home and office:* 7217 Venetian Way, West Palm Beach, Fla. 33406.

CAREER: Elementary education teacher in Pennsylvania; Pequot-sepos Wildlife Sanctuary, Mystic, Conn., director, 1945-57; National Audubon Society, New York, N.Y., nature center director, 1957-61; writer, 1961—. *Military service:* U.S. Army Air Forces, glider pilot, 1940-43; became flight officer. *Member:* Outdoor Writers Association of America, American Birding Association.

WRITINGS: The New Handbook of Attracting Birds, Knopf, 1960; *The Habitat Guide to Birding,* Knopf, 1974. Contributor to magazines.

WORK IN PROGRESS: From Storks to Vultures, an ecological study of the Everglades.

SIDELIGHTS: McElroy writes: "I am interested primarily in functional ecology and environmental interpretations."

* * *

McEVOY, Dennis 1918-

PERSONAL: Born July 27, 1918, in Chicago, Ill.; son of J. P. (a writer) and Mary (O'Crotty) McEvoy; married Nan Tucker (divorced); married Maev Bridget Gallagher, December 16, 1976; children: Nion Tucker. *Education:* Attended Yale University, 1933-34, Waseda University (Tokyo), 1935-36, and Sorbonne, University of Paris, 1937; University of Chicago, B.A., 1940, graduate study, 1940-41. *Home:* Calvo Sotelo 149, Palma de Mallorca, Spain. *Agent:* Julian Bach Literary Agency, 3 East 48th St., New York, N.Y. 10017. *Office:* c/o Office of Editor-in-Chief, *Reader's Digest,* Pleasantville, N.Y. 10570.

CAREER/WRITINGS: San Francisco Examiner, San Francisco, Calif., reporter, 1935; United Press International, Tokyo, Japan, assistant bureau manager, 1938-39; *Chicago Times,* Chicago, Ill., chief correspondent in Moscow, Soviet Union, and Far East, 1941-42; *Reader's Digest,* Pleasantville, N.Y., Far Eastern manager, 1945-51, deputy director of international editions, 1951-57, senior editor, 1958—. Columbia Broadcasting System (CBS), Moscow correspondent, 1941. Notable assignments include coverage of nine wars. Member of American Chamber of Commerce in Japan (first president). *Military service:* U.S. Marine Corps, Infantry and Intelligence, 1943-45; became captain; served as chief of Japanese section in Office of War Information, 1942-43; senior Japanese specialist in Office of Naval Intelligence, 1944-45. *Member:* Dutch Treat Club (New York City). *Awards, honors:* Japan's "Man of the Year" Award, 1947; Order of Isabel la Catolica from Spain, 1967; Prince Henry the Navigator decoration from Portugal, 1969.

WORK IN PROGRESS: An autobiography, *Just Lucky, I Guess.*

SIDELIGHTS: McEvoy founded both the Japanese and the Spanish language editions of *Reader's Digest.* He also speaks and writes Chinese, French, German, Portuguese, Italian, and classical Arabic.

* * *

McFARLAND, Philip (James) 1930-

PERSONAL: Born June 20, 1930, in Birmingham, Ala.; son of Thomas Alfred (a lawyer) and Lucile (a teacher; maiden name, Sylvester) McFarland; married Patricia Connors (a teacher), July 23, 1960; children: Philip James, Jr., Joseph Thomas. *Education:* Oberlin College, B.A., 1951; St. Catharine's College, Cambridge, M.A., 1964. *Home:* 18 Independence Ave., Lexington, Mass. 02173. *Agent:* John Cushman Associates, Inc., 25 West 43rd St., New York, N.Y. 10036. *Office:* Concord Academy, Concord, Mass. 01742.

CAREER: Houghton Mifflin Co., Boston, Mass., textbook editor, 1958-64; traveled and lived in Europe, 1964-66; Concord Academy, Concord, Mass., English teacher, 1966—. *Military service:* U.S. Naval Reserve, active duty, 1951-54; became lieutenant junior grade.

WRITINGS: A House Full of Women (novel), Simon & Schuster, 1960; (with Allan A. Glatthorn, Harold Fleming, and others) *Composition: Models and Exercises,* Harcourt, 1971; (with others) "Focus on Literature" series, Houghton, 1972, revised edition, 1978.

WORK IN PROGRESS: Sojourners: Sketches from Life in Europe and America, 1780-1860, for Atheneum.

* * *

McGINN, Noel F(rancis) 1934-

PERSONAL: Born December 28, 1934, in Colon, Panama; son of Thomas M. (a machinist) and Edith (Bruck) McGinn; married Mary Lou Rasch (a teacher), June 13, 1959; children: Thomas, Mary Margaret, Joseph, Noel Francis, Jr. *Education:* University of California, Santa Barbara, B.A., 1958, M.A., 1960; University of Michigan, Ph.D., 1962. *Politics:* "Christian socialist." *Religion:* Roman Catholic. *Home:* 52 Robbins Rd., Arlington, Mass. 02174. *Office:* Graduate School of Education, Harvard University, Cambridge, Mass. 02138.

CAREER: Psychology trainee at public schools in Devereux, Calif., 1957-58; Institute of Technology and Advanced Studies, Guadalajara, Mexico, professor of psychology and sociology, 1962-64; Harvard University, Cambridge, Mass., research associate, 1964-69, lecturer, 1965-69, associate professor of educational planning, 1969—. Consultant to Ford Foundation in Brazil. *Member:* American Psychological Association, Society for International Development, American Sociological Association, American Educational Research Association, Latin American Studies Association.

WRITINGS: (With Russell G. Davis) *Build a Mill, Build a City, Build a School,* M.I.T. Press, 1969; (with Richard G. King, Alfonso Rangel Guerra, and David Kline) *The Provincial Universities of Mexico,* Praeger, 1971; (with Ernesto Schiefelbein) *El Sistema Escolar y el Problema del Ingreso a la Universidad,* Corporacion de Promocion Universitaria, 1975; *Education in Korea, 1945-1975,* Harvard University Press, 1977. Contributor to psychology and counseling journals.

* * *

McGUIRE, Thomas (Vertin) 1945-

PERSONAL: Born November 10, 1945, in Dearborn, Mich.; son of Edwin Vertin (an engineer) and Olive Ann (DesJardins) McGuire; married Sally Welcome Luick, October 20, 1971; children: Rebecca Leah, Rosemary Desideria. *Education:* Yale University, B.A., 1967; University of Michigan, M.A., 1968. *Religion:* Roman Catholic. *Home address:* Star Route 20086, Fairbanks, Alaska 99701.

CAREER: Deckhand on fishing vessels *Oregon City,* 1973, and *Marcele,* 1976—, both out of Wrangell, Alaska.

WRITINGS: Ninety-Nine Days on the Yukon, Alaska Northwest Publishing, 1977.

SIDELIGHTS: McGuire told *CA:* "I am a fisherman by trade, a canoeist by avocation, but I spend most of my time being a husband and father, cutting wood, and trying to get my car to start. A fairly typical Alaskan. I have written one book in which I tried to show what it was like to move slowly down a big river (did someone else try this? Twain, maybe?) and may never write another since canoeing is all that I know well and I don't intend to be redundant."

* * *

McHAM, David 1933-

PERSONAL: Born July 27, 1933, in Inman, S.C.; son of Clarence O. (a textile worker) and Lois (a textile worker; maiden name, Robbins) McHam; married Wilma Gathings, December 12, 1953 (divorced, 1974); children: Michael, Ritchie. *Education:* Baylor University, B.A., 1958; Columbia University, M.S., 1960. *Politics:* Democrat. *Religion:* Protestant. *Home:* 3226 Daniel, Dallas, Tex. 75205. *Office:* Division of Journalism, Southern Methodist University, Dallas, Tex. 75215.

CAREER: Spartanburg Herald, Spartanburg, S.C., sports writer, 1951-52; *Waco News-Tribune,* Waco, Tex., sports writer, 1956-58; *Houston Post,* Houston, Tex., reporter, 1960-61; Baylor University, Waco, assistant professor, 1961-64, associate professor, 1964-69, professor of journalism, 1969-74; Southern Methodist University, Dallas, Tex., associate professor, 1974-75, professor of journalism, 1975—. *Military service:* U.S. Marine Corps, 1953-56. *Member:* Society of Professional Journalists, Sigma Delta Chi. *Awards, honors:* Newswriting award from Texas Associated Press, 1968.

WRITINGS: Law and the Press in Texas, Texas Daily Newspaper Association, 1972, 3rd edition, 1977.

SIDELIGHTS: McHam told *CA:* "*Law and the Press in Texas* has been used by working journalists and students for more than six years. The book is oriented toward the application of law in Texas, but also looks into national trends. The relationship between the legal authorities and the press has been and continues to be quite good in Texas."

* * *

MC KENNY, Margaret

PERSONAL: Born in Olympia, Wash. *Address:* c/o City Garden Clubs of America, 829 Madison Avenue, New York City, N.Y. 10021.

CAREER: Author.

WRITINGS: Mushrooms of Field and Wood, John Day, 1929; *The Wild Garden* (illustrated by Robert Snedigar), Doubleday, Doran, 1936; (with Edward Loomis Davenport Seymour) *Your City Garden,* Appleton-Century, 1937; *Birds in the Garden and How to Attract Them,* Reynal & Hitchcock, 1939; *A Book of Wild Flowers* (illustrated by Edith F. Johnston), Macmillan, 1939; *A Book of Garden Flowers* (illustrated by Johnston), Macmillan, 1940; *How the Hurricane Helped* (illustrated by Winifred Bromhall), Knopf, 1940; *Trees of the Countryside* (illustrated by Alice Bird), Knopf, 1942; *Abe and His Girl Friend, Amble,* Binfords & Mort, 1945; *A Book of Wayside Fruits* (illustrated by Johnston), Macmillan, 1945; *Wildlife of the Pacific Northwest,* Binfords & Mort, 1954; (with Daniel E. Stuntz) *The Savory Wild Mushroom,* University of Washington Press, 1962, revised and enlarged edition edited by D. E. Stuntz, 1971; (with Roger Tory Peterson) *A Field Guide to Wildflowers of Northeastern and North-Central North America,* Houghton, 1968.

SIDELIGHTS: Ms. McKenny's interest in nature began when she was very young. One of her earlier books, *Your City Garden,* was co-authored with Edward L. D. Seymour and deal with planning and planting a garden in an urban dwelling. A reviewer for *Books* noted: "Both its authors are experienced horticulturists and have first-hand knowledge of the problems the gardener in town must face. They handle their subject straightforwardly and illustrate it freely with fine photographs."

Ms. McKenny has also worked with illustrator Edith F. Johnston in putting out three practical guide books on botany. Their *Book of Wayside Fruits* described over thirty different fruits found in the countryside. "Another nature book from such successful collaborators [McKenny and Johnston] will be greeted with enthusiasm by those who know their previous offerings," wrote a critic for *Weekly Book Review.*

The author's latest book, *A Field Guide to Wildflowers of Northeastern and North-Central North America,* was jointly written with Roger T. Peterson. A *New York Times* reviewer commented:" One of the many very nice things about the book is that common, as well as technical, names are used with illustrations. It is a book for laymen but one having special value for the pros, too."

BIOGRAPHICAL/CRITICAL SOURCES: Books, May 2, 1937; *Weekly Book Review,* July 8, 1945; *New York Times,* May 25, 1968.*

* * *

McKINNEY, Don(ald Lee) 1923-

PERSONAL: Born July 12, 1923, in Evanston, Ill.; son of Guy Doane (a reporter) and Cora (Brenton) McKinney; married Mary Francis Joyce, December 14, 1958; children: Jennifer Joyce, Douglas Guy. *Education:* University of North Carolina, B.A., 1948. *Politics:* Democrat. *Home:* 152 East Rocks Rd., Norwalk, Conn. 06851. *Agent:* Emilie Jacobson, Curtis Brown, Ltd., 575 Madison Ave., New York, N.Y. 10022. *Office:* 230 Park Ave., New York, N.Y. 10022.

CAREER/WRITINGS: John Wiley & Sons, New York City, textbook salesman, 1949-52; free-lance writer of comic books, fiction, and short articles, 1952-54; *True* magazine, New York City, assistant managing editor, 1955-62; *Saturday Evening Post,* New York City, articles editor, 1962-69; *New York Daily News,* New York City, features editor, 1969; *McCall's* magazine, New York City, managing editor, 1969—. Instructor in journalism, New York University, 1975—; lecturer. *Military service:* U.S. Naval Reserve, 1943-46; became ensign. *Member:* American Society of Magazine Editors.

SIDELIGHTS: McKinney told *CA:* "I was always interested in journalism, probably because of my father's reporting career and the fact that many of his friends were reporters or writers. I came to New York to get a job on a magazine, and after five years I got one and have been in magazines ever since. I am and always have been interested in sports—tennis, golf, fishing, etc. Except for my time on a cargo ship during World War II, my travel has been limited to the United States and occasional vacations in the Caribbean."

* * *

MCKINNEY, Gene 1922-

PERSONAL: Born October 2, 1922, in Fort Worth, Tex.; son of B. B. (a composer) and Leila (Routh) McKinney; married Treysa Seely (a teacher), September 1, 1947; children: Mike. *Education:* Baylor University, B.A., 1948, M.A., 1949; attended Columbia University, 1950. *Home:* 423 Fantasia, San Antonio, Tex. 78216. *Office:* Ruth Taylor Theater, Trinity University, 715 Stadium Dr., San Antonio, Tex. 78284.

CAREER: Baylor University, Waco Tex., professor of playwriting, 1948-63; Dallas Theater Center, Dallas, Tex., professor of playwriting and playwright-in-residence, 1963—. Visiting professor of playwriting at Southwest Texas State University, 1973. Script consultant for Radio and TV Commission, 1955-67. *Military service:* U.S. Army, 1942-46; became second lieutenant. *Member:* American Theater Association, Writers Guild of America, Creative Writing Teachers of Texas.

WRITINGS—Plays: "How Are the Mighty Fallen" (one-act), first produced in Waco, Texas at Baylor Theatre, July, 1947; *The Ivory Tower, Two Flights Down* (one-act; first produced in Waco at Baylor Theatre, January, 1948), Baylor University Press, 1948; "The Answer is Two" (three-act), first produced in Waco at Baylor Theatre, January, 1952; *A Different Drummer* (three-act; first produced in Waco at Baylor Theatre, January, 1955), Samuel French, 1966; "Three Zeroes and One One" (one-act), first produced in Waco at Baylor Theatre, July, 1957; "Of Time and the River" (three-act; adaptation of novel by Thomas Wolfe), first produced in Waco at Baylor Theatre, April, 1959; "The Cross-Eyed Bear" (three-act), first produced in Dallas, Tex. at Dallas Theatre Center, February, 1960; "Everybody Plays, Nobody Wins" (one-act), first produced in San Antonio, Tex. at Ruth Taylor Theatre, July, 1970; *The People in the Glass Paperweight* (one-act; first produced in Dallas at Alpha Omega Theatre, January, 1970), Samuel French,

1971; "When You're by Yourself, You're Alone" (one-act), Samuel French, 1975.

Screenplays: "Emergency Signal X," produced by Leake Productions, 1950; "Ministry of Healing," 1951; "Decade of Decision," 1961; "The Mime of Etienne Decroux," 1961.

Also author of television scripts produced independently and by NBC, ABC, and CBS.

WORK IN PROGRESS: A full-length play, untitled as yet.

SIDELIGHTS: McKinney told *CA:* "I try to squeeze in my own writing while dealing with a large group of student writers (I teach at Trinity University in San Antonio, and also at the Dallas Theater Center—so I am one of the few writers-in-residence who commutes). I supervise large and successful playwriting programs at the two theaters, and therefore have little time left for my own creative work. However, each summer I go to Mexico, and spend two months working on my own projects."

* * *

McLAREN, N(orman) Loyall 1892(?)-1977

1892(?)—October 23, 1977; American accountant and author of books on tax laws and management. McLaren died in San Francisco, Calif. Obituaries: *New York Times,* October 25, 1977.

* * *

McLAUGHLIN, David J(ohn) 1936-

PERSONAL: Born April 3, 1936, in Boston, Mass.; son of John and Katherine (McMahon) McLaughlin; divorced; children: Lori, John Randall. *Education:* College of the Holy Cross, B.A., 1958; Fordham University, M.A., 1959. *Home:* 20 East 10th St., New York, N.Y. 10003. *Office:* McKinsey & Co., 245 Park Ave., New York, N.Y. 10017.

CAREER: McKinsey & Co., New York, N.Y., associate, 1963-65; Eastern Airlines, New York City, vice-president of personnel, 1966-67, vice-president of planning, 1967-68; McKinsey & Co. (management consultants), principal, 1969—. Member of advisory board of Erhard Sensitivity Training (EST). *Military service:* U.S. Army National Guard, 1959. *Member:* New York Athletic Club, Sachem Head Yacht Club.

WRITINGS: (With George Foote) *Corporate Retirement Plans,* McKinsey & Co., 1965; *The Executive Money Map,* McGraw, 1975; *Managing People: A Strategic Challenge to the Threshold Company,* McKinsey & Co., 1977; *Some Insights on Life and Love: A Personal Collection of the Writing of J. Krishnamurti,* privately printed, 1977. Contributor to *Encyclopedia of Professional Management,* 1978; contributor to business, finance, and personnel journals.

WORK IN PROGRESS: Research on compensation, career planning, and personnel management.

* * *

McMANUS, Marjorie 1950-

PERSONAL: Born April 13, 1950, in Reading, Pa.; daughter of Frank L. (a corporate manager) and Bernice (Haage) McManus. *Education:* Ohio University, B.S., 1972. *Home:* 220 H, Yonkers Ave., Apt. 19c, Yonkers, N.Y. 10701. *Office:* Folio Magazine Publishing Corp., 125 Elm St., New Canaan, Conn. 06840.

CAREER/WRITINGS: Beverage Industry magazine, New York, N.Y., assistant editor, 1972; *Folio: The Magazine for Magazine Management,* New Canaan, Conn., executive editor, 1972—. Notable assignments include coverage of postal affairs. Free-lance managing editor, *Book Production Industry* magazine, 1974-77. *Awards, honors:* Golden Keys Award, International Association of Printing House Craftsmen, 1974; Jesse H. Neal Editorial Achievement Award, American Business Press, 1975.

WORK IN PROGRESS: Handbook of Magazine Publishing.

* * *

McMILLAN, Bruce 1947-

PERSONAL: Born May 10, 1947, in Boston, Mass.; son of Frank H., Jr. and Virginia M. W. McMillan; married V. Therese Loughran; children: Brett Brownrigg. *Education:* University of Maine, B.S., 1969. *Home address:* Old County Rd., Shapleigh, Me. 04076.

CAREER: Maine Public Broadcasting Network, Orono, director and photographer, 1969, producer-director, 1970-73; caretaker of McGee Island, Me., 1973-75; photographer and writer, 1975—.

WRITINGS—All with own photographs: *Finestkind O'Day: Lobstering in Maine* (juvenile), Lippincott, 1977; *The Alphabet Symphony* (juvenile picture book), Greenwillow Books, 1977; *The Remarkable Riderless Runaway Tricycle* (juvenile), Houghton, 1978; *Punography* (adult photography), Viking, 1978. Contributor to *Down East.*

WORK IN PROGRESS: Books for children and adults, with his own photographs.

SIDELIGHTS: McMillan told *CA:* "I consider myself a photographer who also writes. I find myself high on books and low on television. That is why I am out of television and now working entirely on books.

"In the juveniles field, I am an advocate of more and better photography in children's books. I'm quite pleased with how open juveniles editors are to photography, whether alone or with text.

"My photography has been learned by doing over a period of time, starting as a youngster. Over the past ten years I have exhibited and won contests (a trip to Hawaii) and every time I shoot, I learn more. My writing skills were deficient throughout my school years. During my two-year stay on McGee Island I worked specifically on improving my writing.

"My subject matter so far has come from my immediate surroundings, and my interests."

* * *

MC SWIGAN, Marie 1907-1962

PERSONAL: Born May 22, 1907, in Pittsburgh, Pa.; daughter of Andrew Stephen (a newsman) and Genevieve (Brady) McSwigan. *Education:* University of Pittsburgh, B.A. *Politics:* Democrat. *Religion:* Catholic. *Residence:* Pittsburgh, Pa.

CAREER: Reporter and author. Reporter and feature writer on the staffs of Pittsburgh, Pa. newspapers, 1927-37; assistant publicist for Carnegie Institute, Fine Arts Department; worked in public relations for the University of Pittsburgh; served as director of St. Rosella's Foundling and Maternity Hospital. *Member:* Woman's Press Club, Authors' Club, Catholic Business and Professional Woman's Club, Pi Beta Phi, Alpha Lambda Nu.

WRITINGS—All published by Dutton, except as noted: *The Weather House People* (illustrated by Dorothy Bayley),

Lippincott, 1940; *Snow Treasure* (illustrated by Mary Reardon), 1942, reprinted, 1967; *Five on a Merry-Go-Round* (illustrated by M. Reardon), 1943; *Hi, Barney!* (illustrated by Corinne Dillon), 1946; *Juan of Manila* (illustrated by Margaret Ayer), 1947; *Our Town Has a Circus* (illustrated by Peter Burchard), 1949; *Binnie Latches On* (illustrated by Jessie Robinson), 1950; (contributor with Alma B. Weber and others) *Coonskin for a General,* American Book Co., 1951; *The News Is Good* (illustrated by Jill Elgin), 1952; *Three's a Crowd,* 1953; *All Aboard for Freedom!* (illustrated by E. Harper Johnson), 1954; *Small Miracle* (illustrated by Don Lambo), 1958; *Athlete of Christ: St. Nicholas of Flue, 1417-1487,* Newman Press, 1959; (editor with Leon Anthony Arkus) *John Kane: Painter,* University of Pittsburgh Press, 1971.

Also contributor to various magazines.

SIDELIGHTS: Marie McSwigan began writing children's stories as a diversion from her job. She won national acclaim with the publication of her second book, *Snow Treasure,* in 1942. It tells the story of how Norwegian children loaded gold bullion on their sleds, coasted down the hillside with it under the noses of the Nazis, and hid it under their snowmen.

Many of Marie McSwigan's books are based on fact. *All Abroad for Freedom* relates the story of how Czechs escaped by train into the United States zone of Germany in 1951. The *New York Herald Tribune* said: "Dr. Jan Papanek writes a moving introduction. The illustrations are excellent, giving vivid portraits of young and old, of the train and of Prague." *Kirkus* commented: "At times melodramatic, at times long winded, this has its moments of suspense and serious character study that seem to spring from actual experience. Studied drawings by Harper Johnson add to the picture of a troubled country."

Marie McSwigan made four trips to Europe, three to the Caribbean, two to California, as well as a river cruise from Cincinnati to New Orleans.

BIOGRAPHICAL/CRITICAL SOURCES: Kirkus, September 15, 1950, August 15, 1954; *New York Times,* December 17, 1950; *New York Herald Tribune Book Review,* November 14, 1954.*

(Died July 16, 1962)

* * *

McVAY, Gordon 1941-

PERSONAL: Born April 23, 1941, in North Shields, England; son of James Ramsay (a teacher) and Mary (a teacher; maiden name, Robison) McVay; married Kathleen Adams (a teacher), August 16, 1969; children: Martin James, Mary Elizabeth. *Education:* New College, Oxford, B.A. (honors), 1963, Ph.D., 1969. *Home:* 31 Oakfields Rd., Cringleford, Norwich, Norfolk, England. *Office:* School of European Studies, University of East Anglia, Norwich, Norfolk, England.

CAREER: University of Wales, University College of North Wales, Bangor, assistant lecturer in Russian, 1967-69; University of East Anglia, Norwich, Norfolk, England, lecturer in European studies, 1969—. *Awards, honors:* Leverhulme Award, 1977.

WRITINGS: Esenin: A Life, Ardis, 1976. Contributor to Slavic studies and language Journals.

WORK IN PROGRESS: Esenin and His Friends, with previously unpublished documents and photographs; editing "Esenin Reprint Series," ten volumes, for Mouette Press.

SIDELIGHTS: McVay writes: "My particular area of interest is Russian literature, especially Russian poetry of the 1920's. My first concern was Sergei Esenin; my interests have widened to include Esenin's colleagues, the Imaginist poets (Ivnev, Kusikov, Mariengof, etc.) and peasant poets (Klyuev, Klychkov, etc.). I have visited the Soviet Union seven times, and have spent many months in Soviet archives, unearthing unpublished materials."

AVOCATIONAL INTERESTS: The theater, playing and watching cricket.

* * *

MEBANE, Mary E(lizabeth) 1933-

PERSONAL: Born June 26, 1933, in Durham, N.C.; daughter of Samuel Nathaniel (a farmer) and Carrie (a factory worker; maiden name, Brandon) Mebane. *Education:* North Carolina College at Durham, B.A., 1955; University of North Carolina, M.A., 1961, Ph.D., 1973. *Home address:* P.O. Box 1321, Columbia, S.C. 29202. *Office:* Department of English, University of South Carolina, Columbia, S.C.

CAREER: English teacher in public schools in Durham, N.C., 1955-60; North Carolina College at Durham (now North Carolina Central University), instructor in English, 1960-65; South Carolina State College, Orangeburg, associate professor of English, 1967-74; University of South Carolina, Columbia, professor of English, 1974—. *Member:* International P.E.N., International Platform Association, Authors Guild, Modern Language Association of America, National Council of Teachers of English, College Language Association, South Atlantic Modern Language Association.

WRITINGS: Work anthologized in *A Galaxy of Black Writing,* edited by R. Baird Shuman, Moore Publishing, 1970, and *The Eloquence of Protest,* edited by Harrison E. Salisbury, Houghton, 1972.

Author of "Take a Sad Song" (two-act play), first produced in Columbia, S.C., at Playwrights' Corner, February, 1975.

WORK IN PROGRESS: An autobiography.

SIDELIGHTS: Mebane told *CA:* "My writings center on the black folk of the south, post-1960. It is my belief that the black folk are the most creative, viable people that America has produced. They just don't know it." *Avocational interests:* Reading.

BIOGRAPHICAL/CRITICAL SOURCES: T. G. Rush and Carol F. Myers, editors, *Black American Writers: Past and Present: A Biographical & Bibliographical Dictionary,* two volumes, Scarecrow, 1975; *Esquire,* February, 1976.

* * *

MEDARY, Marjorie 1890-

PERSONAL: Born July 24, 1890, in Waukon, Iowa; daughter of a newspaper editor and publisher. *Education:* Attended Cornell University; Northwestern University, M.A.

CAREER: Teacher in the New England area, 1939-1941, and in Indianapolis, Ind., beginning 1941; worked part-time in the Bookshop for Boys and Girls lending library, Boston, Mass.; became an editor of textbooks for a publishing firm in New York, N.Y.; author of children's books.

WRITINGS: Orange Winter: A Story of Florida in 1880 (illustrated by Harold Sichel), Longmans, Green, 1931; *Prairie Anchorage* (illustrated by John Gincano), Longmans, Green, 1933; *Topgallant: A Herring Gull* (illustrated by Lynd Ward), H. Smith & R. Haas, 1935; *College in Crinoline,* Longmans, Green, 1937; *Joan and the Three Deer* (illustrated by Kurt Wiese), Random House, 1939; *Edra of the Islands* (illustrated by Dorothy Bayley), Longmans, Green, 1940; *Buckeye Boy,* Longmans, Green, 1944; *The Store at Crisscross Corners* (illustrated by Janet Smalley), Abingdon-Cokesbury, 1946; *Prairie Printer,* Longmans, Green, 1949; *Each One Teach One: Frank Laubach, Friend to Millions,* Longmans, Green, 1954; *Under Many a Star,* Peter Pauper Press, 1975.

SIDELIGHTS: Marjorie Medary took an interest in writing at an early age. The author sent out manuscripts of her work throughout her young adult life, but didn't decide to devote her full time to a writing career until she attended a Bread Loaf Writers' Conference during a summer recess from her teaching position.

Ms. Medary is a direct descendent of pioneers who settled in Iowa in the 1850's. Several of the author's books are based on that eventful period when America's frontier was expanding. Ms. Medary's *Crinoline College* tells the story of a young girl who attended a coeducational college in the mid-nineteenth century. "Here is a picture, replete with minute and vivid detail, of an important era in education. Marjorie Medary has caught the flavor of the times in her portrait of very real young people," noted a critic for the *New York Times.*

The author's own childhood adventures also provided her with ideas for her books. Her memory of experiences on Grand Manan Island (off the southeastern coast of Canada) developed into *Joan and the Three Deer.*

Buckeye Boy is about a young orphan boy and his desire to learn the printing trade. A *Kirkus* reviewer observed: "[The book has] interesting bits of canal life, some good gang fights, a glimpse into the printing and politics of the day." In reviewing the same book, a *Saturday Review of Literature* critic wrote; "Clearer than any 'vocational' story, this vivid and well written tale reveals the struggle and the growth of youth."

BIOGRAPHICAL/CRITICAL SOURCES: New York Times, August 29, 1937; *Kirkus,* July 1, 1944; *Saturday Review of Literature,* December 9, 1944, November 12, 1949.*

* * *

MEEK, Loyal George 1918-

PERSONAL: Born September 10, 1918, in Cedar Rapids, Iowa; son of Charles William (a minister and lawyer) and Mina (Armstrong) Meek; married Lois Tankersley, September 28, 1941; children: Jeremy, Andrew, Geoffrey, Margaret. *Education:* Coe College, A.B., 1940. *Office address: Phoenix Gazette,* P.O. Box 1950, Phoenix, Ariz. 85001.

CAREER/WRITINGS: Cedar Rapids Gazette, Cedar Rapids, Iowa, reporter, state editor, editorialist, 1941-60; U.S. Senate, Washington, D.C., special assistant, 1961-62; *Milwaukee Sentinel,* Milwaukee, Wis., editorialist, 1962-73; *Phoenix Gazette,* Phoenix, Ariz., editor, 1973—. Member of Phoenix Public Library advisory board, Arizona Tax Research Association, and Arizona Academy. *Military service:* U.S. Army, 1942-46. *Member:* American Society of Newspaper Editors, Sigma Delta Chi. *Awards, honors:* Sweepstakes award from Iowa Daily Press Association, 1951; editorial writing award from United States Industrial Council, 1970; honor certificate from Freedom Foundation, 1971.

SIDELIGHTS: Meek told *CA:* "I believe the American press should be at least as zealous in exposing foreign government secrets as it is in exposing United States government secrets."

MEEKER, Oden 1919(?)-1976

PERSONAL: Son of Lawrence Meeker; married wife, Olivia (divorced, 1952); married Bertie Moore. *Education:* Princeton University, B.A., 1941. *Residence:* Woodstock, N.Y.

CAREER: Writer and social welfare leader. *Paris Herald Tribune,* columnist with first wife, Olivia, post-World War II period; Cooperative for American Relief Everywhere Inc. (CARE), chief executive, Laos, 1954-55, Hong Kong, 1956, India, 1957-60, Israel, 1965. *War time service:* Worked for British Information Services in the United States during World War II. *Awards, honors:* Anisfield-Wolf award, 1955, for *Report on Africa;* National Council of Christians and Jews citation for promoting understanding between persons of diversified backgrounds.

WRITINGS—All published by Scribner, except as noted: (With wife, Olivia) *And Points South* (illustrated by Barney Tobey), Random House, 1947; *Report on Africa,* 1954; *The Little World of Laos* (photographs by Homer Page), 1959; *Israel Reborn,* 1964; *Israel: Ancient Land, Young Nation,* 1968.

Also contributor to numerous periodicals, including *New Yorker* and *Harper's.*

SIDELIGHTS: Meeker travelled to 130 countries during his lifetime. Many of his writings were based on his trips abroad. His book, *And Points South,* was an account of a ten month trip through Latin America. A *Saturday Review* critic commented: "In this impressionistic book so full of gentle caricatures you may find here and there a strong commentary. The authors give a truthful account of some peculiarities and eccentricities of the Latin American people, but the account is in no way offensive."

The world traveler recorded his observations of the economic, social and political conditions of Laos in his *Little World of Laos.* A critic for the *New York Herald Tribune Book Review* wrote "This reviewer found *The Little World of Laos* particularly pleasant going. A never failing sense of humor, the colloquial style of any good drawing room ranconteur, and original figures of speech paly a large part in the effect."

Meeker's *Report on Africa* covered his trip to that continent in 1952. "The author is offering us a somewhat novel kind of reportage which, besides being immensely informative and genuinely enlightening, has the virtue of being consistently entertaining," noted a reviewer for *Atlantic.*

The author also lived in Israel for several years. In his *Israel Reborn,* Meeker dealt with a brief historical background of present-day Israel.

BIOGRAPHICAL/CRITICAL SOURCES: Saturday Review of Literature, November 22, 1947; *Atlantic,* September, 1954, *New York Herald Tribune Book Review,* March 29, 1959.

OBITUARIES: New York Times, January 20, 1976; *AB Bookman's Weekly,* April 5, 1976.*

(Died January 19, 1976)

* * *

MEER, Fatima 1929-

PERSONAL: Born August 12, 1929, in Durban, South Africa; daughter of Moosa Ismail (a journalist) and Rachael (Farrel) Meer; married Ismail Meer (an attorney), March 11, 1954; children: Shamim Marie, Shehnaz, Rashid. *Education:* University of Natal, B.A. and M.A., 1956. *Religion:*

Muslim. *Home:* 148 Burnwood Rd., Sydenham, Durban, South Africa. *Office:* Department of Sociology, University of Natal, King George V Ave., Durban, Natal 40001, South Africa.

CAREER: University of Natal, Natal, South Africa, senior lecturer in sociology, 1956—. Chairperson, Natal Education Trust, 1973—; executive member, Ghandi Memorial Trust of South Africa. Vice-president and co-founder, Institute for Black Research. *Member;* Black Womens Federation of South Africa (founder and president, 1976, honorary life president, 1977—), Durban District Women's League (secretary, 1952-56). *Awards, honors:* Institute of Advanced Study research fellow, 1971.

WRITINGS: Portrait of Indian South Africans, Avon House, 1970; *Race and Suicide in South Africa,* Routledge & Kegan Paul, 1976; *The Ghetto People,* Africa Trust, 1976. Also author of *Apprenticeship of a Mahatma,* Phoenix Trust.

WORK IN PROGRESS: Sowetto Disturbances; Black Housing in South Africa.

SIDELIGHTS: Meer told *CA:* "My responses have been deeply influenced by my experiences as a Black person in a racist South African society. I am overwhelmed by the injustices that suffocate me, and the disparities that thwart my attempts to find a South African identity in my country. I have now subscribed to the dictum of academia for the sake of academia. Researching and writing means relevance to may social surrounding. In this respect, though a sociologist, I admit my self to being completely involved and hence subjective."

*   *   *

MEERHAEGHE, M.A.G. van
See van MEERHAEGHE, Marcel Alfons Gilbert
*   *   *

MEISLER, Stanley 1931-

PERSONAL: Born May 14, 1931, in New York, N.Y.; son of Meyer (a paperhanger) and Jean (Wolf) Meisler; married Gloria Greenwood, September 28, 1960 (divorced); married Susan Mitchell (a secretary), April 15, 1973; children: Sarah (deceased), Samuel, Joshua, Michael, Michele. *Education:* City College (now of the City University of New York), B.A., 1952; further study at University of California, Berkeley, 1952 and 1962. *Religion:* Jewish. *Home:* Zurbano, 71, Madrid-3, Spain. *Office: Los Angeles Times,* Marques de Cubas-12, Madrid-14, Spain.

CAREER/WRITINGS: Middletown Journal, Middletown, Ohio, newsman, 1953-54; Associated Press, New York, N.Y., correspondent in New Orleans, 1954-57, and Washington, D.C., 1958-64; U.S. Peace Corps, Washington, D.C., deputy director of Office of Evaluation and Research, 1964-67; *Los Angeles Times,* Los Angeles, Calif., correspondent in Africa, 1967-73, Mexico, 1973-76, and Spain, 1976—. Notable assignments include coverage of the U.S. House of Representatives, the Nigerian Civil War, and the dismantling of Franco institutions in Spain. Contributor of articles to *Atlantic, Foreign Affairs, Nation,* and other periodicals.

*   *   *

MELFI, Leonard 1935-

PERSONAL: Born February 21, 1935, in Binghamton, N.Y.; son of Leonard John (a restaurant proprietor) and Louise Marie (Gennarelli) Melfi. *Education:* Attended St. Bonaventure University, 1956-57. *Politics:* Democrat. *Home:* 45 West 89th St., New York, N.Y. 10021. *Agent:* Helen Harvey Associates, 110 West 57th St., New York, N.Y. 10019.

CAREER: Playwright. Lecturer in contemporary theatre, New York University, 1969-70; taught playwright's workshop at Circle in the Square Theatre School (downtown), New York City, 1969-70; instructor in playwrighting at Circle in the Square (uptown), New York City, 1974; actor in "Sweet Suite" and "Beautiful," 1974 and 1975. Painter. Has also worked as a waiter and carpenter. Member of board of Cafe La Mama; panel member of New York State Council on the Arts. *Member:* Dramatists Guild, Playwrights Wing of Actors' Studio, The Forum, New York Theatre Strategy. *Awards, honors:* Selected as outstanding new playwright of the year by Eugene O'Neill Memorial Theatre Foundation, 1966; Rockefeller grant, 1967, 1968.

WRITINGS—Plays: "Birdbath" (one-act), first produced at Theatre Genesis, June 11, 1965; "Ferryboat" (one-act), first produced in New York City at Theatre Genesis, September 2, 1965; "Times Square," first produced in New York City at Cafe La Mama, 1966, produced as a musical at Los Angeles Cultural Center, April, 1977; "Niagra Falls" (full-length), first produced at Cafe La Mama, January 18, 1966; "Lunchtime" (one-act), first produced in London, 1966; "Halloween" (one-act), first produced in New York City, October 27, 1966; "Jack and Jill" (one-act) first produced at Cafe La Mama, December 12, 1967, produced as part of "Oh! Calcutta!" on Broadway at Eden Theatre, June 1, 1969; "The Shirt" (one-act), given as a staged reading at Eugene O'Neill Memorial Theatre in Waterford, Conn., 1967, produced in New York City, June, 1977; "Stars and Stripes" (one-act) produced in New York City at Cafe au Go Go, 1968; "Night" (one-act) produced on Broadway at Henry Miller's Theatre, November 29, 1968; "Cinque" (one-act), first produced in London at Royal Court Theatre, May, 1970, produced as musical "Horse Opera" at Cafe La Mama, December 6, 1974.

Unpublished plays: "Lazy Baby Susan" (one-act), first produced at Cafe La Mama, October 26, 1962; "Sunglasses" (one-act), first produced at Theatre Genesis, June 11, 1965; "Pussies and Rookies" (one-act), first produced at Theatre Genesis, 1965; "Disfigurations" (one-act), first produced in Los Angeles at Mark Taper Forum, 1967; "Stimulation" (one-act), produced in New York City, 1968; "The Breech Baby," produced in New York City at Loft Theatre, 1968; "Having Fun in the Bathroom" (full-length), produced at New York Poets Festival Theatre, 1969; "Wet and Dry" and "Alive" (two one-acts), produced together at Loft Theatre, 1969; "The Jones Man" (full-length), first produced in Provincetown, Mass., at Act IV Theatre, 1969; "Eddie and Susanna in Love" (one-act), first produced in New York City at Manhattan Theatre Club, May 1, 1973; "Ah! Wine!" (full-length), first produced in New York City, January 11, 1974; "Beautiful." (full-length), first produced in New York City at Theatre for the New City, 1974; "Porno Stars at Home" (full-length), first produced in New York City at Courtyard Playhouse, January, 1976; "Fantasies at the Frick" (full-length), produced in New York City at Open Space in Soho, November, 1976; "Butterfaces," first produced at New York Shakespeare Festival, 1977; "Taffy's Taxi," first produced in Pasadena, Calif., at Pasadena Playhouse, July, 1977; "Erotic Behavior Upstate," as yet unproduced.

Collections: *Encounters: Six One-Act Plays* (contains

"Birdbath," "Lunchtime," "Halloween," "Ferryboat," "The Shirt," and "Times Square"), Random House, 1967, revised edition, Samuel French, 1976; (with Israel Horovitz and Terence McNally) *Morning, Noon, and Night,* Random House, 1969. Plays represented in anthologies, including *Best Short Plays of the World Theatre, 1958-1967,* edited by Stanley Richards, Crown, 1967; *Collision Course,* Random House, 1968; *A Methuen Playscript: Three Contemporary Playwrights,* Methuen, 1968; *Oh! Calcutta!,* Grove, 1969; *New Theatre for Now,* edited by Edward Parone, Dell, 1971; *The Off Off Broadway Book,* Bobbs-Merrill, 1972; *Spontaneous Combustion: Eight New American Plays,* edited by Rochelle Owens, Winter House, 1972; *Best American Plays: 1965-1973,* edited by Clive Barnes, Crown, 1975.

Teleplays: "The Rainbow Rest," National Broadcasting Company (NBC), 1967; "Puck! Puck! Puck!," National Educational Television (NET), 1968; "Birdbath," NET, 1970; "Ferryboat," WNYC, 1977.

Author of screenplay "Lady Liberty," 1971. Contributor to *New York.* Also author of two unpublished novels, *The End of Marriage Forever!* and *Bright Angel Bright,* and two unproduced screenplays, "Good Son" and "Gloria Girl."

WORK IN PROGRESS: "The Columbus Day Parade," a play commissioned by the Kennedy Center; two plays, "Paradise Plus" and "Dispossessed"; a musical with songs by Harold Arlen, "Clippety Clop and Clementine"; a play about his father, "Life of a Gentleman"; a play about New Year's Eve in the Bowery, "B.V.M."; "Rusty and Rico and Lena and Louie," a full-length play; "Taxi Tales," three related one-act plays.

SIDELIGHTS: Melfi's father likes to say about his son's vocation: "He does the same thing Shakespeare did." The way Melfi does it was praised by critic Joan Simon, who wrote: "Melfi is essentially a playwright of love, not Luv. He explores not the clashing crudities of modern sex but the subtleties of modern loving, and he does so with wit, wonder and infectious good humor." Clives Barnes commented that Melfi's play "Night" is written with "all the loving twisting and reiteration of Gertrude Stein," and he later recommended "Porno Stars at Home" for "dashes of bright bitchy dialogue and a genuinely intriguing idea."

Although he has written fiction as well as screenplays for movies and television, Melfi remains a man of the theatre, describing its special attraction this way: "There's something about when you put people together and things come out of their mouths one after another, and action happens. And the fact that you think of it coming to life, and there's an audience. This makes me want to write more and more, and the more plays I write the more I dig it. So I can't stop."

BIOGRAPHICAL/CRITICAL SOURCES: Life, October 17, 1967; *New York Post,* November 28, 1968; *New York Times,* November 28, 1968, December 10, 1968, February 7, 1976; Otis Guernsey, editor, *Playwrights, Lyricists, Composers,* Dodd, 1974.

* * *

MENCHER, Melvin 1927-

PERSONAL: Born January 25, 1927, in New York; son of Peter and Theresa (Sherman) Mencher; married Helen Chamberlain, August 27, 1947; children: Thomas Chamberlain, Marianne Theresa, Nicholas Trowbridge. *Education:* Attended University of New Mexico, 1943-44; University of Colorado, B.A., 1947. *Office:* Graduate School of Journalism, Columbia University, New York, N.Y. 10027.

CAREER: United Press Association, New York, N.Y., reporter for Southwest Division, in Santa Fe, N.M., 1947-51; *Albuquerque Journal,* Albuquerque, N.M., statehouse correspondent and reporter, 1952-54; *Fresno Bee,* Fresno, Calif., investigative reporter, 1954-58; University of Kansas, Lawrence, assistant professor of journalism, 1958-62; Columbia University, New York, N.Y., assistant professor, 1962-65, associate professor, 1965-75, professor of journalism, 1975—. Executive secretary of University of Kansas-University of Costa Rica exchange program, 1960-61, associate director of summer program for minority education journalism, 1971. Evaluator for New England Daily Newspaper Survey, 1973.

MEMBER: Association for Education in Journalism, National Council of College Publications Advisers. *Awards, honors:* Nieman fellow at Harvard University, 1952-53.

WRITINGS: FNMA Guide to Buying and Selling Your House, Doubleday, 1973; *News Reporting and Writing,* W. C. Brown, 1977. Costa Rica correspondent for *Christian Science Monitor,* 1962. Contributor to professional journals.

SIDELIGHTS: Mencher writes: "As a journalist, my major interest was in political coverage and investigative reporting, and I have continued that interest as a teacher of journalism at the University of Kansas and at Columbia University. Early in my career I understood that the responsible journalist cannot practice his or her craft in a value-free vacuum, and I have sought to show in my work and in my teaching that the best journalism, the highest achievement of the journalist, is reached by those whose passion is to tell people essential truths about the world they live in."

* * *

MENDOZA, George 1934-

PERSONAL Born June 2, 1934, in New York, N.Y.; son of George and Elizabeth Mendoza; married Nicole Sekora, 1967; children: Ashley. *Education:* Columbia University, B.A., 1953; graduate study at State Maritime College, 1954-56. *Residence:* New York, N.Y.

CAREER: Poet and author of children's books. *Awards, honors:* Lewis G. Carroll Shelf Award, 1968, for *The Hunter I Might Have Been.*

WRITINGS—All children's books: *And Amedeo Asked, How Does One Become a Man?,* Braziller, 1959; (with Wendy Sanford) *The Puma and the Pearl,* Walker & Co., 1962; *The Hawk Is Humming: A Novel,* Bobbs-Merrill, 1964; *A Piece of String,* Astor-Honor, 1965; *Gwot! Horribly Funny Hairticklers,* Harper, 1967; *The Crack in the Wall and Other Terribly Weird Tales,* Dial, 1968; *Wart Snake in a Fig Tree,* Dial, 1968; *The Gillygoofang,* Dial, 1968; *Flowers and Grasses and Weeds,* Funk, 1968; *The Hunter I Might Have Been,* Astor-Honor, 1968; *The Practical Man,* Lothrop, 1968; *And I Must Hurry for the Sea Is Coming In . . . ,* Prentice-Hall, 1969; *A Beastly Alphabet,* Grosset, 1969; *The Digger Wasp,* Dial, 1969; *Herman's Hat,* Doubleday, 1969; *The Starfish Trilogy,* Funk, 1969; (compiler) *The World From My Window: Poems and Drawings* (children's writings), Hawthorn, 1969.

Are You My Friend?, Prentice-Hall, 1970; *The Good Luck Spider and Other Bad Luck Stories,* Doubleday, 1970; *The Inspector,* Doubleday, 1970; *The Marcel Marceau Alphabet Book,* Doubleday, 1970; *The Mist Men and Other Poems,* Doubleday, 1970; *The Christmas Tree Alphabet Book,* World Publishing, 1971; *Big Frog, Little Pond,* McCall Publishing, 1971; *The Fearsome Brat,* Lothrop, 1971; *Fish in the Sky,* Doubleday, 1971; *Goodbye, River, Goodbye,* Doubleday, 1971; *The Hunter, the Tick, and the Gumberoo,* Cowles Book, 1971; *The Marcel Marceau Counting Book,* Doubleday, 1971; *Moonfish and Owl Scratchings,* Grosset, 1971; *Moonstring,* World Publishing, 1971; *The Scarecrow Clock,* Holt, 1971; *The Scribbler,* Holt, 1971; *The Thumbtown Toad,* Prentice-Hall, 1971; *Poem for Putting to Sea,* Hawthorn, 1972; *The Alphabet Boat: A Seagoing Alphabet Book,* American Heritage Press, 1972; *Sesame Street Book of Opposites with Zero Mostel,* Platt, 1974; (with Prasanna Rao) *Shadowplay,* Holt, 1974; *Fishing the Morning Lonely,* Freshet Press, P974; *Norman Rockwell's Americana ABC,* Dell, 1975; (with Carol Burnett) *What I Want to Be When I Grow Up,* Simon & Schuster, 1975; (with Howard Minsky) *Doug Henning's Magic Book,* Ballantine, in press.

Also author of screenplays, including "Petals from a Poem Flower," and "You Show Me Yours and I'll Show You Mine."

SIDELIGHTS: Sea, lapping below the keel of his home-made sloop lost at sea without jib or rudder, led young Mendoza to his decision to be a writer: this rhythm, he found, could be carried into language. Later Mondoza sailed alone across the Atlantic Ocean twice, from Stony Brook to Southampton, and each voyage produced a book. In 1959, encouraged by Fannie Hurst, he decided to "transmute some of the feelings into words," and began writing children's books.

Frequently controversy follows the publication of a Mondoza book: "I've written eight horror books about such things as hairy toads that turn into monsters. My youngsters and their friends love them. The trouble is, adults have come to be covered with so many layers of suspicion and terror, they forget a child's mind is pure.

"They don't realize that what may seem violent to a grown-up, is simply a funny story to a child. When they call fairy tales and children's thrillers the cause of nightmares, they're simply talking too much like adults."

Mendoza's *The Inspector,* a story without words about a "myopic inspector who goes along peering through a magnifying glass at the ground while his increasingly hideous and ravening dog dismembers monsters," came under the severest attacks from critics. Barbara Wersba wrote: "While I am not one of those people who believes children should be shielded from violence, I do believe that they should be shielded from this book. Whatever its allegorical intent, it is sick, tasteless and unnecessary—and the integrity of its publishers is suspect for letting it see the light of day." To such critical response Mendoza responded: "I don't feel that it is a violent book. The underlying humor carries the child but dumps the frigid, myopic adult. *The Inspector* is an allegory . . . the oblivious inspector might represent what is happening in America today."

Mendoza, who has published books with more than twenty-five firms, feels freedom for authors of children's books is often restrained: "many publishers in the children's book field sit on the porch of their teeth and never move off into new and startling directions. Some 'claim' they are doing courageous pieces . . . they make you feel they have just this morning invented the word 'reality' . . . and they cheat children because they present language and meanings in half-tones . . . camouflaging reality and truth."

Mendoza, who has said "children's books are much freer than novels," told Jane O'Reilly: "In years to come I hope I will be a poet. A novelist is a dribbler, a pacing-in-and-out man. A poet dreams he can put the ball through the hoop. To me that is the greatest challenge. I never thought of my books for anybody really, except for myself. I wanted to do the work I believed in. I have a fierce belief in myself. I can usually persuade a publisher I am right—that a work should see the light of day."

BIOGRAPHICAL/CRITICAL SOURCES: New York Times Book Review, May 2, 1971; *San Francisco Examiner,* October 10, 1975.*

*   *   *

MENDRAS, Henri 1927-

PERSONAL: Born May 16, 1927, in Boulogne, France; son of Edmond (a general in the army) and Germaine (Talon) Mendras; married Catherine Hautcoeur (a lawyer), 1955; children: Louis, Marie, Francois, Claire. *Education:* University of Paris, Ph.D., 1950, Doctorat es lettres, 1967; postdoctoral study at University of Chicago, 1950-51. *Home:* 11 rue Cassette, Paris, France 75006. *Office:* Groupe de Recherches Sociologiques, Bt.G Universite de Paris X, 92001 Nanterre, Cedex, France.

CAREER: Centre National de la Recherche Scientifique (CNRS), Paris, France, director of research, 1953-68; University of Nanterre, Paris, head of group for sociological research, 1968-70, director of research, 1970—. Professor at Institut d'Etudes Politiques de Paris, 1957. Consultant to UNESCO, U.N. Food and Agricultural Organization (FAO), and Organization for Economic Cooperation and Development (OECD). *Member:* Societe Francaise de Sociologie, Societe Francaise de Science Politique, Academie d'Agriculture, Association des Ruralistes Francais.

WRITINGS: Etudes de sociologie rurale: Novis et Virgin (title means "Studies in Rural Sociology: Novis and Virgin"), A. Colin, 1953; *Sociologie rurale* (title means "Rural Sociology"), Cours de droit, 1957; (editor) *Les Paysans et la modernisation de l'agriculture* (title means "Peasants and the Modernization of Agriculture"), Centre National de la Recherche Scientifique, 1958; (with J. Fauvet) *Les Paysans et la politique dans la France contemporaine* (title means "Peasants and Politics in Contemporary France"), Fondation Nationale des Sciences Politques, 1958; *Sociologie de la campagne francaise* (title means "Sociology of the French Countryside"), Presses Universitaires de France, 1959.

(With V. Foundoukou and others) *Six villages d'Epire* (title means "Six Villages of Epire"), U.N.E.S.C.O., 1961; (editor) *Les Societes rurales francaises* (title means "French Rural Societies"), Fondation Nationale de Sciences Politiques, 1962; *La Fin des paysans,* A. Colin, 1967, translation by Jean Lerner published as *The Vanishing Peasant: Innovation and Change in French Agriculture,* M.I.T. Press, 1969; *Elements de sociologie* (title means "Elements of Sociology"), A. Colin, 1967; (editor with Yves Tavernier) *Terre, paysans et politique* (title means "Land, Peasants, and Politics"), S.E.D.E.I.S., 1969.

(With Marcel Jollivet) *Les Collectivites rurales francaises* (title means "French Rural Collectives"), A. Colin, 1971; *Les Societes paysannes* (title means "Peasant Societies"), A. Colin, 1976; (editor) *L'Avenir des campagnes en Europe occidentale* (title means "The Future of Rural Areas in Western Europe"), S.E.D.E.I.S., 1977.

Contributor of articles to *Revue francaise de sociologie, Journal of Peasant Studies, Futuribles,* and other journals in his field.

WORK IN PROGRESS: Comparative research on French peasant communities and longitudinal observation of social changes.

SIDELIGHTS: Mendras wonders: "What will a world without peasants be like?"

* * *

MENOLASCINO, Frank J(oseph) 1930-

PERSONAL: Born May 25, 1930, in Omaha, Neb.; son of Phillip and Annie Marie (Ferrante) Menolascino; married Donna Colleen Potthoff, December 28, 1956; children: Michelle, Cynthia, Michael, Scott, Mark, Amy. *Education:* University of Omaha, B.A., 1952; University of Nebraska, M.D., 1957; postdoctoral study at Nebraska Psychiatric Institute, 1958-61. *Politics:* Democrat. *Religion:* Roman Catholic. *Home:* 2318 South 102nd St., Omaha, Neb. 68124. *Office:* Nebraska Psychiatric Institute, 602 South 45th St., Omaha, Neb. 68106.

CAREER: Nebraska Methodist Hospital, Omaha, intern, 1957-58; Nebraska Psychiatric Institute, Omaha, resident, 1958-61, instructor in psychiatry, 1962-65, staff psychiatrist at child development clinic, 1965-70, clinical director, 1970-75, associate director, 1975—. Staff psychiatrist at Lincoln State Hospital, 1961-62. Professor at University of Nebraska at Omaha, 1971—, vice-chairperson of department of psychiatry, 1973—.

MEMBER: American Medical Association, American Psychiatric Association (fellow), American Association on Mental Deficiency (fellow), National Association for Retarded Citizens (president, 1975-77; film consultant), Nebraska Medical Association, Douglas-Sarpy County Medical Society, Alpha Omega Alpha. *Awards, honors:* Edward A. Strecker Memorial Award from Institute of Pennsylvania, 1976.

WRITINGS: Psychiatric Approaches to Mental Retardation, Basic Books, 1970; *Beyond the Limits,* Special Child Publications, 1974; *Challenges in Mental Retardation,* Behavioral Publications, 1976; *Medical Dimensions of Mental Retardation,* University of Nebraska Press, in press. Contributor of about a hundred articles to medical journals.

WORK IN PROGRESS: Modern System for the Retarded.

* * *

MERK, Frederick 1887-1977

August 15, 1887—September 24, 1977; American educator, historian, scholar, and author. Merk was Gurney Professor of History and Political Science Emeritus at Harvard University where he was famous for his "Wagon Wheels" course on U.S. westward expansion. Merk was the author of numerous books on the earlier periods in American history. He died in Cambridge, Mass. Obituaries: *New York Times,* September 27, 1977; *Time,* October 10, 1977. (See index for *CA* sketch)

* * *

MERRILL, John Calhoun 1924-

PERSONAL: Born January 9, 1924, in Yazoo, Miss.; son of J. C. and Irene (Hooter) Merrill; married Dorothy Jefferson (a college assistant dean), September 5, 1948; children: Charles, Judi Merrill McBee, Jon, Linda, Deborah. *Education:* Mississippi Delta State University, B.A., 1949; Louisiana State University, M.A. (journalism), 1950; University of Iowa, Ph.D., 1961; University of Missouri, M.A. (philosophy), 1976. *Home:* 101 South Glenwood Ave., Columbia, Mo. 65201. *Office:* School of Journalism, University of Missouri, Columbia, Mo. 65201.

CAREER: Delta Democrat-Times, Greenville, Miss., reporter, 1946-48; *Jackson Clarion-Ledger,* Jackson, Miss., wire editor, 1950; Northwestern State College of Louisiana, Natchitoches, La., assistant professor of journalism, 1951-62; Texas A & M, College Station, Tex. associate professor of journalism, 1962-64; University of Missouri, Columbia, professor of journalism, 1964—. U.S. Information Agency lecturer abroad, 1970—. Editor of *Natchitoches Times,* summers, 1951-60. Consultant to Central News Agency (Taiwan). *Military service:* U.S. Navy, 1942-46.

MEMBER: International Press Institute, International Institute of Communications, Inter-American Press Association, Association for Education in Journalism, Sigma Delta Chi. *Awards, honors:* Research award from Sigma Delta Chi, 1972, for *Media, Messages, and Men;* named to Journalism Hall of Fame at Louisiana State University, 1975; named distinguished professor of journalism, California State University at Long Beach, 1977.

WRITINGS: The Foreign Press, Louisiana State University Press, 1964, revised edition, 1970; *International Communication,* Hastings House, 1970, revised edition, 1976; *The Imperative of Freedom,* Hastings House, 1974; *Ethics and the Press,* Hastings House, 1975; *Existential Journalism,* Hastings House, 1977. Author of column "Merrill's Maraudings" in *Bryan Daily Eagle,* 1962-64. Special correspondent for *Corriere della Sera,* 1963-68, and *Neue Zuercher Zeitung,* 1965-70.

WORK IN PROGRESS: Revisions of *Elite Press* and *Media, Messages, and Men,* with R. Lowenstein. A book on mass media with M. L. Stein and Dan Garvey.

SIDELIGHTS: Merrill comments: "I have always thought it a good idea to continue to practice journalism, although my main career has been in teaching; I have also travelled widely in the world, conducting journalism seminars, workshops, etc. I have written many books and articles, always trying to fill gaps in existing literature, hoping to provide catalytic prose to stimulate the thinking of students and professional journalists."

* * *

MERRIMAN, Beth
See TAYLOR, Demetria

* * *

MERRITT, Ray E(merson), Jr. 1948-

PERSONAL: Born September 17, 1948, in Atlanta, Ga.; son of Ray Emerson (an architect) and Evelyn (Burdette) Merritt; married Kerida Anne Arnholt (a speech therapist), August 16, 1969; children: Gretchen, Emily. *Education:* Florida State University, B.S., 1970, M.S., 1971. *Home:* 115 Foxcroft Lane, Durham, N.C. *Office:* Department of Political Science, Criminal Justice Program, North Carolina Central University, Durham, N.C. 27707.

CAREER: Florida Division of Youth Services, youth counselor in Titusville, 1972-73, training specialist in Tallahassee, 1973-74; Florida Probation/Parole Commission, Tallahassee, curriculum specialist, 1974-76; Florida Department of Offender Rehabilitation, Tallahassee, curriculum specialist, 1976-77; North Carolina Central University, Durham, instructor in criminology, 1977—. Co-owner and co-director of Personnel Development Associates. Volunteer "crisis home parent" for Florida Division of Youth Services. *Member:* Association of Youth Related Services, Florida Council on Crime and Delinquency, North Carolina Criminal Justice Educators Association.

WRITINGS: (With Donald D. Walley) *The Group Leaders Handbook: Resources, Techniques, and Survival Skills,* Research Press, 1977. Contributor to professional journals.

WORK IN PROGRESS: Training and Staff Development for Correctional Agencies, a "how-to-do-it" book for staff trainers working in the field of corrections.

SIDELIGHTS: Merritt writes that work in "training and staff development led directly to the writing of *The Group Leaders Handbook.* Much of its philosophy and content are applied in my training and teaching experiences. I believe a helping relationship in any group setting can be warm and positive—it does not have to be threatening or negative to effect change. I enjoy people and working in groups has always been very rewarding for me both personally and professionally."

* * *

MERZ, Charles 1893-1977

February 23, 1893—August 31, 1977; American editor and author best known for *Centerville, U.S.A., The Great American Bandwagon,* and *The Dry Decade.* Merz was editor of the *New York Times* from 1938 until 1961, and his editorials against American neutrality in the few years prior to World War II and in opposition to Senator Joseph McCarthy in the 1950's were influential on American thinking. Merz died in New York, N.Y. Obituaries: *New York Times,* September 1, 1977; *AB Bookman's Weekly,* October 10, 1977.

* * *

MESSENGER, Charles (Rynd Milles) 1941-

PERSONAL: Born May 11, 1941, in Fulmer, England; married Anne Falconer; children: Emma, Rawdon, Harriet. *Education:* Oxford University, B.A. (honors), 1965, M.A., 1973. *Address:* c/o Williams & Glyns Bank Ltd., Holts Farnborough Branch, 31-37 Victoria Rd., Farnborough, Hampshire, England. *Agent:* Donald Copeman, 52 Bloomsbury St., London WC1B 3QT, England.

CAREER: British Army, Royal Tank Regiment, career officer, 1959—; present rank, major. Served as lecturer in Near East, Germany, and United States, and held technical and non-technical positions with Ministry of Defence. *Member:* Royal United Service Institute, Army and Navy Club.

WRITINGS: Trench Fighting, 1914-1918, Ballantine, 1972; *The Art of Blitzkrieg,* Ian Allan, 1976; *The Blitzkrieg Story,* Scribner, 1976; *The War in Tunisia, 1942-1943,* Ian Allan, in press; *The Observer's Book of Armoured Fighting Vehicles,* Frederick Warne, in press. Contributor to *Purnell's History of the First World War.*

WORK IN PROGRESS: Paths of Glory, a novel; *British Armoured Cars at War, 1914-1964; A Battalion on the Western Front, 1914-1918; Encyclopedia of Armoured Cars.*

SIDELIGHTS: Messenger told *Ca:* "As a professional tank officer, I am interested in all aspects of armoured warfare. I am also studying the place of armed forces in society and I intend to develop this through the medium of fiction. I plan to extend my writing base in the future by producing non-military works, both fact and fiction."

* * *

MEYER, Bernard C. 1910-

PERSONAL: Born June 26, 1910, in White Plains, N.Y.; son of Max (a manufacturer) and Eugenia (Goodkind) Meyer; married Elly Kassman, June 27, 1936 (deceased); married Leonore Rosenbaum, June 11, 1961; children: (first marriage) Nicholas, Constance, Juliette, Deborah. *Education:* Harvard University, A.B., 1932; Cornell University, M.D., 1936. *Home:* 240 East 62nd St., New York, N.Y. 10021. *Office:* 9 East 96th St., New York, N.Y. 10028.

CAREER: Psychiatrist in private practice, New York City, 1941—; Mount Sinai Hospital, New York City, attending psychiatrist, and clinical professor of psychiatry in Mt. Sinai School of Medicine, 1966—. Lecturer in psychiatry, Columbia University, 1960-66. *Member:* American Psychiatric Association (fellow), American Medical Association, American Psychosomatic Society, American Psychoanalytic Association, New York Academy of Medicine (fellow), New York Psychoanalytic Society and Institute.

WRITINGS: Joseph Conrad: A Psychoanalytic Biography, Princeton University Press, 1967; *Houdini: A Mind in Chains,* Dutton, 1976. Contributor of about forty articles on psychiatry and other subjects to journals.

AVOCATIONAL INTERESTS: Music.

* * *

MEYER, Carol H. 1924-

PERSONAL: Born March 18, 1924, in Brooklyn, N.Y. *Education:* University of Pittsburgh, B.A., 1946; Columbia University, M.S., 1949, D.S.W., 1957. *Home:* 15 West Ninth St., New York, N.Y. 10011. *Office:* School of Social Work, Columbia University, 622 West 113th St., New York, N.Y. 10025.

CAREER: Greenwich House, New York City, group worker, 1944-45; Soho Community House, Pittsburgh, Pa., group worker, 1945-46; Bridgeport Family Society, Bridgeport, Conn., caseworker, 1946-47; caseworker for Community Service Society, 1949-54; director of social service for Shield of David Home for Girls, 1954-55; New York University, New York City, associate professor of social work, 1955-59; Department of Welfare, New York City, assistant to commissioner and director of training, 1959-62; Columbia University, New York City, associate professor, 1962-66, professor of social work, 1966—. *Member:* National Association of Social Workers, Council on Social Work Education (member of board of directors), American Association of University Professors.

WRITINGS: Staff Development in Public Welfare Agencies, Columbia University Press, 1966; *Deprivation: Economic, Social, Emotional—Implications for Social Work Practice* (monograph), Northeast Regional Institute, National Association of Social Workers, 1966; *Social Work Practice: A Response to the Urban Crisis,* Free Press, 1970, revised edition published as *Social Work Practice: Its Changing Landscape,* 1976.

Contributor: Francis J. Turner, editor, *Differential Diagnosis and Treatment in Social Work,* Free Press, 1968; *Current Patterns in Field Instruction in Graduate Social Work Education,* Council on Social Work Education, 1969; Edward J. Mullen and James R. Dumpson, editors, *The Effects of Social Intervention: Implications of Program Evaluators,* Jossey-Bass, 1972; A. J. Kahn, editor, *Shaping the New Social Work,* Columbia University Press, 1973; (author of introduction) Lydia Rapoport, *Creativity in Social Work,* Temple University Press, 1975; B. Ross and S. K. Klinduka, editors, *Social Work in Practice,* National Association of Social Workers, 1976. Contributor of articles and reviews to journals in the social sciences.

MEYER, Erika 1904-

PERSONAL: Born July 7, 1904, in Pomeroy, Iowa; daughter of Henry (a clergyman) and Anna (Schroeder) Meyer; married Sam M. Shiver (a professor of German), June 14, 1960. *Education:* University of Iowa, B.A., 1925, M.A., 1926; University of Wisconsin, Ph.D., 1936. *Home:* 2071 Sylvania Dr., Decatur, Ga. 30033.

CAREER: Allegheny College, Meadville, Pa., instructor in German, 1926-30; Mount Holyoke College, South Hadley, Mass., 1932-60, started as instructor, became professor of German and chairman of department; Agnes Scott College, Decatur, Ga., professor of German, 1962-72, chairman of department, 1964-72. *Member:* Modern Language Association of America, American Association of Teachers of German, American Association of University Professors, Phi Beta Kappa.

WRITINGS—All published by Houghton: *Auf dem Dorfe,* 1949; *In der Stadt,* 1949; *Genialische Jugend,* 1949; *Elementary German,* 1952, 3rd edition, 1975; (editor) Inge Scholl, *Die Weisse Rose,* 1952; *Ein Briefwechsel,* 1954; *Akademische Freiheit,* 1954; *Goslar,* 1954; *Intermediate German,* 1960; (with Jane Mehl) *Fundamentals of German Grammar,* 1975.

WORK IN PROGRESS: Research for a Goethe anthology and biography.

AVOCATIONAL INTERESTS: Travel in Europe (guest of West German Government on one trip, 1957). Spends summers in Vermont.

* * *

MEYER, Lawrence R(obert) 1941-

PERSONAL: Born November 27, 1941, in Chicago, Ill.; son of Ferdnando Kolomon (an engineer) and Gertrude (Weinschank) Meyer; married Aviva Sagalovitch (an executive), June 15, 1968; children: Ariel David, Evan Asher, Noa Anne Sagalovitch. *Education:* University of Michigan, B.A., 1963; Columbia University, M.A., 1964, M.S., 1965. *Religion:* Jewish. *Home:* 3311 Ross Pl. N.W., Washington, D.C. 20008. *Agent:* Hoffman-Sheedy Agency, 145 West 86th St., New York, N.Y. 10024. *Office: Washington Post,* 1150 15th St. N.W., Washington, D.C. 20071.

CAREER: Times-Herald Record, Middletown, N.Y., reporter, 1965-68; *Louisville Times,* Louisville, Ky., reporter, 1968-69; *Washington Post,* Washington, D.C., reporter, 1969—. *Military service:* U.S. Marine Corps, 1966-68; became sergeant.

WRITINGS: A Capitol Crime, Viking, 1977.

WORK IN PROGRESS: False Front, for Viking.

* * *

MEYERS, Jeffrey 1939-

PERSONAL: Born April 1, 1939, in New York, N.Y.; son of Rubin and Judith Meyers; married Valerie Froggatt (a teacher), October 12, 1965; children: Rachel. *Education:* University of Michigan, B.A., 1959; University of California, Berkeley, M.A., 1961, Ph.D., 1967. *Politics:* Socialist. *Religion:* None. *Home:* 2005 Glenwood, Boulder, Colo. 80302. *Agent:* Leresche & Sayle, 11 Jubilee Pl., London SW3 3TE, England. *Office:* Department of English, University of Colorado, Boulder, Colo. 80309.

CAREER: University of California, Los Angeles, assistant professor of English, 1963-65; University of Maryland, Far East Division, Tokyo, Japan, lecturer in English, 1965-66;

Tufts University, Boston, Mass., assistant professor of English, 1967-71; writer in London, England, 1971-74; Christie's, London, in rare books department, 1974; University of Colorado, Boulder, associate professor of English, 1975—. *Awards, honors:* Fellowships from American Council of Learned Societies, 1970, and Huntington Library, 1971; Fulbright fellowship, 1977-78.

WRITINGS: Fiction and the Colonial Experience, Boydell Press, 1973; *The Wounded Spirit: A Study of "Seven Pillars of Wisdom",* Martin, Brian & O'Keefe, 1973; *T. E. Lawrence: A Bibliography,* Garland Publishing, 1974; *A Reader's Guide to George Orwell,* Thames & Hudson, 1975; *George Orwell: The Critical Heritage,* Routledge & Kegan Paul, 1975; *Painting and the Novel,* Barnes & Noble, 1975; *Catalogue of the Library of the Late Siegfried Sassoon,* Christie's, 1975; *A Fever at the Core: The Idealist in Politics,* Barnes & Noble, 1976; *George Orwell: An Annotated Bibliography of Criticism,* Garland Publishing, 1977; *Homosexuality and Literature, 1890-1930,* Athlone Press, 1977; *Married to Genius,* Barnes & Noble, 1977; *Katherine Mansfield: A Biography,* Hamish Hamilton, in press. Contributor to professional and popular magazines, including *London, Sewanee Review,* and *Virginia Quarterly Review.*

WORK IN PROGRESS: A biography of Wyndham Lewis, completion expected in 1979.

SIDELIGHTS: Meyers comments: "I take an inter-disciplinary, comparative, and biographical approach to modern English and European literature, and believe criticism should be based on fact, not theory." *Avocational interests:* Travel (Asia, Africa, the Near East, Europe), tennis.

* * *

MEYNIER, Yvonne (Pollet) 1908-

PERSONAL: Born in France in 1908; married Andre Meynier (a history teacher), August 20, 1927; children: Odette (Mrs. Maurice Touchefeu), Yvette (Mrs. Jean Delaunay), Daniele (Mrs. Yves Treguer). *Education:* Attended Sorbonne, University of Paris. *Home:* 50 Rue de la Palestine, 35000 Rennes, France.

CAREER: Author. Has been a kindergarten teacher, and has worked in radio in France. *Awards, honors:* Grand Prix de la Literature pour les Jeunes, and Enfance au Monde award, both for *The School with a Difference.*

WRITINGS: Maria de l'Assistance, Calmann-Levy, 1946; *Maluories,* Calmann-Levy, 1948; *Comme la Plume au Vent: Dix Ans de Radio* (with a preface by Georges Duhamel), [Blainville-sur-Mer], 1956; *Une Petite Fille Attendait* (illustrated by Pierre Le Guen), Editions G. P., 1961; *L'-Helicoptere du Petit Duc* (illustrated by Raymond Busillet), Magnard, 1962; *Un Lycee pas Comme les Autres* (illustrated by Daniel Dupuy), Societe Nouvelle des Editions G. P., 1962, translation by Patricia Crampton published as *The School with a Difference,* Abelard, 1964; *Erika des Collines* (illustrated by Jacques Pecnard), Societe Nouvelle des Editions G. P., 1963; *La Bonheur est Pour Demain,* Societe Nouvelle des Editions G. P., 1965; *Ou es-tu Antonio?* (illustrated by Michel Gourlier), Magnard, 1970; (with Job de Roince) *La Cuisine Rustique, Bretagne, Maine, Anjou,* R. Morel, 1970; (with husband, Andre Meynier) *Les Cotes de France,* Arthaud, 1972; *Le Voyage Imaginaire* (illustrated by Colette Goulard), Magnard, 1973.*

* * *

MICHAEL, Manfred
See WINTERFELD, Henry

MICHAELS, Carolyn Leopold
See LEOPOLD, Carolyn Clugston

*   *   *

MIDDLEBROOK, David
See ROSENUS, Alan (Harvey)

*   *   *

MIDDLEMISS, Robert (William)   1938-

PERSONAL: Born April 24, 1938, in Hartlepool, England; came to the United States in 1965, naturalized citizen, 1976; son of Robert William (a foreman) and Mary (Kelly) Middlemiss; married Deborah Louise Cass, September 8, 1962 (marriage ended, 1974); married Elizabeth Marie Dixon (a counselor), May 17, 1975; children: (second marriage) Whitney Faulkner (daughter). *Education:* Sir George Williams University, B.A., 1963; McGill University, B.L.S., 1964; Adelphi University, graduate study, 1965-66. *Residence:* Union City, Ga. *Agent:* Charles Byrne, 1133 Avenue of the Americas, New York, N.Y. 10036.

CAREER: Armstrong Cork Co., Montreal, Quebec, laboratory technician, 1953-54; United Aircraft Corp., Longueuil, Quebec, production clerk, 1954-56; Federal Department of Transport, Ottawa, Ontario, marine engineer, 1956-59; York University, Toronto, Ontario, assistant acquisitions librarian, 1964-65; Adelphi University, Garden City, N.Y., acquisitions librarian, 1965-67; Indiana State University, Terre Haute, librarian and head of acquisitions department, 1967-71, lecturer in library science, 1970-71; B. H. Blackwell Ltd., Oxford, England, library services adviser, 1971-72; Media Fair, Inc., Vienna, Va., vice-president, 1973—. *Member:* National Audio Visual Association, American Library Association, Indiana Library Association (president of Junior Members Roundtable).

WRITINGS: The Parrot Man (novel), Fawcett, 1977.

WORK IN PROGRESS: Two spy thrillers, *The Lofoten Run* and *The Lateral Line.*

SIDELIGHTS: Middlemiss told *CA:* "I am interested in using the spy genre as a vehicle for statements on human nature. I want to write for the man on the bus or the woman eating her sandwich in a park, but am trying to couple the escapism of high adventure with provocative and perhaps unpopular inquiries into man's behavior."

*   *   *

MIDGLEY, Graham   1923-

PERSONAL: Born September 29, 1923, in Bradford, England; son of William Edward (a wool merchant) and Edna Louisa (Roberts) Midgley. *Education:* St. Edmund Hall, Oxford, B.A., 1947, B.Litt., 1950. *Politics:* "Feudal." *Religion:* Church of England. *Office:* Vice-principal, St. Edmund Hall, Oxford University, Oxford, England.

CAREER: University of London, London, England, lecturer in English literature at Bedford College, 1949-51; Oxford University, Oxford, England, fellow of St. Edmund Hall and tutor in English, 1951—. *Military service:* British Army, Royal Regiment of Artillery, 1942-46; became lieutenant. *Member:* Johnson Club.

WRITINGS: The Merchant of Venice: A Reconsideration, Macmillan, 1969; *The Life of Orator Henley,* Clarendon Press, 1973; (editor) *The Poetical Works of John Bunyan,* Clarendon Press, in press.

WORK IN PROGRESS: Editing *The Awakening Sermons of John Bunyan,* for Clarendon Press.

AVOCATIONAL INTERESTS: "Main loves, besides one or two special humans, are horses and dogs, skiing and gardening and getting away from cities. My other creative activity is sculpture in wood and stone. I used to collect twentieth century sculpture, but inflation and pay restraint now make it impossible."

*   *   *

MILDO, Albert   1945-

PERSONAL: Born December 25, 1945, in American Fork, Utah; son of Emmett Roman (a juggler) and Lucinda Juanita (a topsoil analyst; maiden name, Klienberg) Mildo; married Gwen Bluff (a mime) July 4, 1965 (marriage ended, 1965); married Ruth Bustod (a plumber), November 22, 1965; children: Delbert, Quince, Beemus, Eunice (Mrs. Robert Pumice). *Education:* Received G.E.D. from American Mystery Writers Technological Institute. *Politics:* "Eisenhoweric." *Religion:* Rosicrucian. *Home:* 221 Lewiston Rd., Grosse Pointe Farms, Mich. 48236.

CAREER: Worked as a janitor, logger, skiing instructor, and wrestling emcee in American Fork, Utah, 1964-65; traveled with "Mildo's Mildew" circus troupe as a mime imitator, 1966; sold herpes salve door-to-door in Gommorah, Fla., 1966-67; curator of dental museum in Buite, Ohio, 1967; worked as license press operator while serving four-year sentence for loitering, Jersey Correctional Institution, 1967-71; founded Mildo's Private Eye Agency where he worked as a private investigator, Detroit, Mich., 1972-73; dishwasher for various fast-food chains in Detroit, 1972-73; writer, 1972—. *Awards, honors:* D.Litt. from Clairmont Correspondence School of Concise Writing School, 1975; Bottom Shelf Award, 1976, from Metropolitan Airport Library, for *Punch My Face, Please.*

WRITINGS: They Can't Talk: A History of Mime from Marcel Marceau to Present, Arty Pubs, 1972; *My Dead Friend,* Shoot-to-Kill, 1972; *Holster to Hell,* Shoot-to-Kill, 1973; *Kiss Me You Beast,* Shoot-to-Kill, 1973; *The Dead Corpse,* Shoot-to-Kill, 1973; *Guilty of Innocence: An Indictment of Penalization,* Parole Publications, 1974; *Sweet Suicide,* Shoot-to-Kill, 1974; (with wife, Ruth Mildo) *Plumbing: One Woman's Story,* Feminque Press, 1975; *The Blood of It All: My Life as a Private Dick,* Shoot-to-Kill Big Books, 1976; *Punch My Face, Please,* Shoot-to-Kill, 1976; *The Naked Bullet,* Shoot-to-Kill, 1977; *I Killed Myself,* Shoot-to-Kill, 1977; *Death Is Lonely,* Shoot-to-Kill, 1978; *Dislocate My Jaw . . . I Beg You,* Mess Press, in press.

WORK IN PROGRESS: A four-volume autobiography, *I Have Lived;* two more detective novels, *Cadavers Don't Talk* and *I Promise Not to Scream When I'm Dead;* a philosophical treatise, *Destiny Is My Fate.*

SIDELIGHTS: "Although I don't take them seriously, I guess I'm most popular for my detective stories," Mildo told *CA.* "I write mostly about masochism because I believe pain is the best learning experience and I want to teach as I'm being read. My pulp stuff isn't your average tripe. I know how to write and I'm damn serious about it. Pain *is* important. If I go a few days without learning anything, I'll put my hand on a burner or step on the end of a rake, and then I'm continuing my quest for knowledge. I once met a man who told me he knew nothing, that he was a fool. I commanded him to step off the curb, whereupon he was struck by a cab. The injury was not too serious, and before the ambulance arrived and he passed out, he thanked me for what I'd done, for the gift of knowledge I'd imparted.

"Of all my writings, I guess I'm most proud of mime history.

I've always loved mime, ever since it was invented, and I hope that my children will become interested in it also. Of course, they may have a small advantage since my two eldest are deaf and mute but, what the hell, they may want to do something else. That's the beauty of this country. They could be presidents, disc jockeys, anything!

"My one motivation in writing is the knowledge that my occupation places me on the same shelves with Tolstoy and Melville, whom I consider my Russian equals. I hope that my readers appreciate their talent as much as I do mime."

AVOCATIONAL INTERESTS: Mime, philosophizing, and "riding my son's wheelchair."

* * *

MILES, Elliot
See LUDVIGSEN, Karl (Eric)

* * *

MILGRAM, Morris 1916-

PERSONAL: Born May 29, 1916, in New York, N.Y.; son of Benjamin and Fanny (Gladstone) Milgram; married Grace Smelo, June 26, 1937 (divorced March 7, 1969); married Jean Babcock Gregg, 1969 (divorced November 5, 1975); married Lorna Riggs Scheide (a prison tutor), December 12, 1975; children: Gene, Betty April. *Education:* Attended City College (now of the City University of New York); University of Newark (now Rutgers University, Newark Campus), B.A., 1939. *Politics:* Democratic Socialist. *Religion:* Jewish. *Home:* 5 Longford St., Philadelphia, Pa. 19136. *Office:* Fund for an Open Society, 9803 Roosevelt Blvd., Philadelphia, Pa. 19114.

CAREER: Workers Defense League, New York, N.Y., national secretary, 1941-47; Milgram Companies, Philadelphia, Pa., housing developer, 1947—. Managing general partner of Partners in Housing; general partner of Housing Partners II; president of Choice Communities, Inc., Affirmative Housing Associates, and Fund for an Open Society; honorary chairman of Job Opportunity in Skill Training; organizer of National Committee on Tithing in Investment (now Sponsors of Open Housing Investment). Special lecturer at New School for Social Research, University of Minnesota, and Brandeis University. Member of board of directors of National Housing Conference, National Sharecroppers Fund, and local unit of American Jewish Committee; member of board of trustees of Rutgers University, 1968-74.

AWARDS, HONORS: Walter White Award from National Committee Against Discrimination in Housing, 1956; D.H.L. from Starr King School for the Ministry, 1967; National Human Rights Award from U.S. Department of Housing and Urban Development (HUD), 1968.

WRITINGS: Developing Open Communities, Association Press, 1963; (author of introduction) Pauli Murray, *Dark Testament and Other Poems,* Silvermine Publishers, 1970; *Good Neighborhood: The Challenge of Open Housing,* Norton, 1977. Contributor to magazines, including *Journal of Intergroup Relations, Common Sense,* and *Integrator.*

SIDELIGHTS: Milgram has worked to increase the availability of low- and modest-cost multiracial housing. One of his companies provides consultation services on affirmative marketing of housing and on economic problems in housing. Another, a construction company, trains disadvantaged people for the housing industry. Another company integrated an all-white community on Long Island with middle-income housing, and without incident. Affirmative Housing Associates acts as a general partner of limited partnerships and can act as a broker-dealer for the sale of integrated housing securities. The Fund for an Open Society is a non-profit mortgage company that provides moderate-interest mortgages to white and minority home buyers making pro-integration housing moves. Sponsors of Open Housing Investment aims at educating individuals to invest in integrated housing when they select housing or investments.

Milgram has written that among the forces which motivated this complex career are the poems of Pauli Murray.

* * *

MILLAR, George Reid 1910-

PERSONAL: Born September 19, 1910, in Boghall, Baldernock, Scotland; son of Thomas Andrew (an architect) and Mary Reid Millar; married Annette Forsyth Stockwell, 1935 (marriage ended); married Isabel Beatritz Paske-Smith, May 28, 1945. *Education:* St. John's College, Cambridge, B.A., 1931. *Politics:* Conservative. *Home:* Sydling Court, Sydling St. Nicholas, Dorset, England.

CAREER: Worked as an architect, 1930-32; *Evening Citizen,* Glasgow, Scotland, reporter, 1934-37; *Daily Telegraph,* London, England, reporter, 1937-38; *Daily Express,* London, Paris bureau chief and war correspondent, 1938-40; farmer, 1962—; writer. *Military service:* British Army, 1939-45; became second lieutenant; received Chevalier de la Legion d'Honneur and Croix de Guerre with palms.

WRITINGS: Maquis, Heinemann, 1945, published as *Waiting in the Night,* Doubleday, 1946; *Horned Pigeon,* Doubleday, 1946; *My Past Was an Evil River* (novel), Heinemann, 1946, Doubleday, 1947; *Isabel and the Sea,* Doubleday, 1948; *Through the Unicorn Gates,* Heinemann, 1950; *A White Boat from England,* Heinemann, 1951, Knopf, 1952; *Siesta,* Heinemann, 1953; *Orellana Discovers the Amazons,* Heinemann, 1954, published as *A Crossbowman's Story,* Knopf, 1955; *Oyster River: One Summer on an Inland Sea,* Bodley Head, 1963, Knopf, 1964; (editor) *Horseman: Memoirs of Captain J. H. Marshall,* Bodley Head, 1970; *Bruneval Raid: Flashpoint of the Radar War,* Bodley Head, 1974, Doubleday, 1975.

SIDELIGHTS: Millar's capture and daring escape as a prisoner of war and his experiences as a parachutist for the French resistance later served as material for *Waiting in the Night* and *Horned Pigeon,* which *Time* praised as being among the "most exciting and intelligent books produced by World War II." Millar has said these war experiences actually strengthened his resolve to write: "I can honestly say that I enjoyed my incarceration in Italy, perhaps the loveliest country on earth; and it was there, when so many around me were repressed and miserable, that I found I could live for writing, if not by it."

Turning to other kinds of adventure after the war, Millar wrote *Isabel and the Sea,* a factual account of a cruise from England to the Greek Islands. Although a post-war chronicle, the observations resonate with all that has gone before, giving what critic Isabel Mallet called "a sense of Europe unsettled and groping, legendary beauty surrounded with man-made threats." A second cruise in 1950 became the subject of *A White Boat from England,* which one critic praised for both its "beautiful flow and simplicity" and the "Chaucerian directness" of Millar's method of introducing fifty or sixty remarkable people.

Millar has turned again to the experience of war for his latest book, *The Bruneval Raid: Flashpoint of the Radar War,* in which he describes the scheme to drop Scottish paratroopers at Bruneval and the dismantling on the spot of an important German radar installation. John Naughton of *The Observer* writes: "George Millar was not personally involved in the raid for the very good reason that he was in a POW camp at the time, but that hasn't prevented him from writing an excellent blow-by-blow account of it."

Millar called *A Crossbowman's Story* an "imaginative reconstruction" of the first exploration of the Amazon in 1541-42. Although of all his works this book reaches the farthest back in time for an adventure, it represents the blend of personal experience, history, and imagination that distinguishes the whole of Millar's work.

Millar told *CA:* "Except when I was (a happy) newspaperman I have never had to write for money. I try to write, and I am a compulsive writer, for myself and for posterity, and when I have something to say.

"I am a physical person, and am as active outdoors aged in the sixties as I was in the twenties. This restricts my output, particularly since in 1962 my wife and I began a 1,000 acre farming enterprise. We are, in every sense, working farmers, producing beef cattle, sheep, and cereals.

"My interests are simple ones, and healthy ones. I put them in this order: marriage, books, sailing my own yacht in strange and preferably solitary waters, wine, foxhunting, cooking, pictures and furniture, travel in France, Ireland, Spain, Italy, and Greece.

"I dislike particularly: telephones, television, socialism and trade unions, jewelry, inverted racial prejudices and snobbery, bad coffee, freezers, bell-bottomed trousers, and the end of elegance in my own and other countries."

BIOGRAPHICAL/CRITICAL SOURCES: Time, January 14, 1946; *New York Times Book Review,* January 19, 1947, August 8, 1948, July 20, 1952; *The Observer,* June 30, 1974; *Times Literary Supplement,* July 26, 1974.

* * *

MILLAR, Ronald (Graeme) 1919-

PERSONAL: Born November 12, 1919, in Reading, England; son of Ronald Hugh and Dorothy Ethel (an actress; maiden name, Dacre-Hill) Millar. *Education:* Attended King's College, Cambridge. *Home:* 7 Sheffield Terrace, London W8, England. *Agent:* Herbert de Leon Ltd., 13 Bruton St., London W1, England.

CAREER: Actor, playwright, and author of screenplays. Began stage career as actor at Ambassador's Theatre, London, 1940; actor in London, 1943-46; playwright, 1942—. *Military service:* Royal Navy, 1940-43.

WRITINGS—All plays; all first produced in London: "Murder from Memory," first produced in 1942; "Zero Hour," first produced in 1944; "The Other Side," first produced in 1946; *Frieda* (first produced in 1946), English Theatre Guild, 1947; "Champagne for Delilah," first produced in 1949; *Waiting for Gillian* (first produced in 1954), Samuel French, 1955; *The Bride and the Bachelor* (first produced in 1956), Samuel French, 1958; *A Ticklish Business* (first produced in 1958), Samuel French, 1959; *The More the Merrier* (first produced in 1960), Samuel French, 1960; *The Bride Comes Back* (first produced in 1960), Samuel French, 1961; *The Affair* (first produced in 1961), Scribner, 1962; "The New Men," first produced in 1962; "The Masters," first produced in 1963; *Robert and Elizabeth* (first produced in 1964), Samuel French, 1967; "On the Level," first pro-

duced in 1966; *Number 10* (first produced in 1967), Heinemann, 1967; *They Don't Grow on Trees* (first produced at Prince of Wales Theatre, December 15, 1968), Samuel French, 1969; *Abelard and Heloise* (first produced in 1970), Samuel French, 1970; "Parents' Day," first produced in 1972; "Odd Girl Out," first produced in 1973; *The Case in Question* (first produced in 1975), Samuel French, 1975; "Once More with Music," first produced in 1976. Also author of *The Affair, The New Men, The Masters: Three Plays Based on the Novels,* Macmillan, 1964.

Screenplays: "Frieda," Universal, 1947; "So Evil My Love," Paramount, 1948; "The Miniver Story," Metro-Goldwyn-Mayer, 1950; "Train of Events," Rank, 1951; "The Unknown Man," Metro-Goldwyn-Mayer, 1951; "Scaramouche," Metro-Goldwyn-Mayer, 1952; "Never Let Me Go," Metro-Goldwyn-Mayer, 1954; "Rose Marie," Metro-Goldwyn-Mayer, 1954; "Betrayed," Metro-Goldwyn-Mayer, 1954.

SIDELIGHTS: Millar discussed the art of dramatizing novels in the *Times Literary Supplement:* "The novel is by nature a discursive, the play a concentrated thing. Distilling the essence of a book, reducing its three or four hundred pages to the two-hour traffic of the stage, is obviously the first task. The danger (one to which critics delight to point) is that in compressing the book you may capture its surface but lose its spirit. But the reverse can also be true. Spoken dialogue and the additional dimensions of the theatre can sometimes highlight and illumine the spirit of a book more clearly than the printed word.

"The boundaries of the stage are both narrower and deeper. By removing the digressions and paring the tangents of a novel (in a play there can be no 'rest passages') the story-line may well be sharpened and intensified. At any rate the temperature *should* go up, not down. And there should be no lack of depth or loss of spirit merely because what took, perhaps, a page of prose can be expressed on the stage by a single line or even a look or gesture. It's simply a matter of technique. In my experience, the greater economy of effect open to the playwright through his actors may help an audience to see the wood *and* the trees.

"But turning a novel into a play is far more than a precis, a breaking up and boiling down. Learning what to leave out is half the story. The other half is learning what to put in. In *The Affair* there is a good example of this."

BIOGRAPHICAL/CRITICAL SOURCES: Times Literary Supplement, September 19, 1968.

* * *

MILLER, Alan Robert 1929-

PERSONAL: Born April 27, 1929, in England; came to the United States in 1931, naturalized citizen, 1951; son of Robert and Mary (Copeland) Miller; married Jean Gifford, August 26, 1951; children: Heather Miller Kilroy, Kendall G., Geoffrey Brooks. *Education:* Boston University, B.S., 1952; University of Massachusetts, M.Ed., 1967. *Politics:* Independent. *Home address:* Cushing St., Winterport, Maine 04496; (summer) 114 Leverett Rd., Shutesbury, Mass. 04473. *Office:* University of Maine, 101 Lord Hall, Orono, Maine 04473.

CAREER: Amherst Journal, Amherst, Mass., editor and publisher, 1952-55; *Stars & Stripes,* Darmstadt, Germany, member of staff, 1955-64; University of Maine, Orono, assistant professor, 1967-70, associate professor of journalism, 1970—. *Military service:* U.S. Army, Infantry, 1946-47.

Member: Association for Education in Journalism, Maine Press Association (member of board of directors, 1970-75).

WRITINGS: (Contributor) Loren Ghiglioni, editor, *Evaluating the Press: The New England Daily Newspaper Survey,* New England Daily Newspaper Survey, 1973; *The History of Current Maine Newspapers,* Eastland Press, 1978. Contributor to journalism magazines and local periodicals, including *Maine* and *Downeast.*

WORK IN PROGRESS: A children's book; short non-fiction articles.

SIDELIGHTS: Miller writes: "Motivation is perhaps the single greatest attribute needed by a topflight journalist. The desire to know what's going on, whether in your home town or in the capitals of the world, an inquiring mind, the wish to learn new things every day, the sheer joy of living a journalist's life because it's the best job in the world—all these *make* the journalist. But the single greatest factor in success (no matter what the field) is self-motivation."

He adds that other characteristics helpful to a journalist include "compassion for your fellow man and an understanding of his plight, self-criticism, a warm sense of humor, and the ability never to take yourself too seriously."

* * *

MILLER, Dorothy (Ryan) 1942-

PERSONAL: Born October 24, 1942, in Lancaster, Pa.; daughter of Clay Miller (an attorney) and Dorothy (Barger) Ryan; married George Eric Miller (a professor of English), September 5, 1964; children: Lisa, Jon, Craig. *Education:* Pennsylvania State University, B.A., 1964, graduate study, 1964-65. *Home:* 91 Ritter Lane, Newark, Del. 19711.

CAREER: Writer, 1973—. *Member:* Phi Beta Kappa.

WRITINGS: (With husband, George Miller) *Picture Postcards in the United States, 1893-1918,* C. N. Potter, 1976. Contributor of articles on postcards and postcard artists to magazines and alumni publications.

WORK IN PROGRESS: A handbook for research in genealogy and local history in southeastern Pennsylvania and Delaware; research on Samuel L. Schmucker and other American postcard artists; editing and writing four volumes of a monograph series on postcard artists for the Gotham Book Mart and Gallery, with husband, George Miller; "a comprehensive study of the American girl in serious and popular art and literature, also with husband."

SIDELIGHTS: Miller told *CA:* "My great-grandfather was President Roosevelt's appointee as postmaster of Lancaster, Pa. I grew up with a heightened awareness of stamps and messages passed through the mail, but soon turned to the images on picture postcards as inherently more interesting than commemorative postal issues. I amassed many shoeboxes of postcards during the 1950's—cards were literally throw-away items then and sold, if at all, for two-for-a-penny at antiques shows.

"During the years when my husband was completing his Ph.D. and I was tied to the house with a new baby, I rediscovered these boxes of pictorial social history and was hooked anew. I collected aimlessly for two or three years—cards were still quite inexpensive—but was constantly frustrated that no reference book was available to answer the hundreds of questions the cards posed. About this point, George, who had also collected stamps as a child, became interested, particularly in issues for American expositions and local celebrations. Together we found many fine examples of turn-of-the-century graphic design on cards and have collected the postcard designs of Alphonse Mucha, undisputed master of art nouveau style; Raphael Kirchner, who achieved international popularity through his postcards, prints, and magazine illustrations; Kolomon Moser and other outstanding artists of the Vienna Sezession; and numerous other lesser-known and unknown artists."

BIOGRAPHICAL/CRITICAL SOURCES: Wilmington Morning News, July 6, 1976; *Lancaster New Era,* July 13, 1976.

* * *

MILLER, George (Eric) 1943-

PERSONAL: Born January 19, 1943, in Buffalo, N.Y.; son of Ralph L. and Lois (Wolfe) Miller; married Dorothy Ryan (a writer and researcher), September 5, 1964; children: Lisa, Jon, Craig. *Education:* Pennsylvania State University, B.A., 1964, M.A., 1966; University of Connecticut, Ph.D., 1969. *Home:* 91 Ritter Lane, Newark, Del. 19711.

CAREER: University of Delaware, Newark, assistant professor, 1969-74, associate professor of English, 1974—. *Member:* Modern Language Association of America, Renaissance Society of America. *Awards, honors:* Folger Shakespeare Library fellow, 1973.

WRITINGS: (With wife, Dorothy Miller) *Picture Postcards in the United States, 1893-1918,* C. N. Potter, 1976; *Edward Hyde, Earl of Clarendon,* Twayne, 1978. Contributor to literature journals. Editor of *Teaching Writing.*

WORK IN PROGRESS: Editing *Mythology in Literature; American Watermarks, 1690 to 1835,* with Thomas Gravell; a book on postcards from Pennsylvania; *Meet Me at the Fair;* an examination of "the image of the American girl in popular and serious literature, art, and music."

* * *

MILLER, J(ohn) D(onald) B(ruce) 1922-

PERSONAL: Born August 30, 1922, in Sydney, Australia; son of Donald G. (a bank officer) and Marion (Carter) Miller; married Margaret Martin; children: Toby. *Education:* University of Sydney, B.Ec., 1944, M.Ec., 1950; London School of Economics and Political Science, London, graduate study, 1952-53. *Politics:* "Radical reformist." *Religion:* "Very little." *Home:* 16 Hutt St., Yarralumla, Australian Capital Territory 2600, Australia. *Office:* Research School of Pacific Studies, Australian National University, Canberra, Australian Capital Territory 2600, Australia.

CAREER: Bank clerk, 1939; Australian Broadcasting Commission, announcer and talks officer in Sydney Canberra, 1939-46; University of Sydney, Sydney, Australia, staff tutor in adult education, 1946-52; University of London, London School of Economics and Political Science, London, England, assistant lecturer in government and international relations, 1953-55; University of Leicester, Leicester, England, lecturer, 1955-57, professor of politics, 1957-62; Australian National University, Canberra, professor of international relations, 1962—. Visiting professor at Indian School of International Studies, 1959, Columbia University, 1962, 1966, and Yale University, 1977; Smuts Visiting Fellow at Cambridge University, 1978. Member of Australian Population and Immigration Council and Australian Research Grants Committee.

MEMBER: Academy of the Social Sciences in Australia (fellow).

WRITINGS: Australian Government and Politics, Duckworth, 1954; Richard Jebb and the Problem of Empire, Athlone Press, 1956; The Commonwealth in the World, Harvard University Press, 1958; The Nature of Politics, Atheneum, 1962; Australia and Foreign Policy, Australian Broadcasting Commission, 1963; Britain and the Old Dominions, Chatto & Windus, 1966; The Politics of the Third World, Oxford University Press, 1966; Australia, Walker & Co., 1966; Survey of Commonwealth Affairs, 1953-1969, Oxford University Press, 1974; The E.E.C. and Australia, Nelson, 1976. Editor of Journal of Commonwealth Political Studies, 1961-62, and Australian Outlook, 1963-69.

WORK IN PROGRESS: The Nature of Foreign Policy, which will consider the special character of foreign policy as opposed to domestic policy; The International Politics of Sugar.

SIDELIGHTS: Miller writes: "I write books about politics mainly to work out problems and clarify my own mind. If they are useful to students and others, well and good; but the main aim is to make a lucid statement about something that has been troubling my understanding. The question of the intellectual level at which an academic book is pitched does not worry me unduly: I think that a book dictates its own form and mode of expression, and that most readers will follow a complicated argument or train of events if it is set out clearly and harmoniously."

* * *

MILLER, Jason 1939(?)-

PERSONAL: Born 1939(?), in Long Island, N.Y.; son of John (an electrician) and Mary (a special education teacher) Miller; married Linda Gleason, 1963 (separated, 1973); children: Jennifer, Jason, Jordan. Education: University of Scranton, B.A., 1961; attended Catholic University of America, 1962-63. Residence: Upper Saddle River, N.J. Office: c/o Public Theater, 425 Lafayette St., New York, N.Y. 10003.

CAREER: Has worked as messenger, waiter, truck driver, welfare investigator, and actor in New York City. Film and television actor appearing in such films as "The Exorcist", 1973, and "Nickel Ride", 1975, also on television in the "Bell System Family Theater," 1975. Playwright. Awards, honors: New York Drama Critics Circle Award, 1972, for "That Championship Season"; Best Play citation, 1972, for "That Championship Season"; Antoinette Perry (Tony) Award, 1973, for "That Championship Season"; Pulitzer Prize in Drama, 1973, for "That Championship Season".

WRITINGS—Plays, except as noted: Stone Step (poetry), privately printed, 1968; "Lou Gehrig Did Not Die of Cancer" (one-act), first produced in New York City at Equity Theater, March 2, 1970; Nobody Hears a Broken Drum (three-act; first produced Off-Broadway at The Fortune Theater, March 19, 1970), Dramatists Play Service, 1971; That Championship Season (first produced Off-Broadway at New York Shakespeare Festival Theatre, May 2, 1972, produced on Broadway at Booth Theatre, September 14, 1972), Dramatists Play Service, 1972. Also author of one-act plays "Perfect Son," and "The Circus Lady."

SIDELIGHTS: Jason Miller's "That Championship Season" was welcomed by critics as a traditional well-made play with a flair for realistic dialogue and characterization.

Miller told Glen Loney of After Dark: "I'm a young writer. I'm not committed to any one style or vision—or one concept of the theater." He does, however, have definite ideas about theatrical form. "For an audience psyche—if there is such a thing as a collective audience psyche—story or plot is necessary," he commented to Loney. "Perhaps that feeling stems from an instinct for design, for an ordering of experience. Roughly, that's what Aristotle said. Perhaps he's right. Again, I don't know.

"But it's absolutely imperative that other forms of theater flourish. Old-fashioned plays and derivative European Absurdism—anything. I think the theater should never strap itself down to one definition, one style or one type of performance. As for the well-made play idea, I prefer to write that way. In terms of 'well-made' having the connotations of 'craft,' I believe in craftsmanship."

"That Championship Season" is about four middle-aged men, once members of a championship high school basketball team, who gather in an annual reunion to honor their coach and relive their memories. In the course of the play their false values and personal failures become apparent.

"'That Championship Season' was born out of my own sense of personal failure," Miller told the New York Times. "When an Off-Off Broadway play of mine, 'Nobody Hears a Broken Drum,' lasted exactly two and one half hours and I had to watch the crew members auctioning off pieces of the set, I started examining the nature of failure. I had to ask myself what type of men would harbor a sense of failure. In the process, I was also forced to account for my own values."

Since the success of this play, Miller himself has concentrated exclusively on acting and finds satisfaction in acting as a career. "When I'm acting," he told the New York Times, "I'm not on an ego trip, so I try to enter into a close collaboration with the writer. And the same applies vice versa. Most good actors have a sense of character and dialogue. The trick is to create it on paper and to live with the discipline. Acting is a communal experience, whereas writing is a solitary one."

The film rights to "That Championship Season" were acquired by Playboy Productions.

BIOGRAPHICAL/CRITICAL SOURCES: New York Times, March 20, 1970, September 15, 1972, May 8, 1973, February 10, 1974; New Yorker, March 28, 1970, May 20, 1972; New York Post, September 23, 1972; Newsweek, September 25, 1972; After Dark, January, 1972; Contemporary Literary Criticism, Volume 2, Gale, 1974.*

* * *

MILLER, John Chester 1907-

PERSONAL: Born December 23, 1907, in Santa Barbara, Calif.; son of Charles Anton (a merchant) and Agnes Albena (Johnson) Miller; married Gladys S. Johnson (an interior decorator), August 26, 1933; children: Charles, John, Jeffrey. Education: Harvard University, B.S., 1930, M.A., 1932, Ph.D., 1939. Home: 7093 Yachthaven Rd., Friday Harbor, Wash. 98250. Office: Department of History, Stanford University, Stanford, Calif. 94305.

CAREER: Bryn Mawr College, Bryn Mawr, Pa., assistant professor, 1939-44, associate professor of history, 1944-49; Stanford University, Stanford, Calif., visiting professor, 1949-50, professor, 1950-51, Robinson Professor of U.S. History, 1951-73, professor emeritus, 1973—. Member: American Historical Association.

WRITINGS: Sam Adams: Pioneer in Propaganda, Little, Brown, 1936; Origins of the American Revolution, Little, Brown, 1943; The Triumphs of Freedom, 1775-1783, Little,

Brown, 1948; *Crisis in Freedom: The Alien and Sedition Acts,* Little, Brown, 1951; *Alexander Hamilton: Portrait in Paradox,* Harper, 1959; *The Federalist Era,* Harper, 1960; *The First Frontier,* Dell, 1965; *Toward a More Perfect Union,* Scott, Foresman, 1969; *This New Man, the American,* McGraw, 1974; *The Wolf by the Ears,* Free Press, 1977.

WORK IN PROGRESS: The Aaron Burr Conspiracy.

* * *

MILLER, Michael M. 1910(?)-1977

1910(?)—August 11, 1977; American psychiatrist, lecturer, and author of books and articles on psychiatry. Miller pioneered the psychiatric technique of hypnoaversion, a technique where hypnosis is used to create an aversion to drinking, smoking, or overeating. Miller was co-founder of the *American Journal of Social Psychiatry.* He died in Pittman, N.J. Obituaries: *Washington Post,* August 20, 1977; *New York Times,* August 21, 1977.

* * *

MILLER, Tom 1947-

PERSONAL: Born August 11, 1947, in Washington, D.C.; son of Morris (a judge) and Sara (an artist; maiden name, Levy) Miller. *Education:* Attended College of Wooster, 1965-68. *Politics:* "Washed-up lefty." *Religion:* None. *Agent:* Theron Raines, Raines & Raines, 475 Fifth Ave., New York, N.Y. 10017. *Office address:* P.O. Box 50842, Tucson, Ariz. 85703.

CAREER: Has worked as an ice cream truck driver; writer. Consultant, Columbia Broadcasting System (CBS) News "Sixty Minutes" program, 1976-77.

WRITINGS: The Assassination Please Almanac, Regnery, 1977. Contributor of articles to *Esquire, Harpers, Rolling Stone, Nation,* and to the alternative press.

WORK IN PROGRESS: A book on culture and conflict along the United States-Mexican border; directing research for Walter Bowart's *Operation Mind Control,* for Delacorte.

SIDELIGHTS: Miller told *CA* his interest in the John F. Kennedy assassination was "not so much hoodunit but rather how it has become part of American culture, folklore and mythology." He cites as early writing influences "a run-in with the Nixon-Mitchell Justice Department in 1971 (I was subpoenaed to testify before a federal grand jury about the political underground; refused to appear), and background with the underground press."

AVOCATIONAL INTERESTS: Country music, cinema, Southwest mythology, and oboe.

* * *

MILLETT, Kate 1934-

PERSONAL: Birth-given name Katherine Murray Millett; born September 14, 1934, daughter of a contractor and an insurance salesperson; married Fumio Yoshimura (a sculptor), 1965. *Education:* University of Minnesota, B.A. (cum laude), 1956; St. Hilda's College, Oxford, earned first class honors, 1958; Columbia University, Ph.D. (with distinction), 1970. *Politics:* Radical Feminist. *Religion:* Born Catholic.

CAREER: Taught English at University of North Carolina for one half semester, resigned and, in the late 1950's, went to New York City to paint and sculpt while supporting herself as a bank clerk and kindergarten teacher; moved to Ja-

pan, taught English at Waseda University, continued sculpting, and held her first one-woman show at Mirami Gallery, 1961-63; returned to New York City, concentrated on furniture sculpture and exhibited her "suite of furniture" at Judson Gallery in Greenwich Village, March, 1967; taught English at Barnard College in 1968, and conducted an experimental communal school of philosophy there in 1969; directed an all-woman crew in a documentary film, 1970; taught a course on the sociology of women at Bryn Mawr College, 1970. Sculptor and writer, 1971—. Exhibited her nine-foot sculptures, "Naked Ladies," at Los Angeles Women's Building, May, 1977. *Member:* National Organization of Women (NOW; chairperson of education committee), Congress of Racial Equality, Phi Beta Kappa.

WRITINGS: Sexual Politics, Doubleday, 1970; *Flying,* Knopf, 1974; *Sita,* Farrar, Strauss, 1977. Writer of filmscript, "Three Lives" documentary; released by Impact Films, 1971.

SIDELIGHTS: A political activist, Kate Millett assumed the role of movement leader upon the publication of her doctoral dissertation, *Sexual Politics,* a book the *New York Times* labeled the "first above-ground political analysis" of the women's liberation movement. Because of the theories expounded in the book—that sexual distinctions are political definitions, that sexual domination in a patriarchal system has artificially maintained women in a dependent, powerless status—it was met, predictably, with hostile reviews. A seminal work published before the basic tenets of women's equality had gained respectability, *Sexual Politics* was received by many critics with ridicule and innuendoes of bra-burning and homosexuality. Critic Irving Howe wrote, for example, that "there are times when one feels the book was written by a female impersonator."

Some critics, though, confronted the content of the book and its social significance. Nancy Allum pointed out that "it is important to put this book in the right perspective. Its main value is that it shows how many of the great opinion moulders throughout history have, deliberately or unconsciously, perpetuated certain myths to the detriment of women." Reviewer Tracy Morley explained that "In a non-sectarian way, Millett sees the power relationship between the sexes as an integral part of the overall social and political oppression in society." And, in a two part interview for *New York Times,* Christopher Lehmann-Haupt stated that "*Sexual Politics* is a radical feminist's study of the infinite variety of man's exploitation of woman, and it should be said at once that the book is supremely entertaining to read, brilliantly conceived, overwhelming in its arguments, breathtaking in its command of history and literature, filled with shards of wit and the dry ice of logic, and written with such fierce intensity that all vestiges of male chauvinism ought by rights to melt and drip away like so much fat in the flame of a blowtorch."

Millett's most recent book is the autobiographical *Sita,* concerning the breakup of a love affair between two women. The work has been met with varied criticism. Some reviewers have accused Millett of over detailization. Sara Sanborn commented: "She conveys absolutely everything. . . . it seems that Kate can't bear to leave out a single meaningful detail." Other critics praise the frankness and feeling of the book. *Kirkus Reviews* stated: "This is primarily a self-masticating explication of the instances in a love affair played out to the last stretches of the soul. Millett can write with the immaculate economy of vision as in the moment of goodbye with Sita moving away 'like the wind of a fast-moving car overtaking.' Stark, severe, exhausting to read—but it demands attention.''

Many reviews of *Sita* combine the two viewpoints—appreciation of the content and annoyance with the form. John Leonard noted: ''While it is impossible not to respect the pain, love, anger, and confusion here, the embarrassment and, I suppose, the bravery, *Sita* is less a book than a tickertape pouring out of a wound.'' Stephen Koch reflected: ''Though completely unimpressed by Millett's *thoughts* about her dilemma, I believed in the dilemma itself and felt its force and dignity.''

BIOGRAPHICAL/CRITICAL SOURCES: Sharon Smith, *Women Who Make Movies,* Hopkinson & Blake, 1975; *Newsweek,* July 27, 1970; *Washington Post,* July 30, 1970; *New Republic,* August 1, 1970, July 6-13, 1974; *New York Post,* August 1, 1970; *Time,* August 3, 1970, December 14, 1970, July 26, 1971, July 1, 1974; *New York Times,* August 5, 1970, August 6, 1970, September 6, 1970, December 18, 1970, November 5, 1971, May 13, 1977; *Ramparts,* November, 1970; *Canadian Forum,* November/December, 1970; *New Leader,* December 14, 1970; *Books and Bookmen,* June, 1971; *Mademoiselle,* February, 1971; *Saturday Review,* June 15, 1974, May 28, 1977; *New York Times Book Review,* June 23, 1974, May 13, 1977; *New Yorker,* August 9, 1974; *National Review,* August 30, 1974; *Kirkus Reviews,* March 1, 1977.*

*   *   *

MILNE, Roseleen 1945-

PERSONAL: Born May 15, 1945, in Aberdeen, Scotland; daughter of Frederick and Barbara (May) Milne. *Education:* Attended secondary school in Aberdeen, Scotland. *Home:* 31 Airyhall Ter., Aberdeen, Scotland.

CAREER: Writer, 1973—. *Awards, honors:* Award of Pitlochry Quaich from Scottish Association of Writers, 1974.

WRITINGS: Borrowed Plumes (novel), Coward, 1977.

WORK IN PROGRESS: Another novel, set in a Spanish winter during the British Expeditionary Force's retreat to Corunna, 1808-09.

SIDELIGHTS: Roseleen Milne told *CA:* ''I have always been interested in the late Georgian/Regency period. What particularly attracts me is the wealth of beauty in architecture, furniture design, and the Grecian 'theme' which influenced the culture of the age. There was such a flowering of talent during the first years of the nineteenth century; it was the England of Jane Austen, Lord Byron, the painters Constable and Turner; the high point, in my view, of English culture before the ugliness of Victorianism took over.

''I particularly deplore the vandalization by modern city planners of those few examples of fine eighteenth-century architecture which are wantonly sacrificed to make way for soulless modern blocks of glass and steel. The old can perfectly well be incorporated with the new, as has happened in the city of Bath, in Somerset, England—perhaps the most complete and unspoilt Georgian city in Europe. Its classical beauty and atmosphere has been retained whilst yet managing to function with all the needs of a large city in this modern age. I understand this policy has been adopted successfully in Williamsburg, Va. I think it immensely important to conserve our historical heritage in this way. Too much has already been sacrificed.''

*   *   *

MILNER, Ron(ald) 1938-

PERSONAL: Born May 29, 1938, in Detroit, Mich. *Educa-*

tion: Attended Columbia University. *Home:* 15865 Monte Vista, Detroit, Mich. 48238. *Agent:* c/o New American Library, 1301 Avenue of the Americas, New York, N.Y. 10019.

CAREER: Playwright. Writer-in-residence, Lincoln University, 1966-67; teacher, Michigan State University, 1971-72; founder and director, Spirit of Shango theatre company. *Awards, honors:* Rockefeller grant; John Hay Whitney fellowship.

WRITINGS—Plays: ''Who's Got His Own'' (three-act), first produced Off-Broadway at American Place Theatre, 1966; ''The Warning: A Theme for Linda'' (one-act), first produced in New York, 1969; (contributor, and editor with Woodie King) *Black Drama Anthology,* New American Library, 1971; *What the Winesellers Buy* (first produced in Los Angeles, 1973), Samuel French, 1974. Also author of ''The Monster'' and ''(M)ego and the Green Ball of Freedom''.

Work represented in anthologies, including *Best Short Stories by Negro Writers,* edited by Langston Hughes, Little, Brown, 1967; *Black Arts: An Anthology of Black Creations,* edited by Ahmed Alhamsi and Hawn K. Wangara, Broadside Press, 1969; *Black Quartet: Four New Black Plays,* edited by Ben Caldwell and others, New American Library, 1970; *Nommo: An Anthology of Modern Black African & Black American Literature,* edited by William R. Robinson, Macmillan, 1972. Also contributed to *Black Poets and Prophets,* edited by Woodie King and Earl Anthony, New American Library.

Contributor to *Negro Digest,* and other periodicals.

SIDELIGHTS: ''The Warning: A Theme for Linda'' was performed in New York in 1969 along with plays by Le Roi Jones, Ed Bullins, and Ben Caldwell. The group was collectively entitled ''A Black Quartet'' and received a wide range of critical reviews, including notices in the *New York Times.* The remarks of a *New York Times* critic in particular offer a good representation of general critical response to the playwright's work. Harry Gilroy found Milner's play the most interesting of the ''quartet'' and explained: ''This is not to derogate the others; but each of them is concerned in some degree with putting over a message, while Mr. Milner's play is devoted to the more complex art of portraying the anguish and the longing for ecstacy of life itself.''

In an essay on current plays by black dramatists, Clive Barnes voiced his mixed though ultimately positive view: ''Ronald Milner's 'The Warning: A Theme for Linda' might well be used as a textbook example on how not to write a play. It digresses, it changes direction, it has undigested fantasy episodes, characters that are undeveloped and themes that get lost on the way to the theatre. Yet the sheer power of the writing—and for that matter the acting—grips you like a vise. Mr. Milner is recreating reality from his own experience, he is writing about people and things he knows, and they tear our hearts to pieces. Having done that, it hardly matters whether he has written a good play or a bad one. It works.''

BIOGRAPHICAL/CRITICAL SOURCES: C. W. Bigsby, editor, *The Black American Writer,* Everett/Edwards, Volume I: *Fiction,* Volume II: *Poetry & Drama,* 1970; Paul C. Harrison, *The Drama of Nommo,* C. Stephens, 1972.*

*   *   *

MILSON, Fred(erick William) 1912-

PERSONAL: Born December 25, 1912, in Sheffield, England; son of Fred (a clerk) and Ada (a waitress; maiden name, Revill) Milson; married Joyce Betty Haggerjudd (a teacher), September 8, 1939; children: Andrew Gordon, Celia Elisabeth Milson Blaszkowicz. *Education:* University of Hull, B.D. (honors), 1950; University of Leeds, M.A., 1958; University of Birmingham, Ph.D., 1964. *Politics:* Liberal. *Religion:* Methodist. *Home:* 1 Kestrel Grove, Bournville, Birmingham, England.

CAREER: Ordained Methodist minister in 1939; served as pastor of churches in Manchester, London, Sheffield, Hull, Stoke, and Leeds, all in England; Westhill College, Selly Oak, Birmingham, England, principal lecturer in sociology, and head of department, 1960—. Research fellow at University of Birmingham, 1972-73. Member of British Broadcasting Corp. "Round Britain Quiz"; member of Gulbenkian Working Group on Community Work, 1972-76; chairperson of Birmingham Local Radio Council, 1973-76, and National Council of Voluntary Youth Service, 1976—; consultant to Commonwealth Conference on Young People in Asia, 1971. *Awards, honors:* Honorary fellow of University of Birmingham.

WRITINGS: Youth and the Cinema, Epworth, 1956; *Living and Loving,* Epworth, 1963; *Social Group Methods and Christian Education,* Chester House Publishers, 1963; *Education,* Methodist Youth Department, 1964; *Group Methods for Christian Leaders: A Study of Group Dynamics,* Religious Education Press, 1965; *Role-Playing in the Youth Club,* Methodist Youth Department, 1966; *His Leadership and Ours,* Epworth, 1968; (editor) *Youth Service and Interprofessional Studies,* Pergamon, 1970; *Youth Work in the 1970's,* Routledge & Kegan Paul, 1970; *Faith and an Evening Paper,* National Christian Education Council, 1970; *Growing with the Job,* National Association of Youth Clubs, 1970; *Church, Youth and Community Development,* Chester House Publishers, 1970; *Youth in a Changing Society,* Routledge & Kegan Paul, 1970; *Sex and a Pastor,* Epworth, 1972; *An Introduction to Group Work Skill,* Routledge & Kegan Paul, 1973; *An Introduction to Community Work,* Routledge & Kegan Paul, 1974; *Community Work and the Christian Faith,* Hodder & Stoughton, 1975. Contributor to magazines and newspapers, including *Guardian, Times Educational Supplement, British Weekly,* and *New Society.*

SIDELIGHTS: Milson writes: "I am mainly interested in the ideological bases of social behaviour. Having worked for many years as a Methodist minister in urban areas I became convinced of the need for an understanding of the Gospel which had a sociological dimension. I have been greatly helped by two American writers—Reinhold Niebuhr and Peter Berger. For me the three most important subjects in life are theology, sociology, and cricket—in that order. My idea of heaven is that there is an endless cricket match being played, I am able to read theological works between the overs, and study the behaviour of the crowd in the lunch interval."

*   *   *

MILTON, David Scott 1934-

PERSONAL: Born September 15, 1934, in Pittsburgh, Pa.; son of S. I. and Gertrude (Osgood) Milton. *Education:* Attended high school in Pittsburgh, Pa. *Home:* 1235 24th St., #1, Santa Monica, Calif. 90404. *Agent:* Shapiro-Lichtman, 9200 Sunset Blvd., Los Angeles, Calif. 90069.

CAREER: Writer, 1960—. Senior lecturer in drama, University of Southern California, 1977-78. *Awards, honors:* The film "Born to Win" was featured at New York Film

Festival; award from *Mark Twain Journal,* 1974, for *Paradise Road.*

WRITINGS: The Quarterback (novel), Dell, 1970; *Paradise Road* (novel), Atheneum, 1974.

Plays: "Metaphysical Cop" (one-act), first produced in New York City at Off Center Theatre, February, 1967; "Scraping Bottom" (one-act), first produced in New York City at New York Theatre Ensemble, November 22, 1968; "Duet for Solo Voice" (one-act), first produced in New York City at American Place Theatre, February, 1970; "Bread" (two-act), first produced in New York City at American Place Theatre, January, 1974; *Duet* (one-act; first produced on Broadway at John Golden Theater, February 11, 1975), Samuel French, 1975.

Screenplays: "Born to Win," United Artists, 1971; "Scraping Bottom," Theatre Guild Films, 1971. Unproduced screenplays include "Kool-Aid Kelly," with Terry Southern; "Cat in the Bag," with Jean-Claude Carrier; "Get the Police," with Dick Richards.

Television: Author of television adaptation of David Hare's "Knuckle," on KCET-Television, 1975, and the documentary presentation "Notes on a Passport: Peggy Stuart Coolidge in Asia," 1969.

WORK IN PROGRESS: Kabbalah, a novel; *The Uncle,* a play in two acts.

SIDELIGHTS: Milton writes: "I've had an astonishing life filled with adventure, plot-like coincidence, villains, heros, desperate characters, comedy, tragedy. If it were a novel one would say it was too Dickensian. There have been scant education from schools, rich lessons from thousands of books, and, most importantly, honest labor with a wide variety of exceptional and fascinating people. I loathe totalitarianism in whatever chic garb it chooses to clothe itself. I am a Jew, albeit a non-observant one, with a passionate love for and commitment to a people whose existence so often has appeared to be only as a blood sacrifice to the barbaric aspect of man's nature.

"I am obsessed by man and his condition: his dreams, his frailties, his bravery, his foolishness. I loathe ideologues, shy away from systems, dislike technocrats, shun those intellectuals possessing thought without wisdom. We are all here for a pathetically short span; we are dust. Greatness is fleeting; deeds are transitory. We must respect and acknowledge each other on this short ride from dark into dark. It is a funhouse ride and we only take it once."

AVOCATIONAL INTERESTS: Lifting weights, playing racquetball, crossword puzzles, modern Russian history.

BIOGRAPHICAL/CRITICAL SOURCES: Pauline Kael, *Deeper into Movies,* 1973.

*   *   *

MINARIK, Else Holmelund 1920-

PERSONAL: Born September 13, 1920, in Denmark; emigrated to the U.S. at age four; married Walter Minarik (died, 1963); married Homer Bigart, 1970; children: (first marriage) Brooke. *Education:* Attended Queens College (now of the City University of New York) and Paltz College of the State University of New York.

CAREER: Has worked as a reporter for a local newspaper, and as a teacher during World War II in Commack, Long Island; author of books for children.

WRITINGS: Little Bear (illustrated by Maurice Sendak), Harper, 1957; *No Fighting, No Biting!* (illustrated by Sendak), Harper, 1958; *Father Bear Comes Home* (illustrated by Sendak), Harper, 1959; *Cat and Dog* (illustrated by Fritz Siebel), Harper, 1960; *Little Bear's Friend* (illustrated by Sendak), Harper, 1960; *Little Bear's Visit* (illustrated by Sendak), Harper, 1961; *The Little Giant Girl and the Elf Boy* (illustrated by Garth Williams), Harper, 1963; *The Winds That Come From Far Away, and Other Poems* (illustrated by Joan P. Berg), Harper, 1964; *A Kiss for Little Bear* (illustrated by Sendak), Harper, 1968.

SIDELIGHTS: As a result of her teaching experience, Else Holmelund Minarik became interested in writing for children. When she couldn't find enough books for her first-graders, she responded to their needs by writing books herself.

Commenting on Else Minarik's first book, *Little Bear,* a *New York Times* critic wrote: "It is difficult to be practical about something charming—one wants only to be charmed. Yet this is a book that must be considered on two counts: its joyousness and its usefulness. It passes on both counts. One look at the illustrations and children will grab it. A second look at the short, easy sentences, the repetition of words and the beautiful type spacing, and children will know they can read it themselves." Wrote *New Yorker:* "What makes this book different from all the other children's books in which animals wear clothes and live in houses is that instead of being a tale told to amuse children it all seems to be happening within a child's head. Also the fact that it is so full of love."

Kirkus commented on *No Fighting, No Biting!:* "Else Holmelund Minarik, whose *Little Bear* indicated a uniquely charming talent, has outdone herself here, and Maurice Sendak's illustrations reaffirm the impression that he is one of the most gifted illustrators of contemporary children's books." The *New York Times* remarked that "Mrs. Minarik has wisely not tried to repeat the tender mood of her first book—that was probably inimitable, even by its own author. This new one may not touch the emotions so sensitively and may not be so durable, but children should find very realistic the sketches of two youngsters engaged in one of those timeless routines of pinching, squeezing, and general teasing."

AVOCATIONAL INTERESTS: Gardening.

BIOGRAPHICAL/CRITICAL SOURCES: New York Times, September 8, 1957, October 5, 1958; *New Yorker,* November 23, 1957; *Kirkus,* July 15, 1958.*

*   *   *

MINARIK, John Paul   1947-

PERSONAL: Born November 6, 1947, in McKeesport, Pa.; son of Rudolph Andrew (an engineer) and Pauline (Babyak) Minarik. *Education:* Carnegie-Mellon University, B.S., 1970; also attended University of Pittsburgh, 1971—, and Community College of Allegheny County, 1972-75. *Residence:* West Mifflin, Pa. *Office:* Academy of Prison Arts, P.O. Box 9901, Pittsburgh, Pa. 15233.

CAREER: U.S. Steel Corp., Pittsburgh, Pa., engineer, 1965-71; Academy of Prison Arts, Pittsburgh, editor, 1973—; Community College of Allegheny County, Pittsburgh, instructor, 1977—. Conducted research on nonlethal gun prototypes for Survival Technology, Inc., 1969-70; has given poetry readings in the Pittsburgh area.

MEMBER: American Society of Mechanical Engineers, American Society of Metals, American Powder Metallurgy Institute, People Concerned for the Unborn Child, Alliance for Consumer Protection, American Dental Assistants As-

sociation, Pennsylvanians for Human Life, Jaycees. *Awards, honors:* Won speaking contests sponsored by American Society of Mechanical Engineers and Society of Automotive Engineers, both 1970; honorable mention from International P.E.N., 1976-77, for a short story.

WRITINGS: A Book (poems), V. Mark Press, 1974, 2nd edition, 1977; *Patterns in the Dusk* (poems), King Publications, 1977. Contributor of technical articles and poems to magazines, including *Greenfield Review, Journal of Popular Culture, Small Pond, Backspace, Occult Americana,* and *Nitty Gritty.*

WORK IN PROGRESS: Measurements and Data; Fear in a Handful of Dust, poems; short stories.

SIDELIGHTS: Minarik writes: "As an engineer and poet, my interdisciplinary interest is in the way people live on this biosphere. My deep concern is for the way our social institutions have been unable to meet the needs of people and I believe no amount of high technology will solve these problems. I feel that people must stay in touch with their basic humanity, and realize that a Super-Presto-Cooker will hardly improve the quality of their lives. It is up to the poet to keep death alive. It is up to the engineer to improve our technology, while keeping a balance with the natural forces of the earth, to allow us to live and die in harmony with the planet. I am against any person who thinks he is not biodegradable."

BIOGRAPHICAL/CRITICAL SOURCES: Ethnic American News, May 15, 1977.

*   *   *

MINTZ, Elizabeth E.   1913-

PERSONAL: Born December 31, 1913, in Minneapolis, Minn.; daughter of William H. (a professor) and Virginia (Cloyd) Emmons; married Alexander Mintz (a professor); children: Ann E., Harvey E. *Education:* University of Minnesota, B.A., 1935; Columbia University, M.A., 1936; New York University, Ph.D., 1956. *Politics:* Liberal. *Religion:* Humanist. *Home:* 21 Pleasant Ave., Hastings-on-Hudson, N.Y. 10706. *Office:* 500 West End Ave., New York, N.Y. 10024.

CAREER: Private practice in psychology, 1953—. Diplomate of American Board of Professional Psychologists. Panel psychologist at Pleasantville Cottage School, 1956-58; supervisor of Pleasantville, N.Y.'s Community Guidance Service, 1958-65; director of group therapy for New York Clinic for Mental Health, 1959-61. Faculty member at Institute for Practising Psychotherapists, 1964-65; visiting professor at Adelphi University, 1971; associate professor at Cornell University, 1971-72.

MEMBER: National Psychological Association for Psychoanalysis, American Academy of Psychotherapists, American Psychological Association, American Group Psychotherapy Association, Eastern Group Therapy Society.

WRITINGS: Marathon Groups: Reality and Symbol, Appleton, 1971; (contributor) Wolberg and Aronson, editors, *Group Therapy 1974,* Postgraduate Center for Mental Health, 1974. Also contributor to *The Psychoanalytic Situation,* edited by Hendrik M. Ruitenbeek, Atherton, and *Confrontation,* edited by L. Blank, G. Gottsegen, and M. Gottsegen, Macmillan. Contributor of about twenty-five articles to psychology journals.

WORK IN PROGRESS: Transpersonal Elements in Conventional Psychotherapy.

MISHAN, E(zra) J(oshua) 1917-

PERSONAL: Born November 15, 1917, in Manchester, England; son of David (a businessman) and Freda (Choueke) Mishan; married Rachel Blesofsky, September, 1951; children: David, Freda, Joseph, Rachel. *Education:* University of London, M.Sc., 1949; University of Chicago, Ph.D., 1951. *Home:* Dormans Park, East Grinstead, Sussex, England. *Office:* Centre for Banking, City University, Saint John St., London EC1, England.

CAREER: University of London, London School of Economics and Political Science, London, England, professor of economics, 1956-75; writer, 1975—. Visiting professor at American University, 1970-72, and University of Maryland, 1974-75; lecturer at Johns Hopkins University, 1971.

WRITINGS: The Costs of Economic Growth, Praeger, 1967; *Twenty-One Popular Economic Fallacies,* Penguin, 1969; *Cost-Benefit Analysis,* Praeger, 1971; *Making the World Safe for Pornography,* Alcove Press, 1973; *The Economic Growth Debate,* Allen & Unwin, 1977. Contributor of more than one hundred articles to economic journals, to *Encounter,* and to newspapers.

WORK IN PROGRESS: An Introduction to Normative Economics.

SIDELIGHTS: Mishan told *CA:* "Economics is just a hobby. My main preoccupation is the appalling world we are moving into." *Avocational interests:* Body building, sculpting.

BIOGRAPHICAL/CRITICAL SOURCES: New York Times Biographical Edition, November 21, 1971.

* * *

MITCHELL, Alexander Ross Kerr 1934-

PERSONAL: Born September 3, 1934, in Edinburgh, Scotland; son of Robert Kay Sabiston (a schoolmaster) and Margaret (Shorthouse) Mitchell; married Rhoda Anderson, November 9, 1959; children: Nicola, Michael. *Education:* University of Edinburgh, MB.Ch.B., 1958, D.P.M., 1962, M.R.C.P., 1971. *Office:* Fulbourn Hospital, Cambridge CB1 5EF, England.

CAREER: Physician in Edinburgh, Scotland, 1958-59; psychiatrist in Sussex, England, 1959-60, and Bristol, England, 1964-66; Fulbourn Hospital, Cambridge, England, consulting psychiatrist, 1966—. Associate lecturer at Cambridge University, 1977—. *Military service:* British Army, Medical Corps, 1960-64; became lieutenant colonel. *Member:* Royal College of Psychiatrists (fellow), Royal College of Physicians (Edinburgh), British Medical Association, Cambridge Medical Society (past president).

WRITINGS: Drugs: The Parents' Dilemma, Priory Press, 1969; *Psychological Medicine in Family Practice,* Balliere, 1971; *Schizophrenia: The Meaning of Madness,* Priory Press, 1972; *Depression,* Penguin, 1975; *What Is a Nervous Breakdown?,* Family Doctor Booklets, 1977.

WORK IN PROGRESS: A book on violence in the family.

SIDELIGHTS: Mitchell writes: "I am primarily interested in making psychiatry and psychological medicine understandable for non-psychiatrists. I believe this complex subject can be presented in an intelligent way, so that interested persons are able to share and understand, and not to be put off by professional mysticism. I am therefore interested in anything that has to do with what people do, what they think, and what they feel."

MITCHELL, Colin W(are) 1927-

PERSONAL: Born October 8, 1927, in London, England; son of Arthur Croft (an artist) and Evelyn (an artist; maiden name, Ware) Mitchell; married Anne Clemency Sarah Phillips (a physician), December 30, 1963; children: Patrick Bernard, David Ware, Julian Gordon, Laura Anna. *Education:* Attended Harvard University, 1944-45; Brasenose College, Oxford, M.A., 1952; University of Liverpool, M.C.D., 1952; University of Aberdeen, cert. soil science, 1956; Cambridge University, Ph.D., 1970. *Religion:* Seventh-Day Adventist. *Home:* 43 Eastern Ave., Reading RG1 5RX, England. *Office:* Department of Geography, University of Reading, Whiteknights, Reading RG6 2AU, England.

CAREER: Government of Sudan, Ministry of Agriculture, soil surveyor in research division, 1952-55; soil survey team leader, Hunting Technical Services, Ltd., 1956-63; University of Cambridge, Cambridge, England, ministry of defense research fellow, 1963-67; University of Reading, Reading, England, lecturer in geography, 1968—. Consultant to government, business, and the United Nations. *Military service:* Royal Air Force, 1945-48. *Member:* International Society of Soil Science, Royal Geographical Society (fellow), British Society of Soil Science, Institute of British Geographers.

WRITINGS: Terrain Evaluation, Longman, 1973. Contributor to scientific journals.

WORK IN PROGRESS: Research on terrain classification schemes and on Saharan geomorphology and soils.

SIDELIGHTS: Mitchell writes: "I have a Christian view of the world which is especially applicable to my interest in development in the Third World. I have worked and managed surveys in Iraq, Jordan, Sudan, Tanzania, Kenya, and Pakistan. I have organized and managed scientific expeditions to Libya, United Arab Emirates, Socotra, Abdul Kuri, Morocco, and elsewhere."

* * *

MITCHELL, Greg 1947-

PERSONAL: Born December 7, 1947, in Niagara Falls, N.Y.; son of Stanley (an accountant) and Edith (Munro) Mitchell. *Education:* St. Bonaventure University, B.A., 1970. *Home:* 85 East 10th St., New York, N.Y. 10003. *Office: Politicks,* 271 Madison Ave., New York, N.Y. 10016.

CAREER/WRITINGS: Niagara Falls Gazette, Niagara Falls, N.Y., reporter, 1968-69; *Zygote,* New York City, news editor, 1970; *Crawdaddy,* New York City, senior editor, 1971-76; *Politicks,* New York City, senior editor, 1977—. Notable assignments include interviews with Joseph Heller, Kurt Vonnegut, Jr., Tom Robbins, Gram Persons, Eugene McCarthy, Han Suyin, Roy Orbison, and Robert Stone. *Awards, honors:* New York State Publishers Association distinguished local reporting award, 1970, for ten-part series on police-black relations in Niagara Falls, N.Y.

WORK IN PROGRESS: The Great American, a novel.

* * *

MITTELMAN, James H(oward) 1944-

PERSONAL: Born November 29, 1944, in Marinette, Wis.; son of Alan W. (a businessman) and Geraldine (Frankel) Mittelman; married Linda Yarr, September 5, 1976; children: Alexandra. *Education:* Michigan State University, B.A. (honors), 1966; graduate study at Georgetown University and Makerere University; Cornell University, M.A., 1970, Ph.D., 1971. *Residence:* New York, N.Y. *Office:* Department of Political Science, Columbia University, New York, N.Y. 10027.

CAREER: Makerere University, Kampala, Uganda, special tutor in political science and research associate at Makerere Institute of Social Science, 1970-71; Cornell University, Ithaca, N.Y., lecturer in political science, 1971-72; Columbia University, New York City, assistant professor of political science, 1972—. Lecturer in Uganda Foreign Service Officers Training Programme, 1970; guest lecturer at Boston University, State University of New York at Albany, University of Rhodesia, University of Witwatersrand, and University of Zambia. Intern at United Nations Institute for Training and Research, 1969; visitor at University of Dar es Salaam, 1975-76; visiting scholar at Centre Universitaire International, 1976; visiting fellow at Princeton University Center for International Studies, 1977-78. Member of board of advisers of Global Center for Community Education. Consultant to United Nations Development Program and United Nations Educational, Scientific and Cultural Organization.

MEMBER: International Studies Association, Society for International Development, African Studies Association, American Political Science Association, Educators to Africa Association, Pi Sigma Alpha, Delta Phi Epsilon, Phi Gamma Mu, 1966 Club. *Awards, honors:* Grants from American Council of Learned Societies, 1973-74, National Science Foundation, 1973-74, University Consortium for World Order Studies, 1975-76, Rockefeller Foundation, 1975-76, and Social Science Research Council, 1977-78.

WRITINGS: The Uganda Coup and the Internationalization of Political Violence, Munger, 1972; (with Onkar S. Marwah) *Asian Alien Pariahs: A Cross-Regional Perspective* (monograph), Center on International Race Relations, University of Denver, 1974; *Ideology and Politics in Uganda: From Obote to Amin,* Cornell University Press, 1975. Contributor of articles and reviews to international studies and African studies journals and to newspapers.

WORK IN PROGRESS: Underdevelopment and the Transition to Socialism: Mozambique and Tanzania, publication expected in 1979.

SIDELIGHTS: Mittelman's studies have taken him to Tanzania, Kenya, and other parts of Africa, Hong Kong, India, the Philippines, Singapore, Taiwan, Europe, the Middle East, Mexico, and South America. *Avocational interests:* Tennis, squash, jogging, basketball, theater, films.

* * *

MIURA, Ayako 1922-

PERSONAL: Born April 25, 1922, in Asahikawa City, Japan; daughter of Tetsuji and Kisa (Satoh) Hotta; married Mitsuyo Miura, May 24, 1959. *Education:* Educated in Japan. *Home:* 4-chome, Toyooka 2-jo, Asahikawa City, Hokkaido 070, Japan. *Agent:* Japan UNI Agency, Inc., Fukuyama Bldg., 1-14 Kanda Jinbocho, Chiyoda-ku, Tokyo 101, Japan.

CAREER: Has worked as an elementary school teacher and manager of a drug store, 1959-61; writer, 1965—.

WRITINGS—In English: *Shiokari Tohge,* 1968, published as *Shiokari Pass,* Fearnehough, Bill and Fearnehough, 1976.

Also author of *Hyoten* (title means "The Freezing Point"), 1965; *Hitsujigaoka* (title means "The Hill of Sleep"), 1966; *Tsumiki No Hako* (title means "A Box of Building

Blocks"), 1968; *Michi Ariki* (title means "The Wind Is Howling"), 1969; *Yameru Toki Mo* (title means "Also in Illness"), 1969; *Kono Tsuchi No Utsawa Omo* (title means "Also This Soil Bowl"), 1970; *Sabaki no Ie* (title means "The House of Judgement"), 1970; *Hikari Aru Uchini* (title means "Within the Light Remains"), 1971; *Zoku Hyoten* (title means "The Freezing Point, Part 2"); *Ikiru Koto, Omou Koto* (title means "To Live, To Think"), 1972; *Kaeranu Kaze* (title means "Ureturned Wind"), 1972; *Jiga No Kohzu* (title means "Composition of Ego"), 1972; *Assate No Kaze* (title means "Wind of the Day After Tomorrow"), 1972; *Shi No Kanata Mademo* (title means "Still Beyond Death"), 1972; *Zanzo* (title means "An Afterimage"), 1973; *Ai Ni Tohku Aredo* (title means "Although Being Far From Love"), 1973; *Tomo Ni Ayumeba* (title means "In Walking Together"), 1973; *Inochi Ni Horikomareshi Ai No Katachi* (title means "The Form of Love Carved in Life"), 1973; *Ishikoro No Uta* (title means "The Song of a Stonelet"), 1974; *Taiyo wa Itumo Kumo no Ue ni* (title means "The Sun is Always Above the Cloud"), 1974; *Kyuyaku Seisho Nyumon* (title means "An Introduction to the Old Testament"), 1974.

Hosokawa Gallaecia Fujin (title means "Madame Gallecia Hosokawa"), 1975; *Ishi No Mori* (title means "A Wood of Stone"), 1976; *Tempoku Genva* (title means "The Tempoku Plain"), 1976; *Deiryu Chitai* (title means "Soil Stream Zone"), 1976; *Hiroki Dohro* (title means "A Broad Road"), 1976; *Hate Tohki Oka* (title means "A Hill on the Far End"), 1977; *Toryo Ichidaiki* (title means "A Personal History of a Master Carpenter"), 1977.

* * *

MOELLER, Charles 1912-

PERSONAL: Born January 18, 1912, in Brussels, Belgium. *Education:* Studied at the seminary of Malines, Belgium; Catholic University of Louvain, Belgium, Ph.D., 1945. *Residence:* Rome, Italy. *Office:* Secretariat pour l'unite des chretiens, via dell'Erba 1, 00193-Rome, Italy.

CAREER: Ordained as a diocesan priest, 1937; Institut Saint-Pierre, Jette, Belgium, professor of poetry, 1941-54; University of Louvain, Belgium, professor, 1956—. Consultant for the theological commission of the Vatican II council, 1962-65; undersecretary of the Curia in Rome for the doctrine of the faith, 1966-73; rector of l'Institut oecumenique in Jerusalem, 1969-73; member of the Royal Academy of French language and literature in Belgium, 1970; secretary of the secretariat for the unity of Christians, 1973—.

WRITINGS—In English: (With Gerard Philips) *Theologie de la grace et oecumenisme,* Editions de Chevetogne, 1957, 2nd edition, 1965, translation by R. A. Wilson published as *The Theology of Grace and the Ecumenical Movement,* St. Anthony Guild Press, 1969; *Mentalite moderne et evangelisation,* Editions Lumen Vitae (Brussels), 1962, translation by E. Mike-Bekassy published as *Modern Mentality and Evangelization,* Alba, Volume I: *God,* 1967, Volume II: *The Church,* 1968, Volume III: *Jesus and Mary,* 1968; *L'Homme moderne devant le salut,* Editions Ouvrieres (Paris), 1965, translation by Charles Quinn published as *Man and Salvation in Literature,* University of Notre Dame Press, 1970.

Other writings: *Humanisme et saintete* (title means "Humanism and Holiness"), Casterman, 1946; *Sagesse grecque et paradoxe chretien* (title means "Greek Wisdom and Christian Paradox"), Casterman, 1948; *Litterature du XXeme siecle et christianisme,* Casterman, Volume 1: *Silence de Dieu* (title means "The Silence of God"), Volume

2: *La Foi en Jesus-Christ* (title means "Faith in Jesus Christ"), Volume 3: *Espoir des hommes* (title means "Hope of Men"), Volume 4: *L'Esperance en Dieu Notre Pere* (title means "Hope in God our Father"), Volume 5: *Amours humains* (title means "Human Loves"), 1953-1975; (Contributor) Adolfo Munoz-Alonzo, editor, *Pesimismo y optimiso en la cultura actual* (title means "Pessimism and Optimism in Modern Culture"), Servicio Español del Profesorado del Movimiento (Madrid), 1963; *L'Elaboration du schema XIII sur l'Eglise dans le monde d'aujourd'hui,* Casterman, 1968; *Culture et apostolat* (title means "Culture and Apostleship"), Apostolat, 1968.

Contributor to *Chalcedon, Geschichte, und Gegenwart, Lexikon fur Theologie und Kirche,* and *Unam Sanctum.* Also contributor to *Irenkon, Revue d'histoire ecclesiastique, Revue nouvelle,* and other journals in his field.

BIOGRAPHICAL/CRITICAL SOURCES: Christian Century, October 7, 1970.

* * *

MOFFETT, Hugh 1910-

PERSONAL: Born August 17, 1910, in Cherryvale, Kan.; son of Adam (a farmer) and Laura (Wilkin) Moffett; married Bette Little; children: Tom, Molly Frederick, Mark. *Education:* University of Missouri, B.J., 1933. *Politics:* Democrat. *Religion:* "Hardly any." *Home:* 69 Park St., Brandon, Vt. 05733.

CAREER/WRITINGS: Des Moines Tribune, Des Moines, Iowa, assistant city editor, 1933-44; *Time,* New York City, bureau head in Denver, Colo., Chicago, Ill., and Tokyo, Japan, 1944-51; *Life,* New York City, news editor, 1944-58, assistant managing editor, 1958-67; Vermont legislature, Montpelier, member of House of Representatives, 1975-78. Contributor of articles to *Life, Smithsonian, Signature, Blair & Ketchum's Country Journal.*

SIDELIGHTS: Moffett told *CA:* "The only way to keep politicians honest is to keep a threat of exposure hanging over their heads. The press is the best agency to accomplish this, more constant than policeman. With skeletons in the closet, it would not be so easy to take this position."

* * *

MOHR, James C(rail) 1943-

PERSONAL: Born January 28, 1943, in Edgewood, Md.; son of Ernest E. (an engineer) and Jean (Wyant) Mohr; married Elizabeth Bushey, July 1, 1967; children: Timothy Crail, Stephanie Elizabeth. *Education:* Yale University, B.A., 1965; Stanford University, Ph.D., 1969. *Home:* 5496 Halflight Garth, Columbia, Md. 21045. *Office:* Department of History, University of Maryland—Baltimore County, Wilkens Ave., Baltimore, Md. 21228.

CAREER: University of Maryland—Baltimore County, Baltimore, assistant professor, 1969-72, associate professor, 1972-77, professor of American history, 1977—. Visiting associate professor at Stanford University, 1973-74; visiting professor at University of Virginia, 1977. *Member:* American Historical Association, Organization of American Historians, Association for the Study of Afro-American Life and History, Southern History Association, Phi Beta Kappa. *Awards, honors:* Danforth associate, 1975—; Rockefeller-Ford Foundation grant, 1975-76.

WRITINGS: The Radical Republicans and Reform in New York During Reconstruction, Cornell University Press, 1973; *Radical Republicans in the North: State Politics During Reconstruction,* Johns Hopkins Press, 1976; *Abortion in America: The Origin and Evolution of National Policy, 1800-1900,* Oxford University Press, 1978. Contributor of articles and reviews to history journals. Member of editorial board of *Journal of Negro History,* 1973-74.

SIDELIGHTS: "My chief purpose in writing books," Mohr told *CA,* "is to try to offer historical perspective—particularly on the formation of social policy—in an era that frequently betrays itself as being perilously ahistorical."

* * *

MONROE, Charles R(exford) 1905-

PERSONAL: Born February 17, 1905, in Iliff, Colo.; son of Charles Thomas (a farmer) and Edna (a farmer; maiden name, Wood) Monroe; married Edith Florence Erickson, August 23, 1928; children: Marilyn Ruth, Eugene Alan. *Education:* University of Colorado, A.B., 1925, M.A., 1926; University of Wisconsin, Madison, Ph.D., 1941. *Politics:* "Democratic as a rule." *Religion:* Methodist. *Home:* 6010 Taft Court, Arvada, Colo. 80004.

CAREER: Bacone College, Muskogee, Okla., instructor in history, 1927-29; Kansas City Junior College, Kansas City, Kan., instructor in history, 1929-38; University of Wisconsin, Madison, instructor in history, 1940-41; Chicago City Colleges, Chicago, Ill., instructor in history, 1941-42; Northwestern University, Evanston, Ill., instructor in history, 1942-43; Chicago City Colleges, professor of history, 1943-48; Chicago Teachers College, Chicago, professor of history, 1948-56; Chicago City Colleges, president of Kennedy-King College, 1956-69; writer, 1969—. Vice-president of Chicago Teachers Union, 1950-56; chairman of education committee, Chicago Commission on Human Relations, 1955-69. *Member:* Kappa Delta Pi. *Awards, honors:* Ford Foundation fellowship, 1954-55.

WRITINGS: (With George Attebury, John Auble, and Elgin Hunt) *Introduction to Social Sciences,* two volumes, Macmillan, 1950; *Profile of the Community College,* Jossey-Bass, 1972. Editor, *Illinois Councilor,* 1948-65.

WORK IN PROGRESS: A revision of *Profile of the Community College.*

SIDELIGHTS: Charles Monroe told *CA:* "Community, junior colleges have become the natural extension of the Americn belief that public education should be available to all citizens. First was the elementary school, then the high school, and now the tuition-free community college. In the past ten years these two-year colleges have begun to emancipate themselves from the traditions and limitations of the four-year academic college and university. Hence, these community colleges have learned to adapt their curricula and instructional practices to the manifold needs of the local community.

"Today the predominant function of these colleges has been to provide the occupational skills which the community needs for its high school graduates and the ever increasing number of adults who wish to upgrade their employment status or to enjoy a richer avocational life.

"Also the community colleges have become the best open door college to provide educational opportunities for the disadvantaged elements of the American society. These colleges find it easier than senior colleges do to break new paths of opportunity for those young people who are the first in their families to attend college, and who are not geared to meet or to want the traditional offerings of the senior colleges."

AVOCATIONAL INTERESTS: International travel, photography.

* * *

MONSARRAT, Ann Whitelaw 1937-

PERSONAL: Born April 8, 1937, in Walsall, England; daughter of Cyril Whitelaw (an accountant) and Marie Patricia (Barnfield) Griffiths; married Nicholas John Turney Monsarrat (a writer), December 22, 1961. *Education:* Educated in Kent, England. *Politics:* Conservative. *Home:* San Lawrenz, Gozo, Malta. *Agent:* Campbell Thomson & McLaughlin Ltd., 31 Newington Green, London N16 9PU, England.

CAREER: West Kent Mercury, Bromley, Kent, England, journalist, 1954-58; *Daily Mail,* London, England, journalist, 1958-61; *Stationery Trade Review,* London, assistant editor, 1961; free-lance writer, 1962—.

WRITINGS: And the Bride Wore ...: The Story of the White Wedding, Gentry, 1973, Dodd, 1974.

WORK IN PROGRESS: A biography of William Makepeace Thackeray, for Dodd.

SIDELIGHTS: Monsarrat told *CA:* "*And the Bride Wore ...* is a social and costume history of the wedding from Greek and Roman times to the present day, with examples drawn from contemporary sources—diaries, letters, fiction, and periodicals. It was sparked off by seeing a television play in which an eighteenth century bride wore a yellow evening dress and no veil: absolutely correct. The white wedding, with all the trimmings we know today, took a long time to evolve and only came into its own at the beginning of last century. It was while working on this book that I became interested in Thackeray—a superb social historian, whose wife went mad, who fell in love with his best friend's wife, who lost his patrimony and made a fortune, and who poured the traumas of his own life into every book he wrote."

* * *

MONTICONE, Ronald Charles 1937-

PERSONAL: Born November 17, 1937, in Pittsburgh, Pa.; son of Charles R. (a professor) and Josephine G. (a teacher; maiden name, Santangelo) Monticone; married Diane T. Kollar (a college professor), June 10, 1967; children: Ronald Charles, Jr., Joanne M. *Education:* University of Maryland, B.A., 1959, M.A., 1962; New York University, Ph.D., 1965. *Politics:* Democrat. *Religion:* Roman Catholic. *Home:* 946 Midland Rd., Oradell N.J. 07649. *Office:* Department of Social Services, Queensborough Community College, Bayside, N.Y. 11364.

CAREER: Bronx Community College, Bronx, N.Y., part-time lecturer in history, 1962-65; Queensborough Community College, Bayside, N.Y., assistant professor, 1965-69, associate professor, 1969-75, professor of government, 1975—. *Member:* American Association for the Advancement of Slavic Studies, Polish Institute of Arts and Sciences in America, Democratic Club (Oradell, N.J.).

WRITINGS: Charles de Gaulle, G. K. Hall, 1975. Contributor of articles and reviews to *Polish Review.* Member of board of editors of *Polish Review.*

WORK IN PROGRESS: A political biography of Georges Pompidou.

SIDELIGHTS: Monticone writes: "My field of interest is primarily comparative European political systems with an emphasis on Eastern Europe. I have traveled extensively in Eastern and Western Europe and in Latin America, and speak Spanish and French and a little Russian. I also teach international politics and American politics."

* * *

MOON, Robert 1925-

PERSONAL: Born November 2, 1925, in Moose Jaw, Saskatchewan, Canada; son of Philip John (an accountant) and Ethel (Kent) Moon. *Education:* University of Saskatchewan, B.A., 1948; Concordia University, Montreal, Quebec, graduate study. *Home address:* P.O. Box 1445, Moose Jaw, Saskatchewan, Canada.

CAREER: Worked as political writer, 1948-55; Saskatchewan Press Gallery, Regina, president, 1955-56; Canadian Parliamentary Press Gallery, Ottawa, Ontario, member of gallery, 1957-66; free-lance journalist, 1966-68; taught at college in Oshawa, Ontario, 1968-71; researcher, 1971—. Alderman of Oshawa, 1970-71. *Military service:* Canadian Army, 1944-45. Canadian Army Reserves; became second lieutenant. *Member:* Canadian Authors Association, Canadian Agricultural Economics Society. *Awards, honors:* Received Kentucky Traveling Fellowship, 1954-55.

WRITINGS: This Is Saskatchewan, Ryerson, 1953; *I Found Canada Abroad,* Ryerson, 1957; *Pearson,* High Hill House, 1962; *Sunday Notebook,* High Hill House, 1963; (editor) *P.M.: Dialogue, Speeches, and Quotations of Prime Minister P. E. Trudeau,* High Hill House, 1972; "*Not Only a Name, A Long Love Letter From Moose Jaw, Saskatchewan,*" Crocus House, 1977.

WORK IN PROGRESS: Writing about Qu'appelle Valley, Saskatchewan.

SIDELIGHTS: Moon told *CA:* "The Trudeau book was unauthorized, and even recorded a roughing up he had from some women over abortion, but the prime minister's office sent me a letter saying thanks.

"Former Prime Minister John Diefenbaker introduced me to the late U.S. President J. F. Kennedy on his only official visit to Canada; I was the only Canadian writer to gain such access—and I had written very critically of Mr. Diefenbaker."

* * *

MOORE, Anne Carroll 1871-1961

PERSONAL: Born July 12, 1871, in Limerick, Me.; daughter of Luther Sanborn (a lawyer) and Sarah Hidden (Barker) Moore. *Education:* Bradford Academy, graduate, 1891; Library School of Pratt Institute, graduate, 1896. *Politics:* Democrat. *Residence:* New York, N.Y.

CAREER: Pratt Institute Free Library, Brooklyn, N.Y., children's librarian, 1896-1906; New York Public Library, supervisor of work with children, 1906-1941. Critic of children's books for *Bookman,* 1918-27, *New York Herald Tribune Books,* 1924-30, and *Atlantic Monthly,* beginning 1930; associate editor, *Horn Book,* 1939-61. Pioneer organizer of children's book departments in libraries; lecturer and consultant on children's literature and librarianship to teachers, librarians, and publishers throughout the United States. *Member:* American Library Association, English Speaking Union, New York State Library Association, New York Library Club. *Awards, honors:* diploma of honor, Pratt Institute, 1932; Constance Lindsay Skinner achievement medal for merit, 1940; L.H.D., University of Maine, 1940; Regina Medal, 1960 and 1963.

WRITINGS: *A List of Books Recommended for a Children's Library,* Iowa Printing Co., 1903; *Joseph A. Altsheler and American History,* [New York], 1919; *Roads to Childhood: Views and Reviews of Children's Books,* Doran, 1920; *New Roads to Childhood,* Doran, 1923; *Nicholas: A Manhattan Christmas Story* (illustrated by Jay Van Everen), Putnam, 1924; *The Three Owls: A Book about Children's Books, Their Authors, Artists, and Critics,* Macmillan, 1925; *Cross-Roads to Childhood,* Doran, 1926; (editor) Washington Irving, *Knickerbocker's History of New York,* Doubleday, Doran, 1928; *The Three Owls Second Book: Contemporary Criticism of Children's Books,* Coward-McCann, 1928; (editor) W. Irving, *Bold Dragoon, and Other Ghostly Tales,* Knopf, 1930; *The Three Owls Third Book: Contemporary Criticism of Children's Books,* Coward, 1931; *Nicholas and the Golden Goose* (illustrated by J. Van Everen), Putnam, 1932; *Seven Stories High,* Compton, 1932.

The Choice of a Hobby: A Unique Descriptive List of Books Offering Inspiration and Guidance to Hobby Riders and Hobby Hunters, Compton, 1934; *Reading for Pleasure,* Compton, 1935; *My Roads to Childhood: Views and Reviews of Children's Books* (illustrated by Arthur Lougee), Doubleday, Doran, 1939; *A Century of Kate Greenaway,* Warne, 1946; (editor with Bertha Mahony Miller) *Writing and Criticism: A Book for Margery Bianco* (illustrated by Valenti Angelo), Horn Book, 1951; (author of appreciation) Beatrix Potter, *The Art of Beatrix Potter,* Warne, 1955.

SIDELIGHTS: Anne Carroll Moore's childhood ambition had been to read law with her father, but his untimely death abruptly ended that plan. She turned to the library and during her lifetime was recognized for her leadership in children's library work. During her ten years at the Pratt Institute Library and her 35 years at the New York Public Library, she affected the practice of librarianship in many ways. According to *Publishers Weekly:* "She toned up the standards of book selection for children, and the professional status of children's work; she expanded the use of storytelling; she attracted the loyal interest of children in libraries and in book reading; she welcomed visitors of similar interests from abroad; she initiated programs of book reviewing, talking, writing, advising about books, traveling, training. In every way she was an able missionary for the world of children's books."

Anne Carroll Moore also greatly influenced the remarkable growth in children's book publishing. She supported new standards of production, encouraged new writing and new art, and pointed out the possibilities of new audiences.

Miss Moore authored several books of criticism of children's books and a few story books for children. Included in the latter category was *Nicholas and the Golden Goose.* The *New York Times* described it: "The book is a historical record for those who have the key, it is a gracious and understanding appreciation of some of the great writers of children's books and it is also a story so full of charm and imagination that it will be loved by children and older readers for the tale's sake alone." *Saturday Review* added: "The charmingly illustrated and well-printed volume has a flavor of its own, indescribable, like all flavors. A strongly marked flavor, too, sure to make some children turn away in bewilderment, sure to be unreasoningly, delightedly savored, and enjoyed by others."

BIOGRAPHICAL/CRITICAL SOURCES: *New York Times,* November 13, 1932; *Saturday Review of Literature,* November 19, 1932; *Publishers Weekly,* July 28, 1951; Carolyn Sherwin Bailey, *Candle for Your Cake,* Lippincott, 1952; *New York Public Library Bulletin,* November, 1956; Aylesa Forsee, *Women Who Reached for Tomorrow,* Macrae, 1960; *Catholic Library Bulletin,* January, 1960; F. C. Sayers, *Anne Carroll Moore: A Biography,* Atheneum, 1972.

OBITUARIES: *New York Times,* January 21, 1961; *Publishers Weekly,* January 30, 1961, February 13, 1961; *New York Public Library Bulletin,* February, 1961; *Catholic Library World,* March, 1961; *Wilson Library Bulletin,* March, 1961.*

(Died January 20, 1961)

* * *

MOORE, James Tice 1945-

PERSONAL: Born August 8, 1945, in Greenville, S.C.; son of William Furman (a teacher) and Aileen (Sylvester) Moore; married Jessie Louise Roberts, November 25, 1965; children: Leslie Anne, Evan Christopher. *Education:* University of South Carolina, B.A., 1966; University of Virginia, M.A., 1968, Ph.D., 1972. *Politics:* Independent. *Home:* 38 Milhaven Sq., Richmond, Va. 23233. *Office:* Department of History, Virginia Commonwealth University, Richmond, Va. 23284.

CAREER: Virginia Commonwealth University, Richmond, instructor, 1970-72, assistant professor of history, 1972—. *Member:* Organization of American Historians, Southern Historical Association, Virginia Historical Association, Phi Beta Kappa. *Awards, honors:* Woodrow Wilson fellowships, 1966, 1969-70; finalist in Frederick Jackson Turner Award competition, sponsored by the Organization of American Historians, 1973.

WRITINGS: *Two Paths to the New South: The Virginia Debt Controversy, 1870-1883,* University Press of Kentucky, 1974. Contributor of articles and reviews to history journals.

WORK IN PROGRESS: A book on the history of the Virginia oyster industry from its colonial origins to the present; historiographical research on the Redeemer Democratic hegemony in the South, 1870-1900.

SIDELIGHTS: Moore comments: "I am particularly interested in reinterpreting the history of the post-Civil War South from a perspective which avoids the ideological-interpretive 'hang-ups' of the Charles A. Beard-C. Vann Woodward 'Progressive' tradition which has for so long shaped our appreciation of the period 1870-1900."

AVOCATIONAL INTERESTS: Collecting stamps, constructing ship models, following the activities of the Washington Redskins, visiting historical sites relevant to Southern history.

* * *

MOORE, Kenneth E(ugene) 1930-

PERSONAL: Born September 19, 1930, in Niagara Falls, N.Y.; son of Gordon Winfield (a civil servant) and Marie (Sinclair) Moore. *Education:* Michigan State University, B.A., 1953; University of Illinois, M.A., 1968, Ph.D., 1970. *Religion:* Roman Catholic. *Home address:* P.O. Box 194, Notre Dame, Ind. 46556. *Office:* Department of Sociology/Anthropology, University of Notre Dame, Notre Dame, Ind. 46556.

CAREER: American Society of Planning Officials, Chicago, Ill., associate editor, 1963-64; University of Notre Dame, Notre Dame, Ind., assistant professor, 1970-76, associate professor of sociology and anthropology, 1976—. *Member:* American Anthropological Association, Society for the Study of Symbolic Interaction, Central State Anthropological Society (member of executive committee). *Awards, honors:* National Institute of Mental Health fellowship, 1967-70; Prize Paper award, Southwestern Anthropological Association, 1967.

WRITINGS: (Editor with James Clemens) *Planning, 1963,* American Society of Planning Officials, 1963; (editor) *Planning, 1964,* American Society of Planning Officials, 1964; *Those of the Street: The Catholic Jews of Mallorca,* University of Notre Dame Press, 1977. Editor of *Bulletin* of Central States Anthropological Society.

WORK IN PROGRESS: Research on urban anthropology, Mediterranean studies, cultural change, Jewish ethnology, and Spanish ethnology.

SIDELIGHTS: Moore writes: "I share in the ongoing probe of those underlying principles which govern much of human behavior. For me anthropology, art, religion, and living are all one. I write to contribute to the understanding of our condition in our time."

* * *

MOORE, Maxine 1927-

PERSONAL: Born December 28, 1927, in Wellington, Kan.; daughter of Harold P. and Clare (Barnard) Stewart; married Francis Harry Moore (an attorney), August 29, 1948; children: Frances, Rebecca, Miranda, Patricia. *Education:* Hockaday Junior College, A.A., 1947; attended Texas Agricultural and Industrial College (now University), 1948; University of Missouri, Kansas City, B.A., M.A., 1969; University of Kansas, Ph.D., 1971. *Home:* 6200 Valley Rd., Kansas City, Mo. 64113. *Office:* Department of Literature, University of Missouri, 51st & Rockhill, Kansas City, Mo. 64110.

CAREER: Worked for various advertising agencies and radio stations; Moore Advertising Associates, Inc., Kansas City, Mo., president, 1961-71; University of Missouri, Kansas City, associate professor of American literature, 1971—. *Member:* Modern Language Association of America, Melville Society. *Awards, honors:* Curator's award from University of Missouri, Kansas City, 1975, for *That Lonely Game.*

WRITINGS: That Lonely Game: Melville, "Mardi", and the Almanac, University of Missouri Press, 1975. Contributor to literature journals.

* * *

MOORE, William Howard 1942-

PERSONAL: Born June 26, 1942, in Harriman, Tenn.; son of Lonnie Henry (a farmer) and Goldie Myrtle Moore; married Mary Elizabeth Galvan, September 27, 1969; children: Adam William. *Education:* University of Tennessee, B.S., 1964, M.A., 1965; University of Texas, Ph.D., 1971. *Home:* 802 University Ave., Laramie, Wyo. 82070. *Office:* Department of History, University of Wyoming, Laramie, Wyo. 82071.

CAREER: Southwest Texas State University, San Marcos, instructor in history, 1971-72; Ohio University, Athens, assistant professor of history, 1972-73; University of Wyoming, Laramie, assistant professor of history, 1973—. *Member:* American Historical Association, Organization of American Historians, Southern Historical Association. *Awards, honors:* National Endowment for the Humanities grant, 1977.

WRITINGS: The Kefauver Committee and the Politics of Crime, 1950-1952, University of Missouri Press, 1974.

WORK IN PROGRESS: A history of American attitudes and policies toward gambling, 1931-1965.

BIOGRAPHICAL/CRITICAL SOURCES: American Historical Review, April, 1977.

* * *

MORAN, Hugh Anderson 1881-1977

1881—August 22, 1977; American clergyman, scholar, and author best known for *Heroes, Creed for College Men,* and *The Alphabet and Ancient Calendar Signs.* He died in Wenatchee, Wash. Obituaries: *New York Times,* August 24, 1977; *AB Bookman's Weekly,* November 21, 1977.

* * *

MORDDEN, Ethan (Christopher) 1947-

PERSONAL: Surname sounds like "*more-*then"; born January 27, 1947, near Wilkes-Barre, Pa.; son of Edgar A. (a building contractor) and Beatrice (a realtor; maiden name, Morgan) Mordden. *Education:* University of Pennsylvania, B.A., 1969. *Politics:* "I am for freedom, tradition, and the rule of merit: a conservative." *Religion:* Society of Friends (Quakers). *Residence:* New York, N.Y. *Agent:* Dorothy Pittman, John Cushman Associates, Inc., 25 West 43rd St., New York, N.Y. 10036.

CAREER: D.C. Comics, New York City, editor of Romance Division, 1970-71; "at-large observer of life's rich pageant and sullen off-Broadway musician," 1971-74; *Opera News,* New York City, assistant editor, 1974-76; free-lance writer, 1976—.

WRITINGS: Better Foot Forward: The History of American Musical Theatre, Viking, 1976; *Opera in the Twentieth Century: Scared, Profane, Godot,* Oxford University Press, 1978; *That Jazz!: An Idiosyncratic Social History of the American Twenties,* Putnam, 1978. Contributor to *Encyclopedia Americana* and *World Book Encyclopedia.*

WORK IN PROGRESS: A beginner's comprehensive symphony handbook, for Oxford University Press, completion expected in 1980; research for "a history of the United States as viewed through the values, ethics, and cultural apprehensions of Jeffersonian Anti-Federalism."

SIDELIGHTS: Mordden writes: "It is a time of specialization, ours, now, and one might well ask how one writer can legitimately move from musical comedy to opera (quasi-plausible) to sociopolitics (not plausible). In answer I can do no better than to quote Jules Michelet: 'All science is one . . . language, literature and history, physics, mathematics and philosophy; subjects which seem the most remote from one another are in reality connected, or rather they all form a single system.' An extreme theory—but, I think, subject to some modification, applicable. Barring physics and math, all these sciences *are* one, for art, thought, and analysis conduce to one study, that of man and his haphazard accommodation to the action and expression of life: to facts and poetry. My field is humanism, and in that context, all—or most—science is indeed one."

* * *

MORDVINOFF, Nicolas 1911-1973
(Nicolas)

PERSONAL: Born September 27, 1911, in St. Petersburg (now Leningrad), Russia; came to the United States, 1946, naturalized citizen, 1952; married Barbara Ellis, 1956; children: Michael, Alexandra, Peter. *Education:* Graduated from the University of Paris. *Residence:* Hampton, N.J.

CAREER: Artist, illustrator, and author. Began drawing at an early age; as a college student, contributed cartoons and illustrations to French magazines and newspapers; traveled to Tahiti where he worked on developing his own artistic style, 1934-1946; illustrator of children's books, New York, N.Y., beginning 1946. His works have been exhibited as one-man shows at various galleries, including the Luyber Gallery in New York, 1949, Wickersham Gallery, 1970, and Galerie 9 in Paris, 1970; works in public collections can be seen at the New York Public Library and the Metropolitan Museum of Art. *Awards, honors:* Caldecott Medal, 1952, for *Finders Keepers;* co-winner of *New York Herald Tribune* award, 1954, for *Alphonse, That Bearded One;* listed among the *New York Times* choice of best illustrated books of the year, 1954, for *Circus Ruckus,* 1955, for *Chaga,* and 1958, for *The Magic Feather Duster;* American Institute of Graphic Arts certificate of excellence, 1955-57.

WRITINGS—Under name Nicolas; all self-illustrated; all published by Harcourt, except as noted: (With Will, pseudonym of William Lipkind) *The Two Reds,* 1950; (with Will) *The Christmas Bunny,* 1953; (with Will) *Circus Ruckus,* 1954; *Bear's Land,* Coward, 1955; (with Will) *Chaga,* 1955; (with Will) *Perry the Imp,* 1956; *Coral Island,* Doubleday, 1957; (with Will) *Sleepyhead,* 1957; (with Will) *The Magic Feather Duster,* 1958; (with Will) *Four-Leaf Clover,* 1959; (with Will) *The Little Tiny Rooster,* 1960; (with Will) *Billy the Kid,* 1961; (with Will) *Russet and the Two Reds,* 1962; (with Will) *The Boy and the Forest,* 1964.

Illustrator: William Standish Stone, *Thunder Island,* Knopf, 1942; Stone, *Pepe Was the Saddest Bird,* Knopf, 1944; Stone, *Ship of Flame: A Saga of the South Seas,* Knopf, 1945; Caroline Guild, *Rainbow in Tahiti,* Doubleday, 1948; Andre Norton (pseudonym of Alice Mary Norton), *Star Man's Son,* Coward, 1952; William Lipkind, *Boy with a Harpoon,* Harcourt, 1952; Willis Lindquist, *Burma Boy,* Whittlesey House, 1953; Lipkind, *Boy of the Islands,* Harcourt, 1954.

Illustrator under name Nicolas: Earl and Marjory Schwalje, *Cezar and the Music Maker,* Knopf, 1951; Will, *Finders Keepers,* Harcourt, 1951; Will, *Even Steven,* Harcourt, 1952; Marie Halun Bloch, *Big Steve,* Coward, 1952; Rudyard Kipling, *Just So Stories,* Doubleday, 1952; Natalie S. Carlson, *Alphonse, That Bearded One,* Harcourt, 1954; Loren D. Good, *Panchito,* Coward, 1955; William Owen Steele, *Davy Crockett's Earthquake,* Harcourt, 1956; Steele, *Daniel Boone's Echo,* Harcourt, 1957; Carlson, *Hortense: The Cow for a Queen,* Harcourt, 1957; Carlson, *Evangeline: Pigeon of Paris,* Harcourt, 1960.

SIDELIGHTS: In the midst of the Russian Revolution, Mordvinoff and his parents fled the country to live in Paris. Besides attending the schools there, Mordvinoff also studied under French painters Fernand Leger and Amedee Ozenfant. After growing up in the fast-paced life of the city, the author-illustrator felt a need to get away, and traveled to the islands of the South Pacific. While in Tahiti, Mordvinoff struck up an association with author, William Stone, who gave the artist his first opportunity to illustrate a book.

A lengthy stay in New York City produced a friendship with William Lipkind, a writer. By 1950, Lipkind and Mordvinoff began collaborating on children's books. *The Two Reds,* their first book together, received favorable reviews.

The team of Will and Nicolas went on to produce a Caldecott Medal winner with their second book, *Finders Keepers.* Mordvinoff's Caldecott award acceptance speech offered this formula for successful picture books: "A picture book must have complete unity in text and pictures. We [Lipkind and Mordvinoff] work in such a close relationship that when a book is finished, it is sometimes hard for us to remember who was responsible for what idea. Story, pictures, design, type, and even color are conceived as one whole. At no time is it a quick or easy process and the work is never in any proportion to the material reward. It is a work of love."

OBITUARIES: Publishers Weekly, May 28, 1973.*

(Died May 5, 1973)

*   *   *

MORGAN, J. Elizabeth 1947-

PERSONAL: Born July 9, 1947, in Washington, D.C.; daughter of William James (a psychologist) and Antionia (a psychologist; maiden name, Bell) Morgan. *Education:* Harvard University, B.A. (magna cum laude), 1967; Somerville College, Oxford, graduate study, 1970; Yale University, M.D., 1971. *Residence:* Brookline, Mass. *Office:* Cambridge Hospital, 1493 Cambridge St., Cambridge, Mass. 02139.

CAREER: Yale New Haven Hospital, New Haven, Conn., resident, 1971-73; Tufts-New England Medical Center, Boston, Mass., resident, 1973-76; Yale New Haven Hospital, plastic surgery resident, 1977; Cambridge Hospital, Cambridge, Mass., plastic surgery resident, 1977——. Trustee of Schefer School, 1973-76. *Member:* American Medical Association, English Speaking Union, Commonwealth Society, Washington Independent Writers Association.

WRITINGS: Spanish-English Medical Conversation Reference, Schering Corp., 1974; (contributor) *Emergency Care of the Hand,* Little, Brown, 1978. Author of "Your Body," a monthly column in *Cosmopolitan,* and "Ask Dr. Elizabeth," syndicated by Register and Tribune Syndicate, 1977. Contributor to magazines.

WORK IN PROGRESS: The Making of a Woman Surgeon, for Bantam.

SIDELIGHTS: Elizabeth Morgan writes: "I am a surgeon interested in writing for the public, as well as in professional medical journals, as I think the American public deserves the best medical information available." *Avocational interests:* Sports, public health, ballet.

*   *   *

MORGAN, (Walter) Jefferson 1940-

PERSONAL: Born March 30, 1940, in Salt Lake City, Utah; son of Thomas Ralph (an executive) and Althea (a pharmacist and nurse; maiden name, Bell) Morgan; married Patricia Williams, 1960 (divorced, 1965); married Jinx Adams (a writer), March 26, 1971; children: Stacy, Derick, Coulter. *Education:* University of California, teaching credential, 1967; also attended Diablo Valley College, Oakland City College, University of Chicago, University of California, Berkeley, Stanford University, and Harvard University. *Home and office:* 867 Sunnyhills Rd., Oakland, Calif. 94610. *Agent:* Carl Brandt, Brandt & Brandt, 101 Park Ave., New York, N.Y. 10017.

CAREER: Oakland Tribune, Oakland, Calif., copyboy, 1957-58, police reporter, 1958-59, assistant state editor, 1959-60, courthouse bureau chief, 1960-63, city desk rewrite man, 1963-69, special writer, 1969-76, author of column

"Dining With Wine," 1976; free-lance writer, 1976—. Western U.S. correspondent for Manchester *Guardian,* 1967—. Instructor at Peralta Colleges, 1967-69. Member of Society of Nieman Fellows. *Member:* Royal Commonwealth Society, Confrerie de la Marmite, San Francisco Press Club, Harvard Club. *Awards, honors:* Newswriting prizes from Associated Press, 1966, 1969, 1971, 1973; William F. Knowland Award, 1966, 1969, 1970; first prize from San Francisco Press Club, 1970, 1973; Nieman fellow at Harvard University, 1971-72; McQuade Award from Association of Catholic Newsmen, 1974; award from California Taxpayers Association, 1974.

WRITINGS: Guide to California Wines, Dutton, 1968, 3rd edition, 1975; *Adventures in the Wine Country,* Chronicle Books, 1971, revised edition, 1976; *Why Have They Taken Our Children?,* Delacorte, 1978. Contributor to popular magazines, including *Reader's Digest, National Wildlife, Bon Appetit, Parade,* and *Travel and Leisure.*

WORK IN PROGRESS: Magazine writing.

* * *

MORGENSTERN, Oskar 1902-1977

1902—July 26, 1977; German-born American economist, logician, theorist, educator, and mathematician. Morgenstern is best known for pioneering efforts in the development of mathematical economics and game theory. Professor at Princeton University until 1970, Morgenstern founded Mathematics Inc., a company whose projects for both government and corporate clients include work on the space shuttle, state lotteries, unemployment studies, and manpower programs. He died in Princeton, N.J. Obituaries: *New York Times,* July 27, 1977; *Newsweek,* August 8, 1977; *Time,* August 8, 1977; *AB Bookman's Weekly,* September 12, 1977. (See index for *CA* sketch)

* * *

MORLAND, Dick
See HILL, Reginald (Charles)

* * *

MORLEY, Patricia (Ann) 1929-

PERSONAL: Born May 25, 1929, in Toronto, Ontario, Canada; daughter of Frederick Charles and Mabel (Winsland) Marlow; married Lawrence Morley (a geophysicist), June 17, 1950 (divorced, 1975); children: Lawrence Charles, Patricia Kathleen, Christopher George, David Boyd. *Education:* University of Toronto, B.A. (honors), 1951; Carleton University, M.A., 1967; University of Ottawa, Ph.D. (summa cum laude), 1970. *Politics:* "Constantly rethought." *Religion:* Christian. *Home address:* P.O. Box 137, Manotick, Ontario, Canada K0A 2N0. *Office:* Department of English, Concordia University, 1455 de Maisonneuve Blvd. W., Montreal, Quebec, Canada.

CAREER: Writer, 1970-71; University of Ottawa, Ottawa, Ontario, part-time lecturer in Canadian literature, 1971-72; Concordia University, Montreal, Quebec, assistant professor, 1972-75; associate professor of English and Canadian studies, 1975—.

MEMBER: International Federation of Modern Language and Literature, European Association of Commonwealth Language and Literature Studies, Canadian Association of Comparative Literatures, Association of Canadian University Teachers of English, Humanities Association of Canada, Canadian Studies Association, Association of Canadian

and Quebec Literatures, Canadian Association of Comparative Literature, Modern Language Association of America. *Awards, honors:* Canada Council fellow, 1969-70; Grants from Humanities Research Council of Canada, 1971 and Social Science Research Council of Canada, 1972.

WRITINGS: The Mystery of Unity: Theme and Technique in the Novels of Patrick White, McGill-Queen's University Press, 1972; *The Immoral Moralists: Hugh MacLennan and Leonard Cohen,* Clarke, Irwin, 1972; *Robertson Davies,* Gage, 1976; *The Comedians: Hugh Hood and Rudy Wiebe,* Clarke, Irwin, 1977; (editor and author of introduction) *Ernest Thompson Seton,* University of Ottawa Press, 1977; *Morley Callaghan,* McClelland & Stewart, in press. Contributor to language and literature journals and to *Canadian Forum.* Book reviewer for *Ottawa Journal,* 1971—.

WORK IN PROGRESS: Margaret Laurence, for Twayne; a comic novel; short plays; a study of Japanese twentieth-century fiction in English translation.

SIDELIGHTS: Patricia Morley writes: "I began to write after completing my doctorate and finding myself unemployed and possibly unemployable: the retrenchment in Canadian universities coincided with my graduation in 1970. My children were increasingly self-sufficient and I needed a new career. Writing was a challenge, then a habit and a way of life. I believe that women need to be more flexible than men in their careers. Life begins at forty. Again."

BIOGRAPHICAL/CRITICAL SOURCES: Ottawa Citizen, May 6, 1977.

* * *

MORLEY, Susan
See CROSS, John Keir

* * *

MORRIS, A(ndrew) J(ames) A(nthony) 1936-

PERSONAL: Born November 7, 1936, in Caerphilly, Wales; son of George (a coalworker) and Minnie (Smart) Morris; married Cicely Alison Rosser (a social worker), December 22, 1958; children: Anthony John Lloyd, Fiona Eleanor. *Education:* London School of Economics and Political Science, LL.B., 1958, M.A., 1963; Institute of Education, London, B.A., 1959, D.Litt., 1967. *Home:* 50 Marlborough Park S., Belfast BT9 6HS, Northern Ireland. *Office:* Department of Philosophy, Politics, and History, Ulster College, Jordanstown, Northern Ireland.

CAREER: Schoolmaster 1959-62, and 1964-66; University of London, London School of Economics and Political Science, London, England, senior research officer, 1967-73; Ulster College, Jordanstown, Northern Ireland, professor of philosophy, politics, and history, 1974—, head of department. Visiting professor at University of North Carolina, Charlotte, 1973.

WRITINGS: Parliamentary Democracy in the Nineteenth Century, Pergamon, 1967; *Radicalism Against War, 1906-14,* Longmans, 1972; (editor and contributor) *Edwardian Radicalism, 1900-1914,* Routledge & Kegan Paul, 1974; *C. P. Trevelyan, 1870-1958: Portrait of a Radical,* Blackstaff, 1977. Contributor of articles and reviews to political science and history journals. Editor of *Moirae.*

WORK IN PROGRESS: A critical study of the formation of the 1905 Liberal Cabinet, with a book expected to result.

MORRIS, J. R. 1914(?)-1977

1914(?)—June 1, 1977; British lecturer, historian, and author. Morris was an authority on later Roman history and Roman Britain, and was founding editor of *Past and Present*. He wrote *Arthur's Britain* and a county-by-county edition of the *Domesday Book*. Morris died in England. Obituaries: *AB Bookman's Weekly*, October 17, 1977.

* * *

MORRIS, Janet E(llen) 1946-

PERSONAL: Born May 25, 1946, in Boston, Mass.; daughter of Cecil R. (in real estate) and Anne H. (a businesswoman) Freeman; married Christopher C. Morris (a musician), October 31, 1971. *Education:* Attended New York University, 1965-66. *Home:* 1 Breakwater Shores, Hyannis, Mass. 02601. *Agent:* Perry Knowlton, Curtis Brown Ltd., 575 Madison Ave., New York N.Y. 10022.

CAREER: Chip Monck Enterprises, New York City, lighting designer, 1963-64; songwriter and recording artist, 1967—. Night manager, Record Plant, 1970. Bass player for Christopher Morris Band, 1975, 1977. *Member:* Science Fiction Writers of America, Costeau Society, Musicians Union, Broadcast Music.

WRITINGS—Novels: *High Couch of Silistra*, Bantam, 1977; *The Golden Sword*, Bantam, 1977; *Wind from the Abyss*, Bantam, 1978; *The Carnelian Throne*, Bantam, 1978.

WORK IN PROGRESS: I, the Sun, a novelized biography of Suppiluliumas I, King of Haiti, about 1379 B.C., including texts translated from the Hittite and letters from Amarna correspondence of Amenophis III, Akhenaten, Tutankhamen, and his widow, as well as excerpts from treaties, and evidence from artifacts of the period.

SIDELIGHTS: Janet Morris writes: "My interests in physics, sociobiology, and cosmology prompted the Silistran world-scheme eventually sold as a quartet. In the tradition of Thomas More, I have used my construct society as a platform from which to comment on and compare moralities applicable to human societies, and to probe the depths of male-female relations. My atavistic Silistrans explore Dr. E. O. Wilson's theory that the gene predisposing to creativity may be inseparably linked to the desire to own and dominate. My current work, *I, the Sun,* allows me to further explore the clashes of divergent moralities through the eyes of a protagonist of the most advanced civilization extant at the time, and to use my studies of Hittite and Egyptian language and ancient Near East history."

* * *

MORRIS, Joe Alex, Jr. 1927-

PERSONAL: Born June 1, 1927, in Denver, Colo.; son of Joe Alex (a writer) and Maxine (Pooler) Morris; married Ursula Kirschbaum, April 4, 1959; children: Maria, Karin, Julia. *Education:* Harvard University, A.B., 1949. *Home:* Diamantidov 72, Psychico, Athens, Greece.

CAREER/WRITINGS: United Press International, New York City, reporter, 1953-57; *New York Herald Tribune,* New York City, reporter, 1957-61; *Newsweek,* New York City, reporter, 1961-65; *Los Angeles Times,* Los Angeles, Calif., reporter, 1965—. Notable assignments include coverage of three Arab-Israeli wars, the Lebanese civil war, the Indo-Pakistani war of 1965, various Cyprus alarums, the Yemeni civil war, and the Kurdish rebellion in Iraq. *Military service:* U.S. Army, 1945-47. *Awards, honors:* Overseas Press Club award for best foreign reporting, 1967.

WORK IN PROGRESS: A novel about Middle East politics.

SIDELIGHTS: Morris writes: "To cover the Middle East properly one should be a prophet with the patience of Job. After many years experience in this region, I lost seventy dollars on two bets that Sadat would not go to Jerusalem. Interestingly, one of the men I bet with was an old-timer in the area. The other was spanking new."

* * *

MORRISEY, George L(ewis) 1926-

PERSONAL: Born December 6, 1926, in Brooklyn, N.Y.; son of Goerge S. and Elizabeth (Pounds) Morrisey; married Carol B. Putnam (a corporate secretary), August 21, 1948; children: Lynn C. Morrisey Rosiska, Steven L. *Education:* Springfield College, B.S., 1951, M.Ed., 1952. *Home:* 8022 San Dimas Circle, Buena Park, Calif. 90620. *Office address:* MOR Associates, P.O. Box 5879, Buena Park, Calif. 90622.

CAREER: Young Men's Christian Association, professional director of organizations in El Paso, Tex., 1952-56, and Los Angeles, Calif., 1956-61; First Western Bank, Los Angeles, administrative assistant, 1961-62; Rockwell International, Downey, Calif., managment development specialist, 1962-68; McDonnell Douglas Corp., Long Beach, Calif., manager of management training, 1968-70; Postal Service Management Institute, Los Angeles, manager of West Coast Center, 1970-72; MOR Associates (management consultants), Buena Park, Calif., founder and president, 1972—. Member of board of directors of local Young Men's Christian Association, 1963— (chairman of board of directors, 1976). *Military service:* U.S. Army, 1945-47.

MEMBER: American Society for Training and Development, National Speakers Association. *Awards, honors:* Publication award from American Society for Training and Development, 1972-73.

WRITINGS—All published by Addison-Wesley: *Effective Business and Technical Presentations: Managing Your Presentations by Objectives and Results,* 1968, 2nd edition, 1975; *Management by Objectives and Results for Business and Industry,* 1970, 2nd edition, 1977; *Appraisal and Development Through Objectives and Results,* 1972; *Management by Objectives and Results in the Public Sector,* 1976.

Also author of numerous cassette kits, with workbooks, including "Management by Objectives and Results Overview," Addison-Wesley, 1972, "Management by Objectives and Results: Self-Teaching Audiocassette Program," MOR Associates, 1975, "Introduction to Management by Objectives and Results," MOR Associates, 1976, "Women and MORe: Winning Techniques for Goal Setting," MOR Associates, 1977, and "Decision-Making and Problem-Solving for MORe Effective Management," MOR Associates, 1977. Contributor to management journals.

SIDELIGHTS: George Morrisey told *CA:* "All publications, teaching and consulting efforts are directed at helping individuals and organizations, in both the public and private sectors, achieve worthwhile results. They are oriented to providing specific tools, techniques and processes in a 'how to' approach. The 'Management by Objective and Results' (MOR) process, which is at the heart of all publications, is a systematic, practical approach to management that recognizes that *people,* not pieces of paper, get the job done."

* * *

MORRISON, James (Harris) 1918-

PERSONAL: Born October 29, 1918, in St. Louis, Mo.; son

of Carl T. (a salesman) and Nellie (Harris) Morrison; married Mary Berthold, January 6, 1942; children: Elaine Morrison Shelby, Kathleen Morrison Cook. *Education:* Washington University, St. Louis, Mo., B.S., 1952; University of Missouri, Kansas City, M.A., 1955; University of Kansas, further study, 1958-62. *Home:* 9804 Hadley, Overland Park, Kan. 66212. *Office:* Lawrence Leiter & Co., 427 West 12th St., Kansas City, Mo. 64105.

CAREER: Western Auto Supply Co., Kansas City, Mo., training and selection specialist, 1950-66; Lawrence Leiter & Co., Kansas City, partner, 1967—. Certified psychologist in Kansas and Ontario. *Military service:* U.S. Navy, electronics technician instructor, 1944-45. *Member:* American Psychological Association, American Society for Training and Development, Institute of Management Consultants (director, 1977—), American Arbitration Association (member of national panel).

WRITINGS: Human Factors in Supervising Minority Group Employees, Public Personnel Association, 1970; *The Human Side of Management,* Addison-Wesley, 1971; (with John J. O'Hearne) *Practical Transactional Analysis in Management,* Addison-Wesley, 1977. Contributor to personnel and psychology journals.

WORK IN PROGRESS: Research on negotiation techniques, conflict management, and stress.

SIDELIGHTS: Morrison writes: "My activity seeks to make the behavioral science findings practically applicable to the science of management and the art of human relationships. In *Practical Transactional Analysis in Management,* we have a treatment of the subject sharply in contrast to the cuteness and fuzziness found in many current writings about transactional analysis. More recently, we are researching cross-disciplinary issues in behavioral studies to relate motivation theory to interpersonal concepts."

*   *   *

MORRISON, James Douglas   1943-1971
(Jim Morrison)

PERSONAL: Born December 8, 1943, in Melbourne, Fla.; son of George Stephen (a rear admiral) and Clara (Clarke) Morrison; married wife, Pamela (died, 1974). *Education:* Attended St. Petersburg Junior College, 1961-62, Florida State University, 1962-63, and University of California at Los Angeles, 1964-65. *Residence:* Paris, France.

CAREER: Singer, songwriter, poet, and filmmaker. Founding member, with Ray Manzarek, John Densmore, and Robbie Krieger, of the "Doors" rock band, 1965-70.

WRITINGS—Under name Jim Morrison: *The Lords and the New Creatures,* privately printed, 1969, Simon & Schuster, 1970; *The Bank of America of Louisiana,* Zeppelin Publishing, 1975. Also author of *An American Prayer,* 1970.

Author of film scripts, including "Feast of Friends," 1970. Contributor of poems to *US, AUM,* and other periodicals.

SIDELIGHTS: Jim Morrison was born in Melbourne, Fla., to a family with a long history of career militarists. His father, then a captain in the U.S. Navy, was transferred several times in Morrison's youth and the family lived near several bases before finally settling in Alexandria, Va. At home, Jim's mother Clara "stood by while the Captain ordered his home-grown recruits around." After graduating from George Washington High School in Alexandria, Morrison attended St. Petersburg Junior College. He was already feeling uneasy about his lifestyle when he transferred to Florida State University in the fall of 1962. A year later he dropped

out, and in February, 1964, he headed west and entered the University of California at Los Angeles to study film. "I was ideally suited for the work I'm doing," Morrison recalled; "it's the feeling of a bowstring being pulled back for 22 years and suddenly being let go."

At UCLA Morrison showed an interest in poetry and philosophy, particularly the work of William Blake and Friedrich Nietzsche. In discussions with his roommate, Dennis Jakob, he anticipated forming a rock group based on some literary works. He decided to call the group the Doors, derived from William Blake's phrase, "There are things that are known and things that are unknown; in between are doors," and the title of Aldoux Huxley's study of mescaline experiments, *The Doors of Perception.* In class, a fellow student recalled, "Morrison was a genius—he knew all about the poets, he knew all about poetry and all about books. He knew more than the teacher even, like sometimes someone would ask a question and the teacher wouldn't know the answer, and Morrison would just blurt it out."

Morrison met future Door member Ray Manzarek in an art class at UCLA. Manzarek, who had played piano since he was ten and studied classical music at the Chicago Conservatory, played on weekends with a local blues-oriented band, Rich and the Ravens. In July, 1965, Morrison met Manzarek again, on the beach in Venice, Calif., and mentioned he had written some songs. "So we sat on the beach and I asked him to sing some of them," Manzarek remembered. "When he sang those first lines—'Let's swim to the moon / Let's climb through the tide / Penetrate the evening / That the city sleeps to hide'—I said, 'That's it.' I'd never heard lyrics to a rock song like that before. We talked a while before we decided to get a group together and make a million dollars." Manzarek recruited jazz drummer John Densmore and former jug-band guitarist Robbie Krieger, both of whom he knew from the Third Street Meditation Center, to complete the Doors.

The Doors practiced for five months and made their debut at the London Fog on Sunset Strip, working for five dollars apiece on weeknights and ten dollars on weekends. The club, increasingly unhappy with the new band, gave them notice after four months. Unable to find bookings, the Doors considered disbanding, but on their last night a talent booker hired them as back-up band at the Whiskey A-Go-Go. At first hardly noticed, the Doors began to draw attention as they added more original songs and Morrison developed into a sensually powerful, extroverted stage performer. Morrison's state performance, in fact, got too strong for the Whiskey one night when he extended the song "The End" to include the Oedipal "Father I want to kill you . . . Mother, I want to . . ." followed by his primal scream. The club fired the group. Whiskey staff member Elmer Valentine remembered Morrison: "He was kinda ahead of his time on certain things—like swearing. But those calls kept coming in. . . . We never had so many calls before for a second group." The Doors found work at Gazzarri's. Jac Ttana, who played with a Los Angeles band, described one night when he and Morrison's wife were the only people in the audience: "He's into 'When the Music's Over,' and he comes to the part where he freaks out and throws the mike stand on the ground—and he really did it. Even more than that. And they went off stage and Pam said, 'Why'd you do all that?' And Jim said, 'You never know when you're giving your last performance.'"

Elektra president Jac Holzman, convinced by promotion man Billy James of the Doors' musical potential, signed the group in late 1966. Producer Paul Rothschild, who worked with the group on their first album, "The Doors," said, "I have never been as moved in a recording studio. I was impressed by the fact that for one of the very first times in rock and roll history sheer drama had taken place on tape. I felt emotionally washed. There were four other people in the control room at the time, when the take was over we realized the tape was still going. And all of us were audience, there was nothing left, the machines knew what to do." The album, which rapidly sold over a million copies, skyrocketed the Doors to fame. *Disk Review* wrote, "In it the Doors laid down their style—hard rock with slippery, psychedelic overtones. Morrison got some of his lyrics from Nietzsche—he always said his main guide to his poetry is 'The Birth of Tragedy' from the 'Spirit of Music'—he combined Nietzsche with a little freshman psychology and a lot of very broad images (the sea, the sun, the earth, death) and came up with Morrison therapy: to become more real, to become a better person, cut your ties to the establishment past, swim in your emotions, suffer symbolic death and rebirth, rebirth as a new man, psychologically cleansed."

By the summer of 1967 the Doors' "Light My Fire" was the top song on the U.S. record charts. It was followed by several hits, including "People Are Strange" and "Love Me Two Times," both in 1967, "The Unknown Soldier" and "Hello I Love You" in 1968 ("Hello I Love You" regaining the top position on the charts for the Doors), and "Touch Me" and "Tell All the People" in late 1968 and early 1969. The Doors played to wildly enthusiastic audiences in every major rock palace in the United States and made appearances on the Ed Sullivan and Jonathon Winters television shows. Morrison was immortalized in the pages of *Vogue* by photographer Richard Avedon. Under Morrison's picture ran a caption which called him "one of the most shaken loose, mind-shaking, and subtle agents of the new music. . . . He gets people. His songs are eerie, loaded with somewhat Freudian symbolism, poetic but not poetry, filled with suggestions of sex, death, transcendence."

The Doors' third album, "Waiting for the Sun," featured the beginning of Morrison's poetic "Celebration of the Lizard" in the song "Not to Touch the Earth." Morrison was named the "Lizard King," partly from the song and the appearance of the poem inside the album's cover, and partly from his wearing reptile skin. He told reporter Salli Stevenson: "I've always liked reptiles. I used to see the universe as a mammoth peristaltic snake and I used to see all the people and objects and landscapes as little pictures of the facets of their skins, their scales. I think the peristaltic motion is the basic life movement. It's swallowing, digestion, the rhythms of sexual intercourse, and even your basic unicellular structures have the same motion."

Morrison's stage antics, his song lyrics, and his reputation as a hard drinker began to attract the attention of the law. "Everybody has to stand for something," Morrison said, "that's what we're here for. If Spiro Agnew stands for law and order, all right, say I stand for sex. Chaos. Movement without meaning. Cop baiting. Fifty-two-week paid vacations with double overtime every year." In December, 1967, Morrison was arrested for obscenity during a concert at the New Haven Arena. According to police, "Morrison apparently became annoyed at the presence of numerous policemen at the concert and made 'obscene objections' to them" in a song. Morrison was acquitted. Later that year concerts in Phoenix and Long Island ended in "riots" and the Doors were banned from returning to those auditoriums. "I always try to get them to stand up," Morrison explained, "to feel free to move around anywhere they want to. It's not to precipitate a

chaos situation. It's . . . how can you stand the anchorage of a chair and be bombarded with all this intense rhythm and not want to express it physically in movement? I like people to be free."

On March 2, 1969, the Doors played a concert to twelve thousand fans in Miami's Dinner Key Auditorium. After the concert the Doors left for a vacation in the Carribean. Charges were made that Morrison committed "lewd and lascivious behavior in public" during the concert, and four days later six warrants, including one felony warrant, were sworn for his arrest. A teenage "Rally for Decency," headlined by Jackie Gleason and Anita Bryant, was staged to show "Miami is really a straight town." After a two month trial in Dade County, Morrison was acquitted of the felony charge and one of three misdemeanors. He was convicted of drunkenness and exposure. Attorney Max Fink was convinced Morrison's appeal would have resulted in an eventual overturn: "The entire situation was unconstitutional," he said. "It would have been an absolute cinch appeal. There was no way in the world for the convictions to stand."

The Dade County concert took its toll on the Doors' career. "It cost us at least a half million dollars," manager Bill Siddens explained. "Ten dates were cancelled immediately and we couldn't work for six months because we could never be sure when we might have to make a court appearance. It almost caused the group to break up." By early 1970, however, the group began to record again, and they produced three gold-record albums by early 1971. "Love Her Madly," a single, made the top of the U.S. charts in early 1971.

Increasingly doubtful of his future as a rock singer, Morrison began working on films and poetry in 1970. He completed the film "Feast of Friends" and began working on a screenplay with poet Michael McClure. *The Lords and the New Creatures,* a book of poems, was published by Simon & Schuster and sold well. "Real poetry," Morrison claimed, "doesn't say anything, it just ticks off the possibilities. Opens all doors. You can walk through any one that suits you." Morrison's poetry, characteristically compact, thematically considers contemporary America—cities, drugs, movies, the hustle for money, the old versus the new. One poem is:

> "They are filming something
> in the street, in front of
> our house."

"People have the feeling that what's going on outside isn't real," Morrison said of the poem, "just a bunch of staged events, all I did was record this feeling. I can't give a plot line because it's what all the people experience all the days, all the meandering happenings."

Late in 1970 Morrison left for a lengthy vacation with his wife Pamela, and after journeying to Spain, Morroco and Corsica, settled in Paris to work on a screenplay and write poetry. Troubled by a respiratory ailment, Morrison saw two doctors and was reportedly back to health. On July 3, 1971, he died of a heart attack. He was quietly buried in Pere Lachaise, near Balzac, Moliere, and Oscar Wilde.

In *An American Prayer,* privately circulated among his friends, Morrison wrote:

> "Death makes angels of us all
> and gives us wings
> where we had shoulders
> smooth as raven's
> claws."

BIOGRAPHICAL/CRITICAL SOURCES: Disk Review,

fall, 1967; *Rolling Stone,* January 20, 1968, April 5, 1969, April 19, 1969, October 15, 1970, March 4, 1971, August 5, 1971; *Crawdaddy,* April, 1969; *Esquire,* June, 1972.*

(Died July 3, 1971, in Paris, France)

* * *

MORRISON, Jim
See MORRISON, James Douglas

* * *

MORROW, Stephen 1939-

PERSONAL: Born January 20, 1939, in New York, N.Y.; son of Dwight W. Morrow, Jr. (a historian) and Margot (Loines) Morrow Wilkie; married Ana Rios Rivas, November 25, 1975; children: Stephen Daniel. *Education:* Amherst College, B.A., 1961. *Office:* United Press International, Jiron Puno 271, Dept. 601, Lima 1, Peru.

CAREER/WRITINGS: Newark Star-Ledger, Newark, N.J., reporter, 1964; *Newark Evening News,* Newark, reporter, 1965; United Press International, New York, N.Y., staffer in Cleveland, Ohio, and Baltimore, Md., 1966-68, bureau manager in Baltimore, 1968-69, and Cleveland, 1969-70, regional editor in Pittsburgh, Pa., 1970-72, correspondent in Rio de Janeiro, 1973, bureau manager in Lima, Peru, 1973—. Notable assignments include coverage of presidential nomination of General Geisels in Brazil, 1973, the October 3, 1974, earthquake, the Peruvian government expropriation of newspapers, 1974, the 1975 coup in Peru, steel strikes in Pittsburgh, Cleveland Browns, and the Baltimore Colts. *Member:* Overseas Press Club.

SIDELIGHTS: Morrow told *CA:* "I'm pleased to be contributing in a modest way to the coverage of Latin America, an under-rated and under-reported part of the world. Latin America is under-reported because its countries lack the economic and political power of Japan, Western Europe and the Near or Middle East, because it has fewer old country ties than Europe, and because its leaders lack the exotic quality of India or Idi Amin. 'Chicano power' may change this."

* * *

MORSE, B. J. ?-1977

?—June 2, 1977; Welsh educator, translator, and poet. Morse was a lecturer in Italian at the University of Wales. In addition to translations of scholarly works and several volumes of poetry, Morse also published criticism of such writers as Rilke, Christina Rossetti, and Dante Gabriel. He died in Cardiff, Wales. Obituaries: *AB Bookman's Weekly,* September 12, 1977.

* * *

MORSE, Hermann Nelson 1887-1977

1887—July 16, 1977; American clergyman, ecumenist, and author of mission textbooks. Morse was one of the chief architects of the National Council of Churches and he was a moderator of the United Presbyterian Church. He died in Washington, D.C. Obituaries: *New York Times,* July 17, 1977.

* * *

MORSE, Peter 1935-

PERSONAL: Born October 29, 1935, in Chicago, Ill. son of John Boit (an artist) and Margaret (McLennan) Morse; married Marcia Maris (a printmaker), July 14, 1972; children: Daniel. *Education:* Yale University, B.A., 1957. *Home:* 2938 Laukoa Pl., Honolulu, Hawaii 96813.

CAREER: Assistant to U.S. Congressman Charles M. Teague, 1957-60; businessman in Santa Barbara, Calif., 1960-65; Smithsonian Institution, Washington, D.C., associate curator of graphic arts, 1965-67; Honolulu Academy of Arts, Honolulu, Hawaii, research associate, 1967—. *Member:* American Society of Composers, Authors and Publishers.

WRITINGS: John Sloan's Prints, Yale University Press, 1969; *Jean Charlot's Prints,* University Press of Hawaii, 1976; *Popular Art,* Capra, in press. Musical compositions include film score for "House Made of Dawn." Contributor of articles on prints and Hawaiian history to magazines.

WORK IN PROGRESS: A book about diabetes for diabetics; *Hokusai's Prints,* with Roger S. Keyes, completion expected in 1985; *The Lahainalvna Engravings.*

AVOCATIONAL INTERESTS: Inventor.

* * *

MORSEY, Royal J(oseph) 1910-

PERSONAL: Born August 2, 1910, in Minster, Ohio; son of Anton J. and Anna (Helmsing) Morsey; married Mary Trottman, August 24, 1940; children: Paul J. *Education:* Ohio State University, B.Sc., 1933, M.A., 1937, Ph.D., 1948. *Home:* 108 Winthrop Rd., Muncie, Ind. 47304.

CAREER: National Cash Register Co., Dayton, Ohio, secretary, 1929-30; Standard Register Co., Dayton, Ohio, in cost work, 1933-36; high school teacher of business in Gambier, Ohio, 1937-39, and of English in Columbus, Ohio, 1939-48; Ball State University, Muncie, Ind., assistant professor, 1948-52, associate professor, 1953-58, professor of English and education, 1959-76; writer, 1977—. *Member:* American Federation of Teachers, National Council of Teachers of English, Indiana Council of Teachers of English (president, 1960-62), Phi Delta Kappa.

WRITINGS: A College Seminar to Develop and Evaluate an Improved High School English Program, Ball State University, 1961; (with Vivian B. Maine) *A Common-Sense Approach to Teaching Spelling,* Ball State University, 1962; *Improving English Instruction,* Allyn & Bacon, 1964, 3rd edition, Rand McNally, 1976.

WORK IN PROGRESS: An autobiography, describing a small midwestern town, 1910-1917.

* * *

MORTON, Carlos 1947-

PERSONAL: Born October 15, 1947, in Chicago, Ill.; son of Ciro (a non-commissioned army officer) and Maria Elena (Lopez) Morton; children: Seth Alexander Frack. *Education:* University of Texas, El Paso, B.A., 1975; University of California, San Diego, M.F.A., 1978. *Politics:* "Active anarchist." *Religion:* "Cosmic." *Home:* 7931 Parral, El Paso, Tex. 79915.

CAREER: Writer, 1971—; *La Luz* magazine, Denver, Colo., associate editor, 1975—; *Revista Chicano-Riquena,* Gary, Ind., contributing editor, 1976—.

WRITINGS: White Heroin Winter, One Eye Press, 1971; *El Jardin,* Quinto Sol, 1974; *Pancho Diablo,* Tonatiuth International, 1976; *Las Many Muertes de Richard Morales,* Tejidos, 1977. Contributor to *Drama Review, Viva, Nuestro,* and other periodicals.

SIDELIGHTS: Morton told *CA:* "I am working on recreating a viable reality for the colonized Chicano-Latino in the United States. Much of my work deals with stereotypes, both mythological and sociological, and my words are a mixture of English and Spanish.

"I am questioning stereotypes, especially in regards to the Latino here in the United States. For example, how could we explore the evolution of the infamous 'frito bandido' on stage? We would have to show the historical transition of the defeated soldier (Mexican) of the War of 1848 to that of the social Robin Hood bandits of the late 19th century (Juan Cortina, Jouquin Murieta) in Texas and California who carried on a type of guerrilla warfare against the Anglo colonizers in the Southwest. We would then have to switch to the Mexican Revolution (1910-21) and the arrival of Pancho Villa and Emiliano Zapata who to the Mexican people are heros and standards of the Revolution, but who to the gringos were nothing more than 'bandits' and 'outlaws'. Throw in a dash of 'machismo' and a bit of the 'sleepy peon' and you got your modern day 'frito bandido.'"

* * *

MORTON, Jocelyn 1912-

PERSONAL: Born June 14, 1912, in Carlisle, England; son of James (a textile manufacturer) and Beatrice (an educator; maiden name, Fagan) Morton; married Katharine Scott (an architect), September 23, 1944; children: Eleanor, Frances Ruck Keene, Emily, Lucy King. *Education:* Attended University of Edinburgh, 1929-30; Oxford University, B.A., 1936. *Politics:* "Floating voter." *Religion:* Church of England. *Home:* 39 Buckland Cres., London NW3 5DJ, England.

CAREER: Morton Sundour Fabrics Ltd. (family textile business), Carlisle, England, director, 1937-44, chairman, 1944-63; researcher and writer, 1963—. Past chairman of Carlisle and District Civic Trust. *Member:* Royal Society of Arts (fellow), Design and Industries Association, William Morris Society, Decorative Arts Society.

WRITINGS: Three Generations in a Family Textile Firm, Routledge & Kegan Paul, 1971.

WORK IN PROGRESS: Miscellaneous lectures on applied design, and civic and rural amenities.

SIDELIGHTS: Morton told *CA* that *Three Generations in a Family Textile Firm* "was written primarily to record the life and achievements in the field of decorative textiles (and allied technical fields) of my grandfather, Alexander Morton, my father, Sir James Morton, my brother, Alastair Morton, and my brother-in-law, Commander R.S.E. Hannay, all of whom were publicly recognised as having made important contributions in these fields, but about whom no single coherent account had been given."

Morton continues: "After early retirement from business owing to the take-over of the family business by a large public corporation, I, in addition to having time to research and write the book in question, also devoted a considerable amount of time to the civic and rural amenity movement in the north of England where I lived until moving to London in 1976."

* * *

MORTON, Marcia Colman 1927-

PERSONAL: Born December 18, 1927, in New York; daughter of Benjamin and Lillian (Siegel) Cohen; married Frederic Morton (a writer), March 28, 1957; children: Re-

becca. *Education:* Hunter College of the City University of New York, B.A., 1948. *Politics:* "Generally so-called liberal; so-called conservative on some issues." *Religion:* Jewish. *Home:* 110 Riverside Dr., New York, N.Y. 10024. *Agent:* Robert Lantz, Lantz Office, Inc., 114 East 55th St., New York, N.Y. 10022.

CAREER: Writer, 1957—. *Awards, honors:* Goldener Rathausmann Award from the City of Vienna, 1965, for writings about Vienna.

WRITINGS: The Art of Viennese Cooking, Doubleday, 1963; *The Art of Viennese Pastry,* Doubleday, 1969; *Pregnancy Notebook,* Workman Publishing, 1972. Contributor to *Woman's Day Cooking Encyclopedia.* Contributor to popular magazines and newspapers, including *Holiday, Mc-Call's, Cosmopolitan,* and *Saturday Review.*

WORK IN PROGRESS: Vienna (tentative title), on Vienna's cultural past, with husband, Frederic Morton, for Little, Brown.

SIDELIGHTS: Marcia Morton writes: "I began to think of myself as a writer—always in nonfiction—at about the age of six, and I have never really thought of doing anything else. I've written about food, travel, marriage, pregnancy, race prejudice—whenever my own experiences made me feel I had something to say about any of these. I spend a good deal of my time in Europe, mostly central Europe, and my great love is the Alps. My husband was born in Vienna and through him I've come to know that city well."

* * *

MOSEL, Tad 1922-

PERSONAL: Born May 1, 1922, in Steubenville, Ohio; son of George Ault (an advertising executive) and Margaret (Norman) Mosel. *Education:* Amherst College, B.A., 1947; attended Yale University, 1947-49; Columbia University, M.A., 1953. *Religion:* Presbyterian. *Home:* 400 East 57th St., New York, N.Y. 10022. *Agent:* William Morris Agency, 1350 Avenue of the Americas, New York, N.Y. 10019.

CAREER: Television dramatist, playwright, 1949—. Clerk, Northwest Airlines, 1951-53. Visiting critic in television writing, Yale University, 1957-58. *Military service:* U.S. Air Force Weather Service, 1943-46; became sergeant. *Member:* Writers Guild (member of executive council), Theta Delta Chi. *Awards, honors:* Pulitzer Prize for Drama, 1961, for "All the Way Home"; New York Drama Critics Circle Award, 1961, for "All the Way Home"; Litt. D., College of Wooster, 1963.

WRITINGS—Published plays: *Other People's Houses: Six Television Plays* (contains "Other People's Houses," "Ernie Barger Is Fifty," televised, 1953, "The Haven," 1953, "The Lawn Party," 1955, "Star in the Summer Night," 1955, "The Waiting Place," 1955), Simon & Schuster, 1956; *The Five-Dollar Bill* (televised, 1957), Dramatic Publishing, 1958; *All the Way Home* (adaptation of James Agee's novel, *A Death in the Family;* first produced in New York at Belasco Theatre, November 30, 1960), Oblensky, 1961; (with P. Kozeka) *Impromptu* (first produced in New York, 1961), Dramatists Play Service, 1961; *That's Where the Town's Going* (televised, 1962), Dramatists Play Service, 1961. Also author of *Jinxed* (televised, 1949), Samuel French.

Plays: "The Happiest Years," first produced in Amherst, Mass., 1942; "The Lion Hunter," first produced in New York, 1952; "Madame Aphrodite," televised, 1953; produced Off-Broadway, December, 1961.

Screenplays: "Dear Heart," 1964; "Up the Down Staircase," 1967.

Teleplays: "The Figgerin' of Aunt Wilma," 1953; "This Little Kitty Stayed Cool," 1953; "The Remarkable Case of Mr. Bruhl," 1953; "Guilty Is the Stranger," 1955; "My Lost Saints," 1955; "The Out-of-Towners," 1956; "The Morning Place," 1957; "Presence of the Enemy," 1957; "The Innocent Sleep," 1958; "A Corner of the Garden," 1959; "Sarah's Laughter," 1959; "The Invincible Teddy," 1960; "Secrets," 1970. Also contributor of scripts to "Goodyear Playhouse," "Philco Playhouse," "Playhouse 90," "Studio One," "Producers' Showcase," "Playwrights '56," "Omnibus," and others.

Anthologies: *Television Plays for Writers: Eight Television Plays,* edited by A. S. Burack, Writer, Inc., 1957; *Best Short Plays, 1957-58,* edited by Margaret Mayorga, Beacon Press, 1958; *Best Television Plays,* edited by Gore Vidal, Ballantine, 1965.

Member of editorial board, *TV Quarterly.*

SIDELIGHTS: Mosel is renowned for his stage adaptation of James Agee's classic *A Death in the Family,* which was called "All the Way Home," and which brought the writer a Pulitzer Prize. Three days after it opened on Broadway the closing notice was posted. Trucks had already arrived to cart away the scenery when the play won the New York Drama Critics Circle Award and was dubbed "The Miracle on Forty-Fourth Street." Shortly thereafter, another closing notice was posted. This time the play was revived by a Pulitzer Prize.

As a writer in several media, Mosel has often transposed one to the other, and understands the complex and often minute problems inherent in each.

BIOGRAPHICAL/CRITICAL SOURCES: New York Times, May 19, 1961, October 28, 1963; *New York Journal-American,* December 30, 1961.

*   *   *

MOSKIN, Marietta D(unston)   1928-

PERSONAL: Born April 30, 1928, in Vienna, Austria; came to the United States in 1946, naturalized citizen, 1952; daughter of Felix C. and Clara (Ettinger) Dunston; married Donald Moskin (in real estate), September 5, 1958; children: James, Linda. *Education:* Barnard College, B.A., 1952; University of Wisconsin, Madison, M.A., 1955. *Residence:* New York, N.Y.

CAREER: Tax Foundation, Inc., New York City, economic research assistant, 1952-53; Savings Bank and Trust Co., New York City, economic research assistant, 1955-56; General Motors Co., New York City, economic research assistant, 1956-58; writer and reviewer of children's books, 1958—. *Awards, honors:* Shirley Kravitz Children's Book Award from Association of Jewish Libraries, 1976, for *Waiting for Mama.*

WRITINGS—For children, except as noted: *The Best Birthday Party,* John Day, 1964; *With an Open Hand,* John Day, 1967; *A Paper Dragon,* John Day, 1968; *Hop, Run, Jump,* translation from German by Rose Demeter, John Day, 1968; *The Bamboo School in Bali,* translation from Dutch by Jef Last and U. P. Tisna, John Day, 1969; *The Different Child Grows Up* (adult), translation from German by Maria Egg, John Day, 1969.

Toto, Coward, 1971; *I Am Rosemarie,* John Day, 1972; *Lysbet and the Fire Kittens,* Coward, 1973; *Waiting for Mama,* Coward, 1975; *Adam and the Wishing Charm,* Coward, 1977.

Work anthologized in *Round About the City,* Crowell, 1966.

WORK IN PROGRESS: A book on religion for young adults; a children's book set in New York City, *The Big Snow,* for Coward.

SIDELIGHTS: Moskin told *CA:* "Having started my working career as an economist, becoming a children's book author was not the most natural progression. But a volunteer job reviewing children's books after my first child was born offered me an invaluable education in children's literature. Suddenly my life-long ambition to become a writer was channeled into books for children. I am still reviewing children's books (for the Child Study Association) and I am still learning from them.

"The current vogue for extreme permissiveness and realism in children's literature is an exciting new trend, provided that the realism is tempered with a sense of hope and that at least one adult in the story is supportive and presents some positive qualities as a counterbalance. If children are to learn anything from their literature, they must be encouraged to believe that life does have good things to offer as well as evil ones, and that young people in even the worst of circumstances must grope for honesty, truth, and a better future.

"I believe that books can and do help children to cope with the problems in their lives, in addition to providing escape and entertainment, and this is one of the reasons why I enjoy writing for young people."

AVOCATIONAL INTERESTS: New York City history, comparative religion, archaeology.

*   *   *

MOTLEY, Mary Penick   1920-

PERSONAL: Born November 18, 1920, in Detroit, Mich.; daughter of Brumal (a building contractor) and Pearl (Parker) Penick; married William Sypret, July, 1939 (divorced, 1942); married Earl H. Motley (a postal clerk), September 3, 1952 (separated). *Education:* Attended University of Michigan, 1937-39, 1943-44, and Wayne State University. *Politics:* "Non-Partisan." *Religion:* Episcopalian. *Home:* 15 East Kirby, #323, Detroit, Mich. 48202.

CAREER: Writer, 1967—. *Member:* University of Michigan Alumni Association. *Awards, honors:* Citation from District of Columbia chapter of 366th Infantry Veterans Association, 1976, for *The Invisible Soldier.*

WRITINGS: Africa: Its Nations, Empires, and People, Wayne State University Press, 1969; *The Invisible Soldier,* Wayne State University Press, 1975.

WORK IN PROGRESS: A book on black soldiers in Korea and Vietnam, completion expected in 1979.

SIDELIGHTS: Mary Motley writes: "My motivation is simple. Afro Americans have never been given a fair and honest place in American history. I am trying to help fill this *chasm* of omission. I chose to write about the black man in the military because of the abysmal ignorance surrounding the black serviceman, even in the contemporary wars; also because books on the subject are very rare and articles on the subject are generally distorted, dishonest, and without a researched background.

"The book *Africa* was to fill the need for an honest-to-goodness textbook on the empires, nations and people of Africa, from which Afro Americans came.

"Perhaps my interest in the black in the military is because my maternal grandfather was a Civil War veteran."

BIOGRAPHICAL/CRITICAL SOURCES: Detroit News, March 3, 1977.

MOUNT, Marshall Ward 1927-

PERSONAL: Born December 25, 1927, in Jersey City, N.J.; son of Elmer Marshall (a physician) and Pauline (an artist; maiden name, Ward) Mount; married Isabel Berkery (a public relations director), September 9, 1950; children: Christopher Ward. *Education:* Columbia University, A.B., 1948, A.M., 1952, Ph.D., 1966. *Residence:* Benin City, Nigeria. *Office:* Department of Creative Arts, University of Benin, Benin City, Nigeria.

CAREER: Finch College, New York, N.Y., professor of art history, 1958-75, chairman of department, 1958-75, director of art history program in San Marino, summers, 1973-75; free-lance writer, 1975-77; University of Benin, Benin City, Nigeria, visiting professor, 1978—. Instructor at New York University, 1960; visiting professor at University of Iowa, summer, 1970, and Parsons School of Design, 1970, 1971; visiting associate professor at Hunter College of the City University of New York, 1972. Leader of study tours to Mali, Cameroon, and India, 1970, 1975—.

MEMBER: African Studies Association (fellow), College Art Association of America, American Association of University Professors, Society of Architectural Historians, African-American Institute. *Awards, honors:* Rockefeller Foundation grants for sub-Saharan Africa, 1961, 1962, 1968; Finch College grant for Africa, 1966; American Council of Learned Societies grant, 1973.

WRITINGS: African Art: The Years since 1920, Indiana University Press, 1973. Contributor to *Oxford Companion to Contemporary Art* and to art and archaeology journals.

WORK IN PROGRESS: Art in African Museums, on material from West, Central, and South Africa that has not been studied, photographed, or written about previously.

SIDELIGHTS: Mount's personal collection includes nearly a thousand examples of traditional African art and about seven thousand color transparencies from Africa. His travels, aside from time spent in Africa, have taken him through Europe and the Near East.

* * *

MUELLER, Robert Kirk 1913-

PERSONAL: Surname is pronounced like Miller; born July 25, 1913, in St. Louis, Mo.; son of E. R. Otto and Lucille (Flaugher) Mueller; married Jane Elizabeth Konesko (an artist), December 27, 1939; children: Lucy Alison (Mrs. Paul White), Patricia Kirk (Mrs. Elmer Hilpert), James Arno. *Education:* Washington University, St. Louis, Mo., B.S., 1934; University of Michigan, M.S., 1935; Harvard University, further graduate study, 1950. *Religion:* Protestant. *Home address:* Huckleberry Hill, Lincoln, Mass. 01773. *Office:* Arthur D. Little, Inc., Acorn Park, Cambridge, Mass. 02140.

CAREER: Monsanto Co., St. Louis, Mo., 1935-68, general manager, 1952-61, vice-president and director of executive committee, 1963-68; Arthur D. Little, Inc., Cambridge, Mass., 1968—, vice-president, 1973-77, chairman of board of directors, 1977—. President of Shawinigan Resins Corp., 1952-61, chairman of board of directors, 1961-63. Member of board of directors of Massachusetts Mutual Life Insurance Co., Massachusetts Mutual Income Investors, Inc. (also member of executive committee), BayBanks, Inc., Plastics Education Foundation, and Salzburg Seminars in American Studies (also member of executive committee). Trustee and vice-chairman of executive committee at Colby-Sawyer College; vice-chancellor of International Academy of Manage-

ment. *Wartime service:* Manager of Longhorn Ordnance Works, Karnack, Tex., 1944-46.

MEMBER: American Management Association (life member; member of international council and president's council), American Institute of Chemical Engineers, American Chemical Society, Society of Chemical Industry, American Association for the Advancement of Science (fellow), Institute of Directors (London, England), New York Academy of Science, Metropolitan Club (New York), Algonquin Club (Boston), Eccentric Club (London), Colony Club (Springfield, Mass.), Harvard Faculty Club.

WRITINGS: Probability Controls, Funk, 1950; *Risk Survival and Power,* American Management Association, 1970; *The Innovation Ethic,* AMACOM, 1971; *Board Life,* AMACOM, 1974; *Buzzwords,* Van Nostrand, 1974; *Metadevelopment: Beyond the Bottom Line,* Lexington Books, in press; *New Directions for Directors: Behind the Bylaws,* Lexington Books, in press.

SIDELIGHTS: Mueller's books have been published in French, German, and Japanese.

* * *

MULCHRONE, Vincent 1919(?)-1977

1919(?)—October 1, 1977; British journalist. Mulchrone was associated with the *London Daily Mail* from 1947 until his death. He was twice named Descriptive Writer of the Year, one of Britain's top journalistic awards. Mulchrone died in London. Obituaries: *New York Times,* October 2, 1977.

* * *

MULKEEN, Anne
See MARCUS, Anne M(ulkeen)

* * *

MULLEN, William Charles 1944-

PERSONAL: Born October 9, 1944, in La Crosse, Wis.; son of Melvin Harold (a telephone technician) and Margaret (Thomley) Mullen; *Education:* Attended University of Wisconsin, La Crosse, 1962-65; University of Wisconsin, Madison, B.A., 1967. *Home:* 435 North Michigan Ave., Chicago, Ill. 60611.

CAREER/WRITINGS: La Crosse Tribune, La Crosse, Wisc., reporter, 1966; *Wisconsin State Journal,* Madison, reporter, 1966-67; *Chicago Tribune,* reporter, 1967—. Notable assignments include coverage of Chicago vote fraud, 1972, police brutality in Chicago, 1973, and world hunger, 1974. Lecturer, Northwestern University, 1975. *Awards, honors:* Edward Scott Beck Award from *Chicago Tribune,* 1972, 1973, 1974; Pulitzer Prize, 1973, for local reporting, 1975, for international reporting; Jacab Scher Award from Women in Communication, 1973.

* * *

MULLER, Herman J(oseph) 1909-

PERSONAL: Born April 7, 1909, in Cleveland, Ohio; son of Joseph John (in real estate) and Julia (Zwilling) Muller. *Education:* John Carroll University, student, 1927-28; Xavier University, Litt.B., 1932; Loyola University, Chicago, Ill., M.A., 1936, Ph.D., 1950; St. Louis University, S.T.L., 1942. *Office:* Department of History, University of Detroit, 4001 McNichols Rd., Detroit, Mich. 48221.

CAREER: Entered Society of Jesus (Jesuits), 1928, ordained Roman Catholic priest, 1941; high school teacher of

Latin and history at Roman Catholic high school in Chicago, Ill., 1935-38; Xavier University, Cincinnati, Ohio, lecturer in history and economics, 1943-47; Loyola University, Chicago, Ill., lecturer in history, 1949-50; West Baden College, West Baden, Ind., instructor in history, 1950-52; John Carroll University, Cleveland, Ohio, lecturer, 1952-53, assistant professor of history, 1953-56; University of Detroit, Detroit, Mich., associate professor, 1956-64, professor of history, 1964—, chairman of department, 1959-67. Visiting lecturer at National University of Ireland Colleges at Dublin, 1968-69, 1971-72, and Cork, 1974-75.

MEMBER: American Historical Association, American Catholic Historical Association, Michigan Academy of Arts and Sciences, Phi Alpha Theta, Alpha Sigma Nu, Alpha Sigma Lambda.

WRITINGS: The University of Detroit, 1877-1977, University of Detroit Press, 1976. Author of about two hundred scripts for educational television programs. Contributor of articles and reviews to scholarly journals.

WORK IN PROGRESS: A book on Jesuit architecture.

SIDELIGHTS: Fr. Muller comments: "Since living in Ireland for three years . . . and after an unbelievable thirty thousand miles of travel in the country I have done much lecturing on Ireland throughout the Detroit area." He also has traveled extensively in Western Europe.

* * *

MULLER, John E.
See FANTHORPE, R(obert) Lionel

* * *

MUMEY, Glen A(llen) 1933-

PERSONAL: Born December 5, 1933, in Minnesota; son of Leo (a farmer) and Olga (Nelson) Mumey; married wife, Lois; children: Brendan, Sol. *Education:* University of North Dakota, B.S.C., 1955, M.A., 1957; University of Washington, Seattle, Ph.D., 1965. *Office:* Department of Finance and Management Sciences, University of Alberta, Edmonton, Alberta, Canada.

CAREER: Former member of faculty at Purdue University, West Lafayette, Ind., University of Saskatchewan, Saskatoon, University of Washington, Seattle, University of Idaho, Moscow, University of North Dakota, Grand Forks; University of Alberta, Edmonton, professor of finance and management sciences, 1970—, chairman of department. Owner and operator of Mumey Farms. *Member:* Administrative Science Association of Canada (president-elect).

WRITINGS: Theory of Financial Structure, Holt, 1969; *Personal Economic Planning,* Holt, 1972; *Canadian Business Finance,* Irwin-Dorsey, 1977.

* * *

MUNARI, Bruno 1907-

PERSONAL: Born October 24, 1907, in Milan, Italy; son of a waiter and innkeeper; married wife, Dilma; children: Alberto, Valeria. *Education:* Attended the Technical Institute of Naples (Italy). *Residence:* Milan, Italy.

CAREER: Painter, sculptor, photographer, illustrator and designer of books, toys, and mobiles. *Awards, honors:* Gold Medal of the Triennale of Milan; several Golden Compasses for industrial designs; *Bruno Munari's ABC* and the *Circus in the Mist* were listed among the New York Times Choice of Best Illustrated Children's Books of the Year in 1960 and 1969, respectively.

WRITINGS: I Libri Munari, Mondadori, 1945; *Nella Notte Buia,* Muggiani, 1956, translation published as *In the Dark of the Night,* G. Wittenborn, 1961; *Alfabetiere Secondo il Metodo Attivo,* Einaudi, 1960; *Il Quadrato* (published with "The Square," a translation by Desmond O'Grady), G. Wittenborn, 1960, translation also published separately as *Discovery of the Square,* G. Wittenborn, 1963; *Vetrine, Negozi Italiani: Modern Design For Italian Show-Windows and Shops* (text in Italian, English, and German), Editrice L'Ufficio Moderno, 1961; *Good Design* (translation from the Italian), All'Insegna del Pesce D'Oro (distributed by G. Wittenborn), 1963; *Supplemento al Dizionario Italiano* (text in English, French, and German), Muggiani, 1963, translation published as *Supplement to the Italian Dictionary,* G. Wittenborn, 1963; *Il Cerchio,* All'Insegna del Pesce D'Oro, 1964, translation by Marcello and Edna Maestro published as *The Discovery of the Circle,* G. Wittenborn, 1965; *Arte come Mestiere,* Laterza, 1966, translation by Patrick Creagh published as *Design as Art,* Penguin, 1971; *Libro Illeggibile,* Museum of Modern Art (New York), 1967; *Design e Comunicazione Visiva,* Laterza, 1968; *Codice Ovvio,* Einaudi, 1971; *Artista e Designer,* Laterza, 1971; *Cappuccetto Verde* (illustrated by the author), Einaudi, 1972.

For children; all illustrated by the author: *Lorry Driver,* Harvill, 1953; *What I'd Like to Be,* Harvill, 1953; *Animals for Sale* (translation from the Italian by Maria Cimino), World Publishing, 1957; *Who's There? Open the Door!* (translation from the Italian by M. Cimino), World Publishing, 1957; *Tic, Tac, and Toc* (translation of *Storie di Tre Uccellini* by M. Cimino), World Publishing, 1957; *The Elephant's Wish* (translation of *Mai Contenti*), World Publishing, 1959; *The Birthday Present* (translation of *L'Uomo del Camion*), World Publishing, 1959; *Jimmy Has Lost His Cap, Where Can It Be?* (translation of *Gigi Cerca il suo Berretto*), World Publishing, 1959; *ABC,* World Publishing, 1960; *Bruno Munari's Zoo.* World Publishing, 1963; *Nella Nebbia di Milano,* Emme Edizioni, 1968, translation published as *The Circus in the Mist,* World Publishing, 1969; *Da Lontano era un'Isola,* Emme, 1971, translation by Pierrette Fleutiaux published as *From Afar It Is an Island,* World Publishing, 1972; *A Flower with Love* (translation from the Italian by Patricia T. Lowe), Crowell, 1974.

Illustrator: Gianni Rodari, *Filastrocche in Cielo e in Terra,* Einaudi, 1960; G. Rodari, *Il Pianeta degli Alberi di Natale,* Einaudi, 1962; G. Rodari, *Favole al Telefono,* Einaudi, 1962; G. Rodari, *Il Libro degli Errori,* Einaudi, 1964; G. Rodari, *La Torta in Cielo,* Einaudi, 1966; Nico Orengo, *A-Uli-Ule: Filastrocche, Conte, Ninnenanne,* Einaudi, 1972.

Editor: *Design Italiano: Mobili* (text in English, French, German, and Italian), C. Bestetti, 1968; (with others) *Campo Urbano: Interventi Estetici Nella Dimensione Collettiva Urbana,* C. Nani, 1969.

SIDELIGHTS: Bruno Munari began his career at age 20 as a member of the Italian Futurist Movement, a group of artists whose efforts were concentrated on giving formal expression to the energy and movement related to mechanical processes. He later became interested in making mobiles, which he calls 'machine inutile'—useless machines. His work has been exhibited in the United States at the New York Public Library and the Museum of Modern Art in New York City. In 1965 he held a one-man show in Tokyo.

In 1970 Munari was invited by Harvard University to teach Basic Design and Advanced Explorations in Visual Communications. There he experimented with a new method of teaching design which he later published in book form, *Design and Visual Communications.*

He began publishing books for children when his own son was small, and in his opinion, there were no good books for children. All of the illustrations in these books were done in tempera. In reviewing *The Circus in the Mist*, a *New York Times Book Review* critic wrote: "Bruno Munari is not only an illustrator but an innovator—a master at introducing us to the delights of abstraction by playing with color and form, and he does it superbly in this experiment in bookcraft. The story is simple—a trip through the foggy city when 'birds make only short flights'. This in black on translucent gray paper evoking a synesthesia of silence till we come to the Grand Circus complete with clowns and the high trapeze where colors are hot and pages laced with cutouts. The limits are those of your imagination. Here is the conscious use of skill, taste, and creative imagination. The effect is exquisite perfection in the graphic arts."

In a review of Bruno Munari's most recent book, *A Flower with Love*, the *Bulletin of the Center for Children's Books* observed: "Handsome color photographs show a dozen examples of ikebana, the Japanese art of flower arrangement. Munari wisely chooses not to stress the technical aspects of balance and design but to show arrangements that exemplify the restraint of ikebana compositions. Each full page photograph is faced by a paragraph of text occasionally adding a line drawing. The book itself is handsome, and it conveys effectively both the idea of choosing a flower lovingly and of expressing love by a gift of inexpensive beauty."

BIOGRAPHICAL/CRITICAL SOURCES: New Yorker, November 19, 1960; *New York Times Book Review,* December 14, 1969; *Saturday Review,* March 21, 1970; *Bulletin of the Center for Children's Books,* April, 1975.*

*   *   *

MUNDELL, William Daniel 1913-

PERSONAL: Born December 30, 1913, in Newfane, Vt.; son of Allie Franklin and Flora May (Gould) Mundell. *Education:* Attended Middlebury College, 1934, Grove City College, 1942, and Marlboro College, 1946. *Residence:* South Newfane, Vt.

CAREER: Self-employed carpenter and mason in Windham County, Vt., 1936-41, 1946-54; Vermont Highway Department, maintenance foreman in Newfane and Marlboro, 1954-69; *Poet Lore,* Washington, D.C., associate editor, 1969—. Photographer; real estate developer. Auditor for town of Newfane, 1939-41, selectman, 1969-72. Member of board of trustees of Moore Free Library, 1941-59 (president of board, 1952-59). Teacher and poet-in-residence at Cooper Hill Writers Conference. *Military service:* U.S. Marine Corps, 1942-45.

MEMBER: Poetry Society of America, Poetry Society of Vermont. *Awards, honors:* Stephen Vincent Benet Narrative Poetry Award from *Poet Lore,* 1968, for "Pasture for Old Horses."

WRITINGS: Hill Journey: Poems from Farm and Forest, Stephen Greene Press, 1970; *Plowman's Earth* (poems), Stephen Greene Press, 1973; *Mundell County* (poems), Greene Press, 1977. Contributor of poems and photographs to literary journals and popular magazines, including *Life, Poetry, American Forest, New Yorker, Atlantic,* and *Saturday Review.*

SIDELIGHTS: Mundell told *CA:* "The poem exists somewhere above the printed page where what the poet intended to communicate and the intellect and the experience of the reader meet in some kind of understanding and recognition. It can happen that the reader, by the suggestiveness of the poet's words, builds into the poem even more than the author's intent. The poet can try to leave enough unstated so that the reader has that invitation to participate in the poem's success."

*   *   *

MUNDY, Max
See SCHOFIELD, Sylvia Anne

*   *   *

MUNN, Glenn (Gaywaine) 1890(?)-1977

1890(?)—September 19, 1977; American economist and author best known for *Meeting at the Bear Market.* Munn died in Riverhead, N.Y. Obituaries: *New York Times,* September 22, 1977.

*   *   *

MUNNELL, Alicia H(aydock) 1942-

PERSONAL: Born December 6, 1942, in New York, N.Y.; daughter of Walter Howe and Alicia (Wildman) Haydock; married Thomas Clark Munnell (an executive), June 8, 1963; children: Thomas Clark, Jr., Hamilton Haydock. *Education:* Wellesley College, B.A., 1964; Boston University, M.A., 1966; Harvard University, Ph.D., 1973. *Home:* 4 Chiltern Rd., Weston, Mass. 02193. *Office:* Federal Reserve Bank of Boston, 600 Atlantic Ave., Boston, Mass. 02106.

CAREER: New England Telephone Co., Boston, Mass., staff assistant in Business Research Division, 1964-65; Boston University, Boston, teaching fellow, 1965-66; Brookings Institution, Washington, D.C., research assistant in Economic Studies Division, 1966-69; Federal Reserve Bank of Boston, Boston, fiscal economist, 1973-76, assistant vice-president, 1976—. Assistant professor at Wellesley College, 1974. Member of Massachusetts governor's task force on unemployment compensation, 1975, special funding advisory committee for Massachusetts pensions, 1976, and Massachusetts Retirement Law Commission, 1976—; vice-chairman of advisory committee of New England Retirement Law Council, 1977. Worked for Committee for Economic Development, summer, 1970.

WRITINGS: (Contributor) Joseph A. Pechman, Henry J. Aaron, and Michael K. Taussig, editors, *Social Security: Perspectives for Reform,* Brookings Institution, 1968; *The Impact of Social Security on Personal Savings,* Ballinger, 1974; (with Robert W. Eisenmenger, Joan T. Poskanzer, Richard F. Syron, and Steven J. Weiss) *Options for Fiscal Reform in Massachusetts,* Federal Reserve Bank of Boston, 1975; *The Future of Social Security,* Brookings Institution, 1977; (contributor) Joseph A. Pechman, editor, *Setting National Priorities: The 1978 Budget,* Brookings Institution, 1977; (contributor) Ann M. Connolly, editor, *Funding Pensions: Issues and Implications for Financial Markets,* Federal Reserve Bank of Boston, 1977; (contributor) Barbara Risman Herzog, editor, *Income and Aging,* Human Sciences Press, 1977. Contributor to professional journals.

WORK IN PROGRESS: Research for a book on issues in the financing of private pensions.

*   *   *

MUNSON, Don 1908-

PERSONAL: Born June 16, 1908, in Bridgeport, Conn.; son

of Frederick L. (a mechanical engineer) and Natalie (Webber) Munson; married Virginia Drew (deceased). *Education:* Attended Hamilton College, 1932. *Religion:* Episcopalian. *Home address:* P.O. Box 182, Chilmark, Martha's Wineyard, Mass. 02535. *Agent:* Lucianne Goldberg, 255 West 84th St., New York, N.Y. 10024.

CAREER: Reporter for *Bridgeport Post-Telegram, Norwalk Sentinal,* and *Westporter,* 1933-40; Raytheon, Inc., Waltham, Mass., supervisor, 1941-44; Ingalls, Mineter Advertising, Boston, Mass., copy writer, 1944-46; Daniel Sullivan Advertising, Boston, copy writer, 1946-48; Little, Brown & Co., Boston, publicity director, 1948-49; free-lance writer, 1950—. Partner of Women's Broadcasting Syndicate. Vice-president of Committee for the Americas, Inc.; chairman of Save Copley Square Committee; member of Boston Committee for Safe Bicycling; co-chairman of New Hampshire Bedell Bridge Committee. Consultant to Media Group, Inc.

MEMBER: Overseas Press Club, Clan MacDougall Society of America. *Awards, honors:* Robert E. Sherwood Award, 1946, for producing "Let Freedom Ring," a series on WBZ-Television.

WRITINGS: (With Allinora Roose) *The Paper Book,* Scribner, 1970; (contributor) *Yankee Anthology,* Yankee, Inc., 1973. Contributor of articles and reviews to magazines and newspapers, including *Printer's Ink, New Yorker,* and *House Beautiful.*

WORK IN PROGRESS: Amazing New Englanders; In Defense of . . .; Women in History; Drinking Made Easy; The Decline of America; with Duncan MacDonald, *Travels in Scotland.*

SIDELIGHTS: Munson comments: "My lifelong friendship with Miss Sally Fairchild of Boston, who had been closely associated with George Bernard Shaw, John Singer Sargent, and other distinguished persons, has had a marked effect on my career. An interest in genealogy developed from a study of my forebear, Thomas Munson, who signed the Fundamental Agreement of the New Haven Colony in the seventeenth century."

AVOCATIONAL INTERESTS: Travel (Soviet Union, Sweden, Belgium, France, Italy, the Netherlands, England, Scotland), fishing, swimming.

* * *

MURAD, Anatol 1904-

PERSONAL: Born December 4, 1904, in Vienna, Austria; came to United States in 1923, naturalized citizen, 1945; son of Gaston (a civil servant) and Gabriele (a painter; maiden name, von Michalkowski) Murad; married Orlene Wettengel (a professor of English), July 13, 1939; children: Anthony, Timothy. *Education:* Columbia University, B.S., 1931, M.S., 1932, Ph.D., 1939. *Home:* 2051 Jubilee Ave., Regina, Saskatchewan, Canada S4S 3T9. *Office:* Department of Economics, University of Regina, Regina, Saskatchewan, Canada S4S 0A2.

CAREER: American Institute of Banking, New York, N.Y., instructor in economics and banking, 1934-39; University of Southern California, Los Angeles, assistant professor of finance and economics, 1939-46; Rutgers University, New Brunswick, N.J., associate professor of economics, 1946-47; University of Puerto Rico, Rio Piedras, professor of economics, 1956, 1958-68; University of Regina, Regina, Saskatchewan, professor of economics, 1968-72, professor emeritus, 1972—. Instructor at Rutgers University, 1937-39;

Fulbright lecturer at University of Muenster, 1957-58; lecturer at University of Southern California, summers, 1955, 1957, 1959. *Member:* American Economic Association.

WRITINGS: The Paradox of a Metal Standard, Graphic Arts Press, 1939; (with Broadus Mitchell and others) *Economics: Experience and Analysis,* William Sloane Associates, 1950; (with Mitchell and others) *Basic Economics,* William Sloane Associates, 1951; *Economics: Principles and Problems,* Littlefield, 1953, 5th edition, 1967; *Private Credit and Public Debt,* Public Affairs Press, 1954; (contributor) K. K. Kurihara, editor, *Post-Keynesian Economics,* Rutgers University Press, 1954; *What Keynes Means,* Bookman Associates, 1962; *Franz Joseph I of Austria and His Empire,* Twayne, 1969. Contributor of articles and reviews to economics and business journals in the United States and Europe.

WORK IN PROGRESS: Research on the theory and history of money.

SIDELIGHTS: Anatol Murad told *CA:* "In all my writings on money I do battle with false theories now prevalent, such as the 'monetarism' of Nobel Laureate Milton Friedman. False theories have led to misinterpretations of the history of money, prices, and inflation." *Avocational interests:* Music, playing the violin.

* * *

MURDEN, Forrest D(ozier), Jr. 1921-1977

March 10, 1921—December 4, 1977; American international public-affairs and management consultant and author of books on world trade and international economic cooperation. He was an aide to Henry Ford II during the 1950's, and was president of his own company since 1967. Murden died in New York, N.Y. Obituaries: *New York Times,* December 5, 1977.

* * *

MURPHY, Michael 1930-

PERSONAL: Born September 3, 1930, in Salinas, Calif.; son of John Andrew (an attorney) and Marie Jeanne (Bedecarre) Murphy; married Dulce Wilmott (formerly director of Esalen Institute in San Francisco), July 11, 1975. *Education:* Stanford University, B.A., 1952, graduate study in philosophy, 1955-56; further study at Sri Aurobindo Ashram (India), 1956-57. *Home:* 103 Hillside Ave., Mill Valley, Calif. 94941.

CAREER: Esalen Institute, Big Sur, Calif., founder and chairman, 1962—. Regents lecturer, University of California, Santa Cruz, 1976. *Military service:* U.S. Army, 1953-54.

WRITINGS: Golf in the Kingdom, Viking, 1972; *Jacob Atabet: A Speculative Fiction,* Celestial Arts, 1977. Also author of *The Appalachian Dulcimer Book,* Folksay Press. Associate editor, *Journal of Transpersonal Psychology,* 1969—.

WORK IN PROGRESS: A book on his "full time research project on the possibilities of bodily transformation through psychological and spiritual disciplines"; a sequel to *Jacob Atabet;* and a book on the spiritual side of sport, with Rhea White.

SIDELIGHTS: Though no longer at the cutting edge of the "new consciousness" movement that began its rapid growth in the hectic and promising sixties, the Esalen Institute has established itself as a tradition in the exploration of "human potential."

The Institute is constructed on some one hundred seventy-five acres of coastline and mountain purchased by grandfather Murphy in 1910 as the sight for a spa based on the European model. Michael Murphy secured right to the land and buildings from his grandmother in 1962, and, despite an initial period of conflict with squatters newly dispossessed, Esalen began, however inauspiciously. It was the sort of beginning that to some degree predetermined the development so characteristic of Esalen. Murphy commented: "I think a lot of the atmosphere of the place came from this outlaw element, having these people around. It may have contributed to the adventurous spirit of the place."

As a consequence of this careful "non-direction," Esalen has become a forum for a variety of ideologies and disciplines. In 1967 Esalen extended itself to San Francisco and today offers nearly three hundred programs a year.

As head of programming, Murphy has had little trouble persuading an impressive list of thinkers, psychologists, therapists and teachers to visit the Institute and instruct. He told *CA:* "Through its successes and failures Esalen has accomplished these three things: It has provided a place where innovative psychological disciplines such as Gestalt Therapy were developed; it helped dramatize the richness of exploration that was possible into neglected aspects of human functioning such as sensory and meditative experience; and it was the model for many similar centers in the United States, Europe, Australia and Canada."

Murphy's first book, a philosophical novel about his favorite game, is entitled *Golf in the Kingdom.* Shivas Irons, its protagonist, was a natural for Murphy who finds it plausible to approach philosophy and mysticism by way of sports.

His second novel, *Jacob Atabet: A Speculative Fiction,* has for its central character a man who "discovers that the body is an opening into the secrets of time, a sort of evolutionary star gate. In it, the universe is remembered, level upon level. And so his lifelong voyage is back to the birth of the universe through his bodily descent."

Living now in Mill Valley, Calif., with his wife, Dulce, Murphy continues to serve as chairman of Esalen, runs eight to ten miles a day, and is working on a third book.

BIOGRAPHICAL/CRITICAL SOURCES: New Yorker, January 5, 1976.

* * *

MURPHY, Robert D(aniel) 1894-1978

October 28, 1894—January 9, 1978; American diplomat, business executive, and author. Highlights of Murphy's forty-year career in the diplomatic service included ambassadorial posts in Belgium and Japan and the third-ranking State Department position of under secretary of state for political affairs. During World War II he served as charge d'affaires at Vichy, which enabled him to develop a network of contacts in France, Algeria, Morocco, and Tunisia to facilitate the 1942 Allied invasion of North Africa. A total of seven presidents made use of Murphy's years of diplomatic experience and skill in negotiation by sending him to world troublespots as a special envoy. After his official retirement from the State Department, he undertook several special diplomatic missions and served as an executive for Corning Glass Works. His memoirs, *Diplomat Among Warriers,* coupled his intimate knowledge of historic events with his personal views about U.S. foreign policy. He died in Manhattan, N.Y. Obituaries: *New York Times,* January 11, 1978; *Washington Post,* January 11, 1978; *Newsweek,* January 23, 1978. (See index for *CA* sketch)

MURRAY, Elwood 1897-

PERSONAL: Born February 3, 1897, in Macomb, Ill.; son of Alonzo Parker (a farmer and stockbroker) and Bessie (Huey) Murray; married Emma Prince; children: Rosalind Meyer, Allen Prince, Maurice Elwood. *Education:* Hastings College, B.A., 1922; University of Iowa, M.A., 1924, Ph.D., 1931. *Politics:* "Independent—tend Democratic." *Home:* 2391 South Clayton, Denver, Colo. 80210. *Office:* Department of Speech Communication, University of Denver, Denver, Colo. 80208.

CAREER: High school debate and English teacher in Ord, Neb., 1922-23, and Council Bluffs, Iowa, 1923-26; Midland College, Fremont, Neb., director of debate and forensics, 1926-27; Purdue University, West Lafayette, Ind., member of faculty of public speaking, 1927-29; University of Denver, Denver, Colo., professor of speech, 1931-69, professor emeritus, 1969—, chairman of department of speech communication, 1931-69, director of School of Speech, 1931-63. Distinguished visiting professor at Southern Illinois University, 1963-64; visiting professor at University of Minnesota, 1965-66, and Murray State University; lecturer at University of Nebraska, University of South Dakota, University of Montana, University of Padua, University of London, University of Bristol, University of Copenhagen, and Karl Marx University. Director of Institute of General Semantics, 1967-69, director emeritus, 1969—. Member of local mayor's Commission on Community Relations, 1958-70; member of Denver Metropolitan Urban Coalition's task force on communications and public opinion, 1969—; member of Balarat Council, 1969—. *Member:* International Communication Association (founding member; president, 1952), American Association of Humanistic Psychology.

WRITINGS: The Speech Personality, Lippincott, 1937, revised edition, 1942; (with Ray Barnard and Joseph Garland) *Integrative Speech,* Dryden Press, 1952; (with Gerald Phillips and David Truby) *Speech: Science-Art,* Bobbs-Merrill, 1970. Contributor of about a hundred fifty articles to speech, psychology, education, and general semantics journals.

* * *

MURRAY, J. Harley 1910(?)-1977

1910(?)—November 15, 1977; American editor and journalist. Murray was editor of the Whaley-Eaton newsletters since 1958. He was an organizer of the Newspaper Guild and one of the original charter organizers of the Wire Service Guild. He died in Washington, D.C. Obituaries: *New York Times,* November 16, 1977.

* * *

MURRAY, K. F.
See CARLISLE, Fred

* * *

MURRAY, Walter I(saiah) 1910(?)-1978

1910(?)—January 10, 1978; American educator and author of books on education. Murray died in New York, N.Y. Obituaries: *New York Times,* January 11, 1978.

* * *

MYERS, (Elliott) Jack 1941-

PERSONAL: Born November 29, 1941, in Lynn, Mass.; son of Alvin George (a salesman) and Ruth Libby (Cohen) Myers; married Nancy Ruth Leppert, May 26, 1967; children: Benjamin Ch'ien, Seth Emmanuel. *Education:* University of Massachusetts, Boston, B.A. (magna cum laude), 1970; University of Iowa, M.F.A., 1972. *Politics:* Liberal Left. *Religion:* Jewish. *Home:* 3004 Dyer St., Dallas, Tex. 75205. *Office:* Department of English, Southern Methodist University, Dallas, Tex. 75275.

CAREER: New England Real Estate Journal, Boston, Mass., news editor, 1963-66; worked as lobster fisherman, cook, mailman, laboratory assistant, typist, and taxi driver, 1967-70; Southern Methodist University, Dallas, Tex., assistant professor of English, 1975—. *Member:* Associated Writing Programs, South Central Modern Language Association, Texas Association of Creative Writers. *Awards, honors:* Award from Academy of American Poets, 1972, for the poem, "Monk"; Voertman Poetry Award from Texas Institute of Letters, 1978, for *The Family War.*

WRITINGS: Black Sun Abraxas (poetry), Halcyone Press, 1970; (with David Akiba) *Will It Burn* (poetry and photography), Falcon Publishing, 1974; *The Family War* (poetry), L'Epervier Press, 1977; (editor) *A Trout in the Milk* (on poet Richard Hugo), Confluence Press, 1978.

WORK IN PROGRESS: The Portable Workshop, an advanced poetry textbook; *What's Left,* poems.

SIDELIGHTS: Myers writes: "Having been deeply influenced by the so-called 'confessional poets,' I now see my task to be one of enlarging upon their breakthroughs by widening the range of my work and admitting some prose techniques (narration, mixed rhythmic structures, less tense lines) into it. The new South American and Continental poets seem to be leading the way in this concern. My new work will, it is hoped, be personal, universal, and easily accessible."

* * *

MYERSON, Michael 1940-

PERSONAL: Born July 2, 1940, in Washington, D.C.; son of Seymour A. (an architect) and Vivien C. (a secretary) Myerson. *Education:* University of California, Berkeley, A.B., 1961. *Politics:* Communist. *Religion:* None. *Home:* 1825 Riverside Dr., New York, N.Y. 10034. *Agent:* Elaine Markson Literary Agency, Inc., 44½ Greenwich Ave., New York, N.Y. 10011.

CAREER: International Publishers, New York, N.Y., editor, 1966-68; writer. Has also worked as a longshoreman and warehouseman.

WRITINGS: These Are the Good Old Days: Coming of Age as a Radical in America's Late, Late Years, Grossman, 1970; *Memories of Underdevelopments,* Grossman, 1974; *Watergate: Crime in theSuites,* International Publishers, 1974; *Nothing Could Be Finer: Repression and Resistance in North Carolina,* International Publishers, 1977. Contributor to magazines, including *Ramparts,* and newspapers.

* * *

MYRICK, William J(ennings, Jr.) 1932-

PERSONAL: Born December 11, 1932, in Dallas, Tex.; son of William J. (a newspaperman) and P. C. Myrick. *Education:* University of Texas, B.A., 1954; Columbia University, M.S., 1960, D.L.S., 1973. *Office:* College Library, Brooklyn, Brooklyn College of the City University of New York, Brooklyn, N.Y. 11210.

CAREER: Brooklyn College of the City University of New York, Brooklyn, N.Y., associate librarian for administrative

services, 1976—. Adjunct assistant professor at Queens College of the City University of New York, autumn, 1973. Chairman of Technical Services Committee, New York Metropolitan Reference and Research Library Agency, 1975—; member of advisory committee, Medical Library Resource Planning Center, 1975; manuscript consultant to Bowker Co. and Neal Schuman Associates.

MEMBER: American Library Association, Association of College and Research Libraries, Library Research Round Table, Continuing Library Education Network and Exchange, American Society for Information Science, Special Libraries Association Association of American Publishers, New York State Library Association, New York Technical Services Librarians (vice-president, 1976-77; president, 1977-78), New York Library Club (member of council, 1976—), Library Association of City University of New York (vice-president, 1973-74; president, 1974-75), Columbia University School of Library Service Alumni Association (first vice-president, 1974-75; president, 1975-76), Columbia University Alumni Federation (treasurer, 1977-79).

WRITINGS: Coordination: Concept or Reality?, Scarecrow, 1975; *Finding Tools for Microfilm Publishing Projects: A Preliminary Union List,* New York Metropolitan Reference and Research Library Agency, 1976. Contributor to library journals.

WORK IN PROGRESS: A survey of the application of the principles of operations research and library management.

* * *

NADEL, Gerald 1945(?)-1977

1945(?)—September 30, 1977; American radio broadcaster, editor, and journalist. Nadel was chief of the Boston bureau of Fairchild Publications from 1970 to 1976, and the broadcaster of a daily radio business commentary. He died in Boston, Mass. Obituaries: *New York Times,* October 3, 1977.

* * *

NAGLER, Michael N(icholas) 1937-

PERSONAL: Born January 20, 1937, in New York, N.Y.; son of Harold (a teacher) and Dorothy (a teacher; maiden name, Nocks) Nagler; married Roberta Ann Robbins, 1959; children: Jessica, Joshua. *Education:* Attended Cornell University, 1954-57; New York University, B.A., 1960; University of California, Berkeley, M.A., 1962, Ph.D., 1966; attended University of Heidelberg, 1962-63. *Politics:* "Non-partisan." *Religion:* "Non-denominational." *Office:* Department of Classics, University of California, Berkeley, Calif. 94720.

CAREER: San Francisco State College, San Francisco, Calif., instructor in foreign languages, 1963-65; University of California, Berkeley, assistant professor, 1966-73, associate professor of classics and comparative literature, 1973—. *Member:* International Comparative Literature Association, American Philological Association. *Awards, honors:* National Foundation for the Arts and Humanities grant, summer, 1967; American Council of Learned Societies grant, 1971-72.

WRITINGS: Spontaneity and Tradition: A Study of the Oral Art of Homer, University of California Press, 1975; *Age of Anger: What You Can Do About Violence Today,* Nilgiri Press, in press. Contributor to scholarly journals and religious magazines. Member of editorial board of *Studia Mystica.*

SIDELIGHTS: Nagler writes: "I am eager to write a book

that would be of use in solving the very serious problems man is confronted with today, and violence seems to be the most urgent of these. My interests in religion and in things cultural converge on this project. In my view the writer has a grave responsibility to use his influence for good (and not merely for self-expression)."

* * *

NAGORSKI, Zygmunt, Jr. 1912-

PERSONAL: Born September 27, 1912, in Warsaw, Poland; came to the United States in 1948, naturalized citizen, 1953; son of Zygmunt J. (a lawyer) and Maria (Cederbaum) Nagorski; married Marie Bogdawszewski (an administrator), November 22, 1938; children: Maria Nagorski LeClere, Andrew, Teresa. *Education:* University of Cracow, M.A., 1935; graduate study at University of Geneva, International Institute of Trade and Patents, and University of Paris. *Politics:* Democrat. *Religion:* Roman Catholic. *Home:* 91 Central Park W., New York, N.Y. 10023. *Office:* Council on Foreign Relations, 58 East 68th St., New York, N.Y. 10021.

CAREER: War correspondent in Germany, 1945; Polish Government in Exile, Ministry of Information, Edinburgh, Scotland, director of Scottish Office, 1946-48; *Chattanooga Times,* Chattanooga, Tenn., reporter, 1948; editor-in-chief, Foreign News Service, Inc., 1949-56; U.S. Information Agency, Washington, D.C., chief of International Branch Office of Research, 1956-59, foreign service reserve officer in Cairo, Egypt, 1959-61, Seoul, Korea, 1961-64, and Paris, France, 1964-66; special assistant to the president, Foreign Policy Association, 1966-68; member of professional staff, Hudson Institute, 1968-69; Council on Foreign Relations, New York, N.Y., director of members' meetings programs, 1969—. Adjunct assistant professor at Queens College of the City University of New York, 1974-75; guest lecturer at colleges and universities, including University of Vermont, University of Indiana, Cornell University, Air Command College, and Foreign Service Institute. Member of board of directors of International University Foundation, National Office of Social Responsibility, and Scarsdale Adult School; past president of American Friends of Wilton Park. *Military service:* Polish Army, 1939-45; served in Poland, England, and France.

MEMBER: International Studies Association, Center for Inter-American Relations, American Academy of Political Science, American Foreign Service Association, American Political Science Association, Council on Foreign Relations, Polish Institute of Arts and Sciences, Mid-Atlantic Club (co-founder; chairperson), University Club. *Awards, honors:* Distinguished service award from U.S. Information Agency, 1966.

WRITINGS: Warsaw Fights Alone, Orbis Books, 1944; *Armed Unemployment,* Orbis Books, 1945; *The Psychology of East-West Trade,* Mason & Lipscomb, 1974. Author of "Report from Eastern Bloc," a monthly column in *Money Manager,* and "Behind the News," in *Boston Globe,* 1954-56. Contributor to magazines and newspapers, including *Newsday, New York Times, Los Angeles Times,* and *Wall Street Journal.*

WORK IN PROGRESS: A biography; research on Eurocommunism and East-West trade.

SIDELIGHTS: Nagorski told *CA:* "My typewriter sits on top of a huge, old English desk. My window offers a skimpy view of Central Park. It is skimpy because snow drifts obstruct my vision. The biggest blizzard of the generation dances outside. Snowflakes whirl around, chase each other within their own world of pleasure and life. It is just beautiful. How can one divorce oneself from nature and write about the trivia of human existence? Of 'current interests and personal views' as prescribed by the editors?

"Man cannot escape everpresent nature. Thank God he cannot. Otherwise my 'specific current interest' would overwhelm me to no end; would make me see nothing but 'me,' nothing but 'us.' And 'me' and 'us' are much less significant than snow flakes. We come and go. They persist and remain. So much for my current interests. So much for human affairs.

"I see a desire to project what bothers me inside. I see my tool to do so ... Words. Typewriter. Thoughts, Paper. Notes. I don't know how to play or to sing or to paint, so I grab at words. They are obedient, fun, sometimes stiff, sometimes warm like lovers whose mood one tries to capture. Like snowflakes without their fragility and softness. And I have an army at my disposal any time I need to go into battle; I fight against myself, or with myself, or against the others, or with them. But without my army of words I would be lost, and lonely, and just plain nobody.

"With that army I form 'personal views.' I worry about the future of New York City and the poverty of Calcutta which I have never seen. It is my army that forms impressions of the Middle East and that allows me to formulate my own reactions to rebellious youth. It is a part of my army which gives me a chance to escape the realities of sadness and to plunge into tunnels of laughter. I love it. Like a child loves going to a movie. Illusions replace realities and I keep forgetting that 'me' matters. I turn into 'me' that is just another tiny dot on the horizon of a never ending dance of beautiful, irreverant, and most seducing snowflakes."

AVOCATIONAL INTERESTS: Cycling, swimming, skiing, foreign travel.

* * *

NAISMITH, Horace
See HELMER, William J.

* * *

NANRY, Charles (Anthony) 1938-

PERSONAL: Born January 6, 1938, in Ann Arbor, Mich.; son of Ambrose James (a farmer) and Frances Isobel (Hoban) Nanry; married Jacqueline Mashioff (a social worker), May 24, 1969; children: Victoria Elizabeth, Abigail Suzzane. *Education:* Sacred Heart College, Detroit, Mich., B.A. (cum laude), 1959; Universita Gregoriana, graduate study, 1959-60; University of Michigan, M.A., 1962; Rutgers University, Ph.D., 1970. *Home:* 4 King Rd., Somerset, N.J. 08873. *Office:* Department of Sociology and Anthropology, University College, Rutgers University, New Brunswick, N.J. 08903.

CAREER: Mercy School of Nursing, Jackson, Mich., instructor in psychology and sociology, 1961; Brooklyn College of the City University of New York, Brooklyn, N.Y., lecturer, 1963, instructor in sociology and anthropology, 1963-64; St. John's University, Jamaica, N.Y., instructor in work and occupations, 1964; Rutgers University, New Brunswick, N.J., instructor, 1966-70, assistant professor, 1970-73, associate professor of sociology, 1973—, chairman of department of sociology and anthropology, 1975—. Rutgers Institute of Jazz Studies, curator, 1968-70, administrator of institute, 1970—, and member of its executive committee, 1971—. President of Jazz Interactions, Inc., 1964-70;

Eastern Conference of Jazz Societies, vice-president, 1967-69, Marshall Stearns Memorial Lecturer, 1967, 1968; chairman of Newport in New York Jazz Festival Conference, 1972. Lecturer at colleges and universities in the United States and Canada; consultant to law firms, hospitals and guidance centers, and local government units.

MEMBER: American Sociological Association, American Association of University Professors, Society for the Solution of Social Problems, Eastern Sociological Society, Alpha Kappa Delta.

WRITINGS: (Editor and contributor) *American Music: From Storyville to Woodstock,* Dutton, 1972; (editor with Irving Louis Horowitz, and contributor) *Sociological Realities II,* Harper, 1975; *The Jazz Text,* Van Nostrand, in press. Contributor to sociology and jazz music journals. Editor of *Journal of Jazz Studies;* guest editor of *Society,* November-December, 1976; review editor for Dorsey.

WORK IN PROGRESS: A study on aging, focusing on the relationship between age and higher education.

*   *   *

NASH, Howard P(ervear), Jr.   1900-

PERSONAL: Born September 8, 1900, in Northport, N.Y.; son of Howard P. (a lawyer) and Emma (Jones) Nash; married Alicia Foster, March 7, 1925; children: Lucinda H. Nash Bell, Ardyth J. Nash Bell. *Education:* Attended New Bedford Textile School. *Politics:* Independent. *Religion:* None. *Home address:* Aucoot Rd., Mattapoisett, Mass. 02739.

CAREER: In textile business, 1924-55; Old Dartmouth Historical Society, New Bedford, Mass., librarian at New Bedford Whaling Museum, 1954-66; Rodman Job Corps, New Bedford, Mass., student librarian, 1966-68; *New Bedford Standard-Times,* New Bedford, Mass., night editor, 1968-73; writer.

WRITINGS: Third Parties in American Politics, Public Affairs Press, 1958; *The Forgotten Wars,* A. S. Barnes, 1968; *Stormy Petrel* (biography), Fairleigh Dickinson University Press, 1969; *A Naval History of the Civil War,* A. S. Barnes, 1972; *Andrew Johnson, Congress, and Reconstruction,* Fairleigh Dickinson University Press, 1972. Contributor of articles and reviews to magazines.

WORK IN PROGRESS: An economic history of the United States, with emphasis on depressions.

SIDELIGHTS: Nash writes: "While employed in the business world, I was a student of history by avocation. Eventually I began writing history in my spare time."

*   *   *

NATANSON, George   1928-

PERSONAL: Born March 7, 1928, in Chicago, Ill.; son of George (an opera singer and artist) and Noreen (an actress; maiden name, Dow) Natanson; married Nelly Esther Rios (a dress designer), July 14, 1970; children: Michael George, Patrick Robert. *Education:* Attended Pomona Junior College, 1941, and University of California, Los Angeles, 1946-48; further study at University of San Marcos, Lima, Peru, 1949-51, University of Buenos Aires, 1952-53, University of San Andres, La Paz, Bolivia, 1954-55, and National Autonomous University of Mexico, 1963-64. *Politics:* "Progressive—subject to my own definition." *Home and office:* Rio Elba 21-6, Mexico 5, D.F., Mexico.

CAREER/WRITINGS: National Broadcasting Company (NBC) News, New York City, radio and television correspondent in Buenos Aires, Argentina, 1951-54; press advisor to president of Bolivia, 1954-56; free-lance writer in La Paz, Bolivia, 1956-59; Business International Corp., New York City, Latin American editor of financial weekly, 1959; *Caracas Daily Journal,* Caracas, Venezuela, special features editor, 1960-61; *Vision* (Spanish language news magazine), New York City, economic-financial editor, 1961-62; *Los Angeles Times,* Los Angeles, Calif., Mexico City bureau chief, 1963-66, Buenos Aires bureau chief, beginning 1966; deputy coordinator for the foreign press for the Mexican Organizing Committee of the XIX Olympic Games in Mexico City, 1968; free lance journalist, 1968-69; Columbia Broadcasting System (CBS) News, New York City, journalist based in Mexico City, 1969—. Notable assignments include an exclusive interview with Argentine General Juan Peron in 1954 which was televised over "Meet the Press." *Military service:* U.S. Navy, 1942-46. *Member:* Overseas Press Club, Foreign Press Association (Mexico City; president, 1975, 1977), Columnist Club (Mexico City). *Awards, honors: Los Angeles Times* annual award for best foreign story, 1964.

WORK IN PROGRESS: Research on the revolution within the Catholic Church in Latin America, for eventual publication in book form.

SIDELIGHTS: Natanson wrote: "The worst speller in the class, I was struck and locked in by journalism as a kid—and I remain a romantic today. God knows, its monetary returns would discourage even a pauper, a class to which I've been attached since entering the profession, but the motivations at the typewriter are, for me, far more compelling—independence, the over-riding factor especially for the free-lancer—and I never did learn to spell."

Natanson shared some of his experiences, adding: "From 1963 until just two years ago, I can safely say I've covered every major breaking news story in Latin America. There are few Latin leaders and U.S. statesmen involved in Latin American affairs I haven't met and written about. More than that, I've come to know intimately the nations and the people—not just their histories, politics, or economics, but their ways of life, customs, folklore, music, joys and sorrow.

"I lived at one time with a poor Indian family on the Bolivian 'altiplano' for two weeks, freezing to death the time I might add, but eating what they ate, working alongside the men in the fields (up to a point—I'm basically lazy). I learned from them and I wrote about it.

"I was instrumental in the escape of the first U.S. citizens ever taken and held hostage in Latin America. There were four of them, U.S. Information Service and Agency for International Development people attached to the U.S. Embassy in La Paz, Bolivia. They had visited the 'Siglo 20' tin mining camp some two hundred miles from La Paz when they were taken and held for about two weeks. Along with correspondents from the *New York Times* and *Time,* I was permitted free access to the hostages to report on their well-being. Finally one day I was visiting them alone in the union hall where they were being held at the camp; I suggested we all just walk out past the dynamite bearing maidens and rifle toting miners—get in my rented jeep and just drive away. Somehow, and to this day I don't know why, it worked. One of the four is Mike Kristula, now public affairs officer at the U.S. embassy in Bogota, Colombia.

"I've managed to live through revolutions, riots, student demonstrations, palace coups, numerous bars where correspondents on a story are wont to meet—and loved many women—a dangerous but fascinating profession which I wouldn't change were I given the chance."

NATHAN, Adele (Gutman)

PERSONAL: Born in Baltimore, Md.; daughter of Louis Kayton and Ida (Newburger) Gutman. *Education:* Goucher College, A.B.; graduate study at Johns Hopkins University, Columbia University, and Peabody Institute. *Residence:* New York, N.Y. *Agent:* Anita Diamant Berke, 51 E. 42nd St., New York, N.Y. 10017.

CAREER: Theatrical director and writer. Began career as founder and director of Vagabond Players, Baltimore, Md., 1916; directed plays in New York, New Jersey, Maryland, and North Carolina; also director of short subjects for Paramount Pictures and Grand National Pictures. Chief script writer, U.S. Department of Education, 1941; director, Operation Independence, Philadelphia, 1950-51. Department chairman, Edwin R. Murrow Memorial Library, 1968. *Member:* American Woman's University Club (Paris), Overseas Press Club, American Theatre Wing, Woman Pays (president, 1967-68). *Awards, honors:* Peabody citation, 1949; National Freedoms Foundation Award, 1953; Eastern Regional Freedoms Foundation Award, 1956.

WRITINGS: (With Margaret S. Ernst) *The Iron Horse,* Knopf, 1931; *The Farmer Sows His Wheat,* Minton, Balch, 1932; *The Building of the First Transcontinental Railroad* (illustrated by Edward A. Wilson), Random House, 1950; *Wheat Won't Wait* (illustrated by Millard McGee), Aladdin, 1952; (with William C. Baker) *Famous Railroad Stations of the World* (illustrated by Graham Bernbach), Random House, 1953; *Seven Brave Companions* (illustrated by Fritz Kredel), Aladdin, 1953; *When Lincoln Went to Gettysburg* (illustrated by Emil Weiss), Aladdin, 1955; *The First Transatlantic Cable* (illustrated by Denver Gillen), Random House, 1959; *Lincoln's America,* Grosset, 1961; *Churchill's England,* Grosset, 1963; *Major John Andre: Gentleman Spy,* F. Watts, 1969; *How to Plan and Conduct a Bicentennial Celebration* (illustrated by Alfred Stern and Ben Edwards), Stackpole, 1971.

Also contributor to numerous periodicals, including *Atlantic Monthly* and *Vogue.**

* * *

NATHAN, Peter E. 1935-

PERSONAL: Born April 18, 1935, in St. Louis, Mo.; son of Emil (a manager) and Kathryn (Kline) Nathan; married Florence Baker, November 26, 1959; children: David Edward, Anne Miller, Laura Carol, Mark Andrew. *Education:* Harvard University, A.B., 1957; Washington University, St. Louis, Mo., Ph.D., 1962. *Politics:* Liberal Democrat. *Religion:* Jewish. *Home:* 28 Beech Hill Circle, Princeton, N.J. 08540. *Office:* Graduate School of Applied and Professional Psychology (GSAPP), Rutgers University, Busch Campus, P.O. Box 819, Piscataway, N.J. 08854.

CAREER: Harvard Medical School Boston, Mass., research fellow to assistant professor, 1962-69; Rutgers University, New Brunswick, N.J., professor of psychology, 1969—, director of clinical training, 1969—, chairman of department of clinical psychology, 1975—, director of Alcohol Behavior Research Laboratory, 1970—. Chairman of alcohol research review committee for National Institute on Alcohol Abuse and Alcoholism, 1973-76; member of National Institute of Mental Health psychological sciences review committee, 1977—. *Military service:* U.S. Army Reserve, 1957-63. *Member:* American Psychological Association (fellow; member of executive board).

WRITINGS: Cues, Decisions, and Diagnoses, Academic Press, 1967; (with S. L. Harris) *Psychopathology and Society,* McGraw, 1975; (with G. A. Marlatt) *Behavioral Approaches to Alcoholism,* Center of Alcohol Studies, 1977; (with Marlatt) *Experimental and Behavioral Approaches to Alcoholism,* Plenum, in press. Contributor to professional journals. Associate editor of *American Psychologist* and *Journal of Clinical Psychology;* member of editorial board of *Journal of Consulting and Clinical Psychology, Addictive Behaviors, Behavior Therapy,* and *Behavior Modification.*

WORK IN PROGRESS: Revising *Psychopathology and Society.*

SIDELIGHTS: Nathan told *CA:* "Ironically, for a person whose career has been built in large part on efforts to understand and treat alcoholism, both my father and grandfather were in the liquor business, as wholesalers, distillers, and executives of large national trade organizations. While some might say this reflects some ambivalence about my identification with them, I see the decision, instead, to reflect their conviction that moderation, rather than alcoholism, was the goal of the ethical purveyor of spirits to mankind."

* * *

NEAL, James M(adison) 1925-

PERSONAL: Born August 6, 1925, in Oklahoma City, Okla.; son of James M. (a rancher) and Tillie B. (a telephone operator; maiden name, Milliken) Neal; married Caroline Dorothy Becker, April 17, 1945 (died December 15, 1974); children: Charles, James W., Jody (Mrs. Albert Rediger), Carolyn. *Education:* University of Colorado, B.A., 1949; University of Oklahoma, further study, 1957-58; South Dakota State University, M.A., 1970. *Religion:* Unitarian-Universalist. *Residence:* Lincoln, Neb. *Office:* 206 Avery Hall, University of Nebraska, Lincoln, Neb. 68508.

CAREER: Alamosa Daily Courier, Alamosa, Colo., chief of Monte Vista Bureau, 1949; *Durango Herald-Democrat,* Durango, Colo., sports editor, 1949-50; *Colorado Springs Free Press,* Colorado Springs, Colo., news editor, 1950-51; *Scottsbluff Star-Herald,* Scottsbluff, Neb., news editor, 1951-53; *Norman Transcript,* Norman, Okla., news editor, 1953-56; *Daily Oklahoman,* Oklahoma City, city desk assistant, 1956-58; *Rapid City Journal,* Rapid City, S.D., wire editor, 1959-67; South Dakota State University, Brookings, instructor in journalism, 1967-71; University of Nebraska, Lincoln, assistant professor, 1971-74, associate professor of journalism, 1974—. Copy editor for *Hartford Courant,* 1969. *Military service:* U.S. Navy, 1942-45; became radio technician first class.

MEMBER: Society of Professional Journalists, Association for Education in Journalism.

WRITINGS: (With Suzanne S. Brown) *Newswriting and Reporting,* Iowa State University Press, 1976.

WORK IN PROGRESS: A program of instruction in grammar, and another in rhetoric.

* * *

NEEF, Elton T.
See FANTHORPE, R(obert) Lionel

* * *

NEILSON, Frances Fullerton (Jones) 1910-

PERSONAL: Born October 21, 1912, in Philadelphia, Pa.; daughter of William (a teacher) and Mary (Fullerton) Jones; married Winthrop Cunningham Neilson, Jr., 1930; children:

Winthrop, John, Mary. *Education:* Attended school in Philadelphia, Pa. *Religion:* Episcopalian.

CAREER: Began producing children's plays for settlement houses and hospitals during the 1930's; became writer for several radio programs, including "Orgets on the Air" and "The Topaz Room"; also served as vice-president of Holiday House (publishing firm). Helped establish libraries in service clubs and hospitals. *Wartime service:* Nurses aide, and member of the Writers' War Board. *Awards, honors:* *New York Herald Tribune* honor award, 1942, for *The Donkey From Dorking.*

WRITINGS: Donkey From Dorking (illustrated by Lidia Vitale and Janet Hopkins), Dutton, 1942; *Mocha the Djuka* (illustrated by Avery Johnson), Dutton, 1943; *Giant Mountain* (illustrated by Mary Reardon), Dutton, 1946; *The Ten Commandments in Today's World* (illustrated by Nils Hogner), Thomas Nelson, 1946; *Look to the New Moon* (Junior Literary Guild selection), Abelard, 1953; *Storm on Giant Mountain,* School Book Services, 1975.

All with husband, Winthrop Neilson: *Dusty for Speed!* (illustrated by Hans Kreis), Dutton, 1947; *Bruce Benson: Son of Fame* (illustrated by Margaret Ayer), Dutton, 1948; *Bruce Benson: Thirty Fathoms Deep* (illustrated by John C. Wonsetler), Dutton, 1949; *Bruce Benson on Trails of Thunder,* Dutton, 1950; *Edge of Greatness,* Putnam, 1951; *Verdict for the Doctor: The Case of Benjamin Rush,* Hastings House, 1958; *Letter to Philemon: Novel of a Man's Search For Faith,* Thomas Nelson, 1962; *Seven Women: Great Painters,* Chilton, 1968; *What's New—Dow Jones: Story of the Wall Street Journal,* Chilton, 1973; *The United Nations: The World's Last Chance for Peace,* New American Library, 1975; *That Lydian Woman,* Revell, 1975.

SIDELIGHTS: Neilson spent most of her childhood in Dorking, England, which provided the backdrop for her first book, *Donkey From Dorking.* The book told the story of Longears the donkey who was taught such entertaining tricks as riding a bicycle.

The author has traveled extensively through the West Indies, Central and South America, Canada, Scotland, France, and Switzerland. *Mocha the Djuka* was inspired by Neilson's expedition into the jungles of Dutch Guiana. "While the jungle background is made vivid with color and sound, this is essentially a story of friendship. It is written warmly and wisely. All friendly and eager youngsters will recognize themselves in this charmingly written and illustrated little book," observed a reviewer for the *Springfield Republican.*

AVOCATIONAL INTERESTS: Swimming, horseback riding, dancing, gardening.

BIOGRAPHICAL/CRITICAL SOURCES: Springfield Republican, September 5, 1943.*

* * *

NELSON, Benjamin 1911-1977

1911—September 17, 1977; American sociologist, historian, and author of books including *Freud and the Twentieth Century* and *Personality—Work—Community: An Introduction to Social Science.* Nelson died in West Germany. Obituaries: *New York Times,* September 20, 1977; *AB Bookman's Weekly,* February 6, 1978.

* * *

NELSON, Joseph Schieser 1937-

PERSONAL: Born April 12, 1937, in San Francisco, Calif.; son of Walter I. (a mining engineer) and Mary Elizabeth (Schieser) Nelson; married Claudine Brenda Stratford-Handcock, August 31, 1963; children: Brenda Denise, Janice Marie, Mark Kent, Karen Elizabeth. *Education:* University of British Columbia, B.Sc. (honors), 1960, Ph.D., 1965; University of Alberta, M.Sc., 1962. *Home:* 7320 156th St., Edmonton, Alberta, Canada T5R 1X3. *Office:* Department of Zoology, University of Alberta, Edmonton, Alberta, Canada T6G 2E9.

CAREER: Indiana University, Bloomington, research associate, 1965-67, assistant director of biological stations for zoology, 1967-68; University of Alberta, Edmonton, assistant professor, 1968-72, associate professor of zoology, 1972—, and associate chairman of department, 1976—. President of Canadian Conference for Fisheries Research, 1977.

MEMBER: Canadian Society of Environmental Biologists (president, 1972-74; member of board of directors, 1975—), Canadian Society of Zoologists, American Society for the Study of Evolution, Society for Systematic Zoology, American Society of Ichthyologists and Herpetologists, American Fisheries Society, Indian Society of Ichthyologists, Federation of Alberta Naturalists, Ottawa Field Naturalists.

WRITINGS: (With M. J. Paetz) *The Fishes of Alberta,* Queen's Printer, 1970; *Fishes of the World,* Wiley, 1976. Contributor of about twenty-five articles to nature magazines and professional journals.

WORK IN PROGRESS: Research on systematics of some New Zealand fishes, and on evolution and evolutionary phenomena in stickleback fishes.

SIDELIGHTS: Nelson writes: "One purpose dominated the writing of *Fishes of the World*—to present a modern introductory systematics treatment of all major fish groups and discuss their evolutionary relationships while mentioning various philosophies and differences of opinion on relationships." *Avocational interests:* Astronomy, swimming.

* * *

NELSON, June Kompass 1920-

PERSONAL: Born June 10, 1920, in Drexel Hill, Pa.; daughter of Frederick Rudolph (a businessman) and Lillian (a merchant; maiden name, Steen) Kompass; married Samuel J. Nelson, Jr. (a chemist), October 25, 1958. *Education:* Drexel University, B.S., 1941; further study at Academia de Belle Arti and University of Florence, both 1957-58; Wayne State University, M.A., 1967; further graduate study at New York University, 1967-68. *Religion:* Protestant. *Home:* 279 McMillan, Grosse Pointe Farms, Mich. 48236. *Office:* Department of Art and Art History, Wayne State University, Detroit, Mich. 48202.

CAREER: Secretary in Philadelphia, Pa., 1941-43; Dravco Corp. (in shipbuilding), Wilmington, Del., secretary and office manager, 1943-44; Time, Inc., secretary in Philadelphia, Pa., 1944-51, and New York, N.Y., 1951-57; Wayne State University, Detroit, Mich., part-time instructor in art history, 1969—. Gives publice lectures on art history. *Member:* College Art Association, American Association of University Women, Smithsonian Institution, Metropolitan Museum of Art, Museum of Modern Art, Archives of American Art, Detroit Institute of Arts.

WRITINGS: Harry Bertoia, Sculptor, Wayne State University Press, 1970.

WORK IN PROGRESS: Research on a Gilbert Stuart portrait in her possession, a seventeenth-century northern Italian painting in her possession, and a small Ingres painting at Detroit Institute of Arts.

SIDELIGHTS: June Nelson writes: "Between 1954 and 1976 I made six trips to Europe of varying durations, the shortest one week and the longest sixteen months. I have visited not only the major cities but many out-of-the-way places. . . . In 1957-58 while studying in Florence, I lived in an Italian home and made many weekend trips to innumerable historically important towns and villages in Tuscany. In addition, I have traveled widely in this country and always with an eye to museums and other places of art historical interest. I plan to continue to travel as often as time and money permit."

AVOCATIONAL INTERESTS: *Tennis.*

* * *

NERLICH, Graham

PERSONAL: Born in Adelaide, Australia. *Education:* University of Adelaide, M.A., 1956; Oxford University, B.Phil., 1958. *Office:* Department of Philosophy, University of Adelaide, South Australia 5067, Australia.

CAREER: University of Adelaide, Adelaide, Australia, professor of philosophy, 1974—.

WRITINGS: The Shape of Space, Cambridge University Press, 1976.

* * *

NESBITT, Elizabeth 1897(?)-1977

1897(?)—August 17, 1977; American educator, specialist in library work with children, and author of *A Critical History of Children's Literature.* Nesbitt was associated with the Carnegie Library School from 1929 to 1962. She died in Atlantic City, N.J. Obituaries: *New York Times,* August 20, 1977; *AB Bookman's Weekly,* September 5, 1977.

* * *

NEWBERRY, Wilma (Jean) 1927-

PERSONAL: Born January 1, 1927, in Covington, Ky.; daughter of Buel F. and Irene (Mayer) Newberry. *Education:* Western Reserve University (now Case Western Reserve University), B.A., 1956; University of Washington, Seattle, M.A., 1959, Ph.D., 1960. *Residence:* Buffalo, N.Y. *Office:* Department of Modern Languages and Literatures, State University of New York at Buffalo, Buffalo, N.Y. 14261.

CAREER: Carthage College, Carthage, Ill., assistant professor of Spanish, 1959-60; University of Oregon, Eugene, assistant professor of Spanish, 1961-63; State University of New York at Buffalo, assistant professor, 1963-67, associate professor, 1967-73, professor of Spanish, 1973—. *Member:* Modern Language Association of America, American Association of Teachers of Spanish and Portuguese, American Association of Teachers of Italian.

WRITINGS: The Pirandellian Mode in Spanish Literature, State University of New York Press, 1973. Contributor to Romance language, comparative literature, and Spanish studies journals.

WORK IN PROGRESS: The Midsummer Theme in Spanish Literature.

* * *

NEWELL, Crosby
See BONSALL, Crosby Barbara (Newell)

NEWELL, Hope Hockenberry 1896-1965
(Hope Hockenberry)

PERSONAL: Born in 1896, in Bradford, Pa. *Education:* Columbia University, B.S. *Residence:* New York, N.Y.

CAREER: Author of books for children. Worked as public health nurse until 1943, when she accepted a position with the national Nursing Council for War Service. *Military service:* U.S. Army Nurse Corps. *Awards, honors:* Lewis Carroll Shelf Award, 1972, for *The Little Old Woman Who Used Her Head.*

WRITINGS: The Little Old Woman Who Used Her Head (illustrated by Margaret Ruse), Thomas Nelson, 1935, reprinted, 1967; *More about the Little Old Woman Who Used Her Head* (illustrated by M. Ruse), Thomas Nelson, 1938; *Steppin and Family* (illustrated by Anne Merriman Peck), Oxford University Press, 1942; *Cider Ike* (illustrated by A. Peck), Thomas Nelson, 1942; *The Story of Christina* (illustrated by A. Peck), Harper, 1947; *The Little Old Woman Carries on* (illustrated by A. Peck), Thomas Nelson, 1947; *A Cap for Mary Ellis,* Harper, 1953; *Penny's Best Summer* (illustrated by W. T. Mars), Harper, 1954; *Mary Ellis, Student Nurse,* Harper, 1958; *Selections from the Little Old Woman Who Used Her Head,* Scholastic Book Services, 1972; *The Little Old Woman Who Used Her Head, and Other Stories* (illustrations from M. Ruse and A. Peck), Thomas Nelson, 1973.

SIDELIGHTS: Newell drew on childhood memories for her book, *Penny's Best Summer.* "There are good humor, an amusing cast of characters, happy family life and plenty of atmosphere in this story," wrote a reviewer for the *New York Times.*

Ms. Newell has also used her experiences as a public health nurse in developing her stories. In reviewing the author's *Cap for Mary Ellis,* a critic for the *New York Herald Tribune* reported: "The training and hospital details are excellent, as they would be when written by an experienced nurse. Girls will find equally fascinating Mary Ellis' home life." *Mary Ellis, Student Nurse* was a sequel to *Cap for Mary Ellis.* It too was highly regarded for its informative storyline. A *Saturday Review* critic noted: "The author has been unusually successful in blending authentic information about the fields of nursing and medical care with a well-sustained plot. Especially commendable is the portrayal of the wide variety of characters who populate a large hospital."

BIOGRAPHICAL/CRITICAL SOURCES: New York Herald Tribune Book Review, January 10, 1954; *New York Times,* November 28, 1954; *Saturday Review,* May 10, 1958.*

(Died, 1965)

* * *

NEWMAN, Andrea 1938-

PERSONAL: Born February 7, 1938, in England; divorced. *Education:* University of London, M.A., 1972. *Agent:* A. D. Peters, 10 Buckingham St., London W.C.2, England.

CAREER: Civil Service, London, England, clerical officer, 1960-62; high school teacher of English in London, England, 1962-64; writer, 1964—.

WRITINGS—Novels: A Share of the World, New American Library, 1964; *Mirage,* Dial, 1966; *The Cage,* Dial, 1967; *Three Into Two Won't Go,* Doubleday, 1968; *Alexa,* Triton, 1968, published as *The City Lover,* Doubleday, 1969; *A Bouquet of Barbed Wire,* Doubleday, 1970; *An Evil Streak,* Doubleday, 1977.

Author of twenty-two plays for British television.

SIDELIGHTS: Three Into Two Won't Go was adapted by Edna O'Brien into a film, starring Rod Steiger and Claire Bloom, for Universal Pictures, 1969.

AVOCATIONAL INTERESTS: Sunbathing, watching films, listening to classical music, seeing friends, sleeping.

*   *   *

NEWMAN, Howard R.   1913(?)-1977

1913(?)—September 8, 1977; American press agent and playwright. Newman was a founding member of the Association of Theatrical Press Agents and Managers, and was author of "Brooklyn Biarritz." Newman died in New York, N.Y. Obituaries: New York Times, September 13, 1977.

*   *   *

NEWSOM, Doug(las Ann)   1934-

PERSONAL: Born January 16, 1934, in Dallas, Tex.; daughter of Jerome Douglas and Grace (Dickson) Johnson; married L. Mack Newsom (a company representative), October 27, 1956; children: Michael Douglas, Kevin Jackson, Nancy Elizabeth, William M. Education: University of Texas, B.J. (cum laude), 1954, B.F.A. (summa cum laude), 1955, M.J., 1956, Ph.D., 1977. Religion: Baptist. Home: 4237 Shannon Dr., Fort Worth, Tex. 76116. Office: Department of Journalism, Texas Christian University, Fort Worth, Tex. 76129.

CAREER: In public relations, 1955-61; University of Texas, Austin, laboratory instructor, 1961-62; Texas Boys Choir, Fort Worth, public relations director, 1964-69; Texas Christian University, Fort Worth, adjunct professor, 1968, instructor, 1969-72, assistant professor, 1972-77, associate professor of journalism, 1977—. Public relations director of Southwest Boat Show, 1966-73; public relations representative for Horace D. Ainsworth Co., 1966-76. Chairman of advisory board of Alcade, 1975-77. Member: Women in Communications (local president, 1968-70), American Women in Radio and Television, Association for Education in Journalism, Kappa Tau Alpha. Mortar Board.

WRITINGS: (With Alan Scott) This Is PR: The Realities of Public Relations, Wadsworth, 1976. Contributor to magazines and newspapers, including Ladies Home Companion, Dallas, and School Musician. Member of board of Public Relations Review.

WORK IN PROGRESS: Public relations writing.

SIDELIGHTS: Doug Newsom writes: "Many of the problems people get into can be traced to communication and the solutions often lie there, too, so my field is never dull. Writing is supposed to be my 'job,' but I still am surprised when it's so defined. I enjoy it too much to ever consider it drudgery; work, yes, but delightful."

AVOCATIONAL INTERESTS: Scuba diving, horseback riding, travel (Italy, Switzerland, Germany, Austria, England, the Philippines, Hong Kong, Thailand, Singapore, Vietnam, Malaysia, Cambodia, Sumatra, Mexico).

*   *   *

NICHOLS, Nina (Marianna) da Vinci   1932-

PERSONAL: Born December 21, 1932, in New York, N.Y.; daughter of Joseph Barbero and Giovanina da Vinci; divorced; children: Peter. Education: Attended Hunter College of the City University of New York and Columbia University; New York University, Ph.D., 1971. Home: 305

West 13th St., New York, N.Y. 10014; and 495 Three Mile Harbor, East Hampton, N.Y. Agent: Ellen Levine, Curtis Brown Ltd., 575 Madison Ave., New York, N.Y. 10022.

CAREER: New York University, New York, N.Y., co-adjutant, 1966-67; Queen's College of the City University of New York, New York City, lecturer, 1968-69; Rutgers University, New Brunswick, N.J., instructor, 1970-71, assistant professor, 1971-77, associate professor, 1977—. Administrative aide for Renaissance Society of America at Columbia University, 1968-69. Free-lance writer, 1968—. Has also worked as a psychotherapist and in advertising agencies. Public lecturer on the theater and on women's writings. Member: Modern Language Association of America, American Institute of Archaeology, Business & Professional Women of America, Renaissance Society of America.

WRITINGS: (Editor with J. Benjamin) Celtic Bull, University of Tulsa, 1968; Man, Myth, Monument, Morrow, 1975. Ghost-writer. Contributor to literary journals and popular magazines, including Ariel, Denver Quarterly, and New Republic.

WORK IN PROGRESS: Love and Neurosis (tentative title), a commentary on contemporary fiction written by and for women, including a cross-country survey of readers and writers.

SIDELIGHTS: Nina Nichols writes: "The work on my present book grew out of my own experience in writing popular fiction, as well as my interest in the relation between art and its audience." Avocational interests: Amateur musician, art, travel (England and Europe).

*   *   *

NICHOLS, Peter
See YOUD, Samuel

*   *   *

NICHOLSON, Paul (Joseph), Jr.   1937-

PERSONAL: Born January 4, 1937, in Oklahoma City, Okla.; son of Paul Joseph (an investment broker) and Dorothy (McCue) Nicholson; married Martha Whitaker, December 24, 1965; children: Kelleigh Elizabeth. Education: Texas Technological College (now Texas Tech University), B.A., 1960; Oklahoma State University, M.A., 1962; attended University of Iowa, 1962-63. Home: 1313 West Fourth St., Flemington, Pa. 17745. Agent: Morris Klein, 63 East Ninth St., Apt. 5-E, New York, N.Y. 10003. Office: Department of English, Lock Haven State College, Lock Haven, Pa. 17745.

CAREER: Texas Christian University, Fort Worth, instructor in English, 1963-66; Jack T. Holmes & Associates (advertising agency), Fort Worth, Tex., creative director, 1967-69; Lock Haven State College, Lock Haven, Pa., assistant professor of English and co-director of creative writing program, 1969—. Has given readings in New York, Texas, Montana, Virginia, and Pennsylvania.

WRITINGS: Memoirs of a Wet Bird (poems), Ice Man's Press, 1965; Odds Without End (short stories), Lock Haven Press, 1972; The Dam Builder (prose poems), Fault Press, 1977.

Co-author of "Sowbelly" (radio series), broadcast by WBPZ-AM-FM Radio, 1974-76.

Work anthologized in New and Experimental Literature, Texas Center for Writers Press, 1975. Contributor of stories, articles, poems, and reviews to popular and literary journals, including *Harper's Weekly, Rolling Stone, Descant,* and *Wormwood Review.* Fiction editor of *Lock Haven Review.*

WORK IN PROGRESS: The King's Freak, a novel.

* * *

NICKEL, Herman 1928-

PERSONAL: Born October 23, 1928, in Berlin, Germany; son of Walter (an officer and businessman) and Wilhelmine (Freund) Nickel; married Phyllis Fritchey (an art critic), May 24, 1958; children: Clayton. *Education:* Union College, B.A., 1951; Syracuse University, J.D., 1956. *Home:* 4448 Hawthorne St. N.W., Washington, D.C. 20016. *Office: Fortune,* 888 16th St. N.W., Washington, D.C. 20006.

CAREER/WRITINGS: Die Neue Zeitung, Berlin, Germany, reporter, 1947; Foreign Policy Association, New York City, head of research unit, 1956-58; Time-Life News Service, New York City, correspondent in Washington and London, 1958-61, Johannesburg, 1961-62, bureau chief in Bonn, 1965-69, diplomatic correspondent in Washington, 1969-71, bureau chief of Tokyo, 1971-74, and London, 1974-77; *Fortune,* New York City, member of board of editors, 1977—. Notable assignments include coverage of Virginia school desegregation, 1958, Britain's decolonization of Africa, the crisis in the Congo, 1961-62, the end of the Adenauer era, Lockheed scandal, the economic crisis in Britain, Kissinger's African shuttle, and interviews with Prime Minister Wilson and Prime Minister Callaghan.

SIDELIGHTS: CA asked Nickel if he foresaw any improvements in the economy of Great Britain. He wrote: "North Sea oil should ease the balance of payments constraints that in the past have dictated the 'stop and go' pattern of British economic policy. But whether the chance will be seized to modernize British industry or wasted like a lottery win remains an open question."

* * *

NIC LEODHAS, Sorche
See ALGER, Leclaire (Gowans)

* * *

NICOLAS
See MORDVINOFF, Nicolas

* * *

NIELSSEN, Eric
See LUDVIGSEN, Karl (Eric)

* * *

NIEMI, Albert (William), Jr. 1942-

PERSONAL: Born August 30, 1942, in Worcester, Mass.; son of Albert W. (a motel operator) and Helen (Powers) Niemi; married Maria Di Sano, February 4, 1967; children: Albert William, Edward Charles. *Education:* Stonehill College, A.B., 1964; University of Connecticut, M.A., 1965, Ph.D., 1969. *Home:* 190 Rolling Wood Dr., Athens, Ga. 30605. *Office:* College of Business Administration, University of Georgia, Athens, Ga. 30602.

CAREER: University of Georgia, Athens, assistant professor, 1968-71, associate professor, 1971-75, professor of economics and associate dean of College of Business Administration, 1975—. *Member:* American Economic Association, Economic History Association, Southern Economics Asso-

ciation, Western Economic Association, Southern Regional Science Association, Southeast Economic Analysis Conference (chairman, 1977-78), Beta Gamma Sigma, Phi Kappa Phi.

WRITINGS: State and Regional Patterns in American Manufacturing, 1860-1900, Greenwood Press, 1974; *Gross State Product and Productivity in the Southeast,* University of North Carolina Press, 1975; *United States Economic History,* Rand McNally, 1975; *Understanding Economics,* Rand McNally, 1978. Contributor to economic journals.

WORK IN PROGRESS: Campus Economics.

* * *

NIMNICHT, Nona 1930-

PERSONAL: Born March 17, 1930, in Loveland, Colo.; daughter of Jacob C. (a farmer) and Ruth (Kroh) Uhrich; married Glen Nimnicht, October 12, 1952 (divorced March 15, 1974); children: Glenda Nimnicht Northrup, Mark, Kara. *Education:* University of Colorado, B.A., 1952; Colorado State University, M.A., 1966; University of California, Berkeley, M.A., 1969. *Politics:* "Humanitarian." *Religion:* "Have none." *Home:* 4370 Townsend Ave., Oakland, Calif. 94602.

CAREER: Rawlins Daily Times, Rawlins, Wyo., reporter, 1952-53; *Northern Wyoming Daily News,* Worland, editor of women's page, 1954-56; Colorado State University, Fort Collins, instructor in English, 1966-67; Merritt College, Oakland, Calif., instructor in English, 1973—.

WRITINGS: In the Museum Naked (poems), Second Coming Press, 1978; (editor with Judith Askew) *Out of the Cellar: Anthology of Women's Poetry,* Thorp Springs Press, 1978. Contributor of poems to literary journals, including *Aldebaron Review, Contemporary Women Poets, Love Lights,* and *Phantasm.*

WORK IN PROGRESS: Letter from Troy, another book of poems, completion expected in 1980.

SIDELIGHTS: Nona Nimnicht writes: "The keen interest in poetry in the San Francisco Bay Area, the range of talents, voices, and audiences here, and the support of other women poets enabled me to write and to make my work public as well. I would like to encourage the dormant giftedness of other women who, like myself, have directed their sensitivity and their creative energy into caring for their children and husbands, instead of developing their own talents."

* * *

NIXON, K.
See NIXON, Kathleen Irene (Blundell)

* * *

NIXON, Kathleen Irene (Blundell)
(K. Nixon)

PERSONAL: Born in London, England; married V. R. Blundell.

CAREER: Author and artist.

WRITINGS—Under name K. Nixon; all self-illustrated: *Pushti,* F. Warne, 1956; *Pindi Poo,* F. Warne, 1957; *Poo and Pushti,* F. Warne, 1959; (with Robert Foran) *Animal Mothers and Babies,* F. Warne, 1960; (with Maurice Burton) *Bird Families,* F. Warne, 1962; *The Bushy Tail Family,* F. Warne, 1963; *Animal Legends,* F. Warne, 1966; *Strange Animal Friendships,* F. Warne, 1967; *Animals and Birds in Folklore,* F. Warne, 1969.

SIDELIGHTS: Nixon has lived in India and has traveled extensively in America, Australia, Canada, China, and Japan. Her animal pictures have been exhibited in several cities, including Melbourne, London, and Paris.*

* * *

NIXON, Richard M(ilhous)   1913-

PERSONAL: Born January 9, 1913, in Yorba Linda, Calif.; son of Francis Anthony and Hannah (Milhous) Nixon; married Patricia Ryan, June 21, 1940; children: Patricia (Mrs. Edward Finch Cox), Julie (Mrs. Dwight David Eisenhower II). *Education:* Whittier College, A.B. (with honors), 1934; Duke University, LL.B. (with honors), 1937. *Residence:* San Clemente, Calif.

CAREER: Thirty-seventh president of the United States. Bewley, Knoop & Nixon, Whittier, Calif., general practice of law, 1937-42; Office of Emergency Management, Washington, D.C., attorney in tire rationing division, 1942; U.S. Representative from 12th District of California, serving on Education and Labor Committee, Select Committee on Foreign Aid, and Committee on Un-American Activities, 1947-50; appointed to vacant seat in U.S. Senate, 1950; elected U.S. Senator from California, serving on Labor and Public Welfare Committee and Expenditures in Executive Departments Committee, 1951-53; vice-president of the United States, serving as chairman of President Eisenhower's Committee on Government Contracts, chairman of the Cabinet Committee on Price Stability for Economic Growth, and as the personal representative of the president on goodwill trips to fifty-four countries, 1953-61; Republican candidate for the presidency, with Henry Cabot Lodge as running mate, 1960; Adams, Duque & Hazeltine, Los Angeles, Calif., counsel, 1961-62; Republican candidate for governor of California, 1962; Mudge, Stern, Baldwin & Todd, New York City, member of firm, 1962-63; Nixon, Mudge, Rose, Guthrie & Alexander (later Nixon, Mudge, Rose, Guthrie, Alexander & Mitchell), New York City, partner, 1964-68; elected president of United States, with Spiro T. Agnew as vice-president, 1968, re-elected to office with landslide majority vote of electoral college, 1972, resigned, 1974. Trustee of Whittier College, 1939-68; honorary chairman of Boys' Clubs of America. *Military service:* U.S. Naval Reserve, 1942-46; served in Pacific theatre of operations; became lieutenant commander.

WRITINGS: The Challenges We Face (excerpts compiled from speeches and papers), McGraw, 1960; *Six Crises* (autobiographical), Doubleday, 1962; *The Inaugural Address of Richard Milhous Nixon,* Achille J. St. Onge, 1969; *Setting the Course, The First Year* (policy statements), Funk, 1970; *U.S. Foreign Policy for the 1970's: Report to Congress,* Harper, 1971; *A New Road for America* (policy statements), Doubleday, 1972; *Four Great Americans* (tributes to Dwight Eisenhower, Everett Dirksen, Whitney M. Young, and J. Edgar Hoover), Doubleday, 1973; *R.N.: The Memoirs of Richard Nixon,* Grosset, 1978.

Yearly collections of State of the Union messages, news conference texts, messages to Congress, and major statements, published by Congressional Quarterly, 5 volumes, 1970-74; reports, speeches, addresses, official papers, and transcript collections published by U.S. Government Printing Office and other publishers.

BIOGRAPHICAL/CRITICAL SOURCES—Books: Richard Nixon, *Six Crises,* Doubleday, 1962; Earl Mazo, *Nixon: A Political Portrait,* Harper, 1968; Gary Wills, *Nixon Agonistes,* Houghton, 1970; Rowland Evans and Robert Novak,

Nixon in the White House, Random House, 1971; Frank Mankiewicz, *Perfectly Clear,* Quadrangle, 1973; Theodore White, *Making of the President 1972,* Athenium, 1973; Carl Bernstein and Bob Woodward, *All the President's Men,* Simon & Schuster, 1974; New York Times, *End of a Presidency,* Holt, 1974; John Osborne, *Last Nixon Watch,* New Republic, 1975; William Safire, *Before the Fall,* Doubleday, 1975; White, *Breach of Faith,* Athenium, 1975; Bob Woodward and Carl Bernstein, *The Final Days,* Simon & Schuster, 1976; James Anthony Lukas, *Nightmare,* Bantam, 1977; Raymond Price, *With Nixon,* Viking, 1978.*

* * *

NORELLI, Martina R(oudabush)   1942-

PERSONAL: Born October 2, 1942, in Washington, D.C.; daughter of Martin Moore (an engineer) and Bettie (a teacher; maiden name, Millett) Roudabush; married, 1962 (divorced, 1968); married Michael Anthony Norelli (a sales representative), November 11, 1970; children: (first marriage) Bettie Ruth; (second marriage) David Anthony (stepchild). *Education:* Attended Mary Washington College, 1960-62; George Washington University, B.A. (with distinction), 1969, M.A., 1972. *Politics:* Democrat. *Religion:* Methodist. *Home:* 115 North Abingdon St., Arlington, Va. 22203. *Office:* National Collection of Fine Arts, Smithsonian Institution, Washington, D.C. 20560.

CAREER: National Collection of Fine Arts, Washington, D.C., secretary, 1970-71, museum technician, 1971-74, assistant curator, 1978, associate curator, 1978—. *Member:* America-Nepal Society.

WRITINGS: American Wildlife Painting, Watson-Guptill, 1975; *Family Treasury of Art,* Ridge Press, 1978.

WORK IN PROGRESS: Continuing research on Abbott Thayer, Louis Agassiz Fuertes, John James Audubon, and other artist-naturalists.

SIDELIGHTS: Martina Norelli writes: "Since I originally began college as a science major and later became an art historian, I was naturally fascinted by those artists who were at the same time natural scientists. My major interest outside my profession is Russian studies. I have traveled to the Soviet Union four times since January, 1976, and have been studying the Russian language since my first trip. I have been interested in Russian history and culture since I was very young, and now devote much of my free time to this interest."

AVOCATIONAL INTERESTS: Reading, music, growing roses.

* * *

NORMAN, Ruth   1903(?)-1977

1903(?)—December 26, 1977; American cooking authority and author of *Cook Until Done.* Norman died in Riverhead, N.Y. Obituaries: *New York Times,* December 28, 1977.

* * *

NORRIS, Hoke   1913-1977

October 8, 1913—July 8, 1977; American journalist and author. Norris was most recently the director of public information for the University of Chicago. For ten years he served as literary editor for the *Chicago Sun-Times.* Norris was the author of two novels and several of his short stories have appeared in national magazines. He died in Chicago, Ill. Obituaries: *New York Times,* July 10, 1977. (See index for *CA* sketch)

NORRIS, Joan 1943-

PERSONAL: Born January 6, 1943, in New York, N.Y.; daughter of Joseph A. (an engineer) and Margaret (an editor; maiden name, Shay) Norris; children: Mark, Jennifer. *Education:* Alfred University, B.A., 1964; further study at University of Dayton, 1966-68, Newton College, 1972, Boston University, 1973, and Brandeis University, 1975. *Home:* 1126 Broadway, Hanover, Mass. 02339.

CAREER: Dayton Art Institute, Dayton, Ohio, director of public relations, 1970-72; Paperback Booksmith, Boston, Mass., director of public relations, 1973-77; WGBH-TV, Boston, public relations specialist, 1977—. Member of steering committee, Boston Literary Hour, 1976—. *Member:* Word Guild, Boston Press Club. *Awards, honors:* Breadloaf Writers Conference Transatlantic scholar in poetry, 1974.

WRITINGS: (Contributor) *Women Poems III,* Women Poems, 1976. Contributor of articles to *Real Paper, Publishers Weekly,* and *Boston Globe,* and poems to *Nation, Ploughshares, Prairie Schooner, Arion's Dolphin,* and *Yes.*

WORK IN PROGRESS: Poetry.

SIDELIGHTS: Norris told *CA:* "I write poems because the exact use of language pleases and challenges me."

* * *

NORTH, Robert
See WITHERS, Carl A.

* * *

NORTHAM, Ray M(ervyn) 1929-

PERSONAL: Born May 28, 1929, in Calgary, Alberta, Canada; son of Lenord Iver (a printer) and Mary Louise (Wilson) Northam; married Joyce Earlene Hout, March 22, 1953; children: Amy Anne, Paul Bruce. *Education:* Oregon State University, B.S., 1953, M.S., 1954; Northwestern University, Ph.D., 1960. *Home:* 3315 Elmwood Dr., Corvallis, Ore. 97330. *Office:* Department of Geography, Oregon State University, Corvallis, Ore. 97331.

CAREER: University of Wisconsin (extension), Kenosha, instructor, 1955; University of Georgia, Athens, instructor, 1956-59, assistant professor of geography, 1959-62, research associate for Institute of Community and Area Development, 1960-62; Portland State University, Portland, Ore., assistant professor, 1962-64, associate professor of geography, 1964-66, director of urban studies program, 1964-65; Oregon State University, Corvallis, associate professor, 1966-70, professor of geography, 1970—. Research associate for Columbian Research Institute, 1963—; visiting associate professor of geography at Yale University, 1965-66. Partner of RNRK Associates (consultants), 1976—. Member of board of directors of Pacific Northwest Regional Development Conference. *Member:* Association of American Geographers, Association of Pacific Coast Geographers, Regional Science Association, Western Regional Science Association, Pacific Regional Science Conference.

WRITINGS: Factors Influencing Recent Industrial Growth in Northeastern Georgia, Institute of Community and Area Development, University of Georgia, 1962; (with James A. Barnes and James E. Lewis) *Regions of Georgia: Their Nature and Delimitation,* Institute of Community and Area Development, University of Georgia, 1963; (contributor) *Atlas of the Pacific Northwest,* Oregon State University Press, 4th edition, 1968, 5th edition, 1974; (with Richard M. Highsmith, Jr.) *World Economic Activities: A Geographic Analysis,* Harcourt, 1968; *Urban Geography,* Wiley, 1975,

2nd edition, 1978; (with Thomas J. Maresh and Mary Lee Nolan) *Oregon Coastal Zone Land: Use, Ownership, and Value Change,* Sea Grant Publications, 1975.

Cartographer of *Atlas of the Pacific Northwest,* Oregon State University Press, 1953; illustrator of *World Regional Geography,* Oregon State University Press, 1954. Contributor to journals in his field.

* * *

NORVILLE, Warren 1923-

PERSONAL: Born October 20, 1923, in Mobile, Ala.; son of Peyton (in real estate) and Angela (Gerow) Norville; married Harriet Durant (a social worker), May 22, 1948; children: Harriet Norville Demeranville, Warren, Jr., Mary Jane. *Education:* Attended Millsaps College, 1943-44; Spring Hill College, B.S., 1947. *Religion:* "I am not much of a church goer. When the weather gets bad enough for the waves to get high enough for me to get scared enough I pray fervently." *Home and Office:* 327 Dalewood Dr., Mobile, Ala. 36608.

CAREER: Owner of a residential construction business in Mobile, Ala., 1948-50; U.S. Air Force, Mobile, civilian trainee, 1955; U.S. Army, Corps of Engineers, Mobile, civilian specifications writer, 1956-58; manager of a real estate and insurance agency in Mobile, 1958-70; writer and marine consultant, 1970—. Owner and operator of sloop rigged charter sailboat "Dancing Girl"; tugboat pilot on the lower Mississippi and other area rivers; navigator and skipper of yachts and fishing vessels on the Atlantic and Pacific Oceans and in the Caribbean; teacher of navigation courses. *Military service:* U.S. Naval Reserve, 1942-71, active duty, 1943-46, 1950-52; became lieutenant commander. U.S. Coast Guard Auxiliary, 1956-65; became district vice-commodore. *Member:* Mardi Gras Society, Mobile Yacht Club.

WRITINGS: Storm Jib and Running Sails (memoirs), Gill Printing, 1970; *Celestial Navigation Step by Step,* International Marine Publishing Co., 1973; *Coastal Navigation Step by Step,* International Marine Publishing Co., 1975; (editor with Fred Townsend and G. H. Hoffman) *Nautical Education for Offshore Extractive Industries,* Sea Grant Publication, 1977. Contributor of articles and recipes to boating and fishing magazines, including *Motor Boat, Sea,* and *Sail.* Regional editor of *Waterway Guide;* Gulf Coast editor of *National Fisherman,* 1974-75.

WORK IN PROGRESS: Stone Quarry Creek, a novel about yacht hijacking and smuggling; *Log of the Li'l Tiger,* narrative of a sail across the Gulf of Mexico in a twenty-two-foot boat during hurricane season; *How to Make Money in the Marine Business.*

SIDELIGHTS: Norville writes: "I am writing *Stone Quarry Creek* to publicize the problems of yacht hijacking and its supposed relation to drug smuggling along the upper Gulf Coast. The fact that these crimes happen is evidence of a failure on the part of someone, in some part of our government, to carry out the duty of protecting our citizens.

"My politics are basically traditional. I think American politics are getting too polarized between the forces of big business and big labor, with additional muddying influences on the waters from other well-organized groups. This leaves the individual entrepreneur, who would rather spend his days working to produce or otherwise doing his or her thing, unrepresented. I am very concerned by what I see as possibly fatal abuses to our political system—a system that is the best yet devised by mankind.

"How to Make Money in the Marine Business is about things individuals or small groups of people can do, on or near the sea, to make sufficient income to survive, meet their responsibilities, and make a contribution to the welfare of their fellow men without enslaving themselves to some job they neither like nor are adapted to.

"Much of my interest is in the marine field because of the influence of five generations of people who either were seamen or near the sea. I could sail before I could ride a bicycle. I believe that the sea and boats offer a discipline and a freedom that is especially good for young people. I am interested in doing all this safely, and for this reason I have spent a good part of my life working for safety afloat in both an official and unofficial status.

"I like to work with my hands. I am a passably good house carpenter and boat carpenter. I have built three boats, and completed a kit boat. I have also built two houses with my own hands, in addition to those built by my construction business. My travels have been primarily in connection with my Navy active duty and my career as navigator and/or skipper of boats I deliver. Countries I have visited are Mexico, Nicaragua, Venezuela, various Caribbean Islands, the Bahamas, Spain, Gibraltar, Italy, Egypt, Saudi Arabia, Bahrein, the Philippines, Cuba, and Japan. I have been through the Panama Canal and the Suez Canal several times.

AVOCATIONAL INTERESTS: Cooking (Southern or Creole style), animals.

* * *

NORWOOD, John
See STARK, Raymond

* * *

NOUWEN, Henri J(osef Machiel) 1932-

PERSONAL: Born January 24, 1932, in Nijerk, Netherlands; came to the United States in 1964; son of Laurent J. M. (a professor) and Maria H. H. (Ramselaer) Nouwen. *Education:* University of Nijmegen, Ph.D. (psychology; cum laude), 1964, Ph.D. (theology), 1971. *Home:* 409 Prospect St., New Haven, Conn. 06510. *Office:* Divinity School, Yale University, New Haven, Conn. 06510.

CAREER: Ordained Roman Catholic priest, 1957; temporary pastor of Roman Catholic churches in United States and Netherlands; Menninger Clinic, Topeka, Kan., fellow in religion and psychiatry, 1964-66; University of Notre Dame, Notre Dame, Ind., visiting professor of psychology, 1966-68; University of Utrecht, Utrecht, Netherlands, staff member of Pastoral Institute in Amsterdam, 1968-69; Catholic Theological Institute, Utrecht, faculty member and chairman of department of behavioral sciences, 1969-70; Yale University, New Haven, Conn., associate professor, 1971-77, professor of pastoral theology, 1977—. Teacher at Gregorian Institute, Rome, Italy, spring, 1978.

WRITINGS: Intimacy: Pastoral Psychological Essays, Fides, 1969; *Bidden om het leven: Het contemplatief engagement van Thomas Merton,* Ambo, 1970, translation by David Schlaver published as *Pray to Live: Thomas Merton, a Contemplative Critic,* Fides, 1972; *Creative Ministry,* Doubleday, 1971; *With Open Hands,* Ave Maria Press, 1972; *The Wounded Healer: Ministry in Contemporary Society,* Doubleday, 1972; (with Walter J. Gaffney) *Aging,* Doubleday, 1974; *Out of Solitude: Three Meditations on the Christian Life* (sermons), Ave Maria Press, 1974; *Reaching Out: The Three Movements of the Spiritual Life,* Double-

day, 1975; *The Genesee Diary: Report from a Trappist Monastery,* Doubleday, 1976; *The Living Reminder: Service & Prayer in Memory of Jesus Christ,* Crossroad Books, 1977.

WORK IN PROGRESS: With Donald McNeil and Douglas Morrison, a book on compassion, for Doubleday.

SIDELIGHTS: Nouwen has made two phonotapes, "Aging and Ministry," for Ave Maria Press, 1973.

* * *

NYE, Robert D(onald) 1934-

PERSONAL: Born November 6, 1934, in Poughkeepsie, N.Y.; son of John Edwin (a building contractor) and Ellen (Jansson) Nye; married S. Lee Siebenlist, 1961 (divorced, 1965). *Education:* Delhi Agricultural & Technical Institute, A.A.S., 1955; Dutchess Community College, A.A., 1961; George Washington University, A.B., 1963, Ph.D., 1969. *Home address:* R.D., Pleasant Valley, N.Y. 12569. *Office:* Department of Psychology, State University of New York College at New Paltz, New Paltz, N.Y. 12561.

CAREER: Naval Medical Research Institute, Bethesda, Md., research psychologist, 1963-65; American Institutes for Research, Silver Spring, Md., research affiliate, 1965-67; Federal City College, Washington, D.C., assistant professor of psychology, 1968-70; State University of New York College at New Paltz, assistant professor, 1970-72, associate professor of psychology, 1972—. Part-time lecturer at University of Virginia and George Washington University, 1967-68; instructor at Poughkeepsie College Center, 1971-72. *Member:* American Psychological Association, Society for the Advancement of Social Psychology, Phi Beta Kappa, Psi Chi.

WRITINGS: Conflict among Humans: Some Basic Psychological and Social-Psychological Considerations, Springer Publishing, 1973; *Three Views of Man: Perspectives from Sigmund Freud, B. F. Skinner, and Carl Rogers,* Brooks/Cole, 1975. Contributor to psychology journals.

WORK IN PROGRESS: Studying theories of personality and psychopathology; research on behavioristic versus humanistic approaches to the study of human behavior.

SIDELIGHTS: Nye comments: "I try to put psychology into simple terms, without oversimplifying. In my teaching, writings, and life I'm after the essentials (not an easy pursuit) and I like to avoid unnecessary complications and vague abstractions." *Avocational interests:* Running and other exercise, reading, going to movies, visiting Boston and the California coast.

* * *

O'BRIEN, Richard 1934-

PERSONAL: Born January 13, 1934, in New York, N.Y.; son of John (an executive) and Milada (Marek) O'Brien; married Mary Ann Shelton (a seismological researcher), June 7, 1958; children: Alison, Sean, Rebecca, Julie. *Education:* Brooklyn College (now of the City University of New York), B.A., 1955. *Home and office:* 173 Midland Ave., Montclair, N.J. 07042. *Agent:* Al Zuckerman, 132 West 31st St., New York, N.Y. 10001.

CAREER: Indemnity Insurance Company of North America, New York, N.Y., resident vice-president, 1958-60; Dorothy Ross Associates, New York City, associate, 1960-65, partner, 1966; Richard O'Brien Publicity, New York City, owner and president, 1966—. *Military service:* U.S. Army, psychologist, 1956-58.

WRITINGS: (With Bill Kaufman and Sean O'Brien) *Jaws Jokes,* Pinnacle Books, 1976; *The Golden Age of Comic Books,* Ballantine, 1977; *Publicity: How to Get It,* Harper, 1977; *Americana Guide to Collectible Toys,* Books American, 1978. Comedy writer for entertainers Woody Allen, Victor Borge, and Joan Rivers. Contributor to comic strips, including "Inside Woody Allen," "Side Glances," "The Treadwells," and "Carnival."

WORK IN PROGRESS: Writing for syndicated comic strips and free-lance cartoonists.

* * *

O'BRIEN, Robert C.
See CONLY, Robert Leslie

* * *

O'CONNELL, Margaret F(orster) 1935-1977

PERSONAL: Born January 7, 1935, in Wilmington, Del.; daughter of Albert E. (an executive) and Margaret (Moir) Forster; divorced. *Education:* Pennsylvania State University, B.S., 1957; Harvard University, certificate in business administration, 1958; graduate study at New York University, 1959. *Home:* 150 East 18th St., New York, N.Y. 10003. *Office:* New York Times Book Review, 229 West 43rd St., New York, N.Y. 10036.

CAREER: Abraham & Straus (department store), in book department, 1958-59; Thomas Y. Crowell Co., New York, N.Y., assistant manager of trade, publicity, and advertising, 1959-61; Random House, Inc., New York City, director of library promotion, 1961-63; *New York Times Book Review,* New York City, associate children's editor, 1963-74, editor, 1974-77. *Member:* National Society of Literature and the Arts, National Book Critics Circle, Overseas Press Club, New York Historical Society, Friends of International Board on Books for Young People.

WRITINGS: The Magic Cauldron: Witchcraft for Good and Evil (juvenile), S. G. Phillips, 1975. Author of column "PTA Books for Children," 1972-74. Contributor to *Crowell-Collier Yearbook.* Contributor to magazines for adults and children, including *ETC: Journal of General Semantics.* Member of advisory board of *Brain/Mind/Bulletin.*

WORK IN PROGRESS: Two novels, one for adults and one for children.

SIDELIGHTS: O'Connell told *CA:* "In writing *The Magic Cauldron,* at first what I found about witches was 'bad.' My newspaperwoman's instinct told me that if something is all bad, or all good—look further. You will find shades of gray. So I did. And I was amply rewarded because a new world opened up with my research. As a matter of fact, if I had looked no further than the subject I researched, it would have been a loss—at least I feel so. Fortunately I was able to extrapolate what I found about witchcraft and myths into other areas of human endeavor. One of them is political philosophy, another is the sociological picture, and more particularly, I have gained a perspective in the human condition, which to me is perhaps the most important gain I made."

BIOGRAPHICAL/CRITICAL SOURCES: Mary Sam Ward, editor, *Delaware Women Remembered,* Modern Press, 1977. Obituaries: *New York Times,* November 9, 1977.

(Died November 6, 1977, in Freeport, Bahamas.)

O'CONNELL, Timothy E(dward) 1943-

PERSONAL: Born August 21, 1943, in Plainfield, N.J.; son of Desmond H. (a businessman) and Rosemary (McGough) O'Connell. *Education:* St. Mary of the Lake Seminary, B.A., 1965, S.T.B., 1967, S.T.L., 1969; Fordham University, Ph.D., 1974. *Home and office:* St. Mary of the Lake Seminary, Mundelein, Ill. 60060.

CAREER: Ordained Roman Catholic priest of Archdiocese of Chicago, Chicago, Ill., 1969; Loyola University, Chicago, director of liturgy, 1967-68; associate pastor of Roman Catholic church in Oak Lawn, Ill., 1969-70; St. Mary of the Lake Seminary, Mundelein, Ill., assistant professor, 1973-76, associate professor of moral theology, 1976—, chairman of department, 1975—. *Member:* American Academy of Religion, Catholic Theological Society of America, American Society of Christian Ethics.

WRITINGS: What a Modern Catholic Believes About Suffering and Evil, Thomas More Association, 1972; *Changing Roman Catholic Moral Theology: A Study in Josef Fuchs,* University Microfilm, 1974; *Contemporary Meditations on Personal Holiness,* Thomas More Association, 1975. Contributor to theology journals and other magazines, including *Chicago Studies, Thought, Critic,* and *America.*

WORK IN PROGRESS: Principles for a Catholic Morality.

* * *

O'CONNOR, John J(oseph) 1918-

PERSONAL: Born June 15, 1918, in Waterbury, Conn.; son of James (a fireman) and Nora (O'Connor) O'Connor; married M. Martha Clancey, June 29, 1943; children: James W., Nancy E., David J. *Education:* Clark University, A.B., 1940; Harvard University, A.M., 1946, Ph.D., 1951. *Home:* 563 Mountain Ave., Bound Brook, N.J. 08805. *Office:* Department of English, Rutgers University, New Brunswick, N.J. 08903.

CAREER: Rutgers University, New Brunswick, N.J., instructor, 1948-52, assistant professor, 1952-58, associate professor, 1958-68, professor of English, 1968—. *Military service:* U.S. Army, Infantry, 1941-43. U.S. Army Air Forces, pilot, 1943-45; became second lieutenant; received Air Medal with clusters. *Member:* Modern Language Association of America, Mediaeval Academy of America, Renaissance Society, Malone Society. *Awards, honors:* Fellowship from Fund for the Advancement of Education, 1954-55.

WRITINGS: Amadis de Gaule and Its Influence on Elizabethan Literature, Rutgers University Press, 1970. Contributor to philology journals.

WORK IN PROGRESS: Translating tales from French Romance.

* * *

ODELL, Robin 1935-

PERSONAL: Born December 19, 1935, in Totton, England; son of Samuel Arthur and Dorothy (Lickfold) Odell; married Joan Bartholomew, September 19, 1959. *Education:* Educated in England. *Politics:* Liberal. *Religion:* Agnostic. *Home:* 15 Churchill Crescent, Sonning Common, Reading RG4 9RU, England. *Office:* Water Research Centre, Medmenham, Marlow SL7 2HD, England.

CAREER: University of Southampton, Southampton, England, laboratory technician in department of zoology, 1951-

54, assistant museum curator, 1956-62; University Institute of Education in Southampton, technical demonstrator, 1962-68; Water Research Centre, Marlow, England, publications manager, 1968—. Member, Institute of Public Relations and Institute of Scientific and Technical Communicators. *Military service:* British Army Medical Service, 1954-56. *Member:* Society of Authors, Crime Writers' Association (Great Britain), Rationalist Press Association, Paternosters, Our Society (crimes club), Southampton Humanist Society (secretary, 1962-68). *Awards, honors:* F.C.C. Watts Memorial Prize, 1957; International Humanist and Ethical Union Prize, 1960.

WRITINGS: Jack the Ripper in Fact and Fiction, Harrap, 1965; (with Tom Barfield) *Humanist Glossary,* Pemberton, 1967; *Exhumation of a Murder,* Harrap, 1975; *Murderer's Who's Who,* Harrap, 1978. Contributor to *Crimes and Punishment Encyclopedia, Psychology, Ethical Outlook, Humanist, New Zealand Rationalist,* and *Pulse.*

SIDELIGHTS: Robin Odell told CA: "I was much impressed in my formative years by Thomas De Quincey's 'Murder Considered as One of the Fine Arts,' an inspired piece of literature. The sinister theme, 'the tiger's heart was masked by the most insinuating and snaky refinement,' motivated my own thinking in my book on Jack the Ripper."

*   *   *

ODOM, William E(ldridge) 1932-

PERSONAL: Born June 23, 1932, in Cookeville, Tenn.; son of John A. (an agricultural researcher) and Callie (an elementary school teacher; maiden name, Everhart) Odom; married Anne Curtis (a college teacher), June 9, 1962; children: Mark Weld. *Education:* U.S. Military Academy, B.S., 1954; Columbia University, M.A., 1962, Ph.D., 1970. *Religion:* Protestant. *Home:* 2343 King Plains N.W., Washington, D.C. 20007. *Office:* White House, Washington, D.C. 20500.

CAREER: U.S. Army, career officer, 1954—; present rank, colonel. Platoon leader and company executive for Seventh Army in Germany, 1955-58; member of U.S. Military Liaison Mission to the Commander of Soviet Forces in Germany, Potsdam, East Germany, 1964-66; U.S. Military Academy, West Point, N.Y., instructor, 1966-67, assistant professor of social science, 1967-69; plans officer, assisting the officer to prime minister of South Vietnam, Saigon, 1970-71; assistant army attache at American Embassy in Moscow, 1972-74; associate professor of social sciences, U.S. Military Academy, 1974-77; National Security Council, Washington, D.C., military assistant to Zbigniew Brzezinski, 1977—. Senior research associate at Columbia University, Institute on International Change, 1974-77.

WRITINGS: The Soviet Volunteers, Princeton University Press, 1973. Contributor of articles to journals.

SIDELIGHTS: Odom told *CA:* "My first tour in Europe gave me a strong sense of the political and military relations between NATO and the Warsaw Pact and set my career interests in the USSR and Germany." Odom's first extensive exposure to a communist state system and to the Soviet Armed Forces came in 1964, while he was posted in Potsdam. At this time, he was one of the few Americans allowed to travel freely in East Germany.

Recalling his post in Saigon, Odom said: "Many of the themes I had developed in my book manuscript—which was essentially complete before I went to Vietnam—seemed vindicated by what I witnessed in an entirely different cul-

ture. Political development and military force structure and policy issues, although different for South Vietnam, shared similar conceptual bases with the issues faced in the USSR during the 1920's. The means and decisions, however, were quite different."

A great highlight in Odom's career was the two years spent in Moscow. It was, he said, "a chance to enrich with first hand observations my knowledge of a society which I had studied for years."

*   *   *

O'DONNELL, (Phillip) Kenneth 1924-1977

March 4, 1924—September 9, 1977; American author and aide to U.S. President John F. Kennedy. O'Donnell began working for Kennedy during his first Senate campaign in 1951, and stayed with him until the President's death in 1963. Aside from his brother Robert, O'Donnell was said to be the president's best friend. O'Donnell was co-author of *Johnny, We Hardly Knew Ye.* He died in Boston, Mass. Obituaries: *New York Times,* September 10, 1977; *Washington Post,* September 10, 1977; *Newsweek,* September 19, 1977; *Time,* September 19, 1977.

*   *   *

O'FLAHERTY, Terrence 1917-

PERSONAL: Born July 15, 1917, in What Cheer, Iowa; son of Leo J. (an investment banker) and Lelia (Thomas) O'-Flaherty. *Education:* University of California, Berkeley, B.A., 1939. *Residence:* San Francisco, Calif. *Office:* c/o *San Francisco Chronicle,* San Francisco, Calif. 94119.

CAREER/WRITINGS: Metro-Goldwyn-Mayer Studios, Culver City, Calif., historical researcher, 1940-42; *San Francisco Chronicle,* San Francisco, Calif., television critic, 1950—. Author of syndicated column "Assignment Television," 1960—. Contributor to *Reader's Digest, McCalls, TV Guide, American Education,* and *Show Magazine.* Co-host (with Mike Wallace) of television series "PM East/PM West," 1961-62; television lecturer. Permanent board member of Peabody Awards for Radio and Television, 1952—. *Military service:* U.S. Naval Reserve, 1942-46; became lieutenant; received Naval Commendation, 1944. *Awards, honors:* Listed as one of the ten most influential television critics in the nation in "Television Critics in a Free Society."

SIDELIGHTS: O'Flaherty writes: "Television is the most beguiling medium of them all—and the most influential. It deserves the keenest continuing appraisal. Reviewing it, however, presents difficulties not shared by cinema critics, book critics, or drama critics who appraise things their readers have not yet seen. *I'm* reviewing something everyone saw last night. They have opinions of their own about it and an adversary relationship is established immediately which is mutually stimulating. Newspaper readers who would never venture strong opinions about art, drama, or literature are not similarly intimidated by TV. It leaves no one neutral. Television is all things to all viewers. For a daily journalist, it is the liveliest beat of all the lively arts."

BIOGRAPHICAL/CRITICAL SOURCES: California Monthly, April, 1975.

*   *   *

O'FLINN, Peter
See FANTHORPE, R(obert) Lionel

O'FLYNN, Peter
See FANTHORPE, R(obert) Lionel

* * *

OGILVIE, Lloyd John 1930-

PERSONAL: Born September 2, 1930, in Kenosha, Wis.; son of Varde Spencer and Kathryn (Jacobson) Ogilvie; married Mary Jane Jenkins, March 25, 1951; children: Heather Anne Ogilvie Scholl, Scott Varde, Andrew Ghlee. *Education:* Lake Forest College, B.A., 1952; Garrett Theological Seminary, M.Div., 1955; further graduate study at New College, Edinburgh, 1955-56. *Home:* 3012 Arrowhead, Los Angeles, Calif. 90068. *Office:* First Presbyterian Church, 1760 North Gower St., Hollywood, Calif. 90028.

CAREER: Student pastor of Presbyterian church in Gurnee, Ill., 1952-56; ordained Presbyterian minister, 1956; pastor of Presbyterian churches in Winnetka, Ill., 1957-62, and Bethlehem, Pa., 1962-72; First Presbyterian Church, Hollywood, Calif., pastor, 1972—. Has delivered sermons on radio and television. Member of board of directors of Hollywood Presbyterian Hospital. *Awards, honors:* D.D. from Whitworth College, 1973; L.H.D. from University of Redlands, 1974; D.Hum. from Moravian College, 1975.

WRITINGS: A Life Full of Surprises, Abingdon, 1969; *Let God Love You,* Word, Inc., 1973; *If I Should Wake Before I Die,* Regal Books (Glendale), 1973; *Lord of the Ups and Downs,* Regal Books, 1974; *Life Without Limits,* Word, Inc., 1975; *You've Got Charisma,* Abingdon, 1975; *Cup of Wonder,* Tyndale, 1976; *Drumbeat of Love,* Word, Inc., 1977; *Loved and Forgiven,* Regal Books, 1977.

WORK IN PROGRESS: Books on First, Second, and Third John, the parables of Jesus, and Old Testament characters.

SIDELIGHTS: Ogilvie comments: "The purpose of my writing is to communicate life as it was meant to be lived. I seek to enable people to grasp the full potential of the adventure of living, to discover self-esteem through an experience of God's love, and to become change agents in society and life's relationships."

* * *

OHASHI, Wataru 1944-

PERSONAL: Born June 11, 1944, in Hiroshima, Japan; came to the United States in 1974; son of Sakei and Yasuyo (Sato) Ohashi; married Bonnie Harrington. *Education:* Chuo University, B.A., 1965. *Home:* 11 West 69th St., New York, N.Y. 10023. *Office:* Harrington-Ohashi Associates, 52 West 55th St., New York, N.Y. 10019.

CAREER: Shiatsu Education Center of America, New York, N.Y., founder and director, 1974—. Partner of Harrington-Ohashi Associates (literary agents), 1976—.

WRITINGS: Shiatsu Acupuncture Needles, Shiatsu Dojo, 1973; *Do-It-Yourself Shiatsu,* Dutton, 1976; *Zen Shiatsu,* Japan Publication, 1977.

WORK IN PROGRESS: A book on Oriental diagnosis.

* * *

OLDER, Julia 1941-

PERSONAL: Born May 25, 1941, in Chicago, Ill.; daughter of David Drake and Martha Louise (Dalrymple) Older. *Education:* University of Michigan, B.A., 1963; Conservatorio Arrigo Boito, diploma, 1966; Instituto San Miguel de Allende, M.F.A., 1969. *Home and office address:* P.O. Box 174, Hancock, N.H. 03449. *Agent:* Mary Jane Higgins, 15½ Appleton St., Boston, Mass. 02116.

CAREER: Institute for Cross-Cultural Research, Washington, D.C., librarian, 1967-68; teacher of English at a pre-school in Celaya, Mexico, 1968-69; G. P. Putnam's Sons, New York, N.Y., assistant to children's book editor, 1969-70; receptionist, 1971; Orchestra de Sao Paulo, Sao Paulo, Brazil, flutist, 1972-73; writer and musician, 1973—. *Awards, honors:* Avery Hopwood Prize from University of Michigan, 1963, for "The Green Bench and Other Poems"; Yaddo residency, 1972; MacDowell Colony residency, 1973; Mary Roberts Rinehart grant, 1974; Ossabaw residency, 1978.

WRITINGS: (With Steve Sherman) *Appalachian Odyssey,* Stephen Greene Press, 1977; (with Steve Sherman) *Soup and Bread du Jour,* Stephen Greene Press, 1978.

Illustrator of *The Wood Stove and Fireplace Book,* Stackpole, 1976. Co-author of review column "Dining in New Hampshire" in *New Hampshire Times,* 1976-78. Contributor of more than fifty poems to magazines and newspapers, including *Appalachia, Organic Gardening, Blue Cloud Quarterly,* and *Hollow Spring Review.* Poetry editor of *New Hampshire Times.*

WORK IN PROGRESS: Trilogy on the Isles of Shoals, a trilogy of historical novels; *Umbanda,* a study of the Afro-Brazilian cult; *Appalachian Root Woman,* about her hike of the Appalachian Trail from Georgia to Maine; *Green and Simple,* poems; *Airstream Odyssey,* poems; *Good-By Small Death,* sonnets; *Oonts and Others,* poems; translations of stories and poems by Boris Vian; two novellas.

SIDELIGHTS: Julia Older writes: "In hiking the two-thousand-mile Appalachian Trail, I learned that the body sometimes leaves the mind behind. I also found that too much self-criticism can be a form of pollution in the quiet of the woods.

"As poetry editor of the *New Hampshire Times,* I have rediscovered how necessary discipline is in any art form. I am a fervent believer in imagination and music in poetry and prose. I have stayed at Yaddo in New York, at the MacDowell Colony in New Hampshire, and at the Ossabaw Island Project in Georgia. My respect and appreciation for these work hideaways grows, even as the National Endowment for the Arts and State arts' councils limp along with scant support. Let us hope that the concerns of artists invited to work at these colonies will focus on filling the spiritual vacuum we are wont to feel in this nuclear world.

"I have lived in France, Italy, Sao Paulo, Brazil, and Mexico; speak Spanish and French, and read and write Italian, Spanish, French, and some Portuguese. I eat Italian, Spanish, French, Chinese, and hope someday to be able to write as well as M.F.K. Fisher in *Gastronomical Me.*"

* * *

OLIVER, Roland Anthony 1923-

PERSONAL: Born March 30, 1923, in Srinagar, Kashmir; son of D. G. and Lorimer Janet (Donaldson) Oliver; married Caroline Florence Linehan, 1947; children: one daughter. *Education:* King's College, Cambridge, M.A. and Ph.D. *Home:* 7 Cranfield House, Southampton Row, London WC1, England; Frilsham Woodhouse, Hermitage, Berkshire, England.

CAREER: Attached to British Foreign Office, 1942-45; School of Oriental and African Studies, London, England, lecturer, 1948-58; University of London, London, England, reader in African history, 1958-63, professor of the history of Africa, 1963-72. Organizer of international conferences on African history and archaeology, 1953-61. Franqui Professor, University of Brussels, 1961; visiting professor, Northwestern University, 1962, Harvard University, 1967. *Member:* Royal African Society (council member), Academie Royale des Sciences d'Outremer (Brussels; corresponding member), Athenaeum Club. *Awards, honors:* Haile Selassie I Prize Trust Award, 1966.

WRITINGS: The Missionary Factor in East Africa, Longmans, Green, 1952, 2nd edition, 1965; *How Christian is Africa?,* Highway Press, 1956; *Sir Harry Johnston and the Scramble for Africa* (illustrated), Chatto & Windus, 1957, St. Martin's, 1958; (editor) *The Dawn of African History,* Oxford University Press, 1961, 2nd edition, 1968; (with John D. Fage) *A Short History of Africa,* Penguin, 1962, New York University Press, 1963, 3rd edition, Penguin, 1970; (with Gervase Mathew) *History of East Africa,* Volume 1, Clarendon Press, 1963, first six chapters reprinted as *History of Africa: The Early Period,* Oxford University Press, 1967; *African History for the Outside World,* School of Oriental and African Studies, 1964; (editor with Caroline Oliver) *Africa in the Days of Exploration,* Prentice-Hall, 1965; (with Anthony Atmore) *Africa Since 1800,* Cambridge University Press, 1967, 2nd edition, 1972; (editor) *The Middle Age of African History,* Oxford University Press, 1967; (compiler and editor with Fage) *Papers in African Prehistory,* Cambridge University Press, 1970.

SIDELIGHTS: Dr. Oliver has traveled in Africa in 1949-50 and 1957-58.

* * *

OLSHAKER, Mark 1951-

PERSONAL: Born February 28, 1951, in Washington, D.C.; son of Bennett (a physician) and Thelma A. (a lawyer) Olshaker; married Carolyn Clemente (an advertising writer), August 28, 1977. *Education:* George Washington University, B.A., 1972. *Home and office:* 2040 North Abingdon St., Arlington, Va. 22207. *Agent:* Edward J. Acton, 288 West 12th St., New York, N.Y. 10014.

CAREER: Worked as a radio disc jockey in Frederick County, Md. and as an advertising copywriter in Washington, D.C.; *St. Louis Post-Dispatch,* St. Louis, Mo., researcher and editor in Washington Bureau, 1974-75; writer and film producer, 1975—. Has worked for television, radio, and industrial films. Consultant to Division of Education Services, Xerox Corp. *Member:* Newspaper Guild, Washington Independent Writers, Sigma Delta Chi. *Awards, honors:* Pulitzer Prize nomination, 1974, for work on magazine-length supplement on the Watergate crisis.

WRITINGS: The Instant Image: Edwin Land and the Polaroid Experience, Stein & Day, in press.

Films: "We All Came to America," Post-Newsweek Television Productions; "A Moment in Time," Post-Newsweek Television Productions; "Patent Pending," Post-Newsweek Television Productions; "Lost in the Everglades" (television drama), Behrens Co.

Contributor to magazines and newspapers, including *Washingtonian* and *New Times.*

WORK IN PROGRESS: A television series on the ideas of Lewis Mumford, for Corporation for Public Broadcasting; a film on volcanoes, for National Park Service; a program on handicapped children, for U.S. Office of Education.

OLSSON, Axel Adolf 1889-1977

1889—October 27, 1977; American paleontologist and author of technical books. Olsson spent most of his adult life in South America and Latin America. He died in Coral Gables, Fla. Obituaries: *New York Times,* October 29, 1977.

* * *

OLSSON, Nils 1909-

PERSONAL: Born June 11, 1909, in Seattle, Wash.; son of Nils Albin and Mathilda (Lejkell) Olsson; married Dagmar T. Gavert, June 15, 1940; children: Karna Barbro (Mrs. Paul Carlson), Nils Greger and Pehr Christopher (twins). *Education:* Attended North Park College, Northwestern University, 1932-34, and University of Minnesota, 1934-35; University of Chicago, A.M., 1938, Ph.D., 1949. *Politics:* Democrat. *Religion:* Lutheran. *Home and office:* Swedish Council of America, 4970 Sentinel Dr., Sumner, Md. 20016.

CAREER: North Park College, Chicago, Ill., instructor in Swedish and admissions counselor, 1937-39; University of Chicago, Chicago, instructor, 1945-50, assistant professor of Swedish, 1950; U.S. Department of State, Washington, D.C., foreign service officer, 1950-67, public affairs officer in Reykjavik, Iceland, 1950-52, attache and public affairs officer at American embassy in Stockholm, Sweden, 1952-55, first secretary of embassy, 1955-57, public affairs adviser in Washington, D.C., 1957-59, chief of American-sponsored schools abroad, 1959-62, first secretary of American embassy in Oslo, Norway, 1962-64, counselor for political affairs, 1964-66, diplomat-in-residence at Indiana University, 1966-67; American Swedish Institute, Minneapolis, Minn., director, 1967-73; Swedish Council of America, Sumner, Md., national coordinator, 1973-74, executive director, 1974—. Member of board of directors of Chicago Evangelical Covenant Historical Commission, 1958. *Military service:* U.S. Naval Reserve, active duty as naval attache to American legation in Stockholm, Sweden, 1943-45; became lieutenant commander.

MEMBER: American Society of Genealogists (fellow), National Genealogical Society, Genealogical Society (Sweden; fellow), Swedish Pioneer Historical Society (executive secretary, 1949-50, 1957-68), Royal Academy of Belles Lettres, History, and Antiquities (Sweden; foreign corresponding member), Pro Fide at Christianismo (Sweden), Royal Society for the Publication of Manuscripts Dealing with Scandinavian History (Sweden), Genealogical Society (Finland; fellow), Skylight Club (Minneapolis), Grolier Club, Cosmos Club, Minneapolis Athletic Club. *Awards, honors:* Knight of Order of Vasa, first class; knight commander of Order of the North Star; Swedish Pioneer Centennial Medal, 1948; Ph.D. from University of Uppsala, 1968; named Swedish American of the Year in Stockholm, 1969; King Carl XVI Gustaf Bicentennial Medal (Sweden), 1976.

WRITINGS: (Editor) *A Pioneer in Northwest America, 1841-1858,* University of Minnesota Press, Volume I, 1950, Volume II, 1959; *Tracing Your Swedish Ancestry,* Royal Swedish Foreign Ministry, 1965, revised second edition, 1974; *Swedish Passenger Arrivals in New York, 1820-1850,* Swedish Pioneer Historical Society, 1967; *Swedish Passenger Arrivals in the United States (Other Than New York), 1820-1850,* Royal Library of Stockholm, 1978. Contributor to history and education journals.

SIDELIGHTS: Olsson writes: "I was the child of Swedish immigrant parents. From my earliest childhood I have had the advantage of a double culture, which has deeply enriched my life. I am unashamedly interested in family history and genealogy. I love to travel and have traversed the greater part of the globe. Primarily, I am interested in people of any culture and intensely curious about them. My reading tends toward travel, discovery, biography, and history."

* * *

O'MALLEY, William J(ohn) 1931-

PERSONAL: Born August 18, 1931, in Buffalo, N.Y.; son of William John (a food distributor) and Beatrice (an office manager; maiden name, Foley). *Education:* Attended College of the Holy Cross, 1949-51; attended seminaries in New York, 1951-55; Fordham University, B.A., 1956, M.A., 1957; Woodstock College, B.Th., 1963, M.Div., 1964; further study at St. Bueno's College, 1964-65, Royal Academy of Dramatic Art, 1967, Northwestern University, 1969, and Jesuit School of Theology (Berkeley), 1974. *Home:* 1800 Clinton Ave. S., Rochester, N.Y. 14618.

CAREER: Entered Society of Jesus (Jesuits), 1951, ordained Roman Catholic priest, 1963; high school teacher in New York, N.Y., 1957-60; McQuaid Jesuit High School, Rochester, N.Y., English and theology teacher, 1965—. Played Father Joe Dyer in "The Exorcist," released by Warner Brothers, 1973. Consultant to American Education Publications, 1964-68, Education Testing Service, and National Assessment of Writing, 1971-72.

WRITING: *An Approach to English* (syllabus and teaching manuals),Buffalo Province Educational Association, 1965; (contributor) Robert Beauchamp, editor, *The Structure of Literature,* American Education Publications, 1969; *Meeting the Living God,* Paulist/Newman, 1973; *The Fifth Week,* Loyola University Press, 1976; *The Roots of Unbelief,* Paulist/Newman, 1976; *A Book About Praying,* Paulist/Newman, 1976. Also author of *The Living Word,* two volumes, as yet unpublished; "Capers," an unproduced filmscript on vocations; "Phoenix," a modernization of the Gospel narratives; and several musical adaptations of books and plays. Contributor of articles to *Jesuit Educational Quarterly, A.E.P. Challenges,* and other educational and Catholic periodicals.

WORK IN PROGRESS: O'Malley reports: "When one is grading senior A.P. essays and sophomore theology quizzes, there hardly seems time for anything worthy of the name research. And yet, every hour I spend with the kids in class or rehearsing a show is really 'research.'"

SIDELIGHTS: O'Malley told *CA:* "I'm a priest-teacher-director, any one of which is enough to exhaust your twenty-four hour day or your forty-five year old cleric. As a Puritan of Kamikaze dedication, I spend my days making certain that I will not die bored." O'Malley has acted in more than twelve plays and has directed more than thirty. Because of his role in "The Exorcist," he has been invited to make several television appearances.

* * *

OMANSKY, Dorothy Linder 1905(?)-1977

1905(?)—July 18, 1977; American magazine executive and journalist. Omansky died in New York, N.Y. Obituaries: *New York Times,* July 19, 1977.

* * *

OMER, Garth St.
See ST. OMER, Garth

O'NEAL, William B(ainter) 1907-

PERSONAL: Born August 21, 1907, in Zanesville, Ohio. *Education:* Carnegie Institute of Technology (now Carnegie-Mellon University), B.Arch., 1930. *Home:* 1716 King Mountain Rd., Charlottesville, Va. *Office:* Division of Architectural History, University of Virginia, Charlottesville, Va. 22903.

CAREER: University of Virginia, Charlottesville, associate professor, 1946-62, professor of architectural history, 1962-72, professor emeritus, 1972—, curator of Museum of Fine Arts, 1950-59, chairman of division of architectural history, 1966-72. Program director, Virginia Museum of Fine Arts, Richmond, 1961-62; member, Art Commission of Virginia, 1974—. *Military service:* U.S. Army, 1942-45. *Member:* American Institute of Architects (fellow), American Association of Architectural Bioliographers, Society of Architectural History (director, 1972—).

WRITINGS: *Jefferson's Fine Arts Library,* University Press of Virginia, 1956; *Charles Smith: Prints and Paintings,* University Press of Virginia, 1958; *Primitive Into Painter: The Life and Letters of John Toole,* University Press of Virginia, 1960; *Jefferson's Buildings at the University of Virginia: The Rotunda,* University Press of Virginia, 1960; *Architecture in Virginia,* Walker & Co., 1968; *Pictorial History of the University of Virginia,* University Press of Virginia, 1968. Editor, *American Association of Architectural Bibliographers Papers,* eleven volumes, University Press of Virginia, 1965-75. Also author of *Architectural Drawings in Virginia, 1819-1969,* 1969.

WORK IN PROGRESS: A work on Alexander Galt, sculptor; a full study of Jefferson's architectural books.

* * *

O'NELL, Carl William 1925-

PERSONAL: Born November 30, 1925, in Pueblo, Colo.; son of Carl William, Sr. (a cooper) and Mary Theresa (Ovechka) O'Nell; married Nancy deLeane Childress (a researcher), April 13, 1956; children: Theresa, Ruth, William, Susan, Maureen. *Education:* Colorado State College (now Northern Colorado State University), B.A., 1956; University of Edinburgh, diploma, 1959; University of Chicago, M.A., 1965, Ph.D., 1969. *Religion:* Roman Catholic. *Home:* 1432 South Bend Ave., South Bend, Ind. 46617. *Office:* Department of Sociology and Anthropology, University of Notre Dame, Notre Dame, Ind. 46556.

CAREER: High school teacher of social studies in Rosamond, Calif., 1956-58; University of Notre Dame, Notre Dame, Ind., assistant professor, 1967-73, associate professor of anthropology, 1973—. *Member:* American Anthropological Association (fellow), American Psychological Association.

WRITINGS: *Dreams, Culture, and the Individual,* Chandler & Sharp, 1976.

WORK IN PROGRESS: A monograph on a Latin American folk illness called Susto, with Arthur J. Rubel.

SIDELIGHTS: O'Nell writes: "I am interested in the study of 'social stress' in different cultures, and the relationship of stress to illness and interpersonal aggression. I am interested in how stress affects personal fantasy, especially dreams. My work has been chiefly among the Zapotec Indians of Mexico."

OOI Jin-Bee 1931-

PERSONAL: Born April 28, 1931, in Malaysia; son of Ooi Choo-Cheng and Yeoh Cheng-Heoh; married Chiu Hui Pin (a lecturer), 1956; children: Su-lin, Yu-lin. *Education:* University of Malaya, B.A., 1953, M.A., 1954; Oxford University, D.Phil., 1956. *Religion:* Christian. *Home:* 12 Binjai Walk, Singapore 21. *Office:* Department of Geography, University of Singapore, Singapore.

CAREER: University of Singapore, Singapore, lecturer, 1957-62, senior lecturer, 1962-68, professor of geography, 1968—, dean of faculty of arts and social sciences, 1977—. Member of Singapore Public Utilities Board. Member of board of directors of Commonwealth Geographical Bureau. *Member:* International Geographical Union (president of national committee). *Awards, honors:* Federal scholarship to University of Malaya, 1949-53; Queen's scholarship to Oxford University, 1954-56.

WRITINGS: (Contributor) T. H. Silcock, editor, *Readings in Malayan Economics,* Donald Moore, 1961; *Land, People, and Economy in Malaya,* Longmans, Green, 1963; (editor with Chiang Hai Ding, and contributor) *Modern Singapore,* University of Singapore, 1969; (editor with Chia Lin Sien) *The Climate of Singapore and West Malaysia,* Oxford University Press, 1974; *Peninsular Malaysia,* Longman, 1976. Contributor to *World Book Encyclopedia, Collier's Encyclopedia,* and *Encyclopaedia Britannica.* Contributor of about twenty articles to Asian and tropical studies journals. Editor of *Journal of Tropical Geography,* 1964—.

WORK IN PROGRESS: Research on the petroleum resources of Indonesia.

AVOCATIONAL INTERESTS: Golf, music, chess, books (fiction and travel).

* * *

OPPENHEIM, Shulamith (Levey) 1930-

PERSONAL: Born September 2, 1930, in Ohio; daughter of Irving M. (a professor of Semitics) and Sara (a teacher; maiden name, Brody) Levey; married Felix Ererra Oppenheim (a professor of political science), May 29, 1949; children: Daniel, Claire, Paul. *Education:* Attended Radcliffe College, 1947-49; University of Delaware, B.A., 1953. *Home:* 41 Arnold Rd., Amherst, Mass. 01002. *Agent:* Marilyn Marlow, Curtis Brown Ltd., 575 Madison Ave., New York, N.Y. 10022.

CAREER: Presented free-lance literary programs on public radio, 1961-70; writer, 1970—. Volunteer nurses' aide. *Member:* Society of Children's Book Writers, Jane Austen Society, Folklore Society of England.

WRITINGS: A Trio for Grandpapa (for children), Crowell, 1974; *The Selchie's Seed* (for children), Bradbury, 1975.

Work anthologized in *Scribner Anthology for Young People,* Scribner, 1976. Children's book reviewer for *New York Times Book Review,* 1960-70.

WORK IN PROGRESS: Mermen: An Un-Natural History, with Jane Yolen, publication by Crowell; *The Laird of Burrafirth;* "The Stranger," to be included in *The Shapeshifters,* publication by Seabury.

SIDELIGHTS: Oppenheim writes that she believes deeply in the idea of "true magic in art, and that it is closely tied with metaphor, in that art itself is a metaphor for life, and this is a kind of magic. Folklore, legend, myth, all are the most rewarding repositories of such metaphors, they are themselves metaphors. I draw my material from these sources, hoping to transmute them into fresh tales, with a new inference, a surprise, which to me is the essential hallmark of genuine originality in any art . . . the putting together of two hitherto unconnected elements.

"Too much material straight from the therapist's couch passes today for art. Too much self-indulgence is allowed in publishing. It is difficult, it often requires hard labor to turn something into another thing. With facility, many writers, painters, etc., get away with mediocre creations. Flaubert often spent months on one paragraph, until it sang out as he wanted it to sing. I find this exhilarating and a more than useful fact to keep before me."

* * *

OPPENHEIMER, George 1900-1977

February 7, 1900—August 14, 1977; American publisher, playwright, screenwriter, editor, and author. Oppenheimer was co-founder of Viking Press, in addition to being a screenwriter for Metro-Goldwyn-Mayer. Collaborating on such films as "A Day at the Races," "Broadway Melody of 1940," and "Two-Faced Woman," he received an Academy Award nomination for "The War Against Mrs. Hadley." Oppenheimer also wrote the pilot and some twenty-nine episodes for the "Topper" series. He contributed to various entertainment and gossip columns, and was drama critic for a Long Island newspaper for many years. He died in New York, N.Y. Obituaries: *New York Times,* August 16, 1977; *AB Bookman's Weekly,* October 17, 1977. (See index for *CA* sketch)

* * *

ORBACH, William W(olf) 1946-

PERSONAL: Born May 30, 1946, in New York, N.Y.; son of Moses (a teacher) and Frieda (Reiss) Orbach; married Fiorella Zippel (a teacher), June 26, 1969; children: Sharon Leah. *Education:* Yeshiva College (now University), B.A., 1967, M.S., 1970; Rabbi Isaac Elchanan Theological Seminary, rabbi, 1970; City University of New York, Ph.D., 1973. *Home:* 2631 McCoy Way, Louisville, Ky. 40205. *Office:* Department of Studies in Religion, University of Louisville, Louisville, Ky. 40208.

CAREER: Lecturer at Brooklyn College of the City University of New York, Bernard M. Baruch College of the City University of New York, and Yeshiva University, 1971-73; University of Louisville, Louisville, Ky., assistant professor, 1973-77, associate professor of studies in religion, 1977—. *Member:* American Political Science Association, American Academy of Religion, Association for Jewish Studies, National Association of Professors of Hebrew (vice-president, 1976—). *Awards, honors:* National Defense Education Act fellowship, 1967-70.

WRITINGS: To Keep the Peace: The United Nations Condemnatory Resolution, University Press of Kentucky, 1977. Contributor to *Journal of Family Law* and *Reconstructionist.* Associate editor, *Hebrew Studies.*

WORK IN PROGRESS: Free Them Now: The American Movement to Aid the Jews Within the Soviet Union.

SIDELIGHTS: Orbach writes: "My basic interest centers around the interaction of politics and religion, especially in the United States. Judaica is obviously my speciality in this regard. I am also very affected by the Nazi destruction of my European Jewry (the Holocaust) and its effects on contemporary American Jewry, both psychologically and theologically. Auschwitz questions the basic core of Judeo-Christian beliefs. In some respects, the American Soviet Jewry movement is a reaction to the Holocaust.''

* * *

O'REGAN, Richard Arthur 1919-

PERSONAL: Born July 15, 1919, in Boston, Mass.; son of Arthur Richard (an army officer) and Amelia (Egbers) O'Regan; married Elizabeth A. Hill (a teacher), March 23, 1946; children: John Kevin, Michael. *Education:* Attended Temple University, 1940-41, and Vienna University, 1953-54. *Home:* 33 Ch. de Grange Canal, Apt. 33, Geneva, Switzerland. *Office:* Associated Press, Palais des Nations, Geneva, Switzerland.

CAREER/WRITINGS: Philadelphia Bulletin, Philadelphia, Pa., reporter and night city editor, 1939-43; United Press, New York City, Russian war specialist, 1943-45; Associated Press, New York City, foreign correspondent, 1945—, chief of bureau in Vienna, 1950-55, Germany, 1955-66, London, 1966-77, director for Europe, Africa and Middle East, 1977—. Notable assignments include all principal European news events since 1945. *Member:* London Press Club, London Directors Club, Frankfurt Press Club.

SIDELIGHTS: CA asked O'Regan if the role of American newspaper men abroad has changed in recent years. He responded: "Foreign correspondents have become better. First, they are better equipped, on the whole, with education, languages and basic knowledge of the world they are reporting. Second, they are doing a better job of informing the American public. They are able today to put national events in a world perspective. Through improved writing and with the correspondent's wider horizons, I feel the American public is better able to understand the fabric of the world economic and political events than was possible 30 years ago.''

When asked what his most memorable experience as a foreign correspondent was, O'Regan wrote: "There's one that never has been fully appreciated. That is, how close the world came to World War III in 1961, when Russian and American tanks faced each other at Checkpoint Charlie on the Berlin Wall. Their guns bristling, the tanks openly challenged each other to take the first step over the brink. Then they withdrew. Frightening that a miscalculation by a single tank commander could have started an atomic war.''

* * *

O'REILLY, Jane 1936-

PERSONAL: Born April 5, 1936, in St. Louis, Mo.; daughter of Archer (an insurance executive) and Mary Margaret (Conway) O'Reilly; children: Jan Fischer. *Education:* Radcliffe College, B.A., 1958. *Agent:* Lois Wallace, 118 East 61st St., New York, N.Y. 10021. *Office:* 333 Central Park West, New York, N.Y. 10025.

CAREER/WRITINGS: New York, New York City, contributing editor, 1968-76; free-lance writer, 1959—. Author of weekly newspaper column, "Jane O'Reilly," for Enterprise Features, 1976—. Contributor to *Atlantic, House and Garden, Ms., New Republic, Oui, New York Times Book Review,* and other publications. *Member:* Society of American Travel Writers, National Book Critics Circle, Washington Independent Writers. *Awards, honors:* Missouri School of Journalism—J.C. Penney Award, 1970.

SIDELIGHTS: In response to a charge frequently raised against contemporary issue periodicals, O'Reilly told *CA:* "*Ms.* has neither capitalized on the cause it represents nor diluted its beliefs in favor of increased profits. An examination of the magazine's profit and loss sheets will certainly not reveal any windfall reaped by going soft on machismo. *Ms.* serves and leads the women's movement, both in the public and the journalistic profession.''

* * *

ORESICK, Peter (Michael) 1955-

PERSONAL: Surname is pronounced O-*res*-sick; born September 8, 1955, in Kittanning, Pa.; son of Peter (a glassworker) and Mary (a glassworker; maiden name, Gernat) Oresick; married Stephanie Lane Flom (a park naturalist), November 26, 1977. *Education:* University of Pittsburgh, B.A., 1977. *Politics:* "Anti-imperialist." *Religion:* Ukranian Catholic. *Home:* 2711 Tilbury Ave., Pittsburgh, Pa. 15217.

CAREER: Keystone Oaks School District, Pittsburgh, Pa., teacher of English, 1977—.

WRITINGS: The Story of Glass (poetry), West End Press, 1977. Contributor to magazines, including *Radical America, Moving On, West End,* and *Iron.*

SIDELIGHTS: Oresick told *CA:* "I grew up in Ford City, Pennsylvania, a small factory town along the Allegheny River north of Pittsburgh. My grandparents were Ukrainian-Ruthenian immigrants (at the turn of the century) who settled there as glassworkers. Glass being the major theme of our lives, so with these poems, my first. They try to place this background in economic, political, and religious perspective. They try to celebrate Slavic-American workers, unsung heroes, the working class.''

* * *

ORGEL, Stephen K(itay) 1933-

PERSONAL: Born April 11, 1933, in New York, N.Y.; son of Samuel Z. (a physician) and Esther (an attorney; maiden name, Kitay) Orgel. *Education:* Columbia University, B.A., 1954; Harvard University, Ph.D., 1959. *Office:* Department of English, Johns Hopkins University, Baltimore, Md. 21218.

CAREER: Harvard University, Cambridge, Mass., instructor in English, 1959-60; University of California, Berkeley, assistant professor, 1960-66, associate professor, 1966-72, professor of English, 1972-75; Johns Hopkins University, Baltimore, Md., professor of English, 1975—. *Member:* Modern Language Association of America, Renaissance Society of America, American Society for Theatre Research, Shakespeare Association. *Awards, honors:* Woodrow Wilson fellowship, 1954-55; American Council of Learned Societies fellowship, 1967-68, 1973-74.

WRITINGS: The Jonsonian Masque, Harvard University Press, 1965; (editor) Ben Jonson, *The Complete Masques,* Yale University Press, 1969; (editor) *Marlowe: Complete Poems and Translations,* Penguin, 1971; (with Roy Strong) *Inigo Jones: The Theatre of the Stuart Court,* two volumes, University of California Press, 1973; (with John Harris) *The King's Arcadia,* Arts Council of Great Britain, 1973; *The Illusion of Power: Political Theater in the English Renaissance,* University of California Press, 1975; (editor) Alexander Ross, *Mystagogus Poeticus; or, The Muses Interpreter,* Garland Publishing, 1976; (editor) P. J. Gordon, *The Renaissance Imagination: Essays and Lectures,* University of California Press, 1976.

WORK IN PROGRESS: Shakespeare and the Kinds of Drama.

ORME, Antony R(onald) 1936-

PERSONAL: Born May 28, 1936, in Weston-Super-Mare, England; came to the United States in 1967, naturalized citizen, 1977; son of Ronald Albert and Anne (Parry) Orme; married Lusanne Becker (a registered nurse), October 1, 1966; children: Mark Antony, Kevin Ronald. *Education:* University of Birmingham, B.A. (first class honors), 1957, Ph.D., 1961. *Office:* Department of Geography, University of California, Los Angeles, Calif. 90024.

CAREER: National University of Ireland, University College, Dublin, lecturer in geography, 1960-68; University of California, Los Angeles, associate professor, 1968-73, professor of geography, 1973—, dean of social sciences, 1977—. Visiting lecturer at University of Natal, 1966. Consultant to timber harvesting and energy companies.

MEMBER: International Geographical Union (member of national committee for Ireland, 1965-68), Association of American Geographers, Geological Society of America, American Quaternary Association, Institute of British Geographers, Geographical Society of Ireland, Association of Geography Teachers of Ireland (president, 1964-68). *Awards, honors:* Grants from Office of Naval Research for Mexico, 1969-71, and southern Africa, 1971-73, Coastal Engineering Research Center, 1972-73, Energy Research and Development Agency/Bendix Corporation for uranium investigations, 1976-77, and National Science Foundation, 1976-79; award of merit from American Institute of Planners, 1975, for "Shorezone Plan for Lake Tahoe."

WRITINGS: (Editor) G. Fahy, *A Regional Geography of Ireland,* Brown & Nolan, 1966; *Ireland,* Aldine, 1970; (contributor) D. R. Coates, editor, *Coastal Geomorphology,* State University of New York at Binghamton, 1973; *Estuarine Sedimentation: South Africa,* Office of Naval Research, 1974; (editor) J. T. Andrews, *Glacier Systems,* Duxbury Press, 1975.

Television scripts: "Natural Forces," 1968; "Vegetation Cover," 1970. Contributor of more than fifty articles to scientific journals. Editor of *Geographical Viewpoint,* 1965-72.

WORK IN PROGRESS: Man, Earth, and Water, publication expected in 1980; continuing scientific research.

SIDELIGHTS: Orme told *CA:* "Much of my work concerns the relationship between environment and society and, whereas I recognize the need for constraint in dealing with our environment, I also believe that the pendulum has often swung too far towards preservation at the expense of the realistic needs and aspirations of the bulk of society. Responsible environmental planning and management should seek to protect the best that nature and society have bequeathed to us from the past while also allowing for the ordered and careful development of our resources and potential in the future."

BIOGRAPHICAL/CRITICAL SOURCES: Geographical Viewpoint, Volume 2, number 3, 1973.

*   *   *

ORMONDROYD, Edward 1925-

PERSONAL: Born October 8, 1925, in Wilkinsburg, Pa.; children: Evan, Kitt, Beth. *Education:* University of California, Berkeley, A.B., 1950. *Residence:* Newfield, N.Y.

CAREER: Author and librarian. *Military service:* Served on a destroyer escort in the Pacific during World War II. *Awards, honors:* Commonwealth Club of California Literature Award, 1957, for *David and the Phoenix.*

WRITINGS: David and the Phoenix (illustrated by Joan Raysor), Follett, 1957; *The Tale of Alain* (illustrated by Robert Frankenberg), Follett, 1960; *Time at the Top* (illustrated by Peggie Bach), Parnassus, 1963; *Jonathan Frederick Aloysius Brown* (illustrated by Suzi Spector), Golden Gate Junior Books, 1964; *Theodore* (illustrated by John M. Larrecq), Parnassus, 1966; *Michael: The Upstairs Dog* (illustrated by Cyndy Szekeres), Dial, 1967; *Broderick* (illustrated by Larrecq), Parnassus, 1969; *Theodore's Rival* (illustrated by Larrecq), Parnassus, 1971; *Castaways on Long Ago* (illustrated by Ruth Robbins), Parnassus, 1973; *Imagination Greene* (illustrated by John Lewis), Parnassus, 1973; *All in Good Time* (illustrated by Robbins), Parnassus, 1975.

SIDELIGHTS: Ormondroyd wrote his first book, *David and the Phoenix,* while he was a student at the University of California, but it took seven years before he could find a publisher for it. A reviewer for the *Chicago Sunday Tribune* observed: "Ormondroyd has written a stimulating, ageless story. It combines beautiful writing, topnotch adventure, and enchanting fantasy."

The author's *Time at the Top* is about a young girl and her unusual elevator ride. An *Atlantic Monthly* reviewer proclaimed, "A book not to miss, beautifully illustrated with black-and-white drawings." In reviewing the same book, a critic for *Junior Bookshelf* commented: "A fresh variation on the 'time slip' theme. The story moves quickly and is interesting, but fantasy of this kind much be carefully thought through, with all its implications, to be convincing."

In *Theodore,* Ormondroyd related the tale of a little girl and her affection for her toy bear. A critic for *Young Readers' Review* wrote: "A recitation of the simple story line cannot do the book justice for the author and artist have really endowed this bear with a personality that is endearing. The very common but hard to capture affection between stuffed animal and child is excellently portrayed."

The author's *Castaways on Long Ago* told the story of three children and their adventurous vacation on a farm. A reviewer for the *Bulletin of the Center for Children's Books* commented: "With high dramatic sense, Ormondroyd saves the most exciting episode and the solution of an unusual mystery-fantasy until the very end of a very good book. What gives the book substance that goes beyond the plot is the quality of characterization: both the children and their farm hosts are highly individual, sharply drawn and consistent in behavior and dialogue, for which the author has a keen ear."

AVOCATIONAL INTERESTS: Collecting books, playing the oboe, recorder, and flute.

BIOGRAPHICAL/CRITICAL SOURCES: Chicago Sunday Tribune, November 17, 1957; *Atlantic Monthly,* December, 1963; *Young Readers' Review,* January, 1967; *Bulletin of the Center for Children's Books,* February, 1974; *Junior Bookshelf,* June, 1976.*

*   *   *

ORMSBY, William (George) 1921-

PERSONAL: Born March 9, 1921, in Toronto, Ontario, Canada; son of Clarence Charles (a plumber) and Irene May (Harris) Ormsby; married Katherine Elizabeth Wise, November 27, 1943; children: Lynne (Mrs. Barry Hargadon), John. *Education:* University of Toronto, B.A., 1948; Carleton University, M.A., 1960. *Home:* 32 Marmac Dr., St. Catharines, Ontario, Canada L2T 2X3. *Office:* Department of History, Brock University, St. Catharines, Ontario, Canada L2S 3A1.

CAREER: Public Archives of Canada, Ottawa, Ontario, archivist, 1948-64; Brock University, St. Catharines, Ontario, associate professor, 1964-66, professor of history, 1966—. Director of Ontario Heritage Foundation. *Military service:* Royal Canadian Navy, 1941-45. *Member:* Canadian Historical Association, Ontario Historical Society (president, 1974-75).

WRITINGS: Crisis in the Canadas, Macmillan (Canada), 1964; *The Emergence of the Federal Concept in Canada,* University of Toronto Press, 1969. Editor of "Ontario" series, Champlain Society. Contributor to Canadian history journals.

WORK IN PROGRESS: A biography of Francis Hincks; research on the assumptions and values of English-speaking groups in Quebec, 1841-1867.

SIDELIGHTS: Ormsby writes: "I am particularly interested in Anglo-French relations in Canada and problems relating thereto, including separatism."

* * *

OTWELL, John H(erbert) 1915-

PERSONAL: Born July 6, 1915, in Van Wert, Ohio; son of Thomas Herbert (a clergyman) and Ida C. (Reber) Otwell; married Marion Grace Knapp, September 17, 1937. *Education:* Attended Kenyon College, 1933-35; DePauw University, A.B. (magna cum laude), 1937; Garrett Biblical Institute, graduate study, 1937; Pacific School of Religion, B.D. (magna cum laude), 1943, Th.D. (summa cum laude), 1947. *Politics:* Republican. *Home:* 1061 Creston Rd., Berkeley, Calif. 94708. *Office:* Department of Old Testament, Pacific School of Religion, 1798 Scenic Ave., Berkeley, Calif. 94709.

CAREER: Ordained Methodist minister, 1941; pastor of Methodist churches in Sardinia, Ohio, 1938-40, Soledad-Fort Romie, Calif., 1940-43, Palo Alto, Calif., 1943-45, and San Francisco, Calif., 1945-47; Pacific School of Religion, Berkeley, instructor, 1947-49, associate professor, 1949-55, professor of Old Testament, 1955—. Pastor of Congregational church in Suisan, Calif., 1950-52. Curator and member of board of directors of Palestine Institute, 1975—. Faculty member at Starr King School for the Ministry, 1956, Perkins Summer School, 1956, Faith and Life Institute, 1964—, and Graduate Theological Union, 1964—. *Member:* Society of Biblical Literature and Exegesis, Theological Study Group of the West Coast, Save the Bay Association.

WRITINGS: (With Margaret Harrison) *C. C. McCown: An Indexed Bibliography,* Pacific School of Religion, 1947; *Ground to Stand On,* Oxford University Press, 1957; (editor with Beatrice McCown Mattison) C. C. McCown, *Man, Morals and History: Today's Legacy from Ancient Times and Biblical Peoples,* Harper, 1958; *I Will Be Your God: A Layman's Guide to Old Testament Study,* Abingdon, 1967, published in England as *A New Approach to the Old Testament,* S.C.M. Press, 1967; (with William Hordern) *Proclamation: Lent,* Fortress, 1976; *And Sarah Laughed: The Status of Women in the Old Testament,* Westminster, 1977. Contributor of articles and reviews to journals.

WORK IN PROGRESS: Research on the attitude toward nature in the Old Testament, the view of the state in the Old Testament, and the relationship between the assumptions of a culture and the interpretation oe the Bible; studying whether or not "ancient Israelite mytho-poetic thinking can be reduced to a system of logic."

SIDELIGHTS: Otwell remarks: "Except for specific assignments, all published works are the result of research undertaken to clarify questions in my mind or in the minds of students. The methods used in all my study of the Old Testament are those called 'Higher Criticism.'" *Avocational interests:* Camping, hiking, sailing, music, photography.

* * *

OUIMETTE, Victor 1944-

PERSONAL: Born April 21, 1944, in Calgary, Alberta, Canada; son of William Mewburn and Freda Lilian (Noble) Ouimette; married Maria Elena Nochera, July 22, 1967. *Education:* Attended University of Victoria, 1961-62; McGill University, B.A., 1965; Yale University, Ph.D., 1968. *Residence:* Montreal, Quebec, Canada. *Office:* Department of Hispanic Studies, McGill University, Montreal, Quebec, Canada H3A 1G5.

CAREER: McGill University, Montreal, Quebec, assistant professor, 1968-73, associate professor of Spanish, 1973—. *Member:* International Association of Hispanists, Canadian Comparative Literature Association, Canadian Association of Hispanists, Modern Language Association of America, American Association of Teachers of Spanish and Portuguese.

WRITINGS: Reason Aflame: Unamuno and the Heroic Will, Yale University Press, 1974. Contributor to Spanish studies journals.

WORK IN PROGRESS: Jose Ortega y Gasset, publication by Twayne expected in 1981.

SIDELIGHTS: Ouimette told *CA:* "*Reason Aflame* is an attempt to examine the nineteenth-century roots of Unamuno's philosophy and the extent to which he applied these to twentieth century concerns. The cult of the hero had been widespread in the last century, particularly because of the influence of Thomas Carlyle. Unamuno was of course aware of this and its subsequent development in the writings of such figures as Tolstoy and William James. The moment when he was writing in Spain was particularly short on heroic figures and this gave a special dimension to the need in any society, but in Spanish society in particular. My book is aimed at tracing these concerns as they are developed by an early existentialist and applied in a highly personal manner to his works of fiction. Spain had, of course, produced the greatest fictitious heroes, Don Quixote, who was also one of the great ethical figures, and it was to him that Unamuno repeatedly turned in his own vision of the heroic in life."

* * *

OVERBEEK, J(ohannes) 1932-

PERSONAL: Born July 17, 1932, in Schiedam, Netherlands; son of Adolf (an executive) and Hendrika (Boeziek) Overbeek; married Chantal Broisin (a nurse), January 28, 1967; children: Bertrand. *Education:* Nijenrode College of Business Administration, diploma, 1956; University of Geneva, M.A., 1961, Ph.D., 1970. *Religion:* None. *Office:* Department of National Development, Pahlavi University, Shiraz, Iran.

CAREER: University of British Columbia, Vancouver, assistant professor of economics, 1968-70; University of Hawaii, Honolulu, assistant professor of economics and research associate at East-West Population Institute, 1970-75; University of Guelph, Guelph, Ontario, associate professor of economics, 1975-76; Pahlavi University, Shiraz, Iran, associate professor of development studies, 1976—. *Military service:* Army of the Netherlands, 1952-54. *Member:* Population Association of America, American Economic Association.

WRITINGS: History of Population Theories, Rotterdam University Press, 1974; *The Population Challenge: A Handbook for Non-Specialists,* Greenwood Press, 1976; (editor) *The Evolution of Population Theory: A Documentary Sourcebook,* Greenwood Press, 1977. Contributor to economics journals.

WORK IN PROGRESS: Population and Canadian Society, a textbook for Canadians.

SIDELIGHTS: Overbeek told *CA:* "I have a strong interest in a number of subjects related to population and development. Examples are 'history of population theories', 'population policy', 'population growth and economic development', and 'migration'. My two year stay in Iran has helped me to become better acquainted with the struggle for economic development/modernization, the population explosion, and life in Asia in general."

*   *   *

OWEN, Clifford
  See HAMITLON, Charles Harold St. John

*   *   *

OWENS, Bill   1938-

PERSONAL: Born September 25, 1938, in San Jose, Calif.; son of Elmo and Molinda (La Mond) Owens; married Janet Louise Betonte, June 1, 1963; children: Andrew, Erik. *Education:* Chico State College (now California State University, Chico), B.A., 1963. *Politics:* Liberal Democrat. *Home:* 268 Yosemite Dr., Livermore, Calif. 94550. *Office address:* P.O. Box 588, Livermore, Calif. 94550.

CAREER: Free-lance news photographer, 1968-77; *Livermore Independent,* Livermore, Calif., free-lance photographer, 1978—. Work has been exhibited at numerous museums and galleries, and with an exhibition currently traveling in Europe. *Member:* American Society of Magazine Photographers, National Press Photographers Association, Society of Photo Education. *Awards, honors:* National Endowment for the Arts grants, 1974, 1978; Guggenheim fellowship, 1976.

WRITINGS: Suburbia, Straight Arrow Books, 1972; *Our Kind of People,* Straight Arrow Books, 1975; *Working: I Do It for the Money,* Simon & Schuster, 1977.

WORK IN PROGRESS: A photographic book on leisure.

SIDELIGHTS: Owens writes: "The documentary photograph is the heart of photography, as it is a record of people, places, and events. The challenge of the documentary photographer is the highest, because the photograph must be technically sharp, contain information, and show the symbols of the society. It must show people and how they live. The documentary photograph, if done properly, will stand the test of time, because it is telling us about ourselves."

*   *   *

OWENS, Pat(rick) J.   1929-

PERSONAL: Born August 5, 1929, in Libby, Mont.; son of James Hill (a forestry laborer) and Rachel (Hoover) Mercedes Williams Owens; divorced; children: James Patrick. *Education:* Attended Harvard University, 1962-63. *Politics:* "Anarco-Syndicalist Whig." *Home address:* Box 492, Northport, N.Y. 11768. *Agent:* Sterling Lord, 660 Madison Ave., New York, N.Y. 10021.

CAREER/WRITINGS: Hungry Horse Dam, Mont., construction laborer, 1946-48, 1951; KLCB-Radio, Libby, Mont. news editor, program director, chief announcer, and assistant general manager, 1952-53; *Daily Inter Lake,* Kalispell, Mont., reporter-photographer, 1953-54; *Columbia Basin News,* Pasco, Wash., city and managing editor, 1954-58; *Arkansas Gazette,* Little Rock, Ark., reporter, 1959-61; *Pine Bluff Commercial,* Pine Bluff, Ark., editorial page editor, 1961-64; *Arkansas Gazette,* associate editor and columnist, 1964-65; *Detroit Free Press,* Detroit, Mich., labor writer, 1965-69; *Newsday,* Garden City, N.Y., chief editorial writer and director of opinion pages, 1969-70, author of column, 1970—. Notable assignments include government, race relations, labor, economics, and coverage of the Little Rock school desegregation crisis and the 1967 auto negotiations. Contributor to magazines, including *Nation, New Republic, Penthouse,* and *More.* Lecturer in conscience in journalism at University of Illinois; guest speaker at universities and colleges. Host of television show in Pasco, Wash.; guest on television news shows. *Military service:* U.S. Army, 1948-51; announcer-writer for Armed Forces Radio Service in Panama and editor of *Caribbean Army News.*

MEMBER: Arkansas Newspaper Mens Association. *Awards, honors:* Sidney Hillman Award, 1961; Nieman fellowship, 1962-63; distinguished reporting citation from American Political Science Association, 1963.

WORK IN PROGRESS: A book on the Black Panthers; editing a book on the state of labor-management relations.

AVOCATIONAL INTERESTS: Pocket Billiards and croquet.

BIOGRAPHICAL/CRITICAL SOURCES: Gerald W. Cormick, editor, *Collective Bargaining Today,* BNA Books, 1971; Stanley Marcus, *Minding the Store,* Little, Brown, 1974; Richard Ney, *The Wall Street Gang,* Praeger, 1974; Edward Jay Epstein, *Between Fact and Fiction: The Problem of Journalism,* Vintage Books, 1975; Richard Rovere, *Arrivals and Departures: A Journalist's Memoirs,* Macmillan, 1976.

*   *   *

OXLEY, William   1939-
  (Jason Hardy)

PERSONAL: Born April 29, 1939, in Manchester, England; son of Harry (a boxer and businessman) and Catherine (a pianist; maiden name, Steel) Oxley; married Patricia Holmes (a writer), April 13, 1963; children: Elizabeth, Katie. *Education:* Attended Manchester College of Commerce, 1953-55. *Politics:* "Individualist." *Religion:* "Pantheist." *Home:* 6 Mount, Furzeham, Britham, South Devonshire, England.

CAREER: Deloitte & Co., London, England, chartered accountant, 1964-68; Lazard Brothers & Co. Ltd., London, chartered accountant, 1968-76; writer and editor, 1976—. Editor of Ember Press. Has given poetry readings and lectures at schools and meetings, including Cambridge College of Arts and Technology, Hull Arts Centre, and City Literary Institute. *Member:* Institute of Chartered Accountants (fellow).

WRITINGS—Poems, except as indicated: The Dark Structures and Other Poems, Mitre Press, 1967; *New Workings,* privately printed, 1968; *Passages from Time: Poems From a Life,* Ember Press, 1971; *The "Icon" Poems,* Ember Press, 1972; *Sixteen Days in Autumn* (travel), privately printed, 1972; *Opera Vetera,* Iconoclast Press, 1973; *The Mirrors of* the Sea, Quarto Press, 1973; (under pseudonym Jason Hardy) "Fightings", Ember Press, 1974; The Mundane Shell, Uldale House Publications, 1975; Eve Free (broadsheet), Sceptre Press, 1975; Country Lass (broadsheet), Words Press, 1975; Superfices, Aquila Publishing, 1976; (translator) L. S. Senghor, Poems of a Black Orpheus, in press.

Work represented in anthologies, including International Who's Who in Poetry Anthology, 1973, International Poetry Society Anthology, 1974, and Words Press Anthology, Volume II, 1974. Contributor of poems, articles, and reviews to journals, including Encounter, Dublin, Outposts, and Scotsman, and to newspapers. Editor of Littack, 1972—, Laissez Faire, and New Headland; associate editor of Orbis, Village Review, 1972-74, Poetry Newsletter (of Temple University), and Lapis Lazuli, 1976—.

WORK IN PROGRESS: Square One, a novel; The Paradise Man, an autobiography.

SIDELIGHTS: Oxley writes: "It is urgent for me to define a new poetry. I have been engaged for five years in propagating a theory of vitalist poetry: a poetry for the whole mind—strong in rhythm, intellect, and imagination. The theory of a vitalist poetry has developed organically and emerged in outline in my poems and various other writings.

"Vitalism or 'neo-vitalism'—terms with a certain weight of traditional definition—began in the United Kingdom in reaction to the academicism of the 50's and against the hysterical and formless thrust of the poetry of the 60's, and against the resultant 'loss of critical centre.' Its uniqueness lies in the fact that what began as a negative impulse manifesting itself in bitter irony . . . ended as a positive and constructive poetic and philosophical theory."

Oxley describes Vitalism as "a firm statement of feeling and ideas in a strong language . . . the philosophy of the new release . . . a poetry of ideas, of feeling." Criticizing the "pallidness of recent English poetry," he declares: "What we need are ideas, not ideologies; original thought, not conformity. An irresistable vocal articulation of affirmative statement . . . a poetry of universal awareness . . . poetry of the Creative Imagination."

* * *

PAANANEN, Victor Niles 1938-

PERSONAL: Born January 31, 1938, in Ashtabula, Ohio; son of Niles Henry and Anni (Iloranta) Paananen; married Donna M. Jones (a teacher and writer), August 15, 1964; children: Karl, Neil. Education: Harvard University, A.B. (magna cum laude), 1960; University of Wisconsin, Madison, M.A., 1964, Ph.D., 1967. Home: 152 Orchard St., East Lansing, Mich. 48823. Office: Graduate School, 246 Administration Building, Michigan State University, East Lansing, Mich. 48824.

CAREER: Continental Insurance Co., Cleveland, Ohio, fidelity and bond underwriter, 1960-62; Wofford College, Spartanburg, S.C., instructor in English, 1962-63; Williams College, Williamstown, Mass., assistant professor of English, 1966-68; Michigan State University, East Lansing, assistant professor, 1968-73, associate professor of English, 1973—, associate chairman of department, 1976-77, assistant dean of Graduate School, 1977—. Member: Modern Language Association of America, Council of Graduate Schools, Association of Graduate Schools, Committee on Institutional Cooperation of Graduate Deans, Midwest Association of Graduate Schools, Michigan Council of Graduate Deans, Phi Beta Kappa.

WRITINGS: William Blake, Twayne, 1977. Contributor to history, literature, and education journals.

WORK IN PROGRESS: Research on political and religious backgrounds of British Romantic literature and the civilization of contemporary England, British studies in general, and graduate education.

SIDELIGHTS: Paananen comments: "My goal, both as an administrator and as a literary critic and scholar, is to make some contribution to the quality of life and consciousness in America—I welcome having access to institutional machinery and to print in pursuit of this goal." Avocational interests: Travel (especially in England).

* * *

PACERNICK, Gary 1941-

PERSONAL: Born May 9, 1941, in Detroit, Mich.; son of Edward (a salesman) and Sally Pacernick; married Dorothea Anton, June 4, 1968; children: Jennifer, Eden. Education: University of Michigan, B.A. (honors), 1963; University of Minnesota, M.A., 1966; Arizona State University, Ph.D., 1969. Religion: Jewish. Home: 5780 Toulon Court, Dayton, Ohio 45424. Office: Department of English, Wright State University, Dayton, Ohio 45435.

CAREER: Wright State University, Dayton, Ohio, assistant professor, 1969-74, associate professor of English, 1974—. Member of literary panel of Ohio Arts Council. Member: Phi Beta Kappa. Awards, honors: Phillips Poetry Award from Stone Country, 1977, for "O Mao."

WRITINGS: Credence (poems), Professor H. Quinn Press, 1974. Work represented in anthology Traveling America With Today's Poets, edited by David Kherdian, Macmillan, 1977. Contributor of poems to magazines, including Choice, Mixed Voices, Poetry Now, and American Poetry Review. Editor of Images.

WORK IN PROGRESS: A book-length series of poems about his family's ethnic Jewish experiences.

SIDELIGHTS: Pacernick told CA: "I got my start rather late as a graduate student at University of Minnesota, when Allen Tate took an interest in my poetry. Since then I have been influenced most perhaps by the less formal, more open poetry of the tradition going back to Whitman and continuing through Williams, the Jewish objectivists, Ginsberg and the Beats, etc. I was also moved by my father's death to explore and discover sources in my Russian Jewish family heritage. I wish to capture dramatic human voices and scenes, the kind of everyday earthy experiences that most people can empathize with."

* * *

PACKARD, Reynolds 1903-1976

PERSONAL: Born in 1903, in Atlantic City, N.J.; married wife, Eleanor (a foreign correspondent). Education: Attended Bucknell College. Residence: Rome, Italy.

CAREER: United Press International, New York City, correspondent in Buenos Aires, 1936-39, bureau chief in Rome, Italy, 1939-47; New York Daily News, New York City, correspondent in Rome, 1948-72. Notable assignments include coverage of both sides of the Spanish Civil War, the Italian invasion of Ethiopia, Hitler's conquest of Czechoslovakia, Allied campaigns in the Mediterranean during World War II, including campaigns in North Africa and the invasion of Italy, and the Chinese Civil War.

WRITINGS: (With wife, Eleanor Packard) Balcony Empire: Fascist Italy at War, Oxford University Press, 1942; The Kansas City Milkman, Dutton, 1950; Rome Was My Beat, Lyle Stuart, 1975.

SIDELIGHTS: Packard, who is best known for his "flamboyant, bylined dispatches with exotic datelines," once said, "My only ambition is to become a literary vagabond with no possessions but a suitcase and a typewriter." A specialist in the "I-was-there" first-person style of reporting, Packard provided readers with accounts of battles, as well as unequivocal forecasts of the outcome of battles still under way. Reporters he had scooped charged Packard with making "less than authentic" reports. "What I want to do," Packard explained, "is to let my readers participate in my experiences in collecting news, whether it's real or phony." On another occasion Packard offered this definition of his reporting: "If you've got a good story, the important thing is to get it out fast. You can worry about details later. And if you have to send a correction, that will probably make another good story."

Packard's novel, The Kansas City Milkman, an account of life in the Paris bureau of an international news wire service, has been "widely regarded by newspapermen as one of the classics of the craft."

OBITUARIES: New York Times, October 16, 1976; Washington Post, October 17, 1976.*

(Died October 15, 1976, in Rome, Italy)

*   *   *

PACKENHAM, Robert Allen   1937-

PERSONAL: Born October 5, 1937, in Watertown, S.D.; son of Floyd E. (a businessman) and Alice Mildred (Staven) Packenham. Education: Augustana College, Rock Island, Ill., B.A., 1958; University of Illinois, M.A., 1959; Yale University, Ph.D., 1964; also attended Harvard University, summer, 1963, and Columbia University, 1963-64. Office: Department of Political Science, Stanford University, Stanford, Calif.

CAREER: Stanford University, Stanford, Calif., assistant professor, 1965-71, associate professor of political science, 1971—. Member: American Political Science Association, American Association for the Advancement of Science, Latin American Studies Association, Phi Beta Kappa. Awards, honors: Brookings Institution fellowship, 1962-63; Ford Foundation fellowship, Federal University of Minas Gerais, 1966-67; Woodrow Wilson fellowship, 1973-74.

WRITINGS: (Contributor) Allan Kornberg and Lloyd Musolf, editors, Legislatures in Developmental Perspective, Duke University Press, 1970; (contributor) Weston Agor, editor, Latin American Legislatures, Praeger, 1971; Liberal America and the Third World, Princeton University Press, 1973; (contributor) Riordan Roett, editor, Brazil in the Seventies, American Enterprise Institute, 1976. Contributor to political science and law journals.

WORK IN PROGRESS: Research on dependency in Brazil since 1964, on legislatures and development, and on theories of development.

SIDELIGHTS: Packenham writes: "I am interested in problems of development in the Third World, especially Latin America, and the ways North Americans relate to this. I am also very much concerned with the actual and desirable impact of social science on public policy, and more broadly with the role of social science and intellectual activity generally in contemporary life."

PAGE, James D.   1910-

PERSONAL: Born May 6, 1910, in Rome, N.Y.; son of Anthony and Margaret (Pace) Page; married Dorothy Skene, September 2, 1937; children: Bruce, Margaret. Education: Columbia University, A.B., 1932, Ph.D., 1935. Home address: P.O. Box 358, Edgartown, Mass. 02539.

CAREER: Temple University, Philadelphia, Pa., professor of psychology, 1941—. Diplomate in clinical psychology of American Board of Examiners in Professional Psychology. Member: American Psychological Association, Sigma Xi.

WRITINGS: Modern Society and Mental Disease, Farrar & Rinehart, 1938; Abnormal Psychology, McGraw, 1947; Approaches to Psychopathology, Columbia University Press, 1966; Psychopathology, Aldine, 1971, 2nd edition, Oxford University Press, 1975.

WORK IN PROGRESS: Psychological Disorders of Children.

*   *   *

PAGE, Robert Collier   1908-1977

1908—September 29, 1977; British-born authority on industrial medicine and author of It Pays to Be Happy. Page was a leading exponent of preventive medicine in companies. He was co-author of Air Commando Doc, a book of his war experiences in Burma. Page died in Ocho Rios, Jamaica. Obituaries: New York Times, October 2, 1977.

*   *   *

PALLEY, Julian I(rving)   1925-

PERSONAL: Born September 16, 1925, in Atlantic City, N.J.; son of Max (a businessman) and Anne (Rosenberg) Palley; married Shirley Wilson (a teacher), September 17, 1950; children: David, Brant, Marl, Daniel. Education: Mexico City College, B.A., 1950; University of Arizona, M.A., 1952; University of New Mexico, Ph.D., 1958. Home: 18112 Gillman St., Irvine, Calif. 92715. Office: Department of Spanish and Portuguese, University of California, Irvine, Calif. 92717.

CAREER: Rutgers University, New Brunswick, N.J., instructor in Spanish and French, 1956-59; Arizona State University, Tempe, assistant professor of Spanish, 1959-62; University of Oregon, Eugene, associate professor of Spanish, 1962-66; University of California, Irvine, professor of Spanish, 1966—, chairman of department, 1970-73. Member: American Association of Teachers of Spanish and Portuguese, Modern Language Association of America. Awards, honors: Jefferson Poetry Award from JNR Publishers, 1976, for Spinoza's Stone and Other Poems.

WRITINGS: La luz no usada: La poesia de Pedro Salinas (title means "A Special Light: The Poetry of Pedro Salinas"), Studium, 1966; (editor and translator) Affirmation: A Bilingual Anthology of Jorge Guillen, University of Oklahoma Press, 1968, 2nd edition, 1970; (editor with Donald Yates and Joseph Sommers) Tres Cuentistas Latinoamericanos (title means "Three Latin Story Writers"), Macmillan, 1969; Spinoza's Stone and Other Poems, JNR Publishers, 1976; El laberinto y la esfera: Cien anos de la novela espanola (title means "The Labyrinth and the Sphere: A Century of the Spanish Novel"), Editorial Insula, 1978. Contributor to periodicals, including Kentucky Romance Quarterly.

WORK IN PROGRESS: Dreams in Spanish Literature; translating poems by Rosario Castellanos.

SIDELIGHTS: Palley writes: "I am interested in writing poetry in English, literary criticism concerned primarily with Spanish peninsular literature, translations from Spanish and Latin American authors.

"*El laberinto y la esfera* is a collection of essays on the Spanish novel, from Perez Galdos in the late nineteenth century to the contemporary Juan Goytisolo, in which the author sees the recurrent motifs of the Labyrinth and the Sphere.

"*Dreams in Spanish Literature* is an attempt at studying the nature and the function of dreams in Spanish literature, from the medieval period to the present. I have been influenced by the depth psychology of Freud, Jung, Adler, etc., and the anthropological studies of Levy-Bruhl, Jackson Lincoln, and others, in my work on dreams in literature."

* * *

PALMER, John L(ogan) 1943-

PERSONAL: Born April 10, 1943, in Darby, Pa.; son of Richard S. (an engineer) and Helen (a teacher; maiden name, Logan) Palmer; married Nancy Hetenyi (an artist and teacher), June 29, 1968. *Education:* Williams College, B.A., 1965; Stanford University, Ph.D., 1970. *Home:* 9112 Potomac Ridge Rd., Great Falls, Va. 22066. *Office:* Brookings Institution, 1775 Massachusetts Ave. N.W., Washington, D.C. 20036.

CAREER: University of Wisconsin, Madison, research associate of Institute for Research on Poverty, 1968; Stanford University, Stanford, Calif., assistant professor of economics and research associate of Institute for Public Policy Analysis, both 1969-71; U.S. Department of Health, Education & Welfare, Washington, D.C., senior staff economist, 1971-73, director of income security policy, 1973-75; Brookings Institution, Washington, D.C., senior fellow of economics studies program, 1975—. Chairman of National Conference on Social Welfare's Task Force on Income Security Policy, 1976-77. Member, National Academy of Sciences Panel for Evaluation of Federal Poverty Research; consultant to government agencies and private foundations. *Member:* American Economic Association, Industrial Relations Research Association.

WRITINGS: Inflation, Unemployment, and Poverty, Heath, 1973; (with Michael C. Barth and George Carcagno) *Toward an Effective Income Support System: Problems, Prospects, and Choices,* Institute for Research on Poverty, 1974; (editor with Joseph A. Pechman) *The Rural Negative Income Tax Experiment,* Brookings Institution, in press; (with Emil Sunley) *Indexing Federal Expenditures for Inflation,* General Accounting Office, in press.

Contributor: Kenneth Boulding and Martin Pfaff, editors, *Redistribution to the Rich and the Poor: The Grants Economics of Income Distribution,* Wadsworth, 1972; Dennis Dugan and William Leahy, editors, *Perspectives on Poverty,* Praeger, 1973; Richard Zeckhauser, editor, *Benefit Cost and Policy Analysis,* Aldine, 1974; Joseph Pechman and Michael Timpane, editors, *Work Incentives and Income Guarantees: The New Jersey Work Incentive Experiment,* Brookings Institution, 1975; Henry Owen and Charles Schultze, editors, *Setting National Priorities: The Next Ten Years,* Brookings Institution, 1976; Richard Burkhauser and George Tolley, editors, *Income Support Policies for the Aging,* Ballinger, 1977; Marilyn Moon and Eugene Finolensky, editors, *Augmenting Measures of Economic Well-Being,* Academic Press, in press; Joseph Peckman, editor, *Setting National Priorities: The 1978 Budget,* Brookings

Institution, in press. Contributor to magazines, including *Public Policy* and *Challenge.*

WORK IN PROGRESS: Labor Market Policies and Income Assistance, a monograph; *Direct Job Creation: Analytic Issues and Policy Implications,* a conference volume; an article for *Redistribution in Growing and Stagnating Economies.*

* * *

PALMER, Ralph Simon 1914-

PERSONAL: Born June 13, 1914, in Richmond, Maine; son of George L. (a driller of artesian wells) and Marion Eleanor (Holmes) Palmer; married Nancy Randerson, June, 1952; children: Keith, Douglas, Shirley. *Education:* University of Maine, B.A., 1937; Cornell University, Ph.D., 1940. *Home and office address:* P.O. Box 74, Tenants Harbor, Maine 04860.

CAREER: New York Department of Conservation, Albany, wildlife researcher, 1940-41; State Conservation Commission, Albany, N.Y., research assistant, 1942; Vassar College, Poughkeepsie, N.Y., instructor, 1942-47, assistant professor of zoology, 1947-49; New York State Museum and Science Service, Albany, state zoologist, 1949-76; University of Maine, Orono, adjunct professor of zoology, 1977—. *Military service:* U.S. Naval Reserve, active duty, 1943-45; served in Normandy; became lieutenant junior grade. *Member:* American Society of Mammalogists, American Ornithologists Union, and approximately twenty other scientific and conservation organizations.

WRITINGS: Maine Birds, Museum of Comparative Zoology, Harvard University, 1949; *The Mammal Guide,* Doubleday, 1952; *Handbook of North American Birds,* Yale University Press, Volume I, 1962, Volumes II and III, 1976; (contributor) G. G. Stout, editor, *Shorebirds of North America,* Viking, 1970. Contributor of about thirty articles and several hundred reviews to scientific journals.

WORK IN PROGRESS: Additional volumes for *Handbook of North American Birds.*

AVOCATIONAL INTERESTS: Photography, fine arts (painting), carpentry, travel.

* * *

PALUDAN, Phillip S(haw) 1938-

PERSONAL: Born January 26, 1938, in St. Cloud, Minn.; son of Paul F. (a hotel manager and truck driver) and Marguerite Catheline (a stenographer; maiden name, Shaw) Paludan; married Marsha Rose McMann (a dancer and teacher), July 26, 1963; children: Karin, Kirsten. *Education:* Occidental College, B.A., 1960, M.A., 1963; graduate study at University of California, Los Angeles, 1962-63; University of Illinois, Ph.D., 1968. *Office:* Department of History, University of Kansas, Lawrence, Kan. 66045.

CAREER: University of Illinois, Champaign-Urbana, instructor in general studies, 1967-68; University of Kansas, Lawrence, assistant professor, 1968-72, associate professor of history, 1973—. Visiting assistant professor at Occidental College, summer, 1969; fellow at Harvard University Law School, 1973-74. Moderator of "History in Today's World," on KANU-Radio. *Member:* Organization of American Historians, Society for the Study of Legal History, Phi Alpha Theta. *Awards, honors:* American Council of Learned Societies fellowship, 1973-74, 1975; American Philosophical Society grant, 1977.

WRITINGS: Covenant with Death: The Constitution, Law and Equality in the Civil War Era, University of Illinois Press, 1975. General editor of "Enduring Issues in the American Past," Heath, 1977—. Contributor to history journals.

WORK IN PROGRESS: Victims: A True Story of the Civil War; The North in the Civil War, completion expected in 1981.

SIDELIGHTS: Paludan comments: "I am avidly interested in teaching—in inducing learning and in helping future teachers of history question why they are doing what they are doing and to whom they are doing it.

"I have been involved in the alternative education reform movement, in reading science fiction, and in sustaining my wife's career as a dancer."

* * *

PAOLUCCI, Anne

PERSONAL: Born in Rome, Italy; came to the United States in 1934, naturalized citizen, 1934; daughter of Joseph and Lucy (Guidoni) Attura; married Henry Paolucci. Education: Barnard College, B.A., 1947; Columbia University, M.A., 1961, Ph.D., 1963; also attended University of Perugia, 1951-52, and University of Rome, 1951-52. Home: 166-25 Powells Cove Blvd., Beachhurst, N.Y. 11357. Office: St. John's University, Jamaica, N.Y. 11349.

CAREER: Teacher of English at private schools in Rye, N.Y., 1955-57, and New York City, 1957-59; City College of the City University of New York, New York City, assistant professor of English, 1959-69; St. John's University, Jamaica, N.Y., university research professor, 1969-77, professor of English and comparative literature, 1977—. Special lecturer at universities throughout U.S. and Canada, and at Universities of Bologna, Catania, Messina, Palermo, Milan, Innsbruck, and Pisa, 1965-67, University of Bari, 1967, University of Urbino, summer, 1967; Fulbright lecturer in American drama at University of Naples, 1965-67. Founder and executive director of Council on National Literatures, 1974—; member of board of directors of World Centre for Shakespeare Studies, 1972—; executive producer and chairman of dramatizations "Rape Italian Style" and "Pirandello: Open-Ended Discussion on Stage." Organized television series "Magazines in Focus," NYC-Television, 1972-73, and "Successful Women: Before, During, and After Women's Lib," ABC-Television, 1973; theatrical producer and director; participated in television programs since 1969. Member of American Commission to Screen Fulbright Applicants for the United States, 1966, 1967; founder of American Playwrights' and Producers' Showcase (Naples), 1967; special guest of Yugoslav Ministry of Culture, 1972; member of advisory board of Casa Italiana at Columbia University, 1975-76. Consultant to National Endowment for the Humanities, 1977—.

MEMBER: International Comparative Literature Association, American Institute of Italian Studies (member of board of advisors, 1977—), American Comparative Literature Association, P.E.N. American Center, Modern Language Association of America (member of executive committee, 1975—), Dante Society of America (member of council, 1974-76; vice-president, 1976-77), Pirandello Society of America (founding member and vice-president, 1968—), Byron Society of America and England (founding member of advisory board, 1973—), Alpha Psi Omega, Barnard Alumni Association, Andiron Club of New York (honorary member). Awards, honors: Fulbright scholar at University of

Rome, 1951-52; Artemesia Award from Quicksilver, 1961, for "Poetry Reading"; New York State grants, 1963, 1964, 1964-65; writer in residence at Yaddo Colony, 1965; award from American-Italian Women of Achievement, 1970; drama award from Medieval and Renaissance Conference at Western Michigan University, 1972, for play "Minions of the Race"; woman of the year award from Herman Henry Scholarship Foundation, 1973; award from Woman's Press Club of New York, 1974.

WRITINGS: (Translator) Machiavelli's Mandragola, Liberal Arts Press, 1957; (translator) Henry Paolucci and James Brophy, Pierre Duhem on Galileo, Twayne, 1962; (with husband, Henry Paolucci) Hegel on Tragedy, Anchor Books, 1962; (editor) Shakespeare Encomium, City College Papers I, 1964; (author of introduction) Eric Bentley, editor, Genius of the Italian Theater, New American Library, 1964; A Short History of American Drama, University of Urbino Press, 1966; Eugene O'Neill, Arthur Miller, Edward Albee, University of Urbino Press, 1967; Commenti critici su Giulio Cesare, Macbeth, Amleto, Otello (title means "Critical Observations on Julius Ceasar, Macbeth, Hamlet, Othello"), University of Urbino Press, 1967.

From Tension to Tonic: The Plays of Edward Albee, Southern Illinois University Press, 1972; Pirandello's Theater: The Recovery of the Modern Stage for Dramatic Art, Southern Illinois University Press, 1974; (editor and author of introduction) Canada, Griffon House Publications, 1977; Eight Short Stories, Griffon House Publications, 1977; Poems for Sbek's Mummies, Marie Mencken and Other People, Places, and Things, Griffon House Publications, 1977; (editor and author of introduction) Dante's Influence on American Writers, Griffon House Publications, 1977.

Plays: "The Short Season" (three-act), first produced in New York, N.Y., at Cubiculo, May, 1970; "Minions of the Race" (one-act), first produced in Kalamazoo, Mich., at Western Michigan University, May, 1972; "In the Green Room (with Machiavelli)" (one-act), first presented as a reading at Ashland Shakespeare Festival, summer, 1974; "Incident at the Great Wall" (one-act), first produced in New York City at Churchyard Theater, January, 1976; (translator) Mario Apollonio, "The Apocalypse According to J.J." (three-act), first produced in New York City at Classic Theatre, Spring, 1976.

Editor of forty-tape cassette series on China, for Edward/Everett Co. Contributor of about eighty poems, stories, articles, and reviews to magazines, including Ararat, Poem, South Carolina Review, Kenyon Review, and Shakespeare Quarterly. Founder and editor of Review of National Literatures and CNL/Report, both 1970—, and CNL/Quarterly World Report, 1978—; member of editorial board of Barnard Alumnae, 1969-71, and Pirandello Newsletter, 1972; member of advisory board of Italian-Americana, 1973—, America-Latina, 1975—, and Gradiva, 1977—.

WORK IN PROGRESS: A book on Hegel and Shakespeare; a book of collected plays.

* * *

PARADIS, Marjorie Bartholomew 1886(?)-1970

PERSONAL: Born about 1886, in Montclair, N.J.; married Adrian F. Paradis. Education: Attended Columbia University.

CAREER: Author of children's books and playwright.

WRITINGS: A Dinner of Herbs, Century, 1928; The Caddis, Century, 1929; The New Freedom: A Comedy in Three

Acts (play), Samuel French, 1931; *It Happened One Day: A Novel*, Harper, 1932; (with Adele Louise De Leeuw) *Golden Shadow*, Macmillan, 1951; *Timmy and the Tiger* (illustrated by Marc Simont), Harper, 1952; *One-Act Plays for All-Girl Casts*, Plays, 1952; *Midge Bennett of Duncan Hall*, Abelard, 1953; *Time Is Now*, Abelard, 1953; (with De Leeuw) *Dear Stepmother*, Macmillan, 1956; *Maid of Honor*, Dodd, 1959; *Mr. De Luca's Horse* (illustrated by Judith Brown), Atheneum, 1962; *Flash Flood at Hollow Creek* (illustrated by Albert F. Michini), Westminster Press, 1963; *Jeanie* (illustrated by Alex Stein), Westminster Press, 1963; *Too Many Fathers* (illustrated by Charles Geer), Atheneum, 1963.

AVOCATIONAL INTERESTS: Portrait painting, hooking rugs.

OBITUARIES: New York Times, July 8, 1970; *Antiquarian Bookman,* September 14, 1970.*

(Died July 2, 1970)

*   *   *

PARENTI, Michael 1933-

PERSONAL: Born September 30, 1933, in New York, N.Y.; son of Michael and Rena (DiLorenzo) Parenti; divorced, 1970; children: Christian. *Education:* City College (now of the City University of New York), B.A. (cum laude), 1955; Brown University, M.A., 1957; Yale University, Ph.D., 1962. *Politics:* "Radical Socialist." *Religion:* "Meditation, cosmology." *Home and office:* 83 North Prospect St., Amherst, Mass. 01002.

CAREER: State University of New York at Stoneybrook, Stoneybrook, assistant professor of political science, 1960-65; Sarah Lawrence College, Bronxville, N.Y., taught political science, 1965-67; University of Illinois, Urbana, visiting associate professor of political science, 1969-70; University of Vermont, Burlington, associate professor of political science, 1970-72; Cornell University, Ithaca, N.Y., visiting professor of government, 1975-76; writer, 1976—. Public lecturer at universities and high schools, and on radio and television programs. *Awards, honors:* Social Science Research Council grant, 1967-68; Ford Foundation grant, 1972-73; and other research grants.

WRITINGS: The Anti-Communist Impulse, Random House, 1969; (editor) *Trends and Tragedies in American Foreign Policy,* Little, Brown, 1971; *Democracy for the Few,* St. Martin's, 1974, 2nd edition, 1977; *Ethnic and Political Attitudes of Italian Americans,* Arno, 1975; *Power and the Powerless,* St. Martin's, 1978. Contributor of about thirty articles to academic journals and periodicals, including *Society, Progressive,* and *Commonweal,* and to newspapers.

WORK IN PROGRESS: A series of autobiographical essays about Italian-American life and political activism; a study of capitalism, socialism, and alternative institutions.

SIDELIGHTS: Parenti told *CA:* "I have developed a critical socialist perspective of American politico-economic institutions and their effects on American life and culture. This has become the basis for much of my recent work. I have been active in the civil rights and anti-war movements and have done political organizing for radical causes in Illinois, Vermont, and Connecticut."

*   *   *

PARISH, David 1932-

PERSONAL: Born October 3, 1932, in Niagara Falls,

N.Y.; son of Wheaton H. and Alma (Kurkowski) Parish; married Ava H. Hughart, November 23, 1963; children: David Andrew. *Education:* Buffalo State Teachers College, B.S., 1954, M.S., 1961; University of Buffalo, Ed.M., 1960; State University of New York College at Geneseo, M.L.S., 1967, graduate study, 1974—. *Religion:* Methodist. *Home:* 5 Crossett Rd., Geneseo, N.Y. 14454. *Office:* Milne Library, State University of New York College at Geneseo, Geneseo, N.Y. 14454.

CAREER: Reading teacher in elementary public schools in Niagara Falls, N.Y., 1957-66; State University of New York College at Geneseo, academic librarian, 1967—, head of government publication section. Co-chairman of State Government Document Planning Committee, 1973-75; member of Geneseo Campus United Ministry Council. *Military service:* U.S. Army, 1956-57.

MEMBER: American Library Association, National Education Association, New York State Library Association, State University Professionals, State University of New York Library Association, Phi Delta Kappa, Masons. *Awards, honors:* Grant from Geneseo Foundation, 1973.

WRITINGS: (With Sally Wynkoop) *Directory of Government Agencies,* Libraries Unlimited, 1969; *Milne Library State Classification Scheme* (pamphlet), Milne Library, State University of New York College at Geneseo, 1969; *State Government Reference Publications: An Annotated Bibliography,* Libraries Unlimited, 1974; *Bibliography of U.S. and State Government Bibliographies* (monograph), State University of New York College at Geneseo, 1975; *The Church in the Valley: History of the Geneseo United Methodist Church,* privately printed, 1975; *Changes in U.S. Society, 1960-1975, as Reflected in Official Government Publications,* Libraries Unlimited, 1976; (editor with Ivan L. Kaldor and Stephen Torok, and contributor) *Proceedings of the First Annual Government Document Workshop,* School of Library and Information Science, State University of New York College at Geneseo, 1976.

Author of a column on popular state publications for *Government Publications Review,* 1976—. Contributor to local and professional journals. Co-editor of *Government Document Task Force Newsletter,* 1973—, and *Livingstone,* 1973—; editor of *Trestle-Board,* 1976—.

WORK IN PROGRESS: History of Livingstone County Mutual Insurance Co.

*   *   *

PARISH, Peggy 1927-

PERSONAL: Born in 1927, in Manning, S.C.; daughter of Herman and Cecil (Rogers) Parish. *Education:* University of South Carolina, graduated, 1948; graduate study at Peabody College, 1950. *Residence:* New York, N.Y.

CAREER: Writer. Has also worked as a teacher in Texas and New York, as an instructor in creative dancing, and in advertising. *Member:* Authors Guild.

WRITINGS: My Golden Book of Manners (illustrated by Richard Scarry), Golden Press, 1962; *Good Hunting Little Indian* (illustrated by Leonard Weisgard), Young Scott Books, 1962; *Let's Be Indians* (illustrated by Arnold Lobel), Harper, 1962; *Willy Is My Brother* (illustrated by Shirley Hughes), W. R. Scott, 1963; *Amelia Bedelia* (illustrated by Fritz Siebel), Harper, 1963; *Thank You, Amelia Bedelia* (illustrated by Siebel), Harper, 1964; *The Story of Grains: Wheat, Corn, and Rice,* Grosset, 1965; *Amelia Bedelia and the Surprise Shower* (illustrated by Siebel), Harper, 1966;

Key to the Rescue (illustrated by Paul Frame), Macmillan, 1966; *Let's Be Early Settlers With Daniel Boone* (illustrated by Lobel), Harper, 1967; *Clues in the Woods* (illustrated by Frame), Macmillan, 1968; *Little Indian* (illustrated by John E. Johnson), Simon & Schuster, 1968; *A Beastly Circus* (illustrated by Peter Parnall), Simon & Schuster, 1969; *Jumper Goes to School* (illustrated by Cyndy Szekeres), Simon & Schuster, 1969; *Granny and the Indians* (illustrated by Brinton Turkle), Macmillan, 1969.

Ootah's Lucky Day (illustrated by Mamoru Funai), Harper, 1970; *Granny and the Desperadoes* (illustrated by Steven Kellogg), Macmillan, 1970; *Costumes to Make* (illustrated by Lynn Sweat), Macmillan, 1970; *Snapping Turtle's All Wrong Day* (illustrated by Johnson), Simon & Schuster, 1970; *Sheet Magic: Games, Toys, and Gifts from Old Sheets* (illustrated by Sweat), Macmillan, 1971; *Haunted House* (illustrated by Frame), Macmillan, 1971; *Come Back, Amelia Bedelia* (illustrated by Wallace Tripp), Harper, 1971; *Granny, the Baby, and the Big Gray Thing* (illustrated by Sweat), Macmillan, 1972; *Play Ball, Amelia Bedelia* (illustrated by Tripp), Harper, 1972; *Too Many Rabbits* (illustrated by Leonard Kessler), Macmillan, 1974; *Dinosaur Time* (illustrated by Lobel), Harper, 1974; *December Decorations: A Holiday How-To Book* (illustrated by Barbara Wolff), Macmillan, 1975; *Pirate Island Adventure* (illustrated by Frame), Macmillan, 1975; *Good Work, Amelia Bedelia* (illustrated by Sweat), Morrow, 1976; *Let's Celebrate: Holiday Decorations You Can Make* (illustrated by Sweat), Morrow, 1976; *Teach Us, Amelia Bedelia* (illustrated by Sweat), Morrow, 1977.*

* * *

PARK, Ed 1930-

PERSONAL: Born February 16, 1930, in Roseburg, Ore.; son of H. N. (a builder) and Helen (Everest) Park; married second wife, Lue Fenn (a writer and photographer), April 14, 1973; children: Alice, Alan, Dale. *Education:* Oregon State College, B.S., 1955, M.S., 1959. *Politics:* "Very independent." *Religion:* Baptist. *Home and office address:* P.O. Box 887, Bend, Ore. 97701.

CAREER: South Dakota Department of Game, Fish & Parks, Pierre, photographer, 1959-61; free-lance writer and photographer, 1961—. *Military service:* U.S. Army, Counter Intelligence Corps, 1951-53. *Member:* Outdoor Writers Association of America (member of board of directors, 1976-79), Northwest Outdoor Writers Association (president, 1976). *Awards, honors:* Several dozen awards for photography since 1961.

WRITINGS: The World of the Bison, Lippincott, 1969; *The World of the Otter,* Lippincott, 1971. Contributor of several hundred articles to magazines, including *Outdoor Life, Field and Stream, Sports Afield, National Wildlife, Outdoors, True, Angler,* and *Audubon.*

WORK IN PROGRESS: The Sportsmans World of Maps, for McKay.

SIDELIGHTS: Park comments: "Most all of my work has been articles and photographs, published in all the major outdoor magazines in this country. Hunting, fishing, wildlife, camping, travel, boating, and other outdoor activities make up the bulk of my writings."

* * *

PARKER, Richard 1915-

PERSONAL: Born in 1915. *Home:* 36 Central Parade, Herne Bay, Kent, England.

CAREER: Formerly employed as a librarian and teacher; novelist and author of fiction for children.

WRITINGS: A Camel from the Desert (illustrated by Biro), Sylvan Press, 1947; *Penguin Goes Home* (illustrated by Biro), Chatto & Windus, 1951; *Six Plays for Boys,* Methuen, 1951; *Only Some Had Guns,* Collins, 1952; *The Gingerbread Man,* Collins, 1953, Scribner, 1954; *A Moor of Spain: The Story of a Rogue* (illustrated by John Harwood), Penguin, 1953; *Seven Plays for Boys,* Methuen, 1953; *A Kind of Misfortune,* Collins, 1954, Scribner, 1955; *Harm Intended,* Collins, 1954, Scribner, 1956; *Draughts in the Sun,* Collins, 1955; *The Three Pebbles* (illustrated by William Ferguson), McKay, 1956; *The Sword of the Ganelon* (illustrated by Ferguson), Collins, 1957, McKay, 1958; *Brother Turgar and the Vikings* (illustrated by Joan Milroy), Ginn, 1959; *The Kidnapped Crusaders* (illustrated by Richard Kennedy), Ginn, 1959.

More Snakes than Ladders (illustrated by Jillian Willett), Brockhampton, 1960, published in America as *Almost Lost* (illustrated by Leonard Shortall), Thomas Nelson, 1962; *The Green Highwayman* (illustrated by Kennedy), Ginn, 1960; *Fiddler's Place,* P. Davies, 1961; *New Home South* (illustrated by Prudence Seward), Brockhampton, 1961; *Voyage to Tasmania* (illustrated by Seward), Bobbs-Merrill, 1961; *Lion at Large* (illustrated by Kurt Werth), Thomas Nelson, 1961; *A Valley Full of Pipers* (illustrated by Kennedy), Bobbs-Merrill, 1962; *Goodbye to the Bush* (illustrated by Kenneth Brown), Ginn, 1963; *Killer,* Doubleday, 1964; *The House That Guilda Drew* (illustrated by Mamoru Funai), Bobbs-Merrill, 1964; *Boy on a Chain,* P. Davies, 1964; *Perversity of Pipers* (illustrated by Kennedy), Van Nostrand, 1964; *Private Beach* (illustrated by Victor Ambrus), Harrap, 1964, Duell, Sloan, 1965; *The Boy Who Wasn't Lonely* (illustrated by James J. Spanfeller), Brockhampton, 1964, Bobbs-Merrill, 1965.

Second-Hand Family (illustrated by Gareth Floyd), Brockhampton, 1965, Bobbs-Merrill, 1966; *M for Mischief* (illustrated by Juan Ballesta), Constable, 1965, Duell, Sloan, 1966; *One White Mouse* (illustrated by Rene Hummerstone), Brockhampton, 1966, published in America as *No House for a Mouse* (illustrated by W. T. Mars), Follett, 1968, and as *The Impossible Pet,* Scholastic Book Services, 1972; *New in the Neighborhood,* Duell, Sloan, 1966; *The Punch Back Gang* (illustrated by John Plant), Harrap, 1966; *The Hendon Fungus,* Meredith Press, 1968; *A Sheltering Tree,* Meredith Press, 1969; *The Old Powder Line,* Thomas Nelson, 1971; *Spell Seven* (illustrated by Trevor Ridley), Thomas Nelson, 1971; *Paul and Etta* (illustrated by Gavin Row), Thomas Nelson, 1973; *A Time to Choose,* Hutchinson, 1973, Harper, 1974; *Three by Mistake,* Thomas Nelson, 1974; *He Is Your Brother* (illustrated by Floyd), Brockhampton, 1974, Thomas Nelson, 1976; *Snatched* (illustrated by Peter Kesteven), David & Charles, 1974; *Boy into Action* (illustrated by Trevor Parkin), Abelard, 1975; *Beyond the Back Gate* (illustrated by Peter Dennis), Abelard, 1975; *The Quarter Boy,* Thomas Nelson, 1976; *In and Out the Window,* Hutchinson, 1976.

SIDELIGHTS: Gingerbread Man, one of Richard Parker's earliest novels, was reviewed by a *New York Times* critic, who wrote; "It's a fine job in every respect—off-trail, refreshing, and exciting. And the excellent depiction of the barely tangential worlds of children and adults may well stay in your mind as long as *High Wind in Jamaica." New Statesman and Nation* commented; "The formula is hackneyed; but Mr. Parker writes well enough to work up a continuous feeling of excitement."

"It's an excellent suspense story in every respect," wrote the *New York Times* of *Harm Intended,* "superlatively written and plotted, with fine examples of detection by the community as a whole. But what you'll remember most is the children, each a fully characterized individual, all wonderfully authentic and alive in their reactions to each other, to their parents, and to the threat of crime."

Commenting on *Lion at Large,* a critic for the *New York Times Book Review* wrote: "This story races along at a fine pace; the dialogue is good, much of it very funny, and there is intrigue, danger and a spine-tingling climax. Through it all the characters seem as real as the youngsters down the block."

"Richard Parker is a vigorous writer with a strong feeling for situation," noted the London *Times Literary Supplement* in its review of *Private Beach.* "In the present book, whose plot is perhaps not intense enough for his energy, he experiments, not unsuccessfully, with that kind of apparently inconsequential spoken thought more usually associated with the style of William Mayne."

BIOGRAPHICAL/CRITICAL SOURCES: New Statesman and Nation, January 9, 1954; *New York Times,* July 25, 1954, July 29, 1956; *New York Times Book Review,* May 14, 1961; *Times Literary Supplement* (London), July 9, 1964.*

* * *

PARKER, Thomas F(rancis) 1932-

PERSONAL: Born October 3, 1932, in Joplin, Mo.; son of Robert Leo (a geologist) and Mary Susan (a teacher; maiden name, Brown) Parker; married Barbara Kathleen Brennan (a registered nurse), August 20, 1955; children: Joseph D., Gregory J., Sara M. *Education:* St. Louis University, student, 1956-59; Tulane University, B.A., 1960, M.A., 1961; University of California, Los Angeles, M.L.S., 1965. *Home:* 306 South Keystone, Burbank, Calif. 91506. *Office:* 3400 West Alameda, Suite 204, Burbank, Calif. 91505.

CAREER: City-County Library, Tulsa, Okla., branch librarian, 1961-63; Burbank Public Library, Burbank, Calif., librarian, 1963-65; University of California, Los Angeles, research librarian, 1965-67, reference librarian, 1967-69, systems librarian, 1969-71; director of research project sponsored by California Institute of Technology, University of California, Los Angeles, and University of Southern California, 1972-74; management systems analyst and consultant in Burbank, Calif., 1974—. *Military service:* U.S. Navy, 1950-53. *Member:* American Library Association, American Association of Information Science, Society for General Systems Research.

WRITINGS: Violence in the United States, 1956-1971, two volumes, Facts on File, 1974. Contributor to library and history journals.

WORK IN PROGRESS: Research on the communication of information in graphic form, and on production of information combining text and visuals.

SIDELIGHTS: Parker writes: "In an age of information explosion there is a dire need for more efficient techniques of information display than text—the linear medium that has carried us so far in the last five hundred years. Visual or graphic information is a simultaneous medium. Combined with text information it offers far more effectiveness in communication. This is the area of my current focus."

* * *

PARLATO, Salvatore J(oseph), Jr. 1936-

PERSONAL: Born February 26, 1931, in Buffalo, N.Y.; son of Salvatore J. (a physician) and Elizabeth (a musician; maiden name, Gugino) Parlato; married Dolores Frates (a radio artist), November 29, 1958. *Education:* Holy Cross College, Worcester, Mass., A.B., 1953; Syracuse University, M.S., 1961. *Politics:* "Constitutional Socialist." *Religion:* Roman Catholic. *Home:* 235 Gould St., Rochester, N.Y. 14610. *Office:* Rochester School for the Deaf, 1545 St. Paul St., Rochester, N.Y. 14621.

CAREER: Encyclopaedia Britannica Films, New York, N.Y., district manager, 1961-69; National Technical Institute for the Deaf, Rochester, N.Y., assistant professor of communications and media coordinator, 1969-73; U.S. Office of Education, Bureau for the Education of the Handicapped, Rochester School for the Deaf, Rochester, N.Y., national coordinator of U.S. Office of Education Captioned Educational Films, 1973—. President of Americanadian Publishers and Producers. Instructor at Rochester Institute of Technology, 1974—, adjunct professor, 1975—. Consultant to World Health Organization. *Military service:* U.S. Marine Corps, 1954-56.

MEMBER: Western New York Educational Communications Association (charter member), Opera Theatre of Rochester (member of board of directors and corporate secretary), Rochester Audio-Visual Association, Rochester and Environs Society for Organizing Unified Resources of Communication and Educational Services.

WRITINGS: Audio Visual Advisor, privately printed, 1960, 2nd edition, 1964; *Films Too Good for Words,* Bowker, 1973; *Superfilms: Educational Award-Winners,* Scarecrow, 1976; *Films Ex Libris: Films from Books,* American Library Association, in press. Contributor to magazines, including *International Development Review, Sightlines, Previews,* and *Media and Methods, A-V Instruction,* and *Lifelong Learning.*

WORK IN PROGRESS: Audio Visual Advisor, 3rd edition; *Filmography on Noise Pollution,* for National Safety Council; *Freeze-Frame,* an analytic monograph on the 16mm film industry.

SIDELIGHTS: Parlato writes: "I always used to wonder about those ads that said, 'Make money writing short paragraphs.' Never did check into them but did manage to find out what they meant when I gave up trying to sell my political fiction novel and concentrated instead on media reference books for libraries and schools. The principal one of these is an annual directory I consider too pivotal and important to identify above—an editor's paranoia I'm still unwilling to part with!"

BIOGRAPHICAL/CRITICAL SOURCES: Rochester Advocate, January, 1977.

* * *

PARRISH, Wendy 1950-

PERSONAL: Born March 2, 1950, in Glencoe, Minn.; daughter of Stanley (a businessman) and Marian Parrish. *Education:* Macalester College, B.A., 1972. *Home:* 171 Vernon St., St. Paul, Minn. 55105.

CAREER: Writer. Teacher at school in St. Paul, Minn., 1971-72, 1975-76, and Macalester College, St. Paul, 1976. Participated in poets-in-the-schools program, St. Paul, 1971-73.

WRITINGS: Conversations in the Gallery (poems), New Rivers Press, 1978. Contributor to magazines, including *Antioch Review, Seneca Review,* and *Northeast.*

WORK IN PROGRESS: Two mystery novels with Deborah Keenan; a second collection of poetry.

* * *

PARSONS, Thornton H(arris)   1921-

PERSONAL: Born September 7, 1921, in Old Town, Me.; son of Charles H. and Martha (Harris) Parsons; married Doris M. Brison, June 16, 1949; children: Alane Rosalind. *Education:* Indiana State College (now University), A.B., 1950; University of Michigan, M.A., 1952, Ph.D., 1959. *Home:* 109 Dorset Rd., Syracuse, N.Y. 13210. *Office:* Department of English, Syracuse University, Syracuse, N.Y. 13210.

CAREER: High school English teacher in Washington, Ind., 1950-51; Eastern Michigan College (now University), Ypsilanti, instructor in English, 1956-58; University of Michigan, Ann Arbor, instructor in English, 1959; Syracuse University, Syracuse, N.Y., assistant professor, 1959-63, associate professor, 1963-69, professor of English, 1969—. Fulbright lecturer at Charles University, 1969-70. *Military service:* U.S. Coast Guard, 1943-46; became radioman first class. *Member:* Modern Language Association of America.

WRITINGS: (Editor with Myron Simon) *Transcendentalism and Its Legacy,* University of Michigan Press, 1966; *John Crowe Ransom,* Twayne, 1969. Contributor to literary journals.

WORK IN PROGRESS: Critical studies of American short fiction and poetry.

* * *

PASINETTI, P(ier-) M(aria)   1913-

PERSONAL: Born June 24, 1913, in Venice, Italy; came to the United States, 1946, naturalized, 1952; son of Carlo and Maria (Ciardi) Pasinetti. *Education:* University of Padua, Dottore in Lettere, 1935; Yale University, Ph.D., 1949. *Home:* 1421 Summitridge Dr., Beverly Hills, Calif. 90210. *Office:* 1259 Dorsoduro, Venice, Italy 30123.

CAREER: Louisiana State University, Baton Rouge, fellow, 1935-36; University of California, Berkeley, fellow, 1936-37; University of Stockholm, Stockholm, Sweden, lecturer, 1942-46; University of California, Los Angeles, lecturer in Italian and humanities, 1949—. *Member:* Authors Guild, Elizabethan Club (Yale University). *Awards, honors:* National Institute of Arts and Letters awards for fiction, 1965.

WRITINGS: (Editor) *Great Italian Short Stories,* Dell, 1959; *Rosso Veneziano* (novel), C. Colombo (Rome), 1959, translation by the author published as *Venetian Red,* Random House, 1960, revised edition of original, Bompiani (Milan), 1965; *La Confusione* (novel), Bompiani, 1964, translation by the author published as *The Smile on the Face of the Lion,* Random House, 1965; *Il ponte dell'Accademia* (novel), Bompiani, 1968, translation by the author published as *From the Academy Bridge: A Novel,* Random House, 1970; *Domani improvvisamente* (novel), Bompiani, 1971, translation by the author published as *Suddenly Tomorrow: A Novel,* Random House, 1973. Author of film scripts. Contributor of articles and reviews to journals.*

* * *

PASTERNAK, Velvel   1933-

PERSONAL: Born October 1, 1933, in Toronto, Ontario, Canada; came to the United States in 1960; son of Hyman (a garment worker) and Annie (Rosengarten) Pasternak; married Goldie Garber, December 29, 1957; children: Shira, Mayer, Naava, Atara, Gadi. *Education:* Yeshiva University, B.A., 1955; attended Juilliard School of Music, 1956; Columbia University, M.A., 1957. *Religion:* Jewish. *Home and office:* 29 Derby Ave., Cedarhurst, N.Y. 11516.

CAREER: Yeshiva University, New York City, instructor at the Cantorial Training Institute, 1959-65; Touro College, New York City, chairperson of music department and associate professor of Jewish music, 1973—. President of Tara Publications. Chief consultant for Hassidic Dance in Ritual and Celebration grant of National Endowment for the Humanities, 1975-76. Member of music council of Jewish Welfare Board. *Member:* Jewish Liturgical Music Society, Guild of Jewish Musicians. *Awards, honors:* Grant from Memorial Foundation for Jewish Culture, 1969-70.

WRITINGS: Songs of the Chassidim, Bloch Publishing, 1968; *Songs of the Chassidim II,* Bloch Publishing, 1971; *Hassidic Favorites,* Tara Publications, 1972; *Rejoice-Songs in Modern Hassidic Style,* Tara Publications, 1973; *Israel in Song,* Tara Publications, 1974; *Great Songs of Israel,* Tara Publications, 1976; *Hassidic Hits,* Tara Publications, 1977.

WORK IN PROGRESS: A documented study of the Hassidic group in the United States and Israel, with particular emphasis on their contribution to the repertoire of Jewish song.

SIDELIGHTS: Pasternak stated that he is the only researcher in the United States working on Hassidic music, an aspect of East European Jewish music beginning in the mid-1700's. "My books are designed to perpetuate an oral tradition of East European Jewry," he explained. "Because these songs make up the musical repertoire of several hundred thousand Orthodox Jews in the United States they have proved extremely functional. This material is now being taught in most Jewish schools throughout the United States and Israel."

* * *

PATEMAN, Kim
See LEVIN, Kim

* * *

PATTERSON, Lillie G.

PERSONAL: Born on Hilton Head Island, S.C.; daughter of Alexander and Maria Patterson. *Education:* Attended Hampton Institute, Catholic University of America, Johns Hopkins University, and New York University. *Home:* 3222 Burleith Ave., Baltimore, Md. 21215.

CAREER: Assistant librarian, Morgan State University, Baltimore, Md.,; began as school librarian, became library specialist, currently educational specialist with Baltimore City Schools. *Awards, honors:* Coretta Scott King Award, 1970, for *Martin Luther King, Jr.: Man of Peace.*

WRITINGS—All published by Garrard, except as noted: *Booker T. Washington: Leader of His People* (illustrated by Anthony D'Adamo), 1962; *Meet Miss Liberty,* Macmillan, 1962; *Francis Scott Key: Poet and Patriot* (illustrated by Vic Dowd), 1963; *Halloween* (illustrated by Gil Miret), 1963; *Birthdays* (illustrated by Erica Merkling) 1965; *Frederick Douglass: Freedom Fighter* (illustrated by Gray Morrow), 1965; *Easter* (illustrated by Kelly Oechsli), 1966; *Lumberjacks of the North Woods* (illustrated by Victor Mays), 1967; *Christmas Feasts and Festivals* (illustrated by Cliff Schule), 1968; *Christmas in America* (illustrated by Vincent Colabella), 1969; *Martin Luther King, Jr.: Man of Peace* (illustrated by Mays), 1969; *Christmas in Britain and Scandinavia* (illustrated by Oechsli), 1970; (editor) *Poetry for Spring* (illustrated by Oechsli), 1973; *Sequoyah: The Cherokee Who Captured Words* (illustrated by Herman B. Vestal), 1975; *Coretta Scott King,* 1977, *Benjamin Bannekec: Genius of Early America,* Abingdon, 1977.

WORK IN PROGRESS: Two biographies for children, one about Daniel Hale Williams, a pioneer in open heart surgery, and another on James Weldon Johnson.

SIDELIGHTS: Patterson wrote to *CA:* "Out of my years of working with children, and training librarians, I feel that I have a solid background on children's reading interests, which grow more and more complex. My topics for writing grow out of gaps that exist in the juvenile book field, and out of my own beliefs in what children will read. Letters reach me weekly from young readers letting me know what one of the books I have written has said to a child. I enjoy research and will make my research as exhaustive for a simple text of less than 10,000 words as I would have done for a multi-volume work on a biographical subject. From this mass of information I try to capture something of the spirit of the individual so that young readers will take inspiration from the life and will be lead to more mature works."

AVOCATIONAL INTERESTS: Reading, sports of all kinds, music, walking, gardening.

BIOGRAPHICAL/CRITICAL SOURCES: New York Times Book Review, May 4, 1969.

* * *

PATTERSON, Robert B(enjamin) 1934-

PERSONAL: Born April 30, 1934, in West Hartford, Conn.; son of Charles McGrath (a chemical sales representative) and Marie (a teacher; maiden name, Schaettle) Patterson; married Ruth Weider (an organization director), May 28, 1960; children: Anne Elizabeth, Robert Benjamin, Jr. *Education:* St. Bernard's College and Seminary, B.A., 1956; Trinity College, Hartford, Conn., M.A., 1958; Johns Hopkins University, Ph.D., 1962. *Home:* 3623 Devereaux Rd., Columbia, S.C. 29205. *Office:* Department of History, University of South Carolina, Columbia, S.C. 29208.

CAREER: University of South Carolina, Columbia, assistant professor, 1962-66, associate professor, 1966-71, professor of history, 1971—. Visiting assistant professor at Trinity College, Hartford, Conn., summer, 1964; visiting associate professor at University of Connecticut, 1965-66; lecturer at Merton College, Oxford, 1975-76. *Military service:* U.S. Marine Corps Reserve, 1958-64, active duty, 1958-59.

MEMBER: American Association of University Professors, American Historical Association, Mediaeval Academy of America, Conference on British Studies, Southern Historical Association, Connecticut Historical Society. *Awards, honors:* Woodrow Wilson fellowship, 1960-62; National Endowment for the Humanities fellowship, 1967.

WRITINGS: (Editor) *Earldom of Gloucester Charters: The Charters and Scribes of the Earls and Countesses of Gloucester to A.D. 1217,* Clarendon Press, 1973. Contributor of articles and reviews to history journals.

WORK IN PROGRESS: A Family of Earls in Norman and Early Angevin England; Robert Earl of Gloucester, William of Malmesbury, and the Emerging English Constitution.

SIDELIGHTS: Patterson told *CA:* "I became interested in the earls of Gloucester in stages. The first earl, Robert, eldest, but illegitimate son of King Henry I of England, first attracted me because he was the principal leader of the civil war which made the succession of Henry II ultimately possible. Earl Robert and his baronial colleagues who opposed King Stephen affected the development of the English 'constitution' by promoting the recognition of theoretical limitations on monarchy and of certain rights enjoyed by freemen (albeit aristocratic ones), not the least being the legitimacy of withholding service or of rebellion as a sanction against broken royal promises. Earl Robert was the epitome of these principles and was the literary patron of one of their most articulate proponents, the historian, William of Malmesbury.

"The next level of interest was the Gloucester family itself, a dynasty which retained its earldom until 1217. For one thing, various members were attractive subjects because they played key roles in English politics between the reign of Henry I and Henry III's accession. The saga of Countess Isabel, Earl Robert's granddaughter, whose career included two royal wardships, three marriages, one divorce, and one widowhood has contributed greatly to a long chapter on the status of aristocratic women in the middle ages. The family's history provides a model of the manner in which England's aristocratic system operated in what historians have regarded as the 'classic' age of English feudalism.

"On yet another level, historians are by nature hunters and detectives; so an added attraction was the sheer enjoyment of what I have called 'manuscript safari,' a systematic search for unprinted and sometimes unknown manuscript sources in private and public collections from Glasgow to Petersfield and from Aberystwyth in Wales to Paris. I found so much manuscript material, particularly charters written for the earls and countesses, that I decided to write a separate paleographical study which would include a critical edition of all of the extant charters and an analysis of the clerical administrations which had produced them."

* * *

PAULSEN, Gary 1939-

PERSONAL: Born May 17, 1939, in Minneapolis, Minn.; son of Oscar and Eunice Paulsen; married second wife, Ruth Ellen Wright (an artist), May 5, 1971; children: James Wright. *Education:* Attended Bemidji College, 1957-58; and University of Colorado, 1976. *Politics:* "As Solzhenitsyn has said, 'If we limit ourselves to political structures we are not artists.'" *Religion:* "I believe in spiritual progress." *Home and office address:* Box 123, Elbert, Colo. 80106. *Agent:* Ray Peekner Literary Agency, 2625 North 36th St., Milwaukee, Wis. 53210.

CAREER: Has worked variously as a teacher, electronics field engineer, soldier, actor, director, farmer, rancher, truck driver, trapper, professional archer, migrant farm worker, singer, and sailor; now a full-time writer. *Military service:* U.S. Army, 1959-62; became sergeant. *Awards, honors:* Central Missouri Award for Children's Literature, 1976.

WRITINGS—Novels: *The Implosion Effect,* Major Books, 1976; *The Death Specialists,* Major Books, 1976; *Winterkill,* Thomas Nelson, 1977; *The Foxman,* Thomas Nelson, 1977; *Tiltawhirl John,* Thomas Nelson, 1977; *C. B. Jockey,* Major Books, 1977; *The Day the White Deer Died,* Thomas Nelson, 1978; *Hope and a Hatchet,* Thomas Nelson, 1978.

Nonfiction: *The Special War,* Sirkay, 1966; *Some Birds Don't Fly,* Rand McNally, 1969; *The Building a New, Buying an Old, Remodeling a Used Comprehensive Home and*

Shelter Book, Prentice-Hall, 1976; *Farm: A History and Celebration of the American Farmer,* Prentice-Hall, 1977; *Hiking and Backpacking,* Simon & Schuster, 1978; *Canoeing and Kayaking,* Simon & Schuster, in press; *Home Repair Book,* Structures Publishing, in press.

Juvenile books: *Mr. Tucket,* Funk & Wagnall, 1968; (with Dan Theis) *The Man Who Climbed the Mountain,* Raintree, 1976; *The Small Ones,* Raintree, 1976; *The Grass Eaters,* Raintree, 1976; *Dribbling, Shooting, and Scoring Sometimes,* Raintree, 1976; *Hitting, Pitching, and Running Maybe,* Raintree, 1976; *Tackling, Running, and Kicking—Now and Again,* Raintree, 1977; *Riding, Roping, and Bulldogging–Almost,* Raintree, 1977; *The Golden Stick,* Raintree, 1977; *Careers in an Airport,* Raintree, 1977; *The CB Radio Caper,* Raintree, 1977; *The Curse of the Cobra;* Raintree, 1977.

Plays: "Communications" (one-act), first produced in New Mexico at a local group theatre, 1974; "Together-Apart" (one-act), first produced in Denver at Changing Scene Theatre, 1976.

Also author of *Meteor, The Sweeper,* and more than two hundred short stories and articles.

WORK IN PROGRESS: "Currently working on the great American novel. Period."

SIDELIGHTS: Paulsen told CA: "I write because it's all I can do. Every time I've tried to do something else I cannot, and have to come back to writing, though often I hate it—hate it and love it. It's much like being a slave, I suppose, and in slavery there is a kind of freedom that I find in writing: a perverse thing. I'm not 'motivated,' as you put it. Nor am I particularly driven. I write because it's all there is."

* * *

PAVITRANDA, Swami 1896(?)-1977

1896(?)—November 18, 1977; Indian-born monk, lecturer, and author of *Common Sense About Yoga* and *Modern Man in Search of Religion.* Pavitranda was spiritual leader of the Vendanta Society of New York and a monk of the Ramakrishna order. He was editor of *Prabuddha Bharata* and the head of the Advaita Ashrama monastery in the Himalayas before coming to the United States in 1948. Pavitranda died in New York, N.Y. Obituaries: *New York Times,* November 22, 1977.

* * *

PAVLAKIS, Christopher 1928-

PERSONAL: Born March 26, 1928, in Haverhill, Mass.; son of Nicholas and Panayota (Theophilos) Pavlakis; married Betty Bohlken, May 5, 1956; children: Ann Elizabeth, John Christopher. *Education:* Chicago Musical College, B.Mus., 1954; DePaul University, M.Mus., 1956; also attended University of Illinois and Roosevelt University. *Politics:* Independent Democrat. *Religion:* Greek Orthodox. *Address:* P.O. Box 52, Inwood Station, New York, N.Y. 10034.

CAREER: Teacher of music theory and composition at private schools in Chicago, Ill., 1959-64; president of music importation firm, New York City, 1964-71; University Music Editions, New York City, co-founder and publisher, 1967—; High Density Systems, Inc., New York City, co-founder and vice-president, 1969—; Molex Microfilm Products, Inc., New York City, co-founder and vice-president, 1973—. Faculty member of Chicago Teachers Col-

lege—North (now Northeastern Illinois State University), 1963-64. *Military service:* U.S. Army, Infantry, 1946-48; served in Japan; became staff sergeant. *Member:* National Micrographics Association, American Musicological Association Central Opera Service, Music Library Association.

WRITINGS: The American Music Handbook, Free Press, 1974.

Musical compositions: "How Do You Do, Sir?" (chamber opera), 1954. Also author of a Noh comedy, a four-movement suite for orchestra, a piano sonata, duets, quintets, and other musical compositions.

Contributor of articles and reviews to music journals. Editor and advertising manager of *Instrumentalist,* 1963-64. Reviewer for *Music Journal* and other music periodicals.

WORK IN PROGRESS: Orchestral symphonies, a string quartet, solo songs, a collection of "Kyrie's" for mixed chorus, and an unnamed stage work.

SIDELIGHTS: Pavlakis told *CA:* "All of my spare time is devoted to music. In the seven years it took to complete the rather massive *Handbook,* which is a topical encyclopedia requiring revision every few years, I would have been able to compose two large-scale symphonic works, one full opera, innumerable small chamber works, songs, solo instrumental pieces, etc. Since I did not, I have a lot of catching up to do. The *Handbook* was written because I could do it, and to satisfy my literary side, which seems to exist in many composers and musicians."

* * *

PAXTON, Robert O(wen) 1932-

PERSONAL: Born June 15, 1932, in Lexington, Va.; son of Matthew W. (a lawyer) and Nell (Owen) Paxton. *Education:* Washington & Lee University, B.A., 1954; Oxford University, B.A., 1956, M.A., 1961; Harvard University, Ph.D., 1963. *Home:* 560 Riverside Dr., #12K, New York, N.Y. 10027. *Office:* Department of History, Columbia University, New York, N.Y. 10027.

CAREER: University of California, Berkeley, instructor, 1961-63, assistant professor of history, 1963-67; State University of New York at Stony Brook, associate professor of history, 1967-69; Columbia University, New York, N.Y., professor of history, 1969—. *Military service:* U.S. Navy, 1956-58. U.S. Naval Reserve, 1951-66; became lieutenant commander. *Member:* American Historical Association, Society for French Historical Studies, Societe d'histoire moderne (Paris). *Awards, honors:* Rhodes scholar, 1954; D.Letters from Washington & Lee University, 1974.

WRITINGS: Parades and Politics at Vichy, Princeton University Press, 1966; *Vichy France: Old Guard and New Order, 1940-44,* Knopf, 1972; *Twentieth-Century Europe,* Harcourt, 1975.

WORK IN PROGRESS: Vichy et les juifs, with Michael Marrus, publication by Calmann-Levy expected in 1980.

* * *

PAYNE, B(en) Iden 1888-1976

PERSONAL: Born September 5, 1888, in Newcastle-on-Tyne, England; son of Alfred (a clergyman) and Sarah (Glover) Payne; married Mona Limerick, May 1, 1906 (divorced, 1950); married Barbara Rankin Chiaroni, January 14, 1950; children: Mrs. Donald Wolfit, Paget. *Education:* Educated in England. *Home:* 2708 Carlton Rd., Austin, Tex. 78703. *Office:* Department of Drama, University of Texas, Austin, Tex. 78712.

CAREER: Actor and director. Began stage career as actor at Theatre Royal, Manchester, England, 1899; Abbey Players, Dublin, Ireland, general manager, 1906-08; Horniman's Manchester Repertory Co., Manchester, organizer, stage director, and producer of more than two hundred plays, 1907-11; formed company with Mona Limerick, organized repertory seasons and toured England, 1911-13; Fine Arts Theatre, Chicago, Ill., director, 1913-14; actor and producer of plays in Chicago, Philadelphia, and New York, 1914-17; Charles Frohman Inc., New York City, general stage director at Empire Theatre, 1917-22; actor and producer of plays in New York and Chicago, 1922-28; Goodman Theatre, Chicago, producer and actor, 1928-32; actor and director in New York, 1931-34; Stratford-on-Avon Shakespeare Memorial Theatre, Stratford-on-Avon, England, general director, 1935-43; University of Texas, Austin, guest professor of drama, 1946-73. Visiting professor of drama, Carnegie Institute of Technology, 1919-34, University of Iowa and University of Washington, 1930-34 and 1943, University of Missouri, 1947, University of Colorado, 1953, University of Michigan, 1954, Banff School of Fine Acts, 1957-64. Director, Shakespeare Summer Festival, San Diego, Calif., 1949-52, 1955, 1957, 1964; director, Oregon Shakespeare Festival, summers, 1956 and 1961.

MEMBER: Players Club, Savage Club. Awards, honors: Southwest Theatre Conference award of merit, 1954; American National Shakespeare Festival and Academy award, 1959, for distinguished service to the theatre; Rodgers and Hammerstein Award, 1962, for distinguished services to theatre; LL.D. from University of Alberta, 1963; Consular Law Society award of merit, 1968; Theta Alpha Phi medal of honor, 1969.

WRITINGS: Where Love Is, Baker, 1956; A Life in a Wooden O (autobiography), Yale University Press, 1977.

Plays: "Dolly Jordan," first produced in New York at Daly's Theatre, October 3, 1922; (with Rosemary Casey) "The Saint's Husband," first produced in 1934; (with Casey) "Mary Goes to See," first produced in London at Haymarket Theatre, February 16, 1938.

SIDELIGHTS: Payne, who directed Ethel and John Barrymore, Otis Skinner, William Gillette, Ruth Chatterton, and Maud Adams, was remembered by one actress whose debut he directed in 1918, Helen Hayes: "On looking back over a lifetime of teachers, I feel sure that B. Iden Payne taught me the most." As a teacher, Payne influenced the careers of dozens of performers, including Kathryn Grant Crosby, Will Geer, Rip Torn, and Pat Hingle.

BIOGRAPHICAL/CRITICAL SOURCES: B. Iden Payne, A Life in a Wooden O, Yale University Press, 1977. Obituaries: New York Times, April 7, 1976; Time, April 19, 1976.*

(Died April 6, 1976, in Austin, Tex.)

* * *

PAYNE, F(rances) Anne 1932-

PERSONAL: Born August 28, 1932, in Harrisonburg, Va.; daughter of Charles F. (a civil servant) and Willie (a civil servant; maiden name, Tarvin) Payne. Education: Shorter College, B.A. and B.Mus., both 1953; Yale University, M.A., 1954, Ph.D., 1960; attended Middlebury College, summer, 1962. Politics: None. Religion: Protestant. Office: Department of English, State University of New York at Buffalo, Clemens Hall, Buffalo, N.Y. 14260.

CAREER: Connecticut College, New London, instructor in English, 1955-56; State University of New York at Buffalo, instructor, 1958-60, lecturer, 1960, assistant professor, 1961-68, associate professor, 1968-75, professor of English, 1975—. Member: Modern Language Association of American, Mediaeval Academy of America, Oxford University Medieval Society, St. Anne's Medieval Society. Awards, honors: American Association of University of Women fellowship, 1966-67; recipient of three State University of New York Research Foundation fellowships.

WRITINGS: King Alfred and Boethius, University of Wisconsin Press, 1968; (contributor) Edward B. Irving and Robert Burlin, editors, Old English Studies in Honor of John C. Pope, University of Toronto Press, 1974. Contributor to Chaucer Review.

WORK IN PROGRESS: Chaucer and Boethius; Chaucer As Menippean Satirist.

* * *

PAZ, Octavio 1914-

PERSONAL: Born March 31, 1914, in Mexico City, Mexico; son of Octavio (a lawyer) and Josephina (Lozano) Paz; married Marie-Jose Tramini, 1964; children: one daughter. Education: Attended National University of Mexico. Politics: "Disillusioned leftist." Religion: Atheist. Office: Plural, Reforma 12, desp. 505, Mexico 1, D.F.

CAREER: Writer. Attended anti-fascist congress in Spain, 1937; aided Spanish Republican refugees in Mexico, 1938-39; secretary at Mexican Embassy in Paris, 1945; Mexican Embassy in Japan, charge d'affaires in 1951, later posted to Secretariat for External Affairs; Mexican ambassador to India, 1962-68. Faculty member at University of Texas; Simon Bolivar Professor of Latin American Studies and fellow of Churchill College at Cambridge University, 1970-71; Charles Eliot Norton Professor of Poetry at Harvard University, 1971-72. Member: American Academy of Arts and Letters (honorary). Awards, honors: Guggenheim fellowship, 1944; Grand Prix International de Poesie, 1963.

WRITINGS: Luna Silvestre, Fabula, 1933; Raiz del hombre, Simbad, 1937; (editor) Voces de Espana, Ediciones Letras de Mexico, 1938; Entre la piedra y la flor, Nueva voz, 1941; (joint compiler) Laurel: Antologia de la poesie moderna en lengua espanola, Editorial Seneca, 1941; Bajo tu clara sombra, Tierra Nueva, 1941; A la orilla del mundo y Primer dia: Bajo tu clara sombra, Raiz del hombre, Noche de resurrecciones, Campania editora y librera ARS, 1942; (contributor) Muriel Rukeyser, editor, The Green Wave, Doubleday, 1948; Libertad abjo palabra, Tezontle, 1949.

El laberinto de la soledad, Fondo de Cultura Economical, 1950, translation by Lysander Kemp published as The Labyrinth of Solitude, Grove, 1961; Aguila o sol?, Tezontle, 1951, translation by Eliot Weinberger published as Aguila o sol? Eagle or Sun?, October House, 1970; (compiler) Anthologie de la poesie mexicaine, Editions Nagel, 1952; Semillas para un himno, Tezontle, 1954; (editor) Antologia poetica: Selection de Octavio Paz, Revista Panoramas, 1956; El arco y la lira: El poema, la revelacion poetica, poesia e historia, Fondo de Cultura Economica, 1956, translation by Ruth L. C. Simms published as The Bow and the Lyre: The Poem, the Poetic Revelation, Poetry and History, University of Texas Press, 1973; Piedra de sol, Tezontle, 1957, translation by Rukeyser published as Sun Stone, New Directions, 1963; Las peras del olmo, Impr. Universidad, 1957; (compiler), Anthology of Mexican Poetry, (translation by Samuel Beckett) Indiana University Press, 1958; La estacion violenta, Fondo de Cultura Economica, 1958; Agua y viento, Ediciones mito, 1959.

Libertad bajo palabra, Fondo de Cultura Economica, 1960; (with Alfonso Medellin) *Magia de la risa,* Universidad Veracruzana, 1962; *Salamandra, 1958-1961,* J. Mortiz, 1962; *Selected Poems* (bi-lingual edition); translation by Rukeyser, Indiana University Press, 1963; (editor with Pedro Sekeli) *Cuatro poetas contemporaneos de Suecia: Martinson, Lundkvist, Ekeloef y Lindegren,* Universidad Nacional Autonoma de Mexico, 1963; *Cuadrivio: Dario, Lopez Velarde, Pessoa, Cernuda,* J. Mortiz, 1965; *Los signos en rotacion,* SUR, 1965; *Vrindaban,* Editions C. Givaudani, 1966; *Puertas al campo,* Universidad Nacion Autonoma de Mexico, 1966; (with Juan Marichal) *E. E. Cummings: Sies poemas yun recuerdo traductor, Octavio Paz,* Papeles de San Armadans, 1966; (compiler) *Poesia en movimiento: Mexico, 1915-1966,* Siglo Veintiuno Editores, 1966; *Claude Levi-Strauss o el nuevo festin de esopo,* J. Mortiz, 1967, translation by J. S. Bernstein and Maxine Bernstein published as *Claude Levi-Strauss: An Introduction,* Cornell University Press, 1970; *Blanco,* J. Mortiz, 1967; *Corriente alterna,* Siglo Veintiuno Editores, 1967, translation by Helen R. Lane published as *Alternating Current,* Viking, 1973; *Marcel Duchamp,* Era, 1968, translation by Donald Gardner published as *Marcel Duchamp or the Castle of Purity,* Gorssman, 1970; *Discos Visuales,* Era, 1968; *Conjunciones y disjunciones,* J. Mortiz, 1969, translation by Lane published as *Conjunctions and Disjunctions,* Viking, 1973; *La centana: Poemas, 1935-1968,* Barral Editores, 1969; *Ladera este: 1962-1968,* J. Mortiz, 1969.

Posdata, Siglo Veintiuno Editores, 1970, translation by Lysander Kemp published as *The Other Mexico: Critique of the Pyramid,* Grove, 1972; *Las cosas en su sitio,* Finisterre, 1971; *Traduccion: Literature y literalidad,* Tusquets Editor, 1971; *Configurations* (translation by G. Aroul and others), New Directions, 1971; (selector and author of notes with others) *New Poetry of Mexico,* Secker and Warburg, 1972; *Renga: Un poema,* J. Mortiz, 1972; *Early Poems: 1935-1955* (translation by Rukeyser and others), New Directions, 1973; *Apariencia des nuda: La obra de Marcel Duchamp,* Era, 1973; (with Julian Rios) *Solo a dos voces,* Editorial Lumen, 1973; *El signo y el garabato,* J. Mortiz, 1973; *Los hijos del limo: Del romanticismo a la vanguardia* (lectures), Seix Barral, 1974, translation by Rachel Phillips published as *Children of the Mire: Modern Poetry from Romanticism to the Avant Garde,* Harvard University Press, 1974; *La busqueda del comienzo,* Editorial Fundamentos, 1974; *Teatro de signos: Transparencias,* Editorial Fundamentos, 1974; *Versiones y diversiones,* J. Mortiz, 1974; *El mono gramatico,* Editorial Seix Barral, 1974; *Pasado en claro,* Fondo de Cultura Economica, 1975; *Vuelta,* Editorial Seix Barral, 1976. Also author of *Topoemas,* 1968.

Founder of *Barandal,* 1931; member of editorial board of *El Popular,* late 1930's; founder of *Taller,* 1939; co-founder of *El hijo prodigo,* 1943; editor of *Plural.*

SIDELIGHTS: Paz is not only a prolific poet, but a critic and a social philosopher as well. Since beginning his literary career at the age of seventeen, Paz has been well received by most international critics. D. R. Gallagher commented that "Paz is never neurotic like Vallejo or like the Neruda of *Residencia.* No edgy splinters, no humid walls menace him. His demand that the world be different is the demand of a healthy man, untroubled by suffering. . . . [A] joyful hedonism often pervades Paz's poetry, and the poems are often celebrations of what he frequently calls a *festin,* a sheer uninhibited feast, where not only clothes, but anything that might inhibit is shed, even one's name. . . ." Gallagher felt that "poems [to Paz] then are journeys, bridges of words

between one 'side and another' and the poet travels across those words like an errant pilgrim. . . . Paz's poetry aims ambitiously at the achievement of fusion, where life, death, body, water, earth, light, darkness are one."

Grace Schulman wrote that "Paz is a living incarnation of those tensions in modern poetry between human commitment and aesthetic concern, a dialectic that is fundamental to the art of all nations. And his poetics is important, for it places the poet at the heart of modern life, singing his solitary song in company with the massed voices of human solitude. In his view, the poet does not speak the language of society but turns away from it, gaining strength in exile. . . . He maintains that the artist, rebuffed by a community that would substitute technological priorities for spiritual growth, trancends those social limitations and ransoms his dying world."

Peter Kerr-Jarrett found Paz to be "a man of exceptional and diverse intelligence, [Paz] has produced works on literature and art, anthropology, culture and politics and has earned the reputation for being one of Mexico's finest poets: but the specialized nature of some of his writings, such as the studies of Levi-Strauss and Marcel Duchamp, and others that deal with cultural issues outside the Anglo-American hemisphere (his *Labyrinth of Solitude* is a classic survey of modern Mexico), have confined him so far to select predominantly academic circles."

Ronald Crisp stated that "Paz establishes himself as a brilliant stylist balancing the tension of East and West, art and criticism, the many and the one in the figures of his writing. Paz is thus not only a great writer: he is also an indispensable corrective to our cultural tradition and a critic in the highest sense in which he himself uses that word."

AVOCATIONAL INTERESTS: Reading books on archaeology, travel, history, philosophy, and studying Mexican Indian mythology.

BIOGRAPHICAL/CRITICAL SOURCES: New Yorker, August 15, 1970; D. P. Gallagher, *Modern Latin American Literature,* Oxford University Press, 1973; *Hudson Review,* Autumn, 1974; *New Statesman,* October 11, 1974; *Nation,* August 2, 1975. *Contemporary Literary Criticism,* Gale, Volume 3, 1975, Volume 4, 1975, Volume 6, 1976.

*   *   *

PEACOCK, James Craig   1888(?)-1977

1888(?)—September 29, 1977; American lecturer, lawyer, and author of *Notes on Legislative Drafting.* Peacock was president of Washington College of Law from 1945 to 1948. Obituaries: *Washington Post,* October 3, 1977.

*   *   *

PEALE, Ruth Stafford   1906-

PERSONAL: Born September 10, 1906, in Fonda, Iowa; daughter of Frank Burton (a minister) and Anna Loretta (Crosby) Stafford; married Norman Vincent Peale (a minister), June 20, 1930; children: Margaret Ann (Mrs. Paul F. Everett), John Stafford, Elizabeth Ruth (Mrs. John M. Allen). *Education:* Syracuse University, A.B., 1928. *Religion:* Dutch (member of Reformed Church in America). *Residence:* New York, N.Y. *Office:* 1025 Fifth Ave., New York, N.Y. 10028.

CAREER: High school mathematics teacher in Syracuse, N.Y., 1928-31; national president of Women's Board of Domestic Missions of the Reformed Church in America, 1936-46; Foundation for Christian Living, Pawling, N.Y., general secretary and editor-in-chief, 1945—; *Guideposts* Magazine, New York, N.Y., co-editor and publisher, 1957—. Appeared on national television program "What's Your Trouble," 1952-68. Member of board and executive committee, New York Theological Seminary; member of board of governors, Help Line Telephone Center, 1970—. Trustee, Hope College, Champlain College, and Syracuse University.

MEMBER: National Council of Churches (member of general board, 1951-66; vice-president, 1952-54), Reformed Church in America (national president of Board of Domestic Missions, 1955-56; Board of North American Missions president, 1967-69; member of general program council, 1968—), American Foundation of Religion and Psychiatry, American Bible Society, Institutes of Religion and Health, Planners of Equal Opportunity, Council of Churches of the City of New York (vice-president, 1964-65), New York Federation of Women's Clubs (former chairman of religion), Sorosis, Alpha Phi.

AWARDS, HONORS: Cum Laude award from Syracuse University Alumni Association of New York, 1965, for outstanding service to the university, church, and community; Honor Iowans' award from Buena Vista College, 1966; Churchwoman of the Year award from Religious Heritage of America, 1969; Champlain College Distinguished Citizen Award; Distinguished Service Award from the Council of Churches of the City of New York; Distinguished Woman of the Year award from National Art Association; Francis W. Willard Award of Achievement from Alpha Phi fraternity; Distinguished Service award from General Federation of Women's Clubs; co-recipient with husband of special citation from Laymen's National Committee; honorary doctor of laws, Syracuse University; honorary doctor of letters, Hope College.

WRITINGS: I Married a Minister, Abingdon-Cokesbury, 1942; (with Arthur Gordon) *The Adventure of Being a Wife,* Prentice-Hall, 1971. Also co-author with husband of syndicated column "There's an Answer." Contributor of articles to *Reader's Digest, Woman's Day, Saturday Evening Post,* and other periodicals.

SIDELIGHTS: In 1964 Ruth Stafford Peale co-starred with her husband in "One Man's Way," a motion picture based on the life of her clergyman husband, Norman Vincent Peale.

* * *

PEAR, Lillian Myers

PERSONAL: Born in Ottawa County, Mich.; daughter of Albert J. (an orchardist) and Mary Ella (Wilde) Myers; married John Robert Pear (an endodontist) children: Robert James, Richard Eugene. *Education:* Earned life certificate from Eastern Michigan University; attended University of Chicago, 1921-23; Wayne State University, B.S., 1937, M.A. (honors), 1948. *Politics:* Republican. *Religion:* Protestant. *Home:* 707 Trombley Rd., Grosse Pointe Park, Mich. 48230.

CAREER: Painter and writer. Began as art teacher in junior high school in Detroit, Mich.; teacher of adult art classes in Grosse Pointe, Mich., 1941-51; art historian for Pewabic Pottery, 1969—. Art director for Red Cross during World War II. Educational director of Grosse Pointe Citizens Association; Secretary of Grosse Pointe Park Planning Commission. Parliamentarian, Cottage Hospital auxiliary. *Member:* International Arts and Letters (Zurich; life fellow), American Association of University Women (president of

Grosse Pointe branch), Smithsonian Institution (charter associate), Questers (national president), League of Women Voters (president of Grosse Pointe league; state parliamentarian), Michigan Cultural Commission (chairperson of fine arts), Michigan Academy of Arts, Science, and Letters (chairperson of fine arts), Grosse Pointe Artists Association (president), Detroit College Women's Club (president), Sigma Phi Epsilon (president of mothers association). *Awards, honors:* First prize from American Association of University Women, 1948, for national art criticism; Founders Award from Questers, 1969; also received awards for paintings from Grosse Pointe Artists Association.

WRITINGS: The Pewabic Pottery: A History of Its Products and Its People, Wallace-Homestead, 1976. Author of column in *Grosse Pointe News.* Contributor to *Spinning Wheel* and *Michigan Historical Magazine.*

WORK IN PROGRESS: A book on Staffordshire pottery, and one on W. H. Barter prints.

SIDELIGHTS: Lillian Pear told *CA:* "I wished to preserve the Pewabic installation and pieces from the wreckers ball, so that future generations could learn and know about the greatest ceramic art legacy left in the United States and Canada."

* * *

PEARL, Ralph 1910-

PERSONAL: Born March 10, 1910, in New York, N.Y.; son of Gustave and Ann (Balaban) Pearl; married Rosalyn Holland, September 23, 1942. *Education:* St. John's University, L.L.B., 1934. *Religion:* Hebrew. *Home:* 176 Columbia, Las Vegas, Nev. 89109. *Office: Las Vegas Sun,* Las Vegas, Nev. 89106.

CAREER: New York American, New York, N.Y., police reporter, 1939-50; *Las Vegas Sun,* Las Vegas, Nevada, entertainment columnist, 1953—; SUN-TV, Henderson, Nevada, television commentator, 1955—.

WRITINGS: Las Vegas Is My Beat, Lyle Stuart, 1973.

SIDELIGHTS: Pearl told *CA:* "For many years I've been known as a most controversial columnist only interested in seeing to it that my readers get the real picture. Consequently, for the first fifteen years of my stay in Las Vegas I feuded constantly with the big stars."

* * *

PEARSON, Bruce L. 1932-

PERSONAL: Born April 30, 1932, in Indianapolis, Ind.; son of Leonard E. (a journalist) and Hildred H. (a teacher; maiden name, Hudson) Pearson; married Kathryn Green (a nursing college instructor), March 31, 1961; children: Sarah Elaine, Thomas Bruce. *Education:* Earlham College, B.A., 1953; Indiana University, M.A., 1963; graduate study at University of California, Los Angeles, 1967-69; University of California, Berkeley, Ph.D., 1972. *Religion:* Quaker. *Home:* 6248 Yorkshire Dr., Columbia, S.C. *Office:* English Department, University of South Carolina, Columbia, S.C. 29208.

CAREER: English teacher in Tokyo, Japan, 1954-58, in Osaka, Japan, 1954-58, and in high school in Indianapolis, Ind., 1958-63; Earlham College, Richmond, Ind., linguistics instructor, 1963-67; California State University, Los Angeles, linguistics instructor, 1969-72; University of South Carolina, Columbia, assistant professor, 1972—. Executive committee member of American Friends Service Committee

(Southeast region). *Member:* Linguistic Society of America; Linguistic Association of Canada and the United States; Southeastern Conference on Linguistics; North and South Carolina Association of Linguists.

WRITINGS: Introduction to Linguistic Concepts, Knopf, 1977; *Workbook in Linguistic Concepts,* Knopf, 1977; *Teaching Linguistic Concepts,* Knopf, 1977. Also author of two plays, "Uncle Tom Andy Bill" and "A Permanent Home," both as yet neither published nor produced. Contributor to *International Journal of American Linguistics.*

WORK IN PROGRESS: Research on American Indian languages, Indian place names of South Carolina, and on other topics.

SIDELIGHTS: Bruce Pearson told *CA:* "My major work in linguistics grows out of my interest in teaching and my dissatisfaction with the unidimensional treatment of the field provided by most textbooks. My own book is an attempt to recapitulate the history of linguistics by analyzing language data in terms of the concepts and analytical tools that have been available at different periods up to the present day. My assumption has been that the best way to learn where we are is to understand how we got here. The best way to plot the course for the future is not to assume that we already have the best of all possible worlds but to recognize that we may have taken a wrong direction along the way and that we need to retrace our steps and start over. Rather than presenting the student with a set of prepackaged conclusions, I have chosen to help students discover for themselves in all its complexities the present situation in their discipline and trust them to work out their own conclusions.

"My ongoing projects center around the study of American Indian languages, both as an end in itself and as a testing ground for linguistic theory. In addition I am interested in using language data as a tool in reconstructing bits and pieces of history that are generally omitted in books drawing on documentary sources. My untangling of the history of the terms Savannah and Shawnee is a case in point. I am also interested in drama and have written two plays, as yet unproduced, dealing with human conflict in the meeting of different languages and cultures on the American frontier. In addition, I am trying to establish a linguistics journal at the University of South Carolina."

AVOCATIONAL INTERESTS: Gardening, coaching baseball.

*   *   *

PEARSON, Lon
   See PEARSON, Milo Lorentz

*   *   *

PEARSON, Milo Lorentz   1939-
   (Lon Pearson)

PERSONAL: Born February 13, 1939, in Murray, Utah; son of Milo Willard (a laborer) and Gulli Vicktoria (Peterson) Pearson; married Janet Stepan, October 7, 1961; children: Russell, Stephanie, Robert, Richard, Sharon. *Education:* University of Utah, B.A., 1965; University of California, Los Angeles, M.A., 1968, C.Phil., 1969, Ph.D., 1973; Johns Hopkins University, postdoctoral study, 1975-76. *Religion:* Church of Jesus Christ of Latter-day Saints (Mormons). *Home:* 933 East Seventh St., Rolla, Mo. 65401. *Office:* Department of Humanities, University of Missouri, Rolla, Mo. 65401.

CAREER: Church of Jesus Christ of Latter-day Saints,

Mexico, missionary, 1959-61; Southeast Builders Supply, Salt Lake City, Utah, accountant, 1962-66; University of California, Los Angeles, associate instructor in Spanish, 1969-70; University of Missouri, Rolla, instructor, 1970-73; assistant professor, 1973-77, associate professor of Spanish, 1977—. *Military service:* U.S. Army National Guard, 1956-66, and 1977; became sergeant first class.

MEMBER: International Institute of Iberoamerican Literature, Modern Language Association of America, American Association of Teachers of Spanish and Portuguese, Midwest Modern Language Association, Foreign Language Association of Missouri (member of executive board, 1973—). *Awards, honors:* National Endowment for the Humanities research fellow, 1975-76; research grants from University of Missouri, 1971, 1973, for South America.

WRITINGS—Under name Lon Pearson: *Nicomedes Guzman: Proletarian Author in Chile's Literary Generation of 1938,* University of Missouri Press, 1976. Contributor of articles and reviews to scholarly journals and newspapers in the United States and South America. Translator for *American Bee Journal,* 1971—; editor of *Missouri Foreign Language Journal,* 1973-78.

WORK IN PROGRESS: A book on Chilean novelist Enrique Lafourcade; a collection of short stories; research on the Chilean "child cult."

SIDELIGHTS: Pearson recently became involved in studying innovative ways for writers to use computers; he has also organized a faculty fiction workshop at University of Missouri for faculty members who are creative writers.

BIOGRAPHICAL/CRITICAL SOURCES: Revista del Sabado, June 30, 1973.

*   *   *

PECK, Abe   1945-

PERSONAL: Legal surname, Peckolick; born January 18, 1945, in Bronx, N.Y.; son of Jacob (a shipping clerk) and Lottie (Bell) Peckolick; married Suzanne Wexler (a staff developer), March 19, 1977. *Education:* New York University, B.A., 1965; also attended City University of New York. *Religion:* Jewish. *Residence:* Chicago, Ill. *Office: Chicago Daily News,* 401 North Wabash Ave., Chicago, Ill. 60611.

CAREER: Held editorial and writing positions with *Chicago Seed,* Chicago, Ill., 1967-71, *Gallery Magazine,* Chicago, 1973, and *Rolling Stone,* San Francisco, Calif., 1975-76; Associated Press, New York, N.Y., music columnist, 1976; *Chicago Daily News,* Chicago, feature writer and editor of "Sidetracks," 1977—. Member of Chicago Media Committee. *Military service:* U.S. Army Reserve, 1966-67.

WRITINGS: (Editor) *Dancing Madness,* Anchor Press, 1976; (editorial Consultant) Linda Rosen Obst, editor, *The Sixties,* Random House, 1977. Contributor to magazines, including *Playboy, Penthouse, Oui,* and *Town and Country.* Contributing editor of *Rolling Stone,* 1976—.

WORK IN PROGRESS: "On going building of 'Sidetracks,' and writing features for the *Daily News.*"

SIDELIGHTS: Peck writes: "I've just started writing for newspapers after several years of magazine work. I'm trying to synthesize magazine style and technique with straightforward time-oriented reporting. Similarly 'Sidetracks' attempts to bring post-sixties style developments into a mainstream newspaper."

PEER, Lyndon A. 1899(?)-1977

1899(?)—October 8, 1977; American plastic surgeon, editor and author of books on tissue transplants. Peer developed a method of rebuilding ears using the natural healing abilities of the human body. He died in Boca Raton, Fla. Obituaries: *New York Times,* October 11, 1977.

* * *

PELADEAU, Marius B(eaudoin) 1935-

PERSONAL: Born January 27, 1935, in Boston, Mass.; son of Marius M. V. (a physician) and Lucienne (a librarian; maiden name, Beaudoin) Peladeau; married Mildred Louise Cole (an author), February 26, 1972. *Education:* St. Michael's College, Winooski Park, Vt., A.B. (cum laude), 1956; Boston University, M.S., 1957; Georgetown University, M.A., 1962. *Home address:* Norris Hill, Monmouth, Maine 04259. *Office:* William A. Farnsworth Library and Art Museum, P.O. Box 466, Rockland, Maine 04841.

CAREER: Public Utilities Fortnightly, Washington, D.C., associate editor, 1962-66; administrative assistant to U.S. Representative Joseph P. Vigorito, in Washington, D.C., 1968-72; Maine League of Historical Societies and Museums, Monmouth, Me., director, 1972-76; William A. Farnsworth Library and Art Museum, Rockland, Me., director, 1976—. Consultant to National Park Service. *Member:* American Association for State and Local History, Company of Military Historians (fellow), White House Correspondents Association, Maine League of Historical Societies, Colonial Society of Massachusetts, Vermont Historical Society, Sigma Delta Chi.

WRITINGS: (Editor) *The Verse of Royall Tyler,* University Press of Virginia, 1968; (editor) *The Prose of Royall Tyler,* Vermont Historical Society, 1972; *Chansonetta: The Life and Photographs of Chansonetta Stanley Emmons, 1858-1937,* Maine Antique Digest, 1977. Contributor of about a hundred articles to scholarly and popular magazines.

WORK IN PROGRESS: The Art of the Drum, on the artistic decoration on military drums from Roman times to the present; research on Maine folk art.

SIDELIGHTS: Peladeau told *CA:* "Royall Tyler was the author of the first American drama professionally produced in this country. He was a prolific writer of plays, poems and prose, and was considered one of the first literary geniuses of the new republic in his lifetime. After his death, however, his reputation declined because of his habit of writing under pseudonyms to protect his legal career (it being considered improper for attorneys to also be authors). Tyler's complete work had not been collected until these two volumes appeared in 1968 and 1972.

"Chansonetta Stanley Emmons was one of America's three pioneer women photographers at the turn-of-the-century. Benjamin Frances Johnson and Alice Austin have received full-length biographies. Mrs. Emmons had not yet achieved the recognition she deserved because the major body of her work had been lost. My re-discovery of it in 1975 led to the publication of the first biography and first comprehensive reproduction of her photos in 1977.

"As to American art and the decorative arts, my interests are catholic, ranging over many subjects. Articles have been commissioned recently on aspects of the arts and crafts of the Shakers in Maine, Maine painted furniture of the 19th century, and several relatively unknown Maine artists of the same period."

PELLOW, Deborah 1945-

PERSONAL: Born March 21, 1945, in Los Angeles, Calif.; daughter of David and Frieda (Kaplan) Pellow. *Education:* University of Pennsylvania, B.A., 1967; Northwestern University, Ph.D., 1974. *Politics:* Democrat. *Religion:* Jewish. *Home address:* P.O. Box 2437, Aspen, Colo. 81611.

CAREER: Council for Community Services, Chicago, Ill., research associate, 1972-76; Colorado Mountain College, Aspen, instructor in anthropology, 1977—. Volunteer worker for Grass Roots Television, 1977—. *Member:* American Anthropological Association, Society for Applied Anthropology, African Studies Association. *Awards, honors:* National Unity Grant, 1968, 1971-72; Fulbright-Hays overseas grant, 1970-71.

WRITINGS: Women in Accra: Options for Autonomy, Reference Book Publications, 1977.

WORK IN PROGRESS: Be My Friend, on the affectual side of anthropological field work; research on innovation among the Bedouin of South Sinai.

SIDELIGHTS: Pellow told *CA:* "The book *Women in Accra: Options for Autonomy* is based upon a study which intended to describe the 'new' urban woman in Ghana. The research was motivated by the West African urbanization literature of the late 1950s and 1960s which reported that greater opportunities and freedoms awaited women in the city, that they could leave their hometowns and kin attachments and go off on their own to seek their fortune. While the author did find that the city offers new roles, these are limited and particularly reserved for men. Women are even more dependent upon men—for status, for subsistence—than in the rural area. They are still forced into sexually-defined roles, as mother, wife, and girlfriend. They are especially limited by their own inability to see beyond traditional models, to conceive of alternatives.

"The book concentrates on ordinary, first and second generation urban dwellers. It portrays them in their daily circumstances of spheres of activity and relationships with others."

* * *

PENA, Humberto J(ose) 1928-

PERSONAL: Born November 10, 1928, in Havana, Cuba; came to the United States in 1961, naturalized citizen, 1970; son of Roman and Maria Teresa (Godinez) Pena; married Delia I. Gomez (a bilingual secretary and translator), February 13, 1955; children: Maria Cristina, Humberto Jorge, Jorge Alberto. *Education:* Colegio Baldor, B.A., 1946; University of Havana, D.Law., 1951; Consejo Superior de Investigaciones Cientificas, D.Lit., 1957. *Politics:* "Center towards the left." *Religion:* Roman Catholic. *Home:* 342 22nd St., Dunbar, W.Va. 25064. *Agent:* Juan Manuel Salvat, P.O. Box 353, Miami, Fla. 33145. *Office:* West Virginia State College, Box 22, Institute, W.Va. 25112.

CAREER: Writer, 1946—. Attorney in Havana, Cuba, 1951-59; professor at University of La Salle, 1955-59; associate professor at West Virginia State College, 1965—. Assistant supervisor of pension and retirement department of Cuban Bank of Social Security. *Member:* Sigma Delta Pi. *Awards, honors:* International Hucha de Plata award from Confederacion Espanola de Cajas de Ahorro (Madrid), 1975, for story "La Inconclusa."

WRITINGS: Yo no habra mas domingos (stories; title means "There Won't Be Any More Sundays"), Ediciones Universal, 1971; *El viaje mas largo* (novel; title means "The Longest Journey"), Ediciones Universal, 1973.

Work represented in anthologies, including *Viente Cuentistas Cubanos* (title means "Twenty Cuban short-story writers"), Ediciones Universal, 1977, and *Espinas al Sol* (poems; title means "Thorns in the Sun"), Ediciones Universal, 1977. Contributor of stories and poems to magazines in Spain, Mexico, Central and South America, and the United States.

WORK IN PROGRESS: Ya es muy tarde (title means "It Is Already Too Late"), a book of stories; studying the literary activity of Jose Marti in the United States and his relations with American writers of his time.

SIDELIGHTS: Pena commented: "It is of extreme importance for a writer to see the things which surround him in a perceptive manner. While in the United States, Spain, and France, I have been able to analyze the Cuban situation and the life of the intellectuals in today's Cuba. The writer needs a stimulus to see his ghosts come alive; injustice, in all of its forms, is my stimulus, and my ghosts are exposed in my literary productions."

*   *   *

PENNINGTON, Robert (Roland) 1927-

PERSONAL: Born April 22, 1927, in Birmingham, England; son of Roland A. (an accountant) and Elsie (Davis) Pennington; married Patricia Irene Rook (a teacher of modern dance), March 14, 1965; children: Elisabeth Ann. *Education:* University of Birmingham, LL.B., 1946, LL.D., 1960. *Politics:* Conservative. *Home:* Gryphon House, Langley Rd., Claverdon, Warwickshire, England. *Office:* Faculty of Law, University of Birmingham, Birmingham 15, England.

CAREER: College of Law, London, England, senior lecturer, 1951-55, reader in law and member of board of management, 1952-62; University of Birmingham, Birmingham, England, senior lecturer, 1962-68, professor of commercial law, 1968—. Solicitor of British Supreme Court, 1951—; government adviser on company legislation in Trinidad, 1967, and Seychelles, 1970; legal adviser to United Nations, 1971—; special British legal adviser to Commission of the European Communities, 1972—. *Military service:* British Army, 1947-49; became lieutenant. *Member:* Law Society, Association of University Teachers.

WRITINGS: Company Law, Butterworth & Co., 1959, 4th edition, 1978; *Companies in the Common Market,* 2nd edition, Oyez Publishing, 1970; *Stannary Law: A History of the Mining Law of Cornwall and Devon,* David & Charles, 1973; (editor) *European Commercial Law Library,* eight volumes, Oyez Publishing, 1973-77.

WORK IN PROGRESS: A ten-volume encyclopedia of European commercial and fiscal law, for Matthew Bender, completion expected in 1988.

SIDELIGHTS: Pennington told *CA:* "My primary interest is British and European commercial law, but I am also interested in the history of commercial law, mining law, and fiscal law; more broadly, the development of the European communities, politically and economically."

*   *   *

PERELLA, Nicholas James 1927-

PERSONAL: Born September 7, 1927, in Boston, Mass.; son of Nicola and Maria (Giovanna) Perella; married wife Vivian, September 7, 1957. *Education:* Suffolk University, B.A., 1952; Harvard University, M.A., 1954, Ph.D., 1957. *Home:* 3 Highland Blvd., Kensington, Calif. 94707. *Office:* Department of Italian, University of California, Berkeley, Calif. 94720.

CAREER: University of California, Berkeley, instructor, 1957-59, assistant professor, 1959-63, associate professor, 1963-68, professor of Italian, 1968—, chairperson of department, 1969-73. *Member:* Modern Language Association of America, American Association of Teachers of Italian, American Association of University Professors.

WRITINGS: The Kiss Sacred and Profane: An Interpretive History of Kiss Symbolism and Related Religio-Erotic Themes, University of California Press, 1969; *Night and the Sublime in Giacomo Leopardi,* University of California Press, 1970; *The Critical Fortune of Battista Guarini's "Il Pastor Fido,"* Olschki, 1973.*

*   *   *

PERELMAN, Lewis J(oel) 1946-

PERSONAL: Born February 13, 1946, in Mt. Vernon, N.Y.; son of Leonard (a merchant) and Ruth (a merchant; maiden name, Price) Perelman. *Education:* City College of the City University of New York, B.S., 1967; Harvard University, Ed.D., 1973. *Politics:* "Ecological Humanism." *Religion:* "Unidentified." *Home:* 435 St. Paul, Denver, Colo. 80206.

CAREER: High school teacher of physics in Mt. Vernon, N.Y., 1968-69; Western Interstate Commission for Higher Education, Boulder, Colo., project director, 1974; Colorado Department of Highways, Denver, policy planner, 1976—; Solar Energy Research Institute, Golden, Colo., senior planner, 1977—. President of PREACT: Strategies for Colorado's Future, 1976-77. *Member:* American Association for the Advancement of Science, Scientists' Institute for Public Information, Zero Population Growth, Phi Beta Kappa.

WRITINGS: The Global Mind: Beyond the Limits to Growth, Mason/Charter, 1976. Contributor to journals, including *Impact, Prospects, Environmental Education Report,* and *Technological Forecasting and Social Change.*

WORK IN PROGRESS: Research on the transformation of U.S. political economy, the passing of the "human" era, and on appropriate technology and energy systems.

SIDELIGHTS: Perelman comments briefly: "*The Global Mind* represents a naive and largely academic five-year effort to devise a process to save the world. The accuracy of my analysis, and the apathy of my audience, both exceeded my expectations."

*   *   *

PERELMAN, S(idney) J(oseph) 1904-

PERSONAL: Born February 1, 1904, in Brooklyn, N.Y.; son of Joseph (a machinist and merchant) and Sophia (Charren) Perelman; married Laura West (a writer), July 4, 1929 (died April 11, 1970); children: Adam, Abby Laura. *Education:* Brown University, B.A., 1925. *Home:* Erwinna, Bucks County, Pa. *Office:* c/o *New Yorker* Magazine Inc., 25 West 43rd St., New York, N.Y. 10036.

CAREER: Judge magazine, New York City, cartoonist and writer, 1925-29; *College Humor* magazine, New York City, cartoonist and writer, 1929-30; full-time writer, 1929—; writer of motion picture scripts, 1930—; *New Yorker* magazine, New York City, regular contributor, 1931—. Manager of radio program, "Author, Author." *Member:* Screen Writers Guild, Dramatists Guild, National Institute of Arts and Letters, Century Association. *Awards, honors:* New York Film Critics award, and Academy of Motion Picture Arts and Sciences award (Oscar), for best screenplay, 1956, for "Around the World in Eighty Days."

WRITINGS: *Dawn Ginsburgh's Revenge,* Liveright, 1929; (with Quentin Reynolds) *Parlor, Bedroom and Bath,* Liveright, 1930; *Strictly from Hunger,* foreword by Robert Benchley, Random House, 1937; *Look Who's Talking,* Random House, 1940; *The Dream Department,* Random House, 1943; *Crazy Like A Fox,* Random House, 1944, reprinted, Vintage, 1973; *Keep it Crisp,* Random House, 1946; *Acres and Pains,* Reynal & Hitchcock, 1947, reprinted, Simon & Schuster, 1972; *The Best of S. J. Perelman: With a Critical Introduction by Sidney Namlerep,* Modern Library, 1947, reprinted, 1962; *Westward Ha! Or, Around the World in Eighty Cliches,* Simon & Schuster, 1947; (contributor) Louis G. Locke, William M. Gibson and George W. Arms, editors, *Readings for a Liberal Education,* Rinehart, 1948, revised edition, 1952; *Listen to the Mocking Bird,* Simon & Schuster, 1949, reprinted, 1970.

The Swiss Family Perelman, Simon & Schuster, 1950; *A Child's Garden of Curses: Containing Crazy Like a Fox, Keep it Crisp, Acres and Pains,* Heinemann, 1951; (contributor) John Lincoln Stewart, editor, *The Essay: A Critical Enthology,* Prentice-Hall, 1952; *The Ill Tempered Clavicord,* Simon & Schuster, 1952; (contributor) P. G. Wodehouse and Scott Meredith, editors, *Best of Modern Humor,* Metcalf, 1952; (contributor) Wodehouse and Meredith, editors, *The Week-end Book of Humor,* Washburn, 1952; *Perelman's Home Companion: A Collector's Item (The Collector Being Perelman) of 36 Otherwise Unavailable Pieces by Himself,* Simon & Schuster, 1955; *The Road to Miltown; or, Under the Spreading Atrophy,* Simon & Schuster, 1957 (published in England as *Bite on the Bullet; or, Under the Spreading Atrophy,* Heinemann, 1957); (contributor) George Oppenheimer, editor, *The Passionate Playgoer: A Personal Scrapbook,* Viking, 1958; *The Most of S. J. Perelman,* introduction by Dorothy Parker, Simon & Schuster, 1958; (contributor) Leslie A. Fiedler, editor, *Art of the Essay,* Crowell, 1958; (contributor) Earle R. Davis and W. C. Hummel, editors, *Reading for Opinions,* Prentice-Hall, 1960; *The Rising Gorge,* Simon & Schuster, 1961; (contributor) Alfred Kazin, editor, *The Open Form: Essays for Our Time,* Harcourt, 1961; *Chicken Inspector No. 23,* Simon & Schuster, 1966; (author of introduction and notes with Richard Rovere) Fred L. Israel, editor, *1897 Sears Roebuck Catalogue,* Chelsea House, 1968; *Baby, It's Cole Inside,* Simon & Schuster, 1970; *The Four Marx Brothers in Monkey Business and Duck Soup,* Lorrimer, 1972, Simon & Schuster, 1973; *Vinegar Puss,* Simon & Schuster, 1975.

Plays: (Contributor of sketches) "The Third Little Show" (revue), produced in New York, 1932; (contributor of sketches with Robert MacGunigle) "Walk a Little Faster" (revue), produced in New York, 1932; (with wife, Laura Perelman) "All Good Americans" (comedy), produced in New York, 1933; (contributor of sketches) "Two Weeks with Pay" (revue), toured, 1940; (with Laura Perelman) *The Night Before Christmas* (comedy; produced in New York, 1941), Samuel French, 1942; (with Ogden Nash) *One Touch of Venus* (comedy; produced in New York, 1943), Little, Brown, 1944; (with Al Hirschfeld) "Sweet Bye and Bye" (comedy), produced in New Haven, Conn., 1946; *The Beauty Part* (two-act comedy; first produced in New Hope, Pa., 1961; produced in New York, 1962), Samuel French and Simon & Schuster, 1963.

Screenplays: "Monkey Business," 1931; "Horse Feathers," 1932; "Paris Interlude," 1934; (with Laura Perelman) "Florida Special," 1936; "Sweet Hearts," 1938; (with Laura Perelman) "Ambush," 1939; (with Laura Perelman) "Boy Trouble," 1939; (with Laura Perelman) "The Golden

Fleecing," 1940; "Larceny, Inc.," 1942; "One Touch of Venus" (based on own play), 1948; (with others) "Around the World in Eighty Days," 1956. Author of television plays for "Omnibus" series, 1957-59, and "Lively Arts" series; author of scripts for television specials in 1950's, including "Aladdin."

SIDELIGHTS: S. J. Perelman has been called the funniest man alive. He has been hailed as the great American humorist, but prefers to think of himself as a *feuilletonist,* a writer of short pieces for popular magazines. He is that. His books are principally collections of his contributions to the *New Yorker.*

Perelman's style is probably most typified by his adept word-play with which he exposes the bizarre inventions of his baroque imagination. Perelman told Roy Newquist that his development as a writer of humorous essays had been influenced by several of his contemporaries and predecessors. He said that one of his most influential contemporaries was Robert Benchley, "with whom I was fortunate enough to be friends during a good portion of my career. Dorothy Parker is another person. Both of these exercised a role in my life which is difficult to put into words. I had great admiration for both as individuals and as artists. I think their standards were very high, indeed, and that just knowing them meant a great deal to me. I'm sure that knowing Groucho Marx has meant a great deal."

When speaking of earlier influences on his development as a humorist, Perelman often mentions George Ade. "George Ade was my first influence as a humorist. He had a social sense of history. His picture of Hoosier life at the turn of the century . . . is more documentary than any of those studies on how much people paid for their coal. Ade's humor was rooted in a perception of people and places. He had a cutting wit and an acerbic wit that no earlier American humorist had." But while Perelman speaks often of those whose work has been influential in his own development, he has been no small influence on the work of others. E. B. White once commented on the consequence of Perelman's presence on the literary humor scene. "I'm sure Sid's stuff influenced me in the early days. His pieces usually had a lead sentence, or lead paragraph, that was as hair-raising as the first big dip on a roller coaster: it got you in the stomach, and when it was over you were relieved to feel deceleration setting in. In the realm of satire, parody, and burlesque, he has, from the beginning, bowed to none. His erudition is as impressive as his flights of fancy." Even Robert Benchley, to whom Perelman claims to be indebted, felt that Perelman had risen to the status of mentor and unchallenged master of the humorous essay. Benchley once said: "It was just a matter of time before Perelman took over the dementia praecox field and drove us all to writing articles on economics."

Stefan Kanfer has credited Perelman with the dubious honor of being the man who has probably "ruined more undergraduate publications than any other living writer . . ." by virtue of his imitability. He wrote that Perelman is "imitable because all masters of the language can be put to the pastiche. It is always the original who attracts the mockingbirds, not the disciple." Perelman's style has come under attack as being simply that—style without significant substance. His work springs from a nostalgic sense of social history and he rarely, to the dismay of some reviewers, deals with the seemingly pressing issues of present importance. In writing about *Baby, It's Cold Inside,* Kanfer reacted strongly to what he called the "strained appeals for Relevant Comedy" directed to Perelman by some critics. He wrote: "In *Baby* there are lambastes of pre-Devlin Dublin, department stores, British snobs, advertising art, television. Or so it seems to the myopic reader. In fact, Perelman must never be examined on a surface level, never considered an adjunct of the editorial page, never read for phase value. . . . His enthusiasms are for language and its unexplored subtleties. . . .

"For years, Perelman has been accused of repeating himself, of following formulae. But they are *his* formulae. To charge him with writing by numbers is like accusing Brillat-Savarin of following nothing but recipes." Perelman's comedic "formula" has developed out of his conception of the nature of humor. He once said: "Humor is purely a point of view, and only the pedants try to classify it. For me its chief merit is the use of the unexpected, the glancing allusion, the deflation of pomposity, the constant repetition of one's helplessness in a majority of situations. One doesn't consciously start out wanting to be a social satirist. You find something absurd enough to make you want to push a couple of anti-personnel bombs under it. If it then seems to have another element of meaning, that's lagniappe. But the main obligation is to amuse yourself."

BIOGRAPHICAL/CRITICAL SOURCES: Saturday Review, September 23, 1961; *Time,* October 13, 1961; *Life,* February 9, 1962; *Newsweek,* January 7, 1963, October 2, 1972; *Vogue,* Feburary 1, 1963; John Wain, editor, *Essays on Literature and Ideas,* Macmillan, 1963; George Plimpton, editor, *Writers at Work,* Viking, 1963; Brooks Atkinson, editor, *Tuesdays and Fridays,* Random House, 1963; Norris W. Yates, editor, *The American Humorist,* Iowa State University Press, 1964; Robert S. Brustein, editor, *Seasons of Discontent,* Simon & Schuster, 1965; *New Statesman,* November 24, 1967; Roy Newquist, editor, *Conversations,* Rand McNally, 1967; *New York Times Magazine,* January 26, 1969; *Atlantic Monthly,* December, 1970; Wilfred Sheed, editor, *The Morning After,* Farrar, Straus, 1971; *New York Times,* January 7, 1971, June 13, 1971; *Harper's Bazaar,* May 2, 1972; Richard Gilman, editor, *Common and Uncommon Masks,* Vintage, 1972; *Contemporary Literary Criticism,* Gale, Volume 3, 1975, Volume 5, 1976.*

* * *

PERKINS, David (Lee)   1939-

PERSONAL: Born January 11, 1939, in Wheeling, W.Va.; son of Virgil Hickman (a teacher) and Dorothy (a teacher; maiden name, Fontaine) Perkins; married Phyllis Haniford (a teacher), August 29, 1964; children: Paul Fontaine. *Education:* University of California, Los Angeles, B.A., 1961; University of Southern California, M.S.L.S., 1969; California State University, Northridge, M.A., 1973. *Home:* 4975 Doman Ave., Tarzana, Calif. 91356. *Office:* Library, California State University, Northridge, Calif. 91330.

CAREER: High school teacher of social studies in Oakdale, Calif., 1965-68; California State University, Northridge, head bibliography librarian, 1969—. *Military service:* U.S. Army, 1961-63. *Member:* American Library Association, Association of College and Research Libraries, Sierra Club, California Library Association (chairman of collection development chapter, 1975), Beta Phi Mu.

WRITINGS: (With Norman E. Tanis) *Native Americans of North America,* Scarecrow, 1975; *Bibliographic Control for Recently Published Books in Anthropology,* ERIC, 1975; (with Carol Bedoian) *A Manual for Collection Developers,* ERIC, 1976.

WORK IN PROGRESS: China: A Bibliography of Basic Works, with Norman E. Tanis and Justine Pinto, for John-

son Associates, Inc.; *India: A Bibliographic Guide,* with Tanis.

* * *

PERKINS, James Ashbrook   1941-

PERSONAL: Born February 7, 1941, in Covington, Ky.; son of Harry Dimmit (an educator) and Juanita (a teacher; maiden name, Ashbrook) Perkins; married Jane Allen, August 17, 1963; children: James Allen, Jeffrey Ashbrook. *Education:* Centre College, Danville, Ky., B.A., 1963; Miami University, Oxford, Ohio, M.A., 1965; University of Tennessee, Ph.D., 1972. *Politics:* Radical Democrat. *Religion:* Presbyterian. *Home:* 118 Prospect St., New Wilmington, Pa. 16142. *Office:* Department of English, Westminster College, New Wilmington, Pa. 16142.

CAREER: Memphis State University, Memphis, Tenn., instructor in English, 1965-67; English teacher and department chairman at Episcopal school in Vicksburg, Miss., 1969-71; University of Tennessee, Knoxville, instructor in English, 1972-73; Westminster College, New Wilmington, Pa., assistant professor of English, 1973—. *Member:* Academy of American Poets, College English Association, Poets and Writers, Associated Writing Programs, South Atlantic Modern Language Association. *Awards, honors:* Senior poetry award from Mississippi Arts Festival, 1971, for "Maps and Highways"; Canaras fellowships from St. Lawrence University, 1975, 1976.

WRITINGS: The Amish: 2 Perceptions (poems), Dawn Valley Press, 1976; *Billy-the-Kid, Chicken Gizzards, and Other Tales* (short stories), Dawn Valley Press, 1977; *The Woodcarver* (poems), Rook Press, 1978. Author of documentary film, "Building a Better Knoxville," and television script, "The World of Henry Fielding," for WMAA-TV. Contributor to literary magazines, including *Druid, Old Hickory Review,* and *Fireweed,* and to professional journals.

WORK IN PROGRESS: Third Persons, stories; a book of poems; a creative writing textbook; a film on poetry for educational television.

SIDELIGHTS: Perkins told *CA:* "Eudora Welty's essay, 'Place in Fiction,' and David Madden's collection of short stories, *The Shadow Knows,* combined to make my personal past a possible subject for literature. In discovering my past, I have learned to write by trying my hand at whatever needed to be done. Coming north into 'exile' gave me a point-of-view, allowed me to see where I left off and the landscape began. Finding out who I am and where I am from has been the whole process up to now. I hope to spend the rest of my life making that discovery interesting to the reading public."

* * *

PERKINS, John (William)   1935-

PERSONAL: Born June 15, 1935, in Torquay, England; son of Wilfred Arthur (a builder) and Phyllis (Blatchford) Perkins; divorced; children: Laura Marie, Rachel Louise. *Education:* University of Manchester, B.A. (honors), 1957; University of Hull, certificate in education, 1958. *Religion:* Church of England. *Residence:* Cardiff, Wales. *Office:* Department of Extra-Mural Studies, University College, University of Wales, 38 Park Pl., Cardiff CF1 3BB, Wales.

CAREER: High school teacher in Lancastershire, England, 1958-60; high school teacher of geography and geology in Plymouth, England, 1960-65; Workers Educational Association, Plymouth, tutor and organizer for Plymouth and West

Devonshire, 1965-70; University of Wales, Cardiff, senior staff tutor in geology, 1970—. *Member:* Royal Geographical Society (fellow), Institute of British Geographers, Geographical Association, Geological Society (London; fellow), Geologists' Association, Devonshire Association, Ussher Society.

WRITINGS: Geology Explained in South and East Devon, David & Charles, 1971; *Geology Explained: Dartmoor and Tamar Valley,* David & Charles, 1972; (with W. E. Minchinton) *Tidemills of Devon and Cornwall,* Exeter Papers in Industrial Archaeology, 1972; (with R. A. Gayer and J. W. Baker) *Geological Guide to Glamorgan Heritage Coast,* Counties of Mid & South Glamorgan, 1975; *Geology Explained in Dorset,* David & Charles, 1977.

WORK IN PROGRESS: Geology Explained in Exmoor and North Devon; Visual Aids in Geology; geological guides to areas in South Wales.

SIDELIGHTS: Perkins told *CA:* "The recurrent theme in my career is the interpretation of geology to the layman. My books reflect my employment doing university extension work. I enjoy writing for adult students and I enjoy teaching them. If I travel abroad it is usually for geological studies." *Avocational interests:* Travel, photography, "rambling and fell walking."

* * *

PERLS, Hugo 1886(?)-1977

1886(?)—August 14, 1977; German-born art dealer, lecturer, and author of books on Plato and an autobiography, *Why Is Camilla Beautiful?* In 1910 Perls gave Mies van der Rohe his first commission to design a private house, and also commissioned Max Pechstein to paint murals in the house's dining room. Perls and his wife were both subjects of portraits by Edvard Munch. He died in New York, N.Y. Obituaries: *New York Times,* August 16, 1977; *AB Bookman's Weekly,* October 10, 1977.

* * *

PESSINA, Giorgio 1902(?)-1977

1902(?)—November 13, 1977; Italian fencing expert and author of books on fencing. Pessina won a gold medal in fencing in the 1928 Olympic Games at Amsterdam. Obituaries: *New York Times,* November 15, 1977.

* * *

PESSO, Albert 1929-

PERSONAL: Born September 19, 1929, in New York, N.Y.; son of Yakov and Esther (Albala) Pesso; married Diane Boyden (a psychomotor therapist), January 15, 1950; children: Tana Martha, Anna Tasmin, Tia Lorraine. *Education:* Goddard College, B.A., 1967. *Home and office address:* Lake Shore Dr., West Franklin, N.H. 03235.

CAREER: Emerson College, Boston, Mass., instructor, 1962-65, assistant professor, 1965-73, associate professor of dance, 1973-75, and director of dance, 1962-75; Psychomotor Institute, Boston, Mass., president, 1970—. Supervisor of psychomotor therapy at McLean Hospital, 1965-73; director of Pesso Psychotherapy Training Program in the Netherlands. *Member:* Association for Humanistic Psychology, American Academy of Psychotherapists.

WRITINGS: Movement in Psychotherapy, New York University Press, 1969; *Experience in Action,* New York University Press, 1973. Contributor to *Voices.*

WORK IN PROGRESS: Books on psychomotor theory; editing his lecture tapes, for publication.

SIDELIGHTS: Pesso comments: "At present I am traveling much of the year, providing training programs in psychomotor therapy for members of the helping professions in the United States and Europe. My wife and I are co-founders of psychomotor therapy."

Pesso described the basic tenets of psychomotor therapy: "Psychomotor is an action-oriented form of therapy and emotional re-education that is based on the theory that a major route to the unconscious is through the body. Feelings, emotions and states of mind affect the way we move, act and hold ourselves. We have found it possible, using PSP (Pesso System Psychomotor) techniques, to enter deeply into the memory and facilitate the re-experiencing of important past events. Positive accommodators as ideal good parents offer new essential emotional experiences which permit new behaviors. One can then transcend one's past without denying or forgetting it."

* * *

PETERS, F(rancis) E(dward) 1927-

PERSONAL: Born June 23, 1927, in New York, N.Y.; son of Frank L. and Marguerite (Quinlan) Peters; married Mary Battistessa (an executive secretary), 1966; children: Peter Paul. *Education:* St. Louis University, A.B., 1950, M.A., 1952; Princeton University, Ph.D., 1961. *Office:* Near East Center, New York University, New York, N.Y. 10012.

CAREER: New York University, New York, N.Y., assistant professor, 1961-64, associate professor of classics, 1964-69, professor of history and Near Eastern language and literature, 1969—. *Member:* American Oriental Society, Middle East Studies Association, Phi Beta Kappa.

WRITINGS: Greek Philosophical Terms, New York University Press, 1968; *Aristotle's Arabus,* E. J. Brill, 1968; *Aristotle and the Arabs,* New York University Press, 1969; *The Harvest of Hellenism,* Simon & Schuster, 1971; *Allah's Commonwealth,* Simon & Schuster, 1974.

WORK IN PROGRESS: The History of the Arabs Before Islam; A Social and Economic History of Medieval Islam.

SIDELIGHTS: Peters writes: "I am a historian of the Near East from 300 B.C. to 1200 A.D., and so also of Hellenistic Judaism, early Christianity, and medieval Islam. I am trained in Greek, Latin, Syriac, and Arabic, with extensive travels in the Islamic world from Morocco to India, but chiefly in Syria.

"My present work is concentrated upon the transition from the world of Greco-Roman antiquity to the new world of Islam. I have spent much of my career studying the passage of ideas from the Greeks to Islam, but more recently I have turned to institutions, and more particularly to the transition of the city and its life from a Greco-Roman milieu to an Islamic one: how the physical shape, functions and classes of the city of late antiquity changed into the present profile of an Islamic city. Much of my travelling is now devoted to an observation of urban geography (quarters, arrangement of street patterns, marketplaces, walls, etc.) as they reflect upon the preindustrial city. Near Eastern cities are rapidly changing and so the historical evidence is equally rapidly being effaced. Dead cities like Petra and Palmyra may remain frozen forever, but the non-industrialized part of living cities like Damascus, Aleppo are being altered faster than the historian can record and study them."

PETERS, H. Frederick 1910-

PERSONAL: Born January 18, 1910, in Dresden, Germany; son of Georg Friedrich (a businessman) and Rosa (Gerisch) Peters; married Helga Charlotte Burkhardt (a teacher), April 9, 1935; children: George Frederick. *Education:* Attended King's College, London, 1929-30; University of Munich, Ph.D., 1933. *Religion:* Episcopalian. *Agent:* Barthold Fles Literary Agency, 507 Fifth Ave., New York, N.Y. 10017. *Office:* Department of Foreign Languages, Portland State University, Portland, Ore.

CAREER: Marlborough College, Wiltshire, England, German master, 1933-35; Tonbridge School, Kent, England, foreign language master, 1935-39; Reed College, Portland, Ore., lecturer, 1940-44, assistant professor, 1944-48, associate professor of German, 1948-49; University of Munich, Munich, Germany, director of American studies and founder of American Institute, 1949-51; Reed College, professor of German, 1951-59; Portland State University, Portland, Ore., professor of German and comparative literature, 1959—, head of department of foreign languages, 1963-70, director, Central European Studies Center, 1965—. Director of Deutsche Sommerschule am Pazifik, 1958—; director of Deutsche Festspiele am Pazific, 1971—. Consultant to Oregon Arts Commission, 1971—. *Wartime service:* U.S. Office of Strategic Services, Washington, D.C., and overseas, 1944-45. U.S. Army, Adjutant General's Office, consultant on Fort Getty Project, 1945; received citation from U.S. Army, 1945.

MEMBER: American Association of Teachers of German, American Association of University Professors, Modern Language Association of America. *Awards, honors:* American Council of Learned Societies grant, 1958; Cross of Merit, Federal Republic of Germany, 1960; Goethe Medal of Goethe Institute, 1962.

WRITINGS: Rainer Maria Rilke: Masks and the Man, University of Washington Press, 1960; *My Sister, My Spouse: A Biography of Lou-Andreas Salome,* Norton, 1962; *Zarathustra's Sister: The Case of Elizabeth and Friedrich Nietzsche,* Crown, 1976. Contributor to *Saturday Review.* Associate editor of *German Quarterly.*

WORK IN PROGRESS: The Life of Friedrich Nietzsche.

AVOCATIONAL INTERESTS: Hiking, swimming, and reading.†

*   *   *

PETERS, Margot 1933-

PERSONAL: Born May 13, 1933, in Wausau, Wis.; daughter of Edgar J. and Elsie (a journalist; maiden name, Merkel) McCullough; children: Marc, Claire. *Education:* University of Wisconsin, Madison, B.A., 1961, M.A., 1965, Ph.D., 1969. *Home:* 511 College St., Lake Mills, Wis. 53551. *Office:* Department of English, University of Wisconsin, Whitewater, Wis. 53190.

CAREER: Northland College, Ashland, Wis., assistant professor of English, 1963-66; University of Wisconsin—Whitewater, assistant professor, 1969-74, associate professor, 1974-77, professor of English, 1977—. *Member:* Modern Language Association of America, Authors Guild of Authors League of America, Bronte Society, Women's Caucus for the Modern Languages, Midwest Modern Language Association. *Awards, honors:* Award from Friends of American Writers, 1975, for *Unquiet Soul;* American Council of Learned Societies fellowship, 1976-77.

WRITINGS: Charlotte Bronte: Style in the Novel, University of Wisconsin Press, 1973; *Unquiet Soul: A Biography of Charlotte Bronte,* Doubleday, 1975; *Shaw and the Actresses,* Doubleday, in press; (contributor) Michael Holroyd, editor, *The Genius of Bernard Shaw,* Rainbird Publishing, in press. Contributor to literature and education journals, and *Southwest Review.*

WORK IN PROGRESS: Love Me Lightly, a novel.

SIDELIGHTS: Margot Peters comments: "My chief interests are Victorian literature and women's studies. My motive for writing about Charlotte Bronte's life from a feminist viewpoint came from a belief that women and their accomplishments must be made visible; for the same reason I am approaching Shaw's career from the viewpoint of the actresses who contributed to it. I hope to write more biographies of women, also for the same reasons."

*   *   *

PETERSEN, Karen Daniels 1910-

PERSONAL: Born March 29, 1910, in St. Peter, Minn.; daughter of Jared Waldo (a physician) and Florence (a teacher; maiden name, Amundson) Daniels; married Sidney Alexander Petersen, June 13, 1935; children: Judith K. (Mrs. Donald Kadidlo), Frederick Sidney. *Education:* University of Minnesota, B.S. (with distinction), 1931. *Religion:* Episcopal. *Home:* 994 Delaware Ave., West St. Paul, Minn. 55118.

CAREER: High school teacher of English and Latin in Mahtomedi, Minn., 1931-35; Science Museum of Minnesota, St. Paul, staff member, 1958-64; free-lance writer, 1964—. Founder of Indian Crafts of the Episcopal Diocese of Minnesota (for marketing Indian craft work). *Member:* National League of American Pen Women, Western History Association, Minnesota Historical Society. *Awards, honors:* Award of merit from American Association for State and Local History; grants from American Philosophical Society and Minnesota Historical Society.

WRITINGS: (With E. Adamson Hoebel) *A Cheyenne Sketchbook,* University of Oklahoma Press, 1964; *Howling Wolf: A Cheyenne Warrior's Graphic History of His People,* American West, 1968; *Plains Indian Art from Fort Marion,* University of Oklahoma Press, 1973. Contributor to anthropology, archaeology, and ethnology journals.

WORK IN PROGRESS: Editing the memoirs of her father, Jared W. Daniels; a book of pictures presenting pre-reservation life as the Plains Indians showed it; a book on the imprisonment of Plains Indians in Fort Marion, Fla., 1875-78.

SIDELIGHTS: Karen Petersen writes: "The motivation for my deep involvement in American Indian culture—craft projects, field work, library research, and writing—had its origin a century before it stirred me to work. I am the third generation since Doctors A. W. and J. W. Daniels became physicians on the Minnesota Sioux Reservation in the 1850's. When many of their patients were hanged or imprisoned for revolting against unbearable wrongs, the brothers joined the few voices lifted in behalf of the Indian. Their sympathies, handed down to me, have started me on a long pathway.

"An attempt to better the economic condition of Minnesota Indian craftworkers by marketing their products led me to investigate craft processes and record nearly vanished techniques. Respect for the crafts moved me into making collections for museums and lecturing to school children. Curiosity over the origin of a family souvenir—a book of drawings by an Indian in 1876—pulled me deep into the dead language of Indian pictography. Another heirloom, this time the memoirs of one of the Daniels brothers, has brought me to my present involvement, the doctor's role in the beginnings of Indian reform.''

AVOCATIONAL INTERESTS: Following the trail of the Fort Marion prisoners up and down the East coast and interviewing their descendants in Oklahoma, camping on the reservations of Minnesota craftworkers, "ferreting out drawings in all sections of the country as well as Canada,'' "travel to far corners of the world to become familiar with other fast-fading simpler cultures, or to study the ruins left by civilizations lost in pre-history.''

*   *   *

PETERSHAM, Maud (Fuller)   1890-1971

PERSONAL: Born August 5, 1890, in Kingston, N.Y.; daughter of a Baptist minister; married Miska Petersham; children: Miki (a son). *Education:* Graduated from Vassar College; studied art at the New York School of Fine and Applied Art. *Residence:* Woodstock, N.Y.

CAREER: Author and illustrator of books for children. *Awards, honors:* Caldecott Medal, 1946, for *The Rooster Crows.*

WRITINGS—With husband, Miska Petersham; all published by J. C. Winston, except as noted: *Miki*, Doubleday, Doran, 1929; *The Ark of Father Noah and Mother Noah*, Doubleday, Doran, 1930; *The Christ Child, as Told by Matthew and Luke*, Doubleday, Doran, 1931; *Auntie and Celia Jane and Miki*, Doubleday, Doran, 1932. *The Story Book of Things We Use*, 1933; *The Story Book of Houses*, 1933; *The Story Book of Transportation*, 1933; *The Story Book of Food*, 1933; *The Story Book of Clothes*, 1933; *Get-a-Way and Hary Janos*, Viking, 1933; *Miki and Mary: Their Search for Treasures*, Viking, 1934.

The Story Book of Wheels, 1935; *The Story Book of Ships;*1935; *The Story Book of Trains*, 1935; *The Story Book of Aircraft*, 1935; *The Story Book of Wheels, Ships, Trains, Aircraft* (collected volume of four previous books), 1935; *The Story Book of Gold*, 1935; *The Story Book of Coal*, 1935; *The Story Book of Oil*, 1935; *The Story Book of Iron and Steel*, 1935; *The Story Book of Earth's Treasures: Gold, Coal, Oil, Iron and Steel* (collected volume of four previous books), 1935; *The Story Book of Wheat*, 1936; *The Story Book of Corn*, 1936; *The Story Book of Rice*, 1936; *The Story Book of Sugar*, 1936, published as *Let's Learn About Sugar*, Harvey House, 1969; *The Story Book of Foods from the Field: Wheat, Corn, Rice, Sugar* (collected volume of four previous books), 1936; *Joseph and His Brothers: From the Story Told in the Book of Genesis*, 1938; *Moses: From the Story Told in the Old Testament*, 1938; *Ruth: From the Story Told in the Book of Ruth*, 1938; *David: From the Story Told in the First Book of Samuel and the First Book of Kings*, 1938; *Stories from the Old Testament: Joseph, Moses, Ruth, David* (collected volume of four previous books), 1938; *The Story Book of Cotton*, 1939; *The Story Book of Wool*, 1939; *The Story Book of Rayon*, 1939; *The Story Book of Silk*, 1939, published as *Let's Learn About Silk*, Harvey House, 1967; *The Story Book of Things We Wear* (collected volume of four previous books), 1939.

An American ABC (illustrated by the authors), Macmillan, 1941, reprinted, 1966; *America's Stamps: The Story of One Hundred Years of U.S. Postage Stamps*, Macmillan, 1947; *The Box with Red Wheels*, Macmillan, 1949, reprinted, 1973; *The Circus Baby*, Macmillan, 1950, reprinted, 1972; *Story of the Presidents of the United States of America*,

Macmillan, 1953; *Off to Bed: Seven Stories for Wide-Awakes*, Macmillan, 1954; *The Boy Who Had No Heart*, Macmillan, 1955; *The Silver Mace: A Story of Williamsburg*, Macmillan, 1956; *The Peppernuts*, Macmillan, 1958.

Illustrator—with husband, Miska Petersham: William Bowen, *Enchanted Forest*, Macmillan, 1920; Carl Sandburg, *Rootabaga Stories*, Harcourt, 1922, reprinted, 1974; Charles Lamb, *Tales from Shakespeare*, Macmillan, 1923; Sandburg, *Rootabaga Pigeons*, Harcourt, 1923; Sisters of Mercy (St. Xavier College, Chicago), *Marquette Readers*, Macmillan, 1924; Mabel Guinnip La Rue, *In Animal Land*, Macmillan, 1924; Margery Clark, *Poppy Seed Cakes*, Doubleday, 1924; Inez M. Howard, Alice Hawthorne, and Mae Howard, *Language Garden: A Primary Language Book*, Macmillan, 1924; Harriott Fansler and Isidoro Panlasigui, *Philippine National Literature*, Macmillan, 1925; Bessie B. Coleman, W. L. Uhl, and J. F. Hosie, *Pathway to Reading*, Silver, Burdette, 1925; Florence C. Coolidge, *Little Ugly Face, and Other Indian Tales*, Macmillan, 1925; John W. Wayland, *History Stories for Primary Grades*, Macmillan, 1925.

Elizabeth C. Miller, *Children of the Mountain Eagle*, Doubleday, 1927; *Everyday Canadian Primer*, Macmillan, 1928; Marguerite Clement, *Where Was Bobby?*, Doubleday, Doran, 1928; Wilhelmina Harper and A. J. Hamilton, compilers, *Pleasant Pathways*, Macmillan, 1928; Harper and Hamilton, compilers, *Winding Roads*, Macmillan, 1929; Harper and Hamilton, compilers, *Heights and Highways*, Macmillan, 1929; Harper and Hamilton, compilers, *Far Away Hills*, Macmillan, 1929; Miller, *Pran of Albania*, Doubleday, Doran, 1929; Miller, *Young Trajan*, Doubleday, 1931; Sydney V. Rowland, W. D. Lewis, and E. J. Marshall, compilers, *Beckoning Road*, J. C. Winston, 1931; Rowland, Lewis, and Marshall, *Rich Cargoes*, J. C. Winston, 1931; Rowland, Lewis, and Marshall, *Wings of Adventure*, J. C. Winston, 1931; Rowland, Lewis, and Marshall, *Treasure Trove*, J. C. Winston, 1931.

Carlo Collodi, *Adventures of Pinocchio*, Garden City Publishing, 1932; Johanna Spyri, *Heidi*, Garden City Publishing, 1932; Jean Young Ayer, *Picnic Book*, Macmillan, 1934; Post Wheeler, *Albanian Wonder Tales*, Doubleday, 1936; Marie Barringer, *Four and Lena*, Doubleday, 1938; Miriam Evangeline Mason, *Susannah, the Pioneer Cow*, Macmillan, 1941; Emilie F. Johnson, *Little Book of Prayers*, Viking, 1941; *Story of Jesus: A Little New Testament*, Macmillan, 1942, reprinted, 1967; Ethan A. Cross and Elizabeth Carney, editors, *Literature*, 1943-46; Mother Goose, *The Rooster Crows: A Book of American Rhymes and Jingles*, Macmillan, 1945; Association for Childhood Education, Literature Committee, *Told Under the Christmas Tree*, Macmillan, 1948; Elsie S. Eells, *Tales of Enchantment from Spain*, Dodd, 1950; Washington Irving, *Rip Van Winkle [and] The Legend of Sleepy Hollow*, Macmillan, 1951; Benjamin Franklin, *Bird in the Hand*, Macmillan, 1951; Eric P. Kelly, *In Clean Hay*, Macmillan, 1953; M. E. Mason, *Miss Posy Longlegs*, Macmillan, 1955.

SIDELIGHTS: Although Maud Petersham did receive some formal art training, she claimed she learned more from working with her husband, Miska. They met at an advertising agency in New York, where both had jobs in the art department.

The Petershams began by illustrating the books of other authors. Often they discovered that the text did not lend itself well to illustrations, so they outlined a book of their own including words and pictures. The pictures were done first and then the text, with the assumption by the Petershams that it would be rewritten by a children's author. To their surprise, *Miki,* their first attempt, was accepted just as it was.

The Petershams did a lot of research for their children's books. They spent three months in Palestine before doing the illustrations for *The Christ Child. Saturday Review* said: "The pictures are soft and delicate in coloring and have all the feeling of Eastern warmth and sunshine. We are glad that the text is not re-told, but taken directly from the Gospels of Matthew and Luke, the only words in which the story of the Nativity should be presented to children." The *New York Times* added, "Here is a picture book that in its reverent and child-like beauty has captured the very spirit of Christmas. Unerringly the artists have put into their illustrations just the details which appeal to a child. The animals, from the small lamb that the shepherd is holding beneath his cloak, to the splendid camels of the Wise Men, interest and please children."

BIOGRAPHICAL/CRITICAL SOURCES: Saturday Review of Literature, December 12, 1931; *New York Times,* November 15, 1931; *Publishers Weekly,* June 22, 1946; Elizabeth Rider Montgomery, *Story Behind Modern Books,* Dodd, 1949.

OBITUARIES: New York Times, November 30, 1971; *Washington Post,* December 3, 1971; *Publishers Weekly,* December 13, 1971.*

(Died November 29, 1971)

*   *   *

PETERSHAM, Miska   1888-1960

PERSONAL: Given name was Petrezselyem Mikaly; born September 20, 1888, in Toeroekszentmiklos, near Budapest, Hungary; emigrated to the United States, 1912, later became a naturalized citizen; married Maud Fuller; children: Miki (a son). *Education:* Attended art school in Budapest and in London. *Residence:* Woodstock, N.Y.

CAREER: Author and illustrator of books for children. *Awards, honors:* Caldecott Medal, 1946, for *The Rooster Crows.*

WRITINGS—With wife, Maud Petersham; all published by J. C. Winston, except as noted: *Miki,* Doubleday, Doran, 1929; *The Ark of Father Noah and Mother Noah,* Doubleday, Doran, 1930; *The Christ Child, as Told by Matthew and Luke,* Doubleday, Doran, 1931; *Auntie and Celia Jane and Miki,* Doubleday, Doran, 1932. *The Story Book of Things We Use,* 1933; *The Story Book of Houses,* 1933; *The Story Book of Transportation,* 1933; *The Story Book of Food,* 1933; *The Story Book of Clothes,* 1933; *Get-a-Way and Hary Janos,* Viking, 1933; *Miki and Mary: Their Search for Treasures,* Viking, 1934.

The Story Book of Wheels, 1935; *The Story Book of Ships,*1935; *The Story Book of Trains,* 1935; *The Story Book of Aircraft,* 1935; *The Story Book of Wheels, Ships, Trains, Aircraft* (collected volume of four previous books), 1935; *The Story Book of Gold,* 1935; *The Story Book of Coal,* 1935; *The Story Book of Oil,* 1935; *The Story Book of Iron and Steel,* 1935; *The Story Book of Earth's Treasures: Gold, Coal, Oil, Iron and Steel* (collected volume of four previous books), 1935; *The Story Book of Wheat,* 1936; *The Story Book of Corn,* 1936; *The Story Book of Rice,* 1936; *The Story Book of Sugar,* 1936, published as *Let's Learn About Sugar,* Harvey House, 1969; *The Story Book of Foods from the Field: Wheat, Corn, Rice, Sugar* (collected volume of four previous books), 1936; *Joseph and His*

Brothers: From the Story Told in the Book of Genesis, 1938; *Moses: From the Story Told in the Old Testament,* 1938; *Ruth: From the Story Told in the Book of Ruth,* 1938; *David: From the Story Told in the First Book of Samuel and the First Book of Kings,* 1938; *Stories from the Old Testament: Joseph, Moses, Ruth, David* (collected volume of four previous books), 1938; *The Story Book of Cotton,* 1939; *The Story Book of Wool,* 1939; *The Story Book of Rayon,* 1939; *The Story Book of Silk,* 1939, published as *Let's Learn About Silk,* Harvey House, 1967; *The Story Book of Things We Wear* (collected volume of four previous books), 1939.

An American ABC (illustrated by the authors), Macmillan, 1941, reprinted, 1966; *America's Stamps: The Story of One Hundred Years of U.S. Postage Stamps,* Macmillan, 1947; *The Box with Red Wheels,* Macmillan, 1949, reprinted, 1973; *The Circus Baby,* Macmillan, 1950, reprinted, 1972; *Story of the Presidents of the United States of America,* Macmillan, 1953; *Off to Bed: Seven Stories for Wide-Awakes,* Macmillan, 1954; *The Boy Who Had No Heart,* Macmillan, 1955; *The Silver Mace: A Story of Williamsburg,* Macmillan, 1956; *The Peppernuts,* Macmillan, 1958.

Illustrator—with wife, Maud Petersham: William Bowen, *Enchanted Forest,* Macmillan, 1920; Carl Sandburg, *Rootabaga Stories,* Harcourt, 1922, reprinted, 1974; Charles Lamb, *Tales from Shakespeare,* Macmillan, 1923; Sandburg, *Rootabaga Pigeons,* Harcourt, 1923; Sisters of Mercy (St. Xavier College, Chicago), *Marquette Readers,* Macmillan, 1924; Mabel Guinnip La Rue, *In Animal Land,* Macmillan, 1924; Margery Clark, *Poppy Seed Cakes,* Doubleday, 1924; Inez M. Howard, Alice Hawthorne, and Mae Howard, *Language Garden: A Primary Language Book,* Macmillan, 1924; Harriott Fansler and Isidoro Panlasigui, *Philippine National Literature,* Macmillan, 1925; Bessie B. Coleman, W. L. Uhl, and J. F. Hosie, *Pathway to Reading,* Silver, Burdette, 1925; Florence C. Coolidge, *Little Ugly Face, and Other Indian Tales,* Macmillan, 1925; John W. Wayland, *History Stories for Primary Grades,* Macmillan, 1925.

Elizabeth C. Miller, *Children of the Mountain Eagle,* Doubleday, 1927; *Everyday Canadian Primer,* Macmillan, 1928; Marguerite Clement, *Where Was Bobby?,* Doubleday, Doran, 1928; Wilhelmina Harper and A. J. Hamilton, compilers, *Pleasant Pathways,* Macmillan, 1928; Harper and Hamilton, compilers, *Winding Roads,* Macmillan, 1929; Harper and Hamilton, compilers, *Heights and Highways,* Macmillan, 1929; Harper and Hamilton, compilers, *Far Away Hills,* Macmillan, 1929; Miller, *Pran of Albania,* Doubleday, Doran, 1929; Miller, *Young Trajan,* Doubleday, 1931; Sydney V. Rowland, W. D. Lewis, and E. J. Marshall, compilers, *Beckoning Road,* J. C. Winston, 1931; Rowland, Lewis, and Marshall, *Rich Cargoes,* J. C. Winston, 1931; Rowland, Lewis, and Marshall, *Wings of Adventure,* J. C. Winston, 1931; Rowland, Lewis, and Marshall, *Treasure Trove,* J. C. Winston, 1931.

Carlo Collodi, *Adventures of Pinocchio,* Garden City Publishing, 1932; Johanna Spyri, *Heidi,* Garden City Publishing, 1932; Jean Young Ayer, *Picnic Book,* Macmillan, 1934; Post Wheeler, *Albanian Wonder Tales,* Doubleday, 1936; Marie Barringer, *Four and Lena,* Doubleday, 1938; Miriam Evangeline Mason, *Susannah, the Pioneer Cow,* Macmillan, 1941; Emilie F. Johnson, *Little Book of Prayers,* Viking, 1941; *Story of Jesus: A Little New Testament,* Macmillan, 1942, reprinted, 1967; Ethan A. Cross and Elizabeth Carney, editors, *Literature,* 1943-46; Mother Goose, *The Rooster Crows: A Book of American Rhymes and Jingles,* Macmillan, 1945; Association for Childhood Education,

Literature Committee, *Told Under the Christmas Tree,* Macmillan, 1948; Elsie S. Eells, *Tales of Enchantment from Spain,* Dodd, 1950; Washington Irving, *Rip Van Winkle* [*and*] *The Legend of Sleepy Hollow,* Macmillan, 1951; Benjamin Franklin, *Bird in the Hand,* Macmillan, 1951; Eric P. Kelly, *In Clean Hay,* Macmillan, 1953; M. E. Mason, *Miss Posy Longlegs,* Macmillan, 1955.

SIDELIGHTS: When Miska Petersham bought his first box of paints at age seven, he decided that he wanted to be an artist instead of a sea captain. As a youth, he walked many miles each day in order to attend art school in Budapest. He had been self-supporting since the age of twelve, went to London when he was twenty, and to the United States a few years later. He would work at any job he could find until he saved some money. Then, he would leave the job and paint until he ran out of money. Following his marriage to Maud Fuller, another illustrator, the Petershams received their big break. Willy Pogany, the illustrator, was a friend of Miska. He had more work than he could possibly do, so he gave Miska and Maud a children's book to illustrate. From that time on, they did nothing else.

Besides illustrating, the Petershams also wrote and illustrated books of their own. The idea for *Circus Baby* came after a visit to the winter headquarters of the Ringling Brothers Circus in Sarasota, Florida. The *New York Times* commented: "Maud and Miska Petersham have combined talents again to make a delightful picture book. The four-color circus scenes are bright and simple. Mother and Baby are wonderfully expressive but still quite real elephants, rather than the stuffed-toy variety so familiar in the nursery books." The *New York Herald Tribune* wrote, describing the Petershams' *The Story of the Presidents of the United States of America:* "The text is excellent, considering the space limitations. Great events are well selected. Personalities are described neatly. There is no room for generalizing on politics or the flow of social history, yet readers of about 11 to 14 would gather much history from the pages."

BIOGRAPHICAL/CRITICAL SOURCES: Publishers Weekly, 1946; Elizabeth Rider Montgomery, *Story Behind Modern Books,* Dodd, 1949; *New York Times,* October 1, 1950; *New York Herald Tribune Book Review,* May 17, 1953.

OBITUARIES: New York Times, May 16, 1960; *Publishers Weekly,* May 23, 1960.*

(Died May 15, 1960)

* * *

PETERSON, Carolyn Sue 1938-

PERSONAL: Born June 23, 1938, in Carthage, Mo.; daughter of Harry A. and Clara (a nutrition aide; maiden name, Johnson) Peterson; children: Angie (adopted). *Education:* Joplin Junior College, A.A., 1957; University of Missouri, A.B., 1959, graduate study, 1964-66; University of Denver, M.A.L.S., 1960; further graduate study at Northwest Missouri State College, 1966-68. *Home:* 3002 Illingworth Ave., Orlando, Fla. 32806. *Office:* Orlando Public Library, 10 North Rosalind, Orlando, Fla. 32801.

CAREER: Town and Country Regional Library, Joplin, Mo., children's librarian, 1960-62; Northwest Missouri State University, Maryville, instructor in library science and librarian at university elementary and high schools, 1962-68; University of Colorado, Boulder, instructor in library science, 1968-70; Orlando Public Library, Orlando, Fla., head of children's department, 1970—.

MEMBER: American Library Association, National League of American Penwomen, National Organization for Women (local vice-president, 1977), Southeastern Library Association, Florida Library Association (president of Children's Caucus, 1976-77), Central Florida Library Association, Orlando League of American Penwomen.

WRITINGS: Reference Books for Elementary and Junior High School Libraries, Scarecrow, 1970, revised edition, 1975.

Author of filmstrip "Sharing Literature with Children," Orlando Public Library, 1974.

Work anthologized in *Start Early for an Early Start,* American Library Association, 1976. Contributor of poems and articles to education and library journals and to children's magazines, including *Jack and Jill* and *Child Life.*

WORK IN PROGRESS: Index to Children's Songs, with Ann D. Fenton; a story program handbook for beginners, with Brenny Hall.

SIDELIGHTS: Carolyn Peterson writes: "Since my professional concerns revolve primarily around children, books, and reading, I have attempted through writing as well as action to promote interest in all three. I believe that children who are reared with a love for books will become reading adults and that adults who read will become enlightened and concerned citizens. With whatever facilities at my disposal, I want to contribute to the welfare and growth of children, for they are our most valuable resources."

AVOCATIONAL INTERESTS: Guitar, archery, sewing, music, collecting sea shells, hiking, the women's movement.

* * *

PETERSON, Eldridge 1905(?)-1977

1905(?)—December 15, 1977; American advertiser, editor, publisher, and author of a book of verse. Peterson was editor and publisher of *Printers Ink* until 1958. He died in New York, N.Y. Obituaries: *New York Times,* December 17, 1977.

* * *

PETERSON, Harold L(eslie) 1922-1978

May 22, 1922—January 1, 1978; American historian, curator, and authority on antique weapons. Peterson, chief curator of the National Park Service, began his career with the park service in 1947 as a historian. He was active in the Eastern National Park and Monuments Association, and served many terms as chairman of the board of directors. Peterson, an authority on weaponry, had an extensive collection of arms and armour. He was named honorary curator of edged weapons at the West Point Museum. Peterson was the author of more than twenty books on weapons and numerous historical publications for the National Park Service. Obituaries: *Washington Post,* January 5, 1978. (See index for *CA* sketch)

* * *

PETERSON, Mendel (Lazear) 1918-

PERSONAL: Born March 8, 1918, in Moore, Idaho; son of Hans Jordan (a professor of psychology) and Fannie (Lish) Peterson; married LaNelle Walker, July 5, 1937 (divorced, May, 1962); married Gertrude A. Auvil (an editor), August 19, 1962; children: (first marriage) LaNelle Hampton (Mrs. Gerald Spence), Mendel Lazear, Jr.; (second marriage) Anna Victoria. *Education:* University of Southern Mississippi, B.S. (honors), 1938; Vanderbilt University, M.A., 1939; attended Lowell Technical Institute, 1945-47. *Politics:* "Horrified observer." *Religion:* "Amused observer." *Home and office address:* P.O. Box 404, McLean, Va. 22101. *Agent:* Julian Bach Literary Agency, Inc., 3 East 48th St., New York, N.Y. 10017.

CAREER: Civilian Conservation Corps (CCC), Nachidoches, Miss., camp educational adviser for Louisiana-Mississippi district, 1939-42; Montgomery Ward, Fort Worth, Tex., management trainee, 1942-43; Smithsonian Institution, Washington, D.C., curator of department of history, 1948-56, chairman of department of armed forces history, 1956-69, curator of Division of Historical Archaeology, 1969-73, director of underwater exploration, 1973—; writer, 1973—. Vice-president of Explorers Research Corp. for Underwater Exploration, 1967—. Consultant to the governments of Bermuda, Jamaica, and Mexico. *Military service:* U.S. Naval Reserve, 1943-70, active duty, 1943-48; became commander.

MEMBER: International Institute for the Conservation of Historic and Artistic Works, International Oceanographic Foundation, American Institute of Archaeology, American Numismatic Association, Nautical Research Association, Company of Military Collectors and Historians, American Association for the Advancement of Science, Society of the South Pole, Club de Exploraciones y Deportes Acuaticos de Mexico (honorary life member), Explorers Club.

WRITINGS: History Under the Sea, Smithsonian Institution Press, 1965, 3rd edition, 1969; *Exploring the Ocean World,* Crowell, 1969, 2nd edition, 1972; *Buried Treasure Beneath the Spanish Main,* U.N.E.S.C.O., 1972; (contributor) George Bass, editor, *A History of Seafaring,* Thames & Hudson, 1972; (contributor) *Underwater Archaeology,* U.N.E.S.C.O., 1972; (contributor) Robert Breeden, editor, *Undersea Treasures,* National Geographic Society, 1974; *Funnel of Gold: Commerce and Warfare in the West Indies,* Little, Brown, 1975. Contributor of articles on underwater exploration, numismatics, and military (especially naval) history to professional journals.

WORK IN PROGRESS: The Undersea Museum, an encyclopedia of underwater discoveries; *Art on Artillery,* on the marking and decoration of muzzle-loading cannon; *Three Hundred Years in Fifty Feet: An Historian Under the Sea,* an autobiography.

SIDELIGHTS: Peterson's travels have taken him to Europe, the Pacific, Antarctica, South America, the Caribbean, and the Philippines. *Avocational interests:* Collecting prints, paintings, antiques, and Roman and Greek coins.

*   *   *

PETERSON, Reona 1941-

PERSONAL: Born May 16, 1941, in New Zealand; daughter of Albert Hector (a sales manager) and Rena (Frobarth) Peterson. *Education:* Auckland Teachers College, certificate, 1960; Auckland University, diploma, 1965. *Religion:* Baptist. *Home address:* P.O. Box 325, 1010 Lausanne, Switzerland.

CAREER: Teacher and music specialist at junior high school in Aukland, New Zealand, 1961-66; international travel and volunteer work, 1967; teacher and music specialist at junior high in Aukland, 1968-69; teacher in Orthodox Jewish grammar school in London, England, 1970-71; Youth With a Mission, Lausanne, Switzerland, secretary and teacher, 1971—.

WRITINGS: Tomorrow You Die, Bible Voice, 1976.

SIDELIGHTS: Reona Peterson told *CA:* "I came to Europe at the beginning of 1970 to study the relevance of the Christian gospel and how it could be effectively communicated to the present generation, regardless of their ideological, philosophical, or religious backgrounds. This necessitated travel as well as study and what began in 1970 has continued throughout the past eight years. Meeting with people on every continent of every persuasion, I am more convinced than ever that Jesus Christ is the way, the truth, and the life for all men. My brief time in Albania—the saga told in *Tomorrow You Die*—served to illustrate this belief even more strongly. If I write again it will be to exhort those who consider themselves Christians to discover the radical life—a changing faith that shook this world in the first century and to see the twentieth century similarly affected."

*   *   *

PETIT, Gaston 1930-

PERSONAL: Born August 16, 1930, in Shawinigan, Quebec, Canada; son of Joseph Arthur and Antoinette (Heroux) Petit. *Education:* Attended Dominican House of Studies, Ottawa, 1953-60, Sophia University, Tokyo, 1961, and Naganuma Japanese School of Language, 1961-63; studied calligraphy under Nankoku Hidai. *Home:* 13, 18 Nampeidai, Shibuya-Ku, Tokyo 150, Japan.

CAREER: Ordained Roman Catholic priest, 1959; Tokyo Atelier, Tokyo, Japan, teacher, 1967-74; Junshin College of Art, Tokyo, print division director, 1968-73; writer, 1973—. Held over fifty one-man art exhibits in eight countries; worked on over twenty Japanese architectural projects.

WRITINGS: 44 Modern Japanese Print Artists, Kodansha, 1973; *Gendai Hanga,* Kodansha, 1974; *Evolving Techniques in Japanese Woodblock Prints,* Kodansha, 1977. Contributor to *Hemisphere, Maintenant,* and other publications.

WORK IN PROGRESS: Japanese Who's Who in Printmaking; Children's Scribblings Lead to Human. Figuration; QWERTYUIOPLKJHGFDSAZXCVBNM; and *The Narrative Image.*

SIDELIGHTS: "As a trilingual Canadian living in Japan," Petit told *CA,* "my thinking reflects my insertion in a Mcluhanesque 20th century coupled with the awareness of a spiritual presence behind the phenomena." *Avocational interests:* Listening to and composing music.

*   *   *

PETROU, David Michael 1949-

PERSONAL: Born November 3, 1949, in Washington, D.C.; son of John (an executive) and Bebe (a sociologist; maiden name, Koch) Petrou. *Education:* University of Maryland, B.A., 1971; Georgetown University, M.A., 1973. *Home:* 7409 Arrowood Rd., Bethesda, Maryland 20034. *Agent:* Kurt Frings Agency, 9440 Santa Monica Blvd., Beverly Hills, Calif. 90210. *Office:* Pinewood Studios, Iver Heath, Buckinghamshire, England.

CAREER: Psychiatric Institutes of America, Washington, D.C., associate director of publicity, 1972; Warner Brothers Inc., Burbank, Calif., publicist for "The Exorcist," 1972-73; Random House, New York City, publicist and editorialist, 1974-75; *In the Know,* New York City, Washington and Los Angeles editor, 1975—. Assistant to the producers for literary projects, Salkind Organization, London, England, 1975—. *Member:* Washington Independent Writers (charter member). *Awards, honors:* Woodrow Wilson fellowship, University of Maryland, 1971.

WRITINGS: The Prince and the Pauper: Fantasy to Film, Grossett & Dunlap, 1978; *Superman—Supermovie: The Making of Superman,* Warner Books, 1978. Also author of short stories and screenplays. Contributor to *In the Know, New York, Newsweek, People, Washingtonian, Washington Post,* and *Village Voice.*

SIDELIGHTS: David Petrou, whose notable assignments include interviews with Marlon Brando and Racquel Welch, told *CA:* "The primary motivating force in shaping the direction of my career has been my pervasive desire to communicate with people, and this, coupled with a long standing fascination with the film industry—in my opinion, the only totally new art form in the last two hundred years—has led to my pursuit of the mastery of filmmaking techniques and a future as a screenwriter."

AVOCATIONAL INTERESTS: Cartooning, tennis, travel.

*   *   *

PETROVA, Olga   1884(?)-1977

1884(?)—November 30, 1977; British-born actress and playwright best known for "The White Peacock" and "The Hurricane." She performed in vaudeville, on Broadway, and in silent films. In 1942 Petrova published her autobiography, *Butter With My Bread.* She died in Clearwater, Fla. Obituaries: *New York Times,* December 7, 1977.

*   *   *

PETROVSKY, N.
See POLTORATZKY, N(ikolai) P(etrovich)

*   *   *

PFADT, Robert Edward   1915-

PERSONAL: Surname is pronounced Faught; born May 22, 1915, in Erie, Pa.; son of George Maxwell (a toolmaker) and Margaret (Illig) Pfadt; married Julia A. VanDeventer, May 27, 1948; children: Kathryn, Margaret, Robert David, Elizabeth. *Education:* University of Wyoming, B.A., 1938, M.A., 1940; University of Minnesota, Ph.D., 1948. *Politics:* Republican. *Religion:* Episcopal. *Home:* 1933 Custer, Laramie, Wyo. 82070. *Office:* Department of Entomology, University of Wyoming, P.O. Box 3354, Laramie, Wyo. 82071.

CAREER: State Fish Commission, Cheyenne, Wyo., field assistant, 1938; U.S. Department of Agriculture, Bureau of Entomology and Plant Quarantine, Bozeman, Mont., field supervisor, 1939; University of Wyoming, Laramie, field assistant, 1940-42, assistant professor, 1943-48, associate professor, 1948-54, professor of entomology, 1954—, head of department of entomology and parasitology, 1952-62. Plant protection adviser and chief of party on U.S. Agency for International Development team in Kabul, Afghanistan, 1967-68; member of Task Force to Review the National Plant Pest Detection and Information Program.

MEMBER: Entomological Society of America, American Association for the Advancement of Science (fellow), Pan American Society of Acridologists, Entomological Society of Canada, Royal Entomological Society (fellow), Association d'Acridologie, Entomological Society of Ontario, Kansas Entomological Society, Sigma Xi, Phi Kappa Phi.

WRITINGS: (Editor and contributor) *Fundamentals of Applied Entomology,* Macmillan, 1962, 3rd edition, in press; *Grasshoppers,* Follett, 1966; *Animals Without Backbones,* Follett, 1967.

WORK IN PROGRESS: Crickets-Their Ways of Living, completion expected in 1979.

SIDELIGHTS: Pfadt writes: "One of the most interesting periods of my life was the two years spent in Afghanistan. Although Kabul, the capital of Afghanistan, has many new buildings and homes as well as ancient structures, the villages appear medieval and are without modern conveniences. The adobe houses have no electricity, running water, or central heating. Restaurants often consist of rough wooden or adobe structures, in which guests sit on wool rugs that cover the earthen floors. The food is cooked on the grill of an adobe-brick stove. As the custom of Afghans is to eat with their hands, village restaurants often have no utensils for their infrequent foreign guests. The menu is limited to a few items, pilou, boiled lamb over rice, or a stew of goat meat, and always plenty of flat bread, called nan, and hot tea.

"Afghanistan, mainly desert and with a temperate to subtropical climate, offers a favorable environment for a large variety of grasshoppers. It was very exciting for me to collect unfamiliar species, not knowing whether they were described already or new to science. Later at the British Museum of Natural History in London, I was able to classify my collection. Three new, undescribed species were represented among the specimens. I enjoyed giving these names.

"Back again in the United States I have a much better appreciation of this blessed country of ours, its abundance of good food, endless variety of consumer products, modern homes, fine hospitals and excellent physicians, great educational systems, replete libraries, great symphony orchestras, and many other forms of art and clean entertainment."

*   *   *

PHELAN, John Martin   1932-

PERSONAL: Born May 1, 1932, in New York, N.Y.; son of John Alfred (a systems accountant) and Irene (Boyhen) Phelan; married Jane Balinong (an editor), July 10, 1971; children: Mary Jo, Regina. *Education:* Fordham University, A.B. (cum laude), 1956, M.A. (education; cum laude), 1958; Woodstock College, Woodstock, Md., M.A. (philosophy; cum laude), 1957, S.T.B. (cum laude), 1962, S.T.L. (cum laude), 1964; New York University, Ph.D. (cum laude), 1968. *Office:* Department of Communications, Fordham University, New York, N.Y. 10458.

CAREER: Entered Society of Jesus (Jesuits), 1950, ordained Roman Catholic priest, 1963, legally released from obligations of the priesthood in 1971; Marine Hospital, Baltimore, Md., senior chaplain, 1963-64; Johns Hopkins University, Baltimore, assistant Newman chaplain, 1963; Rensselaer Polytechnic Institute, Troy, N.Y., assistant Newman chaplain, 1964; Russell Sage College, Troy, assistant Newman chaplain, 1965; Fordham University, New York, N.Y., assistant professor, 1968-72, associate professor, 1972-78, professor of communications, 1978—, chairperson of department, 1969-76, research associate at Institute for Social Research, 1972—, founding director of graduate program in public communications, 1976—. Editor of Jesuit Press, 1965-68.

MEMBER: International Communications Association, Association for Education in Journalism, American Academy of Arts and Sciences, Women in Communications (local founding moderator, 1971), Sigma Delta Chi (local founding moderator, 1970).

WRITINGS: Morality and a Space Program, American

Press, 1962; (editor) *Communications Control,* Sheed, 1969; *Local Advocacy and Delinquency,* Youth Development, U.S. Department of Health, Education & Welfare, 1973; (editor) *Methadone Diversion,* National Institute of Mental Health, 1974; *Mediaworld: Programming the Public,* Continuum Books, 1977; *Mediamyth,* Seabury, 1979; *Entertaining Ethics,* Hastings House, 1979.

SIDELIGHTS: Phelan writes: "As an administrator who directed the five-fold growth of a multi-disciplinary department, as a former clergyman who counseled collegians, medical professionals, and working people, and now as a husband and father (of two adopted teenagers), I have been increasingly impressed by the power of ideas both to create and destroy. Ideas build empires; ideas wreck economies; ideas save careers and marriages; ideas cause ulcers and heartbreak. Further, I have seen that their power is dependent on how effectively they are delivered, expressed, communicated. Without persuasive communication, genius cannot ignite any allegiance; with it, madmen and charlatans can wreck lives and countries. I am professionally committed to communicating effectively the positive insights of the humanities and the social sciences with the hope of bettering lives as well as opening minds. I welcome every opportunity to pursue this vocation in corporate and governmental contexts as well as on the campus."

*   *   *

PHILLIPS, Anne G(arvey)   1929-
(Anne G. Dye)

PERSONAL: Born August 12, 1929, in New York, N.Y.; daughter of Thomas and Olive (Birkett) Garvey; married Henry A. Dye, July 29, 1950 (divorced, February, 1975); married Robert M. Phillips, August 6, 1977; children: (first marriage) Constance, John. *Education:* Wilson College, B.A., 1949; University of Chicago, M.A., 1950; further graduate study at Occidental College, 1951, University of Iowa (Los Angeles extension), 1956-63, and University of California, Los Angeles, 1964-68. *Politics:* Democrat. *Religion:* Unitarian-Universalist. *Home:* 1801 Hill St., Santa Monica, Calif. 90405. *Office:* Department of English, Santa Monica College, 1900 Pico, Santa Monica, Calif. 90405.

CAREER: California Institute of Technology, Pasadena, computer-plotter in wind tunnel, 1950-51; high school teacher in Baldwin Park, Calif., 1951-52; Jet Propulsion Lab, Pasadena, computer-plotter, 1952-53; University of California, Los Angeles, instructor, 1966-67; high school teacher in Beverly Hills, Calif., 1969-70; Los Angeles Trade-Technical College, Los Angeles, part-time instructor, 1970-71, full-time instructor, 1971-72; California State University, Long Beach, study skills counselor at learning assistance center, 1972-73; Santa Monica College, Santa Monica, Calif., instructor in English and reading, 1973—. Part-time instructor at Santa Monica College, 1965-73. *Member:* National Council of Teachers of English, American Association of Junior College Women, Sierra Club, Zero Population Growth, Friends of Animals, Save-the-Redwoods League, Western College Reading Association.

WRITINGS: (With Wanda Miller and Doris Ladd) *Reading Faster and Understanding More,* Winthrop Publishing, 1976.

SIDELIGHTS: Phillips told *CA:* "I am intrigued by studies which show that groups of youngsters who simply read for hours on their own do better in reading and writing than control groups who are led through the usual organized work in reading, grammar, writing, etc. I feel that most of us who are literate—who read and write easily—learned literacy the same way, through long familiarity in our families or on our own with all sorts of interesting things to read. Perhaps 'reading a lot' is more effective than all the experts, dollars, special classes—yes—new textbooks like our own! But until people accept this fact, new courses and textbooks will still be sold—and perhaps will help a little."

*   *   *

PHILLIPS, Dorothy W.   1906-1977

1906—December 15, 1977; American curator, editor, and author of *Ancient Egyptian Animals.* Phillips was curator of Corcoran Gallery of Art from 1958 until 1976. She died in Washington, D.C. Obituaries: *New York Times,* December 17, 1977; *Washington Post,* December 19, 1977.

*   *   *

PHILLIPS, Paul   1938-

PERSONAL: Born November 3, 1938, in Hong Kong; son of Richard G. (an accountant) and Mary D. (a teacher; maiden name, Ricketts) Phillips; married Donna C. Speers (a free-lance writer and broadcaster), September 13, 1958; children: Erin, Nicole. *Education:* Attended Victoria College (now University of Victoria), 1956-58; University of Saskatchewan, B.A. (with distinction), 1962, M.A., 1963; London School of Economics and Political Science, Ph.D., 1967. *Home address:* R.R. 2, Dugald, Manitoba, Canada R0E 0K0. *Office:* University College, University of Manitoba, Winnipeg, Manitoba, Canada.

CAREER: University of Victoria, Victoria, British Columbia, instructor in economics, 1965-66; British Columbia Federation of Labor, Victoria, research director, 1966-68; Simon Fraser University, Burnaby, British Columbia, visiting assistant professor of economics, 1968-69; University of Manitoba, Winnipeg, assistant professor, 1969-75, associate professor of economics, 1975—. Member of Manitoba Economic Development Advisory Board, 1970—, research director, 1974-75; chairman of Milk Control Board of Manitoba, 1975—; member of Dairy Board of Manitoba, 1975—; member of board of directors of Winnipeg Folk Festival, 1976. *Military service:* Royal Canadian Air Force Reserve, pilot, 1956-61; became flying officer. *Member:* Canadian Association of University Teachers.

WRITINGS: No Power Greater: A Century of Labour in British Columbia, Boag Foundation, 1967; (with H. Seldon) *Macro Economic Theory and the Canadian Economy,* Heath, 1972; (with J. Seldon) *Micro Economic Theory and the Canadian Economy,* Heath, 1973; (editor) *Incentives, Location, and Regional Development,* Economic Development Advisory Board, 1975; (editor and contributor) *Manpower Issues in Manitoba,* Economic Development Advisory Board, 1975.

Contributor: G. Shelton, editor, *British Columbia and Confederation,* University of Victoria Press, 1967; Henry C. Klassen and A. W. Rasporich, editors, *Prairie Perspectives II,* Holt, 1973; M. Gunderson, editor, *Collective Bargaining in the Essential and Public Service Sectors,* University of Toronto Press, 1975; A. R. McCormack and I. MacPherson, editors, *Cities in the West,* National Museums of Canada, 1975; W. Gagne, editor, *Nationalism, Technology, and the Future of Canada,* Macmillan, 1976; Klassen, editor, *The Canadian West,* Compoint Publishing, 1977. Contributor to academic journals.

WORK IN PROGRESS: A study of Canadian economic

history; a study of the development of economic dualism in the labor market.

* * *

PIATTI, Celestino 1922-

PERSONAL: Born January 5, 1922, near Zurich, Switzerland; married Marianne Piatti-Stricker (an artist). Education: Attended School for Applied Arts, Zurich, Switzerland, 1937. Residence: Basel, Switzerland.

CAREER: Apprentice in graphic arts, 1938-42; commercial artist in studio of Fritz Buehler, Zurich, Switzerland, 1944-48; opened own studio, 1948; Deutscher Taschenbuch Verlag, Munich, Germany, designer of paperback book covers, 1961-63; author, illustrator, and designer. Awards, honors: Foire Internationale de Lyon award, 1959; Kieler Woche award, 1961; several of Piatti's posters have been given annual awards by the Swiss Federal Department of the Interior.

WRITINGS: (With wife, Marianne Piatti, and Hansbeat Stricker) Reisen mit Pinsel, Stift, und Feder: Skizzenblaetter und Aufzeichnungen, Werner & Bischoff, 1962; The Happy Owls (self-illustrated), Atheneum, 1963; Eulenglueck, Artemis Verlag, 1963; (with Hans Schumacher) ABC der Tiere (self-illustrated), Artemis Verlag, 1965, translation by Jon Reid published as Celestino Piatti's ABC, Atheneum, 1966; (with Ursula Huber) Zirkus Nock (self-illustrated), Artemis Verlag, 1967, translation by Barbara Kowal Gollob published as The Nock Family Circus, Atheneum, 1968; (with Ursula Piatti) Der Kleine Krebs, Artemis Verlag, 1973, translation published as The Little Crayfish, Bodley Head, 1974.

Illustrator: Edzard Hellmuth Schaper, Die Legende vom Vierten Koenig, J. Hegner, 1961; William Saroyan, Zirkusluft, Artemis Verlag, 1968; Aurel von Juechen, Die Heilige Nacht, Artemis Verlag, 1968, translation by Cornelia Schaeffer published as The Holy Night: The Story of the First Christmas, Atheneum, 1968; Max Bolliger, Der Goldene Apfel, Artemis Verlag, 1970, translation by Roseanna Hoover published as The Golden Apple: A Story, Atheneum, 1970.

SIDELIGHTS: As a commercial artist, Celestino Piatti entered exhibits all over the world, winning the poster competition at the Foire Internationale de Lyon in 1959, and at the Kieler Woche in Germany in 1961. After two years of designing paperback book covers, Piatti began illustrating books for children.

BIOGRAPHICAL/CRITICAL SOURCES: Graphis, Number 66, 1956, Number 115, 1964; Saturday Review, June 27, 1964; Book Week, May 15, 1966.*

* * *

PICKERING, George (White) 1904-

PERSONAL: Born June 26, 1904, in Whalton, Northumberland, England; son of George and Ann (Hall) Pickering; married Mary Carola Seward (a physician), April 26, 1930; children: Ann Penelope (Mrs. A. Wright), Jane Marion (Mrs. P. Gillham), Thomas George, Carola Seward (Mrs. N. Haigh). Education: Pembroke College, Cambridge, M.A. (first class honors), 1930, M.B., 1930, M.D., 1955. Home: 5 Horwood Close, Headington, Oxford OX3 7RF, England.

CAREER: St. Thomas Hospital, London, England, casualty officer and house physician, 1926-30; University College Hospital, University of London, London, lecturer in cardio-vascular pathology, 1930-39, professor of medicine, 1939-56; Oxford University, Oxford, England, Regius Professor of Medicine, 1956-69, master of Pembroke College, 1969-74, pro-vice-chancellor, 1967-69; writer, 1974—. Director of medical clinic at St. Mary's Hospital, 1939-56; physician for United Oxford Hospitals, 1956-69. Hertzstein Lecturer at Stanford University and University of California, 1938; visiting professor at numerous American, Canadian, and Australian universities. Member of Medical Research Council and Clinical Research Board, 1954-58; member of Lord Chancellor's Committee on Legal Education, 1967-71, and Council for Scientific Policy, 1968-71; member of board of trustees of Beit Memorial Fellowship and Ciba Foundation; foreign associate of U.S. National Academy of Sciences, 1970.

MEMBER: Royal Society (fellow), Royal College of Physicians (fellow of colleges in London, Edinburgh, and Ireland), British Medical Association (president, 1963-64), Royal Society of Medicine (fellow), American College of Physicians, American Medical Association, Association of American Physicians (honorary member), American Gastroenterological Association, American Academy of Arts and Sciences (foreign corresponding member), American National Academy of Sciences (foreign associate), Academy of Medicine of Mexico, Swedish Medical Society, Australian Medical Association, Deutschen Gesellschaft fuer Innere Medizin (corresponding member), Societe Medical des Hospitaux de Paris (foreign corresponding member), Czechoslovakian Medical Society (foreign corresponding member), Hellenic Cardiac Society (foreign corresponding member), Royal Belgian Academy of Medicine (foreign corresponding member), Danish Society for Internal Medicine (foreign corresponding member), Athenaeum Club. Awards, honors: M.D. from University of Ghent, 1948, University of Siena, 1965, and University of Western Australia, 1965; Sims British Commonwealth traveling professor, 1949; knighted, 1957; Sc.D. from University of Durham, 1957, Dartmouth College, 1960, and University of Hull, 1972; Sc.D. from Trinity College, Dublin, 1962; named honorary fellow of Pembroke College, Cambridge, 1959; LL.D. from University of Manchester, 1964, and University of Nottingham, 1965; D. Univ. from University of York, 1969.

WRITINGS: High Blood Pressure, Churchill, 1955, 2nd edition, 1968; The Nature of Essential Hypertension, Churchill, 1961; (with W. I. Cranston and M. A. Pears) The Treatment of Hypertension, C. C Thomas, 1961; The Challenge to Education, C. A. Watts, 1967; Hypertension: Causes, Consequences, and Management, Churchill, 1970, 2nd edition, 1974; Creative Malady, Oxford University Press, 1974; Tomorrow's Doctors, Oxford University Press, 1978. Contributor to professional journals. Editor of Clinical Sciences, 1939-47.

SIDELIGHTS: Pickering told CA: "My views on hypertension have been regarded as dangerous heresy by such experts as Professor Paren, the Soviet expert on space research, who said they were dangerous because against accepted teaching. However, my views were really a restatement of the facts in logical and connected form and they have steadily gained adherents and may now said to be orthodox."

AVOCATIONAL INTERESTS: Gardening, fishing.

* * *

PIGMAN, William Ward 1910-1977

1910—September 30, 1977; American biochemist specializing in carbohydrates and author of scientific books. Pigman was one of the five men accused by Whittaker Chambers as having been sources of governmental documents which were transmitted by Chambers to a Soviet spy ring. He denied knowing Chambers and no charges were ever brought against him. Pigman died in Woods Hole, Mass. Obituaries: *New York Times,* October 1, 1977; *Washington Post,* October 7, 1977.

* * *

PINSKER, Sanford 1941-

PERSONAL: Born September 28, 1941, in Washington, Pa.; son of Morris David (a salesman) and Sonia (Molliver) Pinsker; married Ann Getson (a teacher), January 28, 1968; children: Matthew, Beth. *Education:* Washington & Jefferson College, B.A., 1963; University of Washington, Seattle, M.A., 1965, Ph.D., 1967. *Religion:* Jewish. *Home:* 700 North Pine St., Lancaster, Pa. 17603. *Office:* Department of English, Franklin & Marshall College, Lancaster, Pa. 17604.

CAREER: Franklin & Marshall College, Lancaster, Pa., assistant professor, 1967-73, associate professor of English, 1973—. *Member:* Modern Language Association of America, Multi-Ethnic Literature of the United States, James Joyce Society, Northeast Modern Language Association.

WRITINGS: The Schlemiel as Metaphor, Southern Illinois University Press, 1971; *Still Life and Other Poems,* Greenfield Review Press, 1975; *The Comedy That "Hoits": An Essay on the Fiction of Philip Roth,* University of Missouri Press, 1975; *When Ozzie Nelson Died,* Seagull Press, in press; *Between Two Worlds: The American Novel in the 1960's,* Whitston Publishing, in press.

WORK IN PROGRESS: Cunning Meditations: Versions of History in Contemporary Fiction.

SIDELIGHTS: Pinsker told *CA:* "Auden once said that the important things to learn were how to laugh and how to pray. For me, poetry seems an ideal place to do both. Criticism, on the other hand, happens when ideas are clear enough to fit into prose."

* * *

PITAVY, Francois L(ouis) 1934-

PERSONAL: Born October 31, 1934, in Le Creusot, France; son of Pierre (an engineer) and Denise (Brill) Pitavy; married Daniele Souques (a university teacher), 1961; children: Bertrand, Christian. *Education:* Attended University of Paris, 1951-55, University of Lyon, 1955-58, and Agregation d'anglais, 1958. *Office:* Faculte de Langues et Civilisations Etrangeres, Universite de Dijon, 2 Blvd. Gabriel, 21000 Dijon, France.

CAREER: High school English teacher in Angers, France, 1958-59, and Besancon, France, 1961-64; Universite de Dijon, Dijon, France, assistant professor, 1964-71, associate professor of American studies, 1971—. *Awards, honors:* Smith-Mundt grants, University of Virginia, 1966 and 1973; American Council of Learned Societies fellowship, 1968-70, for University of Virginia.

WRITINGS: (With Andre Bleikasten) *William Faulkner* (contains "As I Lay Dying" by Bleikasten and "Light in August" by Pitavy), A. Colin, 1970, revised version of Pitavy's contribution (with Gillian E. Cook) published as *Faulkner's Light in August,* Indiana University Press, 1973. Contributor to language and literature journals in the United States and France.

WORK IN PROGRESS: Continuing research on Southern American literature, especially the work of Faulkner.

SIDELIGHTS: Pitavy told *CA:* "Faulkner has attracted the attention of the French ever since the 1930's, and I have long been interested in him—more in his narrative techniques than in his subject matter proper (studied at length in the U.S.), for whose analysis contemporary French criticism provides a fresh and sound approach."

* * *

PLACE, Janey Ann 1946-

PERSONAL: Born January 25, 1946, in Denver, Colo.; daughter of Richard and Peggy (a medical librarian; maiden name, Paddock) Place. *Education:* University of California, B.A. (magna cum laude), 1970, M.A., 1973, C.Phil., 1974, Ph.D., 1975; Immaculate Heart College, M.L.S., 1971. *Home:* 137 Plateau, Santa Cruz, Calif. 95060. *Office:* College V, University of California, Santa Cruz, Calif. 95064.

CAREER: University of California, Santa Cruz, lecturer in film, 1974—, also director of film series. Technical director of audio production for KHET-TV, 1969; producer of radio and television commercials for Fawcett-McDermott Associates, 1969-70; director, sound recordist, and editor of films; film projectionist.

WRITINGS: The Western Films of John Ford, Citadel, 1974; *The Films of John Ford,* Volume II, Citadel, 1977; (contributor) Bill Nichols, editor, *Movies and Methods,* University of California Press, 1977. Contributor to film journals. Managing editor for *Cinema,* 1972-74.

WORK IN PROGRESS: Film Language: Visual and Narrative Codes; The Violent Codes of Sexism and Its Reproduction.

* * *

PLANCK, Carolyn H(eine) 1910-

PERSONAL: Born May 4, 1910; daughter of Richard and Carrie (Weatherly) Heine; married Charles Evans Planck, February 26, 1935; children: Patricia (Mrs. Donald Barber), Charles Robert. *Education:* Rollins College, A.B., 1932. *Politics:* Democrat. *Religion:* Unitarian Universalist. *Home:* 1258 Filton Ct., Fremont, Calif. 94536.

CAREER: League of Women Voters of the United States, Washington, D.C., former editor of *National Voter;* National Education Association, Washington, D.C., member of editorial board, *NEA Journal,* 1956-62. *Member:* League of Women Voters of the United States (former member of Virginia board; member of Fremont board, 1945—).

WRITINGS: (With husband, Charles Evans Planck) *How Two Globetrot on One Retirement Check,* Diablo, 1968; (with C. E. Planck) *Pacific Paradise on a Low Budget,* Acropolis Books, 1973. Editor, *Peace Action,* 1932-35.

* * *

PLANCK, Charles Evans 1896-

PERSONAL: Born October 21, 1896, in Mount Sterling, Ky.; son of Robert Francis and Emma Lewis (Evans) Planck; married Carolyn Heine (an editor and writer), February 26, 1935; children: Patricia (Mrs. Donald Barber), Charles Robert. *Education:* University of Kentucky, A.B., 1919. *Politics:* Democrat. *Religion:* Unitarian Universalist. *Home:* 1258 Filton Ct., Fremont, Calif. 94536.

CAREER: Reporter and aviation editor for *Detroit Free Press,* Detroit, Mich., 1923; public relations work for American Airlines, Seversky Aircraft Corp., Pennsylvania Airlines, and other firms, mostly in the aviation field, 1923-40; employee of Civil Aeronautics Administration, 1940-62, became information officer, 1962. *Military service:* U.S. Marine Corps, 1918-19. *Awards, honors:* Silver Medal, U.S. Department of Commerce, for pilot training activities.

WRITINGS: Women with Wings, Harper, 1943; *How Two Do Europe on One Retirement Check,* William A. Breniman, 1965; (with wife, Carolyn H. Planck) *How Two Globetrot on One Retirement Check,* Diablo, 1968; (with C. H. Planck) *Pacific Paradise on a Low Budget,* Acropolis Books, 1973. Contributor to magazines.

SIDELIGHTS: Charles Evans Planck says that he is interested in local, liberal politics, and has worked long for peace (as has his wife).

* * *

PLUMMER, Kenneth 1946-

PERSONAL: Born April 4, 1946, in London, England. *Education:* Enfield College, B.Sc., 1967; London School of Economics and Political Science, Ph.D., 1973. *Politics:* "Libertarian." *Religion:* None. *Office:* Department of Sociology, University of Essex, Wivenhoe Park, Essex, England.

CAREER: Middlesex Polytechnic, London, England, lecturer, 1968-72, senior lecturer in sociology, 1972-74; University of Essex, Essex, England, lecturer in sociology, 1975—. *Awards, honors:* Social Science Research Council grant, 1975-78.

WRITINGS: Sexual Stigma: An Interactionist Account, Routledge & Kegan Paul, 1975.

WORK IN PROGRESS: Exploring aspects of sexual deviation, with books expected to result.

* * *

POHNDORF, Richard Henry 1916-1977

1916—October 23, 1977; American physical fitness expert and author of books on physical education. Pohndorf's 1958 study of physical fitness, which showed that British children appeared to be in better condition than American children, led to the creation of the President's Council on Physical Fitness under President Kennedy. Pohndorf died in Scottsdale, Ariz. Obituaries: *New York Times,* October 25, 1977.

* * *

POLLAND, Barbara K(ay) 1939-

PERSONAL: Born October 14, 1939, in Milwaukee, Wis.; daughter of Eugene Michael (a surgeon) and Margaret (a writer and nurse; maiden name, Hawtof) Kay; married Peter David Polland, June 24, 1962 (divorced, 1978); children: Mark, Tamy. *Education:* National College of Education, B.Ed., 1961; San Fernando Valley State College, M.A., 1970. *Office:* Department of Child Development and Educational Psychology, California State University, 18111 Nordhoff, Northridge, Calif. 91324.

CAREER: Assistant nursery school teacher in Shorewood, Wis., 1958; kindergarten teacher in Wilmette, Ill., 1961-62; organizer and teacher of kindergarten in Jackson, Wis., 1962-63; substitute teacher in elementary schools in Milwaukee, Wis., 1963-64, and Los Angeles, Calif., 1964-70; California State University, Northridge, assistant professor of child development and educational psychology, 1970—. Volunteer tutor of handicapped children, 1964-66, counselor

and tutor in Santa Monica, Calif., 1968, substitute teacher, 1970—. Licensed marriage, family, and child counselor in California, with a private practice. Member of local Join Hands program, 1969-72.

MEMBER: Association for Childhood Education International, National Association for the Education of Young Children, Congress of Racial Equality (life member), California State Psychological Association, California Association for Neurologically Handicapped Children, United Professors of California, California Women in Higher Education, Southern California Association for the Education of Young Children (member of board of directors), National College of Education Alumni Association, California State University, Northridge, Alumni Club, Kappa Delta Pi (Theta Eta chapter).

WRITINGS: The Sensible Book: A Celebration of Your Five Senses, Celestial Arts, 1974; *Feelings: Inside You and Outloud Too,* Celestial Arts, 1975; *Decisions, Decisions, Decisions,* Celestial Arts, 1976.

WORK IN PROGRESS: Research.

SIDELIGHTS: Barbara Polland writes: "My books have provided the challenge of trying to communicate creatively with children and adults. Questions, statements, and photographs were employed to expand understanding of self and others. Letters expressing enthusiasm have arrived from children and adults and consequently I have felt encouraged to continue.

"Rather than lecture in the college classroom I have developed innovative approaches for learning course material. Adults as well as children like to be *actively* involved in the learning process. I have been invited to present these materials to parents and/or teachers in many cities.

"A small private therapy practice gives me the opportunity to know a few people very well. Because this special kind of sharing so enriches me, I often wonder who gains the most—client or therapist?"

AVOCATIONAL INTERESTS: Arts and crafts, swimming, gardening, psychic phenomena.

* * *

POLONSKY, Antony Barry 1940-

PERSONAL: Born September 23, 1940, in Johannesburg, South Africa; son of Abraham David (a surgeon) and Nina (a physician; maiden name, Abelheim) Polonsky; married Arlene Enid Glickman (a lawyer), August 12, 1964; children: Leah, Jacob. *Education:* University of the Witwatersrand, B.A., 1960; Oxford University, M.A., D.Phil., 1967. *Home:* 27 Dartmouth Park Rd., London, England. *Agent:* Curtis Brown Ltd., 575 Madison Ave., New York, N.Y. 10022. *Office:* Department of International History, London School of Economics and Political Science, University of London, London, England.

CAREER: University of London, London School of Economics and Political Science, London, England, lecturer in history, 1970—. *Member:* Royal Historical Society (fellow). *Awards, honors:* Rhodes scholarship for the Transvaal, 1960.

WRITINGS: Politics in Independent Poland, Clarendon Press, 1972; *The Little Dictators,* Routledge & Kegan Paul, 1975; *The Great Powers and the Polish Quest,* London School of Economics and Political Science, Univeristy of London, 1976.

WORK IN PROGRESS: A History of the Polish Government, 1939-45.

POLTORATZKY, N(ikolai) P(etrovich) 1921-
(N. Petrovsky)

PERSONAL: Born February 16, 1921, in Istanbul, Turkey; came to United States in 1955; naturalized citizen, 1961; son of Peter F. (a priest) and Barbara R. (Kapustian) Poltoratzky; married Tamara Diatlenco, May 24, 1954. *Education:* Attended University of Sofia, 1938-42, and College of Philosophy and Theology (Regensburg, West Germany), 1946-47; Sorbonne, University of Paris, Ph.D., 1954. *Politics:* Independent. *Religion:* Greek-Orthodox. *Home:* 800 Penn Center Blvd., Apt. 408, Pittsburgh, Pa. 15235. *Office:* University of Pittsburgh, Slavic Dept., L.F. 120, Pittsburgh, Pa. 15260.

CAREER: U.S. Army Language School, Monterey, Calif., instructor in Russian, 1955; Brooklyn College (now of the City University of New York), Brooklyn, N.Y., research associate for Inwood Project on Intercultural Communication, 1956-58; Michigan State University, East Lansing, Mich., assistant professor, 1958-60, associate professor, 1960-64, professor of Russian language and literature, 1964-67, director of program, 1962-64; University of Pittsburgh, Pittsburgh, Pa., professor of Slavic languages and literatures, 1967—, chairman of department, 1967-74. Assistant to the director and faculty member of Institute of Soviet Studies, Middlebury College, summers, 1958-65. *Member:* American Association for the Advancement of Slavic Studies, Association of Russian-American Scholars in the United States, Modern Language Association of America, American Association of Teachers of Slavic and East European Languages (Michigan chapter president, 1959-67; Pennsylvania chapter vice-president, 1968, president, 1969-70; national organization vice-president, 1967, secretary, 1972, chairman of Russian Emigre Literature section, 1973). *Awards, honors:* Received research grants from American Philosophical Society, 1960, International Communications Institute of Michigan State University, 1964-65, and International Programs of University of Pittsburgh, 1967-68; University of Pittsburgh faculty research grant, 1971-72.

WRITINGS: (Under pseudonym N. Petrovsky) *Politicheskaia Zhizn' S.Sh.A.* (title means "The Political Life of the U.S.A."), United Nations Relief and Rehabilitation Administration (U.N.R.R.A.), 1947; *Berdiaev i Rossiia* (title means "Berdiaev and Russia"), Society of Friends of Russian Culture, 1967; *I. A. Il'in i polemika vokrug ego idei o soprotivlenii zlu siloi* (title means "I. A. Iljin and the Polemics Concerning His Ideas of Resistance to Evil by Force"), Zaria, 1975.

Editor: (Under pseudonym N. Petrovsky) *Vtoraia mirovaia voina (1939-1945)* (title means "World War II, 1939-45"), U.N.R.R.A., 1946; *Na temy russkie i obshchie* (title means "On Themes Russian and General"), Society of Friends of Russian Culture, 1965; *Russkaia literatura v emigratsii* (title means "Russian Emigre Literature"), Department of Slavic Languages and Literatures, University of Pittsburgh, 1972; *I. A. Il'in: Russkie pisateli, literatura i khudozhestvo* (title means "I. A. Iljin: Russian Writers, Literature, and Art"), Victor Kamkin Book Store, 1973; *Russkaia religiozna-filosofskaia mysl' XX veka* (title means "Russian Religious-Philosophical Thought of the Twentieth Century"), Department of Slavic Languages and Literatures, University of Pittsburgh, 1975.

Contributor of articles to academic journals.

WORK IN PROGRESS: Letopsis' russkoi emigratsii, 1920-1924 (title means "A Chronicle of the Russian Emigration, 1920-1924"), to be published in 1979.

SIDELIGHTS: Poltoratzky writes: "Much in my life was determined by the events of World War II, and also by the fact that my parents were Russians (from the Ukraine) who became emigres because of their opposition to Communism. Born in Turkey and brought up in Bulgaria, I lived after the war in Western Europe, North Africa, and again Europe, while waiting for my visa to emigrate to North America.

"Though formerly active in journalism, I had been intermittently preparing myself for an academic career (in those years by no means certain), in the course of which I hoped to further satisfy my interest in literature, philosophy, history, and contemporary affairs—especially as they relate to Russia and the Soviet Union. The books and monographs which I authored or edited (all in Russian) directly reflect this general background and continued interests."

AVOCATIONAL INTERESTS: Collecting books, travel.

* * *

POMERLEAU, Cynthia S(todola) 1943-

PERSONAL: Born February 19, 1943, in Neptune, N.J.; daughter of Edwin King (an electrical engineer) and Elsa (Dahart) Stodola; married Ovide Felix Pomerleau (a psychologist and writer), September 11, 1965; children: Julie, Aimee. *Education:* Smith College, B.A., 1964; Columbia University, M.A. (honors), 1966; University of Pennsylvania, Ph.D., 1974. *Home:* 7818 Roanoke St., Philadelphia, Pa. 19118. *Office:* Department of Community and Preventive Medicine, Medical College of Pennsylvania, Philadelphia, Pa. 19129.

CAREER: New York City Department of Welfare, New York, N.Y., caseworker, 1964-65; Reader's Digest Association, Pleasantville, N.Y., computer programmer in Educational Division, 1966-67; free-lance writer and researcher, 1975-76; Medical College of Pennsylvania, Philadelphia, director of oral history project on women in medicine, 1976—. Project coordinator for "S.O.S." (smoking cessation program of Educational Services, Inc.), 1975-76.

WRITINGS: (With Ovide F. Pomerleau) *S.O.S.* (therapist's manual), Educational Services, Inc., 1977; (with O. F. Pomerleau) *Break the Smoking Habit: A Behavioral Program for Giving Up Cigarettes,* Research Press, 1977. Contributor to *Women and Health.*

WORK IN PROGRESS: The Rise of Women's Autobiography in England.

* * *

POMERLEAU, Ovide F(elix) 1940-

PERSONAL: Born June 4, 1940, in Waterville, Maine; son of Ovide F. (a physician) and Florence (Beaudet) Pomerleau; married Cynthia Stodola (a writer), September 11, 1965; children: Julie, Aimee. *Education:* Bowdoin College, B.A., 1962; Columbia University, M.S., 1965, Ph.D., 1969. *Residence:* Philadelphia, Pa. *Office:* 1148 Gates Building, Hospital of the University of Pennsylvania, Philadelphia, Pa. 19104.

CAREER: F. D. Roosevelt Veterans Administration Hospital, Montrose, N.Y., research associate in psychology, 1966-69; Temple University, Philadelphia, Pa., assistant professor of psychology, 1969-72, clinical intern in psychology, 1969-71, research director of Temple University unit of Philadelphia State Hospital, 1969-71; University of Pennsylvania, Philadelphia, assistant professor of psychology in psychiatry and director of Center for Behavioral Medicine at university hospital, both 1972—. Licensed clinical psychologist in Pennsylvania; private practice in behavior therapy. Past vice-president of Philadelphia Children's Museum. Consultant, National Heart, Lung, and Blood Institute.

MEMBER: American Psychological Association, American Association for the Advancement of Science, Association for the Advancement of Behavior Therapy, Behavior Therapy and Research Society (clinical fellow), Pavlovian Society, Eastern Psychological Association, Sigma Xi. *Awards, honors:* National Institute of Mental Health grant, 1970-71.

WRITINGS: (With wife, Cynthia S. Pomerleau) *S.O.S.* (self-help smoking cessation program), Educational Services, Inc., 1976; (contributor) J. P. Brady, M. T. Orne, and other editors, *Psychiatry: Areas of Promise and Advancement,* Spectrum, 1976; (contributor) R. J. Haggerty and M. Green, editors, *Ambulatory Pediatrics,* Saunders, 1976; (with C. S. Pomerleau) *Break the Smoking Habit: A Behavioral Program for Giving Up Cigarettes,* Research Press, 1977. Contributor of articles and reviews to professional journals. Review editor for *Journal of Applied Behavior Analysis, Behavior Therapy, Journal of Behavior Therapy and Experimental Psychiatry, Annals of Internal Medicine,* and *New England Journal of Medicine,* and member of editorial board, *Journal of Behavioral Medicine.*

WORK IN PROGRESS: Editing *Behavioral Medicine: Theory and Practice,* with John Paul Brady, publication by Williams & Wilkins expected in 1979.

SIDELIGHTS: Pomerleau writes: "My writing is an outgrowth of my professional activity as a behavior researcher and therapist; I would like to see new techniques derived from the scientific analysis of behavior more widely known."

*   *   *

POPE, Edwin 1928-

PERSONAL: Born April 11, 1928, in Athens, Ga.; son of Henry Louis (a warehouseman) and Rose (a nurse; maiden name, McAfee) Pope; married Eileen Wallace, February 11, 1973; children: David. *Education:* University of Georgia, A.B., 1948. *Politics:* Democrat. *Religion:* Presbyterian. *Residence:* Key Biscayne, Fla. *Office: Miami Herald,* 1 Herald Plaza, Miami, Fla. 33101.

CAREER: Athens Banner-Herald, Athens, Ga., sports editor, 1944-48; United Press, Atlanta, Ga., southern sports editor, 1949-50; *Atlanta Constitution,* Atlanta, sports writer, 1950-53; *Atlanta Journal,* Atlanta, executive sports editor, 1954-55; *Miami Herald,* Miami, Fla., sports editor, 1955—. Sports publicity director at University of Georgia, 1944-46. *Awards, honors:* Named outstanding U.S. sports columnist by Headliners Club, 1962; awards from Thoroughbred Racing Association of American, 1962, for column "Horses Are Only Human," and 1976, for column "The Long Weight for Jockeys"; named superscribe by *Esquire,* 1975.

WRITINGS: Football's Greatest Coaches, McKay, 1954; *Baseball's Greatest Managers,* Doubleday, 1962; *American Greyhound Racing Encyclopedia,* privately printed, 1964; *Ted Williams: The Golden Year,* Prentice-Hall, 1969; (with Norm Evans) *On the Line,* Revell, 1977.

Work anthologized in *Best Sports Stories.* Contributor to national magazines, including *Collier's, Sport, Pageant,* and *Golf Digest.*

SIDELIGHTS: Pope comments that he "began writing as a sports reporter at age eleven, and was the nation's youngest—and worst—sports editor, at fifteen. I was also serving as news editor on D-Day, 1944."

POPE, Thomas Harrington 1913-

PERSONAL: Born July 28, 1913, in Kinards, S.C.; son of Thomas Harrington (a physician) and Marie (Gary) Pope; married Mary Waties Lumpkin, January 3, 1940; children: Mary Waties (Mrs. Robert Hunter Kennedy, Jr.), Thomas Harrington III, Gary Tusten. *Education:* Citadel, A.B., 1935; University of South Carolina, LL.B., 1938. *Religion:* Episcopalian. *Home:* 1700 Boundary St., Newberry, S.C. 29108. *Office:* Pope & Schumpert, 1201 Boyce St., Newberry, S.C. 29108.

CAREER: Admitted to South Carolina bar, 1938, and U.S. Supreme Court bar; attorney in Newberry, S.C., 1938—. Democratic member of South Carolina House of Representatives, 1936-40, 1945-50, speaker of the House, 1949-50. Special circuit judge in Richland and Lexington Counties, 1955-56; member of South Carolina Judicial Council, 1957—. President of South Carolina Democratic Convention, 1958, 1962; chairman of South Carolina Democratic Party, 1958-60; delegate to Democratic National Convention, 1956, 1960. Member of South Carolina State Ports Authority, 1958-65; member of South Carolina Archives Commission, 1965-75, vice-chairman, 1974-75; member of advisory board of National Trust for Historic Preservation, 1967-73. President of South Carolina Foundation of Independent Colleges; member of board of trustees of University of the South, 1965-70, and Newberry College, 1965-75; member of board of visitors at the Citadel, 1939-40, 1946. Member of board of directors of Citizens & Southern National Bank of South Carolina, 1959—, and American Sentinel Life Insurance Co. *Military service:* U.S. Army, 1941-45; served in European theater; became brigadier general. South Carolina National Guard, 1957.

MEMBER: American Law Institute (life member), American College of Trial Lawyers (fellow), American Bar Foundation (fellow), American Bar Association, American Judicature Society, National Association of Railroad Trial Counsel, American Historical Association, Southern Historical Association, South Carolina National Guard Association (president), South Carolina Historical Society; (curator, 1968-74), South Carolina Bar Association (chairman of executive committee, 1956-58; president, 1964), Newberry County Bar Association (president, 1951), Newberry County Historical Society (president, 1966), University of South Carolina Society (curator, 1968-72), Phi Beta Kappa, Omicron Delta Kappa, Phi Delta Phi, Alpha Tau Omega, Caroline Motor Club (member of board of directors; vice-president), Masons (state grand master, 1958-60), Newberry Country Club, Palmetto Club, Summit Club, Pine Tree Hunt Club, Army-Navy Club. *Awards, honors:* Henry Price Medal from Massachusetts Grand Lodge of Masons, 1960; Albert Gallatin Mackey Medal from South Carolina Grand Lodge of Masons, 1965; LL.D. from Newberry College, 1969, and the Citadel, 1977; Algernon Sydney Sullivan Award from Newberry College, 1976; commendation from Association for State and Local History.

WRITINGS: The History of Newberry County, South Carolina, 1749-1860, University of South Carolina Press, 1973.

WORK IN PROGRESS: The History of Newberry County, South Carolina, Volume II.

*   *   *

POPPE, Nicholas N. 1897-

PERSONAL: Born August 8, 1897, in Chefoo, China; son of Nicholas E. and Elizabeth (Morawitz) Poppe; married Natalie V. Belolipskaya, May 11, 1924 (died, 1949); married

Edith O. Ziegler, October 26, 1952. *Education:* University of Petrograd (now University of Leningrad), B.A., 1921, M.A., 1923; University of Leningrad, Ph.D., 1934. *Politics:* None. *Home:* 3220 Northeast 80th St., Seattle, Wash. 98115. *Office:* Department of Far Eastern Languages, University of Washington, Seattle, Wash. 98195.

CAREER: University of Leningrad, Leningrad, Russia, assistant professor, 1921-28, professor, 1928-42; University of Berlin, Berlin, Germany, professor, 1943-49; University of Washington, Seattle, professor of Far East and Slavic languages and literature, 1949-69, professor emeritus, 1969—. *Member:* German Oriental Society, Turkish Oriental Society, American Oriental Society. *Awards, honors:* Guggenheim grant, 1956; Ph.D., University of Bonn, 1968; Indiana University Gold Medal, 1970.

WRITINGS: O rodstvennykh otnoshenijakh chuvashsko-go i tjurko-tatarskikh jazykov, 1925; *Uchebnaja grammatika jakutskogo jazyka,* [Moscow], 1926; *Chuvashi i ikh sosedi,* 1927; *Uchebnik mongol'skogo jazyka,* [Leningrad], 1932; *Lingvisticheskie problemy Vostochnoj Sibiri,* [Moscow], 1933; *Stroj khalkha-mongol'skogo jazyka,* [Leningrad], 1936; *Grammatika pishmenno-mongol'skogo jazyka,* [Moscow], 1937; *Grammatika burjat-mongol'skogo jazyka,* [Moscow], 1938; (editor) *Chal' mg geroichesk epos,* [Moscow], 1940; (editor) G. M. Vasilevich, *Evenkijsko-russkij (tungussko-russkij) slovar',* [Moscow], 1940; *Grammar of Written Mongolian,* O. Harrassowitz (Wiesbaden), 1954; *Introduction to Mongolian Comparative Studies,* Finno-Ugric Society (Helsinki), 1955; *Tatar Manual: Descriptive Grammar and Texts with a Tatar-English Glossary,* Indiana University Press, 1963, revised edition, 1968; *Bashkir Manual,* Indiana University Press, 1964; *Introduction to Altaic Linguistics,* O. Harrassowitz, 1965; *The Twelve Deeds of Buddha,* O. Harrassowitz, 1967; *Diamond Sutra: Three Mongolian Versions of the Vajracchedika Prajnaparamita,* International Publications Service, 1971; *Studies of Turkic Loan Words in Russian,* International Publications Service, 1971. Contributor to *Handbuch der Orientalistik;* contributor of about two hundred articles and reviews to journals in United States, Europe and Asia.

WORK IN PROGRESS: Ancient Buddhist Mongolian texts; translation of Mongolian epics.

SIDELIGHTS: Poppe speaks Russian, German, French, Mongolian, and Finnish. He traveled in Mongolia, 1926-27, 1929, 1940, in East Siberia, 1928, 1930-32, and in Japan, 1958.

BIOGRAPHICAL/CRITICAL SOURCES: Studia Altaica, Festschrift für Nikolaus Poppe zum 60 Geburtstag, O. Harrassowitz, 1957.

* * *

PORTER, Glenn 1944-

PERSONAL: Born April 2, 1944, in New Boston, Tex.; son of Pat Paul (a carpenter) and Mary (Sanders) Porter; married Marilyn Wimberly (an abstractor of technical documents), June 1, 1968. *Education:* Rice University, B.A., 1966; Johns Hopkins University, M.A., 1968, Ph.D., 1970. *Home address:* P.O. Box 3630, Greenville, Del. 19807. *Office:* Eleutherian Mills-Hagley Foundation, Greenville, Del. 19807.

CAREER: Harvard University, Cambridge, Mass., assistant professor of business history, 1970-76; Eleutherian Mills-Hagley Foundation, Greenville, Del., director of Regional Economic History Research Center, 1976—. Adjunct associate professor at University of Delaware, 1976—. Consultant to National Endowment for the Humanities and National Survey of Historic Sites and Buildings.

MEMBER: Organization of American Historians, Economic History Association, Business History Conference, Society for the History of Technology, Historians Film Committee, Phi Beta Kappa. *Awards, honors:* Grants from Alfred P. Sloan Foundation, 1968-69, Ford Foundation, 1968-69, Social Science Research Council, 1971, and National Endowment for the Humanities, 1977-80.

WRITINGS: (With Harold Livesay) *Merchants and Manufacturers: Studies in the Changing Structure of Nineteenth-Century Marketing,* Johns Hopkins University Press, 1971; *The Rise of Big Business, 1860-1910,* Crowell, 1973; (editor with Robert Cuff, and contributor) *Enterprise and National Development: Essays in Canadian Business and Economic History,* Hakkert, 1973; (contributor) Herman Daems and Herman Van der Wee, editors, *The Rise of Managerial Capitalism,* Martimus Nishoff, 1974; (editor and contributor) *Regional Economic History: The Mid-Atlantic Area Since 1700,* Eleutherian Mills-Hagley Foundation, 1976; (contributor) Trevor I. Williams, editor, *The History of Technology: The Twentieth Century,* Oxford University Press, in press; (editor) *The Dictionary of American Economic History,* Scribner, in press. Editor of monograph series "Industrial Development and the Social Fabric," JAI Press. Contributor to economic and history journals. Editor of *Business History Review,* 1970-76; member of editorial board of *Journal of American History,* 1977—.

WORK IN PROGRESS: A study of the social context and consequences of economic change in the Mid-Atlantic states area, 1750-1850.

* * *

PORTER, Joe Ashby 1942-

PERSONAL: Born July 21, 1942, in Kentucky; son of Lawrence (a machinist and coal miner) and Margaret (Wise) Porter. *Education:* Harvard University, B.A., 1964; Pembroke College, Oxford, graduate study, 1964-65; University of California, Berkeley, M.A., 1966, Ph.D., 1973. *Home:* 302 12th Ave. E., Seattle, Wash. 98102.

CAREER: University of Virginia, Charlottesville, assistant professor of English, 1970-73; University of Baltimore, Baltimore, Md., assistant professor of English, 1976-77; Shoreline Community College, Seattle, Wash., assistant professor of English, 1977—. Assistant professor at Towson State College, 1976-77. *Member:* Modern Language Association of America. *Awards, honors:* Fulbright fellowship, 1964-65.

WRITINGS: Eelgrass (novel), New Directions, 1977.

Work anthologized in *The Best American Short Stories.* Contributor of stories to literary journals, including *Occident, Antaeus, Sun and Moon,* and *Triquarterly.*

WORK IN PROGRESS: The Drama of Speech Acts, on four of Shakespeare's plays; a book of stories about Kentucky, some previously published in magazines; a novel.

SIDELIGHTS: Porter, who has lived in France and speaks the language, writes that French literature is one of the major influences on his work. He has also lived in England and North Africa.

* * *

POSPESEL, Howard Andrew 1937-

PERSONAL: Born January 25, 1937, in Dayton, Ohio; son

of Howard I. (a clergyman) and Clara (Robe) Pospesel; married Carmen Miller, August 20, 1960; children: Michael, Amy, Mark. *Education:* Wittenberg University, B.A., 1959; University of Florida, M.A., 1961; University of North Carolina, Ph.D., 1967. *Home:* 16650 Southwest 102nd Pl., Miami, Fla. 33157. *Office:* Department of Philosophy, University of Miami, P.O. Box 248054, Coral Gables, Fla. 33124.

CAREER: University of Miami, Coral Gables, Fla., assistant professor, 1965-71, associate professor, 1971-77, professor of philosophy, 1977—. *Member:* American Philosophical Association, American Association of University Professors, Southern Society for Philosophy and Psychology, Florida Philosophical Association.

WRITINGS: Arguments: Deductive Logic Exercises, Prentice-Hall, 1971, 2nd edition (with David Marans), 1978; *Introduction to Logic: Propositional Logic,* Prentice-Hall, 1974; *Introduction to Logic: Predicate Logic,* Prentice-Hall, 1976. Contributor to philosophy journals.

AVOCATIONAL INTERESTS: Backpacking, poker, painting.

* * *

POST, Gaines, Jr.   1937-

PERSONAL: Born September 22, 1937, in Madison, Wis.; son of Gaines (a professor) and Katherine (Rike) Post; married Jean Bowers, July 19, 1969; children: Katherine, Daniel. *Education:* Cornell University, B.A., 1959; Oxford University, B.A., 1963; Stanford University, M.A., 1965, Ph.D., 1969. *Residence:* Austin, Texas. *Office:* Department of History, University of Texas, Austin, Texas 78712.

CAREER: University of Texas, Austin, assistant professor, 1969-74, associate professor of history, 1974—. *Military service:* U.S. Army, 1959-61; became first lieutenant. *Member:* American Historical Association. *Awards, honors:* Rhodes scholarship, 1961-63.

WRITINGS: The Civil-Military Fabric of Weimar Foreign Policy, Princeton University Press, 1973.

WORK IN PROGRESS: A book on British foreign policy and defense in the 1930's; co-editing a book of essays on modern European and American diplomacy.

SIDELIGHTS: Post told CA, "I inherited my interest in history from my father, a mediaeval historian. I became especially interested in German history and civil-military relations while stationed in Germany." *Avocational interests:* Backpacking, wine tasting, tree pruning.

* * *

POWELL, Clilan B.   1894-1977

1894—September 22, 1977; American radiologist, businessman, editor, and publisher. Powell was among the first black x-ray specialists in the United States and operated a laboratory in Harlem, N.Y., for about twenty-five years. Powell was appointed by New York Governor Thomas Dewey to serve as a member of the New York Athletic Commission. He died in Briarcliff Manor, N.Y. Obituaries: *New York Times,* September 23, 1977.

* * *

POWER, Rex
See LANGLEY, John

POWERS, Edwin   1896-

PERSONAL: Born February 19, 1896, in New York, N.Y.; son of Walter Edwin (a printer and lithographer) and Annie I. (Marshall) Powers; married Carol Gear, June 20, 1931 (divorced, 1953); married Victoria Babcock Karbaum, June, 1969; children: (first marriage) Susan, Martha, Steven. *Education:* Williams College, A.B., 1919; New York Law School, LL.B., 1924; Dartmouth College, M.A., 1930. *Politics:* Independent. *Religion:* Unitarian Universalist. *Home:* 17 Andrina Rd., West Yarmouth, Mass. 02673.

CAREER: Robert College, Constantinople, Turkey, teacher, 1919-21; law clerk in various law firms, New York City, 1921-24; attorney, practicing in New York City, 1924-27; Dartmouth College, Hanover, N.H., 1927-37, began as instructor, became assistant professor of psychology and legal psychology; Bureau of Social Hygiene, New York City, researcher at State Prison Colony, Norfolk, Mass., on leave from Dartmouth College, 1933-35; Cambridge-Somerville Youth Study, Cambridge, Mass., 1937-47, began as counsellor, became director; Judge Baker Guidance Center, Boston, Mass., researcher, 1950; United Prison Association of Massachusetts, Boston, director of research and correctional education, 1953-56; Commonwealth of Massachusetts, deputy commissioner of personnel and training, 1956-66; New England Board of Higher Education, Winchester, Mass., assistant director of project on manpower and training, 1966-67; Massachusetts Correctional Association, Boston, research consultant, 1967—. Teacher of courses in criminology at Boston University and Harvard University. *Military service:* U.S. Navy, 1917-18.

MEMBER: American Psychological Association, American Sociological Association, American Correctional Association, National Council on Crime and Delinquency, American Society of Criminology, Massachusetts Psychological Association, United Prison Association of Massachusetts (past president). *Awards, honors:* Herbert C. Parsons Memorial Award for outstanding achievement in the prevention of crime and in the treatment of offenders, United Prison Association of Massachusetts, 1967.

WRITINGS: (With Helen Witmer) *An Experiment in the Prevention of Delinquency,* Columbia University Press, 1951, reprinted, Patterson Smith, 1972; *The Basic Structure of Administration of Criminal Justice in Massachusetts,* United Prison Association of Massachusetts, 1957, 6th edition, 1973; *Crime and Punishment in Early Massachusetts,* Beacon Press, 1966; (with Gordon Allport and Philip E. Vernon) *Studies in Expressive Movement,* Hafner, 1967. Also author of pamphlets on penal codes for Massachusetts Correctional Association. Contributor to *Encyclopedia Americana* and professional journals.

SIDELIGHTS: Edwin Powers told *CA*: "Interested in almost everything, excepting: Disc jockey talk, television commercials (particularly singing commercials), horror movies, fictional murder mysteries and detective stories." *Avocational interests:* Cycling, skiing, rowing, bowling.

* * *

PRABHUPADA, Bhaktivedanta   1896-
(A. C. Bhaktivedanta Swami, A. C. Bhaktivedanta)

PERSONAL: Born September 1, 1896, in Calcutta, India. *Education:* University of Calcutta, B.A., 1920. *Religion:* "Krishna Conciousness" (Vaisnava). *Address:* c/o Bhaktivedanta Book Trust, 3764 Watseka Ave., Los Angeles, Calif. 90034.

CAREER: Former manager of a chemical company, then proprietor of drug and chemical concern, currently swami and minister of philosophy, religion, and theology. Founder and Acharya of the International Society for Krishna Conciousness in the United States, 1966; founded Vedic farm community in West Virginia, 1968; introduced Vedic system of primary and secondary education to United States in 1972, schools now in Dallas, Tex., Los Angeles, Calif., Port Royal, Pa. and Vrndavana, India; co-founder of Bhaktivedanta Book Trust, 1972.

WRITINGS—Under name A. C. Bhaktivedanta Swami or A. C. Bhaktivedanta; studies on yoga and Vedic philosophy: *Two Essays, Krsna: The Reservoir of Pleasure and Who Is Crazy?*, ISKCON Press, 1967; *Teachings of Lord Caitanya*, ISKCON Press, 1968; *KRSNA: The Supreme Personality of Godhead* (study of *Tenth Canto* of *Srimad Bhagavatam;* see below), ISKCON Press, 1970; *Transcendental Teachings of Prahlad Maharaj,* ISKON Press, 1970; *Krsna Consciousness: The Topmost Yoga System,* ISKCON Press, 1970, Macmillan, 1972; *Easy Journey to Other Planets by Practice of Supreme Yoga,* ISKCON Press, 1970, Macmillan, 1972; *The Perfection of Yoga,* ISKCON Press, 1972, Macmillan, 1973; *Beyond Birth and Death,* Bhaktivedanta Book Trust, 1972; *On the Way to Krsna,* Bhaktivedanta Book Trust, 1973; *Raja-vidya: The King of Knowledge,* Bhaktivedanta Book Trust, 1973; *Elevation to Drsna Consciousness,* Bhaktivedanta Book Trust, 1973; *Perfect Question, Perfect Answers,* Bhaktivedanta Book Trust, 1977.

Translator and author of commentary: *Bhagavad-Gita As It Is,* Macmillan, abridged edition, 1968, complete edition, 1972; *Sri Isopanisad,* ISKCON Press, 1969; *Nectar of Devotion* (translation and study of the "Bhakti-rasamrta-shindhu"), ISKCON Press, 1970, published as *Nectar Of Devotion: The Complete Science of Bhakti Yoga,* Bhaktivedanta Book Trust, 1970; *Srimad Bhagavatam, First Canto,* three volumes, *Second Canto,* two volumes, *Third Canto,* four volumes, *Fourth Canto,* four volumes, *Fifth Canto,* two volumes, *Sixth Canto,* three volumes, *Seventh Canto,* three volumes, *Eighth Canto,* three volumes, *Ninth Canto,* three volumes, Bhaktivedanta Book Trust, 1972—; *Sri Caitanya Caritamrta,* seventeen volumes, Bhaktivedanta Book Trust, 1974-77; *Nectar of Instruction* (translation and study of "Sri Upadesamrta"), Bhaktivedanta Book Trust, 1975.

Editor of *Back to Godhead* magazine, 1944—.

WORK IN PROGRESS: Translating and writing the commentary for 10th-12th cantos of *Srimad Bhagavatam;* a book, *Life Comes from Life.*

* * *

PRAGER, Karsten 1936-

PERSONAL: Born September 3, 1936, in Koenigsberg, Germany; son of Guenther (a horticulturist) and Elisbeth (Opitz) Prager; married LaVerne Lane, January 2, 1960; children: Debra, Karsten, Jr., Nicole, Kevin. *Education:* University of Michigan, B.A. and M.A., 1960. *Home:* 89 Ana Teresa, Aravaca, Madrid, Spain. *Office: Time,* Marques de Cubas 12, 4-B, Madrid 14, Spain.

CAREER/WRITINGS: Bangkok World, Bangkok, Thailand, associate editor, 1960-62; Associated Press, New York City, bureau chief in Southeast Asia, 1962-65; *Time,* New York City, correspondent in Southeast Asia, 1965-68, associate editor, 1969-71, bureau chief in San Francisco, 1971-73, bureau chief in the Middle East, 1973-75, bureau chief in Madrid, Spain, 1976—. Notable assignments include cover-

age of the war in Vietnam and Laos, 1973 Middle East War, the Cyprus War, and civil war in Lebanon. Contributor of articles to *Reporter, Atlantic, Saturday Review,* and other periodicals.

AVOCATIONAL INTERESTS: Politics, economics, energy, skiing, camping, ballet, opera.

* * *

PRESCOTT, Allen 1904(?)-1978

1904(?)—January 27, 1978; American radio announcer and author. Prescott hosted "Wife-Saver" for WNEW-Radio during the 1940's. He also authored *The Wife-Saver's Candy Recipes* and *Aunt Harriet's Household Hints.* Prescott died in New York, N.Y. Obituaries: *New York Times,* January 29, 1978.

* * *

PRESTON, Edward
See GUESS, Edward Preston

* * *

PRICE, Don K(rasher, Jr.) 1910-

PERSONAL: Born January 23, 1910, in Middlesboro, Ky.; son of Don Krasher and Nell (Rhorer) Price; married Margaret Helen Gailbreath, March 3, 1936 (died, 1970); married Harriet Sloane, February, 1971; children: (first marriage) Don C., Linda G. (Mrs. Keith S. Thomson). *Education:* Vanderbilt University, A.B., 1931; Oxford University, B.A., 1934, B. Litt., 1935. *Home:* 114 Irving St., Cambridge 38, Mass. *Office:* Littauer Center, Harvard University, Cambridge, Mass.

CAREER: Nashville Evening Tennessean, Nashville, Tenn., reporter, 1930-32; staff member, Home Owners' Loan Corp., Washington, D.C., 1935-37, Social Science Research Council, New York City, 1937-39, Public Administration Clearing House, Chicago, Ill., 1939-53, U.S. Bureau of the Budget, 1945-46, Hoover Commission on the Organization of the Executive Branch of the Government, 1947-48; U.S. Department of Defense, Washington, D.C., deputy chairman, Research and Development Board, 1952-53; Ford Foundation, New York City, associate director, 1953-54, vice-president, 1954-58; Harvard University, Cambridge, Mass., professor of government and dean, John Fitzgerald Kennedy School of Government, 1958—. Lecturer on political science, University of Chicago, Chicago, Ill., 1946-53. Member of President's Advisory Committee on Government Organization, 1959-61, President's Advisory Panel on a National Academy of Foreign Affairs, 1962-63; chairman of President's Task Force on Government Organization, 1964; special consultant to Executive Office of the President, 1961-72. Member of board of directors, Social Science Research Council, 1949-52, and Committee on Foreign Affairs Personnel, Carnegie Endowment, 1961-63; trustee of RAND Corp. (1961-71), Rhodes Trust, The Weatherhead Foundation, Vanderbilt University, and Twentieth Century Fund. *Military service:* U.S. Coast Guard Reserve, lieutenant, 1943-45.

MEMBER: American Academy of Arts and Sciences (fellow), American Association for the Advancement of Science (past president), American Philosophical Society, Phi Beta Kappa, Cosmos Club (Washington, D.C.), Century Association (New York). *Awards, honors:* Rhodes scholar, 1932; LL.D. from Centre College of Kentucky, 1961, Syracuse University, 1962, Bucknell University, 1970, and Harvard University, 1970; Harvard University Press Faculty Prize, 1966, for *The Scientific Estate;* L.H.D., Case Institute of Technology (now Case Western Reserve University), 1967, and College of Wooster, 1972.

WRITINGS: (With Harold and Kathryn Stone) *City Manager Government in the United States,* Public Administration Service (Chicago), 1940; (with W. Y. Elliott and others) *U.S. Foreign Policy: Its Organization and Control,* Columbia University Press, 1952; *Government and Science,* New York University Press, 1954; (with W. Y. Elliott and others) *The Political Economy of American Foreign Policy,* Holt, 1955; (editor) *The Secretary of State,* Prentice-Hall, 1960; *The Scientific Estate,* Harvard University Press, 1965; *Price Indexes and Quality Change: Studies in New Methods of Measurement,* edited by Z. Griliches, Harvard University Press, 1971.

BIOGRAPHICAL/CRITICAL SOURCES: Saturday Review, April 2, 1966.

* * *

PRIEST, Harold Martin 1902-

PERSONAL: Born July 28, 1902, in Chicago, Ill.; son of Leslie Rue and Katie (Wiglesworth) Priest; married Elizabeth Marshall, February 4, 1930; married Willa Daniels, March 21, 1949; children: (first marriage) Deborah Millay (Mrs. James Edmond Courtney). *Education:* Harvard University, A.B., 1925; Northwestern University, M.A., 1926, Ph.D., 1933; additional study at University of Chicago, 1928-29 and Cornell University, 1931. *Home:* 2459 South Dahlia Lane, Denver, Colo. 80222. *Office:* Department of English, University of Denver, Denver, Colo. 80210.

CAREER: Assistant professor of English at Simpson College, Indianola, Iowa, 1926-29, and Miami University, Oxford, Ohio, 1930-31; Kansas State Teachers College, Emporia, 1933-46, began as assistant professor, became professor of English; University of Denver, Denver, Colo., associate professor, 1946-59, professor of English, 1959-71, professor emeritus, 1971—. *Member:* Modern Language Association of America, American Comparative Literature Association, Renaissance Society of America, Rocky Mountain Modern Language Association (president, 1962-63). *Awards, honors:* Medaglio Culturale from Italian Government.

WRITINGS: Renaissance and Baroque Lyrics, An Anthology of Translations, Northwestern University Press, 1962; (translator, and author of introduction) *Adonis, Selections from L'Adone of Giambattista Marino,* Cornell University Press, 1967. Also author of study guides for Spencer's *Faerie Queene,* 1968, Dante's *Purgatorio,* 1970, and *Paradiso,* 1970, and More's *Utopia,* 1975.

* * *

PRIESTLEY, Harold E(dford) 1901-

PERSONAL: Born May 27, 1901, in Bradford, Yorkshire, England; son of Fred (a cloth manufacturer) and Edna (Bolton) Priestley; married Florence Ethel Hubbard, December 27, 1924. *Education:* University of Leeds, B.A., 1922, diploma in education, 1923, M.A., 1924, M.Ed., 1928; University of London, D.Phil., 1931. *Home and office:* 8 Loten Rd., Benfleet, Exxes SS7 5DD, England. *Agent:* Alec Harrison, International Press Centre, Shoe Lane, London EC4 3JB, England.

CAREER: Assistant teacher at secondary school in Bradford, England, 1924-27; Plaistow Grammar School, London, England, senior history master, 1927-39, headmaster, 1939-

50; free-lance writer and lecturer, 1950—. *Member:* Society of Authors, Benfleet Historical Society (president), Rayleigh Historical Society (president), Upminster Historical Society (vice-president).

WRITINGS: Builders of Europe, Dent, Volume 1: *The Middle Ages,* 1934, Volume 2: *The Renaissance and After,* 1936, Volume 3: *Despotism and Revolution,* 1936; *Song and Verse Mimes* (self-illustrated; juvenile), Macdonald & Co., 1949; *The Pageant of the English People,* Macdonald & Co., Book 1: *The Making of a Nation,* 1949, Book 2: *Days of Change,* 1949, Book 3: *The Common Weal,* 1950, Book 4: *The Machine Age,* 1950; *English History in Play and Picture,* Book 1: *In the Beginning,* Book 2: *Kings and People,* Book 3: *Men and Machines,* Book 4: *The Latest Age,* Macdonald & Co., 1952; (with W. T. Phillips) *When We Leave School* (juvenile), Methuen, 1954, 2nd edition, 1958; *Six Little Punch Plays* (juvenile), Paxton, 1956; *Puppet Plays* (juvenile), E. J. Arnold, 1957; *The Story of Upminster,* privately printed, 1957-62; *Rhymes of a Wibsa Gawby* (poetry), privately printed, 1958.

John Stranger (juvenile historical novel), Harrap, 1960; *Find Out About the Anglo-Saxons* (juvenile), Muller, 1964; *Swords Over Southdowne* (novel based on local history), Muller, 1966; *London: The Years of Change, 1500-1720,* Barnes & Noble, 1966; *Britain Under the Romans,* Warne, 1967; *Voice of Protest: A History of Civil Unrest in Great Britain,* Frewin, 1967; *The Awakening World,* Volume 1: *The Vision of Freedom,* Volume 2: *The Great Uprisings,* 1967, Volume 3: *The Balance of Power,* Volume 4: *The Age of Fear and Hope,* Muller, 1967; *The Evelina: The Story of a London Children's Hospital, 1869-1969,* Guy's Hospital, 1969.

The English Home: A History of Working Class Housing in Great Britain, Muller, 1971; *Heraldic Sculpture: The Work of James Woodford,* Boydell Press, 1972; *Book of the Year 1873,* K. Mason, 1972; *Book of the Year 1874,* K. Mason, 1973; *A Glimpse of Victorian Times,* Threadneedle Press, 1973; *Ancient and Roman Britain,* Warne, 1976; *All-Colour Dictionary* (juvenile), Hamlyn, 1976; *All-Colour Children's Dictionary* (juvenile), Hamlyn, 1977; *A History of Benfleet,* privately printed, 1977. Also author (with J. J. Betts) of *The Momentous Years.*

WORK IN PROGRESS: A book on price levels since 1850, for K. Mason; research on local and parish history; a book on herbs.

SIDELIGHTS: Priestley writes: "My original researches were in diplomatic history (mainly nineteenth-century Italy) in which I am still interested, speaking French, Italian, and German, and having travelled in all three countries.

"I was attracted to local history later as a result of being able more readily to study original records, and this has been my main interest over the last twenty-seven or so years.

"My problem is the dissemination of local history. Owing to the limited market, publication is often difficult or impossible. This prevents people living in a locality from learning about it. My contention is that knowing about the place in which one lives helps one to 'throw down roots' and is of great cultural significance. My own way of dealing with this great shortcoming is to publish books myself at as near cost price as possible, doing the work of preparing, collating, and binding at home."

AVOCATIONAL INTERESTS: Growing herbs.

BIOGRAPHICAL/CRITICAL SOURCES: News Observer, September 16, 1977; *Southend Standard,* September 21, 1977.

PRIMO, Albert T.   1935-

PERSONAL: Born July 3, 1935, in Pittsburgh, Pa.; son of Albert D. (a gardner) and Jeanette (Rovitto) Primo; married Rosina Pregano (a registered nurse), January 21, 1961; children: A. C. Gregg, R. Valeri, Juliet Brooks. *Education:* University of Pittsburgh, B.A., 1958; Carnegie Institute of Technology (now Carnegie-Mellon University), graduate study, 1959-1960. *Residence:* Old Greenwich, Conn. *Agent:* Ira Goldstein, Moses & Singer, Inc., S and H Bldg., Avenue of the Americas, New York, N.Y. *Office:* Primo Newservice, Inc., B-116, Old Greenwich, Conn. 06870.

CAREER: WDTV, Pittsburgh, Pa., cameraman and newsfilm editor, 1953-55; KDKA-TV, Pittsburgh, news correspondent and newscaster, 1955-58, producer and assistant news director, 1958-64; KYW-TV, news director in Cleveland, Ohio, 1964-65, news director in Philadelphia, Pa., 1965-68; American Broadcasting Co. (ABC), New York City, director of news and public affairs for station WABC-TV, 1968-72, vice-president of news, 1972-74, executive producer, 1974—. Primo Newservice, Old Greenwich, Conn., news consultant. Regional correspondent for Columbia Broadcasting System (CBS) News. Notable assignments include coverage of both political conventions in 1968 and interviews with Gerald Ford, Richard Nixon, Barry Goldwater, Robert Kennedy, and William Scranton. *Awards, honors:* Associated Press awards; Peabody Award; Emmy Awards.

SIDELIGHTS: Primo produced material for the first network news program in the country, the Morgan Beatty News. Noted for his innovations in television news, he also developed the first hour long news program and created the eyewitness news concept, a concept now used by more than eighty television stations in the United States.

*   *   *

PRINTZ, Peggy   1945-

PERSONAL: Born November 20, 1945, in Cleveland, Ohio; daughter of James K. and Helene F. Printz; married Paul M. Steinle (a writer), January 11, 1970. *Education:* Smith College, B.A., 1967; Columbia University, M.S.J., 1968, further graduate study, 1976-77.

CAREER: Bank of America, Hong Kong, research assistant and writer for newsletter, 1974; WJAR-TV, Providence, R.I., reporter and producer, 1974-76; *Asian Wall Street Journal,* Hong Kong, staff reporter from Singapore, 1977-78. *Member:* Foreign Correspondents Association of Southeast Asia, Singapore Press Club. *Awards, honors:* Citation from Overseas Press Club, 1973, for article "The Chen Family Still Has Class"; Walter Bagehot fellow in economics and business journalism, Columbia University, 1976-77.

WRITINGS: (Author of revision) Judy Brodie, *Eating Out in Hong Kong,* Longman, 1974; (with husband, Paul Steinle) *Commune: Life in Rural China,* Dodd, 1977.

SIDELIGHTS: Peggy Printz writes: "My husband and I wrote *Commune* to share our experiences on one of China's seventy-five thousand people's communes while filming a television documentary. By observing one people's commune, which is a township of thousands of residents, readers can learn what life is like for the majority of China's peasant farmers, who comprise over eighty per cent of the country's population, and can begin to understand the reality of China today."

PROKOSCH, Frederic   1908-

PERSONAL: Born May 17, 1908, in Madison, Wis.; son of Edouard (a philologist and professor of linguistics) and Mathilde (a concert pianist; maiden name, Dapprich) Prokosch; *Education:* Haverford College, B.A., 1926, M.A., 1928; further graduate study at University of Pennsylvania; Yale University, Ph.D., 1933; post-doctoral study at King's College, Cambridge, 1937. *Home:* "Ma Trouvaille," Plan de Grasse, Alpes Maritimes, France.

CAREER: Poet and novelist. Instructor in English at Yale University, 1932-34; member of faculty at New York University, 1936-37; visiting lecturer at University of Rome, 1950-51. Printer of modern poetry in U.S. and Europe, 1932-40. Cultural attache in Stockholm, Sweden, for U.S. Office of War Information, 1943-44. *Awards, honors:* Guggenheim fellowship, 1937; Harper Novel Award, 1937, for *The Seven Who Fled;* Harriet Monroe Lyric Prize, 1941, from *Poetry* magazine; Fulbright fellowship, 1951; Squash Racquets Champion of France, 1939, and of Sweden, 1944.

WRITINGS: The Asiatics (novel), Harper, 1935; *The Assassins* (poetry), Harper, 1936; *The Seven Who Fled* (novel), Harper, 1937; *The Carnival* (poetry), Harper, 1938; *Night of the Poor* (novel), Harper, 1939; *Death at Sea* (poetry), Harper, 1940; *The Skies of Europe* (novel), Harper, 1942; *The Conspirators* (novel), Harper, 1943; *Age of Thunder* (novel), Harper, 1945; *The Idols of the Cave* (novel), Doubleday, 1946; *Chosen Poems* (poetry), Doubleday, 1947; *Storm and Echo* (novel), Doubleday, 1948; *Nine Days to Mukalla* (novel), Viking, 1953; *A Tale for Midnight* (novel), Little, Brown, 1955; *A Ballad of Love* (novel), Farrar, Straus, 1960; *The Seven Sisters* (novel), Farrar, Straus, 1962; *The Dark Dancer* (novel), Farrar, Straus, 1964; *The Wreck of the Cassandra* (novel), Farrar, Straus, 1966; *The Missolonghi Manuscript* (novel), Farrar, Straus, 1968; *America, My Wilderness* (novel), Farrar, Straus, 1971.

SIDELIGHTS: Prokosch's first novel, *The Asiatics,* was an immense critical and popular success. It was translated into seventeen languages and praised by Thomas Mann and Andre Gide. After publishing several more well-received novels, Prokosch's popularity as a novelist declined, and today he is relatively unknown in the United States. Issac Bashevis Singer, who considers Prokosch "a master of American letters," offered a possible explanation for his being neglected by Americans. Singer wrote: "He has not cared to husband his natural resources. . . . His roots are in this land. If Prokosch, like Faulkner, had limited his creative energies to one milieu, one region, he would certainly be counted today among the pillars of American literature."

One of Prokosch's latest novels has revived critical interest in his work. In *The Missolonghi Manuscript,* Prokosch has devised a diary purportedly written by the poet Byron during the last four months of his life. While reviewers generally felt that Prokosch's work gave readers little additional insight into the life of Byron, most found it to be successful as a work of imagination and craft. Paul West commented "Here and there, it is only fair to say, Prokosch does amplify and extend, retrench and imagine. I just feel that, after reading this insufficiently bold exercise, I've not found out about Byron much that I didn't know, wheras I have found a suave, earthy prose virtuoso imposing on Byron an erotic witness which is vividly his own."

J. A. Cuddon wrote: "It is strong stuff but it is well written. By the end I felt as if I had waded through a kind of congealing stew compounded of excrement, rags of fine clothing, aphorisms, genitalia and urine, out of which exotic blooms rise, over which brilliant butterflies flit, all inhabited by beautiful and prurient shades." A reviewer for *Spectator* found that Prokosch "pulled off the seemingly impossible. He has not only found the perfect and dazzlingly simple form for this task—to have Byron himself tell his own story in a 'lost' manuscript written just before his death and to draw together like the two strings of a bag Byron's present and past—but has succeeded in encompassing his hero completely. Not, I mean, that Byron the poet who actually lived is necessarily caught in these pages, but that Mr. Prokosch's Byron is self-sufficient, he stands up, he speaks, he acts, he thinks; and he is so imaginatively realised that he has as much right to do so as the real Byron."

Commenting on current literary trends in America, Prokosch told *CA:* "I find myself profoundly out of sympathy with the prevalent flavor of the American literary scene. It is actually trendy, obviously commercial, and intensely publicity-conscious (I look back wistfully at the solitude of Emily Dickinson, of Whitman and Melville; our greatest writers). There is enormous talent, but it wilts prematurely in the glare of the fashions. There is a great and varied intelligence, but it is distorted by a greed for notoriety. There is an indigenous integrity, but it is ravaged by a spurious morality, a specious 'contemporaneity' and 'relevance,' and a gradual obliteration of an individual tone of voice. This does not portend favorably for the future. The signs point toward a deepening vulgarization, a widening corruption by the media, by commerce, by vanity, by ostentatiousness, by all that Cyril Connolly meant by 'enemies of promise.' It is difficult, isn't it, quite honestly, to visualize the arrival of a marvelous poet or a magnificent novelist."

BIOGRAPHICAL/CRITICAL SOURCES: Radcliffe Squires, *Frederic Prokosch,* Twayne, 1964; *New York Times Book Review,* January 14, 1968; *Book World,* January 14, 1968; *Chicago Tribune,* January 14, 1968; *Time,* February 9, 1968; *Spectator,* April 12, 1968; *New York Review of Books,* May 23, 1968; *Books & Bookmen,* June, 1968; *Atlantic,* May, 1972; *Contemporary Literary Criticism,* Volume 4, Gale, 1975.

* * *

PUNER, Morton 1921-

PERSONAL: Born November 11, 1921, in New York, N.Y.; son of Jacob (a retailer) and Sarah (Zuckerman) Puner; married Adeline Ramoni, February 4, 1950. *Education:* Attended New York University, 1939-42, and University of Alaska, 1945. *Politics:* Liberal Democrat. *Religion:* Jewish. *Home and office:* La Seraphine, Pierre Plantee, 83990 St. Tropez, France. *Agent:* Sanford J. Greenburger Associates, Inc., 757 Third Ave., New York, N.Y. 10017.

CAREER: Yank, Anchorage, Alaska, staff correspondent, 1943-45; *Reader's Scope,* New York City, editor, 1946-48; Anti-Defamation League, New York City, editor and executive, 1948-53; Praeger Publishers, New York City, editor, 1953-55; Anti-Defamation League, editor of bulletin and executive, 1955-63; Praeger Publishers, book editor, 1963-69; Universe Books, New York City, director, 1969—. Assistant to Vice-President Hubert Humphrey, 1968. Director of Praeger Publishers and Creative Imports. Consultant to U.S. Defense Department. *Military service:* U.S. Army Air Forces, Military Intelligence, 1943-45.

MEMBER: Ligue Internationale Contre Racisme, Authors Guild, Gerontological Society. *Awards, honors:* People-to-people award from U.S. Defense Department; human rights award from B'nai B'rith.

WRITINGS: (Editor with Ernest O. Melby) *Freedom and Public Education,* Praeger, 1953; (editor) *Barriers: Patterns of Discrimination,* Friendly House, 1958; (with Hubert Humphrey) *The Cause Is Mankind,* Praeger, 1964; *To the Good Long Life,* Universe Books, 1974; *Getting the Most Out of Your Fifties,* Crown, 1977. Contributor to popular magazines and newspapers, including *Coronet, Reporter, Holiday,* and *New Republic.*

WORK IN PROGRESS: The Rumor, a documentary novel on French racism.

SIDELIGHTS: Morton Puner writes: "Human rights, specifically minority rights, are my central theme. Nothing much has changed for me since moving to France in 1969, although the complexion of the victims may be a bit different."

* * *

PUTZEL, Michael 1942-

PERSONAL: Born September 16, 1942, in Washington, D.C.; son of Max (a university professor) and Nell (Converse) Putzel; married wife Nancy W., April 8, 1967 (divorced, 1973); married Ann Blackman (a feature writer), February 23, 1974; children: Leila Elizabeth. *Education:* University of North Carolina at Chapel Hill, A.B., 1967. *Politics:* "Nonaligned." *Home:* 3035 O St. N.W., Washington, D.C. 20007. *Office:* Associated Press, 2021 K. St. N.W., Washington, D.C. 20006.

CAREER/WRITINGS: Charleston Gazette, Charleston, W. Va., reporter, 1963-66; Associated Press, New York City, newsman in Raleigh, N.C., 1967, editor on foreign desk, New York City, 1968-69, field correspondent in Saigon, 1969-71, editor in Washington, D.C., 1971, correspondent in Saigon, 1972, editor in Washington, D.C., 1972—. Notable assignments include coverage of the Viet Nam War, including the North Vietnamese offensive, 1972, the Watergate investigation, and Chappaquiddick. *Military service:* U.S. Army, 1964-65.

* * *

QUACKENBUSH, Margery (Carlson) 1943-

PERSONAL: Born July 6, 1943, in Jamestown, N.Y.; daughter of Earle William (a manager) and Eva (Benson) Carlson; married William Leo Quackenbush (an electronic engineer), April 20, 1968; children: Todd William. *Education:* Cornell University, B.A., 1965; University of California, Berkeley, M.A., 1966. *Religion:* Protestant. *Residence:* Palo Alto, Calif. *Office:* Department of Social Sciences, City College of San Francisco, San Francisco, Calif. 94112.

CAREER: International Business Machines Corp., Oakland, Calif., systems engineer, 1966-68; City College of San Francisco, San Francisco, Calif., instructor in political science, 1969—. *Member:* Phi Beta Kappa, Phi Kappa Phi. *Awards, honors:* Woodrow Wilson fellowship, 1965; award from California Society of Pioneers, 1972.

WRITINGS: (With Frieda Porat) *Positive Selfishness,* Celestial Arts, 1977.

* * *

QUEBEDEAUX, Richard (Anthony) 1944-

PERSONAL: Born October 16, 1944, in Los Angeles, Calif.; son of Thomas Crawford (an electrical engineer) and Annette (Scheyer) Quebedeaux. *Education:* University of California, Los Angeles, B.A. (honors), 1966, M.A., 1970;

Harvard University, B.D. (cum laude), 1968; Oxford University, D.Phil., 1975. *Politics:* Democrat. *Religion:* United Church of Christ. *Residence:* Berkeley, Calif.

CAREER: United Church of Christ, Southern California Conference, Pasadena, staff intern for evangelism, 1974-75; United Church Board for Homeland Ministries, New York, N.Y., consultant on church renewal, 1975—. *Member:* American Society of Authors and Journalists. *Awards, honors:* Ecumenical scholarship from World Council of Churches, 1969-70, for Mansfield College, Oxford.

WRITINGS: The Young Evangelicals, Harper, 1974; *The New Charismatics: The Origins, Development, and Significance of Neo-Pentecostalism,* Doubleday, 1976; *The Worldly Evangelicals,* Harper, 1978; *I Found It! The Story of Bill Bright and Campus Crusade for Christ,* Harper, 1979. Contributor to religious magazines and social studies journals.

SIDELIGHTS: Quebedeaux comments: "I have a particular interest in the history, sociology, and theology of contemporary religious movements, and in the relationship between religious belief and experience *and* behavior in the world." *Avocational interests:* Rock, Bach, travel, and "hanging out" in Berkeley.

*   *   *

QUENNELL, Marjorie Courtney   1884-

PERSONAL: Born in 1884, in Bromley Common, Kent, England; daughter of Allen Courtney; married Charles Henry Bourne Quennell (an architect and author), 1904 (died, 1935); children: two sons, one daughter. *Education:* Attended Crystal Palace Art School, Beckenham Technical Art School, and Westminster Art School. *Residence:* Lewes, Sussex, England.

CAREER: Author and artist. Geffrye Museum, London, England, curator, 1935-41. Visited America, 1939, to study museums and education. *Member:* Associate of the Royal Institute of British Architects (honorary).

WRITINGS—With husband, Charles Henry Bourne Quennell; all self-illustrated: *A History of Everyday Things in England,* four volumes, Batsford, 1918-34, Scribner, 1922-35; *Everyday Life in the Old Stone Age,* Batsford, 1921, Putnam, 1922; *Everyday Life in the New Stone, Bronze, and Early Iron Ages,* Batsford, 1922, Putnam, 1923; *Everyday Life in Roman Britain,* Batsford, 1924, Putnam, 1925; *Everyday Life in Prehistoric Times* (originally published in two separate editions as *Everyday Life in the Old Stone Age* and *Everyday Life in the New Stone, Bronze, and Early Iron Ages*), Batsford, 1924, reprinted, Trans World, 1971; *Everyday Life in Anglo-Saxon, Viking, and Norman Times,* Batsford, 1926, Putnam, 1927; *Everyday Things in Homeric Greece,* Batsford, 1929, Putnam, 1930; *Everyday Things in Archaic Greece,* Putnam, 1931, revised edition, Batsford, 1960; *Everyday Things in Classical Greece,* Putnam, 1933; *The Good New Days,* Batsford, 1935; *Everyday Things in Ancient Greece* (originally published in three separate editions as *Everyday Things in Homeric Greece, Everyday Things in Archaic Greece,* and *Everyday Things in Classical Greece*), Putnam, 1954; *Everyday Life in Roman and Anglo-Saxon Times, including Viking and Norman Times* (a revision of *Everyday Life in Roman Britian* and *Everyday Life in Anglo Saxon, Viking, and Norman Times*), Batsford, 1950, Putnam, 1959.

Other: *London Craftsman: A Guide to Museums having Relics of Old Trades,* [London], 1939; (illustrator) Gertrude

Hartman and L. S. Saunders, *Builders of the Old World,* Little, Brown, 1948.

SIDELIGHTS: Reviewing *Everyday Things in Ancient Greece,* a critic for the *Christian Science Monitor* wrote: "There emerges from this effort of text and pictures a clever concept of what living meant to the founders of Western civilization." A reviewer for the London *Times Literary Supplement* commented, "From innumerable scattered references [the Quennells] have succeeded in assembling an astonishing wealth of information, while the illustrations . . . are as skillfully devised as they are pleasing to the eye."

AVOCATIONAL INTERESTS: Painting.

BIOGRAPHICAL/CRITICAL SOURCES: London Times Literary Supplement, November 19, 1954; *Christian Science Monitor,* December 16, 1954; *New York Herald Tribune Book Review,* March 6, 1960.*

*   *   *

QUICK, Armand James   1894-1978

July 18, 1894—January 26, 1978; American hematologist and author of works in his field. Quick was best known for developing tests to diagnose hemophilia and blood clotting. Quick was also among the first doctors to recognize the effects of aspirin on blood clotting. He died in Milwaukee, Wis. Obituaries: *New York Times,* January 27, 1978.

*   *   *

QUICKEL, Stephen (Woodside)   1936-

PERSONAL: Born December 23, 1936, in Harrisburg, Pa.; son of Kenneth Elwood (a physician) and Carolyn (Chick) Quickel; children: Stephen, Jennifer. *Education:* Dartmouth College, A.B., 1958, M.B.A., 1959. *Home:* 7-13 Washington Sq. North, New York, N.Y. 10003. *Office: Institutional Investor,* 488 Madison Ave., New York, N.Y. 10022.

CAREER/WRITINGS: Mellon National Bank and Trust Co., Pittsburgh, Pa., member of staff, 1961-62; *Forbes,* New York City, reporter, 1962-63, staff writer, 1963-64, associate editor, 1964-67, Los Angeles bureau manager, 1967-69, senior editor, 1969-77; *Institutional Investor,* New York City, managing editor, 1977—. Notable assignments include coverage of Saudi Arabia before the oil embargo, and a critical series on the accounting profession. Instructor in writing at New York University; lecturer on finance. *Military service:* U.S. Navy, 1959-61; became lieutenant junior grade.

SIDELIGHTS: Quickel told *CA:* "Business is one of the most pervasive and least understood institutions in America. This makes business and financial journalism a challenging and exciting field."

*   *   *

RAAB, Selwyn   1934-

PERSONAL: Born June 26, 1934, in New York, N.Y.; son of William and Berdie (Glantz) Raab; married Helene Lurie, December 25, 1963; children: Marian. *Education:* City College (now of City University of New York), B.A., 1956. *Office: New York Times,* 249 East 43rd St., New York, N.Y. 10036.

CAREER: New York World-Telegram and Sun, New York City, reporter, 1960-66; National Broadcasting Co. (NBC) News, New York City, producer and television news editor, 1966-71; WNET-News, New York City, executive producer, 1971-74; *New York Times,* New York City, reporter, 1974—. *Awards, honors:* University of Missouri School of

Journalism award, 1969; Sigma Delta Chi Deadline Club awards, 1971 and 1973; New York Press Club award, 1973; New York State Associated Press award, 1973; Heywood Hale Broun Award, 1974; Newspaper Guild of New York Page One award, 1974.

WRITINGS: *Justice in the Back Room,* World Publications, 1967.

* * *

RABDAU, Marianne
See BAKKER-RABDAU, Marianne K(atherine)

* * *

RACINA, Thom 1946-
(Tom Anicar)

PERSONAL: Born June 4, 1946, in Kenosha, Wis.; son of Frank (a dry cleaner) and Esther (Benko) Raucina. *Education:* Attended University of New Mexico, 1964-66; Art Institute of Chicago, B.F.A., 1969, M.F.A., 1971. *Politics:* Democrat. *Home:* 3449 Waverly Dr., Los Angeles, Calif. 90027. *Agent:* Rhoda A. Weyr, William Morris Agency, 1350 Avenue of the Americas, New York, N.Y. 10019.

CAREER: Goodman Theatre, Chicago, Ill., assistant director, 1966-69, playwright-in-residence, 1969-71; writer, 1971—. Children's television writer for Hanna-Barbera, 1972-73. Has worked as a church organist, a price-check boy on roller skates in a discount store, a night club pianist, and a piano teacher. *Awards, honors:* Grant from National Student Association, 1965, to study music and drama in Europe.

WRITINGS—Novels: *Lifeguard,* Warner Paperback, 1976; (under pseudonym Tom Anicar) *Secret Sex,* New American Library, 1976; *The Great Los Angeles Blizzard,* Putnam, 1977; *Quincy, M.E.,* Berkley, 1977; *Kojak in San Francisco,* Berkley, 1977; *Palm Springs,* Seaview Books, 1978; *FM,* Jove, 1978; *Sweet Revenge,* Berkley, 1978.

Musical plays for children: (adaptor) William Shakespeare, "A Midsummer Night Dream," first produced in Chicago, Ill., at Goodman Theatre, 1968; *Allison Wonderland,* Samuel French, 1970; *The Marvelous Misadventure of Sherlock Holmes,* Samuel French, 1971.

Plays: "Allison," first produced in Chicago at Goodman Theatre, January 30, 1970; "Sherlock," first produced in Chicago at Goodman Theatre, July 6, 1971.

WORK IN PROGRESS: *Tomcat,* a novel; *Too Far from the Tree,* a novel with Florence Greenberg; a novel set in contemporary Russia.

SIDELIGHTS: Racina writes: "I have no desire to write literature, only the kind of books I like to read, novels which are real escapist entertainment. The motivation to do much and do it well and be happy at the same time comes from a long history of battling the disease pancreatitis. Having been faced with death several times, it is always a joy to have one more pain-free day to be able to write a few more pages."

AVOCATIONAL INTERESTS: Travel (including the Soviet Union), gourmet cooking, swimming, driving his BMW, playing the piano, and "sharing an eleven room house with two cats, Saxon and Christmas, and a dog named Herschel."

* * *

RAGOSTA, Millie J(ane) 1931-

PERSONAL: Born March 1, 1931, in Huntingdon, Pa.; daughter of Chester Earl (a printer) and Maximilla (Heck) Baker; married Vincent Anthony Ragosta (an insurance agent), February 4, 1950; children: Vincent, Kathleen, Arthur, Kevin, Ruth, Joseph, John, Anthony, Margaret, William, Rosemary. *Education:* Attended high school in Huntingdon, Pa. *Politics:* Liberal Republican. *Religion:* Roman Catholic. *Home:* 337 East Curtin St., Bellefonte, Pa. 16823. *Agent:* William Carrington Guy, 4649 South Atlantic, Daytona Beach, Fla. 32019.

CAREER: Writer, 1966—. *Member:* Bellefonte Women's Club.

WRITINGS: *The Lighthouse* (gothic novel), Avalon, 1971; *House of the Evil Winds* (gothic novel), Bouregy, 1973; *Lorena Veiled* (gothic novel), Ballantine, 1974; *Taverna in Terrazzo* (gothic novel), Ballantine, 1975; *King John's Treasure* (gothic novel), Doubleday, 1976; *Witness to Treason* (historical novel), Doubleday, 1977. Contributor of articles and stories to magazines, including *Family Digest.*

WORK IN PROGRESS: Research for *The White Rose of Scotland* (tentative title), a historical novel based on the life of Katherine Gordon, wife of the most famous of the pretenders to the English throne during the reign of Henry VII.

SIDELIGHTS: Millie Ragosta comments: "I began writing eleven years ago at the age of thirty-five because I was the mother of ten children and was overwhelmed with the need to do something just for myself. But, being convinced a mother is needed at home, it had to be something I could do there. Six years ago, I produced my last baby and the first of eight books. I started with gothics because I had so much to learn, but now I am doing historical fiction, my favorite."

* * *

RAGSDALE, W(arner) B. 1898-

PERSONAL: Born December 21, 1898, in Hiram, Ga.; son of Joseph B. (a farmer) and Emma (Bullard) Ragsdale; married Claribel Kemp, October 21, 1922; children: Warner B., Jr., Ruthmary Ragsdale Reinecke. *Education:* Attended Young Harris College, 1915-17, and Georgia School of Technology, 1918. *Religion:* Baptist. *Home and office:* 406 Dale Dr., Silver Spring, Md. 20910.

CAREER: Employed by *Atlanta Journal,* Atlanta, Ga., *Florida Metropolis* (now *Florida News*), *Hendersonville News,* Hendersonville, N.C., *Charlotte Observer,* Charlotte, N.C., *Philadelphia Evening Ledger,* Philadelphia, Pa., and International News Service, 1919-24; Associated Press, chief of New Orleans Bureau and editor in Atlanta, Ga., 1924-27, night editor, day editor, and reporter in Washington, D.C., 1927-41; *U.S. News & World Report,* Washington, D.C., political editor, 1941-69; free-lance writer, 1969—. Periodical Press Galleries, member of executive committee, 1949-69, chairman, 1963-69. *Member:* National Press Club. *Awards, honors:* Best feature story award from Atlantic City, N.J., Headliners Club, 1937.

WRITINGS: *Politics Inside and Out,* U.S. News & World Report, 1970; *Guide to the '72 Elections,* U.S. News & World Report, 1972; *Three Weeks in Dayton* (on the Scopes trial), American Heritage, 1975.

WORK IN PROGRESS: A history of modern politics, completion expected in 1979.

SIDELIGHTS: Ragsdale writes: "I reported or directed the coverage of twenty-five national political conventions. I traveled with Hoover in 1936, F.D.R. in 1932 and 1944, Truman in 1948, and through the Tennessee Hills with William Jennings Bryan during interludes of the Scopes trial in 1925. As a political reporter, I met, interviewed, and dealt with every Presidential candidate of both major parties between Calvin Coolidge and Jimmy Carter. During almost fifty years of campaign coverage, my hobby was collecting biographies of important figures in American history which now come in handy in the work in which I am now engaged.''

* * *

RAINES, Howell (Hiram) 1943-

PERSONAL: Born February 5, 1943, in Birmingham, Ala.; son of W. S. (a builder) and Bertha (Walker) Raines; married Susan Woodley (a photographer), March 22, 1969; children: Ben Hayes, Jeffrey Howell. *Education:* Birmingham-Southern College, B.A., 1964; University of Alabama, Tuscaloosa, M.A., 1973. *Home:* 1001 58th Ave. S., St. Petersburg, Fla. 33705. *Agent:* Russell & Volkening, Inc., 551 Madison Ave., New York, N.Y. 10017. *Office: St. Petersburg Times,* P.O. Box 1121, St. Petersburg, Fla. 33731.

CAREER: Birmingham Post-Herald, Birmingham, Ala., reporter, 1964-65; WBRC-TV, Birmingham, Ala., staff writer, 1965-67; *Tuscaloosa News,* Tuscaloosa, Ala., reporter, 1968-69; *Birmingham News,* Birmingham, Ala., film critic, 1970-71; *Atlanta Constitution,* Atlanta, Ga., political editor, 1971-74; *St. Petersburg Times,* St. Petersburg, Fla., political editor, 1976—.

WRITINGS: (Contributor) Herbert Alexander, editor, *Campaign Money,* Free Press, 1976; *Whiskey Man* (novel), Viking, 1977; *My Soul Is Rested* (oral history), Putnam, 1977.

* * *

RAINES, John C. 1933-

PERSONAL: Born October 27, 1933, in Minneapolis, Minn.; son of Richard C. (a clergyman) and Lucile (Arnold) Raines; married Bonnie Muir (a teacher), September, 1962; children: Lindsley, Mark, Nathan, Mary. *Education:* Carleton College, A.B., 1955; Union Theological Seminary, New York, N.Y., B.D., 1959, Ph.D., 1966. *Politics:* Democrat. *Religion:* Methodist. *Home:* 423 West Walnut Lane, Philadelphia, Pa. 19144. *Office:* Department of Religion, Temple University, Philadelphia, Pa. 19122.

CAREER: Temple University, Philadelphia, Pa., associate professor of religion, 1967—. *Member:* Authors Guild of Authors League of America, American Academy of Religion, American Society of Christian Ethics, American Association of University Professors. *Awards, honors:* Fulbright fellowship; Columbia University international fellowship; Rockefeller Foundation fellowship.

WRITINGS: (editor) *Marxism and Radical Religion,* Temple University Press, 1971; (editor) *Conspiracy,* Harper, 1972; *Attack on Privacy,* Judson, 1974; *Illusions of Success,* Judson, 1975.

WORK IN PROGRESS: Research on working-class youth, for *Hard Times and the American Dream.*

* * *

RALEY, Patricia E(ward) 1940-

PERSONAL: Born August 21, 1940, in Portland, Ore. *Education:* Stanford University, A.B., 1962; University of California, Los Angeles, M.L.S., 1968. *Agent:* Hoffman-Sheedy Literary Agency, 145 West 86th St., New York, N.Y. 10024.

CAREER: Writer.

WRITINGS: Exploring Human Sexuality, Schenkman, 1975; *Making Love: How to Be Your Own Sex Therapist,* Dial, 1976.

WORK IN PROGRESS: A book on families, with Mel Roman.

* * *

RANK, Hugh (Duke) 1932-

PERSONAL: Born November 3, 1932, in Chicago, Ill.; son of Hugh A. (a salesman) and Margaret (McGreevy) Rank; married Lee Novak (a teacher), August 31, 1958; children: Elizabeth, Christopher, James-Jonathan, David. *Education:* University of Notre Dame, B.A., 1954, M.A., 1955, Ph.D., 1969. *Home:* 834 Pin Oak Lane, Park Forest South, Ill. 60466. *Office:* College of Cultural Studies, Governors State University, Park Forest South, Ill. 60466.

CAREER: Arizona State University, Tempe, instructor in English, 1959-60, 1961-62; St. Joseph's College, Rensselaer, Ind., assistant professor of English, 1962-67; Sacred Heart University, Fairfield, Conn., associate professor of English, 1968-72; Governors State University, Park Forest South, Ill., professor of English, 1972—. *Military service:* U.S. Army, public information officer, 1955-58; served in Germany; became first lieutenant.

MEMBER: National Council of Teachers of English, Conference on College Composition and Communication, Illinois Consumer Educators. *Awards, honors:* Fulbright award, 1967-68; George Orwell Award from National Council of Teachers of English, 1976, for distinguished contribution toward honesty and clarity in public language.

WRITINGS: The American Scene, Gyldendal, 1969, 2nd edition, 1971; *The U.S.A.: A Commentary,* Litton International, 1972; *Edwin O'Connor,* Twayne, 1974; (editor) *Language and Public Policy,* National Council of Teachers of English, 1974; *The Counter-Propaganda File,* privately printed, 1976. Contributor of articles to language and literary journals, including *New England Quarterly,* and poems to ''little'' magazines.

WORK IN PROGRESS: A textbook; editing a book of readings; testing and revising *The Counter-Propaganda File* and similar teaching devices, with commercial publication expected to result.

SIDELIGHTS: Rank writes: ''Trained in 'mainstream' American literature at Notre Dame, my dissertation 'The Soiled Roman Collar' focused on a neglected area of scholarship, analyzing the literary effects of liberalism on American 'Catholic ghetto' literature. This manuscript is still unpublished, but the research produced a dozen related scholarly articles and led to the book *Edwin O'Connor,* which Edmund Wilson (who had read the key chapters in manuscript) termed 'extremely intelligent,' and which reviewers praised.

''Since 1972, my research has centered on propaganda analysis; interest in eighteenth-century rhetoric led me, via Jonathan Edwards and Perry Miller, back to Aristotle's *Rhetoric.* Re-examining my own priorities, I felt that I should apply my own effort to analyze the language and persuasion of our contemporary 'professional persuaders'—especially advertising and political propaganda. When the National Council of Teachers of English created a Committee on Public Doublespeak in 1972 (mandated to help 'prepare children to cope with commercial propaganda'), I became the original chairman, attempting to create a useful technique to teach the young how to analyze sophisticated persuasion. For nearly four years, my main project was the creation of a new schema as a structure to organize propaganda analysis; by re-sorting twenty-five existing taxonomies, eliminating the jargon, I produced a simple pattern, 'Intensify/Downplay,' which can be applied to verbal, nonverbal, and other symbolic human communication. Copyright was released to the public domain so that texts could freely incorporate it. In 1976, the Committee on Public Doublespeak endorsed the schema.''

AVOCATIONAL INTERESTS: "Lieben und arbeiten.''

BIOGRAPHICAL/CRITICAL SOURCES: Daniel Dieterich, *Teaching about Doublespeak,* National Council of Teachers of English, 1976.

* * *

RANSEL, David L(orimer) 1939-

PERSONAL: Born February 20, 1939, in Gary, Ind.; son of Joseph A. (an architect) and Patricia (Lorimer) Ransel; married Therese Holma (a social worker), August 16, 1969; children: Kerstin, Anna-Lisa. *Education:* Coe College, B.A., 1961; Northwestern University, M.A., 1962; Yale University, Ph.D., 1969. *Home:* 1914 David Dr., Champaign, Ill. 61820. *Office:* Department of History, 309 Gregory Hall, University of Illinois, Urbana, Ill. 61801.

CAREER: University of Illinois, Urbana, instructor, 1967-68, assistant professor, 1968-73, associate professor of history, 1973—. *Member:* American Association for the Advancement of Slavic Studies, Phi Beta Kappa, Phi Kappa Phi. *Awards, honors:* Woodrow Wilson fellowship, 1961-62; Soviet-American exchange grant from Inter-University Committee on Travel Grants, for study at Leningrad State University, 1965-66; U.S. Office of Education grants for study abroad, summer, 1970, and spring, 1974; American Council of Learned Societies grant for study in Helsinki, Finland, spring-summer, 1974; Center for International Comparative Studies grant, summer, 1974; National Endowment for the Humanities grant, 1976-77; International Research and Exchange Board grant for research in U.S.S.R., 1979.

WRITINGS: The Politics of Catherinian Russia: The Panin Party, Yale University Press, 1975; (editor) *The Family in Imperial Russia,* University of Illinois Press, 1978. Contributor of articles and reviews to history and Slavic studies journals.

WORK IN PROGRESS: Research on the family and society in imperial Russia, especially the social and economic problems associated with unwanted and abandoned children.

SIDELIGHTS: "I grew up in a town whose politics were dominated by powerful families representing a variety of ethnic styles,'' Ransel told *CA.* "My maternal great-grandfather, William Lorimer, was a boss politician and U.S. senator who built his power on family alliances and patronage networks. These elements of my heritage no doubt sparked my interest in the workings of family and personal clientele systems. My study of Catherinian politics approached this issue from the point of view of the ruling aristocratic family groups. More recently, I have been studying pathologies of the family such as infanticide and child abandonment. I am attempting to plot the economic, social, and psychological factors giving rise to this behavior.

"During the past two centuries the family, both east and west, has undergone enormous changes. We are all vaguely aware of a revolution going on in American family life today.

Yet the causes and impact of these changes need to be better understood. I believe understanding will be much enhanced by historical and cultural comparative perspectives. My recent collection on the family in imperial Russia represents an effort to stimulate further study of this subject in the Russian area and to provide the basis for comparison with the rapidly growing body of western scholarship on the topic.''

Ransel speaks Russian, Swedish, Danish, German, and French.

* * *

RANSOME, Arthur Michell 1884-1967

PERSONAL: Born January 18, 1884, in Leeds, Yorkshire, England; son of Cyril Ransome (a college history professor); married Ivy Constance Walker, 1909 (marriage dissolved); married Euginia Shelepin, 1924; children: (first marriage) one daughter. *Education:* Educated at Rugby School. *Residence:* Suffolk, England.

CAREER: Writer, critic, and journalist. Worked as a war correspondent in Russia for English newspapers during the first World War and the Russian Revolution. *Awards, honors:* Carnegie Medal, 1936, for *Pigeon Post;* Litt.D., University of Leeds, 1952; Commander of the Order of the British Empire, 1953; Caldecott Medal, 1969, for *The Fool of the World and the Flying Ship;* honorary M.A., University of Durham.

WRITINGS—For children: *Nature Books for Children,* Anthony Treherne, 1906; *Old Peter's Russian Tales* (illustrated by Dmitri Mitrokhin), F. A. Stokes, 1917, new edition, Puffin, 1974, excerpt published separately as *The Fool of the World and the Flying Ship,* Farrar, Staus, 1968; *Aladdin and His Wonderful Lamp in Rhyme* (illustrated by Mackenzie), Nisbet, 1920; *Swallows and Amazons,* J. Cape, 1930, Lippincott, 1931, 3rd revised edition, Penguin, 1968; *Swallowdale* (illustrated by C. Webb), J. Cape, 1931, Lippincott, 1932, new edition, Penguin, 1968; *Peter Duck* (self-illustrated), J. Cape, 1932, revised edition, Lippincott, 1933; *Winter Holiday,* J. Cape, 1933, new edition, 1961, Lippincott, 1934; *Coot Club,* J. Cape, 1934, Lippincott, 1935; *Pigeon Post,* J. Cape, 1936, Lippincott, 1937; *We Didn't Mean to Go to Sea* (self-illustrated), J. Cape, 1937, Macmillan, 1938; *Secret Water* (self-illustrated), J. Cape, 1939, Macmillan, 1940; *The Big Six* (self-illustrated), J. Cape, 1940, Macmillan, 1941; *Missee Lee* (self-illustrated), J. Cape, 1941, Macmillan, 1942; *The Picts and the Martyrs; or, Not Welcome at All* (self-illustrated), Macmillan, 1943; *Great Northern?,* J. Cape, 1947, Macmillan, 1948.

Nonfiction: *Bohemia in London* (illustrated by Fred Taylor), Dodd, 1907; *A History of Story-Telling: Studies in the Development of Narrative* (illustrated by J. Gavin), T. C. & E. C. Jack, 1909, reprinted, Folcroft, 1972; *Edgar Allan Poe: A Critical Study,* M. Secker, 1910, reprinted, Haskell House, 1972; *Oscar Wilde: A Critical Study,* M. Secker, 1912, reprinted, Folcroft, 1972; *Portraits and Speculations,* Macmillan, 1913, reprinted, Folcroft, 1972; *Russia in 1919,* B. W. Huebsch, 1919 (published in England as *Six Weeks in Russia in 1919,* Allen & Unwin, 1919); *The Crisis in Russia,* B. W. Huebsch, 1921; *"Racundra's" First Cruise,* B. W. Huebsch, 1923, reprinted, Hart-Davis, 1958; *The Chinese Puzzle,* Allen & Unwin, 1927; *Rod and Line: With Aksakow on Fishing,* J. Cape, 1929; *Mainly about Fishing,* Black, 1959.

Other: *The Souls of the Streets, and Other Little Papers,* Brown, Langham, 1904; *The Stone Lady: Ten Little Papers and Two Mad Stories,* Brown, Langham, 1905; *The Imp and the Elf and the Ogre,* Nisbet, 1910; *The Hoofmarks of the Faun,* Martin Secker, 1911; *The Elixir of Life,* Methuen, 1915; *The Soldier and Death,* B. W. Huebsch, 1922.

Editor: *The World's Story Tellers,* T. C. & E. C. Jack, 1908; *The Book of Friendship,* T. C. & E. C. Jack, 1909; *The Book of Love,* T. C. & E. C. Jack, 1910; John MacGregor, *The Voyage Alone in the Yawl Rob Roy,* Hart-Davis, 1954.

Also translator of a work by Yury N. Libedinsky published as *A Week,* Allen & Unwin, 1923.

SIDELIGHTS: As a boy, Arthur Ransome occupied Lewis Carroll's study at Rugby School. He spent his childhood holidays at Lake Windermere. His first book was published at age 20. A few years later he became interested in criticism, and in 1912, his study of Oscar Wilde appeared.

Ransome went to Russia in 1913 and studied folklore, hoping to obtain enough material for a book of Russian fairy tales. The result was *Old Peter's Russian Tales,* a collection of 21 stories that Russian peasants tell their children. According to the *Springfield Republican,* Ransome said that the stories are "not for the learned nor indeed for grown-up people at all. No people who really like fairy tales ever grow up altogether."

At age 45, Ransome achieved his greatest success with the publication of *Swallows and Amazons.* The story concerns real children, who are likeable and understandable, and who do things every child likes to do. It is based in part on Ransome's childhood memories of the holidays spent at Lake Windermere. *New Statesman* said: "The outward aspect of the book will please the grown-up eye and may raise an expectation that the children in it are psychologically studied for adult reading. But the child-reader will be delighted to find nothing so uninteresting to him as child-psychology, and the things that do interest him treated on a real and serious plane. The ideal reader should certainly be not too old for make-believe about a miniature desert-island."

Swallowdale, the sequel to *Swallows and Amazons,* was reviewed by a *New York Times* critic who said: "Like its predecessor, *Swallows and Amazons,* [it] meets the test of a good book for children, for it can be read with pleasure by adults as well as boys and girls. The book is full of adventure, not artificial excitement, but the kind that a child who has not been too much interfered with will find for himself anywhere, though, in this instance, an island for camping, a sail boat, and a sympathetic and sensible mother furnish an ideal starting point for imaginative play."

Peter Duck has been a favorite among older readers. The *New York Times* said of it: "Mr. Ransome is one of those rare authors who can write for children and about children at the same time. His fine prose style is a delight. The illustrations add to the interest of the book." *Saturday Review* commented: "The story contains all the ingredients necessary to make it not only eminently readable, but also thrilling enough to satisfy the most exacting of tastes. What more could anyone demand than a book about the sea together with a buried treasure in the Caribbean Islands, pirates, storms, sharks, a waterspout, and a happy ending."

AVOCATIONAL INTERESTS: Fishing.

BIOGRAPHICAL/CRITICAL SOURCES: Springfield Republican, December 1, 1917; *New Statesman,* August 2, 1930; *New York Times,* February 14, 1932, May 14, 1933; Roger Lancelyn Green, *Teller of Tales,* Ward, 1953; Hugh Shelley, *Arthur Ransome,* Bodely Head, 1960.

OBITUARIES: New York Times, June 6, 1967; *Publishers Weekly,* June 26, 1967.*

(Died June 3, 1967)

*   *   *

RAO, Raja   1909-

PERSONAL: Born November 21, 1909, in Hassan, Mysore, India; son of H. V. (a professor) and Srimathi (Gauramma) Krishnaswamy; married Katherine Jones (an actress), November, 1965; children: Christopher. *Education:* Attended Hunter College of the City University of New York. *Home:* 1808 Pearl, Austin, Tex. 78701. *Agent:* William Morris Agency, 1350 Avenue of the Americas, New York, N.Y. 10019. *Office:* University of Texas, Austin, Tex. 78712.

CAREER: Professor of philosophy at University of Texas.

WRITINGS: The Serpent and the Rope, Murray, 1960, Pantheon, 1963; *Kanthapura,* New Directions, 1964; *The Cat and Shakespeare,* Macmillan, 1964.

*   *   *

RASMUSSEN, Louis J(ames, Jr.)   1921-

PERSONAL: Born July 16, 1921, in Minneapolis, Minn.; son of Louis J. and Kitty (Bailey) Rasmussen; married Barbara K. Balser, June 24, 1945; children: Diane Louise Rasmussen Myers. *Education:* Attended high school in California and South Dakota. *Politics:* Republican. *Religion:* Methodist. *Home:* 1204 Nimitz Dr., Colma, Calif. 94015. *Office:* San Francisco Historical Records, 1204 Nimitz Dr., Colma, Calif. 94015.

CAREER: San Francisco Examiner, San Francisco, Calif., librarian, 1945-58, assistant on the column "Bay Land," 1958-61; San Francisco Historic Records, Colma, Calif., historical researcher and writer, 1962—. Consultant to business and government. *Military service:* U.S. Army, 1940-45; U.S. Air Force, 1950-52. *Member:* American Historical Writers, Western Historical Society, Military History Society, Association of Professional Researchers.

WRITINGS: San Francisco Ship Passenger Lists, four volumes, San Francisco Historic Records, 1965-70; *Railway Passenger Lists of Overland Trains,* two volumes, San Francisco Historic Records, 1969-60; *California Wagon Train Lists,* San Francisco Historic Records, 1977. Contributor to magazines.

WORK IN PROGRESS: San Francisco Ship Passenger Lists, Volume V, *Railway Passenger Lists of Overland Trains,* Volume III, and *California Wagon Train Lists,* Volume II, all for San Francisco Historical Records.

SIDELIGHTS: Rasmussen writes that his "major interest is research into the movement of humanity to the Western United States during the period from 1849 to 1895. Such movement deals with travel by ship, wagon train, and railroads—from the United States as well as foreign countries."

*   *   *

RASPUTIN, Maria
See BERN, Maria Rasputin Soloviev

*   *   *

RAST, Walter E(mil)   1930-

PERSONAL: Born July 3, 1930, in San Antonio, Tex.; son of Alfred Otto (a clergyman) and Edith Gertrude (a secretary; maiden name, Jordan) Rast; married Suzanne Marie Droege (a flutist), June 5, 1955; children: Joel, Timothy, Rebekah, Peter. *Education:* Concordia Theological Seminary, St. Louis, Mo., M.Div., 1955, M.S.Th., 1956; University of Chicago, M.A., 1964, Ph.D., 1966. *Home:* 303 Valparaiso St., Valparaiso, Ind. 46383. *Office:* Department of Theology, Valparaiso University, Valparaiso, Ind. 46383.

CAREER: Ordained Lutheran minister, 1957; pastor of Lutheran church in Bedford, Mass., 1957-61; Valparaiso University, Valparaiso, Ind., assistant professor, 1961-66, associate professor, 1966-72, professor of theology, 1972—. Co-director of excavations at Bab edh-Dhra, Jordan. Member of board of trustees of American Schools of Oriental Research, 1973-77.

MEMBER: Society of Biblical Literature (member of executive committee, 1976-77), Archaeological Institute of America, Israel Exploration Society, Palestine Exploration Fund, Chicago Society of Biblical Research, Valparaiso Builders Association (president, 1974-76). *Awards, honors:* American Council of Learned Societies fellowship, 1971-72; National Endowment for the Humanities grants, 1975, 1977.

WRITINGS: Tradition History and the Old Testament, Fortress, 1972; *Taanach I: Studies in the Iron Age Pottery,* Scholar's Press, 1978; *Joshua, Judges, Samuel, Kings,* Fortress, in press. Contributor to religious, archaeology, and Oriental studies journals.

WORK IN PROGRESS: Co-directing a series of excavations at Early Bronze Age sites along the southeastern plain of the Dead Sea, in Jordan, with books expected to result.

SIDELIGHTS: Rast told *CA* that his current concern is "interpretation of biblical texts against the background of archaeological activity in the Near East, with a special interest in the ethical and social importance of the Hebrew Bible. I have traveled extensively in the Near East, and lived two years in Jerusalem. I speak and read German, French, Swedish, Hebrew, Greek, Aramaic, and other Semitic languages."

*   *   *

RATTI, John 1933-

PERSONAL: Born February 4, 1933, in Charleston, W.Va.; son of Hugo John, Sr. (a chemist) and Violet (Dodd) Ratti. *Education:* Middlebury College, B.A., 1955; New York University, M.A., 1957. *Religion:* Episcopal. *Home:* 12 Willow Pl., Brooklyn, N.Y. 11201. *Office:* Grolier, Inc., 575 Lexington Ave., New York, N.Y. 10022.

CAREER: Collier's Encyclopedia, New York, N.Y., editorial assistant, 1958-60; American Heritage Publishing Co., New York City, assistant editor, 1960-62; Grolier, Inc., New York City, managing editor, 1962—. Editor for Executive Council of the Episcopal Church.

WRITINGS: A Remembered Darkness (poems), Viking, 1969; *Memorial Day* (poems), Viking, 1974.

Work anthologized in *New Directions 24.* Contributor of poems to magazines, including *Harper's, New Yorker, Shenandoah, Poetry, Salamagundi,* and *Literary Review.*

WORK IN PROGRESS: A third collection of poems; a historical novel for children; research for a book on his Italian relatives who have been artist and artisans in and around Florence since the sixteenth century.

SIDELIGHTS: Ratti writes: "My career in poetry has been an independent venture, divorced from the academic and literary establishments, and divorced from fashion. I am a product of two quite different cultures, long-time rural American on one side, European artists and artisans on the other. I find much of my work springs from the reconciling of these two cultures.

"I am interested in history and the presence of the past in our lives. I read French and French literature. However, I have developed strong ties to England in recent years."

*   *   *

RATTIGAN, Terence 1911-1977

June 10, 1911—November 30, 1977; British playwright and screenwriter. Rattigan is best known for the plays "Separate Tables," "The Browning Version," and "French Without Tears." His plays were quite popular in England and theatre records were broken when both "French Without Tears" and "While the Sun Shines" played more than one thousand performances. Rattigan died in Hamilton, Bermuda. Obituaries: *New York Times,* December 1, 1977; *Washington Post,* December 1, 1977; *Newsweek,* December 12, 1977; *Time,* December 12, 1977; *AB Bookman's Weekly,* February 6, 1978.

*   *   *

RAUF, Abdur 1924-

PERSONAL: Born May 10, 1924, in Amritsar, India; son of Allama Hussain (a journalist) and Hajirah Mir; married Naseem Chughtai (a medical educator), September 2, 1958; children: Asad, Amer, Asim. *Education:* Punjab University, M.A., 1945, M.A. (psychology), 1949; University of London, Ph.D., 1955. *Religion:* Islam. *Home:* 47 Empress Rd., Lahore, Pakistan. *Office:* Additional Education Secretary, Punjab Government, Lahore, Pakistan.

CAREER: Bureau of Education, Lahore, Pakistan, director, 1958-73; Text-Book Board, Lahore, chairman, 1973-74; Curriculum Research & Development Centre, Lahore, director, 1974; Government College of Education, Lahore, chairman of department of psychology, 1974, principal, 1975-76; Punjab Government, Lahore, additional education secretary, 1977—. President of education and social sciences section of Pakistan Science Conference, 1964. Resident Asian senior specialist in education at University of Hawaii's East-West Center, 1966-67.

MEMBER: Pakistan Association for the Advancement of Science, Institute for the Study and Treatment of Delinquency (London, England), Lions International. *Awards, honors:* United Nations social defense fellowship for England, 1952-53.

WRITINGS: West Pakistan: Rural Education and Development, University Press of Hawaii, 1970; *Islamic Culture and Civilization in Pakistan,* Ferozsons Ltd., 1975; *Dynamic Educational Psychology,* Ferozsons Ltd., 1976; *Quran for Children,* Ferozsons Ltd., 1976; *Prophet Muhammad's Guidance for Children,* Ferozsons Ltd., 1977; *Badunwani aur Rishwatstani* (title means "Corruption and Bribery"), Sh. Ghulam Ali & Sons, 1977. Editor of *Sanvi Taaleem* and *Taaleem-o-Tadrees,* both 1967-74.

WORK IN PROGRESS: Human Capital Formation in the Third World; Educational Crises in Pakistan.

SIDELIGHTS: Rauf remarks that "Human capital formation is a great motivational force in my writing and field operations. I strongly believe that in the ultimate analysis technological advancement and economic prosperity are dependent upon human creativity rather than sheer material resources. This belief is reflected in my books as well as policy decision as Pakistan's educational planner. I play an active role in promoting mass awakening on the dignity of human rights, which is also appropriately reflected in my contributions to the Human Rights Days and my community development pursuits as a social work missionary."

Rauf has traveled in England, the United States and Canada, Mexico, Puerto Rico, Japan, Hong Kong, Vietnam, Bangladesh, India, Saudi Arabia, Abu Zahbi, and Egypt, and speaks Urdu, English, Arabic, French, and Spanish.

* * *

RAWLS, Wendell L(ee), Jr. 1941-

PERSONAL: Born August 18, 1941, in Goodlettsville, Tenn.; son of Wendell L. (in textile business) Madolyn (Murphy) Rawls; married: Kathryn Stark, June 19, 1971; children: Amanda Coston, Matthew Bradley. *Education:* Vanderbilt University, B.A., 1970. *Politics:* Independent. *Religion:* Protestant. *Home:* 3800 Mode St., Fairfax, Va. 22030. *Agent:* Morton Janklow Associates, 375 Park Ave., New York, N.Y. *Office:* 1920 L St., N.W., Washington, D.C. 20036.

CAREER/WRITINGS: Nashville Tennessean, Nashville, sportswriter, 1967-70, reporter, 1970-72; *Philadelphia Inquirer,* Philadelphia, Pa., reporter, 1972-77; *New York Times,* New York, N.Y., reporter, 1977—. Notable assignments include coverage of the shooting of George Wallace in 1972, Hurricane Agnes and the 1974 Wilkes-Barre flood, Vietnam refugees in 1975, the capture of Patty Hearst, and the 1976 Republican National Convention. Contributor to *New York Times Magazine. Military service:* U.S. Army Reserves, 1965-71. *Member:* Alpha Tau Omega (president, 1962-63). *Awards, honors:* Thomas L. Stokes Award from Washington Journalism Center, 1975; Keystone (Pa.) Press Award, 1975; Pulitzer Prize, 1977, for special local reporting; Grand Prize from Robert F. Kennedy Journalism Awards Committee, 1977; National Headliner Award, 1977; Heywood Broun Award from Newspaper Guild, 1977; two Associated Press managing editors awards, 1977.

SIDELIGHTS: Rawls commented: "In journalism, every act is a matter of judgement, whether the decision concerns the headline, the length of the story, or the play of the story. Good, logical judgement is essential. Other factors important to my career are courage, quick thinking, a will *never to lose,* an ability to deal with people, ability to handle many different kinds of stories from investigative reporting to features to politics, and a desire to get the story nobody thinks can be gotten."

AVOCATIONAL INTERESTS: Golf, poker, gardening, banjo, all sports, breeding thoroughbred race horses, travel in United States, Mexico, and Canada.

BIOGRAPHICAL/CRITICAL SOURCES: New York Times, April 19, 1977; *Philadelphia Inquirer,* April 19, 1977; *Nashville Tennessean,* April 19, 1977.

* * *

RAWSKI, Conrad H(enry) 1914-

PERSONAL: Born May 25, 1914, in Vienna, Austria; came to the United States in 1939, naturalized citizen, 1948; son of Stanislaus H. (a jurist) and Johanna (Buberl-Maffei) Rawski; married Helen Orr (a teacher); children: Thomas George, Judith Ellen Rawski Kleen. *Education:* University of Vienna, M.A., 1936, Ph.D., 1937; Institute for Austrian Historical Research, certificate, 1936; further study at Peter Pazmany University, 1938-39, and Harvard University, 1939-40; Western Reserve University (now Case Western Reserve University), M.S.L.S., 1957. *Residence:* Chagrin Falls, Ohio. *Office:* School of Library Science, Case Western Reserve University, Cleveland, Ohio 44106.

CAREER: Boston Evening Transcript, Boston, Mass.,

music columnist, 1939-40; Ithaca College, Ithaca, N.Y., assistant professor, 1940-42, associate professor, 1943-50, professor of music and dean of School of Music, 1950-57; Cleveland Public Library, Cleveland, Ohio, head of fine arts department, 1957-62; Case Western Reserve University, Cleveland, associate professor, 1962-65, professor of library science, 1965—, dean of School of Library Science, 1977—. *Military service:* U.S. Army, 1943-46.

MEMBER: Mediaeval Academy of America, American Society for Aesthetics, American Society for Information Science, American Library Association, Cleveland Medical Library Association (fellow), Rowfant Club. *Awards, honors:* Fellow of Fund for the Advancement of Education, Ford Foundation, 1952-53.

WRITINGS: Petrarch: Four Dialogues for Scholars, Press of Western Reserve University, 1967; (contributor) L. E. Bone, editor, *Library School Teaching Methods: Courses in the Selection of Adult Materials,* University of Illinois Press, 1969; (contributor) R. G. Cheshier, editor, *Information in the Health Sciences,* Cleveland Medical Library Association, 1972; *Toward a Theory of Librarianship,* Scarecrow, 1973; (contributor) Aldo Scaglione, editor, *Francis Petrarch: Six Centuries Later,* University of North Carolina Press, 1975; (with T. G. Morris and Tefko Saracevic) *Foundations of Library Science,* Case Western Reserve University, 1976. Contributor of articles, translations, and reviews to library science, historical, and literature journals. Music critic for *Ithaca Journal,* 1945-50.

WORK IN PROGRESS: Modern English translations of Petrarch's *Invective contra medicum* (title means "Invectives Against the Physician") and *De remediis utriusque fortune* (title means "On Remedies for Both Good and Bad Fortune"), completion expected in 1980.

SIDELIGHTS: Rawski writes: "Throughout my professional career as a medieval scholar, information specialist, and teacher, I have been interested in problems of knowledge communication. As a Petrarchan scholar, and one of the few students of Petrarch's Latin works, I have explored the problems of textual analysis, interpretation, and translation posed by historical documents transmitting ideas of distant cultures and times. Ever fascinated by the challenge of the creative message—its grasp and understanding—I have studied the medieval arts and the medieval creative effort as such. As an information specialist I concentrate on the nature of knowledge communication, and particularly, of subject literatures. I have introduced aspects of structural analysis in my work toward algorithmic solutions of metascientific problems concerning knowledge behavior and transmission. My teaching reflects my concern with fundamental issues, insight and understanding. Among my former students are information scientists, academic teachers and leaders in the library profession in the United States and abroad.

As a native of central Europe, I am versed in a number of modern languages, and have specialized in ancient and medieval Latin. I am a trained paleographer and expert in medieval musical notation and rhetorical technique."

AVOCATIONAL INTERESTS: Playing harpsicord and recorder, "dabbling in macro-photography."

* * *

RECK, David 1935-

PERSONAL: Born January 12, 1935, in Texas; son of George B. (a clergyman) and Marie (Heinecken) Reck; married Carol S. Sugerman (a photographer). *Education:* University of Houston, B.Mus., 1958; University of Texas, M.Mus., 1960; studied at University of Pennsylvania, 1960-63, and Tamil Nadu College of Karnatik Music, 1968-70; Wesleyan University, Ph.D., 1975. *Office:* Department of Music, Amherst College, Amherst, Mass. 01002.

CAREER: Free-lance musician and composer in New York, N.Y., 1963—; Amherst College, Amherst, Mass., assistant professor, 1975—. Member of New School for Social Research faculty. *Member:* Canadian Society for Asian Studies, Society for Asian Music, Society for South Indian Studies, Society for Ethnomusicology. *Awards, honors:* Received three Rockefeller arts grants, including 1967 and 1977; Guggenheim fellowship, 1969.

WRITINGS: Music of the Whole Earth, Scribner, 1977.

WORK IN PROGRESS: Music of India.

SIDELIGHTS: Reck told *CA:* "I was born under the sign of Capricorn in south Texas. After a childhood of diverse cultural influences (Mexico, Anglo, the Carter family, fiddling, Grand Ole Opry, baseball, and the Saturday afternoon broadcasts from the Metropolitan Opera—not to mention family connections with India), I worked my way through the universities as a country and jazz musician. Specializing in composition, I studied with Paul Pisk (a disciple of Schoenberg) and George Rochberg. In the 1960's I lived and worked in New York. From 1968 to 1971 I studied in India, documenting folk and ritual music and working under Sri V. T. Ramachandra Iyer, a master musician of the seven-stringed south Indian *veena.* The experience in India was a pivotal one: there were no words, or few words; communication was through sound through music. The richness and variety of musical activity in India made New York seem like just another village somewhere. I returned to the United States to study ethnomusicology.

"I want to be a carpenter of sound, to be surprised (by myself and by others). But I study music, and play it, primarily for that magic touch, that emotional contact with music itself, that mystically makes me (and others) more human, more attuned to the ecology of ourselves and the world."

AVOCATIONAL INTERESTS: Old time music, fiddling.

* * *

REDMONT, Bernard Sidney 1918-

PERSONAL: Born November 8, 1918, in New York, N.Y.; son of Morris Abraham and Bessie (Kamerman) Redmont; married Joan Rothenberg, March 12, 1940; children: Dennis Foster, Jane Carol. *Education:* City College (now of City University of New York), B.A., 1938; Columbia University, M.J., 1939. *Religion:* Unitarian. *Office:* 12/24 Sadova Samotechnaya, Moscow, U.S.S.R. Kv. 38.

CAREER/WRITINGS: Brooklyn Daily Eagle, Brooklyn, N.Y., reporter and book reviewer, 1936-38; free-lance correspondent in Europe, 1939, and Mexico City, 1939-40; *Herkimer Evening Telegram,* Herkimer, N.Y., telegraph editor and editorial writer, 1941-42; U.S. Office of Inter-American Affairs, Washington, D.C., newswriter for shortwave radio broadcasts to Latin America, 1942-43, director of news division, 1944-46; *U.S. News and World Report,* Washington, D.C., correspondent and bureau chief in Buenos Aires and Paris, 1946-51; *Continental Daily Mail,* Paris, columnist, 1951-53; Enlish Language World News Service, Agence France-Presse, Paris, chief correspondent, 1953-65; Westinghouse Broadcasting Co., New York City, European correspondent and Paris bureau chief, 1962-76; Columbia

Broadcasting System (CBS) News, New York City, bureau chief in Moscow, 1976—. *Military service:* U.S. Marine Corps, 1943-44; received Purple Heart. *Member:* Overseas Press Club, National Press Club, Anglo-American Press Association of Paris (president, 1961; treasurer, 1970-73; secretary, 1974-76). *Awards, honors:* Overseas Press Club awards for best reporting from abroad, 1968 and 1973; Chevalier of the Legion of Honor (France), 1974.

* * *

REDWAY, Ralph
　　See HAMILTON, Charles Harold St. John

* * *

REDWAY, Ridley
　　See HAMILTON, Charles Harold St. John

* * *

REED, Kenneth T(errence) 1937-

PERSONAL: Born January 7, 1937, in Grand Rapids, Mich.; son of Kenneth T. (a railway executive) and Ethel V. (Reynalds) Reed; married Emily Beckett (a yoga teacher), September 26, 1961; children: William K., Elizabeth B., Anne B. *Education:* Miami University, Oxford, Ohio, B.A., 1959; State University of Iowa M.A., 1961; University of Kentucky, Ph.D., 1968. *Home:* 341 South D St., Hamilton, Ohio 45013. *Agent:* Jacques de Spoelberch, 1 Point Rd., Wilson Point, South Norwalk, Conn. 06854. *Office:* Department of English, Miami University, Hamilton, Ohio 45011.

CAREER: St. Clair Community College, Port Huron, Mich., instructor in English, 1961-63; Transylvania University, Lexington, Ky., assistant professor of English, 1963-68; Miami University, Hamilton, Ohio, instructor, summer, 1968, assistant professor, 1968-72, associate professor, 1972-77, professor of English, 1977—. Member of board of directors of Family Service of Hamilton and Butler County; member of local Parks and Recreation Board. *Member:* American Association of University Professors, Association of Departments of English, Midwest Modern Language Association, Rossville Historic Association (member of board of trustees).

WRITINGS S. N. Behrman, G. K. Hall, 1975; *Truman Capote,* G. K. Hall, in press. Contributor of about twenty-five articles and reviews to literary journals.

* * *

REES, Meriel
　　See LAMBOT, Isobel

* * *

REESE, Gustave 1899-1977

1899—September 7, 1977; American educator. Reese was author of *Music in the Middle Ages* and *Music in the Renaissance.* He encouraged interest in early music and served as an editorial executive for music publishing houses G. Schirmer and Carl Fischer. He also served as honorary president of American Musicological Society. He died in New York, N.Y. Obituaries: *New York Times,* September 13, 1977.

* * *

REESE, Heloise (Bowles) 1919-1977
　　(Heloise)

1919—December 28, 1977; American newspaper columnist.

"Hints from Heloise," her household hints column, was syndicated in nearly six hundred papers in the United States. Reese also wrote several books, including *Heloise's House-keeping Hints* which became the fastest-selling paperback in the history of Pocket Books, Inc. Her daughter will continue writing the column under the same byline. Reese died in San Antonio, Tex. Obituaries: *New York Times,* December 30, 1977. (See index for *CA* sketch)

*   *   *

REEVES, Joyce
   See GARD, Joyce

*   *   *

RENNER, Thomas C(hoate)   1928-
   (Tom Renner)

PERSONAL: Born October 26, 1928, in Brookline, Mass.; son of George (a manufacturer and stockbroker) and Eleanor (an antique dealer; maiden name, Clancey) Renner; married Nancy LoDuca, November 29, 1952; children: Elaine, Dawn, Sandra, Jacqueline. *Education:* Attended Syracuse University, 1947-48, and Hofstra University, 1954-55. *Politics:* Independent. *Religion:* Roman Catholic. *Residence:* Smithtown, N.Y. *Agent:* Susan Ann Protter, 158 East 52nd St., New York, N.Y. 10022. *Office:* Newsday, 550 Stewart Ave., Garden City, N.Y.

CAREER: Newsday, Garden City, N.Y., organized crime investigator and reporter, 1954—. Past director of Suffolk County Happy Landing Fund. Lecturer about organized crime at schools in Michigan, Massachusetts, Florida, New York, and Rhode Island. *Military service:* U.S. Air Force, 1948-53; became staff sergeant. *Member:* Investigative Reporters and Editors Association. *Awards, honors:* Awards from Bald University, New York University, and Conscience in Journalism, 1977, for "The Arizona Project."

WRITINGS: (Contributor) Nicholas Gage, editor, *Mafia, U.S.A.,* Playboy Press, 1972; (with Vincent Teresa) *My Life in the Mafia,* Doubleday, 1973; (with Teresa) *Vincent Teresa's Mafia,* Doubleday, 1975; (with Michael Hellerman) *Wall Street Swindler,* Doubleday, 1977. Contributor to magazines, including *Saturday Review, Reader's Digest,* and *Science Digest.*

WORK IN PROGRESS: Research for *Code Name Sun: The Making of a Soviet Double Agent* and *The Deputy, the Hood and the Tarnished Star: Corruption Within the U.S. Marshals Service,* both nonfiction.

SIDELIGHTS: Renner writes that he "seeks to expose the growth of organized crime in the United States, to protect the public interest, alerting government enforcement or exposing its or other governmental corruption."

BIOGRAPHICAL/CRITICAL SOURCES: Paul Meskill, *Don Carlo: Boss of Bosses,* Popular Library, 1973; James Dygert, *The Investigative Journalist,* Prentice-Hall, 1976; *The Quill,* March, 1977; *Mother Jones,* June, 1977; *Columbia Journalism Review,* November-December, 1977.

*   *   *

RENNER, Tom
   See RENNER, Thomas C(hoate)

*   *   *

RESNICK, Nathan   1910-1977

June 13, 1910—September 7, 1977; American scholar and educator. An expert on the poet Walt Whitman, Resnick was also chairman of the art department at Long Island University. He died in Kingston, N.Y. Obituaries: *New York Times,* September 8, 1977. (See index for *CA* sketch)

*   *   *

RESNICK, Seymour   1920-

PERSONAL: Born January 15, 1920, in New York, N.Y. *Education:* City College (now of City University of New York), B.A., 1940; New York University, M.A., 1943, Ph.D., 1951. *Home:* 57 Tobin Ave., Great Neck, N.Y. 11021.

CAREER: Office of Censorship, Washington, D.C., examiner and translator, 1942-44; New York University, New York City, instructor in Spanish, 1944-50; City College (now of City University of New York), New York City, lecturer in Romance languages, 1951-52; Rutgers University, New Brunswick, N.J., instructor in Romance languages, 1953-57; high school teacher in Great Neck, New York, 1957-64; Queens College of City University of New York, Flushing, lecturer, 1959-64, associate professor, 1964-66, professor of Romance languages, 1967—. *Member:* Modern Language Association, American Association of Teachers of Spanish and Portuguese, American Council on the Teaching of Foreign Languages.

WRITINGS: Welcome to Spanish: A Grammar and Reader for Beginners, Ungar, 1952; (with Doriane Kurz) *Embarrassing Moments in French, and How to Avoid Them,* Ungar, 1953; *Rapid Spanish,* Ungar, 1960; *Essential French Grammar,* Dover, 1962; *Essential Spanish Grammar,* Dover, 1963.

Editor: Eduardo Barrios, *Cuatro Cuentos,* Harper, 1951, reprinted as *El Nino que Enloquecio de Amor, y Otros Cuentos,* Las Americas Publishing, 1966; (with Jeanne Pasmantier) *An Anthology of Spanish Literature in English Translation,* Ungar, 1958; *Selections from Spanish Poetry* (illustrated by Anne Marie Jauss), Harvey House, 1962; (with J. Pasmantier) *Highlights of Spanish Literature,* Ungar, 1963; *Spanish-American Poetry* (illustrated by Jauss), Harvey House, 1964; (with Pasmantier) *The Best of Spanish Literature in English Translation,* Ungar, 1976.

*   *   *

REY, H(ans) A(ugusto)   1898-1977
   (Uncle Gus)

September 16, 1898—August 26, 1977; German-born illustrator and author of children's books. With his wife, Margret, Rey created the delightful monkey who romped through the books of the "Curious George" series. In addition to the series, Rey wrote more than twenty other children's books, some under the pseudonym Uncle Gus. Rey's books have been translated into more than twelve languages. He died in Boston, Mass. Obituaries: *New York Times,* August 28, 1977; *Publishers Weekly,* October 3, 1977; *AB Bookman's Weekly,* October 17, 1977. (See index for *CA* sketch)

*   *   *

REYNOLDS, Barbara (Ann)   1942-

PERSONAL: Born August 17, 1942, in Columbus, Ohio; daughter of Harvey Reynolds and Mae L. Stewart. *Education:* Ohio State University, B.A., 1966; attended Harvard University, 1976-77, and Boston University. *Politics:* Independent. *Agent:* Julie Fallowfield, McIntosh & Otis, Inc.,

475 Fifth Ave., New York, N.Y. 10017. *Office: Chicago Tribune,* 435 North Michigan Ave., Chicago, Ill. 60611.

CAREER: Cleveland Press, Cleveland, Ohio, reporter, 1967-69; *Chicago Tribune,* Chicago, Ill., staff writer, 1969—. Commentator on WBBM-Radio, 1974—. *Member:* Women in Communications, Media Women. *Awards, honors:* Nieman fellow at Harvard University, 1976-77; National Headliner Award, 1977, for outstanding contribution to journalism.

WRITINGS: Jesse Jackson: The Man, the Movement, and the Myth, Nelson-Hall, 1975. Also contributor to a journalism textbook edited by Deane Lord, Harvard University Press, 1978.

Author of screenplays "The Murder of Fred Hampton" and "Vengeance Is Mine." Correspondent for *National Observer,* 1972-74. Assistant editor of *Ebony,* 1968-69; editor of *Dollars and Sense.*

WORK IN PROGRESS: Research for a book on U.S. ambassador Andrew Young and Coretta Scott King.

SIDELIGHTS: In June, 1977, Barbara Reynolds toured Japan as a guest of the Japanese government, which sparked her interest in studying Oriental history and culture. Another of her interests is screenwriting, which she studied at Boston University, and she hopes that her screenplays will be produced by major studios or independent producers.

BIOGRAPHICAL/CRITICAL SOURCES: Ebony, January, 1977; *Matrix,* October-November, 1977.

* * *

REYNOLDS, Quentin (James) 1902-1965

PERSONAL: Born April 11, 1902, in New York, N.Y.; son of James J. (a public school principal) and Katherine (Mahoney) Reynolds; married Virginia Peine (an actress), March 30, 1942 (divorced). *Education:* Brown University, Ph.B., 1924; Brooklyn Law School, LL.B., 1930. *Politics:* Democrat. *Religion:* Roman Catholic. *Residence:* Bedford Village, New York.

CAREER: Journalist and author. International News Service, New York City, reporter and foreign correspondent, 1932-33; *Collier's,* New York City, associate editor and war correspondent, 1933-45; has also worked as reporter, staff writer, and sportswriter for newspapers, including *Brooklyn Times, New York Evening World,* and *New York World-Telegram. Member:* University Players (New York City), Delta Tau Delta. *Awards, honors:* LL.D., Brooklyn Law School, 1941, University of Western Ontario, 1944; Litt.D., Brown University, 1942.

WRITINGS: Britian Can Take It, Dutton, 1941; *The Wounded Don't Cry,* Dutton, 1941; *A London Diary,* Random House, 1941; *Convoy,* Random House, 1942 (published in England as *Don't Think It Hasn't been Fun,* Cassell, 1942); *American Arms,* Todd, 1942; *Only the Stars are Neutral,* Random House, 1942; *Dress Rehearsal: The Story of Dieppe,* Random House, 1943; *The Curtain Rises,* Random House, 1944; *Officially Dead: The Story of Commander C. D. Smith,* Random House, 1945; *70,000 to 1: The Story of Lieutenant Gordon Manuel,* Random House, 1946, reprinted, Pyramid Publications, 1968; *Leave It to the People,* Random House, 1949.

The Wright Brothers, Pioneers of American Aviation (illustrated by Jacob Landau), Random House, 1950; *Courtroom: The Story of Samuel S. Leibowitz,* Farrar, Straus, 1950, reprinted, Books for Libraries, 1970; *Custer's Last Stand* (il-

lustrated by Frederick T. Chapman), Random House, 1951; *The Man Who Wouldn't Talk,* Random House, 1953; *I, Willie Sutton,* Farrar, Straus, 1953; *The Battle of Britain* (illustrated by Clayton Knight), Random House, 1953; *The Amazing Mr. Doolittle: A Biography of Lieutenant General James H. Doolittle,* Appleton-Century, 1953, reprinted, Arno, 1972; *The F.B.I.,* Random House, 1954, reprinted, 1963; *The Life of Saint Patrick* (illustrated by Douglas Gorsline), Random House, 1955; *Headquarters,* Harper, 1955, reprinted, Greenwood Press, 1972 (published in England as *Police Headquarters,* Cassell, 1956); *The Fiction Factory; or, From Pulp Row to Quality Street: The Story of 100 Years of Publishing at Street & Smith,* Random House, 1955; (with Wilford S. Rowe) *Operation Success,* Duell, Sloan, 1957; *They Fought for the Sky: The Dramatic Story of the First War in the Air,* Rinehart, 1957.

Known but to God, J. Day, 1960; (with Ephraim Katz and Zwy Aldouby) *Minister of Death: The Adolf Eichmann Story,* Viking, 1960; *By Quentin Reynolds* (autobiography), McGraw-Hill, 1963; *Winston Churchill,* Random House, 1963 (published in England as *All about Winston Churchill,* W. H. Allen, 1964); (editor and author of introduction) *With Fire and Sword: Great War Adventures* (illustrated by James Grashow), Dial Press, 1963; (with Geoffrey Bocca) *Macapagal,* D. McKay, 1965.

SIDELIGHTS: While a student at Brown University, Reynolds became a star football player and a heavyweight boxing champion. It was also during this time that he began taking summer and part-time jobs on the staff of newspapers. Though Reynolds received a law degree, he eventually returned to a career in journalism. In 1941 Reynolds was assigned to Moscow as press officer for W. Averill Harriman, a position he resigned six months later in protest of Soviet censorship. As a war correspondent, Reynolds covered North Africa, Sicily, Teheran, Palestine, and battles on the Europian continent. His autobiogrpahy, *By Quentin Reynolds,* focuses primarily on his experiences as a war correspondent.

Reynolds wrote and narrated two motion pictures, "London Can Take It," and "Christmas Under Fire," both produced during World War II.

BIOGRAPHICAL/CRITICAL SOURCES: Quentin Reynolds, *By Quentin Reynolds,* McGraw-Hill, 1963; John Jakes, *Great War Correspondents,* Putnam, 1967. Obituaries: *New York Times,* March 18, 1965; *Time,* March 26, 1965; *Illustrated London News,* March 27, 1965; *Newsweek,* March 29, 1965; *Publishers Weekly,* March 29, 1965; *Current Biography,* April, 1965.*

(Died March 17, 1965)

* * *

RHEINSTEIN, Max 1899-1977

July 5, 1899—July 9, 1977; American educator and author. Rheinstein gained notoriety for his sociological approach to family law. He believed permissive divorce laws threatened family stability. His last major work was *Marriage Stability, Divorce and the Law.* Rheinstein died in Bad Gastein, Austria. Obituaries: *New York Times,* July 11, 1977.

* * *

RHODES, Irwin Seymour 1901-

PERSONAL: Born November 21, 1901, in Cincinnati, Ohio; son of Solomon and Lina (Silberberg) Rhodes; married Mary Elizabeth Frechtling, December 12, 1941. *Educa-*

tion: University of Cincinnati, B.A., 1921; Harvard University, J.D., 1924; Xavier University, M.A., 1962. *Home:* 3815 Erie Dr., Cincinnati, Ohio 45208; and 2122 Massachusetts Ave. N.W., Washington, D.C. 20008.

CAREER: Admitted to Illinois bar, 1924, and Ohio bar, 1925; private practice of law in Chicago, Ill., 1924-29, and Cincinnati, Ohio, 1929—. Chairman of committee for the preservation of the "John Marshall Papers," 1953. Co-director of Irwin S. and Elizabeth F. Rhodes Legal History Collection at University of Oklahoma, member of board of fellows of the university, 1970—.

MEMBER: American Bar Association (chairman of Communist tactics, strategy, and objectives committee, 1962), Federal Bar Association, American Judicature Society, National Historical Society, American Society for Legal History, Maryland Historical Society, Cincinnati Bar Association (chairman of committee for the preservation of legal historical documents, 1961), Cincinnati Law Library Association, Cincinnati Historical Society, Phi Beta Kappa, Cosmos Club, Harvard Club, Harvard Business School Club, Cincinnati Club.

WRITINGS: (Editor) *The Papers of John Marshall: A Descriptive Calendar,* University of Oklahoma Press, 1969. Also editor of *The Papers of Roger Brooke Taney,* Ohio University Press. Contributor to law journals. Editor of *Public Utilities and Carrier Service,* 1926-29; contributing editor of *Ohio Jurisprudence,* 1933-35.

* * *

RICE, Homer C(ranston) 1927-

PERSONAL: Born February 20, 1927, in Bellevue, Ky.; son of S. C. and Nancy Grace (Wilson) Rice; married Phyllis Callison Wardrup, August 12, 1950; children: Nancy Kathryn (Mrs. Steve Hetherington), Phyllis Wardrup, Angela. *Education:* Centre College, A.B.; Eastern Kentucky State University, B.S., 1950, M.Ed., 1951. *Religion:* Methodist. *Office:* Department of Athletics, Rice University, Houston, Tex. 77001.

CAREER: Professional baseball player with the Brooklyn Dodgers, 1948-50; football coach and teacher at high school in Wartburg, Tenn., 1951, Spring City, Tenn., 1952-53, and Fort Thomas, Ky., 1954-61; University of Kentucky, Lexington, instructor in football coaching and head offensive coach, 1962-65; University of Oklahoma, Norman, instructor in football theory, recruiter coordinator, and head offensive coach, 1966; University of Cincinnati, Cincinnati, Ohio, head football coach, 1967-68; University of North Carolina, Chapel Hill, director of athletics, 1969-75; Rice University, Houston, Tex., director of athletics, head football coach, and founder-director of Attitude Technique Institute, 1976—. Instructor at workshops and management institutes; lecturer at clinics. Past president of National Football Foundation and Hall of Fame; member of National Collegiate Athletic Association (NCAA) television committee, statistics and classification committee, and football championship committee. Member of National Association of Collegiate Directors of Athletics management institute staff and executive committee, and of U.S. Congress Joint Committee on Athletics and Education. *Military service:* U.S. Navy, 1944-46; served in Pacific theater.

MEMBER: U.S. Sports Academy, Fellowship of Christian Athletics (past sponsor; member of national conference staff; past member of North Carolina advisory council), Kentucky Colonels, Happenings (member of board of directors). *Awards, honors:* Seven coach of the year awards,

1951-61; award to "winningest football coach in America" from National Statistical Association (NSA), 1961; winner of Carmichael Cup, 1970-71, 1971-72, 1972-73; All-American Award from Pop Warner Little Scholars, 1973, for "Pop Warner Huddle Prayer"; Order of Gimghoul from University of North Carolina; inducted into International Churchmen's Sports Hall of Fame as administrator of the year; named honorary citizen of Texas.

WRITINGS: How to Organize Football Practice, Prentice-Hall, 1962; *The Explosive Short-T,* Prentice-Hall, 1963; *Homer Rice on Triple Option Football,* Parker & Son, 1973; *The Evolution of the Triple Option,* Prentice-Hall, 1974; *The Attitude Technique,* Success Motivation Institute, Inc., 1976; *Motivation,* Medalist Sports, 1976; *Leadership in Athletics,* Success Motivation, 1976. Author of "Pop Warner Huddle Prayer." Contributor to *American Football Coaches Association Manual.* Contributor to athletic journals and sport magazines, including *Sports Digest, Scholastic Coach,* and *Christian Athlete.* Chairman of *American Football Coaches Association Manual,* 1968.

SIDELIGHTS: Rice has headed award-winning teams ever since he began his career in 1951. At University of Cincinnati, his team was number one passing team in the nation, and included that year's college all-star most valuable player and number one scorer in the nation. At University of North Carolina he directed twenty-five Atlantic Coast Conference (ACC) championships.

* * *

RICH, Daniel Catton 1904-1976

PERSONAL: Born April 16, 1904, in South Bend, Ind.; son of Daniel and Martha (Catton) Rich; married Bertha Ten Eyck James (a poet), September 23, 1927; children: Anthony Catton, Michael James, Stephen Ten Eyck, Penelope. *Education:* University of Chicago, Ph.B., 1926; attended Harvard University, 1926-27. *Politics:* Democrat. *Home:* 10 West 66th St., New York, N.Y. 10023. *Office:* Worcester Art Museum, Worcester, Mass.

CAREER: Art Institute of Chicago, Chicago, Ill., editor of *Bulletin,* 1927-39, assistant curator of painting and sculpture, 1929-31, associate curator, 1931-38, curator, 1938-58, director of fine arts, 1938-45, director of Institute, 1945-58, trustee, 1955-58; Worcester Art Museum, Worcester, Mass., director, 1958-70, director emeritus, 1970-76. President, *Poetry,* 1952-76; co-founder, Film Art, Inc.; chairman of Illinois committee, Procurement Division of U.S. Treasury Department; U.S. commissioner to Venice Biennial, 1956; visiting lecturer, Harvard University, 1960-61. Trustee, Solomon R. Guggenheim Museum, Marlboro College (Vt.); member of board of trustees, Chicago Educational TV Council. Member of American national committee, Comite International d'Histoire de l'Art; member, American Committee for Restoration of Italian Monuments, American Committee for the Protection and Salvage of Artistic and Historic Monuments; member of advisory committee on art, U.S. Department of State; member of patrons committee, Federal Art Project of Illinois; member of art juries and numerous selection committees.

MEMBER: International Council of Museums (Paris), American International Academy, Association of Art Museum Directors, American Academy of Arts and Sciences (fellow), American Society of Aesthetics, American Institute of Interior Designers, American Antiquarian Society, American Cultural Society, La Societe des Rosettes et Rubans de France, Phi Beta Kappa, Cliff Dwellers Club, Arts

Club, The Wayfarers Club, Art Directors Club (honorary life), Chicago Club, Tavern Club. *Awards, honors:* Chevalier of the Legion d'Honneur; Officer of the Order of Orange Nassau; Order of Merit (Italy).

WRITINGS: Seurat and the Evolution of La Grande Jatte, University of Chicago Press, 1935, reprinted, Greenwood Press, 1969; *Henri Rousseau,* Museum of Modern Art (New York, N.Y.), 1942, 2nd revised edition, 1946, reprinted, Arno, 1969; *Edgar Hilaire Germain Degas,* Abrams, 1951; (editor) *Seurat, Paintings and Drawings,* University of Chicago Press, 1958; (editor) *Picasso, His Later Works,* 1938-1961, Worcester Art Museum (Mass.), 1962, *The Flow of Art,* Atheneum, 1975. Contributor of articles to *Magazine of Art, Atlantic Monthly,* and of poems to *Poetry* (Chicago).

SIDELIGHTS: Daniel Catton Rich made significant contribution by his work to the benefit of art. The Art Institute of Chicago under his direction assumed a leading role in the exhibition of modern works of art. The Institute's "American Show" in 1947 presented abstract and surrealist art. Though disturbing to the critics, it received popular approval and was well attended. Rich's knowledge of art and diligence in service brought many other important loan exhibitions to Chicago.

OBITUARIES: New York Times, October 18, 1976; *AB Bookmans Weekly,* November 15, 1976.*

(Died October 15, 1976 in New York City)

* * *

RICH, Frank 1949-

PERSONAL: Born June 2, 1949, in Washington, D.C.; son of Frank Hart Rich (a businessman) and Helene (an educational consultant; maiden name, Aaronson) Fisher; married Gail Winston, April 25, 1976. *Education:* Harvard University, A.B., 1971. *Agent:* Sterling Lord, 660 Madison Ave., New York, N.Y. 10021. *Office: Time,* Time-Life Building, Rockefeller Center, New York, N.Y. 10020.

CAREER/WRITINGS: New Times, New York City, senior editor and film critic, 1973-75; *New York Post,* New York City, film critic, 1975-77; *Time,* New York City, cinema and television critic, 1977—. Contributor to *Ms., New York Times, Esquire,* and other periodicals. *Member:* National Society of Film Critics (chairman, 1977), New York Film Critics Circle.

* * *

RICH, Louise Dickinson 1903-

PERSONAL: Born June 14, 1903, in Huntington, Mass.; daughter of James Henry (a newspaper editor) and Florence Myrtie (Stewart) Dickinson; married Ralph Eugene Rich (a businessman), August 27, 1934 (died, 1945); children: Rufus, Dinah. *Education:* Massachusetts State Teachers' College, B.Sc., 1924.

CAREER: Has worked as a high school English teacher; writer.

WRITINGS: We Took to the Woods, Lippincott, 1942; *Happy the Land,* Lippincott, 1946; *Start of the Trail: The Story of a Young Maine Guide,* Lippincott, 1949; *My Neck of the Woods,* Lippincott, 1950; *Trail to the North,* Lippincott, 1952; *Only Parent,* Lippincott, 1953; *Innocence Under the Elms,* Lippincott, 1955; *The Coast of Maine: An Informal History,* Crowell, 1956; *Mindy,* Lippincott, 1959; *The First Book of New World Explorers,* F. Watts, 1960; *The First Book of the Early Settlers,* F. Watts, 1960; *The First*

Book of the Vikings, F. Watts, 1962; *The Natural World of Louise Dickinson Rich,* Dodd, 1962; *The First Book of China Clippers,* F. Watts, 1963; *State O'Maine,* Harper, 1964; *The First Book of the Fur Trade,* F. Watts, 1965; *The First Book of Lumbering,* F. Watts, 1967; *The Kennebec River,* Holt, 1967; *Star Island Boy,* F. Watts, 1968; *Three of a Kind,* F. Watts, 1970; *The Peninsula,* Chatham Press, 1971; *King Philip's War, 1675-76,* F. Watts, 1972.*

* * *

RICHARD, James Robert
See BOWEN, Robert Sydney

* * *

RICHARDS, Frank
See HAMILTON, Charles Harold St. John

* * *

RICHARDS, Hilda
See HAMILTON, Charles Harold St. John

* * *

RICHARDS, Jeffrey (Michael) 1945-

PERSONAL: Born November 5, 1945, in Birmingham, England; son of Joseph Leslie (a works manager) and Peggy (North) Richards. *Education:* Jesus College, Cambridge, B.A., 1967, M.A., 1972. *Office:* Department of History, University of Lancaster, Bailrigg, Lancastershire, England.

CAREER: University of Lancaster, Lancaster, England, lecturer in Byzantine history, 1969—. *Member:* British Film Institute, Association of University Teachers, Ecclesiastical History Society, Sherlock Holmes Society, Cambridge Union Society.

WRITINGS: Visions of Yesterday, Routledge & Kegan Paul, 1973; *Swordsmen of the Screen,* Routledge & Kegan Paul, 1977. Contributor of articles and reviews to magazines, including *Focus on Film, Silent Picture, Cultures,* and *Economist.*

WORK IN PROGRESS: A Social History of the Early Medieval Papacy; a book on John Ford; *The Consul of God,* a biography of Pope Gregory I; editing a series for Routledge & Kegan Paul entitled "Cinema and Society."

SIDELIGHTS: Jeffrey Richards told *CA:* "I have two main research interests: the relationship between Papacy and Empire in the early Byzantine period, and the relationship between cinema and society in Britain and America.

"My basic view on the first is that, contrary to the widely held view that mutual hostility existed between Papacy and Empire, Papal Rome was a loyal subject to the Eastern Emperor in Constantinople until the fall of Ravenna to the Lombards. This view underlies both *A Social History of the Early Medieval Papacy* and the biography of Pope Gregory I, to be called *The Consul of God.*

"I am concerned in the area of cinema to explore the nature of film as artifact rather than as art, a product of its environment, a reflection and influence on that environment. This idea has underlain my film books and is the underlying theme of a series of books I am editing for Routledge & Kegan Paul under the general heading 'Cinema and Society.'"

AVOCATIONAL INTERESTS: Deltiology, railway station architecture, "supporting my local football team, Aston Villa."

RICHTER, Hans 1888-1976

PERSONAL: Born in Berlin, Germany; came to United States, 1941; married. *Education:* Studied classical painting and architecture in Berlin, Germany.

CAREER: Painter, filmmaker, writer. Held first one-man exhibit of his paintings in Germany, 1916; feeling artistically limited by the formal restrictions of Cubism, went to Zurich, Switzerland in 1917 to join Dada (a rebellious art movement), and produced one hundred paintings in that year; abandoned his promising career as a painter in the early 1920's to devote himself to filmmaking; went to New York City in 1941, and became director of Institute of Film Techniques at City College (now of the City University of New York), 1943-56. *Military service:* German Army, served briefly during World War I. *Awards, honors:* Received award from Venice Film Festival, 1947, for "Dreams that Money Can Buy."

WRITINGS: Filmgegner von Heute–Filmfreunde von morgen, Verlag H. Reckendorf, 1929; *Dada Profile,* Verlag Die Arche (Zurich), 1961; *Dada, Kunst und Antikunst,* M. DuMont Schauberg, 1964, translation published as *Dada: Art and Anti-Art,* McGraw, 1965; *Plastic Arts of the Twentieth Century,* edited by Marcel Joray, Editions du Griffon, 1965; *Hans Richter* (autobiographical), Editions du Griffon, 1965; *Dada, 1916-1966,* Goethe Institute (Munich), 1966; *Hans Richter,* edited by Cleve Gray, Holt, 1971; *Begegnungen von Dada bis heute: Briefe, Dokumente,* M. DuMont Schauberg, 1973.

Screenplays: "Rhythm 21," 1921; "Rhythm 22," 1922; "Rhythm 23," 1923; "Filmstudie," 1926; "Vormmittagspuk" (title means "Ghosts Before Breakfast"), 1927; "Dreams that Money Can Buy," 1944; "Eight Times Eight," 1956; "Alexander Calder," 1963.

Art work represented in collections, including *Peinture et cinema,* Goethe Institute, 1971; *The World Between the Ox and the Swine: Dada Drawings by Hans Richter,* Museum of Art, Rhode Island School of Design, 1973; and in numerous U.S. and foreign catalogues.

SIDELIGHTS: Dadaism, an art form exemplified by such incongruities as Mona Lisa with a mustache and fur dinnerware, was described by Linda Greenhouse as "the great artistic upheaval" that "enraged the critics by mocking nearly every accepted artistic convention." Hans Richter, in *Dada: Art and Anti-Art,* called it "a storm that broke over the world of art, as the war did over nations." In a 1965 autobiographical catalogue Richter explained the evolution of Dada: "The law of chance as the last consequence of spontaneous expression led us and became a remedy against war, obedience, banality, and art: Anti-Art as a new art."

Although he was a principal figure behind the movement, Richter's name was not as well known as his friends and fellow Dadaists, Marcel Duchamp, Man Ray, Tristan Tzara, and Jean Arp. Greenhouse offered the opinion that while Richter "was a highly skilled technician, he drew his principal inspiration as a painter from others, and he did not match his early colleagues in innovation."

Richter proved himself an innovative filmmaker, however, and is generally credited with having created the first abstract animated film, "Rhythm 21." His introduction to filmmaking came as his waning enthusiasm for Dada paintings led him to search for a new mode of artistic expression. Influenced by Chinese calligraphy, Richter and Viking Eggling collaborated on painting abstract designs on long paper scrolls. The sequential variations of designs on the scrolls, and the way they forced the eye to move, led Richter to independent experimentation with film.

"Dreams that Money Can Buy," Richter's most well known film, was made in a Manhattan loft on a budget of twenty-five thousand dollars provided largely by art patron Peggy Guggenheim. The film represented artistic visions of six of the leading Dadaist and Surrealist painters. As a dramatization of Marcel Duchamp's "Nude Descending a Staircase," one segment of the film presented a nude woman filmed through a prism as she walked down a set of stairs. In keeping with the spirit of incongruity and irreverence which is Dada, Richter superimposed over the sequence a shot of coal being dumped into a cellar. Critics were puzzled by the film and gave it less than enthusiastic reviews. Bosley Crowther of the *New York Times* told readers: "Maybe you'll get the connection between a misty nude descending a pair of stairs, multiplied by prismatic focus, and a cascade of coal, but we don't."

During the late 1940's Richter resumed painting—mostly anti-Nazi collages, and he continued to paint occasionally from then on. Generally, however, he concentrated his efforts on films.

BIOGRAPHICAL/CRITICAL SOURCES: Hans Richter, *Dada: Art and Anti-Art,* McGraw, 1965; Hans Richter, *Hans Richter,* Editions du Griffon, 1965; *Film Culture,* winter, 1955, issue 11, 1957, winter, 1963-64.

OBITUARIES: New York Times, February 3, 1976; *Time,* February 16, 1976; *Newsweek,* February 16, 1976.*

(Died February 1, 1976, in Locarno, Switzerland)

* * *

RICHTER, Lin 1936-

PERSONAL: Born April 15, 1936, in Paterson, N.J.; daughter of Meyer (a physician) and Evelyn (a teacher; maiden name, Letz) Notkin; married Howard S. Richter (a physician), December 27, 1955; children: Michael, Ronni. *Education:* Attended Wellesley College, 1953-54; Bryn Mawr College, B.A., 1957. *Politics:* Democrat. *Religion:* Jewish. *Home:* 26 Suzanne Rd., Lexington, Mass. 02173. *Office:* Little, Brown & Co., 34 Beacon St., Boston, Mass. 02106.

CAREER: Free-lance medical editor, 1958-65; Lahey Clinic, Boston, Mass., medical writer, 1965-68; Little, Brown & Co., Boston, medical editor, 1968-76, editor-in-chief of Medical Division, 1976—. Member of board of trustees of Lexington Interfaith Corp.

WRITINGS: (With Fred Belliveau) *Understanding Human Sexual Inadequacy,* Little, Brown, 1970.

WORK IN PROGRESS: Revising *Understanding Human Sexual Inadequacy,* based on additional research from Masters and Johnson, with Fred Belliveau.

SIDELIGHTS: Richter told *CA:* "*Understanding Human Sexual Inadequacy* was written at the request of Dr. Masters and Mrs. Johnson who felt that the public interest would be served if some knowledgeable writers could translate their medical material into a short book that would be understandable to the intelligent general reader. They invited us to undertake this, and we agreed gladly. The public response was generally favorable, although we did receive a couple of crank letters from people to whom any writing on sexual matters is taboo. There were also many letters from people seeking help which shows how great the need is for competent sex therapists and factual information about sex."

RIDDER, Marie 1925-

PERSONAL: Born January 27, 1925, in Philadelphia, Pa.; daughter of William (an economist) and Marion (Fleisher) Wasserman; married Walter T. Ridder (a journalist), May 28, 1948; children: Cary, Stephanie, Victor, Pamela. *Education:* Bryn Mawr College, B.A., 1946; George Washington University, M.A., 1947. *Home:* 4509 Crest Lane, McLean, Va. 22101. *Office:* Knight-Ridder Newspapers, National Press Bldg., Washington, D.C. 20045.

CAREER/WRITINGS: Knight-Ridder Newservice, Detroit, Mich., political feature writer, 1944—. Notable assignments include coverage of the Russo-Finnish Pact, 1947, the Hungarian Revolution, 1956, the Portuguese Revolution, 1975, Jimmy Carter and the South. Deputy to the national director, Headstart, Office of Economic Opportunity, 1965-68.

* * *

RIDLEY, Charles P(rice) 1933-

PERSONAL: Born November 16, 1933, in Lewiston, Maine; son of Paul Price (a banker) and Mary (a teacher; maiden name, Briggs) Ridley; married Kyoko Marubayashi, September 11, 1963; children: Marie, Wallace. *Education:* Bates College, B.A., 1955; Stanford University, M.A., 1963, Ph.D., 1973. *Politics:* Democrat. *Home:* 2780 Ross Rd., Palo Alto, Calif. 94303.

CAREER: Jackson Memorial Laboratory, Bar Harbor, Maine, research assistant, 1958-59; Library of Congress, Washington, D.C., technical abstracter, 1965-66; Hoover Institution, Stanford, Calif., research associate, 1966-69; Stanford University, Stanford, lecturer in Chinese, 1973-74; Hoover Institution, research fellow, 1974-76; writer and translator, 1976—. *Military service:* U.S. Army, 1955-58. *Member:* Association for Asian Studies, American Translators Association.

WRITINGS—All published by Hoover Institution: (Translator) C. S. Chen, editor, *Rural People's Communes in Lien-chiang,* 1969; (with Paul H. B. Godwin and Dennis J. Doolin) *The Making of a Model Citizen in Communist China,* 1971; (with Doolin) *A Chinese-English Dictionary of Communist Chinese Terminology,* 1973; *China's Scientific Policies: Implications for International Cooperation,* 1976. Contributor to *Atlantic.*

WORK IN PROGRESS: Satirical essays; a study of moral education in East Asia; translation of and commentary on a classical Chinese text on dream interpretation.

SIDELIGHTS: Charles Ridley speaks French, Chinese, and Japanese. He has lived and traveled in Taiwan and Japan. *Avocational interests:* Photography, musical composition.

* * *

RILEY, Roy, Jr. 1943(?)-1977

1943(?)—October 22, 1977; American journalist. Riley was best known for his sports coverage in Georgia, Alabama, and Tennessee. He died in Birmingham, Ala. Obituaries: *New York Times,* October 23, 1977, October 25, 1977.

* * *

RILEY, Thomas J. 1901(?)-1977

1901(?)—August 17, 1977; American Roman Catholic bishop and columnist. Riley was author of the syndicated "Theology for Everyman" column. He died in Kennebunk Beach, Me. Obituaries: *New York Times,* August 19, 1977.

RIMANOCZY, Richard Stanton 1902-

PERSONAL: Surname is pronounced *Rim*-an-otsy; born March 28, 1902, in Cincinnati, Ohio; son of Alfred William and Daisy Dean (Stanton) Rimanoczy; married Mary Frances Chitwood, 1927 (divorced, 1938); married Ann Degnon, July 12, 1944; children: (first marriage) Anne, Elizabeth. *Education:* Attended Miami University, Oxford, Ohio, 1921-22, and Western Reserve University (now Case Western Reserve University), 1923-24. *Politics:* Independent Conservative. *Religion:* Episcopalian. *Home:* 1220 Park Ave., New York, N.Y. *Office:* American Economic Foundation, 51 East 42nd St., New York, N.Y. 10017.

CAREER: Advertising manager of firms in Cleveland, Ohio, 1925-29; Bayless Kerr Advertising Agency, Cleveland, vice-president, 1930-38; American Economic Foundation, New York City, editorial director, 1938—, president, 1961—. Executive director, Overseas Scholarship Foundation, New York, 1961—. *Member:* American Writers Association (treasurer, 1950-62), Delta Upsilon International (chairman of public relations committee, 1962—), Racquet and Tennis Club and River Club (both New York). *Awards, honors:* Doctor of Semantics, Hillsdale College, 1965.

WRITINGS—All with Fred G. Clark; all published by Van Nostrand, except as noted: *How We Live,* 1944; *Money,* 1947; *How To Be Popular Though Conservative,* 1948; *How to Think about Economics,* 1952; (with Charles Coulter) *Layman's Guide to Educational Theory,* 1955; *Where the Money Comes From,* 1961; (with Leighton A. Wilkie) *The Principles of American Prosperity,* Devin-Adair, 1975. Contributor of numerous articles on economics to periodicals.

WORK IN PROGRESS: Writing on causes and extent of poverty in America, on economic solutions for underdeveloped nations, and on inflation as a trait of human nature.

SIDELIGHTS: Richard Rimanoczy told *CA:* "My work has consisted primarily of finding little, universally understood words of one meaning to replace the technical vocabulary which prevents economics, finance, and accounting from being understood by the layman."*

* * *

RINGER, Fritz (Franz) K(laus) 1934-

PERSONAL: Born September 25, 1934, in Ludwigshafen, Germany; came to the United States in 1949, naturalized citizen, 1956; son of Friedrich (a chemist) and Ernestine (Lorinser) Ringer; married Mary F. Master (a painter), September 17, 1957; children: Monica M., Max K. *Education:* Amherst College, B.A., 1956; Harvard University, Ph.D., 1961. *Home:* 186 Spring St., Lexington, Mass. 02173. *Office:* Department of History, Boston University, 226 Bay State Rd., Boston, Mass. 02215.

CAREER: Harvard University, Cambridge, Mass., instructor, 1960-61, assistant professor of modern European history, 1961-66; Indiana University, Bloomington, associate professor of modern European history, 1966-70; Boston University, Boston, Mass., professor of modern European history, 1970—. *Member:* American Historical Association, American Association of University Professors (local president, 1974-75), National Association for the Advancement of Colored People, American Civil Liberties Union, Phi Beta Kappa. *Awards, honors:* Social Science Research Council fellowships, 1958-60; National Endowment for the Humanities fellowship, 1969-70.

WRITINGS: (Editor) *The German Inflation of 1923,* Oxford University Press, 1969; *The Decline of the German*

Mandarins: The German Academic Community, 1890-1933, Harvard University Press, 1969; *Education and Society in Modern Europe,* Indiana University Press, in press. Contributor to history journals. Member of editorial board of *History of Education Quarterly.*

WORK IN PROGRESS: Ideologies in French Education, 1920-1940.

BIOGRAPHICAL/CRITICAL SOURCES: New Republic, February 22, 1969; *Yale Review,* summer, 1969.

* * *

RINTELS, David 1939-

PERSONAL: Born in Boston, Mass.; son of Jonathan (a lawyer) and Ruth (Wyzanski) Rintels. *Education:* Harvard University, B.A. (magna cum laude), 1959. *Residence:* Los Angeles, Calif. *Office:* Writers Guild of America, 8955 Beverly Blvd., Los Angeles, Calif. 90048.

CAREER: Worked as journalist for *Boston Herald,* 1959-60, news director for WVOX-Radio, New Rochelle, N.Y., and researcher for National Broadcasting Company (NBC), New York, N.Y.; television writer since mid-1960's. *Member:* Writers Guild of America, West (president; chairperson of Committee on Censorship and Freedom of Expression). *Awards, honors:* George Foster Peabody Award from University of Georgia, 1970, for "IBM Presents Clarence Darrow"; Gavel Award from American Bar Association, and Writers Guild of America award, both 1971, both for "A Continual Roar of Musketry" (a two-part segment for "The Senator" series); Emmy Award from National Academy of Television Arts and Sciences, 1974, for "IBM Presents Clarence Darrow", and 1975, for "Fear On Trial"; Writers Guild of America award, American Bar Association award, and Christopher award, all for "Fear on Trial."

WRITINGS: Clarence Darrow (play; based on Irving Stone's novel *Clarence Darrow for the Defense;* first produced on Broadway at Minskoff Theatre, March 3, 1975), Doubleday, 1975.

Author of teleplays, including "IBM Presents Clarence Darrow," 1974, "Fear on Trial," 1975, "The Supreme Court and Civil Liberties," 1976, and "Washington Behind Closed Doors," 1977. Contributor of scripts to television series, including "The Defenders," "Slattery's People," "The Young Lawyers," and "The Senator."

SIDELIGHTS: As chairperson of the Writers Guild of America's Committee on Censorship and Freedom of Expression, Rintels testified before the Senate Judiciary Committee, in 1972. He stated: "Writers want desperately to write about the subjects which interest us as writers and human beings, but we cannot because the men who control television have decreed these matters do not interest the public." He further explained: "They . . . allow laughter but not tears, fantasy but not reality, escapism but not truth."

Discussing his testimony with reporter Holly Hill, Rintels recalled: "I felt it was important to tell the world the conditions under which television writers are working. I once had a production executive say to me about a line with a political reference. . . . 'We hired you to write scripts, not put your ideas in them!'

"Television only presents a single point of view, which states that the status quo is fine and working to the advantage of people," he told Hill. "Such real concerns as the economy, honesty in government, and the cost inadequacies of medical care are somehow felt by the networks to be beyond discussion."

When Rintels' one-man play "Clarence Darrow" opened in 1975, starring Henry Fonda, the author stated: "What attracts me to Darrow is not so much what he did but who he was, the inside of the man, his mind and heart. *Darrow* is not a message play, but a portrait of an honest man concerned with truth who believes that mercy is the highest attribute of man."

BIOGRAPHICAL/CRITICAL SOURCES: Hollywood Reporter, anniversary issue, 1975; Westchester Newspaper Chain, January, 1975; *New York Post,* February 20, 1975.

* * *

RIOTTO, Guy Michael 1943-

PERSONAL: Born October 16, 1943, in Brooklyn, N.Y.; son of Paul Samuel (a police lieutenant) and Guida (a personnel manager; maiden name, Nordstedt) Riotto. *Education:* Attended Paterson State College, 1961-63, and Shimer College, 1964-65. *Politics:* "Decentralized humanistic socialist." *Religion:* Agnostic. *Home address:* Box 233, Andover, N.J. 07821. *Agent:* Laurence Cook, 626 Court St., Hoboken, N.J. 07030. *Office: Wall Street Journal,* 22 Courtland St., New York, N.Y. 10007.

CAREER/WRITINGS: Silver Burdett Co., Morristown, N.J., shipping clerk, 1964-65; Thiokol Chemical Co., Denville, N.J., accounting clerk, 1965-66; *Bergen Evening Standard,* Hackensack, N.J., office assistant, 1966-67; New York Stock Exchange, New York City, transfer clerk, 1968-69; *Wall Street Journal,* New York City, author of "Who's News" daily column, 1969—. Notable assignments include coverage of the Woodstock Festival. Contributor of poems and short stories to *Time Machine. Military service:* U.S. Marine Corps. *Member:* National Geographic Society, Newton Tennis Club. *Awards, honors:* American Legion Award.

WORK IN PROGRESS: This Side Tiber.

SIDELIGHTS: Riotto told *CA:* "I was a child of the sixties and witnessed firsthand the titanic struggle for social justice and human dignity embodied in the anti-war, youth and civil rights movements. In my early working career in the factories, mines and mills of Middle America, I came to comprehend the grim realities of exploitation and class distinctions and the agony of the poor—the forgotten silent lower and working class citizens who in their frustration and deprivation often turn to extremist causes or the pitfall of bigotry. I feel a one-world government run by ecologists and social scientists speaking esperanto is a prerequisite for the avoidance of global disaster."

* * *

RISELING, John J. W. 1888(?)-1977

1888(?)—July 29, 1977; American journalist. Riseling was best known as city editor of *Washington Post.* He died in Rockville, Md. Obituaries: *Washington Post,* July 30, 1977.

* * *

RITCHIE, Barbara Gibbons

PERSONAL: Born in Bemidji, Minn. *Residence:* Denver, Colo.

CAREER: Author, editor, and adapter.

WRITINGS: Ramon Makes a Trade (illustrated by Earl Thollander), Parnassus, 1959; *To Catch a Mongoose* (illustrated by Thollander), Parnassus, 1963; (adapter) Frederick Douglass, *Life and Times of Frederick Douglass,* Crowell,

1966; (adapter) Douglass, *The Mind and Heart of Frederick Douglass: Excerpts from Speeches of the Great Negro Orator,* Crowell, 1968; *The Ghost That Haunted the House That Culpepper Built* (illustrated by Richard M. Powers), Viking, 1968; (editor) *The Riot Report: A Shortened Version of the National Advisory Commission on Civil Disorders,* Viking, 1969; (adapter) Richard Hildreth, *Memoirs of a Fugitive: America's First Antislavery Novel,* Crowell, 1971.

SIDELIGHTS: Barbara Ritchie's picture story, *Ramon Makes a Trade,* is told in both English and Spanish. "This dual text," observed a *Kirkus* reviewer, "affords children of Spanish speaking backgrounds an incentive to increase their English vocabulary, while English speaking children will further be aided by the glossary of Spanish terms which accompanies Ramon's enterprising businesss adventure. A gentle story whose suspense is derived from an accurate understanding of the Mexican delight in bartering."

Another bilingual story is *To Catch a Mongoose,* written in both French and English. M. S. Libby observed in a *Book Week* review: "This is a satisfactory, simple story, but the particular glory of the book is the charming water-color scenes of the island, its inhabitants, palm-fringed shore, streets and market places. They are large and well placed."

BIOGRAPHICAL/CRITICAL SOURCES: Kirkus, November 1, 1959; *New York Times Book Review,* April 12, 1964, May 4, 1969; *Book Week,* May 3, 1964.*

* * *

RIVERS-COFFEY, Rachel 1943-

PERSONAL: Born May 4, 1943, in Boone, N.C.; daughter of Robert C. (a newspaper publisher) and Jean (Lewis) Rivers; married Armfield Coffey (a newspaper editor), May 1, 1965. *Education:* University of Missouri, B.J., 1964. *Politics:* Independent. *Home address:* P.O. Box 526, Boone, N.C. 28607. *Agent:* Oliver Swan, Collier Associates, 280 Madison Ave., New York, N.Y. 10016.

CAREER: Watauga Democrat (family-owned newspaper), Boone, N.C., publisher, 1964—. Member of board of directors of North Carolina Journalism Foundation. *Member:* North Carolina Literary and Historical Association. *Awards, honors:* Newspaper awards include first prizes from North Carolina Press Association, 1974, 1975, and 1976, for articles; first prize from National Newspaper Association, 1976, for an article.

WRITINGS: A Horse Like Mr. Ragman (novel), Scribner, 1977; *The City Man* (novel), Harper, in press.

SIDELIGHTS: Rachel Rivers-Coffey writes: "I do not like to deal with people who are emotionally out of control (yet, how can they know?). Violence fascinates me more than sex, because it frustrates me, whereas sex does not. I know how to be alone without being lonely. I am a poet. Travel greatly interests me, especially a recent trip to Paris where I could speak French—and found the people warm and accommodating—not cold and haughty as my cold and haughty friends told me they would be. I also study Russian and am beginning to pick up Spanish, but enjoy study of wide-ranging subjects on a day-to-day basis. My second-favorite city is New York."

AVOCATIONAL INTERESTS: Pianist (jazz and classics), scuba diving, horses.

* * *

ROBBINS, Harold 1916-

PERSONAL: Name at birth, Francis Kane; born May 21, 1916, in New York, N.Y.; took name Harold Rubin when adopted by the Rubin family in 1927; began using Harold Robbins professionally; married Lillian Machnivitz in 1937 (divorced, 1962); married Grace Palermo; children: Caryn, Adreana. *Education:* Attended public high school in New York, N.Y. *Home:* "Le Cannet," Cannes, France.

CAREER: Supported himself intermittently as a grocery clerk, short-order cook, cashier, errand boy, and bookies' runner, 1927-31; joined the Navy in the early 1930's; later flew his own plane as a food transporter and became a millionaire at age twenty from his business of food factoring, 1935-39; lost his investment in speculation in 1939 and became a shipping clerk for Universal Pictures, 1940-41; promoted to executive director of budget and planning, 1942-57. Novelist.

WRITINGS—All novels: Never Love A Stranger, Knopf, 1948; *The Dream Merchants,* Knopf, 1949; *A Stone for Danny Fisher,* Knopf, 1952; *Never Leave Me,* Knopf, 1953; *79 Park Avenue,* Knopf, 1953; *Stiletto,* Dell, 1960; *The Carpetbaggers,* Trident, 1961; *Where Love Has Gone,* Trident, 1962; *The Adventurers,* Simon & Schuster, 1966; *The Inheritors,* Trident, 1969; *The Betsy,* Trident, 1971; *The Pirate,* Simon & Schuster, 1974; *The Lonely Lady,* Simon & Schuster, 1976. Also author of "The Survivors," a television series for ABC, 1969.

WORK IN PROGRESS: Memories of Another Day, Dreams Die First (film rights already acquired by Universal), *The War Games,* all novels; "79 Park Avenue," "The Pirate," "The Inheritors," all to be television series; a new film version of *A Stone for Danny Fisher.*

SIDELIGHTS: "Robbins doesn't sound like an author, he sounds like a company," the *New Yorker* writers observed after listening to Robbins's agent, Bernard Gitlin, detail the promotion and publicity budget for several of Robbins's books and films. Articles on Robbins almost always include a quantitative evaluation of his work, and the figures are astonishing. None of his thirteen novels has sold fewer than 600,000 copies a year; every one of his books either is or soon will be a film; the books have been translated into thirty-seven languages and guarantee their author an income of at least $500,000 a year until 1981. Although the last Robbins book to receive general critical acceptance was *A Stone for Danny Fisher* in 1952, Robbins points to the statistics and insists, "Critics don't make literary values—readers do." As he explained to the English interviewer David Taylor: "It is a business. I'm a novelist. It's up to me to make you see it my way the best I can. You like what I see and I get paid."

Critics saw Robbins as a serious new writer when *Never Love A Stranger,* his first novel and still his favorite, appeared in 1948. The book was confiscated by the police in Philadelphia but reviewers praised the story of the tough New York City orphan whom Robbins named Francis Kane—the name on his own birth certificate. The book drew heavily from Robbins's experience growing up in New York, and so vividly depicted that world of hustlers and racketeers that one critic called it "a Les Miserables of New York." The following year *The Dream Merchants,* set in Hollywood, won critical praise for its "versimilitude" and "warm humanity." Lewis Gannet wrote in the *New York Post:* "Mr. Robbins knows the great Hollywood art: he keeps his story moving, shifting expertly from tears to laughter and from desperation to triumph." But critic Budd Schulberg, while acknowledging the book's strengths, observed what would become a familiar criticism of Robbins's later and flashier books: "These dream merchants are seen from the outside and characterized in such broad strokes as to qualify as types rather than individuals."

When *The Inheritors* appeared in 1969, Robbins discussed it and his work as a whole in this way: "You can break my writing into three patterns. First, the Depression novels—the social and economic thing. Then, the adventure, picaresque, romantic novels, like *The Carpetbaggers*. And then comes this one, the last novel in a trilogy about the film industry—an industry that no longer exists. In this one, I've scaled down the story, and made it very lean and spare, and now I'm moving into a new thing. I think I'm still evolving as a writer."

Robbins's most recent work has received the sharpest criticism, with *Newsweek*'s assessment of *The Betsy* as "creating the very cliches that it feeds on," and the *New York Times* describing *The Lonely Lady* as sexual exploitation of the very kind Robbins denounces in the novel's four-and-a-half page epilogue. But the author believes his business as a novelist is to "write the modern scene," and leave reflection to others. He explains: "There's a difference between novelists and *writers*. I'm not a writer. I'm a novelist. I don't try to chew up the whole universe. Mailer is a writer. He writes good ideas. But he doesn't write novels."

This candid observation of his own work is typical of the author most interviewers find friendly and unpretentious, and proud of his lasting "twenty years in a business where the average writer lasts eight." Although Robbins insists he is influenced by no other novelists, he admits great admiration for Steinbeck. Of his own reasons and methods for writing, he has said: "I never had writer's block, sweaty palms or anything—I just sit and write. It's the only time I'm doing something for myself. In everything else I do, I'm always doing something that involves the consideration of other people. The only time I'm completely selfish is when I write a book."

Many of Robbins's books have been adapted as screenplays, including "Never Love a Stranger," produced by Allied Artists, 1958, "The Carpetbaggers," produced by Paramount, 1966, "The Adventurers," produced by Paramount, 1970, and "The Betsy," produced by Harold Robbins International, 1978.

BIOGRAPHICAL/CRITICAL SOURCES: Saturday Review, October 29, 1949; *New York Herald Tribune*, November 2, 1949, December 24, 1965; *New York Times*, February 28, 1965; *New York Post*, March 31, 1966, June 24, 1972; *Life*, December 8, 1967; *New York Daily News*, May 19, 1968, May 26, 1968, June 2, 1968, June 9, 1968, June 16, 1968, May 6, 1977; *Variety*, November 5, 1969; *New Yorker*, November 29, 1969; *TV Guide*, April 11, 1970; Alan Whicker, "I'm the World's Best Writer—There's Nothing More to Say" (television documentary), produced by ITV Network, 1971; *Punch*, June 12, 1974; *People*, July 19, 1976; *Contemporary Literary Criticism*, Volume 5, Gale, 1976.*

*   *   *

ROBBINS, Raleigh
    See HAMILTON, Charles Harold St. John

*   *   *

ROBBINS, Ruth   1917(?)-

PERSONAL: Born December 29, 1917 (or 1918, according to some sources), in Newark, N.J.; daughter of Louis Arnold and Bessie (Sofer) Robbins; married Herman Schein,

February 21, 1941; children: Steven. *Education:* Graduated from Pratt Institute, Brooklyn, N.Y., 1939; attended School of Design, Chicago, Ill., 1939-41. *Residence:* Berkeley, Calif.

CAREER: Writer and illustrator. Art director, U.S. Public Health Service, 1941-44, Office of Price Administration, 1944-46; U.S. Army, design consultant, 1946-48; free-lance designer for advertising and industry, 1948-56; Parnassus Press, Emeryville, Calif., founder, vice-president, and art director, 1956—. Teacher, University of California, Berkeley, 1976—. *Member:* National Society of Art Directors, San Francisco Art Directors Club. *Awards, honors:* Caldecott Medal, 1961, for *Baboushka and the Three Kings*.

WRITINGS: Baboushka and the Three Kings (illustrated by Nicolas Sidjakov), Parnassus, 1960; *The Emperor and the Drummer Boy* (illustrated by N. Sidjakov), Parnassus, 1962; *Harlequin and Mother Goose; or, The Magic Stick* (illustrated by N. Sidjakov), Parnassus, 1965; *Taliesin and King Arthur* (illustrated by the author), Parnassus, 1970.

Illustrator: Anne B. Fisher, *Stories California Indians Told*, Parnassus, 1957; Adrien Stoutenberg, *Wild Animals of the Far West*, Parnassus, 1958; Josephine H. Aldridge, *A Penny and a Periwinkle*, Parnassus, 1961; Ernestine N. Byrd, *The Black Wolf of Savage River*, Parnassus, 1961; Theodora Kroeber, *Ishi, Last of His Tribe*, Parnassus, 1964; J. H. Aldridge, *Fisherman's Lock*, Parnassus, 1966; Ursula K. Le Guin, *A Wizard of Earthsea*, Parnassus, 1968; Charlotte Zolotow, *The Beautiful Christmas Tree*, Parnassus, 1972.

SIDELIGHTS: Ruth Robbins' Caldecott Medal-winning story, *Baboushka and the Three Kings*, was reviewed by a *Horn Book* critic who wrote, "Mystery and dignity are in the retelling of the old Russian folk tale. Extraordinary modern drawings, some in rich colors, and a handsome type face which has not been popular for many years combine to make a beautiful picture book." Comments on the award-winning illustrations by Nicolas Sidjakov included this from the *Atlantic*: "The pictures have a translucence and a stylized beauty that is interpretative of the legend."

"Based on history, the author and artist responsible for *Baboushka and the Three Kings* have made another extraordinary book, harmonious in every aspect," wrote *Horn Book* concerning *The Emperor and the Drummer Boy*. "There are no extra words in the direct prose, but no writing down. The pictures, for all their stylization, give a hint of the old books which might have furnished their subjects or been the inspiration for them. Mr. Sidjakov's use of many lines is most suitable in the pictures of ships and rigging and stunning in those of stormy seas. Red and blue are added most effectively. A beautiful book." A *New Yorker* critic observed: "The most unusual and distinguished picture book of the year. The style, which is distinctly 'literary,' has the proper exalted tone of 'la gloire,' and is rich in useful phrases such as 'Back to your duties, all!'"

BIOGRAPHICAL/CRITICAL SOURCES: Horn Book, December, 1960, December, 1962; *Atlantic Monthly*, December, 1960; *New Yorker*, November 24, 1962; *Saturday Review*, November 13, 1965; *New York Times Book Review*, November 28, 1965.*

*   *   *

ROBERTS, Lionel
    See FANTHORPE, R(obert) Lionel

ROBERTS, Richard W. 1935-1978

1935—January 17, 1978; American scientist, inventor, public servant, and author of works in his field. Roberts was best known for his research in ultrahigh-vacuum technology. He died in Wilton, Conn. Obituaries: *Washington Post,* January 19, 1977.

* * *

ROBERTS, Warren (Errol) 1933-

PERSONAL: Born May 8, 1933, in Los Angeles, Calif.; son of H. Cedric (a builder) and Mildred (Howe) Roberts; married Anne Findlay (a librarian), 1957; children: Erin, James, Thomas, Peter. *Education:* University of Southern California, B.S., 1955; University of California, Berkeley, B.A., 1960, M.A., 1961, Ph.D., 1966. *Religion:* Presbyterian. *Home:* 13 Norwood St., Albany, N.Y. 12203. *Office:* Department of History, State University of New York, Albany, N.Y. 12222.

CAREER: State University of New York at Albany, assistant professor, 1963-71, associate professor of history, 1971—. *Military service:* U.S. Army, 1954-56. *Member:* Phi Beta Kappa.

WRITINGS: Morality and Social Class in Eighteenth-Century French Literature and Painting, University of Toronto Press, 1974.

WORK IN PROGRESS: Jane Austen and the French Revolution; Goya, Beethoven Austen, and the Revolutionary Era.

SIDELIGHTS: Warren Roberts told *CA:* "In *Morality and Social Class in Eighteenth-Century French Literature and Painting,* I questioned the supposition that the literature of sensibility was a bourgeois reaction against the degenerate aristocracy. I did not find a bourgeois spirit in this or in any eighteenth-century literature, a conclusion that runs parallel with recent historical studies that emphasize bourgeois acceptance of aristocratic values. Moralistic literature, I argue, came not from the bourgeoisie, but from elitist circles whose values were shaped largely by the aristocracy. But just as the aristocracy gave impetus to sentimental, didactic literature, so too did it produce an erotic-libertine literature, in which perverse nobles act out their sexual fantasies. This literature, I maintain, is not an accurate representation of aristocratic life, but does spring from the tensions and hostilities of a class stripped of its political functions and rendered parasitical. Out of that literature came the myth of the degenerate, sadistic aristocrat that entered into the social atmosphere of pre-Revolutionary France. I reached similar conclusions about painting in my study of the moralistic and erotic themes in Eighteenth-century French art.

"Having examined certain currents of French literature and art before the Revolution, I wondered about the impact of the Revolution on English literature. Inevitably, I ended up reading Jane Austen, even though she never referred to the Revolution, at least directly, in her letters or novels. Just as I questioned certain assumptions about eighteenth-century French literature, so have I done the same with Jane Austen. Arguing against the usual view that Austen was a representative of a backward, rural class that remained aloof from the great events of the day, I have maintained that the stresses and strains of the Revolution entered deeply into her experience and that her novels are an incomparable record of that experience, revealing her ideological responses to the historical forces that were transforming her world.

"My next book, recently begun, will be an extension of my study of Austen. I hope to develop further some ideas about Austen that I only touched upon, and apply those same ideas to two of Austen's contemporaries, Goya and Beethoven. All three of these figures grew up inside the world of the Ancient Regime and reached artistic maturity as that world was coming apart. Moreover, each of them underwent a personal crisis that coincided in time with the public crisis that issued from the French Revolution. What I hope to examine is how their private crises became intertwined with the larger problems of the time, as I feel certain they did. In making these connections I will shed new light on three of the seminal figures of modern culture, and indicate some of the links between artistic change and the historical circumstances in which that change is rooted."

* * *

ROBINSON, Edgar Eugene 1887-1977

April 5, 1887—September 7, 1977; American educator and author. Robinson was an authority on American political parties. He was best known as the author of *The Evolution of the American Political Parties* and *They Voted for Roosevelt.* He died in Palo Alto, Calif. Obituaries: *New York Times,* September 9, 1977; *AB Bookman's Weekly,* November 21, 1977.

* * *

ROBINSON, Haddon W. 1931-

PERSONAL: Born March 21, 1931, in New York, N.Y.; son of William Andrew (a clerk) and Anna (Clementi) Robinson; married Bonnie Vick (a teacher), August 15, 1951; children: Vicki Ann, Terry William. *Education:* Bob Jones University, A.B., 1951; Dallas Theological Seminary, Th.M., 1955; Southern Methodist University, M.A., 1960; University of Illinois, Ph.D., 1964. *Home:* 3909 Swiss Ave., Dallas, Tex. 75204. *Office:* Department of Practical Theology, Dallas Theological Seminary, Dallas, Tex. 75104.

CAREER: Ordained Baptist minister; associate pastor of Baptist church, 1956-58; Dallas Theological Seminary, Dallas, Tex., associate professor, 1958-74, professor of practical theology, 1974—. General director of Christian Medical Society in Oak Park, Ill., 1965—. *Member:* Speech Communication Association of America.

WRITINGS: Psalm Twenty-Three, Moody, 1968; *Grief,* Zondervan, 1976; *Eight Basic Relationships of Christian Life,* Zondervan, 1977. Contributor to theology and speech journals. Editor of *Christian Medical Society Journal.*

* * *

ROBINSON, Selma 1899(?)-1977

1899(?)—August 29, 1977; American author and editor. Robinson published short stories and articles in *New Yorker, Saturday Review of Literature,* and *Harper's.* She also served as editor of *McCall's.* Robinson died in New York, N.Y. Obituaries: *New York Times,* August 31, 1977; *AB Bookman's Weekly,* October 17, 1977.

* * *

ROBINSON, Wayne A(ustin) 1937-

PERSONAL: Born August 13, 1937, in Clinton, Okla.; son of Theodore Ralph (a clergyman) and Minnie Elizabeth (a teacher; maiden name, Pryor) Robinson; children: Laura Beth, Brett, Carol (foster child). *Education:* Southwestern College of Oklahoma City, Th.B., 1959; Oklahoma City University, B.A., 1961; Southern Methodist University,

B.D., 1967. *Politics:* Democrat. *Religion:* Methodist. *Home:* 4725 N.W. 72nd St., Oklahoma City, Okla. 73132. *Office:* 6009 Northwest Expressway, Oklahoma City, Okla. 73132.

CAREER: Oral Roberts Association, Tulsa, Okla., editor-in-chief of *Daily Blessing, Abundant Life,* and *Outreach,* 1967-68, vice-president for communications, 1968-69, executive producer of television programs "Oral Roberts Presents" and "Contact," 1969-70, communications consultant, 1970-71; Oral Roberts University, Tulsa, Okla., vice-president for public affairs, 1971-72; Forum House, Atlanta, Ga., executive editor, 1972-73; free-lance writer, 1973—. *Member:* American Civil Liberties Union, Planned Parenthood of Oklahoma City (vice-president of board of directors).

WRITINGS: I Once Spoke in Tongues, Forum House, 1973; *What's a Nice Church Like You Doing in a Place Like This?,* Word, Inc., 1973; *Oral,* Acton House, 1976. Has also ghost-written two books for other authors.

Films—Documentaries for educational television: "Trial by Community Standards"; "The Other School System."

Editor of *Oklahoma Methodist,* 1969-70.

WORK IN PROGRESS: When the Dream Doesn't Come True; ghost-writing books for other authors.

SIDELIGHTS: Robinson writes: "When I'm finally cranking, the words are flowing, the deadline is imminent, and I finally believe I'm going to make it, it is one of the few times life really makes sense." He has traveled as far south as Chile, and to Europe, the Middle East, and Africa.

* * *

ROCKCASTLE, Verne N(orton) 1920-

PERSONAL: Born January 1, 1920, in Rochester, N.Y.; son of Glenn H. (a teacher) and Grace (a teacher; maiden name, Norton) Rockcastle; married Madeline Thomas (a career information specialist), May 15, 1943; children: Lynn Frances Rockcastle Thye, Diane Jean Rockcastle Wiessinger. *Education:* Syracuse University, A.B., 1942; Massachusetts Institute of Technology, M.S., 1944; Cornell University, Ph.D., 1955. *Religion:* Protestant. *Home:* 102 Sunset Dr., Ithaca, N.Y. 14850. *Office:* 18 Stone Hall, Cornell University, Ithaca, N.Y. 14853.

CAREER: Science teacher in public schools in Rochester, N.Y., 1945-47; State University of New York College at Brockport, assistant professor, 1947-50, associate professor of science, 1950-56; Cornell University, Ithaca, N.Y., associate professor, 1956-59, professor of science education, 1959—. Chairman of Commission on Education for Teachers of Science, 1967-68. *Military service:* U.S. Army Air Forces, 1942-45; became first lieutenant.

MEMBER: American Association for the Advancement of Science (fellow), American Nature Study Society, American Meteorological Society, National Science Teachers Association, New York State Science Teachers Association. *Awards, honors:* Eva L. Gordon Award from American Nature Study Society, 1967, for science writing for children.

WRITINGS: (With Richard E. Ripple) *Piaget Rediscovered,* Cornell University Press, 1964; (with Victor E. Schmidt) *Teaching Science with Everyday Things,* McGraw, 1968; (with Schmidt, Frank R. Salamon, and Betty J. McKnight) *STEM: Elementary School Science,* seven volumes, Addison-Wesley, 1972, North American edition, 1977. Author of forty-three science leaflets for Cornell University Press.

WORK IN PROGRESS: Curriculum in Environmental Education.

AVOCATIONAL INTERESTS: Nature photography.

* * *

RODRIGUEZ O(rdonez), Jaime E(dmundo) 1940-

PERSONAL: Born April 12, 1940, in Guayaquil, Ecuador; came to the United States in 1948, naturalized citizen, 1973; son of Luis A. (an Ecuadorean army officer and military writer) and Beatriz (Ordonez) Rodriguez; married Linda G. Alexander (a historian), November 24, 1965. *Education:* University of Houston, B.A., 1965, M.A., 1966; University of Texas, Ph.D., 1970. *Office:* Department of History, University of California, Irvine, Calif. 92717.

CAREER: California State University, Long Beach, assistant professor of history, 1969-73; University of California, Irvine, assistant professor, 1973-75, associate professor of history, 1975—. *Military service:* U.S. Army, Medical Corps, 1959-62. *Member:* American Historical Association, Conference on Latin American History (chairman of Andean studies committee, 1976), American Academy of Franciscan History (associate), National Academy of History (Ecuador; corresponding member), Pacific Coast Council of Latin American Studies, Centro de Estudios Historicos (Guayaquil; corresponding member). *Awards, honors:* Organization of American States fellowship for Mexico, summer, 1968; Social Science Research Council fellowship for Ecuador, 1971-72, 1972; University of California faculty grants for Ecuador, summer, 1975, and Mexico, summer, 1976.

WRITINGS: (Contributor) Richard Greenleaf and Michael Meyer, editors, *Research in Mexican History,* University of Nebraska Press, 1973; (translator) Romeo Flores Caballero, *Counterrevolution,* University of Nebraska Press, 1974; *The Emergence of Spanish America: Vicente Rocafuerte and Spanish Americanism, 1808-1832,* University of California Press, 1975; *Estudios sobre Vicente Rocafuerte* (title means "Studies about Vincente Rocafuerte"), Archivo Historico del Guayas, 1975; (editor) *Andean Field Research Guide,* Duke University Press, 1977; *El Nacimiento de Hispanoamerica* (title means "The Birth of Spanish America"), Fondo de Cultura Economica, in press. Contributor to Latin American studies journals. Mexico area editor for *The Americas.*

WORK IN PROGRESS: A Socio-Economic History of Quito, Ecuador, 1750-1850.

* * *

ROGERS, H(ugh) C(uthbert) Basset 1905-

PERSONAL: Born June 11, 1905, in Wylam-on-Tyne, England; son of Hugh Stuart (a brigadier general) and Kathleen Mary (Ridley) Rogers; married Eileen Elizabeth Clare Condon, July 10, 1928; children: Sheila Mary (Mrs. J. A. Bird), Hugh Stephen. *Education:* Attended Royal Military College, 1923-24. *Politics:* Conservative. *Religion:* Roman Catholic. *Home:* 209 Reading Rd., Wokingham, Berkshire RG11 16J, England. *Agent,* A. M. Heath, 40-42 William IV St., London S.W.1, England.

CAREER: British Army, career officer, 1924-55, campaigned in Northwest frontier of India, 1929-30, with 2nd Corps Signals in France and Belgium, 1939-40, commander of 2nd Signal Corps, 1942, deputy chief signal officer in South Eastern Command, 1943, chief signal officer in Persia and South Iraq, 1944, commander, signal regiment in Egypt,

1945-46, chief signal officer of Northern Ireland, 1949-52, retiring as colonel; British Foreign Office, London, member of staff, 1956-70; writer, 1955—. *Member:* Society for Army Historical Research, Navy Records Society, Naval Review Society, Irish Military History Society, Army and Navy Club. *Awards, honors:* Officer of the Order of the British Empire, 1940.

WRITINGS: The Pageant of Heraldry, Seeley Service, 1955; *Mounted Troops of the British Army,* Seeley Service, 1959, 2nd edition, 1967; *Weapons of the British Soldier,* Seeley Service, 1960; *Turnpike V: Iron Road,* Seeley Service, 1961; *Troopships and Their History,* Seeley Service, 1963; *Tanks in Battle,* Seeley Service, 1965; *Battles and Generals of the Civil Wars, 1642-1651,* Seeley Service, 1968; *The Last Steam Locomotive Engineer, R. A. Riddles,* Allen & Unwin, 1970; *Artillery through the Ages,* Seeley Service, 1971, published in the United States as *A History of Artillery,* Citadel, 1975; *Chapelon: Genius of French Steam,* Ian Allan, 1972; *Confederates and Federals at War,* Ian Allan, 1973; *Napoleon's Army,* Ian Allan, 1974; *G. J. Churchward: A Locomotive Biography,* Allen & Unwin, 1975; *The British Army of the Eighteenth Century,* Allen & Unwin, 1977; *The Army of Moore and Wellington,* Ian Allan, in press.

WORK IN PROGRESS: The Battle of Amiens: The Eighth of August, 1918; The British Army: Now and in the Future.

SIDELIGHTS: Rogers writes: "My predominant interest is in military and naval history, with a secondary interest in railways and their history. I spent three years at Supreme Headquarters Allied Powers Europe on the staff of Generals Eisenhower and Gruenther, and I hold that North Atlantic Treaty Organization defence in general and British and American defence in particular are of primary importance in the world today. I do not believe anything else is vital, because without adequate defence none of the values we cherish can survive."

*   *   *

ROGERS, Robert
    See HAMILTON, Charles Harold St. John

*   *   *

ROLANT, Rene
    See FANTHORPE, R(obert) Lionel

*   *   *

ROMAGNOLI, G(ian) Franco   1926-

PERSONAL: Born February 1, 1926, in Rome, Italy; came to the United States in 1954, naturalized citizen, 1957; son of Luigi (an architect) and Armida (Baroni) Romagnoli; married Margaret O'Neill (a writer), December 20, 1952; children: Gian Giacomo, Marco, Paolo, Anna. *Education:* Attended University of Rome, 1945-50. *Home and office:* 37 Garfield St., Watertown, Mass. 02172.

CAREER: Independent film producer, director, and cameraman in Italy and the United States, 1949-55; WGBH-Television, Boston, Mass., director of photography, 1955-58, executive producer in film department, 1958-59; independent film producer, director, and cameraman in Italy and the United States, 1959—. Co-host of "Romagnolis' Table" on WGBH-Television. Has had photographic exhibitions in New York City, Boston, and Rome.

WRITINGS: (With wife, Margaret Romagnoli) *The Romagnolis' Table,* Little, Brown, 1975; (with M. Romagnoli) *The Romagnolis' Meatless Cookbook,* Little, Brown, 1976.

Author, director and producer of WGBH-Television series "Layman's Guide to Modern Art." Contributor of articles and photographs to magazines, including *New York Times Magazine* and *Atlantic Monthly.*

WORK IN PROGRESS: A book on modern Italian cooking, with wife, Margaret Romagnoli.

SIDELIGHTS: Some of Romagnoli's films are "Gatecliff," for National Geographic Society; "Let Each Become" (series), Foundation for the Humanities; "Ethiopia: Empire on the Mountain"; "Stone Age to Atom Age," National Educational Television; "The Great Swamp," National Educational Television; "The Vanishing Space," National Educational Television; "The Earth, Our Planet" (series), National Academy of Science; "United Nations at Work"; "The Innocents"; "The Afflicted," American Medical Association; "From Criminal to Citizen"; "Face of America" (series), U.S. Information Agency. He has also produced dozens of television commercials.

BIOGRAPHICAL/CRITICAL SOURCES: TV Guide, March, 1975; *Time,* April, 1975; *McCall's,* May, 1975.

*   *   *

ROMAGNOLI, Margaret O'Neill   1922-

PERSONAL: Born February 25, 1922, in Madison, Wis.; daughter of James Milton (a professor of speech) and Edith (a mathematics teacher; maiden name, Winslow) O'Neill; married G. Franco Romagnoli (a photographer, film producer, and writer), December 20, 1952; children: Gian Giacomo, Marco, Paolo, Anna. *Education:* Attended University of Wisconsin, Madison, and Columbia University. *Politics:* Independent. *Religion:* Roman Catholic. *Home and office:* 37 Garfield St., Watertown, Mass. 02172.

CAREER: Gimbel Brothers, New York, N.Y., copywriter, 1942-43; U.S. Office of War Information, news writer in New York City and Honolulu, Hawaii, 1943-46; *Ladies Home Journal,* Philadelphia, Pa., editorial assistant, 1946-47; American Heritage Foundation, New York, N.Y., publicist, 1947-48; Economic Cooperation Administration, information specialist in Paris, France, and Rome, Italy, 1948-55; writer and editor, 1959-72; writer, 1972—. Co-host of "Romagnolis' Table" on WGBH-Television, Boston.

WRITINGS: (With husband, G. Franco Romagnoli) *The Romagnolis' Table,* Little, Brown, 1975; (with G. F. Romagnoli) *The Romagnolis' Meatless Cookbook,* Little, Brown, 1976. Contributor to *Atlantic Monthly* and *New York Times Magazine.*

WORK IN PROGRESS: A book on modern Italian cooking, with husband, G. Franco Romagnoli.

SIDELIGHTS: Margaret Romagnoli writes: "After years of working and bringing up children on both sides of the ocean, my husband and I returned from a two-year stay in Rome. We gave a series of dinner parties to welcome old friends back to our table and from those parties came the final push to put together our first cookbook, the recipes of which had been collected during work and play in Italy. The same set of parties brought about the suggestion of a television series on Italian cooking. These two projects, completely different from the films we'd worked on, were really motivated by our own enthusiasm for genuine Italian food, a labor of love to preserve some of the traditional dishes no longer made daily at home, and the challenge to do something new professionally.

"It was our work which brought us together and the children who kept us determined to have a solid base in Italy. Our hope to give them a bi-national culture included food, of course."

BIOGRAPHICAL/CRITICAL SOURCES: TV Guide, March, 1975; *Time,* April, 1975; *McCall's,* May, 1975.

* * *

ROME, Anthony
  See ALBERT, Marvin H.

* * *

RONDER, Paul   1940(?)-1977

1940(?)—September 24, 1977; American educator and film-maker. Ronder gained notoriety for his documentary films, including "Second Chance" and "Hiroshima-Nagasaki: August, 1945." He died in New York, N.Y. Obituaries: *New York Times,* September 26, 1977.

* * *

RONKEN, Harriet
  See LYNTON, Harriet Ronken

* * *

ROPER, Robert   1946-

PERSONAL: Born June 10, 1946, in New York; son of Burt W. (a lawyer) and Miriam (a teacher; maiden name, Wickner) Roper; married Susan Bonthron (a writer), March, 1975; children: one. *Education:* Swarthmore College, B.A., 1968; University of California, Berkeley, M.A., 1969. *Residence:* Santa Cruz Mountains of California. *Agent:* Betty Anne Clarke, International Creative Management, 40 West 57th St., New York, N.Y. 10019.

CAREER: Merchant seaman, 1970-71; guitarist and singer. *Member:* Sailors' International Union, Writers Guild of America, Phi Beta Kappa.

WRITINGS: Royo County (novelized stories), Morrow, 1973; *On Spider Creek* (novel), Simon & Schuster, in press. Contributor of stories to magazines.

WORK IN PROGRESS: A novel; a collection of stories.

SIDELIGHTS: Roper writes: "I write because I have to and because it feels good. I try, as best I can, to make my writing musical to the mind's ear and suggestive to its eye.

"I like living in the western United States for the good fishing and mountains and peculiarities of the people. I travel often, mainly to countries where I can speak my crude Spanish."

* * *

ROSDAIL, Jesse Hart   1914(?)-1977

1914(?)—November 7, 1977; American educator and author. Rosdail held the world record for travel by covering more than one million miles and visiting 223 countries. He died in Chicago, Ill. Obituaries: *New York Times,* November 8, 1977.

* * *

ROSE, Betsy
  See ROSE, Elizabeth

* * *

ROSE, Elizabeth   1915-
  (Betsy Rose)

PERSONAL: Born May 28, 1915, in Piedmont, Calif.;

daughter of George E. (a businessman) and Grace (Coughran) Archambeault; married Norman M. Rose (a writer), August 1, 1940 (divorced). *Education:* University of California, Berkeley, B.A., 1937. *Politics:* "Equivocal." *Religion:* "Equivocal." *Home address:* P.O. Box 1124, Laguna Beach, Calif. 92652.

CAREER: Canyon Crier, Hollywood, Calif., editor and co-publisher, 1945-52; *Laguna Beach Post,* Laguna Beach, Calif., editor, 1953-66; free-lance editor and writer, 1966—.

WRITINGS: Grand Jury (novel), Avon, 1974; (editor) *In Search of Noah's Ark,* Schick Sunn Classic Books, 1976; (editor) *The Life and Times of Grizzly Adams,* Schick Sunn Classic Books, 1977; (editor) *The Lincoln Conspiracy,* Schick Sunn Classic Books, 1977. Author of narration for local "Pageant of the Masters," 1974—. Editor and consultant for Sunn Classic Pictures.

WORK IN PROGRESS: What Will the Neighbors Say?, a novel; under name Betsy Rose, a novel, *Tenants;* rewriting *The Sand Meadows.*

SIDELIGHTS: Betsy Rose comments: "My writing seems to center around what I consider a crying need for even-handed justice, and what I hope is an ironic, though fairly loving, look at the human race." *Avocational interests:* Studying small animals, sea creatures, and birds.

BIOGRAPHICAL/CRITICAL SOURCES: Time, January, 1952.

* * *

ROSE, Reginald   1920-

PERSONAL: Born December 10, 1920, in New York, N.Y.; son of William (a lawyer) and Alice (Obendorfer) Rose; married Barbara Langbart, September 5, 1943 (marriage ended); married Ellen McLaughlin, July 6, 1963; children: (first marriage) Jonathan, Richard, Andrew, Steven; (second marriage) Thomas, Christopher. *Education:* Attended City College (now of the City University of New York), 1937-38. *Home:* 30 Kingston House, North Prince's Gate, London SW7, England.

CAREER: Worked as a clerk, publicity writer and advertising copywriter in early 1950's; writer of plays for stage and screen, 1951—. President, Defender Productions, Inc., 1961—, Reginald Rose Foundation, 1963—, Ellrose Equities. *Military service:* U.S. Army, 1942-46; became first lieutenant. *Awards, honors:* Emmy awards from National Academy of Television Arts & Sciences, 1954, for "Twelve Angry Men," 1962, for "The Defender" series, and 1963; Writers Guild of America Awards, 1954, for "Twelve Angry Men," 1962, for "The Defenders" series; Mystery Writers of America award, 1962, for "The Defenders" series.

WRITINGS: Six Television Plays, Simon & Schuster, 1957; (contributor) R. G. Harrison and H. D. Gutteridge, editors, *Two Plays for Study,* McClelland & Stewart, 1967; *The Thomas Book,* Harcourt, 1972.

Plays: "Black Monday," first produced Off-Broadway at Vandam Theatre, 1962; "Twelve Angry Men," first produced in London, England, 1964; "Dear Friends," first produced in Edinburgh, 1968; "This Agony, This Triumph," first produced in California, 1972. Also author of "Baxter," 1973.

Screenplays: "Crime in the Streets," released by Allied Artists, 1956; "Twelve Angry Men," United Artists, 1957; "Dino," Allied Artists, 1957; "Man of the West," United Artists, 1958; "The Man in the Net," United Artists, 1959; "Baxter!," 1973; "The Wild Geese," 1978.

Teleplays: (And creator) "The Defenders" series, Columbia Broadcasting System (CBS), 1961-65; "Dear Friends," CBS, 1967; (and creator) "The Zoo Gang" series, National Broadcasting Co. (NBC), 1975. Also author of scripts including "The Bus to Nowhere," "The Sacco and Vanzetti Case," "The Remarkable Incident at Carson Corners," and others. Contributor of scripts to "Studio One," "Philco Television Playhouse," "Playhouse 90," "CBS Playhouse," "Kraft Television Playhouse," and others.

SIDELIGHTS: Reginald Rose has been an outstanding example to young writers, and has often reminded the television community of their regrettable lack of insight in not encouraging unknowns. While creating "The Defender" series, he received and read hundreds of scripts by unknown writers, and tried to use as many as he could. "There's no place now in television for a new young writer to develop," he said. "There's just too much at stake for a network or sponsor to take a chance on an unknown. All a beginner can do today is try to write for a series. There isn't much fun in that because usually what you see on the screen bears no relation to what you've written."

One of Rose's most successful television dramas has been "Dear Friends." "While the play came out of my life," he commented, "the characters do not represent people in my life. Its a study of truth and illusion in marriage, a study of the modern American marriage. They realize that in order to have a successful marriage each partner will have to be truthful with the other."

A steady, careful craftsman, Rose writes four to five pages a day, six days a week. He concluded: "I like working in New York, living in New York. I hate working in Hollywood. You never see a dirty kid in Beverly Hills."

BIOGRAPHICAL/CRITICAL SOURCES: New York Herald Tribune, June 1, 1960; *New York World Telegram and Sun,* September 2, 1961; *Newark Evening News,* December 3, 1967; *Christian Science Monitor,* December 4, 1967; *New York Times,* July 16, 1975.*

* * *

ROSEN, George 1910-1977

June 23, 1910—July 28, 1977; American educator, medical historian, and author of works in his field. Rosen collected medical data from numerous countries. His books covered a variety of topics, including Roman nurses and physicians' fees during the nineteenth century. He died in Oxford, England. Obituaries: *New York Times,* August 6, 1977; *AB Bookman's Weekly,* October 17, 1977.

* * *

ROSENBLOOM, David H(arry) 1943-

PERSONAL: Born August 27, 1943, in New York, N.Y. *Education:* Marietta College, A.B., 1964; University of Chicago, M.A., 1966, Ph.D., 1969. *Home address:* P.O. Box 162, Winooski, Vt. 05404. *Office:* Department of Political Science, University of Vermont, Burlington, Vt. 05401.

CAREER: University of Kansas, Lawrence, assistant professor of political science, 1969-71; Tel Aviv University, Ramat Aviv, Israel, visiting senior lecturer in political science, 1971-73; University of Vermont, Burlington, assistant professor, 1973-75, associate professor of political science, 1975—. Fellow at U.S. Civil Service Commission, 1970-71; chairman of Percival Wood Clement Prize Essay Competition in Constitutional Law, 1977. *Member:* American Political Science Association, American Society for Public Administration (president of Vermont chapter, 1976-77).

WRITINGS: The United States Civil Service Commission's Role in the Federal Equal Employment Opportunity Program, 1976-1970 (monograph), U.S. Civil Service Commission, 1970; *Federal Service and the Constitution,* Cornell University Press, 1971; (contributor) Joseph A. Uveges, Jr., editor, *The Dimensions of Public Administration,* Holbrook, 2nd edition (Rosenbloom was not included in 1st edition), 1975; *Federal Equal Employment Opportunity,* Praeger, 1977; *Personnel Management in Government,* Dekker, 1977; (with J. M. Shafritz, W. Balk, and A. Hyde) *Public Management: An Illustration,* Praeger, in press. Contributor of about thirty articles to journals in social science and political science.

WORK IN PROGRESS: Public Bureaucracy in the United States and Israel.

* * *

ROSENBLUM, Mort 1943-

PERSONAL: Born June 12, 1943, in Milwaukee, Wis.; son of Martin and Mary (Rakita) Rosenblum; married Randi Slaughter (a writer), October 16, 1971. *Education:* University of Arizona, B.A., 1965; graduate study at Columbia University, 1976-77. *Religion:* Jewish. *Home:* 2, rue de Furstenberg, Paris, France. *Office:* Associated Press, 21, rue de Berri, 75008 Paris, France.

CAREER/WRITINGS: Associated Press, New York, N.Y., correspondent in Kinshasa, Africa, 1967-68, and Lagos, Africa, 1968-70, bureau chief in Singapore, 1970-73, Buenos Aires, 1973-76, and Paris, 1977—. *Member:* Overseas Press Club, Anglo-American Press Club. *Awards, honors:* Edwin R. Murrow fellow, 1976-77.

WORK IN PROGRESS: A book on foreign reporting, for Harper, publication expected in 1978; contribution to a book on human rights by Council on Foreign Relations.

* * *

ROSENFELD, Alvin 1919-

PERSONAL: Born June 8, 1919, in St. Louis, Mo.; son of Maurice G. (a manufacturer and salesman) and Dorothy (Richman) Rosenfeld; married Judith Shepard (a free-lance writer and photographer), July, 1947; children: Michael, Dana, Joel. *Education:* Washington University, St. Louis, Mo., B.A., 1941; Columbia University, M.S., 1942. *Home:* 6120 Broad Branch Rd. N.W., Washington, D.C. 20015. *Agent:* Carl Brandt, Brandt & Brandt, 101 Park Ave., New York, N.Y. 10017.

CAREER: International News Service, New York City, Washington correspondent, 1942-43; United Press International, New York City, on radio news desk, 1943-44; *New York Post,* New York City, rewrite man and correspondent, 1944-48, correspondent and bureau chief in Israel, 1948-50; free-lance writer and lecturer, 1950-52; National Broadcasting Co. (NBC), New York City, stringer correspondent in Israel, 1952-64; *New York Herald Tribune,* New York City, stringer correspondent in Israel, 1959-64; National Broadcasting Co., news bureau chief in Madrid, Spain, 1965-67, and Israel, 1967-70, staff correspondent in Washington, D.C., 1971-73; *Washington Post,* Washington, D.C., special correspondent from Israel (covered the Yom Kippur War and its aftermath), 1973-74; free-lance writer, 1974-75; *Washington Post,* assistant editor of *Outlook,* 1975-77; *Trib,* New York City, senior editor, 1977—. *Member:* Authors League of America, Overseas Press Club, Washington Independent Writers.

WRITINGS: *Ticket to Israel,* Rinehart, 1951; *The Plot to Destroy Israel,* Putnam, 1977. Contributor to magazines, including *New Republic, Reporter,* and *Nation.*

SIDELIGHTS: Rosenfeld was wounded while covering the Greek-Turkish communal warfare in Cyprus, 1964, and lost the use of his left eye and left ear. *The Plot to Destroy Israel,* he told *CA,* "outlines and analyzes the Arab offensive against Israel, ranging from economic warfare through terror."

* * *

ROSENGARTEN, Frank 1927-

PERSONAL: Born June 13, 1927, in New York, N.Y.; son of Herbert and Clae (Peltz) Rosengarten; married Lillian Lebrecht (a social worker), April 28, 1959; children: Philip, Daniel, Lydia. *Education:* Adelphi College (now University), B.A., 1950; Columbia University, M.A., 1951, Ph.D., 1962. *Residence:* New York, N.Y.

CAREER: Case Western Reserve University, Cleveland, Ohio, assistant professor of Italian, 1962-67; Queens College of the City University of New York, Flushing, N.Y., associate professor, 1967-74, professor of romance languages, 1974—. *Military service:* U.S. Navy, 1945-46. *Member:* Modern Language Association of America, American Association of Teachers of Italian, Columbia University Seminar on Modern Italian History (vice-president, 1972-75). *Awards, honors:* American Philosophical Society grant, 1965; junior fellowship from National Foundation for the Humanities, 1968.

WRITINGS: *Vasco Pratolini: The Development of a Social Novelist,* Southern Illinois University Press, 1965; *The Italian Antifascist Press, 1919-1945,* Press of Case Western Reserve University, 1968.

WORK IN PROGRESS: A biography of Italian anti-Fascist jurist, Silvio Trentin, for Feltrinelli.

SIDELIGHTS: Rosengarten told *CA:* "My interest in modern Italian history, especially the anti-Fascist movement, grew out of my doctoral study of Vasco Pratolini, a member of the Resistance movement and communist who, during his teens and early twenties, had been associated with the Fascist movement in Florence. Pratolini's novels stimulated my curiosity about many features of Italian political and social history, to such an extent, in fact, that I gradually began devoting more time in research to strictly historical problems than to literary ones.

"The views I have expressed in both my doctoral thesis on Pratolini and my study of the Italian anti-Fascist press could be characterized as left-liberal or social-democratic. However, since the late 1960's, my political ideas and ideology underwent a change, as a result of the anti-war movement, contacts with friends in Europe, my own thinking. I began to adopt a frankly socialist perspective, and my recent biography of Slivio Trenton, who was a revolutionary socialist, shows strong sympathy on my part for the ideological views of my subject."

* * *

ROSENTHAL, Henry Moses 1906-1977

January 9, 1906—July 29, 1977; American educator and author. Rosenthal wrote *On the Function of Religion in Culture.* He died in Ellsworth, Me. Obituaries: *New York Times,* August 5, 1977; *AB Bookman's Weekly,* October 17, 1977.

ROSENUS, Alan (Harvey) 1940-
(David Middlebrook)

PERSONAL: Surname is pronounced Roe-*zee*-nus; born July 9, 1940, in Chicago, Ill.; son of Isidore (a contractor) and Beatrice (a social and political worker; maiden name, Frey) Rosenus; married Linda Wynne (a sculptress and university teacher), September 12, 1965. *Education:* Brown University, A.B. (cum laude), 1962; Stanford University, graduate study, 1962; San Francisco State College (now University), M.A., 1966; University of Iowa, further graduate study, 1967-69; University of Oregon, D.Arts, 1973. *Residence:* Eugene, Ore. *Agent:* Joan Daves, 515 Madison Ave., New York, N.Y. 10022. *Office:* Urion Press, P.O. Box 2244, Eugene, Ore. 97402.

CAREER: San Francisco State College (now University), San Francisco, Calif., instructor in English and creative writing, 1963-65; College of Marin, Kentfield, Calif., instructor in English and creative writing, 1966-67; Coe College, Cedar Rapids, Iowa, instructor in English, 1968-69; Urion Press, Eugene, Ore., editor-in-chief, 1972—. *Member:* Phi Beta Kappa.

WRITINGS: (Author of introduction) Joaquin Miller, *Unwritten History: Life Among the Modocs,* Urion Press, 1972; (under pseudonym David Middlebrook) *The Old One* (novel), Urion Press, 1974; (editor and author of introduction) *Selected Writings of Joaquin Miller,* Urion Press, 1977. Contributor of articles and reviews (sometimes under pseudonym David Middlebrook) to journals, including *Confluence, Assembling,* and *Margins.*

WORK IN PROGRESS: *The Memoirs of a Well-Hustled Apple-Eater,* a novel; *A Timetable for Dragons,* a novel, completion expected in 1979; *Devil Stories,* short stories; *Modern Man in Search of a Resort,* stories; continuing study of Joaquin Miller and his work.

SIDELIGHTS: Rosenus writes: "While appreciating the new freedoms won by the anti-realists and using some of their methods, *The Old One* may be considered a reaction against the content of anti-realism—I mean the hopeless spiritual landscape. In 1972 I suggested that Joaquin Miller's prose was more important than his poetry and he is being appreciated again for the virtues of his better prose works."

AVOCATIONAL INTERESTS: Ceramics, flute and piano, travel (Japan, Mexico, India, Europe, the Middle East).

* * *

ROSEVEARE, Helen Margaret 1925-

PERSONAL: Born September 21, 1925, in Haileybury, England; daughter of Martin Pearsson (an educator) and Edith Mary (Pearse) Roseveare. *Education:* Newnham College, Cambridge, M.A., M.B., and B.Chir., 1950; Institute of Tropical Medicine (Antwerp, Belgium), D.T.M.H., 1951. *Office:* Worldwide Evangelization Crusade, Bulstrode, Gerrards Cross, Buckinghamshire SL9 8SZ, England.

CAREER: Worldwide Evangelism Crusade, Gerrards Cross, England, medical missionary in the Belgian Congo and Zaire, 1953-73, staff member and deputation worker for the English-speaking world, 1973—.

WRITINGS—Nonfiction: *Doctor Among Congo Rebels,* Lutterworth, 1965; *Give Me This Mountain,* Inter Varsity, 1966; *The Doctor Returns to the Congo,* Lutterworth, 1967; *He Gave Us a Valley,* Inter Varsity, 1976.

WORK IN PROGRESS: Christian devotional booklets and Bible study booklets.

SIDELIGHTS: Helen Roseveare writes that she "became a convinced evangelical Christian as a first-year pre-medical student at Cambridge. My books are all autobiographical, to explain my personal missionary call to service as a doctor to a people who had previously known no Christian medical service, and to explain how it actually 'worked out.'"

BIOGRAPHICAL/CRITICAL SOURCES: Alan Burgess, *Daylight Must Come,* Eerdmans, 1975.

* * *

ROSS, Catherine
  See BEATY, Betty

* * *

ROSS, Floyd H(iatt)   1910-

PERSONAL: Born January 19, 1910, in Indianapolis, Ind.; son of Roy Menzies (a printer) and Anna (Hiatt) Ross; married Mary L. Shields, 1934 (died, 1947); married Frances Dewey Jenney (divorced); married Kashihi Tanaka (a college teacher), June 13, 1968; children: (first marriage) David Roy, Bruce Shields; (third marriage) Floyd Haruhi. *Education:* Butler University, B.A., 1930; Northwestern University, M.A., 1933; Garrett Theological Seminary, B.D., 1933; Yale University, Ph.D., 1935. *Office:* Department of Philosophy, California State Polytechnic University, Pomona, Calif. 91768.

CAREER: Ordained Unitarian-Universalist minister, 1956; Southern Methodist University, Dallas, Tex., instructor in religion, 1935-36; Iowa Wesleyan College, Mount Pleasant, professor of philosophy and religion, 1936-40; University of Southern California, Los Angeles, assistant professor, 1940-45, associate professor, 1945-50, professor of comparative religion, 1950-56, head of department of religion, 1947-55; Claremont School of Theology, Claremont, Calif., professor of world religions, 1956-67; California State Polytechnic University, Pomona, professor of philosophy, 1968—. Director of Blaisdell Institute for Advanced Study of World Cultures and Religions, 1963-67. Minns Lecturer at Boston University, 1958; visiting professor at Occidental College, 1972-77.

MEMBER: Association for Asian Studies, American Society for the Study of Religion, Asia Society, Phi Kappa Phi, Theta Pi. *Awards, honors:* Fulbright grant for India, 1952-53; Rockefeller Foundation grants, 1958, 1960-61; Blaisdell Institute grant for Japan, 1966, 1967.

WRITINGS: Personalism and the Problem of Evil, Yale University Press, 1940; *Addressed to Christians: Isolationism versus World Community,* Harper, 1950; *The Meaning of Life in Hinduism and Buddhism,* Routledge & Kegan Paul, 1952; Beacon Press, 1953; (with Frederick Mayer) *Ethics and the Modern World,* W. C. Brown, 1952; (with Tynette Hill) *Questions That Matter Most: Asked by the World's Religions,* Beacon Press, 1956, reprinted as *The Great Religions by Which Men Live,* Fawcett, 1968; *Man, Myth, and Maturity,* Minns Committee, 1959; *Shinto: The Way of Japan,* Beacon Press, 1965; (contributor) Hatsuo Tanaka, *Senso Dai-Jo-Sai,* Mokuji-sha, 1975.

WORK IN PROGRESS: History of Shinto Thought.

* * *

ROSS, (James) Sinclair   1908-

PERSONAL: Born January 22, 1908, in Shellbrook, Saskatchewan, Canada; son of Peter (a farmer) and Catherine (Foster Fraser) Ross. *Education:* Educated in Saskatche-

wan, Canada. *Religion:* Protestant. *Home:* Apartado 258, Malaga, Spain.

CAREER: Royal Bank of Canada, bank clerk in country branches, 1924-31, in Winnipeg, Manitoba, 1931-42, and Montreal, Quebec, 1946-68. Novelist. *Military service:* Canadian Army, 1942-45.

WRITINGS—All novels, except as indicated: *As for Me and My House,* Reynal & Hitchcock, 1941; *The Well,* Macmillan, 1958; *The Lamp at Noon and Other Stories* (short stories), McClelland & Stewart, 1968; *Whir of Gold,* McClelland & Stewart, 1970; *Sawbones Memorial,* McClelland & Stewart, 1974. Contributor of short stories to *Queen's Quarterly, Journal of Canadian Fiction,* and other periodicals.

* * *

ROSSINI, Frederick A(nthony)   1939-

PERSONAL: Born September 20, 1939, in Washington, D.C.; son of Frederick D. (a scientist) and Anne (Landgraff) Rossini; married Maria Miranda (an architect), June 5, 1964; children: Anthony J., Laura M., Jon D. *Education:* Spring Hill College, B.S., 1962; University of California, Berkeley, Ph.D., 1968. *Residence:* Atlanta, Ga. *Office:* Department of Social Sciences, Georgia Institute of Technology, Atlanta, Ga. 30332.

CAREER: University of California, Berkeley, acting assistant professor of physics, 1968, fellow in philosophy, 1969-71; National Aeronautics & Space Administration, Ames Research Center, Moffat Field, Calif., research associate, 1971-72; Georgia Institute of Technology, Atlanta, assistant professor, 1972-76, associate professor of social sciences, 1976—.

MEMBER: International Society for Technology Assessment, American Association for the Advancement of Science, Philosophy of Science Association, American Association of University Professors, Southern Society for Philosophy and Psychology, Sigma Xi. *Awards, honors:* National Institute of Mental Health fellowship, 1969-71; National Academy of Sciences grant, 1971-72.

WRITINGS: (With Patrick Kelly, Melvin Kranzberg, and others) *Technological Innovation: A Critical Review of Current Knowledge,* San Francisco Press, 1977. Contributor to journals in physics and social sciences.

WORK IN PROGRESS: A Guidebook to Technology Assessment and Impact Analysis, with A. L. Porter, S. R. Carpenter, and R. W. Larson; *Technology, Politics, and Public Policy,* with Barry Bozeman; *On the Epistemology of Interdisciplinary Research.*

SIDELIGHTS: Rossini told *CA:* "My driving intellectual research interest is the question of simultaneously relating to many representations of the world. This occurs, for example, in interdisciplinary research and social conflict. Philosophy has traditionally concerned itself with developing a single set of premises or working toward a single conclusion. It is time to learn to understand and live comfortably with the manifold or alternative representations of the world."

* * *

ROTHENBERG, Alan B(aer)   1907-1977

1907—December 5, 1977; American author, poet, painter, and educator. Rothenberg wrote the novel, *The Mind Reader.* He died in Brooklyn, N.Y. Obituaries: *New York Times,* December 8, 1977.

ROTHMULLER, Aron Marko   1908-
(Jehuda Kinor)

PERSONAL: Born December 31, 1908, in Trnjani, Yugoslavia; came to the United States in 1948, naturalized citizen, 1958; son of Josip and Anna (Hahn) Rothmuller; married Ela Reiss, July 14, 1935 (divorced, 1970); married Catherine Blanchard, January 15, 1971 (divorced); children: (first marriage) Ilan, Daniel. *Education:* Attended Music Academy, Zagreb, Yugoslavia; private study of composition with Alban Berg, and voice with Jan Ourednik and Franz Steiner. *Home:* 1005 East Wylie St., Bloomington, Ind. 47401. *Office:* School of Music, Indiana University, Bloomington, Ind. 47401.

CAREER: Concert and opera singer, with operatic appearances in Hamburg-Altona, Germany, 1932-33, Zurich, Switzerland, 1935-46, Vienna, Austria, 1946-57, London, England, 1948-54, New York, N.Y., 1948-50, (at Metropolitan Opera) 1958-61, 1964-65. Buenos Aires, Argentina, 1952, 1953, and in Berlin, Germany, 1954—. Artist-in-residence at Indiana University, 1955-62, professor of music, 1962—. Recording artist for His Master's Voice, London LP, Decca, and Bartok Records.

WRITINGS: Die Musik der Juden, Pan-Verlag, 1951, English translation by H. S. Stevens published as *The Music of the Jews,* Beechhurst Press, 1954, revised edition, Yoseloff, 1967. Musical compositions of trios, quartets, songs, and ballets, sometimes under pseudonym Jehuda Kinor, include "Divertimento for Trombone, Solo Timpani, and String Orchestra."

*   *   *

ROTHSTEIN, Eric   1936-

PERSONAL: Born March 12, 1936, in New York, N.Y.; son of Emil (a physician) and Charlotte (a teacher; maiden name, Spielberger) Rothstein; married Marian Grunwald (a translator), June 20, 1965. *Education:* Harvard University, A.B. (summa cum laude), 1957; Princeton University, Ph.D., 1962. *Home:* 939 East Gorham St., Madison, Wis. 53703. *Office:* Department of English, University of Wisconsin, 600 North Park St., Madison, Wis. 53706.

CAREER: University of Wisconsin, Madison, instructor, 1961-63, assistant professor, 1963-66, associate professor, 1966-70, professor of English, 1970—. *Member:* Modern Language Association of America, American Society for Eighteenth-Century Studies, Augustan Reprint Society, Johnson Society of the Central Region. *Awards, honors:* American Council of Learned Societies fellowship, 1973-74; American Philosophical Society fellowship, 1976.

WRITINGS: George Farquhar, Twayne, 1967; *Restoration Tragedy: Form and the Process of Change,* University of Wisconsin Press, 1967; (editor) *George Farquhar: The Beaux' Strategem,* Appleton, 1967; (editor with H. K. Miller and G. S. Rousseau, and contributor) *The Augustan Milieu: Essays Presented to Louis A. Landa,* Clarendon Press, 1970; *Systems of Order and Inquiry in Later Eighteenth-Century Fiction,* University of California Press, 1975. Co-editor of "Literary Monographs," University of Wisconsin Press, 1967—. Contributor to language and literature journals.

WORK IN PROGRESS: A history of English poetry, 1660-1780, completion expected in 1979.

*   *   *

ROTHSTEIN, William G(ene)   1937-

PERSONAL: Born February 26, 1937, in Waterbury, Conn.; son of Meyer and Bertha Ann (Goldman) Rothstein. *Education:* Massachusetts Institute of Technology, B.S., 1959; University of Minnesota, M.A., 1961; Cornell University, Ph.D., 1964. *Home:* 2251 Rogene Dr., Apt. T3, Baltimore, Md. 21209. *Office:* Department of Sociology, University of Maryland—Baltimore County, 5401 Wilkens Ave., Baltimore, Md. 21228.

CAREER: Prudential Insurance Co., Newark, N.J., senior research analyst, 1964-66; University of Maryland—Baltimore County, Baltimore, assistant professor, 1966-69, associate professor of sociology, 1969—. *Member:* American Sociological Association, Industrial Relations Research Association, Phi Kappa Phi.

WRITINGS: American Physicians in the Nineteenth Century, Johns Hopkins Press, 1972. Contributor to professional journals.

WORK IN PROGRESS: Research on sociology of occupations and professions.

SIDELIGHTS: Rothstein writes: "My interests are primarily concerned with understanding the social, technical, and economic forces that affect the behavior of workers of all kinds and how workers have responded to these factors, individually and collectively. My approach to this question has been primarily historical, because I am interested in actual worker behavior, and the ways in which it has changed or not changed over time."

*   *   *

ROUNER, Leroy S(tephens)   1930-

PERSONAL: Born August 5, 1930, in Wolfeboro, N.H.; son of Arthur Acy (a clergyman) and Elizabeth Ward (Stephens) Rouner; married Rita Rainsford (a college chaplain), May 21, 1955; children: Stephen Rainsford, Timothy Nichols, Jonathan Kerr, Christina Elizabeth. *Education:* Harvard University, A.B., 1953; Union Theological Seminary, New York, N.Y., M.Div. (summa cum laude), 1958; Columbia University, Ph.D., 1961. *Politics:* Democrat. *Home:* 8 Concord Rd., Wayland, Mass. 01778. *Office:* Boston University, 745 Commonwealth Ave., Boston, Mass. 02215.

CAREER: Harvard University, Cambridge, Mass., coach of lightweight crew, 1953-54, assistant dean of freshmen, 1954-56; Union Theological Seminary, New York City, assistant to the president, 1957-58; ordained minister of United Church of Christ, 1960; United Theological College, Bangalore, India, assistant professor of philosophy and theology, 1961-66; United Church Board of World Ministries, New York City, missionary at large, 1967-69; Boston University, Boston, Mass., professor of philosophical theology, 1970—. Director of Children's Protective Services for Massachusetts Society for the Prevention of Cruelty to Children; member of executive committee and board of directors of Institute for the Philosophy of Religion and Philosophical Theology. *Member:* Phi Beta Kappa.

WRITINGS: (Editor and contributor) *Philosophy, Religion, and the Coming World Civilization,* Nijhoff, 1966; *Within the Human Experience: The Philosophy of William Ernest Hocking,* Harvard University Press, 1970; *The Discovery of Humankind,* Islam and Modern Age Society, in press. Contributor to professional journals.

WORK IN PROGRESS: Editing a book on Christianity and the human community for Harvard University Press, and William Ernest Hocking's *What Does Christianity Mean?,* with Mary Giegengack.

SIDELIGHTS: Rouner told *CA:* "Much of my work has

been influenced by the five years our family lived in India, and by the frequent trips I have made to India since our return home. My doctoral work on Hocking's view of the relationship between Christianity and other world religions provided a framework for both personal and professional relationships with Indian Hindus and Moslims. My present interest in the problem of religious pluralism and the prospect of a global community is really a continuation of an interest held by Hocking and his teachers, Josiah Royce and William James—so my interest is not as discontinuous with my original interest in 20th century American philosophy of religion as it might seem.''

*   *   *

ROUSE, John E(vans) 1892-

PERSONAL: Born September 18, 1892, in Denver, Colo.; son of William L. and Martha (Culbertson) Rouse; married Bess Archer, August 28, 1916 (divorced); married Roma McCormick, September 6, 1956; children: John Taylor, Martha (Mrs. John E. Schalk). Education: Brown University, B.S., 1913. Politics: Republican. Home: One Bar Eleven Ranch, Saratoga, Wyo. 82331.

CAREER: Standard Oil Co., Bayonne, N.J., fireman and still foreman, 1913-14; Continental Oil Co., Florence, Colo., salesman and assistant refinery superintendent, 1915-18; Midwest Refining Co., Casper, Wyo., superintendent of lubrication plant, 1918-23; Standard Oil Co., Casper, and Chicago, Ill., manager of Rocky Mountain division and assistant general manager of manufacturing department, 1923-43; Petroleum Administration for War, Washington, D.C., district director of construction, 1943-44; U.S. Department of the Navy, member of Secretary's Committee on Public Works Projects, 1944-45; Stanolind Oil & Gas Co., Tulsa, Okla., manager of manufacturing department and vice-president of operations, 1945-53; petroleum consultant, Denver, Colo., 1953-55; writer and cattle rancher in Saratoga, Wyo., 1955—. President and member of board of directors of Utah Southern Oil Co., 1957-59. Military service: U.S. Army, 1918.

MEMBER: Alpha Delta Phi, American Legion, Masons, Denver Club. Awards, honors: Distinguished Civilian Service Award from Secretary of the Navy, 1945.

WRITINGS: World Cattle, University of Oklahoma Press, Volume I: Cattle of Europe, South America, Australia, and New Zealand, 1970, Volume II: Cattle of Africa and Asia, 1970, Volume III: Cattle of North America, 1973; The Criollo: Spanish Cattle in the Americas, University of Oklahoma Press, 1977.

SIDELIGHTS: John Rouse has traveled to 110 countries since he went into the cattle business in 1955, studying cattle and man's involvement with them. On his own ranch he has followed modern management practices to improve the size and quality of Angus cattle, and was one of the early commerical cattlemen to use artificial insemination in breeding. His bulls and bred heifers have gained an enviable reputation in the western cattle country.

BIOGRAPHICAL/CRITICAL SOURCES: Denver Post, April 7, 1970.

*   *   *

ROWANS, Virginia
See TANNER, Edward Everett III

ROZHDESTVENSKY, Vsevolod A. 1895(?)-1977

1895(?)—August 31, 1977; Russian poet. Rozhdestvensky often wrote about the city of Leningrad. He wrote his autobiography, Pages of Life. He died in the Soviet Union. Obituaries: New York Times, September 3, 1977; AB Bookman's Weekly, November 21, 1977.

*   *   *

RUBINGTON, Earl 1923-

PERSONAL: Born December 10, 1923, in New Haven, Conn.; son of Herman Harold and Rose Leah (a saleswoman; maiden name, Munves) Rubington; married Sara Anne Sherman (a writer), June 24, 1951; children: Alexandra Gail. Education: Yale University, B.A., 1947, M.A., 1949, Ph.D., 1955. Religion: Jewish. Home: 26 Oakridge Rd., Wellesley Hills, Mass. 02181. Office: Department of Sociology and Anthropology, Northeastern University, Boston, Mass. 02115.

CAREER: Yale University, New Haven, Conn., lecturer in sociology, 1956-62; Rutgers University, New Brunswick, N.J., associate professor of sociology, 1962-69; Northeastern University, Boston, Mass., professor of sociology, 1969—. Military service: U.S. Army Air Forces, 1943-45; became staff sergeant; received Air Medal with three oak leaf clusters. Member: American Sociological Association, Society for the Study of Social Problems, Eastern Sociological Society.

WRITINGS: (With Martin S. Weinberg) Deviance: The Interactionist Perspective, Macmillan, 1968, 2nd edition, 1973; (co-author) The Study of Social Problems, Oxford University Press, 1971, 2nd edition, 1977; (with Weinberg) The Solution of Social Problems, Oxford University Press, 1973; Alcohol Problems and Social Control, C. E. Merrill, 1973. Contributor to sociology journals.

WORK IN PROGRESS: Deviance: The Interactionist Perspective, 3rd edition, with Martin S. Weinberg, for Macmillan; The Solution of Social Problems, 2nd edition, with Weinberg, Oxford University Press.

SIDELIGHTS: Rubington writes: "We put the deviance reader together because at the time no labeling-interactionist anthology was available for teachers of sociology. The Study of Social Problems was a spin-off; material we cut out of the deviance reader came to stand on its own as a text to help teachers who wanted a book that traced sociological theorizing on social problems.''

*   *   *

RUDD, Hughes (Day) 1921-

PERSONAL: Born September 14, 1921, in Wichita, Kan.; son of Hughes Day (a salesman) and Gladys (Burdett) Rudd; married Anna Greenwood, June 10, 1956; children: Jon Demarest. Education: Attended University of Missouri, 1938-41, University of Minnesota, 1950-52, and Stanford University, 1952-55. Politics: None. Religion: "Variable." Agent: Candida Donadio & Associates, 111 West 57th St., New York, N.Y. 10019. Office: 524 West 57th St., New York, N.Y. 10019.

CAREER: Kansas City Star, Kansas City, Mo., reporter, 1946-50; Minneapolis Tribune, Minneapolis, Minn., member of staff, 1950-51; Columbia Broadcasting System (CBS), New York City, correspondent, 1956—, bureau chief in Moscow, 1965-66, and Central Europe, 1966-74, anchorman, "Morning News" program, 1974—. Military service: U.S. Army, 1941-45; became first lieutenant; received Silver Star,

Purple Heart, and Air Medal with six clusters. *Member:* Sigma Alpha Epsilon. *Awards, honors:* Peabody Award for broadcasting, 1976.

WRITINGS: My Escape From the CIA and Other Improbable Events, Dutton, 1966. Contributor of articles to *Harper's, Saturday Evening Post, Esquire, New World Writing,* and *Paris Review.*

WORK IN PROGRESS: A novel; a nonfiction book on life in Southwestern France.

SIDELIGHTS: "A good short story," Rudd told *CA,* "must have an 'epiphany,' as Joyce said. News writing has not affected my fiction style but thirty plus years as a reporter *have* given me a lot of grist for the fiction mill I wouldn't have had otherwise."

* * *

RUELL, Patrick
See HILL, Reginald (Charles)

* * *

RUESCH, Jurgen 1909-

PERSONAL: Born November 9, 1909, in Naples, Italy; came to the United States in 1939, naturalized citizen, 1945; son of Oscar and Vera (Meissner) Ruesch; married Annemarie Jacobson (a physician), December 11, 1937; children: Jeffrey. *Education:* Kantonsschule Trogen, maturitaet, 1928; University of Zurich, M.D., 1935. *Office:* Langley Porter Neuropsychiatric Institute, Medical Center, University of California, San Francisco, Calif. 94143.

CAREER: Kantonsspital, Zurich, Switzerland, intern, 1935; University of Zurich, Zurich, resident at Neurological Institute, 1936-38; University of Basel, Basel, Switzerland, resident at Psychiatric Hospital, 1938-39; Massachusetts General Hospital, Boston, fellow in psychiatry, 1939-41; Harvard University, Cambridge, Mass., fellow in neuropathology, 1941-43; private practice of psychiatry in San Francisco, 1944—. Diplomate of American Board of Psychiatry and Neurology. Research psychiatrist at Langley Porter Neuropsychiatric Institute of University of California, San Francisco, 1943-58, director of treatment research center, 1958-63, director of section for social psychiatry, 1964-75, lecturer, 1943-48, associate professor, 1948-56, professor, 1956—.

MEMBER: International Federation for Medical Psychotherapy (member of board of directors, 1964—), International Association for Social Psychiatry (member of council, 1971—), World Federation for Mental Health, American Medical Association, American Psychiatric Association (fellow), American College of Psychiatrists (fellow), Association for Research in Nervous and Mental Disease (vice-president, 1962), American Association for the Advancement of Science, Royal Society of Medicine (affiliate), German Society for Psychiatry and Neurology (honorary member), California Medical Association, Northern California Psychiatric Society, San Francisco County Medical Society. *Awards, honors:* Rockefeller Foundation fellowship, 1939-41; Macy Foundation fellowship, 1941-43; Hofheimer Award from American Psychiatric Association, 1951.

WRITINGS: (With F. L. Wells) *Mental Examiner's Handbook,* Psychological Corporation, 1942, revised edition, 1945; (with Carole Christiansen, Sally Dewees, R. E. Harris, Susanne H. Heller, Annemarie Jacobson, and M. B. Loeb) *Chronic Disease and Psychological Invalidism,* American Society for Research on Psychosomatic Prob-

lems, 1946, revised edition, University of California Press, 1951; (with Christiansen, Dewees, Harris, Jacobson, and Loeb) *Duodenal Ulcer,* University of California Press, 1948; (with Gregory Bateson) *Communication,* Norton, 1951, revised edition, 1968; (with Weldon Kees) *Nonverbal Communication,* University of California Press, 1956, revised edition, 1972; *Disturbed Communication,* Norton, 1957, revised edition, 1972; *Therapeutic Communication,* Norton, 1961, revised edition, 1973; (with Caroll M. Brodsky and Ames Fischer) *Psychiatric Care,* Grune & Stration, 1964; *Semiotic Approaches to Human Relations,* Mouton & Co., 1972; *Knowledge in Action,* Jason Aronson, 1975.

Contributor to professional journals. Member of editorial board of *Archives of General Psychiatry,* 1961-70, *Psychotherapy and Psychosomatics,* 1964—, *Journal of Nervous and Mental Diseases,* 1966-71, *World Biennial Book on Psychiatry and Psychotherapy,* 1967—, *Communication,* 1971—, *International Encyclopediu of Psychiatry, Psychoanalysis, and Psychology,* 1972—; member of advisory board of *International Journal of Social Psychiatry* and *Social Psychiatry.*

WORK IN PROGRESS: Research on action disturbances of communication, and social factors in mental disease.

* * *

RUGGLES, Joanne Beaule 1946-

PERSONAL: Born May 19, 1946, in New York, N.Y.; daughter of Robert H. and Evelyn (Corzin) Beaule; married Philip Kent Ruggles (a professor of graphic communications), August 31, 1968. *Education:* Attended Akron State University, 1963; Ohio State University, B.F.A., 1968, M.F.A., 1970; further graduate study, University of California, Santa Barbara, 1977. *Home:* 151 Hathaway Ave., San Luis Obispo, Calif. 93401. *Office:* School of Architecture, California Polytechnic State University, San Luis Obispo, Calif. 93406.

CAREER: Ohio State University, Columbus, lecturer in fine arts, 1960-61; Allan Hancock College, Santa Maria, Calif., lecturer in art, 1971-76; Cuesta College, San Luis Obispo, Calif., lecturer in art, 1977—. Lecturer in art and architecture at California Polytechnic State University, 1973—. Artist and printmaker; partner in Beaule-Ruggles Graphics. Member of board of directors of San Luis Obispo Neighborhood Arts Agency. Art works exhibited at colleges and universities, art galleries, and Battelle Memorial Institute; many are in permanent collections. *Member:* American Association of University Professors, American Association of University Women, Artists Equity Association, California Society of Printmakers.

WRITINGS: (With husband, Philip Kent Ruggles) *Darkroom Graphics: Creative Techniques for Artists and Photographers,* American Photographic Book Publishing, 1975; *Historic San Luis Obispo* (serigraphs), Beaule-Ruggles Graphics, 1976.

WORK IN PROGRESS: A text, *Historic San Luis Obispo,* to include historic vignettes and serigraph prints; photographic illustration for *Encyclopedia of Photography,* for Eastern Kodak and American Photographic Book Publishing; studio designs of silkscreen and intaglio prints, drawings, paintings, photographs, and multi-media art works.

* * *

RUGGLES, Philip (Kent) 1944-

PERSONAL: Born October 2, 1944, in Akron, Ohio; son of

Arthur James and Janet (Young) Ruggles; married Joanne Beaule (an artist and professor), August 31, 1968. *Education:* Attended Ohio State University, 1962-63; West Virginia Institute of Technology, B.S., 1965; South Dakota State University, M.S., 1966; also attended Kent State University. *Home:* 151 Hathaway Ave., San Luis Obispo, Calif. 93401. *Office:* Department of Graphic Communications, California Polytechnic State University, San Luis Obispo, Calif. 93406.

CAREER: California Polytechnic State University, San Luis Obispo, lecturer in graphic communications, 1966-67; Arkansas State University, Jonesboro, assistant professor of printing, 1967-68; Columbus Technical Institute, Columbus, Ohio, lecturer in graphic communication and chairman of department of graphic communications, 1968-71; California Polytechnic State University, associate professor of graphic communications, 1971—. Partner in Beaule-Ruggles Graphics; consultant to U.S. Geological Survey and Printing Industry of Central Ohio. *Member:* American Association of University Professors (past local vice-president), Graphic Arts Technical Foundation.

WRITINGS: Budgeted Hourly Cost Rate System, Printing Industry of Central Ohio, 1969; (with wife, Joanne Beaule Ruggles) *Darkroom Graphics: Creative Techniques for Artists and Photographers,* American Photographic Book Publishing, 1975. Author of "Estimating Clinic," a column in *Printing Impressions,* 1977—, and contributing editor.

WORK IN PROGRESS: Printing Estimating Manual (tentative title), a university-level textbook to be used in the instruction of estimating time and cost values related to printing and publishing manufacturing, for Doxbury Press.

* * *

RUIZ-DE-CONDE, Justina (Malaxechevarria) 1909-

PERSONAL: Born November 30, 1909, in Madrid, Spain; came to the United States in 1939, naturalized citizen, 1945; daughter of Andres (a businessman) and Prudencia (a businesswoman; maiden name, Malaxechevarria) Ruiz-de-la-Pena; married Manuel Conde (a physician), October 4, 1934 (divorced, 1962). *Education:* Instituto Nacional del Cardenal Cisneros, B.A., 1926; Universal Central de Madrid, LL.M., 1931; Sorbonne, University of Paris, graduate study, 1937-38; Radcliffe College, M.A., 1943, Ph.D., 1945; also attended Middlebury College, summers, 1940-43. *Home:* 75 Grove St., Apt. 328, Wellesley, Mass. 02181. *Office:* Center for Research on Women, Wellesley College, Wellesley, Mass. 02181.

CAREER: Attorney in Madrid, Spain, 1931-38; Abbot Academy, Andover, Mass., Spanish teacher, 1939-41; Wellesley College, Wellesley, Mass., instructor, 1941-45, assistant professor, 1946-50, associate professor, 1951-57, professor of Spanish, 1957-75, Helen J. Sanborn Professor of Spanish, 1974—, professor emeritus, 1975—, chairman of department, 1946-52, 1954-58, 1961-62, 1964-65, 1967-68, 1969-70, resident research scholar at Center for Research on Women, 1975—. Professor of French at Instituto Nacional de Segunda Ensenanza, 1933-38; instructor at Middlebury College, summers, 1939-41. Member of board of directors of International Institute for Girls in Spain, 1963.

MEMBER: Modern Language Association of America, American Association of Teachers of Spanish and Portuguese (member of executive committee in New England, 1954-55), Hispanic Society of America (corresponding member), American Association of University Professors, American Association of University Women, New England

Association of Teachers of Spanish and Portuguese, Phi Beta Kappa.

WRITINGS: El amor y el matrimonio secreto en los libros de caballerias (title means "Love and Secret Marriage in Romances of Chivalry"), Aguilar, 1948; *Un pueblo mexicano* (title means "Mexican Village"), Norton, 1949; (editor with Ada M. Coe) *Estudios hispanicos: Homenaje a Archer M. Huntington* (title means "Hispanic Studies: Testimonial to Archer M. Huntington"), Department of Spanish, Wellesley College, 1952; *Antonio Machado y Guiomar* (title means "Antonio, Machado, and Guiomar"), Insula, 1964; (contributor) *Spanish Thought and Letters in the Twentieth Century,* Vanderbilt University Press, 1966; *El cantico americano de Jorge Guillen* (title means "The American Song of Jorge Guillen"), Turner, 1973. Also co-author with Stasys Gostautas, Elena Gascon-Vera, and Mary Lusky of *Homenaje a Jorge Guillen,* and author of *Antonio Machado y Robert Frost: Cercania y distancia.* Contributor to Spanish journals in Spain, Mexico, and Puerto Rico.

SIDELIGHTS: Justina Ruiz-de-Conde writes: "I did not want to become a writer, so when I came to the U.S.A. I changed from law to romance languages and found myself jobs as a teacher. While teaching I was able to write on literary subjects, but never fiction. I may, now that I have retired."

* * *

RULE, James B(ernard) 1943-

PERSONAL: Born March 30, 1943, in San Jose, Calif.; son of Calvin J. (a banker) and Ruth (a secretary; maiden name, Lambert) Rule. *Education:* Brandeis University, B.A., 1964; Harvard University, Ph.D., 1969. *Home:* 205 High St., Port Jefferson, N.Y. 11777. *Agent:* Berenice Hoffman, 145 East 86th St., New York, N.Y. 10024. *Office:* Department of Sociology, State University of New York at Stony Brook, Stony Brook, N.Y. 11794.

CAREER: State University of New York at Stony Brook, associate professor of sociology, 1973—. Research fellow, Nuffield College, Oxford, 1969-71; associate, Clare Hall, Cambridge, 1972-73. Consultant to Privacy Protection Study Commission. *Member:* American Sociological Association. *Awards, honors:* Fulbright fellowship, 1971-72; C. Wright Mills Award from Society for the Study of Social Problems, 1973, for *Private Lives and Public Surveillance;* Rockefeller humanities fellowship, 1976-77; Guggenheim fellowship, 1977-78; fellow of Center for Advanced Study in the Behavioral Sciences, 1977-78.

WRITINGS: Private Lives and Public Surveillance, Schocken, 1974; *Insight and Social Betterment,* Oxford University Press, in press.

WORK IN PROGRESS: The Politics of Privacy, for New American Library; further research on privacy and personal record-keeping, and other sociological studies.

* * *

RUSSELL, Clifford S(pringer) 1938-

PERSONAL: Born February 11, 1938, in Holyoke, Mass.; son of Kenneth Clifford (a plant manager) and Helen (a teacher; maiden name, Springer) Russell; married Louise Bennett (an economist), February 3, 1965. *Education:* Dartmouth College, B.A. (summa cum laude), 1960; Harvard University, Ph.D., 1968. *Home:* 4344 Verplanck Pl. N.W., Washington, D.C. 20016.

CAREER: Makerere University, Kampala, Uganda, assistant lecturer in economics, summer, 1964; Social Security Administration, Office of Research and Statistics, Baltimore, Md., economic statistician, summer, 1965; Wayne State University, Detroit, Mich., instructor in economics, summer, 1966; Resources for the Future, Washington, D.C., staff member, 1968-74, director of regional and urban studies program, 1974-75, director of Division of Institutions and Public Decisions, 1975—. Guest researcher at University of Bergen, 1976. Member of executive committee and board of trustees of Environmental Defense Fund. Member of National Academy of Science's environmental research assessment committee; consultant to Organization for Economic Co-operation and Development. *Military service:* U.S. Navy, 1960-63, executive officer of "U.S.S. Nipmuc," 1962-63. *Member:* American Economic Association. *Awards, honors:* Woodrow Wilson fellowship, 1964-68.

WRITINGS: (With David Arey and Robert Kates) *Drought and Water Supply: Implications of the Massachusetts Experience for Municipal Planning,* Johns Hopkins Press, 1970; *Residuals Management in Industry: A Case Study of Petroleum Refining,* Johns Hopkins Press, 1973; (editor) *Ecological Modeling in a Resource Management Framework,* Resources for the Future, 1975; (with William J. Vaughan) *Steel Production: Processes, Products, and Residuals,* Johns Hopkins Press, 1976; (with Walter O. Spofford, Jr. and Robert A. Kelly) *Environmental Quality Management: An Application to the Lower Delaware Valley,* Resources for the Future, 1976.

Contributor: Allen V. Kneese and Blair T. Power, editors, *Environmental Quality Analysis: Theory and Method in the Social Sciences,* Johns Hopkins Press, 1972; Robert Dorfman, Henry Jacoby, and H. A. Thomas, editors, *Models for Managing Regional Water Quality,* Harvard University Press, 1973; *The Management of Water Resources in England and Wales,* Saxon House, 1974; Jerome Rothenberg and I. G. Heggie, editors, *The Management of Water Quality and the Environment,* Macmillan, 1974; Edwin T. Haefele, editor, *The Governance of Common Property Resources,* Johns Hopkins Press, 1974; Edwin Mills, editor, *Economic Analysis of Environmental Problems,* National Bureau of Economic Research, 1975. Contributor of about twenty-five articles and reviews to economic and scientific journals. Member of executive committee and editorial board of *Land Economics;* member of editorial board of *Economic Perspectives.*

*   *   *

RUSSELL, Martin   1934-
(Mark Lester)

PERSONAL: Born September 25, 1934, in Bromley, England; son of Stanley William (a bank official) and Helen Kathleen (Arney) Russell. *Education:* Educated in England. *Home:* 1 Rosehill Cottages, Perrymans Lane, Burwash, Sussex, England.

CAREER: Writer. Has also worked as a reporter in Bromley, England, 1951-58, and as a sub-editor in Croydon, England, 1958-73. *Military service:* Royal Air Force, 1955-57. *Member:* Crime Writers Association.

WRITINGS—All published by Collins except as noted: *No Through Road,* 1965; *No Return Ticket,* 1966; *Danger Money,* 1968; *Hunt to a Kill,* 1969; *Deadline,* 1971; *Advisory Service,* 1971; *Concrete Evidence,* 1972; *Double Hit,* 1973; *Crime Wave,* 1974; *Phantom Holiday,* 1974; *The Client,* 1975; *Murder by the Mile,* 1975; *Double Deal,* 1976; (under pseudonym Mark Lester) *Terror Trade,* R. Hale, 1976; *Mr. T.,* 1977.

SIDELIGHTS: Russell told *CA:* "A desire to explore the workings of the human mind, and to show the bizarre situations these can lead to, motivated me in my choice of the crime or mystery novel as a vehicle. I am intrigued by the Jekyll and Hyde in people."

*   *   *

RUSSELL, Thomas
See LASLETT, Peter

*   *   *

RUTH, John L(andis)   1930-

PERSONAL: Born January 8, 1930, in Harleysville, Pa.; son of Henry Landis (a farmer) and Susan (Landis) Ruth; married Roma Jeanette Jacobs (an elementary school art teacher), May 26, 1951; children: Easter Dawn (Mrs. Paul Nelson), John Allan, Philip Gerhart. *Education:* Eastern Baptist College, B.A., 1956; Harvard University, M.A., 1960, Ph.D., 1968. *Home and office:* 884 Main St., Harleysville, Pa. 19438.

CAREER: Eastern Baptist College, St. Davids, Pa., assistant professor, 1962-68, associate professor, 1968-72, professor of English, 1972-76; Salford Mennonite Church, Harleysville, Pa., associate pastor, 1972—. Ordained Mennonite minister, 1950; pastor of Mennonite churches in Conshohocken and King of Prussia, Pa., 1950-71. Guest professor at University of Hamburg, 1968-69.

MEMBER: Modern Language Association of America, American Studies Association, Melville Society of America, Hymn Society of America, Mennonite Historians of Eastern Pennsylvania. *Awards, honors:* Danforth fellow, 1957-62; Golden eagle from Council on International Nontheatrical Events and gold medallion from Virgin Islands International Film Festival, both 1976, for "The Amish: A People of Preservation."

WRITINGS: Conrad Grebel: Son of Zurich, Herald Press, 1975; *The History of the Indian Valley and Its Bank,* privately printed, 1976; *'Twas Seeding Time,* Herald Press, 1976.

Films: "The Quiet in the Land," 1971; "The Amish: A People of Preservation," 1975. Contributor to *Mennonite Life.*

WORK IN PROGRESS: An autobiographical novel.

SIDELIGHTS: Ruth writes: "I began as a minister among the Mennonites, felt that I needed a broadening of perspective, and studied English literature, which led to more than a decade of teaching literature in college. This vocation has again broadened to include writing, in order to make encounterable the values of my inherited ethos. I have tried to assess and express the meaning of the Mennonite experience in order to fill in a gap in my own and my neighbors' 'education.' I have continued to visit college campuses for lectures on the topics I have written about."

*   *   *

RUUD, Josephine Bartow   1921-

PERSONAL: Born October 16, 1921, in Mitchell, Neb.; daughter of Frank A. (a farmer) and Mina (a teacher; maiden name, Allen) Rusher; married Richard Bartow, June 11, 1943 (died April 11, 1945); married Norman Ruud (a businessman), June 12, 1965; children: (first marriage) Gerald R. *Education:* Chadron State College, diploma, 1940; Iowa State University, B.S., 1950, M.S., 1953; Pennsylvania

State University, Ed.D., 1961. *Home:* 2102 South 17th St., Laramie, Wyo. 82070. *Office:* Agricultural Extension Service, University of Wyoming, P.O. Box 3354, University Station, Laramie, Wyo. 82071.

CAREER: Rural school teacher in Scotts Bluff and Sioux Counties, Neb., 1941-47; high school home economics teacher in Winfield, Iowa, 1950-51; Milwaukee Vocational and Adult Schools, Milwaukee, Wis., director of family life education program, 1953-57; Pennsylvania State University, State College, coordinator of city adult homemaking program, 1957-59; North Dakota State University, Fargo, associate professor, 1961-65, professor of home economics, 1965-73, chairman of home economics education, 1961-73; University of Wyoming, Laramie, professor and state extension leader in home economics at Agricultural Extension Service, 1974—. Member of education committee of North Dakota Commission on the Status of Women, 1963.

MEMBER: American Home Economics Association, Home Economics Education Association (member of publications board), Adult Education Association, Wyoming Home Economics Association (board member), Phi Kappa Phi, Omicron Nu, Soroptimist International (Laramie organizer; member of executive board; past vice-president and president of Fargo, N.D., chapter).

WRITINGS: How to Pot It Now That He's Shot It (wild game cookbook), privately printed, 1969; *Teaching for Changed Attitudes and Values* (monograph), Home Economics Education Association, 1972; (with Olive Hall) *Adult Education for Home and Family Life,* Wiley, 1974; *Handbook on Home and Family Living Through Adult Education,* Interstate, 1977. Contributor to home economics and education journals.

WORK IN PROGRESS: With Cleo Hall, Jane Windson, and Phyllis Worden, an extension bulletin on how to organize groups under varying specific circumstances.

SIDELIGHTS: Josephine Ruud describes herself as a "silly old grandmother" who loves to cook and garden. "I am an organizer," she writes, "and thoroughly enjoy trying to organize some kind of new group or activity. I like to take theory or research results and try to apply them to the teaching of home economics or to adult education."

* * *

RYAN, John Fergus 1931-
(Jack Thames)

PERSONAL: Born June 6, 1931, in Kansas City, Mo.; son of John Fergus (a telephone company employee) and Fay S. (Stukey) Ryan; married Carla J. Smith (an assistant college registrar), August 8, 1952; children: John Bradford, Carla Elizabeth, Andrew David. *Education:* Memphis State College, B.S., 1957. *Politics:* Democrat. *Religion:* Unitarian-Universalist. *Home:* 1937 Lyndale Ave., Memphis, Tenn. 38107. *Agent:* James Brown Associates, Inc., 22 East 60th St., New York, N.Y. 10022.

CAREER: Playwright and novelist, 1957—. Co-chairman of Memphis Anti-Censorship Group, 1961-62. *Military service:* U.S. Army, Infantry, 1952-54; served in Korea; became sergeant. *Member:* Authors Guild of Authors League of America.

WRITINGS—Full-length plays: "The Minor Poet," first produced in Memphis, Tenn., at Workshop Theatre of the Circuit Playhouse, December 8, 1974; "Doctor Holocaust," first produced in Memphis at Circuit Playhouse, July 29, 1976. Also author of "Twyla's Young Man," as yet

unproduced. Author of *The Redneck Bride, Coming Up, Limitus Grogan, McGowan One and Two* (under pseudonym Jack Thames), and a short story collection, *The Nut House Pickings,* all as yet unpublished. Contributor of more than thirty stories to magazines in the United States, England, and France, including *Esquire, Atlantic Monthly,* and *Penthouse.*

WORK IN PROGRESS: A novel about modern city life; a play about Colonel Robert G. Ingersoll.

SIDELIGHTS: Ryan writes that his main interest is the theater. His writings consist of "humorous fiction about people I have known or observed in small towns in Tennessee, Arkansas, and Florida." The novel, *The Red Neck Bride,* is about a wedding in a small Mississippi town.

BIOGRAPHICAL/CRITICAL SOURCES: Phoenix, spring, 1974; *City of Memphis,* August, 1976.

* * *

RYAN, John Julian 1898-

PERSONAL: Born October 5, 1898, in Houston, Tex.; son of John Joseph and Bertha Ida (Bitter) Ryan; married Mary Perkins (a writer and editor); children: John Joseph, Peter Basil, Thomas Edmund, David Paul, Michael Julian. *Education:* Harvard University, A.B., 1921. *Home:* 12 West Union St., Goffstown, N.H. 03045.

CAREER: Instructor in English at Harvard University, Cambridge, Mass., 1925-35, College of the Holy Cross, Worcester, Mass., 1935-39, and Boston College, Chestnut Hill, Mass., 1945-50; instructor in English and philosophy, St. Anselm's College, beginning 1960. Affiliated with summer workshops, Catholic University of America, Washington, D.C., 1940-50; lecturer at colleges and universities, including University of Notre Dame.

WRITINGS: The Idea of a Catholic College, Sheed, 1945; *Beyond Humanism,* Sheed, 1950; *The Humanization of Man,* Paulist/Newman, 1972. Contributor to journals, including *Cross Currents, Critic, Wide World,* and *Catholic Educational Review.*

WORK IN PROGRESS: Books on English composition, the story, the poem, the fallacies of literary criticism, the relationship between science and literature, and the philosophy of prudence.

SIDELIGHTS: Ryan writes: "My main philosophic belief, expressed in my last book, is that man is essentially a creature of skill, and that he will never be happy unless he enjoys the exercise of skill in work, play, *and* behavior. Knowledge is not enough; the *generous exercise* of *skill* is required for happy living."

AVOCATIONAL INTERESTS: Calligraphy.

* * *

RYLE, Gilbert 1900-1976

PERSONAL: Born August 19, 1900, in Brighton, England; son of Reginald John (a physician) and Catherine (Scott) Ryle. *Education:* Graduated from Queen's College, Oxford (first class honors). *Home:* The Orchard, North St., Islip, Oxfordshire, England. *Office:* Magdalen College, Oxford, England.

CAREER: Oxford University, Oxford, England, lecturer in philosophy at Christ Church, 1924, tutor in philosophy at Christ Church, 1925-39, Waynflete Professor of Metaphysical Philosophy at Magdalen College, 1945-68. *Military service:* Welsh Guards, 1939-45; became major. *Awards, hon-*

ors: Honorary fellow of Christ Church, Magdalen College, and Queen's College; D.Litt. from University of Birmingham, University of Warwick, 1969, University of Sussex, 1971, and University of Hull, 1972.

WRITINGS: The Concept of Mind, Hutchinson University Library, 1949, Barnes & Noble, 1959; (contributor) Antony G. N. Flew, editor, *Essays on Logic and Language,* Philosophical Library, 1951; *Dilemmas,* Cambridge University Press, 1954; *Plato's Progress,* Cambridge University Press, 1966; (contributor) P. F. Strawson, editor, *Studies in the Philosophy of Thought and Action,* Oxford University Press, 1968; (contributor) *Phaenomenologie und Sprachanalyse,* Vanderhoeck & Ruprecht, 1971; *Collected Papers,* Volume I: *Critical Essays,* Volume II: *Collected Essays, 1929-68,* Barnes & Noble, 1971.

Editor of congress proceedings. Contributor to scholarly journals. Editor of *Mind,* 1947-71.

BIOGRAPHICAL/CRITICAL SOURCES: Mind, April, 1950; *Philosophical Review,* January, 1951, October, 1958; *Journal of Philosophy,* April 26, 1951; Archana Roy, *A Short Commentary on "The Concept of Mind,"* Naya Prokash (Calcutta), 1973. Obituaries: *AB Bookman's Weekly,* November 15, 1976.*

(Died October 6, 1976, in Yorkshire, England)

* * *

ST. OMER, Garth

PERSONAL: Born in Castries, Saint Lucia, British West Indies; moved to England. *Education:* Attended University of West Indies. *Address:* c/o Faber & Faber Ltd., 3 Queen Square, London W.C.1, England.

CAREER: Novelist, short story and free-lance writer. Lived in France and Ghana.

WRITINGS—Novels, except as noted; all published by Faber: *A Room on the Hill,* 1968; *Shades of Grey* (two novellas, "The Lights on the Hill', and "Another Place, Another Time"), 1968; *Nor Any Country,* 1969; *J–, Black Bam and the Masqueraders,* 1972. Short story included in anthology, *Introduction 2: Stories by New Writers,* Faber, 1964.

SIDELIGHTS: "Garth St. Omer's short novels are distinguished by a quiet and unpretentious simplicity in which the situation of one man is precisely defined," observes Maurice Capitanchik. He goes on to call St. Omer, "a modest and honest author with little illusion about himself, whose patient wish to understand human predicaments is both interesting and significant." Wallace Hildick says: "More than any other living writer, Mr. St. Omer reminds me of Lawrence. He does so not simply in the vivid, subtly rhythmic intensity of many of his passages . . . but also in his themes—of sons and lovers, and of fierce intellectual ambition reinforced and sometimes overforced by economic and cultural necessity."

BIOGRAPHICAL/CRITICAL SOURCES: Punch, December 11, 1968; *Listener,* December 12, 1968; *Observer Review,* December 15, 1968; *Spectator,* December 20, 1968, May 9, 1969; *Books and Bookmen,* February, 1969.*

* * *

SALISBURY, Ruth   1921-

PERSONAL: Born July 5, 1921, in Cleveland, Ohio; daughter of Irvin N. and Ruth (an editor; maiden name, Kelly) Salisbury. *Education:* Allegheny College, B.S., 1942; Carnegie Library School, M.L.S., 1944; University of Pittsburgh,

M.A., 1962, advanced certificate, 1968. *Politics:* Democrat. *Religion:* Protestant. *Home:* 4716 Ellsworth Ave., Pittsburgh, Pa. 15213. *Office:* Historical Society of Western Pennsylvania, 4338 Bigelow Blvd., Pittsburgh, Pa. 15213.

CAREER: University of Pittsburgh, Pittsburgh, Pa., Darlington librarian, 1955-56, coordinator of special collections, 1966-70; Syracuse University, Syracuse, N.Y., rare books librarian, 1971-72; Historical Society of Western Pennsylvania, Pittsburgh, archivist and curator of rare books, 1973—. Member of advisory board for Pennsylvania State Historical Records, 1976—.

MEMBER: Society of American Archivists, Pennsylvania Library Association, Pittsburgh Bibliophiles, Altrusa Club of Pittsburgh. *Awards, honors:* Certificate of merit from Pennsylvania Library Association, 1969, for *Pennsylvania Newspapers.*

WRITINGS: Pennsylvania Newspapers: A Bibliography and Union List, Pennsylvania Library Association, 1969. Contributor to *Western Pennsylvania Historical Magazine.*

WORK IN PROGRESS: Guide to Manuscripts in the Historical Society of Western Pennsylvania, completion expected in 1980.

AVOCATIONAL INTERESTS: Environmental conservation, painting, sketching, hand bookbinding, travel in Canada and England, theater, ballet.

* * *

SALOMON, I(sidore) L(awrence)   1899-

PERSONAL: December 10, 1899, in Hartford, Conn.; son of Joseph (an insurance man) and Elisabeta (Segall) Salomon; married Frances Slobodin, June 28, 1925; children: Joanne (Mrs. H. Lawrence Helfer). *Education:* City College (now City College of the City University of New York), B.A., 1923, M.S., 1924; further study at Columbia University and New School for Social Research. *Politics:* Jeffersonian Democrat. *Religion:* Jewish. *Home:* 12 Stuyvesant Oval, New York, N.Y. 10009.

CAREER: Teacher in New York (N.Y.) public schools, 1923-58. Critic and poet. Conductor of poetry workshop for New York Board of Education, 1948; chairman of New York Public Library "Evenings of Poetry," 1949; poet-in-residence, University of Northern Colorado, 1974; poetry reader at Library of Congress, University of Rochester, Michigan State University, Columbia University, University of Pisa, University of Urbino, and at other colleges and universities. *Member:* Poetry Society of America (executive board, 1959-60), Academy of American Poets, MacDowell Associates, James Joyce Society, Vermont Historical Society, New England Poetry Club. *Awards, honors:* Poetry Society of America annual awards, 1948, 1957; E. A. Robinson fellowship to MacDowell Colony, 1949; National Council on the Arts grant, 1966; Marraki Stuly Gold Metal, 1966; National Endowment for the Humanities grant, 1970-71; American Philosophical Society award, 1974.

WRITINGS: Unit and Universe (poetry), Clarke & Way, 1959; (translator) Carlo Betocchi, *Poems,* Clarke & Way, 1964; (translator) Dino Campana, *Orphic Songs,* October House, 1968; (translator) Alfredo de Palchi, *Sessions with My Analyst,* October House, 1971; (translator) Mario Luzi, *In the Dark Body of Metamorphosis,* Norton, 1975. Contributor of reviews to *Saturday Review* and *Poetry.*

WORK IN PROGRESS: Translating works of Diego Valeri, Vincenzo Carderelli, and Rossana Ombres.

SIDELIGHTS: I. L. Salomon told *CA*: "At heart, I'm a Platonist; in mind, an Aristotelian. My poetry is in the transcendental tradition of Emerson and Thoreau." John Holmes says of his work: "Mr. Salomon is a poet blessed in this earth, returning his blessing to it. His poems have the ease of mastery, and the pride and fire of a man whose sympathies range the world, and the inner self. He is a civilized international, and everywhere he goes, a poet."

* * *

SALTER, Cedric
See KNIGHT, Francis Edgar

* * *

SALTER, James 1925-

PERSONAL: Born June 10, 1925, in New York, N.Y. *Residence:* Aspen, Colo.

CAREER: Writer. *Military Service:* U.S. Air Force, 1945-57.

WRITINGS: The Hunters, Harper, 1957; *The Arm of Flesh,* Harper, 1961; *A Sport and a Pastime,* Doubleday, 1967; *Light Years* (novel), Random House, 1975. Contributor of stories to *Paris Review, Antaeus,* and other literary magazines.

SIDELIGHTS: "The writer's life," Salter told *CA,* "exists for only a small number. It can be glorious, especially after death. There are provincial, national and world writers—one should compete in one's class, despise riches, as Whitman says, and take off your hat to no one."

BIOGRAPHICAL/CRITICAL SOURCES: Contemporary Literary Criticism, Volume 7, Gale, 1977.

* * *

SAMMONS, David 1938-

PERSONAL: Born February 11, 1938, in Chicago, Ill.; son of Joseph Albert and Helen Louise Sammons; married Rosemary Sturtz, August 30, 1959 (divorced October 11, 1973); married Janis Miller (a teacher), January 24, 1974; children: Donna, David, Jr., Michal Ann, Benjamin, Matthew. *Education:* Dartmouth College, A.B., 1960; attended Meadville Theological School, 1961-62; Starr King School for the Ministry, M.Div., 1965; Pacific School of Religion, doctoral study, 1976—. *Politics:* "Independent Democrat most of the time." *Home:* 3441 Morrison Pl., Cincinnati, Ohio 45220. *Office:* St. John's Unitarian Church, 320 Resor Ave., Cincinnati, Ohio 45220.

CAREER: Haggard & Marcusson Co., Chicago, Ill., assistant sales manager, 1960-63; ordained Unitarian-Universalist minister, 1965; associate minister of Unitarian-Universalist church in Rochester, N.Y., 1965-67; St. John's Unitarian Church, Cincinnati, Ohio, senior minister, 1967—. President of Lake Geneva Summer Assembly Planning Council; chairman of Movado Minister's Institute; member of executive board of Free Choice Coalition, Religious Coalition on Abortion Rights, and Independent Voters of Ohio; past president of Cincinnati Action for Peace; adviser to Parents Without Partners and Cincinnati Homophile Organization; member of Neighborhood Support Organization, Clifton Town Meeting, Clergy Consultation Service on Problem Pregnancies, Human Relations Model Subsystems Committee; and Secretary of the Metropolitan Area Religious Coalition. Member of board of directors of Beacon Press.

MEMBER: Unitarian-Universalist Ministers Association, HOME, American Civil Liberties Union, EDUCO, Phi Beta Kappa.

WRITINGS: The Marriage Option, Beacon Press, 1977. Contributor to magazines, including *Single Parent, Brides, Journal of the Liberal Ministry,* and *Cincinnati,* and newspapers.

WORK IN PROGRESS: Rearrangements, dealing with changes in relationships; a report on seminars on ethical perspectives for St. John's business people; a monograph.

SIDELIGHTS: Sammons writes: "I am a liberal minister with particular interests in both human relationships and issues involved in institutional ethics. Often caught out in front on social issues during the confrontations and experiments of the past decade, I've now become concerned about trying to find ways to give perspective to people in the midst of conflict or change. It has not been enough just to raise issues and bitch. People need handles if they are going to respond constructively to the issues facing them and their world. For now, I've given up chasing Zorba's green stones to be a pen-pusher."

BIOGRAPHICAL/CRITICAL SOURCES: Cincinnati, February, 1972; *Queen's Jester,* November 17, 1974; *Cincinnati Post,* October 20, 1977; *Dayton Daily News,* October 20, 1977; *Hamilton Journal Herald,* October 23, 1977.

* * *

SAMSON, Joan 1937-1976

PERSONAL: Born September 9, 1937, in Erie, Pa.; daughter of Edward W. (a physicist) and Helen (a teacher; maiden name, Verrall) Samson; married Warren C. Carberg, Jr. (a library administrator), May 27, 1965; children: Amy Helen, Ethan Linh. *Education:* Attended Wellesley College, 1955-57; University of Chicago, B.A., 1959; Tufts University, M.A., 1968. *Agent:* Patricia S. Myrer, McIntosh & Otis, 475 Fifth Ave., New York, N.Y. 10017.

CAREER: Elementary teacher in the public schools of Chicago, Ill., 1959-60; English teacher in Newton, Mass., 1960-63; free-lance editor in Boston, Mass., 1963-64; elementary teacher in London, England, 1965-66; country day school teacher in Brookline, Mass., 1968-69; manuscript editor of *Daedalus* (journal of American Academy of Arts and Sciences), 1973-75. Co-chairperson of Society of Radcliffe Fellows, 1975. *Awards, honors:* Radcliffe Institute fellowship, 1972-74; *Watching the New Baby* named outstanding science book for children by National Teacher's Association and Children's Council, 1975.

WRITINGS: Watching the New Baby (juvenile), Atheneum, 1974; *The Auctioneer* (young adult novel), Simon & Schuster, 1975. Contributor to *Teacher Paper, American Paper,* and *Daedalus.*

WORK IN PROGRESS: Posthumous publications may be forthcoming.

SIDELIGHTS: Joan Samson wrote: "It was with trepidation one day that I confessed to the headmaster that my baby—my first—was due on June 10, while our final classes were June 11. Surely it was a sign of changing times that he replied cheerfully, 'Well, if we're lucky, we'll make it!' My daughter obliged by arriving ten days late, so until school ended, my all-girl classes watched with many questions and intense interest the increasing evidence of an impending birth. My own interest and curiosity were insatiable and I eagerly researched details concerning the mystery of this newly developing human being. It was only afterward that I had the idea to use my collected data in a book. I found the coming of the new baby into our lives a much more exciting and meaningful experience that I could have ever anticipated. Writing the book, *Watching the New Baby,* was an attempt to express in some small measure how very interesting a new baby can be.''

Samson's husband, Warren Carberg, told *CA:* "*Watching the New Baby* is addressed specifically to children who are about to have a baby sibling and suggests how to react to the newcomer and what to expect. Because it contains a story of the growing fetus, librarians classify it as sex education. But all manner of other folk—notably new mothers—have delighted in the warmth and informativeness of the book.

"The arrival into our family of a son, Ethan Linh, although very different from our daughter's birth, was also an occasion of drama and suspense. After a year's negotiations with adoption agencies and much fingering of a foreign snapshot, Joan and I, with our five-year-old daughter Amy, met the plane from Saigon to welcome our handsome twenty-month-old Vietnamese baby. Bright and alert after a twenty-hour flight, he smiled with pleasure when he saw us. Our mutual appreciation has only increased with time.

"Essentially city dwellers, we nevertheless put down deep roots in our own beautifully wooded land in rural New Hampshire where we spend vacations and weekends. The New England countryside which Joan knew and loved so well is the setting for the novel, *The Auctioneer,* inspired by a vivid dream. Joan awoke one day, she said, with the feeling that the dream had just handed her a situation and an impression that she must write about. What subsequently evolved was a thrilling suspense story which has proved to have a strong appeal for adolescents as well as adults.''

(Died February 27, 1976, in Cambridge, Mass.)

[Sketch verified by husband, Warren C. Carberg, Jr.]

*   *   *

SAMUEL, Alan E(douard) 1932-

PERSONAL: Born July 24, 1932, in Queens, N.Y.; son of Edgar Aaron and Hortense (Kesner) Samuel; married Deborah Hobson, June 13, 1964; children: Deborah Joan, Jean Carol, Katharine Ann, Elizabeth Rose, Alexandra Whitney. *Education:* Hamilton College, B.A., 1953; Yale University, M.A., 1957, Ph.D., 1959. *Address:* 554 Spadina Crescent, Toronto, Ontario, Canada M5S 2J9.

CAREER: Yale University, New Haven, Conn., instructor, 1959-63, assistant professor of classics, 1963-66; University of Toronto, University College, Toronto, Ontario, associate professor, 1966-67, professor of ancient history, 1967—. President of A. M. Hakkert Ltd., and of Rostovtzeff-Welles Library. *Military service:* U.S. Naval Reserve, 1953-56; became lieutenant. *Member:* Comite Internationale de Papyrologie, American Philological Association (former director), Archaeological Institute of America, American Society of Papyrologists (secretary-treasurer, 1968), Classics Association of Canada.

WRITINGS: Ptolemaic Chronology, Beck (Munich), 1962; *The Mycenaeans in History,* Prentice-Hall, 1966; (with John F. Oates and C. Bradford Welles) *Yale Papyri in the Beinecke Rare Book and Manuscript Library,* American Society of Papyrologists, 1967; (with W. Keith Hastings) *Death and Taxes: Ostraka in the Royal Ontario Museum,* A. M. Hakkert, 1971; *Greek and Roman Chronology: Calendars and Years in Classical Antiquity,* Beck, 1972. Contributor of articles to professional journals. Editor of *Bulletin of American Society of Papyrologists.**

SANCHEZ, Ricardo 1941-

PERSONAL: Born March 29, 1941, in El Paso, Tex.; son of Pedro Lucero (a dealer in scrap metals) and Adelina (Gallegos) Sanchez; married Maria Teresa Silva, November 28, 1964; children: Rikard-Sergei, Libertad-Yvonne, Pedro-Cuauhtemoc (deceased), Jacinto-Temilotzin. *Education:* Took extension courses from Alvin Junior College, 1965-69; Union Graduate School, Ph.D., 1975. *Politics:* "Anarcho-Humanist." *Religion:* "Indigenist-non-sectarian." *Home:* 153 East Truman Ave., Salt Lake City, Utah 84115.

CAREER: Incarcerated at Texas Department of Corrections in Huntsville, Tex., 1965-69; Vista community worker, El Paso, Tex., 1969; research director of Project MACHOS, Inc., 1969; *Richmond Afro-American Newspaper,* Richmond, Va., correspondent, 1969; University of Massachusetts, School of Education, Amherst, staff writer, research assistant, and instructor, 1970; Colorado Migrant Council, Denver, director of Itinerant Migrant Health Project, 1970-71; University of Texas, El Paso, consultant, writer, and lecturer for Chicano Affairs Program and Teacher Corps & TTT Program, 1971-72; New Mexico State University, Las Cruces, community staff consultant and lecturer for Social Welfare Teaching Center, 1972-73; El Paso Community College, El Paso, professor of poetry, literature, and critical theory, 1975, National Endowment for the Arts poet-in-residence, 1975-76; University of Wisconsin, Milwaukee, visiting professor and lecturer for Spanish-Speaking Outreach Institute, 1977; University of Utah, Salt Lake City, assistant professor of humanities and Chicano studies, 1977—. Training consultant, writer, and lecturer for American Program Bureau, Boston, Mass., 1970-72, and La Academia de la Nueva Raza, Dixon, N.M., 1971-72; co-founder and counseling supervisor of Trinity-Opportunities Industrialization Center in El Paso, 1972. Board member of Southwest Poets' Conference, 1970—, Father Rahm Health Clinic, El Paso, 1971-73, Trinity Chicano Coalition, El Paso, 1971-73, Texas Council on Alcoholism, El Paso, 1972-73, and La Luz Mexican American Cultural Center of the El Paso diocese, El Paso, 1974-76. Founder and editor of Mictla Publications, 1970-75; chairman of Project TREND, El Paso, 1972-73; co-founder and associate of Chicano Barrio Associates (CHIBAS), El Paso, 1972—; founder and board member of Chicano Light and Power, Inc., El Paso, 1974—. Free lance writer, poet, consultant, and lecturer, 1976-77.

MEMBER: P.E.N. International, Poets and Writers, Inc. (New York City). *Awards, honors:* Ford fellow, Frederick Douglass fellowship in journalism, 1969; Ford Foundation graduate fellow, Union Graduate School, 1973-75.

WRITINGS: Canto y Grito Mi Liberacion/The Liberation of a Chicano Mind, Mictla, 1971, Doubleday-Anchor, 1973; (editor) *Los Cuatro* (title means "The Four"), Barrio Press, 1971; *Obras* (title means "Works"), Quetzal-Vihio Press, 1971; *Mano a Mano* (title means "Hand to Hand"), Conference of Unity & Action, 1971; *HechizoSpells,* Chicano Studies Center, University of California, Los Angeles, 1976; (author of introduction) Bernice Zamora and Jose Antonio Burciaga, *Restless Serpents,* Disenos Lierarios, 1976; (author of introduction) Mario Garza, *Un Paso Mas* (title means "One Step Farther"), Renaissance Publications, 1976. Also author of unpublished manuscripts, "In and Out," "Mexi-Coloured Moods," "With Love & Protest," and "Florimoquiando."

Work represented in several anthologies, including *Points of Departure,* edited by Ernece B. Kelly, Wiley, 1972; and *We Are Chicanos,* edited by Philip D. Ortego, Washington

Square Press, 1973. Contributor to *Publishers' Weekly, De Colores, El Diario, Greenfield Review* and numerous other magazines, reviews, newspapers, and journals. Editor at large, *La Luz* magazine; special issues editor, *De Colores: Journal of Emerging Raza Philosophies,* 1975.

WORK IN PROGRESS: Sojourns & Soulmind Etchings, a collection of poetry, essays, and vignettes; *Milwaukee Blues & Other Things,* poetry monograph for University of Wisconsin, Milwaukee; *CUNA,* a socio/psycholinguistic work in poetry and vignettes.

SIDELIGHTS: Sanchez told *CA:* "I write in order to liberate myself from past inculcations and to enjoin myself with all who want to create a more sanguine society . . . as a Chicano I realize the privation that those who are different must suffer. Writing becomes the vehicle for self expression and the means toward one's humanization. My writings are trilingual, i.e., Spanish, English, or an admixture of both—flowing in and out of the linguistic worlds I am able to inhabit simultaneously . . . creating thus a new world view that contains both. . . . In quest of humanizing liberation do I write, in order to distill from the sordidness of societal oppressiveness a view of being-ness which sings/shouts out love, dignity, and the peacefulness of freedom. . . ."

Besides his writing, Sanchez is engaged in developing television programs and cassette recordings on Chicano culture and literature, and spends much of his time participating and lecturing in symposia, colloquia, and seminars throughout the country.

AVOCATIONAL INTERESTS: Chess, art, dance, dramatics, readings in history, philosophy, folklore, political theory.

BIOGRAPHICAL/CRITICAL SOURCES: Tiempo, December 27, 1976; *Hispano,* January 24, 1977, May 9, 1977; *Revista Chicano-Riquena,* December, 1977.

* * *

SANCHEZ-SILVA, Jose Maria 1911-

PERSONAL: Born November 11, 1911, in Madrid, Spain; son of Lorenzo (a journalist) and Adoracion (Garcia-Morales) Sanchez-Silva; married Maria del Carmen Delgado, 1933; children: six. *Education:* Attended El Dabate (Madrid).

CAREER: Author. Worked as a reporter, editor-in-chief, and assistant director of *Arriba,* Madrid, during late 1930's and early 1940's, and as editor of *Revista de las Artes y los Oficios* during the late 1940's. *Member:* General Society of Spanish Authors (appointed to council, 1963). *Awards, honors:* Francisco de Sales prize, 1942; National Prize for Literature (Spain), 1944 and 1957; National Prize for Journalism (Spain), 1945; Mariano de Cavia prize, 1947; Rodriguez Santamaria prize, 1948; Grand Cross of the Order of Cisneros (Spain), 1959; Virgen del Carmen prize, 1960; award for special services from the Government of Peru, 1962; Grand Cross of Merit (Spain), 1964; Grand Cross of the Order of Alfonso X (Spain), 1968.

WRITINGS: Un Paleto en Londres: La Vuelta al Mundo y Otros Viajes, Editora Nacional (Madrid), 1952; *Adelaida y Otros Asuntos Personales* (illustrated by Lorenzo Goni), Editora Nacional, 1953; *Marcelino Pan y Vino: Cuento de Padres a Hijos* (illustrated by Goni), [Madrid], 1953, translation by Angela Britton published as *Marcelino: A Story from Parents to Children,* Newman Press, 1955, another edition translated by John Paul Debicki published as *The Miracle of Marcelino,* Scepter, 1963; *Historias de Mi Calle,* [Madrid],

1954; *Quince o Veinte Sombras,* Ediciones CID (Madrid), 1955; *El Hereje: Cuento para Mayores* (illustrated by Alvaro Delgado), A. Aguado (Madrid), 1956; *Fabula de la Burrita Non* (illustrated by Goni), Ediciones CID, 1956; *Tres Novelas y Pico,* A. Aguado, 1958.

Cuentos de Navidad (title means "Christmas Stories"; illustrated by Jose Francisco Aguirre), Editorial Magisterio Espanol (Madrid), 1960; *Adios, Josefina!* (illustrated by Goni), Alameda (Madrid), 1962, translation by Michael Heron published as *The Boy and the Whale* (illustrated by Margery Gill), McGraw, 1964; *San Martin de Porres,* Secretariado Martin de Porres (Palencia), 1962; *Colasin, Colason,* Editora Nacional, 1963; *Pesinoe y Gente de Tierra,* [Madrid], 1964; *Cartas a un Nino Sobre Francisco Franco,* [Madrid], 1966; *Tres Animales Son,* Doncel (Madrid), 1966; *Adan y el Senor Dios* (title means "Adam and the Lord"; illustrated by Goni), Escelicer (Madrid), 1967; *Un Gran Pequeno,* Editorial Marfil (Alcoy), 1967, translation by Heron published as *Ladis and the Ant* (illustrated by David Knight), Bodley Head, 1968, McGraw, 1969; *El Segundo Verano de Ladis,* Editorial Marfil, 1968, translation by Isabel Quigly published as *Second Summer with Ladis* (illustrated by Knight), Bodley Head, 1969; (with Luis de Diego) *Luiso* (illustrated by Goni), Doncel, 1969.

Also author of *El Hombre y la Bufanda* (title means "The Man and the Neckcloth"), 1934; *Aventura en Cielo* (title means "Adventures in Heaven"); *El Espejo Habitado* (title means "The Lived-In Mirror"); and *Historias Menores* (title means "Little Stories"). Scriptwriter for motion picture "Ronda Espanola," 1952.

SIDELIGHTS: While a journalist, Sanchez-Silva traveled throughout the world covering stories ranging from discontent in Italy to the 1948 Olympic winter games in England. His books have been translated into twenty-six languages.*

* * *

SANDERS, Marion K. 1905-1977

August 14, 1905—September 16, 1977; American journalist, public relations executive, editor, and biographer. Sanders was senior editor of *Harper's* until her retirement in 1970, but she continued as contributing editor. Sanders was also assistant public relations director for the Port of New York Authority from 1937 to 1944, and then for six years worked as chief of the public relations branch of the International Information Administration. During this period she developed an extensive worldwide publications program. She is best known for her biography of Dorothy Thompson. She died in New York, N.Y. Obituaries: *New York Times,* September 18, 1977; *Time,* October 3, 1977. (See index for *CA* sketch)

* * *

SANFORD, Thomas K(yle), Jr. 1921-1977

PERSONAL: Born July 23, 1921, in Sherman, Tex.; son of Thomas Kyle and Martha (a nurse; maiden name, Thomas) Sanford; married Janet Sliskovich (a woman's editor), April 24, 1952; children: Thomas Kyle III, Michael R., Susan K., Sally Beth. *Education:* Attended Southwestern University, 1939-42. *Politics:* Democrat. *Religion:* None. *Home:* 1907 East Coolidge, Phoenix, Ariz. 85016. *Office: Arizona Republic,* 120 East Van Buren, Phoenix, Ariz. 85012.

CAREER/WRITINGS: Braniff International Airways, Dallas, Tex., co-pilot, 1945-47; *Brownsville Herald,* Brownsville, Tex., managing editor, 1947-51; *Arizona Re-*

public, Phoenix, Ariz., assistant managing editor, 1951—. Contributor of articles to periodicals, including *Quill.* Member of board, Young Mens Christian Association (YMCA), Phoenix. *Military service:* U.S. Air Force, 1942-45; became first lieutenant. *Member:* Society of Professional Journalists (president, 1959), Phoenix Press Club (president, 1961-62). *Awards, honors:* Professional journalism fellow, Stanford University, 1969.

SIDELIGHTS: Sanford told *CA* his "primary career interest has long been in directing hard-hitting news coverage so that the public may be informed in order to intelligently participate in government." *Avocational interests:* Golf, hunting, fishing, hiking, camping.

(Died January 25, 1977)

* * *

SASEK, Miroslav 1916-

PERSONAL: Born November 18, 1916, in Prague, Czechoslovakia; children: Dusan Pedro. *Education:* Educated in Prague, and at l'Ecole des Beaux Arts, Paris. *Residence:* Munich, Germany.

CAREER: Worked for Radio Free Europe, Munich, Germany, 1951-57; author and illustrator. *Awards, honors: New York Times* Choice of Best Illustrated Children's Books of the Year, 1959, for *This Is London,* and 1960, for *This Is New York;* Boys' Clubs of America Junior Book Award, 1961, for *This Is New York.*

WRITINGS—"This Is" series, all illustrated by the author and published by Macmillan: *This Is Paris,* 1959; . . . *London,* 1959, revised edition, 1970; . . . *New York,* 1960; . . . *Rome,* 1960; . . . *Venice,* 1961; . . . *Edinburgh,* 1961; . . . *Munich,* 1961; . . . *San Francisco,* 1962; . . . *Israel,* 1962; . . . *Cape Kennedy,* 1964; . . . *Ireland,* 1964; . . . *Hong Kong,* 1965; . . . *Greece,* 1966; . . . *Texas,* 1967; . . . *the United Nations,* 1968; . . . *Washington, D.C.,* 1969; . . . *Australia,* 1970; . . . *Historic Britain,* 1974.

Other: *Stone Is Not Cold,* Citadel, 1961.

SIDELIGHTS: Born and educated in Czechoslovakia, Miroslav Sasek left the country when the Communists came to power in 1946. He lived and studied in Paris for a while, and then settled in Munich, Germany.

A three-week vacation in Paris gave Sasek the idea for writing travel books for children, and *This Is Paris* appeared in 1959. Sasek had originally intended to write only three books of this nature—about Paris, London, and Rome. However, the success of the first three encouraged him to do more, and in the 1960's, there appeared several Sasek books on European and American cities. He also expanded his scope to include entire countries, as well as points of interest, such as Cape Kennedy and the United Nations.

In 1968, Sasek came to Washington, D.C. to complete the research for a book on that city. He was in the city at the time of the riots which followed the assassination of Martin Luther King, Jr. He was still there when Robert Kennedy was assassinated, and was sketching the gravesite of John F. Kennedy when guards asked him to leave so that they could dig the grave of Robert Kennedy. Sasek described these experiences as a "continuing nightmare," and *This Is Washington, D.C.,* according to critics, reflects this.

BIOGRAPHICAL/CRITICAL SOURCES: New York Times, May 10, 1959; *Times Literary Supplement,* May 29, 1959, December 4, 1959, June 6, 1969; *San Francisco Chronicle,* February 28, 1960.*

SAUNDERS, Thomas 1909-

PERSONAL: Born February 21, 1909, in Crossgates, Scotland; married Janet Agnes Clark, 1940; children: Thomas Glen, James Clark, Allan John. *Education:* University of Manitoba, B.A., 1935; United College, D.D., 1959. *Home:* 527 Oxford St., Winnipeg, Manitoba, Canada.

CAREER: Served as United Church of Canada minister in Manitoba, Canada; *Winnipeg Free Press,* Winnipeg, Manitoba, literary editor, 1960—.

WRITINGS—Poetry: *Scrub Oak,* Ryerson, 1949; *Horizontal World,* Ryerson, 1951; *Something of a Young World's Dying,* Ryerson, 1958; *The Devil and Cal McCabe; or, the Tale of the Cowman's Corns: A Story in Verse,* Ryerson, 1960; *Red River of the North and Other Poems of Manitoba,* Pegius, 1969. Poetry represented in anthology, *Poetry 62,* edited by E. W. Mandel and J. G. Pilon, Ryerson, 1961.*

* * *

SAUTER, Van Gordon 1935-

PERSONAL: Born September 14, 1935, in Middletown, Ohio; son of Freeman and Cornelia (Banker) Sauter; married Patricia Allen, November 22, 1958; children: Mark Allen, Jeremy Banker. *Education:* Ohio University, B.A., 1957; University of Missouri, M.A., 1959. *Office:* 524 West 57th St., New York, N.Y. 10019.

CAREER: New Bedford Standard-Times, New Bedford, Mass., reporter, 1959-63; *Detroit Free Press,* Detroit, Mich., staff writer, 1963-67; *Chicago Daily News,* Chicago, Ill., staff writer, 1967-68; WBBM-CBS radio, Chicago, news and program director, 1968-71; Columbia Broadcasting System News, New York City, executive producer for radio, 1971—. *Member:* Radio-TV News Directors Association, Society of Professional Journalists, Sigma Delta Chi.

WRITINGS: (With Burleigh Hines) *Nightmare in Detroit: A Rebellion and Its Victims,* Regnery, 1968; (with Stephen Feldman) *Fabled Land/Timeless River: Life along the Mississippi,* Quadrangle, 1970.*

* * *

SAUVAGE, Roger 1917-1977

1917—September 26, 1977; French fighter pilot and author. Sauvage's war diary was a best-seller in France. He died in Nice, France. Obituaries: *New York Times,* September 30, 1977.

* * *

SAVAGE, James F(rancis) 1939-

PERSONAL: Born July 23, 1939, in Boston, Mass.; son of James and Hanora (Enright) Savage; married Sharon K. Base (a dental aide), May 29, 1965; children: Sean. *Education:* Boston University, B.S., 1961. *Home:* 1004 Orange Isle, Fort Lauderdale, Fla. 33315. *Office: Miami Herald,* 1 Herald Plaza, Miami, Fla. 33101.

CAREER/WRITINGS: Quincy Patriot Ledger, Quincy, Mass., reporter, 1961-63; *Miami Herald,* Miami, Fla., reporter, 1963-67, investigative reporter, 1967—. Notable assignments include a two year investigative project which led to the disclosure of a systematic collection of political payoffs linked to former Florida Senator Edward Gurney, and other investigative reporting of organized crime and political corruption in Florida. Investigative reporter for *Boston Herald Traveler,* 1967. *Military service:* U.S. Army, 1962. U.S. Army Reserve, 1962-68. *Awards, honors:* National

Headliners Award, 1969; Florida Press Association Award, 1972, 1975; George Polk Memorial Award for Investigative Reporting, 1973; National Associated Press Public Service Award, 1974.

* * *

SAWYER, Ruth 1880-1970

PERSONAL: Born August 5, 1880, in Boston, Mass.; daughter of Francis Milton (an importer) and Ethelinda J. (Smith) Sawyer; married Albert C. Durand, M.D., June 4, 1911; children: David, Margaret (Mrs. Robert McCloskey). *Education:* Columbia University, B.S., 1904. *Religion:* Unitarian. *Home:* Gull Rock, Hancock, Me.

CAREER: Short story writer and author of books for children. Feature writer, New York *Sun;* was sent to Ireland, 1905, 1907, where she began collecting folk tales. Began storytelling professionally for the New York Lecture Bureau, 1908, and started the first storytelling program for children at the New York Public Library. *Awards, honors:* Newbery Medal, 1937, for *Roller Skates;* Caldecott Medal, 1945, for *The Christmas Anna Angel,* and 1954, for *Journey Cake, Ho!;* Regina Medal, 1965; Laura Ingalls Wilder Medal, 1965.

WRITINGS: The Primrose Ring, Harper, 1915; *Seven Miles to Arden,* Harper, 1916; *A Child's Yearbook,* Harper, 1917; *Herself, Himself, and Myself,* Harper, 1917; *Doctor Danny* (illustrated by J. Scott Williams), Harper, 1918; *Leerie* (illustrated by Clinton Balmer), Harper, 1920; *The Silver Sixpence* (illustrated by James H. Crank), Harper, 1921; *Gladiola Murphy,* Harper, 1923; *The Tale of the Enchanted Bunnies,* Harper, 1923; *Four Ducks on a Pond,* Harper, 1928; *Folkhouse: The Autobiography of a Home* (illustrated by Allan McNab), D. Appleton, 1932; *Tono Antonio* (illustrated by F. Luis Mora), Viking, 1934; *The Luck of the Road,* Appleton-Century, 1934.

Picture Tales from Spain (illustrated by Carlos Sanchez), F. A. Stokes, 1936; *Gallant: The Story of Storm Veblen* (published serially as *Hillmen's Gold*), Appleton-Century, 1936; *Roller Skates* (illustrated by Valenti Angelo), Viking, 1936, reprinted, Dell, 1966; *The Year of Jubilo* (illustrated by Edward Shenton), Viking, 1940, reprinted, 1970; *The Least One* (illustrated by Leo Politi), Viking, 1941; *The Way of the Storyteller,* Macmillan, 1942, reprinted, Viking, 1965; *Old Con and Patrick* (illustrated by Cathal O'Toole), Viking, 1946; *The Little Red Horse* (illustrated by Jay Hyde Barnum), Viking, 1950; (contributor) John Gehlmann, editor, *Challenge of Ideas: An Essay Reader,* Odyssey, 1950; *Journey Cake, Ho!* (illustrated by Robert McCloskey), Viking, 1953; *A Cottage for Betsy* (illustrated by Vera Bock), Harper, 1954; *The Enchanted Schoolhouse* (illustrated by Hugh Tory), Viking, 1956; (contributor) *A Horn Book Sampler of Children's Books and Reading,* edited by Norma R. Fryatt, Horn Book, 1959; *How to Tell a Story,* F. E. Compton, 1962; *Daddles: The Story of a Plain Hound-Dog* (illustrated by Robert Frankenberg), Little, Brown, 1964; *My Spain: A Storyteller's Year of Collecting,* Viking, 1967.

Christmas stories: *This Way to Christmas,* Harper, 1916, revised edition, 1970; *The Long Christmas* (illustrated by V. Angelo), Viking, 1941, reprinted, 1966; *The Christmas Anna Angel* (illustrated by Kate Seredy), Viking, 1944; *This is the Christmas: A Serbian Folk Tale,* Horn Book, 1945; *Maggie Rose: Her Birthday Christmas* (illustrated by Maurice Sendak), Harper, 1952; *The Year of the Christmas Dragon* (illustrated by Hugh Tory), Viking, 1960; *Joy to the World: Christmas Legends* (illustrated by Trina S. Hyman), Little, Brown, 1966.

Contributor of over 200 articles, stories, poems, and serials to periodicals, including *Atlantic Monthly* and *Outlook.*

SIDELIGHTS: As a child, Ruth Sawyer developed her love for stories—listening to them, telling them, and finally writing them down—from her Irish nurse, Johanna. The nurse also instilled in Ruth a great love for Irish folklore, an interest which was later extended to other countries. She majored in folklore and storytelling at Columbia University. Following graduation, she told stories twice a week, in all parts of the city, for the New York Public Lecture Bureau.

Ruth Sawyer traveled to Spain and heard tales which she retold in *Picture Tales from Spain.* An *Atlantic* review called it, "A delightful small volume. Carlos Sanchez had made interpretative drawings in black and white which suit the humor and freshness of the tales. Here is a book perfectly adapted for reading aloud—one which will appeal strongly to boys of nine or ten." Another story from Spain was *Tono Antonio.* The *Boston Transcript* described it as, "A quaint and delightful story that, incidentally, leaves the reader feeling that he has just returned from a trip to Spain. F. Luis Mora's charming drawings help a lot in this pleasing illusion."

The Long Christmas is a collection of Christmas stories from several countries. The *New York Times* wrote: "Some of the stories are humorous, some are touching, all have strength and distinction and nearly all will be new to most readers. This is a book that will last a life time, for the truth and charm of these legends and the grace with which Ruth Sawyer has retold them, stand out more clearly with each rereading."

There have been several adaptations made of Ruth Sawyer's works. *The Primrose Ring* was made into a silent motion picture by Lasky Feature Play Company in 1917. Margaret D. Williams adapted a story from *This Way to Christmas* into a two-scene play entitled *Christmas Apple,* published by Samuel French in 1939.

AVOCATIONAL INTERESTS: Sailing, fishing, and berry picking.

BIOGRAPHICAL/CRITICAL SOURCES: Boston Transcript, November 7, 1934; *Atlantic,* October, 1936; *New York Times,* November 16, 1941; Virginia Haviland, *Ruth Sawyer,* Walck, 1965; *Catholic Library World,* January, February, 1965.

OBITUARIES: New York Times, June 6, 1970.*

(Died June 3, 1970)

* * *

SAYERS, Gale 1943-

PERSONAL: Born May 30, 1943, in Wichita, Kan.; son of Roger Earl and Bernice (Ross) Sayers; married Linda Lou McNeil, June 10, 1962 (marriage ended); married Ardythe Elaine Bullard, December 1, 1973; children: Gale Lynne, Scott Aaron, Timothy, Gaylon, Guy, Gary. *Education:* Attended University of Kansas and New York Institute of Finance. *Office:* Allen Fieldhouse, University of Kansas, Lawrence, Kan. 66045.

CAREER: Chicago Bears professional football team, Chicago, Ill., running back, 1965-72; University of Kansas, Lawrence, assistant to athletic director; *Chicago Daily News,* Chicago, Ill., columnist. Co-chairman, Legal Defense Fund for Sports Committee, National Association for the Advancement of Colored People; coordinator, Reach-Out program, Chicago, Ill.; commissioner, Chicago Park District.

Honorary chairman, American Cancer Society. *Member:* Kappa Alpha Psi. *Awards, honors:* Won numerous awards for playing football; holder of numerous National Football League records, including most points rookie season, touchdowns season, and most touchdowns game, all 1965.

WRITINGS: (With Al Silverman) *I Am Third* (autobiography), Viking, 1970; (with Bob Griese) *Offensive Football,* Atheneum, 1972.

* * *

SCHAAL, John H. 1908-

PERSONAL: Born April 28, 1908, in Kalamazoo, Mich.; son of Peter and Grace (Bredeweg) Schaal; married Grace W. Workman; children: Wendell John. *Education:* Attended Hope College, 1926-28; Calvin College, A.B., 1930; Calvin Theological Seminary, B.D., 1933; also attended University of Chicago. *Home:* 1137 Noble St. S.E., Grand Rapids, Mich. 49507.

CAREER: Ordained minister of Christian Reformed Church, 1933; pastor of Christian Reformed churches in Kalamazoo, Mich., 1933-43, and Second Christian Reformed churches in Fremont, Mich., 1943-48; Reformed Bible College, Grand Rapids, Mich., professor of church history and Bible, 1948-73, dean, 1948-73; Grand Rapids Osteopathic Hospital, Grand Rapids, Mich., chaplain, 1973—. Chaplain at Mary Free Bed Rehabilitation Center, 1977—. President of Christian Reformed Board of World Missions, 1965-69, and Wayside Gospel Drive-In Chapel, 1973—; member of board of directors of Forgotten Man Mission, Inc., 1971—, and Children's Radio Bible Hours, 1975—. *Military service:* U.S. Army Reserve, chaplain, 1940-42; became first lieutenant.

WRITINGS: Better Living Through Christ: Studies on Hebrews, Baker Book, 1968; *Three Letters from Prison,* Baker Book, 1970; *The Royal Roman Road,* Baker Book, 1972. Contributor to *Banner.* Editor of church school publications for Christian Reformed Church, 1945-72.

* * *

SCHARPER, Phillip (Jenkins) 1919-

PERSONAL: Born September 15, 1919, in Baltimore, Md.; son of William Albert and Mary Louise (Griffin) Scharper; married Sarah J. Moormann, June 11, 1949; children: Grail, Philip, Katherine, Alice, David, Bede. *Education:* Georgetown University, A.B., 1943, Ph.D., 1944, M.A. (education), 1945; Fordham University, M.A. (English), 1947. *Home:* 1623 Newfield Ave., Stamford, Conn. 06905. *Office:* Orbis Books, Mary Knoll, N.Y. 10545.

CAREER: Xavier University, Cincinnati, Ohio, instructor in English, 1948-50; Fordham University, Bronx, New York, assistant professor of English, 1950-55; *Commonweal,* New York City, associate editor, 1956-57; Sheed & Ward, Inc., New York City, editor-in-chief, 1957-70, vice-president, 1962-70; Orbis Books, Mary Knoll, N.Y., editor-in-chief, 1970—. Adviser for program on pluralism, National Federation of Catholic College Students, 1960-61; delegate, National Conference on Race and Religion, 1962; member of board of directors, Manhattan region of the National Conference of Christians and Jews; member of board of directors, National Committee for Support of the Public Schools; member of national advisory committee, Catholic Council on Civil Liberties; trustee of John XXIII Institute, St. Xavier College. *Member:* Religious Education Association (president, 1963-64; chairman), American Benedictine

Academy. *Awards, honors:* Xavier Award, Xavier University, 1961; Litt.D., Loyola College, 1966, Mt. Mary College, 1966; fellowship for visit to Israel, Jewish Theological Seminary of America.

WRITINGS—Nonfiction: (Editor) Stringfellow Barr and others, *American Catholics: A Protestant-Jewish View,* Sheed, 1959; (with others) *New Horizons in Catholic Thought,* Sheed, 1964; (editor) *Torah and Gospel: Jewish and Catholic Theology in Dialogue,* Sheed, 1966; *Meet the American Catholic,* Broadman, 1969; (with Jacqueline Keller) *Maryknoll Children's Missal,* Orbis Books, 1971; (adaptor with John Eagleson from *Bibel Provokativ*) *The Radical Bible,* Orbis Books, 1972. Also author of television scripts.*

* * *

SCHATTEN, Robert 1911-1977

1911—August 27, 1977; Polish-born American educator, mathematician, and author of works in his field. Schatten wrote *A Theory of Cross Spaces* and *Norm Ideals of Completely Continious Operators.* He died in New York, N.Y. Obituaries: *New York Times,* August 30, 1977.

* * *

SCHELL, Jonathan 1943-

PERSONAL: Born August 21, 1943, in New York, N.Y. *Office: New Yorker,* 25 West 43rd St., New York, N.Y. 10036.

CAREER: New Yorker, New York, N.Y., writer, 1968—.

WRITINGS: The Village of Ben Suc, Knopf, 1967; *The Military Half,* Knopf, 1969; *The Time of Illusion,* Knopf, 1976.

* * *

SCHEURING, Lyn 1937-

PERSONAL: Surname sounds like "sharing"; born November 11, 1937, in New York; daughter of Paul (a contractor) and Philomena (Bonavia) Falzon; married Thomas Scheuring (a campus minister), June 15, 1968; children: Maria Christi, Malissa Ann, Paul Thomas. *Education:* Attended Duquesne University and St. Vincent College, Latrobe, Pa., both 1964-66; Catholic University of America, B.A., 1968. *Religion:* Roman Catholic. *Home:* 129 Home Ave., Rutherford, N.J. 07070.

CAREER: Catholic Charities, Greensburg, Pa., case worker, 1962-66; elementary school teacher in South River, N.J., 1968-69; Office of Economic Opportunity, New York, N.Y., family worker for head-start program, 1969-70; Ignatius House Catholic Charismatic Christian Community, Rutherford, N.J., pastoral leader, 1972—.

WRITINGS: (With husband, Tom Scheuring) *Two for Joy,* Paulist/Newman, 1976. Contributor to *America, New Catholic World,* and *Catholic Charismatic.*

WORK IN PROGRESS: Research on married spirituality and "the call to adoption."

SIDELIGHTS: Lyn Scheuring writes: "We were inspired to encourage others in their search for God, especially married couples. We felt the urgency to break through the limits put on persons because they are married. In fact, we are convinced that a person is as limited as he or she or they together think they are."

BIOGRAPHICAL/CRITICAL SOURCES: Mary Cole, *Summer in the City,* Kenedy, 1968; *Our Sunday Visitor,*

1968; *Living Light,* Summer, 1970; Herb Walker, *God's Living Room,* Logos International, 1972.

* * *

SCHEURING, Tom 1942-

PERSONAL: Surname sounds like "sharing"; born May 23, 1942, in Minnesota; son of Joe A. (a grain elevator operator) and Dorothy (Garry) Scheuring; married Lyn Falzon (an evangelist), June 15, 1968; children: Maria Christi, Malissa Ann, Paul Thomas. *Education:* University of Notre Dame, student, 1960-61; St. Mary's College, Winona, Minn., B.A., 1964; Catholic University of America, M.A., 1967. *Religion:* Roman Catholic. *Home:* 129 Home Ave., Rutherford, N.J. 07070. *Office:* 72 West Passaic Ave., Rutherford, N.J. 07070.

CAREER: Marymount College, Arlington, Va., instructor in theology, 1967-68; principal of elementary school in South River, N.J., 1968-69; William H. Sadlier, Inc. (publisher), New York, N.Y., editor, 1969-70; religious education coordinator of Roman Catholic parish in Beacon, N.Y., 1971-72; Ignatius House Catholic Charismatic Community, Rutherford, N.J., pastoral leader, 1973—. Campus minister at Fairleigh Dickinson University, 1972-77.

WRITINGS: (With wife, Lyn Scheuring) *Two for Joy,* Paulist/Newman, 1976. Contributor to *Catholic Charismatic, America* and *New Catholic World.*

WORK IN PROGRESS: Research on holiness, married spirituality, and "the call to adoption."

SIDELIGHTS: Scheuring writes: "We feel a need to encourage others in their search for God, especially married couples. I experience my marriage as a very concrete way to experience God and grow in wholeness and holiness and want to help other couples, as well as single people, grow in their awareness of God's personal love and the joy-filled effect that can have on their life."

BIOGRAPHICAL/CRITICAL SOURCES: Mary Cole, *Summer in the City,* Kenedy, 1968; *Living Light,* Summer, 1970; Herb Walker, *God's Living Room,* Logos International, 1972.

* * *

SCHILLER, A. Arthur 1902-1977

September 7, 1902—July 10, 1977; American educator, authority on Roman law, and author. Schiller was a member of the Columbia University faculty of law for forty-three years. In addition to being a noted expert on Roman law, Schiller was also an authority on both Coptic law and Adat law. He founded the first Institute of African Law in the United States at Columbia University in 1965. Schiller was a worldwide lecturer on law and the author of several books on ancient and military law. He died in Oneonta, N.Y. Obituaries: *New York Times,* July 11, 1977. (See index for *CA* sketch)

* * *

SCHMALENBACH, Werner 1920-

PERSONAL: Born September 13, 1920, in Goettingen, Germany; son of Herman and Sala (Muentz) Schmalenbach; married Esther Grey, December 15, 1950; children: Peggy, Corinne. *Education:* Basel University, Prof. Dr., 1945. *Home address:* Poststrasse 17, 4005 Meerbusch 1, Germany. *Office:* Kunstsammlung Nordrhein-Westfalen Duesseldorf, Jacobistrasse 2, 4000 Duesseldorf, Germany.

CAREER: Gewerbemuseum Basel, Basel, Switzerland, curator, 1945-55; Kestner-Gesellschaft Hannover, Hannover, Germany, director, 1955-62; Kunstsammlung Nordrhein-Westfalen Duesseldorf, Duesseldorf, Germany, director, 1962—. *Member:* P.E.N., Association Internationale des Critiques d'Art.

WRITINGS: (With Peter Baechlin and George Schmidt) *Der Filmwirtschaftlich, gesellschaftlich, kuenstlerisch,* Holbein-Verlag, 1947, translation by Hugo Weber and Roger Manvell published as *The Film: Its Economic, Social and Artistic Problems,* Falcon Press, 1948; *Die Kunst Afrikas,* Holbein-Verlag, 1953, translation by Glyn T. Hughes published as *African Art,* Macmillan, 1954; *Adel des Pferdes: Kleiner Galopp durch die Kunstgeschichte,* 1959, translation by Daphne M. Goodall published as *The Noble Horse: A Journey Through the History of Art,* J. A. Allen, 1962; *Julius Bissier, farbige Miniaturen,* Piper, 1960; *Bissier,* Abrams, 1963; *Kurt Schwitters,* Verlag DuMont Schauberg, 1967, Abrams, 1970; (editor and author of introduction) *Die Kunstsammlung Nordrhein-Westfalen in Duesseldorf,* Verlag DuMont Schauberg, 1970, translation by Sarah Twohig published as *Picasso to Lichtenstein: Masterpieces of Twentieth-Century Art from This Nordrhein-Westfalen Collection in Duesseldorf,* Tate Gallery Publications, 1974; *Antoni Tapies: Zeichen und Strukturen,* Propylaeen-Verlag, 1974; *Fernand Leger,* Abrams, 1976.

WORK IN PROGRESS: Eduardo Chillida, Drawings.

* * *

SCHMELING, Gareth L(on) 1940-

PERSONAL: Born May 28, 1914, in Algoma, Wis.; son of Walter C. (a nurse) and Tabea (Braem) Schmeling; married Karen Weiss (a reading teacher), December 21, 1963. *Education:* Northwestern College, B.A., 1963; University of Wisconsin—Madison, M.A., 1964, Ph.D., 1968. *Politics:* Democrat. *Religion:* Lutheran. *Home:* 320 Northwest 30th St., Gainesville, Fla. 32607. *Office:* Department of Classics, University of Florida, Gainesville, Fla. 32611.

CAREER: University of Virginia, Charlottesville, assistant professor of Greek and Latin, 1968-70; University of Florida, Gainesville, associate professor, 1970-75, professor of Greek and Latin and chairman of department of classics, 1975—.

MEMBER: American Philological Association, American Classical League, Vergilian Society, Society for the Study of Classics (France), Classical Association of the Middle West and South. *Awards, honors:* American Philosophical Society grants, 1970, 1971, 1972, 1977; National Endowment for the Humanities fellowship, 1973-74; American Council of Learned Societies fellowship, 1974; Rome Prize from American Academy in Rome, Italy, 1977-78.

WRITINGS: (Contributor) *Fons Perennis* (title means "Eternal Fountain"), Baccola & Gili, 1971; (editor) Cornelius Nepos, *Lives of Famous Men,* Coronado, 1971; *Petronius' Satyricon,* Monarch, 1971; *Ovid's Art of Love,* Monarch, 1972; *Chariton,* Twayne, 1974; (with Johanna H. Stuckey) *A Bibliography of Petronius,* E. J. Brill, 1977; *Xenophon of Ephesus,* Twayne, in press. Contributor to classical studies and comparative literature journals.

WORK IN PROGRESS: Apollonius of Tyre, a book on early fiction and its use by the Christian church as propaganda, completion expected in 1980.

SIDELIGHTS: Schmeling writes: "Since both my wife and I are second-generation Americans with strong ties to German culture, art, architecture, and especially music, we have traveled extensively in Germany. One of the few remaining advantages in teaching is the long summer break, and we make use of this almost every year to travel. It is easy for us to visit Germany and avoid France. We have also lived for two years in Italy, and are now beginning to enjoy both the language and the opportunities to speak it.

"Travel in the United States usually takes us to Natchez, Charleston, or Savannah to enjoy the influences of Classical art and architecture. Since moving to the Old South in 1968 we have become hopeless Southerners. The books I have written and those I am now working on have all sprung from professional interest. In the future I hope to do at least one based on personal experiences in traveling."

* * *

SCHMIDT, William E. 1947-

PERSONAL: Born March 15, 1947, in Detroit, Mich.; son of Elmer Frederick and Irene Elsie (Shaver) Schmidt; married Margo Doble (a free-lance writer), November 4, 1972. *Education:* University of Michigan, B.A., 1967. *Religion:* Lutheran. *Home:* 11 Iran St., Dokki, Giza, Egypt. *Office:* 33 Kasr el Nil, 13-3, Cairo, Egypt.

CAREER/WRITINGS: Suffolk Sun, Deer Park, N.Y., reporter, 1968; *Detroit Free Press,* Detroit, Mich., reporter, 1969-73; *Newsweek,* New York, N.Y., correspondent in Chicago, 1973-74, bureau chief in Miami, Fla., 1974-76, Mideast bureau chief, 1976—. Notable assignments include campus dissent of Vietnam era, including Kent State, U.S. narcotics trafficking, tax investigation of Spiro Agnew, 1974 primary campaigns of George Wallace and Ronald Reagan, the war in Lebanon. *Member:* Cairo Foreign Press Association, Detroit Press Club. *Awards, honors:* Detroit Press Club awards, 1969 and 1973; George Polk Award, 1970, for team project on Kent State; Michigan United Press International award, 1972; Overseas Press Club Award, 1976, for reporting the war in Lebanon.

SIDELIGHTS: Schmidt told *CA:* "The greatest difficulty of work in the Middle East—like much of the developing world—is access to reliable information on which to base independent judgements. Reporting in the third world is often a bit like reading tea leaves."

* * *

SCHMITT, Albert R(ichard) 1929-

PERSONAL: Born October 17, 1929, in Mannheim, Germany; son of Albert and Barbara (Mueller) Schmitt; married Barbara L. Gifford (a secretary), May 29, 1954; children: three. *Education:* Colby College, B.A., 1955; University of Pennsylvania, M.A., 1957, Ph.D., 1962. *Office:* Department of German, Brown University, Providence, R.I. 02912.

CAREER: University of Pennsylvania, Philadelphia, instructor, 1961-64, assistant professor of German, 1964-66; University of Colorado, Boulder, associate professor of German, 1966-69; Brown University, Providence, R.I., associate professor, 1969-71, professor of German, 1971—. *Member:* Modern Language Association of America, American Association of Teachers of German, American Association of University Professors, Lessing Society, Goethe-Gesellschaft. *Awards, honors:* M.A., Brown University, 1970; recipient of summer research grants from Deutsche Akademie Austauschdienst (DAAD).

WRITINGS: Catalog of the Programmschriften Collec- tion: *University of Pennsylvania,* G. K. Hall, 1961; *Herder und Amerika,* Mouton, 1967; (with Albert L. Lloyd) *Deutsch und Deutschland Heute* (title means "German and Germany Today"), Van Nostrand, 1967; (editor) Siegfried Lenz, *Zeit der Schuldlosen* (title means "The Innocent—The Guilty"), Appleton, 1967; (editor) *Des Melchior Adam Pastorius Leben und Reisebeschreibungen* (title means "M. A. Pastorius: His Life and Travels"), Delp, 1968; (editor) *Festschrift fuer Detlev W. Schumann,* Delp, 1970; (editor) *Johann Carl Wezel: Kritische Schriften* (title means "J. C. Wezel: Critical Writings"), three volumes, Metzler, 1971-75. Contributor to professional journals.

WORK IN PROGRESS: C. M. Wieland as Literary Critic, 1768-1780; translating a text by Siegfried Lenz; research on German-American literary relations.

* * *

SCHNEIDER, Hans J(uergen) 1935-

PERSONAL: Born April 25, 1935, in Breslau, Germany; came to United States in 1958; permanent U.S. resident; son of Alfred (an industrialist) and Marga (an artist; maiden name, Henkel) Schneider; married Inger Marie Korneliussen (a home economist and lecturer), October 7, 1967; children: Roy, Tom, Helen, Josef John, Rose Sharon. *Education:* Attended commercial trade schools in Germany, 1953-57; Flying School (Bremen, Germany), pilot certificate, 1956; attended sea navigation school in Germany, 1956-57. *Religion:* "Non-denominational, non-affiliated, Bible-reading Christian." *Home and office address:* P.O. Box 105, Ashland, Ore. 97520.

CAREER: Hermann Dauelsberg, Schiffsmakler (a ship broker), Bremen, Germany, apprentice, 1955-57; Schilling & Klett (textile wholesale company), Bielefeld, Germany, foreign representative, 1957-58; Friebe Acro-Accessories, Heidelberg, Germany, export manager, 1958; Schenkers, International Forwarders, Inc., New York City, assistant to import manager, 1958-59; partner in import-export firm, Gerama Buyers Representatives, 1959; Lansen-Naeve Corp. (import-export company), New York City, manager in air freight department, 1959-60; Cosmos Shipping Corp., New Orleans, La., assistant to vice president, 1961; World Wide Evangelism, San Diego, Calif., Salem, Ore., and Ashland, Ore., director, 1961—. President of World Wide Publishing Corp., 1977—. World traveler, private pilot, international lecturer, and consultant. *Awards, honors:* Ph.D. from Laurence University (Sarasota, Fla.).

WRITINGS: Masters of Legalized Confusion and Their Puppets, privately printed, 1968; *Timely and Profitable Help for Troubled Americans,* Hawkes, 1976, 2nd enlarged and revised edition, World Wide Publishing, 1977; *Flying to Be Free,* World Wide Publishing, 1978.

WORK IN PROGRESS: My Life Story.

SIDELIGHTS: Schneider writes: "Hard years under two dictatorships and a complete economic crash generated in me a strong spirit for freedom and liberty which I like to see perpetuated in the United States. However I see many of the mistakes of past empires being repeated in America with catastrophic results.

"I therefore advocate a simpler, less complicated lifestyle, which is not so involved with the intricacies of civilization. The loss of all material gadgets showed us the vanity of striving solely for material things. My father turned from a former multimillionaire into a pauper overnight when World War II ended.

"I now live and write at our mountain ranch, thirty-three miles from the closest town—a good place to raise my children. It is also what my wife and I have been wanting for a long time—to get back to a self-sufficient way of life and educate our children. We have a large organic garden, fruit trees, some goats, and chickens. Our closest neighbor is about two miles away.

"I am sad to see so many people eking out a dull, miserable existence, wasting their time and energies in worthless endeavors when life can be such an exciting, worthwhile experience. My career exemplifies this and I draw on it to lead others into a more challenging direction. I am generally serious minded but very happy in idealistic areas. I have interests along many lines and spend much time in research and field study in different subjects, which helps in my vocation as a free-lance writer.

"I like to utilize and expound the things I have learned in an intense life and during my global travels (about one hundred countries) to help Americans and people of other nations. I strongly advocate living with the natives when visiting foreign lands in order to understand them better. This is also the more enjoyable way to tour the world. My studies included the main religions of mankind as well as five languages. This enables me to converse with people of other cultures more intelligently about their deeper motivations."

AVOCATIONAL INTERESTS: Flying small aircraft, swimming, sailing, hiking in the mountains, good music.

* * *

SCHNEIDER, Isidor 1896-1977

August 25, 1896—August 3, 1977; Ukrainian-born American writer. Although Schneider was known as a left-wing poet and novelist, he admitted that his bourgeois emotions tainted his proletarian poetry. His literary criticism appeared in such periodicals as *New Republic* and *Nation.* He died in New York, N.Y. Obituaries: *New York Times,* August 6, 1977; *AB Bookman's Weekly,* October 17, 1977. (See index for *CA* sketch)

* * *

SCHNESSEL, S. Michael 1947-

PERSONAL: Born April 7, 1947, in Hof, West Germany; came to the United States in 1950, naturalized citizen, 1956; son of Samuel and Gertrude Bertha (Arndt) Schnessel. *Education:* Baltimore Junior College, A.A., 1966; Syracuse University, B.A.J., 1968. *Politics:* "To the left, within reason." *Religion:* "Never touch the stuff." *Residence:* Princeton, N.J. *Office:* P.O. Box 2057, Princeton, N.J. 08540.

CAREER: Robert Rusting Associates (public relations firm), New York, N.Y., account executive, 1969-74; New Jersey State Council on the Arts, Trenton, N.J., public relations director, 1974-75; *Trentonian,* Trenton, art and theater critic, 1975—. President of Exhumation (gallery for antique posters). Active in community theater, as performer and executive.

WRITINGS: A Collector's Guide to Louis Icart, Exhumation, 1973; *Icart,* C. N. Potter, 1976; *Jesse Willcox Smith,* Crowell, 1977. Contributor to journals on antiques and art, and to popular magazines and newspapers, including *Good Housekeeping* and *TV Guide.*

WORK IN PROGRESS: Mr. K. Comes to Ergo, a novel; *Edward Penfield; Eric.*

SCHOEFFLER, Oscar E(dmund) 1899-

PERSONAL: Born March 5, 1899, in Alton, Ill.; son of John W. and Louise L. Schoeffler; married Helen D. Dwight; children: Dwight, John W., Edmund H. (deceased). *Education:* Attended University of Illinois, 1918-20; Columbia University, B.S., 1922. *Politics:* Republican. *Home:* 199 Whispering Sands Dr., Sarasota, Fla. 33581.

CAREER: Fairchild Publications, New York City, reporter, 1923-38; *Esquire,* New York City, fashion editor, 1939-57, fashion director and vice-president, 1957-71; writer, 1971—.

WRITINGS: (With William Gale) *Esquire's Encyclopedia of Twentieth Century Men's Fashions,* McGraw, 1973.

* * *

SCHOFIELD, Sylvia Anne 1918-
(Max Mundy, Sylvia A. Matheson)

PERSONAL: Born May 28, 1918, in London, England; daughter of William Horace (a surveyor and architect) and Anne (a writer and lecturer; maiden name, Terry) Terry-Smith; married Angus Matheson, December, 1941 (divorced, 1951); married Henry Beaumont Schofield (an engineer), August 15, 1956. *Education:* Attended Institute of Archaeology, London, and University of Tehran. *Home:* Casa Beaumont, VA. TS. 60, Javea, Alicante, Spain. *Office:* c/o Vetco International A.G., 350 N. Roosevelt Ave., Tehran, Iran.

CAREER: J. Walter Thompson Co., Bombay, India and London, England, member of staff, 1948-56; guest lecturer on archaeological tours in Iran, Afghanistan, India, Pakistan, and Ceylon; writer. *Member:* Crime Writers Association, Royal Geographic Society, Royal Central Asia Society, Institute of Archaeology (London), British Institute of Persian Studies, Asociacion Ibero Latino-Americana (Tehran), International Press Club.

WRITINGS–Under name Sylvia A. Matheson: *Time Off to Dig,* Odhams, 1961; *The Tigers of Baluchistan,* Arthur Barker, 1967.

Under pseudonym Max Mundy: *Death Is a Tiger* (mystery novel), John Long, 1960; *Dig for a Corpse* (mystery novel), John Long, 1962; *Pagan Pagoda* (mystery novel), John Long, 1965; *Death Cries Ole* (mystery novel), John Long, 1968.

Contributor of articles to periodicals, including *International History, Venture, Geographical Magazine,* and *London Times.* Contributor of short stories, under pseudonym Max Mundy, to *John Creasley's Mystery Bedside Books.*

WORK IN PROGRESS: The Persian Pomegranate, tentative title; *Leathercraft in Ancient Iran; The Pleasures of Persia.*

SIDELIGHTS: "Since childhood," Schofield told *CA,* "I have had an increasing passion for Indian culture, later to include Asia generally. Ancient history, archaeology, anthropology are of particular interest, developing during the past thirty years spent living in India, Burma, Pakistan, Afghanistan, and, for the past eleven years, Iran. I mainly travel alone, using local tranportation, into formerly little-known parts of Baluchistan, the frontier area between present-day Pakistan and Afghanistan, much of Afghanistan itself, and the more remote parts of Iran. I can make myself understood in Urdu, Farsi, Burmese, French, Italian and Spanish, as well as my native English."

SCHOOLER, (Seward) Dean, Jr. 1941-

PERSONAL: Born August 20, 1941, in Coshocton, Ohio; son of Seward Dean (a banker) and Edith (Gardner) Schooler; married Vicki Henderson (an elementary school teacher), January 16, 1950; children: Heather, Matthew. *Education:* Wesleyan University, B.A., 1963; Ohio State University, M.A., 1965, Ph.D., 1969. *Religion:* United Methodist. *Home:* 636 Peakview Rd., Boulder, Colo. 80302. *Office:* Development Center, P.O. Box 2365, Boulder, Colo. 80306.

CAREER: Capital University, Columbus, Ohio, lecturer in political science, 1965-66; University of Arizona, Tucson, assistant professor of government and associate research director of Institute of Government Research, 1968-74; Piney Woods School, Piney Woods, Miss., director of development, 1975-76; Development Center, Boulder, Colo., director, 1976—. Lecturer at Institute of Social Studies (The Hague), 1970, Colorado State University, and University of Colorado at Denver.

MEMBER: American Political Science Association, American Society for Public Administration, Policy Studies Organization, Association for Humanistic Psychology, National Society of Fund-Raisers. *Awards, honors:* Fulbright Advanced Research Scholar in the Netherlands, 1970-71; National Science Foundation grant, 1974.

WRITINGS: Science, Scientists, and Public Policy, Free Press, 1971; (contributor) S. L. Kwee and J. Mullender, editors, *Growing Against Ourselves: The Energy-Environment Tangle,* Lexington Books, 1972; (with Louise J. Dengler) *Science and the Bicentennial,* Institute of Government Research, University of Arizona, 1973. Contributor to professional journals and *Journal of Irreproducible Results.*

WORK IN PROGRESS: An Alternative Process of Land Use Decision-Making: Running Creek Area, Colorado; A Humanistic Approach to the Fund-Raising Process; Citizens and Legislators Attitudes on Policy in Colorado.

AVOCATIONAL INTERESTS: Hiking, fishing, tennis, poetry, creative arts.

* * *

SCHOONMAKER, Ann 1928-
(Ann S. Boyd)

PERSONAL: Born May 14, 1928, in Kalamazoo, Mich.; daughter of Carl B. (in advertising) and Doris (a secretary; maiden name, Newell) Schoonmaker; married Richard C. Boyd, July 3, 1949 (divorced January 3, 1973); children: Nancy, Janet Boyd Gray, John, Laura. *Education:* University of Michigan, B.A., 1949; Drew University, M.R.E., 1965, Ph.D., 1976; American Foundation of Religion and Psychiatry (now Institutes of Religion and Health), certificate, 1972. *Politics:* Independent. *Religion:* Baha'i. *Residence:* Summit, N.J. *Agent:* Donald Cutler, Sterling Lord Agency, Inc., 660 Madison Ave., New York, N.Y. 10021. *Office:* Center for Counseling and Human Development, 33 South Ave. W., Cranford, N.J. 07016.

CAREER: Junior high school teacher of English and social studies in Livingston, N.J., 1949-51; director of religious education at Methodist church in New Providence, N.J., 1964-66; Institutes of Religion and Health, New York, N.Y., therapist, 1972; Plainfield Consultation Center, Plainfield, N.J., marriage counselor and therapist, 1972-73; Center for Counseling and Human Development, Cranford, N.J., staff therapist and coordinator of educational services, 1975—. *Member:* American Association of Marriage Counselors, American Academy of Religion.

WRITINGS: (Under name Ann S. Boyd) *The Devil with James Bond!,* John Knox, 1967; *Me, Myself, and I: Every Woman's Journey to Her Self,* Harper, 1977.

WORK IN PROGRESS: Three novels; books on the phenomenon of travel, psychotherapeutic trends, and the evolution of consciousness.

SIDELIGHTS: Ann Schoonmaker comments: "My main interest is in the stages of the development of consciousness, both in individuals and history. Recent travels to Hong Kong, Israel, Greece, and India are providing the main background for my current projects."

* * *

SCHOR, Lynda 1938-

PERSONAL: Born April 18, 1938, in Brooklyn, N.Y.; daughter of Louis and Julia (Schleifer) Nyfield; children: Alexandra, Timothy, Zachary. *Education:* Cooper Union, B.F.A., 1959; graduate study at New School for Social Research. *Politics:* Feminist and Socialist. *Home and office:* 463 West St., New York, N.Y. 10014. *Agent:* Elaine Markson, 44 Greenwich Ave., New York, N.Y. 10014.

CAREER: Worked as a painter, graphic artist, and textile colorist and designer, made waxes for cast jewelry, and sold crocheted clothing, wallhangings, and other crafts, 1962-71; writer, 1972—. Literary artist with Cultural Council Federation, New York City, 1978—. Fellow at Cummington Community of the Arts, 1973; instructor in English, Pratt Institute, 1974-75; instructor at Womanschool, 1975-76; guest lecturer and reader of own works on radio and at colleges. Fiction juror for literary grant from Maryland Arts Council, 1978. *Member:* P.E.N., Literary Guild, Poets & Writers. *Awards, honors:* Mellon Foundation grant, 1976.

WRITINGS: Appetites (short fiction), Warner Books, 1975. Contributor of numerous stories, articles, and reviews to periodicals, including *Ms., Village Voice, Viva,* and *Redbook.* Work represented in anthologies, including *Bitches and Sad Ladies,* edited by Pat Rotter, Harper's, 1974, *On the Job,* Vintage, 1977, and *Redbook's Famous Fiction,* 1977.

WORK IN PROGRESS: A book of short fiction, *True Love and Real Romance;* two novels, *Phantom Fetus* and *Take a Ride on the Phantom Subway;* a screenplay; short stories.

SIDELIGHTS: "I want to be as vivid, intense, original, and revolutionary as I can be!" Schor told *CA.* "I'm struggling to lead a full life as a mother, writer, and living person without having to choose between them. I hope I make it."

The theme of most of the stories in Schor's book *Appetites* is "superficially, the exploitation of women and the stratagems women devise to ward off or despairingly accommodate exploitation," wrote Lynne Sharon Schwartz. But while the theme Schor explores is common, the stories themselves are not.

The stories are related in their depiction of appetite and fantasy, Schwartz noted. Carole Rosenthal found the stories to be "brilliant." She continued: "*Appetites* pushes the boundaries of conventional good taste, but it also presses the frontiers of the short story form in important new ways, sprawling inventively. The ironies of everyday life become magnified. They begin to clank and rattle like ghosts chained to an unconscious part, groaning of lust and loneliness, comically exaggerated, absurd." And Schwartz commented: "Schor is intelligent, witty, and immensely gifted. She has that quality indispensable to any good writer: the courage to take risks in the pursuit of emotional truth, the courage to go too far rather than not far enough.''

BIOGRAPHICAL/CRITICAL SOURCES: Village Voice, December 11, 1975; Ms., January, 1976.

* * *

SCHORER, Mark 1908-1977

May 17, 1908—August 11, 1977; American novelist, literary critic, biographer, and educator. Schorer was famous for his extensive biography, Sinclair Lewis: An American Life. He was a former chairman of the English department at the University of California, Berkeley. Schorer often reviewed contemporary novels for the New York Times Book Review. He died in Oakland, Calif. Obituaries: New York Times, August 18, 1977; Newsweek, August 29, 1977; Time, August 29, 1977; AB Bookman's Weekly, October 17, 1977. (See index for CA sketch)

* * *

SCHROEDER, Mary 1903-

PERSONAL: Born May 13, 1903, in Sale, Cheshire, England; daughter of William Lawrence (a clergyman) and Katherine (Farquer) Schroeder. Education: Girton College, Cambridge, M.A., 1925; University of Bordeaux, graduate study, 1925-26; University of Leeds, Diploma in Education, 1927; Columbia University, B.Sc., 1935. Home and office: Alnwick College, Alnwick, Northumberland, England.

CAREER: Badminton School, Bristol, England, history mistress, 1927-31, 1932-33; exchange teacher, Seattle, Wash., 1931-32; Yorkshire Post and Leeds Mercury, Leeds, Yorkshire, England, reporter, 1935-39; Girls' County School, Bishop Auckland, England, history and English teacher, 1940-42; Southlands College, London, England, lecturer in English and history, 1942-49; Homerton College, Cambridge, England, senior lecturer in English, 1950-51; Alnwick College, Alnwick, Northumberland, England, senior lecturer in English, 1951—. Member: National Union of Teachers, Association of Teachers in Colleges and Departments of Education, English-Speaking Union, British Federation of University Women.

WRITINGS—History courses for children, with accompanying reference books for teachers; all published by Chatto & Windus: Look at the Past, 1950; Man's Forward March, 1956; Family Tree, 1960; The Storyteller, 1968.

Other juveniles: My Horse Says, 1963, Coward, 1965; The Hunted Prince, Coward, 1969; Hey Robin Hide!, Kaye & Ward, 1974; By Winding Water, Kaye & Ward, 1976.

SIDELIGHTS: Mary Schroeder's stories in her historical series are mostly from sources in Cambridge University Library.*

* * *

SCHULTE, Elaine L(ouise) 1934-
(Elaine L. Young)

PERSONAL: Born November 18, 1934, in Indiana; daughter of Dietrich and Louise (Matthew) Young; married Frank L. Schulte (a business executive and photographer), October 1, 1955; children: Gregory L., Richard M. Education: Purdue University, B.S., 1956. Home address: P.O. Box 746, Rancho Santa Fe, Calif. 92067. Agent: Ruth Cantor, 156 Fifth Ave., New York, N.Y. 10010.

CAREER: J. Walter Thompson (advertising agency), Los Angeles, Calif., member of staff, 1956-57; writer, 1957—.

Lecturer at California community colleges. Member: National League of Pen Women, Alpha Chi Omega.

WRITINGS: Zack and the Magic Factory (juvenile novel), Thomas Nelson, 1976. Contributor of articles, stories, and poems to national and foreign magazines, sometimes under name Elaine L. Young.

WORK IN PROGRESS: A juvenile novel; several juvenile biographies; research and travel in Bryce, Zion, and Grand Canyon National Parks; research on movie concepts.

SIDELIGHTS: Elaine Schulte remarks: ''I lived in Belgium for three years and traveled extensively throughout Europe and Africa. I am interested in archeological sites such as I explored in Turkey and Greece and hope to write about them soon. I am especially interested in history and enjoy making it more interesting so that we might benefit from both errors and what was done well in the past. I have published pieces about Southwestern archeological sites such as Mesa Verde and hope to publish more about them.''

* * *

SCHULTZ, Morton J(oel) 1930-

PERSONAL: Born October 13, 1930, in New York, N.Y.; son of William J. and Dorothy (Meyers) Schultz; married Janice Peck, June 15, 1952; children: Howard, Steven. Education: Rutgers University, B.Letters, 1952, M.A., 1962. Home and office: 6755 West Broward Blvd., Apt. 403A, Plantation, Fla. 33317.

CAREER: U.S. Department of the Army, Edison, N.J., civilian magazine editor, 1954-58; Lockheed Electronics Co., Plainfield, N.J., public relations representative, 1958-63; free-lance writer, 1963—. Military service: U.S. Army, Infantry, 1952-54; became first lieutenant. Member: American Society of Journalists and Authors, National Association of Home Workshop Writers.

WRITINGS: Photographic Reproduction, McGraw, 1963; The Teacher and Overhead Projection, Prentice-Hall, 1965; Teaching Ideas That Make Teaching Fun, Parker & Son, 1969; Practical Handbook of Painting and Wallpapering, Fawcett, 1969; How to Fix It, McGraw, 1971; A Thousand One Questions and Answers About Your Car, McGraw, 1973; Popular Mechanics Complete Car Repair Manual, Hearst Books, 1975; Popular Mechanics Complete Appliance Repair Manual, Hearst Books, 1975.

Contributor of articles to Popular Mechanics, Family Circle, Reader's Digest, Argosy, Popular Science, and others.

WORK IN PROGRESS: McGraw-Hill Illustrated Auto Repair Course.

SIDELIGHTS: Morton Schultz wrote to CA: ''I came to specialize in the field of car repair by having been associated with automobiles practically since day one. My family operated auto sales agencies until Pearl Harbor Day and after V-J Day, and as I was growing up I became experienced in auto mechanics and auto sales. However, cars are by no means my only interest. For example, I write books and magazine articles on home repair and boating, because I am interested in both subjects and I realize that they are important to many people. My background in auto mechanics has made the mastery of home and boat mechanics relatively easy.

''Other subjects that interest me enough to research them thoroughly so I can write about them include aviation, energy, science, technology, and the military.''

SCHULZ, Ernst B(ernhard)   1896-

PERSONAL: Born November 1, 1896, in Cleveland, Ohio; son of Ernst Paul (an artist) and Agnes (Krause) Schulz; married Catherine Lillie, June 21, 1921; children: Robert E., Constance E. (Mrs. Leonard P. Suffredini), Dorothy A. (Mrs. Robert F. McCarty), Mary A. (Mrs. Leverne Sharrer). *Education:* Case Institute of Technology (now Case Western Reserve University), student, 1915-18; University of Michigan, B.S., 1920, M.A., 1921, Ph.D., 1927. *Politics:* Independent. *Religion:* None. *Address:* Box 62, R.D. 1, Coopersburg, Pa. 18036.

CAREER: Instructor at University of Cincinnati, Cincinnati, Ohio, 1922-23, and University of Michigan, Ann Arbor, 1924-27; Lehigh University, Bethlehem, Pa., assistant professor, 1927-31, associate professor, 1931-45, professor of political science, 1945-65, professor emeritus, 1965—. *Member:* National Municipal League, Tau Beta Pi, Kappa Sigma.

WRITINGS: Government: A Phase of Social Organization, Lehigh University Institute of Research, 1929; (with W. L. Godshall) *Principles and Functions of Government in the United States,* Van Nostrand, 1948; *American City Government,* Stackpole, 1949; *Essentials of Government,* Prentice-Hall, 1958; *Democracy,* Barron's, 1966; *Essentials of American Government,* Barron's, 1969, 4th edition, 1975. Contributor to legal and other professional journals.

*   *   *

SCHUMACHER, Ernest Friedrich   1911(?)-1977

1911(?)—September 4, 1977; German-born British economist and author of works in his field. Schumacher's writings often emphasized the importance of small-scale technology. He wrote *Small is Beautiful.* Schumacher died in Zurich, Switzerland. Obituaries: *New York Times,* September 6, 1977; *Washington Post,* September 7, 1977; *Newsweek,* September 19, 1977; *Time,* September 19, 1977; *AB Bookman's Weekly,* November 21, 1977.

*   *   *

SCHUON, Frithjof   1907-

PERSONAL: Born June 18, 1907, in Basle, Switzerland; son of Paul Ludwig (a concert violinist) and Margarethe (Boehler) Schuon; married Catherine Feer (a painter), May 7, 1949. *Education:* Private study in philosophy, comparative religion, and Arabic. *Agent:* c/o Perennial Books Ltd., Pates Manor, Hatton Road, Bedfont, Middlesex TW14 8JP England.

CAREER: Writer, 1934—. Art designer of printed textiles and painter of American Indian subjects.

WRITINGS: Leitgedanken zur Urbesinnung (philosophy; title means "Guidelines for Primordial Meditation"), Orell Fuessli Verlag, 1935; *Tage-und Naechtebuch* (poems; title means "Book of Days and of Nights"), Urs-Graf Verlag, 1947; *Sulamith* (poems), Urs-Graf Verlag, 1947; *De l'Unite transcendante des Religions,* Gallimard, 1948, translation by Peter Townsend published as *The Transcendent Unity of Religions,* Faber, 1953, revised edition, Harper, 1975; *Perspectives Spirituelles et Faits humains,* Les Cahiers du Sud, 1953, translation by Macleod Matheson published as *Spiritual Perspectives and Human Facts,* Faber, 1954; *Sentiers de Gnose,* La Colombe, 1957, translation by G. E. H. Palmer published as *Gnosis: Divine Wisdom,* J. Murray, 1959; *Les Stations de la Sagesse,* Buchet-Chastel, 1958, translation by G. E. H. Palmer published as *Stations of*

Wisdom, J. Murray, 1961; *Language of the Self,* Ganesh, 1959.

Comprendre l'Islam, Gallimard, 1961, translation by Macleod Matheson published as *Understanding Islam,* Allen & Unwin, 1963; *Light on the Ancient World,* Perennial Books Ltd., 1965; *In the Tracks of Buddhism,* Allen & Unwin, 1968; *Dimensions of Islam,* Allen & Unwin, 1970; *Logique et Transcendance,* Editions Traditionnelles, 1972, translation by P. Townsend published as *Logic and Transcendence,* Harper, 1975; *Islam and the Perennial Philosophy,* World of Islam Festival Publishing, 1976; *L'Esoterisme comme Principe et Voie,* Derry-Livres, 1978.

Anthologized in *The Sword of Gnosis,* Penguin, 1974. Contributor to *Studies in Comparative Religion, Etudes Traditionelles,* and *Sophia Perennis.*

SIDELIGHTS: Born a German, Schuon writes that he had to adopt French nationality after Alsace became French. After World War II he became a Swiss citizen.

After studying Islamic esoterism in Algeria and Morocco, he became closely associated with the Algerian Shaykh and Sufi Ahmad Al-Allawi.

Although he has been associated with *Etudes Traditionelles* since 1933, Schuon maintains that he has kept "an independent outlook in many respects, except as regards the main subject of traditional orthodoxy." He has spent much time in North Africa (including Egypt), Turkey, India, and the western United States.

Schuon writes: "From early youth, I was interested above all in religious and metaphysical questions, and fascinated by the problem of the esoteric unity of religions. But I am also an artist and have always been interested in aesthetic matters; my message is not only a metaphysical one, but aesthetic, artistic, moral, and cultural as well.

"I have always taken a keen interest in American Indians and in preserving American Indian religion and culture. I have been adopted by Chief Red Cloud (grandson of the famous Oglala chief) as his brother, with the name Wambli Ohitika (Brave Eagle). I was solemnly adopted by the Sioux Tribe, with the name Wichahpi Wiyakpa (Bright Star)."

*   *   *

SCHUTZ, Anton Friedrich Joseph   1894-1977

April 19, 1894—October 6, 1977; German-born American etcher and author. Schutz published a collection of etchings, *New York in Etchings,* and later wrote his autobiography, *My Share of Wine.* He died in New York, N.Y. Obituaries: *New York Times,* October 7, 1977.

*   *   *

SCHUYLER, George Samuel   1895-1977

February 25, 1895—August 31, 1977; American author and journalist. Schuyler was best known for his conservative stance regarding racial issues. He wrote the satirical *Black No More,* in which blacks are turned white by using a cream. He died in New York, N.Y. Obituaries: *New York Times,* September 7, 1977; *Washington Post,* September 9, 1977; *AB Bookman's Weekly,* November 21, 1977.

*   *   *

SCHWARTZ, Charles

PERSONAL: Born in New York, N.Y.; son of Hyman and Millie (Morros) Schwartz. *Education:* Earned B.A. from Brooklyn College of the City University of New York; New

York University, M.A., 1965, and Ph.D., 1969; private study of composition with Arthur Berger, Roger Sessions, Jacques Ibert, Aaron Copland, Darius Milhaud, and Charles Jones. *Home:* 463 West St., G-219, New York, N.Y. 10014.

CAREER: Free-lance orchestrator and performer (on trumpet), 1950-68; Queens College of the City University of New York, Flushing, N.Y., assistant professor of music, 1967-71; Hunter College of the City University of New York, New York, N.Y., 1972—, began as associate professor, became professor of music. Director of "Composers Showcase" (concert series at Whitney Museum of American Art), 1957—, and "Jazz Profiles," 1958-65. Instructor at New York University, 1969. Commissioned by New York State Council on the Arts to write "Riffs" for Boston Symphony Orchestra and jazz trumpeter Clark Terry, 1973.

MEMBER: American Musicological Society, Authors Guild of Authors League of America, American Society of University Composers, American Association of University Professors, National Association for American Composers and Conductors, American Music Center. *Awards, honors:* MacDowell Colony fellow, 1968.

WRITINGS: Gershwin: His Life and Music (introduction by Leonard Bernstein), Bobbs-Merrill, 1973; *George Gershwin: A Selective Bibliography and Discography,* Information Coordinators, 1974; *Cole Porter: A Biography* (Movie Book Club selection), Dial, 1977.

Compositions: "Comments," Carl Fischer; "Motion," Carl Fischer; "Passacaglia for Orchestra," Carl Fischer; "For Coughers, Sneezers and Snorers." Contributor to *Dictionary of Contemporary Music* and *Grove's Dictionary of Music and Musicians.*

WORK IN PROGRESS: "Mother. . ., Mother. . .," a jazz symphony, for Clark Terry and Zoot Sims.

SIDELIGHTS: Schwartz' jazz symphony, "Professor Jive," has been recorded by Clark Terry and "Collage."

* * *

SCHWARTZMAN, Edward 1927-

PERSONAL: Born December 31, 1927, in New York, N.Y.; son of Isidore (a hatter) and Tillie (Schneider) Schwartzman; married Robin G. Berman (an attorney), May 22, 1971. *Education:* City College (now of the City University of New York), B.S.S., 1949; New York University, M.P.A., 1961. *Politics:* Liberal Democrat. *Religion:* Jewish. *Home:* 333 West 57th St., New York, N.Y. 10019.

CAREER: New York City Planning Department, New York City, principal (urban) planner, 1959-68; New York State Office of Planning Services, New York City, principal planner (planning economist), 1968-75; New York City Off Track Betting Corp., New York City, executive director of corporate development. 1975—. Member of local Citizens Housing and Planning Council. Political campaign consultant in New York and Connecticut. *Military service:* U.S. Army, Corps of Engineers, 1951-52; served in Korea. *Member:* American Society of Planning Officials, American Society of Public Administration, Corporate Planning Society.

WRITINGS: Campaign Craftsmanship: A Professional's Guide to Political Campaigning, Universe Books, 1973.

WORK IN PROGRESS: Research on standards in government: the roles of the judiciary, citizens' groups, political organizations, and legislators in the implementation of standards.

SIDELIGHTS: Schwartzman comments that his goal is "to allow the public to perceive the real options available to public men—to government officials, etc.—and to perceive the limits of leadership."

* * *

SCOTT, J(ohn) Irving E(lias)

PERSONAL: Born in Jamaica, West Indies; came to United States in 1920, naturalized in 1932; son of Joseph (a salesman) and Harriet (Dawkins) Scott; married Helen R. Timms (a teacher); children: Irvlen E., John Irving Elias, Jr. *Education:* Lincoln University, Lincoln University, Pa., A.B., 1927; Wittenberg University, A.M., 1937; University of Pittsburgh, Ph.D., 1942. *Religion:* Baptist. *Home:* 7236 Richardson Rd., Jacksonville, Fla. 32209. *Office:* 2307 Myrtle Ave., Jacksonville, Fla. 32209.

CAREER: Florida Memorial College, St. Augustine, dean, 1927-28; principal of schools in Jacksonville, Fla., 1929-44; Wiley College, Marshall, Tex., dean, 1944-48; Alcorn Agricultural and Mechanical College, Lorman, Miss., dean of instruction, 1948-50; South Carolina State College, Orangeburg, professor of education in graduate school and director of extension service, 1950-53; director of Negro education, Jacksonville and Duval County, Fla., 1953-60; assistant director of education, Duval County, Fla., 1960-65, and director of special services in education, 1965—. Has worked widely in summer extension programs of other southern colleges. President of Citizens Investment Corp. *Member:* National Education Association, Florida Education Association, Alpha Kappa Mu, Phi Beta Sigma, Beta Kappa Chi.

WRITINGS: Living With Others, Meador, 1939; *Finding My Way,* Meador, 1949; *Negro Students and Their Colleges,* Meador, 1949; *Getting the Most Out of High School,* Oceana, 1957, revised edition, 1967; *The Education of Black People in Florida,* Dorrance, 1974. Contributor to education journals. Editor, *Negro Educational Review,* beginning 1950.

* * *

SCUDDER, Kenyon J. 1890-1977

1890—September 26, 1977; American criminologist and author of works in his field. Scudder blamed much of crime on the lack of attention paid to juvenile law-breakers. He wrote *The Twenty Billion Dollar Challenge: A National Program for Delinquency Prevention.* He died in Laguna Hills, Calif. Obituaries: *New York Times,* September 29, 1977.

* * *

SEAGLE, William 1898-1977

January 14, 1898—December 31, 1977; American attorney and writer of books on law. Seagle was a trial examiner for the National Labor Relations Board for many years and senior attorney with the Petroleum Board. He died in Washington, D.C. Obituaries: *New York Times,* January 2, 1978. (See index for *CA* sketch)

* * *

SEAGROATT, Margaret 1920-

PERSONAL: Born February 29, 1920, in Gillingham, Kent, England; daughter of Harold Frank (a chief petty officer in Royal Navy) and Wilhelmina (a civil servant; maiden name, Mackenzie) Vigar; married Edgar Howard Seagroatt (a lecturer in library science), July 9, 1942; children: Ann (Mrs.

Willy Russell), Alastair, Andrew. *Education:* Attended Hammersmith College of Art and Liverpool College of Art, 1952-55; Bolton College of Education, teaching certificate, 1976. *Politics:* "Whatever supports the underprivileged." *Religion:* "Humanitarian." *Home:* 2 Staplands Rd., Liverpool L14 3LL, England. *Office:* Mabel Fletcher Technical College, Sandown Rd., Liverpool L15 4JB, England.

CAREER: Librarian in Thurrock, Fulham, and Leicester, England, 1936-45; National Book League, London, England, researcher, 1945-46; Liverpool College of Art, Liverpool, England, part-time lecturer in weaving, 1956; Bootle School of Art, Bootle, England, part-time lecturer in weaving, 1958-59; Laird School of Art, Birkenhead, England, part-time lecturer in weaving, 1960-68; Kirkby Fields College of Education, Kirkby, England, lecturer in weaving, 1966-72; Mabel Fletcher Technical College, Liverpool, England, lecturer in industrial therapy, 1972—. Part-time lecturer at other schools. Owner of Mersey Yarns. Work has been represented in museums and galleries.

MEMBER: National Association of Teachers in Further Education, National Society for Art Education, National Geographic Society, Cheshire Guild of Weavers (Education), Bluecoat Display Centre, Friends of Liverpool Museums, Embroiderers Guild, British Crafts Center.

WRITINGS: Coptic Weaves, City of Liverpool Museums, 1965, revised edition, Merseyside County Museums, in press; *Rugweaving for Beginners,* Studio Vista, 1971, Watson-Guptill, 1972; (contributor) *Handicrafts,* Volume VI, Octopus Books, 1972; *A Basic Textile Book,* Van Nostrand, 1975.

Author of folk documentary "Lancashire Story." Contributor to *Encyclopaedia of Fabric and Thread,* edited by Constance Howard. Contributor of articles and reviews to craft magazines.

WORK IN PROGRESS: Research for juvenile book on textiles; a comparative study of industrial therapy; research on textile history.

SIDELIGHTS: When her new flat needed rugs, Margaret Seagroatt began making rugs and weaving. Since then she has developed interests in history, ethnology, and archaeology as they relate to weaving, and she collects textiles. At present, her work is oriented toward beginners, children, play groups, and the handicapped.

AVOCATIONAL INTERESTS: Travel, literature, theater, film, folk music, enameling.

*   *   *

SEAMAN, (A.) Barrett 1945-

PERSONAL: Born July 4, 1945, in Long Island, N.Y.; son of Alfred Jarvis (an advertising executive) and Mary Margaret (Schill) Seaman; married Laura Maxwell, April 25, 1970; children: Katherine, Margaret, *Education:* Hamilton College, A.B., 1967; Columbia University, M.B.A., 1971. *Residence:* Bonn, West Germany. *Office: Time,* Godesbergeralee 127, 5300, Bonn-Bad Godesburg, West Germany.

CAREER/WRITINGS: Life, New York City, reporter, 1971-72; *Fortune,* New York City, reporter, 1972; *Time,* New York City, correspondent in New York City, 1973, correspondent in Chicago, Ill., 1973-76, correspondent in Bonn, West Germany, 1976—. Notable assignments include coverage of the Philadelphia street gangs, a Brooklyn, Ill., shoot-out, a profile on Wichita, Kan., Sioux Indians at Pine Ridge, terrorist activities in West Germany, 1977. *Military service:* U.S. Naval Reserve, 1969-71.

SEARLE, Leroy F(rank) 1942-

PERSONAL: Born September 21, 1942, in American Fork, Utah; son of Charles L. (an accountant) and Verda (a mink rancher; maiden name, Woffinden) Searle; married Yvonne Holz, October 23, 1962 (divorced, 1968); married Annie Sowers (an arts administrator), February 14, 1969; children: Cassandra, Sabrina. *Education:* Utah State University, B.A., 1965; University of Iowa, M.A., 1968, Ph.D., 1970. *Office:* Department of English, University of Washington, Seattle, Wash. 98195.

CAREER: University of Rochester, Rochester, N.Y., assistant professor of English, 1970-77; University of Washington, Seattle, assistant professor of English, 1977—. *Member:* Modern Language Association of America, American Society for Aesthetics, Society for Critical Exchange (founding director).

WRITINGS: Language, Literature, and Literary Criticism, State University of New York, Empire State College, 1973; *Lambspring* (poems), Visual Studies Workshop Press, 1974.

WORK IN PROGRESS: The Critical Situation, a history of critical theory; *Vide Infra,* poems.

SIDELIGHTS: Searle comments: "Most of my writing is speculative, concentrating on the philosophical implications of literary criticism. The actual horizon of interest is a coherent presentation of poetry (in a broad sense) as a fundamental mode of conceptualization and form of committed knowledge."

*   *   *

SEARS, Val 1927-

PERSONAL: Born December 5, 1927, in Vancouver, British Columbia, Canada; son of C. J. and Edna Sears; married wife Margaret, 1949; children: Robin, Kit, Kelly. *Education:* University of British Columbia, B.A., 1949. *Home:* 3210 Volta Pl. N.W., Washington, D.C. 20007; and 6 Oaklands Ave., Toronto, Ontario, Canada. *Office:* 715 National Press Bldg., Washington, D.C. 20045.

CAREER/WRITINGS: Toronto Star, Toronto, Ontario, bureau chief in Ottawa, 1960-63, bureau chief in London, England, 1968-71, Washington bureau chief, 1974—.

*   *   *

SEBALD, Hans 1929-

PERSONAL: Born February 22, 1929, in Selb, Germany; came to the United States in 1954, naturalized citizen, 1968; son of Georg (a manual worker) and Anna (Blank) Sebald. *Education:* Manchester College, B.A. (cum laude), 1958; Ohio State University, M.S., 1959, Ph.D., 1963. *Residence:* Apache Junction, Ariz. *Office:* Department of Sociology, Arizona State University, Tempe, Ariz. 85281.

CAREER: Ohio State University, Columbus, assistant instructor, 1961-62, instructor in sociology and anthropology, 1962-63; Arizona State University, Tempe, assistant professor, 1963-67, associate professor, 1967-75, professor of sociology, 1975—. Visiting instructor at University of Manitoba, summer, 1965, and Nevada Southern University (now University of Nevada, Las Vegas), summer, 1967.

MEMBER: American Sociological Association (fellow), National Council on Family Relations (fellow), American Association for the Advancement of Science, Sierra Club, Defenders of Wildlife, Environmental Protection League, Pacific Sociological Association, Alpha Kappa Delta (local vice-president, 1961-63). *Awards, honors:* Lisle fellowship for international studies in Jamaica, 1961.

WRITINGS: Adolescence: A Sociological Analysis, Appleton, 1968, 2nd edition published as Adolescence: A Social Psychological Analysis, Prentice-Hall, 1977; Momism: The Silent Disease of America, Nelson-Hall, 1976. Contributor of articles and reviews to academic journals.

WORK IN PROGRESS: Witchcraft: The Heritage of a Heresy.

SIDELIGHTS: Sebald writes that his basic interests are "teaching and research in sociology; specifically in problems of youth, family, socialization process, and more recently in the psychology and sociology of the occult, especially witchcraft. Research includes witchcraft of Franconian peasants; interracial dating and sexual liaison; selective perception in political affairs; youth's values and attitudes."

AVOCATIONAL INTERESTS: International travel (with emphasis on Iron-Curtain countries), outdoor life and ecology (built his home on the slope of Superstition Mountains), gold panning, Indian-relic hunting, exploring wilderness areas, river floating, wild mushrooms.

* * *

SEIDE, Diane 1930-
(Diane Seidner)

PERSONAL: Born June 15, 1930, in New York, N.Y.; daughter of Alvin (a salesman) and Sylvia (an artist; maiden name, Kessler) Seide; married Joseph Seidner, May 28, 1960 (divorced, January, 1971); children: Michael David, Sabrina Jennifer. Education: Attended Ithaca College, 1948-50; Adelphi University, B.S., 1953; also attended New School for Social Research. Politics: Democrat. Home: 345 East 93rd St., New York, N.Y. 10028.

CAREER: Registered nurse; St. Vincent's Hospital, New York City, head nurse of psychiatry, 1957-58; Mount Sinai Hospital, New York City, instructor in nursing and delivery room head nurse, 1958-59; worked as free-lance writer and editor, 1959-71; St. Luke's Hospital, New York City, head nurse, 1971-72; Parents' Magazine, New York City, associate editor, 1973; writer, 1973—.

WRITINGS: (Under name Diane Seidner) Young Nurse in New York (young adults), Dial, 1967; Careers in Medical Science, Thomas Nelson, 1972; Looking Good: Your Everything Guide to Beauty, Health, and Modeling (young adult), Thomas Nelson, 1977. Author, with Minna Kubie, of Organic Beverages, Bantam; also author of novels under other pseudonyms. Contributor of articles to Parents Magazine and other periodicals. Associate editor, R.N., 1960.

WORK IN PROGRESS: Going It Alone, a novel; Adviser to Kings, on her ancestors; research for a book on the home care industry.

SIDELIGHTS: Diane Seide told CA: "My writing goals are now approaching a crossroads in my life. For a woman, the going-it-alone route produces enormous obstacles, particularly for the creative, brainy, talented woman. Compromises must be made and my children are extremely vital to my life. Therefore, making choices, as Gail Sheehy points out in her excellent book, Passages, does involve often radical changes in midlife crises. Having lost both parents and realizing the aloneness of my position, I have always found the power of creativity—writing in my case—as the single most important force in my life, a force which has kept me going regardless of the obstacles. Basically, my writing objectives are divided between two fields—fiction and nonfiction, particularly health care.

"I have a deep commitment to exposing the health-care-rip-off in our society, which provides medical care for the rich only and often shocking neglect, impersonality, and brutal disregard for the poor as well as the middle class who have been impoverished by escalating medical costs. These costs can be cut in half by closing disreputable nursing homes and for-profit hospitals and creating a viable, humane system of home health care, which is feasible and operable—if the consumer becomes aware of this alternative and how to obtain it. I am currently working on a project which I hope will help to change both federal and state-wide existing legislation so that the old, abandoned, lonely, and infirm and those dying of terminal illness can receive third-party reimbursement through a national health insurance program, and/or medicare and private insurance.

"In fiction I am now taking risks. I am working on projects which express the changes, battles, and solutions to my own life situation that women can relate to—the nitty-gritty truths of going-it-alone, not the absurd panacea formulas of made-to-order-buck books. In addition, I am now aiming at doing the kinds of things that I personally want to do, being good to myself, and working on a variety of projects—books, television, and films.

"Originally, I started out as an actress and eventually I hope to reactivate that passion through writing for the theater and movies. As Saul Bellow, one of my favorite writers, said during an interview a year ago on television, 'a writer's life is hard to achieve in America—perhaps the toughest goal to reach (certainly for a woman) but once you get there, it's the best life.' Indeed it is and worth aiming for. I'd rather aim for the best and fail than aim at nothing, or worse, at mediocrity and always be frustrated."

* * *

SEIDLER, Lee J. 1935-

PERSONAL: Born February 11, 1935, in Newark, N.J.; son of Leo E. (a certified public accountant) and Elizabeth (Ackerman) Seidler; married Lynn Lopatin (executive director of Shubert Foundation), 1959; children: Laurie K. Education: Columbia University, A.B., 1956, M.S., 1957, Ph.D., 1965. Office: Department of Accounting, Graduate School of Business Administration, New York University, 100 Trinity Pl., New York, N.Y. 10006.

CAREER: Price, Waterhouse & Co., New York City, senior accountant, 1956-61; Columbia University, New York City, lecturer in accounting, 1961-64; Robert College, Istanbul, Turkey, assistant professor of accounting, 1964-65; New York University, New York City, assistant professor, 1965-67, associate professor, 1967-69, professor of accounting, 1969—. Deputy chairman of Commission on Auditors' Responsibilities, Member of board of trustees of Foundation for Accounting Education, 1972—; member of board of directors of Shubert Foundation.

MEMBER: American Accounting Association, American Institute of Certified Public Accountants (chairman of international qualification appraisal committee, 1971—), Financial Analysts Federation, New York Society of Certified Public Accountants. Awards, honors: Lindback Foundation award for distinguished teaching, 1969.

WRITINGS: Accounting and Economic Development, Praeger, 1965; (with wife, Lynn L. Seidler) Social Accounting, Wiley, 1975; (with Frederick Andrews and Marc Epstein) The Equity Funding Papers: Anatomy of a Fraud, Wiley, 1977. Contributor to accounting journals. Editor of Accounting Issues, 1968—.

SEIDMAN, Robert J(erome) 1941-

PERSONAL: Born April 1, 1941, in Philadelphia, Pa.; son of Harry S. and Beatrice (Auerbach) Seidman; married Patricia Lynn Magidson (an architect), February 18, 1966. *Education:* Williams College, B.A., 1963; Worcester College, Oxford, M.A., 1965; Columbia University, doctoral study, 1966-70. *Home and office:* 324 Bleecker St., New York, N.Y. 10014. *Agent:* Arnold Goodman, 500 West End Ave., New York, N.Y. 10024.

CAREER: Free-lance writer, 1966—. Columbia University, New York, N.Y., fellow, 1968-69; Boston University, Boston, Mass., writer, 1975-77. *Member:* Authors Guild of Authors League of America, Phi Beta Kappa. *Awards, honors:* Carroll A. Wilson fellowship for Oxford University, 1963-65; Woodrow Wilson fellowship, 1963; prize from Atlanta Film Festival, 1970, for "Touching Ground."

WRITINGS: Notes for Joyce (on *Dubliners* and *A Portrait of the Artist as a Young Man*), Dutton, 1967; (with Don Gifford) *Notes for Joyce: An Annotation of James Joyce's "Ulysses"*, Dutton, 1974; *One Smart Indian* (novel), Putnam, 1977.

Screenplays: "Touching Ground," 1969; "The Beautiful Dolls," 1977.

Contributor of articles and reviews to *New Republic*, *Partisan Review*, and *Ms.*

WORK IN PROGRESS: Bucks County Idyll, a novel.

* * *

SEIDNER, Diane
See SEIDE, Diane

* * *

SEIGNOBOSC, Francoise 1897-1961
(Francoise)

PERSONAL: Born November, 1897, in Lodeve, France; daughter of Henri (an army officer) and Julie (Guerin) Seignobosc. *Education:* College Sevigne (Paris), Baccalaureat Latin-Langues, 1914; also attended Monmouth College, 1926.

CAREER: Author and illustrator of children's books. *Awards, honors:* New York Herald-Tribune award, 1951, for *Jeanne-Marie Counts Her Sheep.*

WRITINGS—All under name Francoise; all self-illustrated; all published by Scribner's, except as noted: *Fanchette and Jeannot*, Grosset, 1937; (editor with Alice Dalgliesh) *The Gay Mother Goose*, 1938; *Mr. and Mrs. So and So*, Oxford University Press, 1939; *The Gay A B C*, 1939; *The Story of Colette*, 1940; *The Thank-You Book*, 1947; *Jeanne-Marie Counts Her Sheep*, 1951; *Small-Trot* (Junior Literary Guild selection), 1952; *Biquette: The White Goat*, 1953; *Noel for Jeanne-Marie*, 1953; *Springtime for Jeanne-Marie*, 1955; *Jeanne-Marie in Gay Paris*, 1956; *What Do You Want to Be?*, 1957; *Chouchou*, 1958; *Jeanne-Marie at the Fair*, 1959; *The Things I Like*, 1960; *The Big Rain*, 1961; *Minou*, 1962; *What Time Is It, Jeanne-Marie?*, 1963.

SIDELIGHTS: The *New York Times* wrote of Francoise's work: "The distinctive charm of Francoise's picture books derives chiefly from a simplicity which is not nearly so naive as it looks at first glance. Her illustrations have a primitive innocent gaiety, as if a child had painted them—if a child could paint so well."

BIOGRAPHICAL/CRITICAL SOURCES: New York Times, March 8, 1953.*

(Died, 1961)

* * *

SELF, Huber 1914-

PERSONAL: Born January 24, 1914, near Bristow, Okla.; son of John Henry (a farmer) and Dolly (Hill) Self; married Audyne Edna Sultenfuss (an executive secretary), November 23, 1942; children: John Dan, Doris Lavone Self Wimmer, Marilyn Joy Self Papez, Stormy Lee Self Kennedy. *Education:* Oklahoma Central State University, B.S., 1941; Oklahoma State University, M.S., 1947; also attended Kansas State University, 1948-50, and University of Nebraska, 1951-53. *Home:* 1508 Wreath Ave., Manhattan, Kan. 66502. *Office:* Department of Geography, Kansas State University, Manhattan, Kan. 66506.

CAREER: Principal of elementary school in Creek County, Okla., 1941-43, and high school in Kiefer, Okla., 1945-46; Kansas State University, Manhattan, instructor, 1947-51, assistant professor, 1953-75, associate professor of geography, 1976—. *Military service:* U.S. Navy.

MEMBER: Association of American Geographers, American Geographical Society, National Council for Geographic Education, Kansas Academy of Science, Sigma Xi, Gamma Theta Epsilon, Pi Gamma Mu, Sigma Gamma Epsilon. *Awards, honors:* Citation from U.S. War Department, 1945, for research in bacteriological warfare.

WRITINGS: Geography of Kansas (junior high school textbook), Harlow Publishing, 1959; *Atlas of Kansas*, Harlow Publishing, 1961; *Introductory Physical Geography* (home study course), Kansas State University Press, 1962; (with Herbert L. Rau) *World Regional Geography* (home study course), Kansas State University Press, 1963; *Geography of Kansas Syllabus and Atlas* (college textbook), W. C. Brown, 1967; (with Homer E. Socolofsky) *Historical Atlas of Kansas*, Oklahoma University Press, 1972; *Environment and Man in Kansas: A Geographical Analysis*, Regents Press of Kansas, 1977. Contributor to *World Book Encyclopedia* and to geography journals.

WORK IN PROGRESS: Minority Population Groups in Kansas.

* * *

SELTZER, George 1924-

PERSONAL: Born June 3, 1924, in Passaic, N.J.; son of William (a biochemist) and Rose (Magill) Seltzer; married Mildred Murstein (a professor of anthropology and sociology), March 29, 1953; children: Judith Ann, Sarah Beth, Lisa Rachel. *Education:* University of Rochester, B.Mus. (with distinction), 1948, M.Mus., 1949, D.M.A., 1956; studied at University of Cincinnati, 1958-60, and Miami University, Oxford, Ohio, 1967; studied the clarinet privately. *Residence:* Oxford, Ohio. *Office:* Department of Music, Miami University, Oxford, Ohio 45056.

CAREER: High school music teacher in Rochester, N.Y., 1947-49; Miami University, Oxford, Ohio, instructor, 1949-51, assistant professor of music, 1951-56; Wilmurs, Inc. (department store), Hamilton, Ohio, controller, 1956-67; Miami University, associate professor, 1968-73, professor of music, 1973—, cataloger for libraries, 1967-68, assistant dean of School of Fine Arts, 1968-71, associate dean, 1971-73. Instructor at Earlham College, 1953-55. Solo and chamber music recitals in the Midwest and Eastern United States, 1945—; performed with professional orchestras in Rochester, N.Y. and Richmond, N.Y., with Dayton Opera Co. and

Dayton Philharmonic Orchestra, both 1968—. Judge of Akron Scholastic Composers Contest, 1972. Vice-president of Hamilton Community Council, 1964, president, 1965-67, member of board of directors, 1957-67; past member of board of directors of Community Action Commission, Family Service of Hamilton, and Hamilton Safety Council. *Military service:* U.S. Army Air Forces, band and orchestra, 1942-45; served in England and France; became sergeant.

MEMBER: American Federation of Musicians, American Symphony Orchestra League, Music Educators National Conference, American Association of University Professors, American Jewish Committee, National Association for the Advancement of Colored People, Ohio Music Educators Association, Ohio Theory-Composition Teachers, Phi Mu Alpha, Pi Kappa Lambda, B'nai B'rith, Rotary International (member of Oxford board of directors, 1977—).

WRITINGS: (Contributor) *The Woodwind Anthology,* Instrumentalist Co., 1972; (contributor) Kenneth L. Neidig, editor, *Music Director's Handbook of Effective Forms,* Instrumentalist Co., 1973; *The Professional Symphony Orchestra in the United States,* Scarecrow, 1975. Contributor of articles and reviews to music journals.

* * *

SENNETT, Richard 1943-

PERSONAL: Born January 1, 1943; married Caroline Rand Herron. *Education:* University of Chicago, B.A. (summa cum laude), 1964; Harvard University, Ph.D., 1969. *Home:* 37 Washington Sq. W., New York, N.Y. 10011. *Agent:* Lynn Nesbit, International Creative Management, 40 West 57th St., New York, N.Y. 10019. *Office:* Center fo Humanistic Studies, New York University, 5 Washington Sq. N., New York, N.Y. 10003.

CAREER: New York University, New York, N.Y., professor of sociology, director of Center for Humanistic Studies, and senior research associate of Center for Policy Research. Sigmund Freud Lecturer at University of London, 1977; guest scholar at Clare College, Cambridge, autumn, 1976; visiting member of Institute for Advanced Study, 1973-74; fellow of Joint Center for Urban Studies, of Harvard University and Massachusetts Institute of Technology, 1967-68. Speechwriter for U.S. Senator Eugene McCarthy, 1968. Co-director of Cambridge Institute, 1969-70; founder and director of Ford Foundation Urban Family Study, 1968-72; member of Agnelli Foundation Commission on Advanced Industrial Societies, 1974—. Member of board of directors of Community Crafts of Roxbury, 1965-67.

MEMBER: New York Council for the Humanities, Humanities Study Group (chairman, 1975—). *Awards, honors:* Nominated for National Book Award, 1973; Guggenheim fellowship, 1973-74; National Endowment for the Humanities senior research fellowship, 1976-77; has also received Woodrow Wilson fellowships and a French Embassy fellowship to France.

WRITINGS: (Editor and contributor) *Classic Essays on the Culture of Cities,* Appleton, 1969; (editor with Stephan Thernstrom, and contributor) *Nineteenth Century Cities,* Yale University Press, 1969; *Families Against the City: Middle Class Homes of Industrial Chicago, 1872-1890,* Harvard University Press, 1970; *The Uses of Disorder,* Knopf, 1970; (with Jonathan Cobb) *The Hidden Injuries of Class,* Knopf, 1972; (editor) *The Psychology of Society: An Anthology,* Random House, 1977; *The Fall of Public Man,* Knopf, 1977; (with Alain Touraine, T. B. Bottomore, and others) *Beyond the Crisis-Society,* Oxford University Press,

1977; (contributor) *Essays in Honor of David Riesman,* Yale University Press, 1977. Contributor to professional journals and other magazines, including *New York Review* and *Partisan Review.* Member of editorial board of *Theory and Society,* 1974—, and *Psychoanalysis and Contemporary Science,* 1976—.

* * *

SEVERO, Richard 1932-

PERSONAL: Born November 22, 1932, in Newburgh, N.Y.; son of Thomas and Mary (Farina) Severo; married Emoke Edith de Papp, April 7, 1961. *Education:* Colgate University, A.B., 1954; graduate study at Columbia University, 1964-65. *Office: New York Times,* 229 West 43rd St., New York, N.Y. 10036.

CAREER/WRITINGS: Columbia Broadcasting System (CBS) News, New York City, news assistant, 1954-55; *Poughkeepsie New Yorker,* Poughkeepsie, N.Y., cub reporter, 1956-57; Associated Press, Newark, N.J., reporter, 1957-61; *New York Herald Tribune,* New York City, rewriter and reporter, 1961-63; CBS-TV News, network writer, 1963-66; *Washington Post,* Washington, D.C., investigative reporter, 1966-68; *New York Times,* New York City, investigative reporter, 1968-71, bureau chief in Mexico City, 1971-73, general, investigative and environmental reporter, 1973—. Contributor of articles to periodicals, including *Reporter, New Republic, New York, Potomac, Book Week, Reader's Digest, New York Times Magazine,* and *Scanlan's.* Poynter fellow-in-residence, Vassar College, 1974-75. *Awards, honors:* CBS News fellowship, 1964-65; Front Page Award from Baltimore-Washington Newspaper Guild, 1967, for human interest reporting; Help Addicts Voluntarily End Narcotics (H.A.V.E.N.) journalistic award, 1969; Schaeffer Gold Typewriter Award from New York Reporters Association, 1969; Page One Award from Newspaper Guild of New York, 1970; George Polk Memorial Award from Long Island School of Journalism, 1975; Hudson River Fishermen's Award, 1976, for environmental reporting; New York Press Club feature award, 1976; James Wright Brown Award from The Deadline Club, 1976; Meyer Berger Award from Columbia University, 1976; Page One Award from Newspaper Guild of New York, 1976.

AVOCATIONAL INTERESTS: Hiking, "serious music (symphonic and chamber)," history (especially ancient), collecting antiques and old books, "also have a fondness for stray dogs and cats."

* * *

SEWELL, James Patrick 1930-

PERSONAL: Born April 5, 1930, in Texas; son of James Alfred and Eunice (Davis) Sewell; married Judith Rutherford, July 6, 1957; children: Bret, Gunnar, Thea. *Office:* Department of Politics, Brock University, St. Catharines, Ontario, Canada.

CAREER: Brock University, St. Catharines, Ontario, member of staff, department of politics.

WRITINGS: Functionalism and World Politics: A Study Based on Programs Financing Economic Development, Princeton University Press, 1966; *UNESCO and World Politics: Engaging in International Relations,* Princeton University Press, 1975.

* * *

SEYMOUR, Raymond B(enedict) 1912-

PERSONAL: Born July 26, 1912, in Boston, Mass.; son of

Waldo Alwynn (a businessman) and Marie E. (Doherty) Seymour; married Frances B. Horan, September 16, 1936; children: David Ray, Peter Jerome, Susan Jayne Seymour Smith, Philip Alan. *Education:* University of New Hampshire, B.S., 1933, M.S., 1935; University of Iowa, Ph.D., 1937; postdoctoral study at Rensselaer Polytechnic Institute, 1963, and University of Utah, 1964. *Home:* 111 Lakeshore Dr., Hattiesburg, Miss. 39401. *Office:* Department of Polymer Science, University of Southern Mississippi, P.O. Box 476, Southern Station, Hattiesburg, Miss. 39401.

CAREER: University of New Hampshire, Durham, instructor in chemistry, 1933-35; University of Iowa, Iowa City, instructor in chemistry, 1935-37; Goodyear Tire & Rubber Co., Akron, Ohio, research chemist, 1937-39; Atlas Mineral Products Co., Mertztown, Pa., chief chemist, 1939-41; Monsanto Co., Dayton, Ohio, research group leader, 1941-45; University of Tennessee, Chattanooga, director of research, 1945-48; Johnson & Johnson, New Brunswick, N.J., director of research, 1948-49; Atlas Mineral & Chemical Products, Mertztown, president, 1949-55; Loven Chemical of California, Newhall, president, 1955-60; Sul Ross State University, Alpine, Tex., associate professor, 1960, professor of chemistry, 1961-64; University of Houston, Houston, Tex., associate professor, 1964-65, professor of chemistry, 1964-76; University of Southern Mississippi, Hattiesburg, professor of polymer science, 1976—. Visiting professor at National Academy of Science (Yugoslavia), 1976. Consultant to U.S. Rubber Reserve, 1941-45, and Agency for International Development (Bangladesh), 1968. Member of U.S. Executive Reserves, 1957—.

MEMBER: American Chemical Society, American Institute of Chemical Engineers, American Association for the Advancement of Science (fellow), American Institute of Chemists (fellow), Society of Plastics Engineers, National Association of Corrosion Engineers, Society of Coatings Technologists, Mississippi Academy of Science, Sigma Xi, Alpha Chi Sigma, Phi Lambda Upsilon, Gamma Sigma Epsilon, Phi Kappa Phi, Hattiesburg Country Club. *Awards, honors:* Award from Western Plastics, 1960; named plastics pioneer by Society of the Plastics Industry, 1973; teaching award from Manufacturing Chemists Association, 1976.

WRITINGS: National Paint Dictionary, Stewart Publications, 1949; (with R. S. Steiner) *Plastics for Corrosion Resistant Applications,* Reinhold, 1955; *Hot Organic Coatings,* Reinhold, 1960; *Introduction to Polymer Chemistry,* McGraw, 1971; *General Organic Chemistry,* Barnes & Noble, 1971; (with Jerry G. Higgins) *Experimental Organic Chemistry,* Barnes & Noble, 1971; *Modern Plastics Technology,* Reston, 1975; (with F. W. Harris) *The Structure-Solubility Relationship in Polymers,* Academic Press, 1977; (with Tom Cassen) *Chemistry and You,* Goodyear Publishing, 1977; *Polymer Chemistry,* Dekker, 1977; *Additives for Plastics,* Academic Press, 1977; *Plastics Versus Corrosives,* Reinhold, 1977; *Advances in Additives for Plastics,* Academic Press, 1978.

Author of columns in *Polymer News* and in *Plastics.* Contributor of more than six hundred articles to journals in the United States, Mexico, England, India, Australia, Italy, Yugoslavia, Czechoslovakia, Germany, France, Belgium, Sweden, and Finland. Technical editor of *Modern Plastics Encyclopedia,* 1960-76. Member of board of editors of *Polymer News, Plastics,* and "Advances in Chemistry," a series for American Chemical Society, all 1976—.

WORK IN PROGRESS: Essential Chemicals, completion expected in 1979.

SIDELIGHTS: Seymour comments: "I am now placing more emphasis in general interest technical and nontechnical writing, including periodical articles on Yugoslavia, Australia education, and America's Centennial."

* * *

SHAH, A(ruind) M(anilal) 1931-

PERSONAL: Born August 23, 1931, in Vaso, India; son of Manilal Chhaganlal (a businessman) and Jadav Shah; married Jyotsna Navnitlal, December 10, 1961; children: Sudhit, Jagan. *Education:* Maharaja Sayajirao University, B.A., 1953, M.A., 1955, Ph.D., 1964. *Religion:* Hindu. *Home:* 38/5 Probyn Rd., Delhi, India 110-007. *Office:* Department of Sociology, University of Delhi, Delhi, India 110-007.

CAREER: Maharaja Sayajirao University, Baroda, India, lecturer in sociology, 1958-60; Center for Advanced Study in the Behavioral Sciences, Stanford, Calif., fellow, 1960-61; University of Delhi, Delhi, India, lecturer, 1961-64, reader, 1964-69, professor of sociology, 1969—, head of department, 1971-76, director of School of Economics, 1973-75, dean of Faculty of Social Sciences, 1973-75, chairman of managing committee of Central Institute of Education, 1974-76, chairman of board of research studies in humanities and social sciences, 1975-76. Lecturer at Maharaja Sayajirao University, summer, 1961. Anthropology fellow at University of Chicago, summer and fall, 1960; visiting fellow at Institute of Development Studies, Sussex, 1976-77. Participant in international conferences; conducted field work in villages in central and eastern Gujarat. *Member:* Indian Sociological Society (member of managing committee, 1967, 1970—), Current Anthropology (associate).

WRITINGS: The Household Dimension of the Family in India, Orient Longman, 1973, University of California Press, 1974; (editor with M. N. Srinivas and M.S.A. Rao, and contributor) *Survey of Research in Sociology and Social Anthropology,* three volumes, Popular Prakashan, 1973-74; (editor with Srinivas and E. A. Ramaswamy, and contributor) *The Fieldworker and the Field,* Oxford University Press, 1978.

Contributor: A. Aiyappan and L. K. Bala Ratnam, editors, *Society in India,* Social Sciences Association, 1956; Milton Singer, editor, *Traditional India: Structure and Change,* American Folklore Society, 1959; Tapan Raychaudhary, editor, *Contributions to Indian Economic History,* Firma K. L. Mukhopadhaya, 1963; Rajeshwar Prasad, G. C. Hallen, and Kusum Pathak, editors, *Conspectus of Indian Society,* Satish Book Enterprise, 1971; Tadashi Fukutake and Kiomi Morioka, editors, *Sociology and Social Development in Asia,* University of Tokyo Press, 1974; Srinivas, S. Seshaya, and V. S. Parthasarthy, editors, *Dimensions of Social Change,* Allied Publishers, 1976.

Contributor to *International Encyclopedia of the Social Sciences* and *Encyclopedia of Social Work in India.* Contributor of about twenty articles to anthropology and sociology journals in India and the United States. Chief editor of *Sociological Bulletin: Journal of the Indian Sociological Society,* 1967, 1969-72, member of editorial board, 1975—; member of editorial board of *I.C.S.S.R. Journal of Abstracts and Reviews: Sociology and Anthropology,* 1975—, and *Social Action,* 1976—.

WORK IN PROGRESS: A book on the sociological history of an Indian village.

SIDELIGHTS: Shah told *CA:* "A major thrust of my writing is integration between sociology and social anthropology and between these two and history. I hope to continue with this thrust.''

*   *   *

SHAH, Diane K(iver) 1945-

PERSONAL: Born April 3, 1945, in Chicago, Ill.; daughter of Milton S. (a publisher) and Ruth (an executive; maiden name, Blum) Kiver; married J. Bruce Shah (a television director), May 12, 1968. *Education:* Indiana University, A.B., 1967. *Agent:* Roslyn Targ Literary Agency, Inc., 250 West 57th St., Suite 1932, New York, N.Y. 10019. *Office:* *Newsweek,* 444 Madison Ave., New York, N.Y. 10022.

CAREER: Bloomington Tribune, Bloomington, Ind., reporter, 1966-67; United Press International, Chicago, Ill., radio writer, 1967-68; *National Observer,* Washington, D.C., staff writer, 1969-77; *Newsweek,* New York, N.Y., associate editor, 1977—.

WRITINGS: The Mackin Cover (suspense novel), Dodd, 1977. Contributor to popular magazines, including *New York, Sport, Vogue,* and *Cosmopolitan.*

WORK IN PROGRESS: A mystery novel.

SIDELIGHTS: Diane Shah comments: ''I have always loved suspense novels. But I found it annoying that there were never any female protagonists I could identify with. The few who existed seemed to talk in exclamation points and swoon a lot. Eventually it occurred to me that maybe I could create a female detective myself. Then I realized I had no role model. So I tried using a reporter instead. I really believe that women are ready for stronger heroines in fiction than they've been given in the past.''

*   *   *

SHANER, Madeleine 1932-

PERSONAL: Born October 13, 1932, in Bolton, England; came to the United States in 1956; daughter of Nathan (a tailor) and Rachel (Posnansky) Weiner; married John Herman Shaner (a writer), December 29, 1957; children: Michael Anthony, Daniel Philip. *Education:* Exmouth College, B.A., 1953; Rose Bruford College of Speech and Drama, teaching diploma, 1954. *Politics:* ''Apolitical.'' *Religion:* Jewish. *Home:* 735 North Orlando Ave., Los Angeles, Calif. 90069. *Agent:* H. N. Swanson, Inc., 8523 Sunset Blvd., Los Angeles, Calif. 90069.

CAREER: Sneiton Dale Secondary School, Nottingham, England, teacher of speech and drama, 1954-56; Pacific Telephone Co., Los Angeles, Calif., drafting clerk, 1957-62; free-lance writer, 1968—. Member of West Hollywood Community Council; member of advisory councils for area schools.

WRITINGS: Halls of Anger (novel), Paperback Library, 1970; *Class of '44* (novel), Warner Paperback, 1973; *So What Do You Do with the Kids?* (nonfiction), Brooke House, 1976; *Goin' South* (novel), Jove Press, 1978.

WORK IN PROGRESS: The Match, a novel, with Oscar Otis; a romantic comedy.

SIDELIGHTS: Madeleine Shaner writes: ''My main interest is in people and their interaction, human relationships, the quirks of character that individualize people. My prime motivation is *money!'' Avocational interests:* The theater, movies, directing community theater, bicycling, travel, health and holistic healing, yoga, music, food, organic gardening, and tap-dancing.

SHANNON, Richard 1945-

PERSONAL: Born August 1, 1945, in San Francisco, Calif. *Education:* Educated in California. *Politics:* ''Devoted to the liberation of the individual.'' *Religion:* ''Organized religion is to faith what painting-by-numbers is to art.'' *Residence:* San Francisco, Calif. *Office:* c/o Celestial Arts, 231 Adrian Rd., Millbrae, Calif. 94030.

CAREER: Poet, philosopher, artist, and writer.

WRITINGS: The Book of Peace, Doubleday, 1971; *The Peacock and the Phoenix,* Celestial Arts, 1976.

WORK IN PROGRESS: Realities, on meditation; *The Book of the Sacred Number,* on numerology; *The EYE,* on the importance of the negative principle; *The Secret Order of Amen-Ra,* on the rebirth of the ancient priesthood.

SIDELIGHTS: Shannon told *CA:* ''I am opposed to all existing systems whether capitalist or communist; but believe that it is the capitalist rather than the communist nations which offer the only hope for the birth of a new society. Freedom must be strengthened wherever it exists; and oppression must be fought to the end. Freedom (which is also the only measure of social justice) can only be measured by the extent of real personal liberty. I am an avid supporter of women, gay men, blacks, and all others in their fight for liberation.''

AVOCATIONAL INTERESTS: Mozart, history.

*   *   *

SHAPIRO, Howard I(ra) 1937-

PERSONAL: Born December 21, 1937, in New York; son of Murray (a certified public accountant) and Esther Shapiro; married Betty Jo Drymer (an artist), January 1, 1975; children: Suzanne, Marjorie. *Education:* Ohio State University, B.A., 1959; Chicago Medical School, M.D., 1963. *Religion:* Jewish. *Office:* 131 Kings Highway N., Westport, Conn. 06880.

CAREER: Brookdale Hospital, New York, N.Y., intern, 1963; Beth Israel Hospital, Boston, Mass., resident in obstetrics and gynecology, 1964-66; Philadelphia General Hospital, Philadelphia, Pa., resident in obstetrics and gynecology, 1967-69; physician in private practice, 1969—. Attending physician at Norwalk Hospital and Yale New Haven Hospital. *Military service:* U.S. Naval Reserve, active duty, 1964-66; became lieutenant, first grade. *Member:* American College of Obstetricians and Gynecologists (fellow), American Cancer Society (local president), Fairfield County Medical Society, Norwalk Medical Society. *Awards, honors:* Ettinger Fellowship for Cancer Research from American Cancer Society, 1973.

WRITINGS: The Birth Control Book, St. Martin's, 1977.

SIDELIGHTS: Shapiro told *CA* his book is ''a consumer's guide, providing accurate information about all forms of contraception, sterilization, and abortion—for women and men about how to determine if care being administered is correct.''

*   *   *

SHARFMAN, Amalie

PERSONAL: Born in Baltimore, Md.; married Warren L. Sharfman (a government lawyer); children: William Lee. *Education:* Attended Goucher College. *Home:* 2901 Cleveland Ave. N.W., Washington, D.C. 20008.

CAREER: Producer and moderator of commercial and educational radio programs in Baltimore, Md., and Washington, D.C. Instructor in creative writing at Assumption College and Clark University, both in Worcester, Mass., and at George Washington University, Washington, D.C. Began as president, became executive director of Worcester Area Mental Health Association. Taught nursery school at a private school and at a day care center during World War II.

WRITINGS: A Beagle Named Bertram (illustrated by Tony Palazzo), Crowell, 1954; *Mr. Peabody's Pesky Ducks* (illustrated by Louis Darling), Little, Brown, 1957; *Papa's Secret Chocolate Dessert* (illustrated by Lilian Obligado), Lothrop, 1972. Contributor of articles to various periodicals.

BIOGRAPHICAL/CRITICAL SOURCES: New York Times, November 17, 1957.

* * *

SHARP, Roger (William) 1935-

PERSONAL: Born May 24, 1935, in Akron, Ohio; son of Ralph Waldo (in advertising) and Marianne (Rodgers) Sharp; married Sandra Sexton, May 26, 1955 (divorced, June 22, 1964); married Joan Churilla, July 4, 1964 (divorced, April 18, 1976); married Gun Algerius (a public relations executive), June 5, 1976; children: John Ralph, Karen Lee. *Education:* Michigan State University, A.B., 1954; graduate study at Wayne State University and University of Miami. *Politics:* Independent. *Religion:* Presbyterian. *Residence:* New York, N.Y. *Agent:* Gerald Dickler, 460 Park Ave., New York, N.Y. 10019. *Office:* ABC, 77 West 66th St., New York, N.Y. 10023.

CAREER/WRITINGS: WTVT, Tampa, Fla., newscaster, 1956-57; WEWS, Cleveland, Ohio, news director, 1957-59; KOTV, Tulsa, Okla., news director, 1959-61; American Broadcasting Company (ABC)-News, New York City, news correspondent, 1961-64; Columbia Broadcasting System (CBS)-News, New York City, executive producer, 1964-65; WNAC-TV, Boston, Mass., newscaster, 1966; ABC News, news correspondent, 1966-72; WABC-TV, New York City, news correspondent, 1972—. Notable assignments include coverage of all political conventions since 1960, the Cuban revolution, President Kennedy's assassination, civil rights in the South, and various space shots from Cape Canaveral. Has narrated documentaries for NASA, the U.S. Army, National Educational Television, and Twentieth Century-Fox. *Military service:* U.S. Air Force Reserve, 1953-57. *Member:* American Federation of Radio & Television Artists (AFTRA), American Radio & Television News Analysts Association (member of executive committee), New York Press Club. *Awards, honors:* AFTRA award for television news coverage of events in Cuba; Headliner Award for best local television news; Associated Press award for best spot news story.

SIDELIGHTS: Sharp told *CA:* "Journalism has offered me a front row opportunity to witness much history over the past twenty years. I find the reporter's job both challenging and fulfilling. The development of television news as the world's most powerful form of information has given me an unusual chance to grow with the many changes in media style. I have an intense interest in travel and have been to all parts of the world and look forward to more free time in the future to return to places I've particularly enjoyed. Fishing of all kinds is a personal passion and like most reporters I hope someday to write a book—perhaps run for political office."

SHEA, Donald F(rancis) 1925-

PERSONAL: Born September 24, 1925, in Maywood, Ill.; son of Frank and Lillie A. (Schmeltzer) Shea. *Education:* DePauw University, A.B., 1947; University of Michigan, A.M., 1947; Loyola University, Chicago, Ill., Ph.D., 1956. *Politics:* Republican. *Religion:* Roman Catholic. *Office:* Department of History, St. Joseph's College, Box 811, Rensselaer, Ind. 47978; and Republican National Committee, 310 First St., S.E., Washington, D.C. 20003.

CAREER: St. Joseph's College, Rensselaer, Ind., instructor, 1947-49, assistant professor, 1955-61, associate professor, 1961-67, professor of history, 1967—, chairman of department, 1961—. Visiting scholar at Columbia University, 1964. Regional director of President Ford Committee, 1976; director of Ethnic/Catholic Division of Republican National Committee, 1977—. *Member:* American Historical Association, American Catholic Historical Association, Phi Beta Kappa.

WRITINGS: The English Ranke: John Lingard, Humanities Press, 1969. Frequent reviewer of historical books.

WORK IN PROGRESS: An oral history of the Congressional side of the 1974 impeachment of Richard Nixon.

BIOGRAPHICAL/CRITICAL SOURCES: American Historical Review, October, 1970; *English Historical Review,* November, 1970.

* * *

SHEA, John 1941-

PERSONAL: Born September 3, 1941, in Chicago, Ill.; son of John Joseph and Ann (Mullarkey) Shea. *Education:* St. Mary of the Lake Seminary, Mundelein, Ill., S.T.D., 1977. *Home:* St. Mary of the Lake Seminary, Mundelein, Ill. 60060.

CAREER: Ordained Roman Catholic priest, 1967; pastor of Roman Catholic parishes in Chicago, Ill., 1967-69; Loyola University, Chicago, Ill., instructor in theology, 1969-73; St. Mary of the Lake Seminary, Mundelein, Ill., instructor in theology, 1974—. *Member:* Catholic Theological Society.

WRITINGS: What a Modern Catholic Believes About Sin, Thomas More Association, 1970; *What a Modern Catholic Believes About Heaven and Hell,* Thomas More Association, 1973; *The Challenge of Jesus,* Thomas More Association, 1975; *The Hour of the Unexpected,* Argus Communications, 1977; *Stories of God,* Thomas More Association, 1978.

WORK IN PROGRESS: A study of the relationship of skills training and theology, for clergymen.

* * *

SHEEHAN, George (Augustine) 1918-

PERSONAL: Born November 5, 1918, in Brooklyn, N.Y.; son of George A. (a physician) and Loretta (Ennis) Sheehan; married Mary Jane Fleming, April 10, 1944; children: George, Mary Jane Sheehan Kroon, Timothy, Ann, Nora, Sarah, Peter, Andrew, John, Stephen, Monica, Michael. *Education:* Manhattan College, B.S., 1940; Long Island College of Medicine, M.D., 1943. *Home:* 55 Rumson Rd., Rumson, N.J. 07760. *Agent:* Mel Sokolow, 6 West 86th St., New York, N.Y. 10028. *Office:* 79 West Front St., Red Bank, N.J. 07701.

CAREER: Resident, Kings County Hospital, Brooklyn, N.Y.; physician in private practice as internist, 1949—. *Military service:* U.S. Navy, Medical Corps, 1944-47; became lieutenant senior grade.

WRITINGS: *Encyclopedia of Athletic Medicine,* World Publications, 1973; *Dr. Sheehan on Running,* World Publications, 1975. Author of weekly column "The Innocent Bystander" in *Red Bank Register,* 1968—, and "Running Wild" in *Physician,* 1974—. Medical editor of *Runner's World,* 1972—.

WORK IN PROGRESS: A book for Simon & Schuster.

SIDELIGHTS: George Sheehan remarks: "I dropped out at forty-five and found running to be a self-renewing inner compulsion. I also had a compulsion to reveal my experiences to others or, at the least, to set them down as truthfully as possible so that I would have a diary."

* * *

SHEEKMAN, Arthur 1901-1978

February 5, 1901—January 12, 1978; American screenwriter. Sheekman wrote many musicals and comedies, including the Marx brothers films, "Monkey Business" and "Duck Soup." He died in Santa Monica, Calif. Obituaries: *New York Times,* January 14, 1978.

* * *

SHELBY, Brit 1949-

PERSONAL: Born April 30, 1949. *Education:* Earned B.A. degree. *Politics:* "Hard to describe—worked in anti-war movement and Goldwater's 1964 campaign." *Religion:* "I usually answer 'Druid,' but that's a lie." *Agent:* William Morris Agency, 1350 Avenue of the Americas, New York, N.Y. 10019.

CAREER: Writer and newspaper reporter. Has worked for U.S. government in various capacities, including grave digger, heavy machinery operator, librarian, and fire hydrant inspector.

WRITINGS: *The Great Pebble Affair,* Putnam, 1976.

* * *

SHENK, Marcia Ann 1953-

PERSONAL: Born June 2, 1953, in New York, N.Y.; daughter of David and Harriet (Skulsky) Shenk. *Education:* Herbert H. Lehman College of the City University of New York, B.A., 1974; New York University, M.A., 1975. *Residence:* New York, N.Y. *Agent:* Samuel French, Inc., 25 West 45th St., New York, N.Y. 10036.

CAREER: New York City Board of Education, New York, N.Y., substitute teacher in elementary schools, 1976—. Stage manager of children's theater at Hudson Guild Theatre. *Member:* American Theatre Association (Children's Theatre Division).

WRITINGS: *Diary* (one-act play; first produced in Mason, Tex., January 21, 1977), Samuel French, 1975.

WORK IN PROGRESS: A collection of short stories.

SIDELIGHTS: Marcia Shenk writes: "My writing is a very personal thing, whether it is based on truth or on an entirely imaginary incident. When I write it is because I want to or need to. As a published author, I am a novice, but I've been writing stories and poems since the second grade.

"As much as who and what I am shapes my writing, my writing shapes who and what I am. It is an extension of myself—the fear, the joy, the hopelessness, and the discovery of growing up. If I didn't write, I'm sure I would have had to develop another outlet for the mental energy that demands to be expressed.

"My goal has never been to teach anyone any lessons through my writing, but just to tell a story. If with that story I can reach something inside, elicit a feeling or any sort of response at all, then I've done something special—I've managed to touch someone whom I may never know. I've communicated. And that, after all, is what it's all about."

* * *

SHEPPARD, Thomas F(rederick) 1935-

PERSONAL: Born June 5, 1935, in Indianapolis, Ind.; son of Francis Sherman and Dorothy (White) Sheppard; married Donna Cox (editor of publications for Colonial Williamsburg Foundation). *Education:* Vanderbilt University, A.B., 1957; University of Nebraska, M.A., 1962; Johns Hopkins University, Ph.D., 1969. *Office:* Department of History, College of William and Mary, Williamsburg, Va. 23185.

CAREER: Western Kentucky University, Bowling Green, teacher of history, 1962-65; College of William and Mary, Williamsburg, Va., assistant professor, 1969-71, associate professor, 1971-77, professor of history, 1977—, chairman of department, 1975—. *Military service:* U.S. Marine Corps, 1957-65, active duty, 1957-60; became captain. *Member:* American Historical Association, Society for French Historical Studies. *Awards, honors:* National Endowment for the Humanities fellow, 1972-73.

WRITINGS: *Lourmarin in the Eighteenth Century,* Johns Hopkins Press, 1971.

WORK IN PROGRESS: *A Social History of the Touraine in the Eighteenth Century and the Revolution.*

SIDELIGHTS: Sheppard writes: "My major area of interest is European history, with particular emphasis on French social and economic history.

"The study of Lourmarin was an attempt to recreate an eighteenth-century village using parish registers, tax rolls, administrative correspondence, letters, council minutes, etc. I am now using the same sources and applying the same techniques in a study of the Touraine, a province with a population of about 250,000 at the time of the French Revolution."

* * *

SHERMAN, Jane 1908-

PERSONAL: Born June 14, 1908, in Beloit, Wis.; daughter of Horace Humphrey (an advertising writer) and Florentine (an opera singer; maiden name, St. Clair) Sherman; married Ned Lehac (a science teacher and musical composer), February 8, 1940. *Education:* Attended high school in Elmhurst, N.Y. *Home:* 116 Huguenot St., New Paltz, N.Y. 12561.

CAREER: Professional dancer; toured the Far East with Ruth St. Denis, Ted Shawn and Denishawn Dancers, 1925-26, and the United States, 1926-27; toured the United States with the Ziegfeld Follies, 1927-28; member of Humphrey-Weidman concert dancers, 1928; performed in Broadway productions "The Third Garrick Gaities," "9:15 Revue," and "Hello, Daddy," 1928-30; danced with Rockettes at Radio City Music Hall in New York, N.Y., 1934-35; traveled and studied in Europe, 1935-44; *Seventeen,* New York City, fiction editor, 1944-45; United Nations Information Center, New York City, secretary to head of Radio Division, 1946; writer, 1946—.

AWARDS, HONORS: De la Torre Bueno Prize from Dance Perspectives Foundation and Wesleyan University Press, 1974-75, for *Soaring: The Diary and Letters of a Den-*

ishawn Dancer in the Far East, 1925-1926; National Endowment for the Humanities grant, 1977-78.

WRITINGS: Soaring: The Diary and Letters of a Denishawn Dancer in the Far East, 1925-1926, Wesleyan University Press, 1976.

For children: *The Real Book about Dogs,* F. Watts, 1951; *The Real Book about Horses,* F. Watts, 1952; *The Real Book about Bugs,* F. Watts, 1952; *The Real Book of Amazing Scientific Facts,* F. Watts, 1953; *The Real Book about Snakes,* F. Watts, 1955; *The Little House that Moved,* Grosset, 1972.

Work anthologized in *The Best in Children's Books,* Doubleday, 1959; *Catch Your Breath,* Garrard, 1973. Contributor of stories, poems, articles, and reviews to magazines, including *Dance, Cue, Eye of Woman,* and *Hudson Valley,* and to newspapers.

WORK IN PROGRESS: The Drama of Denishawn Dance, for Wesleyan University Press.

SIDELIGHTS: Jane Sherman writes: "I have been made aware of the importance to future dance historians of records of dances in the past, particularly those about the work and times of Ruth St. Denis and Ted Shawn. Since I was a part of their company at the peak of their popularity, I am most interested in either writing myself, or helping others of that period write, valid reports of that particular dance period which made such a valuable contribution to American modern dance and American culture in general.

"I am also active with my husband in writing a regular educational newspaper column and other material for the Hudson Valley Citizens Watch on Nuclear Safety, a group organized to fight the spread of atomic energy, especially in our Hudson Valley."

*   *   *

SHERRY, Michael S(tephen) 1945-

PERSONAL: Born January 8, 1945, in Indianapolis, Ind.; son of John Milton (a metallurgist) and Pauline (Griner) Sherry. *Education:* Washington University, St. Louis, Mo., A.B., 1967; Yale University, M.A., 1969, Ph.D., 1975. *Home:* 2212 Sherman, Evanston, Ill. 60201. *Office:* Department of History, Northwestern University, Evanston, Ill. 60201.

CAREER: History teacher at private school in Hamden, Conn., 1969-71; Yale University, New Haven, Conn., teacher of emotionally disturbed students at Psychiatric Institute, 1974-76, lecturer in history, 1975-76; Northwestern University, Evanston, Ill., assistant professor of history, 1976—. *Member:* Organization of American Historians.

WRITINGS: Preparing for the Next War: American Plans for Postwar Defense, 1941-45, Yale University Press, 1977. Contributor of articles and reviews to history journals.

WORK IN PROGRESS: The Enemy in Flames: Fire-Bombing Japan, on strategic bombing and its application against Japan in World War II.

SIDELIGHTS: Sherry told *CA:* "Both my published work and the work in progress reflect my interest in the role played by military force and strategy in American foreign policy. In particular, I'm interested in why the United States, whose official ideology has always been anti-militarist and anti-interventionist, has become the foremost practitioner of the most indiscriminate forms of warfare. In the most personal sense, this interest developed during the 1960s, when my bewilderment and disillusionment about the

Vietnam War led me to explore the origins of the Cold War and to realize that scholars had largely ignored the role played in it by American strategic planners and their ideas. My emphasis has been that, in the militarization of American policy, civilians, rather than officers, have played the greatest role. In particular, strategic bombing of enemy cities has especially appealed to civilian politicians and their constituents, who have viewed such bombing as a cheap and quick means to victory in modern war. My work in progress will attempt to explain the development and application of this notion of warfare."

*   *   *

SHETTY, Sharat 1940-

PERSONAL: Born February 1, 1940, in India; son of Balappa and Adappa Shetty; married Punja, June 18, 1971. *Education:* Karnatak Medical College, M.D., 1964; London School of Hygiene and Tropical Medicine, London, D.T.M.H., 1966. *Religion:* Hindu. *Home:* Kadri Hill, Mangalore 4, Karnataka State, India.

CAREER: Metropolitan Hospital, New York, N.Y., intern, 1966-67, resident in internal medicine, 1970—; Bird S. Coler Hospital, New York City, internist, 1970-74; consulting physician in Mangalore, India, 1975—. *Member:* New York Academy of Medicine (fellow).

WRITINGS: A Hindu Boyhood, M. Evans, 1970.

SIDELIGHTS: Shetty wrote that the purpose for writing his book, *A Hindu Boyhood,* was to enlighten Americans regarding the upbringing of Hindu children. He told *CA:* "Faith and belief in God are necessary. Happiness is a state of mind. Happiness comes from inside rather than from outside. There is great beauty in going through life without anxiety or fear. Half our fears are baseless and the other half discreditable. If a man could have half his wishes he would double his troubles."

*   *   *

SHIERS, George 1908-

PERSONAL: Born October 17, 1908, in Coventry, England; came to the United States in 1948, naturalized citizen, 1954; son of Walter (a watchmaker) and Emily Gertrude (a silk weaver; maiden name, Laxon) Shiers; married May Florence Shackell, October 31, 1936. *Education:* Attended public schools in London, England. *Home:* 3864 Foothill Rd., Santa Barbara, Calif. 93110.

CAREER: Electrician in London, England, 1924-39, electronic specialist, 1939-46, antiquarian bookseller, 1946-48; electrical specialist in Silver Spring, Md., 1948-53; electronic specialist in Santa Barbara, Calif., 1953-58; City College, Santa Barbara, Calif., instructor in electronics and drafting, 1955-68; University of California, Extension, Santa Barbara, instructor in adult education and writing, 1968-75. Writer. *Member:* Institute of Electrical and Electronics Engineers (senior member), Royal Television Society, Friends of the Library (University of California, Santa Barbara).

WRITINGS—For the layman: *Electronic Drafting,* Prentice-Hall, 1962; *Electronic Drafting Techniques and Exercises,* Prentice-Hall, 1963; *Design and Construction of Electronic Equipment,* Prentice-Hall, 1966; *Bibliography of the History of Electronics,* Scarecrow, 1972.

Editor: *The Electric Telegraph: An Historical Anthology,* Arno, 1977; *The Telephone: An Historical Anthology,* Arno, 1977; *The Development of Wireless to 1920,* Arno, 1977; *Technical Development of Television,* Arno, 1977;

Development of Radio After 1920: Basic Technology, Arno, in press; *Facsimile: An Historical Anthology,* Arno, in press. Editor of "Telecommunications," a series of reprints, Arno, 1974. Contributor to professional journals and to *Scientific American.*

WORK IN PROGRESS: Early Television, a bibliography up to 1939; a bibliography of books on television up to 1947, with Christopher H. Sterling; research on the origins of television.

SIDELIGHTS: Shiers comments: "My writing is on technical and scientific subjects, but my approach is slanted toward the layman and beginner as well as the general engineer. On the whole, the material could be classed as semitechnical on a semipopular level.

"I've long been interested in assisting the (usually bewildered) layman and general reader along the path of learning about some of the technical features that are now so important in our daily lives. As a student of readability factors in prose, I strive to match my writing to the intended reader range of understanding, somewhat equivalent to the standard of *Scientific American.* Accuracy and perspective are other foremost factors that I keep in mind in historical writing, consequently a large part of my work involves extensive research."

* * *

SHILLER, Jack G(erald) 1928-

PERSONAL: Born August 17, 1928, in New York, N.Y.; son of Samuel and Beatrice (Greenberg) Shiller; married Doris Joan Barker, July 18, 1954; children: Bethanne, Stephen, Andrew. *Education:* University of North Carolina, A.B., 1947; City College (now of the City University of New York), graduate study, 1947-48; Columbia University, M.D., 1952. *Politics:* Democrat. *Religion:* Jewish. *Home:* 12 Terhune Dr., Westport, Conn. 06880. *Office:* Willows, 129 Kings Highway N., Westport, Conn. 06880.

CAREER: Bellevue Hospital, New York, N.Y., intern, 1952-53; Presbyterian Hospital, New York City, junior assistant resident, 1955-56, senior assistant resident, 1956-57; physician, with private practice of pediatrics, 1957—. Licensed to practice in New York, 1953, and Connecticut, 1957; diplomate of National Board of Medical Examiners, 1953, and American Board of Pediatrics, 1958. Instructor at Columbia University, 1961-68, research associate, 1968-70, assistant clinical professor, 1970-75, associate clinical professor, 1975—. Pediatric assistant at Vanderbilt Clinic; assistant attending physician at Norwalk Hospital, 1957-58, associate attending physician, 1961-66, senior attending physician, 1966—, chief of newborn service, 1967-70, head of department of pediatrics, 1970. Medical examiner for Federal Aviation Agency, 1958-65; director of health for Westport, Conn., 1963-66; member of Connecticut Personal Health Services Commission. *Military service:* U.S. Air Force, flight surgeon in Medical Corps, 1953-55; served in England; became captain.

MEMBER: American Academy of Pediatrics, Hezekiah Beardsley Pediatric Society, Connecticut State Medical Society, Fairfield County Medical Society.

WRITINGS: Infant and Child Care at Sculthorpe (U.S. Air Force dependents' manual), Witley Press, 1955; *Childhood Illness: A Common Sense Approach,* Stein & Day, 1972; *Childhood Injury: A Common Sense Approach,* Stein & Day, 1977. Contributor to pediatric and other medical journals.

SHILLONY, Ben-Ami 1937-

PERSONAL: Born October 28, 1937, in Poland; son of Avraham (a rabbi and farmer) and Judith (a teacher; maiden name, Brum) Shillony; married Helena Kornreich (a lecturer in French literature), April 4, 1962; children: Iris, Ruth. *Education:* Hebrew University of Jerusalem, M.A., 1964; Princeton University, Ph.D., 1970. *Religion:* Jewish. *Home:* 4 Bialik St., Jerusalem, Israel. *Office:* Department of East Asian Studies, Hebrew University of Jerusalem, Jerusalem, Israel.

CAREER: Haboker (newspaper), Jerusalem, Israel, reporter, 1964-65; University of Colorado, Boulder, visiting assistant professor of Japanese history, 1971; Hebrew University of Jerusalem, Jerusalem, Israel, lecturer, 1971-73, senior lecturer in East Asian studies, 1973—. Senior research fellow at Oxford University, 1976-77. *Awards, honors:* Japan Foundation fellow, 1975.

WRITINGS: Revolt in Japan, Princeton University Press, 1973.

WORK IN PROGRESS: Wartime Japan.

SIDELIGHTS: Shillony remarks: "Teaching Japanese history in Hebrew to Israeli students, using English-language teaching materials, while writing in English and Hebrew, is a fascinating challenge. Looking at the history of an extraordinary Eastern nation while drawing on the experience of an unusual Western nation is an exciting experience."

CA asked Shillony what he felt is Japan's future in the world market. He responded: "The two prominent trends in present-day Japan are its enormous economic growth and its expanding ties with China. Japan's role as a leading actor in the world trade will increase and may equal that of the United States by the end of the century. An alliance between China and Japan may create a new power center which could rival that of the U.S. and the Soviet Union."

* * *

SHIRAKAWA, Yoshikazu 1935-

PERSONAL: Born January 28, 1935, in Kawanoe City, Japan; son of Shigeru (a company executive) and Shina (Ishamura) Shirakawa; married Kazuko Miyamoto (a president of a Japanese dancing school); children: Eri. *Education:* Nihon University, B.A., 1957. *Home:* 2-12-15, Takanawa, Minato-ku, Tokyo 108, Japan. *Agent:* Image Bank, Penthouse, 88 Vanderbilt Ave., New York, N.Y. 10017.

CAREER: Nippon Broadcasting System, Literature and Art Division, Tokyo, Japan, producer, 1957-58; Fuji Telecasting Company, Tokyo, chief cameraman, 1958-60; free-lance photographer, 1960—. Special lecturer, Japan Photographic Academy, 1967—; chief instructor and chairman of the board of directors, Kanto Photo Technique Academy, 1974—. Work has been exhibited at fourteen one-man shows, including Konishiroku Gallery, Tokyo, 1957, Nikon Salon, Tokyo, 1970, "The Seat of the Gods" exhibition in ten major Japanese cities, 1971-73, and "Eternal America" exhibition in thirteen Japanese cities, 1975-77. *Member:* Japan Professional Photographers' Society (director, 1967—), Japanese Alpine Club, Nikakai Association of Artists. *Awards, honors:* Annual Minister of Health and Welfare awards, 1956-61; Special Prize at National Park Photo Contest, 1960; Nika Prize at 53rd Nika Exhibition, 1968; Annual Award of the Photographic Society of Japan, 1970; 13th Art Prize from the Mainichi Newspapers, 1972; Minister of Education Award, 22nd Fine Art Grand Prix, 1972.

WRITINGS—In English: *Arupusu,* Kodansha, 1969, translation by J. Maxwell Brownjohn published as *The Alps,* Abrams, 1975; *Himaraya,* Shogakukan, 1971, translation by Thomas I. Elleott published as *The Himalayas,* Abrams, 1973; *America Tairiku,* Kodansha (Tokyo), 1975, translation by T. Uetsuhara published as *Eternal America,* Kodansha (New York), 1975.

Technical books: *Roshutsu no kimetaka* (title means "Exposure and Its Determination"), Ikeda Shoten, 1955; *Camera no Chishiki to utsushi-kata* (title means "Camera and How to Use It"), Ikeda Shoten, 1955; *Sangaku-shashin no giho* (title means "Mountain Photography"), Rikogakusha, 1973.

Photography books: *Shiroi Yama* (title means "White Mountains"), Hobundo, 1960; *Yama* (title means "Mountains"), Chikuma Shobo, 1971; *Kami-gami no za* (title means "The Seats of the Gods"), Asahi Newspapers, 1971; *Shinyaku seisho no sekai* (title means "World of the New Testament"), Shogakukan, 1978.

WORK IN PROGRESS: A book of photography, *Kyuyaku seisho no sekai* (title means "World of the Old Testament"), publication by Shogakukan expected in 1979.

SIDELIGHTS: Shirakawa writes: "Over a period of sixteen years, I have made photographic trips to 130 of the world's countries, seeing with my own eyes, I believe, nearly all of nature's wonderful creations and developing a worldwide point of view. I have photographed from the ground and from the air, my flights having numbered in the thousands, and feel that I am accustomed to seeing nature as a macrocosm.

"To speak of the 'mysteries' and 'wonders' of nature is easy, but I wonder how many people have felt the meaning of those words. How many people have actually experienced those mysteries and those wonders? Very few, I imagine. I feel fortunate in believing that I am one of the few, and it is my earnest wish to pass on to all my deep impressions and barely imaginable experiences. I would like all people to discover anew this earth of ours. It is my fervent desire to show the way to a revitalization of humanity through the pictures I have taken.

"Our age cries, as no other period in the history of mankind has, for the rekindling of the human conscience. Space scientists, medical scientists have taken great strides and made great contributions to mankind; technological advances pile up at a dizzying rate. Yet there is domestic unrest, there are wars between nations, and even in times of peace we are ruining our environment. Day by day our earth is being destroyed, and I have had the fear that in doing my work I may inadvertently have added a stroke to the blueprint of a plan that would make the earth desertic, uninhabitable.

"Recovery of Humanity through rediscovery of the earth is my lifelong theme. *The Alps, Himalayas, Eternal America,* are now in book form. In the future, I want to look at Antarctica, the China continent, the Andes and Patagonia, fjords, one hundred famous mountains of the world and the Japanese Alps. My life work was planned thirteen years ago; I do not know whether I can accomplish my aim. My hope is to introduce to the world the not yet unraveled mysteries of nature. If through my photographs people were to rediscover this earth of ours, my joy could know no bounds."

BIOGRAPHICAL/CRITICAL SOURCES: New York Times, December 2, 1973; *Wall Street Journal,* December 5, 1973, December 3, 1975; *Washington Post,* December 9, 1973; *Newsweek,* December 17, 1973; *Time,* December 17, 1973, December 22, 1975; *Los Angeles Times,* December 8, 1974, December 7, 1975.

SHIRTS, Morris A(lpine) 1922-

PERSONAL: Born April 11, 1922, in Escalante, Utah; son of Morris (a farmer) and Neta (Hall) Shirts; married Dorothy Maxin Baird, 1945; children: Russell, Randy, Andrea, Robert, Steven. *Education:* Dixie College, A.S., 1942; Brigham Young University, B.A., 1947, M.A., 1950; Indiana University, Ed.D., 1952. *Religion:* Church of Jesus Christ of Latter-day Saints (Mormons). *Home:* 570 South 580th W., Cedar City, Utah 84720. *Office:* School of Education, Southern Utah State College, Cedar City, Utah 84720.

CAREER: High school teacher of mathematics, physics, and chemistry in Mount Pleasant, Utah, 1947-50, audiovisual supervisor, 1949-50; Brigham Young University, Provo, Utah, assistant professor of education, 1952-57; National Teachers College, Tehran, Iran, visiting professor of education, 1957-59; Southern Utah State College, Cedar City, associate professor, 1959-64, professor of education, 1965—, chairman of department, 1964-65, dean of School of Education, 1965-72. Member, Utah Bicentennial Commission. *Military service:* U.S. Army Air Forces, 1942-45; received Air Medal. Utah National Guard, 1948-50. *Member:* Society of Motion Picture and Television Engineers.

WRITINGS: Warm-Up for Little League Baseball, Sterling, 1971; *Playing with a Football,* Sterling, 1972; *Call It Right: Umpiring in the Little League,* Sterling, 1977. Contributor to education journals.

WORK IN PROGRESS: The Restless Saint, a series of pioneer stories about his great-great-grandfather; *Past Times,* true stories about the settlement of southern Utah and adjacent areas.

SIDELIGHTS: Shirts writes: "My desire to write in the area of youth athletics stems from a deep urge to improve these activities; I coached Little League baseball for twenty years. I am also involved in Boy Scout activities, and am currently involved in developing a thirteen-hundred-acre Scout camp."

AVOCATIONAL INTERESTS: Collecting and restoring Studebakers (owns five).

*   *   *

SHIVANANDAN, Mary 1932-

PERSONAL: Born January 6, 1932, in Rangoon, Burma; came to the United States in 1960, naturalized citizen, 1971; daughter of Sir John Francis (in Indian Civil Service) and Jean Newton (Simpson) Sheehy; married Kandiah Shivanandan (an astrophysicist), September 17, 1960; children: John Uthya-Surian, Marianne Gauri. *Education:* Newnham College, Cambridge, B.A. (honors), 1954, M.A., 1967. *Politics:* Democrat. *Religion:* Roman Catholic. *Home and office:* 4711 Overbrook Rd., Washington, D.C. 20016. *Agent:* Charlotte Sheedy, 145 West 86th St., New York, N.Y. 10024.

CAREER: Canadian Broadcasting Corp., assistant radio producer in Toronto, Ontario, 1956-58, and Montreal, Quebec, 1958-60; *Mid East,* Washington, D.C., associate editor, 1968-69; American University, Washington, D.C., associate research scientist in foreign area studies, 1969-70; *New American Encyclopedia,* Washington, D.C., associate editor-in-chief, 1971-72; free-lance writer, 1972—. Lecturer to women's groups and schools; has broadcast over Canadian Broadcasting Corp., British Broadcasting Corp., and Australian Broadcasting Corp. *Member:* Washington Independent Writers.

WRITINGS: Bobtail and Bubtail (juvenile), Thacker &

Co., 1945; *Gamal Abdul Nasser*, SamHar Press, 1973; (with Richard F. Nyrop, Beryl L. Benderly, and others, and contributor) *Area Handbook for Pakistan*, U.S. Government Printing Office, 1971, 4th edition, 1975; (with Nyrop, Benderly, and others, and contributor) *Area Handbook for Ceylon*, U.S. Government Printing Office, 1971; (with Nyrop, Benderly, and others, and contributor) *Area Handbook for India*, U.S. Government Printing Office, 3rd edition, 1975. Author of column "Perspectives, News Briefs," in *Marriage & Family Living*, 1977—. Contributor to magazines and newspapers, including *Washingtonian, Rolling Stone*, and *U.S. Catholic*. Contributing editor, *Marriage & Family Living*, 1977—.

WORK IN PROGRESS: Natural Sex (tentative title), on natural methods of family planning, for Rawson.

SIDELIGHTS: Mary Shivanandan writes: "Having traveled since childhood (born in Burma, educated in England and Australia, worked in Canada and the United States . . .) I have a cosmopolitan outlook. Experience, supplemented by research has given me insight into the ways of life and modes of thought of varied cultural and religious groups. This adds more perspective to my present writing on the family.

"After contributing for several years to books, magazines, newspapers and radio on general interest, political, scientific and international topics, I am now writing almost exclusively in the field of marriage, family, feminism, and sex-related topics. The changes in these areas are so vital for the future of society I wish by sound research and creative analysis to illumine trends that are positive and expose those that are destructive. In view of my East/West background I also delight in writing intuitively of both Indian/Sri Lankan and English/American cultures."

BIOGRAPHICAL/CRITICAL SOURCES: CBC Times, Volume XVII, number 10, 1964.

* * *

SHOMON, Joseph James 1914-

PERSONAL: Born October 16, 1914, in Westford, Conn.; son of Joseph and Veronica (Luknar) Shomon; married Vera Bouzane; children: Suzanne, Nancy. *Education:* University of Michigan, B.S.F., 1940, M.S.F., 1947, Ph.D., 1959. *Religion:* Roman Catholic. *Home:* 39-65 52nd St., Woodside, N.Y. 11377.

CAREER: Tennessee Valley Authority, Norris, Tenn., educational forester, 1940-42; Virginia Commission of Game and Inland Fisheries, Richmond, chief of Education Division and editor of *Virginia Wildlife*, 1947-61; National Audubon Society, New York, director of Nature Center Planning Division, 1961-73; American Conservation Planning Associates, New York City, director and principal planning consultant, 1973—. Adjunct assistant professor of environmental studies at New York University, 1965—. *Military service:* U.S. Army Reserve, 1942-72, active duty, 1942-46; served in European theater; became lieutenant colonel; received Distinguished Service Medal, five battle stars.

MEMBER: American Association for the Advancement of Science, American Society of Planning Officials, American Forestry Association, American Nature Study Society, Izaak Walton League of America, Wildlife Society, National Wildlife Federation, National Audubon Society, Nature Conservancy, Smithsonian Associates, New York Zoological Society, Wilderness Society.

WRITINGS: Crosses in the Wind, Stratford House, 1947;

Birdlife of Virginia, Virginia Commission of Game and Inland Fisheries, 1956; *Guidelines to Conservation Education*, Izaak Walton League of America, 1966; *Open Land for Urban America*, Johns Hopkins Press, 1971, *Nature Realms Across America*, American Forestry Association, 1974; *Beyond the North Wind*, A. S. Barnes, 1974. Contributor of more than two hundred articles to professional and popular magazines.

WORK IN PROGRESS: Nature Centers in America for Nellen; *The Wondrous American Forest*.

SIDELIGHTS: Shomon writes that his assignments have taken him to all fifty states, all Canadian provinces, the Arctic, Scandinavia, Russia, Central America, Amazon, Iran, Philippines, Africa, the Bahamas, and Trinidad. He has supervised the planning and consulting efforts of nearly two hundred works involving nature centers, nature parks, urban greenspace areas, wildlife sanctuaries, and arboretums in North America.

* * *

SHOOK, Laurence K(ennedy) 1909-

PERSONAL: Born November 6, 1909, in Toronto, Ontario, Canada; son of Richard Conrad (a businessman) and Mary Ann (Kennedy) Shook. *Education:* University of Toronto, B.A. (honors), 1932, M.A. (philosophy), 1933; Harvard University, A.M. (English philosophy), 1937, Ph.D., 1940. *Home and office:* 59 Queen's Park Cres. E., Toronto, Ontario, Canada M5S 2C4.

CAREER: Entered Congregatio Sancti Basilii (C.S.B.; Basilian Fathers), 1926, ordained Roman Catholic priest, 1935; St. Basil's Seminary, Toronto, Ontario, reader in theology, 1932-36; University of Toronto, Toronto, Ontario, assistant professor, 1940-42, professor of English, 1942-75, head of department, 1942-61, superior and president of St. Michael's College, 1952-58; writer, 1975—. Professor at Pontifical Institute of Mediaeval Studies, 1946—, president of institute, 1961-73; guest lecturer at schools in the United States and Canada. Chairman of International Congress on the Theology of the Renewal of the Church, 1967. *Military service:* Royal Canadian Air Force, chaplain, 1943-45; became flight lieutenant.

MEMBER: Mediaeval Academy of America (fellow; vice-president, 1967-70), Canadian Association of the Sovereign and Military Order of Malta. *Awards, honors:* D.Litt. from Western Michigan University, 1972, and University of Toronto, 1977; officer of the Order of Canada, 1975.

WRITINGS: (Translator) Etienne Gilson, *Heloise and Abelard*, Regnery, 1951; (translator) Gilson, *The Christian Philosophy of St. Thomas Aquinas*, Random House, 1956; (editor) *Theology of Renewal*, two volumes, Herder & Herder, 1968; (editor) *Discussions* (proceedings), Pontifical Institute of Mediaeval Studies, 1968; *Catholic Post-Secondary Education in English-Speaking Canada: A History* (monograph), University of Toronto Press, 1971.

Contributor: John R. Sommerfeldt, editor, *Studies in Medieval Culture*, Western Michigan University, 1964; Millar Maclure and F. W. Watt, editors, *Essays in English Literature from the Renaissance to the Victorian Age: Presented to A.S.P. Wodehouse*, University of Toronto Press, 1964; Jess B. Bessinger, Jr. and Robert P. Creed, editors, *Franciplegius: Medieval and Linguistic Studies in Honor of Francis Peabody Magoun, Jr.*, New York University Press, 1965; Gerard Mulligan, editor, *Were the Dean's Windows Dusty*, two volumes, privately printed, 1967; Beryl Rowland, editor, *Companion to Chaucer Studies,* Oxford University Press, 1968; J. R. O'Donnell, editor, *Essays in Honour of Anton Charles Pegis,* Pontifical Institute of Mediaeval Stuides, 1974. Contributor to *Collier's Encyclopedia* and *New Catholic Encyclopedia.* Contributor of about twenty-five articles to scholarly journals. Member of editorial board of *Mediaeval Scandinavia* and *Mediaevalia et Humanistica.*

WORK IN PROGRESS: The Biography of Etienne Gilson.

* * *

SHORTER, Edward 1941-

PERSONAL: Born October 31, 1941, in Evanston, Ill.; son of Lazar (a civil servant) and Joan (Caperton) Shorter; divorced; children: Matthew, Stephanie, Abigail. *Education:* Wabash College, B.A., 1961; Harvard University, Ph.D., 1967. *Home:* 379 Markham St., Toronto, Ontario, Canada. *Office:* Department of History, University of Toronto, Toronto, Ontario, Canada.

CAREER: University of Toronto, Toronto, Ontario, assistant professor, 1967-71, associate professor, 1971-77, professor of history, 1977—.

WRITINGS: (With Charles Tilly) *Strikes in France,* Cambridge University Press, 1974; *The Making of the Modern Family,* Basic Books, 1975.

WORK IN PROGRESS: The History of Women's Bodies.

* * *

SIEGEL, Ernest 1922-

PERSONAL: Born November 23, 1922, in Savannah, Ga.; son of Abram (a businessman) and Tamara (Cantor) Siegel; married Rita Yohay (in special education), June, 1948; children: Phillip, Paul, Peter. *Education:* Queens College (now of the City University of New York), B.A., 1950, M.A., 1951; Columbia University, Ed.D., 1966. *Religion:* Jewish. *Home:* 14-16 Watersedge Dr., Bayside, N.Y. 11360. *Office:* Department of Education, Adelphi University, Garden City, N.Y. 11530.

CAREER: Elementary school teacher in Newark, N.J., 1950-51, and New York City, 1951-63; Bureau for the Education of the Physically Handicapped, New York City, supervisor, 1963-64; Hunter College of the City University of New York, New York City, assistant professor, 1964-66, part-time lecturer in education, 1964-67; Bureau for the Education of the Physically Handicapped, supervisor, 1967-74; Adelphi University, Garden City, N.Y., associate professor of special education, 1974-77; writer, 1977—. Speaker. Research assistant at Center for Urban Education, 1964-66; faculty member at Queens College of the City University of New York, summers, 1962-67, Lamar Institute of Technology, summer, 1963, Adelphi College, 1965-66, Keene State College, summers, 1968-69, University of New Mexico, summers, 1970-71, Appalachian State University, summer, 1973, and College of New Rochelle, 1973-75. Participant in international congresses.

AWARDS, HONORS: "Professional of the Year" plaque from New York Association for Brain-Injured Children, 1967; "Pioneer of the Year" plaque from Association for Children with Learning Disabilities, 1975.

WRITINGS: Helping the Brain-Injured Child, Association for Brain-Injured Children, 1961; *Who Said It?: A Teaching Aid in Communication,* Educational Activities, Inc., 1966; *More or Less: A Teaching Aid in Arithmetic,* Educational Activities, Inc., 1966; *Special Education in the Regular Classroom,* John Day, 1969; (contributor) Doreen Kromick, editor, *Learning Disabilities: Its Implications to a Responsible Society,* Developmental Learning Materials, 1969; *Teaching One Child: A Strategy for Developing Teaching Excellence,* Educational Activities, Inc., 1972; *The Exceptional Child Grows Up,* Dutton, 1974; (with wife, Rita Siegel) *Creating Instructional Sequences,* Academic Therapy Publishing, 1977; (with R. Siegel and son, Paul Siegel) *Help for the Lonely Child: Strengthening Social Perceptions,* Dutton, 1978. Contributor of articles and reviews to education journals. Member of editorial advisory board of *Journal of Learning Disabilities,* 1973—.

WORK IN PROGRESS: Contemporary Issues in Learning Disabilities.

AVOCATIONAL INTERESTS: Singing, songwriting, theatre-going, traveling.

* * *

SIEGEL, Richard L(ewis) 1940-

PERSONAL: Born October 21, 1940, in New York, N.Y.; son of Samuel (a manufacturer) and Clara Siegel; married Joan Lukin, June 30, 1963; children: Naomi, Daniel, Jordan. *Education:* Brandeis University, B.A., 1961; Columbia University, Ph.D., 1967. *Religion:* Jewish. *Home:* 1230 Rowland Circle, Reno, Nev. 89509. *Office:* Department of Political Science, University of Nevada, Reno, Nev. 89555.

CAREER: University of Nevada, Reno, instructor, 1965-67, assistant professor, 1967-71, associate professor of political science, 1971—. Commentator on KTVN-TV, Reno, 1974-75. *Member:* International Studies Association, American Political Science Association, Policy Studies Association, American Civil Liberties Union (member of national board of directors, 1974—), Northern California Political Science Association (member of executive board).

WRITINGS: Evaluating the Results of Foreign Policy (monograph), Graduate School of International Studies, University of Denver, 1969; (with Leonard Weinberg) *Comparing Public Policies: United States, Soviet Union, and Europe,* Dorsey, 1977. Contributor of articles and reviews to social studies and political science journals.

WORK IN PROGRESS: The Transnationalization of Domestic Policy.

* * *

SIEVERS, Harry J(oseph) 1920-1977

November 14, 1920—October 18, 1977; Jesuit priest, university dean, lecturer, and biographer. Sievers was dean of the Graduate School of Arts and Sciences at Fordham University and a frequent lecturer on the American presidency. A former teacher of history, Sievers served as historical consultant in a boundary dispute between British Guiana and Venezuela. Later he received the Simon Bolivar Medal from Venezuela. He was author of a three-volume biography of Benjamin Harrison. He died in New York, N.Y. Obituaries: *New York Times,* October 20, 1977. (See index for *CA* sketch)

* * *

SILLIPHANT, Stirling (Dale) 1918-

PERSONAL: Born January 16, 1918, in Detroit, Mich.; son of Leigh Lemuel (a sales director) and Ethel May (Noaker) Silliphant; married Tiana Du Long (an actress), July 4, 1974. children: Stirling, Dayle, Loren (deceased). *Education:*

University of Southern California, B.A. (magna cum laude), 1938. *Office:* Burbank Studios, Burbank, Calif. 91505.

CAREER: Walt Disney Studios, Burbank, Calif., publicist, 1938-41; 20th Century Fox, New York, N.Y., publicist, 1942, publicity director, 1946-53; screenwriter and independent producer in Hollywood, Calif., 1953—. President, Pingree Productions. *Military service:* U.S. Navy, 1942-46. *Member:* California Yacht Club, Phi Beta Kappa. *Awards, honors:* Academy Award (Oscar) from Academy of Motion Pictures Arts and Sciences, Mystery Writers of America Edgar Award, and Golden Globe award from Hollywood Foreign Press Association, all 1968, for screenplay "In the Heat of the Night"; Golden Globe award, 1969, for screenplay "Charly"; Image Award from National Association for the Advancement of Colored People (NAACP), 1972, for production of "Shaft"; National Association of Theater Owners box office writer of year award, 1974.

WRITINGS: Maracaibo, Farrar, Straus, 1955; (with Rachel Maddux) *Fiction into Film,* University of Tennessee Press, 1970.

Screenplays: "Five Against the House," Columbia, 1955; "Huk!", United Artists, 1956; "Nightfall," Columbia, 1957; "Damn Citizen," Universal, 1958; "The Line Up," Columbia, 1958; "Maracaibo," Paramount, 1958; "Village of the Damned," Metro-Goldwyn-Mayer, 1960; "The Slender Thread," Paramount, 1965; "In the Heat of the Night," United Artists, 1967; "Charly," Cinerama, 1968; "Marlowe," Metro-Goldwyn-Mayer, 1969; "A Walk in the Spring Rain," Columbia, 1970; "The Liberation of L. B. Jones," Columbia, 1970; "Murphy's War," Paramount, 1971; "The New Centurians," Columbia, 1972; "The Poseidon Adventure," Twentieth Century Fox, 1972; "Shaft in Africa," Metro-Goldwyn-Mayer, 1973; "The Towering Inferno," Twentieth Century Fox, 1974; "The Sailor Who Fell from Grace with the Sea," Avco-Embassy, 1974; "Killer Elite," United Artists, 1974; "The Enforcer," Warner Bros., 1976; "The Swarm," Warner Bros., 1977; "Telefon," Metro-Goldwyn-Mayer, 1977.

Teleplays: (And creator) "Route 66" series, Columbia Broadcasting System (CBS), 1960-64; (and creator) "Naked City" series, American Broadcasting Co. (ABC), 1960-63; (and creator) "Longstreet" series, ABC, 1972-74. Also contributor of teleplays to "Chrysler Theatre," "Schlitz Playhouse," "Suspicion," "Alfred Hitchcock Presents," "G. E. Theatre," and "CBS Playhouse."

BIOGRAPHICAL/CRITICAL SOURCES: Christian Science Monitor, July 9, 1969; *Newsweek,* January 31, 1972; *Women's Wear Daily,* December 18, 1974; *New York Post,* Januray 6, 1975.

* * *

SILVERSTEIN, Charles 1935-

PERSONAL: Born April 23, 1935, in New York; son of Sam and Ida (Berlly) Silverstein. *Education:* State University of New York College at New Paltz, B.S., 1959; Rutgers University, M.A., 1974, Ph.D., 1975. *Religion:* "Sort of Jewish." *Home:* 233 West 83rd St., New York, N.Y. 10024. *Office:* Institute for Human Identity, 490 West End Ave., New York, N.Y. 10024.

CAREER: Institute for Human Identity, New York, N.Y., director, 1973—, director of sex therapy, 1978—. Psychologist. *Member:* American Psychological Association, Association for the Advancement of Behavior Therapy.

WRITINGS: A Family Matter: A Parents' Guide to Homo-

sexuality, McGraw, 1977; (with Edmund White) *The Joy of Gay Sex,* Crown, 1977. Contributor to academic journals. Founding editor, *Journal of Homosexuality.*

WORK IN PROGRESS: Research and clinical work on sex therapy; a book for gay couples.

* * *

SIMON, Linda 1946-

PERSONAL: Born December 12, 1946, in New York; daughter of Samuel and Kay (Pacula) Perlin; married Laurence Simon, August 6, 1966. *Education:* Queens College of the City University of New York, B.A., 1967; New York University, M.A., 1971. *Residence:* Stockbridge, Mass. 01262. *Agent:* Rhoda A. Weyr, William Morris Agency, 1350 Avenue of the Americas, New York, N.Y. 10019.

CAREER: Fordham University, New York, N.Y., instructor in creative writing, 1970-72; free-lance writer, 1972—.

WRITINGS: (Editor) *Gertrude Stein: A Composite Portrait,* Avon, 1974; *The Biography of Alice B. Toklas,* Doubleday, 1977.

WORK IN PROGRESS: Peregrine, short stories; research for a biography of Thornton Wilder, for Doubleday.

SIDELIGHTS: Linda Simon writes that she would someday like to write a biography of Sigrid Undset.

* * *

SIMPSON, Ruth 1926-

PERSONAL: Born March 15, 1926, in Cleveland, Ohio; daughter of Edward and Ethel (Gouldsberry) Simpson. *Education:* Western Reserve University (now Case Western Reserve University), B.A., 1947; also attended Dalcroze School of Music, 1969-71. *Home address:* Zena Rd., Box 422, Woodstock, N.Y. 12498.

CAREER: Hill & Knowlton, Inc., New York City, public relations executive, 1955-58; J. Walter Thompson Company, New York City, public relations executive, 1958-60; Mogul, Williams & Saylor, New York City, public relations executive, 1960-63; N. W. Ayer & Sons, Inc., New York City, public relations executive, 1963-67; Harshe, Rotman & Druck, Inc., New York City, public relations executive, 1967-71; lecturer at colleges throughout the United States, 1971—. *Member:* Daughters of Bilitus (president, 1970-71), Woodstock Gay People (president, 1977—).

WRITINGS: From the Closet to the Courts, Viking, 1976; *Patchwork Majority* (poems), Viking, 1978.

WORK IN PROGRESS: Webscoming, a study of psychic experiences; a collection of short stories for children for Curriculum Concepts.

SIDELIGHTS: Ruth Simpson told *CA:* "As a homosexual I am obligated to my own people; as a woman I am responsible to feminist principles; as a human being I am dedicated to the basic right of human dignity. These responsibilities are met to the best of my ability and on various levels in my writing. I work in the homosexual movement and find the oppression of my gay sisters and brothers particularly illustrative of problems which confront every member of any oppressed group who takes a step away from the hiding place toward that hostile ground known as our society.

"I have worked in a number of movements and have found oppressive action toward all minority groups the same—we all share the same oppressors. Hopefully one day we will understand the similarity of our causes and, from our separate and diverse minorities, form a patchwork majority—a dangerous potential for our shared oppressors."

AVOCATIONAL INTERESTS: Musical composition.

BIOGRAPHICAL/CRITICAL SOURCES: Kay Tobin and Randy Wicker, *The Gay Crusaders,* Paperback Library, 1970; *New York Times,* March 28, 1971; *Woodstock Times,* March 24, 1977; *New York Times-Herald-Record,* July 25, 1977.

* * *

SIMPSON, Stanhope Rowton 1903-

PERSONAL: Born May 7, 1903, in South Wigston, England; son of Herbert (a solicitor) and Sarah Anne (Rowton) Simpson; married Evelyn Constance Adams, August 7, 1930; children: Hugo, Judith, Barbara, Lorna. *Education:* Magdalene College, Cambridge, B.A., 1925, M.A., 1927, Ph.D., 1977. *Politics:* Conservative. *Religion:* Church of England. *Home:* 65 Collington Ave., Bexhill-on-Sea, East Sussex TN39 3NB, England.

CAREER: Sudan Political Service, member of staff in Blue Nile, 1926, Kordofan, 1927-28, Bahr-el-Ghazal, 1929-32, Berber, 1932-33, Mongolla, 1933-36, and Khartoum, 1936-43, commissioner of lands and registrar-general, 1946-53; Colonial Office, London, England, land tenure specialist, 1953-62; Ministry of Quarries Development, London, land tenure adviser, 1962-69; writer, 1969—. Barrister at law; called to the Bar at Inner Temple. *Awards, honors:* Commander of the Order of the British Empire.

WRITINGS: Land Law and Registration, Cambridge University Press, 1976. Contributor to professional journals.

* * *

SIMSON, Eve 1937-

PERSONAL: Born August 7, 1937, in Tallinn, Estonia; came to the United States in 1949, naturalized citizen, 1954; daughter of Aleksander (a civil engineer) and Johanna Maria (a designer of hats and fabrics; maiden name, Kegel) Tammisoo; married Thomas Simson, May 19, 1967. *Education:* Ohio State University, B.Sc., 1959, M.A., 1964, Ph.D., 1969; attended University of Minnesota, 1960. *Home:* 1205 East Wayne St. N., South Bend, Ind. 46615.

CAREER: State of Ohio Health Department, Columbus, statistician, 1960-62; Ohio State University, Columbus, instructor in sociology, 1966-69; St. Mary's College, Notre Dame, Ind., assistant professor of sociology, 1969-72; Indiana University, South Bend, assistant professor of sociology, 1972—. *Member:* American Sociological Association, American Association for the Advancement of Baltic Studies, Popular Culture Association, Estonian Learned Society of America, Authors Guild of Authors League of America, Zeta Tau Alpha.

WRITINGS: The Faith Healer, Concordia, 1977. Contributor of articles and reviews to medical journals, and sociology and library journals; contributor of a play to *El Viento.*

WORK IN PROGRESS: A mystery novel; investigating healing-evangelists; research on Laiuse Gypsies and on the stereotyping of women on television.

SIDELIGHTS: Eve Simson writes: "I became involved in investigating faith healing for my Ph.D. work in medical sociology after having come into personal contact with individuals whose encounters with healer-evangelists ranged from tragedy to conversions and alleged miraculous healings. The great interest shown in my topic by many different groups and individuals motivated me to continue investigating."

AVOCATIONAL INTERESTS: Oil painting, travel (the Soviet Union, Europe, Mexico; especially interested in the Cajun country in and around New Orleans and in London), visiting nature parks and animal preserves in South Africa, reading (everything from Solzhenitsyn to Agatha Christie to nonfiction).

BIOGRAPHICAL/CRITICAL SOURCES: South Bend Tribune, July 16, 1977.

* * *

SINGER, C(harles) Gregg 1910-

PERSONAL: Born June 3, 1910, in Philadelphia, Pa.; son of Arthur Gregg (a bridge architect) and Edith (a teacher; maiden name, Lord) Singer; married Marjorie Pouder, September 6, 1939; children: Marjorie Jean Singer Satterwaite, Richard Gregg, Terrie Elizabeth Singer Speicher, Robert Adams. *Education:* Haverford College, A.B., 1933; University of Pennsylvania, A.M., 1935, Ph.D., 1940. *Politics:* Conservative. *Religion:* Presbyterian. *Home:* 319 Wake Dr., Salisbury, N.C. 28144. *Office:* Department of History, Catawba College, Salisbury, N.C. 28144.

CAREER: Wheaton College, Wheaton, Ill., 1944-48, began as associate professor, became professor of history, chairman of department, 1944-48; Salem College, Winston-Salem, N.C., professor of history, 1948-54, chairman of department, 1954-58; Bellhaven College, Jackson, Miss., professor of history, 1954-58, chairman of department, 1958-75; Catawba College, Salisbury, N.C., professor of history, 1958-77, chairman of department, 1958-75. Area director of War Manpower Commission, 1942-44.

WRITINGS: South Carolina in the Confederation, privately printed, 1941, reissued, Porcupine Press, 1976; *A Theological Interpretation of American History,* Craig Press, 1964; (contributor) Barb Henry, editor, *Christian Faith and Modern Philosophy,* Channel Press, 1964; *Toynbee,* Baker Book, 1965; *John Calvin: His Roots and Fruits,* Presbyterian & Reformed, 1967; (contributor) Ronald Nash, editor, *The Philosophy of Gordon Clark,* Presbyterian & Reformed, 1968; (contributor) E. H. Geehan, editor, *Jerusalem and Athens,* Presbyterian & Reformed, 1971; *The Unholy Alliance,* Arlington House, 1975; (contributor) Gary North, editor, *Foundations of Christian Scholarship,* Ross House Books, 1976. Contributor to *Encyclopedia of Christianity* and *Dictionary of Christianity.* Contributor to professional journals and *Christianity Today.*

WORK IN PROGRESS: The Decline of Western Thought.

SIDELIGHTS: Singer remarks: "I never dreamed I would become a writer. I started to write articles about thirty years ago and in 1964 I produced my first book as a result of my sketches of Augustine, Calvin, the Puritans, and the American Revolution. Its success led to requests to do more writing—and I have done it."

* * *

SINGER, David L(in) 1937-

PERSONAL: Born February 6, 1937, in New York, N.Y.; son of Oscar J. (an attorney) and Esther (a teacher; maiden name, Lin) Singer; married Phyllis Alberts, April 25, 1958 (divorced August 23, 1960); married Mary Beth Whiton (a psychologist), January 12, 1974. *Education:* Brooklyn College (now of the City University of New York), B.A. (cum laude), 1957; Yale University, M.S., 1959, Ph.D., 1964. *Office:* Department of Counseling Psychology, Antioch/New England Graduate School, 1 Elm St., Keene, N.H. 03431.

CAREER: Veterans Administration Hospital, West Haven,

Conn., clinical psychology trainee, 1962-64; Duke University, Durham, N.C., assistant professor of psychology, 1965-67; Columbia University, Teachers College, New York, N.Y., assistant professor, 1967-69, associate professor of psychology, 1967-72, associate director of Psychological Consultation Center, 1967-72; private practice in clinical psychology, 1972-76; Northampton Center for Children and Families, Northampton, Mass., clinical director, 1976-77; Antioch/New England Graduate School, Keene, N.H., counseling psychologist and chairman of department, 1977—. Certified psychologist in Massachusetts and New York. Vice-president of board of directors of A. K. Rice Institute, 1975—; member of board of directors of Institute for Applied Study of Social Systems, 1971—. Director and staff member of group relations conferences, conferences on applied organizational analysis, and workshops; private practice of adult, child, and family therapy in New York City, 1967-72.

MEMBER: International Association of Applied Social Scientists (charter member), American Psychological Association, American Orthopsychiatric Association, American Association for the Advancement of Science, Society for the Psychological Study of Social Issues, American Association of University Professors. *Awards, honors:* Postdoctoral fellow at Judge Baker Guidance Center and Children's Hospital, 1964-65.

WRITINGS: Sleep on It: A Look at Sleep and Dreams (juvenile), Prentice-Hall, 1969; (contributor) Jacob Levine, editor, *Motivation and Humor,* Atherton, 1969; (contributor) Nicholas Long, editor, *Conflict in the Classroom,* Wadsworth, 1975; (contributor) Gordon Lawrence, *Exploring Boundaries,* Wiley, 1978. Contributor of articles and reviews to professional journals and to *Esquire.* Associate editor of *Journal of Personality and Social Systems* (also past member of editorial board).

WORK IN PROGRESS: Research on organizational aspects of human service delivery—especially in mental health services.

SIDELIGHTS: Singer writes that it was his training at Tavistock Institute in London that developed his interest in social systems and organizational theory. *Avocational interests:* Travel, classical music, tennis, "delightfully outrageous people."

* * *

SIRACUSA, Joseph M(arcus) 1944-

PERSONAL: Born July 6, 1944, in Chicago, Ill.; son of John P. (a business executive) and Josephine M. Siracusa; married Sally Johnson (an artist), December 21, 1968; children: Joseph Anthony. *Education:* University of Denver, B.A., 1966, M.A., 1968; University of Colorado, Ph.D., 1971; also attended University of Vienna, 1964-65. *Politics:* Independent. *Religion:* None. *Residence:* St. Lucia, Queensland, Australia. *Office:* Department of History, University of Queensland, St. Lucia, 4067 Queensland, Australia.

CAREER: University of Colorado, Boulder, instructor in history, 1969-71; Merrill Lynch, Pierce, Fenner & Smith, Inc., member of executive training program in Boston, Mass., and New York, N.Y., 1972-73; University of Queensland, St. Lucia, Australia, lecturer, 1973-75, senior lecturer in American diplomatic history, 1976—. Licensed by New York and American Stock Exchanges and Chicago Board of Trade.

MEMBER: American Historical Association, Organization of American Historians, Society for Historians of American Foreign Relations, Australian Institute of International Affairs, Australian-New Zealand American Studies Association. *Awards, honors:* Grants from Australian Government, 1975, 1976, and Harry S Truman Library Institute for National and International Affairs, 1975, 1977.

WRITINGS: (Editor) *New Left Diplomatic Histories and Historians: The American Revisionists,* Kennikat, 1973; *The American Diplomatic Revolution: A Documentary History of the Cold War, 1941-1947,* Holt, 1976; (editor with Glen St. John Barclay) *Australian-American Relations since 1945: A Documentary History,* Holt, 1976; (editor with Barclay, and contributor) *The Impact of the Cold War: Reconsiderations,* Kennikat, 1977; (contributor) John A. Moses, editor, *The Historical Discipline and Culture in Australasia,* University of Queensland Press, 1977; (with Julius W. Pratt and Vincent P. DeSantis) *A History of United States Foreign Policy,* Prentice-Hall, 4th edition (Siracusa was not associated with earlier editions), 1977. Contributor of articles and reviews to history, politics, and international studies journals. Associate editor of *Australian Journal of Politics and History.*

WORK IN PROGRESS: The Intellectual Origins of the Cold War.

SIDELIGHTS: Siracusa writes: "I have been deeply motivated by the erosion of standards in the writing of American history during the past ten years. What was passing for scholarship, not to mention profundity, seemed to me at best rubbish. In fact, the time traveler who unearths our culture in several thousand years will have great difficulty in distinguishing between our fiction and our nonfiction."

AVOCATIONAL INTERESTS: Tennis, walking, "breathing in fresh air."

* * *

SKALLERUP, Harry R(obert) 1927-

PERSONAL: Born March 20, 1927, in Chicago, Ill.; son of Otto R. and Rebecca J. (Rossow) Skallerup; married Marilyn Amy Gage (an editor and indexer), December 31, 1952; children: Thomas M., Susan J., Janet R. *Education:* University of Illinois, B.S. (high honors), 1952; Washington University, St. Louis, Mo., A.M., 1953; University of Minnesota, M.A., 1954. *Office:* Library, Florida Atlantic University, Boca Raton, Fla. 33432.

CAREER: University of Illinois, Urbana, physics librarian, 1954-55; Southern Illinois University, Carbondale, science librarian, 1955-59; W. J. Johnson Antiquarian Books, New York, N.Y., assistant manager, 1959-62; University of Iowa, Iowa City, engineering librarian, 1962-64, head of catalog department, 1964-67; U.S. Naval Academy, Annapolis, Md., associate librarian, 1967-77; Florida Atlantic University, Boca Raton, director of libraries, 1977—. Member of executive steering committee of Federal Library and Information Network, 1976-77. Founder of Runeskald Press, 1974. *Military service:* U.S. Coast Guard, 1945-46. U.S. Merchant Marine, 1946-48.

MEMBER: International Sail, American Library Association, Association of College and Research Libraries, Bibliographical Society of America, Nautical Research Guild, Southeast Library Association, Florida Library Association, Sigma Xi, Beta Phi Mu. *Awards, honors:* H. W. Wilson scholarship from University of Minnesota, 1953-54.

WRITINGS: American State Academy of Science Publica-

tions, Library School, University of Illinois, 1957; *Books Afloat and Ashore: A History of Books, Libraries, and Reading Among Seamen During the Age of Sail,* Archon, 1974; (contributor) *Books for College Libraries,* 2nd edition, American Library Association, 1975. Contributor to library journals.

WORK IN PROGRESS: Research on maritime libraries, the history of American libraries, certain aspects of the history of the book trade, rare book binding, and antique library furniture.

* * *

SLAGHT, Lawrence T(ownsend) 1912-

PERSONAL: Born October 3, 1912, in Sunnyside, Wash.; son of Ralph W. (a farmer) and Elna (a teacher; maiden name, Townsend) Slaght; married Irene Swanson, September 1, 1936; children: Ralph, Dale, Stanley. *Education:* Linfield College, B.A., 1936; Eastern Baptist Theological Seminary, B.D., 1939, Th.M., 1942, Th.D., 1952; University of Pennsylvania, M.A., 1940. *Politics:* Republican. *Home:* 69 Winston Dr., Somerset, N.J. 08873.

CAREER: Ordained Baptist minister, 1940; pastor of Baptist churches in Philadelphia, Pa., 1939-43, Oregon City, Ore., 1943-51, Dover, Del., 1951-60, and Lowell, Mass., 1960-64; *Watchman-Examiner,* New York, N.Y., editor, 1964-70; Community Baptist Church, Somerset, N.J., pastor, 1970—. Professor at Western Baptist Theological Seminary, 1944-49; instructor at Wesley College (Dover, Del.), 1955-60; lecturer at College of the Holy Spirit (Scotland).

WRITINGS: Cornelius Barentse Slecht and Some of His Descendants, privately printed, 1972; *Multiplying the Witness,* Judson, 1974; *Organizing a Church for Action,* Judson, in press. Founder of *American Baptist Fellowship Newsletter.* Contributor to *Baptist Leader.*

SIDELIGHTS: Lawrence Slaght comments: "I have served on the major boards and committees of my denomination for twenty-five years. I have traveled in Finland, Great Britain, and Israel (the latter as a representative of my denomination and the American Jewish Committee)."

* * *

SLATKIN, Charles Eli 1907-1977

1907—July 25, 1977; American art dealer and author of works in his field. Slatkin arranged exhibitions of French sculptors' works, including those of Rodin, Morisot, and Toulouse-Lautrec. He died in New York, N.Y. Obituaries: *New York Times,* July 26, 1977.

* * *

SLAUGHTER, Jane M(undy) 1908-

PERSONAL: Born October 2, 1908, in Buchanan, Va.; daughter of Luther Thomas (a sheriff) and Pearl Carnce (Karnes) Mundy; married Frank G. Slaughter (a writer and physician), June 10, 1933; children: Frank Gill, Jr., Randolph Mundy. *Education:* Jefferson Hospital Training School, R.N., 1926. *Politics:* Independent. *Religion:* Presbyterian. *Home:* 5051 Yacht Club Rd., Jacksonville, Fla. 32210. *Agent:* Brandt & Brandt, 101 Park Ave., New York, N.Y. 10017.

CAREER: Registered nurse in Roanoke, Va., 1926-34; writer, 1972—. Member of board of directors of local Young Women's Christian Association. *Member:* Garden Club of Jacksonville (life member).

WRITINGS: Espy and the Catnappers (juvenile), Doubleday, 1975.

WORK IN PROGRESS: Tess of the Shenandoah, for young people, "based on my own ancestors in the Valley since the mid-1700's."

SIDELIGHTS: Jane Slaughter writes: "Acting on the principle that 'the person who won't read is worse off than one who can't read' I seek to write exciting, suspenseful stories for young readers that will hold their interest and make them want to read more."

* * *

SMART, Carol 1948-

PERSONAL: Born December 20, 1948, in London, England; daughter of Ernest (a hotel proprietor) and Vera (a hotel proprietor; maiden name, Armsden) Pinock; married Barry Smart (a lecturer in sociology), September 22, 1972. *Education:* Portsmouth Polytechnic, B.A. (honors), 1972; University of Sheffield, M.A., 1974. *Home:* 58 Glenalmond Rd., Sheffield S11 7GX, England. *Office:* Department of Social Studies, Trent Polytechnic, Barton St., Nottingham, England.

CAREER: Worked as a social worker, 1972-73; Sheffield University, Sheffield, England, postgraduate tutor in sociology, 1973-74; Trent Polytechnic, Nottingham, England, lecturer in sociology, 1974—. *Member:* British Sociological Association (member of women's caucus), National Association of Teachers in Higher and Further Education.

WRITINGS: Women, Crime, and Criminology: A Feminist Critique, Routledge & Kegan Paul, 1976; (editor with Barry Smart) *Women, Sexuality, and Social Control,* Routledge & Kegan Paul, 1977. Contributor to *British Journal of Sociology.*

WORK IN PROGRESS: Research on women and the criminal process, to document the treatment of women by the courts and the police in the United Kingdom.

SIDELIGHTS: Carol Smart comments: "I wrote *Women, Crime, and Criminology* as a consequence of being a feminist in a master's course in criminology. I realized very quickly that there was little adequate material on women and crime and felt that the whole area needed to be reappraised. I am particularly concerned about the sexist treatment of women in the criminal process (e. g. prostitutes and rape victims) and intend to do more research in this area."

* * *

SMITH, A. Robert 1925-

PERSONAL Born February 13, 1925, in York, Pa.; son of Arthur R. (a textile foreman) and Inez (a painter; maiden name, Dunnick) Smith; married Elizabeth McDowell (a teacher), May 28, 1967; children: Dana Smith, Phillip Morgan, Ted Morgan, Elizabeth Morgan. *Education:* Juniata College, B.S., 1950; further study at George Washington University. *Office:* 121 Second St., N.E., Washington, D. C. 2002.

CAREER: Huntingdon Daily News, Huntingdon, Pa., reporter, 1947; *Evening Star,* Washington, D. C., reporter, 1950; *Bremerton Sun,* Bremerton, Wash., reporter, 1950; *Eugene Register-Guard,* Eugene, Ore., Washington correspondence, 1951—; King Broadcasting Co., Seattle, Wash., Washington, D. C. bureau chief, 1976—. Instructor in journalism at University of Maryland. Member of Town Planning Commission of Washington Grove, Md. *Military ser-*

vice: U.S. Navy, 1943-46. *Member:* National Press Club, American Political Science Association, Association for Research and Enlightenment.

WRITINGS: The Tiger in the Senate, Doubleday, 1962; (with Eric Sevareid) *Washington: Magnificent Capital,* Doubleday, 1965; (with James V. Giles) *An American Rape,* New Republic, 1975.

SIDELIGHTS: Smith writes to *CA:* "My first book, a biography of Senator Wayne Morse, was intended to explain a very complex, controversial political figure. My second was a testimonial not only to a great city but the great experiment, democracy, which succeeds or fails in accord with decisions made here. Both were attempts to illuminate for the citizen reader how our system works. Both grew out of my work as a Washington correspondent for daily newspapers and from the conviction that journalists produce much of the raw material from which historians draw their conclusions.

"My third book was about a case of racial injustice, expressing my personal passion for racial equality and fairness to all citizens under the law. This was the story of three black men accused and convicted of raping a white girl, given the death sentence in Montgomery County, Md., America's most affluent county. The *New York Times* called it the 'Little Scottsboro Case.' It touched off a major legal battle by a white citizens defense committee on behalf of the blacks. It went to the U.S. Supreme Court, which refused to uphold the conviction, forcing the state to reconsider and eventually free and pardon the blacks. I wrote this in collaboration with one of the accused, James V. Giles. The story is currently being considered for a motion picture."

* * *

SMITH, Chard Powers 1894-1977

November 1, 1894—October 31, 1977; American writer, poet, biographer, and educator. Smith, although by education an attorney, gave up the active practice of law in order to become a writer. His poetry, fiction, and history dealt mostly with New England life. He died in Williamstown, Mass. Obituaries: *New York Times,* November 3, 1977; *AB Bookman's Weekly,* February 6, 1978. (See index for *CA* sketch)

* * *

SMITH, Dale O(rville) 1911-

PERSONAL: Born March 7, 1911, in Reno, Nev.; son of Alfred Merritt (a mining engineer) and Ivan (Sessions) Smith; married Virginia Posvar, October 28, 1948; children: Kort Ivy, Voan Ivy (Mrs. Daniel H. Bauer), Drew Givens, Dale Merritt. *Education:* Attended University of Nevada, 1928-30; U.S. Military Academy, West Point, B.S., 1934; graduated from Air War College, 1948; Stanford University, M.A., 1949, Ed.D., 1950. *Politics:* Republican. *Home:* 3055 Heatheridge Lane, Reno, Nev. 89509.

CAREER: Served in U.S. Army and later, U.S. Air Force, 1934-64, retiring as major general; private consultant to various business firms, 1964—. Commissioned second lieutenant, 1934; worked at various assignments in United States and Hawaii, 1935-43; commander of 384th Bombardment Group in England, 1943-44; assigned to work at the Pentagon, 1945-46; Air War College, Maxwell Air Force Base, Ala., instructor, 1946; Air University, Maxwell Air Force Base, director of education and chief of research division, 1946-54; National Security Council, Washington, D.C., sen-

ior military staff member of Operations Coordinating Board, 1954-55; chief of military training in U.S. Mission to Saudi Arabia, advisor to King Saud, and representative of U.S. Department of Defense in bilateral negotiations, 1956-57; commander of 313th Air Division, Okinawa, 1958-60, of 64th Air Division, Stewart Air Force Base, N.Y., 1960-61; Pentagon, Washington, D.C., special assistant for arms control to Joint Chiefs of Staff, 1961-63, member of joint strategic survey council, 1963-64. Executive director, Air Force Historical Foundation, 1965-67; Graham-Eckes School, Palm Beach, Fla., president and vice-chairman of the board of trustees, 1967-70. Chairman, Reno Housing Commission, 1971-75.

MEMBER: Air Force Association, Free and Accepted Masons, Army-Navy Club, Daedalians, Sigma Nu. *Awards, honors*—Military: Twenty service medals and decorations, including Legion of Merit with one oak leaf cluster; Distinguished Flying Cross with three oak leaf clusters; Air medal with four oak leaf clusters; Croix de Guerre with palm.

WRITINGS: U.S. Military Doctrine: A Study and Appraisal, Duell, Sloan & Pearce, 1955; *The Eagle's Talons: A Military View of Civil Control of the Military,* Spartan Books, 1966; (with Curtis LeMay) *America Is in Danger,* Funk, 1968. Contributor of articles on national policy and leadership to various periodicals. Editor, *Aerospace Historian,* 1965-67.

WORK IN PROGRESS: Home of the Brave, a novel.

SIDELIGHTS: Smith told *CA:* "For someone who has devoted his writing efforts to non-fiction, it is a giant step to the fiction medium. I once thought it would be easy to invent a story and not worry about laborious research. Now I know that learning the fiction craft is like learning a new profession."

* * *

SMITH, Douglas 1918-

PERSONAL: Born June 18, 1918, in Success, Ark.; son of William Cortez (a merchant) and Dorcas (Douglas) Smith; married Mary Goding, December 18, 1948 (divorced, 1976); children: Douglas Wilfred. *Education:* University of Arkansas, B.A., 1940. *Home:* 4503 South 31st St., Arlington, Va. 22206. *Office:* 777 14th St. N.W., Rm. 1200, Washington, D.C. 20005.

CAREER/WRITINGS: Russellville Courier-Democrat, Russelville, Ark., editor, 1941-42; *New Orleans Times-Picayune,* New Orleans, La., reporter, 1943-45; *Cleveland Press,* Cleveland, Ohio, Washington correspondent, 1945-52; Scripps-Howard Newspapers, Washington, D.C., editorial writer, 1952-57; *Pittsburgh Press,* Pittsburgh, Pa., Washington correspondent, 1957—. *Military service:* U.S. Air Force, 1942-43; became sergeant. *Member:* National Press Club, Washington Press Club, Sigma Delta Chi.

* * *

SMITH, Emma 1923-

PERSONAL: Born August 21, 1923, in Newquay, England; married R. L. Stewart-Jones in 1951 (died, 1957); children: two. *Agent:* Peter Janson-Smith Ltd., 42 Great Russell St., London WC1, England.

CAREER: Freelance writer. *Awards, honors:* Atlantic Award, 1947; Rhys Memorial Prize, 1949; Black Memorial Prize, 1950.

WRITINGS: Maidens' Trip (novel), Putnam, 1949; *The*

Far Cry (novel), MacGibbon & Kee, 1949, Random House, 1950; *Emily: The Story of a Traveller* (juvenile), Nelson, 1959, published as *Emily: The Travelling Guinea Pig*, McDowell Obolensky, 1959; *Emily's Voyage* (juvenile), Harcourt, 1962; *Out of Hand* (juvenile), Macmillan, 1963, Harcourt, 1964; *No Way of Telling* (juvenile), Atheneum, 1972. Also author of short stories.*

* * *

SMITH, Frederick W(illiam) 1920-

PERSONAL: Born October 21, 1920, in Salmon, Idaho; son of Alvin John (a miner) and Jewel (Landsdale) Smith; married Grace Elizabeth Deaton, June 6, 1945; children: David, Marilyn, Lyle, Neil, Lorita, Lucinda, Kenneth. *Education:* Attended North Manchester College. *Politics:* Independent Democrat. *Religion:* Church of the Brethren. *Home address:* Cedaredge, R.R.1, Box 34, Cedar Mesa, Colo. 81413. *Agent:* Richard Curtis, 156 East 52nd St., New York, N.Y. 10022.

CAREER: Machinist, printer, and rubber stamp maker in Denver, Colo., 1938-43; in prison in Oklahoma and Illinois, 1943-46; farmer in Ohio, 1946-53; plumber in Ohio, 1953-59; plumber and rancher in Cedaredge, Colo., 1959—.

WRITINGS: Journal of a Fast, Ballantine, 1971; *Cattle Mutilation: The Unthinkable Truth* (pamphlet), privately printed, 1976.

WORK IN PROGRESS: Hotevilla: The Traditional Hopi Village; UFO's: Visitors from Beyond Death; Through Death's Door.

SIDELIGHTS: Smith comments: "I am a religiously-oriented, orthodox Christian and Tibetan Buddhist. . . . I have spoken and written on population, but not had anything published on the subject. My views about that are somewhat right of the Pope's, believing that current views and practices will soon be seen to have been catastrophic. . . . I have close friends among the Traditional Hopi, whom we visit often. I am somewhat infamous as an anti-nuclear activist."

AVOCATIONAL INTERESTS: Astronomy (has a small observatory), gardening (in a greenhouse).

* * *

SMITH, Irene 1903-

PERSONAL: Born in 1903, in Columbia, Ky.; married Louis William Green. *Education:* Attended the University of Illinois.

CAREER: Author, librarian, and teacher. Worked in a library in Indianapolis, Ind.; Brooklyn Public Library, children's librarian, superintendent of work with children; lecturer, Pratt Institute Library School.

WRITINGS: A Social Workers's List of Books for Young People, Brooklyn Public Library, 1934; (editor) *The Santa Claus Book* (illustrated by Hertha Depper), F. Watts, 1948; *Lucky Days for Johnny* (illustrated by Kurt Wiese), Whittlesey House, 1950; *Down the Road with Johnny* (illustrated by K. Wiese), Whittlesey House, 1951; *Hubbub in the Hollow* (illustrated by Tony Palazzo), Whittlesey House, 1952; *A History of the Newbery and Caldecott Medals*, Viking, 1957, revised edition, 1963; (editor, with Florence K. Peterson) *A Cavalcade of Horses, in Fact, Fantasy, and Fiction* (illustrated by Wesley Dennis), Thomas Nelson, 1961; *Paris* (illustrated by Emil Weiss), Rand McNally, 1961; *Washington, D.C.* (illustrated by E. Weiss), Rand McNally, 1964.

SIDELIGHTS: About *Lucky Days for Johnny* a *New York*

Times critic commented: "Deceptively simple, this is really an artful little story, written out of a genuine knowledge of the emotions and the humor, both conscious and unconscious, of childhood. It is natural, funny, and easy to read." *Down the Road with Johnny* was the sequel, of which a *New York Times* critic wrote, "As in *Lucky Days for Johnny*, there is nice quiet everyday humor here that children like. It is a good story for very young readers. Kurt Wiese's illustrations on almost every page are delightful."

Of *Hubbub in the Hollow*, the *Christian Science Monitor* wrote that "a simple peaceful charm pervades this tale of adventure in a new way of living." The *New York Times* commented: "This story, though slight, has a certain gaiety. And children will be torn betwixt and between—sympathizing with the city folk who want to get away and with the little animals whose lives were so greatly disturbed. The illustrations in woodsy colors are fun." The *Chicago Tribune* noted: "An appealing and amusing story for beginning readers. They will love the clever pictures of birds and animals, first in protest at all the changes and then happy as the humans in their now peaceful hollow."

Irene Smith has also written *A History of the Newbery and Caldecott Medals*, which *Kirkus* described as a "pleasant and almost chatty book about the awards and their winners which will certainly interest that selected readership which is concerned with the field of children's literature."

BIOGRAPHICAL/CRITICAL SOURCES: New York Times, August 27, 1950, November 11, 1951; *Christian Science Monitor*, September 11, 1952; *Chicago Sunday Tribune*, October 5, 1952; *Kirkus*, August 1, 1957.*

* * *

SMITH, Irwin 1892-1977

June 14, 1892—August 17, 1977; American commercial artist and writer. Smith was the author of two books on Elizabethan theatres, and with the help of John Cranford Adams, constructed a replica of the Globe Playhouse which is on exhibition in the Folger Library in Washington, D.C. He died in Mineola, N.Y. Obituaries: *New York Times*, August 20, 1977; *AB Bookman's Weekly*, October 17, 1977. (See index for *CA* sketch)

* * *

SMITH, Lawrence Berk 1939-

PERSONAL: Born November 10, 1939, in Toronto, Ontario, Canada; son of Isadore (an executive) and Ruth (Berk) Smith; married Marilyn Chapnik (a professor), June 11, 1963; children: Cynthia, Ilyse, Natalie. *Education:* University of Toronto, B.Com., 1962; Harvard University, A.M., 1964, Ph.D., 1966. *Home:* 18 Ormsby Cres., Toronto, Ontario, Canada M5P 2V3. *Office:* Department of Political Economy, University of Toronto, Toronto, Ontario, Canada M5S 1A1.

CAREER: University of Toronto, Toronto, Ontario, assistant professor, 1966-69, associate professor, 1969-72, professor of economics, 1972—, associate chairman, department of political economy, 1975—. Economic consultant, 1966—.

WRITINGS: (Editor with L. H. Officer) *Canadian Economic Problems and Policies*, McGraw, 1970; *Canadian Housing and Mortgage Markets*, Bank of Canada, 1970; *Housing in Canada: Market Structure and Policy Performance*, Central Mortgage & Housing Corp., 1971; (with G. R. Sparks) *Institutional Mortgage Lending in Canada*, Bank of Canada, 1973; *Postwar Canadian Housing and Res-*

idential *Mortgage Markets and the Role of Government,* University of Toronto Press, 1974; (editor with Officer) *Issues in Canadian Economics,* McGraw, 1974; *Anatomy of a Crisis: Canadian Housing Policy in the Seventies,* Fraser Institute, 1977.

WORK IN PROGRESS: Crowding Out in Canadian Capital Markets: Studies of Government Preferential Access, with J. E. Pesando, for Howe Institute.

* * *

SMITH, Lee   1937-

PERSONAL: Born March 17, 1937, in New York, N.Y.; son of Harold A. (in public relations) and Louise (Luyster) Smith; married Angie Rodriguez, September 23, 1961; children: Lee, Matthew, Kevin, Alessandra. *Education:* Yale University, B.A. (cum laude), 1959. *Office: Dun's Review,* 666 Fifth Ave., New York, N.Y. 10019.

CAREER/WRITINGS: Associated Press, New York City, reporter in Seattle and Olympia, Wash., 1962-65; *Newsweek,* New York City, associate editor, 1965-70; *Black Enterprise,* New York City, managing editor, 1970-71; *Dun's Review,* New York City, member of staff. Contributor of articles to *Columbia Journalism Review, More, Skeptic,* and other periodicals. *Military service:* U.S. Army, 1960-62.

* * *

SMITH, Lou   1918-

PERSONAL: Born July 4, 1918, in Heckmondwicke, England; son of Simeon and Lily (Elliot) Smith; married Marguerite Fer, October 23, 1954; children: Sabina. *Education:* Educated in England. *Politics:* "Believes in free enterprise with State taking good care of disabled persons and all those not possessing full faculties." *Home:* 134 Sheen Court, Upper Richmond Rd., Richmond, Surrey, England. *Agent:* Sanford J. Greenburger Associates, 825 Third Ave., New York, N.Y. 10022.

CAREER: U.S. Department of State, Washington, D.C., claims adjustor in Paris, 1948-50; North American Treaty Organization (NATO), Brussels, Belgium, member of international staff, 1968-72. *Military service:* British Army, Airborne Beach Brigade, 1939-46; became sergeant; *Member:* British Legion assistant honorary secretary), American Legion (honorary member).

WRITINGS: Fear and the Dead Man, Collins, 1968; *Psycho in Focus,* Macmillan, 1969; *The Secret of M.1.6.,* Hale, 1975, St. Martin's, 1978; *Master Plot,* Hale, 1976, St. Martin's, 1978; *Primrose: The Fourth Man,* Hale, 1976, St. Martin's, 1976.

WORK IN PROGRESS: The Curse, The Tarantula Syndrome, Traitor With an Old School-Tie.

SIDELIGHTS: "Living abroad has enabled me to see my own countrymen—the British—with objective and analytical eyes," Smith told *CA.* "I condemn British hypocrisy, rigidity of thinking, smallmindedness, whimsy, and lack of factualism."

* * *

SMITH, Marcus J(oel)   1918-

PERSONAL: Born December 14, 1918, in New York, N.Y.; son of Morris (a physician) and Fanny (Edelstein) Smith; married Carol Kander (a physician), June 29, 1941; children: Patricia A., Frederick M., Peter M., Andrew T. *Education:* New York University, B.S., 1938; State Univer-

sity of New York Downstate Medical Center, M.D., 1942; University of Minnesota, postdoctoral study, 1946-48. *Home address:* P.O. Box 1812, Santa Fe, N.M. 87501.

CAREER: Radiologist in Santa Fe, N.M., 1948-76; writer, 1976—. Certified by American Board of Radiology, 1948. Past president of St. Vincent Hospital Medical Staff; founding member of Northern New Mexico Comprehensive Health Care Planning Council. Member of board of directors of Santa Fe Chamber Music Festival. *Military service:* U.S. Army, 1943-46; became captain; received Bronze Star Medal.

MEMBER: Radiological Society of North America (member of council, 1967-71), American College of Radiology (fellow), New Mexico Medical Society, New Mexico Association of Radiologists (past president), Santa Fe County Medical Society (past president), Santa Fe Community Concert Association (past president; member of board of directors), Santa Fe Historical Society (president, 1976-77). *Awards, honors:* Szerlip Medal from State University of New York Downstate Medical Center, 1942.

WRITINGS: Error and Variation in Diagnostic Radiology, C. C Thomas, 1967; *The Harrowing of Hell: Dachau,* University of New Mexico Press, 1972; (with Clark Kimball) *The Hospital at the End of the Santa Fe Trail* (pictorial history of St. Vincent Hospital), Rydal, 1977. Author of "Shadow Or Substance: Radiologic Reflections," a column in *Rocky Mountain Medical Journal,* 1959-68. Contributor of more than thirty articles and reviews to medical journals and *National Observer.* Member of editorial board of *Rocky Mountain Medical Journal,* 1961—.

WORK IN PROGRESS: Malpractice Prevention; Child Abuse; historiography of St. Vincent Hospital, completion expected in 1979.

SIDELIGHTS: Smith writes: "I retired from medical practice in 1976 so that I could spend more time writing. My favorite subjects are the world of the hospital, the malpractice crisis, child abuse, and other paramedical matters." *Avocational interests:* New Mexico history and sociology.

* * *

SMITH, Margaret Chase   1897-

PERSONAL: Born December 14, 1897, in Skowhegan, Me.; daughter of George Emery (a barber) and Carrie (Murray) Chase; married Clyde H. Smith, May 14, 1930 (died, 1940). *Education:* Educated in Skowhegan, Me. *Politics:* Republican. *Religion:* Methodist. *Home and office:* Norridgewock Ave., Skowhegan, Me. 04976. *Agent:* William C. Lewis, Jr., 807 Milestone Dr., Silver Spring, Md. 20904.

CAREER: Teacher in Skowhegan, Me., 1916; office executive for *Independent Reporter,* 1916-28; treasurer of Daniel E. Cummings Co., 1928-30; legislative assistant in Washington, D.C., 1937-40; U.S. Congress, Washington, D.C., representative from 2nd district of Maine, 1940-49, senator from Maine, 1949-73, chairperson of Senate Republican Conference, 1967-73, served on Armed Services Committee, Space Committee, and Appropriations Committee; Woodrow Wilson National Fellowship Foundation, visiting professor at universities, including University of Notre Dame, DePauw University, Colorado College, and University of the South, 1973-76. Received a nomination for president at Republican National Convention, 1964. Charter member of White House Fellows Commission; member of Women's Medical College Board; chairperson of Freedom House, 1970-77; director of Lilly Endowment, 1976—. Appeared frequently on "See It Now," a television documentary series produced by Columbia Broadcasting System (CBS); panelist on "Who Said That?" produced by National Boradcasting Company (NBC). *Military service:* U.S. Air Force Reserve, 1950-58; became lieutenant colonel.

MEMBER: American Academy of Arts and Sciences, Pi Sigma Alpha, Delta Kappa Gamma, Sigma Kappa, Beta Sigma Phi, Theta Sigma Phi. *Awards, honors:* Has received eighty-four honorary degrees from universities and colleges in twenty-four states and in Canada; has received numerous other awards, including award from National Education Association, 1968; Outstanding American Woman Award from National Order of Women Legislators, 1973; Distinguished Leader Award from New York University, 1975.

WRITINGS: (With H. Paul Jeffers) *Gallant Women,* McGraw, 1968; *Declaration of Conscience,* Doubleday, 1972. Author of daily column "Washington and You," syndicated by United Feature Syndicate, 1949-50; author of column "One Woman's Opinion," in *McCall's,* 1965—. Contributor of articles to magazines and newspapers, including *New York Times, Ladies Home Journal, Modern Maturity,* and *Time.*

WORK IN PROGRESS: An autobiography; a critique of the U.S. Senate; commentary on American society; a novel on Washington politics.

SIDELIGHTS: Smith told *CA:* "Activity as a visiting professor beginning in 1973 has been stimulating, revealing, gratifying, and encouraging. The student nihilists of the late sixties and early seventies have been replaced since 1973 by quiet and serious minded students intent on the search for knowledge rather than confrontation. But their 'lecture fare' from the quickly in-and-out high-fee lecturers is heavily imbalanced on the anti-establishment side with too few remaining for in-depth question-and-answer dialogue and sessions.

"Government waste is one of my pet peeves and thus far I view President Carter's record on that score to be practically all talk and no action, all symbolism and no substance. But an even greater pet peeve is the absenteeism in the United States Senate and the rampant 'moonlighting'' by an increasing number of Senators who do not look upon the Senate as an institution to which they should be dedicated (after having been elected to it) but rather as a status symbol by which they can commercialize in getting themselves high lecturer and speech fees while absent and 'moonlighting' from the Senate and the job to which they have been elected. That's why I introduced the constitutional amendment to expel any Senator or Congressman who was absent from more than 40 per cent of the roll call votes."

* * *

SMITH, Richard M(ills) 1946-

PERSONAL: Born December 1, 1946, in Detroit, Mich. *Education:* Albion College, B.A., 1968; Columbia University, M.S.J., 1970. *Office:* Newsweek, Inc., 444 Madison Ave., New York, N.Y. 10022.

CAREER/WRITINGS: *Newsweek,* New York, N.Y., general editor, 1970-74, Asian editor in Hong Kong, 1975-77, managing editor, Newsweek International, 1977—.

* * *

SMITH, Robert Paul 1915-1977

PERSONAL: Born April 16, 1915, in New York, N.Y.; son of Joseph Elkin (a manufacturer) and Esther (Breckstone) Smith; married Elinor Jane Goulding (an artist and writer), February 7, 1940; children: Daniel Paul, Joseph Robert. *Education:* Columbia College (now University), B.A., 1936. *Agent:* Monica McCall, 667 Madison Ave., New York, N.Y. 10022.

CAREER: Author. Wrote continuity for radio for the Columbia Broadcasting System, beginning 1936.

WRITINGS: So It Doesn't Whistle, Harcourt, 1941; *The Man with the Gold-Headed Cane,* Holt, 1943; *The Journey,* Holt, 1943; *Because of My Love,* Holt, 1946; *The Time and the Place,* Simon & Schuster, 1952; (with Max Shulman) *The Tender Trap,* Random House, 1955, three-act play under the same title (first produced on Broadway at the Longacre Theatre, October 13, 1954), Dramatists Play Service, 1956; *"Where Did You Go?" "Out." "What Did You Do?" "Nothing.",* Norton, 1957; *How to Do Nothing with Nobody, All Alone by Yourself* (illustrated by wife, Elinor Goulding Smith), Norton, 1958; *Where He Went: Three Novels,* Viking, 1958; *Translations from the English* (illustrated by Roberta Macdonald), Simon & Schuster, 1958; *And Another Thing* (poems), Norton, 1959; *Jack Mack* (a Junior Literary Guild selection; illustrated by Erik Blegvad), Coward, 1960; *Crank: A Book of Lamentations, Exhortations, Mixed Memories and Desires, All Hard or Chewy Centers, No Creams,* Norton, 1962; *How to Grow Up in One Piece,* Harper, 1963; *When I Am Big* (for children; illustrated by Lillian Hoban), Harper, 1965; *Nothingatall, Nothingatall, Nothingatall* (for children; illustrated by Alan E. Cober), Harper, 1965; *Got to Stop Draggin' that Little Red Wagon Around,* Harper, 1969; *Lost and Found: An Illustrated Compendium of Things No Longer in General Use* (illustrated by Gerald Gersten), Charterhouse, 1973; *Brooklyn at Play: A Social and Cultural History of Brooklyn at the Turn of the Century,* Revisionist Press, 1976. Also author of "Forget This Night," a three-act play.

SIDELIGHTS: Following graduation from Columbia College where he was co-editor of the literary quarterly, the *Columbia Review,* Robert Paul Smith worked for the Columbia Broadcasting System. He wrote radio continuity and made it sound like ad-lib for performers such as Benny Goodman, Frank Sinatra, and Guy Lombardo. In the meantime, he began to write novels.

His first novel was *So It Doesn't Whistle,* which received mixed reviews. According to *Saturday Review:* "This book contains about equal parts of Joyce, Saroyan, and Budd Schulberg; liquor, love, jazz music, and stream-of-consciousness reflections on death and such items are all inextricably mixed in a combination that is somewhat dizzying. The book is extremely funny in its more lucid passages. Anyone who enjoys a 'screwball' story—and anyone with a sufficiently exquisite sense for the incongruous will probably enjoy [it]." *New Republic* commented: "Sometimes the book is a little overwritten, but it has a cocky appeal in the kind of thing it is, and it is the best of its kind since that particular mood appeared in the early Hemingway."

Smith gained fame in 1957 when his book, *"Where Did You Go?" "Out." "What Did You Do?" "Nothing.",* became a best-seller. It has sold over 170,000 copies and was on the best-seller list for almost a year. *Kirkus* described it as "A heartfelt examination of the joys of living [that] reveals the author's boyhood as something more than superior to today's children for on his block the kids did nothing, kept out of the way of their natural enemies, the adults, and filled their days with activities unknown, he thinks, by the current crop."

And Another Thing, a book of poetry, was reviewed by a

Chicago Tribune critic, who wrote: "Robert Paul Smith's new book of verses is the most delightful encountered in its field in a decade or even longer. It probably is obligatory to classify the collection as 'light verse'; it contains so much of genuine humor, and a particularly welcome seasoning of that super-rare commodity, sensible nonsense." The *San Francisco Chronicle* commented: "His point of view is more akin to that of Ogden Nash, although it is entirely his own. Like Nash, Smith is an eminently sane, sophisticated writer, whether he deals in lighthearted poems, or is acidly critical of the public transportation he is forced to endure on New York's Madison avenue. In every case, Smith's survey of American mores, past and present, carries the sound of surprise."

With Max Shulman, Smith wrote *The Tender Trap,* which was produced on Broadway by Clinton Wilder and starred Robert Preston. It ran for 101 performances and for 186 performances on tour. Frank Sinatra, Debbie Reynolds, David Wayne, and Celeste Holm starred in the Metro-Goldwyn-Mayer motion picture based on the play in 1955.

AVOCATIONAL INTERESTS: Building model ships and reading (especially Mark Twain).

BIOGRAPHICAL/CRITICAL SOURCES: Saturday Review, September 6, 1941, June 29, 1957; *New Republic,* September 29, 1941; *Kirkus,* February 15, 1957; *Chicago Sunday Tribune,* August 23, 1959; *San Francisco Chronicle,* September 1, 1959. Obituaries: *New York Times,* January 31, 1977; *Newsweek,* February 14, 1977.*

(Died January 30, 1977, in New York, N.Y.)

* * *

SMITH, Sam(uel Frederic Houston) 1937-

PERSONAL: Born November 24, 1937, in Washington, D.C.; son of Lawrence M. C. (in broadcasting) and Eleanor (Houston) Smith; married Kathryn Jean Schneider (a historian and journalist), October 15, 1966; children: Nathaniel, Benjamin. *Education:* Harvard University, B.A., 1959. *Office:* D.C. Gazette, 1739 Connecticut Ave. N.W., Washington, D.C. 20009.

CAREER: Deadline Washington News Service, Washington, D.C., correspondent, 1959-60; *Roll Call,* Washington, D.C., reporter, 1960; *Idler,* Washington, D.C., editor, 1964-66; *Capitol East Gazette,* Washington, D.C., editor, 1966-69; *D.C. Gazette,* Washington, D.C., editor, 1969—. Reporter for WWDC-Radio, 1959-60; Washington correspondent for WFLN-Radio, 1960, vice-president, 1971—, member of board of trustees, 1976—. Honorary member of board of directors of University Legal Services, 1977—; member of board of directors of Capitol Hill Arts Workshop, 1973-76, United Black Fund, 1973—, and Citizens for City Living, 1974—. Member of District of Columbia Democratic Central Committee, 1968-72; founding member of District of Columbia Statehood Party, member of steering committee, 1971—, neighborhood commissioner, 1976-77. President of John Eaton Home and School Association, 1975-76. Past member of board of directors of Friendship Community Credit Union; handled press relations for Student Nonviolent Coordinating Committees (SNCC) Free D.C. Movement in the 1960's. *Military service:* U.S. Coast Guard Reserve, 1961-67, active duty, 1961-64; became lieutenant.

MEMBER: National Association of Neighborhoods, American Federation of Radio and Television Artists, National Jogging Association, Washington Alliance for Neighborhood Government, Metropolitan Washington Planning and Housing Association (member of board of directors, 1968-76; member of executive committee, 1975-76).

WRITINGS: (Editor) *The Gazette Guides,* District of Columbia Gazette, six volumes, 1971-76; *Captive Capital: Colonial Life in Modern Washington,* Indiana University Press, 1974; *Through D.C. by Bus,* District of Columbia Gazette, 1975. Contributor to magazines and newspapers.

AVOCATIONAL INTERESTS: Playing piano, tenor guitar, and drums (drummer for Crimson Crew, 1956-59, and New Sunshine Jazz Band, 1966-68), weightlifting, jogging.

* * *

SMITH, Terence (Fitzgerald) 1938-

PERSONAL: Born November 18, 1938, in Philadelphia, Pa.; son of Walter W. (a columnist) and Catherine (Cody) Smith; married Ann Charnley (a teacher), June 20, 1964; children: Elizabeth, Christopher. *Education:* University of Notre Dame, B.A., 1960. *Home:* 33 W. Irving St., Chevy Chase, Md. 20015. *Office: New York Times,* 1920 L St. N.W., Washington, D.C. 20036.

CAREER/WRITINGS: Stamford Advocate, Stamford, Conn., reporter, 1960-62; *New York Herald-Tribune,* New York City, political writer, 1962-65; *New York Times,* New York City, correspondent in Israel, 1967-68, and Thailand, 1968-69, Vietnam bureau chief, 1969-70, diplomatic correspondent in Washington, 1970-72, chief correspondent in Israel, 1972-76, deputy foreign editor in New York, 1976-77, national political correspondent, Washington, 1977—. Notable assignments include coverage of the 1967 and 1973 Arab-Israeli wars, and the war in Vietnam. Lecturer. *Military service:* U.S. Army Reserve, 1962. *Member:* Overseas Writers Association.

* * *

SMITHGALL, Elizabeth
See WATTS, Elizabeth (Bailey) Smithgall

* * *

SNEAD, Rodman Eldredge 1931-

PERSONAL: Born May 1, 1931, in Atlantic City, N.J.; son of Eldredge H. (in the lumber business) and Mabelle C. Snead. *Education:* Earlham College, student, 1949-50; University of Virginia, B.A., 1953; Syracuse University, M.A., 1955; Louisiana State University, Ph.D., 1963. *Home:* 412 Ridge Pl. N.E., Albuquerque, N.M. 87106. *Office:* Department of Geography, University of New Mexico, Albuquerque, N.M. 87131.

CAREER: Clark University, Worcester, Mass., assistant professor, 1961-65, associate professor of geography, 1965-68; University of New Mexico, Albuquerque, professor of geography, 1969—. Visiting professor at University of Hawaii, summer, 1965, and Universities of Canterbury and Otago, both 1976. *Military service:* U.S. Army Reserve, 1953-55. U.S. Army, 1955-58, in Intelligence, 1955-56, attache to American Embassy in Karachi, Pakistan, 1956-58.

MEMBER: Association of American Geographers, American Geographical Society, Geological Society of America, American Meteorological Society, Society for Religion in Higher Education (fellow), Explorers Club, Sigma Xi. *Awards, honors:* Grants from Office of Naval Research and National Park Service.

WRITINGS: Physical Geography Reconnaissance: Las Bela Coastal Plain, West Pakistan, Louisiana University Press, 1966; (with Ian Burton and Robert W. Kates) *The Human Ecology of Coastal Hazard in Megalopolis,* University of Chicago Press, 1969; *Physical Geography Reconnaissance: West Pakistan Coastal Zone,* University of New Mexico Press, 1969; *Physical Geography of the Makran Coastal Plain of Iran,* National Technical Information Service, U.S. Department of Commerce, 1970; *Atlas of World Physical Features,* Wiley, 1972. Contributor of about twenty articles to scholarly journals.

WORK IN PROGRESS: Coastal Landforms and Surface Features: A Photographic Atlas and Glossary, for Dowden; revision of *World Atlas of Geomorphic Features,* for Krieger.

SIDELIGHTS: Snead comments: "I became interested in geography very early in my career and loved to travel, first around the United States and Canada, and then to many other countries. Now I have been in ninety-two countries and have lived in Pakistan and Iran for several years. I think the curiosity of what's beyond the hill, over the mountain, or across the ocean has always spurred me on. My main research interests are desert coasts, but I also have an interest in all types of landforms. I have been on a number of geomorphology and archaeological expeditions. My work with archaeologists has mainly been to help determine past environments."

* * *

SNETSINGER, John (Goodall) 1941-

PERSONAL: Born May 12, 1941, in Santa Barbara, Calif.; son of J. I. (a public relations director) and Jo Elise (in publishing business; maiden name, Covelle) Snetsinger. *Education:* University of California, Los Angeles, A.B., 1963; University of California, Berkeley, M.A., 1965; Stanford University, Ph.D., 1969. *Office:* Department of History, California Polytechnic State University, San Luis Obispo, Calif. 93407.

CAREER: San Jose State University, San Jose, Calif., instructor in history, 1967-70; California Polytechnic State University, San Luis Obispo, assistant professor, 1970-74, associate professor of history, 1974—. Researcher at Harry S. Truman Institute of National and International Affairs, 1968, 1973.

WRITINGS: Truman, the Jewish Vote, and the Creation of Israel, Hoover Institution, 1974; (contributor) *Dictionary of American Foreign Policy,* Scribner, 1978.

WORK IN PROGRESS: A book-length manuscript on ethnic politics and American diplomatic history.

* * *

SNOW, (Charles) Wilbert 1884-1977

April 6, 1884—September 28, 1977; American educator, politician, and poet. Snow was professor emeritus at Wesleyan University after being a member of the faculty for thirty-one years. He was a former lieutenant governor of the state of Connecticut and became governor for just twelve days in January, 1947. Life along the Maine seacoast where he grew up was often the theme of Snow's poetry. He died in Spruce Island, Me. Obituaries: *New York Times,* September 30, 1977. (See index for *CA* sketch)

* * *

SOKOLOV, Alexander V(sevolodovich) 1943-
(Sasha Sokolov)

PERSONAL: Born November 6, 1943, in Ottawa, Ontario,

Canada; son of Vsevolod (a Soviet Army officer) and Lydia (an engineer; maiden name, Chernykh) Sokolov. *Education:* Attended Military Institute of Foreign Languages (Moscow), 1962-65; Moscow University, B.A., 1971. *Residence:* Allendale, Mich. *Office:* Department of Foreign Languages, Grand Valley State Colleges, Allendale, Mich. 49401.

CAREER: Staff writer for Soviet periodicals, *Novorossiiskii rabochy* ("The Novorossiisk Worker") in Novorossiisk, Soviet Union, 1967, *Kolkhoznaia pravda* ("Kolkhoz Truth") in Morky, Soviet Union, 1967-68, *Literaturnaia Rossiia* ("Literary Russia") in Moscow, Soviet Union, 1969-71, *Leninskaia pravda* ("Leninist Truth") in Georgievsk, Soviet Union, 1974; Grand Valley State Colleges, Allendale, Mich., writer-in-residence and instructor in Russian, 1977—. Staff writer for *Studencheskii meridian* ("The Student Meridian"), summers, 1970-71.

WRITINGS: Shkola dlia durakov, Ardis, 1976, translation by Carl R. Proffer published as *A School for Fools,* Ardis, 1977. Contributor to *Glagol,* a Russian literary journal.

WORK IN PROGRESS: Mezhdu sobakoi i volkom, translation to be published as *Between the Dog and the Wolf.*

SIDELIGHTS: Although the works of many dissident Soviet authors suffer from a "politicized, one-dimensional perspective which is antithetical to art," George Feifer declared that Sasha Sokolov "is both a disserter and an authentic artist." Feifer praised *A School for Fools* for its "superbly lyrical and mystical descriptions" and "dreamlike fluctuation of time." Sokolov's puzzling story of a schizophrenic pupil provokes "an almost symphonic second reading." Even though disgust with the Soviet system pervades the work, the much broader theme of the meaning, or the meaninglessness, of life qualifies it to be compared with the masterpieces of Russian literature.

Sokolov commented: "*A School for Fools* was written while I was still living in Russia and working as a game warden on the Volga River. Realizing the impossibility of publishing the book in Russia, I had it sent abroad, and it was published by Ardis, a Russian language publishing house."

Sokolov obtained an exit visa from Soviet authorities in 1975 after staging a hunger strike with his Austrian fiancee to protest a ban on their marriage. A bitter family feud had erupted when Sokolov's father opposed his marriage to a foreigner, during which Sokolov accused his father of espionage in Canada and the United States, and his father countered by attempting to have Sokolov declared insane. The international publicity surrounding the ensuing hunger strike made Soviet authorities more than willing to allow Sokolov to leave the country. He emigrated to Canada (where he had been born during his father's diplomatic assignment) and was granted Canadian citizenship.

BIOGRAPHICAL/CRITICAL SOURCES: New York Review of Books, February 19, 1976; *Detroit Free Press,* December 5, 1976; *Newsweek,* July 11, 1977; *Washington Post,* July 24, 1977.

* * *

SOKOLOV, Sasha
See SOKOLOV, Alexander V(sevolodovich)

* * *

SOLBERG, Carl 1915-

PERSONAL: Born March 20, 1915, in Minneapolis, Minn.; son of Carl K. (a Lutheran clergyman) and Sina (a social worker; maiden name, Varland) Solberg; married Barbara

Selmer (a piano teacher), March 5, 1945; children: Carl, Richard, Sara, Andrew. *Education:* St. Olaf College, B.A., 1935; Oxford University, M.A. and B.Litt., both 1939. *Home:* 4 Francis Lane, Port Chester, N.Y. 10573. *Agent:* International Creative Management, 40 West 57th St., New York, N.Y. 10019. *Office:* Roothbert Fund, Inc., 815 Second Ave., New York, N.Y. 10017.

CAREER: Time, Inc., New York, N.Y., member of editorial staff, 1939-70; Roothbert Fund, Inc., New York City, director, 1958—, president, 1970—. Lecturer at Columbia University, 1963-66. *Military service:* U.S. Navy, 1942-45.

WRITINGS: Riding High: America in the Cold War, Mason & Lipscomb, 1973; *Oil Power,* Mason/Charter, 1976.

WORK IN PROGRESS: History of Air Travel, publication by Little, Brown expected in 1979.

* * *

SOLOMON, Barbara H. 1936-

PERSONAL: Born September 25, 1936, in Brooklyn, N.Y.; daughter of Lothar and Rose (Gruber) Hochster; married Stanley J. Solomon (a professor of communication arts and writer of film books), January 26, 1958; children: Nancy Jane, Jennifer Ann. *Education:* Brooklyn College (now of the City University of New York), B.A., 1958; University of Kansas, M.A., 1960; University of Pittsburgh, Ph.D., 1968. *Residence:* New Rochelle, N.Y. *Office:* Department of English, Iona College, New Rochelle, N.Y. 10801.

CAREER: Doane College, Crete, Neb., instructor in English, 1960-62; Temple University, Philadelphia, Pa., instructor in English, 1965-67; Iona College, New Rochelle, N.Y., assistant professor, 1969-76, associate professor of English, 1976—. *Member:* Modern Language Association of America.

WRITINGS: (Contributor) Stanley J. Solomon, editor, *The Classic Cinema: Essays in Criticism,* Harcourt, 1973; (editor) *The Awakening and Selected Stories of Kate Chopin,* New American Library, 1976; (editor) *The Experience of American Women: Thirty Stories,* New American Library, 1978. Contributor to *Conradiana.*

WORK IN PROGRESS: Editing *Modern Women Writers: Essays in Feminist Criticism* (tentative title), with Constance Ayers Denne; editing a book on the writings of Sarah Orne Jewett and Mary Wilkins Freeman, for New American Library, publication expected in 1979; a literary critical study of the American heroine, 1870-1920.

SIDELIGHTS: Barbara Solomon writes briefly: "As a writer and teacher, my major area of special interest is feminist literary criticism—particularly of American literature. I teach courses on the image of women in modern American fiction on both undergraduate and graduate levels."

* * *

SOTOMAYOR, Antonio 1902-

PERSONAL: Surname is pronounced Soto-my-oar; born May 13, 1902, in Chulumani, Bolivia; son of Juan (a businessman) and Carmen (Meza) Sotomayor; married Grace Andrews, May 13, 1926. *Education:* Educated at School of Fine Arts, La Paz, Bolivia, and Hopkins Institute, San Francisco, Calif. *Home and studio:* 3 LeRoy Pl., San Francisco, Calif. 94109.

CAREER: Painter, with work including a number of historical murals in California buildings, churches, and hotels. Instructor in art at Mills College, Oakland, Calif., 1942, and

California School of Fine Arts, San Francisco, 1946-50. Member of San Francisco Art Commission, 1946-50, 1967—. *Member:* Royal Society of Arts (fellow), Bohemian Club and Family Club (both San Francisco). *Awards, honors:* First prize, National Exposition of Painting, 1921.

WRITINGS: Khasa Goes to the Fiesta (juvenile), Doubleday, 1967; *Balloons: The First Two Hundred Years* (juvenile), Putnam, 1972.

Illustrator: Leslie B. Simpson, *Indian Tales from Guatemala,* Scribner, 1936; Victor von Hagen, *Quetzal Quest,* Harcourt, 1939; Carl O. Sauer, *Man in Nature,* Scribner, 1939; von Hagen, *Treasure of the Tortoise Islands,* Harcourt, 1940; Robert O'Brien, *This is San Francisco,* McGraw, 1948; O'Brien, *California Called Them,* McGraw, 1951; Quail Hawkins, *Best Birthday,* Doubleday, 1954; Arturo Torres Rioscco, *Relatos Chilenos,* Harper, 1956; Stanton Delaplane, *Stan Delaplane's Mexico,* Chronicle Books, 1976.

Contributor to *Encyclopedia Americana* and *Arts and Architecture* (magazine).

SIDELIGHTS: Antonio Sotomayor was a member of University of California research expedition in Mexico, 1930; he has traveled elsewhere in Latin America and in Europe and Asia.

* * *

SOWARDS, J(esse) K(elley) 1924-

PERSONAL: Born May 12, 1924, in Clintwood, Va.; son of Leonard Noel (an attorney) and Mary (Kelley) Sowards; married Ardis Elizabeth Rutherford, January 6, 1946; children: Stephen K., Michael L. *Education:* University of Wichita, B.A. (magna cum laude), 1947; University of Michigan, M.A., 1948, Ph.D., 1952. *Home:* 1319 North Edgemoor, Wichita, Kan. 67208. *Office:* Department of History, Wichita State University, Wichita, Kan. 67208.

CAREER: William Woods College, Fulton, Mo., instructor in history, 1950-51; Northwest Missouri State College, Maryville, associate professor of history and humanities, 1951-56; Wichita State University, Wichita, Kan., assistant professor, 1956-60, associate professor, 1960-63, professor, 1963-69, research professor, 1969-73, distinguished professor of history, 1973—, head of department, 1964-65, dean of Fairmount College of Liberal Arts and Sciences, 1965-69. Visiting lecturer at University of Michigan, summer, 1951; visiting professor at University of New Mexico, summer, 1960, and University of Missouri, summer, 1964; adjunct professor at University of Kansas, 1968—. President of Central Renaissance Conference, 1972, member of executive committee, 1973—. *Military service:* U.S. Army, 1943-45; served in European theater.

MEMBER: American Historical Association, Renaissance Society of America, Mediaeval Academy of America, Kansas History Teachers Association, Phi Beta Kappa, Phi Kappa Phi. *Awards, honors:* Ford Foundation grant, 1953-54.

WRITINGS: Western Civilization to 1660, with instructor's manual, St. Martin's, 1964; (with Richard E. Sullivan and Thomas Africa) *Critical Issues in History,* two volumes, Heath, 1967; *The Eve of the Modern World,* Heath, 1967; (with Paul Pascal) *The Julius Exclusus of Erasmus: A Critical Edition with Introduction,* Indiana University Press, 1968; (contributor) K. A. Strand, editor, *Essays on the Northern Renaissance,* Ann Arbor Publishers, 1968; *Makers of the Western Tradition: Portraits from History,* two volumes, St. Martin's, 1975; *Desiderius Erasmus,* Hall, 1975; *A Short History of Civilization,* St. Martin's, 1978. Contributor to history journals.

WORK IN PROGRESS: Erasmus and His Printers; Western Civilization in Film: Instructional Manual; A General History of Renaissance Italy; Renaissance Europe and the Turks: An Essay in Fifteenth-Century Diplomacy; editing *The Collected Works of Erasmus,* Volume XXIII, for University of Toronto Press.

*   *   *

SOWERBY, E(mily) Millicent   1883-1977

September 7, 1883—October 23, 1977; English-born bibliographer and author. An expert on rare books, Sowerby worked as a cataloguer for British bookshops before coming to the United States. Her most notable achievement was the *Catalogue of the Library of Thomas Jefferson,* a ten-year project for the Library of Congress. She died in Muncie, Ind. Obituaries: *New York Times,* October 24, 1977. (See index for *CA* sketch)

*   *   *

SPARTACUS, Deutero
See FANTHORPE, R(obert) Lionel

*   *   *

SPEAR, Benjamin
See HENISCH, Heinz K.

*   *   *

SPITZ, A. Edward   1923-

PERSONAL: Born August 14, 1923, in New York, N.Y.; children: Kenneth, Ellen, Suzanne. *Education:* City University of New York, B.B.A. (cum laude), 1950; Columbia University, M.S., 1953; University of Kentucky, Ph.D., 1969. *Home:* 3324 Tacoma Circle, Ann Arbor, Mich. 48104. *Office:* Department of Marketing, Eastern Michigan University, Ypsilanti, Mich. 48197.

CAREER: Crown Central Petroleum Corp., New York City, assistant sales manager in Branded Lubricants Division, 1946-53; Universal Match Corp., New York City, sales representative in advertising, 1953-54; Lord's Ltd. (retail store chain), Riviera Beach, Fla., president, 1954-64; University of Kentucky, Lexington, instructor in marketing, 1965-67; Indiana State University, Terre Haute, assistant professor of marketing, 1967-70; Eastern Michigan University, Ypsilanti, associate professor, 1970-74, professor of marketing, 1974—.

MEMBER: American Marketing Association, American Economic Association, Financial Management Association, American Institute for Decision Sciences, Midwest Economics Association, Midwest Business Administration Association, Southern Marketing Association, Southern Economics Association, Western Finance Association, Omicron Delta Epsilon, Alpha Iota Delta.

WRITINGS: An Academic Writer's Guide, Bureau of Business Services and Research, Eastern Michigan University, 1972, revised edition, 1974; *Product Planning,* Auerbach, 1972, 2nd edition, 1977; *Marketing Resources: Allocation and Optimization,* Petrocelli, 1974; *Retailing: Case Problems,* Grid, Inc., 1975. Contributor to business and economics journals.

WORK IN PROGRESS: Principles of Retailing, publica-

tion by Winthrop Publishing expected in 1979; *Product Management and Pricing Strategy,* Petrocelli, 1979.

*   *   *

SPRUILL, Steven G(regory)   1946-

PERSONAL: Born April 20, 1946, in Battle Creek, Mich.; son of John Chester (an engineer) and Arleen (a food service manager; maiden name, Camp) Spruill; married Nancy Lyon (a statistician), August 24, 1969. *Education:* Andrews University, B.A., 1968; Catholic University of America, Ph.D., 1978. *Home:* 123 North Park Dr., Arlington, Va. 22203. *Agent:* Kathryne Walters Literary Agents, 316 Fifth Ave., New York, N.Y. 10001. *Office:* Springfield Outpatient Unit, Mount Vernon Community Mental Health Center, 7010 Calamo St., Springfield, Va. 22150.

CAREER: Hazleton Laboratories, Inc., Falls Church, Va., technical writer and editor, 1969-72; Washington Veterans Administration Hospital, Washington, D.C., psychology intern, 1976-77; Mount Vernon Community Mental Health Center, Springfield, Va., psychology intern at Springfield Outpatient Unit, 1977—. *Member:* World Science Fiction Association (charter member, 1977—), Science Fiction Writers of America.

WRITINGS: Keepers of the Gate (novel), Doubleday, 1977; *The Psychopath Plague* (science fiction novel), Doubleday, in press; *The Janus Equation* (science fiction novella), Dell, in press.

WORK IN PROGRESS: Parentheses, a science fiction novel; *The Imperator Plot,* a science fiction novel, second volume of a series beginning with *The Psychopath Plague; Clinician,* a novel revolving around a clinical psychologist; research on the effects of abstract food cues on the subjective hunger response in obese and normal-weighted adult subjects.

SIDELIGHTS: Spruill writes: "At this stage in my writing I want most to entertain—myself and my reader. As a novelist I'd like to do in another way what I attempt to do as a psychotherapist: to free a person for a few hours from the unhappier side of his life and turn him on to the constructive power of his mind. In terms of what happens inside our brains, Captain Queeg is as 'real' as our next door neighbor. Both exist in our minds quite independently of what the neighbor is 'really' like or what Wouk 'really' wanted to portray in Queeg. The wealth of *real* emotion and experience in a good story is why I read and why I write."

AVOCATIONAL INTERESTS: Oil painting, piano playing, choral singing.

*   *   *

STACY, R(obert) H(arold)   1919-

PERSONAL: Born December 22, 1919, in New York, N.Y.; son of George Sydney and Margaret (McKay) Stacy; married Olga Snegyreva, 1969. *Education:* University of Michigan, B.A., 1946, M.A., 1947; Syracuse University, Ph.D., 1965. *Home:* 7267 Mott Rd., Fayetteville, N.Y. 13066. *Office:* Syracuse University, 320 HBC, Syracuse, N.Y. 13210.

CAREER: Syracuse University, Syracuse, N.Y., instructor, 1964-66, assistant professor, 1966-73, associate professor of Russian literature, 1973—. *Military service:* U.S. Army, aerial photograph interpreter in Military Intelligence, 1942-45; became master sergeant. *Member:* American Association of Teachers of Slavic and East European languages.

WRITINGS: (Contributor) William Harkins and Jacob Hursky, editors, *Symbolae in Honorem G. Y. Shevelov,* Logos Verlag, 1971; *Russian Literary Criticism: A Short History,* Syracuse University Press, 1974; *Defamiliarization in Language and Literature,* Syracuse University Press, 1977. Contributor to professional journals. Member of editorial board of *Symposium.*

WORK IN PROGRESS: India and Russian Literature.

SIDELIGHTS: Stacy told *CA:* "My interests lie primarily in the comparative study of literature and the investigation of ultimate or at least significantly influential sources. But I am also interested in such matters as literary realism—seen, however, from the philosophical viewpoints of nominalism and Platonic realism; symbolism and modernism, especially in Russian literature; and a number of Russian Formalist concepts, especially that of *ostranenie* (defamiliarization).

"My book on India and Russian literature is simply an attempt to bring together widely scattered information in this subject and to illustrate the use by Russian prose authors and poets of themes, metaphor, etc., derived from or relating to various aspects of India, especially Hinduism and Sanskrit literature."

*   *   *

STANHOPE, Eric
    See HAMILTON, Charles Harold St. John

*   *   *

STANLEY, Robert
    See HAMILTON, Charles Harold St. John

*   *   *

STANNARD, Una   1927-

PERSONAL: Given name pronounced *Yoo*-na; born December 31, 1927, in Boston, Mass.; daughter of Samuel S. and Miriam (Schneider) Garlitz. *Education:* Boston University, B.A., 1950, M.A., 1953, Ph.D., 1959. *Home address:* P.O. Box 16014, San Francisco, Calif. 94116.

CAREER: Wheaton College, Norton, Mass., instructor in English, 1957-58; University of California, Berkeley, instructor, 1959-60, assistant professor of English, 1960-65; writer, 1965—. *Member:* National Organization for Women, National Woman's Party, Phi Beta Kappa.

WRITINGS: The New Pamela (novel), Ballantine, 1969; (contributor) V. Gornick and B. K. Moran, editors, *Woman in Sexist Society,* Basic Books, 1971; (contributor) H. Z. Lopata, editor, *Marriages & Families,* Van Nostrand, 1973; *Married Women versus Husbands' Names: The Case for Wives Who Keep Their Own Name,* Germainbooks, 1973; *Mrs Man,* Germainbooks, 1977. Contributor to academic journals and popular magazines, including *Ms., Columbia Forum, Medical Aspects of Human Sexuality, Everywoman* and *New Woman.*

WORK IN PROGRESS: Born Unlucky, a novel.

SIDELIGHTS: Stannard told *CA:* "For many years I have been a feminist writer, believing with Elizabeth Cady Stanton that 'The establishing of woman on her rightful throne is the greatest revolution the world has ever known or ever will know.' Although I shall undoubtedly write other feminist articles, the novel I am now working on deals with the distorted world each of us lives in and constantly creates, thinking it to be the real world."

STAR, Jack   1920-

PERSONAL: Born September 17, 1920, in Chicago, Ill.; son of Boris and Leah (Belazerkowsky) Star; married Dorothy Rabin (a researcher), October 19, 1941; children: Amy Leanne (Mrs. Lee Feigon), Merrie (Mrs. Gar Scheuer), Natalie, Vincent. *Education:* Attended Chicago City College, 1938-40 and Central Y.M.C.A. College, Chicago, Ill., 1941. *Home and office:* 18 Wilson Ct., Park Forest, Ill. 60466.

CAREER: Chicago Times, Chicago, Ill., reporter and editor, 1941-48; *Chicago Sun Times,* Chicago, writer and editor, 1948-52; *Look,* New York, N.Y., senior editor, 1952-71; free-lance writer, 1971—; *Chicago* (magazine), Chicago, senior editor, 1977—. Correspondent for *New York Herald Tribune,* 1950-52. Visiting lecturer at Barat College, Columbia College, and Elgin Community College. *Military service:* U.S. Army Air Forces, 1944-45.

MEMBER: American Society of Journalists and Authors, Society of Professional Journalists, Chicago Press Club. *Awards, honors:* Medical journalism award from American Medical Association, 1965, for distinguished journalism; Silver Gavel award from American Bar Association, 1966, for an article in *Look* on police reform; National Headliners Club Award, 1968, for consistently outstanding feature writing; Jacob Scher Award for Investigative Reporting from Women in Communication, 1974, for an article on crime in Chicago subways; certificate of merit from American Bar Association, 1975, for distinguished reporting on the law.

WRITINGS: (Contributor) Berton Roueche, editor, *Together: A Casebook of Physician-Nurse Joint Practice,* National Joint Practice Commission, 1977. Contributor to magazines, including *Saturday Review, Reader's Digest, Catholic Digest, Change, Today's Health,* and *Chicago Tribune Magazine.*

*   *   *

STARK, Raymond   1919-
    (John Norwood)

PERSONAL: Born January 31, 1919, in Bushyhead, Okla.; son of Clint (a clergyman) and Georgia (Stanphil) Stark; married Dolores Donahue, January 31, 1946 (divorced, 1964); children: Carla Rae Stark Teicher, April Renee Stark Brasier. *Education:* Bernadean University, D.Naturopathy, 1968. *Home and office:* 1825 Liberty Rd., Apt. 186, Lexington, Ky. 40505. *Agent:* Elspeth Cochrane Agency, 1 Pavement, London S.W.4, England.

CAREER: Colorado Springs Free Press, Colorado Springs, Colo., city editor and columnist, 1953-65; *Roseburg News-Review,* Roseburg, Ore., city hall reporter, 1965-67; U.S. Government, Washington, D.C., writer and editor in Fort Knox, Ky. and Lexington, Ky., 1967—. Public information officer for Colorado Civil Defense Agency.

MEMBER: International Belles-Lettres Society, International Poetry Centre, World Poetry Library, International Poetry Academy, Clover International Poetry Association, Authors Guild of Authors League of America, Academy of Contemporary Poets, Poetry Society (London), El Paso County Osteopathic Society. *Awards, honors:* Named poet of the year by National Poetry Publishers Association, 1974; named an outstanding lyric poet of the bicentennial era by International Poetry Centre, 1976.

WRITINGS: Crossroads to Nowhere (fiction), Ward, Lock, 1956; (under pseudonym John Norwood) *No Time to Laugh* (fiction), Ward, Lock, 1956; (with April Burk) *Diet-*

ing with Herbs, Barlenmir House, 1977; *New Zealand Herbs,* Viking Sevenseas, 1977; *The Psychedelics Handbook,* Barlenmir House, in press. Author of health column in *Green Revolution.* Contributor to magazines, including *Other Scenes, Fantastic Tales,* and *New Zealand Woman's Weekly.* Kentucky editor of *American Mosaic.*

WORK IN PROGRESS: The Plants of Sexuality, on aphrodisiacs and other sexual botanicals; a comprehensive book listing hundreds of herbs with detailed information, completion expected in 1979.

SIDELIGHTS: Stark writes: "There are those who deem it somewhat strange that I write lyric poetry on the one hand, and offbeat herbal books on the other hand. To me, this seems perfectly normal and logical, since there is a certain lyricism in the offbeat botanicals.

"I am an Anglophile with a number of trips to England to my credit. My only languages are Spanish and Romani, the tongue spoken by the Gypsies of Great Britain. I have travelled in Mexico, and lived in Quito, Ecuador; also I lived in New Zealand."

*   *   *

STARRETT, (Charles) Vincent (Emerson)   1886-1974

PERSONAL: Born October 26, 1886, in Toronto, Ontario, Canada; son of Robert Polk and Margaret Deniston (Young) Starrett. *Education:* Attended public schools in Toronto and Chicago, Ill. *Residence:* Chicago, Ill.

CAREER: Newspaperman, *Chicago Inter-Ocean,* 1905-06; *Chicago Daily News,* Chicago, Ill., newspaperman, 1906-16, war correspondent in Mexico, 1914-15; *Chicago Wave,* Chicago, editor, 1921-22; *Chicago Tribune,* Chicago, columnist, beginning 1942. Instructor, Medill School of Journalism, 1922-23. *Member:* Society of Midland Authors (president, 1933-34), Mystery Writers of America (president, 1961), Arthur Machen Society, Sherlock Holmes Society of England, Baker Street Irregulars (founding member).

WRITINGS: Arthur Machen: A Novelist of Ecstasy and Sin, W. M. Hill, 1918; *The Escape of Alice: A Christmas Fantasy,* privately printed, 1919; *Ambrose Bierce,* W. M. Hill, 1920, reprinted, Kennikat, 1969; *The Unique Hamlet: A Hitherto Unchronicled Adventure of Mr. Sherlock Holmes,* privately printed, 1920; *Ebony Flame* (poems), Convici-McGee, 1922; *Banners in the Dawn: Sixty-Four Sonnets,* W. M. Hill, 1923; *Stephen Crane: A Bibliography,* Centaur, 1923; *Buried Caesars: Essays in Literary Appreciation,* Covici-McGee, 1923, reprinted, AMS Press, 1970; *Coffins for Two,* Covici-McGee, 1924; *Flame and Dust,* Covici, 1924; *Seaports in the Moon: A Fantasia on Romantic Themes,* Doubleday, Doran, 1928; *Penny Wise and Book Foolish,* Covici Friede, 1929; *Murder on "B" Deck,* Doubleday, Doran, 1929.

The Blue Door: Murder, Mystery, Detection in Ten Thrill-Packed Novelettes, Doubleday, Doran, 1930; *All About Mother Goose,* Apellicon Press, 1930; *Dead Man Inside,* Doubleday, Doran, 1931; *The End of Mr. Garment,* Doubleday, Doran, 1932; *The Private Life of Sherlock Holmes,* Macmillan, 1933, revised and enlarged edition, 1960; *The Great Hotel Murder* (originally appeared in *Redbook* under the title, *Recipe for Murder*), Doubleday, Doran, 1935; *Snow for Christmas,* [Glencoe, Ill.], 1935; *Midnight and Percy Jones,* Covici Friede, 1936; *Persons from Porlock, and Other Interruptions* (essays), Normandie House, 1938; *Oriental Encounters: Two Essays in Bad Taste,* Normandie House, 1938.

Books Alive, Random House, 1940, reprinted, Books for Libraries, 1969; *Bookman's Holiday: The Private Satisfactions of an Incurable Collector,* Random House, 1942, reprinted, 1971; *Autolycus in Limbo* (poems), Dutton, 1943; *The Case Book of Jimmie Lavender,* Gold Label Books, 1944, reprinted, Bookfinger, 1973; *Murder in Peking,* Lantern Press, 1946; (with Ames W. Williams) *Stephen Crane: A Bibliography,* J. Valentine, 1948; *Sonnets, and Other Verse,* Dierkes Press, 1949; *Best Loved Books of the Twentieth Century,* Bantam, 1955; *The Great All-Star Animal League Ball Game* (for children; illustrated by Kurt Wiese), Dodd, Mead, 1957; *Book Column,* Caxton Club, 1958; *The Quick and the Dead,* Arkham House, 1965; *Born in a Bookshop: Chapters from the Chicago Renascence* (autobiographical), University of Oklahoma Press, 1965; *Late, Later and Possibly Last: Essays,* Autolycus Press, 1973.

Editor: *In Praise of Stevenson,* Bookfellows, 1919; (and author of introduction) *Men, Women, and Boats,* Boni & Liveright, 1921; *Et Cetera: A Collector's Scrap-Book,* Covici, 1924; *Fourteen Great Detective Stories,* Modern Library, 1928; *A Modern Book of Wonders: Amazing Facts in a Remarkable World,* University of Knowledge, Inc., 1938; (with others) *221B: Studies in Sherlock Holmes,* Macmillan, 1940, reprinted, Biblo & Tannen, 1969; *World's Great Spy Stories,* World Publishing, 1944.

SIDELIGHTS: Born in Toronto of Scotch-Irish parentage, Vincent Starrett was the grandson of the famous Canadian publisher and bookseller, John Young. Starrett wanted to be an illustrator, but began writing stories instead. A $75 check from *Collier's Weekly* for publication of a mystery story sealed his fate. He was an authority on Sherlock Holmes and also wrote poetry, short stories, detective novels, humorous sketches, biographies, and novels.

Commenting on Starrett's *Books Alive, Commonweal* noted: "Mr. Starrett has, apparently, written without any serious intent: he succeeds admirably in giving us an entertaining book. It is a volume of literary gossip, a book not for students or bibliographers, but for those literary ladies—and gentlemen—who appreciate a fund of anecdote and chatty comment. The anecdotes are not, by any means, new; in fact, their familiarity is the chief charm of some: known trivia have a power of solacing by again distracting, which, especially today, many a reader will find welcome."

With Christopher Morley, Elmer Davis, and others, Starrett edited *221B: Studies in Sherlock Holmes. Books* commented: "In this branch of biography nobody ever uses the word definitive. It is an appetite that grows as it eats, and Holmesians will not only feed upon but fall upon this feast, opening the book with a gesture like tucking a napkin under the chin." Starrett also wrote *The Private Life of Sherlock Holmes. Books* described the original edition as, "a book for pleasure, for such peaceful slippered contentment as the two friends found together in Baker Street." The later revision of *Sherlock Holmes* was reviewed by the *Chicago Tribune* which noted, "The volume is rich with enlightenment on every aspect of the lore of Holmes and the period in which he flourished as the world's only consulting detective. The author's scholarship in Holmesiana is supreme, and he writes as if communicating a happy sense of enchantment. The format is a masterpiece of decorative design."

Starrett lived in such cities as St. Louis, Reno, New York, London, Paris, Rome, and Peking. In 1935, the Fox Film Corp. produced "The Great Hotel Murder," based on Starrett's story of the same name.

BIOGRAPHICAL/CRITICAL SOURCES: Books, October 22, 1933, March 31, 1940; *Commonweal,* December 6, 1940; *Chicago Sunday Tribune,* May 1, 1960; Vincent Starrett, *Born in a Bookshop: Chapters from the Chicago Renascence,* University of Oklahoma Press, 1965; Peter A. Ruber, *Last Bookman: A Journey into the Life and Times of Vincent Starrett, Author, Journalist, Bibliophile,* Candlelight Press, 1968.

OBITUARIES: New York Times, January 6, 1974; *Washington Post,* January 13, 1974; *AB Bookman's Weekly,* January 28, 1974; *Publishers Weekly,* February 4, 1974.*

(Died January 5, 1974)

* * *

STATES, Bert O(len) 1929-

PERSONAL: Born August 8, 1929, in Punxsutawney, Pa.; son of Bert Olen (a railroad employee) and Helma (Hellberg) States; married Nancy Beun, June 30, 1951; children: Jerri Beun, Eric Albin. *Education:* Pennsylvania State University, B.A., 1950, M.A., 1955; Yale University, D.F.A., 1960. *Home:* 925 Cayuga Heights Rd., Ithaca, N.Y. 14850. *Office:* Department of English, 212 Lincoln Hall, Cornell University, Ithaca, N.Y. 14853.

CAREER: WKBI-Radio, St. Marys, Pa., announcer, 1950-51; WPXY-Radio, Punxsutawney, Pa., program director, 1953; Human Resources Research Center, Fort Ord, Calif., editorial assistant, 1955-56; Rensselaer Polytechnic Institute, Troy, N.Y., assistant professor of English, 1959-60; Skidmore College, Saratoga Springs, N.Y., assistant professor of English, 1960-64; University of Pittsburgh, Pittsburgh, Pa., assistant professor, 1964-67, associate professor of theater arts, 1967; Cornell University, Ithaca, N.Y., associate professor, 1967-73, professor of English and theater arts, 1973—. *Military service:* U.S. Army, Signal Corps, documentary writer and announcer for Armed Forces Radio Service, 1951-53.

WRITINGS: Irony and Drama: A Poetics, Cornell University Press, 1971; (contributor) Arthur Ganz, editor, *Pinter: A Collection of Critical Essays,* Prentice-Hall, 1972; *The Shape of Paradox: An Essay on "Waiting for Godot",* University of California Press, 1978.

Plays: "The Tall Grass" (one-act), 1958; "A Rent in the Universe" (one-act), 1967; "Ralph" (two-act), first produced in Ithaca, N.Y., at Reader's Theatre, summer, 1975.

Plays anthologized in *Mayorga's Best Plays* and *First Stage.* Contributor to literature journals and literary magazines, including *Yale Review, Southern Review, South Atlantic Quarterly,* and *Hudson Review.*

WORK IN PROGRESS: Research on *Hamlet,* artistry and the dream, and the nature of archetypes.

SIDELIGHTS: States writes: "I am generally interested in the aesthetics and formal nature of dramatic literature, though recently I've gotten interested in myth and its intrusion into fiction, and in the dream as the ur-form of storytelling. My special interest is in Shakespeare and modern drama, examined from the structural viewpoint. I've traveled in Japan, Korea, England, and Mexico. I have written many plays, all of them mediocre to poor, and teach playwriting in addition to my other courses in drama. My work has been heavily influenced by Kenneth Burke and Northrop Frye, whom I seem to mention in almost everything I write."

STEIG, Irwin 1901-1977

1901—November 8, 1977; American businessman, artist, and author. Stein was best known as the author of books on card-playing. He died in Pleasant Beach, N.J. Obituaries: *New York Times,* November 11, 1977.

* * *

STEINER, Barbara A(nnette) 1934-
(Anne Daniel; Kate D'Andrea, Annette Cole, joint pseudonyms with Kathleen Phillips)

PERSONAL: Born November 3, 1934, in Dardanelle, Ark.; daughter of Hershel Thomas (a collector and dealer of Indian relics) and Rachel Julia (a clerk and antiques dealer; maiden name, Stilley) Daniel; married Kenneth E. Steiner (an electrical engineer), August 4, 1957; children: Rachel Anne, Rebecca Sue. *Education:* Henderson State Teachers College (now Henderson State College), Arkadelphia, Ark., B.S.E., 1955; University of Kansas, M.S.E., 1959; attended University of Colorado, 1973 and 1975. *Religion:* Protestant. *Residence:* Boulder, Colo.

CAREER: Writer. Elementary school teacher in the public schools of Independence, Mo., 1955-57, Lawrence, Kan., 1957-58, Wichita, Kan. 1958-59, Nederland, Colo., 1966-68; local church librarian, 1969-74; actor in local religious drama productions, 1971-75; member of task force for Boulder Council of Churches, 1971-75; youth group director, 1972-74. *Member:* Society of Children's Book Writers (vice-president of Rocky Mountain chapter, 1976-77, president, 1977-78), Audubon Society, National Wildlife Association, Colorado Authors League, Evergreen Art Association (president, 1962-63), Evergreen Home Demonstration Club (president, 1961-62), Boulder Tennis Association (secretary, 1970, vice-president, 1977). *Awards, honors:* Top Hand award, 1972, and best juvenile article award, 1973, both from Colorado Authors League; *Biography of a Polar Bear* named best juvenile non-fiction book by Colorado Authors League, and outstanding science book for children by National Science Teachers Association and Children's Book Council, 1973; Top Hand award, 1977, for *Biography of a Kangaroo Rat.*

*WRITINGS—*All for children: *Biography of a Polar Bear,* Putnam, 1972; *Biography of a Wolf,* Putnam, 1973; *Your Hobby: Stamp Collecting,* Schmitt, Hall & McCreary, 1973; *Biography of a Desert Bighorn,* Putnam, 1975; *Biography of a Kangaroo Rat,* Putnam, 1977.

Contributor, sometimes under pseudonyms, of over sixty articles, stories, plays, and poems to children's and teen magazines and religious publications, including *Humpty Dumpty, Ranger Rick, Woman's Day, Childlife,* and *Starwind.*

WORK IN PROGRESS: Biography of a Killer Whale, expected publication, 1978; *Biography of a Bengal Tiger,* 1979; a teen novel, *Imprisoned Splendor;* a novel, *Omu, the Carver and His Whale Brother; America's Story in Quilts;* a picture book, *Desert Trip.*

SIDELIGHTS: Steiner told *CA:* "Man is waking up to how important it is that he preserve his natural environment. He realizes how important each animal is to the balance of nature. I like to tell boys and girls about how interesting an animal's life is and how he has adapted so he can live in sometimes harsh environments, with many other animals or often man as his enemy. Only by learning and working together can we preserve our wildlife, and I find children in the schools where I speak an eager and intelligent audience.

Many are working in wildlife organizations in their schools and clubs elsewhere."

AVOCATIONAL INTEREST: Tennis, backpacking, photography, birding, needlework (especially quilting), stamp collecting, American Indian masks and Navajo rugs, Scout badge teaching (especially creative writing and drama), speaking to school children on endangered species.

* * *

STEINER, George 1929-

PERSONAL: Born April 23, 1929, in Paris, France; came to United States in 1940, naturalized citizen, 1944; son of Frederick George and Elsie (Franzos) Steiner; married Zara Alice Shakow, July 7, 1955; children: David Milton, Deborah Tarn. *Education:* University of Chicago, B.A., 1948; Harvard University, M.A., 1950; Oxford University, Ph.D., 1955. *Home:* 32 Barrow Rd., Cambridge, England.

CAREER: Economist, London, England, member of editorial staff, 1952-56; Institute for Advanced Study, Princeton, N.J., fellow, 1956-58; Princeton University, Princeton, Gauss Lecturer, 1959-60; Cambridge University, Cambridge, England, fellow of Churchill College, 1961—. Visiting professor at New York University, 1966-67; University of California, Regents Lecturer, 1973, Massey Lecturer, 1974; professor of English and comparative literature at University of Geneva, Geneva, Switzerland, 1974. *Member:* Royal Society of Literature (fellow), Athenaeum Club (London), Savile Club (London), Harvard Club (New York City). *Awards, honors:* Bell Prize, 1950; Rhodes scholar, 1955; Fullbright professorship, 1958-59; O'Henry Short Story Prize, 1959; Zabel Award, 1970, from National Institute of Arts and Letters (United States); Guggenheim fellowship, 1971-72; Cortina Ulisse Prize, 1972; D.Litt., 1976, from University of East Anglia.

WRITINGS: Tolstoy or Dostoevsky, Penguin, 1958, Dutton, 1971; *The Death of Tragedy,* Hill & Wang, 1960; (editor with R. Fagles) *Homer,* Prentice-Hall, 1962; *Anno Domini,* Atheneum, 1964; (editor) *The Penguin Book of Modern Verse Translation,* Penguin, 1966; *Language and Silence,* Atheneum, 1967; *Extraterritorial: Literature and the Language Revolution,* Atheneum, 1971; *In Bluebeard's Castle: Notes Toward the Redefinition of Culture,* Yale University Press, 1971; *Fields of Force: Fischer and Spassky at Reykjavik,* Viking, 1974; *After Babel: Aspects of Language and Translation,* Oxford University Press, 1975. Also author of *Nostalgia for the Absolute,* 1974. Contributor of numerous reviews, stories, and articles to periodicals and journals, including *Commentary, Harper's, Nation,* and *New Yorker.*

AVOCATIONAL INTERESTS: Music, chess, mountain walking.

BIOGRAPHICAL/CRITICAL SOURCES: Times Literary Supplement, September 28, 1967; *New Statesman,* October 20, 1967, January 31, 1975; *Yale Review,* Autumn, 1967; *Commonweal,* October 27, 1967; *London* Magazine, December, 1967; *Commentary,* October, 1968, November, 1975; *Time,* July 26, 1971; *New Yorker,* May 5, 1975; *Christian Science Monitor,* May 25, 1975; *New York Times Book Review,* June 9, 1975; *New York Review of Books,* October 30, 1975.

* * *

STEINER, Shari 1941-

PERSONAL: Born March 3, 1941, in Colorado Springs, Colo.; daughter of E. Keith (a highway engineer) and Blanche (Ketzner) Montgomery; married Clyde Lionel Steiner (a photojournalist), June 16, 1962; children: Vienna Kay, Marco Romano. *Education:* Adams State College, B.A., 1962; further study at London School of Economics and Political Science. *Politics:* "Enlightened individualist." *Religion:* "Enlightened individualist." *Residence:* London, England. *Agent:* Alexandria Hatcher, Alexandria Hatcher Agency, 150 West 55th St., New York, N.Y. 10019. *Office:* Media Team Corp., 135 East 55th St., New York, N.Y. 10022.

CAREER: Free-lance writer, 1962—. Rome correspondent for *International Herald Tribune* (Paris, France); public relations representative for Allen, Ingersoll & Weber; lecturer at University of London. *Member:* American Society of Journalists and Authors. *Awards, honors:* Guida Monaci International Journalistic Prize, 1971.

WRITINGS: The Female Factor: A Report on Women in Western Europe, Putnam, 1977. Contributor to magazines and newspapers, including *Saturday Review, Reader's Digest, Ladies Home Journal,* and *Cosmopolitan.*

WORK IN PROGRESS: An illustrated book on women's archetypes through history.

SIDELIGHTS: Shari Steiner writes: "As a journalist who has spent much of my working life in different cultures, I feel that a great many of our questions about how to solve problems can be answered by looking around at how others have tackled the same tasks. To find answers to these questions, I have interviewed government ministers and street sweepers, doctors and hitchikers. I speak Italian and enough French, German, and Spanish to do the relaxed, taped, on-the-spot interviews that have become my specialty.

"The reasons I have focused on the diversity of women are many, and they are rooting in my personal experience of womanhood. I came of age during the era of Women's Liberation. To me, the concept that women are a separate class with common problems that can be attacked and solved by unified action is one of the most centrally important ideas of our time. This belief, coupled with the practical means of achieving universal birth control, will influence our daily lives during this coming century as much as the knowledge of evolution dominated us in the last.

"Probably the main reason I keep writing when editors all seem to be off in Aspen skiing while our last month's heat bill is still unpaid is that my curiosity is a stronger instinct than my practicality. Besides, I've always counted reading as one of life's three great pleasures.

"More seriously, I think the information explosion—both in a journalistic exploration of the outer world and fictional exploration of the inner world—is the most important factor in our age's phenomenal ability to expand materially and to begin coping with the suffering of a large proportion of the world on a scale the past has never witnessed. Hopefully, exchange of information will also make a significant contribution to that most important task—survival of the human race. Perhaps you could say my practical instincts are intact—I'm just one of those who believes in practicality on a long range basis. That's what I tell myself, anyway."

BIOGRAPHICAL/CRITICAL SOURCES: Denver Post, January 28, 1977; *Minneapolis Tribune,* February 17, 1977; *Salt Lake Tribune,* March 1, 1977; *Fort Worth Star Telegram,* March 4, 1977; *Milwaukee Sentinel,* March 15, 1977; *Human Behavior,* May, 1977.

STERLING, Helen
 See HOKE, Helen L.

* * *

STERN, Malcolm H(enry) 1915-

PERSONAL: Born January 29, 1915, in Philadelphia, Pa.; son of Arthur Kaufman (a realtor) and Henrietta (a camp director; maiden name, Berkowitz) Stern; married Louise Bergman (a copy editor), May 25, 1941. *Education:* University of Pennsylvania, B.A., 1935; Hebrew Union College, Cincinnati, Ohio, B.H.L., 1937, M.H.L., 1941, rabbi, 1941, D.H.L., 1957. *Politics:* Liberal. *Home:* 300 East 71st St., New York, N.Y. 10021. *Office:* 790 Madison Ave., New York, N.Y. 10021.

CAREER: Assistant rabbi of Jewish congregation in Philadelphia, Pa., 1941-43, 1946-47, rabbi in Norfolk, Va., 1947-64; Central Conference of American Rabbis, New York, N.Y., director of rabbinic placement, 1964—. Genealogist for American Jewish Archives, 1950—; musical consultant. *Military service:* U.S. Army Air Forces, chaplain, 1943-46; became captain. *Member:* American Society of Genealogists (vice-president, 1973-76; president, 1976—), American Jewish Historical Society (chairman of executive council, 1972—), National Genealogical Society, Jewish Historical Society of England. *Awards, honors:* D.D. from Hebrew Union College, 1966.

WRITINGS: (Editor) *Union Songster,* Central Conference of American Rabbis, 1960; *Americans of Jewish Descent,* Hebrew Union College, 1960, revised edition, American Jewish Historical Society, 1977; (editor) *Uriah Phillips Levy: The Blue Star Commodore,* Norfolk Jewish Community Council, 1961. Also author of *A Jewish Tourist's Guide to the Caribbean,* American Airlines, reprinted as *American Airlines Tourist's Guide to Jewish History in the Caribbean; A Shabbat Manual,* Central Conference of American Rabbis; *A Passover Haggadah,* Central Conference of American Rabbis, *Gates of Prayer,* Central Conference of American Rabbis. Author of program notes for Norfolk Symphony Orchestra, 1948-64. Contributor to magazines, including *Jewish Week.*

WORK IN PROGRESS: Biographical Dictionary of American Jewry, with Jacob R. Marcus; a song book for *Gates of Prayer,* with Raymond Smolover.

AVOCATIONAL INTERESTS: Music, travel (Europe, Israel, the Caribbean, the Orient), making travel scrapbooks.

BIOGRAPHICAL/CRITICAL SOURCES: Dan Rottenberg, *Finding Our Fathers,* Random House, 1977.

* * *

STERNBERG, Cecilia 1908-

PERSONAL: Born September 14, 1908, in England; daughter of Count Cecil and Countess Lillian (Hoyos) Reventlow; married Count Leopold Sternberg (deceased); children: Diana Sternberg Phipps. *Education:* Attended private school in Switzerland. *Politics:* Conservative. *Religion:* Roman Catholic. *Home:* Old Parsonage, Buscot, Oxfordshire, England.

CAREER: Writer, 1976—.

WRITINGS: The Journey (autobiography), Collins, 1977.

* * *

STEWART, Robert T. 1920(?)-1977

1920(?)—October 27, 1977; American journalist. Stewart

was best known for his coverage of tennis and boxing. He died in Glen Rock, N.J. Obituaries: *New York Times,* October 28, 1977.

* * *

STOCKING, George W(ard), Jr. 1928-

PERSONAL: Born December 8, 1928, in Berlin, Germany; son of George Ward (a professor of economics) and Dorothe (Reichhard) Stocking; married Wilhelmina Davis (an anthropologist), August 20, 1949 (divorced, 1965); married Carol Ann Bowman (a social researcher), September 29, 1968; children: Susan Stocking Hallowell, Rebecca, Rachel Louise, Melissa, Thomas Shepard. *Education:* Harvard University, B.A. (cum laude), 1949; University of Pennsylvania, Ph.D., 1960. *Politics:* "(ex-radical) liberal." *Religion:* "(ex-protestant) agnostic." *Home:* 5550 South Dorchester Ave., Chicago, Ill. 60637. *Office:* Department of Anthropology, University of Chicago, Chicago, Ill. 60637.

CAREER: Semi-skilled and unskilled laborer in Massachusetts, 1949-56; University of California, Berkeley, instructor, 1960-61, assistant professor, 1961-66, associate professor of history, 1966-67; University of Chicago, Chicago, Ill., associate professor, 1968-74, professor of anthropology, 1975—. Hill Visiting Professor at University of Minnesota, 1973; visiting professor at Harvard University, 1977. Active in trade union and local political work, 1949-56. Fellow of Center for Advanced Study in the Behavioral Sciences, 1976-77. *Member:* American Anthropological Association, American Historical Association, History of Science Society, Social Science History Association, Royal Anthropological Institute, Cheiron.

WRITINGS: Race, Culture, and Evolution: Essays in the History of Anthropology, Free Press, 1968; (editor) *James C. Prichard's Researches into the Physical History of Man,* University of Chicago Press, 1973; (editor) *The Shaping of American Anthropology, 1883-1911: A Franz Boas Reader,* Basic Books, 1974; (editor) *Selected Papers from the American Anthropologist, 1921-1945,* American Anthropological Association, 1976. Contributor to *Dictionary of American History* and *International Encyclopedia of the Social Sciences.* Contributor of articles and reviews to anthropology, sociology, and history journals. Editor of *History of Anthropology Newsletter;* member of editorial board of *Journal of the History of the Behavioral Sciences.*

WORK IN PROGRESS: Research on the history of British and American anthropology.

SIDELIGHTS: Stocking has traveled in Spain, Mexico, England, Yugoslavia, and Germany.

* * *

STORING, Herbert James 1928-1977

January 29, 1928—September 9, 1977; American educator and author. Storing was recognized as an authority on the United States presidency and government. He died in Charlottesville, Va. Obituaries: *Washington Post,* September 12, 1977.

* * *

STOWE, Richard S(cribner) 1925-

PERSONAL: Born January 2, 1925, in Milwaukee, Wis.; son of Ray and Irene (Scribner) Stowe; married Nancy Marsh (a singer and teacher), June 30, 1962; children: Andrew Marsh, Elizabeth Scribner. *Education:* University of Wisconsin, Madison, B.A., 1949, Ph.D., 1964; University of California, Los Angeles, M.A., 1951. *Religion:* Methodist. *Home:* 423 East Longview Dr., Appleton, Wis. 54911. *Office:* Department of French, Lawrence University, Appleton, Wis. 54911.

CAREER: Park College, Parkville, Mo., instructor, 1952-55, assistant professor of French and Spanish, 1955-56; Lawrence University, Appleton, Wis., instructor, 1957-61, assistant professor, 1961-66, associate professor, 1966-76, professor of French, 1976—. *Military service:* U.S. Army, Infantry, 1944-45; received Bronze Star. *Member:* Modern Language Association of America, American Association of Teachers of French.

WRITINGS: Alexandre Dumas pere, Twayne, 1976.

WORK IN PROGRESS: Arthur de Gobineau, for Twayne; research on nineteenth-century French literature.

SIDELIGHTS: Stowe writes: "In addition to French literature, I am very much interested in English literature of the Romantic and Victorian periods. I have traveled extensively in Europe, with several long stays in France and England." *Avocational interests:* Music, art.

* * *

STRYKER-RODDA, Kenn 1903-

PERSONAL: Born July 7, 1903, in Arlington, N.J.; son of Samuel Hawkins (a carpenter) and Cora Augusta (Stryker) Rodda; married Harriet Mott (a certified genealogist), December 29, 1924; children: Paul Mott, Ellsworth Natton, Andrea. *Education:* Princeton University, A.B., 1923; New York University, M.A., 1927; Webster University, D.Litt., 1929. *Home:* 421 Summit Ave., South Orange, N.J. 07079. *Office:* 122 East 58th St., New York, N.Y. 10022.

CAREER: Pennington Seminary, Pennington, N.J., teacher of drama and mathematics, 1923-25; English teacher and head of department at private school in Woodstock, Va., 1925-27; English teacher at private school in Brooklyn, N.Y., 1927-28, dean, 1928-68; genealogist and writer, 1968—. Adjunct lecturer and coordinator of Institute of Genealogy and Historical Research at Samford University, summers, 1968-74. Charter member of Union County Cultural and Heritage Commission; general chairman of League of Historical Societies of New Jersey, 1968-72.

MEMBER: National Genealogical Society (fellow; president, 1970-74), American Society of Genealogists (fellow), Sons of the American Revolution, Hereditary Order of Loyalists and Patriots, Genealogical Society of New Jersey (fellow; president, 1962-70), New Jersey Historical Society, Long Island Historical Society (life member; member of board of directors, 1952-77), Flagon and Trencher Club (genealogist, 1963—).

WRITINGS: (Compiler with Herbert F. Seversmith) *Long Island Genealogical Source Material,* National Genealogical Society, 1962; *Digging for Ancestors in the Garden State,* Detroit Society for Genealogical Research, 1970; (editor) *Genealogical Research: Methods and Sources,* Volume II, American Society of Genealogists, 1971; *Revolutionary Census of New Jersey,* Polyanthos, 1972; *Genealogy: A Manual,* Boy Scouts of America, 1973; *Denizations, Naturalizations and Oaths of Allegiance in Colonial New York,* Genealogical Publishing, 1975; *Register of Salomon Lachaire,* Genealogical Publishing, 1977.

Privately printed: *Ancestors and Descendants of Abraham Brower Ellsworth,* 1954; *Ancestors and Descendants of Peter A. Bogeart,* 1955; *Case and Related Families,* 1957; *Elliott, Natton and Related Families,* 1957; *A Staten Island Lineage,* 1958; *Harshall and Related Families,* 1959; *Cool, Couwenhoven and Related Families,* 1960; *Probable Ancestry of William M. Todd,* 1961; *Paternal Ancestry of Catriena Hooghlandt,* 1962. Co-editor of "New York Historical Manuscripts: Dutch Series," for Genealogical Publishing, 1974—. Contributor of several hundred articles and reviews to genealogy magazines. Editor for New York Genealogical and Biographical Society, 1965—.

WORK IN PROGRESS: Genealogical research, including some black family history.

SIDELIGHTS: Stryker-Rodda writes briefly: "In articles, reviews, lectures, and courses I am a staunch advocate of sound research methods in family history, genealogy, and local history."

* * *

STUART, Ian 1927-

PERSONAL: Born May 6, 1927, in Royston, England; son of Leslie Charles (a schoolmaster) and Olive Margaret (Wilson) Stuart; married Audrey Joyce Allen, March 7, 1953; children: Bruce Graham, Neil Charles. *Education:* Educated in England. *Religion:* Church of England. *Home:* 218 Watford Rd., St. Albans, Hertfordshire AL2 3EA, England.

CAREER: Writer. Has worked as a bank manager; trustee and treasurer, St. Albans Hostel for the Homeless, 1970-75. *Member:* Crime Writers Association, Society of Authors.

WRITINGS: The Snow on the Ben, Ward, Lock, 1961; *Golf in Hertfordshire,* William Carling, 1972; *Death from Disclosure,* R. Hale, 1976; *Flood Tide,* R. Hale, 1977; *Sand Trap,* R. Hale, 1977; *Fatal Switch,* R. Hale, 1978. Contributor of short stories and articles to periodicals.

WORK IN PROGRESS: A mystery novel.

* * *

SULLIVAN, Mary W(ilson) 1907-

PERSONAL: Born December 25, 1907, in Grants Pass, Ore.; daughter of Roy Stanley (a salesman) and Adelia (a bank clerk; maiden name, Harth) Wilson; married Paul D. Sullivan (a machinery executive), April 15, 1931; children: Mary Anne (Mrs. Raymond Rodolf), Molly (Mrs. David Nicholson), Denis Philip, Francis James, Margaret (Mrs. John Christope Schwarzenbach). *Education:* University of Oregon, student, 1926-28. *Home:* 8811 Pacific Coast Highway, #121, Laguna Beach, Calif. 92651. *Office:* P.O. Box 2865, Pasadena, Calif. 91105.

CAREER: McCormick Steamship Co., Portland, Ore., statistician, 1928-30; *Masonic Analyst* (magazine), Portland, Ore., member of staff, 1930-31; writer, 1965—. *Member:* International P.E.N., Society of Children's Book Writers, United Nations Association, Pacificulture, California Writers Guild, Southern California Council on Literature for Children and Young People, Quill Pen, Alpha Phi.

WRITINGS—Juvenile: Pancho Villa Rebels, Field Enterprises Educational Corp., 1970; *Chili Peppers,* Field Enterprises Educational Corp., 1970; *Rattrap,* Field Enterprises Educational Corp., 1970; *Jokers Wild,* Field Enterprises Educational Corp., 1970; *The Indestructible Old Time String Band,* Thomas Nelson, 1975; *Bluegrass Iggy,* Thomas Nelson, 1975; *Bluegrass Iggy* (different text; Arrow Book Club selection), Scholastic Book Services, 1976; *What's This About Pete?,* Thomas Nelson, 1976; *Brian-Foot-In-the-Mouth,* Thomas Nelson, 1978.

WORK IN PROGRESS: Lectures and research on Asian art.

SIDELIGHTS: Mary Sullivan writes: "As a volunteer librarian in the Catholic Boys School my sons attended, I saw the need for books on subjects other than sports. My first six books are about boys who are into teenage music, the seventh is about a boy who sews, likes it, and questions his masculinity. My next book is about a boy with a disastrous propensity for saying the wrong thing. The one after that deals with and dramatizes speech and image making.

"I feel there can never be too many books published for young people. I like to write them because I seem to have a knack for capturing their interest. Just what it is, I'm not sure, but it may be that the extraordinary richness of my life seeps into my writing.

"Raised by a working mother in the home of grandparents who took pride in having followed the frontier from the Mississippi all the way to Oregon, I inherited their itching foot and married an engineer. His business took us from towns, villages, and crossroads in the northwest to New York and Chicago before returning us west again in Los Angeles."

AVOCATIONAL INTERESTS: International travel (especially the British Isles).

* * *

SUNDERLIN, Sylvia 1911-

PERSONAL: Born September 22, 1911, in Lakeside, Mont.; daughter of Luke Decatur (a rancher) and Alice May (Waterman) Sweetman; married Charles Eugene Sunderlin (a university vice-president), July 8, 1936; children: Elizabeth, Mary Sunderlin Oakley, Katherine, William. *Education:* University of Montana, B.A., 1933; graduate study at Oxford University, 1935-36. *Politics:* Democrat. *Religion:* Episcopalian. *Home:* 3036 P St., Washington, D.C. 20007. *Agent:* Writer's House, Inc., 132 West 31st St., New York, N.Y. 10001.

CAREER: Association for Childhood Education International, Washington, D.C., assistant editor, 1964-66, associate editor, 1966-69, consulting associate editor, 1970-72; American Association for Gifted Children, New York City, editor and staff associate, 1973-75; *House Beautiful,* New York City, editor of monthly column "Address Book," 1976—. Research volunteer for Fine Arts Committee of U.S. Department of the Interior, 1966; president of American Womens' Club in Brussels, 1959-60, 1961-62. *Member:* Delta Gamma. *Awards, honors:* All-American Award from Educational Press Association of America, 1969.

WRITINGS: Antrim's Orange (juvenile), Scribner, 1976. Contributor to magazines, including *Odyssey, Lady's Circle,* and *Better Homes and Gardens.*

WORK IN PROGRESS: Calico the Choosing Cat, for children; *To the Dark Tower Came,* a romantic suspense novel; *The Summer Boy,* for children; *The Queen's Chalice,* a novel.

SIDELIGHTS: Sylvia Sunderlin told *CA:* "For more than twenty years, while my four children were young, I put aside my writing aspirations to devote my time and interests to being wife, mother, hostess, community, civic, and church participant. In 1962, upon return from the last stint abroad, Belgium, I started new phases of life: first, editor, then writer: it took me about three years to get started, short articles, longer articles, stories, then the first book. I'm on my way, a little late but alive. My keen interest in antiquities led to the offer of my present job, a job that found me."

SUTHINEE
See AMBHANWONG, Suthilak

* * *

SVAJIAN, Stephen G. 1906(?)-1977

1906(?)—December 10, 1977; Armenian-born American dentist and author. Svajian wrote many articles about Armenia as well as the book, *A Trip Through Historic Armenia.* He died in Brooklyn, N.Y. Obituaries: *New York Times,* December 15, 1977.

* * *

SWENSON, Peggye 1933-

PERSONAL: Born June 9, 1933, in Wichita Falls, Tex.; daughter of Victor Carroll (a cameraman) and Sybil Mae (Gatlin) Stampfli; married E. Don Swenson (a press photographer), July 8, 1971; children: Penny, Nicki, Kathy, Tony, Ricki, Duane, Becky, Marna. *Education:* Attended high school in Wichita Falls, Tex. *Residence:* Grandbury, Tex. *Agent:* Richard Huttner, 331 East 33rd St., New York, N.Y. 10016.

CAREER: Professional dancer, 1945-52; Dell Detective Magazines, New York, N.Y., area representative, 1954-61; *Laguna Beach News Post,* Laguna Hills, Calif., editor of woman's page and chief photographer, 1975—; writer, 1975—. *Member:* National Press Photographers Association, National League of American Penwomen (past local president), California Press Women (Orange County), Orange County Press Club, Saddleback Valley Photographers Club.

WRITINGS—Novels: *The Double M Factor,* Domina Books, 1977; *Suggestion of Murder,* Domina Books, 1977; *Hell Hath No Fury,* Domina Books, in press. Author of columns "Point of View" and "People & Places" in *Western Photographer.* Contributor to magazines and newspapers. Editor of newsletter of *Saddleback Valley Photographers.*

WORK IN PROGRESS: Juvenile mystery novels, including *Star Jinx, The Puzzle of the Red Hat Box, Secret at the Old Mill;* adult mystery novels, including *Aged in the Vat, Nice Little Town, The Coyote Killer, The Friendly Face of Death, The Gentle Hands of Death.*

SIDELIGHTS: Peggye Swenson writes: "I am a story teller. I am deeply interested in crime due to the fact that I worked (free-lance) with crime magazines when I was first starting my career. In my own work (fiction) I tend to follow that pattern. I have been greatly influenced by the works of Ursula Curtiss and Dolores Hitchens. Of course I am an avid reader of du Maurier, too. I enjoy sharing what I've learned with others; hence, my work as editor on a people-type page for a local newspaper is a great outlet."

* * *

SWIFT, Merlin
See LEEMING, Joseph

* * *

SYVERTSEN, Edythe 1921-

PERSONAL: Born July 8, 1921, in Staten Island, N.Y.; daughter of Theodore and Helga (Johansen) Syvertsen. *Education:* Attended Wagner College, New York University, and City College of the City University of New York. *Politics:* "Always split ticket." *Religion:* Lutheran. *Resi-*

dence: Lincroft, N.J. *Office: New York Post,* 210 South St., New York, N.Y. 10002.

CAREER: Has worked in various positions, including magazine writer, advertising promoter, copywriter, and financial writer, until 1959; *New York Post,* New York, began as copywriter for direct mail, became writer for automotive, real estate, and travel sections, 1959-68, travel editor, 1968—. Ghost writer. *Member:* Sigma Delta Chi.

WRITINGS: Travel Tips, Tempo Books, 1976.

AVOCATIONAL INTERESTS: Photography, horses, dogs (has taught dog obedience classes), gardening, cooking, travel.*

*   *   *

SZEPLAKI, Joseph 1932-

PERSONAL: Surname is accented on first syllable; born April 17, 1932, in Hatvan, Hungary; came to the United States in 1957, naturalized citizen, 1963; son of Joseph, Sr. and Julianna (Gazsi) Szeplaki; married Clara Irmai, January 24, 1957; children: Victor, Aniko. *Education:* Apaczai Csere Janos College of Pedagogy, M.L.S., 1954; also attended Rutgers University, 1962. *Religion:* Roman Catholic. *Home:* 10 Bertrand Island Rd., Mount Arlington, N.J. 07856.

CAREER: Trade-Union Library, Budapest, Hungary, chief librarian, 1955-56; Brandeis University, Waltham, Mass., assistant acquisitions librarian, 1963-65, acting head of department, 1965-66, head of acquisitions, 1966-67; Information Dynamics Corp., Reading, Mass., senior acquisitioner and supervisor of technical services, 1967-68; Ohio University, Athens, head of serials department, 1969-74; University of Minnesota, Minneapolis, assistant professor of library science and head of acquisitions, also consultant for Hungarian collection in Immigration History Research Center, 1974—; Monitor Systems, Inc., Whitehouse, N.J., vice-president, 1974—. Organizer and participant in workshops and seminars; held book exhibitions in Minnesota and Ohio.

MEMBER: International P.E.N., International Social Science Honor Society, American Library Association, American Association for the Study of Hungarian History, American Hungarian Educators Association, Hungarian Association, Arpad Academy. *Awards, honors:* Silver Medal from Cleveland Arpad Academy, 1972, gold medal, 1973, for the bibliography of Louis Kossuth, a third award, 1974, for *The Hungarians in America.*

WRITINGS: Bibliography on Bela Bartok, Ohio University Library, 1972; *Doctoral Dissertations Related to Hungary Accepted in the United States and Canada,* Ohio University Library, 1974; *The Hungarians in America, 1583-1974: A Chronology and Fact Book,* Oceana, 1975; *Louis Kossuth, "The Nation's Guest": A Bibliography on His Trip in the United States, December 4, 1851-July 14, 1852,* Bethlen Press, 1976; *Hungarians in the United States and Canada: Holdings of the Immigration History Research Center, a Bibliography,* Immigration History Research Center, University of Minnesota, 1977; *Bibliography on Cardinal Mindszenty,* Catholic Hungarians' Sunday, 1977; *Hungarian Newspapers in Microform Available in the United States and Canada,* Catholic Hungarians' Sunday, 1977; (editor) *"The Champion of Liberty": The Image of Louis Kossuth in American and English Poetry,* Bethlen Press, in press. Contributor of about a hundred sixty articles to English and Hungarian journals and newspapers, including *The Eighth Tribe: Hungarians in America.*

WORK IN PROGRESS: Abstracts of Doctoral Dissertations Related to Hungary Accepted in the United States and Canada.

SIDELIGHTS: Szeplaki writes: "Being of Hungarian origin, I am continuously involved in observing the many aspects of Hungarian-American life. This includes my constant research on specific topics related to Hungarian-Americanism. My basic efforts are directed toward bibliographical documentation, which has been greatly neglected in the immigration studies areas. Also, I am regularly contributing articles to the Hungarian-American press, which I intend to publish as a collection. However, in the near future, I plan to take up creative writing, my autobiography as the story of an immigrant being my first endeavor."

BIOGRAPHICAL/CRITICAL SOURCES: Boston Globe, October 23, 1966; *Messenger,* April 27, 1972, June 4, 1972.

*   *   *

TABER, Robert W(illiam) 1921-

PERSONAL: Born October 4, 1921, in Marietta, Ohio; son of Harold P. (an auditor) and Carol (Minch) Taber; married Martha Jayne, May 30, 1952; children: Anne Taber Nuhfer, Allen H. *Education:* Marietta College, B.S., 1948; University of Missouri, M.A., 1951. *Home:* 3613 Riviera St., Washington, D.C. 20031. *Office:* National Oceanographic Data Center, 2001 Wisconsin Ave., Washington, D.C. 26235.

CAREER: U.S. Navy Hydrographic Office, Washington, D.C., party chief in oceanography, 1951-56; U.S. Naval Oceanographic Office, Washington, D.C., head of underwater sound section, 1956-57, head of systems analysis group, 1957-61; National Oceanographic Data Center, Washington, D.C., head of geoscience branch, 1961-62, adviser to development programs, 1962-68, chief of production control branch, 1968—. *Military service:* U.S. Army Air Forces, 1944-47; became captain. *Member:* Marine Technology Society.

WRITINGS: (With Harold W. Dubach) *Questions About the Oceans,* U.S. Naval Oceanographic Office, 1968, expanded edition published as *One Thousand One Questions Answered About the Oceans and Oceanography,,* Dodd, 1972.

SIDELIGHTS: Taber writes: "In 1966 my co-author and I designed an educational exhibit at the International Science Fair in Dallas, Tex. Students at the Science Fair used a teletype to ask questions about the oceans to oceanographers in Washington, D.C. and Miami, Fla. As an outgrowth of this, we wrote the book. In 1977 the book was published in Russia, and, according to the Russian oceanographer who translated it, it is now in almost every library in the U.S.S.R."

*   *   *

TAI, Hung-chao 1929-

PERSONAL: Born November 18, 1929, in China; came to the United States in 1956, naturalized citizen, 1970; son of M. C. and T. C. (Chang) Tai; married Julia Chow (a professor), August 14, 1960; children: Eve, Helen, Michael. *Education:* National Taiwan University, B.A., 1954; University of Illinois, M.A., 1958, Ph.D., 1961. *Home:* 25355 Branchester Rd., Farmington Hills, Mich. 48018. *Office:* Department of Political Science, University of Detroit, Detroit, Mich. 48221.

CAREER: University of Montana, Missoula, instructor in political science, 1961-62; University of Detroit, Detroit,

Mich., assistant professor, 1962-66, 1967-68, associate professor, 1968-72, professor of political science, 1972—, chairman of department and director of Asian studies program, 1972—. Research associate at Harvard University, 1966-67, 1968-69, summer, 1973; visiting research associate at University of the Philippines, spring, 1969. Visiting associate professor at National Taiwan University, 1968-69. Founder of Chinese Cultural Center in Detroit, 1971, president, 1971-73, 1976; organizer of Detroit's Summer Far Eastern Ethnic Festivals, 1972—, and Chinese Cultural Festival, 1975. Organizer and project director, Symposium on Chinese and American Culture, Detroit, 1977.

MEMBER: International Studies Association, Association for Asian Studies, American Political Science Association, American Society of International Law, Michigan Association of Chinese Americans (founding member; vice-president, 1972-73). *Awards, honors:* Social Science Research Council grant, summer, 1968; Ford Foundation fellowship, 1968-69.

WRITINGS: (Contributor) Samuel P. Huntington and Clement H. Moore, editors, *Authoritarian Politics in Modern Society,* Basic Books, 1970; (contributor) Norman T. Uphoff and Warren F. Ilchman, editors, *The Political Economy of Development,* University of California Press, 1972; *Land Reform and Politics: A Comparative Analysis,* University of California Press, 1974. Contributor to *Yun-Wu Encyclopedia of Social Sciences.* Contributor to English- and Chinese-language journals and newspapers.

WORK IN PROGRESS: Editing a book on Chinese and American cultures, based on a symposium held in April, 1977.

SIDELIGHTS: Tai writes that he is presently conducting "a study of political systems that belong neither to the typical libertarian-democratic model nor the totalitarian model of the Nazi or Stalinist variety, but that combine in various ways the 'competitive' feature of the democratic model and the 'authoritarian' characteristic of the totalitarian one. The universe of this model may include Yugoslavia, the Republic of China (Taiwan), Zaire, Turkey, Mexico, India, Tanzania, and Tunisia. The study will attempt to identify the ways in which this combination is achieved, and the assess the performance of the political systems in terms of legitimacy, economic development, and stability."

He is also making "an inquiry into the political development of pre-Republican China in terms of political participation, political institutionalization, and growth and distribution of political authority, with other faculty members in Taiwan."

*   *   *

TAINES, Beatrice (Green) 1923-

PERSONAL: Born June 12, 1923, in New York, N.Y.; daughter of Joseph H. (a businessman) and Ruth (Cohen) Green; married Robert Taines (a physician), June 12, 1944; children: Carla, Peter, Andrew, Sarah. *Education:* Hunter College (now of the City University of New York), A.B., 1944; University of California, Berkeley, M.A., 1959, M.J., 1972. *Residence:* Walnut Creek, Calif. *Agent:* Barbara Rhodes Literary Agency, 140 West End Ave., New York, N.Y. 10023. *Office:* English/Journalism Division, Diablo Valley College, Pleasant Hill, Calif. 94523.

CAREER: U.S. Office of War Information, New York, N.Y., news editor, 1944-46; free-lance writer, 1946-48; Diablo Valley College, Pleasant Hill, Calif., instructor in journalism, 1961—. Member of California State School Library

Standards Committee. Past chairman of Concord Arts Festival; member of local cultural commission; member of Contra Costa Grand Jury. Public lecturer. *Member:* American Federation of Teachers, Faculty Association of California Community Colleges, Diablo Valley College Senate.

WRITINGS: (With William Sparke) *Doublespeak: Language for Sale,* Harper, 1975; *Woman of Valor, Man of Honor,* Harper, 1975; (contributor) Sparke, editor, *Prisms: A Self Reader,* Harper, 1975; *Help Help: A Brief Guide to College Reading and Writing,* Diablo Valley College, 1976. Contributor to professional journals and popular magazines, including *Liberty, Woman,* and *Mademoiselle.*

WORK IN PROGRESS: Revising *Help Help;* a textbook; a book about suburban women.

SIDELIGHTS: Beatrice Taines comments: "I teach public relations and magazine article writing; many of my students have published work written in the latter course. During the past academic year, I initiated a new course in doublespeak at my college. Students in the class analyze deceptive uses of language and visuals in public affairs, advertising, and literature, as communicated through all media."

AVOCATIONAL INTERESTS: Travel (England, Spain, Australia, Japan, New Guinea, Israel, Hong Kong, Romania).

*   *   *

TAISHOFF, Sol J(oseph) 1904-

PERSONAL: Born October 8, 1904, in Minsk, Russia; son of Joseph (a salesperson) and Rose (Order) Taishoff; married: Betty Tash (a secretary-treasurer), March 6, 1927 (died, 1977); children: Joanne Taishoff Cowan (died, 1977); Lawrence Bruce. *Education:* Educated in Washington, D.C. public schools. *Politics:* Independent. *Religion:* Jewish. *Home:* 4200 Massachusetts Ave., N.W., Washington, D.C. 20016. *Office:* 1735 DeSales St., N.W., Washington, D.C. 20036.

CAREER: Associated Press, New York City, copyperson at Washington bureau, 1920-21, telegraph operator and member of news staff, 1922-26; *U.S. Daily* (now *U.S. News and World Report*), Washington, D.C., reporter, 1926-31; *Broadcasting* magazine, Washington, D.C., co-founder, editor, 1931—, president and publisher, 1944-71; chairperson, 1971—. Writer of daily radio column, syndicated by Consolidated Press, and appearing in 250 newspapers, 1927-34. Notable assignments include interviews with pioneers in broadcasting Frank Conrad, David Sarnoff, and William S. Paley. Contributor of articles on radio and television to periodicals. Guest lecturer in radio-television at Syracuse University, American University, University of Maryland, and Arizona State University. Vice-president and director of Telecommunications Reports, Inc.; general partner in Jolar Associates; member of board of directors of Washington Journalism Center. *Member:* National Press Club, Broadcast Pioneers (past national president), Broadcasters Club, Institute of Electrical and Electronic Engineers, Sigma Delta Chi (journalism fellow; past national president), Woodmont Country Club.

WORK IN PROGRESS: A book on fifty years in broadcast journalism.

*   *   *

TALARICO, Ross 1945-

PERSONAL: Born March 17, 1945, in Rochester, N.Y.; son of Samuel (a shoemaker) and Regina (Chemuilevski)

Talarico; married June Bird (a public health nurse); children: Joseph. *Education:* Monroe Community College, A.A., 1966; Wisconsin State University—Superior (now University of Wisconsin—Superior), B.A., 1968; Syracuse University, M.A., 1970. *Home:* 6134 North Claremont Ave., Chicago, Ill. 60659. *Office:* Department of English, Loyola University, 6525 North Sheridan Rd., Chicago, Ill. 60626.

CAREER: Southern Connecticut State College, New Haven, writer-in-residence, 1972-73; Loyola University, Chicago, Ill., assistant professor of English, 1974—.

WRITINGS: Snowfires (poetry), Best Cellar Press, 1972; *Simple Truths* (poetry), North Carolina Review Press, 1976; *Trying to Leave* (poetry), Helix House, 1977.

WORK IN PROGRESS: A novel; poems.

SIDELIGHTS: Talarico comments: "As important as it is to become established in the literary community, it is important also, if one is truly a lyric poet, to escape or transcend the confines of its membership. It is my hope that my poetry will help to create new audiences for the lyric poem in America."

*   *   *

TALPALAR, Morris 1900-

PERSONAL: Born May 28, 1900, in Romania; came to the United States in 1909, naturalized citizen, 1925; son of Jacob and Yetta (Weinstein) Talpalar; married Lillian Greenberg, September 28, 1944. *Education:* National University, LL.B., 1929. *Politics:* Democrat. *Religion:* Jewish Orthodox. *Home:* 105-10 62nd Rd., Forest Hills, N.Y. 11375.

CAREER: Owner of a tobacco stand in Washington, D.C., 1925-28; teacher of English to speakers of other languages, 1929-32; U.S. Postal Service, Washington, D.C., postal clerk in New York City, 1943-51; writer. *Military service:* U.S. Army, 1922-25, 1942-43.

WRITINGS: The Sociology of Colonial Virginia, Philosophical Library, 1960, revised edition, 1968; *The Sociology of the Bay Colony* (to 1700), Philosophical Library, 1976.

WORK IN PROGRESS: The Sociology of the Bay Colony Circa 1700, completion expected in 1982.

SIDELIGHTS: Talpalar writes: "The American people today stand in awe of the genius of the past—the Grecian Hellenism, the Latin Renaissance, the classics of Tudor England. The humanities are man's noblest achievement—Aristotle describes the culturally creative person as 'a god amongst men.' We are at present engaged in a mass educational endeavor: we are financing the building and the expansion of institutions of learning—schools, libraries, art centers, museums; this zeal for learning as a normal part of American life may, over the next several generations, bring a Renaissance in America, a flowering of the classical cultural creativity, that will excel the best in man's past; it may possibly even supplant the basic seminal cultures of western civilization, Hebraism and Hellenism, with a universal culture—Anglo-Saxon Scientism."

BIOGRAPHICAL/CRITICAL SOURCES: Choice, October, 1976; *Manas,* November 24, 1976.

*   *   *

TAMPION, John 1937-

PERSONAL: Born July 14, 1937, in Southampton, England; son of William Alfred and Louise G. (Handford) Tampion; married Maureen D. Bailey, March 16, 1962; children: Alan J., Mark J. *Education:* University of Southampton, B.Sc.,

1959, Ph.D., 1964. *Residence:* Sussex, England. *Office:* Dept. of Life Sciences, Polytechnic of Central London, 115 New Cavendish St., London W1M 8JS, England.

CAREER: British Food Manufacturing Industries Research Association, Leatherhead, England, research biochemist, 1963-66; Polytechnic of Central London, London, England, lecturer, 1966-70, senior lecturer in life sciences, 1970—.

WRITINGS: (With Joan Reynolds) *Botany for Flower Arrangers,* Pelham Books, 1971; *The Gardener's Practical Botany,* David & Charles, 1972; *Dangerous Plants,* David & Charles, 1977. Contributor to scientific and popular journals.

WORK IN PROGRESS: Research on microbial enzymology and botany.

SIDELIGHTS: Tampion writes: "I am interested in promoting the study of plants and bringing the latest scientific results to the ordinary citizen.

"My interests in plants range from their submicroscopic biochemical reactions to their interactions in the ecosystem with all types of living organisms. It also ranges from bacteria and viruses to both wild and cultivated plants. Plants have helped to form the world in which man exists and their interaction and exploitation (as raw materials, foodstuffs, medicinally or aesthetically) must clearly be of paramount concern. I like to use every available technique, from the most sophisticated computers and biochemical equipment to the garden spade, in my studies of plants and Man."

*   *   *

TANKARD, James William, Jr. 1941-

PERSONAL: Born June 20, 1941, in Newport News, Va.; son of James William (a surgeon) and Eileen (Looney) Tankard; married Elaine Fuller (a production editor for a journal), July 21, 1973. *Education:* Virginia Polytechnic Institute, B.S., 1963; University of North Carolina, M.A., 1965; Stanford University, Ph.D., 1970. *Home:* 3003 Cherry Lane, Austin, Tex. 78703. *Office:* Department of Journalism, University of Texas, Austin, Tex. 78712.

CAREER: Associated Press, Charlotte, N.C., newsman and broadcast news writer, 1965; *Raleigh Times,* Raleigh, N.C., county government reporter, 1965-66; University of Wisconsin, Madison, assistant professor of journalism, 1970-71; Temple University, Philadelphia, Pa., assistant professor of journalism, 1971-72; University of Texas, Austin, assistant professor, 1972-76, associate professor of journalism, 1976—. Visiting assistant professor at University of Texas, 1970. *Member:* International Communication Association, International Society for General Semantics, Association for Education in Journalism, American Association of University Professors, Sigma Delta Chi.

WRITINGS: (Contributor) Maxwell McCombs, Donald Lewis Shaw, and David Grey, editors, *Handbook of Reporting Methods,* Houghton, 1976; (with Michael Ryan) *Basic News Reporting,* Mayfield, 1977; (contributor) Leonard Sellers and William L. Rivers, editors, *Mass Media Issues: Articles and Commentaries,* Prentice-Hall, 1977. Contributor of articles and reviews to professional journals.

WORK IN PROGRESS: With Werner Severin, *Communication Theory as Applied to the Mass Media.*

SIDELIGHTS: James William Tankard, Jr. told *CA* that his interests are primarily "science reporting, the history of science, the history of statistics and applications of statistics to reporting."

TANNER, Edward Everett III 1921-1976
(Patrick Dennis, Virginia Rowans)

PERSONAL: Born May 18, 1921, in Chicago, Ill.; married Louise Stickney (a writer), December 30, 1948; children: Michael, Elizabeth. Education: Attended private schools in Chicago and Evanston, Ill. Residence: New York City.

CAREER: Employed variously as an account executive for Franklin Spier, Inc. (an advertising agency), as advertising manager for Creative Age Press, and as promotion director for Foreign Affairs, all in New York City, 1945-56; New Republic, New York City, drama critic, 1957-71. Wartime service: American Field Service; served as an ambulance driver during World War II on the Arabian Peninsula and in North Africa, Italy, and France.

WRITINGS—Under pseudonym Patrick Dennis: Auntie Mame: An Irreverent Escapade in Biography, Vanguard, 1955; (with Barbara C. Hooton) Guestward Ho! By Barbara C. Hooton as Indiscreetly Confided to Patrick Dennis, Vanguard, 1956; (with Dorothy Erskine) The Pink Hotel, Putnam, 1957; Around the World with Auntie Mame, Harcourt, 1958; Little Me: The Intimate Memoirs of That Great Star of Stage, Screen, and Television, Belle Poitrine, as Told to Patrick Dennis (fiction), Dutton, 1961; Genius, Harcourt, 1962; First Lady: My Thirty Days Upstairs in the White House, by Martha Dinwiddie Butterfield as Told to Patrick Dennis, Morrow, 1964; The Joyous Season, Harcourt, 1965; Tony, Dutton, 1966; How Firm a Foundation, Morrow, 1968; Paradise, Harcourt, 1971; Three-D, Coward, 1972.

Under pseudonym Virginia Rowans: Oh, What a Wonderful Wedding, Crowell, 1953; House Party, Crowell, 1954; The Loving Couple, Crowell, 1956; Love and Mrs. Sargent, Farrar, Straus, 1961. Contributor of articles and short stories to national magazines.

SIDELIGHTS: "Writing isn't hard; no harder than ditch-digging," Tanner has said. He began his career as a reviser and ghost writer, and was able to preserve his anonymity by using pseudonyms until the immense popularity of his book, Auntie Mame: An Irreverent Escapade in Biography (which was a best-seller for over two years), caused his identity to become known. Auntie Mame was adapted for Broadway production and two movie versions of "Auntie Mame" have also been released, in 1958 and 1973. Another book, Little Me, was adapted for the stage by Neil Simon. Tanner's books have been translated into Spanish, Italian, and German.

AVOCATIONAL INTERESTS: Antique chime clocks, small parties, and listening to music.*

(Died November 6, 1976, in New York City)

* * *

TANNER, Henry 1918-

PERSONAL: Born July 7, 1918, in Bern, Switzerland; son of Victor (an industrialist) and Ann (Muhlemann) Tanner; married Mamoun Tommasi, July, 1944 (divorced); married Paggy Aarup, September 6, 1964; children: Victor. Education: Attended University of Paris, Sorbonne, 1939, and University of Zurich, 1940-44. Politics: "Professional observer." Religion: Protestant. Home: 1, aziz Osman St., Cairo, Egypt. Office: New York Times, 229 West 43rd St., New York, N.Y. 10036.

CAREER/WRITINGS: United Press, New York City, desk editor in Zurich, Switzerland, 1942-43, correspondent in Belgrade, Yugoslavia, 1945-46; Time and Life, New York

City, correspondent in Zurich and Paris, 1946-48; Houston Post, Houston, Tex., foreign affairs columnist, 1949-58; New York Times, New York City, correspondent in North and West Africa, 1958-63; bureau chief in Moscow, 1963-65, Paris, 1965-69, United Nations bureau chief, 1969-71, bureau chief in Cairo, Egypt, 1972—. Notable assignments include coverage of war in Algeria, the anti-Belgian uprising in the Congo, the fall of Khruschev, the student revolution in France, 1968, the war in the Middle East, including the exodus of the Soviets, the 1973 Arab-Israeli war, the Kissinger peace efforts, and the war in Lebanon. Member: Harvard Club. Awards, honors: Nieman fellowship, 1954; Deadline Club Award, 1972, for United Nations coverage.

SIDELIGHTS: Tanner's motivation, he told CA, is "intellectual curiosity, desire to report and if possible interpret contemporary history accurately, fairly, and with compassion."

* * *

TARDIFF, Olive 1916-

PERSONAL: Born January 2, 1916, in Exeter, N.H.; daughter of Edward H. (a salesman) and Maude (Button) Richards; married Joseph A. Tardiff, July 30, 1938; children: Robert J., Nancy E. Tardiff Tavernier, J. Herbert. Education: University of New Hampshire, B.A., 1937; Pratt Institute, M.L.S., 1965. Politics: Independent. Religion: Unitarian-Universalist. Home: 46 Hayes Trailer Park, Exeter, N.H. 03833.

CAREER: Forest Hills Public Library, Forest Hills, N.Y., part-time librarian, 1965-66; Andover Public Library, Andover, Mass., part-time librarian, 1969-70; Exeter Public Library, Exeter, N.H., part-time librarian, 1970-71; North Hampton Public Library, North Hampton, N.H., part-time librarian, 1971-74; writer, 1974—. Member: Sea Quills. Awards, honors: Prizes from State of Maine Writers Conference, 1972, for juvenile fiction, "Story of Molly Stark"; 1973, for humorous verse, "Botanical Dialogue"; 1974, for non-fiction, "Live Free or Die"; 1975, for humorous verse, "Where's the Paint"; 1976, for serious poetry; 1977 for non-fiction article.

WRITINGS: How to Live Happily with Your Retired Husband, Pilot Books, 1973; Molly Stark: Woman of the Revolution, Phoenix Publishing, 1976. Contributor of about a hundred articles to magazines.

WORK IN PROGRESS: A book about women living alone, publication by Pilot Books expected in 1978; research on General Israel Putnam, and Lewis Cass.

SIDELIGHTS: Olive Tardiff writes of her career: "I had lived for three years in Belgium and began to write travel articles, the first published by Boston Globe. On my husband's retirement, I became interested in New Hampshire history."

* * *

TARGAN, Barry 1932-

PERSONAL: Born November 30, 1932, in Atlantic City, N.J.; son of Albert and Blanche (Simmons) Targan; married Arleen Shanken (an artist), March 9, 1958; children: Anthony, Eric. Education: Rutgers University, B.A., 1954; University of Chicago, M.A., 1955; Brandeis University, Ph.D., 1962. Home: 46 Burgoyne St., Schuylerville, N.Y. 12871.

CAREER: Syracuse University, Syracuse, N.Y., assistant professor of English, 1962-67; State University of New

York, Cortland, assistant professor of English, 1967-69; Skidmore College, Saratoga Springs, N.Y., assistant professor, 1969-72, associate professor of English, 1972—, director of external degree program, 1975—. *Military service:* U.S. Army, 1956-58. *Awards, honors:* Short fiction award from University of Iowa, 1975, for *Harry Belten and the Mendelssohn Violin Concerto.*

WRITINGS: Let the Wild Rumpus Start (poetry), Best Cellar Brest, 1972; *Thoreau Stalks the Land Disguised as a Father* (poetry), Greenfield Review Press, 1975; *Harry Belten and the Mendelssohn Violin Concerto* (short stories), University of Iowa Press, 1975.

* * *

TARNAWSKY, Ostap 1917-

PERSONAL: Born May 3, 1917, in Lviv, Ukraine; came to the United States in 1949, naturalized citizen, 1956; son of David and Zenia (Dobrey) Tarnawsky; married Marta Senkowsky (a librarian), March 5, 1949; children: Mark Myron, Maxim David. *Education:* Attended Lviv University, 1935-39, and Lviv Polytechnicum, 1939-41; Technical University, Graz, Austria, diploma, 1947; Drexel University, M.S., 1962; Ukrainian Free University, Munich, Germany, Ph.M., 1975, Ph.D., 1976. *Home:* 6509 Lawnton Ave., Philadelphia, Pa. 19126. *Office:* Community College of Philadelphia, 34 S. 11th St., Philadelphia, Pa. 19107.

CAREER: United Ukrainian American Relief Committee, emigration officer in Salzburg, Austria, 1948-49, and Philadelphia, Pa., 1951-61; Newark Public Library, Newark, N.J., librarian, 1962-63; Temple University, Philadelphia, Pa., librarian, 1964-65; Community College of Philadelphia, Philadelphia, Pa., head cataloger at the library, 1966—, associate professor of library science, 1971—. Member of executive board and teacher at Ridna Shkola (language school), 1961—; executive director of United Ukrainian American Relief Committee, 1964—; founding member and executive officer of Ukrainian Book Center, 1974—.

MEMBER: International P.E.N. (American branch of Writers in Exile Group), Ukrainian Writers Association in Exile (president, 1975—), Ukrainian Library Association of America. *Awards, honors:* Short story awards from *Dilo,* 1938, for "Khlonia", and *Svoboda,* 1958, for "Zrada."

WRITINGS: Slova i mrii (poems; title means "Words and Dreams"), Novi dni, 1948; *Zhyttia* (poems; title means "Live"), Kiev, 1952; *Mosty* (poems; title means "The Bridges"), Slovo, 1956; *Samotnie derevo* (poems; title means "The Solitary Tree"), Slovo, 1960; *Podorozh poza vidome: Shliakhamy modernoi poezii* (title means "Voyage Behind Awareness: On the Trail of Modern Poetry"), Sucasnist, 1965; *Tuha za miton* (essays; title means "The Longing for Myth"), Kluchi, 1966; *Brat-bratovi* (title means "Brother's Helping Hand"), United Ukrainian American Relief Committee, 1971; *Kaminni stupeni* (short stories; title means "Stone Steps"), Sucasnist, 1978.

Contributor: Igor Kostetskii, editor, *Vybranyi Eliot* (title means "Selected Works of T. S. Eliot"), On the Mountain, 1958; Kostetskii, editor, *Vybranyi Ezra Pound* (title means "Selected Works of Ezra Pound"), On the Mountain, 1960; Vasa D. Mihailovich, editor, *Modern Slavic Literature,* F. Ungar, 1972; O. Prokopiv, editor, *The Ukrainian Translations of Shakespeare's Sonnets,* University of Ottawa Press, 1976.

Contributor of articles and reviews to scholarly journals and to newspapers. Co-editor of *Lysty do pryiateliv* (title means "Letters to Friends"), 1953—, *Svoboda,* and *Slovo* (yearbook), 1962—.

WORK IN PROGRESS: A book of sonnets.

AVOCATIONAL INTERESTS: Travel.

* * *

TARRY, Ellen 1906-

PERSONAL: Born, 1906, in Birmingham, Ala.; children: Elizabeth. *Education:* Attended Writers' Laboratory, New York, N.Y. *Residence:* New York, N.Y.

CAREER: Worked as a newspaperwoman, teacher, and social worker; served as deputy assistant to the Regional Administrator for Equal Opportunity, Department of Housing and Urban Development; author of books for children.

WRITINGS: Janie Belle (illustrated by Myrtle Sheldon), Garden City Publishing, 1940; *Hezekiah Horton* (illustrated by Oliver Harrington), Viking, 1942; (with Marie Hall Ets) *My Dog Rinty* (illustrated by Alexander and Alexandra Alland), Viking, 1946, new edition, 1964; *The Runaway Elephant* (illustrated by Harrington), Viking, 1950; *The Third Door: The Autobiography of an American Negro Woman,* McKay, 1955, reprinted, Negro Universities Press, 1971; *Katharine Drexel: Friend of the Neglected* (illustrated by Donald Bolognese), Farrar, Straus, 1958; *Martin de Porres: Saint of the New World* (illustrated by James Fox), Vision Books, 1963; *Young Jim: The Early Years of James Weldon Johnson,* Dodd, 1967.

SIDELIGHTS: Tarry's writings were heavily influenced by her involvement in the civil rights movement. As a result, she became one of the first authors to use blacks as main characters in books for children. One of Tarry's earlier books, *Hezekiah Horton,* told the adventures of a small black child growing up in New York. The book was enthusiastically received by many book critics. "At last we have a realistic, honest book about a negro boy in Harlem," noted a critic for *Saturday Review.*

Tarry's *Runaway Elephant* was based on an actual news story. "We say that fact is stranger than fiction; nevertheless, it takes genius to find such a fact in the news as the escape of a bull elephant from the circus and turn it into a good story. That genius Ellen Tarry has," observed a reviewer for the *New York Herald Tribune.*

In *The Third Door: The Autobiography of an American Negro Woman,* the author describes her experiences in New York and Alabama. Her book, *Young Jim: The Early Years of James Weldon Johnson,* is a biography of a major black poet. A *New York Times* book reviewer noted that "besides offering an inspiring life story, the book gives some penetrating insights into Negro life and problems at the turn of the century."

BIOGRAPHICAL/CRITICAL SOURCES: Saturday Review of Literature, November 14, 1942; *New York Herald Tribune,* October 8, 1950; Ellen Tarry, *The Third Door: The Autobiography of an American Negro Woman,* McKay, 1955, reprinted, Negro Universities Press, 1971; *New York Times,* January 21, 1968.*

* * *

TASCH, Peter A(nthony) 1933-

PERSONAL: Born November 28, 1933, in Brooklyn, N.Y.; son of George Edward and Belle (Crook) Tasch; married Alison Drever (a lecturer in English), June 30, 1961; children: Jeremy, Katharine, Alexandra. *Education:* Bucknell

University, A.B., 1954; Columbia University, M.A., 1959; University of Edinburgh, diploma, 1960; Harvard University, further graduate study, 1961-64. *Home:* 225 Winona St., Philadelphia, Pa. 19144. *Office:* Department of English, Temple University, Philadelphia, Pa. 19122.

CAREER: Temple University, Philadelphia, Pa., instructor, 1964-71, assistant professor, 1971-73, associate professor of English, 1973—. *Military service:* U.S. Army, 1954-57. *Member:* Modern Language Association of America, American Society for Eighteenth Century Studies, American Association of University Professors, Phi Beta Kappa.

WRITINGS: (Editor) *Fables of John Gay,* Imprint Press, 1970; *The Dramatic Cobbler,* Bucknell University Press, 1971. Co-editor, *Scriblerian.*

WORK IN PROGRESS: Research in restoration and eighteenth century drama.

SIDELIGHTS: Tasch told *CA:* "Curiosity and enjoyment motivate me; academic career ambition forces me. Essentially, however, I am a private person." *Avocational interests:* "I enjoy growing trees and shrubs although I am not particularly patient. Puttering cheers me whether it is in eighteenth-century research or in a field."

*   *   *

TASCHDJIAN, Claire L(ouise)   1914-

PERSONAL: Born January 7, 1914, in Berlin, Germany; came to the United States in 1948, naturalized citizen, 1954; daughter of M. (a physician) and Freda (Jaffrey) Martin; married Edgar Taschdjian (a college professor), June 6, 1944; children: Martin Gregory, John Eugene, Sonja Taschdjian Donahue. *Education:* Attended University of Berlin, 1932-33; Catholic University of Peking, B.Sc., 1945; Wagner College, M.Sc., 1960; also attended University of Chicago and University of Illinois. *Politics:* "Demublican." *Religion:* Roman Catholic. *Residence:* Wolcott, Vt. *Office:* Department of Biology, St. Francis College, 180 Remsen St., Brooklyn, N.Y. 11201.

CAREER: Peking Union Medical College, Peking, China, assistant in Cenozoic Research Laboratory, 1940-41; teacher at American high school in Peking, China, 1945-48; University of Chicago, Chicago, Ill., mycologist, 1949-52; New York University, New York, N.Y., clinical assistant in dermatology and syphilology, 1952-56; Maimonides Medical Center, Brooklyn, N.Y., research associate in pediatrics, 1956—. Assistant professor at St. Francis College, 1964-69, associate professor, 1969—; lecturer at State University of New York Downstate Medical Center, 1964-76; visiting professor at University of Ulm, 1970-71.

MEMBER: International Society for Human and Animal Mycology, American Society for Microbiology, Medical Mycology Society of the Americas, American Teilhard Association (charter member), New York Academy of Sciences, New York Medical Mycology Society. *Awards, honors:* Prizes from Maimonides Medical Center, 1961, 1972, and American Society for Obstetrics and Gynecology, 1968, all for research papers in microbiology.

WRITINGS: Biology: Inquiry into Life (high school textbook), Holt, 1960, teacher's manual, 1961; (contributor) *Dermatology,* Harper, 1971; *The Peking Man Is Missing* (suspense novel), Harper, 1977. Contributor of about seventy-five articles to medical and biomedical journals.

WORK IN PROGRESS: Another mystery novel, set in Vermont; research on serology and serodiagnosis of systemic candidiasis.

SIDELIGHTS: Claire Taschdjian writes that her work at Peking Union Medical College involved study of Peking Man. It was she who packed the fossils in 1941, becoming "the last person (presumably) to see them. I was inspired to write a thriller about their loss by the three-ring circus which developed from recent searches for the fossils.

"I am currently trying to write fiction for the fun of it, without sex, violence, and social or psychological problems and messages."

*   *   *

TATE, Robin
    See FANTHORPE, R(obert) Lionel

*   *   *

TAYLOR, Demetria   1903-1977
    (Beth Merriman)

1903—November 18, 1977; American educator, editor, home economics consultant, and author. Taylor was best known as the author of cookbooks, including *The Cook's Blessing* and *The Nutrition Handbook.* She died in New York, N.Y. Obituaries: *New York Times,* November 21, 1977; *AB Bookman's Weekly,* February 6, 1978.

*   *   *

TAYLOR, H. Kerr   1891(?)-1977

1891(?)—December 4, 1977; American missionary, clergyman, and author. Taylor worked as a missionary in China from 1917 to 1931. He died in Charlotte, N.C. Obituaries: *New York Times,* December 5, 1977.

*   *   *

TAYLOR, Samuel (Wooley)   1907-

PERSONAL: Born February 5, 1907, in Provo, Utah; son of John Whitaker and Janet Maria (Woolley) Taylor; married Elizabeth Gay Dimick; children: Sara Taylor Weston. *Education:* Attended Brigham Young University. *Religion:* Church of Jesus Christ of Latter-day Saints (Mormons). *Home:* 1954 Stockbridge Ave., Redwood City, Calif. 94061. *Agent:* Paul R. Reynolds, Inc., 12 East 41st St., New York, N.Y. 10017.

CAREER: Writer, 1932—. Has also worked in carding, spinning, and weaving departments of woolen mills. *Military service:* U.S. Army Air Forces, chief of public relations magazine section, 1943-45; served in European theater; became second lieutenant; received Legion of Merit, Bronze Star, and three battle stars. *Member:* Authors League of America (San Francisco chairman, 1948), Writers Guild of America, California Writers Club.

WRITINGS: (With Eric Friedheim) *Fighters Up* (on U.S. Army Air Forces fighter-plane pilots in Europe), McRae, 1945; *The Man with My Face* (novel), A. A. Wyn, 1948; *Heaven Knows Why* (novel; originally published in *Collier's* as "The Mysterious Way"), A. A. Wyn, 1948; *Family Kingdom* (biography), McGraw, 1951; *The Grinning Gismo* (novel), A. A. Wyn, 1951; *I Have Six Wives* (novel), Greenberg, 1956; *Line Haul* (history), Filmer Publishing, 1959; *Uranium Fever* (biography), Macmillan, 1970; *Nightfall at Nauvoo* (history), Macmillan, 1971; *The Kingdom or Nothing: The Life of John Taylor, Militant Mormon,* Macmillan, 1976.

Screenplays: "The Man With My Face," 1951; "Bait," 1954; "Son of Flubber," released by Walt Disney, 1963; "The Absent Minded Professor," Walt Disney, 1964.

Contributor of hundreds of stories to popular magazines, including *Saturday Evening Post, American, Esquire, Reader's Digest,* and *Family Circle.*

WORK IN PROGRESS: The John Taylor Papers, Volumes I and II, for Peregrine Smith; *The Wasatch Front* (tentative title), on Mormon culture, for Macmillan.

SIDELIGHTS: Taylor writes: "I have been a professional writer since college days, which is longer than I like to remember. My only non-writing work since then was a period of two weeks during the early days of World War II, when I directed the building of a submarine net to save San Francisco from enemy attack.

"I have published an uncounted number of articles and fiction stories in national magazines. My work ranged from short-shorts to serials and one-shot book-lengths. During my misspent youth I ground out pulp-paper stories—detectives, westerns, sports, adventure (even a confession).

"One day I knocked out a routine pulp yarn and on impulse sent it to *Collier's.* When that magazine accepted it—at ten times the pulp rate—I learned a basic fact about the writing business: the only real difference between a high-paying and a penny-ante market is the amount of money involved. Every market requires the best you can do. I also discovered that the better the market, the easier it was to get along with the editor.

"Having learned the great secret, I concentrated on markets that paid top money and were easiest to satisfy.

"My book, *Family Kingdom,* was the story of my father's family of six wives and three dozen kids. It was published in part by *Holiday* and the U.S. State Department distributed this magazine excerpt throughout the world. A considerable amount of my work has been based on the Mormon culture. Six of my published books mined this lode, as well as the two-volume *The John Taylor Papers* and the current project *The Wasatch Front.* A number of my stories have been made into motion pictures. Possibly the most attention came from Walt Disney's 'Absent-Minded Professor,' based on my original story.

"An author doesn't write for his soul; he writes for his public. For many years my public consisted of a midwest chicken farmer. Then the chicken farmer died. This leaves me an author without a public."

*   *   *

TEETER, Don E(l)   1934-

PERSONAL: Born January 7, 1934, in Oklahoma City, Okla.; son of George Earnest (a steelworker) and Dola (Gasseur) Teeter. *Education:* Educated in Moore, Okla. *Politics:* "Registered Democrat but I vote my mind." *Religion:* Christian. *Home and office:* Don's Guitar Shop, 2319 South Stiles, Oklahoma City, Okla. 73129. *Agent:* Sandra Hintz Literary Agency, 2879 N. Grant Blvd., Milwaukee, Wis. 53210.

CAREER: Capitol Steel & Iron Co., Oklahoma City, Okla., warehouseman, 1952-55; Silver Streak Manufacturing Co., Oklahoma City, automotive machinist, 1955, 1957-59; Sharp Auto Supply, Oklahoma City, parts salesman, 1959-61; L & S Bearing Co., Oklahoma City, screw machine operator, 1961-66; Don's Guitar Shop, Oklahoma City, owner, 1966—. *Military service:* U.S. Navy, air force radioman, 1955-57. *Member:* Oklahoma Bluegrass Society.

WRITINGS: The Acoustic Guitar: Adjustments, Care, Maintenance, and Repair, University of Oklahoma Press, 1975. Contributor to *Pickin'.*

WORK IN PROGRESS: A series of outdoor-oriented mysteries.

SIDELIGHTS: Teeter comments: "As a former country boy, writing about the outdoors is a release, a way to get me out of the shop. I am an amateur photographer and, at times, get out in the woods for some nature photography. I have been on trail rides for the past couple of years into primitive areas to quench my thirst for the outdoors and for material for writing, and plan to continue as time and funds permit.

"The guitar repair book was my first venture in writing, and was written out of self-protection. I believe my knowledge was meant to be shared and I was losing many hours of time explaining my techniques to aspiring repairmen, so I decided to write it all down.

"I have put together several manuscripts, all outdoor mysteries, taking place in Arizona and Colorado—the deserts, badlands, mountains, and small towns, etc. Two are aimed at the early teen to young adult market, the other five all center around a nature photographer who seems to keep getting into trouble."

BIOGRAPHICAL/CRITICAL SOURCES: Daily Oklahoman, December 12, 1965.

*   *   *

TEGENFELDT, Herman G(ustaf)   1913-

PERSONAL: Born November 18, 1913, in Bellingham, Wash.; son of Claus G. (a plumber) and Anna E. (a teacher; maiden name, Wahlstrand) Tegenfeldt; married Ruth A. Pearson (a teacher), June 27, 1937; children: Edwin, Judith Tegenfeldt Fenlason, Alice Tegenfeldt Mundhenk, John, Paul, David. *Education:* Western Washington College of Education, B.A., 1934; Bethel Theological Seminary, St. Paul, Minn., B.D., 1940; Northern Baptist Theological Seminary, Th.M., 1947; Fuller Theological Seminary, D.Missiology, 1973. *Politics:* Independent. *Home:* 692 West Eldridge Ave., St. Paul, Minn. 55113. *Office:* Department of Missions, Bethel Theological Seminary, 3949 Bethel Dr., St. Paul, Minn. 55112.

CAREER: Ordained Baptist minister, 1940; teacher in public schools in Seattle, Wash., 1934-37; American Baptist Foreign Mission Society, missionary in Burma and India, 1941-43, and Burma, 1943-66, field secretary, 1961-66; Bethel Theological Seminary, St. Paul, Minn., assistant professor, 1967-70, associate professor, 1970-72, professor of missions, 1973—. Member of Committee to Aid Missionary Education Overseas, 1971—. *Wartime service:* U.S. Army, civilian engaged in refugee work in Burma, 1943-44, honorary chaplain of Burma Rifles and Kachin Rifles, 1944-45. *Member:* Association of Evangelical Professors of Missions, American Society of Missiology, Association of Professors of Missions, Midwest Fellowship of Professors of Missions.

WRITINGS: Hkristan Hpung A Ahtik Labay Laika (title means "A History of the Christian Church"), Burma Baptist Convention, 1962; *Through Deep Waters,* American Baptist Foreign Mission Society, 1968; *A Century of Growth: The Kachin Baptist Church of Burma,* William Carey Library, 1974. Contributor to *Evangelical Missions Quarterly* and *Standard.*

WORK IN PROGRESS: A biographical study of Karl Gutzlaff, missionary and traveler in Thailand, China, and Korea in the early 1800's; research on missionary efforts by the Karens of Burma among other ethnic groups in Burma and Thailand during the nineteenth century.

SIDELIGHTS: Herman G. Tegenfeldt writes: "My service in Burma (and India) provides me with special backgrounds and interests, as well as personal contacts, which enrich the contributions I can make to an understanding of those parts of the world. I enjoy contacts with international students from the Orient, studying in America. Cultural anthropology has a special appeal, as well as questions of cross-cultural communication. I am competent in the Kachin language of Burma, and have some conversational ability in Burmese."

AVOCATIONAL INTERESTS: Photography.

* * *

TENENBAUM, Frances 1919-

PERSONAL: Born September 16, 1919, in New York, N.Y.; daughter of Emanuel (a businessman) and Regina (Musken) Mendelson; married Frank Tenenbaum, May 22, 1943 (deceased); children: Jane, David. *Education:* Skidmore College, student, 1936-38; University of Michigan, B.A., 1941; Columbia University, M.S., 1942. *Residence:* Cambridge, Mass. *Office:* Houghton Mifflin Co., 2 Park St., Boston, Mass. 02107.

CAREER: New York Herald Tribune, New York, N.Y., reporter, 1942-45; free-lance magazine writer, 1945-54; reporter and columnist for *Great Neck Reporter,* 1954-62; worked in editorial and publicity departments at Channel Press, 1962-64; educational columnist for *Great Neck News,* 1964-67; assistant editor for Better Homes and Gardens Book Clubs, 1971-72; Houghton Mifflin Co., Boston, Mass., editor, 1973—.

WRITINGS: Gardening with Wild Flowers, Scribner, 1973; *Nothing Grows for You?,* Scribner, 1975; *Plants from Nine to Five,* Scribner, 1977.

* * *

TENNYSON, Charles Bruce Locker 1879-1977

November 8, 1879—June 22, 1977; British author. Tennyson was best known for his biography of his grandfather, *Alfred Tennyson.* He also wrote his autobiography, *Stars and Markets.* He died in England. Obituaries: *AB Bookman's Weekly,* September 12, 1977.

* * *

TEPPER, Michael 1941-

PERSONAL: Born September 4, 1941, in Baltimore, Md.; son of Jack and Betty (Chodak) Tepper; married Veronica Schofield, November 15, 1972; children: Alexander, Megan. *Education:* University of Maryland, B.A. (special honors), 1963; New York University, M.A., 1965, Ph.D., 1970. *Office:* Genealogical Publishing Co., 521-523 St. Paul Pl., Baltimore, Md. 21202.

CAREER: Mills College of Education, New York, N.Y., instructor in English, 1967-68; Genealogical Publishing Co., Baltimore, Md., managing editor, 1970—. *Member:* Baltimore Bibliophiles.

WRITINGS: (Editor) *Emigrants to Pennsylvania, 1641-1819,* Genealogical Publishing, 1975; (editor) *Passengers to America,* Genealogical Publishing, 1977; *Immigrants to the Middle Colonies,* Genealogical Publishing, in press. Contributor to journals.

WORK IN PROGRESS: A bibliography of American literary annuals and gift books.

TERDIMAN, Richard 1941-

PERSONAL: Born October 18, 1941, in New Rochelle, N.Y.; son of Stanley S. and Selma (Sugerman) Terdiman; married Susan Louise Smith (an art historian), February 26, 1977; children: Daniel William. *Education:* Amherst College, B.A., 1963; Yale University, Ph.D., 1968. *Politics:* "None of the Above Party." *Office:* Department of Literature, University of California—San Diego, La Jolla, Calif. 92093.

CAREER: Swarthmore College, Swarthmore, Pa., instructor, 1967-68, assistant professor of French, 1968-72; University of California, Berkeley, visiting assistant professor of French and comparative literature, 1972-74; Mills College, Oakland, Calif., associate professor of French literature, 1974-76; University of California—San Diego, La Jolla, associate professor of French literature, 1976—. Instructor at Haverford College, summer, 1968; visiting lecturer at San Francisco State University, 1971. *Member:* Modern Language Association of America, Marxist Literary Group, Proust Research Association, Philological Association of the Pacific Coast. *Awards, honors:* Woodrow Wilson fellowship, 1966-67.

WRITINGS: The Dialectics of Isolation, Yale University Press, 1976. Contributor to literary journals.

WORK IN PROGRESS: Literary Theory: Mimesis, Realism, Dialectics; Nineteenth-Century French Fiction.

SIDELIGHTS: Terdiman told *CA:* "My book represented an attempt to provide a materialist and dialectical account of the tradition of French fiction since the Revolution. Since writing it I have worked toward a better understanding of the modalities of relationship between literary production and literature's social and cultural context: both as influencing and as influenced."

* * *

TERR, Leonard B(rian) 1946-

PERSONAL: Born April 26, 1946, in Atlantic City, N.J.; son of H. N. (an executive) and T. B. (a writer) Terr; married Lyndia B. Deckelbaum (an artist), September 1, 1968; children: Jessica Britomart, Jeremy Brendan. *Education:* LaSalle College, A.B., 1967; Brown University, A.M., 1968, Ph.D., 1971; Cornell University, J.D., 1975, Certificate, International Legal Affairs, 1975. *Home:* 1014 Croton Dr., Alexandria, Va. 22308. *Office:* Sutherland, Asbill & Brennan, 1666 K St. N.W., Washington, D.C. 20006.

CAREER: Brown University, Providence, R.I., instructor in English, 1968-71; Wayne State University, Detroit, Mich., assistant professor of English, 1971-72; Elmira College, Elmira, N.Y., assistant professor of English, 1972-73; U.S. Court of Claims, Washington, D.C., law clerk to the chief judge, 1975-76; Sutherland, Asbill & Brennan, Washington, D.C., attorney, 1976—. Visiting writer for Rhode Island Council on the Arts, 1970-71.

MEMBER: American Bar Association, Federal Bar Association, American Civil Liberties Union, American Judicature Society, American Society of International Law, Modern Language Association of America, Pennsylvania Bar Association, District of Columbia Bar Association, Phi Beta Kappa. *Awards, honors:* Prizes from Academy of American Poets, 1970, for *Sitting in Our Treehouse Waiting for the Apocalypse,* and 1971, for "Photographs of a Man in a Burning House"; Deak Prize from American Society of International Law, 1974, for "The Continental Shelf Oil Controversy."

WRITINGS: Sitting in Our Treehouse Waiting for the Apocalypse (poems), Ithaca House, 1975; (with Gordon O. Pehrson, Jr.) *Foreign Corporations: Reorganizations, Liquidations, and Similar Transactions,* Bureau of National Affairs, 1977. Contributor of articles, poems, translations, and reviews to law journals and literary magazines, including *New England Review, Forum,* and *Lace Review.* Managing editor, *Journal of the Associated Writing Programs,* 1969-71; editor of *Criticism,* 1971-72; article and book review editor of *Cornell International Law Journal,* 1974-75.

WORK IN PROGRESS: Another book of poems; a novel; research on freedom of information and the law of privacy, and on literature, law, and the art of language.

SIDELIGHTS: Terr comments that one of the major influences on his development was "my father's death in 1955 at the age of thirty-six when I was nine. I read and reread James Tate's *The Lost Pilot,* about Tate's bomber pilot father who died when Tate was months old and now circles the skies unaged like the rest of his crew but always just out of reach. My mother, a pure Emersonian Transcendentalist, led me to literature and ideas and my wife, a Canadian artist from Montreal, has shown me how these can be understood without words.

"I left teaching partly out of impatience but remain impatient, looking now to Wallace Stevens, Louis Auchincloss, and others for ways of translating the choate precision of law into the inchoate precision of poetry. Sometimes the two languages coalesce, as in a brief in a case involving constitutional liberties. But most often they do not, and I must translate not the language but myself."

AVOCATIONAL INTERESTS: Playing guitar and recorder, singing and composing, sailing, "trying to stay as close as possible to the ocean where I was raised and where I still find the purest peace."

*   *   *

THAMES, Jack
    See RYAN, John Fergus

*   *   *

THANET, Neil
    See FANTHORPE, R(obert) Lionel

*   *   *

THAYER, Frederick C(lifton), Jr.   1924-
    (Jack Walker)

PERSONAL: Born September 6, 1924, in Baltimore, Md.; son of Frederick Clifton (a photographer) and Marian (Walter) Thayer; married Phyllis Dirksen, May 14, 1949 (divorced, 1950); married Carolyn Easley, October 31, 1952; children: Jeffrey, Sarah. *Education:* U.S. Military Academy, B.S., 1945; Ohio State University, M.A., 1954; University of Denver, Ph.D., 1963. *Residence:* Pittsburgh, Pa. *Office:* Graduate School of Public and International Affairs, University of Pittsburgh, Pittsburgh, Pa. 15260.

CAREER: U.S. Air Force, career officer, 1945-69, worked in Aerospace Policies Division, 1963-66, visiting military fellow at Council on Foreign Relations, 1966-67, assistant deputy chief of staff in operations at Military Airlift Command, 1968-69, retiring as colonel; currently associate professor of public and international affairs, at University of Pittsburgh, Pittsburgh, Pa. Visiting lecturer at American University, 1971, George Washington University, 1975, University of North Carolina and York University, 1976, and Pennsyl-

vania State University and California State College, Stanislaus, 1977; visiting associate professor at Syracuse University, spring, 1973, University of Southern California, 1973, 1975, 1976, 1977, and West Virginia University, 1976. Consultant to MITRE Corp. *Member:* American Political Science Association, American Society of Public Administration, Academy of Management.

WRITINGS: Air Transport Policy and National Security, University of North Carolina Press, 1965; *Citizen Participation and Liberal Democratic Government,* Queen's Printer (Canada), 1971; *An End to Hierarchy! An End to Competition!: Organizing the Politics and Economics of Survival,* F. Watts, 1973; (contributor) Frank Trager and Philip Kronenberg, editors, *National Security and American Society,* University Press of Kansas, 1973; (contributor) Bach and Sulzner, editors, *Perspectives on the Presidency,* Heath, 1974; (contributor) Carl Bellone and Lloyd Nigro, editors, *Theoretical Perspectives in Public Administration: A Normative Focus,* Dekker, in press. Contributor of about thirty articles to professional journals, including *Worldview* (sometimes under pseudonym Jack Walker). Member of board of editors of *Public Administration Review,* 1971-76, and *Journal of Comparative Administration,* 1974—.

WORK IN PROGRESS: Research on contradictions in political, economics, and organization theories.

SIDELIGHTS: Thayer writes: "Assuming natural resources to be finite, the world can survive only if a profound social transformation occurs, the first such change since the shift from hunting to agricultural societies some four to five thousand years ago.

"Through an accident of history (the manner in which I had to pursue graduate studies), I was compelled to become interdisciplinary, beginning with studies of air transport policy. I concluded then that competition among airlines was essentially unworkable and inherently wasteful. I now conclude that if resources are finite, and that if we must recognize and act soon on that assumption, we must search for an alternative to the only organized systems with which we are familiar. Neither centralized planning systems (monopoly capitalism, state socialism) nor competitive market systems (capitalist, socialist, or mixed) can possibly work; the former because nobody can possibly command the knowledge required, the latter because it relies upon the absence of planning (except by the individual organization or nation-state). We must search for a global system which combines the total absence of authority and comprehensive planning. Resources simply must be shared, and the agreement on sharing must be arrived at without coercion. Among other things, this must lead to the end of private property as we know it, the end of all superior-subordinate relationships, and the separation of work from income. If we do not do this, the world inevitably faces nuclear holocaust, as we enter the global struggle for possession of the resources that are left. The time is short, perhaps less than a decade."

*   *   *

THAYER, James Stewart   1949-

PERSONAL: Born May 28, 1949, in Eugene, Ore.; son of J. Lewis and Buryl (Stewart) Thayer. *Education:* Washington State University, B.A., 1971; University of Chicago, J.D., 1974. *Home and office:* 417 Harvard Ave. E., Seattle, Wash. 98102. *Agent:* David Hull, James Brown Associates, Inc., 22 East 60th St., New York, N.Y. 10022.

CAREER: Lawyer in private practice, 1974—. *Member:* Phi Beta Kappa.

WRITINGS: The Hess Cross (novel), Putnam, 1977.

WORK IN PROGRESS: The Stettin Secret, a novel.

* * *

THELEN, Gil 1938-

PERSONAL: Born June 24, 1938, in Chicago, Ill.; son of Gilbert Carl (a businessman) and Violet (a businesswoman; maiden name, Okonn) Thelen; married Carol Abernathy, August 23, 1966 (divorced); children: Deborah, Todd. *Education:* Duke University, B.A., 1960; graduate study at Cornell University, 1961-64. *Home:* 11667 Charter Oak Ct., Reston, Va. 22090. *Office: Chicago Daily News,* Suite 300, 1901 Pennsylvania Ave. N.W., Washington, D.C. 20006.

CAREER/WRITINGS: Milwaukee Journal, Milwaukee, Wis., reporter, 1960-61; Associated Press, New York City, newsman, 1965-72; *Consumers Union,* Mt. Vernon, N.Y., Washington editor, 1972-77; *Chicago Daily News,* Chicago, Ill., Washington bureau correspondent, 1977—. Contributor of articles to *Changing Times, New Republic,* and *Nation.* Adjunct lecturer in journalism, George Washington University, 1976—. *Member:* Washington Press Club, Montgomery County Big Brothers (president, 1968). *Awards, honors:* Associated Press Managing Editors Association award, 1972.

SIDELIGHTS: Recent improvements in journalism, Thelen told *CA,* include "opening up of style and topic, increasing commitment to expertise, and welcome focus on issues and developments that really affect people." Investigative journalism, he continued, is "necessary, fraught with land mines, and often frustrating."

* * *

THOMAS, George Finger 1899-1977

1899—September 25, 1977; American educator, theologian, editor, and author. Thomas was past president of the American Theological Society. He taught in India, Japan, and the United States. He died in Princeton, N.J. Obituaries: *New York Times,* September 27, 1977.

* * *

THOMAS, Lewis H(erbert) 1917-

PERSONAL: Born April 13, 1917, in Saskatoon, Saskatchewan, Canada; son of Robert Brenner (a United Church clergyman) and Margaret Mae (Ross) Thomas; married Margaret Eleanor; children: Jean Alice, Robert Telford. *Education:* University of Saskatchewan, B.A. (honors), 1940, M.A., 1941; University of Minnesota, Ph.D., 1953. *Religion:* United Church of Canada. *Home:* 9123 118th St., Edmonton, Alberta, Canada T6G 1T6. *Office:* Department of History, University of Alberta, Edmonton, Alberta, Canada T6G 2H4.

CAREER: Province of Saskatchewan, Regina, archivist, 1948-57; University of Saskatchewan (now University of Regina), Regina, associate professor of history, 1957-64; University of Alberta, Edmonton, associate professor, 1964-65, professor of history, 1965—, chairman of department, 1965-68. Alberta representative on Historic Sites and Monuments Board of Canada, 1968-76. *Member:* Canadian Historical Association. *Awards, honors:* LL.D. from University of Regina, 1972; award from Historical Society of Alberta, 1974; award of merit from American Association for State and Local History, 1976; annual recognition award from Edmonton Historical Board, 1976.

WRITINGS: The Struggle for Responsible Government in the North-West Territories, 1870-97, University of Toronto Press, 1956; *The University of Saskatchewan, 1909-1959,* University of Saskatchewan, 1959; (editor) *Dominion Lands Policy,* McClelland & Stewart, 1973; *The Renaissance of Canadian History: A Biography of A. L. Burt,* University of Toronto Press, 1975; (editor) *William Aberhart and Social Credit in Alberta,* Copp, 1977. Also editor of *Essays in Western History: In Honour of Lewis Gwynn Thomas.* Editor of *Saskatchewan History,* 1949-57.

WORK IN PROGRESS: A History of the Government of Saskatchewan during the Premiership of T. C. Douglas, 1944-62.

SIDELIGHTS: Thomas told *CA:* "My interests have been concentrated on various aspects of the history of higher education in Saskatchewan and Alberta and in the role of the West in Canadian government and society."

* * *

THOMAS, Lorenzo 1944-

PERSONAL: Born August 31, 1944, in the Republic of Panama; son of Herbert Hamilton and Luzmilda (Gilling) Thomas. *Education:* Queens College (now of the City University of New York), B.A., 1967; graduate study at Pratt Institute. *Home address:* P.O. Box 14645, Houston, Tex. 77021.

CAREER: Pratt Institute, New York, N.Y., assistant reference librarian, 1967-68; Texas Southern University, Houston, writer-in-residence, 1973; Black Arts Center, Houston, Ethnic Arts Program creative writing teacher, 1973-75; *Living Blues,* Chicago, Ill., correspondent, 1976—; poet. Member of advisory board, KPFT-FM, Houston, 1973—; member of literature advisory panel, Texas Commission on the Arts and Humanities, 1975—. Has worked with the Poetry-in-the-Schools program in New York, Texas, Oklahoma, Florida, Arkansas, and Georgia. *Military service:* U.S. Naval Reserve, 1968-72. *Member:* Coordinating Council of Literary Magazines (member of board of directors, 1974—). *Awards, honors:* Dwight Durling prize in poetry, 1963; Poets Foundation awards, 1966 and 1974; Committee on Poetry grant, 1973; Lucille Medwick Award, 1974; also received John Golden Award for creative writing.

WRITINGS: Fit Music, Angel Hair Books, 1972; *Dracula,* Angel Hair Books, 1973; (editor) *ANKH: Getting It Together,* HOPE Development, 1974; *Jambalaya,* Reed, Cannon, 1975; *Sound Science,* Sun Be/Am, 1978; *The Bathers: Selected Poems,* Reed, Cannon, 1978. Translator of *Tho Tu Viet-Nam* (poems).

Work represented in anthologies, including *Black Fire,* Morrow, 1968; *The Poetry of Black America,* edited by Arnold Adoff, Harper, 1972; *New Black Voices,* edited by Abraham Chapman, New American Library, 1972; *None of the Above,* edited by Michael Lally, Crossing Press, 1976.

Contributor to *Yardbird, Yardbird Reader, Art & Literature, Angel Hair, C, Massachusetts Review, Umbra,* and other periodicals.

Editor, *Roots,* 1974—; advisory editor, *Nimrod,* 1977—; contributing editor, *Black Focus,* 1977—.

WORK IN PROGRESS: A collection of short stories on rural life in the South; essays on Afro-American music and literature.

SIDELIGHTS: Thomas told *CA:* "I came to New York City speaking Spanish; got beat up on the way home from school because I 'talked funny.' Never forgot it. Went way way way away out of my way to become extra-fluent in English.

"In the late 1950's and early 1960's, I participated in the various avant garde poetry movements in Greenwich Village and Harlem and on the lower East Side: the Umbra Workshop, the Black Arts Theatre, Le Doux Megots, the Poetry Project at Saint Marks-in-the-Bouwerie, and the Metro.

"In recent years, I've spent my time studying languages and revolutionary lifestyles of the Third World, and translating literary works by Vietnamese and Portuguese African poets. Currently I am studying the works of Panamanian poets Roberto MacKay and Chang Marin (Afro- and Asian-Panamanians, respectively). Most of my livelihood comes from working in public schools devising programs that will facilitate our needs for bilingual or multicultural education. I've spent the last five years working in 'problem areas.'

"At the present time, my main interests (and most of the writing I produce) concern bilingual and multicultural education; I study Afro-American (that's the whole hemisphere as far as I'm concerned) folklore and try to produce instructional modules and programs that are effective. I call them poems, articles, and short stories."

* * *

THOMAS, M(ilton) Halsey 1903-1977

February 3, 1903—July 7, 1977; American archivist, librarian, and historical editor. Thomas was the first person to serve as archivist at Princeton University and remained with the university in this position until 1969. He was a contributing editor of *The Papers of Woodrow Wilson.* He died in Princeton, N.J. Obituaries: *New York Times,* July 8, 1977. (See index for *CA* sketch)

* * *

THOMAS, Piri 1928-

PERSONAL: Birth-given name, John Peter Thomas; informally changed name as a youth; born September 30, 1928, in New York, N.Y.; son of John (a laborer) and Delores (Mantanez) Thomas; married Daniela Calo, April 20, 1958; children: Ricardo, San-dee. *Education:* Attended New York City public schools. *Home:* 627 Second St., New York, N.Y. 10016.

CAREER: Author, 1956—. Sent to prison for attempted armed robbery, 1950-56; volunteer worker in prison and drug rehabilitation programs in New York City, 1956—; Center for Urban Education, New York City, staff associate, beginning 1967. Vice-president of Third World Cinema Productions; trustee of Community Film Workshop Council and of American Film Institute. *Member:* Authors Guild. *Awards, honors:* Rabinowitz Foundation grant, 1962; Lever Brothers community service award, 1967.

WRITINGS: Down These Mean Streets (autobiography), Knopf, 1967; "The Golden Streets" (two-act drama), first produced in New York City at Riverside Park by Puerto Rican Traveling Theatre, September 9, 1970; *Saviour, Saviour, Hold My hand* (autobiography), Doubleday, 1972; *Seven Long Times* (autobiography), Praeger, 1974; (author of introduction) Lefty Barretto, *Nobody's Hero: A Puerto Rican Story,* New American Library, 1977.

WORK IN PROGRESS: A novel, *The Man Who Spins the Web; A Matter of Dignity.*

SIDELIGHTS: Piri Thomas began writing in prison, he explained, for a number of reasons. He had decided he could disprove the stereotypes society had placed on his Puerto Rican and black heritage. He also hoped to discover the real person inside, escape his immediate surroundings, and change his life; all through creative writing. He admits it wasn't easy. After his release, the product of four years of writing in prison was accidentally destroyed. "It took me five [additional] years to write *Down These Mean Streets,*" said Thomas, "because I was too much involved in the community work. But at the same time I was very easily threatened with my mind, because I know that when a mind breaks—I've seen it happen too many times, and my mind had to be slowly treated, to get stronger, because you don't just open up Pandora's Box."

Upon publication of this first book, Daniel Stern said: "The book's literary qualities are primitive. Yet it has an undeniable power that I think comes from the fact that it is a report from the guts and heart of a submerged population group, itself submerged in the guts and hearts of our cities. It claims our attention and emotional response because of the honesty and pain of a life led in outlaw, fringe status, where the dream is always to escape."

Thomas wrote the book in his Spanish Harlem dialect mixed with a style of language he picked up in prison. Most critics admired his ability to do this and still retain a highly personal contact with the many readers unfamiliar with this speech. "It is something of a linguistic event," said Stern. "Gutter language, Spanish imagery and personal poetics (sometimes forced, but often richly successful) mingle into a kind of individual statement that has very much its own sound." Through these "rough-hewn words shines a new voice," agreed James Goodsell, "one which may well add significant chapters to ethnic literature in the United States."

Other critics liked the honest attitude in which the book was done, conspicuously lacking sociological and moral judgments. Melvin Maddocks noted: "No alter ego wearing a halo of reform and late success peers over the shoulder of the young punk (age: 12 to 28) who struts angrily across these pages. The reader will never learn—except from the dust jacket—that Piri Thomas is a nearly 40-year-old ex-con, ex-drug addict who, for the past 10 years, has worked at rehabilitating other drug addicts in Spanish Harlem and Puerto Rico. Thomas has willed the past to become the present, clamping it down about his reader and himself as invisibly but as tightly as the walls of his ghetto. Here is the scene, straight and unedited, with no double-vision ironies and no postdated moral judgments—just a mixed bag of now." Nelson Aldrich believes the book "demands to be read as literature, not as raw data for social research. Thomas knows himself; his recollection of his youth is completely honest, and his writing—though occasionally flawed by self-conscious barbaric yawps—is wonderfully powerful. His achievement is to have so thoroughly taken the measure of his individuality that he adds significantly to our sense of the richness and shame of being an American."

The book was not without its adverse criticism. It was banned in some junior high school libraries for giving an unhealthy view of New York City and because it was too explicit in its sex scenes. John Clark is representative of the few who were strongly opposed to the book.

In his review, he said: "The Thomas of the book seems to move from one debauchery to another with little sense of any spiritual turpitude, often detailing his vice with relish and gusto. Certainly a prejudiced society helped to fashion the monster Thomas reveals himself to have been, but his personal laxity and irresponsibility seem equally as reprehensible. His repeated infidelities, his swaggering, his frankly filthy mind seem only incidentally related to the racial injustice upon which he casually blames all his transgressions." Clark does admit the use of language is creative. "Even here, however, the fascinating usages are regrettably smothered in layers of conventional vulgarities and obscenities."

Of Thomas's second book, *Saviour, Saviour, Hold My Hand,* Larry Garvin wrotes: "The telling of this story and its stylistic execution mark a shift in style for Piri. We no longer have the gut experience flung at us for what it's worth. Piri begins to place it within his own developing framework. If the result is tentative and seemingly incomplete at times, it is nevertheless compelling; if it doesn't stand on its own (though by and large, I think it does), it sits well as a transitional work between *Down These Mean Streets* and *Seven Long Times.* For in *Savior,* Piri has taken one step back from his experience; and that one step has provided a developing objectivity which comes to its fruition in *Seven Long Times.*" Garvin believes the chronological narrative used for *Down These Mean Streets* worked well because of its speed and intensity of delivery, "but, it breaks down considerably in *Savior,* which sometimes lacks a consistency of style. The chapters often read like a quest for subject matter; Piri picking his way through the middle years of his life, looking for a viable hook on which to hang his creative expression." *Seven Long Times* was critically better received than *Savior,* but neither of these books reached the wide and favorable reception of *Down These Mean Streets.*

"With the publication of these three books," concludes Garvin, "Piri Thomas has established himself as a writer deserving to be heard. But like many other Third World artists, Piri's publications have not meant economic success, and only sometimes sustenance. . . . But the bumps Piri has received in life have not diminished significantly with publication: the 'brand' society affixes to the 'ex-anything' is permanent. Piri's struggle for survival as a creative artist is necessarily as intense as his struggle to survive the cruelties of his childhood."

BIOGRAPHICAL/CRITICAL SOURCES: Book Week, May 21, 1967; *New York Times Book Review,* May 21, 1967; *Best Sellers,* June 1, 1967; *Life,* June 9, 1967; *Christian Science Monitor,* June 15, 1967; *Crisis,* June-July, 1975.

* * *

THOMAS, Sherilyn 1948-
(Sherry Thomas)

PERSONAL: Born July 7, 1948, in Americus, Ga.; daughter of William R. (a foreign service officer) and Betty (Fox) Thomas. *Education:* Attended Brown University, 1966-69. *Politics:* "Feminist/socialist." *Residence:* P.O. Box 54, Albion, Calif. 95410.

CAREER: National Student Association, Washington, D.C., staff member, 1969-70; sheep rancher, 1970—.

WRITINGS—All under name Sherry Thomas: (With Jeanne Tetrault) *Country Women: Handbook for the New Farmer,* Doubleday, 1976. Author of "Self-Reliance," a column in *Outside.* Contributor to feminist magazines and to *Country Women.*

WORK IN PROGRESS: An oral history of old-time country women; a juvenile novel.

SIDELIGHTS: Sherry Thomas writes: "My confidence and commitment as a writer have risen out of a growing feminist consciousness and with the support of women's publishing. I am also nurtured by my life as a farmer and the rural community that surrounds me. My current work also grows out of these feminist and country roots, though with the movement to fiction I'm moving away from explicity in political statements to an exploration of women's experience."

BIOGRAPHICAL/CRITICAL SOURCES: San Francisco Examiner and Chronicle, September 5, 1976; *New York Times,* January 13, 1977.

* * *

THOMAS, Sherry
See THOMAS, Sherilyn

* * *

THOMAS, William 1906-

PERSONAL: Born April 14, 1906, in Prospect, Ohio; son of Orin Ellsworth (a farmer) and Ruth (Howald) Thomas; married Vera Moren, July 18, 1935 (died November 18, 1948); married third wife, Sara Moyer (a high school counselor), June 18, 1961. *Education:* Ohio State University, B.A., 1929; University of Maryland, M.A., 1931; Bowling Green State University, Ph.D., 1968. *Politics:* Democrat. *Home:* 1904 Greendale Ave., Findlay, Ohio 45840. *Agent:* Charles R. Byrne, 1133 Avenue of the Americas, New York, N.Y. 10036.

CAREER: University of Kansas, Lawrence, instructor in English, 1931-33; free-lance writer, 1945-50; General Motors Institute, Flint, Mich., instructor in English, 1950-57; Michigan State University, East Lansing, editor of *College of Education Quarterly* and coordinator of publications, both 1957-61; Bowling Green State University, Bowling Green, Ohio, instructor in English, 1961-67; Ohio Northern University, Ada, assistant professor of English, 1967-69; Ohio State University, Marion, associate professor of English, 1969-74; writer, 1974—. *Member:* Modern Language Association of America, Ohio State University Faculty Club, Phi Kappa Phi. *Awards, honors:* Florence Roberts Head Memorial Award from American Association of University Women, 1976, for *The Country in the Boy.*

WRITINGS: The Country in the Boy, Thomas Nelson, 1975. Contributor of poems, stories, and articles to literary journals and popular magazines and newspapers, including *Prairie Schooner, Nation, Writer's World,* and *Personalist.*

SIDELIGHTS: Thomas told *CA:* "*The Country in the Boy* is fictionalized autobiography. My intent was to preserve something of a way of life that disappeared with the mechanization of farming in the Midwest in the 1930's. The locale is Marion County, Ohio, and the valley of the Scioto River. The time is 1913 to 1924." *Avocational interests:* Collecting books.

* * *

THOMASON, Tommy 1949-

PERSONAL: Born November 29, 1949, in Magnolia, Ark.; son of Harry Merle (a retail grocer) and Hazel (a grocery clerk; maiden name, Strange) Thomason; married Debbie Presley, December 31, 1976. *Education:* Ouachita Baptist University, B.A., 1971; East Texas State University, M.A., 1972; further study at Dallas Theological Seminary, 1974. *Politics:* Republican. *Religion:* Baptist. *Home:* 5032 San Marcus, Mesquite, Tex. 75150. *Office:* Oates Drive Baptist Church, 2805 Oates Dr., Mesquite, Tex. 75150.

CAREER/WRITINGS: Ouachita Baptist University, Arkadelphia, Ark., sports information director, 1971; East Texas State University, Commerce, Tex., assistant instructor in journalism, 1972-73; South Arkansas University, Magnolia, Ark., instructor in journalism, 1973-76; *Crossroads,* Mesquite, Tex., author of weekly editorial column, 1977—. *Member:* National Council of College Publications Advisers, Association for Education in Journalism, Arkansas College Publications Association (executive officer, 1975-76), Sigma Delta Chi.

SIDELIGHTS: Thomason told *CA:* "My current journalistic interest is in contemporary religious journalism. *Crossroads* is a unique blend of community journalism and Christian perspective. It is intended to appeal to urban secular men with its news and features on the Dallas metroplex, yet the ultimate goal is to share the Christian world-view."

*   *   *

THOMPSON, Duane G(len)   1933-

PERSONAL: Born March 10, 1933, in Washington, Iowa; son of Glen M. and Vaughn (Darbyshire) Thompson; married Milli M. Wright (a teacher), November 26, 1959; children: Carl, Clifford, Lisa, Janni. *Education:* Attended State College of Iowa, 1955-58; University of Oregon, B.S., 1959, M.S., 1964, Ph.D., 1966. *Home:* 438 North Third, Cheney, Wash. 99004. *Office:* Showalter 207, Eastern Washington University, Cheney, Wash. 99004.

CAREER: State Mental Health Institute, Independence, Iowa, special therapist, 1956-58; director of guidance and counseling at a high school in Pleasant Hill, Ore., 1959-63; Project Head Start, Eugene, Ore., research coordinator, 1965-66; Eastern Washington University, Cheney, assistant professor, 1966-67, associate professor, 1969-72, professor of applied psychology, 1972—, chairman of department, 1972-75, director of Child Development Center Clinic, 1967-72, director of Special Education Materials and Training Center, 1967-75, associate dean of graduate studies, 1976-77, vice-provost for undergraduate and graduate studies, 1977—. *Military service:* U.S. Navy, 1951-55. *Member:* American Psychological Association, Council for Exceptional Children, Spokane Psychology Association (past president).

WRITINGS: (Editor) *Readings for Educational Psychology,* Associated Educational Services Corp., 1968; *Writing Long-Range and Short-Range Objectives: A Painless Approach,* Research Press, 1977.

*   *   *

THOMPSON, James   1932-

PERSONAL: Born January 11, 1932, in Newcastle-upon-Tyne, England; son of James and Mary Margaret (Harland) Thompson; married Mary Josephine McAndrew (a teacher), September 20, 1958; children: Rosalind, Gabriel. *Education:* University of Durham, B.A. (first class honors), 1957. *Home:* 94 Elm Rd., Earley, Reading, Berkshire RG6 2TR, England. *Office:* Library, University of Reading, Whiteknights, Reading, England.

CAREER: University of Nottingham, Nottingham, England, chief cataloger at library, 1960-63; University of East Anglia, Norwich, England, senior assistant librarian, 1963-65; University of Glasgow, Glasgow, Scotland, deputy librarian, 1965-67; University of Reading, Reading, England, university librarian, 1967—. Library consultant, member of Berkshire County Library Commission, 1971—. *Member:* Library Association (fellow; member of council, 1972—).

WRITINGS: The Librarian and English Literature, American Library Association, 1968; *Books: An Anthology,* Bingley, 1968; *An Introduction to University Library Administration,* Bingley, 1970, 2nd edition, 1974; *English Studies,* Bingley, 1971; *Library Power,* Bingley, 1974; *A History of the Principles of Librarianship,* Bingley, 1977.

*   *   *

THOMPSON, Mel(vin R.)   1929-

PERSONAL: Born September 14, 1929, in Lansing, Mich.; son of E. Carlyn and Clara (Longworth) Thompson; married Barbara J. Walker, May 17, 1975; children: Jeffrey, Scott, Robert, Jeani. *Education:* Earned Ph.D. from California Pacific University. *Home:* 2204 Plaza de Flores, Carlsbad, Calif. 92008. *Agent:* Barbara Coleman, 2204 Plaza de Flores, Carlsbad, Calif. 92008. *Office:* 525 B St., Suite 2250, San Diego, Calif. 92101.

CAREER: Worked for various banking groups, 1954-68; independent career manager, 1968—. *Military service:* U.S. Army. *Member:* American Federation of Television and Radio Artists, San Diego Press Club.

WRITINGS: Why Should I Hire You?, Venture Press, 1975. Writer of column "Working It Out," syndicated by Field Enterprises.

SIDELIGHTS: Thompson told *CA:* "I am committed to the advancement of personal and career growth. I am a firm believer in the free enterprise system and the power of an informed public."

*   *   *

THOMPSON, Roger Francis   1933-

PERSONAL: Born October 24, 1933, in Harrow, England; son of Cecil Thomas (a banker) and Frances Amy Thompson; married Kathleen Aven Hoey (a social worker), June 19, 1963; children: Damian, Oriel. *Education:* St. John's College, Oxford, B.A., 1957, M.A., 1961; Harvard University, further graduate study, 1967-69. *Home:* 18 Mill Hill Rd., Norwich, England. *Agent:* Curtis Brown Academic, Craven Hill, London W.1, England. *Office:* School of English and American Studies, University of East Anglia, Norwich, England.

CAREER: History master at private school in Windsor, England, 1957-67; high school history teacher in Newton, Mass., 1967-69; University of East Anglia, Norwich, lecturer, 1969-74, senior lecturer, 1974-77, reader in American studies, 1977—. Exchange teacher at private school in Lakeville, Conn., 1962-63; visiting professor at Trinity College (Hartford, Conn.), 1965, and University of Rhode Island, 1977-78. *Military service:* British Army, Royal Artillery, 1952-54; became second lieutenant. *Member:* Association of University Teachers, British Association for American Studies. *Awards, honors:* American Council of Learned Societies fellowship for Harvard University and Yale University, 1974.

WRITINGS: The Golden Door (non-fiction), Allman, 1969; *Women in Stuart England and America,* Routledge & Kegan Paul, 1974; (editor with H. C. Allen, and contributor) *Contrast and Connection,* Ohio State University Press, 1976; (editor) *Samuel Pepys' Penny Merriments,* Columbia University Press, 1976.

Author of "How I Would Have Prevented the American Revolution," broadcast by British Broadcasting Corp. in 1976. Contributor to journals.

WORK IN PROGRESS: Unfit for Modest Ears, an examination of erotic writings in Restoration England; research on Puritan attitudes toward sexuality in the seventeenth century.

* * *

THORMAN, Donald J. 1924-1977

December 23, 1924—November 30, 1977; American publisher, businessman, editor, and author. Thorman had been publisher of the controversial *National Catholic Reporter* since 1965, a year after its founding. He was also president of the National Catholic Reporter Publishing Co., Inc. which publishes books, newsletters, and audio visual materials. Thorman was the author of several books on Catholicism. He died in Kansas City, Mo. Obituaries: *New York Times,* December 1, 1977; *Washington Post,* December 1, 1977. (See index for *CA* sketch)

* * *

THORNTON, Lee 1944-

PERSONAL: Born November 4, 1944, in Virginia; daughter of Lewis F. and Betty M. (Gaskins) Thornton. *Education:* Michigan State University, M.A., 1968; Northwestern University, Ph.D., 1973. *Residence:* Washington, D.C. *Office:* CBS News, 2020 M St., N.W., Washington, D.C.

CAREER: Speech therapist, Washington, D.C. public schools, 1964-66; University of Illinois, Chicago Cir., instructor in speech, 1969-71; Chicago City College, Chicago, Ill., lecturer in communications, 1971-72; Avco Broadcasting, Cincinnati, Ohio, reporter on WLWT, 1972-74; Columbia Broadcasting System (CBS) News, New York, N.Y., Washington bureau reporter, 1974—. Has appeared as substitute co-anchor person on CBS morning news. Lecturer at Ohio State University, 1973-74. *Member:* Washington Press Club, 4-H Club (member of board of advisers), Alpha Kappa Alpha, Alpha Psi Omega. *Awards, honors:* National Association of Broadcasters Award, 1971; Ford Foundation fellow, 1971.

* * *

THORNTON, W. B.
See BURGESS, Thornton Waldo

* * *

THORPE, Trebor
See FANTHORPE, R(obert) Lionel

* * *

THORPE, Trevor
See FANTHORPE, R(obert) Lionel

* * *

THURBER, James (Grover) 1894-1961

PERSONAL: Born December 8, 1894, in Columbus, Ohio; son of Charles Leander (later changed to Lincoln; a politician) and Mary Agnes (Fisher) Thurber; married Althea Adams, May 20, 1922 (divorced); married Helen Wismer, June 25, 1935; children: (first marriage) Rosemary. *Education:* Graduated from Ohio State University, 1919. *Residence:* West Cornwall, Conn.

CAREER: Columbus Dispatch, Columbus, Ohio, reporter, 1920-24; *Chicago Tribune,* Chicago, Ill., reporter for Paris edition, 1924-25; *New York Evening Post,* New York, N.Y.,

reporter, 1925; *New Yorker,* New York City, managing editor, 1927, staff writer, chiefly for "Talk of the Town" column, 1927-1933, regular contributor, beginning 1933. Art works have been exhibited several one-man shows, including shows at the Valentine Gallery, New York City, 1933, and at the Storran Gallery, London, 1937. *Wartime service:* Code clerk, Department of State in Washington, D.C., then at the American Embassy in Paris, 1917-19. *Member:* Author's League of America, Dramatists' Guild, Phi Kappa Psi, Sigma Delta Chi. *Awards, honors:* Caldecott Medal, 1944, for *Many Moons;* Ohioana Book Award, 1946, for *The White Deer;* Litt.D. from Kenyon College, 1950, and Yale University, 1953; L.H.D. from Williams College, 1951.

WRITINGS–Essays and stories: (With E. B. White) *Is Sex Necessary? or, Why You Feel the Way You Do,* Harper, 1929, reprinted 1975; *The Owl in the Attic and Other Perplexities* (self-illustrated), Harper, 1931, reprinted, 1965; *The Seal in the Bedroom and Other Predicaments* (self-illustrated), Harper, 1932, reprinted, 1950; *My Life and Hard Times* (autobiographical), Harper, 1933, reprinted, 1973; *The Middle-Aged Man on the Flying Trapeze: A Collection of Short Pieces* (self-illustrated), Harper, 1935, reprinted, Grosset, 1960; *Let Your Mind Alone! And Other More or Less Inspirational Pieces* (self-illustrated), Harper, 1937, reprinted, 1976; *The Last Flower: A Parable in Pictures* (self-illustrated), Harper, 1939, reprinted, 1971; *Fables for Our Time and Famous Poems Illustrated* (self-illustrated), Harper, 1940, reprinted, 1974; *My World–and Welcome to It* (self-illustrated), Harcourt, 1942, reprinted, 1969 [excerpt from *My World—and Welcome to It* published separately as *The Secret Life of Walter Mitty,* Associated Educational Services, 1967]; *Thurber's Men, Women, and Dogs* (self-illustrated), Harcourt, 1943, reprinted, Dodd, 1975; *The Thurber Carnival* (self-illustrated), Harper, 1945, reprinted, 1975; *The Beast in Me and Other Animals* (self-illustrated), Harcourt, 1948, reprinted, 1973; *Further Fables for Our Time* (self-illustrated), Simon & Schuster, 1956, reprinted, Penguin, 1962; *Alarms and Diversions,* Harper, 1957, reprinted, 1964; *The Years with Ross* (reminiscences; self-illustrated), Little, Brown, 1959, reprinted, Harper, 1975; *Lanterns and Lances,* Harper, 1961; *Credos and Curios* (self-illustrated), Harper, 1962, reprinted, Penguin, 1969; *Thurber and Company* (self-illustrated), Harper, 1966; *Snapshot of a Dog,* Associated Educational Services, 1966; *The Catbird Seat,* Associated Educational Services, 1967.

Plays: (With Elliott Nugent) *The Male Animal* (three-act; first produced on Broadway, January 9, 1940), Random House, 1940 (self-illustrated); "Many Moons," produced in New York, 1947; "A Thurber Carnival," first produced on Broadway at the ANTA Theatre, February 26, 1960. Also author of "Nightingale," a two-act musical, neither published nor produced.

For children: *Many Moons* (illustrated by Louis Slobodkin), Harcourt, 1943, reprinted, 1973 [another edition illustrated by Philip Reed, A. M. & R. W. Roe, 1958]; *The Great Quillow* (illustrated by Doris Lee), Harcourt, 1944, reprinted, 1975; *The White Deer* (illustrated by the author and Don Freeman), Harcourt, 1945, reprinted, 1968; *The 13 Clocks* (illustrated by Marc Simont), Simon & Schuster, 1950; *The Wonderful O* (illustrated by Simont), Simon & Schuster, 1957, reprinted, 1976.

Collected works: *Cream of Thurber,* Hamish Hamilton, 1939; *The Thurber Album: A New Collection of Pieces About People,* Simon & Schuster, 1952, reprinted, 1965; *Thurber Country: A New Collection of Pieces About Males and Females* (self-illustrated), Simon & Schuster, 1953,

Thurber's Dogs: A Collection of the Master's Dogs (self-illustrated), Simon & Schuster, 1955, reprinted, 1963; *The 13 Clocks* [*and*] *The Wonderful O* (for children; illustrated by Ronald Searle), Penguin, 1962; *Vintage Thurber,* two volumes, Hamish Hamilton, 1963.

Illustrator: Margaret Samuels Ernst, *The Executive's in a Word Book,* Knopf, 1939, reprinted, Belmont Books, 1963; Elizabeth Howes, *Men Can Take It,* Random House, 1939; James R. Kinney, *How to Raise a Dog,* Simon & Schuster, 1953 (published in England as *The Town Dog,* Harvill, 1954, reprinted, 1966).

SIDELIGHTS: Brendan Gill has written that Thurber and his *New Yorker* colleague E. B. White had between them "done more than anybody else to set the tone of the *New Yorker.*" Thurber's association with the magazine began when his friend White arranged a job interview with Harold Ross, then the magazine's editor. Thurber was originally hired as managing editor, but within six months managed to work himself down the ladder to a more comfortable position as staff writer. "I thought you were an editor, goddamn it, but I guess you're a writer, so write. Maybe you have something to say," Ross reportedly told him.

While with the *New Yorker,* Thurber established his reputation as twentieth century America's greatest illustrator and humorist. Thurber was a complex figure and while associates bemoaned his notorious bad traits and habits, all were aware of his brilliance as a humorist. His friend Mark Van Doren attempted this description: "He was an extraordinary man . . . with so many quick changes: gentle and fierce, fascinating and boring, sophisticated and boorish, kind and cruel, broadminded and parochial. You can't explain Thurber." His colleague Gill, who called him a "malicious man" and abhored his practical jokes, admired his writing. He wrote that Thurber was "fascinated by the *mana* that seems to reside in words without regard to their overt meanings. As a medium in the great seance of letters he is incomparable; he has only to utter an incantatory moan, and words levitate, phrases rap out unexpected messages, and whole sentences turn into ectoplasm."

Thurber's brand of humor has often been compared to Mark Twain's (although Thurber claimed that he had never read any of Twain's works). But V. S. Pritchett found the comparison untenable because, "the springs of his [Thurber's] manner were too delicate and his mind too inturned for the long masterpiece. One can see this in his brief parodies, in his love of impromtu, in his vision of Walter Mitty, and above all, in those long letters that were written to start useful hares. He was profitably uninventive in the large sense and trapped by autobiography; although he boasted of his powers of total recall, his best things are the result of weeding this deadly faculty."

A reviewer for *Saturday Review* commented that Thurber's stories were essentially "often bitter and cruel; the moral which adorn them cynical (and convulsing). They show . . . that at its worst the human race is viciously silly, while at its best, it is just silly." Most of the laughter in Thurber is friendly laughter," wrote a reviewer for the *New York Times.* "But he is not only a humorist; he is also a satirist who can toss a bomb while he appears to be tipping his hat."

Pritchett wrote of Thurber: "Light humorists run to the facetious, but Thurber was rarely that. He had iron in him. He knew that one lives in peril of what 'may come up in the mind,' as one of the characters in George Eliot says. In the putty-like human beings one saw in Thurber's drawings, one met the Id as one met it, say, in Lear, Carroll, or Saki. We admired the ad-hoc madness, and the care for language."

Numerous movies have been based on Thurber's works, including "Rise and Shine," an adaptation of *My Life and Hard Times,* produced by Twentieth Century Fox, 1941, "The Male Animal," produced by Warner Brothers, 1942, "The Secret Life of Walter Mitty," produced by Samuel Goldwyn Productions, 1947, "She's Working Her Way Through College," an adaptation of *The Male Animal,* produced by Warner Brothers, 1952; "The Battle of the Sexes," an adaptation of *The Catbird Seat,* produced by Continental Distributing, 1960, and "The War Between Men and Women," suggested by several works by Thurber, produced by National General Pictures Corporation, 1972.

Other adaptations of Thurber's writings include "Three by Thurber," a play by Paul Ellwood and St. John Terrell, first produced in New York City at Theater de Lys, 1955, "The Thirteen Clocks," an opera performed on stage and also as a television special, 1954, "The Last Flower," a dance performed by a French ballet company, 1959, and "My World and Welcome to It," a television series, 1969.

BIOGRAPHICAL/CRITICAL SOURCES—Books: James Thurber, *My Life and Hard Times,* Harper, 1933, reprinted, 1973; Thurber, *Thurber Album: A New Collection of Pieces About People,* Simon & Schuster, 1952, reprinted, 1965; Thurber, *Credos and Curios,* Harper, 1962; Robert Eustis Morsberger, *James Thurber,* Twayne, 1964; Norris W. Yates, *The American Humorist: Conscience of the Twentieth Century,* Iowa State University Press, 1964; Thurber, *Thurber and Company,* Harper, 1966; Richard C. Tobias, *Art of James Thurber,* Ohio University Press, 1969; Edwin T. Bowden, compiler, *James Thurber: A Bibliography,* Ohio State University Press, 1969; Stephen Ames Black, *James Thurber: His Masquerades,* Mouton, 1970; Charles S. Holmes, *Clocks of Columbus: The Literary Career of James Thurber,* Atheneum, 1972; Holmes, editor, *Thurber: A Collection of Critical Essays,* Prentice-Hall, 1974; Brendan Gill, *Here at the New Yorker,* Random House, 1975; Burton Bernstein, *Thurber,* Dodd, 1975, reissued as *Thurber: A Biography,* Ballantine, 1976; *Contemporary Literary Criticism,* Volume 5, Gale, 1976.

Articles: *Yale Review,* Autumn, 1965; *Reader's Digest,* September, 1972; *South Atlantic Quarterly,* Autumn, 1974; *Saturday Review,* March 22, 1975; *Newsweek,* March 24, 1975; *Time,* March 31, 1975; *Atlantic,* April, 1975; *New Yorker,* June 23, 1975; *Esquire,* August, 1975; *Smithsonian,* January, 1977.

Obituaries: *New York Times,* November 9, 1961; *Time,* November 10, 1961; *Illustrated London News,* November 11, 1961; *Newsweek,* November 13, 1961; *Publishers Weekly,* November 13, 1961; *Americana Annual,* 1962.*

(Died November 2, 1961)

*   *   *

TIANT, Luis 1940-

PERSONAL: Born November 23, 1940, in Havana, Cuba; came to United States, 1962; naturalized U.S. citizen, 1969; son of Luis Eleuterio (a baseball player) and Isabel (Vega) Tiant; married Maria del Refugio Navarro, 1961; children: Luis, Isabel, Daniel. *Education:* Attended Havana Electro-Mechanical University. *Residence:* Milton, Mass.

CAREER: Mexico City Tigers, Mexico City, Mexico, baseball pitcher, 1959-61; Cleveland Indians, baseball pitcher in franchises in Jacksonville, Fla., Burlington, N.J., and Portland, Ore., 1962-64, baseball pitcher in Cleveland, Ohio, 1964-70; Minnesota Twins, Minneapolis-St. Paul, Minn., baseball pitcher, 1970-71; Boston Red Sox, Boston, Mass., baseball pitcher, 1971—. *Awards, honors:* Player of the Year award from Pacific Coast League, 1964; named American League Comeback Player of the Year by *Sporting News,* 1971; holder of lowest earned run average in the American League, 1972.

WRITINGS: (With Joe Fitzgerald) *El Tiant,* Doubleday, 1976.

SIDELIGHTS: After leading the American League in lowest earned runs averaged in 1968, Tiant developed arm trouble in 1969 and was traded to Minnesota. Considered through in baseball, he was given a final chance with Boston where he made a phenomenal comeback. Tiant has won over twenty games several seasons and was a key player in Boston's 1975 pennant winning season.

* * *

TIDYMAN, Ernest 1928-

PERSONAL: Born January 1, 1928, in Cleveland, Ohio; son of Benjamin (a journalist) and Catherine (Kascsak) Tidyman; married Susan Katherine Gould (a writer), December 25, 1970; children: Benjamin, Nathaniel, Adam, Nicholas. *Education:* Educated in Cleveland. *Agent:* Fred Whitehead, International Creative Management, 8899 Beverly Blvd., Los Angeles, Calif. 90048. *Office:* Ernest Tidyman International, Ltd., Rossiter Rd., Washington, Conn. 06793.

CAREER: Cleveland News, Cleveland, Ohio, newsman, 1954-57; *New York Post,* New York City, newsman, 1957-60; *New York Times,* New York City, editor, 1960-66; *Signature,* New York City, managing editor and writer, 1966-69; free-lance screenwriter, author, and film producer, 1969—. Lecturer. *Military service:* U.S. Army, 1945-46. *Member:* Academy of Motion Picture Arts and Sciences, American Film Institute, British Film Institute, Writers Guild of America, Mystery Writers of America. *Awards, honors:* Academy Award, Writers Guild of America Award, and Edgar Allen Poe Award of Mystery Writers of America, all 1971, all for screenplay "The French Connection"; National Association for the Advancement of Colored People (NAACP) Image Award, 1971, for *Shaft.*

WRITINGS: Flower Power, Paperback Library, 1968; *Shaft,* Macmillan, 1970; *Absolute Zero,* Dial, 1971; *Shaft Among the Jews,* Dial, 1972; *Shaft's Big Score,* Bantam, 1972; *Shaft Has a Ball,* Bantam, 1973; *Goodbye, Mr. Shaft,* Dial, 1973; *High Plains Drifter,* Bantam, 1973; *Dummy,* Little, 1974; *Line of Duty,* Little, 1974; *Shaft's Carnival of Killers,* Bantam, 1974; *The Last Shaft,* Weidenfeld & Nicolson, 1975; *Starstruck,* W. H. Allen, 1975.

Author of screenplays, including "The French Connection," 1971, "Shaft," 1971, "Shaft's Big Score," 1972, "High Plains Drifter," 1973, "Report to the Commissioner," 1975, "The Street People," 1976.

WORK IN PROGRESS: Scenario, a novel; "Vanda," a teleplay; "Giants on the Road," a screenplay; "To Kill a Cop," a screenplay and teleplay.

* * *

TIEN, Hung-Mao 1938-

PERSONAL: Born November 7, 1938, in Taiwan; came to the United States in 1963, naturalized citizen, 1975; son of Chiang-ho and Pien Li Tien; married Amy Kuo (a librarian), January 20, 1968; children: Wendy, Marvin. *Education:* Tunghai University, B.A., 1961; University of Wisconsin, Madison, M.A., 1966, Ph.D., 1969. *Home:* 18285 Le Cha-

teau Dr., Brookfield, Wis. 53005. *Office:* Department of Political Science, University of Wisconsin, 1500 University Dr., Waukesha, Wis. 53186.

CAREER: University of Wisconsin, Waukesha, assistant professor, 1968-72, associate professor, 1972-75, professor of political science, 1975—, chairman of Center System department of history and political science, 1975-78. *Member:* American Political Science Association, Association for Asian Studies. *Awards, honors:* Social Science Research Council grant, 1972.

WRITINGS: Government and Politics in Kuomintang, China, 1927-37, Stanford University Press, 1972. Contributor to political science and Asian studies journals.

WORK IN PROGRESS: Research on the commune system and rural development in the People's Republic of China, and on socio-political changes in Taiwan.

* * *

TIKTIN, Carl 1930-

PERSONAL: Born June 27, 1930, in Brooklyn, N.Y.; son of Nathan (a merchant) and Lena (Lubavitsky) Tuckachinsky; married Barbara Selig, April 10, 1954 (divorced, February, 1968); children: Ross, Michelle, Hope. *Education:* Attended Brooklyn College (now of the City University of New York), 1948-52, 1954-55. *Politics:* "Left leaning." *Religion:* "Jewish—not seriously." *Home:* 59-30 108th St., Corona, N.Y. 11368. *Agent:* Pat Feeley, 52 Vanderbilt Ave., New York, N.Y. 10017. *Office:* New York Life Insurance Co., 166-07 Hillside Ave., Jamaica, N.Y. 11432.

CAREER: New York Life Insurance Co., Jamaica, N.Y., agent, 1955—. *Military service:* U.S. Army, Field Artillery, 1952-54; served in Korea.

WRITINGS: The Hour Glass Man (novel), Arbor House, 1977.

Plays: "Getting Through" (three-act), first produced in New York at Playwrights Horizons, March, 1973; "Once in Love with Amy" (one-act), first produced with two other short plays under title "The Holy Cross" in New York, July, 1974; "Flipping Out" (two-act), first produced in New York at Direct Theatre, October, 1975.

WORK IN PROGRESS: A novel based on "Flipping Out," about a bisexual man.

SIDELIGHTS: Tiktin writes: "Until I became a novelist, I was primarily a playwright. I studied at the HB Studio in Greenwich Village. I had a number of what are called off-off-Broadway experiences. I've belonged, and still to some extent do belong, to the legions of people who are stuck at career choices they made when they were too young and stupid to choose even the right tie. I sell life insurance, which is really not as full of derisive fun as all that because after all, in a capitalistic society, providing dough when the breadwinner dies is a definite social good. But my heart's never been in it, nor was it in the terrible marriage that went along with that career choice. From the moment we separated I resumed writing. I had been a playwright at college.

"If any general theme is prevalent in my work it is the self-imprisonment we inflict upon ourselves—how we get into it and how we try to get out. *The Hour Glass Man* dealt with a man living a life that he was totally incapable of living and finally breaking down because of it, and the second work is the same kind of theme. I've taken the case of a man who is primarily attracted to other men but isn't even quite aware of it himself. He goes through his life making adjustments against that attraction. The adjustments he makes are self-dictated and society-dictated, and of course he winds up adjusting himself out of existence."

* * *

TILLICH, Hannah   1896-

PERSONAL: Born May 17, 1896, in Germany; daughter of Jean (a school superintendent) and Louie (Schulze) Werner; married Paul Tillich (a theologian), 1924 (died, 1965); children: Erdmuthe Tillich Farris, Rene Stephen. *Education:* Attended Koenigliche Kunstschule, 1912-1916. *Home address:* Box 1334, East Hampton, N.Y. 11937.

CAREER: Writer. Worked as an art teacher in Europe.

WRITINGS: From Time to Time, Stein & Day, 1973; *From Place to Place: Travels with Paul Tillich, Travels Without Paul Tillich,* Stein & Day, 1976; *The Harbor Mouse,* Stein & Day, 1978. Contributor of poems to periodicals in Germany and the United States.

WORK IN PROGRESS: Doing research on Wolfram von Eschenbach's *Parsival* for a forthcoming novel.

SIDELIGHTS: Hannah Tillich's first book of memoirs, *From Time to Time,* elicited widely varying opinions from reviewers. Her candor in discussing her marriage to the renowned theologian Paul Tillich—including detailed accounts of their sexual relationships together and with others—was viewed as self-indulgent by some. Diana Trilling, for example, called the book "as narcissistic a document as has come from the pen of women in this century." *Time* criticized Mrs. Tillich for barely mentioning her husband's pioneering work in existential theology and for instead lacing the book with "third-rate poetry and erotic fantasy." Martin Marty found it regrettable that the book had been published at all. He wrote that the author was "a talented but tortured widow. Her gifts are as unmistakable as her wounds; her psychoanalytically-informed memoirs are as blurring as her memories are ambivalent.... Her typescript was full of revelatory I-accused-Paulus-and-he-denied-everything passages. It hardly seems fair that he cannot defend himself now."

However, another group of reviewers, associates and former students of Paul Tillich's among them, defended the book. John Wren-Lewis wrote: "The lofty critics who have tried to argue that Hannah Tillich's book is attracting misplaced notoriety or undeserved attention from prurient interest in its sexual references are guilty, in my view, of hypocritical intellectual snobbery." Harvey Cox, one of Tillich's former students, described Hannah Tillich as "a poet, a witch, a lover, and a mystic. Now full of years," he continued, "she has lived a life crammed with giddy risks, jarring changes, bitter humiliations (some at the hands of her husband) and many, many joys. Her autobiography is a many-faceted collage of surreal fantasies and erotic dreams, of journal excerpts and poetry, of clawing anger and fathomless love. There is not a sentimental sentence in the book, and it is very, very candid indeed."

Reviewer Tom F. Driver commented that the book had the "power of historical fiction, a truth told with a combination of candor and imagination. Of her life with the great theologian she has made a scenario of unforgettable images. The story she tells is not his but hers. Give or take some lurid details, it is also, I think, the story of many women. If there is scandal here, it is the scandal of modern existence spelled out in personal terms."

Wren-Lewis found the book particularly valuable in under-standing Tillich's own work in existential theology. "Existentialism, after all, proclaims the primacy of the personal and concrete in understanding what general, philosophical ideas really mean.... It is from Hannah's story ... that we see the human reality embodied in Tillich's idea of *The Courage to Be,* for it is precisely flesh-and-blood frailty and the tragedies of fallibility that give meaning to the courage of being human." Ultimately though, according to Driver, Hannah Tillich's book is a personal account of "what may happen when the female psyche is liberated from Christian and bourgeois constraint without (for whatever reason) assuming the burden of a new social role. Demons (a favorite word of Tillich's, fully understood by Hannah) are let loose.... Hannah Tillich has let loose the butterflies, as ugly as they are beautiful. Her book made me bleed."

Tillich told *CA:* "When I returned from Chicago to East Hampton, in 1965, I began my first book, *From Time to Time,* with the tales of my husband's first days. From those the tale of *my* life unrolled in an attempt to understand and clarify my own self. My second book, *From Place to Place,* was thought to describe the world around my life and Paul Tillich's as far as he shared it with me, and some events of my life after his death. *The Harbour Mouse* is a fantasy about two women, about femininity and non-femininity as I see it.

"Important to me is *Parsival,* dealing with compassion, defiance, and the ability of the human being to break through 'repetition.'"

BIOGRAPHICAL/CRITICAL SOURCES: Time, October 8, 1973; *New York Times Book Review,* October 14, 1973; *New York Times,* October 27, 1973; *New Republic,* November 24, 1973; *Critic,* November/December, 1973; *Partisan Review,* winter, 1974; *Village Voice,* January 31, 1974; *Psychology Today,* April, 1974.

* * *

TOBEY, Ronald C(harles)   1942-

PERSONAL: Born October 25, 1942, in Plymouth, N.H.; son of George H. (a manager of a hardware store) and Gloria (a nurse; maiden name, Carpenter) Tobey; married Susan E. Sauppee, August, 1964 (divorced, August, 1977); children: Amelia May. *Education:* University of New Hampshire, B.A. (Magna cum laude), 1964; Cornell University, M.A., 1966, Ph.D., 1969. *Politics:* "Patient liberalism." *Religion:* "Lapsed; Calvinist by temperament." *Home:* 5580 Apple Orchard Lane, Riverside, Calif. 92506. *Office:* Department of History, University of California, Riverside, Calif. 92521.

CAREER: University of Pittsburgh, Pittsburgh, Pa., visiting assistant professor of American history, 1969-70; University of California, Riverside, assistant professor, 1970-75, associate professor of history of science, 1975—, coordinator of program in western American studies. Member of National Archives Advisory Council, 1976-77; member of board of trustees of Riverside Municipal Museum, 1977—.

MEMBER: American Historical Association, Organization of American Historians, History of Science Society, Society for Social Studies of Science, American Association for State and Local History, American Studies Association, National Historic Trust. *Awards, honors:* Woodrow Wilson fellowships, 1964-65, 1967-68; National Endowment for the Humanities fellowship, 1975.

WRITINGS: The American Ideology of National Science, 1919-1930, University of Pittsburgh Press, 1971. Contributor to *Dictionary of American History* and to scholarly journals.

WORK IN PROGRESS: The Discovery of Nature Lost: The Science of Ecology in the United States, 1895-1930 (tentative title); a monograph on the ecology of American grasslands.

SIDELIGHTS: Tobey writes: "Generally, I am motivated by a concern that the cultural impact of scientists, the most important group of experts in our society, is not receiving sufficient critical scrutiny. I believe that their ideological posture, which is one of official disconnection with the applied results of their research activity, is generally harmful. It masks the real historical relationships between pure and applied science and between science and the values of our liberal culture. It also inhibits general interest in the ethical and social aspects of the on-going biological revolution among most scientists and relegates popular interest in these matters to a Sunday-supplement spectacle. There simply is insufficient public debate over science among the educated, middle-class public and its leadership.

"I lived in London, England, during 1975, conducting research on nineteenth-century English consciousness of ecological change in, particularly, the fenlands, which were drained by steam-power during the first half of the century."

AVOCATIONAL INTERESTS: Writing poetry, sculpting.

* * *

TODD, Frederick Porter 1903-1977

April 18, 1903—November 9, 1977; American historian and author. Todd was best known for his books on the U.S. military, including *Cadet Gray* and *Soldiers of the American Army, 1775-1954.* He died in Cornwall, N.Y. Obituaries: *New York Times,* November 12, 1977.

* * *

TODOROV, Tzvetan 1939-

PERSONAL: Born March 1, 1939, in Sofia, Bulgaria; son of Todor Borov (a university professor) and Haritina (a librarian; maiden name, Peeva) Todorova; married Martine van Woerkens (a creative writer), August 21, 1972; children: Boris. *Education:* University of Sofia, M.A., 1961; University of Paris, Doctorat de troisieme cycle, 1966, Doctorat es lettres, 1970. *Home:* 2 Sq. Adanson, Paris, France 75005. *Office:* Centre National de la Recherche Scientifique (CNRS), 6 rue de Tournon, Paris, France 75006.

CAREER: Centre National de la Recherche Scientifique (CNRS), Paris, France, director of research, 1968—. *Awards, honors:* Bronze Medal award from Centre National de la Recherche Scientifique, 1974.

WRITINGS: (Editor) *Theorie de la litterature,* Seuil, 1965; (editor) *Recherches semantiques,* Didier, 1966; *Litterature et signification,* Larousse, 1967; *Grammaire du Decameron,* Mouton, 1969; *Introduction a la litterature fantastique,* Seuil, 1970, translation by Richard Howard published as *The Fantastic: A Structural Approach to a Literary Genre,* Cornell University Press, 1973; *Poetique de la prose,* Seuil, 1971, translation by Richard Howard published as *Poetics of Prose,* Cornell University Press, 1977; (with Oswald Ducrot) *Dictionnaire encyclopedique des sciences du langage,* Seuil, 1972; *Poetique,* Seuil, 1973; *Theories du symbole,* Seuil, 1977.

Editor, *Poetique: Revue de theorie et d'analyse litteraires.*

WORK IN PROGRESS: Symbolisme et interpretation (title means "Symbolism and Interpretation"); *Les Genres du discours* (title means "The Genres of Discourse").

SIDELIGHTS: Todorov's books have been translated into Spanish, German, English, Italian, Portuguese, Japanese, Rumanian, Chech, Russian, and Korean.

* * *

TOFTE, Arthur 1902-

PERSONAL: Born June 8, 1902, in Chicago, Ill.; son of Arthur E. (a stockbroker) and Geneva (an artist; maiden name, Steele) Tofte; married Dorothy Anton (a clinical nurse), May 10, 1941; children: Peter, Jean Tofte Harden. *Education:* University of Wisconsin, Madison, B.A., 1925. *Politics:* Republican. *Religion:* Congregationalist. *Home and office:* 7237 Wellauer Dr., Wauwatosa, Wis. 53213. *Agent:* Larry Sternig Literary Agency, 742 Robertson St., Milwaukee, Wis. 53213.

CAREER: Sterling Motor Truck, Milwaukee, Wis., advertising manager, 1934-36; Bucyrus-Erie, South Milwaukee, Wis., editor, 1936-38; Allis-Chalmers Corp., Milwaukee, Wis., advertising manager, 1938-69; writer, 1969—. *Member:* Science Fiction Writers of America, Council for Wisconsin Writers, Wisconsin Regional Writers Association, Raconteurs of Wisconsin, Milwaukee Fictioneers, Allied Authors of Milwaukee. *Awards, honors:* Award from Council for Wisconsin Writers, 1975, for the novel *Walls Within Walls.*

WRITINGS—Science fiction novels: *Crash Landing on Iduna,* Laser Books, 1975; *Walls Within Walls,* Laser Books, 1975; *Survival Planet,* Bobbs-Merrill, 1977; *The Day the Earth Stood Still,* Scholastic Book Services, 1977; *The Ghost Hunters,* Major Books, in press.

Represented in more than fifteen anthologies, including *The Other Side of Tomorrow,* Random House; *Science Fiction Tales,* Rand McNally; *The Night of the Sphinx,* Lerner. Contributor to a wide variety of magazines, including *Esquire, American Heritage, Child Life, Amazing Stories, American Legion,* and *Boy's Life.*

WORK IN PROGRESS: How to Adjust to a Hearing Loss; Timmy, a novel about a hyperactive boy.

SIDELIGHTS: For Tofte, one of the extra advantages of being a successful writer is the time and means to travel. He has made four trips to Europe, and in 1977 searched for and found the farm on which his grandfather lived 110 years ago in Norway.

He spends as much time reading as writing, but believes that much contemporary creativity, in literature, as well as art and music, will not be lasting.

BIOGRAPHICAL/CRITICAL SOURCES: Milwaukee Journal, July 7, 1977; *Wauwatosa News-Times,* July 28, 1977.

* * *

TOLF, Robert W(alter) 1929-

PERSONAL: Born August 3, 1929, in Chicago, Ill.; son of Carl Oscar (a stockbroker) and Margaret (Zeltner) Tolf; married Nancy List (director of Florida Endowment for the Humanities), August 9, 1952; children: Carolyn Anne. *Education:* Harvard University, A.B. (cum laude), 1951; University of Rochester, Ph.D., 1954. *Home and office:* 1980 Sharon St., Boca Raton, Fla. 33432.

CAREER: U.S. Department of State, Washington, D.C., foreign service officer in Scandinavia and Switzerland, engaged in commercial promotion and political-economic reporting, 1957-70; writer, 1971—. Senior research fellow at

Hoover Institution, 1977-78. *Military service:* U.S. Army, Infantry, 1954-57; became first lieutenant. *Member:* Boca Raton Club, Harvard Club of Broward County.

WRITINGS: How to Survive Your First Six Months in Florida, Trend Publications, 1971, 6th edition, 1977; *Guide to Florida Restaurants,* two volumes, Trend Publications, 1972, 2nd edition, 1974; *The Russian Rockefellers: The Saga of the Nobel Family and the Russian Oil Industry,* Hoover Institution, 1976; *Best Restaurants of Florida,* 101 Productions, 1977. Author of columns "Inside Florida Restaurants" in *Florida Trend* and "Table Talk" in *Fort Lauderdale News.* Contributor of travel articles to *New York Times.* Associate editor of *South,* 1973-75; restaurant editor of *Florida Trend,* 1972—.

WORK IN PROGRESS: A comparative analysis of Communism in Scandinavia, detailing the individual party histories and personalities; a selective travel guide for Florida; a biographical study of key leaders in the White Army during the Russian Civil War.

SIDELIGHTS: Tolf told *CA:* "I am strongly motivated to remove the restaurant review/travel article from the Watergate of journalism, to provide honest reportage, albeit it obviously subjective, totally free of pressures and favors and freebies from public relations firms, tourist promotion societies, chambers of commerce, and the establishments/attractions. On a less mundane plane and with the advantage of skills in Swedish, Norwegian, Danish, Icelandic, German, French, and some Spanish—and I'm working on my Russian—I shall continue to research and write on Russian/Soviet affairs, on Scandinavian history and political developments."

*   *   *

TOLNAI, Karoly
    See DE TOLNAY, Charles Erich

*   *   *

TOLNAI, Vagujhelyi Karoly
    See DE TOLNAY, Charles Erich

*   *   *

TOMAS, Andrew Paul

PERSONAL: Born in St. Petersburg, Russia; came to the United States in 1977; Australian citizen; son of an architect; married Heather Elizabeth Hinshaw. *Education:* Educated in northern China and in Los Angeles, Calif. *Home:* 845 East 20th St., Chico, Calif. 95926.

CAREER: Worked in Los Angeles, Calif., 1927-31; Radio Corp. of America, New York, N.Y., assistant accountant in Shanghai, China, 1935-49; internal auditor for a real estate firm in Sydney, Australia, 1949-66; researcher at British Museum Library in London, Bibliotheque Nationale in Paris, and Lenin Library in Moscow, 1966-68; writer, 1968—. *Awards, honors:* Le Cercle du Livre Precieux 1969, for *Atlantis.*

WRITINGS: Signs, Stars, and Seers: An Experiment in Historical Prediction, Llewellyn, 1956; *Les secrets de l'-Atlantide,* Robert Laffont, 1969, translation published as *Atlantis: From Legend to Discovery,* R. Hale, 1972, published in the United States as *Home of the Gods,* Berkeley Publishing Corp., 1974; *La barriere du temps,* Rene Julliard, 1969, translation published as *Beyond the Time Barrier,* Sphere Books, 1974, Berkeley Publishing Corp., 1976; *We Are Not the First: Riddles of Ancient Science,* Putnam,

1971; *On the Shores of Endless Worlds: The Search for Cosmic Life,* Putnam, 1974; *Shambhala: Oasis de Lumiere* (title means "Shambhala: Oasis of Light"), Robert Laffont, 1976.

WORK IN PROGRESS: They Were the First, a sequel to *We Are Not the First.*

SIDELIGHTS: Tomas lived for about twenty years in China. He spent the World War II years there, in great hardship. He moved to Australia two months before the Communist occupation of China. He has since lived in or visited England, France, Portugal, Lebanon, Mexico, Egypt, Spain, West Germany, Austria, Denmark, Switzerland, Italy, Yugoslavia, India, Japan, Singapore, Ceylon, Brazil, Bolivia, Peru, and the Soviet Union. His books have appeared in most of these countries, as well as Sweden, Finland, the Netherlands, Belgium, and Turkey.

AVOCATIONAL INTERESTS: History, archaeology, science.

*   *   *

TOMPKINS, Richard A.   1896(?)-1977

1896(?)—November 18, 1977; American journalist. Tompkins was best known for his coverage of education. He died in Queens, N.Y. Obituaries: *New York Times,* November 21, 1977.

*   *   *

TOOKE, Thomas (Renshaw)   1947-

PERSONAL: Surname is pronounced Took; born May 15, 1947, in North Bay, Ontario, Canada; son of Thomas Renshaw (a salesman) and Marjorie (a teacher; maiden name, Wemp) Tooke; married Elaine Hutcheson (a librarian), August 16, 1975. *Education:* University of Western Ontario, B.A., 1969; University of Toronto, B.Ed., 1970. *Religion:* Anglican. *Home:* 24 Haddon Ave. N., Hamilton, Ontario, Canada L8S 4A3.

CAREER: High school English teacher; writer.

WRITINGS: (With William Gillard) *The Niagara Escarpment,* University of Toronto Press, 1975.

*   *   *

TORRIE, James H(iram)   1908-

PERSONAL: Born August 8, 1908, in Fort Macleod, Alberta, Canada; son of Arthur Edward (a teacher) and Margaret (Bates) Torrie; married Mildred Shield, August 26, 1935; children: Douglas James. *Education:* University of Alberta, B.Sc., 1931, M.Sc., 1934; University of Minnesota, additional study, University of Wisconsin, Ph.D., 1938. *Politics:* Independent. *Religion:* Congregationalist. *Home:* 4723 Sheboygan Ave., Apt. 203, Madison, Wis. 53705.

CAREER: University of Alberta, Edmonton, assistant in plant breeding, 1929-34; University of Wisconsin, Madison, 1935-74, began as assistant professor, professor of agronomy, 1948-74. *Member:* American Statistical Association, American Society of Agronomy, Crop Science Society of America, American Institute of Biological Sciences, American Soybean Association, Biometric Society, Sigma Xi, Phi Sigma, Gamma Sigma Delta. *Awards, honors:* Fulbright research scholar in New Zealand, 1956-57; American Society of Agronomy fellow, 1962; Distinguished Service to Agriculture award, Gamma Sigma Delta, 1971; meritorious service awards from American Soybean Association, and Wisconsin Crop Improvement Association, both 1973.

WRITINGS: (With Robert G. D. Steel) *Principles and Procedures of Statistics,* McGraw, 1960; *Introduction to Statistics,* McGraw, 1976. Also author of scientific papers on the breeding, genetics, and culture of grasses, grains and soybeans; and on the application of statistical methods to biological research.

WORK IN PROGRESS: An elementary book on statistics.

AVOCATIONAL INTERESTS: Gladiolus, rose, and dahlia culture; photography.

* * *

TORRO, Pel
See FANTHORPE, R(obert) Lionel

* * *

TORTORA, Daniel F(rancis) 1947-

PERSONAL: Born January 16, 1947, in New York, N.Y.; son of Daniel (a lawyer) and Gloria (a dietician; maiden name, Salvatore) Tortora; married Angela Arcuni (a high school teacher), August 20, 1966; children: Dawn, Daniel. *Education:* Queens College of City University of New York, B.A., 1968; Michigan State University, M.A., 1970, Ph.D., 1973. *Politics:* "Independent." *Religion:* "What?" *Home address:* P.O. Box 927, Alpine, N.J. 07620. *Agent:* Bill Adler, 1230 Avenue of Americas, New York, N.Y. 10020. *Office:* Department of Psychology, Jersey City State College, Jersey City, N.J. 07350.

CAREER: Michigan State University, East Lansing, Mich., assistant professor of psychology and social science, 1973-74; Jersey City State College, Jersey City, N.J., assistant professor of psychology and director of experimental laboratories, 1974—. Instructor, Lansing Community College, 1972-74. *Member:* American Association for the Advancement of Science, American Psychological Association, Eastern Psychological Association, Midwestern Psychological Association, Michigan Academy of Science, Arts and Letters. *Awards, honors:* Biomedical Science Support grant, 1971; NASA fellowship, 1972.

WRITINGS: Help! This Animal Is Driving Me Crazy, Playboy Press, 1977; (contirbutor) M. R. Denny, editor, *Applied Animal Psychology,* Wiley, 1978. Contributor of articles to *Learning & Motivation* and other periodicals.

WORK IN PROGRESS: Animal Behavior: An Applied Perspective, publication expected in 1979; *Animal Behavior Therapy; Creative Parenting; Beyond the Relaxation Response.*

SIDELIGHTS: Tortora told *CA:* "The treatment of animal behavior problems is an outgrowth of my research on developing animal analogues for human psychotherapy."

"My vocation is psychology. My avocation is psychology," he added.

* * *

TOURTELLOT, Arthur Bernon 1913-1977

July 23, 1913—October 18, 1977; American television executive, historian, and editorial executive. Tourtellot was vice-president and general executive of Columbia Broadcasting Systems and the producer of such historical series as "Crusade in Europe." A former editorial executive for Time Inc. for eleven years, Tourtellot was the director of Time Inc. television productions. He wrote several books on American history and contributed extensively to national magazines. Tourtellot was a trustee of the Museum of Broadcast-ing and the chairman of the editorial board of Columbia University's *Journal of World Business.* He died in Manhattan, N.Y. Obituaries: *New York Times,* October 20, 1977; *Time,* October 31, 1977. (See index for *CA* sketch)

* * *

TOWNSEND, Reginald T. 1890-1977

August 3, 1890—November 12, 1977; American businessman and author. Townsend wrote *Mother of Clubs* and *God Packed My Picnic Basket.* He died in Mount Kisco, N.Y. Obituaries: *New York Times,* November 13, 1977.

* * *

TREE, Christina 1944-

PERSONAL: Born September 1, 1944, in Honolulu, Hawaii; daughter of Alfred E. (an international banker) and Martha (a nurse; maiden name, Rudneski) Tree; married William A. Davis (a travel editor), September 2, 1971; children: Liam, Timothy. *Education:* Mount Holyoke College, B.A., 1965. *Politics:* Liberal. *Religion:* "Liberal Roman Catholic." *Home:* 15 Whittier St., Cambridge, Mass. 02140. *Agent:* Herbert Kenny, 804 Summer St., Manchester, Mass. 01944. *Office: Boston Globe,* Boston, Mass. 02140.

CAREER: Columbia College Today, New York, N.Y., editorial assistant, 1965-66; *Jubilee,* New York City, staff writer, 1966-67; *Boston Globe,* Boston, Mass., assistant travel editor, 1962-72, staff writer, 1977—. *Member:* Society of American Travel Writers.

WRITINGS: How New England Happened, Little, Brown, 1976. Contributor to magazines.

WORK IN PROGRESS: Massachusetts: An Explorer's Guide, for Countryman Press, publication expected in 1979.

SIDELIGHTS: Christina Tree writes: "Before my children were born, I traveled abroad constantly, but at present am content writing about New England, which I do regularly and with ever-increasing enjoyment." *Avocational interests:* "For relaxation I sketch and I collect islands without electricity which our family can retreat to."

* * *

TREMBLE, Freda B. 1894-

PERSONAL: Born October 21, 1894, in Modoe County, Calif.; daughter of Wilson S. (a rancher) and May (Williams) Bayley; married Howard H. Tremble (an engineer), April 21, 1921 (died, 1959). *Education:* University of California, Berkeley, A.B., 1922; graduate study at Boston University, and Pembroke College, Providence, R.I., both 1930. *Home:* 1224 Rossmoor Pkwy., Walnut Creek, Calif. 94595.

CAREER: Writer, broadcaster, and photographer. Women's editor and columnist, *Oakland Times,* Oakland, Calif. *Member:* Photographic Society of America, Society of the Performing Arts, Berkeley Camera Club (member of board), Northbrae Club (past literary chairman), Women's City Club (Grand Rapids, Mich.). *Awards, honors:* Poetry award from *Poet Auslander,* 1959.

WRITINGS: Modoc (juvenile), Warne, 1972. Contributor of articles to periodicals, including *Forbes, Good Housekeeping,* and *Outdoor Guide.*

WORK IN PROGRESS: Generation Gap; Seeing-Eye Pup in a Family; a book on narrow-gauge railroads.

SIDELIGHTS: Recalling her travel experiences, Freda Tremble told *CA:* "With little money and great curiosity, it was *luck* that brought me invitations for six summers with a

German friend in Portugal; surgery requiring five yearly checkups took me to Switzerland. My father, in dry California, loved water so I had to see the Nile and the Aswan Dam. My husband loved ships so I had to cross the Arctic Circle bound for the Land of the Midnight Sun. The high Himalayas were my own idea—I'm glad I did them early."

* * *

TRENT, Olaf
   See FANTHORPE, R(obert) Lionel

* * *

TRIPP, C(larence) A(rthur) 1919-

PERSONAL: Born October 4, 1919, in Denton, Tex.; son of Clarence A. (a merchant) and Lula (Evers) Tripp. *Education:* Rochester Institute of Technology, A.A.S., 1941; New School for Social Research, B.A., 1953; New York University, Ph.D., 1957. *Religion:* None. *Home and office address:* South Blvd., Nyack, N.Y. 10960. *Agent:* Don Congdon, 22 East 40th St., New York, N.Y. 10016.

CAREER: Special assistant to Alfred C. Kinsey in Bloomington, Ind., 1948-56; private practice of psychology in New York, N.Y., 1959—. Instructor at State University of New York Downstate Medical Center, 1955-64. Director of Psychological Research Associates, Inc. *Wartime service:* Secret Service, General Military, 1942-45. *Member:* American Psychological Association.

WRITINGS: The Homosexual Matrix, McGraw, 1975. Contributor to psychiatry and psychology journals.

WORK IN PROGRESS: An analysis of screen phenomena in psychology and anthropology, completion expected in 1982.

SIDELIGHTS: Tripp comments: "All that I write on human sexuality is in line with the Alfred Kinsey-Frank Beach research. The homosexual matrix itself is composed of eight basic items. All of these except two were stabilized by Kinsey and Beach. The two are the addition of import-export psychology to the theory of complementation, and the resistance factor—that is, that sexual motivation is as dependent upon barriers to easy access as it is upon factors of 'drive' and admiration."

* * *

TRIVERS, Howard 1909-

PERSONAL: Born September 30, 1909, in New York, N.Y.; son of Nathan (a merchant) and Anna L. (Lipsit) Trivers; married Mildred Raynolds (a poet), December 22, 1934; children: Aylmer, Robert, Jonathan, Kate, Ruth Ann, Mildred, Howard E. *Education:* Princeton University, A.B., 1930; Harvard University, M.A., 1932, Ph.D., 1941; attended University of Heidelberg, 1932-33, University of Freibourg, 1935-38, and George Washington University, 1943-44; National War College, graduate, 1950. *Religion:* Presbyterian. *Home address:* R.R. 9, Box 446A, Muncie, Ind. 47302. *Office:* Department of Political Science, Ball State University, Muncie, Ind. 47306.

CAREER: U.S. Department of State, Washington, D.C., divisional assistant studying Nazi activities for Division of European Affairs, 1941-43, country specialist for Division of Territorial Studies, 1943-45, German desk officer in Central European Division, 1945-48, assistant chief of the division, 1948-49, acting chief of Division of German Political Affairs, 1949, chief of political section of American Embassy in Copenhagen, Denmark, 1950-52, deputy officer in charge of northern European affairs, 1952-54; National War College, Washington, D.C., professor of international relations, 1954-55; U.S. Department of State, officer in charge of Polish, Baltic, and Czechoslovakian affairs, 1955-57, chief of Eastern Affairs Division of U.S. Mission in Berlin, Germany, 1957-60, political advisor and executive officer of U.S. Mission in Berlin, 1960-62, director of Office of Research and Analysis for the Sino-Soviet Bloc, 1962-65, senior member of board of examiners of foreign service, 1965, American consul general in Zurich, Switzerland, 1966-69; Southern Illinois University, Carbondale, visiting professor of government and diplomat-in-residence, 1969-72; Ball State University, Muncie, Ind., visiting professor, 1972-74; adjunct professor of political science, 1974—. Member of advisory council of philosophy department at Princeton University, 1948-66. *Member:* American Philosophical Association, American Political Science Association, Foreign Service Association.

WRITINGS: (With R. E. Murphy, F. B. Stevens, and J. M. Roland) *National Socialism: Basic Principles,* U.S. Department of State, 1943; *Three Crises in American Foreign Affairs and a Continuing Revolution,* Southern Illinois University Press, 1972; *Lectures on Foreign Affairs,* Ball State University, 1974; *The Community of Man: Four Lectures,* Ball State University, 1977. Contributor to literary, philosophy, and international affairs journals.

SIDELIGHTS: Trivers writes that during his career in diplomacy he "worked on German and Japanese terms of surrender, the U.S. directive for occupation of Germany, and policy proposals for the Potsdam Conference. I participated in the State Department Policy Planning Council and in inter-agency committees, including the Berlin blockade, 1948-49, the Hungarian uprising, 1956-57, and the Cuba missile crisis, 1962.

"As German desk officer, I handled economic, informational, and administrative as well as political problems during the occupation period. I also participated in various international negotiations and conferences, such as the agreement with the British Foreign Office on publication of German Foreign Office archives, the Moscow Conference of 1947, and the Paris meeting of foreign ministers which ended the Berlin blockade in 1949. As officer in charge of Polish-Czech affairs, I was responsible for policy toward Poland at the time of the Gomulka 'revolution.' As political adviser during the Berlin crisis I dealt directly with the Soviet political adviser, handled operational and policy matters with British and French political advisers in a tripartite committee, and maintained liaison with West Berlin authorities.

"As director of the Office of Sino-Soviet Bloc Research, I directed research analysis on political, economic, sociological, and cultural aspects of the Communist world."

* * *

TROFIMENKOFF, Susan Mann 1941-

PERSONAL: Surname is pronounced Tro-*fim*-en-koff; born February 10, 1941, in Ottawa, Ontario, Canada; daughter of Walter Beresford (a teacher) and Marjorie Margaret (a teacher; maiden name, Diehl) Mann; married Nicholas N. Trofimenkoff (a physicist), June 29, 1971; children: Britt-Mari. *Education:* University of Toronto, B.A. (honors), 1963; University of Western Ontario, M.A., 1965; Universite Laval, Ph.D., 1970. *Home:* 149 Drummond St., Ottawa, Ontario, Canada K1S 1K1. *Office:* Department of History, University of Ottawa, Ottawa, Ontario, Canada K1N 6N5.

CAREER: Toyo Eiwa Jogakuin (junior college), Tokyo,

Japan, lecturer in English, 1963-64; University of Montreal, Montreal, Quebec, senior lecturer in history, 1966-70; University of Calgary, Calgary, Alberta, assistant professor of history, 1970-72; University of Ottawa, Ottawa, Ontario, assistant professor, 1972-74, associate professor of history, 1974—, chairman of department, 1977—. *Member:* Canadian Historical Association (member of council, 1971-74), Canadian Research Institute for the Advancement of Women (founding member; member of board of directors, 1976—).

WRITINGS: (Editor) *The Twenties in Western Canada,* National Museum of Man, 1972; (editor) *Abbe Groulx: Variations on a Nationalist Theme,* Copp, 1973; *Action Francaise: French Canadian Nationalism in the Twenties,* University of Toronto Press, 1975; (editor with Alison Prentice) *The Neglected Majority: Essays in Canadian Women's History,* McClelland & Stewart, 1977. Contributor to scholarly journals. Academic editor of *Social Sciences in Canada,* 1975-77.

WORK IN PROGRESS: A biography of Stanley Knowles, Member of Parliament; research on Canadian women's history.

SIDELIGHTS: Dr. Trofimenkoff comments: "French Canadian nationalism sparked my interest in the 1960's; feminism sparks my interest in the 1970's. I adore teaching and writing; administration I seem to do efficiently."

* * *

TROXELL, Eugene A(nthony) 1937-

PERSONAL: Born May 14, 1937, in Eugene, Ore.; son of Emby Ray (a laborer) and Pauline (Kolodejack) Troxell; married Clara Harvey, August, 1961 (divorced, 1969); married Barbara Maloney, May 20, 1972 (divorced, 1977); children: Christopher, Cameron, Keira. *Education:* Gonzaga University, B.A., 1961; University of Chicago, M.A., 1963, Ph.D., 1966. *Residence:* San Diego, Calif. *Office:* Department of Philosophy, San Diego State University, S8n Diego, Calif. 92182.

CAREER: San Diego State University, San Diego, Calif., assistant professor, 1966-72, associate professor of philosophy, 1972—. *Member:* American Philosophical Association. *Awards, honors:* Woodrow Wilson fellowship, 1962.

WRITINGS: (With William S. Snyder) *Making Sense of Things,* St. Martin's, 1976.

WORK IN PROGRESS: "I am working on ways of using visual materials for communicating aspects of our socially constructed reality."

SIDELIGHTS: Troxell writes: "I am primarily interested in aspects of the evolution of the human intellect, as well as in ways in which linguistic patterns appear to influence thought patterns."

* * *

TUCKER, Ann
See GIUDICI, Ann Couper

* * *

TUCKER-FETTNER, Ann
See GIUDICI, Ann Couper

* * *

TURNER, Frederick 1943-

PERSONAL: Born November 19, 1943, in England; came

to the United States in 1967; son of Victor Witter (an anthropologist) and Edith (a writer; maiden name, Davis) Turner; married Mei Lin Chang, June 25, 1966; children: Daniel. *Education:* Christ Chruch, Oxford, B.A., 1965, M.A., 1967, B.Litt., 1967. *Home:* 205 East Woodside Dr., Gambier, Ohio 43022. *Agent:* Virginia Kidd, Box 278, Milford, Pa. 18337.. *Office:* Department of English, Kenyon College, Gambier, Ohio 43022.

CAREER: University of California, Santa Barbara, assistant professor of English, 1967-72; Kenyon College, Gambier, Ohio, associate professor of English, 1972—. *Member:* International Society for the Study of Time, Modern Language Association of America.

WRITINGS: Deep Sea Fish (poetry), Unicorn, 1968; *Birth of a First Son* (poetry), Christopher's Press, 1969; *The Water World* (poetry), Christopher's Press, 1970; *Shakespeare and the Nature of Time,* Oxford University Press, 1971; *Between Two Lives* (poetry), Wesleyan University Press, 1972; (editor) William Shakespeare, *Romeo and Juliet,* University of London Press, 1974; (translator) *Three Poems from the German,* Pothanger Press, 1974. Contributor to *Chaucer Review.*

WORK IN PROGRESS: A Double Shadow, a science fiction novel; *Adventures in Counter-Terra,* poems; *The Garden,* poems and aphorisms; *The Return,* an epic poem.

SIDELIGHTS: Turner comments that his commitment is "to the essential unity of nature and history; a belief in creative evolution. I oppose the distinction between science and the humanities; I believe that language is coterminous with the world." He adds that major influences have been Shakespeare, Eliot, Yeats, Milton, Nabokov, and Pasternak.

AVOCATIONAL INTERESTS: Travel (Europe, Africa), reading (especially science fiction).

* * *

TURNER, Mary
See LAMBOT, Isobel

* * *

TURNEY, Alfred (Walter) 1916-

PERSONAL: Born August 6, 1916, in Mississippi; son of Alfred Walter (plantation manager and writer) and Hazel Waddell (Brown) Turney; married Sarah Chidester (a high school teacher), 1958; children: Mia. *Education:* University of New Mexico, B.A., 1965, M.A., 1966, Ph.D., 1968; also attended Kansas State University. *Politics:* Democrat. *Religion:* Roman Catholic. *Home:* 1529 Pine Ave., Weatherford, Okla. 73096. *Office:* Department of Social Sciences, Southwestern Oklahoma State University, Weatherford, Okla. 73096.

CAREER: U.S. Army, career officer in Corps of Engineers and Military Intelligence, 1938-63, retiring as lieutenant colonel; Southwestern Oklahoma State University, Weatherford, assistant professor, 1968-70, associate professor, 1970-76, professor of history, 1976—. *Member:* Southern Historical Association. *Awards, honors—*Military: Bronze Star Medal.

WRITINGS: Disaster at Moscow, University of New Mexico Press, 1970.

WORK IN PROGRESS: "Researching material pertaining to a hitherto unknown or rather unheralded phase of World War II."

SIDELIGHTS: Alfred Turney told *CA:* "My book, *Disas-*

ter at Moscow, relates the life of one of Germany's most influential but unheralded generals of World War II, General Fedor von Bock, sometimes called the 'MacArthur of Nazi Germany.' Ranking second in senority behind General von Rundstedt in the German Army, Bock was given command of the Wehrmacht's most powerful Army Group during the conquest of Poland in 1939 and the overrunning of France and Western Europe in 1940. In 1941, he took command of the Central Group of Armies, a huge force of about one and a half million highly trained German soldiers, with the mission of destroying Russia's armies in a devastating attack, striking through Western Russia and capturing Moscow, the citadel of Communism, within a matter of weeks. Because of poor strategic planning, overconfidence, inadequate supplies, Russia's backward road and communications networks, and many other factors, Bock's attack bogged down at the gates of Moscow, weeks, even months behind schedule. By November and December 1941, despite enormous losses, the Russian armies managed to counter-attack Bock's forces, which by now were literally frozen to death in the Russian subzero weather. Having lost over half of his huge army, Bock was forced to retreat from Moscow. Hitler then relieved him of command and himself took over command of the German forces in Russia, ordered them ruthlessly to 'stand and fight' and thereby saved them from total destruction in Russia.

"It is believed Bock was attempting to go into exile somewhere in Scandinavia at the time of his death."

* * *

TUROW, Scott 1949-

PERSONAL: Born April 12, 1949, in Chicago, Ill.; son of David D. (a physician) and Rita (a writer; maiden name, Pastron) Turow; married Annette Weisberg (a teacher), April 4, 1971. *Education:* Amherst College, B.A., 1970; Stanford University, M.A., 1974; Harvard University, J.D., 1978. *Politics:* "Leftish." *Religion:* Jewish. *Home:* 920 Pine Tree Lane, Winnetka, Ill. 60093. *Agent:* Elizabeth McKee, McIntosh, McKee & Dodds, Inc., 22 East 40th St., New York, N.Y. 10016.

CAREER: Stanford University, Stanford, Calif., E. H. Jones Lecturer in Creative Writing, 1972-75; writer, 1975—. *Awards, honors:* Writing award from College English Association and Book-of-the-Month Club, 1970.

WRITINGS: One L: An Inside Account of Life in the First Year at Harvard Law School, Putnam, 1977.

Work anthologized in *Best American Short Stories,* 1971, 1972. Contributor of stories, articles, and reviews to literary journals, including *Transatlantic Review, Ploughshares, Harvard, New England,* and *Place,* and to newspapers.

WORK IN PROGRESS: A novel set in the mid-1960's.

SIDELIGHTS: Turow writes: "I hope to practice law and also to maintain a writing career. I went to law school, after six years of writing seriously, because I realized how difficult a writer's life is at this time—especially a writer of fiction—and also due to a recognition that I had, through lawyer-friends and research related to other writing, become keenly interested in law. The idea for *One L*—a nonfiction description of my experience as a first-year law student—came simply because there seemed to me no adequate description elsewhere of what is usually regarded as the most important formative period in a lawyer's life. In the future, I hope to return to writing fiction."

BIOGRAPHICAL/CRITICAL SOURCES: New York

Times, September 15, 1977; *New York Times Book Review,* September 25, 1977; *Washington Post,* October 2, 1977; *Newsweek,* October 17, 1977.

* * *

TUSKA, Jon 1942-

PERSONAL: Born April 30, 1942, in Milwaukee, Wis.; son of Andrew and Florence Tuska. *Education:* Marquette University, B.A., 1966. *Residence:* Los Angeles, Calif. *Agent:* #203, 4555 Fulton Ave., Sherman Oaks, Calif. 91423.

CAREER: Views and Reviews, Milwaukee, Wis., founder and executive editor, 1969-75; writer and film producer, 1969—. Producer of "They Went Thataway" (series) for Public Broadcasting Service, 1969-71.

WRITINGS: The Films of Mae West, Citadel, 1973; *The Filming of the West,* Doubleday, 1976; (editor) *Close-Up: The Contract Director,* Scarecrow, 1976; *The Detective in Hollywood,* Doubleday, 1978, (editor) *Close-Up: The Hollywood Director,* Scarecrow, 1978.

WORK IN PROGRESS: Editing *Close-Up: The Contemporary Director,* publication by Scarecrow expected in 1979; *The Millionaire Cowboy,* a novel set in Hollywood; *Adrian Among the Fleshpeddlers,* a novel dealing with American life from 1965-75.

SIDELIGHTS: Tuska writes: "My work in the area of cinema history led me to found *Views and Reviews* and to publish several books in the field. It was my feeling that while first-hand accounts of people and events were still available, they should be recorded. I found that the majority of books purporting to be cinema history were considerably less than that and so I sought to write histories, or memoirs, of specific genres of film, such as westerns or detective films, calling upon my acquaintance with persons intimately involved in the production of such films.

"The 'Close-Up on the Cinema' series was an attempt to present factually accurate portraits of some thirty directors important in the history and development of the art of the motion picture.

"Because there is no form of communication in the modern world as powerful and as pervasive as the motion picture, a secondary theme, beyond memoirs, is to elucidate and portray the myths and popular, if unfounded, notions such films have infused into the collective consciousness of viewers over the years.

"For me a man's philosophy is not what he writes nor what he says, so much as it is how he has lived. In every portrait I have written, be it biography or fiction, I have concentrated on the individual human being and made, I hope, only one assumption: that a man's old age, and a woman's (provided they have one), is their judge."

AVOCATIONAL INTERESTS: Reading, world travel, classical music, sunlight, fresh air, vitamins, desert air.

BIOGRAPHICAL/CRITICAL SOURCES: Hollywood Reporter, March 19, 1976; *Screen Actor,* April-May, 1976.

* * *

TYLER, Elias S. 1904(?)-1977

1904(?)—September 24, 1977; American educator and author. Tyler was best known for helping underprivileged students obtain business jobs with futures. He died in Long Island, N.Y. Obituaries: *New York Times,* September 25, 1977.

ULLYOT, Joan 1940-

PERSONAL: Born July 1, 1940, in Chicago, Ill.; daughter of Theodore Warren (an architect) and Deborah (Bent) Lamb; married Daniel J. Ullyot (a physician), August 31, 1965 (divorced, 1977). *Education:* Wellesley College, A.B. (honors), 1961; Harvard University, M.D., 1966; postdoctoral study at University of Aberdeen, 1966-67; also attended Free University of Berlin, 1959-60. *Residence:* San Francisco, Calif. *Office:* Division of Aerobics and Physiology, Institute of Health Research, P.O. Box 7999, San Francisco, Calif. 94121.

CAREER: Beth Israel Hospital, Boston, Mass., intern in pathology, 1967-68; University of California, Medical Center, San Francisco, conducted research in electron microscopy, 1969-72; Institutes of Medical Sciences, Institute of Health Research, San Francisco, Calif., director of Division of Aerobics and Physiology, 1972—. Staff member of High Altitude Running Camp in Colorado, 1973-77, and California, 1977; staff member of Sports Clinic at California Surgery Center. Physical fitness adviser to San Francisco Fire Department. Has lectured extensively in the United States and Europe. Long-distance runner and marathoner; member of U.S. National Women's Marathon Team, 1974, 1976; member of Women's National Amateur Athletic Union Long Distance Running Committee; member of West Valley Track Club. *Member:* Phi Beta Kappa. *Awards, honors:* National Institutes of Health special fellowship, 1969-72; RRCA Award for Journalistic Excellence, 1976; Stephen Royce, M.D. award of the American Medical Joggers Association, 1976.

WRITINGS: Women's Running, World Publications, 1976. Contributor to medical journals, *Runner's World,* and other periodicals.

WORK IN PROGRESS: A sequel to *Women's Running.*

SIDELIGHTS: Joan Ullyot writes: "As a woman doctor, who specializes in sports medicine and is also a world-class marathon runner, I have found myself in a unique position as an authority on running and exercise for women. Yet I also feel that I can speak for the average woman, since I only took up my hobby of running at age thirty-one, after a distinctly non-athletic upbringing. I speak German and French and have been able to travel to international sporting events and participate in encouraging women's athletics abroad as well as in the United States."

BIOGRAPHICAL/CRITICAL SOURCES: Runner's World, June, 1976; *Woman Sports,* July, 1977.

* * *

UNDERHILL, Charles
See HILL, Reginald (Charles)

* * *

UNTERMEYER, Louis 1885-1977

October 1, 1885—December 19, 1977; American anthologist, critic, lecturer, poet, and biographer. Untermeyer has been described as being "this century's most notable friend and popularizer of British and American poets and poetry." During his career he edited and compiled more than one hundred books, including such standards as *Modern American Poets* and *Modern British Poetry.* He was poetry consultant to the Library of Congress for two years. He died in Newton, Conn. Obituaries: *New York Times,* December 20, 1977; *Washington Post,* December 20, 1977; *Detroit Free Press,* December 20, 1977; *Time,* January 2, 1978; *Newsweek,* January 2, 1978. (See index for *CA* sketch)

UPTON, Robert

PERSONAL: Born in Chicago, Ill.; married wife, Patricia; children: Kathleen, Jeffrey. *Education:* Attended Florida State University, Northwestern University, Yale University, and University of San Francisco. *Home:* 419 West 22nd St., New York, N.Y. 10011.

CAREER: Novelist and author of screenplays and musicals. *Military service:* U.S. Army.

WRITINGS: Who'd Want to Kill Old George?, Putnam, 1977. Also author of plays, screenplays, and musicals.

WORK IN PROGRESS: Fleece, a novel on international high finance; "Sink the Bank," a screenplay.

* * *

VALENTI, Jack 1921-

PERSONAL: Born September 5, 1921, in Houston, Tex.; married Mary Margaret Wiley, June 1, 1962; children: Courtenay, John, Alexandra. *Education:* University of Houston, B.A., 1946; Harvard University, M.B.A., 1948. *Politics:* Democrat. *Religion:* Roman Catholic. *Agent:* Irving Lazar, Irving Paul Lazar Agency, 211 South Beverly Dr., Beverly Hills, Calif. 90212. *Office:* Motion Picture Association of America, 1600 Eye St. N.W., Washington, D.C. 20006.

CAREER: Weekley & Valenti (advertising agency), Houston, Tex., co-founder and executive vice-president, 1942-63; special assistant to U.S. President in Washington, D.C., 1963-66; Motion Picture Association of America, Washington, D.C., president, 1966—. Member of board of directors of TransWorld Airlines, Kennedy Center, American Film Institute, and *Washington Star. Military service:* U.S. Army Air Forces, 1942-45; served in Italy; received Distinguished Flying Cross, Air Medal with five clusters, Distinguished Unit Citation with one cluster, and three battle stars.

WRITINGS: The Bitter Taste of Glory (nonfiction), World Publishing, 1971; *A Very Human President* (on Lyndon Baines Johnson), Norton, 1976. Contributor to popular magazines, including *Saturday Review, Atlantic Monthly, Reader's Digest, Redbook,* and *Ladies Home Journal,* and to major newspapers.

WORK IN PROGRESS: A novel about Washington, D.C.; a short book on political power.

* * *

VANDENBURG, Mary Lou 1943-

PERSONAL: Born December 18, 1943, in Passaic, N.J.; daughter of Nicholas (an industrial electrician) and Louise (a bookkeeper; maiden name, Rosiello) Yacono; married James Joseph Vandenburg, Jr. (a pharmacist), July 2, 1966; children: James Joseph III. *Education:* William Paterson College of New Jersey, B.A. (magna cum laude), 1965; graduate study at New School for Social Research, 1976-77. *Politics:* "Radical for Capitalism." *Religion:* Atheist. *Home:* 125 Sixth Ave., Apt. 5, Clifton, N.J. 07011.

CAREER: Elementary school teacher in Clifton, N.J., 1965-66, and Glen Rock, N.J., 1966-67; tutor, 1968-75; Hawthorne Public Schools, Hawthorne, N.J., teacher, 1975—. Lecturer on child development, 1969—; volunteer worker with children, including the handicapped. *Member:* Kappa Delta Pi. *Awards, honors:* Honor certificate from Freedoms Foundation, 1972, for essay "Fostering Patriotism in the Home."

WRITINGS: Help!: Emergencies That Could Happen to

You and How to Handle Them (juvenile), Lerner, 1975. Contributor to *Massachusetts Teacher* and *Integrity*.

WORK IN PROGRESS: Fostering Child Development, with accompanying children's series; *Forbidden Fruit.*

SIDELIGHTS: Mary Lou Vandenburg writes: "As a youngster and young adult I was fascinated with nature, human beings, and the creations of man, particularly works of art which integrated truth and beauty. Most inspiring were those art works that concretely displayed the greatness possible to man.

"I have always been involved in a dedicated search to discover the truth and to use these ideas to enlighten myself, enrich my life and to explore my potential. Writing, lecturing, and teaching were the end products of my attempts to utilize my knowledge and experiences concretely.

"While doing volunteer work in Ica, Peru, I met a fellow American who was stranded three days in the Andes. Realizing how important it is to train children for any emergencies they might encounter, I wrote the book *Help!,* for my son and other children, so they could learn to develop self-reliance early in their lives.

"My most enjoyable project so far was writing *Forbidden Fruit*—a fiction story that draws upon my personal experiences and struggles to become enlightened. It is set in the contemporary American battlefield of mysticism versus rationality. The characters and events show these two alternatives, the ultimate consequences of each course of life, and the role of art to enlighten any person determined to discover and utilize the truth to develop personal greatness. This book is a tribute to all those creators who have lived and selected the course of rational self-development, for in that process and as a result of their lives, their innovative creations, and their individual greatness, they have also enlightened the minds and elevated the lives of others."

AVOCATIONAL INTERESTS: Tae Kwon Do (first degree black belt), participated in local theater productions.

* * *

VAN der VELDT, James   1893(?)-1977

1893(?)—August 18, 1977; Dutch-born American Franciscan priest, educator, and author. Van der Veldt had been associated with the psychology faculty of Catholic University since 1945. He died in Washington, D.C. Obituaries: *Washington Post,* August 20, 1977.

* * *

VANDERWERTH, W(illiam) C(onnor)   1904-

PERSONAL: Born October 9, 1904, in Lexington, Tex.; son of Fritz and Bettie (Seattler) Vanderwerth; married Leona Stallings, September 14, 1922 (died May 13, 1973); children: Lila (Mrs. G. A. Fiebig), Billie Ruth (Mrs. Virgil L. Seale; deceased). *Education:* Attended University of Oklahoma. *Religion:* Methodist. *Home:* 930 South Miller, Norman, Okla. 73069.

CAREER: Childress Post, Childress, Tex., shop foreman, 1925-28; *Waco News-Tribune,* Waco, Tex., linotype operator, 1928-30; *Corsicana Sun,* Corsicana, Tex., linotype operator, 1930-32; *Bryan Eagle,* Bryan, Tex., linotype operator and commercial printing supervisor, 1932-45; University of Oklahoma, Norman, superintendent of Journalism Press, 1945-71; writer, 1972—. Correspondent, *Fort Worth Star-Telegram, Wichita Falls Record-News, The Times, Amarillo Globe-Times,* and *The News,* 1925-28; volunteer worker, Norman Municipal Hospital.

WRITINGS: Indian Oratory, University of Oklahoma Press, 1971, 2nd edition, 1972. Contributor of articles and photographs on a wide variety of subjects, including graphic arts, horticulture, and western and Indian history, to magazines.

WORK IN PROGRESS: Gathering material on Indian views of religion, on the Indian as an ally of the white frontier army and the army in its foreign conflicts, and on views of the Indian and "what has been regarded as his liquor 'problem.'"

SIDELIGHTS: Vanderwerth told *CA:* "My interest in Indian affairs was whetted by treaty procedures and negotiations, which were widely written of but invariably gave sketchy accounts of what the Indians said. However, extensive coverage was given to the palavering of the whites. I found that a great number of the Indian speeches had been recorded, so I was able to read the complete orations and not just the excerpts. I felt that this would make very interesting reading and be valuable historical data. I regret that more of these articulate Indians could not have been quoted in my book. All the speeches presented were actually word-of-mouth orations, not written by someone and presented by other persons.

"The American Indian had definite religious concepts long before that famous '1492,' and probably a tremendous mistake was made in the whites trying to ram their brand of religion down the throats of the Indians. The settlers could not understand the Indian religion, and by the same token, the Indians could not understand the religious aims of the whites. Result: conflict. The whites destroyed the Red religion; the Indians never fully accepted the religion of the whites.

"The problems liquor created for the Indians have been long discussed, but the greatest problem was that the dealers in the rot-gut pushed their 'poison' onto the Indians, much as dope peddlers are pushing their wares today. This problem still faces many Indians, but it is not certain, as some observers believe, that Indians cannot resist liquor. This may be a touchy subject, but I feel it is worthy of much study. It is tied up with social and economic conditions."

AVOCATIONAL INTERESTS: Refinishing antique furniture, photography, doing needlepoint and petit point, gardening.

* * *

VAN GELDER, Richard George   1928-

PERSONAL: Born December 17, 1928, in New York, N.Y.; son of Joseph and Clara DeHirsch (Goldberg) Van Gelder; married second wife, Rosalind Rudnick, July 1, 1962; children: Russell Neil, Gordon Mark, Leslie Gail. *Education:* Colorado A & M College, B.S. (with honors), 1950; University of Illinois, M.S., 1952, Ph.D., 1958. *Office address:* American Museum of Natural History, New York, N.Y. 10024.

CAREER: University of Kansas, Lawrence, research assistant, 1954-55, assistant professor, 1955; American Museum of Natural History, New York City, assistant curator, 1956-61, associate curator, 1961-69, curator, 1969—, acting chairperson of department of mammals, 1958-59, chairperson of department, 1959—. Professorial lecturer, Downstate Medical Center, State University of New York, 1970-73; Columbia University, lecturer, 1958-59, assistant professor, 1959-63. Member of board of directors, Archbold Expeditions, 1965—; member of advisory board, Archbold Biological Station; member of technical and editorial advisory board, Population Reference Bureau, 1971—; member of science advisory board, Foundation for Environmental Education, 1972. Participant in Huachuca Mountain Expedition, 1950, Graham Mountain Expedition, 1951, Spotted Skunk Expedition, 1953-54, Puritan Expedition, 1957, Uruguay Expedition, 1962-63, Bolivian Expedition, 1964, Bolivian Expedition II, 1965, Bahama Biological Survey, 1966, Mozambique Expedition, 1968, South West Africa Expedition, 1970, Nyala Expedition, 1971-73.

MEMBER: New York Zoological Society (fellow), American Society of Mammalogists (president, 1968-70), Society of Systematic Zoology, American Academy of Arts and Sciences, Wildlife Society, Sigma Xi, Beta Beta Beta, Phi Sigma, Alpha Gamma Rho.

WRITINGS: (With Henrietta Bancroft) *Animals in Winter,* Crowell, 1963; (editor with William V. Mayer) *Physiological Mammalogy,* Academic Press, 1963; *Biology of Mammals,* Scribner, 1969; *Animals & Man: Past, Present, Future,* Foundation for Environmental Education, 1972.

Juvenile literature; all illustrated: *The Professor and the Mysterious Box,* Harvey House, 1964; *The Professor and the Vanishing Flags,* Harvey House, 1965; *Bats,* Follett, 1967; *Monkeys and Apes,* Follett, 1970.

Author of scholarly reports for the American Museum of Natural History. Member of science advisory board, *Natural History Magazine,* 1958-66 and 1972-73.*

* * *

VAN RENSSELAER, Alexander (Taylor Mason) 1892-1962

CAREER: Editorial writer for several New York newspapers, including the *Sun* and the *Telegram;* joined the publishing firm of Henry Holt & Co. as advertising manager after World War I; later served in the same capacity at Duffield & Co., Century, and Appleton-Century. *Military service:* U.S. Army, World War I.

WRITINGS: (With Frank Butcher) *Yule Light: A Christmas Pageant,* Century, 1930; *Betcha Can't Do It!,* Appleton-Century, 1940; *Try This One!* (illustrated by George Anrig), Appleton-Century, 1941; *Fun with Stunts* (contains *Betcha Can't Do It!* and *Try This One!*), Blackiston, 1945; *The Complete Book of Party Games* (illustrated by M. B. Thompson), Sheridan, 1952, published as *Party Fun and Games,* Fawcett, 1962; *Magic: A Family Activity Book* (illustrated by John N. Barron), Knopf, 1952; *Fun with Ventriloquism* (illustrated by J. N. Barron), Garden City Publishing, 1955; *Fun with Magic* (illustrated by J. N. Barron), Garden City Publishing, 1957; *The Picture History of America* (illustrated by Raymond Lufkin), Doubleday, 1961; *Your Book of Magic* (illustrated by J. N. Barron), Faber, 1966, Transatlantic, 1968. Contributor to *Bookman, St. Nicholas,* and other periodicals.

SIDELIGHTS: Van Rensselaer's study of palmistry, mind reading, and ventriloquism was the outcome of his lifelong dream to be a professional magician. Many of the author's books reflected his interest in the area of illusions and tricks. Van Rensselaer's book, *Betcha Can't Do It!,* contains more than one hundred stunts and practical jokes. A critic for *Books* commented: "Alexander Van Rensselaer is a student of stunts—with coins, matches, milk bottles, brooms, cards, and bewildered witnesses."

BIOGRAPHICAL/CRITICAL SOURCES: Books, October 6, 1940.

OBITUARIES: New York Times, August 22, 1962; *Publishers Weekly,* September 10, 1962.*

(Died August 20, 1962)

* * *

VARGAS LLOSA, (Jorge) Mario (Pedro)   1936-

PERSONAL: Born March 28, 1936, in Arequipa, Peru; son of Ernesto Vargas Maldonaldo and Dora Llosa Ureta; married Julia Urquidi in 1955 (divorced); married Patricia Llosa; children: (second marriage) Gonzalo, Alvaro, Morgana. *Education:* Attended University of San Marcos; University of Madrid, Ph.D., 1959. *Politics:* Democratic Socialist.

CAREER: Employed as a journalist for *La Industria,* Piura, Peru, and La Radio Panamericana and *La Cronica,* both in Lima, Peru; during 1960's, worked in Paris, France, as a journalist with Agence France-Presse, as a broadcaster for the radio-TV network URTF, and as a language teacher; University of London, London, England, faculty member of Queen Mary College and Kings College, 1966-68; University of Washington, Seattle, writer-in-residence, 1968; University of Puerto Rico, Rio Piedras, visiting professor, 1969; *Libre,* Paris, co-founder, 1971; Columbia University, New York, N.Y., Edward Laroque Visiting Professor, 1975. Writer. *Awards, honors:* Premio Leopoldo Alas, 1959, for *Los jefes;* Prix Biblioteca Breve, 1962; Premio Internacionalde Literatura Romulo Gallegos, 1962, for *La casa verde;* Premio de la Critica, 1963, for *La ciudad y los perros;* Premio de la Critica, 1967, for *La casa verde;* Premio Nacional de la novela, 1967, for *La casa verde.*

WRITINGS: Los jefes, Editorial Rocas, 1959; *La ciudad y los perros,* Seix Barral, 1963, translation by Lysander Kemp published as *The Time of the Hero,* Grove, 1966; *La casa verde,* Seix Barral, 1966, translation by Gregory Rabassa published as *The Green House,* Harper, 1968; *Los cachorros,* Editorial Lumen, 1967; *La novela,* Fundacion de Cultura Universitaria, 1968; *Conversacion en la catedral,* Seix Barral, 1969, translation by Rabassa published as *Conversation in the Cathedral,* Harper, 1975; *Lletra de batalla per "Tirant lo Blanc,"* Edicions 62, 1969; *Antologia minima de M. Vargas Llosa,* Editorial Tiempo Contemporaneo, 1969; *En la revolucion en la literatura,* Veintiuno Editores, 1970; *Dia domingo,* Ediciones Amadis, 1971; *Garcia Marquez: Historia de un deicidio,* Barral Editores, 1971; *La historia secreta de una novela,* Tusquets, 1971; *Obras escogidas,* Aguilar, 1973; *Pantaleon y las visitadoras,* Editorial Seix Barral, 1973; *La novela,* America Nueva, 1974; *La orgia perpetua: Flaubert y "Madame Bovary,"* Taurus, 1975.

Contributor to *Casa de las Americas, Primera plana, Expresso,* and *Libre.*

SIDELIGHTS: Vargas Llosa has commented: "Novelists who speak well of their country should be distrusted: patriotism, which is a fruitful virtue in soldiers and in bureaucrats, is usually a poor one in literature. Literature in general and the novel in particular are expressions of discontent. Their social usefulness lies principally in the fact that they remind people that the world is *always* wrong, that life should *always* change."

"One of the most eloquent and conspicuous features of Vargas Llosa's work," according to D. P. Gallagher, "has been his endeavor to evolve the right structure to express this chaos, and he therefore places his reader in a structural labyrinth in his novels that functions as the equivalent of the political, social, and emotional labyrinths his characters inhabit."

Suzanne Jill Levine wrote that Vargas Llosa's books "reflect a world in decay, contaminated by the exploitation of the Indian and the worker, a world victimized by foreign imperialism and by the native bourgeoisie's complicity in this exploitation." His book *Conversation in the Cathedral,* "reveals, as few others have, some of the ugly complexities of the real Latin America," according to Levine.

Vargas Llosa's book *La ciudad y los perros* has been translated into more than twelve languages.

AVOCATIONAL INTERESTS: Tennis, gymnastics, water-skiing, and going to the movies.

BIOGRAPHICAL/CRITICAL SOURCES: D. P. Gallagher, *Modern Latin American Literature,* Oxford University Press, 1973; *New York Review of Books,* March 20, 1975; *New York Times Book Review,* March 23, 1975; *Contemporary Literary Criticism,* Gale, Volume 3, 1975, Volume 6, 1976.*

* * *

VASVARY, Edmund 1888-1977

1888—July 12, 1977; Hungarian-born minister, historian, and author. Vasvary pastored several Hungarian Reformed churches in the United States before becoming comptroller of the Hungarian Reformed Federation of America in Washington, D.C. He was recognized as an authority on the history of Hungarian immigration to the United States. He died in Washington, D.C. Obituaries: *New York Times,* July 17, 1977; *Washington Post,* July 19, 1977.

* * *

VAUGHN, William Preston 1933-

PERSONAL: Born May 28, 1933, in Whiting, Ind.; son of James Carl (a filtration engineer) and Georgiana (Preston) Vaughn; married Virginia Meyer (a mathematics teacher), June 10, 1961; children: Rhonda. *Education:* University of Missouri, A.B., 1955; Ohio State University, M.A., 1956, Ph.D., 1961. *Politics:* Republican. *Religion:* Episcopalian. *Home:* 908 Hilton Pl., Denton, Tex. 76201. *Office:* Department of History, North Texas State University, Denton, Tex. 76203.

CAREER: University of Southern California, Los Angeles, instructor in history, 1961-62; North Texas State University, Denton, assistant professor, 1962-65, associate professor, 1965-69, professor of history, 1969—. *Military service:* U.S. Army Reserve, 1955-63, active duty, 1957; became captain. *Member:* American Historical Association, Organization of American Historians, Southern Historical Association (life member), Texas Lodge of Research (Masons), Texas Association of College Teachers, Phi Beta Kappa, Phi Alpha Theta, Lions. *Awards, honors:* Manuscript award from Phi Alpha Theta, 1972 for *Schools for All.*

WRITINGS: Schools for All: The Blacks and Public Education in the South, University Press of Kentucky, 1974. Contributor to history and social science journals.

WORK IN PROGRESS: The Inflexible Minority, a history of the Antimasonic Party, 1827-43.

SIDELIGHTS: Vaughn writes: "I am active in numerous Masonic organizations—this motivated my interest in political Antimasonry as a subject for historical research." *Avocational interests:* Travel (especially Mexico and Great Britain).

VAYHINGER, John Monroe 1916-

PERSONAL: Born January 27, 1916, in Upland, Ind.; son of Paul Johnson and Hariett Estelle (Palmer) Vayhinger; married Ruth Catherine Imler, September 19, 1939; children: John Earl, Karen Lynn Vayhinger Kuper. *Education:* Taylor University, A.B., 1937; Drew Theological Seminary, B.D. (cum laude), 1940, M.A., 1951; Columbia University, M.A., 1948, Ph.D., 1956; also attended Asbury Theological Seminary, 1937-39, and Butler University, 1939. *Politics:* Republican. *Home:* 1235 Favorite St., Anderson, Ind. 46013. *Office:* Anderson School of Theology, 1123 East Third St., Anderson, Ind. 46011.

CAREER: Licensed clinical psychologist in Indiana, Colorado, and Illinois; ordained United Methodist minister, 1941; pastor of Methodist churches in Indiana, New York, Connecticut, and Colorado, 1938-68; private practice of psycho-therapy, 1958—; Anderson School of Theology, Anderson, Ind., professor of psychology, pastoral counseling, and pastoral care, 1968—. Diplomate of American Board of Professional Psychology and American Association of Pastoral Counselors. Instructor at Drew Theological Seminary, 1948-49; associate professor and head of department at West Virginia Wesleyan College, 1949-51; lecturer at Indiana University (South Bend), 1953-58, and University of Colorado, 1967-68; professor at Garrett Theological Seminary, 1958-64, University of Denver, 1964-67, and Oberlin School of Theology, summers, 1959-61. Chief clinical psychologist at St. Joseph County Adult and Child Guidance Clinic, 1951-58; clinical psychologist at Moffat-Routt Mental Health Center, 1967-68. Regional vice-chairman of World Methodist Family Life Committee; member of International Council of Psychologists and Indiana Conference on Social Welfare; member of advisory council of central Indiana Mental Health Systems; member of Menninger Foundation; chairman of department of institutional ministries of Indiana Council of Churches, 1970—. *Military service:* U.S. Army, 1944-47; served in Pacific theater; became captain.

MEMBER: International Association of Group Psychotherapy, American Psychological Association, American Orthopsychiatric Association (fellow), American Association of Marriage and Family Counselors (clinical member), American Group Psychotherapy Association, Society for Projective Techniques and the Rorschach Institute, National Council on Family Relations, American Association of Pastoral Counselors, Association for Clinical Pastoral Education, Society for the Scientific Study of Religion, Religious Research Association, American Scientific Association (fellow), Christian Association for Psychological Studies, American Association of Sex Educators, Counselors and Therapists, Association of Military Chaplains of the United States, American Society of Psychologists in Private Practice (chairman of committee on professional standards and ethics, 1970—), American Association of University Professors, National Congress of Parents and Teachers (life member), American Association of Retired Persons, Academy of Religion and Mental Health (charter life member), Cousteau Society, Smithsonian Associates, Defenders of Wildlife, American Forestry Association, American Museum of Natural History (associate member), National Wildlife Association, National Audubon Society, Tristate Group Psychotherapy Society, Mid-Western Psychological Association, Indiana Psychological Association, Colorado Psychological Association, Indiana Council on Family Relations, Indiana Correctional Association, Indiana Chaplains Association, Indiana Conference on Social Welfare, Indiana Congress of Parents and Teachers (life member), Madison

County Association for Mental Health (member of board of directors). *Awards, honors:* Grants from Lilly Endowment, 1958-66, and National Institute of Mental Health, 1962-64.

WRITINGS: (With Newman Cryer) *Casebook in Pastoral Counseling,* Abingdon, 1962; *A Psychological Study of Theological Students,* Garrett Theological Seminary, 1964; (contributor) *Counseling,* Baker Book, 1967; (contributor) *Christianity and the World of Thought,* Moody, 1968; *Before Divorce,* Fortress, 1972; *The Single Parent Family,* United Methodist Church, 1972; (contributor) *Direct Psychotherapy: Twenty-Eight Original Americans,* University of Miami Press, 1973; (contributor) *Religious Systems and Psychotherapy,* C. C Thomas, 1973; (contributor) *Sermons from Hell,* Bethany Press, 1975. Contributor to *Baker's Dictionary of Practical Theology.* Contributor of more than twenty articles to religious and scientific journals.

WORK IN PROGRESS: Structure and Dynamics of Pastoral Counseling (tentative title), a textbook; *Moods of Life,* a inspirational book, with Edward Blair.

SIDELIGHTS: Vayhinger writes: "I am involved in many practicums in a state reformatory, a state mental hospital, a community medical hospital, and a health care center for the aging. I spend many weekends in marriage enrichment seminars, family life workshops, and professional enrichment workshops in psychology and theology."

* * *

VERHONICK, Phillis J. 1922(?)-1977

1922(?)—October 1, 1977; American nurse, educator, and author. Her professional positions included research and teaching with the Pan American Health Organization in Latin America and the Caribbean, chief of the nursing department at Walter Reed Army Institute of Research, and professor of clinical nursing at University of Virginia. She died in Charlottesville, Va. Obituaries: *Washington Post,* October 8, 1977.

* * *

VERNY, Tom 1936-

PERSONAL: Born January 26, 1936, in Czechoslovakia; son of Eugene (a lawyer) and Trudy Verny; married Roslyn (Hoffer), August 5, 1961 (divorced, 1978); children: Newton, Louis. *Education:* University of Toronto, M.D., 1961, D.Psych., 1964; Harvard University, postdoctoral study, 1965-66. *Office:* Centre for Holistic Primal Therapy, 93 Harbord St., Toronto, Ontario, Canada M5S 1G4.

CAREER: St. Michael's Hospital, Toronto, Ontario, intern, 1961-62; Clarke Institute, Toronto, clinical instructor, 1966-67; Centre for Holistic Primal Therapy, Toronto, psychiatrist in private practice, 1967—. Instructor at York University. *Member:* Royal College of Physicians (fellow), Canadian Psychiatric Association, Canadian Medical Association, Association for Humanistic Psychology, American Psychiatric Association, Ontario Psychiatric Association, Ontario Medical Association. *Awards, honors:* Eli Lilly international fellowship, 1965.

WRITINGS: Inside Groups, McGraw, 1974; *The Disconnected Self* (on holistic primal therapy), St. Martin's, 1978.

WORK IN PROGRESS: A book on the psychic life of the unborn dealing with tracing memories to conception.

SIDELIGHTS: Verny's first book has been translated into Dutch and Swedish.

VER STEEG, Clarence L(ester) 1922-

PERSONAL: Born December 28, 1922, in Orange City, Iowa; son of John A. and Annie (Vischer) Ver Steeg; married Dorothy Ann De Vries, December 24, 1943; children: John Charles. *Education:* Morningside College, A.B., 1943; Columbia University, M.A., 1946, Ph.D., 1950. *Religion:* Presbyterian. *Home:* 2619 Ridge Ave., Evanston, Ill. 60201. *Office:* Graduate School, Northwestern University, Evanston, Ill. 60201.

CAREER: Columbia University, New York, N.Y., lecturer, 1946-48, instructor in history, 1949-50; Northwestern University, Evanston, Ill., instructor, 1950-52, assistant professor, 1952-55, associate professor, 1955-59, professor of history, 1959—, dean of Graduate School, 1975—. Visiting lecturer at Harvard University, 1959-60; visiting member of Princeton University's Institute of Advanced Study, 1967-68. Member of council of Institute of Early American History and Culture, 1961-64, 1971—, chairman of council, 1970-71. *Military service:* U.S. Army Air Forces, 1942-45; received Air Medal with three oak leaf clusters.

MEMBER: American Historical Association, Organization of American Historians, American Association of University Professors, Southern Historical Association. *Awards, honors:* Albert J. Beveridge Prize from American Historical Association, 1952; George A. and Eliza Gardner Howard Foundation fellowship, 1954-55; Huntington Library fellow, 1955; American Council of Learned Societies senior fellow, 1958-59; Guggenheim fellow, 1964-65.

WRITINGS: Robert Morris: Revolutionary Financier, University of Pennsylvania Press, 1954; *Tailfer's A True and Narrative History of Georgia,* University of Georgia Press, 1960; *The American People: Their History,* Harper, 1961; *The Formative Years, 1607-1763,* Hill & Wang, 1964; *The Story of Our Country,* Harper, 1965; (editor with Richard Hofstadter) *Great Issues in American History: From Settlement to Revolution, 1584-1776,* Random House, 1969; (with John Lee and Clyde Kohn) *Investigating Man's World,* six volumes, Scott, Foresman, 1970; (with Hofstadter) *A People and a Nation,* Harper, 1971; *The Origins of a Southern Mosaic: Studies in the Early Carolinas and Georgia,* University of Georgia Press, 1975; *World Cultures,* Scott, Foresman, 1976. Member of editorial board of *Journal of American History,* 1968—.

WORK IN PROGRESS: Bibliography in Eighteenth Century Southern Colonies; Studies in Eighteenth Century Southern Colonies; An Experimenting Society: The U.S. 1607-1977.

SIDELIGHTS: Ver Steeg told *CA:* "My writings have varied from the highly specialized monographs to textbooks for fifth graders. In each instance my goal has been to enable the reader to understand the subject in terms of his/her educational level and social experience. It is the only way history transcends rote learning or patriotic exhortation. History as taught is often too important for the young because their experience is too limited to invest the subject with their own feeling and understanding. Studies in perception and learning should be made using history as a subject field. I believe in synthesis and prudent interpretation."

* * *

VINTON, Eleanor W(inthrop) 1899-1977

July 25, 1899—September 12, 1977; American poet and writer. Obituaries: *AB Bookman's Weekly,* November 21, 1977. (See index for *CA* sketch)

VINTON, John 1937-

PERSONAL: Born January 24, 1937, in Cleveland, Ohio. *Education:* Attended Ohio State University, 1954-58, New York University, 1958-63, and University of Southern California, 1965-66. *Home:* 167 Hicks St., Brooklyn, N.Y. 11201.

CAREER: Bela Bartok Archives, New York, N.Y., editorial and research assistant, 1962-65; *Washington Evening Star,* Washington, D.C., assistant music critic, 1966-67; Dance Theater Workshop, New York City, general manager, 1971-73; volunteer cataloger for New York Public Library and Dance Notation Bureau, New York City, both 1973-74; "The Yard" (arts colony), Martha's Vineyard, Mass., administrative coordinator, 1974; typesetter, 1975—. *Awards, honors:* Fellowships from Martha Baird Rockefeller Fund for Music, 1970, Mary Duke Biddle Foundation, 1970, 1971, and Ford Foundation, 1971.

WRITINGS: (Editor) *Dictionary of Contemporary Music,* Dutton, 1974; *Essays After a Dictionary: Music and Culture at the Close of Western Civilization,* Bucknell University Press, 1977. Contributor to music journals in the United States, Portugal, Mexico, England, Poland, Sweden, and Hungary. Co-editor of *International Inventory of Musical Sources,* 1963-65.

WORK IN PROGRESS: Storytelling, specializing in traditional myths and legends of contemporary society.

SIDELIGHTS: Vinton writes: "Having confined myself in previous years to a restricted readership, I am in 1977 working to reach a broader public. I feel that books are no longer a vital means of communication (with a few exceptions, such as reference books) and that live public contact, films, and television are the ways to make effective communications. In my new career as a storyteller I am attempting to identify the 'traditional' sources of contemporary entertainment and wisdom—the sources that reflect and shape contemporary values. I have completed full-evening adaptations of Bram Stoker's 'Dracula,' Mark Twain's 'Huckleberry Finn,' and Rudyard Kipling's 'The Jungle Books,' and I am working now on other familiar stories." He has already given public readings of these, on Bartok, and from his own work, including a seven hour presentation of "Diary of Light."

*   *   *

VIOLETT, Ellen 1925-

PERSONAL: Born April 7, 1925, in New York, N.Y.; daughter of Atwood (an insurance broker) and Ellen (McCarter) Violett. *Education:* Barnard College, A.B., 1964. *Residence:* New York, N.Y. *Office:* c/o Writers Guild of America, 22 West 48th St., New York, N.Y. 10036.

CAREER: Worked in editorial departments of *Harper's Bazaar, Hudson Review,* and *Theatre Arts Magazine,* 1947-51; writer for television, 1950—. Playwright for Touring Players Company, 1951-55. *Member:* Writers Guild. *Awards, honors:* Christopher Award, 1950, for "The Lottery."

WRITINGS—Theatre: "The Delicate Ape," first produced in New York City at Fordham University Theatre, 1949; "Copper and Brass," first produced on Broadway at Martin Beck Theatre, October 17, 1957; "Color of Darkness," first produced in New York City at Writer's Stage, 1963.

Television: Author of original scripts and adapter of literary works for series including "Starlight Theatre," "Prudential On Stage," "Cameo Theatre," "Omnibus," "Suspense," "Elgin Hour," "G.E. Theatre," "Producers Showcase," "U.S. Steel Hour," and "CBS Playhouse." Contributor of scripts including "Rebecca," "Go Ask Alice," "The Skin of Our Teeth," "Dear Brutus," and "The Experiment."

SIDELIGHTS: "The main problem of the adaptor," Violett told John Crosby, "is to preserve the original quality of the work. To be an adaptor you need an ear. You find you get so you can write like almost anybody you're adapting. I love words.

"That is why I think good things which have been previously done should be done again and again. I don't object to adaptations when the property is good. An adapter is like an actor—he or she should try to preserve someone else's work and come forward as a person."

*   *   *

VOIGT, William, Jr. 1902-

PERSONAL: Born October 13, 1902, in Atlanta, Ga.; son of William and Cecilia (Volberg) Voigt; married Mary Walker, February 17, 1933 (died, 1947); married Billie Burke Booth (an artist and craftswoman), July 3, 1948. *Education:* Georgia School of Technology (now Georgia Institute of Technology), student, 1920-21. *Politics:* "Independent as can be!" *Religion:* "protestant (lower case)." *Home and office:* Rockin' Cheer Farm, Route 3, Box 3557, Blackshear, Ga. 31516.

CAREER: Blackshear Times, Blackshear, Ga., editor, 1925; *Albany Herald,* Albany, Ga., city editor, 1925-26; *Savannah Morning News,* Savannah, Ga., reporter, 1926-27; reporter and makeup editor for *Atlanta Georgian* and *Atlanta Sunday American,* both Atlanta, 1927-28; *Oklahoma City Times,* Oklahoma City, reporter, 1928-29; Safeway Airlines, Oklahoma City, station agent, 1929-30; Associated Press, reporter-editor in Oklahoma City, 1931, Tulsa, Okla., 1931-35, Kansas City, Kan., 1935, and New York, N.Y., 1935-36, chief of Pittsburgh Bureau, Pittsburgh, Pa., 1936; Carnegie-Illinois Steel Corp., Pittsburgh, public relations manager, 1936-38; *Denver Post,* Denver, Colo., makeup editor, 1938-42; civilian historical writer, Ordinance Department, U.S. Army, 1943-45; Izaak Walton League of America, Chicago, Ill., assistant executive director, 1945-47, western representative, 1947-48, executive director, 1949-55; Pennsylvania Fish Commission, Harrisburg, executive director, 1955-60; Communication Services, Inc., Mechanicsburg, Pa., vice-president and account executive, 1961-63; Interstate Advisory Committee on the Susquehanna River Basin, Harrisburg, executive director, 1963-68; writer, 1968—. Founding member of National Committee on Policies in Conservation Education, 1946-53; member of U.S. Secretary of the Interior's advisory conservation committee, 1949-53; chairman and honorary member of Natural Resources Council of America, 1951-53; member of Pennsylvania Sanitary Water Board and Pennsylvania Water and Power Resources Board, both 1955-60. *Member:* Izaak Walton League of America (life member).

WRITINGS: National Fishing Guide, A. S. Barnes, 1946; (contributor) Charles H. Callison, editor, *America's Natural Resources,* Ronald, 1957, revised edition, 1967; (contributor) Hamilton K. Pyles, editor, *What's Ahead for Our Public Lands?,* Natural Resources Council of America, 1970; *Susquehanna Compact: Guardian of the River's Future,* Rutgers University Press, 1972; *Public Grazing Lands: Use and Misuse by Industry and Government,* Rutgers University Press, 1976. Author of conservation pamphlets. Contributor to popular magazines, including *Sports Afield* and

Field and Stream. Past editor and editorial director of *Outdoor America;* past editorial director of *Pennsylvania Angler.*

WORK IN PROGRESS: *Born with Fists Doubled,* a book on the national actions of the Izaak Walton League of America, the first of a two-part narrative on the Izaak Walton League of America.

SIDELIGHTS: Voigt comments: "I had no kids. So, I've wanted to do something to help other people's kids, not only now but from now on; which is why I've stayed with the natural resources conservation movement. The best thing I've felt I could do to show my appreciation for the good outdoors life I've had the privilege of enjoying was to try to pass on some part of it to youngsters and adults of today and tomorrow. Bathos? I don't think so. Millions unknown and unnamed to me have had the opportunity to enjoy healthful outdoor recreation because of natural resources conservation or restoration or perpetuation projects done by others but stimulated by my writings and hundreds of speeches in nearly all the first forty-eight states. More hordes of outdoors loving people are enjoying fishing and boating on Pennsylvania waters due to my efforts which gave them access to public boat ramp areas and to lakes built during my regime. I cherish a scroll given me by my staff in Pennsylvania in 1960, when I left the Pennsylvania Fish Commission by request of political powers that found I was saying 'no' to people they considered deserving of special privilege; some who wanted my hide were leaders of so-called sportsmen's groups in whose behalf I had been working my tail off."

* * *

VOLKOFF, Vladimir 1932-
(Rholf Barbare, Victor Duloup)

PERSONAL: Born November 7, 1932, in Paris, France; came to the United States in 1966; son of Nicholas and Tatiana (Porokhovstchikoff) Volkoff; children: Tatiana. *Education:* Sorbonne, University of Paris, lic. es lett., 1955; University of Liege, Ph.D. (magna cum laude), 1974. *Religion:* Russian Orthodox. *Residence:* Decatur, Ga.

CAREER: Translator, journalist, lecturer, and professor of French and Russian. *Military service:* French Army Reserve, active duty, 1957-62; became lieutenant; received Military Valor Cross. *Member:* International P.E.N., Modern Language Association of America, South Atlantic Modern Language Association.

WRITINGS: *L'Agent Triple* (novel; title means "The Triple Agent"), Julliard, 1962; *Metro pour l'enfer* (novel; title means "Subway to Hell"), Hachette, 1963; *Les Mousquetaires de la Republique* (novel; title means "Musketeers of the Republic"), Table Ronde, 1964; (under pseudonym Rholf Barbare) *Les trois scorpions* (novel; title means "Three Scorpions"), Alhim Michel, 1965; (under pseudonym Victor Duloup) *La Civilisation Francaise* (title means "French Civilization"), Harcourt, 1970; *Tchaikovsky: A Self-Portrait,* Crescendo, 1975. Contributor of articles, stories, and translations to journals, including *Fiction, Renaissance,* and *La Nation Francaise.*

WORK IN PROGRESS: A biography of St. Vladimir of Russia; novels; poetry; plays.

SIDELIGHTS: Volkoff told *CA* his travels have taken him to England, France, Mexico, Belgium, Luxembourg, Switzerland, Portugal, Spain, Tunisia, Algeria, and Gibraltar. *Avocational interests:* Fencing, shooting, theatricals.

von CUBE, Irmgard 1900(?)-1977

1900(?)—July 25, 1977; German-born screenwriter. Von Cube wrote scripts for motion pictures in Germany, France, and the United States, including the film "Johnny Belinda," for which she received an Academy Award nomination and the 1949 *Look* magazine award. She died in Hollywood. Calif. Obituaries: *New York Times,* July 28, 1977.

* * *

von KLOPP, Vahrah
See MALVERN, Gladys

* * *

VON RAUCH, Georg 1904-

PERSONAL: Surname is pronounced Von Raukh; born August 13, 1904, in Pleskau, Russia; son of Cornelius (a medical doctor) and Frieda (Brock) Von Rauch; married Margaret Reimer; children: Andreas, Hans Heinrich, Georg. *Education:* University of Dorpat, Estonia, M.A., 1927; University of Greifswald, Germany, Ph.D., 1941. *Religion:* Lutheran. *Home:* Birkenweg 2a, Kiel-Kraushagen, Germany.

CAREER: University of Marburg, Marburg, Germany, professor of history, 1946-58; University of Kiel, Kiel, Germany, professor of history, 1958-72.

WRITINGS: *Die Universitaet Dorpat und das Eindringen der Aufklaerung nach Livland,* [Essen], 1943, reprinted, G. Olms, 1969. *Russland: Staatliche Einheit und nationale Vielheit,* [Munich], 1953; *Geschichte des bolschewistischen Russland,* [Wiesbaden], 1955, 5th edition published as *Geschichte der Sowjetunion,* A. Kroener, 1969, translation by Peter Jacobsohn and Annette Jacobsohn published as *A History of Soviet Russia,* Praeger, 1957, 6th edition, 1972; *Lenin: Die Grundlegung des Sowjetsystems,* [Goettingen], 1957, 3rd edition, Muster-Schmidt, 1962; *Studiem zum Verhaeltnis Russlands zu Europa,* [Darmstadt], 1964; *Geschichte der baltischen Staaten,* Kohlhammer, 1970, translation by Gerald Onn published as *The Baltic States: The Years of Independence, Estonia, Latvia, Lithuania, 1917-1940,* University of California Press, 1974.

* * *

WACKER, Charles H(enry), Jr. 1925-

PERSONAL: Born August 19, 1925, in Newark, N.J.; son of Charles Henry and Ida (Meier) Wacker; married Anita Fayen (a teacher), September 8, 1951; children: Charles Henry III, Anita Cecily. *Education:* Columbia University, B.A., 1950; University of California, Los Angeles, M.A., 1965, Ph.D., 1970. *Politics:* Democrat. *Religion:* Episcopalian. *Home:* 1228 San Vicente Blvd., Santa Monica, Calif. 90402. *Office:* Foundation for the Junior Blind, Los Angeles, Calif. 90043.

CAREER: Burroughs, Pasadena, Calif., writer and training specialist, 1957-58; TRW, Inc., Redondo Beach, Calif., writer and training specialist, 1959-65; Litton Industries, Beverly Hills, Calif., writer and training specialist, 1966-68; Xerox, Pasadena, writer and training specialist, 1968-70; Foundation for the Junior Blind, Los Angeles, Calif., educational supervisor, 1972—. Free-lance writer. *Military service:* U.S. Army, 1940-42; became second lieutenant.

WRITINGS: *Lasers: How They Work,* Putnam, 1972.

Technical books: (Editor) *Computer Augmentation of Human Reasoning,* MacMillan, 1965. Contributor to learned journals.

WORK IN PROGRESS: A novel dealing with work and its impact on human development; a biography.

SIDELIGHTS: Wacker told *CA* of his forthcoming novel: "Built around one significant day in the life of the central character, it depicts the socio-economic-personal forces acting on one individual of middle-class society which counterpoint and at the same time shape his life, the choices he makes; the behavior, the attitudes, the barriers, the opportunities created and reacted to. In an ironic cycle, it shows how the distant past of early childhood and youth exert influences which ultimately reemerge and control in old age. Yet, underlying the mundane, is the perpetual dream of breaking out into self-fulfillment, without any real knowledge of what this might be."

*　　*　　*

WADE, Ira Owen   1896-

PERSONAL: Born October 4, 1896, in Richmond, Va.; son of Martin David and Mary Elizabeth Frances (Lyle) Wade; married Mabel Winifred Hamilton, August 9, 1925. *Education:* Johns Hopkins University, A.B., 1916; Columbia University, M.A., 1919; Princeton University, Ph.D., 1923. *Home:* 31 Armour Rd., Princeton, N.J. 08540.

CAREER: John Marshall High School, Richmond, Va., teacher, 1916-17; William and Mary College, Williamsburg, Va., instructor, 1917-18; Marietta College, Marietta, Ohio, head of department of romance languages, 1919-21; Princeton University, Princeton, N.J., instructor in French, 1923-25; University of Western Ontario, London, head of department of romance languages, 1925-27; Princeton University, assistant professor, 1927-31, associate professor, 1931-40, professor of French, 1940—, John N. Woodhull Professor, 1951—, chairperson of department, 1946-58. Director of special program in European civilization, 1958; visiting lecturer or professor at several universities, including University of Chicago, 1945, Harvard University, 1946, 1947, and 1966, University of Pennsylvania, 1955 and 1970, Fordham University, 1967-68, and Boston College, 1971; member of the Committee for the International Exchange of Persons, 1953-56. *Military service:* U.S. Naval Reserve, 1918. *Member:* Modern Language Association of America, American Association of Teachers of French, American Association of University Professors, Nassau Club. *Awards, honors:* Jacobus fellowship from Princeton University, 1922-23; French Legion of Honor, 1955.

WRITINGS: The "Philosophe" in the French Drama of the 18th Century, Princeton University Press, 1926, reprinted, Kraus Reprint Co., 1965; *The Clandestine Organization and Diffusion of Philosophic Ideas in France from 1700 to 1750,* Princeton University Press, 1938, reprinted, Octagon, 1967; *Voltaire and Madame du Chatelet: An Essay on the Intellectual Activity at Cirey,* Princeton University Press, 1941, reprinted, Octagon, 1967; *Studies on Voltaire: With Some Unpublished Papers of Mme. du Chatelet,* Princeton University Press, 1947, reprinted, Russell, 1967.

Voltaire's Micromegas: A Study in the Fusion of Science, Myth, and Art, Princeton University Press, 1950; *The Search for a New Voltaire: Studies in Voltaire Based upon Material Deposited at the American Philosophical Society,* American Philosophical Society, 1958; *Voltaire and Candide: A Study in the Fusion of History, Art, and Philosophy,* Princeton University Press, 1959, reprinted, Kennikat, 1972; *The Intellectual Development of Voltaire,* Princeton University Press, 1969; *The Intellectual Origins of the French Enlightenment,* Princeton University Press, 1971. Contributor of articles to scholarly journals.*

WADEKIN, Karl-Eugen
See WAEDEKIN, Karl-Eugen

*　　*　　*

WADLINGTON, Warwick   1938-

PERSONAL: Born May 2, 1938, in New Orleans, La.; son of Robert L. (in U.S. Army) and Della (Guerin) Wadlington; married Elizabeth Bernard, December 26, 1963; children: Laura, Mark, Paul. *Education:* U.S. Military Academy, B.S., 1961; Tulane University, M.A., 1966, Ph.D., 1967. *Home:* 7210 Lamplight Lane, Austin, Tex. 78731. *Office:* Department of English, University of Texas, Austin, Tex. 78712.

CAREER: University of Texas, Austin, assistant professor, 1967-72, associate professor, 1972-78, professor of English, 1978—. *Military service:* U.S. Army, Infantry, qualified in airborne and ranger training, 1961-64; served in Vietnam; became first lieutenant; received Air Medal with two oakleaf clusters.

WRITINGS: The Confidence Game in American Literature, Princeton University Press, 1975. Contributor to journals, including *Southern Review*.

WORK IN PROGRESS: A book on Faulkner.

SIDELIGHTS: Wadlington told *CA:* "*The Confidence Game in American Literature* deals mainly with Melville, Twain, and Nathanael West as writers representing an important element in American literature, and culture in general. This is a preoccupation with the idea of confidence, especially mutual trust and the belief in oneself, and with the securing and manipulation of confidence. The book shows how this preoccupation manifests itself not only in the themes of these writers but in their rhetoric—their relationship, their 'game,' with their readers. Con-men are often heroes; the writer is often a con-man.

"The dominant themes are of pervasive deception and of lost, grudging, or heroically disabused confidence. The rhetorical controls established by the three writers similarly invite the reader to experience these forms of risky or deceived confidence as he is reading. Combined, theme and rhetoric suggest that not only literary but social and metaphysical realities are grounded mainly or soley upon the persuasions that create trust in these realities."

*　　*　　*

WAEDEKIN, Karl-Eugen   1921-
(Karl-Eugen Wadekin)

PERSONAL: Born May 21, 1921, in Bad Woerishofen, Germany; son of Carl A. F. (a merchant) and Ilse (von Harder) Waedekin; married Irmingard A. Haugg (a writer), August 18, 1945; children: Bernhard, Martina. *Education:* Attended University of Heidelberg, 1940; University of Leipzig, Ph.D., 1950. *Politics:* No affiliation. *Religion:* No affiliation. *Home:* Bahnhofstrasse 29, Starzach-1, Bierlingen, Germany 7245. *Office:* University of Giessen, Otto-Behaghelstrasse 10/D, Giessen, Germany 6300.

CAREER: University of Leipzig, Leipzig, East Germany, assistant to professor of history, 1949-51, lecturer in Russian history, 1951-52; editorial assistant to Klaus Mehnert (a journalist and scholar) in Stuttgart, West Germany, 1953-61; Technical University, Aachen, West Germany, assistant to professor of political science, 1961-65; received grant for independent research from Deutsche Forschungsgemeinshaft (German Research Society), Bonn-Bad Godesberg, West Germany, 1965-68; Technical University at Aachen, lecturer in political science, 1968-69; University of Giessen, Giessen, West Germany, lecturer, 1969-71, professor of international comparative and east European agrarian policies, 1971—. Member of board of the Bundesinstitut fuer ostwissenschaftliche und internationale studien at Cologne, 1974—. *Military service:* German Air Force, 1940-45. *Member:* National Association of Soviet and East European Studies (United Kingdom), Deutsche Gesellschaft fuer Osteuropakunde (German Society of East European Studies), Agrarsoziale Gesellschaft (Society for Socio-economics of Agriculture), Hochschulverband (university association).

WRITINGS: Privatproduzenten in der sowjetischen Landwirtschaft, Verlag Wissenschaft und Politik, 1967, revised and enlarged translation by Keith Bush published as *The Private Sector in Soviet Agriculture,* edited by George Karcz, University of California Press, 1973; *Die sowjetischen Staatsgueter* (title means "The Soviet State Farms"), Verlag Otto Harrassowitz, 1969; *Fuehrungskraefte im sowjetischen Dorf* (title means "Leading Cadres in Soviet Villages"), Duncker & Humblot, 1969.

Die Bezahlung der Arbeit in der sowjetischen Landwirtschaft (title means "The Remuneration of Labor in Soviet Agriculture"), Duncker & Humblot, 1972; *Sozialistische Agrarpolitik in Osteuropa,* (title means "Socialist Agrarian Policies in Eastern Europe and the Soviet Union"), Duncker & Humblot, Volume I: *Von Marx bis zur Vollkollektivierung* (title means "From Marx to Full Collectivization"), 1974, Volume II: *Entwicklung und Probleme 1960-67* (title means "Development and Problems, 1960-1976"), 1977.

Translator of Russian works into German. Contributor to encyclopedias *Staatslexikon* and *Handwoerterbuch der Wirtschaftswissenschaften,* and of articles to journals such as *Soviet Studies, Problems of Communism, Cahiers du monde russe et sovietique, Revue de l'Est, Ostevropa, Osteuropa-Wirtschaft,* and to various conference volumes.

WORK IN PROGRESS: Continuing research on social, economic, and political aspects of agriculture in Eastern Europe and the Soviet Union.

SIDELIGHTS: Waedekin writes: "Having been trained as a historian, and having worked in political science, sociology, and agricultural economics, I combine the approaches of these disciplines in studying and comparing East European (including Soviet), Western, and developing countries' agricultural policies. Independently of one's political stance, I consider it important to know about non-Western systems and to explore not only the ideological but also the historical, social, and economic factors forming these. In more recent publications, I try to write also for a broader public."

Waedekin has traveled widely in the Soviet Union, Eastern Europe, Turkey, Western Europe, the United States, and Canada. Besides his native German, he speaks English, Russian, and French, and reads Latin, Italian, Spanish, Bulgarian, and Turkish.

*   *   *

WALKER, Barbara G(oodwin)   1930-

PERSONAL: Born July 2, 1930, in Philadelphia, Pa.; daughter of Edward W. (a company treasurer) and Dorothy (Goodwin) Jones; married Gordon N. Walker (a research chemist), December 6, 1952; children: Alan C. *Education:* University of Pennsylvania, B.A., 1952. *Home and office address:* Lake Trail W., Mount Kemble Lake, Morristown, N.J. 07960.

CAREER: Teacher of modern dance and fitness exercise, 1954-69; writer, 1965—; free-lance designer of knitwear, 1968—. *Member:* Phi Beta Kappa.

WRITINGS—All published by Scribner: *A Treasury of Knitting Patterns,* 1968; *A Second Treasury of Knitting Patterns,* 1970; *The Craft of Lace Knitting,* 1971; *The Craft of Cable-Stitch Knitting,* 1971; *Charted Knitting Designs,* 1972; *Knitting from the Top,* 1972; *Sampler Knitting,* 1973; *The Craft of Multicolor Knitting,* 1973; *Barbara Walker's Learn-to-Knit Afghan Book,* 1974; *Mosaic Knitting,* 1976.

WORK IN PROGRESS: Research on historical, religious, and social aspects of sexism, women's status, and the position of women in human cultures, past and present.

AVOCATIONAL INTERESTS: Dance (modern, folkdancing, square dancing, preclassic dance), hiking, nature study, animal care, reading, painting.

*   *   *

WALKER, Gregory P(iers) M(ountford)   1942-

PERSONAL: Born December 30, 1942, in Pattingham, Staffordshire, England; son of Colin M. (a civil servant) and Frances (a writer; maiden name, Hodgetts) Walker; married Anne Snow (a teacher of French), March 25, 1972. *Education:* Cambridge University, B.A., 1964, M.A., 1968; University of Sheffield, dip.lib., 1966, M.A., 1971, Ph.D., 1976. *Home:* 12 Orchard Close, Wheatley, Oxford, England. *Office:* Slavonic Section, Bodleian Library, Oxford University, Oxford, England.

CAREER: University of Kent, Canterbury, England, assistant librarian, 1966-68; University of Lancaster, Lancaster, England, assistant librarian, 1968-71; Oxford University, Bodleian Library, Oxford, England, acting head of Slavonic section, 1971-73, head of section, 1973—. Consultant to Pahlavi National Library (Teheran), 1975. *Member:* Library Association, Standing Conference of National and University Libraries (Slavonic and East European Group), Aslib, British Universities' Association of Slavists, National Association for Soviet and East European Studies, Association of University Teachers, Great Britain-Union of Soviet Socialist Republics Association (Oxford representative, 1974—), National Council for Civil Liberties.

WRITINGS: Directory of Libraries and Special Collections on Eastern Europe and the U.S.S.R., Crosby Lockwood, 1971; *Russian for Librarians,* Shoe String, 1973; *Soviet Book Publishing Policy,* Cambridge University Press, 1978. Contributor to Slavic studies, language, and library journals.

WORK IN PROGRESS: A study of information transfer between political systems; continuing research on Russian and Soviet publishing practices and history.

SIDELIGHTS: Walker writes: "My professional concern is primarily with the acquisition and use of Slavonic and East European publications for my library's own collections, but also with national policy affecting library and information services, especially for users of Slavonic materials, and with the cultural, social, and political background of the U.S.S.R. and Eastern Europe. I enjoy travelling in this part of the world (and elsewhere)."

AVOCATIONAL INTERESTS: Architectural history, amateur dramatics, classic detective fiction.

*   *   *

WALKER, Jack
See THAYER, Frederick C(lifton), Jr.

WALKER, Margaret Abigail   1915-

PERSONAL: Born July 7, 1915, in Birmingham, Ala.; daughter of Sigismund (a Methodist minister) and Marion (Dozier) Walker; married Firnist James Alexander, June 13, 1943; children: Marion Elizabeth, Firnist James, Sigismund Walker, Margaret Elvira. *Education:* Northwestern University, A.B., 1935; University of Iowa, M.A., 1940, Ph.D., 1965. *Religion:* Methodist. *Home:* 2205 Guynes St., Jackson, Miss. 39213. *Office:* Department of English, Jackson State College, Jackson, Miss. 39217.

CAREER: Worked as a social worker, newspaper reporter, and magazine editor; Livingstone College, Salisbury, N.C., member of faculty, 1941-42; West Virginia State College, Institute, W.Va., instructor in English, 1942-43; Livingstone College, professor of English, 1945-46; Jackson State College, Jackson, Miss., professor of English, 1949—, director of Institute for the Study of the History, Life, and Culture of Black Peoples, 1968—. Lecturer, National Concert and Artists Corp. Lecture Bureau, 1943-48. *Member:* National Council of Teachers of English, Modern Language Association, Poetry Society of America, American Association of University Professors, National Education Association, Alpha Kappa Alpha. *Awards, honors:* Yale Series of Younger Poets Award, 1942, for *For My People;* Rosenthal fellowship, 1944; Ford fellowship for study at Yale University, 1954; Houghton Mifflin Literary Fellowship, 1966; Fulbright fellowship, 1971; National Endowment for the Humanities, 1972; Doctor of Literature, Northwestern University, 1974; Doctor of Letters, Rust College, 1974; Doctor of Fine Arts, Dennison University, 1974; Doctor of Humane Letters, Morgan State University, 1976.

WRITINGS—Poetry: *For My People,* Yale University Press, 1942; *Ballad of the Free,* Broadside Press, 1966; *Prophets for a New Day,* Broadside Press, 1970; *October Journey,* Broadside Press, 1973.

Other: *Jubilee* (novel), Houghton, 1965; *How I Wrote "Jubilee,"* Third World Press, 1972; (with Nikki Giovanni) *A Poetic Equation: Conversations Between Margaret Walker and Nikki Giovanni,* Howard University Press, 1974.

SIDELIGHTS: Walker told *CA:* "Writers should not write exclusively for black or white audiences, but most inclusively. After all, it is the business of all writers to write about the human condition, and all humanity must be involved in both the writing and in the reading."

BIOGRAPHICAL/CRITICAL SOURCES: Negro Digest, February, 1967, January, 1968; *Times Literary Supplement,* June 29, 1967; *Black World,* December, 1971; *Contemporary Literary Criticism,* Gale, Volume 1, 1973, Volume 6, 1976.

*   *   *

WALLACE, Francis   1894(?)-1977

1894(?)—August 19, 1977; American sportswriter and author of *Kid Galahad* and a biography of Knute Rockne. Wallace wrote "Pigskin Preview" for the *Saturday Evening Post* from 1937 to 1948, and for *Colliers* from 1949 until 1956. He died in Cape Canaveral, Fla. Obituaries: *New York Times,* August 26, 1977.

*   *   *

WALLACE, Nigel
See HAMILTON, Charles Harold St. John

WALLACE, Sylvia

PERSONAL: Born in New York, N.Y.; daughter of Harry (a shopkeeper) and Rose (a shopkeeper; maiden name, Reisman) Kahn; married Irving Wallace (a writer), June 3, 1941; children: David, Amy. *Education:* Attended Columbia University. *Politics:* Liberal. *Religion:* Jewish. *Agent:* Arthur Pine Associates, Inc., 1780 Broadway, New York, N.Y. 10019.

CAREER: Has worked as a copywriter and editor for Dell Publishing Co., New York, N.Y.; free-lance writer, 1947—. Ghost writer for celebrities in the entertainment world.

WRITINGS: The Fountain (novel), Morrow, 1976; (contributor) Irving Wallace, David Wallechinsky, and Amy Wallace, editors, *The Book of Lists,* Morrow, 1977.

WORK IN PROGRESS: A contemporary novel, set in the United States and abroad.

SIDELIGHTS: Sylvia Wallace writes: "My parents owned a Mom and Pop neighborhood candy store in which I worked until I graduated from high school. Now I dwell in a seventeen-room sprawling French country house, midway between Helen Reddy and Gregory Peck. Half of the house is given over to offices for myself, my husband, and children.

"I have never revisited the Bronx. The growing up experience was too traumatic. In 1973, I felt able to cope with it, and asked a taxi driver to take me to 'Scenes of My Childhood.' He refused—said it was too dangerous."

On her writing, she comments: "I wish to depict dilemmas of women—extraordinary women as well as typical—and yearn to present alternatives." Her book, *The Fountain,* will be a major motion picture from Warner Brothers and it will appear, in book form, in France, Germany, Japan, the Netherlands, Turkey, Brazil, Finland, Israel, and Spain. The Wallaces' son David has adopted the original family name, Wallechinsky.

AVOCATIONAL INTERESTS: Politics, skiing, "beach haunting," European travel, the family farmhouse on the island of Menorca.

*   *   *

WALLIS, Ruth O(tis) S(awtell)   1895-1978

March 15, 1895—January 21, 1978; American research anthropologist, educator, and author. Wallis and her husband, Wilson Wallis, wrote books on the Micmac and Malecite Indians of Canada. She was also an author of mystery novels, including *Too Many Bones.* Ruth Wallis died in Putnam, Conn. Obituaries: *New York Times,* January 25, 1978.

*   *   *

WALLNER, Alexandra   1946-

PERSONAL: Born February 28, 1946, in Germany; came to the United States in 1952, naturalized citizen, 1964; daughter of Severin (a physician) and Hildegard (an artist; maiden name, Waltch) Czesnykowski; married John C. Wallner (an illustrator), July 16, 1971. *Education:* Pratt Institute, B.F.A., 1968, M.F.A., 1970. *Home and office:* 19 Seneca Rd., Ossining-on-Hudson, N.Y. 10562.

CAREER: American Home, New York City, assistant art director, 1972-73; *New Ingenue,* New York City, associate art director, 1973-75; free-lance illustrator and writer, 1975—.

WRITINGS: Munch (juvenile; self-illustrated), Crown, 1976.

Illustrator: Martha Gamerman, *Trudy's Straw Hat*, Crown, 1977.

WORK IN PROGRESS: Two juvenile books, *Dangerous Applesauce* and *Little Ugly Face*, both self-illustrated.

SIDELIGHTS: Alexandra Wallner writes: "In my writing of children's books, I'd like to capture the best of good things in the world to retell in my own way. I'd like all my books to have a sense of humor, so that people can have humor about themselves."

* * *

WALLOP, (John) Douglass III 1920-

PERSONAL: Born March 8, 1920, in Washington, D.C.; son of John Douglass, Jr. (an insurance agent) and Marjorie (Ellis) Wallop; married Lucille Fletcher, January 6, 1949; children: Taffy, Wendy. *Education:* University of Maryland, B.S., 1942. *Home:* 3435 South Eighth St., Arlington, Va. 22204. *Office:* 1101 Vermont Ave. N.W., Washington, D.C. 20005.

CAREER: Worked as a rewriter, then as overnight desk rewriter for United Press International (UPI) in Washington, D.C.; radio news writer for National Broadcasting Co. (NBC) in Washington, D.C.; reporter for Associated Press in New York City; insurance agent in Washington, D.C.; writer, 1953—. *Member:* Kappa Alpha, Omicron Delta Kappa.

WRITINGS: Night Light (novel), Norton, 1953; *The Year the Yankees Lost the Pennant* (novel; Book of the Month Club selection), Norton, 1954; (with Jerold Rosenberg) *Damn Yankees* (musical; produced in New York, May 5, 1955), Random House, 1956; *The Sunken Garden*, Norton, 1956; *What Has Four Wheels and Flies?*, Norton, 1959.

Ocean Front, Norton, 1963; *So This is What Happened to Charlie Moe*, Norton, 1965; *The Mermaid in the Swimming Pool*, Norton, 1968; *The Good Life*, Atheneum, 1969; *Baseball: An Informal History*, Norton, 1969; *Stone* (novel), Norton, 1971; *Howard's Bag*, Norton, 1973; *The Girls in Their Tennis Dresses*, Norton, 1977.

AVOCATIONAL INTERESTS: Watching football and baseball, woodworking, and music.*

* * *

WALSH, (Richard) Taylor 1947-

PERSONAL: Born September 25, 1947, in Washington, D.C.; son of Richard Thomas (an insurance agent) and Eugenia (a philosopher; maiden name, Taylor) Walsh. *Education:* Providence College, B.A., 1969. *Home address:* P.O. Box 6313, Washington, D.C. 20015.

CAREER/WRITINGS: Montgomery Journal, Bethesda, Md., writer and photographer, 1973-75; *Daily Star*, Beirut, Lebanon, assistant editor, 1975; *Arab News*, Jeddah, Saudi Arabia, correspondent, 1977—; editor and author of "The Labyrinth" syndicated column, 1977—. Notable assignments include coverage of the Lebanese Civil War, 1975-76. Contributor to *Washington Star, Baltimore Sun, Ski, Sailing, Scanorama,* and *Instructor. Military service:* U.S. Army, 1969-72; became lieutenant. *Member:* Washington Independent Writers, Committee of Small Magazine Editors and Publishers.

SIDELIGHTS: Walsh told *CA:* "The potential of human experience is, I think, for symmetry; not order. It is in the tumbling play, the constant leaping, running and hugging of very small children. So I seek the sweat of a hard run, the dance of basketball. So also a good drenching, by scuba, or under sail or river-running.

"The mechanisms we've built tend to ignore instincts deemed trivial, irrelevant or piddling. We write often about mechanisms, but not enough their essential ingredients. Political American mechanisms, for example; or in the communications industry. How do ideas fare within them? Fostered? South out? Inspired? Not so much today, I fear."

AVOCATIONAL INTERESTS: Historical novels, "compassionate muckraking, discovering Ebla."

* * *

WALTERS, Anna L. 1946-

PERSONAL: Born September 9, 1946, in Pawnee, Okla.; daughter of Luther L. (a laborer) and Juanita M. (Taylor) McGlaslin; married Harry Walters (a museum curator), June 8, 1965; children: Anthony Harold, Daniel A. *Education:* Attended College of Santa Fe, 1972-74. *Office:* Navajo Community College, Tsaile, Ariz. 86556.

CAREER: Institute of American Indian Arts, Santa Fe, N.M., library technician, 1968-74; Dineh Cooperatives, Chinle, Ariz., technical writer, 1975; Navajo Community College, Tsaile, Ariz., technical writer for curriculum development, 1976—.

WRITINGS: (Co-author) *The Sacred: Ways of Knowledge, Sources of Life* (textbook), Navajo Community College Press, 1977; (editor) Chester Hubbard, *Haz Agii BoHo Aah, The Learning of that Which Pertains to the Home*, Navajo Community College Press, 1977; (editor) *Navajo Weaving: From Spider Woman to Synthetic Rugs*, Navajo Community College Press, 1977. Work represented in many anthologies, including *The Man to Send Rainclouds*, edited by K. Rosen, Viking, 1974, *Warriors of the Rainbow*, edited by Rosen, Viking, 1975, and *The Third Woman*, edited by D. Fisher, Houghton, 1978. Contributor of articles to *American Indian Historian, Shantih, Chouteau Review*, and other periodicals. Editor, *Fraueoffensive* (issue on contemporary American Indian Women), [Munich], 1977.

WORK IN PROGRESS: No-Men, a fantasy; untitled history of an American Indian family; poetry.

SIDELIGHTS: Anna Walters told *CA:* "I have been involved in several kinds of writing. I find I am more inclined to be a creative writer rather than a technical writer. I write daily and do not wait for 'inspiration' although it, of course, adds significantly to the content of material when 'inspiration' is there. I write about things I know, people I know. I write because of my need to write. It is my 'true' love."

* * *

WALTON, Robert Cutler 1932-

PERSONAL: Born December 18, 1932, in Jersey City, N.J.; son of Donald James (a clergyman) and Elizabeth (a teacher; maiden name, Ried) Walton; married Charlotte Wilhelmina Kollegger (a realtor), March 25, 1966; children: Alexander, Deborah, Christina. *Education:* Swarthmore College, B.A., 1954; Harvard University, B.D., 1958; Yale University, M.A., 1961, Ph.D., 1964. *Politics:* Republican. *Religion:* Presbyterian. *Home:* 34039 Old Timber Rd., Farmington Hills, Mich. 48018. *Office:* Department of History, Wayne State University, Detroit, Mich. 48202.

CAREER: Duke University, Durham, N.C., instructor in history, 1957-64; University of British Columbia, Vancouver, assistant professor, 1964-68, associate professor of history, 1968-71; Wayne State University, Detroit, Mich., associate professor, 1971-73, professor of history, 1973—. *Member:* American Society for Reformation Research (member of executive committee; vice-president and president), Friends Historical Association, American Society for Church History, Verein fuer Pfaelsische Kirchengeschichte, Detroit Committee on Foreign Relations.

WRITINGS: Zwingli's Theocracy, University of Toronto, 1967; *Over There: European Views of the Americas, 1914-1918,* F. E. Peacock, 1972. Editor of "Studies in the Reformation," a monograph series, for American Society for Reformation Research.

WORK IN PROGRESS: Pietism, Methodism, and Modern Society; a biography of Heinrich Bullinger.

SIDELIGHTS: Walton told *CA:* "*Zwingli's Theocracy* was written to introduce American readers to current European views on the Zwinglian Reformation and to question the old fashioned Protestant Liberal assumptions about the Radical Reformation which typified American scholarship. *Over There* sought to show Americans what they looked like to the European observer."

AVOCATIONAL INTERESTS: Travel (Europe, especially Switzerland), military history, rifle club activities, running, swimming.

*   *   *

WARBURTON, Clark (Abram) 1896-

PERSONAL: Born January 27, 1896, in Shady Grove, N.Y.; son of Melvin Eugene (a clergyman) and Florence Serena (Vough) Warburton; married Amber Arthun, July 5, 1929 (died, 1976); children: Peter. *Education:* Houghton College, Houghton, N.Y., student, 1915-17; Cornell University, B.A., 1921, M.A., 1928; Columbia University, graduate student, 1928-29, Ph.D., 1932. *Home:* 1031 Pine Hill Rd., McLean, Va. 22101.

CAREER: Lecturer in economics at Ewing Christian College and University of Allahabad, Allahabad, India, 1921-24; Rice Institute (now University), Houston, Tex., instructor in economics, 1925-58; Emory University, Atlanta, Ga., associate professor of economics, 1929-31; Brookings Institution, Washington, D.C., member of research staff, 1932-34; Federal Deposit Insurance Corp., Washington, D.C., 1934-65, began as an economist, became chief of Banking and Business Section, Division of Research and Statistics. *Military service:* U.S. Army, American Expeditionary Forces in France, 1918-19; became sergeant. *Member:* American Economic Association, Economic History Association, Southern Economic Association (president, 1963-64), Cosmos Club (Washington, D.C.).

WRITINGS: The Economic Results of Prohibition, Columbia University Press, 1932; (with Maurice Leven and Harold G. Moulton) *America's Capacity to Consume,* Brookings Institution, 1934; *Depression, Inflation, and Monetary Policy,* Johns Hopkins Press, 1966.

Contributor: *Economic Essays in Honor of Wesley Clair Mitchell,* Columbia University Press, 1934; *Five Monographs on Business Income,* American Institute of Accountants, 1950; *Readings in Monetary Theory,* Blakiston Co., 1951; Leland B. Yeager, editor, *In Search of a Monetary Constitution,* Harvard University Press, 1962; Frank M. Tamagna and others, editors, *Monetary Management,* Prentice-Hall, 1963; *The Federal Reserve System After Fifty Years,* Volume II-III, U.S. Government Printing Office, 1964. Also contributor to *Studies in Income and*

Wealth, Volume I, National Bureau of Economic Research, 1937, Volume III, 1939, Volume V, 1943, Volume XXII, Princeton University Press, 1958. About fifty articles published in economic, finance, and political science journals. Managing editor, *Indian Journal of Economics,* 1923-24.

WORK IN PROGRESS: Relation of banking and monetary policy to business fluctuations since 1790; a history of the theory of monetary disequilibrium, 1750-1975.

SIDELIGHTS: Warburton's interests in the relation of banking and monetary policy to business fluctuations began in college when he studied economics under Herbert J. Davenport, some of whose insights, he says, "were truly remarkable." Twenty-five years later he began an examination of the factual record of the role of money supply as related to depression and inflation, coming up with conclusions "confirmed by recent exhaustive analyses by other investigators . . . [but] still regarded by some economists as controversial." His continuing opinion is that U.S. monetary authorities have not yet provided sufficient stability, at an appropriate rate of growth, in the supply of money available to the people and enterprises of the nation.

*   *   *

WARD, Alan Joseph 1936-

PERSONAL: Born May 2, 1936, in Boston, Mass.; son of Joseph Solomon and Rebecca (Myrick) Ward. *Education:* Brandeis University, A.B., 1958; Temple University, A.M., 1960; State University of New York at Buffalo, Ph.D., 1965. *Home:* 5415 North Sheridan Rd., #4301, Chicago, Ill. 60640. *Office:* Henry Horner Children's Center, 6500 West Irving Park Rd., Chicago, Ill. 60634.

CAREER: Public Welfare Department, Boston, Mass., case worker, 1959-60; State University of New York at Buffalo, intern at Psychology Clinic, 1960-62; Veterans Administration Hospital, Buffalo, N.Y., psychology intern for Neuro-Psychiatric Service, 1962-64; Michael Reese Hospital, Chicago, Ill., researcher at Psychosomatic & Psychiatric Institute, 1964-66; Eastern State School and Hospital, Trevose, Pa., supervising clinical psychologist, 1966-70, acting chief psychologist, 1970-71, chief psychologist, 1971-75, research and treatment director of Children's Treatment, Training & Research Service, 1966-75; Chicago-Read Mental Health Center, Chicago, director of Henry Horner Children's Center, 1975—. Certified by American Board of Professional Psychologists; registered psychologist in Illinois, 1966—, licensed in Pennsylvania, 1967—. Instructor at Pennsylvania State University, 1967-68, Temple University, 1968-70, Jefferson Medical College, 1969—, and Roosevelt University, 1976—; adjunct assistant professor at University of Illinois, 1976—. Private practice of psychology in Philadelphia, Pa., 1968-75, and Chicago, Ill., 1975—. Member of Pennsylvania governor's advisory task force on the mental health of children and youth, 1971-75.

MEMBER: American Psychological Association, American Orthopsychiatric Association, National Society for Autistic Children, Psychologists Interested in the Advancement of Psychotherapy, Society of Personality Assessment (fellow), Society of Projective Techniques (fellow), American Society of Clinical Hypnosis, American Association for the Advancement of Science, American Association of Psychiatric Services for Children, Midwestern Psychological Association, Eastern Psychological Association, Illinois Psychological Association, Pennsylvania Psychological Association (fellow), Mental Health Association of Southeastern Pennsylvania, Philadelphia Society of Clinical Psychologists (member of executive committee), Philadelphia Society of Clinical Hypnosis (member of executive board), Sigma Xi. *Awards, honors:* U.S. Public Health Service post-doctoral fellowship, 1964-66.

WRITINGS: (Editor and contributor) *Childhood Autism and Structural Therapy: Selected Papers on Early Childhood Autism,* Nelson Hall, 1976. Contributor of articles are reviews to professional journals. Editor of newsletter of Philadelphia Society of Clinical Psychologists.

WORK IN PROGRESS: Research on the effects of stress upon fetal development and later development of atypical children and childhood psychotherapy.

SIDELIGHTS: Ward has been treating severely disturbed adults and children throughout his career. He comments that his main "areas of vocational interest are adult and child schizophrenia, child development, projective testing, development of the mother-child relationship, psychotherapy, early intervention in childhood disorders of mental health, and community mental health."

AVOCATIONAL INTERESTS: Philosophy, classical music, tennis, fencing, science fiction, travel.

* * *

WARREN, Mary Bondurant 1930-

PERSONAL: Born February 5, 1930, in Athens, Ga.; daughter of John Parnell (a lumber dealer) and Mary Claire (a personnel director; maiden name, Brannon) Bondurant; married James Randolph Warren (a farm equipment dealer), November 27, 1953; children: Eve Bondurant (Mrs. James Corbin Weeks), Mark Standard, Amy Moss (Mrs. Edward Victor Sanders), Stuart Heard, Lisa Brannon. *Education:* University of Georgia, B.S., 1950; attended Oak Ridge Institute of Nuclear Studies, 1953. *Religion:* Methodist. *Home address:* Pocataligo, Route 2, Box 86, Danielsville, Ga. 30633. *Office:* Heritage Papers, Danielsville, Ga. 30633.

CAREER: Union Carbide, Oak Ridge, Tenn., staff member, 1950-51; Oak Ridge Institute of Nuclear Studies, Oak Ridge, Tenn., conducted radio biophysics research in Medical Division, 1951-52; Emory University, Atlanta, Ga., conducted radioisotope research at School of Medicine, 1952-53; Georgia Institute of Technology, Atlanta, technical editor for engineering experiment station, 1954; Veterans Administration Hospital, Atlanta, Ga., radioassay consultant, 1956-57; Heritage Papers, Danielsville, Ga., owner, 1964—. Chairman of Clarke County (Ga.) Civil War Centennial Commission, 1961-65. *Member:* National Genealogical Society, North Carolina Genealogical Society, Georgia Genealogical Society (adviser), Athens Historical Society (charter member; member of board of directors; president, 1962-63).

WRITINGS—Published by Heritage Papers, except as indicated: (contributor) John Stegeman, *These Men She Gave,* University of Georgia Press, 1964; *Jackson Street Cemetery, Athens, Ga.,* 1966; *Mars Hill Baptist Church, Oconee County, Ga.,* 1966; *Marriage Book "A", Clarke County, Ga.,* 1966; *Georgia Genealogical Bibliography, 1963-67,* 1968; *Marriages and Deaths, 1763 to 1820, Abstracted from Extant Georgia Newspapers,* 1968; *Family Puzzlers, 1964-1967,* 1969; *Family Puzzlers, 1968,* 1970; *Family Puzzlers, 1969,* 1970; (editor and author of revision) L. M. Hill, *Hills of Wilkes County, Ga., and Allied Families,* 1972; *Marriages and Deaths, 1820 to 1830, Abstracted from Extant Georgia Newspapers,* 1972; *South Carolina Jury Lists, 1718 Through 1783,* 1977; *Citizens and Immi-*

grants: South Carolina, 1768, 1978. Author of "Athens Lives and Legends," a column in *Athens Daily News,* and "Family Puzzlers," a column in *Athens Banner Herald, Oglethorpe Echo,* and *Athens Daily News,* 1964-67. Editor of *Family Puzzlers,* 1964—, *Carolina Genealogist,* 1970—, and *Georgia Genealogist,* 1970—.

WORK IN PROGRESS: Editing and writing revisions for Bowen's *History of Wilkes Co., Ga.* and Hull's *Annals of Athens, Georgia;* research on post-Revolutionary pensioners of North Carolina, South Carolina, and Georgia, and on special pensions paid by Act of Congress; studying military and alien records from the War of 1812.

SIDELIGHTS: Mary Warren writes: "My interest is *research*—discovering, codifying, and publishing source records of historical and genealogical value. It has been satisfying to locate, recognize, and publish significant federal and state documents in a form useful to researchers. *Family Puzzlers,* my weekly genealogical magazine, strives to increase the research skills of its readers."

* * *

WARWICK, Dennis 1930-

PERSONAL: Surname is pronounced *Wor*-rik; born April 18, 1930, in Wakefield, England; son of Norman (a factory worker) and Fanny (Williams) Warwick; married Margaret Walker (a college lecturer), April 3, 1956; children: David Michael, John Philip. *Education:* University of Durham, B.A. (honors), 1953, diploma, 1954; University of Leeds, Ph.D., 1975. *Politics:* Labour. *Religion:* Anglican. *Home:* 7 Endor Grove, Burley-in-Wharfedale, Ilkley, West Yorkshire LS29 7QJ, England. *Office:* Department of Sociology, University of Leeds, Leeds LS2 9JT, England.

CAREER: Teacher at high schools in Liverpool, England, 1954-62; Margaret Macmillan College of Education, Bradford, England, lecturer, 1963-65, senior lecturer, 1966-68, principal lecturer in sociology, 1969; University of Leeds, Leeds, England, lecturer, 1969-75, senior lecturer in sociology, 1975—. Member of Bradford Metropolitan District Education Committee, 1974-75, and Bradford Youth and Community Consultative Committee. *Military service:* Royal Air Force, 1948-50. *Member:* British Sociological Association, Association of University Teachers.

WRITINGS: Bureaucracy, Longman, 1974. Contributor to sociology journals.

WORK IN PROGRESS: Writing about contemporary British society and culture; research on middle schools in ideology and practice, and on education and race relations.

SIDELIGHTS: Warwick writes that he comes from a working class background. His education took place during wartime, and his national service during the postwar years. "There was an awakening of my sociological interests through early radical politics in the late 1950's, and participation in the educational expansion of the 1960's.

"The book *Bureaucracy* was written at a time of transition theoretically when the interactionist stance of sociologists was beginning to come under attack from Marxists and others who were concerned about the lack of attention paid by phenomenologists and ethnomethodologists to questions of power and class structure in industrial societies. *Bureaucracy* was my response at that time to this transitional phase, and by examining small scale social structures such as schools and colleges, offices and other work situations with references to concepts like bureaucratistion and professionalisation, I was able to point to the obvious links between the macro-and micro levels of analysis. Bureaucracy is shown very much to be a question of power and processes of domination in society.''

* * *

WATANABE, Hitoshi 1919-

PERSONAL: Born November 11, 1919, in Japan; son of Osamu (a physician) and Fusa Watanabe; married wife, Atsuko, October 20, 1946; children: Makoto, Atsumi. *Education:* University of Tokyo, B.Sc., 1946, D.Sc., 1960; attended University of London, 1954-56. *Religion:* Buddhist. *Home:* 4-15-6 Shimo'ochiai, Shinjuku-ku, Tokyo, Japan. *Office:* Archaeological Institute, University of Tokyo, Homgo, Bunkyo-ku, Tokyo, Japan.

CAREER: University of Tokyo, Tokyo, Japan, assistant, 1947-60, lecturer, 1960-67, assistant professor, 1967-72, professor of anthropology and archaeology, 1972—, chairman of Archaeological Institute, 1976—. *Member:* Anthropological Society of Japan (councilor, 1972—), Society of Historical Science (member of board of directors, 1976—), Ethnological Society of Japan, Archaeological Association of Japan, Royal Anthropological Institute (fellow).

WRITINGS: The Ainu Ecosystem: Environment and Group Structure, University of Tokyo Press, 1972 University of Washington Press, 1973; *Bow and Arrow Census in a Papuan Lowland Community: A New Field for Functional-Ecological Study,* Anthropology Museum, University of Queensland, 1975; (editor) *The Human Activity System: Its Spatiotemporal Structure,* University of Tokyo Press, 1977; (editor) *Jinruigaku Kohza* (title means "Anthropology"), Volume XII: *Seitai* (title means "Ecology"), Yuuzankaku Publishing Co., 1977.

WORK IN PROGRESS: Research on the systematization of ecological anthropology as a study of man's life in nature, on hunter-gatherers' ecology, and on an ethnoarchaeological approach to prehistory.

SIDELIGHTS: Watanabe writes: "I have been very much interested in developing an approach to the systematic study of man's life as part of nature, which has been missing even in modern science of man. Man's place in nature has been pursued intensively by anthropologists and other scientists of related fields long since, and there are not a few books using the subject as their titles. In these studies, however, man's place in nature usually means his place in zoological taxonomy only. My problem and concern is his place in nature in terms of ecology.

"Natural historic attitudes and practices were once developing around ethnographic field studies, but modern development of cultural and social sciences, or studies on the nature of culture and society, replaced these with humanistic ones; thus, cultural or social studies of man's modes of life have been developing but naturalistic study of man's life itself, or the structure and function of his life or activity system, has been largely neglected, and therefore, systematization of such a study is an urgent need. I believe that progress in such a study may also be necessary for the better understanding of the nature of culture and society and that such a study would be an efficient key for the integrative study of man.

"Another major interest of mine is in prehistoric archaeology as part of anthropology. My chief concern is the study of method in utilizing ethnographical-ecological data in building up working hypotheses and models for archaeological studies and in archaeological interpretation. The aim is to under-

stand the evolution of the life of peoples in the past in ecological terms. In my point of view, archaeology represents the historical aspect of ecological anthropology as the natural history of man's life.''

BIOGRAPHICAL/CRITICAL SOURCES: Kikan Jinruigaku (title means "Anthropological Quarterly"), Volume VIII, number 1, 1977.

* * *

WATERMEIER, Daniel J(ude) 1940-

PERSONAL: Born August 23, 1940, in New Orleans, La.; son of Daniel J. (a businessman) and Anicetus (Kenny) Watermeier; married Roberta Kane (a teacher), June 17, 1965; children: Aaron, Ethan. *Education:* University of Tennessee, Knoxville, B.A., 1963; University of Maryland, M.A., 1965; University of Illinois, Ph.D., 1968. *Home:* 71 Beckman St., Plattsburgh, N.Y. 12901. *Office:* Department of Theatre, State University of New York College at Plattsburgh, Plattsburgh, N.Y. 12901.

CAREER: Moorhead State University, Moorhead, Minn., assistant professor of theater, 1968-71, acting coordinator of Institute for Minority Group Studies, 1969; State University of New York College at Plattsburgh, associate professor of theater, 1971—, director of theatre, 1973—, chairman of department, 1975—, producing director of summer theater, 1974-76. Member of Clinton County Council on the Arts. *Member:* American Theatre Association, Theatre Library Association, Society for Theatre Research, American Society for Theatre Research, State University of New York Theatre Association, Phi Kappa Phi. *Awards, honors:* State University of New York Research Foundation grant-in-aid, 1971-72; Folger Shakespeare Library fellowship, 1972; Plattsburgh State College Foundation innovative teaching grant, 1973-74; National Endowment for the Humanities pilot program grant, 1978-80.

WRITINGS: Between Actor and Critic: Letters from Edwin Booth to William Winter, Princeton University Press, 1971. Contributor of articles and reviews to *Educational Theatre Journal.*

WORK IN PROGRESS: Editing a book of letters from various personnel to nineteenth-century theatrical impresario, Augustin Daly; research on Edwin Booth's English tours and his "Richelieu"; research on Franklin Haven Sargent, teacher and co-founder of the American Academy of Dramatic Arts.

SIDELIGHTS: Watermeier writes: "A theatre educator, administrator, stage director, and theatre historian, I am particularly interested in the history of American theatre and drama, and Shakespearean stage history. I vew theatre history as a window through which we can perceive and understand our cultural past and relate it to the present. I am keenly interested in the uses of drama in education, and advocate the promotion and development of the arts both in education and in society in general.''

AVOCATIONAL INTERESTS: Drawing, swimming, jogging.

* * *

WATERS, Ethel 1896-1977

October 31, 1896—September 1, 1977; American singer, actress, and author. Once a scullion and chambermaid, Ethel Waters broke into show business as a singer in black clubs and theatres, and became a celebrated stage and screen actress. She made her Broadway debut in "Plantation Revue of 1924," and reached her greatest heights in both the Broadway production and film version of "A Member of the Wedding." Among her other film credits were "Cabin in the Sky" and "Pinky." As a singer she popularized such songs as "Stormy Weather" and "Am I Blue." In later years she became affiliated with the Billy Graham crusades and rededicated her life to Jesus Christ. The hymn she frequently sang at the crusades, "His Eye Is on the Sparrow," was also the title of her best-selling autobiography. She died in Los Angeles, Calif. Obituaries: *New York Times,* September 2, 1977; *Washington Post,* September 2, 1977.

* * *

WATT, Donald Beates 1893-1977

May 3, 1893—November 27, 1977; American organization official and author. Watt founded the Experiment in International Living, an organization designed to foster international understanding by providing opportunities for students to live with families in other countries. The program has grown significantly since its inception in 1932, and now includes a School for International Training at the headquarters in Brattleboro, Vt. Watt also wrote two books about his experience with the Experiment, *Intelligence Is Not Enough* and *Letters to the Founder.* He died in Lancaster, Pa. Obituaries: *New York Times,* November 28, 1977.

* * *

WATTS, Elizabeth (Bailey) Smithgall 1941-
(Elizabeth Smithgall)

PERSONAL: Born May 27, 1941, in Atlanta, Ga.; daughter of Charles Augustus (a newspaper publisher) and Lessie (a journalist; maiden name, Bailey) Smithgall; married John Robert Watts, Jr. (a dentist), June 15, 1968. *Education:* Tulane University, A.B., 1963; University of Pennsylvania, Ph.D., 1971; also attended L'Institute d'Ethnologie and Sorbonne, University of Paris, 1961-62, and Medical College of South Carolina (now Medical University of South Carolina), summer, 1964. *Office:* Department of Anthropology, Tulane University, 1021 Audubon St., New Orleans, La. 70118.

CAREER: Tulane University, New Orleans, La., visiting instructor, spring, 1968, instructor, 1968-70, assistant professor, 1971-73, associate professor of anthropology, 1974—. *Member:* International Association of Human Biologists, American Anthropological Association, American Association of Physical Anthropologists (member of executive committee, 1977—), American Society of Primatologists, Society for the Study of Human Biology, Human Biology Council, Southern Anthropological Society.

WRITINGS: (Contributor) G. H. Bourne, editor, *The Rhesus Monkey,* Volume II, Academic Press, 1975; *Biology of the Living Primates,* W. C. Brown, 1975; (editor with F. E. Johnston and G. W. Lasker) *Biosocial Interrelations in Population Adaptation,* Mouton, 1975. Contributor of articles and reviews, some under name Elizabeth Smithgall, to scientific journals.

WORK IN PROGRESS: Adolescent Growth in Nonhuman Primates, with J. A. Gavan; research on hand-wrist ossification centers in two laboratory colonies of rhesus monkeys.

* * *

WAUTHIER, Claude Rene 1923-

PERSONAL: Born August 22, 1923, in Metz, France; son of Georges (a postal and telegraph service inspector) and Suzanne (Parnaudeau) Wauthier; married Ingrid von Mueller, October 8, 1956; children: Michel, Pierre. *Education:* University of Paris, lic. es lettres, lic. en droit, dipl. en sciences politiques; also attended Cambridge University. *Home:* 44 East Wood-Rd., P.O. Box 3462, Dunkeld, Johannesburg, South Africa.

CAREER: Teacher of French at a school in London, England, 1948-49; attache in Germany for French High Commission, 1950-51; Agence France Presse, journalist, 1952—, bureau chief in Lome, Togo, 1956-58, alternate bureau chief in London, England, 1959-61, bureau chief in Tunis, Tunisia, 1961-62, Algiers, Algeria, 1963-65, and Johannesburg, South Africa, 1965—. *Member:* Association des anciens eleves de la rue Saint-Guillaume, Society of Africanists. *Awards, honors:* Named chevalier de l'Etoile Noir.

WRITINGS: L'Afrique des Africains: Inventaire de la negritude, Editions du Ceuil, 1964, 2nd edition, 1973, English translation by Shirley Kay published as *The Literature and Thought of Modern Africa: A Survey,* Pall Mall Press, 1966, revised edition, Praeger, 1967.

AVOCATIONAL INTERESTS: Collecting African art, swimming.

BIOGRAPHICAL/CRITICAL SOURCES: Nation, June 26, 1967; *London,* Volume VII, number 5, 1967.*

* * *

WEARE, Walter B(urdette) 1938-

PERSONAL: Born December 26, 1938, in Denver, Colo.; son of Walter B. (a pipefitter) and Alice (a seamstress; maiden name, Haight) Weare; married Juanita Stewart (a teacher and artist), 1955; children: Brett, Brenda. *Education:* University of Colorado, B.A., 1963, M.A., 1964; University of North Carolina, Ph.D., 1970. *Home:* 4151 North Prospect, Milwaukee, Wis. 53211. *Office:* Department of History, University of Wisconsin, Milwaukee, Wis. 53201.

CAREER: University of Wisconsin, Milwaukee, instructor, 1968-70, assistant professor of history, 1970—. *Member:* Organization of American Historians, Association for the Study of Afro-American Life and History (state chairman, 1972-75), Southern Historical Association. *Awards, honors:* Fellowships from National Endowment for the Humanities, 1970-71, and American Council of Learned Societies, 1976-77.

WRITINGS: Black Business in the New South: A Social History of the North Carolina Mutual Life Insurance Company, University of Illinois Press, 1973. Contributor to history and social science journals.

WORK IN PROGRESS: Black Kansas: A Study in Community and Diaspora, 1870-1900, for University of Illinois Press.

* * *

WEAVER, Carl H(arold) 1910-

PERSONAL: Born October 15, 1910, in Lima, Ohio; son of William (a farmer) and Della (Simmons) Weaver; married Vera A. Anderson. November 3, 1934; children: Garry Lynn, Kennard Ray, Douglas Alan. *Education:* Bluffton College, B.A., 1936; Ohio State University, M.A., 1950, Ph.D., 1957. *Politics:* None. *Religion:* Methodist. *Home address:* St. Julien Shores, Box 23, Eutanville, S.C. 29048.

CAREER: High school teacher in Green Springs, Ohio, 1936-38, in Fremont, Ohio, 1938-44, and in Kettering, Ohio, 1944-55; Denison University, Granville, Ohio, instructor,

1956-57; Central Michigan University, Mount Pleasant, associate professor, department of speech, 1957-61; University of Maryland, College Park, associate professor and director of general speech, 1961-66; Ohio University, Athens, professor of interpersonal communication, 1966-74, professor emeritus, 1974—, coordinator of graduate studies, School of Speech. Extension teacher, 1947-51, at University of Dayton, Wilmington College, Wright-Patterson Air Force Base, American Banking Institute, and others; visiting summer professor at University of Alberta, 1960, and at Queens College of the City University of New York, 1965, 1966. *Member:* Speech Association of America (member of legislative assembly, 1964-66), National Society for the Study of Communication (executive secretary, 1958-60), American Psychological Association, Central States Speech Association, Ohio Speech Association.

WRITINGS: (With W. L. Strausbaugh) *The Fundamentals of Speech Communication,* American Book Co., 1964, text edition, Van Nostrand, 1968; *Speaking in Public,* American Book Co., 1966; *Human Listening,* Bobbs-Merrill, 1972. Also author of *History of the International Communication Association,* 1974. Contributor of about fifteen articles to speech journals.

*   *   *

WEBER, Jerome C(harles) 1938-

PERSONAL: Born September 1, 1938, in New York, N.Y.; son of Morris and Ethel (Shier) Weber; married Barbara Golden, June 26, 1960 (divorced, 1974); married Lynn Wiley (in Bell System management), July 18, 1975; children: (first marriage) Amy Elizabeth, Jeffrey Glenn. *Education:* Brooklyn College (now of the City University of New York), B.S., 1960; Michigan State University, M.A., 1961, Ph.D., 1966. *Politics:* Democrat. *Religion:* Jewish. *Home:* 1133 Robinhood, Norman, Okla. 73069. *Office:* University College, University of Oklahoma, 650 Parrington Oval, Norman, Okla. 73069.

CAREER: University of Oklahoma, Norman, assistant professor, 1964-68, associate professor, 1968-74, professor of physiology and research methods, 1974—, dean of University College, 1973—. Member of Harvard University's Institute for Education Management, 1973, and Southwest Center for Human Relations Studies. Commissioner of Norman Board of Parks. *Member:* International Society of Sports Psychology, American Association of University Professors, American Association for Higher Education, American College of Sports Medicine (fellow), American Council on Education.

WRITINGS: (With Ronald A. Lee) *The Physical Fitness Status of Oklahoma Youth,* U.S. Office of Health, Education & Welfare, 1969; (with David Lamb) *Statistics and Research in Physical Education,* Mosby, 1970; (contributor) William P. Morgan, editor, *Contemporary Readings in Sport Psychology,* C. C Thomas, 1970. Contributor to academic journals.

SIDELIGHTS: Weber told *CA:* "Various articles on physiological and sports medicine topics are directed to the general question of whether or not regular physical activity is beneficial. There is a consistent and convincing body of information which strongly makes the point that it is. My own studies bear out this conclusion. Of greatest interest is the effect of regular exercise on the performance of the heart in response to stressors of various kinds and its ability to withstand stress. Sports psychology articles speak to the question of transferability of the organism to different types of

stressors and also relate to the general, and generally unanswered, question of how much and what kind of competitive situation is psychologically healthy. Particular interest is related to the questions of age and the responses of younger children to the problems of intense competition. The basic conclusion one might reach at this time is that most of the problems of athletic competition for children can be easily eliminated through more appropriate control of the qualifications and rules of the adults who run these programs."

*   *   *

WEBSTER, James 1925-

PERSONAL: Born March 8, 1925, in New Barhet, Hertfordshire, England; son of James Joscelyn (a bank manager) and May (an organist; maiden name, Spearman) Webster; married Mary Barbara Windeatt (an artist); children: Adrian William, Martin Guy. *Education:* Attended St. Luke's College, Exeter, 1947-49, and Central School of Speech, London, 1949-50; University of London, F.L.C.M., L.R.A.M., 1956. *Politics:* "Very liberal views." *Religion:* "Very liberal views." *Home:* Westward Ho!, St. Ouen, Jersey C.1, United Kingdom.

CAREER: Newton Park College of Education, Bath, England, lecturer in education, 1959-61; Redland College of Education, Bristol, England, senior lecturer in education, 1961-63; University of Bristol, Bristol, England, visiting lecturer, 1963—. *Military service:* Royal Air Force, navigator. *Awards, honors:* Guinness trophy for gliding, 1964, 1965, 1966.

WRITINGS: Practical Reading: Some New Remedial Techniques, Evans Brothers, 1964; *The Red Robber of Larado,* Pitman, 1966; *The Ladybird Book of Tricks and Games and Others* (juvenile), Wiggs & Hepborough, 1966; *Rescue Stories* (juvenile), Ginn, 1967; *More Rescue Stories* (juvenile), Ginn, 1967; *Rescue Adventures* (juvenile), Ginn, 1967; *First Helpings* (juvenile), Thomas Nelson, 1970; *Help Stories* (juvenile), Thomas Nelson, 1970; *Help Yourself Stories* (juvenile), Thomas Nelson, 1970; *Reading Failure, with Particular Reference to Rescue Reading,* revised edition, Ginn, 1971; *Help for Reluctant Readers,* Thomas Nelson, 1975; *Ladybird Readers,* Wiggs & Hepborough, 1975; *Rewards,* Arnold, 1976; *Webster's English Work Books,* Thomas Nelson, 1976. Also author of *The Four Ages,* 1965.

Author of material for British Broadcasting Corp. and Instructional Television (ITV).

WORK IN PROGRESS: "Young Shorty Stories," twelve volumes; "Echoes," series of eight early reading books, completion expected in 1978.

SIDELIGHTS: Webster writes: "My writing stems not so much from creative urge, although I am never free from the disease, as from an obsessive desire to slay the dragon of illiteracy. Much of my work arose from the resident reading clinics for dyslexics (the first in Britain) and is based on I.C.G. (Informant Contextual Guessing)." *Avocational interests:* Gliding, sportscars.

*   *   *

WEIL, Andrew (Thomas) 1942-

PERSONAL: Surname rhymes with "style"; born June 8, 1942, in Philadelphia, Pa.; son of Daniel P. (a store owner) and Jenny (a designer of women's hats; maiden name, Silverstein) Weil. *Education:* Harvard University, A.B. (biology), 1964, M.D., 1968. *Home address:* Route 15, Box 269, Tucson, Ariz. 85715. *Agent:* Lynn Nesbit, International

Creative Management, 40 West 57th St., New York, N.Y. 10019.

CAREER: Botanical Museum of Harvard University, Cambridge, Mass., research associate in ethnopharmacology, 1971—; private practice as a physician specializing in holistic medicine, Tucson, Ariz., 1976—. Lecturer. Fellow, Institute of Current World Affairs, New York City, 1971-75. Wartime service: U.S. Public Health Service, 1969-70; became lieutenant. Member: Linnean Society of London (fellow), Sigma Xi (Harvard-Radcliffe chapter).

WRITINGS: The Natural Mind: A New Way of Looking at Drugs and the Higher Consciousness, Houghton, 1972; Health and Healing in the Year 2000, Houghton, 1978; Mushrooms, Mangoes, Eclipses of the Sun, and Other High Experiences, (a collection of newsletters on plants, drugs, and high states of consciousness), Houghton, 1978. Author of regular column for Journal of Psychedelic Drugs. Contributor of articles to Harper's, Psychology Today, and other periodicals.

Member of editorial advisory board, Journal of Altered States of Consciousness.

WORK IN PROGRESS: Research on the medicinal value of plants and other scientific projects.

SIDELIGHTS: Andrew Weil told CA: "My undergraduate work was on the botany of useful plants, especially psychoactive and medicinal plants. I conduct research on plants still, use herbal preparations in my medical practice, and try to explain to patients and physicians why whole plant drugs are safer than chemical ones. I have a number of scientific research projects in the works, including one on the medicinal value of coca leaves, the South American stimulant and source of cocaine. I have been studying coca in South America and here for a number of years and am working to reintroduce it to the modern pharmacopeia as an herbal treatment for various conditions."

Weil's book, The Natural Mind: A New Way of Looking at Drugs and the Higher Consciousness, is a discussion not only of the real effects of psychoactive drugs, but also of their place in man's natural desire to alter his ordinary perception of reality, to seek higher levels of consciousness. "As a student of psychology and drugs," he wrote, "I have always been interested in the concept of set, the body of expectation that determines experience."

Traveling in 1973 to the Chalbi Desert in Kenya, Africa, to witness a solar eclipse, he witnessed as well a manifestation of the theory that "selective perception of evidence is the basic method by which we construct our models of reality." The Kenyan Government had warned its populace against viewing an eclipse with the naked eye, stating that it caused blindness. Denying this, Weil asserted that it is possible, in fact, to view the entire period of total eclipse without damage to the eye, that only prolonged vision of the exposed sun could cause retinal damage. The natives, however, believed that the eclipse was the work of the government, and when questioned as to what they thought was going to happen, responded, "We have heard that the government is going to cause the sun to die." They secluded themselves accordingly.

Underlying Weil's research is the suggestion that the taboos and false beliefs surrounding psychoactive drugs and those perpetuated by the Kenyan Government concerning solar eclipse are related. The question that occurs, Weil contends, is: Are they not, in their way, "dangerous to the established order of society?" In an article for Harper's magazine, he

concluded: "When events have the potential to get us high by interrupting the ordinary, orderly flow of everyday reality, they are especially threatening to the men in power, who want us to feel threatened along with them."

A frequent traveler, Weil speaks fluent Spanish.

AVOCATIONAL INTERESTS: Nutrition, exercise, yoga, wilderness, and mind-body interaction.

BIOGRAPHICAL/CRITICAL SOURCES: Harper's, November, 1973; Psychology Today, July, 1974.

* * *

WEIL, Gordon L(ee) 1937-

PERSONAL: Surname is pronounced wile; born March 12, 1937, in Mineola, N.Y.; son of Irving (in insurance) and Sadye (in public health; maiden name, Gordon) Weil; married Roberta Meserve (an economic and financial consultant), April 6, 1962; children: Anne Inger, Richard Clement. Education: Bowdoin College, A.B. (magna cum laude), 1958; College of Europe, diploma (with distinction), 1959; Columbia University, Ph.D., 1961. Politics: Democrat. Home and office address: Harpswell, Maine 04079.

CAREER: Rutgers University, New Brunswick, N.J., lecturer in American government, 1962; Drew University, Madison, N.J., assistant professor of political science, 1962-63; Commission of the European Economic Community, Brussels, Belgium, deputy official spokesman, 1963-66; Washington Post, Washington, D.C., economic correspondent from Europe, 1966-68; Twentieth Century Fund, New York, N.Y., research associate in public affairs, 1968-70; executive assistant to Senator George McGovern in Washington, D.C., 1970-72; WNET-Television, New York, N.Y., producer and correspondent, 1973-75; Political Intelligence, Inc., Washington, D.C., president and publisher of Political Intelligence, 1974—. Professorial lecturer at American University, 1963-64; faculty member at College of Europe, 1966-67; lecturer at Bernard M. Baruch College of the City University of New York, 1969-70; visting professor at Bowdoin College, 1973-74; lecturer at Colby College, 1977. Military service: U.S. Army, Adjutant General's Corps, personnel officer, 1961-62; became first lieutenant.

MEMBER: Phi Beta Kappa. Awards, honors: Rockefeller Foundation grant, 1966-68; nominated for New York area Emmy Award by Academy of Television Arts and Sciences, 1974-75, for "The Round Table."

WRITINGS: The European Convention on Human Rights, Sijthoff, 1963; (editor) A Handbook on the European Economic Community, Praeger, 1965; Trade Policy in the Seventies, Twentieth Century Fund, 1969; The Benelux Nations, Holt, 1970; A Foreign Policy for Europe, College of Europe, 1970; (with Ian Davidson) The Gold War: The Story of the World's Monetary Crisis, Holt, 1970; The Long Shot: George McGovern Runs for President, Norton, 1973; American Trade Policy: A New Round, Twentieth Century Fund, 1975; The Consumers Guide to Banks, Stein & Day, 1975, revised edition, 1977; Election '76: A Complete Guide to the Campaign, Political Intelligence, Inc., 1976; Sears, Roebuck U.S.A.: The Great American Catalog Store and How It Grew, Stein & Day, 1977.

Contributor to Encyclopedia Americana and Grolier's Encyclopedia. Contributor to American and foreign journals and newspapers, including New Times, Nation, Newsweek and Politicks.

WORK IN PROGRESS: A book on religious groups and their finances; a book on the Nobel Prize.

SIDELIGHTS: Weil told *CA:* "I am most interested in writing about economic subjects in ways which make them appealing to nonexperts. All too often these important and intriguing stories are not accessible because they are regarded as being too technical or complicated.

"Another matter of concern to me is the relationship between authors and publishers. Authors seem to have too little appreciation or even understanding of the publishing business and the constraints on publishers. On the other hand, publishers trade on authors' vanities and expect them to produce first-rate work on second-rate incomes. There needs to be far more open and frank communication between authors and publishers.

"I am trying to organize a Maine Writers' School, where top writers—investigative reporters, novelists, essayists and others—will teach a program for those interested in improving their skills and seeking to produce marketable material."

* * *

WEINBERG, Helen A(rnstein)   1927-

PERSONAL: Born June 17, 1927, in Orange, N.J.; daughter of Morris Jerome and Jeannette (Tepperman) Arnstein; married Kenneth Gene Weinberg (a lawyer), September 11, 1949; children: Janet S., Hugh B., John A. *Education:* Wellesley College, B.A., 1949; Western Reserve University (now Case Western Reserve University), Ph.D., 1966. *Politics:* Democrat. *Religion:* Jewish. *Home:* 3015 Huntington Rd., Shaker Heights, Ohio 44120. *Office:* Cleveland Institute of Art, Cleveland, Ohio 44106.

CAREER: Cleveland Institute of Art, Cleveland, Ohio, teacher, 1959—. Past chairman of local mayor's committee on culture. *Member:* Modern Language Association of America, American Association of University Professors, Book Critics Circle, Northeast Modern Language Association. *Awards, honors:* National Endowment for the Humanities fellowship, 1977-78.

WRITINGS: The New Novel in America: The Kafkan Mode in Contemporary Fiction (Scholars Library selection), Cornell University Press, 1970.

WORK IN PROGRESS: A book about contemporary American painting and writing.

* * *

WEISBERG, Gabriel P(aul)   1942-

PERSONAL: Born May 4, 1942, in New York, N.Y.; son of Harry I. (a certified public accountant) and Sarah (a high school English teacher; maiden name, Stollak) Weisberg; married Yvonne Marie Louise Herzog, July 23, 1967. *Education:* New York University, B.A., 1963; Johns Hopkins University, M.A. and Ph.D., both 1967. *Home:* 2280 Grandview Ave., Cleveland Heights, Ohio 44106. *Office:* Cleveland Museum of Art, Cleveland, Ohio 44106.

CAREER: University of New Mexico, Albuquerque, assistant professor of art history, 1967-69; University of Cincinnati, Cincinnati, Ohio, associate professor of art history and head of department, 1969-73; Cleveland Museum of Art, Cleveland, Ohio, curator of art history and education, 1973—. Adjunct professor at Case Western Reserve University, 1973—; visiting lecturer at museums, galleries, colleges, and universities. Member of National Endowment for the Humanities subcommittee on educational museum programs.

MEMBER: College Art Association of America, Print

Council of America, American Association of University Professors, Society of Architectural Historians. *Awards, honors:* Kress fellowship, 1966-67; American Philosophical Society grant, summer, 1971, 1974; grants from Ohio Arts Council, 1972-73, National Endowment for the Humanities, 1975, 1977-78, and National Endowment for the Arts, 1977; Fulbright fellowship for France, 1974; Butkin Foundation grant, 1976-77; John P. Murphy Foundation grant, 1976-77; Jennings Foundation grant, 1977.

WRITINGS: The Etching Renaissance in France, 1850-1880, Utah Museum of Fine Arts, 1971; *Social Concern and the Worker: French Prints, 1830-1930,* Utah Museum of Fine Arts, 1973; (with Gerald Needham and Dennis Cate) *Japonisme: Japanese Influence on French Art, 1854-1910,* Cleveland Museum of Art, 1975; (with H. W. Janson) *Traditions and Revisions: Themes from the History of Sculpture,* Cleveland Museum of Art, 1975; *Images of Women: Printmakers in France, 1830-1930,* Utah Museum of Fine Arts, 1978; (contributor) *Essays in Honor of H. W. Janson,* Abrams, 1978; (contributor) Elizabeth G. Holt, editor, *The Triumph of Public Art: Salons and Exhibitions of the Nineteenth Century,* Doubleday, in press. Contributor of about seventy-five articles and reviews to art journals.

WORK IN PROGRESS: Francois Bonvin: French Realist; The Ecole Realist in Nineteenth-Century France, a catalog for Cleveland Museum of Art, completion expected in 1980.

SIDELIGHTS: Weisberg writes: "Continually motivated by works of art, and by when they were created, I have sought to uncover neglected artists or tendencies and develop exhibitions or articles around these. In this way the past can be saved before it is lost forever; many painter's works are unjustly neglected and should be saved and understood before it is too late. Luckily, material from the nineteenth century can still be found and used to create illuminating exhibitions for specialists and the general public."

* * *

WEISBORD, Vera Buch   1895-

PERSONAL: Born August 19, 1895, in Forestville, Conn.; daughter of John Casper (a wood carver and engraver) and Nellie Amelia Louisa (Crawford) Buch; married Albert Weisbord (a teacher, management consultant, labor organizer, and writer), November 29, 1938 (deceased). *Education:* Hunter College (now of the City University of New York), A.B., 1916; attended Art Institute of Chicago, 1952-65. *Politics:* "Marxist, unattached at present." *Religion:* None. *Home:* 4800 South Lake Park, Apt. 812, Chicago, Ill. 60615.

CAREER: Writer, 1919—. Stenographer and translator, 1920-21; substitute teacher of French in New York City high schools, 1924-25; labor organizer and strike leader, 1926-29; factory worker in New York City area, 1928-35; artist (paintings, drawings, collages), 1952-72. *Awards, honors:* Three first prizes from Societe Nationale des Professeurs Francais competition, 1913, for translation and composition.

WRITINGS: A Radical Life (autobiography), Indiana University Press, 1977. Also author of two unpublished novels and about one dozen short stories. Contributor to labor periodicals. Associate editor of *Class Struggle,* 1931-36.

WORK IN PROGRESS: A sequel to *A Radical Life;* research on the early period of the Russian Revolution, 1917-22.

SIDELIGHTS: In her autobiography, Vera Weisbord recounts her experiences as a labor union organizer and Communist Party member during the 1920's and 1930's, contributing significantly to the understanding of the role of women in early American radicalism. Presently she is a registered artist with the Illinois Arts Council, and has sold about half of her four hundred paintings. She writes that she has traveled extensively in Europe, North Africa, the Near East, South and Central America, Mexico, and the islands of the Mediterranean, and would someday like to write a travel book.

*   *   *

WEISSMAN, Benjamin M(urry) 1917-

PERSONAL: Born August 3, 1917, in New York, N.Y.; son of Abraham (a house painter) and Sarah (Solomon) Weissman; married Rae Blum (a research sociologist), September 17, 1939; children: Evelyn Weissman Shatz, Anne Weissman Geiger, Joseph. *Education:* City College (now of the City University of New York), B.S., 1936; City University of New York, M.A., 1964; Columbia University, Ph.D., 1968. *Politics:* "Ruthless humanism without regard to ideology, party, or other conflicting loyalties." *Home:* 265 Briarcliff Rd., Teaneck, N.J. 07666. *Office:* Department of Political Science, Rutgers University, Newark, N.J. 07102.

CAREER: New York Sunday Mirror, New York City, junior editor, 1936-37; clerk for U.S. Railway Mail Service, New York City, 1937, and Department of Welfare, New York City, 1938-41; U.S. Treasury Department, New York City, inspector, 1941-43; free-lance writer, 1946-48; Hoffman's, Union City, N.J., partner, 1948-54; Floor Town, Inc., Paramus, N.J., founder and president, 1954-62; City College of the City University of New York, New York City, lecturer in political science, 1964-68; Rutgers University, Newark, N.J., assistant professor, 1968-74, associate professor of political science, 1974—, head of department, 1975—. Member of regional board of Anti-Defamation League; member of Bergen County Fair Housing Committee; alternate delegate to Democratic National Convention, 1972. *Military service:* U.S. Army Air Forces, 1942-46; served in Asiatic-Pacific theater; became captain. *Member:* Academy of Political Science, American Political Science Association, American Association of University Professors, American Association for the Advancement of Slavic Studies.

WRITINGS: Herbert Hoover and Famine Relief to Soviet Russia, 1921-23, Hoover Institution, 1974. Contributor to Slavic studies journals.

WORK IN PROGRESS: The American Political Contest (tentative title), for Goodyear Publishing.

SIDELIGHTS: Weissman writes: "As you can see, it took me a long time to progress from boy wonder college graduate to late bloomer college professor, In between, I savored (and suffered) a wide variety of what they call today 'life experiences,' ranging from T-man, businessman, free-lance writer, to what I do today, which is teach political science and spend more time on trying to understand it.

"After many years of reading, writing, teaching, and reflecting on politics, I have arrived at a few certainties. (I once told a publisher's representative that I was thinking of writing a book called *Weissman's Eternal, Unchanging Principles of Political Theory.* With a perfectly straight face, I added that it would be a loose-leaf book, subject to yearly revision by simply tearing out 'principles' that no longer worked and adding new ones. With an equally straight face, the rep informed me that his firm did not publish loose-leaf books). One of them is that the only legitimate reason for

preserving such a dangerous, expensive institution as government is the outside chance that it might contribute somehow toward preserving survival and self-realization on a decent human level. *And* any social science discipline or research that is not aimed in the same direction is nothing but high-class hobbyism that I will have no part in fostering. It is just too late in the day for diddling with trivial 'data,' no matter how elegantly worked out or sophisticatedly written up. Sometimes when I hear a colleague carrying on about 'rigor' and 'empirical validity,' I get the feeling that the graduate schools have succeeded in turning out armies of folks who are so addicted to formal 'scholarship' that they would insist on the necessity of announcing the end of the world in perfect grammar.

"Among my more serious hobbies is salt-water fishing. After I get through bending over a hot desk talking to occasionally interested students about politics, there is nothing I like better than to go out and lecture all kinds of groups on the same subject. For me, it is the functional substitute for war. I did a weekly commentary on current events on an evangelist radio station. They loved my light, sourball bleeding-heart approach but canceled the show when sponsors didn't rush in to subsidize it. I also engage in crusades. I don't mean movements—I mean crusades. Arlene Francis had me on her radio talk show, to discuss the notorious Senate Bill #1, which had as its goal the elimination of Amendments #1 through 10. As it turned out, I and a couple of hundred like-minded folk did manage to kill Senate Bill #1, which is the thing I'm proudest of."

BIOGRAPHICAL/CRITICAL SOURCES: American Historical Review, October, 1976.

*   *   *

WELLS, Robert Vale 1943-

PERSONAL: Born July 14, 1943, in Bridgeport, Conn.; son of Ronald Vale (a clergyman) and Patricia (Woodburne) Wells; married Cathie Marie Andersen, September 5, 1964; children: Lisa, Vanessa. *Education:* Denison University, B.A., 1965; Princeton University, Ph.D., 1969. *Home:* 1769 Randolph Rd., Schenectady, N.Y. 12308. *Office:* Department of History, Union College, Schenectady, N.Y. 12308.

CAREER: Union College, Schenectady, N.Y., instructor, 1969, assistant professor, 1969-74, associate professor of history, 1974—. *Member:* American Historical Association, Organization of American Historians, Population Association of America. *Awards, honors:* Fellow of Charles Warren Center at Harvard University, 1974-75; Guggenheim fellowship, 1977-78.

WRITINGS: The Population of the British Colonies in America Before 1776: A Survey of Census Data, Princeton University Press, 1975. Contributor to history and population studies journals.

WORK IN PROGRESS: Revolutions in Americans' Lives: The Impact of Population in American History, completion expected in 1979.

SIDELIGHTS: Wells comments: "My main interest is to establish the importance of birth, death, marriage, and migration in people's lives, and to trace the major historical changes which have occurred with regard to these matters during the past two centuries. The history of the family is also important to my work."

*   *   *

WERSTEIN, Irving 1914(?)-1971

PERSONAL: Born 1914(?), in Brooklyn, N.Y.. *Education:*

Attended New York University.

CAREER: Author of historical stories for children, and journalist. During World War II, served in the U.S. Army as a field correspondent for *Yank* magazine.

WRITINGS—History: *July, 1863,* Messner, 1957, reprinted as *The Draft Riots: July, 1863,* 1971; *Abraham Lincoln Versus Jefferson Davis,* Crowell, 1959; *Danger at Dry Creek: Tales of Wells Fargo* (illustrated by Al Schmidt), Golden Press, 1959; *Marshal Without a Gun: Tom Smith,* Messner, 1959; *The Blizzard of '68,* Crowell, 1960; *Man Against the Elements: Adolphus W. Greely,* Messner, 1960; *The Battle of Midway,* Crowell, 1961; *The Many Faces of the Civil War,* Messner, 1961.

A Nation Fights Back: The Depression and Its Aftermath, Messner, 1962; *The Battle of Aachen,* Crowell, 1962; *Civil War Sailor* (illustrated by Albert Orbaan), Doubleday, 1962; *Kearny, the Magnificent: The Story of General Philip Kearny, 1818-1862,* John Day, 1962; *Guadalcanal,* Crowell, 1963; *Jack Wade: Fighter for Liberty* (illustrated by A. Orbaan), Doubleday, 1963; *The Many Faces of World War I,* Messner, 1963; *Massacre at Sand Creek,* Scribner, 1963; *The Long Escape,* Scribner, 1964; *Turning Point for America: The Story of the Spanish-American War,* Messner, 1964; *Wake: The Story of a Battle,* Crowell, 1964.

The Battle of Salerno, Crowell, 1965; *The Franco-Prussian War: Germany's Rise as a World Power,* Messner, 1965; *The General Slocum Incident: Story of an Ill-Fated Ship,* John Day, 1965; *The Great Struggle: Labor in America,* Scribner, 1965; *Tarawa: A Battle Report,* Crowell, 1965; *The War with Mexico,* Norton, 1965; *The Lost Battalion,* Norton, 1966; *I Accuse: The Story of the Dreyfus Case,* Messner, 1967; *The Plotters: The New York Conspiracy of 1741,* Scribner, 1967; *Sound No Trumpet: The Life and Death of Alan Seeger,* Crowell, 1967; *Ten Days in November: The Russian Revolution,* Macrae Smith, 1967.

Okinawa: The Last Ordeal, Crowell, 1968; *Over Here and Over There: The Era of the First World War,* Norton, 1968; *The Uprising of the Warsaw Ghetto: November 1940-May 1943,* Norton, 1968; *This Wounded Land: The Era of Reconstruction, 1865-1877,* Delacorte, 1968; *All the Furious Battles: The Saga of Israel's Army,* Meredith Press, 1969; *Betrayal: The Munich Pact of 1938,* Doubleday, 1969; *The Cruel Years: The Story of the Spanish Civil War,* Messner, 1969; *The Cruise of the Essex: An Incident from the War of 1812,* Macrae Smith, 1969; *Labor's Defiant Lady: The Story of Mother Jones,* Crowell, 1969.

Pie in the Sky: An American Struggle the Wobblies and Their Time, Delacorte, 1969; *The Stars and Stripes: The Story of Our Flag,* Golden Press, 1969; *Strangled Voices: The Story of the Haymarket Affair,* Macmillan, 1969; *The Trespassers: Korea, June 1871* (illustrated by Joseph Papin), Dutton, 1969; *Year of Turmoil: 1939,* Messner, 1969; *A Proud People: Black Americans* (photos by Bob Adelman), M. Evans, 1970; *Shattered Decade: 1919-1929,* Scribner, 1970; *The Storming of Fort Wagner: Black Valor in the Civil War,* Scholastic Book Services, 1970; *The Supremo: Lord Louis Mountbatten and the Testing of Democracy,* Macrae Smith, 1971; *Land and Liberty: The Mexican Revolution, 1910-1919,* Cowles, 1971; *The Boxer Rebellion: Anti-Foreign Terror Seizes China, 1900,* F. Watts, 1971.

Pictorial works: *1861-1865: The Adventure of the Civil War Told with Pictures,* Pageant Books, 1960; *1776: The Adventure of the American Revolution Told with Pictures,* Cooper Square, 1962; *1914-1918: World War I Told with Pictures,* Cooper Square, 1964; *1898: The Spanish-American War Told with Pictures,* Cooper Square, 1966.

SIDELIGHTS: In a comment upon one of Werstein's books a *New York Times* critic observed: "Werstein's purpose is clear: to show today's young reader that the turmoil of the present did not happen spontaneously."

BIOGRAPHICAL/CRITICAL SOURCES: New York Times Book Review, November 9, 1969, October 11, 1970.

OBITUARIES: New York Times, April 9, 1971; *Publishers' Weekly,* April 26, 1971; *Antiquarian Bookman,* June 24, 1971.*

(Died April 7, 1971)

* * *

WESSEL, Andrew E(rnest) 1925-

PERSONAL: Born November 4, 1925, in Camden, N.J.; son of Norman I. and Mae (Teitelman) Wessel; married Sally Levit, June 27, 1951 (died, 1968); married Hildegard G. Heinrich (a translator), January 7, 1969; children: Madelyn F., Allan E., Markus H., Ingrid D. *Education:* University of Pennsylvania, A.B., 1950, A.M., 1951; University of California, Los Angeles, further graduate study, 1953-54. *Politics:* "In Bavaria: Monarchist; U.S.A.: Democrat." *Religion:* "Antiquarian." *Home and office:* 8891 Adelzhausen, West Germany.

CAREER: Institute for Cooperative Research, University of Pennsylvania, Philadelphia, research associate, 1954-56; Ramo-Wooldridge Corp., Los Angeles, Calif., technical and senior staff member, 1956-61; RAND Corp., Santa Monica, Calif., senior staff member, 1961-69; consultant on information systems and sciences in western Europe, 1969—. *Military service:* U.S. Army, 1943-45; became technical sergeant.

WRITINGS: Computer-Aided Information Retrieval, Wiley, 1975; *The Social Use of Information,* Wiley, 1976. Contributor to professional journals in English and German.

WORK IN PROGRESS: Implementation of Complex Information Systems, publication by Wiley expected in 1979; *Tales for Scienцists and Other Curious Children;* poems.

SIDELIGHTS: Wessel writes: "The 'technology managers'—those involved in the development, application, distribution of the products of technology—often behave as though they were feudal barons, jealous of their prerogatives, protective of their interests within their domains, and preferring only applause or silent acceptance from their public. A small but growing number of scientists and technological innovators have become more broadly concerned with the direct and indirect social impact of what they do. Some of these attempt to create a wider public understanding of and participation in the use and expansion of scientific knowledge. In part this is their attempt to maintain and strengthen the significant forms of democratic processes within their societies. I would hope that *The Social Use of Information* and much of my other work places me within this group so concerned."

* * *

WEST, James
See WITHERS, Carl A.

* * *

WESTON, Alan J(ay) 1940-

PERSONAL: Born February 7, 1940, in New York, N.Y.; married wife Marsha, September 2, 1962; children: Shayne, Marni, Scott. *Education:* University of Alabama, B.A.,

1963, M.A., 1965; University of Kansas, Ph.D., 1969. *Home:* 2201 West Kenboern Dr., Glendale, Wis. 53209. *Office:* School of Allied Health Professions, University of Wisconsin, Milwaukee, Wis. 53201.

CAREER: University of Alabama, University, instructor in speech, 1965-67; University of Kansas, Lawrence, assistant professor of speech, 1969-70; Memphis State University, Memphis, Tenn., associate professor, 1970-72, professor of audiology and speech pathology, 1972-76, chairman of department and director of Memphis Speech and Hearing Center, 1970-76; University of Wisconsin, Milwaukee, professor of speech pathology and audiology, 1976—, dean of School of Allied Health Professions, 1976—. Adjunct professor at University of Tennessee, 1971-76. Member of Mid-South Medical Council; member of Tennessee Board of Education for Certification Standards. Coordinator of audiology and speech pathology for Memphis City Hospitals, 1971-76; member of board of directors of Memphis Oral School for the Deaf and Memphis Speech and Hearing Center.

MEMBER: American Speech and Hearing Association (fellow), Council for Exceptional Children, American Psychological Association, National Association of Executives, National Association of Hearing and Speech Agencies, American Society of Allied Health Professions, Wisconsin Speech and Hearing Association, Tennessee Speech and Hearing Association.

WRITINGS: (Editor and contributor) *Communicative Disorders: An Appraisal,* C. C Thomas, 1972; (contributor) *An Appraisal of Speech Pathology and Audiology: A Symposium,* C. C Thomas, 1973; *The Modification of Articulatory Behavior,* Grune, in press. Contributor to professional journals. Editor of *Allied Health and Behavioral Sciences,* 1977; associate editor of *Journal of the Tennessee Speech and Hearing Association,* 1970-74, and *Journal of Language, Speech, and Hearing Services in Schools,* 1974—; managing editor of *Acta Symbolica,* 1972-76; reviewer for *Journal of Speech and Hearing Research,* 1973-75.

* * *

WETHERBEE, Winthrop (III) 1938-

PERSONAL: Born July 10, 1938, in Boston, Mass.; son of Winthrop, Jr. (a physician) and Carolyn (Hall) Wetherbee; married Andrea Kempf (a curator), March 25, 1962; children: Peter, Jonathan. *Education:* Harvard University, B.A., 1960; University of Leeds, M.A., 1962; University of California, Berkeley, Ph.D., 1967. *Home:* 604 Highland Rd., Ithaca, N.Y. 14850. *Office:* Department of English, Cornell University, Ithaca, N.Y. 14850.

CAREER: Cornell University, Ithaca, N.Y., assistant professor, 1967-72, associate professor, 1972-74, professor of English, 1974—. *Member:* Mediaeval Academy of America, Ithaca Yacht Club. *Awards, honors:* American Council of Learned Societies fellowship, 1970-71; Guggenheim fellowship, 1974-75.

WRITINGS: Platonism and Poetry in the Twelfth Century, Princeton University Press, 1972; *The Cosmographia of Bernardus Silvestris,* Columbia University Press, 1973.

WORK IN PROGRESS: A textbook on medieval Latin; a study of Dante's influence on Chaucer.

* * *

WEXLER, Jerome (LeRoy) 1923-
(Roy Delmar)

PERSONAL: Born February 6, 1923, in New York, N.Y.; son of Lewis (a tailor) and Rose (a clothing designer; maiden name, Leiberman) Wexler; married Gwen Schorr, June 24, 1951 (divorced January 10, 1975); children: Amy, Herbert. *Education:* Attended Pratt Institute and University of Connecticut. *Politics:* "Not interested in politics." *Religion:* Unitarian. *Home and office:* 4 Middle Lane, Wallingford, Conn. 06492.

CAREER: Agricultural Photo Library (stock photograph company), Wallingford, Conn., owner and operator, 1950-58; tool and parts inspector in New Haven, Conn., 1958-73; full-time writer and photographer, 1973—. *Military service:* U.S. Army, 1943-46. *Awards, honors:* American Institute of Graphic Arts certificate of excellence, 1972, for *The Carrot and Other Root Vegetables.*

WRITINGS—Self-illustrated: (With Carolyn Meyer) *Rock Tumbling: From Stones to Gems to Jewelry* (juvenile), Morrow, 1974; *How to Tumble Polish Gemstones and Make Tumbled Jewelry,* Gemac, 1977. Illustrator and photographer for numerous books for children by Millicent E. Selsam. Agricultural photographs have been published under pseudonym Roy Delmar.

WORK IN PROGRESS: Photographic essays on plants, animals, and insects.

SIDELIGHTS: Wexler writes: "I don't know why but almost all nature photographers run around photographing plants only in their flowering and/or fruiting stage. My approach is to study, and photograph the entire life cycle—from seed to seed. When this photo essay is unfolded in a book or in a slide show it entices the reader/viewer with something he can understand and gives me the opportunity of presenting a tremendous amount of botany without the reader/viewer realizing that he's being fed this so-called dull subject.

"The books are directed at children because I believe that if we can get them involved and interested in the world around them now they will never, as adults, be bored, for there is always another plant, insect, or animal to raise and study.

"For many years I owned and ran a stock photo house. I took all of the pictures and showed both good and bad agricultural practices. The pictures were used basically for educational purposes and about four thousand to five thousand were published throughout the world. At present, I am a self-employed writer-photographer specializing in the photography of the world around us: plants, animals, and insects. These photo essays are used in books, magazines, film strips, etc. These pictures, like those for the Agricultural Photo Library, are used basically for educational purposes."

* * *

WEYL, Joachim 1915-1977

1915—July 21, 1977; Swiss-born American scientist, educator, and author. Weyl was chief scientist for the Office of Naval Research and participated in the atomic-bomb tests on the island of Bikini. He died in New York, N.Y. Obituaries: *New York Times,* July 23, 1977.

* * *

WHARTON, David B(ailey) 1914-

PERSONAL: Born February 12, 1914, in Berkeley, Calif.; son of Jay B. (a petroleum engineer) and Leslie (Bailey) Wharton; married Frances Wheaton Booth, September 23, 1937; children: Wendy Wharton Cole, Bailey Frazier. *Education:* Washington & Lee University, J.D., 1937; Stanford University, M.A., 1941. *Home and office:* 1438 Shippee

Land, Ojai, Calif. 93023. *Agent:* Collier Associates, 280 Madison Ave., New York, N.Y. 10016.

CAREER: Colorado State University, Fort Collins, instructor in English and journalism, 1941-43; Office of War Information, San Francisco, Calif., radio newswriter, 1943-46; Department of State, U.S. Foreign Service, Washington, D.C., economic officer in Kabul, Afghanistan, Wellington, New Zealand, and Djakarta, Indonesia, 1947-54, diplomat in India, Pakistan, Japan, Korea, the Philippines, and Taiwan, 1946-62, political officer for British Caribbean, and diplomat in Bermuda, 1962-64; writer and public speaker, 1964—. Professor at Long Island University.

WRITINGS: Thugs on Strike, Korea House, 1962; *Alaska Gold Rush,* Indiana University Press, 1972. Contributor to magazines, including *Asia and the Americas, American Forest, American West,* and *Sea.*

WORK IN PROGRESS: Southeast Alaska: The Inside Passage.

SIDELIGHTS: An authority on emerging societies, Wharton spent two years on a roving assigment inspecting, studying, and reporting on the foreign policy of the United States and the problems of countries in the Far East receiving American assistance. Although he has been received by Mohammed Zahir Shah, King of the Afghans, dined with Nehru and the Mir of Nunza, traveled with Sukarno, played golf with President Garcia of the Philippines, been received by Chiang Kai-shek and entertained by cabinet ministers of Japan and Korea, he has also eaten from the communal pot with tribesmen in the hills and spent more time touring the back country in a jeep than he has in striped trousers at the Foreign Office. He has trekked into Gilgit, been lost in Honduras, threatened with execution in Afghanistan, toured the front lines of Korea by helicopter and jeep, visited Matsu and Quemoy within gun shot of the mainland of China; he is the only westerner ever to travel the hostile unadministered territory between Pakistan and Afghanistan.

*   *   *

WHARTON, John Franklin   1894-1977

July 28, 1894—November 24, 1977; American lawyer and author. Wharton represented many producers, playwrights, and songwriters from the world of the theatre, including Cole Porter and Dwight Wiman. Using his legal talents to aid his friends in the theatre, he devised contracts beneficial to writers and producers, and helped to form the Playwrights Producing Company which enabled writers to maintain control of their material. Among Wharton's writings were two books on economics, a novel, and various articles for *Saturday Review.* He died in Manhattan, N.Y. Obituaries: *New York Times,* November 25, 1977; *Time,* December 5, 1977.

*   *   *

WHEATLEY, Dennis (Yeats)   1897-1977

January 8, 1897—November 11, 1977; British writer of thrillers and books on the occult. One of Wheatley's more than sixty books, *The Devil and All His Works,* is considered to be a modern textbook on satanism. Wheatley's books have been translated into more than twenty-five languages. He died in London, England. Obituaries: *New York Times,* November 12, 1977; *Washington Post,* November 12, 1977; *AB Bookman's Weekly,* February 6, 1978. (See index for *CA* sketch)

WHEELER, David Raymond   1942-

PERSONAL: Born November 6, 1942, in Shreveport, La.; son of David and Mary A. (Worsham) Wheeler. *Education:* Texas Tech University, B.A., 1966, M.B.A., 1968, D.B.A., 1974; also attended New York University and New School for Social Research, 1975—, and Columbia University, 1976. *Home:* 1 Main St., University of Houston, Tex. 77002. *Agent:* Anita Diamant, Writers' Workshop, 51 East 42nd St., New York, N.Y. 10017.

CAREER: U.S. Department of Commerce, Washington, D.C., meteorologist, summers, 1962-64; State of Texas, Austin, auditor, 1968-69; David R. Wheeling Marketing Research, Houston, Tex., president, 1968—. Engineer for LTV Aerospace Corp., 1969-70. Assistant professor at University of North Dakota, 1972-74, Grand Forks Air Force Base, 1973-74, and Bernard M. Baruch College of the City University of New York, 1974-77; visiting professor at Texas Tech University, summers, 1973-74, and Bloomfield College, summer, 1976; associate professor at University of Houston, 1977—. *Member:* American Marketing Association, American Academy of Advertising, Mensa, Southern Marketing Association.

WRITINGS: Journey to the Other Side, Tempo Books, 1976; *Control Yourself,* Nelson-Hall, 1976; *The Lubbock Lights,* Award Books, 1977. Contributor to business, marketing, and advertising journals.

WORK IN PROGRESS: Research on marketing decisions and planning, on gambling, and on secrets and mysteries of the Gulf of Mexico.

SIDELIGHTS: Wheeler stated briefly that *Journey to the Other Side* is a collection of investigative reports of individuals who experienced "clinical" death and then were resuscitated; *Control Yourself* is a behavior modification approach to self-control; *The Lubbock Lights* is an investigation of UFO's and other strange events in western Texas.

AVOCATIONAL INTERESTS: Flying (pilot).

*   *   *

WHITBECK, George W(alter)   1932-

PERSONAL: Born February 17, 1932, in Lewiston, Me.; son of G. Paul (a professor) and Margaret (Lotspeich) Whitbeck; married Ruth Myers, August 27, 1966; children: Margaret R., Paul D. *Education:* Attended Bates College, 1950-52; Columbia University, B.A. (honors), 1957, M.S., 1959, M.A., 1962; Rutgers University, Ph.D., 1970. *Home:* 1911 Montclair Ave., Bloomington, Ind. 47401. *Office:* Graduate Library School, Indiana University, Bloomington, Ind. 47401.

CAREER: United Air Lines, New York City, reservations agent, 1957-58; City College (now of the City University of New York), New York City, library assistant, 1959-61; Levittown Public Library, Levittown, N.Y., reference assistant, 1962-63; State University of New York College at New Paltz, associate director of library for reader services, 1963-67; University of Michigan, Ann Arbor, assistant professor of library science, 1970-73; University of Southern Mississippi, Hattiesburg, professor of library science and chairman of department, 1973-75; Indiana University, Bloomington, professor of library science and associate dean of Graduate Library School, 1975—. *Military service:* U.S. Army, medical corpsman, 1952-55; served in Korea.

MEMBER: American Library Association, Association of College and Research Libraries, Public Library Association, Association of American Library Schools, American

Association of University Professors, American Society for Information Science, Indiana Library Association, Phi Delta Kappa, Catskill 3500 Club.

WRITINGS: The Influence of Librarians in Liberal Arts Colleges in Selected Decision Making Areas, Scarecrow, 1972. Contributor to library science journals.

WORK IN PROGRESS: Research on education for librarianship, public library services, and servicing of government publications collections.

AVOCATIONAL INTERESTS: Hiking, travel, music.

*   *   *

WHITCOMB, Philip W(right) 1891-

PERSONAL: Born November 24, 1891, in Topeka, Kan.; son of George Herbert (a district judge) and Jessie (a lawyer and writer; maiden name, Wright) Whitcomb; married Gertrude Valerie McClintock, August 10, 1914 (deceased); married Genevieve Auriol, August 18, 1942; children: John, Valerie (Mrs. Robert Valaas), Phillida (Mrs. Bond States), Giles MacNair, Gillian Auriol. *Education:* Washburn University, B.A., 1910, further study in law shcool, 1910-11, D.Litt., 1962; Oxford University, B.A., 1914, M.A., 1952. *Politics:* Republican. *Religion:* Presbyterian. *Home:* 42 Terrasse de l'Iris, Apt. 13, Defense-2, 92400 Courbevoie, France.

CAREER: European correspondent for *Harper's Weekly, New York Tribune, Foreign Trade Weekly,* and *Boston Evening Transcript,* 1914-41; war correspondent for Associated Press in France, 1941-42; European correspondent for *Baltimore Sun,* 1942-47; special correspondent, based in Paris, for *Christian Science Monitor,* 1947—. Ex-officio member of board of directors of American Chamber of Commerce in Germany, 1947-67; director of American Chamber of Commerce in France, 1947—; member of the board of American Center for Students and Artists, Paris, 1950—; trustee of American College in Paris, 1962—. *Wartime service:* European war correspondent, 1914-18, 1933 (Riff War), 1941-45; interned twice in Germany during World War II (six months and fifteen months); received U.S. Army award for correspondents, 1945. *Member:* Overseas Press Club of America, Anglo-American Press Association (Paris), American Rhodes Scholars Association, Kappa Sigma, University Club (Paris), Oxford Society, United Oxford and Cambridge University Club (London), Washburn University Alumni Association, Wadham Society, Cercle Interallie, American Club (Paris), American Church in Paris (elder, 1947-67). *Awards, honors:* Rhodes Scholarship, 1911; distinguished service award from Washburn University, 1958; distinguished service award from American Chamber of Commerce in Germany, 1967; Overseas Press Club of America award for best economic reporting from any foreign country to any United States medium, 1970 and 1975; distinguished service award from American Chamber of Commerce in France, 1976.

WRITINGS: (Editor and translator) *France During the German Occupation, 1940-1944,* three volumes, Stanford University Press, 1959; *When You Come to France,* L'-Economie (Paris), 1969; *Seventy-Five Years in the Franco-American Economy,* American Chamber of Commerce in France, 1970.

Editor of *Euromarket News,* 1938-67, *Commerce in France,* 1946-67, *Commerce in Germany,* 1947-67, and *Cross-Channel Trade,* 1960-67.

WORK IN PROGRESS: Research on Benjamin Franklin's seven year road to Yorktown, and on Francisco Suarez at a turning point in the development of Europe's law and philosophy; reminiscences of sixty-three years of journalism in seventeen European and African countries; *A Topeka Whitcomb,* reminiscences of youth and college days.

SIDELIGHTS: Whitcomb shared these reflections about life with *CA:* "No matter how happily an individual may try to escape them, he will discover sooner or later that he is under five obligations. First, and absolutely basic, to maintain in perfect working condition the organism which he has inherited. Second, as a human being to persist in trying to understand the pains and joys, the hopes and discouragements, and the prejudices and tricks of other human beings. Third, as a son or daughter, husband or wife, to make as great an effort to succeed as he makes to succeed in profession, sport, or social life. Fourth, as a citizen, to understand the true needs of his community and then to work for them. Fifth, in business or professional life to be prepared, to watch for openings, and then when luck strikes, to go in fast."

Commenting on his views of his profession, Whitcomb wrote: "Events and statements must be reported in such a way that they also illustrate an essential truth about the country, the people, or the basic situation in that country—if possible, indirectly and unostentatiously—to prevent readers at home from accepting the dangerous adage that 'all countries are basically the same.'"

*   *   *

WHITE, Anthony Gene 1946-

PERSONAL: Born November 8, 1946, in Eugene, Ore.; son of Wallace Eugene (a city manager) and Vivian Arlene (a sales manager; maiden name, Thomson) White; married Carole Ann Price (a life insurance service manager), May 17, 1969. *Education:* Oregon State University, B.S., 1967; Portland State University, M.S., 1971, M.P.A., 1977. *Politics:* Independent. *Religion:* Christian. *Home:* 3270 Forest Court, West Linn, Ore. 97068.

CAREER: City-County Charter Commission, Portland, Ore., research associate, 1971-74; Multnomah County Administrative Services, Portland, property control officer, 1974-75; Portland Area Boundary Commission, Portland, administrative assistant, 1975-76; District Attorney's Office, Portland, program evaluator, 1976-77. Consultant on local government matters. *Military service:* U.S. Army, 1969-72.

MEMBER: American Association for the Advancement of Science, American Mathematical Society, National Municipal League, World Future Society, Futures Information Network, Western Political Science Association, Western Governmental Research Association.

WRITINGS: Reforming Metropolitan Governments, Garland Publishing, 1975. Author of bibliographic monographs for Council of Planning Librarians. Contributor to planning and civic affairs journals.

WORK IN PROGRESS: Research on public administration, boards and commissions, urban problems, and futures studies.

SIDELIGHTS: White comments: "My interest in urban problems developed in the late 1960's, and I was constantly amazed that the federal government could on the one hand call for more urban specialists and on the other hand draft them to fight in Vietnam. By combining my mathematical, bibliographical and futures-related interests, I hope to bring to the urban problems literature a different approach somewhat closer to the scientific method than has been used in the past."

* * *

WHITE, Emmons E(aton) 1891-

PERSONAL: Born April 4, 1891, in Trumbull, Conn.; son of William Franklin (a clergyman) and Bessie (a teacher; maiden name, Eaton) White; married Ruth Parker (a missionary), August 11, 1917; children: Laura (Mrs. John F. Neville), Robin (son), Stephen. *Education:* Yale University, B.A., 1914, B.D., 1917; also studied at Harvard University, 1925. *Politics:* "Republican first, now of no special party." *Home and office:* 669 Harrison Ave., Claremont, Calif. 91711.

CAREER: Ordained a Congregational clergyman, 1917; United Church Board for World Ministries, missionary and teacher in Madura and Ramnad districts of South India, 1917-58; pastor of community church in Russell, Mass., 1959-62; writer, 1963—. Chairman of Madura Church Council, 1946-47; deputy chairman of Madura and Ramnad diocese, 1947-58; president of American College Council, 1947-48. *Member:* University Club (Claremont, Calif.). *Awards, honors:* Named Guardian of Tamil Music by Tamil Theological College of Madura, 1972, for his books and performance of "song-sermons."

WRITINGS: The Kalakshepam as a Method of Evangelism (in Tamil), Christian Literature Society, 1955; *Appreciating India's Music: An Introduction to the Music of India with Suggestions for Its Use in the Churches of India,* Christian Literature Society, 1957, revised edition published as *Appreciating India's Music: An Introduction, with an Emphasis on the Music of South India,* Crescendo, 1971; *The Wisdom of India,* Peter Pauper, 1968; *The Wisdom of the Tamil People, As Illustrated by Translated Selections from Their Ancient Literature,* Munshiram Manoharlal, 1975. Contributor to religious magazines.

WORK IN PROGRESS: Translating the biography of Tamil poet-saint Sundarar, as recorded in *Sacred Tamil Prose Work.*

SIDELIGHTS: White writes: "During my career in South India I became fascinated with the study of Tamil classical literature. Tamil is the language of South India, which we used. I also studied the classical music of South India, using it in the communication of the Christian Gospel to the Tamil people in their own language. I have given over eighty public performances of the 'Kalakshepam' or 'song-sermon'. Without condemnation of any non-Christian faith, I have stressed the importance of accepting Christ."

* * *

WHITE, Jan Viktor 1928-

PERSONAL: Born April 6, 1928, in Prague, Czechoslovakia; came to the United States in 1948, naturalized citizen, 1953; son of Emil (an artist) and Karla (a pianist; maiden name, Kubin) Weiss. married Clare Mallon (a language teacher), July 20, 1962; children: Charles, Alexander, Gregory, Christopher. *Education:* Cornell University, B.Arch., 1951; Columbia University, M.S., 1952. *Home and office:* 213 Wilton Rd., Westport, Conn. 06880.

CAREER: Time, Inc., New York, N.Y., art director for *House and Home,* 1952-64; free-lance consultant, art director, graphic designer, and writer, 1964—. Has designed more than fifty magazine formats in the United States and Latin America; lecturer on editorial presentation. *Military service:*

U.S. Army, Exhibit Unit, 1952-54; became sergeant. *Member:* Society of Publication Designers. *Awards, honors:* More than forty awards for graphic and magazine design, including two silver medals from Society of Publication Designers, 1974, and a gold medal, 1977.

WRITINGS: Editing by Design, Bowker, 1974; *Designing: For Magazines,* Bowker, 1976. Contributor to *Folio.*

WORK IN PROGRESS: Compiling in book form a series of his articles originally published in monthly segments by *Folio* magazine.

SIDELIGHTS: White comments that he has had "twenty-five years' experience in bridging the gap between editors and art directors: teaching editors to become visually sensitive and thus better able to use graphic means to transmit non-graphic thoughts; and persuading designers to expand their vision to include journalism, where the content of the story is more important than its form."

AVOCATIONAL INTERESTS: Carpentry, travel.

* * *

WHITE, Nicholas P. 1942-

PERSONAL: Born July 17, 1942, in New York, N.Y.; son of Morton G. (a professor) and Lucia (a researcher; maiden name, Perry) White; married Merry Isaacs, June 9, 1963 (divorced, December, 1970); married Patricia Denise (an attorney), February 20, 1971; children: Jennifer Robin, Olivia Lawrence. *Education:* Harvard University, B.A., 1963, M.A., 1965, Ph.D., 1970. *Office:* Department of Philosophy, University of Michigan, Ann Arbor, Mich. 48109.

CAREER: University of Michigan, Ann Arbor, lecturer, 1969-70, assistant professor, 1970-75, professor of philosophy, 1975—. *Member:* Society for Ancient Greek Philosophy. *Awards, honors:* National Endowment for the Humanities younger humanist grant, 1974; American Council of Learned Societies fellowship, 1975-76; Guggenheim fellowship, 1977-78.

WRITINGS: Plato on Knowledge and Reality, Hackett, 1976. Contributor to philosophy journals.

WORK IN PROGRESS: Research on Greek ethics, especially Plato's *Republic,* Aristotle's *Nicomachean Ethics,* and Stoic ethics.

* * *

WHITE, Robert Mitchell II 1915-

PERSONAL: Born April 6, 1915, in Mexico, Mo.; son of L. Mitchell (an editor and publisher) and Maude (See) White; married; children: three daughters, one son. *Education:* Washington and Lee University, A.B., 1938. *Home:* 3 Park Circle, Mexico, Mo. 65265. *Office address:* P.O. Box 8, Mexico, Mo. 65265.

CAREER/WRITINGS: United Press International (UPI), Kansas City, Mo., reporter, 1939-40; *Mexico Ledger,* Mexico, Mo., co-editor and publisher, 1946—, president, 1954—. Special consultant to editor and publisher of *Chicago Sun-Times,* 1956-59; president and editor of *New York Herald Tribune,* 1959-61. Notable assignments include studying Soviet press. Contributor to several journalism books and publications. President of Mark Land Co., See Tv Co.; member of board of directors of Associated Press (AP), and other organizations. University lecturer; assistant professor, University of Missouri, 1968-69. *Military:* U.S. Army, Field Artillery, 1940-45; became lieutenant colonel; received Bronze Star Medal. *Member:* International Press Institute,

American Newspaper Publishers Association, National Press Club, American Society of Newspaper Editors, Beta Theta Pi. *Awards, honors:* Sigma Delta Chi Distinguished Service to Journalism Award, 1951 and 1968; Silurian Award, 1959, for best editorial published in New York; University of Missouri Distinguished Service to Journalism Award, 1967; Sigma Delta Chi Wells Key Award, 1970; has also received several regional and state awards.

WORK IN PROGRESS: Journey to China, a compilation of columns written after his first trip to China in 1972; *Second Journey to China,* a compilation of columns about his trip in September, 1977.

* * *

WHITE, T(erence) H(anbury) 1906-1964
(James Aston)

PERSONAL: Born May 29, 1906, in Bombay, India; son of Garrick Hanbury and Constance Edith Southcote (Aston) White. *Education:* Queens' College, Cambridge, B.A. (first class honors), 1928.

CAREER: Teacher at Stowe School in England, resigning at the age of thirty to devote his time to writing. *Member:* British Falconers' Club.

WRITINGS—Fiction, except as noted: *Loved Helen, and Other Poems,* Chatto & Windus, 1929; *The Green Bay Tree; or, The Wicked Man Touches Wood,* Heffer, 1929; (with Ronald M. Scott) *Dead Mr. Nixon,* Cassell, 1931; (under pseudonym James Aston) *First Lesson: A Novel,* Chatto & Windus, 1932, Knopf, 1933; (under pseudonym James Aston) *They Winter Abroad: A Novel,* Viking, 1932, reprinted under author's real name, Chatto & Windus, 1969; *Darkness at Pemberley,* Gollancz, 1932, Century, 1933; *Farewell Victoria,* Collins, 1933, H. Smith & R. Haas, 1934, new edition, Putnam, 1960; *Earth Stopped; or, Mr. Marx's Sporting Tour,* Collins, 1934; *Gone to Ground: A Novel,* Collins, 1935; *Song through Space, and Other Poems,* Lincoln Williams, 1935.

The Sword in the Stone (Book-of-the-Month Club selection), Collins, 1938, Putnam, 1939, reprinted, Collins, 1972; *The Witch in the Wood,* Putnam, 1939, published as *The Queen of Air and Darkness* (also see below), Putnam, 1958; *The Ill-Made Knight,* Putnam, 1940; *Mistress Masham's Repose* (Book-of-the-Month Club selection; illustrated by Fritz Eichenberg), Putnam, 1946; *The Elephant and the Kangaroo,* Putnam, 1947; *The Master: An Adventure Story,* Putnam, 1957; *The Once and Future King* (contains *The Sword in the Stone, The Queen of Air and Darkness, The Ill-Made Knight,* and *The Candle in the Wind*), Putnam, 1958; *Verses,* Alderney, 1962.

Nonfiction: *England Have My Bones,* Macmillan, 1936; *Burke's Steerage; or, The Amateur Gentleman's Introduction to Noble Sports and Pastimes,* Collins, 1938; *The Age of Scandal: An Excursion through a Minor Period,* Putnam, 1950; *The Goshawk,* J. Cape, 1951, Putnam, 1952, new edition, Longman, 1973; *The Scandalmonger,* Putnam, 1952; (editor and translator) *The Book of Beasts: A Translation from a Latin Bestiary of the 12th Century,* Putnam, 1954; *The Godstone and the Blackymor* (illustrated by Edward Ardizzone), Putnam, 1959; *America at Last: The American Journal of T. H. White,* Putnam, 1965; *The White/Garnett Letters,* edited by David Garnett, Viking, 1968; *The Book of Merlyn,* University of Texas Press, 1977.

Author of the periodical publication, *Terence White's Verse-Reel,* 1939— .

SIDELIGHTS: After resigning as a school teacher, White spent time traveling through Western Ireland. The author's account of the journey was told in his book, *The Godstone and the Blackymor.* "The character of the author himself—headstrong, eccentric, humorous, and kind," said a critic for the *Chicago Sunday Tribune,* "is so woven into his descriptions of people and places that it does not seem as tho he were merely describing them for you, but had brought you there. He has the priceless gift of being able suddenly to look at something upside down and make you see it in the same way."

White had a fascination with falconry which led him to the wilds of Northamptonshire in England. There he undertook the task of taming and training a hawk. The author recorded his experience in a log which he later published as *The Goshawk.* A reviewer for the *San Francisco Chronicle* observed: "While *The Goshawk* is rich in the lore and language of a noble art, Mr. White has made it seem far more dramatic and philosophical than technical. Because he has real news of the woods and of the night, something of importance to say about elementals, he has given us a rare and tonic kind of book."

It was the author's fictional works, however, which brought him public recognition. Several of White's writings became popular with both children and adults. *The Master* was a fantasy about two children who were held prisoners on an Atlantic island. "T. H. White exhibits in this book, to a remarkable degree, a gift for being simultaneously funny and frightening, playful and serious, and for driving his narrative at a gallop through a series of sudden shocks and unnerving surprises. *The Master* is not for the incurably solemn or the stubbornly literal-minded. But for any reader, young or old, who is willingly bewitched into a suspension of disbelief, this diversion by a distinguished writer provides rousing entertainment," noted a critic for the *New York Herald Tribune.*

Perhaps White's most well-known piece of work was *The Once and Future King,* influenced by Malory's *Morte d'-Arthur.* Reviewing the book for the London *Times Literary Supplement,* a critic noted: "This ambitious work, so long in the building, now stands complete. It will long remain a memorial to an author who is at once civilized, learned, witty and humane."

In 1963, during the final months of his life, White made a lecture tour across the United States. The author kept a diary of his trip which was published posthumously as *America at Last: The American Journal of T. H. White.*

White's *Once and Future King* was the basis for Alan Jay Lerner's and Frederick Loewe's musical play, "Camelot." First produced at the Majestic Theater in New York in 1960, the play starred Richard Burton, Julie Andrews, Robert Goulet and Roddy McDowell. "Camelot" was later made into a motion picture in 1967 by Warner Brothers and starred Richard Harris, Vanessa Redgrave, and Franco Nero. Walt Disney Productions made White's *The Sword in the Stone* into an animated film under the same title in 1963.

BIOGRAPHICAL/CRITICAL SOURCES: San Francisco Chronicle, March 23, 1952; *New York Herald Tribune,* March 24, 1957; *Times Literary Supplement* (London), April 25, 1958; *Chicago Sunday Tribune,* July 5, 1959; T. H. White, *America at Last: The American Journal of T. H. White,* Putnam, 1965; Sylvia Townsend Warner, *T. H. White: A Biography,* Viking, 1967; T. H. White, *The White/Garnett Letters,* edited by David Garnett, Viking, 1968; John K. Crane, *T. H. White,* Twayne, 1974.

OBITUARIES: New York Times, January 18, 1964; *Illus-*

trated London News, January 25, 1964; *Newsweek,* January 27, 1964; *Publishers Weekly,* January 27, 1964.*

(Died January 17, 1964)

* * *

WICKS, Ben 1926-

PERSONAL: Born October 1, 1926, in London, England; son of Alfred (a printer) and Nell (a charlady; maiden name, Davis) Wicks; married: Doreen Mary Curtis (a nurse), March 31, 1956; children: Vincent, Susan, Kim. *Education:* Educated in England. *Home:* 18 Kellythorne Dr., Don Mills, Ontario, Canada. *Office:* 400 Jarvis St., Toronto, Ontario, Canada.

CAREER: Commercial artist, 1957—; free-lance cartoonist and writer, 1972—. Broadcaster for Canadian Broadcasting Corp. and Global Network, 1967—. Author of "Ben Wicks," syndicated by *Toronto Sun* and *Toronto Star* to about a hundred-fifty daily newspapers, 1967—. As a journalist, covered the Biafra War and events in Australia.

WRITINGS: Ben Wicks' Canada, McClelland & Stewart, 1976. Contributor of articles and cartoons to popular magazines in Canada, England, and the United States, including *Saturday Evening Post, Macleans,* and *Weekend Canada.*

SIDELIGHTS: Wicks has worked as a window cleaner, fruit seller, janitor, milkman, musician, bricklayer's mate, electrician's mate, clerk, and glider pilot. He writes: "The opportunities given me to understanding people of all areas came about through the incredible amount of jobs I was forced to take since leaving school. This mixing has proved invaluable to me whether my occupation has been in print or film. The world is full of experts who have as an horizon a complete set of classroom walls. Would that they and the many newspaper editors could get out into the fresh air and fill their lungs and fingers with much needed truth and freshness."

* * *

WIERZYNSKI, Gregory H(ieronim) 1939-

PERSONAL: Born June 26, 1939, in Warsaw, Poland; son of Casimir (a poet) and Halina (an art historian; maiden name, Pfeiffer) Wierzynski; married: Barbara Braun (a lawyer), April 12, 1969; children: Casimir. *Education:* Brown University, B.A., 1963. *Office:* Time-Life News Service, 888 16th St. N.W., Washington, D.C. 20006.

CAREER/WRITINGS: Business International, New York City, associate editor, 1963-65; *Fortune,* New York City, associate editor, 1965-68; Time-Life News Service, New York City, Washington correspondent, 1969, Boston bureau chief and National Education correspondent, 1969-71, Midwest bureau chief in Chicago, 1971-74, Paris bureau chief, 1974-77, State Department correspondent in Washington, D.C., 1978—. Notable assignments include coverage of campus discontent, 1969-71, U.S. presidential campaign, 1972, and the rise and breakup of the Socialist-Communist alliance in France. *Military service:* U.S. Army, 1960. *Member:* Cercle Interallie.

* * *

WIESE, Arthur E(dward) 1946-

PERSONAL: Born May 13, 1946, in Huntsville, Tex.; son of Arthur Edward (a salesman) and Lola (a teacher; maiden name, Irene) Wiese; married Nanette Arnold (a magazine editor), September 2, 1967; children: Kimberly. *Education:*

Sam Houston State University, B.S., 1967; Southern Illinois University, M.S., 1968. *Religion:* Roman Catholic. *Home:* 920 South Fairfax St., Alexandria, Va. 22314. *Office:* 1136 National Press Bldg., Washington, D.C. 22045.

CAREER/WRITINGS: Houston Post, Houston, Tex., reporter, 1968-70, political reporter in Austin, Tex., 1970-73, Washington bureau chief, 1973—. Notable assignments include coverage of the war in Vietnam, the Sharpstown political scandal, the 1970 and 1972 Senate and gubernatorial campaigns, the 1972 and 1976 national political conventions and campaigns, the funeral of Lyndon Johnson, the White House and Congress. Contributor to periodicals, including *Texas Monthly, Mass Transit,* and *American Journalism Review. Member:* National Press Club (secretary, 1976, treasurer, 1977, vice-president, 1978), White House Correspondents Association, Washington Press Club, Houston Press Club, Chili Appreciation Society Internationale, Red Circle. *Awards, honors:* Headliners Club Award for statewide journalism, 1969, 1970, and 1971; United Press International Managing Editors Association awards, 1970, 1971, and 1973; Texas Associated Press Managing Editors Association awards, 1972 and 1974; Texas Society of Certified Public Accountants award for socially significant journalism, 1976.

SIDELIGHTS: Wiese told *CA* his "hobbies range from baseball to old movies to model railroading to politics."

* * *

WILKINS, Frances 1923-

PERSONAL: Born October 15, 1923, in London, England; married Frank James Wilkins (a lecturer), March 14, 1944; children: Penelope, Sally, Amanda. *Education:* Educated in London, England. *Religion:* Roman Catholic. *Home:* 5 Dene Court, Chelmsford, Essex, England.

CAREER: Teacher. Writer.

WRITINGS—For children: *Speaking and Moving,* Oxford University Press, 1957; *Speaking and Moving at Christmas Time* (rhymes and playlets), Oxford University Press, 1958; *Acting Is Fun: Short Plays for Children,* Blackie & Son, 1958.

Let's Write It Down: A New Approach to Spelling and Composition, University of London Press, 1960; *Six Great Scots,* Hamish Hamilton, 1961; *Six Great Archaeologists: Belzoni, Layard, Schliemann, Evans, Carter, Thompson,* Hamish Hamilton, 1961; *Five Nativity Plays for Junior School Or for Use in Parishes,* Mowbray, 1961; *President Kennedy,* Cassell, 1962; *Six Great Nurses: Louise de Marillac, Florence Nightingale, Clara Barton, Dorothy Pattison, Edith Cavell, Elizabeth Kenny,* Hamish Hamilton, 1962; *The Young Traveller in Spain,* Phoenix House, 1962; *Wizards and Witches,* Oliver & Boyd, 1965, Walck, 1966; *Ancient Crete,* John Day, 1966; *Fairs,* Basil Blackwell, 1967; *Markets and Shops,* Basil Blackwell, 1968; *Unknown Lands,* A. Lynn, 1969.

Bridges in Britain, Basil Blackwell, 1971; *Castles,* Basil Blackwell, 1973; *The Entertainers,* Allman, 1973; *The Shopkeepers,* Allman, 1975; *Symbols and Signs,* Basil Blackwell, 1975; *Magna Carta, June 15, 1215,* Lutterworth, 1975.

Also author of *Mime and Rhyme; The Sailing of the Mayflower,* Lutterworth; *Caves,* Basil Blackwell; *Growing Up in Tudor Times,* Batsford; and *Let's Visit North Africa,* Burke Books.

AVOCATIONAL INTERESTS: Travel (Middle and Far East, Africa, Canada, the United States, the Soviet Union, all of Europe).

WILKS, John 1922-

PERSONAL: Born June 21, 1922, in Manchester, England; son of William Frederick (an accountant) and Lillian (a secretary; maiden name, Barnes) Wilks; married Eileen Mary Austin (a research physicist), June 30, 1951; children: David Robert, Bernard Neville, Andrew Simon, Maureen Elizabeth. *Education:* Brasenose College, Oxford, M.A. and D.Phil., 1950, D.Sc., 1969. *Home:* 219 Woodstock Rd., Oxford, England. *Office:* Clarendon Laboratory, Oxford University, Oxford, England.

CAREER: Oxford University, Oxford, England, fellow of Pembroke College, 1956—, lecturer in physics, 1958—.

WRITINGS: *The Third Law of Thermodynamics,* Oxford University Press, 1961; *The Properties of Liquid and Solid Helium,* Oxford University Press, 1967; *Introduction to Liquid Helium,* Oxford University Press, 1970; (with wife, Eileen Wilks) *Bernard: Bringing Up Our Mongol Son,* Routledge & Kegan Paul, 1974. Contributor to scientific journals.

*   *   *

WILKS, Yorick 1939-

PERSONAL: Born October 27, 1939, in England; son of Alexander (a soldier) and Peggy (Weinel) Wilks; married Ann Snee, January 23, 1965 (died November 3, 1971); married Geraldine de Berly, July 19, 1975. *Education:* Pembroke College, Cambridge, B.A., 1962, M.A., 1964, Ph.D., 1969. *Politics:* Social Democrat. *Religion:* Church of England. *Home:* 402 Old Rd., Clacton, Essex, England. *Office:* Department of Language and Linguistics, University of Essex, Colchester, Essex, England.

CAREER: Cambridge Language Research University, Cambridge, England, research worker, 1963-65; political agent in Cambridge, 1966; television actor in Hollywood, Calif., 1967-69; research associate and lecturer in Stanford, Calif., 1970-74; research fellow in Lugano, Switzerland, 1974-76; University of Essex, Colchester, England, reader in theoretical linguistics, 1976—. *Member:* Aristotelian Society, Mind Association, British Society for the Philosophy of Science, Association for Computational Linguistics, British Linguistic Society.

WRITINGS: *Grammar, Meaning, and Machine Analysis of Language,* Routledge & Kegan Paul, 1972; (editor with Eugene Charniak) *Computational Semantics,* North-Holland Publishing, 1976. Contributor to linguistics, artificial intelligence, and philosophy journals.

WORK IN PROGRESS: A book on communication.

SIDELIGHTS: Wilks comments: "I am interested in the human mind and its relation to the machine; in language; metaphysics; religion; psychoanalysis; Africa; and politics."

*   *   *

WILLARD, Charlotte 1906(?)-1977

1906(?)—October 20, 1977; American art critic, editor, and author of books on art. Willard was an art critic for the *New York Post* from 1964 to 1968. She died in New York, N.Y. Obituaries: *New York Times,* October 23, 1977.

*   *   *

WILLCOX, Sheila 1936-

PERSONAL: Born March 12, 1936, in Warwickshire, England; daughter of Arthur Rex (a director) and Helen (Davies) Willcox; married John Waddington, November, 1959 (divorced, 1966). *Education:* Educated at French convent in Staffordshire, England. *Home and office address:* Shenberrow Hill, Stanton, near Broadway, Worcestershire, England. *Agent:* John Farquharson Ltd., Bell House, 8 Bell Yard, London WC2A 2JR, England.

CAREER: International three-day event equestrian rider, 1957-71; writer, 1971—. International trainer for the Canadian equestrian team, 1975; presently owns Sheila Willcox International, where she trains her own horses for sale on the world market. *Awards, honors:* Won three-day equestrian event in Badminton, 1957, 1958, 1959; European equestrian champion, 1959.

WRITINGS: *Three Days Running* (autobiography), Collins, 1958; *The Event Horse,* Pelham, 1971. Contributor to equestrian journals.

WORK IN PROGRESS: *Riding for a Fall,* an autobiography; a book on horsemanship and stable management.

SIDELIGHTS: *Riding for a Fall* concerns Sheila Willcox's fall in 1971, which resulted in a broken back, paralysis, and an effort to adjust to life with a disability. She writes: "I am a great believer in a logical approach to the equestrian art. I dislike hypocrisy in any form and am determined to take a stand for what I believe is right. All my work is undertaken with the innate desire to produce perfection or its nearest form!"

*   *   *

WILLIAMS, David 1939-

PERSONAL: Born July 3, 1939, in Monmouth, Ore.; son of Wilbur Woodrow (a worker) and Goldie (Smith) Williams; married Barbel M. Nienkarn, September 22, 1963 (divorced, 1974). *Education:* University of Oregon, B.A., 1965, M.A., 1966; further graduate study at University of Hamburg, 1966-67. *Home:* 130 West 71st St., Apt. 10, New York, N.Y. 10023. *Agent:* Paul R. Reynolds, Inc., 12 East 41st St., New York, N.Y. 10017.

CAREER: Popular Library, Inc., New York City, editor, 1968-71; Dell Publishing Co., Inc., New York City, editor, 1971-72; M. Evans & Co., Inc., New York City, editor, 1972-74; writer, 1974—. *Military service:* U.S. Air Force, 1957-62. *Member:* Phi Beta Kappa.

WRITINGS: *Second Sight* (novel), Simon & Schuster, 1977.

WORK IN PROGRESS: A novel.

SIDELIGHTS: Williams writes: "To quote Michel Butor, 'I do not write novels in order to sell them, but in order to unify my life.'"

*   *   *

WILLIAMS, George C(hristopher) 1926-

PERSONAL: Born May 12, 1926, in Charlotte, N.C.; son of George F. and Margaret (an office worker; maiden name, Steuart) Williams; married Doris Lee Calhoun (a librarian), January 25, 1951; children: Jacques, Sibyl (Mrs. Alan Costell), Judith, Phoebe. *Education:* University of California, Berkeley, A.B., 1949; University of California, Los Angeles, M.A., 1952, Ph.D., 1955. *Home:* 7 Yorktown Rd., Setauket, N.Y. 11785. *Office:* Department of Ecology and Evolution, State University of New York at Stony Brook, Stony Brook, N.Y. 11794.

CAREER: Michigan State University, East Lansing, instructor, 1955-57, assistant professor of natural sciences, 1957-60; State University of New York at Stony Brook, associate professor, 1960-66, professor of biological science, 1966—. *Military service:* U.S. Army, 1944-46. *Member:* American Association for the Advancement of Science, American Institute of Biological Sciences, American Society of Ichthyologists and Herpetologists, American Society of Naturalists, American Society of Limnology and Oceanography, American Fisheries Society, Society for the Study of Evolution (vice-president, 1974).

WRITINGS: Adaptation and Natural Selection, Princeton University Press, 1966; *Group Selection,* Aldine-Atherton, 1971; *Sex and Evolution,* Princeton University Press, 1975. Contributor to scientific journals. Editor of *American Naturalist,* 1974—; assistant editor of *Quarterly Review of Biology,* 1967—.

WORK IN PROGRESS: Continuing biological research.

SIDELIGHTS: Williams spent sabbaticals studying fisheries in Iceland, 1966-67, 1973-74, and speaks Icelandic.

*   *   *

WILLIAMS, Melvin D(onald)   1933-

PERSONAL: Born February 3, 1933, in Pittsburgh, Pa.; son of Aaron (a steel worker) and Gladys (Barnes) Williams; married Faye Wanda Strawder, June 20, 1958; children: Aaron Ellsworth, Steven Rodney, Craig Haywood. *Education:* University of Pittsburgh, A.B., 1955, M.A., 1969, Ph.D., 1973; Carlow College, certificate in education, 1973. *Home:* 7029 Apple St., Pittsburgh, Pa. 15206. *Office:* Department of Anthropology, University of Pittsburgh, Pittsburgh, Pa., 15260.

CAREER: Wholesale Periodical Distributing Co., Pittsburgh, Pa., owner and operator, 1955-66; Carlow College, Pittsburgh, instructor, 1969-72, assistant professor of sociology and anthropology, 1969-75, chairperson of department, 1973-75; Colgate University, Hamilton, N.Y., Olive B. O'Connor Professor of American Institutions, 1976—. Assistant instructor at University of Pittsburgh, 1968; staff member at Duquesne University, 1972, and Chatham College, 1975; instructor for Pittsburgh's State Correctional Institution. Member of board of directors of Catholic Social Service of Allegheny County, 1973-76; co-chairperson of project for Urban Redevelopment Authority in Pittsburgh; co-director of project for Western Psychiatric Institute and Clinic, 1973-76; member of ethnic planning committee of Pittsburgh Council on Higher Education. *Military service:* Pennsylvania National Guard, 1956-58; U.S. Army, 1957-58.

MEMBER: American Anthropological Association (fellow), African Studies Association, American Association for the Advancement of Science, American Association of University Professors, American Sociological Association, Association for the Study of Afro-American Life and History, Economic Club of Pittsburgh, Delta Sigma Epsilon. *Awards, honors:* Social Science Research Council grant, 1974; black achiever award from *Talk* Magazine, 1974.

WRITINGS: Community in a Black Pentecostal Church: An Anthropological Study, University of Pittsburgh Press, 1974; (editor and contributor) *Selected Readings in Afro-American Anthropology,* Xerox College Publishing, 1975; *On the Street Where I Lived,* University of Pittsburgh Press, 1978. Contributor to anthropology and religion journals. Associate editor of *Ethnology: An International Journal of Cultural and Social Anthropology.*

WORK IN PROGRESS: The Shadows of My Mind, a book of psychological anthropology and narrative; editing *Ethnic-*

ity in Pittsburgh: A Selective Analysis, with Arthur Tuden and Myrna Silverman; editing *Afro-American Anthropology,* with Yvonne V. Jones; furthur research in neighborhood concerns.

*   *   *

WILLIAMS, Ora (Ruby)   1926-

PERSONAL: Born February 18, 1926, in Lakewood, N.J.; daughter of Charles (proprietor of window cleaning company) and Ida (Bolles) Williams. *Education:* Virginia Union University, A.B., 1950; Howard University, M.A., 1953; University of California, Irvine, Ph.D., 1974; also attended Columbia University, University of California, Berkeley, and New York University. *Home:* 362 Redondo Ave., Long Beach, Calif. 90814. *Office:* Department of English, California State University, 6101 East Seventh St., Long Beach, Calif. 90840.

CAREER: Southern University and Agricultural and Mechanical College, Baton Rouge, La., instructor in English, 1953-55; Tuskegee Institute, Tuskegee, Ala., instructor in English, 1955-57; Morgan State College, Baltimore, Md., instructor in English, 1957-65; Camp Fire Girls, Inc., New York, N.Y., program adviser, 1965-68; California State University, Long Beach, assistant professor, 1968-73, associate professor of English, 1973—. Instructor at Baltimore Junior College, 1963-64; lecturer at Terminal Island. Lyric soprano; has performed in concerts all over the United States; former member of "Overtones" and "Voices, Inc."; has appeared on television in Philadelphia, Pa. Member of advisory councils for Inner City Cultural Centers in Los Angeles and Long Beach.

MEMBER: Modern Language Association of America, College Language Association, Los Angles League of Allied Arts. *Awards, honors:* Danforth fellowship, 1957; Vassie D. Wright Award from Association for the Study of Negro Life and History, 1974, for *American Black Women in the Arts and Social Sciences;* Pearl Tilman Long Beach Central Community Award, 1977.

WRITINGS: American Black Women in the Arts and Social Sciences, Scarecrow, 1973, revised edition, in press. Contributor to language and black studies journals and to Camp Fire Girl magazines.

WORK IN PROGRESS: Selected Collected Works of Alice Dunbar-Nelson; research on musical elements in the works of Angelou, A. Walker, and M. Walker.

SIDELIGHTS: Ora Williams writes: "Much of what I do is undoubtedly a result of my having many excellent teachers, among them an unusual set of parents, who surrounded their nine children with a unique cultural atmosphere. There were animals of every description; dozens of musical instruments; hundreds of books; three or four daily newspapers and several weeklies. . . . My six older brothers and sisters did much to parent the younger members of the family. We all learned to render social services to our fellow man, to be productive."

AVOCATIONAL INTERESTS: Travel (Africa, Puerto Rico, Colombia, Jamaica, the West Indies, Mexico).

*   *   *

WILLIAMS, Patti   1936-

PERSONAL: Born March 17, 1936, in Fort Pierce, Fla.; daughter of Jack (a mechanic) and Lucille (Van Wickler) McGavran; married Harold Page Williams (a clergyman), January 2, 1955; children: Perry Scott, Jacklyn Plythe. *Edu-*

cation: Attended Stetson University, 1956-57, Columbus College, 1969-70, and Presbyterian School of Christian Education, 1973. *Religion:* Presbyterian. *Home:* 3003 South 10th St., Fort Pierce, Fla. 33450.

CAREER: Fort Pierce News Tribune, Fort Pierce, Fla., author of column "White City Social News," 1954-55; teacher of elementary education at elementary schools in Sanford, Fla., Columbus, Ga., and New Orleans, La., 1962-72; marriage counselor at churches in Columbus and Cairo, Ga., 1966-76. Director of youth conferences and seminars.

WRITINGS: Husbands, Logos International, 1976.

WORK IN PROGRESS: Ouch!, a book on hurt feelings.

SIDELIGHTS: Patti Williams writes: "My concern in writing is the desire for our country to get back to the Christian principles it was founded on. I believe this must begin in the home. I feel the need for people to learn the value of the words commitment and responsibility."

* * *

WILLIAMS, Sherley Anne 1944-
(Shirley Williams)

PERSONAL: Born August 25, 1944, in Bakersfield, Calif.; daughter of Jessee Winson (a laborer) and Lena (Silver) Williams; children: John Malcolm. *Education:* California State University, Fresno, B.A., 1966; Howard University, graduate study, 1966-67; Brown University, M.A., 1972. *Home:* 5595 56th Pl., San Diego, Calif. 92114. *Office:* Department of Literature, University of California, San Diego, La Jolla, Calif. 92093.

CAREER: Federal City College, Washington, D.C., community educator, 1970-72; California State University, Fresno, associate professor of English, 1972-73; University of California, San Diego, La Jolla, associate professor of literature and head of department, 1975—. *Member:* Modern Language Association of America. *Awards, honors:* National Book Award nomination, 1976, for *The Peacock Poems.*

WRITINGS: Give Birth to Brightness, Dial, 1972; (under name, Shirley Williams) *The Peacock Poems,* Wesleyan University Press, 1975.

Also author of "Ours to Make," for television, and "Traveling Sunshine Show," a play.

WORK IN PROGRESS: Regular Reefer, poems; *No Rest in My Slumber,* a study of Afro-American poetry; *The Book of Wonder,* poems.

* * *

WILLIAMS, Shirley
See WILLIAMS, Sherley Anne

* * *

WILLIAMSON, Henry 1895-1977

December 1, 1895—August 13, 1977; British writer. Best known for his books on nature, Williamson also wrote novels and introspective works about his experiences during World War I and his rural home life. He died in England. Obituaries: *New York Times,* August 14, 1977; *AB Bookman's Weekly,* October 10, 1977.

* * *

WILLOUGHBY, Hugh
See HARVEY, Nigel

WILSON, Noel Avon 1914-

PERSONAL: Born February 10, 1914, in Weiser, Idaho; son of William T. (a farmer) and Winifred Mae Wilson; married Geraldine Vaughan, August 15, 1965; children: Linda Ellen Stevenson. *Education:* University of Idaho, B.A., 1938; University of Missouri, M.A., 1960; University of Illinois, Ph.D., 1968. *Religion:* United Methodist. *Home:* 1311 Kolb Dr., Jefferson City, Mo. 65101. *Office:* Department of Journalism, Lincoln University, Box 106, Jefferson City, Mo. 65101.

CAREER: Pioneer Press (community newspaper), Cut Bank, Mont., managing editor, 1946-52; *Park County News* (community newspaper), Livingston, Mont., editor, 1954-55; Lincoln University, Jefferson City, Mo., instructor in journalism, 1956-58; Texas Southern University, Houston, assistant professor of journalism and head of department, 1958-66; Lincoln University, assistant professor of journalism, 1966-68, associate professor, 1968—, acting head of department of journalism, 1976-77, coordinator of journalism program, 1977—. *Military service:* U.S. Army Reserve, 1938-66, active duty, 1941-45; served in Mediterranean theater; became lieutenant colonel.

MEMBER: American Academy of Advertising, Association for Education in Journalism (chairman of graphics division, 1967-68), American Society of Journalism School Administrators, American Association of University Professors (past president, Lincoln University chapter; former director, Missouri conference), National Writers Club, Reserve Officers Association, Sigma Delta Chi (president, Mid-Missouri chapter, 1972-73; member of national professional development committee, 1973—), Masons.

WRITINGS: The Urbanization of Man, William F. Wilson Memorial Publishing Fund, 1972; *Say It with Pictures,* William F. Wilson Memorial Publishing Fund, 1972; *A Journalist's Guide to Graphic Design and Planning,* William F. Wilson Memorial Publishing Fund, 1975. Contributor to professional journals including *Quill,* and *Journalism Quarterly.* Former editor, *Journal of Broadcasting* and *The New Age.*

WORK IN PROGRESS: Textbook on newspaper management.

SIDELIGHTS: Noel Wilson told *CA:* "After eighteen years of editing and managing community newspapers, research begun in 1956 in the uses and effects of community media in metropolitan areas led to an awareness of the modern urban complex as a communications system. My theory is that these great areas of humanity with all their agonizing problems and potential for violent disintegration are held in acceptable equilibrium only because the media are able to counteract excesses in specialization. Through the media people are able to explain their usefulness to each other."

Wilson continues: "The difficulty in seeking the good life in the urban environment appears to be in the lags in reaching solutions to rather ordinary problems. The research I would like to free myself to pursue concerns the trends and techniques by which the media might reduce these lags through communications channeling energy and resources where needed."

On an another subject Wilson remarks, "It is incorrect to say that I have dedicated my career to educating blacks for careers in journalism, though my twenty plus years of college teaching have been on faculties of traditionally black universities. I was at first intrigued at the great story I saw in the advent of the Negro revolution. I now find myself greatly challenged by the prospect of being instrumental in the development of a multiracial, multicultural society appropriate to a manageable world community. With neither arrogance nor apology for my Anglo-Saxon origin, I hold my dedication not to a minority but to what appears to be developing into a great new integrated society—a total human entity.''

AVOCATIONAL INTERESTS: Giving lecturers on the Holy Land (Israel), the sacred sites of Rome, and Hawaii, illustrated with his own photographs.

* * *

WILSON, Richard W(hittingham) 1933-

PERSONAL: Born April 7, 1933, in Newark, N.J.; son of Richard Henry and Susan Agnes (Pasley) Wilson; married Amy Auerbacher, July 2, 1955 (divorced August 16, 1976); children: Anne Pasley, Peter Whittingham. *Education:* Princeton University, A.B., 1955, M.A., 1964, Ph.D., 1967. *Home address:* R.D.1, Box 385, Wertsville Rd., Ringoes, N.J. 08551. *Office:* International Center, Rutgers University, 180 College Ave., New Brunswick, N.J. 08903.

CAREER: R. H. Wilson Co., Inc. (inventory control consultants), Mountain Lakes, N.J., vice-president, 1959-62; Princeton University, Princeton, N.J., lecturer in political science, 1967-68; Rutgers University, New Brunswick, N.J., assistant professor, 1968-70, associate professor, 1970-74, professor of political science, 1974—, director of international programs, 1973—. Dean of Chinese summer school at Middlebury College, 1967-68. Member of board of directors of New Jersey World Trade Council; president of New Jersey Asia Seminar; member of board of trustees of Princeton in Asia Foundation; consultant to Mitre Corp. *Military service:* U.S. Naval Reserve, active duty, 1956-59; became captain. *Member:* Association for Asian Studies.

WRITINGS: Learning to Be Chinese, M.I.T. Press, 1970; *The Moral State,* Free Press, 1974; (editor with A. A. Wilson and S. L. Greenblatt) *Deviance and Social Control in Chinese Society,* Praeger, 1977. Contributor to education, sociology, and Asian studies journals.

WORK IN PROGRESS: Editing *Moral Development and Politics,* with G. L. Schochet; *Value Change in Chinese Society,* and *Organizational Behavior in Chinese Society,* with A. A. Wilson and S. L. Greenblatt.

* * *

WILSON, Steve 1943-

PERSONAL: Born February 10, 1943, in Lawton, Okla.; son of George Stanley (a postal worker) and Jessie Marie (a teacher; maiden name, Zorger) Wilson; married Linda Ann Ewing, August 23, 1963; children: Christopher Stephen, Kimberley Ann. *Education:* Central State University, Edmond, Okla., B.A., 1967. *Office:* Museum of the Great Plains, P.O. Box 68, Lawton, Okla. 73502.

CAREER: Museum of the Great Plains, Lawton, Okla., director of library and archives, and editor of *Great Plains Journal,* 1970-73, director of museum, 1973—. *Military service:* U.S. Army, combat correspondent, 1967-69, editor of *Ivy Leaf;* served in Far East. *Member:* Oklahoma Museums Association, Texas Folklore Society, Oklahoma Westerners (Indian Territory Posse).

WRITINGS: Oklahoma Treasures and Treasure Tales, University of Oklahoma Press, 1976. Contributor of more than a hundred-fifty articles to history journals, popular magazines, including *Argosy, True West,* and *Oklahoma Today,* and newspapers.

WORK IN PROGRESS: Research on mining and on the folklore of the American Southwest.

SIDELIGHTS: Wilson writes that he has conducted historical research at libraries and archival repositories in every state in the Southwest, and has made two pack-train expeditions into the Sierra Madre of Mexico to gather material on early Spanish colonial mining and folklore in that region. For more than fifteen years he has been collecting legends and folklore related to mining in the Southwest and Mexico.

* * *

WINER, Richard 1929-

PERSONAL: Born May 14, 1929, in South Dakota; married wife, Peggy (divorced); children: Lee, Frederick, Sharon. *Education:* University of Minnesota, B.S., 1951. *Home:* 812 S.W. 4th Place, Fort Lauderdale, Fla. 33302. *Agent:* Ann Elmo Agency, 52 Vanderbilt Ave., New York, N.Y. 10017. *Office address:* P.O. Box 1673, Fort Lauderdale, Fla. 33302.

CAREER: Worked as reporter and photographer, 1951-59, as a missile photographer at Cape Canaveral, 1959-65, as a television newsreel cameraman, 1965-71, and as a documentary film maker, 1971-75; writer, 1974—. Member of Fort Lauderdale Marine Advisory Board, 1974-75. *Military service:* U.S. Navy. *Member:* Sierra Club, Green Peace Foundation, Authors League, Classic Car Club of America, Antique Automobile Club of America. *Awards, honors:* Golden Eagle Documentary Film Award from Council on International Nontheatrical Events (CINE), 1971, for "The Devil's Triangle."

WRITINGS: The Devil's Triangle, Banta, 1974; *The Devil's Triangle II,* Bantam, 1975; *From the Devil's Triangle to the Devil's Jaw,* Bantam, 1977. Author of documentary film, "The Devil's Triangle," 1971. Contributor of articles to periodicals.

WORK IN PROGRESS: God in a Black Robe, an "expose about erratic judges"; *Cyclops,* about "a large Navy ship that vanished in 1918"; *Super Eight.*

SIDELIGHTS: Winer told *CA:* "To date most of my books and articles have been about the sea and ships. However, two of my present projects are not about the sea. Being a full time author, I write about what inspires me. Most of my current efforts are going into *God in a Black Robe,* for I feel that it's about time people should find out about judges who control their lives. I am also a staunch environmentalist, 'sailor of fortune,' and adventurer.''

Winer's favorite author, he told *CA,* is Jack London.

* * *

WINKLER, Win Ann 1935-

PERSONAL: Born August 29, 1935, in New York, N.Y.; daughter of Nathan B. (a jeweler and teacher) and Lillian (a teacher; maiden name, Kleinman) Winkler. *Education:* Attended Purdue University, Fashion Institute of Technology, School of Visual Arts, and Fashion Art Workshop. *Politics:* "Potpourii." *Religion:* Jewish. *Residence:* New York, N.Y. *Agent:* Bertha Klausner International Literary Agency, Inc., 71 Park Ave., New York, N.Y. 10016. *Office:* Room 1800, 733 Third Ave., New York, N.Y. 10017.

CAREER: Free-lance writer, illustrator, fashion designer, and photographer's stylist, 1957—. Member of advisory committee of Young Women's Christian Association's Encore program; member of rehabilitation committee of Regional Breast Cancer Program for Upper New York and Western Massachusetts.

WRITINGS: Post-Mastectomy: A Personal Guide to Physical and Emotional Recovery, Hawthorn, 1976; (with Ira Victor) *Fathers and Custody,* Hawthorn, 1977. Contributor to *Harper's Bazaar, Dance, American Journal of Nursing, Color Engineering,* and *New York.*

WORK IN PROGRESS: A novel; *Childless Couples,* "focusing on twenty couples married fifteen years or longer; how the childless state (choice or chance) has affected the marriage; the couple's relation to one another, and the problems encountered by having been childless when 'The Feminine Mystique' dominated American culture."

SIDELIGHTS: Win Ann Winkler writes: "When I had my first mastectomy in 1973 I was appalled by the silence which surrounded the subject, even to the degree that the mastectomy patient could not even get any advice on what sort of clothing to take to the hospital. I decided to take action on the situation, and wrote *Post-Mastectomy,* to the annoyance of the 'mastectomy mystique.' I had my second mastectomy in 1976 and since then have been instrumental in setting up supportive services for mastectomy women nationwide.

"As a writer, I seem to specialize in aspects of problems usually overlooked by the general public. Although still active in mastectomy-related services, I would like to lose my mastectomy identity; I am a professional writer, not a professional mastectomee.

"In my private life I would like to lose my writer identity. I am an opera buff, an ardent yoga practitioner. I live in a historical section of New York City, and work with rolled-up sleeves preserving the neighborhood from both encroaching blight and encroaching chic. I still make my own clothes, and I'm a gourmet cook. The only electrical appliance in my kitchen is a refrigerator; my cooking utensils are European or antique. I'm happier poking into research sources for my next book or poking around the community garden than I am with the inevitable publicity hype surrounding every author whose views are controversial."

* * *

WINNICK, Karen B(eth) B(inkoff) 1946-

PERSONAL: Born June 28, 1946, in New York; daughter of Sanford (a certified public accountant) and Miriam (Sclar) Binkoff; married Gary Winnick (a bond broker), December 24, 1972; children: Adam Scott. *Education:* Syracuse University, B.F.A., 1968; graduate study at New York University and School of Visual Arts. *Religion:* Jewish. *Home:* 24 Gramercy Park S., New York, N.Y. 10003.

CAREER: Grey Advertising, New York City, art director, 1970; Lois Holland Calloway, New York City, graphics designer, 1972-75; free-lance artist and writer, 1975—. *Member:* Art Directors Club.

WRITINGS: Patch and the Strings (self-illustrated juvenile book), Lippincott, 1977.

WORK IN PROGRESS: Several self-illustrated books for children.

* * *

WINSLOW, Ola Elizabeth 1885(?)-1977

1885(?)—September 27, 1977; American author and educator. In addition to her biography of Jonathan Edwards, which won a Pulitzer Prize in 1941, Winslow wrote many other historical and biographical works. She was a professor

of English at Wellesley College until her retirement in 1950. Winslow died in Damariscotta, Me. Obituaries: *New York Times,* October 3, 1977. (See index for *CA* sketch)

* * *

WINTER, J. M. 1945-

PERSONAL: Born May 28, 1945, in New York; son of Nathaniel (a dentist) and Bertha (a pianist; maiden name, Heller) Winter; married Tamar De Vries (a jeweler), May 6, 1970; children: Anna Daniella, Jonathan Pierre Abraham. *Education:* Columbia University, B.A., 1966; Cambridge University, Ph.D., 1970. *Home:* 20 Lillington Ave., Leamington Spa, Warwickshire, England. *Office:* Department of History, University of Warwick, Coventry, Warwickshire, England.

CAREER: Hebrew University of Jerusalem, Jerusalem, Israel, lecturer in history, 1970-73; University of Warwick, Coventry, England, lecturer in history, 1913—. *Member:* Royal Historical Society (fellow).

WRITINGS: (Editor) *R. H. Tawney's Commonplace Book,* Cambridge University Press, 1972; *Socialism and the Challenge of War,* Routledge & Kegan Paul, 1974; (editor) *War and Economic Development,* Cambridge University Press, 1975; *Tawney the Historian,* Routledge & Kegan Paul, in press.

WORK IN PROGRESS: The Great War and the British People; a demographic history of World War I.

* * *

WINTERS, Marjorie
See HENRI, Florette

* * *

WINTHROP, Henry 1910-

PERSONAL: Born July 20, 1910, in New York, N.Y.; son of Charles and Rose (Sugar) Winthrop; married Gussie Munk, December 5, 1952; children: Robert. *Education:* City University of New York, B.S., 1935; George Washington University, M.A., 1940; New School for Social Research, Ph.D., 1953; also attended U.S. Department of Agriculture Graduate School, 1936-38, Brooklyn Polytechnic Institute, 1949-50, and American University, 1950-51. *Home:* 1816 Marvy Ave., Tampa, Fla. 33612. *Office:* Department of Interdisciplinary Social Sciences, University of South Florida, 4202 Fowler Ave., Tampa, Fla. 33620.

CAREER: Worked as economist, 1936-41; U.S. Civil Service, Washington, D.C., economist, 1941-46; senior economist for New York State Division of Housing, 1946-47; U.S. Civil Service, economist, 1950-52; Richmond Professional Institute, Richmond, Va., assistant professor of psychology, 1953-54; staff psychologist for Lincoln State School, 1954-55, and Department of Mental Hygiene and Correction, 1955-56; Hollins College, Hollins, Va., assistant professor of psychology, 1956-57; Wichita State University, Wichita, Kan., assistant professor of psychology, 1957-60; University of South Florida, Tampa, associate professor, 1960-62, professor of social science, 1962—. Honorary member of International Council at International Center for Integrative Studies, of India's World Union Council. Member of Center for a Voluntary Society and Centre for Economic and Social Information.

MEMBER: International Union for the History and Philosophy of Science, World Future Society, American Sociological Association, National Planning Association, Society for

General Systems Research, Council on Religion and International Affairs, United Nations Association, Common Cause, British Society for the Study of Artificial Organs.

WRITINGS: Ventures in Social Interpretation, Appleton, 1968; *The Manager's Guide to Good Human Relations,* Motivation, Inc., 1968; *Perspectives on Communication: Some Variations in the Context of Understanding,* MSS Educational Publishing, 1971; *Environment and Man: Some Traditional and Extended Meanings of Ecology,* MSS Educational Publishing, 1971; *Psychological Aspects of Community: Alienation, Identity, and Social Breakdown,* MSS Educational Publishing, 1971; *Vistas of the Future: Prospects and Problems,* University of South Florida, 1971; *Distraction and Responsibility in Mass Society: Some Contemporary Currents in Mass Culture and Mass Leisure,* University of South Florida, 1971; *Education and Culture in the Complex Society: Perspectives on Interdisciplinary and General Education,* University of South Florida, 1971; *Marginal Aspects of Contemporary American Culture,* MSS Educational Publishing, 1972; *The Humanistic Viewpoint in the Social Sciences,* MSS Educational Publishing, 1972.

Author or co-author of monographs for U.S. Department of Labor. Contributor of about eight hundred articles to more than two hundred journals in the areas of psychology, sociology, economics, philosophy, humanities, education, and international studies. Has served as editor of *Journal of Human Relations, Journal of Humanistic Psychology, Journal of Existentialism, Darshana International, Indian Sociological Bulletin, Feedback, Psychics International, Journal of Education, Sociologia Religiosa, International Journal of History and Political Science, Journal of Transpersonal Psychology, Indian Journal of Social Research, Religious Humanism, Existential Psychiatry, Portal: A Journal of Interdisciplinary Thought,* and *International Behavioral Scientist.*

WORK IN PROGRESS: International Studies and World Problems; Distributive Justice and the New International Economic Order; research on international studies.

SIDELIGHTS: Winthrop writes that he is "generally interested in the relationships to one another of specialized areas. I believe that the social sciences will have to reorient themselves *to some extent* to problems of value, particularly in relation to the public interest and the development of a public philosophy. I am greatly interested in contributing to the restoration of a lost balance in the domain of learning—a balance that has always been part of the Western intellectual legacy. I am referring to the humanistic objective of promoting sensitivity not only to the domains of inquiry that fall within the logico-empirical tradition but also to the disciplines which rely on the expressive and non-cognitive functions of language for their proper appreciation. These are disciplines concerned with problems of value and choice in a complex society, with literature and the arts, with religion and morality, and with holistic reconstruction of the life of learning, so that learning may serve as a foundation for action in the life of modern man."

AVOCATIONAL INTERESTS: Literature, music, governmental and consumer problems, travel (England and Mexico).

BIOGRAPHICAL/CRITICAL SOURCES: Futurist, April, 1969.

WITHERS, Carl A.
(Robert North, James West)

PERSONAL: Born near Sheldon, Mo. *Education:* Harvard University, B.A.; graduate work at Columbia University.

CAREER: Writer and researcher in the field of anthropology and folklore. *Member:* American Folklore Society, American Anthropological Association (fellow).

WRITINGS: (Under pseudonym James West) *Plainville, U.S.A.,* Columbia University Press, 1945, reprinted, Greenwood Press, 1970; (with Alta Jablow) *Rainbow in the Morning* (illustrated by Abner Graboff), Abelard, 1956; *Ready or Not, Here I Come* (illustrated by Garry Mackenzie), Grosset, 1964, published as *A Treasury of Games,* 1969; (adapter) *The Tale of a Black Cat* (illustrated by Alan Cober), Holt, 1966; (adapter) *The Wild Ducks and the Goose* (illustrated by Cober), Holt, 1968; (reteller) *Painting the Moon: A Folktale from Estonia* (illustrated by Adrienne Adams), Dutton, 1970; (reteller) *The Grindstone of God: A Fable* (illustrated by Bernarda Bryson), Holt, 1970.

Editor: *The Penguin Book of Sonnets,* Penguin, 1943; *Counting Out* (illustrated by Elizabeth Ripley), Oxford University Press, 1946, published as *Counting-Out Rhymes,* Dover, 1970; *A Rocket in My Pocket* (illustrated by Susanne Suba), Holt, 1948, reprinted, 1968; (under pseudonym Robert North) *The Treasure Book of Riddles* (illustrated by Ruth Wood), Grosset, 1950; (with Sula Benet) *The American Riddle Book* (illustrated by Marc Simont), Abelard, 1954; (with Benet) *Riddles of Many Lands* (illustrated by Lili Cassel), Abelard, 1956; (with Ben Botkin) *The Illustrated Book of American Folklore: Stories, Legends, Tall Tales, Riddles, and Rhymes* (illustrated by Irv Docktor), Grosset, 1958; *I Saw a Rocket Walk a Mile* (illustrated by John E. Johnson), Holt, 1965; *A World of Nonsense: Strange and Humorous Tales from Many Lands* (illustrated by Johnson), Holt, 1968; (with Jablow) *The Man in the Moon: Sky Tales from Many Lands* (illustrated by Peggy Wilson), Holt, 1969.*

(Deceased)

*   *   *

WITTON, Dorothy

PERSONAL: Born in Michigan; became Mexican citizen; married Luis Romero (a forestry engineer). *Education:* Attended University of Michigan and New School for Social Research.

CAREER: Author. Has also worked as a journalist.

WRITINGS: Crossroads for Chela, Messner, 1956; *Treasure of Acapulco,* Messner, 1963; *Our World: Mexico,* Messner, 1969; *Teen-Age Mexican Stories,* Lantern Press, 1972. Contributor of stories to periodicals.

*   *   *

WITTY, Paul   1898-1976

PERSONAL: Born July 23, 1898, in Terre Haute, Ind.; son of William L. and Margaret (Kerr) Witty. *Education:* Indiana State Teachers College (now Indiana State University), A.B., 1920; Columbia University, M.A., 1923, Ph.D., 1931. *Home:* 5555 North Sheridan Rd., Chicago, Ill. 60640.

CAREER: School psychologist in Scarborough-on-Hudson, N.Y., 1922; University of Kansas, Lawrence, associate professor, 1924-25, professor of educational psychology, 1925-30; Northwestern University, Evanston, Ill., professor of education and director of Psycho-Educational Clinic, 1930-

66, professor emeritus, 1966-76. Lecturer. Chief educational consultant, D.C. Heath & Co., 1940-76; consultant, Western Publishing Co. *Military service:* U.S. Army, 1942-44; became major.

MEMBER: International Council for Exceptional Children, International Council for the Improvement of Reading Instruction (president, 1954), American Academy of Arts and Sciences (fellow), American Psychology Association (fellow), American Childhood Education Association, American Educational Research Association, American Association for Gifted Children, National Education Association, National Society for the Study of Education, National Council of Teachers of English, Association for Supervision and Curriculum Development, Society for the Advancement of Education, Sigma Nu, Phi Delta Kappa, Kappa Delta Pi.

WRITINGS: (With Harvay C. Lehman) *The Psychology of Play Activities,* A. S. Barnes, 1927; *A Study of Deviates in Versatility and Sociability of Play Interest,* Columbia University Press, 1931; (with David Kopel) *Reading and the Educative Process,* Ginn, 1939; (editor with Charles E. Skinner) Rose Alschuler, Harold Anderson, Nancy Bayley, and others, *Mental Hygiene in Modern Education,* Farrar & Rinehart, 1939.

The True Book of Freedom and Our U.S. Family, Childrens Press, 1948; *Reading in Modern Education,* Heath, 1949; *Streamline Your Reading,* Science Research Associates, 1949; (editor) *The Gifted Child,* Heath, 1951; *How to Become a Better Reader,* Science Research Associates, 1953; (with Anne Coomer) *Salome Goes to the Fair,* Dutton, 1953; (editor with Miriam E. Peterson and Alfred E. Parker) *Reading Roundup: A Reading-Literature Series,* Heath, 1954; (editor) *Mental Health in Modern Education,* University of Chicago Press, 1955; (with Margaret Ratz) *A Developmental Reading Program for Grades 6 Through 9,* Science Research Associates, 1956; *How to Improve Your Reading,* Science Research Associates, 1956; *Creativity of Gifted and Talented Children: Addresses,* Columbia University Press, 1959.

(With Edith Grotberg) *Developing Your Vocabulary,* Science Research Associates, 1960; (editor) *Development in and Through Reading,* University of Chicago Press, 1961; (editor with Alma Moore Freeland) *Silver Web,* Heath, 1964; (with Freeland) *Peacock Lane,* Heath, 1964; (with Mildred Bebell) *Reading Caravan,* Heath, 1965, revised edition, 1968; (with Grotberg and Freeland) *The Teaching of Reading: A Developmental Process,* Heath, 1966; (editor) *Educationally Retarded and Disadvantaged,* University of Chicago Press, 1967; (with Thomas Barensfeld) *Life and Times of Eight Presidents,* Highlights for Children, 1969; (with Grotberg) *Helping the Gifted Child,* Science Research Associates, 1970; *Adventures in Discovery Program,* Western Publishing, 1970; *Helping Children Read Better,* Science Research Associates, 1970; (editor) *Reading for the Gifted and the Creative Student,* International Reading Association, 1971.

Associate editor, *Highlights for Teachers,* and *Highlights for Children;* advisory editor, *My Weekly Reader;* member of editorial board, *Exceptional Children.*

SIDELIGHTS: As author and educator, Paul Witty pioneered the application of psychological principals to education. His work focused specifically upon gifted children, and served to dispel the myths that a gifted child is unhealthy, asocial, generally undesirable, and necessarily unitalented.

OBITUARIES: New York Times, February 14, 1976; *Publisher's Weekly,* March 22, 1976; *AB Bookman's Weekly,* April 26, 1976.*

(Died February 11, 1976, in Chicago, Ill.)

* * *

WITZE, Claude 1909(?)-1977

1909(?)—December 8, 1977; American journalist. Witze was senior editor of *Air Force* magazine and author of the columns "The Wayward Press" and "Airpower in the News." He died in Bethesda, Md. Obituaries: *Washington Post,* December 10, 1977; *New York Times,* December 16, 1977.

* * *

WOIWODE, Larry (Alfred) 1941-

PERSONAL: Born October 30, 1941, in Carrington, N.D.; son of Everett Carl and Audrey Leone (Johnston) Woiwode; married Carole Ann Peterson, May 21, 1965; children: Newlyn Smith, Joseph William. *Education:* Attended University of Illinois, Champaign-Urbana, 1959-64. *Religion:* Christian. *Agent:* Candide Donadio, 111 West 57th St., New York, N.Y. 10019.

CAREER: Free-lance writer, 1964—. Writer-in-residence, University of Wisconsin, Madison, 1973-74; workshop director, member of fiction panels, or reader of own works at colleges and universities, including University of Illinois, University of Iowa, and City College of City University of New York. Judge for National Book Awards, 1972, and Bush Foundation fellowships, 1977. *Member:* International P.E.N. (executive board member of American chapter). *Awards, honors:* William Faulkner Foundation Award, 1970, for *What I'm Going to Do, I Think;* notable book award, 1970, from American Library Association, for *What I'm Going to Do, I Think;* Guggenheim fellowship, 1971-72; nominated for National Book Award and Critic's Circle Award, both 1976, for *Beyond the Bedroom Wall;* award in fiction, 1976, from Friends of American Writers, for *Beyond the Bedroom Wall;* Doctor of Letters, 1977, from North Dakota State University.

WRITINGS3 What I'm Going to Do, I Think (novel), Farrar, Straus, 1969; (contributor with Richard Lyons, Thomas McGrath, John R. Milton, and Antony Oldknow) *Poetry North: Five North Dakota Poets,* North Dakota Institute for Regional Studies, North Dakota State University, 1970; *Beyond the Bedroom Wall: A Family Album* (novel), Farrar, Straus, 1975; *Even Tide* (poems), Farrar, Straus, 1975.

Contributor of numerous poems, short stories, and reviews to periodicals, including *New Yorker, Atlantic Monthly,* and *New York Times.* Work represented in numerous anthologies, including *Best American Short Stories,* edited by Martha Foley, Houghton-Mifflin, 1971; *Reality in Conflict,* edited by Farrell, Pierce, Pittman, and Wood, Scott, Foresman, 1976; *Mom, the Flag, and Apple Pie: A Bicentennial Salute,* compiled by editors of *Esquire,* Doubleday, 1976.

SIDELIGHTS: Woiwode's novel *Beyond the Bedroom Wall: A Family Album* evoked this response from John Gardner: "It seems to me that nothing more beautiful and moving has been written in years. I was reminded, as I read, of a friend's prediction that the next great movement in literature will be an unashamed return to Victorian copious weeping. That's overoptimistic, probably; but it's a wonderful thing, it seems to me, to laugh and weep one's slow way through an enormous intelligent novel tracing out the life of a family."

The book is a series of shifting moments, done from different sides and different points of view, of five generations of an

American family. The effect of this assemblage is of looking through a family album, as the book's subtitle suggests. Reviewer Peter Prescott wrote that the book's "peculiar construction has its advantages. Through a variety of first-person narrations and third-person points of view, Woiwode can enter the thoughts of all of his characters—he is equally at ease with a young girl rejoicing in her talent and with an old man cursing God. By changing the length and focus of his stories, he can concentrate fully on scenes of either high drama or routine domesticity—a kind of flexibility of intensity that is rare in contemporary fiction. Nevertheless, we cannot read this novel, if that is what it is, without being constantly reminded that its parts once stood separately in magazines, and because each episode requires the structure of a short story, the book as a whole lacks shape and momentum."

Paul Gray had similar problems in accepting the form of the book. "Woiwode's polished images evoke whole landscapes and interiors," he wrote. "But on occasion they leave his characters as rigid as snapshots. Like the subjects of most candid portraits, the Neumillers sometimes appear querulous and unfocused, refugees wrenched by the camera from the context of their lives. The stop-and-start chapters abort their growth and development; some family members are simply dropped or disappear inexplicably for hundreds of pages. Though they struggle with life's standard challenges and disappointments, the stolid Neumillers are rarely compelling enough to carry the massive burden of their saga." Christopher Lehmann-Haupt found Woiwode's attempt to trace a family history through generations "old hat," and commented that "even in Mr. Woiwode's skilled hands, it continues to impose certain burdens on the grace and credibility of his narrative. New material must continually be fed into the plot as the generations pass in review; and even Mr. Woiwode's most vividly realized characters must occasionally deliver expository speeches that sound as if they had been lifted from a well-made play."

However, other reviewers, Roger Sale among them, found the novel to be sufficiently cohesive. Sale wrote: "Woiwode is always evoking, but never in set pieces, and the links we get from episode to episode are never forced because they don't have to be. Home *is* where one starts from and Woiwode's sense of home is strong enough to allow him to be relaxed and unselfconscious when he writes about winters and schools and sex and religion, and tries to make each one fully felt as lived."

Memory is related to both the form and the substance of the novel, as numerous critics have mentioned. Steven Koch commented: "Like narrative itself, memory can mythologize the past or can retrieve the real. Both impulses are inevitable; together they are the warp and woof of Woiwode's narrative texture. His book is, among other things, an anthology of the modes of remembering."

"From beginning to end of this novel," Gardner wrote, "Woiwode's dramatization of the problem of getting a hold on reality—the problem of fully realizing what lies out there at the edge of dreams and memories, *Beyond the Bedroom Wall*—is simply brilliant." Sale found that Woiwode succeeded "by being personal, by putting his imagination at the service of memory, and by realizing in this way that love really is most nearly itself when the here and now cease to matter."

Several reviewers have described the book as sentimental, although few have used the term pejoratively. (Lehmann-Haupt said it is "sentimental in the very best sense of the word.") William Jaspersohn asked Woiwode if he thought his book was sentimental. Woiwode responded: "No. . . . There are depths and types of emotion in *Bedroom Wall* that people haven't encountered in a novel. It's easier to handle if you have a name for it, and 'sentimental' became one. The book is as closely written as most poetry and any emotion in it is 'paid for,' as the Bible says about sin, by the absolute precision of how it's enacted and the precision of what comes before."

BIOGRAPHICAL/CRITICAL SOURCES: New Republic, May 3, 1969, November 29, 1975, December 6, 1975; *Saturday Review,* May 3, 1969, September 6, 1975; *New York Times Book Review,* May 4, 1969, September 28, 1975; *Life,* May 16, 1969; *New York Times,* May 20, 1969, October 14, 1975; *Time,* June 20, 1969, September 29, 1975; *New York Review of Books,* July 10, 1969, November 13, 1975; *Antioch Review,* Summer, 1969; *Book World,* June 21, 1970, August 31, 1975, September 21, 1975, November 14, 1976; *Village Voice,* September 22, 1975; *Newsweek,* September 29, 1975; *Atlantic Monthly,* October, 1975; *New Yorker,* December 29, 1975; *Contemporary Literary Criticism,* Volume 6, Gale, 1976; *Hudson Review,* Spring, 1976; *Yale Review,* March, 1976.

*   *   *

WOLFF, Ernst, 1910-

PERSONAL: Born February 18, 1910, in Tientsin, China; came to the United States in 1960, naturalized citizen, 1971; son of Carl (an importer) and Helene (Kosminski) Wolff; married second wife, Rosalia Li (a nurse), May 28, 1952; children: (second marriage) Martin, Peter. *Education:* University of Berlin, diploma, 1932, LL.B., 1933; University of Washington, Seattle, M.L.S., 1962, Ph.D., 1966. *Home:* 305 West Vermont Ave., Urbana, Ill. 61801. *Office:* Library, University of Illinois, Urbana, Ill. 61801.

CAREER: Kailan Mining Administration, secretary in Tangshan and Tientsin, China, 1936-51; United States Information Office, Hong Kong, translator and editor, 1951-52; commercially employed in Tokyo and Osaka, Japan, 1951-60; University of Washington, Seattle, assistant in Far Eastern Library, 1960-65; University of Illinois, Urbana, head of Far Eastern Library, 1965—.

WRITINGS: Chou Tso-jen, Twayne, 1971. Sub-editor for *Bibliography of Asian Studies,* Association for Asian Studies.

WORK IN PROGRESS: A book on Chinese writer Chu Tzu-ch'ing; a manual of Chinese bibliography.

SIDELIGHTS: Ernst Wolff told *CA:* "My studies of Chou Tso-jen were partly motivated by a compassion for the Chinese—who like myself—had to live through the time of Japanese occupation in North China. We did not like the Japanese military regime but had to make compromises and accommodate ourselves to the situation, unless willing to die a heroic death. Chou Tso-jen was basically a decent character, typically Confucian in manner and philosophy. He lent his name to the North China puppet regime, set up by the Japanese, but never engaged in dishonorable activities.

"In my case, the Germans had disowned me (because I am a Jew); as a stateless person I had to fend for myself as best I could. Certain Japanese contacts were unavoidable. Although in a most unimportant position [with] the Kailan Mining Administration, I had the feeling that remaining at my post as long as the Japanese let me (and they let me indeed) I was doing my humble share to preserve the company for the time that its rightful owners (mostly the British) would come back. May sound corny, but that made me sympathize with Chou Tso-jen (who helped preserve Peking University, and especially its library, during the 'Japanese time')."

AVOCATIONAL INTERESTS: Translating (speaks German, French, Chinese, Japanese), travel (Europe, Far East, Australia).

* * *

WOLFF, Miles 1945-

PERSONAL: Born December 30, 1945, in Baltimore, Md.; son of Miles Hoffman (a newspaper editor) and Anna (Webster) Wolff. *Education:* Johns Hopkins University, A.B., 1965; University of Virginia, M.A., 1967. *Home:* 833 North Elm St., Greensboro, N.C. 27401.

CAREER: Savannah Braves Baseball Club, Savannah, Ga., general manager, 1971-73; Anderson Mets Baseball Club, Anderson, S.C., general manager, 1974; Jacksonville Suns Baseball Club, Jacksonville, Fla., general manager, 1975; Richmond Braves Baseball Club, Richmond, Va., play-by-play announcer, 1977. *Military service:* U.S. Navy, 1967-70; became lieutenant.

WRITINGS: Lunch at the Five and Ten, Stein & Day, 1970.

WORK IN PROGRESS: The Cockatrice, a contemporary fantasy.

SIDELIGHTS: Wolff comments: "I work for minor league baseball teams during the season (April to September) and write in the off-season."

* * *

WOLFF, Richard D(avid) 1942-

PERSONAL: Born April 1, 1942, in Youngstown, Ohio; son of Max (a professor of sociology) and Lotte (an economist; maiden name, Katz) Wolff; married Harriet Fraad (a consultant), September 17, 1965; children: Max Fraad, Theresa Fraad. *Education:* Harvard University, B.A. (magna cum laude), 1963; Stanford University, M.A. (economics), 1964; Yale University, M.A. (history), 1967, Ph.D., 1969. *Home:* 678 Orange St., New Haven, Conn. 06511. *Office:* Department of Economics, University of Massachusetts, Amherst, Mass. 01003.

CAREER: Yale University, New Haven, Conn., instructor in economics, 1967-69; City College of the City University of New York, New York, N.Y., assistant professor of economics, 1969-73; University of Massachusetts, Amherst, associate professor of economics, 1973—. Economic consultant. *Member:* American Economic Association, African Studies Association, Economic History Association, Union of Radical Political Economists.

WRITINGS: (Contributor) *Economics,* 2nd edition, Random House, 1972; *The Economics of Colonialism: Britain in Kenya, 1870-1930,* Yale University Press, 1974. Writer of columns in *Modern Times.* Contributor to economic journals in the United States and Europe.

WORK IN PROGRESS: The Theory of Economic Crisis; The Transition From Federalism to Capitalism in Western Europe; editor of a book of essays by Louis Althusser.

* * *

WOLFF, Robert Jay 1905-1977

July 27, 1905—December 29, 1977; American artist, educator, and writer. Wolff began his art career in the area of sculpture, but soon abandoned this medium to join the movement in abstract painting. His paintings are in numerous permanent collections, including those of the Guggenheim Museum, Brooklyn Museum, Chicago Art Institute, and the Tate Gallery in London. Wolff was professor emeritus at Brooklyn College of the City University of New York. He was the author of educational portfolios for children and books on art. He died in New Preston, Conn. Obituaries: *New York Times,* January 2, 1978. (See index for *CA* sketch)

* * *

WONG, Bing W. 1922-

PERSONAL: Born December 3, 1922, in Amoy, China; son of Boon-yee and Luan (Tsang) Wong; married Helena Poon (an airline ticketing agent), June 18, 1972. *Education:* National Amoy University, B.Sc., 1948. *Politics:* "Nil." *Religion:* "Nil." *Home:* El Moon Fair Mansion, 11 Shiu Fai Terrace, Hong Kong. *Office: Time,* 205 Prince's Bldg., Hong Kong.

CAREER/WRITINGS: Overseas Chinese Daily, Hong Kong, staff reporter, 1950-63, aviation and travel editor, 1963-64; *Time,* New York, N.Y., correspondent in Hong Kong, 1964—. Notable assignments include a portrait of Mao's wife Chiang Ch'ing and her revolutionary operas, the 1969 Chinese Communist and Nationalist Party Congresses, ping pong diplomacy, Mao's heirship problems, successor Hua Kuo-feng's premiership and the fall of Chiang Ch'ing, and the far-flung Chinese overseas.

Contributor to *Mandarin.* Translation supervisor, Time-Life Books' *The Best of Life. Member:* Foreign Correspondents' Club, American Club, Hong Kong Journalists Association.

SIDELIGHTS: When asked about the effect of Mao's death on China, Wong replied: "In my view, the political commentators' claim that China was not prepared for a 'colossal upheaval' has been true as the downfall of Chiang Ch'ing and her 'gang' has not resulted in anything that I can describe as a 'colossal upheaval.' On both Nationalist China and the People's Republic, the effect of Mao's death fundamentally arises from the debilitation of his thought for revolution. You can write a book on that."

* * *

WOODALL, Ronald 1935-

PERSONAL: Born July 5, 1935, in Montreal, Quebec, Canada; son of Walter and Gabrielle (Beaudoin) Woodall; married Heather Maureen Sheppard (a designer), September 9, 1961; children: Jamie, Adam. *Education:* Montreal Museum of Fine Arts School of Art and Design, graduate, 1957; also attended Sir George Williams University. *Home:* 4257 Evergreen Pl., West Vancouver, British Columbia, Canada V7V 1H2. *Office:* 5791 Telegraph Trail, Fisherman's Cove, West Vancouver, British Columbia, Canada.

CAREER: O. E. McIntyre, Ltd., Montreal, Quebec, art director, 1959-60; McKim Advertising, Ltd., Montreal, art director, 1960-64; J. Walter Thompson Co., Vancouver, British Columbia, creative director and vice-president, 1964-75; free-lance creative consultant, writer, painter, and television director and producer, in Vancouver, 1975—. Has held one-man shows of his paintings in Vancouver. *Awards, honors:* Has received approximately one hundred creative advertising awards, including awards from New York, Toronto, and Montreal Art Directors Clubs, Graphica, American TV Festival, Marketing Golds, Canadian Radio-TV Festival, Golden Bessy, U.S. TV Festival, and Hollywood International Broadcast Awards.

WRITINGS: Magnificent Derelicts, J. J. Douglas, 1975; (with T. H. Watkins) *Taken by the Wind,* New York Graphic Society, 1977.

WORK IN PROGRESS: Research for books on architecture of the Yukon goldrush and architecture of the cariboo.

SIDELIGHTS: Woodall told *CA:* "The North American West is a vast repository of forlorn, often bizarre, often elegant abandoned structures that are this continent's equivalent to the ancient ruins of the Old World.

"At the very least, they are high folk sculptures.

"But they are wood. They are rotting, burning, crumbling and being sold for salvage. They won't be saved.

"I intend to record as many of them as I can, *while* I can."

In the past dozen years, Woodall has traveled over 100,000 miles of backroads to paint, photograph, and write about vanishing folk architecture of western North America.

BIOGRAPHICAL/CRITICAL SOURCES: Weekend, February, 1972; *B.C. Motorist,* July/August, 1972; *Leisure,* November, 1972; *Heritage Canada Quarterly,* spring, 1975; *Time,* November 24, 1975; *Macleans,* October 3, 1977.

* * *

WOODARD, Carol 1929-

PERSONAL: Born January 19, 1929, in Buffalo, N.Y.; daughter of Harold A. and Violet (Landsittel) Young; married Ralph Arthur Woodard (an engineer), August 19, 1950; children: Camaron, Carsen, Cooper. *Education:* Hartwick College, B.A., 1950; Syracuse University, M.A., 1952; State University of New York at Buffalo, Ph.D., 1972. *Office:* State University of New York College at Buffalo, 1300 Elmwood Ave., Buffalo, N.Y. 14222.

CAREER: State University of New York College at Buffalo, associate professor of human development and early childhood, 1969—. Consultant to Lutheran Church in America. *Member:* National Association for Education of Young Children, Pi Lambda Theta.

WRITINGS—Adult: *Ways to Teach 3's to 5's,* Lutheran Church Press, 1965.

Juveniles: *Can I Help?,* Lutheran Church Press, 1968; *Time for Fun,* Lutheran Church Press, 1968; *The Busy Family,* Fortress, 1969; *The Very Special Baby,* Fortress, 1969; *It's Fun to Have a Birthday,* Fortress, 1970; *The Wet Walk,* Fortress, 1970; *It's Nice to Have a Special Friend,* Fortress, 1970.

Contributor to magazines.

WORK IN PROGRESS: Developing Concepts of Music and Movement, for Denison.

SIDELIGHTS: "Many of my books for young children concerned the activities and experiences which my own children enjoyed. My children also served as my chief critics and offered invaluable suggestions. My more recent writings concern early childhood material designed to assist the student teacher in the field setting. Teacher education and program development are my major areas of interest related to my vocation while reading and gardening are great for relaxation."

* * *

WOODRUFF, Judy 1946-

PERSONAL: Born November 20, 1946, in Tulsa, Okla.; daughter of William (an army officer) and Anna Lee (Payne) Woodruff. *Education:* Attended Meredith College, 1964-66;

Duke University, B.A., 1968. *Office:* NBC News, 4001 Nebraska Ave. N.W., Washington, D.C. 20016.

CAREER/WRITINGS: WQXI-TV, Atlanta, Ga., secretary and researcher, 1968-69; WAGA-TV, Atlanta, news reporter and anchorwoman, 1970-75; National Broadcasting Co. (NBC) News, New York, N.Y., Washington correspondent, 1976—. Notable assignments include coverage of the Joan Little trial, 1975, and the Jimmy Carter presidential campaign. *Member:* National Academy of Television Arts and Sciences, American Federation of Television and Radio Artists. *Awards, honors:* Emmy Award from National Academy of Television Arts and Sciences, Atlanta chapter, 1975, for outstanding female personality; Woman in Communications award, 1975, for communications excellence.

SIDELIGHTS: Woodruff told *CA:* "The advice I would give to students who want to go into television news is: don't waste your time unless you are very persistent. And don't be timid about fighting for excellence in journalism when there is a conflict with those who believe entertaining the public is more important."

* * *

WOOLF, Robert G(ary) 1928-

PERSONAL: Born February 15, 1928, in Portland, Maine; son of Joseph (a physician) and Anna (a teacher; maiden name, Glousky) Woolf; married Anne Joy Passman, June 2, 1963; children: Stacey Lee, Gary Evan, Tiffany Jill. *Education:* Boston College, A.B., 1949; Boston University, LL.B., 1952. *Politics:* Independent. *Religion:* Jewish. *Home:* 6 Nelson Dr., Chestnut Hill, Mass. 02167. *Office:* 4525 Prudential Tower, Boston, Mass. 02199.

CAREER: Admitted to practice before Supreme Judicial Court, 1952, Federal District Court, 1954, and U.S. Supreme Court, 1956; attorney, specializing in sports law and athlete representation, 1954—. President of Bob Woolf Associates, Inc. Affiliated with International Creative Management. Public lecturer in the area of sports and the law; has appeared on national television sports programs and talk shows, including "Today Show," "Tonight Show," and "Tomorrow Show." Member of Board of directors of Massachusetts Center Repertory Co. and St. Jude's Hospital Foundation. *Military service:* U.S. Army, Judge Advocate Division, 1952-54. *Member:* Shriners, B'nai B'rith.

WRITINGS: Behind Closed Doors (autobiography), Atheneum, 1976.

SIDELIGHTS: Woolf has represented more than three hundred professional athletes since 1964, including John Havlicek, Carl Yastrzemski, Thurman Munson, Marvin Barnes, and Derek Sanderson. At one time, he was being considered for the position of commissioner of American Basketball Association.

* * *

WORMLEY, Stanton Lawrence 1909-

PERSONAL: Born February 7, 1909, in Washington, D.C.; son of Lawrence Riggs (an engineer) and Mary (a registered nurse; maiden name, Burruss) Wormley; married Freida Hare, August 12, 1950; children: Stanton Lawrence, Jr. *Education:* Howard University, A.B., 1930, A.M., 1931; University of Hamburg, diploma, 1932; Cornell University, Ph.D., 1939. *Politics:* Independent. *Religion:* Episcopalian. *Home and office:* 5735 Kansas Ave. N.W., Washington, D.C. 20011.

CAREER: Virginia State College, Petersburg, instructor,

1932-33, assistant professor, 1933-36, associate professor of English, 1936-38, chairman of department of foreign languages, 1933-38, chairman of graduate program in English, 1936-38; Howard University, Washington, D.C., assistant professor, 1938-44, associate professor, 1944-45, professor of German, 1945-71, head of department of German and Russian, 1945-64, director of summer school, 1950-64, acting dean of graduate school, 1952-55, 1960-64, academic vice-president, 1964-69, acting president, 1965-67; writer, 1971—. Visiting professor at City College (now of the City University of New York), summer, 1948. Member of executive committee of Washington Center for Metropolitan Studies (also member of board of trustees), 1965-69, and Consortium of Washington Universities (also vice-chairman), 1965-69; vice-chairman of District of Columbia Police Complaint Review Board, 1965-71; member of Coordinating Council on Education for the Disadvantaged, 1967; member of Health and Welfare Council of the National Capital Area, 1971. Member of board of directors of Center for Community Action Education, 1965-67, WETA-TV, 1966-68, 1969-71, National Harmony Memorial Park (also member of executive committee), 1960—, and national capital area National Conference of Christians and Jews, 1966-73; member of board of trustees of Nathaniel Hawthorne College, 1968—, and Washington Hospital Center, 1973—; member of administrative committee and board of trustees of Meriwether Home for Dependent Children, 1965-69, member of advisory council, 1968. Member of advisory board of WDCA-TV, 1965, and Washington Planetarium and Space Center, 1966; member of interim committee of Central Atlantic Regional Educational Laboratory, 1966. Member of Rock Creek Foundation, 1971 (past president); chairman of board of governors of Rock Creek Cemetery, 1972—. Consultant to U.S. State Department.

MEMBER: Modern Language Association of America, American Association of Teachers of German, College Language Association, Goethe Society of America, American Bible Society (honorary member), Columbian Harmony Society (president, 1964—). *Awards, honors:* Julius Rosenwald Foundation fellowship, 1939-43; named honorary member of Accion Civica Istmena (Panama), 1955; American International Academy fellowship, 1961, Order of the Star and Cross, 1961; Ed.D. from Nathaniel Hawthorne College, 1969; distinguished service award from U.S. Air Force, 1969; Bradford Cross from Rock Creek Parish, 1977.

WRITINGS: Heine in England, University of North Carolina Press, 1943; (editor with L. H. Fenderson) *Many Shades of Black,* Morrow, 1969. Contributor of articles and reviews to journals. Editor of *Virginia State College Gazette* and *Research Journal,* both 1937-38; translator and reviewer for monthly periodical *Hamburg-Amerika Post,* 1931-32.

* * *

WORTH, Sol 1922(?)-1977

1922(?)—August 29, 1977; American filmmaker, scholar, and author. Worth combined the disciplines of anthropology and communications in his research, which culminated in a book about Navajo movie-making techniques that he co-authored. He was a professor of communications at the Annenberg School of the University of Pennsylvania. He died in Boston, Mass. Obituaries: *New York Times,* August 31, 1977; *AB Bookman's Weekly,* October 17, 1977.

* * *

WRIGHT, Jay 1935-

PERSONAL: Born May 25, 1935, in Albuquerque, N.M.

Education: Attended University of New Mexico; earned B.A. from University of California, Berkeley; earned M.A. from Rutgers University; further study at Union Theological Seminary. *Residence:* Penicuik, Scotland.

CAREER: Poet and playwright. Has worked as poet-in-residence at several universities, including Talledega University, Tougaloo University, Texas Southern University, and Dundee University. *Awards, honors:* National Council on the Arts grant, 1967; Hodder fellow in playwriting, Princeton University.

WRITINGS: Death as History (poetry), Kriya Press, 1967; *Homecoming Singer* (poetry), Corinth, 1971.

Work represented in anthologies, including *New Negro Poets: U.S.A.,* edited by Langston Hughes, Indiana University Press, 1964; *For Malcolm: Poems on the Life and Death of Malcolm X,* edited by Dudley Randall and Margaret Burroughs, Broadside Press, 1967; *Black Fire,* edited by LeRoi Jones and Larry Neal, Morrow, 1968; *The Poetry of Black America,* edited by Arnold Adoff, Harper, 1972; *New Black Voices,* edited by Abraham Chapman, New American Library, 1972.

Contributor to *Black World, Journal of Negro Poetry, Negro American Literature Forum, Negro Digest, Evergreen Review, Hiram Poetry Review, Nation,* and other periodicals.

SIDELIGHTS: Howard Junker described Wright's poetry as introspective, outside the Black poetry that "seethes with hatred of whites and the converse, adulation of black beauty." In *Newsweek* Junker wrote: "Jay Wright senses himself as an expatriate, no longer a jazzman with a fixed cultural role, but something else, left to flounder for himself: 'This could have been my town/with light strings that could stand a tempo./Now,/it's the end/of an ethnic dream./I've grown intellectual . . .'"

BIOGRAPHICAL/CRITICAL SOURCES: Newsweek, March 3, 1969; *Black World,* September, 1973.*

* * *

WURFEL, Seymour W(alter) 1907-

PERSONAL: Born October 4, 1907, in Denver, Colo.; son of Walter Conrad (a business executive) and Mabel Clair (Seymour) Wurfel; married Violet Elizabeth Mark (a professor of political science), July 30, 1932; children: David O. D., Walter William. *Education:* Pomona College, B.A. (magna cum laude), 1927; Harvard University, LL.B., 1930; Emory University, J.D., 1950. *Politics:* Republican. *Religion:* Presbyterian. *Home:* 14 Maxwell Rd., Chapel Hill, N.C. 27514. *Office:* School of Law, University of North Carolina, Chapel Hill, N.C. 27514.

CAREER: Admitted to California State Bar, 1930; practiced law in San Diego, Calif., 1930-40; U.S. Army, serving in Infantry, 1940-46, Judge Advocate General's Corps, 1946-60, retired as colonel; University of North Carolina at Chapel Hill, professor of law, 1960—. Member of North Carolina General Statutes Commission, 1972—. *Member:* American Society of International Law, American Bar Association, California State Bar Association, Phi Beta Kappa, Order of the Coif. *Awards, honors*—Military: Legion of Merit. Civilian: Ford Foundation grant for study in Colombia, 1963; U.S. Department of Commerce grant, 1970-72.

WRITINGS: (With William B. Aycock) *Military Law Under the Uniform Code of Military Justice,* University of North Carolina Press, 1955, reprinted, Greenwood Press, 1973; *Foreign Investment in Colombia: Law and Policy,*

University of North Carolina Press, 1965. Contributor to law reviews. Editor, *Law of the Sea,* 1970-75.

WORK IN PROGRESS: Studies in comparative law and conflict of law.

AVOCATIONAL INTERESTS: Golf, swimming, stamp collecting.

* * *

WYATT, Robert John   1931-

PERSONAL: Born September 5, 1931, in London, England; son of John (a food wholesaler) and Elsie (Parker) Wyatt; married Barbara Butler, March 14, 1965 (divorced, 1973); children: Michael Wheeler. *Education:* Attended Ipswich School of Technology, 1948-52; University of London, diploma, 1971. *Politics:* Conservative. *Religion:* Church of England. *Home:* 33 Sturges Rd., Wokingham, Berkshire, England. *Office:* Automobile Association, Basingstoke, Hampshire, England.

CAREER: Automobile Association, Basingstoke, England, transport manager, 1961—. Member of Wokingham Council, 1968-71; vice-chairman of Wokingham Conservatives, 1976-77. *Military service:* British Army, 1952-60. Territorial & Army Volunteer Reserve, Royal Military Police, 1962—; present rank, major. *Member:* Chartered Institute of Transport, Institute of Road Transport Engineers.

WRITINGS: (With Z. E. Lambert) *Lord Austin: The Man,* Sidgwick & Jackson, 1968; *The Austin Seven: The Motor for the Million,* Macdonald & Co., 1968, revised edition, David & Charles, 1972; *Cars,* Macdonald & Co., 1971; *Collecting Volunteer Militaria,* David & Charles, 1974; *The Austin Seven: A Pictorial Tribute,* Motor Racing Publications, 1975; *World Police Vehicles,* Blandford, 1978; *A History of the Austin Motor Company,* David & Charles, 1978. Contributor to motoring magazines.

WORK IN PROGRESS: British School Cadet Forces; Suffolk Volunteer Forces; Uniforms of British Volunteers in Colour, 1797-1908.

SIDELIGHTS: Wyatt writes: "I am mainly involved with the world's largest motoring organisation. My main interests in the writing sphere revolve around motoring history and research, and in British military history, including research in archives. I am able to research archive records on all aspects of British military history."

AVOCATIONAL INTERESTS: European travel, collecting books (especially military books), preparing bibliographies.

* * *

WYCKOFF, Ralph W(alter) G(raystone)   1897-

PERSONAL: Born August 9, 1897, in Geneva, N.Y.; son of Abram Ralph (a lawyer) and Ethel Agnes (Catchpole) Wyckoff; married Laura K. Laidlaw, August 5, 1927; children: Ralph Walter Graystone, Jr., Anne Wyckoff Elias, Grietje Wyckoff Sloan. *Education:* Hobart College, B.S., 1916; Cornell University, Ph.D., 1919. *Office:* Department of Physics, University of Arizona, Tucson, Ariz. 85721.

CAREER: Cornell University, Ithaca, N.Y., instructor in analytical chemistry, 1917-19; Carnegie Institution, Washington, D.C., research associate at geophysical laboratory, 1919-27; Rockefeller Institute for Medical Research, New York, N.Y., associate member, 1927-37; Lederle Laboratories, Pearl River, N.Y., member of staff, 1937-40, associate director of virus research, 1940-42; technical director, Rei-

chel Laboratories, 1942-43; University of Michigan, Ann Arbor, lecturer in physics, 1943-45; National Institutes of Health, Washington, D.C., senior scientist, 1945, scientific director, 1946-52, science attache to U.S. Embassy (London), 1952-54, biophysicist, 1954-59; University of Arizona, Tucson, professor of physics, 1959—. Research associate at California Institute of Technology, 1921-22; research director for Centre National de la Recherche Scientifique, 1959-62, 1969; exchange professor at Sorbonne, University of Paris, 1965; Bragg Memorial Lecturer, 1973; Patterson Memorial Lecturer, 1975. Member of board of directors of Lecomte du Nouy Foundation, 1954—.

MEMBER: International Union of Crystallography (past vice-president; past president), National Academy of Science, American Physical Society (fellow), American Chemical Society, American Academy of Arts and Sciences (fellow), American Association for the Advancement of Science (fellow), American Crystallographic Association (past president), American Society of Electron Microscopy (past president), Royal Netherlands Academy of Sciences (foreign member), Royal Society (London; foreign member), Academie des Sciences (correspondent), Indian Academy of Science (fellow), Royal Microscopical Society (honorary member), Societe Francaise de Microbiologie (honorary member), Societe Francaise de Mineralogie et de Cristallographie (honorary member), Phi Beta Kappa, Sigma Xi. *Awards, honors:* M.D. from Masaryk University, 1947; D.Sc. from University of Strasbourg, 1952, and Hobart College, 1975; medal from Institut Pasteur, 1953.

WRITINGS: An Analytical Expression of the Results of the Theory of Space Groups, Carnegie Institute, 1922, revised edition, 1930; *The Structure of Crystals,* Chemical Catalog Co., 1924, 3rd edition, 1934; *Crystal Structures,* Interscience Publishers, 1948, 14th edition, 1971; *Electron Microscopy,* Interscience Publishers, 1949; *The World of the Electron Microscope,* Yale University Press, 1958; *The Biochemistry of Animal Fossils,* Scientechnica, 1972. Contributor of about four hundred articles to scientific journals.

* * *

WYLIE, Francis E(rnest)   1905-
(Jeff Wylie)

PERSONAL: Born April 25, 1905, in Bloomfield, Ind.; son of William Henry (a clergyman) and Maude (Stout) Wylie; married Elizabeth Johnson, April 8, 1929; children: David A., Richard M. *Education:* Indiana University, A.B., 1928; also attended DePauw University, 1924-25, and University of Grenoble, 1926-27. *Home:* 2 Merrill St., Hingham, Mass. 02043. *Agent:* Boston Literary Agency, P.O. Box 1472, Manchester, Mass. 01944.

CAREER: Louisville Herald-Post, Louisville, Ky., reporter and editor, 1928-36; *Louisville Courier-Journal,* Louisville, reporter and editor, 1937-44; Time, Inc., Boston, Mass., chief of News Bureau, 1944-54; Massachusetts Institute of Technology, Cambridge, Mass., director of public relations, 1955-70; Boston University, Boston, special assistant, 1971-72; Massachusetts Institute of Technology, consultant, 1973-74; writer, 1974—.

WRITINGS: M.I.T. in Perspective, Little, Brown, 1976. Contributor to magazines and newspapers, sometimes under pseudonym Jeff Wylie. Member of editorial board of *Finance,* 1971-76.

WORK IN PROGRESS: Pull of the Moon, on tidal phenomena and lunar lore, for Stephen Greene Press.

WYLIE, Jeff
See WYLIE, Francis E(rnest)

* * *

WYNAR, Christine L(oraine) 1933-

PERSONAL: Born March 14, 1933, in Rockford, Ill.; daughter of Francis W. and Lydia A. (Teuscher) Gehrt; married Bohdan S. Wynar (a book publisher), August 23, 1965. *Education:* Quincy College, B.A., 1955; University of Denver, M.L.S., 1963. *Home:* 6008 South Lakeview St., Littleton, Colo. 80120. *Office:* 6931 South Yosemite St., Englewood, Calif. 80110.

CAREER: Writer. *Member:* American Library Association.

WRITINGS: *Guide to Reference Books for School Media Centers,* Libraries Unlimited, 1973, 1974-75 supplement, 1976.

WORK IN PROGRESS: A second edition of *Guide to Reference Books for School Media Centers.*

* * *

WYNAR, Lubomyr R(oman) 1932-

PERSONAL: Born January 2, 1932, in Lvov, in U.S.S.R.; came to the United States in 1955, naturalized citizen, 1960; son of Ivan (a professor) and Eufrosina (a teacher; maiden name, Doryk) Wynar; married Anna T. Kuzmych (a sociologist), July 15, 1962; children: Natalia. *Education:* Attended University of Munich, 1949-51; Ukrainian Free University, M.A., 1955, Ph.D., 1957; Western Reserve University (now Case Western Reserve University), M.S.L.S., 1959. *Home:* 4984 Pheasant Ave., Ravenna, Ohio 44266. *Office:* School of Library Science, Kent State University, Kent, Ohio 44242.

CAREER: Case Institute of Technology (now Case Western Reserve University), Cleveland, Ohio, instructor in bibliography and periodicals librarian, 1959-62; University of Colorado, Boulder, assistant professor of library science and head of Social Sciences Library, 1962-65; Bowling Green State University, Bowling Green, Ohio, assistant professor and director of Bibliographical Research Center, 1966-68, associate professor of library administration and assistant director of libraries, 1968-69; Kent State University, Kent, Ohio, professor of library science and ethnic studies, 1969—, director of Center for the Study of Ethnic Publication, 1971—. Faculty member at University of Denver, summers, 1961, 1963-65. Research associate at John Carroll University, 1962—.

MEMBER: American Historical Association, American Library Association (chairman of Slavic and East European section, 1971-73), American Association for the Advancement of Slavic Studies, Association for the Study of Nationalities (vice-president, 1977—), Ukrainian Free Academy of Arts and Sciences in the United States (chairman of Commission on Immigration, 1969—), Ukrainian Historical Association, Shevchenko Scientific Society (vice-president of Historical and Philosophical Division, 1973—), Ohio Library Association, Colorado Library Association. *Awards, honors:* Encyclopedia Directory of Ethnic Newspapers and Periodicals was named best reference book of 1972 by American Library Association; grant from U.S. Office of Education, 1977-78.

WRITINGS: *Andrew Voynarovsky: A Historical Study,* Verlag Logos, 1961; *A History of Early Ukrainian Printing, 1491-1600,* Graduate School of Library Science, University of Denver, 1962; *S. Harrison Thomson: A Bio-Bibliography,* Library, University of Colorado, 1963; *History: A Bibliographical Guide,* Library, University of Colorado, 1963; *Prince Dmytro Vyshnevetskyi,* Ukrainian Academy of Arts and Sciences, 1965; *Ukrainian Kozaks and the Vatican in 1594,* Ukrainian Historical Association, 1965; *Guide to Reference Materials in Political Science,* Colorado Bibliographical Institute, Volume I, 1966, Volume II, 1968; *The Early Years of Michael Hrushevsky, 1866-1894,* Ukrainian Historical Association, 1967; *American Political Parties,* Libraries Unlimited, 1969.

Michael Hrushevsky and the Shevchenko Scientific Society, 1895-1930, Ukrainian Historical Association, 1971; *Ethnic Groups in Ohio,* Ethnic Heritage Program, Cleveland State University, 1975; (editor) *Habsburgs and Zaporozhian Cossacks,* Ukrainian Academic Press, 1975; *Encyclopedia Directory of Ethnic Organizations in the United States,* Libraries Unlimited, 1975; (with wife, Anna Wynar) *Encyclopedia Directory of Ethnic Newspapers and Periodicals,* Libraries Unlimited, 1976; (with Lois Butlar) *Building Ethnic Collections,* Libraries Unlimited, 1977; (with Marjorie Murfin) *Reference Services,* Libraries Unlimited, 1977; *Guide to Ethnic Museums, Archives and Libraries in the United States,* Center for Ethnic Studies, Kent State University, 1978.

Managing editor of "Bio-Bibliographical Series" and editor of "Social Science Reference Services" for University of Colorado Library, 1963-65. Contributor of more than two hundred articles and reviews to academic journals. Editor of *Ukrainian Historian,* 1964—. Section editor of ethnic studies in *American Reference Books Annual,* 1974—.

WORK IN PROGRESS: *Introduction to Social Sciences Literature,* publication expected in 1979; editing *Historical Atlas of the Ukraine.*

SIDELIGHTS: Wynar writes that his main interests are history, library science, ethnic studies, and political science. "I am presently involved in library science and library education as these relate to services to ethnic communities and ethnic literature (books, periodicals, and newspapers). In this respect I have attended numerous conferences. I believe that there should be a greater development of the study of ethnicity in the United States in sociological, historical, and various other cultural disciplines." Wynar speaks Ukrainian, German, Polish, Russian, Latin, and Czeck.

* * *

WYNYARD, Talbot
See HAMILTON, Charles Harold St. John

* * *

YANNARELLA, Philip A(nthony) 1942-

PERSONAL: Born December 17, 1942, in Youngstown, Ohio; son of Anthony Charles and Virginia (a legal secretary; maiden name, Barber) Yannarella; married Patricia Carlson (a librarian), August 6, 1971; children: Christopher. *Education:* Youngstown State University, B.A., 1964; Duquesne University, M.A., 1967; further graduate study, Ohio State University, 1967; University of Michigan, A.M.L.S., 1970. *Home:* 18 Alan Court, Apt. 237, Florence, Ky. 41042. *Office:* Library, Northern Kentucky University, Highland Heights, Ky. 41076.

CAREER: Loras College, Dubuque, Iowa, instructor in philosophy, 1967-69; University of Michigan, Ann Arbor, Mich., library science scholar, 1969-71; University of Nebraska, Omaha, reference and document librarian, 1971-77;

Northern Kentucky University, Highland Heights, Ky., documents librarian, 1977—. *Member:* American Library Association (member of Government Documents Round Table), American Association of University Professors, Nebraska Library Association, Omaha Metropolitan Area Librarians Club.

WRITINGS: (With Rao Aluri) *U.S. Government Scientific and Technical Periodicals,* Scarecrow, 1976. Contributor to library journals.

WORK IN PROGRESS: U.S. Government Business and Economic Periodicals, a monograph, with Lowell Greunke; *Historical Statistics: An International Bibliography,* a monograph, completion expected in 1979.

* * *

YARDLEY, Jonathan 1939-

PERSONAL: Born October 27, 1939, in Pittsburgh, Pa.; son of William Woolsey (an educator) and Helen (a bookkeeper; maiden name, Gregory) Yardley; married Rosemary Roberts, June 14, 1961 (divorced, 1975); married Susan Hartt (a publicist), March 23, 1975; children: (first marriage) James Barrett, William Woolsey II. *Education:* University of North Carolina, A.B., 1961; Harvard University, graduate study, 1968-69. *Politics:* Democrat. *Religion:* Episcopalian. *Home:* 9920 North Kendall Dr., Apt. J-401, Miami, Fla. 33176. *Agent:* Elizabeth Darhansoff, 52 East 91st St., New York, N.Y. 10028. *Office: Miami Herald,* 1 Herald Plaza, Miami, Fla. 33101.

CAREER: New York Times, New York, N.Y., assistant to James Reston in Washington, D.C., 1961-62, writer of "News of the Week in Review," 1962-64; *Greensboro Daily News,* Greensboro, N.C., editorial writer and book editor, 1964-74; *Miami Herald,* Miami, Fla., book editor and viewpoint editor, 1974—. Lecturer at University of North Carolina, Greensboro, 1972-73.

WRITINGS: Ring: A Biography of Ring Lardner, Random, 1977.

Author of a weekly book review column syndicated by Knight Newspapers, 1974—. Contributor to magazines, including *New Republic, Life, Sewanee Review,* and *Partisan Review.* Contributing editor of *Sports Illustrated.*

WORK IN PROGRESS: A collection of articles for Random.

* * *

YASHIMA, Taro
See IWAMATSU, Jun Atsushi

* * *

YERIAN, Cameron John

PERSONAL: Born in Michigan; married wife, Margaret A. (a writer); children: Phoebe A., C. Scot. *Education:* Earned degree from University of Michigan. *Residence:* Ann Arbor, Mich. *Office:* Y4 Design Ltd., P.O. Box 1101, Ann Arbor, Mich. 48106.

CAREER: Writer. President of Y4 Design Ltd., Ann Arbor, Mich.

WRITINGS—All children's books; all with wife, Margaret A. Yerian: *ABC's of Aerospace,* Elk Grove Press, 1971; *ABC's of Hydrospace,* Elk Grove Press, 1971; *Rainbows and Jolly Beans: A Look at Drugs,* Elk Grove Press, 1971; *The Yawn Book,* Steck, 1971; *Actor's Workshop,* Children's Press, 1974.

Editor; all children's books; all with M. A. Yerian; all published by Grolier, all 1974: *Creative Activities,* Volume 1: *Making,* Volume 2: *Playing,* Volume 3: *Discovering,* Volume 4: *Performing,* Volume 5: *Creating,* Volume 6: *Collecting,* Volume 7: *Communicating,* Volume 8: *Producing,* Volume 9: *Fooling,* Volume 10: *Organizing,* Volume 11: *Growing,* Volume 12: *Caring,* Volume 13: *Building,* Volume 14: *Searching,* Volume 15: *Foraging,* Volume 16: *Traveling,* Volume 17: *Exploring,* Volume 18: *Sewing,* Volume 19: *Cooking,* Volume 20: *Finding.*

Editor; all children's books; all with M. A. Yerian; all published by Children's Press: *Batik and Tie Dyeing,* 1974; *Competitive Games,* 1974; *Games for One, Two, or More,* 1974; *Group Games,* 1974; *Jewelry, Candles, and Papercraft,* 1974; *Macrame, Knitting, and Weaving,* 1974; *Projects: Earth and Sky,* 1974; *Puppets and Shadow Plays,* 1974; *Showtime,* 1974; *Magnificent Magic,* 1975; *Make-Up and Costumes,* 1975; *Stages, Scenery, and Props,* 1975; *Plays and Special Effects,* 1975; *Easy Tricks and Spooky Games,* 1975; *Codes and Mystery Messages,* 1975; *Money-Making Ideas,* 1975; *Doodling, Drawing, and Creating,* 1975; *Radio and Movie Productions,* 1975; *Community Projects,* 1975; *Easy Sewing Projects,* 1975; *For Campers Only: Sewing and Cooking,* 1975; *Gifts for Everybody,* 1975; *Handmade Toys and Games,* 1975; *Indoor Gardening,* 1975; *Outdoor Gardening,* 1975; *Party Foods,* 1975; *Sew It! Wear It!,* 1975; *Weird Gardens,* 1975; *Working with Wood,* 1975.

* * *

YERIAN, Margaret A.

PERSONAL: Born in Ohio; married Cameron John Yerian (a writer); children: Phoebe A., C. Scot. *Education:* Earned degree from University of Michigan. *Residence:* Ann Arbor, Mich. *Office:* Y4 Design Ltd., P.O. Box 1101, Ann Arbor, Mich. 48106.

CAREER: Writer. Vice-president of Y4 Design Ltd., Ann Arbor, Mich.

WRITINGS—All children's books; all with husband, Cameron John Yerian: *ABC's of Aerospace,* Elk Grove Press, 1971; *ABC's of Hydrospace,* Elk Grove Press, 1971; *Rainbows and Jolly Beans: A Look at Drugs,* Elk Grove Press, 1971; *The Yawn Book,* Steck, 1971; *Actor's Workshop,* Children's Press, 1974.

Editor; all children's books; all with C. J. Yerian; all published by Grolier, all 1974: *Creative Activities,* Volume 1: *Making,* Volume 2: *Playing,* Volume 3: *Discovering,* Volume 4: *Performing,* Volume 5: *Creating,* Volume 6: *Collecting,* Volume 7: *Communicating,* Volume 8: *Producing,* Volume 9: *Fooling,* Volume 10: *Organizing,* Volume 11: *Growing,* Volume 12: *Caring,* Volume 13: *Building,* Volume 14: *Searching,* Volume 15: *Foraging,* Volume 16: *Traveling,* Volume 17: *Exploring,* Volume 18: *Sewing,* Volume 19: *Cooking,* Volume 20: *Finding.*

Editor; all children's books; all with C. J. Yerian; all published by Children's Press: *Batik and Tie Dyeing,* 1974; *Competitive Games,* 1974; *Games for One, Two, or More,* 1974; *Group Games,* 1974; *Jewelry, Candles, and Papercraft,* 1974; *Macrame, Knitting, and Weaving,* 1974; *Projects: Earth and Sky,* 1974; *Puppets and Shadow Plays,* 1974; *Showtime,* 1974; *Magnificent Magic,* 1975; *Make-Up and Costumes,* 1975; *Stages, Scenery, and Props,* 1975; *Plays and Special Effects,* 1975; *Easy Tricks and Spooky Games,* 1975; *Codes and Mystery Messages,* 1975; *Money-Making Ideas,* 1975; *Doodling, Drawing, and Creating,* 1975; *Radio and Movie Productions,* 1975; *Community Projects,* 1975;

Easy Sewing Projects, 1975; *For Campers Only: Sewing and Cooking,* 1975; *Gifts for Everybody,* 1975; *Handmade Toys and Games,* 1975; *Indoor Gardening,* 1975; *Outdoor Gardening,* 1975; *Party Foods,* 1975; *Sew It! Wear It!,* 1975; *Weird Gardens,* 1975; *Working with Wood,* 1975.

* * *

YOLEN, Steven H. 1942-

PERSONAL: Born November 4, 1942, in New York, N.Y.; son of Will H. (an author and publisher) and Isabelle (Berlin) Yolen; married Melinda Allen, May 25, 1965 (divorced); married Maria Lucia Raposa de Almeida (a language instructor), January 10, 1976; children: John Gregory. *Education:* Lafayette College, B.A., 1964. *Home and office:* Rua Sabara, 76 Apt. 81, San Paulo, Brazil.

CAREER/WRITINGS: United Press International, New York City, bureau manager in San Juan, Puerto Rico, 1965-68, executive assistant to the vice-president in Buenos Aires, 1968-70, bureau manager in San Paulo, Brazil, 1970-73, manager for Brazil, 1973-74; Fairchild Publications, New York City, bureau chief in Brazil, 1975—. *Member:* Overseas Press Club, Foreign Press Club in Brazil, San Paulo Foreign Press Society. *Awards, honors:* Overseas Press Club citation for best magazine reporting from abroad, 1976.

* * *

YOORS, Jan 1922(?)-1977

1922(?)—November 27, 1977; Belgian-born artist and author. A celebrated tapistry artist and photographer, Yoors shared his visions of the world through several books, including an account of his travels through Europe with a gypsy tribe during his early youth. He died in New York, N.Y. Obituaries: *New York Times,* November 29, 1977; *AB Bookman's Weekly,* February 6, 1978.

* * *

YORK, Thomas (Lee) 1940-

PERSONAL: Born September 21, 1940, in Washington, D.C.; son of Harold C. (a lawyer) and Alice (Byrd) York; married Lynn Fuller (a teacher), September 9, 1961; children: Paul, Stephen, Rachel, Sarah. *Education:* Tulane University, B.A., 1961, M.A., 1975, doctoral study, 1975—; University of Toronto, B.D., 1967; also attended Duke University. *Home:* 28 Hambly Ave., Toronto, Ontario, Canada M4E 2R6. *Office:* Chapel in the Park, Thorncliffe Park Dr., Toronto, Ontario, Canada M4H 1H4.

CAREER: Ordained Presbyterian minister, 1967; minister to United Church of Canada congregations in Whitby, Ontario, 1964-66, Newmarket, Ontario, 1966-67, Queen Charlotte Island, British Columbia, 1967-68, Bella-Bella, British Columbia, 1968-70, Yellowknife, Northwest Territory, 1970-72, and Chapel in the Park, Toronto, Ontario, 1975—.

WRITINGS: We, the Wilderness (novel), McGraw, 1973; *Snowman* (novel), Doubleday, 1976; *And Sleep in the Woods* (autobiography), Doubleday, in press; *The Musk-Ox Passion* (novel), Doubleday, in press.

WORK IN PROGRESS: Two novels, *Trapper* and *Desireless.*

SIDELIGHTS: York writes that, although a Canadian citizen, he was indicted for draft evasion in 1964, convicted in Little Rock, Ark., in 1973, and sentenced to three years in federal prison. He appealed the conviction and was acquitted in 1974.

He adds that he has traveled twice across the Arctic by canoe, about four thousand miles in all, and is the only known survivor of the whirlpool at Death Rapids on the Canadian side of the Columbia River.

He comments: "I write only from obsessive material, to order it; I would rather not write, but find it a compulsion attendant upon the appetite for living and experiencing fully. I look forward to being less driven: dead."

AVOCATIONAL INTERESTS: Weightlifting (Olympic competition), barrengrounds canoeing, long-distance running, languages (Hebrew, Greek, Latin, German, Old English).

* * *

YOUNG, Elaine L.
See SCHULTE, Elaine L(ouise)

* * *

YOUNGE, Sheila 1945(?)-1977

1945(?)—October 20, 1977; American editor and journalist. Younge was executive editor of *Essence* from 1971 until 1976. She died in Berkeley, Calif. Obituaries: *New York Times,* October 27, 1977.

* * *

ZACHARIS, John C. 1936-

PERSONAL: Born November 29, 1936, in Gardner, Mass.; son of Nicholas (a chef) and Ethel (Costarides) Zacharis; married Marilyn Tufte (an executive secretary), March 18, 1961. *Education:* Emerson College, B.S., 1958, M.S., 1959; Indiana University, Ph.D., 1966. *Home:* 75 Parker Rd., Wellesley, Mass. 02181. *Office:* Department of Speech and Communication, Emerson College, 148 Beacon St., Boston, Mass. 02116.

CAREER: California Polytechnic State University, Pomona, instructor in speech, 1960-62; Lehigh University, Bethlehem, Pa., instructor in speech, 1964-66; professor of speech and communication studies, and head of department, Emerson College, Boston, Mass. *Member:* International Communication Association, Speech Communication Association of America, Eastern Communication Association, Eastern Forensic Association (president).

WRITINGS: Your Future in the New World of Communication, Richards Rosen, 1975; (with Coleman C. Bender) *Speech Communication: A Rational Approach,* Wiley, 1976.

WORK IN PROGRESS: A book on speech communication as it relates to careers.

SIDELIGHTS: Zacharis writes: "I have had heavy background in debate—as a debater and as an instructor. This affects my writing and accounts for the 'rational' approach to communication."

* * *

ZALEZNIK, Abraham 1924-

PERSONAL: Born January 30, 1924, in Philadelphia, Pa.; married wife Elizabeth (a director of special education); children: Dori, Ira. *Education:* Alma College, A.B., 1945; Harvard University, M.B.A., 1947, D.C.S., 1951; postdoctoral study at Boston Psychoanalytic Society and Institute, 1960-65. *Home:* 151 Follen Road, Lexington, Mass. 02173. *Office:* Harvard Business School, Harvard University, Soldiers Field, Boston, Mass. 02163.

CAREER: Harvard University, Harvard Business School, Boston, Mass., instructor, 1948-51, assistant professor, 1951-56, associate professor, 1956-61, professor, 1961-67, Cahners-Rabb Professor of social psychology of management, 1967—. Director of Purity Supreme Supermarkets, Park Electrochemical Corp., Madico Inc., Evans Products Co., Pueblo International, Inc., Gaulin Corp. Trustee, Beth Israel Hospital, Boston. *Military service:* U.S. Navy, 1942-46. *Member:* American Psychoanalytic Association, American Sociological Society, Boston Psychoanalytic Society and Institute.

WRITINGS: (with David Moment) *The Dynamics of Interpersonal Behavior,* Wiley, 1964; (with R. C. Hodgson and D. J. Levinson) *The Executive Role Constellation,* Division of Research, Harvard Business School, 1965; (with G. Dalton and L. B. Barnes) *The Distribution of Authority in Formal Organizations,* Division of Research, Harvard Business School, 1968; *Human Dilemmas of Leadership,* Harper, 1966; (with Manfred F. R. Kets de Vries) *Power and the Corporate Mind,* Houghton, 1975. Contributor of articles to *Harvard Business Review, Behavioral Science, Bulletin of the Menninger Clinic,* and other journals in his field.

WORK IN PROGRESS: Communicating with Business Audiences; research on decision-making and the psychology of the self, on organizations in crisis, and on psychic disequilibria and social change.

*   *   *

ZECKENDORF, William   1905-

PERSONAL: Born June 20, 1905, in Paris, Ill.; son of Arthur William (a merchant) and Byrd (Rosenfield) Zeckendorf; married Irma Levy, September 29, 1928 (divorced, 1934); married Marion Griffin, December 10, 1940 (died, 1968); married Alice K. Bacher, December 21, 1972; children: William Jr., Susan. *Education:* New York University, student, 1922-25. *Religion:* Jewish. *Office:* 383 Madison Ave., New York, N.Y. 10017.

CAREER: Real estate consultant. Samuel Bochard, New York City, assistant purchasing agent, 1925-26; Leonard S. Gans, New York City, associate, 1926-29, partner, 1930—; Webb & Knapp, Inc. (real estate and construction), New York City, vice president, 1938-47, president, 1947-61, chairperson of the board, 1961-65. Director of American Hydrofoil Co., Trizec Co., Webb & Knapp Ltd. (Canada), Gulf States Land & Industries Inc., and Roosevelt Field Inc.; member of board of directors of The Children's Village, New York Infirmary, American Korean Foundation, and Manhattan Eye, Ear, and Throat Hospital; trustee of American Planning and Civic Association; chairperson of the board of Colmar Surinam Oil Co.; Long Island University, chairperson of the board of trustees, 1942-67, trustee, 1968—; honorary chairperson of Realty Foundation of New York. *Member:* Navy League of the United States (life member), Pi Lambda Phi. *Awards, honors:* Chevalier Legion of Honor (France); officer of the Order of Orange Nassau (Netherlands); officer of the Order of Merit (Italy).

WRITINGS: (With Edward McCreary) *Zeckendorf: The Autobiography of William Zeckendorf,* Holt, 1970.

SIDELIGHTS: While associated with Webb & Knapp, Zeckendorf purchased eight acres of land on the East River in New York. In 1946, he sold this land to John D. Rockefeller to be used as the site of the United Nations headquarters.

BIOGRAPHICAL/CRITICAL SOURCES: New York Times, August 20, 1970; *Time,* September 14, 1970.*

ZEIGFREID, Karl
See FANTHORPE, R(obert) Lionel

*   *   *

ZIBART, Carl F.   1907-

PERSONAL: Born February 21, 1907, in Nashville, Tenn.; son of Leon P. (a bookseller) and Celia (Frankland) Zibart; married Grace Herrick (an editor), August 26, 1946; children: Henry H., Rosemary Zibart Barrow, Andrew F. *Education:* Vanderbilt University, B.A., 1929. *Politics:* Democrat. *Religion:* Jewish. *Home:* 3311 Fairmont, Nashville, Tenn. 37203. *Office:* Zibart's Book Store, Nashville, Tenn. 37215.

CAREER: Zibart's Book Store, Nashville, Tenn., owner and operator, 1932—. *Military service:* U.S. Army, Field Artillery, 1942-46; became first lieutenant. *Member:* Torch Club.

WRITINGS: Yesterday's Nashville, E. A. Seemann, 1976.

WORK IN PROGRESS: Guidebook to Nashville; writing for television.

SIDELIGHTS: Zibart comments briefly: "I feel the moribund performance of the Republican Party for the past fifty years leaves the intelligent voter no choice." *Avocational interests:* "I am a lifelong tennis buff who views the emergence of this sport as a major pastime with enthusiasm."

*   *   *

ZIMET, Melvin   1913-

PERSONAL: Born May 29, 1913; son of David (a businessman) and Fanny Zimet; married Joan Gans (a sculptor), October 13, 1935; children: John, Paul. *Education:* New York University, B.S., 1933, M.B.A., 1965, Ph.D., 1972. *Politics:* Independent. *Religion:* Jewish. *Home:* 180 Riverside Dr., New York, N.Y. 10024. *Office:* Manhattan College, Riverdale, N.Y. 10471.

CAREER: Helene Curtis, Inc., Chicago, Ill., manager of New York office, 1946-66; Manhattan College, Riverdale, N.Y., associate professor of management, 1969—, chairman of department. *Member:* Academy of Management, Industrial Relations Research Association, Eastern Academy of Management, Beta Gamma Sigma, Delta Mu Delta.

WRITINGS: Decentralization and School Effectiveness, Teachers College Press, 1973.

WORK IN PROGRESS: Editing *The Collected Papers of Harold Smiddy* with Ronald Greenwood.

*   *   *

ZIMMERMAN, William Dudley   1940-

PERSONAL: Born April 5, 1940, in Washington, D.C.; son of Clarence Mason (an accountant) and Rachel (a teacher; maiden name, Dudley) Zimmerman; married Patricia Moore, September 14, 1963; children: Heather Lynn, William Eric, Brad Moore, Christopher Mason. *Education:* Attended Oklahoma University, 1958-59, and George Washington University, 1959-60. *Home:* Via Cassia 929, Rome, Italy 00189. *Office:* Via Abruzzi 25, Rome, Italy 00187.

CAREER/WRITINGS: WTOP-TV, Washington, D.C., reporter, 1964-69; WHDH-TV, Boston, Mass., reporter, 1969-71; American Broadcasting Co. (ABC) News, New York City, correspondent in Washington, D.C., 1971-75, bureau chief and correspondent in Beirut, 1975-76, and Rome, 1976—. Notable assignments include coverage of

Chappaquiddick, the Thomas Eagleton and R. Sargent Shriver campaigns, the 1968 and 1972 U.S. presidential conventions, the Watergate hearings, and interviews with Anwar Sadat. *Military service:* U.S. Army Reserve, 1957-64; became second lieutenant. *Member:* Overseas Press Club.

*   *   *

ZINDEL, Paul 1936-

PERSONAL: Born May 15, 1936, in Staten Island, N.Y.; son of Paul (a policeman) and Betty (a practical nurse; maiden name, Frank) Zindel; married Bonnie Hildebrand (a screenwriter), October 25, 1973; children: David Jack, Elizabeth Claire. *Education:* Wagner College, B.S., 1958, M.Sc., 1959. *Residence:* New York, N.Y. *Agent:* Curtis Brown, Ltd., 575 Madison Ave., New York, N.Y. 10022.

CAREER: Tottenville High School, Staten Island, N.Y., chemistry teacher, 1959-69; playwright and author of children's books, 1969—. Playwright-in-residence, Alley Theatre, Houston, Tex., 1967. *Member:* Actors Studio. *Awards, honors:* Ford Foundation grant, 1967; received numerous awards for "The Effect of Gamma Rays on Man-in-the-Moon Marigolds" including Obie Award, 1970, Pulitzer Prize in Drama, 1971, New York Critics Award, 1971, and Vernon Rice Drama Desk Award, 1971; honorary doctorate of humanities, Wagner College, 1971.

WRITINGS—Juvenile: *The Pigman,* Harper, 1968; *My Darling, My Hamburger,* Harper, 1969; *I Never Loved Your Mind,* Harper, 1970; *Pardon Me, You're Stepping on My Eyeball,* Harper, 1976; *I Love My Mother,* Harper, 1975; *Confessions of a Teenage Baboon,* Harper, 1977.

Plays: "Dimensions of Peacocks," first produced in New York, 1959; "Euthanasia and the Endless Hearts," first produced in New York, 1960; "A Dream of Swallows," first produced Off-Broadway, April, 1962; *The Effects of Gamma Rays on Man-in-the-Moon Marigolds* (first produced in Houston at Alley Theatre, 1964; produced Off-Broadway at Mercer-O'Casey Theatre, April 7, 1970), Harper, 1971; "And Miss Reardon Drinks a Little," first produced on Broadway at Morosco Theatre, February 25, 1971; "The Secret Affairs of Mildred Wild," first produced in New York City, 1972; "Ladies at the Alamo," first produced at Actor's Studio, 1975, produced on Broadway at Martin Beck Theatre, April 7, 1977; *Let Me Hear You Whisper: A Play,* Harper, 1974.

Screen and television plays include: "The Effect of Gamma Rays on Man-in-the-Moon Marigolds," produced by National Educational Television (NET), 1966, and Twentieth Century-Fox, 1973; "Let Me Hear You Whisper," produced by NET, 1966; "Up the Sandbox," 1972, "Mame," 1973. Also author of "The Pigman" (adapted from his novel), "Mrs. Beneker" (screenplay), and "Farewell to a Mouse Named Mars" (children's teleplay).

Contributor of articles to newspapers and periodicals.

WORK IN PROGRESS: A play entitled "A Destiny on Half Moon Street"; a musical based on Dorothy Parker's, "The Girl Who Wore Glasses"; a novel, *The Undertaker's Gone Bananas.*

SIDELIGHTS: Paul Zindel has always been a writer of plays about women, and has provided actresses with some of the best roles since Tennessee Williams, a writer with whom *Variety* compared him after the opening of "The Effects of Gamma Rays on Man-in-the-Moon Marigolds." But men are beginning to dominate his latest works, Zindel told *CA.*

In a recent television interview Zindel explained that he liked to write about "what's happening," and the fact that his plays are about women does indeed mean that he thinks women are what's happening today. The women, however, are not always very nice. In fact, they are usually women in distress. This has been a central theme in his plays.

"I am virtually desperate for some sign, for any bit of hope, or reason, to make being a human sensible," said Zindel in another interview. "In each of my plays, there is an attempt to find some grain of truth, something to hang onto. In 'Marigolds' it's this: One is composed of matter that's been around for millions of years, matter that comes from other worlds, other galaxies. That's a little thrilling, to be part of that infinity that is so vast and so marvelous that our minds cannot really grasp it."

About his work, Zindel commented: "Whatever I do becomes summarized in my writing. When I have gained a certain quantity of experience which begins to shape itself into something secret and interesting, I feel I must tell others about it. So I sit around and daydream about how I am going to tell it, and when I find a way of condensing it interestingly to myself, and I have a suspicion of a vision those characters will have toward the end of the play, then the excitement and the necessity of wanting to clarify that vision gives me the energy to work indefatigably. I can write a play in a week in those conditions."

Zindel claims that people have told him he is a born playwright, and that he comes at a time when he is most needed, when "the Theatre is dying." His response to this was to describe the unique path which led to his profession. "I evolved into a writer of plays by never having gone near a theatre until I was in my twenties. The fact that I had written two plays by that time makes me believe that the seeds of theatre are born inside us."

BIOGRAPHICAL/CRITICAL SOURCES: Village Voice, April 16, 1970; *New York Times,* April 19, 1970, July 26, 1970, March 8, 1971, February 26, 1971, April 8, 1977; *Time,* April 20, 1970; *Washington Post,* January 27, 1971; *Boston Globe,* January, 1971; *Contemporary Literary Criticism,* Volume 6, Gale, 1976; *Publisher's Weekly,* December 5, 1977; *Top of the News,* December, 1977; *Children's Literature Review,* Volume 3, Gale, 1978.

*   *   *

ZINGARA, Professor
See LEEMING, Joseph

*   *   *

ZIRING, Lawrence 1928-

PERSONAL: Born December 11, 1928, in Brooklyn, N.Y.; son of Israel and Anna (Berg) Ziring; married Raye Marlene Ralph, August 10, 1962; children: Leona, Sarah. *Education:* Columbia University, B.S., 1955, M.I.A., 1957, Ph.D., 1962. *Home:* 5139 Greenhill, Portage, Mich. 49081. *Office:* Department of Political Science, Western Michigan University, Kalamazoo, Mich. 49008.

CAREER: Dacca University, Dacca, East Pakistan, lecturer in political science, 1959-60; Columbia University, New York, N.Y., lecturer in political science, 1960-61; Lafayette College, Easton, Pa., assistant professor of political science, 1961-64; Syracuse University, Syracuse, N.Y., assistant professor of political science, 1964-67; Western Michigan University, Kalamazoo, associate professor, 1967-73, professor of political science, 1973—. Adviser to Pakistan Administrative Staff College, 1964-66. U.S. Information Agency lecturer in Pakistan, 1959-60, 1974-75, 1976; lecturer at Defense Intelligence School, 1964, Foreign Service Institute, 1967, and Canadian Defense College, 1968; external examiner for Karachi University, 1973—, and University of Toronto, 1974. Consultant to U.S. Department of State. *Military service:* U.S. Army, 1951-53.

MEMBER: American Political Science Association, Association for Asian Studies (chairman of Pakistan Studies Development Committee), Asia Society (member of Pakistan Council, 1961—). *Awards, honors:* Fellow of Institute of Oriental Studies, Soviet Union Academy of Sciences, 1974; American Council of Learned Societies fellowship, 1974-75.

WRITINGS: The Ayub Khan Era: Politics in Pakistan, 1958-1969, Syracuse University Press, 1971; (editor with Ralph Braibanti and Howard Wriggins, and contributor) *Pakistan: The Long View,* Duke University Press, 1977; (with C. I. Eugene Kim) *An Introduction to Asian Politics,* Prentice-Hall, 1977; (editor and contributor) *The Subcontinent in World Politics: India, Its Neighbors and the Major Powers,* Praeger, 1978.

Contributor: G. S. Birkhead, editor, *Administrative Problems in Pakistan,* Syracuse University Press, 1966; Anwar Dil, editor, *Toward Developing Pakistan,* Abbottabad Bookservice, 1970; J. Henry Korson, editor, *Contemporary Problems of Pakistan,* E. J. Brill, 1974; Howard Wriggins, editor, *Pakistan in Transition,* Islamabad University Press, 1975; Eric Gustafson, editor, *Pakistan and Bangladesh: Bibliographic Essays in the Social Sciences,* Southern Asian Insitute, Columbia University, 1976. Contributor of more than thirty articles and reviews to learned journals.

WORK IN PROGRESS: The Muslim League, 1947-1958: A Political History; Turkey, Iran, and Afghanistan: The Northern Tier in Transition; research on Jinnah and Pakistan and on Iran and Saudi Arabia; continuing research on politics and foreign policy in South Asia and the Middle East.

SIDELIGHTS: Ziring described his books about Pakistan, saying, "*The Ayab Khan Era* examines the character of Pakistan Army General Ayub Khan's rule (1958-69), his dreams of a new Pakistan, and the reasons for his failure to bring it about—reasons that range from his own errors and inconsistencies in policy and performance to the weight of Pakistan's historic legacies that resisted change. *Pakistan: The Long View* examines the Bhutto period against a background of Pakistan's total experience of independence. The book focuses on the Pakistan that emerged from the disaster of civil war in 1971."

Commenting on the importance of studying Asia, Zirling added, "Asia has affected the course of American history, and it will continue to influence our lives. Our young people need to know a great deal about the vast continent and its turbulent populations. *An Introduction to Asian Politics* acknowledges our responsibility as teachers to present another part of the world to our students."

*   *   *

ZWEIFEL, Frances W.   1931-

PERSONAL: Born May 26, 1931, in Hampton, Va.; daughter of Robert William (an air force officer) and Helen (Huber) Wimsatt; married Richard Zweifel (a museum curator), July 30, 1956; children: Matthew, Kenneth, Ellen. *Education:* Trinity College, B.A., 1952; University of Arizona, M.A., 1956. *Politics:* "Ambiguous." *Religion:* Roman Catholic. *Home:* 412 Glendale Rd., Northvale, N.J. 07647.

CAREER: Free-lance biological illustrator. American Museum of Natural History, New York City, scientific illustrator, 1956-58.

WRITINGS: (Self-illustrated) *A Handbook of Biological Illustration,* University of Chicago Press, 1961; *Bony,* Harper, 1977.

Illustrator: Evelyn Shaw, *Alligator,* Harper, 1972.